SMITHSONIAN INSTITUTION
BUREAU OF AMERICAN ETHNOLOGY
BULLETIN 30

HANDBOOK

OF

AMERICAN INDIANS

NORTH OF MEXICO

EDITED BY

FREDERICK WEBB HODGE

VOLUME III   N to S

WASHINGTON
GOVERNMENT PRINTING OFFICE
(Fourth impression, September, 1912)

SMITHSONIAN INSTITUTION
BUREAU OF AMERICAN ETHNOLOGY
BULLETIN 30

HANDBOOK

OF

AMERICAN INDIANS

NORTH OF MEXICO

EDITED BY

FREDERICK WEBB HODGE

TRADEPAPER:

VOLUME I   A-G   ISBN   1-58218-748-7
VOLUME II   H-M   ISBN   1-58218-749-5
VOLUME III   N-S   ISBN   1-58218-750-9
VOLUME IV   T-Z   ISBN   1-58218-751-7

Digital Scanning and Publishing is a leader in the electronic republication of historical books and documents. We publish many of our titles as eBooks, as well as traditional hardcover and trade paper editions. DSI is committed to bringing many traditional and little known books back to life, retaining the look and feel of the original work.

©2003 DSI Digital Reproduction
First DSI Printing: July 2003

Published by DIGITAL SCANNING, INC.
Scituate, MA 02066
www.digitalscanning.com

CONTRIBUTORS TO PART 2 (Vol. 3 & 4)

A. B. L.	Dr Albert Buell Lewis of the Field Museum of Natural History.
A. C. F.	Miss Alice C. Fletcher of Washington.
A. F. C.	Dr Alexander F. Chamberlain of Clark University.
A. H.	Dr Aleš Hrdlička of the United States National Museum.
A. L. K.	Dr A. L. Kroeber of the University of California.
A. S. G.	The late Dr Albert S. Gatschet of the Bureau of American Ethnology.
A. S. Q.	Mrs Amelia Stone Quinton of New York.
C. B. M.	Mr Clarence B. Moore of Philadelphia.
C. C. W.	Mr C. C. Willoughby of the Peabody Museum, Harvard University.
C. F. L.	Dr Charles F. Lummis of Los Angeles, California.
C. T.	The late Dr Cyrus Thomas of the Bureau of American Ethnology.
C. W.	Dr Clark Wissler of the American Museum of Natural History.
D. I. B.	Mr D. I. Bushnell, jr., of University, Virginia.
D. R.	Mr Doane Robinson of the South Dakota Historical Society.
E. L. H.	Dr Edgar L. Hewett of the School of American Archæology.
E. S.	Dr Edward Sapir of the Geological Survey of Canada.
F. B.	Dr Franz Boas of Columbia University.
F. G. S.	Dr Frank G. Speck of the University of Pennsylvania.
F. H.	Mr Frank Huntington, formerly of the Bureau of American Ethnology.
F. H. C.	The late Frank Hamilton Cushing of the Bureau of American Ethnology.
F. L.	Mr Francis LaFlesche of the Bureau of Indian Affairs.
F. S. N.	Mrs Frances S. Nichols of the Bureau of American Ethnology.
F. W. H.	Mr F. W. Hodge of the Bureau of American Ethnology.
G. A. D.	Dr George A. Dorsey of the Field Museum of Natural History.
G. F.	Mr Gerard Fowke of Saint Louis.
G. P. D.	The Rev. Dr George P. Donehoo of Connellsville, Pa.
G. T. E.	Lieut. G. T. Emmons, United States Navy, retired.
G. W. G.	Judge George W. Grayson of Eufaula, Okla.
H. E. B.	Dr Herbert E. Bolton of Leland Stanford Junior University.
H. W. H.	Mr Henry W. Henshaw, formerly of the Bureau of American Ethnology.
J. A. G.	The Rev. J. A. Gilfillan of Washington.
J. D. M.	Mr Joseph D. McGuire of Washington.
J. M.	Mr James Mooney of the Bureau of American Ethnology.
J. N. B. H.	Mr J. N. B. Hewitt of the Bureau of American Ethnology.
J. O. D.	The late Rev. J. Owen Dorsey of the Bureau of American Ethnology.
J. P. D.	Mr Jacob P. Dunn of Indianapolis.
J. R. S.	Dr John R. Swanton of the Bureau of American Ethnology.
J. W. F.	Dr J. Walter Fewkes of the Bureau of American Ethnology.
L. F.	Dr Livingston Farrand of Columbia University.
M. E. G.	Dr Merrill E. Gates of the United States Board of Indian Commissioners.
M. S. C.	Miss M. S. Cook of the Bureau of Indian Affairs.
O. T. M.	The late Prof. Otis T. Mason of the United States National Museum.
P. E. G.	Dr Pliny E. Goddard of the American Museum of Natural History.
P. R.	Dr Paul Radin of the Bureau of American Ethnology.
R. B. D.	Dr Roland B. Dixon of Harvard University.
S. A. B.	Dr S. A. Barrett of the Milwaukee Public Museum.

W. E.	Mr Wilberforce Eames of the New York Public Library.
W. H.	Dr Walter Hough of the United States National Museum.
W. H. D.	Dr William H. Dall of the United States Geological Survey.
W. H. H.	Mr William H. Holmes of the United States National Museum.
W. J.	The late Dr William Jones of the Field Museum of Natural History.
W. M.	The late Dr Washington Matthews, United States Army.
W. M. B.	The Rev. William M. Beauchamp of Syracuse, N. Y.
W. R. G.	Mr W. R. Gerard of New York.

HANDBOOK OF THE INDIANS

N **A.** For all names beginning with this abbreviation and followed by Sa., Sra., or Señora, see *Nuestra Señora*.

Naagarnep. See *Nagonub*.

Naagetl. A Yurok village on lower Klamath r., just below Ayootl and above the mouth of Blue cr., N. w. Cal.
Naagetl.—A. L. Kroeber, inf'n, 1905. Nai-a-gutl.—Gibbs (1851) in Schoolcraft, Ind. Tribes, III, 138, 1853.

Naahmao (*Nä-ah-mä'-o,* 'turkey'). A clan of the Mahican.—Morgan, Anc. Soc., 174, 1877.

Naai ('monocline'). A Navaho clan.
Naá'í.—Matthews in Jour. Am. Folk-lore, III, 104, 1890. Naá'iȼine.—Ibid. (ȼine = 'people'). Naa'íȼine'.—Matthews, Navaho Legends, 30, 1897.

Naaik (*N'a'iɛk,* or *N'ē'iɛk,* 'the bearberry'). A village of the Nicola band of Ntlakyapamuk near Nicola r., 39 m. above Spences Bridge, Brit. Col.; pop. 141 in 1901, the last time the name appears.
Na-ai-ik.—Dawson in Trans. Roy. Soc. Can., sec. II, 44, 1891. N'a'iɛk.—Teit in Mem. Am. Mus. Nat. Hist., II, 174, 1900. N'ē'iɛk.—Ibid. Ni-ack.—Can. Ind. Aff. 1884, 189, 1885.

Naaish (*Na-aic'*). A Yaquina village on the s. side of the mouth of Yaquina r., Oreg.—Dorsey in Jour. Am. Folk-lore, III, 229, 1890.

Naalgus-hadai (*Naᵋa'lgᴀs xā'da-i,* 'darkhouse people'). A subdivision of the Yadus, a family of the Eagle clan of the Haida.—Swanton, Cont. Haida, 276, 1905.

Naalye (*Na-al-ye*). A division of the Skoton, living, according to the treaty of Nov. 18, 1854, on Rogue r., Oreg.—Compend. Ind. Treaties, 23, 1873.

Naansi. An extinct tribe, probably Caddoan, said by Douay to be numerous in 1687. They were allied with the Haqui and Nabiri in a war against the Kadohadacho and the Hainai at the time La Salle's party were traveling toward the Mississippi after their leader's death.
Naansi.—Douay in Shea, Discov. Miss. Val., 217, 1852. Nansi.—Hennepin, New Discov., II, 41, 1698.

Naapope. See *Nahpope*.

Naas-Glee. Given as a Chimmesyan village at the headwaters of Skeena r., w. Brit. Col.—Downie in Jour. Roy. Geog. Soc., XXXI, 253, 1861.

Naasumetunne ('people dwelling on or near the Naasu'). A clan or band, probably Yakonan, on a small stream called Naasu by the Naltunnetunne, s. of Salmon r. and N. of the mouth of Siletz r., Oreg.
Naaskaak.—Scouler (1846) in Jour. Ethnol. Soc. Lond., I, 233, 1848 (probably identical). Na'-ä-sû me'ȝûnně.—Dorsey in Jour. Am. Folk-lore, III, 231, 1890 (Naltunnetunne name). Naaŭsi.—McKenney and Hall, Ind. Tribes, III, 81, 1854.

Nabatutuei. (*Nabat'hü'-tü'ei,* 'white village'). A traditional pueblo of the Tigua of Isleta, N. Mex.
Nabat'hü'-tü'ei.—Gatschet, Mythic Tale of Isleta, 210, 1891. Nah-bah-tóo-too-ee.—Lummis, Man who Married the Moon, 12, 1894. White Pueblo.—Gatschet, op. cit., 214.

Nabedache (*Nä'-bai-dä'-che,* said to be a fruit resembling the blackberry. Gatschet says the archaic name of the tribe was *Nawadishe*, from *witish,* 'salt'; Joutel (Margry, Déc., III, 390, 1878) corroborates this by saying that *Naoudiche* means 'salt', and that the village bearing this name was so called because of the salt supply near by). One of the 12 or more tribes of the Hasinai, or southern Caddo, confederacy. They spoke the common language of the group. Their main village stood for a century or more 3 or 4 leagues w. of Neches r. and near Arroyo San Pedro, at a site close to the old San Antonio road, which became known as San Pedro. This name clung to the place throughout the 18th century, and seems still to cling to it, since San Pedro cr. and the village of San Pedro, in Houston co., Tex., are in the same general vicinity as old San Pedro. In 1687 a well-beaten path led past this village to the Hasinai hunting grounds beyond the Brazos (Joutel in Margry, Déc., III, 325, 326, 332, 1878). It perhaps became a part of the later San Antonio road.

The Nouadiche mentioned by Bienville in 1700 (Margry, Déc., IV, 441, 1881) and the Amediche mentioned by La Harpe in 1719 (ibid., VI, 262, 1886) are clearly the Nabedache of San Pedro. Joutel (ibid., III, 388, 1878) tells us that the Naodiche village, which he passed through some 15 leagues N. E. of San

Pedro, was allied to the latter, and it seems probable that it belonged to the same tribe. The Naouydiche mentioned by La Harpe in 1719, however, are not so easily identified with the Nabedache, since he associates them with the Tonkawa, calls them a wandering tribe which until La Salle's coming had been at war with the Kadohadacho, and on the same page mentions the Amediche apparently as a distinct tribe (Margry, Déc., vi, 262, 277, 1886). Yet the facts that the "great chief" of the Naouydiches, of whom La Harpe writes, spoke the language of the Nassonites, i. e., Caddoan, and that the Nouadiche of Bienville's account were the Nabedache, make it probable that those of La Harpe's account were the same people. Concerning the Nabedache of San Pedro, always in historic times the chief village of the tribe, the information is relatively full and satisfactory. They are the first Texas tribe of which there is a definite account, and because of their location on the western frontier of the Hasinai group and on the highway from Mexico to Louisiana they are frequently mentioned during the 18th century. La Salle passed through this village in 1686 on his way to the southern Nasoni, and by "the great Coenis village" of Douay's account of this expedition is meant specifically the Nabedache village w. of Neches r. and the Neche village just on the other side (Douay in French, Hist. Coll. La., iv, 204–205, 1852). Joutel's description of the Cenis (Hasinai), as distinguished from the southern Nasoni and the Kadohadacho, is based on his sojourn at the Nabedache and Neche villages (Margry, Déc., iii, 339–356, 1878); likewise Jesus María's invaluable account of the Hasinai was written at his mission near the Nabedache village (Francisco de Jesus María, MS. Relación, Aug. 15, 1691).

The political, social, and economic organization, as well as the general exterior relations of this tribe, were much the same as those of the confederate tribes, and are described under *Neche* (q. v.). Joutel, in 1687, informs us that from the western edge of the Nabedache village to the chief's house it was a "large league" (Margry, Déc., iii, 341, 1878). The houses on the way were grouped into "hamlets" of from 7 to 15, and surrounded by fields. Similar "hamlets" were scattered all the way to the Neches. In the middle of the settlement was a large assembly house, or town house (ibid., 343). Father Damian Massanet (Tex. Hist. Assn. Quar., ii, 303, 1899) thus describes the caddi's or chief's house as he saw it in 1690: "We came to the governor's house, where we found a number of Indians— men, women, and children. . . The house is built of stakes thatched over with grass; it is about 20 varas high, is round, and has no windows, daylight entering through the door only; this door is like a room door such as we have here [in Mexico]. In the middle of the house is the fire, which is never extinguished by day or by night, and over the door on the inner side there is a little mound of pebbles very prettily arranged. Ranged around one-half of the house, inside, are 10 beds, which consist of a rug made of reeds, laid on 4 forked sticks. Over the rug they spread buffalo skins, on which they sleep. At the head and foot of the bed is attached another carpet, forming a sort of arch, which, lined with a very brilliantly colored piece of reed matting, makes what bears some resemblance to a very pretty alcove. In the other half of the house, where there are no beds, there are some shelves about 2 varas high, and on them are ranged large round baskets made of reeds (in which they keep their corn, nuts, acorns, beans, etc.), a row of very large earthen pots like our earthen jars, . . . and 6 wooden mortars for pounding corn in rainy weather (for when it is fair they grind it in the courtyard)." Besides what is learned of Hasinai foods in general we are told by Solís, who visited San Pedro in 1768, that the Nabedache used a root called *tuqui*, which was somewhat like the Cuban cassava. They ground it in mortars and ate it with bear's fat, of which they were particularly fond. Solís also tells us that resident there at this time was an Indian woman of great authority, named *Sanate Adiva*, meaning 'great woman', or 'chief woman'; that she lived in a house of many rooms; that the other tribes brought her presents, and that she had 5 husbands and many servants (Diario, Mem. de Nueva España, xxvii, 280, 281, MS.).

Though the Nabedache were a peaceable people, they had many enemies, and in war they were high-spirited and cruel. In 1687 they and the Neche, aided by some of Joutel's party, made a successful campaign against the "Canohatinno." On the return one female captive was scalped alive and sent back to her people with a challenge (Joutel in Margry, Déc., iii, 377, 1878), while another was tortured to death by the women (ibid., 378). La Harpe reported that in 1714 the Nabedache (Amediches) and other Hasinai tribes were at war with the lower Natchitoch (ibid., vi, 193, 1886). In 1715 a party of Hasinai, including Nabedache, joined St. Denis in an expedition to Mexico. On the way a fierce battle was fought near San Marcos r. (apparently the Colorado) with 200 coast Indians, "always their chief enemies" (San Denis, Declaración, 1715, Mem. de Nueva España, xxvii, 124, MS.). Wars with the Apache were frequent. In 1719 Du Rivage met on Red r. a party of Naouydiches and other tribes who had just won a victory over this enemy (Margry, Déc., vi, 277, 1886). Shortly after this, La Harpe was joined near the Arkansas by the Naouydiche "great chief" and 40 warriors (ibid., 286). We are told that the Nabedache, with other Hasinai, aided the French in 1730 in their war with the Natchez (Mezières in Mem. de Nueva España, xxviii, 229). Early in the 18th century the Nabedache seem generally to have been hostile to the Tonkawan tribes; but later, hatred for the Apache made them frequently allies, and we now hear of the Tonkawans selling Apache captives to the Nabedache. The possession at San Pedro in 1735 of some captive Apache women secured in this way threatened to cause war between the Spaniards and the Apache. The Spaniards, to avoid trouble, ransomed the women and sent them home (Gov. Barrios y Juaregui to the Viceroy, Apr. 17, 1753, MS. Archivo General, Historia, 299). In 1791, after fierce warfare between the Lipan and the combined northern Indians—the Wichita, Hasinai, and Tonkawa—the Apache endeavored to secure the aid of the Hasinai against the Tonkawa, but Gil Ybarbo, Spanish commander at Nacogdoches, prevented it (Ybarbo to the Governor, Apr. 26, 1791, Béxar Archives, Nacogdoches, 1758–93, MS.). Common hostility toward the Apache frequently made the Nabedache and the Comanche friends, but this friendship was unstable. The military relations of the Nabedache in the 19th century have not yet been investigated, but it is known that hostility to the Apache continued well into that period.

In May, 1690, Massanet and Capt. Domingo Ramón founded the first Texas mission (San Francisco de los Texas) at the Nabedache village, and a few months later the second (Santísima Nombre de María) was planted near by (Jesus María, Relación, 1691). On May 25, De León delivered to the Nabedache *caddi* a baston and a cross, and conferred on him the title of "governor of all his pueblos" (De León, Derrotero, 1690). This was done, as Jesus María clearly shows, under the mistaken notion that the Nabedache was the head tribe of the confederacy, and its *caddi* the head chief. These distinctions belonged, however, to the Hainai tribe and the great *chenesi* resident there (ibid., 18). This mistake, it is believed, caused some political disturbance in the confederacy. In 1690–91 an epidemic visited the tribe in common with its neighbors (Jesus María, Relación,

1691). Trouble, fomented by medicine-men and soldiers, soon arose between the missionaries and the Indians. In 1692 the chief, with most of his people, withdrew from the mission to the distant "fields," and refused to return (Massanet, MS., 1692). In 1693 the mission was abandoned (Clark in Tex. Hist. Assn. Quar., v, 200–201, 1902), and when restored in 1716 it was placed at the Neche village on the other side of the river. In 1727 Rivera (Diario, leg. 2093, 1736) reported that San Pedro was then occupied by the Neche, though formerly by the Nabedache. That the Neche had moved to San Pedro is perhaps true; but it seems improbable that the Nabedache had left the place, for long afterward the inhabitants of it continued to be called Nabedache (De Soto Bermudez docs., 1753, MS. Archivo General, Historia, 299; Mezières, Cartas, 1779). When Solís visited the Nabedache in 1768 their customs were still about as first described, except that they had nearly discarded the bow for the firelock, and were very inebriate, due, Solís claimed, to French liquor. In the middle of the 18th century French influence over the Hasinai greatly increased, and Spanish influence declined. In 1753 the Nabedache took part in a gathering of the tribes at the Nadote (Nadaco?) village, in which, it was reported, the Indians proposed killing all the Spaniards in eastern Texas; but St. Denis, of Natchitoches, prevented the attempt (Fr. Calahorra y Sanz, Feb. 23, 1753, MS. Archivo General, Historia, 299). This situation led to a plan, which failed, to have a garrison posted at San Pedro (Barrios y Juaregui to the Viceroy, ibid.). In 1778 or 1779 an epidemic reduced the population, and Mezières, writing from "San Pedro Nevadachos," situated apparently just where Joutel had found it, reported the number of warriors at somewhat more than 160 (Carta, Aug. 26, 1779, Mem. de Nueva España, xxviii, 241). In 1805 Sibley gave the number at 80 men; but about 1809 Davenport, who was at Nacogdoches, gave it as 100 (Report to Manuel Salcedo, copy dated Apr. 24, 1809, in Archivo General, Provincias Internas, 201). Sibley's and Davenport's reports and Austin's map of 1829 all indicate that the tribe had moved up Neches r. after 1779 (original Austin map, in Secretaría de Fomento, Mexico). From a letter in the Béxar Archives it appears that this migration may have occurred before 1784 (Neve to Cabello, Béxar Archives, Province of Texas, 1781–84). In the 19th century the Nabedache shared the fate of the other tribes of the Caddo and Hasinai confed-

eracies, and the survivors are now on the (allotted) Wichita res. in Oklahoma, but are not separately enumerated. (H. E. B.)
Amediche.—La Harpe (1719) in Margry, Déc., III, 194, 1878. **Amedichez.**—Ibid., VI, 266, 1886. **Anabaidaitcho.**—Gatschet, Creek Migr. Leg., I, 43, 1884. **Nabadaches.**—Sibley, Hist. Sketches, 67, 1806. **Nabadachies.**—Pénicaut (1701) in French, Hist. Coll. La., n. s., I, 73, 1869. **Nabádatsu.**—Gatschet, op. cit., 43. **Nabaducho.**—Latham in Trans. Philol. Soc. Lond., 104, 1856. **Nabaduchoe.**—Burnet (1847) in Schoolcraft, Ind. Tribes, I, 239, 1851. **Nabaidatcho.**—Gatschet, Caddo and Yatassi MS., B. A. E., 77. **Na-ba′-i-da′-tŭ.**—J. O. Dorsey, inf'n, 1881 (own name). **Nabato.**—Tex. State Archives, Census, Sept. 16, 1790. **Nabaydacho.**—Jesus María, Relación, MS., 1691. **Nabedaches.**—Sibley, Hist. Sketches, 71, 1806. **Nabedoches.**—Brackenridge, Views of La., 87, 1815. **Nabeidacho.**—Hidalgo, letter, Oct. 6, 1716, MS. in Archivo Gen. **Nabeidátcho.**—Gatschet, Caddo and Yatassi MS., B. A. E., 42. **Nabeidtacho.**—Representación (1716) in Mem. de Nueva España, XXVIII, 163, MS. **Nabidachos.**—Rivera, Diario, leg. 2093, 1736. **Nadatcho.**—Delisle (1687) in Margry, Déc., III, 409, 1878 (identical?). **Nadeches.**—Neill, Hist. Minn., 173, 1858. **Nadeicha.**—Delisle (1687) in Margry, Déc., III, 409, 1878. **Nahodiche.**—La Harpe (1719) in French, Hist. Coll. La., III, 72, 1851. **Nahordikhe.**—Joutel (1687), ibid., I, 163, 1846. **Nahoudikhé.**—Shea, note in Charlevoix, New France, IV, 108, 1870. **Nahudiques.**—Barcia, Ensayo, 278, 1723. **Naodiché.**—Tonti (1690) in French, Hist. Coll. La., I, 71, 1846. **Naonediche.**—De la Tour, map Amérique Septentrionale, 1779. **Naouadiche.**—Tonti (1690) in French, Hist. Coll. La., I, 74, 1846. **Naoudiché.**—Ibid., 75. **Naoudishes.**—Martin, Hist. La., I, 220, 1827. **Naouediches.**—Anville, map N. A., 1752. **Naouidiche.**—Joutel (1687) in Margry, Déc., III, 394, 1888. **Naouydiches.**—La Harpe (1719), ibid., VI, 262, 1886. **Naovediché.**—Tonti (1690) in French, Hist. Coll. La., I, 73, 1846. **Navadacho.**—Bull. Soc. Geogr. Mex., 267, 1870. **Navedachos.**—Morfi quoted by Shea in Charlevoix, New France, IV, 80, 1870. **Navenacho.**—Linarès (1716) in Margry, Déc., VI, 217, 1886. **Navidacho.**—Bull. Soc. Geogr. Mex., 504, 1886. **Nawadíshe.**—Gatschet, Caddo and Yatassi MS., B. A. E., 81 (archaic name, fr. *witish*, 'salt'). **Nebadache.**—Brown, West. Gaz., 214, 1817. **Nebedache.**—Ibid., 215. **Nevachos.**—San Denis (1715) in Mem. de Nueva España, XXVII, 123, MS. **Nevadizoes.**—Mezières (1778) in Bancroft, No. Mex.States, I, 661, 1886. **Noadiches.**—Barcia, Ensayo, 283, 1723. **Nouadiche.**—Bienville (1700) in Margry, Déc., IV, 441, 1880. **Nouidiches.**—De l'Isle, map Amér., 1700. **Novadiches.**—Barcia, Ensayo, 288, 1723. **Ouadiches.**—McKenney and Hall, Ind. Tribes, III, 81, 1854. **Ouidiches.**—Douay (1687) in Shea, Discov. Miss. Val., 218, 1852. **Ouïdiches.**—Hennepin, New Discov., II, 43, 1698. **Yneci.**—Jesus María, Relación, 1691, MS.

Nabesnatana. A division of the Tenankutchin dwelling on the Nabesna branch of Tanana r., Alaska, and having the village of Khiltat at its mouth.—Allen, Rep. Alaska, 79, 1887.

Nabeyxa. A former tribe of Texas, mentioned as being N. E. of the Nabedache by Francisco de Jesus María, a missionary among the latter tribe, in his MS. relation of August, 1691. He included it in his list of Texias ('allies'). Inasmuch as in the same list he mentions the Naviti (apparently the Nabiri), the Nabeyxa must have been supposed by him to be a different tribe. It was probably Caddoan. (H. E. B.)

Nabiri. An extinct village or tribe of Texas, possibly Caddoan, mentioned by Douay in 1687 as populous and as allied with the Haqui and Naansi in a war

against the Kadohadacho and the Hainai. According to De l'Isle's map of 1707 the people then lived N. of Washita r. in s. Arkansas. See Douay in Shea, Discov. Miss. Val., 2d ed, 221, 1903.
Nabari.—McKenney and Hall, Ind. Tribes, III, 81, 1854. **Nabiri.**—Hennepin, New Discov., II, 41, 1698. **Nabites.**—Baudry des Lozières, Voy. à la Louisiane, 243, 1802 (probably identical). **Nabiti.**—De l'Isle, map (1701) in Winsor, Hist. Am., II, 294, 1886. **Nahari.**—Coxe, Carolana, map, 1741. **Nahiri.**—Shea in Charlevoix, New France, IV, 108, note, 1870. **Naviti.**—Francisco de Jesus María, Relación, 1691, MS. (apparently identical).

Nabisippi. A former Montagnais station on the N. shore of the Gulf of St Lawrence, opposite Anticosti id., Quebec.
Nabisippi.—Stearns, Labrador, 269, 1884. **Napissipi.**—Hind, Lab. Penin., II, 180, 1863.

Nabobish. (*Nŭbobish*, 'poor soup.') A Chippewa village, named from a chief, that formerly stood at the mouth of Saginaw r., Mich. The reservation was sold in 1837.
Nababish.—Detroit treaty (1837) in U. S. Ind. Treaties, 245, 1873. **Nabobask.**—Saginaw treaty (1820), ibid., 141, 1837. **Na-bo-bish.**—Detroit treaty (1837), ibid., 249, 1873.

Nabogame (from *Navógeri*, 'where nopals [*navó*] grow.'—Lumholtz). A Tepehuane pueblo in the district of Mina, 17 m. N. of Guadalupe y Calvo, in the s. w. corner of Chihuahua, Mexico, about lat. 26° 20′.
Nabogame.—Orozco y Berra, Geog., 324, 1864. **Navogame.**—Ibid., 322. **Navógeri.**—Lumholtz, Unknown Mex., I, 423, 1902 (Tepehuane name).

Nabowu (named from an unknown plant). A clan of the Chua (Rattlesnake) phratry of the Hopi.
Nabovû wiñwû.—Fewkes in 19th Rep. B. A. E., 582, 1900 (*wiñwû*='clan'). **Na′-bowŭ wuñ-wü.**—Fewkes in Am. Anthrop., VII, 402, 1894.

Nabukak. A Yuit Eskimo village of 48 houses and about 275 people on East cape, N. E. Siberia.
Nabu′qak.—Bogoras, Chukchee, 30, 1904. **Nə′-caklit.**—Ibid., 20 (Chukchee name of people). **Nə′ekan.**—Ibid. (Chukchee name of the village). **Pe′ekit.**—Ibid. (Chukchee derisive name of people.)

Nacachau. One of the 9 tribes mentioned in a manuscript relation by Francisco de Jesus María, in 1691, as constituting the Hasinai confederacy in Texas. They lived just N. of the Neche tribe and on the E. side of Neches r. In 1716 San Francisco de los Texas mission was established, according to Ramón, in their village; and, according to one of Ramón's companions, for them, the Neche, the Nabedache, and the Nacono. The mission soon became known as San Francisco de los Neches and the name Nacachau disappears, the tribe being absorbed, probably, by the Neche. (H. E. B.)
Nacachao.—Hidalgo, letter, Oct. 6, 1716, Archivo General. **Nacachas.**—Representación of the missionaries, 1716, Mem. de Nueva España, XXVII, 163, MS. **Nacoches.**—Ramón, Derrotero, 1716, Mem. de Nueva España, XXVII, 157, MS.

Nacameri ('bat dwelling.'—Och). A former pueblo of the Pima and the seat of a Spanish mission founded in 1638;

situated on the E. bank of Rio Horcasitas, Sonora, Mexico. Pop. 362 in 1678, 62 in 1730.

Nacamere.—Kino, map (1702) in Stöcklein, Neue Welt-Bott, 74, 1726. Rosario Nacameri.—Rivera (1730) quoted by Bancroft, No. Mex. States, 513, 1884. Santa María Nacameri.—Zapata (1678), ibid., 245.

Nacaniche. Possibly a division of the Nabedache, a Caddo tribe with whom they were closely affiliated, although they were not always at peace with the tribes composing the confederacy. They first became known to the French about 1690, and according to La Harpe their villages in 1719 were N. of the Hainai. During the disturbances between the Spaniards and French in the 18th century the Nacaniche seem to have abandoned their more northerly villages and, about 1760, to have concentrated on Trinity r., near the road leading to New Mexico. The tribe was included in the Texas census of 1790 as among those which were under the jurisdiction of Nacogdoches. The Nacaniche were exposed to the same adverse influences that destroyed so large a part of their kindred. They clung to the Nabedache during the trying experiences of the first half of the 19th century, and if any survive they are with the Caddo (q. v.) on the Wichita res., Okla. A stream in E. Nacogdoches co., Texas, preserves their name.   (A. C. F.)

Nacaniche.—Census of 1790 in Tex. State Archives. Nicondiché.—Tonti (1690) in French, Hist. Coll. La., I, 71, 1846.

Nacau. A former tribe of Texas, closely associated with the Nacogdoche. They are mentioned in 1691 by Francisco de Jesus María in his manuscript list of Texias ('allies') as N. E. of his mission among the Nabedache. San Denis, in 1715, gave the Nacao, apparently the same, as one of the Hasinai or Texas tribes (Declaración, MS., 1715, in Mem. de Nueva España, XXVII, 123). In 1716 Nuestra Señora de Guadalupe mission was founded for this tribe and the Nacogdoche (Francisco Hidalgo and Manuel Castellano, letter to Pedro Mesquia, Oct. 6, 1716, MS. Archivo General). This fact, taken with the statement of Jesus María, makes it seem probable that the tribe lived N. of the Nacogdoche. After 1716 the Nacau seem to disappear from history as an independent group; it was perhaps absorbed by the Nacogdoche.   (H. E. B.)

Nacao.—San Denis, 1715, op. cit. Nacau.—Francisco de Jesus María, 1691, MS., op. cit. Nacaxes.—Barrios y Jauregui, 1753, op. cit. (identical?). Nacoho.—Joutel (1687) in Margry, Déc., III, 409, 1878. Nijaos.—Bul. Soc. Geog. Mex., 504, 1869 (identical?). Nocao.—Linares (1716) in Margry, Déc., VI, 217, 1886.

Nacaugna. A Gabrieleño rancheria formerly in Los Angeles co., Cal., at a place later called Carpenter's ranch.

Nacaugna.—Ried quoted by Taylor in Cal. Farmer, Jan. 11, 1861 (cf. Hoffman in Bull. Essex Inst., XVII, 1, 1885). Nicaugna.—Ibid., June 8, 1860.

Nacbuc. A Chumashan village W. of Pueblo de los Canoas (San Buenaventura), Ventura co., Cal., in 1542.

Nacbuc.—Cabrillo, Narr. (1542) in Smith, Colec. Doc. Fla., 181, 1857. Nacbue.—Taylor in Cal. Farmer, Apr. 17, 1863 (misprint).

Nachaquatuck (from Wa′nashque-tuck, 'the ending creek,' because it was the end or boundary of the Eaton's Neck tract.—Tooker). A former Matinecoc village near the present Cold Spring, Suffolk co., Long id., N. Y. The name occurs as early as 1666.

Nachaquatuck.—Thompson, Long Id., I, 501, 1843. Nackaquatok.—Ruttenber, Ind. Geog. Names, 97, 1906.

Nacheninga ('No-heart-of-fear'). The name of at least two prominent Iowa chiefs, commonly called No Heart, both noted for their sterling qualities and highly regarded by both their tribesmen and the whites. Nacheninga the elder

NACHENINGA (AFTER C. B. KING)

died a short time before Catlin's visit to the tribe in 1832, when he was succeeded by his son, who, however, was regarded as subordinate to Mahaskah the younger. The junior Nacheninga has been described as a fine specimen of his race physically, and as "the faithful husband of one wife." His portrait was painted by Catlin in 1832. In behalf of the Iowa he signed the treaty of St Louis, Nov. 23, 1837, and in the same year visited Washington, where his portrait was painted for the War Department by Charles B. King, and is now preserved in the U. S. National Museum (see illustration). Nacheninga was a signer also of the treaty of Great Nemaha agency, Neb., Oct. 19, 1838; the treaty of Washington, May 17, 1854, and that of Great Nemaha agency, Mar. 6, 1861. The name is variously spelled Nachewinga, Nan-chee-ning-a, Nau-che-ning-ga, Non-che-ning-ga, Non-gee-ninga, and Notch-ee-ning-a. Consult Fulton, Red Men of Iowa, 124, 1882; Catlin, North American Indians, II, 1844; Donaldson in National Museum Report for 1885, 1886.

Nachiche ('golden eagle'). A subgens of the Cheghita, the Eagle gens of the Iowa.

Na′tci-tce′.—Dorsey in 15th Rep. B. A. E., 238, 1897. Qra′-qtci.—Ibid.

Nachurituei (*Natchŭ′ri-tü′ei*, 'yellow village'). A traditional pueblo of the Tigua of Isleta, N. Mex.

Na′dshûr′ tü′ei.—Gatschet, Mythic Tale of Isleta, 210, 1891. Nah-choo-rée-too-ee.—Lummis, Man who Married the Moon, 12, 1894. Natchŭ′ri-tü′ei.—Gatschet, op. cit. Yellow Village.—Lummis in St. Nicholas, XVIII, 833, 1891.

Nachvak. An Eskimo missionary station of the Moravians in Labrador, close to C. Chidley.—Duckworth in Proc. Cambridge Philos. Soc., X, 288, 1900.

Nacisi. A small tribe, possibly of Caddoan stock, formerly dwelling in the region of Red r., La. They were first mentioned by Joutel in 1687, at which time they were at enmity with the Cenis (Caddo confederacy). When Bienville and St Denis were exploring Red r. of La., in 1700, they found on that stream a village of the Nacisi consisting of 8 houses. They were still in this neighborhood in 1741, but during the vicissitudes of the 18th century seem to have drifted southward beyond the border of the French province, for in 1790 they are mentioned among the tribes under the jurisdiction of Nacogdoches, in Texas.   (A. C. F.)

Nacachez.—Jefferys, Am. Atlas, map 5, 1776. Nacassa.—Joutel (1687) in Margry, Déc., III, 409, 1878. Nacassé.—La Harpe (ca. 1714) in French, Hist. Coll. La., III, 19, 1851. Nacatches.—Alcedo, Dic. Geog., III, 279, 1788. Nacisi.—Census of 1790 in Texas State Archives. Nagusi.—Coxe, Carolana, map, 1741. Nahacassi.—Joutel, op. cit. Nakasas.—Bienville (1700) in Margry, Déc., IV, 439, 1880.

Nacogdoche (*Na-ko-hodó-tsi*). A tribe of the Hasinai confederacy of Texas. It has been said that their language differed from that of the Hasinai group in general, but there is much evidence to indicate that this is not true. For example, Ramón, who founded missions at the Neche, Hainai, Nasoni, and Nacogdoche villages in 1716, states in his report that "these four missions will comprise from four to five thousand persons of both sexes, all of one idiom" (Representación, July 22, 1716, in Mem. de Nueva España, XXVII, 160, MS.). On the same day the missionaries wrote that the Nacogdoche mission "N. S. de Guadalupe . . . is awaiting people of the same language and customs" as those of the Indians of mission Concepción, i. e., the Hainai (ibid., 163). In 1752, when the governor of Texas was arranging to inspect the villages of the Hainai, Nabedache,

Nacogdoche, Nasoni, and Nadote, Antonio Barrera was appointed interpreter, because he was a person "understanding with all perfection the idiom of these Indians," the implication being that they all spoke a single language (Jacinto de Barrios y Juaregui, Oct. 30, 1752, in Archivo General, Hist., 299, MS.). Mezières said that the Nabedache, Nadaco (Anadarko), Hainai, and Nacogdoche spoke the same language (letter to Croix, Feb. 20, 1778, Mem. de Nueva España, XXVIII, 229, MS.). Other similar evidence might be cited.

Their main village at the opening of the 18th century and for a long time thereafter was approximately on the site of the modern city of Nacogdoches, where four Indian mounds existed until recently. This place seems to have been called Nevantin. The Nacogdoche were mentioned apparently by the Gentleman of Elvas in his account of the De Soto expedition; but they were first made definitely known by Jesus María in 1691, who called them the Nazadachotzi, indicated correctly their location, and classified them as one of the nine Aseney (Hasinai) tribes (Relación, 108, MS.). It seems probable that the Nacogdoche are distinct from the Aquodocez, with whom Pénicaut in 1714 said the Assinaïs were at war (Margry, Déc., V, 504, 1883). At this time San Denis found the Nacogdoche, Hainai, Nadaco (Anadarko), and others at war with the lower Natchitoch, but he restored peace among them (La Harpe in Margry, Déc., VI, 193, 1886; see also letter of Macartij, Nov. 17, 1763, Nacogdoches Archives, MS.). Espinosa tells us that the Nasoni, whose main village was some 25 m. to the N., were especially closely allied with the Nacogdoche, and came to their village for some of their principal religious observances (Chrónica Apostólica, I, 425, 1746).

In July, 1716, the Franciscans of the college at Zacatecas established their first Texas mission at the main Nacogdoche village for this tribe and the Nacao. This mission became the headquarters of the president, Fray Antonio Margil de Jesus (Espinosa, Diario, entries for July 5–8, MS., Archivo General). In 1719 the mission, like all the others of E. Texas, was abandoned through fear of a French attack, but was reestablished in 1721 on the same site (Peña, Diario, Mem. de Nueva España, XXVIII, 44, MS.). The mission continued to exist long after three of its neighbors had been removed; but it had very little success, and in 1773 it was abandoned. The Spanish settlers, who were removed at this time from Adaes, and at whose head was Antonio Gil Ybarbo, were allowed to settle on the Trinity, founding in 1774 a place which they called Pilar de Bucareli. Early in 1779 they migrated, without authority, to the site of the Nacogdoches mission. The modern city of Nacogdoches dates from this time.

The Nacogdoche were nominally within the Spanish jurisdiction, but the French early gained their affection through the unlicensed trade which they conducted with the Indians. The French supplied guns, ammunition, knives, cloth, vermilion, and knickknacks, in return for horses, skins, bear's fat in great quantities, corn, beans, and Apache captives. This trade, particularly that in firearms, was opposed by the Spanish officials, and as a result there were frequent disputes on the frontier, the Indians sometimes taking one side and sometimes the other. In 1733, for example, two Nacogdoche chiefs reported at Adaes that the French had offered them a large reward if they would destroy the Spanish presidio of Adaes (Expediente sobre la Campaña, etc., 1739, Archivo General, Provincias Internas, XXXII, MS.). The charge was denied, of course, by the French. Again, in August, 1750, it was said that the Nacogdoche chief, Chacaiauchia, or Sanchez, instigated as he claimed by San Denis of Natchitoches, went to the Nacogdoches mission, threatened the life of the missionary, Father Calahorra y Sanz, and ordered him to depart with all the Spaniards (Testimonio de Autos de Pesquiza sobre Comercio Ylicito, 1751, Béxar Archives, Adaes, 1739–55, MS.). On the other hand, when in 1752 a gathering of tribes was held at the Nadote village to discuss a plan for attacking all the Spanish establishments, the Nacogdoche chief, apparently Chacaiauchia, and San Denis both appear in the light of defenders of the Spaniards (Testimony of Calahorra y Sanz in De Soto Bermudez, Report of Investigation, Archivo General, Hist., 299, MS.). Chacaiauchia, or Sanchez, seems to have retained the chieftaincy a long time, for in 1768 Solís tells of being visited at the mission by Chief Sanchez, a man of large following (Diario in Mem. de Nueva España, XXVII, 282, MS.).

Some data as to the numerical strength of the tribe are extant. In 1721, when Aguayo refounded the mission, he provided clothing for "the chief and all the rest," a total of 390 (Peña, Diario, in Mem. de Nueva España, XXVII, 44, MS.). This may have included some Nacao, and, on the other hand, it may not have included all of the Nacogdoche tribe. It was reported that in 1733 the two Nacogdoche chiefs mentioned above went to Adaes with 60 warriors (Expediente sobre la Campaña, 1739, op. cit.). It is not known whether the warriors were all Nacogdoche or not, but that is the implication. In

1752 De Soto Bermudez inspected the Nacogdoche pueblo and reported that it consisted of 11 "rancherias grandes," containing 52 warriors, besides many youths nearly able to bear arms (Rep. of Investigation, 1752, Archivo General, Hist., 299). Croix's list of 1778 does not include the Nacogdoche, unless they are his Nacogdochitos, a group of 30 families living on the Attoyac (Relación Particular, Archivo General, Prov. Intern., 182). According to a census of 1790, on the authority of Gatschet, the Nacogdoche were reduced to 34 men, 31 women, 27 boys, and 23 girls. Davenport, in 1809, reported the Nacogdochitos as comprising 50 men (Noticia, Archivo General, Prov. Intern., 201, MS.).

By 1752 the Nacogdoche pueblo had been removed some 3 leagues northward (De Soto Bermudez, op. cit.). When this transfer took place is not clear, but Mezières says that they deserted the mission at once (Carta, Aug. 23, 1779, in Mem. de Nueva España, XXVIII, 225, MS.). In 1771 Gov. Barrios reported them as still near the Hainai (Informe, 2, MS.). It seems probable that a considerable part of the Nacogdoche tribe was absorbed in the general population at Nacogdoches after the settlement of the Spaniards in 1779, for census reports thereafter show a large number of Indians and mixed-bloods at that place. After this time the remnant of the tribe seems sometimes to appear as Nacogdochitos. Morfi, about 1781, located this tribe on the Attoyac. In 1809 Davenport, writing from Nacogdoches, did not name the Nacogdoches in the list of surrounding tribes, but placed the Nacogdochitos on the Angelina, 5 leagues N. of Nacogdoches (Noticia, Archivo General, Prov. Intern., 201, MS.). A Spanish map made between 1795 and 1819 shows the "Nacodoches" above where Davenport put the "Nocogdochitos," i. e., on the E. side of the Angelina about halfway between Nacogdoches and Sabine r. (MS. Mapa Geográfica de las Provincias Septentrionales de esta Nueva España).

In habit, ceremony, and social organization the Nacogdoche resembled the other tribes of the Hasinai confederacy.
(H. E. B.)

Nacado-cheets.—Schoolcraft, Ind. Tribes, I, 239, 1851. Nachodoches.—French, Hist. Coll. La., III, 47, 1851. Nacoocodochy.—La Harpe (1716) in Margry, Déc., VI, 193, 1886. Nacocqdosez.—Jallot (ca. 1720) in Margry, ibid., 233. Nacodissy.—Joutel (1687), ibid., III, 410, 1878. Nacodocheets.—Latham in Trans. Philol. Soc. Lond., 104, 1856. Nacodoches.—Rivera, Diario, leg. 2140, 2602, 1736. Nacodochitos.—Bul. Soc. Geogr. Mex., 504, 1869. Nacogdoches.—Pénicaut (1714) in French, Hist. Coll. La., I, 121, 1869. Nacogdochet.—Drake, Bk. Inds., VI, 1848. Nadacogdoches.—Mezières (1778) quoted by Bancroft, No. Mex. States, I, 661, 1886. Nagcodoches.—Tex. State Archives, 1793. Nagodoches.—La Harpe (1718) in Margry, Déc., VI, 243, 1886. Nagogdoches.—Sibley, Hist. Sketches, 67, 1806.

Nakódōtch.—Gatschet. Caddo and Yatassi MS., B. A. E., 65, 1884. **Nakodō'tche.**—Ibid., 42. **Nakóhodótse.**—Dorsey, Caddo MS., B. A. E., 1882. **Nakúdotche.**—Gatschet, Caddo MS., B. A. E., 1884. **Nakúhědōtch.**—Gatschet, Creek Migr. Leg., I, 43, 1884. **Nasahossez.**—De l'Isle, map (*ca.* 1701) in Winsor, Hist. Am., II, 294, 1886. **Naugdoches.**—Yoakum, Hist. Texas, I, map, 1855. **Nazadachotzi.**—Jesus María (1691), Relacion, 108, MS. **Nocodoch.**—Linarès (1716) in Margry, Déc., VI, 217, 1886.

Nacono. One of the tribes of the Hasinai, or southern Caddo, confederacy. In 1691 Francisco de Jesus María (Relación, 108, MS.) located it s. E. of the Neche and Nabedache tribes. In 1721 the Indians of "el Macono," evidently the same, lived 5 leagues from the Neche tribe. In 1716 San Francisco de los Texas mission was founded near the Neche and Nacachau villages to minister to these two tribes and to the Nabedache and Nacono (Hidalgo, letter, Oct. 6, 1716, MS., Archivo General). Espinosa, who was present at the founding of San Joseph de los Nasones misson, said that it was composed of Nasoni and Nacono, but the latter were more likely the Nadaco (Anadarko). In 1721 Aguayo was visited on the Neches r. by 100 Indians from el Macono, who were still regarded as belonging to San Francisco mission. Peña, in his diary of this expedition, makes the interesting statement that "their chief, who is also chief priest to their idols, is blind. It is presumed that after having been chief many years, he put out his eyes, according to a custom of the Indians, in order to become chief priest among them" (Diario, Mem. de Nueva España, XXVIII, 35, MS.). As their name disappears thereafter, unless they were the Nacomones of Rivera's list (1727), they were, apparently, like numerous other Texan tribes, absorbed by their stronger neighbors.   (H. E. B.)

Macono.—Peña, op. cit., 1721. **Nacomones.**—Rivera (1727), Diario, leg. 2602, 1736 (identical?). **Nacono.**—Francisco de Jesus María, 1691, op. cit.

Nacori. A former Opata pueblo and seat of a Spanish mission founded in 1645; situated on Rio Viejo, an E. tributary of the upper Yaqui, lat. 29° 30′, lon. 109°, E. Sonora, Mexico. Pop. 450 in 1678; 281 in 1730. The town has suffered greatly from Apache depredations, the last attack being made in 1883. The pueblo numbered 339 persons in 1900, of whom a few were Yaqui or Pima, the remainder being classed as Spaniards.

Guadalupe Nacori.—Rivera (1730) quoted by Bancroft, No. Mex. States, I, 514, 1884. **Nacori.**—Orozco y Berra, Geog., 343, 1864. **Nácori Grande.**—Davila, Sonora Histórico, 317, 1894. **Sta María Nacori.**—Zapata (1678) quoted by Bancroft, op. cit., 246.

Nacori. A former Eudeve pueblo and seat of a Spanish mission founded in 1629; situated on the headwaters of Rio Matape, lat. 29°, lon. 110°, Sonora, Mexico. Pop. 394 in 1678, and but 25 in 1730. It is now a civilized settlement, known as Nácori Chico, and contained 337 inhabitants in 1900.

Nacar.—Kino, map (1702) in Stöcklein, Neue Welt-Bott, 74, 1726. **Nacori.**—Rivera (1730) quoted by Bancroft, No. Mex. States, I, 513, 1884. **Sta Cruz (Nacori).**—Zapata (1678), ibid., 246.

Nacosari. A former Opata pueblo, situated in N. E. Sonora, Mexico, on Rio Moctezuma, one of the N. tributaries of Yaqui r., lat. 30° 20′, lon. 109° 25′. It is now a civilized settlement and contained 978 inhabitants in 1900.

Nacosuras.—Ribas (1645) quoted by Bandelier in Arch. Inst. Papers, III, 58, 1890 (name applied to the inhabitants). **Real de Nacosari.**—Orozco y Berra, Geog., 343, 1864.

Nacotchtank. A tribe or band, probably of the Conoy, formerly living on the Anacostia branch of the Potomac, about Washington, D. C. Their principal village, of the same name, was near the present Anacostia (a corruption of the name of the tribe), in 1608. Smith seems to make them of Algonquian stock, but Shea says they were probably Iroquoian. The Conestoga were their enemies.

Anacostan.—White, Relatio Itineris (1642), 85, 1874 (form used by the Jesuits). **Nacochtant.**—Bozman, Md., I, 119, 1837. **Nacostines.**—Ibid. **Nacotchtanks.**—Smith (1629), Va., II, 78, repr. 1819. **Naotchtant.**—Simons in Smith, ibid., I, 177. **Necosts.**—Smith, ibid., II, 87. **Nocotchtanke.**—Ibid., I, 118.

Nadamin. A tribe or settlement mentioned by Joutel in 1687 (Margry, Déc., III, 410, 1878) as an ally of the Hasinai (Caddo). They probably lived at that time in N. E. Texas, near Red r.

Naden-hadai (*Nĕ′dAn xā′da-i*, 'Naden river people'). A subdivision of the Koetas, a family of the Raven clan of the Haida. Unlike the rest of the family this subdivision remained on Queen Charlotte ids. and settled on Naden r.—Swanton, Cont. Haida, 272, 1905.

Nadohotzosn ('point of the mountain'). A band of the Chiricahua Apache (Bourke in Jour. Am. Folk-lore, III, 115, 1890), essentially the same as the Natootzuzn of the White Mountain Apache and the Nagosugn of the Pinal Coyoteros.

Nadowa. A name, expressing utter detestation, applied by various Algonquian tribes to a number of their neighboring and most inveterate enemies. Its use was not limited to the tribes of a single linguistic stock, the historical references showing that it was applied in some instances, in a modified form, to Eskimo, Siouan, and Iroquoian peoples. For synonyms see *Eskimo, Dakota, Iroquois, Iowa, Teton,* and *Nottoway.*

The etymology of the term is in doubt. The analysis proposed by Gerard (Am. Anthrop., VI, 319, 326, 1904), namely, 'he goes to seek flesh to eat,' while grammatically permissible, is historically improbable, being too general. In N. United States the original application of the word appears to have been to various small, dark-colored poisonous rattle-snakes, inhabiting the lake and prairie regions, such as the *Crotalophorus tergeminus* (*Sistrurus catenatus*), and possibly to *C. kirtlandi*, the black massasauga. Cuoq gives as the meaning of the term *natowe*, a "kind of large serpent formerly quite common in the neighborhood of Michillimakina, i. e., Mackinac, the flesh of which the Indians ate; the Algonkin and all nations of the Algonquian tongue give this name to the Iroquois and to tribes of the Iroquoian stock." The Menominee (Hoffman) apply the term to the massasauga rattlesnake, and the Chippewa (Tanner) to a "thick, short rattlesnake." In Tanner's list of Ottawa tribal names are found *Nautowaig*, *Naudoways*, 'rattlesnakes,' and *Matchenawtoways*, 'bad Naudoways,' and in a footnote to the word *Anego*, 'ant,' it is stated that these same Naudoway Indians relate a fable of an old man and an old woman to the effect that these two watched an ant-hill until the ants therein became transformed into white men, and the eggs which these ants were carrying in their mouths were transformed into bales of merchandise. But in none of these references are the people so named thereby defined in such manner that without other information they may be recognized by other nomenclature.

The word "Sioux" is itself an abbreviation of the diminutive of this term, namely, *Nadowe-is-iw*, literally 'he is a small massasauga rattlesnake,' the sensegiving part of the word being dropped, but signifying 'enemy,' 'enemies.' This diminutive form, with the qualifying epithet *Mascoutens*, was a name of the Iowa and the Teton. In Virginia the term, which became Anglicized into "Nottoway," was applied to an Iroquoian tribe resident there. In this locality it is probable that the name was applied originally to the rattlesnake common to this eastern region.   (J. N. B. H.)

Naenshya (*Naě′nsx·a*, 'dirty teeth'). The name of two Kwakiutl gentes, one belonging to the Koskimo, the other to the Nakomgilisala.—Boas in Nat. Mus. Rep. 1895, 329, 1897.

Na-gan-nab. See *Nagonub*.

Nageuktormiut ('horn people'). A tribe of Eskimo who summer at the mouth of Coppermine r. and winter on Richardson r., Mackenzie Ter., Canada.
Deer-Horn Esquimaux.—Franklin, Journ. to Polar Sea, II, 178, 1824. **Na-gè-uk-tor-mè-ut.**—Richardson, Arct. Exped., I, 362, 1851. **Naggiuktoρ-méut.**—Petitot in Bib. Ling. et Ethnog. Am., III, xi, 1876. **Naggœ-ook-tor-mœ-oot.**—Richardson in Franklin, Second Exped., 174, 1828. **Nappa-arktok-towock.**—Franklin, Journ. to Polar Sea, II, 178, 1824.

Nagokaydn ('pass in the mountains'). A band of the Pinal Coyoteros at San Carlos agency, Ariz., in 1881.—Bourke in Jour. Am. Folk-lore, III, 112, 1890.

Nagonabe (*Nagŭnabä*). A former Chippewa village in lower Michigan (Smith in Ind. Aff. Rep., 53, 1851). A chief of this name represented a band on "South Monistic" r. in 1835 (Mich. Pion. Coll., XII, 622, 1888). See also *Nagonub*, *Naguonabe*.

Nagonub (*Nigănŭbĭ*, or *Niganŭb*, 'the foremost sitter'). A Chippewa Indian, born about 1815, and first mentioned as attracting the attention of Gen. Lewis Cass by his sprightliness while but a mere lad. So well pleased was Cass that he gave Nagonub a medal and a written token of his precocity. He attained notoriety through his spirited and often fiery oratory, and his unusually courteous manners won for him the declaration that he was the "beau ideal of an Indian chief" (Morse in Wis. Hist. Soc. Coll., III, 349, 1857). Nagonub is said also to have been an especial favorite with the white ladies, whom he greeted with the ease and grace of a courtier. He signed as first chief of the Fond du Lac Chippewa the treaties of La Pointe, Wis., Oct. 4, 1842, and Sept. 30, 1854. His portrait, painted by J. O. Lewis and copied by King in 1827, hung in the Indian Gallery of the Smithsonian building at Washington, but was destroyed by fire in 1865. His name is also written Naa-gar-nep, Na-gan-nab, and Naw-gaw-nub.   (C. T.)

Nagosugn. A band of the Pinal Coyoteros found in 1881 by Bourke (Jour. Am. Folk-lore, III, 112, 1890) at San Carlos agency, Ariz.; correlated with the Natootzuzn of the White Mountain Apache, and with the Nadohotzosn of the Chiricahua.

Naguatex. A town and province w. of the Mississippi, visited by Moscoso, of De Soto's army, in 1542. Located by Lewis (Narr. De Soto, 238, 1907) on the w. side of Washita r., in the present Clark co., Ark. The tribe was evidently Caddoan.
Nagateux.—Harris, Voy. and Trav., I, 810, 1705. **Naguatex.**—Gentl. of Elvas (1557) in French, Hist. Coll. La., II, 196, 1850. **Naguatez.**—Barton, New Views, app., 9, 1798.

Naguchee (*Nagu′tsĭ′*). A former important Cherokee settlement about the junction of Soquee and Sautee rs., in Nacoochee valley, at the head of Chattahoochee r., in Habersham co., Ga. The meaning of the word is lost, and it is doubtful if it be of Cherokee origin. It may have some connection with the name of the Yuchi Indians.—Mooney in 19th Rep. B. A. E., 526, 1900.
Cauchi.—Pardo (ca. 1598) quoted by Mooney, op. cit., 28 (probably identical). **Nacoochee.**—Common map form. **Nae oche.**—Bartram, Travels, 372, 1792. **Nocoocsee.**—Royce in 5th Rep. B. A. E., map, 1887.

Naguonabe ('feather end,' according to Warren, evidently referring to a feather at the end of a row of others). The civil chief of the Mille Lac Chippewa of Minnesota in the first half of the 19th century, and the principal man of the Wolf clan. He was descended from a Chippewa woman and a Dakota chief. In behalf of his tribe he signed the general treaty of Prairie du Chien, Wis., Aug. 19, 1825, and the treaty between the Chippewa and the United States made at Fond du Lac, Wis., Aug. 6, 1826. His name is also written Nauquanabee and Nagwunabee.

Nagus (*Nă′g₄s*, 'town inhabited'). A town of the Hagi-lanas family of the Haida on an inlet on the s. w. coast of Moresby id., Queen Charlotte ids., Brit. Col.—Swanton, Cont. Haida, 277, 1905.

Nagwunabee. See *Naguonabe*.

Nahaego. A Shoshonean division formerly living in Reese r. valley and about Austin in central Nevada. There were several bands, numbering 530 in 1873.
Na-haé-go.—Powell in Ind. Aff. Rep. 1873, 52, 1874. **Reese River Indians.**—Taylor in Cal. Farmer, June 26, 1863. **Tutoi band.**—Ibid. (named from Tutoi or Totóna, their chief).

Nahane ('people of the west.'—A. F. C.). An Athapascan division occupying the region of British Columbia and Yukon Ter. between the Coast range and the Rocky mts., from the N. border of the Sekani, about 57° N., to that of the Kutchin tribes, about 65° N. It comprises the Tahltan and Takutine tribes forming the Tahltan division, the Titshotina and Etagottine tribes forming the Kaska division, and the Esbataottine and Abbatotine (considered by Petitot to be the same tribe), Sazeutina, Ettchaottine, Etagottine, Kraylongottine, Klokegottine, and perhaps Lakuyip and Tsetsaut. They correspond with Petitot's Montagnard group, except that he included also the Sekani. The language of the Nahane however constitutes a dialect by itself, entirely distinct from Sekani, Carrier, or Kutchin. The western divisions have been powerfully influenced by their Tlingit neighbors of Wrangell, and have adopted their clan organization with maternal descent, the potlatch customs of the coast tribes, and many words and expressions of their language. The two principal social divisions or phratries are called Raven and Wolf, and the fact that Sazeutina and Titshotina seem to signify 'Bear people' and 'Grouse people' respectively, leads Morice to suspect that these groups are really phratries or clans. The eastern Nahane have a loose paternal organization like the Sekani and other Athapascan tribes farther E. According to Morice the Nahane have suffered very heavily as a result of white contact. He estimates the entire population at about 1,000. Consult Morice in Trans. Can. Inst., VII, 517–534, 1904. See *Tahltan*. (J. R. S.)
Dènè des Montagnes-Rocheuses.—Petitot, Dict. Dènè Dindjié, xx, 1876. **Kunânâ.**—McKay in 10th

Rep. N. W. Tribes Can., 88, 1895 (Tlingit name). **Montagnais.**—Petitot, Autour du lac des Esclaves, 362, 1891. **Naa″anee.**—Petitot quoted by Dall in Cont. N. A. Ethnol., I, 32, 1877. **Na-ai′.**—Dawson in Geol. Surv. Can. 1887–8, 201B, 1889. **Na′ane.**—Morice, Notes on W. Dénés, 19, 1893. **Na-anéottiné.**—Petitot, MS. vocab., B. A. E., 1865. **Na′an-nè.**—Petitot in Bull. Soc. de Géog. Paris, chart, 1875. **Na″ annès.**—Petitot, Dict. Dènè-Dindjié, xx, 1876. **Nah′ane.**—Morice in Trans. Can. Inst., VII, 517, 1904. **Nahanés.**—Morice in Proc. Can. Inst., 112, 1889. **Nah′-anésténé.**—Morice, letter, 1890. **Nahanies.**—Dunn, Hist. Oregon, 79, 1844. **Nahanis.**—Duflot de Mofras, Explor. de l'Oregon, II, 183, 1844. **Nahan-'nè.**—Petitot, Autour du lac lac des Esclaves, 362, 1891. **Nahannie.**—Hind, Labrador Penin., II, 261, 1863. **Nahaunies.**—Hardisty in Smithson. Rep. 1866, 311, 1872. **Nah-âw′-ny.**—Ross, MS. notes on Tinne, B. A. E. **Naρi-an-ottiné.**—Petitot, MS. vocab., B. A. E., 1865. **Nathannas.**—Mackenzie cited by Morice in Trans. Can. Inst., VII, 517, 1904. **Nehanes.**—Bancroft, Nat. Races, I, map, 1882. **Nehanies.**—Anderson (1858) in Hind, Labrador Penin., II, 260, 1863. **Nehannee.**—Bancroft, Nat. Races, I, 149, 1882. **Nehannes.**—Ibid., 125, 1874. **Nehanni.**—Latham in Trans. Philol. Soc. Lond., 69, 1856. **Nehaunay.**—Ross, Nehaunay MS. vocab., B. A. E. **Neháunees.**—Dall, Alaska, 429, 1870. **Nohannaies.**—Balbi, Atlas Ethnog., 821, 1826. **Nohannies.**—Gallatin in Trans. Am. Antiq. Soc., II, 19, 1836. **Nohannís.**—Prichard, Phys. Hist., V, 377, 1847. **Nòhhané.**—Richardson, Arct. Exped., I, 179, 1851. **Nohhannies.**—Franklin, Journ. Polar Sea, II, 87, 1824. **Rocky Mountain Indian.**—Mackenzie, Voy., 163, 1801.

Nahankhuotane. A part of the Umpqua living on Cow cr., Oreg., and commonly known as Cow Creeks. By treaty of Sept. 19, 1853, they ceded their lands in s. w. Oregon. They were associated with the Tututni and were among those who opposed the uprising in 1856. They were settled on Grande Ronde res., where 23 were still living in 1906.
Ci′-stă-qwût ni′-li t'çat′ ɉûnnĕ.—Dorsey in Jour. Am. Folk-lore, III, 234, 1890 ('people far from Rogue r.': Naltunnetunne name). **Cow Creek band of Indians.**—U. S. Ind. Treaties, 974, 1873. **Cow Creeks.**—Palmer in Ind. Aff. Rep. 1856, 214, 1857. **Cow Creek Umpquahs.**—Ibid., 219. **Nahanχuótäne.**—Gatschet, Umpqua MS. vocab. B. A. E., 1877 (Umpqua name). **Sê′-qwût ɉûnnĕ.**—Dorsey, Coquille MS. vocab., B. A. E., 1884 (Mishikhwutmetunne name.)

Nahapassumkeck. A Massachuset village, in 1616, in the N. part of Plymouth co., Mass., probably on the coast.—Smith (1616) in Mass. Hist. Soc. Coll., 3d s., VI, 108, 1837.

Nahawas-hadai (*Na xawa′s xă′da-i*, 'watery-house people'). A subdivision of the Salendas, a family of the Eagle clan of the Haida. They used to give away so much grease at their feasts that the floor of their house was said to be "muddy" with it, hence the name.—Swanton, Cont. Haida, 276, 1905.

Nahche (*Na-ai-che*, 'mischievous,' 'meddlesome.'—George Wrattan). An Apache warrior, a member of the Chiricahua band. He is the second son of the celebrated Cochise, and as hereditary chief succeeded his elder brother, Tazi, on the death of the latter. His mother was a daughter of the notorious Mangas Coloradas. As a child Nahche was meddlesome and mischievous, hence his name. He was the leading spirit in the many raids that almost desolated the smaller settlements of Arizona and New Mexico and of northern Chihuahua and Sonora between 1881 and 1886, for which Geronimo, a medicine-man and malcontent rather than a warrior, received the chief credit. In the latter year Geronimo's band, so called, of which Nahche was actually the chief, was captured by General Miles and taken as prisoners of war successively to Florida, Alabama, and finally to Ft Sill, Okla., where Nahche still resides, respected by his own people as well as by the whites. He is now (1907) about 49 years of age. In his prime as a warrior he was described as supple and graceful, with long, flexible hands, and a rather handsome face. His present height is 5 ft. 10¼ in. Col. H. L. Scott (inf'n, 1907),

NAHCHE

for four years in charge of the Chiricahua prisoners in Oklahoma, speaks of Nahche as a most forceful and reliable man, faithfully performing the duties assigned to him as a prisoner, whether watched or not. He was proud and self-respecting, and was regarded by the Chiricahua at Ft Sill as their leader. In recent years, however, he has lost his old-time influence as well as some of his trustworthiness (inf'n from Geo. Wrattan, official interpreter, 1907).

Nahelta (*Na-hel-ta*). A subdivision of the Chasta (q. v.) tribe of Oregon.—Sen. Ex. Doc. 48, 34th Cong., 3d sess., 10, 1873.

Nahltushkan ('town on outside of point'). A former Tlingit town on Whitewater bay, w. coast of Admiralty id., Alaska, belonging to the Hutsnuwu

people. Pop. 246 in 1880, but subsequently abandoned for Killisnoo.

Naltū'ck-ān.—Swanton, field notes, B. A. E., 1904. Neltū'schk'-ān.—Krause, Tlinkit Ind., 118, 1885. Soutskon.—Petroff in Tenth Census, Alaska, 32, 1884.

Nahpooitle. The chief village of the Cathlapotle tribe of the Chinookan family at the mouth of Lewis r., Clarke co., Wash.—Lyman in Oreg. Hist. Soc. Quar., I, 322, 1900.

Nahpope (*Nĕpopᵃ,* 'soup'). A prominent warrior of Black Hawk's band of Sauk and Foxes in the Black Hawk war of 1832. According to Whittlesey (Wis. Hist. Coll., I, 71–2, 84, repr. 1903) Black Hawk was opposed to the war, but was overruled by the young men, who were sustained by Nahpope, who manifested intense hatred of the Americans. He was, however, largely influenced by Waupeshek, the so-called Prophet. Little has been recorded regarding his life. It is known that he took an active part in the Black Hawk war, and special mention is made of his command in the battle of Wisconsin heights, on Wisconsin r., near the present Sauk City, Wis. Here Nahpope's band, reenforced by a score of Black Hawk's warriors, made a valiant stand to cover the flight of the main body of his people down the bluffs and across the river, which was accomplished with slight loss. During the night following the battle the Americans were for a time in a panic, caused by the noise in the Indian camp, which proved to have been only the applause of a speech by Nahpope in which he endeavored to arouse the Winnebago to remain with them in the contest. Nahpope continued in the war to its close, was captured and imprisoned with Black Hawk and his son, and finally released with them. While Nahpope was confined at Jefferson Barracks, Catlin painted his portrait. As his name is not appended to any treaty made by the Sauk and Foxes with the United States, the omission may be attributed to his contempt for the Americans. In the summer preceding the Black Hawk war he visited the English authorities at Ft Malden, Ontario, to consult them in regard to the rights of the Indians to their lands. After his release from prison nothing more is heard of him. His name is also written Naapope and Neapope.   (C. T.)

Nahu (*Na'-hü*). The Medicine clan of the Honani (Badger) phratry of the Hopi.—Stephen in 8th Rep. B. A. E., 39, 1891.

Nahuey. A former Chumashan village near Purísima mission, Santa Barbara co., Cal.

Nahajuey.—Taylor in Cal. Farmer, Oct. 18, 1861. Nahuey.—Ibid.

Naich, Naichi. See *Nahche.*

Naideni. A former Opata pueblo in the vicinity of Fronteras, N. E. Sonora,

Mexico. It is probable that the natives of Naideni were identical with the Neideniba mentioned by Mota-Padilla in 1742.

Naideni.—Bandelier in Arch. Inst. Papers, IV, 530, 1892. **Neideniba.**—Mota-Padilla, Hist. de la Conquista, 361, 1742 (referring to the inhabitants). **Neidenivas.**—Ibid.

Naig. A former village, presumably Costanoan, connected with Dolores mission, San Francisco, Cal.—Taylor in Cal. Farmer, Oct. 18, 1861.

Naikun (*Nā-ikún*, 'house-point'). A semi-legendary Haida town that stood near the famous sand-spit at Graham id., Brit. Col., which ·bears its name. Anciently it was occupied by several families, including the Huados, Kunalanas, and Stlenga-lanas, but owing to internal troubles they separated, abandoning the town. Later on the Naikun-stustai settled there, and still later the Kuna-lanas returned. John Work, in 1836–41, assigned to Naikun 5 houses and 122 inhabitants. This must have been the Kuna-lanas town. It has been long abandoned. (J. R. S.)

Naēku'n.—Boas in 12th Rep. N. W. Tribes Can., 23, 1898. **Nai-koon.**—Dawson, Q. Charlotte Ids., 34B, 1880. **Nā-ikún.**—Swanton, Cont. Haida, 280, 1905. **Nē coon.**—Schoolcraft, Ind. Tribes, V, 489, 1855. **Nē-kón hādē.**—Krause, Tlinkit Indianer, 304, 1885.

Naikun-kegawai (*Nā-iku'n qē'gawa-i*, 'those born at Naikun'). An important family of the Raven clan of the Haida. It seems to have been a sort of aristocratic branch of the Huados, receiving its name from the old town at Naikun, or Rose spit, Queen Charlotte ids., whence the family originally came. They are still fairly numerous. After abandoning Naikun they lived a long time at C. Ball with the Huados, and moved with them to the town of Skidegate. (J. R. S.)

Ellzu cathlans-coon-hidery.—Deans, Tales from the Hidery, 15, 1899 (='noble Gahlins-kun people'). **Naē kun k·erauā'i.**—Boas in 5th Rep. N. W. Tribes Can., 26, 1889; 12th Rep., 25, 1898. **Nā-iku'n qē'gaw-i.**—Swanton, Cont. Haida, 270, 1905. **Nēkwun Kīiwē.**—Harrison in Proc. Roy. Soc. Can., sec. II, 125, 1895.

Naila. A former Chumashan village near Purísima mission, Santa Barbara co., Cal.—Taylor in Cal. Farmer, Oct. 18, 1861.

Nain. A former Moravian mission, built in 1757 near the present Bethlehem, Pa., and named from the ancient town in Galilee. It was established for the converted Indians, chiefly Delawares, who wished to live separately from their tribe, and for this purpose land was obtained from the state government. In May, 1763, a new and enlarged chapel was dedicated, the congregation having increased in numbers and prosperity. This condition, however, was of short duration, for before the year had closed the unfriendly Indians commenced their attacks, and soon the congregation was blockaded on all sides. In November of the same year Nain was abandoned, the Indians remov-

ing to Philadelphia in accordance with the order of the governor of Pennsylvania. Consult Loskiel, Hist. Miss. United Brethren, 1794. See *Missions*.

Nain. A Moravian Eskimo mission on the E. coast of Labrador, lat 56° 40', begun in 1771 (Hind, Lab. Penin., II, 199, 1863; Thompson, Moravian Missions, 228, 1886). See *Missions*.

Naique. A former village, presumably Costanoan, connected with Dolores mission, San Francisco, Cal.—Taylor in Cal. Farmer, Oct. 18, 1861.

Nak. A Kuskwogmiut Eskimo village on the N. bank of Kuskokwim r., Alaska.

Nag-mïout.—Zagoskin in Nouv. Ann. Voy., 5th s., XXI, map, 1850.

Nakai ('white stranger,' i. e., Spaniard). A Navaho clan, the members of which are descended from a white woman who had been captured by the Ute from a settlement in the vicinity of Socorro, N. Mex. Cf. *Nakaydi*.

Nakài.—Matthews in Jour. Am. Folk-lore, III, 103, 1890. **Nakaí.**—Matthews, Navaho Legends, 30, 1897. **Nakàiɣine.**—Matthews in Jour. Am. Folk-lore, op. cit. (ɣine='people'). **Nakaídĭne'.**—Matthews, Navaho Legends, op. cit., 30, 146.

Nakaidoklini (? 'freckled Mexican.'—Matthews). An Apache medicine-man, called Babbyduclone, Bardudeclenny, Bobby-dok-linny, Nakaydoklunni, Nockay-Delklinne, etc., by the whites, influential among the White Mountain Indians in 1881, near Camp Apache, Ariz. He taught them a new dance, claiming it would bring dead warriors to life. In an attempt to arrest him, August 30, the Apache scouts with the troops turned upon the soldiers, resulting in a fight in which several were killed on each side, including the medicine-man himself. See Bourke in 9th Rep. B. A. E., 505, 1892; Mooney in 14th Rep. B. A. E., 704, 1896.

Nakalas-hadai (*Na q!ā'las xā'da-i*, 'clay-house people'). A subdivision of the Koetas, a family of the Raven clan of the Haida, living principally in Alaska.—Swanton, Cont. Haida, 272, 1905.

Nakalnas-hadai (*Na-k·'āl nas xā'da-i*, 'empty-house people'). Given by Boas (Fifth Rep. N. W. Tribes Can., 27, 1889) as a subdivision of the Yaku-lanas, a family of the Raven clan of the Haida; but in reality it is only a house-name belonging to that family.

Na k·'al nas :had'ā'i.—Boas, op. cit.

Nakanawan (*Nä'ka'na'wan*). A division of the Caddo.—Mooney in 14th Rep. B. A. E., 1092, 1896.

Nakankoyo (*Nákan kóyo*). A former village of the Maidu at Big Spring, in Big meadows, on the N. fork of Feather r., Plumas co., Cal. The name is sometimes used for the people of the whole valley. (R. B. D.)

Nakankoyo.—Dixon in Bull. Am. Mus. Nat. Hist., XVII, pt. 3, map, 1905. **Nakû.**—Curtin, MS. vocab., B. A. E., 1885 (recorded as a division).

Nakarori ('many holes in the rocks'). A small rancheria of the Tarahumare near Norogachic, Chihuahua, Mexico.—Lumholtz, inf'n, 1894.

Nakasinena ('sagebrush people'). An important division of the Arapaho, ranging about the headwaters of the South Platte in the region of Pike's Peak and northward along the foot of Bighorn mts. and on Powder r., in Colorado and Wyoming. Although not the largest division, they claimed to be the mother people of the Arapaho. They were commonly known to the whites as Northern Arapaho and to the rest of the tribe as Baachinena. See *Arapaho*.   (J. M.)
Ba'achinĕna.—Mooney in 14th Rep. B. A. E., 954, 1896. Bääküune'naⁿ.—Kroeber in Bull. Am. Mus. Nat. Hist., XVIII, 7, 1902 ('blood-soup men': S. Arapaho name). Bääⁿtctïine'na.—Ibid. ('red-willow men'). Na'kasinĕ'na.—Mooney, op. cit. Na-ka-si'-nin.—Hayden, Ethnog. and Philol. Mo. Val., 321, 1862. Nänäbine'naⁿ.—Kroeber, op. cit. ('northern men'). Näⁿk'hääⁿsēine'naⁿ.—Ibid. ('sagebrush men'). Northern Arapaho.—Mooney, op. cit.

Nakatkhaitunne ('people of the village above'). A former Tututni village on the N. side of Rogue r., Oreg.
Na'-kat-qai'-ꝗûnnĕ.—Dorsey in Jour. Am. Folklore, III, 233, 1890 (own name). Na'-kût-qe'ꝗûnnĕ.—Ibid. (Naltunnetunne name.)

Nakaydi (the name refers to the Mexican mode of walking with toes turned out; cf. *Nakai*). A clan among the White Mountain Apache, composed of descendants of Mexican captives and their Apache captors (Bourke in Jour. Am. Folk-lore, III, 114, 1890). They correspond to the Nakai of the Navaho and the Tidendaye of the Chiricahua.

Nakeduts-hadai (*Na q!ĕ'dᴀts xā'da-i*, ('people of the house that went away discouraged'). A subdivision of the Yaku-lanas, a great family of the Raven clan of the Haida; probably the name was taken from that of a house.—Swanton, Cont. Haida, 272, 1905.

Nakeduxo (*Nakĕ'duxo*). A summer village of the Utkiavinmiut Eskimo in Alaska.—Murdoch in 9th Rep. B. A. E., 83, 1892.

Nakhituntunne (*Na-qi'-tún ꝗûn'nĕ*, 'people at the two roads'). A former village of the Mishikhwutmetunne on Coquille r., Oreg.—Dorsey in Jour. Am. Folk-lore, III, 232, 1890.

Nakhochatunne (*Na'-qo-tcá ꝗûnnĕ*). A former village of the Mishikhwutmetunne on Coquille r., Oreg.—Dorsey in Jour. Am. Folk-lore, III, 232, 1890.

Nakhopani ('brown streak, horizontal on the ground'). A Navaho clan which had its origin s. of Zuñi pueblo, N. Mex., near the salt lake called Naqopà by the Navaho, whence the name.
Naḥopáni.—Matthews, Navaho Legends, 30, 1897. Naqopàni.—Matthews in Jour. Am. Folk-lore, III, 103, 1890.

Nakhotodhanyadi (*Naqotodꝗaaⁿyadi*, 'alligator people'). A Biloxi clan.—Dorsey in 15th Rep. B. A. E., 243, 1897.

Nakhpakhpa ('take down leggings'). A band of the Brulé Teton Sioux.
Naḣpaḣpa.—Dorsey in 15th Rep. B. A. E., 218, 1897. Naqpaqpa.—Ibid.

Nakhtskum. A Yurok village on lower Klamath r., between Meta and Shregegon, N. w. Cal.—A. L. Kroeber, inf'n, 1905.

Nakila (*Na-ꭓi'-lă*). Given as a former Takelma village on the s. side of Rogue r., Oreg., about 10 m. above Yaasitun.—Dorsey in Jour. Am. Folk-lore, III, 235, 1890.

Nakkawinininiwak ('men of divers races'). A mixed tribe of Cree and Chippewa on Saskatchewan r., N. W. Ter., Canada.
Nakkawinininiwak.—Belcourt (ca. 1850) in Minn. Hist. Soc. Coll., I, 227, 1872. Nakoukouhirinous.—Bacqueville de la Potherie, Hist. Am., I, 170, 1753.

Naknahula (*Naxnā'xula*, ? 'rising above other tribes'). A gens of the Koeksotenok, a Kwakiutl tribe.—Boas in Rep. Nat. Mus. 1895, 330, 1897.

Nakoaik. A former Chinook town on the s. side of Columbia r., Oreg.
Naqoā'ix.—Boas, inf'n, 1905. Naꭓuaiꭓ.—Gatschet, MS., B. A. E., 1877.

Nakoaktok (*Nā'q'oaqtôq, or Nā'k!wax·daᵋxᵘ*, 'ten-gens tribe'). A Kwakiutl tribe on Seymour inlet, Brit. Col., with the Gyeksem, Kwakokutl, Sisintlae, Tsitsimelekala, and Walas gentes, according to Boas. According to Dawson the winter town of these people in 1885 was in Blunden harbor, to which they had moved from an older town, Kikwistok. Their summer village was named Mapakum, and they had a fishing station called Awuts. Pop. 104 in 1901, 90 in 1906.
Nahooktaws.—Brit. Col. map, 1872. Nah-keoockto.—Boas in Bull. Am. Geog. Soc., 226, 1887. Nah-keuch-to.—Sproat in Can Ind. Aff., 148, 1879. Nah-knock-to.—Can. Ind. Aff. 1883, pt. I, 190, 1884. Nahkwoch-to.—Sproat, op. cit., 145. Nahwahta.—Can. Ind. Aff., pt. II, 166, 1901. Nā'k·oartok·.—Boas in 6th Rep. N. W. Tribes Can., 53, 1890. Nakoktaws.—Brit. Col. map, 1872. Nakwahtoh.—Tolmie and Dawson, Vocabs. Brit. Col., 118B, 1884. Nakwartᵒq.—Boas in Bull. Am. Geog. Soc., 226, 1887. Nā'ᴋ!wax·daᵋxᵘ.—Boas in Mem. Am. Mus. Nat. Hist., V, pt. II, 322, 1902. Nā'-kwok-to.—Dawson in Trans. Roy. Soc. Can., sec. II, 65, 1887. Nā'q'oaqtôq.—Boas in Rep. Nat. Mus. 1895, 329, 1897. Náqoartoq.—Boas in Petermanns Mitt., pt. 5, 130, 1887. Nar-kock-tau.—Kane, Wand. in N. A., app., 1859. Nuk wul tuh.—Tolmie and Dawson, op. cit., 119B.

Nakolkavik. A Kuskwogmiut Eskimo village on the left bank of Kuskokwim r., near the mouth, Alaska. Pop. 193 in 1880.
Nacholchavígamut.—Spurr and Post quoted by Baker, Geog. Dict. Alaska, 1902. Naghaikhlavigamute.—Petroff, Rep. on Alaska, map, 1884. Naghikhlavigamute.—Ibid., 17. Nakolkavik.—Baker, op. cit.

Nakomgilisala (*Naqó'mg·ilisala*, 'always staying in their country'). A Kwakiutl tribe which formerly lived at C. Scott, at the N. end of Vancouver id., but has since moved to Hope id., farther s. This and the Tlatlasikoala together receive the name of Nawiti from the whites. The two tribes numbered 73 in 1897. The Nakomgilisala gentes are Gyeksem and Naenshya.

Nak·o'mgyilisila.—Boas in 6th Rep. N. W. Tribes Can., 53, 1890. **Naqô'mg·ilisala.**—Boas in Rep. Nat. Mus. 1895, 329, 1897. **Naqomqilis.**—Boas in Bull. Am. Geog. Soc., 226, 1887. **Ne-kum'-ke-līs-la.**—Blenkinsop quoted by Dawson in Trans. Roy. Soc. Can., sec. II, 65, 1887. **Nokumktesilla.**—Brit. Col. map, 1872.

Nakons-hadai (*Na qons xā'da-i*, 'great-house people'). A subdivision of the Yadus, a family of the Eagle clan of the Haida, named from one of their houses. The Yadus were a part of the Stustas (q. v.).—Swanton, Cont. Haida, 276, 1905.

Nakoshkeni (*Nakōshχē'ni*, 'place of the dam'). A former Modoc settlement at the junction of Lost r. with Tule lake, Oreg.—Gatschet in Cont. N. A. Ethnol., II, pt. I, xxxii, 1890.

Nakotchokutchin. A Kutchin tribe dwelling on the lower Mackenzie r., N. of the Kawchodinneh, in lat. 68° N., lon. 133° w. Their hunting grounds are E. of the Mackenzie as far as Anderson r., and their chief game is the caribou. In former days they waged intermittent warfare against the Eskimo of Mackenzie r., with whom, however, they have always traded. Their men numbered 50 in 1866.
Bastard.—Dawson in Rep. Geol. Surv. Can. for 1888, 200B, 1889. **Gens de la Grande Riviere.**—Ross, MS. notes on Tinne, B. A. E. **Loucheux.**—Franklin, Journ. Polar Sea, 261, 1824. **Mackenzie's R. Louchioux.**—Ross, MS. notes on Tinne, B. A. E. **Nakotcho-Kuttchin.**—Petitot in Bull. Soc. de Géog. Paris, chart, 1875. **Nakotchρô-ondjig-Kouttchin.**—Petitot, Autour du lac des Esclaves, 361, 1891 (= 'people of the river with high banks'). **Nakotchρô-ondjig-Kuttchin.**—Petitot, Dict. Dènè-Dindjié, xx, 1876. **Na-kutch-oo-un-jeek.**—Gibbs, MS. notes from Ross (= 'half-caste Indians'). **Nä'-kütch-ū'-ŭn-jŭk kū'tchĭn.**—Ross, MS. notes on Tinne, 474, B. A. E.

Nakraztli ('it flowed with arrows of the enemy'). A village of the Nikozliautin at the outlet of Stuart lake, Brit. Col. Pop. 178 in 1902, 192 in 1906.
Na-ḳa-ztli.—Morice in Trans. Can. Inst., 188, 1890. **Na'kraztli.**—Ibid. **Na'kraztti.**—Morice in Trans. Roy. Soc. Can., x, 109, 1892.

Nakuimana (*Ná'kuimana*, 'bear people'). A local band of the (Southern) Cheyenne.   (J. M.)

Nakuntlun. The original village of the Tsilkotin, on Nakuntlun lake at the head of Salmon r., Brit. Col., and once the most populous, but now almost deserted.
Nakoontloon.—Tolmie and Dawson, Vocabs. Brit. Col., 122B, 1884. **Nakunt'lûn.**—Morice in Trans. Roy. Soc. Can., x, 109, 1892. **Tsoolootum.**—Gamsby in Can. Pac. Ry. Rep., 179, 1877.

Nakwutthume (*Na'-χ́ut-t'ḉu'-me*, 'at the grass higher up the stream'). A former village of the Chetco on Chetco r., Oreg., above all their other villages.—Dorsey in Jour. Am. Folk-lore, III, 236, 1890.

Nalekuitk (*Nā'lekuĭtx*). A clan of the Wikeno, a Kwakiutl tribe.—Boas in Rep. Nat. Mus. 1895, 328, 1897.

Nalkitgoniash. A Micmac village or band in 1760, perhaps in Nova Scotia.—Frye (1760) in Mass. Hist. Soc. Coll., 1st s., x, 115, 1809.

Naltunnetunne ('people among the mushrooms'). An Athapascan tribe for-merly living on the coast of Oregon between the Tututni and the Chetco. They were not divided into villages, and had a dialect distinct from that of the Tututni. The survivors are now on Siletz res., Oreg., numbering 77 in 1877, according to Victor (Overland Mo., VII, 347, 1877).
Nal'-te-ne-me' ʒûnně.—Dorsey, Chetco MS. vocab., B. A. E., 1884. **Nal'tené ʒûnně'.**—Dorsey, Tutu MS. vocab., B. A. E., 1884. **Nal'-tûn-ně' ʒûnně'.**—Dorsey in Jour. Am. Folk-lore, III, 236, 1890. **Noltana.**—Newcomb in Ind. Aff. Rep., 162, 1861. **Noltnacnah.**—Ind. Aff. Rep. 1867, 62, 1868. **Nolt-nat-nahs.**—Ind. Aff. Rep., 470, 1865. **Noltonatria.**—Ind. Aff. Rep., 300, 1877. **Nootanana.**—Ind. Aff. Rep. 1863, 505, 1864. **Nult-nort-nas.**—Ind. Aff. Rep., 495, 1865. **Nul-to-nat-na.**—Siletz agency roll, 1884. **Nûltŏnät'-těne.**—Everette, Tutu MS. vocab., B. A. E., 1883 (trans., 'people by the ocean').

Nama (*Nŭmä*, 'sturgeon'). A gens of the Chippewa. See *Nameuilini*.
Nă-má.—Morgan, Anc. Soc., 166, 1877. **Namă.**—Wm. Jones, inf'n, 1906. **Namé.**—Gatschet, Ojibwa MS., B. A. E., 1882. **Numa.**—Warren (1852) in Minn. Hist. Soc. Coll., v, 45, 1885.

Namabin (*Nŭmäbĭn*, 'sucker'). A gens of the Chippewa.
Nah-ma-bin.—Tanner, Narr., 315, 1830 (trans. 'carp'). **Näm-a'-bin.**—Morgan, Anc. Soc., 166, 1877 (trans. 'carp'). **Namäbin.**—Wm. Jones, inf'n, 1906 (sig. 'sucker'). **Numa-bin.**—Warren (1852) in Minn. Hist. Soc. Coll., v, 45, 1885 ('sucker').

Namakagon. A former village of the Munominikasheenhug division of the Chippewa at upper St Croix lake, w. Wisconsin.
Num-a quag-um.—Ramsey in Ind. Aff. Rep., 86, 1850.

Namanu ('beaver'). A subphratry or gens of the Menominee.—Hoffman in 14th Rep. B. A. E., 42, 1896.

Namasket (from *namaus* 'fish', *aki* 'land,' *et* 'at.'—J. N. B. H). A tribe or band formerly living in a village of the same name about the site of Middleboro, Mass. They were subordinate to the Wampanoag. The village was populous when first known, but the Indians rapidly decreased as the white settlements advanced. In 1794 there were still about 40. One family, named Mitchell, still resides (1907) near Middleboro and claim descent from King Philip. A member of this family wears a so-called Indian costume (see New England Mag., 392, Dec. 1905).   (J. M. F. G. S.)
Lamasket.—Hinckley (1685) in Mass. Hist. Soc. Coll., 4th s., v, 133, 1861 (misprint). **Namascet.**—Dee in Smith (1629), Va., II, 227, repr. 1819. **Namaschet.**—Mourt (1622) in Mass. Hist. Soc. Coll., 2d s., IX, 52, 1822. **Namascheucks.**—Mourt (1622) ibid., IX, 52, 1822. **Namasket.**—Dermer (1620) ibid. **Namassachusett.**—Records (1644), ibid., VII, 137, 1818. **Namassakett.**—Bradford (*ca.* 1650), ibid., 4th s., III, 103, 1856. **Namassekett.**—Cotton (1674), ibid., 1st s., I, 200, 1806. **Nemascut.**—Church (1716) quoted by Drake, Ind. Wars, 75, 1825. **Nemasket.**—Drake, Bk. Inds., bk. 3, 9, 1848. **Nummastaquyt.**—Dermer (1619) quoted by Drake, ibid., bk. 2, 20.

Namassingakent. A village of the Powhatan confederacy existing in 1608 on the s. bank of the Potomac in Fairfax co., Va.—Smith (1629), Va., I, map, repr. 1819.

Namatha (*Na-ma-thä'*, 'turtle'). A gens of the Shawnee.—Morgan, Anc. Soc., 168, 1877.

Namaycush. One of the names of the lake trout (*Salmo namaycush*), Mackinaw trout, or great lake trout, called togue in Maine; from *namekus*, which in the Cree dialect of Algonquian signifies 'trout', the Chippewa word being *namegos*. *Namekus* is a diminutive of *namegw*, 'fish'. The word originated in N. W. Canada. See *Togue*.   (A. F. C.)

Nambe (from *Nam-bé-é*, the native name, probably referring to a round hill or a round valley). A Tewa pueblo,

NAMBE MAN (POTSHUNO)

situated about 16 m. N. of Santa Fé, N. Mex., on Nambe r., a small tributary of the Rio Grande. It became the seat of a Franciscan mission early in the 17th century, but was reduced to a visita of Pojoaque in 1782. Like Santa Clara and Sia this pueblo doubtless owes its decline to the constant intertribal execution for supposed evil practices of witchcraft (Bandelier in Arch. Inst. Pap., III, 35, 1890). Pop. 79 in 1890, 100 (est.) in 1904. The Nambé people claim to have once inhabited the now ruined pueblos of Agawano, Kaayu, Keguayo, Kekwaii, Kopiwari, and Tobhipangge. The Nambe clans, so far as known, are Cloud (Owhu), Birch (Nana),

Fire (Pa), Mountain Lion (Qen), Eagle (Tse), Bear (Ke), Tobacco (Sa), Sun (Tan, extinct), Calabash (Po), Ant (Kungyi), Earth (Nang), Grass (Ta). See *Pueblos, Tewa*.   (F. W. H.)

Mambe.—Ward in Ind. Aff. Rep. 1867, 212, 1868. **Mambo.**—Ward, ibid., 1864, 191, 1865. **Na-im-bai.**—

NAMBE GIRL (PABLA TAFOLLA)

Jouvenceau in Cath. Pion., I, no. 9, 12, 1906. **Na-imbe.**—Bandelier in Arch. Inst. Papers, III, 124, 1890. **Na-im-be.**—Ibid., 260 (own name of pueblo). **Na-i-mbi.**—Ibid., IV, 83, 1892 (or Nambé). **Namba.**—Bent (1849) in Cal. Mess. and Corres., 211, 1850. **Nambe.**—MS. *ca.* 1715 quoted by Bandelier in Arch. Inst. Papers, V, 193, 1890. **Nambè.**—D'Anville, map Am. Sept., 1746. **Nambéhun.**—Gatschet, Isleta MS. vocab., B. A. E., 1885 (Isleta name for the people; sing. Nambe-húide).

Nambi.—Cooper in Ind. Aff. Rep., 161, 1870. **Namburuáp.**—Hodge, field notes, B. A. E., 1895 (Isleta name of pueblo). **Nami Te.**—Simpson, Rep. to Sec. War, 2d map, 1850. **Nampè.**—Domenech, Deserts N. Am., I, 443, 1860. **Nomë'ë.**—Hodge, field notes, B. A. E., 1895 (Acoma name of pueblo). **Númi.**—Stephen in 8th Rep. B. A. E., 37, 1891 (Hano name of pueblo). **San Francisco.**—Villa-Señor, Theatro Am., II, 425, 1748 (mission name). **San Francisco de Nambe.**—Ward in Ind. Aff. Rep. 1867, 213, 1868. **San Francisco Nambe.**—Vetancurt (ca. 1693) in Teatro Mex., III, 317, 1871. **St. Francis.**—Shea, Cath. Miss., 80, 1855. **Vampe.**—Pike, Exped., 3d map, 1810.

Nameaug (Mahican: *name-auk*, 'fishing place,' or 'where fish are taken.'—Trumbull). A former village near the site of New London, Conn., in which some of the conquered Pequot were settled in 1647 under the dominion of the Mahican. The last chief died about 1740, but there were still a considerable number of Indians there in 1755.   (J. M.)
Mameag.—Kendall, Trav., I, 292, 1809. **Mameeag.**—Stiles (1762) in Mass. Hist. Soc. Coll., 1st s., x, 101–103, 1809. **Namcet.**—Mason (1659), ibid., 4th s., VII, 423, 1865. **Nameacke.**—Doc. cited by Trumbull, Ind. Names Conn., 34, 1881. **Nameage.**—Mason (1648), ibid., 413. **Nameaug.**—Hoyt, Antiq. Res., 62, 1824. **Nameeag.**—Deed (1651) quoted by Drake, Bk. Inds., bk. 2, 110, 1848. **Nameock.**—Trumbull, Ind. Names Conn., 34, 1881. **Nameooke.**—Hopkins (1646) in Mass. Hist. Soc. Coll., 4th s., VI, 334, 1863. **Nameoke.**—Drake, Bk. Inds., bk. 2, 95, 1848. **Namêug.**—Williams (1647) in Mass. Hist. Soc. Coll., 3d s., IX, 268, 1846. **Nameugg.**—Doc. cited by Trumbull, Ind. Names Conn., 34, 1881. **Nammiog.**—Ibid. **Namyok.**—Ibid. **Tawawag.**—Ibid., 72. **Tawawog.**—Deed of 1654 in Mass. Hist. Soc. Coll., 1st s., x, 101–103, 1809. **Towawog.**—Kendall, Trav., I, 292, 1809.

Namequa. The only daughter of Black Hawk (q. v.), regarded as one of the handsomest of the Sauk maidens of her time. A young Baltimorean of high social standing, being on a visit to Ft Madison, Iowa, became enamored of her and would have made her his wife but for the opposition of his friends. Namequa appears to have been ever faithful to her father's interests and to his memory, and after reaching maturer years, and even after her marriage, was a constant help to her mother, especially during her father's imprisonment and after his death in 1838.   (C. T.)

Nameroughquena. A village of the Powhatan confederacy in 1608, in the present Alexandria co., Va., on the s. bank of the Potomac, opposite Washington, D. C.—Smith (1629), Va., I, map, repr. 1819.

Names and Naming. Among the Indians personal names were given and changed at the critical epochs of life, such as birth, puberty, the first war expedition, some notable feat, elevation to chieftainship, and, finally, retirement from active life was marked by the adoption of the name of one's son. In general, names may be divided into two classes: (1) True names, corresponding to our personal names, and (2) names which answer rather to our titles and honorary appellations. The former define or indicate the social group into which a man is born, whatever honor they entail being due to the accomplishments of ancestors, while the latter mark what the individual has done himself.

There are characteristic tribal differences in names, and where a clan system existed each clan had its own set of names, distinct from those of all other clans, and, in the majority of cases, referring to the totem animal, plant, or object. At the same time there were tribes in which names apparently had nothing to do with totems, and some such names were apt to occur in clans having totemic names. Most Siouan clans and bands had names that were applied in a definite order to the boys and girls born into them. A Mohave child born out of wedlock received some ancient name, not commonly employed in the tribe. Among the interior Salish, where there were no clans, names were usually inherited in both the male and female lines for several generations, though new names were continually introduced that were taken from dreams or noteworthy events. Loskiel records that a Delaware child was often named in accordance with some dream that had come to its father. According to Ross, a father among some of the northern Athapascan tribes lost his name as soon as a male child was born and was henceforth called after the name of his son; a Thlingchadinne changed his name after the birth of each successive child, while an unmarried man was known as the child of his favorite dog. Among the Maidu infants might be named with reference to some incident occurring at the time of birth, but many received no names other than such general appellations as 'child,' 'baby,' or 'boy,' until they were old enough to exhibit some characteristic which suggested something appropriate. The father and mother addressed a boy all his life by his boyhood name. A girl, however, received different successive names at puberty, childbirth, and in old age. The Kiowa, being without clans, received names suggested by some passing incident or to commemorate a warlike exploit of some ancestor. Sometimes, however, they were hereditary, and in any case they were bestowed by the grandparents to the exclusion of the parents. Young men as they grew up usually assumed dream names, in obedience to visions.

The naming of a rich man's child among the coast Salish was accompanied by a great feast and distribution of property, and an invited chief publicly announced the name given. Names originally belonging to the higher class were sometimes bestowed upon young people among the Haida and Tlingit when their relatives had potlatches, and it thus resulted that names individually acquired became in time hereditary and were added to the list of common names owned by the clan.

The second name, or title, was sometimes, as has been said, bestowed on account of some brave or meritorious action. Thus a Pawnee " was permitted to take a new name only after the performance of an act indicative of great ability or strength of character," and it was done during a public ceremonial. Among the Siouan tribes a similar custom seems to have prevailed, but among the Maidu of California entrance into the secret society took its place as a reason for the bestowal of new titles. On the N. W. coast a man adopted one of the potlatch, or sacred, names of his predecessor when he gave the mortuary feast and erected the grave post. At every subsequent potlatch he was at liberty to adopt an additional title, either one used by his predecessor or a new one commemorative of an encounter with a supernatural being or of some success in war or feast-giving. Along with his place in a secret society a Kwakiutl obtained the right to certain sacred names which had been received by the first holder of his position from the spirit patron of the society and were used only during the season of the ceremonial, like the titles employed in the fraternal and other societies of civilized life. The second name among this people also marks individual excellence rather than the attainment of an hereditary position, for the person did not succeed to the office, but had to pass through a long period of training and labor to be accepted. After a man died his name was held in abeyance for a longer or shorter period, and if it were taken from the name of some familiar object, the name of that object often had to be altered, but the taboo period was not longer than would allow the person's successor to collect his property and give the death feast, and a simple phonetic change often satisfied all scruples. Changes of this kind seem to have been carried to greater extremes by some tribes, notably the Kiowa, where, on the death of any member of a family all the others take new names, while all the terms suggesting the name of the dead person are dropped from the language for a period of years. Among the coast Salish a single name was often used by successive chiefs for four or five generations. Among the Iroquois and cognate tribes, according to Hewitt, the official name of a chieftaincy is also the official name of the officer who may for the time being become installed in it, and the name of this chieftaincy is never changed, no matter how many persons

may successively become incumbents of it. Unlike the Indians of most tribes, a Pueblo, although bearing several names, usually retained one name throughout life. In many tribes a curious custom prohibited a man from directly addressing his wife, his mother-in-law, and sometimes his father-in-law, and vice versa.

Names of men and women were usually, though not always, different. When not taken from the totem animal, they were often grandiloquent terms referring to the greatness and wealth of the bearer, or they might commemorate some special triumph of the family, while, as among the Navaho, nicknames referring to a personal characteristic were often used. The first name frequently refers to something which especially impressed the child's mother at the time of its birth. Often names were ironical and had to be interpreted in a manner directly opposite to the apparent sense. A failure to understand this, along with faulty interpretation, has brought about strange, sometimes ludicrous, misconceptions. Thus the name of a Dakota chief, translated 'Young-man-afraid-of-his-horses,' really signifies 'Young man whose very horses are feared." Where the clan system did not flourish, as among the Salish, the name often indicated the object in nature in which a person's guardian spirit was supposed to dwell. Names for houses and canoes went by families and clans like personal names and property in general.

Names could often be loaned, pawned, or even given or thrown away outright; on the other hand, they might be adopted out of revenge without the consent of the owner. The possession of a name was everywhere jealously guarded, and it was considered discourteous or even insulting to address one directly by it. This reticence, on the part of some Indians at least, appears to have been due to the fact that every man, and every thing as well, was supposed to have a real name which so perfectly expressed his inmost nature as to be practically identical with him. This name might long remain unknown to all, even to its owner, but at some critical period in life it was confidentially revealed to him. It was largely on account of this sacred character that an Indian commonly refused to give his proper designation, or, when pressed for an answer, asked someone else to speak it. Among the Maidu it was not customary, in addressing a person, to use the name descriptive of his personal characteristics.

In modern times the problem of satisfactorily naming Indians for purposes of permanent record has been very puzzling owing to their custom of changing names and to the ignorance on the part of persons in authority of native customs and methods of reckoning descent. According to Mooney, Setimkía, 'Bear bearing down (an antagonist),' the honorable war name of a noted Kiowa chief, is mistranslated 'Stumbling Bear.' Tenepiabi, 'Bird coming into sight', has been popularly known as 'Hummingbird' since he was a prisoner in Florida in 1875, probably a mistake for 'Coming bird.' Hajo, a Creek war title signifying 'recklessly brave,' is popularly rendered 'crazy,' as in the case of Chito Hajo, leader of the Creek opposition to allotment, whose name is popularly and officially rendered 'Crazy Snake.' Even when translated correctly an Indian name often conveys an impression to a white man quite the reverse of the Indian connotation. Thus 'Stinking Saddle Blanket' (Takaibodal) might be considered an opprobious epithet, whereas it is an honorary designation, meaning that the bearer of it, a Kiowa, was on the warpath so continuously that he did not have time to take off his saddle blanket. 'Unable-to-buy,' the name of a Haida chief, instead of indicating his poverty, commemorates an occasion when a rival chief did not have enough property to purchase a copper plate he offered for sale.

In recent years the Office of Indian Affairs has made an effort to systematize the names of some of the Indians for the purpose of facilitating land allotments, etc. By circular issued Dec. 1, 1902, the office set forth the following principles governing the recording of Indian names on agency rolls, etc.: (1) The father's name should be the family surname; (2) the Indian name, unless too long and clumsy, should be preferred to a translation; (3) a clumsy name may be arbitrarily shortened (by one familiar with the language) without losing its identity; (4) if the use of a translation seems necessary, or if a translation has come into such general and accepted use that it ought to be retained, that name should be written as one word.

Consult Boas in Rep. Nat. Mus. 1895, 1897; Cook in Ind. Aff. Rep. 1904, 423–427, 1905; Dixon in Bull. Am. Mus. Nat. Hist., XVII, pt. 3, 1905; J. O. Dorsey in 3d Rep. B. A. E., 1884; Fletcher in Am. Anthrop., Jan. 1899; Hill-Tout (1) in Rep. Brit. A. A. S., 1902, (2) in Am. Anthrop., VII, no. 4, 1905; Gatschet, Creek Migr. Leg., I, II, 1884–88; Loskiel, Hist. of Missions of United Brethren, 1794; Mooney, Calendar Hist. Kiowa, 17th Rep. B. A. E., 1898; Riggs, Dakota-Eng. Dict., 1852; Sapir in Am. Anthrop., IX, no. 2, 1907; Speck, ibid.; Teit in Mem. Am. Mus. Nat. Hist., II, no. 4, 1900.   (J. R. S.)

Nameuilini (*Nŭmäwĭnĭnĭ*, 'sturgeon man.'—W. J.). A band living N. w. of L. Superior, between Rainy lake and L. Nipigon, in Algoma, Ontario, about 1760. Chauvignerie says their totem was a sturgeon. They are probably the Nama gens of the Chippewa.

Kinongeouilini.—St Pierre (1753) in Margry, Déc., VI, 644, 1886. **Nakonkirhirinous.**—Dobbs, Hudson Bay, 23, 1744. **Namäwinini.**—Wm. Jones, inf'n, 1906. **Nameanilieu.**—Schoolcraft, Ind. Tribes, III, 556, 1853 (misprint). **Name8ilinis.**—Chauvignerie (1736) in N. Y. Doc. Col. Hist., IX, 1054, 1855. **Namewilinis.**—Doc. of 1736 in Wis. Hist. Soc. Coll., XVII, 246, 1906. **Sturgeon Indians.**—Dobbs, Hudson Bay, 13, 1744.

Namoit. A village of a tribe of the Chinookan family formerly situated on the Columbia side of Sauvies id., Oreg., near its lower end. According to Lane (Ind. Aff. Rep., 161, 1850) the inhabitants in 1850 were associated with the Cathlacumup and Katlaminimim. Nothing more is known of them.   (L. F.)

Mamnit.—Gairdner, after Framboise (1835), in Jour. Geog. Soc. Lond., XI, 255, 1841. **Nah-mooitk.**—Lyman in Oreg. Hist. Soc. Quar., I, 322, 1900. **Namō'itk.**—Boas, inf'n, 1905. **Namowit.**—Ross, Adventures, 106, 1849. **Naw-moo-it.**—Ibid., 236.

Namontack. A trusted Powhatan Indian whom Powhatan gave to Capt. Newport in 1608 in return for the English boy, Thomas Savage, left with the former for the purpose of gaining knowledge of the language, manners, customs, and geography of tidewater Virginia. Namontack was of shrewd and subtle character, and proved of service to the English in preventing attack and in obtaining needed corn (Smith, Works, Arber ed., 128, 1884). He was subsequently sent to England, and on the way back, in 1610, was murdered in the Bermudas by an Indian companion.

Nampa image. A small human figure of baked clay, 1½ in. in height, apparently intended to represent a female. It is so much injured by exposure that the features are entirely destroyed and the hands and feet are missing. It derives its archeological interest from the fact that it is said to have been brought from a depth of 320 ft by an artesian well sand-pump, at Nampa, Idaho, in 1889. According to Emmons, the formations in which the pump was operating are of late Tertiary or early Quaternary age; and the apparent improbability of the occurrence of a well-modeled human figure in deposits of such great antiquity has led to grave doubt as to its authenticity. It is one of those discoveries which, on account of the importance of the problems involved, requires definitive verification. It is interesting to note that the age of this object, supposing it to be authentic, corresponds with that of the incipient man whose bones were recently recovered by Dubois from the late Tertiary or early Quaternary formations of Java, and it follows that the autochthonous American sculptor had produced this "beautifully formed" figure of a woman at a period when the Master of the Universe had succeeded only in blocking out the first rude suggestion of the human form divine in the Old World.

The history of this specimen is given by Wright in Proc. Boston Soc. Nat. Hist., Jan. 1890, and Feb. 1891. Emmons' statement regarding the age of the formations involved is given in the same connection. Its authenticity is questioned by Powell in Pop. Sci. Monthly, July, 1893. (w. h. h.)

Namskaket. A Nauset village on or near Namskaket cr., Barnstable co., Mass. The Indians sold the site in 1644.
Naamskeket.—Freeman (1792) in Mass. Hist. Soc. Coll., 1st s., I, 232, 1806. **Naemschatet.**—Bradford (ca. 1640), ibid., 4th s., III, 873, 1856. **Namskeket.**—Morton (1668) quoted by Drake, Ind. Wars, 276, 1825. **Naumskachett.**—Bradford (ca. 1650) in Mass. Hist. Soc. Coll., 4th s., III, 219, 1856.

Namukatsup. A former Chitimacha village in St Martins parish, La.
Bayou Chène village.—Gatschet in Trans. Anthrop. Soc. Wash., II, 152, 1883. **Namu kátsup.**—Ibid. (námu='village').

Namumpam. See *Wetamoo.*

Nana (also Nanay, Nané). A subordinate chief and warrior of the Chiricahua Apache during their hostilities against the whites in the latter part of the 19th century. He was Victorio's associate until the death of the latter in Mexico in 1880. In July 1881, with 15 warriors who had been with Victorio, Nana crossed the Rio Grande and made his way into New Mexico, where he was joined by 25 Mescaleros. He then made a rapid and bloody raid across the southern part of the territory, falling upon herders and prospectors, murdering them without mercy. The band was driven back to Mexico by the troops in August of the same year. This was probably the last serious raid made by Nana, who was now an old man. Bourke (Apache Campaign, 99, 1886) describes him as having "a strong face, marked with intelligence, courage, and good nature, but with an under stratum of cruelty and vindictiveness. He has received many wounds in his countless fights with the whites, and limps very perceptibly in one leg." Lummis (Land of Poco Tiempo, 178, 1893) speaks of Nana as fond of wearing in each ear a huge gold watch chain.

Nana. The Birch clan of the Tewa pueblo of Nambe, N. Mex.
Nána-tdóa.—Hodge in Am. Anthrop., IX, 352, 1896 (tdóa='people').

Nanabozho. The demiurge of the cosmologic traditions of the Algonquian tribes, known among the various peoples by several unrelated names, based on some marked characteristic or dominant function of this personage. Among these names are Jamum, Kloskap (Gloskap), Manabozho, Messou, Michabo, Mina-bozho, Misabos, Napiw [a], Nenabozho, Wieska, Wisakedjak, and their dialectic variants. The etymologies proposed for these several names are most probably incorrect, wholly or in material parts.

Nanabozho is apparently the impersonation of life, the active quickening power of 'life—of life manifested and embodied in the myriad forms of sentient and physical nature. He is therefore reputed to possess not only the power to live, but also the correlative power of renewing his own life and of quickening and therefore of creating life in others. He impersonates life in an unlimited series of diverse personalities which represent various phases and conditions of life, and the histories of the life and acts of these separate individualities form an entire cycle of traditions and myths which, when compared one with another, are sometimes apparently contradictory and incongruous, relating, as these stories do, to the unrelated objects and subjects in nature. The conception named Nanabozho exercises the diverse functions of many persons, and he likewise suffers their pains and needs. He is this life struggling with the many forms of want, misfortune, and death that come to the bodies and beings of nature.

The true character of the concept embodied in the personality called Nanabozho has been misconceived. Horatio Hale, for example, calls the Chippewa Nanabozho a fantastic deity, declaring him to have no relation to the Iroquois Te'horon'hiawa'k'hon', whereas he is in everything but minor details identical with the Iroquoian conception embodied in the latter personality. Few, if any, of the characteristic acts and functions of the one may not safely and correctly be predicated of the other, and it is a remarkable parallel if the one is not a concept borrowed by the people of one linguistic family from the thought of the other. If independent creations, they agree in so many points that it is more than probable that the one suggested the other. Even the play of popular interpretation and etymologic analysis have made like errors in the events connected with the life history of each. In the Iroquois legend the brother of Te'horon'hiawa'k'hon is reputed to have been embodied in chert or flint, a statement based on a misconception arising from the common origin of some terms denotive of ice on the one hand and of chert on the other. A like error gave rise to the Chippewa name for chert or flint (?*miskwam*), which signifies 'ice-stone,' and the connection between *malsum*, 'wolf,' and *mă'haliç*, 'a flint or chert,' also a name of Chakekenapok, the brother of Nanabozho. The confusion is that the ruler of winter, the ruler clothed in frost, ice, and snow, is identified with chert or flint, in Iroquois too, because of the identity of origin between the terms for crystal or sparkling ice and the smooth glistening surface of chert or flint.

In Potawatomi and cognate tradition Nanabozho is the eldest of male quadruplets, the beloved Chipiapoos being the second, Wabosbo the third, and Chakekenapok the fourth. They were begotten by a great primal being, who had come to earth, and were born of a reputed daughter of the children of men. Nanabozho was the professed and active friend of the human race. The mild and gentle but unfortunate Chipiapoos became the warder of the dead, the ruler of the country of the manes, after this transformation. Wabosso ('Maker of White'), seeing the sunlight, went to the northland, where, assuming the form of a white hare, he is regarded as possessing most potent manito or orenda (q. v.). Lastly, Chakekenapok, named from chert, flint, or firestone (?fire), was the impersonation originally of winter, and in coming into the world ruthlessly caused the death of his mother.

Having attained the age of manhood, Nanabozho, still feeling deep resentment for the death of his mother, resolved to avenge it by the destruction of his brother Chakekenapok. The two brothers soon grappled with each other. Chakekenapok finally turned and fled, but Nanabozho pursued him over the world, finally overtaking and striking him with a deerhorn or a chert, fracturing or chipping pieces from various parts of his body, and destroying him by tearing out his entrails. The fragments from Chakekenapok's body became huge rocks, and the masses of flint or chert found in various parts of the world show where the conflicts between the two brothers took place, while his entrails became vines. Before the Indians knew the art of fire-making Nanabozho taught them the art of making hatchets, lances, and arrowpoints.

Nanabozho and Chipiapoos dwelt together in a land far removed from the haunts of mankind. They were noted for excellence of body and beneficence of mind, and for the supreme character of the magic power they possessed. These qualities and attributes excited the bitter antagonism of the evil manitos of the air, earth, and waters, who plotted to destroy these two brothers. Nanabozho, who was immune to the effects of adverse orenda and from whose knowledge nothing was barred, knew their snares and devices and hence eluded and avoided them. He, however, warned Chipiapoos, his less-gifted brother, not to leave their lodge or to separate from him even for a

moment. But, disregarding this admonition, one day Chipiapoos ventured out of the lodge and went on the ice of a great lake, probably L. Michigan. This temerity was the opportunity sought by the manitos, who broke the ice, causing Chipiapoos to sink to the bottom of the lake, where his body was hidden by the manitos. Upon returning to the lodge, Nanabozho, missing Chipiapoos and surmising his fate, became inconsolable. Everywhere over the face of the earth he sought for him in vain. Then he became enraged and waged relentless war against all manitos, wreaking vengeance by precipitating a multitude of them into the abyss of the world. He next declared a truce in order to mourn for his brother, disfiguring his person and covering his head to indicate grief, bitterly weeping, and uttering from time to time the name of the lost and unhappy Chipiapoos. It is said Nanabozho secluded himself for six years in his lodge of mourning. During this truce the evil manitos, knowing the unlimited powers of Nanabozho and recollecting the destruction of the vast numbers of manitos by their metamorphosis to gratify his anger, consulted together to devise means for pacifying Nanabozho's wrath; but through fear of their great adversary their plans came to naught. At last four of the manitos, hoary with age and ripe in experience and wisdom, and who had not been parties to the death of Chipiapoos, undertook a mission of pacification. Having built a lodge of condolence near that of Nanabozho, they prepared a feast of welcome, filling with tobacco a pipe the stem of which was a calumet, and then silently and ceremoniously moved toward their antagonist. The four ambassadors severally carried a bag made from the entire skin of an otter, a lynx, a beaver, or of some other animal, which contained magically potent medicines and powerful fetishes. Arriving at the lodge of Nanabozho, they chanted to him with ceremonial formality their good intentions and kind greetings, and asked him to be pleased to accompany them to their lodge. Moved by these greetings, Nanabozho uncovered his head, and, arising, washed himself and then accompanied them. On his entering the lodge the manitos offered him a cup of purification medicine preparatory to his initiation into the Midé, or Grand Medicine Society. Nanabozho partook of the draft, and at once found himself completely freed from feelings of resentment and melancholy. Then the prescribed ritual was performed by the manitos. The proper dances and the chants of the Midé were chanted, and the four manitos, humanized primal beings, gently applied to

Nanabozho their *pindikosan*, or magically potent medicine-bags, which, after ceremonially blowing their orenda or magic power into him, they cast on the ground. At every fall of the medicine-bags Nanabozho became aware that the melancholy, sadness, hatred, and anger that oppressed him gradually left, and that beneficent affection and feelings of joy arose in his heart. On the completion of his initiation he joined in the dances and in the chanting; then they all ate and smoked together, and Nanabozho expressed thanks to his hosts for initiating him into the mysteries of the grand medicine.

To further show their good will, the manitos, by the exercise of their magic powers, brought back the missing Chipiapoos, but, owing to his metamorphosis, he was forbidden to enter the lodge. Having received a lighted torch through a chink in the walls of the lodge, he was required to go to rule the country of the manes, where, with the lighted torch he carried, he should kindle a fire that should never be extinguished, for the pleasure of his uncles and aunts—namely, all men and women—who would repair thither. Subsequently, Nanabozho again descended upon the earth, and at once initiated all his family in the mysteries of the grand medicine. He provided each of them with a medicine-bag, well supplied with potent medicines, charms, and fetishes. He also strictly enjoined upon them the need of perpetuating the accompanying ceremonies among their descendants, explaining to them that these practices faithfully observed would cure their diseases, obtain for them abundance in fishing and hunting, and gain for them complete victory over their enemies.

Some hold to the doctrine that Nanabozho created the animals for the food and raiment of man; that he caused those plants and roots to grow whose virtues cure disease and enable the hunter to kill wild animals in order to drive away famine. These plants he confided to the watchful care of his grandmother, the great-grandmother of the human race, Mesakkummikokwi, and lest man should invoke her in vain she was strictly forbidden ever to leave her lodge. So, when collecting plants, roots, and herbs for their natural and magic virtues, an Algonquian Indian faithfully leaves on the ground hard by the place whence he has taken the root or plant a small offering to Mesakkummikokwi.

It is said that Nanabozho in his many journeys over the earth destroyed many ferocious monsters of land and water whose continued existence would have placed in jeopardy the fate of mankind. It is believed by the faithful that Nanabozho, resting from his toils, dwells on a great island of ice floating on a large sea in the northland, where the seraphim of auroral light keep nightly vigil. It is also believed that should he set foot on the land the world would at once take fire and every living being would share with it a common destruction. As a perversion of an earlier tradition, it is said that Nanabozho has placed four beneficent humanized beings, one at each of the four cardinal points or world-quarters, to aid in promoting the welfare of the human race—the one at the E. supplies light and starts the sun on his daily journey over the sky; the one at the S. supplies warmth, heat, and the refreshing dews that cause the growth of the soothing tobacco plant, and of corn, beans, squashes, and all the herbs and shrubs that bear fruit; the one at the W. supplies cooling and life-giving showers; lastly, the one at the N. supplies snow and ice, enabling the tracking and successful pursuit of wild animals, and who causes them to hibernate, to seek places of concealment from the cold of winter. Under the care of the man-being of the S. Nanabozho placed lesser humanized beings, dominantly bird-like in form, whose voices are the thunder and the flashing of whose eyes is the lightning, and to whom offerings of tobacco are made when their voices are loud and menacing.

Like the Iroquois and Huron sages, the Algonquian philosophers taught that the disembodied souls of the dead, on their journey to the great meadow in which is situated the village of their deceased ancestors, must cross a swift stream precariously bridged by a tree trunk, which was in continual motion. Over this the manes of the justified pass in safety, while the shades of the vicious, overcome by the magic power of adverse fate, fail at this ordeal, and, falling into the abyss below, are lost.

Another and equally credited tradition is to the effect that a manito or primal man-being formed a world which he peopled with man-beings having the form but not the benevolent attributes of man, and that these primal man-beings, doing nothing but evil, finally caused the destruction of the world and themselves by a flood; that having thus satisfied his displeasure the primal man being brought the world again out of the waters and formed anew a fine looking young man, but, being alone, the latter seemed disconsolate and weary of life. Then, pitying him, the primal man-being brought him as he slept a sister for a companion. Awaking, the young man was rejoiced to see his sister, and the two dwelt together for many years in mutual amusement and agreeable discourse. Finally the young man dreamed for the first time, and he related his dream to his sister, saying that it had been revealed to him that five young man-beings would that night visit their lodge, and that she was forbidden to speak to or in any manner recognize any of the first four who would seek admission to the lodge, but that she should welcome the fifth when he would seek admission. This advice she followed. After their metamorphosis these four primal young man-beings became respectively Sama or Tobacco, who, receiving no answer from the sister, died of chagrin; Wapekone or Squash; Eshketamok or Melon, and Kojees or Bean, who shared the fate of the first. But Mandamin or Corn, the fifth, was answered and welcomed by the sister, and he entered the lodge and became her husband. Then Mandamin buried his four comrades, and soon from their graves sprang up respectively tobacco, squashes, melons, and beans in such quantity as to supply them for the year, and tobacco enough to enable them to make offerings to the primal man-beings and to smoke in council. From this union sprang the Indian race.

In one version of the prevailing Algonquian cosmogonic story it is said that before the formation of the earth there was only water; that on the surface of this vast expanse of water floated a large raft on which were the animals of the various kinds which are on the earth and of which the Great Hare was the chief. They sought a fit and firm place on which to disembark; but as there were in sight only swans and other waterfowl, they began to lose hope, and, having no other, they requested the beaver to dive for the purpose of bringing up some earth from the bottom of the water, assuring him in the name of all the animals present that, should he return with only a single particle, it would produce an earth sufficiently spacious to contain and nourish all. But the beaver sought an excuse for refusal, saying that he had already dived around the raft and had failed to reach the bottom. He was pressed so strongly to make anew so worthy an attempt, however, that he took the hazard and dived. He remained without returning for so long a time that the supplicants believed him drowned. Finally they saw him appear nearly dead and motionless. Then all the animals, seeing that he was in no condition to remount the raft, at once interested themselves to take him into it. After examining carefully his paws and tail, they found nothing. But the little hope left them of being able to save their lives compelled them to address themselves to the otter to ask that he make an attempt to find earth at the bottom of the waters. It was told him that his own safety, as

well as theirs, depended on the result of his effort. So the otter yielded to their urging and dived. He remained in the depths of the waters a longer time than did the beaver, but, like him, he came to the surface without success. The impossibility of finding a place to dwell where they could subsist left them nothing more to hope, when the muskrat offered to attempt to find the bottom, and he flattered himself that he would bring back sand. Although the beaver and the otter, much stronger than he, had not been able to accomplish the task, they encouraged him, promising even that, if he succeeded in his attempt, he should be the ruler of the whole world. The muskrat then cast himself into the waters and bravely dived into the depths. After remaining therein nearly an entire day and night he appeared motionless at the side of the raft, belly uppermost and paws closed. The other animals carefully took him out of the water, opened one of his paws, then a second, then a third, and finally the fourth, where there was a small grain of sand between his claws. The Great Hare, who was encouraged to form a vast and spacious earth, took this grain of sand and let it fall on the raft, which became larger. He took a part and scattered it, which caused the mass to increase more and more. When it was of the size of a mountain he willed it to turn, and as it turned the mass still increased in size. As soon as it appeared quite large he gave orders to the fox to examine his work with power to enlarge it. He obeyed. The fox, having learned that the earth was of such size that he could easily take his prey, returned to the Great Hare to inform him that the earth was large enough to contain and nourish all the animals. After this report the Great Hare went over his work, and, on going around it, found it imperfect. He has since not been disposed to trust any one of all the other animals, and ever keeps on enlarging the earth by ceaselessly going around it. The rumblings heard in the caverns of mountains confirm the Indians in the belief that the Great Hare continues the work of enlarging the earth. He is honored by them, and they regard him as the god who has formed the land.

Such is what the Algonquians teach regarding the formation of the earth, which they believe is borne on a raft. Concerning the sea and the firmament, they assert that they have existed for all time. After the formation of the earth all the other animals withdrew into the places most fitted to them, where they could feed and find their prey. The first of these having died, the Great Hare caused men to be born from their cadavers, even from those of the fish which were found along the banks of rivers which he had made in forming the earth, and gave each a different language or dialect. Because some ascribed their origin to the bear, others to the elk, and thus to all the different animals, they believed that they had their being from these creatures. (J. N. B. H.)

Nanahuani. A former Chumashan village on Santa Cruz id., Cal.
Nanahuani.—Taylor in Cal. Farmer, Apr. 24, 1863. Na-na-wa′-ni.—Henshaw, Buenaventura MS. vocab., B. A. E., 1884.

Nanaimo (contraction of *Snanaimux*). A Salish tribe, speaking the Cowichan dialect, living about Nanaimo harbor, on the E. coast of Vancouver id. and on Nanaimo lake, Brit. Col. Pop. 161 in 1906. Their gentes are Anuenes, Koltsiowotl, Ksalokul, Tewetken, and Yesheken.
Nanaimos.—Mayne, Brit. Col., 165, 1861. Nanaimŭk.—Gibbs quoted by Dall in Cont. N. A. Ethnol., I, 241, 1877. Nanainio.—Douglas in Jour. Roy. Geog. Soc., 246, 1854. Snanaimooh.—Tolmie and Dawson, Vocabs. Brit. Col., 120B, 1884. Snanaimuq.—Boas in 5th Rep. N. W. Tribes Can., 32, 1889. Suanaimuchs.—Grant in Jour. Roy. Geog. Soc., 293, 1857.

Nanamakewuk (*Nĕnĕmĕ′kiwŭg i*, 'thunderers.'—W. J.). A gens of the Sauk and Foxes.
Nă-nă-ma′-kew-uk.—Morgan, Anc. Soc., 170, 1877 (trans. 'thunder'). Neneme′kiwạgⁱ.—Wm. Jones, inf'n, 1906.

Nananawi (*Na′-nan-a-wi*, a species of lizard). A clan of the Tuwa (Earth or Sand) phratry of the Hopi.—Stephen in 8th Rep. B. A. E., 39, 1891.

Nanashthezhin ('black-horizontal-stripe aliens', referring to the Zuñi). A Navaho clan, descended from a body of Zuñi who amalgamated with the Navaho.
Nanacǫéjiⁿ.—Matthews in Jour. Am. Folk-lore, III, 104, 1890. Nanastĕ′zin.—Matthews, Navaho Legends, 30, 1897.

Nanatlugunyi (*Nă′nă-tlu ′gŭñ′yĭ*, or, in abbreviated form, *Nă′nă-tlu ′gŭñ′*, or *Nă′nă-tsu ′gŭñ′*, 'spruce-tree place'). A traditional Cherokee settlement on the site of Jonesboro, Washington co., Tenn. The name of Nolichucky r. is probably a corruption of the same word.—Mooney in 19th Rep. B. A. E., 527, 1900.

Nanatsoho. Probably a subdivision of one of the tribes of the Caddo confederacy which resided in a village on Red r. of Louisiana, and, according to Joutel, were allies of the Kadohadacho, Natchitoch, and Nasoni in 1687. They probably drifted southward in the middle of the 18th century, gradually lost their distinctive organization, and became merged with their kindred during the turbulence of that period, suffering distress incident to the introduction of new diseases by the whites. In 1812 a settlement of 12 families was said to exist near the locality of their former villages. (A. C. F.)
Nadsoos.—La Harpe (1718) in Margry, Déc., VI, 243, 1886. Nadsous.—Jefferys, Am. Atlas, map 5, 1776.

Nanatscho.—Trimble (1818) in Morse, Rep. to Sec. War, 259, 1822 (village). Natchoos.—Douay (*ca.* 1687) quoted by Shea, Discov. Miss. Val., 218, 1852. Nathosos.—Joutel (1687) in French, Hist. Coll. La., I, 168, 1846. Nathsoos.—Barcia, Ensayo, 278, 1723. Natsohooks.—Coxe, Carolana, 10, 1741 (also Natchoos). Natsohok.—Ibid., map. Natsohos.—Joutel (1687) in Margry, Déc., III, 409, 1878. Natsoos.—La Harpe (1719), ibid., VI, 263, 1886. Pecan Point.—Trimble (*ca.* 1812) in Morse, Rep. to Sec. War, 259, 1822 (Nanatscho, or).

Nanawonggabe. The principal chief, about the middle of the 19th century, of the Chippewa of Lake Superior. He was born about 1800, and was noted chiefly as an orator, and as the father of Ahshahwaygeeshegoqua ('The Hanging Cloud'), the so-called "Chippewa Princess", who was renowned as a warrior and as the only female among the Chippewa allowed to participate in the war ceremonies and dances, and to wear the plumes of the warriors. Nanawonggabe is described as having been of less than medium height and size, and as having intelligent features. See Morse in Wis. Hist. Soc. Coll., III, 338, 1857.

Nanawu. The Small Striped Squirrel clan of the Tuwa (Earth or Sand) phratry of the Hopi.
Na′-na-wü wüñ-wü.—Fewkes in Am. Anthrop., VII, 404, 1894 (*wüñ-wü*=' clan').

Nanay. See *Nana.*

Nan-chee-ning-ga. See *Nacheninga.*

Nandell. A Tenankutchin village, named from its chief, with 80 inhabitants in 1885; situated on Tetling r., near Wagner lake, about 20 m. from Tanana r., lat. 63° 20′, Alaska.
Nandell.—Baker, Geog. Dict. Alaska, 453, 1906. Nandellas.—Error cited, ibid. Nandell's village.—Allen, Rep., 75, 137, 1885.

Nané. See *Nana.*

Nanepashemet. A Nipmuc chief of considerable note in the early days of the Massachusetts colonies. His home was in Medford, Middlesex co., near Mystic pond. His house, it is said, unlike others, was elevated on a scaffold about 6 ft above the ground, on a hill, at the bottom of which was his fort. He was killed about 1619. His widow, who subsequently married Webcowit, assumed the chieftaincy and was known as the Squawsachem of the Nipmuc. He left 5 children—one known as Sagamore James became sachem of Saugus; another, the sachem of Winnesimet. (C. T.)

Nang. The Earth or Sand clans of the Tewa pueblos of San Juan, Santa Clara, Nambe, and Tesuque, N. Mex., and Hano, Ariz.; that of Tesuque is extinct. Cf. *Nung.*
Naⁿ-tdóa.—Hodge in Am. Anthrop., IX, 350, 1896 (Nambe and Tesuque form; *tdóa*=' people'). Nań-tówa.—Ibid. (Hano form). Na-tdóa.—Ibid. (San Juan and Santa Clara form).

Nang. The Stone clan of the Tewa pueblo of San Juan, N. Mex. Said to be distinct from the Na (Earth or Sand) clan of that pueblo. Cf. *Ku.*
Naⁿ-tdóa.—Hodge in Am. Anthrop., IX, 352, 1896 (*tdóa*=' people').

Nanibas ('fish-eaters'). Probably a Choctaw tribe which early in the 18th century occupied a village near the Mobile and Tohome tribes, about 5 leagues from Ft Mobile, on Mobile bay, Ala. Their earlier home, according to Hamilton (Col. Mobile, 90–91, 1897), was at the bluff on Tombigbee r., still known as "Nanna Hubba," just above its junction with Alabama r. After removal to the vicinity of Ft Mobile they were absorbed by the Mobile tribe.

Namabas.—Pénicaut (1702) in Margry, Déc., V, 427, 1883. **Naniaba.**—Jefferys, Am. Atlas, map 5, 1776. **Naniabas.**—Pénicaut (1702) in French, Hist. Coll. La., n. s., I, 80, 1869.

Nanicksah. One of the chiefs sent by the Ohio Shawnee in 1765 to negotiate a treaty of peace with Sir Wm. Johnson on behalf of the British government. The treaty was signed at Johnson Hall, N. Y., July 13, 1765.—N. Y. Doc. Col. Hist., VII, 755, 1856.

Nanihaba (*nanih* 'hill,' *aba* 'above'). One of the 5 hamlets comprising the former Choctaw town of Imongalasha, in the present Neshoba co., Miss.—Halbert in Pub. Miss. Hist. Soc., VI, 432, 1902.

Nanikypusson. One of the chiefs sent by the Shawnee of Ohio in 1765 to negotiate a treaty of peace with Sir Wm. Johnson in behalf of the British government. The treaty was completed and signed at Johnson Hall, N. Y., July 13, 1765.—N. Y. Doc. Col. Hist., VII, 755, 1856.

Nanipacna (Choctaw: 'high mountain'—Gatschet; 'hill top'—Halbert). An important town visited in 1559–60 by Tristan de Luna, by whom it was named Santa Cruz de Nanipacna; situated in s. Alabama, not far from Alabama r. Halbert (Gulf States Hist. Mag., II, 130, 1903) thinks it was on the E. side of Alabama r. in the present Wilcox co., while Lowery (Spanish Settlements, 361, 1901) places it farther down the river, in Monroe co. It had been visited and partly destroyed by other white men, probably De Soto's expedition, some years before. (J. M.)

Nanipacna.—Barcia, Ensayo, 33, 1723. **Napicnoca.**—Fairbanks, Fla., 59, 1901 (misprint). **Santa Cruz de Nanipacna.**—Barcia, op. cit.

Nannehamgeh (in part from Choctaw *nanih*, 'hill'). The "old town" inhabited by the Natchez.—Adair, Am. Inds., 196, 1775.

Nanortalik. An Eskimo village on a small island in s. Greenland, lat. 60°.

Nannortalik.—Ausland, 162, 1886. **Nanortalik.**—Nansen, First Crossing, 307, 1890. **Nennortalik.**—Koldewey, German Arct. Exped., 182, 1874.

Nanpanta (*Nan'panta,* 'deer'). A Quapaw gens.—Dorsey in 15th Rep. B. A. E., 229, 1897.

Nanpanta. A Deer gens: a division of the Washashewanun gens of the Osage.

Ke ʞa'tsü.—Dorsey in 15th Rep. B. A. E., 234, 1897 ('Turtle with a serrated crest along the shell'). **Naⁿpaⁿta.**—Ibid.

Nansattico. A former Matchotic village on Rappahannock r., s. w. of the present Hampstead, in King George co., Va.

Nansattico.—Herrman, map, 1670. **Nanzaticos.**—Jefferson, Notes, 138, 1801.

Nansemond (from *nansamend,* 'one goes to fish,' or 'one (who) goes to fish (or fishing),' possibly originally a personal name.—Gerard). An important tribe of the Powhatan confederacy (q. v.) formerly occupying a territory on the s. side of lower James r., Va., within the present Nansemond and Norfolk cos., and having their principal town, "Nandsamund," probably about the present Chuckatuck in the former county. They were estimated by Capt. John Smith, in 1608, at 200 warriors, or perhaps a total population of 700 or 800. Like the other tribes of the confederacy they quickly declined after the advent of the whites, and in 1722, when they are mentioned in the Albany treaty with the Iroquois, they numbered, according to Beverley, only 150 in all. A scattered band of about 180 mixed-bloods, mostly truck farmers, still keep up the name near Bowershill, a few miles s. w. from Norfolk. (J. M.)

Nancymond.—Vassall (1667) in N. C. Col. Rec., I, 159, 1886. **Nandsamunds.**—Smith (1624), Va., 347, 1884. **Nanemonds.**—Albany conf. (1722) in N. Y. Doc. Col. Hist., V, 673, 1855. **Nansamond.**—Beverley, Va., bk. 3, 63, 1705. **Nansamund.**—Smith (1629), Va., II, 64, 1819. **Nanseman.**—Winthrop (1647) in Mass. Hist. Soc. Coll., 4th s., VII, 1865. **Nansemond.**—Doc. of 1729 in Martin, N. C., I, app., xvii, 1829. **Nansemun.**—Harrison (1647) in Mass. Hist. Soc. Coll., 4th s., VII, 438, 1865. **Nasamonds.**—Jefferson, Notes, 138, 1801. **Nassamonds.**—Boudinot, Star in the West, 127, 1816. **Nausamund.**—Smith (1629), Va., II, 10, 1819.

Nantahala (*Nûñ'dăyĕ'lĭ* ('middle [i. e. noonday] sun'). Originally the name of a point on Nantahala r. near Jarrett station, Macon co., N. C., where the cliffs are so perpendicular that the sun is not seen at their bases until noon; later applied to the neighboring Cherokee settlement of Briertown (q. v.).

Nantahala.—Mooney in 19th Rep. B. A. E., 528, 1900. **Nantiyallee.**—Doc. of 1799 quoted by Royce in 5th Rep. B. A. E., 144, 1887. **Nuntialla.**—Mooney, op. cit.

Nantapoyac. A village of the Powhatan confederacy in 1608, situated on the s. bank of James r. in Surry co., Va.—Smith (1629), Va., I, map, repr. 1819.

Nantaughtacund. A tribe and village of the Powhatan confederacy, formerly s. of the Rappahannock, in Essex and Caroline cos., Va. In 1608 they numbered about 750.

Nandtaughtacund.—Strachey (ca. 1612), Va., 37, 1849. **Nantaughtacund.**—Smith (1629), Va., I, 117, repr. 1819. **Nantautacund.**—Simons in Smith, ibid., 189. **Naudtaughtacund.**—Purchas, Pilgrimes, IV, map, 1716 (misprint). **Nautaughtacunds.**—Drake, Bk. Inds., bk. 4, 9, 1848 (misprint).

Nanticoke (from *Nentego,* var. of Delaware *Unechtgo, Unalachtgo,* 'tidewater people'). An important Algonquian tribe living on Nanticoke r. of Maryland, on the

E. shore, where Smith in 1608 located their principal village, called Nanticoke. They were connected linguistically and ethnically with the Delawares and the Conoy, notwithstanding the idiomatic variance in the language of the latter. Their traditional history is brief and affords but little aid in tracing their movements in prehistoric times. The 10th verse of the fifth song of the Walam Olum is translated by Squier: "The Nentegos and the Shawanis went to the south lands." Although the Shawnee and Nanticoke are brought together in this verse, it does not necessarily indicate that they separated from the main body at the same time and place; but in both cases the separation appears to have occurred in the region that in verse 1, same canto, is designated Talega land, which was probably in Ohio, since their tradition recorded by Beatty (Brinton, Lenape Leg., 139, 1885) is precisely the same as that of the Shawnee. It is also probable that "south" in the legend signifies some point below the latitude of Pittsburg, Pa., but not s. of the Kanawha. A different and more probable account was given to Heckewelder by the old chief, White, who said that, being great trappers and fishers, they separated from the Delawares after these had reached their eastern seat and wandered s. in search of good fishing and trapping grounds.

The Conoy in 1660 informed the governor of Maryland of a "league that had existed for 13 generations with an emperor of Nanticoke lineage at its head, which embraced all the tribes of the province, and also the Potomac and, as they pretended, even the Iroquoian Conestoga" (Maryland Arch., Proc. Counc., 1636–67, 403). The Tocwogh of Smith, as well as the later Doag, were possibly identical with the Nanticoke.

A short time after its settlement the Maryland colony found the Nanticoke a thorn in its side. As early as 1642 they were formally declared to be enemies, and not until 1678 was the strife composed by treaty. A renewal of hostilities was threatened in 1687, but by prudent measures this was prevented and the peace reaffirmed. In 1698, and from that time forward as long as they remained in the region, reservations were set aside for them. In 1707 they had at least 7 villages. In 1722 their principal village, called Nanduge by Beverley, contained about 100 inhabitants and was the residence of the "empress," who ruled over all the neighboring Indians. At that time they numbered about 500. Soon afterward they began to move N., stopping for a time on the Susquehanna, at the mouth of the Juniata, and about

1748 the greater part of the tribe went up the Susquehanna, halting at various points, and finally settled under Iroquois protection at Chenango, Chugnut, and Owego, on the E. branch of the Susquehanna in s. New York. They were estimated at about 500 in 1765. A part remained in Maryland, where they were still living under the name of Wiwash in 1792, although reduced to about 30. In 1753 a part of those on the upper Susquehanna joined the Iroquois in w. New York, with whom they were still living in 1840, but the majority of the tribe, in company with remnants of the Mahican and Wappinger, emigrated to the W. about 1784 and joined the Delawares in Ohio and Indiana, with whom they soon became incorporated, disappearing as a distinct tribe. A few mixed bloods live on Indian r., Delaware.

The Nanticoke were distinguished from neighboring tribes by a darker color and peculiar customs. They appear to have been devoted to fishing and trapping as a means of subsistence. Heckewelder says: "They are said to have been the inventors of a poisonous substance by which they could destroy a whole settlement of people, and they are accused of being skilled in the arts of witchcraft. It is certain they are dreaded on this account. I have known Indians who firmly believed that they had people among them who could, if they pleased, destroy a whole army by merely blowing their breath toward them. Those of the Lenape and other tribes who pretend to witchcraft say that they learned the science from the Nanticokes." What particular characteristic, art, or knowledge caused them to be looked upon in this light is not stated; but it probably was their knowledge of poisons and the singular custom, which Heckewelder describes, of removing the bones of their dead from place to place during their various shiftings. They appear to have had a head chief, to whom the English, adopting Old World terms, applied the name emperor to distinguish him from the subordinate chiefs whom they called kings. The line of descent of the former was in the female line, and as noted above, if Beverley be correct, a woman might, under certain circumstances, hold the chieftaincy. Their towns appear to have been in some instances fortified, as Smith says: "They conducted us to their pallizadoed towne, mantelled with the barkes of trees, with scaffolds like mounts, brested about with brests very formally."

The Nanticoke confederacy appears to have included, besides the Nanticoke proper, the Arseek, Cuscarawaoc, Nause, Ozinies (?), and Sarapinagh. They had the following villages: Askimimkansen, Byengeahtein (mixed), Chenango (mixed), Conedogwinit (mixed), Locust Necktown, Matchcouchtin, Matcheattochousie, Nanduge, Natahquois, Peixtan (?), Pekoinoke, Pohecommeati, Teahquois, Witichquaom. (J. M. C. T.)

Doages.—Lord Baltimore (1650) quoted by Bozman, Md., I, 119, 1837. **doegs.**—Writer of 1676 in Mass. Hist. Soc. Coll., 4th s., IX, 165, 1871. **Ganniataratich-rone.**—Gatschet in Am. Antiq., IV, 75, 1882 (Mohawk name). **Mantaquak.**—Brownell, Ind. Races, 166, 1853 (misprint). **Naaticokes.**—Peters (1760) in Mass. Hist. Soc. Coll., 4th s., IX, 258, 1871. **Nanduye.**—Beverley, Va., bk. 3, 62, 1705. **Nantaquack.**—Smith (1629), Va., I, map, repr. 1819. **Nantaquaes.**—Rafinesque in Marshall, Ky., I, introd., 37, 1824. **Nantaquak.**—Simons in Smith (1629), Va., I, 175, repr. 1819. **Nantekokies.**—Maumee counc. (1793) in Am. St. Papers, Ind. Aff., I, 357, 1832. **Nantiakokies.**—Perkins and Peck, Annals of the West, 423, 1850. **Nantico.**—Heckewelder in Mass. Hist. Soc. Coll., 2d s., X, 129, 1823. **Nanticook.**—Barton, New Views, app., 5, 1798. **Nanticoes.**—Rafinesque in Marshall, Ky., I, introd., 37, 1824. **Nanticokes.**—Marshe (1744) in Mass. Hist. Soc. Coll., 1st s., VII, 199, 1801. **Nanticooks.**—German Flats conf. (1770) in N. Y. Doc. Col. Hist., VIII, 229, 1857. **Nanticooks.**—Edwards (1788) in Mass. Hist. Soc. Coll., 1st s., IX, 92, 1804. **Nantihokes.**—McKenney and Hall, Ind. Tribes, III, 80, 1854. **Nantikokes.**—Ft Johnson conf. (1757) in N. Y. Doc. Col. Hist., VII, 245, 1856. **Nantikokies.**—Brant (1793) in Am. St. Papers, Ind. Aff., I, 350, 1832. **Nantiocks.**—Macauley, N. Y., III, 39, 1829. **Nantiokes.**—Ft Johnson conf. (1756) in N. Y. Doc. Col. Hist., VII, 173, 1856. **Nantiquacks.** — Heckewelder (1819) quoted by Bozman, Md., I, 177, 1837. **Nantiquaks.**—Bozman, Md., I, 110, 1837. **Nantue.**—Herrman, map, 1670. **Nantycokes.**—Peters (1761) in Mass. Hist. Soc. Coll., 4th s., IX, 440, 1871. **Nautaquake.**—Purchas, Pilgrimes, IV, 1713 (misprint). **Nauticokes.**—Vater, Mith., pt. 3, sec. 3, 312, 1816 (misprint). **Nentégo.**—Heckewelder (1819) quoted by Bozman, Md., I, 174, 1837 (own name). **Nentegowi.**—Brinton, Lenape Leg., 204, 1885. **Nentico.**—Heckewelder in Mass. Hist. Soc. Coll., 2d s., X, 129, 1823. **Otayáchgo.**—Heckewelder (1819) quoted by Bozman, Md., I, 174, 1837 ('bridge people', so called by the Mahican and Delawares because of their custom of felling trees across streams on which to set their traps, and of their skill in fastening logs together to form bridges). **Scanehaderadeyghroones.**—Albany conf. (1748) in N. Y. Doc. Col. Hist., VI, 441, 1855 ('beyond-the-sea people'). **Scaniadaradighroonas.**—Ft Johnson conf. (1756), ibid., VII, 106, 1856. **Scanihaderadighroones.**—Ft Johnson conf. (1753), ibid., VI, 811, 1855. **Schanadarighroones.**—Ft Johnson conf. (1755), ibid., 964. **Schaniadaradighroonas.** — Ibid., 988. **Schani,ha,der,adygh,roon,-ees.**—Clinton (1750), ibid., 548. **Seganiateratickrohne.**—Heckewelder (1819) quoted by Bozman, Md., I, 174, 1837 ('beyond-the-sea people': Iroquois name). **Shaniadaradighroonas.**—Ft Johnson conf. (1756) in N. Y. Doc. Col. Hist., VII, 50, 1856. **Shanihadaradighroones.**—Albany conf. (1754) in Mass. Hist. Soc. Coll., 3d s., V, 30, 1836. **Skanatiarationo.**—Montreal conf. (1756) in N. Y. Doc. Col. Hist., X, 503, 1858. **Skaniadaradighroonas.**—Ft Johnson conf. (1755), ibid., VI, 977, 1855. **Skaniatarati-háka.**—Gatschet, Tuscarora MS., B. A. E., 1885 (Tuscarora name). **Skaniatarationo.**—Montreal conf. (1756) in N. Y. Doc. Col. Hist., X, 500, 1858. **Skanigadaradighroonas.**—Johnson (1756), ibid., VII, 136, 1856. **Skaniodaraghroonas.**—Ft Johnson conf. (1756), ibid., 46. **Skaun-ya-ta-ha-ti-hawk.**—Macauley, N. Y., II, 166, 1829. **Taux.**—Smith (1629), Va., 113, repr. 1884 (from Tawachguano). **Tawachguáns.**—Heckewelder (1819) quoted by Gallatin in Trans. Am. Antiq. Soc., II, 52, 1836 (Delaware name: 'bridge people', from *taiachquoan*, 'a bridge'). **Tawackguáno.**—Schoolcraft, Ind. Tribes, VI, 131, 1857. **Tayachquáns.**—Heckewelder (1819) quoted by Bozman, Md., I, 174, 1837. **Tiawco.**—Easton treaty (1757) in N. Y. Doc. Col. Hist., VII, 294, 1856. **Toags.**—Smith (1629), Va., I, 177, repr.

1819. **Trappers.**—Heckewelder (1819) quoted by Bozman, Md., I, 174, 1837 (name sometimes used by the whites, having reference to their skill in trapping animals). **Unéchtgo.**—Ibid. (Delaware name). **Wenuhtokowuk.**—Aupaumut (1791) quoted by Brinton, Lenape Leg., 20, 1885 (Mahican name).

Nanticoke. A sort of bean; from the name of an Algonquian tribe. Lawson (Hist. Carolina, 76, 1709) mentions *nanticokes* among "the pulse which we found the Indians possessed of when we settled in America." (A. F. C.)

Nantucket. When first settled by the whites this island, s. of the coast of Massachusetts, was occupied by two tribes whose names have not been preserved. One occupied the w. end of the island and was supposed to have come from the mainland by way of Marthas Vineyard; the other tribe lived at the E. end and was said to have come direct from the mainland. The two tribes were independent and were hostile to each other. They had several villages and numbered about 1,500 at the first settlement of the island in 1642 (Mayhew). In 1763 there were only 358 remaining and two-thirds of these died of a fever the next winter. In 1792 there were only 20 left, and these were reduced in 1809 to 2 or 3 persons of pure blood and a few of mixed race. The Indian names of different districts, which were probably the names of villages also, were Shimmoah (also a village), Tetaukimmo, Shaukimmo, Quayz, Podpis, Squam, Sasacacheh, and Siasconsit, and the village Miacomet (Notes on Nantucket (1807) in Mass. Hist. Soc. Coll., 2d s., III, 25–26, 1815). For information concerning the early grants and conveyances of Nantucket lands, see Bull. Nantucket Hist. Assn., I, 1896–1902. (J. M.)

Mantukes.—London Doc. (1682) in N. Y. Doc. Col. Hist., III, 328, 1853. **Mantukett.**—Ibid. **Nantuckett.**—London Doc. (1692–3), ibid., IV, 28, 1854. **Nantucquet.**—London Doc. (1664), ibid., III, 84, 1853. **Nantukes.**—Holland Doc. (1664), ibid., II, 296, 1858. **Nantukett.**—London Doc. (1674), ibid., III, 215, 1853.

Nantuxet. A division of the Unalachtigo (?) branch of the Delawares formerly living in Pennsylvania and Delaware.—Macauley, N. Y., II, 166, 1829.

Nanualikmut ('lake people': Kodiak name). A division of the Knaiakhotana of Cook inlet, Alaska.

Na-nua-li'-q'mūt.—Hoffman, MS., B. A. E., 1882 ('people around the lake': Chugachigmiut name). **Na-nu'-a-lŭk'.**—Ibid. ('lake people': Kaniagmiut name).

Nanumpum. See *Weetamo*.

Nanuntenoo. A sachem of the Narraganset, son of Miantonomo, called also Canonchet or Quananchit. He was the first signer of the treaty of Oct. 1675, but supplied the strength of the Narraganset war against the English, his young men having long secretly supported Philip. He escaped with his life from the fight of Dec. 1675, and in Mar. 1676 defeated the English under Capt. Peirse; but in

April of that year he was surprised by an English force and surrendered. He was taken to Stonington, Conn., and was shot by representatives of his allied enemies under the eyes of the English. His head was sent as a trophy to the magistrates of Hartford (De Forest, Inds. of Conn., 282, 1852). Nanuntenoo was tall and strongly built, and was a man of courage and ability. His fame at times was hardly less than that of King Philip. Some of his sayings have been preserved. (A. F. C.)

Nanusek. An Eskimo settlement in s. E. Greenland.—Meddelelser om Grönland, xxv, map, 1902.

Nanussussouk (*Nĕnuswĭsowŭgⁱ*, 'they go by the name of the buffalo.'—W. J.). A gens of the Sauk and Foxes.
Na-nus-sus'-so-uk.—Morgan, Anc. Soc., 170, 1877. Nenuswisŏwǎgⁱ.—Wm. Jones, inf'n, 1906.

Nanvogaloklak. A Magemiut village on one of the lakes connected with Kvichivak r., Alaska; pop. 100 in 1880.
Nanvogalokhlagamute.—Nelson (1879) quoted by Baker, Geog. Dict. Alaska, 454, 1906 (*mute*= 'people'). Nanvogaloklak.—Baker, ibid. Nauvogalokhlagamute.—Petroff in 10th Census, Alaska, map, 1884 (misprint). Nauwogalokhlagamute.—Petroff, Rep. on Alaska, 54, 1881 (misprint).

Nanyaayi (perhaps 'people of Nanya'). The most important social group among the southern Tlingit. They belong to the Wolf clan, have their winter town at Wrangell, and camp in summer along Stikine r. in Alaska. Ketgohittan and Kutshittan are given as divisions.
Naa-nu-aa-ghu.—Kane, Wand. in N. A., app., 1859. Nanaā'ri.—Boas, 5th Rep. N. W. Tribes Can., 25, 1889. Nān-gohe-āri.—Krause, Tlinkit Ind., 120, 1885. Nanya'ayi.—Swanton, field notes, B. A. E., 1904.

Nanykypusson. See *Nanikypusson.*

Nanzewaspe ('quiet heart'). The principal settlement of the Osage formerly in Neosho valley, s. E. Kans. According to De Smet its inhabitants numbered 600 in 1850.
Çän'ᶻse wáspe.—Dorsey, Osage MS. vocab., B. A. E., 1883. Nän'ᶻse wáspe.—Ibid. Nanze-Waspe.—De Smet, W. Missions, 355, 1856.

Naogeh ('deer'). A clan of the Seneca.
Canendeshé.—French writer (1666) in N. Y. Doc. Col. Hist., IX, 47, 1855. Nä-o'-geh.—Morgan, League Iroq., 46, 80, 1851 (Seneca form).

Napa. A name of doubtful Indian origin, now used to designate a county, a town, a river, and a creek in California. So far as can be learned it was not used as a village name by either the Wintun or the Yukian Wappo, the territories of both of which peoples embrace parts of Napa co., the boundary between them passing just N. of Napa City. Powers (Cont. N. A. Ethnol., III, 218, 1877) lists it as a Patwin tribe. (S. A. B.)

Napai. A mixed Athapascan and Kuskwogmiut village on the N. bank of Kuskokwim r., a little above Kolmakof, Alaska; pop. 23 in 1890.
Napaimute.—Hallock in Nat. Geog. Mag., IX, 91, 1898.

Napai. A Nushagagmiut Eskimo village in the Nushagak district, Alaska; pop. 11 in 1890.
Napaimiut.—11th Census, Alaska, 164, 1893 (Eskimo name for the people).

Napaiskak. A Kuskwogmiut Eskimo village on the left bank of Kuskokwim r., about 4 m. below Bethel, Alaska; pop. 196 in 1880, 97 in 1890.
Napaiskágamut.—Kilbuck quoted by Baker, Geog. Dict. Alaska, 1902. Napaskeagamiut.—11th Census, Alaska, 164, 1893. Napaskiagamute.—Petroff in 10th Census, Alaska, 17, 1884.

Napakiak. A Kuskwogmiut village on the right bank of Kuskokwim r., about 10 m. below Bethel, Alaska; pop. 98 in 1880.
Napachiakáchagamut.—Kilbuck quoted by Baker, Geog. Dict. Alaska, 454, 1906. Napahaiagamut.—Nelson in 18th Rep. B. A. E., pt. 1, 23, map, 1899. Napahaiagamute.—Petroff in 10th Census, Alaska, 17, 1884. Napahayagamiut.—11th Census, Alaska, 104, 1893. Napahayagamute.—Petroff, Resources of Alaska, 53, 1881.

Napaklulik. A Malemiut Eskimo village on Mangoak r., Alaska, s.E. of Selawik lake, about lat. 66° 20', lon. 160° 20'.
Nah-park-lu-lik.—Stoney (1886) quoted by Baker, Geog. Dict. Alaska, 454, 1906. Napaklulik.—Baker, ibid.

Napakutak. An Eskimo village on an island variously called Ettyhren, Ipekut, and Chirluk, off the N. E. coast of Siberia. Pop. 52 in 5 houses about 1895; 37 in 4 houses in 1901.
Napa'kutak.—Bogoras, Chukchee, 29, 1904 (Eskimo name). Nepe'kuten.—Ibid. (Chukchee name).

Napeshneeduta ('Red man who flees not'). A Mdewakanton Sioux, the first full-blood Dakota man to be baptized and received into a Christian church. He was a son of the sister of Mrs Renville, wife of Joseph Renville the trader, and claimed kindred with some of the principal chiefs of the Mdewakanton. He is described as having been above the average height, well formed, and with a countenance indicative of intelligence, kindness, and honesty. He was baptized at Lac-qui-Parle, Minn., Feb. 21, 1840, receiving the name Joseph Napeshnee; his wife was received into the church at the same time, and he brought four children to be baptized, three of them by former wives. His wife died within 5 years, when he married a convert, Pretty Rainbow, who deserted him; he later married another Christian woman and removed to Little Crow's Village, a few miles below Ft Snelling, on the Mississippi, where many of his relatives lived. Here he became ill with fever, and because of his change of religious faith his people refused him food and help. When the outbreak of the Sioux began in 1862, Joseph, like the other Christian Indians, befriended the whites, and in the following spring he was engaged as a Government scout, a position which he held for several years, returning finally to Lac-qui-Parle where he died in July 1870. In his last years Joseph was respected for his piety and industry by both whites and Indians. For nearly 10 years he was a ruling elder in the Presbyterian church, and supported his family, notwithstanding the infirmities of old age, without Government aid. See Williamson in Minn. Hist. Soc. Coll., III, 188, 1880.

Napetaca. A village of the Yustaga tribe or "province" in Florida, the scene of one of the fiercest battles between the Indians and De Soto's troops in 1539. It was probably on one of the head-streams of Suwannee r. (J. M.)
Napetaca.—Gentl. of Elvas (1557) quoted by Bourne, De Soto Narr., I, 41, 1904. Napetuca.—Gentl. of Elvas in Hakluyt Soc. Pub., IX, 39, 1851. Napituca.—Ranjel (ca. 1546) in Bourne, op. cit., II, 73, 1904.

Napeut. A former Pima rancheria on the N. bank of the Rio Gila, s. Ariz.; visited by Father Garcés in 1770.
Napeut.—Arricivita, Chrónica, II, 416, 1792.

Napissa (Choctaw: naⁿpisa, 'spy,' 'sentinel'). A tribe mentioned in 1699 by Iberville as united with the Chickasaw, living in villages adjoining those of the latter, and speaking the same or a cognate language. As they disappear from history early in the 18th century, it is probable that they were absorbed by the Chickasaw, if indeed they were not a local division of the latter. (A. S. G.)
Napissa.—Iberville (1699) in Margry, Déc., IV, 184, 1880. Napyosa.—Ibid., 164. Napyssas.—Ibid., 180.

Napiw^a. See *Nanabozho.*

Napobatin. A name said by Gibbs (Schoolcraft, Ind. Tribes, III, 110, 1853) to signify 'many houses,' and to have been used by the Indians of Big valley, on the s. shore of the main body of Clear lake, for themselves collectively. This is doubtful. (S. A. B.)

Napochies. A tribe living near Coosa r., Ala., at war with the Coças (Creeks) in 1560. They were probably a Muskhogean people, more nearly affiliated to the modern Choctaw. Cf. *Napissa.*
Napaches.—Fairbanks, Hist. Fla., 86, 1871. Napochies.—Barcia, Ensayo, 35–37, 1723.

Napoya. A clan of the Apohola phratry of the Timucua of Florida.—Pareja (ca. 1612) quoted by Gatschet in Proc. Am. Philos. Soc., XVII, 492, 1878.

Nappeckamak ('enclosed or occupied water-place'). The principal village of the Manhattan, on the site of Yonkers, N. Y.
Nappeckamaks.—Bolton quoted by Ruttenber, Tribes Hudson's R., 77, 1872. Nappikomack.—Ruttenber, Ind. Geog. Names, 23, 1906. Nepahkomuk.—Ibid.

Napúchi ('mountain pass'). A small rancheria of the Tarahumare near Norogachic, Chihuahua, Mexico.—Lumholtz, inf'n, 1894.

Naquiscoça. An unidentified town visited by Moscoso's troops in 1542, w. of Mississippi r.—Gentl. of Elvas (1557) in French, Hist. Coll. La., II, 199, 1850.

Narajerachic ('where the dead are dancing'). A burial cave of the Tarahumare in the Arroyo de las Iglesias, on the road from Batopilas to Carichic, in s. w. Chihuahua, Mexico. It has been much despoiled in recent years on account of mining the saltpeter deposits in the cave, in conducting which about a hundred bodies were uncovered.—Lumholtz, Unknown Mex., I, 222, 1902.

Nararachic (probably 'place of tears', or 'weeping place'). Formerly a large pueblo of the Tarahumare, but now an unimportant settlement about 15 m. N. of Norogachic, lat. 27° 40', lon. 107°, Chihuahua, Mexico. With the neighboring ranches the population numbered about 180 families in 1902.
Marrarachic.—Lumholtz in Scribner's Mag., XVI, 311, Sept. 1894 (misprint). Narárachic.—Lumholtz in Internat. Cong. Anthrop., 102, 1894.

Naraticon. A division of the Delawares of s. New Jersey. They have been variously located by writers, but according to Brinton lived on Raccoon cr.
Hattikongy.—De Laet (1633) in N. Y. Hist. Soc. Coll., 2d s., I, 315, 1841. Naratekons.—De Laet (1633), ibid., 303. Naraticons.—Brinton, Lenape Leg., 42, 1885. Naricon.—Doc. of 1656 in N. Y. Doc. Col. Hist., I, 590, 1856 (the creek). Narraticongs.—Proud, Penn., II, 295, 1798. Narraticonse.—Stuyvesant (1608) in N. Y. Doc. Col. Hist., XII, 61, 1877. Narratikonck.—Herrman map, 1670. Nar-rit-i-congs.—Macauley, N. Y., II, 164, 1829.

Narices. A tribe, probably Coahuiltecan or Tamaulipan, at Reinoso, Mexico, near the Rio Grande, below Laredo, Texas, in 1757. They were with the Nazas, Comecrudos, and Tejones. The Narices and the Nazas had been converted at Villa de Pilon, in Nueva Leon (Joseph Tienda de Cuervo, Informe del Reconocimiento e Ynspección de la Colonia de el Seno Mexicano, 1757, MS. in the Archivo General, Historia, LVI; Orozco y Berra, Geog., 294, 1864). (H. E. B.)
Narises.—Tienda de Cuervo, op. cit., 1757.

Nariz (probably Spanish 'nose'). A Papago village, probably in Pima co., s. Ariz.; pop. about 250 in 1863.
Naris.—Browne, Apache Country, 291, 1869 (misquoting Poston). Nariz.—Poston in Ind. Aff. Rep. 1863, 385, 1864.

Narosigak. An Ikogmiut Eskimo village on the left bank of Kwemeluk pass, at Nioklakowik slough, Yukon delta, Alaska.
Narosigagamieut.—Putnam (1899) cited by Baker, Geog. Dict. Alaska, 454, 1906 (mieut='people'). Narosigak.—Baker, ibid.

Narraganset ('people of the small point,' from naiagans, diminutive of naiag, 'small point of land,' with locative ending -et). An Algonquian tribe, formerly one of the leading tribes of New England. They occupied Rhode Island w. of Narragansett bay, including the Niantic territory, from Providence r. on the N. E. to Pawcatuck r. on the s. w. On the N. w. they claimed control over a part of the country of the Coweset and Nipmuc, and on the s. w. they claimed by conquest from the Pequot a strip extending to the Connecticut line. They also owned most of the islands in the bay, some of which had been conquered from the Wampanoag. The Niantic, living in the western part of the country, were a subordinate tribe who became merged with the Narraganset after King Philip's war. The Narraganset escaped the great pestilence that in 1617 desolated the southern New England coast, and, being joined by numbers of the fugitives from the E., became a strong tribe. The early estimates, as usual, greatly exaggerate, but it is certain

NARRAGANSET OF CONNECTICUT, BORN AT BROTHERTON, WISCONSIN. (F. G. SPECK, PHOTO.)

that they numbered, including their dependents, several thousand when first known to the whites. In 1633 they lost 700 by smallpox, but in 1674 they still numbered about 5,000. The next year saw the outbreak of King Philip's war, which involved all the neighboring tribes and resulted in the destruction of the Indian power in southern New England. The Narraganset threw their whole strength into the contest and shared the common fate. In the celebrated swamp fight near Kingston, R. I., on Dec. 19, 1675, they lost nearly 1,000 in killed and prisoners, and soon thereafter the survi-

vors were forced to abandon their country and take refuge in small bands among the interior tribes in the N. and W. It is probable that most of them joined the Mahican and Abnaki, though some may have found their way to Canada. In 1682 a party of about 100 fugitives at Albany asked permission to return in peace. The Niantic had taken no part in the war against the whites, and in this way preserved their tribal organization and territory. The scattered Narraganset, as they surrendered, were settled among them, and the whole body henceforth took the name of Narraganset. They were assigned a tract near Charlestown, R. I., and constantly decreased in numbers, as they were hemmed in by the whites. Many of them joined the Brotherton Indians in New York in 1788. Those who remained numbered about 140 in 1812, and 80 in 1832, but these are now reduced to a few individuals of mixed Indian and negro blood, some of whom have joined the Mohegan near Norwich, Conn.

The Narraganset were ruled by eight chiefs, each of whom had his own particular territory, but was subject to the head chief, who lived at their principal village, called Narraganset, about the site of Kingston. Of the religion of the aborigines of Rhode Island, Roger Williams wrote, Feb. 28, 1638 (Mass. Hist. Soc. Coll., 4th s., VI, 225, 1863) as follows: "They have plenty of Gods or divine powers: the Sunn, Moone, Fire, Water, Earth, the Deere, the Beare, &c. I brought home lately from the Nanhiggonsicks the names of 38 of their Gods, all they could remember." Denison says: "They made no images; their divinities were ghosts; they were extreme spiritualists. Every element and material and object had its ruling spirit, called a god, or Manitou. These divinities seemed ever passionate and engaged in war with each other; hence the passionate and warlike character of the worshippers. They adored not intelligence and virtue, but power and revenge. Every person was believed to be under the influence of some spirit, good or evil—that is, weak or strong—to further the person's desires. These spirits, or Manitous, inhabited different material forms, or dwelt at times in them. The symbolic signature employed by sachems and chiefs, in signing deeds, represented, in many cases, the forms inhabited by their guardian or inspiring spirits; these were bows, arrows, birds, fishes, beasts, reptiles, and the like."

The following were the Narraganset and Niantic villages: Charlestown, Chaubatick, Maushapogue, Mittaubscut, Narraganset, Niantic, Pawchauquet, and Shawomet.

In addition to the writings cited below, consult, for historical data, Rider, Lands of Rhode Island, 1904.   (J. M.)

Amirgankaniois.—Jes. Rel. 1652, 26, 1858. **Anygansets.**—Prince (1632) in Mass. Hist. Soc. Coll., 2d s., VII, 59, 1818. **Marraganeet.**—Jones, Ojebway Inds., 139, 1861 (misprint). **Nahiganiouetch.**—Jes. Rel. 1640, 35, 1858. **Nahiganset.**—Williams (1682) in R. I. Col. Rec., I, 26, 1856. **Nahigganneucks.**—Patent of 1643, ibid., 144. **Nahigconset.**—Williams (1675) in Mass. Hist. Soc. Coll., 4th s., VI, 301, 1863. **Nahiggonsick.**—Williams (1638), ibid., 247. **Nahiggonsjcks.**—Williams (1675), ibid., 304. **Nahigonset.**—Ibid., 300. **Nahigonsick.**—Williams (1638), ibid., 246. **Nanaganset.**—Doc. of 1671 in R. I. Col. Rec., II, 368, 1857. **Nanheygansetts.**—Doc. of 1642, ibid., I, 130, 1856. **Nanhigansets.**—Act of 1644, ibid., 134. **Nanhigga23neuck.**—Williams (1643) in Mass. Hist. Soc. Coll., 1st s., III, 205, 1794 (the true tribal name). **Nanhigganset.**—Williams (1646) in R. I. Col. Rec., I, 33, 1856. **Nanhiggansick.**—Williams (1637) in Mass. Hist. Soc. Coll., 3d s., IX, 299, 1846. **Nanhiggon.**—Williams (1638), ibid., 4th s., VI, 222, 1863. **Nanhiggonset.**—Ibid. **Nanhiggonsicks.**—Ibid., 223. **Nanhiggonticks.**—Williams (1636), ibid., 3d s., I, 160, 1825. **Nanhiggs.**—Williams (1660) quoted by Caulkins, Hist. Norwich, 47, 1866. **Nanhigonset.**—Williams (1668) quoted by Drake, Bk. Inds., bk. 2, 100, 1848. **Nanhigonsick.**—Williams (1638) in Mass. Hist. Soc. Coll., 4th s., VI, 223, 1863. **Nanhygansett.**—Doc. of 1654 in R. I. Col. Rec., I, 131, 1856. **Nanhygansit.**—Gorton and Holden (1667), ibid., II, 234, 1857. **Nanihiggonsicks.**—Williams (1637) in Mass. Hist. Soc. Coll., 4th s., VI, 189, 1863. **Nannogans.**—Mason (1643), ibid., VII, 411, 1865 (abbreviation). **Nannogansetts.**—Ibid. **Nanohiggazneuks.**—Mourt (1622), ibid., 1st s., VIII, 241, 1802. **Nanohigganset.**—Ibid., 239. **Nanohiggunsets.**—Doc. of 1643 quoted by Drake, Bk. Inds., bk. 2, 55, 1848. **Nantigansick.**—Williams (ca. 1640), ibid., 23. **Nantygansick.**—Callender in R. I. Hist. Soc. Coll., IV, 73, 1838. **Nantyggansiks.**—Callender quoted by Drake, Bk. Inds., bk. 2, 23, 1848. **Naragansets.**—Doc. of 1642 in Mass. Hist. Soc. Coll., 3d s., III, 161, 1833. **Naraganset.**—Winthrop (1634), ibid., 4th s., III, 326, 1856. **Naragansicks.**—Peter (ca. 1637), ibid., VI, 95, 1863. **Naraghenses.**—Jes. Rel., 1660, 27, 1858. **Naransett.**—Underhill (1638) in Mass. Hist. Soc. Coll., 3d s., VI, 1, 1837. **Naregansets.**—Patrick (1637) ibid., 4th s., VII, 323, 1865. **Narhigansets.**—Doc. of 1675 in N. Y. Doc. Col. Hist., XIV, 699, 1883. **Narhiggansetts.**—Bradford (1640) in Mass. Hist. Soc. Coll., 4th s., VI, 159, 1863. **Narhiggon.**—Doc. of 1675 in N. Y. Doc. Col. Hist., XIV, 699, 1883. **Naricanset.**—Pynchon (1643) in Mass. Hist. Soc. Coll., 4th s., VI, 373, 1863. **Narigansets.**—Cushman (1622), ibid., III, 122, 1856. **Narigansette.**—Treaty (1644), ibid., 480. **Narigansets.**—Bradford (ca. 1650), ibid., 285. **Narigenset.**—Williams (1654) quoted by Drake, Bk. Inds., bk. 2, 80, 1848. **Nariggansets.**—Williams (1648) in Mass. Hist. Soc. Coll., 3d s., IX, 271, 1846. **Narighansets.**—Bradford (ca. 1650), ibid., 4th s., III, 102, 1856. **Narihgansets.**—Ibid., 113. **Narogansetts.**—Writer of 1676 quoted by Drake, Ind. Chron., 115, 1836. **Narohigansets.**—Patent of 1635 in N. Y. Doc. Col. Hist., XIV, 30, 1883. **Narragancett.**—Doc. of 1668 in R. I. Col. Rec., II, 231, 1857. **Narragangsett.**—Greene (1670) in R. I. Col. Rec., II, 314, 1857. **Narraganses.**—Downing (1630) in Mass. Hist. Soc. Coll., 4th s., VI, 38, 1863. **Narragansett.**—Haynes (1643), ibid., 3d s., I, 230, 1825. **Narraghansets.**—Harris, Voy. and Trav., I, 854, 1705. **Narrangansett.**—Writer of 1644 in R. I. Col. Rec., I, 138, 1856. **Narregansets.**—Patrick (1637) in Mass. Hist. Soc. Coll., 4th s., VII, 323, 1865. **Narrhagansitt.**—Doc. of 1679 in R. I. Col. Rec., III, 63, 1858. **Narricanses.**—Doc. of 1655 in N. Y. Doc. Col. Hist., XIII, 58, 1881. **Narrigansets.**—Bradford (1640) in Mass. Hist. Soc. Coll., 4th s., VI, 160, 1863. **Narrigonset.**—Williams (1638), ibid., 247. **Narrogansets.**—Howes (1644) ibid., 513. **Narrohiggansets.**—Mourt (1622), ibid., 1st s., VIII, 238, 1802. **Narrohiggansets.**—Dee in Smith (1629), Va., II, 227, repr. 1819. **Narrohiggenset.**—Doc. of 1645 in Drake, Bk. Inds., bk. 2, 93, 1848. **Narrohiggin.**—Ibid., 91. **Narrohiggonsets.**—Mourt (1622) in Mass. Hist. Soc. Coll., 2d s., IX, 27, 1822. **Narrowbiggonset.**—Ibid., 68 (misprint). **Narrowgancett.**—Allyn (1670) in R.

I. Col. Rec., II, 347, 1857. **Narrowganneuchs.**—Doc. of 1726, ibid., IV, 371, 1859. **Narrowganneucks.**—Warwick (1643), ibid., 303. **narrow Ganset.**—Johnson (1654) in Mass. Hist. Soc. Coll., 2d s., IV, 42, 1816. **Narrowganssits.**—Ibid., II, 66, 1814. **Narrowganzet.**—Ibid., IV, 28, 1816. **Narrow-Higansetts.**—Patent of 1664 quoted by Thompson, Long Id., 90, 1839. **Narrow Higgansets.**—Patent of 1664 in Vt. Hist. Soc. Coll., II, 501, 1871. **Narygansetts.**—Winthrop (1650) in Mass. Hist. Soc. Coll., 3d s., IX, 289, 1846. **Nayhiggonsiks.**—Williams (1670), ibid., 1st s., I, 278, 1806. **Nazaganset.**—Eliot (1651), ibid., 3d s., IV, 125, 1834. **Nechegansitt.**—Gookin (ca. 1677) quoted by Drake, Bk. Inds., bk. 2, 23, 1848. **Neragonsitt.**—Stanton (1676) in N. Y. Doc. Col. Hist., XIV, 715, 1883. **Norragansett.**—Coddington (1674) in Mass. Hist. Soc. Coll., 4th s., VII, 295, 1865. **Nousaghauset.**—James quoted by Tanner, Narr., 329, 1830.

Narragansett pacer. A breed of horses for which Rhode Island was once famous; so called from the place-name Narragansett, also the appellation of the Algonquian tribe formerly resident in the Rhode Island country.   (A. F. C.)

Narsak. An Eskimo village at the mouth of Ameralik fjord, lat. 64°, w. Greenland.—Nansen, First Crossing of Greenland, II, 252, 1890.

Narsarsuk. An Eskimo village in w. Greenland.—Hartwig, Polar World, 462, map, 1869.

Narsuk. An Eskimo village on the s. E. coast of Greenland, lat. 60° 30′; pop. 20 in 1829.—Graah, Exped. East Coast Greenland, 114, 1837.

Na. Sa. For all names beginning with this abbreviation, see *Nuestra Señora.*

Nasagas-haidagai (*Nạ sagā′s xā′-idạga-i,* 'people of the rotten house'). A subdivision of the Gitins of the Haida of Skidegate, belonging to the Eagle clan. They were unable to restore their house for such a long time that it began to fall to pieces, hence the name. They once occupied a separate town.   (J. R. S.)
Na s′ā′gas qā′edra.—Boas in 12th Rep. N. W. Tribes Can., 24, 25, 1898. **Na sagā′s xā′-idạga-i.**—Swanton, Cont. Haida, 273, 1905. **Na s′ā′yas qā′etqa.**—Boas in 5th Rep. N. W. Tribes Can., 26, 1898. **Nisigas Hāade.**—Harrison in Proc. Roy. Soc. Can., 125, 1895.

Nasaump. See *Samp.*

Nascapee (a term of reproach applied by the Montagnais). The most northeasterly of the Algonquian tribes, occupying the elevated interior of Quebec and Labrador penin. N. of the Gulf of St Lawrence and extending from the vicinity of L. Mistassini to Ungava bay on the N. They call themselves Nanénot, 'true, real men.' Many of them have intermarried with their congeners the Montagnais, and when they visit the coast the two tribes frequent the same stations. When in the neighborhood of Ungava bay they are known as Ungava Indians. They are shorter and of lighter build than the Montagnais, and have delicately formed and clear-cut features, small hands and feet, and large, rather soft, eyes. According to their traditions the Nascapee were driven into their present country in early times by the Iroquois. They assert that originally they lived in a region to the w., N. of a great river (supposed to be the St Lawrence) and toward the E. lay an enormous body of water (believed to be Hudson bay). When they reached the Ungava region their only neighbors were Eskimo, who occupied the coast strip and with whom they became involved in war, which continued until after the arrival of the whites. The two peoples are now on terms of intimacy. The Nascapee do not have the endurance of their Eskimo neighbors against fatigue and hunger, although equally able to withstand the rigors of their harsh climate. The children are obedient; disrespect toward their elders is unknown, and in their dealings one with another there is no quarreling. The Nascapee are generally healthy; their prevailing diseases are of the lungs and bowels—the former resulting from exposure to the extremes of wet and cold and their insanitary houses; the latter due to their gluttony after long fasting from scarcity of food. Those who go to the coast to reside, as many have in recent years, appear to be more subject to diseases than those in the interior. Medical treatment consists of shamanistic incantations and the use of powders and liniments, both native and those procured from traders. Marriage is effected without ceremony and is conditioned on the consent of the parents of the young woman and the ability of the prospective husband to support a wife; after marriage the bond may be severed by either party on slight provocation. Polygamy is common, the number of wives a man may have being limited only by his means of supporting them. The sexual relations of the Nascapee are very loose; but their immorality is confined to their own people. The division of labor is similar to that among most tribes: the women perform all domestic work, including the transportation of game, fetching the fuel, erecting the tipis, hauling the sleds when traveling, etc.; the men are the providers. Girls reach puberty at 14 or 15 years, and are taken as wives at even an earlier age. Mothers usually do not bear more than 4 children; twins are rare.

The Nascapee suspend the bodies of their dead from branches of trees if the ground be much frozen, and endeavor to return when the weather is warm to bury them. Interment, however, has been practised only since the advent of missionaries. A man of distinction is often buried at once, after a fire has been built in a tipi to thaw the earth. They have no horror for the dead, having been known, it is said, to rob Eskimo corpses of their clothing and accompanying implements.

Like other Indians the Nascapee believe that every object, animate or inanimate, is possessed of a form of spirit which, in order that it may perform its services for the welfare of the people, must be propitiated with acceptable offerings. The medicine-men are supposed to be in direct contact with all forms of spirits, and are consulted when it is desired to overcome their baneful influence by means of the shaman's art.

The subsistence of the Nascapee is gained by the chase, which is engaged in chiefly during the winter. In the spring men, women, and children repair to the trading posts, chiefly Ft Chimo, where they trade furs, ptarmigan feathers, etc., for the articles and products of civilization. The reindeer forms the chief source of their food and clothing, although fish, ptarmigan, ducks, geese, hares, rabbits, porcupines, beaver, and, in stress of hunger, an occasional lynx, are also eaten; the eggs of wild fowl are consumed in enormous quantities and in all stages of incubation. Reindeer are speared from canoes while crossing a stream, or snared or shot from ambush while passing through a narrow defile, or, in winter, are driven into a snowbank and speared. In these slaughterings an incredible number of carcasses and skins are left to decay. Wolverenes, wolves, and foxes are never eaten. The flesh of game animals is dried, pounded, made into pemmican, and stored in baskets and bags for future use.

The apparel of the Nascapee is quite distinct for the two sexes; the clothing varies also with the season, as the extremes of climate are very great. That of the men consists of tanned reindeer coat, breeches, leggings, moccasins, gloves or mittens, and cap or headdress. Seams are sewed with sinew, and all the garments except the leggings, which are mostly hidden by the long coat, are ornamented with extravagant painted designs. Moccasins are rarely ornamented, except with beads or with strips of colored cloth. Beaded head-bands are used for bearing burdens, especially for carrying canoes when making portages. In winter the men wear the coat with the fur side inward and with a hood attached. In summer the women wear calico dresses, thin shawls obtained through trade, and moccasins; in winter their apparel consists of a reindeer skin robe, a sleeveless gown reaching a little below the knees, often highly ornamented with painted designs, beadwork, and fringe; and blanket shawl, shoulder cape, leggings, moccasins, and cap.

The dwellings, for both winter and summer, are tents or tipis of reindeer skins sewed together, and measuring 10 to 18 ft at the base and 10 to 14 ft high. The floor is carpeted with young spruce branches, except around the central fire-place; the smoke escapes through an opening in the top of the tipi where the supporting poles are brought together. The place of honor is the side opposite the fire. Poles extend across the tipi for the suspension of pots and kettles, and hunting apparatus, clothing, etc. are hung in convenient places. The outer edge of the interior is slightly raised above the center of the floor, affording a slope for the occupants when sleeping with their feet toward the fire. Sweat lodges of small poles covered with tent skins are in common use, and are heated, as usual, by means of hot stones on which water is poured. The domestic utensils of the Nascapee consist of thin vessels of spruce or birch, of various sizes, for hold-ing liquids and for use as drinking cups; berry dishes or baskets of birchbark, sewed like the wooden vessels with split roots; baskets of birchbark with buck-skin top and draw-string; bags made of the skins of reindeer legs sewed together; and spoons or ladles of wood nicely carved. They are inordinately fond of smoking, chewing, and snuffing tobacco—the lat-ter, however, is practised only among the aged, especially the women. When camped at the trading posts the Indians boil together tobacco and molasses, to which water is added; this compound is drunk until stupefaction ensues. Pipes are made usually of sandstone or slate, with stem of spruce, often ornamented with beadwork, and are valued according to the color of the stone. Transportation and traveling are conducted by means of canoes made of slats or ribs covered with birchbark, sleds or toboggans (*tá-bas-kán*), and snowshoes of four styles framed with wood and netted. Bows and arrows are now almost discarded for guns; but blunt-pointed arrows are still used for killing small game, and by boys. The reindeer spears, already referred to, consist of a shaft 6 ft long with a steel head made from a flat file. Reindeer snares are made of reindeer parchment cut into thin narrow thongs and plaited, or of tanned skin. Beaver are sometimes trapped in a sort of net. Knives, awls, ice scoops and picks, hair combs and comb cases, porcupine tails for cleaning the combs, and fishing tackle are among the neces-sary implements of every Nascapee house-hold.

The chief amusements of the men are games of draughts or checkers, of which they are exceedingly fond, and cup-and-ball. Feasts, accompanied by dance and ceremony, may be given by a man who has been unusually successful in hunt-ing. Drums and drum-like rattles are used for musical accompaniments in their ceremonies; other rattles, as well as bows

and arrows, which are shot at effigy tar-gets, are used by the boys, while elabo-rately costumed dolls are made for the girls. Like other tribes the Nascapee have an abundance of folktales, the chief subject of which are the animals common to their environment. In these tales the wolverene seems to play a prominent part. (See Turner in 11th Rep. B. A. E., 267 et seq., 1894.)

On account of their wandering habits, the nature of their country, and their mixture with the Montagnais, it is im-possible to give an exact statement of their numbers. In 1858 they were esti-mated at about 2,500. In 1884 the Nas-kapee of the lower St Lawrence were officially reported to number 2,860, and the Indians of Labrador and E. Ruperts Land were returned as 5,016. In 1906 there were 2,183 Montagnais and Nasca-pee officially noted as such, and 2,741 unnamed Indians in the interior, 1,253 of whom were in the unorganized territo-ries of Chicoutimi and Saguenay. See *Montagnais, Nitchequon.*

Cuneskapi.—Laure (1731) quoted by Hind, Lab. Penin., I, 34, 1863 (misprint for Ouneskapi). **Es-ko-piks.**—Walch, Map Am., 1805. **Nascopi.**—Stearns, Labrador, 262, 1884. **Nascopie.**—McLean, Hudson Bay, II, 53, 1849. **Nascupi.**—Stearns, Lab-rador, 262, 1884. **Naskapis.**—Hocquart (1733) quoted by Hind, op. cit., 11. **Naskapit.**—Kingsley, Stand. Nat. Hist., pt. 6, 149, 1885. **Naskopie.**—Turner in 11th Rep. B. A. E., 183, 1894. **Nasko-pis.**—Kingsley, Stand. Nat. Hist., pt. 6, 149, 1885. **Naskupis.**—Hocquart (1733) quoted by Hind, Lab. Penin., II, 96, 1863. **Naspapees.**—Stearns, Labra-dor, 262, 1884. **Nasquapees.**—Ibid. (correct form). **Nasquapioks.**—Cartwright (1774) quoted by Hind, Lab. Penin., II, 101, 1863. **Ne né not.**—Turner in 11th Rep. B. A. E., 183, 1894 ('true men': own name). **Neskaupe.**—Kingsley, Stand. Nat. Hist., pt. 6, 148, 1885. **Ounachkapiouek.**—Jes. Rel. for 1643, 38, 1858. **Ounadcapis.**—Stearns, Labrador, 262, 1884. **Ounascapis.**—Hind, Lab. Penin., I, 275, 1863. **Ounescapi.**—Bellin, map, 1755. **Scoffies.**—Gallatin in Trans. Am. Ethnol. Soc., II, ciii, 1848. **Secof-fee.**—Brinton, Lenape Leg., 11, 1885. **Shouda-munk.**—Gatschet in Trans. Am. Philos. Soc., 409, 1885 ('good Indians': Beothuk name). **Skoffie.**—Writer ca. 1799 in Mass. Hist. Soc. Coll., 1st s., VI, 16, 1800. **Unescapis.**—La Tour, map, 1779. **Ungava Indians.**—McLean, Hudson Bay, II, 53, 1849.

Nashamoiess. An Algonquian village in the S. E. part of Marthas Vineyard, Mass., in 1659.—Cotton in Mass. Hist. Soc. Coll., 1st s., I, 204, 1806.

Nashanekammuck. A former Algon-quian village at Chilmark, Marthas Vineyard, Mass. In 1698 the inhabitants numbered 231.

Nashanekammuck.—Rep. of 1698 in Mass. Hist. Soc. Coll., 1st s., X, 131, 1809. **Nashouohkamack.**—Ibid., 1, 204, note, 1806. **Nashouohkamuk.**—Mayhew, Ind. Converts, 13, 1727. **Nashuakemmiuk.**—Cotton in Mass. Hist. Soc. Coll., 1st s., I, 204, 1806.

Nasheakusk ('Loud Thunder'; also spelled Nashashuk, Nasheshuk, Nasues-kuk, Nasheaskusk, Nasheescuck, etc.). The son of Black Hawk and his wife Asshawequa ('Singing Bird'). He was the eldest of Black Hawk's three chil-dren, the others being Nasomsee or Gamesett, a son, and Namequa, a daugh-

ter, who were living at the close of the
Black Hawk war in 1832. Nasheakusk
did not bear a conspicuous part in the
Indian history of the N. W., being of
note chiefly from his association with his
famous father. He was born probably
about the close of the 18th century. He
remained with and followed the fortunes
of his father not only during the war of
1832, but also during his captivity, and
seems also to have lived with his father's
family until the latter's death, Oct. 3,
1838, subsequently remaining with his
mother for some years, probably until
her death, Aug. 29, 1846. Nasheakusk
and his brother made complaint to Gov.
Lucas of Iowa when their father's grave
was desecrated, which resulted in the recovery of the bones. The time of his

NASHEAKUSK

death is not given. A portrait, painted
by Samuel M. Brookes while Nasheakusk
and his father were prisoners of war at
Fortress Monroe, Va., is in possession of
the Historical Society of Wisconsin (see
illustration).   (c. t.)

Nashobah. A former village of Christian Indians in the Nipmuc country, near
Magog pond, in Littleton, Mass. Of it
John Eliot wrote in 1670: "This place
lying in the road-way which the Mau-
quaogs [Mohawk] haunted, was much molested by them, and was one year wholly
deserted, but this year the people have
taken courage, and dwell upon it again."
In 1675 the inhabitants, numbering about
50, were removed to Concord, Mass., on
account of King Philip's war.
Nashoba.—Drake, Bk. of Inds., bk. 2, 54, 1833.
Nashobah.—Gookin (1674) in Mass. Hist. Soc. Coll.,
1st. s., I, 188, 1806. Nasholah.—Writer of 1676

quoted by Drake, Ind. Chron., 125, 1836 (misprint). Nashope.—Eliot quoted by Tooker, Algonq. Ser., x, 24, 39, 1901.

Nashola ('wolf'). A Chickasaw clan
of the Ishpanee phratry.
Nashóba.—Gatschet, Creek Migr. Leg., I, 96, 1884.
Nä-sho-lä.—Morgan, Anc. Soc., 163, 1877.

Nashua ('the land between'). A tribe
formerly living on upper Nashua r., in
Worcester co., Mass., said by some to
have been connected with the Massachuset, but classed by Potter with the
Pennacook. They had a village called
Nashua near the present Leominster, but
their principal village seems to have been
Weshacum, a few miles farther s. The
Nashua tract extended for several miles
in every direction around Lancaster. On
the outbreak of King Philip's war, in
1675, they joined the hostile Indians, and,
numbering several hundred, attempted to
escape at his death in two bodies to the
E. and w. Both parties were pursued and
a large number were killed and captured,
the prisoners being afterward sold into
slavery. A few who escaped eastward
joined the Pennacook, while about 200 of
the others crossed the Hudson to the Mahican or the Munsee, and ceased to exist
as a separate tribe. A few still remained
near their old homes in 1701.   (j. m.)
Nashaue.—Early form cited by Kinnicutt, Ind.
Names, 29, 1905. Nashaway.—Eliot (1651) in Mass.
Hist. Soc. Coll., 3d s., IV, 123, 1834. Nashawog.—
Eliot (1648), ibid., 81. Nashawogg.—Early form
cited by Kinnicutt, op. cit. Nashoway.—Rep. (ca.
1657) in N. H. Hist. Soc. Coll., III, 96, 1832. Nash-
ua.—Writer of 1810 in Mass. Hist. Soc. Coll., 2d s.,
I, 181, 1814. Nashuays.—Drake, Bk. Inds., ix, 1848.
Nashuway.—Hinckley (1676) in Mass. Hist. Soc.
Coll., 4th s., V, 1, 1861. Nashuyas.—Domenech,
Deserts, I, 442, 1860. Nassawach.—Courtland (1688)
in N. Y. Doc. Col. Hist., III, 562, 1853. Nasshaway.—
Pynchon (1677), ibid., XIII, 511, 1881. Nassoway.—
Writer of 1676 quoted by Drake, Ind. Chron., 130,
1836. Naushawag.—Paine (ca. 1792) in Mass. Hist.
Soc. Coll., 1st s., I, 115, 1806.

Nashwaiya ('slanting wolf'). One of
the former Choctaw "Sixtowns," probably in Jasper co., Miss.
Nashoopawaya.—West Fla. map, ca. 1772. Nasho-
weya.—Gatschet, Creek Migr. Leg., I, 109, 1884.
Nashwaiya.—Halbert in Pub. Ala. Hist. Soc., I,
383, 1901.

Nasiampaa. A band of Mdewakanton
Sioux, named from a chief, formerly living E. of Mississippi r., 25 m. from the
agency, near St Paul, Minn.; pop. 139.—
Schoolcraft, Ind. Tribes, III, 612, 1853.

Naskotin. A Takulli sept dwelling in
Chentsithala and Nesietsha villages on
Fraser r., near the mouth of Blackwater
r., Brit. Col. Pop. 65 in 1906, having be-
come reduced from 90 in 1890 through
alcoholic excesses.
Nænscud-dinneh.—Balbi, Atlas Ethnog., 821, 1826.
Nascotins.—Domenech, Deserts, II, 62, 1860. Nas-
cud.—Cox, Columbia R., 327, 1831. Nascud Denee.—
Mackenzie, Voy., II, 175, 1802. Nashkoten.—Smet,
Oregon Miss., 100, 1847. Naskoaten.—Macfie, Van-
couver Id., 428, 1865. Nas-koo-tains.—Harmon,
Jour., 245, 1820. Naskotins.—Cox, Columbia R.,
II, 346, 1831. Na-sku-tenne.—A. G. Morice, inf'n,
1890. Nasrad-Denee.—Vater, Mithridates, III, 421,
1816. Nauscud Dennies.—Gallatin in Trans. Am.
Antiq. Soc., II, 20, 1836. Niscotins.—Hale in U. S.

Expl. Exped., IV, 451, 1845. **Tsistlatho band.**—Can.
Ind. Aff., 214, 1902.

Nasnocomacack. A Massachuset village
in 1616, on the coast of Massachusetts,
probably a few miles N. of Plymouth.—
Smith (1616) in Mass. Hist. Soc. Coll.,
3d s., VI, 108, 1837.

Nasomsee. See *Nasheakusk.*

Nasoni. A former tribe of the Caddo
confederacy. Their principal village
from 1687 to 1752, and probably later, was
about 27 m. N. of Nacogdoches, on or
near an eastern branch of Angelina r., N. E.
Texas. They are possibly identical with
the Nisione of the De Soto narrative of
Biedma. They are mentioned by Joutel
in 1687 and by La Harpe in 1719. The
Spanish mission of San José de los Nazones was established among them in
1716, east of upper Angelina r., but was
transferred to San Antonio r. in 1731.
Being upon the contested Spanish-French
border ground they suffered accordingly
from disease. They are mentioned in
the Texas census of 1790, but seem to
have disappeared as a distinct tribe about
the end of the century. In customs and
religion they resembled their kindred of
the Caddo confederacy.
Nadsonites.—De la Tour, Map Amérique, 1779.
Nasone.—Census of Sept. 16, 1790, in Tex. State
Archives. **Nasonis.**—Barcia, Ensayo, 289, 1723.
Nasony.—Linares (1716) in Margry, Déc., VI, 217,
1886. **Nasoris.**—Barcia, op. cit., 265. **Nasoui.**—
Tonti (1690) in French, Hist. Coll. La., I, 73,
1846. **Nassomtes.**—Boyd, Ind. Loc. Names, 70,
1885. **Nassoni.**—Joutel (1687) in Margry, Déc.,
III, 409, 1878. **Nassonians.**—Hennepin, New Discov., pt. II, 28, 1698. **Nassonit.**—Walche, Charte
von America, 1805. **Nassonites.**—La Harpe (1719)
in Margry, Déc., VI, 263, 1886. **Nazone.**—Tex.
State Archives, Nov. 17, 1763. **Nisione.**—Biedma
(1544) in Hakluyt, Soc. Pub., IX, 197, 1851. **Nis-
sohone.**—Gentl. of Elvas (1557) quoted by Shea,
Early Voy., 149, 1861. **Nissoon.**—Harris, Voy. and
Trav., I, 810, 1705. **Nissoone.**—Gentl. of Elvas
(1557) in French, Hist. Coll. La., II, 198, 1850.
Noachis.—Bancroft, No. Mex. States, I, 614, 1886.
Nossonis.—Hennepin, Discov., Thwaites ed., 416,
1903. **Nozones.**—Rivera, Diario, leg. 2602, 1736.
Sassory.—Cavelier (1687) quoted by Shea, Early
Voy., 39, 1861 (possibly identical).

Nassauaketon ('forked river'). One of
the four Ottawa divisions, living toward
the close of the 17th century in N. Michigan or Wisconsin on a river N. of Green
bay. They were so called from the fact
that they resided then or previous to
leaving Canada on a river having three
branches. See *Negaouichiriniouek.*
Nancokoueten.—Writer of 1695 in N. Y. Doc. Col.
Hist., IX, 627, 1855. **Nansoakouatons.**—Bacqueville
de la Potherie, Hist. Am., IV, 204, 1753. **Nansoua-
ketons.**—Ibid., II, 64. **Nansoüa, Kœtons.**—Ibid.,
48. **Nassauaketon.**—Cadillac (1695) in Minn. Hist.
Soc. Coll., V, 405, 1885. **Nassauakuetoun.**—Cadillac
(1695) in Margry, Déc., V, 80, 1883. **Nassawaketon.**—Verwyst, Missionary Labors, 210, 1886.
Nation de Fourche.—Jes. Rel. 1671, 42, 1858.
Ounasaooetois.—De la Chesnaye (*ca.* 1695) in Margry, Déc., V, 80, 1883. **People of the Fork.**—Montreal
conf. (1700) in N. Y. Doc. Col. Hist., IX, 719, 1855.
Rasaoua koueton.—Jes. Rel. 1640, 35, 1858. **Sassa-
souaoottons.**—Prise de possession (1671) in Perrot,
Mém., 293, 1864. **Sassassouakouetons.**—Perrot,
Mém., 295, note, 1864. **Sassassaouacottons.**—Prise
de possession (1671) in Margry, Déc., I, 97, 1875.
Sassassaoüa Cottons.—Prise de possession (1671)
in N. Y. Doc. Col. Hist., IX, 803, 1855.

Nasskatulok. Given by Krause as a
Yuit Eskimo village at the head of Plover
bay, Siberia (Deutsche Geog. Blätt., V,
80, map, 1882), but it is not mentioned
by Bogoras.

Nastedi ('people of Nass'). A division
of the Wolf phratry of the Tlingit, living
at Kuiu, Alaska. They are said to have
come from Nass r., whence the name.
Nas-tēdi.—Krause, Tlinkit Ind., 120, 1885.

Nasto-kegawai (*Nastŏ′ qē′gawa-i*, 'those
born at Nasto [Hippa] id.'). A branch of
the Skwahladas, one of the most important families of the Raven clan of the
Haida, living on the w. coast of Queen
Charlotte ids., Brit. Col.—Swanton, Cont.
Haida, 270, 1905.

Nasueskuk.—See *Nasheakusk.*

Nasumi. A former Kusan village or tribe
on the s. side of the mouth of Coquille r.,
on the coast of Oregon, near the site of
the present town of Bandon.
Coquille.—Abbott, MS. Coquille census, B. A. E.,
1858. **Lower Coquille.**—Dorsey, Naltûnnetûnně
MS. vocab., B. A. E., 1884. **Masonah.**—Taylor in
Cal. Farmer, June 8, 1860. **Na′-ǫu-mi′ ʝûnnĕ′.**—
Dorsey in Jour. Am. Folk-lore, III, 231, 1890 (Tututni name). **Nas-ah-mah.**—Kautz, MS. Census of
1854, B. A. E., 1855. **Nas-oǫmah.**—Parrish in Ind.
Aff. Rep. 1854, 495, 1855. **Na-son.**—Smith, ibid.,
476. **Nas-sou.**—Abbott, MS. Coquille census, B. A.
E., 1858. **Na′-su-mi.**—Dorsey in Jour. Am. Folk-
lore, III, 231, 1890 (Naltûnnetûnně name).

Natahquois. A Nanticoke village in
1707, probably on the E. shore of Maryland or on the lower Susquehanna.—
Evans (1707) quoted by Day, Penn., 391,
1843. The name is probably only a variant of Nanticoke.

Nataini ('mescal people'). A division
of the Mescalero Apache who claim the
country of the present Mescalero res.,
N. Mex., as their former home.
Nata-hinde.—Mooney, field notes, B. A. E., 1897.
Nata-ï′ni.—Ibid.

Natal rites. See *Child-life.*

Natalsemoch. Given by Kane as the
name of a tribe in Smith inlet, Brit. Col.
It can not be identified with that of any
tribe in this region, but it may have
been applied to a part of the Goasila who
also live on Smith inlet.
Nalal se mooh.—Schoolcraft, Ind. Tribes, V, 488,
1855. **Nalatsenoch.**—Scouler (1846) in Jour. Ethnol.
Soc. Lond., I, 233, 1848. **Natal-se-mooh.**—Kane,
Wand. in N. Am., app., 1859.

Nataotin. A Takulli tribe living on
middle Babine r. and Babine lake, Brit.
Col. Dawson gave their number as
about 300 in 1881. Morice (Notes on
W. Denes, 27, 1892) said that they were
in 3 villages on the N. half of Babine
lake and numbered 310. They are the
people formerly known as Babines, but
Morice gave that name also to the Hwot-
sotenne, as there is perfect community of
language, and both tribes wear labrets.
In 1906 the two bands at Ft Babine and
at the old fort numbered 283. The names
of their villages are Lathakrezla and
Neskollek.
Babinas.—Domenech, Deserts of N. Am., I, 440,
1860. **Babine Indians.**—Hale, Ethnog. and Philol.,

202, 1846. **Babin Indians.**—Latham in Trans. Philol. Soc. Lond., 66, 1856. **Babinis.**—Domenech, op.cit., II, 62, 1860. **Big-lips.**—Kane, Wand. in N. Am.,241, 1859. **Nahto-tin**—Brit. Col. map. **Naotetains.**—Prichard, Phys. Hist., v, 377, 1847. **Nataotin.**—Anderson quoted by Gibbs in Hist. Mag., VII, 76, 1863. **Na-taw-tin.**—Dawson in Geol. Surv. Can. 1879–80, 30B, 1881. **Nâte-ote-tains.**—Harmon, Jour., 203, 1820. **Natotin Tiné.**—Am. Nat., XII, 484, 1878. **Na-to-utenne.**—A. G. Morice, inf'n, 1890. **Ntaauotin.**—Latham in Trans. Philol. Soc. Lond., 66, 1856.

Natarghiliitunne ('people at the big dam'). A former village of the Mishikhwutmetunne on Coquille r., Oreg.

Na′-ta-rxi′-li-i′ ɣûnnĕ.—Dorsey in Jour. Am. Folklore, III, 232, 1890. **Nate′-l′i′-äte tĕne′.**—Everette, Tutu MS. vocab., B. A. E., 1883 (trans. 'people near the waterfall').

Natashquan. A Montagnais rendezvous, visited also by the Nascapee, at the mouth of Natashquan r., on the N. shore of the Gulf of St Lawrence, Quebec. It contained 76 people in 1906.

Natashquan.—Hind, Lab. Penin., II, map, 1863. **Nataskouan.**—Ibid., 180.

Natasi. A former village on Red r. of Louisiana, occupied by one of the tribes of the Caddo confederacy. In 1882 a Caddo Indian gave the Natasi as a division of the Caddo confederacy (Gatschet, Creek Migr. Leg., I, 43, 1884), but as the name does not appear in the revised list of these divisions in 1891 (Mooney in 14th Rep. B. A. E., 1092, 1896) it may be merely a subdivision of the Nabedache. Tonti in 1690 mentioned the villages of the "Nadas" as N. w. of the Natchitoch and near the Yatasi; he also speaks of the Nadouc villages as 12 leagues from Red r. In both instances he probably referred to the same people whose village Iberville learned of in 1699, the name of which was given by his Taensa Indian guide as Nataché. La Harpe in 1719 speaks of the same people by the name Nadassa, saying they were a small nation on Red r. Although the villages of the Natasi lay within the area that was in dispute by the Spaniards, French, and Americans during the 18th and the first half of the 19th centuries, the name of the people is hardly mentioned. Nothing is known of them as a tribe; they had probably mingled with their kindred, whose fate they shared, and if any survive they are now with the Caddo on their reservation in Oklahoma. (A. C. F.)

Nadas.—Tonti (1690) in French, Hist. Coll. La., I, 72, 1846. **Nadassa.**—La Harpe (1719), ibid., III, 19, 1851. **Nadouc.**—Tonti, op. cit., 83. **Nadouches.**—La Harpe, op. cit., 68. **Nataché.**—Iberville (1699) in Margry, Déc., IV, 178, 1880. **Nátassi.**—Gatschet, Creek Migr. Leg., I, 43, 1884 (Caddo name). **Naytasses.**—Robin, Voy. à la Louisiane, III, 3, 1807.

Natatladiltin (*Nata-tla-diltin*, 'agave plant'). An Apache clan or band at San Carlos agency and Ft Apache, Ariz., in 1881.—Bourke in Jour. Am. Folk-lore, III, 112, 1890.

Natche, Natchez. See *Nahche*.

Natchesan Family. A linguistic family established by Powell (7th Rep. B. A. E., 1891), consisting of two tribes, usually known under the names Natchez and Taensa, each comprising several villages. The former dwelt near the present city of Natchez, Miss., the latter near Newellton, La. For the relationship of these two tribes we are dependent entirely on the categorical statements of early French writers, as not a word of Taensa is certainly known to exist. A supposed grammar of this language was published by Adam and Parissot, but it is still under suspicion. For the probable relations of this supposed family with the Muskhogeans, see *Natchez*.

>**Natches.**—Gallatin in Trans. and Coll. Am. Antiq. Soc., II, 95, 306, 1836 (Natches only); Prichard, Phys. Hist. Mankind, v, 402, 403, 1847. >**Natsches.**—Berghaus (1845), Physik, Atlas, map 17, 1848; ibid., 1852. >**Natchez.**—Bancroft, Hist. U.S., 248, 1840; Gallatin in Trans. Am. Ethnol. Soc., II, pt. 1, xcix, 77, 1848 (Natchez only); Latham, Nat. Hist. Man., 340, 1850 (tends to include Taensas, Pascagoulas, Colapissas, and Biluxi in same family); Gallatin in Schoolcraft, Ind. Tribes, III, 401, 1853 (Natchez only); Keane in Stanford's Compend., Cent. and So. Am., app., 460, 473, 1878 (suggests that it may include the Utchees). >**Naktche.**—Gatschet, Creek Migr. Leg., I, 34, 1884; Gatschet in Science, 414, Apr. 29, 1887. >**Taensa.**—Gatschet in The Nation, 382, May 4, 1882; Gatschet in Am. Antiq., IV, 238, 1882; Gatschet, Creek Migr. Leg., I, 33, 1884; Gatschet in Science, 414, Apr. 29, 1887 (Taensas only).

Natchez. A well-known tribe that formerly lived on and about St Catherine's cr., E. and S. of the present city of Natchez, Miss. The name, belonging to a single town, was extended to the tribe and entire group of towns, which included also peoples of alien blood who had been conquered by the Natchez or had taken refuge with them. Iberville, on his ascent of the Mississippi in 1699, names, in the Choctaw language, the following 8 towns, exclusive of Natchez proper: Achougoulas, Cogoucoula, Ousagoucoula, Pochougoula, Thoucoue, Tougoulas, Yatanocas, and Ymacachas. Of these, Tougoulas and perhaps Thoucoue are the Tioux (q. v.) towns. It is probably safe to infer that the 9 towns, including Natchez, represented the entire group, and that the Corn, Gray, Jenzenaque, White Apple, and White Earth villages are only other names for some of the above, with which it is now impossible to identify them. The Tioux and Grigras were two nations under the protection of the Natchez; both were of alien blood. Du Pratz alludes to a tradition that the Taensa and Chitimacha were formerly united with the Natchez, but left them, though the latter had always recognized them as brothers. The Taensa were, indeed, probably an offshoot of the Natchez, but the Chitimacha were of a distinct linguistic family.

It is difficult to form an estimate of the numerical strength of this tribe, as the figures given vary widely. It is probable that in 1682, when first visited by the French, they numbered about 6,000, and were able to put from 1,000 to 1,200 warriors in the field.

The Natchez engaged in three wars with the French, in 1716, 1722, and 1729. The last, which proved fatal to their nation, was caused by the attempt of the French governor, Chopart, to occupy the site of their principal village as a plantation, and it opened with a general massacre of the French at Fort Rosalie, established in 1716. The French, in retaliation, attacked the Natchez villages with a strong force of Choctaw allies, and in 1730 the Natchez abandoned their villages, separating into three bodies. A small section remained not far from their former home, and a second body fled to Sicily id., near Washita r., where they were attacked early in 1731 by the French, many of them killed, and about 450 captured and sold into slavery in Santo Domingo. The third and most numerous division was received by the Chickasaw and built a village near them in N. Mississippi, called by Adair, Nanne Hamgeh; in 1735 these refugees numbered 180 warriors, or a total of about 700. In the year last named a body of Natchez refugees settled in South Carolina by permission of the colonial government, but some years later moved up to the Cherokee country, where they still kept their distinct town and language up to about the year 1800. The principal body of refugees, however, had settled on Tallahassee cr., an affluent of Coosa r. Hawkins in 1799 estimated their gun-men at about 50. They occupied the whole of one town called Nauchee and part of Abikudshi. The Natchez were therefore not exterminated by the French, as has frequently been stated, but after suffering severe losses the remainder scattered far and wide among alien tribes. A few survivors, who speak their own language, still exist in Indian Ter., living with the Cherokee, and in the councils of the Creeks until recently had one representative.

Though the accounts of the Natchez that have come down to us appear to be highly colored, it is evident that this tribe, and doubtless others on the lower Mississippi, occupied a somewhat anomalous position among the Indians. They seem to have been a strictly sedentary people, depending for their livelihood chiefly upon agriculture. They had developed considerable skill in the arts, and wove a textile fabric from the inner bark of the mulberry which they employed for clothing. They made excellent pottery and raised mounds of earth upon which to erect their dwellings and temples. They were also one of the eastern tribes that practised head-flattening. In the main the Natchez appear to have been peaceable, though like other tribes they were involved in frequent quarrels with their neighbors. All accounts agree in attributing to them an

extreme form of sun worship and a highly developed ritual. Moreover, the position and function of chief among them differed markedly from that among other tribes, as their head chief seems to have had absolute power over the property and lives of his subjects. On his death his wives were expected to surrender their lives, and parents offered their children as sacrifices. The nation was divided into two exogamic classes, nobility and commoners or *michmichgupi*, the former being again divided into suns, nobles proper, and esteemed men. Children of women of these three had the rank of their mother, but children of common women fell one grade below that of their father. There were various ways, however, by which a man could raise himself from one grade to another at least as far as the middle grade of nobles. While the commoners consisted partially of subject tribes, the great majority appear to have been as pure Natchez as the nobility. In spite of great lexical divergence, there is little doubt that the Natchez language is a Muskhogean dialect.

Consult Gatschet, Creek Migr. Leg., I, 1884; Mooney, (1) Siouan Tribes of the East, Bull. B. A. E., 1894, (2) in Am. Anthrop., n. s., I, no. 3, 1899, (3) in 19th Rep. B. A. E., 1900, and the authorities cited below. For the archeology of the old Natchez country, see Bull. Free Mus. Univ. Pa., II, no. 3, Jan. 1900.

(H. W. H.   J. R. S.)

Ani'-Na'tsĭ.—Mooney in 19th Rep. B. A. E., 509, 1900 (Cherokee name, abbreviated *Anintsĭ;* sing. *A-Na'tsĭ*). **Chelouels.**—Iberville (1699) in Margry, Déc., IV, 269, 1880. **Innatohas.**—Doc. *ca.* 1721, ibid., VI, 230, 1886. **Nacha.**—Iberville, op. cit., 255. **Nachee.**—Adair, Am. Inds., 225, 1775. **Naches.**—Tonti (1686) in Margry, Déc., III, 556, 1878. **Nachez.**—Schermerhorn (1812) in Mass. Hist. Soc. Coll., 2d s., II, 18, 1814. **Nachis.**—Barcia, Ensayo, 246, 1723. **Nachvlke.**—Brinton in Am. Philos. Soc. Proc., XIII, 483, 1873. **Nachy.**—Tonti (1684) in Margry, Déc., I, 609, 1875. **Nadchés.**—Iberville (1700), ibid., IV, 404, 1880. **Nadechès.**—Ibid., 602. **Nadezès.**—Ibid., 402. **Nahchee.**—Adair, Am. Inds., 353, 1775. **Nahy.**—Tonti (1684) in Margry, Déc., I, 603, 1875. **Naichoas.**—McKenney and Hall, Ind. Tribes, III, 81, 1854 (possibly identical). **Naktohe.**—Gatschet, Creek Migr. Leg., I, 34, 1884. **Natché.**—LaSalle (1682) in Margry, Déc., I, 558, 1875. **Natchee.**—S. C. Gazette (1734) quoted by Rivers, Hist. S. Car., 38, 1856. **Natches.**—Proces verbal (1682) in French, Hist. Coll. La., I, 47, 1846. **Natchese.**—Hervas, Idea dell' Universo, XVII, 90, 1784. **Natchets.**—Bacqueville de la Potherie, Hist. de l'Am., I, 239, 1753. **Natchez.**—Pénicaut (1700) in French, Hist. Coll. La., n. s., I, 57, 1869. **Nattechez.**—Bartram, Voy., I, map, 1799. **Nauchee.**—Hawkins (1799), Creek Country, 42, 1848. **Netches.**—Woodward, Rem., 79, 1859. **Nitches.**—Ibid., 16. **Noatches.**—Domenech, Deserts N. Am., I, 442, 1860. **Notchees.**—Doc. of 1751 quoted by Gregg, Hist. Old Cheraws, 10, 1867. **Notches.**—Glen (1751) quoted by Gregg, ibid., 14. **Pine Indians.**—Mooney in 19th Rep. B. A. E., 509, 1900 (given as incorrect rendering of *Ani'-Na' tsĭ,* op. cit.). **Sunset Indians.**—Swan (1795) in Schoolcraft, Ind. Tribes, V, 260, 1855. **Techloel.**—Iberville (1699) in Margry, Déc., IV, 155, 1880. **Telhoel.**—Ibid., 121. **Theloël.**—Ibid., 179. **Theloelles.**—Ibid., 409. **Tpelois.**—Iberville (1700) in French, Hist. Coll. La., n. s., 26, 1869.

Natchez. The principal village of the Natchez, probably situated on St Catherine's cr., near the Liberty road bridge, about 3 m. from the present city of Natchez, Miss. Later this name was given to a town of the refugee Natchez among the Upper Creeks.

Natchitoch (Caddo form, *Näshi′tosh*). A tribe of the Caddo confederacy which spoke a dialect similar to that of the Yatasi but different from that of the Kadohadacho and its closely affiliated tribes. Their villages were in the neighborhood of the present city of Natchitoches, near those of another tribe called Doustioni (q. v.). Whether the army of De Soto encountered them is unknown, but after La Salle's tragic death among the Hasinai his companions traversed their country, and Douay speaks of them as a "powerful nation." In 1690 Tonti reached them from the Mississippi and made an alliance; and in 1699 Iberville learned of them through a Taensa Indian, but did not visit them in person. Next year, however, he sent is brother Bienville across to them from the Taensa villages. From that time and throughout the many vicissitudes of the 18th century the tribe never broke faith with the French. In 1705 they came to St Denis, commandant of the first French fort on the Mississippi, and asked to be settled in some place where they might obtain provisions, as their corn had been ruined. They were placed near the Acolapissa, and remained there until 1712 when St Denis took them back to their old country to assist him in establishing a new post as a protection against Spanish encroachments, and also in the hope of opening up commercial relations. This post, to which a garrison was added in 1714, remained an important center for trade and travel toward the S. W. for more than a century. St Denis sent messages to the tribes living in the vicinity, urging them to abandon their villages and come to settle near the post, assuring them that he would never forsake them. Some of the tribes yielded to his persuasions, hoping to find safety during the disturbances of the period, but the movement only accelerated the disintegration already begun. In 1731, St Denis, at the head of the Natchitoch and other Indians, besides a few Spaniards, inflicted severe defeat on a strong party of Natchez under the Flour chief, killing about 80 of them. The Natchez, after their wars against the French, had fled to Red r. and were living not far from the trading post and fort. The importance of this establishment and the friendliness of the Natchitoch made the latter so conspicuous in the affairs of the time that during the first half of the 18th century Red r. was known as the Natchitock, a variant of Nashitosh or Natchitoch. Du Pratz states that about 1730 their village near the French post numbered 200 cabins. Owing to wars in which they were forced to take part, to the introduction of new diseases, particularly smallpox and measles, the population of the tribe rapidly declined. In his report to President Jefferson, in 1805, Sibley gives their number as only 50, and adds, "The French inhabitants have a great respect for these natives, and a number of families have a mixture of their blood in them." Shortly afterward they ceased to exist as a distinct tribe, having been completely amalgamated with the other tribes of the Caddo confederacy (q. v.), from whom they differed in no essential of custom, or of ceremonial or social organization.   (A. C. F.   J. R. S.)

Naçacahoz.—Gentl. of Elvas (1557) in French, Hist. Coll. La., II, 199, 1850. **Na-cé-doo.**—J. O. Dorsey, Caddo MS., B. A. E., 1881. **Nachitoches.**—Tonti (1690) in French, Hist. Coll. La., I, 72, 1846. **Nachitock.**—Coxe, Carolana, 10, 1741. **Nachitooches.**—Kingsley, Stand. Nat. Hist., pt. VI, 173, 1885. **Nachitos.**—Joutel (1687) in French, Hist. Coll. La., I, 168, 1846. **Nachittoos.**—Yoakum, Hist. Texas, I, 392, 1855. **Nachittos.**—Ibid., 386. **Nachtichoukas.**—Jefferys, French Dom., pt. I, 164, 1761. **Nacitos.**—Linarès (1716) in Margry, Déc., VI, 217, 1886. **Nactchitoches.**—Du Pratz, Hist. La., II, 242, 1758. **Nactythos.**—Iberville (1699) in Margry, Déc., IV, 178, 1880. **Nadohito.**—Bienville (1700), ibid., 434. **Nadohitoches.**—Ibid., 435. **Nadohitoe.**—Iberville (1700), ibid., 409. **Naguadacó.**—Tex. State Archives, Sept. 16, 1790. **Naguateeres.**—Coxe, Carolana, 10, 1741. **Naketoe's.**—ten Kate, Reizen in N. A., 374, 1885. **Naketosh.**—Gatschet, Caddo and Yatassi MS., 77, B. A. E. **Nakitoches.**—Anduze (after 1825) in Ann. de Prop. de la Foi, III, 501-509. **Napgitache.**—McKenney and Hall, Ind. Tribes, III, 82, 1854. **Napgitoches.**—Coxe, Carolana, map, 1741. **Naquitoches.**—Belle-Isle (1721) in Margry, Déc., VI, 341, 1886. **Nashédosh.**—Gatschet, Creek Migr. Leg., I, 43, 1884. **Näshi′tosh.**—Mooney in 14th Rep. B. A. E., 1092, 1896 (proper Caddo form). **Nasitti.**—Joutel (1687) in Margry, Déc., III, 409, 1878. **Nassitoches.**—Pénicaut (1705), ibid., V, 459, 1883. **Natchetes.**—Hennepin, New Discov., II, 43, 1698. **Natchidosh.**—Gatschet, Creek Migr. Leg., I, 43, 1884. **Natchiloches.**—Domenech, Deserts N. A., I, 442, 1860. **Natchites.**—Douay (1687) quoted by Shea, Discov. Miss., 218, 1852. **Natchitoch.**—Gravier (1701) quoted by Shea, Early Voy., 149, 1861. **Natchitoches.**—Bienville (1700) in Margry, Déc., IV, 437, 1880. **Natchitochis.**—Porter (1829) in Schoolcraft, Ind. Tribes, III, 596, 1853. **Natchitotches.**—Lewis and Clark, Journal, 143, 1840. **Natchitto.**—Joutel (1687) in Margry, Déc., III, 409, 1878. **Natschitos.**—Ibid., 408. **Natsitoches.**—Jefferys, Am. Atlas, map 5, 1776. **Natsshostanno.**—Joutel, op. cit., 409. **Natsytos.**—Iberville (1699), ibid., IV, 178, 1880. **Nazacahoz.**—Gentl. of Elvas (1557) quoted by Shea, Early Voy., 149, 1861. **Neguadoch.**—Güssefeld, Charte von Nord America, 1797. **Nepgitoches.**—Barcia, Ensayo, 289, 1723. **Notchitooches.**—Carver, Travels, map, 1778. **Yatchitoches.**—Lewis and Clark, Journal, 142, 1840.

Nateekin. An Aleut village on Nateekin bay, Unalaska, Aleutian ids., Alaska, with 15 inhabitants in two houses in 1830.

Nateekenskoi.—Elliott, Cond. Aff. Alaska, 225, 1875. **Natieka.**—Sarichef (1792) quoted by Baker, Geog. Dict. Alaska, 296, 1901. **Natiekinskoe.**—Veniaminof (1830) quoted by Baker, ibid., 1906. **Natuikinsk.**—Petroff in 10th Census, Alaska, 34, 1884. **Natykinskoe.**—Veniaminof, Zapiski, II, 202, 1840. **Natykinskoje.**—Holmberg, Ethnog. Skizz., 142, map, 1855.

Natesa (from *ahzingh*, black,' 'dark,'
hence 'dark people'). One of the three
classes or castes into which the Kutchakutchin are divided, the others being the
Chitsa and the Tangesatsa, q. v.
Nah-t'singh.—Hardisty in Smithson. Rep. 1866,
315, 1872 (name of their country). Nate-sa.—Kirby,
ibid., 1864, 418, 1865; Hardisty, ibid., 1866, 315,
1872. Nat-sah-i.—Jones in Smithson. Rep. 1866,
326, 1872. Nat-singh.—Hardisty, op. cit.

Natick ('the place of (our) search.'—
Tooker). A village founded by Indian
converts, mainly Massachuset, under the
supervision of the noted missionary John
Eliot, in 1650, near the present Natick,
Mass. Soon after its establishment it
numbered about 150 inhabitants, who
were given a reserve of 6,000 acres. It
increased in population and after King
Philip's war was the principal Indian village in that region. In 1749 there were
166 Indians connected with the settlement. On the breaking out of the French
and Indian war in 1754 many of the Natick
Indians enlisted against the French. Some
never returned, and the others brought
back an infectious disease which rapidly
reduced the population. In 1764 there
were 37 in the village and some others
connected with it. In 1792 the whole
body numbered but 25 or 30, and soon
thereafter they had become so mixed with
negroes and whites as to be no longer distinguishable. It was reported in Dec.
1821, that Hannah Dexter, 76 years of
age, "the last of the Naticks," had been
murdered by her grandson at Natick.
For a discussion of the name, consult
Tooker, Algonquian Series, x, 1901. See
Missions. (J. M.)
Mawyk.—Salisbury (1678) in N. Y. Doc. Col. Hist.,
XIII, 526, 1881 (misprint). Na-cheek.—Plat of 1677
cited by Tooker, Algonq. Ser., x, 18, 1901. Na-
chick.—Decl. of 1677, ibid. Naitticke.—Salisbury
(1678), op. cit., 524. Natick.—Wilson (1651) in Mass.
Hist. Soc. Coll., 3d s., IV, 177, 1834. Natics.—Barton, New Views, lviii, 1798. Natik.—Eliot (1651) in
Mass. Hist. Soc. Coll., 3d s., IV, 172, 1834. Natique.—
Eliot (1678), ibid., 4th s., VIII, 377, 1868. Nattick.—
Brockholst (1678) in N. Y. Doc. Col. Hist., XIII,
530, 1881. Natuck.—Ibid., 524. Nittauke.—Perry
quoted by Tooker, Algonq. Ser., x, 9, 1901 (given
as Indian name).

Nation, The. A term formerly applied
to several of the larger and more important tribes and confederacies in the Gulf
states, particularly the Creeks, but also to
the Cherokee, Catawba, Choctaw, and
Chickasaw. At present it is an official
term applied to each of the Five Civilized
Tribes (q. v.) in Oklahoma, viz, the Cherokee, Creeks, Choctaw, Chickasaw, and
Seminole. The term *Les Nations* was
used by Canadian French writers of the
17th and 18th centuries (and occasionally in English writings) to designate the
heathen tribes, who were distinguished
into Les grandes Nations and Les petites
Nations. The Rivière des petites Nations in the province of Quebec preserves
this designation. Specifically Le petit
Nation was the Weskarini, q. v.
(H. W. H. A. F. C.)

National Indian Association. A society
for improving the condition of the Indians.
It originated in Philadelphia in 1879 with
a memorial circulated by Mary L. Bon-
ney and Amelia Stone Quinton petition-
ing the Government to prevent the
encroachments of white settlers on Indian
territory and to guard the Indians in the
enjoyment of all the rights guaranteed to
them on the faith of the Nation. A second memorial in 1880 obtained 50,000
signatures, and a third in 1881, signed by
100,000 persons, asked for all Indians
common school and industrial teaching,
land in severalty, and the full status of
citizens. The association, formally constituted in 1880, and taking the name the
National Indian Association in 1882,
changing it to the Women's National
Indian Association in 1883, was the first
body of friends of the Indians to demand
for them citizenship and lands in severalty. For these objects it labored till
1884, when missionary work was added,
and since then it has established for 50
tribes or tribal remnants Christian missions, erecting more than 50 buildings,
which when well established were given
to the various permanent denominational
missionary societies. A home building
and loan department, a young people's
department, libraries, special education
for bright Indians, and hospital work
were added later. The National Indian
Association, which resumed its earlier
name in 1901, has asked for more schools,
an increase in the number of field
matrons, the righting of various wrongs,
and protection and justice to many tribes,
and has constantly advocated the application of civil service reform principles to
the entire Indian service, the gradual
abolition of Indian agencies, the payment
of debts due Indians from the Government, and other measures needed to prepare Indians for civilized self-support
and good citizenship. Since 1888 the
Association has published a periodical
called *The Indian's Friend.* (A. S. Q.)

Natkelptetenk (*N'atqĕlptɛ'tɛnk*, 'yellow-
pine little slope'). A village of the Lytton band of Ntlakyapamuk, on the w.
side of Fraser r., about a mile above
Lytton, Brit. Col.—Teit in Mem. Am.
Mus. Nat. Hist., II, 172, 1900.

Natkhwunche (*Nat-qwûn'-tcě*). A for-
mer village of the Chastacosta on Rogue r.,
Oreg.—Dorsey in Jour. Am. Folk-lore,
III, 234, 1890.

Natleh ('it [the salmon] comes again').
A Natliatin village at the discharge of
Fraser lake into Watleh r., Brit. Col.;
pop. 53 in 1902, 64 in 1906.
Frazer's Lake Village.—Can. Ind. Aff., pt. 2, 78,
1906. Natle.—Morice in Trans. Roy. Soc. Can.
1892, sec. 2, 109, 1893. Natleh.—Morice, Notes on
W. Dénés, 25, 1893.

Natliatin. A Takulli sept inhabiting
the villages Natleh and Stella, one at each

end of Fraser lake, Brit. Col. Pop. 135 in 1892; 122 in 1906.

Chinloes.—Taylor in Cal. Farmer, July 19, 1862. Nantley Tine.—Hamilton in Jour. Anthrop. Inst. Gt. Br., VII, 206, 1878. Natilantin.—McDonald, Brit. Columbia, 126, 1862. Natleh-hwo 'tenne.—Morice, Notes on W. Dénés, 25, 1893 (= 'people of Natleh'). Natliantins.—Domenech, Deserts N. Am., II, 62, 1860. Natliáutin.—Hale, Ethnog. and Philol., 202, 1846. Natlo'tenne.—Morice, Notes on W. Dénés, 25, 1893. Nau-tle-atin.—Dawson in Can. Geol. Surv. 1879–80, 30B, 1881. Œtsœnhwotenne.—Morice, MS. letter, 1890 (= 'people of another kind': Nikozliautin name).

Natootzuzn ('point of mountain'). An Apache clan or band at San Carlos agency and Ft Apache, Ariz., in 1881; correlative with the Nagosugn clan of the Pinal Coyoteros and the Nadohotzosn of the Chiricahua.

Nar-ode-só-sin.—White, Apache Names of Ind. Tribes, MS., B. A. E. Nato-o-tzuzn.—Bourke in Jour. Am. Folk-lore, III, 112, 1890.

Natora. A former pueblo of the Jova in w. Chihuahua, Mexico, near the mission of Teopari, of which it was a visita prior to its abandonment in 1748. The inhabitants moved to within half a league of Arivechi and later settled in the pueblo of Ponida.

Natorase.—Doc. of 18th cent. quoted by Bandelier in Arch. Inst. Papers, IV, 511, 1892.

Natowasepe ('Huron river'). A former Potawatomi village on St Joseph r., about the present Mendon, St Joseph co., s. w. Mich., on a reservation sold in 1833. In addition to the references cited below, see Coffinberry in Mich. Pion. Coll., II, 489, 1880.

Na-to-wa-se-pe.—Treaty of 1832 in U. S. Ind. Treat., 153, 1873. Notawasepe.—Treaty of 1833, ibid., 176. Notawasepe's Village.—Royce in 18th Rep. B. A. E., Mich. map, 1900. Notawassippi.—Council of 1839 in Mich. Pion. Coll., X, 170, 1886. Nottawa Sape.—Treaty of 1827 in U. S. Ind. Treat., op. cit., 675. Nottawasippi.—Douglass (1840) in H. R. Doc. 143, 27th Cong., 2d sess., 3, 1842. Notta-we-sipa.—Treaty of 1832 in U. S. Ind. Treat., 701, 1873.

Natsitkutchin ('strong people'). A Kutchin tribe inhabiting the country from Porcupine r. northward to the Romanzof mts., Alaska. Gibbs (Notes on Ross, Tinne MS., B. A. E.) said that their habitat began in a mountainous region from 50 to 100 m. N. of Ft Yukon. They hunt the caribou as far as the seacoast, being a shifting people. They are chiefly known from their trading with the Kangmaligmiut Eskimo, and for the strong babiche that they make. They resemble the Kutchakutchin in physique and manners. Richardson gave their number as 40 men in 1850; Gibbs (op. cit.) stated that they had 20 hunters; Petroff in 1880 gave the total population as 120. The Teahinkutchin probably belonged to this tribe.

Gens de Large.—Petroff, Rep. Alaska, 62, 1881. Gens du Large.—Ross, MS. Notes on Tinne, B. A. E. Natche'-Kutchin.—Dall, Alaska, 430, 1870. Na-tsikku-chin.—Hardisty in Smithson. Rep. 1866, 197, 1872. Nātsik-kŭtchin.—Dall in Cont. N. A. Ethnol., I, 30, 1877. Natsit-kutchin.—Jones in Smithson. Rep. 1866, 321, 1872. Nā'-ts'ĭt kūtch'-ĭn.—Ross, MS. Notes on Tinne, B. A. E. (= 'outer-country people'). Neyetsè-kutchi.—Richardson, Arct. Exped., I, 399, 1851 (= 'people of the open

country'). Neyetse-Kutchin.—Bancroft, Nat. Races, I, map, 35, 1882. Neyetse-Kutshi.—Latham, Nat. Races, 294, 1854. Tρè-ttchié-dhidié-Koutchin.—Petitot, Autour du lac des Esclaves, 361, 1891 (= 'people who dwell far from the water').

Natsshostanno. An unidentified village or tribe mentioned to Joutel in 1687 (Margry, Déc., III, 409, 1878) by the chief of the Kadohadacho on Red r. of Louisiana as being among his enemies.

Natsushltatunne (Na'-tsúcl-ta'-yúnnĕ', 'people dwelling where they play shinny'). A former village of the Mishikhwutmetunne on Coquille r., Oreg.—Dorsey in Jour. Am. Folk-lore, III, 232, 1890.

Nattahattawants. A Nipmuc chief of Musketaquid, the present Concord, Mass., in 1642. At this time he sold to Simon Willard, in behalf of Gov. Winthrop and others, a large tract of land on both sides of Concord r., in consideration of which he received "six fadom of waompampege, one wastcot, and one breeches" (Drake, Bk. Inds., 54, 1833). Nattahattawants was a supporter and propagator of Christianity among his people, and an honest and upright man. His son, John, usually known as John Tahattawan, lived at Nashobah, Mass., where he was the chief ruler of the Praying Indians. His daughter became the wife of the celebrated Waban (q. v.).

Natthutunne ('people on the level prairie'). A former Tututni village on the s. side of Rogue r., Oreg.

Na-t'ọu' ̣ùnnĕ'.—Dorsey in Jour. Am. Folk-lore, III, 236, 1890. Na-t'qlo' ̣ùnnĕ.—Dorsey, Tutu MS. vocab., B. A. E., 1884 (Tututni and Naltunnetunne name).

Natuhli (Na'dû'lĭ', of unknown meaning). A former Cherokee settlement on Nottely r., a branch of Hiwassee r., at or near the site of the present village of Ranger, Cherokee co., s. w. S. Car. (J. M.)

Na'dû'lĭ'.—Mooney in 19th Rep. B. A. E., 526, 1900. Nantalee.—Royce in 5th Rep. B. A. E., map, 1887. Notley.—Doc. of 1799 quoted by Royce, ibid., 144. Nottely town.—Mooney, op. cit., 332.

Natutshltunne. A former village of the Tututni on the coast of Oregon, between Coquille r. and Flores cr.

Na-tcûl'-tûn.—Dorsey in Jour. Am. Folk-lore, III, 233, 1890. Na-tcûtçl' ̣ùnnĕ'.—Ibid.

Natuwanpika (Ná-tu-wan-pi-ǩa). One of the traditional stopping places of the Bear clan of the Hopi, situated near the present Oraibi, Ariz.

Naugatuck. A former village, subject to the Paugusset, at the falls of Naugatuck r., near Derby, Conn. (Trumbull, Conn., I, 42, 1818). The name refers to a tree, which probably served as a landmark, said to have stood near Rock Rimmon, in what is now Seymour, Conn. (Trumbull, Ind. Names Conn., 36, 1881).

Nauhaught. A Massachusetts Indian, called Elisha and also Joseph, a deacon in 1758 or 1760 of an Indian church that stood on the N. side of Swan's pond, at Yarmouth, Mass. He was a conscientious man and the hero of Whittier's

"Nauhaught the Deacon," in which the poet alludes to his bravery in overcoming temptation. See also Mass. Hist. Soc. Coll., 1st s., v, 56, 1816.

Naujan. A summer settlement of the Aivilirmiut Eskimo on Repulse bay, N. end of Hudson bay.—Boas in 6th Rep. B. A. E., 446, 1888.

Naujateling. An autumn settlement of Talirpingmiut Okomiut Eskimo on an island near the s. w. coast of Cumberland sd., near the entrance; pop. 20 in 1883.— Boas in 6th Rep. B. A. E., map, 1888.

Nauklak. A Kaniagmiut Eskimo village 15 m. E. of Naknek lake, Alaska penin., Alaska.
Naouchlágamut.—Spurr and Post quoted by Baker, Geog. Dict. Alaska, 1902. Nauklak.—Baker, ibid.

Naumkeag ('fishing place,' from *namaas* 'fish,' *ki* 'place,' *-ag* 'at'). A tribe or band, probably belonging to the Pennacook confederacy, which formerly occupied the site of Salem, Mass. It appears, however, that the natives had abandoned the locality before the English reached it, as there is no record that the latter found any Indians on the spot. It has been noticed in regard to the native burials in this locality that the bodies were usually placed in a sitting posture.
Naamhok.—Mather quoted by Drake, Bk. Inds., bk. 3, 99, 1848. Naamkeke.—Doc. of 1676 in N. H. Hist. Soc. Coll., III, 99, 1832. Naembeck.—Smith (1629), Va., II, 177, repr. 1819 (misprint). Naemkeck.— Ibid., 183. Naemkeek.—Smith quoted by Drake, Bk. Inds., bk. 3, 93, 1848. Nahamcok.—Parker (1677) in N. H. Hist. Soc. Coll., III, 100, 1832. Nahum-keag.—Drake, Bk. Inds., bk. 3, 94, 1848. Naiemkeck.—Smith (1629), Va., II, 193, repr. 1819. Namaaskeag.—Potter in Me. Hist. Soc. Coll., IV, 190, 1856. Nambeke.—Bradford (*ca.* 1650) in Mass. Hist. Soc. Coll., 4th s., III, 195, 1856. Namkeake.—Ibid., 241. Namkeg.—Mather quoted by Drake, Bk. Inds., bk. 3, 99, 1848. Naumkeag.—Deed of 1621 in Mass. Hist. Soc. Coll., 2d s., VI, 614, 1815. Naumkeak.—Bartlett (1628), ibid., II, 163, 1814. Naumkeock.—Doc. of 1682, ibid., 3d s., I, 72, 1825. Naumkeek.—Grant of 1635, ibid., 2d s., V, 228, 1815. Naumkek.—Scottow (1694) in Mass. Hist. Soc. Coll., 4th s., IV, 315, 1858. Naumkuk.— Mather quoted by Drake, Bk. Inds., bk. 3, 99, 1848. Nehum-kek.—Higgeson (1629) in Mass. Hist. Soc. Coll., 1st s., I, 123, 1806. Neumkeage.—Bentley (*ca.* 1799), ibid., VI, 231, 1800.

Nauniem (*Naúniĕm,* 'ridge people'). A temporary band of Comanche which is said to have remained near the Rocky mts. to catch horses while the other bands or divisions roamed the plains to the eastward.
Naúniĕm.—Hoffman in Proc. Am. Philos. Soc., XXIII, 299, 1886. No-na-um.—Neighbors in Schoolcraft, Ind. Tribes, II, 128, 1852.

Nauquanabee. See *Naguonabe.*

Nause. A former tribe or probably a subdivision of the Nanticoke in Dorchester co., Md. In 1608 their principal village, of the same name, was on the N. bank of Nanticoke r., near its mouth.— Smith (1629), Va., I, 175, repr. 1819.

Nauset. An Algonquian tribe formerly living in Massachusetts, on that part of C. Cod E. of Bass r., forming a part of or being under control of the Wampanoag.

A writer (Coll. Mass. Hist. Soc., 1st s., VIII, 159, 1802) says: "The Indians in the county of Barnstable were a distinct people, but they were subject in some respects to the chief sachem of the Wampanoags." They probably came in contact with the whites at an early date, as the cape was frequently visited by navigators. From this tribe Hunt in 1614 carried off 7 natives and sold them into slavery with 20 Indians of Patuxet. Champlain had an encounter with the Nauset immediately before returning to Europe. They seem to have escaped the great pestilence which prevailed along the New England coast in 1617. Although disposed to attack the colonists at their first meeting, they became their fast friends, and with few

NAUSET WOMAN OF MASHPEE, MASS.   (F. G. SPECK, PHOTO.)

exceptions remained faithful to them through King Philip's war, even in some instances lending assistance. Most of them had been Christianized before this war broke out. Their estimated population in 1621 was 500, but this is probably below their real strength at that time, as they seem to have numbered as many 80 years afterward. About 1710, by which time they were all organized into churches, they lost a great many by fever. In 1764 they had decreased to 106, living mainly at Potanumaquut, but in 1802 only 4 were said to remain. Their principal village, Nauset, was near the present Eastham. Although their location indicates that fish furnished their chief sustenance, the Nauset were evidently cultivators of the soil, as supplies of corn and beans were obtained from them by the famishing Plymouth colonists in 1622.

The following villages were probably Nauset: Aquetnet, Ashimuit, Cataumut, Coatuit, Cummaquid, Manamoyik, Manomet, Mashpee, Mattakeset, Meeshawn, Namskaket, Nauset, Nobscusset, Pamet, Pawpoesit, Pispogutt, Poponesset, Potanumaquut, Punonakanit, Satucket, Satuit, Skauton, Succonesset, Waquoit, and Weesquobs.　　　　　　　　　　　(J. M.　C. T.)

Cape Indians.—Hubbard (1680) in Mass. Hist. Soc. Coll., 2d s., v, 33, 1815. **Namset.**—Josselyn (1675), ibid., 3d s., III, 317, 1833 (misprint). **Nasitt.**—Hubbard (1680), ibid., 2d s., v, 54, 1815. **Nauset.**—Mourt (1622) quoted by Drake, Bk. Inds., bk. 2, 29, 1848. **Nausit.**—Smith (1616) in Mass. Hist. Soc. Coll., 3d s., VI, 119, 1837. **Nausites.**—Mourt (1622), ibid., 1st s., VIII, 226, 1802. **Nawsel.**—Dermer (1620), ibid., 4th s., III, 97, 1856 (misprint). **Nawset.**—Smith (1616), ibid., 3d s., VI, 108, 1837. **Nawsits.**—Dee in Smith (1629), Va., II, 225, repr. 1819.

Nauvasa. The northernmost of the Catawba towns formerly on Santee r., S. Car.—Byrd (1728), Hist. Dividing Line, 181, 1866.

Nauwanatats (*Nau-wan'-a-tats*). A Paiute band formerly living in or near Moapa valley, s. E. Nev.; pop. 60 in 1873.—Powell in Ind. Aff. Rep. 1873, 50, 1874.

Navaho (pron. *Na'-va-ho*, from Tewa *Navahú*, the name referring to a large area of cultivated lands; applied to a former Tewa pueblo, and, by extension, to the Navaho, known to the Spaniards of the 17th century as Apaches de Navajó, who intruded on the Tewa domain or who lived in the vicinity to distinguish them from other "Apache" bands.—Hewett in Am. Anthrop., VIII, 193, 1906. Fray Alonso Benavides, in his Memorial of 1630, gives the earliest translation of the tribal name, in the form *Nauajó*, 'sementeras grandes'—'great seed-sowings', or 'great fields'. The Navaho themselves do not use this name, except when trying to speak English. All do not know it, and none of the older generation pronounce it correctly, as *v* is a sound unknown in their language. They call themselves *Díné'*, which means simply 'people'. This word, in various forms, is used as a tribal name by nearly every people of the Athapascan stock).

An important Athapascan tribe occupying a reservation of 9,503,763 acres in N. E. Arizona, N. W. New Mexico, and S. E. Utah. Here they are supposed to remain, but many isolated families live beyond the reservation boundaries in all directions. Their land has an average elevation of about 6,000 ft above sea level. The highest point in it is Pastora peak, in the Carrizo mts., 9,420 ft high. It is an arid region and not well adapted to agriculture, but it affords fair pasturage. For this reason the Navaho have devoted their attention less to agriculture than to stock raising. There were for-

merly few places on the reservation, away from the borders of the Rio San Juan, where the soil could be irrigated, but there were many spots, apparently desert, where water gathered close to the surface and where by deep planting crops of corn, beans, squashes, and melons were raised. Within the last few years the Government has built storage reservoirs on the reservation and increased the facilities for irrigation.

It may be that under the loosely applied name Apache there is a record of the Navaho by Oñate as early as 1598, but the first to mention them by name was Zarate-Salmeron, about 1629. They had Christian missionaries among them in the middle of the 18th century (see *Cebolleta, Encinal*), but their teachings did not prevail against paganism. For many years previous to the occupancy of their country by the United States they kept up an almost constant predatory war with the Pueblos and the white settlers of New Mexico, in which they were usually the victors. When the United States took possession of New Mexico in 1849 these depredations were at their height. The first military expedition into their country was that of Col. Alex. W. Doniphan, of the First Missouri Volunteers, in the fall of 1846. On behalf of the United States, Doniphan made the first treaty of peace with the Navaho Nov. 22 of that year, but the peace was not lasting. In 1849, another military force, under the command of Col. John M. Washington, penetrated the Navaho land as far as Chelly canyon, and made another treaty of peace on Sept. 9, but this treaty was also soon broken. To put a stop to their wars, Col. "Kit" Carson invaded their territory in 1863, killed so many of their sheep as to leave them without means of support, and took the greater part of the tribe prisoners to Ft Sumner at the Bosque Redondo on the Rio Pecos, N. Mex. Here they were kept in captivity until 1867, when they were restored to their original country and given a new supply of sheep. Since that time they have remained at peace and greatly prospered.

There is no doubt that the Navaho have increased in number since they first became known to the United States, and are still increasing. In 1867, while they were still prisoners and could be counted accurately, 7,300 of them were held in captivity at one time; but, owing to escapes and additional surrenders, the number varied. All were not captured by Carson. Perhaps the most accurate census was taken in 1869, when the Government called them to receive a gift of 30,000 sheep and 2,000 goats. The Indians were put in a large corral and counted as they went in; only a few herders were absent. The result showed that there were somewhat fewer than 9,000, making due allowance for absentees. According to the census of 1890, which was taken on a faulty system, the tribe numbered 17,204. The census of 1900 places the population at more than 20,000, and in 1906 they were roughly estimated by the Indian Office to number 28,500.

According to the best recorded version of their origin legend, the first or nuclear clan of the Navaho was created by the gods in Arizona or Utah about 500 years ago. People had lived on the earth before this, but most of them had been destroyed by giants or demons. When the

NAVAHO (MANUELITO)

myth says that the gods created the first pair of this clan, it is equivalent to saying that they knew not whence they came and had no antecedent tradition of themselves. It is thus with many other Navaho clans. The story gives the impression that these Indians wandered into New Mexico and Arizona in small groups, probably in single families. In the course of time other groups joined them until, in the 17th century, they felt strong enough to go to war. Some of the accessions were evidently of Athapascan origin, as is most of the tribe, but others were derived from different stocks, including Keresan, Shoshonean, Tanoan, Yuman, and

Aryan; consequently, the Navaho are a very composite people. A notable accession was made to their numbers, probably in the 16th century, when the Thkha-paha-dinnay joined them. These were a people of another linguistic stock—Hodge says "doubtless Tanoan"—for they wrought a change in the Navaho language. A later very numerous accession of several clans came from the Pacific

NAVAHO WOMAN (JUANITA)

coast; these were Athapascan. Some of the various clans joined the Navaho willingly, others are the descendants of captives. Hodge has shown that this Navaho origin legend, omitting a few obviously mythic elements, can be substantiated by recorded history, but he places the beginning at less than 500 years.

The Navaho are classed as belonging to the widespread Athapascan linguistic family, and a vocabulary of their language shows that the majority of their words have counterparts in dialects of Alaska, British America, and California. The grammatical structure is like that of Athapascan tongues in general, but many words have been inherited from other sources. The grammar is intricate and the vocabulary copious, abounding especially in local names.

NAVAHO (CAYATANITA)

The appearance of the Navaho strengthens the traditional evidence of their very composite origin. It is impossible to describe a prevailing type; they vary in size from stalwart men of 6 ft or more to some who are diminutive in stature. In feature they vary from the strong faces with aquiline noses and prominent chins common with the Dakota and other northern tribes to the subdued features of the

Pueblos. Their faces are a little more hirsute than those of Indians farther E. Many have occiputs so flattened that the skulls are brachycephalic or hyper-brachycephalic, a feature resulting from the hard cradle-board on which the head rests in infancy. According to Hrdlicka (Am. Anthrop., II, 339, 1900) they approach the Pueblos physically much more closely than the Apache, notwithstanding their linguistic connection with the latter. In general their faces are intelligent and pleasing. Hughes (Doniphan's Exped.,

NAVAHO

1846) says of them: "They are celebrated for intelligence and good order . . . the noblest of American aborigines." There is nothing somber or stoic in their character. Among themselves they are merry and jovial, much given to jest and banter. They are very industrious, and the proudest among them scorn no remunerative labor. They do not bear pain with the fortitude displayed among the militant tribes of the N., nor do they inflict upon themselves equal tortures. They are, on the whole, a progressive people.

The tribe is divided into a number of

clans, 51 clan names having been recorded, but the number of existing clans may be somewhat more or less. Two of these are said to be extinct, and others nearly so. The clans are grouped in phratries. Some authorities give 8 of these, others 11, with 3 independent clans; but the phratry does not seem to be a well-defined group among the Navaho. Descent is in the female line; a man belongs to the clan of his mother, and when he marries must take a woman of some other clan. The social position of the women is high and their influence great. They often possess much property in their own right, which marriage does not alienate from them. The clans, so far as known, are as follows:

Aatsosni, Narrow gorge; Ashihi, Salt; Bithani, Folded arms; Dsihlnaothihlni, Encircled mountain; Dsihlthani, Brow of the mountain; Dsihltlani, Base of the mountain; Kai, Willows; Kanani, Living arrows; Khaltso, Yellow bodies; Khash-hlizhni, Mud; Khaskankhatso, Much yucca; Khoghanhlani, Many huts; Khon-agani, Place of walking; Kinaani, High standing house; Kinhlitshi, Red house (of stone); Klogi, Name of an old pueblo; Loka, Reeds (phragmites); Mai-theshkizh, Coyote pass (Jemez); Maitho, Coyote spring; Naai, Monocline; Nakai, White stranger (Mexican); Nakhopani, Brown streak, horizontal on the ground; Nanashthezhin, Black horizontal stripe aliens (Zuñi); Notha, Ute; Pinbitho, Deer spring; Theshtshini, Red streak; Thild-zhehi; Thkhaneza, Among the scattered (hills); Thkhapaha, Among the waters; Thkhatshini, Among the Red (waters or banks); Thobazhnaazh, Two come for water; Thochalsithaya, Water under the sitting frog; Thoditshini, Bitter water; Thokhani, Beside the water; Thodho-kongzhi, Saline water; Thotsoni, Great water; Thoyetlini, Junction of the rivers; Tlastshini, Red flat; Tlizihlani, Many goats; Tsayiskithni, Sagebrush hill; Tsezhinkini, House of the black cliffs; Tsenahapihlni, Overhanging rocks; Tse-theshkizhni, Rocky pass; Tsethkhani, Among the rocks; Tsetlani, Bend in a canyon; Tseyanathoni, Horizontal water under cliffs; Tseyikehe, Rocks standing near one another; Tsezhinthiai, Trap dyke; Tsinazhini, Black horizontal forest; Tsinsakathni, Lone tree; Yoo, Beads.

The ordinary Navaho dwelling, or *hogán*, is a very simple structure, although erected with much ceremony (see Mindeleff in 17th Rep. B. A. E., 1898). It is usually conical in form, built of sticks set on end, covered with branches, grass, and earth, and often so low that a man of ordinary stature can not stand erect in it. One must stoop to enter the doorway, which is usually provided with a short passage or storm door. There is no chimney; a hole in the apex lets out the smoke. Some hogans are rude polygonal structures of logs laid horizontally; others are partly of stone. In summer, "lean-to" sheds and small inclosures of branches are often used for habitations. Sweat houses are small, conical hogans without the hole in the apex, for fires are not lighted in them; temperature is increased by means of stones heated in fires outside. Medicine lodges, when built in localities where trees of sufficient size grow, are conical structures like the ordinary hogans, but much larger. When built in regions of low-sized trees, they have flat roofs. Of late, substantial stone structures with doors, windows, and chimneys are replacing the rude hogans. One reason they built such houses was that custom and superstition constrained them to destroy or desert a house in which death had occurred. Such a place was called *chindi-hogan*, meaning 'devil-house'. Those who now occupy good stone houses carry out the dying and let them expire outside, thus saving their dwellings, and indeed the same custom is sometimes practised in connection with the hogan. No people have greater dread of ghosts and mortuary remains.

The most important art of the Navaho is that of weaving. They are especially celebrated for their blankets, which are in high demand among the white people on account of their beauty and utility; but they also weave belts, garters, and saddle girths—all with rude, simple looms. Their legends declare that in the early days they knew not the art of weaving by means of a loom. The use of the loom was probably taught to them by the Pueblo women who were incorporated into the tribe. They dressed in skins and rude mats constructed by hand, of cedar bark and other vegetal fibers. The few basket makers among them are said to be Ute or Paiute girls or their descendants, and these do not do much work. What they make, though of excellent quality, is confined almost exclusively to two forms required for ceremonial purposes. The Navaho make very little pottery, and this of a very ordinary variety, being designed merely for cooking purposes; but formerly they made a fine red ware decorated in black with characteristic designs. They grind corn and other grains by hand on the metate. For ceremonial purposes they still bake food in the ground and in other aboriginal ways. For many years they have had among them silversmiths who fabricate handsome ornaments with very rude appliances, and who undoubtedly learned their art from the Mexicans, adapting it to their own environment. Of late years many of those who have been taught in training schools have learned civilized trades and civilized methods of cooking.

Investigations conducted within the last 25 years show that the Navaho, contrary to early published beliefs, are a highly religious people having many well-defined divinities (nature gods, animal gods, and local gods), a vast mythic and legendary lore, and thousands of significant formulated songs and prayers which must be learned and repeated in the most exact manner. They also have hundreds of musical compositions which experts have succeeded in noting and have pronounced similar to our own music. The so-called dances are ceremonies which last for 9 nights and parts of 10 days, and the medicine-men spend many years of study in learning to conduct a single one properly. One important feature of these ceremonies is the pictures painted in dry powders on the floor of the medicine lodge (see *Dry-painting*). All this cultus is of undoubted antiquity.

The most revered of their many deities is a goddess named Estsánatlehi, or 'Woman Who Changes', 'Woman Who Rejuvenates Herself', because she is said never to stay in one condition, but to grow old and become young again at will. She is probably Mother Nature, an apotheosis of the changing year.

By treaty of Canyon de Chelly, Ariz., Sept. 9, 1849, the Navaho acknowledged the sovereignty of the United States. By treaty of Fort Sumner, N. Mex., June 1, 1868, a reservation was set apart for them in Arizona and New Mexico, and they ceded to the United States their claim to other lands. Their reservation has been modified by subsequent Executive orders.

For the literature pertaining to this tribe see Matthews, (1) Navaho Legends, 1897, and the bibliography therein; (2) Night Chant, 1902.   (W. M.)

Apache Indians of Nabajú.—Zarate-Salmeron (*ca.*1629) trans. in Land of Sunshine, 183, Feb. 1900. Apaches de Nabajoa.—Turner in Pac. R. R. Rep., III, pt. 3, 83, 1856 (so called by Spanish writers). Apaches de Nabaju.—Zarate-Salmeron (*ca.*1629) quoted by Bandelier in Arch. Inst. Papers, IV, 294, 1892. Apaches de Nauajò.—Benavides, Memorial, 56, 1630. Apaches de navaio.—De l'Isle, map Am. Septent., 1700. Apaches de Navajo.—Linschoten, Descr. l'Amérique, map 1, 1638. Apaches de Navajox.—Sanson, L'Amérique, map, 27, 1657. Apaches de Navayo.—Jefferys, Am. Atlas, map 5 (1763), 1776. Apaches Nabajai.—Garcés (1776), Diary, 366, 1900. A'patchu.—Cushing, inf'n ('enemy': Zuñi name). A'patsjoe.—ten Kate, Reizen in N. A., 291, 1885 (or Pátsjoe; Zuñi name). Bágowits.—ten Kate, Synonymie, 8, 1884 (Southern Ute name). Dacábimo.—Stephen in 8th Rep. B. A. E., 35, 1891 (Hopi name). Dávaχo.—Gatschet, MS., B. A. E., 1884 (Kiowa Apache name). Dïné'.—Matthews, Navaho Leg., 210, 1897 (own name, sig. 'people'). Djëné.—Hodge, field notes, B. A. E., 1895 (Laguna name). I'hl-dëné.—Ibid. (Jicarilla name). Iyutagjen-né.—Escudero, Not. Estad. Chihuahua, 212, 1834 (own name). Messen-Apaches.—ten Kate, Reizen in N. A., 241, 1885 (='Knife Apaches', supposedly from Span. *navája*, 'knife'). Moshome.—Bandelier, Delight Makers, 175, 1890 (Keresan name). Nabaho.—Malte-Brun, Geog., V, 326, 1826. Nabahoes.—Pattie, Pers. Narr., 98, 1833. Nabajó.—Alegre, Hist. Comp. Jesus, I, 336, 1841. Nabajoa.—Humboldt, Atlas Nouv.-Espagne, carte 1, 1811. Nabajo Apaches.—Davis, Span. Conq. N. Mex., 358, 1869. Nabajoe.—Barreiro, Ojeada sobre Nuevo-México, app., 9, 1832. Nabbehoes.—Brownell, Indian Races, 483, 1854. Nabijos.—Amer. Pioneer, II, 190, 1843. Nabojas.—Bent (1846) in H. R. Ex. Doc. 76, 30th Cong. 1st sess., 11, 1848. Nabojo.—Davis, Span. Conq. N. Mex., 73, 1869. Nahjo.—Pike, Exped., 3d map, 1810. Namakaus.—Schermerhorn in Mass. Hist. Soc. Coll., 2d s., II, 29, 1814. Nanaha.—Balbi, Atl. Ethnog., 737, 1826. Nanahaws.—Pike, Exped., pt. III, app., 9, 1810. Napao.—Garcés (1776), Diary, 351, 1900. Nauajò.—Benavides, Memorial, 57, 1630 (='sementeras grandes'). Nauajoa.—Alcedo, Dic. Geog., III, 295, 1788. Navago.—Butler, Wild North Land, 127, 1873. Navahœ.—Möllhausen, Pacific, II, 77, 1858. Navahoes.—Parker, Journal, 32, 1840. Navajai.—Garcés (1775) quoted by Orozco y Berra, Geog., 350, 1864. Navajhoes.—Emory, Recon., 27, 1848. Navajo.—Blaeu, Atlas, XII, 62, 1667. Navajoas.—Orozco y Berra, Geog., 59, 1864. Navajoes.—Rivera, Diario, leg. 818, 1736. Navajoos.—Villa-Señor, Theatro Am., pt. 2, 412, 1748. Navajoses.—Ruxton, Adventures, 193, 1848. Navaosos.—Latham, Nat. Hist. Man, 350, 1850. Navejò.—Conklin, Arizona, 211, 1878. Navijoes.—Morgan in N. Am. Rev., 58, Jan. 1870. Navijos.—Gallatin in Nouv. Ann. Voy., 5th s., XXVII, 310, 1851. Navoasos.—Bollaert in Jour. Ethnol. Soc. Lond., II, 276, 1850. Nevajoes.—Mowry in Jour. Am. Geog. Soc., I, 71, 1859. Nodehs.—Deniker, Races of Man, 525, 1900. Novajos.—Cushing in The Millstone, IX, 94, June 1884. Nwasabé.—ten Kate, Synonymie, 8, 1884 (Tesuque name). Oohp.—ten Kate, Reizen in N. A., 160, 1885 (Pima name). Oop.—Ibid. Págowitch.—ten Kate, Synonymie, 8, 1884 (Southern Ute name). Págowits.—Ibid. Pagu-uits.—Gatschet, Yuma-Spr., I, 371, 1883 (Ute name). Pa'-gu-wëts.—Powell, Rep. on Colo. River, 26, 1874 (='reed knives': Ute name). Pátsjoe.—ten Kate, Reizen in N. A., 291, 1885 (or A'patsjoe; Zuñi name). Tacáb-cí-nyu-múh.—Fewkes in Jour. Am. Folk-lore, V, 33, 1892 (Hopi name). Ta'hli'mnïn.—Hodge, field notes, B. A. E., 1895 (Sandia name). Tasámewé.—ten Kate, Reizen in N. A., 259, 1885 (='bastards': Hopi name). Ta-shá-va-ma.—Bourke, Moquis of Ariz., 118, 1884 (Hopi name). Te'liémnim.—Gatschet, MS., B. A. E., 1884 ('without pity': Isleta name). Ten-nai.—Eaton, Navajo MS. vocab., B. A. E. (own name). Tenúai.—Eaton in Schoolcraft, Ind. Tribes, IV, 218, 1854. Tenyé.—ten Kate, Synonymie, 7, 1884 (Laguna name). Wilde Coyotes.—ten Kate, Reizen in N. A., 282, 1885 (Zuñi nickname translated). Yabipais Nabajay.—Garcés (1776), Diary, 457, 1900. Yátilatlávi.—Gatschet, Yuma-Spr., I, 409, 1883 (Tonto name). Yavipai-navajoi.—Orozco y Berra, Geog., 59, 1864. Yavipais-Navajai.—Garcés (1775–76) quoted by Bandelier in Arch. Inst. Papers, III, 114, 1890. Yoetahá.—ten Kate, Reizen in N. A., 197, 1885 (='those who live on the border of the Utes': Apache name). Yu-i'-ta.—Henshaw, Ka'-itch MS. vocab., B. A. E., 1883 (Panamint name). Yutacjen-ne.—Orozco y Berra, Geog., 59, 1864. Yutahá.—Gatschet, Yuma-Spr., I, 370, 1883 (Apache name). Yu-tah-kah.—Eaton, Navajo MS. vocab., B. A. E. (Apache name). Yutajen-ne.—Orozco y Berra, Geog., 41, 76, 1864. Yu-tar-har'.—White, Apache Names of Ind. Tribes, MS., B. A. E., 2, [n. d.] (trans. 'far off': Apache name). Yutíla pá.—Gatschet, Yuma-Spr., III, 86, 1886 (Yavapai name). Yutilatláwi.—Ibid., I, 370, 1883 (Tonto name).

Navahu (*Na-va-hu'*, referring to 'large area of cultivated lands'). A former Tewa pueblo situated in the second valley s. of the great pueblo and cliff village of Puye, w. of Santa Clara pueblo, in the Pajarito Park, N. Mex. The name refers to the large areas of cultivated lands in the vicinity, and by extension was applied to the Navaho (q. v.). Consult Hewett (1) in Am. Anthrop., VIII, 193, 1906; (2) Bull. 32, B. A. E., 16, 1906.

Navasink ('at the promontory'). A tribe of the Unami branch of the Delawares formerly living in the highlands of Navesink, N. J., claiming the land from Barnegat to the Raritan. Hudson, who encountered them immediately after entering the bay of New York, describes them as "clothed in mantles of feathers and robes of fur, the women clothed in hemp; red copper pipes, and other things of copper they did wear about their necks." They appear to have passed out of history soon after their lands were sold. **Na-ussins.**—Nelson, Inds. N. J., 101, 1894 (early form). **Navecinx.**—Tom (1671) in N. Y. Doc. Col. Hist., XII, 493, 1877. **Navesand.**—Needham (1665), ibid., XIII, 398, 1881. **Navesinck.**—Winfield, Hudson Co., 44, 1874. **Navesinks.**—Nelson, op. cit. **Navisinks.**—Schoolcraft, Ind. Tribes, VI, 100, 1857. **Navison.**—Ruttenber, Tribes Hudson R., 159, 1872. **Neuwesink.**—Stuyvesant (1660) in N. Y. Doc. Col. Hist., XIII, 163, 1881. **Neversincks.**—Ruttenber, Tribes Hudson R., 89, 1872. **Neversinghs.**—N. Y. Doc. Col. Hist., XIII, 99, 1881. **Neversink.**—Van der Donck (1656) quoted by Ruttenber, Tribes Hudson R., 51, 1872. **Nevesin.**—Beekman (1660) in N. Y. Doc. Col. Hist., XII, 308, 1877. **Nevesinck.**—Van Werckhoven (1651), ibid., XIII, 29, 1881. **Neve-Sincks.**—Van der Donck (1656) quoted by Ruttenber, Tribes Hudson R., 72, 1872. **Nevesings.**—Doc. of 1674 in N. Y. Doc. Col. Hist., II, 694, 1858. **Nevesinks.**—Doc. of 1659, ibid., XIII, 99, 1881. **Nevisans.**—Lovelace (1669), ibid., 423. **Newasons.**—Ogilby (1671) quoted by Nelson, Inds. N. J., 101, 1894. **Newesinghs.**—Doc. of 1659 in N. Y. Doc. Col. Hist., XIII, 100, 1881. **Newesink.**—Stuyvesant (1658), ibid., 84. **Nieuesinck.**—Doc. of 1652, ibid., 34. **Nieuwesinck.**—Ibid., XIV, 168, 1883. **Novisans.**—Lovelace (1665) quoted by Ruttenber, Tribes Hudson R., 68, 1872.

Navawi (*Na-va-wi'*, 'place of the hunting trap'). A group of ancient Tewa ruins w. of the Rio Grande, situated between the Rito de los Frijoles and Santa Clara canyon, s. w. of San Ildefonso, N. Mex. They consist of two large buildings about 200 yds. apart, several clan houses on the mesa near by, and a cliff village cf considerable extent in the base of the low mesa to the s. and w. The ruin takes its name from a pitfall (*nava*) on the narrow neck of mesa about 300 yds. w. of the pueblo ruin, at the convergence of four trails. **Navakwi.**—Hewett in Am. Anthrop., VI, 645, 1904. **Navawi.**—Hewett in Bull. 32, B. A. E., 22, 1906. **Navekwi.**—Hewett in Am. Anthrop., op. cit., map.

Navialik ('place of the long-tailed duck'). An Ita Eskimo village on Smith sd., N. Greenland. **Navialik.**—Kane, Arctic Explor., II, 199, 1856. **Nerdlă'rin.**—Stein in Petermanns Mitt., no. 9, map, 1902.

Navigation. See *Boats, Travel.*

Navisok. A former Aleut village on Agattu id., Alaska, one of the Near id. group of the Aleutians, now uninhabited.

Navojoa ('prickly-pear house'; from *nabo* 'prickly pear,' *houa* 'house.'— Buelna). One of the principal settlements of the Mayo on Rio Mayo, s. w.

Sonora, Mexico. Of a total population of 8,500 in 1900, 744 were Cahita (Mayo), 69 "Cahuillo," and 28 Yaqui. **Nabojoa.**—Kino map (1702) in Stöcklein, Neue Welt-Bott, 1726. **Natividad Navajoa.**—Orozco y Berra, Geog., 356, 1864. **Navahóa.**—Hardy, Travels in Mexico, 438, 1829. **Navohoua.**—Orozco y Berra, op. cit. **Navojoa.**—Censo de Sonora, 94, 1901 (present official designation).

Nawaas. An unidentified tribe or band occupying a stockaded village, under a chief named Morahieck, on the E. side of Connecticut r. between the Scantic and the Podunk, near the mouth of the latter, in Hartford co., Conn.. in the 17th century. **Nawaas.**—Map of 1616 in N. Y. Doc. Col. Hist., I, 13, 1856. **Nawas.**—Macauley, N. Y., II, 162, 1829. **Nawes.**—De Laet (1633) in N. Y. Hist. Soc. Coll., 2d s., I, 307, 1841. **Newashe.**—Trumbull Ind. Names Conn., 38, 1881.

Nawacaten. A village of the Powhatan confederacy in 1608, on the N. bank of the Rappahannock, in Richmond co., Va.— Smith (1629), Va., I, map, repr. 1819.

Nawake. A place marked as an Indian fort on Lattré's map of 1784, on the upper Scioto, in Ohio. It may have belonged to the Shawnee.

Nawat ('Left-hand'). The principal chief of the Southern Arapaho since the death of Little Raven (q. v.) in 1889. He was born about 1840, and became noted as a warrior and buffalo hunter, taking active part in the western border wars until the treaty of Medicine Lodge in 1867, since which time his people, as a tribe, have remained at peace with the whites. In 1890 he took the lead in signing the allotment agreement opening the reservation to white settlement, notwithstanding the Cheyenne, in open council, had threatened death to anyone who signed. He several times visited Washington in the interest of his tribe. Having become blind, he has recently resigned his authority to a younger man. (J. M.)

Naw-gaw-nub. See *Nagonub.*

Nawiti. A term with three applications: (1) A Kwakiutl town formerly at C. Commerell, N. coast of Vancouver id.; (2) a modern town, properly called Meloopa, a short distance s. of the preceding, from which it received its name; (3) by an extension of the town name it came to be a synonym for the Nakomgilisala and Tlatlasikoala collectively, whose language constitutes the "Newettee subdialect" of Boas. Pop. 69 in 1906. **Mel'oopa.**—Dawson in Trans. Roy. Soc. Can., sec. II, 70, 1887. **Nah-witte.**—Can. Ind. Aff., 145, 1879. **Nah-wittis.**—Scott in Ind. Aff. Rep., 316, 1868. **Nauéte.**—Boas in Bull. Am. Geog. Soc., 227, 1887. **Na-wee-tee.**—Kane, Wand. in N. A., app., 1859. **Nawiti.**—Tolmie and Dawson, Vocabs. Brit. Col., 118B, 1884. **Neu-witties.**—Dunn, Oregon, 242, 1844. **Newatees.**—Sproat, Savage Life, 314, 1868. **Neweetee.**—Irving, Astoria, 107, 1849. **Neweetees.**—Lee and Frost, Oregon, 54, 1844. **Neweetg.**—Taylor in Cal. Farmer, July 19, 1862. **Newettee.**—Dunn, Oregon, 242, 1844. **Newitlies.**—Armstrong, Oregon, 136, 1857. **Newittees.**—Grant in Jour. Roy. Geog. Soc., 293, 1857.

Newitti.—Brit. Col. map, 1872. **Niouetians.**—Nouv. Ann. Voy., IX, 14, 1821. **Ni-wittai.**—Tolmie and Dawson, Vocabs. Brit. Col., 118B, 1884. **Noo-we-tee.**—Can. Ind. Aff. 1883, 190, 1884. **Noo-we-ti.**—Ibid., 145, 1879. **Nouitlies.**—Duflot de Mofras, Oregon, I, 139, 1844. **Nu-witti.**—Can. Ind. Aff. 1894, 279, 1895. **Xumtáspē.**—Boas in Nat. Mus. Rep. 1895, 879, 1897 (own name for the town).

Nawkaw (? 'Wood'). A Winnebago chief, known also as Carrymaunee ('Walking Turtle'), because he was a member of the Walking Turtle family, the ruling family of the tribe. He was born in 1735, and died at the advanced age of 98 years in 1833. His residence was at Big Green lake, between Green Bay and Ft Winnebago (Portage), Wis., and 30 m. from the latter. The earliest recorded notice of Nawkaw relates to his presence, as principal chief of his tribe, at the battle of the Thames, Canada, Oct.

NAWKAW (AFTER McKENNEY AND HALL)

5, 1813, and that he was beside Tecumseh when the latter fell (Wis. Hist. Coll., XIV, 86, 1898). If the statement in regard to his age be correct, Nawkaw was at that time 78 years of age. That he was active in behalf of his tribe in peaceful measures for the remaining years of his life is evident from the fact that he was one of the chief agents of the Winnebago in making settlements and treaties on their behalf. His name, in various forms (Carimine, Karry-Man-ee, Nan-kaw, Nau-kaw-kary-maunie, Karamanu, and Onunaka), is attached to the treaties of St Louis, Mo., June 3, 1816; Prairie du Chien, Wis., Aug. 19, 1825; Butte des Morts, Wis., Aug. 11, 1827; Green Bay, Wis., Aug. 25, 1828; and Prairie du Chien, Aug. 1, 1829. But his most important acts in behalf of peace were his

efforts in keeping his people from taking part in the Black Hawk war in 1832. "The policy of Nawkaw," say McKenney and Hall (Ind. Tribes, I, 316, 1858), "was decidedly pacific, and his conduct was consistent with his judgment and professions. To keep his followers from temptation, as well as to place them under the eye of an agent of our government, he encamped with them near the agency, under the charge of Mr Kinzie." It was chiefly through his exertions that Red Bird and his accomplices in the Gagnier murder were surrendered, and through his influence that clemency was obtained for them, for which purpose he visited Washington in 1829; but the pardon for Red Bird came after he died in prison at Prairie du Chien. Nawkaw was a large man, 6 ft tall and well built. Mrs Kinzie (Wau-Bun, 89, 1856) says he was a stalwart Indian, with a broad, pleasant countenance, the great peculiarity of which was an immense under lip, hanging nearly to his chin; this is seen to some extent in his portrait. He is described as a sagacious man, of firm, upright character and pacific disposition, who filled his station with dignity and commanded respect by his fidelity. One of his daughters, Flight-of-Geese, married Choukeka, or Spoon Dekaury (Wis. Hist. Coll., XIII, 455, 1895). A descendant of Nawkaw was living at Stevens Point, Wis., in 1887.　　　　　　　　　　　　　　　(C. T.)

Nawnautough. A village of the Powhatan confederacy in 1608, on the N. bank of the Rappahannock, in Richmond co., Va.—Smith (1629), Va., I, map, repr. 1819.

Nawotsi. The Bear clan of the Caddo.—Mooney in 14th Rep. B. A. E., 1093, 1896.

Nawunena ('southern men'). The name by which the Southern Arapaho, now associated with the Southern Cheyenne in Oklahoma, are known to the rest of the tribe. They numbered 885 in 1906.

Nanwuine'nan.—Kroeber in Bull. Am. Mus. Nat. Hist., XVIII, 7, 1902 (Northern Arapaho name). **Náwathi'něha.**—Mooney in 14th Rep. B. A. E., 955, 1896 ('southerners': archaic form). **Na'wuněna.**—Mooney, ibid. **Na-wuth'-i-ni-han.**—Hayden, Ethnog. and Philol. Mo. Val., 321, 1862. **Ner-mon-sin-nan-see.**—Schoolcraft, Ind. Tribes, V, 496, 1855. **Southern Arapahoes.**—Official reports. **Southern Band.**—Schoolcraft, op. cit.

Nayakaukaue. A former town on the site of the present St Helens, Columbia co., Oreg. According to Gatschet a band of the Chinookan family settled there in 1877 and were called Nayakaukau by the Clackama.

Nai-a-kook-wie.—Gibbs, MS. no. 248, B. A. E. **Nayakaukau.**—Gatschet, MS., B. A. E., 1877 (Clackama name). **Ne-ah-ko-koi.**—Gibbs, op cit. **Ni-a-kow-kow.**—Lyman in Oreg. Hist. Soc. Quar., I, 322, 1900.

Nayakolole. A Willopah village formerly situated opposite Bay Center, Pacific co., Wash.

Kwulkwul.—Gibbs, Chinook vocab., B. A. E., 23 (Chehalis name). **Nayā'qōlōlē.**—Boaz, inf'n, 1905. **Quer'quelin.**—Swan, N. W. Coast, 211, 1857. **Q!wē'-qolEn.**—Boas, op. cit.

Nayonsay's Village. A former settlement, probably of the Potawatomi, named after a chief, situated in the N. E. part of Kendall co., Ill. By treaty of July 29, 1829, a tract of 960 acres at this village was ceded to Waishkeshaw, a Potawatomi woman, and her child.

Nay-on-say's Village.—Royce in 18th Rep. B. A. E., pt. 2, Ill. map 1, 1900. **Nay-ou-Say.**—Treaty of 1829 in U. S. Ind. Treat., Kappler ed., II, 214, 1903.

Nayuharuke ('where the grass stalk or weed is forked.'—Hewitt). A palisaded town occupied by the hostile Tuscarora in 1713, near Snowhill, Greene co., N. Car. They were defeated here by the colonists with great loss and 800 prisoners taken.

Nahardakha.—Jour. Va. Council (1713) in N. C. Col. Rec., II, 36, 1886. **Naharuke.**—Williamson, Hist. N. C., I, 201, 1812. **Nahasuke.**—Pollock (1713) in N. C. Col. Rec., II, 38, 1886. **Naherook.**—Homann Heirs' map, 1756. **Nahucke.**—Martin, N. C., I, 261, 1829. **Nayuharuke.**—Gatschet, Tuscarora MS., B. A. E., 1885 (Tuscarora form). **No-ho-ro-co.**—Moore (1713) in N. C. Col. Rec., II, 27, 1886. **Nooherolu.**—War map (1711–15) in Winsor, Hist. Am., V, 346, 1887. **Wahasuke.**—Pollock, op. cit.

Nayuhi (*Nŭ-yu'-hĭ*, 'sand place'). A former Cherokee settlement on the E. bank of Tugaloo r., S. Car., nearly opposite the mouth of Panther cr.

Nayowee.—Doc. of 1755 quoted by Royce in 5th Rep. B. A. E., 142, 1887. **Noyoee.**—Royce, ibid., map. **Noyohee.**—Doc. of 1799, ibid., 144. **Nûyu'hĭ.**—Mooney in 19th Rep. B. A. E., 530, 1900.

Nayuuns-haidagai (*Na yū'ʌns xā'i-dʌga-i*, 'people of the great house'). A subdivision of the Gitins of the Haida of Skidegate, Brit. Col., so named from a large house that the family owned at Hlgahet, an old town near Skidegate. The town chief of Skidegate belonged to this division.   (J. R. S.)

Na yū'ans qā'edra.—Boas in 12th Rep. N. W. Tribes Can., 24, 25, 1898. **Nā yū'ans qā'etqa.**—Boas in 5th Rep., ibid., 26, 1889. **Na yū'Ans xā'-idAga-i.**—Swanton, Cont. Haida, 273, 1905.

Naywaunaukauraunah ('they are surrounded by bark or wood.'—Hewitt). The Tuscarora name of a reputed people "encamped on the Lake Erie" at the time of the war between the Iroquois and the Erie, about 1654.

Nay-Waunaukauraunah.—Cusick (1825) in Schoolcraft, Ind. Tribes, V, 643, 1855. **Waranakarana.**—Schoolcraft, ibid., IV, 200, 1854.

Nazan. The present village of the Aleut on Atka id., Alaska. The natives speak a distinct dialect, and are not only the best otter hunters, but surpass all others in making baskets out of grasses. Pop. 236 in 1880; 132 in 1890.

Atkha.—Schwatka, Mil. Recon. in Alaska, 115, 1885. **Nazan.**—Petroff in 10th Census, Alaska, 16, 1884.

Nazas. A tribe, probably Coahuiltecan or Tamaulipan, at Reinosa, Mexico, near the Rio Grande, in 1757. They were with the Narices, Comecrudos, and Tejones. The Nazas and Narices had been baptized at Villa del Pilon, Nueva Leon (Joseph

Tienda de Cuervo, Informe, 1757, MS. in Archivo General, Historia, LVI, Orozco y Berra, Geog., 294, 1864). (H. E. B.)

Nasas.—Tienda de Cuervo, op. cit., 1757.

Nazas. A former Tepehuane pueblo on Rio de Nazas, E. central Durango, Mexico. It was the seat of the mission of Santa Cruz.

Santa Cruz de Nazas.—Orozco y Berra, Geog., 318, 1864.

Nchekchekokenk (*Ntcê'qtcɛqqôkênk*, or *Ntcêqtceqkôkinnk*, 'the red little side hill or slope'). A village of the Lytton band of the Ntlakyapamuk on the w. side of Fraser r., 15 m. above Lytton, Brit. Col.—Teit in Mem. Am. Mus. Nat. Hist., II, 172, 1900.

Nchekus ('red rising ground or eminence'). A village of the Nicola band of the Ntlakyapamuk, about a mile back in the mountains from Kwilchana, Brit. Col.

Ntcê'kus.—Teit in Mem. Am. Mus. Nat. Hist., II, 174, 1900. **Stcê'kus.**—Ibid. **S'tcukôsh.**—Hill-Tout in Rep. Ethnol. Surv. Can., 4, 1899.

Ndeyao ('dog'; probably akin to Chippewa *nĭndai*, 'my pet,' 'my domestic animate possession, a term applied to dogs, horses, and the like.—W. J.). A clan of the Mahican, q. v.

N-de-yä'-o.—Morgan, Anc. Soc., 174, 1877.

Neacoxy. The principal winter village of the Clatsop, formerly at the mouth of Neacoxie cr., at the site of Seaside, Clatsop co., Oreg.

Neacoxa.—Trans. Oregon Pioneer Assn., 86, 1887. **Neacoxy.**—Lee and Frost, Oregon, 283, 1844. **Neah-coxie.**—Lyman in Oreg. Hist. Soc. Quar., I, 321, 1900. **Niā'xaqcē.**—Boas, Chinook Texts, 92, 1894 (correct name).

Neagwaih ('bear'). A clan of the Seneca, q. v.

Atinionguin.—French writer (1666) in N. Y. Doc. Col. Hist., IX, 47, 1855. **Ne-e-ar-gu-ye.**—Morgan, League Iroq., 46, 80, 1851 (Seneca form). **Ne-e-ar-guy'-ee.**—Morgan, Anc. Soc., 153, 1877.

Neah. A permanent town of the Makah on the site of the old Spanish fort, Port Nuñez Gaona, Neah bay, Wash.

Neah.—Treaty of Neah Bay, 1855, in U. S. Ind. Treaties, 461, 1873. **Neeah.**—Swan in Smithson. Cont., XVI, 2, 1870.

Neahkeluk. An important Clatsop village formerly at Point Adams, Clatsop co., Oreg.

Klakhelnk.—Gairdner, after Framboise (1835), in Jour. Geog. Soc. Lond., XI, 255, 1841. **Neahkeluk.**—Lyman in Oreg. Hist. Soc. Quar., I, 321, 1900. **Tiā'kˌēlake.**—Boas, Chinook Texts, 277, 1894 (native name).

Neahkstowt. A former village of the Clatsop near the present Hammond, Clatsop co., Oreg.

Nayā'qotaowē.—Boas, Chinook Texts, 233, 1894. **Ne-ahk-stow.**—Lyman in Oreg. Hist. Soc. Quar., I, 321, 1900.

Neahumtuk. A former village of the Alsea (q. v.) at the mouth of Alsea r., Oregon.

Neamathla. (*Ima'la* is a war and busk title, corresponding nearly to 'disciplinarian'). A Seminole chief who acquired considerable note during the Indian hostilities of 1824–36. He was by birth a Creek, and had come into notice before the war of 1812, but is not mentioned as a chief until 1820. He is spoken of by Gov. Duval, of Florida, as a man of uncommon ability, a noted orator, with great influence among his people, and in 1824 as desirous of being on terms of amity with the United States. Neamathla was one of the signers of the treaty of Camp Moultrie, Sept. 18, 1823, by which about 5,000,000 acres of land were ceded to the United States. This treaty, which was repudiated by a large portion of the tribe, led by Osceola, was the primary cause of the war which shortly followed. His settlement, known also as Ft Town and Nehe Marthla's Town (Woodward, Reminis., 153, 1859) was situated s. of Flint r., Ga., and was destroyed in the war of 1816–17. Because of his treatment by the Florida authorities he returned to the Creek Nation, where he was well received, and became an influential member of the general council held at Tukabatchi. The name Neah Emarthla is signed on behalf of the Hitchiti towns to the Creek treaty of Nov. 15, 1827. See McKenney and Hall, Ind. Tribes, I, 77, 1858.

Neapope. See *Nahpope.*

Nebaunaubay (*Nĭbanabä,* 'sleeping person'). A mythic character whose home is said to be on the floor of the sea; the term is also applied to an under-water bear. Hence the "Merman" gens of the Chippewa (Warren, Ojibways, 44, 1885.)   (w. J.)

Neblazhetama ('blue river village', from *nablezan,* the Kansa name for Mississippi r., and *tanman,* 'village'). An ancient Kansa village on the w. bank of the Mississippi a few miles above the mouth of Missouri r. in the present Missouri. The territory was later occupied by the Sauk and Foxes.
Ne-bla-zhe-tä′-mä.—Morgan in N.Am. Rev.,45,1870.

Nechacokee. A division of the Chinookan family found in 1806 by Lewis and Clark on the s. bank of Columbia r., a few miles below Quicksand (Sandy) r., Oreg. Their estimated number was 100.
Nechacohee.—Lewis and Clark Exped., II, 217, 1814. Nechacoke.—Drake, Bk. Inds., ix, 1848. Nechacokee.—Lewis and Clark, op. cit., 472. Ne-cha-co-lee.—Orig. Jour. Lewis and Clark, iv, 236, 1905. Nechecolee.—Lewis and Clark Exped., II, 222, 1814. Neechaokee.—Ibid., 469.

Nechanicok. A village of the Powhatan confederacy in 1608, on the s. bank of the Chickahominy in the lower part of Henrico co., Va.—Smith (1629), Va., I, map, repr. 1819.

Nechaui. One of the nine tribes mentioned by Francisco de Jesús María as constituting the Hasinai, or southern Caddo confederacy. He described its location as s. e. of the Nabedache tribe, and half a league from the Nacono (Relación, 1691, MS.). In 1721 Peña, in his diary, stated that the Indians of el Macono lived 5 leagues from the crossing of the Neches at the Neche village (Diario, Mem. de Nueva España, xxviii, 36, MS.). The Nechaui apparently are not mentioned thereafter; they were probably absorbed by their neighbors, perhaps the Nabedache.   (h. e. b.)

Neche. A Hasinai tribe that, on the coming of the Europeans in the latter part of the 17th century, lived on Neches r. in e. Texas. Their main village was a league or more e. of that stream, nearly w. of the present city of Nacogdoches and near the mounds s. w. of Alto, Cherokee co. This village was visited by La Salle's party, and it was particularly to it and the Nabedache tribe across the stream that Joutel (Margry, Déc., III, 336 et seq., 1878) applied the name of "Cenis," his rendering of the Indian group name *Hasinai.* This Neche tribe was closely allied by language and culture with about a dozen southern Caddoan tribes, including the well-known Nabedache, Nacogdoche, Hainai, and Nasoni. There are strong indications that these southern tribes, under the headship of the Hainai, formed a subconfederacy fairly distinct from the northern group of Caddoan tribes, which were under the headship of the Kadohadacho.

The enemies of the Neche were the common enemies of this southern Caddoan group. In 1687 some members of La Salle's party went with them in a successful campaign against the "Canohatinno." The Yojuanes sometimes invaded the country of the Neche and their neighbors; relations with the Bidai and Eyeish seem to have been ordinarily unfriendly; but chief of all the enemies were the Apache.

Between the Neche and Nacachau the Querétaran friars, in 1716, established San Francisco de los Neches mission, and at the same time Ramón stationed a garrison there. In 1719 the missionaries, fearing a French attack incident to the outbreak of war between France and Spain, deserted this as well as the other e. Texas missions, and left it to be plundered by the Indians. In 1721 Gov. Aguayo rebuilt the mission; but in 1731 it was removed to San Antonio, where it was known as San Francisco de la Espada (Ramón, Derrotero; Representation by the Missionary Fathers, 1716, MS.; Peña, Diario; Espinosa, Chrónica Apostólica, 418, 153, et seq.).

The Neche tribe, like all of its neighbors, was insignificant in numbers. In 1721 Aguayo, while at the main Neche village, made presents to 188 men, women, and children, which was considered an unusually "general distribution" of gifts (Peña, Diary of Aguayo's expedition, 1721, MS.). The aggregate of Indians of this and the neighboring tribes dependent on the Neches mission (probably including the Nabedache, Nacono, Nechaui, and Nacachau) was estimated by Espinosa, former president of the missions, at about one thousand (see Francisco de Jesús María, Relación; Ramón, Derrotero; Espinosa, Chrónica Apostólica, 439). This estimate must have had a good foundation, for the missionaries kept lists of all the hamlets and households. If Rivera be correct, it would seem that by 1727 part of the Neche tribe had moved across the Rio Neches and occupied the Nabedache site of San Pedro (Rivera, Diario, leg. 2140, 1736). Before the end of the 18th century the tribe apparently became merged with the Nabedache and Hainai tribes, for in the reports of Solís (1767), Barrios (1771), Mezières (1778–79), and others, it was not separately distinguished.

In its main features the social organization of this tribe was similar to that of all the tribes of the group. They lived in agricultural hamlets or single households scattered around a main village. A household consisted of several families living in a large conical grass lodge. The semicommunal households seem to have been organized on the basis of paternal right; but an elder woman served as the economic head. An exogamous clan organization existed, the details of which are not evident. The outlines of the tribal organization are clear. There was an hereditary civil chief (*caddi* or *cää'di*) who also had priestly functions. He ruled through a council composed largely of elder and distinguished men, and was assisted by several grades of administrative functionaries or public servants, such as the *canahas* and the *tammas*. The latter were messengers and overseers, and inflicted the lesser corporal punishments.

The confederate relations of this tribe with its neighbors were more religious than governmental. The caddi of the Hainai tribe ranked as head chief of the group, but of greater authority than any caddi was the head priest, called *chenesi*, or *xinesi*, who kept the central fire temple, situated on the edge of the Hainai domain. From this temple all the households of the surrounding tribes kindled their fires, directly or indirectly. For lesser religious and social functions the Neche and the Hainai tribes (together with the Nabedache, perhaps) formed one group, while the Nasoni and the Nacogdoche were the leading tribes of another subgroup for religious purposes (see Francisco de Jesús María, Relación, 1691, MS.; Terán, Descripción y Diaria Demarcación, 1691, MS.; Espinosa, Chrónica Apostólica, 424, 430, 1746).

Agriculture, semicommunal in method, was an important source of food supply.

The chief crops raised were corn, beans, sunflowers, melons, calabashes, and tobacco. Besides hunting the deer and small game abounding in the vicinity, the Neche hunted buffalo in season beyond the Brazos, and bear in the forests toward the N. (Francisco de Jesús María, Relación; Joutel, Relation, in Margry, Déc., III, 311, 1878; Peña, Diario, 1721, MS.; Espinosa, Chrón. Apostólica, 422). (H. E. B.)

Naches.—Linares (1716) in Margry, Déc., VI, 217, 1886. Naicha.—Espinosa, Chrónica Apostólica, 430, 1746. Naichas.—Ibid., 424, 425, 430. Nascha.—Representation of Missionary Fathers, 1716, MS. Necha.—Francisco de Jesús María, Relación, MS. Nechas.—Ibid.; Rivera, Diario, leg. 2140, 1736; Rivera, Proyecto, 1728, MS.; Peña, Diario of Aguayo's entrada, 1721. Neita.—Francisco de Jesús María, op. cit. (probably identical).

Nechimuasath (*Nɛtcimŭ'asath*). A sept of the Seshart, a Nootka tribe.—Boas in 6th Rep. N. W. Tribes Can., 32, 1890.

Necoes. A town, perhaps of the Cape Fear Indians, in 1663, about 20 m. up Cape Fear r., probably in the present Brunswick co., N. C.

Nachees.—Lawson, Voy., 115, repr. 1860. Necoes.—Long et al. (1663) in N. C. Col. Rec., I, 68, 1886; Martin, Hist. N. C., I, 131, 1829.

Neconga. A former village, probably of the Miami, in Miami co., Ind.—Hough in Ind. Geol. Rep., map, 1883.

Necootimeigh. A tribe formerly living at the Dalles of the Columbia in Oregon (Ross, Fur Hunters, I, 186, 1855). It was probably Chinookan, as it was within Chinookan territory; but the name may have been that of a temporary village of a neighboring Shahaptian tribe.

Necotat. A former Clatsop village at the site of Seaside, Clatsop co., Oreg.

Nakotlā't.—Boas, Chinook Texts, 140, 1894. Neco-tat.—Lyman in Oreg. Hist. Soc. Quar., I, 321, 1900.

Necpacha. The tribal name assigned to an Indian baptized at mission San Antonio de Valero, Tex., Apr. 12, 1728 (Valero Bautismos, partida 221, MS. in the custody of the Bishop of San Antonio). He died shortly after, and the burial record gives his tribal name as Nacpacha. The name may mean Apache; but this latter form was quite well known at San Antonio at the date named. (H. E. B.)

Nacpacha.—Fray Salva de Amaya in Valero Entierros, partida 79, MS. in the custody of the Bishop of San Antonio.

Nedlung. A Talirpingmiut fall village of the Okomiut Eskimo tribe near the S. E. extremity of L. Netilling, Baffin land.—Boas in 6th Rep. B. A. E., map, 1888.

Neecoweegee. An unidentified Dakota band, possibly of the Minneconjou.

Nee-cow-ee-gee.—Catlin, N. Am. Inds., I, 222, 1841.

Needles. The true needle with an eye was extremely rare among the Indians, the awl (q. v.) being the universal implement for sewing. The needle and needle case came to be generally employed only after the advent of the whites, although bone needles 3 to 5 in. long are common in Ontario and the Iroquois area of New York.

The few needles that have been found in western archeological sites are large and clumsy and could have been employed only in coarse work, such as the mats of the Quinaielt, who in making them use a wooden needle to tie the rushes together with cord. A similar needle is used in house building by the Papago. The Eskimo, however, possessed fine needles of ivory, suitable for many of the uses to which the steel needle is put, and the metal thimble was imitated in ivory. Among them the needle case, artistically and in other respects, reached its highest development, like all the objects that were subjected to the ingenuity of this people. Eskimo needle cases were usually carved of ivory or formed from hollow bones (Nelson in 18th Rep. B. A. E., 1899). In the S. W. the sharp spine of the yucca furnished a natural needle, the thread being formed of the attached fiber. Wooden knitting needles were used among the Pueblos. The N. W. coast tribes sometimes made needle cases of copper and later of iron. (W. H.)

Neerchokioon. A Chinookan tribe, said to number 1,340, found by Lewis and Clark in 1806 on the s. side of Columbia r., a few miles above Sauvies id., Oreg. A division of Lewis and Clark's "Shahala nation."
Ne-er-che-ki-oo.—Orig. Jour. Lewis and Clark, IV, 236, 1905. Neerchokioo.—Lewis and Clark Exped., II, 217, 238, 1814.

Neeskotting. The gaffing of fish in shallow water at night with the aid of a lantern. A long pole with a hook at the end is used (Starr, Amer. Ind., 51, 1899). The -ing is the English suffix, and neeskot is probably the equivalent in the Massachuset dialect of Algonquian of the Micmac nigog, 'harpoon' (Ferland, Foy. Canad., 111, 1865), which appears as nigogue in Canadian French. (A. F. C.)

Neeslous. Given as a division of Tsimshian on Laredo canal, N. W. coast of British Columbia. The Haida speak of Níslâs as a Tsimshian chief living in this district.
Neecelowes.—Gibbs after Anderson in Hist. Mag., 74, 1862. Neecelows.—Coues and Kingsley, Stand. Nat. Hist., pt. 6, 136, 1885. Nees-lous.—Kane, Wand. in N. A., app., 1859.

Negabamat, Noël. A converted Montagnais chief, who lived at Sillery, Quebec; born about the beginning of the 17th century. He was baptized, with his wife Marie and his son Charles, in 1639. Although generally peaceful after embracing Christianity, he frequently engaged in war with the Iroquois, always enemies of the Montagnais. In 1652 he was a member of a delegation sent by his tribe to solicit aid from Gov. Dudley, of New England, against the Iroquois. He also appeared in behalf of his people and acted on the part of the French during the convention at Three Rivers, Quebec, in 1645, where a treaty of peace was made with the Iroquois and other tribes. He was selected by Père Druillettes to accompany him on his visit to the Abnaki in 1651, at which time he was alluded to by the French as "Captain Sillery." It was through his efforts that peace was made by the French with one of the tribes on the coast s. of Quebec, neighbors of the Abnaki, seemingly the Malecite or Norridgewock. On his death, Mar. 19, 1666, his war chief, Negaskouat, became his successor. Negabamat was a firm friend of the French, and after his conversion was their chief counsellor in regard to their movements on the lower St Lawrence. (C. T.)

Negahnquet, Albert. A Potawatomi, the first full-blood Indian of the United States to be ordained a Roman Catholic priest. Born near St Marys, Kans., in 1874, he moved with his parents to the Potawatomi res. (now Pottawatomie co., Okla.), where he entered the Catholic mission school conducted by the Benedictine monks at Sacred Heart Mission, making rapid progress in his studies and gaining the friendship of his teachers by his tractable character. Later he entered the College of the Propaganda Fide in Rome, and was there ordained a priest in 1903. The same year he returned to America and has since engaged in active religious work among the Indians.

Negaouichiriniouek ('people of the fine sandy beach.'—A. F. C.). A tribe or band living in 1658 in the vicinity of the mission of St Michel near the head of Green bay, Wis.; probably a part of the Ottawa tribe, possibly the Nassauaketon. They are located by the Jesuit Relation of 1648 on the s. side of L. Huron in the vicinity of the Ottawa. In 1658, fleeing before the Iroquois, they came to the country of the Potawatomi at Green bay precisely as the Ottawa did and at the same time.
Negaouich.—Tailhan in Perrot, Mém., 221, 1864 ("les Illinois Negaouich"). Negaouichiriniouek.—Jes. Rel. 1658, 21, 1858. Negaouichirinouek.—Perrot (ca. 1720), Mém., 221, 1864. Nigouaouichirinik.—Jes. Rel. 1648, 62, 1858.

Negas. A former Abnaki village in Penobscot co., Me.
Negas.—Willis in Me. Hist. Soc. Coll., IV, 108, 1856. Nique.—Alcedo, Dic. Geog., III, 335, 1788 (identical?).

Negro and Indian. The first negro slaves were introduced into the New World (1501–03) ostensibly to labor in the place of the Indians, who showed themselves ill-suited to enforced tasks and, moreover, were being exterminated in the Spanish colonies. The Indian-negro intermixture has proceeded on a larger scale in South America, but not a little has also taken place in various parts of the northern continent. Wood (New England's Prospect, 77, 1634) tells how some Indians of Massachusetts in 1633, coming across a negro in the top of a tree, were frightened, surmising that "he was Abamacho, or the devil." Nevertheless, intermixture of Indians and negroes has occurred in New England. About the middle of the 18th century the Indians of Marthas Vineyard began to intermarry with negroes, the result being that "the mixed race increased in numbers and improved in temperance and industry." A like intermixture with similar results is reported about the same time from parts of C. Cod. Among the Mashpee in 1802 very few pure Indians were left, there being a number of mulattoes (Mass. Hist. Soc. Coll., I, 206; IV, 206; ibid., 2d s., III, 4; cf. Prince in Am. Anthrop., IX, no. 3, 1907). Robert Rantoul in 1833 (Hist. Coll. Essex Inst., XXIV, 81) states that "the Indians are said to be improved by the mixture." In 1890, W. H. Clark (Johns Hopk. Univ. Circ., X, no. 84, 28) says of the Gay Head Indians: "Although one observes much that betokens the Indian type, the admixture of negro and white blood has materially changed them." The deportation of the Pequot to the Bermudas after the defeat of 1638 may have led to admixture there. The Pequot of Groton, Conn., who in 1832 numbered but 40, were reported as considerably mixed with white and negro blood, and the condition of the few representatives of the Paugusset of Milford in 1849 was about the same (De Forest, Hist. Inds. Conn., 356, 1853). Of the Indians in Ledyard we read (ibid., 445): "None of the pure Pequot race are left, all being mixed with Indians of other tribes or with whites and negroes." Long Island presents another point of Indian-negro admixture. Of the Shinnecock on the s. shore, Gatschet in 1889 (Am. Antiq., XI, 390, 1889) observes: "There are 150 individuals now going under this name, but they are nearly all mixed with negro blood, dating from the times of slavery in the Northern states." Still later M. R. Harrington (Jour. Am. Folk-lore, XVI, 37, 1903) notes the occurrence in many individuals of both Indian and negro somatic characters. These Shinnecock evidently have not been so completely Africanized as some authorities believe. The remnant of the Montauk in East Hampton are reported by W. W. Tooker (Ind. Place-names, IV, 1889) to be mixed with negroes, though still recognizable by their aboriginal features. The region of Chesapeake bay furnishes evidences of Indian-negro intermixture. The fact, pointed out by Brinton (Am. Antiq., IX, 352, 1887), that the list of the numerals 1–10 given as Nanticoke in a manuscript of Pyrlæus, the missionary to the Mohawk, dating from 1780, is really Mandingo or a closely related African language, indicates con-

tact or intermixture. Of the Pamunkey and Mattapony of Virginia, Col. Aylett (Rep. Ind., U. S. Census 1890, 602) states that there has been a considerable mixture of white and negro blood, principally the former. Traces of Indian blood are noticeable, according to G. A. Townsend (Scribner's Mag., no. 72, 518, 1871), in many of the freeborn negroes of the E. shore of Maryland. According to Mooney (Am. Anthrop., III, 132, 1890), "there is not now a native full-blood Indian speaking his own language from Delaware bay to Pamlico sound," those who claim to be Indians having much negro blood. We find not only Indian-negro intermixture, but also the practice of negro slavery among the Indians of the s. Atlantic and Gulf states. The Melungeons of Hancock co., Tenn., but formerly resident in North Carolina, are said to be "a mixture of white, Indian, and negro" (Am. Anthrop., II, 347, 1889). The so-called Croatan (q. v.) of North Carolina and Redbones of South Carolina seem to be of the same mixture. The holding of negro slaves by the tribes of the Carolinas led to considerable intermarriage. There has been much negro admixture among the Seminole from an early period, although the remnant still living in Florida is of comparatively pure Indian blood. Of the other Indians of Muskhogean stock the Creeks seem to have most miscegenation, fully one-third of the tribe having perceptible negro admixture. In the time of De Soto a "queen" of the Yuchi ran away with one of his negro slaves. Estevanico, the famous companion of Cabeza de Vaca, the explorer, in 1528–36, was a negro, and the importance of negro companions of Spanish explorers has been discussed by Wright (Am. Anthrop., IV, 217–28, 1902). Of Algonquian peoples the Shawnee, and the Chippewa of Minnesota, etc., furnish some cases of Indian-negro intermarriage—the fathers negro, the mothers Indian. The Canadian Tuscarora of the Iroquoian stock are said to have some little negro blood among them, and Grinnell reports a few persons of evident negro blood among the Piegan and Kainah. Some of the Indian tribes of the plains and the far W. have taken a dislike to the negro, and he often figures to disadvantage in their myths and legends. Marcy, in 1853, reports this of the Comanche, and in 1891 the present writer found it true to a certain extent of the Kutenai of s. E. British Columbia. Nevertheless, a few cases of intermarriage are reported from this region. The Caddo, former residents of Louisiana and E. Texas, appear to have much negro blood, and on the other hand it is probable that many of the negroes of the whole lower Atlantic and Gulf region have much of Indian blood. Lewis and Clark reported that some of the N. W. Indians, for mysterious reasons, got their negro servant to consort with the Indian women, so much were they taken with him. According to Swanton the richest man among the Skidegate Haida is a negro. In the Indiannegro half-breed, as a rule, the negro type of features seems to predominate. The relation of the folklore of the negroes in America to that of the American aborigines has been the subject of not a little discussion. In regard to the "Uncle Remus" stories, Crane (Pop. Sci. Mo., XVIII, 324–33, 1881) and Gerber (Jour. Am. Folk-lore, VI, 245–57, 1893) assume the African origin of practically all these myths, and hold that such borrowing as has taken place has been from the negroes by the Indians. Powell (Harris, Uncle Remus, introd., 1895) and Mooney (19th Rep. B. A. E., 232–34, 1900) entertain the opinion that a considerable portion of the myths in question are indigenous with the Indians of S. E. United States. The latter points out that "in all the southern colonies Indian slaves were bought and sold and kept in servitude and worked in the fields side by side with negroes up to the time of the Revolution." The conservatism of the Indian and his dislike or contempt for the negro must have prevented his borrowing much, while the imitativeness of the latter and his love for comic stories led him, Mooney thinks, to absorb a good deal from the Indian. He also holds that the idea that such stories are necessarily of negro origin is due largely to the common but mistaken notion that the Indian has no sense of humor.

In addition to the writings cited, consult a special study by Chamberlain in Science, XVII, 85–90, 1891. See *Mixed bloods, Race names, Slavery.* (A. F. C.)

Negro Town. A village mentioned in 1836 as near Withlacoochee r., Fla., and burned in that year by the Americans (Drake, Bk. Inds., bk. 4, 135, 1848). It was probably occupied by runaway slaves and Seminole.

Negusset. A former village, probably of the Abnaki, about the site of Woolwich, Me. The site was sold in 1639.
Nassaque.—Smith (1616) in Mass. Hist. Soc. Coll., 3d s., III, 22, 1833. Nauseag.—Sewall (1833) in Me. Hist. Soc. Coll., II, 207, 1847. Neguascag.—Sewall (1833), ibid., 190 (misprint.) Neguaseag.—Willis, ibid., 233. Neguasseag.—Deed of 1648 quoted by Drake, Bk. Inds., bk. 3, 100, 1848. Neguasset.—Sewall (1833) in Me. Hist. Soc. Coll., II, 207, 1847. Negusset.—Deed of 1648 quoted by Drake, Bk. Inds., bk. 3, 100, 1848.

Negwagon. A chief of the Ottawa of the Michilimackinac region of Michigan, commonly known as Little Wing, or Wing, and also called Ningweegon. Although the United States had declined the proffer of Indian services in the war with Great Britain in 1812, Negwagon espoused the American cause and lost a son in battle, whereupon he adopted Austin E. Wing. When the British took possession of Michilimackinac, Negwagon retired with his people to their hunting grounds, hoisting the American flag over his camp. Happening to be alone, he was visited by British soldiers, who ordered him to strike his flag. Obeying the command, he wound the emblem around his arm, and, drawing his tomahawk, said to the officer, "Englishmen, Negwagon is the friend of the Americans. He has but one flag and one heart; if you take one you shall take the other!" Then sounding a war cry he assembled his warriors and was allowed to remain in peace and to hoist the flag again. After the close of the war he annually visited Detroit with his family in two large birchbark canoes with an American flag flying from the stern of each. Lewis Cass, then stationed at Detroit, never failed to reward him on the occasion of these visits with two new flags. By treaty of Mar. 28, 1836, he was granted an annuity of $100, payable in money or goods. Negwagon is described as having been very large in stature. A county of Michigan was named in his honor, but the name was subsequently changed. Consult Wis. Hist. Soc. Coll., III, 1857. (C. T.)

Nehadi (*NexA'dĭ,* 'people of Nĕx'). A Tlingit division living at Sanya, Alaska, peculiar as being outside of both Tlingit phratries and able to marry into any other group. It is said to be of Tsimshian origin. (J. R. S.)

Nehalem. A Salish tribe formerly living on or near Nehalem r., in N. W. Oregon, but now on Grande Ronde res. Pop. 28 in 1871.
Naalem.—Sen. Ex. Doc. 39, 32d Cong., 1st sess., 2, 1852. Naélim.—Framboise quoted by Gairdner (1835) in Jour. Geog. Soc. Lond., XI, 255, 1841. Na-e'-lûm.—Dorsey, Naltûnnetûnnĕ MS. vocab., B. A. E., 1884. Nahelem.—Duflot de Mofras, Oregon, II, 104, 1844. Nehalems.—Palmer in H. R. Ex. Doc. 93, 34th Cong., 1st sess., 111, 1856. Nehalim.—Victor in Overland Mo., VII, 346, 1871. Nehalins.—Geary in Ind. Aff. Rep., 171, 1860. Ne-î'lĕm.—Gatschet, MS., B. A. E. (Nestucca name.)

Nehaltmoken. A body of Salish under the Fraser superintendency, British Columbia.—Can. Ind. Aff., 79, 1878.

Nehemathla. See *Neamathla.*

Nehjao (*Ne-h'-jä-o,* 'wolf'). A clan of the Mahican.—Morgan, Anc. Soc., 174, 1877.

Nehogatawonahs. A band of the Dakota near St Croix r., in Minnesota or Wisconsin, in 1778. It was one of the three river bands.
Nehogatawonaher.—Balbi, Atlas Ethnog., XXXiii, ¶ 774, 1826. Nehogatawonahs.—Carver, Trav., 60, 1778.

Neholohawee. Given by Haywood (Hist. Tenn., 276, 1823) as the name of a

Cherokee clan, signifying 'blind savanna'. No such clan name or meaning exists in the tribe, and the name is evidently a bad corruption either of Ani'-kiláhi or of Ani'-Gatagewi, Cherokee clan names, the latter having a slight resemblance to the word for 'swamp' or 'savanna'.   (J. M.)

Nehowmean (*Nx'ōmī'n*, meaning doubtful). A village of the Lytton band of Ntlakyapamuk, on the w. side of Fraser r., 1½ m. above Lytton, Brit. Col.
Nehowmean.—Can. Ind. Aff., 79, 1878. N'homi'n.—Hill-Tout in Rep. Ethnol. Surv. Can., 4, 1899. Nhumeen.—Can. Ind. Aff. 1892, 312, 1893. Nohomeen.—Brit. Col. Map, Ind. Aff., Victoria, 1872. Nx'ōmī'n.—Teit in Mem. Am. Mus. Nat. Hist., II, 172, 1900.

Neihahat. An unidentified village or tribe mentioned by Joutel in 1689 (Margry, Déc., III, 409, 1878) as an ally of the Kadohadacho.

Neiuningaitua. A settlement of the Aivilirmiut Eskimo on an island N. of the entrance to Lyon inlet, at the s. end of Melville penin., Canada.
Neyūning-Eït-dŭă.—Parry, Second Voy., 162, 1824. Winter Island.—Ibid.

Nekah (*Nī'ka*, 'goose'). A gens of the Chippewa.
Ne-kah.—Warren, Hist. Ojibways, 45, 1885. Ni'ka.—Wm. Jones, inf'n, 1906.

Nekoubaniste. A tribe, probably Montagnais, formerly living N. w. of L. St John, Quebec.
Neconbavistes.—Lattre, map, 1784 (misprint). Nekoubanistes.—Bellin, map, 1755; Alcedo, Dic. Geog., III, 28, 290; IV, 210, 1788. Neloubanistes.—Esnauts and Rapilly, map, 1777 (misprint).

Nekunsisnis ('round isle'). A former Chitimacha village opposite Ile aux Oiseaux, in Lac de la Fausse Pointe, La.
Ne'kun si'snis.—Gatschet in Trans. Anthrop. Soc. Wash., II, 152, 1883.

Nekun-stustai (*Nēku'n stAstā'-i*, 'the Stustas of Naikun'). A subdivision of the Stustas, a family of the Eagle clan of the Haida (q. v.). As their name implies, they lived near the great sand point called Naikun, or Rose spit.   (J. R. S.)
Naēku'n stastaai'.—Boas in 12th Rep. N. W. Tribes Can., 23, 1898. Nēku'n stAstā'-i.—Swanton, Cont. Haida, 276, 1905.

Nelcelchumnee. Given as one of the tribes on Fresno res., Cal., in 1861, numbering 85 (Ind. Aff. Rep., 219, 1861). Apparently the only mention of the tribe, which is presumably Moquelumnan.

Nellagottine ('people at the end of the world'). A division of the Kawchodinne, occupying the country on L. Simpson and along Anderson r., Canada, next to the Eskimo. Anderson and others (Hind, Labrador Penin., II, 260, 1863) called them half Kawchodinne and half Kutchin. Macfarlane (ibid., 259) said they erect lodges of turf on poles. Ross said in 1859 that the Kawchodinne residing in the country around Ft Good Hope extended beyond the Arctic circle on Mackenzie r., coming into contact with the Kutchin, with whom, by intermarriage,

they have formed the tribe Bastard Loucheux.
Bâtard Loucheux.—Hind, Labrador Penin., II, 260, 1863. Bâtards-Loucheux.—Petitot, Dict. Dènè-Dindjié, xx, 1876. Loucheux-Batards.—Ross, MS., B. A. E., 1859. Nnè-la-gottinè.—Petitot in Bul. Soc. Géog. Paris, chart, 1875. Nnè-lla-Gottinè.—Petitot, Autour du lac des Esclaves, 362, 1891. Tρa-pa-Gottinè.—Ibid. (='ocean people'). Vieux de la Mer.—Ibid.

Nellmole. A rancheria belonging to the former Dominican mission of San Miguel de la Frontera, w. coast of Lower California, about 30 m. s. of San Diego, Cal. Its inhabitants spoke a Diegueño dialect.—Taylor in Cal. Farmer, May 18, 1860.

Neluste (*Ne-lus-te*, 'the hollow leaf'). Given by Haywood (Tenn., 276, 1823) as a clan of the Cherokee. No such clan now exists, but there is some evidence of the former existence of a Cherokee clan taking its name from the holly (*ustīstī*); the clan name would probably have been Ani'-Us'tīstī'.   (J. M.)

Nemah. A former Chinook village on the site of the present town of the same name, on the E. side of Shoalwater bay, Wash.
Mar'hoo.—Swan, N. W. Coast, 211, 1857. Māx.—Boas, inf'n, 1905 (Chehalis name). Nē'ma.—Ibid. (own name). TctEmā'x.—Ibid. (Chehalis name for the villagers).

Nemalquinner. A Chinookan tribe, belonging to the Cushook division (q. v.) of Lewis and Clark, which lived in 1806 at the falls of the Willamette, in Oregon, but also had a temporary house on the N. end of Sauvies id., where they went occasionally to collect wappatoo. They numbered 200, in 4 houses.—Lewis and Clark Exped., I, 219, 1814.
Nemalquinner.—Lewis and Clark Exped., II, 219, 1814. Ne-mal-quin-ner's.—Orig. Jour. Lewis and Clark, VI, 116, 1905.

Nemoy. Noted as a Snake band at the head of Madison r., Mont., one of the head forks of the Missouri. This would place the band in Tukuarika territory, though the name is not identified with any known division.
Ne-moy.—Lewis and Clark Exped., I, map, 1814.

Nenabozho. See *Nanabozho*.

Nenekunat. See *Ninigret*.

Nenelkyenok (*Nē'nêlk''ēnôx*, 'people from the headwaters of the river'). A gens of the Nimkish, a Kwakiutl tribe.—Boas in Rep. Nat. Mus. 1895, 331, 1897.

Nenelpae (*Nē'nêlpaē*, 'those on the upper end of the river'). A gens of the Koeksotenok, a Kwakiutl tribe.—Boas in Rep. Nat. Mus. 1895, 330, 1897.

Nennequi. A former village connected with San Carlos mission, Cal., and said to have been Esselen.—Taylor in Cal. Farmer, Apr. 20, 1860.

Nenohuttahe. See *Path Killer*.

Nenoothlect (*Ne-nooth-lect*). A former Chinookan tribe living 28 m. from The Dalles, on Columbia r., Oreg.—Lee and Frost, Oregon, 176, 1844.

Neodakheat (*Ne-o′-däk-he′-ät*, 'head of the lake'). Given by Morgan as a former Cayuga village at the head of Cayuga lake, on the site of Ithaca, N. Y. In 1750, Cammerhoff, Zeisberger's companion, called the lake there Ganiataregechiat, with the same meaning. In 1766 Zeisberger again visited the place and said a Delaware village existed at the end of the lake. Three or 4 m. off was a Tutelo village with a Cayuga chief. The Tutelo had been placed there by the Iroquois. (w. m. b.)
Ne-ó-däk-hé-ät.—Morgan, League Iroq., 470, 1851. Oeyendehit.—Pouchot map (1758) in N. Y. Doc..Col. Hist., x, 694, 1858 (possibly identical). O-nya′-de-a'-kaⁿ'-hyät.—Hewitt, inf'n, 1886 (Seneca form).

Neokautah (Four Legs). The Menominee name of a Winnebago chief whose village, commonly known as Four Legs Village, was situated at the point where Fox r. leaves L. Winnebago, on the site of the present Neenah, Winnebago co., Wis. According to Draper (Wis. Hist. Soc. Coll., x, 114, 1888), while living here Neokautah for a time claimed tribute from Americans who passed his village. With Dekaury and other Winnebago chiefs he joined in the war against the United States in 1812–13, reaching the seat of hostilities in time to join Tecumseh in the fighting at Ft Meigs, Ohio, and later engaged in the attack on Ft Sandusky, so ably defended by Croghan (Grignon's Recollections in Wis. Hist. Soc. Coll., iii, 269, 1857). Neokautah was one of the representatives of his people at the peace conference at Mackinaw, Mich., June 3, 1815, and was a signer of the treaty of Prairie du Chien, Wis., Aug. 19, 1825, under the French name "Les quatres jambes," as leading representative of his tribe. His Winnebago name is given as Hootshoapkau, but it seems to have been seldom used. (c. t.)

Neolithic age. A term, signifying 'new stone age,' applied originally in Europe to the culture period that followed the Paleolithic ('old stone') age and preceded the Bronze or Metal age, the separation, as the name implies, being chronologic. In northern America at the period of discovery the native culture was that of the Stone age in general, all stages of stone art being represented at one and the same time. It is thus not possible to separate the culture as a whole on a time basis, and the terms Neolithic and Paleolithic are not applicable save in a theoretical sense, i. e., on the assumption that each tribe or group of tribes that had achieved the higher stone culture had necessarily at an earlier period passed through the lower. See *Antiquity.* (w. h. h.)

Neomaitaneo (*néomaⁱ*, 'sand piled in hills'; *hetä′neo*, 'men, people': 'sand-hill people'). A band of the Heviqsnipahis division of the Cheyenne, so called from having formerly ranged chiefly in the "sand-hill country" of N. E. Colorado. Not identical with the Cheyenne tribe as a whole, as has been stated. (j. m.)
Néomai-täneo.—Mooney, Cheyenne MS., B. A. E., 1906. Sand-hill people.—Grinnell in Internat. Cong. Americanists, xiii, 139, 1905.

Neomonni (Rain-cloud). An Iowa chief, of inferior grade, during the early half of the 19th century. He claimed to have taken scalps from Kansa, Omaha, Missouri, Sioux, Osage, and Sauk Indians, and Catlin (Fourteen Iowa Indians, 3, 6, 1844), who writes his name "Newmon-ya, Walking rain," says he was much more distinguished as a warrior than White Cloud (under whom he was third chief), one of the most remarkable and celebrated men of the Iowa tribe. Catlin gives Neomonni's age, about 1843, as 54 years, and describes him as nearly 6½ ft tall. He was one of the 14 Iowa who visited England with Melody in 1843, Catlin, who painted his portrait, acting as interpreter. His name appears among the signers to the treaties of Prairie du Chien, Wis., July 15, 1830, as "Niayoo Manie, Walking rain"; Ft Leavenworth, Kans., Sept. 17, 1836, as "Ne-o-mo-na, Raining cloud"; and St Louis, Mo., Nov. 23, 1837, as Ne-o-mon-ni. His portrait was also painted in Washington for the War Department by C. B. King, and is reproduced in McKenney and Hall, Ind. Tribes, ii, 1858.

Nepanet, Tom. A Christian Nipmuc, the faithful and valued friend of the Massachusetts colonists during the King Philip war in the 17th century. The English, desirous of negotiating with the enemy for the release of certain white captives, chose Nepanet as their emissary, and although confined with others on an island in Boston harbor, he consented to undertake the mission. He started for the Indian camp, Apr. 12, 1676, and although unsuccessful in the first attempt, it was chiefly through his initiative and subsequent efforts that the family of Mr Rowlandson and other prisoners were finally released. It was also through his aid that a party of Englishmen under Capt. Henchman were enabled to surprise a body of the enemy at Weshakom ponds, near Lancaster, Mass., in May, 1676. (c. t.)

Nepawtacum. A village of the Powhatan confederacy in 1608, situated on the N. bank of the Rappahannock, in Lancaster co., Va.—Smith (1629), Va., i, map, repr. 1819.

Nephrite. This semiprecious stone, called also jade, was employed by the native tribes of British Columbia and Alaska in the manufacture of implements. Deposits of the stone were found in 1890 by Lieut. Stoney in what is now called the Jade mts., which lie N.. of Kowak r., Alaska, 150 m. above its mouth; and bowlders and erratic fragments have been discovered in lower Fraser valley and at other points in British Columbia and Alaska—facts indicating a wide distribution of the material. Nephrite has not been found, however, so far as known, within the area of the United States proper, with the exception of an erratic bowlder of mottled leek-green color, weighing 47 lbs., obtained by a prospector in auriferous gravels in s. Oregon, and a small pebble from the shores of Puget sd. (Terry). It is usually found associated with metamorphic rocks, but the exact manner of its occurrence is not understood. It is not quite as hard as quartz, but on account of its compact, fibrous structure it is extremely tough and therefore makes very serviceable implements. Though not always fine-grained, nephrite takes a high polish and presents a very handsome appearance. The colors range through various shades of gray, grayish, and olive greens, bright greens, to brownish and blackish hues. It is often streaked and mottled, and is sometimes more or less translucent. Before the introduction of iron in the N. W. nephrite was much employed for hammers, adzes, drills, knives, whetstones, etc., but it seems rarely to have been used for ornaments; and there is no reason for believing that, as in the S., it had any special or mythologic significance. As the stone is too tough to be readily shaped by fracturing, it was divided by sawing—usually, it is believed, with strips of wood used in conjunction with sharp sand. Many of the specimens in our museums show traces of such treatment. The implements were finished by grinding, and sometimes were highly polished. Specimens have been obtained mainly from the coast tribes between Puget sd. in the s. and Point Barrow in the N.; but many are not fully identified as nephrite, and a considerable number are probably pectolite (q. v.). The sources of nephrite and related minerals found in use by the natives has been much discussed, since until recently no deposits had been discovered in America, and it was surmised that the northern specimens might have been brought from Siberia, and the Mexican and Central American from China; but this view is now practically abandoned. Analysis of the northern nephrites gives silica 56 to 58; magnesia, 20 to 22; lime, 11 to 14; oxide of iron, 5 to 8; aluminum, 1 to 3; specific gravity, 2.9 to 3.

For an account of the nephrites and related minerals of British Columbia, consult Dawson in Canadian Rec. of Sci., II, no. 6, 1887. For the Alaskan nephrites see Clark in Am. Jour. Sci., 3d s., XXVIII, 1884; Clark and Merrill in Proc. Nat. Mus. 1888, XI, 1889; Nelson in 18th Rep. B. A. E., 1899; Smith in Mem. Am. Mus. Nat. Hist., IV, Anthrop. III, 1903; Terry in Science, Jan. 3, 1890; Wilson in Rep. Nat. Mus. 1896, 1898. (W. H. H.)

Neponset. A former important Massachuset village on Neponset r. about the present Stoughton, Norfolk co., Mass. John Eliot labored there as a missionary in 1646, and it was one of several temporary residences of Chickataubut, chief of the Massachuset.

Chickatawbut.—Hoyt, Antiq. Researches, 32, 1824 (sachem's name). Naponsett.—Mass. Hist. Soc. Coll., 4th s., III, 325, note, 1856. Narponset.—Hubbard (1680), ibid., 2d s., V, 32, 1815. Neponcett.—Holmes, ibid.,—Ibid., 1st s., VII, 9, 1801. Neponset.—Pincheon (1633), ibid., 2d s., VIII, 232, 1819. Neponsitt.—Gookin (1674), ibid., 1st s., I, 148, 1806.

Nererahhe. A civil or peace chief of that part of the Shawnee living on the Scioto in Ohio, present at the conference between Sir Wm. Johnson and the representatives of the Six Nations at Johnson's Hall, N. Y., in Apr., 1774. He appears to have possessed considerable oratorical power, and at this conference made a strong appeal to the Miami representatives to follow Johnson's advice and remain friendly to the English. Ruttenber (Tribes Hudson R., 306, 1872) mentions him as one of the two or three more prominent chiefs of the Shawnee at that period. Sowanowane, who, Ruttenber thinks, was Cornstalk, was head or war chief of the Shawnee, and when a belt was given to Nererahhe in 1774, he sent it to Sowanowane. (C. T.)

Neron. The "captain general" of the Iroquois, taken near Montreal in 1663, and so called by the French because of his great cruelty. In memory of his brother he had burned 80 captives, besides killing 60 men with his own hand (Jes. Rel., 1656, 1663). He was an Onondaga named Aharihon, suggesting his French name. (W. M. B.)

Nesadi (*NēsA'dî*, 'salt-water people'). A division of the Wolf phratry of the Tlingit, living at Kake, Alaska. (J. R. S.)

Nesaquake. (From *Neese-saqû-auke*, 'land of the second outlet,' i. e., Nesaquake r.—Ruttenber). A settlement to which the Matinecoc retired after the war of 1643, at the present Nissequague, and Nesaquake r., about Smithtown, Suffolk co., Long id., N. Y.

Missaquogues.—Ruttenber, Tribes Hudson R., 74, 1872. Nassaquakes.—Clark, Onondaga, I, 18, 1849. Necoeaquake.—Doc. of 1669 quoted by Thompson, Long Id., I, 255, 1843. Neersaquake.—Ibid. Nesaquack.—Andros (1677) in N. Y. Doc. Col. Hist., XIV, 729, 1883. Nesaquak.—Nicolls (1666), ibid., 576. Nesaquake.—Ibid., 575. Nesaquanke.—Doc. of 1666, ibid., 576. Nesequake.—Doc. of 1650 quoted by Ruttenber, Ind. Geog. Names, 93, 1906. Nessequack.—Doc. of 1686, ibid. Nessequauke.—Skidmore (1675) in N. Y. Doc. Col. Hist., XIV, 702, 1883. Nip-a-qua-ugs.—Macauley, N. Y., II, 164, 1829 (misprint). Nisinckqueghacky.—Doc. of 1645 in N. Y. Doc. Col. Hist., XIV, 60, 1883. Nissaquague.—Wood quoted by Macauley, N. Y., II, 252, 1829. Nissaquogue.—Thompson, Long Id., I, 94, 1843. Nissequake.—Deed of 1666 quoted by Thompson, ibid., 263, ed. 1839. Nissequogue.—Thompson, ibid., I, 466, 1843. Wissiquack.—Doc. of 1704 quoted by Ruttenber, Ind. Geog. Names, 93, 1906.

Nescambioüit. See *Assacumbuit.*

Nescopeck. A mixed Iroquois, Shawnee, and Delaware village formerly at the mouth of Nescopeck r., in Luzerne co., Pa., where a town of the same name now stands. It had been abandoned by 1779. (J. N. B. H.)

Neshamini. A Delaware tribe or band formerly living on Neshaminy cr., Bucks co., Pa.
Neshamani.—Clay quoted by Day, Penn., 485, 1843. Neshaminas.—Boudinot, Star in the West, 127, 1816. Ne-sham-i-nes.—Macauley, N. Y.,II, 166, 1829. Neshaminies.—Proud, Penn., II, 294, 1798. Nishamines.—Sanford, U. S., cxlvii, 1819.

Neshannock. A white-fleshed variety of potato; from the name of the place in Pennsylvania, where it was first produced. *Neshannock*, the name of a village and stream in Mercer co., comes from a word in the Delaware dialect of Algonquian, signifying 'place of two rivers', from *nisha* 'two', *-hanne* 'flowing stream', *-ock* locative suffix. (A. F. C.)

Neshasath (*NE'c'asath*). A sept of the Seshart, a Nootka tribe.—Boas in 6th Rep. N. W. Tribes Can., 32, 1890.

Neshaw. A local word for eel in Massachusetts. Trumbull (Natick Dict., 80, 1903) says: "The name of 'neshaw eel' is yet retained by the fishermen of Marthas Vineyard and perhaps elsewhere in Massachusetts for the silver eel (*Muræna argentea*)." The derivation is from Narraganset *neeshaŭog* 'eels', literally 'pairers,' from *nees* 'two', *auog* 'they go to'. This Algonquian name, Trumbull thinks, may have belonged originally to the lamprey. (A. F. C.)

Nesheptanga. An ancient ruined pueblo situated in Jeditoh valley, in the Hopi country, N. E. Arizona. It seemingly was one of the group of villages built and occupied by the Kawaika people, who were of Keresan stock from the Rio Grande. It was first described, but not named, by V. Mindeleff in 1885 as a ruin between the Bat House (Chakpahu) and the Horn House (Kokopnyama), and was partially excavated by Dr Walter Hough for the National Museum in 1901. See Mindeleff in 8th Rep. B. A. E., 50–51, 1891; Fewkes in 17th Rep. B. A. E., 590, 1898; Hough in Rep. Nat. Mus. 1901, 333 et seq., 1903.
Neshepatanga.—Hough, op. cit., pl. 82.

Neshta. An extinct subgens of the Wazhazhe gens of the Ponca.
Necta.—Dorsey in 15th Rep. B. A. E., 229, 1897 (*c=sh*).

Nesietsha. A Naskotin village at the confluence of Blackwater and Fraser rs., Brit. Col.
Black-Water.—Morice, Notes on W. Dénés, 24, 1893. Nesietcah.—Morice in Trans. Roy. Soc. Can., 109, 1892.

Nesikeep ('little deep hollow or cut', according to Teit; 'destroyed', referring to the incidents of a story, according to Hill-Tout). A village belonging to the Upper Fraser band of Ntlakyapamuk, on the w. side of Fraser r., 38 m. above Lytton, Brit. Col. Pop. 12 in 1901, the last time the name was officially reported. Dawson gives this as a Lillooet town.
N'cēk'p't.—Hill-Tout in Rep. Ethnol. Surv. Can.,4, 1899. Nesikeep.—Can. Ind. Aff., pt. II, 166, 1901. Nes-ī-kip.—Dawson in Trans. Roy. Soc. Can., sec. II, 44, 1891. Nesykep.—Can. Ind. Aff. 1892, 312, 1893. Nisucap.—Ibid., 78, 1878. NsE'qîp.—Teit in Mem. Am. Mus. Nat. Hist., II, 172, 1900.

Neskollek. A Nataotin village on Babine lake, Brit. Col.
Nəs'qôllək.—Morice in Trans. Roy. Soc. Can., x, 109, 1892.

Nespelim. A Salish tribe on a creek of same name, a N. tributary of Columbia r., about 40 m. above Ft Okinakane, Wash. Ross speaks of them as one of the Okinagan tribes, while Winans classes them as part of the Sanpoil. The latter two together numbered 653 on Colville res., Wash., in 1906.
In-as-petsum.—Ross, Fur Hunters, I, 185, 1855. In-spellum.—Ross, Adventures, 290, 1849. Nepeelium.—Ind. Aff. Rep., 253, 1877. Nespectums.—Keane in Stanford, Compend., 525, 1878. Nes-peelum.—Winans in Ind. Aff. Rep., 22, 1870. Nespelim.—Ind. Aff. Rep. 1901, pt. 1, 702, 1902. Nespilim.—Mooney in 14th Rep. B. A. E., pl. 88, 1896. Sin-spee-lish.—Gibbs in Pac. R. R. Rep., I, 414, 1855.

Nesquehonite. A variety of magnesium carbonate, from *Nesquehoning*, the place in Pennsylvania where it was found, and *-ite*, representing the Greek ιτος. Nesquehoning, the name of a stream and village in Carbon co., signifies, in the Delaware dialect of Algonquian, 'at the black deer lick,' from *nisque* 'black', *mahoni* 'deer lick,' *-ing* locative suffix. (A. F. C.)

Nestucca. A branch of the Tillamook, formerly living on and near Nestugga r., N. W. Oreg., now on the Grande Ronde and Siletz res. Their popular name is derived from that of their country; their own name is Stagā'ush ('people of Staga'). Pop. 46 in 1881. They are no longer separately enumerated.
Apáfan.—Gatschet, Kalapuya MS., B. A. E., 30 (Atfalati name for the Oregon Salish; perhaps from *tchápáfan*, 'on the coast'). Nas-tû'-kĭn-me' ɉunnĕ.—Dorsey, MS. Tutu vocab.,1884 (Tututunne name). Naz-tûk'-e-me' ɉunnĕ.—Dorsey, Naltunnetunne MS. vocab., B. A. E., 1884 (Naltunnetunne name). Nestackee.—Condon in Ind. Aff. Rep. 1863, 83, 1864. Nestockies.—Palmer in H. R. Ex. Doc. 93, 34th Cong., 1st sess., 111, 1856. Nestucalips.—Keane in Stanford, Compend., 525,1878. Nestucals.—H. R. Rep. 98, 42d Cong., 3d sess., 374, 1873. Nestuccas.—Huntington in Ind. Aff. Rep. 1867, 71, 1868. Nestucka.—Ibid., 62. Nestuckah.—Victor in Overland Mo., VII, 346, 1871. Nestuckers.—Ind. Aff. Rep., 221, 1861. Nestuckias.—Taylor in Sen. Ex. Doc. 4, 40th Cong., spec. sess., 26, 1867. Nextucas.—Keane in Stanford, Compend., 525, 1878. Neztrucca.—Ind. Aff. Rep., 74, 1874. Nez Tucca.—Ibid., 412, 1872. Neztucca.—Ibid., 346, 1875. Nikaas.—Framboise (1835) quoted by Gairdner in Jour. Geog. Soc. Lond., XI, 255, 1841 (probably identical). Nikas.—Duflot de Mofras, Expl., II, 335, 1844 (probably identical). Nistoki Ampafa amim.—Gatschet, Lakmiut MS., B. A. E., 105 (Lakmiut name). Shibalta.—Gatschet, Shasta vocab., B. A. E., 1877 (Yreka [Kikatsik] name). Si nĭ'-tĕ-lĭ.—Dorsey, Coquille MS. vocab., B. A. E., 1884 ('flatheads': Coquille name). Stagā'ush.—Boas, inf'n, 1906. Tágahosh.—Gatschet, Nestucca MS. vocab., B. A. E., 1884 (own name). Tσqe'-k'qû.—Dorsey, Alsea MS. vocab., B. A. E., 1884 (Alsea name).

Nesutan, Job. One of the Indians chosen by John Eliot to assist him, as interpreter, in translating the Scriptures into the Natick language of Massachusetts. Gookin (Trans. Am. Antiq. Soc., ii, 444, 1836) thus speaks of him: "In this expedition [July, 1675] one of our principal soldiers of the praying Indians was slain, a valiant and stout man named Job Nesutan; he was a very good linguist in the English tongue and was Mr Eliot's assistant and interpreter in his translations of the Bible, and other books of the Indian language." Eliot wrote, Oct. 21, 1650: "I have one [Indian interpreter] already who can write, so that I can read his writing well, and with some pains and teaching, can read mine" (Pilling, Algonq. Bib., 127, 1891).

Neswage. A Delaware chief who, commanding a band of 23 warriors, about 1841, was attacked by the Sioux at a point just n. of the present Adel, Dallas co., Ia., while on their way to visit the Sauk and Foxes, then holding a war dance within the limits of the site of Des Moines. The Delawares offered a brave defense, killing 26 of the Sioux before all but one of their own number fell. This survivor bore the news to the camp of the Sauk and Foxes, a short distance away, among whom were Keokuk and Pashapahs. With 600 warriors they followed the Sioux, inflicting on them severe punishment. Those who visited the scene of the attack on the Delawares found the body of Neswage lying by a tree, his tomahawk at his side and the bodies of four of his warriors immediately about him. Consult Fulton, Red Men of Iowa, 283, 1882.

Netawatwees. A Delaware chief, born about 1677, died at Pittsburg, Pa., in 1776. Netawatwees was one of the signers of the treaty of Conestoga in 1718. As he belonged to the important Unami, or Turtle division of the tribe, he became chief of this division according to usage and in consequence thereof head chief of the tribe. To him were committed all the tokens of contracts, such as wampum belts, obligatory writings, with the sign manual of William Penn and others down to the time that he and his people were forced to leave Pennsylvania and retire to Ohio, where they settled on Cayuga r. He failed to attend the treaty with Bouquet in 1763, and when this officer and Bradstreet with their troops approached his settlement he attempted to escape, but was captured and deposed from his chieftancy until the conclusion of peace, when he was reinstated by his tribe. He became a convert to Christianity in his later years and urged other leaders to follow his example. On his death he was succeeded by White Eyes. (c. t.)

Netchilik. A spring settlement of the Netchilirmiut Eskimo, on the w. side of Boothia land, Canada.

Netchillik.—Boas in 6th Rep. B. A. E., map, 1888.

Netchilirmiut ('people of the place possessing seal'). A large tribe of the Central Eskimo, occupying Boothia Felix, Canada, and the adjoining mainland, in lat. 70°. They have become mixed with the Ugjulirmiut. Their villages are Angmalortuk, Netchilik, North Herndon, and Sagavok. In recent years a large part of the tribe has moved to Hudson bay and lives in the region between C. Fullerton and Repulse bay. Pop. 446 in 1902.

Boothians.—Ross, Second Voy., app., x, 1835. Nachillee.—Schwatka quoted in Science, 543, 1884. Natsilik.—Rink, Eskimo Tribes, i, 33, 1887. Nechjilli.—Amundse in Geog. Jour., xxix, 505, May 1907. Něitchillĕe.—McClintock, Voy. of Fox, 253, 1881. Neitchilles.—Hall, Second Arct. Exped., 277, 1879. Neitschillik.—Boas in Zeitschr. d. Ges. f. Erdk., 1883. Neitschillit-Eskimos.—Ibid. Neitteelik.—Hall, Second Arct. Exped., 256, 1879. Netchillik.—Schwatka in Century Mag., xxii, 76, 1881. Netchillirmiut.—Boas in Trans. Anthrop. Soc. Wash., iii, 101, 1885. Netidlĭ'wi.—Stein in Petermanns Mitt., 198, 1902. Nĕtschilluk Innuit.—Schwatka in Science, iv, 543, 1884. Net-tee-lek.—McClintock, Voy. of Fox, 163, 1881.

Netlek ('sealing place'). An Ita Eskimo village on Murchison sd., n. w. Greenland; pop. 11 in 1892.

Natilivik.—Kroeber in Bull. Am. Mus. Nat. Hist., xii, 269, 1899. Netchiolumi.—Heilprin, Peary Relief Exped., 104, 1893. Netchiolumy.—Peary, My Arct. Jour., 30, 1893. Netelik.—Kane, Arct. Explor., ii, 107, 1856. Netidlĭwi.—Stein in Petermanns Mitt., no. 9, map, 1902 ('young seal'). Netiulūme.—Peary, My Arct. Jour., 129, map, 1893. Netiulumi.—Peary in Geog. Jour., ii, 224, 1898. Netlek.—Markham in Trans. Ethnol. Soc. Lond., 129, 1866. Netlik.—Hayes, Arct. Boat Journ., 130, 1860.

Netop. The word *netop*, used by the English, according to Roger Williams, in saluting the Indians, is a slight corruption of Narraganset *netomp* (=nitaⁿp for nitaⁿpeu), cognate with Abnaki *nidâbé* and southern Renape *nitâpeu* (*netoppew*, Smith), usually interpreted 'my friend,' but meaning, literally, 'my with-man,' i. e., 'my companion.' The words are contracted, respectively, from *ně* 'my' + *wit* 'with' (which loses its *w* in composition) + *-aⁿp(eu)* 'man'; *ně* + *wid* + *aⁿbé;* and *ně* + *wit* + *-âpeu.* Contractions of this kind are not uncommon in Algonquian; for example: Nipissing *nitshĭkwe*, 'my female companion,' lit. 'my co-woman', from *ni* 'my' + *witsh* 'with' + *ikwe* 'woman'; Chippewa *nidji* 'my comrade', from *ni* + *widj* + *i*, 'my co as-I' (or as myself); Delaware *nitis* 'my friend' or 'companion', from *ni* + *wit* + *is;* Cree *nitjiwâm* 'my companion,' lit. 'my with-goer.' Cf. Lat. *comes*, 'companion,' lit. 'with-goer.' (w. r. g.)

Netpinunsh ('red earth'). A former Chitimacha village, 2 m. w. of Charenton, on Bayou Tèche, La.

Nēt Pìnu'nsh.—Gatschet in Trans. Anthrop. Soc. Wash., ii, 151, 1883. Terre Rouge.—Ibid.

Nets, Netting, and Network. In every part of the United States and northward the Indians and the Eskimo used some kind of nets, netting, or network. These were made from animal tissues and vegetal fibers—wool and hair, hide, sinew, and intestines; roots, stems, bast, bark, and leaves. Animal skins were cut into long delicate strips, while sinew and vegetal fibers were separated into filaments and these twisted, twined, or braided and made into openwork meshes by a series of technical processes ranging from the simplest weaving or coiling without foundation to regular knotting. The woman's hands were the most useful implements in net making; but the seine needle, or shuttle, exhibits a variety of forms from the mere stick for winding, as on a bobbin, to the elaborately ornamented needles of the Eskimo. The meshing also shows a variety of processes, through more and more intricate loopings, as in the Maidu netted caps, to the world-wide netting knot (Dixon).

Netting was used for the capture of animals, for the lacings of snowshoes and lacrosse sticks, for carrying-frames and wallets, for netted caps, for the foundation of feather work—in short, for whatever had meshes. Nets for the capture of animals differed with the creatures caught, as bird net, fish net, seal net, crab net; with the form, as rectangular net, circular net, conical net, bag net, or purse net; with the function, as inclosing net, drag net, casting net, dip net, gill net, arresting net, drift net, and hand net.

Beginning at the far N. with the Eskimo, the question of tribal distribution may be considered. Not all the Eskimo used nets for fishing. Boas never saw any among the Central Eskimo, but mentions them as existing in Labrador and westward of Hudson bay; while Murdoch's account of netting at Pt Barrow, Alaska, is full. Netting needles of antler and walrus ivory, and mesh sticks of bone or antler were employed, both of peculiar patterns. The materials are sinew twine (generally braided), rawhide thong, and whalebone. The knot is the usual becket hitch. Small seal are caught in large meshed nets of rawhide, 18 meshes long and 12 deep, with length of mesh 14 in. These nets are set under the ice in winter and in shoal water in summer. Seals are enticed into the nets by whistling, by scratching on the ice, or with rattles. Whitefish are taken in gill nets set under the ice in rivers. A specimen in the National Museum, made of fine strips of whalebone, is 79 meshes long by 21 deep, with meshes 3¼ in. deep. Murdoch, who figures a conical dip net, or fish trap, made of twisted sinew, also gives the spread of various kinds of fish nets, and surmises

that the American Eskimo learned the use of the net from the Siberians.

From native two-strand twine of milkweed and wild hemp fiber the Maidu of California made their nets and netted caps. Fishing nets varied in size, shape, fineness of twine, and in mesh. The Maidu of Sacramento r. used seines, those of the mountains the conical dip net. The knitting was done with a shuttle composed of two slender sticks. The first two or three fingers of the left hand served for mesh stick, and the so-called weaver's knot joined the meshes. Dixon figures and describes the several ways of making the Maidu netted caps, the simplest beginning with the plain coil without foundation, passing through the same coil with a twist or two in it, to the openwork single knot.

Going southward to the California tribes nearer the Mexican border, aboriginal netting is found in both clothing and basketry. In nets of the simplest structure the courses merely hook into one another and resemble coiled basketry, if the foundation be removed. By taking additional half turns and by varying the knotting, artistic patterns are produced. From the simple meshes the work becomes more elaborate and the knots more intricate.

An interesting use of netting has been brought to light by Holmes in his studies of ancient American pottery. In many places have been found vessels and sherds that show net impressions on the surface. In some parts of the Atlantic slope vessels of clay were molded in network, taking the impressions of the texture. In the description of ancient garments, especially those in which feathers bore a conspicuous part, precisely the same methods of netting are described. This furnishes to archeologists an excellent check-off in their studies, since in later times all other forms of textile work, excepting the figure weaving, were abandoned.

Consult Boas (1) in 6th Rep. B. A. E., 1888, (2) in Bull. Am. Mus. Nat. Hist., xv, 1901; Dixon in Bull. Am. Mus. Nat. Hist., xvii, pt. 3, 1905; Goddard in Univ. Cal. Pub., Am. Archæol. and Ethnol., i, 1903; Holmes (1) in 3d Rep. B. A. E., 1884, (2) in Am. Anthrop., ix, no. 1, 1907; Murdoch in 9th Rep. B. A. E., 1892; Teit in Mem. Am. Mus. Nat. Hist., ii, 1900; Turner in 11th Rep. B. A. E., 1894; Willoughby in Am. Anthrop., vii, no. 1, 1905.   (o. t. m.)

Netsekawik. A Kaviagmiut Eskimo village on Golofnin bay, Alaska.—Eleventh Census, Alaska, 162, 1893.

Nettotalis. Given as an Indian village between Yale and Hope, on the w. bank of Fraser r., Brit. Col. (Brit. Col. map,

Ind. Aff., Victoria, 1872). This would be in the country of the Cowichan.

Neusiok. An unclassified tribe, perhaps of Iroquoian stock, found in 1584 occupying the country on the s. side of lower Neuse r., within the present Craven and Carteret cos., N. C. They were at war with the more southerly coast tribes. In the later colonial period the Indians of the same region were commonly known as Neuse Indians and had dwindled by the year 1700 to 15 warriors in two towns, Chattooka and Rouconk. They probably disappeared by incorporation with the Tuscarora. (J. M.)

Neuses.—Martin, Hist. N. Car., 127, 1829. Neus Indians.—Lawson, Hist. Car. 1714, 384, repr. 1860. Neusiok.—Mooney, Siouan Tribes of the East, 7, 1894. Neuusiooc.—De Bry map in Hariot, Brief and True Rep., 1590. Nusiok.—Amadas (1584) in Smith's Works, Arber ed., 309, 1884. Nustoc.—De Bry map (1590), ibid., 342 (misprint).

Neutrals. An important confederation of Iroquoian tribes living in the 17th century N. of L. Erie in Ontario, having four villages E. of Niagara r. on territory extending to the Genesee watershed; the western bounds of these tribes were indefinitely w. of Detroit r. and L. St Clair. They were called Neutrals by the French because they were neutral in the known wars between the Iroquois and the Hurons. The Hurons called them Attiwandaronk, denoting 'they are those whose language is awry', and this name was also applied by the Neutrals in turn to the Hurons. The Iroquois called them Atirhagenrat (Atirhaguenrek) and Rhagenratka. The Aondironon, the Wenrohronon, and the Ongniaahraronon are names of some of the constituent tribes of the Neutrals. Champlain, reporting what he saw in 1616, wrote that the "Nation Neutre" had 4,000 warriors and inhabited a country that extended 80 or 100 leagues E. and W., situated westward from the lake of the Seneca; they aided the Ottawa (Cheueux releuez) against the Mascoutens or "Small Prairie people," and raised a great quantity of good tobacco, the surplus of which was traded for skins, furs, and porcupine quills and quillwork with the northern Algonquian peoples. This writer said that the Indians cleared the land "with great pains, though they had no proper instruments to do this. They trimmed all the limbs from the trees, which they burned at the foot of the trees to cause them to die. Then they thoroughly prepared the ground between the trees and planted their grain from step to step, putting in each hill about 10 grains, and so continued planting until they had enough for 3 or 4 years' provisions, lest a bad year, sterile and fruitless, befall them."

The Rev. Father Joseph de la Roche Daillon, a Récollect, spent the winter of 1626 among this people for the purpose of teaching them Christianity. The first village, Kandoucho, or All Saints, welcomed him. He then went through four other villages, meeting with a friendly reception, and finally reached the sixth, where he had been told to establish himself. He had the villagers call a council of the tribe for the purpose of declaring to them his mission. He was adopted by the tribe, being given to Tsohahissen (Souharissen?), the presiding chief. Daillon says of the Neutrals: "They are inviolable observers of what they have once concluded and decreed." His "father and host," Tsohahissen, had ever traveled among all neighboring tribes, for he was chief not only of his own village, but even of those of the whole tribe, composed of about 28 villages, villas, and towns, constructed like those of the Hurons, besides many hamlets of 7 or 8 lodges for fishing, hunting, or for the cultivation of the soil. Daillon said that there was then no known instance of a chief so absolute; that Tsohahissen had acquired his position and power by his courage and from having been at war many times against 17 tribes, and had brought back heads (scalps?) and prisoners from all. Their arms were only the war club and the bow and arrow, but they were skilful in their use. Daillon also remarked that he had not found in all the countries visited by him among the Indians a hunchback, one-eyed, or deformed person.

But the Hurons, having learned that Father Daillon contemplated conducting the Neutrals to the trading place in the harbor of C. Victory in L. St Peter of St Lawrence r., approximately 50 m. below Montreal, spread false reports about him, declaring to the Neutrals that he was a great magician, capable of filling the air of the country with pestilence, and that he had then already taken off many Hurons by poison, thus seeking to compass his death by fomenting suspicions against him. The bearing of the accusation may be judged when it is known that sorcerers were regarded as public enemies and outlaws and were remorselessly slain on the slightest pretext.

The father declared that there were an incredible number of deer in the country, which they did not take one by one; but by making a triangular "drive," composed of two convergent hedges leading to a narrow opening, with a third hedge placed athwart the opening but admitting of egress at each end of the last one, they drove the game into this pen and slaughtered them with ease. They practised toward all animals the policy that, whether required or not, they must kill all they might find, lest those which were not taken would tell the other beasts that they themselves had been pursued, and that these latter in time of need would not permit themselves to be taken. There were also many elk, beaver, wildcats, black squirrels, bustards, turkeys, cranes, bitterns, and other birds and animals, most of which were there all winter; the rivers and lakes were abundantly supplied with fish, and the land produced good maize, much more than the people required; there were also squashes, beans, and other vegetables in season. They made oil from the seeds of the sunflower, which the girls reduced to meal and then placed in boiling water which caused the oil to float; it was then skimmed with wooden spoons. The mush was afterward made into cakes and formed a very palatable food.

Daillon said that the life of the Neutrals was "not less indecent" than that of the Hurons, and that their customs and manners were very much the same. Like those of the Hurons, the lodges of the Neutrals were formed like arbors or bowers, covered with the bark of trees, 25 to 30 fathoms long and 6 to 8 in breadth, and had a passage running through the middle, 10 or 12 ft wide, from one end to the other. Along the sides was a kind of shelf, 4 ft from the ground, whereon the occupants lay in summer to avoid the fleas. In winter they lay on mats on the ground near the fire. Such a lodge contained about 12 fires and 24 firesides. Like the Hurons they removed their villages every 5, 10, 15, or 20 years, from 1 to 3 or more leagues, when the land became exhausted by cultivation; for as they did not make use of manure to any great degree, they had to clear more new and fertile land elsewhere. Their garments were made from the skins of various wild beasts obtained by the chase or through trade with the Algonkin, Nipissing, and other hunting tribes, for maize, meal, wampum, and fishing tackle.

The Seneca attacked and destroyed a town of the Aondironon in 1647. This seemingly unprovoked invasion was undertaken to avenge the capture among the Aondironon by the Hurons and the subsequent death of a Seneca warrior who had been among the Tionontati for the purpose of committing murder. This seeming rupture of the traditional neutrality existing between the Iroquois and the Neutrals caused the latter to prepare for war, and for a time both sides were on the alert and stood defiant. Finally the Neutrals decided to attempt to recover their captives by some peaceable means, and to await a more favorable opportunity to avenge themselves for this loss. But the sudden and complete destruction of the political integrity of the Hurons by their several defeats in 1648-

49 by the Iroquois caused the Neutrals now to fear the rising power of the Iroquois tribes, and they vainly sought to gain their good will by committing an act of hostility against their unfortunate Huron neighbors. When the Iroquois had sacked the most strongly palisaded towns of the Hurons, the Huron fugitives sought asylum in all directions, and many of them, placing their trust in the long-standing neutrality existing between the Iroquois and the Neutrals, which neither had yet sought to rupture, fled to the Neutral towns for refuge; but instead of affording them protection, the Neutrals seized them as prisoners, and also that portion of the Hurons still remaining in their own country, and led them into captivity (Jes. Rel. 1659-60).

Immediately after the political destruction of the Hurons by the Iroquois the latter again attacked the Neutrals. The entire conquest of the Neutrals in 1650-51 was the result of this war, and some remnants of the Neutral tribes were incorporated chiefly with the Seneca villages in New York.

The Neutrals were visited in 1640-41 by Fathers Brebeuf and Chaumonot. The tribe was then engaged in vigorous war against the western tribes, especially the Mascoutens. These two missionaries visited 18 villages or towns, stopping in 10 of them and expounding their own religious faith whenever they could assemble an audience. In these 10 settlements they estimated about 500 fires and 3,000 persons. On their return journey the fathers remained at Teotongniaton, situated midway between the chief town, Ounontisaston, and the town nearest the Huron country, Kandoucho, where they were compelled to remain on account of snow. While there their hostess was at great pains to shield them from the abuse to which they were constantly subjected; she also aided them to learn the language and to harmonize it with that of these Neutrals. The Awenrehronon, who had formerly lived eastward of the Erie or Panther tribe, took refuge in Khioetoa, or St Michel, a few years before this visit of the two fathers, and they were disposed to listen to the teachings of the missionaries.

As a sign of mourning for their friends and kin the Neutrals customarily blackened not only their own but also the faces of the dead. They tattooed the corpse and adorned it with feathers and other trinkets; if the person died in war, a chief delivered an address over the body, around which were assembled the friends and kin of the dead, who were urged by the orator to hasten to avenge the death. The Neutrals figuratively resurrected the dead, especially great chieftains and persons noted for valor and wisdom, by the substitution of some person who they thought was like the deceased in person, age, and character. The selection was, made in council, by the clan of the deceased person; then all the people except the one chosen arose, and the master of ceremonies, gently lowering his hand to the earth, feigned to raise the illustrious dead from the tomb and to give life to him in the person of the chosen one, on whom he then imposed the name and dignity of the dead chieftain, and the newly made chieftain then arose amid the ceremonial acclaim of the people.

In 1643 the Neutrals sent an expedition of 2,000 warriors against the "Nation du feu," some of whom they attacked in a palisaded village defended by 900 men, who bravely withstood the first assaults; but after a siege of 10 days the Neutrals carried the palisade and killed on the spot many of its defenders and took about 800 captives. After burning 70 of the best warriors of the Nation du feu, they put out the eyes and girdled the mouths of the old men, whom they afterward abandoned to starve (Jes. Rel. 1643–44). The same authority also says that the Nation du feu alone was more populous than all the Neutral nation, all the Hurons, and all the Iroquois, showing that the term had not yet become restricted to those now called Mascoutens, or "Small Prairie people," but included all the so-called Illinois tribes as well.

From the Journal des PP. Jesuites for 1652–53 it is learned that the portions of the Tobacco Nation and of the Neutral Nation then remaining independent bodies of people were assembling with all neighboring Algonquian tribes at A'otonatendie (Akotonatendike?), situated 3 days' journey southward from Skia'e (Sault Sainte Marie); that the Tobacco Nation wintered in 1653 at Tea'on-to'rai, and the Neutrals, numbering 800, at Sken'chio'e (i. e., Fox place) in the direction of Te'o'chanontian, probably Detroit; that these two tribes would rendezvous in the autumn of 1653 at A'otonatendie, where they had assembled more than 2,000 warriors. This is perhaps the last historical mention of the Neutrals as an independent body. It is these Neutrals, apparently, whom Perrot (Mémoire, chap. XIV, 1864) calls "Huron de la nation neutre" and "Hurons neutres."

In 1640 the Hurons offered a present of 9 hatchets (costly articles at that time) to the chieftains of the Neutral council, in the hope of inducing it to order the assassination of Fathers Brebeuf and Chaumonot, but after deliberat-

ing on the proposal all night the council refused to accept the gift.

As has been seen, Daillon said the Neutrals occupied 28 villages in 1626. In 1640 Brebeuf ascribed to them 40 villages with a minimum population of 12,000 persons, including 4,000 warriors. Only a few of the names of these have been preserved, among them being Kandoucho or Tous les Saints, Khioetoa or Saint Michel, Ongniaahra ("Ouororonon," probably on the site of Youngstown, N. Y.; a form of Niagara), Ounontisaston, and Teotongniaton or Saint Guillaume. (J. N. B. H.)

Aragaritkas.—N. Y. Doc. Col. Hist., IV, 908, 1854 (said to be composed of 7 tribes). **Atiaonrek.**—Jes. Rel. 1656, 34, 1858. **Atiouandaronks.**—Ibid., 1635, 33, 1858. **Atiouendaronk.**—Ibid., 1644, 97, 1858. **Atiraguenrek.**—Ibid., 1656, 34, 1858. **Atirhagenrenrets.**—Jes. Rel. quoted by Parkman, Jesuits, xliv, 1867. **Ati-rhagenrets.**—Shea in Schoolcraft, Ind. Tribes, IV, 208, 1854. **Atiwandaronk.**—Shea, Cath. Miss., 24, 1855. **Attenonderonk.**—Schoolcraft, Ind. Tribes, IV, 201, 1854. **Attihouandaron.**—Sagard (1632), Hist. Can., IV, 1866. **Attinoindarons.**—Sagard (1626), Can., II, 408, 1866. **Attionandarons.**—Gallatin in Trans. Am. Ethnol. Soc., II, ciii, 1848 (misprint). **Attionidarons.**—Sagard (1626) quoted by Parkman, Jesuits, xliv, 1867. **Attiouandaronk.**—Jes. Rel. 1641, 72, 1858. **Atti8andarons.**—Ibid., 1639, 88, 1858. **Attiouendarankhronon.**—Ibid., 1640, 35, 1858. **Attiouendaronk.** — Ibid. **Attiuoindarons.** — Sagard (1626), Hist. Can., II, 334, 1866. **Attiwandaronk.**—Shea, Miss. Val., lix, 1852. **Attiwondaronk.**—Royce in Smithson. Misc. Coll., XXV, art. 5, 95, 1883. **Hatiwanta-runh.** — Hewitt, inf'n, 1886 (='their speech is awry'; from *hati* 'they', *owanta* 'voices', *runh* 'is awry': Tuscarora name). **Nation Neuht.**—McKenney and Hall, Ind. Tribes, III, 81, 1854. **Neuter Nation.** — Morgan, League Iroq., 9, 1851. **Neuters.** — Shea, Miss. Val., lx, 1852. **Neutral Nation.**—Ibid., lix. **Neutre Nation.**—Champlain (1616), Œuvres, IV, 58, 1870. **Neutrios.**—Duro, Don Diego de Peñalosa, 43, 1882. **Rhagenratka.**—Shea in Schoolcraft, Ind. Tribes, IV, 208, 1854.

Neutubvig. An unidentified tribe, said to have inhabited the extreme N. end of Whitneys (Whidbey) id., and the country between Skagit r. and Bellingham bay, Wash., in 1852. This territory is Salishan. **Ne-u-lub-vig.**—Starling in Ind. Aff. Rep., 171, 1852. **Ne-u-tub-vig.**—Ibid., 170.

Nevantin. A former village of the Nacogdoche (q. v.) on the site of the present Nacogdoches, Texas.

Nevome. A name applied to the Lower Pima, or Pimas Bajos, living chiefly in Sonora, Mexico, including the middle Yaqui r. region and extending E. somewhat into Chihuahua. They are now almost completely assimilated with the whites, the Nevome ("Pima") population in Sonora and Chihuahua being officially given as only 528 in 1900. Under the same term may be included also one or two small colonies; one known as the Bamoa (q. v.) and the other a former settlement in the Tepehuane territory. The language of the two divisions of the Pima tribe, Upper and Lower, is substantially the same, and there are no marked differences in their physical characteristics; they are generally tall, robust, and well-formed. Their skulls are dolichocephalic. According to Bandelier (Arch. Inst. Papers, III, 54, 1890) their social organization and their religious beliefs and practices were analogous to those of the Yaqui. They were described by Ribas, a missionary of the 17th century, as "on the banks of creeks with good running water, their houses better and more durable than those of neighboring tribes, the walls being formed of large adobes and the roofs flat and covered with earth. Some of their houses were much larger than others and furnished with loopholes like forts, in which the people could take refuge in times of danger." Lumholtz (Unknown Mexico, I, 127, 1902) says they often have connected with their houses a kind of

pueblos of Huexotitlan, Maguina, Tosonachic, Tutuaca, and Yepachic contained a mixed population of Nevome, Tarahumare, and Tepehuane.   (F. W. H.)

Coras.—Bandelier in Arch. Inst. Papers, III, 54, 1890 (Nebomes, or). **Nebome.**—Ribas, Hist. Triumphos, 361, 1645. **Nebomes Baxos.**—Ibid., 370. **Pimas Bajos.**—Orozco y Berra, Geog., 58, 1864. **Pimas de el Sur.**—Rivera, Diario, leg. 1514, 1736. **Southern Pimas.**—Bandelier, op. cit., 76.

Newark works. The most elaborate and complicated group of ancient works E. of the Rocky mts., situated at the junction of South and Raccoon forks of Licking r., near Newark, Licking co., Ohio. They are on a plain elevated 30 to 50 ft above the bottom land bordering the stream, and consist of an extensive series of square, circular, and octagonal inclosures,

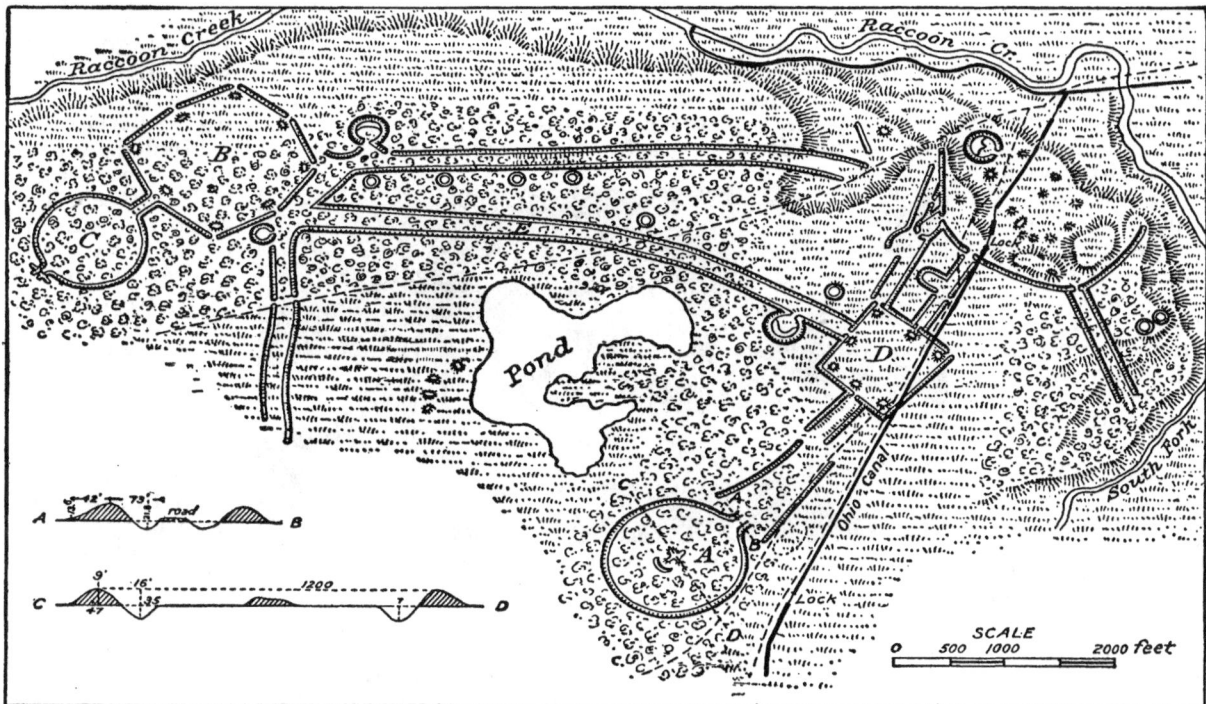

MAP OF NEWARK WORKS.   (AFTER SQUIER AND DAVIS)

outside cellar, covered with a conical roof of dry grass, which serves both as a workroom and as a storeroom for their stock in trade. Like all the converted Indians of this section it is common at the present day for them to fix small crosses in a log and plant them in front of their houses. Their chief and most formidable enemies in former times were the Apache. The divisions of the Nevome, usually so called from the names of the villages at various periods, are: Aivino, Basiroa, Buena Vista, Cumuripa, Ecatacari, Hecatari, Hios, Huvaguere, Maicoba, Moicaqui, Movas, Nuri, Onavas, Onopa, Ostimuri, San Antonio de la Huerta, San José de los Pimas, Sibubapa, Sisibotari, Soyopa, Suaqui, Tecoripa, Tehata, Tehuizo, Tonichi, Ures (in part), and Yecora. The

with mounds, ditches, and connecting avenues spreading over nearly 4 sq. m. A number of the minor structures have been obliterated and a large portion of the remaining walls considerably reduced by the plow. Fortunately, an accurate survey and plat were made by Col. Whittlesey in 1836 while the works were yet comparatively uninjured; and other surveys and plats were made by the Bureau of American Ethnology in 1888 and a partial survey by the U. S. Geological Survey in 1891. The works consist of two groups, nearly 2 m. apart, connected by two walllined avenues. The western group consists of a large circle connected with an octagon. Outside the latter, near the E. corner, there is a small circle, and near the middle of the S. side there is another. From the latter point of the octagon a walled avenue, now almost obliterated, extended directly s. 2 m. or more. From near the E. corner of the octagon two avenues extend eastward with a low wall on each side, one connecting with the square of the eastern group, the other running directly eastward to the descent to the lowland N. of the square. Along these avenues, at one or two points, are small circles. The eastern group consists of a large circle connected with a square by a broad avenue and several adjoining lines of walls. The circle of the western group, which is the westernmost structure of the entire works, is still distinct, being 3 ft high at the lowest point, and averaging 4 to 5 ft, apart from an enlargement on the s. w. side, where for about 170 ft it rises to the height of 14 ft. This enlargement has been called the "observatory," while the circle has been named "the observatory circle." At the N. E. side, directly opposite this observatory, is a gateway leading into an avenue 300 ft long and 80 ft wide, which terminates in one of the gateways of the octagon. The latter, which is symmetrical, has a gateway at each of the 8 corners, opposite which, 60 ft within, is a small mound varying in height from 3 to 6 ft. The mean diameter of the

EMBANKMENT WITH INTERIOR MOAT, NEWARK WORKS

circle, measured from the middle line of the wall, is 1,054 ft. The circumference, measured along the middle of the wall, deviates at no point more than 5 ft from a true circle. The area, including the inner half of the wall, is 20 acres; that of the level interior, 18.6 acres. The parts and angles of the octagon are quite symmetrical. The length of the walls between the centers of the gates averages 621 ft, from which the greatest variation is only 4 ft, except in one wall that falls 8 ft short of the average. The opposite angles do not vary from one another more than 2 degrees in any instance, and the opposite sides do not vary from the same direction more than 2 degrees. The large circle of the eastern group embraces within its circuit the fair grounds of the Licking County Agricultural Society. The wall, in this instance, is accompanied with an inside ditch, varying in width from 28 to 40 ft and in depth from 8 to 13 ft. The width of the wall at the base is from 35 to 55 ft and its height from 5 to 14 ft. There

is one gateway at the N. E. with flanking extensions of the wall into the avenue leading to the square. The square of the eastern group is partially obliterated, yet most of the walls could be distinctly traced in 1888, when the survey on behalf of the Bureau of American Ethnology was made. From this survey it is learned that the sides varied in length from 926 to 951 ft and that the angles at the corners did not in any instance vary from a right angle more than 1 degree. There are now no indications of the inner mounds of the square observed by Whittlesey; but the three-pointed mound in the center of the fair-grounds circle is still visible. There were also, at the time of Whittlesey's survey, 4 or 5 circles that were smaller than those above described. The two or three of these that remain vary from 125 to 200 ft in diameter and have an inside ditch and a semicircular earthen platform on one side. There were also in Whittlesey's time several still smaller circles, which may have been lodge sites. The avenues, except the one connected with the fair-grounds circle, which was wider, were generally about 200 ft wide. Their walls at present do not exceed at any point 2 ft in height, and in many places are almost obliterated.

Consult Harris, Tour to N. W. Ter., 1805; Trans. Am. Antiq. Soc., I, 1820; Smucker in Am. Antiq., III, 261–267, 1881; Thomas, (1) Circular, Square, and Octagonal Earthworks, Bull. B. A. E., 1894, (2) Mound Explorations, 12th Rep. B. A. E., 458–468, 1891. See, also, for list of references, Thomas, Cat. Prehist. Works, Bull. B. A. E., 178, 1891. (C. T.)

Newastarton (?'big waters town'). A Dakota tribe, according to Clark, which roved on the Mississippi above the St Peter's (Minnesota r.), in the present Minnesota. Probably the Mdewakanton. Newastarton.—Lewis and Clark Exped., Coues ed., I, 101, note, 1893. **Ne Was tar ton.**—Orig. Jour. Lewis and Clark, I, 133, 1904.

Newcastle Townsite. The local name for a body of Salish of Cowichan agency, Brit. Col. Pop. 26 in 1896, the last time the name occurs. Newcastle Toronsite.—Can. Ind. Aff. Rep. 1891, 250, 1892 (misprint). **Newcastle Townsite.**—Ibid., 433, 1896.

Newchemass. An unidentified tribe mentioned by Jewitt (Narr., 77, repr.

1849) as living far to the N. of and inland from Nootka sd., early in the 19th century. Their language differed from that of the Nootka, but was understood by the latter. Their complexion was said to be darker, their stature shorter, and their hair coarser than those features of other nations. The locality assigned to them corresponds with that of the Nimkish.

Nuchîmases.—Galiano, Relacion, 94, 1802.

Newcomerstown (named for a female captive). A village of the Delawares in 1766–81, about the site of the present New Comerstown, on Muskingum r., Tuscarawas co., Ohio. The chief's name was Noatwhelama.

New Camero Town.—La Tour, map, 1784 (misprint). New Comers Town.—Hutchins, map in Smith, Bouquet's Exped., 1766. Ville des nouveaux venus.—La Tour, map, 1784 (New Camero town, or).

New Credit. A Missisauga settlement in Tuscarora township of the Six Nations res. on Grand r., Ontario. These Missisauga formerly lived on Credit r., but removed to their present location about the year 1850 by invitation of the Six Nations. They numbered 218 in 1884, 263 in 1906.

New England Company. See *English influence, Missions.*

New Eufaula. A former colony of Upper Creeks from Eufaula, Ala., established in 1767 in N. Florida, lat. 28°.

New Yufala.—Romans, Fla., 280, 1775.

Newhuhwaittinekin. A Shuswap village 4 m. above Cache cr., Bonaparte r., Brit. Col.; pop. 160 in 1906.

Bonaparte Indians.—Can. Ind. Aff. 1885, 91, 1886 (so called by whites). Ne-whuh-wait'-tin-e-kin.—Dawson in Trans. Roy. Soc. Can., sec. II, 44, 1891. Tluh-ta-us.—Can. Ind. Aff. 1885, 196, 1886.

Newichawanoc. A tribe or band of the Pennacook confederacy living on upper Piscataqua r. Their village, of the same name, was situated about the site of Berwick, Me. They were neighbors of the Piscataqua and probably intimately related to them. Their chief is said to have joined in the deed of 1629 to Wheelwright, the genuineness of which is still a mooted question. The tribe early became extinct.

Neahawanak.—Walton (1704) in Me. Hist. Soc. Coll., III, 349, 1853. Nekekowannock.—Potter, ibid., IV, 190, 1856. Newchawanick.—Niles (ca. 1761) in Mass. Hist. Soc. Coll., 4th s., V, 334, 1861. Newgeawanacke.—Rishworth (1656) in Me. Hist. Soc. Coll., I, 397, 1865. Newgewanacke.—Ibid. Newichawanick.—Penhallow (1726) in N. H. Hist. Soc. Coll., I, 81, 1824. Newichawannicke.—Hubbard (1680) in Mass. Hist. Soc. Coll., 2d s., V, 224, 1815. Newichawannock.—Pike (1692) in N. H. Hist. Soc. Coll., III, 44, 1832. Newichawanocks.—Sullivan in Mass. Hist. Soc. Coll., 1st s., IX, 210, 1804. Newichewannock.—Gorges (1678) in Me. Hist. Soc. Coll., II, 257, 1847. Newichuwenoq.—Moodey (1683) in Mass. Hist. Soc. Coll., 4th s., VIII, 362, 1868. Newichwanicke.—Gibbins (1633) in N. H. Hist. Soc. Coll., I, 311, 1824. Newichwannock.—Potter in Me. Hist. Soc. Coll., IV, 190, 1856. Newickawanacks.—McKenney and Hall, Ind. Tribes, III, 80, 1854.

Nuch-a-wan-acks.—Macauley, N. Y., II, 162, 1829. Nuwichawanick.—Potter in Me. Hist. Soc. Coll., IV, 190, 1856.

Newichumni. A division of the Miwok, formerly living between Cosumnes and Mokelumne rs., Cal.

Nevichumnes.—Hale, Ethnog. and Philol., 630, 1846. Newatchumne.—Bancroft, Nat. Races, I, 450, 1874.

New Mikasuky. A former Seminole town, 30 m. w. of Suwannee r., in Lafayette co., Fla., of which Tuskam ha was chief in 1823.—H. R. Ex. Doc. 74, 19th Cong., 1st sess., 27, 1826.

New River Indians. A subsidiary branch of the Shasta who occupied the forks of Salmon r., Siskiyou co., Cal., from a few miles above the junction (the lower parts of those streams being inhabited by the Konomihu), and also the head of New r. They have no names for themselves. Their language is much closer to that of the Shasta proper than is that of the Konomihu, but it is clearly a separate dialect. See Dixon in Am. Anthrop., VII, no. 2, 1905.   (R. B. D.)

Amutakhwe.—A. L. Kroeber, inf'n, 1903 (Hupa name). Djalitason.—Ibid. (Chimariko name).

Newspapers. See *Periodicals.*

Newtown. A former village, probably of the Seneca, on Chemung r., near Elmira, Chemung co., N. Y. It was destroyed by Gen. Sullivan in 1779.

Newton.—Livermore (1779) in N. H. Hist. Soc. Coll., VI, 325, 1850. New Town.—Jones (1780) in N. Y. Doc. Col. Hist., VIII, 785, 1857. Newtown.—Pemberton (ca. 1792) in Mass. Hist. Soc. Coll., 1st s., II, 176, 1810.

Newtown. A former village, probably of the Delawares and Iroquois, on the N. bank of Licking r., about the site of the present Zanesville, Ohio.

Newtown. A former village, probably of the Delawares and Iroquois, on Muskingum r., about the site of the present Newton, Muskingum co., Ohio.

Newtown. A former village, probably of the Delawares and Iroquois, on the w. side of Wills cr., near the site of the present Cambridge, Guernsey co., Ohio.

Newtychanning. A mixed Iroquois village, built in 1778 on the w. bank of Susquehanna r. and on the N. side of Sugar cr., in the vicinity of the present North Towanda, Bradford co., Pa. It was destroyed Aug. 8, 1779, by Colonel Proctor of Sullivan's army, at which time it contained 15 or 20 houses. Near this site was formerly situated the village of Oscalui.   (J. N. B. H.)

Nez Percés ('pierced noses'). A term applied by the French to a number of tribes which practised or were supposed to practise the custom of piercing the nose for the insertion of a piece of dentalium. The term is now used exclusively to designate the main tribe of the Shahaptian family, who have not, however, so far as is known, ever been given to the practice.

The Nez Percés, or Sahaptin of later writers, the Chopunnish (corrupted from Tsútpĕli) of Lewis and Clark, their discoverers, were found in 1805 occupying a large area in what is now w. Idaho, N. E. Oregon, and S. E. Washington, on lower Snake r. and its tributaries. They roamed between the Blue mts. in Oregon and the Bitter Root mts. in Idaho, and according

KALKALSHUATASH, OR JASON—NEZ PERCÉ

to Lewis and Clark sometimes crossed the range to the headwaters of the Missouri. By certain writers they have been classed under two geographic divisions, Upper Nez Percés and Lower Nez Percés. The latter were found by Bonneville in 1834 to the N. and w. of the Blue mts. on several of the branches of Snake r., where they were neighbors of the Cayuse and Wallawalla. The Upper

Nez Percés held the Salmon r. country in Idaho in 1834, and probably also at the same time the Grande Ronde valley in E. Oregon, but by treaty of 1855 they ceded a large part of this territory to the United States.

The reservation in which they were confined at that time included the Wallowa valley in Oregon, as well as a large district in Idaho. With the discovery of gold and the consequent influx of miners and settlers the Oregon districts were in demand, and a new treaty was made by which the tribe was confined to the reservation at Lapwai, Idaho. The occupants of Wallowa valley refused to recognize the treaty, and finally, under their chief, Joseph (q. v.), took active measures of resistance, and the Nez Percé war of 1877 resulted. Several severe defeats were inflicted on the United States troops who were sent against the Indians, and finally, when forced to give way, Joseph conducted a masterly retreat across the Bitter Root mts. and into Montana in an attempt to reach Canadian territory, but he and his band were surrounded and captured when within a few miles of the boundary. Joseph and his followers to the number of 450 were removed to Indian Ter., where their loss from disease was so great that in 1885 they were sent to the Colville res. in N. Washington, where a remnant still resides.

Under the collective name Chopunnish, Lewis and Clark estimated the population to be 7,850. Deducting from this total 1,600 for the Pelloatpallah (Paloos) band, now treated as distinct from the Nez Percés, and 250 for the Yeletpo (Wailetpu, i. e., Cayuse), now supposed to belong to a distinct stock, the total of the Nez Percés in 1805 according to those authors was about 6,000. Wilkes estimated the Chopunnish at about 3,000 in 1849, and Gibbs gave them a population of more than 1,700 in 1853. In 1885 they were estimated officially at 1,437. There are now (1906) somewhat more than 1,600, 1,534 being on the reservation in Idaho and 83 on the Colville res. in Washington.

In general habits of life the Nez Percés as well as the other Shahaptian tribes conform to the inland type of Indians and differ sharply in most respects from their western neighbors, the Chinook. At the time of Lewis and Clark's visit they are reported as living in communal houses, said to contain about 50 families each. There is evidence, however, that the Nez Percés used the typical underground lodge, and that these seldom contained more than 3 or 4 families. A much larger dancing house was built at each permanent winter camp. Salmon constituted their most important food in early times, and with roots and berries made up their entire food supply until the introduction of horses facilitated hunting expeditions to the neighboring mountains. The tribe seems to have been divided into a number of bands or villages, named according to the place where the permanent winter camp was made. Owing to the precarious nature of the food supply the greater portion of the inhabitants of any one of these villages would often be absent for a large part of the year, consequently it is impossible to determine with accuracy the location and population of these divisions in early times. There was no head chief of the tribe, but each band had several chiefs, of whom one was regarded as the leader, and these chiefs were succeeded by their sons as a rule. Expeditions for hunting or war were led by chiefs chosen for the occasion. There are no signs of a clan system in the social organization of the Nez Percés, and marriage is apparently permitted between any couple except in the case of recognized relationship.

The religious beliefs of the Nez Percés, previous to the introduction of Christianity, were those characteristic of the Indians of the interior, the main feature being the belief in an indefinite number of spirits. The individual might procure a personal protecting spirit in the usual way by rigorous training and fasting.

The Nez Percés have always borne a high reputation for independence and bravery, and have been particularly noted for their almost constant friendliness to the whites. Practically the only rupture in these relations was the Nez Percé war of 1877, mentioned above.

The bands and divisions of the Nez Percés are known only approximately. The following are the best defined: Alpowna, on a small branch of the Clearwater, below Lewiston, Idaho; Assuti, on Assuti cr., Idaho; Kamiah, at the town of that name on the Clearwater, Idaho; Lamtama, so called from a branch of Salmon r., Idaho; Lapwai, near the junction of Lapwai cr. and the Clearwater; Willewah, formerly occupying Wallowa valley, Oreg., and now for the greater part on Colville res., Wash. (Joseph's band). In addition a number of bands have been recorded by the names of their chiefs or their supposed places of residence.					(H. W. H. L. F.)

A'dal-k'ato'igo.—Mooney in 14th Rep. B. A. E., 744, 1896 ('people with hair cut across the forehead': Kiowa name). **Aníporspi.**—Gatschet, Kalapuya MS., B. A. E. (Calapooya name). **á-pá-ŏ-pá.**—Long, Exped. Rocky Mts., II, lxxxiv, 1823 (Gros Ventre name). **A-pŭ-pe'.**—Hayden, Ethnog. and Philol. Mo. Val., 402, 1862 ('to paddle', 'paddles': (Crow name). **Asaháptin.**—Gatschet, Kalapuya MS., B. A. E., 31 (Calapooya name). **Blue Earth Indians.**—Coues, Henry and Thompson Jour., 712, 1897. **Blue Mud Indians.**—Orig. Jour. Lewis and Clark (1805), VI, 106, 1905 (probably identical). **Blue Muds.**—Ibid. (name applied by traders).

Chappunish.—Ross, Fur Hunters, I, 306, 1855. **Cheaptin.**—Townsend, Narr., 233, 1839. **Chipunish.**—Kip in Oreg. Hist. Soc. Sources, I, pt. 2, 11, 1897. **Chipunnish.**—Kip, Army Life, 33, 1859. **Choco-nish.**—Gass, Journal, 215, 1807. **Chohoptins.**—Cox, Columbia R., II, 125, 1831. **Chopannish.**—Minto in Oreg. Hist. Soc. Quar., I, 303, 1900 (misprint from Lewis and Clark). **Chopemnish.**—Ind. Aff. Rep., 460, 1854. **Choponiesh.**—Orig. Jour. Lewis and Clark (1805), VII, 115, 1905. **Choponish.**—Ibid., IV, 318, 1905. **Choponnesh.**—Ibid., III, 103, 1905. **Chopunish.**—Kelley, Oregon, 68, 1830. **Chopunmohees.**—Robertson, Oregon, 129, 1846. **Chopunnish.**—Lewis and Clark Exped., I, 455, 1814; II, 587, 1817. **Flathead.**—Gass, Journal, 132, 1807. **Green Wood Indians.**—Coues, Henry-Thompson Jour., 712, 1897. **I'-na-opĕ.**—Dorsey, Kwapa MS. vocab., B. A. E., 1891 (Quapaw name). **Kamŭ'-inu.**—Hoffman, MS., B. A. E., 1884 (own name). **Ko-mun'-i-tup'-i-o.**—Hayden, Ethnog. and Philol. Mo. Val., 264, 1862 (Siksika name). **La-aptin.**—Stevens in Ind. Aff. Rep., 425, 1854 (misprint *L* for *S*). **Mikadeshitchíshi.**—Gatschet, Naisha Apache MS., B. A. E. (Kiowa Apache name). **Nazpercies.**—Hastings, Guide to Oreg., 59, 1845. **Neckpercie.**—Lane (1849) in Sen. Ex. Doc. 52, 31st Cong., 1st sess., 171, 1850. **Neepercil.**—Lane in Ind. Aff. Rep., 159, 1850. **Nenpersaas.**—Meek in H. R. Ex. Doc. 76, 30th Cong., 1st sess., 10, 1848. **Nepercy.**—Irving, Bonneville's Advent., 115, 1868 (name as pronounced by trappers). **Ner Percees.**—Scouler (1846) in Jour. Ethnol. Soc. Lond., I, 237, 1848. **Nes Perces.**—Wilkes, Hist. Oregon, 44, 1845. **Nezierces.**—Farnham, Travels, 69, 1843. **Nez Percé.**—Parker, Journal, 100, 1840. **Nez Percé Flat-Heads.**—Barrows, Oregon, 121, 1884. **Nézperces.**—Wyeth (1848) in Schoolcraft, Ind. Tribes, I, 221, 1851. **Nez Perce's.**—Latham in Jour. Ethnol. Soc. Lond., I, 158, 1848. **Nez percez.**—McKenney and Hall, Ind. Tribes, III, 79, 1854. **Nezpercies.**—Hastings, Guide to Oreg., 59, 1845. **Nezperees.**—Kane, Wanderings in N. A., 290, 1859. **Nez Perse.**—Hines, Oregon, 133, 1851. **Nezpesie.**—Hastings, Guide to Oreg., 59, 1845. **Nez Pierces.**—Coyner, Lost Trappers, 135, 1847. **Nimipu.**—Lyman in Oreg. Hist. Soc. Quar., II, 288, 1901 ('the people': own name). **Numepo.**—Kingsley, Stand. Nat. Hist., pt. VI, 140, 1885. **Nu-me-poos.**—Mattoon in Ind. Aff. Rep. 1905, 199, 1906. **Numipu.**—Mowry, Marcus Whitman, 259, 1901. **Pe ga'-zan-de.**—Dorsey, Kansa MS. vocab., B. A. E., 1882 (Kansa name). **Pe xa'-san-ȼse.**—Dorsey, Osage MS. vocab., B. A. E. ('plaited hair over the forehead': Osage name). **Percés.**—Dunn, Hist. Oregon, 326, 1845. **Pierced Noses.**—Orig. Jour. Lewis and Clark (1805), III, 128, 1905. **Pierced-nose.**—Lewis and Clark Exped., I, 455, 1814. **Pierced Noses.**—Orig. Jour. Lewis and Clark (1805), III, 78, 1905. **Pierce Noses.**—Ibid., 142. **Po'-ge-hdo-ke.**—Riggs, Dak.-Eng. Dict., 423, 1890 (Dakota name). **Sa aptin.**—Lane (1849) in Sen. Ex. Doc. 52, 31st Cong., 1st sess., 170, 1850. **Sa-áptin.**—Gatschet, Okinagan MS., B. A. E. (Okinagan name; pl. Sa-áptinx). **Saaptins.**—Schoolcraft, Ind. Tribes, III, map, 200, 1853. **Sahapotins.**—Gallatin in Trans. Am. Antiq. Soc., II, map, 1836. **Sahaptain.**—Ross, Advent., 217, 1849. **Sahaptan.**—Gatschet misquoted in Congrès des Amér., IV, pt. 1, 285, 1883. **Sahaptanian.**—Brinton, Am. Race, 108, 1891. **Sahaptin.**—Dart in Ind. Aff. Rep., 216, 1851. **Sah haptinnay.**—Featherstonhaugh, Canoe Voy., II, 62, 1847. **Saíduka.**—Gatschet, MS., B. A. E. (Paiute name). **Sapetan.**—Smet, Oregon Miss., 240, 1847. **Sapetens.**—Coues, Henry-Thompson Jour., 709, 1897. **Sapotans.**—Smet, Reisen zu den Felsen-Gebirgen, 205, 1865. **Saptans.**—Armstrong, Oregon, 111, 1857. **Sap'tin.**—Wilkes, West. Am., 97, 1849. **Sha-ap-tin.**—Farnham, Trav., 69, 1843. **Shahaptain.**—Ross, Advent., 217, 1849. **Shahaptan.**—Scouler in Jour. Geog. Soc. Lond., XI, 225, 1841. **Shahaptanian.**—Dorsey in Am. Anthrop., II, 55, 1889. **Shahaptemish.**—Gairdner in Jour. Roy. Geog. Soc. Lond., XI, 256, 1841. **Shahapts.**—Deniker, Races of Man, 532, 1900. **Shaw-ha-ap-ten.**—Ross, Fur Hunters, I, 185, 1855. **Shaw Haptens.**—Ross, Advent., 127, 1849. **Shi'wanish.**—Mooney in 14th Rep. B. A. E., 744, 1896 ('strangers from up the river': Tenino name; applied also to the Cayuse). **Shopumish.**—Kingsley, Standard Nat.

Hist., pt. VI, 140, 1883. **Tchaχsúkush.**—Gatschet, MS., B. A. E. (Caddo name). **Tchútpelit.**—Ibid. (own name). **Thoig′ a-rik-kah.**—Stuart, Montana, 76, 1865 ('kouse-eaters': Shoshoni name). **Tsoi′- gah.**—Ibid., 77. **Tsoo-ah-gah-rah.**—Gebow, Shoshonay Vocab., 16, 1868 (Shoshoni name). **Tsuháru- kats.**—Gatschet, MS., B. A. E. (Pawnee name). **Tsútpĕli.**—Ibid. (own name). **Up-pup-pay.**—Anon. Crow MS. vocab., B. A. E., n. d. (Crow name).

Nhaiiken (*N'haï′ikEn*). A Ntlakyapamuk village near Spences Bridge, Thompson r., Brit. Col. — Hill-Tout in Rep. Ethnol. Surv. Can., 4, 1899.

Niagara. Being of Iroquoian origin, one of the earliest forms of this place-name is that in the Jesuit Relation for 1641, in which it is written *Onguiaahra*, evidently a misprint for *Ongniaahra*, and it is there made the name of a Neutral town and of the river which to-day bears this designation, although *Ongmarahronon* of the Jesuit Relation for the year 1640 appears to be a misprint for *Ongniarahronon*, signifying 'people of Ongniarah.' The Iroquois and their congeners applied it to the place whereon the village of Youngstown, Niagara co., N. Y., now stands. On the Tabula Novæ Franciæ, in Historiæ Canadensis, sev Novæ-Franciæ (bk. 10, Paris, 1664, but made in 1660 by Franciscus Creuxius, S. J.), the falls of Niagara are called "*Ongiara catarractes.*" Much ingenuity has been exercised in attempts to analyze this name. The most probable derivation, however, is from the Iroquoian sentence-word, which in Onondaga and Seneca becomes *O'hniă'gā'*, and in Tuscarora *U'hnia'kā'r*, signifying 'bisected bottom-land.' Its first use was perhaps by the Neutral or Huron tribes.   (J. N. B. H.)

Niagara. A species of grape, well known in the N. E. portion of the United States; so called from its cultivation in the Niagara peninsula. Also the name of a variety of tomato, recorded in Tracy (Am. Var. of Veget. for 1901–2, Wash., 1903); from the place-name *Niagara*, q. v.   (A. F. C.)

Niakewankih. A former village of the Clatsop on the Pacific coast, s. of Pt Adams at the mouth of Ohanna cr., Clatsop co., Oreg. (Boas, Kathlamet Texts, 236, 1901).
Neahkowin.—Lyman in Oreg. Hist. Soc. Quar., I, 321, 1900. **Niā′k¡ewanqîX.**—Boas, Kathlamet Texts, 236, 1901.

Niakla (*Ni-ak′-la*). A former Chumashan village on Santa Cruz id., Cal., E. of the harbor. — Henshaw, Buenaventura MS. vocab., B. A. E., 1884.

Niakonaujang. An Akudnirmiut Eskimo settlement on Padli fjord, Baffin land.
Niaqonaujang.—Boas in 6th Rep. B. A. E., 441, 1888.

Niantic (contr. of *Naïantukq-ut*, 'at a point of land on a [tidal] river or estuary.'—Trumbull). An Algonquian tribe formerly occupying the coast of Rhode Island from Narragansett bay to about the Connecticut state line. Their principal village, Wekapaug, was on the great pond near Charlestown. They were

closely connected with the Narraganset, forming practically one tribe with them. By refusing to join in King Philip's war in 1675 they preserved their territory and tribal organization, and at the close of the war the Narraganset who submitted to the English were placed with

NIANTIC WOMAN.   (F. G. SPECK, PHOTO.)

the Niantic under Ninigret, and the whole body thenceforth took the name of Narraganset.   (J. M.)

Naantucke.—Patrick (1637) in Mass. Hist. Soc. Coll., 4th s., VII, 324, 1865. **Nahantick.**—Charter of 1663 in R. I. Col. Rec., II, 18, 1857. **Nahanticut.**—Underhill (1638) in Mass. Hist. Soc. Coll., 3d s., VI, 1, 1837. **Naiantukq-ut.**—Trumbull, Ind. Names Conn., 36, 1881 (Narraganset and Mohegan form). **Nanteqets.**—Coddington (1640) in Mass. Hist. Soc. Coll., 4th s., VI, 318, 1863. **Nantequits.**—Ibid. **Nayantacott.**—Doc. of 1663 in R. I. Col. Rec., I, 513, 1856. **Nayantakick.**—Williams (1637) in Mass. Hist. Soc. Coll., 4th s., VI, 200, 1863. **Nayantakoogs.**—Ibid., 203. **Nayantaquist.**—Williams (1648), ibid., 3d s., IX, 275, 1846. **Nayantaquit.**—Williams (*ca.* 1636), ibid., I, 160, 1825. **Nayanticks.**—Williams (1638), ibid., 4th s., VI, 248, 1863. **Nayantiks.**—Williams (1670), ibid., 1st s., I, 278, 1806. **Nayantuk.**—Pynchon (1645), ibid., 4th s., VI, 374, 1863. **Nayantuqiqt.**—Williams (1648), ibid., 3d s., IX, 275, 1846. **Nayantuquit.**—Williams (1637), ibid., 4th s., VI, 217, 1863. **Nayhantick.**—Charter of 1663 in R. I. Col. Rec., IV, 371, 1859. **Nayhautick.**—Ibid., 304 (misprint). **Neantick.**—Protest of 1662, ibid., I, 454, 1856. **Neanticot.**—Parsons, R. I. Local Names, 19, 1861. **Neanticutt.**—Hopkins (1646) in Mass. Hist. Soc. Coll., 4th s., VI, 334, 1863. **Neantucke.**—Patrick (1637), ibid., VII, 325, 1865. **Nehanticks.**—Holmes, ibid., 1st s., IX, 79, 1804. **Neyantick.**—Eaton (1647), ibid., 4th s., VI, 347, 1863. **Niantaquit.**—Williams (1636) quoted by Drake, Bk. Inds., bk. 2, 102, 1848. **Niantecutt.**—Doc. of 1659 in R. I. Col. Rec., I, 424, 1856. **Niantic.**—Doc. of 1647 quoted by Drake, Bk. Inds., bk. 2, 109, 1848. **Nianticut.**—Doc. of 1660 in R. I. Col. Rec., I, 450, 1856. **Niantique.**—Eaton (1652) in Mass. Hist. Soc. Coll., 4th s., VII, 468, 1865. **Niantuck.**—Writer after 1686, ibid., 3d s., I, 210, 1825. **Niantucuts.**—Higginson (1637), ibid., 4th s., VII, 396, 1865. **Nihantick.**—Tinker (1659), ibid., 233. **Ninantics.**—Schoolcraft, Ind. Tribes, VI, 112, 1857. **Nocanticks.**—Ibid., 150. **Nyantecets.**—Vincent (1638) in Mass. Hist. Soc. Coll., 3d s., VI, 35, 1837. **Nyantecutt.**—Doc. of 1659 in R. I. Col. Rec.,

I, 418, 1856. **Nyanticke.**—Vincent (1638) in Mass. Hist. Soc. Coll., 3d s., VI, 37, 1837. **Nyhantick.**—Tinker (1660), ibid., 4th s., VII, 241, 1865.

Niantic. An Algonquian tribe formerly occupying the coast of Connecticut from Niantic bay to Connecticut r. De Forest concluded that they once formed one tribe with the Rhode Island Niantic, which was cut in two by the Pequot invasion. Their principal village, also called Niantic, was near the present town of that name. They were subject to the Pequot, and had no political connection with the eastern Niantic. They were nearly destroyed in the Pequot war of 1637, and at its close the survivors were placed under the rule of the Mohegan. They numbered about 100 in 1638, and about 85 in 1761. Many joined the Brotherton Indians in New York about 1788, and none now exist under their own name. Kendall (Trav., 1809) states that they had a small village near Danbury in 1809, but these were probably a remnant of the western Connecticut tribes, not Niantic. According to Speck (inf'n, 1907) several mixed Niantic-Mohegan live at Mohegan, Conn., the descendants of a pure Niantic woman from the mouth of Niantic r. Their voices are commonly said to have been high-pitched in comparison with those of their neighbors. (J. M.)

Naihantick.—Early form cited by Trumbull, Ind. Names Conn., 36, 1881. **Na-ticks.**—Macauley, N. Y., II, 164, 1829 (incorrectly so called). **Nayantiaquet.**—Williams (1648) in Mass. Hist. Soc. Coll., 3d s., IX, 272, 1846. **Nianticks.**—Winthrop (ca. 1642) quoted by Drake, Bk. Inds., bk. 2, 67, 1848. **Niantigs.**—Cobbet (1645), ibid., 83. **Pequot Nayantaquit.**—Williams (1637) quoted by Trumbull, Ind. Names Conn., 36, 1881. **Pequt Nayantaquit.**—Williams (1637) in Mass. Hist. Soc. Coll., 4th s., VI, 220, 1863.

Niantilik ('with the gulls'). An Okomiut Eskimo village of the Kinguamiut subtribe, on Cumberland sd., Canada.

Naintilic.—Howgate, Cruise of Florence, 50, 1877. **Niantilic.**—Kumlien in Bull. Nat. Mus. no. 15, 15, 1879.

Nibakoa. A former village, mentioned in 1777–78, seemingly in the vicinity of Portage, Columbia co., Wis. It contained a mixed population of Chippewa and apparently of Sauk and Foxes.

Nabakoa.—Gautier (1777–78) in Wis. Hist. Soc. Coll., XI, 110, 1888. **Nibakoa.**—Ibid., 109.

Nibowisibiwininiwak ('Death river people'). A subdivision of the Chippewa living in Saskatchewan, N. of L. Winnipeg. Cf. *Onepowesepewenewak.*

Lake Winnipeg band.—Smithson. Misc. Coll., IV, art. 6, 35, 1878. **Nibowi-sibi-wininiwak.**—Gatschet, Ojibwa MS., B. A. E., 1882.

Nicassias. A name applied by early writers (Taylor in Cal. Farmer, Mar. 30, 1860) to a group of Moquelumnan Indians who formerly lived near the coast, in Marin co., Cal. (S. A. B.)

Nichewaug. A village, probably of the Nipmuc, about the present Nichewaug, near Petersham, Worcester co., Mass. The Indians remained until 1754, when they joined the French against the English.—Barber, Hist. Coll. Mass., 597, 1839; Kinnicutt, Ind. Names, 30, 1905.

Nichochi. A Chumashan village on Santa Cruz id., Cal., in 1542.

Nichochi.—Cabrillo (1542) in Smith, Colec. Doc. Fla., 186, 1857. **Nicochi.**—Ibid.

Nicholas. See *Orontony.*

Niciat. The local name for a body of Upper Lillooet around Seton lake, interior of British Columbia. Pop. 50 in 1906.

Necait.—Can. Ind. Aff. Rep., pt. I, 277, 1902. **Niciat.**—Ibid., pt. II, 272.

Nickajack. A former important Cherokee town on the s. bank of Tennessee r., in Marion co., Tenn. It was settled in 1782 by Cherokee who espoused the British cause in the Revolutionary war, and was known as one of the Chickamauga towns. It was destroyed in the fall of 1794. The meaning of the name is lost, and it is probably not of Cherokee origin, although it occurs also in the tribe as a man's name. In the corrupted form "Nigger Jack" it is applied to a creek of Cullasagee r. above Franklin, in Macon co., N. C. See Royce in 5th Rep. B. A. E., map, 1887; Mooney in 19th Rep. B. A. E., 527, 1900.

Nicojack.—Doc. of 1799 quoted by Royce in 5th Rep. B. A. E., 144, 1887. **Nĭkutseg.**—Mooney, op. cit. (abbr. form). **Nĭkutse'gĭ.**—Ibid. **Nikwătse'gĭ.**—Ibid. **Nŭkătse'gĭ.**—Ibid.

Nickomin. A former Chehalis town on North r., which flows into Shoalwater bay, Wash.

Necomanchee.—Swan, N. W. Coast, 211, 1857. **NExumE'ntc.**—Boas, inf'n, 1905, (correct native form).

Nicola Band. One of four subdivisions of the Upper Ntlakyapamuk in the interior of British Columbia.

Cawa'xamux.—Teit in Mem. Am. Mus. Nat. Hist., II, 170, 1900 (' people of the creek,' i. e., Nicola r.). **Nicola band.**—Ibid. **Tcawa'xamux.**—Ibid. **Tcŭā'qamuq.**—Hill-Tout in Rep. Ethnol. Surv. Can., 5, 1899.

Nicola Valley Indians. The official designation of a large number of local groups in British Columbia, principally Cowichan, Lillooet, and Ntlakyapamuk Indians, numbering 522 in 1878.—Can. Ind. Aff., 74, 1878.

Nicomen. A Cowichan tribe on Nicomen slough and at the mouth of Wilson cr., lower Fraser r., Brit. Col. Their villages are Skweahm and Lahaui, but the name has become attached to the latter town of the tribe, which in 1906 had 16 inhabitants. The aggregate population of Nicomen and Skweahm was 44 in 1906.

LEk''ā'mEl.—Boas in Rep. 64th Meeting Brit. A. A. S., 454, 1894. **Nacomen.**—Can. Ind. Aff., 78, 1878. **NEK''ā'mEn.**—Boas, op. cit. **Nicoamen.**—Can. Ind. Aff., 309, 1879. **Nicoamin.**—Ibid., 76, 1878. **Nicomen.**—Ibid., pt. I, 276, 1894.

Nicotowance. When the career of Opechancanough (q. v.) as chief of the Pamunkey tribe, as well as of the Powhatan confederacy, terminated on his death in 1644, he was succeeded as ruler of the Pamunkey Indians by Nicotowance. This chief, desirous of obtaining rest for his people, entered into a treaty of peace with the colonial authorities and was assigned, by an act of the Virginia assembly, Oct. 10, 1649, certain lands for himself and his people. His control, however, appears to have been of short duration, as he soon disappears from history. (c. T.)

Nigaluk. A Nunatogmiut Eskimo village at the mouth of Colville r., Alaska.
Nig-a-lek.—Dall in Cont. N. A. Ethnol., I, map, 1877. Nigaluk.—Baker, Geog. Dict. Alaska, 1902.

Nigco. The tribal name assigned to an Indian baptized in 1730 at San Antonio de Valero mission, Texas. There were both Tonkawan and Coahuiltecan tribes there at the time, but the Nigco can not be identified with any of those known. It may be Sinicu, some of which tribe had been baptized in 1728, and who were probably Coahuiltecan (Valero Bautismos, partida 325, MS. in the custody of the bishop of San Antonio). (H. E. B.)

Nighetanka ('big belly'). A band of the Miniconjou Sioux.
Nige-tanka.—Dorsey in 15th Rep. B. A. E., 220, 1897. Nixe-tañka.—Ibid.

Nightasis. A Haida town of this name is given in John Work's list, 1836–41, with 15 houses and 280 inhabitants. It seems impossible to identify the name with that of any known town. On other grounds Kung, in Naden harbor, would appear to be the town intended.
Nigh tan.—Work (1836–41) in Schoolcraft, Ind. Tribes, V, 489, 1855. Nigh-tasis.—Dawson, Queen Charlotte Ids., 173B, 1880.

Night Cloud. Mentioned by Culbertson (Smithson. Rep. 1850, 142, 1851) as a band of Oglala Sioux. They probably took their name from the chief.

Nigiklik. A former Eskimo village in Alaska at the head of the Yukon delta.
Nigiklik-mïout.—Zagoskin in Nouv. Ann. Voy., 5th s., XXI, map, 1850. Nygykligmjut.—Holmberg, Ethnog. Skizz., map, 1855.

Nigottine ('moss people'). A part of the Kawchogottine division of the Kawchodinne living along the outlet of Great Bear lake, Mackenzie Ter., Canada.
Nì-gottinè.—Petitot in Bul. Soc. de Géog. Paris, chart, 1875. Nnéa-gottine.—Petitot, MS. vocab., B. A. E., 1865. Nni-Gottinè.—Petitot, Autour du lac des Esclaves, 363, 1891. Nni-ottiné.—Petitot, Dict. Dènè-Dindjié, XX, 1876.

Nijuchsagentisquoa (probably 'it is very tall reeds.'—Hewitt). A Cayuga chief, one of the signers, at Albany, N. Y., July 19, 1701, of the "deed from the Five Nations to the King [of England] of their beaver hunting ground."—N. Y. Doc. Col. Hist., IV, 910, 1854.

Nikaomin (*Neqa'umîn*, or *Nqau'mîn*, so named because the water comes from a lake called *Nqauma'tko*, 'wolf lake or water'; from *sqaum*, 'wolf'). A Ntlakyapamuk town on the s. side of Thompson r., 10 m. above Lytton, Brit. Col. It is called Thompson by the whites. Pop. 49 in 1906.
Neqa'umîn.—Teit in Mem. Am. Mus. Nat. Hist., II, 171, 1900. Ni-ca-o-min.—Can. Ind. Aff. 1885, 196,

1886. Nicomen.—Ibid., 309, 1879. Nicomin.—Ibid., map, 1891. Nikaomin.—Ibid., pt. II, 166, 1901. N'kau'men.—Hill-Tout in Rep. Ethnol. Surv. Can., 4, 1899. Nqau'mîn.—Teit, op. cit. Thompson.—Ibid. (modern name).

Nikapashna ('bald head'). The third gens on the Chizhu side of the Ponca tribal circle. Its subgentes are Dtesindeitazhi, Dtedhezedhatazhi, and Dtakhtikianpandhatazhi.
Na-ko-poz'-na.—Morgan, Anc.Soc., 155, 1877 (trans. 'elk'). Nika-ḍa-ona.—Dorsey in 15th Rep.B. A. E., 228, 1897.

Nikhdhitanwan. An ancient Osage village at the junction of the Sac and Osage rs. in Missouri.
Ni-qci' tanwan.—Dorsey, Osage MS. vocab., B. A. E., 1883. Niqdhi tanwan.—Ibid.

Nikhkak. A Knaiakhotana village of about a dozen houses on L. Clark, Alaska. The people, most of whom are of Russian admixture, obtain clothing and other articles of civilized comfort from the trading posts on Cook inlet. Their houses and fish caches are built of hewn logs, floored with planks, and they make windows of parchment. Pop. 42 in 1891; about 25 in 1904.
Keeghik.—Osgood in Nat. Geog. Mag., XV, 329, 1904 (from their name for the lake). Keejik.—Osgood (1902) quoted by Baker, Geog. Dict. Alaska, 364, 1906. Kijik.—Baker, ibid. Nikhak.—Osgood in Nat. Geog. Mag., op. cit. Nikhkak.—Coast Survey map (1898) cited by Baker, op. cit.

Nikiata. A Quapaw gens.—Dorsey in 15th Rep. B. A. E., 230, 1897.

Nikie name. A term employed by Dorsey (3d Rep. B. A. E., 227, 1884) to designate a name "referring to a mythical ancestor, to some part of his body, to some of his acts, or to some ancient rite which may have been established by him"; derived from *nikiē*, the word for such a name in the Omaha dialect of the Siouan stock. According to Francis La Flesche (inf'n, 1907), *nik(a-shi-ga)ie* is derived from *nikashiga* 'people,' and *ie* 'word or utterance,' and a *nikie* name is one given by the people or by the word of the people—a name conferred by the consent of the people. As the chief was the mouthpiece of the people, a *nikie* name is sometimes defined as spoken by a chief, but the primary meaning is that the name is conferred by the word of the people. (A. F. C.)

Nikikouek (from the Chippewa or a cognate dialectic term *nikig* 'otter', with anim. pl. suffix *-ouek*='otter people'. Perrot says the form with initial *m*, *Mikikouet*, is from their own language; such is the case in the cognate Menominee *mikig*). A little known Algonquian tribe that formerly dwelt E. of the Missisauga, among the rock caverns on the N. shore of L. Huron. They are described as lacking in courage, and having much to do with the tribes northward. Twice a year, like the Missisauga, they deserted their village to hunt and fish along the lake for sturgeon and other fish, and there obtained bark for constructing canoes and lodges.

On the approach of winter they frequented the lake shores to kill beaver and elk, whence they returned in the spring to plant and tend their corn. In 1653, jointly with the Saulteurs and the Missisauga, they so completely defeated an Iroquois war-party of 120 men that but few escaped. (J. N. B. H.)

Gens de la Loutre.—Perrot (ca. 1724), Mémoire, 83, 1864. **Mikikoues.**—Ibid., 219. **Mikikoüet.**—Ibid., 83. **Nation de la Loutre.**—Bacqueville de la Potherie, Hist. Amér. Sépt., II, 48, 1753. **Nation of the Otter.**—Heriot, Trav., 209, 1807. **Nigik.**—Kelton, Ft Mackinac, 20, 1884. **Nikicouek.**—Jes. Rel., III, index, 1858. **Nikikouek.**—Jes. Rel. 1658, 22, 1858. **Nikikoues.**—Perrot, Mémoire, index, 1864.

Nikishka. A Knaiakhotana village, of 57 inhabitants in 1880, near the head of Cook inlet, Alaska.—Petroff in 10th Census, Alaska, 29, 1884.

Nikolaief (presumably named by the Russians after Tsar Nikolas). An Aleut village N. of Belkofski, on Alaska penin., Alaska; pop. 43 in 1880.

Nikolaievsky.—Petroff in 10th Census, Alaska, 23, 1884.

Nikolski. An Aleut settlement and trading post for otter skins on Umnak id., Alaska. Pop. 83 in 1834, 127 in 1880, 94 in 1890.

Nikolskoje.—Holmberg, Ethnog. Skizz., map, 1855. **Nikolsky.**—Elliott, Our Arct. Prov., 184, 1886. **Oomnak.**—Ibid., 179. **Recheshnaia.**—Veniaminoff quoted by Petroff in 10th Census, Alaska, 35, 1884. **Retchechnoi.**—Lutke quoted by Baker, Geog. Dict. Alaska, 462, 1906. **Riechesnœ.**—Ibid., 1902. **Rjätscheschnoje.**—Holmberg, op. cit. **Ryochesnoi.**—Veniaminoff (1833) quoted by Elliott, Cond. Aff. Alaska, 225, 1875. **Umnak.**—Eleventh Census, Alaska, 163, 1893.

Nikozliautin ('people of the river covered with the enemy's arrows'). A Takulli clan or division on the s. half of Stuart lake and on Pintce r., Brit. Col. They inhabit two villages, Nakraztli and Pintce. The name comes from a legend of a tribe of dwarfs who once attacked their village in such numbers that the surface of Stuart r. was covered with floating arrows (Morice in Trans. Can. Inst., 188, 1891). The Nikozliautin are devout Catholics, sober, law-abiding, and hospitable. Their main resources are hunting, trapping, and fishing. Pop. 234 in 1906.

Na-kas-le-tīn.—Dawson in Rep. Geol. Surv. Can., 30B, 1881. **Nakazèteo-ten.**—Smet, Miss. de l'Oregon, 63, 1844. **Na-ka-ztli-ṭenne.**—Morice, letter, 1890. **Nakoozétenne.**—Can. Ind. Aff., 215, 1902. **Na-'kraztli-'tenne.**—Morice, Notes on W. Dénés, 26, 1893. **Nancaushy Tine.**—Jour. Anthrop. Inst., VII, 206, 1878. **Nekaslay.**—McLean, Hudson's Bay, I, 262, 1849. **Nekaslayans.**—Ibid., 263. **Nekasly.**—Ibid., 269. **Nikozliantin.**—Macdonald, British Columbia, 126, 1862. **Nikozliantins.**—Domenech, Deserts of N. Am., II, 62, 1860. **Nikozliáutin.**—Hale, Ethnog. and Philol., 202, 1846. **Stewart's Lake Indians.**—Can. Ind. Aff., 79, 1878.

Niktak. A Kaviagmiut Eskimo village on C. Prince of Wales, Alaska.

Nikhtagmut.—Zagoskin, Descr. Russ. Poss. Am., I, 73, 1847 (the people).

Nilakshi ('dawn'). A former Klamath settlement at or below Nilaks mtn., E. shore of Upper Klamath lake, Oreg. The name is now used to designate Modoc

point, but it properly refers to Nilaks mtn. ridge only.—Gatschet in Cont. N. A. Ethnol., II, pt. I, xxx, 1890.

Nílakskní máklaks.—Gatschet, op. cit., pt. II, 243 (name of people).

Nilalhuyu (*Ni-lal-hu'-yu*). A former Chumashan village on Santa Cruz id., Cal., the inhabitants of which are said to have been celebrated for the practice of sorcery.—Henshaw, Buenaventura MS. vocab., B. A. E., 1884.

Nilestunne (*Ni-lĕsṭúnnĕ'*, 'people at the small dam in the river'). A former village of the Mishikhwutmetunne on Coquille r., Oreg.—Dorsey in Jour. Am. Folk-lore, III, 232, 1890.

Niletunne. A former village of the Tututni on the Oregon coast, being the first village s. of the Kusan village of Nasumi, s. of the mouth of Coquille r.

Jake's people.—Dorsey in Jour. Am. Folk-lore, III, 233, 1890 (referring to some man on Siletz res.). **Ni-le' ṭúnnĕ'.**—Ibid.

Nilsumack. A Salish band, probably Cowichan, under the Fraser superintendency, Brit. Col.—Can. Ind. Aff., 78, 1878.

Niltala. A Wikeno village on Rivers inlet, Brit. Col.—Boas in Petermanns Mitt., pt. 5, 130, 1887.

Nim (*neum* or *nüm*, 'people'). A name adopted by Merriam (Science, XIX, 916, 1904) to designate a Mono-Paviotso division on the N. fork of San Joaquin r. and the adjacent region in California. Regarding it, Kroeber (Univ. Cal. Pub., Am. Archæol. and Ethnol., IV, 119, 1907) says: "Nim is not a tribal name but the word for person, *nüm*, which occurs also in other Mono dialects as far s. and E. as Kings r. and Owens r., so that it cannot be regarded as distinctive of these people N. of the San Joaquin." In one or another form it is the common Shoshonean designation for 'men,' 'people.'

Pă-zo-ōds.—Merriam, op. cit. (Holkomah name).

Nimatlala (*Ni-mat-la'-la*). A former Chumashan village on Santa Cruz id., E. of Prisoners harbor.—Henshaw, Buenaventura MS. vocab., B. A. E., 1884.

Nimham, Daniel. A Wappinger chief, noted not only for his active participation in the wars of 1746 and 1754, but especially for his efforts to recover for his tribe the lands lying along the E. side of Hudson r. that had been taken from it while aiding the English. The earliest recorded notice of him is Oct. 13, 1730, the date of an affidavit in which it is stated that the deponent was "a River Indian of the tribe of the Wappinoes" (Ruttenber, Tribes Hudson R., 51, 1872). Nimham was made chief sachem in 1740; his residence after 1746 was at Westenhuck. In 1755, with most of his fighting men, he entered the English service under Sir William Johnson, and about 1762, in company with some Mohegan chiefs of Connecticut, went to England on a mission regarding their land claims. They received a favorable hearing, and on their return to America their claims were brought into court, but were lost to sight during the Revolution. Nimham was killed at the battle of Kingsbridge, N. Y., Aug. 31, 1778, while fighting bravely in the cause of the Americans. Near the entrance to Pelham's Neck, Westchester co., N. Y., were, according to Ruttenber (op. cit., 81), two large mounds, pointed out as the sepulchers of Ann-Hoock and Nimham. The name of Daniel Nimham, as well as those of Aaron, John, and Isaac Nimham, appear in the rolls of New York men enlisted in the service of the Revolution. As Indians are included in the list, Daniel Nimham is doubtless the subject of this sketch. (c. t.)

Nimitapal. A former Chumashan village on Santa Cruz id. (the San Lucas of Cabrillo), Cal., in 1542. Possibly the same as Nimatlala.
Nimetapal.—Taylor in Cal. Farmer, Apr. 17, 1863. Nimitapal.—Cabrillo (1542) in Smith, Colec. Doc. Fla., 181, 1857.

Nimkish (*[8]Nᴇ'mgēs*). A Kwakiutl tribe on and about the river of the same name in N. E. Vancouver id. According to Rev. A. J. Hall they derived their name from that of a mythical halibut, called Num-hyā-lī-gī-yŭ, which caused a tide-rip off the point of the bay. The gentes, according to Boas, are Gyigyilkam, Nenelkyenok, Sisintlae, Tlatlelamin, and Tsetsetloala-kemae. Pop. 151 in 1901, 134 in 1906.
[8]Nᴇ'mgēs.—Boas in Mem. Am. Mus. Nat. Hist., v, pt. I, 133, 1902. Nᴇ'mk·io.—Boas in 6th Rep. N.W. Tribes Can., 54, 1890. Nᴇ·mqic.—Boas in Rep. Nat. Mus. 1895, 331, 1897. Némqisch.—Boas in Petermanns Mitt., pt. 5, 130, 1887. Nim-keesh.—Can. Ind. Aff. 1884, 190, 1885. Nimkis.—Taylor in Cal. Farmer, July 19, 1862. Nim-kish.—Kane, Wand. in N. A., app., 1859. Nimpkish.—Mayne, Brit. Col., 179, 1862. Num-kēs.—Hall quoted by Dawson in Trans. Roy. Soc. Can., sec. II, 72, 1887.

Nimoyoyo. A Chumashan village on San Miguel id. (the Isla de Juan Rodriguez of Cabrillo), Cal., in 1542.
Nimilolo.—Taylor in Cal. Farmer, Apr. 17, 1863. Nimollollo.—Cabrillo (1542) in Smith, Colec. Doc. Fla., 186, 1857.

Nimsewi ('big river'). A division of Maidu living on upper Butte cr., near the edge of the timber in Butte co., Cal.
Nemshan.—Bancroft Nat. Races, I, 450, 1882. Nemshaw.—Hale, Ethnog. and Philol., 631, 1846. Nemshoos.—Bancroft, op. cit. Nemshous.—Taylor in Cal. Farmer, June 8, 1860. Nim Sewi.—Curtin, MS. vocab., B. A. E., 1885. Nim'-shu.—Powers in Cont. N. A. Ethnol., III, 283, 1877 (from *nem-sē-u*, 'big river'). Nim-sirs.—Johnston (1850) in Sen. Ex. Doc. 4, 32d Cong., spec. sess., 45, 1853. Nimskews.—Beale in Sen. Ex. Doc. 57, 32d Cong., 2d sess., 15, 1853. Nim-sus.—Johnston in Ind. Aff. Rep., 124, 1850.

Ninchopan ('bear'). A Tonkawa clan, now nearly extinct.
Nintchopan.—Gatschet, Tonkawe MS. vocab., B. A. E., 1884. Nintropan.—Ibid.

Ningweegon. See *Negwagon*.

Ninibatan (*Niniba-t'aⁿ*, 'keepers of the pipe'). A subgens of the Mandhinka-gaghe gens of the Omaha.—Dorsey in 15th Rep. B. A. E., 228, 1897.

Ninibatan A subgens of the Tapa gens of the Omaha.

Ninibatan. A subgens of the Inshta-sanda gens of the Omaha, consolidated prior to 1880 with another subgens known as the Real Inshtasanda.

Ninigret. A sachem of the Niantic in the region about Westerly, R. I., and a cousin of Miantonomo. Besides the name Ninigret, Nenekunat, etc., he bore earlier that of Janemo or Ayanemo, by which he first became known to the English (Drake, Inds. of N. Am., 131, 1880). He visited Boston in 1637. After the death of Miantonomo he began war against the Mohegan, but the English interfered, and a treaty was signed at Boston in 1647. Contemporary chroniclers have left a detailed account of the appearance of Ninigret before the commissioners and his conduct on that occasion, which was much to his credit. Later (1652) Ninigret visited the Dutch at Manhattan, arousing the suspicions of the English, which were groundless. The next year he made war upon the Long Island Indians. He abstained from personal activity during King Philip's war, but had trouble in keeping terms with the English. He secured to himself and heirs the tribal land near Charlestown; and after the capture of Nanuntenoo (Canonchet), the last chief of the Narraganset, that tribe was consolidated with the Niantic under Ninigret. The latter and Miantonomo were lifelong rivals of Uncas. Notwithstanding his pacific tendencies, Ninigret was drawn into conflict with the Montauk of E. Long Island in 1659. Aptly called by Mather "an old crafty sachem," he seems to have preserved his pride, of which he possessed an inordinate amount, and his property as well, without being obliged to fight for either. Ninigret died full of years some time before the close of the century. He consistently opposed Christianity, and told Mayhew, the missionary, to "go and make the English good first." (a. f. c.)

Ninilchik. A Knaiakhotana village of 18 houses on the E. coast of Cook inlet, s. of the mouth of Kasilof r., Alaska; inhabited in 1890 by 45 natives and 36 Russian creole descendants of the convict colony of 1793.
Munina.—Wosnesenski's map (*ca.* 1840) cited by Baker, Geog. Dict. Alaska, 463, 1906. Ninilchik.—Petroff in Tenth Census, Alaska, 27, 1884.

Ninivois. A Fox chief in command of the warriors of his tribe at the siege of Detroit by Pontiac, in 1763. Ninivois and Take, leader of the Hurons, appear to have been the most active aids of Pontiac at the commencement and during the early part of the siege (Mich. Pion. Coll., VIII, 266–339, 1886), and next to Pontiac were the leaders in the councils of the besiegers and the first to begin the investment of the fort. Fulton (Red Men of Iowa, 477, 1882) writes his name Ninivay and says he was a Potawatomi. (C. T.)

Ninnipaskulgee ('highroad people', from Creek *nini-paski* 'swept road', *algi* 'people'). A former band or tribe of Upper Creeks, probably near Tuckabatchi, Elmore co., Ala.

Ninny-pask-ulgees.—Woodward, Remin., 37, 1859. Road Indians.—Ibid.

Ninstints. A Haida town which formerly stood on Anthony id., at the s. end of Queen Charlotte ids., Brit. Col. The native name was SgA′nguai ('Redcod island'), Ninstints being the white man's corruption of the town-chief's name, Nungstins (*Nañ stíns*, 'he who is two'). All the people from this end of Moresby id. gathered there in comparatively recent times. The remnant have since abandoned the place and settled at Skidegate. It is impossible to identify absolutely the name of this town with that of any given in John Work's list of 1836–41, but it is probably referred to as "Quee-ah," a town to which he assigned 20 houses and a population of 308. At the present day there are probably not a dozen Ninstints people left. The family to which the chief of this town belonged was the Sakikegawai. See Swanton, Cont. Haida, 105, 277, 1905. (J. R. S.)

NEnstǐ′ns.—Boas, 12th Rep. N. W. Tribes Can., 25, 1898. **Ninstance.**—Dawson, Queen Charlotte Ids., 169, 1880. **Ninstence.**—Poole, Queen Charlotte Ids., 195, 1872. **Ninstints.**—Dawson, op. cit. Sg′a′nguai.—Boas, op. cit.

Ninumu. A Chumashan village on one of the Santa Barbara ids., Cal., probably Santa Rosa, in 1542.

Ninimu.—Taylor in Cal. Farmer, Apr. 17, 1863. Ninumu.—Cabrillo (1542) in Smith, Colec. Doc. Fla., 186, 1857.

Ninvok. A Chnagmiut Eskimo village near the delta of Yukon r., Alaska.

Ninvaug.—Zagoskin in Nouv. Ann. Voy., 5th s., XXI, map, 1850.

Ninyuelgual. A former Chumashan village near Purísima mission, Santa Barbara co., Cal.—Taylor in Cal. Farmer, Oct. 18, 1861.

Nio. A small tribe, probably Piman, long extinct, which formerly resided in N. Sinaloa, Mexico, their village, the seat of the mission of San Ignacio de Nio, occupying the site of the present town of the same name. Zapata, in 1678 (Doc. Hist. Mex., 4th s., III, 404, 1854), said that a league and a half N. E. of San Pedro de Guazave was the pueblo of San Ignacio de Nio, in which the language spoken, called Nio, was particular unto itself, though the Mexican was also in common use. Alegre (Hist. Comp. Jesus, I, 294, 1841) states that Father Mendez, who had entered Sinaloa as a missionary, recommended "the pueblos and languages of the Ocoroiri [Ocoroni], Nio, and some others which he had held, to the charge of Father Tapia."

Niowe. Mentioned by Bartram (Travels, 371, 1792) as a Cherokee settlement on the headwaters of Tennessee r. about the year 1775. Possibly intended for Nâyû′hǐ, which signifies 'sand place.' Cf. *Noewe*. (J. M.)

Nipaguay. A Diegueño village near San Diego, s. Cal., about 6 m. from the old presidio to which, in 1774, the mission was removed. See *San Diego*.

Nypagudy.—Taylor in Cal. Farmer, Feb. 22, 1860.

Nipigiguit. A former Micmac village on the site of Bathurst, at the mouth of Nipisiguit r., New Brunswick. The French mission of Sainte Magdalen was there in 1645.

Nepegigoüit.—Jes. Rel. 1645, 35, 1858. **Nipigiguit.**—Vetromile, Abnakis, 59, 1866. **Nipisiguit.**—Membré quoted by Shea, Miss. Val., 86, 1852.

Nipinchen. Given by Bolton (Hist. Westchester Co., 1881) as a former Indian fort on the N. side of Spuyten Duyvil (or Papirinemen) cr., at its junction with Hudson r. from the E., in Westchester co., N. Y. Ruttenber (Ind. Geog. Names, 22, 1906) says the name belongs on the w. side of the Hudson, at Konstable's Hook, and doubts that there was any real settlement there. Cf. *Nipinichsen*.

Nipinichsen. A former Manhattan village on the E. bank of Hudson r., just above Spuyten Duyvil, N. Y.—Ruttenber, Tribes Hudson R., 77, 1872.

Nipissing ('at the little water or lake', referring to L. Nipissing; *Nipisiriniwok*, 'little-water people'). A tribe of the Algonkin. When they first became known to the French, in 1613, they were residing in the vicinity of L. Nipissing, Ontario, which has been their home during most of the time to the present. Having been attacked, about 1650, by the Iroquois, and many of them slain, they fled for safety to L. Nipigon (Mackenzie, Voy., xli, note, 1802), where Allouez visited them in 1667, but they were again on L. Nipissing in 1671. A part of the tribe afterward went to Three Rivers, and some resided with the Catholic Iroquois at Oka, where they still have a village. Some of these assisted the French in 1756. It is their dialect which is represented in Cuoq's Lexique de la Langue Algonquine. They were a comparatively unwarlike people, firm friends of the French, readily accepting the Christian teachings of the missionaries. Although having a fixed home, they were semi-nomadic, going s. in autumn to the vicinity of the Hurons to fish and prepare food for the winter, which they passed among them. They cultivated the soil to a slight extent only, traded with the Cree in the N., and were much given to jugglery and shamanistic practices, on which account the Hurons and the whites called them Sorcerers. Their chiefs were elective, and their totems, according to Chauvignerie (N. Y.

Doc. Col. Hist., x, 1053, 1855), were the heron, beaver, birchbark, squirrel, and blood. No reliable statistics in regard to their numbers have been recorded. The Indians now on a reservation on L. Nipissing are officially classed as Chippewa; they numbered 162 in 1884, and 223 in 1906. A Nipissing division was called Miskouaha. (J. M.)

Askic8aneronons.—Jes. Rel. 1639, 88, 1858 (='sorcerers'—Hewitt). **Askik8anehronons.**—Jes. Rel. 1641, 81, 1858. **Askikouaneronons.**—Ibid. **Aweatsiwaenrrhonon.**—Jes. Rel., Thwaites ed., x, 83, 1897. **Bisserains.**—Champlain (ca. 1624), Œuvres, v, 2d pt., 79, 1870. **Bisseriniens.**—Sagard (1636), Can., I, 190, 1866. **Bissiriniens.**—Jes. Rel.1635,18,1858. **Byssiriniens.**—Charlevoix (1744), New France,II, 95, 1866. **Ebicerinys.**—Sagard (1636), Can., I, 172, 1866. **Epesengles.**—McKenney and Hall, Ind. Tribes, III, 80, 1854. **Epicerinyens.**—Sagard (1636), Can., III, 727, 1866. **Epicerinys.**—Ibid., IV, Huron Dict., 1866. **Epiciriniens.**—Sagard (1636) quoted by Parkman, Pioneers, 351, 1883. **Episingles.**—Dumont, Mem. of La., VI, 135, 1753. **Epissingue.**—Writer of 1756 in N. Y. Doc. Col. Hist., x, 485, 1858. **Ilgonquines.**—La Salle (1682) in French, Hist. Coll. La., I, 46, 1846. **Juskwaugume.**—Jones, Ojebway Inds., 178, 1861. **Kekerannon-rounons.**—Lamberville (1686) in N. Y. Doc. Col. Hist., III, 489, 1853. **Longs Cheveux.**—Jes. Rel. 1671, 35, 1858. **Nation des Sorciers.**—Jes. Rel. 1632, 14, 1858. **Nebicerini.**—Champlain (1613), Œuvres, III, 295, 1870. **Neperinks.**—Clinton (1745) in N. Y. Doc. Col. Hist., VI, 276, 1855. **Nepesangs.**—Pike, Exped., pt. 1, app., 62, 1810. **Nepesinks.**—Clinton (1745) in N. Y. Doc. Col. Hist., VI, 281, 1855. **Nepessins.**—Buchanan, N. Am. Inds., I, 139, 1824. **Nepicerinis.**—Lahontan, New Voy., I, 143, 1703. **Nepicinquis.**—Chauvignerie (1736) quoted by Schoolcraft, Ind. Tribes, III, 554, 1853. **Nepicirenians.**—Heriot, Trav., 195, 1807. **Nepiciriniens.**—Bacqueville de la Potherie, II, 48, 1753. **Nepiscenicens.**—Boudinot, Star in the West, 127, 1816. **Nepiseriniens.**—La Barre (1682) in N. Y. Doc. Col. Hist., IX, 196, 1855. **Nepisin.**—Dobbs, Hudson Bay, map, 1744. **Nepisinguis.**—Mackenzie, Voy., xlii,1801. **Nepisirini.**—Lahontan, New Voy., I, 231, 1703. **Nepisseniniens.**—Doc. of 1695 in N. Y. Doc. Col. Hist., IX, 599, 1855. **Nepissens.**—Boudinot, Star in the West, 127, 1816. **Nepisseriens.**—Du Chesneau (1681) in N. Y. Doc. Col. Hist., IX, 160, 1855. **Nepisseriniens.**—Doc. of 1697, ibid., 669. **Nepissings.**—Doc. of 1695, ibid., 599. **Népissingues.**—Ibid., 602. **Népissiniens.**—Ibid., 596. **Nepissiriens.**—Du Chesneau (1681), ibid., 160. **Nepissiriniens.**—Doc. of 1693, ibid., 566. **Nibissiriniens.**—Parkman, Pioneers, 351, 1883. **Nipeceriniens.**—Colden (1727), Five Nations, 28, 1747. **Nipercineans.**—Schoolcraft, Ind. Tribes, I, 307, 1851. **Nipicirinien.**—Jes. Rel. 1639, 14, 1858. **Nipisierinij.**—Champlain (1615), Œuvres, IV, 21, 1870. **Nipisings.**—Cox, Columbia R., II, 142, 1831. **Nipisingues.**—Henry, Trav., 30, 1809. **Nipisinks.**—German Flats conf. (1770) in N. Y. Doc. Col. Hist.,VIII, 229, 1857. **Nipisiriniens.**—Jes. Rel.1636,69,1858. **Nipissings.**—Doc. of 1741 in N. Y. Doc. Col. Hist., IX, 1080,1855. **Nipissingues.**—Du Chesneau (1679), ibid., 133. **Nipissins.**—Smith, Bouquet's Exped., 69, 1766. **Nipissiriniens.**—Jes. Rel. 1641, 81, 1858. **Nipissirinioek.**—Trumbull, Algonk. Names for Man, 18, 1871 (='small lake men'). **Nipístingues.**—Lettres Edif., I, 696, 1838. **Nippsingues.**—Frontenac (1682) in N. Y. Doc. Col. Hist., IX, 182, 1855. **Nipsang.**—Lear (1792) in Am. St. Pap., Ind. Aff., I, 244, 1832. **Nypissings.**—Lamberville (1686) in N. Y. Doc. Col. Hist., III, 489, 1853. **Nypsins.**—Long, Exped. St Peters R., II, 151, 1824. **Odishk-wa-gami.**—Baraga, Eng.-Otch. Dict., II, 1878 (Chippewa name; Cuoq renders it 'at the last water,' but Chamberlain prefers '[people] on the other side of the lake'). **Odishkwa-Gamig.**—Trumbull, Algonk. Names for Man, 18, 1872 ('people of the last lake'; from *ishkwa* 'at the end of', *gami* 'lake' or 'water': Chippewa name). **O-dish-quag-um-eeg.**—Schoolcraft, Ind. Tribes, II, 139, 1852. **O-dish-quag-um-ees.**—Ramsey in Ind. Aff. Rep., 91, 1850. **Odishquahgumme.**—Wilson, Ojebway Lang., 157, 1874 (= 'Algonquin Indians'). **Otick-waga-mi.**—Cuoq, Lex. Iroq., 42, 1882. **Outiskoüagami.**—

Jes. Rel. 1671, 35, 1858. **Outisquagamis.**—Andre (1671) quoted by Shea, Cath. Miss., 365, 1855. **Pisierinii.**—Champlain (1616), Œuvres, IV, 61, 1870. **Pisirinins.**—Ibid., 63, 1870. **Quiennontateronons.**—Sagard (1636), Can., IV, index, 1866. **Quieunontateronons.**—Ibid., III, 750, 1866. **Skaghnanes.**—Mess. of 1763 in N. Y. Doc. Col. Hist., VII, 544, 1856. **Skaghquanoghronos.**—Johnson (1763), ibid., 582. **Skecaneronons.**—Sagard (1636), Can., III, 727, 1866. **Skekaneronons.**—Ibid., I, 148, 1866. **Skekwanen-hronon.**—Cuoq, Lex. Iroq., 42, 1883 (Mohawk name). **Skequaneronon.**—Sagard (1632), Can., IV, Huron Dict., 1866. **Skighquan.**—Livingston (1701) in N. Y. Doc. Col. Hist., IV, 899, 1854. **Sorcerers.**—Maclean, Can. Savage Folk, 359, 1896 (English rendering of name by which they were known to early French missionaries). **Squekaneronons.**—Sagard (1636), Can., I, 172, 1866 (Huron name). **Tuskwawgomeeg.**—Tanner, Narr., 316,1830 (Ottawa name).

Nipky. Probably a Lower Creek town, as "Appalya, beloved man of Nipky," is mentioned among the Lower Creek chiefs in a document dated Frederica, Ga., in 1747.—McCall, Hist. Ga., I, 367, 1811.

Nipmuc (from *Nipamaug*, 'fresh-water fishing place'). The inland tribes of central Massachusetts living chiefly in the s. part of Worcester co., extending into Connecticut and Rhode Island. Their chief seats were on the headwaters of Blackstone and Quinebaug rs., and about the ponds of Brookfield. Hassanamesit seems to have been their principal village in 1674, but their villages had no apparent political connection, and the different parts of their territory were subject to their more powerful neighbors, the Massachuset, Wampanoag, Narraganset, and Mohegan, and even tributary to the Mohawk. The Nashua, dwelling farther N., are sometimes classed with the Nipmuc, but were rather a distinct body. The New England missionaries had 7 villages of Christian Indians among them in 1674; but on the outbreak of King Philip's war in the next year almost all of them joined the hostile tribes, and at its close fled to Canada or westward to the Mahican and other tribes on the Hudson.

The following villages and bands probably belonged to the Nipmuc: Acoomemeck, Chabanakongkomun, Chachaubunkkakowok, Hadley Indians, Hassanamesit, Magunkaquog, Manchaug, Manexit, Massomuck, Medfield, Menemesseg, Metewemesick, Missogkonnog, Musketaquid, Nashobah, Nichewaug, Okommakamesit, Pakachoog, Quabaug, Quahmsit, Quantisset, Quinebaug, Segunesit, Squawkeag, Tatumasket, Totapoag, Wacuntug, Wenimesset, and Woruntuck. (J. M.)

Neepemut.—Williams (1637) in Mass. Hist. Soc. Coll., 4th s., VI, 190, 1863. **Neepmucks.**—Ibid., 3d s., IX, 300, 1846. **Neepnet.**—Williams (ca. 1636), ibid., 4th s., VI, 188, 1863. **Neipnett.**—Winthrop (1632) quoted by Barber, Hist. Coll., 570, 1841. **Nepmets.**—Higginson (1637) in Mass. Hist. Soc. Coll., 4th s., VII, 396, 1865 (misprint?). **Nep mock.**—Stephens (1675), ibid., 3d s., x, 117, 1849. **Nepnet.**—McKenney and Hall, Ind. Tribes, III, 82, 1854. **Nibenets.**—Maurault, Abenakis, 2, 1866. **Nipmoog.**—Writer of 1675 quoted by Drake, Ind. Chron., 19, 1836. **Nipmucks.**—Williams (1660) in R. I. Col. Rec., I, 40, 1856. **Nipmug.**—Letter of 1675 in N. H. Hist. Soc. Coll., II, 6, 1827. **Nipmuk.**—

Eliot (1659) quoted by Drake, Bk. Inds., bk. 2, 80, 1848. **Nipnet.**—Eliot (1649) quoted by Barber, Hist. Coll., 570, 1841. **Nipnett.**—Dudley (1631) in N. H. Hist. Soc. Coll., IV, 226, 1834. **Nopnat.**—Writer of 1647 quoted by Drake, Bk. Inds., bk. 2, 18, 1848.

Nipoma. A former Chumashan village near Santa Inés mission, Santa Barbara co., Cal. (Taylor in Cal. Farmer, May 4, 1860). Perhaps the same as Nipomo.

Nipomo. A former village under San Luis Obispo mission, 8 m. inland from San Luis Obispo, Cal. Perhaps the same village (Nipoma) given by Taylor as near Santa Inez mission.
Nĭ-pŏ-mŏ.—Schumacher in Smithson. Rep. 1874, 342, 1875.

Niquesesquelua. A Chumashan village on one of the Santa Barbara ids., Cal., probably Santa Rosa, in 1542.
Miquesesquelna.—Wheeler Surv. Rep., VII, 311, 1879. **Nisquesesquelua.**—Cabrillo (1542) in Smith, Colec. Doc. Fla., 186, 1857.

Niquipos. A Chumashan village on either Santa Rosa or Santa Cruz id., Cal., in 1542.
Niquipos.—Cabrillo (1542) in Smith, Colec. Doc. Fla., 181, 1857. **Nquipos.**—Taylor in Cal. Farmer, Apr. 17, 1863.

Nirdlirn. A summer settlement of the Kingnaitmiut subtribe of the Okomiut Eskimo on the N. coast near the head of Cumberland sd., Baffin land.—Boas in 6th Rep. B. A. E., map, 1888.

Nisal (*Nĭsál*). A division of the Chinook tribe formerly residing on Nasal r., Pacific co., Wash.
Gĭ̱ā'lĕlam.—Boas, Chinook Texts, 260, 1894 (own name). **Nasal.**—Swan, N. W. Coast, 211, 1857. **Nisal.**—Boas, op. cit.

Niscak ('bustard'). A tribe or division mentioned with other Algonquian tribes of the region between L. Superior and Hudson bay in the Prise de Possession (1671) in Perrot, Mém., 293, 1864. They were perhaps a gens of the Ottawa.

Nishinam (from *nisenani*, 'our relations'). The southern branch of the Maidu, occupying the valley of Bear r., Cal. While this portion of the Maidu is in some ways distinct from the northern branches, all of this family are so similar in every respect that even without the fact of the complete linguistic unity which they represent it would seem illogical to separate them. The Nishinam divisions and villages, which were once populous and numerous along Bear r., are as follows: *Divisions*—Koloma, Pusune, Vesnak, and Wapumne. *Villages*—Bushamul, Chuemdu, Hamitinwoliyu, Intanto, Kaluplo, Kapaka, Lelikian, Lidlipa, Mulamchapa, Opelto, Pakanchi, Pulakatu, Shokumimlepi, Shutamul, Solakiyu, Talak, Toanimbuttuk, and Yokolimdu. See *Maidu, Pujunan Family.* (R. B. D.)
Nishinam.—Powers in Cont. N. A. Ethnol., III, 282, 1877. **Nis-se-non.**—Merriam in Science, N. s., XIX, 914, 1904 (or, Nishinam). **Tainkoyo.**—Curtin, MS. vocab., B. A. E., 1885. **Tanko.**—Dixon, inf'n, 1903 (northern Maidu name; probably from *tai*, 'west': *Tai-nko*, 'having the west'). **Tankum.**—Chever in Bull. Essex Inst. 1870, II, 28, 1871.

Nishtuwekulsushtun (*Nĭ'-ctu-we-ɥ́ŭl'-sŭc-tŭn*). A former village of the Chastacosta on Rogue r., Oreg.—Dorsey in Jour. Am. Folk-lore, III, 234, 1890.

Nisibourounik. One of the four divisions of the Cree.—Jes. Rel. 1658, 22, 1858.

Niska. The dialectic name for one of the three Chimmesyan divisions, the other two being the Kitksan and the Tsimshian. In tradition, art, and manner of living these three divisions are closely allied, with such geographic differences as would naturally occur. In language less than one-third of the vocabulary is common to all, a like proportion varies in accent, while the remainder is different and more local in character. Dialectic differences are much less marked between the two interior river divisions than between either of them and the Tsimshian of the coast.

The territory of the Niska includes Observatory inlet, Nass bay, and the drainage basin of Nass r. and its tributaries, but those northern sources that interlock with the Iskoot and the Stikine rs. are claimed also by the Tahltan, and over this contention have occurred many wars that have always kept these people apart. The Niska villages have always been on the main river and show evidence of considerable size. The houses, in a single row, follow the contour of the shore; they are built of hewn timbers in the form of a parallelogram, with a central open fireplace of gravel, and a smoke-hole in the roof. Carved heraldic columns stand in front, in which the crest of the deceased is shown at the base and that of the successor at the top, and in one old village grave-houses of logs surmounted by animal and bird forms in wood and stone, representing the totemic emblems of the dead, rest on the river bank in the midst of the columns.

With the establishment of missions the older villages have generally been deserted and the people are being concentrated at three points, under the supervision of missionaries of the Church of England, and small modern dwellings are taking the place of the old communal house. Modern ideas prevail, and the condition of the people is a credit to both their teachers and themselves. The villages, past and present, together with the more important village sites, are: Kincolith, Kitaix, Lakkulzap or Greenville, Gwinwork, Lakungida or Ankeegar, Kisthemuwelgit or Willshilhtumwillwillgit, Qunahhair, Kitwinshilk, Sheaksh, Aiyansh, Kitlakdamix, and Kitwinlkole. Other town names have been given, as follows, but these, wholly or in part, may duplicate some of the above: Kitahon, Kitangata, Kitlakaous, and Andeguale.

The Niska were divided geographically into the Kitkahteen ('people of the lower valley'), including those below the canyon, and the Kitanweliks ('people of the upper river'), comprising those above this point.

Tradition tells that long ago when the principal village was across the river to the southward, some little boys were amusing themselves by catching salmon, cutting slits in their backs in which they inserted flat stones, and then letting them go, playing they were whales. This so incensed the guardian spirit that, rising from the mountain to the southward enveloped in a wide spreading black cloud that changed day into night, with eyes of flame and voice of thunder, he rolled down the mountain side as a river of fire and swept the village away. The people fled across the river and took refuge on the hills until quiet was restored, when they divided, some settling at Kitlakdamix and there retaining the old name of Kitauwiliks, while the others, founding Kitwinshilk on the rocks overlooking the rapids, were ever afterward known by the name of their village as 'The people among the lizards.'

The social organization is founded upon matriarchy, and is dependent upon the existence of four exogamous parties, distinguished by their crests, who intermarry and who supplement one another on all occasions of ceremony. These parties are subdivided into families who are represented by minor crests but who still retain the party emblem. These four parties are: (1) Laghkepo, represented by the Wolf and having as its subdivisions the Brown-bear, Crow, Crane, and Red-wing flicker; (2) Laghkeak, represented by the Eagle and having as its subdivisions the Beaver, Owl, Dog-fish, and Squirrel; (3) Kanhadda, represented by the Raven and having as its subdivisions the Frog, Sea-lion, Sculpin, and Star-fish; (4) Kishpootwada, represented by the Killer-whale and having as its subdivisions the Osprey and the Bear-under-Water. (Boas gives the following subdivisions: Gyitkadok, Lakseel, Laktiaktl, Gyitgyigyenik, Gyitwulnakyel, Gyiskabenak, Lakloukst, Gyitsaek, Laktsemelik, and Gyisgahast. He assigns the first two to the Raven phratry, the next three to the Wolf phratry, the four following to the Eagle phratry, and the last to the Bear phratry.)

The Niska look to the river for their food supply, which consists principally of salmon and eulachon. Indeed it is owing to the enormous number of the latter fish that run in to spawn in the early spring that the name Nass, meaning 'the stomach, or food depot', has been given to the river.

In 1902 the population of the Niska towns was 842; in 1906, 814. (G. T. E.)

Naas River Indians.—Scott in Ind. Aff. Rep. 1869, 563, 1870. **Nascah.**—Brit. Col. map, Ind. Aff., Victoria, 1872. **Nascars.**—Horetzky, Canada on Pac., 126, 1874. **Nasqá.**—Dorsey in Am. Antiq., XIX, 277, 1897. **Náss.**—Dunn, Hist. Oregon, 279, 1844. **Nasχá.**—Boas in Zeit. für Ethnol., 231, 1888. **Nishgar.**—Can. Ind. Aff. Rep., 432, 1896. **Nishka.**—Horetzky, op. cit., 219. **Niska.**—Tolmie and Dawson, Vocabs. Brit. Col., 113B, 1884. **Nîsk·a′.**—Boas in 10th Rep. N. W. Tribes Can., 48, 1895. **Nis-kah.**—Gibbs in Cont. N. A. Ethnol., I, 143, 1877. **Nüss-kā.**—Krause, Tlinkit Ind., 318, 1885. **Oldnass.**—Scott in H. R. Ex. Doc. 65, 36th Cong., 1st sess., 115, 1860 (probably identical).

Niskap. Mentioned with the Smulkamish as bands residing on the Muckleshoot res., Wash. Perhaps a subdivision of the Puyallup.

Nooscope.—Gosnell in Ind. Aff. Rep. 1857, 338, 1858. **White River Indians.**—Gosnell in Ind. Aff. Rep. 1856, 338, 1857.

Nisqualli. A Salish tribe on and about the river of the same name flowing into the s. extension of Puget sd., Wash. The Nisqualli res. is on Nisqualli r. between Pierce and Thurston cos. The name has also been extended to apply to those tribes of the E. side of Puget sd. speaking the same dialect as the above. Such are the Puyallup, Skagit, Snohomish, Snokwalmu, and Stilakwamish. Mitsukwic was a former Nisqualli village. The Nisqualli made a treaty with the United States at Medicine cr., Wash., Dec. 26, 1854, ceding certain lands and reserving others. The Executive order of Jan. 20, 1857, defined the present Nisqualli res.

Askwálli.—Gatschet, Kalapuya MS., B. A. E., 31 (Calapooya name). **Ltsχéals.**—Gibbs, Nestucca vocab., B. A. E. (Nestucca name). **Nasqually.**—White in Ind. Aff. Rep., 460, 1843. **Nesquallis.**—Duflot de Mofras, Expl., II, 335, 1844. **Nesqually.**—U. S. Stat. at Large, XI, 395, 1867. **Nez-quales.**—Smet, Letters, 231, 1843. **Nez qually.**—Hines, Oregon, 29, 1851. **Niskwáli.**—Gatschet in Proc. A. A. A. S., XXXI, 577, 1882. **Niskwalli.**—Gibbs in Cont. N. A. Ethnol., I, 178, 1877 (used collectively). **Nisqualies.**—Domenech, Deserts N. A., I, 442, 1860. **Nisquallis.**—Sterrett (1855) in Sen. Ex. Doc. 26, 34th Cong., 1st sess., 65, 1856. **Nisqually.**—Hale in U. S. Expl. Exped., VI, 211, 1846. **N′squalli.**—Gibbs, MS. no. 248, B. A. E. (name strictly belongs to the village at the first dam on Nisqualli r.). **Qualliamish.**—Schoolcraft, Ind. Tribes, VI, 688, 1857. **Quallyamish.**—Lane quoted by Schoolcraft, ibid., I, 521, 1851. **Skwale.**—Hale in U. S. Expl. Exped., VI, 211, 1846. **Sk′wa-lé-ûbe.**—McCaw, Puyallup MS. vocab., B. A. E., 1885 (Puyallup name). **Skwali.**—Latham in Trans. Philol. Soc. Lond., 71, 1856. **Skwalliahmish.**—Gibbs in Cont. N. A. Ethnol., I, 178, 1877. **Skwalz.**—Gallatin (1846) in Schoolcraft, Ind. Tribes, III, 402, 1853. **Squalliah-mish.**—Gibbs in Pac. R. R. Rep., I, 435, 1855. **Squalli-a-mish.**—Tolmie, ibid., 434. **Squally-ah-mish.**—Starling in Ind. Aff. Rep., 170, 1852. **Squallyamish.**—Scouler in Jour. Geog. Soc. Lond., I, 224, 1841. **Squawlees.**—Meek in H. R. Ex. Doc. 76, 30th Cong., 1st sess., 10, 1848. **Squiath.**—Ind. Aff. Rep. 1856, 265, 1857. **Tsĕ Skuálli amím.**—Gatschet, Lakmiut MS., B. A. E., 105 (Lákmiut-Kalapuya name).

Nissowaquet. An Ottawa chief, known to the French as La Fourche, who during most of his life resided at Michilimackinac, Mich. He is said to have been made head chief of his tribe as early as 1721 (Grignon in Wis. Hist. Coll., III, 198, 1857), at which time Charles DeLanglade, his close friend and aid, married his sister Domitilde. Nissowaquet allied himself with the French in their war with the English, and it is said was present at Ft Duquesne at the time of Braddock's defeat. He is said to have been still living in 1780 (Draper in Wis. Hist. Coll., III, 199, 1857; Mich. Pion. Coll., X, 406, 1888). His name is also spelled Nissaouakouad (Wis. Hist. Coll., VII, 125, 1876).

Nitahauritz. One of the 4 Alibamu towns formerly existing w. of the confluence of Cabo (Cahawba) and Alabama rs., in Dallas co., Ala.

Nitahaurithz.—Lattré, Carte des Etats-Unis, 1784. Nitahauritz.—Jefferys, Am. Atlas, map 5, 1776.

Nitak. A Knaiakhotana village on the E. side of Knik bay, at the head of Cook inlet, Alaska, containing 15 persons in 1880.

Nitak.—Baker, Geog. Dict. Alaska, 1901. Nitakh.—Petroff in 10th Census, Alaska, 29, 1884.

Nitakoskitsipupiks ('obstinate'). A band of the Piegan tribe of the Siksika.

Ne-ta'-ka-ski-tsi-pup'-iks.—Hayden, Ethnog. and Philol. Mo. Val., 264, 1862 (trans. 'people that have their own way'). Nit'-ak-os-kit-si-pup-iks.—Grinnell, Blackfoot Lodge Tales, 209, 1892. Obstinate.—Ibid., 225.

Nitawaliks. Given as a Chimmesyan tribe on upper Nass r., Brit. Col.—Tolmie and Dawson, Vocabs. Brit. Col., 113B, 1884.

Nitawyiks ('lone eaters'). A band of the Piegan tribe of the Siksika.

Lone Eaters.—Grinnell, Blackfoot Lodge Tales, 225, 1892. Ni-taw'-yiks.—Ibid., 209.

Nitchequon. A small tribe or division living about Nicheku lake, Ungava, Canada; probably a Nascapee band.

Nitchequon.—Hind, Labrador Penin., II, 117, 1863. Nitchik Irinionetchs.—Bellin, map, 1755. Nitchik Irinionetz.—La Tour, map, 1779. Nitchiks.—Jefferys, French Dom., pt. 1, map, 1761.

Nitel. A Chumashan village on Santa Cruz id. (the San Lucas of Cabrillo), Cal. in 1542.—Cabrillo (1542) in Smith, Colec. Doc. Fla., 181, 1857.

Nith-songs. The nith-songs (Norwegian *nith*, 'contention') of the Greenland Eskimo are a species of word duel in which the audience present has the deciding voice, a sort of decision by "song and dance" of private quarrels and disputes—primitive arbitration, as it were. As described by Crantz (1767) and Egede (1746) this institution is as follows: When a Greenlander considers himself injured in any way by another person, he composes about him a satirical song, which he rehearses with the help of his intimates. He then challenges the offending one to a duel of song. One after another the two disputants sing at each other their wisdom, wit, and satire, supported by their partisans, until at last one is at his wit's end, when the audience, who are the jury, make known their decision. The matter is now settled for good, and the contestants must be friends again and not recall the matter which was in dispute. Egede styled this song contest "the common mode of avenging one's self in Greenland." To make his opponent the laughing stock of the community is a sweet morsel of revenge for an Eskimo. The general opinion of travelers and others is that the "song duel" was a very useful and even praiseworthy social institution, and Nansen expresses his regret that on the w. coast of Greenland it has been abolished by the missionaries. On the E. coast it lingers, as Nansen reports, in the form of the so-called "drum dance," the only real judicial institution of these Eskimo. The fear of public shame is very powerful as a factor in social betterment. This remarkable restriction of vengeance and modification of the duel has been largely overlooked by sociologists. Boas reports the nith-song as still in vogue among the Eskimo of Baffin land, where "downright hostile feelings and personal grudges are settled by the opponents meeting on a fixed occasion and singing songs at each other"; and Swanton reports an analogous custom among the Tlingit, entered into by opposing phratries. Brinton (Essays of Amer., 287, 1890) gives a specimen of this poetic duel, furnished by Rink. Consult also Egede, Descr. of Greenland, 153, 1745; Crantz, Hist. of Greenland, 178, 1767; Nansen, First Crossing, 337, 1890; Steinmetz, Entwickl. der Strafe, II, 67–76, 1892.   (A. F. C.)

Nitikskiks (*Nit'-ik-skiks*, 'lone fighters'). A band of the Piegan and also of the Kainah tribe of the Siksika.—Grinnell, Blackfoot Lodge Tales, 209, 1892.

Nitinat. A Nootka tribe on a tidal lake of the same name, near the s. w. coast of Vancouver id. Pop. 198 in 1906. Their villages are Carmanah, Clo-oose, Tsooquahna, and Wyah.

Nettinat.—Taylor in Cal. Farmer, Aug. 1, 1862. Niten aht.—Brit. Col. map, Victoria, 1872. Nitinaht.—Sproat, Savage Life, 308, 1868. Nitinat.—Galiano, Viaje, 28, 1802. Ni'tinath.—Boas, 6th Rep. N. W. Tribes Can., 31, 1890. Nittanat.—Kelley, Oregon, 68, 1830 (given as a village). Nitten-aht.—Can. Ind. Aff., 188, 1883. Nittenat.—Scouler (1846) in Jour. Ethnol. Soc. Lond., I. 234, 1848. Nittinahts.—Whymper, Travels, 74, 1869. Nittinat.—Mayne, Brit. Col., 251, 1862.

Nitotsiksisstaniks ('kill close by'). A band of the Piegan tribe of the Siksika.

Kill Close By.—Grinnell, Blackfoot Lodge Tales, 225, 1892. Ni-tot'-si-ksis-stan-iks.—Ibid., 209.

Niudje (*Ni-üdjê*, 'lower part of a stream'). A former village of the Kansa on Kansas r., about 4 m. above the site of Kansas City, Mo.—J. O. Dorsey, Kansa MS. vocab., B. A. E., 1882.

Niueuomokai (*uöm* signifies 'offspring of two sisters'). The Buzzard clan of the Pima.

Ni-ue-Uöm O-kai.—Bandelier in Arch. Inst. Papers, III, 254, 1890. Nuey-kech-emk.—ten Kate, Reizen in N. A., 155, 1885.

Niutang. A village of the Kingnaitmiut subtribe of the Okomiut Eskimo on Kingnait fjord, E. Baffin land.—Boas in 6th Rep. B. A. E., map, 1888.

Niuyaka ('New York'). A subordinate settlement of the Upper Creek town Oak-

fuskee, on the E. bank of Tallapoosa r., 20 m. above Oakfuskee, in Cleburne co., Ala. It was settled in 1777 by Tukpafka Creeks from the Chattahoochee. It was first called by another name, but after the conclusion of the treaty between the United States and the Creeks in New York, Aug. 7, 1790, it received the above appellation. (H. W. H.)
New Yarcau.—Schoolcraft, Ind. Tribes, VI, 371, 1857. New Yaucas.—Pickett, Hist. Ala., II, 339, 1851. New-yau-cau.—Hawkins (1799), Sketch, 45, 46, 1848. New Yauco.—U. S. Ind. Treat. (1825), 326, 1837. New-yau-kau.—Schoolcraft, Ind. Tribes, IV, 381, 1854. New York.—Blount (1793) in Am. State Pap., Ind. Aff., I, 440, 1832. New Youcka.—Flint, Ind. Wars, 202, 1833. Niuyáχa.—Gatschet, Creek Migr. Leg., I, 139, 1884. Nowyawger.—Barnard (1793) in Am. State Pap., Ind. Aff., I, 382, 1832. Nuo Yaucau.—Hawkins (1814), ibid., 860.

Niuyaka. A town of the Creek Nation on New Yorker cr., a s. branch of Deep Fork, about Tp. 13 N., R. 10 or 11 E., Okla.—Gatschet, Creek Migr. Leg., II, 186, 1888.

Niwanshike (*Ni'-wan-ci'-ke*, 'water person'). A subgens of the Pakhtha, the Beaver gens of the Iowa.—Dorsey in 15th Rep. B. A. E., 239, 1897.

Nixora (from *nijor, nixor*, said to mean 'captive'). A term said to have been applied by the Pima of s. Arizona to "those Indians whom the nations beyond capture in their wars among themselves, and whom the Yuma and Papago afterward bring to Altar and other places to sell as captives or slaves, of whatever nation they may be" (Font, 1775-76, cited by Coues, Garcés Diary, 446, 1900; Orozco y Berra, Geog., 350, 1864). According to Garcés, the term Nifores was one of the names which the Pima applied to the Yavapai. Cf. *Genizaros.*
Nichoras.—Mühlenpfordt, Mejico, II, 537, 1844. Niforas.—Garcés (1770) cited by Arricivita, Chrón. Seráfica, II, 455, 1792 (here applied to Yavapai). Nifores.—Garcés (1775-76), Diary, 446, 1900 (applied to Yavapai). Nigoras.—Raynal, Indies, VI, map, 1788. Nijor.—Kino (ca. 1699) in Doc. Hist. Mex., 4th s., I, 349, 1856. Nijoras.—Orozco y Berra, Geog., 350, 1864. Nijores.—Ibid. Nijotes.—Villa-Señor, Theatro Am., pt. 2, 407, 1748. Niojoras.—Alcedo, Dic. Geog., IV, 218, 1788. Nizoræ.—Morelli, Fasti Novi Orbis, 46, 1776. Noraguas.—Garcés (1771) cited by Coues, Garcés Diary (1775-76), 31, 1900.

Nkahlimiluh (*N'-kah-li-mil-uh*). A Ntlakyapamuk village near the mouth of upper Nicola r., Brit. Col.—Dawson in Trans. Roy. Soc. Can., sec. II, 44, 1891.

Nkaih. A Ntlakyapamuk village not far from Stryne, in the interior of British Columbia. Pop. 4 in 1896, after which date it seems to have been confused with a town called Nkya.
Nkaih.—Can. Ind. Aff., 434, 1896. N-wa-ih.—Ibid., 1885, 196, 1886.

Nkakim ('despised', because the people of this place were of low social status and much looked down upon by the Spuzzum people). A village of Ntlakyapamuk in the neighborhood of Spuzzum, Fraser r., Brit. Col.
N'ka'kim.—Hill-Tout in Rep. Ethnol. Surv. Can., 5, 1899.

Nkaktko (*Nqa'ktko*, 'little rotten water', or 'bad water'). A village of the Upper Fraser band of Ntlakyapamuk on the w. side of Fraser r., 28 m. above Lytton, Brit. Col.
Nqa'ktko.—Teit in Mem. Am. Mus. Nat. Hist., II, 172, 1900. N'tā'-kō.—Hill-Tout in Rep. Ethnol. Surv. Can., 4, 1899.

Nkamaplix. A division of Okinagan under the Kamloops-Okanagan agency, Brit. Col.; pop. 232 in 1906.
En-ke-map-o-tricks.—Can. Ind. Aff. 1883, pt. I, 191, 1884. Nkamaplix.—Ibid., pt. II, 166, 1901. Okanagan.—Ibid., pt. II, 68, 1902.

Nkamchin ('confluence', 'entrance'). A village of the Spences Bridge band of Ntlakyapamuk, on the s. side of Thompson r., at its junction with the Nicola, about 24½ m. above Lytton, Brit. Col. Pop. 81 in 1901, the last time the name appears.
Nic-com-sin.—Can. Ind. Aff. 1883, pt. I, 189, 1884. Nicola.—Brit. Col. map, Ind. Aff., Victoria, 1872. Nicola Mouth.—Present white man's name. N'-kam-sheen.—Dawson in Trans. Roy. Soc. Can., sec. II, 44, 1891. Nkamtci'n.—Teit in Mem. Am. Mus. Nat. Hist., II, 173, 1900. Nkumcheen.—Can. Ind. Aff., pt. II, 166, 1901. N'kum'toïn.—Hill-Tout in Rep. Ethnol. Surv. Can., 4, 1899.

Nkamip. An Okinagan division under the Kamloops-Okanagan agency, Brit. Col. Pop. 70 in 1904, 65 in 1906.
En-ke-mip.—Can. Ind. Aff. 1883, pt. I, 191, 1884. N-Kamip.—Ibid., pt. II, 166, 1901. Osoyoos.—Ibid., 79, 1878. Osoyoos.—Ibid., 1882, 259, 1883.

Nkattsim (*Nkattsî'm*, 'log bridge across stream.'—Hill-Tout). A Ntlakyapamuk village on the E. side of Fraser r., about 38 m. above Yale, Brit. Col., near Keefer's station, but on the opposite side of the river. Pop. 87 in 1901, the last time the name appears.
Ne-kat-sap.—Can. Ind. Aff. 1883, pt. I, 189, 1884. Nkatsam.—Ibid., pt. II, 166, 1901. Nkattsî'm.—Teit in Mem. Am. Mus. Nat. Hist., II, 169, 1900. N'ka'tzam.—Hill-Tout in Rep. Ethnol. Surv. Can., 5, 1899.

Nkoeitko (*Nqôe'itko*, 'little lake or pond'—Teit; 'yellow water'—Hill-Tout). A village of the Spences Bridge band of Ntlakyapamuk on the s. side of Thompson r., 30 m. above Lytton, Brit. Col.
N'koakoaē'tkō.—Hill-Tout in Rep. Ethnol. Surv. Can., 4, 1899. Nqôe'itko.—Teit in Mem. Am. Mus. Nat. Hist., II, 173, 1900.

Nkoiam (*N'kō'iam'*, 'eddy'). A Ntlakyapamuk village on Fraser r., below Cisco, Brit. Col.—Hill-Tout in Rep. Ethnol. Can., 5, 1899.

Nkoikin (*Nqoï'kîn*, 'black pine ridge'). A village of the Lytton band of Ntlakyapamuk on the E. side of Fraser r., 8 m. above Lytton, Brit. Col.; so-called because young firs grew thickly there. Pop. 15 in 1897, when last the name appears.
Nkuaikin.—Can. Ind. Aff. 1892, 312, 1893. N'ōkoiē'kEn.—Hill-Tout in Rep. Ethnol. Surv. Can., 4, 1899. Nqakin.—Can. Ind. Aff. 1898, 418, 1899 (in combination with "Stryne-Nqakin", Stryne being another town). Nqoï'kîn.—Teit in Mem. Am. Mus. Nat. Hist., II, 172, 1900. Nquakin.—Can. Ind. Aff., 230, 1886.

Nkukapenach (*N'k·u'kapenatc*, 'canoes transformed to stone'). A Squawmish village community on the right bank of

Squawmisht r., Brit. Col.—Hill-Tout in Rep. Brit. A. A. S., 474, 1900.

Nkuoosai (*Nkuŏ'osai*). A Squawmish gens living on Howe sd., coast of British Columbia.—Boas, MS., B. A. E., 1887.

Nkuoukten (*Nkuŏ'uktẹn*). A Squawmish gens living on Howe sd., coast of British Columbia.—Boas, MS., B. A. E., 1887.

Nkya (*Nqáia*, from *nqa'iɛx*, 'to swim'). A village of the Lytton band of Ntlakyapamuk on the w. side of Fraser r., Brit. Col., 2 m. below Lytton. Pop. 71 in 1901, the last time the name appears.
Macaiyah.—Brit. Col. map, Ind. Aff., Victoria, 1872. **Macayah.**—Can. Ind. Aff., 79, 1878. **Nikai'-a.**—Dawson in Trans. Roy. Soc. Can., sec. II, 44, 1891. **N'kai'ā.**—Hill-Tout in Rep. Ethnol. Surv. Can., 4, 1899. **Nkaih.**—Can. Ind. Aff., 363, 1897 (confused with Nkaih, q. v.). **Nkya.**—Ibid., pt. II, 164, 1901. **Nqa'ia.**—Teit in Mem. Am. Mus. Nat. Hist., II, 171, 1900. **Nyakai.**—Can. Ind. Aff. 1898, 418, 1899.

Nma (*N'-mă'*, 'sturgeon'). A gens of the Potawatomi.—Morgan, Anc. Soc., 167, 1877.

Nmapena (*N'-mă-pe-nă'*, 'carp'). A gens of the Potawatomi.—Morgan, Anc. Soc., 167, 1877.

Ño ('beloved town'). A Calusa village on the s. w. coast of Florida in the latter part of the 16th century.
Ño.—Fontaneda (*ca.* 1575), Mem., Smith trans., 19, 1854. **Non.**—Fontaneda in Doc. Inéd., v, 538, 1866.

Noamlaki (Ilmawi: 'western dwellers.'—Curtin). A Wintun tribe formerly living on Long, Thomes, and Elder crs., in the mountains and on the edge of the plains in Colusa and Tehama cos., Cal.
Nomee Lacks.—Taylor in Cal. Farmer, June 8, 1860. **Nome-Lackees.**—Geiger in Ind. Aff. Rep. 1859, 438, 1860. **Numleki.**—Curtin, Ilmawi MS. vocab., B. A. E., 1889 ('west dwellers': given as Ilmawi name of the Wintun). **Tehamas.**—Hittell, Hist. Cal., I, 731, 1898. **Titkainenom.**—A. L. Kroeber, inf'n, 1903 (Yuki name).

Noatak. A Nunatogmiut settlement on the lower part of Noatak r., in N. W. Alaska.
Noatagamutes.—Petroff in 10th Census, Alaska, 60, 1881. **Noatak.**—Baker, Geog. Dict. Alaska, 464, 1906.

Nobscusset. A village, perhaps of the Nauset, that was subject to the Wampanoag; situated near the present Dennis, Barnstable co., Mass. In 1685 it was a village of the Praying Indians.
Nabsquassets.—Hoyt, Antiq. Res., 89, 1824. **Nobscussett.**—Hinckley (1685) in Mass. Hist. Soc. Coll., 4th s., v, 133, 1861. **Nobsqassit.**—Drake, Bk. Inds., bk. 2, 118, 1848. **Nobsquasitt.**—Gookin (1674) in Mass. Hist. Soc. Coll., 1st s., I, 148, 1806. **Nobsquassit.**—Bourne (1674), ibid., 197.

Nocake. Parched corn-meal, a dish which the English colonists adopted, with its name, from the Algonquian tribes of New England. Roger Williams (Key to Am. Lang., 11, 1643) defines the Narraganset *nokehick* as "parched meal, which is a readie very wholesome food, which they eat with a little water." The Massachuset form as given by Eliot is *nookhic*, the same as *nokhik*. Wood, in 1634, uses the form *nocake;* Palfrey (New Eng., I,

28, 1858) has *nookhik*. The word signifies 'it is soft'. (A. F. C.)

Nochak. A Kuskwogmiut Eskimo village on Chulitna r., Alaska; pop. 28 in 1890.
Noh-chamiut.—Eleventh Census, Alaska, 164, 1893 (the people).

Nochpeem. A tribe or band of the Wappinger confederacy formerly occupying the E. bank of the Hudson about the site of Matteawan, Dutchess co., N. Y. De Laet locates here the Pachami, but Ruttenber says these may have been the Tankitekes, and, indeed, a chief of the latter bore the name Pacham or Pachem. They had a village called Nochpeem, and others called Keskistkonk and Pasquasheck, but their principal one seems to have been called Canopus, from their chief. (J. M.)
Highlanders.—Doc. of 1660 in N. Y. Doc. Col. Hist., XIII, 182, 1881. **Highland Indians.**—Doc. of 1655, ibid., 52. **Hogelanders.**—Breeden Raedt (*ca.* 1630) quoted by Ruttenber, Tribes Hudson R., 80, 1872 (Dutch form). **Noch-Peem.**—Van der Donck (1656) quoted by Ruttenber, ibid., 72. **Nochpeem.**—Treaty of 1644 in N. Y. Doc. Col. Hist., XIII, 17, 1881. **Pachami.**—Map (*ca.* 1614), ibid., I, 1856. **Pachamins.**—De Laet (1633) in N. Y. Hist. Soc. Coll., 2d s., I, 308, 1841.

Nockay-Delklinne. See *Nakaidoklini*.

Nocos. A Chumashan village between Goleta and Pt Concepcion, Cal., in 1542.—Cabrillo (1542) in Smith, Colec. Doc. Fla., 183, 1857.

Nocto. A former Chumashan village near Purísima mission, Santa Barbara co., Cal.—Taylor in Cal. Farmer, Oct. 18, 1861.

Noewe. Mentioned by Bartram (Travels, 371, 1792) as a Cherokee settlement, about 1775, on the upper waters of Tennessee r., apparently in w. North Carolina. The form can not be certainly identified, but it may be intended for Nâyû'hĭ, 'sand place,' or Nûñyâ'hĭ, 'rock place.' Cf. *Niowe*. (J. M.)

Nogaie (*No-ga'-ie*). A Paviotso tribe of four bands, formerly living in N. E. Nevada, in the vicinity of Robinson district, Spring valley, Duckwater, and White r. valley; pop. 200 in 1873.—Powell in Ind. Aff. Rep. 1873, 52, 1874.

Nogal (Span. 'walnut'). A settlement of the Huichol to which emigrated those who once lived at Aguas Azules; situated s. w. of Santa Catarina, in Jalisco, Mexico. The place was afterward taken possession of by Mexican settlers, but now the Huichol are permitted to reside therein.—Lumholtz, Unknown Mex., II, 256, 1902.

Nogales (Span.: 'walnuts'). A ruined pueblo s. of the malpais or lava beds in S. E. New Mexico.—Bandelier in Arch. Inst. Rep., v, 88, 1884.

Nogeling. A Kiatagmiut Eskimo village on the outlet of L. Clark, Alaska; pop. 16 in 1890.
Noghelingamiut.—Eleventh Census, Alaska, 164, 1893 (the people).

Noggai. A former Yukonikhotana village on Yukon r., Alaska, having 10 inhabitants in 1844.—Zagoskin quoted by Petroff in 10th Census, Alaska, 37, 1884.

Nogwats (*No-gwats'*). A Paiute band formerly near Potosi, s. E. Nev. Pop. 56 in 1873, including the Parumpats.—Powell in Ind. Aff. Rep. 1873, 50, 1874.

No Heart. See *Nacheninga*.

Nohioalli. A Costanoan village situated in 1819 within 10 m. of Santa Cruz mission, Cal.—Taylor in Cal. Farmer, Apr. 5, 1860.

Nohulchinta. The highest Koyukukhotana village on Koyukuk r., on the s. fork, 3 m. above the junction. It contained 6 families in 1885.
Nohoolchíntna.—Allen, Rep., 99, 1887.

Nohuntsitk (*Nŏ'xunts'ĭtx*). A Kwakiutl tribe living at the lower end of Wikeno lake, coast of British Columbia.—Boas in Rep. Nat. Mus. 1895, 328, 1897.

Noieltsi (*Noiĕ'ltsi*, 'burnt body'). A Ntlakyapamuk village on the w. side of Fraser r., about 23 m. above Yale, Brit. Col.—Teit in Mem. Am. Mus. Nat. Hist., II, 169, 1900.

Nok. A former Koyukukhotana village on the w. bank of Koyukuk r., Alaska, near its mouth; pop. 50 in 1844.
Nokhakate.—Zagoskin in Nouv. Ann. Voy., 5th s., XXI, map, 1850. Nok-khakat.—Zagoskin quoted by Petroff in 10th Census, Alaska, 37, 1884.

Noka (*No'ke*, 'bear foot'). A gens of the Chippewa.
Noka.—Warren (1852) in Minn. Hist. Soc. Coll., v, 44, 1885. No-kaig.—Ibid., 87 (plural). Nŏk'e.—Wm. Jones, inf'n, 1906.

Noka. A chief of the western Chippewa in the latter half of the 18th century, who attained some celebrity as a leader and hunter. The chief incident of his life relates to the war between the Mdewakanton and the Chippewa for possession of the banks of the upper Mississippi. In 1769, the year following the Lattle of Crow Wing, Minn.—where the Chippewa, though maintaining their ground, were hampered by inferior numbers—they determined to renew the attack on the Mdewakanton with a larger force. This war party, under the leadership of Noka, referred to as "Old Noka" evidently on account of his advanced age, attacked Shakopee's village on Minnesota r., Minn., the result being a drawn battle, the Chippewa retiring to their own territory without inflicting material damage on their enemy. Regarding Noka's skill as a hunter, it is said that he killed in one day's hunt, starting from the mouth of Crow Wing r., Minn., 16 elk, 4 buffalo, 5 deer, 3 bears, a lynx, and a porcupine. Hole-in-the-day was one of Noka's descendants (Warren in Minn. Hist. Soc. Coll., v, 266, 1885).

Nokehick. See *Nocake*.

Nokem (*No'qEm*, from *s'nŏ'k*, 'valley'). A village of the Spences Bridge band of

Ntlakyapamuk at a place called by the whites Drynoch, on the s. side of Thompson r., 16 m. above Lytton, Brit. Col.—Teit in Mem. Am. Mus. Nat. Hist., II, 172, 1900.

Noketrotra. Mentioned as a tribe, seemingly Moquelumnan, formerly on Fresno r., Cal.—Wessels in H. R. Ex. Doc. 76, 34th Cong., 3d sess., 30, 1857.

Nokosalgi ('bear people', from *nokósi* 'bear', *algi* 'people'). A Creek clan.
Nokósalgi.—Gatschet, Creek Migr. Leg., I, 155, 1884. No-kuse'.—Morgan, Anc. Soc., 161, 1877.

Nokrot. A Chnagmiut Eskimo village near C. Romanof, s. coast of Norton sd., Alaska.
Azachagyagmut.—Zagoskin, Descr. Russ. Poss. Am., I, 73, 1847. Nokrotmiut.—Coast Surv., 1868, quoted by Baker, Geog. Dict. Alaska, 1901.

Nokyuntseleta. A former pueblo of the Jemez in New Mexico, the exact site of which is not known.
No-cum-tzil-e-ta.—Bandelier in Arch. Inst. Papers, IV, 207, 1892. No-kyun-tse-le-ta'.—Hodge, field notes, B. A. E., 1895.

Nolcha ('Sun'). Given by Bourke (Jour. Am. Folk-lore, II, 181, 1889) as a clan of the Mohave, q. v.

Nomas (*Nŏ'mas*). The ancestor of a Tlauitsis gens, after whom the gens itself was sometimes called.—Boas in Petermanns Mitt., pt. 5, 130, 1887.

Nomasenkilis (*Nŏmasénχilis*). The ancestor of a Tlatlasikoala gens, after whom the gens itself was sometimes called.—Boas in Petermanns Mitt., pt. 5, 131, 1887.

Nomkolkol (*Nŏm-kŏl'-kŏl*). A former Chumashan village on Santa Cruz id. (the San Lucas of Cabrillo), Cal., E. of the harbor.—Henshaw, Buenaventura MS. vocab., B. A. E., 1884.

Nomoqois. The ancestor of a Nakomgilisala gens, after whom the gens itself was sometimes called.—Boas in Petermanns Mitt., pt. 5, 131, 1887.

Nonantum ('I rejoice,' or 'I am well-minded.'—Trumbull). A Massachuset village on Nonantum hill, near Newton, Middlesex co., Mass. John Eliot began his missionary labors here in 1646, and it was soon after established by law as a village for the converts. In 1650–51 they removed to Natick.
Hoanantum.—Hutchinson in Trans. Am. Antiq. Soc., II, 518, 1836. Nanitomen.—Mass. Hist. Soc. Coll., 1st s., X, 14, 1809. Nonandom.—Harris, ibid., 1st s., IX, 192, 1804. Nonantum.—Gookin (1674), ibid., I, 148, 1806; Eliot (1646) quoted by Pilling, Algonq. Bibliog., 177, 1891. Nonatum.—Gookin (1677) in Trans. Am. Antiq. Soc., II, 518, 1836. Noonanetum.—Shepard (1648) in Mass. Hist. Soc. Coll., 3d s., IV, 38, 1834. Noonatomen.—Eliot (1647), ibid., 20.

Nonapho. A tribal name given in the book of burials at Mission San Antonio de Valero, Texas, in 1726. Only one entry was made under this name, which was for the burial of a child of a Mesquite father and a Nonapho mother. The Mesquites (there appear to have been different tribes by this name) were apparently Tonkawan. At this time there were also Coahuiltecan tribes at the mission, but the Nonapho can not be identified with any of the known tribes (Entierros, San Antonio de Valero, MS. in the custody of the Bishop of San Antonio).　(H. E. B.)

Nonawharitse. A Tuscarora village in North Carolina in 1701, mentioned by Lawson (1709), N. C., 383, 1860.

Non-che-ning-ga. See *Nacheninga*.

Nondas ('steep hill.'—Hewitt). A former Seneca village, visited in 1791 (Am. State Pap., Ind. Aff., I, 151, 1832) by Col. Thomas Procter, who says it lay 8 m. from Squakie hill, which would place it near the present Nunda, Livingston co., N. Y. Mary Jemison, "the white woman," lived there then.　(w. m. b.)

Non-gee-ninga. See *Nacheninga*.

Nongee's Village. A former settlement, probably of the Chippewa, named after a resident chief, situated about the junction of Thornapple cr. with Grand r., Kent co., Mich., a few miles E. of Grand Rapids. The land on which it was situated was ceded to the United States by the treaty of Chicago, Aug. 29, 1821.

Nonharmin (*Nor-har'-min*, 'pulling up stream'). A subclan of the Delawares.—Morgan, Anc. Soc., 172, 1877.

Nonhdeitazhi ('those who touch no charcoal'). A subgens of the Inkesabe gens of the Omaha.
Naqǫeit'a-bajǐ.—Dorsey in 15th Rep. B. A. E., 227, 1897. Non-hde-i-ta-zhi.—F. La Flesche, inf'n, 1906.

Nonhdeitazhi. A subgens of the Tapa gens of the Omaha.
Naqǫe-it'ajǐ.—Dorsey in 15th Rep. B. A. E., 228, 1897. Non-hde-i-ta-zhi.—F. La Flesche, inf'n, 1906.

Nonoava (from *nonó*, 'father.'—Lumholtz). A Tarahumare settlement on the headwaters of Rio Nonoava, s. w. Chihuahua, Mexico. The inhabitants, who numbered 335 in 1900, are becoming completely civilized. Apache raids are still remembered here.
Nonoaba.—Zapata (1678) in Doc. Hist. Mex., 4th s., III, 324, 1857. Nonoava.—Ibid., 327. Nuestra Sonora de Monserrate.—Ibid., 324.

Nonotuc. A village near the present Northampton, on Connecticut r., in Hampshire co., Mass. Its inhabitants seem to have been a part of the Pocomtuc. In 1653 they sold a considerable tract on the w. bank of the river, extending from Hatfield to the falls near Holyoke, but continued to live in the English settlement until King Philip's war in 1675, when they joined the hostiles.　(J. M.)
Nanatan.—Pynchon (1663) in N. Y. Doc. Col. Hist., XIII, 308, 1881. Nonaticks.—Hoyt, Antiq. Res., 91, 1824. Nonotuck.—Ibid., 74. Northampton Indians.—Quanapaug (1675) in Mass. Hist. Soc. Coll., 1st s., VI, 206, 1800.

Nonyishagi (*No-nyish'-ä-gi'*). A former pueblo of the Jemez of New Mexico; definite locality unknown.　(F. W. H.)

Nooachhummilh (*Noo-ach-hum-milh*). A former Chehalis village N. of Grays harbor, on the coast of Washington.—Gibbs, MS. no. 248, B. A. E.

Noohooultch (*Noo-hoo-ultch*). The Chehalis name of an ancient village on the s. side of Grays harbor, Wash.—Gibbs, MS. no. 248, B. A. E.

Noohtamuh (*Nooh-ta-muh*). An unidentified village that anciently stood on the w. end of Harbledown id., Brit. Col., in Kwakiutl territory.—Dawson in Can. Geol. Surv., map, 1887.

Nookalthu (*Noo-kált-hu*). The site of a former Chehalis village N. of Grays harbor, Wash.—Gibbs, MS. no. 248, B. A. E.

Nookhick. See *Nocake*.

Nooksak ('mountain men'). The name given by the Indians on the coast to a Salish tribe, said to be divided into three small bands, on a river of the same name in Whatcom co., Wash. About 200 Nooksak were officially enumerated in 1906, but Hill-Tout says there are only about 6 true male Nooksak. They speak the same dialect as the Squawmish, from whom they are said to have separated.
Neuk-sacks.—Fitzhugh in Ind. Aff. Rep. 1857, 328, 1858. Nook-sáak.—Stevens, ibid., 458, 1854. Nooksac.—Ibid., 17, 1870. Nooksack.—Finkbower, ibid., 1867, 59, 1868. Nook-sâhk.—Stevens, ibid., 455, 1854. Nooksâhk.—Gibbs in Pac. R. R. Rep., I, 433, 1855. Nooksaks.—Keane in Stanford, Compend., 526, 1878. Nootsak.—Hill-Tout in Ethnol. Surv. Can., 55, 1902. Nugh-sahk.—Mallet in Ind. Aff. Rep., 198, 1877. Nŭksahk.—Gibbs in Cont. N. A. Ethnol., I, 180, 1877. Nŭk-sák.—Gibbs, Clallam and Lummi, v, 1863.

Noolamarlarmo (*Nool-ă-mar-lar'-mo*, 'living in water'). A subclan of the Delawares.—Morgan, Anc. Soc., 172, 1877.

Noosiatsks (*Noo-si-átsks*). The Chehalis name of an ancient village on the s. side of Grays harbor, Wash.—Gibbs, MS. no. 48, B. A. E.

Nooskoh (*Noos-kóh*). The Chehalis name of a former village on a creek opposite Whishkah r., Wash.—Gibbs, MS. no. 248, B. A. E.

Noöt (*Nō'ôt*, or *NEró't*, allied to *ró'it*, 'sleep'). A village of the Lytton band of Ntlakyapamuk on the w. side of Fraser r., 12 m. above Lytton, Brit. Col.
NEró't.—Teit in Mem. Am. Mus. Nat. Hist., II, 172, 1900. Nō'ôt.—Ibid. Tent.—Can. Ind. Aff. 1894, 277, 1895 (misprint). Yent.—Ibid., 1898, 418, 1899. Yeó't.—Hill-Tout in Rep. Ethnol. Surv. Can., 4, 1899. Yeut.—Can. Ind. Aff., pt. II, 166, 1901. Yout.—Ibid., 1886, 230, 1887. Ze-ut.—Ibid., 1885, 196, 1885.

Noota. One of the four bands into which Lewis (Trav., 175, 1809) divided the Crows.
Noo'-ta-.—Orig. Jour. Lewis and Clark, VI, 103, 1905. Noo-taa.—Lewis and Clark, Jour., 136, 1840. Nootapareescar.—Lewis and Clark Exped., Coues ed., IV, index, 1339, 1893 (names of two divisions erroneously united).

Noothlakimish. An unidentifiable Bellacoola division on North Bentinck Arm, Brit. Col.; mentioned by Tolmie and Dawson, Vocabs. Brit. Col., 122B, 1884.

Nootka. A name originally applied to the Mooachaht (q. v.) of Nootka sd., w. coast of Vancouver id., and to their principal town, Yuquot (q. v.), but subsequently extended to all the tribes speaking a similar language. These extend from C. Cook on the N. to beyond Port San Juan, and include the Makah of C. Flattery, Wash. Sometimes the term has been so used as to exclude the last-named tribe. The Nootka form one branch of the great Wakashan family and their relationship to the second or Kwakiutl branch is apparent only on close examination. In 1906 there were 435 Makah and 2,159 Vancouver id. Nootka; total, 2,594. They are decreasing slowly but steadily, the reduction in population of the Nootka of Vancouver id. alone having exceeded 250 between 1901 and 1906.

NOOTKA WOMAN.   (AM. MUS. NAT. HIST.)

The Nootka tribes are: Ahousaht, Chaicclesaht, Clayoquot, Cooptee, Ehatisaht, Ekoolthaht, Hachaath (extinct), Hesquiat, Kelsemaht, Klahosaht (probably extinct), Kwoneatshatka (?), Kyuquot, Makah, Manosaht, Mooachaht, Muchalat, Nitinat, Nuchatlitz, Oiaht, Opitchesaht, Pacheenaht, Seshart, Toquart, Uchucklesit, and Ucluelet.   (J. R. S.)
Aht.—Sproat, Savage Life, 312, 1868. **Nootka.**—Hale in U. S. Expl. Exped., VI, 220, 569, 1846. **Nootka-Columbian.**—Scouler in Jour. Roy. Geog. Soc., XI, 221, 1841. **Noutka.**—Duflot de Mofras, Expl., II, 344, 1844. **Nuqueño.**—Galiano, Relación, 30, 1802. **Nutka.**—Ibid. **O'menē.**—Boas in 5th Rep. N. W. Tribes Can., 9, 1889 (Comox name). **Ouakichs.**—Duflot de Mofras, op. cit., 335, 345. **Southern.**—Scouler, op. cit., 224. **Tc'Eā'atq.**—Boas, op. cit., 9 (Skokomish name). **Wakash**—Gallatin in Trans. Am. Antiq. Soc., II, 15, 306, 1836.

Nopeming (for *Nō'pimĭngtashĭnenĭwŭg*, 'people of the bush.'—W. J.). A northern branch of the Chippewa, living in Ontario, N. E. of L. Superior and w. of L. Nipissing, and sometimes ranging E. as far as Ottawa r. From their frequently resorting to Sault Ste Marie they have often been confounded with the band at that place, and they have been likewise confused with the Têtes de Boule, q. v.
Men of the woods.—Maclean, Hudson Bay, I, 74, 1849 (so called by other tribes). **Muskegoag.**—Tanner, Narr., 315, 1830 (applied by the Ottawa to them as well as to the Maskegon). **Noapeeming'.**—Schoolcraft, Miss. Val., 299, 1825. **Nopemen d'Achirini.**—Lahontan, New Voy., I, 231, 1703. **Nopemetus Anineeg.**—Tanner, Narr., 315, 1830 (Ottawa name). **Nopemings.**—Schoolcraft, Ind. Tribes, V, 145, 1855. **Nopemin of Achirini.**—Richardson, Arct. Exped., II, 39, 1851. **Nopemit Azhinneneeg.**—Tanner, Narr., 315, 1830 (Ottawa name). **Nopiming daje inini.**—Cuoq, Lex. Algonquine, 129, 1886 ('men of the interior of the lands': Nipissing name). **Nō'pimingtashineniwag.**—Wm. Jones, inf'n, 1906 (correct name). **Nubenaigooching.**—Can. Ind. Aff., 16, 1875. **Opemens d'Acheliny.**—Du Lhut (1684) in Margry, Déc., VI, 51, 1886. **O'pimittish Ininiwac.**—Henry, Trav., 60, 1809. **Wood Indians.**—Ibid.

Noponne (*No'-pon-ne*, 'face', 'front'). The name of the midmost mesa, directly s. of Zuñi pueblo, N. Mex., so named because the face or front (*no'-pon*) of Kolowissi, the mythical serpent of the sea, appeared above the waters of the flood at that point, when the youth and maiden were sacrificed from the top of Thunder mtn. The southern of the 7 shrines of Ahaiyuta and Matsailema, the twin war gods of the Zuñi, is situated there, but no ruin of any kind.   (F. H. C.)
No-pone.—Fewkes in Jour. Am. Eth. and Arch., I, 100, 1891.

Noptac. A former village connected with San Carlos mission, Cal., and said to have been Esselen.—Taylor in Cal. Farmer, Apr. 20, 1860.

Nopthrinthres. A tribe mentioned by Arroyo de la Cuesta (MS., B. A. E.) as settled at the mission of San Juan Bautista, San Benito co., Cal., during the mission period. A vocabulary given by him shows it to have been Yokuts (Mariposan).
Nopochinches.—Garcia MS. quoted by Bancroft, Hist. Cal., II, 339, 1886.

Noquet (*No'ke*, 'bear foot'; another name for the Bear gens (see *Noka*) of the Chippewa.—W. J.). An Algonquian tribe located by the earliest French writers about Noquet bay, at the mouth of Green bay, extending N. across the peninsula to L. Superior. In 1659 they were attached to the mission of St Michel, together with the Menominee, Winnebago, and others. In 1761 Jefferys, probably on the authority of some recent French writer, says they were on the islands at the mouth of Green bay, formerly occupied by the Potawatomi. They were never prominent as a tribe, and were probably absorbed by the Chippewa or the Menominee.
Nikic.—Coxe, Carolana, 48, 1741. **Nikie.**—Ibid., map. **Nocké.**—Du Lhut (1684) in Margry, Déc., VI, 41, 1886. **Noguets.**—Perrot, Mém., 295, 1864. **Nokes.**—Lahontan (1703), New Voy., I, map, 1703. **Nokets.**—Frontenac (1682) in N. Y. Doc. Col. Hist.,

IX, 182, 1855. **Noquai.**—Kelton, Ft Mackinac, 145, 1884. **Noquets.**—Prise de Possession (1671) in Margry, Déc., I, 97, 1875. **Notketz.**—Vaudreuil (1720), ibid., VI, 511, 1886. **Noukek.**—Jes. Rel. 1658, 21, 1858. **Nouquet.** — Jes. Rel. 1670, 79, 1858. **Roquai.**—Jes. Rel. 1640, 34, 1858.

Noquiquahko. A former Salish band of Fraser superintendency, apparently on or near upper Fraser r., Brit. Col.
No-qui-quahko.—Can. Ind. Aff., 78, 1878.

Norajik. An East Greenland Eskimo village on an island in Angmagsalik fjord, lat. 65° 51′; pop. 47 in 1884.—Meddelelser om Grönland, IX, 379, 1889.

Norbos ('southern house'). A general name applied by the Daupom, or Cottonwood Wintun, to the Nummuk, Noamlaki, Nuimok, Noyuki, and Puimuk tribes of the Copehan family.
Norbos.—Powers in Cont. N. A. Ethnol., III, 230, 1877. **Norboss.**—Powers in Overland Mo., XII, 531, 1874.

Norchean. A Maricopa rancheria on the Rio Gila in 1744.—Sedelmair (1744) cited by Bancroft, Ariz. and N. Mex., 366, 1889.

Normuk ('southern'). A Wintun tribe formerly living on Hay fork of Trinity r., Trinity co., Cal. They were the most southerly Wintun tribe of the Trinity group, hence their name. See *Kashahara*.
Noobimucks.—Taylor in Cal. Farmer, June 8, 1860. **Normoc.**—Powers in Overland Mo., IX, 499, 1872. **Nor'-mok.**—Powers in Cont. N. A. Ethnol., III, 231, 1877. **Nor-rel-mok.**—Ibid.

Norogachic ('where there is a rock in front.'—Lumholtz). A Tarahumare settlement on the headwaters of Rio Fuerte, in the middle of the Sierra Madre, lat. 27° 20′, lon. 107°, Chihuahua, Mexico. Pop. about 3,850 Tarahumare in 1900.—See Orozco y Berra, Geog., 323, 1864; Lumholtz in Scribner's Mag., XVI, 32, July 1894; Lumholtz, Unknown Mex., I, 205, 1902.

Norridgewock (from *Nanrantswak*, 'people of the still water between rapids'). A tribe of the Abnaki confederacy, the typical tribe of the group. Their closest relationship was with the Penobscot, Arosaguntacook, and Wewenoc. Their territory embraced the Kennebec valley nearly to the river's mouth, Norridgewock, their principal village, being on the left bank just below the rapids, near the present Norridgewock, Me. The French established a mission at their village in 1688. In 1695 the Jesuit Father Rasles took up his residence there and succeeded in attaching the tribes so warmly to the French cause that they soon came to be regarded as dangerous enemies of the English colonists. In 1724 an expedition was sent against the Norridgewock, which resulted in the destruction of their village, the dispersion of the tribe, and the death of Rasles. They fled in different parties to the Penobscot and Passamaquoddy, and to St Francis in Canada. A number afterward returned and settled in their old home, but owing to the continued unfriendly disposition of the whites, who again attacked their village in 1749, returned at the breaking out of the French and Indian war in 1754 to St Francis. A few families that remained behind for some years finally found their way also to Canada. See *Abnaki, Missions.*   (J. M.)

Aridgevoak.—Bellin, map, 1755. **Aridgewoak.**—Homann Heirs' map, 1756. **Arransoak.**—Montresor (*ca.* 1775) in Me. Hist. Soc. Coll., I, 459, 1865. **Cambas.**—McKenney and Hall, Ind. Tribes, III, 79, 1854 (misprint). **Canabas.**—Ibid. **Canibas.**—Doc. of 1689 in N. Y. Doc. Col. Hist., IX, 433, 1855. **Cannabas.**—McKeen in Me. Hist. Soc. Coll., V, 327, 1857. **Cannibas.**—Jes. Rel. 1611, 5, 1858. **Carribas.**—Aubery (1720) in N. Y. Doc. Col. Hist., IX, 895, 1855 (misprint). **Kanibals.**—Vetromile, Abnakis, 22, 1866. **Kanibas**—Drake, Bk. Inds., bk. 3, 105, 1848. **Kanibats.**—Frontenac (1691) in N. Y. Doc. Col. Hist., IX, 495, 1855. **Kanibesinnoaks.**—Maurault, Hist. des Abenakis, 5, 1866. **Kanibessinnoaks**—Ibid. **Kenabeca.**—Smith (1631) in Mass. Hist. Soc. Coll., 3d s., III, 22, 1833. **Kenabes.**—Willis in Me. Hist. Soc. Coll., IV, 96, 1856. **Kenebecke Indeans.**—Pateshall (1684), ibid., V, 91, 1857. **Kenebeke.** — Purchas (1625), ibid., 156. **Kennebeck Indians.**—Sewall (1721), ibid., III, 351, 1853. **Kennebecks.**—Gookin (1674) in Mass. Hist. Soc. Coll., 1st s., I, 162, 1806. **Kennebeki.**—La Tour, map, 1779. **Kinnebeck Indians.**—Doc. of 1660 in N. Y. Doc. Col. Hist., XIII, 190, 1881. **Nalatchwániak.**—Gatschet, Penobscot MS., B. A. E., 1887 (Penobscot name). **Namgauck.**—Dudley in Me. Hist. Soc. Coll., V, 429, 1857. **Nanrantsoak.**—Rasles (1712) in Mass. Hist. Soc. Coll., 2d s., VIII, 258, 1819. **Nanrantsouak.**—Rasles (1721) ibid., 252. **Nanrants8ak.**—Vaudreuil (1722) in N. Y. Doc. Col. Hist., IX, 910, 1855. **Nanrantswacs.**—Kendall, Trav., III, 63, 1809. **Nänräntswak.**—Vetromile, Abnakis, 24, 1866. **Nantansoüak.**—Vaudreuil (1724) in N. Y. Doc. Col. Hist., IX, 934, 1855 (misprint). **Naragooe.**—Purchas (1625) in Me. Hist. Soc. Coll., V, 156, 1857. **Naranchouak.**—Jes. Rel. 1652, 24, 1858. **Naranchouek.**—Ibid., 30. **Narangawook.**—Gyles (1726) in Me. Hist. Soc. Coll., III, 357, 1853. **Narangawook.**—Ibid. **Narantsoak.**—Charlevoix (1744) quoted by Drake, Bk. Inds., bk. 3, 126, 1848. **Narantsouak.**—Vaudreuil (1724) in Me. Hist. Soc. Coll., VI, 240, 1859. **Narants8ak.**—Beauharnois (1744) in N. Y. Doc. Col. Hist., IX, 1107, 1855. **Narantsouans.**—Vaudreuil (1724), ibid., 937. **Narants8uk.**—Rasles (1721) in Mass. Hist. Soc. Coll., 2d s., VIII, 262, 1819. **Narantswouak.**—Beauharnois (1744) in N. Y. Doc. Col. Hist., IX, 1107, 1855. **Narautsouak.**—Vaudreuil (1721), ibid., 903. **Narauwings.**—Boudinot, Star in the West, 127, 1816. **Narentoch8an.**—Chauvignerie (1736) in N. Y. Doc. Col. Hist., IX, 1052, 1855. **Narent Chouan.**—Chauvignerie quoted by Schoolcraft, Ind. Tribes, III, 553, 1853. **Naridgewalk.**—Penhallow (1726) in N. H. Hist. Soc. Coll. I, 20, 1824. **Naridgwalk.**—Falmouth treaty (1726) in Mass. Hist. Soc. Coll., 4th s., V, 364, 1861. **Narridgwalk.**—Writer of 1724, ibid., 2d s., VIII, 245, 1819. **Narridgwock.**—Pemaquid treaty (1693) quoted by Drake, Bk. Inds, bk. 3, 121, 1848. **Naurantsoüak.**—Vaudreuil (1724) in N. Y. Doc. Col. Hist., IX, 934, 1855. **Naurautsoak.**—Doc. of 1718, ibid., 880. **Naurautsouak.**—Ibid, 881. **Navidgwock.**—Niles (*ca.* 1761) in Mass. Hist. Soc. Coll., 3d s., VI, 235, 1837 (misprint). **Neridgewalk.**—Niles (*ca.* 1761), ibid., 4th s., V, 335, 1861. **Neridgewok.**—Drake, Bk. Inds., bk. 3, 128, 1848. **Neridgiwack.**—Church (1716) quoted by Drake, Ind. Wars, 201, 1825. **Neridgwook.**—Casco conf. (1727) in N. H. Hist. Soc. Coll., II, 261, 1827. **Neridgwook.**—Ibid. **Nerigwok.**—Drake, Ind. Chron., 175, 1836. **Nerridgawock.**—Falmouth conf. (1727) in Me. Hist. Soc. Coll., III, 407, 1853. **Nerridgewock.**—Ibid., 445. **Nolongewock.**—Pynchon (1663) in N. Y. Doc. Col. Hist., XIII, 308, 1881. **Noridgawook.**—Oakman (*ca.* 1690) quoted by Drake, Bk. Inds., bk. 3, 109, 1848. **Noridgewalk.**—Kendall, Trav., III, 48, 1809. **Noridgewoc.**—Ibid. **Noridgewock.**—Church (1689) in Mass. Hist. Soc. Coll., 4th s., V, 222, 1861. **Noridgwoag.**—Jefferys, Fr. Doms., pt. 1, 123, 1761. **Noridgwock.**—

Pemaquid treaty (1693) quoted by Drake, Bk. Inds., bk. 3, 121, 1848. **Norredgewock.**—McKenney and Hall, Ind. Tribes, III, 82, 1854. **Norridegwock.**—Me. Hist. Soc. Coll., III, 357, 1853 (misprint). **Norridgawock.**—Doc. of 1752, ibid., IV, 170, 1856. **Norridgewalk.**—Colman (1726) in N. H. Hist. Soc. Coll., I, 17, 1824. **Norridgewocks.**—Dummer (1726) in Mass. Hist. Soc. Coll., 1st s., VI, 111, 1800. **Norridgowock.**—Treaty jour. (1749) in Me. Hist. Soc. Coll., IV, 145, 1856. **Norridgwak.**—Güssefeld, map, 1784. **Norridgwalk.**—Homann Heirs' map, 1756. **Norridgwocks.**—Penhallow (1726) in N. H. Hist. Soc. Coll., I, 129, 1824. **Norridgwog.**—Rasles (ca. 1720) in Mass. Hist. Soc. Coll., 1st s., X, 137, 1809. **Norridgwogg.**—Coffin (1796) in Me. Hist. Soc. Coll., IV, 313, 1856. **Norrigawake.**—Portsmouth treaty (1713), ibid., VI, 250, 1859. **Norrigewack.**—Dudley (1704) quoted by Drake, Ind. Wars, 220, 1825. **Norrigewock.**—Niles (ca. 1761) in Mass. Hist. Soc. Coll., 3d s., VI, 247, 1837. **Norrigwock.**—Church (1716) quoted by Drake, Ind. Wars, 247, 1825. **Norrijwok.**—Jefferys, Fr. Doms., pt. 1, map, 119, 1761. **Norriwook.**—La Tour, map, 1782. **Norrywok.**—Jefferys, Fr. Doms., pt. 1, map, 1761. **Norwidgewalks.**—Doc. of 1764 in N. Y. Doc. Col. Hist., VII, 641, 1856. **Nurhântsuaks.**—Maurault, Histoire des Abenakis, 5, 1866. **Quenebec Indians.**—Douglass, Summary, I, 184, 1755. **Wawrigweck.**—Smith (1616) in Mass. Hist. Soc. Coll., 3d s., VI, 107, 1837. **Wawrigwick.**—Smith (1631), ibid., III, 22, 1833.

Norsemen. See *Scandinavian influence.*

Norsit. An East Greenland Eskimo village on an island at the mouth of Angmagsalik fjord, lat. 65° 33′; pop. 25 in 1884.—Meddelelser om Grönland, IX, 379, 1889.

Northern Assiniboin. A division of the Assiniboin as recognized about the middle of the 19th century and earlier. Perhaps the same as the Tschantoga (q. v.), or Gens des Bois of Maximilian, and the Wood Stoneys or Stonies of northern Alberta of the present day, although Denig (1854) says they were so called because they came from the N. in 1839. In Denig's time they numbered 60 lodges under Le Robe de Vent.
Assiniboels of the North.—Jefferys, Am. Atlas, map 8, 1776. **Assiniboins of the North.**—Jefferys, French Dom. Am., pt. 1, map, 1761. **Gens du Nord.**—Hayden, Ethnog. and Philol. Mo. Val., 387, 1862. **Northern People.**—Denig quoted by Dorsey in 15th Rep. B. A. E., 223, 1897. **Tokum′-pi.**—Hayden, op. cit. **Wah-ze-ah we-chas-ta.**—Denig, op. cit. **Wah′-zi-ah.**—Hayden, op. cit.

Northern Comanche. The name by which the Kwahari, Ditsakana, and Detsanayuka were sometimes designated collectively to distinguish them from the Penateka, who were known as Eastern or Southern Comanche.—Mooney in 14th Rep. B. A. E., 1045, 1896.

North Fork. A village in the Canadian district of the Creek Nation, Ind. T., in 1858 (Smith in Ind. Aff. Rep., 149, 1858). The name doubtless refers to the N. fork of Canadian r.

North Herndon. A Netchilirmiut Eskimo village at Felix harbor, Boothia, Can.—Ross, Second Voy., 249, 1835.

Norumbega. A name used by explorers and cartographers of the 16th and the first half of the 17th century to designate the Penobscot r. in Maine, a fabulous great city upon its banks, and a province or "kingdom," including the adjacent New England coast, and sometimes extended in its application to include the whole coast region from Nova Scotia to Virginia. It occurs as Aranbega on the map of Hieronimus Verrazano of 1529, as Auorobagra on a Jomard map of 1543, and as Nurumbega on the Gastaldi map of 1550. With better knowledge of the region the province disappeared and the great city dwindled to a few wigwams at a place called by the Penobscot Indians Agguncia, supposed (Godfrey in Me. Hist. Soc. Coll., VII, 1876) to have been about the present site of Brewer, opposite Bangor, on Penobscot r., Me.

The derivation of the name has been much disputed, but it is generally admitted to be of Indian origin, although attempts have been made to give it a Norse meaning. According to Vetromile, the best recent authority on the Abnaki language, the correct Abnaki form is Nolumbeka, meaning 'a succession of falls and still water', used by the Indians to designate certain parts of Penobscot r., and not the river itself. Father Sebastian Rasles, author of the great Abnaki dictionary, gives the form as Aränmbeg8k, 'au fond de l'eau', from *aränm*, 'au fond'; but which Hewitt thinks means 'at the clay inlet'. According to Gatschet (Nat. Geog. Mag., VIII, 23, 1897), Penobscot *nalambigi* and Passamaquoddy *nalabégik* both refer to the still, quiet (*nala-*) stretch of a river between two riffles, rapids, or cascades; *-bégik*, for *nipégik*, means 'at the water.' A manuscript authority quoted by Winsor (Hist. Am., III, 184, 1884) gives the Penobscot form as Nah-rah-bĕ-gek. De Costa, in the same volume, inclines to a European origin for the name, which Beauvois (1880) derives from Norroenbygda, 'Norway country', and Horsford (Discov. Anc. City Norumbega, 1890) from Norbega, an ancient name for Norway, claiming also to identify the river as Charles r., Mass., and the town site as at the present Watertown.   (J. M.)
Aggoncy.—De Costa in Winsor, Hist. Am., III, 184, 1884. **Agguncia.**—Heylin in Me. Hist. Soc. Coll., VII, 99, 1876. **Agoncy.**—Thevet (1556) quoted by Kohl, Discov. of Me., 416, 1869. **Arambeck.**—Ogilby (1671) in Me. Hist. Soc. Coll., VII, 99, 1876. **Arampec.**—Heylin, ibid., 99. **Aranbega.**—Map of Hieronimus Verrazano (1529) noted by Kohl, op. cit., 291. **Aranmbeg8k.**—Rasles, Abnaki Dict., 1691. **Auorobagra.**—Jomard, map (1543), as reproduced by Kohl, op. cit., 351. **Nah-rah-bĕ-gek.**—Winsor, Hist. Am., III, 184, 1884. **Nolumbeghe.**—Ibid. **Nolumbeka.**—Vetromile, Abnakis, 45, 1866. **Norambegue.**—Jes. Rel. 1611, 2, 1858. **Norembega.**—Blaeu, map (1642), reproduced by Kohl, op. cit., 315. **Norembegua.**—Oldmixon, Brit. Empire, II, 363, 1708. **Norembegue.**—Champlain (1604), Œuvres, III, 26, 1870. **Norimbegue.**—Jefferys, Fr. Doms., I, 98, 1761. **Norombega.**—Mercator, map (1569), reproduced by Kohl, op. cit., 384. **Norumbega.**—Champlain (1605) in Me. Hist. Soc. Coll., VII, 93, 1876; also Hondius map (ca. 1590) reproduced by Kohl, op. cit., 315. **Norumbegua.**—Heylin in Me. Hist. Soc. Coll., 2d s., I, 99, 1869. **Norumbegue.**—Champlain (1636), ibid., VII, 253.

Nurumberg.—Ruscelli, map·(1561), ibid., 2d s., I, 233, 1869 (evidently a form suggested by the name of the German city Nuremberg). **Nvrvmbega.**—Gastaldi, map (1550), as reproduced by·Kohl, op. cit., 226.

Norwalk. A band holding lands on Norwalk and Saugatuck rs., s. w. Conn., which they sold in 1640 and 1641, Mahackemo being then the principal chief (De Forest, Inds. Conn., 177, 1851). No tribal name is given this people, but they were probably closely connected with the Paugusset, about Stratford, or with the more important Quinnipiac about New Haven.   (J. M.)

Norwootuc. An Algonquian tribe or band whose possessions extended from the "great falls" at South Hadley to Mt Sugar Loaf, in the Connecticut valley, Mass. They were attacked by the Mohegan about 1656, and were at war with the Montauk and Narraganset. They were probably a part of the Indians who took part in King Philip's war of 1675 and afterward fled the country, as "Norwootuck plantations" are mentioned in 1678 as if a new English settlement. The Norwootuc were probably the "Nowonthewog or the Eastward Indians," who in 1700 combined with the Mohawk against the English colonists.   (J. M.)

Nalvotogy.—Pynchon (1677) in N. Y. Doc. Col. Hist., XIII, 511, 1881. **Nalwetog.**—Pynchon (1663), ibid., 308. **Narwootuck.**—Leete (1675) in Mass. Hist. Soc. Coll., 4th s., VII, 579, 1865. **Norwootuck.**—Bishop (1678), ibid., VIII, 306, 1868. **Norwottock.**—Doc. (*ca.* 1657) in N. H. Hist. Soc. Coll., III, 96, 1832. **Norwottucks.**—White, Old-time Haunts, 7, 1903. **Norwuthick.**—Quanapaug (1675) in Mass. Hist. Soc. Coll., 1st s., VI, 207, 1800. **Nowonthewog.**—Doc. of 1700 in N. Y. Doc. Col. Hist., IV, 614, 1854.

Noscaric. A Maricopa rancheria on the Rio Gila, Arizona, in 1744.—Sedelmair (1744) cited by Bancroft, Ariz. and N. Mex., 366, 1889.

Nostic. A former settlement of the Tepecano or of a related tribe who may have been replaced by Tlaxcaltec introduced by the Spaniards in the 18th century as a defence against the "Chichimecs." Situated on the Rio de Bolaños, about 4½ m. s. of Mezquitic, in Jalisco, Mexico.—Hrdlicka in Am. Anthrop., V, 388, 409, 1903.

Nastic.—Mota Padilla (1742), Hist. de la Conq., 354, 1870.

Notaloten. A Koyukukhotana village on Yukon r., Alaska, 20 m. above the mouth of Koyukuk r. Pop. 37 in 1844; 15 in 1890.

Natulaten.—Petroff in 10th Census, Alaska, map, 1884. **Nohtalohton.**—Post-route map, 1903. **Notaglita.**—Zagoskin quoted by Petroff, op. cit., 37. **Notaloten.**—Baker, Geog. Dict. Alaska, 1901.

Notched plates. Stone plates of discoidal or rectangular form obtained mainly from ancient mounds in the Ohio valley and the Southern states. Heretofore these plates have been classed with problematical objects (q. v.), and the significance of some specimens remains yet in doubt; but Moore has shown that those obtained in Alabama were undoubtedly used in grinding pigments. It is also observed that a close analogy exists between these tablets and the pigment plates employed by the Pueblos and other Southwestern tribes, and also frequently encountered among the ancient ruins of the S. W. (Fewkes, Russell). The rectangular specimens rarely exceed 10 in. in width by about 15 in length, and the discoidal variety ranges from 6 to 15 in. in diameter. The thickness does not exceed 1½ in. The central portion of one face is often slightly concave, a few are quite flat on both faces, while a smaller number are doubly convex in a slight degree. The margins are square or roundish in section. With rare exceptions the periphery of the discoidal plates is notched or scalloped. In many cases one or more engraved lines or grooves encircle the face of the plate near the margin, and not infrequently the marginal notches extend as shallow grooves inward over

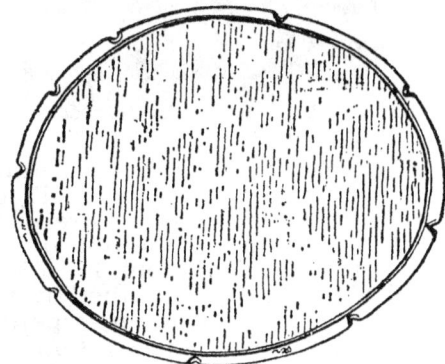

PLAIN PLATE, ALABAMA; DIAM. 7 IN.

the surface of the plate, terminating against the outer encircling band, or connect as loops forming what may be regarded as reversed scallops. The most striking feature of these plates, occurring perhaps in one case in ten, is certain engraved designs occupying the reverse side of the plate, the grinding surface being regarded as the obverse. These subjects are undoubtedly of mythologic origin and include highly conventional representations of the human hand, the open eye, the rattlesnake, death's-head symbols, etc. The rectangular plates have notches or scallops at the ends only, and the surface, excepting in the Ohio specimens (which are tentatively included in this group), has no embellishment other than simple engraved lines extending across the plate near the ends or continuing around the four sides just inside the border.

The most noteworthy of the rectangular plates are the Cincinnati tablet, from a mound in Cincinnati, Ohio, described by

Clark, and by Putnam and Willoughby; the Hurst tablet, found in Pike co., Ohio; the Berlin tablet, found in Jackson co., Ohio, and a number of other decorated specimens from Southern mounds, described by Rau, Moore, and others. Interesting examples of the discoidal plates are the Naples, Ill., speci-

CINCINNATI TABLET, OHIO; LENGTH 5 IN.

men, described by Henderson, and the Arkansas Post specimen, described by Stoddard. These two disks are without marginal notches. Numerous discoidal tablets obtained from mounds in Mississippi and Alabama are described by Moore and Holmes. The feathered serpent tablet from Issaquena co., Miss., the knotted serpent tablet from Moundville, Ala., and other pictured specimens from the latter locality, described by the same authors, are deserving of special mention.

It is observed that these plates are made of sandstone and kindred gritty materials, and this fact confirms Moore's conclusion that they were used in grinding pigments. That they were held in exceptional esteem by their owners is shown by their burial with the dead. These facts indicate clearly that the plates were not intended to serve an ordinary purpose, but rather that they filled some important sacred or ceremonial office, as in preparing colors for shamanistic use or for religious ceremonies. The engraved designs on these plates naturally give rise to speculation, and it is not surprising

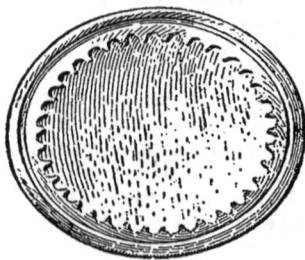

STODDARD PLATE, ARKANSAS; DIAM. 11⅜ IN.

that the very general presence of notched and scalloped margins should suggest the theory that the plates were sun symbols. But a critical examination of the various markings and figures leads to the conviction that all are representative, in a more or less conventional fashion, of animal originals and that all were probably employed because of their peculiar esoteric significance and relationship with the functions of the tablets. It is observed that the notches cut in the edges of the plates are in many instances carried inward over the plate in such a way as to suggest feathers, as these are often formally treated in native art, and this leads to the surmise that the animal original might have been a duck—a symbol of wide distribution among the Indian tribes in the S.; but recalling the

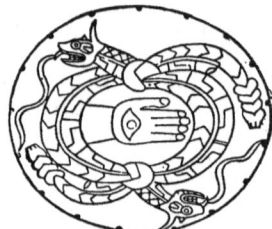

KNOTTED SERPENT PLATE, ALABAMA; DIAM. 12½ IN. (UNIVERSITY OF ALABAMA)

occurrence of the feathered-serpent design engraved on the obverse of the Mississippi tablet, the idea is suggested that the original concept in the mind of the makers of these plates was, at least in some cases, the feathered serpent, a northern form of Quetzalcoatl, a chief deity of the middle American peoples.

A noteworthy feature of the engravings of the serpents and other figures on these mound tablets is the apparent maturity

FEATHERED SERPENT PLATE, MISSISSIPPI; DIAM. 8½ IN. (OHIO STATE ARCHÆOLOGICAL AND HISTORICAL SOCIETY.)

of the art, the intricate forms being skilfully disposed and drawn with a certain hand. The designs are not mere random products, but, like the copper ornaments, the earthenware decorations, and the shell engravings of the Gulf states, were evidently made by skilled artists practising a well-matured art which distinctly suggests the work of the semicivilized nations of Mexico and Central America. These plates may be regarded as furnishing additional proof that the influence of the culture of middle America has been felt all along the northern shores of the Gulf of Mexico and has passed with diminished force still farther to the N.

Consult Clark, Prehist. Remains, 1876; Farquharson in Proc. Davenport Acad. Sci., II, 1877-80; Fewkes in 22d Rep. B. A. E., 1904; Fowke, Archæol. Hist. Ohio, 1902; Henderson in Smithson. Rep. 1882, 1884; Holmes (1) in 2d Rep. B. A. E., 1883, (2) in Am. Anthrop., VIII, no. 1, 1906; Jones, Antiq. So. Inds., 1873; McLean, Mound Builders, 1879; Moore in Jour. Acad. Nat. Sci. Phila., XIII, 1905; Moorehead in Pub. Ohio State Archæol. and Hist. Soc., V, 1897; Putnam and Willoughby in Proc. A. A. A. S., XLIV, 1896; Rau in Smithson. Cont., XXII, 1876; Russell in 26th Rep. B. A. E., 1907; Short, N. Am. Antiq., 1880; Squier and Davis in Smithson. Cont., I, 1848; Stoddard in Am. Antiq., XXIV, no. 3, 1904; Thomas in 12th Rep. B. A. E., 1894; Thruston, Antiq. Tenn., 1897; Wilson in Rep. Nat. Mus. 1896, 1898. (w. H. H.)

Notch-ee-ning-a. See *Nacheninga*.

Notha ('Ute'). A Navaho clan.
Noçà.—Matthews in Jour. Am. Folk-lore, III, 103, 1890. Noçàḍine.—Ibid. Notá.—Matthews, Navaho Legends, 30, 1897. Notáḍine'.—Ibid.

Notomidula. A former village of the Awani, about 400 yds. E. of Machito, in Yosemite valley, Mariposa co., Cal.
Notomidoola.—Powers in Overland Mo., X, 333, 1874. No-to-mid-u-la.—Powers in Cont. N. A. Ethnol., III, 365, 1877.

Notre Dame de Foye. A former mission village near Quebec, settled by some Hurons from Huronia, who removed to Lorette in 1693.—Shea, Cath. Miss., 198, 1855.

Nottoway. An Iroquoian tribe formerly residing on the river of the same name in S. E. Virginia. They called themselves Cheroenhaka, and were known to the neighboring Algonquian tribes as Mangoac (Mengwe) and Nottoway, i. e., Nadowa (q. v.), 'adders,' a common Algonquian name for tribes of alien stock. Although never prominent in history they kept up their organization long after the other tribes of the region were practically extinct. As late as 1825 they still numbered 47, with a "queen," on a reservation in Southampton co. Linguistically they were closely cognate to the Tuscarora. See *Nadowa*. (J. M.)
Che-ro-ha-ka.—Morgan in N. Am. Review, 52, 1870. Mandoages.—Lane (1586) in Smith (1629), Va., I, 91, repr. 1819. Mandongs.—Strachey (ca. 1612), Va., 147, 1849 (misprint). Mangoacks.—Lane (1586) in Smith, Va., I, 87, repr. 1819. Mangoags.—Smith (1629), ibid., 75. Mangoako.—Lane (1586) in Hakluyt, Voy., III, 314, 1810. Mangoangs.—Strachey (ca. 1612), Va., 41, 1849. Moyoacks.—Martin, North Carolina, I, 15, 1829 (misprint). Nâ'tow̌ewok.—Gerard in Am. Anthrop., VI, 319, 1904 (Cree name;

sing. *Nâ'tow̌ĕu*). Notowegee.—Logan, Upper South Carolina, I, 428, 1859. Nottawayes.—Beverley, Va., bk. 3, 63, 1705. Nottoway.—Lawson (1709), North Carolina, 383, 1860. Ontationoué.—N. Y. Doc. Col. Hist., IX, 1057, 1855. Tciruen-haka.—Hewitt, inf'n, 1889 (common name as given by the Iroquois; possibly 'fork of a stream'). Wanjoacks.—Martin, North Carolina, I, 14, 1829 (misprint).

Nouista. An unidentified village or tribe in alliance with the Kadohadacho in 1687.—Joutel in Margry, Déc., III, 410, 1878.

Noutchaoff. An unidentified Bellacoola town on a river of the same name in British Columbia.
Nout-chaoff.—Mayne, Brit. Col., 147, 1862.

Novaculite. A very fine-grained and compact chalcedonic (quartz) rock, ordinarily white or whitish in color, and often distinguished by the archeologist by its somewhat translucent waxen appearance. It occurs in vast bodies in connection with Ordovician (Lower Silurian) strata in Arkansas, especially in the vicinity of Hot Springs, where it was extensively quarried by the aborigines. The ancient excavations here cover many hundreds of acres of the mountain ridges and are surrounded by large bodies of refuse—the result of roughing-out implements by flaking processes. As with the great quarries of Flint Ridge, Ohio, and other localities, the principal product was the leaf-shaped blade, from which arrow- and spear-heads and knives were to be specialized, but the material was used also for axes, celts, ceremonial objects, and ornaments, in the manufacture of which the flaking work was supplemented by pecking and grinding. See *Chalcedony*, *Mines and Quarries*, *Quartz*, *Stonework*.

Consult Griswold in Rep. Geol. Surv. Ark., III, 1890–2; Holmes in Am. Anthrop., V, Oct. 1891; Kunz, Gems and Precious Stones, 1890; Merrill, Rocks, Rock-weathering and Soils, 1897. (w. H. H.)

Novaia. An Ingalik village on the lower Yukon, Alaska; pop. 52 in 1880.—Petroff, Rep. on Alaska, 62, 1881.

Novoktolak. A Kuskwogmiut Eskimo village in the Kuskokwim district, Alaska; pop. 55 in 1890.
Novokhtolahamiut.—Eleventh Census, Alaska, 164, 1893.

Nowadaga. A former Mohawk village on the S. bank of Mohawk r., at the mouth of Nowadaga cr., on the site of Danube, Herkimer co., N. Y. It was the principal Mohawk settlement about 1750. A part of the band here had another village a little lower down the stream, opposite the mouth of East Canada cr. Nowadaga was long the home of Joseph Brant (Thayendanegea).
Nowadaga.—Macauley, N. Y., II, 226, 1829. Nowodaga.—Ibid., 181.

Nowe. Mentioned by Bartram (Travels, 371, 1792) as a Cherokee settlement, about 1775, one of four towns "inland on the branches of the Tanase [Tennessee]." It can not be certainly identified.

Nowi. A Yukonikhotana village on the s. side of Yukon r., at the mouth of Nowikakat r., Alaska, having 107 inhabitants in 1880.
Newi-cargut.—Wymper, Trav. and Advent., map, 1869. Newikargut.—Raymond in Sen. Ex. Doc. 12, 42d Cong., 1st sess., 23, 1871. Nowikakat.—Petroff, Rep. on Alaska, 62, 1881. Noya-kakat.—Petroff, map of Alaska, 1880. Noyokakat.—Petroff in 10th Census, Alaska, 12, 1884.

Noxa. Mentioned by Oviedo (Hist. Gen. Indies, III, 628, 1853) as one of the provinces or villages visited by Ayllon in 1520; probably on the South Carolina coast.

Noyuki ('southern aliens'). The name applied by their northern neighbors to a Maidu tribe formerly occupying the territory about the junction of Yuba and Feather rs., Yuba co., Cal. One of their villages, Yupu, was on the site of the present Yuba city.
Noi-Yucans.—Gieger in Ind. Aff. Rep. 1859, 438, 1860.

Npapuk (*N'på'puk·*). A Squawmish village community on the E. side of Howe sd., Brit. Col.—Hill-Tout in Rep. Brit. A. A. S., 474, 1900.

Npiktim ('white hollow'). A village of the Ntlakyapamuk, so called, according to Hill-Tout, because it was the place where the Indians obtained the white clay they burnt and used for cleaning wool, etc. Pop. 19 in 1897, the last time the name officially appears.
Mpaktam.—Can. Ind. Aff. 1886, 230, 1887. N'pEk'-tEm.—Hill-Tout in Rep. Ethnol. Surv. Can., 5, 1899. Npîktî'm.—Teit in Mem. Am. Mus. Nat. Hist., II, 169, 1900. S'înpûktî'm.—Ibid.

Npokwis (*N'pŏk·wis*). A Squawmish village community on the right bank of Squawmisht r., Brit. Col.—Hill-Tout in Rep. Brit. A. A. S., 474, 1900.

Npuichin (*Npuitci'n*, 'low ridge shore'). A village of the Lytton band of Ntlakyapamuk on the w. side of Fraser r., 8 m. above Lytton, Brit. Col.—Teit in Mem. Am. Mus. Nat. Hist., II, 172, 1900.

Nra Sra. For all references beginning with this abbreviation, or with N. S., see *Nuestra Señora.*

Nsisket (*Nsi'sqEt*, 'the little split or divide', perhaps because near a deep or rocky gulch). A village of the Nicola band of Ntlakyapamuk near Nicola r., a few miles from the w. end of Nicola lake, Brit. Col. Pop. 21 in 1901, the last time the name is given.
Hun-ka-sis-ket.—Can. Ind. Aff. 1883, pt. 1, 191, 1884. N'oïckt.—Hill-Tout in Rep. Ethnol. Surv. Can., 4, 1899. Neyiskat.—Can. Ind. Aff. 1894, 277, 1895. Nsi'sqEt.—Teit in Mem. Am. Mus. Nat. Hist., II, 174, 1900. Nyiskat.—Can. Ind. Aff., 361, 1895. Nzis-kat.—Ibid., 1886, pt. 1, 232, 1887. Nzyshat.—Ibid., pt. II, 166, 1901.

Nskakaulten (*Nsqa'qaultEn*, 'little looking-for-game place'). A village of the Ntlakyapamuk on the s. side of Thompson r., 23 m. above Lytton, and ½ m. below Spences Bridge, Brit. Col.
Nsqa'qaultEn.—Teit in Mem. Am. Mus. Nat. Hist., II, 172, 1900. Spences Bridge [Indians].—Can. Ind. Aff., 79, 1878.

Ntekem (*Ntê'qEm*, 'to make muddy', or 'muddy creek'). A village of the Spences Bridge band of Ntlakyapamuk on the N. side of Thompson r., about 1 m. back from the stream and 39 m. above Lytton, Brit. Col.
N'tāi'kum.—Hill-Tout in Rep. Ethnol. Surv. Can., 4, 1899. Ntê'qEm—Teit in Mem. Am. Mus. Nat. Hist., II, 173, 1900. Oregon Jacks.—Name given by whites.

Nthaich (*N'çai'tc*). A Squawmish village on the right bank of Squawmisht r., Brit. Col.—Hill-Tout in Rep. Brit. A. A. S., 474, 1900.

Ntlaktlakitin (*NLaqLa'kîtîn*, 'the crossing place', 'place for crossing the river'). A village of the Lytton band of Ntlakyapamuk at Kanaka Bar, Fraser r., about 11 m. below Lytton, Brit. Col., with 55 inhabitants in 1906. Some Indians class it with the Lower Ntlakyapamuk.
Hlakklaktan.—Can. Ind. Aff. 1892, 312, 1893. Hlu-hlu-natan.—Ibid., pt. II, 164, 1901. Hlukhluka-tan.—Ibid., 230, 1886. Hluk-kluk-a-tan.—Ibid., 1885, pt. 1, 196, 1886. Kanaka Bar.—Ibid., 1897, 363, 1898. NLaqLa'kîtîn.—Teit in Mem. Am. Mus. Nat. Hist., II, 171, 1900.

Ntlakyapamuk. One of the four great Salish tribes inhabiting the interior of British Columbia and popularly called Thompson Indians, from the river on which a large

NTLAKYAPAMUK MAN.   (AM. MUS. NAT. HIST.)

part of them live. Internally they are divided into the Lower Thompsons, living from a short distance below Spuzzum on Fraser r., nearly to the village of Cisco, and the Upper Thompsons, whose towns extend from the latter point nearly to Lillooet on the Fraser, to within a short distance of Ashcroft on the Thompson, and over all of Nicola valley. The Upper Thompsons are subdivided by Teit into

4 minor bands, the Lytton band, the Nicola band, the Spences Bridge band, and the Upper Fraser band. In addition the following subdivisions are mentioned: Ainslie Creek, Boothroyds, Canoe Lake Indians, Cooks Ferry, Rhaap, Skowtous, and Snakaim. Total population 1,826 in 1902, 1,776 in 1906. The following list of villages was obtained principally from Teit:

Villages of the Lower Thompsons: Chetawe, Kalulaadlek, Kapachichin, Kapaslok, Kimus, Kleaukt, Koiaum, Nkakim, Nkattsim, Nkoiam, Noieltsi, Npiktim, Ntsuwiek, Sintaktl, Skohwak, Skuzis, Skwauyik, Spaim, Spuzzum, Stahehani, Suk, Taqwayaum, Tikwalus, Tliktlaketin, Tzauamuk.

Villages of the Lytton band: Anektettim, Cisco, Kittsawat, Natkelptetenk, Nchekchekokenk, Nehowmean, Nikaomin, Nkoikin, Nkya, Noöt, Npuichin, Ntlaktlakitin, Staiya, Stryne, Tlkamcheen, Tuhezep.

Villages of the Upper Fraser band: Ahulka, Nesikeep, Nkaktko, Ntlippaem, Skekaitin, Tiaks.

Villages of the Spences Bridge band: Atchitchiken, Klukluuk, Nkamchin, Nkoeit-

NTLAKYAPAMUK WOMAN. (AM. MUS. NAT. HIST.)

ko, Nokem, Nskakaulten, Ntekem, Nukaatko, Pekaist, Pemainus, Semehau, Snapa, Spatsum, Stlaz, Tlotlowuk, Zakhauzsiken.

Villages of the Nicola band: Hanehewedl, Huthutkawedl, Koiskana, Kwilchana, Naaik, Nchekus, Nsisket, Ntstlatko, Petutek, Shahanik, Tsulus, Zoht.

To these the following names must be added, although one or two of them

may possibly be synonyms: Cheuek, Kokoiap, Nhaiiken, Nkahlimiluh, Nkaih, Nzatzahatko, Paska, Rhaap, Schaeken, Shkuet, Shkuokem, Shuimp, Skappa, Snakaim, Spapium, Timetl, Tsuzel.

For detailed information consult Teit in Mem. Am. Mus. Nat. Hist., II, pt. IV, 1900, and Hill-Tout in Rep. Ethnol. Surv. Can., Brit. A. A. S., 1899. (J. R. S.)

Cē′qtamux.—Teit in Mem. Am. Mus. Nat. Hist., II, 167, 1900 (Lillooet name, from name of Thompson r.). Clunsus.—Bancroft, Nat. Races, I, 311, 1874. Couteaux.—Taylor in Cal. Farmer, July 19, 1862. Klackarpun.—Survey map, Hydrog. Office, U. S. N., 1882. Knife Indians.—Teit, op. cit. (name given by employees Hudson Bay Co.). Knives.—Anderson quoted by Gibbs in Hist. Mag., VII, 76, 1863. Lükatimü′x.—Teit, op. cit. (Okinagan name). Neklakapamuk.—Can. Ind. Aff., 15, 1879. Neklakussamuk.—Brit. Col. map, Ind. Aff., Victoria, 1872. N-hla-kapm-uh.—Mackay quoted by Dawson in Trans. Roy. Soc. Can., sec. II, 6, 1891. Nicoutameens.—Mayne, Brit. Col., 296, 1862. Nicoutamuch.—Ibid. Nicute-much.—Anderson, op. cit. Nitlakapamuk.—Good, Offices in Nitlakapamuk, 1880. Nko′atamux.—Teit, op. cit., 167 (Shuswap name). N-ku-tam-euh.—Mackay, op. cit., 5. Nkutĕmíχu.—Gatschet, MS., B. A. E. (Okinagan name). NLak′a′pamux.—Teit, op. cit. (own name, sometimes given to Lytton band alone). N′tlaka′-pamuQ.—Hill-Tout in Rep. Ethnol. Surv. Can., 10, 1899. N-tla-kā-pe-mooh.—Dawson in Trans. Roy. Soc. Can., sec. II, 6, 1891. Ntlakya′pamuQ.—Boas in 5th Rep. N.W. Tribes Can., 10, 1889. Sa′lic.—Teit, op. cit. (Okinagan name). Saw-meena.—Anderson, op. cit., 71 (so called by the Tait, a Cowichan tribe). SEmā′mila.—Teit, op. cit. (so called by the Cowichan of Fraser delta). Ske-yuh.—Mackay, op. cit. ('the people': own name). Somena.—Ibid. ('inland hunters': Cowichan name). Thompson River Indians.—Dawson, ibid., 6 (name given by whites). Thompsons.—Ibid.

Ntlippaem (*NLĭp′pa′Em*, 'to extract marrow', according to Teit; 'deep', according to Hill-Tout). A village of the Upper Fraser band of Ntlakyapamuk on the w. side of Fraser r., 22 m. above Lytton, Brit. Col.

Nick-el-palm.—Brit. Col. map., Ind. Aff., Victoria, 1872. Nitlpam.—Can. Ind. Aff., 78, 1878. N′k·lpan.—Hill-Tout in Rep. Ethnol. Surv. Can., 4, 1899. NLĭp′pa′Em.—Teit in Mem. Am. Mus. Nat. Hist., II, 172, 1900.

Ntlkius (*NLki′us*). An Okinagan town on Similkameen r., Brit. Col.—Teit in Mem. Am. Mus. Nat. Hist., II, 174, 1900.

Ntshaautin ('people down against the island'). A Takulli sept dwelling along Blackwater r. and upper Nechaco r., Brit. Col., in the villages of Tluskez, Ilkatsho, and Peltkatchek. Former villages were Tsitsi and Ilrak, now abandoned. Pop. 135 in 1893.

Natcotetains.—Domenech, Deserts N. Am., I, 442, 1860. Nazeteoten.—Smet, Oregon Miss., 100, 1847. Nechao-tin.—Brit. Col. map, Ind. Aff., Victoria, 1872. Neguia Dinais.—Mackenzie, Voy., 309, 1801. Neotetain.—Schoolcraft, Ind. Tribes, V, 59, 1855. Ntshaantin.—Domenech, Deserts N. Am., II, 62, 1860. Ntshaáutin.—Hale, Ethnog. and Philol., 202, 1846. Nu-tcah-′tenne.—Morice in Trans. Can. Inst., IV, 25, 1893. Nu-tca-′tenne.—Ibid.

Ntsiyamis (*Ntsi-ya′-mīs*). A former Kuitsh village on lower Umpqua r., Oreg.—Dorsey in Jour. Am. Folk-lore, III, 231, 1890.

Ntstlatko (*NtsLa′tko*, 'cold water'). A village of the Nicola band of the Ntlak-

yapamuk near Nicola r., a few miles from the w. end of Nicola lake, Brit. Col.
Coldwater.—Teit in Mem. Am. Mus. Nat. Hist., II 174, 1900 (white man's name). **Ntsaɪʼa'tko.**—Ibid. **NtsʟAʼtko.**—Ibid.

Ntsuwiek (*Ntsuwi'ĕk*). A village of the Ntlakyapamuk on the w. side of Fraser r., 27 m. above Yale, Brit. Col.—Teit in Mem. Am. Mus. Nat. Hist., II, 169, 1900.

Nuaguntits (*Nu-a'-gun-tits*). A Paiute band formerly living near Las Vegas, s. E. Nevada; pop. 161 in 1873.—Powell in Ind. Aff. Rep. 1873, 50, 1874.

Nualik. A ruined Eskimo village on the E. coast of Greenland, lat. 67° 16'.—Meddelelser om Grönland, XXVII, map, 1902.

Nubviakchugaluk. A Malemiut Eskimo village on the N. coast of Norton sd., Alaska; pop. 30 in 1880.
Nubviakchugaluk.—Petroff in 10th Census, Alaska, 11, 1884.

Nucassee (*Nĭ'kwăsĭ*, or *Nikw'sĭ'*, meaning lost). An important ancient Cherokee settlement on Little Tennessee r., where now is the town of Franklin, in Macon co., N. C. A large mound marks the site of the townhouse.
Nikwăsĭ.—Mooney in 19th Rep. B. A. E., 527, 1900 (or Nikw'sĭ'). **Nucasse.**—Bartram, Travels, 371, 1792. **Nuckasee.**—Doc. of 1755 quoted by Royce in 5th Rep. B. A. E., 142, 1887. **Nukeza.**—Doc. of 1799, ibid., 144.

Nuchatl. The principal village of the Nuchatlitz on Esperanza inlet, w. coast of Vancouver id.—Can. Ind. Aff., 264, 1902.

Nuchatlitz ('mountain house.'—Sproat). A Nootka tribe occupying the village of Nuchatl and others on Nuchalitz and Esperanza inlets, w. coast of Vancouver id. Pop. 74 in 1902, 62 in 1904, 52 in 1906.
Neu-chad-lits.—Jewitt, Narr., 36, repr. 1849. **Neuchalits.**—Armstrong, Oregon, 136, 1857. **Neuchallet.**—Mayne, Brit. Col., 251, 1862. **Noochahlaht.**—Sproat, Savage Life, 308, 1868. **Nooch-aht-aht.**—Can. Ind. Aff. 1894, 357, 1895. **Nooch-ahtl-aht.**—Ibid., 1896, 430, 1897. **Nooch-alh-laht.**—Ibid., 1883, 188, 1884. **Noochartl-aht.**—Ibid., 1894, 276, 1895. **Noochatl-aht.**—Ibid., 52, 1875. **Nutcā'tlath.**—Boas in 6th Rep. N. W. Tribes Can., 31, 1890.

Nuchawayi. The plural of Nuta, the name applied by the Yokuts in the plains to the Yokuts and Shoshonean tribes of the Sierra Nevada to the E. in California. The Nuchawayi are mentioned as a party to the treaty of Apr. 29, 1851.
New-chow-we.—Royce in 18th Rep. B. A. E., 782, 1899. **Nu-chow-we.**—Barbour in Sen. Ex. Doc. 4, 32d Cong., spec. sess., 255, 1853.

Nuchek. A Chugachigmiut Eskimo village where the Russians established a stockade and trading post, about 1793, known as Ft Konstantine, at Port Etches, Hinchinbrook id., Prince William sd., Alaska. Pop. 74 in 1880, 145 in 1890.
Natcheek.—Baker, Geog. Dict. Alaska, 471, 1906. **Noocheek.**—Ibid. **Nuchek.**—Ibid. (proper form). **Nūchig'mūt.**—Dall in Cont. N. A. Ethnol., I, 21, 1877 (the people). **Nuchusk.**—Mahony in Ind. Aff. Rep. 1869, 575, 1870. **Nutschek.**—Baker, op. cit.

Nuchschi ('descended from heaven'). A Knaiahkhotana clan of Cook inlet,

Alaska.—Richardson, Arct. Exped., I, 407, 1851.

Nuchu. A Miwok division on the s. fork of Merced r., Cal.
Nūt'-chu.—Powers in Cont. N. A. Ethnol., III, 349, 1877.

Nuchumatuntunne ('people in the timber country'). A former Tututni village on the N. side of Rogue r., Oreg., near the mouth.
Nu'-tcu-ma'-tûn ɟûn'nĕ.—Dorsey in Jour. Am. Folklore, III, 233, 1890.

Nuchwugh. A band of Salish, perhaps of the Lummi, on L. Whatcom, Wash.
Neuk-wers.—Ind. Aff. Rep. 1857, 326, 329, 1858. **Núchwugh.**—Gibbs, MS. no. 248, B. A. E. **Sticks.**—Fitzhugh in Ind. Aff. Rep., 326, 1857. **Wood Indians.**—Simmons, ibid., 224, 1858.

Nuculaha. A subdivision or clan of the Apohola or Buzzard phratry of the ancient Timucua of Florida.—Pareja (*ca.* 1613) quoted by Gatschet in Proc. Am. Philos. Soc., XVII, 492, 1878.

Nuculahaquo. A subdivision or clan of the Apohola or Buzzard phratry of the ancient Timucua of Florida.—Pareja (*ca.* 1613) quoted by Gatschet in Proc. Am. Philos. Soc., XVII, 492, 1878.

Nuculaharuqui. A subdivision or clan of the Apohola or Buzzard phratry of the ancient Timucua of Florida.—Pareja (*ca.* 1613) quoted by Gatschet in Proc. Am. Philos. Soc., XVII, 492, 1878.

Nudlung. A summer settlement of the Akudnirmiut Eskimo on Howe bay, Baffin land.
Noodlook.—McDonald, Discov. of Hogarth's Sd., 86, 1841. **Nudlung.**—Boas in 6th Rep. B. A. E., 441, 1888.

Nuestra Señora de Guadalupe. A Franciscan mission established by order of the Viceroy of Mexico on Guadalupe r., Tex., about 1755, with the purpose of gathering the dispersed neophytes who had been at the San Xavier missions on San Gabriel r. Some of the Mayeye from San Xavier de Horcasitas mission were congregated there for a time and two missionaries settled among them; but it does not appear that any mission buildings were erected, nor is it certain that the mission was ever formally founded. Soon afterward the missionaries were ordered to San Saba and the place was abandoned (Informe de Misiones, 1762, MS. in Mem. de Nueva España, XXVIII, 180; Bonilla, Breve Compendio, in Tex. Hist. Ass'n Quar., VIII, 50–51, 1905; Arricivita, Crónica, II, 337, 1792).   (H. E. B.)
N. S. de Guadalupe.—Informe de Misiones, 1762, MS., op. cit.

Nuestra Señora de Guadalupe. A mission established by Padres Ugarte and Helen in 1720–21 on the w. coast of Lower California, lat. 27°. It had 5 visitas in the vicinity in 1726, and 4 in 1745, the others no doubt having become a part of one of the missions founded in the meantime. In 1767 the mission counted 530 baptized natives, speaking a dialect of Cochimi, according to Hervas (Saggio, 79–80, 1787).

Nuestra Señora de Guadalupe.—Venegas, Hist. Cal., II, 198, 1759. **Nuestra Señora de Guadalupe del Sur.**—Buschmann, Spuren, 751, 1859. **Santa Maria de Guadalupe.**—Ibid.

Nuestra Señora de Guadalupe de los Nacogdoches. A mission founded July 9, 1716, by the Franciscans of Zacatecas, at the Nacogdoche village and for the Nacogdoche and Nacau tribes. The site was evidently that of the present city of Nacogdoches, Tex. It was the head Zacatecan mission in E. Texas, being at first in charge of the president, Fray Antonio Margil de Jesus. After him, the most noted missionary there was Joseph Calahorra y Saenz (*ca.* 1750–1770). In 1719 the mission was abandoned, like the others of E. Texas, and when in 1721 Aguayo and Margil de Jesus went to reestablish it, not a sign of church or dwelling remained. On Aug. 18 the new church was dedicated; Fray José Rodriguez was put in charge, and 390 Indians were given presents, having promised to settle in a pueblo, a promise which they evidently never fulfilled. When in 1730–31 the Querétaran missions near by were transferred to San Antonio, this with the other Zacatecan missions was retained, but it was never successful. More than once it was in danger of destruction by the Indians, who were made hostile to the Spaniards by the influence of the French. By 1752 the Nacogdoche Indian village had been removed some 3 leagues northward. In 1767 Rubí reported the mission to be without a single neophyte, either baptized or under instruction. The next year Solís reported that there were an adobe church and several wooden buildings at the mission, but found in the books the record of only 12 baptisms, 8 burials, and 5 marriages. With the cession of Louisiana to Spain in 1762 one of the chief reasons for the mission's existence was removed, and accordingly, on recommendation by Rubí in 1767, its abandonment, together with that of the neighboring establishments, was ordered in 1772 and effected in 1773. Part of the settlers who had been removed in the latter year from E. Texas settled in 1774 on the Trinity, at a place called Pilar de Bucareli; but, because of a flood and attacks by the Comanche, they migrated in 1779 to the site of the Nacogdoche mission, apparently occupying some of its buildings, and became the founders of modern Nacogdoches.

Besides the authorities cited below, see Ramón, Derrotero, 1716, MS. in Mem. de Nueva España, XXVII, 157; Hidalgo to Mesquia, Oct. 6, 1716, MS. in the Archivo General; De Soto Bermudez, Investigación, 1752, MS. in the Archivo General; Rubí, Dictamen, ¶25, 1767, MS. in the Archivo General; Tex. Hist. Ass'n Quar., IX, 67–137, 1906.   (H. E. B.)

Guadalupe.—Bancroft, No. Mex. States, I, 614, 1886. **Guadalupe de los Nacogdoches.**—Ibid., 625. **Mision de Nacogdoches.**—Solís, Diario, 1768, MS. in Mem. de Nueva España, XXVII, 291. **Nacogdoches.**—Bancroft, op. cit., 666. **N. S. de Guadalupe.**—Ramón, Representación, 1716, in Mem. de Nueva España, op. cit., 159. **N. S. de Guadalupe de Alburquerque de los Nacogdoches.**—Solís, 1768, op. cit., 289. **N. S. de Guadalupe de los Nacogdoches.**—Peña, Diario, 1721, MS. in Mem. de Nueva España, XXVIII, 44. **N. S. de Guadalupe de Nacogdoches.**—Ibid., 42.

Nuestra Señora de la Candelaria. One of three Franciscan missions established about 1747–48 on San Xavier (now San Gabriel) r., Tex. For the circumstances of its founding, see *San Francisco de Horcasitas* and consult also *San Ildefonso.* This was the last of these three missions to be put in operation, but it is not known exactly when the neophytes arrived. The principal tribe at the mission was the Coco from the lower Colorado (Arricivita, Crónica, II, 336, 337, 1792). Some time before Mar. 11, 1751, Capt. Joseph de Eca y Musquiz inspected the mission and reported at service 102 neophytes (ibid., 328; Viceroy's decree, Mar. 11, 1751, MS. in Lamar papers). This mission had an unfortunate career. About Dec. 1751, Capt. Rábago y Terán reported the neophytes as already reduced to 25 (Bonilla in Tex. Hist. Ass'n Quar., VIII, 49, 1905). Early in 1752 the Coco took umbrage at the punishment of a slight offense and left in a body for their home on the Colorado (Arricivita, op. cit., 333). A few days afterward Father Ganzabal, minister at San Ildefonso, who had quarreled with the captain of the presidio, was murdered in the door of the Candelaria mission by an unknown person. Later the Coco promised to return to their mission, but apparently they never did so, for the last of the three, San Xavier de Horcasitas, was soon abandoned (ibid., 333, 336). They were taken instead, it seems, to San Antonio de Valero mission, for, beginning in 1755, there were numerous burials there of Coco who had been baptized at Candelaria on Rio San Xavier (Valero, MS. Entierros, entries for the years 1755–1765).   (H. E. B.)

Candelaria.—Bancroft, No. Mex. States, I, 641, 1886.

Nuestra Señora de la Candelaria. A mission founded Feb. 8, 1762, by Capt. Phelipe Rábago y Terán and Fray Diego Ximinez, on the w. side of San Joseph r., now the upper Nueces (not the San Antonio, as has been conjectured), near a site called El Cañon. This mission and San Lorenzo, which was 4 leagues away, were founded for the Lipan after they had been frightened from the San Saba mission by the attack of the Comanche and others in 1758. The chief who asked for this mission and was made "governor'' of it was Texa, or Turnio, who had a following of more than 300 people (Report of Rábago y Terán, Feb. 7 and 8, MS. in Archivo General; also Arricivita, Crónica, II, 385, 386, 1792). The mission was attached to those of the Rio Grande. Before 1767 it was abandoned through the desertion of Turnio and his people (Arricivita, ibid., 391). For further details, see *San Lorenzo*. (H. E. B.)

Candelaria.—Bancroft, No. Mex. States, I, 650, 1886. **Nuestra Señora de la Candelaria.**—Rábago y Terán, Report of the founding, Feb. 7, 8, 1762, MS. in Archivo General.

Nuestra Señora de la Luz. A Franciscan mission established by the Zacatecan friars, among the Arkokisa, on the left bank of lower Trinity r., Tex. A mission for the Arkokisa was proposed as early as 1747 by Capt. Orobio y Basterra, who reported that this tribe, living in five rancherias or pueblos and numbering 300 families, had expressed a desire to settle in a mission between the Sabine and the Trinity, "their fatherland." Some years afterward the plan was carried out, the mission being placed at a site known as Orcoquisac, some distance below modern Liberty. Near it stood the presidio of San Agustin de Ahumada. Within a few years both were moved a short distance upstream to a place called Los Horconsitos. The mission, from the first unsuccessful, was abandoned about 1770, and in 1772 the suppression of the presidio was ordered. (H. E. B.)

Nuestra Señora de la Purísima Concepción. A Franciscan mission, founded July 7, 1716, at the principal Hasinai village, that of the Hainai, on the E. side of Angelina r., Tex., and nearly w. of modern Nacogdoches. It was founded by, and remained for several years in charge of, the president of the Querétaran missions among the Hasinai, Fray Ysidro Felis de Espinosa, later author of the famous work on Franciscan missions, the *Chrónica Apostólica y Seráphica* (1746). The Hainai settlement at the time the mission was founded consisted, it is said, of "an infinite number of ranches, with their patches of maize, melons, watermelons, beans, tobacco," and sunflowers (Ramón, Derrotero, 1716, MS. in Mem. de Nueva España, XXVII, 158). This village was for the missionaries a strategic point in the Hasinai country, for at the Hainai village was the chief temple of the confederacy, presided over by the high priest, the great *Xinesi* (Jesus María, Relación, 1691, MS.), consequently Concepción was made the head mission. Before its removal to San Antonio the mission was sometimes called Nuestra Señora de la Purísima Concepción de los Aynais. The first church and dwellings were built by the Indians of wood and grass, after the manner of the Hasinai grass lodges,

but soon the soldiers and the missionaries, with their own hands, constructed more commodious ones (Ramón, op. cit., 159; Espinosa, Diario, 1716, MS.; and Chrónica, 418, 419, 1746).

The Hasinai Indians were friendly, but they refused to settle permanently in pueblos, and, through the strong influence of their priesthood, were slow to accept baptism. However, within a year Espinosa succeeded in baptizing, on his deathbed, the Hainai chief, which, because of this person's exalted position in the confederacy, presumably made other conversions easier (Espinosa, Chrónica, 440). But success was slight. Supplies for this and the neighboring missions failed to come, some of the soldier guard deserted, and finally, in 1719, the missionaries and soldiers, unaided by home authorities and fearful of a French attack from Natchitoches incident to the rupture between France and Spain, retired with the church ornaments to San Antonio, much to the regret of the Indians (Espinosa, Chrónica, 451–453; see also docs. in French, Hist. Coll. La., III, 67–72, 1851).

In 1721 the Marqués de San Miguel de Aguayo was sent, with Espinosa and Father Margil, to reestablish the missions and to erect presidios for their defense. Espinosa was again put in charge of Concepción, which reoccupied the old church after some repairs were made. On Aug. 8, 1721, the mission was formally reestablished, and to Cheocas, chief of the Hainai and head civil chief of the Hasinai, Aguayo gave "the best suit that he had—blue, heavily embroidered with gold, with waistcoat of gold and silver lace." Cheocas collected the Hainai people, and Aguayo, after exhorting them to come and settle a pueblo, gave presents of clothing and trinkets to 400 persons, including perhaps the 80 Kadohadacho visitors who chanced to be there (Peña, Diario, 1721, MS. in Mem. de Nueva España, XXVIII, 42). Near by Aguayo established an ill-made presidio called Nuestra Señora de los Dolores de los Texas (Peña, ibid.; and Rivera, Diario, leg. 2140, 1736; also Rivera, Proyecto, 1728, MS.).

Success was no greater now than formerly, and in 1731 Mission Concepción, together with San Joseph de los Nasones and San Francisco de los Texas (or Neches), was reestablished on San Antonio r. It was first planned to place them on the San Marcos, and there is some indication that they may have been temporarily located there (MS. in the city clerk's office, San Antonio, dated Aug. 12, 1771). Concepción was placed on the bank of San Antonio r., about 2 m. below San Antonio de Valero, which is now at the center of the city of San Antonio. According to the surviving book of marriage records, it was founded May 5, 1731. The site selected was that which formerly had been assigned to the Ervipiame mission of San Xavier de Náxera (q. v.). The pueblo was called Acuña, and of it the Pajalat chief was made the first governor (Testimonio de Asiento de Misiones, 1730–31, MS.). The mission now sometimes took the name Nuestra Señora de la Purísima Concepción de Acuña.

The tribes served by it were in the main of the Coahuiltecan stock. Their language is preserved in the *Manual* of Bartolome García (1760), who was stationed at the neighboring mission of San Francisco de la Espada. The first marriage recorded was that of "Joseph Flores, of the Patumaco nation, present governor of this pueblo, and chief of the Pajalates, Siguipiles, Tilpacopales, and others." The marriage records show that about 30 so-called tribes (*naciones*) were represented at this mission before 1790. They are here given, with the date of the first appearance of each new name or group of names following: Pajalat, Siquipil, Tilpacopal, Patumaco, Pachalaque, Patalca, Tiloja, Xarame (1733); Pamache (Pamaque?), Cujan (1734); Pacaba (Pacoa? 1735); Guapica (Guapite?), Pausana (1738); Payaya (1739); Pastia (1741); Pacao, Tacame; Orejon (1742); Chayopin (1745); Venado (1746); Apache (1747); Lipan (1751); Sanipao (1755); Piguiqui, Manos de Perro (1756); Yojuan (1758); Pajalache (Pajalat? 1759); Malaquita (1764); Borrado, Copane (1767); Comanche (1770); Pamaque (1775). Of these the Pajalates, Orejones, Pacaos, Pacoas, Pausanas, Tacames, Venados, Pamaques, Pihuiques, Borrados, Sanipaos, and Manos de Perro are named in García's *Manual* as among those speaking Coahuiltecan, and several others are known to have been likewise Coahuiltecans. It is possible that two or three pairs of the names given above are those of identical tribes. It is also to be noted that the Apache and the Yojuane in most cases were captives, while the Pacoa and Chayopin in the list represent neophytes of neighboring missions who intermarried with the neophytes of Concepción (Libro de Casamientos, MS. in the custody of the Bishop of San Antonio).

By Feb. 20, 1740, 250 neophytes had been baptized; but at this date only 120 remained, of whom all but 6 were unbaptized. The explanation is that in the latter part of 1739 a severe epidemic had ravaged all the missions, immediately after which a fresh supply of gentiles was brought in (Descripción de Misiones, Feb. 20, 1740, MS. in Mem. de Nueva España, xxviii, 203). By Mar. 6,

1762, there had been 792 baptisms and 558 burials—a commentary on mortality at the missions. At this time there were 207 persons remaining, largely Pajalates, Tacames, and Sanipaos. There were now a substantial church, apparently the one still standing, a sacristy, cloisters, a workroom where neophytes made cotton fabrics, and a blacksmith shop. The Indian pueblo near by consisted of two rows of stone huts and jacales, surrounded by a wall. The fields were irrigated by means of an acequia leading from a reservoir. On the ranch were 200 mares, 110 horses, 610 cattle, and 2,200 sheep and goats (Ynforme de Misiones, Mar. 6, 1762, MS. in Mem. de Nueva España, xxviii, 168–169). The acequia, known as the "Pajalache or Concepción ditch," is said to have been in use until 1869 (Corner, San Antonio de Bexar, 43, 1890).

Late in 1772 or early in 1773 the Querétaran friars transferred the mission to the Zacatecans, as was true also of the neighboring missions (Libro de Casamientos, MS., first entry for 1773). But the active period of the mission was now past, and the subsequent history was that of decline. Neophytes were difficult to get, government support was withdrawn, and the citizens of San Fernando encroached upon the mission lands. In 1794 the mission was secularized. By 1790 the total number of marriages had reached 249, of which 210 had been contracted before 1770 (Libro de Casamientos). The mission church and vivienda are still fairly well preserved.　　　(H. E. B.)

Nuestra Señora de la Soledad. The thirteenth Franciscan mission founded in California. Father Lasuen himself had explored the region, already known to the Spanish as Soledad, and personally selected the site, which was situated in the Salinas valley, about 4 m. from the present town of Soledad, Monterey co. The native name was Chuttusgelis. Some shelters were erected by neophytes from San Carlos, and on Oct. 9, 1791, the mission of Nuestra Señora de la Soledad was formally established. A few natives witnessed the ceremony. By the end of the year there were 12 converts, and 493 by 1800. In 1797 they had completed an adobe church with straw roof. The greatest number of neophytes, 727, was reached in 1805. In 1810 there were 600, in 1820 435, and about 300 in 1834. The total number of natives baptized was 3,096, of whom 1,306 were children. The total deaths were 2,502, of whom 1,137 were children. The mission was successful in its agricultural operations and well supplied with stock. In 1810 it had nearly 3,000 cattle, 286 horses, and 8,000 sheep, with an average crop for the last decade of 3,660 bushels. By 1820 the livestock had increased considerably, but the crops were smaller. Soledad did not decline so rapidly as some of the other California missions, and in 1834 it still had about 6,000 cattle and 5,000 sheep. The crops, however, were not very good, though there was a certain amount of irrigation. After secularization the decline was rapid, so that in 1840 there were only about 70 natives left, and the livestock had almost entirely disappeared. In 1846 the mission was sold for $800, but its buildings were then in ruins. Portions of adobe walls, some of them 3 ft thick, still remain on the site. The Indians in the neighborhood of Soledad were Chalones, belonging to the Costanoan linguistic stock. In 1817, or thereabouts, according to information given to Taylor (Cal. Farmer, Apr. 20, 1860), approximately a fourth of the neophytes were Chalones, one-fourth Esselen, and one-half from the Tulare lakes. The latter were probably Yokuts (Mariposan). See *California Indians, Costanoan Family, Mission Indians of California, Missions.*   (A. B. L.)

Nuestra Señora de la Soledad. An Apalachee mission settlement established in 1718 near Pensacola, Fla., by Juan Marcos, chief of the tribe, with refugees rescued from captivity among the Creeks, by whom they had been carried away on the destruction of the Apalachee missions by Gov. Moore and his Indian allies in 1704. The effort seems to have been abandoned before 1722.   (J. M.)
Nuestra Señora de la Soledad.—Barcia, Ensayo, 349, 1723. Our Lady of Loneliness.—Shea, Cath. Miss., 75, 1855. Soledad.—Barcia, op. cit., 342.

Nuestra Señora de la Victoria. A Franciscan mission founded in 1677 at Nadadores, within the territory of the present state of Coahuila, Mexico. It was called also Santa Rosa, and familiarly Nadadores. Raids by the Toboso, a wild tribe of northern Mexico, compelled removal from its first site, 40 leagues N. E. of Coahuila, to a position near Nadadores r., 7 leagues N. w. of that city. The Indians collected here were the Cotzales and Manos Prietas, to which, after the removal, 8 Tlascaltec families were added.   (J. R. S.)

Nuestra Señora de los Dolores de la Punta. A mission founded by the Querétaran fathers within the limits of the present Mexican state of Nueva Leon. The Indians gathered here were the Pitas and the Pasalves.

Nuestra Señora de los Dolores del Norte. A Jesuit mission of Lower California, founded early in the 18th century. Venegas (Hist. Cal., II, 198–199, 1759) says: "This mission was joined with that of San Ignacio. Within its district, which lies 30 leagues from S. Ignacio [San Ignacio de Kadakaman] and in the latitude of 29°, were already 548 baptized Indians." Taylor states that this mission was "made as an adjunct to San Ignacio, but a few

years afterward seems to have been absorbed into this last and abandoned, as were two or three pioneer foundations of the same kind, before 1740." See also Browne, Res. Pac. Slope, app., 50, 1869.

Nuestra Señora de los Dolores de los Ais. A Franciscan mission established in 1716 by the Spaniards among the Eyeish, in the vicinity of Sabine r., Tex., 37 leagues from Natchitoches, La., "well toward the E., and near the French settlements already established on Red r." of Louisiana. It was abandoned during the French-Spanish hostilities of 1719 and the mission property destroyed by the Indians, but was reestablished in 1721 with 180 natives. In 1768 it reported only 11 baptisms, and in 1773 was abandoned, probably on account of the decimation of the Eyeish people. See Bancroft, cited below; Garrison, Texas, 1903.
Dolores.—Bancroft, No. Mex. States, I, 615, 666, 1886. Dolores de los Adaes.—Ibid., 625. Santísima Virgen de los Dolores.—Austin in Tex. Hist. Ass'n Quar., VIII, 284, 1905.

Nuestra Señora del Pilar de los Adaes. A presidio established in Sept. and Oct. 1721, by the Marqués de Aguayo, close to the mission of San Miguel de Linares (or de los Adaes), in Texas, and about three-quarters of the way from the Sabine to Natchitoches, La. It was occupied until 1773, when the whole eastern frontier was abandoned. In 1774, however, part of the citizens returned from San Antonio to the Trinity and there founded a village which was called Pilar de Bucareli.   (H. E. B.)
Nuestra Señora del Pilar.—Peña, MS. Diario, 1721, in Mem. de Nueva España, XXVIII, 52. Nuestra Señora del Pilar de los Adaes.—Bonilla, Breve Compendio, 1772, in Tex. Hist. Ass'n Quar., VIII, 34, 1905. Pilar.—Bancroft, No. Mex. States, I, 626, 1886.

Nuestra Señora del Refugio. A mission founded in 1791 by Fray Manuel de Silva, near the mouth of Mission r., flowing into Aransas bay, Tex. It had 62 Karankawa neophytes in 1793. It was maintained until 1828, but in 1824 the mission buildings were abandoned because of the hostility of the Comanche, the baptism of neophytes subsequent to this time being performed at the parochial church. Between 1807 and 1828 the missionaries laboring at Refugio were Fr. José Manuel Gaitán, Fr. Juan María Zepulveda (buried there June 28, 1815), Fr. José Antonio Diaz de Leon, and Fr. Miguel Muñoz. During this period the total number of baptisms was 204, the tribes represented being the Karankawa, Piguique, Copane, Coapite, Pamoque, Cujan, Malaguite, Pajalache, Toboso, Coco, Araname, and Lipan (Libro II de Bautismos, 1807–28, in the archives of the parochial church of Matamoros, Mexico).   (H. E. B.)
Refugio.—Bancroft, No. Mex. States, I, 666, 668, 1886.

Nuestra Señora del Rosario. A Franciscan mission founded in the fall of 1754 about 4 m. s. w. of Espíritu Santo de

Zuñiga mission, nearly opposite modern Goliad and ½ m. from San Antonio r., for the Karankawan tribes, particularly the Cujanes (Kohani), of the Texas coast below this point. Early missionary efforts among the Karankawan tribes had been made at Espíritu Santo, founded in 1722 by the Zacatecan Franciscans near the site of La Salle's settlement on Lavaca r. The hostility of these tribes soon caused the removal of the mission, and subsequently the neighboring presidio, Bahía del Espíritu Santo, to Guadalupe r. The site is now marked by ruins in Mission valley, Victoria co. From this time until 1750 the Karankawan tribes, except the Coco, some of whom before this were attracted to Candelaria mission, were almost unaffected by mission influence; but in the year named, in consequence of José de Escandón's plan to colonize the whole coast country from Pánuco, Mexico, to San Antonio r., renewed efforts were made to missionize them. At first the government ordered that an attempt be made to gather them into Espíritu Santo de Zuñiga mission, which, at Escandón's instance, had been moved in 1749 with the presidio of Bahía to San Antonio r. At the same time the Querétaran missionaries at San Antonio made an effort to gather them there. A quarrel ensued, with the result that Espíritu Santo mission, profiting by the efforts of the Querétarans, succeeded in 1751 in gathering temporarily a number of Karankawans, mainly Cujanes. They deserted in a few weeks, but the missionaries and Captain Ramírez de la Piszina of the presidio continued making efforts to win the Cujanes, Karankawa, Coapites, and Copanes (Kopano).

It being found objectionable to attempt to put these tribes into the Espíritu Santo mission with the Aranames and Tamiques, "since they are of different languages, incompatible dispositions, and do not like to be in their company," an effort was made and permission obtained to transfer mission Nuestra Señora de los Dolores de los Ais from E. Texas to the neighborhood of Espíritu Santo, there to reestablish it for the Karankawan tribes. Objections from E. Texas, however, resulted in an order (Apr. 7, 1755) to found a new mission for the Cujanes (Kohani), Coapites, and Karankawa. The Copanes (Kopano) do not seem to have been included. Already, in consequence of the former plan, the founding of a new mission for these tribes had been begun (Nov. 1754) by Father Camberos and Captain Ramírez de la Piszina. Without waiting for the government to supply funds, work was begun with private donations and borrowed means. The name given the mission was Nuestra Señora del Rosario, with the addition, sometimes, of "de los Cujanes," the addition indicating the prominence of the Cujan tribe in the mission, and also the prevalent usage of the name of this tribe as a generic term for the Karankawan group. As first constructed, the church was built of wood, and was surrounded by a stake palisade. Later this church was replaced by one of stone. Conversions were slow, the total number of baptisms after four years' work being only 21. The Cujanes in particular were hard to manage, and with difficulty were kept from deserting. Adequate government support for the mission was delayed until Apr. 1758, when the supplies that had been asked for were granted, and 10 additional soldiers were added to the garrison at the neighboring presidio. With this aid the mission became more prosperous. In 1768 it was able to report a total of about 200 baptisms, and the indications are that at this time from 100 to 200 Indians lived intermittently, at least, at the mission. Father Solís inspected the mission in that year and reported it in good material condition, but said that the Indians were very hard to subdue, and that the Copanes, some of whom had joined the other tribes there, had entirely deserted it. In the same year charges were made to the government that the Indians were being seriously mistreated by the missionary, Father Escobár, and for that reason were deserting. Solís, however, gave a contrary report. (For a study of the history of Mission Rosario to this point, with citation of authorities for the above statements, see Bolton in Texas Hist. Ass'n Quar., Oct. 1906.) The subsequent history of this mission has never been investigated. Viceroy Revilla Gigedo tells us that it was completely abandoned in 1781; that efforts were made at once to reestablish it, but without success until 1791 (Carta dirigida á la Corte de España, Dec. 27, 1793). Portillo (Apuntes para la Historia Antigua de Coahuila y Texas, 310-11), an unreliable writer, who however had access to documents, says that in 1794 it had 62 neophytes (some of them apparently Coco), and that three years later 97 Coco and Karankawa from the mouth of the Colorado, after failing to gain admission to Espíritu Santo, entered Rosario mission. Ruins of the latter are still to be seen, but little remains of its walls.　　(H. E. B.)

Nuestra Señora del Rosario. A former Cora pueblo and seat of a mission which had Corapa as a visita. Situated near the w. bank of Rio San Pedro, lat. 22° 15′, Jalisco, Mexico.—Orozco y Berra, Geog., 280, 1864.

Nuestra Señora del Valle Humbroso. A Temoris pueblo in Chinipas valley, w. Chihuahua, Mexico.—Orozco y Berra, Geog., 324, 1864.

Nugsoak. A missionary station and trading post opposite Disko id., w. Greenland.

Noogsoak.—Crantz, Hist. Greenland, I, 16, 1767.

Nugumiut ('inhabitants of the cape'). An Eskimo tribe occupying the peninsula between Frobisher bay and Cumberland sd., Baffin land. Sealing on the floes with the harpoon, killing walrus at the floe edge, and hunting deer in the summer are their occupations. Their permanent villages are Nugumiut, Operdniving, Tornait, Tuarpukdjuak, and Ukadlik. Other settlements are Akbirsiarbing, Ekaluin, Kassigiakdjuak, Kekertukjuag, Kodlimarn, and Nuvuktualung. Pop. about 80 in 1883.

New Gummi Lurk.—British Admiralty chart. Nugumeute.—Kumlien in Bull. Nat. Mus. no. 15, 15, 1879. Nugumiut.—Boas in 6th Rep. B. A. E., 422, 1888.

Nugumiut. A winter village of Nugumiut Eskimo at the entrance to Frobisher bay, Baffin land.—Boas in 6th Rep. B. A. E., map, 1888.

Nuhalk (*Nuxa'lk·!*). A Bellacoola division, embracing the following 8 villages, at the mouth of Bellacoola r., Brit. Col.: Atlklaktl, Komkutis, Osmakmiketlp, Peisela, Sakta, Selkuta, Stskeitl, and Tkeiktskune. They include the Keltakkaua, Potlas, Siatlhelaak, Spukpukolemk, and Tokoais gentes.

Nuchalkmχ·.—Boas in Petermanns Mitt., pt. 5, 130, 1887 (-mχ·='people'). Nuqa'lkH.—Boas in 7th Rep. N. W. Tribes Can., 3, 1891. Nuqa'lkmH.—Ibid. (-mH='people of'). Nuxa'lk·!.—Boas in Mem. Am. Mus. Nat. Hist., II, 49, 1898.

Nuiku (*Nū'iku*). A Bellacoola village at the head of South Bentinck arm, Brit. Col. It is one of the Talio towns.

Nū'ik'.—Boas in 7th Rep. N. W. Tribes Can., 3, 1891. Nū'iku.—Boas in Mem. Am. Mus. Nat. Hist., II, 49, 1898.

Nuimok ('southern'). A Wintun tribe formerly living along lower Stony cr., Glenn co., Cal.

Kvmnom.—Kroeber, inf'n, 1903 (Yuki name for Stony Creek Wintun). Noi Mucks.—Geiger in Ind. Aff. Rep., 288, 1858. Nu'-i-mok.—Powers in Cont. N. A. Ethnol., III, 230, 1877.

Nuk ('the point'). A village of the Kinugumiut Eskimo at Port Clarence, Alaska, the site of the reindeer station Teller.

Nooke.—Beechey (1827) quoted by Baker, Geog. Dict. Alaska, 620, 1906. Nookmete.—Jackson in Rep. Bur. Educ., map, 145, 1894. Nookmut.—Dall, Alaska, 408, 1870. Nookmute.—Elliott, Our Arct. Prov., map, 1886. The Nook.—Baker, op. cit. (name given by "the old-timers").

Nukaakmats (*Nuqā'axmats*). A Bellacoola town on Bellacoola r., above Asenane, Brit. Col.

Nuk·ā'aqmats.—Boas in 7th Rep. N. W. Tribes Can., 3, 1891. Nuqā'axmats.—Boas in Mem. Am. Mus. Nat. Hist., II, 49, 1898.

Nukaatko (*Nukaā'tko, Nukaā'tqo,* or *Nɛkaā'tko,* 'one little water'). A village of the Spences Bridge band of Ntlakyapamuk, on the N. side of Thompson r., 43 m. above Lytton, Brit. Col.—Teit in Mem. Am. Mus. Nat. Hist., II, 173, 1900.

Nukchu. Mentioned as a tribe of s. central California, apparently living between San Joaquin and Kings rs. There may be some confusion with a southern Moquelumnan tribe called Nuchu; or the term may be a synonym of Nuchawayi or Nutunutu (q. v.). The Nukchu entered into a treaty with the United States, Apr. 29, 1851, and were placed on a reserve between Chowchilla and Kaweah rs.

Nook-choo.—Royce in 18th Rep. B. A. E., 782, 1899. Nook-choos.—Johnson (1851) in Sen. Ex. Doc. 61, 32d Cong., 1st sess., 22, 1852.

Nukhe ('reddish-yellow buffalo'). A gens of the Ponca, q. v.

Ice.—Dorsey in 15th Rep. B. A. E., 229, 1897 (improperly so called). Nuqe.—Ibid. Nuxe.—Ibid.

Nukhwhaiimikhl (*Nŭkh-whai-i-mikhl*). A Samish village on the s. w. side of Guemes id., N. w. coast of Washington.—Gibbs, Clallam and Lummi, 38, 1863.

Nukhwuchutun (*Nu'-q'wût-tcu'-tûn*). A former village of the Chetco on the s. side of Chetco r., Oreg.—Dorsey in Jour. Am. Folk-lore, III, 236, 1890.

Nukits (*Nŭk·ī'ts*). A Bellacoola village on Bellacoola r., above Snutele, Brit. Col.

Nū'kHits.—Boas in 7th Rep. N. W. Tribes Can., 3, 1891. Nŭk·ī'ts.—Boas in Mem. Am. Mus. Nat. Hist., II, 49, 1900.

Nukitsomk (*Nuχitsō'mχ*). A Wikeno village on Rivers inlet, Brit. Col.—Boas in Petermanns Mitt., pt. 5, 130, 1887.

Nukkehkummees. A village of Praying Indians, probably subject to the Wampanoag, near the site of Dartmouth, Mass., containing about 120 inhabitants in 1698.—Rawson and Danforth (1698) in Mass. Hist. Soc. Coll., 1st s., x, 132, 1809.

Nuklako. A Hankutchin village of 82 inhabitants on Yukon r., near the mouth of Klondike r., just w. of the boundary line between Alaska and British Columbia.

FortReliance.—Petroff in 10th Census, Alaska, map, 1884. Nu-kla-ko.—Schwatka, Rep. on Alaska, 86, 1885. Takon Indians.—Ibid., 84. Tchi-car-gut-ko-tan.—Ibid., 86 (Ingalik name).

Nuklit. A Malemiut Eskimo village near C. Denbigh, Norton sd., Alaska.

Noklich.—Zagoskin in Nouv. Ann. Voy., 5th s., XXI, map, 1850. Noocleet.—Baker, Geog. Dict. Alaska, 473, 1906 (quoted form). Nucleet.—Ibid. Nuklit.—Zagoskin, Descr. Russ. Poss. Am., I, 72, 1847.

Nukluak. An Ikogmiut Eskimo village on the left bank of the Yukon, opposite Ikogmiut mission, Alaska.

Nuchljuagmjut.—Holmberg, Ethnog. Skizz., map, 1855. Nukluag-mïout.—Zagoskin in Nouv. Ann. Voy., 5th s., XXI, map, 1850.

Nuklukayet. A Tenankutchin village, trading post, and mission on the N. bank of the Yukon, Alaska, just below the mouth of the Tanana. Pop. 107 in 1880, 120 in 1890. It is visited for trade by people of various tribes.

Nuclucayette.—Raymond in Sen. Ex. Doc. 12, 42d Cong., 1st sess., 23, 1871. Nuclukayette.—Whymper, Alaska, map, 1869. Nu-klac-i-yat.—Baker, Geog. Dict. Alaska, 473, 1906 (cited form). Nuklakyet.—Ibid. Nuklúkahyét.—Dall, Alaska, 57, 1870. Nuklukaiet.—Petroff in 10th Census, Alaska, 12,

1884. **Nuklukayet**.—Petroff, Rep. on Alaska, 62, 1881. **Nuklukoyet**.—Schwatka, Rep. on Alaska, 97, 1885. **Nuklúkyet**.—Allen, Rep. on Alaska, 86, 1887. **Nuklukyeto**.—Bruce, Alaska, map, 1885.

Nukluktana (*Nukluk-tána*). A Tenankutchin division on Tanana r., Alaska, below Tutlut r.—Allen, Rep. on Alaska, 86, 1887.

Nukwatsamish. A small body of Salish, formerly on a branch of Skagit r., in Whatcom co., Wash., now on Swinomish res.

Do-qua-chabsh.—Mallet in Ind. Aff. Rep., 198, 1877. Nook-na-cham-ish.—Ind. Aff. Rep., 17, 1870. N'qua-cha-mish.—Gibbs in Pac. R. R. Rep., I, 436, 1855. Nū-kwat-samish.—Gibbs in Cont. N. A. Ethnol., I, 180, 1877.

Nulaautin. A sept of the Takulli living in the village of Nulkreh, on Noolke lake, Brit. Col.; pop. 56 in 1879.

Nalo-tin.—Brit. Col. map, 1872. Nool-kē-o-tīn.—Dawson in Rep. Can. Geol. Surv. 1879–80, 30B, 1881. Nulaantins.—Domenech, Deserts N. Am., II, 62, 1860. Nulaáutin.—Hale, Ethnog. and Philol., 202, 1846. Stony Creek band.—Can. Ind. Aff., 214, 1902.

Nulato. A Kaiyuhkhotana village and trading station on the N. bank of Yukon r., Alaska, about 100 m. from Norton sd. and 550 m. by river from the ocean. In 1838 the Russian Malakof built a blockhouse and stockade near here, but shortly afterward, during his absence, it was burned by the Indians. It was rebuilt in 1842 by Lieut. Zagoskin, who was succeeded by Vasili Derzhavin, whose many acts of cruelty led to the massacre of the entire garrison by the Koyukukhotana in 1851. Later Nulato was moved 2 m. up the river to its present site. It is the seat of the Roman Catholic mission of St Peter Claver, and contained 168 inhabitants in 1880, 118 in 1890.

Nalatos.—Schwatka, Rep. on Alaska, 101, 1885. Noulato.—Zagoskin in Nouv. Ann. Voy., 5th s., XXI, map, 1850. Nulato.—Zagoskin, Descr. Russ. Poss. Am., map, 1842. Nūlā'to-kho-tān'ā.—Dall in Cont. N. A. Ethnol., I, 26, 1877.

Nulatok. A Togiagamiut Eskimo village on Togiak r., Alaska; pop. 211 in 1880.

Nulahtuk.—Petroff, Rep. on Alaska, 49, 1881. Nulatok.—Petroff in 10th Census, Alaska, 17, 1884.

Nulkreh. The Nulaautin village on Noolke lake, s. of Nechaco r., Brit. Col.—Morice in Trans. Roy. Soc. Can., x, 109, 1893.

Nuloktolok. A Kaialigmiut Eskimo village on the s. side of Nelson id., Alaska; pop. 25 in 1880.

Nulakhtolagamute.—Petroff, Rep. on Alaska, 54, 1881. Nuloktolgamute.—Nelson (1878) quoted by Baker, Geog. Dict. Alaska, 474, 1906. Nuloktolok.—Baker, ibid. Nulukhtulogumut.—Nelson in 18th Rep. B. A. E., pl. II, 23, 1899.

Num (*Nŭm*). The Earth or Sand clan of the Tigua pueblo of Isleta, N. Mex.

Namtaínin.—Gatschet, Isleta MS. vocab., B. A. E., 1885. Nŭm-t'ai'nin.—Lummis quoted by Hodge in Am. Anthrop., IX, 350, 1896 (*t'ainin*='people').

Numaltachi. A village formerly on Tuolumne r., Tuolumne co., Cal. Judging from its geographic position, it was probably Moquelumnan.

Mul-lat-te-co.—Johnson in Schoolcraft, Ind. Tribes, IV, 407, 1854 (probably identical). Mumaltachi.—

Latham in Trans. Philol. Soc. Lond., 81, 1856. Numal-tachee.—Johnson, op. cit.

Numawisowugi (*Nạmäwiswōagi*, 'they go by the name of the fish'). A phratry of the Sauk and Foxes, including the Sturgeon, Bass, and Ocean gentes; also the name of the Sturgeon gens of this phratry.	(W. J.)

Nă-mă-we'-so-uk.—Morgan, Anc. Soc., 170, 1877 (the gens). Nạmäwisōwagi.—Wm. Jones, inf'n, 1906 (the phratry and the gens).

Numeral systems. See *Counting*.

Numguelgar. A former Chumashan village near Santa Barbara, Cal.—Bancroft, Nat. Races, I, 459, 1874.

Nummuk ('western'). A Wintun tribe that formerly lived on Ruin r., a tributary of Cottonwood r., Shasta co., Cal.

Nommuk.—Powell in 7th Rep. B. A. E., 70, 1891. Num'-mok.—Powers in Cont. N. A. Ethnol., III, 230, 1877.

Numpali. A former division of the Olamentke that probably resided not far from the Olumpali of Marin co., Cal.

Noumpolis.—Choris, Voy. Pitt., 6, 1822. Numpali.—Chamisso in Kotzebue, Voy., III, 51, 1821.

Nun (*Nŭn*). The name of an ancestor of one of the Koskimo gentes, sometimes applied to the gens itself.—Boas in Petermanns Mitt., pt. 5, 131, 1887.

Nuna ('land'). A Nunatogmiut Eskimo village at Pt Hope, Alaska; pop. 74 in 1880.

Noo-nā.—Dall in Cont. N. A. Ethnol., I, 11, 1877. Noona-agamute.—Petroff in 10th Census, Alaska, 4, 1884.

Nunaikak. An Ikogmiut Eskimo village opposite Koserefski, on the lower Yukon, Alaska; perhaps identical with Ukak.

Nunaikagumute.—Raymond in Sen. Ex. Doc. 12, 42d Cong., 1st sess., 25, 1871.

Nunakitit. The northernmost village of the Angmagsalingmiut, on an islet at the entrance of Sermiligak fjord, Greenland, in lat. 65° 53'; pop. 14 in 1884.—Meddelelser om Grönland, XXVII, 22, 1902.

Nunaktak. An Ikogmiut Eskimo village above Anvik, on Yukon r., Alaska.

Nunakhtagamute.—Nelson (1878) quoted by Baker, Geog. Dict. Alaska, 1902. Nunaktak.—Baker, ibid.

Nunaktuau (*Nună'ktuau*). An Utkiavinmiut Eskimo summer village close to Refuge inlet, Alaska.—Murdoch in 9th Rep. B. A. E., 83, 1892.

Nunamiut. A Kaniagmiut Eskimo village on Three Saints harbor, Kodiak id., Alaska; pop. 160 in 1880, 86 in 1890.

Nunjagmjut.—Holmberg, Ethnog. Skizz., map, 142, 1855. Nunochogamute.—Petroff in 10th Census, Alaska, 11, 1884. Old Harbor.—Ibid., 29. Starui gavan.—Eleventh Census, Alaska, 77, 1893 ('old harbor': Russian name).

Nunapithlugak. A Chnagmiut Eskimo village in the Yukon delta, on the right bank of Apoon pass, Alaska.

Fort Hamilton.—Baker, Geog. Dict. Alaska, 1902. Nonapeklowak.—Coast Survey quoted by Baker, ibid., 262, 1906. Nunapithlugak.—Ibid. Old Fort Hamilton.—Ibid.

Nunaria. A deserted Eskimo village of the Sidarumiut near Pt Belcher, Alaska, the occupants of which moved to

Sedaru.—Murdoch in 9th Rep. B. A. E., 44, 1892.

Nunarsuak. An Eskimo settlement in s. e. Greenland, lat. 62° 43′.—Nansen, First Crossing of Greenland, I, 389, 1890.

Nunatak. 'A crest or ridge of rock appearing above the surface of the inland ice in Greenland'—Century Dictionary. From the Eskimo language, in which the word has the same form.   (A. F. C.)

Nunatarsuak. An Eskimo settlement in w. Greenland, near Ameralik fjord.
Nunatarsuak.—Nansen, First Crossing of Greenland, II, 430, 1890. Nunatochsoak.—Peary, My Arctic Jour., 188, 1893.

Nunatogmiut ('mountain people'). An Eskimo tribe inhabiting the banks of Noatak r., Alaska, who formerly ranged the interior as far as Colville r., and established settlements on the Arctic coast. They subsisted by hunting ptarmigan, reindeer, and mountain sheep, and fishing in the mountain streams. The coast they visited only in summer to sell the furs they had trapped. They were a tall, vigorous, rugged people of remarkably fine physique. The tribe proper had 42 members in 1890, while Dall in 1875 estimated them at 300. Their villages are or were Aniyak, Ipnot, Nigaluk, Noatak, Nuna, Shinagrua, and Tikizat.
Noatagamutes.—Elliott, Our Arctic Prov., map, 1886. Nooatoka Mutes.—Kelly, Arctic Eskimos, chart, 1890 ('timber people'). Nooatoks.—Ibid., 14. Noonitagmioots.—Stone in Bull. Am. Mus. Nat. Hist., XIII, 35, 1900. Noyatägameuts.—Hooper, Cruise of Corwin, 26, 1880. Nunatagmut.—Nelson in 18th Rep. B. A. E., map, 1899. Nuna-tangmë-un.—Richardson, Polar Regions, 300, 1861. Nuna-tañmiun.—Murdoch in 9th Rep. B. A. E., 44, 1892. Nünātō′g-mut.—Dall in Cont. N. A. Ethnol., I, 11, 1877. Nuna-tun′g-mëun.—Simpson quoted by Dall, ibid.

Nundawao ('great hill.'—Morgan). An ancient Seneca town near Naples, at the head of Canandaigua lake, Ontario co., N. Y. The name would seem to make it identical with the ancient Seneca town known to the French as Tsonnontouan. Conover, however, thinks the latter was identical with Totiakton (q. v.), near Mendon, Ontario co.
Nun′-da-wä-o.—Morgan, League Iroq., 6, 1851. Onondowä′.—J. N. B. Hewitt, inf′n, 1889 (correct Seneca form). Tenaoutoua.—Charlevoix (1744), New France, III, 122, 1866. Tsonnontouan.—For forms, see *Seneca*.

Nunemasekalis (*Nū′nEmEasqǻlis*, 'old from the beginning'). A gens of the Tlauitsis, a Kwakiutl tribe.
Nunemasek-â′lis.—Boas in 6th Rep. N. W. Tribes Can., 54, 1890. Nū′nEmasEqâlis.—Boas in Rep. Nat. Mus. 1895, 330, 1897.

Nung. The Earth or Sand clan of the Tewa of Hano pueblo, Arizona. Its members numbered 12 in 1893. Cf. *Nang*.
Huc-klic.—Stephen in 8th Rep. B. A. E., 39, 1891 (Navaho name). Nañ.—Fewkes in Am. Anthrop., VII, 166, 1894 (Tewa name). Nuñ.—Stephen, op. cit. (Tewa name). Tcu′-kai.—Ibid. (Hopi name).

Nuniliak. A Kaniagmiut summer village on the s. w. shore of Afognak id., Alaska.
Malinovskie lietnik.—Murashef (1839) quoted by Baker, Geog. Dict. Alaska, 475, 1906 ('raspberry

summer village': Russian name). Nunalik.—Tebenkof quoted by Baker, ibid. Nuniliak.—Ibid. (native name).

Nunivagmiut. A tribe of Eskimo in Alaska, occupying the main part of Nunivak id. and a small district about C. Vancouver on the mainland. They are a trading people; polygamy is rare; the women are not fruitful and fade early; children are taught to work, and a youth is not considered a man until he has killed a deer, a wolf, or a beluga. The kaiak frames are fitted with the nicest skill and covered with the skins of the great maklak seal. Every boy from the age of 10 has his own kaiak, and many maidens and widows have theirs. They make sealskin lines to barter with their neighbors on the continent. The tribe numbered 702 in 1890. The villages are Chulik, Inger, Koot, Kwik, and Tanunak.
Nunivagmut.—Nelson in 18th Rep. B. A. E., map, 1899. Nunivagmute. —Petroff in 10th Census, Alaska, 126, 1884. Nunivak people.—Worman quoted by Dall in Cont. N. A. Ethnol., I, 18, 1877.

Nunkom. A term in local use in Massachusetts in the youth of Rev. Edward Everett Hale (according to his statement at a meeting of the American Antiquarian Society, at Worcester, Mass., Oct. 21, 1903), in the sense of 'boy.' From *nunkomp* (Trumbull, Natick Dict., 96, 228, 233, 1903), 'a young man', 'a boy', in the Massachuset dialect.   (A. F. C.)

Nunnahidihi. See *Path Killer*.

Nunnepoag. A village, probably of the Wampanoag, on Marthas Vineyard, Mass., in 1698, containing about 84 inhabitants.
Numpang.—Drake, Bk. Inds., bk. 2, 118, 1848. Nunnepoag.—Rawson and Danforth (1698) in Mass. Hist. Soc. Coll., 1st s., X, 131, 1809.

Nunni ('fish'). A clan of the Koi phratry of the Chickasaw.
Nánni.—Morgan misquoted by Gatschet, Creek Migr. Leg., I, 96, 1884. Nun-ni.—Morgan, Anc. Soc., 163, 1877.

Nunochok. A Magemiut Eskimo village in the Big Lake region, Alaska; pop. 40 in 1880, 135 in 1890.
Nunachanaghamiut.—Eleventh Census, Alaska, 111, 1893. Nŭnachǎrạ gǎmut.—Baker, Geog. Dict. Alaska, 475, 1906 (quoted from). Nunachogumut.—Nelson in 18th Rep. B. A. E., map, 1899. Nunoch-ogamute.—Tenth Census, Alaska, 11, 1884. Nuno-chok.—Baker, Geog. Dict. Alaska, 475, 1906.

Nuntaneuck. An unidentified tribe, but possibly Siouan, mentioned by Lederer (Discov., 2, 1672) as speaking the common language of the Monacan, Nahyssan, Saponi, and others, and as having occupied the piedmont country of Virginia-Carolina jointly with those tribes after the extinction of the Tacci.
Nuntaly.—Lederer, op. cit.

Nununyi (*Nunû′ñyĭ*, 'wild-potato place,' from *nunu* 'wild potato'). A former Cherokee settlement, sometimes known as Potato Town, on Oconaluftee r., near the present Cherokee, Swain co., N. C. A large mound marks the site.   (J. M.)
Nuanha.—Bartram, Travels, 371, 1792.

Nunvogulukhluguk ('big lake'). An Eskimo village of the Kaialigamiut in the

Big Lake region, Alaska.—Nelson in 18th Rep. B. A. E., map, 1899.

Nuokan. A Yuit Eskimo village at East cape, Siberia.
Nukan.—Humboldt, New Spain, II, 344, 1822. Nuokan.—Krause in Deutsche Geog. Blätt., V, 80, map, 1882.

Nuquiage. A Cayuga village in 1750 at the N. E. corner of Seneca lake, on the outlet, in Seneca co., N. Y.
Nuqiage.—Conover, Kan. and Geneva MS., B. A. E. Nuquiage.—Cammerhoff (1750) quoted by Conover, ibid.

Nurata. A settlement of the Sikosuilarmiut, E. of King cape, Baffin land.— Boas in 6th Rep. B. A. E., 421, 1888.

Nuri. A pueblo of the Nevome and seat of a Spanish mission founded in 1622; situated on a tributary of the Rio Yaqui, lat. 28°, lon. 109°, Sonora, Mex. Pop. 180 in 1678, 41 in 1730. The inhabitants, also called Nuri or Nure, probably spoke a dialect slightly different from the Nevome proper.
Nures.—Orozco y Berra, Geog., 351, 1864 (" habitadores del pueblo de Nuri"). Nuri.—Rivera (1730) quoted by Bancroft, No. Mex. States, I, 514, 1884. S. Joaquin y Sta Ana (Nuri).—Zapata (1678) quoted by Bancroft, ibid., 246.

Nursoorooka. A Tuscarora village in North Carolina in 1701. Johnson, a Tuscarora, thinks the word may be from *Nasurakie*, 'where there are wild parsnips'; Hewitt thinks the termination *ooka* refers to a fork of a stream.
Nursoorooka.—Lawson (1709), North Carolina, 383, 1860. Nyu'-să-ru'-kän.—Hewitt, inf'n, 1886 (Tuscarora form).

Nusatsem (*Nusā'tsEm*). A Bellacoola settlement at the junction of Nusatsem and Bellacoola rs., Brit. Col.—Boas in Mem. Am. Mus. Nat. Hist., II, 49, 1898.

Nusehtsatl. A division of Salish formerly around South bay (Henderson inlet), Wash., now on Nisqualli res. Pop. 30 in 1879.
Noo-seh-chatl.—Stevens in Ind. Aff. Rep., 458, 1854. Nov-seh-chatl.—Gibbs in Pac. R. R. Rep., I, 435, 1855. Nüsehtsatl.—Gibbs in Cont. N. A. Ethnol., I, 178, 1877. South Bay.—Ind. Aff. Rep., 242, 1879.

Nushagagmiut. An Eskimo tribe of Alaska, inhabiting the banks of Igushik, Wood, and Nushagak rs. and the shores of Nushagak bay. Their villages are near together and have large structures in which great festivals are held. Women as well as men perform in the masques. The men are skilful hunters and good ivory carvers. In the interior they build comfortable houses of wood and use birchbark canoes. The tribe numbered 170 in 1890. The villages are: Agivavik, Agulukpuk, Akak, Akuliukpak, Akulivikchuk, Anagnak, Angnovchak, Annugamok, Ekuk, Golok, Igivachok, Igushik, Insiachak, Kakuak, Kalignak, Kanakanak, Kanulik, Mulchatna, Napai, Nushagak, Stugarok, Tikchik, Trinichak, Vuikhtulik, and Yaoherk.
Nushagagmut.—Rink, Eskimo Tribes, 32, 1887. Nushegagmut.—Nelson in 18th Rep. B. A. E., map, 1899. Nushergagmutes.—Dall in Proc. A. A. A. S., 267, 1869.

Nushagak. A Nushagagmiut village, Russian Orthodox mission, and trading post at the mouth of Nushagak r., Alaska. The redoubt and trade station of Alexandrovsk was founded there by Alexander Baranof in 1819, and the Moravian mission of Carmel was established by Americans in 1886 at Kanulik, 1⅜ m. above. Pop. 178 in 1880, 268 in 1890, excluding Bradford (pop. 166), Carmel (pop. 189), and Millerton (pop. 165); including these, 788 in 1900.
Meshagak.—Baker, Geog. Dict. Alaska, 476, 1906 (quoted form). Nushagak.—Ibid. (proper form). Nushegak.—Petroff, Rep. on Alaska, 46, 1881.

Nushaltkagakni ('spring people'). A division of the Modoc at the headwaters of Lost r., s. w. Oreg., near Bonanza.
Nushaltχagakni.—Gatschet in Cont. N. A. Ethnol., II, pt. I, XXXV, 1890. Spring-people.—Ibid.

Nushekaayi ('people back of the fort'). A Tlingit division among the Chilkat, belonging to the Raven clan. They are said to be closely related to the Hlukahadi.
Nucekaa'yî.—Swanton, field notes, B. A. E., 1904. Nüschě-kǎári.—Krause, Tlinkit Ind., 116, 1885.

Nushemouck. An Algonquian village in 1608 about the mouth of Nanjemoy cr., Charles co., Md.—Smith (1629), Va., I, map, repr. 1819.

Nuskek (*Nusxē'q!*). A Bellacoola town on North Bentinck arm, Brit. Col.—Boas in Mem. Am. Mus. Nat. Hist., II, 48, 1898.

Nuskelst (*Nūsq!E'lst*). A Bellacoola village on Bellacoola r. above Tskoakkane, Brit. Col. The people of this place were subdivided into 3 gentes, 2 of which were called Tlakaumoot and Kookotlane.
Nü'sk"Elst.—Boas in 7th Rep. N. W. Tribes Can., 3, 1891. Nusk'E'lstEmH.—Ibid. (-Emh='people'). Nüsq!E'lst.—Boas in Mem. Am. Mus. Nat. Hist., II, 49, 1898.

Nussamek. A village, probably Algonquian, on Potomac r., about Doncaster, Charles co., Md., in 1608. It was leagued with the Nacotchtank and Moyawance in a war against the Potomac.
Nazatica.—Smith (1629), Va., II, 86, repr. 1819. Nussamek.—Ibid., I, map. Pazaticans.—Ibid., II, 78.

Nutltleik (*NuLLē'îx*). A Bellacoola village on Bellacoola r. above Nuskelst, Brit. Col.
NuLLē'îx.—Boas in Mem. Am. Mus. Nat. Hist., II, 49, 1898. Nütltlē'iq.—Boas in 7th Rep. N. W. Tribes Can., 3, 1891.

Nutnur. A former village of the Kalindaruk division of the Costanoan family of California.—Taylor in Cal. Farmer, Apr. 20, 1860.

Nutonto. A former Chumashan village near Santa Inés mission, Santa Barbara co., Cal.—Taylor in Cal. Farmer, Oct. 18, 1861.

Nutqiu (*Nŭ'tqiu*, 'warriors'; sing.: *nŭ'taq*). The warrior organization of the Cheyenne (q. v.), consisting of 6 or more societies.   (J. M.)

Nutrecho. Mentioned as a tribe, seemingly Moquelumman, formerly on Fresno r., Cal.—Wessells in H. R. Ex. Doc. 76, 34th Cong., 3d sess., 30, 1857.

Nutria (Span.: 'otter'; also *Las Nutrias*, 'the otters'; native name *Tŭ'iakwin*, 'seed (corn) place,' or 'planting place'). A Zuñi farming village at the headwaters of an upper branch of Zuñi r., about 23 m. N. E. of Zuñi, Valencia co., N. Mex.; occupied only during the season of planting and harvesting except by one or two families. In the vicinity there are prehistoric ruins, also popularly known by the same name. For plan and description of the pueblo, see Mindeleff in 8th Rep. B. A. E., 94, 1891.

Natrias.—Loew in Ann. Rep. Wheeler Surv., app. LL, 178, 1875 (misprint). Neutrias.—Klett in Pop. Sci. Mo., 588, Sept. 1874. Nutria.—Common map form (also Las Nutrias).—Cushing in Millstone, IX, 55, Apr. 1884 ('people of the planting town': Zuñi name). Tâi'-ya.—Ibid., 225, Dec. 1884. Tola.—Fewkes in Jour. Am. Eth. and Arch., I, 100, 1891 (probably identical). To-ya.—Bandelier in Revue d' Ethnog., 202, 1886. To-y-a.—Bandelier in Arch. Inst. Papers, IV, 340, 1892.

Nutun (*Nŭtŭ'n*). An Ita Eskimo settlement on the s. shore of Inglefield gulf, N. Greenland.—Stein in Petermanns Mitt., no. 9, map, 1902.

Nutunutu. A Yokuts (Mariposan) tribe formerly living on lower Kings r., Cal. They were on the Fresno reserve in 1861, and with the Wimilchi numbered 180. Subsequently they were almost exterminated by white settlers, but two or three Nutunutu survive among neighboring tribes. The name is also pronounced Nutuntu, and in the plural is Nutantisha.

Mon-to-tos.—Wessells (1853) in H. R. Ex. Doc. 76, 34th Cong., 3d sess., 32, 1857 (probably identical). Na-too'-na-ta.—Merriam in Science, XIX, 916, 1904 (or, Nă-toon'ă-tă). No-toan'-ai-ti.—Powers in Cont. N. A. Ethnol., III, 370, 1877. Notonatos.—Bancroft, Nat. Races, I, 456, 1874. No-ton-no-tos.—Johnston (1851) in Sen. Ex. Doc. 61, 32d Cong., 1st sess., 23, 1852 (mentioned as distinct from No-ton-toos, but apparently the same). No-to-no-tos.—McKee et al. in Ind. Aff. Rep., 223, 1851. No-ton-toos.—Johnston, op. cit., 22 (see Notonnotos). Notoowthas.—Henley in Ind. Aff. Rep., 511, 1854. Notototens.—Taylor in Cal. Farmer, June 22, 1860. No-tow-too.—Barbour (1852) in Sen. Ex. Doc. 4, 32d Cong., spec. sess., 254, 1853. Nutonetoos.—Taylor in Cal. Farmer, June 8, 1860. Nutuntu.—A. L. Kroeber, inf'n, 1906. Nutunutu.—Kroeber in Univ. Cal. Pub., Am. Archæol. and Ethnol., II, 360, 1907.

Nutzotin. A band of the Tenankutchin living near the headwaters of Tanana r., Alaska. They occupy the villages of Nandell and Tetling.—Allen, Rep. on Alaska, 137, 1887.

Nuvujalung. A fall settlement of Talirpingmiut Okomiut Eskimo, on the s. w. shore of Cumberland sd., Baffin land.—Boas in 6th Rep. B. A. E., map, 1888.

Nuvujen ('the capes'). An Okomiut Eskimo winter village of the Talirpingmiut on the w. shore of Cumberland sd.; pop. 26 in 1883.

Newboyant.—Kumlien in Bull. Nat. Mus., no. 15, 15, 1879. Nuvujen.—Boas in 6th Rep. B. A. E., 426, 1888.

Nuvuktualung. A summer village of the Nugumiut Eskimo on Frobisher bay,

s. E. Baffin land.—Boas in 6th Rep. B. A. E., map, 1888.

Nuvung. An Aivilirmiut Eskimo winter village on Melville penin., N. E. of the entrance to Lyon inlet.

Noowook.—Lyons, Priv. Jour., 345, 1824. Nuvuk.—Boas in Bull. Am. Mus. Nat. Hist., XV, 6, 1901. Nuvukdjuaq.—Boas in 6th Rep. B. A. E., map, 1888. Nuvung.—Ibid., 449.

Nuwuak. A Kangmaligmiut Eskimo village at Manning pt, Alaska.—Dall in Cont. N. A. Ethnol., I, map, 1877.

Nuwuk ('point'). The principal village of the Nuwukmiut at Pt Barrow, Alaska. Pop., according to Dr Simpson, 309 in 1853; according to Petroff, 200 in 1880; according to Murdoch, 150 or 160 in 1883; according to Kelly, less than 100 in 1890; 152 in 1900, including Ongovehenok, a winter village on Kugrua r., and the refuge and whaling station.

Kokmullit.—Petroff in 10th Census, Alaska, map, 1884 (corrupted from Kunmudlin, 'distant ones', used by the Eskimo of Norton sd.). Noowook.—Kelly, Arct. Eskimos, 14, 1890. Noo'wooh.—Baker, Geog. Dict. Alaska, 476, 1906 (quoted form). Noowook.—U. S. Coast Surv. map, 1898. Nuwŭk.—Murdoch in 9th Rep. B. A. E., 43, 1892.

Nuwukmiut ('people of the point'). An Eskimo tribe of Pt Barrow, Alaska. They belong in race and language to the pure Eskimo stock, and are small in stature, robust and muscular, with full faces, spare bodies, shapely hands and feet, low, broad foreheads, narrowing toward the crown; short, broad noses, high cheek bones, full lips, especially the under one; cheeks often ruddy, and a skin of yellowish brown, varying in some to a brunette almost European, in some to a coppery hue. Their eyes are brown, of various shades, often bright and handsome. The hair is black, perfectly straight, and thick, but short; beards scanty. They are not prolific, and are dying out. Gray hair is uncommon, but wrinkles appear early. The large, regular teeth are worn away by the various uses to which the Eskimo put them, and few of either sex reach the age of 60. Pop. 43 in 1900. Their villages are Isutkwa, Nuwuk, Pernyu, Ongovehenok, and Sinaru.

Kokmalect.—Kelly, Arct. Eskimos, 14, 1890 (given as the name of the old Eskimo dialect of the Arctic coast tribes from Icy cape to Pt Barrow). Noowoo Mutes.—Kelly, ibid., chart. Nugumut.—Zagoskin, Descr. Russ. Poss. in Am., I, 74, 1847. Nŭwŭkmŭt.—Dall in Cont. N. A. Ethnol., I, II, 1877. Nuwung-më-un.—Richardson, Polar Regions, 300, 1861. Nuwŭ'ñmiun.—Murdoch in 9th Rep. B. A. E., 43, 1892.

Nyack (*Naiag*, 'point', 'corner'). A former village, probably of the Unami division of the Delawares, on the w. bank of Hudson r. about the present Nyack, in Rockland co., N. Y. The tract was sold and the Indians were removed in 1652.

Naiack.—Schoolcraft in Proc. N. Y. Hist. Soc., 107, 1844. Naieck.—Doc. of 1652 in N. Y. Doc. Col. Hist., XIV, 190, 1883. Najack.—Doc. of 1660, ibid., XIII, 167, 1881. Najeck.—Treaty of 1660, ibid., 148. Najeek.—Doc. of 1656, ibid., XIV, 365, 1883. Nayack.—Deed of 1657, ibid., 394. **Nayeck.**—Treaty of 1645, ibid., XIII, 18, 1881. **Neyick.**—Doc. of 1649, ibid., 25. **Nyacks.**—Clark, Onondaga, I, 18, 1843. **Nyeck.**—Treaty of 1645 quoted by Ruttenber, Tribes Hudson R., 118, 1872.

Nyack. A settlement in 1680, presumably of the Canarsee, about the present site of Ft Hamilton, Kings co., w. Long id., N. Y. At a later period the occupants removed to Staten id., near by. See Ruttenber, Ind. Geog. Names, 92, 1906.

Nyhatta. An unidentified tribe of Louisiana, apparently populous, reported 3 days' journey up Tassenocogoula (Red) r. from the Huma village in 1699.—Iberville in Margry, Déc., IV, 179, 1880.

Ny Herrnhut. An Eskimo settlement and German Moravian missionary post near Godthaab on the w. coast of Greenland.
New Hernhut.—Kane, Arct. Explor., I, 453, 1856. **New Herrnhut.**—Thompson, Moravian Miss., 203, 1886. **Ny Herrnhut.**—Nansen, First Crossing, II, 172, 1890.

Nyhougoulas. One of the 7 Taensa villages in the 17th century.—Iberville (1699) in Margry, Déc., IV, 179, 1880.

Nyuchirhaan ('openings'). The present Tuscarora village near Lewiston, Niagara co., N. Y.   (J. N. B. H.)
Gä-a-no'-ga.—Morgan, League Iroq., 428, 1851 ('on the mountains': Seneca name). **Gä'-a-no-geh.**—Ibid., 469. **Gä-ä-nŏⁿ-ge'.**—J. N. B. Hewitt, inf'n, 1886 (Seneca form). **Ga-o-no'-geh.**—Morgan, op. cit., 432. **Nyu-tcir-hä''äⁿ.**—Hewitt, inf'n, 1886 (Tuscarora name; tc=ch).

Nzatzahatko (N'zatzahatkō, 'clear water'). A village of the Ntlakyapamuk on Fraser r., Brit. Col., just below Cisco.—Hill-Tout in Rep. Ethnol. Surv. Can., 5, 1899.

Oahgwadaiya (Hot Bread). A Seneca chief who signed the deed to the Tuscarora, Mar. 30, 1808, being then called Captain Hot Bread. The name of another Hot Bread appears on this deed. Oahgwadaiya was short and dark, a leading man and orator, and was chief of a village opposite Avon, N. Y., in 1790, when he was called Gwakwadia. In 1797 his name appears as Ahquatieya. He died of smallpox.   (W. M. B.)

Oakfuskee. A former Upper Creek town on both sides of Tallapoosa r., Ala., about 35 m. above Tukabatchi, possibly on the s. boundary of Cleburne co., where a village of the same name now stands. The Oakfuskee Indians on the E. bank of the river came from 3 villages: Chihlakonini, Huhlitaiga, and Chukahlako. In 1799 Oakfuskee, with its 180 warriors and 7 branch villages on the Tallapoosa (with 270 warriors), was considered the largest community of the Creek confederacy. The 7 villages were Atchinaalgi, Imukfa, Ipisogi, Niuyaka, Sukaispoka, Tallahassee, Tukabatchi, and Tukhtukagi.   (A. S. G.)
Akfaski.—Gatschet, Creek Migr. Leg., I, 139, 1884; II, 185, 1888. **Lower Oakfuske.**—Bartram, Trav., 461, 1791. **Oakbusky.**—Finnelson (1792) in Am. State Pap., Ind. Aff., I, 289, 1832 (misprint). **Oakfuskies.**—Durouzeaux (1792), ibid., 312. **Oak-**

fusky.—Flint, Ind. Wars, 202, 1833. **Oakiuskees.**—Niles (1760) in Mass. Hist. Coll., 4th s., V, 555, 1861. **Oakpuskee.**—U. S. Ind. Treat. (1827), 420, 1837. **Oc-fus-kee.**—Hawkins (1799), Sketch, 45, 1848. **Ockfuskee.**—Jefferys, Am. Atlas, map 5, 1776. **Oekfusaet.**—Lattré, map U. S., 1784. **Okfuski.**—Gatschet, Creek Migr. Leg., I, 139, 1884; II, 185, 1888. **Ok-whûs-ke.**—Adair, Am. Inds., 257, 1775. **Upper Oakfuske.**—Bartram, Travels, 461, 1791.

Oakfuskee. A Creek town on Deep fork of Canadian r., Okla.
Akfáski.—Gatschet, Creek Migr. Leg., I, 139, 1884; II, 185, 1888. **Okfuski.**—Ibid.

Oakfuskudshi ('little Oakfuskee'). A former small Upper Creek village on Tallapoosa r., 4 m. above Niuyaka and 24 m. above Oakfuskee, in E. Ala. The town was destroyed by Gen. White in 1813. It is probable that the people were colonists from Little Oakfuskee (Chihlakonini) on Chattahoochee r., which was destroyed by the Georgians in 1793. See *Chihlakonini.*
Little Ockfuske.—Pickett, Hist. Ala., 557, 1896. **Little Okfuski.**—Pickett, Hist. Ala., II, 299, 1851. **Oc-fus-coo-che.**—Hawkins (1799), Sketch, 51, 1848. **Okfuskū'dshi.**—Gatschet, Creek Migr. Leg., I, 140, 1884.

Oapars. A former Papago rancheria between San Xavier del Bac and the Gila r. in s. Arizona; visited by Father Garcés in 1775, and by Anza and Font in 1780.
Ditt-pax.—Anza and Font (1780) quoted by Bancroft, Ariz. and N. Mex., 392, 1889. **Oapars.**—Arricivita, Crónica Seráfica, II, 416, 1792. **Oitapars.**—Anza and Font (1780) quoted by Bancroft, Ariz. and N. Mex., 392, 1889. **Oytapars.**—Garcés (1775), Diary, 64, 1900. **Oytapayts.**—Anza and Font (1780) quoted by Bancroft, Ariz. and N. Mex., 392, 1889. **Pueblo viejo.**—Ibid.

Oat (Ŏŭt). The Raccoon clan of the Caddo.—Mooney in 14th Rep. B. A. E., 1093, 1896.

Oatka (O'-ät-ka). A former small Seneca village on the site of Scottsville, on the w. bank of Genesee r., Monroe co., N. Y.—Morgan League Iroq., 434, 468, 1851.

O'Bail. See *Cornplanter.*

Obaldaquini. A mission village, probably on the lower Georgia coast, which was among those that revolted against the Spaniards in 1687.—Bárcia, Ensayo, 287, 1723.

Obayos. A tribe formerly living in the province of Coahuila, N. E. Mexico, and gathered into the mission of San Francisco de Coahuila a quarter of a league N. of Monclova (Orozco y Berra, Geog., 302, 1864). It was probably of Coahuiltecan speech.

O'Beal, O'Beel. See *Cornplanter.*

Obidgewong. A Chippewa and Ottawa settlement on the w. shore of L. Wolseley, Manitoulin id. in L. Huron, Ontario, containing 17 inhabitants in 1884, but reduced to 7 in 1906. Their reserve consists of 400 acres. They cultivate the soil, are good bushmen, and in winter cut ties and posts which they peel and sell in summer.
Obidgewong.—Canadian official form. **Wābi'tigwäyäng.**—Wm. Jones, inf'n, 1905 (correct name).

Obodeus. Given by Ker (Travels, 195, 1816), as the name of a tribe living on

upper Red r., apparently in w. Texas.
Not identified, and probably imaginary.

Obozi. One of the 36 tribes of Texas
said by Juan Sabeata, a Jumano Indian, to
have lived in 1683 on "Nueces" r., 3 days'
journey eastward from the mouth of the
Conchos (Cruzate in Mendoza, Viage,
MS. in Archivo General). It has not been
identified, although some of the others in
his list have been. The Nueces r. mentioned by him was not necessarily the
modern Nueces.   (H. E. B.)

Obsidian. A volcanic glass much used
by the Indian tribes for implements and
ornaments. It is generally black or
blackish in color, but some varieties are
brownish, reddish, and greenish in hue,
and sometimes display mottled effects.
Occasionally it is translucent, and in rare
instances fully transparent. It is not
found in the United States E. of the
Rocky mts., but occurs in enormous
bodies in Yellowstone Park, in California and Oregon, and to a lesser extent in
Idaho, Nevada, New Mexico, Arizona,
and in other western states. The more
homogeneous masses of obsidian are easily
broken up, and are flaked into desired
shapes with less difficulty than any other
kind of stone. Considerable evidence of
the shaping of implements is observable
in Yellowstone Park, especially in the
vicinity of Obsidian canyon, where a
body of nearly solid glass 100 ft or more
in thickness, is exposed (Holmes). More
extensive workings have been located in
New Mexico, Arizona, and California,
but no quarries of importance are known.
Implements of obsidian are rare E. of the
Rocky mts. Occasional flaked specimens
have been found in the mounds, and a
remarkable deposit of implements was
discovered in a burial mound on Hopewell farm, near Chillicothe, Ohio. This
deposit, unearthed by Moorehead in
1892 and now preserved in the Field
Museum of Natural History, Chicago,
consists of several hundred beautifully
shaped blades of large size and remarkable
conformation, as well as many smaller objects, not a few of which have been injured
by exposure to fire on an earthen altar.
The material is black throughout, though
slightly translucent when seen in thin
section. Its origin can not be determined.
The nearest deposit of similar character
in place is in the Yellowstone Park, 1,500
miles away; but as no trace of the manufacture of implements of this character
has been found in that section, it seems
probable that the material was brought
from Mexico or from the Pacific coast,
the known deposits in the former country, in the state of Hidalgo, being 1,600
m., and in the latter, Napa and other cos.
in California, 2,000 m. away. Along with
the obsidian implements were found many
implements and ornaments made of copper, shell, and other substances obtained
from distant localities.

Many exceptionally interesting objects
made of obsidian are found in the Pacific
states. These include beautifully shaped
blades, probably used as knives (q. v.),
obtained mostly from the living tribes, the
larger measuring more than 30 in. in
length and 5 in. in width; knife blades
of sickle or hook shape from mounds
near Stockton, Cal. (Meredith, Holmes),
and large numbers of delicately shaped
arrowpoints from the valley of the Columbia. The larger knives were intended for ceremonial rather than for
ordinary use. Of these, Powers says:
"There are other articles paraded and
worn in this and other ceremonial dances
which they will on no account part with,
at least to an American, though they
sometimes manufacture them to order
for one another. One of these is the
flake or knife of obsidian or jasper. I
have seen several which were 15 in. or
more in length and about 2½ in. wide
in the widest part. Pieces as large as
these are carried aloft in the hand in
the dance, wrapped with skin or cloth to
prevent the rough edges from lacer-
ating the hand, but the smaller ones are
mounted on wooden handles and glued
fast. The large ones can not be purchased
at any price, but I procured some about
6 in. long at $2.50 apiece. These are
not properly 'knives,' but jewelry for
sacred purposes, passing current also as
money." More recent and detailed accounts are given by Goddard, Kroeber,
and Rust. Kroeber describes at some
length the use of the knives in ceremonies
and refers to them as primarily objects of
wealth. On account of its brittleness
implements of obsidian were shaped
usually by flaking, but rare specimens
have been produced, or at least finished,
by pecking and grinding. (See *Stonework.*

Consult Goddard in Univ. Cal. Pub.,
Am. Archæol. and Ethnol., I, no. 1, 1903;
Holmes (1) in Rep. Nat. Mus. 1902, 1903,
(2) in Am. Nat., XIII, 1879, (3) in Am.
Anthrop., II, 1900; Kroeber, ibid., VII,
1905; Kunz, Gems and Precious Stones,
1890; Meredith (1) in Moorehead, Prehist.
Impls., 1900, (2) in Land of Sunshine,
II, no. 5, 1899; Moorehead in The An-
tiquarian, I, pts. 10 and 11, 1897; Powers
in Cont. N. A. Ethnol., III, 1877; Ralston in
The Archæologist, II, 1898; Rust in Am.
Anthrop., VII, 1905.   (W. H. H.)

Ocaboa. A former Papago village in
s. Arizona.—Taylor in Cal. Farmer, June
19, 1863.

Ocana. A tribe or subtribe, perhaps
Coahuiltecan, met by Massanet (Diario,
in Mem. Nueva España, XXVII, 92, MS.) a

short distance s. of Nueces r., Tex., in 1691, in a rancheria of Chaguan (Siaguan), Pastulac, Paac, and Quems Indians. In 1706 this tribe was represented at San Francisco Solano mission, near the Rio Grande. About the same time they were entering San Bernardo mission, near by, with the Canuas, Catuxanes, Pazchales, and Pomulumas (Morfi, Viage de Indios, 1777, in Doc. Hist. Mex., 4ª s., III, 442). In their gentile state they intermarried with the Zenizos (Baptismal Rec. of Mission Solano, 1706, partida 226, MS.). For their affiliation, see *Terocodame*, the leading tribe of the locality of the Mission Solano, with whom the Ocana were associated. An Ocana was baptized in 1728 at San Antonio de Valero mission, the successor of San Francisco Solano (ibid., 1728, partida 230). (H. E. B.)

Ocanes.—Rivera, Diario, leg. 2763, 1736.

Ocanahowan. A village where Spaniards are said to have been in 1611; situated five days' journey s. of Jamestown, Va. Perhaps identical with Occaneechi, q. v.

Ocanahowan.—Smith (1629), Va., II, 11, repr. 1819. Ochanahoen.—Strachey (*ca.* 1612), Va., 26, 1849.

Ocatameneton ('village of the gens who dwell at the foot of the lake'). An unidentified eastern Dakota band.

Ocatameneton.—Le Sueur (1700) in Margry, Déc., VI, 86, 1886. Ouatemanetons.—Neill, Hist. Minn., 170, 1858.

Occaneechi. A small tribe of the eastern Siouan group formerly residing in s. Virginia and N. North Carolina. Their history is closely interwoven with that of the Saponi and Tutelo, and there is historical evidence that their language was similar. The first known notice of the Occaneechi is that of Lederer, who visited them in 1670. They then dwelt on the middle and largest island in Roanoke r., just below the confluence of the Staunton and the Dan, near the site of Clarksville, Mecklenburg co., Va. Their fields were on the N. bank of the river, where they raised large crops of corn, having always on hand as a reserve a year's supply. Between the date of this visit and 1676 they were joined by the Saponi and Tutelo, who settled on two neighboring islands. In 1676 the Conestoga sought shelter with them from the attacks of the Iroquois and English. They were hospitably received, but soon attempted to dispossess their benefactors, and, after a battle, were driven out. Being harassed by the Virginians, and Iroquois, they left their island and fled s. into Carolina. In 1701 Lawson found them in a village on Eno r., about the present Hillsboro, Orange co., N. C. They combined later with the Saponi, Tutelo, and others. They were cultivators of the soil and traders. We are assured by Beverley that their dialect was the common language of trade and also of religion over a considerable region. They divided the year into the five seasons of budding or blossoming, ripening, midsummer, harvest, and winter. They were governed by two chiefs, one presiding in war, the other having charge of their hunting and agriculture. Ceremonial feasting was an important feature of their social life. Their tribal totem was a serpent. Consult Mooney, Siouan Tribes of the East, Bull. B. A. E., 1894. See *Patshenin.* (J. M.)

Acconeechy.—Map (1711) in Winsor, Hist. Am., V, 346, 1887. Achonechy.—Lawson (1701), Hist. Car., 96, 1860. Aconeche.—Moll, map, 104, 1720. Aconechos.—Lawson (1701), Hist. Car., 384, 1860. Aconeechy.—Mortier and Covens, États Unis, Amer. maps, II, map 177. Aconichi.—Alcedo, Dic. Geog., I, 19, 1786. Acoonedy.—Vaugondy, map, 1755 (misprint). Akenatzie.—Lederer quoted by Hale in Proc. Am. Philos. Soc., XXI, 10, Mar. 1883. Akenatzy.—Lederer, Discov. (1669-70), 17, repr. 1879. Akoniohi.—Lotter, map, *ca.* 1770. Botshenins.—Hale in Proc. Am. Philos. Soc., XXI, 10, 1883. Ocameches.—Drake, Abor. Race, 13, 1880. Occaanechy.—Byrd (1728), Hist. Dividing Line, I, 187, 1866. Occaneches.—Ibid. Occaneeches.—Beverley, Hist. Va., bk. 3, 24, 1705. Occoneachey.—Fry and Jefferson (1755) in Jefferys, Am. Atlas, map 21, 1776. Ochineeches.—Spotswood (1702) quoted by Hale in Proc. Am. Philos. Soc., XXI, 10, 1883. Ockinagees.—Doc. of 1676 in Mass. Hist. Soc. Coll., 4th s., IX, 167, 1871. Okenechee.—Batts (1671) in N. Y. Doc. Col. Hist., III, 193, 1853; same in Am. Anthrop., IX, 46, 1907. Oscameches.—Domenech, Deserts N. Am., I, 442, 1860. Patshenins.—Hale in Proc. Am. Philos. Soc., XXI, 10, 1883.

Occom, Samson. A Christian convert, called "the pious Mohegan," born in 1723. Converted to Christianity under the influence of Rev. E. Wheelock in 1741, he received in the family of that minister a good education, learning to speak and to write English and obtaining some knowledge of Latin and Greek, and even of Hebrew. Owing to ill health he did not complete the collegiate instruction intended for him. He was successively a school teacher in New London, Conn. (1748); preacher to the Indians of Long id. for some ten years; agent in England (1766-67) for Mr Wheelock's newly established school, where he preached with great acceptance and success; minister of the Brotherton Indians, as those Mahican were called who removed to the Oneida country in the state of New York (1786). On his death at New Stockbridge, N. Y., in 1792, Occom was greatly lamented. He is said to have been an interesting and eloquent speaker, and while in England delivered some 300 sermons. A funeral sermon on Moses Paul, a Mahican executed for murder in 1771, has been preserved in printed form. Occom was the author of the hymn beginning "Awaked by Sinai's Awful Sound," and of another, "Now the Shades of Night are Gone," which gave Bishop Huntington delight that the thought of an Indian was made part of the worship of the Episcopal Church; but it was omitted from the present hymnal. It was through his success in raising funds in England that Mr Wheelock's school was transferred from Lebanon, Conn., to New

Hampshire, where it was incorporated as Dartmouth College. As a man, Occom exhibited the virtues and the failings of his race. He was a regularly ordained minister, having been examined and licensed to preach by the clergymen of Windham co., Conn., and inducted in 1759 by the Suffolk presbytery, Long id. His later years were marred by drunkenness and other vices, but on the whole his life was one of great benefit to his race, though Schoolcraft (Ind. Tribes, v, 518, 1855) praises him perhaps too highly. See J. Edwards, Observations on the Language of the Muhhekaneew Indians, 1789; W. De Loss Love, Samson Occom and the Christian Indians of New England, 1899.   (A. F. C.)

Occow, Okow. The yellow pike perch (*Lucioperca americana*) of the northern great lakes, mentioned by Richardson in Franklin's Narrative (1823) and again in the Fauna Bor. Amer., ii, 1836. The name has since been adopted in ichthyological works. It is from Cree *okaw*, cognate with Chippewa *oka*.   (w. R. G.)

Ocha ('rain-cloud'). Given by Bourke (Jour. Am. Folk-lore, ii, 181, 1889) as a clan of the Mohave, q. v.

Ochechote (Tenino: 'hind dorsal fin [of a salmon]'). A small Shahaptian tribe, speaking the Tenino language, formerly living on the N. side of Columbia r., in Klickitat co., Wash. They were included in the Yakima treaty of Camp Stevens, Wash., June 9, 1855, by which, with other tribes, they ceded their lands to the United States. If any survive they are probably incorporated with other tribes on the Yakima res. Their name has reference to a rock on the N. side of Columbia r., opposite the upper end of an island near the mouth of the Des Chutes.

Ochecholes.——U. S. Stat., xii, 951, 1863. **Uchi'-chol.**——Mooney in 14th Rep. B. A. E., 740, 1896.

Ocheese ('people'). A former Seminole town on the w. side of Apalachicola r., at Ocheese bluff, the site of the present town of Ocheese, Jackson co., Fla. Pop. 220 in 1822, 230 in 1826.

Ocheeses.——Morse, Rep. to Sec. War, 364, 1822. **Ochesos.**——Drake, Bk. Inds., ix, 1848.

Ocheese. A former Lower Creek town on the E. bank of Chattahoochee r., w. central Georgia.

Okesez.——Jeffreys, Am. Atlas, map 5, 1776.

Ochete. A town visited by De Soto in 1539–40, apparently in N. w. Florida, at the head of St Marks bay, 4 leagues from the gulf. Buckingham Smith identifies it with the Aute of Narvaez. It is not the Ocute of Biedma. See Gentleman of Elvas (1557) in French, Hist. Coll. La., ii, 135, 1850.

Ochiakenen. A tribe or band mentioned by Hennepin (New Discov., 313, 1698) as living about 1675 in the same village with the Miami and Mascoutens. See *Ochiatagonga*.

Ochiatagonga. An unidentified tribe mentioned by La Salle, in 1682 (Margry, Déc., ii, 237, 1877) in connection with Islinois (Illinois), Chaouanons (Shawnee), and others, as among those living s. w. from L. Erie and destroyed (?) by the Iroquois. Cf. *Ochiakenen*.

Ochionagueras. An Onondaga war chief, called also Achiongeras, baptized by Father Le Moyne, Aug. 15, 1654, as Jean Baptiste, that being the name of Le Moyne's companion. He successfully led the Iroquois against the Erie. He headed Dablon's escort in Mar. 1656, and the next year was at Montreal in time to refute some Mohawk slanders. Ochionagueras was then described as an Onondaga captain, who "procured by his influence the peace which we have with the upper Iroquois."   (w. m. b.)

Ochoyos. A Costanoan village situated in 1819 within 10 m. of Santa Cruz mission, Cal.——Taylor in Cal. Farmer, Apr. 5, 1860.

Ochuceulga. A former Seminole town of 250 inhabitants E. of Apalachicola r., N. w. Fla. Cothrin was chief in 1822. The name is a form of Ochisi-algi. Cf. *Ocheese*.

O-chuce-ulga.——Morse, Rep. to Sec. War, 307, 1822.

Ochupocrassa. A former Seminole town on "East Florida point," with about 30 warriors in 1820, who had moved down from the Upper Creeks.——Bell quoted by Morse, Rep. to Sec. War, 307, 1822.

Ocilla. A former Seminole town at the mouth of Ocilla r., once called Assilly cr., on the E. bank, in Taylor co., Fla. Latufixico was its chief in 1823.

Oscillee.——H. R. Ex. Doc. 74, 19th Cong., 1st sess., 27, 1826.

Ockneharuse. An unidentified tribe mentioned in 1747 as living in the Ohio valley, and said to number 1,500 or 2,000, exceeding both the Wea and the Missisauga in population (Doc. of 1747 in N. Y. Doc. Col. Hist., vi, 391, 1855). They were possibly the Miami.

Oclackonayahe. A former Seminole village "above Tampa bay," w. Fla.; probably on or near Okliakonkonhee lake, Polk co.——Bell quoted by Morse, Rep. to Sec. War, 306, 1822.

Oclawaha. A former Seminole town on Oclawaha r. in N. central Florida. The Oclawaha division of the Seminole, descended from the Yamasi, betray their origin by the dark color of the skin (McKenney and Hall, Ind. Tribes, i, 272, 1854). Coe Hadjos Town (q. v.), which appears on Taylor's war map of 1839 just E. of Oclawaha r., may be the same.

Oclewahaw.——McKenney and Hall, Ind. Tribes, i, 272, 1854. **Oclawahas.**——Williams, Florida, 231, 1837. **Oc-la-wa-haw.**——Bell quoted by Morse, Rep.

to Sec. War, 307, 1822. **Oc-le-wau-hau-thluc-co.**—Hawkins (1799), Sketch, 25, 1848. **Oklévuaha.**—Penière quoted by Morse, Rep. to Sec. War, 311, 1822. **Oklewaha.**—Brinton, Floridian Penin., 145, 1859.

Ocmulgee (Hitchiti: *óki* 'water', *múlgis* 'it is boiling': 'boiling water'). A former Lower Creek town at the "Ocmulgee old fields," along the E. bank of Ocmulgee r., probably in Pulaski co., Ga., which, according to Adair (Am. Ind., 36, 1775), the South Carolinians destroyed about 1715. According to Creek tradition (Bartram, Trav., 52, 1792) Ocmulgee "old fields" was the site of the first permanent Creek settlement after the migration of the tribe from the w. The Indian trading road passed through this settlement. The "old fields," on which are a number of artificial mounds, terraces, and earthen inclosures, extended along the river for 15 m. The people of the town, who are sometimes mentioned as a tribe, joined those of other settlements in Oct. 1738 in tendering to Oglethorpe their assurances of friendship. (A. S. G.)

Caiomulgi.—Alcedo, Dic. Geog., I, 310, 1786. **Oakmulge.**—Rafinesque, introd. to Marshall, Ky., I, 42, 1824. **Oakmulgee old fields.**—Hawkins (1804) in Am. State Pap., Ind. Aff., I, 691, 1832. **Oakmulgee old towns.**—Am. State Pap. (1802), ibid., 669. **Oakmulge fields.**—Bartram, Travels, 53, 1792. **Oakmulgis.**—Romans, Florida, 90, 1775. **Oakmulgos.**—Ibid., 280. **Ocmulgee.**—Hawkins (1799), Sketch, 83, 1848. **Okmulge.**—Adair, Am. Inds., 36, 1775. **Oxmulges.**—Harris, Voy., II, 335, 1764.

Ocmulgee. The capital and most important town of the Creek Nation, situated on the N. fork of Canadian r., Okla.
Okmúlgee.—Gatschet, Creek Migr. Leg., II, 185, 1888.

Ocmulgee. A former Lower Creek town on the E. side of Flint r., Dougherty co., Ga.; pop. 200 in 1834.
Oakmulges.—Gatschet, Creek Migr. Leg., I, 72, 1884. **Oakmulgo.**—Jefferys, French Dom. Am., I, 134, map, 1761. **Ockmalgo.**—Jefferys, Am. Atlas, map 5, 1776. **Ocumlgi.**—Philippeaux, Map English Col., 1781. **Okmúlgi.**—Gatschet, op. cit., 140.

Ocoee (*Uwagá'hĭ*, 'apricot-vine place'). A former important Cherokee settlement on Ocoee r., near its junction with the Hiwassee, about the present Benton, Polk co., Tenn.—Mooney in 19th Rep. B. A. E., 544, 1900.
Acohee.—Doc. of 1799 quoted by Royce in 5th Rep. B. A. E., 144, 1887.

Ocon. A town, probably of the Hitchiti, formerly on St Marks r., N. w. Fla.—Jefferys, French Dom. Am., 135, map, 1761.

Oconaluftee (from *Egwânul'tĭ*, 'by the river'; from *egwâ'nĭ* 'river', *núlătĭ* or *nul'tĭ* 'near', 'beside'). Mentioned by Bartram as a Cherokee town existing about 1775, probably on the lower course of the river of the same name, at the present Birdtown, on the East Cherokee res., N. C., where was formerly a considerable mound. (J. M.)
Egwânul'tĭ.—Mooney in 19th Rep. B. A. E., 517, 1900 (correct form). **Oconaluftee.**—Present map form. **Ocunnolufte.**—Bartram, Travels, 371, 1792.

Oconee. A small tribe of the Creek confederacy, probably of the Hitchiti division, formerly living on Oconee r., Ga. Oconee, their chief town, was situated, according to Hawkins, about 4 m. below the present Milledgeville. Weekachumpa their chief, known to the English as Long-king, and one of his warriors were among the Indians assembled to welcome Oglethorpe when he arrived in Georgia in 1732. The Oconee formed one of the parties to the treaty between the U. S. and the Creeks at Colerain, Ga., June 29, 1796.
Occouys.—Harris, Voy. and Trav., II, 335, 1764. **Oconas.**—Drake, Bk. Inds., bk. 4, 29, 1848. **Oconees.**—U. S. Ind. Treat. (1797), 69, 1837. **Oconery's.**—Moll, map in Humphrey, Acct., 80, 1730.

Oconee. A former small town on the E. bank of Chattahoochee r., in Georgia, according to Hawkins, and on the w. bank, in Alabama, according to Bartram. It was settled about 1710 by the Oconee who abandoned their old habitat on Oconee r., Ga. Later they established Cuscowilla town on a lake in Alachua co., Fla. According to Bartram, they spoke the "Stincard" language, and were therefore akin to the Hitchiti.
Occone.—Bartram, Travels, 462, 1791. **Ocones.**—Jefferys, Am. Atlas, map 7, 1776. **Oconis.**—Romans, Florida, 90, 1775. **Okonee.**—Jefferys, op. cit., map 5. **Okóni.**—Gatschet, Creek Migr. Leg., I, 67, 1884.

Oconee (*Ukwû'nĭ*). A former Cherokee settlement on Seneca cr., near the present Walhalla, in Oconee co., S. C.—Mooney in 19th Rep. B. A. E., 541, 1900.
Acounee.—Mouzon's map quoted by Royce in 5th Rep. B. A. E., 143, 1887. **Oconnee.**—Royce in 18th Rep. B. A. E., pl. clxi, 1900.

Oconi. A district (subtribe?) in Florida, about 1612, speaking a Timucuan dialect, according to Pareja (Arte Leng. Timuqua, 1886). An ancient Creek town in E. Georgia had the same name. See *Oconee.* (J. M.)

Oconostota (*Â'ganû-stâ'ta*, 'Groundhog-sausage'). A Cherokee war chief in the 17th century. In the French war the Cherokee were at first allies of the English, but the spread of the British settlements and unfair and contemptuous treatment changed their sentiments. When they began to take reprisals for barbarous acts committed by American frontiersmen, and refused to surrender to the perpetrators, Gov. Littleton, of South Carolina, in Nov. 1759, cast into jail a delegation headed by Oconostota that had come to treat for the continuance of peace, saying that he would make peace in the Cherokee country. Attacullaculla obtained the exchange of Oconostota for one of the murderers demanded, and after the return of Littleton from a futile expedition the young war chief laid siege to Ft Prince George in upper South Carolina. He called out the commander, Lieut. Cotymore, for a parley and shot him, whereon the garrison butchered the Cherokee chiefs confined as hostages. Oconostota then fell upon the frontier settlements of Carolina, while the Cherokee warriors over the mountains captured Ft Louden in Tennessee. Col. Montgomery at the head of 1,600 men relieved Ft Prince George and destroyed the lower Cherokee towns, then marched to the succor of Ft Louden, but was routed in a fierce battle. After the war Oconostota became civil chief of the nation. The ancient war between the Cherokee and the Iroquois was terminated by a treaty which Oconostota went to New York to sign in 1768. The contest for their ancestral land, which caused their sympathies to swerve from the English to the French in the earlier war, made the Cherokee eager allies of the British against the Americans in the war of the Revolution. The tribe suffered severely in the contest and at its close Oconostota resigned the chiefship to his son, Tuksi, 'The Terrapin.' He died about 1783. See Mooney, Myths of the Cherokee, 19th Rep. B. A. E., 1900.

Ocota (contraction of *Okotsáli*, 'where there is resinous pine wood'). A small aggregation of Huichol ranches, containing a temple, situated near a small branch of the Rio Chapalagana, about 12 m. E. of the main stream, in Jalisco, Mexico (Lumholtz, Unknown Mex., II, 16, map, 258, 1902). It is distinct from Guadalupe Ocotan.

Okótsali.—Lumholtz, ibid., 258 (proper Huichol name).

Ocotan. A former Tepehuane pueblo in Durango, Mexico, and seat of a Spanish mission.

Huk-tyr.—A. Hrdlicka, inf'n, 1906. Santa María de Ocotan.—Ibid. (present name of town). Santa Maria Ocotan.—Lumholtz, Unknown Mex., I, 469, 1902. S. Francisco Ocotan.—Orozco y Berra, Geog., 318, 1864.

Octashepas. A tribe of the lower Mississippi, mentioned by Bossu in connection with the Taskiki (Tuskegee), Tonica (Tunica), Alibamu, etc. Possibly intended for Okchayi, q. v.

Oaktashippas.—Romans, Fla., 101, 1775. Octashepas.—Bossu (1759), Travels La., I, 229, 1771.

Ocuca. A former rancheria of the Pima in Sonora, Mexico, near Rio San Ignacio, N. w. of Santa Ana.

Occuca.—Orozco y Berra, Geog., 347, 1884. Ocuca.—Rudo Ensayo (ca. 1763), 161, 1863. Oocuca.—Ibid., 152.

Ocute. A town, probably in southern Georgia, entered by De Soto's troops on April 10, 1540. It was situated between Altamaha and Cofaqui.

Cofa.—Garcilasso de la Vega, Florida, 112, 1723. Ocute.—Gentl. of Elvas (1557) in French, Hist. Coll. La., II, 139, 1850; Biedma in Hakluyt Soc. Pub., IX, 179, 1851.

Odanah. A Chippewa settlement on Bad River res., Ashland co., Wis.—Brown in Wis. Archeol., v, 293, 1906; Ind. Aff. Rep., 394, 1906.

Odiserundy. A prominent warrior in the Revolution, often called John the Mohawk, and in chief command of a war party in 1777. The name is now written Deseronto, 'The lightning has struck.' In the New York State Library at Albany is a letter from John Deserontyon, dated Bay of Quinté, Nov. 1796, where he headed a band of Mohawk. He was present at a treaty with the United States after the Revolution. A place in Canada bears his name. (W. M. B.)

Odoesmades. A tribe, evidently Coahuiltecan, living in 1690 a short distance s. of the Rio Grande, on the way from central Coahuila to E. Texas. In the year named many of this tribe were seen in that locality, together with Mescaleros (evidently not the Mescalero Apache) and Momones, but when Terán went through the same country in 1691 he saw none. Many buffalo were seen here by Terán (Descripción y Diario Demarcación, 1691–92, in Mem. de Nueva España, XXVII, 25, MS.). (H. E. B.)

Odshiapofa ('hickory ground'). A town of the Creek Nation, on the North fork of Canadian r., below the mouth of Alabama cr., Okla. (Gatschet, Creek Migr. Leg., II, 186, 1888). The name was formerly applied to a Creek town in Alabama, otherwise known as Little Talasse. See *Talasse.*

Odshisalgi ('hickory-nut people'). One of the extinct clans of the Creeks. Some have regarded the name as representing simply the people of Ocheese, a former town of the Lower Creeks in central Georgia.

O-ché.—Morgan, Anc. Soc., 161, 1878. Odshísalgi.—Gatschet, Creek Migr. Leg., I, 156, 1884.

Odukeo's band (*O-duk-e-o*, 'Tall man'). The name of a Paviotso chief, applied also to his band formerly around Carson and Walker lakes, w. Nev. In 1861 they were said to number 1,261, including the Petodseka band.

Odakeo.—Burton, City of Saints, 576, 1861. O-duk-e-o's (Tall Man) band.—Dodge in Ind. Aff. Rep. 1859, 374, 1860.

Oealitk (*O'ealítx*). A sept of the Bellabella, a Kwakiutl tribe inhabiting the s. shore of Millbank sd., Brit. Col.

O'ēalitq.—Boas in 6th Rep. N. W. Tribes Can., 52, 1890. Ō'ealítx.—Boas in Rep. Nat. Mus. 1895, 328, 1897. Onie-le-toch.—Kane, Wand. in N. A., app., 1859. Owia-lei-toh.—Tolmie and Dawson, Vocabs. Brit. Col., 117B, 1884. Oyelloightuk.—Brit. Col. map, Ind. Aff., Victoria, 1872.

Oetlitk (*Oē'lítx*). A sept of the Bellabella, which, according to Tolmie and Dawson, occupied the middle section of Millbank sd., British Columbia.

Oē'lítx.—Boas in Rep. Nat. Mus. 1895, 328, 1897. Oē'tlitq.—Boas in 6th Rep. N. W. Tribes Can., 52, 1890. Okatlituk.—Brit. Col. map, Ind. Aff., Victoria, 1872. Owīt-lei-toh.—Tolmie and Dawson, Vocabs. Brit. Col., 117B, 1884. Weetle-toch.—Kane, Wand. in N. A., app., 1859. Weitle toch.—Schoolcraft, Ind. Tribes, v, 487, 1855.

Office of Indian Affairs. When the War Department was created by Congress under the act of Aug. 7, 1789, among the duties assigned to it were those "relative to Indian affairs." In 1824 a Bureau of Indian Affairs was organized in the War Department, with Thomas L. Mc-Kenney as its chief. The place was offered him at a salary of $1,600, but with the assurance that the President would recommend the organization of an "Indian department" with a salary for its head equal to that paid the auditors. The functions of the bureau were thus defined in the letter of appointment addressed to Col. McKenney by John C. Calhoun, Secretary of War, dated Mar. 11, 1824:

"To you are assigned the duties of the Bureau of Indian Affairs in this department, for the faithful performance of which you will be responsible. Mr Hamilton and Mr Miller are assigned to you, the former as chief, the latter as assistant clerk. You will take charge of the appropriations for annuities and of the current expenses, and all warrants on the same will be issued on your requisitions on the Secretary of War, taking special care that no requisition be issued, but in cases where the money previously remitted has been satisfactorily accounted for, and on estimates in detail, approved by you, for the sum required. You will receive and examine the accounts and vouchers for the expenditure thereof, and will pass them over to the proper auditor's office for settlement, after examination and approval by you; submitting such items for the sanction of this department as may require its approval. The administration of the fund for the civilization of the Indians is also committed to your charge, under the regulations established by the department. You are also charged with the examination of the claims arising out of the laws regulating the intercourse with Indian tribes, and will, after examining and briefing the same, report them to this department, endorsing a recommendation for their allowance or disallowance. The ordinary correspondence with the superintendents, the agents, and sub-agents, will pass through your bureau."

Col. McKenney had had large responsibility in connection with Indian affairs as superintendent of Indian trade from Apr. 2, 1816, until the United States Indian trading establishment was abolished by act of May 6, 1822. His connection with the Bureau terminated Sept. 30, 1830, by his dismissal, according to his *Memoirs*, on political grounds. Samuel S. Hamilton held the position for about a year, and was succeeded by Elbert Herring.

By the act of July 9, 1832, there was created in the War Department the office of Commissioner of Indian Affairs, at a salary of $3,000, who, subject to the

Secretary of War and the President, should have "the direction and management of all Indian affairs and of all matters arising out of Indian relations." Mr Herring received appointment as Commissioner July 10, 1832. Up to the present time (1907) there have been 28 Commissioners of Indian Affairs, the longest term of office being a little less than 8 years.

On June 30, 1834, an act was passed "to provide for the organization of the Department of Indian Affairs." Under this enactment certain agencies were established and others abolished, and provision was made for subagents, interpreters, and other employees, the payment of annuities, the purchase and distribution of supplies, etc. This may be regarded as the organic law of the Indian department.

When the Department of the Interior was created by act of Mar. 3, 1849, the Bureau of Indian Affairs was transferred thereto, and hence passed from military to civil control. As now organized there is a Commissioner of Indian Affairs (salary $5,000), an Assistant Commissioner ($3,000), a Chief Clerk ($2,250), a Superintendent of Indian Schools ($3,000), a private secretary to the Commissioner ($1,800), and a force of 175 clerks, including financial clerk, law clerk, chiefs of divisions, bookkeepers, architect, and draftsmen; besides 13 messengers, laborers, and charwomen.

The Finance division has charge of all financial affairs pertaining to the Indian Bureau. It keeps ledger accounts, under nearly 1,000 heads, of all the receipts and disbursements of appropriations and other funds for the Indian service, aggregating in late years more than $10,000,000 annually; remits funds to agents and other disbursing officers; attends to the purchase and transportation of supplies for the Indians and the work of the warehouses where these supplies are received and shipped; advertises for bids and prepares estimates for appropriations by Congress. The Treasury Department has estimated that between Mar. 4, 1789, and June 30, 1907, government expenditures on account of the Indian service aggregated $472,823,935. The Indian Office is trustee for more than $35,000,000 in the Treasury of the United States belonging to Indians, on which interest accrues at 4 percent and 5 percent.

The Field Work division has charge of all matters relating to irrigation; prosecutions for sale of liquor to Indians; assisting Indians in obtaining employment, and kindred subjects.

The Land division of the office has charge of everything pertaining to the landed interests of the Indians—allotments, patents, leases, sales, conveyances, cessions of land, or reservation of land for Indian use, railroad rights of way and damages; contracts with Indians for the payment of money; guardianship of minors; settlement of estates; trespassing on Indian reservations and the removal of white persons therefrom; taxation; citizenship and adoption into tribe, and all legal questions growing out of relations between Indians and whites.

The Education division has supervision of Indian school matters, records of school attendance, making plans for school buildings, including their lighting, heating, and sewerage; the selection of school sites, and the issuance of regulations as to the general management of the schools; prepares and supervises bonds of disbursing officers, and has charge of all matters relating to the appointment, transfer, promotion, etc., of employees in the agency and school service.

The Indian Territory division supervises all matters relating to the Five Civilized Tribes in Indian Ter., except railroads, telephones, and pipe-lines; also all timber matters except in the case of the Menominee res., which is in charge of the Land division.

The Accounts division audits the cash and property accounts of agents, school superintendents, and other disbursing officers; has the disposal of unserviceable property; the collection and expenditure of funds coming into the hands of agents from sales of agency property or produce or from other sources; the issuance of livestock, implements, and other supplies to the Indians; sanitary statistics; census; and the preparation and issuance of regulations for all branches of the service.

The Superintendent of Indian Schools inspects the schools personally, supervises methods of instruction, prepares the course of study, both literary and industrial, recommends text-books, and arranges for general and local Indian school institutes.

The Files division briefs, registers, indexes, and files all incoming and indexes all outgoing correspondence.

The Miscellaneous division has charge of business connected with Indian traders and field matrons, leaves of absence granted clerks, the printing required by the office, including the annual report, and the stationery and other supplies needed.

Five special agents and seven school supervisors report to the Commissioner of Indian Affairs their inspections of the work in the field. The employees under the jurisdiction of the office number about 5,000. The annual reports of the Commissioner to the Secretary of the Interior, with reports of agents, inspect-

ors, and school superintendents, and with population, industrial, and other statistics pertaining to the Indians, are published by authority of Congress, and contain much valuable information respecting the various tribes.

For the organization of methods of the Indian service in the field through the agencies and schools, see *Agency system, Education, Governmental policy, Reservations, Treaties.*   (M. S. C.)

Ofogoula (*Ofo,* their own name, and Choctaw *okla* 'people'). A small tribe which formerly lived on the left bank of Yazoo r., Miss., 12 m. above its mouth and close to the Yazoo, Koroa, and Tunica. They are not mentioned in any of the La Salle documents nor, by name at least, in the relations of the priest missionaries De Montigny and La Source who first visited the Yazoo tribes. In 1699 Iberville learned of them and recorded their name from a Taensa Indian among the Huma, but he did not reach their village either on this or on his subsequent expedition. It was probably during the same year that Davion established himself as missionary among the Tunica and necessarily had more or less intercourse with the tribes dwelling with them, i. e., the Yazoo and Ofogoula. Early in 1700 Le Sueur, with whom was the historian Pénicaut, stopped at the village of the combined tribes on his way to the headwaters of the Mississippi, and in November of that year Father Gravier spent some days there. He mentions the Ofogoula under their Tunica name, Ounspik (properly Ŭshpĭ), and states that they occupied 10 or 12 cabins. In 1729 Du Pratz gave the number of cabins in the united village of the Ofogoula, Yazoo, and Koroa, as 60. On the outbreak of the Natchez war the Yazoo and Koroa joined the hostiles, murdered their missionary, and destroyed the French post. The Ofogoula were off hunting at the time, and on their return every effort was made to induce them to declare against the French, but in vain, and they descended the Mississippi to live with the Tunica. There they must have continued to reside, for Hutchins, in 1784, states that they had a small village on the w. bank of the Mississippi, 8 m. above Pointe Coupée, La. Although the name afterward disappears from print, the living Tunica remember them as neighbors to within about 40 years. They are still (1911) represented by a single survivor, from whom it appears that the dialect spoken by this tribe was Siouan.   (J. R. S.)

Affagoula.—Hutchins (1784) in Imlay, West. Terr., 419, 1797. **Nation du Chien.**—Du Pratz, La., II, 226, 1758. **Nation of the Dog.**—Boudinot, Star in the West, 128, 1816. **Ofagoulas.**—Shea, Cath. Miss., 447, 1855. **Ofegaulas.**—Lattré, Map of U. S., 1784. **Offagoulas.**—La Harpe (1721) in French, Hist. Coll. La., III, 110, 1851. **Offegoulas.**—Dumont, ibid., v, 43, 1853. **Offogoulas.**—Pénicaut (1700), ibid., I, 61, 1869. **Ofogoulas.**—Charlevoix, Voy. to Am., II, 250, 1761. **Ofugulas.**—N. Y. Doc. Col. Hist., VII, 641, 1856. **Oofé-ogoolas.**—Keane in Stanford, Compend., 527, 1878. **Opocoulas.**—Iberville (1699) in Margry, Déc., IV, 180, 1880. **Oufé Agoulas.**—McKenney and Hall, Ind. Tribes, III, 80, 1854. **Oufé Ogoulas.**—Du Pratz, La., II, 226, 1758. **Oufé Ogulas.**—Boudinot, Star in the West, 128, 1816. **Oufé-ouglas.**—Jeffreys, French Dom. Am., I, 163, 1761. **Oufi-Ougulas.**—Schermerhorn (1812) in Mass. Hist. Soc. Coll., 2d s., II, 15, 1814. **Ouispe.**—Iberville (1699) in Margry, Déc., IV, 180, 1880. **Ounspik.**—Gravier (1700) quoted by Shea, Early Voy., 3, 133, 1861. **Ouspie.**—French, Hist. Coll. La., III, 106, 1851. **Oussipés.**—Pénicaut (1700), ibid., n. s., 61, 1869. **Ŭshpī.**—Swanton, field notes, B. A. E., 1907 (Tunica name).

Ogeechee. A town or subtribe of the Yuchi, formerly situated at some point on upper Ogeechee r., Ga. The Creeks and other tribes made war on them, and according to Bartram they were finally exterminated by the Creeks and Carolina settlers (?) on Amelia id., Fla., where they had taken refuge after having been driven from the mainland. (J. M.) **How-ge-chu.**—Hawkins (1799), Sketch, 61, 1848. **O-ge-chee.**—Ibid. **Ogechi.**—Alcedo, Dic. Geog., III, 368, 1788. **Ogeeche.**—Bartram, Travels, 64, 1792. **Oghiny-yawees.**—Johnson (1747) in N. Y. Doc. Col. Hist., VI, 359, 1855 ("Senecas, Chenondadees, and the Oghiny-yawees").

Oghgotacton. See *Onockatin.*

Oglala ('to scatter one's own'). The principal division of the Teton Sioux. Their early history is involved in complete obscurity; their modern history recounts incessant contests with other tribes and depredations on the whites. The first recorded notice of them is that of Lewis and Clark, who in 1806 found them living above the Brulé Sioux on Missouri r., between Cheyenne and Bad rs., in the present South Dakota, numbering 150 or 200 men. In 1825 they inhabited both banks of Bad r. from the Missouri to the Black hills, and were then friendly with the whites and at peace with the Cheyenne, but enemies to all other tribes except those of their own nation. They were then estimated at 1,500 persons, of whom 300 were warriors. Their general rendezvous was at the mouth of Bad r., where there was a trading establishment for their accommodation. In 1850 they roamed the plains between the N. and S. forks of Platte r. and w. of the Black hills. In 1862 they occupied the country extending N. E. from Ft Laramie, at the mouth of Laramie r., on North Platte r., including the Black hills and the sources of Bad r. and reaching to the fork of the Cheyenne, and ranged as far w. as the head of Grand r. De Smet (Ind. Aff. Rep., 277, 1865) says: "The worst among the hostile bands are the Blackfeet, the Ogallalas, the Unkpapas, and Santees." The Oglala participated in the massacre of Lieut. Grattan and his men at Ft Laramie in 1854. From 1865 they and other restless bands of western Sioux were the terror of the frontier, constantly attacking emigrant trains on the plains and boats on the river, fighting soldiers, and harassing the forts and stations during several years, under the leadership of Sitting Bull and Crazy Horse. The invasion of the Black hills by gold seekers led to the war of 1876, in which Custer and his command were destroyed. For several months previous thereto stragglers from other tribes had been flocking to Sitting Bull's standard, so that according to the best estimates there were at the battle of Little

OGLALA (AMERICAN HORSE, WASHITATONGA)

Bighorn 2,500 or 3,000 Indian warriors. The victor and his band were soon thereafter defeated by Gen. Miles and fled to Canada. Crazy Horse and more than 2,000 followers surrendered at Red Cloud and Spotted Tail agencies in the May following. These different parties were composed in part of Oglala, of whom the larger part probably surrendered with Crazy Horse.

The Oglala entered into a treaty of peace with the United States at the mouth of Teton (Bad) r., S. Dak., July 5, 1825, and also a treaty signed at Ft Sully, S. Dak., Oct. 28, 1865, prescribing relations with the United States and with other tribes. An important treaty with the Oglala and other tribes was made at Ft Laramie, Wyo., Apr. 29, 1868, in which they agreed to cease hos-

OGLALA (ITESHAPA, DIRTY FACE)

tilities and which defined the limits of their tribal lands. An agreement, confirming the treaty of 1868, was concluded at Red Cloud agency, Neb., Sept. 26, 1876, which was signed on behalf of the Oglala by Red Cloud and other principal men of the tribe.

In 1906 the Oglala were officially reported to number 6,727, all at Pine Ridge agency, S. Dak.

Lewis and Clark (Orig. Jour., VI, 99, 1905) mention only two divisions, the Sheo and the Okandandas. According to the Report of Indian Affairs for 1875 (p. 250), the Oglala were then divided into four bands, "usually called Ogallallas, Kiocsies [Kiyuksa], Onkapas [Oyukhpe], and Wazazies." The Rev. John Robinson in a letter to Dorsey (1879) names the following divisions: Payabya, Tapishlecha, Kiyuksa, Wazhazha, Iteshicha, Oyukhpe, and Waglukhe. These correspond with the seven bands of Red Cloud's pictographs. According to Rev. W. J. Cleveland (1884) they consist of 20 bands, as follow: (1) Iteshicha; (2) Payabya; (3) Oyukhpe; (4) Tapishlecha; (5) Peshla; (6) Chekhuhaton; (7) Wablenicha; (8) Peshlaptechela; (9) Tashnahecha; (10) Iwayusota; (11) Wakan; (12) (a) Igla-

katekhila, (b) Iteshicha; (13) Iteshichaetanhan; (14) Kiyuksa; (15) Wacheonpa; (16) Wachape; (17) Tiyochesli; (18) Waglukhe; (19) Oglala; (20) Ieskachincha. Unidentified bands are: Minisha, Night Cloud, Old Skin Necklace, Red lodge, and the Shorthair band. See *Dakota, Teton.* (J. O. D. C. T.)

Angallas.—Sen. Ex. Doc. 90, 22d Cong., 1st sess., 63, 1832. **Arkandada.**—Brackenridge, Views La., 78, 1815. **Augallalla.**—H. R. Ex. Doc. 117, 19th Cong., 1st sess., 6, 1826. **Chayenne Indians.**—Morse, Rep. to Sec. War, 365, 1822 (error). **Ogabllallas.**—Ind. Aff. Rep., 471, 1838. **Ogalalab Yokpahs.**—Twiss in H. R. Ex. Doc. 61, 36th Cong., 1st sess., 13, 1860 (the latter name probably intended for Oyukhpe, sometimes used to designate the whole people). **Ogalala Dacotas.**—Warren, Dacota Country, 19, 1856. **O-ga-la'-las.**—Hayden, Ethnog. and Philol. Mo. Val., 371, 1862. **Ogalallahs.**—M'Vickar, Hist. Exped. Lewis and Clark, I, 86, 1842. **Ogalallas.**—Ind. Rep. Aff., 296, 1846. **O'Galla.**—U. S. Ind. Treat. (1865), Kappler ed., 692, 1903. **Ogallah.**—Culbertson in Smithson. Rep. 1850, 142, 1851. **Ogallala.**—Ramsey in Ind. Aff. Rep. 1849, 85, 1850. **O'Gallala.**—Treaty of 1866 in U. S. Ind. Treat., 901, 1873. **Ogallalahs.**—Keane in Stanford, Compend., 527, 1878. **Ogallallahs.**—Parker, Jour., 65, 1840. **Ogallallas.**—Sen. Ex. Doc. 56, 18th Cong., 1st sess., 9, 1824. **Ogallallees.**—De Smet, Letters, 37, note, 1843. **Ogeelala.**—Schoolcraft, Ind. Tribes, V, 494, 1855. **Ogellahs.**—Ibid., I, 523, 1851. **Ogellalah.**—Ibid., IV, 252, 1854. **Ogellalas.**—Ind. Aff. Rep., 59, 1842. **Ogillallah.**—Parkman, Oregon Trail, 113, 1883. **O-gla'-la.**—Riggs, Dak. Gram. and Dict., 349, 1890. **Ogllallahs.**—Fremont, Explor.

OGLALA (WAHUIWAPA, EAR OF CORN; WIFE OF LONE WOLF)

Exped., 57, 1854. **Ogolawlas.**—Parker, Minn. Handbook, 141, 1857. **O'Gullalas.**—Treaty of 1867 in U. S. Ind. Treat., 914, 1873. **Ohdada.**—J. O. Dorsey, inf'n (Santee name). **Okadada.**—Robinson, letter to Dorsey, 1879. **Okanandans.**—Bradbury, Trav., 90, 1817. **O-kan-dan-das.**—Lewis and Clark, Discov., table, 34, 1806 (one of the two divisions of the Teton Sioux). **Okdada.**—Dorsey, inf'n (so called by Yankton). **Oknaka.**—Williamson in School-craft, Ind. Tribes, I, 249, 1851. **Onkdaka.**—Ibid. **O-tŏñ'-sŏn.**—Hayden, Ethnog. and Philol. Mo. Val., 290, 1862 ('little stars': Cheyenne name). **Oyer-lal-lah.**—Hoffman in H. R. Ex. Doc. 36, 33d Cong., 2d sess., 3, 1855. **Te'-ton,-o-kan-dan-das.**—Lewis and Clark, Discov., table, 30, 1806. **Teton Okandandes.**—Ramsey in Ind. Aff. Rep. 1849, 87, 1850. **Tetons Okandandas.**—Lewis, Trav., 171, 1809. **Ubchacha.**—Dorsey, Dhegiha MS. Dict., B. A. E., 1878 (Omaha and Ponca name).

Oglala. A subdivision of the Oglala Sioux.
Ogallallas.—Ind. Aff. Rep., 250, 1875 (one of the four divisions of the tribe). **Oglala-hċa.**—Dorsey, inf'n, 1880 ('true Oglala'). **Oglala proper.**—Robinson, letter to Dorsey, 1879.

Oglalaichichagha ('makes himself an Oglala'). A band of the Brulé Teton Sioux.
Og-la'-la.—Hayden, Ethnog. and Philol. Mo. Val., 376, 1862. **Oglala-iċiċaġa.**—Cleveland quoted by Dorsey in 15th Rep. B. A. E., 219, 1897. **Oglala-itc'-itcaxa.**—Ibid.

Ohagi (*O-ha-gi*, 'it compressed it.'—Hewitt). The Seneca name of a Tuscarora (?) village formerly on the w. side of Genesee r., a short distance below Cuylerville, Livingston co., N. Y.—Morgan, League Iroq., 434, 468, 1851.

Ohaguames. A former tribe, probably Coahuiltecan, of the province of Coahuila, N. E. Mexico, members of which were gathered into the mission of San Juan Bautista on Sabinas r.—Orozco y Berra, Geog., 303, 1864.

Ohamil. A Cowichan tribe on the s. side of lower Fraser r., Brit. Col., just below Hope; pop. 55 in 1906.
Ohamiel.—Can. Ind. Aff., 78, 1878. **Ohamil.**—Ibid., pt. II, 160, 1901. **O'Hamil.**—Ibid., 309, 1879. **Ohamille.**—Ibid., 1889, pt. 1, 268, 1890. **Omail.**—Brit. Col. map, Ind. Aff., Victoria, 1872 (given as the name of a town).

Ohanhanska ('long reach in a river'). A former band and village of the Magayuteshni division of the Mdewakanton Sioux, on Minnesota r., consisting, in 1836, of 80 people, under Wamditanka, or Big Eagle, also known as Black Dog.
Big Eagle's band.—Gale, Upper Miss., 251, 1867. **Black-dog.**—Ind. Aff. Rep., 282, 1854. **Black Dog's.**—Long, Exped. St Peter's R., I, 380, 1824. **Black Dog's band.**—Cullen in Ind. Aff. Rep. 1859, 68, 1860. **Oanoska.**—Long, Exped. St Peter's R., I, 385, 1824. **Ohah-hans-hah.**—Prescott in Schoolcraft, Ind. Tribes, II, 171, 1852. **O-hah-kas-ka-tohy-an-te.**—Catlin, N. Am. Inds., II, 134, 1844 (from *ohanhanska taoyate*, 'long reach, its people'). **Shunkasapa.**—Williamson in Minn. Geol. Rep., 110, 1884 ('Black Dog'). **Wah ma dee Tunkah band.**—Schoolcraft, Ind. Tribes, III, 612, 1853 (Wañmditanka, 'Big Eagle').

Ohanoak. An important Chowanoc village in 1586 on the w. side of Chowan r., not far below Nottoway r., probably in Hartford co., N. C.
Blinde Towne.—Lane (1586) in Hakluyt, Voy., III, 312, 1810 (so called by the English). **Ohanoak.**—Ibid. **Ohanock.**—Lane in Smith (1629), Va., I, 87, repr. 1819. **Opanock.**—Martin, N. C., I, 13, 1829 (misprint).

Ohathtokhouchy. A former Seminole town on Little r., 40 m. E. of Apalachicola, in Gadsden co., Fla., in 1823.—H. R. Ex. Doc. 74, 19th Cong., 1st sess., 27, 1826.

Ohdihe (from *ohdihaⁿ*, 'to fall into an object endwise'). A band of the Sisseton

Sioux, an offshoot of the Witawaziyata.—Dorsey in 15th Rep. B. A. E., 217, 1897.

Ohenonpa ('two boilings'). A band of the Brulé Teton Sioux.
O-he-nŏm'-pa.—Hayden, Ethnog. and Philol. Mo. Val., 376, 1862. **Ohe-noⁿpa.**—Cleveland quoted by Dorsey in 15th Rep. B. A. E., 219, 1897. **Ohe-noⁿpa.**—Ibid.

Oherokouaehronon ('people of the grass country.'—Hewitt). An unidentified tribe mentioned with many others in a list of peoples dwelling above the Sault St Louis of St Lawrence r. in 1640 (Jes. Rel. 1640, 35, 1858). The list is imperfect, containing duplicate names given as separate tribes.

Ohetur (*Ohet'ur*). The Yurok name of a Karok village opposite and below Orleans Bar, Klamath r., N. W. Cal.—A. L. Kroeber, inf'n, 1905.

Ohiyesa. See *Eastman, Charles.*

Ohkonkemme. A village in 1698 near Tisbury, Marthas Vineyard, Mass.—Doc. of 1698 in Mass. Hist. Soc. Coll., 1st s., x, 131, 1809.

Ohotdusha (*O-hot-dŭ'-sha*, 'antelope'). A band of the Crows.—Morgan, Anc. Soc., 159, 1877.

Ohrante. A Mohawk warrior in 1776, called Oteroughyanento when he and Joseph Brant met Lord Germain in London, Mar. 14 of the year named. He seems to be the Aruntes whose name appears on one of the Montreal medals, several of which have been connected with Indians of that period.　　　(W. M. B.)

Ohuivo ('the place to which they returned'). A Tarahumare rancheria in a barranca of that name on the extreme headwaters of the Rio Fuerte, in w. Chihuahua, Mexico. The Indians live in both houses and caves, in one of the latter of which, containing the remains of ancient habitations, the Tubare are said once to have dwelt.—Lumholtz, Unknown Mex., I, 187–192, 1902.

Ohytoucoulas. One of the Taensa villages in the 17th century.—Iberville (1699) in Margry, Déc., IV, 179, 1880.

Oiaht. A Nootka tribe on Barclay sd., w. coast of Vancouver id., Brit. Col. Ahadzooas is their principal village. Pop. 159 in 1902, 145 in 1906.
Hō'aiath.—Boas in 6th Rep. N. W. Tribes Can., 31, 1890. **Ohey-aht.**—Can. Ind. Aff. 1880, 315, 1881. **Ohiat.**—Mayne, Brit. Col., 251, 1861. **Ohyaht.**—Sproat, Savage Life, 308, 1868. **Ohyats.**—Mayne, op. cit., 270. **Oiaht.**—Can. Ind. Aff. 1883, 188, 1884. **Oiatuch.**—Grant in Jour. Roy. Geog. Soc., 293, 1857. **Oyty-aht.**—Brit. Col. Map, Ind. Aff., Victoria, 1872.

Oiaur. A former rancheria of the Sobaipuri or Papago, visited by Father Kino in 1697 and 1699, and named by him San Agustin. Situated on the Rio Santa Cruz, 5 or 6 leagues N. of San Xavier del Bac, s. Ariz., of which mission it was a visita in 1732. At the latter date the two settlements had 1,300 inhabitants.
Oiaur.—Mange (1699) quoted by Bancroft, Ariz. and N. Mex., 358, 1889. **S. Agustin.**—Kino, map (1701), ibid., 360. **S. Agustin Oiaur.**—Bernal (1697),

ibid., 356. **S. Augustin.**—Venegas, Hist. Cal., I, map, 1759. **S. Augustinus.**—Kino, map (1702) in Stöcklein, Neue Welt-Bott, 74, 1726.

Oidoingkoyo. A former Maidu village near the headwaters of Feather r. and about 10 m. N. of Prattville, Plumas co., Cal.—Dixon in Bull. Am. Mus. Nat. Hist., XVII, pl. 38, 1905.

Ointemarhen. A village or tribe said to have been in the region between Matagorda bay and Maligne (Colorado) r., Tex. The name was given to Joutel in 1687 by the Ebahamo Indians who dwelt in that country and who were probably Karankawan. See Gatschet, Karankawa Indians, I, 35, 46, 1891. (A. C. F.)
Ointemarhen.—Joutel (1687) in Margry, Déc., III, 288, 1878. **Otenmarhen.**—Joutel (1687) in French, Hist. Coll. La., I, 137, 1846. **Otenmarhen.**—Ibid., 152.

Oitac. A Maricopa rancheria on the Rio Gila in 1744.—Sedelmair (1744) cited by Bancroft, Ariz. and N. Mex., 366, 1889.

Oivimana (*Óivimána*, 'scabby people'; sing. *Óivimán*). A principal division of the Cheyenne; also a local nickname for a part of the Northern Cheyenne.
Hive.—Dorsey in Field Columb. Mus. Pub. 103, 62, 1905. **Ho ïv ï′ ma nah.**—Grinnell, Social Org. Cheyennes, 136, 1905. **Ŏ′ ivimă′ na.**—Mooney in 14th Rep. B. A. E., 1025, 1896. **Scabby band.**—Dorsey in Field Columb. Mus. Pub. 99, 13, 1905.

Ojageght (*Hodjage′/de′*, 'he is carrying a fish by the forehead strap.'—Hewitt). A Cayuga chief, commonly called Fish Carrier, whose name appears on the treaty of 1790. A tract of land a mile square had been reserved for him in 1789, and in that year a letter from Buffalo Creek was signed by Ojageghte or Fish Carrier, and 10 other Cayuga chiefs. In 1792 he had a silver medal from Washington, long preserved. In 1795 his name appears as Ojageghti, and in 1807 as Hojawgata. He was venerated and brave. The later Fish Carriers are Canadian Cayuga, preserving the name. (W. M. B.)

Ojai. A former Chumashan village about 10 m. up Buenaventura r., Ventura co., Cal.
Au-hai′.—Henshaw, Buenaventura MS. vocab., B. A. E., 1884. **Aujay.**—Taylor in Cal. Farmer, July 24, 1863. **Ojai.**—Ibid.

Ojana. A former Tano pueblo s. of the hamlet of Tejon, about lat. 35° 20′, Sandoval co., N. Mex. It was inhabited when visited by Oñate in 1598, and probably as late as 1700.—Bandelier in Arch. Inst. Papers, III, 125, 1890; IV, 109, 1892.
Ojana.—Oñate (1598) in Doc. Inéd., XVI, 114, 1871. **O-ja-na.**—Bandelier, op. cit., III, 125 (aboriginal name).

Ojeegwyahnug ('fisher-skins'). A tribe, probably Athapascan, known to the Ottawa.
Ojeeg Wyahnug.—Tanner, Narr., 316, 1830.

Ojeejok (*Uchïchak*, 'crane'). A gens of the Chippewa.
Ad-je-jawk.—Tanner, Narr., 315, 1830. **Attochingochronon.**—Jes. Rel. 1640, 35, 1858 (Huron name). **Aud-je-jauk.**—Ramsey in Ind. Aff. Rep., 91, 1850. **O-jee-jok′.**—Morgan, Anc. Soc., 166, 1877.

Uj-e-jauk.—Warren in Minn. Hist. Soc. Coll., v, 44, 1885. **Utcitcäk.**—Wm. Jones, inf'n, 1906 (proper form; *tc=ch*).

Ojiataibues. A Maricopa rancheria on Gila r., Ariz., in the 18th century.
Ojia-taibues.—Rudo Ensayo (ca. 1763), 22, 1863. **Oxitahibuis.**—Sedelmair (1744) quoted by Bancroft, Ariz. and N. Mex., 336, 1889. **Santiago.**—Kino map (1701), ibid., 360. **Santiago de Oiadaibuisc.**—Venegas, Hist. Cal., I, map, 1759. **S. Iacobus de Oiadaibuisc.**—Kino, map (1702), in Stöcklein, Neue Welt-Bott, 74, 1726.

Ojio. A former Sobaipuri rancheria visited by Father Kino in 1697; situated on the E. bank of San Pedro r. near its junction with the Gila, s. Arizona, not far from the present Dudleyville.
Ojio.—Bernal (1697) quoted by Bancroft, Ariz. and N. Mex., 356, 1889. **Victoria.**—Ibid. **Victoria de Ojio.**—Kino (1697) in Doc. Hist. Mex., 4th s., I, 280, 1856.

Ojiopas. The Piman name of apparently a Yuman tribe, members of which visited Father Kino while among the Quigyuma of the lower Rio Colorado in 1701. They were probably not the Bagiopa.
Giopas.—Kino (1701) cited in Rudo Ensayo (ca. 1763), Guiteras trans., 132, 1894; Coues, Garcés Diary, 551, 1900; Bancroft, No. Mex. States, I, 497, 1884. **Ojiopas.**—Ibid.

Ojistatara. An Oneida chief in 1776, popularly called The Grasshopper. His name appears as Peter Ojistarara in 1785, and among the Kirkland papers is a speech of The Grasshopper, addressed to Gov. Clinton of New York, Jan. 27, 1785. He was then principal chief, but died that year. There was a later chief of the same name. (W. M. B.)

Ojito de Samalayuca. A mission established among the Suma (q. v.), in 1683; situated 8 leagues below El Paso, in Chihuahua, Mexico.—Escalante (1775) quoted by Bancroft, Ariz. and N. Mex., 192, 1889.

Ojo Caliente (Span.: 'warm spring'; native name, K'iapkwainakwin, 'place whence flow the hot waters'). A Zuñi summer village about 14 m. s. w. of Zuñi pueblo, N. Mex., not far from the ruined town of Hawikuh. See Mindeleff in 8th Rep. B. A. E., 96, 1891.
Aguas Calientes.—Bandelier quoted in Arch. Inst. Rep., v, 43, 1884. **Caliente.**—Donaldson, Moqui Pueblo Inds., 127, 1893. **Hos Ojos Calientes.**—Cushing in Millstone, IX, 19, Feb. 1884 (misprint *Hos* for *Los*). **K'iáp-kwai-na.**—Cushing, ibid., IX, 55, Apr. 1884 (Zuñi name). **K'iap′-kwai-na-kwe.**—Ibid. (='people of the town whence flow the hot waters'). **K'iáp kwai na kwin.**—Cushing in 4th Rep. B. A. E., 494, 1886. **Ojo Caliente.**—Common map form. **Ojos Calientes.**—Cushing in Millstone, IX, 225, Dec. 1884. **Tkäp-quē-na.**—Stevenson in 5th Rep. B. A. E., 542, 1887.

Oka. A modern village of Iroquois, Nipissing, and Algonkin, on L. of the Two Mountains, near Montreal, Quebec. Cuoq says *oka* is the Algonkin name for goldfish or pickerel (see *Occow*). The Iroquois name, *Kanesatake*, signifies 'on the hillside', from *onesata* 'slope or mountain side,' *ke* 'at or on.' The village was settled in 1720 by Catholic Iroquois, who were previously at the Sault au Récollet, and who numbered about 900 at the time of removal. Soon after they were joined by some Nipissing and Algonkin, who removed from a mission on Isle aux Tourtes, the latter place being then abandoned. The two bodies occupy different parts of the village, separated by the church, the Iroquois using the corrupted Mohawk language, while the others speak Algonquian. The total number of both was 375 in 1884, and 461 (395 Iroquois, 66 Algonkin) in 1906. In 1881 a part of them removed to Watha (Gibson), Ontario, where they are now established, numbering 140, making the total number at both settlements about 600. For an account of these Indians see Life of Rev. Amand Parent, Toronto, 1886, in which the religious troubles are related from a Protestant point of view. (J. M. J. N. B. H.)

Canaghsadagaes.—Johnson (1767) in N. Y. Doc. Col. Hist., VII, 958, 1856. Canasadagas.—Johnson (1763), ibid., 582. Canasadauga.—Eastburn (1758) quoted by Drake, Trag. Wild., 283, 1841. Canasadogh.—La Tour, Map, 1779. Canasadogha.—Ibid., 1782. Canasatauga.—Smith (1799) quoted by Drake, Trag. Wild., 181, 1841. Canassadaga.—Colden (1727), Five Nat., 172, 1747. Canassategy.—Weiser (1753) in N. Y. Doc. Col. Hist., VI, 795, 1855. Caneghsadarundax.—Message of 1763, ibid., VII, 544, 1856 (should be Canasasaga, Arundax [Adirondacks]). Canessedage.—Governor of Canada (1695), ibid., IV, 120, 1854. Cannusadago.—Petition of 1764, ibid., VII, 614, 1856. Canossadage.—Romer (1700), ibid., IV, 799, 1854. Conaghsadagas.—Canajoharie Conf. (1759), ibid., VII, 393, 1856. Conasadagah.—Stoddert (1750), ibid., VI, 582, 1855. Conasadago.—Murray (1782) in Vt. Hist. Soc. Coll., II, 357, 1871. Conasadauga.—Eastburn (1758) quoted by Drake, Trag. Wild., 271, 1841. Conessetagoes.—Clinton (1745) in N. Y. Doc. Col. Hist., VI, 276, 1855. Conestauga.—Smith quoted by Day, Penn., 118, 1843. Conissadawga.—Hale in N. H. Hist. Soc. Coll., II, 93, 1827. Connasedagoes.—Bouquet (1764) quoted by Jefferson, Notes, 147, 1794. Connecedaga.—Long, Voy. and Trav., 25, 1791. Connecedegas.—McKenney and Hall, Ind. Tribes, III, 80, 1854. Connefedagoes.—Hutchins (1778) in Schoolcraft, Ind. Tribes, VI, 714, 1857. Connesedagoes.—Croghan (1765) in Monthly Am. Jour. Geol., 272, 1831. Connosedagoes.—Thompson quoted by Jefferson, Notes, 282, 1825. Connosidagoes.—Boudinot, Star in the West, 126, 1816. Connossedage.—Hansen (1700) in N. Y. Doc. Col. Hist., IV, 805, 1854. Ganagsadagas.—German Flats Conf. (1770), ibid., VIII, 229, 1857. Ganesatagué.—Doc. of 1741, ibid., IX, 1079, 1855. Kanassatagi lunuak.—Gatschet, Penobscot MS., B.A.E., 1887 (Penobscot name). Kanesatake.—Cuoq, Lex. Iroq., 10, 1883 (Mohawk name). Kanesatarkee.—King, Journ. Arc. Ocean, I, 11, 1836. Kanossadage.—Freerman (1704) in N. Y. Doc. Col. Hist., IV, 1163, 1854. Lac de deux Montagne.—Stoddert (1750), ibid., VI, 582, 1855. Lac de deux Montagnes.—Johnson (1763), ibid., VII, 582, 1856. Lake of the Two Mountains.—Shea, Cath. Miss., 333, 1855. Oka.—Can. Ind. Aff., 31, 1878. Scawendadeys.—Johnson (1747) in N. Y. Doc. Col. Hist., VI, 359, 1855. Scenondidies.—Stoddert (1753), ibid., 780. Schawendadies.—Ft Johnson Conf. (1756), ibid., VII, 239, 1856. Shoenidies.—Lindesay (1749), ibid., VI, 538, 1855. Shouwendadies.—Ft Johnson Conf. (1756), ibid., VII, 233, 1856. Skawendadys.—Canajoharie Conf. (1759), ibid., 392. Two-Mountain Iroquois.—Morgan, Systems Consang., 153, 1871. Village of the Two Mountains.—Jefferys, Fr. Dom., pt. 1, 14, 1761.

Okaaltakala ('between the waters'). A former Choctaw village that probably stood at the confluence of Petickfa and Yannubbee crs., in Kemper co., Miss.

Oka Altakala.—Halbert in Pub. Miss. Hist. Soc., VI, 424, 1902. Oka-altakkala.—West Florida map, ca. 1775. Oka attakkala.—Romans, Florida, 310, 1775.

Okachippo. A former Choctaw town in Mississippi. It was evidently in Neshoba co., but the exact location is not known. The name may be intended for *Okashippa*, 'water run down.'—Halbert in Pub. Miss. Hist. Soc., VI, 430, 1902.
Oka chippo.—West Florida map, ca. 1775.

Okacoopoly. A former Choctaw town on Ocobly cr., Neshoba co., Miss., from which it probably derived its name. The name may have been *Oka-akobli*, 'water where the biting is,' referring to good fishing there.—Halbert in Pub. Miss. Hist. Soc., VI, 429, 1902.
Oka Coopoly.—West Florida map, ca. 1775.

Okaghawichasha ('man of the south'). A band of the Brulé Teton Sioux.
Okaga-wiċaśa.—Dorsey (after Cleveland) in 15th Rep. B. A. E., 219, 1897. Okaxa-witċaċa.—Ibid.

Okahoki (perhaps *M'okahoki*, 'people of the pumpkin place'). A Delaware band or subclan formerly living on Ridley and Crum crs. in Delaware co., Pa. In 1703 they were removed to a small reservation near Willistown Inn.
M'okahoki.—Brinton, Lenape Leg., 39, 1885. O-kaho'-ki.—Morgan, Anc. Soc., 172, 1877 (said to mean 'ruler').

Okahullo ('mysterious water'). A former scattering Choctaw town on and near the mouth of Sanotee cr., Neshoba co., Miss., and extending into Newton co.—Halbert in Pub. Miss. Hist. Soc., VI, 425, 1902; Brown, ibid., 445.
Oka Hoola.—West Florida map, ca. 1775. Oka Hoolah.—Romans, Florida, 310, 1775. Okha Hullo.—Brown, op. cit.

Okak. A Moravian Eskimo mission on an island in Okak bay, coast of Labrador, established in 1776. The first Christian Eskimo convert in Labrador was baptized here in the same year. In 1851 the natives of the vicinity suffered severely from famine. It is still a flourishing station and the seat of an orphan asylum.
Okak.—Thompson, Moravian Miss., 229, 1890. Ok-kak.—Hind, Labrador Penin., II, 199, 1863. O'Kok.—McLean, Hudson Bay, II, 157, 1849.

Okakapassa. A former Choctaw town that environed the present Pinkney Mill in Newton co., Miss.—Brown in Pub. Miss. Hist. Soc., VI, 443, 1902. Cf. *Acolapissa*.
Little Colpissas.—Jefferys, French Dom. Am., map, 148, 1761. Oka Lopassa.—West Florida map, ca. 1775.

Okalusa ('black water'). The name of a settlement or of settlements of the Choctaw. On d'Anville's map of 1732 one is laid down on the s. side of Blackwater cr., Kemper co., Miss. There are the remains of several other villages along the same stream which may have borne this name at one time or another. The Oaka Loosa of Romans' map (1775) is not on this stream, however, but on White's branch, in the same county, where are still the remains of a town. It is possible that White's branch was also called Okalusa in Romans' time. This writer represents the Black Water warriors as predatory in their habits, often making inroads into the territory of the Creeks. In 1831 the Black Water people numbered 78.—Halbert in Pub. Miss. Hist. Soc., III, 367–368, 1900; VI, 420, 1902.

Black Water.—Jefferys, French Dom., I, 165, 1761. **Oaka Loosa.**—Romans, Florida, map, 1775. **Ogue Loussas.**—Jefferys, French Dom., I, 164, 1761. **Oka Loosa.**—Romans, Florida, 310, 1775. **Okecoussa.**—Lattré, Map U. S., 1784. **Oke Lousa.**—Pub. Miss. Hist. Soc., VI, 420, 1902 (misquotation of d'Anville). **Oké Loussa.**—d'Anville's map in Hamilton, Colonial Mobile, 158, 1897. **Oqué-Loussas.**—Du Pratz, La., II, 241, 1758.

Okanagan Lake. The local name for a body of Okinagan on the w. shore of Okanagan lake in s. w. British Columbia; pop. 37 in 1901, the last time the name appears.

Helowna.—Can. Ind. Aff., pt. II, 166, 1901.

Okapoolo. A former Choctaw village probably in the present Newton co., Miss.—Romans, Florida, map, 1775.

Okatalaya (*Oka-talaia*, 'spreading water'). One of the Choctaw Sixtowns which controlled a large extent of territory in the present Jasper and Smith cos., Miss., but centered on Oka Talaia cr.—Halbert in Pub. Ala. Hist. Soc., Misc. Coll., I, 383, 1901.

Okawasiku ('coot'). A subphratry or gens of the Menominee.—Hoffman in 14th Rep. B. A. E., 42, 1896.

Okchayi. A former Upper Creek town on Oktchayi cr., a w. tributary of Tallapoosa r., 3 m. below Kailaidshi, in Coosa co., Ala. Its inhabitants were of Alibamu origin, as were also those of Okchayudshi. Milfort gives a tradition concerning their migration. Another Creek settlement of the same name was situated on the E. bank of Tombigbee r., at the ford of the trail to the Creek Nation, which was in a bend of the stream a few miles below Sukanatchi junction, probably in Sumter co., Ala. This was probably the mother town of the other Okchayi and of Okchayudshi. (A. S. G.)

Hook-choie.—Hawkins (1799), Sketch, 37, 1848. **Hootohooee.**—Hawkins (1813) in Am. State Pap., Ind. Aff., I, 852, 1832. **Oakchog.**—Sen. Ex. Doc. 425, 24th Cong., 1st sess., 302, 1836. **Oakchoie.**—Pickett, Hist. Ala., II, 341, 1851. **Oakchoys.**—Swan (1791) in Schoolcraft, Ind. Tribes, V, 262, 1855. **Oakgees.**—Galphin (1787) in Am. State Pap., Ind. Aff., I, 32, 1832. **Oakjoys.**—Blount (1792), ibid., 270. **Occha.**—Jefferys, French Dom. Am., I, 134, map, 1761. **Occhoy.**—Romans, Florida, 327, 1775. **Ocka.**—Alcedo, Dic. Geog., III, 361, 1788. **Ockha.**—Jefferys, Am. Atlas, map 5, 1776. **Ockhoys.**—McKenney and Hall, Ind. Tribes, III, 80, 1854. **Ok-chai.**—Adair, Am. Inds., 257, 273, 1775. **Okchoys.**—Romans, Florida, 90, 1775. **Oke-choy-atte.**—Schoolcraft, Ind. Tribes, I, 266, 1851. **Okohoys.**—Carroll, Hist. Coll. S. C., I, 190, 1836. **Oukehaee.**—Schermerhorn (1812) in Mass. Hist. Soc. Coll., 2d s., II, 18, 1814. **Oxiailles.**—Milfort, Mémoire, 266, 1802. **Ozeailles.**—Pickett, Hist. Ala., I, 88, 1851.

Okchayi. A town of the Creek Nation, on Canadian r., near Hillabi, Okla.

Oktcháyi.—Gatschet, Creek Migr. Leg., II, 186, 1888.

Okchayudshi ('little Okchayi'). A former small Upper Creek town in the present Elmore co., Ala., on the E. bank of Coosa r., between Odshiapofa (Little Talassee) and Tuskegee. The village was removed to the E. side of Tallapoosa r. on account of Chickasaw raids.

Hook-choie-oo-che.—Hawkins (1799), Sketch, 37, 1848. **Hookchoioothe.**—Hawkins (1813) in Am. State Papers, Ind. Aff., I, 854, 1832. **Little Oakchoy.**—Creek paper (1836) in H. R. Rep. 37, 31st Cong., 2d sess., 122, 1851. **Little Oakjoys.**—U. S. Ind. Treat. (1797), 68, 1837. **Oakchoieoothe.**—Pickett, Hist. Ala., II, 267, 1851. **Oktchayū'dshi.**—Gatschet, Creek Migr. Leg., I, 141, 1884.

Oke. The principal village of the Ehatisaht (q. v.), on Eperanza inlet, w. coast of Vancouver id., Brit. Col.—Can. Ind. Aff., 264, 1902.

Okechumne. A former Moquelumnan group on Merced r., central Cal.

Ochekhamni.—Kroeber in Am. Anthrop., VIII, 659, 1906. **Okechumne.**—Wessells (1853) in H. R. Ex. Doc. 76, 34th Cong., 3d sess., 30, 1857.

Okehumpkee (probably 'lonely water'). A former Seminole town 30 m. s. w. from Volusia, and N. E. of Dade's battle ground, Volusia co., Fla. Mikanopy was chief in 1823, between which date and 1836 it was abandoned.

Ocahumpky.—Gadsden (1836) in H. R. Doc. 78, 25th Cong., 2d sess., 407, 1838. **Okahumky.**—Scott's map, ibid., 408–9. **Okehumpkee.**—H. R. Doc. 74, 19th Cong., 1st sess., 27, 1826.

Oketo. The Yurok name of Big lagoon on the N. w. coast of Cal., 10 m. N. of Trinidad, as well as of the largest of the several Yurok villages thereon. (A. L. K.)

Okhatatalaya (*Okhata-talaia*, 'spreading pond'). A former Choctaw town in the westernmost part of the present Newton co., Miss. It was named from a pond several acres in extent, near the center of the town, which was a great resort for wild fowl.—Brown in Pub. Miss. Hist. Soc., VI, 445, 1902.

Okilisa (*O-ki'-li-sa*). An extinct Creek clan.—Gatschet, Creek Migr. Leg., I, 155, 1884.

Okinagan (etymology doubtful). A name originally applied to the confluence of Similkameen and Okanogan rs., but extended first to include a small band and afterward to a large and important division of the Salishan family. They formerly inhabited the w. side of Okanogan r., Wash., from Old Ft Okanogan to the Canadian border, and in British Columbia the shores of Okanagan lake and the surrounding country. Later they displaced an Athapascan tribe from the valley of the Similkameen. In 1906 there were 527 Okinagan on Colville res., Wash., and 824 under the Kamloops-Okanagan agency, British Columbia; total, 1,351. Gibbs in 1855 gave the following list of Okinagan bands on Okanogan r.: Tkwuratum, Konekonep, Kluckhaitkwu, Kinakanes, and Milakitekwa. The Kinakanes appear to be the Okinagan proper. He also classed the Sanpoil with them, but says "these are also claimed by the Spokans," and in fact they are still oftener placed by themselves. To Gibbs' list should be added the Intietook band of Ross. The following villages or bands are enumerated in the Canadian Reports of Indian Affairs: Ashnola, Chuchunayha, Keremeus, Nkamaplix, Nkamip, Okanagan Lake, Penticton, Shennosquankin, and Spahamin. Teit gives four others: Kedlamik, Komkonatko, Ntlkius, and Zutsemin. Dawson adds Whatlminek. See also *Skamoynumachs.*

Kānk″utlā′atlam.—Boas in 5th Rep. N. W. Tribes Can., 10, 1889 ('flatheads': Kutenai name). **Kinakanes.**—Gibbs in Pac. R. R. Rep., I, 412, 1855. **KōkEnū′k′kē.**—Chamberlain in 8th Rep. N. W. Tribes Can., 7, 1892 (Kutenai name). **Oakanagans.**—Ross, Fur Hunters, I, 44, 1855. **Oakinaoken.**—Ross, Adventures, 287, 1847 (used collectively and also as applying to a subdivision). **Oakinagan.**—Cox, Columb. R., II, 86, 1831. **Oohinakéin.**—Giorda, Kalispel Dict., I, 439, 1877–79. **Okanagam.**—Duflot de Mofras, Oregon, II, 100, 1844. **Okanagan.**—Parker, Journal, 298, 1840. **Okanagon.**—Teit in Mem. Am. Mus. Nat. Hist., II, 167, 1900. **O-kan-ă-kan.**—Morgan, Consang. and Affin., 290, 1871. **Okanakanes.**—De Smet, Letters, 230, 1843. **Okanaken.**—Boas in 6th Rep. N. W. Tribes Can., map, 1890. **O'Kanies-Kanies.**—Stevens in H. R. Doc. 48, 34th Cong., 1st sess., 3, 1856. **Okenaganes.**—Shea, Cath. Miss., 477, 1855. **Okenakanes.**—De Smet, Letters, 224, 1843. **Okiakanes.**—Stevens in Ind. Aff. Rep. 1856, 190, 1857. **Okinaganes.**—De Smet, op. cit., 37. **Okinagans.**—M'Vickar, Exped. Lewis and Clark, II, 386, 1842. **Okinahane.**—Stevens in Sen. Ex. Doc. 66, 34th Cong., 1st sess., 12, 1856. **OKinakain.**—Gallatin in Trans. Am. Ethnol. Soc., II, 27, 1848. **Okinakan.**—Hale in U. S. Expl. Exped., VI, 205, 1846. **Okinakanes.**—Stevens in Ind. Aff. Rep., 392, 1854. **O'Kinakanes.**—Taylor in Sen. Ex. Doc. 4, 40th Cong., spec. sess., 26, 1867. **Okinā′k′ēn.**—Boas in 5th Rep. N. W. Tribes Can., 10, 1889. **O′kinā′k·ēn.**—Chamberlain in 8th Rep. N. W. Tribes Can., 7, 1892. **Okinekane.**—De Smet, Letters, 215, 1843. **Okin-e-Kanes.**—Craig in H. R. Ex. Doc. 76, 34th Cong., 3d sess., 171, 1857. **O-kin-i-kaines.**—Shaw in H. R. Ex. Doc. 37, 34th Cong., 3d sess., 113, 1857. **Okinokans.**—Watkins in Sen. Ex. Doc. 20, 45th Cong., 2d sess., 5, 1878. **O-ki-wah-kine.**—Ross in Ind. Aff. Rep., 27, 1870. **Oknanagans.**—Robertson (1846) in H. R. Ex. Doc. 76, 30th Cong., 1st sess., 9, 1848. **Okonagan.**—Wilkes, U. S. Expl. Exped., IV, 431, 1845. **Okonagon.**—Dart in Ind. Aff. Rep., 216, 1851. **Okonegan**—Wilkes, ibid., 461, 1854. **Omahanes.**—Stevens in Sen. Ex. Doc. 66, 34th Cong., 1st sess., 10, 1856. **Onkinegans.**—Lane in Sen. Ex. Doc. 52, 31st Cong., 1st sess., 170, 1850. **Oo-ka-na-kane**—Dawson in Trans. Roy. Soc. Can., sec. II, 6, 1891 (Ntlakyapamuk name). **Oukinegans.**—Lane in Ind. Aff. Rep., 159, 1850. **Sohit-hu-a-ut.**—Mackay quoted in Trans. Roy. Soc. Can., sec. II, 6, 1891. **Sohit-hu-a-ut-uh.**—Ibid. **Sinkuaíli.**—Gatschet, MS., B. A. E. (properly Isonkuaíli, 'our people': own name). **Ske-luh.**—Mackay quoted by Dawson in Trans. Roy. Soc. Can., sec. II, 7, 1891 (own name). **Soo-wān′-a-mooh.**—Dawson, ibid., 5 (Shuswap name). **Su-a-na-muh.**—Mackay quoted by Dawson, ibid. **ToitQuā′ut.**—Boas in 5th Rep. N. W. Tribes Can., 10, 1889 (Ntlakyapamuk name). **U-ka-nakane.**—Mackay quoted by Dawson, op. cit., 6.

Okinoyoktokawik. A small Kaviagmiut Eskimo village on the coast opposite Sledge id., Alaska.—11th Census, Alaska, 162, 1893.

Okiogmiut. A name sometimes given collectively to the Eskimo of St Lawrence and the Diomede ids., Alaska. The former belong properly to the Yuit of Asia; for the latter, see *Imaklimiut* and *Inguklimiut.*

Island Innuit.—Dall in Proc. A. A. A. S., XXXIV, 377, 1885. **Kokh′lit innūin.**—Simpson quoted by Dall in Cont. N. A. Ethnol., I, 15, 1877. **Okeeog′-mūt.**—Dall, ibid. **Okeeogmutes.**—Dall in Proc. A. A. A. S., XVIII, 266, 1869. **Okhaganak.**—Petroff in 10th Census, Alaska, map, 1884.

Okiosorbik. A former Eskimo village on Aneretok fjord, E. Greenland; pop. 50 in 1829.

Okkiosorbik.—Graah, Exped. E. Coast Greenland, 114, 1837.

Okisko. A chief of the Weapemeoc of Virginia, in 1585–86, who with Menatonon gave to Ralfe Lane most of the information communicated to Sir Walter Raleigh respecting the surrounding region. Although independent, Okisko was dominated to some extent by Menatonon, who induced him to acknowledge subjection to the English queen. Nevertheless Lane accused him of being the leader in the plot formed by his tribe, the Mandoag (Nottoway), and other Indians, to massacre the colonists. (C. T.)

Okitiyakni (Hitchiti: *Oki-tiyákni*, probably 'whirlpool' or 'river bend'). A former Lower Creek village on the E. bank of Chattahoochee r., 8 m. below Eufaula, in Quitman co., Ga. Pop. 580 in 1822.

Octiyokny.—Woodward, Reminis., 107, 1859. **O-he-te-yoe-on-noe.**—Hawkins (1814) in Am. State Pap., Ind. Aff., I, 859, 1832. **Oka-tiokinans.**—Morse, Rep. to Sec. War, 364, 1822. **Oketayocenne.**—Hawkins, op. cit., 860. **Okete Yocanne.**—Ibid., 845. **O-ke-teyoo-en-ne.**—Hawkins (1799), Sketch, 66, 1848. **Oki-tiyákni.**—Gatschet, Creek Migr. Leg., I, 140, 1884.

Oklafalaya ('the long people'). One of the three great divisions into which the Choctaw (q. v.) were divided for at least a third of a century prior to their removal to Indian Ter. Originally it may have been the name of a town, extended in time to include all the settlements in the region in which it was situated. Unlike those in the eastern divisions, the Indians of this section were scattered in small settlements over a great extent of territory. "The boundary line separating this from the northeastern district began in the vicinity of the present little town of Cumberland, in Webster co. [Miss.]; thence ran southwesterly on the dividing ridge separating the headwaters of Tibbee (Oktibbeha) on the E. from the Big Black waters on the w. down to the vicinity of Dido, in Choctaw co.; thence in a zigzag course on the dividing ridge between the Noxubee and the Yokenookeny waters to the vicinity of New Prospect; thence it zigzagged more or less easterly between the headwaters of Pearl r. and the Noxubee waters to a point on the ridge not far s. of Old Singleton (not the present Singleton); thence southerly on the ridge between the Pearl r. waters on the w. and the Noxubee and Sukenatcha waters on the E.; thence somewhat westerly by Yazoo Town, in Neshoba co.; thence more or less southerly on the ridge between the headwaters of Talasha and the headwaters of Oktibbeha (there are two Oktibbeha crs. in Mississippi) to the ancient town of Kunshak-bolukta, which was situated in the s. w. part of Kemper co., some 2 m. from the Neshoba and about a mile and a half from the Lauderdale co. line. The line separating the western from the southeastern began at Kunshak-bolukta, first going a short distance northwesterly between the Talasha and Oktibbeha waters; thence it zigzagged more or less southwesterly on the dividing ridge between the Pearl and the Chickasawhay waters until it came to the vicinity of Lake Station, in Scott co. Mokalusha Town (Imoklasha), situated on the headwaters of Talasha cr., in Neshoba co., though somewhat s. of the regular line, belonged to the western district. From the vicinity of Lake Station the line ran southward on the dividing ridge between West Tallyhaly and Leaf r. down to the confluence of these two streams. Leaf r. from this confluence down to where it struck the Choctaw boundary line formed the remainder of the line separating the western district from the southeastern."—Halbert in Pub. Ala. Hist. Soc., Misc. Coll., I, 375–376, 1901.

Hattack-falaih-hosh.—Reed in Sturm's Statehood Mag., I, 85, Nov. 1905. **Oaklafalaya.**—U. S. Ind. Treat. (1837), 698, 1837. **Ókla fálaya.**—Gatschet, Creek Migr. Leg., I, 104, 1884. **Olilefeleia.**—Wright in Ind. Aff. Rep., 348, 1843. **Oocooloo-Falaya.**—Romans, Fla., 73, 1775. **Ukla falaya.**—West Florida map, ca. 1775.

Oklahannali ('six towns'). Originally given to 6 closely connected Choctaw towns on several tributaries of Chicasawhay r., in Smith and Jasper cos., Miss., this name finally came to be applied to one of the three principal divisions of the Choctaw which included, besides the "Sixtowns" proper, the districts of Chickasawhay, Yowani, Coosa, and perhaps some others, the names of which have become lost. The towns were also called "English towns" because they espoused the English cause in the Choctaw civil war of 1748–50. Adair (Hist. Inds., 298, 1775) mentions "seven towns that lie close together and next to New Orleans," possibly meaning these. The six towns were Bishkon, Chinakbi, Inkillis Tamaha, Nashwaiya, Okatalaya, and Talla. They spoke a peculiar dialect of Choctaw, and in the Choctaw Nation, where they removed in 1845, they are still known as Sixtown Indians. Although the name "Six Towns" was usually applied to this group, Oskelagna (q. v.) was also mentioned as one of them, which would make a seventh, thus agreeing with Adair's statement. The

population in 1846 (Rutherford in Ind. Aff. Rep., 877, 1847) was 650. For the boundaries of this division, see *Oklafalaya* and *Oypatoocooloo*. (H. W. H.)

Bay Indians.—Rutherford in Ind. Aff. Rep., 877, 1847. **English Towns.**—Gatschet, Creek Migr. Leg., I, 108, 1884. **Oklahaneli.**—Wright in Ind. Aff. Rep., 348, 1843. **Ókla hánnali.**—Gatschet, Creek Migr. Leg., I, 104, 1884. **Okla-humali-hosh.**—Reed in Sturm's Statehood Mag., I, 85, Nov. 1905. **Six-towns.**—Rutherford in Ind. Aff. Rep., 877, 1847. **Six Towns Indians.**—Claiborne (1843) in Sen. Doc. 168, 28th Cong., 1st sess., 192, 1844.

Oknagak. A Kuskwogmiut Eskimo village and seat of a Roman Catholic mission on the N. bank of Kuskokwim r., Alaska. Pop. 130 in 1880, 36 in 1890.

Oh-hagamiut.—11th Census, Alaska, 164, 1893. **Okhogamute.**—Nelson (1879) quoted by Baker, Geog. Dict. Alaska, 1902. **Oknagamut.**—Baker, ibid. **Oknagamute.**—Bruce, Alaska, map, 1885. **Ookhogamute.**—Hallock in Nat. Geog. Mag., IX, 90, 1898.

Okomiut ('people of the lee side'). An Eskimo tribe dwelling on Cumberland sd., Baffin land. They embrace the Talirpingmiut, Kinguamiut, Kingnaitmiut, and Saumingmiut. When whalers first visited them, about 1850, the population amounted to 1,500, but it was reduced to 245 in 1883. Their villages and settlements are: Anarnitung, Aukardneling, Ekaluakdjuak, Ekaluin, Ekalukdjuak, Idjorituaktuin, Igpirto, Imigen, Kangertloaping, Kangertlung, Kangertlukdjuaq, Karmang, Karsukan, Karusuit, Katernuna, Kekertaujang, Kekerten, Kimissing, Kingaseareang, Kingua, Kitingujang, Kordlubing, Koukdjuaq, Naujateling, Nedlung, Niantilik, Nirdlirn, Niutang, Nuvujalung, Nuvujen, Pujetung, Sakiakdjung, Saunutung, Tikerakdjung, Tuakdjuak, Tupirbikdjuin, Ugjuktung, Ukiadliving, Umanaktuak, and Utikimiting.

Oqomiut.—Boas in 6th Rep. B. A. E., 424, 1888. **Oχomiut.**—Boas in Petermanns Mitt., no. 80, 69, 1885.

Okommakamesit. A village of praying Indians in 1674 near the present Marlborough, Mass. It was in the territory of the Nipmuc.

Okkokonimesit.—Gookin (1677) in Trans. Am. Antiq. Soc., II, 435, 1836. **Okommakamesit.**—Gookin (1674) in Mass. Hist. Soc. Coll., 1st s., I, 185, 1806. **Okonhomessit.**—Gookin (1677) in Trans. Am. Antiq. Soc., II, 455, 1836.

Okopeya ('in danger'). A band of the Sisseton Sioux, an offshoot of the Tizaptan.—Dorsey in 15th Rep. B. A. E., 217, 1897.

Okos ('band of bulls'). A former Arikara band under Kunuteshan, Chief Bear.

Bulls.—Culbertson in Smithson. Rep. 1850, 143, 1851. **O-kōs'.**—Hayden, Ethnog. and Philol., 357, 1862.

Okossisak. An Eskimo village on Salmon r., w. Greenland.—Kane, Arctic Explor., II, 124, 1856.

Okow. See *Occow*.

Okowvinjha. A former Gabrieleño rancheria near San Fernando mission, Los Angeles co., Cal. (Taylor in Cal.

Farmer, May 11, 1860). Probably identical with Kowanga or with Cahuenga.

Okpaak. A Malecite village on middle St John r., N. B., in 1769.

Ocpack.—La Tour, map, 1784. **Okpaak.**—Wood (1769) quoted by Hawkins, Miss., 361, 1845. **Ougpauk.**—Jefferys, Fr. Doms., pt. 1, map, 119, 1761.

Okpam. A former Maidu village on the w. side of Feather r., just below the village of Sesum, Sutter co., Cal.—Dixon in Bull. Am. Mus. Nat. Hist., XVII, pl. 38, 1905.

Oktahatke ('white sand'). A former Seminole town 7 m. N. E. of Sampala, probably in Calhoun co., Fla. Menohomahla was chief in 1823.—H. R. Ex. Doc. 74, 19th Cong., 1st sess., 27, 1826.

Oktchunualgi ('salt people'). An extinct Creek clan.

Ok-chŭn'-wä.—Morgan, Anc. Soc., 161, 1878. **Oktchúnualgi.**—Gatschet, Creek Migr. Leg., I, 156, 1884.

Okuwa. The Cloud clans of the Tewa pueblos of San Juan, Santa Clara, San Ildefonso, Tesuque, and Nambe, N. Mex., and of Hano, Ariz.

Kus.—Stephen in 8th Rep. B. A. E., 39, 1891 (Navaho name). **O'-ku-wa.**—Fewkes in Am. Anthrop., VII, 166, 1894 (Hano). **Okuwa-tdóa.**—Hodge in Am. Anthrop., IX, 349, 1896 (Hano and San Ildefonso forms; tdóa ='people'). **O'-ku-wuñ.**—Stephen, op. cit. (Hano). **O'-mau.**—Ibid. (Hopi name). **Oquwa tdóa.**—Hodge, op. cit. (Santa Clara form; q=Ger. ch). **Owhát tdóa.**—Ibid. (Tesuque form). **Owhü tdoa.**—Ibid. (Nambe form).

Okwanuchu (Ok-wa'-nu-chu). A small Shasta tribe formerly occupying the upper part of McCloud r., Cal., as far down as Salt cr., the upper Sacramento as far down as Squaw cr., and the valley of the latter stream. Their language is in part close to that of the Shasta proper, but it contains a number of totally distinct words, unlike any other surrounding language. (R. B. D.)

Ola (O'-la). A former village of the Maidu on Sacramento r., just above Knight's Landing, Sutter co., Cal. The name has also been applied to the inhabitants as a tribal division. If they were the same as the Olashes, who in 1856 lived near Hock farm, Sutter co., there were 20 survivors in 1856. (R. B. D.)

Olashes.—Taylor in Cal. Farmer, Nov. 9, 1860 (probably identical). **Ol'-la.**—Powers in Cont. N. A. Ethnol., III, 282, 1877.

Olabalkebiche (Ulabalkebish, 'Tattooed Serpent,' in French Serpent Piqué, usually but erroneously translated 'Stung Serpent'). A noted Natchez chief and the one oftenest referred to by French writers. He was not the Great Sun, or head-chief of the nation, but occupied the second position of dignity, that of head war-chief, and was so deeply loved by his superior that he was sometimes, as by Dumont's informant, supposed to have been the head-chief himself. He and the Great Sun are usually called brothers, and very likely they were, though it is possibly they were brothers only in the Indian sense—i. e., as children of women belonging to one social group. The first that is heard of Olabalkebiche is in the Natchez war of 1716, when he with his brother and a number of other persons were seized by Bienville and held in captivity until they had agreed to make reparation for the murder of some traders and assist the French in erecting a fort near their villages. From this time until his death Olabalkebiche appears as the friend of the French and peacemaker between his own people and them. He was on intimate terms with all the French officers and the principal settlers, including the historian Le Page Du Pratz. At his death, in 1725, the grief of the Great Sun knew no bounds, and it was with the utmost difficulty that the French could restrain him from committing suicide. They could not, however, avert the destruction of his wives and officers who were killed to accompany his soul into the realm of spirits. Before this took place his body lay in state in his own house for some time surrounded by his friends, the insignia of his rank, and the marks of his prowess, including the calumets received by him, and 46 rings, to indicate the number of times he had counted coup against his enemies. Detailed descriptions of the mortuary ceremonies are given by Du Pratz and Dumont, though the latter, or rather his anonymous informant, is in error in speaking of him as the Great Sun. From all the accounts given of this chief it is evident that he was a man of unusual force of character combined with an equal amount of sagacity in the face of new conditions, such as were brought about by the settlement of the French in his neighborhood. Whether from policy or real regard he was one of the best friends the French possessed among the Natchez, and his death and that of his brother two years later paved the way for an ascendancy of the English party in the nation and the terrible massacre of 1729. (J. R. S.)

Olacnayake. A former Seminole village situated about the extreme N. E. corner of Hillsboro co., Fla.—H. R. Doc. 78, 25th Cong., 2d sess., map, 768, 1838.

Olagale. A "kingdom," i. e. tribe, mentioned by Fontaneda as being, about 1570, somewhere in N. central Florida, E. of Apalachee. By consonantic interchange it appears to be identical with Etocale (Biedma), Ocale (Ranjel), and Cale (Gentl. of Elvas), a "province" through which De Soto passed in 1539 on the road to Potano (q. v.), and is probably also the Eloqualé of the De Bry map of 1591, indicated as westward from middle St John r., perhaps in the neighborhood of the present Ocala, Marion co., Fla. Biedma speaks of it as a small town, probably confusing the tribe with one of its villages, but all the others speak of it as an independent province or kingdom. Ranjel names Uqueten as the first town of the province entered by the Spaniards coming from the s. (J. M.)

Cale.—Ranjel (*ca.* 1546) in Bourne, De Soto Narr., II, 67, 1904; Gentl. of Elvas (1557), ibid., I, 35, 1904. **Eloqualé.**—De Bry map (1591) in Le Moyne Narr., Appleton trans., 1875. **Etocale.**—Biedma (1544) in Bourne, op. cit., II, 5. **Ocala.**—Brinton, Flor. Penin., 19, 1859. **Ocale.**—Ranjel (*ca.* 1546) in Bourne, op. cit., II, 65; De Soto (1539), ibid., 162. **Ocali.**—Garcilasso de la Vega (1591) in Hakluyt Soc. Pub., IX, xxxii, 1851. **Ocaly.**—Garcilasso de la Vega (1591) in Shipp, De Soto and Fla., 281, 1881. **Olagale.**—Fontaneda (*ca.* 1575), Memoir, B. Smith trans., 18–20, 1854.

Olagatano. Named with Otopali by Fontaneda, about 1575, as a village reported to be inland and N. from the coast provinces of "Chicora," about the present Charleston, S. C. Distinct from Onagatano, which he names as a mountain region farther away. (J. M.)

Olacatano.—Fontaneda (1575) quoted by French, Hist. Coll. La., II, 257, 1875. **Olagatano.**—Fontaneda Mem., Smith trans., 16, 1854. **Olgatano.**—Fontaneda quoted by Shipp, De Soto and Fla., 585, 1881. **Olocatano.**—Fontaneda in Ternaux-Compans, Voy., XX, 24, 1841.

Olamentke. A name first applied by some of the earlier writers to a so-called division of the Moquelumnan family inhabiting the country immediately N. of the Golden Gate and San Francisco bay, in Marin, Sonoma, and Napa cos., Cal. The people of this region were among the later neophytes taken to Dolores mission at San Francisco, and among the first of those at San Rafael and San Francisco Solano missions, both of which were in their country. Very few of these so-called Olamentke now survive. See *Moquelumnan.* (S. A. B.)

Bodega.—Ludewig, Am. Aborig. Lang., 20, 1858. **O'-lah-ment'-ko.**—Merriam in Am. Anthrop., IX, 339, 1907. **Olamentke.**—Baer cited by Latham in Proc. Philol. Soc. Lond., 79, 1854.

Olamon ('paint,' usually referring to red paint.—Gerard). A Penobscot village occupying an island in Penobscot r. near Greenbush, Me.

Olamon.—Me. Hist. Soc. Coll., VII, 104, 1876. **Ollemon Indians.**—Vetromile, ibid., VI, 211, 1859. **Ulamánusĕk.**—Gatschet, Penobscot MS., B. A. E., 1887 (Penobscot name).

Olanche. Supposed to be a Mono-Paviotso band of s. E. California, and evidently the people of Olancha, s. of Owens lake.

Olanches.—Taylor in Cal. Farmer, June 8, 1860.

Old Dogs. A society of the Hidatsa.—Culbertson in Smithson. Rep. 1850, 143, 1851.

Old King. See *Sayenqueraghta.*

Old Knife. A prominent chief of the Skidi Pawnee, known among his people as Latalesha ('Knife Chief'), first brought to public notice at St Louis when he signed, as Settulushaa, the treaty of June 18, and, as Letereeshar, the treaty of June 22, 1818. Maj. S. H. Long met him at his camp on Loup fork of Platte r., Nebr., in 1819.

He was the father of Petalesharo (q. v.) and to him is attributed the cessation of the religious custom of burning prisoners. He also signed the treaty of Ft Atkinson, Council Bluffs, Ia., Sept. 30, 1825. An oil portrait, painted by John Neagle in 1821, is in possession of the Historical Society of Pennsylvania.

Old Mad Town. A former village, probably of the Upper Creeks, on an upper branch of Cahawba r., near the present Birmingham, Ala.—Royce in 18th Rep. B. A. E., Ala. map, 1900.

Old Queen. See *Magnus.*

Old Shawnee Town. A village of the Shawnee, situated before 1770 on Ohio r. in Gallia co., Ohio, 3 m. above the mouth of the Great Kanawha.—Washington (1770) quoted by Rupp, West Penn., app., 401, 1846.

Old Sitka. A summer camp of the Sitka Indians on Baranof id., Alaska; pop. 73 in 1880.—Petroff in Tenth Census, Alaska, 32, 1884.

Old Skin Necklace. A former Oglala Sioux band, under Minisa, or Red Water.—Culbertson in Smithson. Rep. 1850, 142, 1851.

Old Smoke. See *Sayenqueraghta.*

Oldtown. A village of the Penobscot on an island in Penobscot r., a few m. above Bangor, Me. It contained 410 inhabitants in 1898.

Indian Oldtown.—Little (1788) in Me. Hist. Soc. Coll., VII, 13, 1876. **Nganudéne.**—Gatschet, Penobscot MS., B. A. E., 1887 (Penobscot name). **Oldtown.**—Conf. of 1786 in Me. Hist. Soc. Coll., VII, 10, 1876. **Panawanscot.**—Ballard (*ca.* 1830), ibid., I, 466, 1865. **Panawapskek.**—Gatschet, Penobscot MS., B. A. E., 1887 (native form of Penobscot).

Olegel. The Yurok name of a Karok village on Klamath r., N. w. Cal., at the mouth of Camp cr., 1 m. below Orleans Bar.—A. L. Kroeber, inf'n, 1905.

Oleharkarmekarto (*Ole-har-kar-me'-kar-to,* 'elector'). A subclan of the Delawares.—Morgan, Anc. Soc., 172, 1877.

Olemos. A former rancheria connected with Dolores mission, San Francisco, Cal.—Taylor in Cal. Farmer, Oct. 18, 1861.

Oler. The Yurok name of a Karok village between Orleans Bar and Red Cap cr., Klamath r., N. w. Cal.—A. L. Kroeber, inf'n, 1905.

Olesino. A Chumashan village between Goleta and Pt Concepcion, Cal., in 1542.

Olesina.—Taylor in Cal. Farmer, Apr. 17, 1863. **Olesino.**—Cabrillo (1542) in Smith, Colec. Doc. Fla., 183, 1857.

Olestura. A former rancheria connected with Dolores mission, San Francisco, Cal.—Taylor in Cal. Farmer, Oct. 18, 1861.

Olhon. A division of the Costanoan family, formerly on San Francisco peninsula and connected with mission Dolores, San Francisco, Cal. The term Costanos, also made to include other groups or tribes, seems to have been applied originally to them.—A. L. Kroeber, inf'n, 1905.

Alchones.—Beechey, Voy., I, 400, 1831. Ohlones.—Taylor in Cal. Farmer, May 31, 1861. Olchone.—Beechey, op. cit., 402. Ol-hones.—Schoolcraft, Ind. Tribes, II, 506, 1852. Oljon.—Taylor in Cal. Farmer, Oct. 18, 1861.

Olitassa (*Holihtasha*, 'fort is there'). A former important Choctaw town, noted by Romans in 1775 on the site of the present De Kalb, Miss. It had two chiefs and more than 100 cabins, and was a kind of capital for the neighboring towns for 20 m. or more around. Once a year delegates from all these towns met there to make new laws.—Halbert in Pub. Miss. Hist. Soc., VI, 426, 1902.

Ollas. See *Pottery, Receptacles*.

Olmolococ. A former rancheria connected with Dolores mission, San Francisco, Cal.—Taylor in Cal. Farmer, Oct. 18, 1861.

Ololopa (*O'-lo-lo-pa*, related to *o'-lo-lo-ko*, 'smoke-hole'). A division or village of the Maidu near Oroville, on Feather r., Butte co., Cal. They numbered between 100 and 150 in 1850, but are now nearly extinct. (R. B. D.)

Holilepas.—Johnson in Schoolcraft, Ind. Tribes, VI, 710, 1857. Holil-le-pas.—Day (1850) in Sen. Ex. Doc. 4, 32d Cong., spec. sess., 39, 1853. Ho-lil-li-pah.—Ind. Aff. Rep., 124, 1850. Holoáloopis.—Powers in Overland Mo., XII, 420, 1874. Hololipi.—Chever in Bull. Essex Inst. 1870, II, 28, 1871. Hol-ó-lu-pai.—Powers in Cont. N. A. Ethnol., III, 282, 1877. Jollillepas.—Day, op. cit. Oleepas.—Delano, Life on Plains, 293, 1854. O-lip-as.—Day, op. cit. O-lip-pas.—Johnston (1850) in Sen. Ex. Doc. 4, 32d Cong., spec. sess., 45, 1853. Ololópai.—Curtin, MS. vocab., B. A. E., 1885.

Olotaraca. A young chief who led the Indian force which accompanied De Gourges in the destruction of the Spanish forts at the mouth of St John r., Fla., in 1568, and distinguished himself by being the first man to scale the breastwork, killing the gunner who had fired on the advancing French. He was the nephew of the chief of the Saturiba (Satourioua) tribe, which held lower St John r. and had welcomed the French under Ribaut in 1562 and Laudonnière in 1564. The name occurs also as Olotoraca, Olotacara, Otocara, etc., and according to Gatschet the proper form is Hola'taraca, *hola'ta* being the title for a subchief in the Timucua language. (J. M.)

Olowitok (*Ol-o'-wi-tok*, from *olowin*, 'west'). A general name applied by the people of the Miwok (Moquelumnan) stock of California to all people living w. of the speaker. (S. A. B.)

Ol-o'-wi-dok.—Powers in Cont. N. A. Ethnol., III, 349, 1877. Ol'-o-wit.—Ibid. (identical, although given as distinct). Olowitok.—S. A. Barrett, inf'n, 1906. Ol-o-wi'-ya.—Powers, op. cit. (identical, although given as distinct). Olwiya.—S. A. Barrett, inf'n, 1906 (alternative form).

Olpen. A former rancheria connected with Dolores mission, San Francisco, Cal.—Taylor in Cal. Farmer, Oct. 18, 1861.

Olposel. A name applied to one of the villages or small divisions of the southern Wintun or Patwin Indians living on the upper course of Cache cr., in Lake co., Cal. (S. A. B.)

Ol'-po-sel.—Powers in Cont. N. A. Ethnol., III, 219, 1877.

Olulato ('above', 'on high'). A Patwin tribe formerly living on Ulatus cr. and about Vacaville, Solano co., Cal.

Hallapootas.—Taylor in Cal. Farmer, Mar. 30, 1860. Ol-u-la'-to.—Powers in Cont. N. A. Ethnol., III, 218, 1877. Ouloulatines.—Choris, Voy. Pitt., 6, 1822. Ullulatas.—Taylor, op. cit. Ululato.—Chamisso in Kotzebue, Voy., III, 51, 1821.

Olumane (*O-lum'-a-ne*, 'vermilion'). A subclan of the Delawares.—Morgan, Anc. Soc., 172, 1877.

Olumpali. A former large Moquelumnan village in the present Marin co., Cal., at a point about 6 m. s. of the town of Petaluma. (S. A. B.)

Olompalis.—Choris, Voy. Pitt., 6, 1822. Olumpali.—Chamisso in Kotzebue, Voy., III, 51, 1821.

Omaha ('those going against the wind or current'). One of the 5 tribes of the so-called Dhegiha group of the Siouan family, the other 4 being the Kansa, Quapaw, Osage, and Ponca. Hale and Dorsey concluded from a study of the languages and traditions that, in the westward migration of the Dhegiha from their seat on Ohio and Wabash rs. after the separation, at least as early as 1500, of the Quapaw, who went down the Mississippi from the mouth of the Ohio, the Omaha branch moved up the great river, remaining awhile near the mouth of the Missouri while war and hunting parties explored the country to the N. W. The Osage remained on Osage r. and the Kansa continued up the Missouri, while the Omaha, still including the Ponca, crossed the latter stream and remained for a period in Iowa, ranging as far as the Pipestone quarry at the present Pipestone, Minn. They were driven back by the Dakota, and after the separation of the Ponca, who advanced into the Black hills, which occurred probably about 1650 at the mouth of Niobrara r., the Omaha settled on Bow cr., Nebr., and may have already been there at the date of Marquette's map (1673). Jefferys (1761) located the Omaha on the E. side of Missouri r., beyond the Iowa, immediately above Big Sioux r. In 1766 they appear to have had friendly relations with the Dakota, as Carver mentions having met both tribes together on Minnesota r. They were at their favorite resort near Omadi, Dakota co., Nebr., in 1800. Lewis and Clark (1804) found them on the s. side of Missouri r. opposite Sioux City, S. Dak., but learned that the tribe in 1802, while living at a point farther up the Missouri, was visited by smallpox, which had greatly reduced their number and caused their removal. Then, as in later years, they were at constant war with the Sioux. They were on the w. side of the Missouri a short distance above the Platte in 1845, but in 1855 removed to what is now Dakota co., Nebr. They joined with other tribes in the treaties of July 15, 1830, and Oct. 15, 1836,

OMAHA MAN

and by the treaty of Washington, D. C., Mar. 16, 1854, ceded all their lands w. of the Missouri and s. of a line running due w. from the point where Iowa r. leaves the bluffs, retaining their lands N. of this line for a reservation. By treaty of Mar. 6, 1865, they sold part of their reservation to the United States for the use of the Winnebago. Many of them learned to cultivate grain and raise stock, and in 1882, through the effort of Miss Alice C. Fletcher, a law was enacted granting lands in severalty and prospective citizenship.

The primitive dwellings of the Omaha were chiefly lodges of earth, more rarely of bark or mats, and skin tents. The earth lodges, similar in construction to those of the Mandan, were intended principally for summer use, when the people were not hunting. The bark lodges were usually elliptical in form, occasionally having two fireplaces and two smoke holes. The skin tent was used when the people were traveling or hunting the buffalo. Pottery was made by the Omaha before 1850, but the art has been forgotten. Their mortars were made by burning a hollow in a knot or round piece of wood, and spoons were made of horn, wood, and pottery. Polygamy was

practised, but the maximum number of wives that any one man could have was three. Until 1880 there were two principal chiefs, usually selected from the Hangashenu subtribe, though there was no law or rule forbidding their selection from other divisions. In addition to these there were subordinate chiefs. Their religion, according to Dorsey (3rd Rep. B. A. E., 1884), was associated with the practice of medicine, mythology, and war customs, and with their gentile system.

The population of the Omaha since their recovery from the great loss by smallpox in 1802, when they were reduced to about 300, has greatly increased. In 1804, according to Lewis (Statist. View, 16, 1807), they numbered 600, including 150 warriors. In 1829 they were estimated at 1,900, and in 1843 at 1,600, both of which estimates were probably excessive. Schoolcraft gives 1,349 in 1851, Burrows 1,200 in 1857, and the same number is given by the census of 1880. In 1906 the population of the tribe was 1,228.

The Omaha gentes as given by Dorsey (15th Rep. B. A. E., 226, 1897) are: A.—Hangashenu half tribe: 1, Wezhinshte; 2,

OMAHA WOMAN

Inkesabe; 3, Hanga; 4, Dhatada; 5, Kanze. B.—Inshtasanda half tribe: 6, Mandhinkagaghe; 7, Tesinde; 8, Tapa; 9, Ingdhezhide; 10, Inshtasanda. (J. O. D. C. T.)
Eromahas.—W. Reserve Hist. Soc. Tracts, I, no. 5, 24, 1871. Ho'-măⁿ-hăⁿ.—Dorsey, Winnebago MS., B. A. E., 1886 (Winnebago name). Hu-úmûi.—Gat-

schet, MS., B. A. E. (Cheyenne name). **La Mar.**—Lewis and Clark, Discov., 20, 1806 (so called by the French). **Maha.**—Marquette, autograph map (1673) in Shea, Discov., 1852. **Mahaer.**—Balbi, Atlas Ethnog., 33, ¶774, 1826. **Mahági.**—Gatschet, MS., B. A. E. (Shawnee name). **Mahahs.**—Carver, Trav., 109, 1778. **Mahan.**—Lewis, Trav., 14, 1809. **Maharha.**—Orig. Jour. Lewis and Clark (1804), I, 203, 1904. **Mahars.**—Whitehouse (1804) in Orig. Jour. Lewis and Clark, VII, 49, 1905. **Maha's.**—Brackenridge, Views La., 70, 1814. **Mahas.**—Iberville (1701) in Margry, Déc., IV, 587, 1880. **Mahaws.**—Pike, Exped., pt. 2, app., 9, 1810. **Makah.**—U. S. Ind. Treaties, Kappler ed., II, 115, 1904 (misprint). **Mama.**—Gale, Upper Miss., 217, 1867 (misprint). **Mawhaws.**—Carver, Trav., 80, 1778. **Mazahuas.**—Rafinesque in Marshall, Hist. Ky., I, 28, 1824. **O'-mâ'-hâ.**—Lewis and Clark, Discov., 20, 1806. **Omaha hcaka.**—Iapi Oaye, XIII, 33, Sept. 1884 ('real Omaha': Yankton name). **Omahahs.**—U. S. Ind. Treat., 639, 1826. **Omahaws.**—Drake, Ind. Chron., pl., 1836. **Omahuas.**—Rafinesque in Marshall, Hist. Ky., I, 30, 1824. **Omalia.**—Schoolcraft, Ind. Tribes, III, 386, 1853 (misprint). **O-maŋ'-ha.**—Cook, Yankton MS. vocab., B. A. E., 184, 1882. **O-maŋ'-ha-hca.**—Ibid. ('true Omaha'). **Omans.**—Jefferys, Fr. Doms. Am., I, 135, 1761. **Omaonhaon.**—Toussaint, Carte de l'Amér., 1839. **Omau'-hau.**—M'Coy, Ann. Reg., no. 4, 84, 1838. **Omawhaw.**—Schoolcraft, Trav., 309, 1821. **Omawhawes.**—Tanner, Narr., 313, 1830. **Omouhoa.**—La Salle (1681) in Margry, Déc., II, 134, 1877 (identical?). **Omowhows.**—Tanner, Narr., 146, 1830. **Omuhaw.**—Hurlbert in Jones, Ojibway Inds., 178, 1861. **O-ni'-ha-o.**—Hayden, Ethnog. and Philol. Mo. Val., 290, 1862 ('drum-beaters': Cheyenne name). **Oni'häº.**—Mooney, Cheyenne Inds., 423, 1907 (Cheyenne name). **Oo-ma-ha.**—Brackenridge, Views La., 76, 1814. **Otomie.**—Schoolcraft, Ind. Tribes, II, 335, 1852 (misprint). **Owáha.**—Gatschet, MS., B. A. E. (Pawnee name). **Owahas.**—Sen. Ex. Doc. 72, 20th Cong., 2d sess., 101, 1829. **Pŭk-tĭs.**—Grinnell, Pawnee Hero Tales, 230, 1889 (Pawnee name). **U'-aha.**—Gatschet, MS., B. A. E. (Pawnee name). **U'-mă-hă.**—Gatschet, Kaw vocab., B. A. E., 27, 1878 (Kansa name). **U-ma "-ha".**—Dorsey in Am. Antiq., 313, Oct. 1888 (misprint). **U-maⁿ-haⁿ.**—Dorsey in Bull. Philos. Soc. Wash., 128, 1880 ('upstream people': Osage name). **U-manhan.**—Ibid., 129 (misprint). **Uwáha.**—Gatschet, MS., B. A. E. (Pawnee name).

Omamiwininiwak ('people of lower part of the river'). The Nipissing name for the Algonkin, properly so called, survivors of whom still live at Bécancour and at Three Rivers, Quebec.—Cuoq, Lexique Algonquine, 193, 1886.

Omanitsenok (*Ŏmanits'ēnôx*, 'the people of Ŏmanis,' a place on Klaskino inlet, Brit. Col.). A gens of the Klaskino, a Kwakiutl tribe.—Boas in Rep. Nat. Mus. 1895, 329, 1897.

Omaskos ('elk'). A subphratry or gens of the Menominee.—Hoffman in 14th Rep. B. A. E., 42, 1896.

Omatl (*Ŏmatl*). The name of an ancestor of a Tlatlasikoala gens, sometimes applied to the gens itself.—Boas in Petermanns Mitt., pt. 5, 131, 1887.

Omaxtux. A former Chumashan village near Purísima mission, Santa Barbara co., Cal.—Taylor in Cal. Farmer, Oct. 18, 1861.

Omegeeze (*Migizi*, 'bald eagle'). A gens of the Chippewa. See *Migichihiliniou.* **Me-giz-ze.**—Tanner, Narr., 314, 1830. **Me-gizzee.**—Warren in Minn. Hist. Soc. Coll., V, 44, 1885. **Mi'-gisi.**—Gatschet, Ojibwa MS., B. A. E., 1882. **Mīgizi.**—Wm. Jones, inf'n, 1907 (correct form). **O-me-gee-ze'.**—Morgan, Anc. Soc., 166, 1877.

Omenaosse. A village or tribe mentioned by Joutel in 1687 as being between Matagorda bay and Maligne (Colorado) r., Texas. The name was given him by the Ebahamo Indians who lived in that region and who were probably Karankawan. See Gatschet, Karankawa Inds., I, 35, 46, 1891. **Omeaoffe.**—Joutel (1687) in French, Hist. Coll. La., I, 137, 1846 (misprint.). **Omeaosse.**—Ibid., 152. **Omeaotes.**—Barcia, Ensayo, 271, 1723. **Omenaossé.**—Joutel (1687) in Margry, Déc., III, 288, 1878.

Omik. A former Aleut village on Agattu id., Alaska, one of the Near id. group of the Aleutians, now uninhabited.

Omisis (*O'mĭ'sĭs*, 'eaters'; sing., *O'mĭ'sĭsts*). A principal division of the Cheyenne. The name is frequently used as synonymous with Northern Cheyenne, because the dominant division in the N. Before the division of the Cheyenne the Omisis occupied that portion of the camp circle immediately N. of the E. entrance.　　　　　　　　　　　　　　(J. M.)

Eaters.—Dorsey in Field Columb. Mus. Pub. 103, 62, 1905. **Hmĭ'sĭs.**—Mooney in 14th Rep. B. A. E., 1026, 1896. **mi'sis.**—Hayden, Ethnog. and Philol. Mo. Val., 290, 1862. **Ŏ missis.**—Grinnell, Social Org. Cheyennes, 136, 1905.

Omitiaqua. A village ("king") in Florida subject to Utina, chief of the Timucua in 1564, according to Laudonnière. The De Bry map places it E. of lower St John r. **Omitaqua.**—De Bry, map (1591) in Le Moyne, Narr., Appleton trans., 1875. **Omitiaqua.**—Laudonnière (1564) in French, Hist. Coll. La., n. s., 243, 1869.

Ommunise (*Omŭnĭse*, 'he gathers firewood.'—W. J.). A Chippewa or Ottawa band formerly living on Carp r., Mich.; also a place between Lake of the Woods and Winnipeg, so called because of the scarcity of wood. **Carp River band.**—Smith in Ind. Aff. Rep., 53, 1851. **Omanisē.**—Wm. Jones, inf'n, 1905 (correct form). **Ommunise.**—Smith, op. cit.

Omowuh. The Rain-cloud clan of the Patki (Water-house) phratry of the Hopi. **Omá-a.**—Bourke, Snake Dance, 117, 1884. **O'-mau.**—Stephen in 8th Rep. B. A. E., 39, 1891. **Omawuu.**—Dorsey and Voth, Mishongnovi Ceremonies, 175, 1902. **O'-mow-ûh wüñ-wû.**—Fewkes in Am. Anthrop., VII, 402, 1894 (*wüñ-wú*=clan).

Ompivromo. A former village, presumably Costanoan, connected with Dolores mission, San Francisco, Cal.—Taylor in Cal. Farmer, Oct. 18, 1861.

Ona. The third village of the Chilula on Redwood cr., Cal. **Oh-nah.**—Gibbs in Schoolcraft, Ind. Tribes, III, 139, 1853 (Yurok name). **Ono.**—Ibid. **Unuh.**—Powers in Overland Mo., VII, 530, 1872.

Onackatin. See *Onockatin.*

Onagatano. A former province N. of Florida peninsula, in snow-clad mountains, where, in the 16th century, it was said the Apalachee obtained their gold. Distinct from Olagatano, q. v. (Fontaneda Mem., ca. 1575, Smith trans., 20, 1854).

Onaghee. An ancient Seneca settlement on the s. side of Fall brook, at Hopewell, Ontario co., N. Y. Before 1720 a number of the inhabitants settled near Montreal, and in 1750 the place had been long deserted.

Onachee.—Cammerhoff (1750) quoted by Conover, Kan. and Geneva MS. **Onaghee.**—Schuyler (1720) in N. Y. Doc. Col. Hist., v, 543, 1855. **Onahe.**—Doc. of 1719, ibid., 528. **Onahee.**—Doc. of 1726, ibid., 797. **Onahie.**—Evans, Map, 1755. **Onnachee.**—Cammerhoff quoted by Conover, op. cit. **Onnaghee.**—Conover, ibid. **Onnahee.**—Riggs (1720) in N. Y. Doc. Col. Hist., v, 570, 1855.

Onaheli. One of five hamlets composing the former Choctaw town of Imongalasha in Neshoba co., Miss.—Halbert in Pub. Miss. Hist. Soc., VI, 432, 1902.

Onancock. A village of the Powhatan confederacy in 1608, about the site of the present Onancock, in Accomack co., Va. Four or five families were still there in 1722.

Onancock.—Beverley, Va., 199, 1722. **Onancock.**—Bozman, Md., I, 149, 1837. **Onancoke.**—Ibid., 148. **Onankok.**—Herrman (1670), Maps to accompany Rep. on the Line between Va. and Md., 1873. **Onaucoke.**—Pory in Smith (1629), Va., II, 61, repr. 1819.

Onapiem. A village or tribe mentioned by Joutel in 1687 as being N. or N. w. of Maligne (Colorado) r., Tex. The region was occupied and controlled largely by Tonkawan tribes, and the name seems to have been given to Joutel by Ebahamo Indians, who were probably Karankawan. See Gatschet, Karankawa Indians, 35, 1891. (A. C. F.)

Onapiem.—Joutel (1687) in Margry, Déc., III, 289, 1878. **Onapien.**—Joutel (1687) in French, Hist. Coll. La., I, 137, 1846. **Onapienes.**—Barcia, Ensayo, 271, 1723.

Onasakenrat ('White Feather'), **Joseph.** A Mohawk chief, noted for his translations of religious works into his native language. He was born on his father's farm, near Oka, Canada, Sept. 4, 1845; at 14 years of age he was sent to Montreal College to be educated for the priesthood, remaining there about 4 years. He was afterward converted to Protestantism and became an evangelical preacher. On June 15, 1877, the Catholic church of Oka was burned, and Chief Joseph was tried for the offense, but was not convicted. He died suddenly, Feb. 8, 1881, at Caughnawaga. Among his translations into the Mohawk dialect are the Gospels (1880) and a volume of hymns. At the time of his death he was engaged in translating the remainder of the Bible, having reached in the work the Epistles to the Hebrews.

Onathaqua (possibly intended for *Ouathaqua*). A tribe or village about C. Cañaveral, E. coast of Florida, in constant alliance with the Calusa (q. v.) in 1564 (Laudonnière). Probably identical in whole or in part with the Ais tribe. Not to be confounded with Onatheaqua, q. v. (J. M.)

Oathkaqua.—De Bry map (1591) in Le Moyne, Narr., Appleton trans., 1875. **Onathaqua.**—Laudonnière (1564) in French, Hist. Coll. La., n. s., 282, 1869 (possibly for Ouathaqua). **Onothaca.**—Brackenridge, La., 84, 1814. **Otchaqua.**—De l'Isle, map, 1700.

Onatheaqua. A principal tribe in 1564, described as living near the high moun-

tains, apparently in upper Georgia, and equal in power and importance to the Timucua, Potano, Yustaga, and Saturiba, according to Laudonnière. Not to be confounded with Onathaqua (q. v.), near C. Cañaveral, Fla. (J. M.)

Onatheaqua.—Laudonnière (1564) in French, Hist. Coll. La., n. s., 244, 1869; De Bry, map (1591) in Le Moyne, Narr., Appleton trans., 1875 (indicated w. of St John r. and beyond Oustaca=Yustaga).

Onava. A former Nevome pueblo and seat of a Spanish mission founded in 1622; situated in lat. 28° 40′, lon. 109°, on the Rio Yaqui, Sonora, Mexico. Pop. 875 in 1678, 457 in 1730. The inhabitants probably spoke a dialect slightly different from the Nevome proper. The town is now completely Mexicanized.

Hare-eaters.—ten Kate in Jour. Am. Eth. and Arch., 142, 1892 (Tchoofkwatam, or: Pima name). **Ohavas.**—Escudero quoted by Bancroft, No. Mex. States, I, 101, 1884. **Onabas.**—Kino map (1702) in Stöcklein, Neue Welt-Bott, 74, 1726. **Onava.**—Balbi (1826) quoted by Orozco y Berra, Geog., 352, 1864. **San Ignacio Onabas.**—Zapata (1678) in Doc. Hist. Mex., 4th s., III, 359, 1857. **Tchoofkwatam.**—ten Kate, op. cit. ('hare-eaters': Pima name).

Onaweron (prob. '[there] are springs of water'). A traditional Iroquois town of the Bear clan; so enumerated in the list of towns in the Chant of Welcome of the Condolence Council of the League of the Iroquois. Nothing definite is known of its situation or of the particular tribe to which it belonged. See Hale, Iroq. Book of Rites, 120, 1883. (J. N. B. H.)

Onawmanient. A tribe of the Powhatan confederacy on the s. bank of the Potomac in the present Westmoreland co., Va., numbering about 400 in 1608. Their principal village, of the same name, was probably on Nominy bay.

Anawmanient.—Bozman, Md., I, 138, 1837. **Nominies.**—Drake, Bk. Inds., bk. 4, 9, 1848. **Onaumanient.**—Smith (1612), Works, Arber ed., 52, 1884 (the village).

Onbi. A Costanoan village situated in 1815 within 10 m. of Santa Cruz mission, Cal.—Taylor in Cal. Farmer, Apr. 5, 1860.

Onchomo (*Ontcomo*). A former Maidu village at Mud Springs, about 5 m. due s. of Placerville, Eldorado co., Cal.—Dixon in Bull. Am. Mus. Nat. Hist., XVII, pl. 38, 1905.

Ondachoe. A Cayuga village mentioned by Cammerhoff, the Moravian, in 1750, as situated on the w. shore of Cayuga lake, N. Y., apparently opposite Aurora. He said it was larger than Cayuga. Gen. Clark placed it at Sheldrake point, but this is too far s. (W. M. B.)

Ondatra. A name for the muskrat (*Fiber zibethicus*), derived from one of the Huron dialects of the Iroquoian language early current in the Hochelaga region of Canada. A more common name is *musquash*, of Algonquian origin. (A. F. C.)

Ondoutaouaka. An Algonquian tribe or division, probably a part of the Montagnais, living in 1644 about 100 leagues above "Saguené," Quebec.

Ondoutaoüaheronnon.—Jes. Rel. 1644, 99, 1858.   **Ondoutaouaka.**—Ibid., 1642, 10, 1858.

Onechsagerat. The "old chief" of Cayuga, mentioned by Cammerhoff in 1750. He was also styled Teiyughsaragarat, the principal chief, when he received Sir Wm. Johnson's belts and went to Canada in 1756. Weiser called him Oyeaghseragearat in 1754, and Oyuchseragarat in 1752. His name appears in 1762 and 1774, the latter year at Onondaga, in November, when "a Cayuga chief named Oyeghseragearat spoke." This may possibly have been a younger man.   (W. M. B.)

Oneida (Anglicized compressed form of the common Iroquois term *tiionĕñ'iote*, 'there it it-rock has-set-up (continuative),' i. e. a rock that something set up and is still standing, referring to a large sienite bowlder near the site of one of their ancient villages). A tribe of the Iroquois confederation, formerly occupying the country s. of Oneida lake, Oneida co., N. Y., and latterly including the upper waters of the Susquehanna. According to authentic tradition, the Oneida was the second tribe to accept the proposition of Dekanawida and Hiawatha to form a defensive and offensive league of all the tribes of men for the promotion of mutual welfare and security. In the federal council and in other federal assemblies they have the right to representation by 9 federal chieftains of the highest rank. Like the Mohawk, the Oneida have only 3 clans, the Turtle, the Wolf, and the Bear, each clan being represented by 3 of the 9 federal representatives of this tribe (see *Clan and Gens*). Insofar as eldership as a member of a clan phratry can give precedence in roll-call and the right to discuss first in order all matters coming before its side of the council fire, the Oneida are the dominant tribe within the tribal phratry, called the Four (originally Two) Brothers and "Offspring," to which they belong. In tribal assemblies the Turtle and the Wolf constitute a clan phratry, and the Bear another. The Oneida have usually been a conservative people in their dealing with their allies and with other peoples. In 1635 they, with the Onondaga, Cayuga, and Mohawk, sought to become parties to the peace concluded in the preceding year between the Seneca and the Hurons. At this period they were called sedentary and very populous, but only from Indian reports.

The Jesuit Relation for 1646 (p. 3, 1858) says that with the exception of the Mohawk there was no treaty, properly speaking, then in existence between the Iroquois tribes inclusive of the Oneida and the French. From the same Relation it is learned that "Onnieoute" (Oneniote), the principal Oneida village of that time, having lost the greater portion of its men in a war with the "upper Algonquin," was compelled to request the Mohawk to lend aid in repeopling the village by granting thereto a colony of men, and that it was for this reason that the Mohawk ceremonially and publicly call the Oneida their daughter or son. This story is probably due to a misconception of the fictitious political kinships and relationships established between the several tribes at the time of the institution and organization of the League (see *Confederation*). The Cayuga and the Tuscarora are likewise called "Offspring," but not for the reason above given. The Jesuit Relation for 1648 (p. 46) first definitely locates the Oneida. From the Relation for 1641 (p. 74) it is gathered that the Jesuit fathers had learned that the Oneida had

HENRY POWLISS (WASTHEELGO, "THROWING UP PINS"), AN ONEIDA

a peculiar form of government in which the rulership alternated between the two sexes. This statement is likewise apparently due to a misconception of the fact that among Iroquois tribes the titles to the chiefships belonged to the women of certain clans in the tribe and not to the men, although men were chosen by the women to exercise the rights and privileges and to perform the duties pertaining to these chiefships, and that there were, and indeed still are, a number of women filling federal chiefships bearing the name of the highest class. These women chieftains have approximately the same rights, privileges, and immunities as the men chiefs, but exercise them fully only in emergencies; they, too, maintain the institutions of society and government among the women.

The Jesuit Relation for 1667 (LII, 145, 1899) declares that the Oneida were at that time the least tractable of the Iroquois tribes. It was at this period that Father Bruyas was stationed at the mission of St François Xavier among the Oneida. It is also learned from this source that the Mohegan and the Conestoga menaced the Oneida. While on this mission Father Bruyas suffered for food for a part of the year and was compelled to sustain life on a diet of dried frogs. By the end of the year 1669 he had baptized 30 persons. In 1660 the Oneida with the Mohawk were the least populous of the Iroquois tribes. The Jesuit Relation for 1669–70 speaks of the Oneida being present at a "feast of the dead" held at the Mohawk village of Caughnawaga, showing that in a modified form at least the decennial ceremony of the so-called "Dead Feast" was practised among the Iroquois when first known. On Jan. 30, 1671, the Oneida began the torture of a captive Conestoga woman, and the torture was prolonged through 2 days and 2 nights because he in whose stead she had been given was burned at Conestoga for that length of time. It is held by some that the town defended by four lines of palisades closely fastened together and attacked by Champlain in 1615 with his Huron and Algonquian allies, was an Oneida village, although other authorities place it elsewhere, in Onondaga territory. In fact, the wars of the Oneida were those of the League, although like the other tribes they seem to have put forth most energy against the tribes who in some manner had given them the greatest offense. The Catawba and the Muskhogean tribes, as well as the Susquehanna r. Indians, the Conestoga, gave most occupation to the Oneida warriors.

After the conquest of the tribes on the Susquehanna and its tributaries and those on the Potomac, chiefly by the warriors of the Oneida, the Cayuga, and the Seneca, and those tribes which had submitted to Iroquois rule, a question arose as to the propriety of the Mohawk, who had not given any aid in subduing these peoples, sharing in the income arising from land sales there. Hence for a time the Mohawk received no emolument from this source, until the Iroquois tribes became divided and the Mohawk sold the lands in the Wyoming Valley region of Pennsylvania to the Susquehanna Land Co. of Connecticut. This, then, in 1728, moved the great federal council of the league at Onondaga to send Shikellamy, an Oneida chief, as a superintendent, to the forks of the Susquehanna for the purpose of watching over the affairs and the interests of the Six Nations of Iroquois in Pennsylvania. At first Shikellamy exercised a general supervision over only the Shawnee and the Dela-

wares, who thereafter were required to consult him in all matters arising between them and the proprietary government. So well did he perform his duty that in 1745 Shikellamy was made full superintendent over all the dependent tribes on the Susquehanna, with his residence at Shamokin. He showed great astuteness in the management of the affairs intrusted to his care, seeking at all times to promote the interests of his people. Such was the influence which the Oneida exercised on the Susquehanna.

In 1687 the Oneida were included in the warrant of the King of Great Britain to Gov. Dongan of New York, authorizing him to protect the Five Nations as subjects of Great Britain. In 1696 Count Frontenac burned the Oneida castle, destroyed all their corn, and made prisoners of 30 men, women, and children.

In 1645–46 the Oneida were at war with the Nipissing, and one band of 17 warriors from "Ononiiote" defeated an Algonkin party under Teswehat, the one-eyed chief of this people, killing the chief's son and taking 2 women prisoners. This Iroquois party was afterward defeated by 30 Hurons and the 2 women were recaptured.

In the Jesuit Relation for 1666–68 Father Bruyas writes that the Oneida were reputed the most cruel of all the Iroquois tribes; that they had always made war on the Algonkin and the Hurons, and that two-thirds of the population of their villages were composed of the people of these two tribes who had become Iroquois in temper and inclination. This missionary adds that the nature of the Oneida was then altogether barbarous, being cruel, sly, cunning, and prone to bloodshed and carnage.

In 1655 a party of 60 Oneida warriors was sent against the Amikwa, or Beaver Indians. This war was still in progress in 1661, for in that year 2 bands, one of 24 and the other of 30 warriors, were encountered on their way to fight the Amikwa.

Chauchetière (letter in Jesuit Relations, Thwaites ed., LXII, 185, 1900) says that "war is blazing in the country of the Outaouaks," that the Iroquois, especially the Oneida, continued their hatred of the Outagami (Foxes) and the Illinois, and so have slain and captured many Illinois. In 1681 they killed or captured about 1,000 of these unfortunate people.

In 1711, about half of the Tuscarora tribe, then dwelling in North Carolina, seems to have conspired with several alien neighboring tribes and bands to destroy the Carolina settlers. The colonists, however, recollecting the ancient feud between the Southern and the Northern Indians, allied themselves with the

Catawba and some Muskhogean tribes. The Tuscarora, sustaining several severe defeats, were finally driven from their homes and hunting grounds. This act of the Southern Indians made the hatred of the Iroquois against the Catawba more bitter and merciless.

The Oneida were at times friendly to the French and to the Jesuit missionaries, while the other Iroquois were their determined enemies. A great part of the Oneida and the Tuscarora, through the influence of Rev. Samuel Kirkland, remained neutral in the Revolutionary war, while the majority of the confederation of the Iroquois were divided and did not act as a unit in this matter. Early in that struggle the hostile Iroquois tribes attacked the Oneida and burned one of their villages, forcing them to take refuge near the Americans in the vicinity of Schenectady, where they remained until the close of the war. Shortly after the main body of the tribe returned to their former homes. At a later period a considerable number emigrated to Canada and settled on Grand r. and Thames r., Ontario. Another small band, called Oriskas, formed a new settlement at Ganowarohare, a few miles from the main body in Oneida co., N. Y. At different earlier periods the Oneida adopted and gave lands to the Tuscarora, the Stockbridges, and the Brothertons. The Tuscarora afterward removed to land granted by the Seneca in w. New York. In 1846, having sold most of their lands in New York, the greater part of the Oneida, together with their last two adopted tribes, removed to a tract on Green bay, Wis., where they now reside. Among those living in New York at the time of removal were two parties known respectively as the First Christian, and the Second Christian or Orchard party.

The Oneida entered into treaties with the United States at Ft Stanwix, N. Y., Oct. 22, 1784; Ft Harmar, O., Jan. 9, 1789; Canandaigua, N. Y., Nov. 11, 1794; Oneida, N. Y., Dec. 2, 1794; Buffalo Creek, N. Y., Jan. 15, 1838; and Washington, D. C., Feb. 3, 1838. They also held no fewer than 30 treaties with the State of New York between the years 1788 and 1842.

The estimates of Oneida population at different periods are no more satisfactory than those relating to the other Iroquois tribes. The earliest account (1660) gives them 500. They are placed at 1,000 in 1677 and 1721. In 1770 they were estimated at 410, in 1776 at 628, and in 1795 at 660, and were said to have been decreasing for a long time. They number at present (1906) about 3,220, of whom 286 are still in New York, 2,151 under the Oneida School Superintendency in Wisconsin, 783 on Thames r., Ontario, besides those settled among the other Iroquois on Grand r., Ontario. There are no means of learning the number of Oneida who joined the several colonies of Catholic Iroquois.

The Oneida towns, so far as known, were: Awegen, Brothertown, Cahunghage, Canowdowsa, Cowassalon, Chittenango, Ganadoga, Hostayuntwa, Oneida, Opolopong, Oriska, Ossewingo, Ostogeron, Schoherage, Sevege, Solocka, Stockbridge, Tegasoke, Teseroken, Teiosweken, and Tkanetota.　　　　(J. N. B. H.)

Anayints.—Pa. Col. Rec., IV, 584, 1851. Anayot hága.—Pyrlæus (ca. 1750) quoted in Am. Antiq., IV, 75, 1881. Annegouts.—Bacqueville de la Potherie, Hist. Amér. Septent., III, 3, 1753. Anoyints.—Mallery in Proc. A. A. A. S., XXVI, 352, 1877. Hogh-na-you-tau-agh-taugh-caugh.—Macauley, N. Y., II, 176, 1829. Honnehiouts.—Hennepin, New Discov., map, 1698. Huniedes.—Doc. of 1676 in N. Y. Doc. Col. Hist., XIII, 500, 1881. Janadoah.—Morse, Am. Geog., I, 454, 1819 (here used for Iroquois generally). Janitos.—Lawson (1700) quoted by Schoolcraft, Ind. Tribes, VI, 326, 1857 (incorrectly given as Lawson's form). Jennitos.—Lawson (1709), Hist. Car., 82, 1860. Nation de la Pierre.—Jes. Rel. 1669, 7, 1858. Ne-ar-de-on-dar-go'-war.—Morgan, League Iroq., 98, 1851 (council name). Neharontoquoah.—Weiser (1750) in Pa. Col. Rec., V, 477, 1851. Ne-haw-re-tah-go.—Macauley, N. Y., II, 185, 1829. Ne-haw-re-tah-go-wah.—Beauchamp in Bull. 78, N. Y. State Mus., 161, 1905. Ne-haw-teh-tah-go.—Cusick, Six Nations. 16, 1828. Ne'yutka.—Gatschet, Seneca MS., B. A. E., 1882 (Seneca name). Ne'yutka-nonu'ndshunda.—Ibid. (another Seneca name). Niharuntagoa.—Pyrlæus (ca. 1750) in Am. Antiq., IV, 75, 1881. Niharuntaquoa.—Weiser (1743), op. cit., IV, 664, 1851. Nihatiloeñdagowa.—J. N. B. Hewitt, inf'n, 1907 ('they are large trees': political name). Nihorontagowa.—Benson quoted by Drake, Bk. Inds., bk. 5, 111, 1848. Niondago'a.—Gatschet, Seneca MS., B. A. E., 1882 ('large trees': Seneca name). Niunda-ko'wa.—Gatschet, Seneca MS., 1882 ('large trees'). Onayauts.—Writer quoted by Drake, Bk. Inds., bk. 5, 4, 1848. Onayiuts.—Colden (1727), Five Nat., app., 58, 1747. O-na-yote'-kä-o-no.—Morgan, League Iroq., 52, 1851. Oncidas.—Keane in Stanford, Compend., 527, 1878 (misprint). Oncydes.—Humphreys, Acct., 294, 1730 (misprint). O-nea-yo-ta-au-cau.—Barton, New Views, app., 6, 1798. Onedes.—Albany Conf. (1737) in N. Y. Doc. Col. Hist., VI, 98, 1855. Onedoes.—Colden (1738), ibid., 123. Oneiadas.—Writer of 1792 in Mass. Hist. Soc. Coll., 1st s., I, 287, 1806. Oneiadds.—Doc. of 1687 in N. Y. Doc. Col. Hist., III, 432, 1853. Oneiades.—Allyn (1666) in Mass. Hist. Soc. Coll., 3d s., X, 63, 1849. Oneidaes.—Dudley (1721) in Mass. Hist. Soc. Coll., 2d s., VIII, 244, 1819. Oneidas.—Doc. of 1676 in N. Y. Doc. Col. Hist., XIII, 502, 1881. Oneides.—Andros (1679), ibid., III, 277, 1853. Oneidoes.—Colhoun (1753), ibid., VI, 821, 1855. Oneids.—Vernon (1697), ibid., IV, 289, 1854. Oneijdes.—Wessels (1693), ibid., 60. Oneiochronon.—Jes. Rel. 1640, 35, 1858. Oneiotchronons.—Ibid., 1646, 34, 1858. Onei8chronons.—Ibid., 1639, 67, 1858. Oneiouks.—Coxe, Carolana, 56, 1741. Oneiouronons.—Courcelles (1670) in Margry, Déc., I, 178, 1875. Oneiout.—Jes. Rel. 1656, 12, 1858 (village). Onei8tcheronons.—Jes. Rel. 1646, 34, 1858. Oneioutchronnons.—Ibid., 1656, 17, 1858. Onei-yu-ta-augh-a.—Macauley, N. Y., II, 185, 1829. Oneiyutas.—Edwards (1751) in Mass. Hist. Soc. Coll., 1st s., X, 146, 1849. Onejda.—Wraxall (1754) in N. Y. Doc. Col. Hist., VI, 857, 1855. Onejdes.—Cortland (1687), ibid., III, 435, 1853. Onejoust.—Louis XIV (1699), ibid., IX, 698, 1855. Oneotas.—Mallery in Proc. A. A. A. S., XXVI, 352, 1877. Oneout.—Jes. Rel. 1656, 10, 1858 (village). Oneoutchoueronons.—Jes. Rel. 1656, 10, 1858. Oneyades.—Doc. of 1679 in N. Y. Doc. Col. Hist., XIII, 536, 1881. Oneydas.—Doc. of 1677, ibid., XIII, 510,

1881. **Oneydays.**—Albany Conf. (1748), ibid., VI, 447, 1855. **Oneyders.**—Markham (1691), ibid., III, 807, 1853. **Oneydes.**—Livingston (1677), ibid., XIII, 510, 1881. **Oneydese.**—Livingston (1720), ibid., V, 565, 1855. **Oneydeys.**—Albany Conf. (1751), ibid., VI, 719, 1855. **Oneydoes.**—Marshe (1744) in Mass. Hist. Soc. Coll., 3d s., VII, 196, 1838. **Oneydos.**—Clarkson (1691) in N. Y. Doc. Col. Hist., III, 814, 1853. **Oneyds.**—Fletcher (1693), ibid., IV, 55, 1854. **Oneyede.**—Dongan (1688), ibid., 521. **Oneyonts.**—Boudinot, Star in the West, 100, 1816. **Oneyoust.**—Denonville (1685) in N. Y. Doc. Col. Hist., IX, 282, 1855. **Oneyuts.**—Macauley, N. Y., II, 176, 1829. **Oniadas.**—Carver, Travels, 172, 1778. **Oniades.**—Coursey (1682) in N. Y. Doc. Col. Hist., XIII, 557, 1881. **Onids.**—Homann Heirs map, 1756. **Oniedas.**—Vetch (1719) in N. Y. Doc. Col. Hist., V, 531, 1855. **Oniedes.**—Albany Conf. (1746), ibid., VI, 317, 1855. **Onioets.**—Coxe, Carolana, 56, 1741. **Onioutcheronons.**—Jes. Rel. 1646, 3, 1858. **Oniouts.**—Schoolcraft, Ind. Tribes, V, 154, 1855. **Oniyouths.**—Boudinot, Star in the West, 128, 1816. **O-ni-yu-ta.**—Macauley, N. Y., II, 176, 1829. **Oniyutaaugha.**—Ibid., 274. **Onneiochronnons.**—Jes. Rel. 1648, 46, 1858. **Onneiotohronnons.**—Jes. Rel. 1658, 3, 1858. **Onneioust.**—Bruyas (1673) in Margry, Déc., I, 242, 1875. **Onneiout.**—Vaudreuil (1712), ibid., 41, 1855. **Onneioutohoueronons.**—Jes. Rel. 1656, 14, 1858. **Onneioute.**—Jes. Rel. 1664, 34, 1858. **Onnei8theronnon.**—Jes. Rel. 1660, 6, 1858. **Onneiouthronnons.**—Jes. Rel. 1657, 34, 1858. **Onnejioust.**—Bellin, map, 1755. **Onnejochronons.**—Jes. Rel. 1652, 35, 1858. **Onnejoust.**—Louis XIV (1699) in N. Y. Doc. Col. Hist., IX, 697, 1855. **Onnejouts.**—Jes. Rel. 1669, 7, 1858. **Onneydes.**—Dongan (1687) in N. Y. Doc. Col. Hist., III, 438, 1853. **Onneyotohronon.**—Jes. Rel., index, 1858. **Onneyouth.**—Charlevoix, Voy to N. Am., II, 25, 1761. **Onnogontes.**—Charlevoix (1736) in Schoolcraft, Ind. Tribes, III, 555, 1853. **Onnoyotes.**—Lahontan, New Voy., I, 157, 1703. **Onnoyoute.**—Ibid., map. **Onodos.**—Coxe, Carolana, map, 1741. **Onoiochrhonons.**—Jes. Rel. 1635, 34, 1858. **Onojake.**—La Montagne (1664) in N. Y. Doc. Col. Hist., XIII, 355, 1881. **Onoyats.**—Mallery in Proc. A. A. A. S., XXVI, 352, 1877. **Onoyauts.**—Greenhalgh (1677) in N. Y. Doc. Col. Hist., III, 252, 1853. **Onoyote.**—Pouchot, map (1758), ibid., X, 694, 1858. **Onoyouts.**—Lahontan, New Voy., I, 23, 1703. **Onoyuts.**—La Tour, map, 1779. **Onyades.**—Greenhalgh (1677) in N. Y. Doc. Col. Hist., III, 250, 1853. **Onydans.**—Harris, Voy. and Trav., II, 311, 1764. **Onyedauns.**—Leisler (1690) in N. Y. Doc. Col. Hist., III, 700, 1853. **Otatsightes.**—Macauley, N. Y., II, 176, 1829 (chief's name). **Ouiochrhonons.**—Jes. Rel. 1635, 34, 1858 (misprint). **Ounéyouths.**—Baudry des Lozières, Voy. à la Le., 243, 1802. **Tau-hur-lin-dagh-go-waugh.**—Macauley, N. Y., II, 185, 1829. **T'wǎ'-rú-nä.**—Hewitt, inf'n, 1886 (Tuscarora name). **Uniades.**—Coursey (1682) in N. Y. Doc. Col. Hist., XIII, 558, 1881. **Uniutáka.**—Gatschet, Tuscarora MS., 1885 (former Tuscarora name). **W'tássone.**—Heckewelder, Hist. Inds., 99, 1876 ('makers of stone pipes': Delaware name; applied also to other Indians who excelled in that art).

Oneida. One of the chief and first known villages of the Oneida people, and which within historical times has been removed to several new situations. It seems to have been originally a town of the Wolf clan, for it is so enumerated in the Chant of Welcome of the Condolence Council of the League of the Iroquois; the Wolf clan constituted one of the two phratries in the tribal council of the Oneida. Arent Van Curler, who visited this town in 1634, wrote that it was situated on a high hill and defended by two rows of palisades; in the ramparts were two gates, one on the w. side, over which were standing "3 wooden images, of cut (carved?) wood, like men," adorned with 3 scalps, and the other, on the E. side, adorned with only one scalp; the western gate was 3½ ft wide, while the other was

only 2 ft. He wrote that this palisade was 767 paces in circumference, and that within it were 66 lodges, "much better, higher, and more finished than all those others we saw." Those seen by Van Curler and his companions were the Mohawk castles. Of the first Mohawk castle Van Curler wrote: "There stood but 36 houses, in rows like streets, so that we could pass nicely. The houses are made and covered with bark of trees, and mostly flat at the top. Some are 100, 90, or 80 paces long, and 22 or 23 ft high. . . . The houses were full of corn that they lay in store, and we saw maize; yes, in some houses more than 300 bushels." His description of the third Mohawk castle, then called Sohanidisse, or Rehanadisse, follows: "On a very high hill stood 32 lodges, like the other ones. Some were 100, 90, or 80 paces long; in every lodge we saw 4, 5, or 6 fireplaces where cooking went on." Some of the lodges were finished with wooden fronts, painted with all sorts of beasts, and in some of them were found very good axes, French shirts, coats, and razors, and lodges were seen where "60, 70 and more dried salmon were hanging." While in the Oneida castle Van Curler witnessed the conclusion of a temporary peace compact between the Oneida and the French Indians for purposes of trade for four years. To this he gave the name "Castle Enneyuttehage, or Sinnekens." The Oneida, the Onondaga, and the Cayuga were named respectively Onneyatte, Onondaga, and Koyockure (for Koyockwe), which indicates that the tribal divisions of the Iroquois were well known to the narrator at this period. This town was probably on one of the early Oneida village sites in the upper valley of Oneida cr., not far from Oriskany cr., and according to Van Curler's estimate, 75 or 80 m. w. of the Mohawk castle of Tenotoge (Tionontogen?); it was situated on the E. side of Oneida cr., and Van Curler saw N. w. of it, on the left bank of the creek, "tremendously high land that seemed to lie in the clouds." Just before reaching the castle he saw three graves, "just like our graves in length and height; usually their graves are round." These graves were surrounded with palisades, nicely closed up, and painted red, white, and black. The grave of a chief had an entrance, and at the top there was "a big wooden bird, and all around were painted dogs, and deer, and snakes, and other beasts." Such was the chief Oneida town of 1634. While with the Oneida Van Curler witnessed apparently a part of the New Year ceremonials of the Iroquois, which he regarded as so much "foolery."

According to Greenhalgh, who visited the Oneida in 1677, they had only one town, "newly settled, double stockadoed," containing about 100 houses and 200 warriors, situated 20 (*sic*) m. from Oneida cr. and 30 m. s. of Mohawk r.; it had but little cleared land, "so that they are forced to send to ye Onondago's to buy corne." This village, therefore, was not situated on the site visited by Van Curler. In Aug. 1696 a principal town of the Oneida was burned by Vaudreuil, a lieutenant of Count Frontenac.

In 1756 Sir William Johnson (N. Y. Doc. Col. Hist., VII, 101, 1856) employed the name Onawaraghhare to designate a place regarded as suitable for the erection of a fort, thus showing that at that time there was a village called "Canowaroghere." In 1762 Lieut. Guy Johnson, starting from German Flats, visited the Oneida (N. Y. Doc. Col. Hist., VII, 512, 1856). The first town reached he called "Upper Oneida Castle," and also simply "Oneida." Thence he went to "Canowaroghere, a new village of the Oneidas." On Sauthier's map of Jan. 1, 1779, 3 Oneida villages are placed in the valley of Oneida cr.: (1) Old Oneyda Cast(le), placed E. of the headwaters of Oneida cr. and N. of the junction of the trails from Ft Schuyler and from Ft Herkermer; (2) Canowaroghare, lower down the valley at the junction of the trails from Ft Schuyler and Ft Stanwix, and on the left bank of Oneida cr.; (3) New Oneyda Castle, on the right bank of Oneida cr., at the junction of the trails from his Canowaroghare and from Ft Stanwix, and on the trail leading from Canowaroghare to the Royal Blockhouse on Wood cr. Two of these, if not all of them, were contemporary. In 1774 the Montauk Indians were to be settled at Canowaroghare. At Oneida in 1667 was founded the mission of Saint François Xavier.

In a note attached to the original of a Paris document of 1757 (N. Y. Doc. Hist., I, 526, 1849) the "great Oneida village" is said to be "two leagues from the Lake," and that within it the English had constructed a "picket Fort with four bastions," which however had been destroyed by the Oneida in pursuance of a promise made by them to the Marquis de Vaudreuil. This note adds that a second Oneida village, called "the little village," was situated "on the bank of the Lake."

It is thus seen that the site and the name have shifted from place to place, but were restricted to the valleys of Oneida cr. and upper Oriskany cr. The name Canowaroghare is the modern name of the city of Oneida and of the Indian settlement situated about 2 m. s., in Madison co., N. Y. In 1666–68 (Jes. Rel., Thwaites ed., LI, 121, 1899) Father Bruyas wrote that "Onneiout" was situated on an eminence whence a great portion of the

surrounding country could be seen, were the environing forest cut away; that "there is no river or lake, except at 5 leagues distant from the town;" that more than half the population was composed of "Algonquins and Hurons," and that the Oneida had never spoken of peace until within two years. The Oneida have settlements in Canada and in Wisconsin at Green Bay, but these are not towns.   (J. N. B. H.)

Anajot.—Schweinitz, Life of Zeisberger, 55, 1870 (error; Oneida, not Tuscarora, town). **Canawaroghare.**—N. Y. Doc. Col. Hist., VII, 611, 1856. **Canowaroghere.**—Johnson (1762), ibid., 512. **Dononiioté.**—Jes. Rel. 1646, Thwaites ed., XXIX, 228, 1898. **Enneyuttehage.**—Van Curler (1634–5) in Rep. Am. Hist. Ass'n 1895, 94, 1896. **Ganó-a-ló-hale.**—Beauchamp, Aborig. Place Names of N. Y., 108, 1907. **Onawaraghhare.**—N. Y. Doc. Col. Hist., VII, 101, 1856. **Oneiout.**—Jes. Rel. 1655, Thwaites ed., XLII, 81, 1899. **Onejoust.**—Paris Doc. (1696) in N. Y. Doc. Hist., I, 330, 1849. **Oneout.**—Jes. Rel. 1655, Thwaites ed., XLII, 77, 1899. **Oneyoté.**—Jes. Rel., index, 1858. **Onieoute.**—Jes. Rel., index, 1858. **Onneiou.**—Ibid., Thwaites ed., LXVI, 187, 1900. **Onneioute.**—Ibid., index, 1901. **Onneyatte.**—Van Curler (1634–5) in Rep. Am. Hist. Ass'n 1895, 95, 1896. **Onnie8te.**—Jes. Rel. 1646, 4, 1858. **Onnonioté.**—Jes. Rel., index, 1858. **Ononiioté.**—Jes. Rel. 1646, 51, 1858. **Ononïoté.**—Jes. Rel. 1647, 9, 1858. **Ononjete.**—Jes. Rel. 1645, 32, 1858. **Ononjoté.**—Ibid., 33. **Ouneiout.**—Jes. Rel., Thwaites ed., LXI, 165, 1900. **Ounejout.**—Ibid., 164. **Ounneiout.**—Ibid., 165. **Sinnekens' Castle.**—Van Curler (1634–5) in Rep. Am. Hist. Ass'n 1895, 92, 1896. **Tkanⁿéohá'.**—Hewitt, inf'n, 1907 (Onondaga name). **Tkanⁿ'warú'há'r.**—Hewitt, inf'n, 1907 (Tuscarora name).

Oneidas of the Thames. A body of Oneida, numbering 783 in 1906, residing on a reservation of 5,271 acres on Thames r., in Delaware tp., Middlesex co., near Strathroy, Ontario. Their principal occupation is day labor, and a few of them are good farmers. They are industrious and law-abiding, and while some of them are progressing well, on the whole their progress is slow.

Oneka. A Mohegan chief of Connecticut, eldest son and successor of the celebrated Uncas; born about 1640, died 1710. In 1659, under the name Owanecco, he joined with his father and his brother, Attawenhood, in deeding a tract 9 m. square for the settlement of the town of Norwich, Oneka signing with the totem of a bird. In 1661 he made an attack, with 70 men, on one of Massasoit's villages, killing 3 persons and taking 6 prisoners. In 1675, at the instance of Uncas, he went to Boston, with two brothers and 50 warriors, to offer their services to the English against the Wampanoag under King Philip, which were accepted, and shortly after his party almost captured this noted leader. In 1679 Uncas and Oneka made a grant of 600 acres to the county for rebuilding the jail, and two years later the General Court gave its consent that Uncas should deed his lands to Oneka. The latter had a son named Mahomet, or Mawhomott.

Onekagoncka. A former Mohawk town, situated on the left bank of Mohawk r., at its confluence with Schoharie r., near the site of the present Fort Hunter, Montgomery co., N. Y. It was visited in 1634 by Arent Van Curler (Corlaer), who referred to it as the first castle, built on a high hill and consisting of "36 houses, in rows like streets. . . The houses were made and covered with bark of trees, and mostly are flat at the top. Some are 100, 90, or 80 paces long and 22 and 23 ft. high. . . The houses were full of corn that they lay in store, and we saw maize; yes, .in some of the houses more than 300 bushels. . . We lived a quarter of a mile from the fort in a small house, because a good many savages in the castle died of smallpox." Speaking of Adriochten, the principal chief of the Onekagoncka castle, Van Curler adds: "The chief showed me his idol; it was a head, with the teeth sticking out; it was dressed in red cloth. Others have a snake, a turtle, a swan, a crane, a pigeon, or the like for their idols, to tell the fortune; they think they will always have luck in doing so." (J. N. B. H.)

Oneniote ('projecting stone.'—Hewitt). A former Cayuga village, on the site of the present Oneida, on Cayuga lake, N. Y. It became greatly reduced in the war with the Hurons in the middle of the 17th century, and resorted to a common Iroquois expedient in perpetuating its people by sending to the Mohawk, their neighbors, "for some men to be married to the girls and women who had remained without husbands, in order that the nation should not perish. This is why the Iroquois (Mohawk) name this village their child." (W. M. B.)
Onneioté. —Jes. Rel. 1653, 18, 1858. **Onneiout.**—Ibid. **Onnie8te.**—Jes. Rel. 1646, 4, 1858. **Ononiioté.**—Jes. Rel. 1646, 51, 1858. **Ononioté.**—Jes. Rel. 1647, 9, 1858. **Ononjete.**—Jes. Rel. 1645, 32, 1858. **Ononjoté.**—Ibid., 33.

Onentisati. A Huron village in Tiny township, Ontario, first mentioned in 1635. (W. M. B.)
Onentisati.—Jes. Rel. 1635, 39, 1858. **Onnentissati.**—Ibid.

Onepowesepewenenewak (*Onipowĭsibĭwinĭnĭwŭg,* 'people of death river'). A former Chippewa band in Minnesota. Cf. *Nibowisibiwininiwak.*
Ónĕpówĕ Sĕpĕ Wenenewok.—Long, Exped. St Peter's R., II, 153, 1824. Ŏnipōwisībīwininiwa̧g.—Wm. Jones, inf'n, 1905 (correct form).

Oneronon. An unidentified tribe living s. of St Lawrence r. in 1640.—Jes. Rel. 1640, 35, 1858.

Onextaco. A former rancheria, presumably Costanoan, connected with San Juan Bautista mission, Cal.—Bancroft, Hist. Cal., I, 557, note, 1886.

Oneyana. Alias Beech Tree. An Oneida chief at the treaty of 1788, and called Peter Oneyana at the treaty of 1785. In 1792

Beech Tree was the principal chief and quite influential, witnessing the Cayuga treaty of 1789 and the Onondaga treaty of 1790, and signing the letters of 1786 and 1787. As Onyanta, or Beech Tree, he signed Col. Harper's deed. He probably died before 1795. (W. M. B.)

Ongniaahra ('bisected bottomland'). A village of the Neutrals, situated in 1626–50 on Niagara r., one day's journey from the Seneca. This is the French spelling of the ancient Huron pronunciation of the name, which, written by English writers from Iroquois utterance, has become "Niagara." (J. N. B. H.)
Ongmarahronon.—Jes. Rel. 1640, 35, 1858 (*m* misprint for *ni;* name of the people). **Onguiaahra.**—Jes. Rel. 1641, 75, 1858 (*ui* misprint for *ni*). **Ouaroronon.**—De la Roche Dallion in Sagard, Hist. du Canada, III, 804, 1866 (*u* misprint for *n,* and second *o* for *a*).

Ongovehenok. A Nuwukmiut Eskimo settlement near Pt Barrow, Alaska.—11th Census, Alaska, 162, 1893.

Onia. A former village of the Papago, probably in Pima co., Ariz., containing 8 families in 1865.—Davidson in Ind. Aff. Rep., 135, 1865.

Onismah. A settlement in Port San Juan, s. w. coast of Vancouver id., Brit. Col., probably inhabited by the Pacheenaht.—Brit. and U. S. Survey Map, 1882.

Onixaymas. A former village, presumably Costanoan, connected with San Juan Bautista mission, Cal.
Onextaco.—Engelhardt, Franc. in Cal., 398, 1897. **Onixaymas.**—Taylor in Cal. Farmer, Nov. 23, 1860.

Onkot (*On'-kot'*). A former Chumashan village in Ventura co., Cal.—Henshaw, Buenaventura MS. vocab., B. A. E., 1884.

Onktokadan. A tribe, not identified, said to have been exterminated by the Foxes. According to Sioux tradition they lived on the St Croix r. in Wisconsin and Minnesota (Neill, Minn., 144, 1858).

Onkwe Iyede ('a human being one is standing'). A traditional Iroquois town of the Tortoise clan; so enumerated in the list of towns in the Chant of Welcome of the Condolence Council of the League of the Iroquois. Nothing is known definitely as to its situation. See Hale, Iroq. Book of Rites, 118, 1883. (J. N. B. H.)

Onnahee. A former Seneca town, placed by Conover (Seneca Villages, 3, 1889) on the E. side of Fall brook, in the w. part of lot 20, town of Hopewell, Ontario co., N. Y. In 1719 this was one of the "furtherest castles of the Cenecas," i. e. farthest westward. (J. N. B. H.)
Onaghee.—Schuyler and Livingston (1719) in N. Y. Doc. Col. Hist., V. 542, 1855. **Onahe.**—Doc. of 1719, ibid., 528. **Onnachee.**—Cammerhoff quoted by Conover, Seneca Villages, 3, 1889.

Onnighsiesanairone. One of the 6 "castles" of the Denighcariages (Amikwa) near Michilimackinac, Mich., in 1723.—Albany Conf. (1723) in N. Y. Doc. Col. Hist., V, 693, 1855.

Onnontare (Mohawk: 'it mountain is present.'—Hewitt). A Cayuga town in 1670 (Jes. Rel. 1670, 63, 1858). From remains found there it seems to have been E. of Seneca r., and at Bluff point, near Fox Ridge, Cayuga co., N. Y. It may have derived its name from the moderate elevation above the marsh, or from Fort hill, which is plainly in sight. In 1670 it was the seat of the mission of Saint René and adjoined the marshes by whose name the river was often known. (w. m. b.)
Onnontare.—Jes. Rel. 1670, 63, 1858. Saint René.—Ibid. (mission name).

Onnontioga ('people of Onontio,' i. e. French Indians, Montreal Indians, Quebec Indians). A people, conquered by the Iroquois, living in 1670 among the Seneca in the village of Kanagaro, which was made up almost entirely of incorporated remnants of the conquered Onnontioga, Hurons, and Neutrals. Gen. J. S. Clark placed them at Waverly, N. Y., at or near Spanish hill, and this seems probable. (j. n. b. h.)
Onnontioga.—Jes. Rel. 1670, 69, 1858. Onnon-Tio-gas.—Shea in Schoolcraft, Ind. Tribes, IV, 208, 1854. Onontiogas.—Conover, Kanadesaga and Geneva MS., B. A. E.

Onoalagona ('big head.'—Hewitt). A Mohawk village, about 1620, on the site of Schenectady, Schenectady co., N. Y. A band, taking its name from the village, occupied the immediate vicinity in more modern times. It is said by Macauley, with little foundation in fact, that the village was built on the site of a still older one, which had been the principal village of the tribe and was called Connoharriegoharrie (Kanon'waro'hă're'?). (j. m.)
Con-no-harrie-go-harrie.—Schoolcraft quoted by Ruttenber, Tribes Hudson R., 398, 1872. Con-nugh-harrie-gugh-harie.—Macauley, N. Y., II, 96, 1829. Ohno-wal-a-gantle.—Ibid. O-no-ä-lä-gone'-na.—Morgan, League Iroq., 474, 1851 (Mohawk name). Oron-nygh-wurrie-gughre.—Ruttenber, Tribes Hudson R., 398, 1872 (quoted form).

Cnockatin. An Esopus chief who signed an agreement with Gov. Nicolls in 1665. He was a chief in the preceding year and one of the five Esopus sachems present at the treaty of 1669. Ruttenber calls him Onackatin or Oghgotacton. (w. m. b.)

Onomio (*O-no'-mi-o*). A former Chumashan village between Pt Concepcion and Santa Barbara, Cal., at a locality now called La Gaviota.—Henshaw, Buenaventura MS. vocab., B. A. E., 1884.

Ononchataronon (Huron name). An Algonkin tribe or band that occupied the district near Montreal, Canada, between St Lawrence and Ottawa rs., and wintered near the Hurons. In 1642 they were but a remnant. They claimed to have been the original occupants of Montreal id. and of a large territory on both sides of the St Lawrence. They said they had been conquered and dispersed by the Hurons, who were then their enemies, and that the survivors of the war had taken refuge with the Abnaki or the Iroquois or had joined the Hurons. Hochelaga, the village found on the island by Cartier in 1535, was occupied by an Iroquoian tribe, but, according to Gatschet, the remains of a second village about 2 m. from its site have been discovered. This would clear the confusion as to the stock of the former occupants of the island. Shea suggests that the names Huron and Iroquois have been transposed, which is likely. Charlevoix says that there was a tradition that the Ononchataronon were at one time at war with the Algonkin, and that they were drawn into an ambuscade and entirely destroyed. He adds that at the time of his visit (1721) they had ceased to exist. This tradition, however, seems doubtful. According to the Jesuit Relations, at the general peace of 1646 the French induced the Ononchataronon to settle again on the island, but they soon scattered on account of the Iroquois. It seems they were met with as early as 1609 by Champlain, as Iroquet, one of their chiefs, was with him at this time. The missionaries described them as arrogant, given to superstition and debauchery, and very cruel. (j. m.)
Nation d'Iroquet.—Jes. Rel. 1633, 29, 1858. Onnoncharonnons.—Jefferys, Fr. Dom. Am., pt. 1, 9, 1761. Onnontcharonnons.—Charlevoix, Jour. Voy., I, 174, 1761. Onontchataranons.—Jes. Rel. 1646, 34, 1858. Onontchataronons.—Jes. Rel. 1641, 57, 1858. Onontchateronons.—Jes. Rel. 1643, 61, 1858. 8natchatazonons.—Jes. Rel. 1641, 29, 1858. Ounontcharonnous.—McKenney and Hall, Ind. Tribes, III, 81, 1854. Ounountchatarounongak.—Jes. Rel. 1658, 22, 1858. Ountchatarounounga.—Jes. Rel. 1640, 34, 1858. Yroquet.—Champlain (1615), Œuvres, IV, 56, 1858.

Onondaga (*Onoñtă''ge*', 'on, or on top of, the hill or mountain'). An important tribe of the Iroquois confederation, formerly living on the mountain, lake, and creek bearing their name, in the present Onondaga co., N. Y., and extending northward to L. Ontario and southward perhaps to the waters of the Susquehanna. In the Iroquois councils they are known as *Hodiseññageta*, 'they (are) the name bearers.' Their principal village, also the capital of the confederation, was called Onondaga, later Onondaga Castle; it was situated from before 1654 to 1681 on Indian hill, in the present town of Pompey, and in 1677 contained 140 cabins. It was removed to Butternut cr., where the fort was burned in 1696. In 1720 it was again removed to Onondaga cr., and their present reserve is in that valley, a few miles s. of the lake (Beauchamp, inf'n, 1907).

The Onondaga of Grand River res., Canada, have 9 clans, namely: Wolf, Tortoise (Turtle?), Bear, Deer, Eel, Beaver, Ball, Plover (Snipe?), and Pigeonhawk. The Wolf, Bear, Plover, Ball, and Pigeonhawk clans have each only one federal chiefship; the Beaver, Tortoise, and Eel clans have each two federal chiefships, while the Deer clan has three. The reason for this marked difference in the quotas of chiefships for the several clans is not definitely known, but it may be due to the adoption of groups of persons who already possessed chiefship titles. In federal ceremonial and social assemblies the Onondaga by right of membership therein take their places with the tribal phratry of the "Three Brothers," of which the Mohawk and the Seneca are the other two members; but in federal councils—those in which sit the federal representatives of all the five (latterly six) Iroquois tribes—the Onondaga tribe itself constitutes a tribal phratry, while the Mohawk and the Seneca together form a second, and the Oneida and the

OTOGDAIENDO, ONONDAGA CHIEF AND FIRE-KEEPER

Cayuga originally, and latterly the Tuscarora, a third tribal phratry. The federal council is organized on the basis of these three tribal phratries. The functions of the Onondaga phratry are in many respects similar to those of a judge holding court with a jury. The question before the council is discussed respectively by the Mohawk and Seneca tribes on the one side, and then by the Oneida, the Cayuga, and, latterly, the Tuscarora tribes on the other, within their own phratries. When these two phratries have independently reached the same or a differing opinion, it is then submitted to the Onondaga phratry for confirmation or rejection. The confirmation of a common opinion or of one of the two differing opinions makes that the decree of the council. In refusing to confirm an opin-

ion the Onondaga must show that it is in conflict with established custom or with public policy; when two differing opinions are rejected the Onondaga may suggest to the two phratries a course by which they may be able to reach a common opinion; but the Onondaga may confirm one of two differing opinions submitted to it. Each chieftain has the right to discuss and argue the question before the council either for or against its adoption by the council, in a speech or speeches addressed to the entire body of councilors and to the public.

Champlain related that in 1622 the Montagnais, the Etchemin, and the Hurons had been engaged for a long time in seeking to bring about peace between themselves and the Iroquois, but that up to that time there was always some serious obstacle to the consummation of an agreement on account of the fixed distrust which each side had of the faith of the other. Many times did they ask Champlain himself to aid them in making a firm and durable peace. They informed him that they understood by making a treaty that the interview of the ambassadors must be amicable, the one side accepting the words and faith of the other not to harm or prevent them from hunting throughout the country, and they on their side agreeing to act in like manner toward their enemies, in this case the Iroquois, and that they had no other agreements or compacts precedent to the making of a firm peace. They importuned Champlain many times to give them his advice in this matter, which they promised faithfully to follow. They assured him that they were then exhausted and weary of the wars which they had waged against each other for more than fifty years, and that, on account of their burning desire for revenge for the murder of their kin and friends, their ancestors had never before thought of peace. In this last statement is probably found approximately the epoch of that historic feud mentioned in the Jesuit Relation for 1660 (chap. II) and by Nicholas Perrot, which made the Iroquois tribes, on the one hand, and the Algonkin on the Ottawa and St Lawrence rs., on the other, inveterate enemies, although this may have been but a renewal and widening of a still earlier quarrel. In 1535 Cartier learned from the Iroquoian tribes on the St Lawrence that they were continually tormented by enemies dwelling to the southward, called Toudamani (probably identical with Tsonnontouan, or Seneca, a name then meaning 'Upper Iroquois'), who continually waged war on them.

In Sept. 1655 the Onondaga sent a delegation of 18 persons to Quebec to confer with Governor de Lauson and with the Algonkin and Hurons. The Onondaga spokesman used 24 wampum belts in his address; the first 8 were presents to the Hurons and the Algonkin, whose leading chiefs were there; each present had its own particular name. The Onondaga professed to speak for the "four upper Iroquois nations," namely, the Seneca, Cayuga, Oneida, and Onondaga, thus leaving only the Mohawk, the "lower Iroquois," from this peace conference, but the Onondaga speaker promised to persuade the Mohawk to change their minds and to make peace. The Onondaga asked for priests to dwell among them and for French soldiers to aid them in their war against the Erie.

In May 1657, 10 years after the dispersion of the Hurons from their motherland, the Onondaga sought by the giving of numerous presents and by covert threats of war to persuade the Hurons who had fled to the vicinity of Quebec to remove to their country and to form with them a single people. The Mohawk and the Seneca also were engaged in this business. Finally, the Hurons were forced to submit to the persistent demands of the Iroquois tribes.

In 1686 the Onondaga were at war against the Cherermons (Shawnee?). They were divided into two bands, one of 50 and another of 250, 50 of the latter being from other tribes. But in 1688 the Onondaga were much under French influence and were regarded as the chief among the Iroquois tribes.

In 1682, at Albany, the Onondaga, with the Mohawk, the Oneida, the Cayuga, and the Seneca, entered into a treaty of peace with the commissioners from the colony of Maryland, who contracted not only for the white settlers, but also for the Piscataway Indians.

With the exception of a part of the Seneca, the Onondaga were the last of the five tribes originally forming the League of the Iroquois to accept fully the principles of the universal peace proposed by Dekanawida and Hiawatha.

Early in 1647 a band of Onondaga on approaching the Huron country was defeated by a troop of Huron warriors, the Onondaga chief being killed and a number taken prisoners. Among the latter was Annenraes, a man of character and authority among the Onondaga. In the following spring he learned that some of the Hurons who had been bitterly disappointed because his life had been spared intended to kill him. To some of his Huron friends he related what he had heard, and that he intended to escape to his own country. His resolution, with the reason for making it, having been reported to the leading Huron chiefs of the council, they concluded to aid him in his purpose, trusting that he would render them some valuable service in return. Giving him some presents and provisions, they sent him off secretly at night. Crossing L. Ontario, he unexpectedly encountered 300 Onondaga making canoes to cross the lake for the purpose of avenging his death (believing he had been killed by the Hurons), and awaiting the arrival of 800 Seneca and Cayuga reenforcements. His countrymen regarded Annenraes as one risen from the dead. He so conducted himself that he persuaded the 300 Onondaga to give up all thought of war for that of peace, whereupon the band, without waiting for the expected reenforcements, returned to Onondaga, where a tribal council was held, in which it was resolved to send an embassy with presents to the Hurons for the purpose of commencing negotiations for peace. The chief of this embassy was by birth a Huron named Soionés, so naturalized in the country of his adoption that it was said of him that "no Iroquois had done more massacres in these countries, nor blows more wicked than he." He was accompanied by three other Hurons, who had not long been captives at Onondaga. The embassy arrived at St Ignace July 9, 1647, finding the Hurons divided as to the expediency of acquiescing in the Onondaga proposals, the Bear tribe of the Hurons justly fearing the duplicity of the enemy even though bearing presents. But the Rock tribe and many villages desired the conclusion of peace in the hope that a number of their kin, then captive at Onondaga, would be returned to them. After many councils and conferences it was found expedient to send an embassy to Onondaga in order the better to fathom this matter. For presents the Hurons took valuable furs, while the Iroquois Onondaga used belts of wampum. The Huron embassy was well received at Onondaga, where a month was spent in holding councils. Finally the Onondaga resolved to send back a second embassy, headed by Skanawati (Scandaouati), a federal chieftain, 60 years of age, who was to be accompanied by two other Onondaga and by 15 Huron captives. One of the Huron embassy remained as a hostage. This embassy was 30 days on the way, although it was in fact only 10 days' journey. Jean Baptiste, the returning Huron delegate, brought back 7 wampum belts of the largest kind, each composed of 3,000 or 4,000 beads. By these belts the Onondaga sought to confirm the peace, assuring the Hurons that they could hope for the deliverance of at least 100 more of their captive kin. The Onondaga desired this peace not only because the life of Annenraes had been spared, but also because they were jealous lest the Mohawk, who had become insolent from their victories and were overbearing even to their allies, might become too much so should the Hurons fail to unite all their forces against them, and further because of fear of the power of the Conestoga. In this Onondaga project of peace the Cayuga and Oneida showed favorable interest, but the Seneca would not listen to it, and the Mohawk were still more averse to it as they were jealous of what had been done by the Onondaga. Hence these last two tribes sent forces to assail the village of St Ignace at the end of the winter of 1647–48. The following incidents show the character of some of the chief men and statesmen of the Onondaga:

Early in Jan. 1648 the Hurons decided to send another embassy to Onondaga. They sent 6 men, accompanied by one of the 3 Onondaga ambassadors then in their country, the other two, including Skanawati, the head of the Onondaga embassy, remaining as hostages. But unfortunately the new Huron embassy was captured and killed by a force of 100 Mohawk and Seneca who had come to the borders of the Huron country. The Onondaga accompanying this embassy was spared, and two Hurons escaped. Early in April, when the distressing news reached the ears of Skanawati, the proud Onondaga ambassador remaining with the Hurons as a hostage, he suddenly disappeared. The Hurons believed that he had stolen away, but, a few days after his disappearance, his corpse was found in the forest lying on a bed of fir branches, where he had taken his own life by cutting his throat. His companion, who was notified in order to exonerate the Hurons, said that the cause of his despair was the shame he felt at the contempt shown for the sacredness of his person by the Seneca and the Mohawk in going to the Huron country and massacring the Huron people while his life was in pledge for the keeping of the faith of his people. Of such men was the great federal council of the Iroquois composed.

The Onondaga had good reason for fearing the Conestoga, for the Jesuit Relation for 1647–48 states that in a single village of the latter people there were at that time 1,300 men capable of bearing arms, indicating for this village alone a population of more than 4,500.

At this time the Conestoga chiefs, through two messengers, informed the Hurons that if they felt too weak to defend themselves they should send the Conestoga word by an embassy. The Hurons eagerly seized this opportunity by sending on this mission 4 Christian Indians and 4 "infidels," headed by one

Charles Ondaaiondiont. They arrived at Conestoga early in June 1647. The Huron deputies informed their Conestoga friends that they had come from a land of souls, where war and the fear of their enemies had spread desolation everywhere, where the fields were covered with blood and the lodges were filled with corpses, and they themselves had only life enough left to enable them to come to ask their friends to save their country, which was drawing rapidly toward its end. This spirited but laconic address moved the Conestoga to send an embassy into the Iroquois country to urge on the Iroquois the advantage of making a lasting peace with their Huron adversaries. Jean Baptiste, a Huron ambassador mentioned before, being at Onondaga at the end of summer, learned that this embassy of the Conestoga had reached the Iroquois country, as he even saw some of the Conestoga presents. It was the purpose of the Conestoga to bring about firm peace with the Hurons and the Onondaga, the Oneida and the Cayuga, and, if possible, the Seneca, and to renew the war against the Mohawk, should they then refuse to become parties to it. The Conestoga did not fear the Mohawk. The Jesuit Relation for 1660 states that about the year 1600 the Mohawk had been greatly humbled by the Algonkin, and that, after they had regained somewhat their former standing, the Conestoga, in a war lasting 10 years, had nearly exterminated the Mohawk, who since, however, had partially recovered from the defeat.

Many of the Onondaga joined the Catholic Iroquois colonies on the St Lawrence, and in 1751 about half the tribe was said to be living in Canada. On the breaking out of the American Revolution in 1775 nearly all the Onondaga, together with the majority of the other Iroquois tribes, joined the British, and at the close of the war the British government granted them a tract on Grand r., Ontario, where a portion of them still reside. The rest are still in New York, the greater number being on the Onondaga res., and the others with the Seneca and Tuscarora on their several reservations.

The Onondaga made or joined in treaties with the state of New York at Ft Schuyler (formerly Ft Stanwix), Sept. 12, 1788; Onondaga, Nov. 18, 1793; Cayuga Ferry, July 28, 1795; Albany, Feb. 25, 1817, Feb. 11, 1822, and Feb. 28, 1829. They also joined in treaties between the Six Nations and the United States at Ft Stanwix, N. Y., Oct. 22, 1784; Ft Harmar, O., Jan. 9, 1789; Canandaigua, N. Y., Nov. 11, 1794, and Buffalo Creek, N. Y., Jan. 15, 1838.

In 1660 the Jesuits estimated the Onondaga at about 1,500 souls, while Greenhalgh in 1677 placed them at 1,750, probably their greatest strength. Later authorities give the numbers as 1,250 (1721), 1,000 (1736), 1,300 (1765), and 1,150 (1778), but these figures do not include those on the St Lawrence. In 1851 Morgan estimated their total number at about 900, including 400 on Grand r. In 1906 those in New York numbered 553, the rest of the tribe being with the Six Nations in Canada.

The Onondaga towns, so far as known, were Ahaouete, Deseroken (traditional), Gadoquat, Gannentaha (mission and fort, Kaneenda), Gistwiahna, Onondaga, Onondaghara, Onondahgegahgeh, Onontacet, Otiahanague, Teionnontatases, Tgasunto, Touenho, and Tueadasso. There were also some transient hunting and fishing hamlets.   (J. N. B. H.)

Anandagas.—Audouard, Far West, 178, 1869. **Desonontage.**—Macauley, N. Y., II, 190, 1829 (quoted from some French source; evidently the name Onondaga with the French article *des*). **Ho-de'-san-no-ge-tä.**—Morgan, League Iroq., 97, 1851. **Honnontages.**—Hennepin, New Discov., 18, 1698. **Hutchistanet.**—Gatschet, Seneca MS., 1882 (Seneca form of council name). **Jenondages.**—Markham (1691) in N. Y. Doc. Col. Hist., III, 808, 1853. **La Montagne.**—Greenhalgh (1677), ibid., 252 (French name for Onondaga Castle). **Let-tegh-segh-nig-egh-tee.**—Macauley, N. Y., II, 185, 1829 (an official name). **Montagneurs.**—Greenhalgh (1677) in N. Y. Doc. Col. Hist. III, 252, 1853 (so called by French). **Montagués.**—Vaudreuil (1760), ibid., X, 1093, 1858 (misprint?). **Mountaineers.**—Hennepin, Cont. of New Discov., 92, 1698 (English translation). **Nation de la Montagne.**—Jes. Rel. 1669, 8, 1858. **Nondages.**—Writer of 1673 in N. Y. Doc. Col. Hist., II, 594, 1858. **'Nontagués.**—Beauharnois (1727), ibid., IX, 968, 1855. **Nontaguez.**—Beauharnois (1734), ibid., 1041. **Omatés.**—Narrative of 1693, ibid., 567 (misprint for Onontaé). **Onadago.**—Deed of 1789 in Am. St. Papers, Ind. Aff., I, 513, 1832. **Onandaga.**—Albany Conf. (1746) in N. Y. Doc. Col. Hist., VI, 319, 1855. **Onandagers.**—Weiser (1748) quoted by Rupp., W. Pa., app., 16, 1846. **Onandages.**—Vernon (1697) in N. Y. Doc. Col. Hist., IV, 289, 1854. **Onandago.**—Rupp, Northampton, etc., Cos., 49, 1845. **Onandagos.**—Procter (1791) in Am. St. Papers, Ind. Aff., I, 156, 1832. **Onandogas.**—Chalmers in Hoyt, Antiq. Res., 159, 1824. **Onantagues.**—Chauvignerie (1736) in Schoolcraft, Ind. Tribes, III, 555, 1853. **Ondages.**—Louis XIV (1699) in N. Y. Doc. Col. Hist., IX, 697, 1855. **Ondiondago.**—Lords of Trade (1754), ibid., VI, 846, 1855 (village). **One-daugh-ga-haugh-ga.**—Macauley, N. Y., II, 185, 1829. **Onendagah.**—Doc. of 1719 in N. Y. Doc. Col. Hist., V, 528, 1855. **O-nĕn-tä'-kĕ.**—Hewitt, inf'n, 1887 (correct form). **Onnandages.**—Deed of 1701 in N. Y. Doc. Col. Hist., IV, 910, 1854. **Onnatagues.**—Lahontan (1703) quoted by Drake, Bk. Inds., bk. 5, 5, 1848. **Onnentagues.**—Hennepin, Cont. New Discov., 93, 1698. **Onnondaga.**—French Doc. (1666) trans. in N. Y. Doc. Col. Hist., III, 125, 1853. **Onnondages.**—Livingston (1677), ibid., XIII, 510, 1881. **Onnondagoes.**—Doc. of 1688, ibid., III, 565, 1853. **Onnondagues.**—Schuyler (1702), ibid., IV, 983, 1854. **Onnonlages.**—Hennepin, Cont. of New Discov., 95, 1698 (misprint). **Onnontaé.**—Jes. Rel. 1654, 8, 1858 (village). **Onnontaehronnons.**—Jes. Rel. 1648, 46, 1858. **Onnontaghé.**—Jes. Rel. 1647, 46, 1858. **Onnontagheronnons.**—Jes. Rel. 1657, 15, 1858. **Onnontagk.**—Narrative of 1693 in N. Y. Doc. Col. Hist., IX, 572, 1855 (village). **Onnontagué.**—Jes. Rel. 1670, 75, 1858 (village). **Onnontaguehronnons.**—Jes. Rel. 1656, 30, 1858. **Onnontaguéronnons.**—Jes. Rel. 1656, 17, 1858. **Onnontaguese.**—Macauley, N. Y., II, 185, 1829. **Onnontaguez.**—Jes. Rel. 1670, 6, 1858. **Onnontatae.**—Denonville? (1688) in N. Y. Doc. Col. Hist., IX, 377,

1855 (village). **Onnontoeronnons.**—Jes. Rel. 1657, 8, 1858. **Onnotagues.**—Lahontan, New Voy., I, 231, 1703. **Ononda-agos.**—Vater, Mith., pt. 8, 314, 1816. **Onondades.**—Leisler (1690) in N. Y. Doc. Col. Hist., III, 700, 1853. **Onondaëronnons.**—Jes. Rel. 1646, 16, 1858. **Onondagaes.**—Doc. of 1765 in N. Y. Doc. Col. Hist., VII, 719, 1856. **Onondagah.**—Doc. of 1719, ibid., V, 529, 1855. **Onondages.**—Dongan (1684) in Mass. Hist. Soc. Coll. 4th s., IX, 187, 1871. **Onondagez.**—Bacqueville de la Potherie, Hist. Am., IV, 128, 1753. **Onondaghas.**—Burnet (1720) in N. Y. Doc. Col. Hist., V, 577, 1855. **Onondaghé.**—Jes. Rel. 1647, 9, 1858 (village). **Onondagheronons.**—Ibid. **Onondagoes.**—Ind. Problem N. Y., 196, 1889. **Onondagos.**—Greenhalgh (1677) in N. Y. Doc. Col. Hist., III, 250, 1853. **Onondagues.**—Doc. of 1676, ibid., XIII, 500, 1881. **Onondajas.**—Johnson Hall Conf. (1765), ibid., VII, 719, 1856. **Onondakes.**—La Montagne (1664), ibid., XIII, 355, 1881. **Onondawgaws.**—Jefferys, Fr. Doms., pt. 1, map and note, 1761. **Onondegas.**—Johnson (1757) in N. Y. Doc. Col. Hist., VII, 278, 1856. **Onontaé.**—Jes. Rel. 1642, 83, 1858 (tribe; in the Relation for 1656, p. 7, it is used as the name of the village). **Onontaehronon.**—Jes. Rel. 1637, 111, 1858. **Onontaerhonons.**—Jes. Rel. 1635, 34, 1858. **Onontaeronons.**—Jes. Rel. 1656, 2, 1858. **Onontaerrhonons.**—Jes. Rel. 1635, 34, 1858. **Onontaez.**—La Salle (*ca.* 1682) in Hist. Mag., 1st s., V, 198, 1861. **Onontager.**—Weiser (1737) in Schoolcraft, Ind. Tribes, IV, 325, 1854. **Onontages.**—Humphreys, Acct., 305, 1730. **Onontaghés.**—Doc. of 1695 in N. Y. Doc. Col. Hist., IX, 596, 1855. **Onontago.**—Weiser in Pa. Col. Rec., IV, 778, 1852–56 (village). **Onontagué.**—Jes. Rel. 1656, 7, 1858 (village). **Onontagueronon.**—Sagard (1632), Hist. Can., IV, 1866 (Huron name). **Onontaguese.**—Harris, Voy. and Trav., II, 928, 1705. **Onontahé.**—Writer of 1695 in N. Y. Doc. Col. Hist., IX, 599, 1855 (village). **Onontaheronons.**—Jes. Rel. 1656, 10, 1858. **Onontake.**—Hennepin, New Discov., 316, 1698. **Onontatacet.**—Bellin, map, 1755. **Onthagues.**—Doc. of 1695 in N. Y. Doc. Col. Hist., IX, 612, 1855. **Onoontaugaes.**—Edwards (1751) in Mass. Hist. Soc. Coll., 1st s., X, 146, 1809. **Onoundages.**—Doc. of 1684 in N. Y. Doc. Col. Hist., III, 347, 1853. **Ontagués.**—Frontenac (1682), ibid., IX, 186, 1855. **O-nun-dä'-ga-o-no.**—Morgan, League Iroq., 52, 1851. **Onundagéga.**—Gatschet, Seneca MS., 1882 (Seneca name). **Onundagéga-nonóⁿdshundä.**—Gatschet, ibid. ('large mountain people': a Seneca name). **Onundawgoes.**—Dudley (1721) in Mass. Hist. Soc. Coll., 2d s., VIII, 244, 1819. **Oonontaeronons.**—Jes. Rel. 1647, 46, 1858. **Sagosanagechteron.**—Weiser in Pa. Col. Rec., V, 477, 1852–56 (council name). **Seuh-nau-ka-ta.**—Cusick, Five Nat., 21, 1848 (council name). **Seuh-no-keh'te.**—W. M. Beauchamp, inf'n, 1907 ('bearing the names': own name). **Seuh-now-ka-ta.**—Macauley, N. Y., II, 185, 1829 (an official name). **Tha-to-dar-hos.**—Ibid., 176 (given as a name for the tribe, but evidently another form of Atotarho, the hereditary title of a chief). **Unedagoes.**—Coursey (1682) in N. Y. Doc. Col. Hist., XIII, 558, 1881. **Yagochsanogéchti.**—Pyrlæus (*ca.* 1750) quoted by Gatschet in Am. Antiq., IV, 75, 1881.

Onondaga. The former chief Onondaga town of central New York, whose site and name were shifted from time to time and from place to place. Within its limits formerly lay the unquenched brands of the Great Council Fire of the League of the Iroquois. During the American Revolution, Washington found it necessary to send an army under Gen. Sullivan to punish the Iroquois tribes for their cruel and bloody work in pursuance of their alliance with Great Britain. The chastisement was so thoroughly administered by the total destruction of more than 40 Iroquois villages and the growing crops surrounding them, that the integrity of the League was disrupted and the scattered remnants forced to seek shelter in Canada and elsewhere. Finally, on Grand r., Ontario, the brands of the Great Council Fire of the League were rekindled by the allied portions of all the tribes of the Six Nations, and here the fire is still burning. The portions of the tribes which elected to remain in New York relighted a fire at Onondaga and sought to reestablish the ancient form of their government there, in order to formulate united action on questions affecting their common interests; but this attempt was only partly successful, since the seat of government had forever departed. The establishment at Onondaga of the seat of federal power by the founders of the League of the Iroquois, made Onondaga not only one of the most important and widely known towns of the Iroquois tribes, but also of North America N. of Mexico. At the zenith of the power of the Iroquois it was the capital of a government whose dominion extended from the Hudson r. on the E. to the falls of the Ohio and L. Michigan on the w., and from Ottawa r. and L. Simcoe on the N. to the Potomac on the s. and the Ohio in the s. w.

Around the Great Council Fire of the League of the Iroquois at Onondaga, with punctilious observance of the parliamentary proprieties recognized in Indian diplomacy and statecraft, and with a decorum that would add grace to many legislative assemblies of the white man, the federal senators of the Iroquois tribes devised plans, formulated policies, and defined principles of government and political action which not only strengthened their state and promoted their common welfare, but also deeply affected the contemporary history of the whites in North America. To this body of half-clad federal chieftains were repeatedly made overtures of peace and friendship by two of the most powerful kingdoms of Europe, whose statesmen often awaited with apprehension the decisions of this senate of North American savages.

The sites with their approximate dates here ascribed to Onondaga are those identified by Clark, Beauchamp, and others, and listed by Beauchamp in the notes to his map (Jes. Rel., Thwaites ed., LI, 294, 1899): The site in 1600 was probably 2 m. w. of Cazenovia and E. of West Limestone cr., Madison co., N. Y. Two sites of towns are accredited to 1620, the one 2½ m. s. w. and the other 1 m. s. of Delphi, Onondaga co., N. Y. The site of 1630 was 1½ m. N. w. of Delphi; that of 1640 was about 1 m. s. of Pompey Center, Onondaga co., on the E. bank of West Limestone cr. That of 1655, in which was established the mission of Saint Jean Baptiste, was about 2 m. s. of the present Manlius, in the same county, on what is called Indian hill; the Jesuit

Relation for 1658 says that this town was large and was called "Onnontaghe . . . because it was on a mountain." This town, with its site, is probably identical with that visited by Greenhalgh in 1677, and described as large, unpalisaded, consisting of about 140 houses, and situated on a very large hill, the bank on each side extending at least 2 m., all cleared land and planted with corn. Greenhalgh learned that there was another village of 24 houses situated 2 m. westward; he estimated the Onondaga warriors at about 350. The site of 1696 was 1 m. s. of Jamesville, E. of Butternut cr., Onondaga co. Count Frontenac burned this town in 1696. The site of 1743 was E. of the creek and N. of the present reservation in Onondaga co., while that of 1756 was w. of the creek. The site of 1779 was that of one of the 3 towns plundered and burned in April by the troops of Col. Van Schaick; they were situated within 2 m. of one another and contained 30 to 40 houses. In 1655 the mission of Saincte Marie de Gannentaa was founded, on the shore of L. Onondaga, 12 m. N. of the mission of St Jean Baptiste; it was also called Saincte Marie du Lac de Gannentaa. To this mission village, which was abandoned in 1658, the Jesuits brought 5 small cannon. For the use of the mission the French Governor Lauson, Apr. 12, 1656, granted to the Jesuit fathers "10 leagues of space in every direction, to wit, 10 leagues of front and 10 leagues in depth—and in the place where they shall choose to establish themselves in the country of the Upper Iroquois called Onondageoronons, be it in the town or near the town of Onondage, or at Gannentae, . . . the said place and extent of 10 leagues square is to be possessed by the said reverend Jesuit fathers, their successors and assigns, in freehold forever." This grant was made evidently without the knowledge or consent of the Onondaga and without any compensation or emolument to them, a course of procedure quite in contrast with that of the Dutch and the English colonists in New York, but on the other hand in close accord with the policy of Gov. Winthrop of Massachusetts, tersely expressed in the formula that "if we leave them sufficient for their use, we may lawfully take the rest, there being more than enough for them and us." This doctrine was embodied into law by the General Court of Massachusetts in 1633, justifying its action by Biblical citation.

From the Jesuit Relations it is learned that under the operation of the principle of conferring citizenship by adoption into some definite stream of kinship common to the Iroquois state, there were colo-nized at Onondaga persons and families from at least 7 different tribes. According to the same authority (Thwaites ed., LXVI, 203, 1900) the Jesuit missions to the Onondaga and the Seneca were abandoned in 1709, and in 1711 a French expedition built a blockhouse at Onondaga, 24½ ft long and 18 ft wide, which Peter Schuyler ordered destroyed along with other building material as "there was other wood ready to build a chappell" (N. Y. Doc. Col. Hist., v, 249, 1855).

Of the Onondaga of 1682, Father Jean de Lamberville (Jes. Rel., Thwaites ed., LXII, 1900) wrote the following interesting facts: "I found on my arrival the Iroquois of this town occupied in transporting their corn, their effects, and their lodges to a situation 2 leagues from their former dwelling-place where they have been for 19 years. They made this change in order to have nearer to them the convenience of firewood, and fields more fertile than those which they abandoned." This was probably the town visited by Greenhalgh in 1677. (J. N. B. H.)

Arnoniogre.—Lamberville, letter, in N. Y. Doc. Col. Hist., III, 488, 1853 (misprint for Onnontaguë). **Känätägö'wä.**—Morgan, League Iroq., II, 87, 1904. **Onendagah.**—N. Y. Doc. Col. Hist., Index, 1861. **Onnondage.**—Jes. Rel., Thwaites ed., XLI, 245, 1899. **Onnondague.**—Ibid., XXX, 259, 1898. **Onnondaqué.**—N. Y. Doc. Col. Hist., Index, 1861. **Onnontaé.**—Jes. Rel., Thwaites ed., XL, 163, 1899.—**Onnonta'e.**—Jes. Rel. 1653, Thwaites ed., XXXVIII, 183, 1899. **Onnontaghé.**—Jes. Rel. 1657, 44, 1858. **Onnontagk.**—N. Y. Doc. Col. Hist., Index, 1861. **Onnontagué.**—Jes. Rel., Thwaites ed., XLII, 179, 1899. **Onontaë.**—N. Y. Doc. Col. Hist., Index, 1861. **Onontagué.**—De la Barre (1684) in N. Y. Doc. Col. Hist., IX, 263, 1855. **Oynondage.**—N. Y. Doc. Col. Hist., Index, 1861. **Saint Jean Baptiste.**—Jes. Rel., Thwaites ed., LII, 153, 1899. **Tagochsanagechti.**—De Schweinitz, Life of Zeisberger, 56, 1870 (name of "lower town").

Onondaghara ('it-mountain top'). A former Onondaga village which, according to Macauley, was the largest of five "in the extent of 8 miles." It was situated on Onondaga r., 3 m. E. of Onondaga Hollow, N. Y., and contained about 50 houses in 1829. (J. N. B. H.)

Onondagharie.—Macauley, Hist. N. Y., II, 177, 1829.

Onondahgegahgeh ('place of the Onondaga'). A former Onondaga village w. of Lower Ebenezer, Erie co., N. Y. Part of the Onondaga lived there after the American Revolution until the Buffalo Creek res. was sold in 1838. (W. M. B.)

Onondakai ('Destroy Town'). A Seneca chief who signed the treaty of 1826. His name is also given as Gonondagie, and, more exactly, as Oshagonondagie. 'He Destroys the Town,' written "Straw Town" in the treaty of 1815, Oosaukaunendauki in 1797. He was one of those whose remains were reinterred at Buffalo in 1884. The name was a favorite one, but, as applied to George Washington and some French governors, has a slightly different form. (W. M. B.)

Onondarka ('on a hill'). A Seneca town N. of Karaghyadirha, on Guy Johnson's map of 1771 (Doc. Hist. N. Y., IV, 1090, 1851). (W. M. B.)

Onontatacet ('one goes around a hill or mountain'). A former Onondaga village located on the Charlevoix map of 1745 on Seneca r., N. Y. It was not a Cayuga village, as some assert. (J. N. B. H.)

Onopa ('salt houses.'—Och). A former Nevome pueblo 9 leagues w. of Bacanora, at the present Santa Rosalia, Sonora, Mexico. It was the seat of a Spanish mission dating from 1677. Pop. 171 in 1678, 76 in 1730.

Santa Rosalia de Onopa.—Zapata (1678) in Doc. Hist. Mex., 4th s., III, 346, 1857. **Sta. Rosalia Onapa.**—Zapata (1678) cited by Bancroft, No. Mex. States, I, 245, 1886.

Onowaragon. An Onondaga who succeeded a chief of the same name. The latter was a French partisan and was condoled in 1728. The former attended a council with Gov. Beauharnois in 1742, being the Onondaga speaker. Weiser, who lodged in his house in 1743, calls him Annawaraogon. He may have been the Kayenwarygoa who attended the Boston council of 1744, but this is doubtful. (W. M. B.)

Ontarahronon ('lake people.'—Hewitt). An unidentified sedentary tribe probably living s of St Lawrence r. in 1640.—Jes. Rel. 1640, 35, 1858.

Ontario'lite. A mineral; according to Dana (Text-book Mineralogy, 435, 1888), "a variety of scapolite occurring in limestone at Galway, Ontario, Canada. Formed with the suffix *-lite*, from Greek λιθος, a stone, from *Ontario*, the name of a lake and a Canadian province. The word is of Iroquoian origin, signifying, according to Hale (Iroq. Book of Rites, 176, 1883) 'the great lake,' from Huron *ontara* or the Iroquois *oniatara*, 'lake,' and *-iō*, a suffix meaning 'great,' or later, 'beautiful,' hence perhaps 'beautiful lake.' (A. F. C.)

Ontianyadi (*Oⁿṭi-aⁿyadi*, 'grizzly-bear people'). A Biloxi clan.—Dorsey in 15th Rep. B. A. E., 243, 1897.

Ontikehomawck. An early village of the Stockbridge tribe in Rensselaer co., N. Y. (W. M. B.)

Ontonagon. A Chippewa band formerly living on Ontonagon r. in upper Michigan. Regarding the origin of the name, Baraga (Otchipwe Dict., 295, 1882) says: "The proper meaning of this word is 'my dish.' An Indian tradition says that a squaw once came to the river, now called 'Ondonagan,' to fetch water with an Indian earthen dish, but the dish escaped from her hand and went to the bottom of the river, whereupon the poor squaw began to lament: *niá nind ondgan, nind ondgan!* Ah, my dish, my dish!

And the river was ever since called after this exclamation.''

Nąntunāgunk.—Wm. Jones, inf'n, 1905 (correct form). **Octonagon band.**—U. S. Stat. at Large, x, 220, 1854 (misprint). **Ontonagon band.**—La Pointe treaty (1854) in U. S. Ind. Treat., 224, 1873.

Ontponea. A tribe of the Manahoac confederacy, formerly living in Orange co., Va.

Ontponeas.—Smith (1629), Va., I, 134, repr. 1819. Ontponies.—Jefferson, Notes, 134, 1794. Outpankas.—Strachey (ca. 1612), Va., 104, 1849. Outponies.—Boudinot, Star in the West, 128, 1816.

Ontwaganha. An Iroquois term, having here the phonetics of the Onondaga dialect, and freely rendered 'one utters unintelligible speech,' hence approximately synonymous with 'alien,' 'foreigner.' Its literal meaning is 'one rolls (or gulps) his words or speech.' This epithet was originally applied in ridicule of the speech of the Algonquian tribes, which to Iroquois ears was uncouth, particularly to the northern and western tribes of this stock, the Chippewa, Ottawa, Miami or Twightwigh, Missisauga, Shawnee, the "Far Indians" including the Amikwa (or Neghkariage (of two castles), the Ronowadainie, Onnighsiesanairone, Sikajienatroene or "Eagle People," Tionontati (only by temporary association with the foregoing), Chickasaw (?), Mascoutens (?), Ronatewisichroone, and Awighsachroene. Thus the term was consistently applied to tribes dwelling in widely separated localities. Sometimes, but rarely, it may have been confounded in use with Tsaganha (q. v.), or Agotsaganha, which had a similar origin but was applied to a different group of Algonquian tribes.   (J. N. B. H.)

At8agannen.—Bruyas, Radices, 40, 1863 ('to speak a foreign language': Mohawk name). Atwagannen.—Bruyas as quoted by Shea in Hennepin, Descr. La., 80, 1880. Dawaganhaes.—Letter (1695) in N. Y. Doc. Col. Hist., IV, 124, 1854. Dawaganhas.—Doc. (1695), ibid., 123. Dewaganas.—Ibid., Gen. Index, 1861. Dewogannas.—Nanfan Narr. (1698), ibid., IV, 407, 1854. Douaganhas.—Cortland (1687), Ibid., III, 434, 1853. Douwaganhas.—Ibid. Dovaganhaes.—Doc. (1691), ibid., 778. Dowaganhaas.—Livingston (1700), ibid., IV, 648, 1854. Dowaganhaes.—Doc. (1693), ibid., 23. Dowaganhas.—Cortland, op. cit. Dowaganhoes.—N. Y. Doc. Col. Hist., Gen. Index, 1861. Dowanganhaes.—Doc. (1691), ibid., III, 776, 1853. Hontouagaha.—Hennepin, Descr. La., 80, 1880. Houtouagaha.—Hennepin, New Discov., 59, 1698 (for Ontwaganha; probably Shawnee). Onkoüagannha.—Jes. Rel. 1670, 5, 1858. Ontôagannha.—Lalement (1661-63) in Jes. Rel., Thwaites ed., XLVII, 145, 1899. Ontôagaunha.—Jes. Rel. 1662, 2, 1858. Ontoouaganha.—MS. 1679 in Jes. Rel., Thwaites ed., LXI, 27, 1900. Ontouagannha.—Le Mercier (1670) in Jes. Rel., Thwaites ed., LIII, 48, 1899. Ont8agannha.—Jes. Rel. 1660, 7, 1858 (="Nation du Feu"). Ontouagennha.—Jes. Rel. 1692, 25, 1858. Ontwagannha.—Shea, Cath. Miss., 285, 1855. Takahagane.—La Salle (1682) in Margry, Déc., II, 197, 1877. Taogarias.—Senex, Map N. Am., 1710. Taogria.—Gravier (1701) quoted by Shea, Early Voy., 124, 1861 (=Shawnee; evidently another form for Ontwaganha). Toagenha.—Gallinée (1670) in Margry, Déc., I, 130, 1875. Toaguenha.—Ibid., 136. Tongarois.—La Harpe (1703) in French, Hist. Coll. La., III, 80, 1851. Tongorias.—Rafinesque in Marshall, Ky., I, introd., 34, 1824. Toüagannha.—Jes. Rel. 1670, III, 30, 76, 1858. Touguenhas.—Gallinée (1670) in Margry, Déc., I, 133, 1875. Towaganha.—Message

of 1763 in N. Y. Doc. Col. Hist., VII, 544, 1856. Twa''ga'hä'.—Hewitt, inf'n, 1907 (Seneca form). Waganhaers.—Doc. (1699) in N. Y. Doc. Col. Hist., IV, 565, 1854. Waganhaes.—Livingston (1700), ibid., 691. Wagannes.—Schuyler and Claese (1701), ibid., 891. Wahannas.—Romer (1700), ibid., 799.

Onuatuc. An Algonquian village in 1608 on the E. bank of Patuxent r. in Calvert co., Md. The inhabitants were probably afterward merged with the Conoy.

Onnatuck.—Bozman, Md., I, 141, 1837. Onuatuck.—Smith (1629), Va., I, map, repr. 1819.

Onuganuk. A Chnagmiut Eskimo village at the Kwikluak mouth of the Yukon, Alaska.

Onúg-anúgemut.—Dall, Alaska, 264, 1870.

Onugareclury. A Cayuga village located on Kitchin's map of 1756 between Cayuga and Seneca lakes, N. Y. Other towns were mentioned there a little earlier, but their names do not resemble this.   (W. M. B.)

Onwarenhiiaki. See *Williams, Eleazer.*

Onyanti. See *Oneyana.*

Onyx. See *Marble.*

Oochukham (*Oo-chuk′-ham*). Given by Morgan (Anc. Soc., 172, 1877) as a subclan of the Delawares, and said to mean 'ground-scratcher.'

Oohenonpa ('two boilings'). A division of the Teton Sioux, commonly known as Two Kettle Sioux, or Two Kettles; also a subdivision thereof. No mention of it is made by Lewis and Clark, Long, or other earlier explorers. It is stated in a note to De Smet's Letters (1843) that the band was estimated at 800 persons. Culbertson (1850) estimated them at 60 lodges, but gives no locality and says they have no divisions. Gen. Warren (1856) found them much scattered among other bands and numbering about 100 lodges. Cumming (Rep. Ind. Aff. for 1856) places them on the s. side of the Missouri. Hayden (1862) says they passed up and down Cheyenne r. as far as Cherry cr. and Moreau and Grand rs., not uniting with other bands. Their principal chief then was Matotopa, or Four Bears, a man of moderate capacity but exercising a good influence on his people. They lived entirely on the plains, seldom going to war, and were good hunters and shrewd in their dealings with the traders. They treated with respect white men who came among them as traders or visitors. They were on the warpath in 1866 at the time of the Ft Phil. Kearney massacre, yet it is not certain that they took an active part in this attack. By treaty made at Ft Sully, Dak., on Oct. 19, 1865, they agreed to cease attacking whites or Indians except in self defense and to settle permanently on designated lands. This treaty was signed on their behalf by chiefs Chatanskah (White Hawk), Shonkahwakkonkedeshkah (Spotted Horse), Mahtotopah (Four Bears), and others, and was faithfully observed by them unless they were in the Sitting Bull uprising of 1876, which is doubtful.

Neither contagion nor war materially reduced the number of the Oohenonpa, which seems to have remained comparatively stationary up to 1887, when it was reported as 642, the last separate official enumeration. They reside on Cheyenne River res., S. Dak., with Sihasapa, Miniconjou, and Sans Arcs.

Only two subdivisions were known to Dorsey, the Oohenonpah and Mawakhota. **Kettle band.**—Culbertson in Smithson. Rep. 1850, 142, 1851. **Kettle band Sioux.**—Cumming in H. R. Ex. Doc. 65, 34th Cong., 1st sess., 4, 1856. **Niḣ'-a-o-ćiḣ'-a-is.**—Hayden, Ethnog. and Philol. Mo. Val., 290, 1862 (Cheyenne name). **Ohanapa.**—

AN OOHENONPA, OR TWO-KETTLE SIOUX

Brackett in Smithson. Rep. 466, 1876. **Ohenonpa Dakotas.**—Hayden, Ethnog. and Philol. Mo. Val., map, 1862. **Ohenonpas.**—Keane in Stanford, Compend., 527, 1878. **Oohenoŋpa.**—Riggs, Dakota Gram. and Dict., xvi, 1852. **Oohe-noⁿpa.**—Dorsey in 15th Rep. B. A. E., 220, 1897; McGee, ibid., 161. **Oohenoupa.**—Hind, Red R. Exped., II, 154, 1860. **Three Kettles.**—Ind. Aff. Rep. 1856, 68, 1857. **Two Cauldrons.**—De Smet, Letters, 37, note, 1843. **Two Kettle.**—Gale, Upper Miss., 226, 1867. **Two Kettles.**—Riggs, Dak. Gram. and Dict., xvi, 1852. **Two Rille band.**—Ind. Aff. Rep., 296, 1846. **Wo-he-nōm'-pa.**—Hayden, op. cit., 371.

Ookwolik. A tribe of Eskimo about Sherman inlet in the Hudson Bay region.—Gilder, Schwatka's Search, 199, 1881.

Oolachan. See *Eulachon.*

Ooltan. A former rancheria, probably of the Papago, visited by Father Kino in 1701; situated in N. w. Sonora, Mexico, 3 leagues N. w. of Busanic (q. v.). **S. Estanislao Octam.**—Bancroft, No. Mex. States, I, 502, 1884 (after Kino). **S. Estanislao Ooltan.**—Bancroft, ibid., 497.

Ooltewah (corruption of *Ultiwä'ï*, of unknown meaning). A former Cherokee settlement about the present Ooltewah, on the creek of the same name in James co., Tenn.—Mooney in 19th Rep. B. A. F, 542, 1900.

Oomiak. The large skin boat or "woman's boat" of the Eskimo; spelled also *umiak;* from the name of this vessel in the eastern Eskimo dialects. (A. F. C.)

Oonilgachtkhokh. A Koyukukhotana village, of 17 persons in 1844, on Koyukuk r., Alaska.—Zagoskin quoted by Petroff in 10th Census, Alaska, 37, 1884.

Oonossoora ('poison hemlock'). A Tuscarora village in North Carolina in 1701.—Lawson, Hist. Car., 383, 1860.

Oony. A former Choctaw town on an affluent of upper Chickasawhay r., s. of the present Pinkney Mill, Newton co., Miss.—Brown in Pub. Miss. Hist. Soc., VI, 443, 1902.

Oosabotsee. A band of the Crows. **Butchers.**—Morgan, Anc. Soc., 159, 1877. **Oo-sä-bot-see.**—Ibid.

Oosaukaunendauki. See *Onondakai.*

Oothcaloga (*Uy'gilä'gï,* abbreviated from *Tsuyu'gilä'gï,* 'where there are dams,' i. e. beaver dams). A former Cherokee settlement on Oothcaloga (Ougillogy) cr. of Oostanaula r., near the present Calhoun, Gordon co., Ga.—Mooney in 19th Rep. B. A. E., 545, 1900.

Ootlashoot. According to Lewis and Clark a tribe of the Tushepaw nation (q. v.) in 1805–06, residing in spring and summer on Clarke r. within the Rocky mts., and in the fall and winter on the Missouri and its tributaries. Pop. 400 in 33 lodges. **Outlashoots.**—Robertson, Oreg., 129, 1846 (misprint). **Eoote-lash-Schute.**—Orig. Jour. Lewis and Clark, III, 54, 1905. **Oate-lash-schute.**—Ibid., VI, 114, 1905. **Oat-la-shoot.**—Lewis and Clark Exped., I, map, 1814. **Oat-lash-shoots.**—Orig. Jour. Lewis and Clark, V, 112, 249, 1905. **Oat-lash-shute.**—Ibid., VI, 120, 1905. **Oleachshoot.**—Gass, Journal, 132, 1807. **Olelachshook.**—Clark in Janson, Stranger, 233, 1807. **Olelachshoot.**—Lewis, Travels, 22, 1809. **Oote-lash-shoots.**—Orig. Jour. Lewis and Clark, III, 103, 1905. **Oote-lash-shutes.**—Ibid., 55. **Ootlashoots.**—Lewis and Clark Exped., I, 440, 1814. **Ootslashshoots.**—Orig. Jour. Lewis and Clark, V, 180, 1905. **Shahlee.**—Lewis and Clark Exped., II, 333, 1814. **Shalees.**—Ibid., 329. **Shallees.**—Ibid., 324 (Chopunnish name).

Opa. The fourth Chilula village on Redwood cr., Cal. **Oh-pah.**—Gibbs in Schoolcraft, Ind. Tribes, III, 139, 1853 (Yurok name).

Opament. An Algonquian village in 1608 on the E. bank of the Patuxent, in Calvert co., Md. The inhabitants were probably absorbed by the Conoy.—Smith (1629), Va., I, map, repr. 1819.

Opassom. See *Opossum.*

Opata (Pima: *o-op* 'enemy', *o-otam* 'people'). A division of the Piman family, formerly inhabiting the country between the w. boundary of Chihuahua and the Rio San Miguel in Sonora, Mexico, and extending from the main fork of the Rio Yaqui, about lat. 28° 30′, to 31°, just below

OPATA MAN.   (AM. MUS. NAT. HIST.)

the s. boundary of Arizona, most of them being settled about the headwaters of Yaqui and Sonora rs. They call themselves Joyl-ra-ua, 'village people.'

Physically the Opata may be considered good specimens of the Indian race. They are not large in stature, but are well-proportioned; their complexion is not so dark as that of the Yaqui; their features are regular and agreeable.

Prior to the advent of the Spanish missionaries, to whose efforts they readily yielded, the habits and customs of the Opata were generally akin to those of the Pima and Papago N. and w. They are described as of a submissive disposition, with much regard for honesty and morality, and have always been friendly to the Mexican Government in all the revolutions and civil dissensions, except in 1820, when a portion of them rebelled in consequence of the injustice of a government officer. After several engagements in which the natives displayed great bravery, they were compelled to submit, owing to the exhaustion of their ammunition and the great superiority in number of the opposing Mexican forces. The humanity and justice shown their prisoners in this rebellion have been the subject of praise.

The Opata houses were formerly constructed of mats and reeds, with foundations of stone, and were more durable than those of most of their neighbors. Caves were also inhabited to some ex-

tent by both the Opata proper and the Jova, even in historic times. Owing to the ruggedness of the country they inhabited, the tribe was divided into petty isolated communities, among which dissension frequently arose, sometimes ending in actual hostility. Thus, the inhabitants of Sinoquipe and Banamichi, in the Sonora valley, were once confederated against those of Huepac and Aconchi, immediately s. This led to the construction outside the villages of defensive works of volcanic rock, where an entire settlement or several allied settlements could resort in event of intertribal irruption. Besides this hostility, the tribe was constantly harassed in former times by the Jano, Jocome, and Suma—warlike tribes believed to have been subsequently absorbed by the Apache. While, as a result of such invasions, a number of Opata villages near the Sonora-Chihuahua frontier were abandoned by their inhabitants, the inroads of these bands made no such lasting impression as those in later years by the Apache proper. When unmolested, the Opata cultivated small garden patches in the canyons, which were nourished by water from the mesas, the drift therefrom being arrested by rows of stones. Hrdlicka (Am. Anthrop., VI, 74, 1904) says there remain no apparent traces of tribal organization among them. They have lost their language, as well as their old religious beliefs and traditions, dress like the Spanish Mexicans, and are not distinguishable in

OPATA GIRLS.   (AM. MUS. NAT. HIST.)

appearance from the laboring classes of Mexico. Their chief occupation is agriculture, their crops consisting principally of maize, beans, melons, and chile. Some of the men are employed as laborers. The Jesuit census of 1730 (Bancroft, No. Mex. States, I, 513–14, 1883) gives the population, including the Eudeve and

Jova, as nearly 7,000. Hardy (Trav. in Mex., 437, 1829) estimated them at 10,000. They are now so completely civilized that only 44 Opata were recognized as such by the national census of 1900.

The chief tribal divisions were Opata proper, Eudeve, and Jova. Other divisions have been mentioned, as the Segui (Tegui), Teguima, and Coguinachi (Velasco in Bol. Soc. Mex. Geog. Estad., 1st s., x, 705, 1863); and Orozco y Berra (Geog., 343, 1864) adds a list of villages included in each. As the divisions last named are merely geographic, without linguistic or ethnic significance, they soon dropped from usage.

The villages of the Opata proper, so far as known, were: Aconchi, Arizpe, Babispe, Bacuachi, Baquigopa, Baseraca, Batepito, Batesopa, Cabora, Comupatrico, Corazones, Corodeguachi (Fronteras), Cuchuta, Cuchuveratzi, Distancia, Guepacomatzi, Huachinera, Huehuerigita, Huepac, Jamaica, Los Otates, Metates, Marysiche, Mochilagua, Motepori, Nacori, Nacosari, Naideni, Oposura, Oputo, Pivipa, Quitamac, Sahuaripa, Suya, Tamichopa, Tepachi, Terapa, Teras, Teuricachi, Tizonazo, Toapara, Ures, Vallecillo, and Yecora. For the villages belonging to the other divisions mentioned above, see under their respective names. See also *Civonároco*. The principal authority on the Opata during the mission period is the Rudo Ensayo, an anonymous account written by a Jesuit missionary about 1763 and published in 1863. (F. W. H.)

Joyl-ra-ua.—Bandelier in Arch. Inst. Papers, III, 57, 1890; Gilded Man, 176, 1893 (own name). Opala.—Ladd, Story of N. Mex., 34, 1891 (misprint). Opate.—Bartlett, Pers. Narr., I, 444, 1854. Opauas.—MS. of 1655 quoted by Bandelier, op. cit., IV, 521, 1892. Ore.—Orozco y Berra, Geog., 338, 1864 (=Ure, used for Opata). Sonora.—Ibid. Teguima.—Ibid. (really an Opata dialect). Ure.—Ibid. (doubtless so named because Opata inhabited the greater portion of the partido of Ures).

Opechancanough. A Powhatan chief, born about 1545, died in 1644. He captured Capt. John Smith shortly after the arrival of the latter in Virginia, and took him to his brother, the head-chief Powhatan (q. v.). Some time after his release, Smith, in order to change the temper of the Indians, who jeered at the starving Englishmen and refused to sell them food, went with a band of his men to Opechancanough's camp under pretense of buying corn, seized the chief by the hair, and at the point of a pistol marched him off a prisoner. The Pamunkey brought boat-loads of provisions to ransom their chief, who thereafter entertained more respect and deeper hatred for the English. While Powhatan lived Opechancanough was held in restraint, but after his brother's death in 1618 he became the dominant leader of the nation, although his other brother, Opitchapan,

was the nominal head-chief. He plotted the destruction of the colony so secretly that only one Indian, the Christian Chanco, revealed the conspiracy, but too late to save the people of Jamestown, who at a sudden signal were massacred, Mar. 22, 1622, by the natives deemed to be entirely friendly. In the period of intermittent hostilities that followed, duplicity and treachery marked the actions of both whites and Indians. In the last year of his life, Opechancanough, taking advantage of the dissensions of the English, planned their extermination. The aged chief was borne into battle on a litter when the Powhatan, on Apr. 18, 1644, fell upon the settlements and massacred 300 persons, then as suddenly desisted and fled far from the colony, frightened perhaps by some omen. Opechancanough was taken prisoner to Jamestown, where one of his guards treacherously shot him, inflicting a wound of which he subsequently died.

Opegoi. The Yurok name of the Karok village opposite the mouth of Red Cap cr., on Klamath r., N. W. Cal. It was the Karok village farthest downstream.—A. L. Kroeber, inf'n, 1905.

Oppegach.—Gibbs (1851) in Schoolcraft, Ind. Tribes, III, 148, 1853. Oppegoeh.—Gibbs, MS. Misc., B. A. E., 1852. Op-pe-o.—McKee (1851) in Sen. Ex. Doc. 4, 32d Cong., spec. sess., 164, 1853. Oppe-yoh.—Gibbs in Schoolcraft, op. cit., 151. Redcaps.—Gibbs, MS., op. cit. Up-pa-goine.—McKee, op. cit., 194. Up-pa-goines.—Meyer, Nach dem Sacramento, 282, 1855. Up-pah-goines.—McKee, op. cit., 161.

Opelousa (probably 'black above', i. e. 'black hair' or 'black skull'). A small tribe formerly living in s. Louisiana. It is probable that they were identical with the Onquilouzas of La Harpe, spoken of in 1699 as allied with the Washa and Chaouacha, wandering near the seacoasts, and numbering with those two tribes 200 men. This would indicate a more southerly position than that in which they are afterward found, and Du Pratz, whose information applies to the years between 1718 and 1730, locates the Oqué-Loussas, evidently the same people, westward and above Pointe Coupée, rather too far to the N. He says that they inhabited the shores of two little lakes which appeared black from the quantity of leaves which covered their bottoms, and received their name, which means 'Black-water people' in Mobilian, from this circumstance. If these were the same as the Opelousas of all later writers it is difficult to understand how the change in name came about, but it is not likely that two tribes with such similar designations occupied the same region, especially as both are never mentioned by one author. When settlers began to push westward from the Mississippi, the district occupied by this tribe came to be called after them, and the name is still retained by the parish seat of St Landry. Of their later history little information can be gathered, but it would seem from the frequency with which this name is coupled with that of the Attacapa that they were closely related to that people. This is also the opinion of those Chitimacha and Attacapa who remember having heard the tribe spoken of, and is partially confirmed by Sibley, who states that they understood Attacapa although having a language of their own. It is most probable that their proper language, referred to by Sibley, was nothing more than an Attacapa dialect, though it is now impossible to tell how closely the two resembled each other. In 1777 Attacapa and Opelousa are referred to at the mouth of the Sabine r. (Bolton in Tex. Hist. Assn. Quar., IX, 117–18, 1905), but the latter are usually located in the s. part of St Landry parish, Sibley stating that in 1806 their village was "about 15 m. from the Appelousa church." At that time they numbered about 40 men, but they have since disappeared completely, owing to the invasion of the whites and the Muskhogean Indians from E. of the Mississippi. (J. R. S.)

Apalousa.—Schoolcraft, Ind. Tribes, III, 529, 1853. Apalusa.—Ker, Travels, 301, 1816. Apéloussas.—Baudry des Lozières, Voy. Louisianes, 241, 1802. Apelusas.—Perrin du Lac, Voyage, 379, 1805. Appalousas.—Sibley, Hist. Sketches, 83, 1806. Appelousas.—Gallatin in Trans. Am. Antiq. Soc., II, 116, 1836. Asperousa.—Brion de la Tour, Map, 1784. Black Water.—Jefferys, French Dom., I, 165, 1761. Loupelousas.—French, Hist. Coll. La., II, 70, 1850. Loupitousas.—Baudry des Lozières, Voy. Louisianes, 243, 1802. Obeloussa.—Philippeaux, Map of Engl. Col., 1781. Ogue Loussas.—Jefferys, French Dom., I, 165, 1761. Opalusas.—Rafinesque in Marshall, Ky., I, introd., 24, 1824. Opelousas.—Sibley (1805) in Am. St. Pap., Ind. Aff., I, 724, 1832. Opeluassas.—Ann. de la Propagation de la Foi, I, 49, 1853. Oppelousas.—Brackenridge, Views of La., 82, 1814. Oqué-Loussas.—Du Pratz, Louisiana, 317, 1774.

Opelto (*O′-pel-to,* 'the forks'). A former Nishinam village in the valley of Bear r., which is the next stream N. of Sacramento, Cal.—Powers in Cont. N. A. Ethnol., III, 316, 1877.

Operdniving ('spring place'). A Nugumiut Eskimo spring village in Countess of Warwick sd., near Frobisher bay, Baffin land.
Oopungnewing.—Hall quoted by Nourse, Am. Explor., 191, 1884. Operdniving.—Boas in 6th Rep. B. A. E., 422, 1888. Oppernowick.—Ross, Voy., 164, 1819.

Opia. A Chumashan village between Goleta and Pt Concepcion, Cal., in 1542.—Cabrillo, Narr. (1542) in Smith, Colec. Doc. Fla., 183, 1857.

Opichiken. A Salish band or village under the Fraser superintendency, Brit. Col.—Can. Ind. Aff., 79, 1878.

Opiktulik. A Kaviagmiut Eskimo village on the N. shore of Norton sd., Alaska; pop. 12 in 1880.
Okpiktalik.—Petroff in 10th Census, Alaska, map, 1884. Okpiktolik.—Ibid., 11. Opiktulik.—Baker, Geog. Dict. Alaska, 1902. Oukviktoulia.—Zagos-

kin in Nouv. Ann. Voy., 5th s., XXI, map, 1850. Upiktalik.—11th Census, Alaska, 162, 1893.

Opilhlako (*Opíl′-′láko,* 'big swamp'). A former Upper Creek town on a stream of the same name which flows into Pakan-Tallahassee cr., N. E. Ala., 20 m. from Coosa r.
Opilika.—H. R. Doc. 452, 25th Cong., 2d sess., 93, 1888. Opilike.—Ibid., 49. Opíl′-′láko.—Gatschet, Creek Migr. Leg., I, 141, 1884. O-pil-thluc-co.—Hawkins (1799), Sketch, 50, 1848.

Opinghaki (*O-ping-ha′-ki,* 'white - face land,' i. e. 'opossum land'). A subclan of the Delawares.
Opinghaki.—W. R. Gerard, inf'n, 1907 (correct form). O-ping′-ho′-ki.—Morgan, Anc. Soc., 172, 1877.

Opiscopank. A village of the Powhatan confederacy in 1608, on the s. bank of the Rappahannock in Middlesex co., Va.—Smith (1629), Va., I, map, repr. 1819.

Opistopia. A Chumashan village between Goleta and Pt Concepcion, Cal., in 1542.
Opistopea.—Taylor in Cal. Farmer, Apr. 17, 1863. Opistopia.—Cabrillo, Narr. (1542) in Smith, Colec. Doc. Fla., 183, 1857.

Opitchesaht. A Nootka tribe on Alberni canal, Somass r., and neighboring lakes, Vancouver id., Brit. Col. Anciently this tribe is said to have spoken Nanaimo (q. v.). The septs, according to Boas, are Mohotlath, Tlikutath, and Tsomosath. Their principal village is Ahahswinnis. Pop. 62 in 1902, 48 in 1906.
Hōpetcisā′th.—Boas, 6th Rep. N. W. Tribes Can., 31, 1890. Opechisaht.—Sproat, Savage Life, 308, 1868. Opecluset.—Mayne, Brit. Col., 251, 1862. Ope-eis-aht.—Brit. Col. map., Ind. Aff., Victoria, 1872. Opet-ches-aht.—Can. Ind. Aff., 308, 1879. Opitches-aht.—Ibid., 187, 1884. Upatsesatuch.—Grant in Jour. Roy. Geog. Soc., 293, 1857.

Opitsat. The permanent village of the Clayoquot (q. v.), on the s. w. shore of Meares id., w. coast of Vancouver id., Brit. Col.; pop. 245 in 1902, 261 in 1906.
Opetsitar.—Gray and Ingraham (1791) quoted in H. R. Doc. 43, 26th Cong., 1st sess., 3, 1840. Opisat.—Can. Ind. Aff., 263, 1902. Opisitar.—Kendrick deed (1791), ibid., 10.

Opodepe. A former pueblo of the Eudeve and seat of a Spanish mission founded in 1649; situated on the E. bank of Rio San Miguel, Sonora, Mexico; pop. 320 in 1678, 134 in 1730. Of a population of 679 in 1900, 26 were Opata and 56 Yaqui.
Asuncion de Opodepe.—Zapata (1678) in Doc. Hist. Mex., 4th s., III, 351, 1857. Opodepe.—Kino, map (1702) in Stöcklein, Neue Welt-Bott, 74, 1726. Opoteppe.—Och, Journey to the Missions (1756), I, 71, 1809.

Opok (*Ô′pok*). A former Maidu settlement on the N. fork of Cosumnes r., near Nashville, Eldorado co., Cal. (R. B. D.)

Opolopong. A former town with a mixed population under Oneida jurisdiction, situated, according to the Evans map of 1756, in Luzerne co., Pa., on the E. branch of the Susquehanna, about 30 m. above Shamokin, at the forks, and about 10 m. below Wyoming. (J. N. B. H.)

Oponays. A former Seminole village "back of Tampa bay," probably in Hillsboro co., w. Fla.—Bell in Morse, Rep. to Sec. War, 306, 1822.

Oponoche. A tribe, probably Yokuts (Mariposan), mentioned as living on Kings r., Cal., in 1853.—Wessells (1853) in H. R. Ex. Doc. 76, 34th Cong., 3d sess., 31, 1857.

Opossian. An unidentified tribe living in the neighborhood of Albemarle sd., N. C., in 1586.

Opossians.—Hakluyt (1600), Voy., III, 312, repr. 1810. **Opossians.**—Lane (1586) in Smith (1629), Va., I, 87, repr 1819.

Opossum (Renape of Virginia *āpäsŭm*, 'white beast', cognate with Chippewa *wâbäsĭm*, applied specifically to a white dog). A North American marsupial, *Didelphys virginiana*, about the size of the domestic cat, with grayish-white hair, with face pure white near the snout, and with black ears. When captured or slightly wounded, it has the habit of feigning death, and by this artifice often escapes from the inexperienced hunter. The name, which was first mentioned in a brief account of Virginia published in 1610, has, with various adjuncts, since been extended to species of the genera *Sarcophilus, Thylacinus, Belideas, Micoureus, Chironectes,* and *Acrobates.* The name enters into several compounds, as: "Opossum mouse," *Acrobates pygmæus,* a pygmy species of opossum of New South Wales; "opossum rug," a commercial name for the skin of an Australian species of *Phalanger;* "opossum shrew,"an insectivorous mammal of the genus *Soledon;* "opossum shrimp," a crustacean, the female of which carries its eggs in pouches between its legs. "Possum," the common aphæretic form of the name, is often used as an epithet with the meaning of "false," "deceptive," "imitative," as in the name "possum haw" (*Viburnum nudum*), the berries of which counterfeit the edible fruit of the black haw (*V. prunifolium*), but differ therefrom in being very insipid; and "possum oak" (*Quercus aquatica*), from the deceptive character of its leaves, which vary in shape and size and often imitate those of *Q. imbricaria,* and thus lead to a confusion between the two species. Used as a verb, the word means "to pretend," "feign," "dissemble," this sense, as well as that of the attributive, being derived from the animal's habit of throwing itself upon its back and feigning death on the approach of an enemy; and hence the expression "playing possum" or "possuming." The opossum of English-speaking people of the West Indies and South America is *Didelphys opossum.* (W. R. G.)

Oposura. A former Opata pueblo and seat of a Spanish mission founded in 1644; situated on the w. bank of Rio Soyopa, N. central Sonora, Mexico. Pop. 334 in 1678, 300 in 1730. The town, now known as Moctezuma, once suffered greatly from Apache raids.

Opasura. — Bandelier, Gilded Man, 179, 1893. **Oposura.**—Croix (1769) in Doc. Hist. Mex., 4th s., II, 25, 1856. **San Miguel de Oposura.**—Zapata (1678), ibid., III, 362, 1857.

Opothleyaholo (properly Hupuehelth Yahólo; from *hupuewa* 'child,' *he'hle* 'good', *yahólo,* 'whooper,' 'halloer,' an initiation title. —G. W. Grayson). A Creek orator. He was speaker of the councils of the Upper Creek towns, and as their representative met the Government commissioners in Feb., 1825, at Indian Springs, Ga., where they came to transact in due form the cession of Creek lands already arranged with venal Lower Creek chiefs. Opothleyaholo informed them that these chiefs had no authority to cede lands, which could be done only by the consent of the whole nation in council, and MacIntosh he warned ominously of the doom he would invite by signing the treaty. Opothleyaholo headed the Creek deputation that went to Washington to protest against the validity of the treaty. Bowing to the inevitable, he put his name to the new treaty of cession, signed at Washington Jan. 24, 1826, but afterward stood out for the technical right of the Creeks to retain a strip that was not included in the description because it was not then known to lie within the limits of Georgia. After the death of the old chiefs he became the leader of the nation, though not head-chief in name. When in 1836 some of the Creek towns made preparation to join the insurgent Seminole, he marched out at the head of his Tukabatchi warriors, captured some of the young men of a neighboring village who had donned war paint to start the revolt, and delivered them to the United States military to expiate the crimes they had committed on travelers and settlers. After holding a council of warriors he led 1,500 of them against the rebellious towns, receiving a commission as colonel, and when the regular troops with their Indian auxiliaries appeared at Hatchechubbee the hostiles surrendered. The United States authorities then took advantage of the assemblage of the Creek warriors to enforce the emigration of the tribe. Opothleyaholo was reluctant to take his people to Arkansas to live with the Lower Creeks after the bitter contentions that had taken place. He bargained for a tract in Texas on which they could settle, but the Mexican government was unwilling to admit them. After the removal to Arkansas the old feud was forgotten, and Opothleyaholo became an important counselor and guide of the reunited tribe. When Gen. Albert Pike, at the beginning of the Civil war, visited the Creeks in a great council near the present town of

Eufaula and urged them to treat with the Confederacy, Opothleyaholo exercised all his influence against the treaty, and when the council decided, after several days of debate and deliberation, to enter into the treaty, he withdrew with his following from the council. Later he withdrew from the Creek Nation with about a third of the Creeks and espoused the cause of the Union. Fighting his way as he went, he retreated into Kansas, and later died near the town of Leroy, Coffey co.　　　　(F. H.　G. W. G.)

Optuabo. A former rancheria, probably of the Sobaipuri, near the present Arizona-Sonora boundary, probably in Arizona, which formed a visita of the mission of Suamca (q. v.) about 1760–64.
Santiago Optuabo.—Bancroft, Ariz. and N. Mex., 371, 1889 (after early docs.).

Oputo. A pueblo of the Opata and seat of a Spanish mission established in 1645; situated on Rio de Batepito, about lat. 30° 30′, Sonora, Mexico. Pop. in 1678, 424; in 1730, 248.
Opoto.—Bandelier in Arch. Inst. Papers, IV, 507, 1892. Oputo.—Orozco y Berra, Geog., 343, 1864. S. Ignacio Opotu.—Zapata (1678) quoted by Bancroft, No. Mex. States, I, 246, 1884.

Oqtogona (*Oqtógonă*, 'bare shins'?; sing. *Oqtógón*). A principal division of the Cheyenne.　　　　(J. M.)
Ŏhk to ŭnna.—Grinnell, Social Org. Cheyennes, 136, 1905 (variously given as meaning 'no leggings,' or as a Sutaio word meaning 'people drifted away'). O'tu'gŭnŭ.—Mooney in 14th Rep. B. A. E., 1026, 1896. Prominent Jaws.—Dorsey in Field Columb. Mus. Pub. 103, 62, 1905.

Oquaga (Mohawk: 'place of wild grapes,' from *onĕⁿhŏkwă'*, 'wild grape.'—Hewitt). An Iroquois village, probably under Tuscarora jurisdiction, formerly on the E. branch of the Susquehanna, on both sides of the river, in the town of Colesville, Broome co., N. Y. It was destroyed by the Americans in 1778. According to Ruttenber, a band of Tuscarora settled there in 1722 and were afterward joined by some Mahican and Esopus Indians who had been living among the Mohawk; but from the records of the Albany Conference in 1722 it appears that they were already at Oquaga at that time. In 1778 it was "one of the neatest Indian towns on the Susquehanna r."; it contained the ruins of an "old fort." O'Callaghan says the inhabitants were Iroquois and chiefly Mohawk. They numbered about 750 in 1765. Cf. *Osquake*.　　　　(J. N. B. H.)
Anaquago.—Butterfield, Washington-Irvine Corresp., 97, 1882. Anaquaqua.—Drake, Bk. Inds., bk. 5, 95, 1848. Aughguagey.—Ft Johnson conf. (1756) in N. Y. Doc. Col. Hist., VII, 104, 1856. Aughquaga.—Ibid., 187. Aughquagahs.—Hutchins (1778) in Jefferson, Notes, 142, 1825. Aughquagchs.—Boudinot, Star in the West, 125, 1816. Aughquages.—Mt Johnson conf. (1755) in N. Y. Doc. Col. Hist., VI, 964, 1855. Augh-quag-has.—Macauley, N. Y., II, 187, 1829. Aughwick.—Johnson (1757) in N. Y. Doc. Col. Hist., VII, 331, 1856 (it may refer to a place of that name in Huntingdon co., Pa.). Aukwick.—Franklin (1755) quoted in N. Y. Doc. Col. Hist., VI, 1008, 1855. Auquaguas.—Ruttenber, Tribes Hudson R., 200, 1872. Ochquaqua.—N. Y.

Doc. Col. Hist., V, 675, note, 1855. Ochtaghquanawicroones.—Albany conf. (1722), ibid. Ochtayhquanawicroons.—Ruttenber, Tribes Hudson R., 200, 1872 ('moccasin people'—Hewitt). Ocquagas.—Clark, Onondaga, I, 223, 1849. Oghguagees.—Johnson (1756) in N. Y. Doc. Col. Hist., VII, 91, 1856. Oghguago.—Johnson (1747), ibid., VI, 361, 1855. Oghkawaga.—Ruttenber, Tribes Hudson R., 272, 1872. Oghkwagas.—Stone, Life of Brant, II, 422, 1864. Oghquaga.—N. Y. Doc. Col. Hist., VII, 49, note, 1856. Oghquago.—Albany conf. (1746), ibid., VI, 324, 1855. Oghquajas.—Johnson (1756), ibid., VII, 42, 1856. Oghquuges.—Albany conf. (1748), ibid., VI, 441, 1855. Ohguago.—Colden (1727), Five Nat., app., 185, 1747. Ohonoguaga.—Coffin (1761) in Me. Hist. Soc. Coll., IV, 271, 1856. Ohonoguages.—Ibid. Ohonoquaugo.—Strong (1747) in Mass. Hist. Soc. Coll., 1st s., X, 56, 1809. Ohquaga.—Johnson (1764) in N. Y. Doc. Col. Hist., VII, 628, 1856. Oneachquage.—Esnauts and Rapilly, Map U. S., 1777. Onehohquages.—Ruttenber, Tribes Hudson R., 200, 1872. Onenhoghkwages.—Ibid. Onĕⁿhokwă'ge.—J. N. B. Hewitt, inf'n, 1888 ('place of wild grapes': Mohawk form). Onoaughquaga.—Tryon (1774) in N. Y. Doc. Col. Hist., VIII, 452, 1857. Onoghguagy.—Map of 1768, ibid., VIII, 1857. Onoghquagey.—Johnson (1767), ibid., VII, 969, 1856. Onohoghquaga.—N. Y. Doc. Col. Hist., VII, 49, note, 1856. Onohoghwáge.—Hawley (1794) in Mass. Hist. Soc. Coll., 1st s., IV, 50, 1795. Onohoquaga.—Hawley (1770), ibid., 3d s., I, 151, 1825. Onohquauga.—Edwards (1751), ibid., 1st s., X, 146, 1809. Ononhoghquage.—Crosby (1775) in N. Y. Doc. Col. Hist., VIII, 551, 1857. Onoquagé.—Shea, Cath. Miss., 211, 1855. Onoquaghe.—N. Y. Doc. Col. Hist., VIII, 551, note, 1857. Oonoghquageys.—German Flats conf. (1770), ibid., 229. Oquacho.—Ruttenber, Tribes Hudson R., 315, 1872. Oquago.—Macauley, N. Y., II, 177, 1829. Ŏtăkwanawĕⁿrunĕⁿ'.—Hewitt, inf'n, 1888 ('moccasin people': correct Mohawk form of Ochtaghquanawicroones). Oughquaga.—Guy Park conf. (1775) in N. Y. Doc. Col. Hist., VIII, 549, 1857. Oughquageys.—Ibid. Oughqũgoes.—Ibid., 554. Ouoghquogey.—Johnson (1764), ibid., VII, 611, 1856. Ouquagos.—Goldthwait (1766) in Mass. Hist. Soc. Coll., 1st s., X, 121, 1809. Skawaghkees.—Morse, System of Modern Geog., I, 164, [1814]. Susquehannah Indians.—Albany conf. (1746) in N. Y. Doc. Col. Hist., VI, 323, 1855 (so called here because living on the upper Susquehanna).

Oquanoxa. An Ottawa village, named from the resident chief, that formerly existed on the w. bank of the Little Auglaize, at its mouth, in Paulding co., Ohio. The reservation was sold in 1831.

Oquitoa. A former Pima rancheria on Rio del Altar, N. W. Sonora, Mexico, and a visita of the mission of Ati (q. v.) dating from about 1694. Pop. 104 in 1730. It is now a civilized town.
Conception del Ukitoa.—Kino, map, 1702, in Stöcklein, Nëue Welt-Bott, 76, 1726. Ognitoa.—Kino, map, 1701, in Bancroft, Ariz. and N. Mex., 360, 1889 (misprint). Oquitoa.—Orozco y Berra, Geog., 347, 1864. Oquitod.—Quijano (1757) in Doc. Hist. Mex., 4th s., I, 53, 1856 (misprint). San Antonio de Uquitoa.—Kino (1694), ibid., 244. San Diepo de Uquitoa.—Venegas, Hist. Cal., I, 303, 1759 (misprint). S. Antonio Oquitoa.—Rivera (1730) quoted by Bancroft, No. Mex. States, I, 514, 1884. Uquiota.—Kino (1696) in Doc. Hist. Mex., 4th s., I, 263, 1856 (misprint).

Oquomock. A former village of the Powhatan confederacy on the N. bank of the Rappahannock, in Richmond co., Va.—Smith (1629), Va., I, map, repr. 1819.

Oraibi (*owa* 'rock,' *obi* 'place': 'place of the rock'). The largest and most important of the villages of the Hopi (q. v.), in N. E. Arizona. In 1629 it became the seat of the Spanish Franciscan mission of San Francisco, which was destroyed in the Pueblo revolt of 1680, the church being reduced to ashes and the two Spanish missionaries killed. During this time the pueblo of Walpi was a visita of Oraibi. Before the mission period Oraibi was reported to contain 14,000 inhabitants, but its population was then greatly reduced, owing to the ravages of a pestilence. Present population about 750. The people of Oraibi are far more conservative in their attitude toward the whites than the other Hopi, an element in the tribe being strongly opposed to civilization. Refusal to permit their children to be taken and entered in schools has been the cause of two recent uprisings, but no blood was shed. As a result of the last difficulty, in 1906, a number

ORAIBI MAN

of the Oraibi conservatives were made prisoners of war and confined at Camp Huachuca, Ariz. Moenkapi is an Oraibi farming village. For a description of the architecture of Oraibi, see Mindeleff in 8th Rep. B. A. E., 76, 1891.

Areibe.—McCook (1891) in Donaldson, Moqui Pueblo Inds., 37, 1893. Craybe.—Hodge, Arizona, map, 1877 (misprint). Espeleta.—Alcedo, Dic.-Geog., II, 92, 1787 (doubtless in allusion to Fray José de Espeleta, killed at Oraibi in 1680). Muca.—Garcés (1776), Diary, 395, 1900 (given as the Zuñi name). Musquins.—Ten Broeck in Schoolcraft, Ind. Tribes, IV, 87, 1854 (Mexican name for). Musquint.—Ten Broeck misquoted by Donaldson, Moqui Pueblo Inds., 14, 1893. Naybé.—Oñate misquoted by Bancroft, Ariz. and N. Mex., 137, 1889. Naybí.—Oñate (1598) in Doc. Inéd., XVI, 137, 1871. Olalla.—Ibid., 207 (doubtless Oraibi; mentioned as the largest pueblo). Orabi.—Keam and Scott in Donaldson, Moqui Pueblo Inds., 14, 1893. Oraiba.—Browne, Apache Country, 290, 1869. Oraibe.—Cortez (1799)

in Pac. R. R. Rep., III, pt. 3, 121, 1856. Oraibi.—Vetancurt (1692), Menolog. Fran., 212, 1871. Oraiby.—Powell in H. R. Misc. Doc. 173, 42d Cong., 2d sess., 11, 1872. Oraiva.—Taylor in Cal. Farmer, June 19, 1863. Oraivaz.—Ten Broeck in Schoolcraft, Ind. Tribes, IV, 87, 1854. Oraive.—Garcés (1775-6) quoted by Bancroft, Ariz. and N. Mex., 137, 395, 1889. Oraivi.—De l'Isle, Carte Mexique et Floride, 1703. Orambe.—Bandelier in Arch. Inst. Papers, IV, 369, 1892 (misprint). Orante.—Escudero, Not. de Chihuahua, 231, 1834 (probably identical). Orawi.—Senex, Map, 1710. Oraybe.—Villa Señor, Theatro Am., II, 425, 1748. Oraybi.—Vargas (1692) quoted by Davis, Span. Conq. N. Mex., 367, 1869. Orayha.—Disturnell, Map Méjico, 1846. Orayve.—Alcedo, Dic.-Geog., III, 246, 1788. Orayvee.—Eastman, map in Schoolcraft, Ind. Tr., IV, 24, 1854. Orayvi.—D'Anville, Map Am. Sept., 1746. Orayxa.—Ruxton, Adventures, 195, 1848. Orehbe.—Keane in Stanford, Compend., 527, 1877. Oreiba.—Goodman in Ind. Aff. Rep., 997, 1893. O-rey-be.—Palmer, ibid., 133, 1870. Oriabe.—Clark and Zuck in Donaldson, Moqui Pueblo Inds., 14, 1893. Oribas.—Vandever in Ind. Aff. Rep., 262, 1889. Oribe.—Platt, Karte Nord-America, 1861. Oribi.—Carson (1863) in Donaldson, Moqui Pueblo Inds., 34, 1893. Oriva.—Schoolcraft. Ind. Tribes, I, 519, 1853. Orribies.—Irvine in Ind. Aff. Rep., 160, 1877. Oryina.—French, Hist. Coll., La., II, 175, 1875. Osaybe.—Bourke in Proc. Am. Antiq. Soc., n. s., I, 244, 1881 (misprint). Osoli.—Arrowsmith, Map N. A., 1795, ed. 1814 (possibly identical). O-zái.—Stevens, MS., B. A. E., 1879 (Navaho name; corrupted from Oraibi). Ozí.—Eaton in Schoolcraft, Ind. Tribes, IV, 220, 1854 (Navaho name). Rio grande de espeleta.—Villa-Señor, Theatro Am., II, 425, 1748. San Francisco de Oraibe.—Bancroft, Ariz. and N. Mex., 349, 1889. San Francisco de Oraybe.—Vetancurt (1692) in Teatro Am., III, 321, 1871. San Miguel Oraybi.—Bancroft, Ariz. and N. Mex., 173, 1889. U-lè-ò-wà.—Whipple, Pac. R. R. Rep., III, pt. 3, 13, 1856 (Zuñi name). Yabipai Muca.—Garcés (1776), Diary, 444, 1900 (or Oraibe). Yavipai muca oraive.—Garcés (1775-6) quoted by Orozco y Berra, Geog., 41, 1864.

Orapaks. A former village of the Powhatan confederacy, between the Chickahominy and Pamunkey rs., in New Kent co., Va. Powhatan retired thither about 1610 when the English began to crowd him at Werowacomoco.

Orakakes.—Drake, Bk. Inds., bk. 4, 7, 1848 (misprint). Orapack.—Strachey (ca. 1612), Va., map, 1849. Orapakas.—Drake, op. cit., 9. Orapakes.—Smith (1629), Va., I, 142, repr. 1819. Orapaks.—Strachey, op. cit., 36. Oropacks.—Harris, Voy. and Trav., I, 848, 1705. Oropaxe.—Ibid., 831.

Oratamin. A Hackensack chief in the 17th century, prominent in the treaty relations between the Hackensack and neighboring tribes and the Dutch. After the butchery of the Indians at Pavonia, N. J., by the Dutch in Feb. 1643, 10 or 11 of the surrounding tribes arose in arms against the latter to avenge the outrage, but concluded a treaty of peace Apr. 22 of the same year, "Oratamin, sachem of the savages living at Achkinheshacky [Hackensack], who declared himself commissioned by the savages of Tappaen [Tappan], Rechgawawanc [Manhattan], Kichtawanc [Kitchawank], and Sintsinck [Sintsink]," acting on their behalf. This treaty was immediately followed by a new outbreak on the part of the Indians, but peace was restored and another treaty, in which Oratamin took a prominent part, was made at Ft Amsterdam [New York],

Aug. 30, 1645 (N. Y. Doc. Col. Hist., XIII, 18, 1881). On July 19, 1649, a number of leading Indians, including Oratamin, made further proposals for a lasting peace. At the close of the conference, held at Ft Amsterdam, a special gift of tobacco and a gun was made to Oratamin, while "a small present worth 20 guilders was then given to the common savages" (ibid., 25). He also took part in the treaty of Mar. 6, 1660, in behalf of his own tribe and of the chief of the Highlands, N. Y., and was present May 18, 1660, when peace was concluded with the Wappinger. A few weeks later he interceded for the Esopus Indians, and had the satisfaction of being present at the conclusion of peace with them (Nelson, Inds. N. J., 106, 1894). In 1662 Oratamin complained to the Dutch authorities of the illicit sale of brandy to his people, and on Mar. 30 of that year was authorized to seize the liquor brought into his country for sale, as well as those bringing it. On June 27, 1663, Oratamin was again called into consultation by the whites in an effort to limit the Esopus war. Two weeks later chiefs of several tribes N. of the Hackensack appeared and ratified all that had been said and done by the aged chief, primarily through whose efforts the Esopus war was brought to a close and peace declared May 16, 1664, Oratamin and three other chiefs becoming security therefor. He was asked by Gov. Carteret, in 1666, to attend a conference regarding the purchase of the site of Newark, N. J., but was then so old and feeble that he could not undertake the journey from Hackensack to that place. He probably died in 1667. His name is also written Oratam, Oratamy, Oratan, Oraton (Nelson, Names of Inds. N. J., 44, 1904).   (C. T.)

Oratory. In Indian tribal life the orator held a distinguished place. To be able to state clearly and to urge eloquently one's views on a question before a council of the tribe raised a man to power and influence among his fellows. The government of a tribe was generally vested in a council composed of the chiefs of the different bands or clans, or of the elders of the tribe, and, as unanimous consent to any proposition was usually required before it could be accepted, much argumentation was characteristic of their deliberations. In the higher circle of chiefs, as well as in the societies of warriors or leading men, the orator had his function. To speak well, to plead well, to tell a story effectively was accounted a desirable gift for a man. Many occasions arose when facility in address was required, as in formal tribal negotiations or visits, in certain parts of religious ceremonies, or in purely social intercourse.

Some of the Eastern tribes had an official orator for state occasions, which office was hereditary in certain Western tribes. The native languages lent themselves to oratory. A picture full of detail and movement could be given in comparatively few words, while the symbolism inherent in the Indian's outlook upon nature gave poetry to his speech. His vivid conceptions seemed often to thrill his frame, governing his attitude, the folds of his robe, his glance, and his gestures. The Indian's oratory early impressed the white race, and scattered through the historical records of our country are bits of powerful native utterance. We have the speeches of Cornplanter, Red Jacket, Big Elk, Logan, and a host of others, all of which have the ring of true eloquence. This gift still lingers, but now, as in the past, it is most often heard in protest against unfair dealing. Standing before a commission the members of which had been using many arguments in favor of their project, the Wichita chief who had listened in silence stooped, and gathering a handful of the dry soil of his reservation, straightened himself and said, as he threw the myriad particles into the air, "There are as many ways to cheat the Indian!" Consult Mooney in 14th and 17th Rep. B. A. E.   (A. C. F.)

Orcan. A village mentioned by Joutel in 1687 as situated N. or N. w. of the Maligne (Colorado) r., Texas, the name seemingly having been given him by Ebahamo Indians, who were probably of Karankawa affiliation. In some editions of Joutel's relation the name is combined with Piou, or Peinhoum. The two names may have belonged to one village or to two closely related villages.   (A. C. F.)
Orcamipias.—Barcia, Ensayo, 271, 1723. Orcampion.—Joutel (1687) in French, Hist. Coll. La., I, 138, 1846. Orcampiou.—Shea, note in Charlevoix, New France, IV, 78, 1870. Orcan.—Joutel (1687) in French, Hist. Coll. La., I, 152, 1846.

Orchard Party. A part of the Oneida as recognized by the treaty of Albany, Feb. 2, 1827.—Indian Problem, 301, Albany, 1889.

Ordeals. An ordeal is strictly a form of trial to determine guilt or innocence, but the term has come to be applied in a secondary sense to any severe trial or test of courage, endurance, and fortitude. In accordance with these two usages of the term, ordeals among the North American tribes may be divided into (1) those used to establish guilt and to settle differences, and (2) those undergone for the sake of some material or supernatural advantage.
The ordeals corresponding closest to the tests to which the name was originally applied were those undertaken to determine witches or wizards. If it was

believed that a man had died in consequence of being bewitched, the Tsimshian would take his heart out and put a red-hot stone against it, wishing at the same time that the enemy might die. If the heart burst, they thought that their wish would be fulfilled; if not, their suspicions were believed to be unfounded. A Haida shaman repeated the names of all persons in the village in the presence of a live mouse and determined the guilty party by watching its motions. A Tlingit suspected of witchcraft was tied up for 8 or 10 days to extort a confession from him, and he was liberated at the end of that period if he were still alive. But as confession secured immediate liberty and involved no unpleasant consequences except an obligation to remove the spell, few were probably found innocent. This, however, can hardly be considered as a real ordeal, since the guilt of the victim was practically assumed, and the test was in the nature of a torment to extract confession.

Intimately connected with ordeals of this class were contests between individuals and bodies of individuals, for it was supposed that victory was determined more by supernatural than by natural power. A case is recorded among the Comanche where two men whose enmity had become so great as to defy all attempts at reconciliation were allowed to fight a duel. Their left arms having been tied together, a knife was placed in the right hand of each, and they fought until both fell. A similar duel is recorded in one of the Teton myths, and it is probable that the custom was almost universal. Resembling these were the contests in vogue among Eskimo tribes. When two bodies of Eskimo met who were strangers to each other, each party selected a champion, and the two struck each other on the side of the head or the bared shoulders until one gave in. Anciently Netchilirmiut and Aivilirmiut champions contested by pressing the points of their knives against each other's cheeks. Such contests were also forced on persons wandering among strange people and are said to have been matters of life and death. Chinook myths speak of similar tests of endurance between supernatural beings, and perhaps they were shared by men. Differences between towns on the N. Pacific coast were often settled by appointing a day for fighting, when the people of both sides arrayed themselves in their hide and wooden armor and engaged in a pitched battle, the issue being determined by the fall of one or two prominent men. Contests between strangers or representatives of

different towns or social groups were also settled by playing a game. At a feast on the N. Pacific coast one who had used careless or slighting words toward the people of his host was forced to devour a tray full of bad-tasting food, or perhaps to swallow a quantity of urine. Two persons often contested to see which could empty a tray the more expeditiously.

Ordeals of the second class would cover the hardships placed upon a growing boy to make him strong, the fasts and regulations to which a girl was subjected at puberty, and those which a youth underwent in order to obtain supernatural helpers (see *Child life*), as well as the solitary fasts of persons who desired to become shamans, or of shamans who desired greater supernatural power. Finally, it is especially applicable to the fasts and tortures undergone in preparation for ceremonies or by way of initiation into a secret society.

The first of these may best be considered under *Education* and *Puberty customs*, but, although some of the ceremonies for the purpose of initiating a youth into the mysteries of the tribe took place about the time of puberty, their connection therewith is not always evident, and they may well be treated here. Thus Pueblo children, when old enough to have the religious mysteries imparted to them, went through a ceremonial flogging, and it is related of the Alibamu and other Indian tribes of the Gulf states that at a certain time they caused their children to pass in array and whipped them till they drew blood. The *huskanaw* (q. v.), or *huskany*, was an ordeal among Virginia Indians undertaken for the purpose of preparing youths for the higher duties of manhood. It consisted in solitary confinement and the use of emetics, "whereby remembrance of the past was supposed to be obliterated and the mind left free for the reception of new impressions." Among those tribes in which individuals acquired supernatural helpers a youth was compelled to go out alone into the forest or upon the mountains for a long period, fast there, and sometimes take certain medicines to enable him to see his guardian spirit. Similar were the ordeals gone through by chiefs among the Haida, Tlingit, Tsimshian, and other N. Pacific coast tribes when they desired to increase their wealth, or success in war, or to obtain long life, as also by shamans who wished increased powers. At such times they chewed certain herbs supposed to aid them in seeing the spirits. The use of the "black drink" (q. v.) by Muskhogean tribes was with similar intent, as also were the emetics just referred to in use among the Virginian peoples.

While undergoing initiation into a secret society on the N. Pacific coast a youth fasted, and for a certain period disappeared into the woods, where he was supposed to commune with the spirit of the society in complete solitude. Any one discovering a Kwakiutl youth at this time could slay him and obtain the secret society privileges in his stead. On the plains the principal participants in the Sun dance (q. v.) had skewers run through the fleshy parts of their backs, to which thongs were attached, fastened at the other end to the Sun-dance pole. Sometimes a person was drawn up so high as barely to touch the ground and afterward would throw his weight against the skewers until they tore their way out. Another participant would have the thongs fastened to a skull, which he pulled around the entire camping circle, and no matter what obstacles impeded his progress he was not allowed to touch either thongs or skull with his hands. During the ceremony of Dakhpike, or Nakhpike, among the Hidatsa, devotees ran arrows through their muscles in different parts of their bodies; and on one occasion a warrior is known to have tied a thirsty horse to his body by means of thongs passed through holes in his flesh, after which he led him to water, restrained him from drinking without touching his hands to the thongs, and brought him back in triumph. The special ordeal of a Cheyenne society was to walk with bare feet on hot coals. A person initiated into the Chippewa and Menominee society of the Midewiwin was "shot" with a medicine bag and immediately fell on his face. By making him fall on his face a secret society spirit or the guardian spirit of a N. W. coast shaman also made itself felt. When introduced into the Omaha society, called Wash-ashka, one was shot in the Adăm's apple by something said to be taken from the head of an otter. As part of the ceremony of initiation among the Hopi a man had to take a feathered prayer-stick to a distant spring, running all the way, and return within a certain time; and chosen men of the Zuñi were obliged to walk to a lake 45 m. distant, clothed only in the breech-cloth and so exposed to the rays of the burning sun, in order to deposit plume-sticks and pray for rain. Among the same people one of the ordeals to which an initiate into the Priesthood of the Bow was subjected was to sit naked for hours on a large ant-hill, his flesh exposed to the torment of myriads of ants. At the time of the winter solstice the Hopi priests sat naked in a circle and

suffered gourds of ice-cold water to be dashed over them. Ordeals of this kind enter so intimately into ceremonies of initiation that it is often difficult to distinguish them.

Certain regulations were also gone through before war expeditions, hunting excursions, or the preparation of medicines. Medicines were generally compounded by individuals after fasts, abstinence from women, and isolation in the woods or mountains. Before going to hunt the leader of a party fasted for a certain length of time and counted off so many days until one arrived which he considered his lucky day. On the N. W. coast the warriors bathed in the sea in winter time, after which they whipped each other with branches, and until the first encounter took place they fasted and abstained from water as much as possible. Elsewhere warriors were in the habit of resorting to the sweat-lodge. Among the tribes of the E. and some others prisoners were forced to run between two lines of people armed with clubs, tomahawks, and other weapons, and he who reached the chief's house or a certain mark in safety was preserved. Inasmuch as the object behind most tortures was to break down the victim's self-command and extort from him some indication of weakness, while the aim of the victim was to show an unmoved countenance, flinging back scorn and defiance at his tormentors until the very last, burning at the stake and its accompanying horrors partook somewhat of the nature of an ordeal.   (J. R. S.)

Oregon jargon, Oregon trade language. See *Chinook jargon*.

Orehaoue. A Cayuga chief who opposed the Jesuits and caused Father Carheil's withdrawal. He aided the English of Albany in preventing Penn's purchase of Susquehanna lands, and visited De la Barre in 1684. In 1687 Denonville seized him and sent him to France. He was then called Goiguenha [Cayuga]-Oreouahe, and often Taweeratt; also Wahawa by the Onondaga. In 1688 the Cayuga wished for "Taweeratt, the chief warrior of Cayouge, who is lamented amongst them every day." Returning in 1689, Orehaoue became attached to Count Frontenac and fought for the French. He died in 1698 and was buried with high honors as "a worthy Frenchman and good Christian."   (W. M. B.)

Orejones (Span.: 'big-eared people'). Indians of the N. W. coast. As the wearing of lip, nose, and ear ornaments is common among Indians on the northern coasts, Taylor (Cal. Farmer, Aug. 24, 1863) believes there can be little doubt that the word *Oregon* is derived from the Spanish nickname, used to distinguish them from the California Indians. Carver (Trav., ix, 76, 1778) seems, however, to be the first to employ the term Oregon to designate his great "River of the West"—the Columbia—of which he learned from the Sioux, Assiniboin, and Cree Indians.

Orejones. A former division of the Faraon Apache.—Orozco y Berra, Geog., 59, 1864.

Orejones. A former Coahuiltecan tribe dwelling near the coast between the Nueces and San Antonio rs., Texas. Their residence between these rivers was made the basis of a claim to them and their relatives by San Juan Capistrano mission in a quarrel, in 1754, with Vizarron mission (Ynforme of the College of Querétaro to the Commissary General, 1754, MS.). That they lived near the coast is evident. In 1760 the San Antonio missionaries reported them in a list of coast tribes (Ynforme de Misiones, 1762, MS.). In 1780 Governor Cabello included them in the tribes along the coast between the Nueces and Ysla de los Copanes (Cabello to Croix, May 28, 1780, MS.). But that they were not the tribe nearest to the gulf appears from the statement that when, in 1754, their very near neighbors, the Pamaques, deserted their mission, Father Arricivita sought them first in their native country, but, failing to find them, "he went in to the islands inhabited by the barbarous and uncultured tribes, of which the best known are those named Manos de Perro" (Ynforme, 1754, op. cit.).

That they were Coahuiltecan rests on the enumeration, on the title-page of García's Manual (1760), of tribes in the San Antonio and Rio Grande missions speaking the same language. Of their intimate affiliation with some of these tribes there is other evidence. They were closely bound by intermarriage with the Pamaques, and in 1731 each spoke "both languages so perfectly that they were not distinguished" (Ynforme, 1754, op. cit.). According to García they spoke the same language, with only minor differences. They lived "almost together" and went together to the missions (Ynforme, 1754). They seem also to have been closely related to the Piguiques and Panascánes (or Pasnaćanes), likewise close neighbors.

The Orejones were the basis of the foundation of San Juan Capistrano mission in 1731, but with them came numerous Pamaques (Ynforme, 1754, op. cit.). Testimony given by Andrés, a Sayopin (Chayopin), in a manuscript dated May 13, 1752, states that there were Orejones at Candelaria mission on San Xavier r. (Béxar Archives), but other evidence shows that they were neophytes from San Antonio serving as interpreters. Some time before 1754 the mission of

Vizarron, s. of the Rio Grande, asserted a claim to the Orejones, but this was disputed by San Juan Capistrano mission (Ynforme, 1754).

In 1762 a total of 203 "Orejones, Sayopines, Pamaques, and Piguiques" was reported at San Juan Capistrano mission (Ynforme, 1762). It was said in 1754 that the Pamaques and their neighbors, removed from their native soil to the missions, had become almost extinct. It is probable that this assertion applied also to the Orejones (Camberos, missionary at Bahía, letter to the Viceroy, MS.), although Cabello's report of 1780 indicates that some were still living near the coast between the San Antonio and the Nueces. (H. E. B.)

Orenda. The Iroquois name of the fictive force, principle, or magic power which was assumed by the inchoate reasoning of primitive man to be inherent in every body and being of nature and in every personified attribute, property, or activity, belonging to each of these and conceived to be the active cause or force, or dynamic energy, involved in every operation or phenomenon of nature, in any manner affecting or controlling the welfare of man. This hypothetic principle was conceived to be immaterial, occult, impersonal, mysterious in mode of action, limited in function and efficiency, and not at all omnipotent, local and not omnipresent, and ever embodied or immanent in some object, although it was believed that it could be transferred, attracted, acquired, increased, suppressed, or enthralled by the orenda of occult ritualistic formulas endowed with more potency. This postulation of a purely fictitious force or dynamic energy must needs have been made by primitive man to explain the activities of life and nature, the latter being conceived to be composed of living beings, for the concept of force or energy as an attribute or property of matter had not yet been formed, hence the modern doctrine of the conservation of energy was unknown to primitive thought. As all the bodies of the environment of primitive man were regarded by him as endowed with life, mind, and volition, he inferred that his relations with these environing objects were directly dependent on the caprice of these beings. So to obtain his needs man must gain the goodwill of each one of a thousand controlling minds by prayer, sacrifice, some acceptable offering, or propitiatory act, in order to influence the exercise in his behalf of the orenda or magic power which he believed was controlled by the particular being invoked. Thus it came that the possession of orenda or magic power is the distinctive characteristic of all the gods, and these gods in earlier time were all the bodies and beings of nature in any manner affecting the weal or woe of man. So primitive man interpreted the activities of nature to be due to the struggle of one orenda against another, put forth by the beings or bodies of his environment, the former possessing orenda and the latter life, mind, and orenda only by virtue of his own imputation of these things to lifeless objects. In the stress of life, coming into contact or more or less close relation with certain bodies of his environment, more frequently and in a more decided manner than with the other environing bodies, and learning to feel from these relations that these bodies through "the exercise of their orenda controlled the conditions of his welfare and in like manner shaped his ill fare," man gradually came to regard these bodies as the masters, the arbiters, the gods, of the conditions of his environment, whose aid, goodwill, and even existence were absolutely necessary to his well-being and to the preservation of his life. In the cosmogonic legends, the sum of the operations of this hypothetic magic power constitutes the story of the phenomena of nature and the biography of the gods, in all the planes of human culture. From the least to the greatest, there are incomparable differences in strength, function, and scope of action among the orendas, or magic powers, exercised by any group of such fictitious beings. Therefore it is not remarkable to find in many legends that for specific purposes man may sometimes possess weapons whose orenda is superior to that possessed by some of the primal beings of his cosmology. It is likewise found that the number of purposes for which a given orenda may be efficient varies widely.

The Algonquian *manito*, the Shoshonean *pokunt*, the Siouan *mahopá*, *χubé* or rather *hopádi*, correspond approximately, if not exactly, with this Iroquois term *orenda* in use and signification. Those who interpret these terms as denotive simply of what is expressed by the English words 'mystery,' 'immortal,' 'magic,' 'sorcery,' or 'wonderful,' fail to appreciate the true nature and functions of the assumed power denoted by these terms as conceived by the Indians who devised these terms.

The following are compound terms occurring in the Jesuit Relations, in which *orenda* is the noun element: Arendiowane, Arendio8ane, Arendioguanne, Arendioauanné, Arendiouane, Arendiwané, Arendaonatia. See *Mythology, Otkon, Oyaron, Religion.*

Consult Powell, introd. to Cushing's Zuñi Folk Tales, 1901; Hewitt in Am. Anthrop., IV, 33–46, 1902. (J. N. B. H.)

Orestaco. A former village, probably Costanoan, situated to the E. of San Juan Bautista mission, Cal.—Bancroft, Hist. Cal., I, 559, 1886.

Orientation. The entrance way of Indian dwellings in the open country generally faced the E. When a tribal ceremony was to take place, the Indians of the plains camped in a circle and the line of tents was broken on the E. side so as to leave an open space. If, within this circle, a smaller one was constructed of boughs and for the special rites, this also had its opening to the E. Articles used for sacred purposes in ceremonies were arranged so as to conform to the idea of orientation, and their ornamentation was made to serve that thought. For instance, the colored band on the basket drum used in the Night Chant of the Navaho was "not continuous but intersected at one point by a narrow line of uncolored wood" in order "to assist in the orientation of the basket at night in the medicine lodge" when the light was dim. The placing of prayer-sticks and other symbolic devices, as well as their colors, referred to the points of the compass (see *Color symbolism*). Even the drumstick used in the Navaho Night Chant ceremony must be made of four yucca leaves, which, while on the plant, pointed to the four quarters; that which was toward the E. must first be plucked, and with that from the W. forms the core of the drumstick. Again, during the initial acts of a religious ceremony the priest and his assistants must face the E. In the busk ceremony of the Creeks the four logs with which the new fire was kindled were laid crosswise with reference to the cardinal points. Tents and dwellings, except on the seacoast, generally face the E. Among the Pueblos the communal dwellings usually face the sun, and additions are rarely made toward the N.; in the older pueblos the kivas (q. v.) also were oriented. In burials orientation was not universally observed, although it was common among some of the tribes. Among the Tlingit of Alaska it was regarded as of importance, for it was believed that if the dead were not placed with their heads to the E. they could not be "reborn." In myths, legends, and rituals the E. was spoken of as "the place where dwelt the dawn and the sun." These two, the dawn and the sun, were regarded as distinct and unrelated. The dawn was the child of "mother darkness," or night, and the animating power which pervades all things; it was born anew each day, while the sun came into existence once for all in the ancient days, and was one of the lesser and visible gods. He was always the same, and was appointed to make his daily journey through the sky. In the mythical region of the sun's abode the house wherein he dwelt was oriented, so that the sun itself faced a mysterious E., whence came to it potency from the all-pervading power. From the customs of the people, from their myths and rituals as well as from their language, it is learned that the E. not only stood for the gift of physical light but symbolized the region whence men received supernatural help and guidance (Matthews, Navaho Legends; C. Mindeleff in 17th Rep. B. A. E.; Fletcher in 22d Rep. B. A. E.). As the point where the sun appeared on the E. horizon shifted with the seasons, some of the tribes set up marks to assist in observing the time of the winter or the summer solstice, when important rites took place and orientation was closely observed (see Fewkes in 15th Rep. B. A. E.). In ceremonial processions, either when entering or when within the lodge, kiva, or the field to be consecrated, the start was usually from a point facing the E., and the movement was from left to right. This "ceremonial succession" has been traced by Cushing (Am. Anthrop., v, 1893) as resulting in part from "hand usage in left and right finger counting." Among peoples where the orientation of dwellings, etc., was not observed, as on the N. Pacific coast and in mountainous and forest regions, traces of orientation are found in some of their ceremonies. Where the custom was closely observed, consciousness of the E. seemed to have been deeply seated in the native mind, and they observed an abstract orientation when not outwardly practising it. For instance, the Omaha tribal circle was composed of 10 gentes, 5 occupying the half N. of the eastern opening and 5 the southern half. When camping on the annual tribal hunt, the opening was in the direction they were going, which might be w. of their camping site, in which case the circle would be as if it had turned on a hinge at the western part, and the 5 gentes of the northern half would still be on the N. and in the same order as if the opening were at the E., and the 5 gentes at the s. would preserve their old relative position. The orientation of the tribal circle was thus at all times preserved, although the camp might not actually be so placed upon the prairie. See *Cross.*

For further information, consult Mooney in 15th and 17th Reps. B. A. E.; J. O. Dorsey in 3d and 15th Reps. B. A. E.; DuBois in Am. Anthrop., IX, no. 1, 178, 1907; Fletcher in Pubs. Peabody Museum; Hawkins, Sketch (1799), 75, 1848; Hewett in Am. Anthrop., VI, no. 5, 1904; Lewis in Mem. Internat. Cong. Anthrop., 1894; McGee in 19th Rep. B. A. E.; Matthews in Mem. Am. Mus. Nat. Hist., VI; Mindeleff in 8th Rep. B. A. E.; Mooney in Mem. Am.

Anthrop. Ass'n, I, no. 6, 1907; Speck, ibid., II, no. 2, 1907, and the writings of Fewkes in the Reports of the Bureau of American Ethnology and the American Anthropologist.			(A. C. F.)

Orkua. A settlement of East Greenland Eskimo, now deserted.—Meddelelser om Grönland, XXV, 23, 1902.

Orlova (Russian: 'Orlof's'). A Kaniagmiut Eskimo settlement at Eagle harbor, Ugak bay, Kodiak id., Alaska; pop. 147 in 1880, 77 in 1890.

Eagle harbor.—11th Census, Alaska, 76, 1893. **Orlova.**—Coast Surv. map, 1898. **St. Orloff.**—Coast Surv. maps.

Ormejea. The name of two former Pima villages in s. Arizona; pop. of one in 1858, 212; of the other, 643.—Bailey in Ind. Aff. Rep., 208, 1858. Cf. *Hermho, Hormiguero.*

Ornament. In treating of the decorative art of the tribes of northern North America it may be briefly stated at the outset that the earliest manifestations of the phenomena of embellishment were probably of instinctive kinds in which design, as we understand it, had no part. These manifestations consisted rather in the assembling of attractive objects for the pleasure they gave, the attachment of such objects to the person, or the addition of colors to the skin, the motives being to please the savage fancy, to attract the attention of others, or to simulate animals by imitating their markings. These forms of esthetic activity were supplemented in time by the application of embellishments to the dress, when that came into use, and to all kinds of possessions having close relations with the person or which were otherwise intimately associated with the life and thought of the people. Among the tribes the person was subject to varied decorative treatment. The skin was tattooed, colors were applied in various ways, and ornamental objects were attached in every possible manner. Feathers and other articles were added to the hair; pins, plugs, and pendants to the ears; labrets to the lips; and encircling bands to the waists, arms, and legs. The costume was elaborated for decorative effect and the headdress especially became a marvel of gaudy display, well illustrated in the so-called war bonnet of the Plains tribes and the still more highly developed headdresses shown in the paintings and sculptures of the middle Americans (see *Adornment*). But it is the embellishment of things made and used that calls for particular attention in this place, and in this field the American aborigines, and more especially the semicivilized peoples of middle America, were hardly excelled by any other known people of corresponding culture grade. Nothing with which they had to deal was left without some kind of decorative treatment, and their appreciation of the esthetic values of form and line compares favorably with that of the eastern Asiatics.

The native ornament may first be considered with respect to the several methods of execution or utilization of the elements:

(1) The sculptor's art (see *Sculpture and Carving*) was employed in shaping and

a

b

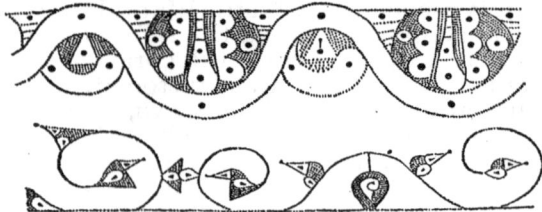

c

d

ENGRAVED DESIGNS—POTTERY OF THE MOUND-BUILDERS. *a, b,* MISSISSIPPI; *c,* FLORIDA; *d,* ARKANSAS

decorating objects of stone, wood, bone, horn, and shell, and in some sections this branch is still practised with exceptional skill. Among the N. W. coast tribes totem poles, house posts, mortuary columns, masks, batons, pipes, and various implements and utensils represent the forms of beasts, men, and monsters, in

relief and in the round. Although these motives usually have primarily a symbolic or other special significance and rarely take wholly conventional forms, they are employed with remarkable skill and appreciation of their decorative values. The carvings in stone, bone, and ivory of the Eskimo are particularly noteworthy, and taste is exercised in the shaping of objects of every class. The motives employed are apparently not so generally symbolic as among the Indian tribes, and life-forms are executed with the simply artistic idea more definitely in view. The excellence of this far-northern work is no doubt due in part to the introduction of implements of steel and to the influence of the art of the whites. Among the tribes of middle North America sculptural embellishment of minor works was common, and the mound-building tribes, for example, showed decided cleverness, especially in the decoration of their tobacco pipes, carving the forms of birds and beasts and even men with excellent taste. Sculpture and sculptural embellishment deal largely with symbolic and ceremonial subjects, and are almost exclusively the work of the men.

(2) Plastic ornament, the work of the modeler (see *Pottery*), is confined to pottery-making tribes, such as the mound-builders and the Pueblos. In pottery, as in sculpture, various beasts, as well as men and fanciful beings, were rendered in the round and in all degrees of relief in connection with utensils, implements, and other objects, and their utilization is probably due largely to the association of religious notions with the creatures represented. All were introduced under the supervision of taste, and are thus properly classed as embellishments. Formal geometric decorations were rarely executed by plastic methods, save the simple incised varieties, better classed with engraving, and the impressed or stamped varieties, which bear somewhat the same relation to the plastic art proper that engraving bears to sculpture. The potter's art, relating primarily to household affairs, is practised almost exclusively by the women. Ornamental designs worked out in the native metals, excepting where the methods of the whites have been introduced, are essentially plastic in character and execution. North of Mexico the work of the early days was confined very largely to repoussé figures executed in sheet metal. The working of metal, so far as known, is a man's art (see *Metalwork*).

(3) Engraved ornament (see *Engraving*) is executed with pointed tools on surfaces of various kinds, and has characteristics in common with both sculpture

and painting. In certain branches of art it deals principally with geometric figures, but in others life motives are employed with considerable freedom, the representations running through the entire scale of convention. The work of the Eskimo executed on bone and ivory illustrates the more decidedly pictorial phases of this branch, although there are apparent traces of an earlier geometric stage of engraved design. That of the N. W. coast tribes, executed on wood,

ENGRAVED DESIGNS—SLATE PLAQUE OF THE HAIDA

bone, stone, and metal, embodies animal forms almost exclusively, and is always highly conventional though never fully geometric in style. That of the mound-builders, while employing life forms to

ENGRAVED DESIGNS—SILVER BRACELETS OF THE HAIDA, WITH ANIMAL FIGURES. (NIBLACK.)

some extent, is largely geometric. The Pueblos relied on the brush rather than on the graver for their ornament. Pictographic inscriptions executed in incised lines on rock, birchbark, and other surfaces, are not properly classed as ornament. Engraved decoration has closely associated with it in the potter's art a range of imprinted and stamped figures which are usually quite formal, as in the ancient pottery of the Southern and Eastern states and in the coil ware of the ancient Pueblos. Engraved design employed in heraldic, totemic, and religious art is usually the work of the men; applied to domestic art, as in ceramics, it is the work of the women.

(4) Embellishments in color (see *Painting, Dry-painting, Dyes and Pigments,*

Tattooing) are applied to objects or surfaces by means of a great variety of implements and devices, and in the form of paints, dry pigments, stains, and dyes, or are pricked into the skin. They take a prominent place in the art of the northern aborigines. Color ornament, in its simplest form, consists in the application of plain colors to the person and to the surface of objects, but more commonly it takes the form of pictorial and conventional designs of wide range; and,

ANCIENT PUEBLO BOTTLE　　　ARCHAIC ZUÑI OLLA

not infrequently, sculptured and modeled life forms, as in masks, totem poles, earthen vases, etc., are colored in imitation of nature, although generally in formal fashion. By far the most important branch of color decoration embraces conventional delineations of life forms on manufactured articles and constructions. These decorations, usually symbolic, are characteristically displayed on articles of skin among the hunter tribes, as the Sioux; on the pottery of the more seden-

PAINTED DESIGNS FROM POTTERY OF THE ANCIENT PUEBLOS

tary peoples, as the Pueblos; and on houses, utensils, and ceremonial objects among the N. W. coast tribes. Although the free-hand methods employed in the painter's art are favorable to flowing lines and the graphic reproduction of life forms, the color ornament of some of the tribes is almost exclusively geometric, good illustrations appearing on the pottery of the ancient Pueblos and in the decoration of articles of skin by some of the Plains tribes. It is probable that the geometric character in the first of these instances is in a measure due to copyism from textile designs and, in the second, to the use of rigid coloring implements instead of brushes. The mound-builders, skilful with the graver's point, seem to have had slight mastery of the brush, although some good examples of their work in this branch have been obtained from the ancient key settlements of the Florida coast. In painting, as in engraving, symbolic designs seem to originate largely with the men and the nonsymbolic with the women, although the distinctions between the work of the sexes probably vary with the social organization and state of culture. A peculiar method of color decoration practised by some of the tribes consisted in the cutting or scraping away of portions of the surface coloring of an object, developing the design in the contrasting color beneath. It has often been assumed that native taste in the use of colors was instinctive and that harmonious results were a matter of course; but there is apparently little evidence on this point, and it is probable that the pleasing combinations observed are in large measure due to the fact that the colors available to the tribes are

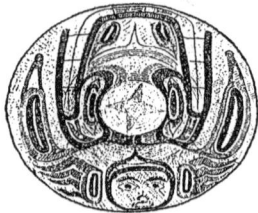

PAINTED DESIGNS OF THE HAIDA

generally quiet in tone rather than brilliant. Colors were often symbolic, being associated with particular concepts: as, for example, green with summer; white with winter; blue with death; yellow with the east, and red with the west (see *Color symbolism*).

(5) Textile ornament (see *Weaving*), elaborated in the constructive features or units of the art and in colors associated with these, is displayed to good advantage in the weaving of the ancient and modern Pueblos and the Navaho of to-day, and also among some of the tribes of the N. W., the Shoshoni, Shahaptin, and Chilkat, for example. It is usually highly geometric in style as a result of the peculiar technic. In this art even life forms take on characteristics of the

construction or combination of parts, and geometric characters necessarily prevail. The same is true in general of the decorations in the allied arts of basketry, featherwork, beadwork, quillwork, netting, and embroidery (q. v.). The last named, although assuming some of the characteristics of the textile foundation

CEREMONIAL CHILKAT GARMENT WITH DESIGNS IN GOBELIN STYLE. (NIBLACK)

on which it is superposed, frequently expresses its designs in flowing graphic forms, and the same is true to a lesser degree in the Gobelin style of weaving practised by the N. W. coast tribes. As already stated, the decorative motives of the last-mentioned tribes are in the main representative of life forms, but, with the exception of the Nootka and other of the more southern tribes, their basketry decoration is almost exclusively geometric. Featherwork had a prominent place in native art and is still common in the W., the feather-decked baskets of some of the Pacific coast tribes being marvels of tasteful and brilliant ornament. The basketry designs of the western tribes furnish striking illustrations of the native genius for decoration. So far as known the mound-building tribes had made no considerable progress in this branch. Textile art of all forms is largely the work of the women.

(6) Inlaying (see *Mosaic*) was

DESIGN WOVEN IN TULAREÑO BASKET. (POWERS)

employed by the more advanced tribes in the decoration of objects of wood, stone, and bone, but these decorations were usually of a very simple nature and are of no particular importance in the discussion of the native ornament of the N.; the ancient Mexicans, however, executed many superb works by this method.

Associated ornaments are appended or otherwise attached to articles of dress, accouterments, utensils, etc., and consist of tassels, fringes, beads, feathers, buttons, bells, and the like (see *Adornment*). They are, however, not usually employed in the elaboration of designs, though effective as ornaments.

The embellishments introduced by the various methods described above into the native arts include or represent several classes of motives which, although not always readily distinguished from one another, may be grouped in a general way, as follows:

(1) The technic, having its immediate origin in technic features of the arts themselves and primarily nonideographic; (2) the simply esthetic, introduced from various sources solely for the purpose of adornment and also primarily nonideographic; (3) the simply ideographic, portraying pictorially some scene, object, or incident, or expressing in more or less formal manner some ordinary or nonsacred idea, as a name, a number, purpose, ownership, title, rank, achievement, a personal or tribal device, etc.; (4) the sacred, expressive of some religious concept, very generally delineative, and present because the concept has a significant relationship with the person or the object decorated. Employed in the various arts these diversified elements are subject to many mutations of *form* and *meaning*. Applied to objects of art or to the person, the *forms* of all classes of motives, significant and nonsignificant, are, to a greater or less degree, under the supervision of taste, and undergo modifications to satisfy the esthetic sense. The simplest denotive signs, for example, are not cut on an implement or utensil without attention to spacing, uniformity of outline, and neatness of finish, while realistic representations are adapted to or brought into harmony with the varying conditions under which they are employed. Motives of all classes take on different forms or receive distinct treatment in each of the arts with which they are associated, on account of differences in technic and in the material, shape, and size of the objects to which they are applied. These changes are in the direction of elaboration where this is called for, as in the filling of large spaces, and in the direction of simplicity as influenced by restricted spaces, by haste in execution, or by defective skill; and when the shapes or available spaces demand it, figures are distorted and divided without regard to representative consistency. Representations of natural forms introduced into embellishment have, in general, a tendency to become more conventional with repetition, and under the influence of the technic of some of the

arts, as in weaving, they pass readily into purely conventional forms. It does not follow, however, that geometric forms necessarily originate in this way. It appears that with many primitive tribes geometric ornament comes into general use at a very early stage of culture progress, arising in technical features of the arts, in suggestions of fancy, and possibly in other ways. Graphic delineations of life forms coming into use later combine with or take the place of the conventional decorations, and in so doing are forced into the conventional mold, assuming various degrees of simplification and geometricity. There is also, no doubt, a reciprocal elaboration of the geometric forms to meet the requirements of the new associations. That highly geometric phases of decoration in many cases come into use quite early is apparent from a glance at the work of the northern tribes. In the Pueblo region the handsome earthenware of the olden time displays mainly nonrealistic geometric phases of embellishment; that of the middle period has a considerable percentage of representative elements, while that of the later time is rich in realistic motives. In the Mississippi valley and the Atlantic woodlands simple geometric decorations seem to prevail more fully among the more primitive tribes and the realistic among the more cultured. The change from the formal to the realistic is no doubt due somewhat to the gradual adaptation of decorated articles at first purely practical in function to sacred ceremonial uses. The ideas associated with ornament are greatly diversified in derivation and character, and subject to profound changes with lapse of time, with advance in culture, and with tribal mutations. The simple technic and esthetic motives are without particular ideographic associations, although ideas may be attached to or read into them at any stage of their utilization by the imaginative, symbol-loving aborigines. With all tribes devoted to the embellishing arts there is necessarily a large body of nonideographic motives which had no significance originally or which have lost it, but it is a common practice to give to the figures names suggested by their form, often perhaps for convenience of reference merely; thus a triangular figure woven in a basket or painted on a leather case may be called a "tipi" by one people, a "mountain" by another, and an "arrowhead" by a third; a simple cross may become the morning star, a mythic animal, or a sign of the four quarters of the world. And these simple designs employed in basketry or beadwork may be so associated as to tell or suggest a story, which may be elaborated indefinitely by the primitive fancy. Again, any simple motive may suggest some symbol or sacred creature; thus a mere crooked line previously meaningless may become a serpent with a whole train of superstitions attached; or it may be made to stand for lightning, the shaft of the gods; or it may be assumed to represent a river about which the fathers have fabricated a myth. Ornament belonging to or derived from religious and other symbolic forms of art, however, is originally fully burdened with associated ideas. The art of a highly religious people is thus especially rich in ideographic elements, and the character of these elements is in a large measure determined by the nature of the particular environment. An agricultural people, for example, occupying an arid region and devoting much attention to the ceremonial bringing of rain, employs a great number of symbols representing clouds, lightning, rain, water, and water animals, and these are introduced freely into its decorative art. A maritime people, depending on the products of the sea for subsistence, embodies in its mythology the creatures of the sea and the birds and the beasts that prey upon them, and symbols depicting these have a prominent place in its ornamental art. The dominant thought of a people in other than the religious realm finds expression in pictography and in this form passes into ornament. It is observed that warlike peoples, as the tribes of the plains, devoted to military achievement, are wont to embody in their art, in association more or less intimate with their religious symbols, the signs and emblems of daring deeds, and with some of these tribes a system of military devices has arisen which constitutes a primitive phase of heraldry (q. v.). These devices, applied to shields, costumes, and dwellings, take their place in the decorative arts of the people.

Considerable diversity in the ideas associated with decoration arises from differences in the spheres of activity of the men and the women. Delineative elements having their origin in myth and ceremony, in military occupations and the chase, and in pictography generally, are largely the creations of the men; the activities of the women are connected in a great measure with the domestic establishment, and embellishments employed in the strictly domestic arts consist in large part of designs derived from nonsymbolic sources or those which have associated meanings obtained traditionally, or from dreams, or such as are invented to please the fancy. However, articles made by the women for the men, as clothing and certain ceremonial objects, may be embellished with subjects pertaining to masculine activities. So different is the point of view of the two sexes

that designs identical in origin and appearance, used by the men and the women respectively, have wholly distinct interpretations. It would seem that where a marked difference exists between the decorative work of the men and the women, especially among the more primitive tribes, that of the women is less distinctly symbolic than that of the men, less graphic in character, and more fully dominated by simple esthetic requirements.

Generally speaking it may be said that each tribe employs in its ornament a group of elements or motives, ideographic and nonideographic, more or less distinctly its own and variously derived, and having characteristics determined largely by the grade and kind of culture and the nature of the immediate environment. The ornament of one tribe acts upon that of a neighboring tribe and is reacted upon according to the degrees of tribal intimacy and culture relationship, and the motives with or without their associated significance pass from one to the other, undergoing changes more or less radical and giving rise to endless variants. The ornamental art of any tribe is thus, as a rule, highly composite in style and significance, being derived through a plexus of channels and conditioned at all times by the particular environment.

In view of these facts it behooves the student of ornament to approach the subjects of origin and significance with due caution. He should remember that identical or closely analogous conventional forms may have diverse origins, and that the exact significance of a given ornament, formal or graphic, must be sought, not in analogous devices of other peoples and not in explanations previously obtained, but from the particular tribe, clan, society, or individual found using it, and that a search for ultimate meanings, if not necessarily futile, is fraught with peculiar difficulties.

Consult Balfour, Evolution of Decorative Art, 1893; Barrett in Am. Anthrop., VII, no. 4, 1905; Beauchamp, Metallic Ornaments of N. Y. Inds., 1903; Boas (1) in Pop. Sci. Mo., LXIII, no. 6, 1903, (2) in Bull. Am. Mus. Nat. Hist., IX, 1897; Culin in Bull. Free Mus. Univ. Pa., II, 235, 1900; Cushing in Proc. Am. Philos. Soc., XXXV, 1896; Dixon in Bull. Am. Mus. Nat. Hist., XVII, pt. 3, 1905; Emmons in Mem. Am. Mus. Nat. Hist., III, Anthrop. II, pt. 2, 1903; Farrand, ibid., II, Anthrop. I, pt. 5, 1900; Haddon, Evolution in Art, 1895; Hamlin in Am. Architect, LIX, no. 1160, 1898; Holmes (1) in 4th Rep. B. A. E., 1886, (2) in Am. Anthrop., III, no. 2, 1890, (3) in 6th Rep. B. A. E., 1888, (4) in Am. Anthrop., V, no. 1, 1892; Kroeber (1) in Am. Anthrop., n. s., III, no. 2, 1901, (2) in Bull. Am. Mus. Nat.

Hist., XVIII, pt. 1, 1902, (3) in Univ. Cal. Pub., Am. Archæol. and Ethnol., II, no. 4, 1905; Laufer in Mem. Am. Mus. Nat. Hist., VII, pt. 1, 1902; Lumholtz, (1) ibid., III, Anthrop. II, pt. 1, 1900, (2) ibid., pt. 3, 1904, (3) Unknown Mexico, 1902; Schmidt, Indianer-studien in Zentral-Brasilien, 1905; Schurtz, Das Augenornament, Abh. Phil. Hist., 11, K. Sächsische Ges. der Wissenschaften, XV, no. II; Stolpe, Studier i Amerikansk Ornamentik, 1896; Swanton in Mem. Am. Mus. Nat. Hist., VIII, 1905; Teit, ibid., II, Anthrop. I, pt. 4, 1900; Von den Steinen, Unter den Natur-Völkern Zentral Brasiliens, 1894; Wissler in Bull. Am. Mus. Nat. Hist., XVIII, pt. 3, 1904.　　(W. H. H.)

Oronhyatekha ('It [is a] burning sky'). A noted Mohawk mixed-blood, born on the Six Nations res., near Brantford, Ontario, in 1841; died at Augusta, Ga., Mar. 4, 1907. In his childhood he attended a mission industrial school near his home, and later entered the Wesleyan Academy at Wilbraham, Mass., and Kenyon College at Gambier, Ohio, where he remained two years, fitting himself for Toronto University, which he afterward entered. To cover expenses during his college vacation, he hired some white men, whom he dressed in Indian garb and exhibited with himself in a "Wild West" show. While a student at Toronto, in 1860, the chiefs of the Six Nations deputized Oronhyatekha to deliver an address to the Prince of Wales (King Edward VII) on the occasion of his visit to America, the Prince inviting him to continue his studies at Oxford, which he entered under the tutelage of Sir Henry Acland, regius professor of medicine. Returning to America a graduated physician, he practised for a time in Toronto. He married a granddaughter of Joseph Brant (Thayendanegea), the celebrated Mohawk, by whom he had a son and a daughter. Oronhyatekha was an enthusiast in secret society work. He was a prominent member of the Good Templars and of the Masonic fraternity, and in 1902, at Chicago, was elected president of the National Fraternal Congress. He was founder of the Independent Order of Foresters and held the office of Grand Ranger from 1881 until the time of his death. He delivered an address at the Indian centennial at Tyendinaga, Canada, Sept. 4, 1884. One who knew him personally described Oronhyatekha as "a man of extraordinary parts. He impressed all with his remarkable refinement. The stranger would take him for a high-class Englishman, were it not for those racial marks which betrayed his Indian origin. He was an expert parliamentarian, of dignified and suave yet forceful address. He was a keen debater, poignant and witty when occasion demanded, could tell a good story, and had

a faculty of withdrawing from any situation without leaving behind him rancor or injured feelings" (New Indian, Stewart, Nev., Mar. 1907). Oronhyatekha was the author of an article on the Mohawk language, printed in the Proceedings of the Canadian Institute (n. s., X, 182–194, 1865; XV, 1–12, 1878).

Orono. A Penobscot chief, born, according to tradition, on Penobscot r., Me., in or about 1688. According to one tradition he was a descendant of Baron de Castine, and although Williamson, who seems to have seen him and was familiar with his later career, is disposed to reject this story (Mass. Hist. Soc. Coll., 3d s., IX, 82–91, 1846), yet from Orono's own admissions it is possible that he was a son of Castine's daughter, who married a Frenchman, and with her children was taken captive in 1704. Nickolar, who was related to Orono by marriage, asserted, according to Williamson, that Orono was in some way related to old Castine; moreover he asserts that Orono was not of full blood, but part white—"a half breed or more." Orono informed Capt. Munsell (Williamson, op. cit., 83) that his father was a Frenchman and his mother half French and half Indian. He had none of the physical characteristics of an Indian save that he was tall, straight, and well proportioned. Very little is known of him until he had passed his 50th year. That he embraced the Roman Catholic faith while comparatively young, and that he was only a subordinate chief until he had reached his 75th year, are confirmed by the scanty records of his history. Until 1759 Tomasus, or Tomer, was head-chief of the Penobscot, when he was succeeded by Osson, who in turn was succeeded by Orono about 1770 or 1774. These three were ardent advocates of peace at the commencement of the French and Indian war in 1754, and until war was declared against the tribe by the English colonists. In 1775 Orono and three of his colleagues went, with one Andrew Gilman as interpreter, to profess their friendship and to tender their services to the Massachusetts government. They met the Provincial Congress at Watertown on June 21, where they entered into a treaty of amity with that body and offered assistance, and afterward proved faithful allies of the colonists during their struggle for independence. Orono was held in as high esteem after the war as before; and in 1785 and 1796 entered into treaties with Massachusetts, by which his tribe ceded certain portions of their lands and fixed permanent limits to the parts reserved. At the time of the latter treaty Orono is said to have reached his 108th year. He died at his home at Oldtown, Me., Feb. 5, 1802. His wife, who was a full blood

Indian and his almost lifelong companion, survived him a few years. Orono had a son, who was accidently shot about 1774, aged 25 years; and a daughter who married Capt. Nickolar. Orono was buried in the cemetery at Stillwater, Penobscot co., Me., in the vicinity of the town that bears his name. (C. T.)

Oroysom. Said to have been the native name of the site of San José mission, Cal. The territory was Costanoan.
Oroysom.—Engelhardt, Franc. in Cal., 390, 1897.
Oroyson.—Ibid.

Osacalis. A Costanoan village situated in 1819 within 10 m. of Santa Cruz mission, Cal.
Osacalis.—Taylor in Cal. Farmer, Apr. 5, 1860.
Souquel.—Ibid.

Osachile. An inland town of w. Florida, apparently belonging to the Yustaga tribe, situated probably not far E. from Ocilla r., and visited by De Soto in 1539. (J. M.)

ever, and the Osage recognize three more closely amalgamated divisions which seem, from the traditional account of them, to represent as many formerly independent tribes. According to this account, as gathered by J. O. Dorsey, the beings which ultimately became men originated in the lowest of the four upper worlds which Osage cosmology postulates and ascended to the highest where they obtained souls. Then they descended until they came to a red-oak tree on which the lowest world rests and by its branches reached our earth. They were divided into two sections, the Tsishu, or peace people, who kept to the left, living on roots, etc.; and the Wazhazhe (true Osage), or war people, who kept to the right and killed animals for their food. Later these two divisions exchanged commodities, and after some time the Tsishu

GROUP OF OSAGE.   (ELEVENTH CENSUS)

Ossachile.—Garcilasso de la Vega (1591) quoted by Shipp, De Soto and Florida, 299, 1881. Uçachile.—Ranjel (ca. 1546) in Bourne, De Soto Narr., II, 73, 1904. Uzachil.—Gentl. of Elvas (1557) in French, Hist. Coll. La., II, 133, 1850. Uzela.—Gentl. of Elvas quoted in Hakluyt Soc. Pub., IX, xxxii, 1851.

Osage (corruption by French traders of *Wazhazhe*, their own name). The most important southern Siouan tribe of the western division. Dorsey classed them, under the name Dhegiha, in one group with the Omaha, Ponca, Kansa, and Quapaw, with whom they are supposed to have originally constituted a single body living along the lower course of the Ohio r.

Geographically speaking, the tribe consists of three bands: the Pahatsi or Great Osage, Utsehta or Little Osage, and Santsukhdhi or Arkansas band. These appear to be comparatively modern, how-

people came into possession of four kinds of corn and four kinds of pumpkins, which fell from the left hind legs of as many different buffaloes. Still later the tribe came upon a very warlike people called Hangka-utadhantse, who lived on animals, and after a time the Tsishu people succeeded in making peace with them, when they were taken into the nation on the war side. Originally there were seven Tsishu gentes, seven Wazhazhe gentes, and seven Hangka gentes, but, in order to maintain an equilibrium between the war and peace sides after adopting the Hangka, the number of their gentes was reduced to five and the number of Wazhazhe gentes to two. In camping the Tsishu gentes are on the left or N. side of the camping circle, and the Hangka or Wazhazhe gentes on the right or S. side, the entrance to the circle being eastward. Beginning at this entrance the arrangement of gentes is as follows: Tsishu gentes (from E. to w.·): 1, Tsishusintsakdhe; 2, Tsedtukaindtse; 3, Minkin; 4, Tsishuwashtake; 5, Haninihkashina; 6, Tsetduka; 7, Kdhun. Hangka gentes (from E. to w.): 8, Washashewanun; 9, Hangkautadhantsi; 10, Panhkawashtake; 11, Hangkaahutun; 12, Wasapetun; 13, Upkhan; 14, Kanse.

The gentile organization appears to have been very similar to that of the Omaha and other southern tribes of this division, involving paternal descent, prohibition of marriage in the gentes of both father and mother, and probably gentile taboos. The functions of the various gentes were also differentiated to a certain extent. Matters connected with war were usually undertaken by the war gentes and peace-making by the peace gentes, while it was the duty of the chief of the Tsishuwashtake gens to defend any foeman who might slip into the camp-circle and appeal to him for protection. The Tsishu gentes are also said to have had the care and naming of children. Heralds were chosen from certain special gentes, and certain others monopolized the manufacture of moccasins, war standards, and war pipes. On the death of a head-chief the leading man called a council and named four candidates, from whom the final selection was made. Seven appears as a sacred number in the social organization of the Osage, but from the war and other customs of the tribe it appears that the sacred ceremonial number was usually four (Dorsey in Am. Nat., Feb. 1884).

The first historical notice of the Osage appears to be on Marquette's autograph map of 1673, which locates them apparently on Osage r., and there they are placed by all subsequent writers until their removal westward in the 19th century. Douay (1686) assigns them 17 villages, but these must have been nothing more than hunting camps, for Father Jacques Gravier, in a letter written in 1694 from the Illinois mission, speaks of but one, and later writers agree with his statement, though it must be understood as applying only to the Great Osage. Gravier interviewed two Osage and two Missouri chiefs who had come to make an alliance with the Illinois, and says of them: "The Osage and Missouri do not appear to be so quick-witted as the Illinois; their language does not seem very difficult. The former do not open their lips and the latter speak still more from the throat than they" (Jes. Rel., LXIV, 171, 1900). Iberville in 1701 (Margry, Déc., IV, 599, 1880) mentions a tribe of 1,200 to 1,500 families living in the region of Arkansas r., near the Kansa and the Missouri,

and, like these, speaking a language that he took to be Quapaw. The name of this tribe through errors in copying and printing became Crevas, but the description indicates the Osage. In 1714 they assisted the French in defeating the Foxes at Detroit. Although visits of traders were evidently quite common before 1719, the first official French visit appears to have been in that year by Du Tisné, who learned that their village on Osage r. then contained 100 cabins and 200 warriors. The village of the Missouri was higher up, and a short distance s. w. of the latter was another Osage village which from later maps is shown to have been occupied by the Little Osage. Then,

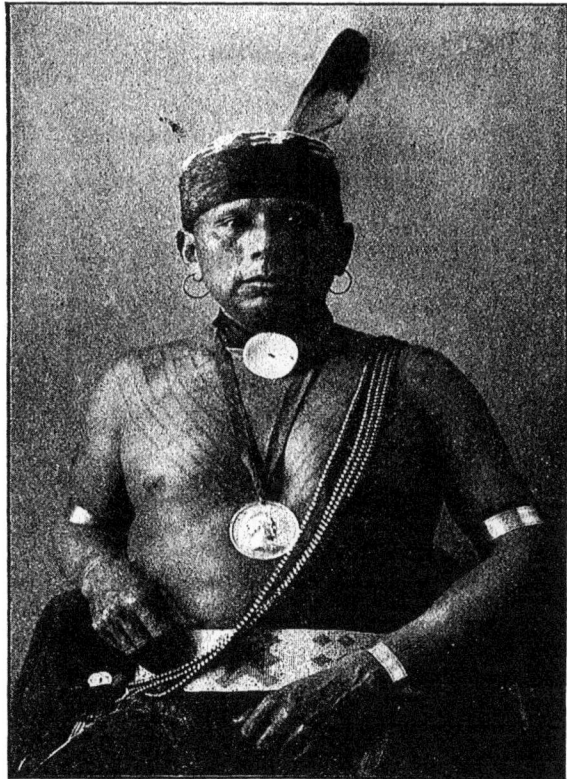

OSAGE MAN

as always, the tribe was at war with most of the surrounding peoples, and La Harpe witnesses to the terror in which they were held by the Caddoan tribes. The Illinois were also inveterate enemies, though at one time, when driven w. of the Mississippi by the Iroquois, they fled to the Osage for protection. Charlevoix met a party of Osage at the Kaskaskia village on Oct. 20, 1721. Regarding them he wrote: "They depute some of their people once or twice every year to sing the calumet among the Kaskasquias, and they are now actually here at present." The French officer Bossu met some Osage at Cahokia (q. v.) in 1756. About 1802, according to Lewis and Clark, nearly half of the Great Osage under a chief named Big-track migrated to Arkansas r., thus constituting the Arkansas band. The same explorers (1804) found the Great Osage, numbering about 500 warriors, in a village on the s. bank of Osage r., the Little Osage, nearly half as numerous, 6 m. distant, and the Arkansas band, numbering 600 warriors, on Vermilion r., a branch of the Arkansas.

On Nov. 10, 1808, by a treaty with the United States concluded at Ft Clark, Kans., near Kansas City, Mo., the Osage ceded to the United States all their lands E. of a line running due s. from Ft Clark to Arkansas r., and also all of their lands w. of Missouri r., the whole comprising the larger part of what is now the state of Missouri and the N. part of Arkansas. The territory remaining to them, all of the present state of Oklahoma N. of Canadian and Arkansas rs., was still further reduced by the provisions of treaties at St Louis, June 2, 1825; Ft Gibson, Ind. T., Jan. 11, 1839; and Canville, Kans., Sept. 29, 1865; and the limits of their present reservation were established by act of Congress of July 15, 1870. This consisted (1906) of 1,470,058 acres, and in addition the tribe possessed funds in the Treasury of the United States amounting to $8,562,690, including a school fund of $119,911, the whole yielding an annual income of $428,134. Their income from pasturage leases amounted to $98,376 in the same year, and their total annual income was therefore about $265 per capita, making this tribe the richest in the entire United States. By act of June 28, 1906, an equal division of the lands and funds of the Osage was provided for.

Estimates of Osage population later than that of Lewis and Clark are the following: Sibley, 1,250 men (including 400 Great Osage, 250 Little Osage, and 600 of the Arkansas band); Morse (1821), 5,200 (including 4,200 Great Osage and 1,000 Little Osage); Porter (1829), 5,000; U. S. Indian Office (1843), 4,102; Schoolcraft (1853), 3,758 (exclusive of an important division known as Black Dog's band). According to the Indian Office census of 1877, they numbered 3,001; in 1884, 1,547; 1886, 1,582; 1906 (after the division of the tribal lands and trust funds had been provided for), 1,994.

The following villages were occupied by the Osage at different times: Big Chief, Black Dog, Heakdhetanwan, Intapupshe, Khdhasiukdhin, Little Osage Village, Manhukdhintanwan, Nanzewaspe, Nikhdhitanwan, Pasukdhin, Paghuukdhinpe, Santsukdhin, Takdheskautsiupshe, Tanwakanwakaghe, Tanwanshinka, Wakhakukdhin, and White Hair Village. The following bands and divisions have not been identified: Shapei-nihkashina, Petkhaninihkashina, and Tatseinihkashina. (J. R. S.)

A-ha-chae.—Hamilton in Schoolcraft, Ind. Tribes, IV, 406, 1854. Ä'lähó.—Mooney in 17th Rep. B. A. E., 394, 1898. Anahons.—La Harpe (1719) in Margry, Déc., VI, 261, 1886 (probable misprint for Anahou). Anahous.—Ibid., 284. Ani'-Wasa'sĭ.—Mooney in 19th Rep. B. A. E., 509, 1900 (Cherokee name). Annaho.—Joutel (1687) in Margry, Déc., III, 410, 1878. Assenjigun.—Schoolcraft, Ind. Tribes, IV, 304, 1854 (error). Assigunaigs.—Ibid., 592 (error; see Assegun). Autreohaha.—Thevenot quoted by Shea, Discov., 268, 1852. Bone Indians.—Schoolcraft, Ind. Tribes, IV, 592, 1854. Crevas.—Iberville (1702) in Margry, Déc., IV, 599, 1880 (misprint). Guasachis.—Escudero, Noticias Nuevo Méx., 83, 1849. Huashashas.—Rafinesque in Marshall, Ky., I, 28, 1824. Huzaas.—Long, Exped. Rocky Mts., II, 311, 1823. Huz-zau.—Pénicaut (1719) in French, Hist. Coll. La., n. s., I, 151, 1869. Huz-zaws.—Long, Exped. Rocky Mts., II, 244, 1823. Oçages.—Barcia, Ensayo, 242, 1723. Orages.—Coxe, Carolana, 15, 1741. Osage.—Hennepin, New Discov., pt. I, 141, 1698. Osarge.—Orig. Jour. Lewis and Clark (1804), I, 36, 1904. Osasi'gi.—Gatschet, Shawnee MS., B. A. E. (Shawnee name). O-saw-ses.—Long, Exped. Rocky Mts., II, 244, 1823. Osayes.—Morse, N. Am., map, 1776 (misprint?). Osédshi maḱlaks.—Gatschet, MS., B. A. E. (Modoc name). Ossage.—Schermerhorn (1812) in Mass. Hist. Soc. Coll., 2d s., II, 31, 1814. Ouasoys.—Croghan (1759) in Rupp, West. Penna., 146, note, 1846. Ouchage.—Marquette map (1673) in Shea, Discov., 268, 1852. Ouichaatcha.—Bowles, Map of America, ca. 1750. Ous.—Pénicaut (1719) in French, Hist. Coll. La., n. s., I, 151, 1869. Ousasons.—Boudinot, Star in the West, 128, 1816. Ousasoys.—Croghan (1759) in Jefferson, Notes, 145, 1825 (probably a French corruption of Washashe). O-ŭχtχitan.—Gatschet, Cheyenne MS., B. A. E. ('hair cropped short': Cheyenne name). Ozages.—Hennepin, New Discov., pt. II, 47, 1698. Ozajes.—Barcia, Ensayo, 298, 1723. Ozanges.—Hennepin, New Discov., pt. II, 47, 1698. Ozas.—Amer. Pioneer, II, 190, 1843. Tsíwiltzha-e.—Gatschet, Na-isha Apache MS., B. A. E. (Kiowa Apache name). Uzajes.—Barcia, Ensayo, 299, 1723. Waoaoe.—Dorsey, Osage MS. vocab., B. A. E., 1883 (own name). Wahashas.—Rafinesque in Marshall, Hist. Ky., I, 30, 1824. Wahsash.—Keane in Stanford, Compend., 542, 1878. Wajáje.—Dorsey, Çegiha MS. Dict., B. A. E., 1878 (Ponca, Omaha, Kansa, and Quapaw name). Waraye.—Ibid. (Iowa, Oto, and Missouri name). Wasāāzj.—ten Kate, Reizen in N. A., 383, 1885. Wasagè.—Hunter, Captivity, 18, 1823. Wasashe.—Brackenridge, Views of La., 72, 1815. Wā'sassa.—Gatschet, MS., B. A. E. (name given by Foxes and many other tribes). Wasawsee.—Gale, Upper Miss., map facing 49, 1867. Wasbasha.—Lewis and Clark Exped., I, 9, 1814. Washas.—Balbi, Atlas Ethnog., 56, 1826. Wa-sha-she.—Pitchlynn (ca. 1828) quoted by Smith, Cabeça de Vaca, 171, note, 1871. Washbashaws.—Schoolcraft, Ind. Tribes, VI, 689, 1857. Wash-sashe.—Marcy, Explor. Red R., 273, 1854 (Comanche and Wichita name). Wássash.—Gatschet, Arapaho MS., B. A. E. (Arapaho name). Wassashsha.—Brown, West. Gaz., 193, 1817. Wausashe.—Gallatin in Trans. Am. Antiq. Soc., II, 126, 1836. Wa-wha.—Pénicaut (1719) in French, Hist. Coll. La., n. s., I, 151, 1869. Wawsash.—Balbi, Atlas Ethnog., 56, 1826. Waw-sash-e.—Long, Exped. Rocky Mts., I, 328, 1823. Wažaža.—Riggs, MS. letter to Dorsey (Dakota name). Wa-zha-zhe.—Dorsey in Am. Naturalist, 113, note, Feb. 1884. Wos-sosh-e.—M'Coy, Annual Register, no. 2, 17, 1836. Wû-sa-sĭ.—Grayson, MS. vocab., B. A. E., 1885 (Creek name). Zages.—Harris, Coll. Voy. and Trav., I, map of America, 685, 1705.

Osage. A former Miami village on Wabash r., just w. of the Mississinewa, in Miami co., Ind. It was so called from its being the residence of an Osage Indian domiciliated among the Miami, and whose name appears in treaties as Osage and Osage the Neutral (J. P. Dunn, inf'n, 1907). In 1838 the site was included in an individual reserve granted to Richardville, the Miami chief.

Osaga.—Hough, map in Indiana Geol. Rep., 1882 (misprint). **Osage town.**—Royce, map in 1st Rep. B. A. E., 1881. **Osage village.**—Treaty of 1838 in U. S. Ind. Treat., 508, 1873.

Osage orange. The bois d'arc (*Toxylon pomiferum*), native in the Osage mts.; from the ethnic term *Osage*, applied in particular to a people of Siouan stock. The wood was commonly used by western tribes for making bows, hence the French name. Cf. *Ozark*. (A. F. C.)

Osamekin. See *Massasoit*.

Osanalgi (*Osán-algi*, 'otter people'). A Creek clan.—Gatschet, Creek Migr. Leg., I, 155, 1884.

Osass (*O''sass*, 'muskrat'). A subphratry or gens of the Menominee.—Hoffman in 14th Rep. B. A. E., 42, 1896.

Oscalui. A former town of the Conestoga, probably situated near the mouth of Sugar cr., on the right bank of Susquehanna r., in Bradford co., Pa.

Ogehage.—Hendrickson's map (1616) in N. Y. Doc. Col. Hist., I, 1856. **Oscalui.**—Jour. Mil. Exped. Gen. Sullivan, 1779, 124, 1887.

Osceola (also spelled Oseola, Asseola, Asseholar, properly *Asi-yaholo*, 'Blackdrink halloer,' from *asi*, the 'black drink' (q. v.), *yaholo*, the long drawn-out cry sung by the attendant while each man in turn is drinking). A noted Seminole leader to whom the name Powell was sometimes applied from the fact that after the death of his father his mother married a white man of that name. He was born on Tallapoosa r., in the Creek country, about 1803. His paternal grandfather was a Scotchman, and it is said the Caucasian strain was noticeable in his features and complexion. He was not a chief by descent, nor, so far as is known, by formal election, but took his place as leader and acknowledged chieftain by reason of his abilities as a warrior and commander during the memorable struggle of his people with the United States in the Seminole war of 1835. Secreting the women, children, and old men of his tribe in the depths of a great swamp, where the white troops were for a long time unable to find them, Osceola turned his energy to the work of harassing the Government forces. Maj. Dade and his detachment, the first to attack him, were cut off, only two or three wounded men escaping. Beginning with Gen. Gaines, one after another officer was placed in charge of the army sent against this intrepid warrior and his followers. These were successively baffled, owing largely to the physical difficulties to be overcome on account of the nature of the Seminole country, until Gen. Jesup, maddened by the public cry for more energetic action, seized Osceola and his attendants while holding a conference under a flag of truce—an act condemned as inexcusable treachery by the same public that had urged him on. The loss of freedom, and brooding over the manner in which he had been betrayed, broke the spirit of the youthful chief, who died a prisoner in Ft Moultrie, S. C., in Jan. 1838. In physique Osceola was described as tall, slender, and straight, with a countenance pleasing, though of somewhat melancholy cast. See Sketch of the Seminole War, by a Lieutenant, 1836; Barr, Narr. Ind. Wars in Fla., 1836; McKenney and Hall, Ind. Tribes, 1854; Potter, The War in Florida, 1836; Ellis, Indian Wars of the United States, 1892. (C. T.)

OSCEOLA. (AFTER CATLIN)

Oschekkamegawenenewak (*Oshă'kŭmĭgawĭnĭnĭwŭg*, 'people of the transverse ridge.'—W. J.). A former Chippewa band in Minnesota, living in 1753 near Rainy lake. The name is applied also to some Chippewa once living E. of Mille Lac but now at White Earth.

Oschekkamega Wenenewak.—Long, Exped. St Peter's R., II, 153, 1824 ("or those of the cross or transverse ridge"). **Oshä'kamigãwininiwag.**—Wm. Jones, inf'n, 1906.

Oscouarahronon. The Iroquois name of an unidentified but probably Algonquian tribe s. of St Lawrence r. in the 17th century.—Jes. Rel. 1640, 35, 1858.

Osetchiwan ('place of the headless'). An ancient Zuñi pueblo, now in ruins, situated N. w. of Hawikuh (q. v.) in w. New Mexico.

O''setchiwan.—Cushing, inf'n, 1891. **Osh-a-chewan.**—Fewkes in Jour. Am. Eth. and Arch., I, 101, 1891. **O'shetchiwan.**—Cushing, op. cit.

Osguage. A former village of the Mohawk, consisting in 1634, when it was visited by Van Curler, of 9 houses. For a description of these, see *Onekagoncka*.

It was situated near a large confluent of Mohawk r., between the third and fourth castles of the Mohawk, E. of the village of Cawaoge, which was about 1 m. E. of the fourth castle of that date. This may have been a town of the Wolf clan, as Van Curler learned that the principal chief of this village was known as Oguoho, i. e. 'Wolf.' It was probably distinct from Osquake. (J. N. B. H.)

Ohquage.—Van Curler (1634–35) in Rep. Am. Hist. Ass'n 1895, 98, 1896.

Oshach. The Sun clans of the Keresan pueblos of Laguna, Acoma, Sia, San Felipe, and Cochiti, N. Mex. The Sun clan of Laguna claims to have come originally from San Felipe; that of Acoma forms a phratry with the Huwaka (Sky) clan. (F. W. H.)

Hano Oshatch.—Lummis, New Mex. David, 48, 1891 (evidently applied here to the Acoma in general). Ohshǎhch-hǎno^ch.—Hodge in Am. Anthrop., IX, 352, 1896 (Laguna form; hǎnoch= 'people'). Osǎch-hǎno.—Ibid. (Sia form). Osǎch-hǎnoq^ch.—Ibid. (Acoma form). O'shach-hǎno.— Ibid. (San Felipe form). O'shach-hǎnuch.— Ibid. (Cochiti form). O'-sharts.—Stevenson in 11th Rep. B. A. E., 19, 1894 (Sia form). Oshatsh.— Bandelier, Delight Makers, 243, 1890 (Cochiti form).

Oshagonondagie. See *Onondakai.*

OSHKOSH. (WISCONSIN HISTORICAL SOCIETY)

Oshkosh ('his hoof', or 'his nail'; cf. *Oshkushi*). Head-chief of the Menominee in the first half of the 19th century; born 1795, died Aug. 31, 1850. He was of the Owasse gens, and grandson of Chakauchokama, called "The Old King," long head-chief of the tribe. Oshkosh became a warrior when 17 years of age, being one of the hundred of his tribesmen under

Tomah who joined Col. Robert Dickson of the British army and participated in the capture of Ft Mackinaw, Mich., from the Americans in July, 1812. He was with the party who in 1813 made an unsuccessful attack on Ft Sandusky, Ohio, then in charge of Maj. Geo. Croghan. It was at the treaty of Butte des Morts, Mich. Ter. (now Wisconsin), Aug. 11, 1827, that he was first officially recognized as chief of the Menominee, when, in fact, he was named as chief by Cass and McKenney, the United States commissioners, in order that he might represent his tribe. Oshkosh is described as having been of medium size, possessing good sense, ability, and bravery, but a slave to strong drink, which led him, at least in one instance, deliberately to murder, without provocation or excuse, an inoffensive Indian. His name is also written Oiscoss, Oskoshe, and Oskashe. His portrait, painted by Samuel M. Brookes, is in possession of the State Historical Society of Wisconsin. See Hoffman in 14th Rep. B. A. E., 1896. (C. T.)

Oshkushi (*Uskasha^a*). The animate form of an inanimate word referring to 'hoof,' 'claw,' 'nail'; applied to a member of the social divisions of the Sauk, Foxes, and Kickapoo. The division is irrespective of clan and is the cause of intense rivalry in sport. Their ceremonial color is black. (W. J.)

Oshonawan ('musty town'). An ancient Zuñi settlement, now in ruins, situated E. of Ojo Caliente, N. Mex. (F. H. C.)

O-sho-na.—Fewkes in Jour. Am. Eth. and Arch., I, 101, 1891.

Oshtenuhlawan (*Osh'-te-nu'-hla-wan,* 'dwelling place of the rock or cave shelter surrounded'). A companion ruin to Hlauhla, which is situated 10 m. N. N. E. of Zuñi, N. Mex. (F. H. C.)

Osiquevede. Mentioned by Fontaneda, about 1575, in connection with Mogoso, Tocobaga, Carlos (Calusa,) Ais, and Sonsobe, as a village or tribe of Florida below (S. from) Apalachee, Fla. (J. M.)

Osiguevede.—Fontaneda in Ternaux-Compans, Voy., XX, 40, 1841. Osiquevede.—Fontaneda Memoir, Smith trans., 27, 1854.

Oskakumukchochikam (*Os Kǎ'kǎmǎk Tcótcikǎm,* 'arrow-bush standing'). A former Pima village in S. Arizona.—Russell, Pima MS., B. A. E., 16, 1902.

Oskawaserenhon ('dead branches have fallen'). A traditional Iroquois town of the Wolf clan; so enumerated in the list of towns in the Chant of Welcome of the Condolence Council of the League of the Iroquois. Nothing definite is known as to its situation or to what tribe it belonged. See Hale, Iroq. Book of Rites, 1883. (J. N. B. H.)

Oskelagna (*yagena*='land'). Recorded on the West Florida map (*ca.* 1775) as one of the former Choctaw "Sixtowns," situated probably in Jasper co., Miss. It is not, however, one of the Sixtowns recorded by Gatschet. See *Oklahannali*.

Oskenotoh (*Os-ken'-o-toh*). The Deer clan of the Hurons.—Morgan, Anc. Soc., 153, 1877.

Oskquisaquamai. A fish-eating people mentioned in connection with Assiniboin, Cree, and Maskegon, in the middle of the 18th century; probably a band of Cree.

Oskquisaquamai.—Bacqueville de la Potherie, Hist. Am., I, 176, 1753. Osquisakamais.—Dobbs, Hudson Bay, 25, 1744.

Oskuk (*Os' kük*, 'tree standing'). A small Pima village on Gila r., s. Arizona.—Russell, Pima MS., B. A. E., 18, 1902.

Osmakmiketlp (*Ōsmaxmik·é'lp*). A Bellacoola village on the N. side of Bellacoola r., at its mouth, in British Columbia; it was one of the eight Nuhalk towns.—Boas in Mem. Am. Mus. Nat. Hist., II, 49, 1898.

Osonee. A former village, probably of the Upper Creeks, on Cahawba r., in Shelby co., Ala.

Old Osonee.—Royce in 18th Rep. B. A. E., Ala. map, 1900.

Osotchi. A former Lower Creek town on the w. bank of Chattahoochee r., Russell co., Ala., 2 m. below Uchee town and adjoining Chiaha. It was settled prior to 1791 by people from Flint r., Ga., and in 1832 had 168 heads of families. In Oklahoma the descendants of the people of Osotchi and Chiaha are settled in one village.

Hooseche.—Bartram, Travels, 462, 1791. Hoositchi.—Bartram as cited by Gatschet, Creek Migr. Leg., I, 142, 1884. Ocsachees.—Harris, Voy., II, 335, 1764. Odsinachies.—McKenney and Hall, Ind. Tribes, III, 80, 1854 (probably identical). Ooscooches.—Hawkins (1813) in Am. State Pap., Ind. Aff., I, 854, 1832. Oosechu.—Adair, Am. Inds., 257, 1775. Oo-se-oo-che.—Hawkins (1799), Sketch, 25, 63, 1848. Ooseoochee.—U. S. Ind. Treat. (1814), 163, 1837. Oscoochee.—Gallatin in Trans. Am. Antiq. Soc., II, 95, 1836. Oseooche.—Wilkinson (1802) in Am. State Pap., Ind. Aff., I, 677, 1832. Ositchy.—Pickett, Hist. Ala., II, 104, 1851. Oso-chee.—Am. State Papers, Ind. Aff., II, 837, 1834. Ósotchi.—Gatschet, Creek Migr. Leg., I, 142, 1884. Ossuchees.—Am. State Papers, Ind. Aff., I, 383, 1832. Ostretchees.—H. R. Ex. Doc. 276, 24th Cong., 1st sess., 308, 1836. Ósudshi.—Gatschet, Creek, Migr. Leg., I, 142, 1884. Ósutchi.—Ibid. Oswichees.—Woodward, Reminis., 38, 1859. Oswichu.—U. S. Ind. Treat. (1827), 419, 1837. Oswitcha.—H. R. Ex. Doc. 276, 24th Cong., 1st sess., 300, 1836. Oswitche.—H. R. Doc. 452, 25th Cong., 2d sess., 49, 1838. Oswitchee.—Schoolcraft, Ind. Tribes, IV, 578, 1854. Ousauches.—Barnard (1793) in Am. State Pap., Ind. Aff., I, 382, 1832. Owitchees.—McCall, Hist. Georgia, I, 364, 1811. Owseecheys.—Harris, Voy., II, 327, 1764. Usechees.—Kinnard (1793) in Am. State Pap., Ind. Aff., I, 388, 1832. Usuchees.—Seagrove (1793), ibid., 387. Úsutchi.—Gatschet, Creek Migr. Leg., I, 142, 1884.

Osotchi. A town of the Creek Nation, on Deep fork, below Ocmulgee, Okla.

O'sudshi.—Gatschet, Creek Migr. Leg., II, 186, 1888.

Ospo. A Yamasee mission on the coast of Georgia in the latter part of the 16th century. In 1597, in a general attack on the missions, the church was destroyed and the priest in charge, Father Avila, taken prisoner, but he was finally rescued after having once been condemned to the stake. See *Tolemato*.　　　　　(J. M.)

Ospa.—Shea, Cath. Miss., 70, 1855. Ospo.—Barcia, Ensayo, 171, 1723.

Osquake (from *Otsquago*, 'under the rock,' Mohawk name of the creek.—Hewitt). A Mohawk band and village formerly at Ft Plain and on Osquake cr., Montgomery co., N. Y. (Macauley, N. Y., II, 296, 1829). Cf. *Osguage*.

Ossaghrage (Iroquois: 'place of beaver dams.'—Hewitt). An Abnaki village in 1700.—Bellomont (1700) in N. Y. Doc. Col. Hist., IV, 758, 1854.

Ossahinta ('Frost'). The principal chief of the Onondaga from 1830 until his death in 1846; he was born in 1760 and belonged to the Turtle clan. Ossahinta was of high character and an eloquent speaker, and was commonly known as Captain Frost.　　　　　(W. M. B.)

Osse (*Os'-se*, 'old squaw duck'). A subphratry or gens of the Menominee.—Hoffman in 14th Rep. B. A. E., 42, 1896.

Ossewingo. A town with a mixed population under Oneida jurisdiction, formerly situated, according to the Evans map of 1756, a few miles above Chenango, Broome co., N. Y. The report of Thompson and Post in 1758 (Pa. Archives, III, 413, 1853) says, with reference to Chenango, that it is a "town of the Nanticokes, on Susquehanna, about half way between Owegey and Ossewingo," which indicates apparently that Chenango lay between the two towns mentioned and is not identical with Ossewingo, as some writers assert. See Halsey, Old N. Y. Frontier, 276, 1901.　　　　　(J. N. B. H.)

Ossingsing (Delaware: *assinesink*, 'at the little stone,' probably referring to the heaps of small stones that the Indians were accustomed to form at certain places, especially at the foot of a hill.—Gerard). A former village of the Sintsink (q. v.) on the site of Ossining, N. Y.—Ruttenber, Tribes Hudson R., 79, 1872.

Ossipee ('lake formed by the enlargement of a river.'—Maurault). A small tribe of the Pennacook confederacy formerly living on Ossipee r. and lake in Carroll co., N. H., and Oxford co., Me. Their village, of the same name, was probably on the lake.　　　　　(J. M.)

Osipees.—Kendall, Trav., III, 45, 1809. Ossepe.—Treaty of 1690 in Mass. Hist. Soc. Coll., 3d s., I, 113, 1825. Ossipee.—Penhallow (1726) in N. H. Hist. Soc. Coll., I, 71, 1824.

Ossossané ('a mound'). A former important Huron village, belonging to the Bear clan, situated between L. Simcoe and Georgian bay, Ontario. It was known under various names at different periods. In 1639 the mission of La Conception was removed there from Ihonatiria.　　　　　(J. N. B. H.)

Immaculate Conception.—Shea, Cath. Miss., 177, 1855. La Conception.—Jes. Rel. 1640, 63, 1858. La Rochelle.—Jes. Rel. 1636, 123, 1858. Ossonane.—

Jes. Rel. 1639, 88, 1858 (changed in *errata* to Ossossane). **Ossosandué.**—Jes. Rel. 1637, 70, 1858. **Ossosané.**—Ibid., 131. **Ossossandue.**—Ibid., 70. **Ossossané.**—Jes. Rel. 1636, 123, 1858. **Ossossarie.**—Jes. Rel. 1640, 63, 1858 (misprint). **Quevindoyan.**—Mémoire of 1637 in Margry, Déc., I, 4, 1875 (sig. 'at the base of the mountain.'—Hewitt). **Quieuindohain.**—Sagard (1686), Can., II, 422, 1866. **Quieuindohian.**—Ibid., I, 200, 1866. **Sainct Gabriel.**—Ibid., note. **Tequenonquiaye.**—Champlain (1615), Œuvres, IV, 28, 1870. **Tequeunoikuaye.**—Sagard (1636), Can., I, 200, 1866. **Tequeunonkiaye.**—Sagard misquoted in Champlain, Œuvres, IV, 28, note, 1870.

Ossuary. See *Mortuary customs*.

Osswehgadagaah ('hawk'). A clan of the Seneca.
Canonchahonronon.—French writer (1666) in N. Y. Doc. Col. Hist., IX, 47–48, 1855. **Os-sweh-gä-dä-gä′-ah.**—Morgan, League Iroq., 80, 1851.

Ostimuri. A pueblo of the Nevome, with 57 inhabitants in 1730; apparently situated in Sonora, Mexico, E. of lon. 109° and N. of lat. 29. It seems to have been a visita of and near the mission of (Santa Rosalia) Onopa, q. v.
S. Ildefonso Ostimuri.—Rivera (1730) quoted by Bancroft, No. Mex. States, I, 514, 1884.

Ostogeron. A former Iroquois village, apparently under Oneida jurisdiction, situated, according to the Brion de la Tour map of 1781, above Tuskokogie, on the E. bank of the E. branch of the Susquehanna r. This is probably an error for Chenango r. in N. Y. (J. N. B. H.)
Octageron.—Lattré, Map, 1784. **Ostogeron.**—Esnauts and Rapilly, Map, 1777.

Ostonwackin. A village occupied by Delaware, Cayuga, Oneida, and other Indians under Iroquois control on the w. branch of the Susquehanna, at the mouth of Loyalsock cr., at the site of the present Montoursville, Lycoming co., Pa. It was at one time the home of the celebrated Madam Montour, q. v.
French Town.—Darlington, Christopher Gist's Jour., 155, 1893. **Ostanghaes.**—Albany conf. (1722) in N. Y. Doc. Col. Hist., V, 675, 1855 (the inhabitants). **Ostonwackin.**—Loskiel (1794) quoted by Day, Penn., 525, 1843. **Ots-on-wacken.**—Darlington, op. cit. **Otstonwackin.**—Loskiel, Hist. Miss. United Breth., pt. 2, 32, 1794. **Otstuago.**—Darlington, op. cit.

Ostrovki (Russian: 'little islands'). A Kaniagmiut Eskimo village on Kachemak bay, w. coast of Kenai penin., Alaska; pop. 74 in 1880.—Petroff in 10th Census, Alaska, 29, 1884.

Ostyalakwa. A former pueblo of the Jemez of New Mexico; definite location unknown. Asserted to be distinct from Astialakwa.
Osht-yal-a.—Bandelier in Arch. Inst. Papers, IV, 207, 1892. **Ost′-yal-a-kwa.**—Hodge, field notes, B. A. E., 1895.

Osuktalaya (*Osak-talaya*, 'hickory grove'). A former Choctaw town of the Oklafalaya, or Western party, on the headwaters of Chickasawhay r., in Neshoba or Kemper co., Miss. See Halbert in Pub. Miss. Hist. Soc., VI, 427, 1902.

Osunkhirhine, Pierre Paul. An Abnaki Indian of St Francis, near Pierreville, Quebec, noted for his translations, especially of religious works, into the Penobscot dialect of the Abnaki language, published from 1830 to 1844. He received a good education at Moore's Charity School, Hanover, N. H., and returned to his home as a Protestant missionary. In some of his published works (Pilling, Bibliog. Algonq. Lang., 539–40, 1891) his name appears as Wzokhilain, because it could not be more exactly transliterated into the Abnaki language.

Oswegatchie ('at the very outlet'). A former village of Catholic Iroquois under French influence, on the site of Ogdensburg, St Lawrence co., N. Y., at the mouth of the Oswegatchie. In 1748 Father Picquet began there La Presentation mission, which grew so rapidly, mainly by recruits from the Onondaga and Cayuga, that three years later the settlement numbered 3,000. The French fort La Gallette was built there about the same time. In spite of the opposition of the Iroquois confederation the mission prospered, and at the breaking out of the French and Indian war in 1754 the Oswegatchie and other Catholic Iroquois sided with the French against their former brethren. The settlement was invaded the next year by smallpox, which carried off nearly half the population. In 1763 they were estimated at about 400. They joined the British in the Revolution and at the close of the war the disorganized remnant was settled temporarily at Johnstown and later at Indian Point near Lisbon, not far from their old settlement. About the year 1806 the survivors finally joined the Onondaga and St Regis. (J. N. B. H.)
La Gallette.—Writer of 1756 in Mass. Hist. Soc. Coll., 1st s., VII, 99, 1801. **La Gattell.**—Johnson (1763) in N. Y. Doc. Col. Hist., VII, 573, 1856 (transposed). **La Présentation.**—Quebec conf. (1751), ibid., X, 237, 1858 (mission name). **Osevegatchies.**—Imlay, West. Ter., 293, 1797 (misprint). **Osswegatche.**—Johnson (1763) in N. Y. Doc. Col. Hist., VII, 573, 1856. **Oswagatches.**—Boudinot, Star in the West, 128, 1816. **Oswagatic.**—Writer of 1756 in Mass. Hist. Soc. Coll., 1st s., VII, 99, 1801. **Osweatchies.**—Jefferson, Notes, 282, 1825. **Osweegachio.**—Albany conf. (1754) in N. Y. Doc. Col. Hist., VI, 862, 1855. **Osweegchie.**—Ibid., 887. **Oswegachys.**—Johnson (1763) in Schoolcraft, Ind. Tribes, VI, 270, 1857. **Oswegatches.**—Croghan (1765) in Monthly Am. Jour. Geol., 272, 1831. **Oswegatchie.**—Wraxall (1754) in Mass. Hist. Soc. Coll., 3d s., V, 23, 1836. **Oswegatchy.**—Eastburn (1758) in Drake, Trag. Wild., 270, 1841. **Oswegatsy.**—Ft Johnson conf. (1756) in N. Y. Doc. Col. Hist., VII, 47, 1856. **Soegatzy.**—Document of 1749, ibid., X, 203, 1858. **Sweegachie.**—Mt Johnson conf. (1755), ibid., VI, 968, 1855. **Sweegassie.**—Albany conf. (1754), ibid., 856. **Sweegochie.**—Wraxall (1756), ibid., VII, 20, 1856. **Swegaachey.**—Johnson (1753), ibid., VI, 779, 1855. **Swegä′-che.**—Morgan, League Iroq., 26, 1851. **Swegachee.**—Johnson (1756) in N. Y. Doc. Col. Hist., VII, 90, 1856. **Swegachey.**—Mt Johnson conf. (1753), ibid., VI, 811, 1855. **Swegachie.**—Johnson (1756), ibid., VII, 132, 1856. **Swegachy.**—Canajoharie conf. (1759), ibid., 382. **Swegatsy.**—Stoddert (1753), ibid., VI, 780, 1855. **Swetgatchie.**—Jefferys, Fr. Doms, pt. 1, 141, 1761. **Usuokĕ-hága.**—Gatschet, Mohawk MS., 1877 (Mohawk name).

Oswego tea. A name applied to *Monarda didyma*, a plant used for medicinal purposes by Indians, and after them by the whites, particularly the Shakers of New York state. From the place name Oswego. (A. F. C.)

Otacite. See *Outacity*.

Otaguottouemin. An Algonquian tribe mentioned by Champlain (Œuvres, IV, 20, 1870), who heard of them during his passage up the Ottawa r. in 1615. They dwelt in a sparsely inhabited desert and lived by hunting, and by fishing in rivers, ponds, and lakes. The Jesuit Relation of 1640 describes them as dwelling N. of the Kichesipirini. They seldom descended to trade with the French.
Kotakoutouemi.—Jes. Rel. 1640, 34, 1858. Otokotouemi.—Jes. Rel., III, index, 1858. 8ta8kot8emi8ek.—Jes. Rel. 1650, 34, 1858.

Otai. A former Diegueño rancheria near San Diego, s. Cal.—Ortega (1775) quoted by Bancroft, Hist. Cal., I, 254, 1884.

Otaki (*O'-ta-ki*). A former Maidu village between Big and Little Chico crs., in the foothills of Butte co., Cal., a few miles E. of Michopdo. (R. B. D.)
O-tá-ki.—Powers in Cont. N. A. Ethnol., III, 282, 1877 (the people). O-ta-kūm'-ni.—Ibid. (the village).

Otakshanabe. A former Choctaw village of the "Sixtowns" district; probably in Jasper co., Miss.—West Fla. Map, *ca.* 1775.

Otassite. See *Outacity*.

Otat. A former Diegueño settlement, tributary to the mission of San Miguel de la Frontera, on the gulf coast of Lower California, about 30 m. s. of San Diego, Cal. (A. S. G.)

Otates (from Aztec *otatli*, a species of cane). A ruined pueblo of the Opata, near Guachinera, E. Sonora, Mexico, about lat. 30°.
Los Otates.—Bandelier in Arch. Inst. Papers, IV, 517, 1892.

Otatshia ('crane'). A phratry of the Menominee; also a subphratry or gens.
Otä'tshia wi'dishi'anun.—Hoffman in 14th Rep. B. A. E., 42, 1896.

Otchek, Otchig. See *Pekan*.

Otekhiatonwan ('village in the thicket'). A band of the Wahpeton Sioux.
O-ta-har-ton.—Lewis and Clark, Discov., 34, 1806. Oteñatoŋwaŋ.—Riggs, letter to Dorsey, 1882. Oteñiatoŋwaŋ.—Dorsey (after Ashley) in 15th Rep. B. A. E., 216, 1897. Oteqi-atoⁿwaⁿ.—Ibid.

Otenashmoo. A former Chumashan village at "Las Possas," about 2 m. from Santa Barbara mission, Cal.—Taylor in Cal. Farmer, May 4, 1860.

Oteroughyanento. See *Ohrante*.

Otherday, John (*Angpetu-tokecha*). A Wahpeton Sioux, son of Zitkaduta, or Red Bird, and nephew of Big Curly, chief of the Wahpeton at Lac qui Parle, Minn.; born at Swan lake, Minn., in 1801. It is said that when a young man he was "passionate and revengeful, and withal addicted to intemperance, and he lived to lament that he had slain three or four of his fellows in his drunken orgies"

(Sibley). Yet at times he manifested the same devotion to his tribesmen as he afterward showed to the whites, on one occasion, in a battle with the Chippewa at St Croix r., bearing from the field "One-legged Jim," who had been severely wounded, and, during the same action, saving the life of another Indian called Fresnière's Son. But he early became desirous of following the ways of the white men, adopting their dress, later becoming a devoted member of Dr Williamson's church, and abandoning his intemperate habits. When in 1857 the wily Inkpaduta, "too vile to be even countenanced by the Sioux," fell upon and massacred the settlers at Spirit lake, in the present South Dakota, and carried Miss Abigail Gardner and Mrs Noble into

JOHN OTHERDAY. (SOUTH DAKOTA HISTORICAL SOCIETY)

captivity, Otherday and Paul Mazakutemani volunteered to follow the outlaw's trail, rescuing Miss Gardner, but arriving too late to save the life of the other captive. At the time of the Sioux outbreak of 1862, Otherday, who had married a white woman, resided on the reservation near Minnesota r., in a comfortable dwelling built for him by the agent. When he learned that hostilities were imminent, he hastened to the upper agency and there gathered 62 of the whites, whom he guided in safety through the wilderness to St Paul, then hastened back to the frontier to save other lives and to aid in bringing the murderers to justice. To him and the other Christian Indians who aided in the rescue the missionary party of 43 were indebted for their escape to an extent not then known (Riggs). In the military campaign organized to quell the outbreak Otherday was employed by Gen. Sibley as a scout, in which capacity he rendered valued service. He participated in the battles of Birch Coolie and Wood lake, taking with his own hands two horses from the enemy and slaying their riders. "He was often in their midst and so far in advance of our own men that they fired many shots at him in the belief that he was one of the foe. No person on the field compared with him in the exhibition of reckless bravery. He was clothed entirely in white: a belt around his waist, in which was placed his knife; a handkerchief was knotted about his head, and in his hand he lightly grasped his rifle" (Heard). Otherday signed the Sisseton and Wahpeton treaty at Washington, Feb. 19, 1867. Congress granted him $2,500, with which he purchased a farm near Henderson, Sibley co., Minn.; here he resided for three or four years, but not being successful as a farmer he sold his land at a sacrifice and removed to the Sisseton and Wahpeton res., S. Dak., where the agent built a house for him. He died of tuberculosis in 1871, and was buried in a pasture on the N. side of Big Coule cr., 75 ft from the stream, about 12 m. N. W. of Wilmot, Roberts co., S. Dak.

Consult Heard, Hist. Sioux War, 1863; Riggs in Minn. Hist. Soc. Coll., III, 1880; Doane Robinson (1) in Monthly South Dakotan, III, Oct. 1900, (2) in S. Dak. Hist. Coll., II, 1904; De Lorme W. Robinson in S. Dak. Hist. Coll., I, 1902; Bryant and Murch, Hist. Massacre by Sioux Inds., 1872.　　　　　(C. T.)

Otiahanague. An Onondaga village at the mouth of Salmon r., Oswego co., N. Y., in the 18th century.　(W. M. B.)

Otituchina (prob. 'three islands'). A former Upper Creek town on Coosa r., probably in or near Talladega co., Ala.

O tee toochinas.—Swan (1791) in Schoolcraft, Ind. Tribes, v, 262, 1855.

Otkialnaas-hadai (ᵂot ḱiál náas xā′da-i, 'Eagle's-legs-house people'). A subdivision of the Yadus, a branch of the Stustas, one of the greatest of the Haida families. It belonged to the Eagle clan.—Swanton, Cont. Haida, 276, 1905.

Otkon. The common Iroquois descriptive epithet and name applied to any object or being which performs its functions and exercises its assumed magic power or *orenda* (q. v.) in such manner as to be not only inimical to human welfare, but hostile to and destructive of human life; it is the name in common use for all ferocious and monstrous beings, animals, and persons, especially such as are not normal in size, power, and cunning, or such things in which there is marked incongruity between these properties of beings. The term is often applied to fetishes and to similar things. As a qualifier it is equivalent to the English mysterious, monstrous, devilish, or rather demoniac; but as a noun, or name, to monster, demon, devil, goblin, witch, wizard. The term has found a peculiar use in a translation of the Gospels by one Joseph Onasakenrat into the Iroquois tongue (Montreal, 1880), where it is employed to translate Spirit and Holy Spirit; this is done also in a Mohawk Catechism by the Abbé F. Piquet (Paris, 1826). In both it is made the equivalent of the English 'spirit', and in both works Holy Spirit or Holy Ghost is rendered *Rotkon*, 'he, a human being, is an *otkon*', i. e. 'a demon, or spirit,' modified either by *Roiatatokenti*, 'his body is holy,' or by *Ronikonratokenti*, his mind is holy.' The initial o– in *otkon* is a pronominal affix, denotive of number, person, and gender, and meaning here the singular number, third person, and zoic gender. When the term is to be used with reference to persons or anthropic beings, the affix changes to *ro–, ago–, hoñna–*, or *koñna–*, signifying respectively, 'he,' 'one,' 'they (masculine),' and additionally to every one of these last definitions, the anthropic gender. So that *Rotkon* denotes 'he, a human being, is an *otkon*,' i. e. a demon or spirit. In grammatic form the term *otkon* is an adjective or attributive; its correct nominal form requires the suffix *–tcera, –tsera*, or *–tchä'*, according to dialect, denoting state of being; whence *otkontcera*, etc., usually written *otkonsera*, is formed; by missionary influence, the latter, modified by the attributive *–ksĕñ*, 'bad', 'evil', 'wicked', 'ugly', is the common name for the Devil of Christian belief. The following are some of the forms of this term found in the Jesuit Relations (Thwaites ed.): *ocki, okhi, oki, onkaqui* (pl.), *oqui, oski, otkis;* and in Lafitau's Mœurs des Sauvages Amériquains, 1724, *okki* and *otkon* occur. Preceded by an expression denoting 'verily' the term *otkon* is used as an expletive, or, perhaps, mild curse.　　　　　(J. N. B. H.)

Otnaas-hadai (ᵂot náas xā′da-i, 'Eagle-house people'). A subdivision of the Yadus, a Haida family on the Eagle side, which was in turn a branch of the Stustas.—Swanton, Cont. Haida, 276, 1905.

Oto (from *Waťóta*, 'lechers'). One of the three Siouan tribes forming the Chiwere group, the others being the Iowa and Missouri. The languages differ but slightly. The earliest reference to this tribe is found in the tradition which relates to the separation of the Chiwere group from the Winnebago. This tradition is given by Maximilian, who states that it was communicated to Maj. Bean, the Indian agent, by an old Oto chief. He related that, before the arrival of the whites a large band of Indians, the Hotonga ('fish-eaters'), who inhabited the lakes, migrated to the s. w. in pursuit of buffalo. At Green bay, Wis., they divided, the part called by the whites Winnebago remaining, while the rest continued the journey until they reached the Mississippi at the mouth of Iowa r., where they encamped on the sand beach and again divided, one band, the Iowa, concluding to remain there, and the rest continuing their travels reached the Missouri at the mouth of Grand r. These gave themselves the name of Neutache ('those that arrive at the mouth'), but were

CHIEF GEORGE—ARKEKETAH—OTO

called Missouri by the whites. The two chiefs, on account of the seduction of the daughter of one by the son of the other, quarreled and separated one from the other. The division led by the father of the seducer became known as Waghtochtatta, or Oto, and moved farther up the Missouri. While the Winnebago settled in Wisconsin, the Iowa, after they ceded to the United States all the lands on which they first settled, moved w. between Missouri r. and the Little Platte. The Missouri, having been unfortunate in a war with the Osage, divided, and a part of them lived with the Iowa and a part with the Oto. The Oto continued up the Missouri until they crossed the Big Platte and lived for some time a short distance above its mouth; later they resided on Platte r.,

about 80 m. by water from the Missouri. The same tradition was obtained by Maj. Long several years before Maximilian's visit. Dorsey was informed by the Iowa chiefs who visited Washington in 1883 that their people once formed part of the Winnebago. The Oto seem to have been most intimately associated with the Iowa. That they were ever at the mouth of Missouri r., where, according to one tradition, they were with the Missouri, is not likely. The fact that they were with the Iowa in the vicinity of Blue Earth r., Minn., immediately preceding Le Sueur's visit in 1700, indicates that their movement was across the Mississippi into s. Minnesota instead of down that stream. Le Sueur was informed by some Sioux whom he met that "this river was the country of the Sioux of the West, of the Ayavois [Iowa] and the Otoctatas [Oto]." Messengers whom he sent to invite the Oto and Iowa to settle near his fort at the mouth of Blue Earth r. found that they had moved w. toward the Missouri r., near the Omaha. Marquette, in 1673, apparently locates the tribe on his autograph map on upper Des Moines or upper Iowa r. Membré (1680) places them 130 leagues from the Illinois, almost opposite the mouth of the Wisconsin. Iberville (1700) said that the Oto and Iowa were then with the Omaha between the Missouri and Mississippi rs., about 100 leagues from the Illinois. The last two statements agree substantially with that of Le Sueur. It is therefore not probable, as given in one statement, that the Oto were on Osage r. in 1687. That they were driven farther s. by the northern tribes at a later date will appear from the list of localities given below. Lahontan claims to have visited their village in 1690 on the "Otentas [Iowa or Des Moines] river at its junction with the Mississippi," perhaps referring to a temporary camp. In 1721, according to Charlevoix, the Oto were below the Iowa, who were on the E. side of Missouri r., and above the Kansa on the w. side. Le Page du Pratz (1758) mentions the Oto as a small nation on Missouri r. Jefferys (1761) placed them along the s. bank of "Panis river," probably the Platte between its mouth and the Pawnee country; but in another part of his work he locates them above the Kansa on the w. side of Missouri r. Lewis and Clark (1804) locate the tribe at the time of their expedition on the s. side of Platte r., about 30 m. from its mouth, but state that they formerly lived about 20 m. above the Platte, on the s. bank of the Missouri. Having diminished, probably through wars and smallpox, they migrated to the neighborhood of the Pawnee, under whose protection they lived, the Missouri being incorporated with them. From 1817 to 1841 they were on Platte r. near its mouth. In the latter year they consisted of 4 villages. In 1880 a part of the tribe removed to the lands of the Sauk and Fox Indians in Indian Ter., and in 1882 the remainder left their home in Nebraska and went to the same reservation.

The Oto tribe has never been important, their history being little more than an account of their struggles to defend themselves against their more powerful enemies, and of their migrations. That they were not noted for their military prowess, notwithstanding Long's statement of the deeds of bravery of some of their warriors, seems evident from their inability to cope with their enemies, although, according to Lewis and Clark, they were once "a powerful nation." They were cultivators of the soil, and it was on this account, and because they were said to be industrious, that Le Sueur wished them and the Iowa to settle near his fort. Lewis and Clark speak of those they saw, at or near Council Bluffs, as almost naked, having no covering except a sort of breechcloth, with a loose blanket or painted buffalo robe thrown over their shoulders. Their permanent villages consisted of large earthen lodges similar to those of the Kansa and Omaha; when traveling they found shelter in skin tipis. One of their musical instruments was a stick notched like a saw, over the teeth of which a smaller stick was rubbed forcibly backward and forward.

The Oto and Missouri made a treaty of peace with the United States, June 24, 1817. They joined with other tribes in the treaty of Prairie du Chien, Wis., July 15, 1830, by which were ceded all rights to lands E. of Missouri r. up to the mouth of Big Sioux r. By the treaties of Oto village, Nebr., Sept. 21, 1833; Bellevue, Nebr., Oct. 15, 1836; Washington, Mar. 15, 1854, and Nebraska City, Nebr., Dec. 9, 1854, they ceded to the United States all their lands except their reservation on Big Blue r., Nebr. Here they remained until about 1882, when, with the Missouri, they were removed to Indian Ter. and placed under the Ponca, Pawnee, Oto, and Oakland agency. Their reserve contained 129,113 acres.

Morgan gives the Oto and Missouri gentes together, as follows: Mejeraja (Wolf), Mooncha (Bear), Ahrowha (Cow Buffalo), Hooma (Elk), Khaa (Eagle), Luteja (Pigeon), Waka (Snake), Makotch (Owl). Dorsey obtained the following list of Oto gentes: Patha (Beaver), Tunanpi (Black Bear) or Munchirache, Arukhwa (Buffalo), Rukhcha (Pigeon), Makache (Owl), Wakan (Snake), Cheghita (Eagle).

Lewis and Clark gave their number in 1805 as 500; Catlin, in 1833 (including the Missouri), as 1,200; Burrows, in 1849,

900; the Indian Report of 1843 (including the Missouri), as 931. In 1862 the two tribes numbered 708; in 1867, 511; in 1877, 457; in 1886, 334; in 1906, 390.

Anthoutantas.—Hennepin, New Discov., 132, 1698. **Authontantas.**—Shea, Early Voy., 101, note, 1861. **Che-wæ-ræ.**—Hamilton in Trans. Neb. State Hist. Soc., I, 75, 1885 (own name). **Hoctatas.**—Le Sueur (1700) in Margry, Déc., VI, 91, 1886. **Hotos.**—Bourgmont (1724), ibid., 396. **Houatoctotas.**—Bienville (1721), ibid., 386. **Huasiotos.**—Rafinesque in Marshall, Ky., I, introd., 28, 1824. **Huatoctas.**—Ibid. **La Zóto.**—Lewis and Clark, Discov., 14, 1806. **Mactotatas.**—Jefferys, French Dom. Am., pt. 1, 139, 1761. **Malatautes.**—McKenney and Hall, Ind. Tribes, III, 82, 1854. **Matokatági.**—Gatschet, MS., B. A. E. (Shawnee name). **Matontenta.**—La Salle Exped. (1680) in Margry, Déc., II, 95, 1877. **Matotantes.**—Hennepin, New Discov., II, 47, 1698. **Matoutenta.**—La Salle (1682) in Margry, Déc., I, 487, 1876. **Metotonta.**—Hennepin, New Discov., II, 309, 1698. **Motantees.**—La Métairie (1682) in French, Hist. Coll. La., II, 25, 1875. **Motútatak.**—Gatschet, MS., B. A. E. (Fox name). **Octata.**—De l'Isle, map (1701) in Neill, Hist. Minn., 1858. **Octoctatas.**—Iberville (1702) in Margry, Déc., IV, 598, 1880. **Octolacto.**—Adelung, Mithridates, III, 271, 1816. **Octolatas.**—Jefferys (1763), Am. Atlas, map 5, 1776. **Octootatas.**—Minn. Hist. Coll., I (1850-56), 342, 1872. **Octotales.**—McKenney and Hall, Ind. Tribes, III, 82, 1854. **Octotas.**—Doc. of 1701 in Margry, Déc., IV, 587, 1880. **Octotata.**—De l'Isle, map of La. (1701) in Neill, Hist. Minn., 1858. **Octotota.**—Vaugondy, Map, 1778. **Ollo's.**—Brackenridge, Views of La., 70, 1815. **Ontotonta.**—Cavalier (1687) in Shea, Early Voy., 28, 1861. **Otenta.**—Hennepin, New Discov., map, 1698. **Ote-toe.**—Donaldson in Smithson. Rep. 1885, II, Catlin Gallery, 75, 1886. **Otheues.**—McKenney and Hall, Ind. Tribes, III, 80, 1854. **Otho.**—Bourgmont (1723) in Margry, Déc., VI, 402, 1886. **Othoe.**—Smithson. Misc. Coll., XIV, art. 6, 29, 1867. **Othonez.**—Dunbar in Mag. Am. Hist., IV, 248, 1880. **Othoues.**—Jefferys, French Dom. Am., pt. 1, 139, 1761. **Othouez.**—Le Page du Pratz, Hist., II, 251, 1758. **Othoves.**—Alcedo, Dic. Geog., III, 410, 1788. **Otoctatas.**—Le Sueur (1700) in Neill, Hist. Minn., 162, 1858. **Otocototas.**—Margry, Déc., VI, 396, 1886. **Otoe.**—Irving, Sketches, 10, 1835. **Otoetata.**—Long, Exped. St Peter's R., II, 320, 1824. **Otontanta.**—Marquette, autograph map, 1673, in Shea, Discov. Miss., 1852. **Otopplata.**—Margry, Déc., VI, 747, 1886 (misprint). **Otoptata.**—Bruyère (1742), ibid., 449. **Ototantas.**—Margry, Déc., II, 191, 1877. **Ototata.**—Crepy, Carte de l'Am. Sépt. **Otoutanta.**—La Salle (1682) in Margry, Déc., II, 215, 1877. **Otoutantas Paoté.**—Margry, ibid., 249. **Ottoas.**—Arrowsmith, Map, 1795. **Ottoas.**—McKenney in Ind. Aff. Rep., 90, 1825. **Ottoes.**—Lewis and Clark, Discov., 14, 1806. **Ottoos.**—Schermerhorn (1812) in Mass. Hist. Coll., 2d. s., II, 10, 1814. **Otto's.**—Ibid. **Ottotatocs.**—Du Lac, Voy. dans les Louisianes, vii, 1805. **Ottotatoes.**—Du Lac (1802), ibid., map. **Ottowas.**—Hunter, Captivity, 24, 1823. **Otutaches.**—Adelung, Mithridates, III, 271, 1816. **Outantes.**—Harris, Coll. Voy. and Trav., I, map, 685, 1705. **Outentontes.**—Coxe, Carolana, map, 1741. **Toctata.**—Iberville (1702) in Margry, Déc., IV, 601, 1880. **Waǥútada.**—Dorsey in Cont. N. A. Ethnol., VI, pt. 1, 420, 1892 (Omaha and Ponca name). **Wâd-doké-tâh-tâh.**—Lewis and Clark, Discov., 14, 1806. **Wa-dook-to-da.**—Brackenridge, Views of La., 75, 1815. **Wa-do-tan.**—Long, Exped. Rocky Mts., I, 338, 1823. **Wadótata.**—Dorsey, Kansa MS. vocab., B. A. E., 1882 (Kansa name). **Wagh-toch-tat-ta.**—Maximilian, Trav., 507, 1843. **Wah-teh-ta-na.**—Long, Exped. Rocky Mts., I, 338, 1823. **Wahtohtanes.**—Keane in Stanford, Compend., 542, 1878. **Wahtohtata.**—Long, Exped. Rocky Mts., I, 338, 1823. **Wäh-tŏk-tä-tä.**—Ibid., II, lxxx. **Wah-tooh tah-tah.**—Ibid., 363. **Washō'χla.**—Gatschet, Kaw MS. vocab., B. A. E., 27, 1878 (Kansa name). **Watohtata.**—Dorsey, Tciwere MS. vocab., B. A. E., 1879 (Dakota name). **Watóta.**—Ibid. (own name). **Waǥútata.**—Dorsey, Osage MS. vocab., B. A. E., 1883 (Osage name).

Otoacte. A former village, presumably Costanoan, connected with Dolores mission, San Francisco, Cal.—Taylor in Cal. Farmer, Oct. 18, 1861.

Otocara. See *Olotaraca.*

Otocomanes. Mentioned with the Aitacomanes as a people occupying a province which had been visited by the Dutch, where gold and silver was abundant. The locality is not given, and the province is probably as imaginary as the expedition in connection with which it is mentioned. See Freytas, Exped. of Peñalosa (1662), Shea trans., 67, 1882.

Otontagan. An Ottawa band living before 1680 on Manitoulin id., L. Huron, Ontario, whence they were driven out by the Iroquois.

Otontagans.—Lahontan, New Voy., I, 93, 1703. Outaouas of Talon.—Ibid.

Otopali. A village mentioned by Fontaneda, about 1575 (Memoir, Smith trans., 16, 1854), as reputed to be inland and northward from the coast province of Chicora (q. v.), which was about the present Charleston, S. C.

Otowi. An extensive prehistoric pueblo situated on a mesa about 5 m. w. of the point where the Rio Grande enters White Rock canyon, between the Rito de los Frijoles and Santa Clara canyon, in the N. E. corner of Sandoval co., N. Mex. The pueblo consisted of a cluster of five houses situated on sloping ground and all except one connected by a wall. They were terraced structures, each house group having from two to four stories, altogether containing about 450 rooms on the ground floor and probably 700 rooms in all. The settlement was provided with ten subterranean circular kivas, all except two detached from the walls of the dwellings. A reservoir was placed so as to receive the drainage from the village. According to the traditions of certain clans of the present Tewa of San Ildefonso, Otowi was the oldest village occupied by their ancestors. They hold in an indefinite way that prior to the building of Otowi their clans occupied small scattered houses on the adjacent mesas, and they claim that, owing to the failure of the mesa water supply, removal to the valley eventually became necessary, a detachment of the Otowi people founding Perage on the w. side of the Rio Grande about a mile w. of the present San Ildefonso. Associated with Otowi are numerous cliff-dwellings excavated in the soft volcanic walls of the adjacent canyons. These consist of two types: (1) open-front dwellings, usually single-chambered, in most cases natural caves enlarged and shaped artificially; (2) wholly artificial dwellings with closed fronts of the natural rock in situ, usually multi-chambered, with floors, always plastered, below the level of the entrances; crude fireplaces beside the doorway; rooms commonly rectangular and well-shaped. From about ½ m.

to 1 m. above Otowi is a cluster of conical formations of white tufa, some 30 ft high; they are full of caves, both natural and artificial, some of which have been utilized as habitations. See Hewett (1) in Am. Anthrop., VI, 641, 1904; (2) Bull. 32, B. A. E., 1906.

Otreouati. See *Grangula.*

Otshpetl. The second Chilula village on Redwood cr., N. W. Cal.

Ot-teh-petl.—Gibbs in Schoolcraft, Ind. Tribes, III, 139, 1853 (Yurok name).

Otsinoghiyata ('The Sinew'). An old and prominent Onondaga chief, commonly called The Bunt, a man of strong yet genial character. Ziesberger first mentioned him, in 1752, as the principal chief, living in the upper town. He was called Ozinoghiyata in the Albany treaty of 1754, and was mentioned almost yearly afterward. In 1762 he was called chief sachem of Onondaga, and was at the Pontiac council at Oswego in 1766. He signed the Fort Stanwix treaty in Oct. 1768, and was at conferences at German Flats in 1770 and Onondaga in 1775. In 1774 he retired from the chieftaincy on account of his advanced age, and was succeeded by Onagogare.   (W. M. B.)

Otsiquette, Peter. An Oneida chief who signed the treaty of 1788. He was a well educated man and had visited Lafayette in France, but returned to savage life. He was a member of the delegation of chiefs to Philadelphia in 1792, where he died and was buried with military honors. He is also called Peter Otzagert and Peter Jaquette. Elkanah Watson described him at the treaty of 1788. Peter Otsiequette, perhaps the same Indian, witnessed the Onondaga treaty of 1790.   (W. M. B.)

Otskwirakeron ('a heap or collection of twigs'). A traditional Iroquois town of the Bear clan; so enumerated in the list of towns in the Chant of Welcome of the Condolence Council of the League of the Iroquois. Nothing definite is known of its situation or to what tribe it belonged. See Hale, Iroq. Book of Rites, 120, 1883.   (J. N. B. H.)

Ottachugh. A village of the Powhatan confederacy in 1608, on the N. bank of Rappahannock r., in Lancaster co., Va.—Smith (1629), Va., I, map, repr. 1819.

Ottawa (from *ădāwe*, 'to trade', 'to buy and sell,' a term common to the Cree, Algonkin, Nipissing, Montagnais, Ottawa, and Chippewa, and applied to this important Algonquian tribe because in former times they were noted among their neighbors as intertribal traders and barterers, dealing chiefly in corn-meal, sunflower oil, furs and skins, rugs or mats, tobacco, and medicinal roots and herbs).

On French r., near its mouth, on Georgian bay, Champlain in 1615 met 300 men of a tribe which, he said, "we call *les cheueux releuez.*'' Of these he said that their arms consisted only of the bow and arrow, a buckler of boiled leather, and the club; that they wore no breechclout, and that their bodies were much tattooed in many fashions and designs; that their faces were painted in diverse colors, their noses pierced, and their ears bordered with trinkets. The chief of this band gave Champlain to understand that they had come to that place to dry huckleberries to be used in winter when nothing else was available. In the following year Champlain left the Huron villages and visited the "Cheueux releuez" (Ottawa), living westward from the Hurons, and he said that they were very joyous at "seeing us again." This last expression seemingly shows that those whom he had met on French r. in the preceding year lived where he now

OTTAWA MAN

visited them. He said that the Cheueux releuez waged war against the Mascoutens (here erroneously called by the Huron name Asistagueronon), dwelling 10 days' journey from them; he found this tribe populous; the majority of the men were great warriors, hunters, and fishermen, and were governed by many chiefs who ruled each in his own country or district; they planted corn and other things; they went into many regions 400 or 500 leagues away to trade; they made a kind of mat which served them for Turkish rugs; the women had their bodies covered, while those of the men were uncovered, saving a robe of fur like a mantle, which was worn in winter but usually discarded in summer; the women lived very well with their husbands; at the catamenial period the

women retired into small lodges, where they had no company of men and where food and drink were brought to them. This people asked Champlain to aid them against their enemies on the shore of the fresh-water sea, distant 200 leagues from them.

In the Jesuit Relation for 1667, Father Le Mercier, reporting Father Allouez, treated the Ottawa, Kiskakon, and Ottawa Sinago as a single tribe, because they had the same language and together formed a common town. He adds that the Ottawa (Outaoüacs) claimed that the great river (Ottawa?) belonged to them, and that no other nation might navigate it without their consent. It was, for this reason, he continues, that although very different in nationality all those who went to the French to trade bore the name Ottawa, under whose auspices the journey was undertaken. He adds that the ancient habitat of the Ottawa had been a quarter of L. Huron, whence the fear of the Iroquois drove them, and whither were borne all their longings, as it were, to their native country. Of the Ottawa the Father says: "They were little disposed toward the faith, for they were too much given to idolatry, superstitions, fables, polygamy, looseness of the marriage tie, and to all manner of license, which caused them to drop all native decency."

According to tradition (see *Chippewa*) the Ottawa, Chippewa, and Potawatomi tribes of the Algonquian family were formerly one people who came from some point N. of the great lakes and separated at Mackinaw, Mich. The Ottawa were located by the earliest writers and also by tradition on Manitoulin id. and along the N. and s. shore of Georgian bay.

Father Dablon, superior of the missions of the Upper Algonkin in 1670, said: "We call these people Upper Algonkin to distinguish them from the Lower Algonkin who are lower down, in the vicinity of Tadousac and Quebec. People commonly give them the name Ottawa, because, of more than 30 different tribes which are found in these countries, the first that descended to the French settlements were the Ottawa, whose name remained afterward attached to all the others." The Father adds that the Saulteurs, or Pahoüiting8ach Irini, whose native country was at the Sault Sainte Marie, numbering 500 souls, had adopted three other tribes, making to them a cession of the rights of their own native country, and also that the people who were called Noquet ranged, for the purpose of hunting, along the s. side of L. Superior, whence they originally came; and the Chippewa (Outcibous) and the Marameg from the N. side of the same lake, which they regarded as their native land. The Ottawa were at Chagaouami-gong or La Pointe de Sainte Esprit in 1670 (Jes. Rel. 1670, 83, 1858).

Father Le Mercier (Jes. Rel. 1654), speaking of a flotilla of canoes from the "upper nations," says that they were "partly Ondataouaouat, of the Algonquine language, whom we call 'les Cheueux releuez.'" And in the Relation for 1665 the same Father says of the Ottawa that they were better merchants than warriors.

In a letter of 1723, Father Sébastien Rasles says that he learned while among the Ottawa that they attributed to themselves an origin as senseless as it was ridiculous. They informed him that they were derived from three families, each composed of 500 persons. The first was that of Michabou (see *Nanabozho*), or the Great Hare, representing him to be a gigantic man who laid nets in 18 fathoms of water which reached only to his armpits and who was born in the island of Michilimackinac, and formed the earth and invented fish-nets after carefully watching a spider weaving its web for taking flies; among other things he decreed that his descendants should burn their dead and scatter their ashes in the air, for if they failed to do this, the snow would cover the ground continuously and the lakes would remain frozen. The second family was that of the Namepich, or Carp, which, having spawned its eggs on the shore of a river and the sun casting its rays on them, a woman was thus formed from whom they claimed descent. The third family was that of the Bear's paw, but no explanation was given of the manner in which its genesis took place. But when a bear was killed a feast of its own flesh was given in its honor and an address was made to it in these terms: "Have thou no thoughts against us, because we have killed thee; thou hast sense and courage; thou seest that our children are suffering from hunger; they love thee, and so wish to cause thee to enter their bodies; and is it not a glorious thing to be eaten by the children of captains?" The first two families bury their dead (Lettres Edif., iv, 106, 1819).

It has been stated by Charlevoix and others that when they first became known to the French they lived on Ottawa r. This, however, is an error, due to the twofold use of the name, the one generic and the other specific, as is evident from the statements by Champlain and the Jesuit Relations (see Shea in Charlevoix, New France, ii, 270, 1866); this early home was N. and W. of the Huron territory. No doubt Ottawa r., which they frequently visited and were among the first western tribes to navigate in trading expeditions to the French settlements,

was named from the Ottawa generically so called, not from the specific people named Ottawa. There is unquestioned documentary evidence that as early as 1635 a portion of the Ottawa lived on Manitoulin id. Father Vimont, in the Jesuit Relation for 1640, 34, 1858, says that "south of the Amikwa [Beaver Nation] there is an island [Manitoulin] in that fresh water sea [L. Huron], about 30 leagues in length, inhabited by the Outaouan [Ottawa], who are a people come from the nation of the Standing Hair [Cheueux Releuez]." This information he received from Nicolet, who visited the Ottawa there in 1635. On the DuCreux map of 1660, on a large island approximating the location of Manitoulin id., the "natio surrectorum capillorum," i. e. the Cheveux Releves, or Ottawa, is placed. They were allies and firm friends of the French and the Hurons, and conducted an active trade between the western tribes and the French. After the destruction of the Hurons, in 1648–49, the Iroquois turned their arms against the Ottawa, who fled with a remnant of the Hurons to the islands at the entrance of Green bay, where the Potawatomi, who had preceded the Ottawa and settled on these islands, received the fugitives with open arms and granted them a home. However, their residence here was but temporary, as they moved westward a few years afterward, a part going to Keweenaw bay, where they were found in 1660 by Father Menard, while another part fled with a band of Hurons to the Mississippi, and settled on an island near the entrance of L. Pepin. Driven away by the Sioux, whom they had unwisely attacked, they moved N. to Black r., Wis., at the head of which the Hurons built a fort, while the Ottawa pushed eastward and settled on the shore of Chaquamegon bay. They were soon followed by the missionaries, who established among them the mission of St Esprit. Harassed by the Sioux, and a promise of protection by the French having been obtained, they returned in 1670–71 to Manitoulin id. in L. Huron. According to the records, Father Allouez, in 1668–69, succeeded in converting the Kiskakon band at Chaquamegon, but the Sinago and Keinouche remained deaf to his appeals. On their return to Manitoulin the French fathers established among them the mission of St Simon. There is a tradition that Lac Court Oreilles was formerly called Ottawa lake because a band of the Ottawa dwelt on its shores, until they were forced to move by the attacks of the Sioux (Brunson in Wis. Hist. Coll., iv). Their stay on Manitoulin id. was brief; by 1680 most of them had joined the Hurons at Mackinaw, about the station established by Marquette in 1671.

The two tribes lived together until about 1700, when the Hurons removed to the vicinity of Detroit, while a portion of the Ottawa about this time seems to have obtained a foothold on the w. shore of L. Huron between Saginaw bay and Detroit, where the Potawatomi were probably in close union with them. Four divisions of the tribe were represented by a deputy at the treaty signed at Montreal in 1700. The band which had moved to the s. e. part of the lower Michigan peninsula returned to Mackinaw about 1706. Soon afterward the chief seat of a portion of the tribe was fixed at Waganakisi (L'Arbre Croche), near the lower end of L. Michigan. From this point they spread in every direction, the majority settling along the e. shore of the lake, as far s. as St Joseph r., while a few found their way into s. Wisconsin and n. e. Illinois. In the n. they shared Manitoulin id. and the n. shore of L. Huron with the Chippewa, and in the s. e. their villages alternated with those of their old allies the Hurons, now called Wyandot, along the shore of L. Erie from Detroit to the vicinity of Beaver cr. in Pennsylvania. They took an active part in all the Indian wars of that region up to the close of the War of 1812. The celebrated chief Pontiac was a member of this tribe, and Pontiac's war of 1763, waged chiefly around Detroit, is a prominent event in their history. A small part of the tribe which refused to submit to the authority of the United States removed to Canada, and together with some Chippewa and Potawatomi, is now settled on Walpole id. in L. St Clair. The other Ottawa in Canadian territory are on Manitoulin and Cockburn ids. and the adjacent shore of L. Huron.

All the Ottawa lands along the w. shore of L. Michigan were ceded by various treaties, ending with the Chicago treaty of Sept. 26, 1833, wherein they agreed to remove to lands granted them on Missouri r. in the n. e. corner of Kansas. Other bands, known as the Ottawa of Blanchard's fork of Great Auglaize r., and of Roche de Bœuf on Maumee r., resided in Ohio, but these removed w. of the Mississippi about 1832 and are now living in Oklahoma. The great body, however, remained in the lower peninsula of Michigan, where they are still found scattered in a number of small villages and settlements.

In his Histoire du Canada (ɪ, 190, 1836), Fr Sagard mentions a people whom he calls "la nation du bois." He met two canoe loads of these Indians in a village of the Nipissing, describing them as belonging to a very distant inland tribe, dwelling he thought toward the "sea of the south," which was probably L. Ontario. He says that they were dependents of the Ottawa (Cheueux Releuez) and formed with them as it were a single tribe. The men were entirely naked, at which the Hurons, he says, were apparently greatly shocked, although scarcely less indecent themselves. Their faces were gaily painted in many colors in grease, some with one side in green and the other in red; others seemed to have the face covered with a natural lace, perfectly well-made, and others in still different styles. He says the Hurons had not the pretty work nor the invention of the many small toys and trinkets which this "Gens de Bois" had. This tribe has not yet been definitely identified, but it may have been one of the three tribes mentioned by Sagard in his *Dictionnaire de la Langve Hvronne*, under the rubric "nations," as dependents of the Ottawa (Andatahoüat), namely, the Chisérhonon, Squierhonon, and Hoindarhonon.

Charlevoix says the Ottawa were one of the rudest nations of Canada, cruel and barbarous to an unusual degree and sometimes guilty of cannibalism. Bacqueville de la Potherie (Hist. Am. Sept., 1753) says they were formerly very rude, but by intercourse with the Hurons they have become more intelligent, imitating their valor, making themselves formidable to all the tribes with whom they were at enmity and respected by those with whom they were in alliance. It was said of them in 1859: "This people is still advancing in agricultural pursuits; they may be said to have entirely abandoned the chase; all of them live in good, comfortable log cabins; have fields inclosed with rail fences, and own domestic animals." The Ottawa were expert canoemen; as a means of defense they sometimes built forts, probably similar to those of the Hurons.

In the latter part of the 17th century the tribe consisted of 4, possibly 5, divisions. It is repeatedly stated that there were 4 bands, and no greater number is ever mentioned, yet 5 names are given, as follows: Kishkakon, Sinago, Keinouche, Nassauaketon, and Sable. La Mothe Cadillac says there were 4 bands: Kiskakon, Sinago, Sable, and Nassauaketon (Verwyst, Miss. Labors, 210, 1886). Outaoutiboy, chief of the Ottawa, speaking at the conference with Gov. de Callières, Sept. 3, 1700, said: "I speak in the name of the four Outaouais nations, to wit: The Outaouaes of the Sable, the Outaouaes Sinago, the Kiskakons, and the people of the Fork" (Nassawaketon). In addition to these chief divisions there were minor local bands, as Blanchard's Fork, Kajienatroene, Maskasinik, Negaouichiriniouek, Niscak, Ommunise, Otontagan, Talon, and Thunder Bay. Chauvignerie in 1736 distinguished the Ottawa of Grand River, L. Nipissing, Michilimackinac, Detroit, and Saginaw. According to Morgan the names of the Ottawa gentes are unknown, but Chauvignerie in 1736 mentioned the bear, otter, gray squirrel, and black squirrel as the totems of different bands of the tribe. According to Charlevoix the Ottawa signed with a hare the provisional treaty concluded at Montreal in 1700. At the great conference on the Maumee in 1793 they signed with the otter totem. In Tanner's Narrative is given a list of 18 totems among the Ottawa and Chippewa, but there is nothing to indicate which are Ottawa and which Chippewa.

The Ottawa entered into numerous treaties with the United States, as follows: Ft McIntosh, Jan. 21, 1785; Ft Harmar, Ohio, Jan. 9, 1789; Greenville, Ohio, Aug. 3, 1795; Ft Industry, July 4, 1805; Detroit, Mich., Nov. 17, 1807; Brownstown, Mich., Nov. 25, 1808; Greenville, Ohio, July 22, 1814; Spring Wells, Mich., Sept. 8, 1815; St Louis, Mo., Aug. 24, 1816; on the Miami, Ohio, Sept. 29, 1817; St Mary's, Ohio, Sept. 17, 1818: L'Arbre Croche and Michilimackinac, Mich., July 6, 1820; Chicago, Ill., Aug. 29, 1821; Prairie du Chien, Wis., Aug. 19, 1825; Green Bay, Wis., Aug. 25, 1828; Prairie du Chien, Wis., July 29, 1829; Miami Bay, Ohio, Aug. 30, 1831; Maumee, Ohio, Feb. 18, 1833; Chicago, Ill , Sept. 26, 1833; Washington, D. C., Mar. 28, 1836; Council Bluffs, Iowa, June 5 and 17, 1846; Detroit, Mich., July 31, 1855, and Washington, D. C., June 24, 1862.

The population of the different Ottawa groups is not known with certainty. In 1906 the Chippewa and Ottawa on Manitoulin and Cockburn ids., Canada, were 1,497, of whom about half were Ottawa; there were 197 Ottawa under the Seneca School, Okla., and in Michigan 5,587 scattered Chippewa and Ottawa in 1900, of whom about two-thirds are Ottawa. The total is therefore about 4,700.

The following are or were Ottawa villages: Aegakotcheising, Anamiewatigong, Apontigoumy, Machonee, Manistee, Menawzhetaunaung, Meshkemau, Michilimackinac, Middle Village, Obidgewong (mixed), Oquanoxa, Roche de Bœuf, Saint Simon (mission), Shabawywyagun, Tushquegan, Waganakisi, Walpole Island, Waugau, Wolf Rapids.

(J. M.   J. N. B. H.)

Ahtawwah.—Kane, Wanderings of an Artist, 23, 1859. **Algonquins Superieurs.**—Jes. Rel. 1670, 78, 1858. **Andata honato.**—McKenney and Hall, Ind. Tribes, III, 79, 1854. **Andatahouats.**—Sagard (1632), Hist. du Can., I, 192, 1866 (Huron name). **Andatohats.**—Coxe, Carolana, map, 1741. **Atawawas.**—Colden (1727), Five Nations, 29, 1747. **Atowas.**—Schoolcraft, Ind. Tribes, v, 143, 1855. **Attawas.**—Askin (1812) in Minn. Hist. Soc. Coll., v, 460, 1885. **Attawawas.**—Parkman, Pioneers, 347, 1883. **Autawa.**—Abnaki Speller (1830) in Me. Hist. Soc. Coll., VI, 247, 1859. **Autouacks.**—Clark, Onondaga, I, 204, 1849. **Cheueux ou poils leué.**—Sagard, Hist. du

Can., I, 192, 1866. **Cheueux releues.**—Champlain (1616), Œuvres, IV, 58, 1870. **Courterrielles.**—Lapham, Inds. Wis., II, 1870. **Dewagamas.**—McKenney and Hall, Ind. Tribes, III, 79, 1854. **Dewaganas.**—Colden (1727), Five Nations, 42, 1747 ('mumblers': Iroquois name). **Ku'taki.**—Gatschet, Fox MS., B. A. E. (Fox name). **Oadauwaus.**—Parkman, Pioneers, 347, 1883. **Octogymists.**—Fort James conf. (1683) in N. Y. Doc. Col. Hist., XIV, 773, 1883. **Odahwah.**—Jones, Ojebway Inds., 178, 1863. **Odahwaug.**—Warren (1852) in Minn. Hist. Soc. Coll., v, 31, 1885. **Odawas.**—Schoolcraft, Ind. Tribes, v, 145, 1855. **Ondataouaouat.**—Jes. Rel. 1654, 9, 1858. **Ondataouatouat.**—Charlevoix, New France, II, 270, note, 1866. **Ondatauauat.**—Bressani quoted in note to Charlevoix, ibid. **Ondatawawat.**—Jes. Rel. 1656, 17, 1858 (Huron name, probably derived from the Algonkin). **Ondatouatandy.**—Jes. Rel. 1648, 62, 1858 (probably identical, though Lalement supposed them to be a division of the Winnebago). **Ondoutaoüaheronnon.**—Jes. Rel. 1644, 99, 1858. **Ond8ta8aka.**—Jes. Rel. 1642, 10, 1858. **Onontakaës.**—Doc. of 1695 in N. Y. Doc. Col. Hist., IX, 596, 1855 (confounded with the Onondaga). **Ontaanak.**—Jes. Rel. 1648, 62, 1858. **Ontaonatz.**—Hennepin (1683), La., Shea ed., 276, 1880. **Ontdwawies.**—Clarkson (1766) in Schoolcraft, Ind. Tribes, IV, 269, 1854. **Onttaouactz.**—Hennepin (1683), La., Shea ed., 52, 1880. **Otahas.**—Smith (1785) quoted by Schoolcraft, Ind. Tribes, III, 554, 1853. **Otaoas.**—Denonville (1687) in N. Y. Doc. Col. Hist., IX, 336, 1855. **Ota8ais.**—Conf. of 1751, ibid , X, 232, 1858. **Otaoüaks.**—Jes. Rel. 1670, 6, 1858. **Otaous.**—Denonville (1687) in N. Y. Doc. Col. Hist., IX, 336, 1855. **Otauas.**—Doc. of 1668 in French, Hist. Coll. La., II, 138, 1875. **Ota'wa.**—Gatschet, Ojibwa MS., B. A. E., 1882 (Chippewa name). **O-ta'-wa.**—Hewitt, Onondaga MS., B. A. E., 1888 (Onondaga name). **Otawas.**—Denonville (1687) in N. Y. Doc. Col. Hist., III, 466, 1853. **Otawaus.**—Albany conf. (1726), ibid., v, 791, 1855. **Otawawas.**—Ibid., 795. **Otoways.**—Pike, Exped., pt. 1, app., 63, 1810. **Ottah-wah.**—Warren (1852) in Minn. Hist. Soc. Coll., v, 193, 1885. **Ot-tah-way.**—Ibid., 282. **Ottaouais.**—Doc. of 1759 in N. Y. Doc. Col. Hist., X, 982, 1858. **Ottaouets.**—Perkins and Peck, Annals of the West, 33, 1850. **Ottauwah.**—Macauley, N. Y., II, 174, 1829. **Ottawacks.**—Albany conf. (1726) in N. Y. Doc. Col. Hist., v, 791, 1855. **Ottawacs.**—Courcelles (1671), ibid., IX, 85, 1855. **Ottawaes.**—Johnson (1763), ibid., VII, 525, 1856. **Ottawagas.**—Goldthwait (1766) in Mass. Hist. Soc. Coll., 1st s., X, 122, 1809. **Ottawaies.**—Croghan (1760), ibid., 4th s., IX, 249, 1871. **Ottawak.**—Long, Exped. St. Peter's R., II, 151, 1824. **Ottawas.**—Writer of 1684 quoted by Ruttenber, Tribes Hudson R., 171, 1872. **Ottawawa.**—Doc. of 1695 in N. Y. Doc. Col. Hist., IV, 122, 1854. **Ottawawaas.**—Livingston (1687), ibid., III, 443, 1853. **Ottawawe.**—Dongan (1687), ibid., 476. **Ottawawooes.**—Doc. of 1688, ibid., 565. **Ottawaws.**—Croghan (1760) in Mass. Hist. Soc. Coll., 4th s., IX, 250, 1871. **Ottaway.**—Schuyler (1698) in N. Y. Doc. Col. Hist., IV, 406, 1854. **Ottawwaws.**—Tanner, Narr., 36, 1830. **Ottawwawwag.**—Ibid., 315 (Ottawa name). **Ottawwawwug.**—Parkman, Pioneers, 347, 1883. **Ottewas.**—Lang and Taylor, Rep., 23, 1843. **Ottoawa.**—Livingston (1687) in N. Y. Doc. Col. Hist., III, 443, 1853. **Ottova.**—Markham (1691), ibid., 808. **Ottowaes.**—Johnson (1764), ibid., VII, 674, 1856. **Ottowais.**—Dongan (ca. 1686), ibid., III, 395, 1853. **Ottowas.**—Chauvignerie (1736) quoted by Schoolcraft, Ind. Tribes, III, 554, 1853. **Ottowata.**—Treaty of 1829 in U. S. Ind. Treat., 164, 1873. **Ottowaus.**—Edwards (1788) in Mass. Hist. Soc. Coll., 1st. s., X, 92, 1804. **Ottowauways.**—Doc. of 1747 in N. Y. Doc. Col. Hist., VI, 391, 1855. **Ottowawa.**—Lamberville (1686), ibid., III, 490, 1853. **Ottowawe.**—Valiant (1688), ibid., 522. **Ottowaws.**—Carver, Trav., 19, 1778. **Ottowayer.**—Vater, Mith., pt. 3, sec. 3, 406, 1816. **Ottoways.**—Lords of Trade (1721) in N. Y. Doc. Col. Hist., v, 622, 1855. **Ottowose.**—Valiant (1688), ibid., III, 522, 1853. **Ottwasse.**—Dongan (1686), ibid., IX, 318, 1855. **Ouatawais.**—Jefferys, Fr. Doms., pt. 1, map, 1761. **Ouatouax.**—La Barre (1683) in N. Y. Doc. Col. Hist., IX, 202, 1855. **Outaois.**—Vaudreuil (1703), ibid., 743. **Outaoise.**—Doc. of 1748, ibid., X, 151, 1858. **Outaonacs.**—Warren (1852) in Minn. Hist. Soc. Coll., v, 407, 1885. **Outaoüacs.**—Jes. Rel. 1671, 25, 1858.

Outa8acs.—Doc. of 1693 in N.Y. Doc. Col. Hist., IX, 562, 1855. 8ta8acs.—Doc. of 1695, ibid., 604. Outaoü-aes.—Frontenac (1673), ibid., 95. 8ta8aës.—Montreal conf. (1700), ibid., 719. Outa8aës.—Ibid., 720. Outaouagas.—La Galissonière (1748), ibid., x, 182. 1858. Outaouaies.—Denonville (1687), ibid., IX, 365, 1855. Outaouais.—Talon? (1670) quoted by Neill, Minn., 120, 1858. Outa8ais.—Doc. of 1695 in N.Y. Doc. Col. Hist., IX, 598, 1855. 8ta8ais.—Doc. of 1695, ibid., 601. Outaouaks.—Jes. Rel. 1656, 38, 1858. Outaouan.—Jes. Rel. 1640, 34, 1858. Outaou-aos.—Frontenac (1681) in N.Y. Doc. Col. Hist., IX, 146, 1855. Outaouas.—Writer of 1660 in Margry, Déc., I, 55, 1875. Outa8as.—Doc. of 1746 in N.Y. Doc. Col. Hist., x, 51, 1858. 8ta8as.—Denonville (1688), ibid., IX, 384, 1855. Outaouats.—Doc. of 1757, ibid., x, 630, 1858. Outaouaus.—Doc. of 1691, ibid., IX, 521, 1855. Outaouax.—La Barre (1683), ibid., 201. Outaouays.—Writer of 1690 in Margry, Déc., I, 59, 1875. Outaoues.—Frontenac (1682) in N.Y. Doc. Col. Hist., IX, 176, 1855. Outaoüois.—Courcelles (1670), ibid., 788. Outa8ois.—Doc. of 1695, ibid., 611. Outaoutes.—Lamberville (1684), ibid., 259. Outa8uas.—Beauharnois (1744), ibid., 1112. Outaovaos.—Crepy, Map, ca. 1755. Outaovas.—Hennepin (1683) in Harris, Voy., II, 917, 1705. Outaowaies.—Boudinot, Star in the West, 212, 1816. Outarwas.—Lords of Trade (1721) in N.Y. Doc. Col. Hist., v, 621, 1855. Outauaes.—Frontenac (1682), ibid., IX, 180, 1855. Outauas.—Denonville (1686), ibid., 295. Outauies.—Parkman, Pioneers, 347, 1883. Outau-ois.—Frontenac (1682) in N.Y. Doc. Col. Hist., IX, 182, 1885. Outavis.—Writer of 1761 in Mass. Hist. Soc. Coll., 4th s., IX, 428, 1871. Outavois.—Tonti (1694) in Margry, Déc., IV, 4, 1880. Outawacs.—Courcelles (1671) in N.Y. Doc. Col. Hist., IX, 79, 1855. Outawais.—Jefferys, Fr. Dom., pt. 1, 47, 1761. Outawas.—Talon (1670) in N.Y. Doc. Col. Hist., IX, 65, 1855. Outawase.—Doc. of 1671, ibid., IX, 84, 1855. Outawawas.—Writer of 1756 in Mass. Hist. Soc. Coll., 1st s., VII, 117, 1801. Outaway.—Charlevoix, Voy. to N. Am., II, 47, 1766. Outawies.—Boudinot, Star in the West, 100, 1816. Outawois.—Doc. of 1746 in N.Y. Doc. Col. Hist., x, 34, 1858. Outduaois.—Bouisson (1699) quoted by Shea, Early Voy., 45, 1861. Outeonas.—Chauvignerie (1736) quoted by Schoolcraft, Ind. Tribes, III, 554, 1853. Outimacs.—Imlay, West. Ter., 292, 1797. Outontagans.—Lahontan (1703) in N.Y. Doc. Col. Hist., IX, 606, note, 1855. Outouacks.—Coxe, Carolana, 46, 1741. Outouacs.—N.Y. Doc. Col. Hist., III, 489, note, 1853. Outouais.—Parkman, Pioneers, 347, 1883. Outouaouas.—St Cosme (ca. 1700) in Shea, Early Voy., 47, 1861. Outouvas.—Perkins and Peck, Annals of the West, 33, 1850. Outowacs.—Jefferys, Fr. Dom., pt. 1, map, 1761. Outtamacks.—Croghan (1765) in Monthly Am. Jour. Geol., 272, 1831. Outtaois.—Vaudreuil (1703) in N.Y. Doc. Col. Hist., IX, 743, 1855. Outtaouacts.—Hennepin, Cont. of New Discov., 129, 1698. Outtaouatz.—Ibid., 85. Outta8es.—De Callières (1700) in N.Y. Doc. Col. Hist., IX, 708, 1855. Outtaouis.—Vaudreuil (1707), ibid., 810. Outtauois.—Vaudreuil (1704), ibid., 760. Outtawaats.—Parkman, Pioneers, 347, 1883. Outtawas.—Denonville (1686) in N.Y. Doc. Col. Hist., IX, 300, 1855. Outtoaets.—Parkman, Pioneers, 347, 1883. Outtouatz.—Hennepin, New Discov., 87, 1698. Sontaouans.—Doc. of 1691 in N.Y. Doc. Col. Hist., IX, 518, 1855 (confounded with the Seneca). Tawaa.—Campbell (1760) in Mass. Hist. Soc. Coll., 4th s., IX, 357, 1871. Tawas.—Bouquet (1760), ibid., 322. Tawaws.—Trader of 1778 quoted by Schoolcraft, Ind. Tribes, III, 560, 1853. Taways.—Croghan (1760) in Mass. Hist. Soc. Coll., 4th s., IX, 275, 1871 (Delaware form). Touloucs.—Lamberville (1686) in N.Y. Doc. Col. Hist., III, 489, 1853 (misprint). Towako.—Walam Olum (1833) in Brinton, Lenape Leg., 206, 1885 (old Delaware name). Towakon.—Ibid., 198. Traders.—Schoolcraft, Ind. Tribes, v, 145, 1855. Uda'wak.—Gatschet, Penobscot MS., B. A. E., 1887 (Penobscot name). Ukua'-yata.—Gatschet, Wyandot MS., B. A. E., 1877 (Huron name). Utaobaes.—Barcia, Ensayo, 297, 1723. Utawas.—La Tour, Map, 1779. Utawawas.—Colden (1727), Five Nations, 29, 1747. Utovautes.—Barcia, Ensayo, 236, 1723. Uttawa.—Colden (1764) in N.Y. Doc. Col. Hist., VII, 667, 1856. Waganhaers.—Doc. of 1699, ibid., IV, 565, 1854. Waganhaes.—Livingston (1700), ibid., 691.

Waganha's.—Hunter (1710), ibid., v, 168, 1855 ('stammerers': Iroquois name). Waganis.—Markham (1691), ibid., III, 808, 1853. Wagannes.—Bleeker (1701), ibid., IV, 891, 1854. Wagenhanes.—Wessels (1693), ibid., IV, 61, 1854. Wagunha.—Colden (1727), Five Nations, 108, 1747. Wahannas.—Romer (1700) in N.Y. Doc. Col. Hist., IV, 799, 1854. Watawawininiwok.—Baraga, Eng.-Otch. Dict., 300, 1878 (trans.: 'men of the bulrushes'; so called because many rushes grew in Ottawa r.). Wdowo.—Abnaki Spelling Book (1830) quoted in Me. Hist. Soc. Coll., VI, 247, 1859 (Abnaki name). W'tawas.—Heckewelder in Mass. Hist. Soc. Coll., 2d s., x, 128, 1823.

Otter Tail. A band of the Pillager Chippewa on White Earth res., Minn., numbering 726 in 1906.

Otusson (probably from *ŭtasŭn*, 'bench' or 'platform' in the lodge.—W. J.) A former Chippewa village, taking its name from a chief, on upper Huron r. in Sanilac co., Mich., on a reserve sold in 1837.

Otzagert, Peter. See *Otsiquette.*

Otzenne ('intermediate people'). A Sekani tribe living between the Saschutkenne and the Tselone on the w. side of the Rocky mts., Brit. Col.

Otzen-ne.—Morice in Trans. Can. Inst., 29, 1893.

Ouabanghirea. One of several towns situated close together, apparently on Ohio r. or one of its tributaries, on Marquette's map of 1673 as given by Thevenot (but not on the true map as given by Shea, Discov. and Expl. Miss. Val., 1852). It is possible that the name refers to the Ouabano; but the way in which these towns are located on the map shows that their situation is mere guesswork.

Ouabano (Algonquian: 'eastern'; cf. *Abnaki*). An unidentified tribe or band, probably Algonquian, encountered by La Salle in 1683. They traded with the Spaniards, and at La Salle's solicitation visited Fort St Louis on Illinois r. in company with the Shawnee and Chaskpe. They appear to have come from the S.

Oabano.—La Salle (1683) in Margry, Déc., II, 314, 1877. Ouabans.—Memoir of 1706 in N.Y. Doc. Col. Hist., IX, 799, 1855.

Ouachita. A former tribe, apparently Caddoan, residing on Black or Ouachita r., in N. E. Louisiana. Bienville in 1700 encountered some of them carrying salt to the Taensa, with whom he says they were intending to live. Later he reached the main Ouachita village, which he found to comprise about 5 houses and to contain about 70 men. It would seem that the tribe subsequently retired before the Chickasaw and settled among the Natchitoch, their identity being soon afterward lost. They are not to be confounded with the Wichita. (J. R. S.)

Ouachibes.—Boudinot, Star in the West, 128, 1816. Ouachita.—La Harpe (1719) in French, Hist. Coll. La., III, 18, 1851. Ouachites.—Du Pratz, Hist. Louisiane, 318, 1774. Ouasitas.—Tonti (1690) in French, Hist. Coll. La., I, 72, 1846. Oüassitas.—Pénicaut (1712) in Margry, Déc., v, 497, 1883. Ouatchita.—Iberville (1700), ibid., IV, 414, 1880. Quachita.—Royce in 18th Rep. B.A.E., La. map, 1900. Wouachita.—Ann. de la Prop. de la Foi, II, 384, ca. 1825.

Ouadaougeounaton. Mentioned by Alcedo (Dic. Geog., III, 416, 1788) as an Indian settlement of Louisiana, "in the territory of the Sioux of the west." The name is possibly a synonym of Wea.

Ouade. A village in Georgia, about 1564, near the coast, apparently on or near lower Altamaha r. De Bry (Brev. Narr., II, map, 1591) locates it on the coast of South Carolina, s. of Ft St Helena. The name may be a dialectic form of Guale, q. v.

Oualeanicou. A tribe mentioned by Coxe (Carolana, 48, 1741), in connection with the Foxes and Menominee, as living on Wisconsin r., Wis. The word may be a corrupted form of Iliniouec (Illinois) or may possibly refer to the Winnebago.

Oualuck's Band (*Ou-a-luck*). The local name of a Snake band formerly in Eureka valley, E. Oreg.—Drew in Ind. Aff. Rep., 59, 1863.

Ouanakina. Mentioned by Smith (Bouquet's Exped., 70, 1766) as a tribe probably associated with the Creeks and numbering 300. Schoolcraft includes them under the heading "Upper, Middle, and Lower Creeks." It is possible that they are identical with the Wewoka (q. v.) who lived on Wenoka cr., Elmore co., Ala. (C. T.)

Onanikins.—Boudinot, Star in the West, 128, 1816. Ouanikina.—Schoolcraft, Ind. Tribes, III, 557, 1853.

Ouananiche. A species of salmon (*Salmo salar ouananiche*) found in the waters of E. Quebec and part of Labrador. Chambers (The Ouananiche, 50, 1896) cites 26 different spellings, literary and popular, French Canadian and English, including *wananish, ouininiche, wininish,* and *winanis,* all of them corruptions of the French Canadian *ouananiche,* which form appears in the documents of the old Jesuit missionaries. An English *winanis* dates back to the first decade of the 19th century; *awenanish* is used by Bouchette somewhat later. The source of the word is *wananish* in the Montagnais dialect of Algonquian, which seems to be a diminutive in -*ish* of *wanans* or *awanans,* one of the words for salmon in the older language. Dr Wm. Jones suggests a cognate form of the Chippewa *winīnīsh,* 'unpleasant fat' (*ish* referring to unpleasantness), and says the same language has *wininsī* (animate), 'is unclean.' (A. F. C.)

Ouapou. A tribe mentioned by La Salle in 1680 (Margry, Déc., II, 60, 1877) as living in lower Michigan. Probably *Poues,* or *Poux,* i. e. Potawatomi, with the demonstrative prefix *ona.* (J. M.)

Ouasouarini (probably for *Awasīsiwinīnīwŭg,* 'people of the Bullhead clan.'—W. J.). A Chippewa tribe living in 1640 on Georgian bay, Ontario, N. of the Hurons (Jes. Rel. 1640, 34, 1858). They are probably identical with the Ouassi, found in the vicinity of Nipigon r. in 1736; also with the Ouasaouanik, spoken of in 1658 as a well-known tribe living near the Sault Ste Marie. The Ouassi were found by J. Long in 1791, mixed with other Chippewa, on the N. shore of L. Superior, almost exactly in the locality assigned them by Dobbs in 1744. Chauvignerie estimated their number in 1736 at about 300 souls, and stated that the catfish (bullhead) was their totem, which was also the totem of the Awausee (q. v.).

Aouasanik.—Jes. Rel. 1648, 62, 1858. Awasatciu.—Wm. Jones inf'n, 1905 (correct Chippewa form). Ouacé.—Chauvignerie (1736) in N.Y.Doc.Col.Hist., IX, 1054, 1855. Ouali.—Chauvignerie (1736) quoted by Schoolcraft, Ind.Tribes, III, 556, 1853 (misprint). Ouasaouanik.—Jes. Rel. 1658, 22, 1858. Ouasouarim.—Jes. Rel. 1640, 34, 1888. Ouassi.—Dobbs, Hudson Bay, 32, 1744. Wasawanik.—Jes. Rel., III, index, 1858. Wasses.—Long, Voy. and Trav., 45, 1791.

Ouenrio. A Huron village, situated, according to the Jesuit Relation for 1635, about 1 league from Ossossané. Father Jones (Jes. Rel., XXXIV, 255, 1898) places it in Tiny tp., about 3 m. N. E. of La Fontaine, Ontario. Its people had previously been a part of those of Toanche and Ihonatiria. In 1635 three feasts were held here to satisfy a dream, the description of the accompanying ceremonies giving a fair idea of such performances (Jes. Rel., X, 201, 1897). In 1637 an epidemic caused great distress to the inhabitants of Ouenrio, carrying off many and creating a desire to have the Jesuit missionaries dwell among them. In his Relation for 1635 Le Jeune says their cabins were better than the hovels of the Montagnais and were constructed like bowers, or garden arbors, of which, instead of branches and grass, some were covered with cedar bark, others with broad strips of ash, elm, fir, or spruce bark; and although those of cedar were regarded as best, they were very inflammable, wherefore so many similar villages had been burned. (J. N. B. H.)

Oenrio.—Jes. Rel. 1635, 31, 1858. Oüenrio.—Jes. Rel. 1637, 153, 1858. 8enrio.—Jes. Rel. 1636, 123, 1858 Wenrio.—Shea, Cath. Miss., 176, 1855.

Oueschekgagamiouilimy (possibly for *Ushashă'tagamiwinīnīwŭg,* 'people of the ridge'). The Caribou gens of the Chippewa of Rainy r., Minn. St Pierre in 1753 (Margry, Déc., VI, 649, 1886) spoke of them as near Rainy lake, Ontario. (W. J.)

Oughetgeodatons ('dung village'). A village or subdivision of one of the western Sioux bands.

Oiudachenaton.—Jefferys (1763), Am. Atlas, map 5, 1776. Onghetgechaton.—De l'Isle, map of La. (1700), in Neill, Hist. Minn.,164, 1858. Onghetgéodatons.—Le Sueur (1700) in Margry, Déc., VI, 87, 1887. Oughetgeodatons.—Le Sueur (1700) in Neill, Hist. Minn., 170, 1858. Ouidachenaton.—De l'Isle, op. cit. Ouidaougeouaton.—Jefferys, op. cit. Ouidaougeoumaton.—De la Tour, map, 1779 (misprint of m for n). Ouidaougeounaton.—Carte des Poss. Angl., 1777. Ouidaugeounaton.—De l'Isle, op. cit.

Ouheywichkingh. An Algonquian village on Long id., N. Y., probably near the western end.—Doc. of 1645 in N. Y. Doc. Col. Hist., XIV, 60, 1883.

Ouiatenon (abbr. of *wawiiatanong*, 'at *wawiiatan*,' i. e. 'the current goes round': whence the name of the Wea tribe.—Gerard). The principal village of the Wea, situated on the s. E. bank of the Wabash, just below the mouth of Wea cr., in what is now Tippecanoe co., Ind. It was headquarters for the French traders in that section, the French Ft Ouiatenon having been nearly opposite the mouth of the creek. It is described as extending 3 m., though the number of houses it contained was but 70, exclusive of the French dwellings. In 1777 this was the principal Indian center on the Wabash, Ouiatenon and a Kickapoo town on the opposite side of the river together containing 1,000 fighting men. It was destroyed by the United States troops under Gen. Scott in 1791. For forms of the name, see *Wea*. (J. M.   J. P. D.)

Ouikaliny (misprint of *Onikaliny*). A tribe N. of L. Superior in 1697, who sometimes traded with the French, but generally with the English on Hudson bay. They may have been the Maskegon.
Gens de l'Outarde.—La Chesnaye (1697) in Margry, Déc., VI, 7, 1886. Ouikaliny.—Ibid., 7.

Ouinebigonhelini (probably for *Winibigowininiwŭg*, 'people of the unpleasant water.'—W. J.). A tribe or band, doubtless of the Maskegon, living on Hudson bay at the mouth of Nelson r. in the middle of the 18th century.
Ouenebegonhelinis.—Dobbs, Hudson Bay, 24, 1744. Ouinebigonhelini.—Ibid., 23.

Ouininiche. See *Ouananiche*.

Oujatespouitons. A band of one of the Dakota tribes w. of Mississippi at the close of the 17th century.
Oujalespious.—La Harpe (1700) in French, Hist. Coll. La., III, 27, 1851. Oujalespoitons.—Le Sueur (1700) in Neill, Hist. Minn., 170, 1858 (sig.: 'village divided into many small bands'). Oujalespoitous.—Le Sueur quoted by Shea, Early Voyages, 104, 1861. Oujatespouetons.—Shea, ibid., 111 (sig.: 'village dispersed in several little bands'). Oujatespouitons.—Le Sueur (1700) in Margry, Déc., VI, 80, 1886. Ouyatespony.—Pénicaut in Minn. Hist. Soc. Coll., II, pt. 2, 6, 1864.

Oukesestigouek (Cree: *ukĭsĭstĭgwek*, 'swift-water people.'—Gerard). A Montagnais tribe or band, known to the French as early as 1643. They lived about the headwaters of Manicouagan r., N. of the Papinachois, with whom they appear to have been in close relation. They are spoken of as a quiet and peaceable people, willingly receiving instructions from the missionaries. (J. M.)
Ochessigiriniooek.—Keane in Stanford, Compend., 526, 1878. Ochessigiriniouek.—Albanel (*ca.* 1670) quoted by Hind, Lab. Penin., II, 22, 1863. Ochestgooetoh.—Keane in Stanford, Compend., 526, 1878. Ochestgouetoh.—Hind, Lab. Penin., II, 20, 1863. Ochestigouecks.—Crepy, Map, *ca.* 1755. Ouchessigiriniouek.—Jes. Rel. 1670, 13, 1858. Ouchestigoüek.—Jes. Rel. 1665, 5, 1858. Ouchestigouetch.—Jes. Rel. 1664, 13, 1858. Ouchestigouets.—Bellin, Map, 1755. Oukesestigouek.—Jes. Rel. 1643, 38, 1858.

Oukiskimanitouk (probably for *Okiskimanisiwog*, 'whetstone-bird people', i. e. 'kingfisher people'). A clan of the Chippewa of L. Superior. Chauvignerie in 1736 noted the Oskemanettigons, an Algonquian tribe of 40 warriors on Winnipeg r., having the fisher as its totem. This may be identical.
Oskemanettigons.—Chauvignerie (1736) in N. Y. Doc. Col. Hist., IX, 1054, 1855. Oskemanitigous.—Chauvignerie (1736) quoted by Schoolcraft, Ind. Tribes, III, 556, 1853. Oukiskimanitouk.—Jes. Rel. 1658, 22, 1858. Ushkimani'tigōg.—Wm. Jones, inf'n, 1906.

Oukotoemi. A Montagnais band, part of whom gathered at Three Rivers, Quebec, in 1641 (Jes. Rel. 1641, 29, 1858). Doubtless a part of the Attikamegue.

Oumamiwek (Montagnais: *umámiwek*, 'down-stream people.'—Gerard). A tribe or band of Montagnais, closely related to, if not identical with, the Bersiamite. It is possible that the two were members of one tribe, each having its distinct organization. Shea (Charlevoix, New France, II, 243, 1866), following the Jesuit Relations, says the Bersiamite were next to Tadoussac and the Oumamiwek inland in the N. E. The Relation of 1670 places them below the Papinachois on the St Lawrence. It is, however, certain that the Papinachois were chiefly inland, probably about the headwaters of Bersiamite r. From a conversation with an Oumamiwek chief recorded by Father Henri Nouvel (Jes. Rel. 1664) it is learned that his people and other tribes of the lower St Lawrence were in the habit at that early day of visiting the Hudson Bay region. The people of this tribe were readily brought under the influence of the missionaries.
Oumamiois.—Jes. Rel. 1670, 13, 1858. 8mami8ek.—Jes. Rel. 1650, 41, 1858. 8mami8ekhi.—Jes. Rel. 1641, 57, 1858. Oumamiwek.—Bailloquet (1661) in Hind, Lab. Penin., II, 20, 1863. Oumaniouets.—Homann Heirs map, 1756 (located about head of Saguenay r., and possibly a distinct tribe). Oumanois.—Hind, Lab. Penin., II, 21, 1863 (perhaps quoting a writer of 1664). Ouramanichek.—Jes. Rel. 1644, 53, 1858 (identical?).

Oumatachi. An Algonquian band living between Mistassini and Abittibi lakes, Quebec, in the 18th century.
Oumatachi.—Jefferys, French Dom., pt. 1, map, 1761. Oumatachiiriouetz.—La Tour, Map, 1779 (should be Oumatachiriniouetz).

Ounnashattakau. A Seneca chief, usually called Ounneashataikau, or Tall Chief, born in 1750. He signed the treaties of 1797 and Aug. 31, 1826, his name appearing as Auashodakai in the latter. He lived alternately at Squakie hill (Dayoitgao), near Mt Morris, N. Y., and at the latter place. He died and was buried at Tonawanda in 1828, but his remains were removed, June 11, 1884, to Mt Morris, where a monument bearing his name in the form A-wa-nis-ha-dek-ha (meaning 'burning day') has been erected to his memory. He is described as having been a graceful and fine-looking man. (W. M. B.)

Ounontisaston ('at the foot of the mountain.'—Hewitt). An important Huron village visited by De la Roche Dallion in 1626 (Shea, Cath. Miss., 170, 1855) and mentioned by Sagard (Can., III, 805, 1866) in 1636. Its location is uncertain, but it was probably not far from Niagara r., and the name may refer to its situation on the ridge facing the N.   (W. M. B.)

Ouray (said by Powell to be the Ute attempt to pronounce the name *Willie*, given him by the white family to which he was attached as a boy; other authorities give the meaning 'The Arrow'). A chief of the Uncompahgre Ute, born in Taos, N. Mex., in 1833. He was engaged in a fierce struggle with the Sioux in his early manhood, and his only son was captured by the Kiowa, never to be restored. His

OURAY

relations with the United States government, so far as recorded, began with the treaty made by the Tabeguache band at Conejos, Colo., Oct. 7, 1863, to which his name is signed "U-ray, or Arrow." He also signed the treaty of Washington, Mar. 2, 1868, by the name U-re; though to the amendment, Aug. 15, 1868, it is written Ou-ray. He is noted chiefly for his unwavering friendship for the whites, with whom he always kept faith and whose interests he protected as far as possible, even on trying occasions. It was in all probability his firm stand and the restraint he imposed upon his people that prevented the spread of the outbreak of the Ute in Sept. 1879, when agent N. C. Meeker and others were killed and the women of the agency made captives.

As soon as Ouray heard of this outbreak he commanded the cessation of hostilities, which the agent claimed would have stopped further outrage had the soldiers been withheld. Ouray at this time signed himself as "head chief" of the Ute, though what this designation implied is uncertain. For his efforts to maintain peace at this time he was granted an annuity of $1,000 as long as he remained chief of the Ute. Ouray had a fair education, speaking both English and Spanish. His death occurred Aug. 24, 1880, at which time he was residing in a comfortable, well-furnished house on a farm which he owned and cultivated.   (C. T.)

Ousagoucoula (Choctaw: 'hickory people,' from *ossak*, 'hickory'). One of the 9 Natchez villages in 1699.
Noyers.—Richebourg in French, Hist. Coll. La., III, 248, 1851. Ousagoucoula.—Iberville (1699) in Margry, Déc., IV, 179, 1880. Walnut Village.—Gayarré, La., I, 156, 1851.

Ousint. A former village, presumably Costanoan, connected with Dolores mission, San Francisco, Cal.—Taylor in Cal. Farmer, Oct. 18, 1861.

Outacity. Given in documents as the name or title of a prominent Cherokee chief about 1720; also spelled Otacite, Otassite, Outassatah, Wootassite, Wrosetasatow.—Mooney in 19th Rep. B. A. E., 529, 546, 1900.

Outainink (*utĕnink*, 'site of the town', or 'place where the town was'). A former Munsee Delaware village, otherwise known as Old Town, formerly on White r., a short distance above the present Muncie, Delaware co., Ind. The proper name was Wapicomekoke (q. v.), or Wapikahmekunk, which was given also to the new village at the present Muncie on the abandonment of the other.   (J. P. D.)
Old Town.—Dunn, True Ind. Stories, 286, 1909. Outainink.—Ibid. Ou-tau-nink.—Hough, map, in Ind. Geol. Rep., 1882. Wah'-pi-cŏm-ĕ'-kŏke.—Dunn, op. cit. Wah-pi-kah-mĕ'-kunk.—Ibid.

Outaouakamigouk (probably for *Utäwäkämĭguk*, 'people of the open country or land.'—Gerard). A tribe or band on the N. E. coast of L. Huron in 1648; probably a part of the Ottawa.
Ouraouakmikoug.—Jes. Rel. 1658, 22, 1858. Outaouakamigouk.—Jes. Rel. 1648, 62, 1858.

Outassatah. See *Outacity*.

Outchichagami (Montagnais: *Utchĭkägämi*, 'people near the water.'—Gerard). The name of a small tribe living N. of Albany r., in Keewatin, Canada. They speak a Chippewa dialect fairly well understood by the Chippewa of the N. shore of L. Superior.   (W. J.)
Otcitcā'kŏnsag.—Wm. Jones, inf'n, 1906. Outchichagami.—Jefferys, French Dom. Am., I, map, 1761. Outchichagamiouetz.—La Tour, Map, 1779.

Outchougai. A band that lived in 1640 on the E. side of Georgian bay, Ontario r., and probably S. of French r. They were connected with the Amikwa. In 1736 they were living at Oka, Quebec, and were described by Chauvignerie as a clan of the Nipissing, with the heron as their totem.

Achagué.—Chauvignerie (1736) in N. Y. Doc. Col. Hist., IX, 1053, 1855. Achaque.—Chauvignerie (1736) quoted by Schoolcraft, Ind. Tribes, III, 554, 1853. Archouguets.—Jes. Rel. 1643, 61, 1858. Atchougek.—Jes. Rel. 1658, 22, 1858. Atchoughe.—Jes. Rel. 1648, 62, 1858. Atchouguets.—Jes. Rel., III, index, 1858. Outchougai.—Jes. Rel. 1640, 34, 1858. Outchouguets.—Jes. Rel., III, index, 1858.

Outimagami(Nipissing: 'deep-water people'). An unidentified Algonquian tribe or band formerly living N. of L. Nipissing, toward Hudson bay (Jes. Rel. 1640, 34, 1858). The name appears to be identical with that of L. Temagami.   (A. F. C.)

Outurbi *uturĭbi*, 'turibi [*Coregonus artedii*, a congener of the white-fish] people.'—Gerard). A former Algonquian tribe or band in Ontario, living N. of L. Nipissing and wandering to the region of Hudson bay.

Otaulubis.—Bacqueville de la Potherie, Hist. Am., II, 49, 1753. Outouloubys.—Du Lhut (1684) in Margry, Déc., VI, 51, 1886. Outurbi.—Jes. Rel. 1640, 34, 1858.

Ouwerage (Iroquois name). One of the 5 Abnaki villages in 1700.—Bellomont (1700) in N. Y. Doc. Col. Hist., IV, 758, 1854.

Ovens. The pit oven, consisting of a hole excavated in the ground, heated with fire, and then filled with food which was covered over and allowed to cook, was general in America, though as a rule it was employed only occasionally, and principally for cooking vegetal substances. This method of cooking was found necessary to render acrid or poisonous foods harm-

A PUEBLO OVEN

less and starchy foods saccharine, and as a preliminary in drying and preserving food for winter use. Rude camp devices, such as baking in a cavity in the ashes, sometimes incasing in clay the substance to be cooked, were in common use; simple pit ovens, charged according to a definite plan, and ovens with a draft hole, the latter occurring among the Pueblos, comprise the varieties of this invention in northern America.

The Taculli cook roots in a pit oven, placing a layer of heated stones in the bottom, then a layer of food, and finally a covering of earth. Powers says the Pomo extract the toxic principle from buckeyes by steaming them underground for two or three days; they first excavate a large hole, pack it watertight around the sides, burn a fire therein for a space of time, then put in the buckeyes with water and heated stones, and cover the whole with a layer of earth. The Hupa, Maidu, Yurok, and perhaps most of the acorn-consuming Indians of California, cooked acorn mush in small sand pits, and the Tlelding made soap-root (*Chlorogalum pomeridianum*) palatable by cooking it in an earth-covered heap. The Hupa cook the same plant for about two days in a large pit, lined with stones, in which a hot fire is maintained until the stones and surrounding earth are well heated; the fire is then drawn, the pit lined with leaves of wild grape and wood sorrel to improve the flavor of the bulbs, and a quantity of the bulbs thrown in; leaves are then placed on top, the whole is covered with earth, and a big fire built on top (Goddard). The Indians of British Columbia, including Vancouver id., roasted clams in a pit oven, in much the same way as the New England Indians followed in the well-known "clambake" early adopted by the whites. Wherever camas (q. v.) is found, the Indians roasted it in pits. A cavity is made in the ground large enough to hold 10 to 20 bushels, and lined with pebbles; the pit is then filled in order with roots, pebbles, and grass, upon which is formed a hearth of wet clay, over which a fire is kept up for about seventy hours; if the fire burns through the hearth, which is indicated by steam rising through the camas, the oven is again covered with clay (Gibbs).

Speaking of the Powhatan Indians, Capt. John Smith says: "The chief root they have for food is called Tockawhoughe. It groweth like a flagge in Marishes. In one day a Salvage will gather sufficient for a weeke. These roots are much of the greatnesse and taste of Potatoes. They use to cover a great many of them with Oke leaves and Ferne, and then cover all with earth in the manner of a Cole-pit; over it, on each side, they continue a great fire 24 houres before they dare eat it. Raw it is no better then poyson, and being rosted, except it be tender and the heat abated, or sliced and dryed in the Sunne, mixed with sorrell and meale or such like, it will prickle and torment the throat extreamely, and yet in sommer they use this ordinarily for bread."

The Panamint Indians of California roasted cactus joints in pits, also mescal, and the Paiute and Siksika cooked poison root (tobacco root) in the same way (Schoolcraft, Ind. Tribes, VI, 697, 1857; Maximilian, Trav., 252, 1843); the Kutchin cooked roots in the same fashion, and even the Alaskan Eskimo roasted roots of the wild parsnip in underground ovens. Some tribes, as the Pawnee, Karankawa, and Sioux, simply roasted small portions of corn and meat in ashes; and the Yuma, Zuñi, and others encase a dead rat or a rabbit in clay and then put the ball in the fire until the meat is roasted.

The Pueblos carried the art of cooking in pit ovens much farther than any other Indians. They had large community ovens consisting of a bottle-shaped cavity excavated in the ground and provided with a draft-hole; in these great quantities of green corn ears are roasted. Similar ovens, 12 to 15 ft in diameter, found among the ancient ruins of the Salt River valley in Arizona, show the effect of great heat; the Apache employ such ovens for roasting maguey. Small family ovens with draft hole, and others consisting merely of a jar set in the ground and covered with a stone, are still used by the Hopi. These are heated with a fire of twigs; a jar of mush is set in them, the orifice of the oven covered with a stone luted down with clay, and a fire built over the top and kept burning for about 12 hours. The Zuñi had such ovens lined with stone slabs but without draft hole, and also a pit oven in which mush was baked between slabs of heated stones. The dome-shape ovens of stone plastered with clay are in common use among the Pueblos (except the Hopi), and the Mexicans of the Southwest, but this form of cooking apparatus was introduced from Spain by way of Mexico. Some of the Pueblos had an oven cult, in Zuñi represented by the demon inspector of ovens. See *Food*.

Consult Boas in Proc. Brit. A. A. S. 1890, 15, 1891; Chesnut in Cont. Nat. Herb., VII, no. 3, 1902; Cushing in The Millstone, IX, 1884; Coville in Am. Anthrop., V, 354, 1892; Dixon in Bull. Am. Mus. Nat. Hist., XVII, pt. 3, 1905; Gibbs in Cont. N. A. Ethnol., I, 194, 1877; Goddard in Univ. Cal. Pub., Am. Archæol. and Ethnol., I, no. 1, 1903; Hudson in Am. Anthrop., II, 775, 1900; Loskiel, Hist. Miss. United Breth., pt. 1, 108–9, 1794; Maximilian, Travels, 252, 1843; Mindeleff in 8th Rep. B. A. E., 1891; Morice in Proc. Canadian Inst., 135, Oct. 1889; Powers in Cont. N. A. Ethnol., III, 49–50, 89, 150, 1877; Schoolcraft, Ind. Tribes, VI, 697, 1857; Smith, Works, Arber ed., 1884.   (W. H.)

Owaiski. A former Seneca village near the site of Wiscoy, on the w. bank of Genesee r., in Allegany co., N. Y.

57009°—Bull. 30, pt 2—12——12

Hishhue.—Procter (1791) in Am. State Papers, Ind. Aff., I, 158, 1832. **Ohhisheu.**—Procter, ibid., 152. **O-wa-is'-ki.**—Morgan, League Iroq., 467, 1851.

Owasse ('bear'). A phratry and also a subphratry or gens of the Menominee. **Owa'sse wi'dishi'anun.**—Hoffman in 14th Rep. B. A. E., 42, 1896 (*wi'dishi'anun*='phratry').

Owassissas. A former Seminole town on an E. branch of St Marks r., N. W. Fla.; pop. 100 in 1822.—Morse, Rep. to Sec. War, 364, 1822.

Owego. A former town with a mixed population, under Cayuga jurisdiction, situated on the right bank of Owego cr., about 2 m. from the Susquehanna, in Tioga co., N. Y. In 1779 the village consisted of about 20 houses, which were burned by Gen. Poor of Sullivan's army, Aug. 20 of that year.   (J. N. B. H.)
Awegen.—Esnauts and Rapilly Map, 1777. **Owago.**—Livermore (1779) in N. H. Hist. Soc. Coll., VI, 322, 1850. **Owegé.**—Map of 1768 in N. Y. Doc. Col. Hist., VIII, 1857. **Owegey.**—Guy Park conf. (1775), ibid., 561. **Owegi.**—Güssefeld Map, 1784. **Owego.**—Johnson Hall conf. (1765) in N. Y. Doc. Col. Hist., VII, 728, 1856. **Owegy.**—Homann Heirs Map, 1756. **Oweigey.**—Mt Johnson conf. (1755) in N. Y. Doc. Col. Hist., VI, 984, 1855.

Owendos ('an island', or possibly for *Ouendat*, 'Hurons'). A village marked on early maps on the headwaters of Tuscarawas or Beaver cr., in Ohio or Pennsylvania.
Ovvendoes.—Alcedo, Dic. Geog., III, 274, 1788. **Owendoes.**—Esnauts and Rapilly Map, 1777. **Owendos.**—Homann Heirs Map, 1756.

Owhyhee. Mentioned by Ross (Fur Hunters, I, 83, 130, 1855), with Iroquois and Abnaki, as if the name of an Indian tribe, members of which formed a party of voyageurs on Columbia r., Oregon. The name however, is simply an early form of Hawaii, Kanakas having made their influence felt on the N. W. coast in the early half of the 19th century and later. The name, spelled Owyhee, survives as that of a river in Nevada, Oregon, and Idaho, and a range of mountains, a county, and a postoffice in the state last mentioned. See *Hawaiian influence*.

Owiyekumi (*Ow'-i-yē-kumī*). The principal town of the Quatsino on Forward inlet, Quatsino sd., N. W. coast of Vancouver id.—Dawson in Trans. Roy. Soc. Can. for 1887, sec. II, 65, 1888.

Owl's Town. A former village, probably of the Delawares, on Mohican r. in Coshocton co., Ohio.—Hutchins map in Smith, Bouquet's Exped., 1766.

Oxidoddy. An Indian name, of uncertain origin, preserved by herbalists and "herb doctors" for black-root, Culver's-root, or Culver's-physic, *Veronica virginica*.   (W. R. G.)

Oyak. A Kuskwogmiut Eskimo village on the E. shore of Kuskokwim bay, Alaska, just N. of the mouth of Kanektok r.
Oyágamut.—Spurr and Post quoted by Baker, Geog. Dict. Alaska, 1902.

Oyaron (*o-i-ä′-ro*ⁿ′). The common Iroquois name of the personal, and sometimes the gentile and tribal, tutelary, guardian genius, or guiding spirit believed to protect and watch over the destiny and welfare of every person or kindred.

The doctrines connected with the concept of the *oyaron* lie at the base of the activities comprehended under the rubric totemism, the key to which is the idea of guardianship or voluntary protection, based on the concept of primitive man that the earth and all that it contains was brought into being by the primal beings of his cosmogony solely for the welfare and glory of man, and that therefore these owed to him the duty of voluntarily making provision for his welfare. It was a dogma of this early philosophy that the *oyaron* was revealed or manifested itself to the subject in a vision or dream, either before or after birth. After birth it could be ceremonially acquired in the following general manner: At the age of puberty, the boy under the tutorship of an old man, usually a diviner or prophet, and the girl under that of a matron, withdrew to some secluded spot, in which tutor and pupil lived in a lodge built for the purpose, from which all persons except the novice and the tutor were rigidly excluded. During this period of strict seclusion, the novice was subjected to a rigorous fast and dosed with prescribed powders and decoctions, and his face, shoulders, and breast were blackened to symbolize the mental darkness in which the novice or initiate then was and also his physical want of occult power. The initiate was directed carefully to observe his or her dreams or visions during this fast and to report them in minutest detail to his tutor, whose duty it was to give attention to the behavior of his charge. In the fulfilment of his duty, the tutor frequently conferred with the ancients, the elders and chief women of the clan and tribe, concerning his charge, in order the better to choose from the occult hints embodied in the dreams and visions what should be selected, or rather what had been suggested in the dreams as the tutelary or guardian genius of the initiate, on which would in the future depend the welfare and security of his life, his *oyaron*, and, lastly, what vocations he should choose to be successful in after life. The *oyaron* revealed in one of these mysterious dreams or visions consisted usually of the first trifle that impressed the imagination of the dreamer—a calumet, a pipe, a knife, a bow or an arrow, a bearskin, a plant, an animal, an action, a game: in a word, anything might become, if suggested in a dream or vision, a tutelary or an *oyaron*. But what is fundamental and important is that it was not

believed that the object itself was in fact a spirit or genius, but that it was its embodiment, the symbol or outward sign of the union subsisting between the soul and its tutelary or guardian genius, through the guidance and potency of which the soul must know and do everything; for, by virtue of the *oyaron* a person could transform himself in shape and size, and could do what he pleased, unless checked by a more powerful orenda (q. v.) guided by a more astute *oyaron;* it was the subjective being which was the means of his metamorphoses, his enchantments, whether he regarded these changes real or whether he was persuaded that it was the soul alone that detached itself, or the genius that acted in conformity with his own intention and according to his will.

Tutelaries had not the same efficiency, nor the same scope of action. There were persons more favored, more enlightened, than the common people, through the guidance of genii of superior potency, enabling the souls of such persons to feel and to see not only what concerned their possessors personally, but to see even into the very bottom of the souls of other persons, to pierce through the veil which covered them, and there to perceive the natural and the innate desires and promptings which those souls might have had, although these souls themselves had not perceived them, or at least had not expressed them by dreams and visions, or although so expressed in this peculiar manner, those revelations had been entirely forgotten. It was this ability of seeing into the bodies of men that gave these persons the name *saïotkatta* (Huron), or *shagotgathwas* (Onondaga), or *agotsinnachen* (by both Hurons and Iroquois), the first signifying 'One who examines another by seeing,' literally, 'one customarily looks at another.' But beyond this occult knowledge of hidden things, they professed the further ability to perform still other wonders by means of certain chants, songs, and dances, through which they were enabled to put forth their own orenda. In this capacity, a person of this class received the name *arendiouanen* (for *harendiowanen*), a compound of the noun orenda and the qualifier *-wanen*, 'large,' 'great,' 'powerful,' together signifying 'his orenda is powerful,' or 'one whose orenda is powerful.' Lastly, the intercourse of the persons having potent orenda and superior *oyaron*, with spirits, especially those regarded as monstrous in form and disposition and as hostile to the welfare of man, gave them the name of *agotkon*, 'one who is an otkon' (q. v.).

Those having powerful orenda and possessing the protection of a potent and resourceful *oyaron* were regarded as wise men, knowing both human and divine things, the efficacy of plants, rocks, ores, and all the occult virtues and secrets of nature; not only could they sound the depths of the hearts of other persons, but they could foresee what would come to pass in the future, read the fate of men in the signs, wonders, and omens of the earth, claiming to maintain intimate intercourse with the gods, a favor of which less-gifted persons were quite unworthy. These reputed favors of the gods added to an austerity of life and a well-regulated code of manners, at least in appearance, and a conduct above suspicion, or at least censure, gained them the respect if not the fear of all persons, who consulted them as oracles, as sources of truth, and the favored mediators between man and the gods. They could foresee the success or failure of war or a journey, could divine the secret source or cause of illness, could suggest what would make a hunting or a fishing trip successful, could discover things lost by theft, the source of evil and of spells and enchantments, and they could apply their art to exorcise them, to drive them away and to apply the proper remedies to thwart their purposes. They were also adepts in making their calling one of power and authority, and a source of profit and remuneration.

The person whose life was regarded as being under the protection of some being embodied in a material thing, in this occult manner, had less reason for apprehension than he whose life was so protected by some particular animal, for should the animal die, it was a foregone conclusion that he himself incurred the risk of a like fate. This belief was so strong that many seemingly proved its truth by dying soon after the known death of the tutelary animal. This connection of things, which, although alien to man, had nevertheless such an intimate relation to his life, sprang from a motion, an innate impulse, or from a natural desire of the soul, which drew it toward the object and established a moral union between the two, upon the maintenance of which depended the welfare of the person and the peace of his soul. This desire or longing for something seen in a dream or vision was very different from the momentary or voluntary craving which sprang from a knowledge of the object toward which the mind was directed; for it was innate, intrinsic, to the soul, and did not rest on any knowledge of the need of the thing by the mind itself, although it had so much interest in knowing what the soul desired or needed; and, indeed, it would not be strange that the mind should not know anything about it, should the tutelary fail to express itself through dreams or visions.

The unfortunate consequences to which, it was believed, one would be exposed, should he or she fail to provide the soul with what it desired or required as indicated in a dream or vision, compelled the people scrupulously to observe all dreams with the utmost care and diligence, and engaged not only the dreamer but all his tribesmen to obtain for him all the satisfaction that he could desire in the fulfilment of his dream. This was done in such manner that, on these occasions, not only did they not refuse anything asked of them (a refusal being a stigma of the utmost infamy), but they went even farther than that which would have given satisfaction, and sacrificed their most precious possessions.

In addition to those tutelaries belonging to every person, there were *oyaron* common to the family, the gens, or the clan, and probably to the tribe, which were placed in the lodge. Sacrifices and offerings were made to them of dogs, other animals, and various articles of food, raiment, and adornment. Warriors carried their personal *oyaron* carefully wrapped in some sacred skin, and they did not cease from invoking it to give them victory over their enemies. The *oyaron* was an efficient aid to the shaman in all things: in making medicines, in healing wounds, in performing the miracles of his art, and in exorcising the spells cast by other shamans and in thwarting their enchantments. The sacrifice or offering was a very important part of the cult of the *oyaron*, for should one have failed to make in its honor a feast, an offering, or a sacrifice, to feed it, keep it alive, and give it renewed strength, at stated periods, the *oyaron* would have become angry, and, if too long neglected, would have turned on its owner or owners and caused him or them troubles, illness, and probably death. It was a doctrine of this philosophy of the *oyaron* that if it suggested the prohibition of anything during the treatment of a patient by a shaman and this prohibition was neglected or disregarded, the patient would invariably have a relapse. Of such a patient the Tuscarora say "one is be-*oyaron*-ed" (if such a hybrid be permitted for illustration), and is in origin and application like the English "bewitched." These prohibitions are what are commonly called *taboo*. This transgression of the dictum of some *oyaron*, or god, becomes sin in the higher cults of man, and this fact leads to the understanding of the nature and genesis of the concept of the *taboo*.

There was a class of shamans of both sexes who cast spells and enchantments solely for the purpose of doing evil, for the intent of executing private vengeance, or for the gratification of malice, and justly were they regarded with awe and fear. In Iroquois, they received the name *agotkon*, or *hoññatkon*—i. e. 'they are *otkons*,' or persons having the magic power of monstrous beings. There were also shamans of both sexes who exerted their magic power under the guidance of their several *oyaron* to secure and promote the welfare of their cotribesmen by consenting to attempt to correct and undo the wrongs and evils devised and perpetrated by the other class. In either class the ability to do what was not normal sprang from the same principle, the conjectured possession of orenda, or magic power.

By the combined astuteness and potency of the *oyaron* of persons added to that of their own inherent orenda, some highly favored individuals became immune to all powers and influences belonging to the earth, since they knew all things, saw all things, and could do all things. Such personages or beings were naturally shunned and feared, because of this imputed invulnerability and immunity from all causes having their origin or the earth. (J. N. B. H.)

Oyateshicha ('bad nation'). A band of the Mdewakanton Sioux. Neill gave their habitat as on Rice cr., Minn., 7 m. above the falls of St Anthony. In 1853 their village was on Minnesota r., 7 m. from the agency in Minnesota. In 1858 they removed to Oak Grove, and subsequently to Nebraska with other Santee Sioux.

Bad.—Prescott in Schoolcraft, Ind. Tribes, II, 171, 1852. **Goodroad's band.**—Ind. Aff. Rep., 282, 1854. **Goodrod's band.**—Schoolcraft, Ind. Tribes, III, 613, 1853 (misprint). **O-ya-tay-shee-ka.**—Neill in Minn. Hist. Soc. Coll., I, 263, 1872. **Oyate-citca.**—Dorsey in 15th Rep. B. A. E., 216, 1897. **Oyate šiĉa.**—Ibid. **Tah-chunk wash taa.**—Schoolcraft, Ind. Tribes, III, 612, 1853 (correctly. Tachanku washte, 'Good road', their chief in 1836). **Wa-kpa-a-ton-we-dan.**—Neill, Hist. Minn., 144, 1858 (='those who dwell on the creek').

Oyateshicha. A band of the Yankton Sioux.

Oyate-citca.—Dorsey in 15th Rep. B. A. E., 217, 1897. **Oyate-šiĉa.**—Ibid.

Oydican. A tribe or subtribe, possibly Coahuiltecan, represented in 1706 and later at San Francisco Solano mission, near the lower Rio Grande. For their affiliation, see *Terocodame*, a tribe of the same locality with whom they intermarried and with whom they were associated at the mission. The Oydican seem to have belonged to what was called the Terocodame band (MS. Baptismal Rec., 1706–07, partidas 181, 239, 261, 271, 316). (H. E. B.)

Oydica.—MS. Baptismal Rec., op. cit., partida 261.

Oyeghseragearat. See *Onechsagerat*.

Oyike (*Oyi-ké*, 'winter people', from Tewa *oyi*, 'frost'). One of the two branches into which each well-regulated Tewa village is divided in consequence of certain traditional beliefs regarding the religious organization of that people.

Oyi-ké.—Bandelier in Arch. Inst. Papers, III, 304, 1890. **Oyique.**—Bandelier in Century Cyclop. cf Names, 1894.

Oypatukla (*Ahepat-okla*, 'potato-eating people', referring to the native hogpotato). The northeastern of the three divisions into which the Choctaw were distinguished for some time previous to their removal w. of the Mississippi. By Romans the name is mistranslated 'small nation.' For the dividing line between this district and that to the w., see *Oklafalaya*. For about 9 m. the dividing line between it and the southeastern district was formed by a trail running from Concha to Ayanabi, i. e. from the former place to the dividing ridge between the N. E. prong of Chickasawhay and Yanubbee crs., about 1 m. from Ayanabi, in Kemper co., Miss. "From this point in the trail on the dividing ridge, the line ran southerly on the ridge some 3 m. until it struck the 'divide' between Petickfa and Black Water. It kept this divide easterly down to the confluence of these two creeks." From this point to Ponta cr. the line was continued by a trail leading to Coosha. "Ponta cr. from the trail-crossing, downward and eastward, constituted the remainder of the line separating the two districts."—Halbert in Pub. Ala. Hist. Soc., Misc. Coll., I, 378–79, 1901.

Ahepat Okla.—Halbert, op. cit. **Oy-pat-oo-coo-la.**—Pickett, Hist. Ala., I, 137, 1851. **Oypat oocooloo.**—Romans, Fla., 74, 1775.

Oyuchseragarat. See *Onechsagerat*.

Oyukhpe ('unloaded'). A band of the Oglala Sioux.

Oiyurpe.—Robinson, letter to Dorsey, 1879 (r = h; trans. 'where they put down their packs'). **Onkapas.**—Ind. Aff. Rep., 250, 1875. **Oyuhpe.**—Dorsey in 15th Rep. B. A. E., 220, 1897. **Oyuqpe.**—Ibid. **Yokpahs.**—Twiss in Sen. Ex. Doc. 35, 36th Cong., 1st sess., 7, 1860 (probably identical).

Ozanbogus. A tribe formerly living on lower Mississippi r., seen by Tonti in 1688. They were probably the Uzutiuhi (q. v.).

Ozanbogus.—Douay in Shea, Discov., 226, 1852. **Ozembogus.**—McKenney and Hall, Ind. Tribes, III, 81, 1854. **Zembogu.**—Barcia, Ensayo, 261, 1723.

Ozark. A term at one time applied to a local band of Quapaw, from their residence in the Ozark mountain region of Missouri and Arkansas. The spelling *Ozark* is an American rendering of the French *Aux Arcs,* intended to designate the early French post among the Arkansa (Quapaw) about the present Arkansas Post, Ark. (J. M.)

Osark tribe.—Ker, Trav., 40, 1816. **Ozark.**—Nuttall in Jour. Phil., 61, 1821.

Ozatawomen. A village of the Powhatan confederacy, situated in 1608 on the s. bank of the Potomac in King George co., Va.—Smith (1629), Va., I, map, repr. 1819.

Ozenic. A village of the Powhatan confederacy, situated in 1608 on Chickahominy r. in New Kent co., Va.

Ozenick.—Smith (1629), Va., I, map, repr. 1819. **Ozinieke.**—Ibid., II, 91.

Ozette. A Makah village and reservation 1 m. square at Flattery Rocks, coast of Washington. The reservation, comprising 23,040 acres, created under the provisions of the Neah Bay treaty of Jan. 31, 1855, and by Executive orders of Oct. 26, 1872, and Jan. 2 and Oct. 21, 1873, contained 44 Indians in 1901, 35 in 1906.

Hosett.—Swan, Indians of C. Flattery, Smithson. Cont., XVI, 6, 1870. **Osett.**—U. S. Ind. Treat., 461, 1873. **Osette.**—Land Office map of Washington, 1891. **Ozette.**—Ind. Aff. Rep., pt. I, 385, 1901.

Ozinies. A former tribe or village, probably a part of the Nanticoke, living on the s. side of Chester r., Md., about 15 m. from its mouth. Smith estimated them at the time of his visit, in 1608, at 60 warriors, or about 220 souls. They were allies of the Conestoga in 1633.

Osinies.—Bozman, Md., I, 127, 1837. **Ozenies.**—Smith (1629), Va., II, 77, repr. 1819. **Ozimies.**—Drake, Bk. Inds., x, 1848 (misprint). **Ozinies.**—Smith, op. cit., I, map.

Ozinoghiyata. See *Otsinoghiyata*.

Pa. The Fire clan of the Tewa pueblos of San Ildefonso and Nambe, N. Mex.

Pa-tdóa.—Hodge in Am. Anthrop., IX, 350, 1896 (*tdóa*='people').

Pa (*Pa'*). The extinct Deer clan of the former pueblo of Pecos, N. Mex.

Pa'+.—Hodge in Am. Anthrop., IX, 350, 1896 (+=*ash*, 'people').

Paac. A tribe or subtribe, probably Coahuiltecan, met by Massanet in 1691 on an arroyo 6 leagues s. w. of Nueces r., Texas, which the Spaniards called San Lucas, or Arroyo del Carmichael, and which the Indians called Guanapacti (Massanet, Diario, in Doc. Hist. Texas, I, 92, MS.). This tribe was in a rancheria together with Quems, Pachules, Ocanas, Chaguanes, and Pastalucs (Pastalacs?). Cf. *Pakawa*.   (H. E. B.)

Paachiqui. A tribe, apparently Coahuiltecan, mentioned in 1690 by Massanet in a list of tribes met by him between the presidio of Coahuila in Mexico and the Hasinai country of Texas. In the same list he named Parchaques, which would indicate their distinctness (Velasco, Dictamen Fiscal, 1716, in Mem. de Nueva España, XXVII, 183, MS.). On his expedition in 1691 from San Salvador del Valle mission, Massanet found them on the right bank of "Rio Hondo," 11 leagues E. of the Nueces, with the Patchal, Papañaca, Pacuáchiam, Aguapálam, Samampác, Vánca, Payaván (Payaban), and Patavó (Pataguo) tribes. At the same point, a few hours later, he was visited by the Pitahay, Apaysi, and Patsau. These Indians called Rio Hondo "Puanapapac" (Massanet, Diario, 1691, in Mem. de Nueva España, XXVII, 94, MS.). Several of the tribes named above were later gathered at San Francisco Solano and San Antonio de Valero missions, Texas, but the name of Paachiqui does not appear among them.   (H. E. B.)

Parchiquis.—Massanet, op. cit., 1690.

Paako. A former pueblo, evidently of the Tanos, s. of the mining camp of San Pedro, in lat. 35° 15', Santa Fé co., N.

central N. Mex. The village was of the compact communal type, and its houses, which were generally of 2 stories, were apparently constructed of rubble. It contained 3 circular kivas and as many stone inclosures which doubtless had been corrals for flocks, and which in themselves, if not of modern origin, would point to the occupancy of the pueblo in historic times. From its situation and the available evidence there is doubt as to whether the pueblo was the home of the Tigua or Tanos people. Regarding this Bandelier has learned that Paako was the term applied to the pueblo by the Tanos of Santo Domingo (the same name also having been used by Oñate in 1598), who claim that it was a village of their people, while the early Spanish documents refer to it as a Tigua settlement with the additional Spanish designation "San Pedro." Having been situated on the borderland of these two tribal divisions it is not improbable that the village was made up of members of both, and was referred to at various times as pertaining to the Tigua. Since the ruins are claimed by the Tanos to be those of one of the pueblos of their ancestors, however, and since it was separated from the nearest Tigua villages to the southward by the lofty and densely wooded Sierra de Carnué at a time when intertribal disturbances were common, the settlement is classed as that of the Tanos people. According to Bandelier the pueblo was inhabited at least as late as 1626, but was abandoned prior to 1670. Shea (Cath. Missions, 82, 1855) states that a mission was founded at San Pedro del Cuchillo (which seems to be the same) in 1661. See Bandelier in Arch. Inst. Papers, IV, 112 et seq., 1892.

Paáco.—Oñate (1598) in Doc. Inéd., XVI, 118, 1871. **Pa-a-ko.**—Bandelier in Arch. Inst. Papers, IV, 112, 1892 (Tanos name). **Pä-qu.**—Bandelier, Gilded Man, 221, 1893. **San Pablo.**—Zarate-Salmeron (*ca.* 1629) quoted by Bandelier in Arch. Inst. Papers, IV, 113, 1892 (apparently the original Saint name). **San Pedro.**—Niel (*ca.* 1629) quoted by Bandelier, ibid. (so changed from "San Pablo" by Niel). **San Pedro del Cuchillo.**—Shea, Cath. Miss., 82, 1855.

Paauwis (*Pa-au'-wĭs*). A former Siuslaw village on Siuslaw r., Oreg.—Dorsey in Jour. Am. Folk-lore, III, 230, 1890.

Pabaksa ('cut heads'). A division of the Upper Yanktonai Sioux, formerly roaming, with other bands, the country from L. Traverse, Minn., to Devils lake, N. Dak. They are now with the Sisseton and Wahpeton on Devils Lake res., N. Dak., where, under the designation Devil's Lake Sioux, the three bands numbered 985 in 1906.

Cut Beards.—Ind. Aff. Rep., 109, 1850. **Cut heads.**—Culbertson in Smithson. Rep. 1850, 141, 1851. **Pabaska Sioux.**—Ind. Aff. Rep., 482, 1906. **Pah Baxa.**—Ind. Aff. Rep., 109, 1850. **Pah-bax-ahs.**—Schoolcraft, Ind. Tribes, II, 169, 1852. **Tete Coup.**—Sen. Ex. Doc. 90, 22d Cong., 1st sess., 63, 1832. **Tête-Coupées.**—Hayden, Ethnog. and Philol. Mo. Val., 371, 1862. **Tetes Coupes.**—Culbertson, op. cit. **Wan-**

naton.—Sen. Ex. Doc. 90, 22d Cong., 1st sess., 63, 1832. **Yanctonnais Cutheads.**—Ind. Aff. Rep., 53, 1858.

Pabor. A tribe or subtribe, possibly Coahuiltecan, members of which were at San Francisco Solano mission, near the Rio Grande, in 1706–07. They seem to have belonged to the Terocodame (q. v.) band or confederacy, for a Pabor was interpreter for this band at the mission (MS. Baptismal Rec., 1706–07, partidas 161, 210, 248, 249, 291, 301). (H. E. B.)
Babor.—Ibid., partida 210. **Bobor.**—Ibid., partida 161.

Pac. See *Shoe-pack*.

Pacana. A small tribe of unknown affinity, but probably belonging to the same group as the Alibamu and Koasati, mentioned by Adair in 1775 as one of those incorporated with the Muscogee or Creek confederacy. Their town may have been that known as Pakan-tallahassee (q. v.), i. e. 'Pacana old town,' on the E. side of Lower Coosa r., Ala. In connection with several other small tribes in the French interest they crossed the Mississippi on the withdrawal of the French from the Alabama region in 1764, and in 1805 were described by Sibley as living on Calcasieu r., La., having then about 30 men and speaking a language different from those around them, but using also the Mobilian trade jargon. The various renderings of the name are all guesses, ranging from 'pecan,' 'mayapple,' and 'peach orchard,' to 'high,' 'superior,' and 'upper ones.' (J. M.)
Pacamas.—Warden, Account U. S. A., III, 551, 1819 (misprint *m* for *n*). **Pacanas.**—Sibley, Hist. Sketch, 62, 1806. **Pakanas.**—Romans, Florida, I, 90, 1775. **Pak-ka′-na.**—Adair, Am. Inds., 257, 1775. **Panacas.**—Coues and Kingsley, Stand. Nat. Hist., pt. VI, 156, 1883. **Pasquenan.**—d'Anville, Map Mex. and Florida, 1703 (misprint ?).

Pacane. See *Pecan*.

Pacaruja. Mentioned by Uhde (Länder, 121, 1861) as a tribe living in the 18th century on the Texas coast between the Nueces and the Rio Grande.

Paccamagannant. An unidentified Indian village probably near Patuxent r., Md., about 1610.
Paccamagannant.—Pory in Smith (1629), Va., II, 62, repr. 1819. **Paccamagannat.**—Bozman, Md., 151, 1837.

Pachade. A village of Christian Indians near Middleboro, Mass., in 1703, probably connected with the Wampanoag.—Cotton (1703) in Mass. Hist. Soc. Coll., 3d s., II, 244, 1830.

Pachal. A tribe, apparently Coahuiltecan, which in the latter part of the 17th century ranged on both sides of the Rio Grande below the present Eagle Pass, Texas. Massanet met some of them at rancherias 10 and 6 leagues s. w. of Nueces r. with Quems, Ocana, Chaguan (Siaguan), Pastaluc, and Paac Indians, and at "Rio Hondo", 11 leagues N. E. of the Nueces, with Sanpanal, Vánca, Payaván, Aguapálam, Samampác, Patavó

(Pataguo), Pitahay, Apaysi, and Patsau Indians (Massanet, Diario, 1691, in Mem. de Nueva España, XXVII, 92, 94, MS.). In 1699 Fray Diego de Salazar founded San Juan Bautista mission on Sabinas r. with Pachal and Chaguan (Siaguan), Mescal, and Xarame Indians from near the Sabinas (Portillo, Apuntes para la Historia Antigua de Coahuila y Texas, 278–79, 1888). Shortly afterward the mission was reestablished on the Rio Grande near Presidio del Rio Grande, with the same and other tribes (Morfi, Viage de Indios, 1778, in Doc. Hist. Mex., 3d s., IV, 440–41, 1856). In 1703 members of the tribe were connected with San Bernardo mission (Portillo, op. cit., 288). In 1728 Rivera reported Pachoches (Pachules?), then a fragmentary tribe, at Caldera mission, s. of Sabinas r. (Diario, leg. 2763, 1736). The name Pachal is much like Patzau, but since Massanet mentions both in the same list, they are probably distinct. (H. E. B.)
Pachales.—Diego de Salazar y San Buenaventura, 1691, in Portillo, op. cit. **Pachoches.**—Rivera (1728), Diario, leg. 2763, 1736 (identical?). **Pachules.**—Massanet, op. cit., 92, 1691. **Patchal.**—Massanet, 1691, op. cit. **Paxchales.**—Orozco y Berra, Geog., 303, 1864.

Pachalaque. A Coahuiltecan tribe at Nuestra Señora de la Purísima Concepción de Acuña mission, Texas, in the 18th century. That these people belonged to the Coahuiltecan family is evidenced not only by the form of the name and the fact that members thereof were taken to the mission with tribes unquestionably Coahuiltecan, but by more direct testimony. A missionary, in doubt, recorded one convert as either "Pachalaque or Orejona" (Libro de Casamientos, partida 62, MS.). Both of these tribes were well known at the mission, and must have spoken the same language, or this doubt would not have arisen. That the Orejones were Coahuiltecan is proved by the fact that they are contained in the García list of 1760 as among the tribes speaking that language. That the Pachalaque were distinct from the Pajalat is also clear, for they are frequently distinguished on the same page of the records by a single missionary, and even in a single entry one party to a marriage is entered as a Pajalat and the other a Pachalaque (Libro de Casamientos, partidas 1–62, MS.). That they were distinct from the Pastaluc (q. v.) is not so certain. They entered Nuestra Señora de la Purísima Concepción de Acuña mission as early as 1733 with the Pajalat, Tilpacopal, Patumaco, Patalca, Tiloja, Siquipil, and Xarame tribes (ibid.), and there is evidence that before this time they intermarried with the Patumaco particularly (ibid., partida 2). While at the mission they intermarried most frequently with these and the Tilpacopal. A Pachalaque was married to a Tilpacopal at this mission as late as 1773 (ibid., partida 214). Orozco y Berra (Geog., 304, 1864) locates the Pajalaques, who may be the same, on San Antonio r. · (H. E. B.)

Pachalaca.—Morfi, Hist., bk. II, ca. 1781, MS. Pachalate.—Libro de Casamientos, partida 214, 1773, MS. Pachalgagu.—Ibid., partida 61, 1743 (perhaps a miscopy). Pajalache.—Ibid., partidas 162, 163, 1759; and testimony, May 13, 1752, Béxar Archives, 1751–69, MS. (identical?). Pajalaques.—Orozco y Berra, Geog., 304, 1864.

Pachaloco. A former tribe of N. E. Mexico, probably Coahuiltecan, which was gathered into the mission of San Juan Bautista, Coahuila, at its second foundation in 1701 (Orozco y Berra, Geog., 303, 1864). Evidently a division of the Pachal. Cf. *Pachalaque.*

Pachawal. A Kawia village in the San Jacinto mts., s. Cal. Los Coyotes, a name which appears to have been applied to this place, is now a reservation of non-arable mountainous land, comprising 22,640 acres, 85 m. from Mission Tule River agency, transferred in 1903 to the Pala agency. It contains also the Agua Caliente settlement of San Ysidro or Wilakal, and the Diegueño settlement of San Ignacio. The total population of the reservation in 1903 is given as 106.

Cayote.—Heintzelman (1853) in H. R. Ex. Doc. 76, 34th Cong., 3d sess., 41, 1857. Coyotes.—Lovett in Ind. Aff. Rep., 124, 1865. Los Coyotes.—Ind. Aff. Rep., 175, 1902. Pá-cha-wal.—Barrows, Ethno-Bot. Coahuilla Ind., 34, 1900. San Ignacio.—Ibid.

Pacheenaht. A Nootka tribe on San Juan harbor, Vancouver id. Their village is Pacheena, at the mouth of San Juan r. Pop. 71 in 1897, 54 in 1906.

Pacheena.—Can. Ind. Aff., pt. II, 158, 1901. Pacheenaht.—Sproat, Savage Life, 308, 1868, Pacheenett.—Mayne, Brit. Col., 251, 1862. Pachenah.—Whymper, Alaska, 79, 1869. Patcheena.—Grant in Jour. Roy. Geog. Soc., 293, 1857. Patcinā'ath.—Boas in 6th Rep. N. W. Tribes Can., 31, 1890.

Pachera. A small division of the Tarahumare, and the name of their principal village at the extreme headwaters of the N. branch of the Rio Nonoava, under the municipality of Guerrero, w. Chihuahua, Mexico. According to Orozco y Berra (Geog., 34, 1864) they spoke a dialect slightly different from that of the Tarahumare proper.

Pachera.—Zapata (1678) in Doc. Hist. Mex., 4th s., III, 333, 1857. Santa Rosa de Santa María.—Ibid.

Pachgantschihilas. See *Buckongahelas.*

Pachhepes. A former village in California, said to have been Esselen.—Taylor in Cal. Farmer, Apr. 20, 1860.

Pack. See *Shoe-pack.*

Pacohamoa ('trout'). A society or gens of the Sauk.

Pá-cŏ-hä-mŏ-ä.—Long, Exped. St Peter's R., II, 231, 1824.

Pacpul. A Coahuiltecan tribe at Caldera mission, Coahuila, in 1689. It was a chief of this tribe, called Juan, who assisted in taking one of the survivors of La Salle's party from N. of the Rio Grande to the presidio of Coahuila (Massanet in Texas Hist. Ass'n Quar., II, 284, 1899).

In 1691 Massanet had with him a Pacpul guide who explained to the Payaya Indians at San Antonio the meaning of the mass and interpreted Massanet's discourse (Diario, Mem. de la Nueva España, XXVII, 96, MS.). This indicates that the Coahuiltecan language extended to the San Antonio, at least. (H. E. B.)

Pacpoles.—Rivera, Diario, leg. 2763, 1736.

Pacsiol. A former Chumashan village near Purísima mission, Santa Barbara co., Cal.—Taylor in Cal. Farmer, Oct. 18, 1861.

Pacuaches. A former tribe of N. E. Mexico or s. Texas, evidently Coahuiltecan, members of which were gathered into San Bernardo mission on the lower Rio Grande, although their proper habitat was 15 leagues distant.

Paachiquis.—Massanet (1690), Dictamen Fiscal, Nov. 30, 1716, MS. cited by H. E. Bolton, inf'n, 1906 (probably identical). Pachagues.—Revilla-gigedo (1793) cited by Bancroft, Nat. Races, I, 611, 1886. Pachaques.—Fernando del Bosque (1675) in Nat. Geog. Mag., XIV, 347, 1903. Pachoches.—Padilla quoted by Orozco y Berra, Geog., 306, 1864. Pacúaches.—Revillagigedo, op. cit. Paguaches.—Orozco y Berra, op. cit., 307. Paguachis.—Ibid., 304. Parchaques.—Massanet (1690), op. cit.

Pacuáchiam. A tribe or subtribe, probably Coahuiltecan, met by Massanet in 1691 on Rio Hondo, Texas, which was called by the Indians Guanapajac. They were with other tribes or bands which Massanet called Sanpanal, Patchal, Papañaca, Parchiquis, Aguapálam, Samampác, Vánca, Payaván, and Patavó. At the same point Massanet was visited by the Pitahay, Apaysi, and Patsan or Patzau (Diario, in Doc. Hist. Tex., I, 94, MS.). The Colton map of Texas (1878) gives "Paguache crossing" just above Presidio San Juan Bautista, on the Rio Grande. Cf. *Pacuaches.* (H. E. B.)

Pacuchianis.—Massanet (1690) in Dictamen Fiscal, Nov. 30, 1716, MS. (identical?).

Paddle tablets. See *Duck tablets, Problematical objects.*

Padjegadjin (*Pa-dje'-ga-djin'*, 'forest extending across'). A former Kansa village on Kansas r., Kan. (J. O. D.)

Padli. A Padlimiut Eskimo settlement at the head of the fjord of the same name where the Akudnirmiut and Padlimiut gather in summer to catch salmon.—Boas in 6th Rep. B. A. E., map, 1888.

Padlimiut. A tribe of Central Eskimo occupying the E. coast of Baffin land from Exeter to C. Hooper and numbering 43 in 1883. Their villages are Ekaloaping, Idjuniving, Itijarelling, Karmakdjuin, Kekertakdjuin, Kingnelling, Padli, and Siorartijung.—Boas in 6th Rep. B. A. E., 441, 1888.

Padshilaika (Creek: 'pigeon roost'). A former Yuchi town at the junction of Patchilaika cr. with Flint r., Macon co., Ga. According to Hawkins the Yuchi moved there from Savannah r. soon after 1729.

Pad-gee-li-gau.—Hawkins (1799), Sketch, 62, 1848.

Padshiläïka.—Gatschet, Creek Migr. Leg., I, 142, 1884. **Pigeon Roost.**—Ibid.

Pafallaya. A province traversed by De Soto and his army in Nov. 1540, after the battle of Mauvila and before reaching Taliepatava, Cabusto, and Chicaça. It was probably in E. Mississippi. Pickett places it in Green, Marengo, and Sumter cos., w. Ala., and considers its people to have been Choctaw. See Gentl. of Elvas (1557) in French, Hist. Coll. La., II, 160, 1850.

Pagaichi. A former Tarahumare settlement on the headwaters of Rio Nonoava, s. w. Chihuahua, Mexico, 6 leagues N. of Carichic, and near Nonoava.
Pagaichi.—Zapata (1678) in Doc. Hist. Mex., 4th s., III, 329, 1857. **Paguichic.**—Orozco y Berra, Geog., 323, 1864. **Paguichique.**—Censo del Estado de Chihuahua, index, 11, 1904 (name of present pueblo).

Pagaits (*Pa-ga'-its*, 'fish-creek people'). A Paiute tribe formerly near Colville, s. E. Nevada; pop. 34 in 1873.—Powell in Ind. Aff. Rep. 1873, 50, 1874.

Pagantso (*Pa'-gan-tso*). A Paviotso division of 3 bands formerly living in Ruby valley, N. E. Nevada; pop. 172 in 1873.— Powell in Ind. Aff. Rep. 1873, 52, 1874.

Pagatsu (*Pä'gatsû*, 'head of the stream'). Mentioned by Mooney (14th Rep. B. A. E., 1045, 1896) as an extinct division of the Comanche. Cf. *Parkenaum*.

Pagayuats (*Pa-ga-yu-ats*). One of the tribes, known under the collective term Gosiute, formerly on Otter cr., s. w. Utah.—Powell and Ingalls in Ind. Aff. Rep. 1873, 51, 1874.

Paghuukdhinpe (*ʗaxu'-uʗɸiɴ'-de*, 'where they dwelt on a mountain'). A Santsukdhin Osage village on the E. side of Verdigris r., Ind. T.   (J. O. D.)

Pagmi. Described in 1554 (Ibarra cited by Bancroft, Ariz. and N. Mex., 73, 1889) as a most beautiful city adorned with very sumptuous edifices, extending over 3 leagues, with great houses of 3 stories, and with extensive plazas, and the houses surrounded with walls that appeared to be of masonry. The imaginary town was also represented as abandoned, the inhabitants having gone eastward. The locality was seemingly in what is now s. w. United States or N. w. Mexico.

Paguan. A tribe reported by Massanet (Dictamen Fiscal, Nov. 30, 1716, MS.) on the road from Coahuila to the Tejas (Texas) country in 1690, and probably affiliated with the Coahuiltecan stock. Cf. *Paguanan*.

Paguanan. A tribe or subtribe, members of which were baptized at San Antonio de Valero mission, Texas, in 1743–48. They may have been the same as the Payuguan (q. v.), as the two names are not found to have been used by the same writer. They were associated with the Caguas, Tou, Zana, Sijame, Ujuiape, and Hierbipiamo (Ervipiame) tribes, and

their language, some words of which are preserved, seems to have been the same as that of most of these other tribes (MS. Baptismal Rec., partidas 653, 681, 711, 782).   (H. E. B.)
Pahuanan.—Baptismal Rec., op. cit., 852, 1751.

Paguate (native name *Kwístyi*, 'take it down,' referring to an ancient tradition). A former summer village of the Lagunas, now a permanently occupied pueblo of that tribe; situated 8 m. N. of Laguna, Valencia co., N. Mex. Next to the parent pueblo it is said to be the oldest and largest of the Laguna villages, the population numbering 350 or 400. Not to be confounded with Pojoaque, although authors have confused the two names. See *Keresan Family, Laguna, Pueblos*. (F. W. H.)
Kvishti.—Loew (1875) in Wheeler Survey Rep., VII, 345, 1879. **Kwístyi.**—Hodge, field-notes, B. A. E., 1895. **Pagnati.**—Calhoun (1849) in Cal. Mess. and Corresp., 218, 1850. **Paguate.**—G. H. Pradt, letter to B. A. E., 1891. **Pahuata.**—Gwyther in Overland Mo., 262, Mar. 1871. **Pahuate.**—Collins in Ind. Aff. Rep. 1902, 255, 1903. **Pajuate.**—Donaldson, Moqui Pueblo Inds., 94, 1893. **Pogouaté.**—Gallatin in Nouv. Ann. Voy., 5th s., XXVII, 297, 1851. **Poguaque.**—Gallegos (1844) in Emory, Recon., 478, 1848. **Poguaté.**—Gallatin in Trans. Am. Ethnol. Soc., II, xciv, 1848. **Pohanti.**—Ten Broeck in Schoolcraft, Ind. Tribes, IV, 77, 1854. **Pojnati.**—Simpson in Smithson. Rep. 1869, 328, 1871. **Pojuaque.**—Parke, Map New Mexico, 1851. **Pojuate.**—Abert in Emory, Recon., 469, 1848. **Pojuato.**—Emory, ibid., 133. **Poquaté.**—Latham, Var. of Man, 395, 1850. **Povate.**—Loew (1875) in Wheeler Survey Rep., VII, 339, 1879. **Povuate.**—Ibid., 418. **Provate.**—Kingsley, Stand. Nat. Hist., VI, 183, 1883. **Pujuaque.**—Bancroft, Ariz. and N. Mex., 64, 1889. **Queesché.**—Pradt quoted by Hodge in Am. Anthrop., IV, 346, 1891.

Paguemi. Described by Ibarra in 1554 (Bancroft, Ariz. and N. Mex., 72, 1889) as an abandoned pueblo whose houses were of several stories, and where there were traces of metals having been smelted. Situated in a great plain "adjoining those of the *vacas*—the buffalo plains." It is apparently imaginary.

Paguits (*Pa-gu'-its*, 'fish people'). A Paiute band about Pagu (Fish) lake, s. w. Utah; pop. 68 in 1873.—Powell in Ind. Aff. Rep. 1873, 50, 1874.

Pagwiho (*Pa-gwi'-ho*). A Paviotso tribe formerly living in the adobe meadows near Mono lake, E. Cal.—Powell, Paviotso MS., B. A. E., 1881.

Pahatsi ('campers at the mountain top'). One of the three principal divisions of the Osage tribe, commonly known as Great Osage.
Bar-har-cha.—Pénicaut (1719) in French, Hist. Coll. La., I, 151, note, 1869. **Elder Osages.**—Dorsey in Am. Nat., 114, Feb. 1884. **Grand Eaux.**—Boudinot, Star in the West, 126, 1816. **Grandes eaux.**—French trader in Smith, Bouquet Exped., 70, 1776. **Grand Osâge.**—Lewis and Clark, Discov., 11, 1806. **Grand Tuo.**—Croghan (1759) quoted by Jefferson, Notes, 145, 1825. **Grand Zo.**—Lewis and Clark, Discov., 11, 1806. **Grand Zue.**—Croghan (1759) in Rupp, Hist. W. Pa., 146, note, 1846. **Great Osage.**—Fisher, New Trav., 15, 1812. **Great Ossage.**—Schermerhorn (1812) in Mass. Hist. Soc. Coll., 2d s., II, 31, 1814. **Great Ozages.**—Jefferys (1763), Am. Atlas, map 5, 1776. **Pa-ha-sca.**—Schoolcraft, Ind. Tribes, VI, 540, 1857. **ʗaɥsi.**—J. O. Dorsey, inf'n (own

name).　ꞯahéꞱsi.—Dorsey, Osage MS. vocab., B.
A. E., 1883.

Pahkanu. A band of Indians, probably
Moquelumnan, formerly frequenting the
banks of Stanislaus and Tuolumne. rs.,
central California.—Wessells (1853) in
H. R. Ex. Doc. 76, 34th Cong., 3d sess.,
30, 1857.

Paho. See *Prayer-sticks.*

Pahoc. Mentioned by Oviedo (Hist.
Gen. Indies, III, 628, 1853) as one of the
provinces or villages, probably on the
South Carolina coast, visited by Ayllon
in 1520.

Pahosalgi. An extinct Creek clan, the
name of which can be traced only in war
titles, as Pahós'-hádsho.—Gatschet, Creek
Migr. Leg., I, 155, 1884.

Pahquetooai ('rainbow town'). A vil-
lage of the ancestors of the present Tigua
pueblo of Isleta, N. Mex.
P'ah-que-too'-ai.—Lummis, Man who Married the
Moon, 161, 1894. **Piaqui.**—Oñate (1598) in Doc.
Inéd., XVI, 102, 1871 (possibly identical).

Pahshapaha. See *Pashipaho.*

Pahuirachic. A former rancheria of the
Tarahumare in the district and municipality of Guerrero, Chihuahua, Mexico,
but now a civilized rancho, with 662 inhabitants in 1900.
Pahuirachic.—Censo del Estado de Chihuahua, 12,
1904. **Paquirachic.**—Orozco y Berra, Geog., 323,
1864.

Pahvant. A Ute division occupying a
considerable territory in w. central Utah,
their chief seat being Corn cr. According
to Powell they speak the same language
as the Uintah, and socially affiliate and
intermarry with them. Some are now on
Uintah res., and are classed officially with
the Ute. There were said to be 134 in
Utah in 1885, not under an agent.
Pagampache.—Escalante (1776) quoted by Duro,
Peñalosa, 142, 1882 (probably identical). **Pagam-
pachis.**—Dominguez and Escalante (1776) in Doc.
Hist. Mex., 2d s., I, 537, 1854. **Paguampe.**—Esca-
lante quoted by Simpson (1859), Expl. Across
Utah, 494, 1876. **Pah-Vantes.**—Simpson, ibid., 459.
Pahvants.—Remy and Brenchley, Jour. to Great
Salt Lake, II, 349, 1841. **Pah Vauts.**—Morris (1853)
in H. R. Doc. 18, 33d Cong., 1st sess., 5, 1854 (mis-
print). **Pah Vents.**—Head in Ind. Aff. Rep., 149,
1868. **Pahvontee.**—Doty, ibid., 1864, 175, 1865.
Parant Utahs.—Wilson in Ind. Aff. Rep., 67, 1860.
Paravan Yuta.—Burton, City of Saints, 577, 1861.
Parvain.—Carvalho, Travels, 187, 1857. **Parvan.**—
Simpson, op. cit., 51. **Par Vans.**—Hatch in Ind.
Aff. Rep. 1863, 116, 1864. **Pauvans.**—Call (1856) in
H. R. Ex. Doc. 29, 37th Cong., 2d sess., 40, 1862.
Pauvante.—Bradley (1856), ibid., 36. **Pavant
Utahs.**—Wilson (1849) in Cal. Mess. and Corresp.,
185, 1850. **Pavant Yuta.**—Burton, City of Saints,
577, 1861. **Pohbantes.**—Hurt in Ind. Aff. Rep.
1855, 200, 1856. **Povantes.**—Collins, ibid., 125, 1861.
Puaguampe.—Dominguez and Escalante (1776) in
Doc. Hist. Mex., 2d s., I, 468, 1854 (trans. 'hechi-
ceros,' i. e. 'sorcerers').

Paiinkkhwutthu (*Pai'-in-kqwŭ'-t'çû*). A
former Yaquina village on the s. side of
Yaquina r., Oreg.—Dorsey in Jour. Am.
Folk-lore, III, 229, 1890.

Paimiut ('mouth-of-river people'). A
Kuskwogmiut Eskimo village on Kuskokwim r., 25 m. above Bethel, Alaska; pop.
30 in 1880.

Paimut.—Russian form cited by Baker, Geog.
Dict. Alaska, 487, 1906. **Paimute.**—Petroff, Rep.
on Alaska, 17, 1884.

Paimiut. An Ikogmiut Eskimo village
on the s. bank of Yukon r., 38 m. above
Russian Mission, Alaska, lat. 62°, 10',
lon. 160° 10'. Pop. 89 in 1880, 65 in 1890.
Paimiut.—11th Census, Alaska, 165, 1893. **Pai-
mjut.**—Holmberg, Ethnog. Skizz., map, 1855.
Paimut.—Zagoskin in Nouv. Ann. Voy., 5th s.,
XXI, map, 1850. **Paimute.**—Petroff in 10th Census,
Alaska, map, 1884.

Painting. The tribes N. of Mexico, as
well as those of every part of the continent except, perhaps, the higher arctic
regions, delighted in the use of color. It
was very generally employed for embellishing the person and in applying decorative and symbolic designs to habitations,
sculptures, masks, shields, articles of bark,
skin, pottery, etc., in executing pictographs upon natural surfaces of many
kinds, as on cliffs and the walls of caverns,
and in preparing the symbolic embellishments of altars and sacred chambers (see
Dry-painting, Graphic art). Color was
applied to the person for decorative purposes as an
essential
feature of
the toilet:
for impress-
ing behold-
ers with ad-
miration or
fear; for
purposes of
obscurity
and decep-
tion; in ap-
plying tri-
bal, person-

ESKIMO BRUSHES AND PAINTING STICKS

al, or other denotive devices; in the application of symbolic designs, especially on
ceremonial occasions; and as a means of
protection from insects and the sun (see
Adornment). The native love of color
and skill in its use were manifested especially in decorative work. This is illustrated by the wonderful masks and totem
poles of the N. W. coast tribes (Boas),
and in the artistic polychrome pottery
(q. v.) of the Pueblos (Fewkes). Little
advance had been made in representative
or pictorial art, yet some of the productions are noteworthy, as illustrated in the
Hopi *katcina* work (Fewkes) and in the
Kiowa ceremonial paintings on skins described by Mooney, although some of the
latter show unmistakable evidence of the
influence of the whites.

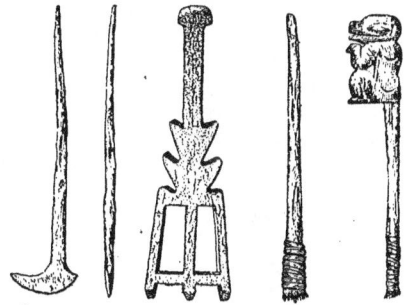

The pigments were derived from many
sources, but were mainly of mineral origin (see *Dyes and Pigments*), especially
the oxides of iron (see *Hematite*) and carbonate of copper. The aborigines were
skilled in preparing the mineral colors,
which were usually ground in small mortars or rubbed down on a flat stone, and

in extracting stains and dyes from vegetal substances. The colors were applied with a dry point or surface, as with a piece of chalk, charcoal, or clay; or, when mixed with water or oil, with the fingers or hand, or a stick, brush, or pad, and also sprayed on with the mouth, as in Pueblo mask painting. Brushes were rude, consisting often of fibrous substances, such as bits of wood, bark, yucca, or reeds, chewed, beaten, or rubbed at one end until sufficiently pliable to deliver the color; and great skill was shown by many of the tribes in the use of these crude tools. Hair was not in general use, although excellent brushes are now made by the more advanced tribes. The brushes used by the tribes of the N. W. coast were often provided with beautifully carved handles. Very interesting painting implements are seen in some sections. Paddle-shaped or spatulate bits of wood are used, applied edgewise for thin lines and flatwise for covering spaces; and striping tools having two or three points and neatly carved of bone and ivory are in use by the Eskimo (Turner). The Plains tribes employed a flat piece of spongy bone from the knee joint of a buffalo or an ox; it has a sharp edge of rounded outline which serves for drawing lines, while the flat side serves for spreading the color over large areas. These tools, being porous, have the advantage of holding a quantity of liquid color. Shells were frequently used for paint cups, while for this purpose the Pueblos made miniature jars and bowls of pottery, sometimes in clusters. Colors in the form of powder, sand, clay, and meal were used, and are still used, by several tribes in preparing dry-paintings (q. v.) for ceremonial purposes which are executed on the floors of ceremonial chambers or altars (Matthews, Stevenson, Fewkes). See *Art, Ornament.*

Consult Boas (1) in 6th Rep. B. A. E., 1888, (2) in Mem. Am. Mus. Nat. Hist., II, Anthrop. I, 1898; Dorsey in 11th Rep. B. A. E., 1894; Fewkes in 17th, 21st, and 22d Reps. B. A. E.; Hoffman in 7th Rep. B. A. E., 1891; Holmes in Smithson. Rep. 1903, 1904; Mooney in 17th Rep. B. A. E., 1898; Niblack in Nat. Mus. Rep. 1888, 1890; Stevenson (1) in 5th Rep. B. A. E., 1887, (2) in 11th Rep. B. A. E., 1894; Turner in 11th Rep. B. A. E., 1894. (W. H. H.)

Paint Town. A Cherokee settlement on lower Soco cr., within the reservation in Jackson and Swain cos., N. C.—Mooney in 19th Rep. B. A. E., 509, 1900.
Ani'-Wâdihï'.—Mooney, ibid. ('place of the Paint people or clan': native name).

Paisin. A former Kalindaruk village near Monterey bay, Cal., whose inhabitants were connected with San Carlos and San Juan Bautista missions.
Pagnines.—Taylor in Cal. Farmer, Nov. 23, 1860. **Pagosines.**—Engelhardt, Franc. in Cal., 398, 1897.

Pagsin.—A. L. Kroeber, inf'n, 1903. **Paycines.**—Engelhardt, op. cit. **Paysim.**—Taylor in Cal. Farmer, Apr. 20, 1860.

Paiuiyunitthai (*Pai'-u-i-yu'-nĭt-t'çai*). A former Kuitsh village on lower Umpqua r., Oreg.—Dorsey in Jour. Am. Folklore, III, 231, 1890.

Paiute. A term involved in great confusion. In common usage it has been applied at one time or another to most of the Shoshonean tribes of w. Utah, N. Arizona, s. Idaho, E. Oregon, Nevada, and E. and s. California. The generally ac-

PAIUTE MAN

cepted idea is that the term originated from the word *pah*, 'water,' and *Ute*, hence 'water Ute'; or from *pai*, 'true,' and *Ute*—'true Ute'; but neither of these interpretations is satisfactory. Powell states that the name properly belongs exclusively to the Corn Creek tribe of s. w. Utah, but has been extended to include many other tribes. In the present case the term is employed as a convenient divisional name for the tribes occupying s. w. Utah from about the locality of Beaver, the s. w. part of Nevada, and the

N. w. part of Arizona, excluding the Chemehuevi.

With regard to the Indians of Walker River and Pyramid Lake reservations, who constitute the main body of those commonly known as Paiute, Powell claims that they are not Paiute at all, but

PAIUTE WOMAN

another tribe which he calls Paviotso. He says: "The names by which the tribes are known to white men and the department give no clue to the relationship of the Indians. For example, the Indians in the vicinity of the reservation on the Muddy and the Indians on the Walker River and Pyramid Lake reservations are called Pai or Pah Utes, but the Indians know only those on the Muddy by that name, while those on the other two reservations are known as Paviotsoes, and speak a very different language, but closely allied to, if not identical with, that of the Bannocks" (Powell and Ingalls in Ind. Aff. Rep. 1873). The Indians of Walker r. and Pyramid lake claim the Bannock as their cousins, and say that they speak the same language. The different small bands have little political coherence, and there is no recognized head-chief. The most influential chiefs among them in modern times have been Winnemucca, who died a few years ago, and Natchez. As a rule they have been peaceable and friendly toward the whites, although in the early sixties they several times came into collision with miners and

emigrants, hostility being frequently provoked by the whites themselves. The northern Paiute were more warlike than those of the S., and a considerable number of them took part with the Bannock in the war of 1878. Owing to the fact that the great majority of the Paiute (including the Paviotso) are not on reservations, many of them being attached to the ranches of white men, it is impossible to determine their population, but they may be safely estimated at from 6,500 to 7,000. In 1906 those on reservations in all Nevada were reported to number, at Walker River res., 486; at Moapa res., 129; at Pyramid Lake res., 554; at Duck Valley (Western Shoshoni agency), 267; not under an agency (1900), 3,700. In Utah there were 76 Kaibab, 154 Shivwits, and 370 Paiute not under an agency; in Arizona, 350 Paiute under the Western Nevada School Superintendent.

As a people the Paiute are peaceable, moral, and industrious, and are highly commended for their good qualities by those who have had the best opportunities for judging. While apparently not as bright in intellect as the prairie tribes, they appear to possess more solidity of character. By their willingness and efficiency as workers they have made themselves necessary to the white farmers and

GROUP OF PAIUTE

have been enabled to supply themselves with good clothing and many of the comforts of life, while on the other hand they have steadily resisted the vices of civilization, so that they are spoken of by one agent as presenting the "singular anomaly" of improvement by contact with the whites. Another authority says: "To these habits and excellence of character may be attributed the fact that they are annually increasing in numbers, and that they are strong, healthy, active people. Many of them are employed as laborers on the farms of white men in all seasons, but they are especially serviceable during the time of harvesting and haymaking." Aside from their earnings among the whites, they derive subsistence from the fish of the lakes, jackrabbits and small game of the sage plains and mountains, and from piñon nuts and other seeds, which they grind into flour for bread. Their ordinary dwelling is the wikiup, or small rounded hut, of tule rushes over a framework of poles, with the ground for a floor and the fire in the center, and almost entirely open at the top. Strangely enough, although appreciating the advantages of civilization so far as relates to good clothing and to such food as they can buy at the stores, they manifest no desire to live in permanent houses or to procure the furniture of civilization, and their wikiups are almost bare of everything excepting a few wicker or grass baskets of their own weaving.

Following are the Paiute bands so far as known: Hokwaits, Ichuarumpats, Kaibab, Kwaiantikwokets, Kwiengomats, Kwiumpus, Moapariats, Moquats, Movwiats, Nauwanatats, Nogwats, Nuaguntits, Pagaits, Paguits, Paraniguts, Paruguns, Parumpaiats, Parumpats, Paspikaivats, Pawipits, Pintiats, Sauwontiats, Shivwits, Timpashauwagotsits, Tsuwarits, Uainuints, Uinkarets, Unkakaniguts, Unkapanukuints, Utumpaiats, and Yagats.   (H. W. H. J. M.)

Auölasús.—ten Kate, Reizen in N. A., 160, 1885 (='Mezcal-Schoenen': Pima name). Ca-hualchitz.—Whipple, Pac. R. R. Rep., III, pt. 3, 16, 1856 (this and the various forms by Garcés are from Kohoaldje, the Mohave name of the Virgin r. Paiute.—Kroeber). Cajualas.—Garcés quoted by Escudero, Not. Estad. de Chihuahua, 228, 1834. Cajuales.—Garcés (1776), Diary, 472, 1900. Chemebet Quajala.—Ibid., 303. Chemegue cajuala.—Orozco y Berra, Geog., 349, 1864 (misprint from Garcés). Chemegué Cuajála.—Garcés, op. cit., 444. Chemeguet Cajuala.—Ibid., 475. Chemeque-caprala.—Cortez (1799) quoted in Pac. R. R. Rep., III, pt. 3, 126, 1856 (misprint of Garcés' Chemegué Cuajála). Da-da'-ze ni'-ka-cin'-ga.—Dorsey, Kansas MS. vocab. B. A. E., 1882 (= 'grasshopper people': Kansa name). Diggers.—Howe, Hist. Coll., 419, 1851. Hogăpa'goni.—Mooney in 14th Rep. B. A. E., 1048, 1896 ('rush-arrow people': Shoshoni name). Kohoaldje.—Kroeber, inf'n, 1905 (Mohave name of Virgin r. Paiute). Nüma.—Mooney in 14th Rep. B. A. E., 1048, 1896 ('people', 'Indians': own name). Pa'gonotch.—Gatschet, MS., B. A. E. (Southern Ute name). Pah-Edes.—Head in Ind. Aff. Rep., 122, 1866. Pahmetes.—Wilson, ibid., 1849, 67, 1850. Pahnutes Utahs.—Wilson (1849) in Cal. Mess. and Corresp., 185, 1850. Pah-rú-sá-páh.—Whipple in Pac. R. R. Rep., III, pt. 3, 16, 1856 (Chemehuevi name). Pah-Touts.—Sen. Misc. Doc. 53, 45th Cong., 3d sess., 78, 1879. Pahusitahs.—Remy and Brenchley, Journ. to Great Salt Lake, II, 388, 1841. Pah-Utah.—Möllhausen, Journ. to Pacific, I, 46, 1858. Pah-Utes.—Forney in Ind. Aff. Rep. 1859, 366, 1860. Paiá'ti.—Henshaw, Panamint MS. vocab., B. A. E. (Panamint name). Pai-Ides.—Audouard, Far West, 182, 1869. Pai-

uches.—Farnham, Mexico, map, 1846. Paiulee.—Remy and Brenchley, op. cit., I, 38. Paiutes.—Poston in Ind. Aff. Rep. 1863, 387, 1864. Pai-yu'chimŭ.—Mooney in 14th Rep. B. A. E., 1048, 1896 (Hopi name). Pai-yúdshi.—Corbusier, inf'n ('all eyes': Yavapai name; corrupted from "Paiute"). Pai-yu'tsĭ.—Mooney in 14th Rep. B. A. E., 1048, 1896 (Navaho name). Pan-Utahs.—Domenech, Deserts N. Am., II, 64, 1860. Parusi.—Escalante et al. (1775) in Duro, Peñalosa, 142, 1882 (probably identical). Pasuchis.—Escudero, Not. Nuevo Méx., 83, 1849. Pa-uches.—Collins in Ind. Aff. Rep., 125, 1861. Pa-u-da.—Ibid. Pa-utes.—Hinton, Handbook Ariz., 361, 1871. Paynutes.—Wilson (1849) in Cal. Mess. and Corresp., 185, 1850. Payoche.—Ten Broeck (1852) in Schoolcraft, Ind. Tribes, IV, 82, 1854. Payuchas.—Garcés (1776), Diary, 405, 1900. Payuches.—Ibid., 351. Páyukue.—Gatschet, MS., B. A. E. (Zuñi name). Payutas.—Platt, Karte Nord-Am., 1861. Payutsín dinné.—Gatschet, MS., B. A. E. (Navaho name). Pazuchis.—Orozco y Berra, Geog., 59, 1864. (Pey) metes Utahs.—Wilson in Ind. Aff. Rep. 1849, 67, 1850. Pey-ute.—Forney, ibid., 1859, 364, 1860. Piedes.—Carvalho, Travels, 213, 1857. Pi-Edes.—Beadle, Undeveloped West, 658, 1873. Pie Edes.—Hatch in Ind. Aff. Rep. 1863, 116, 1864. Pi-eeds.—Simpson (1859), Rep. of Expl. Across Utah, 35, 1876. Pieutes.—Barney (1857) in H. R. Ex. Doc. 29, 37th Cong., 2d sess, 78, 1862. Pi-u-chas.—Graves in Ind. Aff. Rep., 386, 1854. Piute.—Mooney in 14th Rep. B. A. E., 1048, 1896 (popular name, Eng. pron.). Py-eeds.—Simpson, Rep., op. cit., 35. Pyentes.—Palmer, Travels, 35, 1847. Snake Diggers.—Simpson, op. cit., 460 (Pah-Utahs or). Ute Diggers.—Ibid. Yabipai Cajuala.—Garcés (1776), Diary, 444, 1900. Yavipai cajuala.—Garcés misquoted by Orozco y Berra, Geog., 41, 1864. Yavipais-caprala.—Garcés misquoted by Cortez (1779) in Pac. R. R. Rep., III, pt. 3, 126, 1856.

Paiute Snakes. Given as a Shoshoni band on Klamath res., Oreg.
Piute Snakes.—Ind. Aff. Rep., 344, 1873.

Pajalat. One of three tribes mentioned by Espinosa (Chrónica Apostolica, I, 459, 1746) as living near San Antonio r., Texas, when the Franciscan missions were removed thither in 1730–31. The other two were the Pacao and Pitalaque (probably the same as the Pachalaque). There were numerous Pajalat in Concepción mission before 1748, and they intermarried there freely with the Patumacas, Pujanes (Cujanes?), Patalcas, and Tilpacopales (MS. records of the mission). They are given as a tribe distinct from the Pachalaque in the records of Concepción mission; for instance, one missionary records marrying a Pajalat and a Pachalaque, which is evidence that these were not considered merely two forms of the same name, though they were probably closely related. According to Gatschet there was a Tonkawa gens or subtribe bearing the same name (Páχalatch, 'mouth open').   (H. E. B.)

Paalat.—Espinosa, Chrónica Apost., I, 459, 1746. Pajalaches.—MS., May 13, 1752, in Béxar Archives, Texas. Pajalames.—Orozco y Berra, Geog., 384, 391, 1864. Pajalaques.—Ibid., 304. Pajalât.—Rivera, Diario, leg. 2602, 1736. Pajalatames.—Padilla quoted by Orozco y Berra, op. cit., 306. Pajalites.—Informe, 1762, in Mem. de Nueva España, XXVIII, 167, MS. Pallalat.—Uhde, Länder, 121, 1861. Páχalatch—A. S. Gatschet, Tonkawe MS. vocab., B. A. E., 1884 (given as a Tonkawa gens).

Pajarito (Span.: 'little bird'). A tribe, evidently Coahuiltecan, at Camargo, on the Rio Grande, in 1757, with Venados, Tejones, Tareguanos, and Cueros Quemados. Of the Pajaritos, 56 individuals were in the mission (Joseph Tienda de Cuervo, Revista of Camargo, July 13, 1757, in Archivo Gen., Hist., LVI). The Venados were given by García in 1760 as one of the tribes speaking the language of his Manual, i. e. Coahuiltecan. In 1780 Gov. Cabello reported the Paxahitos, evidently the same as the Pajaritos, as a coast tribe s. of the mouth of the Rio Grande. With them he enumerated the Comecrudos, Texones, Guianapaqueños (*sic*), Manyateños, Cotanans, Aguichachas, and Cueros Quemados (Rep. on coast tribes, May 28, 1780, Béxar Archives, Province of Texas). (H. E. B.)

Pajarito Park (Span. : 'little bird', adapted from the Tewa *Tshirege*, 'bird', the name of an important ruin within the limits of the tract). Geographically, this term stands for a high, park-like tableland about 40 m. in length and from 15 to 25 m. in width, on the w. side of the Rio Grande in N. New Mexico. It is limited on the N. by the Rio Chama, on the w. by the Jemez mts., and on the s. by the Cañada de Cochiti. It forms the E. side of the Jemez plateau. The tableland is of volcanic origin, its surface from the base of the mountains eastward being capped by a sheet of volcanic tufa, varying in thickness from 100 to 2,000 ft, which had its origin as volcanic ash deposited from the ancient craters of the Jemez range. These great tufa beds vary in color from gray to yellow, and geologically are of vast age. On the E. rim of the s. part of the tableland, along the Rio Grande, are extensive basaltic extrusions of comparatively recent origin, while the bluffs forming the E. rim of the N. half are formed of the conglomerates which mark the w. shore-line of the Miocene lake that once occupied the basin now known as Española valley. Recent basaltic extrusions also occur on the N. rim of the park along the Rio Chama. The mean altitude of the park is about 7,000 ft. The high w. side is heavily forested with pine and spruce; along the Rio Grande side the mesas are covered only with buffalo grass, while between these two extremes lies a zone lightly covered with piñon and juniper, interspersed with stretches of open land. This zone, now comparatively barren from lack of water, was evidently covered with tilled fields at some remote time. Torrential erosion in past ages has dissected this once continuous level tableland into a series of narrow elevated parallel mesas, better described by the Spanish term *potreros*, extending out from the mountains toward the Rio Grande. These potreros vary in width from a few yards to 2 or 3 m. and from ½ m. to 5 m. in length. They present, especially on the s. side, perpendicular

escarpments of from 50 to 500 ft in height, at the base of which is invariably a long talus slope. The canyons lying between the potreros are usually little valleys from ¼ m. to 1 m. in width, divided by a now dry arroyo bordered by a narrow, level and very fertile floodplain. These little valleys are now lightly wooded, but show every evidence of tillage in remote times. Pajarito Park is now for the greater part devoid of water except on the side at the base of the mountains. The only streams that carry their water to the Rio Grande for any considerable part of the year are the Santa Clara, the Bravo, and the Rito de los Frijoles. Others sink in the sand within a few miles of their source, and a vast number carry water at all only in flood season. There are very few perennial springs in the park. The principal canyons that cut through it from w. to E. are as follows, beginning at the N.: the Santa Clara, the Chupadero, the Guages, the Alamo, the Pajarito, the Rito de los Frijoles. Between them are hundreds of smaller canyons.

Ethnologically Pajarito Park is of great importance. It stands for a plainly marked, prehistoric ethnic area, the investigation of which throws much light on the ethnological problems of the S. W. The zone of ancient habitation extends from N. to s. the entire length of the park. It is only from 5 to 10 m. in width, and lies between the high timbered western slope and the narrow barren eastern rim overlooking the Rio Grande. The inhabited area did not exceed 300 sq. m. in extent.

The characteristic archeological remains are the ancient pueblo ruins and excavated cliff-dwellings. The latter class of remains exists in vast numbers. Almost every escarpment that presents a southern exposure is honeycombed with these dwellings (see *Cliff-dwellings*). Many natural caves, originally formed by water and wind erosion, have been utilized for dwelling purposes, either with or without modification, though usually there has been some shaping by excavation to render the home more commodious or convenient. In the form of lodge generally found in the softer tufa formations, the entire front of the cave is open. In some instances the front is closed by a wall of masonry which is entered through a small doorway with stone casing. Another form of cliff-houses of this same general class, which exists here in even greater numbers than those just described, is the wholly excavated dwelling. These are found in the firmer strata of tufa where the walls are less liable to crumble. In these a small doorway has been cut into the perpendicular face of the cliff to a depth of from 1 to 4 ft. The excavation is then expanded into a room usually of sufficient height only to permit of standing erect, varying from roughly circular to rectangular. These rooms rarely exceed 10 ft in the greatest dimension, except those which were used for ceremonial purposes. In these dwellings the main living room usually contains prayer-meal niches, alcoves, and in many cases small back rooms, probably for storage, are connected with them. There is usually a crude fireplace beside the doorway, a ventilating aperture at the floor level and another for a smoke vent above the door. There are no windows. In front of the dwellings, against the cliffs, verandas were built of poles and stone that doubtless served for living rooms during a considerable part of the year. The entire number of excavated cliff-dwellings in Pajarito Park would reach several thousand.

Of the other general class of archeological remains, viz, ancient Pueblo ruins, there are two forms: (1) The "small house" ruins, containing from 2 to 100 rooms, that never exceeded one story in height, of which there are large numbers scattered over the mesa tops and in the valleys. They are of great age and seem to belong to an epoch when the mesas were well watered and the population diffused over considerable areas. (2) The great community houses contained from 1,000 to 1,200 rooms, and 2 to 4 stories. The most noteworthy of these, named from N. to S., are Chipiinuinge, Kwengyauinge, Teeuinge, Poihuuinge, Puye, Shufinne, Tshirege, Otowi, Tsankawi, Tyuonyi, Yapashi, Haatse, Kuapa, and Kotyiti. We find in these the prototype of the present terraced community houses of Taos, Zuñi, and the Hopi villages. Many of the ancient buildings were of much greater size than any of the Pueblo houses of the present day. They were built in nearly all cases of stone rudely dressed and laid in adobe mortar. Ceilings and roofs were made of poles, brush, bark, and clay. Floors were made of adobe firmly tamped and smoothed. Walls were plastered with abobe mud, over which a thin wash made of "white earth" was laid from time to time. Doors were small and cased with stone, rarely with wood. There were no real windows. Small circular apertures near the floor aided ventilation. Fireplaces were usually placed beside the doors. These buildings differ from the large Pueblo houses of the present day in having no large and fairly commodious rooms, all apartments being mere rectangular cells ranging in size from 6 × 8 ft to 8 × 14 ft. Exterior rooms in all cases were entered by ladders from above. The type form of these great houses is that of four rectangular structures surrounding a squarish court. Many are found with one or more of the sides open. With the increase of the community additional courts were developed.

The circular kiva, always wholly or in great part subterranean, accompanies all the larger pueblos, from 1 to 15 being found in and about each village. Small reservoirs and other vestiges of primitive irrigation works are found about the large buildings only. The entire district is rich in pictography, the best specimens of which are found etched upon the vertical walls of the cliffs.

The principal collections of archeological material from Pajarito Park are to be found in the National Museum at Washington and the Southwest Museum at Los Angeles, Cal. Noteworthy facts shown by these collections are that the art of decorative glazing was quite advanced among these people, and that their system of symbolism was distinct from any other known. The study of the skeletal remains discloses the fact that the ancient inhabitants of Pajarito Park were a homogeneous people, of medium stature, and of rather inferior muscular development. The prevailing cranial type was dolichocephalic. In view of the fact that the predominant cranial type among the people of all the adjacent Pueblo villages at the present time is brachycephalic, this is of great ethnologic interest. As yet nothing further can be said concerning the relationship of these ancient people to any existing tribes. The time of occupancy of the ancient pueblo and cliff houses is conjectural. Excavations have yielded not a single vestige of Spanish influence, and traditions reaching back of four centuries are of questionable value in determining even approximate chronology. However, both archeological and geological evidence point to long occupancy and remote abandonment of these sites. Tentatively, from 2 to 4 centuries may be assigned as the length of time they had been abandoned before the Spanish invasion in 1540, and it may be said that the accumulating evidence now points to the lengthening of that period. There are no evidences of events of catastrophic character to have caused the disappearance of their inhabitants. In all probability their migration was caused by progressive desiccation of the country and the pressure of predatory enemies.

For further information, with ground plans and other illustrations, see Hewett in Bull. 32, B. A. E., 1906. Consult also the articles on the several ruins above mentioned.   (E. L. H.)

Pajassuck. A village in central Massachusetts, apparently on Connecticut r., in 1663.—Pynchon (1663) in N. Y. Doc. Col. Hist., XIII, 308, 1881.

Pakab. The Reed (*Phragmites communis*) phratry of the Hopi, which includes the following clans: Pakab, Kwahu (Eagle), Kwayo (Hawk), Koyonya (Turkey), Tawa (Sun), Paluna (Twin Brother of Puhukonghoya), Shohu (Star), Massikwayo (Chicken-hawk), Kahabi (Willow), and Tebi (Greasewood). The Reed phratry of Fewkes corresponds with the Eagle phratry of Stephen (8th Rep. B. A. E., 39, 1891). According to tradition this people came to Tusayan from the w. and s., apparently settling first at Mishongnovi.
Pa'-kab nyû-mû.—Fewkes in Am. Anthrop., VII, 403, 1894 (*nyû-mû*='phratry').

Pakab. The Reed or Arrow clan of the Hopi.
Bakab.—Voth, Hopi Proper Names, 75, 1905. Pákab.—Voth, Oraibi Summer Snake Ceremony, 282, 1903. Pakab wiñwû.—Fewkes in 19th Rep. B. A. E., 584, 1900 (*wiñwû*='clan'). Pa'-kab wüñwû.—Fewkes in Am. Anthrop., VII, 403, 1894.

Pakachoog. A former Nipmuc village near Worcester, Mass., probably in Millbury. It was occupied in 1674 by Praying Indians.
Boggachoag.—Kinnicutt, Ind. Names, 33, 1905. Packachoog.—Ibid. Packachooge.—Gookin (1677) in Trans. Am. Antiq. Soc., II, 467, 1836. Pakachoag.—Worcester Spy, Aug. 7, 1885. Pakachoog.—Gookin (1674) in Mass. Hist. Soc. Coll., 1st s., I, 192, 1806. Pakashoag.—Letter of 1676 quoted by Drake, Ind. Chron., 131, 1836. Pakaskoag.—Ibid. (misprint). Pakodch-oog.—Tooker, Algonq. Ser., X, 43, 1901 (given as probably original form; trans. 'they are finished, completed, perfect').

Pakadasank. An important village, probably of the Munsee, formerly about the site of Crawford, Orange co., N. Y.
Pakadasank.—Ruttenber, Tribes Hudson R., 392, 1872. Pekadasank.—Doc. of 1756 quoted by Ruttenber, Tribes Hudson R., 393, 1872.

Pakamali. Probably the Maidu of Big Meadows, Cal., from *Paqā'mali*, the name by which the Maidu are known to most of the Achomawi.
Pá-ka-mal-li.—Powers in Cont. N. A. Ethnol., III, 274, 1877. Paqāmali.—Dixon in Bull. Am. Mus. Nat. Hist., XVII, 123, 1905.

Pakan. See *Pecan*.

Pakanchi (*Pa'-kan-chi*). A former Nishinam village in the valley of Bear r., N. of Sacramento, Cal.
Pácanche.—Powers in Overland Mo., XII, 22, 1874. Pakanchi.—Powers in Cont. N. A. Ethnol., III, 316, 1877.

Pakani (*Pa'-ka-ni*). A Tonkawa gens of which there were only 5 survivors in 1884. (A. S. G.)

Pakan-Tallahassee (*ipákan* 'may-apple'(?), *itálua* 'town', *hássi* 'ancient' in the sense of waste). A former Upper Creek town on Pakan-Tallahassee cr. (Corn cr.?), which joins Coosa r. from the E. about 4 m. above the present Wetumpka, Elmore co., Ala.
Buknatallahassa.—Robin, Voy., II, map, 1807. Old Peach Orchard Town.—J. W. Stidham, inf'n to A. S. Gatschet (*ipákana*='peach'). Pákan'-Talahássi.—

Gatschet, Creek Migr. Leg., I, 142, 1884. Pockentallahassee.—Creek paper (1836) in H. R. Rep. 37, 31st Cong., 2d sess., 122, 1851. Pockentalleehassee.—Sen. Ex. Doc. 425, 24th Cong., 1st sess., 299, 1836. Pocontallahasse.—Bartram, Travels, 461, 1791. Pocuntullahases.—Swan (1791) in Schoolcraft, Ind. Tribes, V, 262, 1855. Puo-cun-tal-lau-has-see.—Hawkins (1799), Sketch, 41, 1848. Puckantala.—Bartram, Voy., I, map, 1799. Puckautalla.—Philippeaux, Map Engl. Col., 1781. Puckuntallahasse.—Pickett, Hist. Ala., II, 267, 1851. Tuecuntallauhassee.—Schoolcraft, Ind. Tribes, IV, 380, 1854.

Pakan Tallahassee. A town of the Creek Nation on Canadian r. below Hilabi, Okla.
Pákan-Talahássi.—Gatschet, Creek Migr. Leg., II, 186, 1888.

Pakataghkon (probably for *pachatachan*, 'split wood.'—Gerard). A former Delaware village, situated a mile from the present Margaretsville, Delaware co., N. Y., at the mouth of Bush Kill. This village is located on the Popachton or Papotunk branch on Sauthier's map of 1779. (W. M. B.)

Pakawa (from *Pakawai*, referring to tattooing.—Gatschet). Specifically a division of the Coahuiltecan family living not far from San Antonio r., Texas, in the 18th century. Espinosa says that when the missions were removed from E. Texas to this river in 1730–31 there were "in sight three tribes of very docile gentile Indians, the Pacaos, Pajalat, and Pitalaque, who together number more than a thousand persons" (Chrónica Apostolica, I, 459, 1746). Some of them entered San Francisco de la Espada mission with the Axcahomos, but deserted in 1737 (Ysasmendi to the Governor, Nov. 22, 1737, MS.). In 1738 Pedro, a "Pachao," was "governor" of this mission (MS. of 1738 in the Archivo General). Some of the tribe were also at Concepción, according to manuscript records of the mission, and "Pacuas" were also at San Bernardo mission, on the Rio Grande (Morfi, Viage de Indios, 442, 1856). (H. E. B.)

Generically the term Pakawa has been applied by Gatschet to include a linguistic family formerly living on both sides of the lower Rio Grande, and practically identical with the Coahuiltecan family (q. v.). Its numerous dialects, according to Gatschet, were spoken in the w. as far as the Sierra Madre and in the E. to or beyond San Antonio r. One dialect of it is preserved in the Manual of Padre Bartholomé García (1760). The tribe to which the name Pakawa appears to apply is that mentioned as the Pintos (Span. 'painted' or 'tattooed'), Pacaos, or Pacuas, etc., their name in their own language, according to Gatschet, being Estok-pakawaila or Newasol-pakawai or, without the prefix, Pakawai or Pakawaila. The only survivors of the tribe in 1886 were two women who were found by Gatschet on the s. bank of the Rio

Grande near Reynosa, at a place called La Volsa. They were sometimes called Tompacuas by the Comecrudo, which is or was the name of a rancheria in Hidalgo co., Texas, 20 m. N. of the Rio Grande. (C. T.)

Estók pakawaíle.—Gatschet, Comecrudo MS., B. A. E. (own name). **Newasol pakawai.**—Ibid. (Comecrudo name). **Pacahuches.**—Taylor in Cal. Farmer, Apr. 17, 1863. **Pacaos.**—Rivera, Diario, leg. 2602, 1736. **Pachao.**—Doc. of 1738 in Archivo Gen., cited by H. E. Bolton, inf'n, 1906. **Pachoches.**—Orozco y Berra, Geog., 308, 1864. **Pacoas.**—García, Manual, title, 1760. **Pacos.**—Orozco y Berra, Geog., 304, 1864. **Pacuaches.**—García, Manual, title, 1760. **Pacuas.**—Orozco y Berra, Geog., 303, 1864. **Paguachis.**—Ibid., 304. **Paikawa.**—Gatschet, Karankawa Indians, 38, 1891. **Paíkawan.**—Ibid. **Pakawá.**—Buschmann (1859) quoted by Gatschet, ibid., 33. **Pintos.**—18th century MS. quoted by Orozco y Berra, Geog., 294, 1864. **Tompacuas.**—Gatschet, MS., B. A. E., 1886 (Comecrudo name.)

Pakhpuinihkashina. A society of the Osage, q. v.

ɋaqpú'i'niqk'äciⁿ'a.—Dorsey in 15th Rep. B. A. E., 235, 1897.

Pakhtha ('beaver,' probably archaic). An Iowa gens, now extinct, having joined the Patha gens of the Oto (Dorsey, Tciwere MS. vocab., B. A. E., 1879). Its subgentes were Rawekhanye, Rathroche, Raweyine, and Niwanshike.

Beaver.—Morgan, Anc. Soc., 156, 1877. **Pä-kuh'-thä.**—Ibid. **Pa'-qɋa.**—Dorsey in 15th Rep. B. A. E., 239, 1897.

Paki. A former Maidu village on Mud cr., or near Cusa lagoon, N. of Chico, Butte co., Cal. (R. B. D.)

Paiki.—Curtin, MS. vocab., B. A. E., 1885. **Pake.**—Dixon in Bull. Am. Mus. Nat. Hist., XVII, pl. 38, 1905.

Pakwa. The Frog clan of the Patki or Cloud phratry of the Hopi.

Pá-kua.—Bourke, Snake Dance, 117, 1884. **Pakwa wiñwû.**—Fewkes in 19th Rep. B. A. E., 583, 1900 (wiñwú = clan). **Pa'-kwa wüñ-wû.**—Fewkes in Am. Anthrop., VII, 402, 1894.

Pala ('water'). A Luiseño village N. E. of San Luis Rey, San Diego co., Cal. Latterly the name was applied to a reservation of 160 acres of allotted arable land, under Mission Tule River agency. By court decision in 1901 the Indians of Warner's ranch were dispossessed of their lands, and by act of Congress of May 27, 1902, Pala res. was enlarged by purchase to 3,598 acres, and the Warner ranch people removed thereto in 1903. In the latter year the Tule River agency was divided into the Pala and San Jacinto agencies. In 1865 the pop. of Pala was 162; in 1902, 76; in 1903, after its enlargement, 258; in 1906, 138. See Ind. Aff. Rep., 124, 1865; 175, 1902; 146, 1903; 205, 1906; Hayes MS. quoted by Bancroft, Nat. Races, I, 460, 1886; Jackson and Kinney, Rep. Mission Inds., 29, 1883. Cf. *Palin*.

Palacheho (*Phalacheho*). A former Chickasaw town in N. Mississippi, forming part of a large settlement of 5 towns.— Adair, Am. Ind., 353, 1775.

Palaihnihan (Klamath: from *p'laikni*, 'mountaineers'). Formerly recognized as a linguistic family in N. E. California, but probably to be regarded, as the result of recent studies by Dixon (Am. Anthrop., VII, 213, 1905), as only a branch of the Shastan ("Shasta-Achomawi") family. Their habitat embraced the drainage area of Pit r. above Montgomery cr. except Goose Lake valley, of which only the s. end was in their territory. Linguistically the group falls into two rather sharply contrasted and numerically unequal divisions, the Achomawi and the Atsugewi. The tribal and minor divisions recognized were the Achomawi, Astakiwi, Atsugewi, Atuami, Chumawi, Hantiwi, Humawhi, Ilmawi, and Puisu. Physically there were considerable differences between these tribes. The Astakiwi and Humawhi have been described by Powers as "most miserable, squalid, peak-faced, mendicant, and mendacious wretches." Their faces were skinny, foreheads low and retreating, bodies lank, and abdomens protuberant. The Atuami were much superior in physique. All the tribes were indifferent hunters. They trapped game by digging pitfalls with fire-hardened sticks and covered them with brush, grass, and earth. These pits were so numerous they gave its name to Pit r., after which these Indians have generally been called. The Humawhi and Astakiwi, having no acorns or salmon, as most other California tribes, were hard pressed for a food supply. Game birds were abundant, but they captured and killed few. Grasshoppers, crickets, trout and suckers, camas, clover blossoms, and bearberries formed their chief diet. The Achomawi of Fall r. subsisted largely on salmon. Among the Palaihnihan woman is said to have held a servile and degraded position; whether maiden or widow she was owned by her father or brother, to be sold, with her children, if any, at his pleasure. Marriage was a matter of bargain and sale, and polygamy was common. A woman was seldom held responsible for adultery, but if a wife deserted her husband and refused to return to him he was allowed to take her life. However, a husband had no control over his wife's personal property, which at her death was claimed by her relatives. In case of the birth of twins, one was almost always destroyed. Cremation was generally practised in cases where persons died of unknown diseases; in all other cases the dead were buried in a sitting posture; the Ilmawi however never burned their dead. The Palaihnihan Indians dwelt chiefly in bark and brush houses of an irregularly quadrangular form, similar to those of the Shasta, or in semisubterranean dwellings like sweat-houses. During the summer these dwellings were abandoned and the people lived in brush shelters while hunting and collecting food. Their social organization was rather loose, the authority of the chief or leader being but nominal. Like the Shasta, whom they resembled in many of their customs and practices, it was not rare for a woman to be a shaman or priest. They had but few religious ceremonies and dances, but like the Maidu had an elaborate creation myth in which the coyote played the most important rôle. Very few individuals of the family remain. Some of them were removed to Round Valley res., Cal., and these, with some natives from Potter valley, numbered 34 in 1889. (R. B. D. F. W. H.)

Mo-e-twas.—Palmer in Ind. Aff. Rep., 470, 1854. Palaihnih.—Hale in U. S. Expl. Exped., VI, 218, 1846. Palaiks.—Ibid., 199. Pitt river Indians.—Russell (1853) in H. R. Ex. Doc. 76, 34th Cong., 3d sess., 74, 1857. Yuca's.—Ibid. (='enemies').

Palakahu. A division of the Umpqua according to Parker (Jour., 257, 1840); not identified, but evidently either Athapascan or Yakonan.

Palaquesson. A village or tribe visited by La Salle in Feb. 1687, w. of Brazos r., Texas, having a chief named Palaquechaure. According to La Salle the speech of the people resembled that of the Ceni (Asini, Hasinai=Caddo) whom he had visited the year before. Joutel states that the Palaquesson had no fixed dwelling place, but hunted over a considerable stretch of country, yet when the people came to a fertile tract they settled there, the men preparing the soil for planting and the women sowing the maize. So long as the crops were good the people remained sedentary, but when these failed hunting was resumed, at which times they divided into groups to insure greater success. It is probable that the French encountered these people during one of their hunting periods, as Douay says they were in 10 villages. They knew the Spaniards, from whom they obtained horses, and were allies of the Ceni, joining their war excursions to the s. and E.

The houses of the Palaquesson were of dried grass. On the death of an occupant the dwelling was burned and the survivors erected a new one on another site. Men and women tattooed their faces in lines and their bodies with plant and animal figures. Their boats were similar to those used on the Missouri—a skin stretched over a light framework of wood. Nothing is known of their beliefs. (A. C. F.)

Alakea.—Cavelier (1687) quoted by Shea, Early Voy., 39, 1861. Palagueques.—Orozco y Berra, Geog., 293, 1864. Palaguessons.—Coxe, Carolana, map, 1741. Palaquechaune.—Charlevoix, New France, IV, 90, 1870. Palaquechauré.—Joutel (1687) in Margry, Déc., III, 305, 1878. Palaquechone.—Barcia, Ensayo, 271, 1723. Palaquesones.—Ibid., 273. Palaquesson.—Douay (1687) quoted by Shea in French, Hist. Coll. La., IV, 212, 1852. Palaquessous.—McKenney and Hall, Ind. Tribes, III, 81,

1854. Paloguessens.—Coxe in French, Hist. Coll. La., II, 241, 1850. Palquesson.—Charlevoix, New France, IV, 90, 1870.

Palatki (Hopi: 'red house'). A prehistoric cliff village in the valley of Oak cr., in the "Red-rock" country, s. of Flagstaff, Ariz.; believed to have been one of the stopping places of the Patki or Cloud clans of the Hopi in their migration from the S.—Fewkes in 17th Rep. B. A. E., 553-58, 1898.

Palatkwabi ('red land of the south'). The place inhabited by the Patki or Cloud clans of the Hopi prior to their settlement in Tusayan, N. E. Ariz. The locality is somewhere in the great cactus region of s. Arizona.

Pa-lat'-kwa-bi.—Fewkes in Am. Anthrop., VII, 402, 1894, and 17th Rep. B. A. E., 568, 1898. Palát-kwapi.—Voth, Traditions of the Hopi, 47, 1905.

Paleolithic implements. The term applied to implements, usually of stone, belonging to the Paleolithic age as first defined in Europe and afterward identified in other countries. In America the Paleolithic, as chronologically distinct from the Neolithic age, is not established, and the more primitive forms of implements, corresponding in general to the Paleolithic implements of Europe, can be properly referred to only as of Paleolithic type. In this connection it should be noted that implements of the most primitive type were made and used by the American tribes, whatsoever their stage of culture progress. See *Antiquity, Neolithic age.* (W. H. H.)

Paleuyami. A Yokuts (Mariposan) tribe, now extinct, formerly living on Poso cr., Cal. Recorded by Powers, under the name Paleummi, as the Yokuts name of a tribe related to the Paiute. Their dialect was quite different from that of the other Yokuts tribes. See *Altinin.*

Bŏdĕr'wĭŭmĭ.—Hoffman in Proc. Am. Philos. Soc., XXIII, 301, 1886. Pal-e'-um-mi.—Powers in Cont. N. A. Ethnol., III, 393, 1877. Paleuyami.—Kroeber in Univ. Cal. Pub., Am. Ethnol. and Archæol., II, 5, 1907.

Palewa (*pe-le-wa'*, 'turkey'). A gens of the Shawnee.

Pa-la-wä'.—Morgan, Anc. Soc., 168, 1877. Palēwa.—Wm. Jones, inf'n, 1906.

Palin. A former Luiseño village in lower San Luis Rey valley, San Diego co., Cal. (Grijalva, 1795, cited by Bancroft, Hist. Cal., I, 563, 1886). Possibly identical with the present Pala (q. v.), in which event the name was seemingly corrupted by the Spaniards.

Palisades. See *Fortification and Defense.*

Palisema. A district w. of the Mississippi, five days' march from the province of Coligoa; visited in 1541 by De Soto's troops.—Gentl. of Elvas (1557) in French, Hist. Coll. La., II, 178, 1850.

Palladium. This term was the name of the statue of the goddess Pallas or Minerva, preserved in the ancient city of Troy, and supposed to hold protecting watch over the destinies of its people. The use of the term has been broadened to include any similar sacred object of national or tribal veneration. Several of our Indian tribes had such palladiums, which were venerated with ceremonial forms and regarded with zealous care and upon whose continued safe possession the existence and prosperity of the tribe were believed to depend. As a rule the true origin of the object of tribal veneration was lost in obscurity, but was accounted for by a sacred myth which represented it as having been given to the people by their mystic culture-hero at the beginning of the world. A priest was appointed to watch over it, a special depository was provided for it, prayer and sacrifice were made to it, and it was rarely or never exposed to public view except on the occasion of certain great tribal gatherings when it was made the central figure of the ceremony. Like the Hebrew ark of the covenant, it was sometimes carried in the battle front to insure victory over the enemy.

Notable instances are the sacred box of the Cherokee (Mooney in 19th Rep. B. A. E., 1900), the metal tablets of the Creeks (Gatschet, Creek Migr. Leg., I, II, 1884, 1888), the *taime* of the Kiowa (Mooney in 17th Rep. B. A. E., 1898), the medicine arrows of the Cheyenne (Dorsey in Am. Anthrop., V, 644, 1903; Mooney in Mem. Am. Anthrop. Ass'n, I, no. 6, 1907), the "ark" of the Mandan (Maximilian, Trav., 1843; Matthews, Hidatsa, 1877), and the *seicha* or flat pipe of the Arapaho (Mooney in 14th Rep. B. A. E., 1896; Scott in Am. Anthrop., IX, no. 3, 1907).

The Cherokee sacred box is still remembered in the traditions of their old men, who say that it contained the most sacred belongings of the tribe, and that the prosperity of their people departed after its capture by the Delawares. Their account of its exterior agrees with that given by Adair from the statement of a white man who saw it with them in 1756. It was a rectangular box, about 3 ft long, covered with a dressed deerskin and resting upon blocks to keep it from the earth. It was watched by a sentinel with bow and arrows, who drew an arrow to the head and warned the stranger away when he attempted a closer inspection.

The sacred metal plates of the Creeks were kept by priests of the Wind clan in Tukabatchi town in a depository on one side of the public square. They were said to be 7 in all, 5 of copper and 2 of brass, with engraved characters resembling letters. At times they were said to give out a miraculous ringing sound without being touched. Once a year, at the annual Green Corn dance, they were exhibited to the people from a distance, after which they were washed in the stream, rubbed and cleaned, and put away again for another year. As usual with such things, the Tukabatchi people claimed to have received them from a supernatural being at the beginning of their existence as a people, but it is more likely that they were a relic of some early Spanish expedition, perhaps a trophy from the great battle of Mavila in 1540. They are noted by Adair as early as 1775 and are still preserved in the Creek Nation, Okla.

The *taimé* of the Kiowa is a small stone image bearing resemblance to the head and bust of a man, decorated with down feathers and with images of the sun and the crescent moon painted upon its breast. It is kept in a parflèche box of peculiar shape and decoration, and, like the Creek plates, was exposed only once a year, at the annual Sun dance. It is still sacredly preserved, but as the dance has not been performed since 1887 the box has not been opened since, not even the custodian being permitted to undo the wrappings.

The medicine arrows of the Cheyenne are 4 in number, of different colors, and were kept together in charge of a special priest from the earliest traditional period, before the tribe had removed from the head of the Mississippi r. They have no connection with the Sun dance, antedating that ceremony in the tribe, but are exposed only on occasion of a solemn purification rite when a Cheyenne has been killed by one of his own tribe. They are still preserved among the Southern Cheyenne, by whom the rite of blood atonement was performed as late as 1904.

The "flat pipe" of the Arapaho is kept by a priest of the Wyoming branch of the tribe, together with an ear of corn and a stone turtle, all of which, according to their tradition, they have had from the beginning of the world. Around these centers the tribal genesis tradition, which is recited when the package is opened, as may be done on special occasions, without regard to other ceremonial periods. The box in which the sacred objects were kept was never allowed to touch the ground, and when on the march the priest in charge, even though mounted, was not allowed to rest it upon his horse, but must carry it upon his own back. See *Fetish*. (J. M.)

Palm. Only two representatives of the palm family occur in the United States. One of these has a limited distribution in s. California, and is employed somewhat in basketry; but among the Piman tribes of Sonora and Sinaloa, especially, palm leaves were extensively used for making mats for inclosing houses and for hats and basketry. The other variety of palm is the palmetto *Sabal*, which entered largely into the life of the Indians of s. w. Florida. The Seminole still use the palmetto trunk in house building, and the leaves for thatching, beds, basketry, twine, and rope, and the bud is eaten, raw or baked (5th Rep. B. A. E., 517, 1887). Biedma (1540) speaks of the use of palmetto leaves for thatching, and Dickenson, writing of Florida, says that "an Indian brought a fish boiled on a palmetto leaf and set it down amongst us" (Narr. of a Shipwreck, 1803). According to Bartram (Trans. Am. Ethnol. Soc., iii, pt. 1, 49–50, 1853) the Creeks of Alabama had several species of palms which they used for food. One of them (*Sabal minus* Pers.) is a low plant, without stalk or stem, that bears a vast collection of plumes or drupes with fibrous farinaceous pulpy coating resembling manna. Another species (*Serenoa sereulata*) was used for medicine. Empty pods of the palm were used in dances as ankle rattles by the Tepehuane (Lumholtz, Unknown Mex., i, 477, 1902). (w. h.)

Palomas (Span.: 'doves'). One of the three large villages in the vicinity of Trinity r., Tex., visited by La Salle in 1687. Cavelier states that the village was surrounded by a palisade of cane. The people seemed to be fairly well supplied with horses and were hostile to the Spaniards. Their affiliation is not known.
Palomas.—Cavelier (1687) in Shea, Early Voy., 38, 1861. Palona.—Douay quoted by Shea, Discov. Miss. Val., 212, 1852. Palonnas.—Coxe in French, Hist. Coll. La., ii, 241, 1850.

Palonies (said to have been so called by the Spaniards because they wore their hair so short as to suggest baldness). Mentioned as a division of the Chemehuevi that occasionally went to the north of Los Angeles, Cal., in 1845.—Ried quoted by Hoffman in Bull. Essex Inst., xvii, 28, 1885.

Paloos (*Pä-lus'*). A Shahaptian tribe formerly occupying the valley of Palouse r. in Washington and Idaho, and the n. bank of Snake r. as far as its junction with the Columbia. They were found by Lewis and Clark in 1805 on the Clearwater in Idaho. Their closest connection was with the kindred Nez Percés, and they still hold close relations with that tribe. They were included in the Yakima treaty of 1855, but have never recognized the treaty obligations and have declined to lead a reservation life. They have 4 villages, all on Snake r., as follows: Almotu, Palus, Tasawiks, and Kasispa. They are active adherents of the Smohalla (q. v.) doctrine. Lewis and Clark estimated their number in 1805 at 1,600; in 1854 they were said to number 500; at present

the population is unknown. See Mooney in 14th Rep. B. A. E., 735, 1896. (L. F.)
Pallatapalla.—Lee and Frost, Ten Years in Oreg., 51, 1844. Pallet-to Pallas.—Ross, Fur Hunters, I, 185, 1855. Palloatpallah.—Lewis and Clark Exped., ii, 333, 1814. Pallotepallers.—Ibid., vii, 341, 1905. Pallotepallors.—Lewis, Travels, 11, 1809. Pallotepellows.—Orig. Jour. Lewis and Clark (1806), v, 187, 1905. Paloas.—Lane in Sen. Ex. Doc. 52, 31st Cong., 1st sess., 171, 1850. P a l o o c h e.—Ross, Fur Hunters, ii, 6, 1855. Paloose.—Parker, Journal, 284, 1840. Palouse.—Treaty of 1855 in U. S. Stat. at Large, xii, 951, 1863. Pälus.—Mooney in 14th Rep. B. A. E., 735, 1896. Palvas.—Lane in Ind. Aff. Rep., 159, 1850. Pel-late-pal-ler.—Orig. Jour. Lewis and Clark, v, 117, 1905. Pelloatpallah.—Lewis and Clark Exped., ii, 471, 1814. Pelloat pallahs.—Orig. Jour. Lewis and Clark, v, 187, 1905. Pel-lote-pal-ler.—Lewis and Clark Exped., Coues ed., 1070, 1893. Peloose.—Hale in U. S. Expl. Exped., vi, 213, 1846. Pelouches.—Gairdner (1835) in Jour. Geog. Soc. Lond., xi, 252, 1841. Pelouse.—Stevens in Ind. Aff. Rep., 462, 1854. Pelouze.—Lord, Nat. in Brit. Col., 105, 1866. Pelus.—Hale in U. S. Expl. Exped., vi, 569, 1846. Peluse.—Gibbs in Pac. R. R. Rep., i, 418, 1854. Polanches.—Powell in 7th Rep. B. A. E., 106, 1891. Pollotepallors.—Janson, Stranger in Am., 233, 1807. Polonches.—Gairdner (1835) in Jour. Geog. Soc. Lond., xi, 256, 1841. Selloat-pallahs.—Lewis and Clark Exped., map, 1814. Se wat palla.—Schoolcraft, Ind. Tribes, v, 706, 1855.

Palseta ('alkali water'). An important Kawia village in Cahuilla valley, s. Cal. Its Spanish name (Cabezon, from a former chief) has been applied to a reservation of 640 acres occupied in 1906 by 76 Indians under the San Jacinto agency.
Cabazon.—Wright in Ind. Aff. Rep. 1902, pt. 1, 175, 1903. Cabeson.—Stanley, ibid., 194, 1869 (name of chief and valley). Cavesons.—Denver, ibid., 406, 1857. Pal se-ta.—Barrows, Ethno-Bot. Coahuilla Ind., 33, 1900.

Paltatre. A Chumashan village between Goleta and Pt. Concepcion, Cal., in 1542.
Paltatre.—Cabrillo, Narr. (1542) in Smith, Colec. Doc. Fla., 183, 1857. Paltatro.—Taylor in Cal. Farmer, Apr. 17, 1863.

Paltchikatno. A former Kaiyuhkhotana village on Innoko r., Alaska.
Paltchikatno.—Zagoskin in Nouv. Ann. Voy., 5th s., xxi, map, 1850. Tichaïchachass.—Ibid.

Paltewat (*Pal te-wat*, 'water and pine tree'). A Kawia village at Indio, in Coahuilla valley, s. Cal.—Barrows, Ethno-Bot. Coahuilla Ind., 33, 1900.

Paluna. One of the War-god clans of the Hopi.
Palaña wiñwû.—Fewkes in 19th Rep. B. A. E., 584, 1900. Pa-lüñ-am wüñ-wû.—Fewkes in Am. Anthrop., vii, 403, 1894.

Palus. A village of the Paloos tribe on the n. bank of Snake r. just below its junction with the Palouse, in Washington.
Palus.—Mooney in 14th Rep. B. A. E., 735, 1906. Paw-luch.—Ross, Fur Hunters, I, 185, 1855.

Palux (Chehalis: *L!pē'lEqc*, 'slough covered by trees.'—Boas). A division of the Chinook tribe living on Palux r., emptying into Shoalwater bay, Pacific co., Wash.
Gitlā'tlpē'leks.—Boas, MS., B. A. E. (Chinook name). L!pē'lEqc.—Ibid. (Chehalis name). Palux.—Swan, N. W. Coast, 211, 1857.

Palwunun (or Badwunun, from *pal-u* 'down-stream,' *-inin* 'people of.'—Kroeber). A collective name applied by the

Yokuts of Kern r. to the Indians about
Kern lake, s. E. Cal.

Pal-wu′-nuh.—Powers in Cont. N. A. Ethnol., III,
393, 1877.

Pamacocack. A former village of the
Powhatan confederacy, on the w. bank
of Potomac r., about 30 m. below the
present Alexandria, in Prince William
co., Va. Another and apparently more
important village of the same name was
directly opposite, on the Maryland side,
from which it is probable that the name
properly belonged to the river stretch
rather than to the settlement.   (J. M.)

Pamacocack.—Smith (1629), Va., Arber ed., map,
1884.

Pamacocack. A former village on the
Maryland side of the Potomac, opposite
that of the same name on the Virginia
side, and about the mouth of Mattawo-
man cr. and the present Pomonkey,
Charles co. It was of some importance,
having 60 warriors, or perhaps 250 souls,
when visited by Capt. John Smith in
1608. The boy Spelman confuses it with
Nacotchtank, which he makes ''Nacottawtanke.''   (J. M.)

Camocacocke.—Spelman (*ca.* 1615) in Smith, Va.,
Arber ed., civ, 1884 (misprint form and incorrectly identified with ''Nacottawtanke ''=Na-
cotchtank). **Pamacacack.**—Bozman, Md., I, 39,
1837. **Pamacaeack.**—Smith (1629), Va., Arber ed.,
348, 1884 (misprint). **Pamacocack.**—Smith (1629),
ibid., map.

Pamame. A former Luiseño village in
lower San Luis Rey valley, San Diego
co., Cal.—Grijalva (1795) cited by Bancroft, Hist. Cal., I, 563, 1886.

Pamamelli. A former Luiseño village
in Santa Margarita valley, San Diego co.,
Cal.—Grijalva (1795) cited by Bancroft,
Hist. Cal., I, 563, 1886.

Pamaque. A tribe mentioned by Fray
Bartholomé García (1760) as one of those
speaking the language of his Manual,
i. e. Coahuiltecan. They dwelt near the
Texas coast between the Nueces and San
Antonio rs. Their residence between
these streams was made the basis of a
claim to them and their relatives, the
Piguiques and the Pasnacanes, by San
Juan Capistrano mission, in a quarrel
with Vizarron mission in 1754 (Ynforme
of the College of Querétaro to the Commissary Gen., 1754, MS.). That they
lived near the coast is evident. A Spanish manuscript of 1752 says: ''The Pamaques are from the mouth of the said
river [Nueces].'' In 1762 the San Antonio missionaries reported them in a
list of coast tribes. In 1780 Governor
Cabello, naming the coast tribes from the
Nueces to Ysla de los Copanes, put the
''Pamacas'' (undoubtedly the Pamaques) first in the list, which was given in
a w. to E. order. This would put them
near the mouth of the Nueces (Cabello
to Croix, May 28, 1780, MS.). The tribe
is evidently the same as Orozco y Berra's
Panagues, which he puts on the Nueces.

The Pamaques were closely related to
the Piguiques and the Pasnacanes, who
lived in the same locality. Indeed, the
last two tribes seem sometimes to have
been considered as subdivisions of the
first. They were together in San Juan
Capistrano mission, whence they fled
together in 1754 (Ynforme, 1754, op. cit.).
They were also closely related to the
Orejones (q. v.). The wider affiliation of the Pamaques may perhaps be
indicated by Cabello's list of their neighbors, cited above. It includes Pamacas
(Pamaques), Malaguitas, Orejones,
Chayopines (in San Juan Capistrano
mission); Pacagues, Borrados (in San
Francisco de la Espada); Pajalates,
Tacames, Manos de Perro, Copanes, and
Cujanes (in Concepción mission). As it
was a general policy of the missions, not
always carried out, to keep closely related
tribes together, it is not improbable that
this grouping has ethnological significance.

In 1733 the Pamaques entered San Juan
Capistrano mission, and by 1754 the
records showed 196 baptisms of this tribe,
including, apparently, the Piguiques, but
not the Pasnacanes, who entered in 1743
(Ynforme, 1754, op. cit.; Santa Ana to
the Viceroy, Mar. 4, 1743, MS.). Before
1748 there were numerous ''Pamaches''
at Concepción mission; these may be the
same, although it is not certain (MS.
mission records). According to Camberos, missionary at Bahía, the Pamaques
were nearly extinguished by 1754 (Letter
to the Viceroy, May 6, 1754, MS.), but
the tribe was still being missionized at
San Juan Capistrano in 1762. At that
time a total of 203 ''Orejones, Sayopines,
Pamaques, and Piguiques '' was reported
there (Ynforme, 1762, op. cit.). According to Cabello, they were still living on
the coast in 1780.   (H. E. B.)

Pamacas.—Cabello, op. cit. **Pamâques.**—García,
op. cit. **Panagues.**—Orozco y Berra, Geog., 304,
1864. **Panego.**—Joutel Jour. (1687), Eng. trans.,
90, 1716. **Panequo.**—Joutel in Margry, Déc., III,
289, 1878 (identical?).

Pamawauk. A village of the Powhatan
confederacy, perhaps identical with Pamunkey.—Strachey (*ca.* 1616), Va., 26,
1849.

Pamet. A former village near Truro,
Barnstable co., Mass., probably belonging
to the Nauset.

Pamet.—Dee in Smith (1629), Va., II, 235, repr. 1819.
Pamit.—Freeman (1685) in Mass. Hist. Soc. Coll.,
4th s., V, 132, 1861. **Pamnit.**—Treaty of 1687, ibid.,
186. **Paomet.**—Mourt (1622), ibid., 1st s., VIII, 256,
1802. **Paumet.**—Hinckley (1685), ibid., 4th s., V,
133, 1861. **Pawmet.**—Smith (1616), ibid., 3d s., VI,
108, 1837. **Powmet.**—Dee in Smith (1629), Va., II,
235, repr. 1819.

Pamiadluk. An Eskimo mission and
trading post in s. Greenland, lat. 61°.—
Koldewey, German Arctic Exped., 183,
1874.

Pamissouk (*Pämĭsähŭgĭ*, 'they that fly
past'). A gens of the Sauk; not the Eagle

gens necessarily, as Morgan states, since the term is applicable to any of the "winged" clans. (w. j.)

Pämisähagi.—Wm.Jones,inf'n,1906 (correct form). Pă-mis'-so-uk.—Morgan, Anc. Soc., 170, 1877.

Pamitoy (*Pam'-mi-toy*, 'western tule-eaters'). A Paviotso band formerly in Mason valley, w. Nev.; so called because a lake in this valley, now dry, formerly yielded tule.—Powers, Inds. W. Nevada, MS., B. A. E., 1876.

Pamlico. An Algonquian tribe formerly living on Pamlico r., in Beaufort co., N. C. They were nearly destroyed by smallpox in 1696. The survivors, numbering about 75, lived in 1710 in a single village. They took part in the Tuscarora war of 1711, and at its close that portion of the Tuscarora under treaty with the English agreed to exterminate them. The remnant was probably incorporated as slaves with that tribe. (J. M.)

Pamlico.—Drake, Bk. Inds., x, 1848. Pamlicough.—Doc. of 1718 in N. C. Col. Rec., II, 315, 1886. Pamphleco.—Doc. of 1676, ibid., I, 228, 1886. Pampleco.—Doc. of 1676, ibid., 233. Pamplicoes.—Doc. of 1699, ibid., 514. Pamptaco.—Gale (1711), ibid., 827. Pamptecough.—Doc. of 1705, ibid., 629. Pamptego.—Graffenried (1711), ibid., 924. Pamptichoe.—Urmstone (1718), ibid., II, 310, 1886. Pampticoes.—Doc. of 1696, ibid., I, 472, 1886. Pampticoke.—Brinton, Lenape Leg., 11, 1885. Pampticough.—Lawson (1709), Hist. Carolina, 384, repr. 1860. Pamptucough.—Lawson (1709), map, in Hawks, N. C., II, 1858 (misprint). Pamtico.—Blair (1704) in N. C. Col. Rec., I, 603, 1886. Pamticough.—Doc. of 1719, ibid., II, 342, 1886. Pantico.—Linschoten, Description de l'Amér., 6, 1638. Panticoes.—Keane in Stanford, Compend., 529, 1878. Panticoughs.—Ibid. Pemblicos.—Hewat, S. C. and Ga., II, 279, 1779. Pemlico.—Oldmixon (1708) quoted by Carroll, Hist. Coll. S. C., II, 459, 1836. Pemlicoe.—Archdale (1707) quoted by Carroll, ibid., 89. Pemplico.—Doc. of 1681 in N. C. Col. Rec., I, 333, 1886. Pemptico.—Ogilby (1671), map, in Hawks, N. C., II, 1858. Phampleco.—Doc. of 1676 in N. C. Col. Rec., I, 228, 1886.

Pamoranos. Given by Orozco y Berra (Geog., 299, 1864) as a Tamaulipan tribe living in Texas, N. of Laredo. They are mentioned in 1732 by Fr. Juan Lozada as one of numerous tribes who had made peace with the Spaniards. (H. E. B.)

Pamozanes.—Orozco y Berra, op. cit., 294.

Pampopas. A Coahuiltecan tribe formerly living on Nueces r., Tex., 22 leagues from San Juan Bautista mission, with the Tilijaes on the same stream immediately below them. It is one of several tribes mentioned by García (Manual, title, 1760) as speaking the same, i. e. Coahuiltecan, language. They appear to have been in the same territory in 1701 (Orozco y Berra, Geog., 303, 1864).

Manuscripts dated in 1736–38 confirm the above statements as to their residence on the Nueces (indicating that they some-times established themselves to the E., even across Rio Frio) and fix their latitude as probably above the junction of Rio Frio with the Nueces (Gov. Sandoval, Aug. 25, 1736, Lamar Papers, Span. MS., no. 31; Testimony of Aug. 29, 1736; Yndiferente de Guerra, 1736–37, Misiones, XXI,

Archivo Gen.; Orobio y Basterra, letter of Apr. 26, 1738, Historia, LXXXIV, Archivo Gen.). Rivera (Proyecto, 1728) calls them a roving tribe. In the early part of the 18th century Pampopas were in San Juan Bautista mission, on the Rio Grande, 9 families being there in 1738, together with Tilijyas (Tilijaes), Pitas, Pastalocos, and Mescales (Portillo, Apuntes para la Historia Antigua de Coahuila y Texas, 283, 1888; Morfi, Viage de Indios, Doc. Hist. Mex., 3d s., IV, 441, 1856). Fray Antonio de Buenaventura de Olivares, who in 1718 moved San Francisco Solano mission from the Rio Grande and reestablished it as San Antonio de Valero, mentioned the Pampoas (Pampopas) as one of the tribes he intended to gather there (undated MS. letter to the Viceroy), but they went rather to San José de Aguayo mission (q. v.), founded shortly after, where they were settled with Pastias, Sayopines, and Tacasnanes (Pasnacanes?). Apparently all these tribes soon deserted the mission, but some Pampopas were taken back. In 1736 some were recovered from rancherias on the Rio Frio, and in 1737 others from the Medina (Documents, op. cit.). In 1738 Orobio y Basterra (op. cit.) located them "on the banks of Rio de las Nuezes," and suggested enlisting them in a campaign against the Apache, thus indicating their hostility toward that tribe, which seems to have been the rule with the Coahuiltecan group of the Texas coast. The tribe must have been small then, for Orobio y Basterra counted on only 200 warriors from this and three other tribes of a different region. In 1750 Fr. Santa Ana speaks of the Pampopas as quite generally "reduced and attached" to their mission (Petition, Feb. 20, 1750, in Mem. de Nueva España, XXVIII, 140, MS.); in 1768 Solís wrote as though they comprised a part of the 350 adult men at San José mission (Diario, ibid., XXVII, 270); and in 1793 Revilla-Gigedo implied that they formed a part of the 114 neophytes still at the latter mission (Carta, Dec. 27, 1793, in Dic. Univ. de Hist. y de Geog., V, 447, 1853–56). (H. E. B.)

Pampapas.—Revilla-Gigedo (1793) quoted by Bancroft, Nat. Races, I, 611, 1886. Pampoas.—Olivares, 1718, op. cit. Pampopas.—Gov. Sandoval (1736), op. cit. Pampos.—Santa Ana (1750), op. cit.

Pamuncoroy. A village of 50 inhabitants, belonging to the Powhatan confederacy, situated in 1608 on the s. bank of Pamunkey r. in New Kent co., Va.

Pamuncoroy.—Smith (1629), Va., I, map, repr. 1819. Paraconos.—Strachey (ca. 1612), Va., 62, 1849.

Pamunkey (from *päm*, 'sloping,' slanting; *-anki*, 'hill', 'mountain', 'highland': 'sloping hill', or 'rising upland', referring to a tract of land in what is now King William co., Va., beginning at the junction of Pamunkey and Mattapony rs. "Where the river is divided the country is called Pamaunke'' (Smith).— Gerard). The leading tribe of the Powha-

KEIZIAH DENNIS—PAMUNKEY.

tan confederacy (q. v.) of Virginia, and still keeping up a recognized tribal organization.

THEODORA OCTAVIA COOK—PAMUNKEY.

At the time of the first settlement of Virginia they occupied the territory about the junction of the Pamunkey and Mattapony

rs., in King William co., being estimated by Smith in 1608 to number nearly 300 warriors, or perhaps a total of 1,000 souls. Their principal town, destroyed by the English in 1625, was probably not far from the present West Point. They took a leading part in the early wars with the English up to the death of Opechancanough (q. v.), and in consequence were among the greatest sufferers. In 1654 they suffered another heavy loss in the death of their chief Totopotomoi (q. v.), with nearly 100 of his warriors, who had marched to the assistance of the English in repelling an invasion of the mountain tribes. In 1675 their "queen," known as Queen Anne (q. v.), widow of Totopotomoi, again furnished help against the frontier raiders in Bacon's rebellion. For

TERRILL BRADBY IN DANCE COSTUME—PAMUNKEY.

her services on this occasion she received special recognition from the English government. In 1722, when the Pamunkey last appear in a public treaty, they were said to number only about 200. In 1781 Jefferson reported them to number only about 60, of tolerably pure blood, but this estimate is probably too low. They were then occupying a state reservation of about 300 acres in a bend of Pamunkey r., in King William co., opposite White House. Quite a number at that time retained their language. They still occupy the same reservation and keep up their tribal organization under state supervision, with a mixed-blood population of about 140. They live chiefly by fishing, with some small farming, and have entirely lost their language and original characteristics.   (J. M.)

Chepecho.—Strachey (*ca.* 1612), Va., 62, 1849. **Pamanuk.**—Harris, Voy. and Trav., I, 833, 1705. **Pamanuke.**—Ibid., 831. **Pamaomeck.**—Herrman, map (1670) in Rep. on line between Va. and Md., 1873. **Pamareke.**—Strachey (*ca.* 1612), Va., 62, 1849 (misprint). **Pamauke.**—Smith (1629), Va., II, 66, repr. 1819. **Pamaunk.**—Pots in Smith, ibid., I, 216. **Pamaunkes.**—Pory in Smith, ibid., II, 68. **Pamaunkie.**—Beverley, Va., 199, 1722. **Pamavukes.**—Smith, (1629), Va., II, 82, repr. 1819. **Pamonkies.**—Percy in Purchas, Pilgrimes, IV, 1689, 1626. **Pamunkeys.**—Writer of 1676 in Mass. Hist. Soc. Coll., 4th s., IX, 165, 1871. **Pamunkies.**—Jefferson, Notes, 137, 1794.

Pan.   The Coyote gens of the Pima. See *Stoamohimal*.
Pahn-kech-emk.—ten Kate, Reizen in N. A., 155, 1885. **Pan.**—Bandelier in Arch. Inst. Papers, III, 254, 1890.

Panachsa (*Pá-nach-sa*).   A former Kawia village in the San Jacinto mts., s. Cal. — Barrows, Ethno-Bot. Coahuilla Inds., 27, 1900.

Panalachic (corruption of Tarahumare *Banalachic*, 'face place', from *banalá* 'face', *chic* the locative, referring to the outline of a large rock near by.—Lumholtz, Unknown Mex., I, 211, 1902). A Tarahumare settlement near the headwaters of the s. branch of Rio Nonoava, lat. 27° 40', lon. 107° 15', Chihuahua, Mexico. Pop. 380 in 1900.

Panamenik.   A Karok village on the w. bank of Klamath r., Cal., where the town of Orleans Bar now stands. In 1852 it had 4 houses.
Koomen.— A. L. Kroeber, inf'n, 1903 (Yurok name). **Panamenik.**—Ibid. (correct name). **Panom-nik.**—Gibbs, MS. Misc., B. A. E., 1852.

Panamint.   A Shoshonean division formerly occupying a considerable area in and around Panamint valley, s. E. Cal., and extending s. in scattered rancherias toward Mohave r. Henshaw found a few individuals living at the mining town of Darwin (Panamint) in 1883, and learned that about 150 still survived, scattered here and there, in the desert country E. of Panamint valley. It is uncertain whether their affinities are with the Ute-Chemehuevi or Mono-Paviotso group of Shoshoneans, but are here placed tentatively with the former. The Matarango are mentioned as a subdivision. See Coville in Am. Anthrop., Oct. 1892.   (H. W. H.)
Coitch.—Bancroft, Nat. Rac. I, 456, 1874. **Kaitc'.**—Henshaw, Panamint MS. vocab. B. A. E., 1883 (asserted by a Panamint to be their own tribal name, but given as their name for the Shoshoni proper). **Ke-at.**—Gatschet in Wheeler Surv. Rep., VII, 411, 1879.

Panequo.   A village or tribe mentioned by Joutel in 1687 as being N. or N. w. of the Maligne (Colorado) r., Texas. The country was the abode of Tonkawan tribes, although Karankawan Indians also sometimes roamed there. The name seems to have been given to Joutel by the Ebahamo, who were probably of Karankawan affinity.   (A. C. F.)
Panego.—Joutel (1687) in French, Hist. Coll. La., I, 138, 1846. **Panequo.**—Joutel (1687) in Margry, Déc., III, 289, 1878.

Pang (*Pän* or *Pä*).   The Deer clans of the Tewa pueblos of San Ildefonso and Santa Clara, N. Mex.
Päⁿ-tdóa.—Hodge in Am. Anthrop., IX, 350, 1896 (San Ildefonso form; *tdóa*='people'). **Pä-tdóa.**—Ibid. (Santa Clara form).

Pangwa.   The Mountain-sheep clan of the Ala (Horn) phratry of the Hopi.
Pa'n-wa.—Stephen in 8th Rep. B. A. E., 38, 1891. **Pañ'-wa wüñ-wü.**—Fewkes in Am. Anthrop., VII, 401, 1894 (*wüñ-wü*='clan'). **Pañwû wiñwû.**—Fewkes in 19th Rep. B. A. E., 583, 1901 (*wiñwû*-'clan').

Panhkawashtake ('Ponca peacemakers').   The 10th Osage gens, the third on the right or Hangka side of the tribal circle, one of the original Osage fireplaces (Dorsey in 15th Rep. B. A. E., 234, 1897). Its subgentes are Tsewadhe, Washape, Wakedhe, Wasetsi, and Khundtse.
Naⁿpaⁿta.—Dorsey, Osage MS. vocab., B. A. E., 1883. **Naⁿpaⁿtaqtsi.**—Ibid. **Paⁿh'ka wacta'ᶍe.**—Dorsey in 15th Rep. B. A. E., 234, 1897.

Pani.   A slave of Indian race. According to Hamilton (quoted by Hale in Proc. Can. Inst., n. s., I, 23, 1897), "Pani and Pawnee are undoubtedly the same word in different orthographies," the Pawnee being the tribe from whom the Algonquian and other Indians of the great lakes and the middle west obtained their slaves. It is thought by some that the Pawnee (q. v.) received their name from this fact; but Dunbar believes that Pawnee is derived from *pariki*, signifying 'horn' in the language of these Indians. Cuoq says: "As most of the Indian slaves belonged to the nation of the Panis (English *Pawnees*), the name *panis* (*pawnee*) was given in the last [18th] century to every Indian reduced to servitude." In the literature of the 17th and 18th centuries relating to Canada and the W. the word appears as *pawnee*, *pannee*, *pani*, and in other forms. See also Hamilton, Slavery in Canada, Trans. Can. Inst., I, 102, 1889–90.   (A. F. C.)

Pani Blanc.   A former band of the Cree living N. E. of L. Winnipeg, Can.
Panis Blanc.—Dobbs, Hudson Bay, map, 36, 1744.

Paniete.   A pueblo of either the Tigua or the Tewa of New Mexico about the close of the 16th century.—Oñate (1598) in Doc. Inéd., XVI, 102, 1871.

Panisee.   An Indian medicine-man or shaman. The word is used by Whittier (Bridal of Pennacook) after Hubbard and Winslow. The former makes *panisee* a synonym of *powah* or *powow* in the language of the Algonquian tribes of New England.   (A. F. C.)

Panit (*ᒉa'-nĭt*).   A former Alsea village on the s. side of Alsea r., Oreg.—Dorsey in Jour. Am. Folk-lore, III, 230, 1890.

Panka ('Ponca').   A division of the Kansa tribe.—Dorsey in Am. Nat., 671, July 1885.

Pannee.   See *Pani*.

Panpakan (*Pan'-pa-kan*).   A Maidu village on Deer cr., near Anthony House, Nevada co., Cal. (R. B. D.)

Panpacans.—Powers in Overland Mo., XII, 420, 1874. Pan'-pa-kan.—Powers in Cont. N. A. Ethnol., III, 282, 1877.

Panquechin. A band of Sanetch in the s. E. part of Vancouver id.; pop. 64 in 1906.

Panquechin.—Can. Ind. Aff. Rep., 66, 1902. Paukwechin.—Ibid., 308, 1879.

Panthe. A former Choctaw town, noted in 1775 by Romans, by whom it was erroneously located, its position having evidently been transposed with that of Coosha (q. v.). It was at the head of Ponta cr., Lauderdale co., Miss. This town and Coosha were collectively known as the Coosha towns.—Halbert in Pub. Miss. Hist. Soc., VI, 416, 1902.

Paonte.—Romans, Florida, 308, 1775.

Paor. A province on the E. side of ancient Florida, near Chicora; seen by Ayllon in 1520.—Barcia, Ensayo, 5, 1723.

Paouites. An unidentified tribe, living probably in Texas in 1690, said to be at war with the inhabitants of Toho or Teao village. Mentioned in the testimony concerning the death of La Salle, by the French captives, Pierre and Jean Talion. See Margry, Déc., III, 612, 1878.

Lemerlauans.—Ibid.

Papago (from *papáh* 'beans', *ɓotam* 'people': 'beansmen,' 'bean-people' (Kino, 1701, in Doc. Hist. Mex., 4th s., I, 360, 1856; McGee in Coville and Macdougal, Des. Bot. Lab., 1903); hence Span. *Frijoleros*. The name is often erroneously connected with 'cut-hair,' 'baptized,' etc.). A Piman tribe, closely allied to the Pima, whose original home was the territory s. and s. E. of Gila r., especially s. of Tucson, Ariz., in the main and tributary valleys of the Rio Santa Cruz, and extending w. and s. w. across the desert waste known as the Papaguería, into Sonora, Mexico. From San Xavier del Bac to Quitovaquita, one of their westernmost rancherias, it is about 120 m., and this may be considered as the extent of the settlements in the 17th and 18th centuries, during which period, owing to the inhospitality of their habitat, they were less inclined to village life than the Pima. Like the latter, the Papago subsist by agriculture, maize, beans, and cotton formerly being their chief crops, which they cultivated by means of irrigation; but many desert plants also contribute to their food supply, especially mesquite, the beans of which are eaten, and the saguaro, pitahaya, or giant cactus (*Cereus giganteus*), from the fruit of which preserves and a sirup are made. An extensive trade in salt, taken from the great inland lagoons, was formerly conducted by the tribe, the product finding ready sale at Tubac and Tucson. Their present principal crops are wheat and barley. They are also stock-raisers; and in recent years many of them

have gained a livelihood by working as laborers, especially on railroads and irrigation ditches. The Papago are tall and dark-complexioned; their dialect differs but little from that of the Pima, and their habits and customs are generally similar except that the men wear the hair only to the shoulders. Their traditions also bear close resemblance save where varied by local coloring. Like the Pima, the Papago women are expert basket makers. Their pottery is far inferior to that of the Pueblos, and the designs and patterns of both the pottery and the basketry are the same as those of the Pima. One of their favorite games, played with 4 sticks, was that known as *kints* (Spanish *quince*, 'fifteen'), called by them *ghin-skoot* (probably derived from the same word).

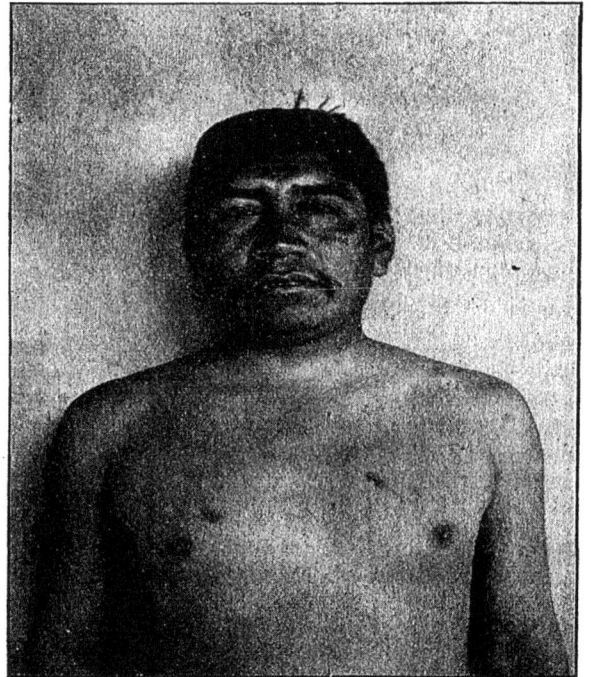

PAPAGO OF SAN XAVIER, ARIZONA. (AM. MUS. NAT. HIST.)

From early times the Papago have been known as a frugal and peaceable people, although they by no means lacked bravery when oppressed by their enemies, the Apache, from whose raids they suffered severely. Their typical dwelling is dome shaped, consisting of a framework of saplings, thatched with grass or leafy shrubs, with an adjacent shelter or ramada. These lodges are from 12 to 20 ft in diameter, and sometimes the roof is flattened and covered with earth.

The Papago in the U. S. numbered 4,981 in 1906, distributed as follows: Under the Pima school superintendent (Gila Bend res.), 2,233; under the farmer at San Xavier (Papago res.), 523 allottees on reserve, and 2,225 in Pima co. In addition, 859 Papago were officially reported in Sonora, Mexico, in 1900, but this is probably a low estimate of their true number in that state.

The Papago subdivisions and settlements, so far as known, are: Acachin, Alcalde, Ana, Anicam, Areitorae, Ati, Babasaqui, Bacapa, Baipia, Bajio, Batequi, Boco del Arroyo, Caborca, Caca Chimir, Cahuabi, Canoa, Casca, Charco, Chioro, Chuba, Coca, Comohuabi, Cops, Cubac, Cuitciabaqui, Cuitoat, Cujant, Cumaro, Elogio, Fresnal, Guadalupe, Gubo, Juajona, Junostaca, Macombo, Mesquite, Milpais, Nariz, Oapars, Ocaboa, Oiaur, Onia, Ooltan, Otean, Perigua, Perinimo, Piato, Poso Blanco, Poso Verde, Purificación (?), Quitovaquita, Raton, San Bonifacius, San Cosme, Sand Papago, San Ignacio (?), San Lazaro, San Luis Babi (?), San Martin, San Rafael, Santa Barbara (?), Santa Rosa, Saric (?), Saucita, Shuuk, Sicobutobavia, Sierra Blanca, Soba, Sonoita, Tachilta, Tacquison, Tecolote, Tubasa, Tubutama, Valle, Zuñiga. 　(F. W. H.)

Bean-people.—McGee in Coville and Macdougal, Des. Bot. Lab., 16, 1903 (transl. of aboriginal name). Beansmen.—Ibid. Hute-pa.—Thomas, Yuma MS. vocab., B. A. E., 1868 (Yuma name). Págago.—ten Kate, Reizen in N. A., 28, 1885 (misprint). Papabi-cotam.—Balbi quoted by Orozco y Berra, Geog., 352, 1864 (c=o). Paṗabi-Ootam.—Pfefferkorn (1794) quoted by Bandelier in Arch. Inst. Papers, III, 72, 1890. Papábi-Otawas.—Mexico, II, 300, 1853. Papabos.—Mota-Padilla, Hist. de la Conq., 519, 1742. Papabotas.—Kino (ca. 1699) in Doc. Hist. Mex., 4th s., I, 360, 1856 (or "pimas frijoleros," because their chief crop is beans—papavi). Papaga.—Forbes, Hist. Cal., 162, 1839. Papagi.—Morelli, Fasti Novi Orbis, 46, 1776. Papago-cotam.—Latham in Trans. Philol. Soc. Lond., 92, 1856 (c=o). Pa-Pagoe.—Box, Advent., 257, 1869. Papagoes.—Taylor in Cal. Farmer, June 13, 1862. Papagoose.—White, MS. Hist. Apaches, B. A. E., 1875. Papagos.—Villa-Señor, Theatro Am., pt. 2, 395, 1748. Papah-a′atam.—McGee, op. cit. (name applied by neighboring peoples, accepted by Papago as their tribal name). Papahi-Ootam.—Mayer, Mexico, II, 38, 1850. Papah′o.—McGee, op. cit. (given as early Spanish pronunciation). Papahotas.—Orozco y Berra, Geog., 58, 353, 1864. Papajos.—Platt, Karte Nord-Am., 1861. Papalotes.—Sedelmayr (1746) quoted by Bandelier in Arch. Inst. Papers, III, 74, 1890. Papani.—A. L. Pinart, inf'n (Seri name). Papa-Otam.—MS. of 1764 quoted by Bandelier in Arch. Inst. Papers, III, 72, 1890. Papapootam.—Rudo Ensayo, ca. 1762, ibid., 73. Papap Ootam.—Bandelier, Gilded Man, 150, 1893. Papap-Otam.—Bandelier in Arch. Inst. Papers, op. cit., 72. Papavicotam.—Orozco y Berra, Geog., 353, 1864. Papavos.—Mota-Padilla, Hist. de la Conq., 361, 1742. Papawar.—Pattie, Pers. Narr., 83, 1833. Papayos.—Mayer, Mexico, II, 300, 1853. Papelotes.—Orozco y Berra, Geog., 353, 1864. Papigo.—Gray, So. Pac. R. R. Surv., 55, 1856. Pima-Papabotas.—Mange (1699) quoted by Bancroft, Ariz. and N. M., 358, 1889. Pimas frijoleros.—Kino (ca. 1699) in Doc. Hist. Mex., 4th s., I, 360, 1856. Saikinné.—ten Kate, Reizen in N. A., 197, 1885 (='sand houses': Apache name). Si-ke-na.—White, MS. Hist. Apaches, B. A. E., 1875 (trans. 'bare-footed Indians': Apache name for Pima, Papago, and Maricopa). Tá′hba.—Gatschet, Yuma Sprachstamm, 86, 1886 (Yavapai name). Táxpa.—Ibid. Techpamāis.—ten Kate, Reizen in N. A., 160, 1885 (Maricopa name). Texpamaís.—ten Kate, Synonymie, 5, 1884 (Maricopa name). Tóno-Oöhtam.—ten Kate, Reizen in N. A., 23, 1885 ('people of the desert': own name). Vassconia.—Poston in Ind. Aff. Rep., 153, 1864 (='Christians'). Widshi

itikapa.—White quoted by Gatschet, Yuma-Sprachstamm, 1886 (Tonto name).

Papagonk (Lenape: papegonk, 'at the pond.'—Gerard). A band found in Ulster co., N. Y., doubtless the same as is placed on Lotter's map of 1777 on the E. branch of Delaware r., near the present Pepacton, Delaware co. They were probably a part of the Munsee.

Papaconck.—Lotter, Map of N. Y. and N. J., 1777. Papagonck.—Tryon (1778) quoted by Ruttenber, Tribes Hudson R., 255, 1872. Papagonk.—Tryon (1774) in N. Y. Doc. Col. Hist., VIII, 451, 1857. Popaghtunk.—Johnson (1771), ibid., 287.

Papajichic ('drinking - much - beer place.'—Lumholtz). A Tarahumare pueblo near Norogachic, Chihuahua, Mexico; pop. 838 in 1900.

Papagichic.—Lumholtz, inf'n, 1894. Papajichic.—Orozco y Berra, Geog., 323, 1864.

Papakeecha ('flat belly', i. e. a bedbug). A Miami chief whose village, commonly known as Flat Belly's Village, was E. of Turkey lake, at the present Indian Village, Noble co., Ind. 　(J. P. D.)

Flat Belly's Village.—Mississinewa treaty (1826) in U. S. Ind. Treat., 495, 1873. Pa-hed-ke-teh-a Village.—Hough, map in Ind. Geol. Rep., 1882 (misprint). Pă-pă-kēē′-cha.—J. P. Dunn, inf'n, 1907.

Papanacas. A former tribe of N. E. Mexico or S. Texas, probably Coahuiltecan, members of which were gathered into San Bernardo mission in Coahuila.—Orozco y Berra, Geog., 303, 1864. See Paachiqui, Pacuáchiam.

Papasquiaro. A former Tepehuane pueblo in W. Durango, Mexico, on the S. branch of Rio Nazas, probably on the site of the present Santiago. It was the seat of a Jesuit mission founded by Geronimo Ramirez in 1596, but was abandoned in 1616 on account of Toboso raids, and was subsequently temporarily repeopled with Eudeve.

Santiago Papasquiaro.—Orozco y Berra, Geog., 318, 1864.

Papiak (Pápĭăk·). A Squawmish village community on Burrard inlet, Brit. Col.—Hill-Tout in Rep. B. A. A. S., 474, 1900.

Papigochic ('snipe town.'—Froebel). A former Tarahumare settlement on the site of the present Villa de la Concepción, on the upper Rio Papigochi, in S. W. Chihuahua, Mexico, about lat. 28° 45′, lon. 108° 30′.—Orozco y Berra, Geog., 323, 1864.

Papinachois (Opápinagwa, 'they cause you to laugh.'—Hewitt). A Montagnais tribe or division living in the 17th century about the headwaters of Papinachois r., N. of the Bersiamite. They visited Tadoussac and received religious instruction from the missionaries, and by 1664 the latter had penetrated their country, finding them tractable and inoffensive. Charlevoix believed that this and other tribes of the same section had become extinct in his day. As late as 1721 they joined in a letter to the governor of Massachusetts.

Chauvignerie mentions a people of the same name living N. of L. Superior in 1736, numbering 20 warriors and having the hare as their totem, but these were a distinct people.						(J. M.)

Oupapinachiouek.—Jes. Rel. 1643, 38, 1858. **8papina-chi8ekhi.**—Jes. Rel. 1641, 5, 1858. **Oupapinachi8kü.**—Ducreux in N. Y. Doc. Col. Hist., x, 170, note, 1858. **Papenachois.**—McKenney and Hall, Ind. Tribes, III, 81, 1854. **Papinachaux.**—Chauvignerie (1736) quoted by Schoolcraft, Ind. Tribes, III, 556, 1853. **Papinaches.**—Doc. of 1748 in N. Y. Doc. Col. Hist., x, 170, 1858. **Papinachiois.**—Jes. Rel. 1666, 3, 1858. **Papinachi8ekhi.**—Jes. Rel. 1642, 39, 1858. **Papinachois.**—Bailloquet (1661) quoted by Hind, Lab. Penin., II, 20, 1863. **Papinakioises.**—Jes. Rel. 1666, 3, 1858. **Papinakois.**—Chauvignerie (1736) in N. Y. Doc. Col. Hist., IX, 1054, 1855. **Papinan-chois.**—Bacqueville de la Potherie, I, 207, 1753. **Papipanachois.**—Lahontan, New Voy., I, 207, 1703. **Papiragad'ek.**—Jes. Rel. 1640, 12, 1858. **Papivaches.**—Barcia, Ensayo, 184, 1723. **Papone-ches.**—Ibid., 183. **Popinoshees.**—Schoolcraft, Upper Miss., 93, 1834.

Papiscone. A village of the Powhatan confederacy in 1608, on the N. bank of the Rappahannock, in King George co., Va.—Smith (1629), Va., I, map, repr. 1819.

Papka. A Kuskwogmiut Eskimo village on the N. shore of Kuskokwim bay, Alaska.

Pápkamut.—Spurr and Post quoted by Baker, Geog. Dict. Alaska, 1902 (*mut=miut,* 'people').

Pappoose. An Indian infant, a child; written also *papoose.* Roger Williams (1643) gives *papoos* as the word for child in the Narraganset dialect of Algonquian; Wood (1634) has *pappouse;* Eliot uses for child or infant *peisses,* and Trumbull (Words derived from Ind. Languages, 27, 1872) thinks that pappoose may be derived from *papeisses,* a reduplicative of *peisses.* Eliot also has *papeississu,* 'he is very small.' On the origin of the word Mr W. R. Gerard (inf'n, 1907) says: "The infantine utterances *papa* and *mama* are very widely distributed the world over; and it is not improbable that *papu* was the Narraganset infant's way of uttering the syllables that in the mouths of most infants are heard as *pápa.* To this the Indians may have added the diminutive suffix *-es,* making *papúes,* and used the word as the name for a little child. *Papúes* comes very near in sound to *papoose,* a word which cannot be referred to any known Algonquian root. There is a curious resemblance between the word and the Latin *púpus,* 'child'. The word has become widely known and applied. Burton (Highlands of the Brazil), in speaking of the young of the tapir, says: 'and the calf [is called] Tapy'ra Curumim Ocu, Papoose of the big Tapir.' Peter Smith, in his Medical Facts (1813), applied it to the root of *Caulophyllum thalictroides,* the blue cohosh, because it was used by Indian women to facilitate parturition. The word has also been used as a verb, thus, Winthrop (Canoe and Saddle, 1862) has: ' This fash-ionable [infant] was *papoosed* in a tight-swathing wicker-work case.'" The word pappoose has been carried by white settlers to the extreme W., and has found lodgment in local varieties of the Chinook jargon. From pappoose have been named *pappoose frame,* an Indian cradle, and *pappoose root,* the blue cohosh (*Caulophyllum thalictroides*).						(A. F. C.)

Paraje (Span.: 'place,' 'residence'). A former summer village of the Laguna Indians, now a permanently occupied pueblo of that tribe, situated 6 m. N. NW. of Laguna, Valencia co., N. Mex. Native name, Tsimuná, referring to a black hill near by.

Paraje.—Pradt quoted by Hodge in Am. Anthrop., IV, 346, 1891. **Paraji.**—Ind. Aff. Rep. 1903, 514, 1904. **See-mun-ah.**—Pradt, op. cit. **Tsimuná.**—Hodge, field notes, B. A. E., 1895.

Paraniguts (*Pa-ran'-i-guts,* 'people of the marshy spring'). A Paiute band formerly living in the valley of the same name in S. E. Nevada; pop. 171 in 1873.—Powell in Ind. Aff. Rep. 1873, 50, 1874.

Pah Ranagats.—Head in Ind. Aff. Rep. 1867, 174, 1868. **Pah-rán-nè.**—Whipple in Pac. R. R. Rep., III, pt. 3, 16, 1854. **Pah-Reneg-Utes.**—Sale in Ind. Aff. Rep., 153, 1865. **Paranagats.**—Gatschet in Wheeler Surv. Rep., VII, 410, 1879.

Parantones. A tribe of which 21 were reported in 1794 at Espiritu Santo de Zúñiga mission, Texas, by Fr. Juan José Aguilar. They were with Jaranames (Aranames), Tamiques, Prietos, Brazos largos, Vende flechas, and Gumpusas, all of which were said to have been subtribes of the Jaranames (Portillo, Apuntes para la Hist. Antigua de Coahuila y Texas, 308, 1888).						(H. E. B.)

Parathees. Given by Ker (Travels, 113, 1816) as the name of a tribe living apparently on Red r., N. W. Texas. Not identifiable and probably mythical.

Parchaque. A tribe, evidently Coahuiltecan, mentioned in 1675 by Fernando del Bosque. They, with the Catujanos, Tilijaes, and Apes, are said to have occupied the country N. E. from Monclova across the Rio Grande (Exped., in Nat. Geog. Mag., XIV, 347, 1903). They were mentioned by Massanet in 1690 in his list of tribes, and in 1691 were said by him to have lived between the Sabinas and the Rio Grande. On his expedition to the Hasinai country from San Salvador del Valle de Santiago, he met them about 10 leagues S. of the Rio Grande. They, with Mescaleros, Yoricas, Chomes, Ala-chomes, and Pamais (Pamayes?) accompanied the Spanish party several days. Massanet said they were wanderers, without agriculture, living on buffalo meat and wild products. Some words of these tribes Massanet recorded; thus, *asaguan* meant 'heart,' and *ganapetuan,* their name for the Rio Grande, meant 'large body of water' (Diario, 1691, in Mem. de Nueva España, XXVII, 90, MS.; Velasco,

Dictamen Fiscal, Nov. 30, 1716, ibid., 183).   (H. E. B.)

Pachaques.—Fernando del Bosque (1675), op. cit.

Parchacas.—Massanet, 1691, op. cit.

Parched Corn Indians. A name indefinitely applied. "In most of our American colonies there yet remain a few of the natives, who formerly inhabited those extensive countries . . . We call them 'Parched-corn-Indians,' because they chiefly use it for bread, are civilized and live mostly by planting."—Adair, Am. Inds., 343, 1775.

Parchinas. Mentioned by Rivera (Diario, leg. 2602, 1736) as a tribe or village apparently near the lower Rio Grande in s. Texas. Probably Coahuiltecan.

Parflêche (pron. *par'-flesh*). The ordinary skin box of the Plains and Rocky mtn. tribes, made of stiff-dressed rawhide from which the hair has been removed. It is usually of rectangular shape, varying from 2 by 3 ft in size for the largest boxes—used as clothes trunks, for storing food, etc.—to small pouches

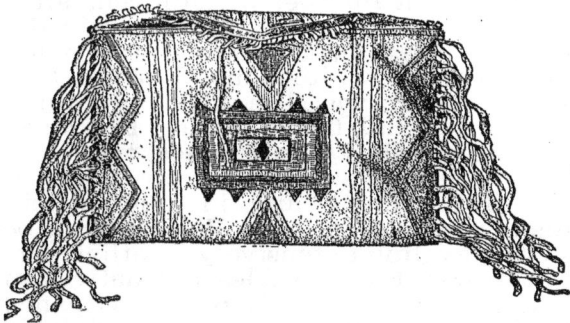

PARFLÊCHE PACKING-CASE OF THE PLAINS TRIBES.   (MASON)

for holding paints, mirrors, or other toilet articles. Those used for storing clothing are made in pairs, two to each bed in the tipi, by trimming the rawhide to proper form while still pliable, folding over the edges upon each other, and fastening them in place by means of strings of skins passed through holes near the sides. The surface is painted with designs in various colors, and at times a fringe is added. Round boxes, somewhat resembling a quiver in shape, are made of the same material for holding feathers and decorative war-bonnets. In other sections baskets of various kinds, boxes of bark or matting, or bags of grass or soft-dressed skin, took the place of parflêche. The word is of doubtful origin, but as commonly spelled appears in French narratives as early as 1700, and is probably from some old French root, possibly from *parer* ' to parry,' *flêche* 'arrow,' in reference originally to the shield or body-armor of rawhide. See *Boxes and Chests, Rawhide, Receptacles, Skin-dressing*.   (J. M.)

Pariscar. One of the four divisions of the Crow tribe, according to Lewis and Clark.

Pa-rees-car.—Lewis and Clark, Discov., 40, 1806; Orig. Jour. Lewis and Clark, VI, 103, 1905.

Parka. A dress of bird or seal skin worn as an outside garment by the Eskimo of the N. W. coast of America; from the name of this article in the Aleut dialect of the Eskimo language.   (A. F. C.)

Parkeenaum (*Par-kee-na-um*, 'water people'). Given by Neighbors (Schoolcraft, Ind. Tribes, II, 127, 1852) as a division of the Comanche. The name, which is not recognized by the Comanche, may possibly have been intended for Pagatsu, q. v.

Parker, Ely Samuel. A mixed-blood Seneca of the Wolf clan, son of Chief William Parker, whose wife was a descendant of a Huron captive; born on the Tonawanda res., N. Y., in 1828. His Seneca name was Hasanoanda, 'Coming to the Front,' but on receiving the official title Deionin, hogä´,wĕⁿ ('it holds the door open'), when he became eighth chief of the tribe, he laid the other aside. Parker received an academic education, studied law and civil engineering, and at the outbreak of the Civil War was employed as engineer on a Government building at Galena, Ill., then the home of Ulysses S. Grant. A friendship sprung up between the two which continued after both joined the Union Army at the outbreak of the Civil War. Parker's distinguished service in the Vicksburg campaign led to his selection by Grant as a member of his staff. In May, 1863, he became assistant adjutant-general, with the rank of captain, and was afterward secretary to Gen. Grant until the close of the war. On Apr. 9, 1865, he became brigadier-general of volunteers; in 1866, a first lieutenant of cavalry in the United States Army, and on Mar. 2, 1867, captain, major, lieutenant-colonel, and brigadier-general. By reason of their intimate relations, as well as of Parker's excellent handwriting, Grant intrusted him while his secretary with both his personal and official correspondence. It was thus that at Lee's surrender Parker engrossed the articles of capitulation. Parker resigned from the Army in 1869 to accept from President Grant an appointment as Commissioner of Indian Affairs. He retired in 1871, but subsequently held several positions under the city government of New York, and at the time of his death at Fairfield, Conn., Aug. 31, 1905, was connected with the police department. General Parker was an intimate friend of Lewis H. Morgan, the ethnologist, and his efficient coworker in preparing his "League of the Iroquois," first published in 1851. "The recognized authority and value of this book are due to the work of Parker, as well as to that of Morgan. As a sachem Parker had full knowledge of the institutions of his people, and as a man of education and culture he had both the interest and ability necessary to make those institutions known to civilized man as no ordinary interpreter could have done." Parker had a sister, Miss Caroline G. Parker (Gahano, 'Hanging Flower'), and a younger brother, Nicholas, both of whom the General survived. Miss Parker (sometimes, without reason, referred to as "Queen of the Senecas") married John Mountpleasant, a Tuscarora. Consult Morgan, League of the Iroquois, a new edition edited and annotated by Herbert M. Lloyd, New York, 1904.

Parker, Quana (from Comanche *kwaina*, 'fragrant,' joined to his mother's family name). A principal chief of the Comanche, son of a Comanche chief and a white captive woman. His father, Nokoni, 'wanderer,' was the leader of the Kwahadi division, the wildest and most hostile portion of the tribe and the most inveterate raiders along the Texas border. In one of the incursions, in the summer of 1835, the Comanche attacked a small settlement on Navasota r., in E. Texas, known from its founder as Parker's Fort, and carried off 2 children of Parker himself, one of whom, Cynthia Ann Parker, then about 12 years of age, became later the wife of the chief and the mother of Quana, born about 1845. The mother, with a younger infant, was afterward rescued by the troops and brought back to Texas, where both soon died. Quana grew up with the tribe, and on the death of his father rapidly rose to commanding influence. The Kwahadi band refused to enter into the Medicine Lodge treaty of 1867, by which the Comanche, Kiowa Apache, Cheyenne, and Arapaho were assigned to reservations, and continued to be a disturbing element until 1874, when, in consequence of the depredations of an organized company of white buffalo hunters, Quana himself mustered the warriors of the Comanche and Cheyenne, with about half the Kiowa and some portion of the other two tribes, for resistance. The campaign began June 24, 1874, with an attack led by Quana in person at the head of 700 confederate warriors against the buffalo hunters, who were strongly intrenched in a fort known as the Adobe Walls, on the South Canadian in the Texas panhandle. In addition to the protection afforded by the thick walls, the white hunters had a small field-piece which they used with such good effect that after a siege lasting all day the Indians were obliged to retire

with considerable loss. The war thus begun continued along the whole border s. of Kansas until about the middle of the next year, when, being hard pressed by the troops under Gen. Mackenzie, most of the hostiles surrendered. Quana, however, kept his band out upon the Staked plain for 2 years longer, when he also came in. Recognizing the inevitable, he set about making the best of the new conditions, and being still young and with the inherited intelligence of his white ancestry, he quickly adapted himself so well to the white man's road as to become a most efficient factor in leading his people up to civilization. Through his influence the confederated tribes adopted the policy of leasing the surplus pasture lands, by which a large annual income was added to their revenues. He popularized education, encouraged house building and agriculture, and discouraged dissipation and savage extravagances, while holding strictly to his native beliefs and ceremonies. Polygyny being customary in his tribe, he had several wives and a number of children, all of whom, of proper age, have received a school education, and one or two of whom have married white men. For nearly 30 years Parker was the most prominent and influential figure among the 3 confederated tribes in all leases, treaty negotiations, and other public business with the Government, and in this capacity made repeated visits to Washington, besides traveling extensively in other parts of the country. Besides his native language he spoke both English and Spanish fairly well. Before his death, Feb. 23, 1911, he lived in a large and comfortable house, surrounded by well-cultivated fields, about 12 m. w. of Ft Sill, Okla. Quanah, a town in N. Texas, was named in his honor. (J. M.)

Partocac. A Chumashan village w. of Pueblo de las Canoas (San Buenaventura), Ventura co., Cal., in 1542. Placed by Taylor at the Indian cemetery on the mesa of the Goleta farm.

Paltocac.—Taylor in Cal. Farmer, Apr. 17, 1863. Partocac.—Cabrillo (1542) in Smith, Colec. Doc. Fla., 181, 1857. Partocac.—Taylor, op. cit.

Paruguns (*Pa-ru'-guns*, 'marsh people'). A Paiute band formerly near Parawan, s. w. Utah; pop. 27 in 1873.

Parawan.—Smithson. Misc. Coll., XIV, 39, 1878. Parawat Yutas.—Burton, City of Saints, 578, 1861. Pa-ru'-guns.—Powell in Ind. Aff. Rep. 1873, 50, 1874.

Parumpaiats (*Pa-room'-pai-ats*, 'people of the meadows'). A Paiute band formerly in or near Moapa valley, s. E. Nev.; pop. 35 in 1873.—Powell in Ind. Aff. Rep. 1873, 50, 1874.

Parumpats (*Pa-room'-pats*). A Paiute band formerly at Parum spring, s. E. Nev.; pop. 56 in 1873, including the Nogwats.—Powell in Ind. Aff. Rep. 1873, 50, 1874.

Pasakunamon (*Pä-sa-kun-ä'-mon*, 'pulling corn,' according to Morgan; but properly *paskunemen*, 'pulling by hand' and referring to corn or anything else inanimate.—Gerard). A sub-clan of the Delawares.—Morgan, Anc. Soc., 172, 1877.

Pasalves. A former tribe of N. E. Mexico or S. Texas, probably Coahuiltecan, members of which were gathered into Nuestra Señora de los Dolores de la Punta mission, at Lampazos, N. Nuevo Leon.
Pasalves.—Orozco y Berra, Geog., 303, 1864. Pastalve.—Massanet (1690) in Dictamen Fiscal, Nov. 30, 1716, MS. cited by H. E. Bolton, inf'n, 1906.

Pasara. Given as a Karok village on Klamath r., Cal., inhabited in 1860.
Pas-see-roo.—Taylor in Cal. Farmer, Mar. 23, 1860.

Pasaughtacock. A village of the Powhatan confederacy in 1608, on the N. bank of York r., in King and Queen co., Va.—Smith (1629), Va., I, map, repr. 1819.

Pascagoula (Choctaw: 'bread people', from *paska* 'bread,' *okla* 'people'). A small tribe of Indians formerly living on Pascagoula r. in S. Mississippi, in intimate connection with the Biloxi, but now extinct as a separate division. As no vocabulary of their language has been preserved, nor their own tribal name, their ethnic relations are conjectural; it is not unlikely, however, that they belonged to the Muskhogean linguistic family.

The first mention of them is that of Iberville in 1699 (Margry, Déc., IV, 193, 1880), who refers to the village of the Bilocchy (Biloxi), Pascoboula (Pascagoula), and Moctobi, to reach which from Biloxi bay took 2½ days. There were really three villages, and a little farther on (ibid., 195), he speaks of the three as being on Pascagoula r., a short distance apart. As the three together, according to Sauvole (ibid., 451), did not contain more than 20 cabins, the estimate of 100 families is ample. About 1764, in company with the Biloxi and several other tribes, they determined to leave the neighborhood of Mobile, and in 1784 were found settled on the E. side of the Mississippi, 10 m. above the village of the Tunica. Together with the neighboring Biloxi they were estimated at 20 warriors, probably about 75 souls. Before 1791, however, they had moved up Red r. and settled at the confluence of that stream with Bayou Rigolet du Bon Dieu. The name of their chief at that time was Du Blanc. About 1795 they sold their lands here to Miller and Fulton, and followed the Biloxi to Bayou Bœuf, settling between them and the Choctaw. Later they sold these lands to the same parties, the sale being confirmed by the United States in 1805, but probably continued to reside in the neighborhood, where they died off or became incorporated with the Biloxi and Choctaw. Morse in 1822 enumerated three distinct bands of Pascagoula, two on Red r. and a third on a branch of the Neches, aggregating 240 souls; but probably some mistake was made, as the Biloxi are given as numbering only 70. (A. S. G.   J. R. S.)
Bread Nation.—Gallatin in Trans. Am. Antiq. Soc., II, 115, 1836. Breed Nation.—Boggs (1793) in Am. St. Papers, Ind. Aff., I, 449, 1832 (misprint). Miskigúla.—Gatschet, Biloxi MS., 1886 (Biloxi name). Nation of Bread.—Boudinot, Star in West, 128, 1816. Pacha-oglouas.—Jefferys, Fr. Doms. Am., pt. I, 162, 1761. Pacha-Ogoulas.—Le Page du Pratz, La., II, 214, 1758. Pasagoula.—Coxe, Carolana, map, 1741. Pascaganlas.—Schermerhorn (1812) in Mass. Hist. Soc. Coll., II, 27, 1814 (misprint). Pascagolas.—Sibley, Hist. Sketches, 83, 1806. Pascagoulas.—Pénicaut (1699) in French, Hist. Coll. La.. n. s., I, 38, 1869. Pasca Ogoulas.—Gallatin in Trans. Am. Antiq. Soc., II, 115, 1836. Pasca Ooco-las.—McKenney and Hall, Ind. Tribes, III, 81, 1854. Pasca-Oocoolos.—Romans, Florida, 101, 1775. Pascoboula.—Iberville (1700) in Margry, Déc., IV, 427, 1880. Pascoogoulas.—Sibley (1805) in Am. St. Papers, Ind. Aff., I, 725, 1832. Paskagoulas.—Dumont, La., I, 135, 1753. Paskaguna.—Gatschet, inf'n (Caddo form). Paspagolas.—Woodward, Reminis., 25, 1859. Pescagolas.—Lewis, Trav., 208, 1809.

Pascegna. A former Gabrieleño rancheria in Los Angeles co., Cal., at the site of the present San Fernando.
Pascegna.—Reid (1852) quoted by Taylor in Cal. Farmer, June 8, 1860. Pascog-na.—Ibid., Jan. 11, 1861. Pasheckna.—Ibid., May 11, 1860. Pashingmu.—A. L. Kroeber, inf'n, 1905 (Luiseño name).

Pashagasawissouk (*Peshegesiwäg*, pl. for 'deer'). Given as the Elk gens of the Sauk.
Pä-sha'-ga-sa-wis-so-uk.—Morgan, Anc. Soc., 170, 1877. Pecegesiwag.—Wm. Jones, inf'n, 1906 (correct form; *c* = *sh*).

Pasharanack (apparently *pesharinäk*, 'near the cove, or bay.'—Gerard). A village of the Abnaki in 1616, probably on the coast of Maine.—Smith (1616) in Mass. Hist. Soc. Coll., 3d s., VI, 107, 1837.

Pashashe. A Cholovone village E. of lower San Joaquin r., Cal.—Pinart, Cholovone MS., B. A. E., 1880.

Pashasheebo (Montagnais: *pàshashibu*, 'swollen river.'—Gerard). A Montagnais village on the N. shore of the Gulf of St Lawrence.—Stearns, Labrador, 271, 1884.

Pashipaho (*Päshipahowa*, 'He touches lightly in passing.'—W. J.). A prominent Sauk chief, belonging to one of the Fish clans, whose name is usually but improperly translated "Stabber." He was born about 1760, and first came into public notice when he signed, as principal chief of the Sauk, the treaty of St Louis, Mo., Nov. 3, 1804, by which the allied Sauk and Foxes ceded to the United States their lands in Illinois and Wisconsin. This was the treaty repudiated by Black Hawk and which ultimately brought on the so-called Black Hawk war of 1832. Little is known of Pashipaho's career as a warrior, but it is probable that he was highly regarded by his tribesmen as a fighting man, for it was under his leadership that the Iowa were defeated in a decisive battle on Des

Moines r. in May 1823, in which engagement Black Hawk was second in command. He was also the leader in the plot to destroy Ft Madison, Iowa, in 1809, an effort that failed because the whites were forewarned. He is said to have been vindictive and implacable in his resentments, on one occasion undertaking a long journey for the purpose of killing the Indian agent at Prairie du Chien, Wis., because the latter had offended him; but his attempt was thwarted by Taimah. Pashipaho supported Keokuk in opposing Black Hawk's war against the whites, and took no part in it. In addition to signing the St Louis treaty of 1804, he was a leading participant in negotiating subsequent treaties with the United States at Ft Armstrong, Rock Island, Ill., Sept. 3, 1822; Washington, D. C., Aug. 4, 1824, and Ft Armstrong, Sept. 21, 1832. Pashipaho was again at Ft Armstrong in Aug. 1833, on the occasion of the liberation of Black Hawk and his companions, when in a speech he advocated the peace policy of Keokuk, remarking that at one time he had taken prisoner the "great chief of the Osages," but had voluntarily released him. While in Washington, Pashipaho's portrait was painted by Charles B. King for the Indian gallery of the War Department, and is reproduced in McKenney and Hall's Indian Tribes; ten years later his portrait was again painted by George Catlin. Mention is made of Pashipaho's presence with other Sauk and Fox chiefs in camp on Des Moines r. in 1841, when news of a massacre of some of their people by the Sioux was received. Although Keokuk was present, and Pashipaho was then so old that he had to be aided in mounting his horse, the latter led the pursuit of the marauders. It is probable that his death occurred not long thereafter, though but little is known of his last years other than that he was much given to intemperate habits. He moved with his people to their reservation in Kansas. Other recorded forms of the name are Pahshapaha, Pasheparho, Pashepawko, Pashepiho, and Pushee Paho. (C. T.)

Pashir. The Water-pebble clan of the Tigua pueblo of Isleta, N. Mex.

P'áshir-t'aínin.—Lummis quoted by Hodge in Am. Anthrop., IX, 352, 1896 (t'aínin = 'people').

Pashka. A former Modoc settlement on the N. W. shore of Tule or Rhett lake, s. w. Oreg.

Páshχa.—Gatschet in Cont. N. A. Ethnol., II, pt. I, XXXII, 1890. Páshχanuash.—Ibid. (name of people). Pásχa.—Ibid. Pásχanuash.—Ibid., XXXIV (name of people).

Pasinogna. A former Gabrieleño rancheria in Los Angeles co., Cal., at a locality later called Rancho del Chino.

Pasinog-na.—Ried (1852) quoted by Hoffman in Bull. Essex Inst., XVII, 2, 1885. Passinogna.—

Ried quoted by Taylor in Cal. Farmer, June 8, 1860.

Pasion. A former group of Mohave rancherias on the E. bank of the Rio Colorado, below the present Ft Mohave, in Arizona, visited and so named by Fray Francisco Garcés in 1776.

Rancherias de la Pasion.—Garcés, Diary, 228, 416, 1900.

Paska. A Ntlakyapamuk village on or near Thompson r., Brit. Col.; pop. 17 in 1897, the last time the name appears.

Pasha.—Can. Ind. Aff., 363, 1897. Paska.—Ibid., 230, 1886.

Paskwawininiwug ('prairie people'). The Plains Cree, one of the two great subdivisions of the Cree, subdivided into Sipiwininiwug and Mamikininiwug.

Ammisk-watcheé'-thinyoowuc.— Franklin, Journ. to Polar Sea, I, 168, 1824. Beaver Hill Crees.—Ibid. Cree of the Prairie.—Morgan, Consang. and Affin., 286, 1871. Grandes pagnes.—Petitot, in Jour. Roy. Geog. Soc., 649, 1883. Mus-ko-tá-we-ne-wuk.—Morgan, Consang. and Affin., 286, 1871. Paskwawiyiniwok.—Lacombe, Dict. de la Langue des Cris, x, 1874. People of the Prairie.—Morgan, Consang. and Affin., 286, 1871. Plain Crees.—Robinson, Great Fur Land, 186, 1879. Prairie-Crees.—Petitot in Jour. Roy. Geog. Soc., 649, 1883. Prairie Indians.—Hind, Red River Exped., 151, 1860.

Pasnacanes. A tribe or subtribe living in the 18th century with the Pamaques, near the Texas coast between the Nueces and San Antonio rs. They were probably Coahuiltecan, since they were very closely related to the Pamaques, of which tribe they seem sometimes to have been regarded as a subdivision (Ynforme of the College of Querétaro to the Commissary General, 1754, MS.). In the early history of San José mission, Tacasnanes, perhaps the same, were taken there, together with Pampopas, Pastias, and Chayopines, but they soon deserted (Altamira, opinion of Feb. 27, 1750, Mem. Hist. Tex., Archivo Gen., XXVIII, 140, MS.). In 1743 the Pasnacanes were being "reduced" at the Querétaran missions near San Antonio, where their kinsmen, the Pamaques, had already been gathered (Fr. Santa Ana to the Viceroy, Mar. 4, 1743, MS.). (H. E. B.)

Panascán.—Ynforme of 1754, op. cit. Pasnacanes.—Ibid., 136. Tacasnanes.—Altamira, op. cit. (identical?).

Pasos. An unidentified tribe or band having horses and living on lower Missouri r. in 1680; probably Siouan.—La Salle (ca. 1680) in Margry, Déc., II, 168, 1878.

Paspahegh. A tribe of the Powhatan confederacy that lived between Chickahominy and James rs., Va., and numbered 200 in 1608. It was with the people of this tribe that the settlers of Jamestown came into most direct contact.

Paspahegas.—Boudinot, Star in the West, 128, 1816. Paspaheghes.—Strachey (ca. 1612), Va., 35, 1849. Paspaheghs.—Smith (1629), Va., II, 6, repr. 1819.

Paspahegh. The principal village of the Paspahegh, situated on the N. bank of James r., in Charles City co., Va. It was burned by the English in 1610.

Paspahege.—Smith (1629), Va., II, 77, repr. 1819. **Paspahegh.**—Ibid., 6. **Paspaheigh.**—Harris, Voy. and Trav., I, 836, 1705. **Paspihae.**—Percy (ca. 1606) in Purchas, Pilgrimes, IV, 1687, 1626. **Paspihe.**—Ibid.

Paspahegh. A village of the Powhatan confederacy in 1608, situated on the s. bank of Chickahominy r., in Charles City co., Va., above Providence Forge.—Smith (1629), Va., I, map, repr. 1819.

Paspikaivats (*Pa-spi'-kai-vats*, 'water spring mountain people'). A Paiute band formerly living near Toquerville, s. w. Utah; pop. 40 in 1873.—Powell in Ind. Aff. Rep. 1873, 50, 1874.

Pasquasheck. A former Nochpeem village, probably on the E. bank of Hudson r., in Dutchess co., N. Y.

Pasquasheck.—Ruttenber, Tribes Hudson R., 80, 1872. **Pasquuasheck.**—Van der Donck (1656) quoted by Ruttenber, ibid., 72.

Pasquayah. An Assiniboin village situated where Carrot r. enters the Saskatchewan, in E. Saskatchewan, Canada. The elder Henry says that at the time of his visit, in 1775, it consisted of 30 tipis. The younger Henry (Coues, New Light, II, 470, 1897) found it in 1808, previous to the smallpox epidemic, a place of general rendezvous for different tribes.

Pasquayah.—Henry, Trav., 256, 1809. **Poscoiac.**—Coues, New Light, II, 469, note, 1897. **Poskoyac.**—Jefferys, Fr. Dom. Am., pt. 1, map, 1744.

Pasquenoc (seemingly a corrupt form of *pasakwen* 'to be close together,' + *ok* 'people.'—Gerard). A Weapomeioc village in 1586, on the N. shore of Albemarle sd., perhaps in Camden co., N. C.

Pasquenock.—Smith (1629), Va., I, map, repr. 1819. **Pasquenoke.**—Dutch map (1621) in N. Y. Doc. Col. Hist., I, 1856. **Passaquenock.**—Lane (1586) in Smith (1629), Va., I, 87, repr. 1819. **Passaquenoke.**—Hakluyt, Voy. (1600), III, 312, repr. 1810. **Woman's town.**—Lane (1585) quoted by Hawks, N. C., I, 112, 1859. **Womens towne.**—Lane (1586) in Smith (1629), Va., I, 87, repr. 1819.

Pasqui. Mentioned by Oviedo (Hist. Gen. Indies, III, 628, 1853) as one of the provinces or villages, probably on the South Carolina coast, visited by Ayllon in 1520. See *Tasqui.*

Pasquotank. An Algonquian tribe or band living in 1700 in North Carolina on the N. shore of Albemarle sd.

Paspatank.—Lawson (1714), Hist. Car., 383, repr. 1860. **Pasquotank.**—Mooney, Siouan Tribes of the East 7, 1894.

Passaconaway. A chief of the region about Pennacook on Merrimac r. as early as 1632 (Drake, Inds. of N. Am., 278, 1880). In 1629 his daughter married Winnepurget, sachem of Saugus, as told in Whittier's "Bridal of Pennacook." His son, Wannalancet, was afterward sachem of Pennacook. According to the chronicler Hubbard, Passaconaway was "the most noted powwow and sorcerer of all the country." He formally submitted to the English in 1644, and died at a very advanced age. (A. F. C.)

Passadumkeag (probably from *pasidämkik*, 'beyond the sandy beach', from *pasid* 'beyond', *amk* 'sand', *ik* locative.—Gerard). A Penobscot village at Nicolas id. in Penobscot r., near the present Passadumkeag, Penobscot co., Me. The village was destroyed by the English in 1723, and the inhabitants retired to Mattawamkeag.

Passadumkeag.—Vetromile, Abnakis, 22, 1866. **Passadunkee.**—Conf. of 1786 in Me. Hist. Soc. Coll., VII, 10, 1876.

Passamaquoddy (*Peskĕdĕmakădi*, 'plenty of pollock.'—Gatschet). A small tribe belonging to the Abnaki confederacy, but speaking nearly the same dialect as the Malecite. They formerly occupied all the region about Passamaquoddy bay and on St Croix r. and Schoodic lake, on the boundary between Maine and New Brunswick. Their principal village was Gunasquamekook, on the site of St Andrews, N. B. They were restricted by the pressure of the white settlements, and in 1866 were settled chiefly at Sebaik, near Perry, on the s. side of the bay, and on Lewis id. They had other villages at Calais, on Schoodic lake in Washington co., Me., and on St Croix r. in New Brunswick. They were estimated at about 150 in 1726, 130 in 1804, 379 in 1825, and from 400 to 500 in 1859. The Passamaquoddy and Penobscot tribes send to the Maine legislature a representative who is permitted to speak only on matters connected with the affairs of the Indian reservations (Prince in Proc. Am. Philos. Soc., XXXVI, 481, 1897). See *Abnaki.* (J. M.)

Machias Tribe.—Winthrop (1633) in Mass. Hist. Soc. Coll., 4th s., III, 292, 1856. **Machies tribe.**—Gyles (1726) in Me. Hist. Soc. Coll., III, 357, 1853 (applied to a part of the Passamaquoddy living on Machias r.). **Pasamaquoda.**—Pownall (1759), ibid., V, 368, 1857. **Passamacadie.**—Willis (ca. 1830), ibid., I, 27, 1865. **Passamaquoda.**—Pownall (1759), ibid., V, 371, 1857. **Passamaquodda.**—Penhallow (1726) in N. H. Hist. Soc. Coll., I, 33, 1824. **Passamaquoddy.**—Penhallow (1726) in N. H. Hist. Soc. Coll., I, 92, 1824. **Passamaquodie.**—Williamson in Me. Hist. Soc. Coll., VII, 203, 1876. **Passamequado.**—Dudley (1704) quoted by Drake, Ind. Wars, 220, 1825. **Pas-sam-ma-quod-dies.**—Ind. Aff. Rep., app., 2, 1824. **Passammaquoddies.**—Macauley, N. Y., II, 162, 1829. **Passemaquoddy.**—Church (1716) quoted by Drake, Ind. Wars, 200, 1825. **Passimaquodies.**—Trumbull, Conn., II, 64, 1818. **Pennoukady.**—Vaudreuil (1721) in N. Y. Doc. Col. Hist., IX, 904, 1855. **Peskadam8kkan.**—Aubery (1720), in N. Y. Doc. Col. Hist., IX, 895, 1855. **Peskadamukotik.**—Gatschet, Penobscot MS., B. A. E., 1887 (Penobscot name). **Peskadaneeoukkanti.**—McKenney and Hall, Ind. Tribes, III, 79, 1854. **Peskamaquonty.**—Vetromile, Abnakis, 54, 1866. **Pesmaquady.**—Gyles (1726) in Me. Hist. Soc. Coll., III, 357, 1853. **Pesmocady.**—Cadillac (1692), ibid., VI, 279, 1859. **Pesmokanti.**—Abnaki letter (1721) in Mass. Hist. Soc. Coll., 2d s., VIII, 262, 1819. **Pĕs-ta-moka'tiŭk.**—Chamberlain, Malesit MS., B. A. E., 1882 (Malecite name). **Pestumagatiek.**—Prince in Proc. Am. Philos. Soc., XXXVI, 479, 1897 (own name). **Quaddies.**—James quoted by Tanner, Narr., 327, 1830. **Quaddy Indians.**—Ind. Aff. Rep., 144, 1827. **Quoddies.**—Drake, Bk. Inds., X, 1848. **Quoddy Indians.**—Ind. Aff. Rep., 99, 1828. **St. Croix Indians.**—Hoyt, Antiq. Res., 220, 1824. **Scootuks.**—Keane in Stanford, Compend., 534, 1878. **Unchagogs.**—Drake, Bk. Inds., XII, 1848. **Unchechauge.**—Andros (1675) in N. Y.

Doc. Col. Hist., XIV, 709, 1883. **Uncheckauke.**—Doc. of 1677, ibid., 733. **Unquechauge.**—Andros (1675), ibid., 695. **Unshagogs.**—Keane in Stanford, Compend., 541, 1878. **Vncheckaug.**—Doc. of 1667 in N. Y. Doc. Col. Hist., XIV, 602, 1883. **Vnquechauke.**—Doc. of 1668, ibid., 605.

Passaunkack. A village of the Powhatan confederacy in 1608, on the s. bank of Mattapony r., in the N. w. part of King William co., Va.—Smith (1629), Va., I, map, repr. 1819.

Passayonk ('in the valley.'—Hewitt). A Delaware village on Schuylkill r., Pa., in 1648. Macauley calls the band a part of the Manta, and says that they lived along the w. bank of the lower Delaware, extending into Delaware.
Passajonck.—Beekman (1660) in N. Y. Doc. Col. Hist., XII, 310, 1877. **Passajongh.**—Beekman (1660), ibid., 302. **Passajonk.**—Macauley, N. Y., II, 166, 1829. **Passayonk.**—Hudde (1648) in N. Y. Doc. Col. Hist., XII, 36, 1877. **Passayunck.**—Ibid., 309.

Passing Hail's Band. A band of Mdewakanton Sioux formerly living on Yellow Medicine r., Minn., and taking its name from its chief, Wasúwicaxtanxi, or Wasuihiyayedan, otherwise known as Bad Hail, Passing Hail, and Traveling Hail. The band numbered 193 in 1863. See Ind. Aff. Rep., 314, 1863; Minn. Hist. Soc. Coll., VI, pt. 3, 386, 1894.

Passycotcung. A former village of the Munsee or the Delawares, but subject to the Seneca, on Chemung r., N. Y.—Hamilton (1760) in Mass. Hist. Soc. Coll., 4th s., IX, 280, 1871.

Pastaloca. A tribe, evidently Coahuiltecan, met by Massanet, in 1691, at points 6 and 10 leagues s. w. of Nueces r., Texas, with Quems, Pachul, Ocana, Chaguan (Siaguan), and Paac Indians (Diario, 1691, in Mem. de Nueva España, XXVII, 92, MS.). It was evidently given in his list of 1690 and miscopied in Mem. de Nueva España (XXVII, 183) as Pastalve. In 1703 this was one of the tribes at San Bernardo mission, and in 1738 61 families of the tribe were at San Juan Bautista (Portilla, Apuntes, 283, 288, 1888). In 1720 a woman of this tribe was baptized at San Antonio de Valero mission and her name written Pastaloca and Pastoloca. In the burial record her name is entered Pastalac (Valero Bautismos, 1720, partida 76, MS.). In 1730 a daughter of two gentiles, a Papan(ac?) and a Pastalath, was baptized there.   (H. E. B.)
Pastalac.—Valero Entierros, partida 249, MS. **Pastaloca.**—Valero Bautismos, partida 76, MS. **Pastalocos.**—Orozco y Berra, Geog., 303, 1864. **Pastaluc.**—Massanet, op. cit., 1691. **Pastalve.**—Velasco, Dictamen Fiscal, in Mem. de Nueva España, XXVII, 183, MS. (miscopy). **Pastoloca.**—Valero Bautismos, partida 76, MS. **Patacales.**—Orozco y Berra, Geog., 304, 1864 (identical?).

Pastancoyas. A tribe, probably Coahuiltecan, at San Bernardo mission, on the Rio Grande in Coahuila, in or after 1703.—Orozco y Berra, Geog., 303, 1864.

Pastanza. A village of the Potomac tribe of the Powhatan confederacy on or near Potomac r. in Virginia in 1608, ruled by a brother of the chief of the Potomac tribe. It may have been one of the villages on Aquia cr. in Stafford co., marked on Capt. John Smith's map but not named.   (J. M.)
Paspatanzie.—Spelman (ca. 1615) misquoted by Tooker, Algonq. Ser., VIII, 21, 1901. **Pasptanzie.**—Spelman (ca. 1615) in Smith, Va., Arber ed., civ, 1884. **Pastanza.**—Strachey (ca. 1612), Hist. Va., 39, 1849.

Pasteal. A tribe, evidently Coahuiltecan, given in Massanet's list (1690) of tribes between central Coahuila and the Hasinai country, a route most of which he had four times passed over (Velasco, Dictamen Fiscal, Nov. 30, 1716, in Mem. de Nueva España, XXVII, 183, MS.). The name is probably distinct from Pastalac, a synonym of Pastaloca, q. v.   (H. E. B.)
Pastias.—Rivera, Diario, leg. 2602, 1786 (identical?).

Pastoliak. A Chnagmiut Eskimo village on the right bank of Pastoliak r., near the s. shore of Norton sd., Alaska; pop. 80 in 1880.
Pastoliak.—Tebenkof (1849) quoted by Baker, Geog. Dict. Alaska, 490, 1906. **Pastoliakh.**—Petroff in 10th Census, Alaska, 11, 1884.

Pastoligmiut. A subdivision of the Unaligmiut Eskimo of Alaska, formerly camping at the head of Pastolik bay.
Paschtoligmeuten.—Wrangell quoted by Richardson, Arct. Exped., I, 370, 1851. **Paschtoligmjuten.**—Holmberg, Ethnog. Skizz., 6, 1855. **Paschtoligmüten.**—Wrangell, Nachr., 122, 1839. **Paschtuligmüten.**—Ibid. **Pashtolegmutis.**—Latham (1845) in Jour. Ethnol. Soc. Lond., 183, 1848. **Pashtolits.**—Keane in Stanford, Compend., 529, 1878. **Pastoligmut.**—Holmberg quoted by Dall, Alaska, 407, 1870.

Pastolik. A Chnagmiut Eskimo village on Pastolik r., Alaska; pop. 113 in 1890.—Nelson in 18th Rep. B. A. E., map, 1899.

Pastolik. A former Unaligmiut Eskimo camp for hunting beluga, at the head of Pastol bay, Alaska.
Pachtolik.—Zagoskin in Nouv. Ann. Voy., 5th s., XXI, map, 1850. **Paschtolik.**—Holmberg, Ethnog. Skizz., map, 1855. **Pastólik.**—Dall, Alaska, 236, 1870.

Pasukdhin ('village on a hilltop'). An ancient village of the Osage. The name was afterward given to a settlement of the Pahatsi, or Great Osage, on Verdigris r., Okla. In 1850, when visited by De Smet, it numbered 600 souls.
Bif-hill.—De Smet, W. Miss., 355, 1856 (misprint). **Big Hills.**—Keane in Stanford, Compend., 470, 1878. **Passoi-Ougrin.**—De Smet, op. cit. ꟼasuꟼḍiⁿ.—Dorsey Osage MS. vocab., B. A. E., 1883. **Pasukdhiⁿ.**—Ibid.

Pasulin (Pasúliⁿ, 'village on a hilltop'). A former village on Kansas r., occupied about 1820 by the Kansa, when the tribe had 4 villages.   (J. O. D.)

Pataguo. A Coahuiltecan tribe, first mentioned by Massanet, Nov. 16, 1690, in his list of tribes met between the presidio of Coahuila and the Hasinai country of Texas. The tribes were given in the list in geographical order, and the indication is that this tribe then lived N. E. of the Rio Grande (Velasco, Dictamen Fiscal, Nov. 30, 1716, Mem. de Nueva España, XXVII, 183, MS.). This view is supported by the fact that in 1691 Massanet found the tribe at Rio Hondo, 11 leagues N. E. of the Rio Nueces. They were with Indians of the "Sanpanal, Patchal, Papañaca, Parchiquis, Pacuáchiam, Aguapálam, Samampác, Vánca, and Payaván" tribes (ibid., 94). One of these is in García's list of Coahuiltecan tribes (1760), and Massanet records the statement that the language of this country was the same (i. e. Coahuiltecan) all the way from his starting point to beyond San Antonio r. (ibid., 98; and Espinosa, Diario, May 8, 1716). In 1716 Ramón and Espinosa found three rancherias of the tribe in the same locality (Derrotero, 1691, in Mem. de Nueva España, XXVII, 145, MS.). Members of this tribe were baptized at San Francisco Solano mission after 1704 (Valero Bautismos), where they frequently intermarried with the Xarames, and between 1720 and 1763 numbers of them were at San Antonio de Valero (ibid., passim). In 1738 Lorenzo, a Pataguo, was "governor" of this mission (Testimony, June 3, 1738, in Archivo Gen., Yndiferente de Guerra, 1736–37, fol. 88, MS.). In their gentile state they intermarried with the Payayas and Patzaus (Valero Casamientos, partidas 128, 157, MS.).　　　　　(H. E. B.)

Pachajuen.—Valero Entierros, partida 257, 1739, MS. (identical?). Patagahan.—Ibid., partida 255, 1739. Patagahu. — Ibid., 1739. Patagua.—Espinosa, Diario, 1716, MS. in Archivo Gen. Pataguan.—Valero Casamientos, 1716, partida 9, MS. Patague.—Valero Entierros, 1704, partida 25. Pataguita.—Morfi, Hist., ca. 1781, MS. (identical?). Pataquakes.—Hernando del Bosque, Exped., 1675, in Nat. Geog. Mag., XIV, 343, 1903 (identical?). Pataque.—Valero Bautismos, 1728, partida 220. Patavo.—Massanet, Nov. 16, 1690, cited in Mem. de Nueva España, XXVII, 183, MS.

Pataheuhah. Given by Schoolcraft (Ind. Tribes, III, 612, 1853) as a former village of the Mdewakanton Sioux, with 229 inhabitants, on Minnesota r., 25 m. from the agency in Minnesota; perhaps that of Chetanduta, 'Scarlet hawk,' chief of the Tintaotonwe.

Patakeenothe (*Pä-täke-e-no-the'*, 'rabbit'). A gens of the Shawnee.—Morgan, Anc. Soc., 168, 1877.

Patameragouche. Given by Alcedo (Dic. Geog., IV, 117, 1788) as an Indian [Micmac] village on the E. coast of Nova Scotia, near Canso str. Not identified.

Pataotrey. A large village of the Jumano in New Mexico in 1598; doubtless situated in the region of Abo, E. of the Rio Grande.

Pataotrey.—Oñate (1598) in Doc. Inéd., XVI, 114, 1871. Patasce.—Ibid., 123 (believed by Bandelier to be probably identical).

Pataquilla. A rancheria near the presidio of La Bahía and the mission of Espíritu Santo de Zúñiga, on the lower Rio San Antonio, Tex., in 1785, at which date it contained only 3 inhabitants (Bancroft, No. Mex. States, I, 659, 1886).

Its people were possibly of Karankawan or Coahuiltecan affinity. Cf. *Pastaloca.*

Pataunck. A tribe or subtribe of the Powhatan confederacy on Pamunkey r., Va., numbering about 400 in 1612.—Strachey, Va., 62, 1849.

Patchoag ('where they divide in two,' referring to two streams forming one river.—Trumbull). A tribe on the S. coast of Long id., N. Y., extending from Patchogue to Westhampton. Besides their principal village, bearing the same name, they had others at Fireplace, Mastic, Moriches, and Westhampton. The Cannetquot Indians were a part of this tribe. The survivors are known as Poosepatuck, q. v.

Patchoag. The principal village of the Patchoag, near the present Patchogue, Suffolk co., Long id., N. Y.

Onchechaug.—Patent of 1680 quoted by Thompson, Long Id., I, 413, 1843. Pachough.—Ruttenber, Ind. Geog. Names, 81, 1906. Patchague.—Wood in Macauley, N. Y., II, 252, 1829. Patchogue.—Ibid. Pochoug.—Writer of 1752 quoted by Thompson, Long Id., I, 414, 1843. Pochoughs.—Ruttenber, Ind. Geog. Names, 81, 1906. Unachog.—James quoted by Tanner, Narr., 328, 1830. Uncachage.—Deed of 1664 quoted by Thompson, Long Id., I, 410, 1843. Unquachog.—Trumbull, Ind. Names Conn., 74, 1881 (trans. *uhque-adchuauk,* 'end of a mountain'). Vnchechange.—Doc. of 1676 in N. Y. Doc. Col. Hist., XIV, 717, 1883.

Patha ('beaver'). An Oto gens.

Beaver.—Dorsey, Tciwere MS. vocab., B. A. E., 1879. Pa-ça'.—Dorsey in 15th Rep. B. A. E., 240, 1897.

Path Killer (corrupted translation of *Núñnä'hĭ-dihĭ',* 'he kills [habitually] in the path'). A former prominent Cherokee chief who signed the treaties of Tellico in 1804 and 1805, and the treaty of Turkeytown (Chickasaw Council House) in 1816. See *Ridge, Major.*　　　(J. M.)

Patica. The name of two villages in N. E. Florida at the period of the French Huguenot occupancy in 1564. One was on the coast, 8 leagues S. of Ft Caroline, which stood near the mouth of St John r.; its chief was friendly with the French and was probably of the Saturiba, or possibly of the Timucua tribe. The other village was on the w. bank of St John r., apparently about midway between the present Jacksonville and Palatka, and probably belonged to the Timucua. It appears on the De Bry map of 1591 as Patchica. Bartram mentions the "Paticas," with "Yamasees," "Utinas," and others, as early enemies to the Carolina colony until their strength was broken by the Creeks.　　　(J. M.)

Patchica.—De Bry, map (1591) in Le Moyne, Narr., Appleton trans., 1875 (on St John r.). Patica.—Laudonnière (1564) in French, Hist. Coll. La., n. s., 275, 1869 (used for both villages). Paticas.—Bartram, Trav., 54, 1792. Paticos.—Schoolcraft, Ind. Tribes, V, 98, 1855.

Patiquilid. A Chumashan village on one of the Santa Barbara ids., Cal., probably Santa Rosa, in 1542.—Cabrillo, Narr.

(1542), in Smith, Colec. Doc. Fla., 186, 1857.

Patiquin. A Chumashan village on one of the Santa Barbara ids., Cal., probably Santa Rosa, in 1542.—Cabrillo, Narr. (1542), in Smith, Colec. Doc. Fla., 186, 1857.

Patiri. An unidentified tribe given by Morfi (Hist. Tex., bk. II, *ca.* 1781, MS.) in his list of Texas tribes.

Patki. . The Cloud or Water-house phratry of the Hopi, which comprises the following clans: Patki, Kau (Corn), Omowuh (Rain-cloud), Tangaka (Rainbow), Talawipiki (Lightning), Kwan (Agave), Sivwapi (*Bigelovia graveolens*), Pawikya (Aquatic animal [Duck]), Pakwa (Frog), Pavatiya (Small aquatic creatures), Murzibusi (Bean), Kawaibatunya (Watermelon), and Yoki (Rain). This people claims to have come from the greatcactus region in the "red land of the south," called by them Palátkwabi. The Water-house phratry of Fewkes and the Rain (Yoki) phratry of Stephen are identical.
Pat-ki-nyû-mû.—Fewkes in Am. Anthrop., VII, 402, 1894 (*nyû-mû*='phratry'). Yo'-ki.—Stephen in 8th Rep. B. A. E., 39, 1891.

Patki. The Cloud or Water-house clan of the Patki phratry of the Hopi.
Batki.—Dorsey and Voth, Mishongnovi Ceremonies, 175, 1902. Batkiñyamu.—Ibid. Pa'jeh.—Bourke, Snake Dance, 117, 1884. Patki wiñwû.—Fewkes in 19th Rep. B. A. E., 583, 1901 (*wiñwû*='clan'). Pat'-ki wüñ-wû.—Fewkes in Am. Anthrop., VII, 402, 1894.

Patnetac. A former village, presumably Costanoan, connected with Dolores mission, San Francisco, Cal.—Taylor in Cal. Farmer, Oct. 18, 1861.

Pato. A town between Aguacay and Amaye, w. of the Mississippi, probably in the present Clark co., Ark.; visited by Moscoso's troops, after De Soto's death, in July 1542.—Gentl. of Elvas (1557) in French, Hist. Coll. La., II, 195, 1850.

Patofa. A former district and town, probably Uchean, named after its chief, situated in Georgia and visited by De Soto's expedition in Apr. 1540 (Gentl. of Elvas, 1557, in French, Hist. Coll. La., II, 139, 1850). If Uchean, the name is possibly related to the Yuchi term *padófa*, 'dark,' 'obscure' (F. G. Speck, inf'n, 1907).

Patoqua ('village of the bear'). Formerly one of the western group of Jemez pueblos, situated on a ledge of the mesa that separates Guadalupe and San Diego canyons, 6 m. N. of Jemez pueblo, N. central New Mexico. It seems to have been the seat of the Spanish mission of San Joseph de los Jemez (which contained a church as early as 1617), but was abandoned in 1622 on account of hostility of the Navaho. In 1627, however, it and Gyusiwa were resettled by Fray Martin de Arvide with the inhabitants of a number of small pueblos then occupied by the Jemez. It was permanently abandoned prior to the Pueblo revolt of 1680. The people of this pueblo claimed to have dwelt at the lagoon of San José, 75 m. N. w. of Jemez, and that they removed thence to a place between Salado and Jemez rs., where they built the pueblo of Anyukwinu. See Bandelier in Arch. Inst. Papers, IV, 205, et seq., 1892; and cf. Century Cyclopedia of Names, 1894, art. *Patoqua*.   (F. W. H.)
Batokvá.—Loew (1875) in Wheeler Surv. Rep., VII, 343, 1879. Patoqua.—Bandelier in Arch. Inst. Papers, IV, pt. 2, 207, 1892. San Joseph de Jemez.—Bandelier (1888) in Compte-rendu Cong. Am., VII, 452, 1890. S. Iosepho.—Crepy, Map Am. Sept., *ca.* 1783. S. Josef.—D'Anville, Map Am. Sept., 1746. S. Josefo.—Jefferys, Am. Atlas, map 5, 1776. Sᵗ Josef.—D'Anville, Map N. A., Bolton's ed., 1752. St. Joseph.—Shea, Cath. Missions, 80, 1870.

Patshenin. A tribe or band formerly living with the Saponi and Tutelo under Iroquois protection on Grand r., Ontario. They probably came from the S. with those tribes, and Hale thinks they may have been the Occaneechi.
Botshenins—Hale in Proc. Am. Philos. Soc., Mar. 2, 1883. Patshenins.—Ibid.

Pattali. One of the Apalachee towns mentioned in a letter of 1688 addressed by a number of Apalachee chiefs to Charles II of Spain. A facsimile of the original letter was reproduced and published by Buckingham Smith in 1860.—Gatschet, Creek Migr. Leg., I, 76, 1884.

Patung. The Squash phratry of the Hopi, consisting of the Squash, Crane, Pigeon-hawk, and Sorrow-making clans. They claim to have come from a region in southern Arizona called Palatkwabi.
Batánga.—Voth, Trad. of Hopi, 40, 1905. Patuñ.—Fewkes in 19th Rep. B. A. E., 583, 1901.

Patung. The Squash clan of the Patung phratry of the Hopi.
Batang.—Voth, Oraibi Summer Snake Ceremony, 283, 1903. Batang-a.—Dorsey and Voth, Mishongnovi Ceremonies, 176, 1902. Patuñ wiñwû.—Fewkes in 19th Rep. B. A. E., 583, 1900 (*wiñ-wû*='clan'). Pa'-tuñ-wuñ-wü.—Fewkes in Am. Anthrop., VII, 402, 1894.

Patuterajuit. A former settlement of the Angmagsalingmiut Eskimo of the E. coast of Greenland.—Meddelelser om Grönland, IX, 382, 1889.

Patuxent (probably related in meaning to *Patuxet*, q. v.). An Algonquian tribe formerly living in what is now Calvert co., Md., their principal village bearing the same name. It is probable that they were closely related to the Conoy, if not a part of them. They met the Maryland colonists, on their first arrival, on terms of friendship, which continued without serious interruption as long as the tribe existed. As early as 1639 the colonial authorities proclaimed the Patuxent as friends and declared them under the protection of the colony. In 1651 they, together with other Indians, were placed on a reservation at the head of Wicomico r. The following is an account of a religious ceremony in their temple, from the Relatio Itineris of White: "On an appointed day all the men and women of every age, from several districts, gathered together round a large fire; the younger ones stood nearest the fire, behind these stood those who were older. Then they threw deer's fat on the fire, and lifting their hands to heaven and raising their voices they cried out Yaho! Yaho! Then making room some one brings forward quite a large bag; in the bag is a pipe and a powder which they call Potu. The pipe is such a one as is used among us for smoking tobacco, but much larger; then the bag is carried round the fire and the boys and girls follow it, singing alternately with tolerably pleasant voices, Yaho! Yaho! Having completed the circuit the pipe is taken out of the bag and the powder called Potu is distributed to each one as they stand near; this is lighted in the pipe and each one drawing smoke from the pipe blows it over the several members of his body and consecrates them."

Patuxents.—Bozman, Md., II, 421, 1837. **Pautuxuntes.**—Smith (1629), Va., I, 135, repr. 1819.

Patuxent. The principal village of the Patuxent, situated on the E. bank of Patuxent r., Md. Capt. John Smith estimated the number of warriors at 40 in 1608.

Barchuxem.—White (1634), Relatio Itineris, 41, 1874. **Barcluxen.**—White quoted by Shea, Cath. Miss., 487, 1855. **Patuxent.**—Writer of 1639 quoted in Relatio Itineris, 63, 1874. **Patuxunt.**—Yong (1634) in Mass. Hist. Soc. Coll., 4th s., IX, 105, 1871. **Pawtuxunt.**—Smith (1629), Va., I, 118, repr. 1819.

Patuxet (prob. *Pátukeset*, 'at the little fall.'—Gerard). A Massachuset village on the site of Plymouth, Mass. It was depopulated by the great pestilence of 1617, which seems not to have extended much farther south.

Acawmuck.—Smith, map (ca. 1616), cited in Mass. Hist. Soc. Coll., 2d s., III, 175, 1846 ('to go by water': used in describing a place more easily reached by water than by land). **Accomack.**—Smith (1616), ibid., 3d s., VI, 108, 1837. **Accoomeek.**—Winthrop (ca. 1625), ibid., III, 175, 1846. **Apaum.**—Williams' deed (ca. 1635) in R. I. Col. Rec., I, 18, 1856 (Narragansetname). **Ompaäm.**—Cotton (1708) in Mass. Hist. Soc. Coll., 3d s., II, 232, 1830 (Massachuset name). **Patuckset.**—Pratt (1662), ibid., 4th s., IV, 480, 1858. **Patusuc.**—Kendall, Trav., II, 45, 1819. **Patuxet.**—Smith (1629), Va., II, 183, repr. 1819. **Patuxite.**—Dermer (1620) in Mass. Hist. Soc. Coll., 4th s., III, 97, 1856. **Patuyet.**—Dee in Smith (1629), Va., II, 228, repr. 1819. **Umpame.**—Writer of 1815 in Mass. Hist. Soc. Coll., 2d s., III, 175, 1846 (so called by Mashpee Indians).

Patwin ('man,' 'person'). A name adopted by Powers to designate a division of the Copehan family (q. v.). They occupied the area extending from Stony cr., Colusa co., to Suisun bay, Solano co., Cal., and from Sacramento r. to the boundary of the Kulanapan family on the w., but excluding the so-called Coyote Valley Indians on the headwaters of Putah cr. in the s. part of Lake co., determined by Barrett to be Moquelumnan and not Copehan. The dialects of this division differ considerably from those of the Wintun. Powers believed the Patwin were once very numerous. The manners and customs of the tribes in the interior and on the mountains differed greatly from those near the shore. On the plains and in the valleys in building a dwelling they excavated the soil for about 2 ft, banked up enough earth to keep out the water, and threw the remainder on the roof in a dome. In the mountains, where wood was more abundant and rain more frequent, no roofing of earth was used. In war the Patwin used bows and arrows and flint-pointed spears; no scalps were taken, but the victors are said often to have decapitated the most beautiful maiden they captured. They had a ceremony for "raising evil spirits" and dances to celebrate a good harvest of acorns or a successful catch of fish. The dead were usually buried, though cremation was practised to some extent by some of the tribes. For the Patwin villages, see *Copehan Family*.

Patchawe.—Powers in Cont. N. A. Ethnol., III, 95, 1877 (Chimariko name). **Patwae.**—Ibid. **Patweens.**—Powers in Overland Month., XIII, 543, 1874. **Pat-win.**—Powers in Cont. N. A. Ethnol., III, 218, 1877.

Patzau. A tribe, probably Coahuiltecan, mentioned as early as 1690 by Massanet in his list of tribes met between the presidio of Coahuila and the Hasinai country of Texas. The tribes were given in the list in geographical order, and the indication is that the Patzau then lived N. E. of the Rio Grande (Velasco, Dictamen Fiscal, Nov. 30, 1716, in Mem. de Nueva España, XXVII, 183, MS.). In the following year Massanet found them 11 leagues E. of Nueces r. with the Pataguos, Pachales, and others (ibid., 94). This tribe is evidently distinct from the Putzai as well as from the Pachales, but it is difficult to distinguish some of the variants of these two names. Some of the Patzau entered San Francisco Solano mission on the Rio Grande as early as 1712, and between 1723 and 1750 a number of them were baptized at San Antonio de Valero (Valero Bautismos, passim). (H. E. B.)

Pacha.—Valero Bautismos, 1730, partida 327, MS. **Pachà.**—Ibid., 1737, partida 433. **Pachac.**—Ibid., 1735, partida 407. **Pachai.**—Ibid., 1732, partida 363. **Pachaug.**—Ibid., 1731, partida 351. **Pachaxa.**—Ibid., 1728, partida 227. **Paisau.**—Ibid., 1723, partida —. **Paiztat.**—Ibid., 1733, partida 878. **Pasaju.**—Ibid., 1728, partida 239. **Pasxa.**—Ibid., partida 432. **Pattsau.**—Massanet (1690) in Dictamen Fiscal, Nov. 30, 1716, MS. (miscopy). **Patzar.**—Valero Bautismos, 1727, partida 178. **Paza.**—Ibid., 1741, partida 540. **Pazac.**—Ibid., 1732, partida 367. **Pazajo.**—Ibid., 1733, partida 371. **Pazaju.**—Ibid., partida 374. **Pazaug.**—Ibid., 1732, partida 356. **Pazhajo.**—Ibid., 1712, partida 7. **Psaupsau.**—Ibid., 1730, partida 319 (identical?).

Paughaden. See *Pauhagen*.

Paugie. See *Porgy*.

Paugusset ('where the narrows open out.'—Trumbull). A small Algonquian tribe in Connecticut, on Housatonic r., near the mouth of the Naugatuck. Their principal village, Paugusset, was on the E. side of the river. They had a fortress on the E. bank about half a mile above the Naugatuck, and another in Milford. Ruttenber makes them a part of the Wappinger confederacy, and says they were subject to the Mattabesec. They claimed a tract on both sides of the lower Housatonic, extending up to Newtown, but sold most of their lands about 1660. Besides their principal village they had Turkey Hill Village, Pauquaunuch, Naugatuck, and Poodatook. The whole tribe numbered perhaps 700 or 800. In 1762 they had mainly retired to Scaticook, farther up the river, where the survivors then numbered 127, while about 60 were still in their old homes. Several mixed-blood families are said to survive near Bridgeport, Conn.   (J. M.   C. T.)
Pagasett.—Conn. Rec. cited by Trumbull, Ind. Names Conn., 46, 1881. Paugassett.—N. H. Rec. (1642), ibid. Paugussetts.—De Forest, Inds. Conn., 51, 1853. Pawgasset.—New Haven Rec. (1642) quoted by Trumbull, op. cit. Pawgasuck.—Donn. Rec. quoted, ibid. Pawghksuck.—Stiles (1761), ibid. Wepawaugs.—Ibid., 49. Wopowage.—Trumbull, Conn., I, 42, 1818.

Paugusset. The chief village of the Paugusset, situated on the E. bank of Housatonic r., in New Haven co., Conn., about a mile above Derby. It contained about 300 inhabitants.
Pagasett.—Conn. Rec. quoted by Trumbull, Ind. Names Conn., 46, 1881. Paugasset.—Birdsey (1761) in Mass. Hist. Soc. Coll., 1st s., x, 111,1809. Paugusset.—Trumbull, Conn., I, 42, 1818. Pawgassett.—New Haven Rec. (1642) quoted by Trumbull, Ind. Names Conn., op. cit. Pawgasuck.—Conn. Rec., ibid. Pawghkeesuck.—Stiles (1761), ibid.

Paugwik. An Aglemiut and Unalaskan village at the mouth of Naknek r., Alaska, on the S. side. Pop. (including Kingiak) 192 in 1880, 93 in 1890.
Kennuyak.—Petroff, Rep. on Alaska, 45, 1881. Kinuiak.—Petroff, ibid., map. Naugvik.—Sarichef quoted by Baker, Geog. Dict. Alaska, 1902. Pakwik.—11th Census, Alaska, 164, 1893. Paugwik.—Petroff in 10th Census, Alaska, 17, 1884. Pawik.—Baker, op. cit. Suworof.—Ibid. Taugwik.—Petroff, Rep. on Alaska, 45, 1881.

Pauhagen. One of the New England names of the menhaden, or mossbunker (*Alosa menhaden*); also a sort of mackerel bait made of chopped or ground fish. Trumbull (Natick Dict., 69, 1903) derives the word from *pŏkangan* (*pwkangan*) in the Abnaki dialect of Algonquian, said to signify 'fertilizer'; but this is regarded as very doubtful by Gerard, who says the fish called by Rasles *pŏkangané* cannot be identified. Other spellings are paughaden, poghaden, pauhaugen. See *Menhaden, Pogy, Porgy*.   (A. F. C.)

Pauhuntanuc. An Abnaki village in 1614, probably on or near the coast of Maine.
Paghhuntanuck.—Smith (1616) in Mass. Hist. Soc. Coll., 3d s., VI, 107, 1837. Pauhuntanuck.—Smith (1631), ibid., III, 22, 1833.

Paukauns. See *Pecan*.

Paul; Little Paul. See *Mazakutemani*.

Pauma. A former Luiseño rancheria on San Luis Rey r., San Diego co., Cal.; pop. 106 in 1865. The name is now also applied to a reservation of 250 acres of unpatented land, with 67 inhabitants, which was under the Mission-Tule consolidated agency until 1903, when the agency was divided and Pauma placed under the Pala agency (Ind. Aff. Rep., 125, 1865; ibid., 175, 1902). The Pauma rancheria seems to have existed at least as early as 1795 (Grijalva cited by Bancroft, Hist. Cal., I, 563, 1886), when it is mentioned under the form Pamua.
Palma.—Ames, Rep. Miss. Indians, 6, 1873.

Paupattokshick. A village of 15 houses on lower Thames r., in New London co., Conn., occupied in 1638 by some of the conquered Pequot assigned to the Mohegan.—Williams (1638) in Mass. Hist. Soc. Coll., 4th s., VI, 251, 1863.

Pauquaunuch. A village of the Paugusset in Stratford township, Fairfield co., Conn. It contained 25 wigwams about 1710, but before 1761 the Indians had removed up the river to Scaticook.
Golden Hill tribe.—De Forest, Inds. Conn., 49,1853. Pauquaunuch.—Birdsey (1761) in Mass. Hist. Soc. Coll., 1st s., X, 111, 1809. Pughquonnuck.—Trumbull, Conn., 109, 1818.

Pausanes. A Coahuiltecan tribe formerly living on San Antonio r., Texas; mentioned by García as one of the tribes speaking the language of his Manual.
Pamanes.—Taylor in Cal. Farmer, Apr. 17, 1863. Pames.—Ibid. Pausanas.—Shea, Cath. Miss., 86, 1855. Pausanes.—García, Manual, title, 1760. Pauzanes.—Doc. of 1737 cited by Orozco y Berra, Geog., 304, 1864.

Paushuk (*pau-shŭk′*, 'cutthroats'). An Arikara band.—Hayden, Ethnog. and Philol. Mo. Val., 357, 1862.

Pavatiya. The Tadpole clan of the Hopi.
Pavatiya wiñwû.—Fewkes in 19th Rep. B. A. E., 583, 1901 (*wiñwû*='clan'). Pa-va-ti-ya wüñ-wû.—Fewkes in Am. Anthrop., VII, 402, 1894.

Paviotso. A name applied originally by Powell to a group of small Shoshonean tribes in w. Nevada, and extended for convenience to all related bands in that region. For their names, see *Mono-Paviotso*.
Athlets.—Gatschet in Wheeler Surv. Rep., VII, 410, 1879. Báloh.—Powers, Inds. W. Nevada, MS., B. A. E., 1876 (Washo name). Pa'lu.—Henshaw, Washo MS. vocab., B. A. E., 1883 (Washo name). Paviotso.—Ind. Aff. Rep., 251, 1877. Pa-vi-o-tsos.—Powell in H. R. Misc. Doc. 86, 43d Cong., 1st sess., 5, 1874. Payutes.—Taylor in Cal. Farmer, Jan. 31, 1862. Pey-ute.—Forney in Ind. Aff. Rep., 365, 1859. Pi-utah.—Holeman in Ind. Aff. Rep., 151, 1852. Piutahs—Holeman, ibid., 444, 1853. Pi-utes.—Taylor in Cal. Farmer, June 26, 1863. Plai'kni.—Gatschet in Cont. N. A. Ethnol., II, pt. I, XXXV, 1890 (collective name for Snakes, Klamath, and Modoc on Sprague r., Oreg.). Py-ute.—Hurt in Ind. Aff. Rep. 1856, 228, 1857. Say-do-carah.—Hopkins, Life Among Piute, 75, 1882 (trans. 'conquerors' or 'enemy'). Sidocaw.—Campbell in Ind. Aff. Rep., 119, 1866. Taniyumu'h.—Powers, Inds. W. Nevada, MS., B. A. E., 1875 (own ancient name). Ti'vati'ka.—Hoffman in Proc. Am. Philos. Soc., XXIII, 298, 1886 (='pine-nut eaters').

Paviye. A rancheria, probably Cochimi, connected with Purísima (Cadegomo) mission, Lower California, in the 18th century.—Doc. Hist. Mex., 4th s., v, 189, 1857.

Pavlof. An Aleut village at Selenie pt., Pavlof bay, Alaska penin., Alaska. Pop. 59 in 1833, according to Veniaminof.
Pavlooskoi.—Elliott, Cond. Aff. Alaska, 225, 1875. **Pavlovsk.**—Petroff in 10th Census, Alaska, 35, 1884. **Pavlovskoe.**—Veniaminof, Zapiski, II, 203, 1840. **Pawlowskoje.**—Holmberg, Ethnog. Skizz., map, 1855. **Selenie.**—Dall (1880) quoted by Baker, Geog. Dict. Alaska, 1902 (Russian: 'settlement').

Pavuwiwuyuai (*Pa-vu'-wi-wu'-yu-ai*). A Paviotso band formerly about Mammoth City, Utah.—Powell, Paviotso MS., B. A. E., 1881.

Paw. The Water clan of the pueblo of Taos, N. Mex.
Pâ-taína.—Hodge, field notes, B. A. E., 1899 (*taína* = 'people').

Pawating (*Bawi'ting*, a cognate form of *Bawi'tigunk*, 'at the rapids.'—W. J.). An ancient Chippewa village at Sault Ste Marie, on the s. bank of St Marys r., Chippewa co., Mich. According to Dr Wm. Jones the old village site is the most sacred spot known to the old-time Chippewa. A Chippewa who has been to the rapids has made a holy pilgrimage, because there his ancestors were created, there the manitos blessed the people, and from there was the dispersion round about L. Superior. The people, from the situation of their village, were called Saulteurs by the early French writers, and as the French became acquainted with more remote bands of Chippewa the term came to designate the whole tribe. The Jesuit mission of Sainte Marie du Sault was established at Pawating in 1669.   (J. M.)
Bahwetego-weninnewug.—Tanner, Narr., 63, 1830. **Bahwetig.**—Ibid., 64. **Baouichtigouin.**—Jes. Rel. 1640, 34, 1858. **Bawateeg.**—Schoolcraft in Minn. Hist. Soc. Coll., v, 398, 1885. **Bawating.**—Ibid. **Bawitigowininiwag.**—Kelton, Ft Mackinac, 145, 1884. **Bǎwi'tigunk.**—Wm. Jones, inf'n, 1906. **Bǎwit'ing.**—Ibid. **Bawiting.**—Baraga, Eng.-Otch. Dict., 206, 1878. **Bow-e-ting.**—Warren (1852) in Minn. Hist. Soc. Coll., v, 38, 1885. **Bunger.**—McLean, Twenty-five Years' Service, I, 195, 1842. **Cascade people.**—Richardson, Arct. Exped., II, 37, 1851. **D'Achiliny.**—Neill in Minn. Hist. Soc. Coll., v, 413, 1885. **Fall Indians.**—Tanner, Narr., 63, 1830. **Gens du Sault.**—Jes. Rel. 1640, 34, 1858. **Habitans du Sault.**—Jes. Rel. 1642, 97, 1858. **Opendachiliny.**—La Chesnaye (1697) in Margry, Déc., VI, 6, 1886. **Pagouitik.**—Jes. Rel. 1658, 22, 1858. **Pahouitingdachirini.**—N. Y. Doc. Col. Hist., IX, 161, note, 1855. **Pahouiting8ach Irini.**—Jes. Rel. 1670, 79, 1858. **Pah-witing-dach-irini.**—Shea, Cath. Miss., 362, 1852. **Pahwittingdach-irini.**—Shea, Discov. Miss. Val., xlvii, 1852. **Panoirigoueiouhak.**—Charlevoix (1744), Jour., I, 285, 1761 (misprint). **Paouitagoung.**—Jes. Rel. 1648, 62, 1858. **Paouitigoüeieuhak.**—Jes. Rel. 1642, 97, 1858. **Paouitikoungraentaouak.**—Gallinee (1669) in Margry, Déc., I, 163, 1875. **Patroniting Dach-Irini.**—Heriot, Trav., 206, 1807. **Paüoirigoüeieuhak.**—Charlevoix (1744), New Fr., II, 137, 1866. **Pauoitigoueieuhak.**—Jes. Rel. 1642, 97, 1858. **Pauotigoueieuhak.**—Warren (1852) in Minn. Hist. Soc. Coll., v, 397, 1885. **Pawateeg.**—Schoolcraft in Minn. Hist. Soc. Coll., v, 398, 1885. **Pawating.**—Ibid. **Pǎwêtěkǒ Wěněněwǎk.**—Long, Exped. St Peter's R., II, 154, 1824. **Pawichtigouek.**—Trumbull (1870) in Minn. Hist. Soc. Coll., v,

398, 1885. **Pawistucienemuks.**—Domenech, Deserts, I, 443, 1860 (misprint). **Pawitagou-ek.**—Trumbull (1870) in Minn. Hist. Soc. Coll., v, 398, 1885. **Sainte Marie de Sault.**—Shea, Cath. Miss., 361, 1855 (the mission). **Sault Sainte Marie.**—Henry, Trav., 60, 1809. **Saut Indians.**—Kelton, Ft Mackinac, 145, 1884.

Pawcatuck. A village, probably on Pawcatuck r., Washington co., R. I., occupied in 1657 by a remnant of the conquered Pequot. Regarding the name, Trumbull (Ind. Names Conn., 48, 1881) says: "If the name belonged first to the territory—the eastern part of the Pequot country—it certainly stands for *Paquatauke*, i. e. 'Pequot land'; but if, as is on the whole more probable, it belonged to the river, the first two syllables stand either for *pauqua* 'clear, open', or for *pagwa* 'shallow', and the last syllable, *tuk*, denotes a 'tidal river.' Yet neither analysis satisfactorily disposes of the name of Paucatuck or Pacatuck (1688) brook, in West Springfield, Mass."
Pacotucke.—Hopkins (1646) in Mass. Hist. Soc. Coll., 4th s., VI, 334, 1863. **Pakatucke.**—Brewster (1657), ibid., VII, 82, 1865. **Paquatuck.**—Rec. of 1658 quoted by Trumbull, Ind. Names Conn., 48, 1881. **Paquatucke.**—Record (*ca.* 1651) in Mass. Hist. Soc. Coll., 4th s., VII, 127, 1865. **Paucatuck.**—R. I. Col. Rec. cited by Trumbull, Indian Names Conn., 48, 1881. **Paucatucke.**—Record (1662) in R. I. Col. Rec., I, 499, 1856. **Pauquatuck.**—Wharton (1683) in Mass. Hist. Soc. Coll., 1st s., v, 234, 1806. **Pawcatuck.**—Charter of 1663 in R. I. Col. Rec., II, 19, 1857. **Pawkeatucket.**—Hopkins (1648) in Mass. Hist. Soc. Coll., 4th s., VI, 341, 1863. **Pocatocke.**—Record (1653) quoted by Drake, Bk. Inds., bk. 2, 76, 1848. **Poccatuck.**—Uncas deed (1650) cited by Trumbull, Ind. Names Conn., 48, 1881. **Poquatocke.**—Minor (1656) cited by Trumbull, ibid. **Poquatucke.**—Record (1659), ibid., 110. **Powcatuck.**—Mason (1648) in Mass. Hist. Soc. Coll., 4th s., VII, 414, 1865. **Pwacatuck.**—Williams (1648), ibid., 3d s., IX, 274, 1846. **Pwoakatuck.**—Williams (1648), ibid., 284. **Pwocatuck.**—Williams (1649), ibid., 286. **Pwockatuck.**—Williams (1648), ibid., 283. **Pwouacatuck.**—Williams (1648), ibid., 274.

Pawchauquet. A village, probably Narraganset, in w. Rhode Island in 1655.—Williams (1655) in Mass. Hist. Soc. Coll., 3d s., x, 10, 1849.

Pawcocomac. A village of the Powhatan confederacy in 1608, on the N. bank of Rappahannock r., at the mouth of the Corotoman, in Lancaster co., Va.—Smith (1629), Va., I, map, repr. 1819.

Pawikya. The Aquatic Animal (Duck) clan of the Patki phratry of the Hopi.
Pawikya wiñwû.—Fewkes in 19th Rep. B. A. E., 583, 1901 (*wiñwû* = 'clan'). **Pa'-wi-kya wüñ-wû.**—Fewkes in Am. Anthrop., VII, 402, 1894.

Pawipits. Given as a Paiute band on Moapa res., s. E. Nevada.
Pa-Weapits.—Ingalls (1872) in H. R. Ex. Doc. 66, 42d Cong., 3d sess., 2, 1873. **Pawipits.**—Ind. Aff. Rep., 251, 1877.

Pawnee. A confederacy belonging to the Caddoan family. The name is probably derived from *pariki*, a horn, a term used to designate the peculiar manner of dressing the scalp-lock, by which the hair was stiffened with paint and fat, and made to stand erect and curved like a horn. This marked feature of the Pawnee gave currency to the name and its application to cognate tribes. The people called themselves Chahiksichahiks, 'men of men.'

In the general northeastwardly movement of the Caddoan tribes the Pawnee seem to have brought up the rear. Their migration was not in a compact body, but in groups, whose slow progress covered long periods of time. The Pawnee tribes finally established themselves in the valley of Platte r., Nebr., which territory, their traditions say, was acquired by conquest, but the people who were driven out are not named. It is not improbable that in making their way N. E. the Pawnee may have encountered one or more waves of the southward movements of Shoshonean and Athapascan tribes. When the Siouan tribes entered Platte valley they found the Pawnee there. The geographic arrangement always observed by the four leading Pawnee tribes may give a hint of the order of their northeastward movement, or of their grouping in their traditionary southwestern home. The Skidi place was to the N. W., and they were spoken of as belonging to the upper villages; the Pitahauerat villages were always downstream; those of the Chaui, in the middle, or between the Pitahauerat and the Kitkehahki, the villages of the last-named being always upstream. How long the Pawnee resided in the Platte valley is unknown, but their stay was long enough to give new terms to 'west' and 'east,' that is, words equivalent to 'up' or 'down' that eastwardly flowing stream.

The earliest historic mention of a Pawnee is that of the so-called "Turk" (q. v.), who by his tales concerning the riches of Quivira (q. v.) allured and finally led Coronado, in 1541, from New Mexico over the plains as far as Kansas, where some Pawnee (see *Harahey*) visited him. The permanent villages of the tribes lay to the N. of Quivira, and it is improbable that Coronado actually entered any of them during his visit to Quivira, a name given to the Wichita territory. It is doubtful if the Apane or the Quipana mentioned in the narrative of De Soto's expedition in 1541 were the Pawnee, as the latter dwelt to the N. W. of the Spaniards' line of travel. Nor is it likely that the early French explorers visited the Pawnee villages, although they heard of them, and their locality was indicated by Tonti, La Harpe, and others. French traders, however, were established among the tribes before the middle of the 18th century.

How the term Pani (q. v.), or Pawnee, as applied to Indian slaves, came into use is not definitely known. It was a practice among the French and English in the 17th and 18th centuries to obtain from friendly tribes their captives taken in war and to sell them as slaves to white settlers. By ordinance of Apr. 13, 1709, the enslavement of negroes and Pawnee was recognized in Canada (Shea's Charlevoix, v, 224, 1871). The Pawnee do not seem to have suffered especially from this traffic, which, though lucrative, had to be abandoned on account of the animosities it engendered. The white settlers of New Mexico became familiar with the Pawnee early in the 17th century through the latter's raids for procuring horses, and for more than two centuries the Spanish authorities of that territory sought to bring about peaceful relations with them, with only partial success.

As the Pawnee villages lay in a country remote from the region contested by the Spaniards and French in the 17th and 18th centuries, these Indians escaped for a time the influences that proved so fatal to their congeners, but ever-increasing contact with the white race, in the latter part of the 18th century, introduced new diseases and brought great reduction in population together with loss of tribal power. When the Pawnee territory, through the Louisiana Purchase, passed under the control of the U. S., the Indians came in close touch with the trading center at St Louis. At that time their territory lay between the Niobrara r. on the N. and Prairie Dog cr. on the s., and was bounded on the w. by the country of the Cheyenne and Arapaho, and on the E. by that of the Omaha, on the N. of the Platte, and on the s. of the Platte by the lands of the Oto and Kansa tribes. The trail to the S. W., and later that across the continent, ran partly through Pawnee land, and the increasing travel and the settlement of the country brought about many changes. Through all the vicissitudes of the 19th century the Pawnee never made war against the U. S. On the contrary they gave many evidences of forbearance under severe provocation by waiting, under their treaty agreement, for the Government to right their wrongs, while Pawnee scouts faithfully and courageously served in the U. S. army during Indian hostilities. The history of the Pawnee has been that common to reservation life— the gradual abandonment of ancient customs and the relinquishment of homes before the pressure of white immigration.

The first treaty between the Pawnee and the U. S. was that of the several bands made at St Louis, June 18–22, 1818, when peace was concluded with all the tribes of the region disturbed by the War of 1812. By treaty of Ft Atkinson, Neb., Sept. 28, 1825, the Pawnee acknowledged the supremacy of the United States and agreed to submit all grievances to the Government for adjustment. By treaty of Grand Pawnee Village, Nebr., Oct. 9, 1833, they ceded all their lands s. of Platte r. By that of Ft Childs, Nebr., Aug. 6, 1848, they sold a 60-mile strip on the Platte about Grand Island. By treaty of Table cr., Nebr., Sept. 24, 1857, all lands N. of the Platte were assigned to the Government, except a strip on Loup r. 30 m. E. and w. and 15 m. N. and s., where their reservation was established. This tract was ceded in 1876, when the tribes removed to Oklahoma, where they now live. In 1892 they took their lands in severalty and became citizens of the U. S.

The tribal organization of the Pawnee was based on village communities representing subdivisions of the tribe. Each village had its name, its shrine containing sacred objects, and its priests who had charge of the rituals and ceremonies connected with these objects; it had also its hereditary chiefs and its council composed of the chiefs and leading men. If the head chief was a man of unusual character and ability he exercised undisputed authority, settled all difficulties, and preserved social order; he was expected to give freely and was apt to be surrounded by dependents. Each chief had his own herald who proclaimed orders and other matters of tribal interest.

The tribe was held together by two forces: the ceremonies pertaining to a common cult in which each village had its place and share, and the tribal council composed of the chiefs of the different villages. The confederacy was similarly united, its council being made up from the councils of the tribes. In the meetings of these councils rules of precedence and decorum were rigidly observed. No one could speak who was not entitled to a seat, although a few privileged men were permitted to be present as spectators. The council determined all questions touching the welfare of the tribe or of the confederacy.

War parties were always initiated by some individual and were composed of volunteers. Should the village be attacked, the men fought under their chief or under some other recognized leader. Buffalo hunts were tribal, and in conducting them officers were appointed to maintain order so as to permit each family to procure its share of the game. The meat was cut in thin sheets, jerked, and packed in parflêche cases for future use. Maize, pumpkins, and beans were cultivated. The maize, which was regarded as a sacred gift, was called "mother," and religious ceremonies were connected with its planting, hoeing, and harvesting. Basketry, pottery, and weaving were practised. The Pawnee house was the earth

lodge (q.v.), the elaborate construction of which was accompanied with religious ceremony, and when after an absence from home the family returned to their dwelling the posts thereof were ceremonially anointed. Men shaved the head except for a narrow ridge from the forehead to the scalp-lock, which stood up like a horn. Frequently a scarf was tied around the head like a turban. Both beard and eyebrows were plucked; tattooing was seldom practised. The breechcloth and moccasins were the only essential parts of a man's clothing; leggings and robe were worn in cold weather and on gala occasions. Face painting was common, and heraldic designs were frequently painted on tent-covers and on the robes and shields of the men. Women wore the hair in two braids at the back, the parting as well as the face being painted red. Moccasins, leggings, and a robe were the ancient dress, later a skirt and tunic were worn. Descent was traced through the mother. There were no totems belonging to the confederacy. After marriage a man went to live with his wife's family. Polygamy was not uncommon.

The religious ceremonies were connected with the cosmic forces and the heavenly bodies. The dominating power was Tirawa, generally spoken of as "father." The heavenly bodies, the winds, thunder, lightning, and rain were his messengers. Among the Skidi the morning and evening stars represented the masculine and feminine elements, and were connected with the advent and the perpetuation on earth of all living forms. A series of ceremonies relative to the bringing of life and its increase began with the first thunder in the spring and culminated at the summer solstice in human sacrifice, but the series did not close until the maize, called "mother corn," was harvested. At every stage of the series certain shrines, or "bundles," became the center of a ceremony. Each shrine was in charge of an hereditary keeper, but its rituals and ceremonies were in the keeping of a priesthood open to all proper aspirants. Through the sacred and symbolic articles of the shrines and their rituals and ceremonies a medium of communication was believed to be opened between the people and the supernatural powers, by which food, long life, and prosperity were obtained. The mythology of the Pawnee is remarkably rich in symbolism and poetic fancy, and their religious system is elaborate and cogent. The secret societies, of which there were several in each tribe, were connected with the belief in supernatural animals. The functions of these societies were to call the game, to heal diseases, and to give occult powers. Their rites were elaborate and their ceremonies dramatic.

Four tribes of the Pawnee confederacy still survive: the Chaui or Grand Pawnee, the Kitkehahki or Republican Pawnee, the Pitahauerat or Tapage Pawnee, and the Skidi or Wolf Pawnee.

In 1702 the Pawnee were estimated by Iberville at 2,000 families. In 1838 they numbered about 10,000 souls, according to an estimate by houses by the missionaries Dunbar and Allis, and the estimate is substantially confirmed by other authorities of the same period, one putting the number as high as 12,500. The opening of a principal emigrant trail directly through the country in the '40's introduced disease and dissipation, and left the people less able to defend themselves against the continuous attacks of their enemies, the Sioux. In 1849 they were officially reported to have lost one-fourth their number by cholera, leaving only 4,500. In 1856 they had increased to 4,686, but 5 years later were reported at 3,416. They lost heavily by the removal to Indian Ter. in 1873–75, and in 1879 numbered only 1,440. They have continued to dwindle each year until there are now (1906) but 649 survivors.

Messrs Dunbar and Allis of the Presbyterian church established a mission among the Pawnee in 1834, which continued until 1847 when it was abolished owing to tribal wars. In 1883 the Woman's National Indian Association established a mission on the Pawnee reservation in Oklahoma, which in 1884 was transferred to the Methodist Episcopal Church, under whose auspices it is still in operation.

Consult Dunbar, Pawnee Indians, 1880–82; Grinnell, Pawnee Hero Stories, 1889; G. A. Dorsey, (1) Traditions of the Skidi Pawnee, 1904, (2) The Pawnee: Mythology, pt. 1, 1906; Fletcher, (1) in Am. Anthrop., IV, no. 4, 1902, (2) The Hako, 22d Rep. B. A. E., 1903; Winship, Coronado Exped., 1896.   (A. C. F.)

Aches.—Rafinesque in Marshall, Hist. Ky., I, 36, 1824. **Aḣ-i'-hi-nin.**—Hayden, Ethnog. and Philol. Mo. Val., 326, 1862 ('wolf people': Arapaho name). **Ahuachés.**—La Harpe (1719) in Margry, Déc., VI, 310, 1886. **Apani.**—Schoolcraft, Ind. Tribes, VI, 495, 1857. **Áwahe.**—Gatschet, Wichita MS., B.A.E., 1884 (Wichita name). **Awáhi.**—Gatschet, Wichita and Caddo MSS. B. A. E., 1884 (Caddo and Wichita name). **Awó.**—Gatschet, Tonkawe MS., B. A. E., 1884 (Tonkawa name, originally used by the Wichita). **Aχehinén.**—Gatschet, Arapaho MS., B. A. E., 1879 (Arapaho name). **Aχihínen.**—Ibid. ('wolf people': Arapaho name). **Ća'-hiks-i-ća'-hiks.**—Hayden, Ethnog. and Philol. Mo. Val., 349, 1862 (sig. 'men of men,' or 'last of men,' i. e. 'Indians': own name). **Çahiksi-çahiks.**—Hayden in Proc. Am. Philos. Soc., X, 401, 1869 (sig. 'Red man,' 'Indian'). **Dárāzhazh.**—Gatschet, Naisha Apache MS., B. A. E., 1884 (Kiowa Apache name). **Franceses.**—Doc. of 1727 quoted by Bandelier in Arch. Inst. Papers, V, 191, 1890 (Pananas, or). **Harahey.**—For forms of this name, see *Harahey.* **Ho-di-hi-dăn'-ne.**—ten Kate, Synonymie, 8, 1884 (sig. 'wolves': Cheyenne name). **Ho-ni'-i-ta-ni-o.**—Hayden, Ethnog. and Philol. Mo. Val., 290, 1862 (sig. 'little wolf people': Cheyenne name). **Hu'-tab Pa-da'-niɲ.**—Cook, Yankton MS. vocab., B. A. E., 184, 1882 (sig. 'Pawnees along the edge

or shore' [?]). **Kuitare'-i.**—Gatschet, Comanche MS., B. A. E., 1884 ('wolf people': Comanche name). **Kwitara'-a.**—ten Kate, Synonymie, 9, 1884 (Comanche name; incorrectly said to mean "skinned buttocks"). **Pa-dai'-na.**—Hoffman in Proc. Am. Philos. Soc., 295, 1886 (dialectic form of "Pawnee"). **Pa-da'-ni.**—Riggs, Dakota Gram., 173, 1852 (Dakota name). **Padani Maśteta.**—Iapi Oaye, XIII, no. 9, 33, Sept. 1884 (sig. 'Pawnee in the warm land' [Ind Ter.]). **Ꞁaḋiⁿ.**—Dorsey, Çegiha MS. Dict., B. A. E., 1879 (Omaha and Ponca name). **Páḋiⁿ.**—Dorsey, Osage MS. vocab., B. A. E., 1883 (Osage name; also Páyiⁿ). **Pahneug.**—Tanner, Narr., 316, 1830 (Ottawa name). **Pa'-i.**—Gatschet, Kaw MS. vocab., B. A. E., 27, 1878 (Kansa name). **Pāiné.**—Ruxton, Advent., 245, 1848. **Pa-la'-ni.**—Hoffman in Proc. Am. Philos. Soc., 295, 1886 (Teton form of "Padani"). **Panana.**—MS. of 1685–93 quoted by Bandelier in Arch. Inst. Papers, V, 185–6, 1890. **Pánanan.**—Hodge, field notes, B. A. E., 1895 (Tigua name). **Paneas.**—Lewis, Travels, 13, 1809. **Panes.**—Bowen, Am. Discov. by Welsh, 91, 1876. **Pani.**—Schoolcraft, Ind. Tribes, III, 50, 1853. **Panias.**—Sibley, Hist. Sketches, 23, 1806. **Panies.**—Henry, Trav. in Canada, 80, 1809. **Paⁿ-iⁿ.**—Gatschet, Kaw MS. vocab., B. A. E., 27, 1878 (Kansa name; also Pá-i). **Panis.**—De l'Isle, map of La. (1718) in Neill, Hist. Minn., 164, 1858. **Panis-Blancs.**—Hutchins (1764) in Schoolcraft, Ind. Tribes, III, 557, 1853. **Panyi.**—Dorsey, Tciwere MS. vocab., B. A. E., 1879 (Oto, Iowa, and Missouri name). **Panys.**—Perrot (*ca.* 1718), Mémoire, 63, 1864. **Panzas.**—Lewis and Clark Exped., II, 572, 1817. **Paoneneheo.**—R. Petter, inf'n, 1907 ('the ones with projecting front teeth': early Cheyenne name). **Paoninihiéu.**—Gatschet, Cheyenne MS., B. A. E., 1879 ('having the front teeth projecting': given as a Cheyenne division, but according to Petter, the Pawnee). **Paonis.**—Perkins and Peck, Annals of the West, 670, 1850. **Par-lar-nee.**—Corliss, Lacotah MS. vocab., B. A. E., 106, 1874 (Dakota form of "Padani"). **Pauanas.**—Bancroft, Ariz. and N. Mex., 236, 1889 (misprint). **Paunee.**—Writer of 1786 in Mass. Hist. Soc. Coll., 1st s., III, 24, 1794. **Pawnawnees.**—Carver, Travels, 118, 1778. **Pawne.**—Balbi, Atlas Ethnog., 54, 1826. **Pawnee.**—Pike, Travels, 165, 1811. **Pawneer.**—Audouard, Travers l'Amérique, 182, 1869. **Pawni.**—Latham, Essays, 400, 1860. **Páwnye.**—Abert in Emory, Recon., 536, 1848. **Páyiⁿ.**—Dorsey, Kansa MS. vocab., B. A. E., 1882 (Kansa name). **Pedanis.**—Warren (1855), Neb. and Dak., 50, 1875 (misprint for Padanis). **Pe-nai-na.**—Hoffman in Proc. Am. Philos. Soc., 295, 1886 (dialectic variant of "Padani"). **Pi-ta'-da.**—Grinnell, Pawnee Hero Stories, 240, 1889 (name given by southern tribes). **Poenese.**—Gass, Journal, 18, 1847. **Ponis.**—Gass, Voyage, 406, 1810. **Quipana.**—Biedma (1544) in French, Hist. Coll. La., II, 106, 1850. **Quipano.**—Schoolcraft, Ind. Tribes, VI, 67, 1857; cf. IV, 310, 1854. **Shaved heads.**—Sage, Scenes in Rocky Mts, 155, 1846. **Tcháhiksi-tcáhiks.**—Gatschet, MS., B. A. E. ('men of men': own name). **Tschihri.**—Maximilian, Trav., II, 247, 1841 (Arikara name). **Tśé-śa do ḣpa ka.**—Matthews, Ethnog. Hidatsa, 208, 1877 ('wolf people': Hidatsa name). **Tśe' śa no ḣpa ka.**—Ibid. **White Pani.**—Le Page du Pratz, Hist. La., map, 1774. **White Pania.**—Lewis, Travels, 181, 1809. **Wóhesh.**—Gatschet, Wichita MS., B. A. E., 1884 (Wichita name). **Xaratenumanke.**—Will and Spinden, Mandans, 215, 1906 (Mandan name).

Pawokti. One of the four Alibamu towns situated in 1798 on the E. bank of Alabama r., 2 m. below Tawasa (Toowassau), near the present Montgomery, Ala.

Pau-wag-ta.—Royce in 18th Rep. B. A. E., Ala. map, 1900. **Pau-woo-te.**—Hawkins (1799), Sketch, 36, 1848. **Pawactas.**—Swan (1791) in Schoolcraft, Ind. Tribes, V, 262, 1855. **Pawokti.**—Hawkins, op. cit.

Pawpoesit. A former village near Barnstable, Mass., occupied by Christian Indians, probably the Nauset.—Bourne

(1674) quoted by Drake, Bk. Inds., bk. 2, 118, 1848.

Paxinos. A Minisink and subsequently a Shawnee chief of the 17th and 18th centuries. He appears first in history in 1680, when as sachem of the Minisink he sent 40 men to join the Mohawk in an expedition against the French, and 10 years later was sent by his tribe to confer with Gov. Dongan of New York in regard to engaging in the war against the same nation. About 1692 or 1694 a small body of Shawnee settled among the Munsee, of whom the Minisink formed a division, and possibly Paxinos may have been one of this party. He was married about 1717. As early at least as 1754 he is referred to as the "old chief" of the Shawnee (Loskiel, Miss. United Breth., pt. 2, 157–160, 1794), and is so designated in the New York Colonial Documents wherever referred to. Heckewelder (Ind. Nations, 88, 1876), confirmed by Brinton, also says he was the chief of the Shawnee. He removed from Minisink to the Delaware country, but at what date is unknown, his next appearance being in connection with the difficulties which grew out of the removal of the Delawares to Wyoming, Pa. After the death, in 1749, of Shekellimus, the father of Logan, who had been a friend of the Moravian missionaries, the latter were fortunate in gaining the friendship of Paxinos. In 1754 he, with Tedyuskung, warned the people of Gnadenhuetten to remove to Wajomick (Wyoming), Pa.; but for this their lives would have been in danger. The next year Paxinos renewed the warning and demanded an answer in the name of the Hurons. His wife, for whom he had great affection and to whom he had been married for 38 years, was converted and baptized with Paxinos' consent. Soon after his last visit the Moravian settlement at Shamokin was attacked, and hearing of the danger to which the missionary Kiefer was exposed, Paxinos sent his two sons to conduct him to a place of safety. He was present with chiefs of other tribes at Ft Johnson, N. Y., Apr. 15–19, 1757, in conference with Sir Wm. Johnson regarding lines of travel and trade (N. Y. Doc. Col. Hist., VII, 245–47, 1856), and also at the conference with Gov. Denny at Easton, Pa., in August of the same year (ibid., 316–20). Paxinos removed with his family to Ohio in 1755 or 1758, where his tribesmen joined in the war against the English. It is probable that he died shortly after this time. He left two sons, Kolapeka and Teatapercaum, the latter a chief of some note in the war of 1764 (Ruttenber, Tribes Hudson R., 306, 1872). His name is given in various forms, as Paxihos, Paxinosa, Paxnos, Paxnous, Paxowan, Paxsinos, etc.   (C. T.)

Paxpili. A former Chumashan village near Purísima mission, Santa Barbara co., Cal.
Axpitil.—Taylor in Cal. Farmer, Oct. 18, 1861. Paxpili.—Ibid.

Paya. A rancheria, probably Cochimi, under Purísima (Cadegomo) mission, Lower California, in the 18th century.
Emetgale axá cang.—Doc. Hist. Mex., 4th s., v, 189, 1857 (sig. 'great trees of the white earth'). Paya.—Ibid.

Payabya ('pushed aside'). An Oglala band under Young-man-afraid.
Pa-a'-bi-a.—Hayden, Ethnog. and Philol. Mo. Val., 376, 1862 (trans. 'those who camp at the end'). Pa-ha-hi'-a.—Ibid. Payabya.—Robinson (1879) quoted by Dorsey in 15th Rep. B. A. E., 220, 1897 (sig. 'pushed aside'). Payabyeya.—Cleveland (1884) quoted by Dorsey, ibid.

Payanmin. A Costanoan village situated in 1819 within 10 m. of Santa Cruz mission, Cal.—Taylor in Cal. Farmer, Apr. 5, 1860.

Payaya. A prominent Coahuiltecan tribe living in the latter part of the 17th century on San Antonio r., Texas. In 1691 Father Massanet, when on his way to E. Texas, passed through their village, which was then apparently near the site of the present city of San Antonio. There he erected an altar, and, through a Pacpul interpreter, explained the Christian doctrine. For the native name of their stream, *Yana guana*, he substituted the Christian name San Antonio de Padua. As early as 1706 some of the Payaya were baptized at San Francisco Solano mission, on the Rio Grande, and this was one of the principal tribes for which Father Olivares founded San Antonio de Valero mission in 1718. They ranged at least from the Rio Grande to the Brazos. In 1716 Espinosa met them near the latter stream, and in 1717 Derbanne met them near the San Marcos (Colorado?). According to Rivera, writing in 1727, their most usual home was near the Medina, on an arroyo bearing the tribal name. At San Antonio de Valero mission the Payaya mingled particularly with the Xarame, who had been moved with the mission from the Rio Grande. These two tribes were the most constant inhabitants at the mission, and members of both were there as late as 1776 (Massanet, Diario, 1691, MS. in Mem. de Nueva España, XXVII, 95; Teran, Descripción y Diaria Demarcación, 1691, MS., ibid., 28; Olivares, Carta, 1716, MS., ibid., 169; Derbanne, 1717, in Margry, Déc., VI, 206, 1886; Rivera, 1727, Diario, leg. 1957, 1736; Baptismal Records of San Antonio de Valero mission, MS., passim).   (H. E. B.)
Paia.—Baptismal Rec. San Antonio de Valero, 1718, MS. Paiaia.—Ibid., 1716. Paialla.—Ibid., 1720. Paiaya.—Ibid., 1718. Paillailles.—Derbanne (1717) in Margry, Déc., VI, 206, 1886. Pay-

aguas.—Mota-Padilla, Hist. de la Conq., 383, 1742. **Payai.**—Baptismal Rec. San Antonio de Valero, 1726, MS. **Payaia.**—Ibid., 1724. **Payalla.**—Ibid., 1728. **Payay.**—Massanet, op. cit., 1691. **Payaya.**—Olivares, op. cit., 1716. **Payayas.**—Rivera, Diario, leg. 1994, 2602, 1736. **Payayasa.**—Baptismal Rec. San Antonio de Valero, 1728. **Payayes.**—Salinas (1693) cited in Dictamen Fiscal, 1716, Mem. de Nueva Espana, XXVII, 185. **Payseyas.**—Uhde, Länder, 121, 1861. **Peyaya.**—Terán (1691), op. cit.

Payne's Town. A refugee negro slave settlement formerly in Alachua co., Fla., named from King Payne, a Seminole chief.—Bell in Morse, Rep. to Sec. War, 309, 1822.

Payojke (*Pay-oj-ké*, 'summer people'). One of the two branches into which each well regulated Tewa village is divided in consequence of certain traditional beliefs regarding the religious organization of that people (Bandelier in Arch. Inst. Papers, III, 304, 1890). See *Tewa*.

Payuguan. A tribe or subtribe, probably Coahuiltecan, at San Francisco Solano mission, near the Rio Grande, Mexico, after 1703. They were associated with the Piniquu, Pataguo, Xarame, Siaban, Terocodame (q. v.), and other tribes. After this mission became San Antonio de Valero, on San Antonio r., Texas, members of this tribe entered it, as records of their baptism there between 1720 and 1741 still exist. Their identity with the Payuhan tribe, mentioned in 1735, is evidenced by the fact that in the baptismal records both names are in one case applied to the same individual (Baptismal Rec. of San Francisco Solano and San Antonio de Valero missions, MS.). Rivera (Diario, leg. 2763, 1736) mentions them in 1727 as a Coahuila tribe, which would indicate that they did not extend E. of Medina r. Cf. *Paguan.* (H. E. B.)
Paiugan.—Baptismal Rec., 1726, partida 170, MS. **Paiuguan.**—Ibid., 1713, 24. **Pajuguan.**—Ibid., 1728, 213. **Payaguanes.**—Rivera (1727), Diario, leg. 2763, 1736. **Payavan.**—Massanet (1690) in Dictamen Fiscal, Nov. 30, 1716, MS. (identical?). **Payugan.**—Baptismal Rec., 1720, 59, MS. **Payuguan.**—Ibid., 1706, 230. **Payuhan.**—Ibid., 1735, 418. **Payuhuan.**—Ibid., 1721, 92.

Payupki. A ruined pueblo on a point of Middle mesa, 6 m. N. of Mishongnovi, N. E. Arizona. It was built and occupied by discontented Tanos, Tewa, and Tigua from the Rio Grande, who left their homes between the Pueblo rebellion of 1680 and 1696. In 1706 the Payupki villagers were attacked and defeated by Capt. Holguin, who in turn was driven by the Hopi from their territory. In 1742 padres Delgado and Pino visited the Hopi country and returned to the Rio Grande with 441 Indians, said to have been Tigua originally from Sandia and Alameda, and established them in the refounded pueblo of Sandia, to which village the Hopi still apply the name Payupki. See Mindeleff in 8th Rep. B. A. E., 1891; Fewkes in 17th Rep. B. A. E., 583, 1898; Meline, Two

Thousand Miles, 1867; Bancroft, Ariz. and N. Mex., 243, 1889. (F. W. H.)
Mesa de las Tiguas.—Menchera map cited by Fewkes in 22d Rep. B. A. E., 19, 1904.

Pe (*Pë*). The Firewood or Timber clans of the Tewa pueblos of San Juan, Santa Clara, and San Ildefonso, N. Mex., and of Hano, Ariz. That of Hano is extinct.
Pè.—Fewkes in Am. Anthrop., VII, 166, 1894. **Pë-tdóa.**—Hodge, ibid., IX, 350, 1896 (San Juan and Santa Clara form; *tdóa*='people'; San Ildefonso form, Pe-tdóa.)

Pe (*Pe'*). The Sun clan of the pueblo of Jemez, N. Mex. A corresponding clan existed also at the former related pueblo of Pecos.
Pe.—Hewett in Am. Anthrop., VI, 431, 1904 (Pecos form). **Pe'+.**—Hodge, ibid., IX, 352, 1896 (Pecos form; += *ash* = 'people'). **Pe-tsaá.**—Ibid. (Jemez form; *tsáa* or *tsaásh* = 'people').

Peace. See *War and War discipline*.

Peace Policy. The Indian policy which is now accepted as the settled policy of the Government and is sustained by the common sentiment of the American people, was inaugurated by President Grant at the beginning of his first administration. On his recommendation Congress enacted the law, approved Apr. 10, 1869, providing for the appointment of a "Board of Commissioners," to consist of not more than 10 persons, to be selected by him (the President) "from men eminent for their intelligence and philanthropy, to serve without pecuniary compensation, who may under his direction exercise joint control with the Secretary of the Interior over the disbursement of the appropriations made by this Act, or any part thereof, as the President may designate." William Welsh of Philadelphia, John B. Farwell of Chicago, George H. Stuart of Philadelphia, Robert Campbell of St Louis, E. S. Tobey of Boston, William E. Dodge of New York, Felix R. Brunot of Pittsburg, Nathan Bishop of New York, and Henry S. Lane of Indiana were the Board of Commissioners as at first appointed. They were at that time called "The Peace Commission." In his first annual message, Dec. 1869, President Grant said: "From the foundation of the Government to the present, the management of the original inhabitants of this continent, the Indians, has been a subject of embarrassment and expense, and has been attended with continuous robberies, murders, and wars. From my own experience upon the frontiers and in Indian countries, I do not hold either legislation, or the conduct of the whites who come most in contact with the Indians, blameless for these hostilities. The past, however, can not be undone, and the question must be met as we now find it. I have adopted a new policy toward these wards of the nation (they can not be regarded in any other light than as wards) with fair results, so far as tried, and which I hope will be attended ultimately with great success."

For nearly 40 years the Board of Indian Commissioners has cooperated with the Government, favoring such legislation and administration in Indian affairs as by peaceful methods should put an end to Indian discontent, make impossible Indian wars, and fit the great body of Indians to be received into the ranks of American citizens. For the measures which they have proposed, to effect these reforms, see *United States Board of Indian Commissioners*. The Mohonk Indian Conference (q. v.), inaugurated and maintained by one of the present members of the Peace Commission, by its marked influence in guiding public opinion has added a strong element of popular support to this Peace Policy. It is interesting to note that the inauguration of a distinctive Peace Policy toward the Indians is due to one of the greatest of American warriors, President Ulysses S. Grant. The wisdom of this plan is shown in the fact that the policy advocated by the Peace Commission has resulted in an entire cessation of Indian warfare for the last score of years. (M. E. G.)

Pea Creek Band. A band of Florida Seminole, part of whom shared in the massacre of Maj. Dade and his command on Withlacoochee r. in Dec. 1835.—Schoolcraft, Ind. Tribes, VI, 469, 1857.

Peag. By the Massachusetts Indians, strings of white and dark purple shell beads (put among animate objects) were termed respectively *waⁿpaⁿpiag*, 'white strings,' and *sŭkaⁿpiag*, 'black strings' (=Abnaki *waⁿbaⁿbiag* and *sĕgaⁿbiag*). The English settlers, unused to French nasal sounds, pronounced and wrote the first of these words *wampampeag*. The word is from *wamp* (*waⁿp*), 'white,' *ampi* (*-aⁿpi*), 'string,' and the animate plural *-ag*. Finding the word too cumbersome, the colonists divided it and formed the two terms "wampum" and "piag," neither of which has any meaning, since the first consists of the root *wamp* 'white,' with a suffixed nasalized vowel, *am* (=*aⁿ*), belonging to and forming an essential part of *-ampe* (*aⁿpi*) 'string,' while the generic suffix *aⁿpi* 'string' has no meaning without the prefix *aⁿ*. See *Wampampeag, Wampum.* (W. R. G.)

Peantias. Mentioned by Buchanan (Sketches of N. Am. Ind., I, 138, 1825) as a wandering tribe on both sides of the Mississippi, numbering 800 souls. Probably imaginary.

Pearls. On the arrival of Europeans in Florida, Louisiana, and Virginia, pearls were found to be in great favor for personal embellishment among the natives, and this gem at once became a factor of importance in the avaricious schemes of promoters of conquest and colonization. Fabulous stories were told of the abundance and beauty of the pearls, which were eagerly sought by barter and by plundering the graves of the natives where they had been buried with the dead. The Knight of Elvas relates that De Soto obtained from burial places at the town of Cofitachique on Savannah r., below the present Augusta, Ga., 350 pounds of pearls, and a member of the first Virginia colony "gathered together from among the savage people aboute five thousande: of which number he chose so many as made a fayre chaine, which for their likenesse and uniformitie in roundnesse, orientnesse, and pidenesse of many excellente colours, with equalitie in greatnesse, were verie fayre and rare" (Hariot, Narrative of Virginia, 18, 1893). But the supply was really limited, and the majority of those obtained were ruined as jewels by perforation for suspension or by the heat employed in opening the shellfish from which they were abstracted. It also appears that many of the larger specimens referred to by the early writers were probably really not pearls, but polished beads cut from the nacre of sea shells and quite worthless as gems. It has been found that the real pearls were obtained from bivalve shells—from the oyster along the seashore and in tidewater inlets, and from the mussel on the shores of lakes and rivers. The pearls were probably not especially sought and collected by the natives, but obtained in the course of food consumption, which resulted in the accumulation of the vast deposits of shells known as shell-heaps (q. v.). The very general use of pearls by the pre-Columbian natives is amply attested by archeologists who in recent years have explored the mounds of the interior valleys, Professor Putnam having obtained more than 60,000 pearls—nearly 2 pecks—drilled and undrilled, from a single burial mound near Madisonville, Ohio. It appears that pearls were rarely used by the tribes w. of the Mississippi and on the Pacific coast, although the most important American pearl fisheries of the present day are on the coast of the Gulf of California. The primitive tribes of that region were not sufficiently ambitious to seek and make use of these gems.

Consult Dall in Am. Naturalist, XVII, no. 7, 1883; Kunz, Gems and Precious Stones, 1890; Jones, Antiq. Southern Inds., 1873; Putnam in 18th Rep. Peabody Mus., 1886; Rau in Smithson. Rep. 1872, 1873; Stearns in Nat. Mus. Rep. 1887, 1889. (W. H. H.)

Peashtebai. A Montagnais village on the s. coast of Labrador.—Stearns, Labrador, 271, 1884.

Pebulikwa (*Pe'-bu-li-kwa*). A former pueblo of the Jemez in New Mexico, the exact site of which has not been determined.

Pe'-bu-li-kwa.—Hodge, field notes, B. A. E., 1895.
Pem-bul-e-qua.—Bandelier in Arch. Inst. Papers, IV, 207, 1892.

Pecan. The nut of *Carya olivæformis*, one of the largest and most majestic trees of the river bottoms of s. Indiana, s. Illinois, Iowa, Louisiana, and Texas. The nut, the name of which has been spelled *pecan* from at least the time of Capt. Carver (1778), and is pronounced *pĕkáwn* in the W. and S., was early known also as "Illinois - nut." It is thin - shelled, smooth, and olive-shaped, much superior in flavor to the nuts of the rest of the genus, and has been held in great esteem for more than a century. The word *pecan*, as is shown by its pronunciation, was derived, not from the Creole *pacane*, but directly from Algonquian, in the various dialects of which *päká'n*, *púká'n*, *págá'n*, *púgá'n*, *päká*ⁿ*n*, is a general term for a hard-shelled 'nut'; hence the name "pecan-nut," sometimes used, is tautological. To the Illinois Indians the pecan was the nut par excellence, hence their designation of it simply as "nut," without any qualificative. The word is a radical one, and, as is the case with all Algonquian radical words, can be derived from no known root. The suggestion that it is from a root *päk*, 'to strike,' is untenable, for the reason that if such were the case *päkán* would necessarily be derived from a verb *päke* or *päkeu*, which could not possibly be formed from the root just mentioned.	(w. r. g.)

Peccarecamek (?'hickory town.'—Hewitt). A reported Indian settlement on the s. Virginia border, which, according to Indian information, had stone houses, of more than one story, which the inhabitants had been taught to build by the survivors of Raleigh's colony who escaped the massacre at Roanoke (Strachey, Va., 26, 1849).

Pechquinakonck (possibly from *pechuwi* 'near', *nak* 'island', *unk* the locative.—Gerard). An unidentified village in North Salem, Westchester co., N. Y., noted on Van der Donck's map of 1655. See Shonnard, Hist. Westchester Co., N. Y., 48, 1900.	(w. m. b.)

Peckikery. See *Hickory*.

Pecking implements. One of the four principal shaping processes employed by the tribes in the manufacture of implements and other objects of stone is known as pecking, and the implements used are stone hammers (q. v.) of various shapes; some are mere fragments of hard, tough rock with suitable points or edges, while others are more or less completely specialized, the typical implement being somewhat discoidal in form, with periphery convex or angular in profile, and with the sides slightly pitted for the accommodation of the opposing thumb and fingers, which hold it lightly. The operation consisted of repeated blows rapidly delivered with the periphery or edge of the implement upon the surface to be shaped, and the crumblings which resulted, although minute, gradually reduced undesirable parts, formed grooves, ridges, pits, nodes, etc., giving such approximation to the form desired that the grinding and rubbing processes, which usually followed, readily produced the finished work. Consult the citations under *Stonework*.	(w. h. h.)

Peckwes. A village in New Jersey, about 10 m. from Hackensack, in 1694. It probably belonged either to the Munsee or to the Shawnee, who were about that time removing from the S. to the Delaware country.—Schuyler (1694) in N. Y. Doc. Col. Hist., IV, 98, 1854.

Pecos (from *P'e'-a-ku'*, the Keresan name of the pueblo). Formerly the largest and most populous of the pueblos of New Mexico in historic times, occupied by a people speaking the same language of the Tanoan family, with dialectic variations, as that of Jemez; situated on an upper branch of Pecos r., about 30 m. s. E. of Santa Fé. In prehistoric times the Pecos people occupied numerous pueblos containing from 200 to 300 rooms each, and many compactly built single-story house groups of from 10 to 50 rooms each. These were scattered along the valley from the N. end of Cañon de Pecos grant to Anton Chico, a distance of 40 m. At the time of the arrival of the first Spaniards under Coronado, in 1540, the tribe had become concentrated in the great communal structure popularly known as Pecos. According to Bandelier, the Pecos declare that they came into their valley from the s. E., but that they originated in the N. and shifted across the Rio Grande, occupying successively the pueblos now in ruins at San José and Kingman previous to locating at their final settlement. The principal pueblo of the tribe, according to the same authority, was Tshiquité, or Tziquité (the pueblo of Pecos), which he identifies with the Acuique, Cicuic, Cicuye, etc., of the early Spanish chroniclers. Gatschet (Isleta MS. vocab., B. A. E., 1879), however, records Sikuyé as an Isleta name of Pecos pueblo, and as the Isleta people are Tigua and Coronado went from Tiguex (Tigua) province directly to Pecos in 1540, it seems more likely that Cicuye in its various forms was the Tigua name of Pecos pueblo in the 16th century. Bandelier thinks it possible that the ruins at Las Ruedas and El Gusano are those of pueblos also occupied by the Pecos people contemporaneously with their principal town at the time of the Spanish advent, and, indeed, Zarate-Salmeron, about 1629, mentions that the tribe at that date occupied also the pueblo of Tuerto, near the present Golden. At the time of Coronado's visit Pecos contained 2,000 to 2,500 inhabitants. It consisted of two great communal dwellings, built on the terrace plan, each 4 stories high, and containing 585 and 517 rooms respectively in its ground plan. Two Franciscan friars remained there after Coronado's departure in 1542, but both were probably killed before the close of the year. Pecos was visited also by Espejo in 1583, Castaño de Sosa in 1590-91, and Oñate in 1598, the last calling it Santiago. During the governorship of Oñate the first permanent missionaries were assigned to Pecos, and the great church, so long a landmark on the Santa Fé trail, was erected about 1617. The pueblo suffered severely first at the hands of the Querecho, or Apache of the plains, and after 1700 through raids by the Comanche. In the revolts of 1680-96 against Spanish authority (see *Pueblos*) Pecos played an important part, and its actual decline may be said to have begun at this time. In 1760 Galisteo was a visita of its mission, and, including the latter pueblo, Pecos contained 599 inhabitants in that year. In 1782, however, the Pecos mission was abandoned, its people being ministered by a priest from Santa Fé. Its population had dwindled to 152 in 1790-93, probably on account of a Comanche raid in which nearly every man in the tribe was killed. Epidemics, brought about apparently by the proximity of the cemetery to the source of water supply, also hastened the diminution of the Pecos people. In 1805 they had become reduced to 104, and in 1838 the pueblo was finally abandoned, the 17 survivors moving to Jemez, where there are now perhaps 25 Indians of Pecos blood, only one of whom however was born at the mother pueblo. The names of Pecos ruins, so far as recorded, are Kuuanguala, Pomojoua, San José (modern Spanish name of locality), Seyupa, and Tonchuun. The Pecos clans were as follows: Waha (Cloud), Pe (Sun), Ya (Coyote), Seé (Eagle), Kyunu (Corn), Sohl (Badger), Sungti (Turquoise), Daahl (Earth or· Sand), Wahaha (Calabash), Kiahl (Crow), Pa (Deer), Shiankya (Mountain lion), Whala (Bear), Fwaha (Fire), Amu (Ant), Kotsaa (Pine), Petdelu (Wild Turkey), Tashtye (Buffalo), Gyuungsh (Oak), Alawahku

(Elk), Alu (Antelope), Morbah (Parrot), and Hayah (Snake).

Consult Bandelier in Arch. Inst. Papers, I, pt. 2, 1881; III, 127, 1890; IV, 125, 1892; Hodge in Am. Anthrop., Oct. 1896; Hewett, ibid., n. s., VI, 426, 1904. (F. W. H.)

Acuique.—Coronado (1541) in Doc. Inéd., XIV, 325, 1870. **A-cu-lah.**—Simpson, Recon. Navaho Country, 143, 1850. **Acuyé.**—Bandelier in Arch. Inst. Papers, I, 114, 1881 (probably proper name for Cicuyé). **Âgin.**—Ibid., 20 (aboriginal name in the Jemez language). **Agiu?.**—Bancroft, Ariz. and N. Mex., 53, 1889 (the possible proper name). **A-gu-yu.**—Bandelier in Ritch, N. Mex., 201, 1885. **Âqiu.**—Bandelier in Arch. Inst. Papers, I, 114, 1881 (Pecos and Jemez name). **A-q'iu.**—Bandelier in Arch. Inst. Bull., I, 18, 1883. **Aqui.**—Bancroft, Ariz. and N. Mex., 53, 1889 (misquoting Bandelier). **Aquiu.**—Bandelier in Arch. Inst. Papers, III, 127, 1890 (name of the Pecos tribe). **Chichuich.**—Zaltieri, map (1566) in Winsor, Hist. Am., II, 451, 1886. **Cicoua.**—Schoolcraft, Ind. Tribes, IV, 39, 1854. **Cicui.**—Barcia, Ensayo, 21, 1723. **Cicuic.**—Gomara (1554) quoted by Hakluyt, Voy., 455, 1600, repr. 1810. **Cicuica.**—Wytfliet, Hist. des Indes, 114, 1605. **Cicuich.**—Ramusio, Nav. et Viaggi, III, 455, map, 1565. **Cicuick.**—Heylyn, Cosmography, 967, 1703. **Cicuie.**—Ladd, Story of N. Mex., 52, 1891. **Cicuio.**—Bancroft, Ariz. and N. Mex., 135, 1889. **Cicuiq.**—Bandelier in Arch. Inst. Papers, IV, 118, 1892. **Cicuique.**—Coronado (1541) in Doc. Inéd., XIV, 323, 1870. **Cicuya.**—Marcy, Army Life, 18, 1866. **Cicuyan Indians.**—Schoolcraft, Ind. Tribes, IV, 27, 1854. **Cicuyé.**—Castañeda (1596) in Ternaux-Compans, Voy., IX, 67, 1838. **Cicuyo.**—Benavides, Memorial, 99, 1630. **Ciquique.**—Espejo (1583) in Doc. Inéd., XV, 123, 1871. **Circuio.**—Hakluyt Society Pub., XXX, 227, 1862. **Coquite.**—Mota-Padilla (1742), Conq. N. Galicia, 164, 165, 1870. **Cucuye.**—Simpson in Trans. Am. Geog. Soc., V, map, 1871. **Cycuyo.**—Benavides, Memorial, 99, 1630. **Hiokŭö'k.**—Hodge, field notes, B. A. E., 1895 (Isleta Tigua name). **Hyó-quahoon.**—Lummis, Man Who Married the Moon, 145, 1894 (Isleta Tigua name of Pecos people). **K'ok'-o-ro-t'ŭ'-yu.**—Hodge, field notes, B. A. E., 1895 (Pecos name of pueblo). **Los Angeles.**—Bancroft, Ariz. and N. Mex., 281, 1889 (mission name). **N. S. de los Angeles de Pecos.**—Alencaster (1805) quoted by Prince, N. Mex., 37, 1883. **N. S. de los Angeles de Tecos.**—Bancroft, Native Races, I, 599, 1882 (misquoting Meline). **N. Senora de Pecos.**—Jeffery's Am. Atlas, map 5, 1776. **Nuestra Señora de los Angeas de Pecos.**—Ward in Ind. Aff. Rep. 1867, 213, 1868. **Nuestra Señora de los Angeles de Porciúncula.**—Vetancurt (1693) in Teatro Mex., III, 323, 1871 (church name). **Nuestra Señora de Pecos.**—D'Anville, map Am. Sept., 1746. **Nuestra Señora de Portiuncula de los Angeles de Pecos.**—Bandelier in Ausland, 815, 1882 (mission name). **Paego.**—Bandelier in Arch. Inst. Papers, I, 20, 1881 (Keresan name of pueblo). **Pae-qo.**—Ibid., 114 (Keresan name of tribe). **Paequiu.**—Ibid., III, 127, 1890 (alternative form of Pae-quiua-la, aboriginal name of tribe). **Pae-quiua-la.**—Ibid. **Pae-yoq'ona.**—Ibid., I, 114, 1881 (Keresan name of pueblo). **Pago.**—Bandelier in N. Y. Staatszeitung, June 28, 1885. **Pagos.**—Falconer in Jour. Roy. Geog. Soc., XIII, 216, 1843. **P'a-qu-láh.**—Hewett in Am. Anthrop., VI, 430, 1904 (Jemez name). **P'a-tyu-lá.**—Hodge, field notes, B. A. E., 1895 (Jemez name). **Pa-yo-go-na.**—Bandelier in Revue d'Ethnographie, 203, 1886 (Keresan name). **Payoqona.**—Bandelier in N. Y. Staatszeitung, June 28, 1885 (Keresan name). **Péahko.**—Hodge, field notes, B. A. E., 1895 (Santa Ana name). **Peakŭní.**—Hodge, ibid. (Laguna name of pueblo; Peakŭnimi=Pecos people). **Pecas.**—Edwards, Campaign, map, 1847. **Peccos.**—Oñate (1598) in Doc. Inéd., XVI, 258, 1871. **Peco.**—Mühlenpfordt, Mejico, II, 528, 1844. **Pecos.**—Oñate (1598) in Doc. Inéd., XVI, 109, 1871 (first use of the term). **Pegóa.**—Mühlenpfordt, Mejico, II, 528, 1844. **Peici.**—Sanson, L'Amérique, map, 27, 1657. **Peicis.**—De l'Isle, Map Am. Septentrionale, 1700. **Peicj.**—Linschoten, Descrip. de l'Amérique, map

1, 1638. **Péku.**—Hodge, field notes, B. A. E., 1895 (Sandia Tigua name). **Piecis.**—Blaeu, Atlas, XII, 62, 1667. **Santiago.**—Oñate (1598) in Doc. Inéd., XVI, 259, 1871. **Sikoua.**—Schoolcraft, Ind. Tribes, IV, 40, 1854. **Sikuyé.**—Gatschet, Isleta MS. vocab., B. A. E., 1879 (Isleta name of pueblo; the people are called Sikuyén). **Suco.**—Galvano (1563) in Hakluyt Society Pub., XXX, 227, 1862 (applied also to Acuco=Acoma). **Tamos.**—Espejo (1583) in Doc. Inéd., XV, 123, 1871 ("el gran pueblo de los Peccos, y es el que Espejo llama la provincia de Tamos."—Oñate, 1598, in Doc. Inéd., XVI, 258, 1871). **Tanos.**—Bandelier in Arch. Inst. Papers, IV, 126, 1892 (misquoting Espejo). **Tichuico.**—Wytfliet, Hist. des Indes, 114, 1605. **Ticuic.**—Vaugondy, map Amérique, 1778. **Ticuique.**—Jaramillo (1540) in Doc. Inéd., XIV, 309, 1870. **Tienique.**—Jaramillo, ibid. **Tshi-quit-é.**—Bandelier in Arch. Inst. Papers, III, 121, 127, 1890 (given as proper name). **Tzi-quit-é.**—Ibid., 127.

Pectolite. A somewhat rare mineral, resembling nephrite, found in British Columbia and Alaska, and used by the native tribes for implements. It is hard and tough and made excellent hammers, which were sometimes ground into cylindrical shape and somewhat polished, showing to advantage the structure of this handsome stone, which is greenish gray and slightly translucent. Little is known of the distribution or manner of occurrence of pectolite. Analysis gives silica 54, lime 32, soda 9, water 4, magnesium, 1. For illustrations see Murdoch in 9th Rep. B. A. E., 1892; Nelson in 18th Rep. B. A. E., 1899.   (W. H. H.)

Pedee. A small tribe, probably Siouan, formerly living on the middle course of Pedee r., S. C. Nothing is known of its language and little of its history. On a war map of 1715 its village is placed on the E. bank, considerably below that of the Cheraw, about the present Cheraw. In 1744 they with others killed several Catawba, which led to their being driven from their lands into the white settlements. Two years later they and the Sara are named as tribes which had long been incorporated with the Catawba. In 1751 they were mentioned at the Albany conference as one of the small tribes living among the white people in South Carolina, against whom the Iroquois were asked not to war. While most of the Pedee joined the Catawba, there were some who remained among the white settlements as late as 1755. See Mooney, Siouan Tribes of the East, 1894.   (J. M.)
Peadea.—Brion de la Tour, map, 1784. **Pedees.**—War map (ca. 1715) in Winsor, Hist. Am., v, 364, 1887. **Pidees.**—Glen (1751) in N. Y. Doc. Col. Hist., VI, 709, 1855.

Pedilonians. Mentioned by Buchanan (Sketches N. Am. Ind., I, 138, 1825) as a tribe, numbering 500 souls, living w. of the Mississippi. Probably imaginary.

Pedro's Village. Given by Bancroft (Nat. Races, I, 460, 1882, quoting Hayes' MS.) as a former Luiseño village 5 m. from Agua Caliente, s. Cal. It may equally well have belonged to the Agua Calientes or to the Diegueños.

Peekishe. A tribe which, according to a tradition of the Kansa, lived near them in Missouri, near the mouth of Kansas r. They had long hair which they wrapped around their heads like turbans, and they shaved the tops of their heads. The tribe is said to have gone S., none of them remaining near the Kansa.
Pe-e′-ki-ce.—Dorsey, Kansa MS. vocab., B. A. E., 1882.

Peepchiltk (*Pe-éptcĭlt'k'*, 'concave'). A Pima village N. E. of Casa Blanca, s. Arizona; so called from a family with "concave" noses.
Pe-éptcĭlt'k'.—Russell, Pima MS., B. A. E., 18, 1902. **Pepchalk.**—Dudley in Ind. Aff. Rep. 1871, 58, 1872. **Peptchörl.**—ten Kate quoted by Gatschet, MS., B. A. E., xx, 199, 1888.

Peeyou. Given as one of the Calapooya tribes on Willamette r., Oreg. Not identified.
Pecyou.—Bancroft, Nat. Races, I, 309, 1882. **Peeyou.**—Ross, Adventures, 236, 1847.

Pehir. A village mentioned by Joutel as being w. or N. w. of the Maligne (Colorado) r., Texas, in 1687. The territory was controlled largely by tribes of the Caddoan family.   (A. C. F.)
Pehir.—Joutel (1687) in French, Hist. Coll. La., I, 137, 1846. **Pehires.**—Barcia, Ensayo, 271, 1723. **Pihir.**—Joutel, op. cit., 152.

Peiltzun ('buckskin'). An Apache clan or band at San Carlos agency and Ft Apache, Ariz., in 1881.
Pe-iltzun.—Bourke in Jour. Am. Folk-lore, III, 112, 1890.

Peinhoum. A village mentioned by Joutel in 1687 as being N. or N. w. of the Maligne (Colorado) r., Texas. The name seems to have been given him by Ebahamo Indians, who were probably of Karankawan affinity. The locality was controlled principally by Caddoan tribes. See *Orcan.*   (A. C. F.)
Pehumas.—Barcia, Ensayo, 271, 1723. **Peihoum.**—Joutel (1687) in French, Hist. Coll. La., I, 138, 1846. **Peihoun.**—Ibid., 152. **Piohum.**—Joutel (1687) in Margry, Déc., III, 289, 1878. **Piou.**—Joutel in French, op. cit., 152.

Peisela (*Pē′ĭsEla*). A Bellacoola town at the entrance to the valley opening on the N. side of the mouth of Bellacoola r., Brit. Col. It was one of the Nuhalk villages (Boas in Mem. Am. Mus. Nat. Hist., II, 48, 1898).

Peisiekan (*Pe-i-si-e-kan*, 'striped'). A band of Cree, occupying 40 or 50 tipis and roving and hunting near Tinder mts., Canada, in 1856.—Hayden, Ethnog. and Philol. Mo. Val., 237, 1862.

Peissaquo. A village or tribe spoken of by Joutel in 1687 as being N. or N. w. of the Maligne (Colorado) r., Texas. The name seems to have been given him by Ebahamo Indians, who were probably of Karankawan affinity. The locality mentioned was controlled mainly by Caddoan tribes.   (A. C. F.)
Peisacho.—Joutel (1687) in French, Hist. Coll. La., I, 138, 1846. **Peissaquo.**—Joutel (1687) in Margry, Déc., III, 288, 1878.

Peixolóe. Mentioned as a pueblo of the province of Atripuy (q. v.), in the vicinity of the lower Rio Grande, New Mexico, in 1598.—Oñate (1598) in Doc. Inéd., XVI, 115, 1871.

Peixtan. A former Shawnee or Nanticoke village on or near the lower Susquehanna, in Dauphin co., Pa., possibly on the site of the present Paxton or Paxtonville.—Evans (1707) quoted by Day, Pa., 391, 1843.

Pekaist (*Pe'qaist*, 'white stone'). A village of the Spences Bridge band of the Ntlakyapamuk, on the s. side of Thompson r., 32 m. above Lytton, Brit. Col.; pop. 5 in 1897 (the last time the name appears), including Pemainus.
Pakeist.—Can. Ind. Aff., 230, 1886. Pe'qaist.— Teit in Mem. Am. Mus. Nat. Hist., II, 173, 1900. 'P'kâi'st.—Hill-Tout in Rep. Ethnol. Surv. Can., 4, 1899. Pukaist'.—Dawson in Trans. Roy. Soc. Can. 1891, sec. II, 44, 1892.

Pekan. A name of the fisher (*Mustela pennanti*). The word is used by Charlevoix (Nouv. France, III, 134, 1744) and came into English through Canadian French, where it occurs also as *pécan*. It seems to be of Algonquian origin, though not western, for the animal is called in Chippewa *otchig*, in Cree *otchek*. It is referred by some to an Abnaki *pékané*, mentioned by Rasles, which Trumbull (Natick Dict., Bull. 25, B. A. E., 260, 1903) thinks means this animal. (A. F. C.)

Pekickery. See *Hickory*.

Pekoinoke. A village of the Nanticoke still existing in Maryland in 1755.—Mt Johnson conf. (1755) in N. Y. Doc. Col. Hist., VI, 983, 1855.

Pekwan. A Yurok village on lower Klamath r., at the mouth of Pekwan cr., N. W. Cal.
Pack-wans.—McKee (1851) in Sen. Ex. Doc. 4, 32d Cong., spec. sess., 162, 1853. Påhk-wans.—Meyer, Nach dem Sacramento, 282, 1855. Pak-wan.— McKee op. cit., 194. Pec-quan.—Gibbs (1851) in Schoolcraft, Ind. Tribes, III, 138, 1853. Pek'-wan.— Powers in Cont. N. A. Ethnol., III, 44, 1877. Tirip'- ama.—A. L. Kroeber, inf'n, 1904 (Karok name).

Pekwiligii (possibly 'place of the Picuris people'). A former pueblo of the Jemez in New Mexico, the exact site of which is not known.
Pe-cuil-a-gui.—Bandelier in Arch. Inst. Papers, IV, 207, 1892. Pe'-kwïl-i-gi-i'.—Hodge, field notes, B. A. E., 1895.

Pekwuteu. A Yurok village on lower Klamath r., on the tongue of land jutting out between it and the Trinity where they join, opposite Weitspus (Weitchpec), N. W. Cal. It is called also Pekwututl.—A. L. Kroeber, inf'n, 1905.

Pelchiu. Mentioned as a pueblo of New Mexico in 1598, possibly Keresan.
Pelchin.—Bancroft, Ariz. and N. Mex., 136, 1889 (misquoting Oñate). Pelchiu.—Oñate (1598) in Doc. Inéd., XVI, 115, 1871.

Pelheli (*Pe'lǫeli*). Said by the Kwantlen to have been a division of their people who settled on the Pacific opposite Alert bay, Brit. Col. Probably, as Hill-

Tout suggests (Ethnol. Surv. Can., 55, 1902), they were identical with the Bellacoola.

Pelkatchek ('wherewith one catches fat'). A village of the Ntshaautin on Tchestata lake, Brit. Col.
Pel'catzék.—Morice in Trans. Roy. Soc. Can., 109, 1892. Pe-ʇ'ka-tcék.—Morice, Notes on W. Dénés, 25, 1893.

Pelones (Span.: 'the hairless ones'). Mentioned by Rivera (Diario, leg. 2602, 1736) as a tribe or village apparently near the lower Rio Grande in s. Texas. Probably Coahuiltecan. Mota Padilla (Conq. Nueva Galicia, 514, 1870) mentioned the Pelones in 1742 as a people connected with the missions of Nuevo León, Mexico.

Pemainus (*Pemai'nus:* according to Teit, 'the flat underneath or near the brow or steep,' because a low flat extends along the river here for some distance; according to Hill-Tout, 'grassy hills'). A village of the Spences Bridge band of Ntlakyapamuk, on the s. side of Thompson r., 28 m. above Lytton, Brit. Col. Pop. 5 in 1897, including Pekaist.
PEmai'nus.—Teit in Mem. Am. Mus. Nat. Hist., II, 173, 1900. Pimaî'nüs.—Hill-Tout in Rep. Ethnol. Surv. Can., 4, 1899. Piminos.—Can. Ind. Aff., 196, 1885.

Pemaquid (? 'it is precipitous land.'— Hewitt). An Abnaki village in 1614 about the present Pemaquid, Lincoln co., Me. Fort Charles was built there in 1677, after the English occupancy became prominent in the colonial history of New England. It was taken and burned by the Abnaki on Aug. 2, 1689.
Panaquid.—Strachey (ca. 1612), Va., 27, 1849. Pema- quid.—Strachey, ibid., 169 (the river). Pemma- quid.—Smith (1616) in Mass. Hist. Soc. Coll., 3d s., VI, 97, 1837. Pemmayquid.—Smith, map (ca. 1614) in Me. Hist. Soc. Coll., V, 162, 1857. Penaquid.— Smith (1631) in Mass. Hist. Soc. Coll., 3d s., III, 20, 1833.

Pematuning ('at the Wry-mouth's.'— Hewitt). A village, probably of the Delawares, near Shenango, Pa., in 1764.— Hutchin's map (1764) in Smith, Bouquet's Exped., 1766.

Pemberton Meadows. The local name for a body of Lower Lillooet living N. of Lillooet lake, Brit. Col.; pop. 261 in 1906.

Pembina. A Canadian name for the acid fruit of *Viburnum opulus*, the high-bush cranberry, a plant growing in low ground, along streams, from New Brunswick, far westward, and s. to Pennsylvania. The word is a corruption of Cree *nipiminán*, 'watered-berry,' i. e. the fruit of a plant growing in, or laved by, water; not 'water-berry,' as has been stated, since that would be *nipimin;* and, besides, the fruit is not watery. The name of the fruit is derived from the habitat of the plant that bears it. (W. R. G.)

Pemmican. A food preparation (also spelled *pemican*) used in the wilds of the northern parts of North America, and made by cutting the meat of the reindeer into thin slices, drying the latter in the sun or over the smoke of a slow fire, pounding them fine between stones, and incorporating the material with one-third part of melted fat. To this mixture dried fruit, such as choke or June berries, is sometimes added. The whole is then compressed into skin bags, in which, if kept dry, it may be preserved for four or five years. Sweet pemmican is a superior kind of pemmican in which the fat used is obtained from marrow by boiling broken bones in water. Fish pemmican is a pemmican made by the Indians of the remote regions of the N. W. by pounding dried fish and mixing the product with sturgeon oil. The Eskimo of Alaska make a pemmican by mixing chewed deer meat with deer-suet and seal-oil. "This food," observes Lieut. Ray, "is not agreeable to the taste, probably owing to the fact that the masticators are inveterate tobacco-chewers." The word is from Cree *pĭmĭkân*, 'manufactured grease,' from *pĭmĭkeu*, 'he (or she) makes (or manufactures) grease,' that is, by boiling crude fat, *pĭmĭ*, in water and skimming off the supernatant oil. The verb is now used by the Cree in the sense of 'he makes pemmican.' The word is cognate with Abnaki *pĕmĭkân*. (w. R. G.)

Pemveans. Mentioned by Boudinot (Star in the West, 128, 1816) in a list of tribes; unidentified.

Penah ('turkey'). A former village of the Fox tribe, situated on the site of Cassville, Grant Co., Wis.—Snyder, VanVechten & Co., Hist. Atlas Wis., 209, 1878.

Peñasco Blanco (Span.: 'large white rock'). One of the most important ruins of the Chaco Canyon group, N. w. N. Mex., and one of the most remarkable of all known prehistoric Indian structures N. of Mexico. It is situated on a high mesa at the s. side of the canyon, about 3 m. below Pueblo Bonito. In plan it is an almost perfect ellipse; the long diameter is 500 ft, the short 365 ft. The w. half of the ellipse is occupied by the pueblo proper, which was 5 tiers of rooms deep and probably 4 stories high. The E. half consists of a continuous series of single-story rooms. The outer wall is in a ruinous condition, but little of it remaining. As in almost every one of the Chaco canyon buildings, there is no uniformity of structural skill displayed in the masonry, some portions being of the crudest kind while in other parts are beautiful examples of horizontal alternations of thick and thin blocks. There are 7 kivas on the w. side of the court, and a large one, 50 ft in diameter, outside the s. end. The rooms in the main building are larger, averaging 20 ft in length, varying in width from 10 to 20 ft, the width of the

rooms in each tier being uniform throughout the entire length of the building. In addition to the writings cited below, consult Jackson in 10th Rep. Hayden Surv., 1878. (E. L. H.) **Peñasca Blanca.**—Simpson, Exped. Navajo Country, 82, 1850. **Penasco Blanca.**—Hardacre in Scribner's Mag., 275, Dec. 1878 (misprint). **Señasca Blanca.**—Domenech, Deserts N. Am., I, 200, 1860 (misprint).

Peñas Negras (Span.: 'black rocks'). A small communal pueblo on an eminence w. of the Pecos road, near the edge of a forest, 8 m. s. s. E. of Santa Fé, N. Mex. It was inhabited in prehistoric times by the Tanos or the Tewa, but its aboriginal name is unknown.—Bandelier in Arch. Inst. Papers, IV, 97, 1892.

Penateka (*Pénätĕka*, 'honey eaters'). An important division of the Comanche, formerly ranging on the edge of the timber country in E. Texas, and hence frequently known to the whites as Eastern or Southern Comanche. They had but a loose alliance with their western kinsmen and sometimes joined the Texans or troops against them. They are now with the rest of the Comanche in s. w. Oklahoma.—Mooney in 14th Rep. B. A. E., 1045, 1896. **Hoesh.**—Smithson. Misc. Coll., II, art. 3, 53, 1862. **Ho-is.**—Neighbors in Ind. Aff. Rep., 579, 1848. **Honey Eaters.**—Butler and Lewis (1846) in H. R. Doc. 76, 29th Cong., 2d sess., 6, 1847. **Honigeters.**—ten Kate, Reizen in N. A., 377, 1885 ('honeyeaters': Dutch form). **Hoo-ish.**—Butler and Lewis, op. cit. **Jū-ī.**—Butcher and Leyendecher, Comanche MS. vocab., B. A. E., 1867 (='woodman'). **Ku'baratpat.**—Mooney in 14th Rep. B. A. E., 1045, 1896 (='steep climbers'; another Comanche name). **Orientales.**—Bol. Soc. Geog. Mex., V, 318, 1857 (apparently identical). **Pe-nă-döj-kā.**—Butcher and Leyendecher, op. cit. **Penandé.**—Pimentel, Lenguas, II, 347, 1865. **Pen-a-tacker.**—Leavenworth (1868) in H. R. Misc. Doc. 139, 41st Cong., 2d sess., 6, 1870. **Penatakas.**—Leeper in Ind. Aff. Rep. 1859, 256, 1860. **Penelakas.**—Penney in Ind. Aff. Rep., 101, 1870. **Penelethkas.**—Keane in Stanford, Compend., 530, 1878. **Penetakees.**—Neighbors in Ind. Aff. Rep., 577, 1848. **Penetakers.**—Walkley (1868) in Sen. Ex. Doc. 18, 40th Cong., 3d sess., 15, 1869. **Peneteghka.**—Alvord (1868), ibid., 9. **Penetéka.**—ten Kate, Reizen in N. A., 384, 1885. **Pe-netéka-Comanches.**—Ibid., 373. **Pene-teth-ca.**—Sanders (1870) in H. R. Ex. Doc. 7, 42d Cong., 1st sess., 3, 1871. **Penetethka.**—Ind. Aff. Rep., 334, 1873. **Penetoghkos.**—Alvord, op. cit., 7. **Penhatethka.**—Battey, Advent., 200, 1875. **Pen-ha-teth-kahs.**—Ibid., 307. **Pĕñ'-ha-tĕth'-kas.**—Ibid., 284. **Pennelakas.**—Penney in Ind. Aff. Rep. 1869, 101, 1870. **Penne-taha.**—Comanche and Kiowa treaty in Sen. Ex. Doc. O, 39th Cong., 1st sess., 4, 1866. **Pennetekas.**—Walkley (1868) in Sen. Ex. Doc. 18, 40th Cong., 3d sess., 18, 1869. **Penttakers.**—McKusker (1868), ibid., 14. **Sugar Eater band.**—Comanche and Kiowa treaty, op. cit. **Sugar or Honey Eaters.**—Schoolcraft, Ind. Tribes, I, 522, 1851. **Tĕ'kăpwai.**—Mooney in 14th Rep. B. A. E., 1045, 1896 (='no meat': another Comanche name). **Te'yuwĭt.**—Ibid. (='hospitable': another Comanche name).

Pencoana. Mentioned as a pueblo of the province of Atripuy, in the vicinity of the lower Rio Grande, New Mexico, in 1598.—Oñate (1598) in Doc. Inéd., XVI, 115, 1871.

Pendants. See *Adornment, Gorgets, Ornament, Plummets.*

Penelakut. A Cowichan tribe on Kuper and Galiano ids., off the s. E. end of

Vancouver id. The Lilmalche and Tsussie are perhaps parts of the same. Pop. of the Penelakut proper, 181 in 1902, 145 in 1906.

Pa-nel-a-kut.—Can. Ind. Aff., 308, 1879. Penâlahuts.—Ibid., lix, 1877. Pēnā′leqat.—Boas, MS., B. A. E., 1887. Penalikutson.—Mayne, Brit. Col., 165, 1861. Penduhuts.—Brit. Col., map, Ind. Aff., Victoria, 1872. Penelakut.—Can. Ind. Aff., 164, 1901.

Pengnok. An Utkiavinmiut Eskimo village near C. Smythe, Alaska.—11th Census, Alaska, 162, 1893.

Penikikonau ('fish hawk'). A subphratry or gens of the Eagle phratry of the Menominee.—Hoffman in 14th Rep. B. A. E., 42, 1896.

Peninsular Shellmound. One of the 5 principal shell deposits of Damariscotta r., Me., situated on a broad peninsula formed by a bend in the river about 1 m. N. of Newcastle. The mound extends along the w. bank for about 400 ft, and consists almost wholly of closely-packed oyster shells in an irregular mass varying from a few inches in thickness at the northern end to a height of about 22 ft near its southern extremity. The shells are exposed throughout its length on the river side, and a considerable portion of the mound has been undermined and washed away by the water. The mound is covered by a dense growth of pine and spruce. Large quantities of shell have been carried away for road making and other purposes, and many tons have been burned in the kiln which stands near its southern end. The mound has never been systematically explored, and but few artifacts have been found during the superficial examinations that have been made. Its structure and general contents are apparently the same as in the Whaleback mound (q. v.) on the opposite side of the river. Consult Wyman in 2d Rep. Peabody Mus., 1869; Berry in N. E. Mag., xix, 1898–99. (c. c. w.)

Penjeacú. Mentioned as a pueblo of the province of Atripuy, in the region of the lower Rio Grande, New Mexico, in 1598.—Oñate (1598) in Doc. Inéd., xvi, 115, 1871.

Penna (*Pen′-nă*, 'turkey'). A gens of the Potawatomi.—Morgan, Anc. Soc., 167, 1877.

Pennacook (cognate with Abnaki *pĕnắkuk*, or *penaⁿkuk*, 'at the bottom of the hill or highland.'—Gerard). A confederacy of Algonquian tribes that occupied the basin of Merrimac r. and the adjacent region in New Hampshire, N. E. Massachusetts, and the extreme s. part of Maine. They had an intermediate position between the southern New England tribes, with whom the English were most directly interested, and the Abnaki and others farther N., who were under French influence. Their alliances were generally with the northern tribes, and

later with the French. It has been supposed that they were an offshoot of the southern tribes, as they spoke substantially the same language as the Massachusetts and Rhode Island Indians, and are generally classed with the Mahican. We know the confederacy only as constituted under the influence and control of Passaconaway, who probably brought into it elements from various tribes of the same general stock. The tribes directly composing the confederacy were: Agawam, Wamesit, Nashua, Souhegan, Amoskeag, Pennacook proper, and Winnipesaukee. The first three of these were in Massachusetts, the others in New Hampshire. The Accominta of Maine and the Naumkeag of Essex co., Mass., were merged in larger tribes and disappeared at an early period. Besides these, the following tribes were more or less connected with the confederacy and usually considered a part of it: Wachuset, Coosuc, Squamscot, Winnecowet, Piscataqua, and Newichawanoc. Some writers also include the Ossipee, Sokoki, Pequawket, and Arosaguntacook, but these four tribes had their closest relations with the Abnaki group. The Arosaguntacook were certainly connected with the Abnaki confederacy. Pentucket village also belonged to the Pennacook confederacy, although the Indians there do not seem to have been designated as a distinct tribe. The Pennacook were reduced by smallpox and other causes to about 2,500 in 1630, and in 1674 had decreased to about 1,250. On the outbreak of King Philip's war the next year the Nashua and Wachuset joined the hostile tribes, but the greater part of the Pennacook, under the chief Wannalancet, kept on friendly terms with the whites until the treacherous seizure of about 200 of their number by Waldron in 1676. They then abandoned their country, the greater part with their chief removing to Canada, while a considerable number fled westward. The latter were pursued by the English and overtaken at Housatonic r., and a number of them killed. The survivors escaped to the Mahican of the Hudson, and were afterward settled at Scaticook, Rensselaer co., N. Y. Those who had removed to Canada were first settled near Quebec, but being afterward joined by some of their relatives from Scaticook, they were given, in 1685, a tract at Côte de Lauzun, whence they removed in 1700 to St Francis, where they met the Abnaki, who were also exiles from New England. The St Francis Indians soon became noted as the bitterest foes of the English colonies, and so continued until the fall of the French power in America. Their descendants still reside at the same place. Soon after their settlement at St Francis they endeavored to persuade those at Scaticook to join them, but without success.

The following were Pennacook villages and bands: Accominta, Agawam, Amoskeag, Coosuc, Nashua, Newichawanoc, Ossipee, Pennacook, Pentucket, Piscataqua, Souhegan, Squamscot, Wachuset, Wamesit, Weshacum, Winnecowet, Winnipesauki. (J. M. C. T.)

Merrimacks.—Drake, Bk. Inds., bk. 2, 62, 1848. **Nechegansett.**—Gookin (*ca.* 1675) quoted by Vater, Mith., pt. 3, sec. 3, 377, 1816. **Owaragees.**—Colden (1727), Five Nations, 104, 1747. **Panukkog.**—Hogkins (1685) in N. H. Hist. Soc. Coll., I, 220, 1824. **Peenecooks.**—McKeen in Me. Hist. Soc. Coll., III, 323, 1853. **Penacook.**—Writer, *ca.* 1680, quoted by Drake, Bk. Inds., bk. 3, 115, 1848. **Penagooge.**—Record of 1675 quoted by Drake, ibid., 96. **Penakook.**—Letter of 1676 quoted by Drake, ibid., 84. **Penecooke.**—Nicholson (1688) in N. Y. Doc. Col. Hist., III, 551, 1853. **Penicoock.**—Moll, map in Humphrey, Account, 1730. **Penicook.**—Sabin (1699) in N. Y. Doc. Col. Hist., IV, 619, 1854. **Penikook.**—Jefferys, Fr. Doms., pt. 1, map, 1761. **Pennacokes.**—Bellomont (1700) quoted by Ruttenber, Tribes Hudson R., 184, 1872. **Pennacooke.**—Hubbard (1680) in Mass. Hist. Soc. Coll., 2d s., v, 242, 1815. **Pennagog.**—Gookin (1677) in Trans. Am. Antiq. Soc., II, 464, 1836. **Pennakooks.**—Gookin (1674), ibid., 1st s., I, 149, 1806. **Pennecooke.**—Doc. of 1659 in N. H. Hist. Soc. Coll., III, 212, 1832. **Pennekokes.**—Livingston (1702) in N. Y. Doc. Col. Hist., IV, 996, 1854. **Pennekook.**—Ibid. **Pennekooke.**—Courtland (1688), ibid., III, 562, 1853. **Pennicook.**—Rawson (1668) in N. H. Hist. Soc. Coll., III, 223, 1832. **Pennikook.**—Schuyler (1700) in N. Y. Doc. Col. Hist., IV, 662, 1854. **Pennokook.**—Schuyler (1687), ibid., III, 482, 1853. **Penny Cook.**—Douglass, Summary, I, 185, 1755. **Penny-Cooke.**—Rawson (1668) in N. H. Hist. Soc. Coll., III, 223, 1832. **Pennykoke.**—Livingston (1702) in N. Y. Doc. Col. Hist., IV, 996, 1854. **Pinnekooks.**—Albany treaty (1664), ibid., III, 68, 1853. **Ponacooks.**—McKenney and Hall, Ind. Tribes, III, 79, 1854. **Ponacoks.**—Colden (1727), Five Nations, 95, 1747.

Pennacook. A tribe of the Pennacook confederacy. They occupied both banks of Merrimac r. for some miles above and below Concord, N. H. They were the strongest and most influential tribe of the confederacy and the last to preserve their tribal name, having incorporated most of the other tribes before King Philip's war in 1675.

Pennacook. The principal village of the Pennacook tribe, situated on the site of the present Concord, N. H.

Penobscot (derived by Vetromile from *Pănnawănbskek*, 'it forks on the white rocks,' or *Penaubsket*, 'it flows on rocks'; Godfrey and Ballard practically agree with Vetromile, the name applying directly to the falls at Oldtown, but Ballard says it has also been rendered 'rock land,' from *penops* [*penopsc*] 'rock,' and *cot* [*ot*] locative, applied to the bluff at the mouth of the river near Castine. Gerard gives the aboriginal form as *Pĕnobskăt*, lit. 'plenty stones'). A tribe of the Abnaki confederacy (q. v.), closely related in language and customs to the Norridgewock. They are sometimes included in the Malecite group, but this is an error. They were probably the most numerous tribe of the Abnaki confederacy, and for a time more influential than the Norridgewock.

They occupied the country on both sides of Penobscot bay and r., and claimed the entire basin of Penobscot r. Their summer resort was near the sea, but during the winter and spring they inhabited lands near the falls, where they still reside, their principal modern village being Oldtown, on Indian id., a few miles above Bangor, in Penobscot co. A band living on Moosehead lake, Me., was popularly known as Moosehead Lake Indians. That Indians of this tribe were encountered by navigators before the middle of the 16th century appears to be certain. Kohl (Discov. East Coast Am., 1869) says that Norumbega on the Penobscot was often visited by French navigators and fishermen from the Great Bank and that they built there before 1555 a fort or settlement. When more thorough exploration began in the 17th century the Penobscot chief, known as Bashaba (a term probably equivalent to head-chief), seems to have had primacy over all the New England tribes southward to the Merrimac. The residence of Bashaba at this period appears to have been somewhere in the region of Bangor, possibly at the Norumbega of early travelers. Champlain, who sailed up the Penobscot (called by him Norumbega) in 1605, says: "Now I will leave this discourse to return to the savages who had led me to the rapids of Norumbega, who went to inform Bessabes, their captain, and gave him warning of our arrival." His residence must therefore have been in the neighborhood of the rapids. The Penobscot at this period seem to have been distinct from the "Tarratine," or Abnaki of Norridgewock, and at war with them, although since the English occupancy of the country they have always been known as a part of the Abnaki and have sometimes been specifically designated as Tarratine. The principal village, from which the tribe derived its name, seems to have been identical with Pentagouet of early French and English writers, situated on or near the site of Castine, Me. The various forms of Pentagouet and Penobscot are constantly confused in literature. Other settlements at that period were at Mattawamkeag, Olamon, and Passadumkeag. All of these appear to have been temporary stations until the French gave a permanent character to Penobscot by the establishment of a mission there in 1688. The Penobscot took an active part in all the wars on the New England frontier up to 1749, when they made a treaty of peace, and have remained quiet ever since. This treaty brought them into disfavor with the Abnaki of St Francis, who continued hostilities in the French interest, for which reason very few of the Penobscot ever joined their emigrant tribesmen in Canada, and they now constitute the only important body of Indians remaining in New England excepting the Passamaquoddy. Different estimates gave them about 650 (1726), 1,000 (Chauvignerie, 1736), 700 (1753), 400 (1759), 700 (1765), and 350 (1786). Most of the estimates within the present century give them from 300 to 400 souls. They now number about 410.   (J. M.)

Pamnaouamske.—Godfrey in Me. Hist. Soc. Coll., VII, 3, 1876. **Pamna8amske.**—Doc. of 1693 in N. Y. Doc. Col. Hist., IX, 571, 1855. **Panagamsdé.**—Vaudreuil (1724) in Me. Hist. Soc. Coll., VI, 240, 1859. **Panahamsequit.**—Iberville (1701) in N. Y. Doc. Col. Hist., IX, 731, 1855. **Panampskéwi.**—Gatschet, Penobscot MS., B. A. E., 1887 (Penobscot form; pl. Panampskéwiak). **Panamské.**—Vaudreuil (1710) in N. Y. Doc. Col. Hist., IX, 851, 1855. **Pana-ómpskek.**—Gatschet, Penobscot MS., B. A. E., 1887. **Panaomské.**—Longueuil (1726) in N. Y. Doc. Col. Hist., IX, 955, 1855. **Panaonke.**—Jefferys, French Doms., pt. 1, map, 1761. **Panaouameské.**—Bacqueville de la Potherie, III, 189, 1753. **Panaouamké.**—Doc. of 1724 in N. Y. Doc. Col. Hist., IX, 940, 1855. **Pana8amsdé.**—Ibid., 939. **Panaouamsde.**—Godfrey in Me. Hist. Soc. Coll., VII, 3, 1876. **Panaouamské.**—Vaudreuil (1721) in N. Y. Doc. Col. Hist., IX, 905, 1855. **Pana8amské.**—Doc. of 1697, ibid., 676. **Pana8amsket.**—Chauvignerie (1736), ibid., IX, 1052, 1855. **Panaouamsquée.**—Vaudreuil (1724), ibid., 937. **Panaouanbskek.**—Rasles (ca. 1720) in Me. Hist. Soc. Coll., IV, 102, 1856. **Panaouanké.**—Doc. of 1750, ibid., X, 211, 1858. **Panaouaske.**—Memoir of 1718 in N. Y. Doc. Col. Hist., IX, 881, 1855. **Panaoumski.**—Chauvignerie (1736) in Schoolcraft, Ind. Tribes, III, 553, 1853. **Panaounké.**—Doc. of 1727 in N. Y. Doc. Col. Hist., IX, 989, 1855. **Panaouské.**—Montcalm (1757), ibid., X, 619, 1858. **Panawamské.**—Beauharnois (1744), ibid., IX, 1107, 1855. **Panawamskik.**—Ballard (ca. 1830) in Me. Hist. Soc. Coll., I, 466, 1865. **Panawaniské.**—Shea, Cath. Miss., 143, 1855. **Panawanskek.**—Godfrey in Me. Hist. Soc. Coll., VII, 2, 1876. **Panawopskéyal.**—Gatschet, Penobscot MS., B. A. E., 1887. **Pannaouamské.**—Doc. of 1747 in N. Y. Doc. Col. Hist., X, 99, 1858. **Panna8amské.**—Doc. of 1746, ibid., 54. **Panna8anskeins.**—Rasles (1724) in Mass. Hist. Soc. Coll., 2d s., VIII, 246, 1819. **Pännawänbskek.**—Vetromile, Abnakis, 24, 1866. **Pann8anskeans.**—Rasles (1724) in Mass. Hist. Soc. Coll., 2d s., VIII, 247, 1819. **Panouamké.**—Writer of 1723 quoted in Me. Hist. Soc. Coll., VII, 5, 1876. **Panouamsdè.**—Writer of 1723, ibid., 4. **Panoüamské.**—Vaudreuil (1724) in N. Y. Doc. Col. Hist., IX, 934, 1855. **Pan8amské.**—Vaudreuil (1721) in N. Y. Doc. Col. Hist., IX, 904, 1855. **Pan8maské.**—Vaudreuil (1721), ibid., 904. **Panoümsqué.**—Vaudreuil (1725), ibid., 495. **Panouske.**—Godfrey in Me. Hist. Soc. Coll., VII, 3, 1876. **Pánwâpskik.**—Ballard in Rep. Coast. Surv., 256, 1871. **Peimtegouët.**—Champlain (1613) in Me. Hist. Soc. Coll., VII, 253, 1876. **Pemetegoit.**—Champlain (1632), Œuvres, v, pt. 1, 72, 1870. **Pemptagoiett.**—Aulney (1644) in Mass. Hist. Soc. Coll., 3d s., VII, 94, 1838. **Pemtegoit.**—Jefferys, Fr. Doms., pt. 1, map, 1761. **Penaské.**—Vaudreuil (1704) in N. Y. Doc. Col. Hist., IX, 762, 1855. **Penaubsket.**—Vetromile, Abnakis, 48, 1866. **Fenboscots.**—Falmouth conf. (1727) in Me. Hist. Soc. Coll., III, 409, 1853. **Penboscut.**—Treaty rep. (1726), ibid., 386. **Pennobscot.**—Smith (1616) in Mass. Hist. Soc. Coll., 3d s., VI, 97, 1837. **Penobcsutt.**—Falmouth treaty (1726) in Me. Hist. Soc. Coll., III, 386, 1853 (misprint). **Penobscotes.**—Dee in Smith (1629), Va., II, 238, repr. 1819. **Penobscotts.**—Treaty of 1749 in Me. Hist. Soc. Coll., IV, 146, 1856. **Penobscut.**—Prince (1631) in Mass. Hist. Soc. Coll., 2d s., VII, 34, 1818. **Penobskeag.**—Willis in Me. Hist. Soc. Coll., IV, 108, 1856. **Penobsots.**—Falmouth conf. (1727), ibid., III, 410, 1853. **Pentacoet.**—Cadillac (1692), ibid., VI, 281-2, 1859. **Pentagoets.**—Maurault, Hist. des Abenakis, 5, 1866. **Pentagoiett.**—Mass. Hist. Soc. Coll., 3d s., VII, 94, 1838. **Pentagonett.**—Ibid., note. **Pentagouetch.**—Jes. Rel. 1640, 35, 1858. **Pentagovett.**—Willis in Me. Hist. Soc. Coll., IV, 108, 1856. **Pentegoët.**—Jes. Rel. 1611, 15, 1858. **Pentug8et.**—

Rasles (1721) in Mass. Hist. Soc. Coll., 2d s., VIII, 262, 1819. **Penobscot.**—Georgetown treaty rep. (1717) in Me. Hist. Soc. Coll., III, 363, 1853. **Ponobscut.**—Ibid., 362.

Penobscot. The summer village of the Penobscot at the mouth of Penobscot r., on or near the site of Castine, Me. For the name, see *Penobscot* (tribe).

Panawanske.—Godfrey in Me. Hist. Soc. Coll., VII, 46, 1876. **Panna8apské.**—Lauverjat (1718) in Mass. Hist. Soc. Coll., 2d s., VIII, 259, 1819. **Pañnasañbskek.**—Rasles quoted by Ballard in Me. Hist. Soc. Coll., I, 466, 1865. **Pentagouet.**—Doc. of 1638 in N. Y. Doc. Col. Hist., IX, 4, 1855. **Pintagoné.**—Lauverjat, op. cit.

Penointikara ('honey eaters'). A Bannock band. Cf. *Penateka*.

Honey-Eaters.—Schoolcraft, Ind. Tribes, I, 522, 1853. **Penointik-ara.**—Ibid. **Sugar-Eaters.**—Ibid.

Peñon (Span.: *El Peñon*, 'the great rock'). A former Indian settlement on an island 13 leagues N. of Rio de Mosquitos, E. Florida, at the entrance of the Rio Matanzas.—Roberts, Florida, 23, 1763.

Penoy. An unidentified village or tribe mentioned by Cavelier in 1687 (Shea, Early Voy., 39, 1861) as being next to Akasquy and a day's journey from the Sassory (Nasoni). This proximity to Caddoan people makes it probable that they were kindred.   (A. C. F.)

Pensacola (Choctaw: 'hair-people,' from *pansha* 'hair', *okla* 'people'). A tribe once inhabiting tracts around the present city and harbor of Pensacola, w. Fla. According to Barcia (Ensayo, 316, 1723) they had been destroyed by tribal wars before the Spaniards became established there in 1696, but from a reference in Margry it appears that a few still remained at a later period.   (J. M.)

Pançacola.—Barcia, Ensayo, 316, 1723. **Pansacolas.**—Gravier (1701) in Shea, Early Voy., 159, 1861 (local reference). **Panzacola.**—B. Smith, Colec. Doc. Fla., 30, 1857. **Passacolas.**—Pénicaut (1723) in Margry, Déc., v, 378, 1883. **Pençacola.**—Fairbanks, Hist. Fla., 168, 1871. **Pençocolos.**—Barcia, Ensayo, 316, 1723. **Pensacolas.**—Pénicaut (1699) in French, Hist. Col. La., n. s., I, 38, 1869. **Pensicola.**—Coxe, Carolana, 28, 1741. **Penzocolos.**—Shea, note in Charlevoix, New France, v, 118, 1871.

Penticton. An Okinagan village at the outlet of Okanagan lake, Brit. Col.; pop. 158 in 1906. See Can. Ind. Aff., pt. II, 68, 1902; 75, 1906.

Pentucket. A Pennacook village on the site of Haverhill, Mass. It was sold to the whites in 1642.

Pennatuckets.—Kidder in Me. Hist. Soc. Coll., VI, 236, 1859. **Penticutt.**—Ward (1639) in Mass. Hist. Soc. Coll., 4th s., VII, 27, 1865. **Pentuckett.**—Firmin (1639), ibid., 2d s., IV, 126, 1816.

Peñunde. An unidentified tribe spoken of in 1683 by Juan Sabeata, a Jumano Indian from the mouth of Conchos r., N. E. Chihuahua, Mexico. It was one of 36 tribes, friendly to his own, and said by him to live on Nueces r., 3 days' journey E. of his home (Mendoza, Viage, 1683-84, MS. in Archivo General). It was Juan Sabeata's report that led to Domingo de Mendoza's expedition into Texas in 1683-84.   (H. E. B.)

Peoria (through French *Peouarea*, from Peoria *Piware^a*, 'he comes carrying a pack on his back': a personal name.—Gerard). One of the principal tribes of the Illinois confederacy. Franquelin in his map of 1688 locates them and the Tapouaro (q. v.) on a river w. of the Mississippi above the mouth of Wisconsin r., probably the upper Iowa r. Early references to the Illinois which place them on the Mississippi, although some of the tribes were on Rock and Illinois rs., must relate to the Peoria and locate them near the mouth of the Wisconsin. When Marquette and Joliet descended the Mississippi in 1673, they found them and the Moingwena on the w. side of the Mississippi near the mouth of a river supposed to be the Des Moines, though it may have been one farther N. When Marquette returned from the S., he found that the Peoria had removed and were near the lower end of the expansion of Illinois r., near the present Peoria. At the close of the war carried on by the Sauk and Foxes and other northern tribes against the Illinois, about 1768, the Kickapoo took possession of this village and made it their principal settlement. About the same time a large part of the Peoria crossed over into Missouri, where they remained, building their village on Blackwater fork, until they removed to Kansas. One band, the Utagami, living near Illinois r., was practically exterminated, probably by the northern tribes, during the Revolutionary war (Gatschet, Sauk and Fox MS., B. A. E., 1882). Utagami, according to Dr Wm. Jones, may mean the Foxes who were known to the northern Algonquians as *Utŭgamig*, 'people of the other shore.' The Foxes claim to have annihilated the Peoria for the help they gave the French and other tribes in the wars against them (the Foxes). The main body of the Peoria remained on the E. bank of Illinois r. until 1832, when, together with the other tribes of the old Illinois confederacy, they sold to the United States their claims in Illinois and Missouri, and to the consolidated tribes, under the names of Peoria and Kaskaskia, was assigned a reservation on Osage r., Kans. In 1854 the Wea and Piankashaw united with them, and in 1868 the entire body removed to Indian Ter. (Oklahoma), where they now reside. The Peoria made or joined in the treaties with the United States at Edwardsville, Ill., Sept. 25, 1818; Castor Hill, Mo., Oct. 27, 1832; Washington, D. C., May 30, 1854, and Feb. 23, 1867.

The early estimates of the numbers of the Peoria are altogether unreliable, and later estimates shed no light on their population from the fact that several Illinois tribes were then consolidated under the same name. In 1736 Chauvignerie esti-

mated the Peoria at about 250 souls. They were so nearly exterminated soon afterward by the northern tribes that about the year 1800 Gov. William Henry Harrison of the Northwest Ter. could find only 4 men of the tribe living. In 1829 the Indians consolidated under that name numbered 120. According to the report of the Indian Office the Peoria and allied tribes in Oklahoma numbered 192 in 1906.   (J. M.   C. T.)

Opea.—Whiteside (1811) in Am. St. Papers, Ind. Aff., I, 804, 1832. **Payories.**—Volney, View of U. S. A., 352, 1804. **Peaouarias.**—Cadillac (1695) in Margry, Déc., V, 124, 1883. **Pecuarias.**—Jefferys, Fr. Doms., pt. 1, map, 1761. **Peoiras.**—Hunter, Narr., 178, 1823. **Peola.**—Long, Exped. Rocky Mts., II, 285, 1823. **Peonas.**—Sen. Misc. Doc. 53, 45th Cong., 3d sess., 73, 1879. **Peonies.**—Porter (1829) quoted by Schoolcraft, Ind. Tribes, III, 592, 1853. **Peores.**—Writer of 1812 quoted by Schoolcraft, ibid., 555. **Peorians.**—Knox (1792) in Am. St. Papers, Ind. Aff., I, 319, 1832. **Peorias.**—Joutel (1687) in Margry, Déc., III, 481, 1878. **Peouarewi.**—Shea, Rel. de la Mission du Miss., 26, 1861. **Peouarias.**—Homann Heirs' Map, 1756. **Peouarius.**—Jefferys, Fr. Doms., pt. 1, 138, 1761. **Peoüaroüa.**—Gravier (ca. 1680) in Shea, Early Voy., 116, 1861. **Peoucaria.**—La Salle (1681) in Margry, Déc., II, 134, 1877. **Peoueria.**—La Salle (1682), ibid., 201. **Peouria.**—Allouez (1680), ibid., 96. **Péouryas.**—Vater, Mith., pt. 3, sec. 3, 351, 1816. **Perouacca.**—Marquette (ca. 1673), Discov., 349, 1698. **Perouasca.**—Ibid., 333. **Peroueria.**—Joutel (1688) in French, Hist. Coll. La., I, 185, 1846. **Pianrias.**—Imlay, West. Ter., 290, 1797. **Piantias.**—Smith (1785) quoted by Schoolcraft, Ind. Tribes, III, 555, 1853. **Piorias.**—Bouquet (1764) quoted by Jefferson, Notes, 143, 1825. **Pioüaroüa.**—Gravier (1701) in French, Hist. Coll. La., II, 88, 1875. **Pronaria.**—Morse, Hist. N. Am., 256, 1776. **Proneseas.**—La Salle (ca. 1682) quoted in Hist. Mag., 1st s., V, 197, 1861. **Pronevoa.**—Hennepin, New Discov., 310, 1698. **Prouaria.**—Coxe, Carolana, map, 1741.

Pepatlenok (*P'ē'paʟēnȏx*, 'the flyers'). A gens of the Tenaktak (q. v.).—Boas in Rep. Nat. Mus. 1895, 331, 1897.

Pepawitlenok (*Pē'pawiʟēnȏx*, 'the flyers'). A gens of the Klaskino, a Kwakiutl tribe.—Boas in Rep. Nat. Mus. 1895, 329, 1897.

Pepegewizzains (Chippewa: *pipikiwise^ns*, 'pigeon-hawk.'—Gerard). A gens or society of the Chippewa and also of the Ottawa.—Tanner, Narr., 314, 1830.

Pepikokia. An Algonquian tribe or band mentioned in the latter part of the 17th century as a division of the Miami. In 1718 both they and the Piankashaw were mentioned as villages of the Wea. That the relation between these three groups was intimate is evident. They were located on the Wabash by Chauvignerie (1736) and by other writers of the period. They are spoken of in 1695 as Miamis of Maramek r., that is, the Kalamazoo. A letter dated 1701 (Margry, Déc., IV, 592, 1880) indicates that they were at that time in Wisconsin. Chauvignerie says that Wea, Piankashaw, and Pepikokia "are the same nation, though in different villages," and that "the devices of these Indians are the Serpent, the Deer, and the Small Acorn." They were sometimes called Nation de la Grüe, as though the crane was their totem. They disappear from history before the middle of the 18th century and may have become incorporated in the Piankashaw, whose principal village was on the Wabash at the junction of the Vermilion. (J. M.)

Kipikavvi.—St Cosme (1699) in Shea, Rel. de la Mission du Miss., 17, 1861. **Kipikawi.**—St Cosme (1699) in Shea, Early Voy. Miss., 50, 1861. **Kipikuskvvi.**—St Cosme (1699) in Shea, Rel. de la Mission du Miss., 18, 1861. **Pegoucoquias.**—Memoir of 1701 in Margry, Déc., IV, 592, 1880. **Pepepicokia.**—Coxe, Carolana, 12, 1741. **Pepepoaké.**—La Salle (1682) in Margry, Déc., II, 216, 1877. **Pepicoquias.**—Bacqueville de la Potherie, IV, 56, 1753. **Pepicoquis.**—Writer of 1695 in N.Y. Doc. Col. Hist., IX, 621, 1855. **Pepikokia.**—La Salle (1683) in Margry, Déc., II, 319, 1877. **Pepikokis.**—Bacqueville de la Potherie, II, 261, 1753. **Pepiᴋoukia.**—Jes. Rel., LVIII, 40, 1899. **Pepikoukia.**—Tailhan, Perrot Mém., 222, 1864. **Petikokias.**—Chauvignerie (1736) in N. Y. Doc. Col. Hist., IX, 1057, 1855. **Petitscotias.**—Memoir (1718), ibid., 891. **Pettikokias.**—Chauvignerie (1736) quoted by Schoolcraft, Ind. Tribes, III, 555, 1853. **Tepicons.**—Longueuil (1752) in N.Y. Doc. Col. Hist., X, 246, 1858 (identical?).

Pequaock. See *Pooquaw*.

Pequawket (a name of disputed etymology, the most probable rendering, according to Gerard, being 'at the hole in the ground,' from *pekwakik*). A tribe of the Abnaki confederacy, formerly living on the headwaters of Saco r. and about Lovell's pond, in Carroll co., N. H., and Oxford co., Me. Their principal village, called Pequawket, was about the present Fryeburg, Me. The tribe is famous for a battle fought in 1725 near the village, between about 50 English under Capt. Lovewell and 80 Indians, the entire force of the tribe, under their chief, Paugus. Both leaders were killed, together with 36 of the English and a large part of the Indian force. By this loss the Pequawket were so weakened that, together with the Arosaguntacook, they soon after withdrew to the sources of Connecticut r. After being here for a short while, the Arosaguntacook removed to St Francis in Canada, while the Pequawket remained on the Connecticut, where they were still living under their chief at the time of the Revolution. Some of them seem to have found their way back to their old home some time after the Lovewell fight. (J. M.)

Pâgwâki.—Kendall, Trav., III, 173, 1809 (correct form). **Paquakig.**—Gyles (1726) in Me. Hist. Soc. Coll., III, 358, 1853. **Peckwalket.**—Sullivan in N.H. Hist. Soc. Coll., I, 27, 1824. **Peg8akki.**—French letter (1721) in Mass. Hist. Soc. Coll., 2d s., VIII, 262, 1819. **Pegouakky.**—Vaudreuil (1721) in N.Y. Doc. Col. Hist., IX, 904, 1855. **Pegwacket.**—Denison (1676) in Me. Hist. Soc. Coll., I, 223, 1865. **Pegwackit.**—Georgetown treaty (1717), ibid., III, 373, 1853. **Pegwackuk.**—Martin (1676), ibid., I, 223, 1865. **Pegwaggett.**—Winthrop in N. H. Hist. Soc. Coll., I, 27, 1824. **Pegwakets.**—Kidder in Me. Hist. Soc. Coll., VI, 235, 1859. **Pehqwoket.**—Drake, Ind. Chron., 173, 1836. **Pequakets.**—Drake, Bk. Inds., x, 1848. **Pequaquaukes.**—Potter in Schoolcraft, Ind. Tribes, V, 222, 1855. **Pequauket.**—Writer in N. H. Hist. Soc. Coll., V, 207, 1837. **Pequawett.**—Willis in Me. Hist. Soc. Coll., IV, 109, 1856. **Pequawket.**—Pike (1703) in N. H. Hist. Soc. Coll., III, 51, 1832. **Pickpooket.**—Pike (1704), ibid., 54. **Pickwacket.**—Doc. of 1749 in Me. Hist. Soc. Coll., IV, 155, 1856. **Pickwooket.**—N. H. Hist. Soc. Coll., I, 27, note, 1824. **Picqwaket.**—Freeman (ca. 1830) in Me. Hist. Soc. Coll., I, 333, 1865. **Picwocket.**—Kendall, Trav., III, 173, 1809. **Piggwacket.**—Symmes (ca. 1725) quoted by Drake, Bk. Inds., bk. 3, 131, 1848. **Pigocket.**—Jefferys, Fr. Doms., pt. 1, 123, 1761. **Piguachet.**—McKeen in Me. Hist. Soc. Coll., III, 324, 1853. **Pigwachet.**—Sullivan in Mass. Hist. Soc. Coll., 1st s., IX, 210, 1804. **Pigwacket.**—Penhallow (1726) in N. H. Hist. Soc. Coll., I, 20, 1824. **Pigwackitt.**—Wendell (1749) in N. Y. Doc. Col. Hist., VI, 542, 1855. **Pigwocket.**—Portsmouth treaty (1713) in Me. Hist. Soc. Coll., VI, 250, 1859. **Pigwoket.**—Drake, Bk. Inds., bk. 3, 135, 1848. **Pigwolket.**—Kendall, Trav., III, 173, 1809. **Piquachet.**—Me. Hist. Soc. Coll., III, 358, note, 1853.

Pequea (*Piqua*, 'dust,' 'ashes'). A Shawnee village on Susquehanna r., at the mouth of Pequea cr., in Lancaster co., Pa. It was settled by the tribe on its removal from the S. about the year 1694, and abandoned about 1730 for another location. (J. M.)

Pequa.—Lewis (1824) quoted by Day, Penn., 208, 1843. **Pequea.**—Barton, New Views, xxxii, 1798. **Pequehan.**—Evans (1707) quoted by Day, op. cit., 381. **Piqua Town.**—Johnston (1812) in Am. St. Papers, Ind. Aff., I, 807, 1832. **Piqued.**—Putnam, Mid. Tenn., 365, 1859.

Pequen. An unidentified pueblo in New Mexico in 1598.—Oñate (1598) in Doc. Inéd., XVI, 103, 1871.

Pequimmit. A village of Christian Indians near Stoughton, Norfolk co., Mass., in 1658.—Homer (ca. 1798) in Mass. Hist. Soc. Coll., 1st s., V, 267, 1806.

Pequot (contr. of *Paquatauog*, 'destroyers.'—Trumbull). An Algonquian tribe of Connecticut. Before their conquest by the English in 1637 they were the most dreaded of the southern New England tribes. They were originally but one people with the Mohegan, and it is possible that the term Pequot was unknown until applied by the eastern coast Indians to this body of Mohegan invaders, who came down from the interior shortly before the arrival of the English. The division into two distinct tribes seems to have been accomplished by the secession of Uncas, who, in consequence of a dispute with Sassacus, afterward known as the great chief of the Pequot, withdrew into the interior with a small body of followers. This body retained the name of Mohegan, and through the diplomatic management of Uncas acquired such prominence that on the close of the Pequot war their claim to the greater part of the territory formerly subject to Sassacus was recognized by the colonial government. The real territory of the Pequot was a narrow strip of coast in New London co., extending from Niantic r. to the Rhode Island boundary, comprising the present towns of New London, Groton, and Stonington. They also extended a few miles into Rhode Island to Wecapaug r. until driven out by the Narraganset about 1635. This country had been previously in possession of the Niantic, whom the Pequot invaded from the N. and forced from their central position, splitting them into two bodies, thenceforth known as Eastern and Western Niantic. The Eastern Niantic put themselves under the protection of the Narraganset, while the western branch became subject to the Pequot and were settled on their w. border. The conquerors rapidly extended their dominion over the neighboring tribes, so that just previous to the Pequot war Sassacus was the head over 26 subordinate chiefs and claimed control over all Connecticut E. of Connecticut r. and the coast westward to the vicinity of Guilford or New Haven, while all of Long Island except the extreme w. part was also under his dominion. Nearly all of this territory, excepting Long Island, was claimed by Uncas, the Mohegan chief, after the conquest of the Pequot. At the period of their greatest strength the Pequot probably numbered at least 3,000 souls, but have been estimated much higher.

By the murder of a trader who had treated them harshly, followed by several other acts of hostility, the Pequot became involved in a war with the colonists in 1637. Through the influence of Roger Williams and of Uncas the English secured the assistance, or at least the neutrality, of the neighboring tribes, and then marched against the Pequot. Their principal fort, near Mystic r., was surprised and set on fire, and probably 600 Pequot men, women, and children perished in the flames or were shot down while trying to escape. This terrible slaughter so crippled the Pequot that after a few desperate but unsuccessful efforts at resistance they determined to separate into small parties and abandon their country. Some went to Long Island, others fled to the interior, while a large party headed by Sassacus attempted to reach the Mohawk, but were intercepted near Fairfield, Conn., and almost the entire party were killed or captured. The prisoners became slaves to the colonists or were sold into the West Indies. The few who escaped to the Mohawk, including Sassacus, were put to death by that tribe. The scattered fugitives were shot down wherever found by the neighboring tribes, until the survivors at last came in and asked for mercy at the hands of the English. A party of 70 had previously made submission to the Narraganset and become a part of that tribe.

In 1638 the surrendered Pequot were distributed among the Mohegan, Narraganset, and Niantic, and forbidden longer to call themselves Pequot. Although it has been customary to regard the Pequot as exterminated in this war, such was far from being the case. They numbered 3,000 or more at the beginning of the war, and only about 700 or 800 are known to have been killed. The rest joined other tribes or finally submitted to the English. Several years afterward a Pequot chief was found living on Delaware r., and there can be no question that many others had found refuge with the Mahican and other western tribes. In June 1637, after the dispersion of the tribe, those about New Haven and on Long Island were reported to number 350 warriors, or about 1,250 souls. Those portioned out among the friendly tribes in September 1638, numbered 200 warriors, with their families, or about 700 in all. Of these, one-half went to the Mohegan, 80 warriors to the Narraganset, and 20 warriors to the Niantic. They occupied six separate villages among these tribes, in addition to those villages which were occupied jointly. At the same time there were a large number on Long Island who remained there in subjection to the English; others were in the vicinity of New Haven and among the Nipmuc and neighboring tribes; many were scattered as slaves among the English settlements, and others had been sent to the West Indies.

The Pequot who had been given to the Indian allies of the colonists were treated so harshly by their masters that it was finally necessary, in 1655, to gather them into two villages near Mystic r., in their old country, and place them under the direct control of the colonial government. Here they numbered about 1,500 in 1674. They decreased rapidly, as did the other tribes, and in 1762 the remnant numbered 140 souls, living in Maushantuxet, at Ledyard, Conn. In 1832 these were reduced to about 40 mixed-bloods, who still occupied their reserve and cherished the old hatred of the Mohegan, who lived a few miles distant. It appears from an article by Prince and Speck (Am. Anthrop., Apr. 1903) that there are still in Connecticut about 100 persons of Pequot-Mohegan blood. A colony of about 50 individuals of this group are employed chiefly as farm and factory workers a few miles s. of Norwich; the others live in adjacent towns. About 25, according to Speck (inf'n, 1907), are still on the old Groton tract near Ledyard and keep themselves distinct from the Mohegan, but they retain practically nothing of their former culture. The following were Pequot villages: Aukumbumsk, Cosattuck, Cuppunaugunnit, Mangunckakuck, Maushantuxet, Mystic, Nameaug, Paupattokshick, Pawcatuck, Sauquonckackock, Stonington, Tatuppequauog, and Weinshauks. (J. M.)

Maquot.—Randolph (1676) in N. Y. Doc. Col. Hist., III, 242, 1853. Pakauds.—McKenney and Hall, Ind. Tribes, III, 79, 1854. Paquatauog.—Trumbull, Ind. Names Conn., 50, 1881. Peacott.—Record of 1645 quoted by Drake, Bk. Inds., bk. 2, 91, 1848. Peaquitt.—Parker (1654) in Mass. Hist. Soc. Coll., 4th s., VII, 446, 1865. Peaquods.—Johnson (1654), ibid., 2d s., IV, 28, 1816. Peaquots.—Doc. of 1638 quoted by Drake, Bk. Inds., bk. 2, 61, 1848. Pecoates.—Dudley (1631) in N. H. Hist. Soc. Coll., IV, 225, 1834. Pecoats.—Winslow (1637) in Mass. Hist. Soc. Coll., 4th s., VI, 164, 1863. Pecods.—Johnson (1654), ibid., 2d s., II, 66, 1814. Pecoites.—Stanton (1676) in N. Y. Doc. Col. Hist., XIV, 715, 1883. Pecoits.—Ibid. **Pecotts.**—Record of 1644 quoted by Drake, Bk. Inds., bk. 2, 90, 1848. **Peequots.**—Rawson (1663) in R. I. Col. Rec., I, 517, 1856. **Pegod.**—Johnson (1654) in Mass. Hist. Soc. Coll., 2d s., VII, 46, 1818. **Pekash.**—Prince (1631), ibid., 25. **Pekoath.**—Winthrop (1631), ibid., 4th s., III, 312, 1856. **Pekoct.**—Esopus Treaty (1665) in N. Y. Doc. Col. Hist., XIII, 401, 1881. **Pekot.**—Peter (ca. 1639) in Mass. Hist. Soc. Coll., 4th s., VI, 105, 1863. **Pek8atsaks.**—Maurault, Abnakis, 3, 1866. **Pequants.**—Vincent (1638) in Mass. Hist. Soc. Coll., 3d s., VI, 35, 1837. **Pequatit.**—Williams (1637), ibid., 4th s., VI, 200, 1863. **Pequatoas.**—Map of 1659 cited by Schoolcraft, Ind. Tribes, VI, 116, 1857. **Pequatoos.**—Opdyck (1640) in N. Y. Doc. Col. Hist., II, 141, 1858. **Pequatt.**—Writer of 1654 quoted by Trumbull, Conn., I, 326, 1818. **Pequeats.**—Underhill (1638) in Mass. Hist. Soc. Coll., 3d s., VI, 3, 1837. **Pequente.**—Treaty (1645), ibid., 4th s., III, 438, 1856. **Pequents.**—Prince (1633), ibid., 2d s., VII, 93, 1818. **Pequetans.**—Vincent (1638), ibid., 3d s., VI, 40, 1837. **Pequets.**—Vincent (1638), ibid., 35. **Pequett.**—Brewster (1650), ibid., 4th s., VII, 70, 1865. **Pequid.**—Lechford (1641), ibid., 3d s., III, 103, 1833. **Pequims.**—Prince (1632), ibid., 2d s., VII, 58, 1818. **Pequin.**—Williams (1637), ibid., 3d s., IX, 301, 1846. **Pequite.**—Coddington (1651), ibid., 4th s., VII, 282, 1865. **Pequitóog.**—Williams quoted by Vater, Mith., pt. 3, sec. 3, 378, 1816. **Pequitts.**—Gardiner (1636) in Mass. Hist. Soc. Coll., 4th s., VII, 53, 1865. **Pequoadt.**—Caulkins, Hist. Norwich, 49, 1866. **Pequod.**—Nowell (1637) in Mass. Hist. Soc. Coll., 4th s., VII, 325, 1865. **Pequoids.**—Macauley, N. Y., II, 225, 1829. **Pequoite.**—Goodwin (1653) in Mass. Hist. Soc. Coll., 4th s., VII, 48, 1865. **Pequoits.**—Downing (1637), ibid., VI, 48, 1863. **Pequote.**—Downing (1654), ibid., 83. **Pequotoh.**—Stuyvesant (1650), ibid., 533. **Pequots.**—Vane (1636), ibid., 582. **Pequoyts.**—Hooker (1637), ibid., 388. **Pequts.**—Williams (1636), ibid., 3d s., I, 159, 1825. **Pequtt.**—Gardiner (1636), ibid., 4th s., VII, 57, 1865. **Pequttôog.**—Williams (ca. 1643) quoted by Trumbull, Ind. Names Conn., 50, 1881. **Pequuts.**—Williams (ca. 1643) in Mass. Hist. Soc. Coll., 1st s., V, 103, 1806. **Pequuttoog.**—Williams (1643), ibid., III, 205, 1794. **Peqvats.**—Map of 1616 in N. Y. Doc. Col. Hist., I, 1856. **Peqwit.**—Gardiner (1650) in Mass. Hist. Soc. Coll., 4th s., VII, 59, 1865. **Sickenames.**—Dutch deed (1633) quoted by Ruttenber, Tribes Hudson R., 83, 1872.

Pequottink. A village of the Moravian Delawares established in 1788 on the E. bank of Huron r., near the present Milan, Erie Co., Ohio. It was still occupied in 1805.

New Salem.—Loskiel, Hist. Missions, map, 1794. **Pequottink.**—Harris, Tour, 135, 1805. **Petquottink.**—Loskiel, op. cit. **Pettquotting.**—Zeisberger (1786), Diary, 234, 275, 1885 (the stream).

Pera. A tribe mentioned by McKenney and Hall (Ind. Tribes, III, 81, 1854), with "Naansi, Naichoas, Ouadiches, Cabinoios, Mentous, Ozotheoa, Dogenga, Panivacha, and Panaloga," as if one of the tribes mentioned by early French explorers in the southwestern plains. Unidentified.

Perage (Pe-ra-ge). A prehistoric pueblo claimed by certain clans of the Tewa inhabitants of San Ildefonso to have been inhabited by their ancestors. Its ruins lie a few rods from the w. bank of the Rio Grande, about 1 m. w. of San Ildefonso pueblo, N. Mex.—Bandelier in Arch. Inst. Papers, IV, 78, 1892; Hewett in Bull. 32, B. A. E., 17, 1907.

Percoarson. See Poquosin.

Perebluk. A Kaviagmiut Eskimo village at Port Clarence, Alaska.—11th Census, Alaska, 162, 1893.

Perforated stones. A name applied to certain forms of prehistoric objects the purpose of which is not fully determined,

but so much is known or safely assumed with respect to the majority of those in collections that they may be removed from the problematical class without danger of serious error. It is intended here to refer only to such perforated objects as may not with safety be regarded as spindle whorls, drill disks, sinkers, ear ornaments, and beads. Perforated stones are widely distributed over the country, but are not found in considerable numbers save in s. California, where they are very numerous and display considerable diversity of form and size. They are found with burials and also on occupied sites generally, and are made of stone of many varieties and of differing degrees of hardness. A prevailing form throughout the country is somewhat ring-like, and the name "doughnut-stone," sometimes applied, is sufficiently descriptive. Many of them are only ordinary water-worn pebbles or bowlders, unworked except for the hole drilled through the shortest diameter or for some slight alteration in the direction of greater symmetry, others are of various degrees of elaboration, and a few show incised decorative lines. Few are finished, however, in such a way as to suggest decidedly that they were other than mere objects of common use. It is not assumed that all of these perforated objects served like or even kindred purposes, and similar objects are known to have been used in different parts of the world for club-heads, hammers, sinkers, missiles, as weights for digging sticks, in playing games, etc. The California specimens, however, on account of the uniformity of their essential features and the very general traces of wear, may well be regarded as having served a single purpose, and that a practical one. They vary from highly conical or globular forms to flattish rings or disks, and in size from such as might have served as beads to others weighing 3 or 4 pounds. The majority are of medium or large size. The perforation is usually somewhat biconical and a little larger at one end than at the other, and varies from $\frac{1}{2}$ to $1\frac{1}{2}$ in. in diameter at the narrowest part. In most cases the perforation is polished or worn smooth by use and in such a way as practically to demonstrate that the objects were mounted on sticks or handles, and that thus mounted they were subjected to prolonged usage as implements. It is further observed that one face of the flattish forms became polished in this use from the perforation outward to the periphery, and the globular and conical ones for an inch or more outward and downward from the opening. This use was so gentle and involved surfaces so soft that a high polish resulted, without the least tendency to abrade or roughen. In fact this polishing is just such as would result from continued contact with the hand resting on the perforated stone in wielding a digging stick on which it served as a weight. The fact that this wear occurs always on the side of the smaller opening seems to indicate that the stones were slipped down on a shaft until arrested by an enlargement, enough of the shaft remaining above for a hand-hold. That most of these stones served in this manner as weights for digging sticks may be regarded as practically demonstrated. The smaller, toy-like specimens were probably employed by children or were made especially for burial with the dead. It is noted that the periphery of some of the discoidal forms shows traces of rough usage, such as would result from employment as hammers, but this may be the result of usage not originally intended.

Consult Henshaw, Perforated Stones, Bull. 2, B. A. E., 1887; Meredith in Moorehead's Prehist. Impls., 1900; Powers in Cont. N. A. Ethnol., III, 1877; Putnam in Rep. Surv. West 100th Merid., VII, 1879; Rau in Smithson. Cont., XXII, 1876; Schumacher in 11th Rep. Peabody Mus., 1878; Yates in Moorehead's Prehist. Impls., 1900.   (w. h. h.)

Perforating implements. See *Awls, Drills and Drilling.*

Perignak. A Sidarumiut Eskimo village on Seahorse ids., near Pt Belcher, Alaska (11th Census, Alaska, 162, 1893). Cf. *Pernyu.*

Perigua. A former Papago village s. of the Rio Gila, in s. Arizona; pop. 400 in 1863.

Del Pirique.—Bailey in Ind. Aff. Rep., 208, 1858.
Perigua.—Browne, Apache Country, 291, 1869.
Periqua.—Poston in Ind. Aff. Rep. 1863, 385, 1864.
Pirigua.—Taylor in Cal. Farmer, June 19, 1863.

Perinimo. A former Papago village, probably in Pima co., s. Ariz., having 46 families in 1865.

Perinimo.—Davidson in Ind. Aff. Rep., 135, 1865.
Pisañomo.—Bailey, ibid., 208, 1858.

Periodicals. The first periodical printed in any of the North American Indian languages was the *Cherokee Phœnix*, a weekly newspaper in English and Cherokee, edited by Elias Boudinot (q. v.), a native Indian, and published in Georgia at New Echota, the capital of the Cherokee Nation, from Feb. 21, 1828, to Oct. 1835. A religious magazine printed entirely in Cherokee, called the *Cherokee Messenger*, edited by Evan Jones and J. Bushyhead, was issued in twelve numbers from the Baptist Mission Press at Park Hill, Ind. T., between Aug. 1844, and May 1846; and a new series under the same title, edited by J. Buttrick Jones, appeared in 1858, but was soon discontinued. On Sept. 26, 1844, the first number of the *Cherokee Advocate* was published at Tahlequah, Ind. T. This was a weekly newspaper, published every Saturday morning, half in English and half in Cherokee.

The first series was discontinued in Sept. 1853. A new series was begun in 1870, and a third series in 1876. Of it, Mooney (19th Rep. B. A. E., 111, 1900) says: "It is still continued under the auspices of the Nation, printed in both languages and distributed free at the expense of the Nation to those unable to read English—an example without parallel in any other government." The *Cherokee Almanac* was an annual publication for many years.

The first number of a small semimonthly or monthly newspaper in the Shawnee language, called *Shau-wau-nowe Kesauthwau* (*Shawnee Sun*), was published from the Shawnee Baptist Mission Press, Ind. T., on Mar. 1, 1835, and was continued under the editorship of Johnston Lykins until 1839, when it was discontinued. This was the first newspaper printed entirely in an Indian language. In the Seneca language the Rev. Asher Wright edited a small magazine called *Ne Jaguhnigoagesgwathah, or The Mental Elevator*, of which were printed at the Buffalo Creek and Cattaraugus reservations in New York from Nov. 30, 1841, to Apr. 15, 1850, nineteen numbers in all.

The fourth Indian language to have a newspaper of its own was the Dakota. In Nov. 1850, the first number of *Dakota Tawaxitku Kin*, or the *Dakota Friend*, was published in Santee Dakota and English, edited by G. H. Pond, and printed at St Paul, Minn. The paper was issued monthly until Aug. 1852. Another newspaper, called *Iapi Oaye* (*The Word-Carrier*), in Santee and Yankton Dakota, was started in May 1871, and has been continued monthly under successive editors at Greenwood, S. Dak., and at the Santee agency, Nebr., the present (1907) editor being Rev. A. L. Riggs. In Jan. 1878, the Niobrara Mission issued the first number of a monthly paper called *Anpao, The Day Break*, which was printed mostly in Yankton Dakota, and was continued afterward at Madison, S. Dak., under the title *Anpao Kin, The Daybreak*. The Catholic mission at Fort Totten, N. Dak., also publishes a monthly paper in the Santee Dakota, entitled *Sina Sapa Wocekiye Taeyanpaha*, the first number of which was issued in Feb. 1892, with the Rev. Jerome Hunt, of the Benedictine order, as editor. It is now (1907) in its eleventh volume.

The earliest periodical for the Chippewa Indians was entitled *Petaubun, Peep of Day*, published monthly at Sarnia, Ont., by the Rev. Thomas Hurlburt, beginning in Jan. 1861. It was in English and Chippewa, and was continued through 1862 or later. The *Pipe of Peace*, a Chippewa newspaper, edited by the Rev. E. F. Wilson in English and Chippewa, was published monthly at the

Shingwauk Home in Sault de Ste Marie from Oct. 1878, till Sept. 1879. A fortnightly paper called *The Indian* was published at Hagersville, Ont., from Dec. 30, 1885, till Dec. 29, 1886, the editor being the chief Kahkewaquonaby (Dr Peter E. Jones). Although it was printed mainly in English, some Chippewa articles were included. There were, moreover, two periodicals in English edited by the Rev. E. F. Wilson, one entitled *Our Forest Children*, published monthly at the Shingwauk Home from Feb. 1887, to Sept. 1890, and the other entitled *The Canadian Indian*, published monthly at Owen Sound, Ont., from Oct. 1890, to Sept. 1891. Beginning with Mar. 1896, the publication of "a monthly journal [chiefly in Chippewa language] devoted to the interests of the Franciscan missions among the Ottawa and Chippewa Indians," under the title *Anishinabe Enamiad*, was commenced at Harbor Springs, Mich., by Father Zephyrin Engelhardt, and is still conducted by the Franciscan fathers at that place.

The periodicals of the Creek and Choctaw Indians begin with the one called *Our Monthly*, printed almost entirely in Muskogee, of which the first volume was issued in manuscript in 1870–72. From Jan. 1873, to Oct. 1875, the numbers were printed at Tullahasse, Creek Nation, the editors being the Rev. W. S. and Miss A. A. Robertson. A weekly newspaper, *The Vindicator*, "devoted to the interests of the Choctaws and Chickasaws," printed mostly in English, with occasional articles in Choctaw, was started at Atoka, Ind. T., in 1872. This paper was united with the *Oklahoma Star* about 1877 and was continued as the *Star Vindicator* at McAlester, Ind. T. In May 1876, another weekly newspaper, entitled *Indian Journal*, was started at Muscogee, Ind. T., and published in English and Muskogee. This paper was at one time the official organ of the Creek Nation. *Our Brother in Red*, first a monthly and afterward a weekly paper, printed in English, Muskogee, and Choctaw, was published at Muscogee, Ind. T., from 1882 to 1889 or later. A newspaper called *The Indian Champion*, "Official Paper of the Choctaw Nation," written in English and Choctaw, was published weekly at Atoka, Ind. T., beginning in 1884, but was discontinued at the close of 1885. *The Indian Missionary*, a monthly paper in English, Choctaw, and Muskogee, was begun at Eufaula, Ind. T., in Aug. 1884, and continued at Atoka. Another weekly paper, called *The Muskogee Phœnix*, also printed in English, Choctaw, and Muskogee, began to appear Feb. 16, 1888, at Muscogee, Ind. T. The *Indian Chieftain*, "devoted to the interests of the Cherokees, Choctaws, Chickasaws,

Seminoles, Creeks, and all other Indians of the Indian Territory," was published weekly at Vinita, Ind. T., from 1882 to 1888. The *Indian Herald* was published weekly at Pawhuska, Osage Nation, Ind. T., from 1875 to 1877 or later. The *Indian Moccasin*, published monthly at Afton, Ind. T., by Jeremiah Hubbard, a native Indian, was begun in Jan. 1893, and continued through 1894.

Four periodicals printed by the Indian missions near the Pacific coast are worthy of mention. One of these, *The Youth's Companion*, of which the Rev. J. B. Boulet was editor, a juvenile monthly magazine, published for the benefit of the Puget Sound Catholic mission, was set in type, printed, and in part was written by the pupils of the industrial boarding schools on the Tulalip res. in Snohomish co., Wash., from May 1881, to May 1886. Another, the *Kamloops Wawa*, is a little magazine in the Chinook jargon, written in stenographic characters reproduced by a mimeograph, published irregularly by Father J. M. R. Le Jeune at Kamloops, British Columbia, from May 1891, to Dec. 1904. Another is *The Paper that Narrates*, a monthly printed for two years at Stuart's Lake, Brit. Col., in the Déné syllabic characters invented by Father A. G. Morice, the first number of which appeared in Oct. 1891. The fourth is *Haǵaǵa*, printed in Nass and English at Aiyansh Mission, Nass r., Brit. Col., from June 1893 until at least as late as Feb. 1895.

Several Indian periodicals have been published at the Indian Industrial School at Carlisle, Pa., among them being *Eadle Keahtah Toh*, monthly, Jan. 1880, to Mar. 1882; *School News*, monthly, June 1880, to May 1883, edited first by Samuel Townsend, a Pawnee boy, and later by Charles Kihega, an Iowa Indian boy; *The Morning Star*, monthly, Apr. 1882, to Dec. 1887; *The Red Man*, monthly, Jan. 1888, to June 1900; *The Indian Helper*, weekly, Aug. 14, 1885, to July 6, 1900; the last two were consolidated under the name *The Red Man and Helper*, published weekly from July 13, 1900, to July 29, 1904; *The Arrow*, weekly, Sept. 1, 1904, and still issued.

Of a kindred nature are *The Moqui Mission Messenger*, established by Rev. C. P. Coe, missionary among the Hopi of Arizona, and published first at the Hopi mission in typewriting on a manifolding machine in Jan. 1894, then printed at Chicago until Apr. 1895; *The Indian School Journal*, printed by the boys of the Chilocco Indian Industrial School at Chilocco, Okla.; *The Albuquerque Indian*, published monthly by the Albuquerque (N. Mex.) Indian School, June 1905, to May 1906; *The Mission Indian*, published monthly, later semimonthly, at the Banning (Cal.)

mission, from 1885 to 1900; the *Indian Advocate*, published monthly by the Benedictine Fathers of Sacred Heart Mission, Okla., beginning in Jan. 1889; *The New Indian*, monthly organ of the Indian Training School at Stewart, Nev., beginning in 1903; *The Indian Advance*, published monthly by the Carson Indian School, Carson, Nev., from Sept. 1899; and two magazines recently established, one *The Native American*, published by the Indian School at Phœnix, Ariz., the other *The Indian Outlook*, published monthly by Rev. J. B. Rounds at Darlington, Okla.

The only periodical in the Greenland Eskimo, entitled *Atuagagdliutit*, an 8-page quarto paper, with woodcuts, has been published irregularly at Nungme (Godthaab), since Jan. 1861.　　　　(w. e.)

Perkoson. See *Poquosin*.

Pernyu. A Nuwukmiut Eskimo summer village on the w. shore of Elson bay, close to Pt Barrow, Alaska. Cf. *Perinak*.
Pergniák.—Officers (1849–53) cited by Baker, Geog. Dict. Alaska, 494, 1906. **Perignak.**—Baker, ibid. **Perignax.**—Ray (1885) quoted by Baker, ibid. **Pernyû.**—Murdoch in 9th Rep. B. A. E., 84, 1892.

Perquiman. An Algonquian tribe or band living in 1700 on the n. side of Albemarle sd., N. C.—Mooney, Siouan Tribes of the East, 7, 1894.

Persimmon (an apocopated form of Renâpe *pasĭmĕnan*, 'dried fruit,' i. e. fruit dried artificially; from *pasĭmĕneu*, 'he (or she) dries fruit.' Fruit dried spontaneously would be *pasĭmĕn*, 'dry fruit.' The word is cognate with Nipissing *pasĭmĭnan*, a name in that dialect for a raisin or a dried huckleberry; Cree *pasĭmĭnan*, a name for any fruit dried artificially. According to J. P. Dunn (inf'n, 1907), among the Miami and western Algonquian tribes generally it is *pĭáhkemĭn*). The fruit of *Diospyros virginiana*, of the Ebenaceæ or Ebony family, known also as date-plum, or possum-wood. The tree is found over a large part of the United States from Connecticut to Florida and from Ohio to Texas. A species (*Diospyros texana*) is known as Mexican persimmon, black persimmon, chapote, etc. The Creole name, *plaquemin*, is a corruption of Illinois *piakimin* (cf. Miami *piahkimin*). The early writers on the Virginian country spelled the word in divers ways, as *putchamin* (Capt. John Smith, 1632), *pessemmin* (Strachey, 1610–1613), *persimena* (1648), *parsimon, posimon, putchimon, pitchumon, persimon* (Clayton, Flora Virg., 43, 156, 1743). This fruit, which resembles a yellow plum, but is globular and about an inch in diameter, is exceedingly austere and astringent before maturity, and, as Capt. John Smith (who was the first to notice it, under the name of *putchamin*) observes, draws "a man's mouth awry with much torment"; but, in the fall, after bletting, and being softened by the frost, it becomes sweet and fine-flavored. In the S. the fruit remains adherent to the branches long after the leaves have been shed (a fact to which the name mentioned by Smith alludes), and, when it falls to the ground, is eagerly devoured by wild and domestic animals. It was much esteemed by the Virginia Indians, who preserved it by drying it upon mats spread upon frames or barbecues. It is from the berries in the form of prunes that the name, after undergoing many vicissitudes of spelling, has been handed down to us, that probably being the condition in which the fruit was locally first seen, by the English settlers, in use among the Indians. The name of the fruit in a fresh or growing state (*putchamin* or *pitchamin*) became obsolete at the beginning of the third quarter of the 18th century. The fruit is used in the S. for making a beverage called "persimmon (or simmon) beer," which is much liked by country folk. "Persimmon wine" is a spirituous liquor obtained by distilling persimmon beer.

"Huckleberry above the persimmon" is a Southern phrase meaning to excel (Bartlett). "To rake up the persimmons" is a Southern gambling term for pocketing the stakes, or gathering in the "chips." "The longest pole knocks down the most simmons" is a Southern adage meaning that the strongest party gains the day. "That's persimmons" is a Southernism for "that's fine." The hard flat seeds of the persimmon were used by the Algonquian Indians of Virginia in playing their *mamantuwákan*, or dice game.　　　(a. f. c.　w. r. g.)

Peruka. The Frog or Toad clan of San Felipe pueblo, N. Mex.
Pë'rŭka-háno.—Hodge in Am. Anthrop., ix, 350, 1896 (*háno* = 'people').

Pesawa (*Mĕshäwä*, 'elk,' from which comes the word for 'horse.'—W. J.). Given as the Horse gens of the Shawnee.
Mecäwä.—Wm. Jones, inf'n, 1906. **Pe-sa-wä'.**—Morgan, Anc. Soc., 168, 1877.

Pescadero (Span. 'fisherman'). A former Yuma rancheria on the n. bank of Gila r., s. w. Arizona, visited by Anza and Font in 1775.
El Pescadero.—Anza and Font cited by Bancroft, Ariz. and N. Mex., 392, 1889.

Pescadero. A former pueblo of the Pima, with 237 inhabitants in 1730. Situated in N. Sonora, Mexico; definite locality unknown.
San Pablo del Pescadero.—Orozco y Berra, Geog., 347, 1864. **S. Pablo Pescadero.**—Rivera (1730) quoted by Bancroft, No. Mex. States, i, 513, 1884.

Pescado (contr. from Span. *Ojo Pescado*, 'fish spring,' on account of numerous small fish in a spring there; native name Heshotatsinan, or Heshotatsinakwin, 'place of the pictographs'). A Zuñi summer village about 15 m. e. of Zuñi pueblo, N. Mex. The pueblo was built on the foundations of an ancient town, on the walls of which may still be seen sculptured pictographs, whence the native name. See Mindeleff in 8th Rep. B. A. E., 95, 1891.

Héshota Izina.—Bandelier in Revue d'Ethnog., 200, 1886 (misprint). **He-sho-ta-tsi'-na.**—Cushing in The Millstone, IX, 55, Apr. 1884. **He-sho-ta-tsi'-na-kwe.**—Ibid. ('people of the pictured town'). **Hé sho ta tsí nan.**—Cushing in 4th Rep. B. A. E., 494, 1886. **Hesh-o-ta-tzi-na.**—Fewkes in Jour. Am. Eth. and Arch., I, map, 1891. **Heshota Tzinan.**—Bandelier in Arch. Inst. Papers, IV, 333, 1892 (referring to the ruin). **Ojo de Pescado.**—Gatschet in Mag. Am. Hist., 260, Apr. 1882. **Ojo Percado.**—Eaton in Schoolcraft, Ind. Tribes, IV, 220, 1854 (misprint). **Ojo Pescado.**—Whipple, Pac. R. R. Rep., III, pt. 3, 44, 1856. **Ojo Pesoado.**—Eastman, map in Schoolcraft, Ind. Tribes, IV, 1854 (misprint). **Pescado.**—Common map form. **Piscao.**—Hughes, Doniphan's Exped., 197, 1848. **Prescado.**—Donaldson, Moqui Pueblo Inds., 127, 1893 (misprint).

Pescado. An unidentified tribe, spoken of in 1683 by Juan Sabeata, a Jumano Indian from the mouth of Conchos r., N. E. Chihuahua, Mexico. It was one of 36 tribes, friendly to his own, said by Sabeata to live on Nueces r., 3 days' journey from his home (Mendoza, Viage, 1683–84, MS. in Archivo General). (H. E. B.)

Peshewah (*Pi-zhe'-wa*, The Lynx). A Miami chief, better known on the frontier as John B. Richardville; born on St Marys r., Ind., near the present Ft Wayne, about 1761. After the death of Little Turtle the chiefship fell to Peshewah. Inheriting noble French blood on his father's side, his abilities were such, it is said, as well adapted him to direct the affairs of the Miami. He spoke French and English fluently, as well as his native tongue; and for many years his house on the bank of St Marys r., about 4 m. from Ft Wayne, was known as the abode of hospitality. At the time of his death, Aug. 13, 1841, Peshewah was about 80 years of age and was regarded as the wealthiest Indian in North America, his property, it is said, being valued at more than a million dollars. The town of Russiaville, Ind., takes its name, in corrupted form, from him. (C. T.　J. P. D.)

Peshla ('bald head'). A band of the Oglala Teton Sioux.

Pe-cla.—Dorsey (after Cleveland) in 15th Rep. B. A. E., 220, 1897. **Pe-śla.**—Ibid. **Short hair.**—Culbertson in Smithson. Rep. 1850, 142, 1851.

Peshlaptechela ('short bald head'). A band of the Oglala Teton Sioux.

Pe-cla-ptcetcela.—Dorsey (after Cleveland) in 15th Rep. B. A. E., 220, 1897. **Pe-hi'-pte-ci-la.**—Hayden, Ethnog. and Philol. Mo. Val., 376, 1862 (trans. 'short hair band'). **Pe-śla-ptecela.**—Dorsey, op. cit. **Short hair band.**—Hayden, op. cit.

Pesquis. Mentioned as a pueblo of the province of Atripuy, in the region of the lower Rio Grande, in New Mexico, in 1598.—Oñate (1598) in Doc. Inéd., XVI, 115, 1871.

Pessacus. A noted chief of the Narraganset (1623–77), brother of Miantonomo. In 1645–58 war was threatened between his people and the English, but was avoided after much talk and conference, chiefly by the diplomacy of Ninigret. Pessacus met his death in an expedition against the Mohawk. The unlatinized form of his name appears as Pessacks. (A. F. C.)

Pessemmin. See *Persimmon.*

Pestles. Implements used by the aborigines in combination with mortars and grinding plates for pulverizing foods, paints, and other substances. The use of pestles was general, and they are still constantly employed by tribes retaining their primitive customs. They are made of stone, wood, and more rarely of other materials. Bowlders and other natural stones of suitable shape are very generally employed in the grinding work, and the less perfectly adapted forms are modified to accommodate them to the hand and to the particular grinding surface. Pestles for use on flat surfaces are cylindrical and used with a rolling motion, or are flattish beneath for use after the manner of a muller (q. v.). For use in a depression or a deep receptacle the grinding end of the implement is round or conical, while the upper part or handle is shaped for convenience in grasping or is carved to represent some esoteric concept associated in the primitive mind with the function of the apparatus. In many cases the shape of the implement was such that it could be used in one position as a muller and in another as a pestle (indeed, the Seneca apply the same name to both pestle and mortar, but modified by the terms "upper" and "lower"), while some examples have a concave surface, available as a mortar. The same stone becomes also on occasion a nut cracker and a hammer. Long, slender, cylindrical pestles are common in the Eastern states, a length of 2 ft being common, while the diameter rarely exceeds 3 in. In the Ohio and adjacent valleys a short, somewhat conical or bell-shaped form prevails, while on the Pacific slope the shapes are remarkably varied. The prevalent type of California pestle is somewhat cylindrical, but tapers gracefully upward, the length varying from a few inches to nearly 3 ft. They are sometimes encircled by a ridge near the base to keep the hand from slipping down, and frequently terminate above in a similar encircling ridge or a conical knob. On the N. W. coast the shapes are still more noteworthy, occasional examples being carved to represent animal forms. Some are T-shaped, suggesting the conventional pillow of the Egyptians, while still others have perforate or annular handles. Stone pestles are found on inhabited sites, but were rarely buried with the dead. They are less common in portions of the S. where stone was not plentiful, and in the Pueblo country, where the metate and muller were in general use.

Wooden pestles were used with wooden mortars, and were often maul-shaped, although both ends were sometimes enlarged, the implement being so long as to be held midway in its length, the operator standing upright. Very commonly the smaller end was used in the mortar, and the receptacle was deep and sharply conical to suit. Schoolcraft illustrates an ingenious use of pestles by the Indians of New Hampshire, the implement being suspended from the elastic branch of a tree, by which means the arduous task of lifting the heavy weight was avoided.

For references to writings relating to pestles, see *Mortars*. (w. h. h.)

Petaikuk (*Petá′ĭkŭk*, 'where the *petai* [ash tree?] stands'). A former Pima village in s. Arizona.—Russell, Pima MS., B. A. E., 16, 1902. Cf. *Pitac*.

Petalesharo (*Pitarésharu*, 'chief of men'). A Skidi Pawnee chief, son of Old Knife (Letalesha), born about 1797. Long describes him as a man of fine physique and prepossessing countenance, and as the most intrepid warrior of his tribe. It was he who, at one time, when his tribesmen were assembled for the purpose of sacrificing a captive Comanche woman, stepped forward and declared that it was his father's wish to abolish this practice, and that he presented himself for the purpose of laying down his own life on the spot or of releasing the victim. He then cut the thongs that bound the woman to a cross, bore her swiftly through the crowd to a horse, which he presented to her, and, having mounted another himself, conveyed her beyond the reach of immediate pursuit; after having supplied her with food, and admonishing her to make the best of her way to her own tribe, which was at the distance of at least 400 m., he returned to his village. "This daring deed," says Long, "would, almost to a certainty, have terminated in an unsuccessful attempt under the arm of any other warrior, and Petalesharo was, no doubt, indebted for this successful and noble achievement to the distinguished renown which his feats of chivalry had already gained for him and which commanded the high respect of all his rival warriors." He signed, in behalf of his tribe, the treaty of Grand Pawnee village on Platte r., Nebr., Oct. 9, 1833, as Pe-tah-lay-shah-rho. The treaty of Table cr., Nebr., Sept. 24, 1857, was signed by "Petanesharo, the man and the chief." (c. t.)

Petaluma. A former Moquelumnan village about 2 m. E. of Petaluma, Sonoma co., Cal. (s. a. b.)
Petaluma.—Taylor in Cal. Farmer, Mar. 30, 1860. Yol-hios.—Ibid.

Petangenikashika ('those who became human beings by the aid of a crane'). A Quapaw gens.
Crane gens.—Dorsey in 15th Rep. B. A. E., 229, 1897. Peʼtaⁿ eʼnikaciʼ꜓a.—Ibid.

Petaniqwut. See *Mahabittuh*.

Petao. A village or tribe mentioned by Joutel as living in 1687 N. or N.W. of the Maligne (Colorado) r., Texas. The region was the abode of Caddoan tribes, and also of a few intrusive Tonkawan and Karankawan Indians. The name seems to have been mentioned to Joutel by the Ebahamo Indians, who were probably affiliated with the Karankawa. (a. c. f.)
Petao.—Joutel (1687) in French, Hist. Coll. La., I, 138, 1846. Petaro.—Joutel (1687) in Margry, Déc., III, 289, 1878. Petaz.—Shea in Charlevoix, New France, IV, 78, 1870. Petçares.—Barcia, Ensayo, 271, 1723. Petsaré.—Joutel (1687) in Margry, Déc., III, 289, 1878. Petzare.—Joutel (1687) in French, Hist. Coll. La., I, 152, 1846.

Petchaleruhpaka (*Pe-tchale-ruh-pä′-ka*, 'raven'). Given by Morgan (Anc. Soc., 159, 1877) as a gens of the Crow tribe, but more probably it was a society or a local band.

Petchenanalas. See *Buckongahelas*.

Petdelu. The extinct Turkey clan of the former pueblo of Pecos, New Mexico.
Pe-dâhl-lu.—Hewett in Am. Anthrop., n. s., VI, 431, 1904. P'etdelŭ′+.—Hodge in Am. Anthrop., IX, 352, 1896 (+ = *ash* = 'people').

Petenegowats. A Mono tribe formerly living in Esmeralda co., w. Nev.; pop. 150 in 1870. They were found by Merriam in 1903 just across the line, in Owens valley, Cal.
Ma-haʼ-bĭt-tuh.—Powers, Inds. W. Nev., MS., B. A. E., 1876 (= 'pine-nut eaters'). Owens Valley Paiutes.—Merriam in Science, XIX, 916, June 15, 1904.—Petenegowat Pah-Utes.—Campbell in Ind. Aff. Rep., 113, 1870. Petonaquats.—Merriam, op. cit. Pet-tán-i-gwut.—Powers, op. cit.

Peticado (probably Fr. *Petit Caddo*, 'little, or lower, Caddo'). The name given by Mezières in 1770 to one of the Caddoan tribes between the Adai and the Kadohadacho, in Texas. Having left the Adai, Mezières passed through the Yatasi village, thence to the Peticado, thence to the Kadohadacho. The context of the reports makes it appear that the Peticado, also called "the Cado," were nearer to the Yatasi than to the Kadohadacho, and that their village was on or near Red r. At this time the Peticado village was dominated by French traders, particularly one Du Pain, who opposed the Spanish intrusion (Mezières, Relazion, Oct. 21, 1770, MS. in Archivo General, Provincias Internas, 100; Fray Santa María to the Viceroy, July 21, 1774, MS. in Archivo General). (h. e. b.)
Cados.—Carabaxal, Oct. 30, 1770, Relazion, op. cit. Piticado.—Santa María, 1774, op. cit.

Petkhaninihkashina ('crane people'). A social division of the Osage, said by Dorsey to be a subgens.
Peʼtqaⁿ iʼniqkʼäciⁿʼa.—Dorsey in 15th Rep. B. A. E., 235, 1897.

Petodseka (*Pe-tod-se-ka*, 'white spot'). A Paviotso band formerly about Carson and Walker lakes, w. Nev.—Dodge in Ind. Aff. Rep. 1859, 374, 1860.

Petroglyphs. See *Pictographs*.

Petukqunnunk. See *Tuckernuck*.

Petutek (*Pɛtu'tᴱk*, or *Ptŭ'tɛk*, 'little spring [of water]'). A village of the Nicola band of the Ntlakyapamuk, 41 m. above Spences Bridge, Brit. Col.—Teit in Mem. Am. Mus. Nat. Hist., ii, 174, 1900.

Pewikwithltchu (*Pe'-wi-kwĭthl-tchu,* 'grass swallowers,' in allusion to their drinking dew and rain water). An aboriginal people, mentioned in Zuñi tradition as having lived at a settlement about 13 m. s. of the present Zuñi pueblo. See *Shuminkyaiman.*   (F. H. C.)

Peyotan ('peyote place'). A Cora pueblo and seat of a mission near the E. bank of Rio San Pedro, about lat. 22° 40', Jalisco, Mexico. Santa Rosa was its visita.

S. Juan Peyotan.—Orozco y Berra, Geog., 280, 1864.

Peyote (Spanish derivative from the Nahuatl *peyotl,* 'caterpillar,' referring to the downy center of the "button"). A species of small cactus, variously classified as *Anhalonium* or *Lophophora* (Coulter), found in the arid hills along the lower Rio Grande and southward in Mexico; formerly and still much used for ceremonial and medicinal purposes by all the tribes between the Rocky mts. and the Gulf of Mexico, from Arkansas r. southward, almost to the City of Mexico. Among the various tribes it is known under different names, as *señi* (Kiowa); *wokowi* (Comanche); *hikori* or *hikuli* (Tarahumare). By the whites it is commonly but incorrectly known as "mescal," from a confusion with the maguey cactus of the S. W. from which the fiery intoxicant mescal is prepared. In appearance the peyote plant resembles a radish in size and shape, the top only appearing above ground. From the center springs a beautiful white blossom, which is later displaced by a tuft of white down. N. of the Rio Grande this top alone is used, being sliced and dried to form the so-called "button." In Mexico the whole plant is cut into slices, dried, and used in decoction, while the ceremony also is essentially different from that of the northern tribes.

Some chemical study of the plant was made by the German chemist Lewin as early as 1888, but the first knowledge of its ritual use was given to the world in 1891 by James Mooney, of the Bureau of American Ethnology, who had witnessed the ceremony while engaged in ethnologic investigations among the Kiowa, and brought back to Washington a large quantity for medical and psychologic experimentation. Tests thus far made indicate that it possesses varied and valuable medicinal properties, tending to confirm the idea of the Indians, who regard it almost as a panacea.

Among the Tarahumare and others of Mexico the chief feature of the ceremony, as described by Lumholtz, is a dance. Among the Kiowa, Comanche, and other Plains tribes it is rather a ceremony of prayer and quiet contemplation. It is usually performed as an invocation for the recovery of some sick person. It is held in a tipi specially erected for the purpose, and begins usually at night, continuing until the sun is well up in the morning. As many men as can sit comfortably within the tipi circle may participate, but, as a rule, women do not take part in the ceremony proper, but occupy themselves with the preparation of the sacred food and of the feast in which all join at the close of the performance. A fire is kept burning in the center of the tipi, inclosed within a crescent-shaped mound, on the top of which is placed a sacred peyote. Following an opening prayer by the chief priest, four peyotes are distributed to each participant, who chews and swallows them, after which the sacred songs begin to the accompaniment of the drum and rattle, each man singing four songs in turn, and are kept up all night, varied by the intervals of prayer and other distributions of peyote, with a peculiar baptismal ceremony at midnight. The number of "buttons" eaten by one individual during the night varies from 10 to 40, and even more, the drug producing a sort of spiritual exaltation differing entirely from that produced by any other known drug, and apparently without any reaction. The effect is heightened by the weird lullaby of the songs, the constant sound of the drum and rattle, and the fitful glare of the fire. At some point during the ceremony the sick person is usually brought in to be prayed for, and is allowed to eat one or more specially consecrated peyotes. At daylight the Morning Star song is sung, when the women pass in the sacred food, of which each worshiper partakes, and the ceremony concludes with the Meat song. The rest of the morning is given to friendly gossip, followed by a dinner under leafy arbors, after which the various families disperse to their homes.

Consult Lewin, Ueber Anhalonium Lewinii, 1888; Lumholtz (1) Tarahumari Dances and Plant Worship, 1894, (2) Symbolism of the Huichol Indians, 1900, (3) Unknown Mexico, 1902; Mooney, The Mescal Plant and Ceremony, and Prentiss and Morgan, Therapeutic Uses of Mescal Buttons, 1896; Mooney, Calendar History of the Kiowa, 17th Rep. B. A. E., 1898; Ellis, Mescal, 1898; Urbina, El Peyote y el Ololiuhqui, 1900.   (J. M.)

Peytre. Mentioned as a pueblo of the province of Atripuy (q. v.), in the region of the lower Rio Grande, N. Mex., in 1598.—Oñate (1598) in Doc. Inéd., xvi, 115, 1871.

Pfia (*Pfiä'-taĭina*, 'feather people'). A clan of the pueblo of Taos, N. Mex.—Hodge, field notes, B. A. E., 1899.

Pfialola (*Pfiälóla-taĭina*, 'earring people'). A clan of the pueblo of Taos, N. Mex.—Hodge, field notes, B. A. E., 1899.

Pfiataikwahlaonan (*Pfiätaĭkwa'hláonan*). A clan of the pueblo of Taos, N. Mex.—Hodge field notes, B. A. E., 1899.

Philip. See *King Philip*.

Phillimees. A Seminole town on or near Suwannee r., w. Fla., in 1817.—Drake, Bk. Indians, x, 1848.

Physiology. While practically nothing is known of the physiology of the Eskimo, with the exception of their great capacity for animal food, recent investigations have yielded definite information in this line regarding the Indians. It has been supposed that in his physiologic functions the Indian differs considerably from the white man, but the greater our knowledge in this direction the fewer the differences appear; there is, however, a certain lack of uniformity in this respect between the two races.

The period of gestation of Indian women is apparently the same as that of the whites, and the new-born child is in every way comparable to the white infant. It begins to suckle as soon as it is given the breast, generally shows excellent nutrition, and has from the beginning a good voice. In 6 to 8 months the first teeth appear; during the 7th or 8th month the child begins to sit up; at 1 year it stands alone, and soon after begins to walk; at the age of about 18 months it commences to talk, and when 4 years of age it has a good command of language. During its first year the Indian child spends as much time in sleeping as does a healthy white child, and after the first year is very playful. It cries, on the average, less than the white child, but the principal reason for this seems to be the fact that it is generally well nourished and not sickly. The infant is nursed usually much later than among whites, not infrequently up to its 3d or 4th year, but after its 6th to 9th month it also partakes of most of the foods of its parents. Up to the 7th year incontinence of urine is quite frequent, apparently without pathological cause, but this disappears spontaneously thereafter.

As among whites, the period of puberty in the Indian is earlier in the low and hot regions than in those that are elevated or cold. In such very hot regions as the lower Colorado valley many of the girls begin to menstruate between the ages of 11 and 13; while among tribes that live at a considerable altitude, as the Apache of Arizona and the Indians farther N., this function begins usually during the 13th or 14th year, and delays are more numer-

ous; precise data from many localities are as yet lacking. The development of the breast in the girl commences usually at about the 12th year, and except among individuals there appears to be no great variation among the tribes of which there is most knowledge. Full development of the breast is seldom attained in the unmarried young woman before the 18th year. The time of puberty in Indian boys differs apparently but little, if any, from that in whites. Scanty growth of mustache is noticeable from about the 16th year, sometimes much later.

Marriage is generally entered into earlier than among American whites; only few girls of more than 18 years, and few young men of more than 22 years, are unmarried. Now and then a girl is married at 14 or 15, and there is an instance of a Comanche girl of 11 years who married a Kiowa. Among the latter tribe it is not exceptional for girls to be married at 13. Indian women bear children early, and the infants of even the youngest mothers seem in no way defective. The birth rate is generally high, from 6 to 9 births in a family being usual. Twins are not very uncommon, but triplets occur very rarely. One or more naturally sterile women may be met in every large band.

The adult life of the Indian offers nothing radically different from that of ordinary whites. The supposed early aging of Indian women is by no means general and is not characteristic of the race; when it occurs, it is due to the conditions surrounding the life of the individual. Gray hairs in small numbers may occasionally be found, as in brunette whites, even in children, but such occurrence is without significance. Senile grayness does not commence earlier than among healthy whites, and it advances more slowly, seldom, if ever, reaching the degree of complete whiteness. Baldness not due to disease is extremely rare. A common phenomenon observed in the aged Indian is pronounced wrinkling of the skin of the face and other parts. Little is known as to the exact period of menopause in the women, for but few of them know their actual age. Men remain potent, at least occasionally, much beyond 50 years. The longevity of the Indian is very much like that of a healthy white man. There are individuals who reach the age of 100 years and more, but they are exceptional. Among aged Indians there is usually little decrepitude. Aged women predominate somewhat in numbers over aged men. Advanced senility is marked by general emaciation, marked wrinkling of the skin, forward inclination of the body, and gradual diminution of muscular power as well as of acuteness of the senses. The teeth are often much worn down, or are lost mainly through the absorption of the alveolar processes.

Among the more primitive tribes, who often pass through periods of want, capacity for food is larger than in the average whites. Real excesses in eating are witnessed among such tribes, but principally at feasts. On the reservations, and under ordinary circumstances, the consumption of food by the Indian is usually moderate. All Indians readily develop a strong inclination for and are easily affected by alcoholic drinks. The average Indian ordinarily passes somewhat more time in sleep than the civilized white man; on the other hand, he manifests considerable capability for enduring its loss. Yawning, snoring, eructation, and flatus are about as common with Indians as with whites. Sneezing, however, is rare, and hiccough even more so. Dreams are frequent and variable. Illusions or hallucinations in healthy individuals and under ordinary conditions have not been observed. Lefthandedness occurs in every tribe, and with nearly the same frequency as among whites (approximately 3 per cent). The sight, hearing, smell, and taste of the Indian, so far as can be judged from unaided but extended observation, are in no way peculiar. In the ordinary Indian with healthy eyes and ears, the sight and hearing are generally very good, but in no way phenomenal. To those who receive education above that of the common school, glasses are often necessary. In the old, eyesight is generally weakened, and in some the hearing is more or less blunted. The physical endurance of Indians on general occasions probably exceeds that of the whites. The Indian easily sustains long walking or running, hunger and thirst, severe sweating, etc.; but he often tires readily when subjected to steady work. His mental endurance, however, except when he may be engaged in ceremonies or games, or on other occasions which produce special mental excitement, is but moderate; an hour of questioning almost invariably produces mental fatigue. Respiration and temperature are nearly the same as in healthy whites, the latter perhaps averaging slightly lower; but the pulse is somewhat slower, the general average in adult men approximating 66. Muscular force in the hands, tested by the dynanometer, is somewhat lower than with whites in the males and about equal in the females. The shoulder strength shows less difference, and the strength, or at least the endurance, of the back and lower limbs, judging from the work and other pursuits to which the Indians are accustomed, probably exceeds that of the whites.

The mental functions of the Indian should be compared with those of whites reared and living under approximately similar circumstances. On closer observation the differences in the fundamental psychical manifestations between the two races are found to be small. No instincts not possessed by whites have developed in the Indian. His proficiency in tracking and concealment, his sense of direction, etc., are accounted for by his special training and practice, and are not found in the Indian youth who has not had such experience. The Indian lacks much of the ambition known to the white man, yet he shows more or less of the quality where his life affords a chance for it, as in war, in his games, art, adornment, and many other activities.

The emotional life of the Indian is more moderate and ordinarily more free from extremes of nearly every nature, than that of the white person. The prevalent subjective state is that of content in wellbeing, with inclination to humor. Pleasurable emotions predominate, but seldom rise beyond the moderate; those of a painful nature are occasionally very pronounced. Maternal love is strong, especially during the earlier years of the child. Sexual love is rather simply organic, not of so intellectual an order as among whites; but this seems to be largely the result of views and customs governing sex relations and marriage. The social instinct and that of self-preservation are much like those of white people. Emotions of anger and hatred are infrequent and of normal character. Fear is rather easily aroused at all ages, in groups of children occasionally reaching a panic; but this is likewise due in large measure to peculiar beliefs and untrammeled imagination.

Modesty, morality, and the sense of right and justice are as natural to the Indian as to the white man, but, as in other respects, are modified in the former by prevalent views and conditions of life. Transgressions of every character are less frequent in the Indian. Memory (of sense impressions as well as of mental acts proper) is generally fair. Where the faculty has been much exercised in one direction, as in religion, it acquires remarkable capacity in that particular. The young exhibit good memory for languages. The faculty of will is strongly developed. Intellectual activities proper are comparable with those of ordinary healthy whites, though on the whole, and excepting the sports, the mental processes are probably habitually slightly slower. Among many tribes lack of thrift, improvidence, absence of demonstrative manifestations, and the previously mentioned lack of ambition are observable;

but these peculiarities must be charged largely, if not entirely, to differences in mental training and habits. The reasoning of the Indian and his ideation, though modified by his views, have often been shown to be excellent. His power of imitation, and even of invention, are good, as is his aptitude in several higher arts and in oratory. An Indian child reared under the care of whites, educated in the schools of civilization, and without having acquired the notions of its people, is habitually much like a white child trained in a similar degree under similar conditions.

Consult Boteler, Peculiarities of the American Indian from a Physiological and Pathological Standpoint, 1880–81; Mays, Experimental Inquiry, 1887; Holder, Age of Puberty of Indian Girls, 1890; Currier, Study Relative to Functions of Reproductive Apparatus, 1891; Parker, Concerning American Indian Womanhood, 1891–92; Eleventh Census, Rep. on Indians, 1894; Hrdlicka (1) Physical and Physiological Observations on the Navaho, 1900, (2) Bull. 34, B. A. E., 1908. See also the bibliographies under *Anatomy* and *Health and Disease.*   (A. H.)

Pia (*Pi-ă*). A former Siuslaw village on Siuslaw r., Oreg.—Dorsey in Jour. Am. Folk-lore, III, 230, 1890.

Piacaamanc. A rancheria, probably Cochimi, formerly connected with Purísima (Cadegomo) mission, which was near the w. coast of Lower California, about lat. 26° 20′.—Doc. Hist. Mex., 4th s., v, 189, 1857.

Piachi. A walled town, probably of the Choctaw, formerly on Tombigbee r., w. Ala.; visited by De Soto in 1540. Lewis thinks it probable that it was on Black Warrior r., Ala.

Piache.—Gentl. of Elvas (1557) in French, Hist. Coll. La., II, 156, 1850. **Piachi.**—Gentl. of Elvas in Lewis, Exped. De Soto, 188, 1907.

Piagadme. A rancheria, probably Cochimi, formerly connected with Purísima (Cadegomo) mission, Lower California.—Doc. Hist. Mex., 4th s., v, 189, 1857.

Piamato. A pueblo of the Tigua or the Tewa of New Mexico in 1598.

Piamato.—Oñate (1598) in Doc. Inéd., XVI, 102, 1871. **Xiomato.**—Ibid., 116.

Pianbotinu (*Piänbötinŭ-taíina*, 'white mountain people'). A clan of the pueblo of Taos, N. Mex.—Hodge, field notes, B. A. E., 1899.

Piankashaw (possibly connected with *Päyangitchaki*, 'those who separate,' from *pevangiani*, 'I separate from,' according to Gatschet; the Miami form, according to J. P. Dunn, is *Payŭnggïsh′ah*). Formerly a subtribe of the Miami, but later a separate people. In an account of the rivers and peoples of the W., La Salle, about 1682, mentions the Piankashaw as one of the tribes gathered about his Illinois fort; these were bands brought from

their usual habitat. In the account by Cadillac (1695) they are spoken of as being w. of the Miami village on St Joseph r., Mich., with the Mascoutens, Kickapoo, and other tribes. It is probable they were then on Vermillion r., in Indiana and Illinois. St Cosme (1699) says that the village of the Peanzichias Miamis was on Kankakee r., Ill., but that they formerly lived on the Mississippi. They had possibly been driven w. by the Iroquois. Their ancient village was on the Wabash at the junction of the Vermillion; at a later period they established another settlement, Chippekawkay, lower down the river, at the present site of Vincennes, Ind. About 1770 they gave permission to the Delawares to occupy the E. part of their territory. Chauvignerie (1736) says that the Wea, the Piankashaw, and the Pepicokia were the same nation in different villages, and gives the deer as the Piankashaw totem. In the beginning of the present century they and the Wea began to cross over into Missouri, and in 1832 the two tribes sold all their claims in the E. and agreed to remove to Kansas as one tribe. About 1854 the consolidated tribe united with the remnant of the Illinois, then known as Peoria and Kaskaskia, and in 1867 the entire body sold their lands in Kansas and removed to the present Oklahoma, where they are now known under the name of Peoria. The Piankashaw made or participated in treaties with the United States at Greenville, O., Aug. 3, 1795; Ft Wayne, Ind., June 7, 1803; Vincennes, Ind., Aug. 7, 1803, Aug. 27, 1804, and Dec. 30, 1805; Portage des Sioux, Mo., July 18, 1815; Vincennes, Ind., Jan. 3, 1818 (not ratified); Castor Hill, Mo., Oct. 29, 1832; Washington, D. C., May 30, 1854, and Feb. 23, 1867.

The Piankashaw probably never numbered many more than 1,000 souls. In 1736 Chauvignerie estimated the Piankashaw, Wea, and Pepicokia together at about 1,750. In 1759 the Piankashaw alone were estimated at 1,500, and five years later at 1,250. This was reduced to 950 in 1780, and 800 in 1795. In 1825 there were only 234 remaining, and in 1906 all the tribes consolidated under the name of Peoria numbered but 192, none of whom was of pure blood.   (J. M.)

Hopungieasaw.—Woodward, Reminisc., 23, 1859 ('dancing Indians,' from *opŭnga*, 'to dance': Creek name). **Hopungiesas.**—Ibid., 94. **Miankish.**—Gatschet, Caddo MS., B. A. E., 1884 (Caddo name). **Päyangitchaki.**—Gatschet, Miami MS., B. A. E., 1888 (correct Miami form). **Peahushaws.**—McKenney and Hall, Ind. Tribes, III, 79, 1854. **Peanghichia.**—La Salle (1682) in Margry, Déc., II, 201, 1877. **Peanguicheas.**—McKenney and Hall, Ind. Tribes, op. cit. **Peanguichias.**—Doc. of 1718 in N. Y. Doc. Col. Hist., IX, 891, 1855. **Peanguischias.**—Beauharnois (1745), ibid., X, 25, 1858. **Peanguiseins.**—Cadillac (1695) in Margry, Déc., v, 124, 1883. **Peankshaws.**—Lang and Taylor, Rep., 23, 1843. **Peanquichas.**—Chauvignerie (1736) quoted by Schoolcraft, Ind. Tribes, III, 555, 1853. **Peanzichias Miamis.**—St Cosme (1699) quoted by Shea,

Early Voy., 58, 1861. **Peauguicheas.**—McKenney and Hall, Ind. Tribes, III, 79, 1854. **Pecankee-shaws.**—Hough in Indiana Geol. Rep., map, 1883. **Pehenguichias.**—McKenney and Hall, Ind. Tribes, III, 80, 1854. **Pelagisía.**—Gatschet, Shawnee MS., B. A. E., 1879 (Shawnee name; plural, Pelagis-íagi). **Peouanguichías.**—Bacqueville de la Potherie, II, 335, 1753. **Piancashaws.**—Vater, Mith., pt. 3, sec. 3, 351, 1816. **Piangeshaw.**—Jones, Ojeb-way Inds., 178, 1861. **Pianguichia.**—Coxe, Caro-lana, map, 1741. **Pianguisha.**—Croghan (1757) in N. Y. Doc. Col. Hist., VII, 268, 1856. **Pianka-shaws.**—Johnson (1763),ibid.,583. **Piankaskouas.**—Tailhan, Perrot Mém., 222, note, 1864. **Pianke-shas.**—McCoy, Ann. Reg., 21, 1836. **Pianke-shaws.**—German Flats conf. (1770) in N. Y. Doc. Col. Hist., VIII, 233, 1857. **Piankichas.**—Vater, Mith., pt. 3, sec. 3, 351, 1816. **Piànkishas.**—Croghan (1759) quoted by Jefferson, Notes, 146, 1825. **Pian-kishaws.**—Harrison (1814) quoted by Drake, Tecum-seh, 160, 1852. **Piankshaws.**—De Butts (1795) in Am. St. Papers, Ind. Aff., I, 582, 1832. **Pianquicha.**—Smith, Bouquet's Exped., 64, 1766. **Pianquiches.**—Perkins and Peck, Annals of the West, 687, 1850. **Pianquishaws.**—Croghan (1759) quoted by Rupp, West. Penn., 146, 1846. **Pi-auk-e-shaws.**—Beckwith in Indiana Geol. Rep., 41, 1883. **Piawkashaws.**—Vater, Mith., pt.3, sec. 3, 344, 1816. **Pinkeshaws.**—Kelton, Ft Mackinac, 38, 1884. **Piouanguichias.**—Bacqueville de la Potherie, II, 346, 1753. **Plan-kishaws.**—Dalton (1783) in Mass. Hist. Soc. Coll.,1st s., X, 123, 1809 (misprint). **Poüankikias.**—Tailhan, Perrot Mém., 222, note, 1864. **Pyankashees.**—Es-nauts and Rapilly Map, 1777. **Pyankeeshas.**—Croghan (1765) in N. Y. Doc. Col. Hist., VII, 781, 1856. **Pyankehas.**—Croghan (1765) quoted in Am. Jour. Geol., 272, 1831. **Pyankeshaws.**—Croghan (1765), ibid., 265. **Pyankishaws.**—Volney, View of U. S. A., 352, 1804. **Tukachohas.**—Loskiel (1794) quoted by Ruttenber, Tribes Hudson R., 336, 1872.

Piankatank. A tribe of the Powhatan confederacy on Piankatank r., Va. They numbered about 200 in 1608. Their prin-cipal village, also called Piankatank, was on the river of the same name in Middle-sex co.

Payankatanks.—Simons in Smith (1629), Va., I, 160, 1819. **Payankatonks.**—Jefferson, Notes, 138, 1801. **Piankatanks.**—Drake, Bk. Inds., bk. 4, 9, 1848.

Piasa (probably cognate with Cree *piyesiw*, referring to an imaginary bird, a name of the thunderbird, and also cognate with the Chippewa *binéssi*, 'a large bird.'—Hewitt). The name given to a prehistoric pictograph formerly on the face of the rocky bluff where Alton, Ill., is now situ-ated. It was first mentioned and described by Marquette, in the account of his journey down the Mississippi in 1673, who, how-ever, speaks of two (Jes. Rel. 1673–75, Thwaites ed., LIX, 139, 1900; Shea, Discov. Miss., 39, 1852): "While skirting some rocks, which by their height and length inspired awe, we saw upon one of them two painted monsters which at first made us afraid, and upon which the boldest savages dare not long rest their eyes. They are as large as a calf; they have horns on their heads like those of deer, a horrible look, red eyes, a beard like a tiger's, a face somewhat like a man's, a body covered with scales, and so long a tail that it winds all around the body, passing above the head and going back between the legs, ending in a fish's tail. Green, red, and black are the three colors

composing the picture." Marquette fur-ther says that the painting was well done. Douay, who visited the locality on his jour-ney from Texas in 1686, considers this de-scription as exaggerated, saying: "This frightful monster is a horse painted on a rock with matachia [an old term for paint] and some other wild beasts made by the Indians" (Shea, Discov. Miss., 223, 1852). He says he reached them without diffi-culty, and adds: "The truth is that Miamis pursued by Mitchigamias having been drowned here the Indians since then offer tobacco to these figures." St Cosme, who journeyed down the Mississippi in 1699, says that the figures were then almost erased (Shea, Early Voy., 66, 1861). In 1836 John Russell published what he claimed to be the Indian "tradition of the Piasa," which is copied by McAdams in his Records of Ancient Races, 1887. The tradition is admitted to be chiefly imaginary, and is substantially the same as that given by Jones (Illinois and the West, 54–56, 1838). McAdams, who had studied the literature and local traditions relating to these figures, states that a figure made in 1825 by a Mr Dennis represented the animal as winged, and adopts this form in his book. The figure as seen by Marquette appears to have been almost precisely of the form and detail of the "medicine animal of the Winnebago" given by Schoolcraft (Ind. Tribes, II, pl. 55, fig. 224, 1852), and hence is probably connected with some myth. The latter author says the figure was drawn for him by Little Hill, a Winne-bago chief, who stated that the animal was seen only by medicine-men. Park-man (Discov. Great West, 59, 1874) says that when he passed the place in 1867 "a part of the rock had been quarried away, and instead of Marquette's mon-ster, it bore a huge advertisement." See also Mallery in 10th Rep. B. A. E., 77–79, 1893; Armstrong, The Piaza, or, the Devil among the Indians, 1887; Bayliss in Rec. of the Past, VII, pt. 2, 1908.   (C. T.)

Piato. Mentioned as a division of the Pima who inhabited the region of Ca-borca and Tubutama, in Sonora, Mexico (Orozco y Berra, Geog., 348, 1864). They were really a branch of the Papago, and probably the same as the Soba.

Piattuiabbe (*Pi-at-tui'-ab-be*). A tribe of the Paviotso, consisting of five bands, near Belmont, s. central Nevada; pop. 249 in 1873.—Powell in Ind. Aff. Rep. 1873, 52, 1874.

Piba. The Tobacco phratry of the Hopi, which comprises the Piba and Chongyo (Pipe) clans. According to Stephen these form part of the Rabbit (Tabo) phratry. The Piba people were strong at Awatobi before its destruction.

Piba.—Bourke, Snake Dance, 117, 1884. **Pi-ba nyû-mû.**—Fewkes in Am. Anthrop., VII, 405, 1894 (*nyúmû*=phratry). **Pieb.**—Fewkes, ibid., VI, 367, 1893.

Piba. The Tobacco clan of the Hopi. **Pi′ba.**—Stephen in 8th Rep. B. A. E., 39, 1891. **Piba wiñwû.**—Fewkes in 19th Rep. B. A. E., 583, 1900 (*wiñwû*=clan). **Pib-wün-wu.**—Fewkes in Am. Anthrop., VII, 405, 1894. **Pip.**—Voth, Oraibi Summer Snake Ceremony, 282, 1903. **Piva.**—Dorsey and Voth, Oraibi Soyal, 12, 1901.

Picachos (Span.: 'peaks'). A Tepehuane pueblo in Jalisco, Mexico.—Orozco y Berra, Geog., 281, 1864.

Pichikwe (*Pi-chi kwe*, 'parrot people'). A clan of the pueblo of Zuñi, N. Mex.; also called Mulakwe, 'Macaw people.'—Cushing in 13th Rep. B. A. E., 368, 1896.

Pickaway anise. An herbalist's name, of Ohio origin, for *Ptelea trifoliata*. For the name, see *Piqua*. (w. r. g.)

Pickawillanee. A village on Miami r., at the site of the present Piqua, Miami co., Ohio, destroyed about 1750. It was occupied by the Miami, who were driven out in 1763 by the tribes adhering to the English interest. The site was afterward occupied by the Shawnee as Piqua Town (q. v.). The Picts, mentioned about that time as a western tribe, are located on old maps in this vicinity. (J. M.) **Pickawillanees.**—Carver, Trav., map, 1778. **Pickawillany.**—Esnauts and Rapilly Map, 1777. **Picts.**—Stobo (1754) quoted by Rupp., W. Penn., app., 295, 1846. **Tawixtwi.**—La Tour Map, 1784 (for Twightwee, a name for the Miami).

Picks. Digging implements of the pick type were in very general use among the

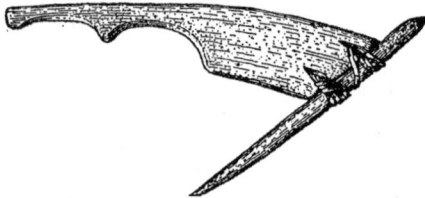

ESKIMO ROOT PICK OF BONE. (NELSON)

aborigines, and native examples are still found among tribes most remote from the influence of the whites. Usually these implements are made of wood, bone, or shell, points of antler and walrus tusks being especially adapted for the purpose. They may well be regarded as in a measure filling the functions of the pick, the hoe, the spade, and, for that matter, the plow of civilized peoples. Stone picks were in somewhat common use in many sections, and numerous examples are preserved in our museums. It appears, however, that their employment was confined largely to mining and quarrying operations where the substances dealt with were too compact to be successfully managed with tools of less durable kind. These stone picks are often rude in shape and are not always readily distinguished from ruder forms of the ax, adz, chisel, and gouge, which served at times, no doubt, a somewhat similar range of functions. The simplest forms were unmodi-

fied fragments of stone of convenient shape, used in the hand or rudely hafted. The most primitive artificial forms were suitable pieces of stone slightly altered by chipping, pecking, and grinding, to make them more effective.

The most important class of stone picks are such as were used in getting out soapstone and rough-shaping the utensils made from it, and in working quarries of mica and iron oxides. These quarry implements

PAINT QUARRY PICK; MISSOURI. (LENGTH, 7¾ IN.)

are of different degrees of elaboration, ranging from the fragment or bowlder brought to a point by a few blows of the hammerstone to neatly shaped forms flaked or pecked and ground over the entire surface. Many are

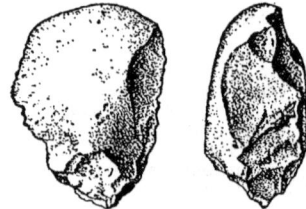

STEATITE QUARRY PICK; DISTRICT OF COLUMBIA

chisel-like and have flat edges, instead of points, and symmetric blades, though often rough at the upper end as if intended to be inserted in a socket. (See *Stonework*.) These could with equal propriety be classed with chisels or even with adzes. In the soapstone quarries are found also many examples of celts, gouges, and grooved axes adapted by various kinds and degrees of remodeling to the work of extracting masses of the stone used in blocking out the vessels.

(w. h. h.)

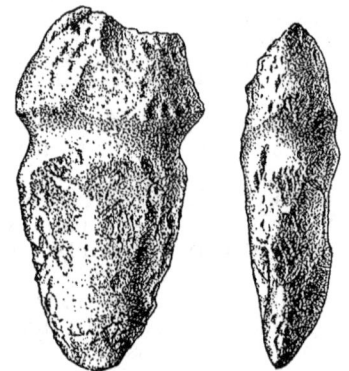

STEATITE QUARRY PICK; MARYLAND

Picolata. Originally a Timucua, later a Seminole, town, on the E. bank of St Johns r., w. of St Augustine, Fla.—H. R. Doc. 78, 25th Cong., 2d sess., map, 768–69, 1838.

Picquemyan. An Algonquian tribe living on lower St Lawrence r., Canada, in 1534.—Cartier (1536), Bref Récit, 40, 1866.

Pic River. A Chippewa settlement at the mouth of Pic r., on the N. shore of L. Superior, Ontario, occupied in 1884 by 245 and in 1906 by 210 Indians.

Pictographs. Pictography may be defined as that form of thought-writing which seeks to convey ideas by means of picture-signs or marks more or less suggestive or imitative of the object or idea in mind. Significance, therefore, is an essential element of pictographs, which are alike in that they all express thought, register a fact, or convey a message. Pictographs, on the one hand, are more or less closely connected with sign language (q. v.), by which they may have been preceded in point of time. Some, indeed, see in pictography a later stage of gesture speech, but the evidences assumed to be indicative of such genetic connection fall far short of proof, and it is believed that pictography may have had a more or less independent origin and career. Pictographs, on the other hand, are closely connected with every varying form of script and print, past and present, the latter being, in fact, derived directly or indirectly from them.

Although the earliest use of picture-signs is shrouded in the mists of antiquity, and although they have been employed by all uncivilized peoples, it is chiefly to the American Indian we must look for a comprehensive knowledge of their use and purpose, since among them alone were both pictographs and sign language found in full and significant employ.

Pictographs have been made upon a great variety of objects, a favorite being the human body. Among other natural substances, recourse by the pictographer has been had to stone, bone, skins, feathers and quills, gourds, shells, earth and sand, copper, and wood, while textile and fictile fabrics figure prominently in the list.

The tools by which and materials of which pictographs have been made are almost as various as the objects upon which they have been found. For carving upon hard substances, including cutting, pecking, scratching, and rubbing, a piece of hard pointed stone, frequently perhaps an arrowpoint, was an effective tool. For carving bone and ivory the Eskimo had learned to use the bow-drill. For incising bark and similar substances a pointed bone was employed. A piece of charcoal, or more often a bit of red ocher, served for drawing. Dyes of various shades of brown, red, and yellow, which were extracted from plants, were available for painting. The Zuñi and Navaho employed corn-meal for ceremonial marking of their bodies, and for their famous dry-paintings (q. v.) used sand, ashes, and powdered mineral and vegetal substances of various hues.

For the Indian skilled in sign language it was natural and easy to fix signs upon bark, skin, or rock, but the evolution of pictographs into sound signs or a true phonetic alphabet must have been very slow, and its accomplishment was limited to a few peoples who already were pressing upon the confines of, if they had not entered, the civilized state. On this continent, so far as known, this stage of thought writing had been reached only by the Aztec and Maya, who in this, as in some other directions, had far outstripped other tribes. Had the coming of the Spaniard been delayed a few centuries it is probable that he would have found these peoples in possession of a written sound language.

In the earlier stages of picture-writing, when the savage artist sought to record facts and ideas, his picture signs assumed a literal form and, so far as his limited skill sufficed, natural and artificial objects were portrayed realistically. Neither in modeling nor sculpture, however, was the skill of the Indian artist sufficient for the accurate delineation of animate or inanimate objects, nor was such accuracy essential to his purpose; hence, when attempting the specific portrayal of animals, his end was attained chiefly by emphasizing prominent and unmistakable features, a method which soon

ANCIENT PUEBLO PICTOGRAPHS, DRAWN IN COLOR ON ROCK SURFACE; ARIZONA. (MINDELEFF)

led to the elimination of everything but essentials.

From the earliest form of picture-writing, the imitative, the Indian had progressed so far as to frame his conceptions ideographically, and even to express abstract ideas. Later, as skill was acquired, his figures became more and more conventionalized till in many cases all semblance of the original was lost, and the ideograph became a mere symbol. While the great body of Indian glyphs remained pure ideographs, symbols were by no means uncommonly employed, especially to express religious subjects, and a rich color symbolism likewise was developed, notably in the S. W.

Among the Indians of the United States the use of pictographic signs reached highest development among the Kiowa and the Dakota tribes in their so-called calendars. These calendars are painted on deer, antelope, and buffalo hides, and constituted a chronology of past years. The Dakota calendars have a picture for each year, or rather for each winter, while that of the Kiowa has a summer symbol and a winter symbol, with a picture or device representing some noteworthy event. The origin of the calendar, or "winter count," dates back probably only a few generations, and while the method of transcription is purely aboriginal it is to be inferred that contact with the whites had stimulated the inventive powers of the Indian in this direction without prescribing

DAKOTA PICTOGRAPH; DRAWN IN COLOR ON PAPER. (MALLERY)

its form, just as Sequoya was stimulated to the invention of the Cherokee syllabary by the observed use of writing. (In addition to Mallory, consult Mooney in 17th and 19th Reports B. A. E., and see *Sequoya*.)

Tattooing (q. v.) is a form of picture-writing more widespread than any other and perhaps more commonly practised. Originating in very ancient times, it persists to-day among certain classes of civilized peoples. Besides the permanent

incised, or painted; occasionally they are rendered both permanent and conspicuous by being first incised and then painted. They appear on sea-worn bowlders, on glacier-polished rocks, on canyon cliffs, and within caves. Mallery states that petroglyphs of the incised form are more common in the N., while colored ones are more numerous in the S., and that petroglyphs of any kind are less common in the central part of the United States. The general absence in the interior of suitable media upon which to inscribe glyphs doubtless explains their general absence there, but the significance of the former facts of distribution is not apparent.

Our present knowledge of Indian petroglyphs does not justify the belief that they record events of great importance, and it would seem that the oft-expressed belief that a mine of information respecting the customs, origin, and migrations of ancient peoples is locked up in these generally indecipherable symbols must be abandoned. In the above connection it is of interest to note that similar and sometimes identical pictographic symbols ap-

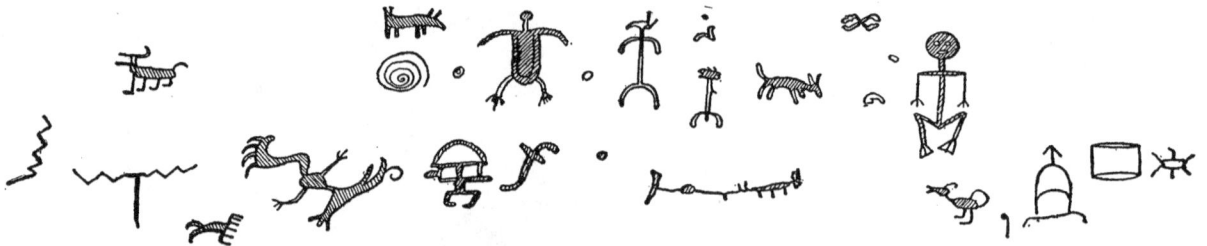

PETROGLYPHS INCISED ON ROCK SURFACE; NEW MEXICO. (MALLERY)

marking of the body by means of coloring matter introduced under the skin, tattooing includes scarification and body painting. Whether the practice of tattoo had its origin in a desire for personal adornment or, as concluded by Spencer and others, as a means of tribal marks, its final purposes and significance among our Indians were found by Mallery to be various and to include the following: Tribal, clan, and family marks; to distinguish between free and slave, high and low; as certificates of bravery in passing prescribed ordeals or in war; as religious symbols; as a therapeutic remedy or a prophylactic; as a certificate of marriage in the case of women, or of marriageable condition; as a personal mark, in distinction to a tribal mark; as a charm; to inspire fear in an enemy; to render the skin impervious to weapons; to bring good fortune, and as the design of a secret society.

The form of picture-writing known as the petroglyph is of world-wide distribution and is common over most of North America. Petroglyphs may be pecked or

pear in widely remote parts of the world, and Mallery notes that the pictographs of Central and South America show remarkable resemblances to some from New Mexico, Arizona, and California. Bearing in mind the racial identity, similar culture status, and, in a general way, the similar environment of their makers, such resemblances, and even identities, in pictographic representation are in no wise surprising. Even were it possible to establish for these similar and widely separated symbols a common significance, which is not the case, such facts are best interpreted as coincident, and as closely analogous to the occurrence of identical words in unrelated languages. Upon this head Col. Mallery pertinently remarks that in attempts to prove relationship identity of symbols is of less importance than general similarity of design and workmanship. His further statement, conservative though it be, that by the latter criteria it is possible, to a limited extent, to infer migrations and priscan habitat is less convincing. It is thought that criteria like these should be employed with great caution, and that in such studies their chief value must ever be as aids in connection with other and corroborative evidence.

When interrogated, modern Indians often disclaim knowledge of or interest in the origin and significance of the petroglyphs, and often explain them as the work of supernatural beings, which explanation in the minds of many invests them with still deeper mystery. Beyond the fact that by habits of thought and training the Indian may be presumed to be in closer touch with the glyph maker than the more civilized investigator, the Indian is no better qualified to interpret petroglyphs than the latter, and in many respects, indeed, is far less qualified, even though the rock pictures may have been made by his forbears.

That, as a rule, petroglyphs are not mere idle scrawls made to gratify a fleeting whim, or pass an idle moment, is probably true, although sometimes they are made by children in play or as a pastime. Nevertheless their significance is more often local than general; they pertain to the individual rather than to the nation, and they record personal achievements and happenings more frequently than tribal histories; petroglyphs, too, are known often to be the records of the visits of individuals to certain places, signposts to indicate the presence of water or the direction of a trail, to give warning or to convey a message. However important such records may have seemed at the time, viewed historically they are of trivial import and, for the greater part, their interest perished with their originators. Many of them, however especially in s. w. United States, are known on the authority of their makers to possess a deeper significance, and to be connected with myths, rituals, and religious practices.

Whatever the subjects recorded by Indian glyphs, whether more or less important, the picture signs and their symbolism were rarely part of a general system, unless perhaps among the Aztec and the Maya, but are of individual origin, are obscured by conventionalism, and require for their interpretation a knowledge of their makers and of the customs and events of the times, which usually are wanting.

From the above appears the futility of serious attempts to interpret, without extraneous aid, the rock writings of ancient man, since in most cases it is almost certain that only the writer and his intimate compeers possessed the key.

While pictographs in general have not yielded the rich fund of information of past peoples and times expected by students, and while the historic import and value of many of them are slight or al-together wanting, their study is important. These pictures on skin, bark, and stone, crude in execution as they often are, yet represent the first artistic records of ancient, though probably not of primitive, man. In them lies the germ of achievement which time and effort have developed into the masterpieces of modern eras. Nor is the study of pictographs less important as affording a glimpse into the psychological workings of the mind of early man in his struggles upward.

See memoirs by Mallery in 4th and 10th Reps. B. A. E., from which much of the above is taken.   (H. W. H.)

Pictou. A Micmac village or band at the northern end of Nova Scotia in 1760.—Frye (1760) in Mass. Hist. Soc. Coll., 1st s., x, 116, 1809.

Picuris (from *Pikuria*, its Keresan name). A Tigua pueblo about 40 m. N. of Santa Fé, N. Mex., identified by Bandelier with the Acha of the chroniclers of Coronado's expedition in 1540–42. It early became the seat of the Franciscan mission of San Lorenzo and was said to have contained 3,000 inhabitants in 1680, when, in the Pueblo revolt of that year, the natives killed their missionary, burned the church, and abandoned the pueblo, but it was rebuilt near its former site in or soon after 1692. In 1704 the Picuris people, on account of some superstition, again deserted their pueblo and fled to Quartelejo (q. v.), a Jicarilla settlement 350 leagues N. E. of Santa Fé, but were induced to return 2 years later. On this account and by reason of their proximity to the Jicarillas in later times, the Picuris tribe has a considerable infusion of Apache blood. Pop. 125 in 1900, 101 in 1904. Consult Bandelier in Arch. Inst. Papers, v, 182–83, 1890. See *Khahitan, Pueblos, Tigua.*   (F. W. H.)

Acha.—Castañeda (1596) in Ternaux-Compans, Voy., IX, 168, 1838. **Pecari.**—Hervas (*ca.* 1800) quoted by Prichard, Phys. Hist. Man., v, 341, 1847. **Pecora.**—Calhoun in Cal. Mess. and Corresp., 215, 1850. **Pecucio.**—Pike, Exped., 2d map, 1810. **Pecucis.**—Ibid., 3d map. **Pecuri.**—MS. of 1683 quoted by Bandelier in Arch. Inst. Papers, III, 88, 1890. **Pecuries.**—Vetancurt (*ca.* 1693) in Teatro Mex., III, 300, 1871. **Pecuris.**—Humboldt, Atlas Nouv.-Espagne, carte 1, 1811. **Pe″kwilitâ′.**—Hodge, field notes, B. A. E., 1895 (Jemez and Pecos name). **Picaris.**—Simpson, Exped. to Navajo Country, 2d map, 1850.. **Piccuries.**—Ladd, Story of N. Mex., 201, 1891. **Picoris.**—Calhoun in Cal. Mess. and Corresp., 211, 1850. **Pictoris.**—Curtis, Children of the Sun, 121, 1883. **Picuni.**—Powell in Am. Nat., XIV, 605, Aug. 1880. **Picuri.**—Bancroft, Ariz. and N. Mex., 176, map, 1889. **Picuria.**—Ind. Aff. Rep., 506, 1889. **Picuries.**—Oñate (1598) in Doc. Inéd., XVI, 109, 257, 1871. **Picux.**—Hinton, Handbook to Ariz., map, 1878. **Pikuri′a.**—Hodge, field notes, B. A. E., 1895 (Keresan name). **Ping-gwi′.**—Ibid. ('gateway of the mountains': Tewa name). **Ping-ul-tha.**—Bandelier in Arch. Inst. Papers, III, 123, 260, 1890 (aboriginal name; see *Ualana*). **Pinuéltâ.**—Hodge, field notes, B. A. E., 1895 (own name). **Sam-nâ′i.**—Ibid. (another Isleta name). **Samnán.**—Ibid. (Sandia name). **San Lorenzo de los Pecuries.**—Vetancurt (*ca.* 1693) in Teatro Mex., 318,

1871 (mission name). **San Lorenzo de Pecuries.**—Ward in Ind. Aff. Rep. 1867, 213, 1868. **San Lorenzo de Picuries.**—Alencaster (1805) quoted by Prince, New Mexico, 37, 1883. **Sant Buenaventura.**—Oñate (1598) in Doc. Inéd., XVI, 257, 1871 (first saint name applied). **S. Lorenzo.**—Bancroft, Ariz. and N. Mex., 281, 1889. **S. Lorenzo de los Picuries.**—Bowles, Map America, 17..? **S. Lorenzo de Picuries.**—Jefferys, Am. Atlas, map 5, 1776. **S͏͆ Laurence.**—Kitchin, Map N. A., 1787. **Ticori.**—Gatschet in Mag. Am. Hist., 259, Apr. 1882 (misprint). **Tók'elé.**—Hodge, field notes, B. A. E., 1895 (Jicarilla name). **Ualana.**—Bandelier in Arch. Inst. Papers, III, 123, 260, 1890 (aboriginal name; see *Ping-ul-tha*, above). **Vicuris.**—Lane in Schoolcraft, Ind. Tribes, V, 689, 1855. **We-la-tah.**—Jouvenceau in Cath. Pion., I, no. 9, 12, 1906 (own name). **Wílana.**—Hodge, field notes, B. A. E., 1899 (Taos name).

Piechar. A village or tribe mentioned by Joutel as being N. or N. W. of the Maligne (Colorado) r., Texas, in 1687. The name seems to have been furnished to Joutel by Ebahamo Indians, who were probably affiliated with the Karankawa. The locality was occupied chiefly by Caddoan tribes. (A. C. F.)
Pechir.—Joutel (1687) in Margry, Déc., III, 289, 1878. **Pichar.**—Joutel (1687) in French, Hist. Coll. La., I, 137, 1846. **Pichares.**—Barcia, Ensayo, 271, 1723. **Pickar.**—Joutel (1687) in French, op. cit., 152. **Piechar.**—Joutel (1687) in Margry, op. cit., 288.

Piedras Blancas (Span. 'white stones'). An unidentified tribe, named in 1693 by Gregorio Salinas (Velasco, Nov. 30, 1716, in Mem. de Nueva España, XXVII, 185, MS.) among those seen by him in Texas or Mexico on the way from the Hasinai to Coahuila. They were in Coahuiltecan territory, and perhaps belonged to that group. (H. E. B.)

Piegan (*Pikuni*, referring to people having badly dressed robes). One of the 3

WHITE CALF, A PIEGAN MAN

tribes of the Siksika (q. v.) or Blackfoot confederacy. Its divisions, as given by

Grinnell, are : Ahahpitape, Ahkaiyiko-kakiniks, Kiyis, Sikutsipumaiks, Sikopoksimaiks, Tsiniksistsoyiks, Kutaiimiks, Ipoksimaiks, Sikokitsimiks, Nitawyiks,

NATÚKA (TWO MEDICINE), A PIEGAN WOMAN

Apikaiyiks, Miahwahpitsiks, Nitakoskitsipupiks, Nitikskiks, Inuksiks, Miawkinaiyiks, Esksinaitupiks, Inuksikahkopwaiks, Kahmitaiks, Kutaisotsiman, Nitotsiksisstaniks, Motwainaiks, Mokumiks, and Motahtosiks. Hayden (Ethnog. and Philol. Mo. Val., 264, 1862) gives also Susksoyiks.

In 1858 the Piegan in the United States were estimated to number 3,700. Hayden 3 years later estimated the population at 2,520. In 1906 there were 2,072 under the Blackfeet agency in Montana, and 493 under the Piegan agency in Alberta, Canada.

Muddy River Indians.—Franklin, Journ. to Polar Sea, 97, 1824. **Paegan.**—Umfreville (1790) in Me. Hist. Soc. Coll., VI, 270, 1859. **Pa-e-guns.**—Prichard, Phys. Hist. Mankind, 414, 1847. **Pagans.**—Ind. Aff. Rep., 593, 1837. **Paygans.**—Kane, Wanderings in N. A., 366, 1859. **Peagan.**—Henry, MS. vocab., Bell copy, B. A. E., 1812. **Peagin.**—Robinson, Great Fur Land, 195, 1879. **Peaginou.**—Ibid., 188. **Pe-ah-cun-nay.**—Crow MS. vocab., B. A. E. (Crow name). **Pecaneaux.** — Schoolcraft, Ind. Tribes, V, 179, 1855. **Pedgans.**—Ind. Aff. Rep., 292, 1846. **Peegans.**—Proc. Brit. A. A. S., Sept. 1885, 2 (pronunciation). **Pegan.**—De Smet, Oregon Miss., 326, 1847. **Peganes.**—Domenech, Deserts, I, 443, 1860. **Pe-gan-o.**—Warren (1852) in Minn. Hist. Soc. Coll., V, 34, 1885 (Chippewa name). **Peganœ'-koon.**—Franklin, Journ. Polar Sea, 97, 1824 (form used by themselves). **Peganoo-eythinyoowuc.**—Ibid. **Peigans.**—Keane in Stanford, Compend., 531, 1878. **Pe-kan-ne.**—Morgan, Consang. and Affin., 240, 1871. **Pekanne-koon.**—Alex. Henry, MS., 1808. **Picaneaux.**—Mackenzie, Voy., lxvii, 1802. **Picaneux.**—Hayden, Ethnog. and Philol. Mo. Val., 256, 1862. **Pickan.**—Gallatin in Trans. Am. Ethnol. Soc., II, 21, 1848. **Piedgans.**—Culbertson in Smithson. Rep. 1850, 144, 1851. **Pië-**

gan.—Maximilian, Trav., 508, 1843. **Piekané.**—Proc. Brit. A. A. S., Sept. 1885, 2. **Piekann.**—Maximilian, Trav., 227, 1843. **Pigans.**—Duflot de Mofras, Explor., II, 342, 1844. **Pikani.**—Wilkes, U. S. Expl. Exped., IV, 471, 1845. **Pikun'-i.**—Hayden, Ethnog. and Philol. Mo. Val., 256, 1862. **Pilgans.**—Wilkes, U. S. Expl. Exped., IV, 471, 1845 (misprint). **Teagans.**—Ind. Aff. Rep., 473, 1838 (misprint).

Piekouagami (a form seemingly cognate with the Cree *Piyakwagami* and with *Pakwagami*, the Algonkin name of the Montagnais, the elements of which are *påkkwa* 'shallow (water),' 'flat,' and *-gami* 'lake,' 'expanse of water,' the two elements together signifying 'flat lake.' The so-called vocalic change transforms *påkkwa* into *piyakkwa*, which with *-gami* forms *Piyakkwagami*, or, as sometimes written, *Piakwagami*, originally the name given to L. St John, Canada, by the Kakouchaki, or Porcupine tribe. From the Jesuit Relation for 1672 (44, 1858) it is learned that the country around L. St John was beautiful, and the soil was good and land abounded in otter, elk, beaver, and especially in porcupines. For this reason the people who dwelt on the shores of this lake received the name Kâkouchac (*Kâkkasewok*, 'porcupines,' not from *kâkwa*, 'porcupine,' but rather from a term which is the source of both, namely, *kâkk*, 'rude, rough, or harsh to the touch'; whence, *Kâkkasewok*, 'they have skin harsh to the touch').

According to the Jesuit Relation for 1641 (57, 1858), the Kakouchaki, or Porcupine people, were one of a number of inland tribes which, having heard the gospel in their own countries, were expected to remove to the residence of St Joseph at Sillery, although the fear of the Iroquois, the common enemy of all these tribes, was a great obstacle to the contemplated removal and consolidation of small tribes. The Porcupines were reputed good, docile, and quite easily won to the Christian faith.

From the Jesuit Relation for 1672 (44, 1858), it appears that at that early time (1641–72) L. St John was a trading center for all the tribes dwelling between Hudson bay and St Lawrence r.; that more than 20 tribes had been seen at this place; that the Porcupines were greatly reduced in numbers by their recent wars with the Iroquois and by smallpox; but that since the general peace of 1666 the population had increased by small additions from other tribes arriving there from various places.

The Jesuit Relation for 1647 (65, 1858), in describing the lake, says: "It is surrounded by a flat country ending in high mountains distant from 3, 4, or 5 leagues from its banks; it is fed by about 15 rivers, which serve as highways to the small tribes which are inland to come to fish therein and to maintain the trade and friendship which exist among them.

. . . . We rowed for some time on this lake, and finally we arrived at the place where the Indians of the 'nation of the Porcupine' were." This would indicate that the dwelling-place of the Kakouchaki, or Porcupine people, was some distance from the outlet of the lake. (J. N. B. H.)

Nation du Porc-Epic.—Jes. Rel. 1641, 57, 1858. **Peikuagamiu.**—Arnaud (1880) quoted by Rouillard, Noms Géog., 83, 1906. **Peok8agamy.**—Crespieul (1700) quoted, ibid. **Peyakwagami.**—Laflèche quoted, ibid. (Cree name). **Piagouagami.**—Jes. Rel. 1652, 16, 1858. **Piakouakamy.**—Normandin (1732) quoted, ibid. **Piakuakamits.**—Lemoine (1901) quoted, ibid. **Pichouagamis.**—Toussaint, Map of Am., 1839. **Pickovagam.**—Alcedo, Dic. Geog., IV, 205, 1788. **Piekouagamiens.**—Jefferys, Fr. Doms., pt. I, 18, 1761. **Piekouagamis.**—La Tour, Map, 1779. **Piekovagamiens.**—Esnauts and Rapilly, Map, 1777. **Pikogami.**—Homann Heirs' Map, 1784. **Pockaguma.**—Schoolcraft (1838) in H. R. Doc. 107, 25th Cong., 3d sess., 9, 1839.

Pierced tablets. A numerous and widely distributed class of prehistoric objects of problematical significance and use. The typical forms are flat, oblong tablets of stone, and more rarely of copper, shell, and bone. They are often rectangular in outline, but the margin is

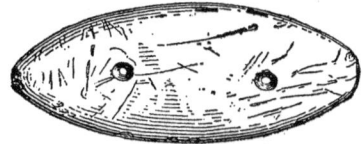

BANDED SLATE; MICHIGAN (¼)

modified in many ways, and sometimes shows ornamental notchings, and, occasionally, rude ornamental or symbolic designs are engraved on the flat surfaces.

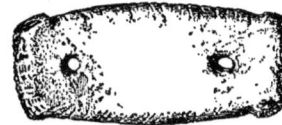

STEATITE; NORTH CAROLINA

The ends of the tablets are in cases pointed or rounded, and again they expand like ax blades or the spread wings of a bird. Rarely the outline of the tablet assumes the shape of a bird; these forms approach the banner stones (q. v.). Others are convex on one face and flat or concave on the other, suggesting relationship with the boat-stones (q. v.). Generally there are two perforations, occasionally one, and in a few cases three or even more. Those having

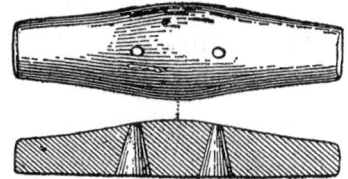

BANDED SLATE; OHIO (¼)

one perforation placed near one end are often somewhat celt shaped, but being thin and fragile may be classed as pendants; they seem to be allied to the spade stones (q. v.). Those with two or more holes were probably fixed to some part of the costume, or to some article of ceremony. The holes are usually countersunk from both sides of the plate, and often show decided effects of wear by cords of suspension or attachment. Many of these objects are made of slate. Their distribution is general, and their use must have extended at one time or another to most of the tribes E. of the plains, and well northward into Canada. They average only a few inches in length, but the largest are as much as 14 in. long. See *Problematical objects.*

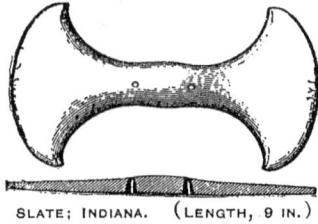

SLATE; INDIANA. (LENGTH, 9 IN.)

Consult Abbott, (1) Prim. Indus., 1881, (2) in Smithson. Rep. 1875, 1876; Fowke, (1) Archæol. Hist. Ohio, 1902, (2) in 13th Rep. B. A. E., 1896; Jones, Antiq. So. Inds., 1873; Mercer, Lenape Stone, 1885; Moorehead, Prehist. Impls., 1900; Rau (1) in Smithson. Rep. 1872, 1873, (2) in Smithson. Cont. Knowl., XXII, 1876; Read and Whittlesey in Ohio Centennial Rep., 1877; Squier and Davis, Ancient Monuments, Smithson. Cont., I, 1848; Thruston, Antiq. of Tenn., 1897; Ward in Bull. Wis. Nat. Hist. Soc., IV, 1906. (W. H. H.)

Pierrish. A former Potawatomi village, commonly known as Pierrish's Village, on the N. bank of Eel r., just above Laketon, Wabash co., Ind. It took its name from a resident French half-breed interpreter, Pierrish Constant, known to the Miami as Pahtash, 'Miring Down' (J. P. Dunn, inf'n, 1907).

Pierishe's Village.—Royce in 18th Rep. B. A. E., Indiana map, 1899.

Pierruiats (*Pi-er-ru-i-ats*). One of the tribes known under the collective term Gosiutes, living at Deep cr., s. w. Utah, in 1873.—Powell and Ingalls in Ind. Aff. Rep. 1873, 51, 1874.

Pieskaret. The Algonkin name, often written Piskaret, of a noted Algonkin (Adirondack) chief, who lived on the N. bank of the St Lawrence, below Montreal, Canada, in the first half of the 17th century. According to Schoolcraft (W. Scenes and Remin., 87, 1853) the dialectic form in his own tribe was Bisconace ('Little Blaze'). Although he became noted by reason of his daring, comparatively few incidents of his life have been recorded. Charlevoix (New France, II, 181, 1866) says he was "one of the bravest men ever seen in Canada, and almost incredible stories are told of his prowess." His most noted exploit occurred during an excursion into the Iroquois country with but four followers, well armed with guns, when they encountered on Sorel r., in five boats, a band of 50 Iroquois, most of whom they killed or captured. On another occasion Pieskaret ventured alone within the Iroquois domain, and coming to one of their villages, by secreting himself during the day succeeded in killing and scalping the

members of a household each night for three successive nights. He was ultimately brought under the influence of Catholic missionaries and in 1641 was baptized under the name Simon, after which he was commonly known among the whites as Simon Pieskaret. After his acceptance of Christianity so much confidence was placed in his prudence and ability that he was commissioned to maintain peace between the French and the Indians, as well as between the Hurons and Algonkin; he was authorized to punish delinquents, "and especially those who committed any fault against religion. It is wonderful how he discharged his office." (Jes. Rel. 1647, XXXI, 287, 1898.) He was present and made a speech at the conference between the French governor and the Iroquois and other tribes at Three Rivers, Canada, in 1645. Two years later, while a large body of Iroquois were going on a pretended visit to the governor, some of their scouts met Pieskaret near Nicolet r., and treacherously killed him while off his guard. (C. T.)

Pigeon Town. One of the former villages of the Mequachake or Spitotha division of the Shawnee, situated on Mad r., 3 m. N. w. of West Liberty, Logan co., Ohio. This and the others were destroyed by Gen. Benj. Logan in 1786. See Howe, Hist. Coll. Ohio, II, 98, 1896; Royce in 18th Rep. B. A. E., Ohio map, 1899.

Pigment plates. See *Notched plates.*

Pigments. See *Dyes and Pigments.*

Pigmies. See *Popular fallacies.*

Piguique. A tribe or subtribe, mentioned by Fray Bartholomé García (1760), under the name of Pihuiques, as one whose young people understood the language of his Manual, i. e. Coahuiltecan. They lived near the Texas coast, between Nueces and San Antonio rs., and were closely related to the Pamaques, of which tribe they seem sometimes to have been regarded as a subdivision. García's statement suggests a recent attachment of the Piguique to the Pamaque. In 1766 part of them were reported as living on the Isla de Culebras with the Copane and Karankawa tribes. This fact, taken with García's statement, might indicate that they were of Karankawan stock, but had recently mingled much with the Coahuiltecans and had learned their language. Previous to 1766 the Piguique had suffered greatly from measles and smallpox (Diligencias Practicadas por Diego Orttiz Parrilla, 1766, MS.). Their history, so far as it is known, is the same as that of the Pamaque (q. v.), unless the Piguicanes are the same. Some of the Piguicanes entered Espíritu Santo de Zúñiga mission, which does not seem to be true

of the Pamaque (Solís, Diario, 1767–68, MS.).　　　　(H. E. B.)
Piguicanes.—Solís, op. cit. (identical?). **Pihniques.**—Taylor in Cal. Farmer, Apr. 17, 1863 (misprint). **Pihuiques.**—García, op. cit., 1760.

Pihcha. The Skunk clan of the Chua (Snake) phratry of the Hopi.
Pi'h-tca.—Stephen in 8th Rep. B. A. E., 38, 1891.

Pihkash. The Young Corn Ear clan of the Hopi.
Píhkash.—Dorsey and Voth, Mishongnovi Ceremonies, 175, 1902.

Piiru. A former Chumashan village on Piru cr. or arroyo emptying into Saticoy r., Ventura co., Cal.—Taylor in Cal. Farmer, July 24, 1863.

Pikakwanarats (*Pi-ka-kwa'-na-rats*). A division of the Ute, of whom 32 were found in 1873 on the Uinta res., Utah, where they were known under the general name of Uinta Ute.—Powell in Ind. Aff. Rep. 1873, 51, 1874.

Pikalps. A former village of the Semiahmoo Salish at Camp Semiahmoo, on Semiahmoo bay, N. W. Wash.—Gibbs, Clallam and Lummi, 37, 1863.

Pikiiltthe (*Pĭ'-ki-ĭl'-t'çĕ*). A former Yaquina village on the s. side of Yaquina r., Oreg.—Dorsey in Jour. Am. Folk-lore, III, 229, 1890.

Pikirlu. An Ita Eskimo winter village on Foulke fjord, N. Greenland.—Markham in Trans. Ethnol. Soc. Lond., 126, 1866.

Pikiulak. A winter and spring settlement of the Aivilirmiut Eskimo on Depot id., N. E. of Chesterfield inlet, Hudson bay.
Pikiulaq.—Boas in 6th Rep. B. A. E., map, 1888.

Pikiutdlek. A southern settlement of the Angmagsalingmiut Eskimo in E. Greenland, who there seek stone for making lamps and vessels.
Pikiudtlek.—Nansen, First Crossing, I, 250, 1890. **Pikiutdlek.**—Meddelelser om Grönland, X, 369, 1888.

Pikmiktaligmiut. A subdivision of the Unaligmiut Eskimo of Alaska, whose village is Pikmiktalik.
Pikmikta'lig-mūt.—Dall in Cont. N. A. Ethnol., I, 17, 1877.

Pikmiktalik. An Unaligmiut Eskimo village near the mouth of Pikmiktalik r., Alaska, just N. of C. Romanoff; pop. 10 in 1880.
Pichmichtalik.—Holmberg, Ethnog. Skizz., map, 1855. **Pietmiektaligmiut.**—Baker, Geog. Dict. Alaska, 1902 (Russian spelling). **Pikmigtalik.**—Whymper, Alaska, 269, 1869. **Pikmiktal'ik.**—Dall in Cont. N. A. Ethnol., I, 17, 1877.

Pikta. A coast village of the Kinugumiut Eskimo near C. Prince of Wales, Alaska.
Pikhta.—Zagoskin in Nouv. Ann. Voy., 5th s., XXI, map, 1850.

Pikyaiawan (Zuñi: *Pi-k'yai-a-wan*, 'town of the water-cresses'). An ancient pueblo which, with Kyatsutuma, was the northernmost home of the Snail people and one of the outposts or strongholds of Matyata (q. v.) that were conquered by the Zuñi in prehistoric times. See *Kyamakyakwe.*　　　(F. H. C.)

Pilaklikaha. A former Seminole town in the E. part of Sumter co., Fla., near Dade's battle ground of Dec. 28, 1835. A town of the same name is shown on Taylor's war map of 1839. It was burned by the U. S. troops in 1836. Here chief Micanopy lived, and the town was often called by his name, from the Creek *miko*, 'chief'; *unapa*, 'above'. Ft Defiance was established here. There is a Micanopy town now in Alachua co., Fla., 12 m. s. of Gainesville.　　　(H. W. H.)
Inicanopa.—Belton (1836) in Drake, Bk. Inds., bk. 4, 77, 1848 (misprint of Micanopa). **Inocanopy.**—Drake, Ind. Chron., 206, 1836. **Micanopy.**—Call (1835) in Sen. Doc. 278, 26th Cong., 1st sess., 30, 1840. **Micanopy's town.**—Drake, Bk. Inds. bk. 4, 76, 1848. **Miconopy.**—H. R. Doc. 78, 25th Cong., 2d sess., map, 768–69, 1838. **Pe-lac-le-ka-ha.**—Bell in Morse, Rep. to Sec. War, 307, 1822. **Pelaklekaha.**—Scott's map in H. R. Doc. 78, 25th Cong., 2d sess., 408–09, 1838. **Pelaklikhaha.**—Gadsden (1836), ibid., 399. **Pilaklikaha.**—Drake, Bk. Inds., bk. 4, 92, 1848. **Pinclatchas.**—Swan (1791) in Schoolcraft, Ind. Tribes, V, 262, 1855. **Pyaklékaha.**—Penière quoted by Morse, Rep. to Sec. War, 311, 1822.

Pilalt. A Cowichan tribe on lower Chilliwack r. and part of Fraser r., Brit. Col. According to Hill-Tout they numbered 25 in 1902. Their villages were Chutil, Kwalewia, Skelautuk, Skwala, and Schachuhil. Boas adds Cheam, but if he is right that town must contain several tribes.
Pallalts.—Mayne, Brit. Col., 295, 1862. **PElā'tlQ.**—Boas in Rep. 64th Meeting B. A. A. S., 454, 1894. **Pilalt.**—Tolmie and Dawson, Vocabs. Brit. Col., 120B, 1884. **Pila'tlq.**—Hill-Tout in Ethnol. Surv. Can., 48, 1902.

Pilatka ('going into the water'). A former town, probably Seminole, on the w. bank of St Johns r., Fla., N. w. of Drums (now Crescent) lake, on or near the site of the present Palatka.—H. R. Doc. 78, 25th Cong., 2d sess., map, 768, 1838.

Pilawa (*Pĭ-la-wä'*, 'turkey'). A gens of the Miami.—Morgan, Anc. Soc., 168, 1877.

Pile dwellings. Primitive dwellers along the shallow margins of the sea, on the banks of bayous, tide-water rivers,

SEMINOLE HOUSE, FLORIDA.　(MACCAULEY)

and lands in general subject to inundation found it necessary to raise the floors of their dwellings above the reach of tide and flood. This was done by erecting mounds of earth or shells, or by planting poles or piles in the yielding earth to which floor timbers could be attached at suitable levels. Pile dwellings were observed by early Spanish explorers of the Caribbean sea, and Venezuela ('Little

Venice') received its name from the fact that the native dwellings, like those of Venice, were built in the midst of the waters. Dwellings of this type are still used by natives of the Venezuelan lagoons, and the Indians of Florida, occupying lands subject to overflow, build houses of nearly identical construction. As described by MacCauley, the typical Seminole house is approximately 9x16 ft in horizontal extent and is made partly or wholly of products of the palmetto tree. Eight palmetto piles support the roof, which is strongly framed of poles and thatched with leaves of the same tree, the eaves being about 7 ft and the ridge pole about 12 ft from the ground. The platform is 3 or 4 ft from the ground and is supported by split palmetto logs lying transversely, flat side up, upon beams which extend lengthwise

ESKIMO FISHERMAN'S SUMMER HOUSE, ALASKA. (NELSON)

of the building, and are lashed to the uprights with ropes of palmetto fiber. The thatching of the roof is quite a work of art inside, the regular laying of the leaves displaying much skill and taste on the part of the builder. The sides are open at all seasons of the year. In recent years traces of pile dwellings have been discovered by Cushing on Key Marco, on the gulf coast of Florida, and he was of the opinion that the key dwellers generally built their villages in this manner, digging artificial canals and water courts to accommodate their boats, and erecting mounds and platforms for the more ambitious religious and civic structures. A unique use of timbers in the construction of habitations is observed on the island of St Michael, Alaska, where the Eskimo fishermen have built pile dwellings against the rugged and precipitous cliffs far above

the reach of the waves. Niblack refers to houses raised on high logs or stilts. He states that, "according to Vancouver, amongst the Kwakiutl of Johnstone strait, there were dwellings 'raised and supported near 30 ft. from the ground by perpendicular spars of very large size' with 'access formed by a long tree in an inclined position from the platform to the ground, with notches cut in it by way of steps about a foot and a half asunder.'" According to Boas the Bellacoola also erected pile dwellings. See *Architecture, Cliff-dwellings, Habitations.*

Consult Cushing in Proc. Am. Philos. Soc., 1896; MacCauley in 5th Rep. B.A.E., 1887; Nelson in 18th Rep. B. A. E., 1899; Niblack in Rep. Nat. Mus. 1888, 1890. Vancouver, Voy., 1801.   (w. h. h.)

Pilidquay. A Chumashan village on one of the Santa Barbara ids., Cal., probably Santa Rosa, in 1542.

Peledquey.—Taylor in Cal. Farmer, Apr. 17, 1863. Pilidquay.—Cabrillo, Narr. (1542), in Smith, Colec. Doc. Fla., 186, 1857.

Pilingmiut. A tribe of Eskimo in w. Baffinland, on the N. E. coast of Fox basin. Their village is Piling, whence their name.

Peelig.—Parry, Sec. Voy., 355, 449, 1824 (the village). Piling.—Boas in 6th Rep. B. A. E., 444, 1888 (the village). Pilingmiut.—Ibid. (the tribe).

Pillagers (translation of their own name, *Ma'kŭndwäwĭnĭnĭwŭg,* 'robber people,' so called because at one time they were the most formidable robbing unit of the Chippewa.—W. J.). A division of the Chippewa, formerly living in N. Minnesota on Leech and Ottertail lakes and in the intermediate country. They are now gathered on the reservation at Leech lake, formerly their principal rendezvous, and on White Earth res. They formed the advance guard of the Chippewa in the invasion of the Sioux country, establishing themselves first on Leech lake, and gradually pushing westward from that point. Morse (Rep. to Sec. War, 32, 1822) says these Indians were in bands, each having its own chief. The Pillagers made or joined in treaties with the United States at Leech lake, Minn., Aug. 21, 1847, and at Washington, D. C., Feb. 22, 1855, Mar. 11, 1863, and May 7, 1864. In 1855 they numbered about 1,200, under 7 chiefs. In 1884 they were reported at 1,556. The official census for 1906 makes the number 2,377: 837 Leech Lake and 464 Cass and Winibigoshish Pillagers at Leech lake, and 726 Ottertail, 289 Leech Lake Pillagers, and 61 Cass and Winibigoshish at White Earth.

Chippeways of Leach Lake.—Lewis and Clark, Discov., 28, 1806. Cypowais plunderers.—Beltrami quoted by Neill, Hist. Minn., 372, 1858. Ma'kandwä-wininiwag.—Wm. Jones, inf'n, 1905 (correct form). Makandwewininiwag.—Baraga Otchipwe-Eng. Dict., 207, 1880 (from Makandwéwini, a pillager: Chippewa name). Muk-im-dua-win-in-e-wug.—Warren (1852) in Minn. Hist. Soc. Coll., v, 256, 1885. Mukkundwas.—Schoolcraft, Ind. Tribes, v, 145, 1855.

Muk-me-dua-win-in-e-wug.—Warren (1852) in Minn. Hist. Soc. Coll., v, 39, 1885. **Mukundua.**—Schoolcraft, Ind. Tribes, II, 59, 1852. **Muk-un-dua-win-in-e-wing.**—Ramsey in Ind. Aff. Rep., 88, 1850. **Muk-un-dua-win-in-e-wug.**—Schoolcraft, Ind. Tribes, II, 153, 1852. **Mukundwa.**—Ibid., v, 98, 1855. **Pillagers.**—Fond du Lac treaty (1847) in U. S. Ind. Treat., 221, 1873. **Pilleurs.**—Henry, Trav., 245, 1809. **Pilliers.**—Franklin, Journ. Polar Sea, 56, 1824. **Robbers.**—Ibid. **Rogues.**—Henry, Trav., 245, 1809.

Pilteuk (*Pil-tē'-uk*, 'white earth'). A Shuswap village at Clinton, on a w. affluent of Bonaparte r., a N. tributary of Thompson r., interior of British Columbia; pop. 50 in 1906.
Clinton.—Can. Ind. Aff., pt. II, 162, 1901 (white man's name). **Pil-tē'-uk.**—Dawson in Trans. Roy. Soc. Can., sec. II, 44, 1891.

Pilumas (*Pi'-lŭm-ăs'*). A former Siuslaw village on Siuslaw r., Oreg.—Dorsey in Jour. Am. Folk-lore, III, 230, 1890.

Pima ('no,' in the Nevome dialect, a word incorrectly applied through misunderstanding by the early missionaries.—B. Smith in Shea, Lib. Am. Ling., III, 7, 1861). As popularly known, the name of a division of the Piman family living in the valleys of the Gila and Salt in s. Arizona. Formerly the term was employed to include also the Nevome, or Pimas Bajos, the Pima as now recognized being known as Pimas Altos ('Upper Pima'), and by some also the Papago. These three divisions speak closely related dialects. The Pima call themselves *Â'-ä'tam*, 'the people.'

PIMA MAN

According to tradition the Pima tribe had its genesis in the Salt River valley, later extending its settlements into the valley of the Gila; but a deluge came, leaving a single survivor, a specially favored chief named Cího, or Sóho, the progen-

itor of the present tribe. One of his descendants, Sivano, who had 20 wives, erected as his own residence the now

SAVEITA, A PIMA WOMAN

ruined adobe structure called Casa Grande (called Sivanoki, 'house of Sivano') and built numerous other massive pueblo groups in the valleys of the Gila and Salt. The Sobaipuri, believed to have been a branch of the Papago, attributed these now ruined pueblos, including Casa Grande, to people who had come from the Hopi, or from the N., and recent investigations tend to show that the culture of the former inhabitants, as exemplified by their art remains, was similar in many respects to that of the ancient Pueblos. Sivano's tribe, says tradition, became so populous that emigration was necessary. Under one of the sons of that chief a large body of the Pima settled in Salt River valley, where they increased in population and followed the example of their ancestors of the Gila by constructing extensive irrigation canals and reservoirs and by building large defensive villages of adobe, the remains of which may still be seen.

The Pima attribute their decline to the rapacity of foreign tribes from the E., who came in three bands, destroying their pueblos, devastating their fields, and killing or enslaving many of their inhabitants. Prior to this, however, a part of the tribe seceded from the main body and moved s., settling in the valleys of Altar, Magdalena, and Sonora rs., as well as of adjacent streams, where they became known as Pimas Bajos or Nevome, and

Opata. The others descended from the mountains whence they had fled, resettled the valley of the Salt, and again tilled the soil. They never rebuilt the substantial adobe dwellings, even though needed for defense against the always aggressive Apache; but, humbled by defeat, constructed dome-shaped lodges of pliable poles covered with thatch and mud, and in such habitations have since dwelt. The names applied to the Pima by the Apache and some other tribes furnish evidence that they formerly dwelt in adobe houses. Early in the 19th century the Pima were joined by the Maricopa, of Yuman stock, who left their former home at the mouth of the Gila and on the Colorado owing to constant oppression by the Yuma and Mohave. Although speaking distinct languages the Maricopa and Pima have since dwelt together in harmony. They intermarry, and their general habits and customs are identical.

How much of the present religious belief of the Pima is their own is not known, though it is not improbable that the teachings of Kino and other missionaries in the 17th and 18th centuries influenced more or less their primitive beliefs. They are said to believe in the existence of a supreme being, known as the "Prophet of the Earth," and also in a malevolent deity. They also believe that at death the soul is taken into another world by an owl, hence the hooting of that bird is regarded as ominous of an approaching death. Sickness, misfortune, and death are attributed to sorcery, and, as among other Indians, medicine-men are employed to overcome the evil influence of the sorcerers. Scarification and cauterization are also practised in certain cases of bodily ailment.

Marriage among the Pima is entered into without ceremony and is never considered binding. Husband and wife may separate at pleasure, and either is at liberty to marry again. Formerly, owing to contact with Spaniards and Americans, unchastity prevailed to an inordinate degree among both sexes. Polygamy was only a question of the husband's ability to support more than one wife. The women performed all the labor save the hunting, plowing, and sowing; the husband traveled mounted, while the wife laboriously followed afoot with her child or with a heavily laden burden basket, or *kiho*, which frequently contained the wheat reaped by her own labor to be traded by the husband, often for articles for his personal use or adornment.

The Pima have always been peaceable, though when attacked, as in former times they frequently were by the Apache and others, they have shown themselves by no means deficient in courage. Even with a knowledge of firearms they have only in recent years discarded the bow and arrow, with which they were expert. Arrowpoints of glass, stone, or iron were sometimes employed in warfare. War clubs of mesquite wood also formed an important implement of war; and for defensive purposes an almost impenetrable shield of rawhide was used. The Pima took no scalps. They considered their enemies, particularly the Apache, possessed of evil spirits and did not touch them after death. Apache men were never taken captive; but women, girls, and young boys of that tribe were sometimes made prisoners, while on other occasions all the inhabitants of a besieged Apache camp were killed. Prisoners were rarely cruelly treated; on the contrary they shared the food and clothing of their captors, usually acquired the Pima language, and have been known to marry into the tribe.

Agriculture by the aid of irrigation has been practised by the Pima from prehistoric times. Each community owned an irrigation canal, often several miles in length, the waters of the rivers being diverted into them by means of rude dams; but in recent years they have suffered much from lack of water owing to the rapid settlement of the country by white people. Until the introduction of appliances of civilization they planted with a dibble, and later plowed their fields with crooked sticks drawn by oxen. Grain is threshed by the stamping of horses and is winnowed by the women, who skilfully toss it from flat baskets. Wheat is now their staple crop, and during favorable seasons large quantities are sold to the whites. They also cultivate corn, barley, beans, pumpkins, squashes, melons, onions, and a small supply of inferior short cotton. One of the principal food products of their country is the bean of the mesquite, large quantities of which are gathered annually by the women, pounded in mortars or ground on metates, and preserved for winter use. The fruit of the saguaro cactus (*Cereus giganteus*) is also gathered by the women and made into a sirup; from this an intoxicating beverage was formerly brewed. As among most Indians, tobacco was looked upon by the Pima rather as a sacred plant than one to be used for pleasure. Formerly they raised large herds of cattle in the grassy valleys of the upper Gila. The women are expert makers of water-tight baskets of various shapes and sizes, decorated in geometric designs. They also manufacture coarse pottery, some of which, however, is well decorated. Since contact with the whites their native arts have deteriorated.

The Pima are governed by a head chief, and a chief for each village. These officers are assisted by village councils, which do not appoint representatives to the tribal councils, which are composed of the village chiefs. The office of head-chief is not hereditary, but is elected by the village chiefs. Descent is traced in the male line, and there are five groups that bear some resemblance to gentes, though they exert no influence on marriage laws, nor is marriage within the group, or gens, prohibited (Russell, Pima MS., B. A. E., 313–15, 1903). These five groups are Akol, Maam, Vaaf, Apap, and Apuki. The first three are known as Vultures or Red People, the other two as Coyotes or White People. They are also spoken of respectively as Suwuki Ohimal ('Red Ants') and Stoam Ohimal ('White Ants').

The Pima language is marked by the constant use of radical reduplication for forming the nominal and verbal plural. It is also distinguished by a curious laryngeal pronunciation of its gutturals, which strangers can imitate only with great difficulty.

The Pima within the United States are gathered with Papago and Maricopa on the Gila River and Salt River res. The Pima population was 3,936 in 1906; in 1775 Father Garcés estimated the Pima of the Gila at 2,500. Their subdivisions and settlements have been recorded as follows, those marked with an asterisk being the only ones that are not extinct. Some of the names are possibly duplicated.

Agua Escondida(?), Agua Fria(?), Aquitun, Aranca, Arenal(?), Arivaca(?), Arroyo Grande, Bacuancos, Bisani, *Blackwater, Bonostac, Busanic, Cachanila(?), *Casa Blanca, Cerrito, Cerro Chiquito, Chemisez, Chupatak, *Chutikwuchik, Chuwutukawutuk, Cocospera, Comac, Estancia, Gaibanipitea(?), Gutubur, *Harsanykuk, *Hermho, *Hiatam, Hormiguero(?), Hueso Parado, *Huchiltchik, Imuris, Judac, *Kamatukwucha, Kamit, *Kawoltukwucha, Kikimi, Kookupvansik, Mange, Merced, Nacameri, Napeut, Ocuca, Oquitoa, Ormejea, Oskakumukchochikam, *Oskuk, *Peepchiltk, Pescadero, Petaikuk, Pintados(?), Pitac(?), Potlapiguas, Remedios, *Rsanuk, *Rsotuk, *Sacaton, San Andrés Coata, San Fernando, San Francisco Ati, San Francisco de Pima, San Ignacio, San Serafin, *Santan, Santos Angeles, *Saopuk, Sepori, *Shakaik, *Statannyik, Stukamasoosatick, Sudacson, *Tatsituk, Taumaturgo, Tubuscabors, Tucson(mixed), Tucubavia, Tutuetac(?), Uturituc, *Wechurt. (F. W. H.)

Â'-â'tam.—Russell, Pima MS., B. A. E., 8, 1902 (own name: 'men,' 'the people'). **Â'-â'tam Â'kimûlt.**—Ibid. ('river people'; used to distinguish themselves from the Papago). **A'kémorl-Ôōhtam.**—ten Kate, Reizen, 24, 1885 ('river people': own name). **Aquira-Otam.**—Bandelier in Arch. Inst. Papers, III, 103, 1890 (or Pimas proper).

Arizonian Pimas.—Bandelier, ibid., 54. **Âw-o-tum.**—Grossman, Pima and Papago vocab., B. A. E., 1871 (own name). **Gila Pimas.**—Font (1775) cited by Schoolcraft, Ind. tribes, III, 301, 1853. **Jatapaiña.**—Garcés (1776), Diary, 402, 1900 (Yavapai name). **Narsh-*tiz'*-a.**—White, Apache Names of Ind. Tribes, MS., B. A. E. ('live in mud houses': Apache name). **Nashteíse.**—White, Apache vocab., B. A. E., 1875 (Apache name). **Northern Pimas.**—Bandelier, Gilded Man, 150, 176, 1893 (Ootam, or). **Ohotoma.**—Velarde in Doc. Hist. Mex., 4th s., I, 345, 1856 (own name; pl. form). **Ootam.**—Bandelier, Gilded Man, 150, 176, 1893. **Otama.**—Velarde in Doc. Hist. Mex., 4th s., I, 345, 1856 (own name; sing. form). **Paymas.**—Venegas, Hist. Cal., I, 286, 1759. **Pema.**—U. S. Statutes at Large, II, 401, 1863. **Pemos.**—White, MS. Hist. Apaches, B. A. E., 1875. **Pijmos.**—Gailatin in Trans. Am. Ethnol. Soc., II, lxxxix, 1848. **Pimahaitu.**—18th cent. MS. quoted by B. Smith in Shea, Lib. Am. Ling., III, 7, 1861. **Pimas.**—Kino (1692) in Doc. Hist. Mex., 4th s., I, 226, 1856. **Pimases.**—De l'Isle, Map Am. Sept., 1700. **Pimas Gileños.**—Font (1775) in Ternaux-Compans, Voy., IX, 384, 1838 (=Pima of Gila r.). **Pimas Ileños.**—Hinton, Handbook to Ariz., map, 1878. **Pime.**—Hervas, Idea dell' Universo, XVII, 75, 1784. **Pimera.**—Venegas, Hist. Cal., I, 408, 1759 (the tribal range; misprint of Pimeria). **Pimes.**—Alcedo, Dicc. Geog., IV, 218, 1788 (also Pimas). **Pimese.**—Morse, Hist. Am., 68, 1798. **Pimez.**—Taylor in Cal. Farmer, Apr. 11, 1862. **Pimi.**—Clavijero, Storia della Cal., I, 260, 1789. **Pimicas.**—Sedelmayr (1746) quoted by Bandelier in Arch. Inst. Papers, III, 74, 1890; Villa-Señor, Theatro Am., pt. 2, 408, 1748. **Pimo.**—Johnston in Emory, Recon., 598, 1848. **Pimo Galenos.**—Mayer, Mexico, II, 300, 1853 (=Pimas Gileños). **Pimoles.**—Stratton, Captiv. Oatman Girls, 49, 1857. **Pimos Illnos.**—Hinton, Handbook to Arizona, 27, 1878 (=Pimas Gileños). **Pincos.**—Marcy, Prairie Trav., 307, 1861 (misprint). **Pininos.**—Smart in Smithson. Rep. 1868, 417, 1869. **Pipos-altos.**—Mayer, Mex., II, 38, 1853 (misprint). **Pirnas.**—Venegas, Hist. Cal., II, 208, 1759 (misprint). **Pomo.**—Emory, Recon., pl., 84, 1848 (misprint). **Primahaitu.**—18th cent. doc. quoted by B. Smith in Shea, Lib. Am. Ling., III, 7, 1861 (mistake for *Pimahaitu*, sig. 'nothing'; applied erroneously). **Puma.**—Brackenridge, Mex. Letters, 83, 1850 (also Pimo). **Saikiné.**—Gatschet, Piñal Apache MS., B. A. E., 1883 ('living in sand [adobe] houses': Apache name). **Saikinné.**—ten Kate, Reizen in N. A., 197, 1885 ('sand houses': Apache name). **Si-ke-na.**—White, MS. Hist. Apaches, B. A. E., 1875 (Apache name for Pima, Papago, and Maricopa). **Simas.**—Domenech, Deserts, II, 305, 1860 (misprint). **Techpás.**—ten Kate, Reizen, 160, 1885 (Maricopa name). **Tĕχ-păs'.**—ten Kate, Synonomie, 5, 1884 (Maricopa name). **Tihokáhana.**—Gatschet, Yuma-Sprachstamm, 86, 1886 (Yavapai name). **Tzekinne.**—Bourke in Jour. Am. Folk-lore, III, 114, 1890 ('stone-house people': Apache name). **Widshi íti'kapa.**—White quoted by Gatschet, Yuma MS., B. A. E. (Tonto-Yuma name). **Ze-*gar'*-kin-a.**—White, Apache Names of Ind. Tribes, MS., B. A. E. ('live in villages': Apache name).

Piman Family. One of the northern branches of the Nahuatl or Aztec family of Buschmann, and of the Sonoran branch of the Uto-Aztecan family of Brinton, but regarded by Powell as a distinct linguistic stock. The extensive ramifications which the former authorities assign to this group, in which they include also the Shoshonean tribes, are not yet accepted as fully proven. With the exception of most of the Pima, part of the Papago, and the now extinct Sobaipuri, all the tribes composing this family inhabit or inhabited N. W. Mexico, including the greater portions of the states of Sonora, Chihuahua, Sinaloa, and Durango, as well as parts of Jalisco and Zacatecas. Besides the tribes mentioned the family includes the Nevome, Opata (including Eudeve and Jova), Tarahumare, Cahita, Cora, Huichol, Tepecano, Tepehuane, Nio, Tepahue, and Zoe, with their numerous branches. For further information see under the divisional names. Consult Powell in 7th Rep. B. A. E., 98, 1891, and authorities thereunder cited; Orozco y Berra, Geog., 58, 1864; Brinton, Am. Race, 123, 1891; Kroeber in Univ. Cal. Pub., Am. Archæol. and Ethnol., IV, no. 3, 1907; Hrdlicka in Am. Anthrop. Jan.-Mar., 1904; Rudo Ensayo (ca 1763), 1863; Ribas, Hist. Triumphos, 1645; Documentos para la Hist. Mex., 4th s., I, III, 1856.

Pimitoui. A village of the Illinois confederacy on Illinois r., near the mouth of Fox r., in Lasalle co., Ill. In 1722 the inhabitants abandoned it and removed to Cahokia and Kaskaskia. The band occupied different localities at different periods; in 1699 they were but 8 leagues from the Mississippi. They clung to their old belief after other bands of the Illinois had accepted missionary teachings. On some old maps the Pimitoui and Peoria villages near Peoria lake are given as identical.   (J. M.)

Pamitaris' town.—Rupp, West. Penn., 327, 1846. Peniteni.—St Cosme (1699) in Shea, Early Voy., 65, 1861. Permavevvi.—St Cosme (1699), ibid., 59. Pimeteois.—Nuttall, Jour., 250, 1821. Pimitconis.—Boudinot, Star in the West, 128, 1816. Pimiteoui.—Du Pratz (1758), La., II, map, 1774. Pimiteouy.—Shea, Cath. Miss., 428, 1855. Pimitoui.—De l'Isle, map (ca 1720) in Neill, Hist. Minn., 1858. Pimytesouy.—Memoir of 1718 in N. Y. Doc. Col. Hist., IX, 890, 1855.

Pimocagna. A former Gabrieleño rancheria in Los Angeles co., Cal., at a locality later called Rancho de Ybarra.

Pimocagna.—Ried (1852) quoted by Taylor in Cal. Farmer, Jan. 11, 1861. Piniocagna.—Ibid., June 8, 1860.

Pimtainin (*Pim-t'aïnïn*, 'deer people'). A clan of the Tigua of Isleta, N. Mex.—Lummis quoted by Hodge in Am. Anthrop., IX, 350, 1896.

Pinal Coyoteros. A part of the Coyotero Apache, whose chief rendezvous was the Pinal mts. and their vicinity, N. of Gila r. in Arizona. They ranged, however, about the sources of the Gila, over the Mogollon mesa, and from N. Arizona to the Gila and even southward. They are now under the San Carlos and Ft Apache agencies, where they are officially classed as Coyoteros. According to Bourke, there were surviving among them in 1882 the following clans (or bands): Chisnedinadinaye, Destchetinaye, Gadinchin, Kaihatin, Klokadakaydn, Nagokaydn, Nagosugn, Tegotsugn, Titsessinaye, Tutsoshin, Tutzose, Tziltadin, and Yagoyecayn.

They are reputed by tradition to have been the first of the Apache to have penetrated below the Little Colorado among the Pueblo peoples, with whom they intermarried (Bourke in Jour. Am. Folklore, III, 112, 1890). They possessed the country from San Francisco mt. to the

CHIQUITO, A PINAL COYOTERO MAN

Gila until they were subdued by Gen. Crook in 1873. Since then they have peaceably tilled their land at San Carlos.

WIFE OF CHIQUITO

White (Hist. Apaches, MS., B. A. E., 1875), for several years a surgeon at Ft Apache, says that they have soft, musical voices, uttering each word in a sweet, pleasant tone. He noted also their light-hearted, childish ways and timid manner, their pleasant expression of countenance, and the beauty of their women. Married women tattooed their chins in three blue vertical lines running from the lower lip. **Pinal Coyotero.**—Steck in Ind. Aff. Rep. 1859, 346, 1860. **Piñal Coyotero.**—Steck in Cal. Farmer, June 5, 1863. **Pinals Apaches.**—Ind. Aff. Rep. 1869, 94, 1870.

Pinaleños (Span: 'pinery people'). A division of the Apache, evidently more closely related to the Chiricahua than to any other group. Their principal seat was formerly the Pinaleño mts., s. of Gila r., s. E. Arizona, but their raids extended far into Sonora and Chihuahua, Mexico. They were noted for their warlike character and continued their hostility toward the United States (notwithstanding 1,051, including Arivaipa, were on the San Carlos reserve in 1876), until forced by Gen. George Crook to surrender in 1883. They are now under the San Carlos and Ft Apache agencies, Ariz., being officially known as Pinals, but their numbers are not separately reported. The Pinaleños and the Pinal Coyoteros have often been confused. See *Apache.*
Chokonni.—Bourke in Jour. Am. Folk-lore, III, 115, 1890 (= 'juniper,' a Chiricahua division). **Ha-hwad′-ja.** — Corbusier, Apache-Mojave and Apache-Yuma vocab., B. A. E., 1875 (Yavapai name). **Ha-hwadsha.**—Gatschet, Yuma-Spr., II, 124, 1883 (Yavapai name). **Penal Apaches.**—White, MS. Hist. Apaches, B. A. E., 1875. **Pendeña.**—Ind. Aff. Rep., 122, 1861. **Pimal.**—Ind. Aff. Rep., 306, 1877. **Piñal.**—Bartlett, Pers. Narr., I, 308, 1854 (= Piñols, = Pinaleños). **Pinal.**—Ind. Aff. Rep., 187, 1858. **Pinal Apache.**—Ind. Aff. Rep., 141, 1868. **Pinal Apachen.**—Ind. Aff. Rep., 209, 1875 (misprint). **Pinaleno.**—Gibbs, letter to Higgins, 1866. **Pinaleños.**—Bartlett, Pers. Narr., I, 308, 1854 (= Piñal, = Piñols). **Pinalino.**— Bancroft, Nat. Races, v, index, 1874. **Pinal Leñas.**—Whipple in Pac. R. R. Rep., III, pt. 3, 119, 1856. **Pinal Leño.**—Turner, ibid., 81. **Pinal Leno.**— Haines, Am. Ind., 159, 1888. **Pinal Llanos.**—Browne, Apache Country, 290, 1869. **Pinelores.**—Hamilton, Mexican Handbook, 48, 1883. **Pinery.**—Gatschet, Zwölf Sprachen, 65, 1876. **Piñoleno.**—Möllhausen, Tagebuch, 146, 1858. **Pinolero.**—Emory, Recon., 78, 1848 (trans. 'pinole-eaters'). **Pinoles.**—Haines, Am. Ind., 159, 1888. **Piñol - Indianer.**—Möllhausen, Tagebuch, 146–147, 1858. **Pinols.**—Morgan in N. A. Rev., 58, 1870. **Piñols.**—Bartlett, Pers. Narr., I, 308, 1854 (= Piñal, = Pinaleños). **Piñon Lano.**—Emory, Recon., 78, 1848 (=piñon wood tribe'; regarded as distinct from Pinoleros, 'pinole-eaters'). **Pinon, Lanos.**—Haines, Am. Ind., 159, 1888. **Piñon Llano Apaches.**—Parke, Map N. Mex., 1851. **Tchĭ-kûn′.**—Corbusier, Apache Mohave and Apache Yuma vocab., B. A. E., 1875. **Tinalenos.**—Haines, Am. Ind., 134, 1888 (misprint).

Pinanaca. An unidentified tribe, met by Fernando del Bosque in Texas, in 1675, about 7 leagues N. of the Rio Grande. They are possibly the Pamaque.
Pinanacas.—Bosque (1675) in Nat. Geog. Mag., XIV, 344, 1903. **Pinnancas.**—Ibid., 340.

Pinashiu (*Pinäsh′iu*, 'bald eagle'). A subphratry or gens of the Menominee.—Hoffman in 14th Rep. B. A. E., pt. 1, 42, 1896.

Pinawan ('windy place'). A ruined pueblo of the Zuñi, about 1½ m. s. w. of Zuñi pueblo, on the road to Ojo Caliente, N. Mex. The name has been associated with Aquinsa, mentioned by Oñate in 1598, on account of the possible misprinting of Apinawa, a form of the name Pinawan, but there is no other evidence, and the ruins have every appearance of being those of a prehistoric village. For plan and description see Mindeleff in 8th Rep. B. A. E., 86, 1891.   (F. W. H.)
A′-pi-na.—Cushing in Proc. Cong. Int. Amér., VII, 156, 1890 (or Pi′-na-wan). **A-pinaua.**—Bandelier in Jour. Am. Eth. and Arch., III, 84, 1892. **Pinaua.**—Peet in Am. Antiq., XVII, 852, 1895 (misprint). **Pin-a-au.**—Fewkes in Jour. Am. Eth. and Arch., I, 101, note, 1891. **Pinana.**—Bandelier, Gilded Man, 195, 1893. **Pî-na-ua.** —Bandelier in Revue d'Ethnog., 201, 1886. **Pin-a-ua.**—Bandelier in Arch. Inst. Papers, III, 133, 1890. **Pi′-na-wa.**—Cushing in Millstone, X, 22, Feb. 1885. **Pi-na-wan.**—Ibid., 4, Jan. 1885. **Town of the Winds.**—Ibid., 2. **Village of the Winds.**—Cushing, Zuñi Folk Tales, 104, 1901.

Pinbitho ('deer spring'). A Navaho clan.
Pinbiọò′.—Matthews in Jour. Am. Folk-lore, III, 103, 1890. **Pinbiọòɖine.**—Ibid. **Pin bĭtó′.** — Matthews, Navaho Legends, 30, 1897. **Pin bĭtó′ dĭne′.**—Ibid.

Pincers. Little or nothing exists to show that the Indians had pincers before the coming of white men, though the presence of this tool generally among less modified tribes argues its employment in precolumbian times, and specimens have not survived because the elastic properties of wood or horn were doubtless utilized in the manufacture of pincers and these substances easily decay. Tribes in the environment of the prickly-pear (*Opuntia*) handled its spiny fruit with pincers made of a single piece of elastic withe moistened and bent over into the proper form, or a straight stick with a wide slit extending almost its entire length, after the fashion of a clothespin. Tribes which used hot stones for cooking or for the sweat-bath usually handled them with pincers of bent wood or of two pieces of wood held together near one end with a ring of tough splint, or the pincers were merely two sticks held one in each hand.

Small pincers or tweezers were almost universally used, on account of the custom of removing coarse hair from the body, and it is probable that the primitive form was two valves of shell or simply two small pieces of wood, bone, or horn. Later they were commonly home-made of a bit of sheet-iron or brass, but the trader found the commercial article a desirable addition to his stock. The Ntlakyapamuk of Thompson r., Brit. Col., have pincers made of two pieces of horn, in construction like the pincers for handling hot stones, or made of a single piece of wood or copper.

Consult Holmes in Nat. Mus. Rep. 1900, pl. 15, 33, 1901; Teit in Mem. Am. Mus. Nat. Hist., I, pt. IV, p. 227, May 1900.   (W. H.)

Pinder Town. A settlement formerly on Flint r., Ga. Woodward, in 1817, stated that the Indians were "Chehaws," in which event the settlement was probably a part of Chiaha on Chattahoochee r. There was also a Chiaha on Flint r., perhaps identical with Pinder.
Fulemmy's.—Woodward, Reminisc., 155, 1859. Pinder Town.—Ibid.

Pine Log (from the native name *Na'tsasûñ'tlûñyĭ*, 'pine foot-log place'). A former Cherokee settlement on the creek of the same name in Bartow co., Ga.
Pine Log.—Doc. of 1799 quoted by Royce in 5th Rep. B. A. E., 144, 1887. Na'ts-asûñ'tlûñyĭ.—Mooney in 19th Rep. B. A. E., 527, 1900.

Pineshow. A Dakota band, probably of the Wahpeton, named from the chief. They numbered 150 in 1820, and lived on Minnesota r., 15 m. from its mouth.
Panisciowa.—Coues in Pike, Exped., I, 86, 1895. Penechon.—Ibid. Penichon. Pinchon.—Ibid. (French form). Perition.—Ibid. Pinchow.—Ibid. Pinechon.—Ibid. Pineshow's band.—Morse, Rep. to Sec. War, 365, 1822. Piniohon.—Coues, op. cit. Pinneshaw.—Ibid. Tacokoquipesceni.—Ibid. Takopepeshane.—Ibid.

Pineshuk. A former Choctaw town on a branch of Pearl r., Winston co., Miss.—Gatschet, Creek Migr. Leg., I, 108, 1884.

Pingitkalik. A winter settlement of Iglulirmiut Eskimo in N. Melville penin.—Lyons, Priv. Jour., 403, 1824.

Pinguishuk. A Sidarumiut Eskimo village on Seahorse id., Arctic coast, Alaska; pop. 29 in 1880.
Pingoshugarun.—Brit. Adm. chart (1882) cited by Baker, Geog. Dict. Alaska, 499, 1906. Pinguishugamiut.—11th Census, Alaska, 162, 1892. Pinoshuragin.—Petroff in 10th Census, Alaska, map, 1884.

Pinhoti (*Pin'-hóti*, from *pinua* turkey, *húti*, *hóti*, 'home': 'turkey home'). A former Upper Creek town in the s. part of Cleburne co., Ala., a short distance E. of Oakfuskee. The trail from Niuyaka to Kawita old town passed through it.
Pin-e-hoo-te.—Hawkins (1799), Sketch, 50, 1848. Pin'-hóti.—Gatschet, Creek Migr. Leg., I, 142, 1884. Turkey-Home.—Ibid. Turkey Town.—Pickett, Hist. Ala., II, 298, 1851.

Pinini (from *Pininéos*, the New Mexican corruption of Spanish *Pigméos*, 'pigmies'). A mythic tribe to which, according to San Felipe tradition, is attributed the slaughter of many of the inhabitants of the former Cochiti town of Kuapa in New Mexico, in consequence of which the pueblo was permanently abandoned. The Cochiti themselves assert that the destroyers of the ancient settlement mentioned were the Tewa.—Bandelier in Arch. Inst. Papers, IV, 166, 1892. See *Ishtuayene*.

Pininicangui ('place of the corn-flour'). A prehistoric Tewa pueblo on a knoll in a valley about 2 m. s. of Puye and 3 m. s. of Santa Clara cr., on the Pajarito plateau, Sandoval co., N. Mex. It was built of volcanic tufa blocks, roughly dressed, its ground-plan forming a large rectangle about 150 by 210 ft. The pueblo probably antedated the great Puye settlement

by many years. See Hewett in Bull. 32 B. A. E., 1907. (E. L. H.)

Piniquu. A tribe or subtribe, probably Coahuiltecan, represented at San Francisco Solano mission, near the Rio Grande, in Coahuila, Mexico, in 1704, with the Xarame, Payuguan, Siaban, Siaguan, Pataguo, and Apache. (H. E. B.)
Minicau.—Baptismal Rec. 1705, MS. Piniquu.—Ibid., 1704.

Pinnokas. Mentioned by Schoolcraft (Travels, viii, 1821) as one of the tribes seen by Lahontan on his imaginary journey up "Long r." in 1703. Misquoted, and the name intended not determinable.

Pins. Slender cylindrical pieces of pointed and headed bone, shell, wood, horn, and metal were made by the Indians for special purposes as well as for ordinary fastening. In many instances awl-like worked bones, found in ancient sites, were blanket fasteners such as are used by the N. W. coast tribes, and probably such pins were common among tribes that wore robes and blankets. Pins also were employed in joinery, in the fastening of bags and tent flaps, for stretching skins in drying, and as pickers for the pipe. Until recently they were stuck in holes made in the lobe and rim of the ear by a number of tribes E. of the Mississippi, and nose and ear pins were seen by explorers among California and Oregon tribes. Large and small pins of shell have been found in sites in the E. and on the Pacific coast (Holmes, Putnam). Thorns serve as pins among the Ntlakyapamuk of Thompson r., Brit. Col. (Teit). The most general use of the pins was as a support for the plumes worn in the hair. A pin was used by the Eskimo for closing wounds in game to prevent loss of blood, which is a delicacy among this people.
Consult Holmes in 2d Rep. B. A. E., 213, 1883; Niblack in Rep. Nat. Mus. 1888, 1890; Putnam in Wheeler Surv. Rep., VII, 1879; Smith in Mem. Am. Mus. Nat. Hist., VII, pt. ii, 424, 1900; Teit, ibid., I, pt. iv, 187, 1900. (W. H.)

Pintados (so called by the Spaniards because of their custom of tattooing or painting their bodies). A tribe, some members of which visited Fray Marcos de Niza while at Matape, a town of the Eudeve in central Sonora, Mexico, and who claimed to live E. of that place. Bandelier (Arch. Inst. Papers, v, 133, 1890) has been unable to determine whether the original narration refers to the custom of tattooing or painting; if the latter, he is inclined to the opinion that they were Pima or Sobaipuri; otherwise they are not identifiable.
Painted Indians.—Bandelier, op cit., 133. Pintadi.—Niza (1539) in Ramusio, Nav. et Viaggi, III, 357, 1565 (Italian form). Pintados.—Niza in Hakluyt, Voy., III, 440, 1600.

Pintahae. A Saponi town visited by Lederer in 1670; according to Lawson (Hist. Car., 1709), the residence of the "king."

Pintce ('confluence of Pin river'). A village of the Nikozliautin on Stuart lake, Brit. Col., at the mouth of Pintce r.; pop. 42 in 1906.
Pinchy.—Harmon, Jour., 205, 1820. **Pintce.**—Morice in Trans. Roy. Soc. Can., x, 109, 1892.

Pinthlocco. A former Creek town on Pinthlocco cr., in Coosa co., Ala.—Royce in 18th Rep. B. A. E., Ala. map, 1899.

Pintiats (*Pin'-ti-ats*). A Paiute band formerly living in or near Moapa valley, s. E. Nev.; pop. 47 in 1873.—Powell in Ind. Aff. Rep. 1873, 50, 1874.

Pintos (Span.: 'the piebald ones'). A tribe living in 1757 on the N. side of the Rio Grande, opposite Reynosa, in Texas. Across the river, in Tamaulipas, lived the Alapaguemes (Pedro de Estrada, in Cuervo, Revista, 1757, MS. in Archivo Gen., Hist., LVI). At the same time a part of the tribe was under a mission at the villa of San Fernando, near by. In 1780 Cabello said they were at the mission of Nuevo Santander (Rep. on Coast Tribes, MS. in Béxar Archives). The tribe was reported to have been always peaceful.					(H. E. B.)

Pinutgu (*Pĭ'nătgû'*, 'Penateka Comanche'). A contemptuous term applied by the Cheyenne to those of their own tribe who remained quiet during the outbreak of 1874–75.					(J. M.)
Outlaw.—Dorsey in Field Columb. Mus. Pub. 103, 62, 1905.

Pioge. A prehistoric Tewa pueblo at the site of the village of Los Luceros (now called Lyden) on the E. bank of the Rio Grande, in the S. E. part of Rio Arriba co., N. Mex. The present inhabitants of San Juan claim it as one of their ancient settlements, whence their ancestors settled in the locality which they to-day occupy. Consult Bandelier (1) in Ritch, New Mex., 202, 1885, (2) in Arch. Inst. Papers, IV, 63, 1892.

Piomingo. See *Colbert, William*.

Pipe, Captain. See *Hopocan*.

Pipes. A tube in which tobacco was smoked is to-day called a pipe. Some pipes were straight, others curved; still

CALIFORNIA; SERPENTINE. (LENGTH, 9¼ IN.)

others had a bowl at a right angle to the stem, and in certain instances the angle was acute; some pipes had two or more bowls or stems. In North America the shape of pipes varied according to local-

ity; some were of a single piece, others had detachable stems. The pipe most widely distributed was a straight tube, usually plain on the outside, but occasionally elaborately ornamented. The rudest pipes of this type were made from the leg-bone of a deer

NEW MEXICO; CLAY. (LENGTH, 6 IN.)

or other animal, and were often reenforced with a piece of rawhide, which, wrapped on wet, contracted in drying and thus aided in preventing the bone from splitting. The tubular stone pipe had one end enlarged to hold the tobacco, the stem being inserted in the opposite end. Pipes of this form had necessarily to be smoked by throwing back the head, a position which had a tendency to cause the to-

COLORADO RIVER; CLAY. (LENGTH, 3½ IN.)

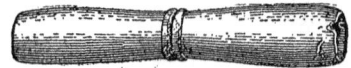

KENTUCKY; CHLORITE. (LENGTH, 7¼ IN.)

bacco to be drawn into the mouth, to prevent which, in some localities, a small pellet of pottery was often inserted in the bowl. The cloud-blower of the Pueblos is a straight tubular pipe, varying from a few inches to a foot in length.

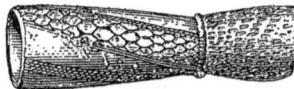

GEORGIA; CHLORITE. (LENGTH, 6 IN.)

Those of small size are usually made of clay in the same manner as pottery. Large cloud-blowers are usually made of stone, and do not differ in form, decoration, or use from those of clay. This form of pipe is used solely for ceremonial purposes, the smoke being blown to the cardinal directions by medicine-men. Though there is evidence of reeds or other tubes having been used for

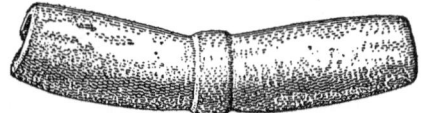

SOUTHERN FORM; STEATITE. (LENGTH, 9 IN.)

KENTUCKY; CHLORITE. (LENGTH, 9 IN.)

inhaling smoke for medicinal purposes prior to the Christian era in Europe, there is little doubt that the tobacco pipe, now common over the world, is of American origin. Pipes were made of pottery, wood, bone, metal, or stone, or a combination of two or more of these materials. Many pipes have figures delicately engraved on their surfaces; others have elaborately carved or modeled human and other figures on or forming the bowl or the stem. A striking characteristic of pipes is that figures on stems or bowls from a given area commonly face in one direction. Some pipes are diminutive, weighing scarcely an ounce; others weigh several pounds. Pipes of great size have been found, suggesting use on special occasions, as to seal a treaty or other important agreement. In every community there were artisans who possessed special skill in pipe making, and there were sources of supply the ownership of which was recognized and respected. The material most commonly used for pipes was soapstone, though many other stones, many of them incapable of resisting great heat, were also employed, even for the most elaborate specimens. The capacity of the pipe bowl varied in different localities and at different periods; some would hold but a thimbleful of tobacco, others would contain an ounce or more. The most diminutive pipes now used are those of the Alaskan Eskimo. Those of the greatest capacity are the flat-bottomed monitor pipes, found along the Atlantic coast and inland to Ohio and Tennessee. Among many Indian tribes the pipe was

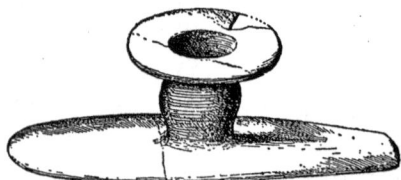
TENNESSEE; LIMESTONE. (LENGTH, 6½ IN.)

TENNESSEE; CHLORITE. (LENGTH, 7 IN.)

KENTUCKY; STEATITE. (LENGTH, 10¾ IN.)

SIOUX CALUMET; CATLINITE

ILLINOIS; CATLINITE. (LENGTH, 8 IN.)

TENNESSEE; CLAYSTONE. (LENGTH, 5 IN.)

held in great veneration. Some pipes were guarded by a specially appointed official and were kept in fur with the greatest care in specially designated tents, or contained in a case made for the purpose. The palladium (q. v.) of the Arapaho is a flat stone pipe which has been seen by only one white man (Mooney (1) in 14th Rep. B. A. E., 961, 1896, (2) in Mem. Am. Anthrop. Ass'n, I, no. 6, 1907; Scott in Am. Anthrop., IX, no. 3, 1907). Certain of their dance pipes are also flat, i. e. the stem and the bowl are in the same plane.

The word "calumet" (q. v.) was early employed as the name of a dance. Marquette referred to the calumet in 1675, not only in the latter sense, but also as a pipe. Father Biard, in 1616, and Father Hennepin, in 1679, applied the term to the pipe, in which sense it is still employed. Various early writers refer to a calumet of peace and one of war, the former being white, the latter red. Lafitau (Mœurs des Ameriquains, II, 327, 1724) refers to the calumet as a true altar where sacrifice was made to the sun; he also speaks of the calumet of peace. The bowl of the calumet pipe of the Sioux is at a right angle to the stem, and has a solid projection extending in front of the bowl. In the older specimens of this type high polish and carved figures are unusual; with modern examples, however, high polish is common and the stems are often elaborately carved. In comparatively recent time inlaying became usual, geometrical or animal figures being cut in the stone into which thin strips of lead were inlaid.

Pipestems are straight, curved, or twisted; round or flat; long or short. Elaborate ornaments for the stems have been said to be made by the women with beads, porcupine quills, feathers, hair, etc., but it is probable that they were put on by the men. The design of the pipe

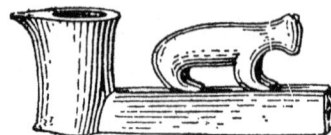
NORTH CAROLINA; CHLORITE. (LENGTH, 3¾ IN.)

NEW YORK. (LENGTH, 3⅜ IN.)

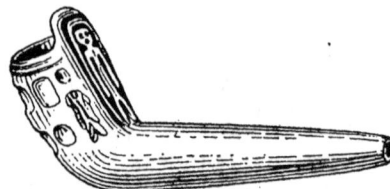
NEW YORK; STALAGMITE. (LENGTH, 4 IN.)

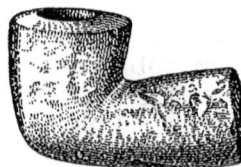
GEORGIA; STEATITE. (LENGTH, 5 IN.)

was characteristic of the tribe using it and was readily recognized by friends or enemies. George Catlin, after whom pipestone was named (see *Catlinite*), truthfully says that the stems of pipes were carved in many ingenious forms, quite staggering the unenlightened to guess how they were bored until the process was explained. The simplest way was to split a suitable piece of wood lengthwise, remove the heart, and glue the two parts together again. One of the most elaborately modeled of all the varieties of American pottery pipes is that found in the region

formerly occupied by the Iroquois. The pottery was usually burned hard and the bowls elaborately ornamented with figures of birds and animals. In one specimen both bowl and stem are covered with a number of human faces; another is in form of the head and neck of a bird, probably a pigeon, the beak projecting above the bowl on the side farthest from the smoker, the bowl being formed of the bird's head and the stem representing the neck. Another graceful specimen is in the form of a snake. Stone pipes also were found in this region, including those of marble of a rich saffron color. North of the Iroquois area, extending from Labrador to the Rocky mts., there is found a pipe of uniform pattern, the bowl of which, having the form of an acorn, rests on a keel-like base which has

ARKANSAS; QUARTZITE. (LENGTH, 7 IN.)

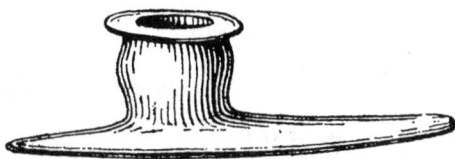

WEST VIRGINIA; STEATITE. (LENGTH, 5 IN.)

one to five holes bored through its narrowest part, one of which was designed for holding a string attached to the stem to prevent it from being lost in the snow, the others for the suspension of ornaments.

The Alaskan Eskimo pipe is of peculiar shape and apparently owes its origin to Asiatic influence. The bowl, made of metal, stone, bone, or ivory, holds but a pinch of tobacco, while the large curved stem often consists of two pieces of wood held together by rawhide. Some of these pipes have small plates set in their stems which can be opened for the purpose of cleaning or to collect the liquid in order to mix it with fresh tobacco. Some Eskimo pipes are made from walrus or fossil ivory, and are elaborately engraved with fishing and hunting scenes. Pipes of this character are now made for sale, as is the case with very elaborately carved specimens made by the Haida and Tlingit. Among the many American pipes none is more remarkable than those belonging to the biconical type, found in Canada and along the Mississippi. Some of these are perfectly plain, others are elaborately carved in imitation of men and animals. The term "biconical" has been employed for the reason that both bowl and stem perforations are of cone shape, the smaller end of the cones meeting at approximately the center of the specimens, at a right angle to each other. The most artistically finished of all American pipes are those of the mound type, of which Squier and Davis (Ancient Monuments, 152, 1848) found more than 200 in a single mound in Ohio. These pipes apparently were smoked without

OHIO; STONE; LENGTH, $3\frac{1}{4}$ IN. (SQUIER AND DAVIS)

stems, although they show no marks of the teeth. The stems as a rule are not ornamented, though the bowls are carved with great skill in imitation of birds, frogs, turtles, beaver, men, etc.

Another typical and delicately fashioned stone pipe is found in the middle Atlantic states; it has a flat base, the bowl being generally but not always at a right angle to the stem. The bowl, which is large in comparison with other pipes from this section, is rarely ornamented but is usually highly polished.

The tomahawk or hatchet pipe is made of metal; it is provided with an eye to receive a handle, and a sharp blade for use in cutting wood or as an offensive weapon. The poll of the hatchet, shaped like an acorn, is hollow and has a hole in the base, connecting with an opening extending through the helve, through which the smoke was drawn. Many of these pipes were inlaid with silver in ornamental design. These tomahawk or hatchet pipes

OHIO; STONE; LENGTH, $3\frac{1}{4}$ IN. (SQUIER AND DAVIS)

largely displaced the stone pipe and the stone ax, relieving the natives of much weight while traveling. Who first made use of the metal tomahawk it is impossible to say; but from the shape of the blade it is probable that the crescent form was of Spanish origin, the blade resembling the lily was of French derivation, while the simple hatchet was English, for each of these nations armed their Indian allies with these most effective weapons.

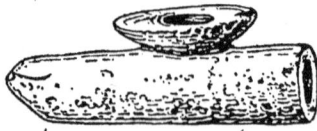

KENTUCKY; LIMESTONE. (LENGTH, 3¼ IN.)

There are unique types of pipes found in various parts of the country, particularly in Georgia and the Carolinas, some of which appear to have followed copper originals and some to have been influenced by European models. In Maryland shell-heaps there has been found a type of pipe, to which it is difficult to assign a date, resembling the trade pipes that were made in large quantities in England, France, Italy, Holland, and Germany to supply the demand during the early colonial period, many of the latter being distinguishable by designs or initials. See *Smoking, Tobacco*.

WEST VIRGINIA; METAL; WORK OF WHITES. (LENGTH, 8 IN.)

Consult McGuire, Pipes and Smoking Customs, Rep. U. S. Nat. Mus., 1897, and authorities therein cited; Abbott, (1) Prim. Indus., 1881; (2) in Surv. W. 100th Merid., VII, 1879; Beauchamp in Bull. N. Y. State Mus., IV, no. 18, 1897; Berlin in Proc. and Coll. Wyo.

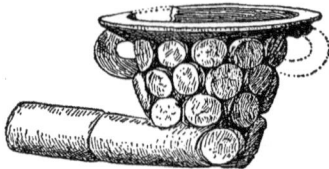

GEORGIA; CLAY; LENGTH, 3⅜ IN. (MOORE)

Hist. and Geol. Soc., IX, 1906; Dorsey and Voth in Field Columb. Mus. Pub., Anthrop., III, no. 1, 1901; Morgan, League of the Iroquois, 1904; Palmer in Bull. 2,

NORTH CAROLINA; STEATITE. (LENGTH, 11 IN.)

S. W. Soc. Archæol. Inst. Am., 1905; Scott in Am. Anthrop., IX, no. 3, 1907; Smith in Am. Anthrop., VIII, no. 1, 1906; Squier and Davis in Smithson. Cont., I, 1848; Archæol. Reps. Ontario, app. to Rep. Minister of Education; Thruston, Antiq. of Tenn., 1897; West, Aborig. Pipes Wis., 1905.　　　　　　　　　　　(J. D. M.)

Pipestone. See *Catlinite*.

Pipiaca. A Maricopa rancheria on the Rio Gila, Arizona, in 1744.—Sedelmair (1744) cited by Bancroft, Ariz. and N. Mex., 366, 1889.

Pipsissewa. A popular name for *Chimaphila umbellata*, first mentioned by Dr B. S. Barton, in his Collections towards a Materia Medica of the United States (1798), and since variously corrupted to *pkipsessiwa, psiseva, pipsisseway*, etc. The plant once enjoyed a great reputation as a lithontriptic among some of the Wood Cree, who raised it to the dignity of an animate object and spoke of as *pipisisi-kweu*, 'it reduces it (stone in the bladder) to very fine particles.' Pipsissewa beer is a decoction of *Chimaphila*, with the addition of sugar to sweeten it, ginger to flavor it, and yeast to produce fermentation. This drink has been used in scrofulous affections.　　　　　　　　　　(W. R. G.)

Piqosha. The Hide Carrying-strap clan of the Hopi.
Hide Strap clan.—Voth, Traditions of the Hopi, 22, 1905. Piqö'sha.—Ibid., 37.

Piqua (contr. of *Bi-co-we-tha*, of indefinite meaning, but referring to ashes). One of the five principal divisions of the Shawnee. Their villages at different periods were Pequea, in Pennsylvania; Lick Town, on Scioto r. in Pickaway co., Ohio; Piqua, on Mad r., and Piqua, on Miami r., Ohio. On being driven from the last place by the Kentuckians they removed to Wapakoneta and St Marys r.　(J. M.)
Bi-co-we-tha.—W. H. Shawnee in Gulf States Hist. Mag., I, 415, 1903. Paquea.—Schoolcraft, Ind. Tribes, I, 90, 1851. Pecawa.—Drake, Ind. Chron., 189, 1836. Pecuwési.—Heckewelder quoted by Brinton, Lenape Leg., 30, 1885. Pékoweu.—Heckewelder, ibid. Pĕkuégi.—Gatschet, Shawnee MS., B. A. E., 1879 (Shawnee name, plural form). Pequea.—Schoolcraft, Ind. Tribes, I, pl. 27, 1851. Pickawa.—Marshall, Ky., I, 109, 1824. Pickaway.—Harmar (1790) in Am. St. Papers, Ind. Aff., I, 105, 1832. Pickawee.—Harris, Tour., III, 111, 1805. Pickawes.—Barton, New Views, xxxii, 1798. Pícoweu.—Heckewelder quoted by Brinton, Lenape Leg., 30, 1885. Picque.—La Tour, Map, 1784. Pikoweu.—Johnston (1819) quoted by Brinton, Lenape Leg., 30, 1885.

Piqua. The name of two or more former Shawnee villages in Ohio, occupied by the Piqua division of the tribe: (1) The earlier town, which was the birthplace of the noted Tecumtha, was situated on the N. side of Mad r., about 5 m. w. of the present Springfield, in Clark co. It was destroyed by the Kentuckians under Gen. G. R. Clark in 1780, and never rebuilt, the Indians removing to the (Great) Miami r., where they established two new towns known as Upper and Lower Piqua. (2) Upper Piqua was on Miami r., 3 m. N. of the present Piqua in Miami co., and on the site of the former Miami town of Pickawillanee, q. v. (3) Lower Piqua was a smaller village on the site of the great town of that name. Both villages were within the territory ceded by the treaty of Greenville in 1795, after which the Shawnee retired to Wapakoneta. See Howe, Hist. Coll. Ohio, 1896–98. For synonyms see *Piqua*, above.   (J. M.)

Little Pickaway.—Flint, Ind. Wars, 151, 1833. Pikkawa.—Harmar (1790) quoted by Rupp, West. Penn., app., 227, 1846.

Piros. Formerly one of the principal Pueblo tribes of New Mexico, which in the early part of the 17th century comprised two divisions, one inhabiting the Rio Grande valley from the present town of San Marcial, Socorro co., northward to within about 50 m. of Albuquerque, where the Tigua settlements began; the other division, sometimes called Tompiros and Salineros, occupying an area E. of the Rio Grande in the vicinity of the salt lagoons, or salinas, where they adjoined the eastern group of Tigua settlements on the s. The western or Rio Grande branch of the tribe was visited by members of Coronado's expedition in 1540, by Chamuscado in 1580, by Espejo in 1583 (who found them in 10 villages along the river and in others near by), by Oñate in 1598, and by Benavides in 1621–30, the latter stating that they were in 14 pueblos along the river. Judging from the numerous villages of the province of Atripuy (q. v.) mentioned by Oñate, which appears to have been the name applied to the range of the Rio Grande division of the Piros, Benavides' number does not seem to be exaggerated. The establishment of missions among the Piros began in 1626. In that year the most southerly church and monastery in New Mexico were built at Senecú by Arteaga and Zuñiga (to whom are attributed the planting of the first vines and the manufacture of wine in this region), and during the same year missions at Sevilleta, Socorro, and probably also at Alamillo were founded. It is not improbable that the Piros of the Rio Grande, although said to number 6,000 in 1630, were already seriously harassed by the persistent hostility of the Apache, for Sevilleta had been depopulated and destroyed by fire "in consequence of intertribal wars" prior to the establishment of the missions, and was not resettled until about 1626. Moreover, the 14 villages along the Rio Grande occupied by the Piros in 1630 were reduced to 4 half a century later. "This was due not only to the efforts of the missionaries to gather their flock into larger pueblos," says Bandelier, "but also to the danger to which these Indians were exposed from the Apaches of the 'Perrillo' and the 'Gila,' as the southern bands of that restless tribe were called."

The area occupied by the Piros of the Salinas extended from the pueblo of Abo s. E. to and including the pueblo of Tabira, commonly but improperly called "Gran Quivira," a distance of about 25 m. The habitat of the eastern Piros was even more desert in character than that of the eastern Tigua, which bounded it on the N., for the Arroyo de Abo, on which Abo pueblo was situated, was the only perennial stream in the region, the inhabitants of Tabira and Tenabo depending entirely on the storage of rain water for their supply. In addition to the 3 pueblos named, it is not improbable that the now ruined villages known by the Spanish names Pueblo Blanco, Pueblo Colorado, and Pueblo de la Parida were among the 11 inhabited settlements of the Salinas seen by Chamuscado in 1580, but at least 3 of this number were occupied by the Tigua. Juan de Oñate, in 1598, also visited the pueblos of the Salinas, and to Fray Francisco de San Miguel, a chaplain of Oñate's army, was assigned the Piros country as part of his mission district. The headquarters of this priest being at Pecos, it is not likely that much active mission work was done among the Piros during his incumbency, which covered only about 3 years. The first actual missions among the Piros pueblos of the Salinas were established in 1629 by Francisco de Acevedo at Abo and Tabira, and probably also at Tenabo, but before the massive-walled churches and monasteries were completed, the village dwellers of both the Salinas and the Rio Grande suffered so seriously from the depredations of the Apache, that Senecu on the Rio Grande, as well as every pueblo of the Salinas, was deserted before the Pueblo insurrection of 1680. Prior to the raid on Senecu by the Apache in 1675, 6 of the inhabitants of that village were executed for the massacre of the alcalde-mayor and 4 other Spaniards. Probably on account of the fear with which the Spaniards were known to be regarded by the Piros after this occurrence, they were not invited by the northern Pueblos to participate in the revolt against the Spaniards in 1680; consequently when Otermin, the governor, retreated from Santa Fé to El Paso in that year, he was joined by nearly all the inhabitants of Socorro, Sevilleta, and Alamillo. These, with the former occupants of Senecu, who, since the destruction of their village by the Apache had resided at Socorro, were afterward established in the new villages of Socorro, Texas, and Senecu del Sur in Chihuahua, on the Rio Grande below El Paso, where their remnants still survive. In attempting to reconquer New Mexico in the following year, Otermin caused Alamillo to be burned, because the few remaining inhabitants fled on his approach. Only 3 families remained at Sevilleta when the Spaniards retreated, but these had departed and the pueblo was almost in ruins on their return in 1681.

The entire Piros division of the Tanoan family probably numbered about 9,000 early in the 17th century. Of these, only about 60 individuals are known to survive.

Living with or near the Piros of the Salinas in the 16th and 17th centuries were a band of Jumano (q. v.), a seminomadic tribe of which little is known. The proximity of these Indians to the Piros pueblos led to the error, on the part of cartographers of that period, of confounding the Jumano and Piros, hence the references on many early maps to the "Humanos de Tompiros," etc.

Following is a list of Piros pueblos, so far as known, all of them being now extinct with the exception of Senecu del Sur, while Socorro has become "Mexicanized": Abo, Agua Nueva, Alamillo, Barrancas, Qualacu, San Felipe, San Pascual, Senecu, Senecu del Sur (also Tigua), Sevilleta, Socorro or Pilabo, Socorro del Sur, Tabira, Tenabo, Teypana, Tenaquel.

The following pueblos, now extinct, were probably also occupied by the Piros: Amo, Aponitre, Aquicabo, Atepua, Ayqui, Calciati, Canocan, Cantensapue, Cunquilipinoy, Encaquiagualcaca, Huertas, Peixoloe, Pencoana, Penjeacu, Pesquis, Peytre, Polooca, Preguey, Pueblo Blanco, Pueblo Colorado, Pueblo de la Parida, Pueblo del Alto, Queelquelu, Quialpo, Quiapo, Quiomaqui, Quiubaco, Tecahanqualahamo, Teeytraan, Tercao, Texa, Teyaxa, Tohol, Trelagu, Trelaquepu, Treyey, Treypual, Trula, Tuzahe, Vumahein, Yancomo, Zumaque.

The following pueblos, now also extinct, were inhabited either by the Piros or the Tigua: Acoli, Aggey, Alle, Amaxa, Apena, Atuyama, Axauti, Chein, Cizentetpi, Couna, Dhiu, Hohota, Mejia, Quanquiz, Salineta, San Francisco, San Juan Bautista, Xatoe, Xiamela, Yonalus.

Consult Bandelier in Arch. Inst. Papers, Am. ser., IV, 236–253, 268–292, 1892; Lummis, Land of Poco Tiempo, 283–310, 1893. See also *Chealo, Pueblos, Salineros, Tanoan Family, Tigua, Tompiros, Tutahaco*. (F. W. H.)

Biroros.—Blaeu, Atlas, XII, 61, 1667. Norteños.—Froebel, Seven Years' Travel, 353, 1859 (= 'northerners,' so named because inhabiting the region of El Paso del Norte; may also refer to Tigua). Picos.—Benavides (1630) misquoted by Bancroft, Ariz. and N. Mex., 163, 1889 (Piros, or). Pir.—Senex, Map, 1710. Pira.—Benavides, Memorial, 14, 1630. Piri.—Sanson, l'Amérique map, 27, 1657. Pirj.—Linschoten, Description de l'Amérique, map 1, 1638. Piros.—Benavides, Memorial, 1630. Piruas.—Ladd, Story of New Mex., 15, 1891. Pyros.—Perea, Verdadera Rel., 2, 1632. Siros.—Villa-Señor, Theatro Am., II, 360, 1748. Tükahun.—Gatschet, Isleta MS. vocab., B. A. E., 1885 (= 'southern Pueblos': Isleta Tigua name for all Pueblos below their village; cf. *Tutahaco*).

Pisa (*Pi'-sa*, 'white sand'). A clan of the Lizard (Earth or Sand) phratry of the Hopi.—Stephen in 8th Rep. B. A. E., 39, 1891.

Piscataqua. A former small tribe connected with the Pennacook confederacy, living on Piscataqua r., the boundary between Maine and New Hampshire. Their principal village, also called Piscataqua, seems to have been near the present Dover, Stafford co., N. H. For the Maryland form of the name, see *Conoy*, and also *Piscataway*, following. (J. M.)

Pascataquas.—Barstow, New Hamp., 22, 1853. Pascatawayes.—Gookin (1674) in Mass. Hist. Soc. Coll., 1st s., I, 149, 1806. Passataquack.—Smith (1616), ibid., 3d s., VI, 107, 1837. Piscataquas.—Sullivan, ibid., 1st s., IX, 210, 1804. Piscataquaukes.—Potter quoted by Schoolcraft, Ind. Tribes, V, 223, 1855.

Piscataway. A former Conoy village situated on Piscataway cr., in Prince George co., Md., the residence of the Conoy chief at the time of the English occupancy of Maryland in 1634. It was the seat of a Jesuit mission established in 1640, but was abandoned two years later through fear of the Conestoga. A garrison was stationed there in 1644. Piscataway is seemingly identical with Kittamaquindi (q. v.), which received its name from a resident chief. (C. T.)

Pascataway.—White, Relatio Itineris, 82, 1874. Pascatawaye.—Ibid., 33. Pascatoe.—Ibid., 76. Piscattoway.—Bozman, Hist. Md., II, 290, 1837.

Pischenoas. A people met by Tonti in 1686 (Margry, Déc., III, 557, 1878) between the Natchez and the Quinipissa tribes on the Mississippi, who chanted the calumet to them because they were "gun-men."

Picheno.—Douay (ca. 1688) quoted by Shea, Discov. Miss., 226, 1852. Tichenos.—McKenney and Hall, Ind. Tribes, III, 82, 1854.

Pisha (*Pi'-ca*). The Field-mouse clan of the Asa phratry of the Hopi.—Stephen in 8th Rep. B. A. E., 39, 1891.

Pishaug. Defined by the Standard Dictionary (1895) as a young or female surf-scoter (*Œdemia perspicillata*): apparently identical with the Massachuset *a'pishaug*, widgeons, given by Trumbull (Natick Dict., 249, 1903), a plural form, the singular of which is *a'pish(a)*, or *apish'*. (A. F. C.)

Pishla-ateuna (*Pi'shla áteuna*, 'those of the northernmost'). A phratry embracing the Aingshi (Bear), Kalokta (Heron or Crane), and Tahluptsi (Yellow wood) clans of the Zuñi. (F. H. C.)

Pishquitpah. A Shahaptian tribe mentioned by Lewis and Clark as living in 1805 on the N. side of Columbia r. at Muscleshell rapid and wintering on Tapteal (Yakima) r., Wash. They numbered 2,600 (1,600?), in 71 mat houses, subsisted by hunting and fishing, and did not flatten their heads so much as the tribes farther down the river. They are described as of good stature, "pleasantly featured," and well proportioned. Both men and women rode well. The women wore skirts reaching to the knees, long leggings and moccasins, and large robes. Mooney (14th Rep. B. A. E., 739, 1896) regards them as probably identical with the Pisko band of the Yakima. (L. F.)

Pisch quit pás.—Orig. Jour. Lewis and Clark, III, 137, 1905. **Pishquitpah.**—Lewis and Clark Exped., II, 252, 1814. **Pishquitpaws.**—Ibid., 23. **Pishquitpows.**—Ibid., II, 319, 1817. **Pisquitpahs.**—Morse, Rep. to Sec. War, 370, 1822. **Pisquitpaks.**—Domenech, Deserts N. A., I, 443, 1860.

Piskakauakis (*Apistikákákis*, magpie, lit. 'small raven.'—Hewitt). A Cree band living in the vicinity of Tinder mtn., Northwest Ter., Canada, in 1856. They occupied 30 earth lodges and log cabins, and cultivated small patches of corn and potatoes; during the winter they hunted buffalo and traded the hides to the Hudson's Bay Co.—Hayden, Ethnog. and Philol. Mo. Val., 237, 1862.

Piskaret. See *Pieskaret*.

Piskitang. An unidentified Algonquian tribe or band formerly living near the Nipissing in Canada.

Piskatang.—Jes. Rel., Thwaites ed., XLV, 105, 1899. **Piskitang.**—Jes. Rel. 1653, 32, 1858.

Pisko ('river bend'). A Yakima band occupying a village on the s. side of Yakima r. between Toppenish and Setass crs., on the Yakima res., Wash.

Pispizawichasha ('prairie-dog people'). A band of the Brulé Teton Sioux.

Pispiza-wićáśa.—Dorsey in 15th Rep. B. A. E., 218, 1897. **Pispiza-witoaca.**—Ibid.

Pispogutt. A village of Christian Indians, probably Nauset, in 1674 (Bourne, 1674, in Mass. Hist. Soc. Coll., 1st s., I, 198, 1806). It seems to have been in w. Barnstable co., Mass., near Buzzards bay, and may be identical with Pocasset.

Pisqueno. A Chumashan village on one of the Santa Barbara ids., Cal., probably Santa Rosa, in 1542.—Cabrillo, Narr. (1542), in Smith, Colec. Doc. Fla., 186, 1857.

Pisquows (probably from the Yakima *pisko*, 'bend in the river'). Originally a Salish tribe on Wenatchee or Pisquows r., a western tributary of the Columbia in the present Kittitas and Okanogan cos., Washington. Gibbs states that by 1853 they were so largely intermarried with the Yakima as to have almost lost their identity. Gibbs, Hale, and most subsequent authors have employed the term in a collective sense. The former made it include "the Indians on the Columbia between the Priest's and Ross' rapids on the Pisquouse or Winatshapam r., the En-te-at-kwu, Chelan lake, and the Methow or Barrier r." The Pisquows proper or the remnant of them are now on the Yakima res., Wash. Their bands were Camiltpaw, Siapkat, Shallattoo, Shanwappom, Skaddal, and Squannaroo. See Mooney in 14th Rep. B. A. E., 736, 1896.

Pichons.—Wilkes, West Am., 104, 1849. **Piscahoose.**—Lane in Sen. Ex. Doc. 52, 31st Cong., 1st sess., 174, 1850. **Piscaous.**—Duflot de Mofras, Expl., II, 335, 1844. **Pischoule.**—Stevens (1856) in H. R. Ex. Doc. 37, 34th Cong., 3d sess., 55, 1857. **Pischous.**—Irving, Astoria, map, 1849. **Piscous.**—Hale in U. S. Expl. Exped., VI, 210, 1846. **Piskwas.**—Gallatin in Trans. Am. Ethnol. Soc., II, 20, 1848.

Piskwaus.—Latham in Trans. Philol. Soc. Lond., 71, 1856. **Pisquous.**—Hale, op. cit., 224. **Pisquouse.**—U. S. Stat. at Large, XII, 951, 1863. **Piss-cows.**—Ross, Adventures, 290, 1847.

Pissacoac. The chief village of the Pissasec in 1608, situated on the N. bank of Rappahannock r. above the present Leedstown, in Westmoreland co., Va.

Pisacack.—Simons in Smith (1629), Va., I, 185, repr. 1819. **Pissacoack.**—Smith, ibid., map.

Pissasec. A tribe or band of the Powhatan confederacy living on the N. bank of Rappahannock r. in King George and Westmoreland cos., Va. They formed part of the Matchotic tribe. Their principal village was Pissacoac.

Pissaseck.—Smith (1629), Va., I, map, repr. 1819. **Pissassack.**—Simons, ibid., 185. **Pissassees.**—Boudinot, Star in the West, 128, 1816 (misprint).

Pissuh (cognate with Chippewa *pijiᵘ*, 'lynx.'—W. J.). A gens of the Abnaki.

Pezo.—J. D. Prince, inf'n, 1905 (modern St Francis Abnaki form). **Pijiᵘ.**—Wm. Jones, inf'n, 1906 (Chippewa form). **Pis-suh'.**—Morgan, Anc. Soc., 174, 1877.

Pistchin. A Clallam village on Pysht r., Wash., which flows into Juan de Fuca strait. Starling erroneously states that the "Macaws and Pist-chins speak the same language."

Pisht.—Eels in Smithson. Rep. 1887, 608, 1889. **Pishtot.**—Stevens in Ind. Aff. Rep., 450, 1854. **Pishtst.**—U. S. Ind. Treat., 800, 1873. **Pist-chin.**—Starling in Ind. Aff. Rep., 170, 1852. **Pist chins.**—Ibid., 172.

Pitac. A former rancheria of the Pima on the Gila r., s. Ariz., visited by Father Garcés in 1770 (Arricivita, 1791, quoted by Bancroft, Ariz. and N. M., 387, 1889). Cf. *Petaikuk*.

Pitahauerat ('down stream,' or 'east.'—Grinnell). One of the tribes of the Pawnee confederacy. The French spoke of them as Tapage Pawnee, and in a treaty with the U. S. in 1819 the tribe is designated as Noisy Pawnees. The Pitahauerat always placed their villages toward the E., or downstream, from the Chaui, and are spoken of as the lower villages. At one time the tribe lived on Smoky Hill r., w. Kans., and later rejoined their kindred on Loup r., Nebr., where their reservation was established in 1857. In 1876 they were removed to Oklahoma, where they now live. Their lands have been allotted in severalty, and they are citizens of the U. S. In their village organization, customs, and beliefs, they did not differ from the other Pawnee. According to Grinnell the tribe is divided into the Pitahauerat proper and the Kawarakish. (A. C. F.)

Noisy Pawnees.—Treaty of 1819 in U. S. Stat., VII, 172, 1846. **Pawnee Tappage.**—Treaty of 1849 in U. S. Ind. Treat., 647, 1873. **Pawnee Tappahs.**—Treaty of 1858, ibid., 650. **Pawnee Tappaye.**—Treaty of 1834, ibid., 648. **Pe-tä-hä'-ne-rat.**—Morgan in Smithson. Cont., XVII, 196, 1871. **Pethahanerat.**—Keane in Stanford, Compend., 530, 1878. **Pethowerats.**—Ibid. **Pe-tou-we-ra.**—Long, Exped. Rocky Mts., II, lxxxv, 1823. **Pit-a-hau'-ĕ-rat.**—Dunbar in Mag. Am. Hist., IV, 251, 1880. **Pitaháwiratá.**—Sanssouci quoted by Dorsey in Cont. N. A. Ethnol., VI, 381, 1892 (prob. Omaha notation of Pawnee name). **Pitavirate Noisy Pawnee.**—Treaty of 1819 in U. S. Ind. Treaties, 645, 1873. **Tapage.**—Parker, Journal, 51, 1840. **Tapahowerat.**—Ind. Aff. Rep., 213, 1861. **Tapaje.**—Grinnell, Pawnee Hero Stories, 240, 1889. **Tappa.**—Ind. Aff. Rep., 213, 1861. **Tappage.**—Long, Exped. Rocky Mts., I, 351, 1823. **Tappage Pawnee.**—Irving, Ind. Sketches, II, 13, 1835. **Tappaye Pawnee.**—Treaty of 1834 in U. S. Ind. Treaties, 649, 1873 (misprint). **Witaháwiǫatá.**—La Flesche quoted by Dorsey in Cont. N. A. Ethnol., VI, 413, 1892 (Omaha name).

Pitahauerat. One of the two divisions of the Pitahauerat, or Tapaje Pawnee, the other being the Kawarakish.—Grinnell, Pawnee Hero Stories, 241, 1889.

Pitahay. A tribe, evidently Coahuiltecan, met by Massanet (Mem. de Nueva España, XXVII, 94, MS.), in 1691, 11 leagues E. of middle Nueces, r., Texas, together with Pacuache, Payavan, Patavo, Patsau, and other tribes. (H. E. B.)

Pitas. A former tribe of N. E. Mexico or S. Texas, probably Coahuiltecan, gathered into the mission of Nuestra Señora de los Dolores de la Punta, at Lampazos, Nuevo Leon.—Orozco y Berra, Geog., 303, 1864.

Pitaya (local contraction of *pitahaya*, the fruit of the *Cereus giganteus*, and the cactus itself). A former Maricopa rancheria on the Rio Gila, in S. Arizona, in 1744.—Sedelmair (1744) cited by Bancroft, Ariz. and N. Mex., 366, 1889.

Pitchibourenik. A tribe or supposed tribe formerly residing near the E. side of James bay, Canada; probably a band of the Cree.

Pitchiboucouni.—La Tour Map, 1784. **Pitchiboueouni.**—La Tour Map, 1779. **Pitchib8renik.**—Jes. Rel. 1660, 11, 1858. **Pitehiboutounibuek.**—Jes. Rel. for 1672, 54, 1858.

Pitchlynn, Peter Perkins. A prominent Choctaw chief of mixed blood, born at the Indian town of Hushookwa, Noxubee co., Miss., Jan. 30, 1806; died in Washington, D. C., Jan. 17, 1881. His father, John Pitchlynn, was a white man and an interpreter commissioned by Gen. Washington; his mother, Sophia Folsom, a Choctaw woman. While still a boy, seeing a partially educated member of his tribe write a letter, he resolved that he too would become educated, and although the nearest school was in Tennessee, 200 m. from his father's cabin, he managed to attend it for a season. Returning home at the close of the first quarter, he found his people negotiating a treaty with the general Government. As he considered the terms of this treaty a fraud upon his tribe, he refused to shake hands with Gen. Jackson, who had the matter in charge in behalf of the Washington authorities. Subsequently he entered an academy at Columbia, Tenn., and finally was graduated at the University of Nashville. Although he never changed his opinion regarding the treaty, he became a strong friend of Jackson, who was a trustee of the latter institution. On returning to his home in Mississippi, Pitchlynn became a farmer, built a cabin, and

married Miss Rhoda Folsom, a Choctaw, the ceremony being performed by a Christian minister. By his example and influence polygamy was abandoned by his people. He was selected by the Choctaw council in 1824 to enforce the restriction of the sale of spirituous liquors according to the treaty of Doaks Stand, Miss., Oct. 18, 1820, and in one year the traffic had ceased. As a reward for his services he was made a captain and elected a member of the National Council, when the United States Government determined to remove the Choctaw, Chickasaw, and Creeks w. of the Mississippi. His first proposition in that body was to establish a school, and, that the students might become familiar with the manners and customs of white people, it was located near Georgetown, Ky., rather than within the limits of the Choctaw country. Here it flourished for many years, supported by the funds of the nation. Pitchlynn was appointed one of the delegation sent to Indian Ter. in 1828 to select the lands for their future homes and to make peace with the Osage, his tact and courage making his mission entirely successful. He later emigrated to the new reservation with his people and built a cabin on Arkansas r. Pitchlynn was an admirer of Henry Clay, whom he met for the first time in 1840. He was ascending the Ohio in a steamboat when Mr Clay came on board at Maysville. The Indian went into the cabin and found two farmers earnestly engaged in talking about their crops. After listening to them with great delight for more than an hour, he turned to his traveling companion, to whom he said: "If that old farmer with an ugly face had only been educated for the law, he would have made one of the greatest men in this country." He soon learned that the "old farmer" was Henry Clay. Charles Dickens, who met Pitchlynn on a steamboat on the Ohio r. in 1842, gives an account of the interview in his American Notes, and calls him a chief; but he was not elected principal chief until 1860. In this capacity he went to Washington to protect the interests of his tribesmen, especially to prosecute their claims against the Government. At the breaking out of the Civil War Pitchlynn returned to Indian Ter., and although anxious that his people should remain neutral, found it impossible to induce them to maintain this position; indeed three of his sons espoused the Confederate cause. He himself remained a Union man to the end of the war, notwithstanding the fact that the Confederates raided his plantation of 600 acres and captured all his cattle, while the emancipation proclamation freed his 100 slaves. He was a natural orator, as his address to the President at the White House in 1855, his speeches before the congressional committees in 1868, and one delivered before a delegation of Quakers at Washington in 1869, abundantly prove. In 1865 he returned to Washington, where he remained as the agent of his people until his death, devoting attention chiefly to pressing the Choctaw claim for lands sold to the United States in 1830. In addition to the treaty of 1820, above referred to, he signed the treaty of Dancing Rabbit, Miss., Sept. 27, 1830, and the treaty of Washington, June 20, 1855; he also witnessed, as principal chief, that of Washington, Apr. 28, 1866. Pitchlynn's first wife having died, he married, at Washington, Mrs Caroline Lombardy, a daughter of Godfrey Eckloff, who with two sons and one daughter survive him, the children by the first marriage having died during their father's litetime. Pitchlynn became a member of the Lutheran Memorial Church at Washington, and was a regular attendant until his last illness. He was a prominent member of the Masonic order, and on his death the funeral services were conducted in its behalf by Gen. Albert Pike. A monument was erected over his grave in Congressional Cemetery by the Choctaw Nation. In 1842 Pitchlynn was described by Dickens as a handsome man, with black hair, aquiline nose, broad cheek-bones, sunburnt complexion, and bright, keen, dark, and piercing eyes. He was fairly well read, and in both speaking and writing used good English. He was held in high esteem both by the members of his tribe and by all his Washington acquaintances. See also Lanman, Recollections of Curious Characters, 1881.   (C. T.)

Pitchumon. See *Persimmon.*

Pithlkwutsiaus (*Pi̧çl'-kwŭ-tsi-aus'*). A former Siuslaw village on Siuslaw r., Oreg.—Dorsey in Jour. Am. Folk-lore, iii, 230, 1890.

Pitic. A settlement of the Soba on the Rio Altar in n. w. Sonora, Mexico. It was a visita of the Spanish mission Caborca from prior to 1701, with 313 inhabitants in 1730, and the seat of a presidio established about 1753–54. The name was subsequently changed to Altar. A writer in 1702 (Doc. Hist. Mex., 4th s., v, 138, 139, 1857) says: "This rancheria [Soba] is called Pitquin in the Pima tongue because there is the junction of the two rivers of Tubutama and that of San Ignacio." Rivera, in 1730 (Bancroft, No. Mex. States, i, 514, 1884), classifies it as a pueblo of the Pimas Altos.

Natividad Pitiqui.—Rivera (1730) quoted by Bancroft, No. Mex. States, i, 514, 1884. Piquitin.—Kino (1696) in Doc. Hist. Mex., 4th s., i, 263, 1856. Pitic.—Anza (1774) quoted by Bancroft, Ariz. and N. Mex., 389, 1889. St. Diego de Pitquin.—Venegas, Hist. Cal., i, map, 1759. San Diepo de Pitquin.—Ibid., 303 (misprint). Soba.—Writer *ca.* 1702 in Doc. Hist. Mex., 4th s., v, 138-9, 1857.

Pitiktaujang. A summer village of the Aivilirmiut Eskimo on Repulse bay, n. extremity of Hudson bay.—Boas in 6th Rep. B. A. E., 446, 1888.

Pitkachi. One of the northern Yokuts (Mariposan) tribes of s. central California, on the s. side of San Joaquin r., below Millerton, their territory thus adjoining that of the Chukchansi (Powers in Cont. N. A. Ethnol., iii, 370, 1877; Merriam in Science, xix, 915, June 15, 1904). They were spoken of in 1851 as a large and warlike tribe inhabiting the foothills of the Sierra Nevada, on the headwaters of the Mariposa, Chowchilla, Fresno, and San Joaquin (Barbour in Sen. Ex. Doc. 4, 32d Cong., spec. sess., 61, 1853).

Pik-cak-ches.—Barbour, op. cit., 252. Piscatchees.—Taylor in Cal. Farmer, June 8, 1860. Pit-cach-es.—Ind. Aff. Rep., 223, 1851. Pit-cat-chee.—Sen. Ex. Doc. 4, 32d Cong., spec. sess., 93, 1853. Pitcatches.—Lewis in Ind. Aff. Rep. 1856, 252, 1857. Pitchackies.—Barbour, op. cit., 61. Pit-cuch-es.—Johnston in Sen. Ex. Doc. 61, 32d Cong., 1st sess., 22, 1852. Pitiaches.—Henley in Ind. Aff. Rep., 512, 1854. Pit'-ka-chi.—Powers in Cont. N. A. Ethnol., iii, 370, 1877. Pit-kah'-che.—Merriam in Science, xix, 915, June 15, 1904. Pit-kah'-te.—Ibid.

Pits. Excavations made in the ground for ovens, houses, reservoirs, caches, traps, shrines, graves, and for other purposes, are very generally found in the neighborhood of Indian habitations, and even for centuries after the abandonment of villages traces of these pits remain. In the W. some tribes still practise the custom of making pits for various purposes. By reason of the numerous roasting pits excavated along its banks, Pit r. in n. California and the Achomawi or "Pit River Indians" of the neighborhood were so named. The practice of roasting food in a small pit (the so-called Gipsy oven) appears to have been a common one among Indians, and such excavations are probably most numerous (see *Ovens*). Within the habitat of the agave, especially in s. Arizona and n. Sonora, pits several feet in diameter have long been used for roasting the plants to produce mescal (q. v.). The Maidu of n. California gathered grasshoppers and locusts, of which they were very fond, by digging a large shallow pit in a meadow or flat, and then, by setting fire to the grass on all sides, drove the insects into the pit; their wings being burned off by the flames, they were helpless, and were thus collected by the bushel (Dixon). Abandoned field ovens of the Pueblos for roasting at once immense quantities of green corn become mere pits by the falling in of the earth sides, leaving no superficial clew to their former purpose. Some of the depressions around ancient ruins are likewise enigmatic, although some probably were dug originally as reservoirs, as ovens, or for obtaining material for adobe (see *Adobe, Food, Irrigation*). Storage pits were in general use. Such pits, filled with refuse, have been found on the Baum and Gartner village sites in Ohio (Mills), and from them have been taken much material connected with the daily life of the people; they surrounded the habitations and were lined with straw or bark to receive corn in the ear compactly laid in, or shelled corn in woven bags. The Creek Indians built large storage pits in the ground (see *Receptacles, Storage and Caches*). Quarry pits for extracting copper, stone, clay, ocher, turquoise, etc., have been observed in localities where these substances occur, and sometimes, as in the L. Superior region, the Flint Ridge deposit in Ohio, and the pipestone quarry of Minnesota, an immense amount of work of this sort has been done (see *Mines and Quarries*). Occasionally pit traps were made, those of the Navaho consisting of a pocket at the end of a cul de sac of stakes. Burials were often made in pits, in which sometimes a number of bodies were deposited (see *Mortuary customs*). Cairn graves were formed by scooping a hole in the ground, placing the body therein, and covering with stones. This custom had a wide range. Pit houses are comparatively rare, but are found among the Eskimo, the Maidu of California, and a prehistoric tribe of w. New Mexico (see *Habitations*). Pits were sometimes dug for use as sweat houses, and the kivas (q. v.) of the Pueblos were usually at least partly underground. Consult Dixon in Bull. Am. Mus. Nat. Hist., XVII, pt. 3, 1905; Jones in Smithson. Rep. 1885, 900, 1886; Holmes, ibid., 1903, 723–26, 1904; Hough in Bull. 35, B. A. E., 1907; Loskiel, Hist. Miss. United Breth., pt. I, 108, 1794; Mills, Certain Mounds and Village Sites in Ohio, I, pt. 3, 211–22, 1907; Powers in Cont. N. A. Ethnol., III, 1877; Yarrow in First Rep. B. A. E., 113, 142, 1881.   (w. H.)

Pitsokut. A former Maidu village near Roseville, Placer co., Cal.—Dixon in Bull. Am. Mus. Nat. Hist., pl. 38, 1905.

Pitted stones. See *Cupstones, Hammers*.

Pituarvik. A village of the Ita Eskimo on Whale sd., w. Greenland, where the tribe assembles for the spring walrus hunt.

Peterárwi.—Stein in Petermanns Mitt., no. 9, map, 1902. **Peteravak.**—Markham in Trans. Ethnol. Soc. Lond., 129, 1866. **Peteravik.**—Bessels, Am. Nordpol. Exped., 1898. **Petowach.**—Ross., Voy. of Discov., 134, 1819. **Petowack.**—Ibid., 196. **Pituarvik.**—Kroeber in Bull. Am. Mus. Nat. Hist., XII, 269, 1899.

Pivanhonkapi (*Pivánhonkapi*). A traditionary village about 4 m. N. w. of Oraibi pueblo, N. E. Ariz. According to Hopi story Pivanhonkapi and Hushkovi (q. v.) were destroyed by a fire that had been kindled in the San Francisco mts., 90 m. away, at the instance of the chief of Pivanhonkapi and with the aid of the Yayaponchatu people, who are said to have been in league with supernatural forces, because the inhabitants of Pivanhonkapi had become degenerate through gambling. Most of the inhabitants were also destroyed; the survivors moved away, occupying several temporary villages during their wanderings, the ruins of which are still to be seen.—Voth, Traditions of the Hopi, 241, 1905.

Pivipa. A former pueblo of the Opata, on the Rio Soyopa, a western branch of the Yaqui, in N. E. Sonora, Mexico (Orozco y Berra, Geog., 343, 1864). Pivipa is now a civilized rancho of 173 inhabitants.

Pivwani (*Pi-vwa'-ni*). The Marmot clan of the Chua (Snake) phratry of the Hopi.—Stephen in 8th Rep. B. A. E., 38, 1891.

Pizhiki ('Buffalo'). A Chippewa chief, often called Buffalo, his English name, formerly residing on La Pointe or Madeline id., Wis.; born about 1759, died Sept. 7, 1855. He is spoken of as one of the most distinguished chiefs of the Chippewa tribe (Wis. Hist. Coll., III, 365, 1857); but Warren indicates more closely the scope of his authority by referring to him as "Kechewaishkeen (Great Buffalo), the respected and venerable chief of the La Pointe band [Shaugaumikong] and principal chief of all the Lake Superior and Wisconsin bands" (Minn. Hist. Coll., v, 48, 1885). In one instance he signed a treaty as representative of the St Croix band, and in another in behalf of both the St Croix and La Pointe bands. According to Warren (p. 87) he was the grandson of chief Augdaweos, which seems to have been also the name of his father. When Buffalo was about 10 years of age his family removed to the vicinity of the present Buffalo, N. Y., where they remained two years, then went to Mackinaw, there residing several years, and thence returned to La Pointe. But few of the important incidents of Pizhiki's life are recorded, but he was an informant of Warren, the historian of the Chippewa. His name is signed to the treaties of Prairie du Chien, Wis., Aug. 19, 1825 ("Gitspee Waskee, le bœuf of La Pointe"); Fond du Lac, Wis., Aug. 5, 1826 ("Peezhickee"); St Peters r. (Wisconsin side), July 29, 1837 ("Pezheke"); La Pointe, Wis., Oct. 4, 1842 ("Gitchiwaisky"); Fond du Lac, Aug. 2, 1847 ("Ke-che-wash-keen"), and La Pointe, Wis., Sept. 30, 1854 ("Ke-che-waish-ke"). Schoolcraft (Personal Mem., 103, 1851) says that "Gitchee Waishkee, the Great First-born" was familiarly called "Pezhickee, or the Buffalo." By the last treaty a section of land was granted to him out of the territory then ceded to the United States. Previous to his death, in 1855, Pizhiki was baptized in the Roman Catholic faith.

To Commissioner Manypenny, who was with him when he died, he presented his pipe and tobacco pouch, desiring him to take them to Washington. He was buried, Sept. 9, in the Catholic cemetery at La Pointe.

A Chippewa chief of the St Croix band, also named "Peezhickee," or Buffalo, signed the treaties of Prairie du Chien, Wis., Aug. 19, 1825; Fond du Lac, Wis., Aug. 5, 1826, and St Peters r., Wis., July 29, 1837. (C. T.)

Pkhulluwaaitthe (*Pkqŭl-lu′-wa-ai-t′çĕ*). A former Yaquina village on the s. side of Yaquina r., Oreg.—Dorsey in Jour. Am. Folk-lore, III, 229, 1890.

Pkipsissewa. See *Pipsissewa*.

Pkuuniukhtauk (*Pku-u′-ni-uqt-auk′*). A former Yaquina village on the s. side of Yaquina r., Oreg.—Dorsey in Jour. Am. Folk-lore, III, 229, 1890.

Plaikni (*P′laĭkni*, 'uplanders'). A collective name given by the Klamath to all the Indians on Sprague r., above and below Yaneks, on the Klamath res., s. w. Oreg. They comprise the majority of the Modoc, many Klamath, and the Shoshonean Walpapi and Yahuskin settled in these parts.—Gatschet in Cont. N. A. Ethnol., II, pt. I, xxxv, 1890.
Uplanders.—Gatschet, ibid.

Plaquemine. See *Persimmon*.

Plaques. See *Receptacles*.

Playwickey ('town of the turkey'). A former Delaware village in Bucks co., Pa. It probably belonged to the Unalachtigo division, and may have been on Neshaminy cr.
Planwikit.—Brinton, Lenape Leg., 39, 1885. Playwickey.—Deed of 1737 quoted by Day, Penn., 507, 1843.

Pluggy's Town. A former village, named from its chief, which occupied the site of Delaware, Delaware co., Ohio, in 1776. It belonged to a marauding band of Indians, who seem to have been chiefly Mingo. See Butterfield, Washington-Irvine Corr., 9, 1882.

Plummets. A group of prehistoric pendant-like objects of stone, bone, shell, hematite ore, copper, and other materials the origin and use of which have been much discussed (see *Problematical objects*). The name plummet is applied because of the resemblance of many specimens to the ordinary builder's plummet, but the shapes are greatly diversified, numerous variants connecting the well-established type forms with other groups of objects, as net sinkers, club heads, pestles, birdstones, boat-stones, pendant ornaments, etc. Numerous specimens are rudely shaped, but the greater number are highly finished and symmetric, and often graceful in contour. Eccentric forms are sometimes encountered, especially in Florida, and rather rarely the body is carved to

represent in formal fashion the head of a duck. Usually there is a shallow encircling groove; occasionally there are two, at the upper end; and in rare cases one or more grooves or ridges encircle the body of the longer specimens at different points, giving a spindle-like effect. Some are grooved at both ends, while many terminate below in conical or nipple-like points. A few are truncated or have a slight depression at the upper end, and rare specimens of the long slender variety have one side flat or slightly hollowed out, suggesting the form of a dugout canoe. Perforations for suspension are observed in numerous cases, indicating affiliation with ordinary pendant ornaments, while some well-finished specimens have neither grooves nor perforations.

COPPER; FLORIDA; ⅓ (MOORE)

The plummets are widely distributed over the country, occurring in great profusion in Florida, in the Mississippi valley, and in California, and are often found associated with human remains in burials. Some were undoubtedly worn on the person, after the manner of pendant ornaments, but there is good reason to believe that many of them were devoted to magic

COPPER; FLORIDA; ⅓ (MOORE)   STONE; FLORIDA; ⅓ (MOORE)

and ceremony, being invested by their owners with extraordinary powers as charms, talismans, amulets, fetishes, etc., capable in one way or another of exerting profound influence on the welfare of the individual, the society, the clan, or the tribe. The Indians of s. California, in whose possession some of these objects are found, believe them to be helpful in war and the chase, in producing rain, in curing the sick, in games of chance, etc. (Henshaw, Yates). It has been suggested that the original plummets may have been net sinkers, or other objects having at first only practical functions, which in time came to be regarded as luck stones or charms, passing gradually into general use as such, with many shades of significance and widely divergent forms. It is worthy of note that the aborigines generally are disposed to attribute magical significance to all old worked stones as well as to all

a   *b*

a SPECULAR IRON; LOUISIANA (1-4); *b* SPECULAR IRON; TENNESSEE (¼).

unusual natural shapes. According to Dr Wm. Jones the Chippewa regard these objects with deep veneration. The ancient name of the plummet type was *mōjābäwasin*, 'a stone (*-asin*) of human attributes (*-äbä-*) that casts a spell (*moj-*).' Its present name is *shĭngābä-wasin*, stone of human attributes lying at rest (*shing-*). *Kĭsis*, 'sun,' was applied to a circular disk; and *tibi'ki kĭsis*, 'night sun or moon,' to a crescent perforated at the horns. These three types—plummet, circular, and crescent—went under the general name of *ubawānāganan*, 'dream objects.' The phrase *tibi'ki kĭsis wäba-wānaganit* means 'one who (wearing the crescent as a necklace) dreams of the moon,' literally, 'one who wears the moon dream object (for his necklace).'

These objects are found in large numbers in the mounds of Florida, and Moore has illustrated numerous specimens in his works. The range of form is apparently greater here than in any other section of the country, each of the several materials used having given rise to peculiar features, although the elongated plummet and spindle shapes prevail. Suspension was apparently effected by passing a knotted cord through the center of a bit of hide, with the knot underneath, and then folding the margins of the hide down over the head of the plummet, where it was fastened by means of a groove cord. Asphaltum was used in completing the work. The occurrence of a number of these plummets of diversified shapes about the waist of a skeleton in a mound seems to indicate that they had been attached to the girdle. A cache of 12 or more specimens of exceptional beauty of form and finish—one carved to represent a duck's head—was obtained by Moore from a mound in Brevard co., Fla. Cushing describes specimens which bear evidence of having been suspended by means of filaments attached to the groove band and brought together in a knot above.

In the mound region of the Mississippi valley plummets are mostly of stone and hematite ore (Squier and Davis, Fowke, Moorehead). They are rare in the Pueblo region, but many are found in California, and much attention has been given to their study (Abbott, Henshaw, Meredith, Putnam, Yates). From the dry bed of a small lake in Sonoma co., drained for agricultural purposes in 1870, many hundreds of these objects were collected, indicating their use either as sinkers for fishing lines or nets or as offerings to the spirits of the water, the keepers of the fish. Perhaps the stones themselves were believed to possess magical power over the finny tribes. It is a noteworthy fact that a number of these objects appear among the collections obtained from sup-posedly very ancient auriferous gravel deposits in California.

Closely allied to the plummets is a unique group of objects, mostly of slate, resembling half-plummets. The small head, tapering body, and spike-like base or tail suggest somewhat the form of the common lizard; but the analogy is rather closer in many examples with the duck-head plummets, which have one flat side. Although some are slightly grooved at the top for suspension, the presence of a flat side suggests the possibility that they were attached when in use to the surface of some object, as a tablet, a calumet, or a baton. A few examples of kindred objects have the upper end carved to represent the head of some mammal, as a wolf.

Consult Abbott, (1) in U. S. G. and G. Surv. West of 100th Merid., VII, 1879, (2) Prim. Indus., 1881; Beauchamp in Bull. N. Y. State Mus., IV, no. 18, 1897; Cushing in Proc. Am. Philos. Soc., XXXV, 1896; Eells in Smithson. Rep. 1886, 1889; Foster, Prehist. Races, 1878; Fowke, Archæol. Hist. Ohio, 1902; Henderson in Am. Nat., 1872; Henshaw in Am. Jour. Archæol., I, no. 2, 1885; Jones, Aborig. Remains of Tenn., 1876; Meredith in Moorehead's Prehist. Impl., 1900; Moore, various papers in Jour. Acad. Nat. Sci. Phila., 1894–1905; Moorehead, Prehist. Impl., 1900; Peabody in Bull. Mus. Sci. and Art, Univ. Pa., III, no. 3, 1901; Putnam in U. S. G. and G. Surv. W. 100th Merid., VII, 1879; Rau, (1) Archæol. Coll. Nat. Mus., 1876, (2) Prim. Fishing, 1884; Squier and Davis, Aborig. Mon., 1848; Willoughby in Peabody Mus. Papers, I, no. 6, 1898; Wilson in Rep. Nat. Mus. 1896, 1898; Yates in Smithson. Rep. 1886, 1889.   (w. h. h.)

Po. The Calabash clans of the Tewa pueblos of San Juan, Santa Clara, San Ildefonso, Nambe, and Tesuque, N. Mex. That of Tesuque is extinct.
Po-tdóa.--Hodge in Am. Anthrop., IX, 349, 1896 (*tdóa*=‘people’).

Po (*P'o*). The Water clans of the Tewa pueblos of San Juan and San Ildefonso, N. Mex.
P'ho.--Bandelier, Delight Makers, 379, 1890. P'ho doa.--Ibid. (*doa*=‘people’). P'o-tdóa.--Hodge in Am. Anthrop., IX, 352, 1896.

Poaquesson. See *Poquosin*.

Poatsituhtikuteh (*Poát-sit-uh-ti-kút-teh*, ‘clover-eaters’). A Paviotso band formerly residing on the N. fork of Walker r., w. Nevada.—Powers, Inds. W. Nevada, MS., B. A. E., 1876.

Poblazon (‘large town,’ ‘a population’). The Spanish name of a ruined pueblo on Rio San José, a tributary of the Puerco, in Valencia co., N. Mex. It may have been Keresan.
Poblaçon.—Emory, Recon., 133, 1848. Poblacon.—Simpson in Smithson. Rep. 1869, 332, 1871. Po-blazon.--Abert in Emory, Recon., 467, 1848.

Pocahontas (*Pocahantes*, for *Pokahantesu*, a verbal adjective meaning 'he (or she) is playful,' 'sportive,' apparently a cognate of Chippewa *pagaandisi*, contracted to *pagándisi*, and the vowel preceding the one dropped lengthened by compensation, as always happens in such cases. The aspirate *h* is not a radical element and is not employed in Chippewa. The Chippewa adj. suffix -*si* becomes -*su* in the eastern Algonquian dialects. The Chippewa word is used of a person, male or female, who dislikes to work and prefers to spend his or her time in frivolous amusements. The root is adjectival and trisyllabic.—Gerard). The daughter of Powhatan, chief of a group of Virginian tribes, 1595–1617. Her real name was Matoaka (Matowaka), a word found also in the misspelled form of Matoka and Matoaks. The sole Algonquian root from which the name can be derived is *mĕtaw*, 'to play,' 'to amuse one's self;' whence *Mĕtawáke*, 'she uses (something) to play with,' or 'she amuses herself playing with (something).' It was undoubtedly to her innate fondness for playthings, play, and frolicsome amusement that was due the name given her by her parents, as well as the expression "Pokahantes" used by her father when speaking of her (Gerard).

By reason of the alleged romance of her life, Pocahontas is one of the most famous of American women. Her father's "dearest daughter," a mere girl at the time, she is said to have saved Capt. John Smith from a cruel and ignominious death at the hands of Powhatan's people, whose prisoner he then was; and she is credited with enabling many other Englishmen to escape the wrath and vengeance of her tribespeople. What the truth is about some of her alleged exploits can never be known; some writers have even doubted the episode with Capt. Smith. After the departure of Smith for England in 1609, faith was not kept with the Indians as promised, and Pocahontas, by the aid of a treacherous chief, was decoyed on board the ship of Capt. Argall in the Potomac, carried off to Jamestown (1612), and afterward taken to Werawocomoco, Powhatan's chief place of residence, where a sort of peace was effected and the ransom of Pocahontas agreed upon. While among the Englishmen, however, Pocahontas had become acquainted with John Rolfe, "an honest gentleman, and of good behaviour." These two fell in love, an event which turned out to the satisfaction of everybody, and in Apr. 1613, they were duly married, Pocahontas having been previously converted to Christianity and baptized under the name of "the Lady Rebecca." This alliance was of great advantage to the colonists, for Powhatan kept peace with them until his death. In 1616, Mr and Mrs Rolfe, with her brother-in-law Uttamatomac and several other Indians, accompanied Sir Thomas Dale to England, where, owing to the prevalent misunderstanding of those times concerning the character and government of the American tribes, Mrs Rolfe was received as a "princess." In Mar. 1617, while on board ship at Gravesend ready to start for America with her husband, she fell ill of smallpox, and died about the 22d year of her life. In July 1907, a skeleton, believed to be the remains of Pocahontas, was unearthed within the site of Gravesend Parish church. She left behind her one son, Thomas Rolfe, who was educated by his uncle, Henry Rolfe, in England. Thomas Rolfe afterward went to Virginia, where he ac-

POCAHONTAS. (THE BOOTON HALL PORTRAIT)

quired wealth and distinction, leaving at his death an only daughter, from whom was descended, on the mother's side, John Randolph of Roanoke (1773–1833). Other distinguished Virginians are also said to claim descent from Pocahontas. She was called Pocahontas, Capt. John Smith says, "because that the savages did think that, did we know her real name, we should have the power of casting an evil eye upon her."

Strachey, the first secretary of the colony, gives some details (Hist. Trav. Va. Brit., 1849) regarding the early life and marriage of Pocahontas to an Indian chief, named Kocoum, previous to her union with Rolfe.

In addition to the authorities cited, consult the Works of Capt. John Smith, Arber ed., 1884; the biographies of Pocahontas by E. L. Dorsey (1906), Robertson and Brock (1887), and Seelye and

Eggleston (1879); Adams, Chapters of Eden, 1871; Bushnell in Am. Anthrop., IX, no. 1, 1907. (A. F. C. J. N. B. H.)

Pocan. One of the names of the poke-weed (*Phytolacca decandra*), also known as pocan-bush; practically the same word as *puccoon* (q. v.) and of the same origin, from a Virginian dialect of Algonquian. See *Poke.* (A. F. C.)

Pocapawmet. A Massachuset village, in 1614, on the s. shore of Massachusetts bay.—Smith (1616) in Mass. Hist. Soc. Coll., 3d s., VI, 108, 1837.

Pocasset ('where a strait widens out'; cf. *Paugusset*). A former Wampanoag village about the site of Tiverton, Newport co., R. I., and Fall River, Mass., ruled in 1675 by the woman chief Westamore, sister-in-law of King Philip. A part of the site, within the boundaries of Massachusetts, was afterward set aside as a reservation under the name of Freetown or Fall River res., and contained 59 mixed-blood inhabitants in 1764 and 37 in 1848. They were sometimes also known as Troy Indians. Consult Dubuque, Fall River Ind. Res., 1907.

Pocasicke.—Deed (*ca.* 1638) quoted by Drake, Bk. Inds., bk. 2, 60, 1848. Pocasset.—Trumbull, Ind. Names Conn., 46, 1881. Pocassett.—Records (1639) in R. I. Col. Rec., I, 88, 1856. Pocassitt.—Sanford (1671), ibid., II, 427, 1857. Pokeesett.—Deed of 1659 quoted by Drake, Bk. Inds., bk. 3, 3, 1848. Powakasick.—Deed of 1638 in R. I. Col. Rec., I, 47, 1856. Troy Indians.—Rep. of 1865 cited by Dubuque, op. cit. Weetemore Indians.—Church (1716) quoted by Drake, Ind. Wars, 67, 1825.

Pocasset. A former village near the present Pocasset, Barnstable co., Mass.; perhaps identical with Pispogutt.

Pocasset.—Trumbull, Ind. Names Conn., 46, 1881. Pokeset.—Kendall, Trav., II, 127, 1809. Pokesset.—Freeman (1792) in Mass. Hist. Soc. Coll., 1st s., I, 231, 1806.

Pocatamough. A village in 1608 on the w. bank of Patuxent r., in St Marys co., Md.—Smith (1629), Va., I, map, repr. 1819.

Poccon. See *Puccoon.*

Pochotita (Nahuatl: 'where there are silk-cotton trees'). A sacred place of the Huichol, containing a temple; situated 5 m. N. of Santa Catarina, in the Sierra de los Huicholes, near the upper waters of the Rio Chapalagana, in Jalisco, Mexico.

Pochotita.—Lumholtz, Unknown Mex., II, 138, 1902. Rawéyapa.—Ibid. (Huichol name).

Pochougoula (prob. Choctaw: 'pond-lily people'). One of the 9 villages formerly occupied by the Natchez.—Iberville (1699) in Margry, Déc., IV, 179, 1880.

Pocoan. See *Puccoon.*

Pocol. A former Diegueño rancheria near San Diego, s. Cal.—Ortega (1775) cited by Bancroft, Hist. Cal., I, 254, 1884.

Pocomtuc. A tribe formerly living on Deerfield and Connecticut rs., in Franklin co., Mass. Their principal village, of the

same name, was near the present Deerfield, and they were frequently known as Deerfield Indians. They had a fort on Ft Hill in the same vicinity, which was destroyed by the Mohawk after a hard battle in 1666. They were an important tribe, and seem to have ruled over all the other Indians of the Connecticut valley within the limits of Massachusetts, including those at Agawam, Nonotuc, and Squawkeag. They combined with the Narraganset and Tunxis in the attacks on Uncas, the Mohegan chief. All these joined the hostile Indians under King Philip in 1675, and at the close of the war in the following year fled to Scaticook, on the Hudson, where some of them remained until about 1754, when they joined the Indians in the French interest at St Francis, Quebec. (J. M.)

Pacamteho.—Ft Orange conf. (1664) in N. Y. Doc. Col. Hist., XIII, 379, 1881. Pacamtekock.—Dareth (1664), ibid., 380. Pacamtekookes.—Albany treaty (1664), ibid., III, 68, 1853. Pacomtuck.—Pynchon (1663), ibid., XIII, 308, 1881. Patrantecooke.—Courtland (1688), ibid., III, 562, 1853. Paucomtuck.—Williams (1648) in Mass. Hist. Soc. Coll., 3d s., I, 178, 1825. Paucomtuckqut.—Williams (1648), ibid. Pawcompt.—Mason (1648), ibid., 4th s., VII, 413, 1865. Pecompticks.—Caulkins, Norwich, 45, 1866. Pecomptuck.—Drake, Bk. Ind., bk. 3, 81, 1848. Pocompheake.—Hubbard (1682) in Mass. Hist. Soc. Coll., 2d s., V, 462, 1825. Pocomptuck.—Mason (1659), ibid., 4th s., VII, 423, 1865. Pocomtakukes.—Gookin (1674), ibid., 1st s., I, 160, 1806. Pocomtock.—Addam (1653) quoted by Drake, Bk. Inds., bk. 2, 79, 1848. Pocomtuck.—Mason (*ca.* 1670) in Mass. Hist. Soc. Coll., 2d s., VIII, 153, 1819. Pocumptucks.—Hubbard (1682), ibid., V, 462-3, 1815. Pocumtuck.—Hoyt, Antiq. Res., 76, 1824. Pocomtucks.—Macauley, N. Y., II, 162, 1829 (misprint). Pokomtakukes.—Ibid., 189. Pokomtock.—Stanton (1676) in N. Y. Doc. Col. Hist., XIV, 715, 1883. Powcomptuck.—Mason (1648) in Mass. Hist. Soc. Coll., 4th s., VII, 413, 1865.

Pocon. See *Puccoon.*

Pocopassum. An Abnaki village in 1614, in Maine, probably on the coast.—Smith (1616) in Mass. Hist. Soc. Coll., 3d s., VI, 107, 1837.

Pocosan, Pocosin, Pocoson. See *Poquosin.*

Pocotaligo (Creek: possibly *Apókitaläíki*, 'settlement extending' or 'town situated [there]'). The largest town of the Yamasi before the revolt of 1715; situated in Beaufort co., S. C., between Combahee and Savannah rs. Pocotaligo is now a township in Beaufort co. (A. S. G.)

Pocataligo.—Drake, Ind. Chron., 175, 1836. Pocotaligat.—Humphreys, Acct., 97, 1730. Pocotaligo.—Mills, S. C., 370, 1826. Poketalico.—Gallatin in Trans. Am. Antiq. Soc., II, 84, 1836.

Podunk. Defined by Bartlett (Dict. of Americanisms, 791, 1877) as "a term applied to an imaginary place in burlesque writing or speaking." This word appears as a place name in both Connecticut and Massachusetts, occurring as early as 1687 in its present form, and in the forms *Potaecke* and *Potunke* in 1636 and 1671 respectively. It is the name of a brook in Connecticut and of a pond in Brookfield, Mass., and the meadows thereabout had also this name. It is derived from either the Mohegan or the Massachuset dialect of Algonquian. The word is identical with *Potunk*, a Long Island place-name which, according to Ruttenber (Ind. Geog. Names, 100, 1906), is presumably a corruption of *P'tuk-ohke*, 'a neck or corner of land '. (A. F. C.)

Podunk. A band or small tribe on Podunk r., in Hartford co., Conn., closely related to the Poquonnoc. Their principal village, also called Podunk, was at the mouth of that river. They seem to have gone off with the hostile Indians at the close of King Philip's war in 1676, and never to have returned. (J. M.)

Podunck.—Willis (1666) in N. Y. Doc. Col. Hist., III, 121, 1853. Podunks.—Stiles (1761) in Mass. Hist. Soc. Coll., 1st s., X, 105, 1809. Windsor Indians.—McClure (1797), ibid., V, 170, 1806.

Poele. A Chumashan village on one of the Santa Barbara ids., Cal., probably Santa Rosa, in 1542.—Cabrillo, Narr. (1542), in Smith, Colec. Doc. Fla., 186, 1857.

Poelo (*Po-e'-lo*). Said by Powers (Cont. N. A. Ethnol., III, 393, 1877) to be a tribe, related to the Paiute, on Kern r. slough, s. E. Cal., but it is more probably merely a place name. The section mentioned is in Mariposan (Yokuts) territory.

Poetry. Most Indian rituals can be classed as poetry. They always relate to serious subjects and are expressed in dignified language, and the words chosen to clothe the thought generally make rhythm. The lines frequently open with an exclamation, a word which heralds the thought about to be uttered. Prose rituals are always intoned, and the delivery brings out the rhythmic character of the composition. Rituals that are sung differ from those that are intoned in that the words, in order to conform to the music, are drawn out by vowel prolongations. If the music is in the form of the chant, but little adjustment is required beyond the doubling or prolonging of vowels; but if the music is in the form of the song, the treatment of the words is more complex; the musical phrase will determine the length of a line, and the number of musical phrases in the song the number of lines to the stanza. To meet the requirements of the musical phrase the vowels in some of the words will be prolonged or doubled, or vocables will be added to bring the line to the measure required by the music. In many instances similar or rhyming vocables are placed at the close of recurring musical phrases. This device seems to indicate a desire to have the word sound recur with the repetition of the same musical phrase, affording an interesting suggestion as to one of the possible ways in which metric verse arose. Where vocables are added to fill out the measure of a line, or are exclusively used in the singing of a phrase

or a song, they are regarded as being unchangeable as words, and no liberties are ever taken with them.

The same treatment of words in their relation to the musical phrase is observed in the secular songs of tribes. In those sung by the various societies at their gatherings, or those which accompany the vocations of men or women in love songs, war songs, hunting songs, or mystery songs, the musical phrase in every instance fixes the rhythm and measure, and the words and vocables are made to conform to it. In many of these songs the words are few, but they have been carefully chosen with reference to their capability of conveying the thought of the composer in a manner that, to the native's mind, will be poetic, not prosaic. Moreover, the vocables used to fill out the measure are selected so as to harmonize with the thought that the words and music jointly seek to convey; they are flowing when the emotion is gentle or supplicating, but broken and sharp when defiance or aggression is the theme. The picturesque quality of Indian speech lends itself to poetic conceits and expressions. The few words of a song will, to the Indian, portray a cosmic belief, present the mystery of death, or evoke the memory of joy or grief; to him the terse words project the thought or emotion from the background of his tribal life and experience, and make the song vibrant with poetic meaning.

Many of the rites observed among the natives, from the Arctic ocean to the Gulf of Mexico, are highly poetic in their significance, symbolism, and ceremonial movements; the rituals and accompanying acts, the songs whose rhythm is accentuated by the waving of feathered emblems, the postures and marches, and the altar decorations combine to make up dramas of deep significance, replete with poetic thought and expression.

The peculiarities of Indian languages and the forms in which the Indian has cast his poetic thought, particularly in song, make it impossible to reproduce them literally in a foreign language; nevertheless they can be adequately translated. In the poetry of the Indian are blended his beliefs, social usages, traditions of ancient environment, and his views of nature, making a record of great human interest. See *Music and Musical instruments.*

Consult Cushing, Zuñi Creation Myths, 1896; Matthews, Navaho Night Chant, 1902; Mooney, Ghost-Dance Religion, 1896; Fletcher, (1) The Hako, 1904, (2) Study of Omaha Music, 1893, (3) Indian Story and Song, 1900. (A. C. F.)

Pogamoggan. A club, cudgel, war-club: from Chippewa *pägämägan* or *pŭgŭmägan* (according to dialect), meaning, literally, '(what is) used for striking'. The cognate word, *päkämàgan*, is used by the Cree as a name for a hammer or mallet. See *Clubs, Tomahawks*.   (w. r. g.)

Pogatacut. A sachem of the Manhasset of Long Id., who signed the deed of East Hampton in 1648. In the same year his name was written Poygratasuck. He was a brother of the chief of the same name who died in 1651, and whose body, on the way to the grave, was set down between Sag Harbor and East Hampton. At the spot where his head rested was made the "Sachem's Hole," which was kept clear by the Indians until destroyed in building a turnpike. Consult Ruttenber, Tribes Hudson R., 75, 1872; N. Y. Doc. Col. Hist., I, 676, 1853.   (w. m. b.)

Poggie, Poggy. See *Pogy, Porgy*.
Poghaden. See *Pogy, Pauhagen*.
Pogie. See *Pogy, Porgy*.
Pogonip. A Shoshonean term used in Nevada to designate a peculiar fog that occasionally visits the mountain country in winter. The sun is obscured, usually during the entire day, and sometimes for days, while the air is charged with a heavy fog in which fine particles of snow seem to be flying. Although the temperature may not be low, intense cold is felt on account of the unusual humidity that prevails. It is said that the Indians greatly fear these fogs.

Pogoreshapka (Russian: 'burnt cap'). An Ikogmiut Eskimo village on the right bank of the lower Yukon, about 20 m. from Koserefski, Alaska; pop. 121 in 1880.
Gagara-Shapka.—Dall, inf'n (Russian: 'loon cap; name applied to a village where the natives made birdskin caps, for which Pogoreshapka is a mistake). Pogoreshapka.—Petroff in Tenth Census, Alaska, 12, 1884.

Pogromni (Russian: 'desolation'). An Aleut village near Pogromni volcano, on the n. shore of Unimak id., e. Aleutian ids., Alaska.—Lutke (1828) quoted by Baker, Geog. Dict. Alaska, 1902.

Pogy. A northern New England name for the menhaden; also applied to a fishing boat. A trap for menhaden fishing is known as pogy-catcher. The word is either identical with *porgy* (q. v.) or corrupted from *poghaden*, a variant of *pauhagen*, another name of this fish. It is spelled also *pogie* and *poggie*.   (a. f. c.)

Pohallintinleh (*Pohalin tinliu*, 'at the squirrels' holes.'—A. L. K.). A name given by Powers (Cont. N. A. Ethnol., III, 370, 1877) as that of a Mariposan (Yokuts) tribe living a little n. of Ft Tejon, near Kern lake, Cal., but it is really only the name of a locality.

Pohemcomeati. A Nanticoke village in 1707 on the lower Susquehanna in Pennsylvania.—Evans (1707) quoted by Day, Penn., 391, 1843.

Pohickery. See *Hickory*.

Pohkopophunk (*Puchapuchung*, 'at the cleft rock.'—Gerard). A Delaware village about 1740 in e. Pennsylvania, probably in Carbon co.
Pochapuchkung.—Loskiel (1794) quoted by Day, Penn., 517, 1843. Pohkopophunk.—Scull (ca. 1737) quoted by Day, ibid., 475.

Pohoi (*Po'-hoi*, 'wild-sage people'). The Comanche name for the Shoshoni, of whom a few are incorporated in the former tribe; early referred to as a Comanche band.   (j. m.)
Po'-hoi.—Mooney in 14th Rep. B. A. E., 1045, 1896. Po̅-jo̅.—Butcher and Leyendecker, Comanche MS. vocab., B. A. E., 1867 (trans. 'of the mute tribe'). Tre̅s-qu̅i-tă̆.—Ibid. (trans. 'spare evacuators').

Pohomoosh. A Micmac village or band in 1760, probably in Nova Scotia.—Frye (1760) in Mass. Hist. Soc. Coll., 1st s., X, 116, 1809.

Pohonichi. A name applied to those Indians of the Moquelumnan family who formerly lived during the summer months in Yosemite valley, Cal. The name is derived from *Pohono*, the Indian name for Bridalveil fall in Yosemite valley. These people lived during the cold season in the Sierra foot-hills along Merced r. Of the original group of people to which the term was applied there are now (1906) but two or three survivors.   (s. a. b.)
Fonechas.—Bancroft, Nat. Races, I, 363, 1874. Openoches.—Taylor in Cal. Farmer, June 8, 1860. Pah-huh-hach-is.—Johnston in Sen. Ex. Doc. 61, 32d Cong., 1st sess., 23, 1852. Phonecha.—Henley in Ind. Aff. Rep., 512, 1854. Po-ha-ha-chis.—Johnston, op. cit., 22. Poho-neche.—Royce in 18th Rep. B. A. E., 822, 1899. Po-ho-ne-chees.—Barbour in Sen. Ex. Doc. 4, 32d Cong., spec. sess., 252, 1853. Pohoneechees.—Bancroft, Nat. Races, I, 456, 1874. Po-ho-neech-es.—McKee et al. (1851) in Sen. Ex. Doc. 4, 32d Cong., spec. sess., 74, 1853. Po-ho-neich-es.—McKee in Ind. Aff. Rep., 223, 1851. Po'-ho-ni-chi.—Powers in Cont. N. A. Ethnol., III, 350, 1877. Pohuniche.—Savage (1851) in Sen. Ex. Doc. 4, 32d Cong., spec. sess., 231, 1853. Po-ko-na-tri.—Wessells (1853) in H. R. Ex. Doc. 76, 34th Cong., 1st sess., 30, 1857. Powhawneches.—Barbour et al. in Sen. Ex. Doc. 4, 32d Cong., spec. sess., 61, 1853.

Pohulo (*Po-hu'-lo*, a species of herb). An extinct clan of the Tewa pueblo of Hano, Ariz.—Fewkes in Am. Anthrop., VII, 166, 1894.

Poiam. A Squawmish village community on the right bank of Squawmisht r., w. Brit. Col.
Po̅ia'm.—Hill-Tout in Rep. B. A. A. S., 474, 1900. P'o̅yăm.—Boas, MS., B. A. E., 1887.

Poihuuinge. A large prehistoric Tewa pueblo, now ruins, on the summit of a small but lofty mesa about 1 m. s. of Chama r. and 4 m. w. of its confluence with the Rio Grande, in Rio Arriba co., N. Mex. The pueblo was built of adobe and irregular blocks of the heavy black lava of which the mesas in this region are composed. It was built in three sections, about a court, the s. side being open. There were two circular kivas within the court and two outside at some distance from the building. The site is strongly defensive, but the water and food supply must have been precarious, there being no possibility of agriculture and no stream nearer than the valley a mile away. Consult Hewett in Bull. 32, B. A. E., 33, 1907. (E. L. H.)

Poisons. Plant and animal poisons were known generally among the Indians, this knowledge growing out of the familiarity with the environment characteristic of American tribes. Plant poisons were commonly employed as an aid in capturing fish. The Cherokee pounded walnut bark and threw it into small streams to stupefy the fish so that they might be easily dipped out in baskets as they floated on the surface of the water (Mooney). Among other Southeastern Indians fishing was carried on by poisoning the streams with certain roots (a species of Tephrosia was most commonly used), so that the stupefied fish could be secured by means of bows and long-shafted arrows (Speck). Powers says of the California Indians: " When the summer heat dries up the streams to stagnant pools they rub poisonous soap root in the water until the fish are stupefied, when they easily scoop them up, and the poison will not affect the tough stomachs of the aborigines." The root is pounded fine and mixed into the water; buckeyes were used in the same manner by both western and eastern Indians. Goddard states, however, that the Hupa do not use fish poisons. Heckewelder says that the Nanticoke invented fish poison, and were reputed skilful in destroying human life by means of poison. Obviously the use of poison for taking human life is a subject that yields little confirmatory evidence. Powers states that he could not discover that the Indians of California "ever used poisons to any considerable extent to rid themselves of their enemies; if they did, it was the old shamans, and they kept the matter a secret." He also says that the Indians were very much afraid of poison. According to Mooney, among the Cherokee the poisonous wild parsnip was used for conjuration and poisoning, and individuals are said to have eaten it in order to commit suicide. Pope (q. v.), the leader of the Pueblo Indians in the insurrection of 1680, is said to have been killed by poison, but the character of the poison is not stated. Cushing says the Zuñi poisoned certain springs at the entrance of their valley with yucca juice and cactus spines, which caused suffering and death among the forces of Diego de Vargas, as recorded by the narrators of his expedition in 1692. Priests among the Yokuts of California drank a decoction of roots of *Datura metaloides* to produce religious frenzy, and this poisonous drink sometimes caused death from overdose (Powers). The Hopi, Navaho, and other

tribes of the S. W. are acquainted with the poisonous properties of the Datura, which the Hopi say was used by their sorcerers. Arrow poison of vegetal and animal origin was generally known. The Lipan Apache dipped their arrows into the sap of *Yucca angustifolia*, which they say is poisonous (Hoffman), and the Kaniagmiut Eskimo and the Aleut poisoned their arrows and lance-points with a preparation of aconite, by drying and pulverizing the root, mixing the powder with water, and, when it fermented, applying it to their weapons (Mason). The Rudo Ensayo (*ca.* 1763) describes a plant, called *mago* by the Opata of Sonora, the milk of which was used by these Indians for arrow poison. The character indicates a euphorbia. Castañeda relates that a member of Coronado's expedition of 1540 was wounded by a poisoned arrow; "the skin rotted and fell off until it left the bones and sinews bare, with a horrible smell. The wound was in the wrist, and the poison had reached as far as the shoulder when he was cured. The skin on all this fell off." The antidote used was the juice of the quince. The expedition lost 17 men from arrow wounds during a punitive raid in Sonora. "They would die in agony from only a small wound, the bodies breaking out with an insupportable pestilential stink." Hoffman says the Jova, Seri, Apache, Blackfeet, Kainah, Piegan, and Teton Sioux employ rattlesnake venom. "The Shoshoni and Bannock Indians state that the proper way to poison arrows, as formerly practised by them, is to secure a deer and cause it to be bitten by a rattlesnake, immediately after which the victim is killed, the meat removed and placed in a hole in the ground. After the mass has become putrid the arrowpoints are dipped into it. By this method the serpent venom is supposed to be the most essential in the operation; but it is extremely doubtful if the venom has time to fully enter into the circulation in the short interval between the time that the victim is bitten and then killed. If the method was actually practised by these Indians, as they affirm it was, and only for the destruction of noxious beasts, the poison of the putrescent matter may have caused death by septicemia." Hoffman cites many other instances of the use of arrow poison and concludes that some of the Indian tribes applied to their arrows harmful substances which from observation they knew were deadly. McGee asserts that the Seri did not use arrow poison as such, but rather as a substance which by magic power produced death and that this power was given the substance through conjuration employed in its preparation, though he says the Seri arrow preparation is "sometimes septic in fact" on account of the decomposing matter of which it is made.

Consult Bandelier in Arch. Inst. Papers, III, 77, 1890; Bourke in Am. Anthrop., IV, 74, 1891; Chesnut in Cont. U. S. Nat. Herb., VII, 3, 330, 1902; Cushing in 13th Rep. B. A. E., 331, 1896; Goddard in Pub. Univ. Cal., Am. Arch. and Eth., I, pt 1, 30, 1903; Hoffman (1) in Am. Anthrop., IV, 67–71, 1891, (2) in 14th Rep. B. A. E., pt 1, 284, 1896; Jones, Antiq. So. Inds., 248, 1873; McGee in 17th Rep. B. A. E., pt 1, 54, 256–59, 1898; Mason in Smithson. Rep. 1892, 666, 1893; Mooney in 19th Rep. B. A. E., pt 1, 1900; Powers in Cont. N. A. Ethnol., III, 1877; Speck in Am. Anthrop., IX, 293, 1907; Winship in 14th Rep. B. A. E., pt 1, 500, 502, 1896.   (W. H.)

Poitokwis. A former village of the so-called Kalendaruk division of the Costanoan family, connected with San Carlos and San Juan Bautista missions, Cal.
Poitoiquis.—Taylor in Cal. Farmer, Nov. 23, 1860. **Poytoquis.**—Bancroft, Nat. Races, III, 653, 1882. **Poytoquix.**—Engelhardt, Franc. in Cal., 398, 1897 (at San Juan Bautista). **Pytoguis.**—Taylor in Cal. Farmer, Apr. 20, 1860.

Pojiuuingge. A prehistoric pueblo of the Tewa of San Juan, the ruins of which are situated at La Joya, about 10 m. N. of San Juan pueblo, N. N. Mex. The name is probably identical with Poihuuinge (q. v.). Cf. *Poseuingge.*
Pho-jiu Uing-ge.—Bandelier in Arch. Inst. Papers, IV, 64, 1892.

Pojoaque (*Po-hwa'-ki*). The smallest pueblo occupied by the Tewa of New Mexico in recent times; situated on a small eastern tributary of the Rio Grande, about 18 m. N. w. of Santa Fé. It became the seat of the Spanish mission of San Francisco early in the 17th century. After the Pueblo rebellions of 1680 and 1696 it was abandoned, but was resettled with 5 families by order of the governor of New Mexico in 1706, when it became the mission of Nuestra Señora de Guadalupe. In 1760 it was reduced to a visita of the Nambe mission; but in 1782 it again became a mission, with Nambe and Tesuque as its visitas. In 1712 its population was 79; in 1890 it was only 20; since 1900 it has become extinct as a Tewa pueblo, the houses now being in possession of Mexican families. See *Pueblos, Tanoan, Tewa.*   (F. W. H.)
Guadalupe.—Villaseñor (1748) cited by Shea, Cath. Miss., 83, 1855. **Nuestra Señora de Guadalupe de Pojuaque.**—Ward in Ind. Aff. Rep. 1867, 213, 1868. **Ohuaqui.**—Ruxton, Adventures, 196, 1848. **Ohuqui.**—Ruxton in Nouv. Ann. Voy., 5th s., XXI, 84, 1850. **Ojuaque.**—Escudero, Noticias Estad. Chihuahua, 180, 1834. **Pajoaque.**—Loew (1875) in Wheeler Survey Rep., VII, 345, 1879. **Pajuagne.**—Domenech, Deserts N. A., II, 63, 1860 (misprint). **Pajuaque.**—Ibid., I, 183, 1860. **P'asuiáp.**—Hodge, field notes, B. A. E., 1895 (Tigua name). **Pasúque.**—Alcedo, Dic. Geog., IV, 114, 1788. **Payuaque.**—Meriwether (1856) in H. R. Ex. Doc. 37, 34th Cong., 3d sess., 146, 1857. **Pejod-**que.—Schoolcraft, Ind. Tribes, VI, 688, 1857. **P'Ho-zuang-ge**——Bandelier in Arch. Inst. Papers, III, 260, 1890 (aboriginal name of the pueblo). **Pofuaque.**—Ind. Aff. Rep. 1864, 191, 1865. **Pogodque.**—Calhoun in Schoolcraft, Ind. Tribes, III, 633, 1853. **Pohuaque.** Brühl in Globus, LV, no. 9, 129, 1889. **Pojake.**—Stevenson in 2d Rep. B. A. E., 328, 1883. **Pojanque.**—Curtis, Children of the Sun, 121, 1883. **Pojanquiti.**—Stevenson in Smithson. Rep. 1880, 137, 1881. **Pojaugue.**—Parke, Map of New Mex., 1851. **Pojoague.**—Morrison in Ann. Rep. Wheeler Surv., app. NN, 1276, 1877. **Pojoaque.**—Gatschet in Wheeler Survey Rep., VII, 417, 1879. **Pojodque.**—Calhoun (1851) in Schoolcraft, Ind. Tribes, VI, 709, 1857. **Pojouque.**—Wallace, Land of the Pueblos, 42, 1888. **Pojuague.**—Bandelier in Revue d'Ethnog., 203, 1886. **Pojuaque.**—MS. *ca.*1715 quoted by Bandelier in Arch. Inst. Papers, V, 193, 1890. **Pokwádi.**—Stephen in 8th Rep. B. A. E., 37, 1891 (Hano Tewa name). **Po'kwoide.**—Fewkes in 19th Rep. B. A. E., 614, 1900 (Hano Tewa name). **Po-suan-gai.**—Jouvenceau in Cath. Pion., I, no. 9, 12, 1906. **Potzua-ge.**—Bandelier in Revue d'Ethnog., 203, 1886 (aboriginal name). **Poujuaque.**—Arny in Ind. Aff. Rep. 1871, 383, 1872. **Poχuáki.**—Gatschet, Isleta MS. vocab., 1885 (Isleta name). **Po-zuan-ge.**—Bandelier in Ritch, New Mexico, 201, 1885 (proper name). **Pozuang-ge.**—Bandelier in Arch. Inst. Papers, III, 124, 1890. **P'o-zuang-ge.**—Ibid., IV, 83, 1892 (or Pojuaque). **Pozuaque.**—Ind. Aff. Rep. 1864, 193, 1865. **Projoaque.**—Taylor in Cal. Farmer, June 19, 1863. **Pujuaque.**—Villa-Señor, Theatro Am., II, 418, 1748. **Pusuaque.**—Hezio (1797–98) quoted by Meline, Two Thousand Miles, 208, 1867. **San Francisco Pajagüe.**—Villagran (1610), Hist. Nueva México, app. 3, 96, 1900.

Pokagon. A Potawatomi village, taking its name from a prominent chief, in Berrien co., Mich., near the w. bank of St Joseph r. just N. of the Indiana line. The tract on which it was situated was ceded to the United States by the treaty of Chicago, Sept. 26–27, 1833.
Parc aux Vaches.—Royce in 18th Rep. B. A. E., Mich. map, 1899. **Po-ca-gan's village.**—Tippecanoe treaty (1832) in U. S. Ind. Treat., 701, 1873. **Pocagons Vill.**—Royce in 1st Rep. B. A. E., map, 1881. **Pokagon.**—Chicago treaty (1833) in U. S. Ind. Treat., 176, 1873.

Pokagon, Simon. The last chief of the Pokagon band of Potawatomi, born in 1830 at their old village 1 m. from St Joseph r., Berrien co., Mich.; died near Hartford, Van Buren co., Mich., Jan. 27, 1899. His father, Leopold Pokagon, was chief for 12 years and signed several important treaties with the United States in behalf of his tribe, that of Tippecanoe r., Oct. 26, 1832, being the one by which the site of Chicago came into possession of the whites. Simon was 10 years of age when his father died, and on reaching his 14th year was sent to school at Notre Dame, Ind., for 3 years; then, encouraged by his mother in his desire for education, attended Oberlin College, Ohio, for a year, and next went to Twinsburg, Ohio, where he remained 2 years. It is said that he was educated for the priesthood, spoke four or five languages, and bore the reputation of being the best educated full-blood Indian of his time. He wrote numerous articles for the leading magazines, and delivered many addresses of merit during the last quarter of the 19th century. In 1899 he published in book form "Ogimawkwe Mitigwäkî (Queen of the Woods),'' an account of the wooing of his first wife, and at the World's Fair in Chicago, in 1893, "The Red Man's Greeting,'' a booklet of birch-bark. He was a poet, and the last of his verses, both in its English and Potawatomi versions, appeared in the Chicago Inter-Ocean, Jan. 23, 1899, just before his death. Pokagon was credited with ably managing the affairs of his 300 tribesmen scattered through Michigan, and, inspired by enlightened views, was the means of promoting their welfare. He pressed and finally collected a Potawatomi claim for $150,000 from the United States. He was a man of sturdy character, unostentatious in manner, of simple habit, and a consistent Catholic. A monument has been erected by the citizens of Chicago in Jackson Park to the memory of Simon and his father. (C. T.)

Pokaiosum (*Pō'kaiŏ'sum*, 'slide'). A Squawmish village on the left bank of Squawmisht r., Brit. Col.—Hill-Tout in Rep. B. A. A. S., 474, 1900.

Pokanoket. The principal settlement of the Wampanoag tribe, and the residence of Massasoit and King Philip; situated on the E. side of Narragansett bay, on the Bristol peninsula, Rhode Id. The site has been variously described as at Mount Hope, Bristol, Warren, and Barrington, all of which may easily be correct, as Indian settlements were seldom compactly built, and all the places named are within 3 m. of a central point. The etymology of the name is uncertain, one writer making it mean 'a wood,' while another makes it 'a clearing,' and a third 'land over the water.' It was also sometimes known to the English under variant forms of Sowams, which Tooker, with apparent reason, makes a general term for 'southwest' (i. e. from Plymouth), rather than the specific name of a settlement. It was abandoned on the breaking out of King Philip's war in 1675. A brochure, Massasoit's Town Sowams in Pokanoket, by Virginia Baker, was issued at Warren in 1904. (J. M.)

Chawum.—Smith (1616) in Mass. Hist. Soc. Coll., 3d s., VI, 108, 1837. Chawun.—Ibid., 119. Pacanacot.—Prince (1632), ibid., 2d s., VII, 58, 1818. Pacanaukett.—Doc. of 1668, ibid., IV, 266, 1816. Pacanawkite.—Bradford (ca. 1650), ibid., 4th s., III, 97, 1856. Pacanokik.—Prince (1633) quoted by Freeman, ibid., 1st s., VIII, 159, 1802. Packanoki.—Dee in Smith (1629), Va., II, 227, repr. 1819. Packanokick.—Mourt (1622) in Mass. Hist. Soc. Coll., 2d s., IX, 27, 1822. Paconekick—Smith (1631), ibid., 3d s., III, 22, 1833. Pakanawkett.—Record of 1673 quoted by Drake, Bk. Inds., bk. 3, 16, 1848. Pakanoki.—Dee in Smith (1629), Va., II, 227, repr. 1819. Pakanokick.—Mourt (1622) in Mass. Hist. Soc. Coll., 1st s., VIII, 235, 1802. Paukanawket.—Deed of 1646 in R. I. Col. Rec., I, 31, 1856. Pawkanawkuts.—N. Y. Doc. Col. Hist., IV, 615, note, 1854. Pawkunnawkuts.—Morton (1617), New Eng. Memorial, 38, 1855. Pawkunnawkutts.—Gookin (1674) in Mass. Hist. Soc. Coll., 1st s., I, 148, 1806. Pek8anokets.—Maurault, Abenakis, 2, 1866. Pocanakets.—Morton (1620), New Eng. Memorial, 42, 1855. Pocanakett.—

Morton (1662) quoted by Drake, Bk. Inds., bk. 3, 17, 1848. Pocanauket.—Deed of 1649 in Mass. Hist. Soc. Coll., 2d s., VII, 139, 1818. Pocanawkits.—Bradford (ca. 1650), ibid., 4th s., III, 96, 1856. Pocanoket.—Thompson, Long Id., I, 456, 1843. Pocanokit.—Dermer (1619) quoted by Drake, Bk. Inds., bk. 2, 20, 1848. Pockanockett.—Morton in Mass. Hist. Soc. Coll., 1st s., VIII, 159, 1802. Pockanoky.—Johnson (1654), ibid., 2d s., II, 66, 1814. Pockonockett.—Hinckley (1682), ibid., 4th s., V, 78, 1861. Pokanacket.—Hubbard (1680), ibid., 2d s., V, 32, 1815. Pokanocket.—Hutchinson quoted by Freeman, ibid., 1st s., VIII, 159, 1802. Pokanokik.—Callender (1739) in R. I. Hist. Soc. Coll., IV, 73, 1838. Puckanokick.—Mourt (1622) in Mass. Hist. Soc. Coll., 1st s., VIII, 243, 1802. Sawaams.—Mourt (1622), ibid., 263. Sowaams.—Winslow (ca. 1623) quoted by Drake, Bk. Inds., bk. 2, 31, 1848. Sowam.—Hoyt, Antiq. Res., 34, 1824. Sowame.—Hubbard (1680) in Mass. Hist. Soc. Coll., 2d s., V, 32, 1815. Sowames.—Writer of 1627, ibid., 1st s., III, 52, 1794. Sowams.—Letter of 1627, ibid., 4th s., III, 225, 1856. Sowamsett.—Mason (1661) quoted by Drake, Bk. Inds., bk. 2, 100, 1848. Sowans.—Josselyn (1675) in Mass. Hist. Soc. Coll., 3d s., III, 309, 1833. Sow-wames.—Clark (1652), ibid., VIII, 290, 1843. Sowwams.—Williams (1638), ibid., I 176, 1825.

Poke. The pigeon-berry (*Phytolacca decandra*); also called poke-weed, poke-berry, pocan, pocan-bush, Indian poke, poke-root, etc. It was not named after President Polk, but the name was evidently derived from the same source as *puccoon*. See also *Pocan*. (A. F. C.)

Pokegama. A former Chippewa village on Pokegama lake, Pine co., Minn.
Pa'kēgạmāng.—Wm. Jones, inf'n, 1905 (correct form). Pokagomin.—Washington treaty (1863) in U. S. Ind. Treat., 215, 1873. Po-ka-guma.—Warren (1852) in Minn. Hist. Soc. Coll., V, 165, 1885. Pokegama.—Ind. Aff. Rep. 1862, 354, 1863. Po-ke-gom-maw.—Treaty of 1842 in Minn. Hist. Soc. Coll., V, 491, 1885. Pokeguma.—Neill, ibid.

Pokekooungo (*Poke-koo-un'-go*). The Turtle clan of the Delawares.—Morgan, Anc. Soc., 172, 1877.

Pokeloken. Defined by Bartlett (Dict. of Americanisms, 478, 1877) as "an Indian word used by hunters and lumbermen in Maine and New Brunswick to denote a marshy place or stagnant pool extending into the land from a stream or lake." A New Brunswick place name, Popelogan, Pocologan, or Poclagain, is derived from *pecelaygan*, 'a place for stopping' (?) in the Malecite dialect of Algonquian, by Ganong (Roy. Soc. Can., 263, 1896). Tooker, in his discussion of *poquosin*, considers *pokeloken* to be derived from the same radical. See *Bogan*. (A. F. C.)

Poke-weed. See *Pocan*, *Poke*.

Pokickery. See *Hickory*.

Police. See *Agency system*.

Polished Stone age. See *Neolithic age*.

Polishing implements. Many of the implements, ornaments, and other artifacts of the native tribes were given a high degree of finish by the use of polishing implements. These necessarily varied in form, material, and texture, according to the material and form of the object treated. Wood, bone, stone, metal, and earthenware each required distinct treatment, and special forms of polishing implements were employed. The arrowshaft of wood was polished with an implement of stone grooved for the purpose; the earthen vessel was given its even surface by rubbing with a smooth pebble or bit of wood, gourd, bone, or shell. The countless implements, ornaments, pipes, and miscellaneous sculptures of the aborigines were finished with the aid of polishers of varying forms and textures, while many objects received their finishing touches by rubbing with a piece of deerskin, fishskin, or other variously textured but pliable material, or even with the hand, and the high polish of many forms of implements comes from long-continued use, as in digging in the soil, or in contact with a haft or the hand. In many cases natural objects, such as pebbles, shells, etc., were employed in the polishing work; but it is not always easy to identify these, and the same is true of many polishers that have been artificially shaped. An interesting form of rubbing implement of clay is found occasionally in Tennessee: the discoid base, a few inches in diameter, has a convex undersurface, and above it is supplied with a cylindrical or looped handle; the convex surface is usually worn quite smooth from use, hence it is surmised that the implement was employed in smoothing earthenware or the clay plastering of walls. A few examples are of stone. In the shaping of stone the polishing work usually follows the more roughly abrading or grinding operations, the implements as well as the processes employed in the one passing by insensible gradations into those of the other.

Polishing implements are described incidentally in numerous works and articles on ethnology and archeology, many of which are referred to under *Archeology* and *Stonework*. See also *Abrading implements*.　　　　　　　　　　　(W. H. H.)

Polooca. Mentioned as a pueblo of the province of Atripuy (q. v.) in the region of the lower Rio Grande, N. Mex., in 1598.—Oñate (1598) in Doc. Inéd., XVI, 115, 1871.

Polotkin. See *Saulotken*.

Polynesian influence. See *Hawaiian influence*.

Pomeioc. An Algonquian palisaded village in 1585, about the mouth of Gibbs cr., in the present Hyde co., N. C. It was one of the villages drawn in color by John White during his visit to Virginia in 1585 as a member of Raleigh's first expedition, now preserved in the British Museum, and illustrated by De Bry. The houses of the village were "covered and enclosed, some wth matts, and some wth barcks of trees. All compassed about wth small poles stock thick together in stedd of a wall." For a photograph of the original of White's drawing, see Bushnell in Am. Anthrop., IX, 32, 1907.

Pameik.—Strachey (*ca.* 1612), Va., 143, 1849. **Pomecock.**—Martin, N. C., I, 11, 1829 (misprint). **Pomeiock.**—Amadas and Barlow in Smith (1629), Va., I, 84, repr. 1819. **Pomeioke.**—Strachey (*ca.* 1612), Va., 145, 1849. **Pomejock.**—Dutch map (1621) in N. Y. Doc. Col. Hist., I, 1856.

Pomo. The name of the Indian linguistic stock, technically known as Kulanapan (q. v.), living in parts of Sonoma, Lake, Mendocino, Colusa, and Glenn cos., Cal. In the northern Pomo dialect *Pomo* means 'people,' and added to a place name forms the name for a group of people. Although *Poma* is almost as frequently heard as *Pomo*, the latter has come into general use in both scientific and popular literature.

The territory occupied by the Pomo is in two parts: a main area which extends, generally speaking, from w. to E., from the coast to the crest of the main range of the Coast Range mts., and from s. to N., from the vicinity of Santa Rosa to Sherwood valley on the upper course of Eel r.; the second area is a very small one, lying wholly within the Sacramento valley drainage and comprising only a limited area on the headwaters of Stony cr. in Colusa and Glenn cos., and is occupied by a people speaking a dialect differing from any of those spoken in the main area to the w. The Pomo thus occupied all of Russian River valley except two small areas, one between Geyserville and Healdsburg, the other at the extreme head of Potter valley, both of which were occupied by people of the Yukian stock. On the w. of the main Pomo area is the Pacific, on the s. is Moquelumnan territory, on the E. are Yukian-Wappo and Wintun areas, and on the N. the Yuki and the Athapascan Kato areas, from which it is separated by the watershed between Cahto and Sherwood valleys.

Certain peoples living to the N. of the Pomo area, generally known by their Pomo names (Kai, Kastel, Kato, and Yusal Pomo), are not, as supposed, Pomo, but Athapascan.

There are in all seven dialects, one being found exclusively in the small Pomo area in the Sacramento valley drainage, the remainder lying within the limits of what has been designated as the main Pomo area. Of the latter six dialects two are confined to the vicinity of Clear lake, one to the southern part of the coast held by the Pomo, and one almost entirely to the lower course of Russian r., while the other two occupy portions of the interior valley region along Russian and Eel rs. and also portions of the Pomo coast.

In appearance the Pomo resemble the other Indians of N. central California; they are comparatively short, though on the whole they are taller and of more powerful build than their Yuki and Athapascan neighbors immediately to the N. Both men and women, especially the latter, are often fat, with large faces. The women tattoo very slightly, and this chiefly upon the chin. They are noted for their basketry, which in variety of technique and range of patterns is probably unrivaled in North America, while its fineness of finish and elaborateness of decoration, especially with feathers, are remarkable. In their general culture the Pomo are similar to such peoples as the Wintun, Maidu, and Yuki. They are essentially unwarlike.

The Pomo were the most southerly stock on the coast not brought under the mission influence of the Franciscans in the 18th and early 19th centuries, their contact with the mission fathers being only very slight and then in the extreme southern part of their territory. However, Franciscan missionaries have more recently been active among them. A few, especially the so-called Little Lakes and Big Lakes, are at present on the Round Valley res., but the majority are living free from governmental control in or near their old homes, supporting themselves by civilized pursuits, especially farming. Their number at present is about 800. As throughout the greater part of California, true tribes do not exist among the Pomo, their largest political and geographical division being the village and the surrounding land controlled by it. (s. a. b.)

The following names are mentioned by Powers as those of divisions and villages of the Pomo. In many instances, however, this writer attached to village names the significance of those of tribal divisions, while in others the names are those used by whites to designate the Indians of a certain village or a certain valley. The names here given represent a very small portion of the number of villages actually inhabited by the Pomo in aboriginal times: Ballokai Pomo, Bidamarek, Boalkea, Bokea, Buldam, Cahlahtel Pomo, Chamkhai, Chomchadila, Dahnohabe, Danokha, Dapishul, Erio, Erusi, Gallinomero, Gualala, Haukoma, Hopitsewah, Kaiachim, Kaime, Keliopoma, Khabemadolil, Khabenapo, Khana, Khawina, Khoalek, Khwakhamaiu, Koi, Komacho, Kulanapo, Laguna, Lema, Makhelchel, Makoma, Masut, Mayi, Mitomkai Pomo, Moiya, Musalakun, Napobatin, Salan Pomo, Shiegho, Shigom, Shnalkeya, Shodakhai Pomo, Shokhowa, Shutaunomanok, Tabahtea, Tyuga, Ubakhea, Venaambakaia, Yapiam, Yokaia Pomo.

As elsewhere in California, villages and larger groups are difficult to distinguish, and true tribes do not exist. The preceding list is therefore not only incomplete, but unsystematic. For further information consult Barrett, Ethno-geography of the Pomo and Neighboring Indians, Univ. Cal. Pub. in Am. Archæol. and Ethnol., VI, no. 1, 1908.

Nokonmi.—A. L. Kroeber, inf'n, 1903 (Yuki name). Pomo.—Powers in Cont. N. A. Ethnol., III, 146, 1877.

Pomoacan. See *Half-King*.

Pomojoua. One of two pueblos, formerly occupied by the Pecos tribe, near San Antonio del Pueblo, 3 m. s. e. of San Miguel, San Miguel co., N. central N. Mex.
Pom-o Jo-ua.—Bandelier in Arch. Inst. Papers, IV, 129, 130, 1892.

Pomouic. An Algonquian tribe, living in 1585 on the coast of North Carolina. They were seated on Pamlico r., w. of the Secotan, in what is now Beaufort co. Their principal village, named Pananaioc on White's map, seems to have been about Pungo r. Amadas said of them: "Adjoyning to Secotan beginneth the country Pomouik, belonging to the King called Piamacum, in the Country Nusiok [Neusiok] upon the great river Neus. These have mortall warres with Wingina, King of Wingandacoa. Betwixt Piemacum and the Lord of Secotan a peace was concluded; notwithstanding there is a mortall malice in the Secotans, because this Piemacum invited divers men and 30 women to a feast, and when they were altogether merry before their Idoll, which is but a meere illusion of the Devill, they sudainly slew all the men of Secotan and kept the women for their use" (Smith, 1629, Va., I, 85, repr. 1819). In later times the same region was occupied by the Pamlico, and it is not improbable that the two names refer to the same people.
Pamauuaioc.—De Bry, map, in Hawks, N. C., I, 1859. Pananaioc.—Smith (1629), Va., I, map, repr. 1819. Pananarocks.—Martin, N. C., I, 14, 1829 (misprint). Pananojock.—Dutch map (1621) in N. Y. Doc. Col. Hist., I, 1856. Pananuaioc.—Hakluyt (1600), Voy., III, 306, repr. 1810. Pomonick.—Martin, N. C., I, 12, 1829 (misprint). Pomouik.—Amadas and Barlow (ca. 1585) in Smith (1629), Va., I, 85, repr. 1819.

Pomperaug ('place of offering,' referring to an ancient stone-heap "on which each member of the tribe, as he passed that way, dropped a small stone."—Trumbull). A village near Woodbury, Conn., in 1704, and the name of the tract on both sides of Pomperaug r., a branch of the Housatonic, bought by the first planters of Woodbury in 1673 (Trumbull, Ind. Names Conn., 53, 1881). The inhabitants were allied with those at Scaticook, in Litchfield co.
Pomparague.—Trumbull, Conn., I, 83, 1818. Pomperaug.—Ibid., 325.

Pompton. A Munsee band formerly residing on Pompton r., in N. New Jersey. They are first mentioned in a deed of 1695. Memerescum was their chief in 1710. In 1758, when they joined in the treaty of Easton, they were residing at Otsiningo under Seneca protection. In that treaty they are called also Waping or Oping, signifying "eastern," probably either from their former position on the eastern Munsee frontier or perhaps from their having incorporated some remnants of the Wappinger. The meaning of the name is unknown.   (J. M.)

Opings.—Easton treaty (1758) quoted by Ruttenber, Ind. Geog. Names, 113, 1906. **Pompeton.**—N. Y. records quoted, ibid. **Pompton.**—N. Y. Doc. Col. Hist., VIII, 811, 1857. **Ponton.**—Deed of 1695 quoted by Nelson, Inds. N. J., 112, 1894. **Pumpton.**—N. Y. records quoted by Ruttenber, op. cit. **Wapings.**—Easton treaty (1758) quoted by Nelson, op. cit., 118. **Wappings.**—Easton treaty (1758) quoted by Ruttenber, op. cit.

Pomuluma. A tribe of N. E. Mexico, brought in to San Bernardo mission, founded in 1703. They are perhaps mentioned by Peñalosa, under the name Poluluma, in connection with the Jumano. Their language was probably Coahuiltecan.

Polulumas.—Duro, Don Diego de Peñalosa, 134, 1882. **Pomulumas.**—Orozco y Berra, Geog., 303, 1864.

Ponak (a variety of large plant). A Hopi clan.

Pönakñyamu Pöna.—Dorsey and Voth, Mishongnovi Ceremonies, 260, 1902.

Ponca. One of the five tribes of the so-called Dhegiha group of the Siouan family, forming with the Omaha, Osage, and Kansa, the upper Dhegiha or Omaha division. The Ponca and Omaha have the

GARHOGARSHEGAR (HAIRY BEAR), A PONCA CHIEF

same language, differing only in some dialectic forms and approximating the Quapaw rather than the Kansa and Osage languages. The early history of the tribe is the same as that of the other tribes of the group, and, after the first separation, is identical with that of the Omaha. After the migration of the combined body to the mouth of Osage r. the first division of the

Omaha group took place, the Osage settling on that stream, and the Kansa continuing up Missouri r., while the Omaha and Ponca crossed to the N. side. The course of the latter is given from the tradition recorded by J. O. Dorsey (Am. Nat., Mar. 1886) as follows: The Omaha and Ponca, after crossing the Missouri, ascended a tributary of that river, which may have been Chariton r., and finally reached the pipestone quarry in s. w. Minnesota. All the traditions agree in stating that the people built earth lodges or permanent villages, cultivated the soil, and hunted buffalo and other animals. When game became scarce they abandoned their villages and moved N. W. On reaching a place where game was plentiful, other villages were built and occupied for years. Thus they lived and moved until they reached the pipestone quarry. After reaching Big Sioux r. they built a fort. The Dakota made war on the Omaha and their allies, defeating them and compelling them to flee s. w. until they reached L. Andes, S. Dak. There, according to Omaha and Ponca tradition, the sacred pipes were given and the present gentes constituted. From this place they ascended the Missouri to the mouth of White r., S. Dak. There the Iowa and Omaha remained, but the Ponca crossed the Missouri and went on to Little Missouri r. and the region of the Black hills. They subsequently rejoined their allies, and all descended the Missouri on its right bank to the mouth of Niobrara r., where the final separation took place. The Ponca remained there and the Omaha settled on Bow cr., Nebr., while the Iowa went down the Missouri to the site of Ionia, Dixon co., Nebr. The Pana, who on Marquette's autograph map (1673) are placed near the Omaha, apparently on the Missouri about the mouth of the Niobrara, are supposed to be the Ponca. If so, this is the earliest historical mention of the tribe. They were met by Lewis and Clark in 1804, when their number, which had been greatly reduced by smallpox toward the close of the 18th century, was estimated at only 200. This number, however, may not include those who had taken refuge with the Omaha. Lewis and Clark (Orig. Jour. Lewis and Clark, VI, 88, 1905) say that they formerly resided on a branch of Red r. of the North, but as this statement is at variance with all other authorities, and as the wording of the sentence is almost identical with that relating to the Cheyenne (ibid., 100), there is probably a confusion of tribes. They increased rapidly, however, reaching about 600 in 1829 and some 800 in 1842; in 1871, when they were first visited by Dorsey, they numbered 747. Up to this time the Ponca and Sioux were amicable, but a dispute grew out of the cession of lands, and the Sioux made annual raids on the Ponca until the enforced removal of the tribe to Indian Ter. took place in 1877. Through this warfare more than a quarter of the Ponca lost their lives. The displacement of this tribe from lands owned by them in fee simple attracted attention, and a commission was appointed by President Hayes in 1880 to inquire into the matter; the commission visited the Ponca settlements in Indian Ter. and on the Niobrara, and effected a satisfactory arrangement of the affairs of the tribe, through which the greater portion (some 600) remained in Indian Ter., while some 225 kept their reservation in Nebraska. The two bands now (1906) number, respectively, 570 and 263; total, 833. Their lands have been allotted to them in severalty. For the treaties made by the Ponca, see *Treaties*. The divisions or gentes as given by Morgan (Anc. Soc., 155, 1877) are as follows, the names following in parentheses being the proper forms or definitions according to La Flesche: 1, Wasabe, 'grizzly bear' (properly black bear); 2, Deagheta (Dhihida), 'many people'; 3, Nakopozna (Nikapashna), 'elk'; 4, Mohkuh, 'skunk' (Moukou, 'medicine'); 5, Washaba, 'buffalo'; 6, Wazhazha, 'snake'; 7, Nohga, 'medicine' (Noóghe, 'ice'); 8, Wahga, 'ice' (Waga, 'jerked meat'). According to Dorsey, the tribe is divided into two half-tribes, Chizhu and Wazhazhe. Each half-tribe contains 4 gentes: I. Chizhu half-tribe: 1, Hisada; 2, Wasabehitazhi; 3, Dhighida; 4, Nikapashna. II. Wazhazhe half-tribe: 5, Makan; 6, Washabe; 7, Wazhazhe; 8, Nukhe. (J. O. D. C. T.)

Díhit.—Gatschet, MS., B. A. E. (Pawnee name). **Kañ′kaⁿ.**—Dorsey, Winnebago MS. vocab., B. A. E., 1886 (Winnebago name). **la Pong.**—Lewis and Clark, Discov., 21, 1806 (French traders' name). **Les Pongs.**—Lewis quoted by Coues, Lewis and Clark Exped., I, 108, note 20, 1892. **Li-hit′.**—Dunbar in Mag. Am. Hist., 252, 1880 (Pawnee name of the Dhegida division, applied to the tribe). **Pana.**—Marquette map (1673) cited by Gale, Upper Miss., 219, 1867. **Pana′s.**—Coxe, Carolana, 16, 1741. **Pancas.**—Ind. Aff. Rep., 16, 1842. **Pancaws.**—Ind. Aff. Rep. 1854, 295, 1855. **Pangkaws.**—Hamilton in Schoolcraft, Ind. Tribes, IV, 406, 1854. **Paⁿqka.**—Dorsey, Osage MS., B. A. E., 1883 (Osage name). **Pania.**—Orig. Jour. Lewis and Clark, V, 366, 1905. **Panka.**—Riggs in Iapi Oaye, Feb. 10, 1881 (Dakota name). **Pañka.**—Dorsey, Dhegiha MS. Dict., 1878 (own name). **Paŋ′-ka.**—Cook, Yankton MS. vocab., B. A. E., 184, 1882. **Pañ′-kă.**—Dorsey, Kwapa MS. vocab., B. A. E. (Quapaw name). **Pañ′kaⁿ.**—Dorsey, Tciwere MS. vocab., B. A. E., 1879 (Iowa, Oto, and Missouri name). **Pocan.**—Fisher, Interesting Acct., 29, 1812. **Ponars.**—Orig. Jour. Lewis and Clark, V, 366, 1905. **Poncahs.**—Long, Exped. Rocky Mts., II, 364, 1823. **Poncan.**—Lewis, Trav., 14, 1809. **Poncar.**—H. R. Ex. Doc. 117, 19th Cong., 1st sess., 6, 1826. **Poncarars.**—Lewis and Clark Exped., I, map, 1814. **Poncaras.**—Lewis and Clark, Discov., 30, 1806. **Poncare.**—Orig. Jour. Lewis and Clark, VI, 88, 1905. **Poncarer.**—Ibid., I, 132, 1904. **Poncaries.**—Ibid. **Pon′cârs.**—Lewis and Clark, Discov., 21, 1806. **Poncas.**—Floyd (1804) in Orig. Jour. Lewis and Clark, VII, 10, 1905. **Poncaw.**—Bean in H. R. Ex. Doc. 87, 21st Cong., 1st sess., 40, 1829. **Ponchas.**—Balbi, Atlas Ethnog., 56, 1826. **Poncrars.**—Orig. Jour. Lewis and Clark, I, 29, 1904. **Poncye.**—Floyd (1804), ibid., VII, 10, 1905. **Pongkaws.**—Gale, Upper Miss., 183, 1867. **Poniars.**—Am. St. Papers, Ind. Aff., I, 711, 1832. **Ponka.**—Nicollet, Rep. on Upper Miss. R., map, 1843. **Ponkahs.**—Ramsey in Ind. Aff. Rep. 1849, 84, 1850. **Ponkas.**—Orig. Jour. Lewis and Clark, VI, 271, 1905. **Pons.**—Maximilian, Reise, II, 632, 1841. **Ponsars.**—Farnham, Trav., 31, 1843. **Poong-câr.**—Lewis and Clark, Discov., 21, 1806 (own name). **Poukas.**—Lewis, Trav., 3, 1809. **Puncah.**—M'Coy, Ann. Reg., no. 2, 4, 1836. **Puncas.**—De l'Isle, map (ca. 1703) in Neill, Hist. Minn., 164, 1858. **Puncaw.**—Long, Exped. Rocky Mts., I, 343, 1823. **Punchas.**—Domenech, Deserts N. Am., II, 306, 1860. **Punchaws.**—Sen. Ex. Doc. 47, 16th Cong., 1st sess., 4, 1820. **Punka.**—Morgan in N. Am. Rev., 45, Jan. 1870. **Ríhit.**—Gatschet, MS., B. A. E. (Pawnee name). **Tchiáχsokush**—Gatschet, Caddo and Yatassi MS., B. A. E., 71 (Caddo name).

Pone. Among the Powhatan tribes, a ball or flat round cake made of a paste of corn-meal and hot water, covered with hot ashes in a fire-bed until baked, then immediately dipped in water to clean it, and afterward allowed to dry by its own heat; or, a similar cake made from the flour obtained from certain edible roots and seeds, and sometimes "buttered" with deer's suet (*rûnga*). The cake was sometimes put into a pot and boiled, and afterward laid upon a smooth stone and allowed to harden. (2) A kind of bread or cake made of corn-meal, milk, and eggs; called also corn pone. (3) A cake made of grated sweet potatoes, sugar, and spices, and called sweet-potato pone. The word is from Powhatan *âpân* '(something) baked', from *äpen* 'she bakes'; cognate with Middle States Lenape *äpân*, Munsee *ächpân*, Caniba (Norridgewock) *abäⁿn*, Passamaquoddy *äbân*. (W. R. G.)

Poniards. See *Daggers*.

Ponida (*Po′-ni-da*). A former Jova pueblo situated on a small stream between the Rio Batepito and the Chihuahua boundary, lat. 29° 10′, lon. 110° 50′, E. Sonora, Mexico (Doc. of 1764 quoted by Bandelier in Arch. Inst. Papers, IV, 510, 1892). The place, which is now civilized, contained 153 inhabitants in 1900.

Poningo. The principal village of the Siwanoy in 1640, situated near the present Rye, Westchester co., N. Y.—Ruttenber, Tribes Hudson R., 367, 1872.

Ponoetaneo ('lower men', i. e. 'down-river men'). A local name now used by the Cheyenne of Cantonment and the upper Canadian, Okla., to designate those living farther down the river, in the neighborhood of Darlington. In Hayden's time (*ca.* 1860) it appears to have been employed by the Northern Cheyenne to designate those of the Southern group. It is not a true divisional name. (J. M.)

Ponoetaneo.—R. Petter, inf'n, 1906. **Po-no-i′-ta-ni-o.**—Hayden, Ethnog. and Philol. Mo. Val., 290, 1862.

Ponokix (*Po-no-kix′*, 'elk'). Given by Morgan (Anc. Soc., 171, 1877) as a division of the Kainah tribe of the Siksika. Cf. *Siksinokaks*, 'Black Elks'.

Ponpon. A former village of the Yuchi

in s. w. South Carolina.—Hawkins (1799), Sketch, 61, 1848.

Pontiac. An Ottawa chief, born about 1720, probably on Maumee r., Ohio, about the mouth of the Auglaize. Though his paternity is not positively established, it is most likely that his father was an Ottawa chief and his mother a Chippewa woman. J. Wimer (Events in Ind. Hist., 155, 1842) says that as early as 1746 he commanded the Indians—mostly Ottawa—who defended Detroit against the attack of the northern tribes. It is supposed he led the Ottawa and Chippewa warriors at Braddock's defeat. He first appears prominently in history at his meeting with Maj. Robert Rogers, in 1760, at the place where Cleveland, Ohio, now stands. This officer had been dispatched to take possession of Detroit on behalf of the British. Pontiac objected to the further invasion of the territory, but, learning that the French had been defeated in Canada, consented to the surrender of Detroit to the British, and was the means of preventing an attack on the latter by a body of Indians at the mouth of the strait. That which gives him most prominence in history and forms the chief episode of his life is the plan he devised for a general uprising of the Indians and the destruction of the forts and settlements of the British. He was for a time disposed to be on terms of friendship with the British and consented to acknowledge King George, but only as an "uncle," not as a superior. Failing to receive the recognition he considered his due as a great sovereign, and being deceived by the rumor that the French were preparing for the reconquest of their American possessions, he resolved to put his scheme into operation. Having brought to his aid most of the tribes N. w. of the Ohio, his plan was to make a sudden attack on all the British posts on the lakes at once —at St Joseph, Ouiatenon, Michilimackinac, and Detroit—as well as on the Miami and Sandusky, and also attack the forts at Niagara, Presque Isle, Le Bœuf, Venango, and Pitt (Du Quesne). The taking of Detroit was to be his special task. The end of May 1763 was the appointed time when each tribe was to attack the nearest fort and, after killing the garrison, to fall on the adjacent settlements. It was not long before the posts at Sandusky, St Joseph, Miami (Ft Wayne), Ouiatenon, Michilimackinac, Presque Isle, Le Bœuf, and Venango were taken and the garrison in most cases massacred; but the main points, Detroit and Ft Pitt, were successfully defended and the Indians forced to raise the siege. This was a severe blow to Pontiac, but his hopes were finally crushed by the receipt of a letter from M. Neyon, commander of Ft Chartres, advising him to

desist from further warfare, as peace had been concluded between France and Great Britain. However, unwilling to abandon entirely his hope of driving back the British, he made an attempt to incite the tribes along the Mississippi to join in another effort. Being unsuccessful in this attempt, he finally made peace at Detroit, Aug. 17, 1765. In 1769 he attended a drinking carousal at Cahokia, Ill., where he was murdered by a Kaskaskia Indian. Pontiac, if not fully the equal of Tecumseh, stands closely second to him in strength of mind and breadth of comprehension.

Consult Parkman, Conspiracy of Pontiac; Randall, Pontiac's Conspiracy, in Ohio Archæol. and Hist. Quar., Oct. 1903; Hough, Diary of the Siege of Detroit in the War with Pontiac, 1860.   (c. t.)

Pontotoc. A former Chickasaw settlement in N. Mississippi, apparently at or near the site of the present Pontotoc, Pontotoc co.

Ponyinumbu (*Po-nyi Num-bu*). A very ancient pueblo of the Tewa, the ruins of which are in the vicinity of the Mexican settlement of Santa Cruz, in N. Santa Fé co., N. Mex.—Bandelier in Arch. Inst. Papers, IV, 83, 1892.

Ponyipakuen (*P'o-nyi Pa-kuen*). A former pueblo of the Tewa in the vicinity of Ojo Caliente and El Rito, about the boundary of Taos and Rio Arriba cos., N. Mex.—Bandelier in Arch. Inst. Papers, IV, 83, 1892.

Poodatook (Mohegan: *Powntuckuck*, 'country about the falls.'—Trumbull). A former village, subject to the Paugusset, on Housatonic r., near Newtown, Fairfield co., Conn. About 1660 it contained about 250 inhabitants, who afterward decreased and joined the Scaticook farther up the river. In 1761 only 2 or 3 families remained in Newtown. Ruttenber calls it a Stockbridge village. The Moravians had a mission there.

Poodatook.—Birdsey (1761) in Mass. Hist. Soc. Coll., 1st s., X, 111, 1809. Potatik.—Ruttenber, Tribes Hudson R., 86, 1872. Potatuck.—Trumbull, Ind. Names Conn., 56, 1881. Totatik.—Ruttenber, op. cit., 197 (misprint).

Pooquaw. A name used on the island of Nantucket for the round clam (*Venus mercenaria*). As its earlier form *pequaock* indicates, this word is a reduction of the Indian name of this shellfish in the Algonquian dialects of New England, the Narraganset *poquaûhock* or the Massachuset *poquahoc* signifying literally 'thick or tightly closed shell', from *poquaû*, 'thick or tightly closed', and -*hock*, 'that which covers.' Roger Williams (1643) calls the Narraganset *pooquaûhock* a horsefish.   (a. f. c.)

Pooscoostekale (probably *Puskus Takali*, 'hanging child.'—Halbert). A former Choctaw town, mentioned by Romans as having been deserted in 1771. It was

s. w. by w. from Concha, and so seems to have been in the s. w. corner of Kemper co., Miss., though possibly in Neshoba co.
Pooscoos te Kalè.—Romans, Florida, 311, 1775. Rooskoos Tokali—Ibid., map.

Poose-back. A word reported as used in w. Connecticut to designate the Indian woman's manner of carrying a child on the back (Babbitt, Dial. Notes, 342, 1894); from *pappoose*. The second component is the English *back*.   (A. F. C.)

Poosepatuck. Also called *Uncachogue*. One of the 13 tribes of Long Island, N. Y., probably subordinate to the Montauk. They occupied the s. shore from Patchogue E. to the Shinnecock country. In 1666 a reservation was ceded to their

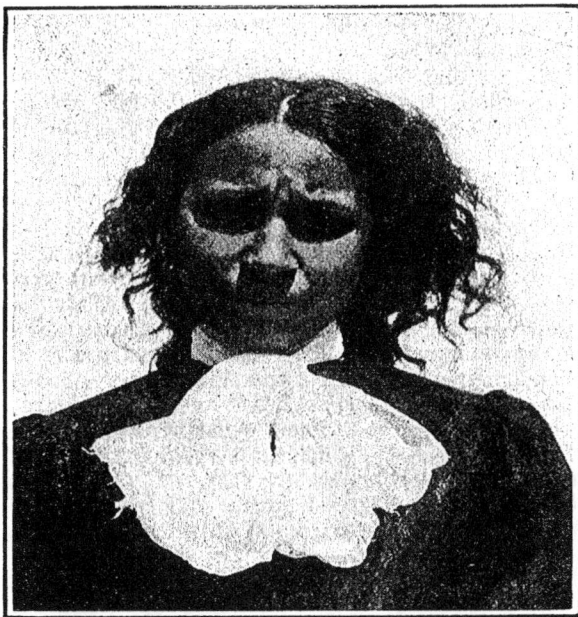

POOSEPATUCK WOMAN.   (F. G. SPECK, PHOTO.)

sachem, Tobaccus, on Forge r., a short distance above the town of Mastic, where a few mixed-bloods still survive, with no knowledge of their language or customs, on a state reservation of 50 acres. Elizabeth Joe, their woman sachem and last chief, died in 1832. In 1890 they numbered 10 families, governed by 3 trustees. See *Patchoag*.   (F. G. S.)

Pooshapukanuk. A former Choctaw settlement, including Mt Dexter, probably in Marion co., Miss. It was the scene of the treaty of Nov. 16, 1805.—Am. State Papers, Ind. Aff., I, 749, 1832.

Pope (*Po-pé*). A celebrated Tewa medicine-man, native of the pueblo of San Juan, who first appears in New Mexico history in 1675 as a leader either of some prisoners charged with witchcraft, and with killing several missionaries, or of a party that visited the Spanish governor at Santa Fé in that year demanding their release. Later making Taos the seat of his efforts, he quietly preached the doctrine of in-

dependence of Spanish authority and the restoration of the old Pueblo life, which developed into a plot to murder or drive from the country the 2,400 Spanish colonists and priests. Chief among Pope's adherents were Catiti of Santo Domingo, Tupatú of Picuris, and Jaca of Taos. The plot quickly spread among the Pueblos, meeting with enthusiasm as it went. Aug. 13, 1680, was the day set for the onslaught, and the news was communicated by runners, even to the far-off Hopi in Arizona, by means of a knotted string; but for some reason the Piros of the lower Rio Grande were not invited to join in the massacre. Every precaution was taken to keep from the Spaniards all news of the proposed revolt; no woman was permitted to know of it, and, because suspected of treachery, Pope put his own brother-in-law to death. Nevertheless the news leaked out, and Pope's only hope of success was to strike at once. The blow came on Aug. 10. Four hundred Spanish colonists, including 21 priests, were murdered, and Santa Fé was besieged, its thousand inhabitants taking refuge with Gov. Antonio de Otermin in the official buildings. Here they remained until the 20th, when a sortie made by 100 of the men resulted in the rout of the Indians, 200 being killed and 47 captured and hanged in the plaza of the town. The following day the Spaniards abandoned Santa Fé and began their long retreat down the Rio Grande to El Paso.

Having accomplished this much, Pope set about to realize the rest of his dream. Those who had been baptized as Christians were washed with yucca suds; the Spanish language and all baptismal names were prohibited; where not already consumed by the burning of the churches, all Christian objects were destroyed, and everything done to restore the old order of things. This project of obliterating everything Spanish from the life and thought of the Indians met with the same enthusiasm as that with which the plan of revolt had been received, and for a time Pope, dressed in ceremonial garb as he went from pueblo to pueblo, was everywhere received with honor. His success, however, had been more than he could stand. Assuming the rôle of a despot, he put to death those who refused to obey his commands, and took the most beautiful women for himself and his captains. Then the old enemies of the Pueblos intervened—drought, and the Apache and Ute, who took advantage of the absence of the Spaniards to resume their forays. Internal dissension also arose. The Keresan tribes and the Taos and Pecos people fought against the Tewa and Tanos, and the latter deposed Pope on account of his lordly demands, electing

to his place Luis Tupatú, who ruled the Tewa and Tanos until 1688, when Pope was again elected; but he died before the reconquest of the province by Vargas in 1692. See *Prophets, Pueblos.*
Consult Bancroft, Ariz. and N. Mex., 1889; Bandelier in Arch. Inst. Papers, III, IV, 1890–92. Davis, Span. Conq. N. Mex., 1869.   (F. W. H.)

Popelout. Said to have been the name of the site of San Juan Bautista mission, in Costanoan territory, Cal.
Popelout.—Engelhardt, Franc. in Cal., 397, 1897.
Popeloutechom.—Ibid.

Popkum. A Cowichan tribe in a town of the same name on Popkum res., lower Fraser r., Brit. Col.; pop. 12 in 1906.
Pā'pk'um.—Boas in Rep. Brit. A. A. S., 454, 1894.
Popoum.—Can. Ind. Aff., pt. II, 160, 1901. Popkum.—Ibid., 309, 1879.

Popof (named for Vasili and Ivan Popof, traders and hunters in 1762–63). An Aleut fishing settlement at Pirate cove, Popof id., one of the Shumagins, Alaska; pop. 7 in 1880, 146 in 1890 (including another settlement at Humboldt harbor).—11th Census, Alaska, 85, 1893.

Poponesset. A village of Christian Indians in 1674 near Poponesset bay, Barnstable co., Mass. Its inhabitants were probably a part of the Nauset.
Pawpoesit.—Bourne (1674) in Mass. Hist. Soc. Coll., 1st s., I, 197, 1806. Popponeeste.—Freeman (1792), ibid., 231. Popponessit.—Freeman (1792), ibid., 231.

Popotita ('where there is popote', a stiff straw). A Huichol rancheria and religious place about 15 m. s. w. of San Andrés Coamiata, q. v.
Epithápa.—Lumholtz, Unknown Mex., II, 72, 1902 (Huichol name, referring to a kind of stiff grass).
Popotita.—Ibid.

Popular fallacies. Since the day when Columbus miscalled the aborigines of America "Indians," believing that he had discovered India, popular fallacies respecting them have been numerous and widespread. Some of the more important of them will be discussed here.

Origin of the Indians.—As soon as, or even before, the newly discovered continent was found to be not connected with Asia, theories of the origin of the Indians began to be formulated by the learned, and, consistently with the religious spirit of the age, a solution of the problem was sought in Hebrew tradition. In the Indians were recognized the descendants of the "lost tribes of Israel." The latest and most earnest supporters of the Hebrew origin are the Mormons, whose statements are alleged to have the authority of direct revelation. Absurd as the theory is in the light of present knowledge, anthropology owes to it several valuable treatises on the habits and characteristics of the Indians, which it could ill afford to lose, notably Lord Kingsborough's Mexican Antiquities (1830–48) and Adair's History of the North American Indians (1775), the lat-

ter book being filled with fancied similarities to Jewish customs, rites, and even traditions. (See *Lost Ten Tribes.*)

Equally absurd, but less widespread, was the myth of a tribe of Welsh Indians, descendants of a colony reputed to have been founded by Prince Madoc about 1170. The myth placed them, with their Welsh language and Welsh Bible, first on the Atlantic coast, where they were identified with the Tuscarora, and then farther and farther w., until about 1776 we find the Welsh, or "white," Indians on the Missouri, where they appeared as the Mandan (according to Catlin), and later on Red r. Later still they were identified with the Hopi of Arizona, and finally with the Modoc of Oregon, after which they vanish. (See *Croatan; White Indians;* consult Mooney in Am. Anthrop., IV, 393, 1891, and Bowen, America Discovered by the Welsh, 1876.)

Other seekers of a foreign origin for the American aborigines have derived them in turn from Greeks, Chinese, Japanese, Phenicians, Irish, Polynesians, and even from the peoples of Australasia. Most of these theories are based on fortuitous analogies in habits, institutions, and arts; but the attempt is frequently made to strengthen them by alleged similarities of language. The general similarity of the human mind in similar stages of culture in every part of the world, with its proneness to produce similar arts, institutions, religious ideas, myths, and even material products, sufficiently explains the former class of facts, whilst the hypotheses of identity of language, based, as they invariably are, on a small number of verbal similarities in the nature of coincidences, are wholly disproved on adequate examination and analysis.

Indian languages.—Indian languages are so utterly unlike European speech in sound and so different in structure and character that it is not surprising that erroneous conceptions concerning them should arise. The unlearned conceived the idea that the speech of all Indians of whatsoever tribe was practically the same, that it was little more than a sort of gibberish, that it contained but a small number of words, that to eke out its shortcomings the Indian was compelled to use gestures, that it was hardly human speech, much less orderly and well developed language.

A comprehension of the manifold variety of Indian linguistic families, embracing a multitude of languages and dialects, of their rich vocabularies, flexible grammatical methods, and general sufficiency to express any and all concepts the Indian mind is capable of entertaining, above all, of their capacity, shared with more advanced tongues, of indefinite expansion corresponding to culture growth, was reserved for a later period and more complete study. The intricacies of Indian languages are even yet but partially understood; their proper study has hardly begun, so vast is the field.

Indians not nomadic.—One of the common fallacies of early historians, by no means yet entirely dissipated, was the idea that the Indians were generally nomadic, having no fixed place of abode, but wandering hither and yon as fancy or the necessities of existence demanded. The term nomadic is not, in fact, properly applicable to any Indian tribe. Every tribe and every congeries of tribes, with exceptions to be noted, laid claim to and dwelt within the limits of a certain tract or region, the boundaries of which were well understood, and were handed down by tradition and not ordinarily relinquished save to a superior force. Between many of the tribes, indeed, were debatable areas, owned by none but claimed by all, which from time immemorial formed the cause of disputes and intertribal wars. Most or all of the tribes E. of the Mississippi except in the N., and some W. of it, were to a greater or less extent agricultural and depended much for food on the products of their tillage. During the hunting season such tribes or villages broke up into small parties and dispersed over their domains more or less widely in search of game; or they visited the seashore for fish and shellfish. Only in this restricted sense may they be said to be nomadic. The so-called "horse Indians" and the Plains Indians, at least after the latter acquired the horse, wandered very widely in search of their chief dependence, the buffalo. Though most of these had no fixed and permanent villages, they yet possessed some idea as to the extent of their own territory as well as that of their neighbors. The Athapascan and Algonquian tribes of the far N., where absence of agriculture, the wide expanses of desolate territory, and the nature of the game necessitated frequent changes of abode and forbade any form of fixed village life, most nearly approached nomadic life.

Indian ownership of land.—The exact nature of Indian ownership of land appears not to have been understood by the early settlers, and the misunderstanding was the fruitful source of trouble and even bloodshed. Neither the individual Indian nor the family possessed vested rights in land. The land belonged to the tribe as a whole, but individual families and clans might appropriate for their own use and tillage any portion of the tribe's unoccupied domain. Hence it was impossible for a chief, family, clan, or any section of a tribe legally to sell or to give away to aliens, white or red, any part of the tribal domain, and the inevitable consequence of illegal sales or gifts was bad feeling, followed often by repudiation of the contract by the tribe as a whole. Attempts by the whites to enforce these supposed legal sales were followed by disorder and bloodshed, often by prolonged wars. (See *Land Tenure.*)

Ideas of royalty.—It is perhaps not strange that the early emigrants to America, habituated to European ideas of royal descent and kingly prerogative, should describe the simple village and tribal organizations of the Indians with high-sounding phrases. Early treatises on the Indians teem with the terms "king," "queen," and "princess," and even with ideas of hereditary privilege and rank. It would be difficult to imagine states of society more unlike than one implied by such terms and the simple democracy of most of the Indians. On the N. W. coast and among some tribes of the s. Atlantic region ideas of cáste had gained a foothold, principally founded on a property basis, but this was exceptional. Equality and independence were the cardinal principles of Indian society. In some tribes, as the Iroquois, certain of the highest chieftaincies were confined to certain clans, and these may be said in a modified sense to have been hereditary, and there were also hereditary chieftaincies among the Apache, Chippewa, Sioux, and other tribes. Practically, however, the offices within the limits of the tribal government were purely elective. The ability of the candidates, their courage, eloquence, previous services, above all, their personal popularity, formed the basis for election to any and all offices. Except among the Natchez and a few other tribes of the lower Mississippi, no power in any wise analogous to that of the despot, no rank savoring of inheritance, as we understand the term, existed among our Indians. Even military service was not compulsory, but he who would might organize a war party, and the courage and known prowess in war of the leader chiefly determined the number of his followers. So loose were the ties of authority on the warpath that a bad dream or an unlucky presage was enough to diminish the number of the war party at any time or even to break it up entirely.

The idea prevalent among the colonists of a legal executive head over the Indians, a so-called king, was acceptable on account of the aid it lent to the transaction of business with the Indians, especially to the enforcement of contracts. It enabled the colonists to treat directly and effectively with one man, or at most with a few, for the sale of land, instead of with the tribe as a whole. The fact is that social and political organization was of the lowest kind; the very name of tribe, with implication of a body bound together by social ties and under some central authority, is of very uncertain application. (See *Chiefs*.)

Knowledge of medicine.—Many erroneous ideas of the practice of medicine among the Indians are current, often fostered by quacks who claim to have received herbs and methods of practice from noted Indian doctors. The medical art among all Indians was rooted in sorcery; and the prevailing idea that diseases were caused by the presence or acts of evil spirits, which could be removed only by sorcery and incantation, controlled diagnosis and treatment. This conception gave rise to both priest and physician. Combined with it there grew up a certain knowledge of and dependence upon simples, one important development of which was what we know as the doctrine of signatures, according to which, in some cases, the color, shape, and markings of plants are supposed to indicate the organs for which in disease they are supposed to be specifics. There was current in many tribes, especially among the old women, a rude knowledge of the therapeutic use of a considerable number of plants and roots, and of the sweating process, which was employed with little discrimination. (See *Medicine and Medicine-men*.)

The Great Spirit.—Among the many erroneous conceptions regarding the Indian none has taken deeper root than the one which ascribes to him belief in an overruling deity, the "Great Spirit." Very far removed from this tremendous conception of one all-powerful deity was the Indian belief in a multitude of spirits that dwelt in animate and inanimate objects, to propitiate which was the chief object of his supplications and sacrifices. To none of his deities did the Indian ascribe moral good or evil. His religion was practical. The spirits were the source of good or bad fortune whether on the hunting path or the war trail, in the pursuit of a wife or in a ball game. If successful he adored, offered sacrifices, and made valuable presents. If unsuccessful he cast his manito away and offered his faith to more powerful or more friendly deities.

In this world of spirits the Indian dwelt in perpetual fear. He feared to offend the spirits of the mountains, of the dark wood, of the lake, of the prairie. The real Indian was a different creature from the joyous and untrammeled savage pictured and envied by the poet and philosopher. (See *Mythology, Nanabozho, Religion*.)

Happy hunting ground.—If the term be understood to imply nothing more than a belief of the Indian in a future existence, it answers, perhaps, as well as another. That the Indian believes in a future life his mortuary rites abundantly testify. It

may be confidently stated that no tribe of American Indians was without some idea of a life after death, but as to its exact nature and whereabouts the Indian's ideas, differing in different tribes, were vague. Nor does it appear that belief in a future life had any marked influence on the daily life and conduct of the individual. The American Indian seems not to have evolved the idea of hell and future punishment.

Division of labor.—The position of woman in Indian society, especially as regards the division of labor, has been misunderstood. Historians have generally pictured her as a drudge and slave, toiling incessantly, while her indolent husband idles away most of the time and exists chiefly by the fruits of her labor. While the picture is not wholly false, it is much overdrawn, chiefly because the observations which suggest it were made about the camp or village, in which and in the neighboring fields lay the peculiar province of woman's activity. In addition to the nurture of children, their duties were the erection and care of the habitation, cooking, preparation of skins, and the making of clothing, pottery, and basketry, and among many tribes they were expected also to help bring home the spoils of the chase. Among agricultural tribes generally tillage of the fields was largely woman's work. Thus her tasks were many and laborious, but she had her hours for gossip and for special women's games. In an Indian community, where the food question is always a serious one, there can be no idle hands. The women were aided in their round of tasks by the children and the old men. Where slavery existed their toil was further lightened by the aid of slaves, and in other tribes captives were often compelled to aid in the women's work.

The men did all the hunting, fishing, and trapping, which in savagery are always toilsome, frequently dangerous, and not rarely fatal, especially in winter. The man alone bore arms, and to him belonged the chances and dangers of war. The making and administration of laws, the conduct of treaties, and the general regulation of tribal affairs were in the hands of the men, though in these fields woman also had important prerogatives. To men were intrusted all the important ceremonies and most of the religious rites, also the task of memorizing tribal records and treaties, as well as rituals, which involved astonishing feats of memory. The chief manual labor of the men was the manufacture of hunting and war implements, an important occupation that took much time. The manufacture of canoes, also, was chiefly man's work, and, indeed, in some tribes the men did the skin dressing and even made their wives' clothing.

Thus, in Indian society, the position of woman was usually subordinate, and the lines of demarcation between the duties of the sexes were everywhere sharply drawn. Nevertheless, the division of labor was not so unequal as it might seem to the casual observer, and it is difficult to understand how the line could have been more fairly drawn in a state of society where the military spirit was so dominant. Indian communities lived in constant danger of attack, and their men, whether in camp or on the march, must ever be ready at a moment's warning to seize their arms and defend their homes and families.

Where Indian communities adopted settled village life, as did the Pueblo peoples, or where the nature of tribal wealth was such as to enable women to become property holders on a large scale, as among the Navaho, whose women own the sheep, or where slavery was an established institution and extensively practised, as among the N. W. coast tribes, the position of women advanced, and there ensued, among other social changes, a more equal division of laborious tasks. (See *Labor, Women.*)

Degeneracy of mixed-bloods.—It has long been an adage that the mixed-blood is a moral degenerate, exhibiting few or none of the virtues of either, but all the vices of both of the parent stocks. In various parts of the country there are many mixed-bloods of undoubted ability and of high moral standing, and there is no evidence to prove that the low moral status of the average mixed-bloods of the frontier is a necessary result of mixture of blood, but there is much to indicate that it arises chiefly from his unfortunate environment. The mixed-blood often finds little favor with either race, while his superior education and advantages, derived from association with the whites, enable him to outstrip his Indian brother in the pursuit of either good or evil. Absorption into the dominant race is likely to be the fate of the Indian, and there is no reason to fear that when freed from his anomalous environment the mixed-blood will not win an honorable social, industrial, and political place in the national life. (See *Mixed-bloods.*)

Indian pigmies and giants.—All times and all peoples have had traditions of pigmies and giants. It is therefore nowise surprising that such myths were early transplanted to American soil. The story of an ancient race of pigmies in Tennessee, familiar to most archeologists, owes its origin to the discovery, in the early half of the last century, of numerous small stone coffins or cists containing skeletons. The largest, measured by Featherstonhaugh, was 24 in. long by 9 in. deep. The small size of the

cists was assumed by their discoverers to be proof of the existence of a race of dwarfs, and the belief gained ready credence and exists to the present day in the minds of a few. In many cases the skeletons of the supposed dwarfs proved to be those of children, while, as pointed out by Jones and Thomas, the skeletons of the adults found in the cists had been deprived of flesh, a common Indian mortuary custom throughout the mound region, and then disjointed, when the bones of an adult could be packed into very small space.

A race of dwarfs has also been popularly ascribed to the cliff-dweller region of New Mexico and Arizona, partly owing to the finding of shriveled and shrunken mummies of children, too hastily assumed to be those of dwarfs, and partly owing to the discovery of small apartments in the cliff-dwellings, of the nature of cubby-holes for the storage of property, the entrances to which were too small to permit the passage, erect, of an ordinary man; hence, in the mind of the discoverers, they must have been used by dwarfs. The Pueblo peoples are, indeed, of relatively small stature, but they are as far from being dwarfs as other Indians from being giants. (For details respecting the dwarfs of Tennessee, see Haywood, Natural and Aboriginal History of Tennessee, 1823; Jones, Antiquities of Tennessee, 10, 1876.)

The myth of the discovery of giant skeletons, perennial in newspapers, is revived at times by the finding of huge fossil mammalian remains of ancient epochs, erroneously supposed by the ignorant to be human; at others by the discovery of buried skeletons the bones of which have in the course of time become separated, so as to give the impression of beings of unusual height. There was considerable diversity of stature among Indian tribes, some, as the Pueblos, being of rather small size, while among the tribes of the lower Colorado and the Plains were many men of unusual size. Now and then, too, as among other peoples, a man is found who is a real giant among his kind; a skeleton was exhumed in West Virginia which measured $7\frac{1}{2}$ ft in length and 19 in. across the shoulders. (See *Anatomy, Physiology.*)

Mound-builders and Cliff-dwellers.—The belief was formerly held by many that the mound-builders of the Mississippi valley and the cliff-dwellers of the S. W. border were racially distinct from the Indians or had reached a superior degree of culture. The more thoroughly the mounds and cliff ruins have been explored and the more carefully the artifacts, customs, and culture status of these ancient peoples are studied, the more apparent is it that their attainments were nowise superior to those of the later Indian. There is no evidence incompatible with the theory that the builders of the mounds and the dwellers in the cliffs are the ancestors of the tribes now or recently in possession of the same regions.

Stolidity and taciturnity.—The idea of the Indian, once popular, suggests a taciturn and stolid character, who smoked his pipe in silence and stalked reserved and dignified among his fellows. Unquestionably the Indian of the Atlantic slope differed in many respects from his kinsmen farther w.; it may be that the forest Indian of the N. and E. imbibed something of the spirit of the primeval woods which, deep and gloomy, overspread much of his region. If so, he has no counterpart in the regions w. of the Mississippi. On occasions of ceremony and religion the western Indian can be both dignified and solemn, as befits the occasion; but his nature, if not as bright and sunny as that of the Polynesian, is at least as far removed from moroseness as his disposition is from taciturnity. The Indian of the present day has at least a fair sense of humor, and is very far from being a stranger to jest, laughter, and repartee.   (H. W. H.)

Population. The question of the number of the native population of America, and particularly of the United States and British America, at the coming of the white man, has been the subject of much speculation. Extremists on the one hand have imagined a population of millions, while on the other hand the untenable claim has been made, and persistently repeated, that there has been no decrease, but that on the contrary, in spite of removals, wars, epidemics, and dissipation, and the patent fact that the aboriginal population of whole regions has completely disappeared, the Indian has thriven under misfortune and is more numerous to-day than at any former period. The first error is due in part to the tendency to magnify the glory of a vanished past, and in part to the mistaken idea that the numerous ancient remains scattered over the country were built or occupied at practically the same period. The contrary error—that the Indian has increased—is due to several causes, chief of which is the mistake of starting the calculation at too recent a period, usually at the establishment of treaty relations. The fact is that between the discovery of America and the beginning of the federal government the aboriginal population had been subjected to nearly three centuries of destructive influences, which had already wiped out many tribes entirely and reduced many others to mere remnants. Another factor of apparent increase

is found in the mixed-blood element, which is officially counted as Indian, although frequently representing only $\frac{1}{16}$, $\frac{1}{32}$, or even $\frac{1}{64}$ of Indian blood, while in the late Indian Ter. (Oklahoma) it is well known that the tribal rolls contain thousands of names repudiated by the former tribal courts. The Indian of the discovery period was a full-blood; the Indian of to-day is very often a mongrel, with not enough of aboriginal blood to be distinguishable in the features, yet, excepting in a few tribes, no official distinction is made.

The chief causes of decrease, in order of importance, may be classed as smallpox and other epidemics; tuberculosis; sexual diseases; whisky and attendant dissipation; removals, starvation and subjection to unaccustomed conditions; low vitality due to mental depression under misfortune; wars. In the category of destroyers all but wars and tuberculosis may be considered to have come from the white man, and the increasing destructiveness of tuberculosis itself is due largely to conditions consequent upon his advent. Smallpox has repeatedly swept over wide areas, sometimes destroying perhaps one-half the native population within its path. One historic smallpox epidemic originating on the upper Missouri in 1781–82 swept northward to Great Slave lake, eastward to L. Superior, and westward to the Pacific. Another, in 1801–02, ravaged from the Rio Grande to Dakota, and another, in 1837–38, reduced the strength of the northern Plains tribes by nearly one-half. A fever visitation about the year 1830 was officially estimated to have killed 70,000 Indians in California, while at about the same time a malarial fever epidemic in Oregon and on the Columbia—said to have been due to the plowing up of the ground at the trading posts—ravaged the tribes of the region and practically exterminated those of Chinookan stock. The destruction by disease and dissipation has been greatest along the Pacific coast, where also the original population was most numerous. In California the enormous decrease from about a quarter of a million to less than 20,000 is due chiefly to the cruelties and wholesale massacres perpetrated by the miners and early settlers. The almost complete extermination of the Aleut is attributable to the same causes during the early Russian period. Confinement in mission establishments has also been fatal to the Indian, in spite of increased comfort in living conditions. Wars in most cases have not greatly diminished the number of Indians. The tribes were in chronic warfare among themselves, so that the balance was nearly even until, as in the notable case of the Iroquois, the acquisition of firearms gave one body an immense superiority over its neighbors. Among the wars most destructive to the Indians may be noted those in Virginia and southern New England, the raids upon the Florida missions by the Carolina settlers and their savage allies, the wars of the Natchez and Foxes with the French, the Creek war, and the war waged by the Iroquois for a period of thirty years upon all the surrounding tribes.

A careful study of population conditions for the whole territory N. of Mexico, taking each geographic section separately, indicates a total population, at the time of the coming of the white man, of nearly 1,150,000 Indians, which is believed to be within 10 per cent of the actual number. Of this total 846,000 were within the limits of the United States proper, 220,000 in British America, 72,000 in Alaska, and 10,000 in Greenland. The original total is now reduced to about 403,000, a decrease of about 65 per cent. The complete study is expected to form the subject of a future Bulletin of the Bureau of American Ethnology. (J. M.)

Poquim, Poquoiam. See *Uncas.*

Poquonnoc (from *pauqu'un-auke*, 'a clearing'). A tribe formerly living about the mouth of Farmington r. in Hartford co., Conn. Their principal village, called also Pequonnoc, was near the present Windsor. **Paquaanocke.**—Windsor Rec. (1636–59) cited by Trumbull, Ind. Names Conn., 55, 1881. **Paquanaug.**—Plymouth deed (1687), ibid. **Paquaniock.**—Windsor Rec., op. cit. **Pequanucke.**—R. I. Col. Rec. (1644) cited by Trumbull, ibid. **Poquan'noc.**—Trumbull, ibid., 54. **Poquannock.**—McClure (1797) in Mass. Hist. Soc. Coll., 1st s., v., 169, 1806. **Poquonock.**—Windsor Rec., op.cit. **Powquaniock.**—Ibid.

Poquosin. A name applied in eastern Maryland, Virginia, and North Carolina to a low wooded ground or swamp, which is covered with shallow water in winter and remains in a miry condition in summer. Some of these swamps in North Carolina, such as the "Holly Shelter pocoson," are 40 m. in length, and overgrown with great bodies of valuable timber trees, rendered inaccessible to the outer world by reason of overflow and the perpetual miry state of the ground. In Duplin co. in the same state, in which *pocosons*, or "dismals" as they are also called, abound, there are 105 sq. m. of pure mud swamps, and in Pender co. 206 sq. m. of overflowed land. The name is sometimes applied to a reclaimed swamp. The name is from Renape *påkwesen*, a verbal adjective meaning 'it (the land) is in a slightly watered condition.' The word is common to all Algonquian dialects, and in Wood Cree is used substantively as a name for a 'shoal' or 'shallow'. The name is spelled also *poaquesson, poquoson, pocoson, perkoson.* (W. R. G.)

Porgy. According to Bartlett (Dict. Americanisms, 484, 1877), a name given in New York to a fish (*Sparus argyrops*) called in Rhode Island and E. Connecticut scup, and in some other parts of New England scuppaug. The dictionaries give *porgy* the following meanings: 1. Braize (*Pagrus vulgaris*), scup, pinfish, and margate-fish. 2. Surf-fish of the Pacific coast. 3. Angel-fish. 4. Toad-fish and menhaden. *Porgy*, spelled also *poggy, pogy, pogie, paugie,* etc., is a reduction of *mishcuppaûog*, plural of *mishcup*, in the Narraganset dialect of Algonquian, which Roger Williams (1643) rendered 'breames.' The whites took the plural as a singular and decapitated it, hence *porgy, paugie*, etc. The decaudated form appears as *mishcup* in some parts of New England. Gerard, on the other hand, asserts that *porgy* is "not a corruption of an Indian word, but a name in England for a fish allied to our porgy. It was introduced at an early period, and is mentioned by Josselyn. Catesby gives it also as the name of a Bermuda fish. It was evidently derived from *pargus*, one of the forms of *pagrus*, a word of Greek origin." See *Mishcup, Pogy.* (A. F. C.)

Porphyry. Rock of igneous origin and resembling granite, but characterized by the presence of crystals of quartz and feldspar which, when large and contrasting with the somber matrix, give a very attractive appearance. It was often used by the native tribes in making their heavier implements, and the more showy varieties were selected for the manufacture of ornaments and objects of ceremony. (W. H. H.)

Portage Band. A Winnebago division that resided in 1811 at the portage of Fox and Wisconsin rs., at the present site of Portage, Wis.—Gale, Upper Miss., 185, 1867.

Porter, Pleasant. One of the last chiefs of the Creek Nation; born at the family home near the present Coweta, N. of Arkansas r., in the Creek Nation, Okla., Sept. 26, 1840, died of paralysis at Vinita, Cherokee Nation, Sept. 3, 1907, while en route to Missouri. His father was a white man, Pleasant Porter inheriting his Indian blood from his mother, who, through her father, Tulope Tustunuggee, of the Big Spring town of Creeks, had a decided strain of negro blood. He was a bright boy, but acquired only a limited education at the old Tallahassee mission school; from wide reading, however, after he became of age, he was regarded as one of the best informed Indians in the entire Indian Ter. When the Civil War broke out many of Porter's relatives and friends espoused the cause of the North and enlisted in its service, but with the majority of the Creeks he entered the service of the Confederacy and at the close of the war was a first lieutenant of Company A, Second Creek regiment. In an engagement with the Creeks who had taken sides with the North, Porter received a wound which subjected him to a slight lameness throughout the remainder of his life. Soon after peace was restored he took an active part in shaping the affairs of the Creek Nation; first becoming one of the clerks of the National council, he was soon promoted to a seat in that body, which he retained for twelve or sixteen years, and for one term was president of the upper house. He also served one or two terms as superintendent of schools of the Nation, and has sometimes been credited with the fatherhood of the school system of the Creek Nation of that time. On twenty or more occasions he was a delegate of the Nation to Washington, where he was intrusted with important interests, being a member of the particular delegation that concluded the last agreement between the Creeks and the United States in 1902. At the most critical period in the history of his tribe Porter was elected to the chieftaincy, and after serving a term of four years to their satisfaction, was again elected to the office and was serving the term due to terminate Dec. 5, 1907, when death came. Porter was ever true to his people, and amid the perplexing conditions attending the surrender of their tribal government and the assumption of that of the whites he led them perhaps more successfully than any other Creek leader could have done. He was the seventh and last Creek chief elected by the people after the adoption in 1867 of the national constitution. He left a son William, two daughters, Mrs Mainie Farnesworth and Miss Lenora, and also a sister, Mrs Nancy Yargee, residing at Red Fork, Okla.

Port Essington. A modern town, occupied by Tsimshian and whites, at the mouth of Skeena r., Brit. Col. It is important as a port and as a center of the canning industry. Pop. in 1908, with Kitzumgaylum and Kitzelas, 191.

Port Simpson. A modern town, formerly called Fort Simpson, on the N. w. coast of British Columbia between Metlakatla and the mouth of Nass r., built up around a Hudson's Bay Co.'s stockade. In 1908 it contained 703 Tsimshian Indians.

Portuguese. See *Croatan Indians*.

Poruptanck. A village of the Powhatan confederacy in 1608, situated on the N. bank of York r. in Gloucester co., Va.—Smith (1629), Va., I, map, repr. 1819.

Poseuingge. A ruined Tewa pueblo at the Rito Colorado, about 10 m. w. of the hot springs near Abiquiu, N. Mex. It was the home of Poseueve, a shaman or successful wizard, who, according to na-

tive tradition, was subsequently deified, and "around whose figure the story of Montezuma has latterly been woven." The aboriginal name of the village was Po-se or P'ho-se, Poseuingge referring to the ruins. Cf. *Pojiuuingge*, and consult Bandelier in Arch. Inst. Papers, III, 61, 310, 1890; IV, 37 et seq., 1892.

Another ruined pueblo bearing the same name, and called also Posege, is situated at Ojo Caliente, about 14 m. above its mouth and about the same distance N. E. of Abiquiu. The ruins are on a hill about 140 ft above the stream; they are of adobe and stone, and the remains of 13 circular kivas are still to be seen. See Hewett in Bull. 32, B. A. E., 38–39, 1906.
P'ho-se.—Bandelier, op. cit., IV, 42. Po-se.—Ibid.

Poshiwu. The Magpie clan of the Hopi.
Pociwû wiñwû.--Fewkes in 19th Rep. B. A. E., 584, 1900. Po-si'-o.—Stephen in 8th Rep. B. A. E., 39, 1891. Pósiwuu.—Voth, Hopi Proper Names, 101, 1905. Po'-si-wûwüñ-wû.—Fewkes in Am. Anthrop., VII, 405, 1894.

Poskesa. A Mono tribe that lived between San Joaquin and Kings rs., Cal. Not mentioned since the first period of American occupancy, when they were said to have been one of four tribes under the chief Towoquiet. They ceded their lands to the U. S. by treaty of Apr. 29, 1851, and were placed on a reserve between Chowchilla and Kaweah rs.
Boshgisha.—A. L. Kroeber, inf'n, 1906 (Yokuts name). Pas-ke-sa.—Royce in 18th Rep. B. A. E., 782, 1899. Pas-ke-sas.—Barbour in Sen. Ex. Doc. 4, 32d Cong., spec. sess., 252, 1853. Po-ke-as.—Johnston in Sen. Ex. Doc. 61, 32d Cong., 1st sess., 22, 1852. Pos-ke-as.—Ibid., 23. Pos-ke-sas.—McKee in Ind. Aff. Rep., 223, 1851.

Poso Blanco (Span.: 'white well or water-hole'). A Papago village in s. Arizona, s. of Gila r.; pop. about 300 in 1863.—Poston in Ind. Aff. Rep. 1863, 385, 1864.

Posos (Span.: 'water holes'). A former Yuma rancheria near the s. bank of Gila r., above its mouth, in the present Arizona; visited by Anza and Font in 1776.
Posos.—Font, map (1777), in Bancroft, Ariz. and N. Mex., 393, 1889. Pozos de Enmedio.—Anza and Font cited by Bancroft, ibid. Zacatal Duro.—Ibid.

Poso Verde (Span.: 'green well or water hole'). A Papago village s. of the Arizona-Sonora boundary, opposite Oro Blanco, Ariz.; pop. about 350 in 1863 (Poston in Ind. Aff. Rep. 1863, 385, 1864), when it was regarded as in the United States.
Chutukivahia.—J. W. Fewkes, inf'n, 1907 ('green spring': native name).

Possum. A popular form of *opossum* (q. v.).

Posta. See *La Posta*.

Potam. A Yaqui settlement on the N. bank of lower Rio Yaqui, s. w. Sonora, Mexico.
Potam.—Velasco (1850) quoted by Bancroft, Nat. Races, I, 608, 1882. Potan.—Alcedo, Dic. Geog., IV, 288, 1788. Santísima Trinidad de Potam.—Orozco y Berra, Geog., 355, 1864.

Potano. A tribe of Timucuan stock formerly occupying an inland territory in N. Florida, about the upper waters of Suwannee r. De Soto passed through their territory in 1539, the French Huguenots found them at war with the Timucua in 1564, and Pareja mentions them in 1612 as speaking a Timucuan dialect. They were later Christianized and gathered into mission villages, which, with those of the Apalachee, were destroyed by the incursions of the savages from the northward in 1701–08. (J. M.)

Patanou.—Laudonnière (1564) misquoted by Shipp, De Soto and Fla., 518, 1881. **Potano.**—Gentl. of Elvas (1557) in Bourne, De Soto Narr., I, 38, 1904; Ranjel (*ca.* 1546), ibid., II, 70, 1904; Pareja (1612) as quoted by Gatschet in Proc. Am. Philos. Soc., XVII, 479, 1880. **Potanou.**—Laudonnière (1564) in French, Hist. Coll. La., n. s., 243, 1869. **Potavou.**—Brinton, Fla. Penin., 119, 1859 (misprint *v* for *n*).

Potanumaquut. A former Nauset village on Pleasant bay, near Harwich, Barnstable co., Mass. In 1762 it still contained 64 Indians and was, next to Mashpee, the largest Indian village in the county.

Ponanummakut.—Rawson and Danforth in Mass. Hist. Soc. Coll., 1st s., X, 133, 1809. **Potanumacut.**—Treaty of 1687, ibid., 4th s., V, 186, 1861. **Potanumaquut.**—Freeman (1792), ibid., 1st s., I, 230, 1806. **Potenumacut.**—Writer (*ca.* 1767), ibid., 2d s., III, 14, 1815. **Poterrummecout.**—Stiles (1762), ibid., 1st s., X, 112, 1809.

Potaucao. A village of the Powhatan confederacy in 1608, in New Kent co., Va., between the Chickahominy and Pamunkey rs.

Potaucao.—Smith (1629), Va., I, map, repr. 1819. **Potavncak.**—Pots, ibid., 219.

Potawackati. A band, probably Moquelumnan, so called from their chief, formerly residing near the headwaters of Mariposa, Merced, and Tuolumne rs., Cal.

Potawackaties.—Barbour et al. (1851) in Sen. Ex. Doc. 4, 32d Cong., spec. sess., 60, 1853.

Potawatomi (J. B. Bottineau, speaking Chippewa and Cree fluently, gives *Potawatamiñk* or *Potawaganiñk*, i. e. 'People of the place of the fire,' as the primary form of the name. This derivation is strongly confirmed by the Huron name *Asistaguerouon* (Champlain, 1616), for *Otsistä'ge-'roñnoñ'*, likewise signifying 'People of the place of fire,' which was applied by them to their enemies who dwelt in 1616 on the w. shores of L. Huron. The Jesuit Relation for 1671 (42, 1858) has the following passage: "Four nations make their abode here, namely, those who bear the name Puans (i. e., the Winnebago), who have always lived here as in their own country, and who have been reduced to nothing from being a very flourishing and populous people, having been exterminated by the Illinois, their enemies; the Potawatomi, the Sauk, and the Nation of the Fork (la Fourche) also live here, but as strangers (or foreigners), driven by the fear of Iroquois [The Neuters and Ottawa] from their own lands which are between the lake of the Hu-

rons and that of the Illinois." The Jesuit Relations employ the expression "Nation of Fire," until in the one for 1670 (p. 94) occurs the first use of "Makskouteng," who are represented as living then on Fox r. in what is now Wisconsin. Hence, it seems clear that the term "nation of fire" was originally applied to the Potawatomi and their close neighbors, the Sauk and the "Nation of the Fork," dwelling on the w. shore of L. Huron. And since a part at least of the Potawatomi tribe bears the name *Maskotens*, officially known as the "Prairie Band," and the tribe as a whole was a part of those who were called "People of the Fire," a natural confusion arose as to the application of these two names,

POTAWATOMI MAN

and so the term "Fire Nation" at last became permanently affixed to a people whose proper name was "People of the Small Prairie," latterly known as the Mascoutens.—Hewitt). An Algonquian tribe, first encountered on the islands of Green bay, Wis., and at its head. According to the traditions of all three tribes, the Potawatomi, Chippewa, and Ottawa were originally one people, and seem to have reached the region about the upper end of L. Huron together. Here they separated, but the three have sometimes formed a loose confederacy, or have acted in concert, and in 1846 those removed beyond the Mississippi, asserting their former connection, asked to be again united. Warren conjectured that it had been less than three centuries since the Chippewa became disconnected as a distinct tribe from the Ottawa and Potawatomi. In the Jesuit Relation for 1640 the Potawatomi are spoken of as living in the vicinity of the Winnebago. Verwyst (Missionary Labors, 211, 1886) says that in 1641 they were at Sault Ste Marie, fleeing before the Sioux. The Jesuit Relation of 1642, speaking of the meeting of Raymbault and Jogues with the tribes at Sault Ste Marie, says that "a certain nation farther away, which they called Pouteatami, had abandoned its country and taken refuge with the inhabitants of the Sault in order to escape from some other hostile nation which was continually harassing them." At the "feast of the dead" attended by Raymbault and Jogues in 1641, somewhere E. or N. E. of L. Huron, the Chippewa and Potawatomi appear to have been present. In 1667, Allouez met 300 of their warriors at Chaquamegon bay. A portion of them were dwelling in 1670 on the islands in the mouth of Green bay, chiefly about the Jesuit mission of St François Xavier. They were then moving southward, and by the close of the 17th century had established themselves on Milwaukee r., at Chicago, and on St Joseph r., mostly in territory that had previously been held by the Miami. (For their migration from Michigan, see *Sauk*.) After the conquest of the Illinois, about 1765, they took possession of the part of Illinois lying N. E. of the country seized by the Sauk, Foxes, and Kickapoo, at the same time spreading eastward over southern Michigan and gradually approaching the Wabash. At the treaty of Greenville, in 1795, they notified the Miami that they intended to move down upon the Wabash, which they soon afterward did, in spite of the protests of the Miami, who claimed that whole region. By the beginning of the 19th century they were in possession of the country around the head of L. Michigan, from Milwaukee r. in Wisconsin to Grand r. in Michigan, extending s. w. over a large part of N. Illinois, E. across Michigan to L. Erie, and s. in Indiana to the Wabash and as far down as Pine cr. Within this territory they had about 50 villages. The principal divisions were those of St Joseph r. and Huron r., Mich., Wabash r., and the Prairie band of Potawatomi in Illinois and Wisconsin.

The Potawatomi sided actively with the French down to the peace of 1763; they were prominent in the rising under Pontiac, and on the breaking out of the Revolution in 1775 took arms against the United States and continued hostilities until the treaty of Greenville in 1795. They again took up arms in the British interest in 1812, and made final treaties

of peace in 1815. As the settlements rapidly pressed upon them, they sold their land by piecemeal, chiefly between the years 1836 and 1841, and removed beyond the Mississippi. A large part of those residing in Indiana refused to leave their homes until driven out by military force. A part of them escaped into Canada and are now settled on Walpole id. in L. St Clair. Those who went w. were settled partly in w. Iowa and partly in Kansas, the former, with whom were many individuals of other tribes, being known as Prairie Potawatomi, while the others were known as Potawatomi of the Woods. In 1846 they were all united on a reservation in s. Kansas. A part of them was known as the Keotuc band. In 1861 a large part of the tribe took lands in severalty and became known as Citizen Potawatomi, but in 1868 they again removed to a tract in Indian Ter. (Oklahoma), where they now are. The others are still in Kansas, while a considerable body, part of the Prairie band, is yet in Wisconsin, and another band, the Potawatomi of Huron, is in lower Michigan.

The Indians of this tribe are described in the early notices as "the most docile and affectionate toward the French of all the savages of the west." They were also more kindly disposed toward Christianity, besides being more humane and civilized than the other tribes. Tailhan says: "Their natural politeness and readiness to oblige was extended to strangers, which was very rare among these peoples. Up to this time (1864) they have resisted the rum and brandy with which the Anglo-Saxons have poisoned the other tribes." Sir William Johnson, however, complained in 1772 of robberies and murders committed by them through the intrigues and jealousy of the French traders. Their women were more reserved than was usual among Indians, and showed some tendency toward refinement in manners. The Potawatomi of Milwaukee r., who were considerably intermixed with Sauk and Winnebago, were described about 1825 as being lazy fellows, as a rule preferring to fish and hunt all summer long rather than to cultivate corn, and noted players of the moccasin game and lacrosse, heavy gamblers and given to debauchery. Polygamy was common among the Potawatomi when they were visited by the early missionaries.

According to Schoolcraft, it is believed by the Potawatomi that there are two spirits who govern the world: one is called Kitchemonedo, or the Great Spirit; the other Matchemonedo, or the Evil Spirit; the first is good and beneficent, the other wicked. But all this is the result of Christian teaching. In former times the Potawatomi worshiped the sun to some extent—at least they sometimes offered sacrifice in honor of the sun in order that the sick might recover or that some desire might be obtained. They were accustomed, as were several other tribes of the N. W., to hold what has been called the "feast of dreams," during which their special or individual manito was selected. Dog meat was the flesh chiefly used at this feast. Burial was probably chiefly by inhumation, though there is some evidence that scaffold exposure was practised by the western part of the tribe. Sir Daniel Wilson alludes to certain graves surmounted by small mounds, which the surveyors informed him were Potawatomi burial places. Other graves of the same character found in Iowa are also known to have been burial places of people of the same tribe. Cremation was sometimes resorted to, but this appears to have been limited exclusively to those belonging to the Rabbit gens. About the year 1825 many of them took up the doctrine of the Kickapoo prophet Kanakuk. The Potawatomi have a tendency to elide vowels and syllables, due to the rapidity with which the dialect is spoken as compared with that of the Ottawa and the Chippewa (W. Jones, inf'n, 1906).

Chauvignerie (1736) mentions among the Potawatomi totems the golden carp, frog, tortoise, crab, and crane. According to Morgan (Anc. Soc., 167, 1877) they have 15 gentes, as follows: (1) Moah, 'Wolf'; (2) Mko, 'Bear'; (3) Mukh, 'Beaver'; (4) Misshawa, 'Elk'; (5) Maak, 'Loon'; (6) Knou, 'Eagle'; (7) Nma, 'Sturgeon'; (8) Nmapena, 'Carp'; (9) Mgezewa, 'Bald Eagle'; (10) Chekwa, 'Thunder'; (11) Wabozo, 'Rabbit'; (12) Kakagshe, 'Crow'; (13) Wakeshi, 'Fox'; (14) Penna, 'Turkey'; (15) Mketashshekakah, 'Black Hawk.'

The tribe probably never greatly exceeded 3,000 souls, and most estimates place them far below that number. The principal estimates give them about 1,500 in 1765, 1,750 in 1766, 2,250 in 1778, 2,000 in 1783, 1,200 in 1795, 2,500 in 1812, 3,400 in 1820, and 1,800 in 1843. The last estimate does not include those who had recently fled to Canada. In 1908 those in the United States were reported to number 2,522, distributed as follows: Citizen Potawatomi in Oklahoma, 1,768; Prairie band in Kansas, 676; and Potawatomi of Huron, in Calhoun co., Mich., 78. A few besides these are scattered through their ancient territory and at various other points. Those in British territory are all in the province of Ontario and number about 220, of whom 176 are living with Chippewa and Ottawa on Walpole id. in L. St Clair, and the remain-

der (no longer officially reported) are divided between Caradoc and Rivière aux Sables, where they reside by permission of the Chippewa and Munsee.

The Potawatomi have participated in the following treaties with the United States: Ft Harmar, Ohio, Jan. 9, 1789; Greenville, Ohio, Aug. 3, 1795; Ft Wayne, Ind., June 7, 1803; Ft Industry, Ohio, July 4, 1805; Grouseland, Ind., Aug. 21, 1805; Detroit, Mich., Nov. 17, 1807; Brownstown, Mich., Nov. 25, 1808; Ft Wayne, Ind., Sept. 30, 1809; Greenville, Ohio, July 22, 1814; Portage des Sioux, Mo., July 18, 1815; Spring Wells, Mich., Sept. 8, 1815; St Louis, Mo., Aug. 24, 1816; Miami, Ohio, Sept. 29, 1817; St Mary's, Ohio, Oct. 2, 1818; Chicago, Ill., Aug. 29, 1821; Prairie du Chien, Wis., Aug. 19, 1825; Wabash, Ind., Oct. 16, 1826; St Joseph, Mich., Sept. 19, 1827; Green Bay, Wis., Aug. 25, 1828; St Joseph River, Mich., Sept. 20, 1828; Prairie du Chien, Wis., July 29, 1829; Camp Tippecanoe, Ind., Oct. 20, 1832; Tippecanoe River, Ind., Oct. 26 and 27, 1832; Chicago, Ill., Sept. 26, 1833; Lake Maxeeniekuekee, Ind., Dec. 4, 1834; Tippecanoe River, Ind., Dec. 10, 1834; Potawattimie Mills, Ind., Dec. 16, 1834; Logansport, Ind., Dec. 17, 1834; Turkey Creek Prairie, Ind., Mar. 26, 1836; Tippecanoe River, Ind., Mar. 29 and Apr. 11, 1836; Indian Agency, Ind., Apr. 22, 1836; Yellow River, Ind., Aug. 5, 1836; Chippewanaung, Ind., Sept. 20, 22, and 23, 1836; Washington, D. C., Feb. 11, 1837; Council Bluffs, Iowa, June 5 and 17, 1846; Kansas River, Kan., Nov. 15, 1861; Washington, D. C., Feb. 27, 1867.

The following were the Potawatomi villages at various periods: Abercronk (?), Ashkum's Village, Assiminehkon, Aubbeenaubbee's Village, Chechawkose's Village, Chekase's Village, Chichipe Outipe, Chippoy, Comoza's Village, Kewigoshkeem's Village, Kinkash's Village, Little Rock, Macon, Macousin, Mangachqua, Maquanago (?), Masac's Village, Matchebenashshewish's Village, Maukekose's Village, Menoquet's Village, Mesheketeno's Village, Mesquawbuck's Village, Mickkesawbee, Milwaukee, Minemaung's Village, Mota's Village, Muskwawasepeotan, Natowasepe, Nayonsay's Village, Pierrish's Village, Pokagon, Prairie Ronde, Rock Village, Rum's Village, St Joseph (mission), St Michael (mission), Sawmehnaug, Seginsavin's Village, Shaytee's Village, Shobonier's Village, Soldier's Village, Tassinong, Toisa's Village, Tonquish's Village, Topenebee's Village, Waisuskuck's Village, Wanatah, Wimego's Village, Winamac's Village, Wonongoseak.   (J. M.   J. N. B. H.)

Adawadenys.—Canajoharie conf. (1759) in N. Y. Doc. Col. Hist., VII, 384, 1856 (probably an Iroquois corruption). **Asistagueronon.**—Champlain (1616), Œuvres, v, pt. 1, 275, 1870. **Asistagueroüon.**—Ibid. (1616), IV, 58, 1870. **Assestagueronons.**—Schoolcraft, Ind. Tribes, IV, 206, 1854. **Assistaeronons.**—Jes. Rel. 1670–71, as quoted by Schoolcraft, ibid., 244. **Assistagueronon.**—Sagard (1636), Hist. Can., I, 194, 1864; Champlain (1632), Œuvres, v, map, 1870. **Assistaqueronons.**—Champlain (ca. 1630), as quoted by Schoolcraft, Ind. Tribes, IV, 244, 1854. **Athistaëronnon.**—Jes. Rel. 1646, 77, 1858. **Atowateany.**—Post (1758) quoted by Proud, Penn., II, app., 113, 1798. **Atsistaehronons.**—Jes. Rel. 1641, 72, 1858. **Atsistahéroron.**—Champlain, Œuvres, IV, 58, note, 1870. **Atsistarhonon.**—Sagard (1632), Hist. Can., Huron Dict., 1866 (Huron name). **Attistae.**—Schoolcraft, Ind. Tribes, IV, 244, 1854 (misquoted from Jes. Rel. 1640, 35, 1858). **Attistaehronon.**—Jes. Rel. 1640, 35, 1858. **Attistaeronons.**—Jes. Rel. 1640 quoted by Schoolcraft, Ind. Tribes, IV, 244, 1854. **Fire Nation.**—Schoolcraft, ibid., 206. **Gens de Feu.**—Champlain (1616), Œuvres, IV, 58, 1870; Sagard, Grande Voyage, I, 53, 1865. **Gens feu.**—Sagard, Hist. Can., I, 194, 1836 (misprint). **Kúnu-hayánu.**—Gatschet, Caddo MS., B. A. E., 1884 ('watermelon people,' from kúnu, 'watermelon': Caddo name). **Nation du Feu.**—Jes. Rel. 1641, 72, 1858. **Nation of Fire.**—Jefferys, French Doms., pt. I, 48, 1761. **Ndaton-8atendi.**—Potier, Racines Huron, MS., 1751 (Huron name). **Ondatouatandy.**—Jes. Rel. 1648, 62, 1858. **Oupouteouatamik.**—Jes. Rel. 1658, 21, 1858. **Patawatamies.**—Greenville treaty (1795) quoted by Harris, Tour, 249, 1805. **Patawattamies.**—Turkey Creek treaty (1836) in U. S. Ind. Treaties, 648, 1837. **Patawattomies.**—Hunter, Captivity, 14, 1823. **Pattawatamies.**—Hamtranck (1790) in Am. St. Papers, Ind. Aff., I, 87, 1832. **Pattawatima.**—Ft Harmar treaty (1789), ibid., 6. **Pattawatimees.**—Jones, Ojebway Inds., 238, 1861. **Pattawatimy.**—De Butts (1795) in Am. St. Papers, Ind. Aff., I, 565, 1832. **Pattawatomie.**—Washington treaty (1868) in U. S. Ind. Treat., 691, 1873. **Pattawattamees.**—Wilkinson (1791) quoted by Rupp, W. Penn., app., 236, 1846. **Pattawattomies.**—Hunter, Narr., 192, 1823. **Pattawattomis.**—Heckewelder quoted by Barton, New Views, app., 3, 1798. **Pattiwatima.**—Knox (1789) in Am. St. Papers, Ind. Aff., I, 8, 1832. **Pa-tu-átami.**—Gatschet, Kaw MS. vocab., B. A. E., 27, 1878 (Kansa form). **Pautawatimis.**—Doc. of 1712 quoted by Gale, Upper Miss., 61, 1867. **Pautawattamies.**—Conf. of 1766 in N. Y. Doc. Col. Hist., VII, 854, 1856. **Pauteauamis.**—Chauvignerie (1736) quoted by Schoolcraft, Ind. Tribes, III, 556, 1853. **Pedadumies.**—Schoolcraft, ibid., v, 196, 1855. **Peki'neni.**—Gatschet, Fox MS. vocab., B. A. E., 1882 (Fox name; plural Pekineni'hak, 'grouse people,' from peki, 'grouse'). **Peoutewatamie.**—Ft Harmar treaty (1789) in U. S. Ind. Treat., 27, 1837. **Po-da-wand-um-ee.**—Schoolcraft, Ind. Tribes, II, 139, 1852. **Po-da-waud-umeeg.**—Warren (1852) in Minn. Hist. Soc. Coll., v, 32, 1885. **Poes.**—Long, Voy. and Trav., 144, 1791. **Ponkeontamis.**—Morse, N. Am., 256, 1776 (misprint). **Ponteatamies.**—Gage (1764) in N. Y. Doc. Col. Hist., VII, 656, 1856. **Ponteotamies.**—Bouquet (1764) quoted by Jefferson, Notes, 148, 1825. **Pontewatamis.**—Lattré, map, 1784. **Pontowattimies.**—Carver, Trav., 19, 1778. **Poodawahduhme.**—Jones, Ojebway Inds., 180, 1861. **Potavalamia.**—Tonti, Rel. de la Le., 100, 1720. **Potawahduhmee.**—Jones, Ojebway Inds., 178, 1861. **Potawatama.**—Perkins and Peck, Annals of the West, 295, 1850. **Potawatamies.**—Ind. Aff. Rep., 144, 1827. **Potawatamis.**—Johnson (1765) in N. Y. Doc. Col. Hist., VII, 711, 1856. **Potawatimie.**—Spring Wells treaty (1815) in U. S. Ind. Treat., 173, 1837. **Pŏ-tă-w'ă-tŏ'-mĕ.**—Long, Exped. St Peter's R., I, 91, 1824 (own name). **Potawatomis.**—Ibid., 81. **Potawattamies.**—Wilkinson (1791) quoted by Rupp, W. Penn., app., 236, 1846. **Potawattimie.**—Tippecanoe treaty (1836) in U. S. Ind. Treat., 709, 1873. **Potawattomies.**—Tanner, Narr., 245, 1830. **Potawatumies.**—Warren (1852) in Minn. Hist. Soc. Coll., v, 124, 1885. **Pŏ-tă-waw-tŏ'-mĕ.**—Dunn, True Indian Stories, 299, 1908 (given as Keating's pronunciation). **Pŏ-tă-wŏt-mĕ.**—Ibid. (given as a Potawatomi pronunciation). **Potawtumies.**—Lindesay (1749) in N. Y. Doc. Col. Hist., VI, 538, 1855. **Poteotamis.**—Montcalm (1757), ibid., x, 553, 1858. **Poté-**

oüatami.—Jes. Rel. for 1671, 25, 1858. **Poteouatamis.**—Vater, Mith., pt. 3, sec. 3, 351, 1816. **Potewatamies.**—Gallatin in Trans. Am. Ethnol. Soc., II, civ, 1846. **Potewatamik.**—Gatschet, Ojibwa MS., B. A. E., 1882 (Chippewa name). **Potiwattimeeg.**—Tanner, Narr., 315, 1830 (Ottawa name). **Potiwattomies.**—Ibid. **Pō-tŏsh'.**—Dunn, True Indian Stories, 299, 1908 (Miami nickname). **Potowatameh.**—Du Ponceau in Mass. Hist. Soc. Coll., 2d s., IX, xv, 1822. **Potowatamies.**—Croghan (1765) in N. Y. Doc. Col. Hist., VII, 784, 1856. **Potowatomies.**—Trader (1778) quoted by Schoolcraft, Ind. Tribes, III, 561, 1853. **Potowotamies.**—Gallatin in Trans. Am. Antiq. Soc., II, 121, 1836. **Pottawatameh.**—Barton, New Views, xxxiii, 1797. **Pottawatamie.**—Treaty of 1821 in U. S. Ind. Treat., 152, 1873. **Pottawataneys.**—Hopkins (1766) in N. Y. Doc. Col. Hist., VII, 993, 1856. **Pottawatimies.**—Treaty (1806) in U. S. Ind. Treat., 371, 1873. **Pottawatomies.**—De Smet, Letters, 26, 1843. **Pottawattamies.**—Brown, W. Gaz., 348, 1817. **Potta-wat-um-ies.**—Warren (1852) in Minn. Hist. Soc. Coll., v, 81, 1885. **Pottawaudumies.**—Ibid., 218. **Pottawattamies.**—Shea, Cath. Miss., 397, 1855. **Pottawottomies.**—Brownstown treaty (1809) in U. S. Ind. Treat., 194, 1873. **Pottewattimies.**—Hildreth, Pioneer Hist., 75, 1848. **Pottiwattamies.**—Harris, Tour, 195, 1805. **Pottowatamies.**—Rupp, W. Penn., 345, 1846. **Pottowatomy.**—Smith (1799) quoted by Drake, Trag. Wild., 221, 1841. **Pottowattomies.**—Flint, Ind. Wars, 89, 1833. **Pottowautomie.**—Council Bluffs treaty (1846) in U. S. Ind. Treat., 182, 1873. **Pottowotomes.**—Treaty (1836), ibid., 150, 1873. **Poueatamis.**—Boisherbert (1747) in N. Y. Doc. Col. Hist., x, 84, 1858. **Pouës.**—Cadillac (1695) in Margry, Déc., v, 120, 1883 (abbreviated form used by French). **Pouhatamies.**—Boudinot, Star in the West, 128, 1816. **Poulteattemis.**—Prise de Possession (1671) in Margry, Déc., I, 97, 1875. **Poulx.**—Montreal conf. (1756) in N. Y. Doc. Col. Hist., x, 447, 1858. **Poulx teattemis.**—Prise de Possession (1671) in N. Y. Doc. Col. Hist., IX, 803, 1855. **Pous.**—Dunn, True Ind. Stories, 299, 1908 ('lice': French name, of accidental meaning; see Poux, Pouz). **Poutauatamis.**—Vaudreuil (1712) in N. Y. Doc. Col. Hist., IX, 863, 1855. **Poutawatamies.**—Johnson (1772), ibid., VIII, 292, 1857. **Poutawottamies.**—Imlay, W. Ter., 372, 1793. **Poutéamis.**—Lamberville (1682) in N. Y. Doc. Col. Hist., IX, 798, 1855. **Poüteaoüatami.**—Allouez (1677) quoted by Shea, Discov. Miss. Val., 71, 1852. **Pouteatami.**—Jes. Rel. 1642, 97, 1858. **Pouteatimies.**—Lamberville (1682) in N. Y. Doc. Col. Hist., IX, 192, 1855. **Pouteauatamis.**—Doc. of 1748, ibid., x, 150, 1858. **Pouteotamis.**—Harris, Voy. and Trav., II, 919, 1705. **Pouteoüatami.**—Jes. Rel. for 1667, 18, 1858. **Pouteouatamiouec.**—Jes. Rel. for 1667, 18, 1858. **Pouteouatamis.**—Chauvignerie (1736) in N. Y. Doc. Col. Hist., IX, 1058, 1855. **Poute8atamis.**—Doc. of 1695, ibid., 619. **Pouteouatimi.**—Doc. of 1748, ibid., x, 171, 1858. **Pouteouetamites.**—Gallinèe (1661) in Margry, Déc., I, 144, 1875. **Pouteouitamis.**—La Galissonière (1748) in N. Y. Doc. Col. Hist., x, 182, 1858. **Pouteouotamis.**—Coxe, Carolana, 19, 1741. **Poutewatamies.**—Doc. of 1746 in N. Y. Doc. Col. Hist., x, 34, 1858. **Poutoualamis.**—Tonti, Rel. de la Le., 100, 1720. **Poutoüamis.**—Writer of 1756 in N. Y. Doc. Col. Hist., x, 401, 1858. **Poutouatamis.**—Du Chesneau (1681) IX, 161, 1855. **Poutouatamittes.**—Gallinèe (1669) in Margry, Déc., I, 142, 1875. **Poutouotamis.**—Coxe, Carolana, map, 1741. **Poutouwatamis.**—Le Sueur (1700) quoted by Neill, Minn., 156, 1858. **Poutowatomies.**—Pike, Trav., 18, note, 1811. **Poutuatamis.**—Le Sueur (1700) quoted by Shea, Early Voy., 94, 1861. **Poutwatamis.**—Duquesne (1754) in N. Y. Doc. Col. Hist., x, 263, 1858. **Pouutouatami.**—Jes. Rel. 1640, 35, 1858. **Poux.**—Frontenac (1682) in N. Y. Doc. Col. Hist., IX, 182, 1855. **Pouz.**—Doc. of 1748, ibid., x, 142, 1858. **Powtawatamis.**—Trader of 1766 quoted by Schoolcraft, Ind. Tribes, III, 556, 1856. **Powtewatamis.**—Jefferys, Fr. Doms., pt. 1, 144, 1761. **Powtewattimies.**—Council of 1786 in Am. St. Papers, Ind. Aff., I, 8, 1832. **Powtowottomies.**—Carver, Trav., 349, 1778. **Puotwatemi.**—York (1700) in N. Y. Doc. Col. Hist., IV, 749, 1854. **Putavatimes.**—Croghan (1759) quoted by Rupp, W. Penn., app., 138, 1846. **Putawatame.**—Ft Wayne treaty (1810) in U. S. Ind. Treat., 374, 1873. **Putawatimes.**—

Croghan (1759) quoted by Proud, Penn., II, 296, 1798. **Putawatimies.**—Treaty of 1806 in U. S. Ind. Treat., 373, 1873. **Putawatimis.**—Ibid. **Putawatomie.**—Brown, W. Gaz., 45, 1817. **Putawawtawmaws.**—Dalton (1783) in Mass. Hist. Soc. Coll., 1st s., X, 123, 1809. **Pú-te-wa-ta.**—Riggs, Dak. Gram. and Dict., 184, 1852 (Sioux form). **Pú-te-wa-taḍaɲ.**—Ibid. (Santee form). **Putewatimes.**—Croghan (1759) quoted by Rupp, W. Penn., app., 132, 1846. **Putowatomey's.**—Croghan (1760) in Mass. Hist. Soc. Coll., 4th s., IX, 289, 1871. **Puttawattimies.**—Grouseland treaty (1803) in U. S. Ind. Treat., 370, 1873. **Puttcotungs.**—Beatty, Jour., 63, 1798 (misprint). **Puttewatamies.**—Croghan (1765) in N.Y. Doc. Col. Hist., VII, 781, 1856. **Puttowatamies.**—Bouquet (1760) in Mass. Hist. Soc. Coll., 4th s., IX, 295, 1871. **Puttwatimees.**—Croghan (1760), ibid., 262. **Tchĕshtalálgi.**—Gatschet, Koassati MS., B. A. E., 1885 ('watermelon people,' from Creek *tchĕ'stali*, 'watermelons': Koassati name adopted from the Creeks). **Undatomátendi.**—Gatschet, Wyandot MS., B. A. E., 1881 (Wyandot name). **Wah-hō'-na-hah.**—Dunn, True Ind. Stories, 299, 1908 (Miami name). **Wáhiúɖaqá.**—Dorsey in Cont. N. A. Ethnol., VI, pt. 2, 664, 1890 (Omaha name). **Wáhiúyaha.**—Dorsey, Kansas MS. vocab., B. A. E., 1882 (Kansa name). **Wă'ă-h'ò-nă-hă.**—Long, Exped. St Peter's R., I, 92, 1824 ('fire-makers': Miami name). **Wapoos.**—La Salle (1680) quoted by Parkman, La Salle, 180, 1883 (identical?). **Woraqa.**—Dorsey, Tciwere MS. vocab., B. A. E., 1879 (Iowa, Oto, and Missouri name). **Wo-rá-qĕ.**—St Cyr, inf'n, 1886 (Winnebago name).

Potawatomi of Huron. A division of the Potawatomi, formerly living on Huron r., in s. E. Michigan. They participated in the treaty of Greenville, Ohio, Aug. 3, 1795, and they are also specially mentioned in the treaty of Detroit, Nov. 17, 1807. Their number has been small from the time they first came into notice. The population given in 1871 is 50; in 1886, 79; in 1888, the last enumeration, 77. An itinerary of about 1770 (Mich. Pion. Coll., XIII, 49, 1889) says their village then consisted of six large cabins, and gives the distance from Detroit as 40 m. By 1886 these Potawatomi had all taken lands in severalty and had become citizens. When the Potawatomi ceded the greater portion of their lands to the United States and moved w. of the Mississippi, this band and some of the tribe living in Indiana refused to join in the movement and have remained on their early home lands. (c. t.)

Potawatomi of the Wabash. A group of Potawatomi bands having their villages on the headwaters of Tippecanoe r., Ind. By the treaty of Chippewaynaung (U. S. Ind. Treat., 713, 1873) they sold their reserves in 1836 and agreed to remove within two years across the Mississippi. They were the bands under the chiefs known as Ashkum, Chechawkose, Menoquet, Mota, Kinkash, Weesionas, and Wesaw.

Potchushatchi (*potchúsua* 'hatchet', *hátchi* 'stream'). A former Upper Creek town on Hatchet cr., probably in Coosa co., Ala.

Hatchet-Creek.—Parsons (1833) in Schoolcraft, Ind. Tribes, IV, 578, 1854. **Po chis hach cha.**—Ibid. **Pochuse-hat-che.**—Hawkins (1799), Sketch, 50, 84, 1848. **Pookuschatche.**—Pickett, Hist. Ala., II, 267,

1851. **Pótchus'-hátchi.**—Gatschet, Creek Migr. Leg., I, 143, 1884.

Poteskeet. An Algonquian tribe or band living in 1700 on the N. shore of Albemarle sd., N. C.—Mooney, Siouan Tribes of the E., 7, 1894.

Potic (probably an equivalent of Abnaki and Mohegan *Powntuckúk*, 'country about the falls'). A Mechkentowoon village w. of the present Athens, Greene co., N. Y. It was temporarily occupied by the fugitive Pennacook after their flight from New England about 1676.

Potateuck.—Ruttenber, Ind. Geog. Names, 173, 1906. **Potatik.**—Ibid. **Potic.**—Ibid. **Potick.**—Deed of 1678 in N. Y. Doc. Col. Hist., XIII, 545, 1881. **Potik.**—Ruttenber, Tribes Hudson R., 86, 1872.

Potlapigua. Mentioned by Orozco y Berra (Geog., 58, 348, 1864) as a division of the Pima Alta, inhabiting the region about Babispe, Baserac, and the frontier, in Sonora, Mexico. This was Opata territory. The name was also applied to their principal settlement.

Patlapiguas.—Hamy in Bull. Soc. d'Anthropologie, VI, 787, map, 1883. **Potlapiguas.**—Mange (1716) in Doc. Hist. Mex., 4th s., I, 401, 1856.

Potlas (*Pŏ'tlas*). A gens of the Nuhalk people, a Bellacoola subdivision of the coast of British Columbia.—Boas in 7th Rep. N. W. Tribes Can., 3, 1891.

Potlatch. The great winter ceremonials among the tribes of the N. Pacific coast from Oregon to Alaska. The word has passed into popular speech along the N. W. coast from the Chinook jargon, into which it was adopted from the Nootka word *patshatl*, 'giving,' or 'a gift.' Although varying considerably in different parts of the coast, these potlatches were mainly marked, as the name implies, by the giving away of quantities of goods, commonly blankets. The giver sometimes went so far as to strip himself of nearly every possession except his house, but he obtained an abundant reward, in his own estimation, in the respect with which his fellow-townsmen afterward regarded him, and when others "potlatched" he, in turn, received a share of their property with interest, so that potentially he was richer than before. During the festival in which the gifts were made, houses and carved poles were raised, chiefs' children were initiated into the secret societies, their ears, noses, and lips were pierced for ornaments, and sales of copper plates, which figured prominently in the social and economic life of the people of this region, took place. Among the Haida, children were then tattooed. All was accompanied with dancing, singing, and feasting. Consult Boas in Rep. Nat. Mus. for 1895. See *Fasting, Feasts, Hospitality.* (J. R. S.)

Potoashees. A division of the Salish mentioned by Lewis and Clark as resid-

ing in 1804 on the coast of Washington, n. w. of the Klumaitumsh. They numbered 200 people, in 10 houses.
Potoashees.—Lewis and Clark Exped., II, 119, 1814. **Potoashs.**—Orig. Jour. Lewis and Clark, VI, 70, 1905 (also Potoash's, p. 118).

Potoltuc. A Chumashan village w. of Pueblo de las Canoas (San Buenaventura), Ventura co., Cal., in 1542.—Cabrillo, Narr. (1542), in Smith, Colec. Doc. Fla., 181, 1857.

Potomac. An Indian town, the name of which, when heard by the discoverers and first explorers of the river, was supposed by them to be that of the stream, and was erroneously written *Patowomek*. This town was situated about 55 m. in a straight line from Chesapeake bay, on a peninsula, in what is now Stafford co., Va., formed by Potomac r. and Potomac cr. It was the principal residence of a werowance who is said to have been as powerful as Powhatan, but whose name has not been preserved. On his return from a visit to Powhatan's son, Parahunt ('One who misses his aim,' otherwise called Tanx Powhatan, or 'The lesser Powhatan'), this werowance was accompanied by Henry Spelman, once interpreter to the Jamestown colony, who took the occasion now offered him to escape from the bondage into which he had been sold to Parahunt by Capt. John Smith. Spelman, in his Relation of Virginia (*ca.* 1613), styles his new master "King Patomecke" and his people the "Patomeck."

The word Patomeck (*Pätómĕk*) is a verbal noun meaning 'something brought,' and, as a designation for a place, may perhaps be short for, say, *Enda Pätómĕk*, 'where something is brought.' Verbal nouns of this kind, for which one grammarian has proposed the name of "gerundives," are found only in the eastern Algonquian dialects. They are formed from both transitive and intransitive verbs by suffixing thereto, after a slight change in the termination, the syllable *-mĕk*, *-mŭk*, or *-mĭk*, according to dialect. Thus, in Abnaki, from *bägäsi'tun*, 'he cooks it,' is formed *bägäsi'tumĕk*, 'something cooked;' from *tsäkĕsáwĕ'tun*, 'he ignites with it,' *tsäkĕsáwĕ'tumĕk*, 'with what is ignited' (a match.) In Natick, from *womássu*, 'he descends,' is formed *womássimŭk*, 'a descent.' In Delaware, from *wuläptoneu*, 'he speaks favorably,' is formed *wuläptonämĭk*, 'good tidings.' In like manner, from *päton*, 'he brings it,' is formed *pätómĕk*, 'what is brought.'

The town so called may have been the place to which the tribes along the river and in its vicinity brought the tribute which was expected from them by the werowance of the country. (W. R. G).
Patomek.—Religion in Va., by R. G., quoted by Hart. Am. Hist. told by Contemporaries, I, 294, 1902. **Potomac.**—Martin, N. C., I, 97, 1829. **Potomeack.**—White (*ca.* 1634), Relatio Itineris, 33, 1874.

Potomac. An important tribe of the Powhatan confederacy, formerly occupying the s. bank of Potomac r., in Stafford and King George cos., Va. In 1608 they numbered about 800. Their principal village bore the same name. The Conoy stated in 1660 that they were among those over whom the Potomac chief at one time had dominion (Maryland Archives, Proc. Council, 1636–67, 403, 1885).
Patamack.—De la Warre (1611) in Mass. Hist. Soc. Coll., 4th s., IX, 5, 1871 (the chief). **Patawoenicke.**—Writer of 1649, ibid., 2d s., IX, 110, 1822. **Patawomeck.**—Smith (1629), Va., II, 39, repr. 1819. **Patawomekes.**—Ibid., I, 118. **Patomacs.**—Thompson quoted by Jefferson, Notes, 277, 1825. **Patowamack.**—Drake, Bk. Inds., bk. 4, 17, 1848. **Patowmeck.**—Map (*ca.* 1640) in Rep. on the Line between Va. and Md., 1873. **Patowomacks.**—Boudinot, Star in the West, 128, 1816. **Patowomeek.**—Harris, Voy. and Trav., I, 839, 1705. **Patowomek.**—Simons in Smith (1629), Va., I, 177, repr. 1819. **Pattawomekes.**—Smith., ibid., 135. **Petawomeek.**—Harris, Voy. and Trav., 842, 1705. **Potomack Indians.**—Philadelphia treaty (1701) quoted by Proud, Penn., I, 431, 1797. **Potowmack.**—Md. patent (1632), ibid., 117. **Satawomeck.**—Strachey (*ca.* 1612), Va., 38, 1849. **Satawomekes.**—Ibid., map.

Potopaco (*Potŏpäkw*, equivalent of Massachuset *potûpagw*, Abnaki *podĕbägw*, 'bay,' 'cove'). A village on the left bank of Potomac r., in Charles co., Md., w. of Port Tobacco, the name of which is a corruption of the Indian word. About 1642 the Jesuit mission was removed to that place from Piscataway, and the village then contained 130 converts. It was extinct in 1722.
Portobacco.—Writer of 1642, Relatio Itineris, 82, 1874. **Porto-Back.**—Bozman, Md., II, 468, 1837. **Portobacke.**—Map (*ca.* 1640) in Rep. on Line between Va. and Md., 1873. **Portobaco.**—Herrman, map (1670), ibid. **Port Tabago.**—Beverley, Va., 199, 1722. **Potapaco.**—Smith (1629), Va., I, map, repr. 1819. **Potapoco.**—Strachey (*ca.* 1612), Va., 38, 1849. **Potopaco.**—Bozman, Md., I, 139, 1837.

Potoyanti. A band, probably Moquelumnan, formerly living about the headwaters of Tuolumne, Merced, and Mariposa rs., central Cal. During the mission period they were neophytes of Dolores mission, and prior to 1851 were placed by United States authorities on a reserve between the Tuolumne and the Merced. There were 110 of them on Fresno reserve in 1861.
Pota-aches.—Bancroft, Nat. Races, I, 455, 1874. **Potoachos.**—Taylor in Cal. Farmer, June 8, 1860. **Potoancies.**—Lewis in Ind. Aff. Rep. 1856, 252, 1857. **Potoencies.**—Ind. Aff. Rep., 219, 1861. **Potoyantes.**—Barbour et al. (1851) in Sen. Ex. Doc. 4, 32d Cong., spec. sess., 69, 1853. **Po-to-yan-ti.**—Johnston in Sen. Ex. Doc. 61, 32d Cong., 1st sess., 22, 1852. **Po-to-yan-to.**—Barbour (1852), op. cit., 252. **Potoyau-te.**—McKee et al. (1851), ibid., 74. **Po-toy-en-tre.**—Wessells (1853) in H. R. Ex. Doc. 76, 34th Cong., 3d sess., 30, 1857.

Potre. Mentioned by Juan de Oñate as a pueblo of the Jemez (q. v.) in New Mexico in 1598. The name has not been identified with the native name of any ruined settlement in the vicinity of the present Jemez.
Potre.—Oñate (1598) in Doc. Inéd., XVI, 114, 1871. **Poze.**—Ibid., 102.

Potrero (a Spanish word with several meanings, here referring to pasture ground). A Luiseño village in San Diego co., s. Cal.; pop. 177 in 1865. The name was subsequently given to a reservation of 8,329.12 acres of allotted land, 75 m. from Mission Tule River agency, on which were situated the settlements of La Joya and La Piche, containing 225 people. In 1905 the Potrero res. was consolidated with that of Morongo, in Riverside co., Cal., under the San Jacinto superintendency.

Pots. See *Receptacles*.

Pottery. Many of the more cultured American tribes were skilful potters. The Peruvians are generally regarded as having taken the lead in this art, but the Colombians, Central Americans, and Mexicans were not far behind, and some excellent work was done also in Brazil and Argentina. Within the area of the United States the art had made very considerable advance in two culture centers— the Pueblo region of the S. W. and the great mound province of the Mississippi valley and the Gulf states. Over the remainder of North America, N. of Mexico, the potter's art was limited to the making of rude utensils or was practically unknown. The Pueblo tribes of New Mexico and Arizona, as well as some of the adjacent tribes to lesser extent, still practise the art in its aboriginal form, and the Cherokee and Catawba of North and South Carolina have not yet ceased to manufacture utensils of clay, although the shapes have been much modified by contact with the whites. The Choctaw of Mississippi and the Mandan of the middle Missouri valley have but recently abandoned the art.

It has been observed that pottery is not among the earlier arts practised by primitive peoples. With nomads it is not available because of the fragility of the utensils, but sedentary life encourages its development. Among the more primitive peoples stone-boiling in baskets and in bark and wooden vessels was and is practised, and even with some fully sedentary tribes, as those of the N. W. coast, these vessels have not yet been replaced by earthenware. The introduction or rise of the potter's art among primitive peoples is believed to correspond somewhat closely with the initial stages of barbarism; but this idea must be liberally interpreted, as some tribes well advanced toward higher barbarism are without it.

CHEROKEE POT WITH STAMP DESIGNS.   HEIGHT 10 IN.

The clay used was mixed with various tempering ingredients, such as sand or pulverized stone, potsherds, and shells; the shapes were extremely varied and generally were worked out by the hand, aided by simple modeling tools. The building of the vessel, the principal product of the potter's art, varied with the different tribes. Usually a bit of the clay was shaped into a disk for the base, and the walls were carried up by adding strips of clay until the rim was reached. When the strips were long they were carried around as a spiral coil. As the height increased the clay was allowed to set sufficiently to support the added weight. The Pueblo potters, to facilitate the work of modeling, sometimes placed the incipient vessel in a shallow basket, or upon the bottom fragment of an old vessel, or, as for example the Zuñi, upon a specially made dish. As a rule, the baking was done in open or smothered fires or in extremely crude furnaces, and the paste remained comparatively soft. In Central America a variety of ware was made with hard paste somewhat resembling our stoneware. Notwithstanding the remarkable aptness of the Americans in this art, and their great skill in modeling, they had not achieved the wheel, nor had they fully mastered the art of glazing.

MANDAN POT.   HEIGHT 7¼ IN.

ROULETTE USED IN DECORATING EARTHENWARE.   (RESTORATION)

In New Mexico and Arizona a variety of pottery is found on deserted village sites showing rather crude decorative designs executed in a medium usually of brownish and greenish hues having the effect of a glaze, and while the nature of the mixture is not well known, chemical examination shows that in some cases at least this is a salt glaze. Women were the potters, and the product consisted mainly of vessels for household use, although the most cultured tribes made and decorated vases for exclusively ceremonial purposes. In some communities a wide range of articles

SAN JUAN PUEBLO WOMAN POLISHING A BOWL

was made, the plastic nature of the material having led to the shaping of many fanciful forms. Florida burial mounds contain many rudely shaped vessels, often

The ornamentation of vases included the modeling of various life forms in the round and in relief, and incising, imprinting, and stamping designs of many kinds in the soft clay. The more advanced potters employed color in surface finish and in executing various designs. The designs were often geometric and primitive in type, but in many sections life forms were introduced in great variety and profusion, and these were no doubt often symbolic, having definite relation

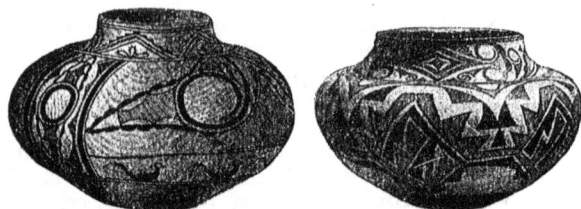

MODERN ZUÑI OLLAS

to the use of the object, ceremonial or otherwise. Unbroken examples of earthenware are preserved mainly through burial with the dead, and the numerous specimens in our collections were obtained mainly from burial places. On inhabited sites the vessels are usually broken, but even in this form they are of great value to the archeologist for the reason that they contain markings or other features peculiar to the tribes concerned in their manufacture.

PADDLE STAMPS FOR DECORATING POTTERY. a, FIGURES CUT IN WOOD, CHEROKEE; b, CORD COVERED (RESTORATION)

toy-like, besides other articles of clay in great variety, manifestly intended as mortuary offerings and not to serve any practical end (Moore).

ZUÑI DECORATING WITH DESIGNS IN COLOR.   SANTA FE RY.)

The ancient potters of the Pueblo country excelled those of the historic period in the quality and beauty of their ware, as in Tusayan, and some varieties are without a rival in the art N. of the valley of Mexico. We here recognize numerous groups of products representing different communities, tribes, or groups of tribes, but there is a general resemblance throughout in form, material, method of manufacture, and ornament. This is true of the pottery of the present tribes; the ware of the Zuñi, for example, although having a family resemblance to the wares of the Hopi, the Acoma, the Sia, and the Cochiti, is readily distinguished from them. Apparently the most primitive pottery of the region is the coiled ware, which is built up of strips of clay so coiled and indented as to give the effect of basketry. This and the white ware with decorations in black lines and figures are apparently connected more especially with the cliff-dwelling period (see *Cliff-dwellings*). The beautiful polychrome vases of the ancient Hopi of Arizona are

ZUÑI.   BUILDING AND SMOOTHING PROCESSES

the most artistic of northern ceramic products. They are well illustrated by collections from the ancient sites of Homolobi, Sikyatki, and Shongopovi (Fewkes).

The tribes of the plains did not practise the art save in its simplest forms, but

ZUÑI FIRING EARTHENWARE.   (SANTA FE RY.)

the ancient tribes of the middle and lower Mississippi valley and the Gulf states were excellent potters. The forms of the vessels and the styles of decoration are exceedingly varied, and indicate a remarkable predilection for the modeling

of life forms—men, beasts, birds, and fishes; and the grotesque was much affected. Aside from plastic embellishment, the vases were decorated in color, and more especially in incised and stamped designs, those on the Gulf coast presenting slight suggestions of the influence of the semi-civilized cultures of Yucatan, Mexico, and the West Indies. The pottery of the tribes of the N. Atlantic states and Canada consists mainly of simple culinary utensils, mostly round or conical bodied bowls and pots decorated with angular incised lines and textile imprintings. The best examples are recovered from burial places in central-southern New York and northern Pennsylvania—the region occupied from the earliest times by the Iroquois. The clay tobacco

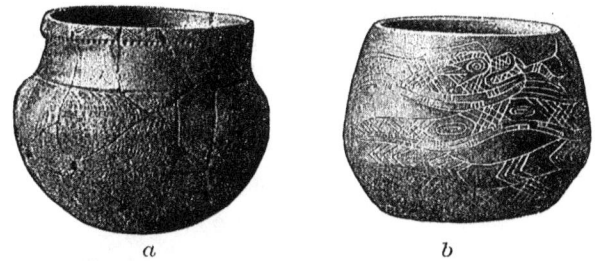

MOUND WARE.   *a*, WISCONSIN; HEIGHT 6½ IN.   *b*, SOUTH CAROLINA; HEIGHT 5 IN.

pipes of this section are unusually interesting, and display decided skill in modeling, although this work has been in-

MOUND WARE, ARKANSAS.   HEIGHT 10 IN.

fluenced to some extent by the presence of the whites (Holmes). The practical absence of pottery from the Pacific states and British Columbia is noteworthy. The few rude vessels found in central and southern California are believed to be of somewhat late origin, and may be due to the influence of the Pueblo tribes on the E. The principal earthen relics of well-determined antiquity are clay pellets, probably intended for use in slings, labret-like forms, beads, etc., obtained from mounds in the San Joaquin valley (Holmes). According to Culin, clay pellets are still used by the Pomo with the sling for hunting birds. The early and very general use of basketry and of stone vessels in this region may have operated to retard the development of the potter's art. N. of the Canadian boundary conditions were not favorable to the development of this art, although specimens of rude earthenware are obtained from mounds and other sites in New Brunswick (Matthew and Kain), the Lakes provinces (Boyle), the Red r. country (Montgomery), and in Alaska as far as Pt Barrow (Murdoch). Nelson describes the manufacture of pottery at St Michael, on Norton sd., and Hough mentions the occurrence of earthenware lamps in the Yukon valley and on St Lawrence id. See *Art, Ornament.*

ANCIENT PUEBLO COILED WARE.

a, HEIGHT 12 IN.; *b*, HEIGHT 6 IN.

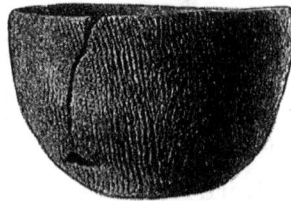

MOUND WARE, NORTH CAROLINA. CORD AND NET DECORATION. *a*, HEIGHT 4¾ IN.; *b*, HEIGHT 3¾ IN.

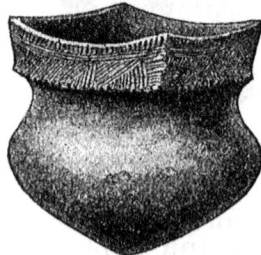

IROQUOIS, PENNSYLVANIA

IROQUOIS, VERMONT

ESKIMO, ALASKA. (NELSON)

ANCIENT HOPI POLYCHROME WARE

Cushing in 4th Rep. B. A. E., 1886; Dellenbaugh, North Americans of Yesterday, 1901; Evers in Cont. St Louis Acad. Sci., pt. I, 1880; Fewkes (1) in 17th Rep. B. A. E., 1898, (2) in 22d Rep. B. A. E., 1903; Foster, Prehist. Races, 1878; Fowke, Archæol. Hist. Ohio, 1902; Harrington in Am. Anthrop., x, no. 4, 1908; Harrison in Proc. and Coll. Wyoming Hist. and Geol. Soc., 1886; Holmes (1) in Bull. Geog. and Geol. Surv. Terr., II, no. 1, 1876, (2) in 3d Rep. B. A. E., 1884, (3) in 4th Rep. B. A. E., 1886, (4) in 20th Rep. B. A. E., 1903; Hough in Rep. Nat. Mus. 1901, 1902; C. C. Jones, Antiq. So. Inds., 1873; J. Jones in Smithson. Cont., XXII, 1876; Matthew in Bull. Nat. Hist. Soc. New Brunswick, no. 3, 1884; Matthew and Kain, ibid., v, no. 23, 1905; Mills in Ohio Archæol. and Hist. Quar., XIII, no. 2, 1904; Moore, various reports on explorations, in Jour. Acad. Nat. Sci. Phila., 1894–1908; Moorehead, Prehist. Impls., 1900; Morgan, League Iroq., 1904; Murdoch in 11th

Consult Abbott, Prim. Indus., 1881; Ann. Archæol. Reps. Ontario, 1888–1907; Beauchamp in Bull. N. Y. State Mus.;

Rep. B. A. E., 1894; Nelson in 18th Rep.

B. A. E., 1899; Nordenskiöld, Cliff Dwellers of the Mesa Verde, 1893; Putnam in Peabody Mus. Reps.; Read and Whittlesey in Ohio Centen. Rep., 1877; Schoolcraft, Ind. Tribes, I–VI, 1851–57; Squier and Davis in Smithson. Cont., I, 1848; J. Stevenson (1) in 2d Rep.

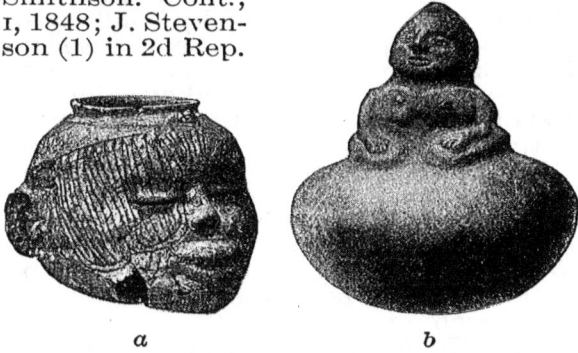

MOUND VASES; HUMAN FORMS. *a*, ARKANSAS; HEIGHT 6¾ IN. *b*, MISSOURI; HEIGHT 9¼ IN.

B. A. E., 1883, (2) in 3d Rep. B. A. E., 1884; M. C. Stevenson in 11th Rep. B. A. E., 1894; Stites, Economics of the Iroquois, 1905; Thomas in 12th Rep. B. A. E., 1894; Thruston, Antiq. Tenn., 1897;

ANCIENT PUEBLO WARE; DESIGNS IN BLACK ON WHITE GROUND *a*, HEIGHT 8 IN.; *b*, HEIGHT 6 IN.

Will and Spinden in Peabody Mus. Papers, III, no. 4, 1906; Willoughby (1) in Jour. Am. Folk-lore, x, no. 36, 1897, (2) in Putman Mem. Vol., 1909; Wyman in Mem. Peabody Acad. Sci., I, no. 4, 1875. (W. H. H.)

Pottery Hill. The local name of a prehistoric pueblo ruin, oval in shape, measuring 228 by 150 ft, situated on the N. side of the Salt and Little Colorado r. watershed, in the White mts., near Linden, Navajo co., Ariz.—Hough in Nat. Mus. Rep. 1901, 297, 1903.

Potzuye (*Po-tzu-ye*). A prehistoric pueblo of the Tewa, on a mesa w. of the Rio Grande in N. New Mexico, between San Ildefonso pueblo on the N. and the Rito de los Frijoles on the s.—Bandelier in Arch. Inst. Papers, IV, 78, 1892.

Pouches. See *Bags, Receptacles.*

Pouxouoma. A former Costanoan village, said to have been connected with San Juan Bautista mission, Cal.—Engelhardt, Franc. in Cal., 398, 1897.

Powcomonet. A village of the Powhatan confederacy in 1608, on the N. bank of Rappahannock r., in Richmond co., Va.— Smith (1629), Va., I, map, repr. 1819.

Powell. See *Osceola.*

Poweshiek (properly *Păwĭshĭka*, 'he who shakes [something] off [himself],' a masculine proper name in the Bear clan, the ruling clan of the Foxes). A Fox chief at the period of the Black Hawk war in 1832. It was he, rather than Keokuk, to whom was due the weakening of Black Hawk's fighting power. The tie which held together the Sauk and Foxes had for some time been growing weak, and when Kwaskwamia, a subordinate Sauk chief, ceded away the Rock River country in Illinois, without the knowledge or consent of the rest of the people, Poweshiek with most of the Foxes withdrew from the others and crossed the Mississippi to the vicinity of the present Davenport, Iowa. When the fighting began they were joined here by Keokuk and the fleeing Sauk, and later also by the defeated hostiles, to whom they gave protection. Poweshiek died in Kansas. In behalf of his tribe he signed the treaty of Ft Armstrong, Rock Island, Ill., Sept. 21, 1832; treaties made in the same locality, Sept. 27 and 28, 1836; Washington, Oct. 21, 1837; and Sac and Fox agency, Iowa, Oct. 11, 1842. A county of Iowa takes its name from him. (W. J.)

Powhatan (Southern Renape *pawä'tan*, 'falls in a current' of water.—Gerard). A confederacy of Virginian Algonquian tribes. Their territory included the tidewater section of Virginia from the Potomac s. to the divide between James r. and Albemarle sd., and extended into the interior as far as the falls of the principal rivers about Fredericksburg and Richmond. They also occupied the Virginia counties E. of Chesapeake bay and possibly included some tribes in lower Maryland. In the piedmont region w. of them were the hostile Monacan and Manahoac, while on the s. were the Chowanoc, Nottoway, and Meherrin of Iroquoian stock. Although little is known in regard to the language of these tribes, it is believed they were more nearly related to the Delawares than to any of the northern or more westerly tribes, and were derived either from them or from the same stem. Brinton, in his tentative arrangement, placed them between the Delawares and Nanticoke on one side and the Pamptico on the other.

When first known the Powhatan had nearly 200 villages, more than 160 of which are named by Capt. John Smith on his map. The Powhatan tribes were visited by some of the earliest explorers of the period of the discovery, and in 1570 the Spaniards established among them a Jesuit mission, which had but a brief existence. Fifteen years later the southern tribes were brought to the notice of the English settlers at Roanoke id., but little was known of them until the establishment of the Jamestown settlement in 1607. The Indians were generally friendly until driven to hostility by the exactions of the whites, when petty warfare ensued until peace was brought about through the marriage of Powhatan's daughter to John Rolfe, an Englishman. (See *Pocahontas*). A few years later the Indians were thinned by pestilence, and in 1618 Powhatan died and left the government to Opechancanough. The confederacy seems to have been of recent origin at the period of Powhatan's succession, as it then included but 7 of the so-called tribes besides his own, all the others having been conquered by himself during his lifetime.

Opechancanough was the deadly foe of the whites, and at once began secret preparations for a general uprising. On Mar. 22, 1622, a simultaneous attack was made along the whole frontier, in which 347 of the English were killed in a few hours, and every settlement was destroyed excepting those immediately around Jamestown, where the whites had been warned in time. As soon as the English could recover from the first shock, a war of extermination was begun against the Indians. It was ordered that three expeditions should be undertaken yearly against them in order that they might have no chance to plant their corn or build their wigwams, and the commanders were forbidden to make peace upon any terms whatever. A large number of Indians were at one time induced to return to their homes by promises of peace, but all were massacred in their villages and their houses burned. The ruse was attempted a second time, but was unsuccessful. The war went on for 14 years, until both sides were exhausted, when peace was made in 1636. The greatest battle was fought in 1625 at Pamunkey, where Gov. Wyatt defeated nearly 1,000 Indians and burned their village, the principal one then existing.

Peace lasted until 1641, when the Indians were aroused by new encroachments of the whites, and Opechancanough, then an aged man, organized another general attack, which he led in person. In a single day 500 whites were killed, but after about a year the old chief was taken and shot. By his death the confederacy was broken up, and the tribes made separate treaties of peace and were put upon reservations, which were constantly reduced in size by sale or by confiscation upon slight pretense. About 1656 the Cherokee from the mountains invaded the lowlands. The Pamunkey chief with 100 of his men joined the whites in resisting the invasion, but they were almost all killed in a desperate battle on Shocco cr., Richmond. In 1669 a census of the Powhatan tribes showed 528 warriors, or about 2,100 souls, still surviving, the Wicocomoco being then the largest tribe, with 70 warriors, while the Pamunkey had become reduced to 50.

In 1675 some Conestoga, driven by the Iroquois from their country on the Susquehanna, entered Virginia and committed depredations. The Virginian tribes were accused of these acts, and several unauthorized expeditions were led against them by Nathaniel Bacon, a number of Indians being killed and villages destroyed. The Indians at last gathered in a fort near Richmond and made preparations for defense. In Aug., 1676, the fort was stormed, and men, women, and children were massacred by the whites. The adjacent stream was afterward known as Bloody run from this circumstance. The scattered survivors asked peace, which was granted on condition of an annual tribute from each village. In 1722 a treaty was made at Albany by which the Iroquois agreed to cease their attacks upon the Powhatan tribes, who were represented at the conference by four chiefs. Iroquois hostility antedated the settlement of Virginia. With the treaty of Albany the history of the Powhatan tribes practically ceased, and the remnants of the confederacy dwindled silently to final extinction. About 1705 Beverley had described them as "almost wasted." They then had 12 villages, 8 of which were on the Eastern shore, the only one of consequence being Pamunkey, with about 150 souls. Those on the Eastern shore remained until 1831, when the few surviving individuals, having become so much mixed with negro blood as to be hardly distinguishable, were driven off during the excitement caused by the slave rising under Nat Turner. Some of them had previously joined the Nanticoke. Jefferson's statement, in his Notes on Virginia, regarding the number and condition of the Powhatan remnant in 1785, are very misleading. He represents them as reduced to the Pamunkey and Mattapony, making altogether only about 15 men, much mixed with negro blood, and only a few of the older ones preserving the language. The fact is that the descendants of the old confederacy must then have numbered not far from 1,000, in several tribal bands, with a considerable percentage still speaking the language. They now number altogether about 700, including the Chickahominy, Nandsemond, Pamunkey, and Mattapony (q. v.), with several smaller bands. Henry Spelman, who was prisoner among the Powhatan for some time, now in the house of one chief and then in that of another, mentions several interesting customs. The priests, he says, shaved the right side of the head, leaving a little lock at the ear, and some of them had beards. The common people pulled out the hairs of the beard as fast as they grew. They kept the hair on the right side of the head cut short, "that it might not hinder them by flappinge about their bowstringe when they draw it to shoott; but on ye other side they let it grow and haue a long locke hanginge doune ther shoulder." Tattooing was practised to some extent, especially by the women. Among the better sort it was the custom, when eating, for the men to sit on mats round about the house, to each of whom the women brought a dish, as they did not eat together out of one dish. Their marriage customs were similar to those among other Indian tribes, but, according to Spelman, "ye man goes not unto any place to be married, but ye woman is brought unto him wher he dwelleth." If the presents of a young warrior were accepted by his mistress, she was considered as having agreed to become his wife, and, without any further explanation to her family, went to his hut, which became her home, and the ceremony was ended. Polygamy, Spelman asserts, was the custom of the country, depending upon the ability to purchase wives; Burk says, however, that they generally had but one wife. Their burial customs varied according to locality and the dignity of the person. The bodies of their chiefs were placed on scaffolds, the flesh being first removed from the bones and dried, then wrapped with the bones in a mat, and the remains were then laid in their order with those of others who had previously died. For their ordinary burials they dug deep holes in the earth with very sharp stakes, and, wrapping the corpse in the skins, laid it upon sticks in the ground and covered it with earth.

They believed in a multitude of minor deities, paying a kind of worship to everything that was able to do them harm beyond their prevention, such as fire, water, lightning, and thunder, etc. They also had a kind of chief deity variously termed Okee, Quioccos, or Kiwasa, of whom they made images, which were usually placed in their burial temples. They believed in immortality, but the special abode of the spirits does not appear to have been well defined. The office of werowance, or chieftaincy, appears to have been hereditary through the female line, passing first to the brothers, if there were any, and then to the male descendants of sisters, but never in the male line. The Chickahominy, it is said, had no such custom nor any regular chief, the priests and leading men ruling, except in war, when the warriors selected a leader.

According to Smith, "their houses are built like our arbors, of small young sprigs, bowed and tied, and so close covered with mats or the bark of trees very handsomely, that notwithstanding wind, rain, or weather they are as warm as stoves, but very smoky, yet at the top of the house there is a hole made for the smoke to go into right over the fire." According to White's pictures they were oblong, with a rounded roof (see *Habitations*). They varied in length from 12 to 24 yds., and some were as much as 36 yds. long, though not of great width. They were formed of poles or saplings fixed in the ground at regular intervals, which were bent over from the sides so as to form an arch at the top. Pieces running horizontally were fastened with withes, to serve as braces and as supports for bark, mats, or other coverings. Many of their towns were inclosed with palisades, consisting of posts planted in the ground and standing 10 or 12 ft high. The gate was usually an overlapping gap in the circuit of palisades. Where great strength and security were required, a triple stockade was sometimes made. These inclosing walls sometimes encompassed the whole town; in other cases only the chief's house, the burial house, and the more important dwellings were thus surrounded. They appear to have made considerable advance in agriculture, cultivating 2 or 3 varieties of maize, beans, certain kinds of melons or pumpkins, several varieties of roots, and even 2 or 3 kinds of fruit trees.

They computed by the decimal system. Their years were reckoned by winters, *cohonks*, as they called them, in imitation of the note of the wild geese, which came to them every winter. They divided the year into five seasons, viz, the budding or blossoming of spring; earing of corn, or roasting-ear time; the summer, or highest sun; the corn harvest, or fall of the leaf, and the winter, or cohonk. Months were counted as moons, without relation to the number in a year; but they arranged them so that they returned under the same names, as the moon of stags, the corn moon, first and second moon of cohonks (geese), etc. They divided the day into three parts, "the rise, power, and lowering of the sun." They kept their accounts by knots on strings or by notches on a stick.

The estimate of population given by Smith is 2,400 warriors. Jefferson, on the basis of this, made their total population about 8,000.

The tribes, in the order of their location on Smith's map, were as follows: Tauxenent, Fairfax co.; Potomac, Stafford and King George cos.; Cuttatawomen, King George co.; Pissasec, King George and Richmond cos.; Onawmanient, Westmoreland co.; Rappahannock, Richmond co.; Moraughtacund, Lancaster and Richmond cos.; Secacawoni, Northumberland co.; Wicocomoco, Northumberland co.; Nantaughtacund, Essex and Caroline cos.; Mattapony, Mattapony r.; Mummapacune, York r. (mentioned by Strachey); Pamunkey, King William co.; Werowocomoco, Gloucester co.; Piankatank, Piankatank r.; Pataunck (mentioned by Strachey) and Youghtanund, Pamunkey r.; Chickahominy, Chickahominy r.; Powhatan, Henrico co.; Arrohattoc, Henrico co.; Weanoc, Charles City co.; Paspahegh, Charles City and James City cos.; Chiskiac, York co.; Kecoughtan, Elizabeth City co.; Appomattoc, Chesterfield co.; Quioucohanoc, Surry co.; Warrasqueoc, Isle of Wight co.; Nansemond, Nansemond co.; Chesapeake, Princess Anne co.; Accohanoc, Accomac and Northampton cos.; Accomac, Northampton co. Several other names appear in later times as the broken tribes formed new combinations.

The following were Powhatan villages: Accohanoc, Accomac, Acconoc, Accoqueck, Accossuwinck, Acquack, Anaskenoans, Appocant, Appomattoc, Arrohattoc, Askakep, Assaomeck, Assuweska, Attamtuck, Aubomesk, Aureuapeugh, Cantaunkack, Capahowasic, Cattachiptico, Cawwontoll, Chawopo, Checopissowo, Chesakawon, Chesapeak, Chiconessex, Chincoteague, Chiskiac, Cinquack, Cinquoteck, Cuttatawomen (1), Cuttatawomen (2), Gangasco, Kapawnich, Kerahocak, Kiequotank, Kupkipcock, Machapunga (1), Machapunga (2), Mamanahunt, Mamanassy, Mangoraca, Mantoughquemec, Martoughquaunk, Massawoteck, Matchopick, Matchut, Mathomauk, Matomkin, Mattacock, Mattacunt, Mattanock, Maysonec, Menapucunt, Menaskunt, Meyascosic, Mohominge, Mokete, Moraughtacund, Mouanast, Mutchut, Muttamussinsack, Myghtuckpassu, Namassingakent, Nameroughquena, Nansemond, Nantapoyac, Nantaughtacund, Nawacaten, Nawnautough, Nechanicok, Nepawtacum, Onancock, Onawmanient,

Opiscopank, Oquomock, Orapaks, Ottachugh, Ozatawomen, Ozenic, Pamacocac, Pamawauk, Pamuncoroy, Pamunkey, Papiscone, Pasaughtacock, Paspahegh, Paspanegh, Passaunkack, Pastanza, Pawcocomac, Peccarecamek, Piankatank, Pissacoac, Pissasec, Poruptanck, Potaucao, Potomac, Powcomonet, Powhatan, Poyektauk, Poykemkack, Pungoteque, Quackcohowaon, Quioucohanock, Quiyough, Rappahannock, Rickahake, Righkahauk, Ritanoe, Roscows, Secacawoni, Secobec, Shamapa, Skicoak, Sockobeck, Tantucquask, Tauxenent, Teracosick, Utenstank, Uttamussac, Uttamussamacoma, Waconiask, Warrasqueoc, Weanoc, Wecuppom, Werawahon, Werowacomoco, Wicocomoco, Winsack.

In addition to the authorities found in Arber's edition of Smith's Works, consult Mooney, Willoughby, Gerard, and Bushnell in Am. Anthrop., IX, no. 1, 1907.   (J. M.)

Pouhatan.—Hennepin, Cont. of New Discov., map, 1698. **Powhatan.**—De la Warre (1611) in Mass. Hist. Soc. Coll., 4th s., IX, 5, 1871. **Powhatanic confederacy.**—Kingsley, Stand. Nat. Hist., pt. 6, 151, 1885. **Powhattans.**—Gallatin in Trans. Am. Ethnol. Soc., II, civ, 1848. **Sachdagugh-roonaw.**—Ibid., 59 (Iroquois name). **Sachdagughs.**—Ibid.

Powhatan. The ruling chief and practically the founder of the Powhatan confederacy (q. v.) in Virginia at the period of the first English settlement. His proper name was Wahunsonacock, but he was commonly known as Powhatan from one of his favorite residences at the falls of James r. (Richmond). According to Smith, of some 30 cognate tribes subject to his rule in 1607, all but six were his own conquests. At the time of the coming of the English, Powhatan is represented to have been about 60 years of age, of dignified bearing, and reserved and stern disposition. His first attitude toward the whites was friendly although suspicious, but he soon became embittered by the exactions of the newcomers. On the treacherous seizure of his favorite daughter, Pocahontas (q. v.), in 1613, he became openly hostile, but was happily converted for the time through her marriage to Rolfe. He died in 1618, leaving the succession to his brother, Opitchapan, who however was soon superseded by a younger brother, the noted Opechancanough (q. v.).   (J. M.)

Powhatan. The tribe which gave name to the Powhatan confederacy. Its territory was in what is now Henrico co., Va., and the tribe numbered about 150 in 1608. The chief of the tribe at the time the English commenced the settlement at Jamestown was called Wahunsonacock, but was commonly known to the whites as Powhatan from his place of residence, and the name was extended to the confederacy.   (J. M.)

Powhatan. The village of the Powhatan tribe, situated on the N. bank of James r., Va., at the falls, on ground now forming an eastern suburb of the city of Richmond.

Powitch. A western name of the Oregon crab-apple (*Pyrus rivularis*), known also as powitch-tree, from *pówitsh*, the Chinook name of this plant, through the Chinook jargon. (A. F. C.)

Powow. A term to which is now assigned the following meanings: 1. A medicine-man. 2. The conjuring of a medicine-man over a patient. 3. A dance, feast, or noisy celebration preceding a council, expedition, or hunt. 4. A council. 5. A conference. The most recent use by the whites is in the sense of a political conference or talk. It is now used both as a noun and as a verb. In Narraganset *powáw* and in Massachuset *pauwau*, cognate with the Micmac *bû'uin*, signifies priest, wizard, magician. As Bartlett (Dict. of Americanisms, 488, 1877) remarks, "the name was also given by the early chronicles to the feasts, dances, and other public doings of the red men, preliminary to a grand hunt, a war expedition, or the like," and was soon adopted by the whites "in political talk, to signify any uproarious meeting, etc." In certain parts of the Southern states the terms "powow doctor," and "to powow," meaning to practise witchcraft, are still in use. Brinton (Lenape Leg., 71, 1885) correctly considers this Algonquian word to be from the same root as Chippewa *bawâdna*, 'he dreams of him,' and the Cree *pâwâmiw* 'he dreams,' the *powow* obtaining his art from dreams. The Massachuset *pauwau*, 'he uses divination,' would then mean, more primitively, 'he dreams.' (A. F. C.)

Poxen. Mentioned, in connection with Puaray, apparently as a pueblo of the Tigua (q. v.) of New Mexico in 1598.—Oñate (1598) in Doc. Inéd., XVI, 115, 1871.

Poyektauk. A village of the Powhatan confederacy in 1608, on the N. bank of the Rappahannock, in Richmond co., Va.—Smith (1629), Va., I, map, repr. 1819.

Poygratasuck. See *Pogatacut.*

Poyi. The Chaparral-cock or Roadrunner clan of Zuñi, New Mexico. It is nearly if not quite extinct.
Póye-kwe.—Hodge in Am. Anthrop., IX, 349, 1896 (*kwe*='people'). Póyi-kwe.—Cushing in 13th Rep. B. A. E., 368, 1896 (given as "Grouse or Sagecock people").

Poykemkack. A village of the Powhatan confederacy in 1608, on the N. bank of the Rappahannock, in Richmond co., Va.—Smith (1629), Va., I, map, repr. 1819.

Prairie Band of Potawatomi. The division of the Potawatomi formerly residing s. of L. Michigan, in Wisconsin, Illinois, and Indiana. They adhered more closely to their old ways than the bands of the Wabash, the St Joseph, and Huron. Some authors have supposed them to be the old Mascoutens. The majority of them, numbering 676 in 1908, are now in Kansas, but a large number are still scattered over s. Wisconsin. See *Potawatomi.*
Bluff Indians.—Clarke in Ind. Aff. Rep. 1855, 97, 1856. M'shkudän'nik.—Gatschet, Potawatomi MS., B. A. E., 1878 (Potawatomi name). Potawatamie tribe of Indians of the prairie.—Tippecanoe treaty (1832) in U. S. Ind. Treat., 697, 1873.

Prairie Kickapoo. The Kickapoo formerly living in E. Illinois, called the Prairie band to distinguish them from the Vermilion band on the Wabash.
Kickapoos of the prairies.—Am. St. Papers, Ind. Aff., 135, 1832. Prairie Indians.—Shea, Cath. Miss., 395, 1855.

Prairie la Crosse. A Winnebago village in s. E. Wisconsin to which Black Hawk fled in 1832.—Drake, Bk. Inds., bk. 5, 158, 1848.

Prairie Ronde. A Potawatomi village about the boundary of the present Cass and Van Buren cos., s. w. Michigan, on a tract of land ceded to the United States by the treaty of St Joseph, Mich., Sept. 19, 1827.

Prayer. In their endeavors to secure the help of the supernatural powers, the Indians, as well as other peoples, hold principally three methods: (1) The powers may be coerced by the strength of a ritualistic performance; (2) their help may be purchased by gifts in the form of sacrifices and offerings; or (3) they may be approached by prayer. Frequently the coercing ritualistic performance and the sacrifice are accompanied by prayers; or the prayer itself may take a ritualistic form, and thus attain coercive power. In this case the prayer is called an incantation. Prayers may either be spoken words, or they may be expressed by symbolic objects, which are placed so that they convey the wishes of the worshipper to the powers. The rituals of the Plains tribes and those of the Pueblos contain many prayers. Thus in the Hako ceremony of the Pawnee occurs a prayer-song in which the father of the powers is invoked to send needed help; in the Sun dance (q. v.) of the Arapaho occur prayers to the "Man-Above" for assistance in the performance of the ceremony; the Zuñi ceremonials contain prayers for rain, food, and health; the Hupa of California offer a prayer accompanying their ceremonials asking for health. Prayers accompanying rituals are rather rare on the N. Pacific coast. Very often prayers accompany sacrifices. They are given when tobacco smoke is offered to the gods; they accompanied bloody sacrifices of the Pawnee and the Iroquois, as well as the sacrifices of pollen among the Navaho. Prayers of this kind very commonly accompany the sacrifice of food to the souls of the deceased, as among the Algonquian tribes, Eskimo, and N.W. coast Indians. The custom of expressing prayers by means of symbolic objects is found principally among the Southwestern tribes (see *Prayer sticks*). Prayers are often preceded by ceremonial purification, fasting, the use of emetics and purgatives, which are intended to make the person praying agreeable to the powers. Among the North American Indians the prayer cannot be considered as necessarily connected with sacrifice or as a substitute for sacrifice, since in a great many cases prayers for good luck, for success, for protection, or for the blessing of the powers, are offered quite independently of the idea of sacrifice. While naturally material benefits are the object of prayer in by far the majority of cases, prayers for an abstract blessing and for ideal objects are not by any means absent. Among the northern Californian tribes and among the Eskimo the prayer is often pronounced in a set form, the effectiveness of which is not due to the willingness of the supernatural powers to take pity on the mortal, but to the set form in which the prayer is delivered, the prayer formula or the incantation being a charm by means of which the fulfillment of the prayer can be secured. The incantation may be effective through its power to coerce the supernatural powers to comply with the wish of the person praying, or it may act as a charm which gives fulfillment by its own inherent power. The Indians pray not only to those supernatural powers which are considered the protectors of man—like the personal guardians or the powers of nature—but also to the hostile powers that must be appeased. See *Ceremonies, Mythology, Religion, Sacrifice*.   (F. B.)

Prayer sticks. Sticks to which feathers are attached, used as ceremonial supplicatory offerings. The most familiar prayer sticks are those made by the Pueblo Indians of New Mexico and Arizona, who use them extensively for a definite purpose, but analogous objects representing the same idea are employed in the ceremonies of nearly all American tribes. A great variety of prayer sticks of different sizes are employed by the Pueblos, though perhaps the greatest number measure the length of the hand with fingers extended, differing in form, number, painting, and carving, and having different kinds of feathers and objects attached to them, according to their destination and the person or persons offering them.

The making of prayer sticks among the Pueblos is a complicated ceremony, having a multitude of minute details to be observed. Cord of native cotton is used to attach the feathers, herbs, meal, etc., to the sticks, which, as a rule, are made of cottonwood shoots. The feathers are those of particular birds, and they must be perfect and come from particular parts of the plumage. The paints used must be ceremonially gathered, prepared, and applied. In paho-making even the refuse—chips of wood, ends of cord, etc.—is disposed of in a prescribed manner. Prayer sticks are often consecrated by being moistened with medicine, sprinkled with sacred meal, and fumigated with tobacco, and by other rites; and after prayers have been breathed into them they are sent out in the hands of messengers to be deposited in shrines, springs, or fields. Prayer sticks for family offerings are made on the occasion of ceremonies and are deposited also by authorized persons. Individual offerings of prayer sticks are also made.

The sticks to which the plumes are attached indicate the gods to whom the prayers are offered, and the feathers convey to the gods the prayers which are breathed into the spiritual essence of the plumes. This conception is materialized in the "breath feather," generally the downy plume of the eagle. Prayers are also breathed into sacred meal, pollen, and other objects offered.

The idea of feeding the gods is expressed by one form of the Hopi prayer stick, the *páho*, 'water prayer,' to which a small packet of sacred meal is tied. The prayer stick may be regarded as a symbolic substitute for human sacrifice (Fewkes in 16th Rep. B. A. E., 297, 1897). Prayer sticks, nearly always painted green or blue, are frequently found with the dead in ancient Pueblo cemeteries, and great deposits of them occur in ceremonial caves in s. Arizona. Navaho and Apache prayer sticks are similar to those of the Pueblos. The ornamented wands placed in the sod of the Pawnee Hako altar, and the feathered wands planted round the skull of the buffalo in the Cheyenne sun dance are examples of prayer sticks, and the Eskimo make use of similar wands. The so-called prayer stick of the Kickapoo was a mnemonic device for Christian prayer.

Consult Fewkes, Tusayan Snake Ceremonies, 1897; Fletcher, The Hako: A Pawnee Ceremony, 1904; G. A. Dorsey, Arapaho Sun Dance, 1903; Dorsey and Voth in Field Columb. Mus. Pubs., Anthrop. ser.; Mason in Science, VIII, no. 179, 1886; Matthews, (1) Mountain Chant, 1887, (2) Night Chant, 1902; Mooney, Ghost Dance Religion, 1896; Nelson in 18th Rep. B. A. E., 414, 415, 1897; Solberg, Über die Bâhos der Hopi, in Archiv für Anthropologie, IV, 48–74, 1905; M. C. Stevenson, (1) The Sia, 1893, (2) The Zuñi Indians, 1905.   (W. H.)

Praying Indians. Indians of different tribes who accepted the teachings of the missionaries, Catholic Iroquois, Moravian Indians, and, more especially, those Indians of E. Massachusetts and the adjacent region who were organized into Christian .congregations by John Eliot and his successors. The missionary work was begun by Eliot in 1646 at Nonantum, a small village a few miles from Boston. His efforts were so successful that he soon had a considerable number of converts, who removed in 1650–51 to Natick, where a tract was reserved for them, and a new town was established under English regulations. These converts were some of the remnants of the Massachuset. The powerful tribes of the Wampanoag, Narraganset, and especially the Mohegan opposed the work and generally refused to allow the missionaries within their territories. The work went on rapidly along the E. coast and on the islands. In a few years the greater part of the natives of Marthas Vineyard and Nantucket were classed as Christians, while there were also numerous congregations on the peninsula E. of Buzzards bay and others in the interior farther N. In 1674, just before the outbreak of King Philip's war, there were in E. Massachusetts, excluding the peninsula, 7 principal praying towns: Hassanamesit, Magunkaquog, Nashobah, Natick, Okommakamesit, Punkapog, and Wamesit. There were also 7 new praying towns in the Nipmuc country, whose inhabitants had more recently been brought under missionary influence: Chabanakongkomun, Manchaug, Manexit, Wacuntug, Pakachoog, Quantisset, and Wabaquasset. The last three were in N. E. Connecticut. Wamesit, and perhaps Nashobah, were within the territory of the Pennacook, the others being occupied by the Massachuset and Nipmuc. The 14 villages numbered about 1,100 souls. Around Plymouth and on C. Cod were about 500 more, distributed among 23 villages. Those in Nantucket and Marthas Vineyard numbered perhaps 1,000 more, and there were a few others among the Mohegan. The entire number of professed Christian Indians in S. New England at the outbreak of King Philip's war was thus about 2,500. When the general Indian rising occurred in 1675, the Praying Indians found themselves in danger from both sides. The hostiles viewed them as traitors and renegades, while the whites despised them for their apparent weakness and suspected them to be secret allies of the enemy. The contemptuous treatment and harsh dealing of the English had already rendered the converts restive, and the result was that a great part of them joined the enemy, the inhabitants of several villages going off in a body. The others offered their services to the English, who accepted the help of a few, but had those remaining in the 7 original praying towns removed to an island in Boston harbor until the war was ended. These were soon reduced to 300 souls by starvation and exposure. The war practically ended the mission work. In 1682 only 4 of the 14 first-named praying towns remained, and only about 300 of their 1,100 inhabitants. The Indians E. of Buzzards bay also suffered, though in a less degree, but from their isolated position had generally remained quiet. Those on Marthas Vineyard and Nantucket refrained from hostilities, mainly on account of their affection for the missionary, Mayhew. After the dispersion or destruction of the more powerful tribes through this war, the remaining Indians ceased to be of importance, and the term "Praying Indians" lost its distinctive meaning. (J. M.)

Precaute. An Abnaki village in 1602 on the N. E. coast of Maine.—Purchas (1625) in Me. Hist. Soc. Coll., V, 156, 1857.

Preguey. Mentioned as a pueblo of the province of Atripuy (q. v.), in the region of the lower Rio Grande, N. Mex., in 1598.—Oñate (1598) in Doc. Inéd., XVI, 115, 1871.

Presentación. A former settlement on the W. side of the Rio Colorado, in Lower California, doubtless belonging to the so-called Quiquyuma (Quigyuma), visited by Father Kino in Nov. 1701.—Bancroft, No. Mex. States, I, 497, 1884.

Preservation of Collections. Fur, skin, feathers, woolen fabrics, and other organic materials subject to attack by insects enter so largely into ethnological collections that much attention is given to their preservation. Specimens are first subjected to the vapor of gasoline in an air-tight receptacle, where they may remain for several hours, after which they are removed and aired. Gasoline used freely will not injure specimens, and is efficient in destroying the eggs, larvæ, and adults of all insects, as well as molds and other low forms of life. The second step is dampening the sterilized specimens with a solution of corrosive sublimate, made by dissolving one-fourth ounce of bichloride of mercury in a pint of alcohol and adding a pint of soft water. A brush is used to apply the solution, which is used sparingly on colors that will "run." Some specimens may be dipped in the solution, but delicate articles are sprayed by means of an atomizer. Experience and judgment are necessary in the use of the poisonous and explosive preservatives. Before specimens having feathers, fur, or the like become quite dry they are brushed, rubbed, and shaken to restore them to their former condition. Specimens that have been poisoned are kept under observation for some time in order to ascertain the thoroughness of the treatment, which sometimes must be repeated. Gnawing insects are quickly detected by the droppings which fall from the specimens attacked. In the spring, cases are tested by the introduction of a little formaldehyde, which drives the insects from their hiding places. Specimens in which organic material is used for mounting or hafting receive careful attention to insure the thorough penetration of the poison to every part of the joints or interstices. Fur skins retaining animal oils are cleaned and made pliable by a taxidermist, who macerates them in a solution of equal parts of saltpeter, alum, borax, and Glauber's salt in water (2 oz. of each to the gallon) for 2 weeks, stirring once in a while. When removed, the skins are washed and worked till dry. Furriers steep and scour pelts in a bath of alum, bran, and salt to remove grease from the skin, and then in a bath of soap and soda to remove oil from the fur. By this process the skin is tanned.

The most difficult pests to eradicate are the wood-boring insects, which prey upon baskets, sapwood, and wood containing fecula. For plain wooden articles baking is necessary, followed by treatment with corrosive sublimate, as described above. In some museums specimens are subjected to dry heat in a sterilizing oven. The dangers of gasoline are thus avoided. But all specimens can not be treated by heat, and when specimens are placed in the oven in masses the heat does not sufficiently penetrate the interior to kill germs. Baskets, if soiled from use, may be scoured with a stiff brush and soap and water previous to fumigation and poisoning. They may also, when dry, be rubbed with a preparation made by dissolving an ounce of paraffin in a pint of turpentine and adding a little drying oil. This gives a slight gloss to the surface, brings out the design, and repels insects. It will also preserve, to some extent, unglazed pottery from dust and the effects of dampness, which sometimes, especially in mortuary pottery, cause exfoliation and the ultimate destruction of the vessels. In more serious cases vessels may be submerged in gasoline containing 6 oz. of paraffin to the gallon. Samples of foodstuffs and food preparations are placed in glass jars, a little gasoline is poured into each, and the jars are tightly closed. Moth balls may subsequently be placed in the jars. Moth balls of crude naphthol may be laid among specimens, some of which may have spots

to which the poison has not adhered. Except in nearly air-tight spaces, however, moth balls do not protect unpoisoned articles from attacks of insects, while camphor, tobacco, pepper, and essential oils are practically valueless. It is found of advantage to brush the interior of drawers where specimens are stored with corrosive sublimate solution to prevent the harboring of insects in the corners and crevices, where they commonly undergo metamorphosis. Flags or other textiles of historic or ethnologic value which are fragile may be preserved by dampening them with a weak solution of alum and gum arabic in water. The alum preserves the colors and the gum arabic gives strength. Such specimens should be draped on wire netting or some other suitable support. Specimens of animal or vegetal origin must generally be poisoned to prevent the attacks of insects, placed in dust-proof cases, kept dry, and in some instances guarded against direct sunlight or strong reflected light, and against extremes of heat and cold.

Spears, swords, and other objects of iron are oiled with kerosene to soften rust, which then easily yields to gentle scraping with a knife blade. This is followed by a rubbing with emery cloth until the metal is clean, since the discolored layer beneath is the seat of continued oxidation. When clean, the metal is coated with the turpentine-paraffin solution and lightly wiped. Objects eaten by rust are warmed and dipped in the solution. If the objects are thin and fragile, they must be handled with care until the solution dries. The same treatment is given to exfoliating or verdigrised bronzes. Ancient pottery having incrustations on the exterior and chemical infiltrations is dipped in a 1-to-5 mixture of commercial muriatic acid in water, washed for 2 hours in plenty of pure water, and dried.

Among numerous materials used for repairing, cements and glues are important. For wooden articles a mixture of equal parts of white and brown glue, applied hot, suffices, or some of the trade liquid glues may be used. Plaster casts are mended with shellac dissolved in alcohol. Objects of stone, bone, shell, glass, porcelain, earthenware, etc., are preferably mended with casein cement.

Consult Hough, Preservation of Museum Specimens from Insects and the Effects of Dampness, Rep. U. S. Nat. Mus. 1887, 1889; Hrdlička, Directions for Collecting Information and Specimens for Physical Anthropology, Bull. U. S. Nat. Mus., No. 39, 1904; Jones in Am. Anthrop., VII, no. 4, 1905; Wilder, ibid., VI, no. 1, 1904; Willoughby, ibid., X, no. 2, 1908. (W. H.)

Presumpscot (commonly interpreted 'river of many shallows,' but more probably derived in part from *ompsk* 'stone,' *ut* the locative). An unidentified Abnaki tribe or subtribe on Saco r., Me.; perhaps the Sokoki or Wawenoc.

Presumscott.—Sullivan in Mass. Hist. Soc. Coll., 1st s., IX, 210, 1804.

Prickaway. One of the Diegueño rancherias represented in the treaty of 1852 at Santa Isabel, s. Cal.—H. R. Ex. Doc. 76, 34th Cong., 3d sess., 132, 1857.

Priests. See *Chiefs, Medicine and Medicine-men, Religion, Secret societies, Shamans and Priests, Social organization.*

Prietos (Span.: *prieto,* 'dark,' hence 'dark ones'). Given in 1794 by Father José Aguilar as a subtribe of the Jaranames (Aranama). Twelve of the Prietos were then in Espiritu Santo de Zúñiga mission, Texas, with Jaranames, Tamiques, and others, all said to be subdivisions of the Jaranames (Portillo, Apuntes para la Historia Antigua de Coahuila y Texas, 308, 1888). (H. E. B.)

Prisoners. See *Captives.*

Problematical Objects. There are several groups or classes of prehistoric art objects, mainly of stone, many of them of wide distribution, the purpose and significance of which are not fully determined. The possible uses, however, have been much discussed, and in a few cases the solution has become so nearly complete that the groups have been withdrawn from the problematical class. In archeological literature some of these groups of objects are referred to as "ceremonials," but, besides having a distinct and well-established application, this term is inappropriate, since there is no absolute assurance that the objects were used ceremonially. At the same time there is a strong probability that many of them had such use as a primary or a secondary function. It is equally clear that some of them served practical purposes. These groups of objects have been variously named from their form or supposed use, but in the absence of definite knowledge respecting their use or purpose it seems better, so far as possible, to assign names suggested by form only, as these are not seriously misleading and serve the purposes of classification and description. As our knowledge increases and uses become known, appropriate names will readily be suggested.

The names employed for the more fully segregated groups, most of which are already in use, are Banner stones, Birdstones, Boat-stones, Cache disks and blades, Cones, Cupstones, Discoidal stones (chunkey stones?), Footprint sculptures, Hook-stones, Hemispheres, Inscribed tablets, Notched plates, Duck tablets, Pierced tablets (gorgets?), Plummets, Pulley-stones (ear ornaments?), Perforated stones (digging weights?), Spade-stones (ceremonial axes?), Spineback stones, Spools, Tubes (cupping tubes?). See the articles under these heads respectively. The hyphen used in this list indicates the omission of the word "shaped."

To this list could be added numerous less fully differentiated groups of objects in chipped and polished stone, in clay, bone, shell, wood, and metal, the significance and use of which can as yet only be surmised. Some of these are of formal and others of eccentric shape, while many represent men, beasts, and monsters; in fact, nearly all classes of prehistoric sculptured life forms could be assigned to the problematical class, since the motives which led to their manufacture, the particular significance attached to them, and the manner of their use, are and must remain largely subjects of conjecture. It is also true that many of the things of common use, as ornaments, implements, and pipes, have had associated with them ideas of a mystic nature known only to the individual or to the social or religious group to which they pertained. As already stated, some of the objects included in the list given above probably served practical uses, but objects designed for a definite practical use are necessarily measurably uniform in pattern and size, while many of the groups of objects under discussion show almost limitless variation as if subject to the free play of fancy, untrammeled save by those nebulous or plastic ideas that cluster about a primitive symbol of general use. It would appear also that some specimens were employed on occasion in practical work for which they were not originally intended, while others had their origin in implements of utility and probably retained in part their original functions; but in the majority of instances they doubtless had definite, well-established functions or purposes, the history of which is connected with the history of native religious beliefs and practices. The majority, however, can be interpreted, in a general way, through knowledge of the employment by historic tribes of similar classes of objects, variously referred to as amulets, charms, divinatory and gaming devices, emblems, fetishes, insignia, luck stones, medicine stones, symbols, talismans, tutelaries, etc. This affords but little aid, however, since full and clear explanations regarding the ceremonial and sacred objects of living peoples are difficult to obtain, if obtainable at all. This is exemplified by objects of such widespread use as the calumet, in very general use among the eastern tribes in colonial days, and the mysterious "coppers" of the

N. W. coast tribes, many of which have been handed down for generations and appear to be but imperfectly understood even by their present owners.

It may be observed, however, that none of these groups of objects can owe their origin to the play of fancy merely, for individual selections of talismans and tutelary deities are made at random and do not constitute or develop into groups of objects of well-established and widespread types with numerous variants. Such established types must be the outgrowth of customs of wide extent and affecting a large body of people. That some of the classes of objects devoted to esoteric uses had their origin in common implements, as axes, clubs, sinkers, mortars, pestles, etc., is highly probable, and it is equally likely that some of them had not been divorced wholly from their original application. Such transfers from practical to symbolic use are common with primitive peoples, the process being an easy and a natural one. It is not unlikely, therefore, that some of these classes of objects, exhibiting marked diversity of form, size, and finish, had multiple offices, serving on occasion or with different communities as implements, ornaments, and symbols. It may fairly be assumed, also, that such of these objects as embody conventional life forms had their origin in some animal fetish, totem, or other form of mythological symbol.

Most of the objects here referred to have been described and discussed by various writers, especially in archeological and other scientific journals, as the American Anthropologist, American Antiquarian, Antiquarian, Archæologist, Wisconsin Archeologist, Science, American Naturalist, etc.; in publications of institutions, societies, and the Government, as reports of the Smithsonian Institution, National Museum, Bureau of American Ethnology, Geographical and Geological Surveys, American Museum of Natural History, Peabody Museum of Archæology and Ethnology, Free Museum of Science and Art of the University of Pennsylvania, New York State Museum, Academy of Natural Sciences of Philadelphia, American Ethnological Society, Ohio Archæological and Historical Society, Canadian Institute, Education Department of Ontario, etc.; and in various works most of which are referred to in the articles treating of the individual varieties of problematical objects. Prominent among the latter are Abbott, Prim. Indus., 1881; Ann. Archæol. Reps. Ontario, 1888–1907; Brown in Wis. Archeol., II, no. 1, 1902; Clark, Prehist. Remains, 1876; Foster, Prehist. Races, 1878; Fowke, Archæol. Hist. Ohio, 1902; Jones, Antiq.

So. Inds., 1873; MacLean, Mound Builders, 1879; Moorehead, (1) Prehist. Impls., 1900, (2) Bird-stone Ceremonials, 1899; Peabody in Bull. Mus. Univ. Pa., III, no. 3, 1901; Read and Whittlesey, Ohio Centen. Rep., 1877; Thruston, Antiq. of Tenn., 1897; Yates in Bull. Santa Barbara Soc. Nat. Hist., I, no. 2, 1890. (w. h. h.)

Projectiles. See *Bows, Arrows, and Quivers; Rabbit sticks; Slings; Throwing Sticks.*

Property and Property right. Broadly speaking, Indian property was personal. Clothing was owned by the wearer, whether man, woman, or child. Weapons and ceremonial paraphernalia belonged to the man; the implements used in cultivating the soil, in preparing food, dressing skins, and making garments and tent covers, and among the Eskimo the lamp, belonged to the women. In many tribes all raw materials, as meat, corn, and, before the advent of traders, pelts, were also her property. Among the tribes of the plains the lodge or tipi was the woman's, but on the N. W. coast the wooden structures belonged to the men of the family. Communal dwellings were the property of the kinship group, but individual houses were built and owned by the woman. While the land claimed by a tribe, often covering a wide area, was common to all its members and the entire territory was defended against intruders, yet individual occupancy of garden patches was respected. (See *Land tenure.*) In some instances, as among the Navaho, a section of territory was parceled out and held as clan land, and, as descent in the tribe was traced through the mother, this land was spoken of by members of the clan as "my mother's land." Upon such tract the women worked, raising maize, etc., and the product was recognized as their property. The right of a family to gather spontaneous growth from a certain locality was recognized, and the harvest became the personal property of the gatherers. For instance, among the Menominee a family would mark off a section by twisting in a peculiar knot the stalks of wild rice growing along the edge of the section chosen; this knotted mark would be respected by all members of the tribe, and the family could take its own time for gathering the crop. On the Pacific slope, as among the Hupa, varying lengths of river shore were held as private fishing rights by heads of families, and these rights passed from father to son, and were always respected. Clan rights to springs and tracts of land obtained among the Pueblos. The nests of eagles were also the property of the clan within whose domain they were found. The eagle never permanently left the vicinity of the nest where it was born, so, although the bird remained in freedom, it was regarded as the property of the clan claiming the land on which its nest was situated. This claim upon the eagles held good after the clan had left the region and built a new village even 40 m. away. (See *Eagle*.)

Names (q. v.) were sometimes the property of clans. Those bestowed on the individual members, and, as on the N. W. coast, those given to canoes and to houses, were owned by "families." Property marks were placed upon weapons and implements by the Eskimo and by the Indian tribes. A hunter established his claim to an animal by his personal mark upon the arrow which inflicted the fatal wound. Among both the Indians and the Eskimo it was customary to bury with the dead those articles which were the personal property of the deceased, either man or woman. In some of the tribes the distribution of all the property of the dead, including the dwelling, formed part of the funeral ceremonies. There was another class of property, composed of arts, trades, cults, rituals, and ritual songs, in which ownership was as well defined as in the more material things. For instance, the right to practise tattooing belonged to certain men in the tribe; the right to say or sing rituals and ritual songs had to be purchased from their owner or keeper. Occasionally a spectator with quick memory might catch a ritual or a song, but he would not dare to repeat what he remembered until he had properly paid for it. The shrine and sacred articles of the clan were usually in charge of hereditary keepers, and were the property of the clan. The peculiar articles of a society were in the custody of an appointed officer; they were property, but could not be sold or transferred. Songs and rites pertaining to the use of healing herbs were property, and their owner could teach them to another on receiving the prescribed payment. The accumulation of property in robes, garments, regalia, vessels, utensils, ponies, and the like, was important to one who aimed at leadership. To acquire property a man must be a skilful hunter and an industrious worker, and must have an able following of relatives, men and women, to make the required articles. All ceremonies, tribal festivities, public functions, and entertainment of visitors necessitated large contributions of food and gifts, and the men who could meet these demands became the recipients of tribal honors. (See *Potlatch*.)

Property right in harvest fields obtained among the tribes subsisting mainly on maize or on wild rice. Among the Chippewa the right in wild-rice lands was not based on tribal allotment, but on occupancy. Certain harvest fields were habit-

ually visited by families that eventually took up their temporary or permanent abode at or near the fields; no one disputed their ownership, unless an enemy from another tribe, in which case might established right. Among the Potawatomi, according to Jenks, the people "always divide everything when want comes to the door."

Consult Boas in Rep. Nat. Mus. 1895, 1897; McGee in 15th Rep. B. A. E., 1897; Fletcher in Pub. Peabody Mus., Harvard Univ.; Fewkes in Am. Anthrop., II, 690, 1900; Goddard in Univ. of Cal. Pub., I, no. 1, 1903; Jenks in 19th Rep. B. A. E., 1900; Mindeleff in 17th Rep. B. A. E., 1898. (A. C. F.)

Prophets. From time to time in every great tribe and every important crisis of Indian history we find certain men rising above the position of ordinary doctor, soothsayer, or ritual priest to take upon themselves an apostleship of reform and return to the uncorrupted ancestral belief and custom as the necessary means to save their people from impending destruction by decay or conquest. In some cases the teaching takes the form of a new Indian gospel, the revolutionary culmination of a long and silent development of the native religious thought. As the faithful disciples were usually promised the return of the earlier and happier conditions, the restoration of the diminished game, the expulsion of the alien intruder, and reunion in earthly existence with the priests who had preceded them to the spirit world—all to be brought about by direct supernatural interposition—the teachers have been called prophets.

While all goes well with the tribe the religious feeling finds sufficient expression in the ordinary ritual forms of tribal usage, but when misfortune or destruction threatens the nation or the race, the larger emergency brings out the prophet, who strives to avert the disaster by molding his people to a common purpose through insistence upon the sacred character of his message and thus furnishes support to the chiefs in their plans for organized improvement or resistance. Thus it is found that almost every great Indian warlike combination has had its prophet messenger in the outset, and if all the facts could be known we should probably find the rule universal.

Among the most noted of these aboriginal prophets and reformers within our area, all of whom are noted elsewhere under the appropriate titles, are: Popé, of the Pueblo revolt of 1680; the Delaware prophet of Pontiac's conspiracy, 1762; Tenskwatawa, the Shawnee prophet, 1805; Kanakuk, the Kickapoo reformer, 1827; Tavibo, the Paiute,

1870; Nakaidoklini, the Apache, 1881; Smohalla, the dreamer of the Columbia, 1870–1885; and Wovoka, or Jack Wilson, the Paiute prophet of the Ghost Dance, 1889 and later. Consult Mooney, Ghost Dance Religion, in 14th Rep. B. A. E., pt. ii, 1896.   (J. M.)

Proqueu. A former village, presumably Costanoan, connected with Dolores mission, San Francisco, Cal.—Taylor in Cal. Farmer, Oct. 18, 1861.

Proven. An Eskimo missionary station in w. Greenland.—Kane, Arct. Explor., ii, 126, 1856.

Pructaca. A former village, presumably Costanoan, connected with Dolores mission, San Francisco, Cal.—Taylor in Cal. Farmer, Oct. 18, 1861.

Pruristac. A former village, presumably Costanoan, connected with Dolores mission, San Francisco, Cal.—Taylor in Cal. Farmer, Oct. 18, 1861.

Psakethe (*Pĭshĕkĕthĕ*, 'deer'). A gens of the Shawnee.
Pishekethe.—Wm. Jones, inf'n, 1906 (correct form). Psake-the'.—Morgan, Anc. Soc., 168, 1877.

Psaupsau. A small tribe represented at San Antonio de Valero mission, Texas, in the 18th century.

Pseudo-Indian. As "pseudo-Indian" may be included forgeries of American Indian objects, implements, etc., on the one hand, and, on the other, objects, implements, etc., imitative of or closely resembling real American Indian things into whose manufacture the idea of forgery does not necessarily enter. These "pseudo-Americana" have been the subject of much archeological discussion, and some very patent frauds have long managed to maintain their existence in the field or the museum. Objects manufactured for trade purposes in imitation of real Indian articles belong here also. Of some of these last, Indians themselves have been the makers. There might be mentioned the imitations of European objects in American material, which, however, are rather pseudo-European than pseudo-American. According to McGuire (Rep. Nat. Mus. 1897, 493, 1899), a large number of the tobacco pipes of the American aborigines are in part or wholly pseudo-American—"in almost every pipe of the Iroquoian area may be traced forms distinctly copied from European sources." Pseudo-American also are the "trade pipes," "trade tomahawks," etc. This view of the pseudo-American character of many Indian pipes is not shared by David Boyle, who, however, considers many of the wampum belts now in existence to have been "entirely made by Europeans, with just enough 'Indian' in the make-up to make them pass muster among the natives for commercial and treaty purposes" (Archæol. Rep. Ontario,

55, 1901; 28, 1903). Beauchamp follows Morgan and Brinton in thinking that with the Iroquois "no existing belts antedated the Dutch settlement and trade" (Bull. N. Y. State Mus., 340, Mar. 1901). After the colonization of New York, wampum beads were manufactured by the European settlers in prodigious quantities for trade and treaty purposes. Several of the aboriginal names of Long Island refer to its importance as a wampum center. In 1844 wampum was still manufactured by whites in New Jersey and sold to Indian traders of the far W., and the best of this article was still made at Babylon, L. I., in 1850, according to Beauchamp. The great spread of the use of wampum, like that of tobacco, has been thought to be due to white influence. Beauchamp (Archæol. Rep. Ontario, 86, 1903) does not consider the bone combs found in the state of New York as really aboriginal, believing that "no New York or Canadian Indian ever made a bone comb until he had European hints." Boyle takes an opposite view. Forged and pseudo-American flint implements, pottery, and steatite images are well known to archeologists. An interesting account of the achievements of one man in the making of spurious fishhooks, spear and arrow points, cutting implements, etc., in Wisconsin, is given by Jenks (Am. Anthrop., n. s., ii, 292–96, 1900), while those of a man in Michigan who has attempted to produce objects with a biblical meaning have been exposed by Kelsey (Am. Anthrop., x, no. 1, 1908). Several centers of manufacture of "antiquities" have been discovered by the experts of the Bureau of American Ethnology in various parts of the country. As pseudo-American may be classed the numerous pictographic frauds and controverted pictographs, especially those cited by Mallery (10th Rep. B. A. E., 759–67, 1893). Among these may be mentioned the Kinderhook (Ill.) copper plates, the Newark (Ohio) inscribed stone, the Pemberton (N. J.) inscribed stone ax, the Grand Traverse (Mich.) inscribed stone, the inscribed stone maul from Isle Royal (Mich.), and probably also such "mound builders' relics" as the famous Grave cr. stone. In this class may also be placed the Abbé Domenech's "Manuscript pictographique Américain," published in 1860, which Petzholdt, the German orientalist, declared to be "only scribbling and incoherent illustrations of a local German dialect" (Pilling, Algonq. Bibl., 114, 1891). Pseudo-American may also be called those "pictographs" due to weathering and other natural causes, such as those in New Brunswick described by Ganong (Bull. Nat. Hist. Soc. N. B., 175–78, 1904), and, according to

Mallery, the pictured rocks of Monhegan (Me.), the mica plates of Sandusky, etc. Mallery also observes (p. 759): "With regard to more familiar and portable articles, such as engraved pipes, painted robes, and like curios, it is now well known that the fancy prices paid for them by amateurs have stimulated their unlimited manufacture by Indians at agencies, who make a practice of sketching upon ordinary robes or plain pipes the characters in common use by them, without regard to any real event or person, and selling them as significant records." The wood and stone arts of the Haida have also suffered from forgery and imitation.

There is even a pseudo-American language, the so-called Taensa of Parisot, of which an alleged grammar and vocabulary were published in Paris in 1882. The evidence seems to prove this document an entire fabrication (see Brinton, Essays Am., 452, 1890; Swanton in Am. Anthrop., x, no. 1, 1908). See *Popular fallacies*. (A. F. C.)

Psinchaton ('village of red wild rice'). An unidentified Dakota tribe or band in Minnesota, one of the divisions of the so-called Sioux of the West.—Le Sueur (1700) in Margry, Déc., vi, 87, 1886.

Psinoumanitons ('village or gatherers of wild rice'). A Dakota tribe or band, probably in Wisconsin, one of the divisions of the Sioux of the East.—Le Sueur (1700) in Margry, Déc., vi, 86, 1886.

Psinoutanhinhintons ('the great wild-rice village'). A Dakota tribe or band in Minnesota, a division of the so-called Sioux of the West.
Psinontanhinhintons.—Shea, Early Voy., 111, 1861.
Psinoutanhhintons.—Neill, Hist. Minn., 170, 1858.
Psinoutanhinhintons.—Le Sueur (1700) in Margry, Déc., vi, 87, 1886.

Psiseva. See *Pipsissewa*.

Psychology. The psychological differences between the various divisions of mankind have always been objects of speculation and ingenious inference, but out of it all has come little that can be considered definite or satisfactory. Direct positive data are scarcely to be had, and the indirect data available are far from sufficient for definite conclusions. Hence, the specific question of psychological differences between Indians and other races is still an unsolved problem. There are, however, certain points of view and some suggestive data that may be discussed under three heads:

A. Observation by psychologists.

B. Observations by teachers and other officials.

C. Evidences of differences, observable in culture.

A. Modern psychology has developed experimental methods for the study of differences in mental life, practically all of which can be successfully applied to representatives of the various races. The probability that differences will be found among them has been greatly increased by the work of Myers, Rivers, and McDougall, members of the Cambridge Anthropological Expedition to Torres straits, since the Papuans as tested for visual acuity, color vision, visual spatial perception, auditory acuity, upper limit of hearing, smallest perceptible tone-difference, olfactory acuity, discrimination of odor-strengths, memory and discrimination of odors, delicacy of tactile discrimination, localization of points touched, temperature spots, sensibility to pain, discrimination of small differences of weight, degree of size-weight illusion, reaction times, showed differences in most cases from Whites. Unfortunately, we have on record but one successful attempt to apply the methods of psychology to American natives. This is the work of Prof. R. S. Woodworth and Dr F. G. Bruner, upon such representatives of the less civilized races as were on exhibition at the Louisiana Exposition at St Louis in 1904. A full and comprehensive report on the tests for hearing has been made by Dr Bruner. He tested Indians, Whites, Filipinos, Ainu, and Congo natives as to the upper limit of hearing and auditory acuity. The results for the right ear in the test for the upper limit were as follows:

	No.	Average		
Congo natives	6	33,223	D. V.	2468
Whites	156	32,285	"	2344
Cocopa	10	32,123	"	977
School Indians	63	31,975	"	2663
Tehuelche	3	30,240	"	3551
Filipinos	97	29,916	"	2180
Ainu	7	28,846	"	1873
Kwakiutl	7	28,296	"	1413

The results for the left ear vary slightly from the above; but not sufficiently to make any material changes in the order as given above. Though the differences are small, the table, as a whole, indicates that, while Indians are inferior to Whites and Congo natives, they differ greatly among themselves. In the tests for acuity, the rank for the right ear was: Whites, Cocopa, School Indians, Congo natives, Tehuelche, Kwakiutl, Ainu, Filipinos; for the left ear, Whites, Congo natives, School Indians, Cocopa, Kwakiutl, Ainu, Tehuelche, Filipinos. While there is some shifting of position for the left ear, the relative positions of Whites, School Indians, and Filipinos remains the same throughout. As due allowance has been made for accidental variations in making these tests, the results may be regarded as reasonably certain. In general, they indicate that, in the ability to perceive high tones and to distinguish faint sounds, the Indians are superior to Filipinos, but inferior to Whites and Congo natives.

In addition to the above, the results of a few other tests have been reported. Color blindness has been found in three cases from a group of 250 which, so far as it goes, does not differ much from the proportion among the Whites. A few tests in reaction-time, made by Witmer, show the Indian superior to Whites and American Negroes. As previously stated, the results of these few tests suggest that, with a more extended series, numerous differences will be found between Indians and other races, as well as between the different tribes of Indians themselves.

On more general psychological grounds, unusual tendencies to hysteria and similar psychic phenomena have been assigned to the Indian. This is made probable by the readiness with which many Indians yield to suggestion in disease, jugglery, and religious activities, and has been offered as a cause for the large part played by the medicine-man on such occasions. This impression, of course, concerns Indians as compared to Whites, and not to other less civilized races. (See *Physiology*.)

B. Since the schools for Indians are essentially the same as those used by white children, the relative progress of Indian and white children may be taken as evidence of their respective mental powers. However, a satisfactory comparative study of Indian children in the school seems not to have been made; so that we are forced to fall back upon some general impressions and less direct evidence. It has been asserted by teachers in Indian schools that the children under their charge showed more aptitude and greater skill in many kinds of hand work than was usually encountered among white children of the same age. This is often strongly asserted with respect to drawing and penmanship. On the other hand, no critical examination of this point has been made, so that judgment must be suspended. The general experience has been that, when Indian children have passed normally from our lower schools to the college and the university, they average up to the level of the Whites; but, again, many of the cases cited are of mixed blood, and no estimates have been made of the relative number of failures to reach such a standard. Thus, while there is no direct evidence that Indians can not do the work of the school and of life as efficiently as Whites, this fact can not be taken as proof that they have the requisite ability to the same degree. The tests of Dr Bruner on the Indians in the model school at St Louis showed that, while in the auditory sense these Indians were superior to their unschooled representatives, they were still inferior to Whites selected at random. While it is true that the data for hearing prove nothing with respect to the other senses, they do suggest the presence of differences so far not overcome by education and a change of environment. Hence, the question must remain open until more data are available.

In addition to these somewhat definite systematic observations, we have the opinions of educated persons resulting from extended official or philanthropic labors among the Indians. A general statement of such opinions on the general psychological characteristics of the Indians has been given in the article on *Physiology*, the import of which seems to be that no definite differences exist except perhaps in the objective form of emotional reactions. Yet, so far, no one seems to have collected enough individual statements from competent persons to say what is the approximate consensus of such opinion and, even if they had, such a consensus could not be taken alone as a satisfactory solution of the problem.

C. It is customary to speak of the customs and thought prevailing among a people as their culture. Since, in all cultural activities, ideas and judgments play important parts, it has often been assumed that a detailed comparison of cultures would reveal psychological differences between the peoples to whom the cultures belonged. Indeed, some persons go so far as to assert that the existence of cultural differences necessitates the existence of psychological differences. Yet when the subject is taken on its merits, several difficulties are encountered. In the first place, some definite method of grading cultures must be devised before satisfactory conclusions as to corresponding psychological differences can be formed. As yet, no consistent way of grading as to higher and lower has been found. Further, anthropologists now believe in the existence of a tendency to conventionalize thought and the association of ideas as a factor in the differentiation of culture. Such a tendency appears when the symbolic art of such tribes as the Arapaho, Dakota, and Shoshoni are compared, each using similar designs, but associated with different kinds of ideas. Also, some claim has been made, but on less definite grounds, that Indian mythology as a whole is less closely associated with creators and gods than is the case with other peoples. In a more general way, we find everywhere among the Indians a marked tendency to inter-associate the sociological, religious, and artistic aspects of their lives to such a degree that they can scarcely be unraveled. This has sometimes been taken as one of the most characteristic aspects of Indian modes of thought. The claim is made, however, that such conventions of thought can not in themselves be taken as indications of functional differences between the minds (as such) of Indians and other races; since, on *a priori* grounds, what has become conventional or habitual for one may in turn become conventional for another. This theory, that all cultural differences are in no wise due to psychological differences, but to causes entirely external, or outside of the conscious life, places the inherent worth of a Pigmy, an Indian, a Mongol, and a European upon the same level, and considers culture as the sum of habits into which the various groups of mankind have fallen. While strong arguments in support of this interpretation of culture are offered by many anthropologists, together with plausible reasons for doubting the existence of fundamental psychological differences in function, so far nothing has been brought forward to render doubtful the existence of psychological differences between races analogous to those between individuals among ourselves. Modern psychological science is gradually solving the puzzle as to the kind and degree of individual psychological differences, and it is reasonable to suppose that, when these investigations have made more progress, the same methods may be successfully adapted to the comparison of tribal and other ethnic divisions of humankind.

In conclusion, it appears that we have no satisfactory knowledge of the elemental psychological activities among Indians, because they have not been made the subjects of research by trained psychologists. On the other hand, it may be said that in all the larger aspects of mental life they are qualitatively similar to other races.

Consult Bruner, Hearing of Primitive Peoples, 1908; Reports of the Cambridge Anthropol. Exped. to Torres Straits, II, 1901–03; Bache, Reaction Time with Reference to Race, Psychol. Rev., II, 475, 1895; Farrand, Basis of American History, 1904; Boas, Human Faculty as Determined by Race, Proc. Am. Ass'n Adv. Sci., 1894; Hrdlička in Bull. 34, B. A. E., 1908. (c. w.)

Ptansinta ('otter tail'; from *ptan* 'otter', *sinte* 'tail'). A former village of the Santee Sioux at the head of L. Traverse, Minn.—Williamson in Minn. Geol. Rep. for 1884, 110, 1885.

Pteyuteshni ('eat no buffalo cows'). A band of the Hunkpatina division of the Yanktonai Sioux.

Band that eats no buffalo.—Culbertson in Smithson. Rep. 1850, 141, 1851. Pte-yute-oni.—Dorsey in 15th Rep. B. A. E., 218, 1897. Pte-yute-śni.—Ibid.

Ptolme. A tribe once mentioned (Henley in Ind. Aff. Rep., 511, 1854) as living on Kings r., Cal. It was probably Yokuts (Mariposan).

Pualnacatup. A Chumashan village on one of the Santa Barbara ids., Cal., probably Santa Rosa, in 1542.—Cabrillo, Narr. (1542), in Smith, Colec. Doc. Fla., 186, 1857.

Puaray ('village of the worm'). A former pueblo of the Tigua, the ruins of which have been identified by Bandelier as those on a gravelly bluff overlooking the Rio Grande in front of the s. portion of the town of Bernalillo, N. Mex. At the time of Coronado's expedition (1540–42) it was the principal settlement of the province of Tiguex, and was known to the chroniclers of the expedition by the name of the province. It was one of the two pueblos in which the Tigua took refuge and fortified themselves against the Spaniards during a siege of 50 days (see *Tigua*), and was the seat of the missionary labors of two of the Franciscan friars escorted to New Mexico in 1581 by Francisco Sanchez Chamuscado, but who were killed shortly afterward. The identification of Puaray with the Tiguex village of the Tiguex province of the chroniclers of Coronado's expedition is determined by statements made by the Indians to Espejo in 1583, and by the discovery there by Oñate, in 1598, of a partially effaced painting representing the murder of the missionaries. It was the seat of the mission of San Bartolomé, and had 200 inhabitants at the time of the Pueblo revolt of 1680; but the pueblo was destroyed before 1711, and was never rebuilt. (F. W. H.)

Coofer.—Mota-Padilla (1742), Hist. Nueva Galicia, 160, 1870 (cf. Bancroft, Ariz. and N. Mex., 55, 1889). Coofert.—Ibid., 165. Paola.—Espejo misquoted by Whipple, Pac. R. R. Rep., III, pt. 3, 114, 1856. Paray.—Jefferys, Am. Atlas, map 5, 1776. Pauray.—Bowles, Map Am., 1784. Poala.—Espejo (1583) in Hakluyt, Voy., III, 468, 1600. Poalas.—Bancroft, Ariz. and N. Mex., 135, 1889. Pruara.—Ladd, Story of N. Mex., 79, 1891. Puala.—Espejo (1583) in Doc. Inéd., XV, 175, 1871. Puála.—Oñate (1598), ibid., XVI, 208, 1871. Pualas.—Espejo (1583), ibid., XV, 112, 1871. Puara.—Espejo quoted by Bancroft, Ariz. and N. Mex., 135, 1889. Púarái.—Villagran, Hist. Nueva Mex., 137, 1610. Puaray.—Oñate (1598) in Doc. Inéd., XVI, 109, 115, 1871. Puary.—Doc. of 1681 quoted by Bandelier in Arch. Inst. Papers, IV, 169, 1892. Puray.—Vetancurt (1696) in Teatro Mex., III, 312, 1871 ("el nombre Puray quiere decir gusanos, que es un género de que abunda aquel lugar"). Puruai.—Salmeron (1629) quoted by Bancroft, Nat. Races, I, 600, 1882. Puruay.—Bancroft, Ariz. and N. Mex., 172, 1889. San Bartolomé.—Vetancurt (1696) in Teatro Mex., III, 312, 1871 (mission name). Sant Antonio de Padua.—Oñate (1598) in Doc. Inéd., XVI, 254, 1871 (first saint name applied). Tehoua.—Schoolcraft, Ind. Tribes, IV, 40, 1854. Tigouex.—Coronado misquoted by Schoolcraft, Ind. Tribes, IV, 26, 1854. Tigouex-on-the-rock.—Ibid., 28. Tiguex.—Castañeda (1596) in 14th Rep. B. A. E., 497, 1896. Village of the Worm or Insect.—Bandelier in Arch. Inst. Papers, IV, 226, 1892 (Puar-ay, or).

Pubea. See *Evea*.

Puberty customs. The significance of a girl's entrance into womanhood was not only appreciated by all American tribes, but its importance was much exaggerated. It was believed that whatever she did or experienced then was bound to affect her entire subsequent life, and that she had exceptional power over all persons or things that came near her at that period. For this reason she was usually carefully set apart from other people in a small lodge in the woods, in a separate room, or behind some screen. There she remained for a period varying from a few days, preferably 4, to a year or even longer—the longer isolation being endured by girls of wealthy or aristocratic families—and prepared her own food or had it brought to her by her mother or some old woman, the only person with whom she had anything to do. Her dishes, spoons, and other articles were kept separate from all others and had to be washed thoroughly before they could be used again, or, as with the Iroquois, an entirely new set was provided for her. For a long period she ate sparingly and took but little water, while she bathed often. Salt especially was tabooed by the girl at this period. A Cheyenne girl purified herself by allowing smoke from sweet grass, cedar needles, and white sage to pass over her body inside of her blanket. She was also forced to sit up for long periods to prevent her from becoming lazy, and among the Haida she had to sleep on a flat rock with a bag of gravel or something similar for a pillow. If she ate too much, it was thought that she would be greedy in later life; if she talked too much, that she would become garrulous, and if she laughed, that she would become too much inclined to hilarity. A Shuswap girl would climb trees and break off their tips in order to become strong, and play with gambling sticks that her future husband might be a successful gamester. A Hupa girl must not tell a lie during this time or she would become forever untruthful. Among the Tsimshian if a girl desired a certain number of sons when married, the same number of men chewed her food for her; if she desired daughters, that office was performed by women. At the end of her fast she was covered with mats and held over a fire in order that her children might be healthy. The Shuswap, Ntlakyapamuk, Apache, Hupa, and other tribes did not allow a girl to touch her head or scratch her body except with a comb or stick. On the N. W. coast she usually wore a broad-brimmed hat to protect the sky, sun, sea, and other objects in nature from pollution and to protect herself from the deleterious influences which they in turn

might exert. Often the hole for the labret was bored about this time. Among the Haida a girl was not allowed to gaze on the sea lest her face and eyes should acquire nervous, twitching movements from the motion of its waves, or on fire for fear that her face would become red. If she looked upon red salmon, her eyes would become inflamed. If a girl ate fresh salmon, the Bellacoola feared that her mouth would be transformed into a long beak; and if a Ntlakyapamuk girl ate bear meat, it was thought she would be childless. There was, in addition, a long series of food taboos in each tribe, governed by some supposed resemblance between the article of diet and phenomena of certain diseases. On the N. Pacific coast as much property as the family could afford was hung about the girl while fasting so that she might become rich in after years; and she was not allowed to do any work, so that she might become a chief's wife and be waited on by slaves. Quite different was the custom among the Ntlakyapamuk and other tribes wanting the institution of slavery where the girl spent her time in imitating various useful employments in order not to be lazy when she grew up. Among the latter people the girl was supposed to be under the special care of the Dawn, to which she continually prayed, and she made a record of her offerings and the ceremonials she had passed through by painting pictures of them on bowlders and on small stones. This, according to Teit, was believed to insure long life. Kroeber also records the execution of paintings by Luiseño Indian girls in s. California.

Among many tribes it was believed that the supernatural beings were especially offended by menstrual blood. Therefore a Haida girl at this time must not go down to the beach at low tide, lest the tide come in and cover one of the chief sources of food supply. She must not step across a small stream, lest the old woman who resides at its head leave and take all the fish with her. When her people went to a salmon creek to dry fish she must get out of the canoe just before they reached it and approach the smokehouse from behind, for if she saw a salmon jump all the salmon might leave. If a hunter's glance happened to fall upon her, blood would be injected into his eye, preventing him from seeing game, and a crust of blood would surround his spear, making it unlucky. The Alaskan Eskimo supposed that a girl was surrounded by a sort of film at this time which would attach itself to a hunter who came too near and enable every animal to see him. Fishing tackle and gambling sticks might be affected in the same way, and therefore gambling sticks and hunting and fishing implements were removed from the house, at least temporarily, when the girl had occasion to come from behind her screen. Armed with the blood of a menstruant woman a man would attack and destroy hostile supernatural powers or put to flight any by which he was himself assailed. If a menstruant girl scratched any place where one felt pain, the pain would stop. The whole period of isolation and fast usually ended with a feast and public ceremonies as a sign that the girl was now marriageable and that the family was open to offers for her hand. Although Hopi girls appear to have been spared the multifarious taboos imposed upon their sisters elsewhere, the attainment of puberty was marked by a change in the arrangement of their hair, which was then gathered into two whorls, one on each ear, symbolizing the flower of the squash; after marriage it was worn in simple braids (see *Hair dressing*). Among the Diegueños, girls were laid down upon green herbs caused to steam by means of a fire underneath. They were then covered with blankets and left for four days and nights, while dancing and feasting went on about them to drive away the evil spirits. Symbolic acts were also performed, such as throwing seeds over them that they might be prolific, and scattering property among the onlookers that they might be generous. According to Wissler, the Teton Dakota still perform a ceremony for girls called "singing over girls that bleed." It is rather long, and is based on the buffalo, one of the dances representing the mating of the buffalo.

Although not so definitely connected with the period of puberty, certain ordeals (q. v.) were undergone by a boy at about that period which were supposed to have a deep influence on his future career. Among these are especially to be noted isolation and fasts among the mountains and woods, sweat bathing and plunging into cold water, abstinence from animal food, the swallowing of medicines sometimes of intoxicating quality, and the rubbing of the body with fish spines and with herbs. As in the case of the girl, numbers of regulations were observed which were supposed to affect the boy's future health, happiness, and success in hunting, fishing, and war. Like the girls, Ntlakyapamuk youths made paintings upon rocks during this period in order to insure long life, and all except those who desired to become successful warriors, who addressed the Sun, also directed their prayers to the Dawn. The regulations of a boy were frequently undergone in connection with ceremonies introducing him into the mysteries of the tribe or of some secret society. They were not as wide-spread in North America as the regulations imposed upon girls, and varied more from tribe to tribe. It has also been noticed that they break down sooner before contact with whites.

The most detailed account of puberty customs among North American tribes is given by Teit in Mem. Am. Mus. Nat. Hist., II, Anthrop. I, pt 4, 1900. An interesting account of a puberty ceremony for girls among the Diegueños is given by Rust in Am. Anthrop., n. s., VIII, no. 1, 1906. See also Boas in Reps. on N. W. Tribes Canada, 1889–98; Dixon in Bull. Am. Mus. Nat. Hist., XVII, pt. 3, 1905; Goddard in Pub. Univ. Cal., Am. Archæol. and Ethnol., I, no. 1, 1903; Grinnell in Am. Anthrop., n. s., IV, no. 1, 1902; Hearne, Travels, 1795; Hill-Tout (1) in Reps. Ethnol. Surv. Can., 1898–1903, (2) in Jour. Anthrop. Inst. G. B., XXXIV, 1904; Loskiel, Missions United Brethren, 1794; Nelson in 18th Rep. B. A. E., 1899; Owen, Musquakie Folk-lore, 1904; Sapir in Am. Anthrop., IX, no. 2, 1907; Speck in Mem. Am. Anthrop. Ass'n, II, no. 2, 1907; Swanton in Mem. Am. Mus. Nat. Hist., V, pt 1, 1905. (J. R. S.)

Pubugna. A former Gabrieleño rancheria in Los Angeles co., Cal., at a place later called Alamitos. — Ried (1852) quoted by Taylor in Cal. Farmer, June 8, 1860.

Puccoon. Any one of various plants whose juice was used by the Indians for staining and dyeing; also any one of some others to which the term has been transferred by the whites. The chief ones are: 1. *Lithospermum vulgare*, the puccoon of the Virginia Indians. 2. The bloodroot (*Sanguinaria canadensis*), called red puccoon. 3. The yellow root (*Hydrastis canadensis*), or yellow puccoon. The word *puccoon*, spelled earlier puccon, poccon, pocon, pocoan, pocones, etc., is derived, as the "poccons, a red dye," in Strachey's and Smith's vocabularies indicates, from one of the Virginian dialects of Algonquian. In s. w. Virginia puccoon is locally abbreviated 'coon.' According to Trumbull and Gerard the word is from, or from the same root as, the name for blood. (A. F. C.)

Puchkohu (*Pútc-ko-hu*). The Rabbit-stick clan of the Asa phratry of the Hopi. — Stephen in 8th Rep. B. A. E., 39, 1891.

Puckna. A former village of the Upper Creeks in the s. w. part of Clay co., Ala. — Royce in 18th Rep. B. A. E., Ala. map, 1899.

Pueblito (Span.: 'little village'). A small settlement of the Tewa of San Juan pueblo, opposite the latter, on the w. bank of the Rio Grande in Rio Arriba co., N. Mex. — Bandelier in Arch. Inst. Papers, IV, 63, 1892.

Pueblito. An Acoma summer village about 15 m. N. of the pueblo of Acoma, Valencia co., N. Mex.

Titsiap.—Hodge, field notes, B. A. E., 1895 (native name).

Pueblo Alto (Span.: 'high village'). Two pueblo ruins, about 500 ft apart, but both belonging to a single ancient village, situated on the top of the mesa N. of Chaco canyon, N. W. N. Mex., about ½ m. N. of Pueblo Bonito. The main building is rectangular in form, facing S., the court inclosed by the usual semicircular double wall which was really a series of one-story apartments. The N. wall is 360 ft long, the wings 200 and 170 ft, respectively. The rooms are from 15 to 20 ft long and 8 to 12 ft wide. The walls are almost entirely thrown down. The smaller building is about 75 ft square and much better preserved, some second-story walls being still intact. This building contains some of the best plain masonry to be found in the Chaco Canyon group. There is a large circular kiva in the small building and traces of 7 in the large one. A quarter of a mile E. of the ruins is a wall extending N. and S. 1,986 ft. Other walls extend toward this from the main building but do not connect with it. Pueblo Alto is reached from the canyon by a tortuous stairway through a narrow crevice just back of Pueblo Bonito. See Jackson in 10th Rep. Hayden Surv., 1878.　　　　　　　　　　　(E. L. H.)

Ki-a-a.—Lummis in Land of Sunshine, XV, 425, 1901.

Pueblo Blanco (Span.: 'white village'). A ruined pueblo of the Tano on the S. border of the Galisteo plain, N. central New Mexico.—Bandelier in Arch. Inst. Papers, IV, 116, 1892.

Pueblo Blanco. A former pueblo, presumably of the Piros, on the W. rim of the Médano, or great sand-flow, E. of the Rio Grande, about lat. 34° 30′, New Mexico. It was probably inhabited in historic times.—Bandelier in Arch. Inst. Papers, IV, 278, 281, 1892.

Pueblo Bonito (Span.: 'beautiful village'). The central and most important ruin of the Chaco Canyon group in N. W. New Mexico. The building, which stands within 70 ft of the N. wall of the canyon, is of dark brown sandstone, semielliptical in form. Its length E. and W. is 667 ft, greatest depth N. and S. 315 ft. It was originally 5 stories high, there being portions of the fifth-story wall still standing. The greatest height of standing wall at present is 48 ft, 39 ft being above the detritus; probably half of the original walls remain standing. The rooms are mostly rectangular, but there are many of irregular form, semicircular, trapezoidal, elliptical, triangular, etc., owing to the subsequent addition of rooms to the original structure, several such additions and remodelings being evident. In fact, no unit of original plan is discernible, and additions seem to have been made within, without, and upward as needed. The masonry of Pueblo Bonito ranges from plain rubble to what appears to be ornamental mosaic in places. Every type of masonry known to Pueblo architecture is found in this building, and not fewer than 27 circular kivas, varying from 10 to 50 ft in diameter, have been uncovered in it. The kiva is in every instance a circular room built within a square or rectangular one, the space between the walls being filled with earth and masonry. In some cases the interior of the kivas is of fine tablet masonry, alternating with bands of larger blocks, giving an ornamental finish. The fireplaces are of the most primitive character. The timbering is exceptionally heavy, logs 40 ft in length and 18 in. in diameter having been found. The doorways vary from 24 by 36 to 30 by 50 in.; the lintels are straight, smooth poles about 3 in. in diameter; windows vary from 6 by 12 to 12 by 16 in. Extensive excavations have been made in Pueblo Bonito by the Hyde Exploring Expedition; the collections found are now in the American Museum of Natural History, New York.

Consult Simpson, Exped. to Navajo Country, 80, 1850; Hardacre in Scribner's Mag., 276, Dec. 1878; Jackson in 10th Rep. Hayden Surv., 1878; Pepper (1) in Am. Anthrop., VII, no. 2, 1905, (2) in Putnam Anniv. Vol., 1909.　(E. L. H.)

Pueblo Caja del Rio. A very ancient pueblo on a rocky bluff 3 m. N. E. of Cochiti, in the so-called Caja del Rio, so named from the "boxing" of the canyon of the Rio Grande here, in Sandoval co., N. Mex. Concerning it Bandelier (Arch. Inst. Papers, IV, 80, 1892) says: "Whether the Tehuas [Tewa], the Tanos, or some other unknown tribe were the builders of it I am unable to say. The people of Cochiti disclaimed all knowledge of its former occupants. The amount of arable land in the vicinity is sufficient; for the population, as I estimate it, could not have exceeded 400."

Chin-a Ka-na Tze-shu-ma.—Bandelier, op. cit., 80 ('the old houses on the river': Cochiti name.) Ti-tji Hän-at Ka-ma Tze-shu-ma.—Ibid. ('the old houses in the north': another Cochiti name).

Pueblo Colorado (Span.: 'red village'). A ruined pueblo of the Tano on the S. border of the Galisteo plain, N. central New Mexico.—Bandelier in Arch. Inst. Papers, IV, 116, 1892.

Pueblo Colorado. A former pueblo, presumably, of the Piro on the W. rim of the Médano, or great sand-flow, E. of the Rio Grande, about lat. 34° 30′, New Mexico. It was probably inhabited in historic times.—Bandelier in Arch. Inst. Papers, IV, 278, 281, 1892.

Pueblo del Alto (Span.: 'village of the height,' so called on account of its situation above the reach of inundation). A prehistoric village, probably of the Piro, the ruins of which lie on the E. side of the Rio Grande, 6 m. s. of Belen, N. Mex.—Bandelier in Arch. Inst. Papers, IV, 237, 1892.

Pueblo de la Parida (Span.: 'village of the woman lately delivered'). A former pueblo, presumably of the Piro, on the w. rim of the Médano, or great sandflow, E. of the Rio Grande, about lat. 34° 30′, New Mexico. It was probably inhabited in historic times.—Bandelier in Arch. Inst. Papers, IV, 278, 281, 1892.

Pueblo del Arroyo (Span.: 'village of the gulch'). An important ancient pueblo less than ⅛ m. below Pueblo Bonito, in Chaco canyon, N. w. N. Mex. It is on the N. side of the arroyo, on its very brink, is rectangular in form, and faces eastward. The western wall is about 270 ft long, and the 2 wings 125 and 135 ft respectively. The extremities of the wings are connected by a semicircular double wall, the space between being occupied by a series of rooms. Portions of the third-story wall are standing. The original height was probably 4 stories. The heavy floor timbers, averaging about 10 in. in thickness, are still in place. There are 2 kivas in the court, 3 built within the pueblo walls, and 4 outside the main building. The largest is 37 ft in diameter. The masonry is of dull brown sandstone, well laid in adobe mortar. Consult Jackson in 10th Rep. Hayden Surv., 1878, and Hardacre and Simpson, cited below. (E. L. H.)

Del Orroyo.—Domenech, Deserts of N. A., I, 200, 1860. Pueblo del Arroya.—Hardacre in Scribner's Mag. 275, Dec. 1878 (misprint). Pueblo del Arroyo.—Simpson, Exped. to Navajo Country, 81, 1850.

Pueblo del Encierro (Span.: 'village of the inclosure'). A former pueblo, probably Keresan, described as being some distance above Tashkatze, which is opposite Cochiti, in N. central New Mexico. The Tano of Santo Domingo disclaim its former occupancy by their people.—Bandelier in Arch. Inst. Papers, IV, 179–81, 1892.

Pueblo de los Jumanos. A former large village of the Jumano (q. v.), situated in the "Salinas" E. of the Rio Grande. central New Mexico, in the vicinity of Tabira, or the so-called Gran Quivira. The definite location of the pueblo is not known, although it is supposed to have been situated near the base of the elevation called Mesa de los Jumanes. In 1598 the northern division of the Jumano occupied 4 villages in this region, but before 1629 they lived in tipis and were semi-nomadic. In the latter year they were

gathered in a "great pueblo" to which the name San Isidoro was applied by the Franciscan missionaries, and an attempt made at their conversion. The Pueblo de los Jumanos was mentioned by Escalante in 1778—fully a century after the abandonment of the Salinas by the Tigua and the Piro. According to Escalante the pueblo was destroyed by the Apache, who were the scourge of the Pueblos during this period. (F. W. H.)

Jumancas.—Escalante (1778) quoted by Bandelier in Arch. Inst. Papers, III, 132, 1890. Numanas.—De l'Isle, Carte Mex. et Floride, 1703. Pueblo de Jumanos.—Bandelier, op. cit., 131. San Isidoro.—Benavides (1630) trans. in Land of Sunshine, XIII, 285, 1900. S. Isidoro Numanas.—Benavides (1630) as cited by Bancroft, Ariz. and N. Mex., 164, 1889. Xumanos (great pueblo of the).—Benavides trans. in Land of Sunshine, op. cit.

Pueblo de los Silos. A large Tano village situated in the Galisteo basin, between the Keresan pueblos of the Rio Grande and Pecos, N. Mex., in 1540; so called by the Spaniards of Coronado's expedition because of the large underground cellars found there stored with corn. The village had the appearance of newness, but because of depredations by the Teya, a Plains tribe, 16 years before, only 35 houses were inhabited, the remainder having been destroyed. See Castañeda in 14th Rep. B. A. E., 453, 523, 570, 1896.

Pueblo de los cilos.—Castañeda, op. cit., 453. Zitos. Mota-Padilla (1742), Hist. Nueva Galicia, 164, 1870 (apparently identical).

Pueblo Largo (Span.: 'long village'). A former Tano pueblo of the compact, communal type, situated about 5 m. s. of Galisteo, N. Mex. It was possibly occupied in the 16th and the beginning of the 17th centuries.—Bandelier (1) in Ritch, N. Mex., 201, 1885; (2) in Arch. Inst. Papers, III, 125, 1890; IV, 106, 1892; (3) Gilded Man, 222, 1893.

Hishi.—Bandelier in Arch. Inst. Papers, III, 125, 1890 (native name).

Pueblo Nuevo (Span.: 'new village'). A Tepehuane pueblo in s. Durango, Mexico, near Mezquital r.—Orozco y Berra, Geog., 319, 1864.

Pueblo Pintado (Span.: 'painted village'). An important ancient pueblo ruin, of yellowish gray sandstone, situated near the head of the Chaco wash, on the low mesa to the s., in Chaco canyon, N. w. N. Mex. It is the most easterly of the Chaco Canyon group. The building is L-shaped, the 2 wings measuring 238 ft and 174 ft, exterior measure. The extremities of the wings are connected by a row of small apartments. The inclosed court was occupied by 2 kivas and other semisubterranean structures, while just outside the court is another large kiva. The standing outer walls are still about 28 ft high; the original height was probably about 40 ft. This ruin is surrounded by about 10 ruins of minor pueblos, all within a mile of the main building. The surrounding region is an absolute desert.

The site is an exceedingly interesting one because of its situation, being well toward the top of the continental divide and likely to contain important evidences of contact with the Pueblos of the Rio Grande drainage, particularly Jemez. See Simpson, Exped. to Navajo Country, 81, 1850; Jackson in 10th Rep. Hayden Surv., 1878.   (E. L. H.)

Kinkale.—E. L. Hewett, inf'n, 1905 ('large houses surrounded by small ones': Navaho name). **Kinkyel.** — Ibid.   **Pueblo Colorado.** — Simpson, Exped. Navajo Country, 75, 1850 (trans. 'red town'). **Pueblo de Montezuma.**—Ibid. ('town of Montezuma,' said to be so called by some of the Pueblos). **Pueblo de Ratones.**—Ibid. ('rat town': trans. of Jemez name). **Pueblo Grande.**—Ibid. ('great town': so called by a Navaho). **Pueblo Pintado.**—Ibid. (Spanish name).

Pueblo Quemado (Span.: 'burnt village'). An abandoned pueblo of the Tano or the Tewa, 6 m. s. w. of Santa Fé, N. Mex. See *Tzenatay.*

Agua Frio.—Eastman, map (1853) in Schoolcraft, Ind. Tribes, IV, 24–25, 1854 (misprint). **Pueblo quemado.**—Oñate (1598) in Doc. Inéd., XVI, 114, 1871 (possibly identical). **Quimado.**—Ritch, N. Mex., 166, 1885 (Agua Fria, or).

Pueblo Raton (Mex.-Span.: 'rat village'). An Indian village in 1763 on Cayo Ratones, about New r. inlet, s. E. coast of Florida (Roberts, Fla., 21, 1763). The inhabitants were probably a remnant of the ancient Tequesta tribe.   (J. M.)

Pueblos ('towns', 'villages', so called on account of the peculiar style of compact permanent settlements of these people, as distinguished from temporary camps or scattered rancherias of less substantial houses). A term applied by the Spaniards and adopted by English-speaking people to designate all the Indians who lived or are living in permanent stone or adobe houses built into compact villages in s. Colorado and central Utah, and in New Mexico, Arizona, and the adjacent Mexican territory, and extended sometimes to include the settlements of such tribes as the Pima and the Papago, who led an agricultural life. The Pueblo people of history comprise the Tanoan, Keresan (Queres), and Zuñian linguistic families of New Mexico, and the Hopi, of Shoshonean affinity, in N. E. Arizona. These are distributed as follows, the tribes or villages noted being only those now existent or that recently have become extinct:

LINGUISTIC STOCK.	GROUP.	TRIBES OR VILLAGES.
Tanoan	Tewa	Nambe, Tesuque, San Ildefonso, San Juan, Santa Clara, Pojoaque (recently extinct), Hano.
	Tigua ...	Isleta, Sandia, Taos, Picuris, Isleta del Sur (Mexicanized).
	Jemez ...	Jemez, Pecos (extinct).
	Tano	Practically extinct.
	Piro	Senecu, Socorro del Sur (both Mexicanized).

LINGUISTIC STOCK.	GROUP.	TRIBES OR VILLAGES.
Keresan (Queres) .	Eastern..	San Felipe, Santa Ana, Sia, Cochiti, Santo Domingo.
	Western .	Acoma, Laguna, and outlying villages.
Zuñian	Zuñi	Zuñi and its outlying villages.
Shoshonean	Hopi	Walpi, Sichomovi, Mishongnovi, Shipaulovi, Shongopovi, Oraibi.

Habitat.—The Pueblo tribes of the historical period have been confined to the area extending from N. E. Arizona to the Rio Pecos in New Mexico (and, intrusively, into w. Kansas), and from Taos on the Rio Grande, New Mexico, in the N., to a few miles below El Paso, Texas, in the s. The ancient domain of Pueblo peoples, however, covered a much greater territory, extending approximately from w. Arizona to the Pecos and into the Texas panhandle, and from central Utah and s. Colorado indefinitely southward into Mexico, where the remains of their habitations have not yet been clearly distinguished from those of the northern Aztec.

History.—Of the Pueblo tribes the Zuñi were the first to become known to civilized people. In 1539 Fray Marcos of Niza, a Franciscan, journeyed northward from the City of Mexico, accompanied by a Barbary negro known as Estevan, or Estevanico, who had been a companion of Cabeza de Vaca and the two other Spanish survivors of Narvaez's expedition, shipwrecked in the Gulf of Mexico in 1528. The negro went ahead of the friar to prepare the way, but contrary to instructions reached a province that became known as the Seven Cities of Cibola, unquestionably identified with the Zuñi villages of w. New Mexico, far in advance of Fray Marcos. Here Estevanico, with some of the Indians who had followed him, was killed by the Zuñi. A few days later the friar viewed from an adjacent height a town identified as Hawikuh, the first one seen in journeying toward the N. E.; then planting a cross and taking formal possession of the new country in the name of Spain, he hastened back to the City of Mexico, where he presented a glowing report of what he had seen and heard.

Fired with enthusiasm at the report of riches in the northern country, the Viceroy Mendoza organized an expedition, under Francisco Vasquez de Coronado, which, for wealth of equipment and for the prominence of the men who accompanied it, has never been equaled in the annals of American exploration. Guided by Fray Marcos of Niza, the expedition departed from Compostela, Feb. 23, 1540, and reached Culiacan Mar. 28. On Apr.

22 Coronado departed from the latter place with 75 horsemen, leaving the main force to follow, and reached Hawikuh, which he named Granada, on July 7. The Indians showing hostility, the place was stormed by the Spaniards and the inhabitants were routed after Coronado had almost lost his life in the attack. Exploring parties were sent in various directions—to the Hopi villages of Tusayan, the Grand Canyon of the Colorado, the Rio Grande valley, and the buffalo plains—nowhere finding the expected wealth but always encouraged by news of what lay beyond. The main army reached Cibola in September, and departed for Tiguex (the country and chief village of the present Tigua Indians), about the present Bernalillo, on the Rio Grande, where winter quarters were established. The natives revolted owing to atrocities committed by the Spaniards, but the uprising was quelled after a long siege and the killing of many Indians. In the following April (1541) Coronado started with his entire force, under the guidance of an Indian nicknamed "The Turk," evidently a Pawnee, whom he had found living among the Pueblos, to explore a province to the far eastward called Quivira (q. v.). The Spaniards were led astray by the guide, whom they later executed; the main force was sent back to the Rio Grande, and a picked body finally reached the buffalo country of E. Kansas. In the spring of 1542 Coronado's force started on their return to Mexico. Two missionaries were left behind—Fray Juan de Padilla, who went to Quivira, and Fray Luis, a lay brother, who remained at Pecos. Both were killed by the natives whom they expected to convert. In Coronado's time the Pueblos were said to occupy 71 towns, and there may have been others which the Spaniards did not enumerate.

The Pueblos were visited successively by several other Spanish explorers. Francisco Sanchez Chamuscado, in 1581, escorted three Franciscan missionaries to the Tigua country of the Rio Grande, but they were killed soon after. Antonio de Espejo, late in 1582, started with a small force from San Bartolomé in Chihuahua for the purpose of determining the fate of the missionaries. He traversed the Pueblo country from the Hopi villages of N. E. Arizona to Pecos in New Mexico, and returned to San Bartolomé by way of Pecos r. Espejo's itinerary is traceable with no great difficulty, and most of his tribal names are readily identified. His estimates of population, however, are greatly exaggerated—in some cases at least ten times too large. Following Espejo, in 1590, was Gaspar Castaño de Sosa, who with a party of 170 persons followed up the Pecos as far as the pueblo

of that name, which is described as having five plazas and sixteen kivas; the pueblo was provided with much maize, and the pottery and the garments of the men and women aroused admiration. One of the most important of all the expeditions was that of Juan de Oñate, the colonizer of New Mexico in 1598 and founder of Santa Fé seven years later; for by reason of it the Pueblo tribes were first definitely influenced by civilization. Traveling northward, Oñate reached on May 22 the first pueblos of the Rio Grande—those of the Piro in the vicinity of the present Socorro. A party was sent to visit the pueblos of the Salinas, E. of the Rio Grande, and the main body reached the Tigua country a few weeks later, finding there, at Puaray village, evidences of the murder of the friars in 1581. Other pueblos were visited, the natives taking the oath of obedience and homage in each instance, and several saint names were applied that have remained to this day. The Pueblo country was divided into districts, to each of which a priest was assigned, but little was done toward the founding of permanent missions during Oñate's stay. The first settlement of the Spaniards was established, under the name San Gabriel de los Españoles, on the Rio Grande at the Tewa village of Yukewingge, at the mouth of the Rio Chama, opposite San Juan pueblo; it remained the seat of the colony until the spring of 1605, when it was abandoned and Santa Fé founded.

Active missionary work among the Pueblos was commenced early in the 17th century, and although many baptisms were made by the few resident friars little was done toward actual conversion. The condition of affairs in 1629 is set forth in the Memorial written by Fray Alonso Benavides, the custodian of the Franciscan Order in the province, published in the following year. The appeal of Benavides resulted in the sending of 30 new missionaries and the founding of many new missions from the Hopi country and the Zuñi in the w. to the pueblos of the Salinas in the E. Substantial churches and monasteries were erected with the aid of the natives, and much was done toward concentrating the Indians with a view of more readily effecting their Christianization. Toward the middle of the century difficulties arose between the civil officials and the missionaries, in which the Indians became involved. Finally the latter, led by a native of San Juan named Popé (q. v.), arose in revolt in August, 1680, killing 21 of the 33 missionaries, about 375 other colonists of a total of about 2,350, and destroying the missions, together with their furnishings and records. Governor Otermin and the surviving colonists took refuge in the government buildings at Santa Fé, and withstood a siege by about 3,000 Indians for 10 days, when, after a desperate sortie, the Indians were forced back with a loss of 300 killed and 47 captured. The prisoners were hanged, and the next day (Aug. 21) the Spaniards, numbering about 1,000, commenced their long retreat to El Paso. Evidently in fear lest the Spaniards should return at any time with a strong force, many of the Pueblos abandoned their settlements and took refuge in new ones on less pregnable sites, leaving the former villages to crumble. For 12 years the Pueblos remained independent of the Spaniards, but not free from dissension among themselves or from depredations by their old enemies, the Navaho and the Apache. In 1692 Diego de Vargas reconquered the province after severely chastising many of the natives and destroying some of their towns. Of all the pueblos of New Mexico at the beginning of the revolt (at which time there were 33 active missions, while others were mere visitas) only Acoma and possibly Isleta continued to occupy their former sites after the conquest. In 1696 some of the Pueblos once more rebelled, killing several missionaries, but they surrendered after having been again severely punished by Vargas. From this time the Pueblos have been notably peaceful toward the whites, the only exception being in Jan., 1847, when the Taos Indians, instigated by some misguided Mexicans, killed Gov. Charles Bent and some other Americans and took refuge in their fortified town and mission church, which were stormed by troops with a loss to the Indians of about 150 killed outright, while a number were later tried and hanged.

Arts and industries.—While the material culture of the sedentary people of this great territory, as revealed by ethnological and archeological investigations, is sufficiently homogeneous to warrant its designation as "the Pueblo culture," there are many local differences in architecture and in building materials, due chiefly to the influence of environment. In the northern portions particularly, and scattered here and there almost through-

out the area, are the remains of dwellings built in recesses of cliffs or canyon walls, in some cases the natural cavities having been enlarged or modified by artificial means, in others the cliff face having been practically honeycombed to serve as habitations. These are the cliff-dwellings (q. v.) built and occupied by the ancestors of the present Pueblos, no doubt for purposes of defense against ancient enemies. In the valleys and on the mesa tops the structures varied according to the available building materials and to the exigencies of the sites. In the northern parts of the Pueblo area the houses were generally of sandstone, readily quarried near at hand; in some places blocks of lava, or tufa, were used. In the southern valleys, especially along the Gila and the Salt, adobe (q. v.) was the material usually employed. The groups of dwellings were generally compact structures of several stories, with many small rooms made necessary owing partly to the scarcity of suitable timber for roofing larger structures and partly to the lack of means of transporting it, for, like other Indians, the Pueblos had no horses or donkeys before the coming of the whites. The villages were often rectangular, with open courts, but usually there was little fixed plan of outline, new dwellings being

CLIFF-DWELLINGS IN NEW MEXICO

added wherever and whenever need demanded (although sometimes influenced by the direction of the sun), often resulting in great community groups of houses forming irregularly oblong, square, semicircular, circular, and elliptical ground-plans, with wings and minor projections. The pueblos were generally built in terrace fashion; i. e., the upper tiers of houses were set back of those next below, so that the roofs of the lower stories formed a kind of front yard for those next above. Unlike the dwellings of to-day, the lower stories were without doors, entrance being gained by means of ladders and a hatchway in the roof. The upper houses were and still are reached by means of movable ladders, or by masonry steps built against the outer walls and resting on the roofs of the houses below. In the ancient pueblos the fireplace was generally in the form of a shallow box or pit in the middle of the floor, the smoke finding egress through the hatchway as in some of the kivas to-day. Corner fireplaces were also in use, but chimneys, as well as the dome-shaped ovens built on the ground or on the roofs, and paneled doors and shutters, were doubtless derived from the Spaniards. Floors were paved with stone slabs or plastered smooth with adobe mortar like the walls and roofs. Accompanying each pueblo was at least one kiva (q. v.); indeed the belief has been advanced that the kiva formed the nucleus of the ancient pueblo, which grew up around it. The houses are constructed and owned by the women, the men helping with the heavy work, such as quarrying stone and hauling and emplacing the beams. The Pueblos made good basketry (q. v.), but it is not the equal of that of some of the tribes of N. California, although some of the Hopi manufacture basket placques in two distinct styles of weaving, excellently ornamented with anthropomorphic and other figures in harmonious colors derived from native substances, now largely superseded by the dyes of commerce. As potters and weavers the Pueblos have not been excelled by any Indians N. of Mexico (see *Pottery, Weaving*). Their earthenware vessels, ancient and modern, consist of practically every form known to the aborigines, from large rough cooking and storage vessels to delicately modeled and elaborately painted jars, bowls, platters, bottles, ladles, and box-shaped utensils.

Many of the ancient Pueblos, especially those of the northern area, may be designated as horticulturists rather than as agriculturists, so intensive was their method of cultivation. Their small fields were irrigated from living streams or from storage reservoirs, the chief crop being corn. Cotton also was raised, the product being woven into everyday clothing and ceremonial cloaks, kilts, and leggings, which were extensively traded to other tribes. The Hopi were and still are the principal cotton weavers of all the Pueblos, but the native cotton has given place almost entirely to trade stuffs. After the introduction of sheep by the Spaniards, the weaving of native wool, as well as of strands of bayeta on rude hand looms, became an important

industry. It is believed that weaving was introduced among the Navaho by Pueblo women adopted into that tribe. Many so-called "Navaho blankets" are really the product of Hopi and Zuñi looms, operated by both men and women. In the southern Pueblo area especially, agriculture was conducted on a large scale, and elaborate and extensive systems of irrigation (q. v.) were employed. Such works, utilized by an entire community, were constructed under a communal system; and indeed this method is still largely followed by all the Pueblos. In addition to fields of corn, wheat, pumpkins, melons, etc., small garden patches of onions, beans, chile, etc., near the houses are cultivated, water being daily conveyed to them in jars by the women, to whom the gardens belong.

In addition to their agriculture the Pueblos hunted to some extent, and there are still some excellent hunters among them. The deer, antelope, bear, and mountain lion were the larger game sought, and the eastern Pueblos hunted also the buffalo on the plains. Rabbits abound throughout the Pueblo country, and are hunted individually as well as by large groups of men and boys, who surround a wide area and gradually drawing

PUEBLO ON A MESA TOP—WALPI, ARIZONA

together entrap the rabbits and dispatch them with boomerang-shaped hunting sticks. Traps also are employed, especially for catching small mammals and birds, including eagles, which are highly prized on account of their feathers, so largely used in ceremony. Fish and other products of the water are never eaten, and various animals are tabooed as food by the members of certain clans. In early times the turkey was domesticated, and there is evidence that large flocks were "herded" in much the same manner as are sheep and goats at the present time. A few turkeys, as well as eagles, are still kept in captivity, but only for their feathers. The only other domestic animal was the dog, but there is no evidence that the Pueblos employed this animal as a beast of burden like the tribes of the plains (see *Domestication, Travois*). Horses, asses, horned cattle, sheep, and goats, like wheat, grapes, peaches, and apples, now more or less extensively grown, were not known to the Indians before the coming of the Spaniards in the 16th century. In s. Arizona, in association with ancient ruins, pictographs and figurines representing a llama-like quadruped have been found, the rock-pictures indicating the animals as being herded by men with bolas.

The ancient clothing of Pueblo men consisted typically of a short tunic of deerskin and trousers of the same material reaching to the knees; leggings of skin or of cotton, fastened at the knees, held in place by a narrow garter woven in pattern; and moccasins of deerskin with rawhide soles neatly sewn with sinew. Knitted footless stockings of yarn are now commonly worn by both men and women, with or without leggings. A piece of skin (now usually fresh goatskin), with hairy side inward and entirely incasing the foot, was used over the moccasin in snowy weather. The breechcloth is universally worn by males. The warriors wore a close-fitting cap of skin, ventilated with numerous holes and decorated with feathers; this cap is still worn as a part of the ceremonial costume of the Priests of the Bow, of Zuñi. Evidence produced by excavation in the cliff-dwellings indicates that garments woven of yucca fiber, as well as of cotton with feathers, were also used in early times. Sandals of yucca or other fibers were worn instead of moccasins. The hair of the Pueblo men is "banged" above the eyes, cut horizontally at the neck line, and the back hair gathered and tied with a woven band into a tight knot behind. A headband, now usually a bandana handkerchief, is always worn by men and boys of the western Pueblos, but those of the Rio Grande valley, except during ceremonies, wear the hair in side plaits and require no headband. After the introduction of sheep, woven woolen garments largely replaced the skin tunics and trousers of the men, and the cheap cotton fabrics of commerce in time superseded woolen goods to a great extent. Robes of twisted strands of rabbit skin and wildcat skin were worn in cold weather, and were employed also as bedding; but these have given place almost entirely to the bright-colored blankets,

identical with the so-called "Navaho blankets," of native wool, bayeta, or commercial yarn, woven by both men and women among the Zuñi and the Hopi, and worn especially on gala occasions. The ornaments of the men consist of necklaces of ground and drilled shell and turquoise beads, turquoise being mined in considerable quantity at Los Cerillos, N. Mex. (the Queres of San Felipe serving as the chief traders in the product); and of ear and neck pendants of the same materials, and beautifully executed mosaics of shell and turquoise and other colored stones. Leather belts and wrist-guards ornamented with large disks of coin silver are commonly worn and are highly prized, and leggings and moccasins are usually studded with silver buttons. German silver and copper are sometimes employed for ornamentation, but these metals are not highly regarded by the Pueblos. Their metal-working process was derived from the Spaniards.

The clothing of the women now consists of a woolen dress of native weave, knee-length, made in the form of a blanket, the two ends being sewn together; the garment is worn over the right shoulder and under the left, and belted at the waist with a very long woven sash, usually of red and green wool, fringed at the ends and tucked in; a cotton shirt extending to the knees; for indoor use, knitted leggings of yarn; for outdoor use, and especially on gala occasions, leggings consisting of an entire deerskin wrapped round and round from below the knee to the ankle and forming part of the moccasins of the same material. The leggings and moccasins, unlike those of the men, are not dyed. The women wear also a light cotton mantle, and when the weather demands, a woolen blanket similar to the blankets above mentioned. A valued possession is the "ceremonial blanket" of white cotton, embroidered, knotted, and fringed. Among some of the Pueblos the hair of the married women is banged slightly in front, parted in the middle, and wrapped in two coils back of the ears; girls who had reached the marriageable age had the hair arranged in two large whorls at the sides of the head: these

VALLEY PUEBLO—ZUÑI, NEW MEXICO

among the Hopi (who alone among the Pueblos now employ this method of hairdressing) represent squash blossoms, symbols of fertility. Other Pueblo women do not bang the hair, but part it in the middle and wear it in a braid at each side. Necklaces, pendants, bracelets, earrings, and finger rings of silver are commonly worn, particularly during outdoor ceremonies, and on gala occasions Hopi girls wear as ear pendants small tablets ornamented with turquoise mosaic.

Social and religious organization.—Every Pueblo tribe is composed of a number of clans or gentes, these terms here being employed to indicate descent in the female or the male line, respectively. The clans vary greatly in number. The little pueblo of Sia, for example, with only about a hundred inhabitants, is represented by 16 existing clans, while 21 others are traceable though extinct. Among some of the Pueblos, notably the Hopi, there is evidence of a phratral grouping of the clans. Most of the clans take their names from natural objects or elements, especially animals and plants, and are divided into regional or seasonal groups, depending more or less on the habits and habitat of the related animals, plants, or other objects or elements from which they take their names, and on various religious beliefs. There is evidence that originally a priest or religious chief presided over each clan. (For the names of the clans, see under the several tribes.)

Of the mythology, religion, and ceremonies of the Pueblos comparatively little has been recorded thus far except in so far as the Zuñi, Hopi, and Sia are concerned. Among the Zuñi there are many organizations embracing secret orders whose functions pertain to war, healing, hunting, agriculture, magic, religion, etc., although it should be said that the religious motive enters largely into all their activities. In these ceremonial organizations the cardinal directions play a prominent part, each important society, according to Cushing, representing a distinct region; for example, the Pihlakwe, or Bow priesthood of the Zuñi, represent the west, the Shumekwe the east, the Newekwe or Galaxy people the upper region, the Chitolakwe or Rattlesnake people the lower region, etc. Each society has its own series of rites and ceremonies, some of which are performed in secret, while others, in the form of public dances, are elaborate and impressive. The origin of these organizations and the mythology and religious beliefs underlying them are too complicated to admit of even an outline here. On this subject the reader should consult (for the Zuñi) Cushing, (1) Zuñi Creation Myths, in 13th Rep.

B. A. E., (2) Zuñi Folk Tales, 1901, and Mrs Stevenson in 5th and 23d Reps. B. A. E.; (for the Hopi) Fewkes in the 15th, 16th, 19th, and 21st Reps. B. A. E., and various articles in Am. Anthr., Jour. Am. Folk-lore, and Jour. Am. Eth. and Arch.; (for the Sia) Mrs Stevenson in 11th Rep. B. A. E.

All the Pueblos are monogamists, and the status of women is much higher than among most tribes. Among the tribes in which descent is reckoned through the mother, at least, the home is the property of the woman, and on the marriage of her daughters the sons-in-law make it their home. Marriage is effected with little ceremony, and divorce is lightly regarded, the wife having it in her power to dismiss her husband on a slight pretext, the latter returning to his parents' home, sometimes for a trifling cause; in such cases either is free to marry again. There are many instances, however, in which men and women marry but once, spending their lives together in perfect accord and happiness. Labor is divided as equitably as possible under the circumstances. As among other tribes, the women perform all domestic duties as well as some of the lighter farm work, especially at harvest time; but unlike most Indian women those of the Pueblos are helped by the men in the heavier domestic work, such as house-building and the gathering of fuel, while men also weave blankets, make their wives' moccasins, and perform other labors usually regarded in Indian life as a part of women's work. Like the houses, the small garden patches are the property of the women, who alone cultivate them, and the carrying of water and the making of pottery are also strictly women's functions. The children are spoken of as belonging to the mother; i. e., among most of the Pueblos they belong to the clan of the mother; and in this case, at least, if the father and the mother should separate, the children remain with the latter. Children are very obedient and only on very rare occasions are they punished.

Originally the government of the Pueblos was controlled by the priesthood, the various functions of government, as war and peace, witchcraft, hunting, husbandry, etc., being regulated by representatives of the societies pertaining thereto. On the advent of the Spaniards the outward form of the government of most of the tribes was changed by the establishment of a kind of elective system and the control of strictly civil affairs by a governor, a lieutenant-governor, and a body of aldermen, so to call them. All the Pueblos except the Hopi still successfully maintain this system of local government; but all affairs of a religious or ceremonial nature are controlled by the priesthood.

Population.—The statistics of population of the Pueblo tribes are not satisfactory, owing to the unreliability of some of the estimates, especially in the earliest period of Spanish exploration, due in part to the desire to exaggerate the Indian population in order to attract greater attention to the country from Spain and Mexico. The table on the opposite page, compiled from various sources, gives the population of the various Pueblos from 1630 to the present time. In some instances the figures are approximate estimates only, and may be regarded as little more than broad guesses; at other times the count was evidently closely made.

As will be seen, the table does not include the Piro and Tigua pueblos of the lower Rio Grande in Texas and Chihuahua, nor the Hopi (q. v.) of Arizona. In 1725 the total population was given at 9,747; in 1749, 11,942; in 1793, 7,455, and in 1794, 9,495. These figures include the lower Rio Grande villages. In 1885 the Indians of 19 pueblos of New Mexico, including Zuñi, were reported to number 7,762. In 1887 the population of all the New Mexican pueblos was given as 8,357. From these figures it is evident that the Pueblo population has varied little during the last two centuries.

Following is a list of pueblos, now extinct or Mexicanized, which are as yet either unidentified or unclassified: Acacagua, Acoti ("birthplace of Montezuma"), Atica, Aychini, Baguacat, Casa Blanca, Casa del Eco, Casa Grande, Casa Montezuma, Castildavid, Chettrokettle, Chichilticalli, Cristone, Hungopavi, Kinnazinde, Kintyel, Nogales, Pagmi, Paguemi, Peñasco Blanco, Pequen, Poblazon, Pueblo Alto, Pueblo Bonito, Pueblo del Arroyo, Pueblo de los Silos, Pueblo Pintado, Pueblo Viejo, San Rafael de los Gentiles, Sargarría, Siemas, Triati, Una Vida, Urraca, Viní, Wejegi, Xutis, Yncaopi, Ytriza. For pueblos classified by tribes, see *Hopi, Jemez, Keresan, Piro, Tano, Tewa, Tigua, Zuñi.* (F. W. H.)

Biǎǎlpahéko.—Mooney, inf'n, 1893 ('beardless people': Kiowa ancient name). Catholic Indians.—Gregg, Commerce of Prairies, I, 122, 1844 (Pueblos, or). Chiǎlan.—Curtis, Am. Ind., I, 135, 1907 ('have burros': Jicarilla Apache name). Christian Indians.—Calhoun (1849) in Cala. Mess. and Corresp., 207, 1850. Cow Nation.—Cabeza de Vaca cited by Wallace in Atlantic Mo., 217, Aug. 1880 (misapplied by Wallace to all the Pueblos). Ho-pi'-ci-nu-me.—ten Kate, Synonymie, 7, 1884 (Hopi name). Hopíshinome.—ten Kate, Reizen in N. Am., 259, 1885 ('good people': Hopi name). Indios Manzos.—Ruxton in Nouv. Ann. des Voy.,5th s., XXI, 80, 1850 (or Pueblos). Kis'ándinné.—Gatschet, Navaho MS., B. A. E., 1887 (Navaho name). Kisani.—Stephen, MS., B. A. E. (Navaho name). Ki-žǎ'n-ne—ten Kate, Synonymie, 6, 1884 ('many houses': Navaho name; ž=zh, ę=e mute of Latin). Koksawópalĭm.—

Curtis, Am. Ind., II, 110, 1908 ('tie their hair back': Pima name). Mexicans.—Haines, Am. Ind.,160, 1888 ("All the Pueblo Indians are called Mexicans, who make the striped blanket"). Myǎlaname.—Hodge, field-notes, B. A. E., 1895 (Taos name). Parblos.—Gallatin in Trans. Am. Eth. Soc., II, lxx, 1848. Pau'-ę-rǎts'.—ten Kate, Synonymie, 8, 1884 (Ute name). Pôbǎlo.—Mooney, inf'n, 1893 (Kiowa pronunciation of "Pueblo"). Purblos.—Garrard, Wahtoyah, 131, 1850. Purbulo.—Coyner, Lost Trappers, 171, 1847. Sedentary Village Indians.—Morgan in 1st Rep. Arch. Inst. Am., 43, 1880. Ta'-ide.—Gatschet, Isleta MS., B. A. E., 1882 (Isleta name for one Pueblo Indian). Táinin.—Ibid. (Isleta name for the Pueblos). Tai'-wa.—ten Kate, Synonymie, 9, 1884 ('little men': Comanche name). Thluëlla'kwe.—ten Kate, Reizen in N. Am., 291, 1885 (Zuñi name). T'lu-ĕl-la'-kwe.—ten Kate, Synonymie, 7, 1884 ('people of the towns': Zuñi name). Town Builders.—Wallace, Land of the Pueblos, 240, 1888 (Pueblo, or). Town-building Indians.—Ibid., 236. Town Indians.—Wallace in Atlantic Mo., 216, Aug. 1880. Towns-people.—Bancroft, Nat. Races, I, 526, 1882. Tu Tlŭnĭ.—Curtis, Am. Ind., I, 134, 1907 ('much water': Apache name for Pueblos of the Rio Grande). Village Indians.—Morgan in N. Am. Rev., 463, Apr. 1869.

Pueblo Viejo (Span.: 'old village'). The name given to that portion of Gila valley from Pima to San José, between Mt Graham and the Bonita mts., s. Ariz., on account of the ruins of prehistoric habitations there. The name was earlier applied to an important ruin (see *Buena Vista*) and later to the settlement of San José near its site. See Fewkes (1) in Am. Anthr., XI, June 1898; (2) 22d Rep. B. A. E., 168, 172, 1904.

Pueblo Viejo. A village of mixed Tepehuane and Aztec population, in the N. part of the Territory of Tepic, Mexico. Although Spanish is here largely used, outsiders are not permitted to settle in the village. Only the old people speak Nahuatl correctly; the Tepehuane influence is strong, even in the ancient religion of the people.—Lumholtz, Unknown Mex., I, 473, 1902.

Puerta Chiquita (Span.: 'little port or gateway'). A rancheria of 18 Mission Indians on Gov. Gage's ranch, San Diego co., Cal. By act of Congress of May 27, 1902, these and others on Warner's ranch were removed in 1903 to a new reservation purchased for them at Pala. They are probably Diegueño or Luiseño.

Puerta de la Cruz (Span.: 'gateway of the cross'). A former Diegueño rancheria on upper San Luis Rey r., San Diego co., s. Cal., later on Agua Caliente res. No. 1, occupied by Warner's ranch. By court decision the 14 survivors were compelled to vacate, and, under act of Congress of May 27, 1902, were assigned a new tract purchased for them at Pala in 1903.—Ind. Aff. Rep., 175, 1902; 118, 1903.

Puerta de San José (Span.: 'gateway of St Joseph'). A former Diegueño rancheria on upper San Luis Rey r., San Diego co., Cal.—Jackson and Kinney, Rep. Miss. Ind., 20, 1883.

POPULATION OF THE VARIOUS PUEBLOS FROM 1630.

Pueblo	Language	1630	1680	1760	1788	1790-3	1797-8	1805	1809	1850	1856	1860	1864	1871	1874	1889	1901-5
Abiquiu	[Genízaros, mixed.]			166	1,181	216	176	134	126		"Mexicanized."					300	300
Abo	Piro		800	Abandoned about 1675.													
Alameda	Tigua		300	Abandoned about 1675.													
Acoma	Keres	2,000	1,500	1,052		820	757	731	816	350	1,200	523	491	436	500	582	739
Alamillo	Tigua		300	(a)													
Belen	[Genízaros, mixed.]						107	"Mexicanized."									
Chilili	Tigua		500	Abandoned about 1675.													
Cochiti	Keres		300	450		720	505	656	697	254	800	172	229	243	400	300	300
Cuyamunque	Tewa		(b)														
Galisteo	Tano		c 800	(d)	Abandoned between 1760 and 1805.												
Hano l	Tewa				375(?)						600	250				161	
Isleta (N. M.)	Tigua		2,000	e 304	e 2,103	410	e 603	419	487	751	800	440	786	768	1,200	1,037	989
Jemez	Jemez	3,000	5,000	373		485	272	264	297	365	450	650	346	344	800	474	450
Laguna	Keres			600	1,368	668	802	940	1,022	749	800	927	988	927	900	970	1,384
Nambé	Tewa		f 600	204		155	178	143	133	111	500	103	94	78	100	81	100
Pecos	Jemez	2,300	2,000	g 599		152	189	104		Moved to Jemez in 1838.							
Picuris	Tigua		3,000	328	212	254	251	250	313	222	800	143	122	127	150	120	125
Pojoaque	Tewa			99	368	53	79	100		48	500	37	29	32	20	18	(h)
Puaray	Tigua		200	Abandoned about 1675.													
Quarai	Tigua		600	Abandoned about 1696.													
San Cristóbal	Tano		(i)	Abandoned about 1696.													
Sandia	Tigua		3,000	291	596	304	116	314	364	241	500	217	197	186	225	150	74
San Felipe	Keres		j 600	458		532	282	289	405	800	800	360	427	482	400	501	475
San Ildefonso	Tewa		800	484	k 1,566	240	251	175	283	500	500	154	161	156	570	189	250
San Juan	Tewa		300	316		260	202	194	208	568	500	341	385	426	350	373	425
San Marcos	Tano		600	Abandoned in 1680.													
Santa Ana	Keres			404	452	356	634	450	550	399	500	316	298	373	500	264	226
Santa Clara	Tewa		300	257		134	193	186	220	279	600	179	144	189	50	187	325(?)
Santa Cruz	Tewa			316	k 1,076	Abandoned and reestablished.				"Mexicanized."							
Santo Domingo	Keres			424	1,035	650	1,483	333	720	666	800	261	604	735	1,000	930	1,000
Sia	Keres		150	568	608	275	262	254	286	124	450	117	103	121	125	113	125
Socorro (N. M.)	Piro		600	Abandoned in 1680; moved to Texas.													
Tajique	Tigua		300	Abandoned about 1675.													
Taos	Tigua	2,500	2,000	505	578	518	531	508	527	361	800	363	361	397	375	324	425
Tesuque	Tewa		200	232	138	138	155	131	160	119	700	97	101	98	125	94	100
Zuñi	Zuñi	10,000	2,500	664	1,617	1,935	2,716	1,470						1,530	1,500	1,547	1,514

a See Isleta.　b See Nambé.　c Probably includes San Cristóbal.　d See Pecos.　e Includes Tomé and Belen.　f Probably includes Cuyamunque and Jacona.
g Includes Galisteo.　h "Mexicanized."　i Established about 1700.　j Includes Santa Ana.　k Includes Spaniards.　l See Galisteo.

Puerto (Span.: 'gateway'). Mentioned by Oñate (Doc. Inéd., xvi, 114, 1871) in 1598 with a number of other Keresan and Tano pueblos of New Mexico, to one of which groups it doubtless belonged. See *Tuerto*.
Puerito.—Bandelier in Arch. Inst. Papers, iv, 97, 1892 (misprinted from Oñate).

Puguviliak. A Yuit Eskimo village at Southwest cape, St Lawrence id., Bering sea.
Poogooviliak.—Elliott, Our Arct. Prov., 457, 1886. Poogovellyak.—Ibid. Pugupiliak.—Baker, Geog. Dict. Alaska, 1902 (quoted as erroneous). Puguviliak.—Nelson in 18th Rep. B. A. E., map, 1899.

Puhksinahmahyiks ('flat bows'). A band of the Siksika, or Blackfeet.
Flat Bows.—Grinnell, Blackfoot Lodge Tales, 208, 1892. Puh-ksi-nah'-mah-yiks.—Ibid.

Puichon. A former village, presumably Costanoan, connected with Dolores mission, San Francisco, Cal.—Taylor in Cal. Farmer, Oct. 18, 1861.

Puimem (*pui* 'east', *měm* 'water': 'eastern water,' the local native name for Pit r.). A Wintun tribe formerly living on Pit r., Shasta co., Cal.
Pu'-i-mim.—Powers in Cont. N. A. Ethnol., iii, 230, 1877.

Puimuk (*pu-i* 'east', *mok* 'people': 'eastern people'). A Wintun tribe formerly occupying lower Elder and Thomes crs., Tehama co., Cal., and a strip of country on the e. side of Sacramento r. They were almost constantly at war with the Noamlaki, a highland tribe, and were finally forced by them to abandon their own country.
Pooemoos.—Powers in Overland Mo., xii, 581, 1874. Pu'-i-mok.—Powers in Cont. N. A. Ethnol., iii, 230, 1877.

Puisascamin. An unidentified tribe or band formerly in the neighborhood of Hudson bay or the upper lakes, trading with the French.—La Barre (1683) in N. Y. Doc. Col. Hist., ix, 798, 1855.

Puisu (Wintun: 'people living east'). A tribe or subtribe of the Shastan family (Curtin), or of mixed Copehan and Shastan (Powers), formerly living at the great bend of Pit r., in Shasta co., Cal. Curtin makes them a part of the Ilmawi tribe. According to Powers they were a mixed people resulting from intermarriage between the Wintun and Shastan tribes.
Madéqsi.—Curtin, Ilmawi vocab., B. A. E., 1889. Pooesoos.—Powers in Overland Mo., xii, 530, 1874. Pu'-i-su.—Powers in Cont. N. A. Ethnol., iii, 230, 1877. Pu'-shüsh.—Ibid.

Pujetung. A spring settlement of Kingua Okomiut Eskimo on an island in Cumberland sd., near the entrance to Nettilling fjord, Baffin land.—Boas in 6th Rep. B. A. E., map, 1888.

Pujunan Family. A linguistic family named by Powell (7th Rep. B. A. E., 99, 1891) from a former Nishinam settlement, properly called Pusune, between American and Sacramento rs., Cal. As the family includes only a single group, known as Maidu (q. v.), a description of the tribal group serves also for the family. The Maidu constitute one of the larger stocks of n. California and occupy the area e. and w. between Sacramento r. and the e. boundary of the state, and n. and s. from the vicinity of Lassen peak to the n. fork of the Cosumnes. Within this area three divisions of the Maidu may be recognized, a Northwestern, a Northeastern, and a Southern, each differing from the others to some degree in language and culture.

In all probability the Spaniards, during their occupancy of California, came in contact with representatives of the Maidu, but little has been recorded in regard to them. The first appearance of these people in literature dates practically from the time of the U. S. exploring expedition in 1838–1842, when the overland party traversed the entire Sacramento valley, coming in contact with the Maidu and with the other families of the region. The acquisition of California by the U. S. soon after this time, and the great impetus to immigration given by the discovery of gold, put an end to the isolation of the family, and, as the territory occupied by the Maidu lay in the heart of the mining district, led to their rapid decrease. A few were transferred at an early date to reservations nearer the coast, but to-day almost all the survivors are scattered through the sierra and foothills near the sites of their old homes.

In general culture the Maidu may be regarded as typical of the Indians of central California. Living in permanent villages they depended mainly on acorns, seeds, and other natural vegetal products for food, although fish and game, particularly in the mountains, formed a portion of their diet. Their dwellings were circular, conical-roofed lodges built of poles, bark, brush, and grass, and often covered, particularly in the Sacramento valley region, with a heavy layer of earth. The floor was sunk a foot or more in the ground, and access was by a door at one side, sometimes prolonged into a passageway, while a smoke hole at the top of the structure gave light and ventilation. Similar but larger structures served as dance or assembly houses. Their arts were few and simple. Where any method of navigation was employed, they made use of rude balsas, or of dugouts, propelled by poles. Bows and arrows were their chief weapons, although spears and slings were also used. In summer they wore little clothing, the men often going entirely naked. The men wore knitted net caps, the women basket caps. Carving and painting were unknown, and the chief means of expressing the esthetic sense was in basketry, in the manufacture of which the Maidu were very skilful, making baskets of several types and ornamenting them with many interesting designs. No trace of a clan system has been found among them, and their social organization seems to have been very loose. They were divided into many small village communities whose chiefs or headmen had little actual power. The dead were buried as a rule, although cremation was sometimes practised. The most notable feature of their religious beliefs and ceremonies was the autumnal "burning," or sacrifice of property to the dead, in which large offerings of all sorts of property were made by friends and relatives. They had also many dances, in which elaborate and costly feather headdresses were worn. The object of many of these dances was the increase of food animals. The mythology of the Maidu is rich, the most distinctive feature being a long and detailed creation myth. The present survivors of the Maidu probably number fewer than 500. Sixty years ago their number was doubtless considerable; a conservative estimate of the total population just previous to the gold rush would be 5,000 to 6,000. For the villages see *Maidu, Nishinam.* Consult Dixon, The Northern Maidu, Bull. Am. Mus. Nat. Hist., xvii, pt. 3, 1905.   (R. B. D.)

Pukwaawun. One of the principal villages of the Betonukeengainubejig Chippewa of w. Wisconsin, in 1850.
Pukwaawun.—Ramsey in Ind. Aff. Rep., 85, 1850. Puk-wa-wanuh.—Minn. Hist. Soc. Coll., v, 191, 1885.

Pulacuam. An unidentified tribe named in Massanet's list of tribes between central Coahuila and the Hasinai country of Texas in 1690. The tribes are given in geographical order in general, and the indication is that this one resided near the border between the Coahuiltecan and the Tonkawan groups, falling rather in the latter district (Velasco, Dictamen Fiscal, 1716, in Mem. de Nueva España, xxvii, 183, MS.). The only known tribe suggested by the name is the Sulujame, which was at San Antonio de Valero mission, Texas (Valero Bautismos, MS., passim.).   (H. E. B.)

Pulakatu (*Pu'-lak-a-tu*). A former Nishinam village in the valley of Bear r., which is the next stream N. of Sacramento, Cal.
Púlacatoo.—Powers in Overland Mo., xii, 22, 1874. Pú-lak-a-tu.—Powers in Cont. N. A. Ethnol., iii, 316, 1877.

Pumham (contraction of *Pumoham,* 'he goes by water.'—Gerard). A sachem of the region about Warwick, R. I. (Drake, Inds. of N. Am., 257, 1880), described by Hubbard as "one of the stoutest and most valiant sachems that belonged to the Narragansetts." It was in his country that the Rev. Samuel Gorton took refuge in 1642, to the displeasure of the authorities of Massachusetts. Pumham joined in King Philip's war, and his

town was burned by the English in 1675. He escaped in the defeat of the following year, but was soon afterward captured and slain.   (A. F. C.)

Pummy ('fish oil or grease'). A New England term. Used by Holman F. Day in Ainslee's Magazine (xiv, 81, 1904): "If that ain't porgy *pummy* I'm smellin'." From one of the Algonquian languages of the New England region, the derivation is seen from Massachuset *pummee,* Abnaki *pemi,* Lenape *pomih,* oil, fat, grease.   (A. F. C.)

Puna. The Cactus Fruit clan of the Chua (Snake) phratry of the Hopi.
Póna.—Voth, Trad. of Hopi, 34, 1905. Pü-nañ'-nyu-mû.—Fewkes in Am. Anthr., vi, 364, 1893 (*nyu-mû* = people, usually applied by this author to designate a phratry). Pü-na'wuñ-wü.—Fewkes in Am. Anthr., vii, 402, 1894 (*wuñ-wii* = clan). Pü'n-e.—Stephen in 8th Rep. B. A. E., 38, 1891.

Punames (Keresan: *Pu-na-ma,* 'people in the west,' referring to the western division of the Rio Grande branch of the Keresan stock). Mentioned by Espejo in 1583 as a province comprising 5 towns, of which Sia (q. v.) was the largest. In Hakluyt's version of Espejo's narrative the name is misprinted "Cunames," which in turn is corrupted into "Cuames" in Ogilby's America, 1671. Strangely enough these corrupted forms closely resemble the Keresan term *Cuame,* signifying 'people in the south,' but they bear no relation to that word. Santa Ana formed one of the other pueblos of the group. See Espejo in Doc. Inéd., xv, 115, 178, 1871; Bandelier in Arch. Inst. Papers, iv, 193, 1892.   (F. W. H.)
Cuames.—Ogilby, America, 291, 1671 (misprint). Cunames.—Whipple, Pac. R. R. Rep., iii, pt. 3, 114, 1856 (misquoting Hakluyt). Cunames.—Mendoça, Hist. of China (1586), in Hakluyt, Voy., iii, 461, 469, 1600 (after Espejo, 1583). Cunanes.—Dobbs, Hudson Bay, 163, 1744. Cuuames.—Purchas, Pilgrimes, v, 855, 1626. Pumames.—Espejo (1583) in Doc. Inéd., xv, 115, 1871. Punames.—Ibid., 178. Punanes.—Dobbs, op. cit. Purames.—Hinton, Handbook to Ariz., 387, 1878.

Punaryou (*Pun-ar'-you,* 'dog standing by the fireside'). A subclan of the Delawares.—Morgan, Anc. Soc., 172, 1877.

Pung. An old New England term for a rude sort of box sleigh, a cutter or jumper. Bartlett (Dict. of Americanisms, 504, 1877) cites one description of a pung: "Sledges, or pungs, coarsely framed of split saplings, and surmounted with a large crockery crate." Prof. W. F. Ganong (inf'n, 1903) states that *pung* is very much used now in New Brunswick, applied to box sleighs, especially of a rather good kind. The word is a reduction of *Tom Pung,* itself a corruption of *toboggan* (q. v.).   (A. F. C.)

Pungoteque (from *pungotekw,* 'sand-fly river.'—Gerard). A village of the Powhatan confederacy in Accomac co., Va., probably near Metomkin inlet. It was nearly extinct in 1722.

Pungoteque.—Beverley, Va., 199, 1722. **Punkotink.**—Herrman, map (1670) in Rep. on Bdy. Line between Va. and Md., 1873.

Punishment. See *Captives, Ordeals.*

Punk. See *Punkie.*

Punkapog (probably from *pankwapog*, 'shallow pond.'—Gerard). A former village of Praying Indians near Stoughton, Norfolk co., Mass. It was settled originally by some Indians who removed from Cohannet in 1654 and who numbered about 60 souls in 1674, and was one of the few Praying towns in existence after King Philip's war in 1675–76. A few Indians were still there in 1792.

Packemitt.—Gookin (1677) in Trans. Am. Antiq. Soc., II, 518, 1836. **Pakemit.**—Harris in Mass. Hist. Soc. Coll., IX, 160, 1804. **Pakemitt.**—Gookin (1674) in Mass. Hist. Soc. Coll., 1st s., I, 184, 1806. **Pakomit.**—Gookin, ibid., 435. **Pankapog.**—Gookin, ibid., 465. **Penkapog.**—Ibid. **Ponkipog.**—Eliot (1655) in Mass. Hist. Soc. Coll., 3d s., IV, 270, 1834. **Puncapaugs.**—Schoolcraft, Ind. Tribes, VI, 150, 1857. **Puncapoag.**—Hubbard (1680) in Mass. Hist. Soc. Coll., 2d s., VI, 544, 1815. **Punckapaug.**—Nicholson (1688) in N. Y. Doc. Col. Hist., III, 551, 1853. **Punkapoag.**—Gookin (1674) in Mass. Hist. Soc. Coll., 1st s., I, 148, 1806. **Punkapog.**—Gookin (1677) in Trans. Am. Antiq. Soc., II, 435, 1836. **Punkapoge.**—Walker (1671) in Mass. Hist. Soc. Coll., 1st s., VI, 198, 1800. **Punkepaog.**—Hoyt, Antiq. Res., 95, 1824. **Punkipaog.**—Cotton (1678) in Mass. Hist. Soc. Coll., 4th s., VIII, 245, 1868. **Punkipoag.**—Harris, ibid., 1st s., IX, 160, 1804. **Punkipog.**—Ibid. **Punkqu.**—Leverett (1677) in N. Y. Doc. Col. Hist., XIII, 514, 1881 (part illegible in MS.). **Punquapoag.**—Rawson (1675) quoted by Drake, Ind. Chron., 17, 1836. **Punquapog.**—Rawson (1675) in Trans. Am. Antiq. Soc., II, 451, 1836.

Punkie (also *punky, punk*). A minute gnat, called also sand-fly or midge (*Simulium nocivum*), the bite of which produces an intolerable itching and smarting sensation as if a spark of fire had dropped upon the naked skin. These winged atoms are, says Loskiel, "called by the [Lenape] Indians *ponk*, or 'living ashes,' from their being so small that they are hardly visible, and their bite as painful as the burning of red-hot ashes." Another species is the black fly, so well known as the scourge of travelers in the N., of which pest Sir Alexander Mackenzie remarks that "it is the most tormenting insect of its kind in nature." *Punky*, or *punkie*, is from the Dutch of New York and New Jersey *púnki*, pl. *púnkin*, from (by vocalic addition) Lenape *púnk* or *ponk*, short for *púnkus*, cognate with Chippewa *píngosh*, Cree *píkkus*, Abnaki *pĕkus*, etc., all names for the sand-fly, and from the root *púnkw, píngw, píkkw, pĕkw*, 'to be pulverulent,' 'asheslike.'	(w. r. g.)

Punonakanit. A Nauset village near Wellfleet, Barnstable co., Mass. Some Praying Indians were there in 1764.

Pononakanit.—Hist. of Eastham in Mass. Hist. Soc. Coll., 1st s., VIII, 159, 1802. **Punonakanit.**—Bourne (1764), ibid., I, 196, 1806.

Puntlatsh. A Salish tribe on Baynes sd. and Puntlatsh r., E. coast of Vancouver id. In 1893 they numbered 45; in 1896, the last time their name appears in the Canadian Reports on Indian Affairs, the "Punt-ledge, Sail-up-Sun, and Comox" numbered 69, since which time they have apparently been classed with the Comox. The Puntlatsh dialect embraces the Puntlatsh, Saamen, and Hwahwatl.	(J. R. S.)

P·E′ntlatc.—Boas in 5th Rep. N. W. Tribes Can., 10, 1889. **Puntlatsh.**—Tolmie and Dawson, Vocabs. Brit. Col., 119B, 1884. **Punt-ledge.**—Can. Ind. Aff. for 1893, 302, 1894.

Punuk. A Yuit Eskimo village on Punuk id., E. of St Lawrence id., Bering sea, Alaska.

Poonook.—Elliott, Our Arct. Prov., 443, 1886.

Punxsutawny (Lenape: *Punksuteney*, 'gnat town.'—Gerard). A former Delaware village under the jurisdiction of the Six Nations of New York; situated on Big Mahoning cr., in Jefferson co., Pa., in 1755. It was deserted in 1758.	(J. N. B. H.)

Eschentown.—Guss, Hist. Juniata and Susquehanna Val., chap. ii, 61, 1885. **Ponchestanning.**—Post, Jour. (1758), in Pa. Archives, III, 542, 1853. **Puncksotonay.**—Guss, op. cit.

Punyeestye (Keresan: 'place to the west on the bank of a stream'). Formerly a summer village of the Laguna Indians (q. v.), now a permanently inhabited pueblo of that tribe, situated 3 m. w. of Laguna, N. Mex.

Pun-yeest-ye.—Pradt quoted by Hodge in Am. Anthr., IV, 346, 1891. **Punyístyi.**—Hodge, field notes, B. A. E., 1895. **Santa Ana.**—Pradt, op. cit. (common Spanish name).

Puretuay. A former Tigua pueblo on the summit of the round mesa of Shiemtuai, or Mesa de las Padillas, 3 m. N. of Isleta, N. Mex. According to tradition it was abandoned on account of witchcraft before the Spanish discovery of New Mexico, part of the inhabitants moving N. W., the remainder settling at Isleta, where their descendants still dwell. According to Bandelier it probably formed one of the pueblos of the province of Tiguex, visited by Coronado in 1541. If this be the case it may be indentical with the Pura of Oñate in 1598.

Hyem Tu-ay.—Bandelier in Arch. Inst. Papers, III, 130, 1890; IV, 232, 1892 (probably a misprint of the name of the mesa). **Para.**—Columbus Mem. Vol., 155, 1893 (misprint of Oñate's Pura). **Poo-reh-tú-ai.**—Lummis, Man Who Married the Moon, 130, 1894. **Pura.**—Oñate (1598) in Doc. Inéd., XVI, 115, 1871 (probably identical). **Pur-e Tu-ay.**—Lummis quoted by Bandelier in Arch. Inst. Papers, IV, 232, 1892.

Purificación. A ranchería, probably Papago, 12 leagues from Agua Escondida, near the Arizona-Sonora boundary, probably in a S. E. direction; visited by Anza in 1774.—Anza quoted by Bancroft, Ariz. and N. Mex., 389, 1889.

Purísima Concepción. The eleventh Franciscan mission founded in California. Its establishment was postponed for the same reason as that of Santa Barbara, but on Dec. 8, 1787, the formal ceremonies were performed by Lasuen and the new mission dedicated to La Purísima Concepción. Owing to its being the rainy season the party returned to Santa Barbara and work was not begun until the spring. The site chosen, which was called by the natives Algsacupí, was near the present town of Lompoc, Santa Barbara co. There were numerous villages in this vicinity; the natives were intelligent and industrious, and within the following twenty years nearly all the population in the district had been baptized. In 1790 there were 234 neophytes; in 1800, 959, and in 1804, 1,522, the highest number reached. In live stock this was one of the most prosperous missions in California, having 10,015 large stock and 10,042 small stock in 1810. The average crop for the preceding decade was 3,300 bushels. Though the population decreased after 1804, numbering 1,297 in 1810, and 1,127 in 1820, the material prosperity increased till after the latter date, and the cattle continued to increase until after 1830, when 13,430 large stock were reported. The first church erected was a very crude structure, and in 1802 a better one, of adobe roofed with tile, was completed. This, together with most of the other buildings, was almost entirely destroyed by an earthquake in 1812. After this a new site, called Amun by the natives, 5 or 6 m. away on the other side of the river, was selected, and here a new church was built, being finished in 1818. In 1824 the neophytes, in conjunction with those at Santa Inés, revolted and took possession of the mission, but the fathers were not molested, and the soldiers and their families were allowed to retire; four white men and several Indians however were killed. An expedition was sent down from Monterey, and the Indians, who in the meantime had fortified themselves within the mission buildings, were attacked and forced to surrender, after a battle in which six of them were killed and a large number wounded. Several Indians were condemned to death for the killing of the white men, and others imprisoned or banished. The buildings were much damaged during the trouble, and in 1825 a new church was dedicated. Five years later there were 413 neophytes, and 407 in 1834. Up to that time the total number of baptisms was 3,232, of whom 1,492 were children. In 1844 the mission was reported as without property or agricultural land, but with a vineyard and about 200 neophytes. Most of these died of smallpox shortly afterward. In 1845 the mission was sold for $1,110. The buildings were deserted and allowed to decay, although a considerable portion of the walls is still standing. In 1905 the Landmarks Club acquired possession of the buildings and the immediate grounds, with the intention of preserving the church from further decay. The Indians of this neighborhood belonged to the Chumashan linguistic family (q. v.). See also *California Indians; Mission Indians of California; Missions.* (A. B. L.)

Purísima Concepción de Acuña. A Franciscan mission established in 1731 on San Antonio r., about 1 m. below the present San Antonio, Texas, under the protection of the presidio of San Antonio de Béjar. Prior to this time it was situated near Angelina r., in E. Texas, and was known as La Purísima Concepción de los Ainai (q. v.). Pop. 207 in 1762, the number of baptisms having been 792; it had also 600 cattle, 300 horses, and 2,200 sheep. In 1785 the population was only 71, and in 1793, 51. It ceased to exist as an independent mission before the close of the century. In 1785 it was said to have the best church in the province, being valued, with other property, at $35,000. See Bancroft, No. Mex. States, I, 1886; Garrison, Texas, 1903.

Purísima Concepción de los Ainai. A mission established in July 1716 among the Hasinai, near Angelina r., 9 leagues from San Francisco de los Neches, Texas. It was abandoned during the French-Spanish hostilities of 1719, when the mission property was destroyed by the Indians. In Aug. 1721 it was reestablished with 400 Indians, and new buildings were erected. It was transferred to San Antonio r. in 1731, becoming known as La Purísima Concepción de Acuña (q. v.). The designation of this mission as "Purísima Concepción de los Asinais" came from a miscopy of the word "Ainai" in Mem. de Nueva España, XXVII, fol. 163. See Bolton in Texas Hist. Quar., XI, no. 4, 259, note 5, 1908; Garrison, Texas, 50, 1903; and Bancroft cited below. (H. E. B.)

La Concepcion.—Bancroft, No. Mex. States, I, 614, 625, 1886. Purisima Concepcion.—Ibid., 614. Purisima Concepcion de los Asinais.—Mem. de Nueva España, XXVII, fol. 163, MS. compiled *ca.* 1791.

Purutea. A former village, presumably Costanoan, connected with Dolores mission, San Francisco, Cal.—Taylor in Cal. Farmer, Oct. 18, 1861.

Pushee Paho. See *Pashipaho.*

Pushmataha (*Apushim-alhtaha*, 'the sapling is ready, or finished, for him.'—Halbert). A noted Choctaw, of unknown ancestry, born on the E. bank of Noxuba cr. in Noxubee co., Miss., in 1764; died at Washington, D. C., Dec. 24, 1824. Before he was 20 years of age he distinguished himself in an expedition against the Osage, w. of the Mississippi. The boy disappeared early in a conflict that lasted all day, and on rejoining the Choctaw warriors was jeered at and accused of cowardice, whereon Pushmataha replied, "Let those laugh who can show more scalps than I can," forthwith producing five scalps, which he threw upon the ground—

the result of a single-handed onslaught on the enemy's rear. This incident gained for him the name "Eagle" and won for him a chieftaincy; later he became mingo of the Oklahannali or Six Towns district of the Choctaw, and exercised much influence in promoting friendly relations with the whites. Although generally victorious, Pushmataha's war party on one occasion was attacked by a number of Cherokee and defeated. He is said to have moved into the present Texas, then Spanish territory, where he lived several years, adding to his reputation for prowess, on one occasion going alone at night to a Tonaqua (Tawakoni?) village, killing seven men with his own hand, and setting fire to several houses. During the next two years he made three more expeditions against the same people, adding eight scalps to his trophies. When Tecumseh visited the Choctaw in 1811 to persuade them to join in an uprising against the Americans, Pushmataha strongly opposed the movement, and it was largely through his influence that the Shawnee chief's mission among this tribe failed. During the War of 1812 most of the Choctaw became friendly to the United States through the opposition of Pushmataha and John Pitchlynn to a neutral course, Pushmataha being alleged to have said, on the last day of a ten days' council: "The Creeks were once our friends. They have joined the English and we must now follow different trails. When our fathers took the hand of Washington, they told him the Choctaw would always be friends of his nation, and Pushmataha can not be false to their promises. I am now ready to fight against both the English and the Creeks." He was at the head of 500 warriors during the war, engaging in 24 fights and serving under Jackson's eye in the Pensacola campaign. In 1813, with about 150 Choctaw warriors, he joined Gen. Claiborne and distinguished himself in the attack and defeat of the Creeks under Weatherford at Kantchati, or Holy Ground, on Alabama r., Ala. While aiding the United States troops he was so rigid in his discipline that he soon succeeded in converting his wild warriors into efficient soldiers, while for his energy in fighting the Creeks and Seminole he became popularly known to the whites as "The Indian General." Pushmataha signed the treaties of Nov. 16, 1805; Oct. 24, 1816; and Oct. 18, 1820. In negotiating the last treaty, at Doak's Stand, "he displayed much diplomacy and showed a business capacity equal to that of Gen. Jackson, against whom he was pitted, in driving a sharp bargain." In 1824 he went to Washington to negotiate another treaty in behalf of his tribe. Following a brief visit to Lafayette, then at the capital, Pushmataha became ill and

died within 24 hours. In accordance with his request he was buried with military honors, a procession of 2,000 persons, military and civilian, accompanied by President Jackson, following his remains to Congressional Cemetery. A shaft bearing the following inscriptions was erected over his grave: "Pushmataha a Choctaw chief lies here. This monument to his memory is erected by his brother chiefs who were associated with him in a delegation from their nation, in the year 1824, to the General Government of the United States." "Push-ma-taha was a warrior of great distinction—He was wise in council—eloquent in an extraordinary degree, and on all occasions, and under all circumstances, the white man's friend." "He died in Washington, on the 24th of December, 1824, of the croup, in the 60th year of his age." General Jackson frequently expressed the opinion that Pushmataha was the greatest and the bravest Indian he had ever known, and John Randolph of Roanoke, in pronouncing a eulogy on him in the Senate, uttered the words regarding his wisdom, his eloquence, and his friendship for the whites that afterward were inscribed on his monument. There is good reason to believe, however, that much of Pushmataha's reputation for eloquence was due in no small part to his interpreters. He was deeply interested in the education of his people, and it is said devoted $2,000 of his annuity for fifteen years toward the support of the Choctaw school system. As mingo of the Oklahannali, Pushmataha was succeeded by Nittakechi, "Day-prolonger." Several portraits of Pushmataha are extant, including one in the Redwood Library at Newport, R. I., one in possession of Gov. McCurtin at Kinta, Okla. (which was formerly in the Choctaw capitol), and another in a Washington restaurant. The first portrait, painted by C. B. King at Washington in 1824, shortly before Pushmataha's death, was burned in the Smithsonian fire of 1865. Consult Lanman, Recollections of Curious Characters, 1881; McKenney and Hall, Indian Tribes, 1854; Halbert in Trans. Ala. Hist. Soc., ii, 107–119, 1898, and authorities therein cited; Lincecum in Pub. Miss. Hist. Soc., ix, 115, 1906.

Puskita. See *Busk*.

Pusune (*Pu-su′-ne*). A former Nishinam settlement near Barnard slough, between American and Sacramento rs., Cal. The name, in the form Pujunan (q. v.), was adopted by Powell for the family designation of the Maidu. (R. B. D.)

Poosoonas.—Powers in Overland Mo., xii, 22, 1874. Pujuni.—Hale, Ethnog. and Philol., 631, 1846. Punjuni.—Powell in Cont. N. A. Ethnol., iii, 587, 1877 (misprint). Pushune.—Sutter (1847) quoted by Bancroft, Nat. Races, i, 450, 1874. Pu-su′-na.—Powers in Cont. N. A. Ethnol., iii, 315, 1877. Pu-su′-ne.—R. B. Dixon, inf'n, 1905. Puzhune.—

Hale, op. cit., 222. **Puzlumne.**—Keane in Stanford, Compend., 532, 1878. **Tuzhune.**—Gallatin in Trans. Am. Ethnol. Soc., II, 20, 1848 (misprint).

Putaay. A former tribe, probably Coahuiltecan, met on the road from Coahuila to the Texas country.—Massanet (1690) in Dictamen Fiscal, Nov. 30, 1716, MS.

Putchamin, Putchimon. See *Persimmon*.

Putetemini ('sweat lip', 'upper lip'). A Yanktonai Sioux band of the Hunkpatina division, formerly occupying an earth-lodge village on James r., S. Dak. **Drifting Goose band.**—Hayes(1879)in Ind. Aff. Rep., 317, 1886 (named from chief). **Mag-a-bo-das.**—Ibid. **Maxa-bomdu.**—Dorsey in 15th Rep. B. A. E., 218, 1897 (='drifting goose').

Puukong. One of the War-god clans of the Hopi. **Püükoñ wiñwû.**—Fewkes in 19th Rep. B. A. E., 584, 1900 (*wiñ-wû*='clan').

Puuntthiwaun. A former Yaquina village on the s. side of Yaquina r., Oreg. **Pu'-un-t'çi-wa'-ŭn.**—Dorsey in Jour. Am. Folk-lore, III, 229, 1890.

Puyallup. An important Salish tribe on Puyallup r. and Commencement bay, w. Wash. According to Gibbs, their designation is the Nisqualli name for the mouth of Puyallup r., but Evans (Bancroft, Hist. Wash., 66, 1890) says the name means 'shadow,' from the dense shade of its forests. By treaty at Medicine creek, Wash., Dec. 26, 1854, the Puyallup and other tribes at the head of Puget sd. ceded their lands to the United States and agreed to go upon a reservation set apart for them on the sound near Shenahnam cr., Wash. In 1901 there were 536 on Puyallup res., Wash.; in 1909, 469. See *Niskap*. **Pee-allipaw-mich.**—Starling in Ind. Aff. Rep., 171, 1852. **Picanipalish.**—Schoolcraft, Ind. Tribes, VI, 688, 1857 (misprint). **Puallip.**—Lane in Ind. Aff. Rep., 162, 1850. **Puallipamish.**—Lane in Sen. Ex. Doc. 52, 31st Cong., 1st sess., 173, 1850. **Puallipaw-mish.**—Starling in Ind. Aff. Rep., 170, 1852. **Pualliss.**—Ibid. **Pugallipamish.**—Schoolcraft, Ind. Tribes, V, 701, 1855. **Pugallup.**—Sterrett in Sen. Ex. Doc. 26, 34th Cong., 1st sess., 65, 1856 (misprint). **Puiâle.**—Hale in U. S. Expl. Exped., v, 221, 1846. **Puyallop.**—Ford in H. R. Ex. Doc. 37, 34th Cong., 3d sess., 94, 1857. **Puyallup.**—Treaty of 1854 in U. S. Indian Treaties, 561, 1873. **Puyallupahmish.**—Gibbs in Cont. N. A. Ethnol., I, 178, 1877. **Pu-yallup-a-mish.**—Gibbs in Pac. R. R. Rep., I, 435, 1855. **Puyalûp.**—Mooney in 14th Rep. B. A. E., pl. lxxxviii, 1896.

Puycone. A former village, presumably Costanoan, connected with Dolores mission, San Francisco, Cal.—Taylor in Cal. Farmer, Oct. 18, 1861.

Puye (Tewa: *Pu-ye'*, 'assembling place of cottontail rabbits.'—J. P. Harrington). A large ruined pueblo of worked blocks of tufa on a mesa about 10 m. w. of the Rio Grande and a mile s. of Santa Clara canyon, near the intersection of the boundaries of Rio Arriba, Sandoval, and Santa Fé cos., N. Mex. Along the southern face of the mesa, extending for many hundreds of yards, is a series of cliff-dwellings or cavate lodges excavated in the tufa, and formerly provided with porches or shelters, the roof-beams of which were set in holes in the wall of the cliff. The pueblo and the cliff-dwellings are attributed to certain clans of the Tewa, and the cliff-dwellings have been occupied in part at least during the historical period, although they are doubtless of prehistoric origin. See 7th Rep. B. A. E., xxiv, 1891; Bandelier (1) Delight Makers, 377, 1890, (2) in Arch. Inst. Papers, IV, 67, 1892; Hewett (1) in Am. Anthr., VI, 649, 1904, (2) in Bull. 32, B. A. E., 1906, (3) in Out West, XXXI, 693, 1909. See *Shufinne*.

Pygmies. See *Popular Fallacies*.

Pyquaug (from *pauqui-auke*, 'clear land,' 'open country.'—Trumbull). A former village, subject to the Mattabesec, near Wethersfield, Conn. **Panquiaug.**—Hoyt, Antiq. Res., 41, 1824 (misprint). **Pauquiaug.**—Hubbard (1680) in Mass. Hist. Soc. Coll., 2d s., VI, 307, 1815. **Pauquog.**—Kendall, Trav., I, 84, 1809. **Pequeag.**—Ibid. **Piquag.**—Field, Middlesex Co., 35, 1819. **Piquaug.**—Kendall, op. cit., 84. **Piquiag.**—Ibid. **Pyquaag.**—Doc. cited by Trumbull, Ind. Names Conn., 44, 1881. **Pyquag.**—Ibid. **Pyquaug.**—Trumbull, Conn., I, 40, 1818. **Weathersfield Indians.**—Field, Middlesex Co., 35, 1819.

Pyrite, or Iron pyrites. The glistening yellow crystals of disulphid of iron, sometimes called "fool's gold," occurring plentifully in many sections of the country. The crystals, which present a handsome appearance, were occasionally employed by the Indians for ornaments and amulets, and are found now and then in the kit of the medicine-man. They were also used in connection with stone as strike-a-lights. See *Iron*. (w. h. h.)

Pythagoreans. A name applied by Lahontan to certain Indians he claimed to have met on his "Long" r. Probably imaginary, although Barcia refers to them apparently in good faith. **Pitagoriciens.**—Lahontan, Nouv. Voy., I, 158, 1703 (French form). **Pitagoricos.**—Barcia, Ensayo, 292, 1723 (Span. form). **Pythagoreans.**—Lahontan, New Voy., I, 121, 1703.

Qailertetang (*Khai-ler-te'-tang*). Amazons of Central Eskimo mythology. They have no men among them, but masked figures of them mate the couples in a Saturnalian festival.—Boas in 6th Rep. B. A. E., 605, 640, 1888.

Qanikilak (*Q'ānikīlaq*). An ancestor of a Nakomgilisala gens, after whom the gens itself was sometimes called.—Boas in Petermanns Mitt., pt. 5, 131, 1887.

Quabaug (said to be contracted from *Msquabaug*, or *Msquapaug*, 'red (or bloody) pond'). A tribe or band, probably of the Nipmuc group, formerly living in Worcester co., Mass. Their principal village, near the site of Brookfield, bore their name. They joined the revolt under King Philip in 1675, abandoned their territory, and never returned. **Quabaag.**—Pynchon (1700) in N. Y. Doc. Col. Hist., IV, 616, 1854. **Quabaconk.**—Writer (*ca.* 1661) quoted by Drake, Bk. Inds., bk. 2, 98, 1848. **Quabage.**—Gookin (1677) in Trans. Am. Antiq. Soc., II, 450, 1836.

Quabagud.—Eliot (1651) in Mass. Hist. Soc. Coll., 3d s., IV, 125, 1834. **Quabakutt.**—Record of 1661 quoted by Drake, Bk. Inds., bk. 2, 100, 1848. **Quabaog.**—Writer of 1676 quoted by Drake, Ind. Chron., 54, 1836. **Quabâquick.**—Dunster (*ca.* 1648) in Mass. Hist. Soc. Coll., 4th s., I, 252, 1852. **Quabaugs.**—Gookin (1674), ibid., 1st s., I, 160, 1806. **Quabauk.**—Mason (1661) quoted by Drake, Bk. Inds., bk. 2, 100, 1848. **Quaboag.**—Drake, Ind. Chron., 129, 1836. **Quaboagh.**—Cortland (1688) in N. Y. Doc. Col. Hist., III, 562, 1853. **Quabog.**—Drake, Ind. Chron., 59, 1836. **Quaboug.**—Writer of 1676 quoted by Drake, ibid., 126. **Quawbaug.**—Leete (1675) in Mass. Hist. Soc. Coll., 4th s., VII, 576, 1865. **Quawbawg.**—Writer of 1675 quoted by Drake, Ind. Chron., 19, 1836. **Quawpaug.**—Williams (1675) in Mass. Hist. Soc. Coll., 4th s., VI, 310, 1863. **Quebaug.**—Hinckley (1676), ibid., v, 1, 1852. **Quoboag.**—Hutchinson (*ca.* 1680), ibid., 1st s., I, 260, 1806. **Quoboge.**—Ibid., 77. **Squabage.**—Temple quoted by Kinnicutt, Ind. Names, 39, 1905. **Squabang.**—Moll, map, in Humphreys, Acct., 1730 (misprint). **Squabaug.**—Temple, op. cit. **Squabauge.**—Ibid. **Squaboag.**—Paine (*ca.* 1792) in Mass. Hist. Soc. Coll., 1st s., I, 115, 1806. **Squabog.**—Nicholson (1688) in N. Y. Doc. Col. Hist., III, 552, 1853. **Squapauke.**—Temple quoted by Kinnicutt, Ind. Names, 39, 1905. **Wabaage.**—Gookin (1677) in Trans. Am. Antiq. Soc., II, 467, 1836.

Quackcohowaon. A village of the Powhatan confederacy in 1608, on the s. bank of Mattapony r., in King William co., Va.—Smith (1629), Va., I, map, repr. 1819.

Quacoshatchee. A former Cherokee settlement in the N. w. part of Pickens co., S. C.; destroyed during the Revolutionary war.
Quacoratchie.—Royce in 18th Rep. B. A. E., pl. clxi, 1899. **Quacoretche.**—Mouzon's map (1771) quoted by Royce in 5th Rep. B. A. E., 143, 1887.

Quahatika. A small Piman tribe, closely allied to the Pima, of whom they are an offshoot and with whom they still intermarry to some extent. They live in the desert of s. Arizona 50 m. s. of the Gila r., speak a dialect slightly different from that of the Pima, and subsist by agriculture. They manufacture better pottery than that of their congeners, and are said to have introduced cattle among the Pima from the Mexicans about 1820. They formerly made arrows of yucca stalks which they bartered to their neighbors. It is said that about the beginning of the 18th century the Quahatika occupied with the Pima the village of Aquitun (*Akuchini*, 'creek mouth'), w. of Picacho, on the border of the sink of Santa Cruz r., but abandoned it about 1800. Their chief settlement is Quijotoa.
Kohátk.—Curtis, Am. Ind., II, 112, 1908 (Papago name). **Kwahadk'.**—Russell in 26th Rep. B. A. E., passim, 1908. **Kwohatk.**—Hrdlička in Am. Anthr., VIII, 39, 1906 (proper name, originally the name of their village). **Qahatika.**—Curtis, op. cit. **Quarities.**—Hrdlička, op. cit. (local name).

Quahaug. See *Quahog.*

Quahmsit. A village, probably Nipmuc, perhaps identical with Quantisset, whose warriors were with other hostile Indians in 1675 at Manexit, N. E. Conn.—Quanapaug (1675) in Mass. Hist. Soc. Coll., 1st s., VI, 205, 1800.

Quahog. A name in use in New England for the round or hard clam (*Venus mercenaria*); spelt also *quahaug*. This word is probably a reduction of *poquaû-*

hock in the Narraganset, the same as *poquahoc* in the Massachuset dialect of Algonquian, the Indian name for this shellfish. The last half of the word has survived in English, while in Nantucket the first part has come down as *pooquaw.* The word appears also as *cohog*, and even in the truncated form *hog.* As a place name it appears in Quogue, a village in Suffolk co., N. Y.   (A. F. C.)

Quaiapen. See *Magnus.*

Quaitso. A Salish division on the coast of Washington, N. of the Quinaielt, of which tribe they are probably a part. In the time of Lewis and Clark (1806) they numbered 250, in 18 houses. In 1909 there were 62, under the Puyallup school superintendency, Wash.
Kéh-chen-wilt.—Gibbs, MS. no. 248, B. A. E. (Makah name). **Kweet.**—Ind. Aff. Rep., 254, 1877. **Kwéhts-hū.**—Gibbs, op. cit. **Kwetso.**—Mooney in 14th Rep. B. A. E., pl. lxxxviii, 1896. **Lóh-whilse.**—Gibbs, op. cit. (Makah name). **Quai'tso.**—Swan, N. W. Coast, 211, 1857. **Queets.**—Simmons in Ind. Aff. Rep., 233, 1858. **Queet-see.**—Ind. Aff. Rep., 180, 1907 (alternative form). **Quehts.**—Ford in Ind. Aff. Rep. 1857, 341, 1858. **Quieetsos.**—Lewis and Clark Exped., II, 474, 1814. **Quits.**—Ind. Aff. Rep., 61, 1872. **Quoitesos.**—Kelley, Oregon 68, 1830.

Quakers. See *English influence.*

Qualacu. Mentioned by Oñate in 1598 as the second pueblo of the province of Atripuy (q. v.), traveling northward. It was the most southerly of the Piro settlements on the E. bank of the Rio Grande, being situated near the foot of the Black mesa, on or near the site of San Marcial, N. Mex. Trenaquel was the most southerly of the Piro villages on the w. bank of the river. Consult Oñate (1598) in Doc. Inéd., XVI, 115, 250, 1871; Bandelier in Arch. Inst. Papers, III, 131, 1890; IV, 252, 1892.   (F. W. H.)

Qualatchee (correct form unknown). A former Cherokee town on the headwaters of Chattahoochee r., Ga. Another settlement of the same name was situated on Keowee r., S. C.—Mooney in 19th Rep. B. A. E., 529, 1900.
Qualatche.—Bartram, Travels, 372, 1792 (given as on Flint r.).

Qualla (*Kwa'lĭ*, Cherokee pronunciation of "Polly", from an old woman who formerly lived near by). The former agency of the East Cherokee and now a P. O. station, just outside the reservation, on a branch of Soco cr., in Jackson co., N. C.—Mooney in 19th Rep. B. A. E., 526, 1900.
Kwalûñ'yĭ.—Mooney, op. cit. (='Polly's place'). **Quallatown.**—Ibid.

Quamash. See *Camas.*

Quamichan. A Salish tribe in Cowitchin valley, s. E. Vancouver id., speaking the Cowichan dialect; pop. 300 in 1901, 260 in 1909.
Kwaw-ma-chin.—Can. Ind. Aff., 308, 1879. **Quamichan.**—Ibid., pt. II, 164, 1901. **Xuámitsan.**—Boas, MS., B. A. E., 1887.

Quamish. See *Camas.*

Quana. See *Parker, Quana.*

Quananchit. See *Nanuntenoo.*

Quanataguo. The tribal name given in 1728 for an Indian woman at San Antonio de Valero mission, Texas. The only clue to her tribe's affiliation is that she was married to a Pazac or a Patzau (Valero Entierros, 1728, part. 87, MS.) (H. E. B.)

Quanaukaunt. See *Quinney.*

Quane. Given by Kane (Wand. in N. A., app., 1859) as the name of a tribe at C. Scott, N. w. end of Vancouver id., but Boas explains it as merely the native name for the cape. The people included under the designation, said to number 260, must have been part of the Nakomgilisala. (J. R. S.)

Quanmugua. A Chumashan village w. of Pueblo de las Canoas (San Buenaventura), Ventura co., Cal., in 1542. In the Muñoz MS. this name is given, but in the Cabrillo narration (Smith, Colec. Doc. Fla., 181, 1857) the name is divided, probably erroneously, and stands for two towns, Quanmu and Gua.

Quanquiz. Mentioned by Oñate as a pueblo of New Mexico in 1598. It was doubtless situated in the Salinas, in the vicinity of Abó, E. of the Rio Grande, and in all probability belonged to the Tigua or the Piro.
Quanquiz.—Oñate (1598) in Doc. Inéd., XVI, 113, 1871. Zuanquiz.—Columbus Mem. Vol., 154, 1893 (misprint).

Quantisset. A Nipmuc village, about 1675, on Thompson hill, Quinebaug r., near Thompson, Windham co., Conn. The ruins of an "old Indian fort" stood on this hill in 1727.
Quanatusset.—Tooker, Algonq. Ser., X, 41, 1901. Quantisick.—Quanapaug (1675) in Mass. Hist. Soc. Coll., 1st s., VI, 207, 1800. Quantisset.—Gookin (1674), ibid., I, 190, 1806. Quánutusset.—Eliot quoted by Trumbull, Ind. Names Conn., 61, 1881. Quatiske.—Mass. Rec. quoted by Trumbull, ibid. Quatissik.—Ibid. Quinetus'set.—Trumbull, ibid., 61, 1881.

Quapa. A former Gabrieleño village in Encino or San Fernando valley, Los Angeles co., Cal.—Padre Santa María (1796) cited by Bancroft, Hist. Cal., I, 553, 1886.

Quapaw (from *Ugákhpa*, 'downstream people'). A southwestern Siouan tribe, forming one of the two divisions of the Dhegiha group of Dorsey. At the time of separation the Quapaw are supposed to have gone down the Mississippi, and the Omaha group, including the Omaha, Kansa, Ponca, and Osage, up the Missouri. There is undoubtedly a close linguistic and ethnic relation between the Quapaw and the other four tribes. The recorded history of this tribe is commonly supposed to begin with the chronicles of De Soto's expedition (1539–43). In the relation of the Gentleman of Elvas and that of Biedma, they or their chief band are mentioned under the name Pacaha, and in that by Garcilasso de la Vega under the name Capaha, the latter being nearer the true pronunciation, though the author wrote only from information and manuscripts furnished, while the former two were members of the expedition. The people of the tribe, or rather of one portion or division of it, were found in a strongly fortified village, which one of the chroniclers, probably with some exaggeration, describes as "very great, walled, and beset with towers." He adds: "Many loopholes were in the towers and wall . . . a great lake came near unto the wall, and it entered into a ditch that went round about the town, wanting but little to environ it around. From the lake to the great river [Mississippi] was made a weir by which the fish came into it" (French, Hist. Coll. La., pt. 2, 172,

QUAPAW MAN

1850). He further says: "And in the town was great store of old maize and great quantity of new in the fields [the date was June 19]. Within a league were great towns, all walled." Their village was on the w. bank of the Mississippi, N. of Arkansas r., within the limits of the present Arkansas, probably in Phillips co. There are archeological remains and local conditions in this county which suit exactly the description of Pacaha: the lake on one side, Mississippi r. on the other, the connecting channel, and the island near by. There is, it is true, a locality in Crittenden co. where the ancient works, lake, channel, river, and island are all found, but this locality does not agree so well with the narration. The statement by early French explorers, who found them below the mouth of St Francis r., that they had removed from their old town, where the outworks were still to be seen, a short distance to the N., indicates that they had been in that region for many years. Their traditional history seems to have a substantial basis. Father Gravier, in the description of his voyage down the Mississippi in 1700, remarks (Shea's trans., 120, 1861) that Wabash and lower Ohio rs. were called by the Illinois and Miami the river of the Akansea (Quapaw), because the Akansea formerly dwelt on their banks. Three branches were assigned to it, one of them coming from the N. W. and passing behind the country of the Miami, called the river St Joseph, "which the Indians call properly Ouabachci." The Quapaw

QUAPAW WOMAN

are known historically and from other evidence to have been mound builders, and also builders of mounds of a given type. A mound group containing mounds of this type is found in s. w. Indiana on the Ohio near its junction with the Wabash; and further, there is a map of the War Department showing the territory claimed by the Quapaw, which borders the Ohio from this point downward. Dorsey found traditions among the tribes composing his Dhegiha group asserting a former residence E. of the Mississippi, and the separation of the Quapaw from the other tribes, apparently in s. Illinois, the former going down the Mississippi and the other tribes up Missouri r., whence the names Quapaw (*Ugákhpa*), 'those going downstream or with the current,' and

Omaha, 'those going upstream or against the current.' Whether the Akansea of the tradition include also the other tribes of the Dhegiha is uncertain.

It was not until about 130 years after De Soto's visit, when the French began to venture down the Mississippi, that the Quapaw again appear in history, and then under the name Akansea. The first French explorer who reached their country was the missionary Marquette, who arrived at the village of the Akansea in June 1673, accompanied by Joliet. On his autograph map (Shea, Discov. and Expl. Miss., 1852) the name Papikaha, apparently on Arkansas r. some distance above its mouth, is a form of Quapaw; but Akansea, on the E. bank of the Mississippi, apparently opposite the mouth of the Arkansas, must have been another Quapaw village, not the one visited by Marquette, which was on the opposite side, as Gravier found them on the w. side and said that he "cabined a league lower down, half a league from the old village of the Akansea, where they formerly received the late Father Marquette, and which is discernible now only by the old outworks, there being no cabins left" (Shea, Early Voy., 126, 1861). Biedma, one of the chroniclers of De Soto's expedition, says that a village on the E. bank was tributary "like many others" to the sovereign of Pacaha. La Salle (1682) found three villages of the tribe along the Mississippi r., one on the w. bank, the next 8 leagues below on the E. bank, and another 6 leagues below on the w. bank at the mouth of the Arkansas r. This order is given in describing the descent and ascent of the stream. Tonti mentions as Akansea villages Kappa on the Mississippi, and Toyengan, Toriman, and Osotony inland (French, Hist. Coll. La., I, 60, 1846). La Métairie, La Salle's notary, in his expedition down the Mississippi in 1682, mentions the Akansea villages as follows: "On the 12th of March we arrived at the Kapaha village, on the Arkansas. Having established a peace there and taken possession, we passed on the 15th another of their villages situated on the border of their river, and also two others farther off in the depth of the forest, and arrived at that of Imaha, the largest village of this nation" (French, Hist. Coll. La., 2d s., II, 21, 1875). In July, 1687, 2 of their villages were, according to Joutel, on Arkansas r., the others being on the Mississippi. St Cosme, who descended the Mississippi with Tonti in 1698, found the tribe, or at least 2 of the villages, decimated by war and smallpox, the disease having destroyed "all the children and a great part of the women." He estimated the men of the 2 villages at 100. De l'Isle's map of 1700 places the Acansa village on the s. side of Arkansas r. Gravier (1700) locates the village of Kappa on the Mississippi half a league from the water's edge and 8 leagues above the mouth of the Arkansas. Tourima seems to have been close by. Gravier says: "The Sitteoui Akansea are five leagues above its [the Arkansas'] mouth and are much more numerous than the Kappa and Tourima; these are the three villages of the Akansea." A document of 1721 (N. Y. Doc. Col. Hist., v, 622, 1855) says, on what authority is unknown, that the "Acansa" who were on the E. side of the Mississippi, as has been noted above, differed from the "Acansia" who dwelt on the w. side. Nuttall says the people called Arkansa by Charlevoix were then (1761) made up of confederated remnants of ruined tribes.

At the time Le Page Dupratz visited that section, a few years later, it seems the Akansea had retired up the Arkansas r. and were living about 12 m. from the entrance of White r., and had been joined by the Michigamea and some Illinois. Sibley (1805) states that the Arkensa were then in 3 villages on the s. side of Arkansas r. about 12 m. above Arkansas Post. They claimed to be the original proprietors of the country on Arkansas r., extending up it about 300 m. to the Osage country. According to a Mexican document there were 150 families on Sulfur cr., a southern affluent of Red r. of Texas, in 1828. Porter in 1829 said they were then in the Caddo country on Red r. in Louisiana. In 1877 they were on their reservation in the N. E. corner of Indian Ter., and in that year the Ponca tribe was brought on their reservation for a short time, being removed to the present Ponca res., w. of the Osage, in 1878. Most of the Quapaw soon left their reservation and removed to that of the Osage.

On account of the great change wrought in the condition of these Indians by contact with the whites, their true character and customs can be learned only by reference to the accounts of the early explorers. Father Zenobius (Le Clercq, Estab. Faith, Shea ed., 2, 168, 1881) says: "These Indians do not resemble those at the north, who are all of a morose and stern disposition; these are better made, civil, liberal, and of a gay humor." Joutel says they are strong, well made, and active; "the females better made than those of the last village [Cahinnio?] we passed." That the people had made considerable advance in culture is evident from the accounts given of their structures; as, for example, the walled village described above. They also built large mounds—the height of one is given as 40 feet—on which they placed, in some instances, their chief buildings. Joutel (Margry, Déc., III, 442, 1878) mentions a house "built on a place a little elevated [mound]," of great pieces of wood jointed one with another dovetailed to the top, of beautiful cedar (cedre) wood (cypress?), and covered with bark. Their village houses he describes as long, with "domed" roofs, each containing several families. Mention is made of a fish weir near one of their villages, in an artificial canal, and of nets which De Soto's followers utilized on their arrival for procuring a supply of fish. The Akansea were active tillers of the soil, and also manufacturers of pottery, many of the finest specimens taken from the mounds of E. Arkansas in all probability having been made by this tribe. Their drum was made by stretching skin over a large pottery vessel. Du Poisson (1727) speaks of their painted designs on skins. A matachee, he says, "is a skin painted by the Indians with different colors, and on which they paint calumets, birds, and animals. Those of the deer serve as cloths for the table, and those of the buffalo as coverings for the bed." The same author describes their dress of ceremony as "well matché, that is having the body entirely painted of different colors, with the tails of wildcats hanging down from places where we usually represent the wings of Mercury, the calumet in their hands, and on their bodies some little bells" (Kip, Early Miss., 258, 1866). Their method of disposing of their dead was by burial, often in the floor of their houses, though usually they were deposited in graves, sometimes in mounds; sometimes the body was strapped to a stake in a sitting position and then carefully covered with clay. Though polygamy was practised to some extent, it was not common.

The population of the Quapaw at the time of De Soto's visit in 1541 must have been considerable, as the number of those of the village of Pacaha, who fled to the island on the approach of the Spaniards, is given as 5,000 or 6,000. Father Vivier (1750) speaks of the "Akansas" as "an Indian tribe of about 400 warriors," equaling 1,400 to 1,600 souls (Kip, Early Miss., 318, 1866). Porter (Schoolcraft, Ind. Tribes), gives 500 as their number in 1829. In 1843 they numbered 476. In 1885 there were 120 on the Osage res. and 54 on the Quapaw res.; and in 1890 the total number on both reservations was given as 198. The population in 1909, including all mixed-bloods, was 305, all under the Seneca School superintendency, Okla.

The following are the gentes of the Quapaw as obtained by J. O. Dorsey: Zhawe (beaver), Wazhingka (small bird), Wasa (black bear), Te (buffalo), Petang (crane), Nanpanta (deer), Shangke (dog),

Khidh (eagle), Anpan (elk), Hu (fish), Mantu (grizzly bear), Hangka (ancestral), Tangdhangtanka (panther), Wesa (snake), Mikakh (star), Mi (sun), Tukhe (reddish yellow buffalo), Wakanta (thunder-being), Ke (turtle), Nikiata (meaning unknown), Tizhu (meaning unknown), Makhe (upper world). Other subdivisions are: Grands Akansas, Epiminguia, Ozark, Petits Acansas, and possibly the Casqui.

The Quapaw participated in the following treaties with the United States: St Louis, Aug. 24, 1818; Harrington's, Ark., Aug. 15, 1824; at an unnamed locality, May 13, 1833; Camp Holmes, Ind. Ter., Aug. 24, 1835; Washington, Feb. 23, 1867.

The Quapaw villages were Imaha, Tongigua, Tourima, Ukakhpakhti, and Uzutiuhi, but it is probable that Imaha and Tourima were identical.   (C. T.)

Acansa.—La Salle (1680) in Hist. Mag., 1st s., v, 197, 1861. Acansas.—Joutel (1687) in Margry, Déc., IV, 121, 1880. Acansea.—Gravier (1700) in Shea, Early Voyages, 131, 1861. Acanseas.—St Cosme (1699) in Shea, Early Voyages, 65, 1861. Acansias.—Lond. Doc. XXII (1721) in N. Y. Doc. Col. Hist., v, 622, 1855. Accanceas.—Joutel (1687) in French, Hist. Coll. La., I, 176, 1846. Accances.—Bacqueville de la Potherie, Hist. Amérique, II, 222, 1753. Akama.—Carte de Taillée des Poss. Angl., 1777. Akamsca.—Hennepin, New Discov., II, 345, 1698. Akamsea.—Shea, Discov., 254, 1852. Akamsians.—Boudinot, Star in the West, 125, 1816. Akancas.—French, Hist. Coll. La., I, 60, 1846. Akanças.—N. Y. Doc. Col. Hist., IX, 623, 1855. A Kansea.—Bacqueville de la Potherie, Hist. Amérique, I, map, 1753. Akanceas.—Barcia, Ensayo, 265, 1723. Akansa.—Hennepin, Descr. La. (1683), Shea's trans., 186, 1880. Akansaes.—Coxe, Carolana, 11, 1741. Akansas.—Métairie (1682) in French, Hist. Coll. La., II, 21, 1875. Akanscas.—St Cosme (1699) in Shea, Early Voy., 47, 1861. Akansea.—Marquette, map (1673) in Shea, Discov., 1852. Akansis.—D'Anville, Carte Amérique Septentrionalis, 1756. Akanssa.—Hennepin, New Discov., map, 1698 (river). Akanzas.—Bossu, (1751), Trav. La., 70, 1771. Akensas.—Lettres Édifiantes, I, 745, 755, 1838. Akinsaws.—Trumbull, Ind. Wars, 185, 1851. Alkansas.—La Harpe (1720) in Margry, Déc., VI, 241, 1886. Aquahpa.—Adair, Am. Inds., 269, 1775. Aquahpah.—Ibid., 320. A-qua-pas.—Hadley, Quapaw vocab., B. A. E., 1882. Arcanças.—Dumont, La., I, 134, 1753. Arcansa.—Sibley, Hist. Sketches, 138, 1806. Arc Indians.—Schoolcraft, Ind. Tribes, III, 537, 1853. Arkansas.—Pénicaut, Rel. (1700) in Margry, Déc., v, 402, 1883. Arkansaws.—Pike, Trav., 173, 1811. Arkansea.—Baldwin in Am. Antiq., I, no. 4, 237, note, 1879 (misprint). Arkanses.—French trader in Smith, Bouquet Exped., 70, 1766. Arkanzas.—Jefferson, Notes, 141, 1825. Arkensas.—Sibley (1805), Hist. Sketches, 85, 1806. Arkensaw.—Schermerhorn in Mass. Hist. Soc. Coll., II, 23, 1814. Arkensea.—Baldwin in Am. Antiq., I, no. 4, 237, note, 1879. Atcansas.—La Harpe (1720) in Margry, Déc., VI, 311, 1886. Beaux Hommes.—Gallatin in Trans. Am. Antiq. Soc., II, 130, 1836 (French name). Bow Indians.—Schoolcraft, Ind. Tribes, III, 537, 1853. Canceas.—N. Y. Doc. Col. Hist., IX, 673, 1855. Capa.—Barcia, Ensayo, 279, 1723. Capaha.—Garcilasso de la Vega, Florida, 181, 1723. Cappas.—Pénicaut (1700) in French, Hist. Coll. La., I, 62, 1869. Copatta.—Rafinesque in Marshall, Ky., I, introd., 28, 1824. Cuapas.—Bol. Soc. Geog. Mex., 268, 1870. Enansa.—Tonti (1684) in Margry, Déc., I, 599, 1876. Gappa.—H. R. Ex. Doc. 43, 19th Cong., 2d sess., 8, 1827. Gnapaws.—Keane in Stanford, Compend., 513, 1878. Handsome Men.—Jefferys, French Dom., I, 144, 1761. I'ma.—Gatschet, Caddo and Yatassi

MS., B. A. E., 82 (Caddo name). Imahans.—La Harpe (1718) in Margry, Déc., VI, 261, 1886. Inapaw.—Hayden, Ethnog. and Philol. Mo. Val., 447, 1862 (misprint). Ká'hpagi.—Gatschet, Shawnee MS., B. A. E., 1885. Kapaha.—Le Métairie (1682) in French, Hist. Coll. La., 2d s., pt. 2, 21, 1875. Kapahas.—Schoolcraft, Ind. Tribes, IV, 310, 1854. Kapas.—Le Page Dupratz, Hist. La., map, 1757. Kappa Akansea.—Gravier (1700) in Shea, Early Voy., 125, 1861. Kappas.—Tonti (1688) in French, Hist. Coll. La., I, 71, 1846. Kappaws.—Lynd in Minn. Hist. Soc. Coll., II, pt. 2, 58, 1864. Kappawson-Arkansas.—Ann. de la Propag. de la Foi, II, 380, 1841 (misprint of "Kappaws on Arkansas"). Kiapaha.—Schoolcraft, Ind. Tribes, VI, 66, 1857. Kwapa.—Powell in 1st Rep. B. A. E., xvii, 1881. Kwapa Ǫegiha.—Dorsey in 3d Rep. B. A. E., 211, 1885. Kwapa-Dhegiha.—Am. Naturalist, 829, Oct. 1882. Ocansa.—Hennepin, New Discov., 310, 1698 (erroneously called a part of the Illinois). Ocapa.—Sibley, Hist. Sketches, 85, 1806. O-ga-pa.—Hadley, Quapaw vocab., B. A. E., 1882. Ogoh pæ.—Fontenelle in Trans. Neb. State Hist. Soc., I, 77, 1885. O-guah-pah.—Balbi, Atlas Ethnog., 56, 1826. O-guah-pas.—Nuttall, Jour., 81, 1821. Oguapas.—Shea, Discov., 170, note, 1852. Onyapes.—McKenney and Hall, Ind. Tribes, III, 81, 1854. Oo-gwapes.—Shea, Cath. Missions, 447, note, 1855. Oo-yapes.—Ibid. O-qua-pas.—Gale, Upper Miss., 202, 1867. Oquapasos.—Bollaert in Jour. Ethnol. Soc. Lond., II, 282, 1850. Ougapa.—French, Hist. Coll. La., III, 107, 1851. Ouguapas.—Shea, Cath. Miss., 449, 1855. Oupapa.—Harris, Coll. Voy. and Trav., I, 685, map, 1705 (prob. misprint for Oucapa or Ougapa). Ouyapes.—Charlevoix, Voy. to Am., II, 249, 1761. Ouyapez.—Jefferys (1765), Am. Atlas, map 25, 1776. Pacaha.—Gentl. of Elvas (1557) in French, Hist. Coll. La., II, 169, 1850. Papikaha.—Marquette, autograph map (1673), in Shea, Discov., 268, 1852. Qaupaws.—Johnson in Rep. Sen. Com. 379, 33d Cong., 1st sess., 1, 1854. Qawpaw.—Pike, Trav., map, 1811. Quapás.—Nouv. Ann. des Voy., XI, 12, 1823. Quapau.—Hunter, Captivity, 415, 1823. Quapaw.—Ibid., 190. Quapaws-Arkansas.—Shea, Cath. Miss., 452, 1855. Quapois.—Whipple in Pac. R. R. Rep., III, pt. 1, 16, 1856. Quappas.—Gallatin in Trans. Am. Antiq. Soc., II, 126, 1836. Quappaws.—Shea, Early Voy., 76, note, 1861. Quaupaw.—Hurlbert in Jones, Ojebway Inds., 178, 1861. Quawpa.—Balbi, Atlas Ethnog., 56, 1826. Quawpaw.—Tanner, Narrative, 328, 1830. Quepâs.—Nouv. Ann. des Voy. XIX, 12, 1823. Queppa.—Balbi, Atlas Ethnog., 56, 1826. Querphas.—N. Y. Doc. Col. Hist., VII, 641, 1857. Quppas.—Schoolcraft, Ind. Tribes, v, 98, 1855. Qwapaws.—Bollaert in Jour. Ethol. Soc. Lond., II, 265, 1850. Savansa.—Margry, Déc., I, 616, 1876 (prob. the Quapaw). Ugakhpa.—Dorsey in Bull. Philos. Soc. Wash., 129, 1880. Ugaqpa.—Dorsey, Dhegiha MS. Dict., B. A. E., 1880 ('down stream people': so called by the Omaha, Ponca, and Kansa). U-gá-qpa-qti.—Dorsey, Kwapa MS. vocab., B. A. E., 1883 (='real Quapaws'). Ŭgáχpa.—Gatschet, Kaw MS. vocab., B. A. E., 27, 1878 (Kansa name). Ugaχ-páχti.—Gatschet, Creek Migr. Leg., I, 30, 1884 (own name). Ŭ-kăh-pû.—Grayson, Creek MS. vocab., B. A. E., 1885 (Creek name). Uӊáqpa.—Dorsey, Osage MS. vocab., B. A. E., 1883 (Osage and Quapaw name). Uӊaqpaqti.—Dorsey, Kwapa MS. vocab., B. A. E., 1891. Utsúshuat.—Gatschet, Wyandot MS., B. A. E. ('wild apple,' the fruit of Carica papaya: Wyandot name). Wiapes.—Jefferys, French Dom. Am., pt. 1, 143, 1760. Wyapes.—Ibid., 144.

Quarai. A former pueblo of the Tigua, about 30 m. E. of the Rio Grande in an air line, in the E. part of Valencia co., N. Mex. At the time of its occupancy it was the southernmost Tigua pueblo of the Salinas region. Quarai was the seat of a Spanish mission from 1629, and contained a monastery and a church dedicated to the Immaculate Conception, the walls of which are still standing. According to Vetancurt, Quarai had 600 inhabitants immediately prior to its abandonment. Between 1664 and 1669 the people of this pueblo connived with the Apache, during a moment of friendliness of the latter, to rout the Spaniards, but the plot was discovered and the leader executed. About 1674 the Apache compelled the Quarai people to flee to Tajique, 12 m. northward. The latter village remained inhabited probably a year longer, when its occupants were also forced to succumb to the persistent hostility of the Apache, and to flee to El Paso, Texas, being afterward settled in the village of Isleta del Sur, farther down the Rio Grande, where their descendants, almost completely Mexicanized, now reside. Consult Bandelier in Arch. Inst. Papers, IV, 258, 261 et seq., 1892; Lummis, Land of Poco Tiempo, 1893. (F. W. H.)

Coarac.—Salas (1643) quoted by Bandelier in Arch. Inst. Papers, IV, 261, 1892. Cuarac.—Llana (ca. 1631) quoted by Vetancurt, Menolog. Fran., 240, 1871. Cuaraí.—Lummis in Scribner's Mo., 470, Apr. 1893. Cuaray.—Bandelier in Arch. Inst. Bull., I, 31, 1883. Cua-ray.—Bandelier in Arch. Inst. Papers, III, 129, 1890. Cuarrá.—Ibid., IV, 261, 1892. Cuarry.—Bandelier quoted in Arch. Inst. Rep., V, 50, 1884. Cuerrò.—Moïse in Kans. City Rev., 480, Dec. 1881. Cuzá.—Oñate (1598) in Doc. Inéd., XVI, 113, 1871 (apparently identical with his Cuzayá). Cu-za-ya.—Oñate, ibid., 118 (believed by Bandelier, Arch. Inst. Papers, IV, 113, 258, 1892, to be possibly Quarai). La Concepcion de Quarac.—Vetancurt (1693), Crónica, III, 324, 1871. N. D. de Querca.—Vaugondy, Map Amérique, 1778. Qouarra.—Gallatin in Nouv. Ann. Voy., 5th s., XXVII, 298, 1851. Quara.—Llana (1759) quoted by Bandelier in Arch. Inst. Papers, IV, 259, 1892. Quarac.—Bandelier in Arch. Inst. Papers, I, 24, 1881. Quarra.—Abert in Emory, Recon., 487, 1848. Quarro.—Loew (1875) in Wheeler Survey Rep., VII, 340, 1879. Querra.—Cozzens, Marvelous Country, 268, 1873. Quouarra.—Gallatin in Nouv. Ann. Voy., 5th s., XXVII, 298, 1851.

Quaras. An Indian village on the "first cane river" 3 days' journey E. of Matagorda bay, Texas; visited by La Salle in Jan. 1688. This territory was occupied by the Karankawa.

Kouaras.—Gravier (1688) in Shea, Early Voy., 34, 1861. Quaras.—Shea, ibid.

Quarries. See *Mines and Quarries.*

Quartelejo. An outpost mentioned in Spanish documents of the 17th and 18th centuries as situated on the buffalo plains, N. E. of New Mexico, at which dwelt a band of Jicarilla Apache. A part of the Taos Indians of New Mexico emigrated there in the middle of the 17th century, but were later brought back; and in 1704 the Picuris Indians fled there on account of some superstition, remaining two years. In 1900 Williston and Martin excavated a typical pueblo ruin in Beaver cr. valley, Scott co., Kans., which may have been the site of the Quartelejo. The band of Jicarillas formerly settled in this neighborhood were usually called Apaches de Quartelejo, or de Cuartelejo. See Bandelier in Arch. Inst. Papers, III, 181, 212, 1890; IV, pt. 2, 138, 1892; V, 181–185, 1890; Williston and Martin in Kans.

Hist. Soc. Coll., VI, 1900; Hodge in Am. Anthr., II, 778, 1900. (F. W. H.)

Cuartelejos.—Mota-Padilla, Hist. de la Conq., 516, 1742. Quartelejo.—MS. of 1713 quoted by Bandelier in Arch. Inst. Papers, V, 182, 1890. Quartelexo.—MS. of 1720, ibid., 183. Santo Domingo.—Bancroft, Ariz. and N. Mex., 229, 1889 (saint name applied in 1706).

Quartz. A widely distributed mineral, very generally white or whitish in color, and having a glassy fracture. It is the hardest of the common minerals, is infusible under the blowpipe, and resists all acids except hydrofluoric. It was in very general use by the aborigines. Quartz crystals — transparent, smoky, amethystine, etc.—were sometimes employed unmodified as ornaments, or as fetishes and charms, and the larger crystals were utilized in some sections in the manufacture of arrowheads, knives, and ornaments. White vein quartz occurs very generally along the Appalachian highland, where it was obtained from outcropping veins or from the surface, where weathered out and broken into fragments. Pebbles and bowlders, which occur plentifully in river and shore deposits, were also much used. Choice pieces were in somewhat rare cases employed in the manufacture of polished objects, as bannerstones, plummets, chunkey disks, etc., in which the beauty of the stone was an important consideration. Popularly, white quartz is often erroneously called flint. See *Flint, Chalcedony, Quartzite.* (W. H. H.)

Quartzite. A metamorphosed sandstone in which, although often quite glassy, the granular structure is still traceable. Its appearance is usually described as saccharoidal—that is, resembling sugar in its crystallized state. Its color varies greatly, brownish and purplish gray varieties prevailing. It occurs in massive strata in many parts of the country, and on account of its great hardness and toughness is a prominent constituent of river, beach, and glacial gravels and bowlder beds. It was extensively employed by the native tribes of the N., as it is sufficiently brittle to be flaked into desired implement forms and yet very generally so tough and heavy as to be used for sledges, hammers, axes, picks, chisels, chunkey disks, etc. In the suburbs of Washington, D. C., there are extensive ancient quarries where Cretaceous bowlder beds made up chiefly of this material were worked by the prehistoric aborigines, the product of the flaking shops which surround the quarries being principally a leaf-shaped blade suited for specializing into knives, spear and arrow points, drills, and scrapers (Holmes in 15th Rep. B. A. E., 1897). In Converse co., Wyo., there are extensive quarries where massive outcrops of Cretaceous quartzite were worked by the native tribes, and numerous flaking shops where the manufacture of implements was carried on (Dorsey in Pub. 51, Field Columb. Mus., 1900).   (w. h. h.)

Quasky. A name of the blueback, or oquassa trout (*Salmo oquassa*): derived from the Algonquian appellation of Oquassa or Oquassac lake, Me., where this fish is found.   (a. f. c.)

Quasquen. An unidentified tribe, possibly the Kaskaskia, living formerly beside the Shawnee and Delawares on a branch of the Ohio r. and with them in alliance with the Seneca. — Iberville (*ca.* 1702) in Margry, Déc., iv, 544, 1880.

Quatsino (*Guáts'ēnôx*, 'people of the north country'). A Kwakiutl tribe living at the entrance of the sound of the same name at the n. end of Vancouver id., Brit. Col. Their gentes are Hamanao and Quatsino (or Guatsenok). Their principal winter village in 1885 was Owiyekumi, and another called Tenate was occupied in summer. Pop. 22 in 1909.   (j. r. s.)
Gua′ts′ēnoq.— Boas in 6th Rep. N. W. Tribes Can., 53, 1890. **Gua′ts′ēnôx.**—Boas in Rep. Nat. Mus. 1895, 329, 1897. **Kwat-se-no.**—Can. Ind. Aff., 279, 1894. **Kwats′ēnoq.**—Boas in Petermanns Mitt., xxxiii, 131, 1887. **Kwatsino.**—Tolmie and Dawson, Vocabs. Brit. Col., 118b, 1884. **Kwat-zi-no.**—Ibid. **Kwawt-se-no.**—Can. Ind. Aff., 189, 1884. **Quatsenos.**—Can. Ind. Aff., 113, 1879. **Quatsino.**—Mayne, Brit. Col., 251, 1862. **Quat-si-nu.**—Kane, Wand. in N. A., app., 1859.

Quawqualalp. A Cowichan town on lower Fraser r., opposite Yale, Brit. Col.— Brit. Col. map, Ind. Aff., Victoria, 1872.

Queeah. Given in John Work's list (Schoolcraft, Ind. Tribes, v, 489, 1885) as the name of a Haida town of 20 houses with 308 inhabitants in 1836–41. It was perhaps Ninstints (q. v.), which was on an island, Queeah being merely *Guai-a*, 'it is an island.'   (j. r. s.)

Queelquelu. Mentioned by Oñate (Doc. Inéd., xvi, 115, 1871) as a pueblo of the province of Atripuy (q. v.), in the region of the lower Rio Grande, N. Mex., in 1598.

Queen Anne. The name given by the English to the woman chief of the Pamunkey tribe (q. v.) of Virginia from about 1675 to 1715 or later. She was the widow of Totopotomoi (q. v.), chief of the tribe, who lost his life in the English service while aiding in repelling an invasion by the wilder inland tribes. She first appears prominently in connection with Bacon's rebellion in 1675, when the colonial government called on her for a contingent of men to cooperate with the governor's forces. She appeared at the council in Indian costume, accompanied by her son, and with dramatic expression of grief and scorn, rejected the proposal on the ground that for 20 years no reward but neglect had been meted out to her or her people for the death of her husband and his warriors. On promise of better

treatment she finally consented to furnish the aid required. It was probably in return for her help on this occasion that she received from Charles II the silver headpiece, or "crown," inscribed to the "Queen of Pamunkey," now in possession of the Society for the Preservation of Virginia Antiquities, at Richmond. Her last appearance in history seems to have been in 1715 as a petitioner on behalf of her oppressed people.   (j. m.)

Queenashawakee. A Delaware village on upper Susquehanna r., Pa., about 1758. According to Gerard (inf'n, 1908) the forms of the name as recorded are abortive attempts to write from memory the word *Kwinishûkûneihäki*, 'panther land (or country).'
Queenashawakee.—Post (1758) quoted by Rupp, West Penn., app., 77, 1846. **Quenishachshachki.**—Loskiel (1794) quoted by Day, Penn., 526, 1843.

Queen Esther. See *Montour*.

Queequehatch. See *Quickhatch*.

Quelaptonlilt. A former Willopah village on the s. side of Willapa r., near its mouth, in Pacific co., Wash.
Kulā′ptEnᵍEt.—Boas, field notes (Chehalis name). **Niā′ktcixupenēqē.**—Ibid. (Chinook name). **Quelap′ton-lilt.**—Swan, N. W. Coast, 211, 1857.

Quelotetrey. Mentioned by Oñate in 1598 as a large pueblo of the Jumano (q. v.), in the vicinity of Abo, e. of the Rio Grande, in New Mexico.
Cuelóce.—Oñate (1598) in Doc. Inéd., xvi, 123, 1871 (probably identical). **Cuelotetrey.**—Bandelier in Arch. Inst. Papers, iii, 167, 1890. **Quelotetreny.**—Ibid. (misprint). **Quelotretrey.**—Oñate, op. cit., 114. **Zuelotetrey.**—Columbus Mem. Vol., 155, 1893 (misprint).

Quelqueme. A Chumashan village w. of Pueblo de las Canoas (San Buenaventura), Ventura co., Cal., in 1542.
Quelqueme.—Cabrillo, Narr. (1542), in Smith, Colec. Doc. Fla., 181, 1857. **Quelquimi.**—Taylor in Cal. Farmer, Apr. 17, 1863.

Quelshose. Given officially (Can. Ind. Aff., 78, 1878) as a Salish band or village of Fraser superintendency, Brit. Col.; perhaps identical with Clahoose.

Quemelentus. A former Costanoan village on San Francisco bay, Cal.—Taylor in Cal. Farmer, Oct. 18, 1861.

Quemocac. A village situated in 1608 on the e. bank of Patuxent r., in Calvert co., Md.—Smith (1629), Va., i, map, repr. 1819.

Quems. A former tribe of Coahuila, Mexico, probably belonging to the Coahuiltecan family.
Cems.—Valero Mission baptismal rec., 18th century. **Quems.**—Manzanet, letter (1689), in Tex. Hist. Ass'n Quar., viii, 205, 1905. **Quimis.**—Doc. quoted by Orozco y Berra, Geog., 306, 1864. **Quims.**—Valero Mission baptismal records, 18th century.

Queptahua. A former Diegueño village near the headwaters of San Diego r., San Diego co., Cal.—Sanchez (1821) cited by Bancroft, Hist. Cal., ii, 442, 1886.

Querecho. A Pueblo name for the buffalo-hunting Apache of the plains of e. New Mexico and w. Texas, first encountered by Coronado's expedition in 1541 on its journey to Quivira. They were described as enemies of the Teyas, another hunting tribe of the plains, and were well built and painted; they lived in buffalo-skin tipis, used dogs and travaux for transporting their effects, and subsisted entirely on the buffalo, of which they killed all they wished, "and tan the hides, with which they clothe themselves and make their tents, and they eat the flesh, sometimes raw, and they also even eat the blood when thirsty." Bandelier identifies the Querecho with the Kirauash, or Q'irauash, the Keresan name of a wild tribe which had destroyed the Tano villages s. of Santa Fé, N. Mex., and also threatened the pueblos of Santo Domingo and Pecos in pre-Spanish time. In this connection Hodge has determined that the Pecos name for the Navaho is *Keretsá*, and for the Apache *Tagukerésh*.

The Querecho were therefore most likely the plains Apache, later known by the names Mescaleros, Jicarillas, Faraones, Llaneros, etc.; in short, all the Apache who subsisted on the bison, excepting possibly the Kiowa Apache.　(F. W. H.)

Apaches orientaux.—ten Kate, Synonymie, 8, 1884. **Apaches Vaqueros.**—Benavides, Memorial, 71, 1630. **Apaches Vasqueras.**—Senex, Map, 1710. **Baqueros.**—Oñate (1599) in Doc. Inéd., XVI, 308, 1871. **Buffalo Hunters.**—Schoolcraft, Ind. Tribes, VI, 72, 1857. **Eastern Apache.**—ten Kate, Synonymie, 8, 1884. **Guerechos.**—Coronado (1541) in Doc. Inéd., XIV, 327, 1870. **Kirauash.**—Bandelier in Arch. Inst. Papers, IV, 116, 1892. **Muχ-tzi'-ĕn-tăn.**—ten Kate, Synonymie, 8, 1884. **Oi-ra-uash.**—Bandelier, Gilded Man, 226, 1893 (misprint). **People-of-the-flat-roof-houses.**—Smith, Cabeça de Vaca, 163, 1871 (misquoting Jaramillo and confusing these with the Pueblos). **Q'i-ra-vash.**—Bandelier in Ausland, 813, 1882. **Queerchos.**—Ladd, Story of N. Mex., 88, 1891. **Querchos.**—Schoolcraft, Ind. Tribes, VI, 72, 1857. **Querechaos.**—Simpson in Smithson. Rep. 1869, 321, 1871. **Quereches.**—Oñate (1599) in Doc. Inéd., XVI, 308, 1871. **Querechos.**—Coronado et al. in 14th Rep. B A. E., passim, 1896. **Querehos.**—Kern in Schoolcraft, Ind. Tribes, IV, 35, 1854. **Quirireches.**—La Harpe (1720), Jour. Hist., 200, 1831 (possibly identical). **Vagueros.**—Smith, Cabeça de Vaca, 163, 1871 (misprint). **Vaqueros.**—Sosa (1590) in Doc. Inéd., XV, 207, 1871.

Queres. See *Keresan Family*.

Quesal. An unidentified tribe or subtribe some of whose members were living in 1706–07 in Coahuila, Mexico, near the Rio Grande, at San Francisco Solano and Nadadores missions. One of those at the former mission was married to a Tepehuane, q. v. (Valero Bautismos, entries for 1706 and 1707, MS.).　(H. E. B.)
Quisal.—Valero Bautismos, 1707, op. cit.

Quesinille. A former Luiseño village near Las Flores, San Diego co., Cal.—Grijalva (1795) cited by Bancroft, Hist. Cal., I, 563, 1886.

Quet. A former village, presumably Costanoan, connected with Dolores mission, San Francisco, Cal.—Taylor in Cal. Farmer, Oct. 18, 1861.

Quguas. A native village, probably Shoshonean, formerly situated not far

from the headwaters of San Luis Rey r., San Diego co., Cal.—Grijalva (1795) cited by Bancroft, Hist. Cal., I, 563, 1886.

Quialpo. Mentioned by Oñate (Doc. Inéd., XVI, 115, 1871) as a pueblo of the province of Atripuy (q. v.), in the region of the lower Rio Grande, N. Mex., in 1598. Compare *Quiápo*.

Quiana. Given by De l'Isle as one of the Hopi pueblos of Arizona, and mentioned also as such by Villa-Señor. The name is not identifiable with that of any former or present pueblo of the Hopi.
Quiana.—De l'Isle, Carte Mexique et Floride, 1703. **Quianna.**—Villa-Señor, Theatro Am., II, 425, 1748.

Quiápo. Mentioned by Oñate (Doc. Inéd., XVI, 115, 1871) as a pueblo of the province of Atripuy (q. v.), in the region of the lower Rio Grande, N. Mex., in 1598. Compare *Quialpo*.

Quiburi ('houses', the plural of *ki* in the Nevome dialect). A former Sobaipuri rancheria, in 1760–64 a visita of the mission of Suamca (q. v.), established as such by Father Kino about 1697; situated on the w. bank of the Rio San Pedro, perhaps not far from the present town of Benson, s. Ariz.
Giburi.—De l'Isle, Map Am., 1703. **Kiburi.**—Kino, map (1702) in Stöcklein, Neue Welt-Bott, 74, 1726. **Quiburi.**—Kino (1697) in Doc. Hist. Mex., 4th s., I, 277, 1856. **Quiburio.**—Venegas, Hist. Cal., I, map, 1759. **Quiburis.**—Bernal (1697) quoted by Bancroft, Ariz. and N. Mex., 356, 1889. **San Ignacio Guibori.**—Writer *ca.* 1702 in Doc. Hist. Mex., 4th s., V, 136, 1857. **San Pablo de Quiburi.**—Apost. Afanes quoted by Coues, Garcés Diary, 153, 1900. **San Pablo de Quipuri.**—Ibid. **S. Juan Quiburi.**—Docs. of 1760–64 in Bancroft, No. Mex. States, I, 563, 1884. **S. Pablo Quiburi.**—Kino (1696–97) quoted by Bancroft, No. Mex. States, I, 263, 1884.

Quickhatch (also *quickehatch, quiquihatch, queequhatch*). A name, first mentioned by Ellis in 1748, applied by the English residents of the Hudson Bay country to the wolverene, *Gulo luscus*. The word is from Cree *kwĭkkwáhaketsh*=Prairie Cree *kĭkkwáhakes*=(minus the derogative suffix -*s* or -*sh*) Chippewa *qwĭngwáage*, the 'scathless' or 'invulnerable' beast; from the root *kwĭkkw, kĭkkw*, 'to be just grazed', but not hit, by a blow or shot aimed at; 'hard to hit' would be a concise interpretation.　(W. R. G.)

Quide. One of 36 tribes, friends of the Jumano, said by Juan Sabeata (q. v.) in 1683 to have lived in the present Texas, three days' travel E. of the mouth of the Conchos, and to have desired missionaries.—Mendoza (1683–84), MS. in Archivo Gen., Mex.　(H. E. B.)

Quigalta. An Indian province of which De Soto's army first heard while at Anilco, the Anicoyanque of Biedma. The army journeyed thence to Guachoya, on the Mississippi, where it arrived Apr. 17, 1541. From there messengers were sent to the cacique of Quigalta, 3 days' journey s., probably in N. w. Mississippi. There is reason for believing that this may have been the Natchez.

Chigantalgi.—Schoolcraft, Ind. Tribes, IV, 148, 1854 (error). Chigantualga.—Ibid., V, 99, 1855; VI, 197, 626, 1857. Quigalta.—Gentl. of Elvas (1557) in French, Hist. Coll. La. II, 186, 1850. Quigualtanji.— Schoolcraft, Ind. Tribes, IV, 123, 1854. Quigualtanqui.—Garcilasso de la Vega, Florida, 207, 1723. Quiguas.—Rafinesque in Marshall, Ky., I, introd., 32, 1824. Quiqualtangui.—Herrera, Hist., Eng. trans., VI, 8, 1726. Quiqualthangi.—Margry, Déc., II, 198, 1877. Wiwas.—Rafinesque, op. cit., 36.

Quigaute. A town and province w. of the Mississippi at which De Soto's army arrived Aug. 4, 1541, when marching s. from Pacaha (Quapaw). The people were sun-worshipers. According to the Gentleman of Elvas this was the largest town the Spaniards saw in the province of Florida. It was in E. Arkansas, N. of Arkansas r.

Quigata.—Biedma (1544) in French, Hist. Coll. La., II, 106, 1850. Quigaute.—Gentl. of Elvas (1557), ibid. 175. Quiguata.—Biedma in Hakluyt Soc. Pub., IX, 193, 1851. Quiguate.—Garcilasso de la Vega, Florida, 187, 1723.

Quigyuma. A Yuman tribe, which, with the Cajuenche, spoke a dialect close to that of the Yuma proper. In 1604–05 they occupied 6 rancherias on the Rio Colorado below the mouth of the Gila and above the Cocopa; in 1762 (Rudo Ensayo, Guiteras trans., 131, 1894) they dwelt in a fertile plain, 10 or 12 leagues in length, on the E. bank of the Colorado, and here they were found by Father Garcés in 1771 in a group of rancherias which he named Santa Rosa. By 1775, however, when Garcés revisited the tribe, which he designates as the "Quiquima or Jalliquamay," they had moved to the w. side of the river. Their first rancherias on the N. were in the vicinity of Ogden's landing, about lat. 32° 18′, where they met the Cajuenche. On the s. their territory bordered that of their kindred, but enemies, the Cocopa. The Rudo Ensayo (ca. 1762) mentions them as the most populous tribe on the river. Garcés (1775) estimated their number at 2,000, and described them as being a generous people, with abundant provisions; they were more cleanly than the Cajuenche or the Yuma, "and as the women do not paint so much, they appear middling white" (Diary, 1775, 181, 1900). It is possible that the Quigyuma were finally absorbed by the Cocopa or by some other Yuman tribe. Their rancherias, so far as recorded, were Presentacion, San Casimiro, San Felix de Valois, San Rudesindo, and Santa Rosa. (F. W. H.)

Halliquamayas.—Bandelier in Arch. Inst. Papers, III, 110, 1890 (classed as the Comoyei). Jallicuamai.—Orozco y Berra, Geog., 59, 353, 1864. Jallicuamay.—Garcés (1775–6) cited, ibid., 38. Jallicumay.—Escudero, Not. Estad. de Chihuahua, 228, 1834. Jalliquamai.—Garcés (1775–6), Diary, 434, 1900. Jalliquamay.—Ibid., 176 (or Quiquima). Quicama.—Alarcon (1540) in Ternaux-Compans, Voy., IX, 326, 1838 (evidently identical). Quicam-

opa.—Sedelmair (1744) quoted by Bancroft, Nat. Races, III, 684, 1882 (probably Pima name of same; opa= 'people'). Quicimas.—Venegas, Hist. Cal., I, 304, 1759. Quicoma.—Alarcon in Hakluyt, Voy., III, 514, 1810. Quigyamas.—Browne quoted by Bancroft, Nat. Races, I, 598, 1882. Quihuimas.— Orozco y Berra, Geog., 59, 353, 1864. Quimac.— Sedelmair cited by Bancroft, Ariz. and N. Mex., 368, 1889. Quinquimas.—Venegas, Hist. Cal., I, 308, 1759. Quiquimas.—Kino (1701) cited, ibid., 301. Quiquimo.—Baudry des Lozières, Voy. Louisiane, map, 1802. Quiquionas.—Rudo Ensayo (ca. 1762), Guiteras trans., 131, 1894 (Quiquimas, p. 132). Tallignamay.—Forbes, Hist. Cal., 162, 1839. Talliguämais.—Domenech, Deserts, I, 444, 1860. Talliguamayue.—Cortez (1799) in Pac. R. R. Rep., III, pt. 3, 18, 1856. Talliguamays.—Ibid., 124. Tlalliguamayas.—Zarate-Salmeron (ca. 1629) cited by Bancroft, Ariz. and N. Mex., 156, 1889. Tlalliquamallas.—Zarate-Salmeron (ca. 1629) in Land of Sunshine, 106, Jan. 1900.

Quijotoa (kiho 'carrying basket,' toak 'mountain,' because of the shape of a mountain in the vicinity.—Fewkes). A village of the Quahatika, in the w. part of Pima co., s. Arizona. Pop. about 500 in 1863; present number unknown.

Kihâtoak'.—Russell in 26th Rep. B. A. E., 217, 1908 (Pima name). Kihotoak.—Ibid., 43. Quejotoa.— Poston in Ind. Aff. Rep. 1863, 385, 1864. Quejoton.— Poston misquoted by Browne, Apache Country, 291, 1869. Tnijotobar.—Bailey in Ind. Aff. Rep. 208, 1858.

Quileute. A Chimakuan tribe, now the only representative of the linguistic stock, whose main seat is at Lapush, at the mouth of Quillayute r., about 35 m. s. of C. Flattery, w. coast of Washington. A small division of the tribe, the Hoh, live at the mouth of the river of the same name, 15 m. s. of Lapush. Since they have been known to the whites the Quileute have always been few in number, but being of an independent and warlike disposition and occupying an easily defended situation, they have successfully resisted all the attempts of neighboring tribes to dislodge them. Their most active enemies have been the Makah, of Neah bay, and until they came under the control of the United States petty warfare between the two tribes was constant. The Quileute are noted for their skill in pelagic sealing and are the most successful in that pursuit of all the tribes of the coast. They are also daring whalers, but have not attained the proficiency of the Makah. Salmon are caught in considerable numbers and constitute an important article of food. Roots and berries of various kinds are also much used. Although the woods in their vicinity abound with deer, elk, and bear, the Quileute seem to have hunted them but little and have confined themselves to a seafaring life. There is evidence that a clan system of some sort formerly existed among them, but is now broken down. Their customs as well as their mythology indicate a possible connection with the tribes of Vancouver id. The Quileute, together with the Quinaielt, by treaty at

Olympia, July 1, 1855, and Jan. 25, 1856, ceded all their lands to the United States and agreed to remove to a reserve to be provided for them in Washington Ter. The tribe has gradually diminished until now it numbers but slightly more than 200. They are under the jurisdiction of the Neah Bay agency.   (L. F.)

Kuille-pates.—Ford in H. R. Ex. Doc. 37, 34th Cong., 3d sess., 103, 1857. Kwe-dee'-tut.—Gibbs in Cont. N. A. Ethnol., I, 173, 1877. Kwille-hates.— Ford, op. cit., 102. Kwille'hiūt.—Gibbs, op. cit., 172. Kwilleut.—Eells in Am. Antiq., X, 174, 1888. Kwilleyhuts.—Stevens in H. R. Ex. Doc. 37, 34th Cong., 3d sess., 49, 1857. Kwilléyute.—Swan in Smithson. Cont., XVI, 17, 1869. Ouileute.—Gosnell in Ind. Aff. Rep., 183, 1861. Que-lai'-ūlt.—Swan, N. W. Coast, 211, 1857. Quellehutes.—Hay in Ind. Aff. Rep., 46, 1870. Quilahutes.—Milroy, ibid., 339, 1872. Quilehutes.—Ford, ibid., 1857, 341, 1858. Quileutes.—Gosnell, ibid., 189, 1861. Quil-i-utes.— Kendall, ibid., 307, 1862. Quillalyute.—Swan, N. W. Coast, 343, 1857. Quillayutes.—Wickersham in Am. Antiq., XXI, 371, 1899. Quil-leh-utes.—Treaty of 1856 in U. S. Stat. at Large, XII, 10, 1863. Quilleutes.—Farrand in Mem. Am. Mus. Nat. Hist., IV, 80, 1902. Quilleyutes.—Simmons in Ind. Aff. Rep., 225, 1858. Quillihute.—Taylor in Sen. Ex. Doc. 4, 40th Cong., spec. sess., 4, 1867. Quilliutes.—Milroy in Ind. Aff. Rep., 341, 1872. Quilloyaths.—Browne in H. R. Ex. Doc. 39, 35th Cong., 1st sess, 21, 1858.

Quillwork. Embroidery worked with quills of the porcupine or sometimes with those of bird feathers. The two kinds of embroidery bear a superficial resemblance. In both cases the stiffness of the quill limits freedom of design, making necessary straight lines and angular figures.

The gathering of the raw materials, the hunting of porcupines or the capture of birds, was the task of the men, who also in some tribes prepared the dyes. Sorting and coloring the quills, tracing the design on dressed skin or birchbark, and the embroidering were exclusively the work of women.

In sorting porcupine quills the longest and the finest were first selected and laid in separate receptacles. Another selection was made, and the long or fine quills of the second quality were laid away. The remaining quills were kept for common work. Bladders of the elk or buffalo served as quill cases. The dyes, which varied in different parts of the country, were compounded variously of roots, whole plants, and buds and bark of trees. The quills were usually steeped in concoctions of these until a uniform color was obtained—red, yellow, green, blue, or black. No variegated hues were made, and rarely more than one shade of a color. The natural color of whitish quills afforded a white, and sometimes those of a brownish cast were used. The quills of feathers were split, except the fine pliant tips. The porcupine quills were not split, nor were they used in the round state. They were always flattened. This was done by holding one end firmly between the teeth, pressing the edge of the thumb-nail against the quill held by the forefinger, and drawing it tightly along the length of the quill, the process being repeated until the quill became smooth and flat. This flattening process was never done until the quill was required for immediate use. It was not uncommon for a woman to have in her workbag several patterns drawn on bits of skin, bark, or paper, cut through to make a stencil. These patterns were stenciled or drawn with a bone paint-brush, a stick, or a dull knife, on the skin or bark that was to be worked. A woman who was skilled in or had a natural gift for drawing would copy a design by the free-hand method, except that she had first made some measurements in order that the pattern should be in its proper place and proportions. Some even composed designs, both the forms and arrangement of colors, and worked them out as they embroidered. Among most tribes the awl was the only instrument used in quill-working. The Cheyenne, Arapaho, and Sioux, the principal quill-working tribes, had a specially shaped bone for flattening, bending, and smoothing (Mooney). A small hole was made with it in the skin or bark, through which the sharp point of the quill was thrust from the back and drawn out on the front side. An end of the flattened quill was left at the back, and this was bent and pressed close to the skin or bark to serve as a fastening, like a knot on a thread. Another hole was made, perpendicular to the first, and through this the quill was passed to the back, thus making the stitch. The distance between the holes determined not only the length of the stitches, but also the width of the lines forming the design. All designs in quillwork were made up of wide or narrow lines, each composed of a series of upright stitches lying close together. As quills were always so short that one could make only a few stitches at most, the fastening of ends and uniformity in the length of stitches were important points in the technic of the work. The width of the lines varied from a sixteenth to a quarter of an inch. Very rarely was more than one width employed in one design. The banded fringe usually attached to the border of tobacco-bags was made on strips of dressed skin, cut in the desired width, around which flattened quills were closely and evenly bound, care being taken to conceal the ends of the quills in order that the binding, even when various colors were used to form the design, might look as though it was one band. Different colors on the different strands of the fringe were so arranged that when the strands hung in place the meeting of the colors made the figure.

The stems of pipes were decorated with fine flattened quills, closely woven into a long and very narrow braid, which was wound about the wooden stem.' Different colors were sometimes so disposed along the length of these braids that when they were wound around the stem they made squares or other figures. Careful calculations as well as deftness of finger were required for this style of work.

Porcupine quills were employed for embroidery from Maine to Virginia and w. to the Rocky mts. N. of the Arkansas r. On the N. W. coast they were used by tribes which had come in contact with the Athapascans. So far as known, this style of work was not practised by the tribes of California, nor by those of the southern plains, as the Kiowa, Comanche, Apache, and Wichita, the porcupine not being found in their country. Quills seem to have been an article of barter; hence their use was not confined to regions where the animal abounded. This style of decoration was generally put on tobacco and tinder bags, workbags, knife and paint-stick cases, cradles, amulets, the bands of burden-straps, tunics, shirts, leggings, belts, arm and leg bands, moccasins, robes, and sometimes on the trappings of horses. All such objects were of dressed skin. Receptacles and other articles made of birch-bark also were frequently embroidered with quills.

Nearly every tribe has its peculiar cut for moccasins, often also its special style of ornamentation, and these were carefully observed by the workers. The dress of the men was more ornate than that of the women, and the decorations the women put on the former were generally related to man's employments—hunting and war. The figures were frequently designed by the men, and a man very often designated what particular figure he desired a woman to embroider on his garment. Some designs belonged exclusively to women; there were, moreover, some that were common to both sexes. The decorative figures worked on the garments of children not infrequently expressed prayers for safety, long life, and prosperity, and usually were symbolic. There was considerable borrowing of designs by the women through the medium of gifts exchanged between tribes during ceremonial observances or visits, and thus figures that were sacred symbols in some tribes came to be used merely as ornaments by others. Some of the designs in quillwork were undoubtedly originated by men, while others were invented by women. These were frequently credited to dreams sent by the spider, who, according to certain tribal mythic traditions, was the instructor of women in the art of embroidery.

Technical skill as well as unlimited patience was required to make even,

smooth, and fine porcupine quillwork, and proficiency could be acquired only by practice and nice attention to details. The art seems to have reached its highest development among those tribes to whose territory the porcupine was native, and especially among those which had an abundant food supply and whose men were the principal providers—conditions that made it possible for the women to have the leisure necessary for them to become adept in the working of quills. This art, which formerly flourished over a wide area, is rapidly dying out. It is doubtful whether any woman at the present day could duplicate the fine embroidery of a hundred years ago. The use of the split quills of bird-feathers for embroidery was common among the Alaskan Eskimo, and was also practised by some other tribes.

The hair of animals was sometimes combined with the quills in forming the figures. The northern Algonquian tribes, as well as the Eskimo of Alaska and of N. E. Siberia, employed the hair of the moose, its pliancy permitting freedom of design, while its texture seems to make it susceptible of taking delicate hues in dyeing; undyed hair was used to blend the colors and to outline the curved, flowing lines of the figures. A few examples of this beautiful aboriginal work are preserved in museums. (A. C. F.)

Quilmur. A tribe hostile to the Alchedoma, the border of whose territory was visited by Fray Francisco Garcés in 1774, when he explored the valleys of the Gila and the Colorado, in Arizona. They were apparently N. of the Alchedoma, and from their locality might possibly be the Mohave. See Garcés, Diary (1774), 45, 1900; Bancroft, Ariz. and N. M., 390, 1889. Cf. *Gueymura.*

Quiman. A Chumashan village between Goleta and Pt Concepcion, Cal., in 1542.—Cabrillo, Narr. (1542), in Smith, Colec. Doc. Fla., 183, 1857.

Quina. A former village, probably Salinan, connected with San Antonio mission, Monterey co., Cal.—Taylor in Cal. Farmer, Apr. 27, 1860.

Quinahaqui. A town on a large river between Guatari (Wateree) and Issa (Catawba), probably in South Carolina; visited by the expedition of Juan Pardo in 1567.—Juan de la Vandera (1569) in Smith, Colec. Doc. Fla., 15–19, 1857.

Quinaielt. A Salish tribe on Quinaielt r., Wash., and along the coast between the Quileute and the Quaitso on the N. (the latter of which probably formed a part of the tribe), and the Chehalis on the s. Lewis and Clark described them in two divisions, the Calasthocle and the Quiniilt, with 200 and 1,000 population, respectively. In 1909 they numbered 156, under the Puyallup school superintendency.

For their treaty with the United States, see *Quileute*.

Calasthocle.—Lewis and Clark Exped.,II,474,1814. Ca-lâst-ho-cle.—Orig. Jour. Lewis and Clark, VI, 118, 1905. Calasthorle.—Swan, letter of Oct. 28, 1885. Calasthorte.—Lewis and Clark, op. cit., 120. Kuin-ae-alts.—Ford in H.R.Ex.Doc.37,34th Cong., 3d sess.,102,1857. Kwaiantl.—Hale in U. S. Expl. Exped., VI, 212, 1846. Kwenaiwitl.—Ibid. Kwinaith.—Stevens in Ind. Aff. Rep.,448, 1854. Kwinaitl.—Gibbs in Pac. R. R. Rep., I, 428, 1855. Kwinaiult.—Swan in Smithson. Cont., XVI, 8,1870. Kwinaiutl.—Gibbs in Cont. N. A. Ethnol., I, 167, 1877. Quaiantl.—Keane in Stanford, Compend., 532, 1878. Queenhithe.—Kelley, Oregon, 68, 1830. Queen Hythe.—Hale in U.S. Expl. Exped., VI, 212, 1846 (corrupted form used by whites). Queenioolt.—Scouler (1846) in Jour. Ethnol. Soc. Lond., 235, 1848. Quemults.—Taylor in Cal. Farmer, Aug, 1, 1862. Queniauitl.-Keane in Stanford, Compend., 532,1878. Que'-ni-ült.—Swan, N.W. Coast, 210, 1857. Quenoil.—Lane in Sen. Ex. Doc. 52, 31st Cong., 1st sess., 174, 1850. Quenoith.—Ford in Ind. Aff. Rep., 341, 1857. Quevoil.—Lane, ibid., 162, 1850 (perhaps misprint for Quenoil). Qui-dai-elt.—Eells, letter of Feb. 1886. Quilaielt.—Gosnell in Ind. Aff. Rep., 183,1861. Qui-nai-elts.—Treaty of 1855 in U.S.Ind.

QUINAIELT MAN   (AM. MUS. NAT. HIST.)

Treaties, 723, 1873, Quin-aik.—Gibbs in Pac. R.R. Rep., I, 435, 1855. Quinailee.—Schoolcraft, Ind. Tribes, V,490,1855. Quin-aitle.—Stevens in Ind. Aff. Rep.,457,1854. Quinaiult.—Stevens in H.R.Ex.Doc. 37,34th Cong.,3d sess., 43,1857. Quinaiutl.—Ibid., 49. Quinault.—Farrand in Mem. Am. Mus. Nat. Hist.,IV, 80, 1902. Quinayat.—Duflot de Mofras, Expl., II, 335, 1844 Quinielts.—Orig. Jour. Lewis and Clark, VI, 70, 1905. Quiniilts.—Lewis and Clark Exped.,II, 474, 1814. Quinilts.—Domenech, Deserts of N. A., I, 443, 1860. Quiniltz.—Kelley, Oregon, 68, 1830. Quiniult.—Taylor in Cal. Farmer, July 25, 1862. Quiniutles.—Lee and Frost, Ten Years in Oreg., 99, 1844. Quinults.—Lewis and Clark Exped., II, 119, 1814. Qumault.—Ind. Aff. Rep., 219, 1861. Qweenylt.—Framboise quoted by Gairdner (1835) in Jour. Geog. Soc. Lond., XI, 255, 1841.

Quinaouatoua. A former Iroquois village in Ontario, w. of L. Ontario, between Hamilton and Grand rs.

Quinaouatoua.—Bellin, Map, 1755. Quinaoutoua.—La Tour, Map,1784. Tinaoutoua.—Homann Heirs Map, 1756.

Quincajou. See *Carcajou*.

Quinebaug ('long pond'). A former tribe or band, classed with the Nipmuc but subject by conquest to the Pequot, living on Quinebaug r. in E. Connecticut. They extended from the upper falls to the falls near Jewett City.

Plainfield Indians.—Trumbull, Conn., I, 469,1818. Qinaboags.—Gookin (1674) quoted by Hoyt, Antiq. Res., 91, 1824. Quannepague.—Mason (1699) in R. I. Col. Rec., III, 380, 1858. Queenapaug.—Record of 1669 quoted by Caulkins, Norwich, 256, 1866. Quenebage.—Writer ca. 1690 in Mass. Hist. Soc. Coll., 3d s., I, 210,1825. Quenebaug.—Cranfield et al. (1683), ibid., 1st s., V, 239,1816. Quenibaug.—Trumbull, Conn., I, 33, 1818. Quinabaag.—Gookin (1674) in Mass. Hist. Soc. Coll., 1st s., I, 147, 1806. Quinaboag.—Gookin (1674) quoted by Hoyt, Antiq. Res.,88,1824. Quinebage.—Brereton (1663) in R.I. Col. Rec., I, 518, 1856. Quinebaugs.—Bulkley (1724) in Mass. Hist. Soc. Coll., 1st s., IV, 174, 1795. Quineboag.—Writer of 1830, ibid., 3d s., II, 76, 1830. Quinepage.—Coddington (1639), ibid., 4th s., VII, 278, 1865. Quinibaug.—Trumbull, Conn., I, 469, 1818. Quinibauge.—Col. Rec. (1671) quoted by Trumbull, Ind. Names Conn., 60, 1881. Quinnabaug.—Col. Rec. (1701), ibid. Quinnuboag.—Endecott (1651) in Mass. Hist. Soc. Coll., 4th s., VI, 153, 1863. Qunnubbágge.—Endecott (1651), ibid., 3d s., IV, 191, 1834.

Quinebaug. The chief Quinebaug village, situated near Plainfield, Windham co., Conn. According to De Forest, there were 25 Indians, probably the remnant of the band, at Plainfield in 1774.

Quinequaun. See *Quinney*.

Quinet. A tribe living near Matagorda bay, Texas, with whom La Salle made peace in Jan. 1687, as he was leaving that region for the Mississippi. The Quinet were then living in what was then Karankawan territory and were at war with the Quoaquis, or Coaque (Hennepin, New Discov., 30, 1698; Shea, Early Voy., 21, 1861).

Quinnapin (probably an abbreviation of *kwínúpínúm*, 'he turns (something) around.'—Gerard). A chief of the Narraganset, nephew of Miantonomo. He sided with his brother-in-law, King Philip, in the war of 1675, and was present at the attack on Lancaster. The next year he was captured by the English, tried by court-martial at Newport, R. I., sentenced to death, and shot. Quinnapin was the Indian who purchased Mrs Rowlandson from her captor at the taking of Lancaster. Her narrative contains interesting information about him. (A. F.•C.)

Quinnat. An economically important species of salmon (*Salmo quinnat*) of the Pacific coast of North America: the common salmon of the Columbia, known also as tyee salmon, Chinook salmon, etc. From *t'kwinnat*, the name of this fish in Salishan dialects current in the Columbia r. region. According to Boas, the Upper Chinook form is *igúnat*. (A. F. C.)

Quinney, John. An Indian of the Mohegan or Stockbridge tribe, who lived about the middle of the 18th century. He was probably an assistant or interpreter to the Rev. John Sergeant the elder, missionary at Stockbridge, Mass., from 1735 to 1749, whom he aided in translating into Mohegan various prayers and other works, including the Assembly's Catechism, printed at Stockbridge in 1795. Nothing is known of his personal history; but his descendants were prominent in the later history of the tribe.

His son, JOSEPH QUINNEY, whose name is also spelled Quanaukaunt and Quinequaun, was town constable of Stockbridge in 1765; and in 1777, after the death of the sachem Solomon Unhaunnauwaunnutt, was made chief of the Mohegan tribe. Another JOSEPH QUINNEY, perhaps a son, was chosen deacon of the new Stockbridge (N. Y.) church in 1817, and in the following year was one of the leaders in the emigration of his people from the State of New York to their new home in the W.

Quinney, John W. A Stockbridge Indian of the early half of the 19th century, born in 1797, and chief of the tribe in Wisconsin for three years previous to his death, July 21, 1855. When a boy he was one of three who received a common English education under the patronage of the United States, being placed under the tuition of Caleb Underhill, of Westchester, N. Y., where he pursued his studies with alacrity and proficiency. By degrees he gained the confidence of his people, until almost the entire tribal business was intrusted to him. In 1822, he, with two others, formed a deputation to Green Bay, Wis., where a treaty was made and concluded with the Menominee, by which was purchased all the Green Bay lands designed for the future home of the New York Indians. In 1825 he procured the passage of a law by the New York legislature granting the Stockbridge tribe full value for the New York lands, thus enabling them subsequently to remove to Green Bay. The lands of the New York Indians purchased from the Menominee being endangered by a repurchase made by United States officers, Quinney was sent in 1828 to petition Congress, in behalf of the united New York tribes, for the recognition of their landed rights. In this, however, he failed, and the Stockbridge tribe lost their home at Kaukana, Fox r., but the Government allowed them $25,000 for their improvements. Quinney next entered at once into a new plan, and finally, after protracted efforts, he obtained, in 1832, the grant of two townships on the E. side of L. Winnebago, Wis., where the tribe still resides. About the year 1833 Quinney framed a constitution, as the basis of a tribal government, which was adopted by his people and led to the abandonment of hereditary chieftainship. In 1846 he effected the repeal of an act of Congress of 1843 which made citizens of his tribesmen, thus permitting his people

to enjoy their own customs and government; he also obtained for them $5,000 on account of their old claims. The tribe made a treaty in 1843, in concluding which Quinney took a prominent part, the Government agreeing to find the tribe a new home w. of the Mississippi, and to remove them thither; but after many unsuccessful attempts on their part to select the lands and remove, in which Quinney engaged with untiring zeal, he finally conceived the plan of reacquiring the township of Stockbridge. Efforts immediately commenced finally terminated in the ratification of a new treaty by which the Government receded to the tribe its old home. In 1854, Quinney succeeded in obtaining the passage of a law by Congress which granted to him the title to 460

JOHN W. QUINNEY. (FROM A PAINTING IN THE WISCONSIN HISTORICAL SOCIETY.)

acres in Stockbridge. At the election held in 1852, he was chosen grand sachem of the tribe, which office he filled honorably until his death, encouraging everything calculated to improve his people (Wis. Hist. Soc. Coll., IV, 309–311, 1859).

The prominence of the Quinney family in the history of the Stockbridge tribe is shown by the presence of from one to three of the family names signed to every treaty made by these Indians with the United States from Oct. 27, 1832, to Feb. 5, 1856.

Quinnipiac ('long-water people.'—Gerard). A tribe formerly occupying the country on both sides of Quinnipiac r. about its mouth, in New Haven co., Conn. Their principal village bore the same name. Ruttenber makes them a part of the Wappinger group and subject to the

Mattabesec, while Gookin says they were subject to the Pequot. De Forest includes in this tribe the Guilford Indians as well as those of New Haven, East Haven, and Branford. The Hammonasset might also be included. They were estimated in 1730 at 250 to 300 persons. In 1638 they numbered 47 warriors, but in 1774 there were only 38 souls. Some of them had removed in 1768 to Farmington, where land was bought for them among the Tunxi. Some Quinnipiac graves have been examined, in which skeletons were found at the depth of 3½ ft, stretched on bare sandstone with no indication of wrappings or inclosures. For an account of the labors of the Rev. Abraham Pierson at Branford and of his translations into the Quiripi, or Quinnipiak, language of various works for the use of the Indians, see Pilling, Bibliog. Algonq. Lang., 396–402, 1891, and consult also Townshend, Quinnipiak Inds., 1900. (J. M.)

Kinnipiaks.—Maurault, Abnakis, 3, 1866. Panaquanike.—Haynes (1639) in Mass. Hist. Soc. Coll., 4th s., VI, 355, 1863. Qinnepioke.—Trumbull, Conn., I, 95, 1818. Queenapiok.—Underhill (1638) quoted by Townshend, Quinnipiak Inds., 8, 1900. Queenapoick.—Underhill (1638) in Mass. Hist. Soc. Coll. 3d s.,VI,1, 1837. Quenepiage.—Patrick (1637), ibid., 4th s., VII, 324, 1865. Quenepiake.—Davenport (1637) quoted by Townshend, Quinnipiak Inds., 8, 1900. Quenopiage.—Patrick (1637) in Mass. Hist. Soc. Coll., 4th s., VII, 323, 1865. Querepees.—De Laet (1633) quoted by Trumbull in Conn. Hist. Soc. Coll., III, 9, 1895. Quiliapiack.—Ruggles in Mass. Hist. Soc. Coll., 1st s., IV, 182, 1795. Quilipiacke.—Haynes (1639), ibid., 4th s., VI, 355, 1863. Quillipeage.—Stoughton (1637) quoted by Trumbull, Ind. Names Conn., 61, 1881. Quillipiacke.—Hopkins (1648) in Mass. Hist. Soc. Coll., 4th s., VI, 340, 1863. Quillipieck.—Early record cited by Trumbull in Conn. Hist. Soc. Coll., III, 10, 1895. Quillipiog.—Dunster (ca. 1648), in Mass. Hist. Soc. Coll., 4th s., I, 252, 1852. Quillipiuk.—Hubbard (1680), ibid., 2d s., VI, 318, 1815. Quillipyake.—Rogers (1640), ibid., 4th s., VII, 217, 1865. Quillypieck.—Davenporte (1639), ibid., 3d s., III, 166, 1833. Quimipeiock.—Eliot (1647), ibid., IV, 7, 1834. Quinapeag.—Lechford (1641), ibid., III, 98, 1833. Quinapeake.—Gookin (1674), ibid., 1st s., I, 147, 1806. Quinipiac.—Kendall, Trav., I, 276, 1809. Quinipieck.—Early record cited by Trumbull in Conn. Hist. Soc. Coll., III, 10, 1895. Quinipiuck.—Clark (1652) in Mass. Hist. Soc. Coll., 3d s., VIII, 290, 1843. Quinnepaeg.—Niles (1761), ibid., VI, 169, 1837. Quinnepas.—McKenney and Hall, Ind. Tribes, III, 81, 1854. Quinnepauge.—Niles (1761) in Mass. Hist. Soc. Coll., 3d s., VI, 169, 1837. Quinnepiack.—Prince (1735), ibid., 2d s., VIII, 122, 1819. Quinne-pyooghq.—Stiles quoted by Trumbull, Ind. Names Conn., 61, 1881. Quinnipauge.—Kendall, Trav., I, 276, 1809. Quinnipiak.—Drake, Ind. Chron., 156, 1836. Quinnipiĕuck.—Williams quoted by Trumbull in Conn. Hist. Soc. Coll., III, 9, 1895. Quinnipiog.—Peters (ca. 1637) quoted by Drake, Bk. Inds., bk. 2, 102, 1848. Quinnipioke.—Kendall, Trav., I, 276, 1809. Quinnopiage.—Patrick (1637) in Mass. Soc. Coll., 4th s., VII, 323, 1865. Quinnypiag.—Mason (ca. 1670), ibid., 2d s., VIII, 146, 1819. Quinnypiock.—Agreement of 1638 quoted by Trumbull in Conn. Hist. Soc. Coll., III, 10, 1895. Quinnypiog.—Mason (1637) quoted by Townshend, Quinnipiak Inds., 10, 1900. Quinopiocke.—Trumbull, Ind. Names Conn., 9, 10, 1881. Quinypiock.—Eaton (1640) in Mass. Hist. Soc. Coll., 4th s., VI, 345, 1863. Quirepeys.—Van der Donck (1656) quoted by Ruttenber, Tribes Hudson R., 82, 1872. Quiripeys.—Trumbull, Ind. Names Conn., 61, 1881 (early Dutch form). Quiripi.—Trumbull in Conn. Hist. Soc. Coll., III, 9, 1895. Qunnipiĕuk.—Williams quoted by Vater, Mith., pt. 3, sec. 3, 378, 1816. Qunnipiuck.—Williams (1638) in Mass. Hist. Soc. Coll., 4th s., VI, 251, 1863. Qunnipiug.—Williams (1640), ibid., 265. Qunnippiuck.—Vater, Mith., pt. 3, sec. 3, 344, 1816. Quunnipieuck.—Williams (1643) in Mass. Hist. Soc. Coll., 1st s., III, 205, 1794 (name used by the tribe). Qvinipiak.—Peter (ca. 1637), ibid., 4th s., VI, 94, 1863.

Quinnipiac. The principal village of the Quinnipiac, occupying the site of New Haven, Conn. For details of its situation and history, see Townshend, Quinnipiak Inds., 1900.

Quioborique. One of 36 tribes reported in 1683 as living in Texas, 3 days' travel N. E. of the mouth of the Rio Conchos. This information was given to Domingo de Mendoza by his Jumano guide, Juan Sabeata (Mendoza, Viage, 1683–84, MS. in Archivo General of Mexico). (H. E. B.)

Quiomaquí. Mentioned by Oñate (Doc. Inéd., XVI, 115, 1871) as a pueblo of the province of Atripuy (q. v.), in the region of the Rio Grande, N. Mex., in 1598.

Quiotráco. A pueblo of the Tigua or the Tewa in New Mexico in 1598 (Oñate in Doc. Inéd., XVI, 116, 1871). Bandelier (Ritch, New Mexico, 201, 1885) identifies it with ruins in Rio Arriba co., and it appears to be identical with Quioyaco, mentioned by Oñate (op. cit., 102) as a Chigua (Tigua) pueblo.

Quioucohanock ('gull river people.'—Gerard). A former tribe of the Powhatan confederacy on the s. bank of James r. in Surry co., Va. They numbered about 125 in 1608.

Quioughcohanock was understood to be the name of two streams about 11 m. apart, afterward called Upper and Lower Chipoak creeks. The name of the people was understood by the settlers of Jamestown to be Tapahanock, 'people of the stream that ebbs and flows'—a characteristic of all creeks of tidewater Virginia, which depend for their water on the tides of the rivers into which they flow, and not on the drainage of the surrounding land. Their chief town and residence of the werowance was probably upon an eminence now called Wharf Bluff, just E. of Upper Chipoak cr., in Surry co. It was visited, May 5, 1607, by Capt. Archer, who gives an entertaining account of the werowance of the country. (W. R. G.)

Quiocohànoes.—Jefferson (1785), Notes, 129, 1802. Quiocohanses.—Boudinot, Star in the West, 128, 1816. Quiyougcohanocks.—Smith (1629), Va., I, 116, repr. 1819. Quiyoughcohanocks.—Strachey (ca. 1612), Va., 35, 1849 (the river). Quiyoughqnohanocks.—Pots in Smith (1629), Va., I, 230, repr. 1819 (misprint).

Quioucohanock. The chief village of the Quioucohanock (q. v.).

Coiacohanauke.—Strachey (ca. 1612), Va., 56, 1849. Quiyonghcohanock.—Smith (1629), Va., I, map, repr. 1819 (misprint). Tapahanock.—Strachey (ca. 1612), Va., 56, 1849 (commonly, but corruptly, so called by the English).

Quiquiborica. A former rancheria, probably of the Sobaipuri, visited by Kino and Mange in 1699 (Mange cited by

Bancroft, Ariz. and N. Mex., 358, 1889). Situated on the Rio Santa Cruz, 6 leagues s. of Guevavi (q. v.), near the Arizona-Sonora boundary. Probably the later Buenavista. See *Bacuancos.*

Quiquihatch. See *Quickhatch.*

Quirogles. A former Costanoan village on or near San Francisco bay, Cal.
Quirogles.—Taylor in Cal. Farmer, Oct. 18, 1861. Quirotes.—Humboldt, New Spain, I, 321, 1811.

Quisabas. A tribe mentioned in 1684 by Domingo de Mendoza (Viage, 1683–84, MS. in Archivo Gen.) among those he expected to see in central Texas.

Quisaht (prob. 'people on the other side'). A name given to the Nootka settlements "beyond the Yuclulaht" (Ucluelet).—Sproat, Savage Life, 303, 1868.

Quiscat. The name of a chief of the lower Tawakoni village, and of the village itself, in the latter part of the 18th century. The settlement was on the w. side of the Brazos, on a bluff or plateau above some springs, not far from modern Waco, Texas. In 1778, immediately after an epidemic, it contained 150 warriors, or about 750 people (Mezières in Mem. de Nueva España, XXVIII, 273, MS.). In 1779, Mezières, while at the village, called it the "first village of the Taucanas, named that of Quiscat" (Noticia de los Efectos, etc., Sept. 13, 1779, in Mem. de Nueva España, XXVIII, 248, MS.). Morfi erroneously says that this village was one of Kichai and Yscani (Hist. Tex., *ca.* 1781, MS.). The name El Quiscat was applied to the village as late as 1795 (Manuel Muñoz in Lamar Papers, Mar. 13, 1795, MS.). Chief Quiscat went to San Antonio with Mezières to make peace with the Spaniards, apparently in 1772, and remained thereafter generally friendly, particularly using his influence to aid the Spaniards in restoring the apostate Aranames to Espíritu Santo mission, and inducing the Tonkawa to settle in a permanent village (Vial, Diario, 1787, in Archivo Gen., Hist., XLIII, MS.). Pedro Vial, when on his expedition from San Antonio to Santa Fé, having been severely injured by a fall from his horse, stayed three weeks at the lodge of Chief "Quiscate" to recover. See *Flechazos.* For the name, cf. *Kishkat,* given as a Wichita subtribe. (H. E. B.)
Guiscat.—Morfi, MS. Hist. Tex., II, *ca.* 1781. Quiscat.—Mezières (1779), op. cit. Quiscate.—Vial (1787), op. cit. Quisquate.—Ibid.

Quisiyove. A Calusa village on the s. w. coast of Florida, about 1570.
Luiseyove.—Fontaneda as quoted by French, Hist. Coll. La., 2d s., II, 255, 1875 (misprint). Quiseyove.—Fontaneda as quoted by Ternaux-Compans, Voy., XX, 22, 1841. Quisiyove.—Fontaneda Memoir (*ca.* 1575), Smith trans., 19, 1854.

Quitacas. One of the tribes the members of which accompanied Domingo de Mendoza on his expedition from the middle Rio Grande to the interior of Texas in 1683–84.—Mendoza, Viage (1683–84), MS. in Archivo Gen. Mexico. (H. E. B.)

Quitamac. A ruined pueblo of the Opata about 12 m. s. E. of Baserac, on the headwaters of Rio Yaqui, lat. 30°, E. Sonora, Mexico.
Quit-a-mac.—Bandelier in Arch. Inst. Papers, III, 62, 1890; IV, 517, 1892.

Quitoles. A tribe mentioned by Cabeza de Vaca (Smith trans., 84, 1851) as dwelling on the coast during his sojourn in Texas in 1527–34. The locality given is indefinite, and the ethnic relations of the tribe can not be determined with certainty, but they were probably Karankawan or Coahuiltecan. Cf. *Guisoles.*
Quitoks.—Cabeza de Vaca, Smith trans., 137, 1871.

Quitovaquita. The westernmost Papago village, situated on the headwaters of Rio Salado of Sonora, near the Arizona-Sonora boundary, lon. 112° 40'. Pop. 250 in 1863, 314 in 1900.
Quitobaca.—Garcés, Diary (1775-6), 487, 1900 (here confused with Bacapa). Quito Vaqueta.—Browne, Apache Country, 291, 1869. Quotovaquita.—Poston in Ind. Aff. Rep. for 1863, 385, 1864.

Quittaub. A village having some Praying Indians in 1698, apparently in s. w. Plymouth co., Mass. It may have been subject to the Wampanoag. See Rawson and Danforth (1698) in Mass. Hist. Soc. Coll., 1st s., X, 129, 1809.

Quiubaco. Mentioned by Oñate (Doc. Inéd., XVI, 115, 1871) as a pueblo of the province of Atripuy, in the region of the lower Rio Grande, N. Mex., in 1598. Possibly an attempt at Shiewibak, the native name of Isleta pueblo.

Quiutcanuaha. An unidentified tribe mentioned by Jesus María (Relación, Aug. 15, 1691, folio 112, MS.) as among the "Texias," or allies of the Hasinai of Texas. He said that they were s. w. of the Nabedache, and named them with Vidix (Bidai?), Toaha, Cantouhaona, Mepayaya, and others. They evidently lived beween Trinity and San Antonio rs. (H. E. B.)

Quivers. See *Arrows, Receptacles.*

Quivi. An unidentified tribe mentioned by Morfi in his list of Texas tribes (MS. Hist. Tex., bk. II, *ca.* 1781)

Quiviquinta. A Tepehuane pueblo in N. Jalisco, Mexico, 38 m. N. w. of Jesus María, and about 40 m. s. w. of Lajas.
Quiaviquinta.—Orozco y Berra, Geog., 281, 1864.

Quivira (possibly a Spanish corruption of *Kidikwiús,* or *Kirikurus,* the Wichita name for themselves, or of *Kirikuruks,* the Pawnee name for the Wichita). An Indian "province" of which Coronado learned from an Indian of the plains, evidently a Pawnee, known as "The Turk," while on the Rio Grande among the Pueblos of New Mexico in 1540–41. Quivira being reported as populous and of great wealth, Coronado started with his army, in the spring of 1541, to find it, with The Turk as a guide; but the Spaniards finding they were being misled by the Indian, who hoped to lose them on the great plains and cause them to perish, The Turk was put in irons, the main force sent back from the upper waters of the Rio Colorado of Texas, where they then were, and another Indian, Ysopete, chosen as guide for the rest of the journey due N. to Quivira, of which province he was a native. Proceeding northward for about thirty days with 30 picked horsemen, Coronado reached a river, which he called SS. Peter and Paul (identified as the Arkansas), the last of June, and proceeded up its N. bank within the present Kansas. This was the beginning of the Quivira country. The surrounding region was traversed during the remainder of the summer, but great disappointment met the Spaniards at the finding of only villages of grass lodges occupied by a semi-agricultural tribe, identified as the Wichita. The Turk was strangled to death as a punishment for his deception. An invitation was sent to the chief, Tatarrax, of the neighboring province of Harahey, believed to have been the Pawnee country, and every effort was made by the Spaniards to find traces of the gold in which the region was reputed to abound, but of course without result. The explorers returned to the Rio Grande by a more direct route, evidently following, from the Arkansas r., what later became the Santa Fé trail. Coronado continued to Mexico with his army in 1542, leaving behind Fray Juan de Padilla, who returned to Quivira, but was murdered by the natives because he planned to leave them and minister to another tribe. The name Quivira soon appeared on the maps of the period, but by reason of the indefiniteness of the knowledge of its situation the locality shifted from the region of the Great Plains to the Pacific coast, and finally settled, in the form La Gran Quivira, at the ruins of the forgotten Piro settlement of Tabira, E. of the Rio Grande in New Mexico, at which a Franciscan mission was established in 1629.

Consult Bandelier (1) in Arch. Inst. Papers, I, 1883; III, v, 1890; (2) in The Nation, Oct. 31 and Dec. 7, 1889; Winship in 14th Rep. B. A. E., 1896; Hodge (1) in Brower, Harahey, 1899; (2) in Span. Expl. in the Southern U. S., 1907; Mooney in Harper's Mag., May, 1899; Ritchey in Kans. Hist. Soc. Coll., VI, 1900; Dunbar, ibid., X, 1908; Brower, Quivira, 1898.   (F. W. H.)

Aguivira.—Coronado (1541) in Doc. Inéd., XIV, 324, 1870. Cuivira.—Castañeda (1596) misquoted in Am. Geog. Soc. Trans., v, 213, 1874. Cuybira.—Losa (1582–83) in Doc. Inéd., XV, 145, 1871. Gran Quivira.—Kino (ca. 1699) in Doc. Hist. Mex., 4th s., I, 347, 1856 (confused with Tabira). Mivera.—Pennant, Arctic Zoology, 3, 1792 (misprint). Qnivira.—Mota-Padilla, Hist. de la Conquista, 164, 1742 (misprint). Quebira.—Doc. of 1542 in Smith, Colec. Doc. Fla., I, 151–54, 1857. que Vira.—Jaramillo as quoted in Doc. Inéd., XIV, 310, 1870.

Quibira.—Coronado (1541), ibid., 326. Quinira.—Demarcación y Division, etc., ibid., XV, 461, 1871 (also Quinira). Quiriba.—Jaramillo (ca. 1560), ibid., XIV, 313, 1870 (misprint). Quiuira.—Gomara (1554) quoted by Hakluyt, Voy., III, 455, 1600); Galvano (1563) in Hakluyt Soc. Pub., XXX, 227, 1862; Munster, Cosmog., 1st map, 1598. Quiuiriens.—Gomara, Hist. Gen., 470a, 1606. Quivera.—Schoolcraft, Ind. Tribes, IV, 28, 1854. Quivica.—Hornot, Anec. Amér., 221, 1776. Quivina.—Dobbs, Hudson Bay, 163, 1744 (misprint). Quivira.—Coronado (1541) in Ternaux-Compans, Voy., IX, 362, 1838; Doc. Inéd., XIII, 264, 1870. Quiviræ.—Morelli, Fasti Novi Orbis, 23, 1776. Quivirans.—Prince, N. Mex., 166, 1883 (the people). Quivirenses.—Alcedo, Dic. Geog., IV, 389, 1788 (the people). Qvivira.—Wytfliet, Hist. des Indes, map, 114–16, 1605. Tindan.—Bonilla (1776) quoted by Bancroft, Ariz. and N. Mex., 108, 1889; Bandelier in Arch. Inst. Papers, III, 174, 1890 (Quivira and Teton confused). Xaqueuria.—Galvano (1563) in Hakluyt Soc. Pub., XXX, 227, 1862 (apparently Axa and Quivira).

Quiyough ('gulls.'—Hewitt). A village of the Powhatan confederacy in 1608, on the s. bank of Aquia cr., near its mouth, in Stafford co., Va. (Smith, 1629, Va., I, map, repr. 1819). The name Aquia is derived therefrom.

Quizquiz. A former town on or near the Mississippi r. in N. w. Miss. De Soto (1541) found its people at war with those of a town called Alibamo, and he assaulted the place before crossing the Mississippi into the Quapaw country.

Chisca.—Garcilasso de la Vega, Fla., 175, 1723. Quizquiz.—Gentleman of Elvas in Hakluyt Soc. Pub., IX, 89, 1851. Quiz Quiz.—Biedma (1544) in French, Hist. Coll. La., II, 104, 1850.

Qunahair ('pleasant place'). An inhabited Niska village of 5 old-fashioned houses with totem-poles in front; situated on a gravel flat at the edge of the woods, on the s. bank of Nass r., Brit. Col., just below the canyon. In 1906 the inhabitants were about to leave it and to settle several miles above, at the lower end of the canyon.   (G. T. E.)

Qunnoune. See *Canonicus*.

Quoddy. A variety of large herring found in Passamaquoddy bay, Me. From the place and ethnic name Passamaquoddy, *Peskĕdĕmakádi*, according to Gatschet (Nat. Geog. Mag., VIII, 23, 1897), which signifies 'abundance of pollock' in the Passamaquoddy dialect. The truncated form *Quoddy* appears also in place nomenclature. There are also "quoddy boats" in this region.   (A. F. C.)

Quoits. See *Chunkey*.

Quoratean Family. A term derived from Kworatem, the Yurok name of a small area of flat land at the confluence of Klamath and Salmon rs., just below the mouth of the latter, N. w. Cal. This name, proposed by Gibbs (Schoolcraft, Ind. Tribes, III, 422, 1853), was adopted by Powell (7th Rep. B. A. E., 100, 1891) for the linguistic family consisting of the Karok (q. v.) tribe or group.

Quotough. A village situated in 1608 on the w. bank of Patuxent r., in Prince George co., Md.—Smith (1629), Va., I, map, repr. 1819.

Qyan. The name of a place at the N. point of Gray's harbor, coast of Washington (Gairdner, 1835, in Jour. Geog. Soc. Lond., XI, 255, 1841). Unidentified.

Rababou. See *Robbiboe*.

Rabbit Assiniboin. A small band of Assiniboin living in 1829 in Assiniboia, Canada, w. of the Red River band.—Henry, Jour., II, 522, 1897.

Rabbit Lake Chippewa. A Chippewa band on Rabbit lake, Minn.—Washington treaty (1863) in U. S. Ind. Treat., 215, 1873.

Rabbit stick. The flat, curved rabbit club, *pútshkohu* of the Hopi, often called a boomerang, is not self-retrieving like the Australian weapon, though it shares the aeroplane nature of the latter; it is similar in form, but has not the delicate curves shaped to cause a return flight. Not all the Australian aeroplane clubs, however, are self-retrieving, a property probably discovered through practise with sailing clubs. The Hopi rabbit stick is delivered in the same way as the Australian, and its course after it strikes the ground often brings it to the right or left of the thrower and nearer to him than the farthest point reached in its flight. It makes one or more revolutions in its flight toward a rabbit, and if it does not strike the animal directly, its rapid gyration when it touches the ground makes probable the hitting of any object within several feet. So far as is known this is the only aeroplane club used in America. The material is Gambell's oak (*Quercus gambelii*), and a branch of the proper curve is selected for its manufacture. One end is cut out to form a handle, and the club is usually varnished with resin and painted with an invariable design in black, red, and green. Of late years a rabbit figure is frequently painted thereon. The weapon has a religious significance, probably arising from its use in ceremonial rabbit hunts, and it is the symbol of the sacred dance personage named Makto, 'hunt.'

The Gabrieleños of s. California used a rabbit stick similar to that of the Hopi; it was 2 ft in length in a straight line, 1¼ in. across at the handle, and 1¾ in. across at the broadest part, with an average thickness of ¾ in. It was made of hard wood, and ornamented with markings burnt in the surface.

See Fewkes in 21st Rep. B. A. E., pl. xlix, 1903; Dellenbaugh, North Americans of Yesterday, 270, 1901; Hoffman in Bull. Essex Inst., XVII, 29, 1885; Parry in Proc. Am. Asso. Adv. Sci. for 1872, 397–400.   (W. H.)

Rabbit Trap. A Cherokee settlement in upper Georgia about the time of the removal of the tribe to the W. in 1839.—Doc. of 1799 quoted by Royce in 5th Rep. B. A. E., 144, 1887.

Raccoon. A well-known quadruped, *Procyon lotor*, of the Ursidæ, or bear family, esteemed alike for its flesh and its pelt, which was one of the skins used by the southern Indians for making their loose winter mantles, or matchcoats. The first mention of the name in a recognizable form, that of *arocoun*, was made in 1610, and the second, in that of *aroughcun*, in 1612. The animal, which is nocturnal in its habits, sleeps in the daytime in some hollow tree (the sweet gum, *Liquidambar styraciflua*, in the S.) during the successive climbings of which to seek its abode the sharp nails with which its forepaws are provided leave long scratches upon the bark. Such a tree is hence called by the Indians by a name signifying 'raccoon tree.' It was from such tree-scratching custom that the animal received from the Virginia Indians the name by which it is universally known to English-speaking people, viz, *ärä῾kun*, an apocopated form of *ärä῾kunĕm*, 'he scratches with the hands.' The name is sometimes applied in British Guiana to the coatimondi (*Nasua fusca*), and, along with its apheretic form of 'coon' (which also is a humorous name for a negro, and in 1844 was a nickname applied to members of the Whig party, that adopted the raccoon as an emblem), enters into several combinations, as, 'raccoon-berry,' the fruit of *Podophyllum peltatum* and *Symphoricarpus racemosus*, on which the animal feeds; 'raccoon dog,' a kind of dog (*Nyctereutes procyonoides*) of Japan and China, and also a dog trained to hunt raccoons; 'raccoon grape,' a species of grape (*Vitis æstivalis*) of which the animal, and his relative the bear, are very fond; 'raccoon (or coon) oyster,' a small southern variety of the mollusk on which the animal subsists when vegetable food is scarce; 'raccoon perch,' the yellow perch (*Perca flavescens*), the dark bands upon the sides of which bear a remote resemblance to those of a raccoon's tail; 'coon bear,' a large carnivore of Tibet, and 'coon-heel,' a name in Connecticut for a long, slender oyster. In the Presidential campaign of 1844, 'Coonery' was a derogative synonym for Whiggery or Whiggism, meaning the doctrines of the Whig party. The animal has the reputation of being very knowing; hence the simile 'as sly as a coon,' and the metaphor 'he is an old coon,' said of a person who is very shrewd. Finally, 'to coon' is to creep, cling close, to creep as a coon along a branch; a 'gone coon' is a person whose case is hopeless, and a 'coon's age' is a southern figurative expression meaning a long time; while to be 'as forlorn as an unmated coon' is to be extremely wretched.   (W. R. G.)

Race names. The names given to the white man by the various Indian tribes exhibit a wide range of etymological signification, since the newcomers received appellations referring to their personal appearance, arrival in ships, arms, dress, and other accouterments, activities, merchandise and articles brought with them, as iron, and fancied correspondence to figures of aboriginal myth and legend. A few tribes borrowed words to designate the white man, probably before they actually saw him. Some others extended the term at first employed for Englishmen or Frenchmen to include all white men with whom they afterward had to do. In the following examples the native names have been simplified so far as possible.

Algonquian names.—Among the various languages of the Algonquian stock a number of different terms for white man are to be found. The Arapaho has *niatha*, *nanagakanet*, *nihanatayeche*, etc. The last signifies 'yellow hide,' the second 'white-skinned.' Of *niatha* Mooney (14th Rep. B. A. E., 1020, 1896) says: "The word signifies literally expert, skillful, or wise, and is also the Arapaho name for the spider." Kroeber (Trad. of Arapaho, 8, 1902) says the name is given to the character in Arapaho traditions corresponding to the Algonquian Nanabozho, Napi, etc., and the Siouan Ishtinike, while at the same time it is now "the ordinary word for white men in Arapaho just as in Cheyenne the name of the mythical character *Vihho*, has been applied to the whites." (See also Wake, Nihancan, the White Man, Am. Antiq., XXVI, 224–31, 1904.) In Siksika a white man is called *napiekwan*, in which -*ekwan* is a kind of ethnic suffix of the person. As a general term for 'white man' we have the Chippewa *wayabĭshkiwäd*, 'one who is white' (generally referring to Englishmen only); Miami, *wâbkĕlokéta*, 'white skin' (a white man); equally common with these terms for whites in general is *misha'kĭganäsiwŭg*, 'they of the hairy chest' (Wm. Jones, inf'n, 1906). The former Chippewa term corresponds with the Cree *wapiskisiw* and related words in cognate dialects. The Delaware *woapsit*, 'white person,' signifies literally 'he is white.' Delaware also has for 'European' *schwonnach*, 'person from the salt (sea).' The Chippewa term for 'Englishman,' *shaganash*, has been extended to mean 'white man,' just as has also the Micmac word for 'Frenchman,' *wenooch*, Penobscot *awenoch*, Abnaki *awanoch*, cognate with such other Algonquian terms for 'white man' as the Narraganset *awaunagus*, Scaticook *wanux*, Pequot-Mohegan *wonnux*, Passamaquoddy *wenoch*, etc., primarily derived from *awan*, 'who,' 'somebody,' the European being looked upon as 'somebody coming.'

Athapascan names.—According to Morice (Anthropos, I, 236, 1906), the Western Déné call the whites *neto*, and the French *su-neto*, i. e. 'the true white men.' The Navaho term for whites is *Belagana*, a corruption of the Spanish word *Americano*.

Eskimo names.—The representative Eskimo term for 'white man' is *kablunak*, according to Rink (Am. Anthr., XI, 181–87, 1898), a corruption by Europeans of *keydlunak*, 'wolf,' preserved in this sense only in the Eskimo language of the far west, the name having been given with reference to the myth of "the girl and the dogs." Another etymology derives the word from the root *qauk*, 'daylight,' 'white day,' so that it ultimately signifies 'having very light skin.' Petitot favors a derivation which indicates the European fashion of "wearing a cap or hat covering their foreheads down to the eyebrows (*kablut*)." In the secret language of the Central Eskimo medicinemen (Boas in Bull. Am. Mus. Nat. Hist., XV, 35, 1901) the word for 'European' is *kidlatet*, evidently a derivative of *kidlak*, the secret term for 'iron.' When the crew of the *Plover* reached Pt Barrow (Richardson, Polar Reg., 300, 1861), they were termed by the Eskimo *shakenatanagmeun*, 'people from under the sun,' and *emakhlin*, 'sea men,' but commonly *nelluangmeun*, 'unknown people.' The Greenland Eskimo called the Danes *ukissut*, 'winterers.'

Iroquoian names.—The Cherokee, according to Mooney, call the white man *yûñwunega*, from *yûñwi* 'person,' and *unega* 'white.' Cuoq (Lex. Iroq., 112, 1882) gives for 'white man,' *kihnaraken*, 'my skin is white,' from *keraken* 'I am white,' and *ohna* 'skin.' Another Iroquoian term is *asseroni*, 'he makes axes,' the name applied by the Iroquois to the first Dutch colonists, and in Canada, in the form *onseronni*, to the French. Other Iroquoian names now or formerly in use are: Wyandot or Caughnawaga *tulhaesaga*, said to mean 'morning-light people,' and *ashalecoa*, or *assaricol*, said to mean 'big knife'; Huron *agnonha*, 'Frenchman.'

Kiowan names.—A Kiowa term for 'white men' is *bedalpago*, 'hairy mouths,' from *bedal* 'lip,' *pa* 'downy hair,' and *go* tribal terminal. Another is *ta-'ka-i*, 'ears sticking out,' which, according to Mooney (14th Rep. B. A. E., 1091, 1896) applies to the ears of a white "as compared with the Indian's, which are partly concealed by his long hair." It is also the Kiowa name for a mule or a donkey. Another term is *hañpogo*, 'trappers,' because some of the first whites known to them were American trappers (Mooney, 17th Rep. B. A. E., 397, 1898). Still other names in use among the Kiowa for white men, according to Mooney, are *ganoñko*, 'growlers,' in allusion to their rougher voices; *gañtonto*, 'capwearers,' and *boyoñko*, 'blonds.' The word *bedal-pago*, while designating whites in general, applies more particularly to Americans, who are also known as *t'o-ta'ka-i*, 'cold whites,' that is, northern white men, as distinguished from the Mexicans to the s. The Texans are distinguished as *Tehä'-nego*, from the Spanish *Tejano*.

Kitunahan names.—The Kutenai call a white man *suyapi*, a term identical with *sueapo*, given by Parker (Jour., 381, 1840) as the Nez Percé word for 'American.' Another Kutenai term is *nutlukene*, 'stranger.' A third expression, *kamnuqtlo aktsmakinik*, 'white man,' is probably a translation of the English term.

Maidu name.—According to Gatschet the term for white man is *sakini*, i. e. 'ghosts,' 'spirits'.

Shoshonean names.—In Shoshoni and Comanche the word for 'white man' is *taivo;* in Paiute and Bannock, *tavibo*. This, as Mooney (14th Rep. B. A. E., 1056, 1896) has pointed out, seems to be derived from *täbi*, 'the sun.' The Washo name for 'white man,' *tabaa*, may have been borrowed from the neighboring Paviotso. The idea of sun men, or easterners, is met with elsewhere, as among the Hopi of Shoshonean stock.

Siouan names.—Long (Exped. Rocky Mts., II, lxxx, 1823) gives the name for 'white man' in Oto as *mazonkka*, 'ironmakers,' and the Omaha name as *wahta*, 'makers.' A vocabulary of about 1819 has Omaha *wahe*, Hidatsa *washi*, i. e. *masi*. More modern vocabularies and dictionaries give the following Siouan words for 'white man': Dakota, *washechu;* Mandan, *wuashi;* Assiniboin, *wahsheechoon*. These and related words signify 'rich people,' or perhaps 'generous people.' The Hidatsa term (Matthews, Hidatsa Ind., 183, 1877) for 'white' (American) is *maetsihateki*, or *maetsiictia*, i. e. 'long or big knife.'

Skittagetan names.—The Skidegate dialect of Haida has for 'white man' *kelgadaa*, 'man white,' and *yets-haidagai*, 'iron people,' the latter being the usual term.

Wakashan names.—The Nootka word for 'white man' or 'European,' *mamatlne*, signifies really 'house adrift on water,' in reference to the ships of the newcomers. The word in the Clayoquot dialect is *mamatle*.

The examples cited show the variety existing in the names for 'white man' among the linguistic stocks N. of Mexico and the interesting ways in which such appellations have been made up from peculiarities of a physical, mental, or social character.

Yuchi name.—The Yuchi term for white man (American) is *kuyáχka*, from *ku* 'man,' *wiaχka* 'white' (Gatschet).

Muskhogean name.—The Choctaw term for white man is *naⁿhullo*.

Americans.—The American, or inhabitant of the English colonies in what is now the United States, received from the Indians during and after the wars which preceded and followed the Revolution, names which distinguished him from the Frenchman and the Englishman. Probably from the swords of the soldiery several tribes designated Americans as 'big knives,' or 'long knives.' This is the signification of the Chippewa and Nipissing *chĭmo'koman*, from *kechimo'koman*, 'great knife,' Cree *kitchimokkuman*, Delaware *m'chonsikan*, 'big knife' (i. e., Virginian), and cognate terms in some of the Algonquian dialects. In Menominee is found *mokuman* (*mo'koman*, 'knife'); in Wyandot (1819), *saraumigh;* in Shawnee, *shĕmanĕse*, 'big knife'; in Oto (1823), *mahehunjeh;* in Omaha (1823), *mahhetunguh;* in Dakota (1823), *menahashah;* in Hidatsa (1823), *manceechteet*. These, like the Yankton *minahanska* and Teton *milahanska*, signify 'long or big knife.' In 1871 Roehrig gave the Dakota word for 'American' as *isangtanka*, 'big knife.' The Siksika term *omak kistoapikwan* signifies 'big-knife person'; *ommakistowan* has about the same meaning. The prominence of Boston in the early history of the United States led to its name being used for 'American' on both the Atlantic and the Pacific coast. The Micmac to-day call the United States *Bostoon*, and an American *Bostoonkawaach;* the Nipissing *Bastone*, the Canadian Abnaki *Bastoni*, and the Mohawk Iroquois *Wastonronon*, signify not merely the inhabitants of Boston, but the New Englanders or the people of the United States in general. The share of the men in Boston in the development of the Oregon country is recalled by the term *Boston*, which in the Chinook jargon designates 'American.' From the jargon this word passed into a number of the languages of the Pacific coast region: Klamath, *Boshtin;* Kutenai, *Bosten;* Déné (Carrier), *Boston*. The eastern Déné name is *Bestcorh-o'-tinne*, 'people of the big knives.' The Navaho have adopted *Pelikano*, or *Melikano*, from the Spanish 'Americano.' The Hopi name is *Mellycawno* (Bourke, Moquis of Arizona, 317, 1884), but among themselves they use the term *Pahana*, 'eastern water people.' The Zuñi call Americans *Melikanakwe* (Cushing, in Millstone, x, 100, June 1885). The Cherokee called Americans *Aniwatsini*, 'Virginians,' from *Watsini* 'Virginia' (Mooney).

English.—One of the earliest terms for 'Englishman' is the Natick *wautacone*, 'coat man,' 'he who wears clothing.' Others, the Pequot, *waunnux*, 'somebody coming,' the term used also for 'Frenchman' in several eastern Algonquian dialects; and the Narraganset *chauquaquock*, 'knife men.' In the latter language Roger Williams cites *Englishmannuck*, and the form *Englishmansog*, both plurals, as also in use. The modern Canadian Abnaki has *Iglizmon*. A Shawnee vocabulary of 1819 (Trans. Am. Antiq. Soc., I, 290, 1820) has *Englishmanake*. To another group belong the Micmac *Aglaseaoo*, the Abnaki *Anglis*, the Nipissing *Aganesha*, the Prairie Cree *Akaydsiw*, the Chippewa *Shăganāsh* (which possibly is connected with 'spearman' or the 'contemptible spearman'—Wm. Jones, inf'n, 1906), the Ottawa *Saganash*, the Cree *Akaias*, etc., all of which are thought to be corruptions of the French 'Anglais' or 'les Anglais.' The older forms of these words, as the Missisauga (1801) *Zaganassa*, the Montagnais (1800) *Agaleshou*, the Micmac (1800) *Angalsheeau*, Nascapee *Naggaleshou*, and the Nipissing *Angalesha*, seem to justify this belief, although it is possible some of these words may have been corrupted from 'English' instead of from 'Anglais.' The Abnaki corruption of 'Englishman' was *Iglismon* (Maurault, Abenakis, vii, 1866), Delaware *Ingelishman*. Long (Exped. Rocky Mts., 1823) gives for 'British' in Oto *ragarrashing*, and in Omaha *sukanash*, both loan words from the Algonquian. In the language of the Siksika 'Englishman' is *nitapiapikwan*, 'real white man.' The Canadian Mohawk of Lake of Two Mountains, Quebec, call an 'Englishman' *tiorhensaka*, 'inhabitant of the east.' Long, early in the century, gave for 'British' in Hidatsa *bosheittochresha*, which he interprets as meaning 'the men who bring black cloth.' In the Chinook jargon the word for 'English' is *Kintshautsh*, and for 'Englishmen' *Kintshautshman*, from 'King George,' the reigning monarch at the period in which the jargon arose. From the jargon these terms have passed into a number of the languages of the Pacific Coast region: Klamath, *Sking dshudsh* or *King Dshutch;* Kutenai, *Skindjatsh*, 'Canadian,' 'Englishman.' The western Déné, according to Morice (Anthropos, I, 236–7, 1906) call the English *sagœnaz*, an Algonquian loan-word; the eastern Déné term them *tsé-o'tinne*, 'inhabitants of the rocks.' In Creek (of the Muskhogean stock) Gatschet cites for Englishmen *mikĭlisi*, 'subjects of the great king,' with which goes Choctaw and Chicasaw *minkĭlisi*.

Scotch.—According to Cuoq (Lex. Iroq., 166, 1882), the Mohawk of Lake of Two Mountains, Quebec, called the first Scotchmen (settlers) with whom they came into contact *kentahere*, in reference to their headdress, 'Tam O'Shanter,' which reminded them of a cow-dropping (*ota*). Wilson (Ojebway Lang., 343, 1874) gives *Scotchmun* as the term in Canadian Chippewa. Another Chippewa name is *Opitotowew*, 'he who speaks differently.' Rand gives in Micmac *Skŏjemĕn*.

French.—The Algonquian languages in particular furnish several special words for 'Frenchman,' individuals of that nationality having come into very close contact with many of the tribes of this stock, as settlers, coureurs des bois, and hunters and trappers, often having Indian wives and becoming members of aboriginal communities. The Micmac term was *wenjooch* (in composition *wenjoo*), applied to white men, sometimes even to the English, but originally and specifically to the Frenchman and signifying 'somebody coming.' That this was its original signification the related eastern Algonquian words for 'white man' indicate, as the Penobscot *awenoch*, the Pequot *wanux*, the Passamaquoddy *wenoch*, etc. Another Algonquian term for Frenchman is the Cree *wemistikojiw*, Chippewa *wemĭtigoshĭ*, 'people of the wooden canoes,' probably akin to the Fox *wämĕ̆tĕgowĭsĭta*, 'one who is identified with something wooden,' probably referring to something about clothing or implements. The Fox name for a Frenchman is *wämĕ̆tĕgoshĭa* (Wm. Jones, inf'n, 1906); Menominee, *wameqtikosiu;* Missisauga, *wamitigushi*, etc. Lahontan translated the old Algonkin *mittigouchiouek*, 'builders of vessels,' which Trumbull (Trans. Am. Philol. Asso., 154, 1871) considered incorrect, though he saw in it a reference to the 'wooden boats' of the French, *mitigo* meaning 'wooden.' An aged Missisauga woman related (Chamberlain, Lang. of Mississagas, 60, 1892) that the word referred to the boxes carried by the early French traders, but this may have been merely a folk etymology suggested by *mitigwash*, 'trunk,' 'valise.' The Siksika word for 'Frenchman' is *nitsappekwan*. A Shawnee vocabulary of 1819 gives *Tota*, and Cotton's old Massachuset vocabulary has the plural form *Punachmonog*, evidently taken from the English 'Frenchman.' The Abnaki corruption of 'Frenchman' was *Pelajemon* (Maurault, Abenakis, viii, 1866). An Hidatsa name is *masik'ti*, 'true white.' The Hasinai of Texas, according to Bolton, called the French *Canos;* in allusion to this fact the Spaniards named an Arkokisa partisan of the French, *Canos*.

The Mohawk of Lake of Two Mountains, Quebec, call a Frenchman *onseronni*, which Cuoq (Lex. Iroq., 69, 1882) interprets as 'maker of hatchets,' from *konnis* 'I make,' and *osera* 'hatchet.' This is the same name as *aseronni*, the appellation conferred on the first Dutch colonists of New York by the Iroquois, and apparently a more or less general term for 'white man.'

The term in Chinook jargon for Frenchman is *Pasaiuks*, which Hale (Chinook Jarg., 49, 1890) derives from 'Français' with the Chinook plural suffix *uks*. It has been used to signify also 'foreigners,' and has passed into several Indian languages of the Pacific Coast region, e. g., the Klamath *Pasháyuks*. The Kutenai call a Frenchman *notlukene*, 'foreigner,' 'stranger.' According to Grossman (Smithson. Rep. 1871, 412, 1873) the Pima called a Frenchman *parlesick* (plural, *paparlesick*), from *parle* (Spanish, *padre*), 'priest.' The Athapascan Takulli call a Frenchman *neto* or *nado*.

German.—Some of the Indian tongues have special words for 'German.' The Chippewa term is *Anima*, a modification of the French Allemand, introduced by traders or missionaries. Baraga (Otchipwe Dict., pt. 2, 36, 1880), says: "The Indians also call a German 'Detchman,' a corruption of 'Dutchman,' as the Germans are improperly called in some parts of this country." From the French comes also the Micmac *Alma*. The Sauk and Fox have *Tŭchiᶜa*, from 'Dutch.' In Klamath the term for 'German' is *Detchmal*, while in the Modoc dialect of the Lutuamian stock the name applied to the German settler is *muni tchuleks gitko*, 'thickset fellow' (Gatschet, Klamath Inds., II, 1890). Mooney (Myths of Cherokee, 141, 1902) mentions a noted Cherokee chief about 1830 who was named *Tahchee*, or 'Dutch.' He gives the plural Cherokee name as *Anitŭtsi* (Cherokee MS. vocab., B. A. E., 1887). A Blackfoot word for 'German' is *kistappekwan*. The Creek name for a German, according to Adair (Am. Inds., 66, 1775), was *yah yah algeh*, 'those whose talk was ja ja.' The Chickasaw name was *kish kish tarakshe* (ibid., 7).

Spanish.—The contact of the Indian tribes of the Southern states with Spanish explorers, settlers, and colonizers gave rise to several names for them. The Algonquian dialects of the Great Lakes and the E. have taken their words for Spaniard from the English or French: Nipissing *Espaniio*, from the French Espagnol, as also the Chippewa *Eshpayo* and the Siksika *Spiokwan*, or *Spiokuwin*, 'Mexican,' 'Spaniard.' The Sauk and Foxes have *Aᶜpayoᶜa* for Spaniard, and *Mähikoᶜa* for Mexican. The Cherokee term for Spaniard is *Askwani*, derived from the Spanish Español, to which was added the tribal prefix *ani*, making *Aniskwani*, 'Spaniards.' The Arkokisa called the Spaniards *Yegsa*. The Klamath have *Spaniolkni*, from Español, with the Indian suffix. The Mohawk of Lake of Two Mountains, Quebec, use *Eskwanior*, from the French Espagnol. For Mexicans of various districts the Indians along the border have developed special terms: Kiowa *ä-ta-ᶜka-i*, literally 'timber Mexicans,' applied to inhabitants of Tamaulipas; *do kañi-taᶜka-i*, 'bark Mexicans,' inhabitants of Santa Rosa mts.; *ko p-taᶜka-i*, 'mountain whites,' used for New Mexicans and sometimes generally for Mexicans; *tsoñ-taᶜka-i*, 'light-haired Mexicans'; *tso-taᶜka-i*, 'rock white men,' Mexicans about Silver City, N. Mex.; *pa-edal-taᶜka-i*, 'great-river whites,' Mexicans of the Rio Grande, etc. (Mooney in 17th Rep. B. A. E., 435, 1898). The Navaho term for Mexicans is *naakai*, 'white foreigners' and for Spaniards, *naakai-diyini*, 'holy white foreigners.' The Olamentke of California called the Spaniards by the name, *Olingo*, that they applied to the Aleut brought thither by the Russians, which seems to be the same word, *Ullenego*, as that which they applied to themselves as Indians. The Russians they call by another term, *levuyume*. The Mohave Indians call a Mexican or a Spaniard *haiko tahana*, 'long white man,' while the Zuñi, who received their first knowledge of the white man in the person of the early Spanish explorers from Mexico, call the Mexicans *tsipolo-kwe*, 'mustached people.' The old Tonkawa term for a Mexican is *tóptcho*, the newer one *kanushá-akon*.

Negro.—Among certain Indian tribes the name of the negro signifies simply 'black flesh.' This is the meaning of the Chippewa *maᶜkadäwiyas*, the Cree *kaskite wiyas*, etc. The Delaware *nescalenk* signifies 'black face.' Some others designate him as 'black man,' which is the sense of the Nipissing *makatewinini*, the Yuchi *kúispi*, etc. 'Black Indian' is the meaning of the Kutenai *kamkokokotl aktsemakinek*, the latter term signifying 'Indian' as distinguished from 'man,' *titkat*, and *kitonaqa*, 'Kutenai.' The Delaware *nesgessit lenape* has a similar signification. Sometimes the word for 'black' alone is used, as the Kutenai *kamkokokotl*, etc. With several tribes 'black white man,' or, in some cases, 'black foreigners,' is the real meaning of the term for negro, as the Mohave *waiko kwanil* and the Comanche *duqtaivo*, from *duq*, black, and *taivo*, 'white man' or 'foreigner'; also the Siksika *siksapikwan*, *napikwan* signifying 'white man'; and the Kiowa *koñkyäoñ-kᶜia*, 'man with black on, or incorporated into, him.' The Narraganset of Roger Williams's time "called a blackamoor *suckauttacone*, a coal-black man, for *sucki* is black and *wautacone* one that wears clothes"; according to Trumbull (Natick Dict., 226) *sucki* means 'dark-colored,' not 'black,' and *Wautacone* was one of the names by which an Englishman was designated; hence, 'black Englishman' might be a fair rendering of the word. Analogous is the Menominee word for negro, *apésen wameqtikosiu*, 'black Frenchman.' According to Gatschet the Kiowa Apache word for negro, *lizhena*, means 'buffalo-black-haired.' In Klamath *waiha*, applied to the negro, signifies 'servant,' and the Timucua *atemimachu* means 'his black slave.' The Klamath have besides adopted from the whites the term *nigga*, from which is derived *niggalam shaamoksh*, the term for monkey, meaning literally 'negro's kinsman.'

Dutch.—The Iroquoian tribes of New York called a Dutchman *aseronni*, a term identical with *onseronni*, by which the Mohawk of Lake of Two Mountains, Quebec, designate a Frenchman to-day. Its literal signification seems to be 'maker of hatchets.' The Iroquois used the word as an adjective to designate several things, as *ooskah asseroni*, 'flax,' in Onondaga, literally, 'Dutchman's thread'; *ossaheta asseroni*, 'peas,' literally, 'Dutch beans' (Beauchamp in Jour. Am. Folk-lore, xv, 96, 98, 1902). The Delawares of New Jersey called the Dutch by a name spelled by the early writers *swannekins*. Without the English *s* this is evidently identical with the Delaware *schwonnachquin*, 'white people,' literally, 'people from the salt sea (*schwon*),' a term used to designate Europeans in general.

Chinaman.—Some of the Indian tribes, through the actual presence among them of the Oriental, others by indirection only, have come to have special names for the Chinaman. The Kutenai, who know him from actual observation, call the Chinaman *gooktlam*, the chief component of which is *aqkoktlam*, 'hair,' in reference to his queue. The Chinook jargon has adopted the English word. The Siksika name is *apotsepista*. The Kiowa name signifies 'yellow man.'   (A. F. C.)

Racket. See *Ball play, Games.*

Rahasálali ('oak wood'). A Tarahumare rancheria near Palanquo, Chihuahua, Mexico.—Lumholtz, inf'n, 1894.

Rahaughcoon. See *Raccoon.*

Rahun. An important Yaqui settlement on the N. bank of the lower Rio Yaqui, s. w. Sonora, Mexico. Escudero estimated its population at 6,000 in 1849, but its present number is not known.
Asuncion de Raum.—Orozco y Berra, Geog., 355, 1864. Racum.—Escudero, Not. Son. y Sin., 100, 1849. Rahum.—Velasco (1850) quoted by Bancroft, Nat. Races, I, 608, 1882. Raún.—Mühlenpfordt, ibid.

Rahway. See *Rockaway.*

Raiabó ('the slope,' or 'the hillock'). The name of several distinct rancherias of the Tarahumare not far from Norogachic, Chihuahua, Mexico.—Lumholtz, inf'n, 1894.

Rain-in-the-Face. A noted Sioux warrior and chief, born near the forks of Cheyenne r., N. Dak., about 1835, died

at Standing Rock res., in the same state, Sept. 14, 1905. He was a full-blood Hunkpapa, one of a family of six brothers, one of whom was known as Iron Horse. Shortly before his death, he said: "My father was not a chief; my grandfather was not a chief, but a good hunter and a feast-maker. On my mother's side I had some noted ancestors, but they left me no chieftainship. I had to work for my reputation" (Eastman in Outlook, Oct. 27, 1906). He received his common name as the result of a personal encounter, when about 10 years of age, with a Cheyenne boy, whom he worsted; he received several blows in the face, however, causing it to be spattered with blood and streaked where the paint had been washed away. When a young man, he joined a war-party against the Gros Ventres, some of whose horses they stole, but the Sioux party was overtaken and had to fight for their lives. Rain-in-the-Face had his face painted to represent the sun when half covered with darkness—half black and half red. Fighting all day in the rain, his face became partly washed and streaked with red and black, so again he was named Rain-in-the-Face. He had been many times on the warpath, but his first important experience as a warrior was in the attack on the troops near Ft Phil Kearny, Wyo., in Dec. 1866, in which Capt. Fetterman and his entire command of 80 men were killed. He participated also in a fight, two years later, near Ft Totten, Dak., in which he and his horse were wounded. About three years before the Custer massacre in 1876, Rain-in-the-Face was accused of killing a surgeon and a trader of Gen. Stanley's expedition, for which he was arrested by Col. Thomas Custer. Having confessed his guilt, he was imprisoned for a time, but was allowed by his guard to escape and joined Sitting Bull's band of hostiles in the spring of 1874, declaring that he would "cut the heart out of Tom Custer and eat it." Rain-in-the-Face was a leading participant in the Little Bighorn fight, and although it has frequently been stated that he personally killed Gen. Custer, this is now generally doubted, and was denied by him. From wounds received in this battle he was permanently lamed, yet he followed Sitting Bull into Canada, where he remained until 1880, when most of the fugitives surrendered to Gen. Miles at Ft Keogh, Mont. He had seven wives, few of whom lived long or happily with him; the last wife was found in his tipi with her throat cut.

Ramah. An Eskimo mission established on the E. coast of Labrador by the Moravians in 1871.—Thompson, Moravian. Miss., 230, 1890.

Ramcock. The village of the Rancocas, on Rancocas cr., N. J., in the 17th century.

Ramcock.—Evelin (ca. 1648) quoted by Proud, Penn., I, 113, 1797. Rancokeskill.—Newcastle conf. (1675) in N. Y. Doc. Col. Hist., XII, 523, 1877 (Rancokus creek; kill=creek). Rankokus.—Doc. of 1674, ibid., III, 223, 1853 (applied to the hill).

Ramushonok. A Chowanoc (?) village in 1585, apparently between the Meherrin and Nottoway rs., in Hertford co., N. C.

Ramushonoq.—Smith (1629), Va., II, map, repr. 1819. Ramushouug.—DeBry, map, in Hawks, N. C., I, 1859.

Rancheria Grande. The name applied to a large aggregation of Indians who lived during the greater part of the first half of the 18th century near the middle Brazos r., Texas. It was closely associated with the Tonkawan tribes of the region, but in origin it was a curious composite. To the Ervipiame, perhaps natives of the region, there were added (1) the remains of numerous broken-down tribes from near and even beyond the Rio Grande, who had moved eastward and settled with the Ervipiame for defence and protection against the Apache, and to escape punishment at the hands of the Spaniards for damages done on the frontier, and (2) many apostates from the missions of the Rio Grande and the San Antonio missions. Because of the prominence of the Ervipiame in the group, it was sometimes called "Rancheria Grande de los Ervipiames." The presence of the apostates in the settlement made it especially obnoxious to the missionaries (Arch. Col. Santa Cruz de Querétaro, K, leg. 19, doc. 19, 1729, MS.). Rancheria Grande is mentioned in the Spanish records as early as 1707, when Diego Ramón, captain at San Juan Bautista, set out to punish it for disturbances at the missions (Diego Ramón, Diario, 1707, MS.). It was then said to be on the San Marcos, perhaps the Colorado. Again, in 1714, he recovered from it apostates from the missions (Arch. Col. Santa Cruz de Querétaro, op. cit.).

In 1716, when Capt. Ramón and Fr. Espinosa passed through it, it was 2 or 3 leagues w. of the Brazos, above the junction of its two arms, and above the mouth of the San Xavier, now the San Gabriel and the Little r. This would apparently put the rancheria above Cameron, in Milam co. According to Ramón there were more than 2,000 Indians, mostly gentile but some apostate, of various tribes, the most important being the Ervipiame. Espinosa noted also Ticmanares, Mesquites, Pamayes, Payayes, Mescales, Cantonaes, Xarames, and Sijames (Ramón, Derrotero, 149–152, 1716, MS.; Espinosa, Diario, entries from May 30 to June 14, MS.).

In 1722 the mission of San Xavier de Náxera was founded at San Antonio for the Ervipiame of Rancheria Grande, and their settlement became known as the Ervipiame suburb. Among those baptized there, the Ervipiames, Muruames, and Ticmamares were the most numerous. A Guerjuatida "from Rancheria Grande" was in the list. Other tribal names, some of which may represent intermarriages at the missions, were Tucara (Tawakoni?), Pamaya, Pazaguan, Gabilan, and Cantunal. Rancheria Grande continued to be mentioned as near San Xavier r., and it was four chiefs of the Yojuanes, Maieyes (unquestionably Tonkawan tribes), Deadozes, and Rancheria Grande who asked for the missions later founded (ca. 1749) on San Xavier r. (Dispatch of the Viceroy, Mar. 26, 1751, Lamar Papers, MS.). The Tonkawa tribe also offered to enter these missions, and were assigned to that of San Francisco Xavier, with the Yojuanes, Mayeyes, and Ervipiames, or Rancheria Grande Indians, apart from the Karankawan and the Bidai-Arkokisa groups which entered the other two missions near by. These facts, together with the additional one that the Apache were enemies of the San Xavier group, are only a few of numerous indications that Rancheria Grande was largely Tonkawan in its affiliation. The Indians had dogs and horses, engaged in only a little agriculture, were expert hunters and fighters, traded in skins, and made rafts of skins and of poles and reeds. (H. E. B.)

Ranchos (Span.: Los Ranchos, 'the ranches'). A former pueblo of the Taos Indians, about 3 m. from Taos pueblo, N. N. Mex., which in 1854 had become a Mexicanized town.—Lane in Schoolcraft, Ind. Tribes, v, 689, 1855. It is now known as Ranchos de Taos.

Rancocas. A division of the Delawares formerly living on the E. bank of Delaware r., in the present Burlington co., N. J. Their village was Ramcock. They were estimated at 100 warriors about 1648.

Chichequaas.—Proud, Penn., II, 294, 1798. Lamikas.—Ibid. Ramkokes.—Deed of 1649 in N. Y. Doc. Col. Hist., XII, 49, 1877. Ramocks.—Sanford, U. S., cxlvi, 1819. Rancokas.—Boudinot, Star in the West, 128, 1816. Rankokas.—Proud, Penn., II, 294, 1798. Remkokes.—De Laet (1633) in N. Y. Hist. Soc. Coll., 2d s., I, 315, 1841.

Rappahannock (Renape: Răpĕhănĕk, 'the alternating stream.' In Northern Lenape the addition of k to -häne gave the stream name a specific meaning, and this terminal letter had the same force as the definite article 'the'. The termination -ock in the Southern Renape word may be the animate plural suffix; if so, the word would mean "people of the alternating (ebb and flow) stream.' However this may be, the suffix is not locative, since the Renape characteristic of the locative is -nk, not -k. The cognate name of the river, Tappahannock, is still preserved as a place name in Essex co., Va. See Am. Anthr., VI, 315, 320–29, 1904; VII, 238, 1905.—Gerard). A tribe of the Powhatan confederacy formerly living on Rappahannock r. in Richmond co., Va. In 1608 they numbered about 400.

Rapahanna —Percy in Purchas, Pilgrimes, IV, 1687, 1626. **Rapahanocks.**—Smith (1629), Va., I, 74, repr. 1819. **Rappahanoc.**—Writer of 1676 in Mass. Hist. Soc. Coll., 4th s., IX, 162, 1871.

Rappahannock. The principal village of the Rappahannock, situated at the mouth of a creek, on Rappahannock r. It was extinct in 1722.

Toppahanock.—Strachey (ca. 1612), Va., 37, 1849.

Raquette. See *Ball play, Games*.

Rararachi (*Ra-ra'-ra-chi*, 'bought'). A small rancheria of the Tarahumare, near Norogachic, Chihuahua, Mexico. Also called Rarárachic, but mainly by the Mexicans.—Lumholtz, inf'n, 1894.

Rarenaw. See *Roanoke*.

Raritan (a corruption, by the Dutch of New Jersey, of *ĕräriiwitan*, or by apheresis, *'räruwitan*, 'the stream overflows so (or in such a way)'. The form *Raritang* represents the participle *'räruwitank*, 'the stream which overflows so (or in such a way)'. Owing to the frequent inundation of the land by the overflow of the river due to freshets, the Indians inhabiting its banks were, according to Van Tienhoven, compelled to remove farther inland.—Gerard). A former important division of the New Jersey Delawares, occupying the valley of Raritan r. and the left bank of Delaware r. as far down as the falls at Trenton, where they seem to have had an important settlement (see *Assunpink*). They are frequently mentioned as a confederacy, and one writer says they had "two sachemdoms and about 20 chieftaincies." They were estimated at 1,200 warriors about 1646, but this is doubtless a gross exaggeration. Owing to troubles with the Dutch and the inroads of the southern Indians, they retired soon afterward to the mountains. They gradually sold their lands, until in 1802 they, with remnants of other New Jersey tribes, were reduced to a small reservation called Brotherton, in Eversham, Burlington co. By invitation of the Stockbridges and Brothertons, then in Oneida co., N. Y., they joined them in that year. In 1832, being then reduced to about 40 souls, they sold their last rights in New Jersey and afterward removed with the other tribe to Green bay, Wis.   (J. M.)

Raretangh.—Doc. of 1640 in N. Y. Doc. Col. Hist., XIII, 7, 1881. **Raritan.**—Doc. of 1644, ibid., I, 150, 1856. **Raritangs.**—Van Tienhoven (1650), ibid., 366. **Raritanoos.**—Doc. of 1649, ibid., XIII, 25, 1881. **Raritanus.**—Doc. (ca. 1643), ibid., I, 198, 1856.

Raruta. Mentioned by Lawson (Hist. Car., 383, 1860) as a Coree village in 1701. It was probably on the coast of North Carolina, s. of Neuse r., in the present Carteret co.

Rasanachic ('large white rock') A small pueblo of the Tarahumare, not far from Norogachic, Chihuahua, Mexico.—Lumholtz, inf'n, 1894.

Rasawek. The chief village of the Monacan confederacy in 1608, situated in the fork of Rivanna and James rs., Fluvanna co., Va.

Rasauweak.—Smith (1629), Va., I, 134, repr. 1819. **Rassawek.**—Strachey (ca. 1612), Va., 102, 1849. **Rassaweak.**—Pots in Smith (1629), Va, I, 216, 1819. **Rassawek.**—Ibid., map.

Rat. See *Adario*.

Rathroche (*Ra-5ro'-ṛe*). A subgens of the Pakhtha or Beaver gens of the Iowa.—Dorsey in 15th Rep. B. A. E., 239, 1897.

Rations. See *Agency system*.

Raton (Span.: 'mouse,' but in the S. W. usually 'rat'). A Papago village in s. Arizona, with 140 inhabitants in 1858.

Del Raton.—Bailey in Ind. Aff. Rep., 208, 1858.

Ratontita (Span.-Mex.: 'place of the rat,' from a sacred stuffed mouse that hangs in the temple). A Huichol rancheria, with a temple and adjoining god houses, situated in the Sierra de los Huicholes, about 12 m. w. of Bolaños, in Jalisco, Mexico.—Lumholtz, Unknown Mex., II, 262, 1902.

Taquitzata.—Lumholtz, op. cit. ('the silk of corn is falling': Huichol name).

Rattles. Instruments for producing rhythmic sound, used by all tribes except some of the Eskimo. The rattle was generally regarded as a sacred object, not to be brought forth on ordinary occasions, but confined to rituals, religious feasts, shamanistic performances, etc. This character is emphasized in the sign language of the plains, where the sign for rattle is the basis of all signs indicating that which is sacred. Early in the 16th century, Estevan, the negro companion of Cabeza de Vaca, traversed with perfect immunity great stretches of country in northwestern Mexico, occupied by numerous tribes, bearing a cross in one hand and a gourd rattle in the other. Eskimo used rattles for enticing seals into the water.

Rattles may be divided into two general classes, those in which objects of approximately equal size are struck together, and those in which small objects, such as pebbles, quartz crystals, or seeds, are inclosed in hollow receptacles. The first embraces rattles made of animal hoofs or dewclaws, bird beaks, shells, pods, etc. These were held in the hand, fastened to blankets, belts, or leggings, or made into necklaces or anklets so as to make a noise when the wearer moved. On the N. W. coast, puffin beaks were strung on a frame composed of pieces of wood bent into two concentric rings and held together by crosspieces. From the Eskimo a similar rattle has been obtained in which the puffin beaks are replaced by bear claws. In the W., pecten shells were strung together to make rattles, while among some California tribes olivella shells took the place of the deer hoofs used by others. The Pueblos make rattles of conus and olivella shells, as well as of antelope hoofs, tortoise shells, and gourds. One Omaha rattle mentioned by Dorsey was made of the molars of the elk. The Tepehuane used the empty pods of the palm for ankle rattles. In this connection may be mentioned the clappers of bone and wood used by the Tlingit, Haida, and other peoples.

The second type of rattle was made of a gourd, of the entire shell of a tortoise, of pieces of rawhide sewed together, or, as on the N. W. coast, of wood. It was usually decorated with paintings, carvings, or feathers and pendants, very often having a symbolic meaning.

GOURD RATTLE; KIOWA

The performer, besides shaking these rattles with the hand, sometimes struck them against an object. Women of the Gulf tribes fastened several tortoise-shell rattles to each leg where they were concealed by their clothing. Little drums inclosing pebbles were used by the Mandan and the Pueblos, as well as by children among the Labrador Eskimo. Many tribes made rattles of loop shape out of dried buffalo tails, and one has been found in Tennessee, made of pottery. The copper tinklers of the S. W., and ceramic vessels with heads containing loose clay pellets, are other varieties. Pueblo children found a natural rattle provided for them in the pods of the rattlebox plant. Most curious of all was a rattle used by the Pima and the Indians of California, which consisted of a number of cocoons strung together containing small stones.

On the N. W. coast, besides common rattles for festive occasions, there were oval wooden rattles, which were the property of shamans, and wooden rattles having many designs around a central figure of the raven, which were used almost exclusively by chiefs. The carving on shamans' rattles generally represented supernatural helpers, and it may be noted

CHIPPEWA GOURD RATTLE (HOFFMAN)

that Tlingit shamans often had special rattle spirits, separate from their other helpers. For illustrations of rattles, see *Music and Musical Instruments.*

Consult Boas in Rep. Nat. Mus. 1895, 1897; Curtis, N. Am. Ind., II–v, 1908–09; Dawson, Q. Charlotte Ids., 1880; Dorsey (1) in 3d Rep. B. A. E., 1884, (2) in 13th Rep. B. A. E., 1896; Fewkes in 22d Rep. B. A. E., 1903; Hoffman in 7th Rep. B. A. E., 1891; Lumholtz, Unknown Mex., 1902; Mooney in 14th Rep. B. A. E. 1896; Morgan, League Iroq., 1904; Murdoch in 9th Rep. B.A.E., 1892; Speck in Mem. Am. Anthr. Asso., II, pt. 2, 1907. (J. R. S.)

Rattling Moccasin Band. A band of the Udewakanton Sioux, taking its name from the chief (known also as Rattling Runner), formerly resident on Minnesota r., below L. Traverse, Minn.—Ind. Aff. Rep. 1859, 102, 1860; Coll. Minn. Hist. Soc., III, 85, 1880.

Raudauquaquank. The only village of the Bear River Indians of North Carolina in 1701, then containing 50 warriors.—Lawson (1709), N. C., 383, 1860.

Rawekhangye (*Ra-we′ qanʸ-ye*, 'big beaver'). A subgens of the Pakhtha or Beaver gens of the Iowa.—Dorsey in 15th Rep. B. A. E., 239, 1897.

Raweyine (*Ra-we′ yiñ′-e*, 'young beaver'). A subgens of the Pakhtha or Beaver gens of the Iowa.—Dorsey in 15th Rep. B. A. E., 239, 1897.

Rawhide. The great strength and toughness of rawhide rendered it useful to the Indian in an almost equal degree with sinew, and among all tribes it was prized for these qualities. The skins of various large land and aquatic animals were made into rawhide, varying, according to the animal, in thinness, color, strength, etc. In preparing rawhide the skin was fleshed, dehaired, and stretched till it dried, when it was ready for use. Whole buffalo or cow skins were used as covers for the bull-boats of the Sioux and other tribes of the upper Missouri, and deerskins and seal and sea-lion skins, joined by sewing, covered the canoes, kaiaks, and umiaks of the tribes of the far N. Pieces of rawhide were folded or sewn to form the parflèche trunks and knife, feather, and arrow cases, pouches, and pemmican bags of the Plains tribes, who used also circular pieces of thick hide for pemmican or fruit mortars. Buckets, dippers, cups, drumheads, rattles, shields, cradles, etc., were made of rawhide by many tribes, and helmet masks were made of the same material by the Pueblos.

The property which green rawhide has of greatly shrinking in drying was made use of in many ways—notably for casing handles and heads of stone clubs, for mending broken articles, and for making drumheads and lacing them. Sometimes rings of rawhide from the tails of animals were shrunk on club handles or pipestems, like bands of iron. Soles of moccasins were made of this material in the W., and the Plains tribes often utilized old parflèche cases for this purpose. Cut in strips of differing sizes, rawhide was used for harness, thongs, whiplashes, wattling, for making cages, fencing, etc. Narrow strips, called babiche by the French, were employed for fishing and harpoon lines, nets, lacing for snowshoes, rackets, ball sticks, and gaming wheels. Bags (sometimes called by their Algonquian name *muskemoots*) of fine workmanship were knit of babiche. Braided babiche was the material of reatas, halters, cinches, and carrying-straps. See *Parflèche, Shaganappi, Skins and Skin-dressing.* (w. h.)

Rawranoke. See *Roanoke.*

Rayon. A former village of the Opata in Sonora, Mexico, but now a civilized settlement. Besides Opata and Pima (Hrdlička in Am. Anthr., vi, 72, 1904), the settlement contained 63 Yaqui in 1900.

Razboinski (Russian: 'robbers'). A Chnagmiut Eskimo village on the right bank of the Yukon, Alaska, near the head of the delta; pop. 151 in 1880. Kinegnagmiut.—Baker, Geog. Dict. Alaska, 337, 1902 (native name) Rasbinik —Dall, Alaska, 229, 1870. Razbinsky.—Nelson in 18th Rep. B. A. E., map, 1899. Razboinik. — Petroff in 10th Census, Alaska, 12, 1884. Razboinikskaia —Petroff, Rep. on Alaska, 57, 1881. Razboiniksky.—Petroff in 10th Census, Alaska, map, 1884.

Rchaketan. Given by Krause (Tlinkit Indianer, 116, 1885) as a Tlingit division of the Raven clan in the Chilkat town of Klukwan, Alaska. Unidentified.

Rchauutass-hade. Quoted by Krause (Tlinkit Indianer, 304, 1885) as the name of a branch of the Haida of Queen Charlotte ids., Brit. Col. It is not identifiable with any known group.

Reaum's Village. A former Chippewa village, so called after the chief, on Flint r., Mich., on a tract about the boundary of Genesee and Saginaw cos., ceded to the United States under the treaty of Jan. 14, 1837. The Reaum family, from which the chief evidently derived his name, was prominent in the early history of Michigan.

Receptacles. Objects of mineral, vegetal, or animal material, the chief function of which is merely to contain things. The term receptacle includes all that is meant by the following terms: bag, basin, basket, boat, bottle, bowl, box, cache, canteen, case, with many names (awl-case, bow-case, plume-case, food-case, etc.), chest, coffin, cradle, cup, dish, gourd, granary, grave, jar, ladle, mortar, net, olla, oven, parflèche, pit, platter, pot, pouch, purse, quiver, reservoir, sack, scabbard, spoon, tinaja, tray, trough, trunk, urn, vase, vessel, wallet—a vast family of utensils, wonderfully varied in form, material, and size, whose functions include, beside the simple one of holding, those of gathering, carrying, serving, sifting, boiling, baking, mixing, grinding, pounding, pouring, evaporating, sprinkling, etc.

Men, even in the lowest known stages of culture, employ receptacles for food and drink, relying largely on those furnished by nature, as fruit cases, shells of mollusks and turtles, bladders, etc., while others, for varied purposes, are improvised of bark, leaves, skins of animals, and the like. The inventive genius of the tribes was constantly called into requisition to improve on and multiply the natural facilities. Strands of bark, grass, leaves, hair, and other filaments, employed originally in holding and carrying solid objects, were also combined in various ways, supplying nets, baskets, cradles, quivers, and hammocks; and pliable branches, twigs, and leaves served for the construction of shelters, dwellings, caches, and granaries. Nature furnished varied receptacles for water, as lakes, ponds, springs, and cavities in rocks, and the tribes constructed reservoirs and cisterns, making residence possible on many arid sites. Stone vessels in the form of concretions were available in some sections, and these were modified and used as cups and dishes, and with advanced communities the softer stones, and with some even the harder varieties, were carved into vessels of many forms. The use of baked clay made it possible to shape receptacles for many purposes which, in their highest development, took graceful shapes and were tastefully embellished. A joint of cane, readily severed, formed an exceptionally neat cup, and wooden utensils shaped by means of charring, scraping, and cutting were in almost universal use by the tribes, serving countless useful purposes. The more important varieties of receptacles are herein treated under their individual names. (w. h. h.)

Rechquaakie (contr. and corruption of *rekawihaki*, 'sandy land.'—Gerard). A former Rockaway village near the present Rockaway, Long id., N. Y. Rechquaakie.—Ruttenber, Tribes Hudson R., 110, 1872. Reckheweck.—Ibid., 155. Rockaway.—Ibid., 110.

Rechtauck. A former Manhattan village on Manhattan id., N. Y. In 1643 it was temporarily occupied by some fugitive Wecquaesgeek, who were attacked and massacred by the Dutch.— Ruttenber, Tribes Hudson R., 106, 1872.

Red Bank. A former Cherokee settlement on Etowah r., at or near the present county seat of Canton, Cherokee co., Ga.—Doc. of 1799 quoted by Royce in 5th Rep. B. A. E., 144, map, 1887.

Red Bird (*Wănig-suchkă*). A Winnebago war chief, so named, according to one authority, because he habitually wore a red coat and called himself English, and by another because he wore on each shoulder, "to supply the place of an epaulette, a preserved red-bird." He was born about 1788 and was the leading spirit in the Winnebago outbreak of 1827. He was friendly with the settlers of Prairie du Chien, Wis., who regarded him as a protector until two Winnebago, who had been arrested for the murder of a family of maple-sugar makers, were erroneously reported to have been turned over to the Chippewa by the military authorities at Ft Snelling and clubbed to death while running the gauntlet. The Winnebago chiefs, on the receipt of this news, met in council and determined upon retaliation, selecting Red Bird to carry out their decree. With this purpose in view he, with two companions, after visiting the house of Lockwood, a trader at Prairie du Chien, proceeded to the house of Registre Gagnier, who with his hired man they shot down after being hospitably entertained by them. An infant was torn from the mother (who made her escape), and was stabbed and left for dead, though subsequently restored. Red Bird and his companions proceeded the same day, June 26, 1827, to the rendezvous of his band, consisting of 37 warriors with their wives and children, at the mouth of Bad Axe r., Minn. A day or two later they attacked a boat on the Mississippi, killing 4 and wounding 2 of the crew, and losing a third of their own number. When the troops arrived and prepared to attack the Winnebago, Red Bird and his accomplices gave themselves up and were tried and convicted, but sentence was deferred until the last day of the general court, and then, for some unknown cause, was not pronounced. With his companions Red Bird was remanded to prison to await sentence, where he died, Feb. 16, 1828. The others were condemned to death, but were pardoned by President John Quincy Adams, in Nov. 1828, at the instance of Nawkaw, who, with a deputation of his tribesmen, visited Washington in their behalf.

Redbones. See *Croatan Indians.*

Red Cedar Lake. A Chippewa village on Red Cedar lake, Barron co., Wis.—Warren (1852) in Minn. Hist. Soc. Coll., v, 191, 1885.

Red Clay (free translation of *Elăwă′di*, abbreviated form of *Elăwă′diyĭ*, 'red earth place'). A Cherokee settlement, popularly known as Yellow-hill settlement, and now officially called Cherokee. It is the post-office and agency headquarters for the East Cherokee, and is situated on Oconaluftee r., in Swain co., N. C.—Mooney in 19th Rep. B. A. E., 517, 1900.

Red Cliff. A Chippewa band formerly attached to La Pointe agency, near the w. end of L. Superior, in Wisconsin or Minnesota.—Ind. Aff. Rep. 1873, 332, 1874.

Red Cloud (*Makhpíya - lúta*, 'Scarlet Cloud,' frequently known among his people as *Makhpia-sha*, 'Red Cloud'). A principal chief of the Oglala Teton Sioux of Pine Ridge res., the largest band of the Sioux nation, and probably the most famous and powerful chief in the history of the tribe. The origin of the name is disputed, but is said by ex-agent McGillycuddy (inf'n, 1906) to refer to the way in which his scarlet-blanketed warriors

RED CLOUD

formerly covered the hillsides like a red cloud. If this be true, the name was bestowed after he had obtained recognition as a leader.

Red Cloud was born at the forks of Platte r., Nebr., in 1822, and died at Pine Ridge, S. Dak., Dec. 10, 1909. He was a member of the Snake family, the most distinguished and forceful of his tribe, and rose to prominence by his own force of character, having no claim to hereditary chiefship, which in the Oglala band rested with the family represented by They-fear-even-his-horse ("Young-man-afraid-of-his-horses"), the latter being more conservative and more friendly toward civilization. Red Cloud's father died of drunkenness brought about by the introduction of liquor into the tribe without stint, commencing about 1821. When in 1865 the Government undertook to build a road from Ft Laramie, Wyo., on the North Platte, by way of Powder r. to the gold regions of Montana, Red Cloud headed the opposition for his tribe, on the ground that the influx of travel along the trail would destroy the best remaining buffalo ground of the Indians. The first small detachment of troops sent out to begin construction work were intercepted by Red Cloud with a large party of Oglala Sioux and Cheyenne, and held practically as prisoners for more than two weeks, but finally were allowed to proceed when it seemed to the chief that they might be massacred by his young men. In the fall of the same year commissioners were sent to treat with the Oglala for permission to build the road, but Red Cloud forbade the negotiations and refused to attend the council.

On June 30, 1866, another council for the same purpose was called at Ft Laramie, Red Cloud this time attending and repeating his refusal to endanger the hunting grounds of his people. While he was speaking, a strong force of troops under Gen. Carrington arrived, and on being told, in reply to a question, that they had come to build forts and open the road to Montana, he seized his rifle and with a final defiant message left the council with his entire following. Carrington then set out on his mission, which included the rebuilding and garrisoning of Ft Reno, on Powder r., and the establishment of Ft Phil Kearny and Ft C. F. Smith, the last named being on Bighorn r., in Montana. Another protest to Carrington himself proving ineffectual, Red Cloud surrounded the troops and working force at Ft Kearny with perhaps 2,000 warriors and harassed them so constantly that not even a load of hay could be brought in from the prairie except under the protection of a strong guard, while it was made impossible to venture out after the game that was abundant all around. On Dec. 21, 1866, an entire detachment of 81 men under Capt. Fetterman was cut off and every man killed. On Aug. 1, 1867, another severe engagement occurred near the post. In all this time not a single wagon had been able to pass over the road, and in 1868 another commission was appointed to come to terms with Red Cloud, who demanded as an ultimatum the abandonment of the three posts and of all further attempts to open the Montana road. A treaty was finally made on this basis, defining the limits of the Sioux country as claimed by the Sioux, Red Cloud refusing to sign or even to be present until the garrisons had actually been withdrawn, thus winning a complete victory

for the position which he had taken from the beginning. He finally affixed his signature at Ft Laramie, Nov. 6, 1868. From that date he seems to have kept his promise to live at peace with the whites, although constantly resisting the innovations of civilization. He took no active part in the Sioux war of 1876, although he is accused of having secretly aided and encouraged the hostiles. Being convinced of the hopelessness of attempting to hold the Black hills after the discovery of gold in that region, he joined in the agreement of cession in 1876. In the outbreak of 1890–91 also he remained quiet, being then an old man and partially blind, and was even said to have been threatened by the hostiles on account of his loyal attitude toward the Government.

As a warrior Red Cloud stood first among his people, having counted 80 coups (q. v.) or separate deeds of bravery in battle. As a general and statesman he ranked equally high, having been long prominent in treaties and councils, and several times a delegate to Washington, his attitude having been always that of a patriot from the Indian standpoint. Unlike Indians generally, he had but one wife, with whom he lived from early manhood. Personally he is described by one well acquainted with him as a most courtly chief and a natural-born gentleman, with a bow as graceful as that of a Chesterfield. For some years before his death he was blind and decrepit, and lived in a house built for him by the Government. His immediate band is known as Iteshicha (q. v.)   (J. M.)

Red Eagle. See *Weatherford, William.*

Red Fish. A prominent Oglala Sioux chief about 1840. He led his people against the Crows in 1841, and met a serious repulse which cost him his position and influence. Father De Smet met him at Ft Pierre, in the present South Dakota, in the latter year.   (D. R.)

Red Head. A prominent Onondaga, whose English name was borne by an earlier chief, but his native name is not mentioned. He drew a map of the St Lawrence for Sir Wm. Johnson in Aug. 1759, and was an active war chief. A creek E. of Oswego, N. Y., was called Red Head's cr. Sir William "condoled" his death at Oswego, Aug. 1764, he having fallen dead in the fort before the baronet's arrival. See Stone, Life of Sir William Johnson, II, 219, 402, 409, 1865.

Red Horn. A Piegan chief. The border troubles caused by lawless whites and horse-stealing Indians reached such a pitch in the fall of 1869 that Col. E. M. Baker took out an expedition in the winter to punish the truculent bands of Piegan. He surprised the camp of Red Horn on Marias r., Mont., Jan. 23, 1870, while smallpox was raging among the inmates, and the soldiers killed Red Horn and 172 others. The number of women and children among these was later a subject of controversy. See Dunn, Massacres of the Mountains, 509–42, 1886.

Red Iron Band. A former Sisseton Sioux band, named from its chief, Mazahsha, residing at the mouth of Lac qui Parle r., Minn. They were friendly in the outbreak of 1862, and after the massacre prevented the escape of Little Crow with 276 captives into the far N. W. This band was a part of the so-called Traverse des Sioux band. (D. R.)

Red Jacket. A noted Seneca orator and chief of the "merit" class (see *Chiefs*) of the Wolf clan, born about 1756, probably at Canoga, in Seneca co., N. Y., where a monument commemorates his

RED JACKET

birth; died on the former "Buffalo reservation" of the Seneca, on lands now within the limits of Buffalo, N. Y., Jan. 20, 1830. In civil life his Indian name was Otetiani, probably meaning 'prepared' or 'ready'. On his elevation to a chiefship, he received the name 'Shagoië′wāthă' (commonly spelled Sa-go-ye-wat-ha), signifying literally 'he them causes to be awake,' and, as a name, 'he who causes them to be awake,' a designation having no reference to his reputed ability as an effective speaker, although this seems to be the popular inference. Being a member of the Wolf clan of the Seneca, the Indian names received by Red Jacket belonged, according to custom, exclusively to this important clan. And, institutionally, clan names were in large measure designations descriptive of

some distinctive feature, attitude, habit, or other phenomenon characteristic of the clan tutelary. So it being one of the marked habits of the wolf to disturb or awaken people at night by howling or by other means, there naturally would be a personal name belonging to the Wolf clan which embodied this lupine trait and which in this case became the name of a tribal but not federal chiefship therein. This is also an official name among the Cayuga. In the American Revolution, his tribe, the Seneca, having reluctantly espoused the cause of Great Britain, Red Jacket, although strongly opposed to this course of his people, took the field with his fellow warriors. At once his ability and intelligence attracted the attention of British officers, one of whom gave him a brilliant red jacket, which, when worn out, was replaced by a second, and so on until this distinctive dress became a characteristic feature of its wearer, whence his popular name. Red Jacket was frequently employed in carrying dispatches, but he took no very active part in the actual fighting; indeed, he was even reproached with being a coward for certain conduct in the field by the great fighting chief, Cornplanter. During the invasion of the Seneca country by Gen. Sullivan in 1779, Cornplanter sought to make a stand against the American forces on the shore of Canandaigua lake, but on the approach of the American troops, a number of Indians, including Red Jacket, began to retreat. Seeing the ill effect of this movement, Cornplanter endeavored to rally the fugitives. Placing himself in front of Red Jacket, he sought to persuade him and his fellow refugees to turn back to fight, but his efforts were fruitless; in anger, the baffled chief, turning to Red Jacket's young wife, exclaimed, "Leave that man; he is a coward!"

Red Jacket was reputed to have had a most tenacious memory and a quick wit, and, being a ready and effective speaker, he possessed a remarkable gift for defensive debate; but, judging from his interpreted speeches and from his course in life, it is evident he was not a deep, broad-minded thinker, and so justly he could hardly be called a great orator. He was at all times an egotist, and his mind was of so narrow a cast that he failed to see that he and his people had reached a point where they had to strive to adjust themselves so far as practicable to the new conditions brought about by the coming of the white race. And so he likewise failed to read aright the lesson taught by the cataclysm that engulfed the institutions of the Iroquois of the League when the avenging army of Sullivan desolated their homes, their orchards, and their harvests in 1779. The meager measure of importance that finally attached to Red Jacket arose largely from his usefulness in communicating officially with the whites after his tribe had unfortunately lost the greater number of its leading warriors and noted chieftains. This usefulness lay in his ready utterance, in his remarkable memory of the events and transactions between his people and the white men, where written records were wanting or of little use for the lack of ability to read and write, and, lastly, in his inordinate fondness to be in the public eye. In no other respect was his influence or usefulness among his people great. They recognized in him merely a fluent speaker; not a reformer or a great leader, but rather a man who was an adept in giving utterance to the thoughts of others or to the common opinion of his tribe or immediate followers rather than to something new and constructive.

It is commonly believed that Red Jacket was present at the treaty of Ft Stanwix in 1784, and that he made a great speech there in opposition to it. But this is a mistake, since there is no authentic evidence that he was in attendance there in any capacity, and, indeed, he was not then a chief. The speech of Red Jacket at the great council of the confederated Indians held at the mouth of Detroit r. two years later, was, according to authentic records, his first formal public address, and it has been characterized as a "masterpiece of oratory." In it the speaker eloquently opposed the burying of the hatchet, and because it voiced the predominant feeling of the assembled warriors it received warm approval. The formal address of this council to the Congress of the United States, however, was pacific yet firm in tone. It was framed and written apparently by Thayendanegen, or Captain Joseph Brant, then recently from England, whose views were evidently largely shaped by the contents of a letter written to him by Sidney, one of the British secretaries of state, dated at Whitehall, Apr. 6, 1786; hence, it would seem that Thayendanegen dominated the action of this council notwithstanding the alleged hostile fulminations of Red Jacket, mentioned above. Red Jacket was a staunch conservative, and, aided by his natural gifts, became the great advocate and defender of the faith and the institutions of his people, and the bitter opponent of the changes suggested and introduced by the culture of the white race. In this emergency, Red Jacket, a product of the institutions and culture of the Seneca—the so-called paganism of the Iroquois—championed

the customs, the religion, and the institutions of his tribesmen, and, in addition, at least in appearance, strove manfully to prevent the sale of the lands of his people. In his chosen position he yielded nothing to persuasion, and he was unmoved by bribery or threats. Red Jacket carried his unreasoning conservatism to such a degree that he bitterly antagonized all educational, industrial, and missionary efforts designed for the betterment of his people, believing, he protested, that such instruction wholly unfitted an Indian for any kind of useful endeavor. In this belief he was not alone. Addressing himself to a young man who had been educated among the whites, he derisively exclaimed, "What have we here? You are neither a white man nor an Indian; for heaven's sake tell us, what are you?" It is even asserted that he treated with unconcealed contempt any Indian who made use of a stool or a chair in his cabin. Finally, however, the force of circumstances compelled him reluctantly to acquiesce in measures designed to ameliorate the condition of his people.

In 1821 the legislature of New York enacted a law forbidding the residence of white men on Indian lands. In the following year, the chief of the Christian party among the Seneca and the "friends of Christianity and civilization in this and adjoining counties" sought to have this law changed in such manner that ministers of the Gospel and mechanics of good moral character might be exempted from its operations. In this, however, they failed, whereupon the pagan party among the Seneca, abetted by "some white pagans," led by Red Jacket, entered complaint against the further residence of the missionary on the Seneca reservation, and in 1824 the mission was abandoned. The law, however, was later amended, and Mr Harris, the missionary, had the satisfaction of returning to the reservation in June 1825.

When the Seneca Christian party had grown in numbers and included many influential chiefs, and the schools had gained a fair foothold, its members became impatient under the dictation of one whose intemperance and profligacy had lessened him in their esteem, and in Sept. 1827 they, including 26 chiefs, took steps which resulted in the deposition of Red Jacket from his chiefship; but he was afterward relieved of this humiliation by his reinstatement through the mediation of the Office of Indian Affairs. In the document setting forth the reasons, among many, for his deposition, signed by 26 leading chiefs of his tribe, Red Jacket is charged among other things with sending, by the solicited aid of white men, falsehoods to the President; with creating and fomenting divisions and disturbances among his people; with having "a bad heart" for having in a time of famine among his people hidden the body of a deer which he had killed instead of sharing it with them; with stealing and appropriating to his own use goods which as annuities belonged to orphan children and to old people; and with being a traitor to the United States, since, in the War of 1812, they charged, "you divided us—you acted against our Father, the President, and his officers, and advised with those who were not friends."

Replying to a question asking the reasons for his unyielding opposition to the establishment of missionaries among his people, Red Jacket said, with a sarcastic smile: "Because they do us no good. If they are not useful to the white people, why do they send them among the Indians; if they are useful to the white people, and do them good, why do they not keep them at home? They are surely bad enough to need the labor of every one who can make them better. These men know that we do not understand their religion. We can not read their book; they tell different stories about what it contains, and we believe they make the book talk to suit themselves. . . . The Great Spirit will not punish for what we do not know. . . . These black coats talk to the Great Spirit, and ask light, that we may see as they do, when they are blind themselves, and quarrel about the light which guides them. These things we do not understand. . . . The black coats tell us to work and raise corn; they do nothing themselves, and would starve to death if somebody did not feed them. All they do is to pray to the Great Spirit; but that will not make corn or potatoes grow; if it will, why do they beg from us, and from the white people. . . . The Indians can never be civilized; they are not like white men. . . . We are few and weak, but may for a long time be happy, if we hold fast to our country and the religion of our fathers." The atheistic notions expressed in this reply were clearly adopted from white men.

In 1821, a woman named Caughquawtaugh, after being tried by the Seneca council, was executed as a witch by Tommy Jemmy, otherwise called Soonongize (Shonón'gaiz). This act coming to the knowledge of the neighboring whites, they had the executioner arrested and imprisoned. The plea of Tommy Jemmy at the trial was that the Indians were an independent people and so exercised original jurisdiction over their criminals.

At this trial Red Jacket was called as a witness to testify concerning the customs of his people. At an opportune moment, however, it is alleged, he gave utterance to the following sentiments as a rebuke to those who were inclined to ridicule the Indian belief in witchcraft: "What? Do you denounce us as fools and bigots, because we still believe that which you yourselves believed two centuries ago? Your black coats thundered this doctrine from the pulpit, your judges pronounced it from the bench, and sanctioned it with the formalities of law; and you would now punish our unfortunate brother, for adhering to the faith of *his* fathers and of yours! Go to Salem! Look at the records of your own government, and you will find that hundreds have been executed for the very crime which has called forth the sentence of condemnation against this woman and drawn down upon her the arms of vengeance. What have our brothers done, more than the rulers of your own people have done? And what crime has this man committed, by executing in a summary way the laws of his country and the command of the Great Spirit?" It is very doubtful that Red Jacket possessed all the facts stated in this alleged speech; it seems rather an extract from the brief of the defendant's attorney than the off-hand allocution of an Indian who could not write his own name and who studiously avoided the company of white men.

Red Jacket in his life was charged with want of courage and resolution, and even with timidity; with duplicity, treachery, and even with treason; and with so far forgetting the proprieties as not to hesitate to rob his friends. Stone says of him that he "had been known to exert his eloquence to enkindle a war-spirit in the bosoms of the braves of his nation, and provoke them to take up the hatchet, while he ingeniously avoided the war-path, and availed himself of the absence of the warriors, thus procured, to plunder the goods, and even live-stock, wherever he could—not caring to discriminate between the property of any enemy and that of the absentees of his own people." In a letter to the Duke of Northumberland, in 1805, Brant bestowed on Red Jacket the name "Cow-killer," because, during the Revolution, having exhorted his fellow warriors to behave with courage in an approaching battle and promising to be in the thick of the fight himself, and being missed from the engagement, he was found cutting up a cow belonging to an Indian. Subsequent to the Revolution Brant often openly blamed Red Jacket with causing him trouble and embarrassment during Sullivan's invasion, "being," he asserted, "the principal cause of the disasters of his people." Indeed, during this campaign Red Jacket had sought to induce the young warriors and the less resolute chiefs to agree to submission to the American army. A runner was sent to Sullivan's camp for this purpose, but the astute Brant, having knowledge of this treason, frustrated the purposes of Red Jacket by having the bearer of the American flag of truce killed and his papers taken.

Although nominally and officially at peace with the United States after the treaty of Ft Stanwix in 1784, the Six Nations were nevertheless dissatisfied with some of its terms, and for ten years subsequently had to be conciliated with great care and at much expense. During this period, 1786–94, Red Jacket sought to thwart the Indian policy of the United States in regard to the hostile western tribes, but Wayne's victory over the confederated tribes in 1794 sobered the thoughts of the malcontents among the Indian tribes.

In pursuance of the invitation to the chiefs of the Six Nations to visit the President, given by Col. Pickering at Painted Post in June 1791, two months after the remarkable council held with these Indians at Buffalo Creek by Col. Proctor, a friendly delegation, consisting of 50 chiefs of the Six Nations, in the spring of 1792 visited Philadelphia, then the seat of government. It was during this conference that President Washington, as a token of friendship and esteem, gave a silver medal, bearing his own likeness, to Red Jacket, who then and in later life showed his appreciation of this gift with the care he bestowed on it and with the pride with which he was accustomed to wear it. This medal is now in the custody of the Buffalo Historical Society.

Even after the solemn assurances of lasting friendship for the United States by the New York Indians in the War of 1812, the vacillating character and inconstancy of Red Jacket and other prominent chiefs are made plain in a letter addressed to Farmer's Brother and other chiefs by Gen. Porter, dated Chippewa, Canada, July 25, 1814, inviting the Indians to join him at once at that place. Among other things, he wrote: "We shall soon drive the enemy, who dare not show their heads where we go. We want your aid to assist us in the pursuit. You have already lost one glorious opportunity by being absent. We are aware of the conduct of three of your chiefs—Red Jacket, Cornplanter, and Blue Sky. If they do not choose to act for themselves, they should not dissuade others." By this it is seen that at least one American officer openly charged Red Jacket with treasonable conduct, notwithstanding Stone's unintentionally ironical statement that Red Jacket "was no more suspected of treachery than he was of courage, by the American officers in the service."

In 1827 Red Jacket's wife, together with 22 of her Seneca neighbors, joined the church, notwithstanding her husband's threat to leave her should she take such a step. He therefore sullenly carried out his threat, and gave himself over to renewed and unbridled dissipation. But after a few months' absence he meekly returned to his wife, who condescended to receive him on condition that he would not in future interfere with her religious duties. Afterward he faithfully kept his word, and, indeed, at times he even aided her in these duties.

In 1828, at the request of Dr J. W. Francis, of New York city, R. W. Weir painted a likeness of Red Jacket; and in 1829 Catlin also painted a full length life-size portrait of him, representing him standing on Table Rock, Niagara Falls, in accordance with Red Jacket's wishes.

The project of reinterring the remains of Red Jacket and the chiefs contemporary with him, lying forsaken in graves on the former Buffalo res., had its inception about 1863, but it did not take definite shape until 1876, when W. C. Bryant, of the Buffalo Historical Society, obtained the consent of the Seneca council to the removal of the bodies. On Oct. 9, 1884, with appropriate ceremonies, the remains were reinterred in Forest Lawn Cemetery, Buffalo, N. Y., where a handsome memorial was unveiled June 22, 1891.

Consult Hubbard, Red Jacket and his People, 1886; Ketchum, Buffalo and the Senecas, 1864–65; McKenney and Hall, Indian Tribes, I, 1858; Stone (1) Life of Brant, 1838, (2) Life and Times of Red Jacket, 1841; Trans. Buffalo Hist. Soc., III, 1885.   (J. N. B. H.)

Red Legs' Band. A former band of the Wahpekute Sioux in Minnesota, named from its chief, Hushasha.—Ind. Aff. Rep. 1859, 100, 1860; Coll. Minn. Hist. Soc., VI, 394, 1887.

Red Lodge. A former Oglala Sioux band under Yellow Eagle.—Culbertson in Smithson. Rep. 1850, 142, 1851.

Red Man; Red Man and Helper. See *Carlisle School; Periodicals.*

Red Men, Improved Order of. A society of American citizens, originally composed of advocates of individual rights and admirers of Indian character, who adopted as their patron and exemplar the Delaware chief Tammany; but, as it is constituted at the present day, its primary objects are the promotion among men of the exercise and practice of the principles of benevolence and charity, the care and protection of widows and orphans, and the cultivation of friendly relations among those who have entered its circle. The democratic influence which attended its birth has caused the idea that all men are equal to remain its fundamental tenet. There were several patriotic societies at the close of the 18th and the commencement of the 19th century which may have contributed to the rise of the present order. There was organized in Philadelphia, about 1772, a society known as the Sons of Tammany, that may be considered its direct ancestor, the first recorded notice of which is in the Philadelphia Chronicle of May 4, 1772: "On Friday, the 1st instant, a number of Americans, Sons of King Tammany, met at the house of Mr James Byrn, to celebrate the memory of that truly noble chieftain whose friendship was most affectionately manifest to the worthy founder and first settlers of this province. After dinner the circulating glass was crowned with wishes, loyal and patriotic, and the day concluded with much cheerfulness and harmony. It is hoped from this small beginning a society may be formed of great utility to the distressed, as this meeting was more for the purpose of promoting charity and benevolence than mirth and festivity." Subsequently it was the custom of the society to hold a regular festival every year on May 12. On that day the members walked in procession through the streets of Philadelphia, with hats decorated with bucks' tails, to a handsome rural place in the direction of Schuylkill r. which they called the "wigwam," where, after a "long talk," according to Indian custom, and after the "pipe of peace" had been smoked, they spent the day in festivity and mirth. The association continued in this form for some years after the peace with Great Britain, when the owner of the "wigwam," who had generously lent it every year in honor of Tammany, having met with misfortune was compelled to sell it to satisfy his creditors. After the discontinuance of the festive association other societies of a similar character were formed in Philadelphia and New York, bearing the name Tammany; the only one of these continued to the present day is the Tammany Society of New York city. See *Tammany*.

The present Order of Red Men, like the original society, is a social, fraternal, and benevolent organization commemorating the customs, traditions, and history of the Indians, and is purely American. Its proceedings are secret only in so far as secrecy is expedient and proper. Its organization, proceedings, and mode of initiating members imitate Indian customs, and Indian terms are used to designate the officers and in conducting ceremonies. The Order of Red Men has passed through three phases. The first was its existence as originally organized in Philadelphia. After the colonies declared for separate government began the second phase, when it is said these societies became intensely popular, and their anniversaries bade fair to excel Independence day in public esteem. They were thus auspiciously continued until a short time before the second war with Great Britain, when Gen. Dearborn, Secretary of War, looking on them as demoralizing to soldiers, issued orders prohibiting them in the army. It is asserted that the third phase of the order began in 1813 at Ft Mifflin, on Delaware r., 4 m. below Philadelphia, among volunteer soldiers called Junior Artillerists. An unbroken chain in the existence of the society thus formed continued in Pennsylvania and neighboring states, but without an attempt at concurrent action until 1857. On Oct. 21 of that year a grand demonstration, including a public parade in full regalia, with banners and other insignia, took place at Lancaster, Pa. But the Order of Red Men as now existing seems to have taken its form from the Red Men's Society, Tribe No. 1, of Maryland, organized Mar. 12, 1834, at the house of D. McDonald, in Baltimore. This tribe subsequently assumed supreme authority, which was not challenged by the older tribe in Pennsylvania, and its authority has been acknowledged ever since. In a charter granted by the Maryland legislature on Mar. 14, 1835, the name was changed to the "Improved Order of Red Men." The organization is now represented in every state and territory in the Union. The total membership in 1905 was 382,121, the number of tribes 4,206, and the assets of the organization about $4,000,000. (C. T.)

Red Mouths. A band or society of the Crow tribe.—Culbertson in Smithson. Rep. 1850, 144, 1851.

Red River Assiniboin. An Assiniboin band, estimated in 1829 at 24 tipis (Coues, Henry-Thompson Jour., II, 522, 1897), living w. of the Otaopabine, w. Canada.

Red River Chippewa. A former Chippewa band in w. Minnesota.—Ind. Aff. Rep., 332, 1873.

Red Sticks. Among the Creeks and their cousins, the Seminole, all warlike functions, including the declaration of war, the organizing of war parties, and the burning of captives, were in charge of the officers of certain clans, which clans were designated for this reason 'bearers of the red' in contradistinction to the 'white' or peace clans, in the towns of which all peace treaties were negotiated and where it was forbidden to shed human blood. The symbol of the declaration of war was the erection of a tall pole, painted red, in the public square, as a rallying point for the warriors, whence the popular term "Red Sticks" applied by writers both to these towns and to the hostile war element which at various periods made headquarters in them, particularly during the Creek and Seminole war. The most noted towns controlled by the war clans were Atasi of the Upper Creeks, Kawita of the Lower Creeks, and Mikasuki of the Seminole. See *Baton Rouge*.   (J. M.)

Red Thunder. A chief of the Pabaksa or Cuthead band of Yanktonai Sioux in the early part of the 19th century; also known as Shappa, the Beaver. Lieut. Z. M. Pike saw him at the great council at Prairie du Chien, Wis., in Apr. 1806, and pronounced him the most gorgeously dressed of any chief he met. With his famous son Waneta he enlisted with the British in the War of 1812, and fought at Ft Meigs and at Sandusky, Ohio. He was killed under tragic circumstances by the Chippewa on Red r. of the North in 1823. Col. Robert Dickson, the British agent in the W. during 1812–15, married a sister of Red Thunder.   (D. R.)

Red Town. A former Seminole town on Tampa bay, w. Florida.—Bell in Morse, Rep. to Sec. War, 306, 1822.

Redwing. The name of a succession of chiefs of the former Khemnichan band of Mdewakanton Sioux, residing on the w. shore of L. Pepin, Minn., where the city of Redwing now stands. At least four chiefs in succession bore the appellation, each being distinguished by another name. The elder Redwing is heard of as early as the time of the Pontiac war, when he visited Mackinaw, and was in alliance with the English in the Revolution. He was succeeded by his son, Walking Buffalo (Tatankamani), who enlisted in the British cause in 1812. The name was maintained during two succeeding generations, but disappeared during the Sioux outbreak of 1862–65. The family was less influential than the Little Crows or the Wabashas of the same tribe.   (D. R.)

Ree Band. According to Grinnell (Soc. Org. Cheyennes, 144, 1905) a local nickname for a part of the Northern Cheyenne.

Reechochic (*re-e-cho'* 'play' or 'the act of playing', *chic* 'place of'). A small Tarahumare rancheria near Norogachic, Chihuahua, Mexico.—Lumholtz, inf'n, 1894.

Rekeachic (*re-ke-a'* 'white earth', *chic* 'place of'). A small rancheria of the Tarahumare near Norogachic, Chihuahua, Mexico.—Lumholtz, inf'n, 1894.

Rekorichic (*re-ko-ri'* 'water jar', *chic* 'place of'). A Tarahumare rancheria about 15 m. N. E. of Norogachic, in Chi-

huahua, Mexico. Called by the Mexicans Tecorichic.—Lumholtz, inf'n, 1894.
Tecorichic.—Orozco y Berra, Geog., 322, 1864.

Rekuvirachic ('place of the stone pillars'). A small rancheria of the Tarahumare in the Sierra Madre, w. Chihuahua, Mexico.—Lumholtz, inf'n, 1894.

Rekuwichic ('place of the high stone pillars'). A small rancheria of the Tarahumare not far from Norogachic, Chihuahua, Mexico.—Lumholtz, inf'n, 1894.

Rekwoi. A Yurok village on the N. side of the mouth of Klamath r., N. w. Cal. It has given name to the present American settlement of Requa, a mile upstream from the old village site, at which there now live only two or three Yurok families.   (A. L. K.)
Rek-qua.—Gibbs (1851) in Schoolcraft, Ind. Tribes, III, 138, 1853. Requa.—Powers in Overland Mo., VII, 530, 1872. Ri-kwa.—Powers in Cont. N. A. Ethnol., III, 44, 1877. Sufíp.—A. L. Kroeber, inf'n, 1904 (Karok name).

Relationship. See *Clan and Gens, Family, Kinship.*

Religion. For the purpose of a brief description of the religion of the American Indians we may define religion as that group of concepts and acts which spring from the relation of the individual to the outer world, so far as these relations are not considered as due to physical forces the action of which is accounted for by purely rationalistic considerations. The scope of religious concepts will depend to a certain extent, therefore, on the knowledge of the laws of nature; and, since the border-line of the natural and the supernatural, as conceived in the mind of primitive man, does not coincide with our view of this subject, there will be marked differences between the scope of religion among civilized nations and that among less advanced peoples. For instance, the causal relations determining the movements of the stars are recognized by civilized man; but at an earlier time it was believed that the positions of the stars influenced in a mysterious manner the fates of man and that their movements could be controlled by his will. Among tribes which held to the latter opinion, views relating to the heavenly bodies would form part of the religion of the people; while among those peoples to which the causal relations determining the motions of the stars are known, these motions are no longer subject to religious interpretations.

Owing to the different point of view, it may also happen that certain ideas of primitive man, which from our standpoint would have to be considered as religious in character, are interpreted by the people holding them as purely rationalistic. In our judgment, for instance, sympathetic cures, which are believed in by most primitive tribes and even by uneducated people among ourselves, can not be considered as due to any physical effect, while among primitive tribes they may be so viewed. The same is true of certain mythological concepts. If an Indian tribe explains the markings on the skin of the chipmunk as due to the fact that at an early time the grizzly bear scratched its back, this may be to the mind of the Indian a perfectly rationalistic explanation, while to us it would be entirely mysterious. Thus it appears that the general views of nature—the explanations given for the occurrence of natural phenomena—necessarily enter into a consideration of the religions of primitive tribes, even if these explanations should be based on a purely rationalistic attitude on the part of primitive man. The less clear the line between observation and reasoning on the one hand and imagination and inference due to emotional states on the other, the less sharply drawn will be the line between what may be called science and religion. In accordance with the definition given before, those concepts that spring from the relation of the individual to the outer world, and the form of which depends on imagination and emotion, may be said to form the tenets of religion.

When religious acts are considered in greater detail, it appears that here also acts prompted by rationalistic considerations are not sharply separated from others dictated by imagination and emotion. Thus, when a medicine-man pursues and captures the fleeing soul of a sick man, he may follow out by his acts in a rational way opinions based largely on reasoning, although deeply affected in their origin by such emotions as fear and love. When, on the other hand, he tries to gain greater efficiency by putting himself into a state of emotional excitement, in which he believes his chances of success are enhanced, his acts become religious, in the stricter sense of the term. This lack of sharp division between rationalistic and religious forms of activity is found everywhere. Furthermore, it must be borne in mind that many actions are performed without any conscious reason, except so far as they are required by custom. This is true particularly of actions that are considered as proper, like those determined by rules regulating the behavior of the young to the old, or of the common people to the nobility; or also of actions that are considered as ethical, like those of hospitality and of pity. Here the line of demarcation between religious activities and others not connected with religion becomes even less sharp, because it often happens that actions originally performed without any particular reason or for purely rationalistic purposes are secondarily given religious mo-

tives. It thus follows that religious views and actions are not primarily connected with ethical concepts. Only in so far as man in his religious relations to the outer world endeavors to follow certain rules of conduct, in order to avoid evil effects, is a relation between primitive religion and ethics established.

The religious concepts of the Indians may be described in two groups—those that concern the individual, and those that concern the social group, such as tribe and clan. The fundamental concept bearing on the religious life of the individual is the belief in the existence of magic power, which may influence the life of man, and which in turn may be influenced by human activity. In this sense magic power must be understood as the wonderful qualities which are believed to exist in objects, animals, men, spirits, or deities, and which are superior to the natural qualities of man. This idea of magic power is one of the fundamental concepts that occur among all Indian tribes. It is what is called *manito* by the Algonquian tribes; *wakanda*, by the Siouan tribes; *orenda*, by the Iroquois; *sulia*, by the Salish; *naualak*, by the Kwakiutl, and *tamanoas*, by the Chinook. Notwithstanding slight differences in the signification of these terms, the fundamental notion of all of them is that of a power inherent in the objects of nature which is more potent than the natural powers of man. This idea seems adequately expressed by our term "wonderful"; and it is hardly necessary to introduce an Indian term, as has often been attempted. Among the American terms, the word *manito* (q. v.; see also *Orenda, Otkon, Oyaron*) has been most frequently used to express this idea. The degree to which the magic power of nature is individualized differs considerably among various tribes. Although the belief in the powers of inanimate objects is common, we find in America that, on the whole, animals, particularly the larger ones, are most frequently considered as possessed of such magic power. Strong anthropomorphic individualization also occurs, which justifies us in calling these powers deities. It seems probable that among the majority of tribes, besides the belief in the power of specific objects, a belief in a magic power that is only vaguely localized, exists. In cases where this belief is pronounced, the notion sometimes approaches the concept of a deity, or of a great spirit which is hardly anthropomorphic in its character. This is the case, for instance, among the Tsimshian of British Columbia and among the Algonquian tribes of the Great Lakes, and also in the figure of the Tirawa of the Pawnee.

As stated before, the whole concept of

the world—or, in other words, the mythology of each tribe—enters to a very great extent into their religious concepts and activities. The mythologies are highly specialized in different parts of North America; and, although a large number of myths are the common property of many American tribes, the general view of the world appears to be quite distinct in various parts of the continent. Taking into consideration the continent of America as a whole, we find a type of explanation of the world which is psychologically quite different from the familiar Semitic type. In the Semitic religions eternal existence appeared as an unintelligible problem, and the mind preferred to assume a beginning which was accounted for by transferring the existing world, as it was known by observation, into the thought of a creator, and interpreting the creation as a projection of his thoughts by his will-power into objective existence. The Indian mind, on the other hand, accepts the eternal existence of the world, and accounts for its specific form by the assumption that events which once happened in early times settled for once and all the form in which the same kind of event must continue to occur. For instance, when the bear produced the stripes of the chipmunk by scratching its back, this determined that all chipmunks were to have such stripes; or when an ancestor of a clan was taught a certain ceremony, that same ceremony must be performed by all future generations. This idea is not by any means confined to America, but is found among primitive peoples of other continents as well, and occurs even in Semitic cults.

Considering American mythologies in their broadest outlines, the following areas may be distinguished: (1) The Eskimo area, the mythology of which is characterized by an abundance of purely human hero-tales, and a very small number of traditions accounting for the origin of animals, and these generally largely in human setting. (2) The North Pacific Coast area, characterized by a large cycle of transformer myths, in which the origin of many of the arts of man is accounted for, as well as the peculiarities of many animals; the whole forming a very disconnected heterogeneous mass of traditions. (3) Allied to these appear the traditions of the Western plateau and of the Mackenzie basin area, a region in which animal tales abound, many accounting for the present conditions of the world, the whole being very disconnected and contradictory. (4) The Californian area, the mythologies of which are characterized by a stronger emphasis laid on creation by will-power than is found in most other parts of the American continent. (5) The principal characteristic of the mythologies of the area of the Great Plains,

the eastern woodlands, and the arid Southwest, is the tendency to systematization of the myths under the influence of a highly developed ritual. This tendency is more sharply defined in the S. than in the N. and N. E., and has perhaps progressed further than anywhere else among the Pueblos, to whom the origin of the clans and societies seems to give the keynote of mythological concepts; and among the Pawnee, whose contemplation of the stars seems to have given the principal tone to their mythology (see also article *Mythology*). The religious concepts of the Indians deal largely with the relation of the individual to the magic power mentioned above, and are specialized in accordance with their general mythological concepts, which determine largely the degree to which the powers are personified as animals, spirits, or deities.

Another group of religious concepts, which are not less important than the group heretofore discussed, refers to the relations of the individual to his internal states, so far as these are not controlled by the will, and are therefore considered as subject to external magic influences. Most important among these are dreams, sickness, and death. These may be produced by obsession, or by external forces which compel the soul to leave the body. In this sense the soul is considered by almost all tribes as not subject to the individual will; it may be abstracted from the body by hostile forces, and it may be damaged and killed. The concept of the soul itself shows a great variety of forms. Very often the soul is identified with life, but we also find commonly the belief in a multiplicity of souls. Thus, among the Eskimo, the name is considered as one of the souls of man, another soul belongs to the body, a third one is independent of the body. The soul is also identified with the blood, the bones, the shadow, the nape of the neck (see *Soul*). Based on these ideas is also the belief in the existence of the soul after death. Thus, in the belief of the Algonquian Indians of the Great Lakes, the souls of the deceased are believed to reside in the far west with the brother of the great culture-hero. Among the Kutenai the belief prevails that the souls will return at a later period, accompanying the culture-hero. Sometimes the land from which the ancestors of the tribe have sprung, which in the S. is often conceived of as underground, is of equal importance.

Since the belief in the existence of magic powers is very strong in the Indian mind, all his actions are regulated by the desire to retain the good will of those friendly to him, and to control those that are hostile.

The first means of retaining the good

will of the friendly power is the strict observance of a great variety of proscriptions. An important group of these may be combined under the term "taboo" (q. v.). Among these, furthermore, food taboos are particularly common. Every tribe of America, no matter how scanty their means of subsistence may have been, had certain kinds of tabooed food— that is, food forbidden, either permanently or at certain seasons, or on certain occasions. Thus, one division of the Omaha were forbidden to eat the shoulder of the buffalo, while another one was forbidden to eat the elk; the Iroquois were forbidden to eat the animal from which their family name was taken, and the same is true of Pueblo and other clans; the Eskimo must not eat caribou and walrus at the same season; the Navaho must not touch flesh of the bear, nor the Zuñi anything that lives in the water.

Not less numerous are the taboos of work. These are perhaps nowhere so highly developed as among the Eskimo, among whom work on caribou-skins, seal-skins, metals, ice, and heather is forbidden under certain conditions. Here belong, also, the taboos of story-telling, and of playing certain games at certain seasons, which are quite common. Of great importance are the taboos intended to prevent the evil effects of impurity. Thus we find a large number of taboos forbidding menstruating women, murderers, and mourners from performing certain kinds of work. They must not touch fresh food lest the magic powers controlling the food supply may be offended.

Social taboos, which are very common in Polynesia, are not so markedly developed in América, although the strict secrecy with which certain sacred actions are performed by privileged members of a tribe is akin to this institution. Thus it is forbidden, except on certain occasions, for any member of the tribe to touch or even see the contents of sacred bundles (see *Palladium*), and even then only the keeper of the bundle is allowed to open it to view. While all these taboos are essentially negative in their character, forbidding certain actions in order to avoid giving offense, there are positive acts which are required for the same purpose. Some of these might well be called rules of ethical conduct, although the one reason given for them is the endeavor to retain the good will of the wonderful powers of nature. All the numerous regulations which are found all over the continent, and intended to retain the good will of the food animals, and which are essentially signs of respect shown to them, belong to this class. Dogs must not gnaw the bones of food animals, because this is a sign of disrespect.

The bear, after having been killed, receives marks of reverence; and the first game animals obtained at the beginning of the hunting season must be treated with particular care. The complicated customs relating to buffalo hunting, and the salmon ceremonials of the N. W. Indians, as well as the whale ceremonials of the Eskimo, may also be given as examples. Respectful behavior toward old people and generally decent conduct are also often counted among such required acts. Here may also be included the numerous customs of purification that are required in order to avoid the ill will of the powers. These, however, may better be considered as constituting one of the means of controlling magic power, which form a very large part of the religious observances of the American Indians.

The Indian is not satisfied with the attempt to avoid the ill will of the powers, but he tries also to make them subservient to his own needs. This end may be attained in a variety of ways. Perhaps the most characteristic of North American Indian methods of gaining control over supernatural powers is that of the acquisition of one of them as a personal protector. Generally this process is called the acquiring of a manito; and the most common method of acquiring it is for the young man during the period of adolescence to purify himself by fasting, bathing, and vomiting, until his body is perfectly clean and acceptable to the supernatural beings. At the same time the youth works himself by these means, by dancing, and sometimes also by means of drugs, into a trance, in which he has a vision of the guardian spirit which is to protect him throughout life. These means of establishing communication with the spirit world are in very general use, also at other periods of life (see *Black drink, Dance, Ordeals, Peyote, Tobacco*). The magic power that man thus acquires may give him special abilities; it may make him a successful hunter, warrior, or shaman; or it may give him power to acquire wealth, success in gambling, or the love of women.

While the above is the most common method of acquiring magic power, other means are well known among the American Indians, particularly among those tribes in which strong clan organizations prevail. They believe that wonderful power may be attained by inheritance. There are also numerous cases, as among the Arapaho and Blackfeet (Siksika), where the privilege of acquiring it and the control over it may be purchased. Among the American Eskimo the idea prevails that it may be transmitted by teaching and by bodily contact with a person who controls such powers. Ordinarily its possession is considered so sacred that it must not be divulged except in cases of extreme danger, but among other tribes it may be made known to the whole tribe. In a few cases the opinion prevails that such powers exist in certain localities, but can not be acquired by individuals.

Another means of controlling the powers of nature is by prayer, which may be directed either to the protecting spirit of the individual or to other powers. Objects of prayer may be protection in danger, removal of sickness, the obtaining of food or other material benefits, or a more general and abstract request for the blessing of the powers. Many prayers are addressed in fixed form or contain at least certain old formulas.

Another way of invoking the protection of the powers is through the use of charms (also called fetishes, q. v.). The charm is either believed to be the seat of magic power, or it may be a symbol of such power, and its action may be based on its symbolic significance. Of the former kind are presumably many objects contained in the sacred bundles of certain Indians, which are believed to be possessed of sacred powers; while symbolic significance seems to prevail in charms like the stones worn by the North Pacific Coast Indians, which are believed to harden the skin against missiles of hostile shamans, or the magic whip of wolf-skin of the Eskimo, which is believed to have the power of driving away spirits.

Symbolic actions are also made use of. Such acts are, for instance, the setting-up of prayer-sticks (q. v.), which are meant to convey man's wishes to the powers. Often these wishes are indicated by special attachments, expressing in symbolic or pictographic manner the thing wished for. Somewhat related to such symbolic actions are also all processes of divination, in which, by a symbolic act, the propitiousness of the proposed undertaking is ascertained.

Still more potent means of influencing the powers are offerings and sacrifices. On the whole, these are not so strongly developed in North America as they are in other parts of the world. In many regions human sacrifices were common— for instance, in Mexico and Yucatan— while in northern America they are known only in rare instances, as among the Pawnee. However, many cases of torture, particularly of self-torture, must be reckoned here (see *Ordeals, Sun Dance*). Other bloody sacrifices are also rare in North America. We may mention the sacrifice of the dog among the Iroquois. Only to a limited extent do we find the

tendency of considering the killing of game as a bloody sacrifice. On the other hand, sacrifices of tobacco smoke, of corn, and of parts of food, of small manufactured objects, and of symbolic objects, are very common. These gifts may be offered to any of the supernatural powers with the intent of gaining their assistance and avoiding their enmity.

Still another way of gaining control over supernatural powers is by incantations, which in a way are related to prayers, but which act rather through the magic influence of the words. Therefore the traditional form of these incantations is rigidly adhered to. They occur frequently among the Arctic tribes of the continent, but are not by any means lacking among others, who believe that the recitation of a short formula may aid in reaching a desired end. In the same way that incantations are related to prayer, certain acts and charms are related to offerings. We find among almost all Indian tribes the custom of performing certain acts, which are neither symbolic nor offerings, nor other attempts to obtain the assistance of superior beings, but which are effective through their own potency. Such acts are the use of lucky objects intended to secure good fortune; or the peculiar treatment of animals, plants, and other objects, in order to bring about a change of weather.

There is also found among most Indian tribes the idea that the supernatural powers, if offended by transgressions of rules of conduct, may be propitiated by punishment. Such punishment may consist in the removal of the offending individual, who may be killed by the members of the tribe, or the propitiation may be accomplished by milder forms of punishment. Of particular interest among these is confession as a means of propitiation, which is found among the Athapascans, the Iroquois, and the Eskimo. Other forms of punishment are based largely on the idea of purification by fasting, bathing, and vomiting. Among the Plains Indians the vow to perform a ceremony or another act agreeable to the powers is considered an efficient means of gaining their good will or of atoning for past offenses.

Protection against disease is also sought by the help of superhuman powers. These practices have two distinct forms, according to the fundamental conception of disease. Disease is conceived of principally in two forms—either as due to the presence of a material object in the body of the patient, or as an effect of the absence of the soul from the body. The cure of disease is intrusted to the shamans or medicine-men, who obtain their powers generally by the assistance of guardian spirits, or who may personally be endowed with magic powers. It is their duty to discover the material disease which is located in the patient's body, and which they extract by sucking or pulling with the hands; or to go in pursuit of the absent soul, to recover it, and to restore it to the patient. Both of these forms of shamanism are found practically all over the continent, but in some regions—for instance, in California—the idea of material bodies that cause sickness is particularly strongly developed; while in other regions the idea of the absence of the soul seems to be more marked. In treating the patient, the shamans almost everywhere use various means to work themselves into a state of excitement, which is produced by singing, by the use of the drum and rattle, and by dancing. The belief also widely prevails that unpropitious conditions may counteract the work of the shaman, and that for this reason particular care must be taken to remove all disturbing and impure elements from the place where the shamanistic performance is held. When the shaman has to have intercourse with the spirits, whom he visits in their own domain, or when he has to pursue the soul of the patient, we find frequently sleight-of-hand employed, such as the tying of the hands of the shaman, who, when his soul leaves the body, is believed to free himself with the help of the spirits. (See *Magic, Medicine and Medicine-men, Shamans and Priests.*)

The belief that certain individuals can acquire control over the powers has also led to the opinion that they may be used to harm enemies. The possession of such control is not always beneficial, but may be used also for purposes of witchcraft (q. v.). Hostile shamans may throw disease into the bodies of their enemies, or they may abduct their souls. They may do harm by sympathetic means, and control the will-power of others by the help of the supernatural means at their disposal. Witchcraft is everywhere considered as a crime, and is so punished.

Besides those manifestations of religious belief that relate to the individual, religion has become closely associated with the social structure of the tribes; so that the ritualistic side of religion can be understood only in connection with the social organization of the Indian tribes. Even the fundamental traits of their social organization possess a religious import. This is true particularly of the clans (q. v.), so far as they are characterized by totems (q. v.). The totem is almost always an object of more or less religious reverence to the clan; and there are many cases in which taboos relating to the totemic animal exist, like those previously referred to among the Omaha. Also in cases where the clans have definite political functions, like those of the Omaha and the Iroquois, these functions are closely associated with religious concepts, partly in so far as their origin is ascribed to myths, partly in so far as the functions are associated with the performance of religious rites. The position of officials is also closely associated with definite religious concepts. Thus, the head of a clan at times is considered as the representative of the mythological ancestor of the clan, and as such is believed to be endowed with superior powers; or the position as officer in the tribe or clan entails the performance of certain definite religious functions. In this sense many of the political functions among Indian tribes are closely associated with what may be termed "priestly functions." The religious significance of social institutions is most clearly marked in cases where the tribe, or large parts of the tribe, join in the performance of certain ceremonies which are intended to serve partly a political, partly a religious end. Such acts are some of the intertribal ball-games, the busk of the Creeks, the sun-dance of the Plains Indians, performances of the numerous warrior societies of the Plains, which will be found treated under these headings. Here also belong the secret societies, which are highly developed among the Pueblos, in California, and on the North Pacific coast. It is characteristic of rituals in many parts of the world that they tend to develop into a more or less dramatic representation of the myth from which the ritual is derived. For this reason the use of masks (q. v.; see also *Ceremony*) is a common feature of these rituals, in which certain individuals impersonate supernatural beings. In those tribes among which very complex rituals have developed we find the ceremonies frequently in charge of certain officers, who are at the same time the keepers of the sacred objects belonging to the tribe or to the societies (see *Altar, Palladium*); and it would seem that the whole system of religious beliefs and practices has developed the more systematically, the more strictly the religious practices have come to be in charge of a body of priests. This tendency to systematization of religious beliefs may be observed particularly among the Pueblos and the Pawnee, but it also occurs in isolated cases in other parts of the continent; for instance, among the Bellacoola of British Columbia, and those Algonquian tribes that have the Midewiwin ceremonial fully developed. In these cases we find that frequently an elaborate series of esoteric doctrines and practices exists, which are known to only a small portion of the tribe, while the mass of the people are familiar only with part of the ritual and with its exoteric features. For this reason we often find the religious beliefs and practices of the mass of a tribe rather heterogeneous as compared with the beliefs held by the priests. Among many of the tribes in which priests are found, we find distinct esoteric societies, and it is not by any means rare that the doctrines of one society are not in accord with those of another. All this is clearly due to the fact that the religious ideas of the tribe are derived from many different sources, and have been brought into order at a later date by the priests charged with the keeping of the tribal rituals. Esoteric forms of religion in charge of priests are found among the tribes of the arid region in the Southwest, the tribes of the southern Mississippi basin, and to a less extent among the more northerly tribes on the Plains. It would seem that, on the whole, the import of the esoteric teachings decreases among the more northerly and northeasterly tribes of the continent. It is probably least developed among the Eskimo, the tribes of the Mackenzie basin, and the tribes of the great plateau region, in so far as these have remained uninfluenced by the Plains Indians and by those of the Pacific coast.

On the whole, the Indians incline strongly toward all forms of religious excitement. This is demonstrated not only by the exuberant development of ancient religious forms, but also by the frequency with which prophets (q. v.) have appeared among them, who taught new doctrines and new rites, based either on older religious beliefs, or on teaching partly of Christian, partly of Indian origin. Perhaps the best known of these forms of religion is the Ghost-dance (q. v.), which swept over a large part of the continent during the last decade of the 19th century. But other prophets of similar type and of far-reaching influence were numerous. One of these was Tenskwatawa (q. v.), the famous brother of Tecumseh; another, the seer Smohalla (q. v.) of the Pacific coast; and even among the Eskimo such prophets have been known, particularly in Greenland.   (F. B.)

Relosoa (*Re-lo-soa*, 'place of many potatoes'). A rancheria of the Tarahumare, 20 m. E. of Chinatu, in the Sierra Madre, w. Chihuahua, Mexico.—Lumholtz, inf'n, 1894.

Remahenonc. A village, perhaps belonging to the Unami Delawares, in the vicinity of New York city in the 17th century.—Doc. of 1649 in N. Y. Doc. Col. Hist., XIII, 25, 1881.

Remedios. A former Spanish mission established among the Pima by Father Kino, about 1697, on the San Ignacio branch of Rio Asuncion in Sonora, Mexico. A new church was erected there in 1699–1700. Pop. 20 in 1730.
Los Remedios.—Orozco y Berra, Geog., 347, 1864. Nuestra Señora de los Remedios.—Kino (1697) in Doc. Hist. Mex., 4th s., I, 275, 1856 (full mission name). Remedios.—Bernal (1697) quoted by Bancroft, Ariz. and N. Mex., 356, 1889.

Renape (contraction of *Erendpeu*, 'true or native man', 'man properly so called,' man in contrast with anthropomorphic beings). An individual belonging to one of the largest linguistic groups into which the Algonquian family of languages is divided; which has, from a phonetic viewpoint, a closer affinity with Chippewa than with any other group; and which, since the change of *r* to *l*, which took place in historic time, has been distinguished as "Lenape". The word is from (1) *ĕrĕn*, 'true', 'genuine', 'properly so called', cognate with Abnaki *ärĕn*, *älĕn*, Micmac *ĕlĕn*, Narraganset and Menominee *ĕnĭn*, Chippewa *ĭnĭn*, Cree dialects *ĭyĭn*, *ĭthĭn*, *ĭrĭn*, *ĭtĭn*, etc.; and (2) *-ápeu*, 'man,' from (by the regular loss of initial *n* in composition) the radical word *nápeu*, meaning (*a*) 'man', (*b*) 'male'. "*Renapoaks*, for so they [the Roanok] call by that general name all the inhabitants of the whole maine, of what province soever." (Lane, *ca.* 1586, in Hakluyt, Voy., III, 260, 1600.)   (W. R. G.)

Renapoak (from *renape*, q. v., and *-ak*, plural suffix). The Indians formerly of the interior of North Carolina, so called by the Algonquian tribes on Albemarle sd., N. C.—Lane (1586) in Hakluyt, Voy., III, 317, repr. 1810.

Renville, Gabriel. The last chief of the Sisseton Sioux, to which position he was appointed in 1866 by the War Department. He was a son of Victor and a nephew of the celebrated Joseph Renville. He was born at Sweet Corn's village, Big Stone lake, S. Dak., in Apr. 1824, and died at Sisseton agency, Aug. 26, 1902. His mother was Winona Crawford, daughter of Captain Crawford of the English army and of a daughter of Walking Buffalo Redwing (Tatankamani), chief of the Khemnichan. Gabriel was a valued friend of the whites during the massacre and resulting war of the Sioux outbreak in 1862–65.   (D. R.)

Renville, Joseph. The half-Sioux son of a French fur-trader, born at Kaposia (St Paul), Minn., in 1779. His early childhood was passed in the tipi of his mother, but when about 10 years of age he was taken by his father to Canada and placed under the care of a Catholic priest, from whom he received knowledge of the French language. He came into prominence as a guide to Lieut. Z. M. Pike in 1805, and entered the service of the British in the War of 1812 as interpreter to the Sioux, with the rank of captain. He was present at Ft Meigs and Ft Stephenson, Ohio, and the good conduct of the Indians there was due largely to his influence. He went to the great council at Portage des Sioux (mouth of the Missouri) in 1815 as interpreter, and resigned his British commission and half pay to attach himself thenceforth to the American interest. He organized the Columbia Fur Co., with headquarters on L. Traverse, Minn., and, calling to his assistance many of the bold characters released from other service by the consolidation of the Hudson's Bay and N. W. Fur Cos., was able to meet the American Fur Co. on its own grounds with a competition so strong that the latter was glad to make terms and place the Columbia Co.'s men in charge of its Upper Missouri outfit. At the time of the consolidation Renville established an independent business at Lac qui Parle which he conducted until his death. In 1834 he met Dr. T. S. Williamson, the famous missionary, at Prairie du Chien, out on his first reconnoissance, and arranged with him to go to Lac qui Parle and establish a mission the next year. Williamson returned to Ohio for his family, and the next spring met Renville at Ft Snelling, whence he proceeded to Lac qui Parle, which became the scene of most of his long service with the Sioux. They were soon after joined by Dr S. R. Riggs, and engaged, with Renville's assistance, in the translation of the Scriptures. Renville translated every word of the Bible into the Dakota language, and the missionaries faithfully recorded it; he also rendered them invaluable assistance in the construction of the grammar and dictionary of the Dakota language. In 1841 Renville was chosen and ordained a ruling elder, discharging the duties of his office until his death at Lac qui Parle in Mar. 1846. Many descendants still reside among the Sisseton Sioux in South Dakota. (D. R.)

Rerawachic (*re-ra'-wa* 'giant woodpecker,' *chic* 'place of'). A Tarahumare rancheria not far from Norogachic, Chihuahua, Mexico.—Lumholtz, inf'n, 1894.

Reservations. A natural result of land cessions by the Indians to the U. S. Government was the establishment of reservations for the natives. This was necessary not only in order to provide them with homes and with land for cultivation, but to avoid disputes in regard to boundaries and to bring them more easily under control of the Government by confining them to given limits. This policy, which has been followed in Canada under both French and English control, and also to some extent by the colonies,

was inaugurated by the United States in 1786. It may be attributed primarily to the increase of the white population and the consequent necessity of confining the aboriginal population to narrower limits. This involved a very important, even radical, change in the habits and customs of the Indians, and was the initiatory step toward a reliance upon agricultural pursuits for subsistence. Reservations in early days, and to a limited extent more recently, were formed chiefly as the result of cessions of land; thus a tribe, in ceding land that it held by original occupancy, reserved from the cession a specified and definite part thereof, and such part was held under the original right of occupancy, but with the consent of the Government, as it was generally expressly stated in the treaty defining the bounds that the part so reserved was "allotted to" or "reserved for" the given Indians, thus recognizing title in the Government. However, as time passed, the method of establishing reservations varied, as is apparent from the following return, showing the method of establishment of the various reservations, given by the Commissioner of Indian Affairs in his Report for 1890: By Executive order, 56; by Executive order under authority of Congress, 6; by act of Congress, 28; by treaty, with boundaries defined or enlarged by Executive order, 15; by treaty or agreement and act of Congress, 5; by unratified treaty, 1; by treaty or agreement, 51.

The setting aside of reservations by treaty was terminated by the act of Mar. 3, 1871, which brought transactions with the Indians under the immediate control of Congress and substituted simple agreements for solemn treaties. By sundry subsequent laws the matter has been placed in control of the President. Reservations established by Executive order without an act of Congress were not held to be permanent before the general allotment act of Feb. 8, 1887, under which the tenure has been materially changed, and all reservations, whether created by Executive order, by act of Congress, or by treaty, are permanent. Reservations established by Executive order under authority of Congress are those which have been authorized by acts of Congress and their limits defined by Executive order, or first established by Executive order and subsequently confirmed by Congress. The Indian titles which have been recognized by the Government appear to have been (1) the original right of occupancy, and (2) the title to their reservations, which differs in most cases from the original title in the fact that it is derived from the United States. There have been some titles, and a few of them still exist, which the Indian Bureau deems exceptions to this rule, as where the reservation was formed by restricting the original areas or where reservations have been patented to tribes by the Government. Examples of the latter class are the patents to the Cherokee, Choctaw, and Creek nations. In a few instances the Indians purchased the lands forming in whole or in part their reservations. The construction given to these by the Indian Bureau and the courts is that they are not titles in fee simple, for they convey no power of alienation except to the United States, neither are they the same as the ordinary title to occupancy; they are "a base, qualified, or determinable fee," with a possibility of reversion to the United States only, "and the authorities of these nations may cut, sell, and dispose of their timber, and may permit mining and grazing, within the limits of their respective tracts, by their own citizens." The act of Mar. 1, 1889, establishing a United States court in Indian Territory, repealed all laws having the effect of preventing the Five Civilized Tribes in said Territory (Cherokee, Choctaw, Chickasaw, Creek, and Seminole) from entering into leases or contracts with others than their own citizens for mining coal for a period not exceeding ten years. As a general rule the Indians on a reservation could make no leases of land, sales of standing timber, or grants of mining privileges or rights of way to railways without the authority of Congress. On the other hand, it was obligatory upon the Government to prevent any intrusion, trespass, or settlement on the lands of any tribe or nation of Indians unless the tribe or nation had given consent by agreement or treaty.

The idea of removing the Indians residing E. of the Mississippi to reservations w. of that river was a policy adopted at an early date. The first official notice of it appears in the act of Mar. 26, 1804, "erecting Louisiana into two territories, and providing the temporary government thereof." By treaty with the Choctaw in 1820 they had been assigned a new home in the W., to include a considerable portion of w. Arkansas, with all that part of the present Oklahoma s. of the South Canadian and Arkansas rs. In 1825 President Monroe reported to the Senate a formal "plan of colonization or removal" (see Schoolcraft, III, 573 et seq., 1853), of all tribes then residing E. of the Mississippi, to the same general western region. In accordance with this plan the present Oklahoma, with the greater portion of what is now Kansas, was soon after constituted a territory, under the name

of "Indian Territory," as a permanent home for the tribes to be removed from the settled portions of the United States. Most of the northern portion of the territory was acquired by treaty purchase from the Osage and Kansa. A series of treaties was then inaugurated by which, before the close of 1840, almost all the principal Eastern tribes and tribal remnants had been removed to the "Indian Territory," the five important Southern tribes— Cherokee, Creek, Choctaw, Chickasaw, and Seminole—being guaranteed autonomy under the style of "Nations." By subsequent legislation Kansas was detached from the Territory, most of the emigrant tribes within the bounds of Kansas being again removed to new reservations s. of the boundary line. By other and later treaties lands within the same Territory were assigned to the actual native tribes—Kiowa, Comanche, Wichita, Cheyenne, etc.—whose claims had been entirely overlooked in the first negotiations, which considered only the Osage and Kansa along the eastern border. Other tribes were brought in at various periods from Texas, Nebraska, and farther N., to which were added, as prisoners of war, the Modoc of California (1873), the Nez Percés of Oregon and Idaho (1878), and the Chiricahua Apache of Arizona (1889), until the Indian population of the Territory comprised some 40 officially recognized tribes.

An unoccupied district near the center of the Territory, known as Oklahoma, had become the subject of controversy with intruding white settlers, and was finally thrown open to settlement in 1889. In 1890 the whole western portion of Indian Territory was created into a separate territory under the name of Oklahoma. In the meantime, under provisions of an allotment act passed in 1887 (see *Land tenure*), agreements were being negotiated with the resident tribes for the opening of the reservation to white settlement. In 1906 a similar arrangement was consummated with the five autonomous tribes of the eastern section, or Indian Territory—the Cherokee, Creek, Choctaw, Chickasaw, and Seminole—together with the several small tribes in the N. E. corner of Indian Territory. In the following year, 1907, the whole of the former Indian Territory was created into a single state under the name of Oklahoma.

According to the report of the Commissioner of Indian Affairs, the number of reservations in the United States in 1908, including the 19 Spanish grants to the Pueblo Indians, was 161, aggregating 52,013,010 acres, as follows:

Schedule showing each Indian Reservation in 1908, under what Agency or School, Tribes occupying or belonging to it, Area not Allotted or Specially Reserved, and Authority for its Establishment. (Compiled by the Office of Indian Affairs.)

Reservation.	Tribes.	Acres.	Established by—
ARIZONA:			
Camp McDowell	Yavapai (Mohave Apache)	24,971	Executive order, Sept. 15, 1903; act of Apr. 21, 1904 (XXXIII, 211).
Colorado River ^a	Chemehuevi, Kawia, Cocopa (not on res.), Mohave.	240,640	Act of Mar. 3, 1865 (XIII, 559); Executive orders, Nov. 22, 1873, Nov. 16, 1874, and May 15, 1876. (See sec. 25, Indian appropriation act, approved Apr. 21, 1904, XXXIII, 224.)
Fort Apache	Arivaipa, Chiricahua, Coyotero, Mimbreño, Mogollon, Pinaleño, Tsiltaden.	1,681,920	Executive orders, Nov. 9, 1871, July 21, 1874, Apr. 27, 1876, Jan. 26 and Mar. 31, 1877; act of Feb. 20, 1893 (XXVII, 469); agreement made Feb. 25, 1896, approved by act of June 10, 1896 (XXIX, 358), supplemented by act of June 7, 1897 (XXX, 64).
Gila Bend	Papago	22,391	Executive order, Dec. 12, 1882.
Gila River	Maricopa, Pima	357,120	Act of Feb. 28, 1859 (XI, 401); Executive orders, Aug. 31, 1876, Jan. 10 and June 14, 1879, May 5, 1882, and Nov. 15, 1883.
Havasupai	Havasupai	518	Executive orders, June 8 and Nov. 23, 1880, and Mar. 31, 1882.
Hopi	Hopi	2,472,320	Executive order, Dec. 16, 1882.
Navaho ^b	Navaho	9,586,323	Treaty of June 1, 1868 (XV, 667), and Executive orders, Oct. 29, 1878, Jan. 6, 1880, May 17, 1884 (two), and Nov. 19, 1892. 1,769,600 acres in Arizona and 967,680 acres in Utah were added to this reservation by Executive order of May 17, 1884, and 46,080 acres in New Mexico were restored to the public domain, but were again reserved by Executive orders, Apr. 24, 1886, Jan. 8, 1900, and Nov. 14, 1901. By Executive orders of Mar. 10 and May 15, 1905, 61,523 acres were added to the reservation, and by Executive order of Nov. 9, 1907, as amended by Executive order of Jan. 28, 1908, 82,560 acres were added.
Papago	Papago	27,566	Executive order, July 1, 1874, and act of Aug. 5, 1882 (XXII, 299). 41,622.65 acres were allotted to 291 Indians, and 14 acres reserved for a schoolsite; the residue, 27,566 acres, unallotted.
Salt River	Maricopa and Pima	46,720	Executive orders, June 14, 1879, and Sept. 15, 1903. (See S. Doc. 90, 58th Cong., 2d sess.)
San Carlos	Arivaipa, Chiricahua, Coyotero, Mimbreño, Mogollon, Mohave, Pinaleño, San Carlos, Tonto, Tsiltaden, Yuma Apache.	1,834,240	Executive orders, Nov. 9, 1871, Dec. 14, 1872, Aug. 5, 1873, July 21, 1874, Apr. 27, 1876, Oct. 30, 1876, Jan. 26 and Mar. 31, 1877; act of Feb. 20, 1893 (XXVII, 469); agreement made Feb. 25, 1896, approved by act of June 10, 1896 (XXIX, 358). (See act of June 7, 1897, XXX, 64, and act of Mar. 2, 1901, XXXI, 952.) Executive order of Dec. 27, 1902.
Walapai	Walapai	730,880	Executive orders, Jan. 4, 1883, Dec. 22, 1898, and May 14, 1900.
		17,025,609	
CALIFORNIA:			
Digger	"Digger"	330	Act of Mar. 3, 1893 (XXVII, 612), provides for purchase of 330 acres; not allotted.
Hupa Valley	Hupa, Yurok, Redwood (Chilula), Saiaz (Saia).	99,051	Act of Apr. 8, 1864 (XIII, 39); Executive orders, June 23, 1876, and Oct. 16, 1891. There have been allotted to 639 Indians 29,143.38 acres, reserved to 3 villages 68.74 acres, and opened to settlement under act of June 17, 1892 (XXVII, 52), 15,096.11 acres, the former Klamath River reservation.
Mission (28 reserves)	Diegueños, Kawia, Luiseños, Serranos, Temecula.	187,958	Executive orders, Jan. 31, 1870, Dec. 27, 1875, May 15, 1876, May 3, Aug. 25, Sept. 29, 1877, Jan. 17, 1880, Mar. 2, Mar. 9, 1881, June 27, July 24, 1882, Feb. 5, June 19, 1883,

(continued) Jan. 25, Mar. 22, 1886, Jan. 29, Mar. 14, 1887, and May 6, 1889. 270.24 acres have been allotted to 17 Indians and for church and cemetery purposes on Sycuan res., 119.99 acres allotted to 15 Indians on Pala res., 1,299.47 acres allotted to 85 Temecula Indians, and 2.70 acres reserved for school purposes. Proclamations of President, Apr. 16, 1901 (xxxii, 1970), and May 29, 1902 (xxxii, 2005); act of Feb. 11, 1903 (xxxii, 822). Warner's ranch of 3,353 acres purchased. 3,742.45 acres have been purchased under acts of June 21, 1906 (xxxiv, 325-333), and Mar. 1, 1907 (xxxiv, 1015-1022). Area subject to change by additions under above acts.

Reservation	Tribes occupying it	Area in acres	When and how established
Round Valley	Clear Lake (Pomo), Concow (Konkau), Little Lake, Nomelaki, Pit River (Achomawi), Potter Valley, Redwood, Wailaki, Yuki.	32,282	Acts of Apr. 8, 1864 (xiii, 39), and Mar. 3, 1873 (xvii, 634); Executive orders, Mar. 30, 1870, Apr. 8, 1873, May 18, 1875, and July 26, 1876; act of Oct. 1, 1890 (xxvi, 658). 5,408.72 acres were allotted to 619 Indians, 180 acres reserved for school purposes, 3 acres for a mission, 10.43 acres for a cemetery, and 177.13 acres for agency purposes; the residue, 32,282 acres, unallotted and unreserved. (See act of Feb. 8, 1905, providing for a reduction of area of res. xxxiii, 706.)
Tule River	Kawia (not on res.), Kings River Indians (Choinimni, Chukaimina, Iticha, Tiseechu, Wichikik, and Wimilchi), Moache (Mono), Tejon (Southern Yokuts), Tule (Tulareños), Wichumni (Wikchamni).	48,551	Executive orders, Jan. 9 and Oct. 3, 1873, and Aug. 3, 1878.
Yuma	Yuma Apache (Yuma)	45,889	Executive order, Jan. 9, 1884; agreement, Dec. 4, 1893, ratified by act of Aug. 15, 1894 (xxviii, 332). See Indian appropriation act, Apr. 21, 1904, sec. 25 (xxxiii, 224).
		414,061	
COLORADO: Ute*b*	Capote, Moache, Wiminuche	483,750	Treaties of Oct. 7, 1863 (xiii, 673), and Mar. 2, 1868 (xv, 619); act of Apr. 29, 1874 (xviii, 36); Executive orders, Nov. 22, 1875, Aug. 17, 1876, Feb. 7, 1879, and Aug. 4, 1882; acts of June 15, 1880 (xxi, 199), July 28, 1882 (xxii, 178), May 14, 1884 (xxiii, 22), Aug. 15, 1894 (xxviii, 337), and Feb. 20, 1895 (xxviii, 677). 65,450.33 acres were allotted to 352 Indians, and 360 acres reserved for the use of the Government; also 7,360.32 acres allotted to 39 Indians, and 523,079 acres opened to settlement by President's proclamation, Apr. 13, 1899. The residue, 483,750 acres, retained as a reservation for the Wiminuche Ute.
		483,750	
IDAHO: Cœur d'Alène	Cœur d'Alène (Skitswish), Kutenai, Pend d'Oreille (Kalispel; not on res.), Spokan.	404,480	Executive orders, June 14, 1867, and Nov. 8, 1873; agreements made Mar. 26, 1887, and Sept. 9, 1889, and confirmed in Indian appropriation act approved Mar. 3, 1891 (xxvi, 1026-1029); agreement of Feb. 7, 1894, ratified by act of Aug. 15, 1894 (xxviii, 322).
Fort Hall	Bannock, Shoshoni	447,940	Treaty of July 3, 1868 (xv, 673); Executive orders, June 14, 1867, and July 30, 1869; agreement made July 18, 1881, and approved by Congress July 3, 1882 (xxii, 148); acts of Sept. 1, 1888 (xxv, 452), Feb. 23, 1889 (xxv, 687), and Mar. 3, 1891 (xxvi, 1011); agreement made Feb. 5, 1898, ratified by act of June 6, 1900 (xxxi, 672), ceding 416,060 acres, of which 6,172.44 have been allotted to 90 Indians; remainder of ceded tract opened to settlement June 17, 1902 (President's proclamation of May 7, 1902, xxxii, 1997), act of Mar. 30, 1904 (xxxiii, 153).

a Partly in California.

b Partly in New Mexico.

SCHEDULE SHOWING EACH INDIAN RESERVATION IN 1908, UNDER WHAT AGENCY OR SCHOOL, TRIBES OCCUPYING OR BELONGING TO IT, AREA NOT ALLOTTED OR SPECIALLY RESERVED, AND AUTHORITY FOR ITS ESTABLISHMENT—Continued.

Reservation.	Tribes.	Acres.	Established by—
IDAHO—Continued. Lapwai	Nez Percés		Treaty of June 9, 1863 (XIV, 647); agreement of May 27, 1887, ratified by act of Sept. 1, 1888 (XXV, 452); agreement of May 1, 1893, ratified by act of Aug. 15, 1894 (XXVIII, 326). 180,370.09 acres were allotted to 1,895 Indians, 2,170.47 acres reserved for agency, school, mission, and cemetery purposes, and 32,020 acres of timber land reserved for the tribe; the remainder opened to public settlement by President's proclamation, Nov. 8, 1895 (XXIX, 873).
Lemhi	Bannock, Sheepeater (Tukuarika), Shoshoni	64,000	Unratified treaty of Sept. 24, 1868; Executive order, Feb. 12, 1875; agreement of May 14, 1880, ratified by act of Feb. 23, 1889 (XXV, 687). (See 34 Stat. L., 335, and agreement executed Dec. 28, 1905, approved by President Jan. 27, 1906.)
		916,420	
IOWA: Sauk and Fox	Potawatomi, Sauk and Foxes of the Mississippi, Winnebago.	2,965	By purchase. See act of Mar. 2, 1867 (XIV, 507), and act of Feb. 13, 1891 (XXVI, 749). Deeds of 1857, 1865, 1867, 1868, 1869, 1876, 1880, 1882, 1883, June, July, and Oct., 1888, 1892, 1893, 1894, 1895, and 1896.
		2,965	
KANSAS: Chippewa and Munsee	Chippewa, Munsee		Treaty of July 16, 1859 (XII, 1105). 4,195.31 acres were allotted to 100 Indians; the residue, 200 acres, allotted for missionary and school purposes. Patents issued to allottees; balance of allotments sold and proceeds paid to heirs. (See ninth section.) (Act of June 7, 1897, XXX, 92.)
Iowa	Iowa		Treaties of May 17, 1854 (X, 1069), and Mar. 6, 1861 (XII, 1171). 11,768.77 acres were allotted to 143 Indians, and 162 acres reserved for school and cemetery purposes.
Kickapoo	Kickapoo	398	Treaty of June 28, 1862 (XIII, 623). 18,619 acres allotted to 233 Indians, 120 acres reserved for church and school; the residue, 398.87 acres, unallotted. (Acts of Feb. 28, 1899, XXX, 909, and Mar. 3, 1903, XXXII, 1007.)
Potawatomi	Prairie band of Potawatomi	500	Treaties of June 5, 1846 (IX, 853), and Nov. 15, 1861 (XII, 1191); treaty of relinquishment, Feb. 27, 1867 (XV, 531). 76,536.95 acres allotted to 811 Indians; 319 acres reserved for school and agency, and 1 acre for church; the residue, 500.62 acres, unallotted. (Acts of Feb. 28, 1899, XXX, 909, and Mar. 3, 1903, XXXII, 1007.)
Sauk and Fox	Sauk and Foxes of the Missouri	24	Treaties of May 18, 1854 (X, 1074), and Mar. 5, 1861 (XII, 1171); acts of June 10, 1872 (XVII, 391), and Aug. 15, 1876 (XIX, 208). 2,843.97 acres in Kansas and 4,194.33 acres in Nebraska were allotted to 84 Indians, and under act of June 21, 1906 (XXXIV, 324–349), 960.91 acres were allotted to 37 Indians, leaving 24.03 acres unallotted.
		922	

	Acres	
MICHIGAN:		
Isabella	2,373	Executive order, May 14, 1855; treaties of Aug. 2, 1855 (XI, 633), and Oct. 18, 1864 (XIV, 657). 96,213 acres were allotted to 1,934 Indians.
L'Anse	1,029	Treaty of Sept. 30, 1854 (X, 1109). 47,216 acres allotted to 645 Indians; the residue, 1,029 acres, unallotted.
L'Anse and Vieux Desert bands of Chippewa of L. Superior.		
Ontonagon band of Chippewa of L. Superior.		Treaty of Sept. 30, 1854 (X, 1109); Executive order, Sept. 25, 1855. 2,561.35 acres were allotted to 36 Indians.
	3,402	
MINNESOTA:		
Bois Fort band of Chippewa		Treaty of Apr. 7, 1866 (XIV, 765); act of Jan. 14, 1889 (XXV, 642). 55,211.79 acres were allotted to 693 Indians, and 434.63 acres reserved for agency and other purposes; the residue of 51,863 acres to be opened to public settlement.
Deer Creek	do	Executive order, June 30, 1883; act of Jan. 14, 1889 (XXV, 642). 295.55 acres were allotted to 4 Indians; the residue of 22,744 acres to be opened to public settlement. (Executive order of Dec. 21, 1858.)
Fond du Lac	Fond du Lac band of Chippewa of L. Superior.	Treaty of Sept. 30, 1854 (X, 1109); act of May 26, 1872 (XVII, 190). 23,283.61 acres were allotted to 351 Indians by act of Jan. 14, 1889 (XXV, 642); the residue, 76,887 acres, was opened to settlement. Agreement of Nov. 21, 1889. (See act of Jan. 14, 1889, XXV, 642.)
Grand Portage (Pigeon r.)	Grand Portage band of Chippewa of L. Superior.	Treaty of Sept. 30, 1854 (X, 1109); act of Jan. 14, 1889 (XXV, 642). 24,191.31 acres were allotted to 304 Indians, 208.24 acres reserved for agency and wood purposes, and the residue of 16,041.97 acres was to be opened to public settlement.
Leech Lake	Cass Lake, Pillager, and Lake Winnibigoshish bands of Chippewa.	Treaty of Feb. 22, 1855 (X, 1165); Executive orders, Nov. 4, 1873, and May 26, 1874; act of Jan. 14, 1889 (XXV, 642), 37,683.06 acres were allotted to 536 Indians, and 321.60 acres reserved for agency and school purposes; 1,381.21 acres were allotted to 17 Cass Lake Indians, and the residue of 55,054 acres was to be opened to public settlement. (Act of June 27, 1902, XXXII, 402.)
Mdewakanton	Mdewakanton Sioux	By purchase. See acts of Congress, July 4, 1884, Mar. 3, 1885, June 29, 1888, Mar. 2, 1889, Aug. 19, 1890. 339.70 acres were deeded to 47 Indians; 12,242.76 acres allotted to 88 Indians and held in trust by the United States; 8.90 acres reserved for school.
Mille Lac	Mille Lac and Snake River bands of Chippewa.	61,014	Treaties of Feb. 22, 1855 (x, 1165), and May 7, 1864 (XIII, 693, 695); act of Jan. 14, 1889 (XXV, 642); joint resolution No. 5, Dec. 19, 1893 (XXVIII, 576); joint resolution No. 40, approved May 27, 1898 (XXX, 745). The lands composing this reservation have been ceded to the Government, but are not yet open to sale or settlement.
Red Lake	Red Lake and Pembina bands of Chippewa	543,528	Treaty of Oct. 2, 1863 (XIII, 667); act of Jan. 14, 1889 (XXV, 642); agreement, July 8, 1889 (H. R. Ex. Doc. 247, 51st Cong., 1st sess. 27, 32); Executive order, Nov. 21, 1892. Act of Mar. 3, 1903 (XXXII, 1009), and act of Feb. 20, 1904, ratifying agreement made Mar. 10, 1902 (XXXIII, 46), for sale of 256,152 acres. Act of Feb. 8, 1905 (XXXIII, 708), granting 320 acres as right of way for the Minneapolis, Red Lake and Manitoba Ry. Co.
Vermilion Lake	Bois Fort band of Chippewa	1,080	Executive order, Dec. 20, 1881; act of Jan. 14, 1889 (XXV, 642).
White Earth	Chippewa of the Mississippi, Pembina, and Pillager Chippewa.	78,178	Treaty of Mar. 19, 1867 (XVI, 719); Executive orders, Mar. 18, 1879, and July 13, 1883; act of Jan. 14, 1889 (XXV, 642). See agreement of July 29, 1889 (H. R. Ex. Doc. 247, 51st Cong., 1st sess., 34, 36). Under act of Jan. 14, 1889 (XXV, 642), 402,516.06 acres have been allotted to 4,868 Indians, and 1,899.61 acres reserved for agency, school, and religious purposes; and under act of Apr. 28, 1904

SCHEDULE SHOWING EACH INDIAN RESERVATION IN 1908, UNDER WHAT AGENCY OR SCHOOL, TRIBES OCCUPYING OR BELONGING TO IT, AREA NOT ALLOTTED OR SPECIALLY RESERVED, AND AUTHORITY FOR ITS ESTABLISHMENT—Continued.

Reservation.	Tribes.	Acres.	Established by—
MINNESOTA—Continued. White Earth (Continued).	Chippewa of the Mississippi, Pembina, and Pillager Chippewa—Continued.		(XXXIII, 539), 223,928.91 acres have been allotted to 2,794 Mississippi and Otter Tail Pillager Chippewa, being additional allotments to a part of the allottees under act of Jan. 14, 1889, leaving unallotted and unreserved 78,178.19 acres. Lands now in process of allotment under both acts.
White Oak Point and Chippewa.	Lake Winnibigoshish and Pillager bands of Chippewa, and White Oak Point band of Mississippi Chippewa.	683,800	Treaties of Feb. 22, 1855 (x, 1165), and Mar. 19, 1867 (XVI, 719); Executive orders, Oct. 29, 1873, and May 26, 1874; act of Jan. 14, 1889 (XXV, 742); 14,389.73 acres were allotted to 180 Lake Winnibigoshish Indians, the residue, 112,663.01 acres, of Winnibigoshish reserve to be opened to public settlement; 38,090.22 acres were allotted to 479 Chippewa Indians; the residue of 154,855 acres was restored to the public domain.
MONTANA: Blackfeet.	Blackfeet (Siksika), Blood (Kainah), Piegan.	959,644	Treaty of Oct. 17, 1855 (XI, 657); unratified treaties of July 18, 1866, and July 13 and 15 and Sept. 1, 1868; Executive orders, July 5, 1873, and Aug. 19, 1874; act of Apr. 15, 1874 (XVIII, 28); Executive orders, Apr. 13, 1875, and July 13, 1880; agreement made Feb. 11, 1887, approved by Congress, May 1, 1888 (XXV, 129); agreement made Sept. 26, 1895, approved by act of June 10, 1896 (XXIX, 353); act of Feb. 27, 1905, confirming grant of 856.11 acres, and 120 acres of unsurveyed land. (See XXXIII, 816.) Lands now in process of allotment.
Crow	Mountain and River Crows	1,844,182	Treaty of May 7, 1868 (XV, 649); agreement made June 12, 1880, and approved by Congress Apr. 11, 1882 (XXII, 42); agreement made Aug. 22, 1881, approved by Congress July 10, 1882 (XXII, 157); Executive orders, Oct. 20, 1875, Mar. 8, 1876, Dec. 7, 1886; agreement made Dec. 8, 1890, ratified and confirmed in Indian appropriation act approved Mar. 3, 1891 (XXVI, 1039-1040); agreement made Aug. 27, 1892. (See Ind. Aff. Rep., 1892, p. 748; also President's proclamation, Oct. 15, 1892, XXVII, 1034.) Act of Apr. 27, 1904 (XXXIII, 352), to amend and ratify agreement of Aug. 14, 1899. Under act of Feb. 8, 1887 (XXIV, 388), and act of Feb. 28, 1891 (XXVI, 794), and Executive order, June 8, 1901 (modifying Executive order of Mar. 25, 1901) 447,914.90 acres have been allotted to 2,272 Indians, and 1,822.61 acres reserved for administration, church, and cemetery purposes, leaving unallotted and unreserved 1,844,182.49 acres, and 14,711.96 acres on ceded part have been allotted to 81 Indians.
Fort Belknap.	Grosventres (Atsina), Assiniboin	497,600	Treaty of Oct. 17, 1855 (XI, 657); unratified treaties of July 18, 1866, and July 13 and 15 and Sept. 1, 1868; Executive orders, July 5, 1873, and Aug. 19, 1874; act of Apr. 15, 1874 (XVIII, 28); Executive orders, Apr. 13, 1875, and July 13, 1880; agreement made Jan. 21, 1887, approved by Congress May 1, 1888 (XXV, 124); agreement made Oct. 9, 1895, approved by act of June 10, 1896 (XXIX, 350).
Fort Peck.	Assiniboin, Brulé, Santee, Teton, Hunkpapa, and Yanktonai Sioux.	1,776,000	Treaty of Oct. 17, 1855 (XI, 657); unratified treaties of July 18, 1866, and July 13 and 15 and Sept. 1, 1868; Executive orders, July 5, 1873, and Aug. 19, 1874; act of Apr. 15, 1874 (XVIII, 28); Executive orders, Apr. 13, 1875, and July 13, 1880; agreement made Dec. 28, 1886, approved by Congress May 1, 1888 (XXV, 113).

Reservation	Tribes	Acres	Authority
Jocko	Bitter Root, Carlos band, Kutenai, Lower Kalispel, Pend d'Oreille.	1,128,182	Treaty of July 16, 1855 (XII, 975). Under acts of Apr. 23, 1904 (XXIII, 302), Feb. 8, 1887 (XXIV, 388), and Feb. 28, 1891 (XXVI, 794), 2,378 Indians have been allotted 220,950.12 acres, and under act of Apr. 23, 1904, 2,524.70 acres have been reserved for tribal uses, and under act of Apr. 23, 1904, as amended by act of Mar. 3, 1905 (XXXIII, 1049–1080), 6,774.92 acres have been reserved for agency purposes, 4,977 acres for water power, etc., and 431.62 for town-site purposes, and 69,760 acres (approximately) were granted by the act of Apr. 23, 1904, to the State of Montana for school purposes, aggregating 305,418.36 acres, leaving unallotted and unreserved 1,128,181.64 acres. These lands, and the lands reserved for town-site purposes, are, with the exception of timber lands, to be disposed of as provided for by section 8 of the act of Apr. 23, 1904 (XXXIII, 302).
Northern Cheyenne	Northern Cheyenne	489,500	Executive orders, Nov. 26, 1884, and Mar. 19 1900; act of Mar. 3, 1903 (XXXII, 1000).
		6,695,108	
NEBRASKA: Niobrara	Santee Sioux		Act of Mar. 3, 1863 (XII, 819); treaty of Apr. 29, 1868 (XV, 637); Executive orders, Feb. 27, July 20, 1866, Nov. 16, 1867, Aug. 31, 1869, Dec. 31, 1873, and Feb. 9, 1885. 32,875.75 acres were selected as homesteads, 38,908.01 acres as allotments, and 1,130.70 acres for agency, school, and mission purposes; unratified agreement of Oct. 17, 1882. (For modification see sundry civil appropriation act approved Mar. 3, 1883, XXII, 624. For text, see misc. Indian doc., vol. 14, p. 305.) Act of Apr. 30, 1888 (XXV, 94), not accepted.
Omaha	Omaha	12,421	Treaty of Mar. 16, 1854 (X, 1043); selection by Indians with the President's approval, May 11, 1855; treaty of Mar. 6, 1865 (XIV, 667); act of June 10, 1872 (XVII, 391); act of June 22, 1874 (XVIII, 170); deed to Winnebago Indians, dated July 31, 1874; act of Aug. 7, 1882 (XXII, 341); act of Mar. 3, 1893 (XXVII, 612); 129,470 acres allotted to 1,577 Indians; the residue, 12,421 acres, unallotted.
Ponca	Ponca	640	Treaty of Mar. 12, 1858 (XII, 997), and supplemental treaty Mar. 10, 1865 (XIV, 675); act of Mar. 2, 1889 (XXV, 892). 27,202.08 acres were allotted to 167 Indians, and 160 acres reserved and occupied by agency and school buildings. (See President's proclamation, Oct. 23, 1890, XXXVI, 1559.)
Sioux (additional)	Oglala Sioux		Executive order, Jan. 24, 1882.
Winnebago	Winnebago	1,711	Act of Feb. 21, 1863 (XII, 658); treaty of Mar. 8, 1865 (XIV, 671); act of June 22, 1874 (XVIII, 170); deed from Omaha Indians, dated July 31, 1874 (Indian Deeds, VI, 215). 106,040.82 acres were allotted to 1,200 Indians; 480 acres reserved for agency, etc.; the residue, 1,710.80 acres, unallotted.
		14,772	
NEVADA: Duck Valley *a*	Paiute, Western Shoshoni	312,320	Executive orders, Apr. 16, 1877, and May 4, 1886.
Moapa River	Chemehuevi, Kaibab, Pawipits, Paiute, Shivwits.	1,000	Executive orders, Mar. 12, 1873, and Feb. 12, 1874; act of Mar. 13, 1875 (XVIII, 445); selection approved by the Secretary of the Interior, July 3, 1875; Executive order, July 31, 1903.
Pyramid Lake	Paiute	322,000	Executive order, Mar. 23, 1874. (See Sec. 26, Indian appropriation act, approved Apr. 20, 1904 (XXXIII, 225).

a Partly in Idaho.

SCHEDULE SHOWING EACH INDIAN RESERVATION IN 1908, UNDER WHAT AGENCY OR SCHOOL, TRIBES OCCUPYING OR BELONGING TO IT, AREA NOT ALLOTTED OR SPECIALLY RESERVED, AND AUTHORITY FOR ITS ESTABLISHMENT—Continued.

Reservation.	Tribes.	Acres.	Established by—
NEVADA—Continued. Walker River	Paiute		Executive order, Mar. 19, 1874; joint resolution of June 19, 1902 (XXXII, 744); act of May 27, 1902 (XXXII, 245–260); act of Mar. 3, 1903 (XXXII, 982–997); act of June 21, 1906 (XXXIV, 325); proclamation of President, Sept. 26, 1906, opening ceded part to settlement. It contains 268,005.84 acres, leaving in diminished reserve 50,809.16 acres. Allotted to 492 Indians, 9,783.25 acres; reserved for agency and school, 80 acres; reserved for cemetery, 40 acres; reserved for grazing, 37,390.29 acres; reserved for timber, 3,355.62 acres; reserved for church purposes, 160 acres. Subject to disposition under President's proclamation, 268,005.84 acres.
		635,320	
NEW MEXICO: Jicarilla Apache	Jicarilla Apache	286,400	Executive orders, Mar. 25, 1874, July 18, 1876, Sept. 21, 1880, May 15, 1884, and Feb. 11, 1887. 129,313.35 acres were allotted to 845 Indians, and 280.44 acres reserved for mission, school, and agency purposes. The residue, 268,400 acres, unallotted. Lands now in process of allotment.
Mescalero Apache	Mescaleros, Mimbreños, Lipan	474,240	Executive orders, May 29, 1873, Feb. 2, 1874, Oct. 20, 1875, May 19, 1882, and Mar. 24, 1883.
Pueblo— Jemez	Pueblos	17,510	Confirmed by United States patents in 1864, under old Spanish grants; acts of Congress approved Dec. 22, 1858 (XI, 374), and June 21, 1860 (XII, 71; see Gen. Land Off. Rep. for 1876, p. 242, and for 1880, p. 658); Executive orders of June 13 and Sept. 4, 1902, setting apart additional lands for San Felipe and Nambe Pueblos, and Executive order of July 29, 1905, setting apart additional lands for Santa Clara Pueblo.
Acoma		95,792	
San Juan		17,545	
Picuris		17,461	
San Felipe		34,767	
Pecos (extinct)		18,763	
Cochiti		24,256	
Santo Domingo		74,743	
Taos		17,361	
Santa Clara		49,369	
Tesuque		17,471	
San Ildefonso		17,293	
Pojoaque (extinct)		13,520	
Sia		17,515	
Sandia		24,187	
Isleta		110,080	
Nambe		13,586	
Laguna		125,225	
Santa Ana		17,361	
Zuñi		215,040	Executive orders, Mar. 16, 1877, May 1, 1883, and Mar. 3, 1885. The original Spanish grant comprised 17,581.25 acres.
		1,699,485	

Reservation	Tribe	Acres	Authority
NEW YORK:			
Allegany	Onondaga, Seneca	30,469	Treaties of Sept. 15, 1797 (VII, 601), and May 20, 1842 (VII, 587).
Cattaraugus	Cayuga, Onondaga, Seneca	21,680	Treaties of Sept. 15, 1797 (VII, 601), June 30, 1802 (VII, 70), and May 20, 1842 (VII, 587).
Oil Spring	Seneca	640	By arrangement with the State of New York (see Ind. Aff. Rep. for 1877, 166). Seneca agreement of Jan. 3, 1893, ratified by act of Feb. 20, 1893 (XXVII, 470); act of June 7, 1897 (XXX, 89).
Oneida	Oneida	350	Treaty of Nov. 11, 1794 (VII, 44); arrangement with the State of New York. (See Ind. Aff. Rep. for 1877, 168.)
Onondaga	Oneida, Onondaga, St. Regis	6,100	Treaty and arrangement with the State of New York.
St. Regis	St. Regis	14,640	Treaty of May 13, 1796 (VII, 55). They hold about 24,250 acres in Canada.
Tonawanda	Cayuga and Tonawanda bands of Seneca	7,549	Treaties of Sept. 15, 1797 (VII, 601), and Nov. 5, 1857 (XII, 991); purchased by the Indians and held in trust by the comptroller of New York; deed dated Feb. 14, 1862.
Tuscarora	Onondaga and Tuscarora	6,249	Treaty of Jan. 15, 1838 (VII, 551); arrangement (grant and purchase) between the Indians and the Holland Land Co.
		87,677	
NORTH CAROLINA:			
Qualla boundary and other lands.	Eastern band of Cherokee	48,000 / 15,211	Deeds to Indians under decision of the United States circuit court for the western district of North Carolina, entered at November term, 1874, and acts of Congress approved Aug. 14, 1876 (XIX, 139), and Aug. 23, 1894 (XXVIII, 441); deeds to Indians dated Oct. 9, 1876, and Aug. 14, 1880; now held in fee by Indians who are incorporated. Act of Mar. 3, 1903 (XXXII, 1000). (See Opinions of Asst. Atty. Gen., Mar. 14, 1894, and Feb. 3, 1904. 35,000 acres of the 98,211 acres sold. Deeds dated Oct. 4, 1906; approved Dec. 12, 1906.)
		63,211	
NORTH DAKOTA:			
Devils Lake	Assiniboin, Cuthead (Pabaksa), Santee, Sisseton, Yankton, and Wahpeton Sioux.	92,144	Treaty of Feb. 19, 1867 (XV, 505); agreement of Sept. 20, 1872, confirmed in Indian appropriation act approved June 22, 1874 (XVIII, 167). 135,824.33 acres were allotted to 1,193 Indians, 727.83 acres reserved for church, and 193.61 acres reserved for Government purposes. Act of Apr. 27, 1904 (XXXIII, 319), to amend and ratify agreement made Nov. 2, 1901. President's proclamation of June 2, 1904 (XXXIII, 2368).
Fort Berthold	Arikara, Hidatsa, Mandan	884,780	Unratified agreement of Sept. 17, 1851, and July 27, 1866; Executive orders, Apr. 12, 1870, July 13, 1880, and June 17, 1892; agreement of Dec. 14, 1886, ratified by act of Mar. 3, 1891 (XXVI, 1032). (See Pres. proc. May 20, 1891, XXVII, 979). 80,340 acres were allotted to 940 Indians; the residue, 884,780 acres, unallotted. Lands now in process of allotment.
Standing Rock	Blackfeet (Sihasapa), Hunkpapa, Lower and Upper Yanktonai Sioux.	1,847,812	Treaty of Apr. 29, 1868 (XV, 635); Executive orders, Jan. 11 and Mar. 16, 1875, and Nov. 28, 1876; agreement ratified by act of Feb. 28, 1877 (XIX, 254); Executive orders, Aug. 9, 1879, and Mar. 20, 1884 (1,520,640 acres in South Dakota); unratified agreement of Oct. 17, 1882. (For modification see sundry civil appropriation act approved Mar. 3, 1883, XXII, 624; for text see Misc. Indian Doc. XIV, 305.) Act of Congress of Apr. 30, 1888 (XXV, 94), not accepted. Act of Congress of Mar. 2, 1899 (XXV, 888). President's proclamation of Feb. 10, 1890 (XXVI, 1554). Under act of Mar. 2, 1899 (XXV, 884), and authority of the President of Sept. 26, 1905, 2,489 Indians have been allotted 824,828.44 acres, leaving unallotted 1,847,811.56 acres. Lands now in process of allotment.

SCHEDULE SHOWING EACH INDIAN RESERVATION IN 1908, UNDER WHAT AGENCY OR SCHOOL, TRIBES OCCUPYING OR BELONGING TO IT, AREA NOT ALLOTTED OR SPECIALLY RESERVED, AND AUTHORITY FOR ITS ESTABLISHMENT—Continued.

Reservation.	Tribes.	Acres.	Established by—
NORTH DAKOTA—Cont'd. Turtle Mountain	Pembina Chippewa	2,824,736	Executive orders, Dec. 21, 1882, Mar. 29 and June 3, 1884. Agreement made Oct. 2, 1892, amended by Indian appropriation act approved and ratified Apr. 21, 1904, (xxxiii, 194). 45,894 acres allotted to 326 Indians, and 186 acres reserved for church and school purposes under the above-named act.
OKLAHOMA: Cherokee	Cherokee	877,229	Treaties of Feb. 14, 1833 (vii, 414), Dec. 29, 1835 (vii, 478), and July 19, 1866 (xiv, 799); agreement of Dec. 19, 1891, ratified by act of Mar. 3, 1893 (xxvii, 640); agreement ratified by act of July 1, 1902 (xxxii, 716). [Lands subsequently allotted.]
Cheyenne and Arapaho	Southern Arapaho, and Northern and Southern Cheyenne.		Executive order, Aug. 10, 1869; unratified agreement with Wichita, Caddo, and other tribes, Oct. 19, 1872; Executive orders of Apr. 18, 1882, and Jan. 17, 1883, relative to Fort Supply military reserve (relinquished for disposal under act of Congress of July 5, 1894, by authority of Executive order of Nov. 5, 1894; see Gen. Land Off. Rep., 1899, p. 158). Executive order of July 17, 1883, relative to Fort Reno military reserve. Agreement made in October, 1890, confirmed in Indian appropriation act approved Mar. 3, 1891 (xxvi, 1022-1026). 529,682.06 acres were allotted to 3,294 Indians, 281,828.55 acres for Oklahoma school lands, 32,343.93 acres are reserved for military, agency, mission, and other purposes, and the residue of 3,500,562.05 acres was opened to settlement by the President's proclamation of Apr. 12, 1892 (xxvii, 1018), and Executive order of July 12, 1895. See President's proclamation of Aug. 12, 1903 (xxxiii, 2317).
Chickasaw	Chickasaw	1,690,964	Treaty of June 22, 1855 (xi, 611); agreement of Apr. 23, 1897, ratified by act of June 28, 1898 (xxx, 505); act of July 1, 1902 (xxxii, 641), ratifying agreement of Mar. 21, 1902; act of Apr. 21, 1904 (xxxiii, 209); act of Apr. 28, 1904 (xxxiii, 544). Lands now in process of allotment.
Choctaw	Choctaw	3,505,766	Do.
Creek	Creek, Yuchi	626,044	Treaties of Feb. 14, 1833 (vii, 417), and June 14, 1866 (xiv, 785), and deficiency appropriation act of Aug. 5, 1882 (xxii, 265); agreement of Jan. 19, 1889, ratified by act of Mar. 1, 1889 (xxv, 757); President's proclamation of Mar. 23, 1889 (xxvi, 1544); agreement of Sept. 27, 1897, ratified by act of June 28, 1898 (xxx, 514); agreement of Mar. 8, 1900, ratified by act of Mar. 1, 1901 (xxxi, 861); President's proclamation of June 25, 1901 (xxxii, 1071); agreement of Feb., 1902, ratified by act of June 30, 1902 (xxxii, 500); President's proclamation of Aug. 8, 1902 (xxxii, 2021). (See act of May 27, 1902, xxxii, 258; act of Apr. 21, 1904 (xxxiii, 204).) Lands now in process of allotment.
Iowa	Iowa, Tonkawa		Executive order, Aug. 15, 1883; agreement of May 20, 1890, ratified by act of Feb. 13, 1891 (xxvi, 753). 8,685.30 acres were allotted to 109 Indians, 20 acres held in common for church, school, etc.; the residue was opened to settlement by proclamation of the President, Sept. 18, 1891 (xxvii, 989).

Kansa	Kansa, or Kaw		Act of June 5, 1872 (XVII, 228). 260 acres reserved for cemetery, school, and town site. Remainder, 99,877 acres, allotted to 247 Indians; act of July 1, 1902 (XXXII, 636), ratifying agreement, not dated.
Kickapoo	Mexican Kickapoo		Executive order, Aug. 15, 1883; agreement of June 21, 1891, ratified by act of Mar. 3, 1893 (XXVII, 557). 22,529.15 acres were allotted to 283 Indians, 479.72 acres reserved for mission, agency, and school purposes; the residue was opened to settlement by proclamation of the President, May 18, 1895 (XXIX, 868); act of Mar. 3, 1903 (XXXII, 1001),
Kiowa and Comanche	Apache, Comanche, Kiowa		Treaty of Oct. 21, 1867 (XV, 581, 589); agreement made Oct. 6, 1892, ratified by act of June 6, 1900 (XXXI, 676). The cession embraced 2,488,893 acres, of which 443,338 acres have been allotted to 2,759 Indians and 11,972 acres reserved for agency, school, religious, and other purposes; the residue of 2,033,583 acres was opened to settlement. President's proclamations of July 4, 1901 (XXXII, 1975), June 23, 1902 (XXXII, 2007), Sept. 4, 1902 (XXXII, 2026), and Mar. 29, 1904 (XXXIII, 2340). Of the 480,000 acres grazing land set apart under act of June 6, 1900, 1,841.92 acres were reserved for town sites under act of Mar. 20, 1906 (XXXIV, 801), 82,059.52 acres were allotted to 513 Indians under act of June 5, 1906 (XXXIV, 213), and 480 acres allotted to 3 Indians under act of June 5, as amended by act of Mar. 7, 1907 (XXXIV, 1018). The remaining 395,618.56 acres were turned over to the General Land Office for disposal under acts of June 5 and June 28, 1906, and proclamation of Sept. 19, 1906.
Modoc	Modoc		Agreement with Eastern Shawnee made June 23, 1874, and confirmed in Indian appropriation act approved Mar. 3, 1875 (XVIII, 447). The lands were all allotted, 3,976 acres to 68 Indians, 8 acres reserved for church and cemetery purposes, 2 acres for school, and 24 acres for timber.
Oakland	Tonkawa, Lipan		Act of May 27, 1878 (XX, 84). Obtained by deeds from Cherokee, dated June 14, 1883 (Indian Deeds, VI, 476), and from Nez Percés, dated May 22, 1885 (Indian Deeds, VI, 504). 11,273.79 acres were allotted to 73 Indians, 160.50 acres reserved for Government and school purposes, and the residue of 79,276.60 acres was opened to settlement. Agreement made Oct. 21, 1891, ratified by Indian appropriation act approved Mar. 3, 1893 (XXVII, 644).
Osage	Great and Little Osage, Quapaw	1,470,058	Cherokee treaty of July 19, 1866 (XIV, 804); order of Secretary of the Interior, Mar. 27, 1871; act of June 5, 1872 (XVII, 228); deed from Cherokee, dated June 14, 1883 (Indian Deeds, VI, 482). Lands now in process of allotment.
Oto	Oto, Missouri		Act of Mar. 3, 1881 (XXI, 381); order of the Secretary of the Interior, June 25, 1881; Cherokee deed, dated June 14, 1883 (Indian Deeds, VI, 479). Under acts of Feb. 8, 1887 (XXIV, 388), Feb. 28, 1891 (XXVI, 794), and Apr. 21, 1904 (XXXIII, 189), 127,711.22 acres were allotted to 514 Indians (885 allotments). 720 acres were reserved for agency, school, church, and cemetery purposes, and 640 acres set aside for tribal uses.
Ottawa	Ottawa of Blanchards Fork and Roche de Bœuf.	1,587	Treaty of Feb. 23, 1867 (XV, 513), 12,714.80 acres were allotted to 157 Indians; 557.95 acres were authorized to be sold by act of Mar. 3, 1891 (XXVI, 989); the residue, 1,587.25 acres, unallotted.
Pawnee	Pawnee		Act of Apr. 10, 1876 (XIX, 29). Of this 230,014 acres are Cherokee and 53,006 acres are Creek lands (see Indian Deeds, VI, 470); 112,859.84 acres were allotted to 821 Indians, 840 acres reserved for school, agency, and cemetery purposes, and the residue of 169,320 acres was opened to settlement. Agreement made Nov. 23, 1892, ratified by act of Mar. 3, 1893 (XXVII, 644).
Peoria	Kaskaskia, Miami, Peoria, Piankashaw, Wea..		Treaty of Feb. 23, 1867 (XV, 513), 43,450 acres allotted to 218 Indians. The residue, 6,313.27 acres, sold under act of May 27, 1902 (XXXII, 245).

SCHEDULE SHOWING EACH INDIAN RESERVATION IN 1908, UNDER WHAT AGENCY OR SCHOOL, TRIBES OCCUPYING OR BELONGING TO IT, AREA NOT ALLOTTED OR SPECIALLY RESERVED, AND AUTHORITY FOR ITS ESTABLISHMENT—Continued.

Reservation.	Tribes.	Acres.	Established by—
OKLAHOMA—Continued.			
Ponca	Ponca	320	Acts of Aug. 15, 1876 (XIX, 192), Mar. 3, 1877 (XIX, 287), May 27, 1878 (XX, 76), and Mar. 3, 1881 (XXI, 422). Obtained by deed from Cherokee, dated June 14, 1883 (Indian Deeds, VI, 473); there have been allotted to 784 Indians 101,050.75 acres, and reserved for agency, school, mission, and cemetery purposes 523.56 acres, leaving unallotted and unreserved 320 acres. Indian appropriation act, approved Apr. 21, 1904 (XXXIII, 217).
Potawatomi	Absentee Shawnee, Potawatomi		Treaty of Feb. 27, 1867 (XV, 531); act of May 23, 1872 (XVII, 159); agreements with citizen Potawatomi, June 25, and absentee Shawnee, June 26, 1890, ratified and confirmed by the Indian appropriation act of Mar. 3, 1891 (XXVI, 1016-1021). 222,716 acres are Creek ceded lands and 365,851 acres Seminole lands. 215,679.42 acres were allotted to 1,489 Potawatomi, 70,791.47 acres to 563 absentee Shawnee, 510.63 acres were reserved for Government purposes, and the residue was opened to settlement by the President's proclamation of Sept. 18, 1891 (XXVII, 989).
Quapaw	Quapaw		Treaties of May 13, 1833 (VII, 424), and Feb. 23, 1867 (XV, 513). 56,245.21 acres were allotted to 247 Indians, 400 acres reserved for school, and 40 acres for church purposes. Agreement of Mar. 23, 1893, ratified in Indian appropriation act approved Mar. 2, 1895 (XXVIII, 907). Agreement of Jan. 2, 1899, ratified in Indian appropriation act approved Mar. 3, 1901 (XXXI, 1067). Act of Mar. 3, 1903 (XXXII, 997),
Sac and Fox	Ottawa, Sauk and Foxes of the Mississippi		Treaty of Feb. 18, 1867 (XV, 495); agreement of June 12, 1890, ratified by act of Feb. 13, 1891 (XXVI, 749). 87,683.64 acres were allotted to 548 Indians and 800 acres reserved for school and agency purposes; the residue was opened to settlement by the President's proclamation, Sept. 18, 1891 (XXVII, 989).
Seminole	Seminole	21,374	Treaty of Mar. 21, 1866 (XIV, 755); Creek agreement, Feb. 14, 1881, and deficiency act of Aug. 5, 1882 (XXII, 265). Agreement of Mar. 16, 1889 (see Indian appropriation act approved Mar. 2, 1889). Agreement recorded in treaty book, vol, 3, p. 35. Agreement of Oct. 7, 1899, ratified by act of June 2, 1900 (XXXI, 250). Agreement made Dec. 16, 1897, ratified by act of Congress approved July 1, 1898 (XXX, 567).
Seneca	Seneca		Treaties of Feb. 28, 1831 (VII, 348), Dec. 29, 1832 (VII, 411), and Feb. 23, 1867 (XV, 513). 25,821.55 acres were allotted to 302 Indians, and 104.22 acres reserved for Government, church, and school purposes. Agreement of Dec. 2, 1901, ratified by act of May 27, 1902 (XXXII, 262).
Shawnee	Seneca, Eastern Shawnee		Treaties of July 20, 1831 (VII, 351), Dec. 29, 1832 (VII, 411), and Feb. 23, 1867 (XV, 513); agreement with Modoc, made June 23, 1874, and confirmed by Congress in Indian appropriation act approved Mar. 3, 1875 (XVIII, 447). 10,484.81 acres were allotted to 84 Indians, and 86 acres reserved for agency purposes; the residue, 2,543 acres, sold (agreement of Dec. 2, 1901, ratified by act of May 27, 1902, XXXII, 262).

Reservation	Tribes	Acres	Authority and history
Wichita	Caddo, Delawares, Ioni (Hainai), Kichai, Towakoni, Waco, Wichita.	1,511,576	Treaty of July 4, 1866, with Delawares (XIV, 794); unratified agreement of Oct. 19, 1872; agreement made June 4, 1891, ratified by act of Mar. 2, 1895 (XXVIII, 895). 152,991 acres were allotted to 965 Indians, 4,151 acres reserved for agency, school, religious, and other purposes, and the residue of 586,468 acres was opened to settlement. President's proclamation of July 4, 1901 (XXXII, 1975). Act of May 4, 1896 (XXIX, 113); President's proclamation of Mar. 16, 1896 (XXIX, 878). Unoccupied Chickasaw and Choctaw leased lands west of the North Fork of the Red river.
Wyandot	Wyandot	3,651,518 / 535	Treaty of Feb. 23, 1867 (XV, 513). 20,695.54 acres were allotted to 241 Indians, and 16 acres reserved for churches, etc., leaving 534.72 unallotted.
OREGON: Grande Ronde	Kalapuya (Calapooya), Clackamas, Cow Creek (Nahankhuotana), Lakmiut, Mary's River (Chepenafa), Molala (Molalla), Nestucca, Rogue River (Chasta), Santiam, Shasta (Chastacosta), Tumwater, Umpqua, Wapato, Yamhill (Yamel).	9,705,453	Treaties of Jan. 22, 1855 (X, 1143), and Dec. 21, 1855 (XII, 982); Executive order, June 30, 1857. 440 acres were reserved for government use and 33,148 acres allotted to 269 Indians. Act of Apr. 28, 1904 (XXXIII, 567), amending and ratifying agreement of June 27, 1901.
Klamath	Klamath, Modoc, Paiute, Pit River (Achomawi), Walpape (Walpapi), and Yahuskin band of Snakes (Shoshoni).	872,186	Treaty of Oct. 14, 1864 (XVI, 707). 177,719.62 acres were allotted to 1,174 Indians, and 6,094.77 acres reserved for agency, school, and church purposes. The residue, 872,186 acres, unallotted and unreserved. Act of May 27, 1902 (XXXII, 260); Indian appropriation act approved Apr. 21, 1904 (XXXIII, 202); act of Mar. 3, 1905 (XXXIII, 1033). Lands now in process of allotment.
Siletz	Alsea, Coquille (Mishikhwutmetunne), Kusan, Kwatami, Rogue River (Chasta), Skoton, Shasta (Chastacosta), Saiustkea (Shiitwauk?), Siuslaw, Tututni, Umpqua, and thirteen others.	3,200	Unratified treaty of Aug. 11, 1855; Executive orders, Nov. 9, 1855, and Dec. 21, 1865; act of Mar. 3, 1875 (XVIII, 446); agreement of Oct. 31, 1892, ratified by act of Aug. 15, 1894 (XXVIII, 323). 47,716.34 acres were allotted to 551 Indians; the residue of 177,563.66 acres, except 5 sections, was ceded to United States (President's proclamation of May 16, 1895, XXIX, 866). Acts of May 31, 1900 (XXXI, 233), and Mar. 3, 1901 (XXXI, 1085).
Umatilla	Cayuse, Umatilla, Wallawalla	79,820	Treaty of June 9, 1855 (XII, 945); act of Aug. 5, 1882 (XXII, 297); act of Mar. 3, 1885 (XXIII, 340); act of Oct. 17, 1888 (XXV, 559); orders of Secretary of the Interior, Dec. 4, 1888. 76,923.90 acres were allotted to 893 Indians and 980 acres reserved for school and mission purposes. Act of July 1, 1902 (XXXII, 730).
Warm Springs	Des Chutes (Tyich), John Day, Paiute, Tenino, Warm Springs (Tilkuni), Wasco.	322,108	Treaty of June 25, 1855 (XII, 963). 140,696.45 acres were allotted to 969 Indians, and 1,195 acres reserved for church, school, and agency purposes. The residue, 322,108 acres, unalloted and unreserved.
		1,277,314	
SOUTH DAKOTA: Crow Creek and Old Winnebago.	Lower Yanktonai, Lower Brulé, Miniconjou, and Two Kettle (Oohenonpa) Sioux.	111,711	Order of department, July 1, 1863; treaty of Apr. 29, 1868 (XV, 635); and Executive order, Feb. 27, 1885, annulled by the President's proclamation of Apr. 17, 1885; act of Mar. 2, 1889 (XXV, 888); President's proclamation of Feb. 10, 1890 (XXVI, 1554). There have been allotted to 840 Indians 172,733.81 acres, and reserved for agency, school, and religious purposes 1,076.90 acres, leaving a residue of 111,711 acres. Lands are now in process of allotment.

SCHEDULE SHOWING EACH INDIAN RESERVATION IN 1908, UNDER WHAT AGENCY OR SCHOOL, TRIBES OCCUPYING OR BELONGING TO IT, AREA NOT ALLOTTED OR SPECIALLY RESERVED, AND AUTHORITY FOR ITS ESTABLISHMENT—Continued.

Reservation.	Tribes.	Acres.	Established by—
SOUTH DAKOTA—Cont'd. Lake Traverse	Sisseton and Wahpeton Sioux		Treaty of Feb. 19, 1867 (xv, 505); agreement of Sept. 20, 1872, confirmed in Indian appropriation act approved June 22, 1874 (xviii, 167); agreement of Dec. 12, 1889, ratified by act of Mar. 3, 1891 (xxvi, 1035–1038). 309,904.92 acres were allotted to 1,339 Indians, 32,840.25 acres reserved for school purposes, 1,347.01 acres for church and agency purposes, and the residue, 574,678.40 acres, was opened to settlement by the President's proclamation of Apr. 11, 1892 (xxvii, 1017).
Cheyenne River	Blackfeet (Sihasapa), Miniconjou, Sans Arcs, and Two Kettle (Oohenonpa) Sioux.	2,547,209	Treaty of Apr. 29, 1868 (xv, 635); Executive orders, Jan. 11, Mar. 16, and May 20, 1875, and Nov. 28, 1876; agreement, ratified by act of Feb. 28, 1877 (xix, 254); Executive orders, Aug. 9, 1879, and Mar. 20, 1884; unratified agreement of Oct. 17, 1882. (For modification see sundry civil appropriation act approved Mar. 3, 1883 (xxii, 624); for text see Misc. Indian Docs. xiv, 305.) Act of Apr. 30, 1888 (xxv, 94), not accepted. Act of Mar. 2, 1889 (xxv, 888); President's proclamation of Feb. 10, 1890 (xxvi, 1554); act of Feb. 20, 1896 (xxix, 10). President's proclamations of Feb. 7, 1903 (xxxii, 2035), and Mar. 30, 1904 (xxxiii, 2340). 320,631.05 acres have been allotted to 934 Indians, leaving unallotted 2,547,208.95 acres.
Lower Brulé	Lower Brulé and Lower Yanktonai Sioux	199,730	Treaty of Apr. 29, 1868 (xv, 635); Executive orders, Jan. 11, Mar. 16, and May 20, 1875, and Nov. 28, 1876; agreement, ratified by act of Feb. 28, 1877 (xix, 254); Executive orders, Aug. 9, 1879, and Mar. 20, 1884. Unratified agreement of Oct. 17, 1882. (For modification see sundry civil appropriation act approved Mar. 3, 1883 (xxii, 624); for text see Misc. Indian Docs. xiv, 305.) Act of Apr. 30, 1888, (xxv, 94), not accepted. Act of Mar. 2, 1889 (xxv, 888); President's proclamation of Feb. 10, 1890 (xxvi, 1554); act of Feb. 20, 1896 (xxix, 10); agreement made Mar. 1, 1898, ratified by act of Mar. 3, 1899 (xxx, 1362), ceding 120,000 acres to the United States. 151,856 acres were allotted to 555 Indians, and 964.06 acres reserved for agency, school, and religious purposes, leaving unallotted and unreserved 199,729.94 acres. See act of Apr. 21, 1906 (xxxiv, 124), and President's proclamation of Aug. 12, 1907.
Pine Ridge	Brulé and Oglala Sioux, Northern Cheyenne	1,943,121	Treaty of Apr. 29, 1868 (xv, 635); Executive orders, Jan. 11, Mar. 16, and May 20, 1875, and Nov. 28, 1876; agreement ratified by act of Feb. 28, 1877 (xix, 254); Executive orders, Aug. 9, 1879, and Mar. 20, 1884. Unratified agreement of Oct. 17, 1882. (For modification see sundry civil appropriation act approved Mar. 3, 1883, xxii, 624; for text see Misc. Indian Docs. xiv, 305.) Act of Apr. 30, 1888 (xxv, 94), not accepted. Act of Mar. 2, 1889 (xxv, 888). President's proclamation of Feb. 10, 1890 (xxvi, 1554). (See act of Feb. 20, 1896 xxix, 10.) A tract of 32,000 acres in Nebraska was set apart by Executive order of Jan. 24, 1882, and was restored to the public domain by Executive order of Jan. 25, 1904, and by Executive order of Feb. 20, 1904, 640 acres of this land were set apart for Indian school purposes, constituting the Sioux additional tract. (See Nebraska.) Under act of Mar. 2, 1889 (xxv, 888), and authority of President of July 29, 1904, 854,989.51 acres have been allotted to 2,604 Indians, and 11,333.68 acres reserved for agency

Reservation	Tribes	Area (acres)	Authority and history
Rosebud	Loafer (Waglukhe), Miniconjou, Oglala, Two Kettle (Oohenonpa), Upper Brulé, and Wah-zhazhe Sioux.	1,524,210	school, and church purposes, aggregating 866,323.19 acres, leaving unallotted and unreserved 1,943,120.74 acres. Lands in process of allotment. Treaty of Apr. 29, 1868 (XV, 635); Executive orders, Jan. 11, Mar. 16, and May 20, 1875, and Nov. 28, 1876; agreement ratified by act of Feb. 28, 1877 (XIX, 254); Executive orders, Aug. 9, 1879, and Mar. 20, 1884. Unratified agreement of Oct. 17, 1882. (For modification see sundry civil appropriation act approved Mar. 3, 1883, XXII, 624; for text see Misc. Indian Docs., XIV, 305.) Act of Apr. 30, 1888 (XXV, 94) not accepted. Act of Mar. 2, 1889, XXV, 888). President's proclamation of Feb. 10, 1890 (XXVI, 1554). (See act of Feb. 20, 1896, XXIX, 10.) 1,258,558.35 acres allotted to 4,914 Sioux Indians. 416,000 acres opened to settlement, 29,392.01 acres reserved for Government purposes, churches, cemeteries, etc. The residue, 1,524,209.64 acres, unallotted and unreserved. Lands now in process of allotment. Agreement made Mar. 10, 1898, ratified by act of Mar. 3, 1899 (XXX, 1364). Act of April 23, 1904 (XXXIII, 254) ratifying agreement made Sept. 14, 1901. President's proclamation of May 16, 1904 (XXXIII, 2354).
Yankton	Yankton Sioux	6,325,980	Treaty of Apr. 19, 1858 (XI, 744). 263,567.72 acres were allotted to 2,649 Indians, and 1,252.89 acres reserved for agency, church, and school purposes, pursuant to an agreement made Dec. 31, 1892, ratified by act of Congress approved Aug. 15, 1894 (XXVIII, 314); the residue was opened to settlement by the President's proclamation of May 16, 1895 (XXIX, 865).
UTAH: Uinta Valley	Gosiute, Pavant (Pahvant), Uinta, Yampa, Grand River, Uncompahgre, and White River Ute.	179,194	Executive order, Oct. 3, 1861; acts of May 5, 1864 (XIII, 63), June 18, 1878 (XX, 165), and May 24, 1888 (XXV, 157); joint resolution of June 19, 1902 (XXXII, 744); act of Mar. 3, 1905 (XXXII, 997); Indian appropriation act, approved Apr. 21, 1904 (XXXIII, 207); President's proclamations of July 14, 1905, setting aside 1,010,000 acres as a forest reserve, 2,100 acres as town-sites, 1,004,285 acres opened to homestead entry, 2,140 acres in mining claims; 103,265.35 acres allotted to 1,283 Indians, and 60,160 acres under reclamation, the residue, 179,194.65 acres, unallotted and unreserved.
Uncompahgre	Tabequache (Tabeguache) Ute	179,194	Act of Congress approved June 15, 1880, ratifying the agreement of Mar. 6, 1880 (XXI, 199); Executive order, Jan. 5, 1882. 12,540 acres allotted to 83 Indians and the rest of the reservation restored to the public domain by act of June 7, 1897 (XXX, 62). Joint resolution of June 19, 1902 (XXXII, 744).
WASHINGTON: Chehalis	Chinook, Clatsop, Chehalis		Order of the Secretary of the Interior, July 8, 1864; Executive order, Oct. 1, 1886. 471 acres set aside for school purposes; the residue, 3,753.63 acres, was restored to the public domain for Indian homestead entry. 36 Indians made homestead selections, covering all the land.
Columbia	Moses's band (Sinkiuse)		Executive orders, Apr. 19, 1879, Mar. 6, 1880, and Feb. 23, 1883; Indian appropriation act of July 4, 1884 (XXIII, 79). Agreement made July 7, 1883, ratified by act of July 4, 1884 (XXIII, 79). Executive orders, May 1, 1886, Mar. 9, 1894; department orders of Apr. 11 and Apr. 20, 1894, and Executive order of Jan. 19, 1895. 25,172.30 acres allotted to 40 Indians (see Executive order of May 21, 1886, and act of Mar. 8, 1906, XXXIV, 55).

Schedule showing each Indian Reservation in 1908, under what Agency or School, Tribes occupying or belonging to it, Area not Allotted or Specially Reserved, and Authority for its Establishment—Continued.

Reservation.	Tribes.	Acres.	Established by—
WASHINGTON—Continued.			
Colville	Cœur d'Alène (Skitswish), Colville, Kalispel, Okinagan, Lake (Senijextee), Methow, Nespelim, Pend d'Oreille, Sanpoil, Spokan.	1,300,000	Executive orders, Apr. 9 and July 2, 1872; agreement made July 7, 1882, ratified by act of July 4, 1884 (XXIII, 79); act of July 1, 1892 (XXVII, 62); acts of Feb. 20, 1896 (XXIX, 9), and July 1, 1898 (XXX, 593). 50,900.30 acres in the northern half were allotted to 648 Indians; the rest of the northern half, estimated at 1,449,268 acres, was ordered to be opened to settlement on Oct. 10, 1900, by a proclamation of the President dated Apr. 10, 1900 (XXXI, 1963); the residue, estimated at 1,300,000 acres, is unallotted. Act of Feb. 7, 1903 (XXXII, 803).
Hoh River	Hoh	640	Executive order, Sept. 11, 1893.
Lummi	Dwamish, Etakmur (Etakmehu), Lummi, Snohomish, Sukwamish (Suquamish), Swiwamish (Samamish).	598	Treaty of Pt. Elliot, Jan. 22, 1855 (XII, 927); Executive order, Nov. 22, 1873. Allotted 11,634 acres to 85 Indians; reserved for Government school 80 acres; unallotted and unreserved 598 acres.
Makah	Makah, Quileute	23,040	Treaty of Neah Bay, Jan. 31, 1855 (XII, 939); Executive orders, Oct. 26, 1872, Jan. 2 and Oct. 21, 1873. Lands now in process of allotment, except timber lands.
Muckleshoot	Muckleshoot (Niskap, Skopamish, Smulkamish, etc.).	169	Executive orders, Jan. 20, 1857, and Apr. 9, 1874. 39 Indians have been allotted 3,191.97 acres.
Nisqualli	Muckleshoot, Nisqualli, Puyallup, Skwawksnamish (Squaxon), Stailakoom (Steilacoomamish), and five others.		Treaty of Medicine cr., Dec. 26, 1854 (x, 1132); Executive order, Jan. 20, 1857. The land was all allotted, 4,718 acres, to 30 Indians.
Osette	Osette (part of the Makah).	640	Executive order, Apr. 12, 1893.
Port Madison	Dwamish, Etakmehu (Etakmehu), Lummi, Snohomish, Sukwamish (Suquamish), Swiwamish (Samamish).	1,375	Treaty of Pt. Elliot, Jan. 22, 1855 (XII, 927); order of the Secretary of the Interior, Oct. 21, 1864. 5,909.48 acres were allotted to 39 Indians, and the residue of 1,375 acres was not allotted.
Puyallup	Muckleshoot, Nisqualli, Puyallup, Skwawknamish (Squaxon), Stailakoom (Steilacoomamish), and five others.		Treaty of Medicine cr., Dec. 22, 1854 (x, 1132); Executive orders, Jan. 20, 1857, and Sept. 6, 1873. 17,463 acres were allotted to 169 Indians. Agreement made Nov. 21, 1876, ratified by act of Feb. 20, 1893 (XXVII, 464). (For text see Ind. Aff. Rep., 1893, p. 518.) The residue, 599 acres, laid out as an addition to the city of Tacoma, has been sold, with the exception of 39.79 acres reserved for school, and 19.43 acres for church and cemetery purposes, under acts of Mar. 3, 1893 (XXVII, 612), June 7, 1897 (XXX, 62), and June 21, 1906 (XXXIV, 377).
Quileute	Quileute	837	Executive order, Feb. 19, 1889.
Quinaielt	Quaitso, Quinaielt	214,262	Treaties of Olympia, July 1, 1855, and Jan. 25, 1856 (XII, 971); Executive order, Nov. 4, 1873. Under acts of Feb. 8, 1887 (XXIV, 388), and Feb. 28, 1891 (XXVI, 794), 121 Indians have been allotted 9,737.94 acres, leaving unallotted 214,262.06 acres, now in process of allotment.
Shoalwater	Shoalwater (Lower Chehalis), Chehalis	335	Executive order, Sept. 22, 1866.
Skokomish	Clallam, Skokomish, Twana		Treaty of Pt No Point, Jan. 26, 1855 (XII, 933); Executive order, Feb. 25, 1874. Allotted in treaty reserve, 4,990 acres; residue, none. Allotted in Executive order, addition, known as the Fisher addition, 814 acres; residue, none. 62 allotments.

Reservation	Tribes	Acres	Authority
Snohomish, or Tulalip	Dwamish, Etakmur (Etakmehu), Lummi, Snohomish, Sukwamish (Suquamish), Swiwamish (Samamish).	8,930	Treaty of Pt Elliot, Jan. 22, 1855 (XII, 927); Executive order, Dec. 23, 1873. 13,560 acres were allotted to 94 Indians, leaving the residue of 8,930 acres unallotted.
Spokan	Spokan	153,600	Executive order, Jan. 18, 1881. Agreement made Mar. 18, 1887, ratified by Indian appropriation act approved July 13, 1892 (XXVII, 139). Joint resolution of Congress of June 19, 1902 (XXXII, 744). Lands now in process of allotment.
Squaxon Island (Klahchemin).	Nisqualli, Puyallup, Skwawksnamish (Squaxon) Stailakoom (Steilacoomamish), and five other tribes.		Treaty of Medicine cr., Dec. 26, 1854 (x, 1132). The land was all allotted, 1,494.15 acres, to 23 Indians.
Swinomish (Perrys island)	Dwamish, Etakmur (Etakmehu), Lummi, Snohomish, Sukwamish, Swiwamish (Samamish).		Treaty of Pt Elliot, Jan. 22, 1855 (XII, 927); Executive order, Sept. 9, 1873. 7,172 acres were allotted to 71 Indians; reserved for school 89.80; unallotted 0.35 acre.
Yakima	Klikitat, Paloos, Topnish, Wasco, Yakima	837,753	Treaty of Walla Walla, June 9, 1855 (XII, 951). Agreement made Jan. 13, 1885, ratified by Indian appropriation act approved Mar. 3, 1893 (XXVII, 631). Executive order, Nov. 28, 1892; agreement, Jan. 8, 1894, ratified by act of Congress approved Aug. 15, 1894 (XXVIII, 320). 255,056.03 acres were allotted to 2,823 Indians, and 1,020.24 acres reserved for agency, church, and school purposes; the residue of 543,916.13 acres is held in common. Act of Dec. 21, 1904 (XXXIII, 595), recognizing claim of Indians to 293,837 acres additional land subject to the right of bona fide settlers or purchasers, acquired prior to Mar. 5, 1904.
		2,542,179	
WISCONSIN:			
Lac Court Oreille	Lac Court Oreille band of Chippewa of L. Superior.	20,096	Treaty of Sept. 30, 1854 (x, 1109); lands withdrawn by General Land Office, Nov. 22, 1860, Apr. 4, 1865 (see report by Secretary of the Interior, Mar. 1, 1873). Act of May 29, 1872 (XVII, 190). 57,746 acres allotted to 1,003 Indians; the residue, 20,096 acres, unallotted. Act of Feb. 3, 1903. (XXXII, 795).
Lac du Flambeau	Lac du Flambeau band of Chippewa of L. Superior.	26,153	Treaty of Sept. 30, 1854 (x, 1109), lands selected by Indians. Department order of June 26, 1866. Act of May 29, 1872 (XVII, 190). 43,558 acres allotted to 520 Indians; act of Feb. 3, 1903 (XXXII, 795), 120 Indians were allotted 7,512.40 acres, leaving unallotted 26,153.40 acres.
La Pointe (Bad r.)	La Pointe band of Chippewa of L. Superior.	46,613	Treaty of Sept. 30, 1854 (x, 1109). 368.91 acres patented under art. 10; 195.71 acres fishing ground. 76,256.92 acres allotted to 959 Indians. Under acts of Feb. 11, 1901 (XXXI, 766), and Mar. 2, 1907 (XXXIV, 1217), 880 acres were allotted to 11 Indians, leaving unallotted and unreserved 46,613.58 acres.
Red Cliff	La Pointe band (Buffalo Chief) of Chippewa of L. Superior.		Treaty of Sept. 30, 1854 (x, 1109); Executive order, Feb. 21, 1856. The lands were withdrawn by the General Land Office, May 8 and June 3, 1863. 2,535.91 acres were allotted to 35 Indians under the treaty; of the residue, 11,566.90 acres were allotted to 169 Indians pursuant to the joint resolution of Feb. 20, 1895 (XXVIII, 970), and 40.10 acres were reserved for school purposes.
Menominee	Menominee	231,680	Treaties of Oct. 18, 1848 (IX, 952), May 12, 1854 (X, 1064), and Feb. 11, 1856 (XI, 679).
Oneida	Oneida		Treaty of Feb. 3, 1838 (VII, 566). 65,402.13 acres were allotted to 1,501 Indians, and the remainder, 84.08 acres, was reserved for school purposes.
Stockbridge	Stockbridge, Munsee.	11,803	Treaties of Nov. 24, 1848 (IX, 955), Feb. 5, 1856 (XI, 663), and Feb. 11, 1856 (XI, 679); act of Feb. 6, 1871 (XVI, 404); for area see act of June 22, 1874 (XVIII, 174).
		336,345	

SCHEDULE SHOWING EACH INDIAN RESERVATION IN 1908, UNDER WHAT AGENCY OR SCHOOL, TRIBES OCCUPYING OR BELONGING TO IT, AREA NOT ALLOTTED OR SPECIALLY RESERVED, AND AUTHORITY FOR ITS ESTABLISHMENT—Continued.

Reservation.	Tribes.	Acres.	Established by—
WYOMING: Wind River	Northern Arapaho and Eastern Band of Shoshoni.	95,307	Treaty of July 3, 1868 (XV, 673); acts of June 22, 1874 (XVIII, 166), and Dec. 15, 1874 (XVIII, 291); Executive order, May 21, 1887; agreement made Apr. 21, 1896, amended and accepted by act of June 7, 1896 (XXX, 93); amendment accepted by Indians July 10, 1897. Act of Mar. 3, 1905, ratifying and amending agreement with Indians of Apr. 21, 1904 (XXXIII, 1016). President's proclamation, June 2, 1906, opening ceded part to settlement. It contains 1,472,844.15 acres, leaving in diminished reservation 282,115.85 acres; allotted therein to 358 Indians, 34,010.49 acres. Reserved for Mail Camp, 120 acres; reserved for Mail Camp Park, 40 acres; reserved for bridge purposes, 40 acres. Subject to disposition under President's proclamation, 1,438,653.66 acres. 92.44 acres reserved by Secretary to complete allotments to Indians on ceded part. Of the diminished reserve, 185,016.65 acres were allotted to 1,781 Indians, and 1,792.05 acres were reserved for agency, school, church, and cemetery purposes, under acts of Feb. 8, 1887 (XXIV, 388), as amended by act of Feb. 28, 1891 (XXVI, 794), and treaty of July 3, 1868 (XV, 673), leaving unallotted and unreserved 95,307.15 acres.
		95,307	
Total		52,013,010	

There are some small State reservations in Maine, New York (including Long Island), Virginia, and South Carolina.

Indian reservations in Canada, especially in the western part, appear to have been formed for bands or minor divisions, seldom for entire tribes, and the land set apart was usually a small area, sometimes not exceeding 4 acres, due to the fact that the Indians were simply confirmed in possession of their residence tracts instead of being collected on reservations especially established for such purpose. These tracts appear to have been reserved in some instances in accordance with treaties, in some by special act of Parliament, in some by the decision of the military council, and in others by an Indian commissioner. Special names were usually given, but the reservations of each province or district were numbered. The reservations in the Dominion number several hundred. (C. T.)

Reservoirs. See *Irrigation, Receptacles.*

Resochiki (*Res-o-chĭ′-kĭ*, 'cave place'). The name of several small independent rancherias of the Tarahumare in Chihuahua, Mexico.—Lumholtz, inf'n, 1894.

Restigouche. An important Micmac village on the N. bank of Restigouche r., near its mouth, in Bonaventure co., Quebec. The French mission of Sainte Anne was established there in the 17th century. In 1884 the village contained 464 souls; in 1909, 498.
Cross Point.—Bradley, Atlas, 1885. **Mission Point.**—Can. Ind. Aff. for 1884, xxv, 1885. **Misti-gouche.**—Beauharnois (1745) in N. Y. Doc. Col. Hist., x, 15, 1858. **Octagouche.**—Coffen (1754), ibid., VI, 835, 1855. **Ouristigouche.**—De Levis (1760), ibid., x, 1100, 1858. **Papechigunach.**—Vetromile, Abnakis, 59, 1866 (='place for spring amusements'). **Restigouche.**—Can. Ind. Aff. 1880, 32, 1881. **Ristigouche.**—Le Clercq (ca. 1685) quoted by Shea, Discov. Miss. Val., 86, 1852. **Ristigutch.**—Vetromile, Abnakis, 59, 1866. **Sainte-Anne de Ré-stigouche.**—Roy, Noms Géographiques Québec, 336, 1906.

Retawichic (*Ret-a-wĭ′-chic*, 'warm land'). A small pueblo of the Tarahumare on the "Camina Real" toward Batopilas, Chihuahua, Mexico.
Retawíchi.—Lumholtz, inf'n, 1894. **Tetagui-chic.**—Orozco y Berra, Geog., 323, 1864 (Mexican name).

Reyata Band. A Santee Sioux band under Sky Man in 1853 and 1862.—Hinman, Jour., 3, 1869.

Reyes (Span.: *Los Reyes*, 'twelfth-night'). Apparently a rancheria of the Sobaipuri on the Rio Santa Cruz, in the present s. Arizona, in Spanish colonial times.—Kino, map (1701), in Bancroft, Ariz. and N. Mex., 360, 1889; Venegas, Hist. Cal., I, map, 1759.

Rgheyinestunne (*Rxö′-yi-nĕs-ṛŭnnĕ′*). A former village of the Mishikhwutmetunne on Coquille r., Oreg.—Dorsey in Jour. Am. Folk-lore, III, 232, 1890.

Rhaap. Given as the name of a subdivision of the Ntlakyapamuk residing on

or near the middle course of Fraser r., Brit. Col., in 1880. The initial letter in the name is probably a misprint.

Rhombus. See *Bull-roarer.*

Rhyolite. A variously colored volcanic rock having a glassy ground-mass, extensively employed by the tribes of the Middle Atlantic states for making the larger varieties of flaked implements. It occurs in large bodies in South mtn. and other Eastern Slope ranges to the N. and S., where it is usually grayish, sometimes purplish-gray in color, and shows scattered whitish crystals of feldspar. Native quarries have been located on the mountain slope near Fairfield, Pa., and it is assumed that the countless implements of this material found throughout an extensive region to the S. and E. down to the Atlantic coast came largely from this source. Noteworthy in the distribution of these quarry products are numerous caches of long slender unspecialized blades ranging from a few specimens to two hundred or more. Consult Holmes in 15th Rep. B. A. E., 1897. (W. H. H.)

Ribnaia (Russian: 'fish'). A Chnagmiut Eskimo village on the right bank of the lower Yukon, Alaska; pop. 40 in 1880.
Ruibnaia.—Petroff, Rep. on Alaska, 57, 1881. **Rybnia.**—Petroff in 10th Census, Alaska, 12, 1884.

Rice Lake. A settlement of the Mississauga in the county of Northumberland, Ontario, usually called "Rice Lake Indians" on account of their proximity to that body of water. In 1909 they numbered 93. In the first half of the 19th century they were noted for their skill in "medicine."
Indians of Rice Lake.—Chamberlain in Jour. Am. Folk-lore, I, 151, 1888. **Rice Lake band.**—Can. Ind. Aff. Rep. 1906, 17, 1907.

Rice Lake Band. A Chippewa band residing on Rice lake, Barron co., Wis. Their settlement, according to Warren, was made as early as the year 1700. They numbered 184 in 1909, under La Pointe agency.
Rice Lake.—Warren (1852) in Minn. Hist. Soc. Coll., v, 164, 1885. **Rice Lake band.**—Washington treaty (1863) in U. S. Ind. Treat., 215, 1873.

Richardville, John B. See *Peshewah.*

Richibucto. A Micmac village at the mouth of Richibucto r., in Kent co., N. B.
Elagibucto.—Vetromile, Abnakis, 58, 1866. **Richi-bouctou.**—Bollan (1748) in Mass. Hist. Soc. Coll., 1st .s, VI, 136, 1800. **Richibuctos.**—Keane in Stanford, Compend., 533, 1878. **Rigibucto.**—Vetromile, Abnakis, 58, 1866. **Rishebouctou.**—Frye (1760) in Mass. Hist. Soc. Coll., 1st s., x, 116, 1809. **Rishe-bucta.**—Ibid., 115.

Richuchi (*Ri-chu-chi′*, from the name of a small red aquatic animal called by the Mexicans *sandifuela*). A small rancheria of the Tarahumare, not far from Norogachic, s. w. Chihuahua, Mexico.—Lumholtz, inf'n, 1894.

Rickahake. A village of the Powhatan confederacy in 1612, probably in the present Norfolk co., Va. It was occupied by some renegades who had formed a plot against a ruling chief and fled to escape punishment. The account is given by Pory in Smith (1629), Va., II, 64, repr. 1819. Cf. *Righkahauk*.

Riddle, Toby. See *Winema*.

Riechesni (Russian: 'brook village'). A former Aleut village on Little bay, Akun, Krenitzin ids., Alaska; pop. 37 in 1830.
Raicheshnoe.—Veniaminof, Zapiski, II, 202, 1840. **Raychevsnoi.**—Veniaminof cited by Elliott, Cond. Aff. Alaska, 235, 1875.

Righkahauk. A village in 1608, possibly of the Chickahominy tribe, on the w. bank of Chickahominy r., in New Kent co., Va.—Smith (1629), Va., I, map, repr. 1819. Cf. *Rickahake*.

Rincon (Span: 'corner,' in the S. W. usually referring to a corner, angle, or recess in a valley). A Luiseño village w. of San Luis Rey, San Diego co., Cal., in 1883; not to be confounded with Rincon in Riverside co. The name is now given to a tract of 2,552.81 acres of patented and allotted land, with 119 inhabitants, under the Pala agency. See Ind. Aff. Rep. for 1902, 175; for 1903, 147, 1904; Jackson and Kinney, Rep. Mission Ind., 29, 1883; Kelsey, Spec. Rep. Cal. Inds., 33, 1906.

Ring stones. See *Perforated stones*.

Rique ('place of panthers.'—Hewitt). An important palisaded town of the ancient Erie, situated probably near the present site of Erie, Erie co., Pa. In 1658 it was said to have been sacked by 1,200 Iroquois, although defended by between 2,000 and 3,000 combatants.
Erie.—Jes. Rel. 1641, 71, 1858. **Erige.**—Macauley, N. Y., I, 119, 1829. **Erike.**—Ibid. **Rigué.**—Jes. Rel. 1656, 32, 1858. **Rique.**—Shea, note in Charlevoix, New France, II, 266, 1866 (Onondaga name).

Rirak. A Yuit Eskimo village in Plover bay, N. E. Siberia; pop. 24 in 4 houses about 1895; 9 in 2 houses in 1901. The people are of the Aiwan division and are very poor.
I'en.—Bogoras, Chukchee, 29, 1904 (Chukchi designation.) **Ri'rak.**—Ibid. (Eskimo name). **Tirik.**—Nelson in 18th Rep. B. A. E., map, 1899.

Rising Moose. See *Tamaha*.

Ritanoe. A village, probably of the Powhatan confederacy, in Virginia or North Carolina about 1612, near some copper mines.—Strachey (*ca.* 1612), Va., 26, 1849.

Ritenbenk. A missionary station and Danish trading post in N. Greenland, just across the bight from Disko id.
Ritenbenk.—Meddelelser om Grönland, XXV, map, 1902. **Rittenbenk.**—Crantz, Hist. Greenland, I, pl. I, 15, 1767.

Rito (Span.: 'rite,' 'ceremony'). A former pueblo of the Laguna Indians on the s. bank of San José r., Valencia co., N. Mex. It was deserted prior to 1848, because those who lived higher up on the Arroyo de Rito cut off all the water of the stream in seasons when they wanted to irrigate their lands, thus depriving the people of Rito of it (Abert in Emory Recon., 474, 1848). It is now a small Mexican village, but there are a few old Laguna houses there.

Ritual. See *Ceremony, Religion*.

River Desert. A band of Algonkin occupying the Maniwaki res., comprising about 44,537 acres, on Desert r., at its confluence with Gatineau r., Quebec. The members of this band, numbering 409 in 1909, gain their livelihood by "shantying," driving, hunting, and lumbering, and engage to a limited extent in agriculture. The women make moccasins, mittens, baskets, etc., while the men manufacture snowshoes and ax-handles. The older men drink to excess and are rather dependent on the whites for employment.

River Indians. Used by Hubbard in 1680 (Mass. Hist. Soc. Coll., 2d s., V, 33, 1815) as a collective term for the Indians formerly living on Connecticut r. above the coast tribes.

River Rouge. An Algonkin settlement in Ottawa co., Quebec, containing 31 Indians in 1884.—Can. Ind. Aff. 1884, 184, 1885.

River that Flies. A former band of the Miniconjou Sioux.—Culbertson in Smithson. Rep. 1850, 142, 1851.

Roanoak (*Roanok*, 'northern people'). The first people with whom Amadas and Barlowe came into contact after landing, in July, 1584, on the island of Wococon (*wákákan* 'curve' or 'bend,' from its shape as shown on White's map), in what is now North Carolina. The language of the inhabitants being unintelligible, it was but natural for them to mistake the word *Wingandacoa* for the name of the country, and the name *Roanoak* for that of the island which these Indians inhabited. On visiting this island (about 12 m. long) a few days after their arrival, Barlowe and his companions found at its northern end (a location whence possibly the name of the people) "a village of nine houses built of Cedar, and fortified round about with sharpe trees to keepe out their enemies, and the entrance into it made like a turne pike very artificially." This was the residence of Wingina, the werowance of the Roanoak, and of Granganameo, his brother. White marks this village "Roanoac," in accordance with the custom of the early settlers, but not of the natives, of designating Indian villages by the names of their inhabitants.

The name Roanoak, having been made known in England by Barlowe, in his report to Sir Walter Raleigh, became fixed, in the form Roanoke, in geographical nomenclature as the name, primarily, of an island; later it was applied to a river of Virginia and North

Carolina, a city and county of Virginia, and villages in other states.

According to Mooney, the application of the name *Roanoak* (*roanoke*, *ronoke*, *ronoak*, the Virginia and North Carolina term from some Algonquian dialect, which the records of Maryland, Virginia, and North Carolina constantly use to designate wampum (q. v.) and for which Lawson employs the form *rawrenoc*) should be restricted to the village described above, one of those of the Secotan tribe, in 1585–89, under jurisdiction of Wingina. (w. R. G.)

Roanoke. A name applied, with several variants, by the Virginia colonists, to the shell beads employed by the neighboring Indians as articles of personal adornment or media of exchange; a case of substitution of a familiar word for one that was ill understood and probably more difficult to pronounce. Capt. John Smith (1612 and 1624) gives the Powhatan name for shell beads in the form of *rawrenock* and *rawranoke*, and William Strachey defines *rarenaw* as 'a chain of beads.' The root *rár* means to 'rub,' 'abrade,' 'smooth,' 'polish.' The original word may have been *rárenawok*, 'smoothed shells,' pl. of *rarenaw*. See *Shellwork*, *Wampum*. (w. R. G.)

Robbiboe. A sort of pemmican soup stated by Schele de Vere (Americanisms, 44, 1872) to be in use throughout the N. W. among hunters, trappers, and others. This is the Canadian French *rababou*, a soup of flour and pemmican used by the voyageurs and early settlers. The word is probably derived from *nabob*, or *napop*, which signifies 'broth' in the Chippewa and closely related dialects of Algonquian, with *n* converted into *r* as in some languages of this stock. (A. F. C.)

Robesco. A rancheria of the Eudeve and the seat of a mission dating from 1673. Situated in central Sonora, Mexico, about lat. 29°, lon. 110°. Pop. 330 in 1678, and but 8 in 1730.

Robesco.—Rivera (1730) quoted by Bancroft, No. Mex. States, I, 513, 1884. **San Francisco de Javier Reboyco.**—Zapata (1678) in Doc. Hist. Mex., 4th s., III, 355, 1857. **S. Fran. Javier Reboico.**—Zapata (1678) quoted by Bancroft, No. Mex. States, I, 246, 1884.

Robinson, Alexander. A chief of the Potawatomi, known also as Cheecheebingway; born at Mackinaw, Mich., in 1789. His father was a Scotch trader, his mother an Ottawa. Although but 5 years of age when Gen. Anthony Wayne fought the battle of the Miami in 1794, of which he was an accidental observer, Robinson retained a vivid recollection of what he saw on that occasion. He was present at the surrender of the fort at Chicago during the War of 1812, and tried in vain to prevent the massacre of the troops, succeeding in carrying off Capt. Helm, the commandant, and his wife, in a canoe,

traversing the entire length of L. Michigan and placing them in safety at Mackinaw (Wis. Hist. Soc. Coll., VII, 328, 1876). It is stated that, probably in 1827, he prevented the young men of his tribe from making an attack on Ft Dearborn. In the Black Hawk war of 1832 Robinson and his people espoused the cause of the whites, and, so far as they actively participated, formed part of the force under Gen. Atkinson and Gen. Henry. He served as interpreter for Gen. Lewis Cass during his treaty negotiations with the Chippewa, June 6, 1820, and his name, in the form Cheecheepinquay, is signed to the treaty of Prairie du Chien, Wis., July 29, 1829; also, as Tshee-tshee-beengguay, to the supplementary treaty of Oct. 1, 1834. The sum of $5,000 was allowed him, and $400 granted his children. (C. T.)

Rocameca (contraction of Old Abnaki *Näräkämïguk*, 'at (or on) the land upstream.'—Gerard). A former tribe of the Abnaki confederacy on Androscoggin r., on the border of Oxford and Franklin cos., Me. Their plantation extended for several miles along both banks of the stream. It is possible that they belonged to the Arosaguntacook. (J. M.)

Arockamecook.—Ballard in Rep. U. S. Coast Surv. 1868, 247, 1871. **Arrockaumecook.**—McKeen in Me. Hist. Soc. Coll., III, 323, 1853. **Merocomecook.**—Coffin (1797), ibid., IV, 340, 1856. **Narakamig8.**—French letter (1721) in Mass. Hist. Soc. Coll., 2d s., VIII, 262, 1819. **Narrackomagog.**—Niles (ca. 1761), ibid., 3d s., VI, 246, 1837. **Narrahamegock.**—Penhallow (1726) in N. H. Hist. Soc. Coll., I, 83, 1824. **Narrakamegook.**—Portsmouth treaty (1713) in Me. Hist. Soc. Coll., VI, 250, 1859. **Rocameca.**—Russell, ibid., II, 167, 1847. **Roccamecco.**—McKeen, ibid., III, 323, 1853 (the tract). **Rockamagug.**—Penhallow (1726) in N. H. Hist. Soc. Coll., I, 122, 1824. **Rockamecook.**—Perepole in Me. Hist. Soc. Coll., III, 333, 1853 (village). **Rocomeco.**—Coffin (1797), ibid., IV, 340, 1856 (the point). **Rouameuo.**—McKeen, ibid., III, 323, 1853 (village).

Rocheachic ('fish place'). A small pueblo of the Tarahumare in Chihuahua, Mexico.—Lumholtz, inf'n, 1894.

Roche de Bœuf (French: 'buffalo rock'). An Ottawa village on the N. w. bank of Maumee r., near Waterville, Lucas co., Ohio. In 1831 the reservation was sold and the Indians removed to Kansas, where they joined the Ottawa of Blanchard Fork, and by treaty agreement were to become citizens in 1867.

Fondagame.—Detroit treaty (1807) in Am. St. Papers, Ind. Aff., I, 747, 1832 (misprint for Tondaganie, the chief). **Roche de Bœuf.**—Detroit treaty (1807) in U. S. Ind. Treat., 193, 1873. **Rocher de Bout.**—Hutchins, map (1778), in Butterfield, Washington-Irvine Corr., 354, 1882. **Tendaganee's village.**—Brown, West. Gaz., 164, 1817. **Tondaganie.**—Maumee treaty (1819) in U. S. Ind. Treat., 203, 1873 (chief's name).

Rockahominy. An Indian food preparation (the "cold flour" of Western hunters), used under different names (*psitamun*, *nuk'hik*, *yok'hig*, *rok'hig*, *pinole*, *tiste*, etc.) from Canada to Peru, and made of parched corn (called by the Powhatan

Indians of Virginia *äpärumĕnăn*, 'parched grain') pounded into a very fine powder. At the N. maple sugar is sometimes mixed with it, and, in Texas, powdered mesquite beans, while still farther s. chocolate and cane sugar enter into its composition. This preparation is carried in a skin bag or pouch by the hunter, who is able to subsist on it alone for several days at a time. It was formerly the principal food of Indian war parties going on distant expeditions, its bulk being reduced to the smallest possible compass, and it being so light that the Indians could, without inconvenience, carry a supply sufficient for a long journey. Under the name of *mashika*, it forms an important part of the rations furnished to the soldiers of the Peruvian army. From Powhatan of Virginia (with a vocalic suffix due to English-speaking people) *rokahamĕn*, a verb meaning, in its indefinite sense, 'softened'; cognate with Lenape *lok'hamĕn*, and Abnaki *nuk'hamĕn*. (W. R. G.)

Rockaway (Renape: *regawihäki*, 'sandy land.'—Gerard.) A tribe formerly living about Rockaway and Hempstead, on the s. coast of Long id., N. Y. They were scattered over the plains and extended N. W. to Newton. Their principal village was Rechquaakie, besides which they had another on Hog id., in Rockaway bay.

Rackeaway.—Doc. of 1662 in N. Y. Doc. Col. Hist., XIV, 512, 1883. **Rechkewick.**—Deed of 1647, ibid., 68. **Rechouwhacky.**—Deed of 1639, ibid., 15. **Rechowacky.**—Stuyvesant (1663), ibid., XIII, 322, 1881. **Reckkeweck.**—Deed of 1647, ibid., XIV, 66, 1883. **Reckkouwhacky.**—Deed of 1669 quoted by Ruttenber, Ind. Geog. Names, 87, 1906. **Reckomacki.**—Stuyvesant (1660) in N. Y. Doc. Col. Hist., XIV, 474, 1883. **Reckonhacky.**—Doc. of 1644, ibid., 56. **Reckowacky.**—Doc. of 1660, ibid., XIII, 184, 1881. **Roakaway.**—Doc. of 1657, ibid., XIV, 416, 1883. **Rockaway.**—Deed of 1643, ibid., 530. **Rockeway.**—Doc. of 1675, ibid., 705. **Rockway.**—Andros (1675), ibid., 709.

Rockaway. A two-seated pleasure carriage with a canopy top, named after Rockaway, a river and a village in New Jersey, derived from the Delaware dialect of Algonquian prevalent in this region. (A. F. C.)

Rock Village. A former Potawatomi village in N. E. Illinois, on a reservation sold in 1837.—Tippecanoe treaty (1832) in U. S. Ind. Treat., 698, 1873; Washington treaty (1837), ibid., 715.

Rocky Point. A former Micmac village on Prince Edward id., Canada.

Roenoke. See *Roanoke*.

Rokeag. An Indian food preparation made of finely powdered parched corn: spelled also *roucheag* and *rokee*. The word is from Quiripi (Quinnipiac) *rok'hig*, abbreviated from *rokĕhigan*, and, like its Massachuset and Pequot-Mohegan cognates, *nokehĭk* and *yokeag*, means '(what is) softened.' (W. R. G.)

Rokohamin. See *Rockahominy*.

Roktsho. The highest of the Chilula villages on Redwood cr., N. Cal.

Rooktsu.—Kroeber, MS., Univ. Cal. (Yurok name). Roque-choh.—Gibbs in Schoolcraft, Ind. Tribes, III, 139, 1853.

Rolfe, Thomas. The son and only child of the celebrated Pocahontas (q. v.) of Virginia, by her husband John Rolfe. He was born in England in 1617, shortly before the death of his mother, and was educated in London by his uncle, Henry Rolfe. On reaching manhood he came to America, where, in 1641, he petitioned the Virginia government for permission to visit his mother's sister and uncle among their people, then at war with the English. He is styled by one writer "a gentleman of great distinction and possessed of ample fortune," but his name is not conspicuous in the records of his time. He left one daughter, who in turn left one son, through whom certain families trace descent from Pocahontas. (J. M.)

Romaine (*Orămänĭshipu*, 'vermilion river,' from Montagnais *orămän* 'vermilion', *shipu* 'river.'—Gerard). A Montagnais village and trading station on the coast of Labrador, at the mouth of Romaine r. In 1884 the inhabitants numbered 287.

Grand Romaine.—Can. Ind. Aff. Rep. 1884, pt. 1, 185, 1885. Olomanosheebo.—Stearns, Labrador, 264, 1884. Romaine.—Ibid.

Roman Nose (*Woqĭnĭ*, 'hook nose'). A former noted chief of the Himoiyoqis warrior society of the Southern Cheyenne. The name "Roman Nose" was given him by the whites; his proper name was Sauts, 'Bat.' He was prominent in the Indian wars along the Kansas frontier between 1864 and 1868, and led the attack at the celebrated battle of Aricaree Fork or Beecher's Island, E. Colorado, Sept. 17–25, 1868, in which a company of 52 scouts under command of Col. (Gen.) G. A. Forsyth successfully held off several hundred Cheyenne warriors for 8 days until help arrived. Roman Nose was shot in the afternoon of the first day's fight and died that night in the Indian camp, to which he had been removed by his friends. See *Cheyenne*. (J. M.)

Romonan. A division of the Costanoan family of California, presumably on San Francisco peninsula and connected with Dolores mission, San Francisco. Sometimes included under the term Costanos.

Romanons.—Taylor in Cal. Farmer, May 31, 1861. Ro-mo-nans.—Schoolcraft, Ind. Tribes, II, 506, 1852. Rowanans.—Hittell, Hist. Cal., I, 731, 1898.

Ronatewisichroone. The Iroquois name of a tribe, probably Algonquian, formerly living about the upper Great Lakes. They sent a friendly message to the Seneca in 1715.—Livingston (1715) in N. Y. Doc. Col. Hist., V, 445, 1855.

Ronowadainie. One of the 6 "castles" of the Amikwa, near Michilimackinac,

Mich., in 1723.—Albany Conf. (1723) in N. Y. Doc. Col. Hist., v, 693, 1855.

Root Diggers. A band, probably Shoshoni, but given by Culbertson (Smithson Rep. 1850, 144, 1851) as a Crow clan. See *Digger.*

Roots. For economic as well as for religious purposes the Indians used the various parts of plants to a greater extent than substances of animal or mineral character. This was the case even in the arid region, although plants with edible roots are limited mainly to areas having abundant rainfall. The more important uses of roots were for food, for medicine, and for dyes, but there were many other uses, as for basketry, cordage, fire-sticks, cement, etc., and for chewing, making salt, and flavoring.

Plants of the lily family furnished the most abundant and useful root food of the Indians throughout the U. S. The Eskimo of Kowak r. ate roots of the wild parsnip, which they secured from the caches in the nests of field-mice. The Indians of C. Flattery ate camas bulbs, procured by trade from tribes to their southward, as well as equisetum roots, and roots of fern, grass, water plants, clover, cinquefoil, and eelgrass. Equisetum tubers and eelgrass roots were eaten raw; other roots were boiled by means of hot stones or baked in pit ovens. Camas (q. v.) was a staple root-food from the Wasatch mts. in Utah, northward and westward; it was an article of widespread commerce, influenced the migration of tribes, and might have become in time the basis of primitive agriculture, especially in the valley of Columbia r. Leiberg says: "Every meadow was a camas field. The plant was so plentiful in many places that it is no exaggeration to say that in the upper St Mary basin more than half of the total herbaceous vegetation in the lowlands was composed of this one species." The Skitswish people congregated here in the summer to dig camas and to hunt deer. The root was dug with a sharp-pointed stick. In part of this area the kouse root (q. v.), second only to camas in importance, was dug in April or May, before camas was in season. This root is the *racine blanc* of the Canadian voyageurs. It was pounded and made into thin cakes, a foot wide and 3 ft long, which were ribbed from the impression of the poles on which they were laid over the fire to smoke-dry or bake.

The tubers of the arrowhead plant (*Sagittaria arifolia* and *S. latifolia*), wappatoo (q. v.) in Algonquian, were widely used in the N. W. for food. When passing across Chewaucan marsh of the Oregon plains, E. of the Klamath res., Frémont noticed large patches of ground

that had been torn up by Indian women in digging the roots of the wappatoo. The Chippewa and Atlantic Coast Indians also made use of them. The roots of the cattail flag and bur reed were eaten by the Klamath of Oregon, who used also the roots of carum, calochortus, and valerian. The Nez Percés of Idaho ate the balsam root (*Balsamorrhiza incana* and *B. sagittata*), as well as the roots of *Carum gairdneri, Callirrhoë pedata,* and *Ptilocalais* sp.

The pomme blanche, Indian turnip, or prairie potato (*Psoralea esculenta*) was prized by tribes living on high plains from the Saskatchewan to Louisiana and Texas. The root was dug by women by means of a pointed stick, then dried, pounded to meal, and cooked with jerked meat and corn. For winter use these roots were cut in thin slices and dried. The Sioux varied their diet with roots of the Indian turnip, two kinds of water lily, the water grass, and the *mdo* of the Sioux, called by the French pomme de terre, the ground-nut (*Apios apios*). To these may be added the tuber of milkweed (*Asclepias tuberosa*), valued by the Sioux of the upper Platte, and the root of the Jerusalem artichoke (*Helianthus tuberosa*), eaten by the Dakota of St Croix r. Other Plains tribes gathered esculent roots to eke out their food supply; among them the immense roots of the wild potato (*Ipomœa leptophylla*) were dug with great labor and eaten by the Cheyenne, Arapaho, and Kiowa. The Miami, Shawnee, and other tribes of the middle W. ate the "man of the earth" (*Ipomœa pandurata*) and Jerusalem artichoke (*Helianthus tuberosus*). From the universal habit among Californian tribes, especially the Paiute, of gathering food roots, the name "Diggers" was applied to them by the early settlers and has remained to this day in popular usage. The esculent roots growing in great variety in California were a considerable addition to the Indian larder. Among the plants thus utilized were the brake, tule, calochortus, camas, and various lilies. Calochortus bulbs, called wild sago, were eaten also by the tribes of Utah and Arizona. The bulbs are starchy and palatable, and it is said that the Mormons, during their first five years in Utah, consumed this root extensively.

In the S. W. few edible roots are found, though many medicinal roots are gathered. The Hopi, Zuñi, and other tribes eat the tubers of the wild potato (*Solanum jamesii*). The Southern and Eastern tribes also made use of the potato. Though this acrid tuber is unpalatable and requires much preparation to render it suitable for food, many tribes recognized its value. The Navaho, especially, dug and consumed large quantities of it, and on account of the griping caused by eating it, they ate clay with it as a palliative. The Pima, Hopi, and other Arizona tribes habitually chewed the roots of certain plants having sweet or mucilaginous properties.

The Seminole of Florida possessed a valuable plant called *coonti* (q. v.), the bulbous starchy root of which was converted into flour. The apparatus employed in the coonti industry comprised mortars and pestles, platforms, mash vessels, strainers, and vats. The starch, separated from the mashed root by washing and sedimentation, was fermented slightly, dried on palmetto leaves, and made into bread. A demand among the whites for coonti flour has led to the establishment of several mills in Florida The coonti industry is similar to the cassava industry of the West Indies and South America, and it seems probable that the method of manufacture in Florida did not originate there. Hariot mentions 6 plants the roots of which were valued as food by the Virginia Indians, giving the native names, appearance, occurrence, and method of preparation. Many of the medicinal roots of eastern and southern U. S. were adopted by the whites from the Indian pharmacopeia; some of these are still known by their native names, and about 40 are quoted in current price lists of crude drugs. Indians formerly gathered medicinal roots to supply the trade that arose after the coming of the whites. Many roots were exported, especially ginseng, in which there was an extensive commerce with China; and, curiously enough, the Iroquois name for the plant has the same meaning as the Chinese name. Ginseng was discovered in America by Lafitau in 1716, and under the French régime in Canada many thousands of dollars' worth were sent yearly to the Orient. In Alaska ginseng was used by sorcerers to give them power. Although the use of edible roots by the Indians was general, they nowhere practised root cultivation, even in its incipient stages. In the U. S. the higher agriculture, represented by maize cultivation, seems to have been directly adopted by tribes which had not advanced to the stage of root cultivation. See *Basketry, Dyes and Pigments, Food, Medicine and Medicine-men.*

Consult Palmer, Food Products of the North American Indians, U. S. Agric. Rep. 1870, 1871; Chamberlain in Vehr. d. Berliner Gesel. f. Anthr., 551, 1895; Chesnut, Plants used by the Indians of Mendocino co., Cal., Cont. U. S. Nat. Herb., VII, no. 3, 1902; Coville, Notes on the Plants used by the Klamath Indians of Oregon, ibid., v, no. 2, 1897; Leiberg,

ibid., v, no. 1, p. 37; J. O. Dorsey in 3d Rep. B. A. E., 308, 1884; MacCauley in 5th Rep. B. A. E., 1887; Hariot, Briefe and True Report, 1590; Hrdlička in Bull. 34, B. A. E., 1908.   (w. h.)

Rosario. See *Nuestra Señora del Rosario.*

Roscows. A former Kecoughtan settlement in Elizabeth City co., Va.—Jefferson (1781), Notes, 129, 1802.

Ross, John. Chief of the Cherokee; born in Rossville, Ga., Oct. 3, 1790; died in Washington, D. C., Aug. 1, 1866. He was the son of an immigrant from Scotland by a Cherokee wife who was herself three-quarters white. His boyhood name of Tsan-usdí, 'Little John,' was exchanged when he reached man's estate

JOHN ROSS

for that of Guwisguwi, or Cooweescoowee, by which was known a large white bird of uncommon occurrence, perhaps the egret or the swan. He went to school in Kingston, Tenn. In 1809 he was sent on a mission to the Cherokee in Arkansas by the Indian agent, and thenceforward till the close of his life he remained in the public service of his nation. At the battle of the Horseshoe, and in other operations of the Cherokee contingent against the Creeks in 1813–14, he was adjutant of the Cherokee regiment. He was chosen a member of the national committee of the Cherokee Council in 1817, and drafted the reply to the U. S. commissioners who were sent to negotiate the exchange of the Cherokee lands for others w. of the Mississippi. In the contest against the removal his talents found play and recognition. As president of the national committee from 1819 till 1826 he was instrumental in the introduction of school and mechanical training, and led in the development of the civilized autonomous government embodied in the republican constitution adopted in 1827. He was associate chief with William Hicks in that year, and president of the Cherokee constitutional convention. From 1828 till the removal to Indian Ter. in 1839 he was principal chief of the Cherokee Nation, and headed the various national delegations that visited Washington to defend the right of the Cherokee to their national territory. After the arrival in Indian Ter., he was chosen chief of the united Cherokee Nation, and held that office until his death, although during the dissensions caused by the Civil War the Federal authorities temporarily deposed him. See Mooney, Myths of the Cherokee, 19th Rep. B. A. E., 122, 150, 224, 225, 1900.

Roucheag. See *Rokeag.*

Rouconk. A Neusiok village in 1701, probably on lower Neuse r., in Craven co., N. C.—Lawson (1709), Hist. Car., 384, 1860.

Roundhead (*Stiahta*). A Wyandot (Huron) chief who espoused the British cause in the War of 1812, being connected chiefly with Col. Proctor's command. Nothing is known of his early history, and though spoken of as a fine-looking man and a celebrated Indian chief, his history as recorded refers only to the time of the war mentioned. He was with Maj. Muir, of Proctor's command, on the Miami near Ft Miami, Ohio, Sept. 27–28, 1812, and urged in vain the English commander to hold his position and fight the American forces. In Oct. following he accompanied Maj. Muir to River Raisin, where Proctor was gathering his forces, and later in the same year he met his death. Gen. Proctor, in a letter dated Oct. 23, 1813, states that "the Indian cause and ours experienced a serious loss in the death of Round Head." A village in the s. w. corner of Hardin co., Ohio, his early home, bore his name, which survives in that of the present town of Roundhead built on its site. Roundhead had a brother known as John Battise, a man "of great size and personal strength," who was killed at Ft Meigs while fighting for the British.　　　　　　(c. t.)

Roymount. A Delaware village with 14 warriors, existing about 1648, near C. May, N. J.—Evelin (*ca.* 1648) quoted by Proud, Penn., i, 114, 1797.

Rsanuk (*Rsá'nŭk,* 'beginning'). A Pima village about 1 m. E. of Sacaton station, on the Maricopa and Phœnix R. R., s. Arizona.—Russell in 26th Rep. B. A. E. 23, 1908.

Rsotuk (*Rsótŭk'*, 'water standing'). A Pima village N. w. of Casa Blanca, s. Arizona.—Russell in 26th Rep. B. A. E., 23, 1908.

Ruche ('pigeon'). An Iowa gens. Lu'-chih.—Morgan, Anc. Soc., 156, 1877. **Pigeon.**—Ibid. **Ru'-tce.**—Dorsey in 15th Rep. B. A. E., 239, 1897.

Rukhcha ('pigeon'). An Oto gens. Lute'-ja.—Morgan, Anc. Soc., 156, 1877. **Ru'-qtca.**—Dorsey in 15th Rep. B. A. E., 240, 1897.

Rumsen. A division of the Costanoan family, formerly about Monterey, Cal., inhabiting Monterey, Sur, and Carmel r. The term has been made to include also, as a subdivision, the so-called Kalendaruk of the lower Salinas and Pajaro rs. As early as 1602 Vizcayno wintered among the Rumsen at Monterey, though he does not mention them by name. The first mission founded in California, after that of San Diego, was established as Carmelo in Rumsen territory in 1770. Six or eight Rumsen, mostly old women, survived about Monterey and Carmel in 1903. The following villages of the Rumsen are mentioned: Achasta, Echilat, Guayusta, Kakonkaruk, Karmentaruka, Sargentaruka, Tukutnut, Wachanaruka.　(a. l. k.)
Achastas.—Taylor in Cal. Farmer, Apr. 20, 1860. Achastli.—Latham in Proc. Philol. Soc. Lond., vi, 79, 1852–53. Achastlians.—Chamisso in Kotzebue, Voy., iii, 49, 1821. Achastliens.—Lamanon in Perouse, Voy., ii, 291, 1797. Achastlier.—Adelung, Mithridates, iii, 204, 1816. Achastlies.—Mayer, Mexico, ii, 39, 1853. Achistas.—Taylor in Cal. Farmer, Apr. 20, 1860. Rumsenes.—Mayer, op. cit. Rumsien.—Humboldt, Essai Pol., i, 321, 1811. Runcienes.—Hittell, Hist. Cal., i, 797, 1898. Runsenes.—Taylor in Cal. Farmer, Apr. 20, 1860. Runsienes.—Galiano, Relacion, 164, 1802. Ruslen.—Latham in Proc. Philol. Soc. Lond., vi, 79, 1854.

Rum's Village. A former village of the Potawatomi, about 4 m. s. of South Bend, St Joseph co., Ind. It was included in the lands ceded to the U. S. by treaty of Chicago, Aug. 29, 1821.

Running Water. A former Cherokee town on the s. E. bank of Tennessee r., below Chattanooga, near the N. w. Georgia line, and 4 m. above Nickajack. It was settled in 1782 by Cherokee who espoused the British cause in the Revolutionary war, and was known as one of the Chickamauga towns. It was destroyed in the fall of 1794. See Royce in 5th Rep. B. A. E., map, 1887; Mooney in 19th Rep. B. A. E., 54, 78, 1900.

Runonvea. An Iroquois village formerly situated near Big Flats, Chemung co., N. Y., and burned Aug. 31, 1779, by the troops under Gen. Sullivan.—Cook, Jour. Sullivan's Exped., 381, 1887.

Runtee. A circular piece of flat shell drilled edgeways and probably strung and originally used as an ornament. The name *runtee* was first mentioned, a century after the settlement of Virginia, by Beverley, who says of the objects so called: "Runtees are made of the Conch-Shell as the Peak is, only the Shape is flat and round like a Cheese, and drill'd

Edge-ways'' (Hist. Va., bk. III, 145, 1705). Holmes says of these objects (2d Rep. B. A. E., 230, 1883): "The fact that they are found in widely separated localities indicates that they were probably used in trade since the advent of the whites." The word *runtee* is not Algonquian, but evidently an English corruption of French *arrondi*, 'rounded,' 'made round,' short, perhaps, for *écaille arrondie*, 'shell made round.' Mr Holmes further remarks that "this is probably some form of bead held in high esteem by tribes of the Atlantic coast when first encountered by the whites, who have taken up its manufacture for purposes of trade." Râle mentions shell ronds (*paganrank*) worn at the neck by Abnaki men, one of which was worth one beaver, and ronds (*paghiganak*) of the women, six small ones or three large ones of which were worth one beaver. See *Beads, Shell-work*. (W. R. G.)

Ruptari. One of the two villages of the Mandan (q. v.) on the upper Missouri in North Dakota in 1804. When the Mandan were almost destroyed by the ravages of smallpox in 1837, the remnant abandoned their villages to the Arikara and established a new settlement nearer Knife river. They subsequently removed to Ft Berthold.

Nuptadi.—Matthews, Ethnog. Hidatsa, 14, 1877. Rooptahee.—Lewis and Clark Exped., I, 120, 1814. Roop-tar-ha.—Lewis and Clark, Discov., 24, 1806. Roop-tar′-har.—Lewis and Clark, Trav., 19, 1807. Roop-tar-he.—Orig. Jour. Lewis and Clark, I, 256, 1904. Roop-tar-hee.—Ibid., 212. Rop-tar-ha.—Am. St. Papers, Ind. Aff., I, 710, 1832. Ruhptare.—Maximilian Trav., 335, 1843. Rùptari.—Matthews, loc. cit.

Russian influence. Russian influence on the natives of N. W. America began with the voyage of Bering (1741), which revealed the wealth of peltries to the traders of E. Siberia. The Siberian region had been mostly subjected by the traders at the end of the 17th century, but the processes of intertribal trade had carried the wrought iron of the Yakut, the pipes and tobacco of Mongolia, among these people much earlier than the advent of Russians, who were the first to introduce firearms. But the intense hostility between the Siberian and American Eskimo at Bering strait restricted the trade and the intercontinental influences for many years later.

The traders conquered the Aleut, but were checked by the more warlike Kodiak Eskimo and by internal dissensions; only with the formation of a general trading association (1781) and its sequel, a government monopoly (1790 and 1799), were exploration and trade systematically organized. S. and E. of Cook inlet the Russians had to meet the opposition of the Spaniards, the English, and the free American traders as well as the

well-armed and warlike Tlingit tribes, Haida, etc. In the eastern interior the Hudson's Bay Company began to draw away trade as early as 1810. Owing to the hostile attitude of the Spanish authorities and the need of food supplies, the Russians bought, in 1811, a small tract of land from the natives at Bodega bay, Cal., and later one at Russian r., where they raised cereals for the support of the more northerly colonies and did a little trading. In this way they came in contact with the natives of California. As they found the Tlingit would not trade with them, they brought Aleut sea-otter hunters from the N., with their kaiaks, to hunt on the otter grounds of the Alexander archipelago, the California coast, and on at least one occasion came with one of these parties as far s. as the Santa Barbara ids., the visit lingering in the mind of the last surviving Santa Rosa islander late in the eighties. With the progress of exploration direct trade and contact with the natives on the N. W. coast proceeded about as follows:

Aleutian islands (Russian), 1741–1867.

Southeastern Alaska (Russian), 1804–1867.

California (Russian), 1811–1841.

Norton sound and Yukon delta (Russian vessels), 1818–1822.

Norton sound (permanent trading posts, R. A. Co.), 1832–1867.

St Matthew and St Lawrence islands, 1810–1867.

Upper Yukon (permanent posts, H. B. Co.), 1839–1867.

Lower Yukon (permanent posts, Russian), 1838–1867.

Bering strait, Kotzebue sound, and coast northward, first trade, 1820.

Bering strait, Kotzebue sound, and coast northward, beginning of regular annual trade, 1848.

Arctic coast w. of Return reef, first trade, 1825.

Arctic coast E. of Return reef (English), 1825.

Tanana river people, first contact (English), 1863.

Cook inlet and Kodiak, introduction of cattle, 1850.

First school by Russians (at Kodiak) for Eskimo, by order of Shelikoff, 1795.

First school by Russians for Tlingit (at Sitka), by order of Etolin, about 1844.

Second school at Kodiak, by order of Resanoff, 1805.

Desultory mission work (Aleut and at Kodiak), 1793–1816.

Systematic mission work (Sitka, Kodiak, Aleut), 1816–1908.

Systematic mission work (Lower Yukon), about 1860.

Distribution.—Aleut were transported

E. and s. and in later years as servants at the trading posts. Each trading post of importance had a Yakut fisherman in charge of salmon traps. Californian natives were taken to Kodiak in 1841, where there was a small village of superannuated Company's servants as late as 1870—now, probably, all dead. Some Kanaka from Oahu took part (*ca.* 1850) in the Company's whaling expeditions, which had no great success.

Changes of sustenance, and stimulants.— The art of distilling was introduced among the Tlingit by Russian convicts about 1796, and, though forbidden under severe penalties by the Company, was secretly practised at many of the isolated trading posts. The use of cereals as food was hardly known until the sixties, except among the Company's servants at posts. The same may be said of sugar and tea. They were known as gifts or luxuries, not as trading goods. The natives until 1867 lived entirely off the natural food resources of the country, as did most of the Russians and Hudson's Bay Company's men.

Clothing.—Cotton drill, cloth, and blankets took the place of the more valuable furs early in the history of the trade, but till recently skins and native footwear held their own as vastly better for winter wear.

Tools, utensils, and guns.—The first iron tools were made in imitation of the stone and native copper tools and weapons (iron celts were called "toes"); exotic forms came very slowly into use. The native, as late as 1866, preferred to buy malleable iron or wood-files, and to make his own tools in ancient shapes. Kettles and frying-pans were first adopted of exotic utensils. Guns came first from the Hudson's Bay Company and free traders; percussion guns came only in the sixties. Flint-and-steel was eagerly accepted from the very first, matches only about 1867. Axes, sheath knives, and saws were always sought in trade; other tools made their way much more slowly.

Ornaments.—These, except pearl buttons (among the Tlingit) and Chinese cash, were hardly salable among the practical Alaskan natives. There was practically no sale for such things except dentalium shell, small mirrors, and copper or brass wire for rings or bangles, which the natives made themselves. Bright-colored blankets and striped drilling were a good deal used, and certain kinds of beads, which were used as a sort of currency quite as much as for ornament.

Tobacco.—This probably reached the Bering strait region (with pipes) by intertribal commerce from Mongolia before the Russians brought it. The American type of pipe was not found there until much later, and was rarely seen until after 1867. The Mongolian type of pipe is not known s. and E. of Bristol bay, where the Russians first introduced tobacco, but was universal N. and w. of that locality. Tobacco is not mentioned in early lists of trading goods, and was probably only in general use after the Russians had made permanent settlements or trading posts.

Language.—The Chinook jargon was introduced, almost as soon as it was formed, by free traders in s. E. Alaska, and was also more or less used in this region by the Russian traders. In the Eskimo region a jargon arose, composed of Russian, Eskimo, and Hawaiian words, corrupted, and used without inflection. This jargon has been in use from Bristol bay to Pt Barrow and on the Eskimo coast of Siberia, and has been frequently mistaken by hasty travelers and recorded in vocabularies as an Eskimo dialect. The Vega vocabularies were partly of this kind. The Aleut used Russian, and so far as is known never had a jargon.

Myths and religion.—The Aleut were converted to the Greek Church, of which they are, so far as they understand it, devoted members, though retaining secretly much of their ancient religion. On the rest of the people of Alaska the influence of the Greek Church was infinitesimal, and consisted in a purely nominal adherence by rare individuals to a few formalities. From what is known of the myths and mythology of either Tlingit or Eskimo, there was in them, up to 1868, no trace of Christian teaching. With the first introduction of Russian priests in 1793, it is probable that native children were taught to repeat the responses and catechism and join in the intoned service. The teaching of reading, writing, and other secular branches did not come in most cases till much later, but the dates are not recorded.

Population.—Zymotic diseases, normally unknown in the region, at various times have been introduced by traders and have proved very fatal in approximately the order following: scarlet fever, measles, smallpox, syphilis. The last-named was introduced into the Norton Sound region by the American Telegraph Expedition in 1866, the Russians having been successful in excluding it up to that time. A disease affecting the bones is noticeable in many prehistoric skeletons, but seems not to have been syphilitic. After the warfare with the early traders ceased, the natives under Russian auspices, when friendly, were carefully protected as purveyors of peltries, and probably did not seriously diminish in numbers under the conditions then existing.

In general the Russians endeavored to maintain the *status quo* among the natives (other than Aleut and Tlingit), and succeeded fairly well in so doing. The Russian law attaching the individual to the soil (*zemlia*) of his commune operated to prevent legal marriages between native Americans, whose "zemlia" was American, and Russian servants of the company whose "zemlia" was Russian; since when the latter finished his term of service (if not in debt to the company) he was obliged to go back to his original domicile, while he could not take his native wife away from her legal domicile or "zemlia." In this way numerous unions not legally sanctioned grew up, and the women who entered into them were apparently regarded socially as in no way less respectable than the occasional Russian wives with whom they associated on apparently equal terms, and they made as devoted partners and mothers. At the transfer of Alaska to the United States, many of these unions were legalized by authority of the Czar in compliance with the terms of the treaty, which permitted Russian residents to remain and become American citizens if they saw fit. The children of these unions with Tlingit, Eskimo, Aleut, or Californian natives formed a large and intelligent class on the N. W. coast, known to the Russians as "creoles," a class which gave many officials and at least one governor (Etolin) to Russian America. The Russo-Tlingit and Russo-Eskimo crosses were the most numerous and fertile. The issue of casual and mercenary unions was a small factor, as the women in the case were usually infertile. The purity of the Aleut blood probably suffered most from this cause, as that of a subject people; while the quasi-legitimate unions above referred to frequently produced large families which later formed an important element of the civilized population. (W. H. D.)

Russian River Pomo. A collective term for the inhabitants of the numerous Pomo villages lying in the valley of Russian r., Cal.

Sa. The Tobacco clan of the Tewa pueblos of Nambe, N. Mex., and Hano, Ariz.

Cä.—Stephen in 8th Rep. B. A. E., 39, 1891 (Hano name). Na′-to.—Ibid. (Navaho name). Pi′-ba.—Ibid. (Hopi name). Sà.—Fewkes in Am. Anthr., VII, 166, 1894 (Hano form). Sä-tdóa.—Hodge, ibid., IX, 352, 1896 (Nambe form; *tdóa* = 'people').

Saamen. A Salish tribe on Kwalekum r., E. coast of Vancouver id. They speak the Puntlatsh dialect. Probably identical with the Qualicum cited below, who numbered 14 in 1909.

Kwa-le-cum.—Can. Ind. Aff. 1880, 316, 1881. Kwan-le-cum.—Ibid., 308, 1879. Qualicum.—Ibid., pt. II, 164, 1901. Quawlicum.—Ibid., 120, 1880. Quhli-cum.—Ibid., map, 1891. Sáamen.—Boas, MS., B. A. E., 1887.

Sabassa. A collective term applied to the Indians of Laredo and Principe chan-

nels, Brit. Col. By Kane it was made to include the Kitkatla, Kitkahta, and Neeslous of the Tsimshian, and the Kitamat and Kitlope of the Kwakiutl.

Sabassa.—Dunn, Hist. Oreg., 273, 1844. Sabassas Indians.—Kane, Wand. in N. A., app., 1859. Sebassa.—Dunn, op. cit.

Sabeata. A Jumano (Tawehash) chief from the mouth of the Rio Conchos in Chihuahua, born in New Mexico. In Oct. 1683, he went to Paso del Norte, Texas, and asked Gov. Cruzate for missions for his people and their friends, and for protection against the Apache. His native name was Sabeata, but he had been baptized Juan, at Parral. It was his story of the "great kingdom of the Texas" that led to Domingo de Mendoza's expedition to the interior of Texas in 1683–84. Sabeata accompanied the expedition, but before it returned he gained the ill-will of the Spaniards and absconded. Meanwhile missions were established for his people at the mouth of the Conchos (Mendoza, Viage, 1683–84, MS. in Archivo Gen.). In 1691 Sabeata was met on the Rio Guadalupe at the head of a band of his people on their annual buffalo hunt. He still carried his Spanish commission as "governor," and he asked Massanet for more missionaries (Massanet, Diario que hicieron los padres misioneros, Mem. de Nueva España, XXVII, 98–103, MS.). His name appears also as Labiata, Safiata, and Saveata. (H. E. B.)

Sabino. An Abnaki village in 1608 at the mouth of Kennebec r., Me., probably on the w. side of the main channel.

Sabino.—Strachey (1618) in Me. Hist. Soc. Coll., III, 301, 1853. Sebanoa.—Sewell, ibid., VII, 304, 1876 (the chief). Sebeno.—Ballard in Rep. U. S. Coast Surv. 1868, 257, 1871 (trans. 'where the river makes into the land'). Sebenoa.—Strachey (1618) in Me. Hist. Soc. Coll., III, 301, 1853.

Sable. One of the divisions of the Ottawa. Toward the close of the 17th century they were settled at Mackinaw, Mich.

Gens du Sable.—Bacqueville de la Potherie, IV, 59, 1753. Outaouak of the Sable.—Doc. of 1695 in N. Y. Doc. Col. Hist., IX, 627, 1855. Outaoüasinagouc.—Jes. Rel. 1667, 17, 1858. Sables.—Doc. of 1698, ibid., 683. Sablez.—Bacqueville de la Potherie, IV, 94, 1753.

Saboba. A Luiseño village, said to have been the principal one of San Jacinto res., Cal. Though Luiseño, the dialect differs somewhat from that at San Luis Rey. San Jacinto res., established 6 m. from San Jacinto, consists of 2,960 acres of poor, almost waterless land. The original dwellings of the Saboba people were jacales, but these gave place in turn to adobe and frame houses. They gain a livelihood chiefly by laboring for white people, and by cultivating the 150 acres of irrigable land contained in their reservation. Saboba village contains a Catholic church, and a Government school that was the first to be established among the s. California Indians. The Saboba people formerly made baskets in considerable numbers. They are said to have a noticeable strain of Mexican blood. They are inclined to drunkenness, especially on the feast day held in celebration of Mexican independence, owing to the introduction of liquor by the whites. In 1909 the population was 140.

Laboba.—Lovett in Ind. Aff. Rep., 124, 1865 (misprint). Matale de Maño.—Williamson in Ann. Pub. Hist. Soc. S. Cal., II–III, 139, 1909. Saboba.—Jackson and Kinney, Rep. Miss. Ind., 17, 1883. San Jacinto.—Burton (1853) in H. R. Ex. Doc. 76, 34th Cong., 3d sess., 117, 1857; Ind. Aff. Rep., 175, 1902. Savova.—Kroeber in Univ. Cal. Pub., Am. Archæol. and Ethnol., VIII, 35, 1908 (Serrano name). Savovoyam.—Ibid. (name for inhabitants). Soboba.—Ind. Aff. Rep. 1905, 191, 1906 (said to mean 'cold'). Sovovo.—Kroeber in Univ. Cal. Pub., Am. Archæol. and Ethnol., VIII, 39, 1908 (native form).

Sacagawea. A Shoshoni woman who accompanied Lewis and Clark. She was the wife of Toussaint Charbonneau, a French Canadian voyageur living among the Hidatsa, who was engaged by the explorers as interpreter, and she was desirous of returning to her own people, the Shoshoni of the Rocky mts., from whom she had been captured by the Hidatsa and sold to Charbonneau when about 14 years of age. On the Missouri r. her husband, by his bad seamanship, overturned the boat on which were the records of the expedition, but as they floated in the river they were seized by Sacagawea and thus preserved. The leaders of the expedition have recorded praises of the fortitude and serviceableness exhibited on many occasions by Birdwoman, as she was called, the English rendering of her Hidatsa name (*tsakaka*, 'bird'; *mia*, otherwise *wia*, *bia*, 'woman'), though she was encumbered by an infant, born during the journey. When Lewis and Clark came to the first band of Shoshoni, of which her brother had become chief, Sacagawea acted as interpreter and enabled the expedition to obtain ponies, without which they could not have crossed the divide. Of her, Lewis wrote: "Sah-cah-gar-we-ah our Indian woman was one of the female prisoners taken at that time tho' I cannot discover that she shews any immotion of sorrow in recollecting this event, or of joy in being again restored to her native country; if she has enough to eat and a few trinkets to wear I believe she would be perfectly content anywhere." (Orig. Jour. Lewis and Clark, I, 283, 1904.) On the return journey she guided Capt. Clark's party, when they were lost, through the mountain passes of Montana. She remained among the Shoshoni in Wyoming, and when the Wind River res. was created took up her abode there with her son, and there she died, near Ft Washakie, Apr. 9, 1884, almost a hundred years of age. Her grave is marked with a brass tablet, presented by Timothy F. Burke, of Cheyenne, Wyo. The last heard of her husband was in 1838, when Larpenteur saw him in the Hidatsa country. He was then an old man. A bronze statue of this heroine of the expedition was erected in City Park, Portland, Oreg., in the summer of 1905, and another statue is to be placed in the State capitol at Bismarck, N. Dak. Consult Orig. Jour. Lewis and Clark, 1904–05; Hebard in Jour. Am. Hist., I, no. 3, 1907; Fletcher in Out West, XXIII, no. 2, 3, 1905; Coues, Forty Years a Fur Trader, 1898; Wheeler and Brindley in Cont. Hist. Soc. Mont., VII, 1910.   (F. H.)

Sacahayé. An unidentified village or tribe mentioned to Joutel in 1687 (Margry, Déc., III, 410, 1878), while he was staying with the Kadohadacho on Red r. of Louisiana, by the chief of that tribe, as one of his allies.

Sacaspada. A Calusa village on the s. w. coast of Florida, about 1570.—Fontaneda Memoir (*ca.* 1575), Smith trans., 19, 1854.

Sacaton (from Nahuatl *sacaton*, 'small grass', dim. of *zacatl*, Hispanized *zacate*, 'grass', 'hay'). A former small settlement and trading station of the Pima, on the Gila r., about 22 m. E. of Maricopa station and 16 m. N. of Casa Grande station on the S. P. R. R., s. Arizona. In 1858 it had 204 inhabitants, and in 1863, 144. On the opposite bank of the river is now the seat of the Pima agency, which controls the Pima, Maricopa, and Papago tribes, numbering about 6,500, and has a flourishing boarding school. See *Uturituc*.

Kü'-ü-ki.—Russell, Pima MS., B. A. E., 18, 1902 ('big house': Pima name). Sacatone.—Brown, Apache Country, 114, 1869. Saketon.—Box, Adventures, 325, 1869. Socatoon.—Bailey in Ind. Aff. Rep., 207, 1858. Tótsik.—ten Kate quoted by Gatschet, MS., B. A. E., XX, 199, 1888 (Pima name).

Sachal. Given by Wilkes (U. S. Expl. Exped., V, 132, 133, 1844) as the name of a tribe, numbering 40, on a lake of the same name and on Chehalis r., s. w. Wash., into which the lake flows "through a river also called Sachal."

Sachem. (1) In the form of government of the Indians of Massachusetts, the supreme ruler of a territory inhabited by a certain number of tribes, each governed by an inferior sachem generally called by the colonists a *sagamore* (a cognate word of Abnaki origin), and acting under his command and protection. The dignity was hereditary, never elective. (2) By extension, a name given by writers to the chief of a tribe of other North American Indians. (3) One of a body of high officials in the Tammany Society of New York city.

The name *sachim* first occurs in Mourt's Relation (1622), and next in Winslow's Good Newes from New England (1624).

The plural form given by Roger Williams (1643) shows that the word is an abbreviation of *sâchimau*. The name is from the Narraganset dialect, one of the prominent phonetic peculiarities of which was the assibilation of gutturals. *Sâchimau* (=*sâtshimau*) is by assibilation of original *k* from *sâkimau*=Abnaki *sang'man* (whence, by corruption, *sagamore*)=Passamaquoddy *sogmo*=Lenape *sakimau*=Chippewa *sâgima*, all radical words—words that cannot now be referred to any known root.

The word has given rise to the adjective *sachemic*, and the substantives *sachemdom* and *sachemship* (Gookin, 1674). A Long Island serpent, probably the milk-snake, has been called *sachem-snake*. See *Chiefs, Government, Sagamore*.   (w. r. g.)

Sacheriton (*Sa-cher-i-ton*). A division of the Skoton, mentioned in the treaty of Nov. 18, 1854 (U. S. Ind. Treat., 23, 1873), as dwelling on Rogue r., Oreg.

Sâchim. See *Sachem*.

Sachuen. A Costanoan village situated in 1819 within 10 m. of Santa Cruz mission, Cal.—Taylor in Cal. Farmer, Apr. 5, 1860.

Sackagoming. See *Sagakomi*.

Sackhoes (*Sukhoos*, 'Black Kettle,' a chief's name.—Ruttenber). A Kitchawank village in 1684, on the site of Peekskill, Westchester co., N. Y.
Sackhoes.—Ruttenber, Tribes Hudson R., 79, 1872; see also Ruttenber, Ind. Geog. Names, 30, 1906. Saeckkill.—Van der Donck (1658) quoted by Ruttenber, ibid., 72.

Saclan. A former group or division of the Costanoan family inhabiting the shore of San Francisco bay, Cal., opposite San Francisco, at Oakland or somewhat to the s. They were subject to the Dolores mission. Their dialect appears to have been very different from other Costanoan dialects.
Chaclan.—Taylor in Cal. Farmer, Oct. 18, 1861. Chaclanes.—Bancroft, Hist. Cal., I, 709, 1884. Sacalanes.—Ibid. Saclan.—Arroyo de la Cuesta, Idiomas Californias, 1821, MS. trans., B. A. E. Saklans.—Choris, Voy. Pitt., 6, 1822. Soclan.—Chamisso in Kotzebue, Voy., III, 51, 1821.

Saconnet. A band or small tribe living near Sakonnet pt., Newport co., R. I., connected with the Wampanoag or the Narraganset. Under the woman chief Ashawonks they took the side of the English in King Philip's war of 1675, and from her their land was purchased by the whites. In 1700 they numbered about 400; but in 1763 they were visited by an epidemic which considerably diminished their numbers, so that by 1803 they had dwindled to a dozen persons, living near Compton. Their chief village bore the name of the tribe.   (j. m.)
Saconet.—Williams (1649) in Mass. Hist. Soc. Coll., 3d s., IX, 281, 1846. Saconnet.—Parsons, Ind. Names R. I., 25, 1861 (the point). Sagkonate.—Mass. Hist. Soc. Coll., 1st s., IX, 199, 1804. Sakonett.—Cotton (1674), ibid., I, 200, 1806. Saugkonnet.—Stiles (1672), ibid., X, 114, 1809. Scato

neck.—Doc. of 1676 quoted by Drake, Ind. Chron., 53, 1836. Seaconet.—Winslow (1676) in Mass. Hist. Soc. Coll., 4th s., v, 10, 1861. Seaconnet.—Walley (1690), ibid., 247. Seakonnet.—Ibid., 1st s., IX, 199, 1804. Seconett.—Hinckley (1682), ibid., 4th s., v, 78, 1861. Seconnett.—Mayhew (1671), ibid., 1st s., VI, 196, 1800. Sekonett.—Hinckley (1685), ibid., 4th s., v, 133, 1861. Sekunnet.—Hinckley (1685), ibid., 134. Sogkonate.—Church (1716), ibid., 1st s., IX, 199, 1804.

Sacrifice. In spite of the present very general application of this term, its original connection with religion is shown by the meaning of the word itself, "to make sacred." Instead of the simple dedication of objects to a deity or deities, however, such as this would imply, it is associated in the minds of most people with the idea of self-abnegation, or the giving up of something valuable on the part of the sacrificer. Yet this is but one of several ideas pertaining to sacrifice in the minds of primitive people, and Tylor in his standard work on Primitive Culture has put the matter in a nutshell while summing up the evolution—or perhaps we should rather say devolution—of sacrifice when he states that "the ruder conception that the deity takes and values the offering for itself, gives place on the one hand to the idea of mere homage expressed by a gift, and on the other to the negative view that the virtue lies in the worshipper depriving himself of something prized." "These ideas," he adds, "may be broadly distinguished as the gift-theory, the homage-theory, and the abnegation-theory." From what follows it will be seen that the gift-theory was the dominant one among Indian tribes, yet the ordeals of such a ceremony as the Sun-dance show plainly that the abnegation-theory occupied a prominent position in the thought of some tribes; nor can we deny that the homage-theory was also entertained, however difficult it may be to isolate it thoroughly from the others. In all this the differences in point of view between North American Indians and the lower classes of so-called civilized races on the subject of sacrifice is not very great. A far greater distinction is that between the view that sacrifice produces a change in the deity beneficial to the worshipper, and the view that sacrifice produces a beneficial change in the worshipper himself.

To understand each sacrifice properly, six questions need to be answered: (1) who sacrifices, (2) to what being or beings the sacrifice is offered, (3) the nature of the sacrifice, (4) the method of offering it, (5) the time when it was performed, and (6) its object.

In that part of North America N. of Mexico by far the greater number of sacrifices were offered by individuals, either male or female, as when bits of food were thrown into the fire during meals, or articles were laid upon sacred rocks or upon shrines. The offering of first-fruits among the Natchez was made by each father of a family, and on certain occasions when a live stag was sacrificed by the Iroquois it was the oldest man of the hut or village that gave the death-blow. At the moose feast of the Montagnais the sacrifice was made by him who had killed the animal. Among the Muskhogean tribes a special sacrifice was offered by the war leader and his religious assistant before starting out upon an expedition, and in general it may be said that the leaders of war or hunting parties took the lead also in sacrifices and all other observances having in view the success of the enterprise. But just as the Muskhogean war leader had a religious assistant to share his duties, so warriors on the N. Pacific coast were always accompanied by at least one shaman. In prescribing what offerings should be made in case of sickness, the shaman was an absolute guide, though the offerings were actually furnished by the family of the sick man and were often a mere payment to the shaman himself. Society and tribal rites and ceremonies were oftener than not themselves considered as sacrifices, and thus furnish us with examples of sacrifices participated in by large bodies of people. Not as frequently as in the Old World, and yet occasionally (witness, for instance, the White Dog ceremony of the Iroquois and the human sacrifice of the Skidi Pawnee), there is a special national sacrifice consummated by chosen individuals to whom the title of "priest" may very properly be applied.

A complete answer to the second question would necessitate a catalogue of all the superhuman beings conceived of by every Indian tribe, as well as those material beings and objects which were supposed to possess supernatural power in the slightest degree. Nevertheless it may be of interest to mention some of those of which there is direct information. The most prominent are: the sky, the earth, the sun, the moon, the four cardinal points, the winds, the thunder, the mountains, rocks of all sizes and shapes, particularly those of peculiar appearance or such as resemble things animate, certain animals and trees, springs, places where paint was obtained, eddies and rapids in rivers, and a number of monsters supposed to dwell beneath the surface of lakes, rivers, and the ocean. In the case of the natural objects mentioned, it is to be understood that it was not the object itself in any case which was thus approached, but the animating soul of each. In addition, offerings were made to personal manitos and medicine bundles by the possessors of the same, by shamans

to their guardian spirits, and even by the laity to shamans, though in this last case the shaman was perhaps considered only as an intermediary. In several cases, even by christianized Indians, sacrifices were offered to missionaries, to the crosses which they carried or set up, and to the mission churches.

The article by far the most widely used in sacrifice was native tobacco. Next came articles of food, and then articles of clothing and adornment, particularly the latter. Hunting and fishing implements are mentioned less frequently, evidently because it would be more agreeable to the deity to receive food outright than the means for obtaining it. Dogs, particularly white ones, were sacrificed by the Iroquois, Cree, Ottawa, Illinois, and related tribes, and in at least one feast by the Arikara and the Skidi Pawnee. In the buffalo country its place seems to have been taken in a measure by the buffalo, the skin of a white animal being again preferred. In one early narrative a buffalo-skin is mentioned among sacrifices offered by the Illinois, while the skull of a buffalo was hung at the top of an Arapaho medicine-lodge erected by youths just previous to their first war expedition. The greatest importance, however, seems to have been attached to it by the Mandan, who preferred the skin of a young white cow buffalo, or, failing that, the skin of a white bull or an old cow. The offal of a buffalo was sacrificed by the Arikara. Offerings of bears, or rather the skins and skulls of these animals, are referred to among the Iroquois and Algonquian tribes of the N. E. forest country, being mentioned as far w. as the Illinois. A kind of bear sacrifice also existed along the N. Pacific coast and the neighboring mountain region. Deer, elk, and moose were sacrificed by the Iroquois and Algonquian tribes of the N. and E. Deer-hoofs were held in great esteem by the N. W. tribes, and were used to make fringes for the dancing skirt or apron of a shaman; it is natural, therefore, to find them mentioned in a list of articles sacrificed by the Cœur d'Alênes. In the same list wolf-tails also occur. On the N. Pacific coast we find cuts of whale, pieces of fresh or dried fish, and grease of all kinds. A Montagnais sacrifice consisted of eels, while the Mistassin sacrificed fish-bones. Among birds the first place is taken by the eagle, which appears to have been employed everywhere, the part offered being the down, wings, or tail. Feathers of other birds, especially those of a red color, like the flicker-feathers of the N. Pacific coast, are also mentioned. In this connection reference should be made to the feathered prayer-sticks (q. v.) of the Pueblos, Navaho, and Apache. It is possible that similar devices were employed elsewhere, since Maximilian mentions in a Mandan sacrifice "little sticks or rods to which some feathers were attached." Sticks without any such attachment the Iroquois were accustomed to throw upon a certain sacred stone whenever they passed. Among Iima offerings Russell mentions twigs of the creosote bush, and small stones. Next to tobacco, corn was the most highly prized vegetal product in most of North America, and we consequently find it used in sacrifices and ceremonies by most of the agricultural tribes. Adair states that the only sacrifice of corn among the Creeks was at their annual festival which corresponds to the harvest feast, or feast of ingathering, in the Old World (see *Busk*). In some form or other it is probable that this was represented among all the corn-raising tribes of the E. and S. As might have been expected, this form of sacrifice also assumes important proportions among the tribes of the S. W.—the Pueblos, Navaho, and Apache—a constant sacrifice among them being sacred meal, while among the Pawnee of the plains mush was used. Among other sacrifices of vegetal character should be mentioned the red cedar-bark which figures so prominently in the secret-society performances of the Indians on the N. Pacific coast. A large Iroquois sacrifice, made in response to a dream, contained, among other articles, four measures of sunflower seed and as many of beans. The incense root of the Hupa should also be noted in this connection. Manufactured articles were represented by blankets, arrows, powder and lead, shell beads and articles made of them, pans, kettles, elk-skin fishing-lines, cloth of various kinds, especially red cloth, rings, bracelets, pipes, knives, wooden and clay images, guns, and hatchets. The predilection for red, already remarked in connection with feathers and cloth, finds expression also in a very wide use of red paint for sacrificial purposes. Paint, like any other article, might be offered loose to a supernatural being, but usually it was daubed upon the stone, tree, or other object to which it was desired to show respect. In their own ceremonies Dakota women use blue paint oftener than red, but this is not a constant indication of sex.

Unless the customary immolation of a number of captives at the end of a war expedition may be considered sacrificial, human sacrifices do not seem to have been particularly common N. of Mexico, though there are a number of instances. Perhaps the best known is that of the sacrifice of a female captive to the morning star by the Skidi Pawnee. An early missionary tells of the sacrifice of a female captive by the Iroquois, and states that parts of her body were sent to the other villages of the tribe to be eaten. It appears from Cuoq that the Nipissing formerly offered a young female captive upon an elevated platform as a sacrifice to "the god of war," but the wording leaves us somewhat in doubt whether the sacrifice was anything more than symbolic. In ancient times Kansa Indians put the hearts of slain foes into the fire as a sacrifice to the winds, but later, animals such as deer and grouse were substituted. The Hurons burned the viscera and a portion of the flesh of one who had been drowned or had died of a cold as a sacrifice to the Sky god, who was supposed to be angry. In 1700, when Iberville was among the Taensa villages, their temple was struck by a thunderbolt and burned, upon which five women threw their infants into the flames as a sacrifice to the offended deity, and more would have done the same had not the French interposed. On another occasion the Iroquois drove arrows into the body of a new-born babe, ground up its bones, and swallowed a little of the resultant powder before starting out to war; but this may have been a war-medicine rather than a true sacrifice. Since the highest class of nobles among the Natchez and Taensa were supposed to be of divine origin, the slaughter of a number of servants, and of other members of their families, to wait on them in the hereafter, was of the nature of a sacrifice, although of an unusual character. Another form of human sacrifice was the offering of scalps. Among the Arapaho these were hung up in the medicine lodge, and on one occasion De Smet passed a pole on the bank of the Missouri on which hung a scalp offered by the Arikara. He assumed that this was a sacrifice to the sun, but more likely it was to some river monster. At the time of the Sun-dance, pieces of flesh were cut from their bodies by the participants, offered to the sun, and then placed under a buffalo chip. In fact all the mutilations inflicted at the Sun-dance and related ceremonies, such as cutting off finger-joints and slitting the flesh for the attachment of thongs, partook of the character of sacrifices. It is said that the blood shed in tearing these thongs through the flesh was acceptable to Tiráwa, chief deity of the Pawnee. On one occasion each member of a war-party sacrificed a small piece of flesh cut from his tongue. Hair—presumably human hair—is mentioned among sacrifices offered by the Arikara and the Ntlakyapamuk, but more often it was cut or singed off out of respect for the dead. Before passing from this subject it should be noted that certain other sacrifices are believed to have been substituted for an earlier sacrifice of human beings, just as the Kansa substituted animals of various kinds for human hearts. Hewitt is of the opinion that the white dog of the Iroquois has been substituted in this way; while Fewkes regards the prayer-sticks of the S. W. as representing animals or human beings. There are many points in favor of such views, but it will not do to theorize too far on the basis of general resemblances. Finally, it is important to remark that the object of sacrifice being usually to please a supernatural being by acting in accordance with his supposed desires, it is obvious that songs, dances, feasts, and ceremonies generally may be employed for the same end and in such cases properly fall within the same category. They are viewed in this light by the Indians themselves.

The method of sacrificing depended on the nature of the sacrifice itself and the being who was supposed to receive it. Offerings were generally made to sacred stones by laying the articles on or near them, inserting them in crevices, or throwing them in their direction. As already noted, red paint was usually smeared upon objects considered sacred, and Ntlakyapamuk women always painted their faces red when they went to gather berries or to dig roots on certain mountains, or just before they came in sight of certain lakes. When mountains or rocks were close to some body of water, however, they might be considered, as among the Haida, the dwellings of subaqueous beings, and sacrifices were then thrown into the water in front of them. The Haida always placed on a paddle the articles to be sacrificed, repeated a prayer or request, and let them slide into the sea. Sacrifices to more distant beings or those not so distinctly localized were put into the fire. Sometimes, as in the case of the white dog of the Iroquois, the human victim of the Skidi, and a Muskhogean deer sacrifice mentioned by Adair, in which the animal was burned on a fire of green boughs, complete cremation took place. Usually, however, only part of the animal or article was consumed, the rest being eaten or otherwise employed or thrown away. At feasts or even ordinary repasts a little meat, fish, grease, etc., was often thrown into the fire, though sometimes merely on the ground. Among the Kiowa any drink-offering, such as water or coffee, was poured out on the ground as a sacrifice to the earth, but by the N. W. coast tribes the same thing was done for the benefit of the departed. An early missionary observes that the Hurons threw tobacco on the red-hot stones in their

sweat-lodge when bathing. Still another method of offering sacrifices was to place them on trees or poles. Dogs were hung on trees or tall poles by the central Algonquians and some of the Plains tribes, and white buffalo-skins were treated in the same manner by the Mandan and by other tribes of the northern plains. These were offered to the sun, the lord of life, or to other principal or celestial deity, but offerings were made in the same manner to beings in lakes, rivers, and springs, except that in such cases the poles were placed at the edge of the water. One case of sickness is recorded in which three dogs were hung to the door of the house as an offering for recovery. Such sacrifices, as well as those placed upon rocks and other natural features, were allowed to remain until they rotted to pieces, though they were sometimes plundered by foreign tribes and quite uniformly by white people. In other cases valuable objects were simply presented or allowed to remain for a time and afterward removed. Vessels or utensils so offered may have been regarded as lent to the deity, but in the case of food the idea was usually present that supernatural beings partook only of the spirit of the food and man could very properly devour its substance. Fewkes states this to be the belief of the Hopi; and a missionary to one of the Eastern tribes remarks that during a certain feast they would ask their deity to take food, yet offered him nothing. A large number of feasts among American Indian tribes doubtless had this communion character. In other cases the deity might be fed by placing food in the mouth of a mask representing him. At most sacrificial feasts the food was devoured by all alike. Only occasionally do we find that function appropriated by shamans, priests, or some special class of persons as was so frequently the case in the Old World. The Natchez, however, present an example to the contrary, food being taken to the temple, offered to the gods there, and then sent to the houses of the chief and his principal men. Tobacco was sometimes offered loose, but oftener in a pipe, the stem of the pipe being presented to the deity, or whiffs of smoke directed toward him, a common custom being to offer it to the four cardinal points, zenith, and nadir, successively. Even without any accompanying actions it was often supposed that the spiritual part of tobacco, when smoked ceremonially, was wafted to the presence of the gods. Powdered tobacco was sometimes blown into the air or upon some sacred object, and eagle down was treated in the same manner. Not infrequently the sacrifice bore a symbolic resemblance to the object desired by the person sacrificing. Thus the Hupa offer dry incense root upon a rock, near which dwells a being supposed to have control of the weather, when they desire the rains to cease, but incense root mixed with water when they wish the frosts to melt and disappear. In the same way Alaskan Eskimo, when animals of a certain species are scarce, offer the skin of such an animal to the moon in order that the being who resides there may send them more.

Sacrifices to rocks, rapids, eddies, and other natural features were usually made every time a person passed them, and offerings at meals and feasts were of course governed by the time these occurred, the latter being often held as the result of a dream or a vow. The white dog feast of the Iroquois was celebrated five days after the first appearance of the new moon following the winter solstice. The harvest feast of the Southern tribes and the corn-planting sacrifice of the Quapaw were in the same way dependent on the succession of the seasons, as was the Ntlakyapamuk sacrifice of the first berries of the season. Sacrifices to the thunder-beings were naturally most common during thunderstorms, and periods of want, war, or disease determined others. The Pawnee and the Creeks sacrificed part or sometimes the whole of the first buffalo or deer killed during both their summer and winter hunts. The first buffalo killed by a young Pawnee boy was also offered, and a special offering was made in this tribe when the first thunder was heard in the spring and it was known that winter was over. The Skidi Pawnee made their human sacrifice "about corn-planting time," but it was not annual. According to Cushing there was annually among the Zuñi a grand sacrifice of prayer-sticks by the "Prey Brotherhood Priesthood of the medical societies," and at the full moon of each month lesser sacrifices of the same kind by the male members of the Prey clans.

The objects for which sacrifices were made were as numerous and varied as the desires of the suppliants. The sum and substance of all was, as usual, to escape evils and secure benefits. Naturally enough, considering the economic conditions among Indian tribes, food was asked for most frequently. Second only to this came freedom from illness. Other petitions were for good weather, the cessation of storms, a calm sea, rain, good crops of corn, increase of courage and success in war, hunting, or fishing, assistance in passing rapids or dangerous reefs, and the preservation of the home and the family. A full consideration of this question, however, comes rather under the head of Prayer (q. v.).

As on mythology and prayer, a discussion of sacrifice borders closely also on mortuary customs, the shades of the dead being invoked and presented with food, clothing, etc., much as in the case of higher powers. There are many cases in which supernatural beings are said to have been men originally, but a real worship of ancestors as such appears to be altogether absent in spite of the almost divine honors which were paid dead chiefs among the Natchez. In dealing with tobacco we touch on the subject of incense, which may be defined as a sacrifice to please the sense of smell of the deity just as food pleases his palate, and songs, dances, and ceremonies please his ears and eyes. On another side we approach the question of taboos, which are nothing more or less than prohibitions against doing certain things displeasing to the gods; and we find ourselves even concerned with confession, since among the Eskimo confession of the transgression of a taboo secures immunity from its harmful consequences. Consecration confronts us in the Natchez custom of presenting seed to the temple before planting, and atonement is suggested ·by the case of the Iroquois, who, having dreamed that he had been captured and burned at the stake, assisted by his friends went through a mimic representation of burning at the stake, but substituted a dog for his own person. Finally, from the sacrifice, prayer, feast, dance, and ceremony designed to ·please, placate, and secure the interest of supernatural beings, we find ourselves passing over into the charms, magic formulæ, and observances by which it is believed that his power can be compelled almost independently of his own volition. Such a transition is indicated by the Lillooet belief that cold weather, snow, or rain may be brought on by burning the skin of an animal having control over it.

One of the best discussions of sacrifice among lower races generally is given by Tylor (Primitive Culture, II, 375–410). Material regarding American tribes in particular must be gathered from a large number of works, of which the following are a few: Reports of the Bureau of American Ethnology, Smithsonian Institution, and National Museum; Contributions to North American Ethnology, IX; Memoirs and Bulletins of the American Museum of Natural History; University of California Publications in American Archæology and Ethnology; Reports of the Peabody Museum of Harvard University; American Anthropologist (old and new series); Journal of American Folk-lore; Reports of the Committee of the British Association for the Advancement of Science to investigate the Northwestern Tribes of Canada, and Reports of the

Ethnological Survey of Canada; Transactions of the Royal Society of Canada; Transactions of the Canadian Institute; Jesuit Relations; Thwaites, Early Western Travels; Gatschet, Creek Migration Legend, 1884–88; Adair, History of the American Indians, 1775; Curtis, North American Indian, i–v, 1907–09. (J. R. S.)

Sacsiol. A Chumashan village formerly near Purísima mission, Santa Barbara co., Cal.—Taylor in Cal. Farmer, Oct. 18, 1861.

Sacspili. A Chumashan village formerly near Purísima mission, Santa Barbara co., Cal.—Taylor in Cal. Farmer, Oct. 18, 1861.

Sadammo. Given by Jesus María (Relacion, MS., 1691) as a synonym for Apache. Jesus María and Belisle (Margry, Déc., vi, 344, 1886) evidently heard the same name for Apache when among the Hasinai of Texas. La Harpe, however, makes Sadamons synonymous with Toyals, which would seem to have been a Tonkawa tribe. Perhaps it was a general term for the hostile tribes N. and W. of the Hasinai.
Sadammo.—Jesus María, op. cit. Sadamon.—Belisle, op. cit. Sadamons.—La Harpe, Jour. Hist., 271, 1831. Sadujames.—Rivera, Diario, leg. 2763, 1736.

Sadaues. A former rancheria connected with Dolores mission, San Francisco, Cal.

Sadekanaktie. A principal Onondaga chief and speaker, first mentioned at a council at Onondaga, N. Y., Jan. 29, 1690. His name is variously spelled, and was the national council name. He was speaker at Albany, Feb. 25, 1693, and then announced Gov. Fletcher's name of Cayenquiragoe, or Swift Arrow. He was prominent in the councils of 1698 and 1699, and went to Albany in 1700 through fear of poisoning. Colden thought his lameness a convenient excuse, but he was carried into a council in 1693 by four men. Sakoghsinnakichte (a fuller form of the name) died in 1701, and at his condolence in June another chief bearing the same name was nominated. His name appears in many forms, including Adaquarande, Adaquarondo, Aqueendera, Aqueendero, Aqtienderonde, Kaqueendera, Kaqueendero, Sadaganacktie, Sadeganaktie, Sadeganastie, Sadegeenaghtie, Sadekanaktie, Sakoghsinnakichte, Sudagunachte. (W. M. B.)

Sadekanaktie. An Onondaga chief who succeeded another of that name in 1701, and signed the Beaver land deed of that year and its renewal in 1726. In the first the name is written Sadeganastic; in the second, Sadegeenaghtie, Wolf tribe, his totem being a bent arrow. He made two long speeches at Albany in Aug. 1710, when he was called Kaquendero, but he was not so prominent in council as his predecessor had been. (W. M. B.)

Sadjugahl-lanas (*Sᵉadjū'gal lā'nas*). A family of the Eagle clan of the Haida. They claim to be descended from a woman named Hehlu-keingans, along with the Kona-kegawai, Djiguaahl-lanas, Stawashaidagai, and Kaiahl-lanas. Until recently they did not stand very high in the social scale, but owing to his personal popularity their chief in 1901 had become town chief of Masset. This family is said to have had 4 unnamed subdivisions.—Swanton, Cont. Haida, 275, 1905.
Sahājūgwan alth Lennas.—Harrison in Proc. Roy. Soc. Can., sec. ii, 125, 1895. Sg·adzē'guatl lā'nas.—Boas, Twelfth Report N. W. Tribes of Canada, 23, 1898.

Safiata. See *Sabeata.*

Sagadahoc (Abnaki: *Saⁿgedéhok,* 'at the river mouth or outflow.'—Gerard). A village at the mouth of Kennebec r., in Sagadahoc co., Me., in 1614. Kendall, about 1807, found some Indians living at St Francis, Canada, who said they had formerly lived at the mouth of the Kennebec. They were probably a part of the Wewenoc or Arosaguntacook.
Ozanghe'darankiac.—Kendall, Trav., iii, 144, 1809. Sagadahock.—Smith (1631) in Mass. Hist. Soc. Coll., 3d s., iii, 22, 1833. Zanghe'darankiac.—Kendall, op. cit.

Sagaiguninini ('lake people', from *sagaïgŭn* 'lake', *ĭnĭnĭ* 'man'). A tribe which lived s. w. of Ottawa r., Ontario, about 1640.
Sagachiganirini8ek.—Jes. Rel. for 1646, 34, 1858. Sagahiganirini.—Jes. Rel. for 1640, 34, 1858. Sāgaïganinini.—Wm. Jones, inf'n, 1906 (correct form). Sakahiganiriouek.—Jes. Rel. for 1648, 62, 1858.

Sagakomi. The name of a certain smoking mixture, or substitute for tobacco, applied also to the bearberry bush (*Arctostaphylos uva-ursi*) or other shrubs the leaves and bark of which are used for the same purpose. The word, which has come into English through Canadian French, is not, as some have supposed (Richardson, Arctic Exped., ii, 303, 1851), a corruption of the *sac-à-commis* of the voyageurs and coureurs de bois of the N. W., but is of Algonquian origin. It is derived from *sagákomin,* which, in Chippewa and closely related dialects, signifies 'smoking-leaf berry.' The form *sagakomi* occurs in Lahontan (Voy., ii, 53, 1703) and other writers of the early years of the 18th century. (A. F. C.)

Sagamite. A porridge of boiled corn, a favorite dish of the early settlers, derived from the Indians. The word occurs early in Canadian French, being found in Sagard-Théodat (1632), and survives still in Louisiana, whither it was carried from New France. As Cuoq (Lex. Algonq., 15, 1886) points out, the term never meant 'soup' or 'porridge' in the language from which it was taken. The word *kisagamite* signifies in Nipissing, Chippewa, and closely related Algonquian dialects, 'the broth (*agami*) is hot' (*kisâgamitew,* 'it is a hot liquid'—Baraga). In English the word occurs also as *sagamity*, as in Lewis and Clark (Trav., III, 2, 1817). (A. F. C.)

Sagamore. A corruption of *sang'man*, the Abnaki name for the chief or ruler of a tribe, the dignity of which was elective, the choice usually falling on an individual who was at the head of a prominent clan. Other spellings are *sagomoh* (Rosier, 1603), *sogomo, sagomo, sagamo,* and *sagamour*. (2) A term applied by early writers to the lesser sachems among the Massachuset Indians. Josselyn uses the word *sagamorship* (of which he apparently was the author) as a synonym for sachemship. See *Chiefs, Government, Sachem*. (W. R. G.)

Sagangusili (*Sᵉagā'ñusĭlĭ*). A family belonging to the Raven clan of the Haida. They lived at one time in Naden harbor, Queen Charlotte ids., Brit. Col., and are said to have been related to the Skidaokao.—Swanton, Cont. Haida, 271, 1905. Sahāḡungūsilĭ.—Harrison in Proc. Roy. Soc. Can., 125, 1895. Sg·āḡa'ngsilai.—Boas, Twelfth Rep. N. W. Tribes Can., 23, 1898.

Sagarissa. See *Sakarissa*.

Sagaunash ('Englishman'). A mixedblood Potawatomi chief, better known as Billy Caldwell, born in Canada about 1780. His father, according to report, was an Irish officer in the British service, and his mother a Potawatomi. Sagaunash was educated in Roman Catholic schools, learned to write English and French with facility, and was master of several Indian dialects. From 1807 to the battle of the Thames in Oct. 1813, he was in the British interest and was intimately associated with Tecumseh, whose secretary he is said to have been. After the battle referred to he transferred his allegiance to the United States, establishing his residence at Chicago in 1820. In 1826 he held the office of justice of the peace, and during the Winnebago excitement of 1827 was, with Shabonee, of great service to the Americans. His wife was a daughter of Neescotnemeg. Sagaunash died at Council Bluffs, Iowa, Sept. 28, 1841, aged about 60 years. (C. T.)

Sagavok. A Netchilirmiut Eskimo village on Boothia penin., s. of Felix harbor. Sagavoq—Boas in 6th Rep. B. A. E., map, 1888. Shag-a-voke.—Ross, Second Voy., 324, 1835.

Sagawamick. (Chippewa: *Shâgawámika*, 'there is a long shallow place in the lake'; probably a contraction of *Shâgawámikang*, 'at the long shallow place in the lake.'—Gerard. The principal village of the Misisagaikaniwininiwak, or Mille Lac band of Chippewa, numbering about 300 persons, situated on the s. shore of Mille Lac, Minn., and during the month of May 1900, consisting of about 30 matcovered wigwams. The village occupies the site of an ancient settlement of the Mdewakanton (q. v.), who occupied the country until they were driven southward

by the Chippewa, probably about the middle of the 18th century. Near the village is a group of more than 60 burial mounds, which, together with fragments of pottery and implements of stone and copper found upon the surface, was considered by the Chippewa to have been of Mdewakanton origin. The Chippewa at the present time utilize these mounds as burial places for their own dead, and on the top and sides of one were 13 ancient graves. Deeply worn trails lead from Sagawamick toward the E., S., and W., and the indications are that the site has long been occupied. (D. I. B.) Sa-ga-wah-mick.—Bushnell in Science, 408, Sept. 23, 1904.

Sagdlet. A Danish station and Eskimo village on an island off the s. w. coast of Greenland, lat. 60° 15'.—Meddelelser om Grönland, XVI, map, 1896.

Sagdlirmiut. An exceedingly primitive Eskimo tribe, having had little intercourse with neighboring people, formerly inhabiting Southampton id. and the islands of Fox basin (Boas in 6th Rep. B. A. E., 444, 451, 1888). In 1900 they were estimated to number about 300, but owing to the establishment of a whaling station on their island soon afterward and the introduction of outside natives with modern guns and superior appliances, by which the food supply of the islanders was quickly destroyed, the Sagdlirmiut became extinct by the spring of 1903 (Boas in Am. Anthr., VI, 746, 1904). Sead-ler-me-oo.—Parry, Second Voy., 250, 464, 1824.

Sagem. See *Sachem*.

Sagenomnas. A tribe of California, apparently of the central portion, and probably about San Joaquin r. It belonged either to the Yokuts (Mariposan) or to the Moquelumnan family. Sage-nom-nas.—Johnston in Sen. Ex. Doc. 61, 32d Cong., 1st sess., 20, 1852. Sage-nom-nis.—Ryer in Sen. Ex. Doc. 4, 32d Cong., spec. sess., 199, 1853.

Sagewenenewak (contr. and abbrev. of Chippewa *Sâginawĭnĭnĭwäk*, 'people of the river-mouth.'—Gerard. See *Saginaw*). A Chippewa division living at the mouth of Red r., Manitoba. Sâgĕ Wenenewak.—Long, Exped. St Peters R., II, 153, 1824. Sāgitawāwininiwag.—Wm. Jones, inf'n, 1906 (correct name).

Saghwareesa. A Tuscarora chief. Conrad Weiser placed him in his list of influential men in 1752, styling him "the wisest and best Daniel," and calling him Achsaquareesory. He was at Ganatisgoa in the same year, and in 1753 appeared in Pennsylvania. In 1755 he was styled Segwarusa, chief of the Tuscarora; in the following year as Sequareesa—the most frequent form. He had a conference with Sir William Johnson at Oneida lake in 1761, was at Onondaga in the same year, and signed the Ft Stanwix treaty in 1768. Zeisberger called him

Shequallisere in 1752. Several chiefs bore the same name. Cf. *Sakarissa, Sequareesere.* (w. m. b.)

Sagi ('bear'). A Yuchi clan.

Sag⁸ĕ'.—Speck, Yuchi Inds., 70, 1906. Sagí tahá.— Gatschet, Uchee MS., B. A. E., 70, 1885 (= 'bear gens').

Sagin. A Costanoan village situated in 1819 within 10 m. of Santa Cruz mission, Cal.—Taylor in Cal. Farmer, Apr. 5, 1860.

Saginaw (*Sâginawa*, 'mouth of a river.' — Gerard. Cf. *Saguenay*). A former village situated near the present Saginaw, Mich. It was first occupied by the Sauk, and when deserted by that tribe it was settled by a band of Ottawa and Chippewa, known as Saginaw, who continued to reside there until 1837, when they removed beyond the Mississippi. The term was also officially employed to designate all the Chippewa of eastern lower Michigan from Thunder bay southward. (J. M.)

Osaginang.—Kelton, Ft. Mackinac, 9, 1884 (Chippewa name). Osāgināwᵉ.—Wm. Jones, inf'n, 1906. Sacenong.—N. Y. Doc. Col. Hist., IX, 293, note, 1855. Saganaws.—Detroit treaty (1837) in U. S. Ind. Treat., 248,1873. Sagina.—Croghan (1765) in N. Y. Doc. Col. Hist., VII, 784, 1856. Sāginãng.— Wm. Jones, inf'n, 1905 (correct form). Saginaw.— Detroit treaty (1855) in U. S. Ind. Treat., 234, 1873. Saguina.—Detroit treaty (1807) in Am. St. Papers, Ind. Aff., I, 747, 1832. Saguinam.—Doc. of 1747 in N. Y. Doc. Col. Hist., x, 119, 1858. Saguinan.— Denonville (1686), ibid., IX, 295, 1855. Saguinau.— Doc. of 1747, ibid., x, 128, 1858. Sakiman.— Denonville (1688), ibid., IX, 378, 1855. Sakinam.— Hennepin, New Discov., 83, 1698. Sakinan.—Doc. of 1695 in N. Y. Doc. Col. Hist., IX, 604, 1855. Saki- nang.—Frontenac (1690), ibid., 450. Saquinam.— Memoir of 1718, ibid., 888. Saquinan.—Denonville (1686), ibid., 293. Sau-ge-nong.—Tanner, Narr,. 30, 1830. Saw-ge-nong.—Ibid., 239.

Sagnitaouigama. An Algonkin tribe or band living in 1640 s. w. of Ottawa r. in Ontario (Jes. Rel. 1640, 34, 1868). They were possibly the same as the Sinago.

Sagonaquade ('he angers them'), commonly known as Albert Cusick. A descendant of the Tuscarora chief Nicholas Cusick, but an Onondaga by mother-right. He was born on the Tuscarora res., N. Y., Dec. 25, 1846, and lost his chiefship through being a Christian. He has aided various workers in linguistics and folk-lore, and Horatio Hale esteemed him highly. He was ordained deacon by Bishop Huntington, Oct. 1, 1891, and still lives (1909) on the Onondaga res., N. Y., where he is influential for good. His notes on Indian life are of high value to ethnology. (w. m. b.)

Sagoquas. A Massachuset village s. of Cohasset, Norfolk co., Mass., in 1614.— Smith (1616) in Mass. Hist. Soc. Coll., 3d s., VI, 97, 1837.

Sagua-lanas (*Sa'gua lā'nas*, 'people of the town up the inlet'). A family of the Eagle clan of the Haida. The inlet referred to in their name is probably Virago sd. or Naden harbor. They are said to have branched off from the Tohlka-gitunai, but were afterward so closely asso-

ciated with the Stustas as to be usually regarded among the Stustas families. Their town was Kung, at the entrance of Naden harbor. A subdivision was called Dotuskustl.—Swanton, Cont. Haida, 275, 1905.

Sa'gua lā'nas.—Swanton, op. cit. Sak'lā'nas.— Boas, Twelfth Rep. N. W. Tribes Can., 22, 1898. Shāgwau Lennas.—Harrison in Roy. Soc. Can., sec. II, 124, 1895.

Saguarichic (probably 'place of the saguaro,' or giant cactus). A Tarahumare settlement near San Francisco de Borja, in the district of Iturbide, Chihuahua, Mexico.—Orozco y Berra, Geog.,323,1864; Censo del Estado de Chihuahua, 1904.

Saguenay (French corruption of *Sâginawa*, 'river-mouth,' variously spelled *sagina, saguinau,* and *saguina.*—Gerard. Cf. *Saginaw*). A group of Nascapee bands that lived on Saguenay r., Quebec.

Saguenay.—Dutch map (1616) in N. Y. Doc. Col. Hist., I, 1856. Saquenets.—French writer in Me. Hist. Soc. Coll., VI, 212, 1859.

Sagui-gitunai (*Saguî' gîtAnā'-i*, 'GitAns living up the inlet'). A family of the Eagle clan of the Haida. They originally formed one family with the Djahuigitinai, but separated from them on account of some internal differences and settled in Masset inlet; hence their name. They occupied half of the town of Kayang, just above Masset. A part of them was called Kialdagwuns.—Swanton, Cont. Haida, 274, 1905.

Saguî' gîtAnā'-i.—Swanton, op. cit. Saqguî' gyit'- inai'.—Boas, Twelfth Rep. N. W. Tribes Can., 23, 1898. Shāgwikitonĕ.—Harrison in Proc. Roy. Soc. Can., sec. II, 125, 1895.

Saguikun-lnagai (*Saguîkun lnagā'-i*, 'up the inlet point-town people'). A branch of a Haida family called Kunalanas, belonging to the Raven clan.—Swanton, Cont. Haida, 271, 1905.

Sagunte. A former village, presumably Costanoan, connected with Dolores mission, San Francisco, Cal.—Taylor in Cal. Farmer, Oct. 18, 1861.

Sagwaycangwalaghtton. See *Sayenquenaghta.*

Sa-haidagai (*Sa xā'-idAga-i*, 'people living on the high ground'). A subdivision of the Stawas-haidagai, a family of the Eagle clan of the Haida, so called from the nature of the ground on which their houses stood.—Swanton, Cont. Haida, 273, 1905.

Saheoquiaudonqui. See *Sequidongquee.*

Sahewamish. A Salish division on Hammersly inlet, at the s. end of Puget sd., Wash. Not to be confused with the Sawamish.

Sahawahmish.—Stevens in H. R. Ex. Doc. 37, 34th Cong.,3d sess.,45,1857. Sa-heh-wamish.—U.S. Ind. Treaties, 561,1873. Sahewamish.—Gibbs quoted by Dall in Cont. N. A. Ethnol., I, 241, 1877. Sahhih- wish.—Ind. Aff. Rep. 1856, 265, 1857. Say-hah-ma- mish.—Schoolcraft, Ind. Tribes, IV, 600, 1854. Say- hay-ma-mish.—Starling in Ind. Aff. Rep., 170, 1852. Sayhaynamish.—Lane in Sen. Ex. Doc. 52, 31st Cong., 1st sess., 173, 1850. Sayhaywamish.—DeHarley quoted by Schoolcraft, op. cit., V, 700, 1855. **Se-hĕhwa-mish.**—Tolmie quoted by Gibbs in Pac. R. R. Rep., I, 434, 1855.

Sahldungkun (*Sᵉā'ĭdʌñ kun*). A former town of the Sagui-gitunai family of the Haida, on the w. side of Yagun r., at its mouth.—Swanton, Cont. Haida, 281, 1905.

Sahtlilkwu (*Saht-lil-kwu*). An Okinagan band in Washington.—Gibbs in Pac. R. R. Rep., I, 413, 1855.

Sahuaripa ('at the [place of the] saguaro,' referring to the *Cereus giganteus*). A former Jova pueblo, containing also some Opata and Eudeve, situated on an E. branch of Yaqui r., lat. 29° 30', lon. 109°, Sonora, Mexico. It was the seat of a Spanish mission founded in 1627. Pop. 682 in 1678; 150 in 1730. The inhabitants, also called Sahuaripa, probably spoke a language slightly differing from Opata proper. Sahuaripa is now a civilized community of nearly 3,000 inhabitants.

Saguaripa.—Zapata (1678) in Doc. Hist. Mex., 4th s., III, 342, 1857. Sahuaripa.—Rivera (1730) quoted by Bancroft, No. Mex. States, I, 513, 1884. Samaripa.—Zapata, op. cit., 341 (misprint). Santa María de los Angeles de Saguaripa.—Zapata, op. cit., 344. Sauaripa.—Early doc. quoted by Bandelier in Arch. Inst. Papers, III, 56, 1890. Sta María Sahuaripa.—Catálogo (1658) quoted by Bancroft, No. Mex. States, I, 245, 1884.

Saia. The name which the Hupa employ, when speaking to white people, to designate the Athapascans to the S. of themselves, on Mad r. and the tributaries of Eel r., Cal. Through misunderstanding this name was given these people when they were taken prisoners by the military in 1862 and removed to a reservation on Smith r., in what is now Del Norte co., where some of them remained until that reservation was abandoned in 1868. They were then removed to Hupa valley, where, ill-treated by the Hupa, they eked out a pitiful existence for 10 years, finally drifting back to their old neighborhood. They closely resembled the Wailaki in language and customs. Spalding (Ind. Aff. Rep., 82, 1870) gave their population as 27 men and 46 women. In 1877 they were nearly extinct. They were once among the bravest of the California Indians. (P. E. G.)

Noan'-kakhl.—Powers in Cont. N. A. Ethnol., III, 124, 1877 (Wailaki name). Sai'-az.—Ibid., 122. Siahs.—Gibbs in Schoolcraft, Ind. Tribes, III, 139, 1853. Sians.—Ibid. Siaws.—Spalding in Ind. Aff. Rep., 82, 1870. S-yars.—Stevens in Ind. Aff. Rep., 132, 1867.

Saikez. A Takulli village, probably of the Tatshiautin, s. of Nechaco r., Brit. Col., about lat. 53° 55' N., lon. 124° w.

Sai'kaz.—Morice in Trans. Roy. Soc. Can., X, 109, 1892. Sy-ous.—Harmon, Jour., 202, 1820.

Sailupsun. A body of Salish of Cowichan agency, Brit. Col.; pop. 69 in 1896, including the Puntlatsh and Comox, but no longer separately enumerated.

Pail-uk-sun.—Can. Ind. Aff. 1894, 278, 1895. Sailk-sun.—Ibid., 1884, 188, 1885. Sail-up-sun.—Ibid., 1895, 360, 1896.

Saint. For additional saint names, see the Synonymy at the end of this volume.

Saint Andre. A dependency of the Mission des Apôtres which was founded in 1640 and abandoned in the following year; situated in one of the 9 towns of the Tionontati, an Iroquoian tribe inhabiting the hill country s. and s. w. of Nottawasaga bay, in Grey, Bruce, and Huron counties, Ontario. The only known reference to this mission is given in the Jesuit Relation for 1640, 95, ed. 1858.

Saint Anne. A Malecite mission in 1760 on an island in St John r., near the present Frederickton, N. B.—Shea, Cath. Miss., 154, 1855.

Saint Antoine. A Huron village in 1640, and one of the dependencies of Mission de la Conception, established among the Bear tribe; situated probably in Simcoe co., Ontario (Jes. Rel. 1640, 78, 1858). Nothing is known of its history or of its exact position. (J. N. B. H.)

Saint Augustine. A Nascapee and Montagnais station at the mouth of St Augustine r., on the N. shore of St Lawrence gulf, Quebec.

Sainte Elisabeth. An Algonquian village among the Hurons in Ontario in the 17th century.

Saincte Elizabeth.—Jes. Rel. 1640, 90, 1858.

Saint Francis. A Catholic mission village, occupied principally by Abnaki, on St Francis r., near Pierreville, Yamaska district, Quebec. After the removal of the Christian Indians hither from Chaudiere r. they received constant accessions from the Abnaki and Pennacook, especially the former, who had been driven out of New England by the advance of the English settlements. After the death of Père Rasles in 1724 the greater part of the Abnaki fled to St Francis, which thus became an Abnaki village. The Arosaguntacook acquired the leading position, and their dialect is that now used in the village. At the beginning of the French and Indian war in 1754 a large number of the hostile Scaticook joined the settlement. As the St Francis Indians had been driven from their homes, they retaliated upon the New England settlers at every opportunity and soon became noted as the bitterest enemies of the English colonies. In 1759 a force was organized and sent under Maj. Rogers against the village, which then contained about 700 inhabitants. St Francis was surprised and burned, 200 of the Indians—men, women, and children—being killed, and the remainder scattered. These afterward returned, and the village was rebuilt, but the fall of the French power in America put an end to further hostility on the part of the Indians. A number of them joined the British forces in the Revolution, and again in the War of 1812.

They numbered 360 in 1821, 387 in 1858, 335 in 1908, and 293 in 1909. They still spend a great part of their time in hunting, as well as in making and selling baskets, moccasins, and other Indian wares. See *Missions*. (J. M.)

Alsigôntegok.—J. D. Prince, inf'n, 1905 (present Abnaki name). Arsikantekok.—Ibid. (old Abnaki name). Nessa8akamíghé.—Rasles (1691), Abnaki Dict., 458, 1833 ('where fish is dried by smoke': Abnaki name). Saint-François.—Kendall, Trav., II, 53, 1809. S. François de Sales.—Le Sueur (1734) quoted by Kendall, ibid., 294. St. Francis.—Chauvignerie (1736) in N. Y. Doc. Col. Hist., IX, 1052, 1855. St. Francis de Sales.—Shea, Cath. Miss., 142, 1855. St. Francoi.—Clinton (1745) in N. Y. Doc. Col. Hist., VI, 281, 1855. St. François.—Albany conf. (1724), ibid., V, 713, 1855. Saint François du Lac.—Jes. Rel., LXXI, 311, 1901. Skensowahneronon.—Cuoq., Lex., 155, 1882 ('people at St Francis,' from *skensowah*, a corruption of St François, *ne* 'at', *ronon* 'people': Caughnawaga name). Za Plasua.—Wzokhilain quoted by Pilling, Bibl. Algonq. Lang., 539, 1891 (Abnaki pronunciation of "St. Francis").

Saint Francis. A mission village founded in 1683 by some Algonkin and Montagnais converts from Sillery at the falls of Chaudiere r., Beauce district, Quebec. They were soon joined by the remaining inhabitants of Sillery, which was then abandoned. In 1700 they removed to the new village.

St. françois de Sales.—Jes. Rel., LXIII, 123, 1901.

Saint Francis. A Menominee mission established in 1844 on Wolf r. or L. Poygan, Winnebago co., Wis., and abandoned in 1852 on the removal of the tribe to a reservation in Shawano co., where the new mission of St Michael was established.

Saint Francis Xavier. A French Catholic mission established by Bruyas in 1667 at the Oneida village of Ganowarohare.

Saint Francis Xavier. A Jesuit mission established by Allouez in 1669 at a village of Miami and Mascoutens on Fox r., Wis., near De Pere, Brown co., where the Mascoutens had a village a few m. from Green bay. Among the Indians attached to it were Miami, Mascoutens, Illinois, Kickapoo, Sauk, Foxes, Potawatomi, and Winnebago.

Saint Francis Xavier. A former mission, established in 1852 among the Chippewa on Mille Lacs, Aitkin co., Minn.

Mascoutens.—Shea, Cath. Miss., 372, 1855.

Saint George. An Aleut village on St George id., Pribilof group, Alaska. The inhabitants, who tend the fur seals, were brought originally from Atka and Unalaska. Pop. 88 in 1880, 92 in 1890. See Petroff, 10th Census, Alaska, 23, 1884.

Saint Helena. A large island off the coast of Beaufort co., S. C., taking its name from the Spanish post of Santa Elena established there by Menendez in 1566. The Indians were among those known collectively as Cusabo (q. v.), and were probably of the Muskhogean stock. In 1684 "the queen of St Helena" made sale of lands to the English. (J. M.)

Saint Ignace. A Huron mission established by Marquette in 1670 on Mackinac id., Mich., but which was removed soon after to Pt Ignace, on the mainland to the N.

St. Ignatius.—Shea, Cath. Miss., 364, 1855.

Saint Jacques. A Jesuit mission established about 1670 among the Mascoutens, Illinois, Kickapoo, Miami, and Wea, about the site of Berlin, Wis.

Saint Jacques.—Lamberville (1673) in Jes. Rel., LVIII, 21, 1899.

Saint Jacques. A former village of the Tionontati (q. v.) in Ontario.

Sainct Iacques.—Jes. Rel. 1640, 95, 1858.

Saint Jacques et Saint Philippe. A village of the Tionontati (q. v.) in Ontario in 1640.

sainct Iacques et sainct Philippe.—Jes. Rel. 1640, 95, 858.

Saint Jean. The chief town of the Wolf clan or phratry of the Tionontati in 1649, in which the Jesuit fathers had maintained a mission for some years; situated probably in the hill country of Bruce co., Ontario, on the E. frontier of the Tionontati territory, fronting their enemies, the Iroquois. According to the Jesuit Relation for 1650 (p. 8, ed. 1858) this town contained 500 or 600 families, which, following the rate of $7\frac{1}{2}$ to 8 persons to a family (ibid., p. 3), would give a total population of 3,750 to 4,800, apparently a rather high estimate. In Nov. 1649 the Jesuit fathers then resident on Christian id., Georgian bay, Canada, learned from two Huron converts who had just escaped from a band of 300 Iroquois warriors that the enemy was undecided whether to attack the Tionontati or the Jesuit fathers and their converts on the island. This information was conveyed to the Tionontati, who received the news with joy, for, exulting in their prowess, they regarded the hostile troop as already conquered. Having awaited the attack of the Iroquois for some days, the Tionontati, and especially the men of St Jean, resolved, on Dec. 5, to go against the enemy lest they escape; but the Iroquois having learned from two captives the practically defenseless condition of St Jean, hastened to attack it before the return of its warriors, whom they had failed to meet. On Dec. 7 they appeared before the town, set fire to the bark cabins, and slaughtered the defenseless inhabitants. According to the Jesuit Relation for 1650, Father Garnier refused to attempt to escape, but ran everywhere to give absolution to the Christians he met, and to seek in the burning cabins the children, the sick, and the neophytes, whom he baptized. While thus engaged he was shot twice, and later his skull was crushed by hatchet blows. In the Récit d'un Ami de l'Abbé de Gallinée (Margry, Déc., I, 366, 1875) it is said that before being killed, Father Garnier shot 3 Iroquois with a gun. Two days later the Tionontati warriors returned to find their town in ashes, and the mutilated bodies of their people. This disaster caused them to abandon their country. (J. N. B. H.)

Saint Jean Baptiste. A mission in Ontario about 1640, visited by the Hurons and Totontaratonhronon.

S. Iean Baptiste.—Jes. Rel. 1640, 90, 1858.

Saint Joachim. A mission village among the Hurons in Ontario in 1640.

S. Ioachim.—Jes. Rel. 1640, 90, 1858.

Saint Joseph. A Cayuga mission established in New York by the French in 1668.—Shea, Cath. Miss., 261, 1855.

Saint Joseph. A Potawatomi mission established by Allouez about 1688 on St Joseph r., near the s. end of L. Michigan. The mission and the river gave rise to the designation "Saint Joseph Indians," and "Potawatomis of St. Joseph's." See Shea, Cath. Miss., 375, 1855; Croghan (1765) in N. Y. Doc. Col. Hist., VII, 786, 1856.

Saint Mark. A mission established by Allouez about 1670 among the Foxes of Wolf r., Wis.—Shea, Cath. Miss., 365, 1855.

Saint Mary. A former Potawatomi mission and village on the N. bank of Kansas r., in Pottawatomie co. Kan. The mission was established by the Jesuits on Pottawatomie cr., Miami co., in 1838, but was removed to Linn co. in the following year, thence in 1847–48 to its final site. Under the act of Nov. 15, 1861, 320 acres of land, including the church, schools, and fields, were set apart for the mission's use. It continued to be a mission school until 1869.

Saint Michael. A town on an island of the same name, s. coast of Norton sd., Alaska, where the Russians in 1833 established a stockaded post. Pop. 109 in 1880, 101 in 1890.

Michaelovski Redoubt.—Dall, Alaska, 9, 1870. Redoubt St. Michael.—Baker, Geog. Dist. Alaska, 543, 1906.

Saint Michael. A Jesuit mission existing in 1658 at a Potawatomi village in s. Wisconsin, containing about 3,000 inhabitants, including about 500 fugitive Tionontati.

Saint-Michel.—Jes. Rel. 1658, 21, 1858.

Saint Michael. A Menominee mission established in 1852 on Shawano lake, Shawano co., Wis., on the removal of the tribe from Poygan lake.—Shea, Cath. Miss., 393, 1855. See *Saint Francis.*

Saint Michaels. A Franciscan mission among the Navaho in the N. E. corner of Arizona, just s. of the Navaho res. line, about 3 m. w. of the New Mexico boundary, and 27 m. N. w. of Gallup, N. Mex. It is situated in a well-watered valley called by the Navaho Tsohotso ('large meadow'), and by the early Spaniards Cienega Amarilla ('yellow swamp', or 'yellow meadow'), probably on account of the numerous yellow flowers that flourish there toward the end of summer. The mission had its inception in 1896, when the site was purchased for $3,000 by the late Rev. J. A. Stephan, director of the Bureau of Catholic Indian Missions, with funds supplied by Rev. Mother Katharine Drexel, foundress of the Sisters of the Blessed Sacrament. On Oct. 13, 1897, Rev. Juvenal Schnorbus was placed in charge, assisted by Rev. Anselm Weber, and the lay-brother Placidus Buerger. Arriving at Tsohotso, Oct. 11, 1898, the fathers changed the name to St Michaels, and almost immediately the task of reducing the Navaho language to writing was begun. In 1900 Father Schnorbus was transferred to Cincinnati, Father Weber becoming his successor, with Rev. Leopold Ostermann and Rev. Berard Haile as assistants. In May 1901 Mother Katharine purchased two ranches contiguous to the mission for $4,000, increasing the mission lands to 440 acres, about one-half of which is suitable for agriculture. In March of the following year the erection of a commodious school building was commenced, and was finished in December, with accommodations for 150 pupils. Much of the laboring work in connection with the new building was done by the Indians. At the time of the opening 57 pupils were enrolled; the next year there were 87, in 1906 the number had increased to 118, and in 1908 to 127. The pupils are instructed in the Christian faith in their own tongue by the fathers. A community of 13 Sisters of the Blessed Sacrament have charge of the school and are making marked progress, the Navaho children bearing fair comparison with white children in intelligence. At the present writing (1908) more than 100 children at their own request and with the consent of their parents were baptized after due instruction. In 1903 a new residence and a chapel were erected, and a post-office has been established at the mission. A Navaho ethnologic dictionary, by the fathers, was published by the St Michaels Press in 1910.

Saint Paul. An Aleut village on the Pribilof id. of that name, settled with natives of other islands employed in caring for the fur seals. Pop. 298 in 1880, 244 in 1890. See Petroff, 10th Census, Alaska, 23, 1884.

Saint Regis. A settlement of Catholic Iroquois, situated on the s. bank of the St Lawrence, at the boundary between the United States and Canada, with a reservation extending several miles along the river on both sides of the line. They call the place Akwesasne, 'where the partridge drums,' referring to sounds made by a cascade at that point. The village was established about 1755, during the French and Indian war, by a party of Catholic Iroquois from Caughnawaga,

Quebec, and it became the seat of the Jesuit mission of Saint Francis Regis. The village rapidly increased in population, and in 1806 received a considerable part of those who had been driven from Oswegatchie. When the boundary between the two countries was surveyed the village was found to be thereon, and since then a part of the reservation has been under control of the United States, while the rest is under the Canadian government. The St Regis Indians numbered 2,850 in 1909, having 1,501 in Quebec and 1,349 in New York. They have sometimes been known as "Praying Indians," and formed a part of the "Seven Nations of Canada." 　　　　(J. M.)

Aghquessaine.—Ft Stanwix Treaty (1768) in N. Y. Doc. Col. Hist., VIII, 129, 1857. **Aghquissasne.**—Johnson (1763), ibid., VII, 582, 1856. **Ah-qua-sos′-ne.**—Morgan, League Iroq., 474, 1851. **Akusash-rónu.**—Gatschet, Caughnawaga MS., B. A. E.,

CHARLES WHITE, A SAINT REGIS CHIEF

1882 (Caughnawaga name for tribe). **Akwe-sasne.**—Cuoq, Lex. Iroquois, 2, 1883 (Caughnawaga name). **Aquasasne.**—Shea, Cath. Miss., 339, 1855. **Oughquissasnies.**—Johnson (1775) in N. Y. Doc. Col. Hist., VIII, 660, 1857 (the band). **Qua-sos-ne.**—Morgan, League Iroq., map, 1851. **St. Bigin.**—Writer of 1756 in N. Y. Doc. Col. Hist., X, 405, 1858 (misprint). **Saint Francis Regis.**—Shea, Cath. Miss., 340, 1855. **St. Regis.**—Pouchot map (1758), in N. Y. Doc. Col. Hist., x. 694, 1855. **Wakui-saskeóno.**—Gatschet, Seneca MS., B. A. E., 1882 (Seneca name of tribe).

Saint Simon. An Ottawa mission about 1670 on Manitoulin id. in L. Huron.—Shea, Cath. Miss., 365, 1855.

Saint Simon et Saint Jude. A village of the Tionontati (q. v.) in 1640.
Sainct Simon et sainct Jude.—Jes. Rel. 1640, 95, 1858.

Saint Thomas. A village of the Tionontati in 1640.
Sainct Thomas.—Jes. Rel. 1640, 95, 1858.

Saint Xavier. A mission village of the Hurons in Ontario in 1640.
Sainct Xavier.—Jes. Rel. 1640, 81, 1858.

Saitinde ('sand people'). A division of the Jicarilla Apache, who claim the vicinity of the present Española, N. Mex., as their original home. 　　　(J. M.)
Sait-ĭndĕ.—Mooney, field notes, B. A. E., 1897.

Saitkinamuks ha Shumahadletza (*Sä′itkĭ-namuxs ha CumaxaтIE′tza*, 'people of (chief) CumaxaтIE′tza'). The inhabitants of 2 or 3 small villages on Fraser r., Brit. Col., just above Spences Bridge.—Teit in Mem. Am. Mus. Nat. Hist., II, 171, 1900.

Saitok. The name of two Eskimo villages in w. Greenland, one situated in lat. 73° 32′, the other in lat. 73° 7′.—Science, XI, 259, 1888.

Saituka ('camas eaters'). A collective term applied in various forms by the Paiute and other Shoshonean tribes to the camas-eating Indians of Oregon and Idaho, especially to the tribes of the Shahaptian family (q. v.).

Saiyiks (*Sai′-yiks*, 'liars'). A band of the Siksika, or Blackfeet.—Grinnell, Blackfoot Lodge Tales, 208, 1892.

Sajiuwingge (*Sä-jiu Uing-ge*). A prehistoric pueblo of the Tewa Indians of San Juan, the ruins of which are situated at La Joya, about 10 m. N. of San Juan pueblo, Rio Arriba co., N. Mex.

Sakaedigialas (*Saqai′dᴀgialas*, 'he threw grease, dropping from a bird split open, around the house'). A Haida town formerly on or near Kuper id., Queen Charlotte ids., Brit. Col. It was owned by the Kas-lanas, who were subsequently exterminated, it is said, by the people of Kaisun. 　　　　　　(J. R. S.)
SaqaĭdA-gialas.—Swanton, Cont. Haida, 280, 1905. Saqai′dᴀgî′lgaña Inagā′-i.—Ibid.

Sakagawea. See *Sacagawea*.

Sakahl. A band of Cowichan at Hope, on Fraser r., Brit. Col.; pop. 80 in 1909.
Fort Hope.—Can. Ind. Aff. Rep., 78, 1878. Hope.—Ibid., 309, 1879. Sakahl.—Brit. Col. map, Ind. Aff., Victoria, 1872. Tskaus.—Wilson in Trans. Ethnol. Soc. Lond., 278, 1866.

Sakaikumne. A division of the Miwok formerly living between Cosumne and Mokelumne rs., Cal.
Sagayayumnes.—Hale, Ethnol.and Philol.,630,1846.

Sakamna. An Utkiavinmiut Eskimo summer village inland from Pt Barrow, Alaska.—Murdoch in 9th Rep. B. A. E., 83, 1892.

Sakapatayi (*Sa-ka-pa-ta′-yi*, probably referring to water-lilies covering the surface of a pond). A former Upper Creek town on a tributary of Hatchet cr., Coosa co., Ala., at a place now called Socopathy. 　　　　　　　(A. S. G.)
Sakapatáyi.—Gatschet, Creek Migr. Leg., I, 143, 1884. Sakapató-i.—Ibid. (sometimes so pronounced by Creeks). Sock-o-par-toy.—Schoolcraft, Ind. Tribes, IV, 578, 1854.

Sakarissa ('Spear-dragger'). A Tuscarora chief who attended the Canandaigua treaty of 1794. He was probably the Oghshigwarise present at Niagara Landing in 1789, and Osequirison at Queenstown in 1813. The chief Sakarissa was one of the founders of the Tuscarora Congregational church in 1805, and accompanied Solomon Longbeard in 1802 to North Carolina, where land claims were settled. At Canandaigua the Quakers said: "He appears to be a thoughtful man, and mentioned a desire he had, that some of our young men might come among them as teachers." See Elias Johnson, Six Nations, 134, 1881; Savery, Journal, 359, 1837. Cf. *Saghwareesa, Sequareesere*.   (W. M. B.)

Sakaweston. An Indian seized by Capt. Harlow in 1611 from one of the islands off the coast of New England, who, after he had lived many years in England, went as a soldier to the wars in Bohemia, as Capt. John Smith relates.

Sakawithiniwuk ('people of the woods'). The Wood Cree, one of the several divisions of the Cree. They are divided into the Sakittawawithiniwuk and the Athabaskawithiniwuk.

Ayabāskawiyiniwag.—Wm. Jones, inf'n, 1906 (own name). Cree of the Woods.—Morgan, Consang. and Affin., 286, 1871. Na-he'-ah-wuk.—Ibid. Northern Crees.—Franklin, Journ. Polar Sea, II, 213, 1824. People of the Woods.—Morgan, op. cit., 286. Sackaweéthinyoowuc.—Franklin, op. cit., 168. Sakawiyiniwok.—Lacombe, Dict. de la Langue des Cris, X, 1874. Strongwood Cree.—Maclean, Hudson Bay, II, 264, 1849. Thick Wood Crees.—Franklin, op. cit., 168, 1824. Upper Cree.—Cox, Columbia R., II, 207, 1831. Wood Crees.—Hind, Lab. Penin., II, app., 262, 1863.

Sakaya. A former unidentified village situated a little w. of Sentinel Rock, Yosemite valley, Mariposa co., Cal.

Sáccaya.—Powers in Overland Mo., X, 333, 1874. Sak'-ka-ya.—Powers in Cont. N. A. Ethnol., III, 365, 1877.

Sakayengwalaghton. See *Sayenqueraghta*.

Sakeyu (*Sä-ke-yu*). A prehistoric pueblo of the Tewa on a mesa w. of the Rio Grande in N. New Mexico, between San Ildefonso pueblo and Rito de los Frijoles (Bandelier in Arch. Inst. Papers, IV, 78, 1892). Possibly the same as Tsankawi (q. v.).

Sakhauwotung ('the mouth of a creek where one resides'). A former small village of Delawares who moved from New Jersey about 1737; situated on the w. bank of Delaware r., near the site of Allen Ferry, about 7 m. below the Gap, in Northampton co., Pa. It was visited by Zinzendorf in 1742. David Brainerd built a cabin at this place in 1744, when he was preaching to the Indians "at the Forks." At that time he had about 30 or 40 Indians present at the services, and the following year baptized Moses Tatemy, who had acted as his interpreter. Brainerd preached here for the last time Feb. 23, 1746. Consult Brodhead, Delaware Water Gap, 1867; Memoirs of Rev. David Brainerd, 1822; Memorials of Moravian Church, 1870.   (G. P. D.)

Sakhone A former Costanoan village on the site of Soledad mission, Cal.

Sakhones.—Taylor in Cal. Farmer, Apr. 20, 1860.

Sakiakdjung. A spring settlement of Kingua Okomiut Eskimo at the head of Cumberland sd., Baffin land.

Sakiaqdjung.—Boas in 6th Rep. B. A. E., map, 1888.

Saki-kegawai (*Sa'ki qē'gawa-i*, 'those born up the inlet'). A prominent family of the Eagle clan of the Haida. They belonged to the Gunghet-haidagai, or Ninstints people, and were said to be a part of the Gunghet-kegawai. Their chief was town chief of Ninstints, which received its name among the whites from one of his names, Nungstins (*Nañ stins*, 'One who is two').—Swanton, Cont. Haida, 272, 1905.

Sakittawawithiniwuk ('people of the mouth of the river.'—W. J.). A subdivision of the Sakawithiniwuk, or Wood Cree.

Sakoghsinnakichte. See *Sadekanaktie*.

Saksinahmahyiks (*Sak-si-nah'-mah-yiks*, 'short bows'). A subtribe of the Kainah.—Grinnell, Blackfoot Lodge Tales, 209, 1892.

Sakta (*Sáqta*). A Bellacoola town on the N. side of the mouth of Bellacoola r., Brit. Col. It was one of the 8 Nuhalk villages.—Boas in Mem. Am. Mus. Nat. Hist., II, 49, 1898.

Sakuma. A band formerly inhabiting the lower Colorado valley in the present Arizona or California, who were conquered, absorbed, or driven out by the Mohave.—Bourke in Jour. Am. Folklore, II, 185, 1889.

Sakumehu. A Salish division on the headwaters of Skagit r., Wash., numbering 250 in 1852. The remnant is now on Swinomish res.

Sachimers.—Stevens in Ind. Aff. Rep., 17, 1870. Sac-me-ugh.—Mallet, ibid., 198, 1877. Sah-ku-méhu.—U. S. Stat. at Large, XII, 927, 1863. Saku-mé-hu.—Stevens in Ind. Aff. Rep., 458, 1854. Sock-a-muke.—Starling, ibid., 170, 1852.

Sakutenedi (*SАqutē'nedi*, 'grass people'). A Tlingit division at Kake, Alaska, belonging to the Raven clan.   (J. R. S.)

Salabi. The Spruce clan of the Kachina phratry of the Hopi.

Sa-la'-bi.—Stephen in 8th Rep. B. A. E., 39, 1891. Salab wiñwû.—Fewkes in 19th Rep., B. A. E., 584, 1900 (*wiñwû*='clan'). Sa-lab' wŭñ-wü.—Fewkes in Am. Anthr., VII, 404, 1894.

Salachi. A Chumashan village formerly near Purísima mission, Santa Barbara co., Cal. Twice mentioned in mission archives; seemingly two villages of the same name.—Taylor in Cal. Farmer, Oct. 18, 1861.

Salal. A berry-bearing evergreen plant (*Gaultheria shallon*) of the Columbia r. region, the fruit of which has been an important source of food for the Indians; written also *sallal*, the name of this fruit in the Chinook jargon, from Chinook *kl'kwu-shalla*.   (A. F. C.)

Salan Pomo. A name given by Ford (Ind. Aff. Rep. 1856, 257, 1857), in the form Salan Pomas, as that of a division of the Pomo which inhabited Potter valley, Mendocino co., Cal. It is probable that this name is a corruption of Shanel, the name of one of the largest of the old villages in this valley. (s. A. B.)

Salapaque. One of the tribes of w. Texas, some at least of whose people were neophytes of the mission of San José y San Miguel de Aguayo.—Texas State archives, Nov. 1790.

Salem. A village of the Moravian Delawares, established in 1781 on the w. bank of Tuscarawas r., 1½ m. s. w. of Port Washington, Tuscarawas co., Ohio. The Indians were driven out during the Revolution, but returned after the war. The mission was abandoned in 1781. (J. M.)

Salendas (*S̯ⁱalᴀ′ndas*). A family of the Eagle clan of the Haida; one of those that migrated to Alaska. One branch settled among the Tongass and another at Sitka, while the Haida portion became subdivided into two house groups, the Hlimul-naas-hadai and the Nahawas-hadai.—Swanton, Cont. Haida, 276, 1905. S'alɛ′ndas.—Boas, Twelfth Rep. N. W. Tribes Can., 22, 1898.

Salinan Family. A linguistic stock of California, named by Latham (1856) and Powell (1891) from Salinas r. The Salinan Indians inhabited parts of San Luis Obispo, Monterey, and perhaps San Benito cos., their territory extending from the sea to the main ridge of the Coast range and from the head of the Salinas drainage to a short distance above Soledad. Little is known about them; no name for themselves as a body, for their language, or for any division, either in their own or in any other Indian language, is known; nor is it known what any such divisions may have been. The name of the place at which the mission of San Miguel was established was Vahia, or Vatica, and that of the mission of San Antonio, Sextapay. The Tatche (Tachi) or Telame Indians, mentioned by Duflot de Mofras as at San Antonio, are Yokuts tribes that were brought to that mission. Cholame cr. and town in San Luis Obispo co. possibly take their name from a Salinan word, and the same may be the case with Jolon in Monterey co.

The missions of San Antonio and San Miguel (q. v.) were established in Salinan territory in 1771 and 1797. The total baptisms at these missions reached 4,400 and 2,400 respectively, and it appears that these numbers included Yokuts. Like all the other tribes, the Salinan Indians decreased rapidly during mission times, the numbers at each mission having fallen to fewer than 700 by 1831, and more rapidly after secularization. At present their total number is perhaps 20, most of them near Jolon. See *California Indians, Mission Indians, Missions.*

The Salinan language is very irregular in its structure and more complex than most languages of California. Two dialects, those of San Antonio and San Miguel, which do not differ much, are known, and it is probable that there were others. The Salinan Indians appear to have lived in houses of brush or grass and to have had no canoes. They hunted more than they fished, but depended for their subsistence principally on vegetal food, such as acorns and grass seed. They used stone mortars and coiled baskets, and burned the dead. Of their religion and mythology nothing is known, except that they regarded the eagle, the coyote, and the humming-bird as creators. (H. W. H.   A. L. K.)
×**Runsiens.**—Keane in Stanford's Compend., Cent. and S. Am., 476, 1878 (San Miguel of his group belongs here). =**Salinan.**—Powell in 7th Rep. B. A. E., 101, 1891. <**Salinas.**—Latham in Trans. Philol. Soc. Lond., 85, 1856. >**San Antonio.**—Powell in Cont. N. A. Ethnol., III, 568, 1877. <**Santa Barbara.**—Gatschet in Mag. Am. Hist., 157, 1877 (cited here as containing San Antonio); Gatschet in U. S. Geog. Surv. W. 100th Mer., VII, 419, 1879 (contains San Antonio and San Miguel). >**Sextapay.**—Taylor quoted by Shea, Lib: Am. Ling., VII, vii, 1861.

Salinas. Mentioned by Rivera (Diario, leg. 2602, 1736) as a tribe or village apparently near the lower Rio Grande in Texas. It was possibly Coahuiltecan.

Salineros. A Spanish collective designation for the Piro and Tigua occupying, until 1675–80, the pueblos of Abo, Chilili, Quarai, Tabira, Tenabo, etc., near the salt lagoons E. of the Rio Grande, central New Mexico. See also *Chealo, Tompiros.* Salineros.—Benavides, Memorial (1630), in Land of Sunshine, XIV, 46, 1901. Salmeros.—Benavides misquoted by Bancroft, Ariz. and N. Mex., 164, 1889.

Salineta. Probably a pueblo of the Piro or the Tigua, 4 leagues from Guadalupe mission at El Paso, in the present Texas, in 1680.—Otermin (1680) quoted by Bancroft, Ariz. and N. Mex., 182, 1889.

Salish (Okinagan: *sälst*, 'people'). Formerly a large and powerful division of the Salishan family, to which they gave their name, inhabiting much of w. Montana and centering around Flathead lake and valley. A more popular designation for this tribe is Flatheads, given to them by the surrounding people, not because they artificially deformed their heads, but because, in contradistinction to most tribes farther w., they left them in their natural condition, flat on top. They lived mainly by hunting. The Salish, with the cognate Pend d'Oreille and the Kutenai, by treaty of Hell Gate, Mont., July 16, 1855, ceded to the United States their lands in Montana and Idaho. They also joined in the peace treaty at the mouth of Judith r., Mont., Oct. 17, 1855. Lewis and Clark estimated their population in 1806 to be 600; Gibbs gave their probable number in 1853 as 325, a diminution said to be due to wars with the Siksika; number of Flatheads under Flathead agency, Mont. (1909), 598.

SALISH MAN (AM. MUS. NAT. HIST.)

Ah-shu-ah-har-peh.—Crow MS. vocab., B. A. E., n. d. **A-shu′-e-ka-pe.**—Hayden, Ethnog. and Philol. Mo. Val., 402, 1862 ('flatheads': Crow name). **å-too-hå-pĕ.** — Long, Exped. Rocky Mts., II, lxxxiv, 1823 (Hidatsa name). **Cootstooks pai tah pee.**—Henry, MS. vocab., 1808 (Blackfoot name). **Faux Tetes-Plates.**—Duflot de Mofras, Expl., II, 335,1844. **Flatheads.**—Lewis and Clark, Discov., 35, 1807. **Flathead-Selish.**—Gatschet in Proc. A. A. A. S., XXXI, 577, 1883. **Hohilpo.**—Lewis and Clark Exped., I, map, 1814. **Ka-ka-i-thi.** — Hayden, Ethnog. and Philol. Mo. Val.,326, 1862 ('flathead people': Arapaho name). **Ka-ko′-is-tsi′-a-ta′-ni-o.**—Ibid., 290 ('people who flatten their heads': Cheyenne name). **Ko-tŏh′-spi-tup′-i-o.** — Ibid., 264 (Blackfoot name). **Nebagindibe.**—Baraga, Otchipwe-Eng. Dict., 281, 1880 ('flat head': Chippewa name; "properly Nebagindibed"—identical?). **Pa Bda-ská.**—Cook, Yankton MS. vocab., B. A. E., 184, 1882. **Pa O-bde′-ca.** — Ibid. ('heads cornered or edged': Yankton name). **Saalis.**—Duflot de Mofras, Expl., II, 335, 1844. **Sae-lies.**—Mayne, Brit. Col., 297, 1862. **Sälish.**—Gatschet, MS., B. A. E. (own name). **Têtes-Plates.**—Common French form, applied to various tribes. **Whull-e-mooch.**—Deans in Am. Antiq., 41, 1886 (applied to Puget sd. tribes).

Salishan Family. A linguistic family inhabiting the N. portions of Washington, N. Idaho, w. Montana, a small strip of the N. w. coast of Oregon, and in Canada the S. E. part of Vancouver id. from Thurlow id. to Sooke bay, and all the s. mainland of British Columbia as far as Bute inlet and Quesnelle lake, with the exception of that portion held by the Kutenai, although within the Kutenai area, at the Columbia lakes, is a small settlement of Salish. An isolated division of the family,

the Bellacoola, had established itself farther N. on Dean inlet, Burke channel, and Bellacoola r. The name Salish was originally applied to a large tribe in w. Montana popularly known as Flatheads, thence it was finally extended to cover all those speaking a similar language.

Although lexically distinct from one another, the Salish, Chimakuan, and Wakashan languages belong to the same structural type and have remote points of resemblance with Algonquian. Physically and culturally the coast and interior Salish belong to different groups, the former being affiliated to some extent with the other coast people to the N., and the interior Salish resembling interior stocks in their own neighborhood.

If his own statements may be relied upon, Juan de Fuca (1592) was probably the first white man to visit the country inhabited by people of this family. After his time several Spanish navigators passed along their coasts, but their position exposed them less frequently to visits from vessels than that of the Nootka and tribes farther N. Later British and American vessels came to trade, the most notable expedition being that of Geo. Vancouver (1792–94), whose name became attached to Vancouver id. The first detailed information regarding the Salishan tribes was obtained, however,

SALISH MAN (AM. MUS. NAT. HIST.)

from the account of the expedition of Lewis and Clark (1804–06), and knowledge of them was extended by the establishment of Astor's fort in 1811 at the mouth of the Columbia, although the fort itself was not within Salish territory. From that time until 1846 most of this region, known as the Oregon Territory, was a subject of dispute between Great Britain and the United States, and it was not until after its settlement and until the California gold fever had somewhat subsided that settlers began to come into this region in numbers. On the Canadian side employees of the Hudson's Bay Company were among the first to enter the country. The establishment of a post at Victoria in 1843 was one of the most momentous events to the Indians of the entire coast.

The coast Salish form the southern arm of the N. W. Coast culture, which fades away southward from Bute inlet and Comox (where it resembles that of the more highly developed Kwakiutl) to the semi-Californian Tillamook and the Nestucca of Oregon. Unlike the more northern Haida, Tlingit, and Tsimshian, descent is usually reckoned through the father.

The Salish dwellings in the northern part of this area are of the Nootka type, longer than those farther N., and containing several families each with its own fire. They are also built in the same way of heavy planks and beams. They resemble the other coast tribes in the important part fish and shellfish play in their diet, and in the extent to which canoes are employed. The interior Salish depended more on hunting, but so many large salmon streams flow through this country that even they were more given to a fish diet than were the interior tribes generally. The houses of the interior Salish of British Columbia differed considerably from those on the coast. To construct them, holes were dug and poles set up in conical form around their edges; the whole was covered with poles on which was laid grass, and sometimes cedar bark, and over all earth was thrown.

War, slavery, and the potlatch (q. v.) were regular institutions on the coast. One of the most characteristic customs, especially prevalent along the coasts of Washington and British Columbia, was artificial head-flattening, but it did not obtain, curiously enough, among the Indians now called Flatheads (see *Salish*).

Population (1909): Coast Salish in United States, 3,600; coast Salish in Canada, 4,874; total, 8,474. Interior Salish in United States, 4,988; interior Salish in Canada, 5,390; total, 10,378. Total Salish in United States, 8,366; total Salish in Canada, 10,264; grand total, 18,630.

The Salishan dialects may be grouped as follows:

I. DIALECTS OF THE INTERIOR: 1, *Lillooet* in w. British Columbia; 2, *Ntlakyapamuk* (Thompson Indians) in s. w. British Columbia; 3, *Shuswap* in s. central

British Columbia; 4, *Okinagan* in s. E. British Columbia, extending into the United States, the subdivisions of which are the Okinagan proper, Colville, Nespelim or Sanpoil, Senijextee (Snaichekstik) of the Arrow lakes and Columbia r. below the lakes; 5, *Flathead* in E. Washington, Idaho, and Montana, subdivisions of which are the Spokan, Kalispel or Pend d'Oreilles, and Salish or Flathead; 6, *Skitswish* or *Cœur d'Alènes* in N. Idaho; 7, *Columbia groups* in the w. part of the interior of Washington, including the Pisquows or Wenatchi, Sinkiuse, Methow, and other local divisions.

II. COAST DIALECTS: 8, *Bellacoola*, a group of tribes on Bentinck Arm and Deans inlet, Brit. Col.; 9, *Comox group* on the N. part of the Gulf of Georgia, with two subdivisions—(*a*) the Comox proper, including the Comox and Eëksen, Homalko, Kaäke, Kakekt, Seechelt of Jervis inlet, Sliammon, and Tatpoös; and (*b*) the Puntlatsh, including the Hwahwatl, Puntlatsh, and Saämen; 10, *Cowichan group* in the neighborhood of Nanaimo on Vancouver id., and in the delta of Fraser r. It embraces, on Vancouver id., the Clemclemalats, Comiakin, Hellelt, Kenipsim, Kilpanlus, Koksilah, Kulleets, Lilmalche, Malakut, Nanaimo, Penelakut, Quamichan, Siccameen, Snonowas, Somenos, Tateke, Yekolaos; and, in the Fraser valley, the Chehalis, Chilliwack, Coquitlam, Ewawoos, Katsey, Kelatl, Kwantlen, Matsqui, Musqueam, Nehaltmoken, Nicomen, Ohamil, Pilalt, Popkum, Samahquam, Scowlitz, Sewathen, Siyita, Skwawalooks, Snonkweametl, Squawtits, Sumass, and Tsakuam; 11, *Squawmish group*, including the Squawmish of Burrard inlet and Howe sd. and probably the Nooksak of N. Washington; 12, *Songish group*, on Juan de Fuca str., San Juan id., and parts of the coasts of Washington and British Columbia. It includes the Clallam (Wash.), Lummi (Wash.), Samish (Wash.), Sanetch (Brit. Col.), Semiahmoo (Brit. Col. and Wash.), Songish (Brit. Col.), Sooke (Brit. Col.); 13, *Nisqualli group*, embracing all tribes E. of Puget sd. and s. to Mt Tacoma, and, on the west side, the region up to Olympia, except Hood canal. It includes two dialectic divisions, the Nisqualli and the Snohomish. Well-known divisions are the Nisqualli proper, Dwamish, Puyallup, Skagit, Snoqualmu or Snoquamish, and Squaxon. Following are the names of some of the numerous bands of the Nisqualli: Etakmehu, Kwehtlmamish (?), Nukwatsamish, Nusehtsatl, Potoashees, Sahewamish, Sakumehu, Samamish, Sawamish, Sekamish, Shomamish, Shotlemamish, Skihwamish, Skopamish, Smulkamish, Squacum, Stehtsasamish, Steila-

coomamish, Suquamish, and Towah-hah. Other bands which may belong here, but which cannot be identified, are Neutubvig, Nuchwugh, Opichiken, Sinslikhooish, Sintootoolish, and Sktehl-mish; 14, *Twana group*, on Hood canal, Puget sd., including the Twana and Sailupsun; 15, *Chehalis group*, embracing six dialects, which show considerable variation. These are the Quinault and Quaitso of N. W. Washington; the Humptulips of the N. part of Grays harbor; the Lower Chehalis of Grays harbor and Shoalwater bay; the Satsop E. and N. E. of Grays harbor; the Upper Chehalis E. of Shoalwater bay; and the Cowlitz on the river of that name southward to Columbia r.; 16, *Tillamook* on the coast of Oregon, including the Tillamook or Nestucca, and the Siletz. Tillamook is the Chinook name for the tribe whose territory is called in Chinook, Nehalem.
>**Salish.**—Gallatin in Trans. Am. Antiq. Soc., II, 134, 306, 1836 (or Flat Heads only); Latham in Proc. Philol. Soc. Lond., II, 31–50, 1846 (of Duponceau; said to be the Okanagan of Tolmie). ×**Salish.**—Keane in Stanford's Compend., Cent. and S. Am., app., 460, 474, 1878 (includes Flatheads, Kalispelms, Skitsuish, Colvilles, Quarlpi, Spokanes, Pisquouse, Soaitlpi). =**Salish.**—Bancroft, Nat. Races, III, 565, 618, 1882. >**Selish.**—Gallatin in Trans. Am. Ethnol. Soc., II, pt. 1, 77, 1848 (vocab. of Nsietshaws); Tolmie and Dawson, Comp. Vocab., 63, 78, 1884 (vocabularies of Lillooet and Kullëspelm). >**Jelish.**—Gallatin in Schoolcraft, Ind. Tribes, III, 402, 1853 (obvious misprint for Selish; follows Hale as to tribes). =**Selish.**—Gatschet in Mag. Am. Hist., 169, 1877 (gives habitat and tribes of family); Gatschet in Beach, Ind. Miscel., 444, 1877. <**Selish.**—Dall, after Gibbs, in Cont. N. A. Ethnol., I, 241, 1877 (includes Yakama, which is Shahaptian). >**Tsihaili-Selish.**—Hale in U. S. Expl. Exped., VI, 205, 535, 569, 1846 (includes Shushwaps, Selish or Flatheads, Skitsuish, Piskwaus, Skwale, Tsihailish, Kawelitsk, Nsietshawus); Gallatin in Trans. Am. Ethnol. Soc., II, pt. 1, c, 10, 1848 (after Hale); Berghaus (1851), Physik. Atlas, map 17, 1852; Buschmann, Supren der aztek. Sprache, 658–661, 1859; Latham, Elem. Comp. Philol., 399, 1862 (contains Shushwap or Átna Proper, Kuttelspelm or Pend d'Oreilles, Selish, Spokan, Okanagan, Skitsuish, Piskwaus, Nusdalum, Kawitchen, Cathlascou, Skwali, Chechili, Kwaintl, Kwenaiwtl, Nsietshawus, Billechula). >**Atnahs.**—Gallatin in Trans. Am. Antiq. Soc., II, 134, 135, 306, 1836 (on Fraser r.); Prichard, Phys. Hist. Mankind, v, 427, 1847 (on Fraser r.). >**Atna.**—Latham in Trans. Philol. Soc. Lond., 71, 1856 (Tsihaili-Selish of Hale and Gallatin). ×**Nootka - Columbian.**— Scouler in Jour. Roy. Geog. Soc. Lond., XI, 224, 1841 (includes, among others, Billechoola, Kawitchen, Noosdalum, Squallyamish of present family). ×**Insular.**—Scouler, ibid. (same as Nootka-Columbian family). ×**Shahaptan.**—Scouler, ibid., 225 (includes Okanagan of this family). ×**Southern.**— Scouler, ibid., 224 (same as Nootka-Columbian family). >**Billechoola.**—Latham in Jour. Ethnol. Soc. Lond., I, 154, 1848 (assigns Friendly Village of Mackenzie here); Latham, Opuscula, 250, 1860 (gives Tolmie's vocabulary). >**Billechula.**—Latham, Nat. Hist. Man, 300, 1850 (mouth of Salmon r.); Latham in Trans. Philol. Soc. Lond., 72, 1856 (same); Latham, Opuscula, 339, 1860. >**Bellacoola.**—Bancroft, Nat. Races, III, 564, 607, 1882 (Bellacoola only; specimen vocabulary). >**Bilhoola.**—Tolmie and Dawson, Comp. Vocab., 62, 1884 (vocab. of Noothlākimish). >**Bilchula.**—Boas in Petermanns Mitteilungen, 130, 1887 (mentions Sātsq. Nūteʼl, Nuchalkmχ, Taleómχ). ×**Naass.**— Gallatin in Trans. Am. Ethnol. Soc., II, pt. 1, c, 77, 1848 (cited as including Billechola). >**Tsihaili.**— Latham, Nat. Hist. Man, 310, 1850 (chiefly lower

part of Fraser r. and between that and the Columbia; includes Shuswap, Salish, Skitsuish, Piskwaus, Kawitchen, Skwali, Checheeli, Kowelits, Noosdalum, Nsietshawus). ×**Wakash.**—Latham, Nat. Hist. Man, 301, 1850 (cited as including Klallems). ×**Shushwaps.**—Keane in Stanford's Compend., Cent. and S. Am., app., 460, 474, 1878 (quoted as including Shewhapmuch and Okanagans). ×**Hydahs.**—Keane, ibid., 473 (includes Bellacoola of present family). ×**Nootkahs.**— Keane, ibid., 473 (includes Komux, Kowitchans, Klallums, Kwantlums, Teets of present family). ×**Nootka.**—Bancroft, Nat. Races, III, 564, 1882 (contains the following Salishan tribes: Cowichin, Soke, Comux, Noosdalum, Wickinninish, Songhie, Sanetch, Kwantlum, Teet, Nanaimo, Newchemass, Shimiahmoo, Nooksak, Samish, Skagit, Snohomish, Clallam, Toanhooch). <**Puget Sound Group.**—Keane in Stanford's Compend., Cent. and S. Am., app., 474, 1878 (comprises Nooksahs, Lummi, Samish, Skagits, Nisqually, Neewamish, Sahmamish, Snohomish, Skeewamish, Squanamish, Klallums, Classets, Chehalis, Cowlitz, Pistchin, Chinakum; all but the last being Salishan). >**Flatheads.**—Keane, ibid., 474, 1878 (same as Salish, above). >**Kawitshin.**—Tolmie and Dawson, Comp. Vocab., 39, 1884 (vocabs. of Songis and Kwantlin sept, and Kowmook or Tlathool). >**Qauitschin.**—Boas in Petermanns Mitteilungen, 131, 1887. >**Niskwalli.**—Tolmie and Dawson, Comp. Vocab., 50, 121, 1884 (or Skwalliamish vocab. of Sinahomish).

Sallal. See *Salal.*

Salmon River Indians. A Salish division on Salmon r., w. Oregon, between the Siletz and the Nestucca. Part of them were on Grande Ronde res. in 1863.
Ci′-cĭn-xau′.—Dorsey, Alsea MS. vocab., B. A. E., 1884. **Kaouaï.**—Duflot de Mofras, Explor., II, 104, 1844. **Kowai.**—Gairdner (1835) in Jour. Geog. Soc. Lond., XI, 255, 1841 (either the above tribe or the Nestucca). **Salmon River.**—Ind. Aff. Rep., 221, 1861. **Tsän tcha′-ishna amím.**—Gatschet, Lakmiut MS., B. A. E., 105 (Lakmiut-Kalapuya name).

Salnahakaisiku (*Sal-na-ha-kai′-sĭ-ku*). A Chumashan village formerly in Ventura co., Cal., at a locality now called El Llano de Santa Ana.—Henshaw, Buenaventura MS. vocab., B. A E., 1884.

Salpilel. A Chumashan village formerly on the Patera ranch, near Santa Barbara, Cal.
Salpilel.—Taylor in Cal. Farmer, Apr. 24, 1863. **Sa-pi′-li.**—Henshaw, Santa Barbara MS. vocab., B. A. E., 1884. **Saughpileel.**—Taylor in Cal. Farmer, May 4, 1860 (at San Miguel, 6 m. from Santa Barbara mission). **Silpaleels.**—Gatschet in Chief Eng. Rep., pt. III, 553, 1876. **S′pi′-lil.**—Henshaw, Buenaventura MS. vocab., B. A. E., 1884.

Salsona. Mentioned as a Costanoan division hostile to those Indians among whom Dolores mission at San Francisco, Cal., was established. In 1776 the latter, being attacked by the Salsona, fled to the islands in the bay or to the eastern shore. The Salsona are said to have lived 6 leagues to the s. E., which would put them near San Mateo. They may be identical with the Olhones. See Engelhardt, Franc. in Cal., 295, 1897.
Salsen.—Humboldt, New Spain, II, 345, 1811. **Salses.**—Mayer, Mexico, II, 39, 1853. **Salsona.**—Clavijero, Hist. Baja Cal., 206, 1852. **Salzon.**—Taylor in Cal. Farmer, Oct. 18, 1801.

Salt. Not all tribes of Indians were accustomed to use salt, whether from the difficulty of procuring it, the absence of the habit, a repugnance for the mineral, or for religious reasons, it is not always possible to say. Salt was eaten as a condiment, the only instance of its use as a preservative being its addition to yeast to prevent putrefaction. The desire for salt is presumed to arise from a physiological need, and it is thought that the demand for it is greatest when cereal or vegetal food is eaten, and decreases as the diet is more and more of animal substance. Baegert says the tribes of Lower California ate "everything unsalted, though they might obtain plenty of salt," and gives as a reason that since they moved about constantly, salt was too cumbersome to carry with them. The Gabrieleños of s. California used salt sparingly; the Hupa, the Achomawi, and perhaps other California Indians, do not eat salt; the Eskimo regard it as an abomination, while the Achomawi believe its use in food would cause sore eyes (Dixon). The Creeks tabooed its use in the busk ceremony until after the ball play (Speck). Other tribes used substitutes for salt, as the Karankawa of Texas, who, Gatschet says, used chile instead; and the Virginia Indians, who made a form of lye by burning to ashes the stalk of a certain plant. "They season their broth with it, and they know no other salt," says Capt. John Smith. The Cherokee used lye, and even now among the Eastern Cherokee salt is almost unused by them. Indeed it is probable that none of the Southern tribes used salt before the coming of the whites. According to Hariot, the people of Roanoak used as a condiment the saline ashes of a plant taken to be orage, and resembling the melden of the Germans (*Atriplex patulum*), a species of saltwort, which runs into many varieties and is common to Europe and America. All the Algonquian names for salt are formed from a root meaning "to be sour" or "acid." There is no root "to be saline." The water of the ocean was known as "sour water."

Salt exists in enormous quantities in the United States, and it was not difficult for the Indians to obtain it. The Omaha took up salt incrustations with feathers and transferred it to bags, or broke up rock salt with sticks and pounded it to the desired fineness. The source of their supply was near Lincoln, Nebr., and the headwaters of a stream s. w. of Republican r., probably Saline r., Kans. The Shawnee were famed as salt makers, and the great spring on Saline cr., below the mouth of Walnut cr., on the Ohio, was purchased from them by treaty. The large vessels of very thick pottery found near the salines and elsewhere are found to have been used as evaporating pans by the Indians. The Quapaw made salt from the water of saline springs near the mouth of Arkansas r., evaporating it in earthen

pans made for the purpose, which left the salt formed into square cakes (Giddings). C. C. Jones says: "The Knight of Elvas informs us that natural salt and the sand with which it was intermixed were thrown into baskets made for the purpose. These were large at the mouth and small at the bottom, or, in other words, funnel-shaped. Beneath them—suspended in the air on a ridge pole—vessels were placed. Water was then poured upon the admixture of sand and salt. The drippings were strained and boiled on the fire until all the water was evaporated, and the salt left in the bottom of the pots." Fragments of these leaching baskets have been found in the salt deposits of Petit Anse id., La. An important salt-making site was uncovered in 1902 by the Peabody Museum at Kimmswick, Mo., where the salt pans were found in place (Bushnell).

The Rio Grande Pueblos acquired salt principally from the Manzano salines, in central New Mexico; the Zuñi obtained their supply from a salt lake many miles s. w. of their pueblo. There was early discrimination by the Pueblos in the quality of salt, and long journeys were made to obtain the best kind. In this pursuit many trails led to the Zuñi salt lake, where a number of towns were built by a tribe or tribes which were exterminated by the Zuñi immediately anterior to the advent of the Spaniards in 1539–40. The salt naturally deposited from the supersaturated waters of the Zuñi salt lake was collected and carried long distances to the settlements, having been found, it is said, in cliff-ruins in s. Colorado, 200 m. from the source of supply. Among the Pueblos, pottery vessels of special form were used to contain salt, and mortuary vessels which contained food for the dead are frequently saturated with this substance, causing exfoliation of the surface of the ware.

The Navaho myth of the origin of Dsilydje Qaçál relates that "next day they traveled up the stream to a place called Tse'çqáka, and here again they halted for the night. This place is noted for its deposits of native salt. The travelers cut some out from under a great rock and filled with it their bags, made out of the skins of the squirrels and other small animals which they had captured" (Matthews).

The Hopi have obtained their salt from time immemorial from the Grand Canyon of the Colorado, westward from their villages about 100 m. Here salt is gathered with ceremony by making sacrifice to the Goddess of Salt and the God of War, whose shrines are there (Fewkes). The Pueblos have important salt deities, that of the Hopi being Hurúng Wuhti, "The Woman of the Hard Substances," who was a sea deity, like the Mexican salt goddess Huitocilmatl. The myth concerning the latter relates that she was sister of the rain gods, with whom she quarreled; in their resentment they drove her to salt water, where she invented the art of panning the mineral and became Goddess of Salt. The Zuñi "Salt Mother" was Mawe, genius of the sacred salt lake. At certain seasons war parties were sent to the lake for salt, and while there ceremonies were performed and offerings made. See *Chaunis Temoatan, Food.*

Consult Baegert in Smithson. Rep. 1863, 366, 1864; Bushnell in Man, 13, 1907; ibid., 35, 1908; Collinson in Jour. Geog. Soc. Lond., 1st s., xxv, 201, 1855; Cushing (1) in 13th Rep. B. A. E., 353–54, 1896, (2) in Millstone, ix, no. 12, 1884; Dixon in Am. Anthr., x, no. 2, 1908; Dorsey in 3d Rep. B. A. E., 309, 1884; Gatschet, Karankawa Inds., 1891; Giddings in Pop. Sci. Mo., June 1891; Hariot in Holbein Soc. Pub., 14, 1888; Hoffman in Bull. Essex Inst., xviii, 9–10, 1885; Jones, Antiq. So. Inds., 45, 1873; Mason in Smithson. Rep. 1886, 225, 1889; Matthews in 5th Rep. B. A. E., 388, 1887; Mooney in 7th Rep. B. A. E., 330, 1891; Speck in Mem. Am. Anthr. Asso., ii, pt. 2, 1907; Stevenson in 23d Rep. B. A. E., 60, 1904; Thomas in 12th Rep. B. A. E., 695, 696, 1894; Wilson in Rep. Nat. Mus. 1888, 673, 1890.   (w. h.)

Salt Chuck Indians (Chinook jargon: *salt-tchuk*, 'salt-water'). A general term applied indiscriminately to coast tribes by inland Indians in the N. W. In 1884, J. O. Dorsey, when at Siletz agency, Oreg., heard this term applied, not only by the inland tribes (as Takelma) to the coast peoples (Athapascan, Kusan, etc.), but even by Athapascans to themselves. See Fitzhugh in Ind. Aff. Rep. 1857, 329, 1858.

Saltketchers. A former Yuchi village in s. South Carolina, about the present Salkehatchie. It seems to have been a village of the Yamasee at the time of the war with that tribe in 1715.
Saltketchers.—Hawkins (1799), Sketch, 61, 1848.
Sol-ke-chuh.—Ibid.

Salt Lick. A village, probably of the Delawares, on Mahoning cr., near Warren, Trumbull co., Ohio, about 1760 (Croghan (1760) in Mass. Hist. Soc. Coll., 4th s., ix, 289, 1871). The "old salt works" here were operated by the whites before the survey of the E. part of the Western Reserve in 1796. In 1800 the chief of the settlement, "Captain George," was killed during a fight with settlers (Howe, Hist. Coll. Ohio, ii, 659, 1896).

Saltwater Pond. A village in 1685, probably in Plymouth co., Mass.—Hinckley (1685) in Mass. Hist. Soc. Coll., 4th s., v, 133, 1861.

Saluda. A small tribe formerly living on Saluda r., S. C. According to Rivers

(Hist. S. C., 38, 1856) they removed to Pennsylvania probably early in the 18th century, which, if true, would indicate that they were probably connected with the Shawnee. In addition to that of the river, the name survives in Saluda gap in the Blue Ridge.

Salutation. In general Indian salutation was accompanied by less demonstration than is usual among Europeans, particularly the inhabitants of southern Europe, but it would be a mistake to assume that less feeling existed. Mallery, who devoted much attention to this subject, says:

"The North American Indians do not have many conventional forms of salutation. Their etiquette generally is to meet in silence and smoke before speaking, the smoking being the real salutation. But a number of tribes—e. g., the Shoshoni, Caddo, and Arikara—use a word or sound very similar to *How!* but in proper literation *Hau* or *Hao.* Most of the Sioux use the same sound in communication with the whites, from which the error has arisen that they have caught up and abbreviated the 'How are you?' of the latter. But the word is ancient, used in councils, and means 'good,' or 'satisfactory.' It is a response as well as an address or salutation. The Navaho say, both at meeting and parting, '*Agalani,*' an archaic word the etymology of which is not yet ascertained. Among the Cherokee the colloquy is as follows: No. 1 says, '*Siyú*' [properly *Âsiyu*], 'good'; No. 2 responds, *Âsiyú; tá-higwatsú?*' 'good; are you in peace?' To this No. 1 says, 'I am in peace, and how is it with you?' No. 2 ends by 'I am in peace also.' Among the Zuñi happiness is always asserted as well as implored. In the morning their greeting is, 'How have you passed the night?' in the evening, 'How have you come unto the sunset?' The reply always is 'Happily.' After a separation of even short duration, if more than one day, the question is asked, 'How have you passed these many days?' The reply is invariably, 'Happily,' although the person addressed may be in severe suffering or dying."

The greeting *Hao!* or some variant was found over a much wider area than Mallery indicates. What Mallery says of smoking applies only to ceremonial visitings. The ordinary passing greeting among the Plains tribes and probably most others is "Good" in the various languages (Mooney).

Close relations or very dear friends on meeting after a considerable absence would throw their right arms over each other's left shoulders and their left arms under each other's right arms, embrace gently and allow their heads to rest against each other for an instant. The ceremonial form of salutation consisted principally in rubbing with the hands, and is thus described by Iberville as practised on the lower Mississippi: "When I arrived where my brother was, the chief or captain of the Bayogoulas came to the shore of the sea to show me friendship and civility after their manner, which is, being near you, to stop, pass the hands over their face and breast, and afterward pass their hands over yours, after which they raise them toward the sky, rubbing them and clasping them together" (Margry, Déc., IV, 154–55, 1880). Although varying to a certain extent, substantially the same ceremony is reported from the Indians of Carolina and the plains, the Delawares, the Iroquois, the Aleut, and the Eskimo proper; it was therefore widespread throughout North America. Rubbing of noses by two persons is referred to by early writers, and an old Haida Indian affirmed it to have been the ancient custom among his people, but well authenticated cases are rare, although the rubbing of the nose with the hand was often observed among Eskimo tribes. Mooney says that most of these instances, as in the case of the Comanche, may have been nothing more than misconceptions of the hugging described above. Not infrequently the rubbing ceremonies were accompanied by the shedding of tears. Friederici finds two areas in America in which this prevailed, one in the central and south-central part of South America among the Tupi tribes of São Paulo, Minas Geræs, and Bahia, the Charrua of Banda Oriental, and some of the Chaco tribes; the second in North America w. of the Mississippi from the sources of that river to the Texas coast. This was particularly conspicuous near the Gulf of Mexico, from which circumstance the tribes there were often called "weepers." Mooney states that he has noted the custom only where persons meet after a considerable absence, and it was explained to him as due to memories of events, particularly deaths, which had taken place since the previous meeting and which the figure of the long absent one calls to mind. In some cases, however, this has been observed on the first meeting of Indians with white men, when it perhaps had some religious significance.

Consult Friederici in Globus, LXXXIX, 30–34, 1906; Mallery (1) in Am. Anthr., III, 201–16, 1890, (2) in Pop. Sci. Month., XXXVIII, 477–90, 629–44, 1891.   (J. R. S.)

Salwahka (*Sal-wa'-kha*, prob. 'at the foot of the creek.'—Sapir). A former Takelma village near the mouth of Illinois r. or one of its tributaries in Oregon.

Illinois Creek.—Dorsey, Takelma MS. vocab., B. A. E., 1884. Illinois Valley (band).—Ibid. x̣us ǫla' ǫûnně'.—Dorsey, Tutu MS. vocab., B. A. E., 1884 ('plenty-of-camas people': Tutu name). Săl-wă'-qă.—Dorsey in Jour. Am. Folk-lore, III, 235, 1890 (own name). Salwáxa.—Sapir in Am. Anthr., IX, 254, 1907.

Samahquam. A body of Salish of Fraser River agency, Brit. Col.; pop. 67 in 1909.
Samackman.—Can. Ind. Aff., 138, 1879 (probably identical). Samahquam.—Can. Ind. Aff., pt. 2, 160, 1901. Semaccom.—Can. Ind. Aff. 1884, 187, 1885.

Samamish (Skagit: *samena*, 'hunter.'—Gibbs). A Salish division on Samamish and Dwamish lakes, w. Wash., numbering 101 in 1854. Gibbs classed them as of Dwamish connection. They are not to be confounded with the Sawamish of Totten inlet.
Mon-mish.—Starling in Ind. Aff. Rep., 171, 1852 (separated by misprint from Say-hay-mon-mish). Sababish.—Gibbs in Pac. R. R. Rep.; I, 432, 1855. Sahmamish.—Starling, op. cit., 170. Sam-ab-mish.—Ross in Ind. Aff. Rep. 1869, 135, 1870. Sam-áhmish.—U. S. Ind. Treaties, 378, 1873. Samamish.—Gibbs, op. cit. Say-hay.—Starling, op. cit., 171 (see *Mon-mish*, above). Sim-a-mish.—Ross, ibid., 17, 1870.

Samampac. A tribe, evidently of the Coahuiltecan family, met by Massanet (Diario, in Mem. de Nueva España, XXVII, 94, MS.) in 1691 w. of Rio Hondo, Tex., with Patchal, Papanac, Patsau, and other tribes.   (H. E. B.)

Sambella. A former Upper Creek town on the N. side of Tallapoosa r., in Elmore co., Ala.—Royce in 18th Rep. B. A. E., Ala. map, 1899.

Samboukia. An unidentified tribe formerly living on the E. side of Yazoo r., Miss. Mentioned only by Coxe, who places them between the Koroa and the Tihiou (Tioux).
Samboukas.—Coxe in French, Hist. Coll. La., III, 59, 1851. Samboukia.—Coxe, Carolana, 10, map, 1741.

Samish. A Salish division formerly on a river and bay of the same name in Washington, now on Lummi res. Aseakum and Nukhwhaiimikhl were among their villages.
Isamishs.—Domenech, Deserts N. A., I, 441, 1860. Kahmish.—Ross in Ind. Aff. Rep., 135, 1869. Sabsh.—Mallet, ibid., 198, 1877 (said to be subordinate to Nugh-lemmy). Sahmish.—Stevens in H. R. Ex. Doc. 37, 34th Cong., 3d sess., 46, 1857. S'ã'mic.—Boas in 5th Rep. N. W. Tribes Can., 10, 1889. Samish.—Gibbs in Pac. R. R. Rep., I, 436, 1855. Sawish.—Simmons in Ind. Aff. Rep., 224, 1858. Sohmish.—Stevens, op. cit., 70.

Samoset (possibly from *Osamoset*, 'he who walks over much.'—Gerard). A native and sagamore of Pemaquid, and the original proprietor of the site of Bristol, Me. It is stated that he appeared among the Pilgrims soon after their landing in 1620 and greeted them with the words "Welcome, Englishmen!"—showing that he was more or less acquainted with their language—and informed them that he was a sagamore of Moratiggon (q. v.). As he had been in the C. Cod country for 8 months, it is probable that he went thither with Capt. Dermer, who left Monhegan for C. Cod a few months previous to the date mentioned. Samoset introduced the Pilgrims to Massasoit (q. v.), with whom it seems he was in friendly relation at that time. Moved to pity by his apparent destitution, the Pilgrims gave him "a horseman's coat" and also "strong water and biskit and butter, and cheese and pudding, and a piece of a mallard." Samoset repaid this kindness by the services he rendered the new colonists. He is next heard of two years later at Capmanwogen (Southport, Me.), with Capt. Levett, whom he esteemed as his special friend. In July, 1625, he, with Unongoit, executed the first deed made between the Indians and the English, conveying to John Brown, of New Harbor, 12,000 acres of the Pemaquid territory. Nothing further is recorded of Samoset until 1653, when he signed a deed conveying 1,000 acres to William Parnell, Thomas Way, and William England. He probably died soon thereafter, and was buried with his kindred on his island homestead near Round pond, in the town of Bristol. He is described as having been tall and straight, with hair long behind and short in front; his only dress "a leather" about his waist with a fringe about a span long. Mention is made of one son born to him about 1624, but his name is not given. Consult Mourt in Mass. Hist. Soc. Coll., 1st s., VIII, 226, 1802; Thornton in Me. Hist. Soc. Coll., v, 167–201, 1857; Sewell in Mag. Am. Hist., VIII, 820–25, 1882.   (C. T.)

Samp. A maize porridge, once a very important article of food in New England and elsewhere. In 1677 the treasurer of Massachusetts was ordered to procure, among other things to be given as presents to the king, "two hogsheads of speciall good *sampe*." Roger Williams (Key to Am. Lang., 33, 1643) defines the *nasaump* of the Narraganset dialect of Algonquian as "a kind of meale pottage unparched," adding that "from this the English call their *samp*, which is Indian corn beaten and boiled, and eaten hot or cold with milke or butter." Josselyn (1672) describes *sampe* as "a kind of loblolly of blue corn to eat with milk." The Narraganset *nasaump*, 'softened with water,' is cognate with the Abnaki *tsanbann*, corn mush, etc.   (A. F. C.)

Sampala. A former Seminole town, 26 m. above the forks of Apalachicola r., on the w. bank, in Calhoun co., Fla.—H. R. Ex. Doc. 74 (1823), 19th Cong., 1st sess., 27, 1826.

Sampanal. A tribe, evidently of the Coahuiltecan family, met by Massanet's party in 1689, when on the way from Coahuila to Texas, at Sacatsol mts., 20 leagues N. of the Rio Grande, in Texas. They were with the Mescal, Yorica, Chomene (Jumano), Tilpayay, and other tribes (Manzanet, Carta, *ca.* 1690, in Quar. Tex. Hist. Asso., II, 284, 1899). In 1691 Massanet met the same tribe near Rio Hondo (Diario, in Mem. de Nueva España, XXVII, 94, MS.).   (H. E. B.)

Sanpanal.—Massanet (1691), Diario, op. cit. Sanpanale.—Massanet, List of Tribes dated Nov. 16, 1690, in Mem. de Nueva España, XXVII, 183, MS.

Sampe. See *Samp.*

Sana. A central Texas tribe, apparently Tonkawan. It was known as early as 1691, when Massanet mentioned it in one of the most important passages bearing on the ethnology of early Texas. When about 25 m. N. E. of San Antonio r., apparently at Arroyo del Cibolo, and about opposite Seguin, he wrote: "I may note that from the mission [San Salvador, in Coahuila] to this place there is still one language [the Coahuiltecan] . . . From this place to the Texas there are other languages. There follow the Catqueca, Cantona, Emet, Cavas, Sana, Tojo, Toaa, and other tribes of Indians. At the said place, it being on the boundary between the Indians, they speak different languages, although they are all friendly and do not have wars." The Coahuiltecan tribes called the place Xoloton, and the tribes to the E. called it Bata Coniquiyoqui (Mem. de Nueva España, XXVII, 98, MS.).

In 1716 the Chanas, evidently identical, are mentioned by Ramón, together with Apaches, Yojuanes, and Chuuipanes, as enemies of the Texas (Orig. MS. in Archivo Gen. de Mex.). An imperfect copy of Ramón's report give "Jumanes" and "Chivipanes" in place of Yojuanes and Chuuipanes (Representación, Mem. de Nueva España, XXVII, 160, MS.). In 1716 the same list is given as the Apaches, Yojuanes, Cibipanes, and Canas (Dictamen Fiscal, Nov. 30, ibid., 193), and a few days later as Apaches, Jojuanes, Huvipanes (Ervipiames), and Chanas (Junta de Guerra, Dec. 2, 1716, ibid., 217). If the last list be correct, it is one of several indications of the Tonkawan affiliation of the Sana. Shortly after this period Llano r. was known as Rio de los Chanes, but it is not known that there is any connection between this and the name of the Sana tribe.

In 1721 the Sana are again met and dealt with. Late in January, it seems, some of the tribe (Samas) came from the E. to San Antonio and reported to Capt. García that Saint Denis, the French commandant at Natchitoches, had called a meeting of many tribes 30 leagues from San Antonio (Peña, Diario, Mem. de Nueva España, XXVII, 6, MS.). When Aguayo passed through San Antonio he made the Sana presents. Later he met part of the tribe, apparently in their home, halfway between the Guadalupe and the Colorado, in the neighborhood of modern San Marcos (ibid., 18).

Late in 1739 or early in 1740 a severe epidemic visited the San Antonio missions, and in Feb., 1740, the missionaries, wishing to replenish the supply of Indians, declared their intention of bringing in "the Zanas and Mayeyes, since they are related to those already converted" (ibid., xxviii, 203). As Massanet distinctly tells us that the Sana did not speak the Coahuiltecan language, and as the Mayeyes were quite evidently Tonkawan, the conclusion is that the Sana also were Tonkawan. A considerable list of words spoken by the Sana and their congeners is extant, and a careful study of it will perhaps settle the point (San Antonio de Valero Bautismos, beginning with 1740, MS.). In 1740 gentile Sana began to enter San Antonio de Valero mission in considerable numbers, and continued coming till about 1749. A study of the records shows that before entering the mission they were very closely interrelated by marriage with the Tojo (Tou, Too), Mayeye, Sijame, Tenu, and Aujuiap tribes or subtribes. In 1743, "Numa, of the Tou tribe, chief of the Zanas," was baptized at the mission (San Antonio de Valero Bautismos, partidas 494, 549, 579, 581, 608, 633, 635, 647, 675, 714, etc.). In 1793 the Sana were mentioned as one of the main tribes at San Antonio de Valero (Revilla-Gigedo, Carta, 195, in Dic. Univ. de Hist. y de Geog., v, 1854).

The native pronunciation of the name was perhaps Chanas, but the most frequent spelling in the mission records is Zanas. Cf. *Sanukh*.   (H. E. B.)

Canas.—Ramón (1716), Derrotero, in Mem. de Nueva España, xxvii, 193, MS. Chanas.—Junta de Guerra, 1716, ibid., 217; also Father Zarate (1764), Valero Bautismos, partidas 1495-96. Chanes.—Ramón, op. cit.,160. Sanas.—Massanet (1691), op. cit. Zana.—Valero Bautismos, partida 494, MS.

San Agustin de Ahumada. A Spanish presidio established in 1756 near the mouth of Trinity r., Texas, to prevent the French from trading and settling among the Arkokisa and Bidai Indians, who lived along the lower courses of that stream and the Rio San Jacinto. Its establishment was the direct result of the arrest in 1754 (not 1757, as Morfi says) of one Blancpain (or Lanpen), who was trading in that vicinity among the Arkokisa. Bancroft gives the date of the founding as 1755, but an official report says that it was effected in consequence of an order of Feb. 12, 1756. It is true, however, that a temporary garrison was considered in 1755. Bancroft also fixes the first site about 100 m. up the Trinity, but official documents show that it was only about 2 leagues' distance from the mouth. Near it was established, at about the same time, Nuestra Señora de la Luz, or Orcoquisac (Arkokisa), mission.

Because of the unhealthfulness of the site, a plan to remove the presidio to the arroyo of Santa Rosa de Alcazar, a branch of the Rio San Jacinto, in the center of the Arkokisa country, was soon proposed;

in 1757 the Viceroy ordered the plan carried out; and, according to an official statement, it was accomplished before Aug., 1760, but this seems to be an error. Later, apparently in 1764, the presidio was ordered moved to Los Horconsitos, 2 or 3 leagues N. of the original site, but it appears that the removal was never made. A few years afterward the presidio was burned as the result of a quarrel, and in 1772 its abandonment was ordered, although this, as well as that of the mission, had already taken place (see Lamar Papers, Span. MS. no. 25; Nacogdoches Archives, Span. MS. no. 488; Valcarcel, Expediente sobre Variaciones, etc., Aug. 7, 1760, MS. in Archivo Gen.; Abad to the Viceroy, Nov. 27, 1759, and Dictamen Fiscal, Feb. 7, 1760, both in Béxar Archives, San Agustin de Ahumada; Viceroy Cruillas to Gov. Martos y Navarrete, Aug. 30, 1764, MS. in Béxar Archives; Bonilla, Breve Compendio, in Quar. Tex. Hist. Asso., viii, 11, 56, 57, 61, 1904; Bancroft, No. Mex. States and Tex., i, 615 (map), 653, 655–656, 1886).   (H. E. B.)

Orcoquisac.—Rubi, Dictamen, 1767, MS. San Agustin de Aumada.—Barrios y Jauregui (1756) in Nacogdoches Archives, Span. MS. no. 488. San Augustin de Ahumada.—Ibid. San Augustin de Ahumada Rio de la Trinidad.—Valcarcel (1760), op. cit.

San Andrés (Saint Andrew). A former village of the Tubar on the extreme headwaters of the Rio Fuerte, 3 m. from Morelos, s. w. Chihuahua, Mexico; now largely Mexicanized. — Lumholtz, Unknown Mex., i, 442, 1902.

San Andrés Coamiata. A Huichol village near the upper waters of the Rio Chapalagana, on a plain in the sierra in the w. part of the tribal territory, in N. w. Jalisco, Mexico.

San Andrés Coamiata.—Lumholtz, Huichol Ind., 5, 1898. Tátéíkia.—Lumholtz, Unknown Mex., ii, 27, 1902 ('house of our mother,' alluding to a mythical serpent: Huichol name).

San Andrés Coata. A former Pima rancheria, visited and so named by Father Kino in 1697, and probably as early as 1694 (Bancroft, No. Mex. States, i, 259, 1884); situated near the junction of the Gila and Salado, s. Ariz. Taylor (Cal. Farmer, June 13, 1862) mentions it as a mission founded by Kino in 1694, but this is evidently an error.

San Andrés.—Garcés (1775), Diary, 142, 1900. San Andrés Coata.—Mange in Doc. Hist. Mex., 4th s., i, 306, 1856.

San Angelo. A rancheria of the Sobaipuri, near the w. bank of Rio Santa Cruz, below its mouth in s. Arizona, first visited and doubtless so named by Father Kino in the latter part of the 17th century.

S. Angel.—Kino, map (1701), in Bancroft, Ariz. and N. Mex., 360, 1889. S. Angelo.—Kino, map (1702), in Stöcklein, Neue Welt-Bott, 74, 1726.

San Antonio (Saint Anthony). A former pueblo of the Tigua, situated E. of the present settlement of the same name, about the center of the Sierra de Gallego, or Sierra de Carnué, between San Pedro and Chili-li, E. of the Rio Grande, N. Mex. Accord-ing to Bandelier (Arch. Inst. Papers, IV, 253, 1892), the only mention of the settle-ment is made in the Carnué land grant in the 18th century, and it must have been occupied within historic times.

San Antonio. A former group of Al-chedoma rancherias, situated on the Rio Colorado in Arizona, 35 or 40 m. below the mouth of Bill Williams fork. Visited and so named by Fray Francisco Garcés in 1776.—Garcés, Diary, 423, 1900.

San Antonio. A Tepehuane pueblo, and formerly the seat of a Spanish mission, at the N. boundary of Durango, Mexico, lon. 105°.

S. Antonio.—Orozco y Berra, Geog., 319, 1864.

San Antonio de la Huerta. A pueblo of the Nevome, situated at the junction of the Rio Batepito and Rio Soyopa, tribu-taries of the Rio Yaqui, about lat. 29°, lon. 109°, Sonora, Mexico (Orozco y Berra, Geog., 351, 1864). It is now a civilized pueblo, and contained 171 inhabitants in 1900.

San Antonio de Padua. The third Fran-ciscan mission established in California. The place was chosen by Father Junípero Serra in the well-wooded valley of the stream now known as San Antonio r., about 6 m. from the present town of Jolon, Monterey co. The native name of the place was Texhaya, or Teshaya. Here the mission was founded by Serra with great enthusiasm on July 14, 1771, though only one native was present. The Indians, however, proved friendly; they brought food and helped in the work of con-structing the church and other necessary buildings. The first native was baptized a month later, and by the end of 1772, 158 baptisms were reported. In 1780 the neophytes numbered 585, while by 1790 they had reached 1,076, making it the largest mission community at that time in California. By 1800 there was a slight increase to 1,118, while the greatest num-ber in the history of the mission, 1,124, was reached in 1805. The wealth of the mission was not so great as that of some others. The land was reported as rather sterile and difficult to irrigate, although the average crop for the decade ending 1810 was 3,780 bushels. In the year last named there were 3,700 cattle, 700 horses, and more than 8,000 sheep. Though the number of the neophytes gradually de-creased, reaching 878 in 1820 and 681 in 1830, the mission live stock continued to multiply and the crops were nearly as good as before. In 1830 Robinson (Life in California, 81, 1846) reported that everything at the mission was in the most perfect order, and the Indians cleanly and well dressed. Beyond an attack on the mission converts by some outside na-tives in 1774, in which one Indian only

was wounded, there does not seem to have been any trouble with the natives in this region. By 1830 there were said to be no more gentiles within 75 m. Up to 1834 the total number of Indians baptized was 4,348, of whom 2,587 were children. The earlier buildings of the mission were of adobe, but a new and larger church with arched corridors and a brick front was begun about 1809, and completed within the next ten years. The mission was formally secularized in 1835, and during the next few years declined rapidly, losing a large part of its stock. There was much friction between Padre Mer-cado and the civil administrator, and many of the Indians deserted because of bad treatment. As with the other mis-sions, the control was restored to the padres in 1843, but too late to accomplish much good. There seems to be no record of the sale of the mission. Padre Doroteo Ambris remained there for several years, and at his death the mission was deserted, except for an occasional service by a visit-ing priest from San Miguel. The place remained in ruins until 1904, when the Landmarks Club of California undertook its preservation. The Indians in the neighborhood of the San Antonio mission belonged to the Salinan linguistic stock, but the mission also had neophytes from the San Joaquin valley, probably Yokuts. The following names of villages have been taken from the old mission books (Taylor, Cal. Farmer, Apr. 27, 1860): Atnel, Chacomex, Chitama, Cholucyte, Chunapatama, Chuquilin (San Miguelita), Chuzach, Cinnisel, Ejmal, Ginace, Iolon, Lamaca, Lima, Quina (Quinada), Sapay-wis, Seama, Steloglamo, Subazama, Teco-lom, Teshaya, Tetachoya (Ojitos), Texja, Tsilacomap, Zassalete, Zumblito. The rancherias, it is said, were generally named after their chiefs. (A. B. L.)

San Antonio de Valero. A mission, com-monly known as the The Alamo (Ah′-lah-mo), transplanted in 1718 from the Rio Grande to the site of the present city of San Antonio, Texas. It, together with the ad-jacent presidio and villa, was founded as an intermediate center of operations between the Rio Grande and the E. Texas mis-sions, which had been reestablished in 1716. The missionary part of the enter-prise was planned and directed by Fray Antonio de San Buenaventura de Oli-vares. In 1700 he had founded San Fran-cisco Solano mission near the Rio Grande, in Valle de la Circumcisión (Portillo, Apuntes para la Historia Antigua de Coahuila y Texas, 269–70, 1888). It was subsequently moved to San Ildefonso, thence to San Joseph, on the Rio Grande, a short distance from Presidio del Rio Grande (Valero Bautismos, folio 1). The principal tribe baptized at these places was the Xarame, although the Siaguan,

Payuguan, Papanac, and perhaps others were represented. By 1716, 364 baptisms had been performed (Valero Bautismos). In this year, when the government was planning a settlement between the Rio Grande and E. Texas, Olivares proposed transplanting this mission, with its Indians, to the river then called San Antonio de Padua, maintaining that his Xarames, since they were well versed in agriculture, would assist in teaching and subduing new neophytes (Olivares to the Viceroy, Mem. de Nueva España, 169–70, MS.). This plan was carried out in 1718, possession of the new site being formally given on May 1. The transfer was no doubt facilitated by the close affinity of the tribes at the new site with those at the old. The mission was founded near the E. frontier of the Coahuiltecan group. The tribes or bands near by were extremely numerous and in general correspondingly small. One of the chief ones was the Payaya. This was not the first time they had heard the gospel, for in 1691 Massanet had entered their village on San Antonio r. (which they had called Yanaguana), set up a cross, erected an altar in a chapel of boughs, said mass in the presence of the natives, explained its meaning, and distributed rosaries, besides giving the Payaya chief a horse. This tribe, Massanet said, was large, and their rancherias deserved the name of pueblo (Diario, Mem. de Nueva España, XXVII, 95–96, MS.).

Within about a year the mission, now called San Antonio de Valero, was removed across the river, evidently to the site it still occupies (Espinosa, Chrónica Apostolica, 450, 1746). From the records it seems that only one baptism was performed in 1718. In 1719 there were 24, mainly of Xarames and Payayas, but representing also the Cluetau, Junced (Juncal?), Pamaya, Siaguan, Sijame, Sumi, and Terocodame tribes. The first decade resulted in about 250 baptisms, representing some 40 so-called tribes. By Feb. 1740, there had been 837 baptisms. Shortly before this an epidemic had gone through all the San Antonio missions, and left at Valero only 184 neophytes; but immediately afterward (1739–40) 77 Tacamanes (Tacames?) were

brought in (Mem. de Nueva España, XXVIII, 203–04, MS.). A report made Dec. 17, 1741, showed 238 persons resident at the mission (Urrutia to the Viceroy, MS.). On May 8, 1744, the first stone of a new church was laid, but in 1762 it was being rebuilt, a work that seems never to have been completed (Diego Martín García, 1745, op. cit., and Ynforme de Misiones, 1762, Mem. de Nueva España, XXVIII, 164, MS.). According to a report made in 1762, the books showed 1,972 baptisms (evidently an exaggeration), 247 burials, and 454 marriages. There were then 275 persons, of the Xarame, Payaya, Sana, Lipan (captives mainly), Coco, Tojo (Tou), and Karankawa tribes. Of this number 32 were gentiles of the last-named tribe, whose reduction was then being attempted, notwithstanding the opposition of the Zacatecan missions (see *Nuestra Señora del Rosario*). The same report, besides describing the monastery workshops, church, chapel, and ranch, says of the Indian quarters: "There are 7 rows of houses for the dwellings of the Indians; they are made of stone and supplied with doors and windows; they are furnished with high beds, chests, metates, pots, flat earthen pans, kettles, cauldrons, and boilers. With their arched porticoes the houses form a broad and beautiful plaza through which runs a canal skirted by willows and fruit trees, and used by the Indians. To insure a supply of water in case of blockade by the enemy a curbed well has been made. For the defense of the settlement, the plaza is surrounded by a wall. Over the gate is a large tower with its embrasures, 3 cannons, some firearms, and appropriate supplies (Trans. by E. Z. Rather, in Bolton and Barker, With the Makers of Texas, 64–65, 1904). For a description of the massive walls, see Bancroft, No. Mex. States, II, 207–08, 1889.

After 1765 the activity of this mission suddenly declined, even more rapidly than that of the neighboring missions. This decline was contemporaneous, on the one hand, with the lessening of political activity in Texas after the acquisition of Louisiana by the Spaniards, and, on the other hand, with a growing hos-

CHURCH OF SAN ANTONIO DE VALERO, "THE ALAMO"

tility on the part of the northern tribes. It seems also true that the docile tribes on which the mission had largely depended were becoming exhausted. Moreover the growing villa of San Fernando encroached upon the mission lands and injurious quarrels resulted. From 1764 to 1783 only 102 baptisms were recorded for Valero, while a number of these were of Spaniards. In 1775 Inspector Oconor reported fewer than 15 families there (quoted by Portillo, op. cit., 297–98). In 1793 there were still 43 Payaya, Sana, and others, evidently survivors of families brought there long before (Revilla Gigedo, Carta, Dec. 27, 1793, MS.).

In 1793 this mission was secularized, and the lands were divided among the neophytes and some of the citizens (not Indians) who had abandoned Adaes in 1773. The walled inclosure and the buildings were later occupied by the company del Alamo de Parras, whence the name Alamo (Revillo-Gigedo, op. cit.; Portillo, op. cit., 353–54), and in 1836 they became the scene of one of the most heroic events in all history—the famed resistance and annihilation of Travis and his men, Mar. 6, 1836. The chapel is now the property of the State of Texas.

The baptismal records show the surprising number of about 100 apparently distinct tribes or subtribes represented at this mission during its whole career after the removal to the San Antonio. These are: Apache, Apion, Caguas, Camai, Cantuna (Cantanual), Cems (Quems?), Chaguantapam, Chapamaco, Chuapas, Cimataguo, Cluetau, Coco, Cocomeioje (Coco), Colorado, Comanche, Cupdan, Emet, Gabilan, Guerjuatida, Huacacasa, Hyerbipiamo, Jancae (Tonkawa?), Juamaca (Juampa?), Juancas, Jueinzum, Juncatas (Juncataguo), Junced, Karankawa, Lipan, Macocoma (Cocoma), Manos Coloradas, Manos Prietas, Maquems, Matucar, Mayeye, Menequen, Merhuan, Mescales, Mesquites, Mulato, Muruam, Natao, Necpacha (Apache?), Nigco, Ocana, Pachaquen (cf. Pacuaches), Pachaug, Paguanan, Pamaya, Papanac (Panac), Paquache, Pasqual, Pastaloca, Pataguo, Patan, Patauium, Patou, Patzau, Pausaqui, Pausay, Payaya, Payuguan (Payuhuan), Peana, Piniquu, Pita, Psaupsau, Quesal, Quimso (Quems?), Secmoco, Sencase, Siaban, Siaguan, Siaguasan, Siansi, Sijame, Sinicu, Siniczo (Senisos, Cenizos), Sulujame, Sumi, Tacames (Tacamane), Tenu, Terocodame, Tetzino, Texa (Hainai?), Ticmamar, Tishim, Tonkawa, Tonzaumacagua, Tucana, Tuu, Ujuiap (Aujuiap), Uracha, Xarame, Xaraname (Araname), Yman, Yojuan, Yorica, Yuta (Yute), Zorquan.

(H. E. B.)

San Antonio de Velero.—Bancroft, No. Mex. States, I, 618, 1886 (misprint).

Sanate Adiva (said to mean 'great woman,' or 'chief woman'). A priestess or chieftainess at the Nabedache village on San Pedro cr., Houston co., Texas, in 1768. See *Nabedache*.

San Athanasio (Saint Athanasius). A Cochimi pueblo and visita 5 leagues from San Ignacio de Kadakaman mission, Lower California, in 1745.—Venegas, Hist. Cal., II, 198, 1759.

San Benito (Saint Benedict). A former Serrano village of 80 inhabitants near the source of the Rio Mohave, 3 leagues N. E. over the mountains from San Bernardino valley. It was visited and so named by Fray Francisco Garcés in 1776.—Garcés, Diary (1776), 246, 1900.

San Bernabé (Saint Barnabas). A former Tepehuane pueblo of Durango, Mexico, and the seat of a mission.—Orozco y Berra, Geog., 319, 1864.

San Bernardino (Saint Bernardinus). The name of "an island that the [Gila] river makes temporarily when it rises," where there are some Maricopa rancherias. The place was visited by Anza, Font, and Garcés in 1774–75. Not to be confounded with a Maricopa rancheria of the same name on the Gila, 4 leagues above. See Coues, Garcés Diary, 119, 126, 1900.

San Bernardino. A former Maricopa rancheria at Agua Caliente, or the hot springs, near the Rio Gila, s. Ariz., about 24 leagues above its mouth. It was visited by Anza in 1774, and by Garcés, Anza, and Font in 1775.
Agua Caliente.—Anza and Font (1780) cited by Bancroft, Ariz. and N. Mex., 392, 1889. San Bernardino del Agua Caliente.—Font (1775) quoted in Coues, Garcés Diary, 120, 1900.

San Bernardo (Saint Bernard). A name applied by Mezières in 1778 to one of two Tawehash villages visited by him on upper Red r., Texas. See Mezières, letter to Croix, Apr. 19, 1778 (in which he reports having given the village this name in honor of the Governor of Louisiana), MS. in Archivo Gen. Mex. (H. E. B.)

San Bonifacio (Saint Boniface). Apparently a former rancheria of one of the Piman tribes, probably Papago, situated s. of the Rio Gila between San Angelo and San Francisco, in the present Arizona, at the beginning of the 18th century.
S. Bonifacius.—Kino, map (1702), in Stöcklein, Neue Welt-Bott, 74, 1726.

San Buenaventura. The ninth Franciscan mission founded in California, and the last by Father Junípero Serra. The site was chosen within the limits of the present Ventura, Ventura co., near the beach and adjoining one of the native villages, and the usual founding ceremonies took place Mar. 31, 1782. The natives seemed pleased with the prospect and readily aided in the construction of the new buildings. The increase in the number of neophytes was not so rapid as at some of the missions. In 1790 there were 385; in 1800, 715; in 1810, 1,297; while the highest number, 1,328, was reached in 1816. In other respects the mission was very successful; it had more cattle (10,013 head) and raised more grain (9,400 bushels) in 1800 than any other place in California. Vancouver visited the mission in Nov. 1793, and remarked on the quantity, variety, and general excellence of its vegetables and fruits. The buildings also were excellent, though the new stone church was not completed and dedicated until 1809. During the first decade of the 19th century the mission continued the most prosperous in California. In 1810 there were 21,221 cattle, 3,276 horses and mules, and 8,543 small stock, with an average crop for the decade of 6,400 bushels. Though losing somewhat by 1820, the mission still retained first place. The earthquake of 1812, which destroyed the church at San Juan Capistrano, also severely injured the new church of San Buenaventura, and it was feared that the whole mission site was settling into the sea, so that all the inhabitants removed to higher ground for three months. After 1820 the mission declined rapidly, both in converts and in material prosperity. In 1830 there were 726 neophytes, and 626 in 1834. Up to that time the total number of natives baptized was 3,805, of whom 1,909 were children. Secularization does not seem to have been carried out here until 1837. Bancroft estimates that in 1840 there were about 250 Indians in the community and as many more scattered in the district. In 1844 the mission was reported as still fairly prosperous; in 1846 the lands were sold for $12,000. The buildings remained in the possession of the Catholic Church, and since 1843 the mission has been the regular parish church of Ventura, which in garbled form was named from the mission. In 1893 the old church was so renovated as to lose much of its historic interest. The Indians among whom San Buenaventura mission was established belonged to the Chumashan (q. v.) linguistic family, which probably furnished the major portion of the neophytes.   (A. B. L.)

San Carlos (Saint Charles). The second Franciscan mission founded in California. Even before the founding of San Diego an expedition started N. under Portolá, in 1769, to explore the country and find the port of Monterey, previously described by Vizcaino (1602), where it was intended to establish the next mission. They reached the port, but did not recognize it, and returned, after setting up a cross on the

shore of the bay. The following spring two expeditions started, one by land and one by sea. Both expeditions arrived safely, and the port was this time recognized beyond a doubt. The cross was found still standing, but surrounded and adorned with arrows, sticks, feathers, fish, meat, and clams, placed there by the natives, apparently as offerings. The bells were hung and the Mission of San Carlos Borromeo de Monterey was formally founded June 3, 1770. Some huts were built and a palisade erected, but for several days no natives appeared. Father Junípero Serra soon became dissatisfied with the site of the mission, and in December, after the necessary buildings had been constructed, it was removed to Carmelo valley. The mission was henceforth known as San Carlos Borromeo del Carmelo, sometimes in later days merely as Carmelo. The old site became the presidio of Monterey. The native name of the new site, according to Taylor (Cal. Farmer, Feb. 22, 1860) was Eslenes. The number of converts gradually increased, 165 being reported in 1772, and 614 in 1783. Serra made San Carlos his headquarters, and here he died, Aug. 24, 1784, and was buried in the mission church. In 1785 Lasuen was chosen padre presidente, and made his residence chiefly at San Carlos, Palou having temporarily taken charge after Serra's death. Monterey being an important port, San Carlos was visited by a number of travelers, including La Perouse (1786) and Vancouver (1793). The mission never had a large number of neophytes; the highest, 927, was reached in 1794, after which there was a gradual decline. In livestock and agriculture the mission was fairly successful, the average crop for the decade ending 1800 being 3,700 bushels. Cattle and horses in 1800 numbered 2,180, and sheep more than 4,000. There was considerable increase during the next decade, but before 1820 the decline had begun, though it was less marked for a time than at many other missions. In 1797 a new stone church, the ruins of which are still to be seen, was completed. The number of neophytes was 758 in 1800, 513 in 1810, 381 in 1820, and about 150 in 1834. There was but little of the mission property left at the time of secularization in the year last named, while by 1840 the ruined buildings were all that remained. The mission church was entirely neglected until about 1880, when it was restored and roofed, and was rededicated in Aug. 1884. The neophytes of San Carlos belonged chiefly to the Costanoan and Esselenian linguistic stocks. Representatives of most of the Esselen villages were doubtless included, as well as of the Rumsen, Kalindaruk, and Sakhone divisions of the

Costanoan, some of the Chalones, with probably also some of the Mutsun. The following names of villages are given by Taylor (Cal. Farmer, Apr. 20, 1860), most of them being taken from the mission books: Achasta, Alcoz, Animpayamo, Aspasniagan, Cakanaruk, Capanay (Kapanai), Carmentaruka, Chachat, Coyyo, Culul (Kulul), Ecgeagam, Echilat, Eslanagan, Excellemaks, Fyules, Gilimis, Guayusta, Ichenta, Jappayon, Lucayasta, Mustac, Nennequi, Noptac, Nutnur, Nuthesum (Mutsun), Pachhepes, Paisin, Pytoguis (Poitokwis), Santa Clara (Esselenes proper), Sapponet, Sargentarukas, Soccorondo, Tebityilat, Tiubta, Triwta, Tucutnut (or Santa Teresa), Tushguesta, Wachanaruka, Xaseum, Xumis, Yampas, Yanostas, Ymunacam.   (A. B. L.)

Carmelo.—Taylor in Cal. Farmer, Apr. 20, 1860. San Carlos.—Ibid. San Carlos de Carmelo.—Ibid. San Cárlos del Carmelo.—Bancroft, Hist. Cal., I, 170, 1886. San Cárlos de Monterey.—Ibid.

San Carlos Apache. A part of the Apache dwelling at the San Carlos agency, Ariz.,

SAN CARLOS APACHE

numbering 1,172 in 1909. The name has little ethnic significance, having been applied officially to those Apache living on the Gila r. in Arizona, and sometimes referred to also as Gileños, or Gila Apache (q. v.).

Bin-i-ette She-deck-a.—White, MS. Hist. Apaches, B. A. E., 1875 (Chiricahua name). Háhel-topa-ipá.—Gatschet, Yuma Sprachstamm, I, 370, 1877 ('men with bows and arrows who live on the river': Tonto name).

San Casimiro (Saint Casimir). A rancheria of the so-called Quiquima (Quigyuma), visited by Father Kino in Feb.–Mar. 1702. Doubtless situated on the E. bank

of the Rio Colorado, above tidewater, in N. w. Sonora, Mexico.—Bancroft, No. Mex. States, I, 500, 1884; Coues, Garcés Diary, 178, 1900.

Sanchecantacket. A village in 1698 near Edgartown, on the island of Marthas Vineyard, Mass.

Sahnchecontuckquet.—Doc. of 1698 in Mass. Hist. Soc. Coll., 1st s., X, 132, 1809. Sanchecantacket.—Ibid., I, 204, note, 1806. Sengekontakit.—Cotton (1674), ibid.

Sanchines. A former village, presumably Costanoan, connected with Dolores mission, San Francisco, Cal.—Taylor in Cal. Farmer, Oct. 18, 1861.

San Clemente (Saint Clement). A former rancheria, probably of the Sobaipuri, visited and so named by Kino and Mange in 1699. Situated on the w. bank of Rio Santa Cruz, N. of the present Tucson, Ariz.—Mange (1699) in Doc. Hist. Mex., 4th s., I, 316, 1856.

San Cosme (Saint Cosmas). A former rancheria, probably of the Papago, directly N. of San Xavier del Bac, on Rio Santa Cruz, s. Ariz.

S. Cosmas.—Kino, map (1702), in Stöcklein, Neue Welt-Bott, 74, 1726. S. Cosme.—Venegas, Hist. Cal., I, map, 1759.

San Cristóbal (Saint Christopher). Once the principal pueblo of the Tano (q. v.), situated between Galisteo and Pecos, Santa Fé co., N. Mex. The natives of this pueblo and of San Lazaro were forced by hostilities of the Apache, the eastern Keresan tribes, and the Pecos to transfer their pueblos to the vicinity of San Juan, where the towns were rebuilt under the same names (Bancroft, Ariz. and N. Mex., 186, 1889). This removal (which was more strictly to a place called Pueblito, near the present Potrero, about 2 m. E. of Santa Cruz, on the Rio Santa Cruz), occurred after the Pueblo revolt of 1680, and prior to 1692, at which latter date the natives were found by Vargas in their new locality. The pueblo was abandoned in 1694, but was later reoccupied, and was finally deserted in 1696 after the murder of their missionary in June of that year. Most of their descendants are now among the Hopi of Arizona. See Bandelier in Arch. Inst. Papers, IV, 83, 103, 1892; Meline, Two Thousand Miles, 220, 1867.

Christobal.—Arrowsmith, Map N. A., 1795, ed. 1814. Christoval.—Crepy, Map Amér. Sept., 1783 (?). Pânt-hâm-ba.—Bandelier, Gilded Man, 221, 1893 (misprint). San Christóval.—Alcedo, Dic. Geog., I, 557, 1786. San Cristóbal.—Sosa (1591) in Doc. Inéd., XV, 25 et seq., 1871. San Cristobel.—Meline, Two Thousand Miles, 220, 1867. San Cristoforo.—Columbus Mem. Vol., 155, 1893. San Cristóval.—Bandelier in Arch. Inst. Papers, I, 101, 1881. Sant Chrpstobal.—Oñate (1598) in Doc. Inéd., XVI, 114, 1871. Sant Xpoval.—Ibid., 259. Sant Xupal.—Ibid., 258. S. Christoval.—D'Anville, Map Am. Sept., 1746. Yam-p'ham-ba.—Bandelier in Arch. Inst. Papers, III, 125, 1890 (aboriginal name). Yam P'hamba.—Ibid., IV, 83, 1892.

Sandals. In America, as among Oriental nations, the sandal was anciently used, following in its distribution generally the warmer isotherms, but often being carried by migration and retained through tribal custom in regions where extremes of temperature prevailed. In both hemispheres the sandal formed a part of the costume of the peoples more advanced in culture; it was the characteristic footwear of the Peruvians, Central Americans, Mexicans, and Pueblos, and especially of Indians living in the cactus region generally. In its simplest form the Pueblo sandal consisted of a sole braided from tenacious leaves, held to the foot by a toe and heel cord, or by a cord roved through loops on the margin of the sole and passing over the foot. Other sandals have flaps at the toe and heel, and in some cases the entire foot is covered, when the sandal becomes a sort of rude moccasin. Sandals occur in considerable variety, designed for men, women, and children, and for different seasons. The material is almost exclusively derived from the yucca plant—either the plain leaves, hanks of the extracted fiber, or cord of various sizes twisted from the fiber. Sandals consisting of a half-inch pad of yucca fibers, held to the foot with strips of the same material or by thongs, are said to be worn by Kawia men at night. Putnam found sandals in Mammoth Cave, Ky., thus determining their former use in E. United States. A few tribes of California, the Ute of the interior basin, the Mohave, the Pima, and perhaps the tribes around the Gulf of Mexico, wore sandals. Within recent years the older people among the Pima have commonly worn sandals of undressed hide, especially when traveling, to protect the feet from cactus spines. A similar sandal is worn by the Chemehuevi. Among some of the ancient Pueblos a sandal was buried with the body of an infant to "guide" the deceased to the *sípapu* or entrance to the underworld. See *Clothing, Moccasin.*

Consult Fewkes in 17th Rep. B. A. E., 573, 1898; Holmes in 13th Rep. B. A. E., 34, 1896; Kroeber in Univ. Cal. Pub., Am. Archæol. and Ethnol., VIII, no. 2, 1908; Mason in Rep. Nat. Mus. 1894, 1896; Mindeleff in 8th Rep. B. A. E., 133, 1891; Nordenskiöld, Cliff Dwellers of the Mesa Verde, 1893.   (W. H.)

Sandatoton ('those who eat by themselves'). A clan or band of the Chiricahua Apache, supposed to be a part of the Pinaleño now under San Carlos and Fort Apache agencies, Ariz.

Kassilúda.—Gatschet, MS., B. A. E., 1883 (from the name or their chief). San-da-to-tons.—White, MS. Hist. Apaches, B. A. E., 1875. Sandedotán.—Gatschet, MS., B. A. E., 1883.

Sandbanks. A Hatteras village on Hatteras id., N. C., E. of Pamlico sd., in 1701.—Lawson (1709), Hist. Car., 383, 1860.

Sanderstown. A former Cherokee settlement in N. E. Alabama, probably taking its name from some prominent mixed-blood.   (J. M.)

Sandia (Span.: 'watermelon'). A Tigua pueblo on the E. bank of the Rio Grande, N. Mex., 12 m. N. of Albuquerque. It evidently formed one of the pueblos of the Province of Tiguex of the chroniclers of Coronado's expedition in 1540–42; and is the Napeya (a corruption of Nafiat, the native name of the pueblo) of Juan de Oñate in 1598. Sandia became the seat of the Franciscan mission of San Francisco early in the 17th century, but it was abandoned during the Pueblo revolt of 1680, most of the inhabitants fleeing for safety to the Hopi country in N. E. Arizona, where, probably

A SANDIA MAN

with other refugees, they built the village of Payupki, on the Middle mesa, the walls of which are still partly standing. Payupki is the name by which the Sandia pueblo is still known to the Hopi. In 1681 Gov. Otermin, during his attempt to reconquer New Mexico, burned Sandia. The people remained among the Hopi until 1742, when Fathers Delgado and Pino brought 441 of them and their children to the Rio Grande; but it would seem that some of these returned to Arizona, since Father Juan Miguel Menchero, in a petition to the governor in 1748, stated that for six years he had been engaged in missionary work among the Indians, and had "converted and gained more than 350 souls from here to the Puerco r., which I have brought from the Moqui pueblos—bringing with me the cacique of these Moqui pueblos, for the purpose of establishing their pueblo at the place called Sandia," and thereupon asked for possession of the land at that point "so as to prevent my converts from returning to apostacy." The governor made the desired grant (which now consists of 24,187 acres, confirmed by Congress), and the new pueblo was established in due form under the name Nuestra Señora de los Dolores y San Antonio de Sandia (see Meline, Two Thousand Miles, 214, 1867; Prince, New Mexico, 38, 1883). The population of Sandia was 78 in 1910. See *Pueblos, Tigua.* (F. W. H.)

Asumpcion.—Bancroft, Ariz. and N. Mex., 281, 1889 (or Dolores; mission name). **Çandia.**—Zárate-Salmeron (ca. 1629) quoted by Bandelier in Arch. Inst. Papers, IV, 220, 1892. **Deis.**—Pike, Exped., app., pt. iii, 13, 1810. **Dolores.**—Bancroft, Ariz. and N. Mex., 281, 1889 (Asumpcion or; mission name). **Kĭn Nodózi.**—Curtis, Am. Ind., I, 138, 1907 ('striped houses': Navaho name). **Mapeya.**—Columbus Memorial Vol., 155, 1893 (misprint of Oñate's "Napeya"). **Na-fhi-ap.**—Bandelier in Arch. Inst. Papers, III, 130, 1890 (native name of the pueblo). **Nafiad.**—Gatschet, Isleta MS. vocab., B. A. E., 1885 ('dusty place': Isleta name of the pueblo). **Na-fi-ap.**—Bandelier in Arch. Inst. Papers, III, 260, 1890 (native name of the pueblo). **Nafíat.**—Hodge, field notes, B. A. E., 1895 (native name of pueblo). **Nafíhuide.**—Gatschet, Isleta MS. vocab., B. A. E., 1885 (pl. Nafíhun: Isleta name of the people). **Napeya.**—Oñate (1598) in Doc. Ined., XVI, 115, 1871 (corruption of Na-fi-ap). **Nâ'pfĕ'ta.**—Hodge, field notes, B. A. E., 1899 (from *nä* 'hill,' *pfä'na* 'cloud,' referring to the wind-blown sand-dunes in the vicinity: Taos name). **Naphíat.**—Hodge, field notes, B. A. E., 1895 (also Nafiat; Isleta name). **Ña-pĭ-ăp.**—Bandelier in Arch. Inst. Bull., I, 18, 1883 (native name). **Na-pi-hah.**—Jouvenceau in Cath. Pion., I, no. 9, 13, 1906. **Na-si-ap.**—Bandelier, Gilded Man, 149, 1893. **N. S. de los Dolores de Sandia.**—Alencaster (1805) quoted in Prince, Hist. N. Mex., 37, 1883 (mission name). **Nuestra Señora de los Dolores de Sandia.**—Ward in Ind. Aff. Rep. 1867, 213, 1868 (mission name). **Our Lady of Sorrow and Saint Anthony of Sandia.**—Meline, Two Thousand Miles, 218, 1867. **Our Lady of Sorrows and Saint Anthony of Sandia.**—Prince, Hist. N. Mex., 38, 1883. **Payüpki.**—Fewkes in Am. Anthr., VI, 397, 1894 (Hopi name). **Sandea.**—Meriwether (1856) in H. R. Ex. Doc. 37, 34th Cong., 3d sess., 146, 1857. **Sandia.**—Rivera, Diario, leg. 784, 1736. **San-Diaz.**—Malte-Brun, Geog., V, 328, 1826. **Sandilla.**—Arny in Ind. Aff. Rep. 1871, 382, 1872. **San Francisco de Sandia.**—Benavides, Memorial, 20, 1630. **Saudia.**—Davis, El Gringo, 428, 1857 (misprint). **SDiaz.**—Mühlenpfordt quoted by Buschmann, Neu-Mexico, 272, 1858. **S Dies.**—Pike, Exped., 3d map, 1810. **Sendia.**—D'Anville, Map Amér. Sept., 1746. **St. Dies.**—Pike, Exped., app., pt. iii, 222, 1810. **Sundia.**—Calhoun (1840) in Cal. Mess. and Corresp., 206, 1850. **Washrotsi.**—Hodge, field notes, B. A. E., 1895 ('dusty': Laguna name). **Wā'shutse.**—Gatschet, Laguna MS. vocab., B. A. E., 1879 (Laguna name). **Wash-ŭ'tsi.**—Hodge, field notes, B. A. E., 1895 (Acoma name). **We'-suala-kuin.**—F. H. Cushing, inf'n, 1884 ('foot village', referring to the large feet of the inhabitants [?]: Zuñi name; *s=hl*). **Zandia.**—Zarate-Salmeron (ca. 1629) quoted by Bancroft, Nat. Races, I, 600, 1882.

San Diego (Saint James). The first mission established within the present state of California. After the expulsion of the Jesuits in 1767, the Spanish authorities determined to found a number of military and missionary establishments in Califor-

nia. The mission work was placed in the hands of the Franciscans, and Father Junípero Serra, who was already president of the missions of Lower California, took charge. Two vessels and two land expeditions were dispatched northward from the settlements in Lower California, and reached the harbor of San Diego, named and described in 1602 by Vizcaino, in the early summer of 1769. Serra arrived with the last land division on July 1, and on July 16 he formally founded the mission, dedicating it to San Diego de Alcalá. The place chosen was at the present Old Town, on a hill near the bay, at or near the native village of Cosoy. The natives were by no means timid; indeed they soon became so bold in their thievish operations that they made a concerted attempt to plunder the settlement. In the conflict which followed, Aug. 15, 1769, one Spaniard and a number of Indians were killed. After this a stockade was built around the mission, and the natives became more respectful. The missionary work was at first without success, and it was a year or more before the first neophyte was enrolled, while for several years the work progressed but slowly. During the first few years the mission also suffered much from lack of supplies, and at one time was on the point of being abandoned when the supplies arrived. Owing to lack of knowledge of local conditions the crops of the first two or three years were not successful. In 1774 the mission was moved N. E. up the valley about 6 m. to a place called by the natives Nipaguay, while the old site at Cosoy became the presidio. At the new locality various buildings were erected, including a wooden church, 18 × 57 ft, with roof of tules. At the end of this year there were 97 neophytes; the crops had been fairly successful and the livestock were increasing. During the summer of 1775 the prospects seemed bright: on one day 60 new converts were baptized; but a little later, on the night of Nov. 4, 1775, the mission was attacked by nearly 800 Indians. The total number of persons at the mission was only 11—4 soldiers, the two priests, and 5 others, two of whom were boys. Father Jayme and two of the men were killed, and most of the buildings burned. This uprising seems to have been due largely to two of the recently baptized neophytes, who incited the neighboring rancherias to make the attack. For several years after there were reports of intended hostilities, but aside from an expedition sent against the hostile Indians of Pamó in 1778, there seems to have been no open conflict. Meanwhile the mission building had been rebuilt and the number of neophytes increased rapidly. In 1783 there were 740; in 1790, 856; and in 1800, 1,523, the mission at that time being the most populous in California. In 1797 there were 554 baptisms, the second largest number recorded for a single year at any California mission. Fages reported in 1787 that on account of the sterility of the soil not more than half the neophytes lived at the mission, and indeed it seems that the converts lived more independently than at the other missions, occupying to a large extent their own rancherias. About the year 1800 extensive irrigation works were begun, including a large dam, still in existence, which was constructed about $3\frac{1}{2}$ m. above the mission, though this may not have been finished before 1817 or even later. A new church was built and dedicated Nov. 12, 1813. During the decade ending with 1820 the death rate among the neophytes was 77 per cent of baptisms and 35 per cent of population. The greatest number of neophytes, 1,829, was reached in 1824, while by 1830, the number had decreased to about the same as in 1820. During this decade the mission attained its greatest prosperity and had several ranches and cattle stations in the neighboring valleys. One of the most important was at Santa Isabel, where a chapel was built in 1822 for the 450 neophytes of that place. From the time of its founding to its secularization in 1834, when statistics ceased, the total number of Indians baptized numbered 6,036, of whom 2,685 were children. As the neophytes here had never been so closely attached to the mission as elsewhere, the change due to secularization was not great, the decay of the mission having begun a decade before. The opportunity was given the Indians in 1833 to become independent of the mission and take up lands for themselves, but very few accepted the offer. In Nov. 1834, the native pueblo of San Pascual was reported to contain 34 families. In 1840 there were still about 800 ex-neophytes nominally under the control of mission authorities, though but 50 at the mission proper. The mission building and orchards still remained in charge of the padres till about 1846, when they were sold by Governor Pico. In 1852 the buildings were used as barracks by United States troops. Of the old adobe church but little now remains excepting the façade and some crumbling walls, but steps have been taken by the Landmarks Club of California to prevent further decay. The Indians in the neighborhood of San Diago, from whom the mission drew most of its neophytes, belong to the Yuman linguistic stock, and have been given the collective name Diegueños (q. v.).   (A. B. L.)

San Diego. A Cora pueblo and formerly a visita of the mission of Santa Fé.; situated on the w. bank of Rio San Pedro, lat. 22° 10′, Jalisco, Mexico, 12 m. s. of Rosa Morada.
S. Diego.—Orozco y Berra, Geog., 280, 1864.

San Diego del Rio (Saint James of the River). A former Tepehuane pueblo in Durango, Mexico, and the seat of a Spanish mission.
S. Diego del Rio.—Orozco y Berra, Geog., 319, 1864.

San Dieguito (Little Saint James). A Diegueño settlement, established after the secularization act of 1834, about halfway between San Diego and San Luis Rey missions, s. Cal.
San Dieguito.—Arguello (1856) in H. R. Ex. Doc. 76, 34th Cong., 3d sess., 117, 1857. San Dieguito.—Kroeber in Univ. Cal. Pub., Am. Arch. and Eth., IV, 146, 1907. Sinyaupichkara.—Ibid. 149 (native name). Unov.—Ibid. (Luiseño name).

San Dionysio (Saint Dennis). A former Yuma rancheria on the N. bank of Gila r., near its mouth, in Arizona, visited and so named by Father Kino in 1700. It was directly across the Colorado from Concepcion mission, the site of the subsequent Ft Yuma. See Coues, Garcés Diary, 1900.
Palma's rancheria.—Anza (1774) in Bancroft, Ariz. and N. Mex., 389, 1889 (named from the Yuma chief). San Dionysio.—Venegas, Hist. Cal., I, 301, 1759. S. Dionísio.—Anza (1774) cited by Bancroft, Ariz. and N. Mex., 389, 1889. S. Dionysio.—Venegas, Hist. Cal., I, map, 1759. S. Dionysius.—Kino, map (1702), in Stöcklein, Neue Welt-Bott, 74, 1726. S. Doonysio.—Kino, map (1701) in Bancroft, Ariz. and N. Mex., 360, 1889 (misprint).

Sand Painting. See *Dry Painting*.

Sand Papago. A term formerly locally applied to the Indians around Sonoita, called by the Spaniards Papagos Arenanos, from their frequenting, at certain seasons of the year, the wild wastes which stretch away along the shores of the Gulf of California, feeding principally on fish, jaivas, and a singular root which is found in the sand drifts.—Taylor in Cal. Farmer, Dec. 28, 1860.

Sand Town. A former Upper Creek town on the right bank of Chattahoochee r., at the mouth of Sweetwater cr., Douglas co., Ga. The land was ceded to the United States by treaty of Washington, D. C., Jan. 24, 1826.—Royce in 18th Rep. B. A. E., pt. 2, 714, and Ga. map, 1899. See *Uktahasasi*.

Sand Town. A former Upper Creek town on Chattahoochee r. near the present Sand Town, Campbell co., Ga.—Royce in 18th Rep. B. A. E., Ga. map, 1899.

Sandusky (Huron: *Otsaandosti*, 'cool water'). Two Wyandot villages formerly in Ohio; the one, sometimes called Lower Sandusky, was on the site of the present Sandusky, Erie co., and was settled in 1751 by a party of Hurons from near Detroit. The other village, commonly known as Upper Sandusky, was near the

present town of that name, in Wyandot co.
Ostandousket.—Doc. of 1748 in N. Y. Doc. Col. Hist.,
X, 151, 1858. **Sandesqué.**—Boisherbert (1747) in
N. Y. Doc. Col. Hist., X, 84, 1858. **Sandoské.**—Doc.
of 1747, ibid., 114. **Sandosket.**—Doc. of 1748, ibid.,
138. **Sandoski.**—Crepy Map, *ca.* 1755. **Sandosky.**—
Johnson (1763) in N. Y. Doc. Col. Hist., VII, 583, 1856
(the fort). **Sandouski.**—Homann Heirs' map, 1756.
Sandousky.—Johnson (1763) in N. Y. Doc. Col.
Hist., VII, 526, 1856 (the fort). **Sanduskee.**—
La Galissonière (1748), ibid., X, 182, 1858. **San-
duski.**—Watts (1763) in Mass. Hist. Soc. Coll., 4th
s., IX, 483, 1871. **Sanduskians.**—Clark (1782) in Butterfield, Washington-Irvine Corr., 402, 1882. **Sandusky.**—Johnson (1763) in N. Y. Doc. Col. Hist.,
VII, 533, 1856. **Sᵗ 'd'osquet.**—French Rep. (1761)
in Mass. Hist. Soc. Coll., 4th s., IX, 428, 1871.
St. Douskie.—Writer of 1782 in Butterfield, Washington-Irvine Corr., 375, 1882. **St. Dusky.**—Ibid.

Sandy Hill. A band, probably Missisauga, living E. of Georgian bay, Ont.—
Hind, Lab. Penin., II, 170, 1863.

San Emidio. A Chumashan division,
named after the land grant and present
Rancho Emidio, formerly occupying "the
country from Buena Vista and Carises
lakes and Kern r. to the Sierra Nevada
and Coast range," Cal. By treaty of June
10, 1851, these tribes, which had been
greatly reduced by smallpox and by conflict with Spaniards and neighboring Indians, reserved a tract between Tejon
pass and Kern r., and ceded the remainder of their lands to the United States.
The treaty, however, was made inopera-
tive through its rejection by the Senate.
San Imiri.—Royce in 18th Rep. B. A. E., 782, 1899.
San Imirio.—Ibid., 788. **San Juris.**—Barbour in
Sen. Ex. Doc. 4, 32d Cong., spec. sess., 256, 1853.

Sanetch. A Salish tribe speaking the
Songish dialect and living on Saanich
peninsula and the neighboring ids., s. w.
Vancouver id. According to Wilson
(Jour. Ethnol. Soc. Lond., 238, 1866), they
numbered about 600 in 1858; in 1909 the
population was 249. There are 5 bands:
Mayne Island, Panquechin, Tsawout,
Tsartlip, and Tsehump. The Saturna Is-
land Indians also belong to the Sanetch.
Eus-ā-nioh.—Kane, Wand. in N. A., 239, 1859.
Isanisks.—Shea, Cath. Miss., 475, 1855. **Nanitch.**—
Wilkes, U. S. Expl. Exped., IV, 483, 1845.
Saanitch.—Mayne, Brit. Col., 165, 1861. **Sāmtsh.**—
Tolmie and Dawson, Vocabs. Brit. Col., 120B,
1884. **Sanetch.**—Grant in Jour. Roy. Geog. Soc.,
293, 1857. **Sanich.**—Can. Ind. Aff. Rep, map, 1891.
Sq̇sā'nitc.—Boas, MS., B. A. E., 1887.

San Felipe (Saint Philip). A Keresan
pueblo on the w. bank of the Rio Grande,
about 12 m. above Bernalillo, N. central
New Mexico. Before the advent of the
Spaniards into New Mexico in the 16th
century, the ancestors of the inhabitants
of this pueblo and of Cochiti formed a
single tribe occupying successively a
number of pueblos, the last of which was
Kuapa. Owing to the aggressiveness of
the Tewa, whose territory formed their
northern boundary, these people were
forced to separate into two divisions,
one, the Cochiti, retiring to the Potrero
Viejo, the other branch going farther
down the Rio Grande to the site of the
present Mexican settlement of Cubero,

just w. of that stream, where they built
the pueblo of Katishtya. Subsequently,
however, this village was abandoned and
a new one, bearing the same name, was
constructed at the foot of the mesa of
Tamita. Here the San Felipe lived when
Coronado visited New Mexico in 1540.
In 1591 Castaño de Sosa visited the
pueblo and probably gave it the saint
name by which it is now commonly
known; and in 1598 Oñate also visited it,
a document bearing on his expedition
applying the name "Castixes" (Katishtya) collectively to the pueblos of
San Felipe and "Comitre." This, however, is doubtless an error in copying,
the latter name being apparently a misprint or corruption of Tamita, the name
of the mesa at the foot of which the

A SAN FELIPE MAN

pueblo of San Felipe stood. It became
the seat of a Spanish mission early in the
17th century, and its first church was
erected by Fray Cristóbal de Quiñones,
who died at the pueblo in 1607 or 1609,
and was buried in the church he had
founded. San Felipe was also the residence of the Father Custodian in 1636,
but not as a permanent seat. The San
Felipe Indians took an active part in the
Pueblo revolt of 1680, and as there was
then no resident priest at their pueblo,
they aided in killing the missionaries of
Cochiti, Santo Domingo, and San Felipe
(the latter residing at the monastery of
Santo Domingo), as well as in the massacre of the Spanish colonists in the
neighboring haciendas and of some of the
members of their own tribe who re-

mained faithful to the Spaniards. In the latter part of 1681 the pueblo was deserted by its inhabitants, who fled with the Cochiteños and others to Potrero Viejo, but returned in 1683 (see *Cochiti*). Between the latter date and 1692, when Vargas made his appearance in New Mexico, they again retreated with the other tribes to the Potrero, but the San Felipes were induced by the Spaniards to return. When Vargas appeared the following year he found the San Felipe Indians in a new pueblo at the northern end of the summit of the long Black mesa (Pŭ'nyi Chátya) w. of the present village, which had been built subsequent to 1683. Here a church was erected in 1694, the walls of which are still partly standing. Soon after the beginning of the 18th century, when there was no further necessity of a defensive site, the tribe left its mesa settlement and erected at its base the San Felipe of the present time—the fourth pueblo that has borne the aboriginal name Katishtya. No remains of the old village near the mesa of Tamita are traceable. San Felipe was made a visita of Santo Domingo in 1782. Population, 554 in 1890, 475 in 1905, and 514 in 1910.

Following are the San Felipe clans, those marked * being quite extinct, and those marked † having only one or two survivors in 1895: Yaka (Corn), Dyami (Eagle), Kuuts (Antelope), Haami (Tobacco), Oshach (Sun), Tanyi (Calabash), Hakanyi (Fire), Tsina (Turkey), Huuka (Dove), Showati (Parrot), Peruka (Frog or Toad), Waiushr (Duck), Tsits (Water), Sii) Ant), †Isi (a red and white flower), Shrotsona (Coyote), *Tawash (Moon), †Miitsr (Hummingbird), †Sisika (Swallow), Yascha (Coral bead), Hapanyi (Oak), Kohai (Bear), *Dyani (Deer), *Ishto (Arrow), *Mina (Salt), *Haatsu (Earth), *Shuwimi (Turquoise), Soshka (Roadrunner), *Schilra (Crow), Mokaich (Mountain-lion).

Consult Bandelier in Arch. Inst. Papers, III, 126, 1890; IV, 187 et seq., 1892. See *Keresan Family, Pueblos.* (F. W. H.)

Cachichi.—Oñate (1598) in Doc. Inéd., XVI, 102, 1871 (probably identical). Castixes.—Oñate (1598), ibid., 114 (corruption of *Katistya*: Bandelier in Arch. Inst. Papers, IV, 189, 1892). Catriti.—Bandelier in Arch. Inst. Bull., I, 18, 1883 (from an early source). Kacht'yá.—Hodge, field notes, B. A. E., 1895 (Laguna name). Ka-lis-cha.—Simpson in Rep. Sec. War, 143, note 1850 (given as proper name; misprint?). Kalistcha.—Loew in Wheeler Surv. Rep., VII, 418, 1879 (old name; misprint?). Kátihcha.—Voth, Trad. Hopi, 11, 1905 (Hopi name). Ka-tish-tya.—Bandelier in 7th Internat. Cong. Amér., VII, 451, 1890 (aboriginal name). Kat-ish-tya.—Bandelier in Arch. Inst. Papers, III, 126, 1890. Kat-ist-ya.—Ibid., IV, 189, 1892. Ka-ti-tya.—Jouvenceau in Cath. Pion., I, no. 9, 12, 1906. Oâ-tish-tye.—Bandelier, Gilded Man, 215, 1893 (misprint, O for Q). P'ătŭ'ak.—Hodge, field notes, B. A. E., 1895 (Isleta name; probably 'deep water'). Q'ash-trĕ-tye.—Bandelier in Arch. Inst. Bull., I, 18, 1883 (proper name). San Felepe.—Davis, Span. Conq. N. Mex., map, 1869. San Felipe.—Doc. of

1604 quoted by Bandelier in Arch. Inst. Papers, VI, 189, 1892. San Felipe de Keres.—Mühlenpfordt, Mejico, II, 533, 1844. San Felipe de Queres.—Kern in Schoolcraft, Ind. Tribes, IV, 35, 1854. San Felipo.—Kingsley, Stand. Nat. Hist., VI, 183, 1883. San Felippe.—Gallegas (1844) in Emory, Recon., 478, 1848. San Fellipe.—Bandelier in Arch. Inst. Papers, IV, 193, 1892 (misprint). San Filipé.—Hughes, Doniphan's Exped., 96, 1848. San Phelipe.—Villa-Señor, Theatro Am., II, 420, 1748. San Phelippe.—Falconer in Jour. Roy. Geog. Soc. Lond., XIII, 217, 1843. San Philippe.—Johnston (1846) in Emory, Recon., 567, 1848. San Phillippe.—Abert, ibid., 461. Sant Phelipe.—Oñate (1598) in Doc. Inéd., XVI, 114, 254, 1871. Sant Philepe.—Oñate misquoted by Bandelier in Arch. Inst. Papers, IV, pt. 2, 97, 1892. S. Felip.—D'Anville, Map N. A., Bolton's ed., 1752. S. Felipe.—D'Anville, Map Am. Sept., 1746. S. Felipe de Cueres.—Humboldt, Atlas Nouv. Espagne, carte 1, 1811. S. Felipe de Cuerez.—Humboldt quoted by Simpson in Smithson. Rep. 1869, 334, 1871. Sn Phelipe.—Doc. of 1693 quoted by Bandelier in Arch. Inst. Papers, IV, 190, 1892. Sᵖ Philip de queres.—Pike, Exped., 3d map, 1810. S. Phelipe.—Rivera, Diario, leg. 784, 1736. St. Philip.—Pike, Travels, 273, 1811. St. Philippe.—Abert in Emory, Recon., 462, 1848. St. Philips.—Pike, Exped., app., pt. III, 13, 1810. St. Phillipe.—Abert in Emory, Recon., 469, 1848. St. Phillippe.—Ibid., 461. To Háchĕle.—Curtis, Am. Ind., I, 138, 1907 ('pull up water': Navaho name). Wé-thlu-ella-kwin.—Cushing in The Millstone, IX, 151, Sept. 1884 (Zuñi name of "Old San Felipe"). Wi'-li-gi.—Hodge, field notes, B. A. E., 1895 (Pecos name). Wi'-li-gi-i'.—Ibid. (Jemez name).

San Felipe. A former Diegueño ranchería about 70 m. N. E. of San Diego, s. Cal. As the Indians failed to prove title, the land was confirmed to white settlers by court decision, and in 1903, under act of Congress of May 27, 1902, the 40 occupants of San Felipe were removed to a new reservation at Pala. See *Melejo.*

Puerta San Felipe.—Jackson and Kinney, Rep. Mission Inds., 24, 1883. San Feilpe.—Kelsey, Report, 29, 1906 (misprint). San Felipe.—Taylor in Cal. Farmer, June 12, 1863.

San Felipe. A former pueblo of the Piro, on the Rio Grande, probably near the present San Marcial, Socorro co., N. Mex. Mentioned only in a document of 1582–83 (Doc. Inéd., XV, 83, 90, 1871). Not to be confounded with the Keresan pueblo of the same name farther N. See *Qualacú.*

Sant Felipe.—16th cent. doc., op. cit.

San Felipe. A former Sobaipuri ranchería at the junction of Santa Cruz and Gila rs., s. Arizona; first visited by Father Kino and doubtless so named by him. Not to be confounded with the San Felipe (see *Terrenate*) near the headwaters of the Santa Cruz.

San Felipe.—Kino, map (1701), in Bancroft, Ariz. and N. Mex., 360, 1889. San Philippi.—Cooke in Emory, Recon., 559, 1848. S. Philip.—Kino, map (1702), in Stöcklein, Neue Welt-Bott, 74, 1726.

San Felipe. A former small pueblo of the Opata on the Rio Sonora, Sonora, Mexico. The settlement is now civilized, but it still retains some pure Opata.—Hrdlička in Am. Anthr., VI, 72, 1904.

San Felipe. A mission village, probably on the lower Georgia coast, which was among those revolting against the Spaniards in 1687.—Barcia, Ensayo, 287, 1723.

San Felix de Valois. Mentioned in the 18th century as the first rancheria of the Quiquima (Quigyuma), traveling southward; apparently situated on the E. bank of the Rio Colorado, between its mouth and the junction of the Gila, probably about the present Arizona-Sonora boundary.—Bancroft, No. Mex. States, I, 497, 1884; Coues, Garcés Diary, 177, 1900.

San Fernando (Saint Ferdinand). A Franciscan mission, founded Sept. 8, 1797, in Los Angeles co., Cal. The site chosen is said to have been that of a native rancheria called Pasecgna, but the place had already been occupied as a private ranch, with a house which the missionaries appropriated for their dwelling. Bancroft says that the name of the site was Achois Comihavit. The new mission was dedicated by Father Lasuen to San Fernando, Rey de España, the ceremonies being witnessed by a large gathering of natives. On the first day 10 children were baptized. By the close of the year there were 55 neophytes, and 310 in 1800. In 1806 an adobe church with tiled roof was consecrated. The number of neophytes reached 955 in 1810, while the death-rate was lower than at most of the missions. The mission seems to have been somewhat cramped for lands, at least numerous protests were made against the granting of neighboring ranches to private individuals. Nevertheless the mission was prosperous, the average crop for the decade ending 1810 being 5,220 bushels. The greatest number of neophytes, 1,080, was reached in 1819. After this there was a decided decline in both population and prosperity. In 1834 the natives numbered 792. Up to this time there had been baptized 2,784 Indians, of whom 1,367 were children. The effect of secularization was not so disastrous here as at most of the missions, the administrators in charge giving general satisfaction, so that in 1840 there were still 400 Indians in the ex-mission community. In 1843 San Fernando was returned to the control of the padres, but in 1845 was leased to private individuals, and in the following year was sold by Gov. Pico for $1,120. The last resident minister left in 1847. The old mission church was built of adobe and is now in ruins, though the walls are still standing; the monastery has been repaired by the Landmarks Club of California. The Indians in the neighborhood of San Fernando belong to the Shoshonean linguistic stock and have been included under the name Gabrieleños (q. v.), though more distant tribes to the N. E. doubtless furnished many neophytes. The following villages are recorded as having existed in the neighborhood of San Fernando: Kowanga, Mapipinga, Okowvinjha, Pascegna, Quapa, Sawayyanga, Tacuenga, Tuyunga. (A. B. L.)

San Fernando. A former Pima rancheria, 9 leagues E. of the ruins of Casa Grande, near Rio Gila, s. Arizona; visited and so named by Father Kino about 1697.—Bernal (1697) in Bancroft, Ariz. and N. Mex., 356, 1889.

San Fernando Vellicata. A Franciscan mission founded in 1769 by Padre Junípero Serra in the N. w. interior part of Lower California, lat. 30° (Browne, Pac. Slope, app., 50, 1869; Shea, Cath. Miss., 91, 1855). Vellicata is probably identical with Guiricata (see *San Juan de Dios*). Its inhabitants are described as peaceful, and, judging from the locality, were Cochimi.
San Fernando Villacata.—Taylor in Cal. Farmer, Jan. 24, 1862. San Fernando Villacatta.—Browne, op. cit. St. Ferdinand.—Shea, op. cit.

San Francisco (Saint Francis). A Cora pueblo and formerly a visita of the mission of Jesus María; situated on the upper waters of the Rio Jesus María, in the N. part of the territory of Tepic, Mexico. See Orozco y Berra, Geog., 280, 1864; Lumholtz, Unknown Mex., I, 508; II, map, 1902.

San Francisco. A rancheria near the presidio of La Bahía and the mission of Espíritu Santo de Zúñiga, on the lower Rio San Antonio, Texas, in 1785, at which date it had 17 inhabitants. These Indians were probably of Karankawan affinity. See Bancroft, No. Mex. States, I, 659, 1886.

San Francisco. A mission station on the lower Rio Grande, between El Paso, Tex., and San Lorenzo, in 1680 (Otermin quoted by Bancroft, Ariz. and N. Mex., 182, 1889). It probably pertained to the Tigua or the Piro, or to both.

San Francisco Ati (A-ti′). A Pima village, visited by Kino and Mange in 1698; situated w. of the Rio Santa Cruz, in s. Arizona. It was the seat of a mission established in 1756 by Father Pfefferkorn, according to Och (Nachrichten, I, 71, 1809). Not to be confounded with the Papago settlement of Ati (q. v.) farther s., on the Rio Altar, in Sonora.
Atí.—Arricivita (1771) quoted by Bancroft, Ariz. and N. Mex., 387, 1889. Atison.—Anza and Font (1780), ibid., 392 (doubtless identical; i. e., the "spring" (*son* or *zoni*) of Atí). San Francisco Atí.—Mange (1698) in Doc. Hist. Mex., 4th s., I, 318, 1856. S. Francisco.—Kino, map (1701), in Bancroft, Ariz. and N. Mex., 360, 1889. S. Franciscus.—Kino, map (1702), in Stöcklein, Neue Welt-Bott, 74, 1726.

San Francisco Borja. A mission established among the Cochimi by Padre Winceslao Link in 1762; situated in lat. 29°, near the E. coast of Lower California. It was apparently only a visita of San Ignacio (lat. 28°) in 1745, Venegas mentioning it as such in 1759.

San Borja.—Venegas, Hist. Cal., II, 198, 1759. **San Francisco Borja.**—Taylor in Browne, Res. Pac. Slope, app., 50, 1869. **S. Borgia.**—Clavigero, Storia della Cal., II, 146, 1789. **S. Francesco Borgia.**—Taylor, op. cit.

San Francisco de la Espada. A Franciscan mission, founded Mar. 5, 1731, on the abandonment of San Francisco de los Neches (see *San Francisco de los Tejas*), about 9 m. below San Antonio, Texas, on the w. bank of San Antonio r. Its ruins are now known at San Antonio as "fourth mission." It was at this mission that Fr. Bartolomé García wrote his famous Manual (1760), which preserves for us the Coahuiltecan language. There were brought from the Frio and Nueces rs. (Espinosa conveys a wrong impression when he says they were "in sight") to this and the neighbor missions three docile native tribes, unused to agriculture, the Pacao, Pajalat, and Pitalac, which together were

CHURCH OF SAN FRANCISCO DE LA ESPADA

said to number about 1,000 persons. This mission was founded with the Pacao tribe, its chief being made "governor" of the pueblo, called Pueblo de Acuña (Testimonio de Asiento de Misiones, Gen. Land Office, Texas, Span. Archives, XL, folios 13, 21–22). Since most of the records for this mission have disappeared, our knowledge of its tribal history is fragmentary. In June 1737 there were 137 neophytes, mainly Pacaos and Arcahomos (apparently those better known as Tacames), 80 of them having been baptized. These two tribes seem to have been for some time the chief ones there. On June 7 of that year all deserted, the missionaries charging the flight to fear of the Apache, while Indians and soldiers said the cause was bad treatment. By Nov. 22 only 7 had returned, in spite of the

fact that three efforts had been made to reclaim them. In January a fourth embassy sent for them brought back 108 more (Lamar Papers, Span. MS. no. 33; Expediente sobre la campaña, Archivo Gen., Prov. Intern., XXXII; Testimony, Aug. 5, 1737, Archivo Gen., Misiones, XXI, MS.). In June 1738 the mission still had a Pacao "governor" (Archivo Gen., Yndiferente de Guerra, 1736–37, folio 93; this volume has recently been transferred to Sección de Historia). This year the Apache made a raid on the neophytes while they were gathering fruit in the neighborhood, near the Medina, killed a number, and took others captive (Expediente sobre la campaña, 6). By Feb. 20, 1740, there had been 233 baptisms at the mission, and at that time, which was immediately after an epidemic, there were 120 neophytes remaining (Descripción, Mem. de Nueva España, XXVIII, 203, MS.). Between 1740 and 1762 the success of the mission was considerable, for by Mar. 6 of the latter year the number of persons baptized had reached 815. Of these 513 had been buried at the mission. These figures are a telling commentary on the death-rate. There were now 52 families, or 207 persons, mainly Pacaos, Borrados, and Maraquites or Maraguitas, the last two of which tribes were still being brought in. A church of stone, begun some time before, was at this time in process of construction. The Indian pueblo consisted of three rows of stone huts. On the ranch there were 1,262 head of cattle, 4,000 sheep and goats, 145 horses, besides burros and working oxen (Ynforme de Misiones, in Mem. de Nueva España, XXVIII, 172–78, MS.).

This mission was conducted by the Querétaran fathers up to about 1773, when it was turned over to the Zacatecans. In 1778 Father Morfi wrote in his diary that there were 133 neophytes and 4,000 head of stock, which had much decreased owing to the attack of the Lipan and Comanche. The church, having fallen into ruins, had been razed; apparently it had never been finished. Morfi commented particularly on the excellent lands and irrigating facilities of the mission (Viage de Indios, 1778, in Doc. Hist. Mex., 464–65, 1856). About 1781 Governor Cabello proposed that the buildings of this mission should be destroyed and the neophytes sent to San Antonio de Valero or San José, but this was not done (Revilla-Gigedo, Carta, 1793, ¶ 223). In 1785 the neophytes numbered 57, and in 1793 only 46. On Apr. 10, 1794, the commandant general of the Provincias Internas, Pedro de Nava, ordered this and the neighbor missions secularized, and the order was in part carried out in June and July by Gov. Manuel Muñoz. On July 11 the movables and lands were distributed among the Indians, each of the 15 adult males being given about 10 acres as private property, and about 100 acres being assigned to the Indians in common (Ynventario de los bienes, etc., in Gen. Land Office, Texas, Span. Archives, L, folios 29–40). It seems, however, that the Zacatecan friars continued their ministry there well into the 19th century. In 1804 there were 39 persons living at the pueblo, and 107 at the mission of San Francisco de la Espada. They were probably not all Indians (census of 1804 in Béxar Archives). (H. E. B.)

San Francisco de los Tejas (or Neches). A Franciscan mission, established in May-June 1690, among the Nabedache tribe, a short distance w. of Neches r., and about 40 m. s. w. of Nacogdoches, Texas. The Nabedache village and the stream near which the mission was founded both became known to the Spaniards as San Pedro. The name of the general locality is still preserved by San Pedro cr. and by the post village of San Pedro N. E. of Crockett, Houston co. A recent personal examination of the country by the writer, in the light of the documents, has fixed the location of the mission at a point from one to two miles N. w. of the present village of Weches. The mission, the first in Texas, was founded by Capt. Alonso de León and Father Damian Massanet, sometimes called Manzanet (Manzanet, letter in Quar. Tex. Hist. Asso., II, 281–312, 1899). The padres founded near by another small establishment called Santísimo Nombre de María, at which Francisco de Jesus María wrote his valuable report on the Hasinai Indians, Aug. 15, 1691. The missionaries worked zealously and succeeded in baptizing the *xinesi*, or high-priest, of the confederacy, and 80 or more others; but, owing to pestilence, the refusal of the Indians to live in a pueblo of the Spanish sort, their growing hostility, and the excesses of the soldiers, the missions were abandoned, Oct. 25, 1693, by order of the Viceroy (Velasco, Dictamen Fiscal, Nov. 30, 1716, in Mem. de Nueva España, XXVII, 188, MS.). In 1716 San Francisco mission was refounded a few leagues farther inland, across the Neche r. and among the Neche and Nacachau tribes. The site was evidently s. w. of Alto, Cherokee co., near the Neche Indian mounds. While here the mission was known as San Francisco de los Neches, or de los Texas. It was put in charge of a pioneer in that country, Fr. Francisco Hidalgo, and was designed to serve the Nabedache, Neche, Nacachau, and Nacono tribes (Hidalgo and Cas-

tellano to Mesquía, Oct. 6, 1716, MS. in Archivo Gen.), but it apparently did not succeed any better than before. In 1719 it was abandoned, like all of the E. Texas missions, because of fear of an attack by the French. On Aug. 5, 1721, it was reestablished by the Marquis de Aguayo and Espinosa, and put in charge of Fr. José Guerra. On this day Aguayo gave the Neche chief the *baston*, the symbol of authority conferred by the Spaniards, and clothed 180 Indians of all ages. Espinosa exhorted them to gather into a pueblo, to be named San Francisco Valero (Peña, Diario, Mem. de Nueva España, XXVIII, 39, MS.). This they promised to do as soon as they could harvest their corn (ibid.). Still the mission failed to succeed. In 1727 Rivera found it without Indians, and described the settlement as one of huts (Diario, leg. 2,140, 1736; Proyecto, folio 50, 1728, MS. in Archivo Gen.). In 1729 the presidio on the Angelina was withdrawn, and as a result the mission, together with those of San José de los Nazones and Nuestra Señora de la Purísima Concepción (q. v.), was removed in 1730. After an attempt had been made to find a site on the San Marcos, Nueces, and Frio rs., the mission was reestablished, in 1731, on San Antonio r. as San Francisco de la Espada (q. v.). The buildings of the mission were evidently mainly of wood, hence no remains have been identified. (H. E. B.)

Francisco de Necha.—Rep. de los Religiosos, 1729, MS. in Mem. de Nueva España, XXVIII, 65, MS. **Nuestro Padre San Francisco de los Tejas.**—Espinosa, Diario, 1716, MS. in Archivo Gen., Prov. Intern., 181. **San Francisco.**—Francisco Hidalgo, Oct. 6, 1716, Letter to Mesquía, MS. **San Francisco de los Nechas.**—Bonilla, Breve Compendio (1772), in Quar. Tex. Hist. Asso. VIII, 35, 1904. **San Francisco de los Neches.**—Ibid., 38. **San Francisco de los Techas.**—Massanet, Letter, Aug. 20, 1691, MS. in Archivo Gen., Prov. Intern., 182. **Señor San Francisco.**—Ramón (1716), Derrotero, in Mem. de Nueva España, XXVII, 216, MS.

San Francisco de Pima. A Pima rancheria, 10 or 12 leagues above the Rio Asunción from Pitic, about lat. 31°, Sonora, Mexico. Depopulated many years prior to 1763 (Rudo Ensayo, ca. 1763, 159, 1863).

San Francisco de Valero. The name assigned in 1721 to the Indian pueblo attached to San Francisco de Los Neches (or Tejas) mission, near Neches r., in Cherokee co., Texas (Peña, Diario, 1721, in Mem. de Nueva España, XXVIII, 39, MS.). See *San Francisco de los Tejas*, and *Neche*. (H. E. B.)

San Francisco Solano. The last Franciscan mission established in California. The removal of the sick Indians to San Rafael had proved so beneficial that the proposal was made to move the San Francisco (Dolores) mission to some more favored spot on the N. shore of the bay. The country was explored and the Sonoma valley favorably reported. The cross was first planted July 4, 1823, but work did not begin until Aug. 25, when a party arrived from San Francisco. Objections were raised to the transfer, however, and it was finally compromised by founding a new mission, the old ones not being disturbed. Neophytes were to be allowed to go to the new mission from San Francisco, San Rafael, and San José, provided they originally came from the Sonoma region, and new converts might come from anywhere, but no force was to be used. The mission church, 24 by 105 ft, was dedicated, Apr. 4, 1824, to San Francisco Solano. To avoid confusion it was commonly called Solano, and later Sonoma. At the close of 1824 there were 693 neophytes, of whom 322 had come from San Francisco, 153 from San José, 92 from San Rafael, and 96 were baptized at the new mission. In 1830 there were only 760 neophytes, though 650 had been baptized, and as only 375 had been buried, many must have run away. The highest number, 996, was reached in 1832. The mission was not particularly prosperous. The large stock numbered 2,729 in 1830, small stock 4,000; but these numbers were about doubled by 1834. The crops for several years averaged more than 2,000 bushels. There were 650 neophytes in 1834. The total number of baptisms was 1,312, of whom 617 were children. The mission was secularized in 1835–36 under Vallejo and Ortega. The movable property was given the neophytes, who were free to go where they pleased. Owing to troubles with hostile Indians they seem later to have restored their stock to the care of Vallejo, who managed it for the general welfare. Affairs seem to have prospered under his care, and Bancroft estimates that in 1840 there were still 100 ex-neophytes at Sonoma and 500 others in the neighborhood. Vallejo conducted several campaigns against hostile Indians. The pueblo of Sonoma was organized in 1835. In 1845, when Gov. Pico was planning the sale of the missions, Solano was declared without value. The buildings and immediate grounds, of course, as with all the missions, remained in the possession of the church. In 1880 these were sold, and for a time the old church was used as a barn. In 1903 the old buildings and grounds were purchased by William R. Hearst and deeded to the state of California. Some work has since been done to preserve the buildings from further ruin. The Indians in the neighborhood of this mission belong to the Olamentke division of the Moquelumnan family (q. v.), but many of the neophytes came from more distant

stocks, the Copehan especially being well represented. The following names of villages, taken from the mission books, are given by Bancroft (Hist. Cal., II, 506, 1886): Aloquiomi, Atenomac, Canijolmano, Canoma, Carquin, Caymus, Chemoco, Chichoyomi, Chocuyem, Coyayomi (or Joyayomi), Huiluc, Huymen, Lacatiut, Linayto (Libayto?), Loaquiomi, Locnoma, Malaca, Mayacma, Muticolmo, Napato, Oleomi, Paque, Petaluma, Polnomanoc, Putto or Putato (Pulto or Pultato or Pultoy = Putah cr. ?), Satayomi, Soneto, Suisun, Tamal, Tlayacma, Topayto, Ululato, Utinomanoc, Zaclom. (A. B. L.)

San Francisco Solano. A Franciscan mission founded in March, 1700, s. of the Rio Grande, below Eagle Pass, Texas. In 1718 it was transferred to San Antonio, and refounded as San Antonio de Valero (q. v.), now the famous Alamo Mission. (H. E. B.)

San Francisco Vizarron. A Franciscan mission founded in 1737 in N. Mexico among Coahuiltecan Indians (Portillo, Apuntes, 313–17, 1888). The first tribes gathered there were Piguiques and Pausanes; later the Pasnacanes, Tinapihuayas, and Julimeños followed. In 1754 the mission was involved in a bitter dispute with the San Juan Capistrano mission over the Pamaques (Informe of 1754 in Mem. de Nueva España, XXVII, 307–11, MS.). (H. E. B.)

San Francisco Xavier de Horcasitas. The first of three Franciscan missions founded by the College of the Santa Cruz de Querétaro in 1748–49 on San Xavier (now San Gabriel) r., Texas, the others of the group being San Ildefonso and Nuestra Señora de la Candelaria. Their location has not hitherto been definitely known, but the remains of the irrigation plant connected with these missions were in 1907 identified by the writer 9 miles N. w. of Rockdale, Milam co. As early as 1744 or 1745 Fr. Francisco María Ano de los Dolores y Viana, missionary at San Antonio de Valero, began making visits to the tribes of central Texas, and soon those of the San Xavier region asked for missions in their own territory, although they refused to enter the missions at San Antonio (Arricivita, Crónica, pt. II, 321–22, 1792; Decree of the Viceroy, Mar. 26, 1751, MS. in Lamar Papers). While the request was being considered in Mexico, Fr. Dolores ministered to the petitioners on the San Xavier and attracted thither other tribes from the E. and s. In Dec. 1746 three missions were authorized, but they were not formally established until 1748–49, the first one (San Francisco Xavier) being founded early in 1748.

The records of these missions are highly

important for the ethnology of the tribes of middle and southern Texas, as they show that the tribes gathered at San Xavier were distributed among the three missions avowedly on the basis of linguistic grouping. In San Francisco Xavier were placed the group of Tonkawan affiliation, including the Tonkawa, Yojuane, Mayeye, and Ervipiame; to San Ildefonso were assigned the Bidai, Arkokisa, Deadose, and Patiri; and to Nuestra Señora de la Candelaria the Karankawan group, including Coco, Karankawa, and Tops (Documents in the College of Santa Cruz de Querétaro, K. leg. 6, nos. 12 and 18).

The successful beginning of these missions is proved by the fact that when Capt. Joseph de Eca y Musquiz inspected them some time before Mar. 11, 1751, he counted 431 neophytes—161 at San Xavier, 176 at San Ildefonso, and 102 at Candelaria. By that time 253 persons had been baptized, of whom 77 had died (Arricivita, op. cit.; Viceroy's decree, op. cit.). Some time before Musquiz had made his report (the chronology is not clear) an epidemic of smallpox attacked the Indians, carrying off 40 at San Ildefonso alone (Arricivita, op. cit., 328–29). Four times within one year the Apache molested San Xavier mission, killing 3 soldiers and 4 Indians, and stealing some horses. Soon after the epidemic the Indians of San Ildefonso were all induced by the Nabedache and other eastern tribes to desert and join in a general campaign against the Apache. When they returned they settled some leagues from the mission and did not reënter it (Arricivita, op. cit., 326). These misfortunes proved the necessity of a stronger military force to protect the missions and to control the neophytes. Accordingly, on Mar. 11, 1751, a presidio named San Xavier, garrisoned by 50 soldiers, was authorized (Decree of this date, in the Lamar Papers). It was assigned to Don Felipe Rábago y Teran, who took charge in December of that year (Dolores to the Viceroy, Oct. 28, 1760, MS. in Archivo Gen. de Mex.). A quarrel arose between Rábago and the missionaries; early in 1752 the Coco of Candelaria deserted; and a few days later (May 11) the missionary at San Ildefonso was murdered by an unknown hand. The addition of drought, strange natural phenomena, and another epidemic, to these misfortunes, caused the abandonment of the place in 1755 or 1756, the garrison and missionaries removing to San Marcos r. Shortly afterward some of the Mayeye of San Xavier mission were reassembled by the missionaries and taken to Guadalupe r., where they were ministered to for a short time (Arricivita, op. cit., 337; Dolores, Escrito, June 1756,

MS. in the College of Santa Cruz de Querétaro). In the latter part of 1756 the garrison was removed from the Rio San Marcos to become a part of the new presidio at San Sabá (Arricivita, op. cit., 367). See *Nuestra Señora de la Candelaria; San Francisco Xavier de Náxera; San Ildefonso.* (H. E. B.)

San Javier.—Bancroft, No. Mex. States, I, 641, 1886.

San Francisco Xavier de Náxera. A Querétaran mission, nominally founded Mar. 10, 1722, on San Antonio r., Texas, between San Antonio de Valero and San José missions, under the protection of the presidio of San Antonio de Béjar, and put in charge of Fr. José Gonzales. It was founded for the Ervipiame Indians of Ranchería Grande (q. v.) near the Brazos, at the request of their chief, called by the Spaniards Juan Rodriguez, who, before Feb. 1721, brought 50 families of his followers to San Antonio. When Aguayo went to reestablish the E. Texas missions, he took Juan Rodriguez with him as a guide, and when he returned to San Antonio in 1722 he founded the mission, as stated. Juan Rodriguez was made "governor of the suburb (*barrio*) of the Hyerbipiamos." It seems that the material part of the mission was never supplied, and that the baptisms of the Ervipiame which followed were made at Valero mission. They were first entered in a separate book, and later transferred to the Valero records as "Baptisms of the Hyerbipiamos, whom it was attempted to place in a new mission with the name San Francisco Xavier, an attempt which failed because they remained in this mission of San Antonio." These entries, 32 in number, began Mar. 12, 1721 (before the mission was founded), and ended July 20, 1726 (Libro en que se Assientan los Bauptismos de los Indios de esta Mision de S. Antº). Of these baptisms 24 were of persons of Ervipiame, Maruam, or Ticmamar blood. About 1748 a new mission, called San Xavier, was established on San Xavier r. for Ranchería Grande and other tribes, and it may be regarded, therefore, as the revived San Francisco Xavier de Náxera. (H. E. B.)

San Javier de Nájera.—Bancroft, No. Mex. States, I, 666, 1886. San Xavier de Náxera.—Garrison, Texas, 70, 1903.

San Francisco Xavier de Viggé-Biaundo. A Jesuit mission, commonly known as Biaundo, or Viaundo, founded in 1699 by Padre Picolo in Lower California. The 11 Indian settlements which belonged to it in 1702 are enumerated in Picolo's memoir of 1702 (Lettres Edifiantes, II, 62, 1841). Eight of these lay s. of the seat of the mission, which was in 25° 45′ lat., a few m. s. w. of Loreto. According to Hervas, the natives spoke Cochimi. According to Venegas (Hist. Cal., II, 196, 1759) it had only five visitas in 1745, one of which was doubtless Jacuencacahel (q. v.). The population was 485 in 1768, including that of its subordinate villages.   (A. S. G.)

Biaundo.—Picolo in Stöcklein, Neue Welt-Bott, num. 72, p. 35, 1726. Francisco Xavier.—Venegas, Hist. Cal., I, 259, 1759. Saint-François-Xavier.—Picolo (1702) in Lettres Edifiantes, II, 63, 1841 (Biaundo, or). Saint-François-Xavier-de-Biaundo.—Picolo (1702), ibid., 62. San Francisco Javier.—Clavijero, Hist. Baja Cal., 109, 1852. San Francisco Xavier.—Venegas, Hist. Cal., I, 261, 1759. San Francisco Xavier de Vigge.—Taylor quoted by Browne, Res. Pac. Slope, app., 49, 1869. San Javier de Viggé.—Clavijero, Hist. Baja Cal., 46, 1852. San Xavier de Viaundo.—Venegas, op. cit., 264. San Xavier de Vigge.—Ibid., 325. St. Xavier.—Ibid., 396. Vigge Biaundo.—Ibid., 258.

San Gabriel Arcangel. The fourth Franciscan mission established in California. It was founded Sept. 8, 1771, at a place called by the natives Sibagna (or Tobiscagna, according to Taylor, Cal. Farmer, Feb. 22, 1860), a fertile and well-wooded spot on a stream afterward known as San Gabriel r., in Los Angeles co. The party with supplies had been sent up from San Diego, and included 10 soldiers for the protection of the new mission. The natives were at first friendly, and assisted in bringing timber and in helping to construct the buildings and stockade. Friction soon arose with the Indians, however, probably due to the outrages of the soldiers, and one native chieftain was shot. Owing to these troubles with the natives the number of soldiers was increased. These seem to have been an unruly lot, and their actions appear to have hindered the early growth of the mission, the whole number baptized during the first two years being only 73. In Fr. Junípero Serra's first annual report of 1773 he declared the native population in that region was larger than elsewhere, but that the various villages were hostile to one another, so that those near the mission, for example, could not go to the sea for fish. Situated as it was in a fertile region, the agricultural returns seem to have been very successful after the first year, so that later San Gabriel frequently furnished the other missions with supplies. Occupying also a position where the overland route from Sonora and the Colorado met that from Lower California, it soon became one of the most important of the missions. The natives seem to have been soon conciliated. The number of neophytes was 638 in 1783, and 1,040 in 1790. An uprising of the natives, including the neophytes, was threatened in 1785, but the scheme was frustrated without bloodshed, and the leaders were imprisoned. During the following years San Gabriel continued to flourish, despite the large number of deaths among the neophytes, nearly as many as the number of baptisms. There were numerous reports of threatened hostilities, but nothing serious occurred. The harsh treatment of the neophytes led many of them to escape, and some of these doubtless plotted revenge. The greatest number of neophytes, 1,701, was reached in 1817, after which there was a somewhat irregular but gradual decrease. The largest crop, amounting to 29,400 bushels, was raised in 1821. Among industrial experiments tried was a grist mill (the building for which is still standing), which, however, did not prove an entire success, as after about two years its use seems to have been abandoned. Later another mill was built. There were four chapels attached to this mission; that of the pueblo of Los Angeles was dedicated in 1822, though begun many years before. The others were Puente, San Antonio de Santa Ana, and San Bernardino (Guachama). This last seems to have been established about 1822 at the special request of the natives, and flourished till about 1834, when it was destroyed by hostile Indians. In the latter year there were 1,320 neophytes. Up to that time 6,814 natives had been baptized, of whom 2,459 were children. After secularization the wealth of the mission rapidly decreased, thousands of cattle being destroyed merely for their hides and tallow, so that by 1840 the livestock had practically disappeared. Most of the neophytes left the mission, though in 1844, 300 were reported as helping to attend the vineyards, all that was left of the productive property. In 1846 Gov. Pico sold the mission for debt, but the title was finally declared invalid. Since 1850 the church has been a regular parish church. The Indians in the neighborhood of this mission belong to the Shoshonean linguistic family, and have been given the collective name of Gabrieleños (q. v.); included among these are those at San Fernando mission. There were also many neophytes from the Serrano (q. v.) villages farther E., and probably representatives of other groups also. The names of the rancherias associated with San Gabriel mission were: Acuragna, Alyeupkigna, Awigna, Azucsagna, Cahuenga, Chokishgna, Chowigna, Cucomogna, Hahamogna, Harasgna, Houtgna, Hutucgna, Isanthcogna, Maugna, Nacaugna, Pascegna, Pasinogna, Pimocagna, Pubugna, Sibagna, Sisitcanogna, Sonagna, Suangna, Tibahagna, Toviscanga, Toybipet, Yangna.   (A. B. L.)

San Geronimo (Saint Jerome). A former rancheria, probably of the Maricopa, situated 20 leagues from Merced and 27 leagues from the Rio Gila, s. Arizona. It was visited by Father Kino in Sept. 1700.

San Geronymo.—Venegas, Hist. Cal., I, 300, 1759. S. Gerónimo.—Bancroft, Ariz. and N. Mex., 359, 1889.

Sangmisok. A settlement of East Greenland Eskimo near C. Farewell.—Ausland, LIX, 161, 1886.

Sangona ('shot at some white object').

A band of the Hunkpatina division of the Yanktonai Sioux.

Sah-own.—Lewis and Clark, Discov., 34, 1806. **San-ona.**—Dorsey in 15th Rep. B. A. E., 218, 1897. **San-ona.**—Ibid. **Saone.**—J. O. Dorsey, inf'n, 1897.

San Gorgonio. A former village of s. California, in the pass of the same name in San Bernardino co. It is mentioned by Burton (H. R. Ex. Doc. 76, 34th Cong., 3d sess., 117, 1857) as belonging to the Kawia, but it is more likely to have been Serrano.

San Ignacio (Saint Ignace). A Pima rancheria on the N. bank of Rio San Ignacio, lat. 30° 45′, lon. 111°, Sonora, Mexico, and the seat of a presidio and mission from early times. It was visited by Father Kino in 1694, and by Kino and Mange in 1699. Pop. 94 in 1730. In 1749–50 it was reported to be ''more Pápago than Pima.'' Not to be confounded with San Ignacio de Tubac. (See Kino, 1694, in Doc. Hist. Mex., 4th s., I, 254, 1856; Mange in Bancroft, Ariz. and N. Mex., 358, 1889; Bancroft, No. Mex. States, I, 533, 1884.)

San Ignacio.—Kino, op. cit. **San Ygnacio.**—Rudo Ensayo (ca. 1763), 152, 1863.

San Ignacio. A village, apparently of the Tubare (q. v.), in the upper fork of the Rio Sinaloa, lon. 107° 50′, lat. 26° 45′, Sinaloa, Mexico.—Orozco y Berra, Geog., map, 1864.

San Ignacio. A small Cahuilla settlement on Los Coyotes res., s. Cal. See *Pachawal*.

San Ignacio de Kadakaman (*Kadakaman*, 'sedge brook.'—Venegas). A former Cochimi village and Spanish mission, situated in the Sierra de San Vicente, lat. 28°, 40 leagues N. w. of Santa Rosalia Mulege, and 25 leagues N. E. of Guadalupe, Lower California. The mission of San Ignacio Kadakaman, or San Ignacio Loyola, was established in 1728 by Padre Luyando, but it was later consolidated with Nuestra Señora de los Dolores del Norte, 60 m. northward. In 1745 it had 9 visitas.

Cada-kaaman.—Venegas, Hist. Cal., I, 421, 1759. **Kada-Kaaman.**—Ibid., II, 89. **Kadakaamang.**—Clavigero, Storia della Cal., I, 107, 1789. **San Ignacio.**—Venegas, op. cit., I, 422; II, 198, 1759. **San Ignacio de Kadakaman.**—Taylor quoted by Browne, Res. Pac. Slope, app., 50, 1869. **S. Ignazio di Kadakaaman.**—Clavigero, op. cit., II, 48.

San Ildefonso. The second of three Franciscan missions established in 1748–49 by the College of Santa Cruz de Querétaro on San Xavier (now San Gabriel) r., 9 m. N. w. of Rockdale, Milam co., Texas. The circumstances of its establishment are given under San Francisco Xavier de Horcasitas (q. v.). The principal tribes at San Ildefonso mission were the Arkokisa, Bidai, and Deadose, all of which spoke the same language. Another tribe located there was the Patiri, probably of the same linguistic group, since the tribes were distributed among the three missions avowedly on the basis of lin-

guistic differences. About **1750,** it seems (the chronology is not clear), an epidemic visited the mission, during which about 40 persons died, all baptized. Some time before Mar. 11, 1751, Capt. Joseph de Eca y Musquiz counted at the mission 176 neophytes. Four months after the epidemic the remaining Indians deserted in a body, to join the Nabedache and other eastern tribes in a general campaign against the Apache, their mortal enemy (Arricivita, Crónica, 329, 1792). Later they returned and camped, to the number of 66 families, near San Xavier mission, where their minister served them for some time. They expressed a willingness to return to San Ildefonso, but this course was discouraged, because of the bad state of affairs at the establishments (Arricivita, op. cit., 337). Thus it seems that the San Ildefonso mission was not in operation after 1751. On May 11, 1752, Father Ganzabal, missionary of San Ildefonso, already deserted, was murdered at the Candelaria mission by an unknown hand. In 1756–57 a new mission, called Nuestra Señora de la Luz (q. v.), was founded for this group of tribes on the lower Trinity. (H. E. B.)

San Ildefonso. A Tewa pueblo near the E. bank of the Rio Grande, about 18 m. N. w. of Santa Fé, N. Mex. It became the seat of a Spanish mission at least as early as 1617, and had Santa Clara and San Juan as its visitas in 1680, but was itself reduced to a visita of Santa Clara in 1782. Bandelier has identified the Bove of Oñate with the pueblo of San Ildefonso, which in 1598 was situated about a mile from the present village. The Indians of this pueblo took a prominent part in the uprising against Spanish authority in 1696, and it was not until after the fourth assault of their nearby mesa stronghold by Vargas that they surrendered. In this revolt the two missionaries were killed and the church was burned (Bandelier in Arch. Inst. Papers, IV, 82, 1892). The pueblo now (1910) numbers 110 inhabitants. The clans of San Ildefonso, so far as their names have been recorded, are Tan (Sun), Pe (Firewood), Tse (Eagle), Ton (Antelope), Po (Calabash), Pa (Fire), P'o (Water), Ku (Stone), Kuping (Coral), Kungye (Turquoise), Okuwa (Cloud), Kea (Badger), Te (Cottonwood), D'ye (Gopher), Kang (Mountain lion), Ye (Lizard), De (Coyote), Whapi (Red-tail hawk), Kwatsei (White bead), Tse (a mountain tree), Pang (Deer), Se (Blue bird), Kungtsa (White corn), Kungtsoa (Blue corn), Kungpi (Red corn), Kungtsei (Yellow corn), Kungfetdi (Black corn), Kungaii (Sweet corn), Kyunggang (Hawk), Koo (Buffalo). See *Pueblos, Tanoan Family, Tewa*. (F. W. H.)

Bove.—Oñate (1598) in Doc. Inéd., XVI, 256, 1871. **Ildefonso.**—Calhoun in Cal. Mess. and Corresp., 213, 1850. **O-po-que.**—Bandelier in Ritch, New Mex., 201, 1885 (native name). **O-po-que.**—Bandelier in Ausland, 925, 1882 (native name). **P'áhwia'hlíap.**—Hodge, field notes, B. A. E., 1895 (Isleta name). **Pákwiti.**—Ibid. (Santa Ana name). **Pâwhá'hlita.**—Ibid. ('where the river enters a canyon': Taos name). **P'Ho-juo-ge.**—Bandelier in Arch. Inst. Papers, III, 260, 1890 (native name). **Po-hua-gai.**—Jouvenceau in Cath. Pion., I, no. 9, 12, 1906. **Po-juo-ge.**—Bandelier in Arch. Inst. Papers, IV, 82, 1892. **Po-juo-que.**—Ibid., III, 124, 1890 (aboriginal name). **Poo-joge.**—Bandelier, Gilded Man, 232, 1893. **Posonwû.**—Fewkes in 19th Rep. B. A. E., 614, 1900 (Hano Tewa name; probably identical). **Posówe.**—Stephen in 5th Rep. B. A. E., 37, 1891 (Hano name; probably identical). **Powhoge.**—Hewett in Am. Anthr., VI, 630, 1904. **San Aldefonso.**—Simpson, Rep. to Sec. War, 140, 1850. **San Il de Conso.**—Lane (1854) in Schoolcraft, Ind. Tribes, V, 689, 1855 (misprint). **San Ildefonso.**—MS. of 1719 quoted by Bandelier in Arch. Inst. Papers, v, 190, 1890; Villa-Señor, Theatro Am., II, 418, 1748. **San Ildefonzo.**—Brevoort, New Mexico, 20, 1874. **San Ildephonso.**—Villa-Señor, Theatro Am., II, 413, 1748. **San Ilefonso.**—Benavides, Memorial, 26, 1630. **San Jldefonso.**—Wislizenus, Memoir, map, 1848. **Sant Yldefonso.**—Bandelier in Arch. Inst. Papers, I, 19, 1881 (correcting Oñate). **Sant Ylefonso.**—Oñate (1598) in Doc. Inéd., XVI, 116, 1871. **San Yldefonso.**—Davis, El Gringo, 88, 1857. **San Yldefonso.**—Curtis, Children of the Sun, 121, 1883. **S. Ildefonse.**—Vaugondy, Map Amérique, 1778. **S. Ildefonsia.**—Simpson in Rep. Sec. War, 2d map, 1850. **S. Ildefonso.**—D'Anville, Map N. A., Bolton's ed., 1752. **Tsĕ Tŭ Kĭnnĕ.**—Curtis, Am. Ind., I, 138, 1907 ('houses between rocks': Navaho name).

San Ildefonso. A former rancheria, apparently of the Soba, visited by Anza in 1774, and by Anza and Font in 1776; situated 4 leagues N. W. of Caborca, Sonora, Mexico. See Anza, cited by Bancroft, Ariz. and N. Mex., 389, 1889.

San Ildefonso de Cieneguita. Mentioned by Bancroft (No. Mex. States, I, 524, 1884), together with Tubac, Pitiqui, Caborca, Cocospera, etc., as a mission of Sonora, Mexico. Whether it was inhabited by Pima, Papago, or Opata has not been determined.

Sanipao (*Sa-ni-pa'-o*). A former Coahuiltecan tribe, part of whom were Christianized at Nuestra Señora de la Purísima Concepción mission (q. v.), Texas. In Mar. 1755 a band of them, the first of the tribe recorded in the marriage book, appeared at Concepción, and in one day were instructed, baptized, and remarried to the wives "whom they had taken in the forests" (Concepción Casamientos, partidas 111–17). During the next two or three years there were numerous baptisms and marriages of persons of this tribe, some evidently newcomers, and thereafter an occasional one is recorded down to 1790, when the extant record ceases (ibid., passim). The language of the tribe is preserved in the Manual (1760) of Bartholomé García, who was stationed at the neighbor mission of San Francisco de la Espada. The Sanipao are mentioned in the Informe de Misiones of Mar. 6, 1762 (Mem. de Nueva España, XXVIII, 167, MS.). Portillo's statement that this tribe was at Concepción at its foundation is probably incorrect, and is apparently based on the misleading statement in Revilla-Gigedo's Carta of 1793 (Portillo, Apuntes, 304, 1888).　　　　　(H. E. B.)

Samipoas.—Taylor in Cal. Farmer, Apr. 17, 1863. **Sanipaó.**—Concepción Casamientos, partida 248, 1790, MS.

San Jacome. A rancheria, apparently of the Cajuenche, in the 18th century, situated near the mountains, about lat. 33° 08', central s. California.—Garcés (1775), Diary, 167, 1900.

San Javier. See *San Francisco Xavier de Horcasitas; San Xavier.*

San Joaquin (Saint Joachim). An Indian settlement and mission visita in 1745, situated 3 leagues from the parent mission of San Ignacio de Kadakaman, Lower California.

S. Gioachino.—Clavigero, Storia della Cal., I, 107, 1789 (Italian form). **S. Joachin.**—Venegas, Hist. Cal., II, 198, 1759.

San Joaquin. A collective name for the Costanoan, Moquelumnan, and Yokuts tribes on San Joaquin r., Cal., estimated to number about 400.

San Joaquin's Band. A Paviotso band, named from its chief, formerly in Carson valley, at the forks, in w. Nevada. They were said to have numbered 170 in 1859.—Dodge in Ind. Aff. Rep. 1859, 373, 1860.

San José (Saint Joseph). The fourteenth Franciscan mission founded in California, and the first one of the five new missions established by Fr. Lasuen in 1797–98 to fill the gaps between the older ones. The site chosen was about 15 m. N. of Santa Clara, and about 3 m. from the present town of Irvington, Alameda co. The native name of the site was Oroysom. The formal ceremonies of foundation were performed by Fr. Lasuen on June 11, 1797, and by the end of that year there were 33 baptisms, and 286 by 1800. In 1810 there were 545, but 1,104 deaths were reported during the decade. In 1820 there were 1,754 neophytes. The highest number, 1,886, was reached in 1831. The mission was prosperous from the beginning and continued so long after many of the others declined. In 1820 there were 6,859 large stock and 1,200 small stock; in 1830, 13,300 and 13,030, respectively. The average crop for the decade ending 1820 was 6,020 bushels, and for that ending 1830, 5,409 bushels. The first church was a wooden structure with a grass roof, but in 1809 a new church was dedicated. Even before the founding of the mission the Indians of its neighborhood, especially to the eastward, were somewhat feared, and San José seems to have had more trouble with the Indians than any other in California. The rather forceful methods used by the padres in obtaining neophytes, together with the ease with which they could escape to gentile or hostile villages, doubtless increased the difficulties. More than once expeditions to recover runaway neophytes were attacked. In 1826 a party of neophytes got into trouble with the Cosumni, and a punitive expedition was sent out, which brought in 40 captives. In 1829 there was an extensive campaign into the San Joaquin valley against rebellious natives headed by Estanislas, a former neophyte of the mission. After 1830 San José was more prosperous than any other mission in California. In 1834 the neophytes numbered about 1,400. The number of natives baptized up to that time was 6,670, of whom 2,488 were children. In 1840, 580 were still at the mission, with possibly 200 more scattered in the district. The mission was secularized in 1836, when the inventory showed a total valuation, excluding lands and church property, of $155,000. After 1840 the decline was rapid. In 1843 the mission was restored to the control of the padres. Two years later it was estimated that about 250 Indians still lived in the vicinity. In 1846 the mission was sold by Gov. Pico for $12,000, but this sale was not confirmed, and the Catholic Church retained control. The old mission church has now completely disappeared and a modern parish church has been built on the site. The only part of the old buildings remaining is a portion of the monastery. The Indians in the neighborhood of the mission belonged to the Costanoan linguistic stock, the Saklan, Karkin, and Mutsun divisions being doubtless represented. A large part of the neophytes, however, especially during the later years of its existence, came from San Joaquin and Sacramento valleys, and included representatives of the Moquelumnan, Copehan, and Mariposan (Yokuts) linguistic stocks.	(A. B. L.)

San José. A former Diegueño village on upper San Luis Rey r., in San Diego co., Cal. It later became a part of Agua Caliente No. 1 res., on which Warner's ranch was situated. By court decision, the Indians, numbering only 14, were evicted in 1903, when they were assigned to a new reservation purchased for them at Pala. See Jackson and Kinney, Rep. Miss. Ind., 24, 1883; Ind. Aff. Rep., 175, 1902; 118, 1903.

San José. A group of Huichol rancherias under the jurisdiction of San Andrés Coamiata, situated about 10 m. N. w. of the latter place, in the Sierra de los Huicholes, Jalisco, Mexico. It is a religious center and the seat of a temple or "god house of the sun."—Lumholtz, Unknown Mex., II, 28, 1902.
Háiokalita.—Lumholtz, ibid. ('where there are springs': Huichol name).

San José. A rancheria of one of the Yuman tribes, which was selected as the site of a mission, on the Rio Gila near its mouth in s. w. Arizona; visited and named by Fr. Sedelmair in 1748.—Bancroft, Ariz. and N. Mex., 367, 1889.

San José. A ruined pueblo near Pecos, New Mexico, formerly occupied by the Pecos Indians.—Bandelier in Arch. Inst. Bull., I, 15, 1883.

San José. A Tepehuane pueblo and the seat of a mission in E. Durango, Mexico.—Orozco y Berra, Geog., 318, 1864.

San José de Comondu. A Cochimi settlement in the central mountainous part of Lower California, lat. 26° 5', and the seat of the Jesuit mission founded by Padre Mayorga in 1708. In 1745 it had 3 visitas, one lying a league to the w., another 7 leagues N., and another 10 leagues E. on the Gulf shore (Venegas). In 1767 the population of the mission was 360, according to Clavigero, probably including the inhabitants of the visitas.
Comondú—Clavijero, Hist. Baja Cal., 61, 1852. San José Commondu.—Taylor quoted by Browne, Res. Pac. Slope, app., 50, 1869. San José de Comondú.—Clavijero, op. cit., 109. San Joseph de Comondu.—Venegas, Hist. Cal., II, 197, 1759. San Joseph de Comonda.—Ibid., I, 399.

San José de los Nazones. A Franciscan mission founded July 10, 1716, by Fray Isidro Felix de Espinosa, author of the Chrónica Apostólica among the Nazoni and for the Nazoni and Nadaco, E. of Angelina r. and about 20 m. N. w. of Nacogdoches, on a small stream flowing N., evidently one of the southern branches of Shawnee cr., Texas. The statement that it was between the Neches and the Trinity is incorrect, as is also the assertion that it was founded for the "Noaches," a tribe which did not exist in Texas. After three years of little success, the mission was abandoned in 1719, in common with all the others of E. Texas, through fear of a French invasion. On Aug. 13, 1721, it was reestablished on the same site by the Marqués de Aguayo and Father Espinosa. The church and the dwelling, which were found in ruins, were rebuilt, the chief of the Nazoni was reinstated as "governor," and Fray Benito Sanchez left in charge (Peña, Derrotero, folio 18, Mexico, 1722). In 1729 the presidio near the Angelina, which protected this mission, was withdrawn, and as a result the mission was suppressed in 1729–30. An attempt was first made to reestablish it on San Marcos r., then on the Nueces and the Frio, but finally a site was chosen on the San Antonio, 12 m. below the present city of that name. Here, on Mar. 5, 1731, the mission of San José was rechristened San Juan Capistrano (q. v.). While in E. Texas, the mission had never been very successful, for while the Indians were in the main friendly, they were indifferent to the faith, and refused to give up their life in scattered villages to live in mission pueblos. (H. E. B.)

San José.—Bancroft, No. Mex. States, I, 614, 635, 665, 1886. San Joseph.—Garrison, Texas, 50, 1903.

San José de los Pimas. A former small settlement of the Nevome, situated 20 leagues from Pitic, on the Rio de Matape, in Sonora, Mexico. It was formerly a visita of the mission of Tecoripa. The place, which is now civilized, contained 150 inhabitants in 1900, 65 of whom were of Yaqui blood.

San Jose de los Pimas.—Hardy, Travels, 437, 1829. San Joseph de los Pimas.—Rudo Ensayo (*ca.* 1763), 125, 1863.

San José y San Miguel de Aguayo (Saint Joseph and Saint Michael). A Franciscan mission established in 1720 near Rio San Antonio, about 6 m. below the

THE CHURCH OF SAN JOSÉ Y SAN MIGUEL DE AGUAYO

present San Antonio, Texas, under the protection of the presidio of San Antonio de Béjar. It was long considered the most flourishing of the Texas missions, and in 1778 its church, worth $40,000, was said to be the finest in New Spain. The Indian population was 350 in 1762, up to which year there had been 1,054 baptisms. The mission also possessed 1,500 yoke of oxen. In 1785 the population was 106; in 1793, 114. It ceased to exist as an independent mission before the close of the century. See Bancroft, No. Mex. States, I, 1886; Garrison, Texas, 1904.

San Juan (Saint John). A Tewa pueblo near the E. bank of the Rio Grande, 25 m. N. W. of Santa Fé, N. Mex., before the establishment of which the Indians occupied and abandoned successively 3 other pueblos, immediately previous to the 16th century (Bandelier in Arch. Inst. Papers, IV, 21, 61, et seq., 1892). When Oñate visited it in 1598, he established there the headquarters of the provincial government, and preparations were even made for building the permanent city of "San Francisco" in its vicinity (see *Yugeuingge*). It was the seat of a Franciscan mission from an early date, and, owing partly to the generous character of its inhabitants

in 1598 in receiving the people of Yugeuingge after the voluntary relinquishment of their pueblo to the Spaniards, gained from the latter for their village the designation "San Juan de los Caballeros." In 1782, 500 of the inhabitants of San Juan and Santa Clara died of pestilence in two months. Besides the main pueblo of San Juan the Indians held a portion of the arable lands about Chamita, and a small colony of them dwell on the w. side of the Rio Grande at the so-called Pueblito. They claim Pioge, Sajiuwingge, and Pojiuuingge as ruins of their ancient villages. Pop. 404 in 1910.

The clans of San Juan are: Tan (Sun), Nan (Stone), Kopin (Coral), Na (Earth), Kunya (Turquoise), Pe (a mountain tree), Sepin ("Painted Eagle"), Oquwa (Cloud), Po (Calabash), Ta (Grass), Kun (Corn), Po' (Water), De (Coyote), Ke (Bear), Kan (Mountain lion), Keya (Badger), Ye (Lizard), Dye (Gopher), Te (Cottonwood). See *Pueblos, Tanoan Family, Tewa.* (F. W. H.)

Jyuo-tyu-te Oj-ke.—Bandelier in Arch. Inst. Papers, III, 260, 1890 (proper name of the pueblo). Kaj-kai.—Jouvenceau in Cath. Pion., I, no. 9, 12, 1906 (given as native name). Kin Klĕchini.—Curtis, Am. Ind., I, 138, 1907 ('red house people': Navaho name). Ochi.—Gatschet in Mag. Am. Hist. 259, Apr. 1882. Ohke.—Hodge, field notes, B. A. E., 1895 ('up-stream place': Tewa name). Ohque.—Smith, Caeça de Vaca, 163, 1871. Oj-ke.—Bandelier in Arch. Inst. Papers, III, 123, 1890. Oj-qué.—Bandelier in Ritch, N. Mex., 201, 1885. Orke'.—Fewkes in 19th Rep. B. A. E., 614, 1900 (Hano Tewa name). Pâkabalŭyŭ.—Hodge, field notes, B. A. E., 1895 ('where the Rio Grande opens into a plain': Tao name).

A CHIEF OF SAN JUAN, NEW MEXICO

Pakŭ'parai.—Hodge, field notes, B.A.E., 1895 (Isleta name). **Pakuqhalai.**—Ibid (Picuris name). **Saint-Jean des Chevaliers.**—Cordova (1619) trans. in Ternaux-Compans, Voy., x, 440, 1838 (French form). **San Juan.**—Villa-Señor (1748) quoted by Shea, Cath. Miss., 82, 1855. **San Juan de Cabalenos.**—Donaldson, Moqui Pueblo Inds., 91, 1893 (misprint). **San Juan de los Caballeros.**—Cordova (1619) trans. in Ternaux-Compans, Voy., x, 440, 1838; Villa-Señor, Theatro Am., II, 418, 1748. **San Juan de los Cabelleros.**—Shea, Cath. Miss., 82, 1870 (misprint). **San Juaneros.**—ten Kate, Reizen in N. A., 221, 1885. **San Juaners.**—Davis, Span. Conq. of N. Mex., 289, 1869. **Sant Joan.**—Oñate (1598) in Doc. Inéd., XVI, 256, 1871. **Sant Joan Batista.**—Ibid., 109, 116. **S. Iean.**—Crepy, Map Amér. Sept., 1783(?). **S. Jean.**—Vaugondy, Map Amérique, 1778. **S. Joanne.**—Morelli, Fasti Novi Orbis, 31, 1776. **S. John.**—D'Anville, Map N. A., Bolton's ed., 1752. **St. Johns.**—Heyleyn, Cosmography, 1072, 1703.

San Juan. A Timucua mission town in 1688, named in a letter from the chiefs of the tribe to the King of Spain (see copy and translation in Gatschet, Timucua Lang., in Proc. Am. Philos. Soc., XVIII, 497, 1880). It was visited by Dickenson in 1699, and was apparently situated on Little Talbot id., N. from St Augustine, Fla.   (J. M.)

San Juan. An Apalachee mission town in N. w. Florida during the latter half of the 17th century. It was destroyed, with others of the same tribe, by the English and their Indian allies in the war of 1702–06.   (J. M.)

San Juan. An Opata village of Sonora, Mexico, mentioned by Hrdlička (Am. Anthr., VI, 72, 1904) as one of the pueblos at which full-blood Opata may still be found.

San Juan. A collective term used to designate the Indians formerly under San Juan Bautista mission, San Benito co., Cal.—Taylor in Cal. Farmer, Apr. 20, 1860.

San Juan. A Cochimi visitation town of the mission of San José de Comondu, in lat. 26°, central Lower California, in 1708.—Venegas, Hist. Cal., I, 404, 1759.

San Juan Bautista (Saint John the Baptist). The fifteenth Franciscan mission established in California. The site was chosen between San Carlos and Santa Clara, about 6 m. from the present town of Sargent, Santa Clara co. The native name was Popelout, or Popeloutchom. Here some buildings had already been erected by men from Monterey, and on June 24, 1797, President Lasuen founded the new mission. By the end of the year there had been 85 baptisms, and in 1800 the neophytes numbered 516. These increased to 702 in 1810, 843 in 1820, and 1,248 in 1823, after which the decline began. The stock and crops prospered from the beginning. In 1810 there were 6,175 large stock and 9,720 small stock; in 1820, 11,700 and 9,530 respectively. The average crop for the decade ending 1810 was

3,700 bushels; for that ending 1820, 3,300 bushels. In 1830 there was a considerable decrease in stock, but the crops remained good. For the first two or three years after its founding the mission had considerable trouble with the Ansaime, who lived in the mountains about 25 m. to the E. These were finally defeated and a number of captives brought to the mission. A new mission church, begun in 1803, was dedicated in 1812. In 1832 there were 916 neophytes. The total number of baptisms from the time of its founding was 3,913, of whom 2,015 were children. In 1835, 63 Indians were emancipated, but after that time there is no further record. A number of whites settled in the region, and the place became known as the pueblo of San Juan de Castro. In 1846 the orchard, all that remained of the land improvements, was sold. The buildings continued in possession of the Catholic Church, and are still in use. The Indians in the neighborhood of San Juan Bautista belonged to the Costanoan linguistic family. In its later years it drew many of its neophytes from San Joaquin valley, and the Yokuts were probably well represented. García, according to Bancroft (Hist. Cal., II, 339, 1886), speaks of an expedition to the Mariposas, the rancheria of Nopochinches being named, in which 300 Indians of all ages and sexes were brought to San Juan Bautista. A list of the villages from which neophytes were drawn follows (Bancroft, op. cit., I, 557, 1886; Taylor in Cal. Farmer, Nov. 25, 1860), although several of them also supplied neophytes to San Carlos: Absayme (Ausaimas, Ausaima = Ansaimes), Absayruc, Asystarca, Calendaruc (Kalindaruk), Chapana, Echantac, Giguay, Guachurrones (Wacharones), Iratae, Jasniga, Jeboaltae, Lithenca, Mitaldejama, Motssum (Mutsun), Onextaco, Onixaymas, Paisin (Pagosines or Paysines), Popelout, Pouxouoma, Poitokwis, Suricuama, Tamarox, Teboaltac (=Jeboaltae), Thithirii, Tipisastac (Tipsistana=Tipsistaca), Trutca, Uñijaima, Utchuchu, Xisca (or Xixcaca), Xivirca, Yelmus.   (A. B. L.)

San Juan Bautista (so named by Oñate, who reached it on St John's day, June 24, 1598). Formerly a small pueblo on the Rio Grande, 16 m. above Sevilleta, N. Mex., at the site of the present Sabinal. Whether it was a Piro or a Tigua settlement is not known, since it was near the boundary of the territory of those two groups. In 1626 Sevilleta was mentioned as the last Piro settlement to the N.; therefore if San Juan Bautista belonged to that tribe it was abandoned between 1598 (the date of Oñate's visit) and 1626.   (F. W. H.)

San Iuan Baptista.—Villagran, Hist. N. Mex., 136, 1610.　San Juan Baptista.—Bandelier in Arch. Inst. Papers, IV, 238, 1892.　Sant Joan Baptista.—Oñate (1598) in Doc Inéd., XVI, 252, 1871.

San Juan Bautista. A Cora pueblo and formerly a visita of the mission of Santa Fé; situated near the w. bank of Rio San Pedro, lat. 22° 20′, Jalisco, Mexico.— Kino in Doc. Hist. Mex., 4th s., I, 300, 1856.

San Juan Capistrano. A Franciscan mission established by Fr. Junípero Serra, Nov. 10, 1776, at a place called in the native tongue Sajirit, or Quanis-Savit, at the present San Juan, Orange co., Cal. As soon as Franciscan missionaries, who were superseded by Dominicans in Lower California, arrived in San Diego, the ardent apostle to Alta California sent two friars to institute a mission at a roadstead 26 leagues N. of San Diego. They raised a cross on Oct. 30, 1775, but hastily returned when they learned that in the absence of the soldiers the natives had burned San Diego mission. No sooner was it rebuilt than Fr. Junípero proceeded to inaugurate the projected second mission, then hurried to San Gabriel and brought down the requisite stock of cattle escorted by a single soldier, and when a band of yelling, painted Indians threatened his life he won their confidence and friendship. The natives of this coast, well supplied by prolific nature, were not covetous of food or gifts, but remarkably eager for baptism. The inhabitants of the valley came from the other side of the Santa Ana mts., where they had a large rancheria called Sejat. About 2 m. from the mission they had one called Putuidem, and in its immediate vicinity they settled at Acagchemem (Geronimo Boscana in Cal. Farmer, Oct. 11, 1861). The fruitful plain soon yielded an exchangeable surplus of wheat, corn, and legumes. Juicy grasses nourished herds and flocks that doubled each year. The vine was first planted there and it grew wonderfully, and pomegranates, quinces, peaches, nectarines, and other fruits of Old Spain throve as well. By 1783 there were 383 converts; in 1790 there were 741, and the mission herds had increased to 2,473 head, the small stock to 5,500, the grain crop to upward of 3,000 bushels. Houses for 40 neophyte families were constructed in 1794, some of them roofed with tiles. The weaving industry was introduced in 1797, and woolen blankets and cloth of native dye were produced, while the wool clip was abundant enough to supply other missions also. A stone church, the finest in California, that was nine years in building, was completed in 1806. It had a high tower and five interior arches of stone, all the work of the neophytes. Illegal sales of provisions to American and Russian trading vessels filled the coffers of the mission. The number of neophytes increased to 1,138 in 1810, the average crop to 5,570 bushels, and the large stock to 10,213 head, while the number of sheep, though still the largest among the missions, decreased in ten years from 17,030 to 11,500, but at the end of the following decade there were 15,000, with 11,500 cattle and nearly 1,000 horses, while the neophyte population, after reaching 1,361 in 1812, declined to 1,064. On Dec. 8, 1812, the new church was destroyed by an earthquake, and nearly 50 natives who were attending early mass were buried beneath the ruins. In 1830 the number of neophytes had declined to 926, cattle to 10,978, sheep to 5,000. Torrents gullied the fertile soil and weeds choked the crops, while the affairs of the mission were mismanaged. The missionary quarreled with the captain of the guard, and the neophytes grew lazy and insolent. In 1833 the earlier scheme of secularization was carried out at this mission as an experiment. The neophytes, of whom there were 861, were all released from mission restriction, provided with farms and farm stock, and constituted into a pueblo. In the following year their new liberties were abrogated and they were placed on a footing with the people of other missions. From the founding of the mission till 1834 the number of natives baptized was 4,317, 1,689 adults and 2,628 children. The number of deaths was 3,153. The civilian administrator was avaricious, and the neophytes deserted until only 80 were found at the mission in 1839. They clamored to be formed again into a pueblo, and the Government acceded to their desire on the condition of their working faithfully during a period of probation under the direction of the padre, but he was unwilling to take charge unless citizens were allowed to come in and the Indian alcaldes were held in control. During the next few years most of the Indians left for Los Angeles or elsewhere. In 1841 the Indians were fully emancipated and land was assigned to those who desired it in the newly founded pueblo of San Juan, but not more than 20 to 30 seem to have settled there. What remained of the mission grounds was sold in 1845 for $710. The ruins of the old stone church still remain as when overthrown. The Landmarks Club of California has secured a lease of the buildings and grounds, placed a roof, with the original tiles, on the old adobe church, supposed to have been built by Serra, besides making other repairs to preserve the buildings from further decay. The

Indians in the neighborhood of this mission belong to the Shoshonean linguistic stock and are known as Juaneños (q. v.), though it is probable that the mission included neophytes from more distant groups.　(F. H.　A. B. L.)

Quanis Savit.—Taylor in Cal. Farmer, Feb. 22, 1860 (the name of the site of San Juan Capistrano mission). **Sajirit.**—Bancroft, Hist. Cal., I, 304, 1886 (native name of mission site). **San Capistrano.**—Shea, Cath. Miss., 98, 1855. **San Juan Capestrano.**—Hale, Ethnog. and Philol., 222, 1846. **San Juan Capistrano.**—Proper name of mission.

San Juan Capistrano. A mission established in 1731 on San Antonio r., about 7 m. below the present San Antonio, Texas, under the protection of the presidio of San Antonio de Béjar. Prior to this time it was situated between Trinity and Neches rs., and was known as San José de los Nazones (q. v.). The population was 203 in 1762, up to which time there had been 847 baptisms. The mission contained also 1,000 cattle, 500 horses,

SAN JUAN CAPISTRANO MISSION, TEXAS

and 3,500 sheep. The inhabitants had become reduced to 58 in 1785, and to only 34 in 1793. It ceased to exist as an independent mission before the close of the century. See Bancroft, No. Mex. States, I, 1886; Garrison, Texas, 1903.

San Juan de Dios (Saint John of God). A former mission on the w. side of Lower California.

Guiricatà.—Clavigero, Storia della Cal., II, 173, 1789. **St. John of God.**—Shea, Cath. Miss., 90, 1855.

San Juan de los Jemez. A mission or the visita of a mission established by the Franciscans between 1627 and 1680 at one of the pueblos of the Jemez, probably Amushungkwa (q. v.), at the junction of the Guadalupe and San Diego branches of Jemez r., in N. central New Mexico. It contained a church. See Bandelier in Arch. Inst. Papers, IV, 208, 1893.

San Juan de los Jemes.—Lara (1696) quoted by Bandelier, op. cit., 209. **San Juan de los Jemez.**—Doc. of 1692, ibid. **S. Jua.**—Ibid., 208.

San Lázaro (Saint Lazarus). A former Tano pueblo 12 m. s. w. of the present Lamy, on the s. bank of the Arroyo del Chorro, Santa Fé co., N. Mex. Prior to the Pueblo uprising in 1680 it was a visita of the mission of San Marcos, but between that date and 1692 the inhabitants were forced

to abandon it by the combined forces of the Pecos and the Rio Grande Keresan tribes and to transfer their pueblo to the neighborhood of the present Santa Cruz, where the town was rebuilt under the same name, but was abandoned in 1694. See Bancroft, Ariz. and N. Mex., 186, 1889; Bandelier in Arch. Inst. Papers, I, 22; IV, 83, 105, 1892.　(F. W. H.)

I-pe-re.—Bandelier in Arch. Inst. Papers, III, 125, 1890 (aboriginal name). **San Cázaro.**—Bandelier in Ritch, N. Mex., 201, 1885 (misprint). **San Lasaro.**—Ladd, Story of N. Mex., 92, 1891. **San Lázaro.**—Vetancurt (1696) in Teatro Mex., III, 324, 1871. **S. Lazaro.**—D'Anville, Map Am. Sépt., 1746. **S! Lazarus.**—Kitchin, Map N. A., 1787.

San Lázaro. A former settlement, probably of the Papago, and the seat of a Spanish mission; situated on the Rio Santa Cruz, in lon. 110° 30′, just below the Arizona-Sonora boundary, at the site of the present town of that name. The mission was doubtless established by Father Kino about 1697. It was abandoned in 1845 on account of Apache depredations.

San Lázaro.—Kino (1697) in Doc. Hist. Mex., 4th s., I, 276, 1856. **San Lorenzo.**—Orozco y Berra, Geog., 347, 1864. **S. Lázaro.**—Bernal (1697) in Bancroft, Ariz. and N. Mex., 356, 1889. **S. Lazarus.**—Kino, map (1702) in Stöcklein, Neue Welt-Bott, 74, 1726. **S. Lorenzo.**—Mange in Bancroft, Ariz. and N. Mex., 358, 1889 (identical?).

San Lorenzo (Saint Lawrence). A Franciscan mission, founded in Texas, Jan. 26, 1762 (not in 1761 as Arricivita says), for the Lipan after they were frightened from San Saba mission by the attack of the Comanche and others in 1758. The site was at El Cañon, on the Rio San Joseph, now the upper Nueces, and not the San Antonio, as has been conjectured (El Cañon is shown on the La Fora map, ca. 1767). The principal chief concerned was Cabezón, who was made "governor" of the pueblo of neophytes, called Santa Cruz. He stipulated and was granted three conditions before entering the mission. These were that the Spaniards should (1) protect his people from the Comanche during a great buffalo hunt, (2) aid them in a campaign against that tribe, and (3) deliver to him the captive daughter of the Natagé (Kiowa Apache) head chief (Report of Rábago y Terán, Jan. 31, 1761, MS. in Archivo Gen.). Two weeks afterward Nuestra Señora de la Candelaria (q. v.) was founded nearby.

A year after their establishment, Ximinez (quoted by Arricivita, Crónica 388, 1792) reported that about 400 Indians were in the two missions, of which this one was the more prosperous. El Cañon had been chosen as a retreat from the Comanche, and for some time it was unmolested, it seems; but in 1766 and 1767, in retaliation for two hostile campaigns by the Lipan, the Comanche three times attacked San Lorenzo mission (Candelaria was already abandoned). In the last attack it is said they killed and captured more than 30 Lipan and ran off

more than 1,000 horses (Arricivita, op. cit., 392–93). In 1767 the Viceroy, on the recommendation of the Marqués de Rubi, ordered the mission abandoned. What are apparently the ruins of this mission are still plainly visible in Edwards co., about 40 m. N. W. of Uvalde.   (H. E. B.)
Santa Cruz.—Rábago y Terán, Feb. 7, 1762, MS. in Archivo Gen. (properly the name of the Indian pueblo, not of the mission).

San Lorenzo. A former Suma pueblo, probably containing also some Piro and Tigua, near El Paso, on the Rio Grande, in Chihuahua. It was the seat of a Spanish mission from 1712, and had 440 inhabitants in 1790, but became a Mexicanized town on the extermination of the tribe.   (F. W. H.)
San Lorenzo.—Villa-Señor, Theatro Am., II, 360, 423, 1748. San Lorenzo del Real.—Ward in Ind. Aff. Rep. 1867, 213, 1868. San Lorenzo el Real Pueblo de Zumas.—18th Cent. doc. cited by Bandelier in Arch. Inst. Papers, III, 88, 1890. S. Lorenzo.—Rivera, Diario, leg. 684, 1736. S. Lorenzo del Realito.—Bonilla (1776) quoted by Bancroft, Ariz. and N. Mex., 191, 1889.

San Lucas. A Cora pueblo on the upper waters of the Rio Jesus María, on the E. border of the Cora country, in the N. part of the territory of Tepic, Mexico.—Lumholtz, Unknown Mex., II, 16, map, 1902.

San Luis (Saint Louis). The district in w. Kansas once inhabited by the Apaches del Quartelejo; so named by Juan Uribarri in 1706 (Bancroft, Ariz. and N. Mex., 229, 236, 1889). At this time, or shortly afterward, it was within the range of the Jicarillas. See *Quartelejo*.

San Luis. A former Diegueño rancheria near San Diego, s. Cal.—Ortega (1775) quoted by Bancroft, Hist. Cal., I, 253, 1884.

San Luis Babi. A rancheria, probably of the Papago, visited by Father Kino in 1701; situated in N. w. Sonora, Mexico, between Busanic and Cocospera.
S. Luis Babi (?).—Bancroft, No. Mex. States, I, 497, 1884.

San Luis de Apalache. A principal town and mission of the Apalachee, formerly situated, according to Fairbanks (Hist. Fla., 123, 1901), 2 m. w. of the present Tallahassee, Fla. The settlement is named in a letter of the chiefs to the King of Spain in 1688, and was destroyed, with the mission church and fort, by the English and their Indian allies under Gov. Moore in 1704.   (J. M.)
San Luis.—Fairbanks, Fla., 123, 1901. San Luis de Apalachi.—Doc. of 1688 quoted by Gatschet, Creek Migr. Leg., I, 76, 1884. St. Lewis.—Carroll, Hist. Coll. S. C., II, 575, 1836 (the fort). St. Lewisses.—Ibid., 353. St. Louis.—Brackenridge (1827) in Williams, West Fla., 107, 1827.

San Luis de las Amarillas. A presidio established in 1757 on San Saba r., Texas, for the protection of San Saba mission (q. v.), on the other side of the stream. The ruins of this presidio are still to be seen at Menardville, Menard co.   (H. E. B.)

San Luis Obispo. The fifth Franciscan mission established in California, on a site, called Tixlini by the natives, now in-cluded in the city of the same name. The mission, dedicated to San Luis Obispo de Tolosa, was founded by Fr. Junípero Serra on Sept. 1, 1772, the place being near the Cañada de los Osos, where Fages had earlier in the year spent three months hunting bears to supply the northern establishments with food. The natives were well disposed, willing to work, and offered their children for baptism, although the number of neophytes increased slowly. There was no rancheria near the mission, and the natives being well supplied with food, such as deer, rabbits, fish, and seeds, were not particularly desirous of settling at the mission. Crops seem to have been fairly successful from the first. In 1776 all the buildings except the church and the granary were burned by Indians who were enemies of those attached to the mission, the tule roofs of the buildings being fired by means of burning arrows. This led to the general adoption of tiles for roofing. In 1794 an unsuccessful attempt was made by outside Indians to cause the converts to revolt, but it ended with the imprisonment of five of the leaders. There were 492 neophytes in 1780, and 605 in 1790, while the highest number, 946, was reached in 1794. Want of water was reported as the chief drawback of the mission, though the average crop for the decade ending 1800 was 3,200 bushels, and for the next decade 4,456 bushels. About 1809 a chapel seems to have been built at San Miguelito. One was also established at Santa Margarita, the ruins of which still remain. Though the population of the mission gradually decreased after 1794, industries seem to have thriven for a time. Both woolen and cotton cloth was woven, and the Indians were reported as always well dressed. After 1820 the decline was more marked, so that by 1830 there were only 283 neophytes remaining, and marks of neglect were everywhere visible (Robinson, Life in Cal., 84, 1846). In 1834 there were 264 neophytes. The total number of natives baptized to 1834 was 2,608, of whom 1,331 were children. In 1840 there were still 170 ex-neophytes at the mission. The decline in wealth exceeded 50 percent. All the horses were stolen in 1840, and thenceforward the decline was rapid, so that in 1844 the mission was reported as having neither land nor cattle, while the neophytes were demoralized and scattered for want of a minister. The mission was sold in 1845 by Gov. Pico for $510. The ownership of the buildings was later confirmed of course to the Catholic Church, but both monastery and church have been so much rebuilt that they have little resemblance to the original structures. The Indians in the neighborhood of the mission belonged to the Chumashan (q. v.) linguistic family, though speaking a dialect rather different from the others. The following are a few of the villages: Chapule, Chiminer, Chofuate, De Impimu, De Qmchechs, Lteguie, Sesjala, Sespala, Tchena, Tgmaps, Walekhe (A. B. L.)

San Luis Rey de Francia (Saint Louis, King of France, commonly contracted to San Luis Rey). A Franciscan mission founded June 13, 1798, in San Diego co., Cal. It was the last mission established in California s. of Santa Barbara, and the last one by Fr. Lasuen, who was aided by Frs. Santiago and Peyri. The native name of the site was Tacayme. Occupying an intermediate position between San Juan Capistrano and San Diego, it seems to have been chosen chiefly because of the great number of docile natives in the neighborhood. On the day of the founding, 54 children were baptized, and the number of baptisms by the end of the year reached 214. Fr. Peyri, the head of the new mission, was most zealous and energetic, the natives were willing to work, and by July 1, 6,000 adobes were made for the new church, which was completed in 1802. Other buildings also were constructed, and neophytes rapidly gathered in, so that by 1810 the number reached 1,519, a more rapid growth than in any other mission, while the death-rate was the lowest. The mission also prospered materially, having in 1810, 10,576 large stock, 9,710 small stock, and an average crop for the preceding decade of 5,250 bushels. During the next decade the mission continued to prosper, the population reaching 2,603 in 1820, while the large stock numbered 11,852, the small stock 13,641, and the average crop was 12,470 bushels. In 1816 Fr. Peyri founded the branch establishment, or asistencia, of San Antonio de Pala, about 20 m. up the river. Here a chapel was built, a padre stationed, and within a year or two more than a thousand converts gathered. The mission attained its greatest prosperity about 1826, when it had 2,869 neophytes, but from this time it gradually declined. The mission lands were extensive, including ranches at Santa Margarita, Las Flores, Temecula, San Jacinto, and Agua Caliente, all of which were tended by the neophytes. At the time of secularization in 1834 San Luis Rey had the greatest number of neophytes of all the missions, namely 2,844, and also the greatest number of livestock. After secularization the decline was rapid, both in population and wealth. The Indians managed to retain partial control of some of the mission ranches for a few years longer, but soon had to give them up.

The total number of natives baptized up to 1834 was 5,401, of whom 1,862 were children. In 1846 Gov. Pico sold what was left of the mission buildings and ground for $2,437. Their agent was dispossessed by Frémont, and during most of 1847 the place was garrisoned by United States troops. It was also held as a sub-Indian agency for some time afterward. As with the other missions, the title to the buildings and the immediate grounds was finally confirmed to the Catholic Church. In 1892 the church was repaired, and the next year rededicated. Other buildings also have been repaired or rebuilt, and San Luis Rey is now a college for the training of missionaries. The chapel at Pala has likewise been restored, and while the original inhabitants have entirely disappeared, Pala has recently become the home of the Hot Springs Indians from Warner's ranch (see *Agua Caliente*), having 252 inhabitants in 1908. The Indians in the neighborhood of the San Luis Rey mission belong to the Shoshonean linguistic stock, and have been given the collective name of Luiseños (q. v.). (A. B. L.)

San Manuel (Saint Emanuel). A reservation of 640 acres of worthless land, consisting of dry hills, which has been patented to its 125 Mission Indian inhabitants; situated 10 m. from San Bernardino, Cal.—Ind. Aff. Rep. 1902, 175, 1903; ibid., 1903, 147, 1904; Kelsey, Rep. Cal. Inds., 31, 1906.

San Marcos (Saint Mark). A ruined pueblo, 18 m. s. sw. of Santa Fé, N. Mex., which, according to Vetancurt, was formerly occupied by Keresan Indians. Bandelier, however, makes the statement that the aboriginal occupants were Tano, although there may have been Keres among them. A Spanish mission, with 600 neophytes, existed there at the time of the Pueblo rebellion of 1680, having as its visitas the pueblos of San Lázaro and Ciénega. The churches were destroyed during the revolt, the missionary, Padre Tinoco, was killed while at Galisteo, and the pueblo permanently abandoned. Twelve years later (1692), when Vargas visited the country, the pueblo was in ruins, with only a few of the walls standing. According to Meline (Two Thousand Miles, 220, 1867), the inhabitants joined the Tewa at San Juan. The name San Marcos was first applied by Gaspar de Sosa in 1591. The pueblo should not be confused with Kuakaa (q. v.), a prehistoric ruin 5 m. s. of Santa Fé, although San Marcos apparently bore the same Tano name. (F. W. H.)

Cua-ka.—Bandelier in Arch. Inst. Papers, III, 125, 1890 (Tano name). Kua-kaa.—Ibid., IV, 92, 1892 (Tano name). Ku-kua.—Ibid., III, 125. San Marcos.—Sosa (1591) in Doc. Inéd., XV, 251, 1871. Sant Marcos.—Oñate (1598), ibid., XVI, 114, 1871. S. Mark.—Bowles, Map America, 1784. S! Marco.—

Crepy, Map Amér. Sept., 1783 (?). **Ta-tze.**—Ladd, Story of N. Mex., 79, 1891 (misprint). **Ya-atze.**—Ritch, New Mexico, 166, 1885 (aboriginal name). **Yaa-tze.**—Bandelier, Gilded Man, 283, 1893. **Yates.**—Oñate (1598) in Doc. Inéd., XVI, 102, 1871. **Ya-tze.**—Bandelier in Arch. Inst. Papers, IV, 92, 1892 (Keresan name). **Yâtzé.**—Bandelier, Gilded Man, 221, 1893.

San Marcos. A Cochimi visitation town of Santa Rosalia Mulege mission in 1745, on the E. shore of Lower California, 8 leagues N. of Mulege, probably on San Marcos id.—Venegas, Hist. Cal., II, 198, 1759.

San Marcos de Apalache. The principal town and mission station of the Apalachee in the 17th century, situated about the present St Marks, Wakulla co., Fla. It is mentioned in a letter of the chiefs of the tribe to the King of Spain in 1688. In 1704 it was taken and entirely destroyed, with the church and other mission buildings, by the English and their Indian allies under Gov. Moore. (J. M.)
San Marcos.—Gatschet, Creek Migr. Leg., I, 76, 1884. **San Marcos de Apalache.**—Barcia, Ensayo, 389, 1723. **St. Mark de Appalachee.**—Brackenridge (1827) in Williams, West Fla., 107, 1827. **St. Marks.**—Shea, Cath. Miss., 74, 1855.

San Martin. A former Maricopa rancheria on Gila r., w. of the great bend, in s. w. Arizona; visited by Anza, Font, and Garcés in 1775. See Garcés (1775), Diary, 117, 1900.
S. Martin of the Opas.—Bancroft, Ariz. and N. Mex., 392, 1889.

San Martin. A former rancheria, probably Papago, visited by Father Kino in 1701; situated in s. w. Sonora, Mexico, between Busanic and Sonoita.—Kino cited by Bancroft, No. Mex. States, I, 497, 1884.

San Mateo (Saint Matthew). A Timucua mission town in 1688, named in an address from the chiefs of the tribe to the King of Spain (see copy and translation by Gatschet in Proc. Am. Philos. Soc., XVIII, 497, 1880). There appears to have been another town of the same name, possibly a Spanish settlement, in w. Florida at a later date. (J. M.)

San Mateo. A former Jova pueblo and seat of a Spanish mission founded in 1677; situated in E. Sonora, Mexico, about lat. 29°. It was temporarily deserted in 1690, owing to Apache depredations. Pop. 596 in 1678, and only 95 in 1730.
San Mateo.—Zapata (1678) in Doc. Hist. Mex., 4th s., III, 349, 1857. **San Mateo de Saguaripa.**—Ibid. **San Mateo Malzura.**—Orozco y Berra, Geog., 345, 1864. **S. Mateo.**—Bancroft, No. Mex. States, I, 513, 1884.

San Mateo. A pueblo, probably Keresan, in New Mexico in 1590.—Sosa (1590) in Doc. Inéd., XV, 254, 1871.

San Miguel (Saint Michael) The sixteenth Franciscan mission established in California. The site chosen was at a place called by the natives Vahia, in the upper Salinas valley, between San Antonio and San Luis Obispo, in the N. part of the present San Luis Obispo co. Taylor (Cal.

Farmer, Apr. 27, 1860) says the name of the rancheria at the site of the mission was Chulam, or Chalomi. At this place Fr. Lasuen, on July 25, 1797, "in the presence of a great multitude of gentiles of both sexes and of all ages," formally founded the mission. The natives were very friendly, and 15 children were offered for baptism the same day. The mission grew rapidly in population and wealth. By 1800 there were 362 neophytes, and 973 in 1810, while the greatest number, 1,076, was reached in 1814. At the end of the first three years the mission had 372 horses and cattle, and 1,582 small stock, while the crops for that year (1800) were 1,900 bushels. In 1810 there were 5,281 cattle and horses, 11,160 small stock, with an average crop for the preceding decade of 3,468 bushels. During the next decade the stock increased considerably, but the crops began and continued to decline. In 1806 the mission lost a number of its buildings and a large quantity of supplies by fire, but the roof only of the church was injured. Shortly after 1818 a new church was completed. In 1828 the mission lands were reported as extending from the ocean to Tulare lake. In 1834 there were 599 neophytes. Up to this time the total number of natives baptized was 2,562, of whom 1,277 were children. The mission was secularized in 1836, and was generally prosperous until 1840, as its ranches and vineyards had not been granted to private individuals. The Indians lived at the mission and on the ranches, and in 1840 still numbered 350. In 1844, however, San Miguel was reported as without lands or cattle, while its neophytes were demoralized and scattered for want of a minister. The mission was sold in 1845, but the purchase was later declared invalid. The church and monastery were preserved and are still in use. The church is particularly interesting because of the interior decorations, which have been practically undisturbed since the days of the first padres. The Indians of this mission belonged to the Salinan (q. v.) linguistic family, though among the neophytes were many, probably Yokuts, from San Joaquin valley, with whom the natives around the mission are said to have been on intimate terms. (A. B. L.)

San Miguel. A former village of the Tubar on the extreme headwaters of the Rio Fuerte, in s. w. Chihuahua, Mexico. Although now largely Mexicanized, it is still the chief seat of the Tubar people.—Lumholtz, Unknown Mex., I, 443, 1902.

San Miguel. A Cochimi settlement and visita of Nuestra Señora de Guadalupe mission in Lower California, from which it was distant 6 leagues s. E., in 1745.—Venegas, Hist. Cal., II, 198, 1759.

San Miguel de la Frontera (Saint Michael of the Frontier). A Dominican mission established by Fathers Valdellon and Lopez, in 1782, about lat. 32° 10′, Lower California, 30 m. s. E. of San Diego, Cal. The rancherias connected with the mission in 1860 were Otat, Hawai, Ekquall, Hassasei, Inomassi, Nellmole, and Mattawottis. The inhabitants spoke a Diegueño dialect. See Taylor in Cal. Farmer, May 18, 1860.

San Miguel of the frontiers.—Taylor cited by Browne, Res. Pac. Slope, app., 51, 1869.

San Miguel de Linares. A Franciscan mission established among the Adai, near Sabine r., La., in 1716. In 1719 a force of French, with Natchitoch and Caddo allies, took possession of it, and the Indians destroyed the buildings, but the mission was reestablished by the Spaniards with 400 Adai 2 years later. It reported 103 baptisms in 1768, and was abandoned in 1773.

Adaes.—Garrison, Texas, 75, 1903. Los Adeas.—La Harpe (1719) quoted by Bancroft, No. Mex. States, I, 618, 1886. San Miguel.—Bancroft, ibid., 626. San Miguel de Cuellar.—Ibid., 615, 666. San Miguel de los Adais.—Pelaez, Mem. Guatemala, III, 52, 1852. San Miguel de los Adeas.—Ibid., 618.

San Miguel de los Noches ('Saint Michael of the Noches,' here referring to a Yokuts tribe sometimes called Noches, who lived in the vicinity). A rancheria situated probably on the site of the present Bakersfield, Kern co., s. Cal., in 1776.

San Miguel de los Noches por el Santo Principe.—Garcés, Diary (1775-76), 299, 1900.

San Miguel Zuaque. A settlement of the Zuaque division of the Cahita, on the s. bank of Rio del Fuerte, 20 m. above its mouth, in N. w. Sinaloa, Mexico. The inhabitants used both the Zuaque and the Vacoregue dialects.

San Miguel Zuaque.—Orozco y Berra, Geog., 332, 1864. S. Michaël.—Kino, map (1702), in Stöcklein, Neue Welt-Bott, 1726. S. Miguel.—Orozco y Berra, Geog., map, 1864.

Sannak. A fishing settlement of Aleut on Sannak id., E. Aleutians, Alaska; pop. 132 in 1890.—Eleventh Census, Alaska, 163, 1893.

Sannio. A Cayuga village on the E. side and at the foot of Cayuga lake, N. Y., in 1750.—De Schweinitz, Life of Zeisberger, 57, 1870.

Sannup. A word said to have been used in Massachusetts as a designation for an Indian married man. It is mentioned first in the Voyages into New England of Levett (1628), whose travels did not extend southward beyond the boundaries of Maine, and who remarks, "The sagamores will scarce speak to an ordinary man, but will point to their men and say "sanops must speak to sanops and sagamores to sagamores." Cotton Mather, in his Magnalia (ca. 1688), uses the word in his classification of Indian society, in which he states that the highest class consisted of the "nobles," comprising all those who were descended from blood royal, those who were invested with authority by the sachem and who had always been considered as noble; and, second, the "yeomen" or "sannups," who formed the mass of the community, and possessed a right in the lands of the tribe, etc.; and, third, the "villains" or "serfs," who had no property in the land, and were in some degree subject to the sannups or ordinary citizens. The word was not known to the Massachuset Indians, but by the whites who used it, like the words skunk, wigwam, musquash, and sagamore, was borrowed from the dialects of the Abnaki, in which it occurs in the following forms: Norridgewock *seenanbe*, Passamaquoddy *senanbe*, Penobscot *sananba*, 'man,' *vir* (in contradistinction to *ărĕnanbe*, *ălĕnanbe*, 'true man,' *homo*). The suffix -*anbe* means 'man,' but the meaning of the prefix *seen-*, *sen-*, is not known. (W. R. G.)

San Pablo (Saint Paul). A former Yuma rancheria on the Rio Colorado, 8 or 10 m. below the present Yuma and about a league s. of Pilot Knob, in California. It was visited by Garcés, Anza, and Font in 1775, and was on or near the site of the later mission of San Pedro y San Pablo (q. v.). See Coues, Garcés Diary (1775-76), 19, 163, 1900.

Laguna del Capitan Pablo.—Coues, op. cit., 163. Laguna de San Pablo.—Ibid.

San Pablo. A former Yuma rancheria on the s. bank of the Rio Gila, Ariz., 3 leagues above its mouth. It was visited by Father Kino in 1699.

S. Pablo.—Kino, map (1701), in Bancroft, Ariz. and N. Mex., 360, 1889. S. Paulus.—Kino, map (1702), in Stöcklein, Neue Welt-Bott, 74, 1726. S! Pablo.—Venegas, Hist. Cal., I, map, 1759 (located where San Pedro should be).

San Pascual (Holy Easter). A small band of Diegueño Indians in San Diego co., S. Cal. "The maps show an Indian reservation named San Pascual, but actually there is no such reservation. A reservation was selected for these Indians comprising certain descriptions of land in township 12 s., range 1 w., in San Diego co. By some inexcusable error, the land was actually reserved in township 11 s., range 1 w. None of the San Pascual Indians ever lived on the land actually reserved, as that was considered to be Shoshonean territory, and the San Pascual are Yuman. Both pieces of land are barren and of little value. The Indians actually occupied the land in township 12. In the years that have passed, all the land in the intended reservation worth filing on has been taken up by the whites in the usual manner" (Kelsey, Rep. Cal. Inds., 30, 1906). In 1909 the San Pascual Indians numbered 71, under the Mesa Grande school superintendent.

San Pascual.—Burton (1856) in H. R. Ex. Doc. 76, 34th Cong., 3d sess., 114, 1857. San Pasqual.—Sleigh in Ind. Aff. Rep. 1873, 32, 1874.

San Pascual. A former pueblo of the Piro on the E. bank of the Rio Grande, opposite the present San Antonio village (which occupies the site of Senecú), Socorro co., N. Mex. Shea (Cath. Miss., 82, 1855) states that a mission existed there and that it was destroyed during the rebellion of 1680. According to Bandelier, however, the village in all probability was abandoned about 1675, since Senecú, on the opposite side of the river, was destroyed early in that year by the Apache. Consult Bandelier in Arch. Inst. Papers, IV, 250, 1892. See also *Piro*.

San Pascual. A former Yuma rancheria on Gila r., Ariz., 16 to 20 leagues above its mouth, visited by Anza and Font in 1775.—Bancroft, Ariz. and N. Mex., 392, 1889.

San Pascual. A village of the Gidanemuk, a branch of the Serranos of s. California, visited and so named by Fray Francisco Garcés in 1776.

San Pasqual.—Garcés, Diary, 273, 1900.

San Pedro (Saint Peter). A Yuma rancheria on the Rio Gila in Arizona, 3 leagues above its junction with the Colorado. It was visited by Father Eusebio Kino in 1699.

S. Pedro.—Kino, map (1701), in Bancroft, Ariz. and N. Mex., 360, 1889 (see p. 359). S. Petrus.—Kino, map (1702), in Stöcklein, Neue Welt-Bott, 74, 1726. S? Peter.—Venegas, Hist. Cal., I, map, 1759 (located where San Pablo should be).

San Pedro. A Mohave rancheria, visited and so named by Fray Francisco Garcés in 1776; situated on or near the w. bank of the Rio Colorado, lat. 35° 01′, about 8 m. N. W. of Needles, S. E. Cal.—Garcés, Diary (1776), 234, 416, 1900.

San Pedro de los Jamajabs.—Garcés, op. cit.

San Pedro. A Timucua mission on the present Cumberland id., Fla., named in 1688 in an address from the chiefs of the tribe to the King of Spain, a translation of which appears in Proc. Am. Philos. Soc., XVIII, 497, 1880.

San Pedro. A rancheria of the Tejas (Hainai), on a stream of the same name, at which the Franciscan mission of San Francisco de los Tejas (q.v.) was founded in 1690. It contained 80 men in 1782 (Bancroft, No. Mex. States, I, 665, 1886). See *Nabedache*.

San Pedro. One of the principal settlements of the Mayo, situated in s. Sonora, Mexico.—Hrdlička in Am. Anthr., VI, 59, 1904.

San Pedro Guazave. A former settlement of the Guazave (Vacoregue) on the E. bank of Rio Sinaloa, about lat. 25° 40′, N. W. Sinaloa, Mexico.

Guasave.—Orozco y Berra, Geog., map, 1864. San Pedro Guasave.—Ibid., 332.

San Pedro Martire (Saint Peter the Martyr). A Dominican mission, founded May 28, 1794, by Father Pallas, about 40 m. E. of Santo Tomás mission, lat. 31° 50′, Lower California.

San Pedro Martyr.—Taylor in Browne, Res. Pac. Slope. app.. 50. 1869.

San Pedro y San Pablo (Saint Peter and Saint Paul). A mission established by Fray Francisco Garcés in 1780 among the Yuma on the w. bank of Colorado r., near the site of modern Fort Defiance (Pilot Knob), 8 or 10 m. below Yuma, in extreme s. E. California. On July 17-19, 1781, the mission was sacked and burned by the natives, about 50 Spaniards, including Garcés, three other friars, and Capt. Rivera y Moncada were killed, and the women and children made captives. See *Concepción, Missions, San Pablo*.

Bicuñer.—Coues, Garcés Diary, 21, 1900. San Pedro-Pablo.—Taylor in Browne, Res. Pac. Slope, app., 51, 1869. San Pedro y San Pablo.—Arricivita, Crón. Seraf., 504-511, 539, 1792; Bancroft, Ariz. and N. Mex., 397, 1889; Coues, cited above. San Pedro y San Pablo de Bicuñer.—Coues, Garcés Diary, 19, 1900.

San Pedro y San Pablo. A Cochimi settlement and visita in 1745, situated 8 leagues E. of the parent mission of Nuestra Señora de Guadalupe, lat. 27°, Lower California.

San Pedro and San Pablo.—Venegas, Hist. Cal., II, 198, 1759.

Sanpet. A body of Ute formerly occupying San Pete valley and Sevier r., central Utah. Powell found 36 on the Uinta res., Utah, in 1873, although they are said to have numbered 500 in 1865. They are now included under the collective name of Uinta Ute.   (H. W. H.)

Land Pitches.—Farnham, Travels, 58, 1843. Sampeetches.—De Smet, Letters, 37, 1843. Sampiches.—Prichard, Phys. Hist. Man., V, 430, 1847. Sampichya.—Burton, City of Saints, 578, 1861. Sampuches.—Collins in Ind. Aff. Rep., 125, 1861. San-Petes.—Humphreys in Ind. Aff. Rep. 1859, 381, 1860. Sanpiche Utahs.—Wilson (1849) in Cal. Mess. and Corresp., 185, 1850. San Pitch.—Correll (1856) in H. R. Ex. Doc. 29, 37th Cong., 2d sess., 37, 1862. San Pitches.—Cooley in Ind. Aff. Rep., 18, 1865. Sanpits.—Gebow, Shoshonay Vocab., 5, 1868 (Shoshoni name). Sempiche Utahs.—Wilson in Ind. Aff. Rep. 1849, 67, 1850.

Sanpoil. A body of Salish on Sans Poil r. and on the Columbia below Big bend, Wash. Gibbs classed them as one of the 8 bands of Spokan and also as one of the 6 bands of Okinagan, they being claimed by both tribes. In 1905 they were reported to number 324, on the Colville res., but in 1909 their population was given as only 178, the disparity being attributed to duplication in previous counts. No treaty was ever made with these Indians for their lands, the Government taking possession of their country except such portions as have been set apart by Executive order for their occupancy.

Cingpoils.—De Smet, Letters, 220, 1843. Hai-ai′-nĭma.—Mooney in 14th Rep. B. A. E., 733, 1896 (Yakima name). He-high-e-nim-mo.—Gibbs in Pac. R. R. Rep., I, 417, 1855. Hihighenimmo.—Lewis and Clark Exped., II, 475, 1814. Hihighenimo.—Kelley, Oregon, 68, 1830. Ipoilq.—Mooney in 14th Rep. B. A. E., 733, 1896 (Yakima name). Linpoilish.—Schoolcraft, Ind. Tribes, III, 200, map' 1853. N'pochele.—Gibbs in Pac. R. R. Rep., I, 414, 1855. N'poch-le.—Stevens in Ind. Aff. Rep., 429, 1854. N'pookle.—Gibbs, op. cit., 412. San Poels.—Shanks in Sen. Misc. Doc. 32, 43d Cong., 1st sess., 3, 1874. Sanpoil.—Ind. Aff. Rep. 1901, 702, 1902. Sanpoils.—

Stevens, ibid., 22, 1870. **Sanspoële.**—Wilson in Trans. Ethnol. Soc. Lond., 292, 1866. **Sans Puelles.**—Gibbs in Pac. R. R. Rep., I, 414, 1855. **Sapwell.**—Parker, Jour., 293, 1840. **Sempoils.**—Lane in Sen. Ex. Doc. 52, 31st Cong., 1st sess., 170, 1850. **Sinapoil.**—Cox, Columbia R., II, 38, 1831. **Sinapoiluch.**—Anderson quoted by Gibbs in Hist. Mag., VII, 77, 1863. **Sinipouals.**—Duflot de Mofras, Oregon, II, 335, 1844. **Sinpaivelish.**—M'Vickar, Exped. Lewis and Clark, II, 386, 1842. **Sinpauēlish.**—Parker, Jour., 313, 1842. **Sin-poh-ell-ech-ach.**—Ross, Adventures, 290, 1849. **Sinpoil.**—De Smet, Letters, 169, 1843. **Sin-poil-er-hu.**—Suckley in Pac. R. R. Rep., I, 300, 1855. **Sin-poil-schne.**—Gibbs, ibid., 414. **Siur Poils.**—Mooney in 14th Rep. B. A. E., 733, 1896 (variant form). **Sklarkum.**—Suckley, op. cit., 300. **Snpoiliᵡiᵡ.**—Gatschet, MS., B. A. E. (Okinagan form). **Snpuélish.**—Ibid. (Salish form).

San Rafael. The next to the last Franciscan mission established in California; founded as an asistencia or branch of San Francisco (Dolores). The mortality among the Indians in San Francisco had become so great that a panic was feared, and a transfer of a portion of the survivors to some situation on the N. side of the bay was proposed. At first they were sent over without a priest, but after several had died it was determined to found a new establishment; this was done, Dec. 14, 1817, the new mission being dedicated to San Rafael Arcángel. The native name of the place was Nanaguami. About 230 neophytes were transferred from San Francisco, most of whom, however, originally came from the N. side of the bay. An adobe building, 87 by 42 ft, divided into rooms for chapel, dwelling-rooms, etc., was finished in 1818. Two years later there were 590 neophytes, and 1,140, the highest number reached, in 1828. By 1823 the establishment was recognized as a separate mission. Its wealth was never very great, though it was prosperous, having in 1830, 1,548 large stock and 1,852 sheep, with an average crop for the preceding decade of 2,454 bushels. In 1830 there were 970 neophytes, the number decreasing about 50 percent in the next four years. At the time of secularization considerable property was distributed among the Indians; but in 1837, under the plea that the natives were not making good use of it, this was again brought together, with a promise of redistribution under more favorable circumstances. In 1839 the Indians were reported to be greatly dissatisfied, and in 1840 a distribution of the livestock was ordered. There were then 190 Indians near the mission, and probably 150 more scattered elsewhere. In 1846 Frémont took possession of the mission. After he left, it seems to have been unoccupied, and it has now entirely disappeared. The neophytes probably belonged chiefly to the Olamentke division of the Moquelumnan family. (A. B. L.)

San Rafael. Formerly a rancheria of the Papago in s. Arizona, near the headwaters of the Rio Salado of Sonora, Mexico; visited in 1701 and 1702 by Father Kino and so named by him. Possibly identical with the modern Mesquite or Quijotoa (q. v.), but not to be confounded with the mission of Guevavi, which bore the same saint name, nor with San Serafin (Actum). **San Rafael.**—Kino (1700) in Doc. Hist. Mex., 4th s., I, 318, 1856. **S. Rafael.**—Kino, map (1701), in Bancroft, Ariz. and N. Mex., 360, 1889; Venegas, Hist. Cal., I, map, 1759. **S. Rafael Actun.**—Bancroft, No. Mex. States, I, 502, 1884. **S. Raphaël.**—Kino, map (1702), in Stöcklein, Neue Welt-Bott, 74, 1726.

San Rafael. A former rancheria in s. Arizona, probably Maricopa, visited by Kino and Mange in 1699 (Mange cited by Bancroft, Ariz. and N. Mex., 358, 1889). Not to be confounded with the San Rafael in the Pima country.

San Rafael de los Gentiles. Mentioned by Bancroft (Ariz. and N. Mex., 281, 1889) as a pueblo settlement of New Mexico with 15 inhabitants, about 1765. Locality not known.

San Rudesindo. A rancheria of the Quigyuma, visited and so named by Father Kino in Mar. 1702. Doubtless situated on the E. bank of the Rio Colorado, just above its mouth, in N. W. Sonora, Mexico. See Venegas, Hist. Cal., I, 310, 1759; Bancroft, No. Mex. States, I, 500, 1884; Coues, Garcés Diary, 178, 1900.

San Sabá. A Franciscan mission established on the Rio San Sabá in Texas, in Apr. 1757, among the Lipan Apache, under the protection of the presidio of San Luis de las Amarillas, 1½ leagues distant, named in honor of the Viceroy of Mexico. The Spaniards were induced by the Lipan to found the mission in order that they might gain the aid of the former against their enemies the Comanche, but after its establishment the Lipan refused under various pretexts to become concentrated under mission influence. On Mar. 2, 1758, the Comanche and their allies (Wichita and others) raided the Spanish horse herd and captured 62 head, and on the 16th 2,000(?) mounted hostiles gained entrance to the mission under protestations of friendship, murdered nearly all the occupants, and burned the buildings. But few of the Lipan were killed, most of them having fled to the mountains on the approach of the Comanche. In the following year an expedition against the raiders was made, and in an attack on a rancheria 150 leagues away, 55 of the foe were killed, but little else was accomplished, the Spaniards fleeing when a band of warriors, said to number 6,000, of different tribes, at a place called San Teodoro in the Wichita (Taovayases) country, made a stand against them. See Bancroft, No. Mex. States, I, 646, 1886; Garrison, Texas, 1904.

San Sabas. A visitation town in 1745, situated 3 leagues from the parent mission of San Ignacio de Kadakaman, about lat.

28° 40′, Lower California. Its inhabitants spoke a Cochimi dialect. See Venegas, Hist. Cal., II, 198, 1759.

San Salvador (Holy Savior). A former rancheria, evidently of the Sobaipuri, on San Pedro r., above Quiburi, s. Ariz.—Kino, map (1701), in Bancroft, Ariz. and N. Mex., 360, 1889.

Sans Arcs (French trans. of *Itazipcho*, 'without bows,' from *itazipa*, 'bow,' and *cho*, abbrev. of *chodan*, 'without'). A band of the Teton Sioux. Hayden, about 1860, says that they and the Hunkpapa and Sihasapa "occupy nearly the

YELLOW HAWK, A SANS ARC

same district and are so often camped near each other, and are otherwise so connected in their operations as scarcely to admit of being treated separately." On the other hand, Warren (Dacota Country) indicates that their closest relations were with the Miniconjou.

Their divisions as given by Swift in a letter to Dorsey (1884) are: 1 Itazipcho (Without bows); 2 Shinalutaoin (Scarlet-cloth earring); 3 Wolutayuta (Eat-dried-venison-from-the-hind-quarter); 4 Mazpegnaka (Wear-metal-in-the-hair); 5 Tatankachesli (Dung-of-a-buffalo-bull);

6 Shikshichela (Bad-ones-of-different-kinds); 7 Tiyopaoshanunpa (Smokes-at-the-entrance-to-the-lodge).

The Sans Arcs entered into a peace treaty with the United States at Ft Sully, S. Dak., Oct. 20, 1865, and were a party also to the treaty of Ft Laramie, Wyo., Apr. 29, 1868.

Bowpith.—Warren, Dacota Country, 16, 1856. Ee-ta-sip-shov.—Catlin, N. A. Inds., I, 223, 1841. Itahzipchois.—Warren, Dacota Country, 16, 1856. Itazipchos.—Ibid., index, vi. Itazipóo.—Riggs, Dakota Gram, xvi, 1852 (trans. 'bow pith,' or 'without bows'). Itazipcoes.—Keane in Stanford, Compend., 516, 1878. Itazipko.—Burton, City of Saints, 119, 1861. Lack-Bows.—De Smet, Letters, 37, note, 1843. Ma'-i-sin-as.—Hayden, Ethnog. and Philol. Mo. Val., 290, 1862 (Cheyenne name). Nobows.—Hoffman (1854) in H. R. Doc. 36, 33d Cong., 2d sess. 3, 1855. Sans Arcs.—Schoolcraft, Ind. Tribes, III, 629, 1853. Sansarcs Dakotas.—Hayden, Ethnog. and Philol. Mo. Val., map, 1862. Sarsarcs.—Cleveland in Our Church Work, Dec. 4, 1875 (misprint). Taze-char.—Corliss, Lacotah MS. vocab., B. A. E., 106, 1874 (trans. 'bows from the heart of a tree'). Taze-par-war-nee-cha.—Corliss, ibid. Without-Bows.—Hayden, Ethnog. and Philol. Mo. Val., 371, 1862.

San Sebastian. A Kawia rancheria in the 18th century; situated in central southern California, lat. 33° 08′, evidently near Salton lake. Father Font referred to it as "a small rancheria of the mountain Cajuenches, or more properly of the Jecuiches." See Coues, Garcés Diary (1775), 167, 1900.

San Sebastian.—Font (1775) cited by Coues, Garcés Diary (1775), 167, 1900. San Sebastian Peregrino.—Garcés (1774), ibid., 42. San Sevastian.—Garcés (1775), ibid., 167.

San Sebastian. A pueblo of the Huichol, situated about 5 m. s. of Santa Catarina, and 10 m. e. of Rio Chapalagana, in the Sierra de los Huicholes, Jalisco, Mexico.—Lumholtz, Unknown Mex., II, 16, map, 257, 1902.

San Serafin (Holy Seraph; also St Francis of Assisi). A former Pima rancheria n.w. of San Xavier del Bac, s. Ariz.; visited by Kino and Mange in 1699.

Guactum.—Mange (1701) quoted by Bancroft, Ariz. and N. Mex., 359, 1889. San Serafin.—Venegas, Hist. Cal., I, map, 1759. San Serafin de Actum.—Mange (1700) in Doc. Hist. Mex., 4th s., I, 318, 1856. Seraphim.—Kino, map (1702), in Stöcklein, Neue Welt-Bott, 74, 1726. S. Serafin.—Kino, map (1701), in Bancroft, Ariz. and N. Mex., 360, 1889. S. Serafin Actum.—Bancroft, ibid., 358. S. Serafino del Napcub.—Anza and Font (1780) quoted by Bancroft, ibid., 392.

San Simon. A mission village, probably on St Simon id., Georgia coast, the inhabitants of which were among those revolting against the Spaniards of Florida in 1687.—Barcia, Ensayo, 287, 1723.

San Simon y San Judas. A former Papago rancheria, visited and so named by Father Kino in 1700; situated in Sonora, Mexico, about lon. 111°, lat. 31°, between Cocospera and Busanic.

San Simon y San Judas.—Mange cited by Bancroft, Ariz. and N. Mex., 359, 1889. S. Simon.—Bancroft, No. Mex. States, I, 497, 1884.

Santa Aguida. A Cochimi rancheria in 1706, probably in the vicinity of San Ignacio Kadakaman mission, on the

shore of Amuna in Lower California.—
Venegas, Hist. Cal., I, 421, 1759.

Santa Ana (Saint Ann). A Keresan
pueblo on the N. bank of the Rio Jemez, a
w. affluent of the Rio Grande, in central
New Mexico. The original pueblo of
the tribe, according to Bandelier, stood
near the Mesa del Cangelon, w. of the
Rio Grande and N. of Bernalillo; but this
was abandoned prior to the Spanish explorations in the 16th century, and
another pueblo built on an elevation that
rises about midway between Santa Ana
and San Felipe, on the great Black mesa
of San Felipe. This was the village visited in 1598 by Oñate, who referred to it
as Tamy and Tamaya—the latter being
the name applied by the inhabitants to

A NATIVE OF SANTA ANA

both this pueblo and its predecessor. It
was early the seat of a Spanish mission;
but at the outbreak of the Pueblo rebellion in 1680 it had no priest, yet was not
without a church and monastery. In that
revolt the Santa Ana people joined those
of San Felipe in the massacre of the missionaries at Santo Domingo and the colonists in the Rio Grande valley. As the
pueblo was situated w. of the Rio Grande,
it was not molested by Gov. Otermin
during his attempt to reconquer New
Mexico in 1681, but in 1687 Pedro Rene-
ros de Posada, then governor at El Paso,
carried the pueblo by storm after a desperate resistance, and burned it, several Indians perishing in the flames.
When Vargas made his appearance in

1692 the Santa Ana tribe occupied a mesa
known as Cerro Colorado, some 10 m. N.
and eastward from Jemez, but were
induced by Vargas to return to their
former locality, where they constructed
the pueblo occupied to-day. This, like
the two former villages, is also known to
the natives as Tamayá. In 1782 Santa
Ana was a visita of the mission of Sia.
Population 253 in 1890, 226 in 1905, and
211 in 1910. The clans of Santa Ana are:
Tsinha (Turkey), Dyami (Eagle), Yak
(Corn), Hooka (Dove), Shutson (Coyote),
Showita (Parrot), Hakan (Fire).

Consult Bandelier in Arch. Inst. Papers,
III, 126, 1890; IV, 193 et seq., 1892; Bancroft, Ariz. and N. Mex., 200, 1889. See
also *Keresan Family, Pueblos*. (F. W. H.)

Hwerói.—Hodge, field notes, B. A. E., 1895 (Tigua
name). Ramaya.—Columbus Mem. Vol., 155,
1893 (misprint of Onate's Tamaya). S. Anna.—
Blaeu, Atlas, XII, 62, 1667. Santa Ana.—Oñate
(1598) in Doc. Inéd., XVI, 114, 1871. Santa Anna.—
Villa-Señor, Theatro Am., II, 415, 1748. Santana.—
Hezio (1797–98) in Meline, Two Thousand Miles,
269, 1867. Sta. Ana.—Alcedo, Dic. Geog., I, 85,
1786. Sta Ana.—D'Anville, Map Am. Sept., 1746.
St Ana.—Arrowsmith, Map N. A., 1795, ed. 1814.
Támaiya,—Hodge, field notes, B. A. E., 1895
(San Felipe and Cochiti form of name). Tam-
ayá.—Ibid. (name of pueblo in Santa Ana and
Sia dialects). Tamaya.—Oñate (1598) in Doc.
Inéd., XVI, 115, 1871. Ta-mă-yǎ.—Bandelier in
Arch. Inst. Bull., I, 18, 1883. Tamy.—Oñate (1598),
op. cit., 102. Tamya.—Coronado [Oñate] quoted
by Bandelier in Arch. Inst. Bull., I, 18, 1883.
Tan-a-ya.—Bandelier in Arch. Inst. Papers, IV,
194, 1892 (misprint). To-Mia.—Loew in Ann.
Rep. Wheeler Surv., app. LL, 178, 1875. Tom-
i-ya.—Simpson in Rep. Sec. War, 143, 1850. Tu'-
na-ji-i'.—Hodge, field notes, B. A. E., 1895 (Jemez
and Pecos name).

Santa Ana. A pueblo of the Opata in
1730, with 34 inhabitants (Rivera, 1730,
cited by Bancroft, No. Mex. States, I, 513,
1884); situated in one of the eastern
Sonora valleys, Mexico, but definite locality unknown. At the present time
there are five settlements called Santa
Ana in Sonora.

Santa Ana. A pueblo, inhabited by
both Tarahumare and Tepehuane, on
the headwaters of the Rio del Fuerte,
about lat. 26° 30′, s. w. Chihuahua, Mexico.—Orozco y Berra, Geog., 322, 324,
map, 1864.

Santa Ana. A former pueblo of the Va-
rohio division of the Tarahumare, be-
tween Batopilas and Guachochic, s. w.
Chihuahua, Mexico.—Orozco y Berra,
Geog., 324, 1864; Lumholtz, Unknown
Mex., I, 446, 1902.

Santa Barbara. The tenth Franciscan
mission founded in California. The presidio of Santa Barbara was established in
1782, soon after the founding of San
Buenaventura mission, and it was the intention to found a mission at Santa Barbara also, but owing to lack of agreement
between the civil authorities and the
padres as to the method of organization
of the proposed seat, it was not founded

till several years later. Finally, on Dec. 4, 1786, the cross was raised and blessed by Fr. Lasuen at a place called Taynayan by the natives, a mile or so from the presidio. Owing to it being the rainy season, buildings were not begun until later. By 1790 there were 438 neophytes. A church 18 × 90 ft, and numerous other buildings, all roofed with tiles, had been completed. In the next 10 years the number of neophytes increased to only 864, though 1,237 were baptized and only 624 had died. Probably some of the others had been allowed to live in their own villages away from the mission. A new church was finished in 1794, and by 1800 quite a number of new buildings had been erected. At that time there were 60 neophytes engaged in making and weaving cloth, while a carpenter and a tanner were regularly employed to teach the natives those trades. Within the next few years 234 adobe houses were erected for the neophytes. In 1803 a mission chapel was built at San Miguel. In 1801 an epidemic carried off a great number of the natives and caused the neophytes, through a pretended revelation of their old deities, temporarily to renounce Christianity, though the Fathers knew nothing of this until later. The greatest number of neophytes, 1,792, was reached in 1803; in 1810 there were 1,355. The crops were good, averaging 6,216 bushels for the preceding decade; the large stock numbered 5,670, and small stock 8,190. During the following decade the crops increased somewhat, but the stock declined. The earthquake of 1812 injured rather seriously the church, and a new one, 40 × 165 ft, was begun in 1815, and completed and dedicated in 1820. This is still standing. The walls are 6 ft thick, of irregular sandstone blocks laid in cement, while the towers, 20 ft square, are, with the exception of a narrow passageway in one of them, solid masses of stone and cement to a height of 30 ft. In 1820 there were 1,132 neophytes, in 1830 only 711. In 1824 there was considerable trouble with the neophytes; a revolt had arisen at Santa Inés, and the Indians from Santa Barbara demanded that the soldiers at the mission leave their arms and withdraw to the pre-

sidio. This demand finally led to a conflict, and the natives fled to the hills and later to San Joaquin valley. After the revolt at Santa Inés and Purísima had been quelled, the Indians were finally induced to return by the granting of a general pardon. The padres and the church property were at no time interfered with. In 1834 there were 556 neophytes. The total number of natives baptized up to that time was 4,658, of whom 2,168 were children. In 1840 there were still probably 250 ex-neophytes at the mission. The mission continued prosperous even after its secularization, and the buildings were kept in better condition than at other places. In 1843 it was returned to the control of the padres, who, in 1844, reported that they had the greatest difficulty in supporting the 285 souls dependent on them. In 1846 the mission was sold for $7,500, though the principal buildings, as elsewhere, remained in the possession of the Church, and have been better preserved than at any other California mission. The Indians connected with Santa Barbara belonged chiefly to the Chumashan (q. v.) linguistic family, though Yokuts were also probably represented, as many neophytes are reported as coming from the "Tulares." (A. B. L.)

MISSION OF SANTA BARBARA, CALIFORNIA

Santa Barbara. A former rancheria, probably of the Papago, visited by Father Kino in 1706; situated 4 m. s. w. of Busanic, near the headwaters of the N. branch of Altar r., in Sonora, Mexico.—Kino cited by Bancroft, No. Mex. States, I, 501, 1884.

Santa Catalina (Saint Catherine). A mission town, probably Yamasee, perhaps on St Catherine id., Ga. Its inhabitants revolted in 1687 against the Spaniards, destroyed the mission, and fled to the English in Carolina.

Santa Catalina.—Barcia, Ensayo, 287, 1723. St. Catherine's.—Shea, Cath. Miss., 73, 1855.

Santa Catalina. A former Tepehuane pueblo in lat 25° 10′, lon. 106°, N. w. Durango, Mexico, the seat of a Jesuit mission founded by Geronimo Ramirez in 1596, but abandoned in 1616.—Orozco y Berra, Geog., 318, 1864.

Santa Catalina de los Yumas. A mission founded by the Dominican Father Lorient, May 18, 1797, in the N. part of Lower California, 50 m. E. of Santo Tomás mission, about lat. 31° 20′. It was destroyed by the Indians between 1827 and 1833. This was the last mission established in Lower California. According to Duflot de Mofras (Voy., I, 217, 228, 1844) the Indians living there were the Gueymura. See also Taylor in Browne, Pac. Slope, app., 51, 1869.

Santa Catarina. A settlement of the Huichol, consisting of only 11 houses and a temple, in the valley of the middle Rio Chapalagana, a N. E. tributary of the Rio Grande de Santiago, in Jalisco, Mexico.—Lumholtz, Unknown Mex., II, 16, map, 147, 1902.
Tōapúli.—Lumholtz, ibid., 147 ('where there is amole : Huichol name).

Santa Clara. The eighth Franciscan mission established in California. The site first chosen was near Guadalupe r., not far from the head of San Francisco bay, and about 3 m. from its present position. This site was called Thamien by the natives. Here the mission was founded, Jan. 12, 1777, and dedicated to Santa Clara de Asis. Cattle and supplies arrived from Monterey and San Francisco, and work on the buildings was immediately begun. The Indians were at first friendly, but soon began to steal cattle, and did not entirely desist even after 3 were killed and several flogged. By the end of the year there had been 67 baptisms, mostly children. In 1779 the mission was twice flooded, and it was decided to rebuild at another site on higher ground. A new church was begun in 1781 and finished in 1784, the finest erected in California up to that time. This church was considerably damaged by earthquakes in 1812 and later, and a new one was finally built on the present site in 1825–26. Shortly after 1800 there was considerable trouble with the natives. Many of the neophytes seem to have run away at different times, and the expeditions sent out to bring them back were attacked in a few cases. The wealth of the mission increased rapidly. In 1790 the large stock numbered 2,817, small stock 836; in 1800 there were about 5,000 each, while in 1810 the numbers were 8,353 and 10,027, respectively, with average crops for the two decades of 4,600 and 4,970 bushels. The converts also increased rapidly, numbering 927 in 1790, 1,247 in 1800, 1,332 in 1810, and 1,357 in 1820. The highest figure, 1,464, was reached in 1827, after which the decline was very rapid. The stock and the yearly crops of the mission had decreased considerably before this time. The total number of natives baptized up to 1834 was 7,711, of whom 3,177 were children. The death-rate at the mission was very high. In 1834 there were about 800 neophytes, while in 1840 there were only 290, with possibly 150 more scattered in the district. The mission was secularized in 1837. By 1840 two-thirds of the stock and apparently all of the available property had disappeared. The mission was returned to the control of the padres in 1843, and two years later there were about 150 ex-neophytes connected with the mission. After this Santa Clara mission became a regular parish church, and in 1851 Santa Clara College was established in the old mission buildings. The growth of the college necessitated the renovation and enlargement of the buildings, so that now there is little remaining of the old adobe structures. The Indians in the neighborhood of the mission belonged to the Costanoan linguistic family, and these doubtless furnished the majority of the neophytes, yet it is probable that the Mariposan (Yokuts) and Moquelumnan stocks were also represented.　　(A. B. L.)

Santa Clara. A Tewa pueblo on the w. bank of the Rio Grande, about 30 m. above Santa Fé, in Rio Arriba co., N. Mex. The native name of the pueblo is K'hapóo, said to mean "where the roses (?) grow near the water." The natives assert that their ancestors dwelt in the clusters of

A NATIVE OF SANTA CLARA

artificial grottos excavated in cliffs of pumice-stone (Puye and Shufinne) w. of the Rio Grande, and this may be true of both historic and prehistoric times; but the Santa Clara people probably were not the only Tewa occupants of these cliff-lodges. Santa Clara was formerly the seat of a Spanish mission, with a church and monastery erected between 1622 and 1629, and was a visita of the mission of San Ildefonso (q. v.) until 1782, when it was again made a mission with San Ildefonso as its visita. Like Sia and Nambe, this pueblo, according to Bandelier, doubtless owed its decline to the constant inter-killing going on for supposed evil practices of witchcraft, or to the ravages of disease, for in 1782 500 deaths occurred in this and San Juan pueblos alone within two months (Bandelier in Arch. Inst. Papers, IV, 23, 1892). Not to be confounded with the Tano pueblo of Tuerto, whose aboriginal name is the same as that of Santa Clara. The Santa Clara clans are: Tang (Sun), Khung (Corn), Tse (Eagle), Kea (Badger), Pe (Tree or Firewood), Te (Cottonwood), Na (Earth), Po (Calabash), D'ye (Gopher), Kunya (Turquoise), Kupi (Coral), Yan (Willow), and Pa (Deer). There are also an Oak and probably a Cloud clan. Pop. 277 in 1910.　　　(F. W. H.)

Āk'-e-ji.—Hodge, field notes, B. A. E., 1895 (Pecos name). Ána Sǔshǐ.—Curtis, Am. Ind., I, 138, 1907 ('tribe like bears,' so named from their skunk-skin moccasins, at first thought to be of bear-skin: Navaho name). Ca-po.—Bandelier in Ritch, New Mexico, 201, 1885 (native name). Capo.—Vetancurt (1696), Crónica, 317, 1871. Capoo.—Benavides, Memorial, 59, 1630. Caypa.—Oñate (1598) in Doc. Inéd., XVI, 256, 1871 (confounded with San Juan). Giowaka-ā'.—Stevenson, Pecos MS. vocab., B. A. E., 1887 (Pecos name of the pueblo). Giowatsa-ā'.—Ibid. Hai'bata.—Hodge, field notes, B. A. E., 1895 (Taos name). Hâibă'yŭ.—Ibid., 1899 (another form of Taos name). Haiphahá.—Ibid. (Picuris name). Kah-po.—Jouvenceau in Cath. Pion., I, no. 9, 12, 1906. Kaïïpa.—Hodge, field notes, B. A. E., 1895 (Acoma name). Kai'p'a.—Ibid. (Cochiti name). Kap-ho'.—Ibid. (San Juan and San Ildefonso form). Ka-Po.—Bandelier (1888) in Proc. Cong. Am., VII, 457, 1890. Ka-po.—Bandelier in Arch. Inst. Papers, III, 124, 260, 1890 (native name of pueblo). Ka-Poo.—Bandelier, Gilded Man, 232, 1893. Ka-pou.—Bandelier in Arch. Inst. Papers, IV, 64, 1892. Kápung.—Stephen in 8th Rep. B. A. E., 37, 1891 (Hano name). K'haibhaí.—Hodge, field notes, B. A. E., 1895 (Isleta name). K'ha-po'-o.—Ibid. (own name). Santa Clara.—Oñate (1598) in Doc. Inéd., XVI, 116, 1871. S. Clara.—Crepy, Map Amér. Sept., 1783 (?). Shi-ap'-a-gi.—Hodge, field notes, B. A. E., 1895 (Jemez name). Stᵃ Clara.—D'Anville, Map Amér. Sept., 1746. S⁺ Clara.—De l'Isle, Carte Mex. et Flor., 1703.

Santa Clara. A collective term used to designate the Indians formerly living within the territory or under the influence of Santa Clara mission, Santa Clara co., Cal. They were Thamien, with their divisions into Gergecensens and Socoisukas (Taylor in Cal. Farmer, Nov. 23, 1860).

Santa Clara. A former village in California, so called by the padres of San Carlos mission. Its people are said to have been Esselen.—Taylor in Cal. Farmer, Apr. 20, 1860.

Santa Coleta. A group of rancherias, evidently of the Alchedoma, near the Rio Colorado in w. Arizona, about 50 m. below the mouth of Bill Williams fork. They were visited and so named by Fray Francisco Garcés in 1776.

Rancherias de Santa Coleta.—Garcés (1776), Diary, 424, 1900.

Santa Cruz (Holy Cross). The twelfth Franciscan mission established in California. The proposed site was personally examined by Fr. Lasuen, who found the natives friendly and ready to help. Supplies and native assistants were sent from the neighboring missions, especially Santa Clara, and the mission was formally founded Sept. 25, 1791, at the place where is now situated the town of Santa Cruz, Santa Clara co. At the end of the year there were 84 neophytes. In 1792 there were 224, and the highest number, 523, was reached in 1796. In 1800 there were 492. At this time the mission had 2,354 head of cattle and horses, and 2,083 of small stock, while the crop for the year amounted to 4,300 bushels. The church, 30 by 112 ft and 25 ft high, with stone front, was completed and dedicated in 1794. In 1797 a number of colonists arrived from Mexico and settled just across the river Lorenzo from the mission. This settlement caused the missionaries much trouble, and seems to have demoralized the Indians. In 1798 the padre in charge was much discouraged with the outlook and reported that 138 neophytes had deserted. He protested against the settlement, but without effect. The number of neophytes remained about the same for the next 20 years, being 507 in 1810, and 461 in 1820. The livestock increased and the crops continued good. In 1812 one of the fathers was murdered by some of the neophytes, who plead in defense that he was excessively cruel, had flogged two of them to death, and was inventing further instruments of torture. In 1818 and 1819 there was considerable friction between the mission fathers and the authorities at Brancifort, all but three of the neophytes leaving the mission at one time for fear of attack. After 1820 the mission continued prosperous, but the population decreased, there being 320 neophytes in 1830, and about 250 in 1834. The total number of natives baptized up to that time was 2,216, of whom 939 were children. Within 4 years after its secularization most of the property had disappeared. In 1839 there were 70 Indians reported at the mission, with perhaps as many more scattered in the district. In 1840 a number of buildings were destroyed and the church was injured by an earthquake. After 1842 the mission was regarded as a part of Brancifort; the buildings had then entirely disappeared. The Indians in the neighborhood of the mission belong to the Costanoan linguistic family. The mission had neophytes from the following villages, all in the present county of Santa Cruz (Taylor, Cal. Farmer, Apr. 5, 1860): Achilla, Aestaca, Agtism, Apil, Aulintac, Chalumü, Chanech, Chicutae,

Choromi, Coot, Hauzaurni, Hottrochtac, Huachi, Hualquilme, Huocom, Locobo, Luchasmi, Mallin, Nohioalli, Ochoyos, Onbi, Osacalis (Souquel), Payanmin, Sachuen, Sagin, Shiuguermi, Shoremee, Sio Cotchmin, Tejey, Tomoy, Turami, Utalliam, Wallanmi, Yeunaba, Yeunata, Yeunator.			(A. B. L.)

Santa Cruz. A former Tewa pueblo, situated E. of the Rio Grande, 30 m. N. w. of Santa Fé, at the site of the present town of the same name. It was abandoned probably about the time of the Pueblo revolt of 1680–92, but was refounded with 29 families in 1706 and a mission established. The place gradually became civilized, and is now a "Mexican" town.
La Cañada.—Prince, Hist. N. Mex., 319, 1883 (or Santa Cruz). Santa Cruz de la Cañada.—Villa-Señor, Theatro Am., pt 2, 413, 1748. Santa María de Grado.—Cuervo (1706) quoted by Bancroft, Ariz. and N. Mex., 228, 1889 (mission name from 1706); Jefferys, Am. Atlas, map 5, 1776.

Santa Cruz. A settlement, chiefly of Lipan, at which a Spanish mission was established in 1762; situated in the valley of San José, halfway between San Sabá and the Rio Grande, in Texas.
San Lorenzo de la Santa Cruz.—Arricivita quoted by Buschmann, Spüren d. aztek. Spr., 307, 1859.

Santa Cruz. A former Opata pueblo of Sonora, Mexico, the inhabitants of which were called Contla (Orozco y Berra, Geog., 344, 1864). Probably situated on the Rio Sonora, about lat. 30°.

Santa Cruz. One of the Apalachee towns of Florida, mentioned in the letter of Apalachee chiefs to Charles II, King of Spain, in 1688.—Gatschet, Creek Migr. Leg., I, 76, 1884.

Santa Cruz de Mayo. A settlement of the Mayo on the w. bank of Rio Mayo, about 12 m. above its mouth, s. w. Sonora, Mexico.
Santa Cruz de Mayo.—Orozco y Berra, Geog., 356, 1864. S. Crux.—Kino, map (1702), in Stöcklein, Neue Welt-Bott, 1726.

Santa Eulalia. A former rancheria, probably of the Sobaipuri, visited by Father Kino in 1700. Situated slightly N. w. of Busanic, immediately s. of the present Arizona-Sonora boundary.
Santa Tulalia.—Venegas, Hist. Cal., I, 300, 1759 (misprint). Sta Eulalia.—Early writer quoted by Bancroft, Ariz. and N. Mex., 359, 1889. St. Eulalia.—Kino, map (1701), in Bancroft, Ariz. and N. Mex., 360, 1889.

Santa Fé (Holy Faith). A former Cora pueblo and seat of a mission with San Diego and San Juan Bautista as its visitas. Situated near the N. bank of the Rio Grande de Santiago, lon. 104° 40', Jalisco, Mexico.—Orozco y Berra, Geog., 280, 1864.

Santa Fé. A Seminole town on the E. fork of Suwannee r., Fla., in 1822.
Santa Fé.—Romans, Fla., 280, 1775. Santa-fee-talofa.—Bell in Morse, Rep. to Sec. War, 306, 1822.

Santa Gertrudis (Saint Gertrude). A mission founded in 1751 by Father Consag on the E. side of Lower California, lat. 27° 58'. The Indians, who spoke a Cochimi dialect, numbered about 1,000 in 1767. (See Hervas, Saggio, 79–80, 1787; Taylor in Browne, Res. Pac. Slope, app., 50, 1869.)

Santa Gertrudis. A small Huichol rancheria, with a temple, in Jalisco, Mexico.
Santa Gertrudes.—Lumholtz, Unknown Mex., II, 16, map, 1902.

Santa Inés (Saint Agnes). The nineteenth Franciscan mission established in California; founded Sept. 17, 1804, at a place called by the natives Alajulapu, about 25 m. from Santa Barbara, and nearly as far from Purísima. A large number of neophytes from Santa Barbara and Purísima attended the opening ceremony, and many remained at the new mission. On the same day 27 children were baptized. By the end of the first year there were 225 neophytes, in 1810 there were 628, while the highest number, 768, was reached in 1816. In material things the mission prospered, having 7,720 head of large stock in 1820, 5,100 of small stock, and an average annual crop for the preceding decade of 4,340 bushels. The stock increased and the crops continued good for another decade, between 1822 and 1827 supplies to the value of $10,767 being furnished the presidio at Santa Barbara. The first church was seriously injured by an earthquake in 1812, and a new one of adobe lined with brick, which still stands, was completed in 1817. In 1824 there was a revolt of the neophytes at Santa Inés, and a conflict between them and the soldiers, a large part of the mission buildings being burned, and the hostile Indians fleeing, apparently to Purísima (q. v.). In 1830 there were 408 neophytes, but the number decreased to 344 in 1834. Up to that time 1,323 natives had been baptized, of whom 757 were children. In 1840 there were still about 300 Indians in the neighborhood, and the affairs of the mission were generally prosperous. In 1844 Santa Inés was reported to have had 264 neophytes, with sufficient resources for their support. After this the property of the mission rapidly declined, and in 1846 the land was sold for $7,000, but the building and church property remained in the charge of the padre. In 1844 an ecclesiastical college was opened at Santa Inés, but it was abandoned 6 years later. The Indians in the neighborhood of the mission belonged to the Chumashan (q. v.) linguistic family, to which most of its neophytes probably belonged. Many came from the Channel islands, especially Santa Rosa. Some of the neophytes were skilled workers in silver and carved leather, and their work and productions were and still are highly prized for their excellence and artistic merit.			(A. B. L.)

Santa Inés. A reservation of unsurveyed, unpatented land, occupied by 52 Mission Indians in 1909; situated 240 m. from Mission Tule River agency, in Santa Barbara co., not far from the old Sànta Inés mission, s. Cal. These Indians were located on lands belonging to the Catholic Church and also what is known as the college grants. Legal steps were taken several years ago to obtain for the use of these Indians the lands on which they had resided, and which they had cultivated for many years, but the question has not yet been determined.
Santa Ynez.—Ind. Aff. Rep. 1902, 175, 1903.

Santa Isabel. A Diegueño village about 50 m. N. E. of San Diego, s. Cal. Pop. 125 in 1873. The name is now given to a reservation of 29,845 acres of waterless, mountainous stock land, with 284 inhabitants.
Santa Isabella.—Audubon (1849), Western Jour., 169, 1906. Santa Ysabel.—Ames, Rep. Miss. Inds., 5, 1873. St. Isabella.—Emory, Recon., 614, 1848.

Santa Isabel. A group of Mohave rancherias, visited and so named by Fray Francisco Garcés in 1776; situated at or in the vicinity of the present Needles, s. E. Cal.—Garcés, Diary (1776), 234, 1900.

Santa Isabel. Mentioned as the last Yuma rancheria on the s. side of the Rio Gila; visited by Father Kino in Nov. 1701.—Bancroft, No. Mex. States, I, 497, 1884.

Santa Lucia. A former visitation town of San Ignacio de Kadakaman mission, situated 10 leagues distant from it, about lat. 28°, Lower California. Its inhabitants were Cochimi. See Venegas, Hist. Cal., I, 421; II, 198, 1759.

Santa Lucia de Acuera. A Spanish mission of the 17th century, established at the Timucuan town of Acuera, on the E. coast of Florida, s. of Cape Cañaveral. It was probably destroyed, with the other Timucuan missions, in the invasion of the hostile Creeks and Carolina troops about 1705. Distinct from Acquera. (J. M.)

Santa Margarita. A name applied by Fray Francisco Garcés (Diary, 411, 1900) in 1776 to a rancheria, probably of the Walapai, near the Cerbat mts. of w. Arizona.

Santa Margarita. Given by Bancroft (Nat. Races, I, 460, 1874) as a Luiseño village of California, but it perhaps belonged to the Shoshonean Kawia.

Santa María (Saint Mary). A settlement, probably of a people speaking a Cochimi dialect, situated 5 leagues N. of the mission of Nuestra Señora de Guadalupe, above lat. 27°, Lower California. In 1745 it was a visita of the mission mentioned. See Venegas, Hist. Cal., II, 198, 1759.

Santa María de los Dolores (Saint Mary of the Sorrows). A former pueblo of the Jova, with 180 inhabitants in 1730; situated in E. Sonora, Mexico, near Rio Viejo, a tributary of the Yaqui. It formed a visita of the mission of Teopari prior to the abandonment of that pueblo on account of Apache depredations in the latter part of the 18th century.
Dolores.—Rivera (1730) quoted by Bancroft, No. Mex. States, I, 514, 1884. Los Dolores.—Orozco y Berra, Geog., 345, 1864. Santa Maria de los Dolores.—Rivera (1730) cited by Bandelier in Arch. Inst. Papers, IV, 510, 1892.

Santa María de Palaxy. A settlement at the mouth of Yellow r., Santa Rosa co., w. Fla., probably one of the villages into which the remnant of the Apalachee was gathered after 1718.

Santa María Magdalena. A mission founded by Father Linck's two associates, Arnes and Diez, at Cabujakaamang, in lat. 30° or 31°, Lower California. It was the last Jesuit mission established in that territory. For reference to its language, see Buschmann, Spuren, 472, 1858, and consult also Venegas, Hist. Cal., II, 199, 1759.
Cabujacaamang.—Clavijero, Hist. Baja Cal., 108, 1852. Cabujakaamang.—Clavigero, Storia della Cal., II, 181, 1789. Cabujakamang.—Shea, Cath. Miss., 90, 1855. Santa Maria.—Taylor quoted by Browne, Res. Pac. Slope, app., 50, 1869. Santa Maria de los Angeles de Kabu Juacama.—Taylor in Cal. Farmer, Jan. 24, 1862. St. Mary's.—Shea, op. cit.

Santa María Magdalena. A former Temoris pueblo in Chinipas valley, w. Chihuahua, Mexico; pop. 585 in 1678.—Orozco y Berra, Geog., 324, 1864.

Santa Marta (Saint Martha). A visita of San Ignacio de Kadakaman mission and situated 11 leagues from it, in lat. 28°, Lower California, in 1745.
Santa Martha.—Venegas, Hist. Cal., II, 198, 1759.

Santa Monica. A visita of San Ignacio de Kadakaman mission, situated 7 leagues from it, about lat. 28°, Lower California, in 1745.—Venegas, Hist. Cal., II., 198, 1759.

Santan (corruption of Span. Santa Ana). A Pima settlement on the N. bank of Rio Gila, opposite the Pima agency, s. Ariz.
Ao'pohiûm.—Russell in 26th Rep. B. A. E., 23, 1908 (native name, of unknown meaning).

Santa Nynfa. A visita of San Ignacio de Kadakaman mission, situated 5 leagues from it, about lat. 28°, Lower California, in 1745.
Santa Nympha.—Venegas, Hist. Cal., I, 421, 1759. Santa Nynfa.—Ibid., II, 198, 1759.

Santa Olalla. A "laguna," or perhaps more strictly a flat subject to inundation, which in the 18th century contained some Yuma rancherias; situated in N. Lower California, lat. 32° 33', somewhat above the entrance of New r. to the main floodplain of the Rio Colorado, 6 to 10 m. w. of the latter and about 8 leagues w. s. w. of the mouth of the Gila. It was notable, at the time named, as the end of the Yuma and the beginning of the Cajuenche settlements. The Comeya also descended "to this land to eat calabashes and other fruits of the river." See Coues, Garcés Diary (1775–6), 165 et seq., 1900.

Santa Eulalia.—Coues, op. cit., 165. **Santa Olalla.**—Ibid. **Santa Olaya.**—Ibid., passim. **St. Eulalie.**—Ibid.

Santa Rita (Holy Rite). The Spanish name of what was probably an ancient settlement of the Tepecano, or of a related tribe, but occupied since early in the 18th century by Tlaxcaltec introduced by the Spaniards for defense against the "Chichimecs"; situated about 15 m. s. e. of Bolaños, in Jalisco, Mexico.—Hrdlička in Am. Anthr., v, 425, 1903.

Santa Rosa (Saint Rose). A Papago village s. of the Rio Gila and w. of Tucson, Ariz. It contained 120 inhabitants in 1858, 160 families under Chief Anastasio in 1865, and about 400 people in 1869 (see Ind. Aff. Reps. for dates given, also Taylor in Cal. Farmer, June 19, 1863; Browne, Apache Country, 291, 1869). The adjacent mountain of Santa Rosa is a sacred place in Pima and Papago mythology.

Santa Rosa. A name applied by Fray Francisco Garcés, in 1771, to a group of Quigyuma ("Jalliquamay") rancherias on the e. side of the lower Rio Colorado, about lat. 32° 18', in n. w. Sonora, Mexico. When he revisited the place in 1775 the settlements were abandoned, the Quigyuma having moved to the w. side of the river in Lower California.—Garcés, Diary (1775), 182, 1900.

Santa Rosa. A former Cora pueblo and a visita of the mission of Peyotan, near the w. bank of the Rio San Pedro, lat. 22° 45', Jalisco, Mexico (Orozco y Berra, Geog., 280, 1864). The place now consists of a few houses occupied by Mexicans.

Santa Rosa. A small Kawia settlement on a reservation of unsurveyed, unpatented land under the San Jacinto agency, in Riverside co., s. Cal. The reservation contained 77 inhabitants in 1909.

Santa Rosa. A Cora settlement on the upper waters of the Rio Jesus María, in the n. part of the territory of Tepic, Mexico.—Lumholtz, Unknown Mex., ii, 16, map, 1902.

Santa Rosalia Mulege. A former Indian settlement and Spanish mission on the e. shore of Lower California, half a league from Mulege r., lat. 26° 55'. The mission was founded in 1705 by Padre Juan M. Basualda, and in 1745, according to Venegas (Hist. Cal., ii, 197-198, 1759), had two visitas, Santísima Trinidad and San Marcos. The old settlement was abandoned in 1815 by the few remaining inhabitants on account of the establishment there of a depot for exiles from Sonora and Sinaloa. See Venegas, Hist. Cal., i, 381; ii, 197, 1759.
Carmaañe Galexá.—Doc. Hist. Mex., 4th s., v, 186, 1857 (after early document). Molejé.—Duflot de Mofras, Expl., i, 219, 228, 238, 1844. Mulege.—Vene-

gas, Hist. Cal., i, 335, 1759. **Santa Rosalia de Moleje.**—Taylor in Browne, Res. Pac. Slope, app., 49, 1869. **S. Rosalia di Mulegè.**—Clavigero, Storia della Cal., ii, 185, 1789.

Santa Teresa. The northernmost Cora pueblo and formerly the seat of a mission; situated in the Sierra de Nayarit, in the n. part of the territory of Tepic, Mexico. Quemalúsi.—Lumholtz, Unknown Mex., i, 489, 1902 (native name, after a mythical personage). Santa Teresa.—Orozco y Berra, Geog., 280, 1864.

Santa Ynéz. See *Santa Inés.*

Santee (*Isañyati*, from *isañ* 'knife,' contraction of *isañta-mde* 'knife lake,' Dakota name for Mille Lacs, and *ati*, 'to pitch tents at'). An eastern division of the Dakota, comprising the Mdewakanton and Wahpekute, sometimes also the Sisseton and Wahpeton. Hennepin (1680), who probably included only the Mdewakanton, says (Descr. La., Shea's trans., 203, 1880): "In the neighborhood of L. Buade are many other lakes, whence issue several rivers, on the banks of which live the Issati, Nadouessans, Tinthonha (which means prairie-men), Ouadebathon River People, Chongaskethon Dog, or Wolf tribe (for *chonga* among these nations means dog or wolf), and other tribes, all which we comprise under the name Nadouessiou [Sioux]." In Le Sueur's list (1700) the Issati are omitted and the Mdewakanton (written Mendeoucantons) inserted, for the first time. The name Santee was applied by the Missouri River Dakota to all those of the group living on Mississippi and lower Minnesota rs., the Mdewakanton, Wahpekute, Wahpeton, and Sisseton. Ramsey (Rep. Ind. Aff. for 1849, 74, 1850) and Riggs limit the use of the term to designate the Mdewakanton. McGee (15th Rep. B. A. E., 160, 1897) includes only the Wahpekute, which has been the usual application of the term since 1862, when the two tribes were gathered on the Santee res. in Knox co., Neb. Reyata is mentioned as a band and Ptansinta as a village of the Santee.

The tribes forming this group joined under the collective name in the following treaties with the United States: Prairie du Chien, Wis., July 15, 1830; St Louis, Mo., Oct. 13, 1830; Bellevue, Neb., Oct. 15, 1836; Washington, D. C., Feb. 19, 1867; Fort Laramie, Wyo., Apr. 29, 1868. See *Dakota*, and the Santee divisions above given.
Dacotas of the St. Peter's.—Warren, Dacota Country, 17, 1856. **Eastern Sioux.**—Jefferys, French Dom. Amer., pt. i, 45, 1761. **Esanties.**—Riggs, Dakota Gram. and Dict., 92, 1852. **E. Scihous.**—Coxe, Carolana, map, 1741. **Es-sah'-ah-ter.**—Ramsey in Ind. Aff. Rep. for 1849, 78, 1850 (pronunciation). **Esson.**—Ibid. **Hizantinton.**—Jefferys (1763), Am. Atlas, map 5, 1776. **Isanati.**—Neill, Hist. Minn., 51, 1858. **Isantie Dakotas.**—Hayden, Ethnog. and Philol. Mo. Val., map, 1862. **Isanties.**—Riggs, Dakota Gram. and Dict., 92, 1852. **I-saŋ'-tis.**—Hayden, op. cit., 371. **Isantiton.**—De l'Isle (1700), map of La., in Neill, Hist.

Minn., 164, 1858. **Isanyate.**—Seymour, Sketches Minn., 17, 1850. **Isanyati.**—Williamson in Schoolcraft, Ind. Tribes, I, 248, 1851. **Isatis.**—Barcia, Ensayo, 238, 1723. **Isaunties.**—Morgan in N. Am. Rev., 44, Jan. 1870. **Issanti.**—Seymour, op. cit., 152. **Issaqui.**—La Chesnaye (1697) in Margry, Déc., VI, 6, 1886. **Issaquy.**—Ibid. **Issati.**—Hennepin, New Discov., 174, 1698. **Issatie.**—Bowles, Map Am., 1784. **Issatrians.**—Hennepin, op. cit., 99. **I-tsá'-ti.**—Matthews, Ethnog. Hidatsa, 161, 1877 (Hidatsa name). **Izatys.**—Du Lhut (1678) in Margry, Déc., VI, 22, 1886. **Lower Sioux.**—Ind. Aff. Rep., 52, 1858. **Nad8esseronons sédentaires.**—Tailhan in Perrot, Mém., 340, note, 1864. **Nation du boeuf.**—Minn. Hist. Soc. Coll., II, pt. 2, 31, note, 1864. **Santas.**—Parker, Jour., 45, 1842. **Santees.**—Ind. Aff. Rep., 554, 1837. **Santee Sioux.**—Poole, Among Sioux, 31, 1881. **Santie.**—Ramsey in Ind. Aff. Rep. for 1849, 86, 1850. **Santie bands.**—U. S. Stat. at Large, IV, 464, 1860. **Santie Sioux.**—H. R. Doc. 57, 25th Cong. 2d sess., 2, 1837. **Saux of the Wood.**—Trumbull, Ind. Wars, 185, 1851. **Scioux of the East.**—Le Sueur (1700) quoted by Neill, Hist. Minn., 170, 1858. **Scioux of the Woods.**—Chauvignerie (1736) quoted by Schoolcraft, Ind. Tribes, III, 557, 1853. **Sedentary Nadouesserons.**—Minn. Hist. Soc. Coll., II, pt. 2, 31, note, 1864. **Sioux de L'Est.**—Le Sueur (1700) in Margry, Déc., VI, 78, 1886. **Sioux of the River.**—Seymour, Sketches Minn., 135, 1850. **Sioux of the Woods.**—Smith, Bouquet Exped., 70, 1766. **Sioux orientaux.**—Perrot, Mémoire, 232, notes, 1864. **Sioux sédentaires.**—Ibid. **Sioux of the River St. Peter's.**—Treaty of 1815 in U. S. Ind. Treat., 869, 1873. **Upper Dakotas.**—Ramsey in Minn. Hist. Soc. Coll., I, 49, 1872.

Santee. A tribe, probably Siouan, formerly residing on middle Santee r., S. C., where Lawson in 1700 found their plantations extending for many miles. One of their villages was called Hickerau. While friendly to the white people, they were at war with the coast tribes. According to Rivers (Hist. S. C., 94, 1874), they had two villages with 43 warriors in 1715, and were then settled 70 m. N. of Charleston. Bartram (Trav., 54, 1791) tells us that in 1715 they sided with the Yamasee against the British, and that they were attacked and reduced by the Creeks, who were allies of the British. It appears from South Carolina colonial documents that the Santee and Congeree were cut off by the "Itwans and Cossaboys," coast tribes in the English interest, and the prisoners sold as slaves in the West Indies in 1716. Those that escaped were probably incorporated with the Catawba. Lawson states that their chief was an absolute ruler with power of life and death over his tribe, an instance of despotism very rare among Indians. Their distinguished dead were buried on the tops of mounds, built low or high according to the rank of the deceased, with ridge roofs supported by poles over the graves to shelter them from the weather. On these poles were hung rattles, feathers, and other offerings from the relatives of the deceased. The corpse of an ordinary person was carefully dressed, wrapped in bark, and exposed on a platform for several days, during which time one of his nearest kinsmen, with face blackened in token of grief, stood guard near the spot and chanted a

mournful eulogy of the dead. The ground around the platform was kept carefully swept, and all the dead man's belongings—gun, bow, and feather robes—were placed near by. As soon as the flesh had softened it was stripped from the bones and burned, and the bones themselves were cleaned, the skull being wrapped separately in a cloth woven of opossum hair. The bones were then put into a box, from which they were taken out annually to be again cleaned and oiled. In this way some families had in their possession the bones of their ancestors for several generations. Places where warriors had been killed were sometimes distinguished by piles of stones or sticks, to which every passing Indian added another. After the manner of the Cherokee and other Southern tribes the Santee kept corn in storehouses raised on posts and plastered with clay. They made beautiful feather robes and wove cloth and sashes of hair. Consult Lawson, Hist. Carolina, repr. 1860; Mooney, Siouan Tribes of the East, 80, 1894. (J. M.)

Santee.—Lawson (1700), Hist. Carolina, 34, 1860. **Seratees.**—Mills, Stat. S. C., 735, 1826. **Seretee.**—Lawson (1700), op. cit., 45. **Zantees.**—Howe in Schoolcraft, Ind. Tribes, IV, 155, 1854.

San Teodoro (Saint Theodore). A name applied by Mézières, in 1778, to one of two Tawehash villages visited by him on upper Red r., Texas.—Bancroft, No. Mex. States, I, 649, 663, 1886.

Santiago (Saint James). A Tigua pueblo in New Mexico in 1626 (Zárate-Salmerón, ca. 1629, cited by Bancroft, Nat. Races, I, 600, 1882). According to Bandelier (Arch. Inst. Papers, IV, 227, 1892) it was situated about 5½ m. above Bernalillo, on the Mesa del Cangelon.

Santiam. A Kalapooian tribe formerly residing on the river of the same name, an E. tributary of the Willamette, in Oregon. They are now on Grande Ronde res., where they numbered 23 in 1906. In 1909 the number officially reported was only 5, the remainder evidently having received patents for their lands and become citizens. In 1877 Gatschet was able to learn of 4 bands, Chamifu, Chanchampenau, Chanchantu, and Chantkaip, which had formerly existed in the tribe. **Ahálpam.**—Gatschet, Atfalati MS., B. A. E., 1877 (Atfalati name). **Santaims.**—Ind. Aff. Rep., 469, 1865. **Santainas.**—Taylor in Sen. Ex. Doc. 4, 40th Cong., spec. sess., 27, 1867. **Santiam.**—Dayton treaty, 1855, in U.S.Ind. Treat., 18, 1873. **Santian.**—Ind. Aff. Rep., 205, 1851. **Sautains.**—Ind. Aff., Rep. 1864, 503, 1865. **Tsan halpam amím.**—Gatschet Lakmiut MS., B. A. E., 1877 (Lakmiut name).

Santísima Trinidad (Most Holy Trinity). A Cochimi village and visita of Santa Rosalia Mulege mission in 1745, situated 6 leagues S. SE. therefrom, lat. 26° 55′, Lower California.—Venegas, Hist. Cal., II, 198, 1759.

Santísimo Nombre de María (Most Holy Name of Mary). A Franciscan mission founded among the Caddo by Padre Francisco de Jesus María in 1690, on Arcangel San Miguel r. (the Rio Neches), a few miles N. E. of the mission of San Francisco de los Tejas, in the present Texas. After San Francisco had been abandoned this mission was not heard of again.—Austin in Tex. Hist. Asso. Quar., VIII, 281, 1905.

Santo Domingo (Saint Dominic, also Holy Sabbath). A Keresan pueblo on the E. bank of the Rio Grande, about 18 m. above Bernalillo, N. central N. Mex. The earliest traditions of the pueblo locate it at the Potrero de la Cañada Quemada, whence the inhabitants in prehistoric times removed successively to two villages, each named Gipuy (q. v.), the later one of which they occupied when visited by Oñate in 1598. The earlier Gipuy stood on the banks of the Arroyo de Galisteo, more than a mile E. of the present station of Thornton, but was partially destroyed by a rise of that dangerous torrent in one night, the inhabitants being compelled to move farther westward, where the second Gipuy was built. This pueblo, also destroyed by a flood, was succeeded by Huashpatzena, on the Rio Grande, which suffered the fate of its predecessors. The present Santo Domingo, the aboriginal name of which is Kiua, has had three disasters from flood since its establishment 200 years ago, the latest occurring in 1886 when both churches were destroyed. The first Gipuy is the only pueblo of the Santo Domingo Indians E. of the Rio Grande of which any trace remains. At the time of Oñate's visit in 1598 Santo Domingo was chosen as the "monastery of the advocation of Nuestra Señora de la Asunción" (Doc. Inéd, XVI, 254, 1871). It also became the seat of a mission early in the 17th century, and after 1782 had San Felipe and Cochiti as its visitas. According to Bandelier 18 clans are represented in this pueblo. Pop. 819 in 1910. Consult Bandelier in Arch. Inst. Papers, III, 260, 1890; IV, 184 et seq., 1892. See also *Keresan Family, Pueblos.* (F. W. H.)

Dji'wi.—Hodge, field notes, B. A. E., 1895 (Laguna name). Domingo.—Vaugondy, Map Amérique, 1778. Dyi'-wa.—Hodge, field notes, B. A. E., 1895 (Cochiti name). Ge-e-way.—Simpson in Rep. Sec. War, 143, 1850. Ge-e-wē.—Simpson (1850) quoted in Wheeler Surv. Rep., VII, 418, 1879 (old name). Ki-hua.—Jouvenceau in Cath. Pion., I, no. 9, 12, 1906. Kĭn Klĕkái Nĭ.—Curtis, Am. Ind., I, 138, 1907 ('white houses': Navaho name). Ki'-o-a-me.—Whipple, Pac. R. R. Rep., III, pt. 3, 90, 1856 (or Ki'-wo-mi; name by which they call themselves). Ki'-o-wummi.—Ibid., 9 (given as tribal name; incorrectly identified with Tiguex). Ki-ua.—Bandelier in Arch. Inst. Papers, III, 260, 1890 (aboriginal name of pueblo). Kivome.—Pimentel cited by Cubas, Repub. Mexico, 65, 1876 (Kiwomi or). Ki'-wa.—Hodge, field notes, B. A. E., 1895 (San Felipe form). Ki'-wo-mi.—Whipple, Pac. R. R. Rep., III, pt. 3, 90, 1856 (or Ki'-o-a-me; own name). Saint Domingo.—Möllhausen, Pacific, I, 331, 1858. San Domingan.—Wallace, Land of the Pueblos, 55, 1888 (applied to the language). San Domingo.—Mühlenpfordt, Mejico, II, 533, 1844.

Santa Dominga.—Calhoun in Schoolcraft, Ind. Tribes, III, 633, 1853. Santa Domingo.—Abert in Emory, Recon., 484, 1848 (misprint). Santo Domingo.—Vetancurt (1696) cited by Bandelier in Arch. Inst. Papers, IV, 168, 1892 (misprint). Santo Domingo.—Sosa (1590) in Doc. Inéd., XV, 258, 1871; Oñate (1598), ibid., XVI, 102 et seq., 1871 ("just as likely to have been the former pueblo of San Felipe as Guipuy or old Santo Domingo."—Bandelier in Arch. Inst. Papers, IV, 123, 1892). Sț Domingo.—Kitchin, Map N. A., 1787. Sto Dom. de Cochiti.—Bancroft, Ariz. and N. Mex., 281, 1889 (said to be so called after 1782; distinct from Cochiti, however). Sto. Domingo.—Rivera, Diario, leg. 784, 1736. Sto. Domingo de Cuevas.—Escudero, Not. Estad. de Chihuahua, 180, 1834. Ta'-wi-gi.—Hodge, field notes, B. A. E., 1895 (Jemez name; Pecos form Ta-wi'-gi). Te'-wi-gi.—Ibid. (Tewa name, said to mean 'pueblo place'). Tihua.—Bandelier, Gilded Man, 216, 1893 (misprint T for K). Ti'wï.—Hodge, field notes, B. A. E., 1895 (Acoma name). Tu-a-wi-hol.—Gibbs, MS. vocab., B. A. E., 1868 (Isleta name for pueblo). Tu'-iai.—Gatschet Isleta MS. vocab., B. A. E., 1885 (Isleta name of pueblo). Tüwi'-ai.—Ibid. (Isleta name of pueblo). Túwii.—Stephen in 8th Rep. B. A. E., 30, 1891 (Hopi name of pueblo). Tŭwita.—Hodge, field notes, B. A. E., 1895 ('haliotis place': Taos name). Tŭ-wit-ha'.—Ibid. (Picuris name). Tüwiχuide.—Gatschet, Isleta MS. vocab., B. A. E., 1885 (pl. Tüwiχun: Isleta name for the people). T'wi'wi.—Hodge, field notes, B. A. E., 1895 (Santa Ana name). You-pel-lay.—Wallace, Land of the Pueblos, 56, 1888 (erroneously so called from one of their dances).

Santos Angeles (Holy Angels). Mentioned as a Pima pueblo of Sonora, Mexico, by Orozco y Berra (Geog., 347, 1864). Definite locality unknown.

Santotin. A division of the Tenankutchin, occupying the territory about a lake on White r., Alaska, and westward, extending down Tanana r. to a point nearly opposite the head of Forty Mile cr. Mantotin.—Allen, Rep. on Alaska, 137, 1887. Santo-tin.—Dawson in Rep. Geol. Surv. Can., n. s., III, 203B, 1889.

Santo Tomás (Saint Thomas). A Dominican mission established in 1790 in the N. part of Lower California, lat. 31° 40', near Todos Santos bay. Its inhabitants, sometimes called San Tomaseños, were visited in Apr. 1867 by Dr Wm. M. Gabb, who found their language to be a dialect of Diegueño or Comeya, closely related to Htaam and Kiliwi. Santo Tomas.—Taylor in Browne, Res. Pac. Slope, app., 51, 1869.

Santo Tomás. A settlement of the Jova on the upper waters of Papigochic r., 4 m. s. of Metachic, in w. Chihuahua, Mexico.—Orozco y Berra, Geog., 345, 1864.

Santsukhdhin ('campers in the highland grove'). One of the three larger divisions of the Osage, commonly known as the Arkansas band. Originally a part of the Grand Osage, or Pahatsi, living successively on Sac r., and on Little Osage r. in Vernon co., Mo., they were induced by the trader Choteau, about 1802, to secede from the main body under White Hair and remove to the Arkansas r., Manuel Lisa, another trader, having obtained a monopoly of the Missouri traffic from the Spanish authorities. At the time named Clermont and Casesagra were their principal men. In 1810 their village was on the Verdigris branch of the Arkansas, 60 m. above its mouth, in the present Oklahoma; in 1820 they were at the mouth of the river, then numbering 600. When met by De Smet in 1850 their number was reported at 700.

Arkansa band.—McGee in 15th Rep. B. A. E., 162, 1897. **Arkansaw band.**—Lewis and Clark Exped., I, 8, 1814. **Arkansaw Osages.**—Pike, Trav., 430, 1811. **Big Track.**—Schermerhorn (1812) in Mass. Hist. Soc. Coll., 2d s., II, 31, 1814 (name of a chief). **Chamers.**—Balbi, Atlas Ethnog., 56, 1826. **Chancers.**—Long, Exped. Rocky Mts., III, 274, repr. 1905 (misprint). **Chaneers.**—Long, Exped. Rocky Mts., II, 244, 1823. **Chaniers band.**—Brackenridge, Views La., 293, 1815. **Chêniers.**—De Smet, W. Miss., 355, 1856. **Clamore.**—Keane in Stanford, Compend., 470, 1878 (name of chief). **Clermont's band.**—Long, Exped. Rocky Mts., Thwaite's ed., XVI, 280, 1905. **Clermo's band.**—Long, Exped. Rocky Mts., II, 244, 1823. **Osage des Chenes.**—Long, ibid., 237. **Osages of the Oaks.**—Ibid. **Santsĕ'pasŭ'.**—Dorsey, Osage MS. vocab., B. A. E., 1883 (their ancient village: 'point of a timbered highland'). **ṣan-ʇsu'-ɥʤiⁿ.**—McGee, after Dorsey, in 15th Rep. B. A. E., 162, 1897. **Sanze-Ougrin.**—De Smet, loc. cit.

Sanukh (*Sänux*). A former Tonkawa clan or band (Gatschet, Tonkawe MS. vocab., B. A. E., 1884). Possibly the Sana or Zana of mission archives.

Sanup. See *Sannup*.

San Xavier del Bac (the Jesuit mission name, combined with the Piman *bak, vak, váaki,* its native designation, signifying 'house,' 'adobe house,' also 'ruined house,' 'ruin': probably given because of the remains of ancient adobe structures in the vicinity). A former important Sobaipuri rancheria on Rio Santa Cruz, 9 m. s. of Tucson, Ariz., in the N. E. corner of what is now the Papago res. It was first visited and the Saint name applied in 1692 by Father Kino, a celebrated Jesuit, who next visited it perhaps in 1694, again in 1697 (at which date it numbered 830 persons in 176 houses), and many times thereafter. In 1700 he founded a church, built of light porous stone, the construction of which was possibly begun in the previous year. In its earlier years the mission flourished under the Jesuits, of whom 22 served San Xavier until 1767, when they were succeeded by Franciscans. In 1751–53, during a revolt of the Pima, the mission was plundered and abandoned, but was reoccupied two years later under the protection of the presidio of Tubac. Between 1760 and 1764 it contained 400 inhabitants—less than half its population 60 years before—and these had dwindled to 270 by 1772. When Fray Francisco Garcés, its first Franciscan missionary, took charge in 1768 he found the mission in a neglected state, but it again began to flourish on the establishment of the presidio of Tucson in 1776. In 1783 the erection of a new church of plastered brick, commodious and of architectural merit, was begun by Padre Baltasar Cavillo near the site of that built by Kino, and was brought to its present state of completeness by Padre Narciso Gutierres in 1797—

a date still legible over the portal. The remains of these priests are buried in the church. In 1810 San Xavier again began to decline, and came to an end as an independent mission with the expulsion of the Franciscans on the fall of the Colonial government, Dec. 2, 1827, from which time it struggled along as a visita of Magdalena, Sonora, until 1859, when Arizona was segregated ecclesiastically from the diocese of Santa Fé, N. Mex. In 1852 Bartlett described it as "truly a miserable place, consisting of from 80 to 100 huts, or wigwams, made of mud or straw," but "in the midst of these hovels stands the most beautiful church in the State of Sonora." In 1865 the population was 80 Papago families. In the preceding year a school was established at San Xavier by the Catholic Church; this contained 125 day pupils in 1908. In 1873 a Government school was begun, but was closed in 1876 when the Papago were consolidated under the Pima agency. It is now a scattered but large and flourishing Papago settlement. There are numerous adobe houses, and the Indians are advancing toward civilization. The people are under the supervision of a white farmer, who acts as subagent. A number of the San Xavier Papago within recent years have settled in the outskirts of Tucson. Consult Bartlett, Pers. Narr., II, 185, 1854; Rudo Ensayo (*ca.* 1763), 1863; Salpointe, Brief Sketch, 1880; Bancroft, Ariz. and N. Mex., 1889; Coues, Garcés Diary, 1900; Curtis, N. Am. Ind., II, 1908.   (F. W. H.)

Bac.—Bernal (1697) quoted by Bancroft, Ariz. and N. Mex., 356, 1889. **Batosda.**—Ibid. (or S. Javier). **San Javier del Bac.**—Bancroft, ibid., 362. **San Xabier del Bac.**—Rudo Ensayo (*ca.* 1763), 106, 1863. **San Xavier de Báca.**—Hardy, Travels, 421, 1829. **San Xavier del Bác.**—Garcés (1775), Diary, 64, 1900. **San Xavier de Zac.**—Poston in Ind. Aff. Rep. 1864, 154, 1865. **San Zavier de Bac.**—Donaldson, Moqui Pueblo Inds., 3, 1893. **S. Cayetano de Bac.**—Writer of 1754 quoted by Bancroft, No. Mex. States, I, 270, 1884 (confused with Tumacacori). **S. Francisco Xavier de Bac.**—Venegas, Hist. Cal., I, map, 1759. **S. Javier.**—Bernal (1697), op. cit. **S. Javier Bac.**—Kino, map (1701), in Bancroft, Ariz. and N. Mex., 360, 1889. **S. Javier del Bacel.**—Escudero, Not. Chihuahua, 228, 1834. **S. Xaver du Bac.**—Kino, map (1702), in Stöcklein, Neue Welt-Bott, 74, 1726. **S. Xavier.**—Font, map (1777), in Bancroft, Ariz. and N. Mex., 393, 1889. **S. Xavier del Bac.**—Villa-Señor, Theatro Am., II, 403, 1748.

Sanyakoan. A Tlingit tribe formerly inhabiting a town named Gash, at C. Fox, Alaska, and often confused with the neighboring Tongas. Pop. 177 in 1839. In the census of 1880 they are erroneously placed on Prince of Wales id., and are given a population of 100. Their social divisions are Nehadi and Tekoedi.   (J. R. S.)

Cape Fox Indians.—Kane, Wand. in N. A., app., 1859. **Lugh-se-le.**—Ibid. **Lukhselee.**—Petroff in Tenth Census, Alaska, 37, 1884 (after a Hudson's Bay Co. census of 1889). **Sanakhanskoe.**—Veniaminoff, Zapiski, II, pt. III, 30, 1840. **Sā'nak'oan.**—Boas, 10th Rep. on N. W. Tribes of Can., 34, 1895. **S!ā'nya koan.**—Swanton, field notes, B. A. E., 1904. **Ssángha-kŏn.**—Krause, Tlinkit Ind., 120, 1885.

Saone (probably the same as Sanona). A division of the Teton Sioux, comprising the Sans Arcs, Sihasapa, Oohenonpa, and sometimes the Hunkpapa, first mentioned by Lewis and Clark, and under the form Souon-Teton in Clark's MS., where they are called "people of the prairie" and made one of the 12 tribes of the Dakota, while the Souon are another. Riggs informed Dorsey that the name "Sanoni-wicasa" was used as a nickname, and wrote (Word Carrier, 14, June–July, 1889) that the Brulés and Oglala formerly applied it to the Sans Arcs, Miniconjou, and Hunkpapa. Lewis and Clark did not include the Miniconjou, but included the rest of the Teton found along Missouri r. except the Brulés and Oglala, and estimated them at 300 men, or 900 souls—three-tenths of the whole. There was a Sangona, or Sahown, band of the Hunkpatina, with which they have been confused (see Coues in Lewis and Clark Exped., I, 101, note, 1897). The Hunkpapa were probably not counted as Saone proper by Lewis, for in his table (Discov., 34, 1806) he distinguishes from these the Saone Hunkpapa. The Saone, under the name Sioune, joined the Oglala in the treaty with the United States at the mouth of Teton r., S. Dak., July 5, 1825. As the "Siounes of the Fire-hearts band" are mentioned and the Hunkpapa are not, it is probable the latter were not included under the term Sioune.

Sahohes.—McKenney and Hall, Ind. Tribes, III, 81, 1854. Sa-hone.—Brackenridge, Views La., 78, 1815. Sah-o-ne.—Lewis and Clark, Discov., 34, 1806. Sahonies.—Bradbury, Trav., 90, 1817. Saones.—Sen. Ex. Doc. 90, 22d Cong., 1st sess., 63, 1832. Saoynes.—De Smet, Letters, 37, note, 1843. Sawons.—Ind. Aff. Rep., 471, 1838. Scione Sioux.—H. R. Ex. Doc. 2, 18th Cong., 1st sess., 68, 1823. See-oo-nay.—Ramsey in Ind. Aff. Rep. 1849, 69, 1850 (pronunciation). Sioane.—Ramsey, ibid., 84. Siones.—H. R. Ex. Doc. 117, 19th Cong., 1st sess., 6, 1826. Sionne.—Ramsey in Ind. Aff. Rep. 1849, 85, 1850. Sioune.—Treaty of 1825 in U. S. Ind. Treat., 339, 1826. Siouones.—Sen. Ex. Doc. 56, 18th Cong., 1st sess., 9, 1824. Siowes.—Parker quoted by M'Vickar, Hist. Exped. Lewis and Clark, I, 86, note, 1842. Souon.—Clark, MS., codex B, Amer. Philos. Soc., 57. Souon-Teton.—Ibid. Sowans.—Ind. Aff. Rep., 59, 1842. Tetans Saone.—Ramsey in Ind. Aff. Rep. 1849, 85, 1850. Te'-ton-sâh-o-ne'.—Lewis and Clark, Discov., 30, 1806. Teton Saone.—Ibid., 34. Tetons Sahone.—Lewis, Trav., 171, 1809. Tetons Saone.—Lewis and Clark Exped., I, 61, 1814.

Saone Hunkpapa. A part of the Hunkpapa Sioux.

Sah-o-ne-hont-a-par-par.—Lewis and Clark, Discov., table, 34, 1806. Sanoni-Hunkpapa.—Riggs in Word Carrier, 14, June–July, 1889.

Saopuk (S'áopük, 'many trees'). A Pima village at The Cottonwoods, on Gila r., s. Ariz.

S'a'opuk.—Russell in 26th Rep. B. A. E., 23, 1908. Saufpak.—ten Kate quoted by Gatschet, MS., B. A. E., XX, 199, 1888 (trans. 'cottonwoods').

Sapa Chitto (Osapa chitto, 'big corn field'). A former large Choctaw settlement about Dixon, Neshoba co., Miss.—Halbert in Pub. Miss. Hist. Soc., VI, 432, 1902.

Sapala. A mission village, perhaps on Sapelo id., coast of Georgia, which was one of those revolting against the Spaniards of Florida in 1687.—Barcia, Ensayo, 287, 1723.

Sapaquonil. A Chumashan village formerly on Jimeno's rancho, Ventura co., Cal.—Taylor in Cal. Farmer, May 4, 1860.

Sapaywis. A former Salinan village connected with San Antonio mission, Monterey co., Cal.—Taylor in Cal. Farmer, Apr. 27, 1860.

Sapechichic ('place of bats'). A small rancheria of the Tarahumare, not far from Norogachic, Chihuahua, Mexico.—Lumholtz, inf'n, 1894.

Sapeessa. A former Choctaw town on the N. side of Black Water cr., Kemper co., Miss., apparently about midway between Shomotakali and the branch emptying into Black Water known as Mineral Spring branch. Its exact location has not been identified.—Halbert in Pub. Miss. Hist. Soc., VI, 416, 1902.

Sapa-Pesah.—Romans, Florida, 309, 1775. Sapeessa.—West Florida map, ca. 1775.

Sapelek. A Chumashan village formerly near Santa Inés mission, Santa Barbara co., Cal.—Taylor in Cal. Farmer, May 4, 1860.

Sapohanikan (Delaware: Awäsopoðkän-chan, 'over against the pipe-making place,' i. e., Hoboken, a remnant of the native name Hopoðkänhäking, 'at the tobacco-pipe land'). Hoboken was the outlet for peltries collected in the interior by the Indians, who took them in their canoes directly across the river and landed with them in a cove north of "Sapokanichan Point," near the present Gansevoort st., New York city. The adjoining land was not the site of an Indian village. Van Twiller purchased a tract in the vicinity and established on it a tobacco plantation, with buildings inclosed in a stockade, and called his Dutch settlement "Sapokanikan." See Ruttenber, Ind. Geog. Names, 17, 1906.   (W. R. G.)

Sapohanikan.—Hall (1639) in N. Y. Doc. Col. Hist., XIV, 19, 1883. Sapokanikan.—Van Tienhoven (1641), ibid., 35. Saponickan.—Ibid., 27. Sappokanican.—Deed of 1640, ibid.

Saponi. One of the eastern Siouan tribes, formerly living in North Carolina and Virginia, but now extinct. The tribal name was occasionally applied to the whole group of Ft Christanna tribes, also occasionally included under Tutelo. That this tribe belonged to the Siouan stock has been placed beyond doubt by the investigations of Hale and Mooney. Their language appears to have been the same as the Tutelo to the extent that the people of the two tribes could readily understand each other. Mooney has shown that the few Saponi words recorded are Siouan.

Lederer mentions a war in which the Saponi seem to have been engaged with the Virginia settlers as early as 1654–56, the time of the attack by the Cherokee, probably in alliance with them. The first positive notice is by Lederer (1670), who informs us that he stopped a few days at Sapon, a town of the Tutelo confederacy, situated on a tributary of the upper Roanoke. This village was apparently on Otter r., s. w. of Lynchburg, Va. Pintahae is mentioned also as another of their villages near by. It is evident that the Saponi and Tutelo were living at that time in close and apparently confederated relation. In 1671 they were visited by Thomas Batts and others accompanied by two Indian guides. After traveling nearly due w. from the mouth of the Appomattox about 140 m., they came to Sapong, or Saponys, town. Having been harassed by the Iroquois in this locality, the Saponi and Tutelo at a later date removed to the junction of Staunton and Dan rs., where they settled near the Occaneechi, each tribe occupying an island in the Roanoke in what is now Mecklenburg co., Va. Lawson, who visited these Indians in 1701, found them dwelling on Yadkin r., N. C., near the present site of Salisbury, having removed to the s. to escape the attacks of their enemies. Byrd (1729) remarks: "They dwelt formerly not far below the mountains, upon Yadkin r., about 200 miles west and by south from the falls of Roanoak. But about 25 years ago they took refuge in Virginia, being no longer in condition to make head not only against the northern Indians, who are their implacable enemies, but also against most of those to the south. All the nations round about, bearing in mind the havock these Indians used formerly to make among their ancestors in the insolence of their power, did at length avenge it home upon them, and made them glad to apply to this Government for protection."

Soon after Lawson's visit in 1701 the Saponi and Tutelo left their villages on the Yadkin and moved in toward the settlements, being joined on the way by the Occaneechi and their allied tribes. Together they crossed the Roanoke, evidently before the Tuscarora war of 1711, and made a new settlement, called Sapona Town, a short distance E. of that river and 15 m. w. of the present Windsor, Bertie co., N. C. Soon after this they and other allied tribes were located by Gov. Spotswood near Ft Christanna, 10 m. N. of Roanoke r., about the present Gholsonville, Brunswick co., Va. The name of Sappony cr., in Dinwiddie co., dating back at least to 1733, indicates that they sometimes extended their excursions N. of Nottoway r. Their abode here was not one of quiet, as they were at war with neighboring tribes or their old enemies, the Iroquois. By the treaty at Albany

(1722) peace was declared between the northern Indians and the Virginia and Carolina tribes, the Blue Ridge and the Potomac being the boundary line. Probably about 1740 the Saponi and Tutelo went N., stopping for a time at Shamokin, in Pennsylvania, about the site of Sunbury, where they and other Indians were visited by the missionary David Brainard in 1745. In 1753 the Cayuga formally adopted the Saponi and Tutelo, who thus became a part of the Six Nations, though all had not then removed to New York. In 1765 the Saponi are mentioned as having 30 warriors living at Tioga, about Sayre, Pa., and other villages on the northern branches of the Susquehanna. A part remained here until 1778, but in 1771 the principal portion had their village in the territory of the Cayuga, about 2 m. s. of what is now Ithaca, N. Y. When the Tutelo fled to Canada, soon after 1779, they parted with the Saponi (Hale was informed by the last of the Tutelo) at Niagara, but what became of them afterward is not known. It appears, however, from a treaty made with the Cayuga at Albany in 1780 that a remnant was still living with this tribe on Seneca r. in Seneca co., N. Y., after which they disappear from history. Consult Mooney, Siouan Tribes of the East, Bull. B. A. E., 1894; Bushnell in Am. Anthr., IX, 45–46, 1907, and the authorities cited below. (J. M.)

Paanese.—Cayuga treaty, Albany, 1789, quoted by Hall, N. W. States, 70, 1849. Sapenys.—Batts, Jour. (1671), in Am. Anthr., IX, 47, 1907. Sapiny.—Ibid., 46. Sapon.—Lederer, Discov., 2, map, 1672. Sapona.—Martin, N. Car., I, 253, 1829. Saponas.—Lawson (1701), Hist. Car., 82, 1860. Saponees.—Knight (1712) in N. Car. Rec., I, 866, 1886. Sapones.—Croghan, Jour. (1765), 36, 1831. Saponeys.—Johnson (1763) in N. Y. Doc. Col. Hist., VII, 582, 1856. Sapongs.—Batts (1671), ibid., III, 194, 1853. Saponi.—Byrd (1728), Hist. Dividing Line, I, 75, 1866. Saponie. — Spotswood (1711) quoted by Burk, Virginia, III, 89, 1805. Saponys.—Batts, Jour. (1671), in Am. Anthr., IX, 47, 1907. Sapoonies.—Hutchins (1768) in Jefferson, Notes, 142, 1825. Sappona.—Pollock (1712) in N. Car. Rec., I, 884, 1886. Sapponces.—Albany conf. (1717) in N. Y. Doc. Col. Hist., V, 490, 1855. Sapponees.—N. Car. council (1727) in N. Car. Rec., II, 674, 1886. Sapponeys.—Doc. of 1709 in Va. State Papers, I, 131, 1875. Sapponi.—Burk, Hist. Virginia, III, 17, 1805. Sapponie.—N. Car. Council (1726) in N. Car. Rec., II, 643, 1886 (town). Sappony.—N. Car. Council (1727), ibid., 674. Saps.—Lawson (1701), Hist. Car., 89, 1860.

Sapponet. A former village connected with San Carlos mission, Cal., and said to have been Esselen.
Sepponet.—Taylor in Cal. Farmer, Apr. 20, 1860.

Saptuui (Saph'-tu-u'-i). A former Chumashan village in the interior of Ventura co., Cal., at a place called El Conejo.—Henshaw, Buenaventura MS. vocab., B. A. E., 1884.

Saquerisera. See Sequareesere.

Saracachi. A Eudeve pueblo of Sonora, Mexico, with 31 inhabitants in 1730; situated near the present Cucurpe. The comisaria of Saracachi y Dolores, which contained 401 inhabitants in 1900, is the outgrowth of the former pueblo.

Sacarachi.—Rivera (1730) quoted by Bancroft, No. Mex. States, I, 513, 1884. **Saracatzi.**—Orozco y Berra, Geog., 344, 1864.

Saracuam. One of the tribes enumerated by Massanet (Dictamen Fiscal, Nov. 30, 1716, MS.) as on the road from Coahuila to the Texas country. The affinities of the tribe are uncertain.

Saraise. A former village, presumably Costanoan, connected with Dolores mission, San Francisco, Cal.—Taylor in Cal. Farmer, Oct. 18, 1861.

Sarapinagh. A tribe or division living in 1608 on Nanticoke r., on the eastern shore of Maryland. It is probable that they were a part of the Nanticoke tribe.

Sarapinagh.—Simons in Smith (1629), Va., I, 175, repr. 1819. **Soraphanigh.**—Purchas, Pilgrimes, IV, 1713, 1626.

Sarasota. Mentioned by Armistead (H. R. Doc. 247, 27th Cong., 2d sess., 14, 1842) as a Seminole settlement in Florida in 1841; pop. 30 or 40. Doubtless situated at or near the site of the present town of that name in Manatee co.

Saratoga ('the place where ashes or alkaline substances float.'—Hewitt). According to Macauley, the name of a Mohawk band (village?) formerly occupying the w. bank of the Hudson, about Saratoga and Stillwater, in Saratoga co., N. Y.

Oh-sa-ra-kas.—Macauley, N. Y., II, 174, 1829. **Saratogas.**—Bollan (1748) in Mass. Hist. Soc. Coll., 1st s., VI, 135, 1800.

Saratoga. A kind of trunk. Bartlett (Dict. of Americanisms, 551, 1877) says: "The enormous trunks carried by fashionable ladies to Saratoga Springs have obtained for them the specific name of 'Saratoga trunks,' or Saratogas." From the place-name Saratoga (q. v.), a word of Iroquois origin. Another term from this region is "Saratoga chips"—potatoes sliced thin and fried crisp in hot fat—so-called because they were first made popular in the Saratoga hotels. (A. F. C.)

Sarauahi. Apparently the name of two villages in N. E. Florida in the 16th century. One marked on the De Bry map of 1591 as Sarrauahi (river) is described by Laudonnière in 1564 as on an inlet N. of St John r., and about 2 leagues from the French Ft Caroline on the s. bank of the river, near its mouth. This probably belonged to the Saturiba tribe. The other, probably Calanay of the De Bry map, is described by Fontaneda, about 1575, as 50 or 60 leagues up St John r. and subject to Utina, the Timucua chief. Laudonnière also notes "Calany" as subject to Utina. The printed synonym forms for both are interchangeable. (J. M.)

Azavay.—Fontaneda (ca. 1575) in Ternaux-Compans, Voy., XX, 35, 1841 (middle St John r.; misprint for Zaravay in same passage of Smith trans.). **Calanay.**—De Bry, map (1591), in Le Moyne Narr., Appleton trans., 1857 (middle St John r.; identical?). **Calanio.**—Barcia, Ensayo, 48, 1723 (identical?). **Calany.**—Laudonnière (1564) in French, Hist. Coll. La., n. s., 243, 1869 (the Calanany of De Bry map, and noted as subject to Utina). **Saranay.**—Fontaneda (ca. 1575) in French, Hist. Coll. La., 2d s., II, 264, 1875 (middle St John r.). **Sarauahi.**—Laudonnière (1564) quoted by Shipp, De Soto and Fla., 519, 1881 (N. of St John r.). **Saraurahi.**—Laudonnière (1564) in French, Hist. Coll. La., n. s., 315, 1869 (N. of St John r.; misprint second r for v). **Saravay.**—Fontaneda Memoir (ca. 1575), Smith trans., 25, 1854 (mentioned as on middle St John and subject to Utina, chief of the Timucua). **Sarrauahi.**—De Bry, map (1591), in Le Moyne Narr., Appleton trans., 1875 (river short distance N. of St John r.). **Serranay.**—Laudonnière (1564) in French, Hist. Coll. La., n. s., 257, 1869 (identical?). **Zaravay.**—Fontaneda Memoir (ca. 1575), Smith trans., 25, 1854.

Sardlok. An Eskimo village on the w. coast of Greenland, lat. 64° 20′.—Nansen, Eskimo Life, 166, 1894.

Sarfalik ('place of guillemots'). An Ita Eskimo village near Smith sd., N. Greenland.—Heilprin, Peary Relief Exped., 104, 1893.

Serwådling.—Stein in Petermanns Mitt., 198, 1902. **Severnik.**—Kane, Arct. Explor., II, 125, 1856.

Sargarría. Mentioned as a New Mexico mission in 1742.—Mendoza et al. (1742–3) quoted by Bancroft, Ariz. and N. Mex., 244, 1889.

Sargentaruka. A former village of the Rumsen division of the Costanoan family, 21 m. E. of Carmelo r., Cal. It is said to have been populous.

Sargenta rucas.—Taylor in Cal. Farmer, Apr. 20, 1860. **Sargentarukas.**—Ibid. **Sirkhintaruk.**—Kroeber, Costanoan MS., Univ. Cal., 1902 (Sirkhinta, name of place with locative ending -ta; ruk, 'houses,' 'village': said to have been the same as Kakontaruk, or Kakonkaruk, at Pt Sur, s. of Monterey).

Saric. A rancheria, probably of the Papago, visited by Kino in 1694; the seat of a mission from about 1700 (Bancroft, Ariz. and N. Mex., 357, 1889). Situated on the w. bank of Rio Altar, in N. Sonora, Mexico.

Nuestra Señora de los Dolores del Saric.—Orozco y Berra, Geog., 347, 1864. **Oacpuaguigua.**—Quijano (1757) in Doc. Hist. Mex., 4th s., I, 52, 1856. **Saric.**—Kino (1699), ibid., 294. **Sarie.**—Box, Adventures, 270, 1869. **Sário.**—Hardy, Travels, 422, 1829. **Sarique.**—Keler (1752) in Doc. Hist. Mex., 4th s., I, 26, 1856. **Sarrii.**—Venegas, Hist. Cal., I, 304, 1759. **Sta. Gertrudis Saric.**—Kino (1706) quoted by Bancroft, No. Mex. States, I, 501, 1884.

Sarkak. A Danish Eskimo village on the Waigat, N. Greenland.—Wyckoff in Scribner's Mag., XXVIII, 450, 1900.

Sarkarmiut. A ruined Angmagsalingmiut village on the E. coast of Greenland, lat. 66° 19′.—Meddelelser om Grönland, XXVII, map, 1902.

Sarontac. A former village, presumably Costanoan, connected with Dolores mission, San Francisco, Cal.—Taylor in Cal. Farmer, Oct. 18, 1861.

Sarrochau. A former Winnebago village on the site of Taycheedah, Fond du Lac co., Wis.—Grignon in Wis. Hist. Soc. Coll., III, 288, 1857.

Sarrope. According to information of a former Spanish captive among the Calusa (q. v.) in Florida, as related to

Laudonnière in 1564, a great lake about 2 or 3 days journey N. E. from the Calusa territory and situated between that and C. Cañaveral. It had an inhabited island whose people were warlike and independent and traded coonti root to the neighboring tribes. This body of water was probably Kissimmee or, possibly, Okeechobee lake. (J. M.)

Sarrope.—Laudonnière (1564) in Basanier, Historie, in French, Hist. Coll. La., n. s., 282, 1869. Serrope.—De l'Isle, map, 1700 (incorrectly marked as a town on the s. w. coast of Florida).

Sarsi (from the Siksika *sa arsi*, 'not good'). A tribe of the eastern group of the northern division of the Athapascan family. There is a myth or tradition found among the Tsattine, according to which their secession from the tribe is said to have been the sequel of a blood feud. According to this story, a dog belonging to a member of one division was killed by a young man of the other division, who was slain by the owner and avenged by his relatives. The animosity engendered between the two factions became so rooted and vindictive that the weaker party migrated. The explanation the Sarsi themselves give is one common in the Plains region. The people were crossing a lake when the hand of a boy became attached to a horn protruding from the ice. When the horn was struck the ice broke. Those who had not reached the neighborhood remained in the N. as the Tsattine, those who had already passed went on to the s. and became the Sarsi, and those near by were engulfed in the lake and became mythical water beings. At the beginning of the 19th century the Sarsi numbered 120 warriors, in 35 tents (Mackenzie, Voy., I, lxx, 1801). Their hunting grounds were on the upper Saskatchewan, toward the Rocky mts. Umfreville, in 1790 (Maine Hist. Soc. Coll., VI, 270, 1859), spoke of them as one of the leading tribes trading with the Hudson's Bay Co. Mackenzie found them on the N. branch of Saskatchewan r., few in number and appearing to have come from the N. W. He identified them with the Sekani. Richardson (Arct. Exped., II, 6, 1851) said they lived near the Rocky mts., between the sources of Athabasca and Saskatchewan rs. Their customs have been greatly modified by their long residence among the Siksika, but their language remains fairly constant. Gallatin said that the Tsattine and Sarsi together numbered 150 hunters. Wilson, in 1888, found two bands, the Blood Sarsi and the real Sarsi. In 1897 two divisions were reported, one at Ft Calgary, on Bow r., lat. 51°, and the other near Battleford. In 1909 there were 197 engaged in farming, stock-raising, and woodcutting on the reserve at Calgary, Alberta, mingling little

with other Indians except on occasions of ceremony. Rev. E. F. Wilson, who visited them in 1888, describes them as inferior in mental capacity to the Siksika, not so fine and tall a race, and less communicative, having no liking for white people.

Their dress consists of the breechclout, blanket, leggings, beaded moccasins, and a gray, white, or colored blanket thrown loosely over one or both shoulders. Both men and women paint the upper part of their faces with ocher or vermilion. They wear brooches and earrings of steel, and bracelets and necklaces of beads, bones, claws, teeth, and brass wire, and finger-rings of coiled brass wire. They live in conical tipis in summer, and in low log huts, plastered with mud, in winter. Their chief handicrafts are the preparation of skins, of which they make their clothing and saddles for their numerous ponies, and the making of bows of cherry wood and arrows of willow, which are winged with feathers and pointed with sharp filed pieces of scrap-iron, the shaft having four shallow grooves down its entire length. Some of the men have from two to four wives, whom they can divorce at pleasure, restoring the presents received with the wife, or their equivalent. Girls are often betrothed at 10 years of age and married at 14. After betrothal they must look no man in the face. A man must not meet his mother-in-law, and if he accidentally touch her he must give her a present. The Sarsi have little knowledge of medicinal roots and herbs; most of their physicians are women. As among many other Indian tribes, a doctor when called in heats a stone in the fire, touches it with his finger, and with the same finger presses various parts of the patient's body in order to divine the seat and character of the malady. He then sucks the affected place, pretending to draw out the disease and spit it from his mouth, the performance being accompanied with the beating of a drum and the shaking of a rattle. The Sarsi know how to cauterize efficaciously with burning touchwood, and they use the vapor bath, building a low bower of bent green saplings covered with blankets, within which red-hot stones are placed in a hole in the ground, and over these the patient pours water that is handed him from outside. When thoroughly steamed he rushes out and plunges into cold water, sometimes with fatal result. The dead are wound in tent cloths and blankets and deposited on scaffolds in a burial ground. A warrior's pony is shot, and blankets, clothing, utensils, and food are left beside the corpse. The bodies of distinguished warriors or chiefs are placed in tipis (4th Rep.

N. W. Tribes Canada, 242–255, 1889). The language of the Sarsi is uncorrupted, notwithstanding association with the Siksika. (J. O. D. P. E. G.)

Bongees.—Chappell, Hudson's Bay, 166, 1817 (possibly a misprint). **Castors des Prairies.**—Petitot, Autour du lac des Esclaves, 362, 1891. **Circee.**—Franklin, Journ. Polar Sea, I, 170, 1824. **Ciriés.**—Gairdner (1835) in Jour. Geog. Soc. Lond., XI, 257, 1841. **Isashbahátse̊.**—Curtis, N. Am. Ind., 180, 1909 ('bad robes': Crow name). **Lurcees.**—Can. Ind. Rep. 1872, 63, 1873 (misprint). **Mauvais Monde, des Pieds-Noirs.**—Petitot, op. cit. **Sa arcez.**—Petitot in Jour. Roy. Geog. Soc., 652, 1883 ('not good': Siksika name). **Sa-arcix.**—Petitot, Autour du lac des Esclaves, 362, 1891. **Sarcees.**—Tanner, Narr., 293, 1830. **Sarcess.**—Ibid., 390. **Sarois.**—Maximilian, Trav., 242, 1843. **Sarcix.**—Petitot, Autour du lac des Esclaves, 362, 1891. **Sarsees.**—Mackenzie, Voy., lxx, 1801. **Sarséwi.**—Petitot in Jour. Roy. Geog. Soc., 652, 1883 (Cree name). **Sarxi.**—Wilson in 4th Rep. N. W. Tribes Can., 11, 1888. **Sassee.**—Franklin, Journ. Polar Sea, I, 170, 1824. **Sassis.**—Maximilian, Trav., 242, 1843. **Searcies.**—Ind. Aff. Rep., 473, 1838. **Sircie.**—Robinson, Great Fur Land, 188, 1879. **Sorsi.**—Richardson, Jour., II, 6, 1851. **Soténná.**—Wilson in 4th Rep. N. W. Tribes Can., 11, 1888 (own name). **Surcee.**—Smet, Oregon Miss., 327, 1847. **Surci.**—Richardson, Jour., II, 6, 1851. **Surcie.**—Smet, Miss. de l'Oreg., 252, 1848. **Sursis.**—Duflot de Mofras, Oregon, II, 342, 1844. **Sussee.**—Umfreville (1790) in Maine Hist. Soc. Coll., VI, 270, 1859. **Sussekoon.**—Henry, Blackfoot MS. vocab., 1808 (Siksika name). **Sussez.**—Armstrong, Oregon, 114, 1857. **Sussi.**—Latham in Trans. Philol. Soc. Lond., 66, 1856. **Swees.**—Chappell, Hudson's Bay, 166, 1817. **Tcō'kō.**—Chamberlain in Rep. on N. W. Tribes Can., Brit. A. A. S., 8, 1892 (Kutenai name). **Tsô-Ottinè.**—Petitot, Autour du lac des Esclaves, 362, 1891 ('people among the beavers'). **Tsū'qōs.**—Chamberlain in Rep. on N. W. Tribes Can., Brit. A. A. S., 8, 1892 (Kutenai name). **Ussinnewudj Eninnewug.**—Tanner, Narr., 316, 1830 ('stone mountain men': Ottawa name).

Sasabac. A rancheria of the Maricopa on Gila r., Ariz., in 1744.—Sedelmair (1744) cited by Bancroft, Ariz. and N. Mex., 366, 1889.

Sasabaithi (*Säsábäithi*, 'looking up,' or 'looking around,' i. e. 'watchers'). A band of the Arapaho, q. v.

Saschutkenne ('people of the black bear'). A tribe of the Sekani who hunt on the w. declivity of the Rocky mts., about lat. 56° and northward, and before 1892 traded at Ft Connolly, Brit. Col. Dawson (Rep. Geol. Surv. Can., 200B, 1889) stated that they had recently returned to the headwaters of Black r. after having abandoned the region for a number of years. In 1890 Morice gave their habitat as Thutage lake and northward, w. of the Rocky mts.

Al-ta'-tin of Bear Lake.—Dawson in Rep. Geol. Surv. Can., 1887–8, 200B, 1889. **Bear Lake Indians.**—Ibid. **Sas-chu-tqéne.**—Morice, inf'n, 1890. **Saschût-'qenne.**—Morice in Trans. Can. Inst., 1892–93, 29, 1895. **Sat-e-loo'-ne.**—Dawson, op. cit. (so called by the Titshotina).

Saskatchewan Assiniboin. An Assiniboin band of 50 lodges that dwelt in 1808 about Eagle hills and s. Saskatchewan r., Assiniboia.—Henry-Thompson Jour., II, 523, 1897.

Saskatoon. A name in use in the Canadian N. W. for the service berry (*Amelanchier canadensis*): probably a corruption of *misáskwatomin*, which is the name applied to the fruit in the Cree dialect of Algonquian, signifying 'fruit of *misáskwat*, the tree of much wood,' from *mis* 'much', and *áskwat* 'wood'. Saskatoon occurs also as a place-name in the above-named region. (A. F. C.)

Sassaba. A minor Chippewa chief of the Crane gens, who first appears in history as a member of Tecumseh's forces at the battle of the Thames, Canada, Oct. 5, 1813, in which his brother, to whom he seems to have been greatly attached, was killed while fighting by his side. This incident embittered Sassaba against the Americans during the remainder of his life. When Lewis Cass visited Sault Ste Marie, Mich., in 1820, to negotiate a treaty with the Chippewa for purchasing a small tract of land, Sassaba, who was one of the chiefs assembled on this occasion, not only manifested his bitter animosity toward the United States authorities, but displayed his eccentric character as well. During the council he hoisted the British flag over his tent, which was torn down by Gen. Cass in person. On this occasion he was thus dressed: "Beginning at the top an eagle's feather, bear's grease, vermilion and indigo, a red British military coat with two enormous epaulets, a large British silver medal, breech-clout, leggins, and moccasins." He arose in council and remarked gruffly that the Chippewa did not wish to sell their land; and refusing the pipe, kicked over the presents that had been placed before him, and rushed from the tent under its side. He refused to sign the treaty (Wis. Hist. Soc. Coll., v, 414–15, 1868). On Sept. 25, 1822, Sassaba and his wife and child were drowned at Sault Ste Marie. He had been drinking heavily at Point aux Pins, 6 m. above the rapids, and was intoxicated during the trip. According to Schoolcraft (Pers. Mem., 119, 1851) he would often walk through the village where he resided, divested of every particle of clothing except a large gray wolf's skin, which he had drawn over his body in such manner as to let the tail dangle behind. From this habit the name Myeengun ('wolf') was sometimes applied to him. He was also known as The Count. (C. T.)

Sassacus (perhaps the equivalent of Massachuset *Sassakusu*, 'he is wild' (untamed), 'fierce.'—Gerard). The noted and last chief of the Pequot tribe while yet in their integrity; born near Groton, Conn., about 1560, killed by the Mohawk in New York, June 1637. He was the son and successor of Wopigwooit, the first chief of the tribe with whom the whites had come in contact, who was killed by the Dutch, about 1632, at or near the site of Hartford, Conn., then the principal Pequot settlement. Soon after assuming the chiefship, in Oct. 1634 Sassacus sent an emissary to the governor of the Massachusetts Bay colony to ask for a treaty of friendship, offering as an inducement to surrender all the rights of the Pequot to the lands they had conquered, provided the colonists would settle a plantation among his people, an offer which he must have known he could not carry out, and perhaps had no intention of trying to fulfill, as he nourished bitter enmity toward the whites. This proposal had the effect of turning against him Uncas, the Mohegan chief, who was related to him by both blood and marriage. The domain of the Pequot during Sassacus's chiefship extended from Narragansett bay to Hudson r., including the larger part of Long id., and it is said that at the height of his prosperity no fewer than 26 sachems were subordinate to him. Because of his depredations, especially on the neighboring tribes, the colonists decided in 1636 to make war on the Pequot. The name of Sassacus had inspired such terror among the surrounding tribes that the Indian allies of the whites could not believe the latter would dare to make a direct attack on the stronghold of this wily chief. The war was soon ended, and Sassacus, having suffered defeat and the loss of a large portion of his people, fled with 20 or 30 of his warriors to the Mohawk country. Even here he found no safety, for before the close of 1637 his scalp and those of his brother and five other Pequot chiefs were sent to the governor of Massachusetts by the Mohawk. As Sassacus had carried with him in his flight a large quantity of wampum, a desire on the part of the Mohawk to possess this treasure may have led to the death of himself and his followers. Sassacus was spoken of by the commissioners in 1647 as "the malignant, furious Piquot," while, on the other hand, De Forest styles him "a renowned warrior and a noble and high-spirited man." Consult De Forest, Inds. Conn., 1852; Stone, Uncas and Miantonomoh, 1842; Coll. Mass. Hist. Soc., 1st s., IX, 1804; Drake, Inds. N. A., 1880.   (C. T.)

Sastaretsi. See *Adario*.

Sastean. A linguistic family established by Powell (7th Rep. B. A. E., 105, 1891) to include a single tribe, known as Shasta, formerly occupying a part of the drainage area of Klamath and Sacramento rs., N. California. The name is based on the form Saste, given the tribe by Hale (U. S. Expl. Exped., VI, 218, 1846). See *Shasta, Shastan Family*.

Sasthut ('black-bear bathing place'). A Tatshiautin village on Connolly lake, Brit. Col.

Sas-thût.—Morice, Notes on W. Dénés, 27, 1893, Sést'sethût.—Morice in Trans. Roy. Soc. Can., x. 109, 1893.

Sasuagel. A Chumashan village formerly on Santa Cruz id., Cal.
Sasaguel.—Bancroft, Nat. Races, I, 459, 1874. Sasuagel.—Taylor in Cal. Farmer, Apr. 24, 1863. Swa-hŏl.—Henshaw, Buenaventura MS. vocab., B. A., E., 1884.

Satank. See *Setangya*.

Satanta (properly *Set-t'aiñ'-te*, 'White Bear'). A noted Kiowa chief, born about 1830; died by suicide in prison, Oct. 11, 1878. For about 15 years before his death he was recognized as second chief in his tribe, the first rank being accorded to his senior, Setängyä, or Satank, and later to Lone Wolf, although probably neither of these equaled him in force and ability. His eloquence in council gained for him the title of "Orator of the Plains," while his manly boldness and directness and his keen humor made him a favorite with army officers and commissioners in spite of his known hostility to the white man's laws and civilization. He was one of the signers of the Medicine Lodge treaty of 1867, by which his tribe agreed to go on a reservation, his being the second Kiowa name attached to the document. The tribe, however, delayed coming in until compelled by Custer, who seized Satanta and Lone Wolf as hostages for the fulfilment of the conditions. For boastfully avowing his part in a murderous raid into Texas in 1871, he, with Setangya and Big Tree, was arrested and held for trial in Texas. Setangya was killed while resisting the guard. The other two were tried and sentenced to life imprisonment in the Texas State penitentiary. Two years later they were released, conditional upon the good behavior of their people, but in the fall of 1874, the Kiowa having again gone on the warpath, Satanta was rearrested and taken back to the penitentiary where he finally committed suicide by throwing himself from an upper story of the hospital.

In appearance Satanta was a typical Plains warrior, of fine physique, erect bearing, and piercing glance. One who saw him in prison in 1873 describes him as "a tall, finely formed man, princely in carriage, on whom even the prison garb seemed elegant," and meeting his visitor "with as much dignity and grace as though he were a monarch receiving a foreign ambassador." His memory is cherished by the Kiowa as that of one of their greatest men. See Mooney, Calendar History of the Kiowa Inds., 17th Rep. B. A. E., 1898.   (J. M.)

Satapo (probably Creek: *sáta* 'persimmon,' *api* 'tree'). A town, possibly of the Upper Creeks, mentioned by Juan de la Vandera in 1567 (Smith, Colec.

Doc. Fla., I, 18, 1857); apparently on the N. border of the Creek country.

Satayomi. A former village connected with San Francisco Solano mission, Cal.—Bancroft, Hist. Cal., II, 506, 1886.

Satchin ('red rock'). An Apache clan or band at San Carlos agency and Ft Apache, Ariz., in 1881.
Char-cheiné.—White, Apache Names of Ind. Tribes, MS., B. A. E. (= 'country with red rocks'). Satchin.—Bourke in Jour. Am. Folk-lore, III, 111, 1890.

Satchotugottine ('people of the lake of bears of the plains'). A part of the Kawchodinne living immediately N. of Great Bear lake, Mackenzie Ter., Canada.
Sa-tchô-gottinè.—Petitot in Bul. Soc. de Géog. Paris, chart, 1875 ('people of bear lake'). Satchô t'u gottiné.—Petitot, Dict. Dèné-Dindjié, xx, 1876.

Satechi. A former rancheria of the Jova, containing also some Tarahumare, situated in E. Sonora, on the headwaters of the Rio Yaqui, about 30 m. w. sw. from Bacadeguachi, of which it was a visita in 1762. It was abandoned between 1764 and 1800 on account of Apache depredations. See Bandelier in Arch. Inst. Papers, III, 56, 1890; IV, 511, 1892; also, Rudo Ensayo (ca. 1763), Guiteras trans., 217, 1894.

Sathlrekhtun (*Saçl'-rĕq-tûn*, 'village on the dark side of a canyon where the sun never shines'). A former village of the Mishikhwutmetunne on Coquille r., Oreg.—Dorsey in Jour. Am. Folk-lore, III, 232, 1890.

Saticoy. A Chumashan village, containing about 20 Indians in 1863, on the lower part of Santa Paula r., Ventura co., Cal., about 8 m. from the sea.
Sa-ak-ti'-kâ-i.—Henshaw, Buenaventura MS. vocab., B. A. E., 1884. Saticoy.—Taylor in Cal. Farmer, July 24, 1863.

Satquin. An Abnaki village on the coast of Maine, s. w. of Kennebec r., in 1614.—Smith (1631) in Mass. Hist. Soc. Coll., 3d s., III, 22, 1833.

Satsk (*Sätsq*). A Bellacoola town on Dean inlet, Brit. Col.; one of the five still inhabited. See *Kinisquit*.
Satskōmilh.—Tolmie and Dawson, Vocabs. Brit. Col., 122B, 1884 (= 'people of Satsk'). Sätsq.—Boas in Mem. Am. Mus. Nat. Hist., II, 49, 1900.

Satsop. A Salish division on Satsop r., emptying into Chehalis r., Wash. Usually classed under the collective term Lower Chehalis.
Sachap.—Wilkes, U. S. Expl. Exped., v, 132, 1845. Satcap.—Ross in Ind. Aff. Rep., 18, 1870. Satchap.—Swan, N. W. Coast, 309, 1857. Sat-sa-pish.—Eells, letter of Feb. 1886. Satsop.—Ford in Ind. Aff. Rep. 1857, 341, 1858.

Satucket (abbrev. of *Sâkitûkut*, 'at the mouth of tidal river'). A village, probably of the Nauset, near Brewster, Barnstable co., Mass., in 1687. Gookin says it was subject to the Wampanoag.
Sahquatucket.—Rawson and Danforth (1698) in Mass. Hist. Soc. Coll., 1st s., x, 133, 1809. Saquatucket.—Treat (1687), ibid., 4th s., v, 186, 1861. Saquetuckett.—Hinckley (1685), ibid., 133. Satucket.—Freeman (1685), ibid., 132. Satuket.—Ibid., III, 97, note, 1856. Saughtughtett.—Dermer

(1620), ibid., III, 97, 1856 (misprint). Saukatucket.—Freeman. ibid., 1st s., VIII, 151, 1802. Sawkattukett.—Gookin (1674), ibid., I, 148, 1806.

Satuit. A village, probably of the Nauset, existing in 1674 on Cotuit r., near Mashpee, Barnstable co., Mass.
Sanctuit.—Mass. Hist. Soc. Coll., 1st s., I, 197, note, 1806. Satuit.—Bourne (1674), ibid.

Satumuo. A former rancheria connected with Dolores mission, San Francisco, Cal.
Satumuo.—Taylor in Cal. Farmer, Oct. 18, 1861. Saturaumo.—Ibid.

Saturiba. A Timucuan tribe in Florida, occupying, about 1565, the territory on both sides of lower St John r., with the adjacent coast territory, northward to Satilla r., Ga., including Cumberland (Tacatacuru) id., beyond which was Guale (Yamasee) territory. The statement quoted in Brinton (Fla. Penin., 120, 1859) making St. Helena, S. Car., their northern boundary, is incorrect. They were at war with the Timucua, their nearest neighbors higher up on the river, and afterward with the Spaniards, but welcomed and aided the French during the short stay of the latter. Their chief was said to rule 30 subchiefs, each perhaps representing a different village. The name may have been properly that of the head chief rather than of the tribe, the two being frequently confused by the early explorers. It does not occur in Pareja's list of Timucuan dialects in 1612, the tribe being probably noted under one of the unidentified names in the list, viz, Itafi, Tucururu, or Mocama, the last two being specially designated as located on the coast. All the Indians of this region were Christianized by Franciscan missionaries before the end of the 16th century. See *Patica, Timucua, Timucuan Family*. (J. M.)
Satiroua.—Anon. author of Reprinse (ca. 1568) in Ternaux-Compans, Voy., xx, 324, 1841. Satoriva.—Fontaneda (ca. 1575) in French, Hist. Coll. La., 2d s., II, 264, 1875. Satouriona.—B. Smith, note to Fontaneda Mem., 46, 1854 (misprint n for u). Satourioua.—Laudonnière (1565) in French, Hist. Coll. La., 315, 1869. Saturiba.—Barcia, Ensayo, 100, 1723 (ordinary Spanish form). Saturiora.—Brackenridge, Views of La., 48, 1815 (misprint second r for u). Sotoriva.—Fontaneda (ca. 1575) as quoted by Ternaux-Compans, Voy., xx, 34, 1841; also as quoted in B. Smith trans., 24, 1854. Soturiba.—Brinton, Fla. Penin., 120, 1859.

Saturna Island Indians. The local name for a small body of Sanetch on Saturna id., off the s. E. coast of Vancouver id. Pop. 5 in 1892, the last time the name is officially noted.

Satwiwa (*Sat-wi'-wa*). A Chumashan village formerly in the interior of Ventura co., Cal., at a place called Rancho Alazuna.—Henshaw, Buenaventura MS. vocab., B. A. E., 1884.

Sauchu. A Chumashan village formerly near Santa Inés mission, Santa Barbara co., Cal.
Sanchu.—Bancroft, Nat. Races, I, 459, 1874. Sauchu.—Taylor in Cal. Farmer, Oct. 18, 1861.

Saucita. A Papago village in s. Arizona, with 250 inhabitants in 1863.

San Laida.—Browne, Apache Country, 291, 1869 (misquoting Poston). Sou Saida.—Poston in Ind. Aff. Rep. 1863, 385, 1864.

Saucon. A former village, presumably Costanoan, connected with Dolores mission, San Francisco, Cal.—Taylor in Cal. Farmer, Oct. 18, 1861.

Saugahatchi (*sauga* 'gourd', *hatchi* 'creek'). A former Upper Creek town on an E. branch of Tallapoosa r., 10 m. below Eufaula, Ala., probably in Talladega or Clay co.

Sauga Hátchi.—Gatschet, Creek Migr. Leg., I, 143, 1884. Sogahatches.—Swan (1791) in Schoolcraft, Ind. Tribes, v, 262, 1855. Sougahatchee.—Campbell (1836) in H. R. Doc. 274, 25th Cong., 2d sess., 20, 1838. Sou-go-hat-che.—Hawkins (1779), Sketch, 49, 1848. Sowgahatcha.—H. R. Doc. 274, 25th Cong., 2d sess., 152, 1838. Sow ga hatch cha.—Parsons (1833) in Schoolcraft, Ind. Tribes, IV, 578, 1854.

Saugiesta. A tribe named by Le Sueur in 1700 as about the L. Superior region; possibly the Sauk, but thought by Shea to be the Saulteurs, i. e., the Chippewa.

Sangiestas.—Le Sueur (1700) as quoted by Shea, Early Voy., 92, 1861. Saugiestas.—Le Sueur, as quoted by Neill, Minn., 154, 1858.

Saugus ('small outlet.'—Hewitt). A former village near Lynn, Essex co., Mass. It seems to have belonged to the Massachuset, but may have been Pennacook. The chief of Saugus ruled also the Indians at Marblehead.

Cawgust.—Josselyn (1675) in Mass. Hist. Soc. Coll., 3d s., III, 322, 1833. Sagus.—Humfrey (1630), ibid., 4th s., VI, 10, 1863. Sagust.—Peter (1639), ibid., VII, 202, 1865. Sangut.—Josselyn (1675), ibid., 3d s., III, 322, 1833. Saugus.—Prince (1631), ibid., 2d s., VII, 31, 1818. Saugust.—Williams (ca. 1638), ibid., 4th s., VI, 252, 1863. Sawgus.—Prince (1631), ibid., 2d s., VII, 33, 1818.

Sauk (*Osā'kiwŭgⁱ*, 'people of the outlet,' or, possibly, 'people of the yellow earth,' in contradistinction from the Muskwakiwuk, 'Red Earth People', a name of the Foxes). One of a number of Algonquian tribes whose earliest known habitat was embraced within the eastern peninsula of Michigan, the other tribes being the Potawatomi, the "Nation of the Fork," and probably the famous Mascoutens and the Foxes. The present name of Saginaw bay (*Săgină'we*, signifying 'the country or place of the Sauk') is apparently derived from the ethnic appellative Sauk. There is presumptive evidence that the Sauk, with the tribes mentioned above, were first known to Europeans under the general ethnic term "Gens de Feu" or that of "Asistagueronon," the latter being the Huron translation of the specific name Potawatomi, both the terms in question being first recorded by Champlain and Sagard. In 1616 Champlain, while in what is now Ontario, learned from the Tionontati, or Tobacco Nation, that their kindred, the Neutral Nation, aided the Ottawa (Cheueux releuez) in waging war against the Gens de Feu, i. e. 'People of the Fire,' and that the Ottawa carried on a warfare against "another nation of savages who were called Asista-

gueronon, which is to say, 'People of the Place of the Fire,'" who were distant from the Ottawa 10 days' journey; and lastly, in more fully describing the country, manners, and customs of the Ottawa, he added, "In the first place, they wage war against another nation of savages who are called Asistagueronon, which is to say, 'people of the fire,' distant from them 10 days' journey." He supplemented this statement with the remark that "they pressed me strongly to assist them against their enemies, who are on the shore of the Mer Douce [Lake Huron], distant 200 leagues." Sagard, who was in Canada during the years 1623–26, wrote in his Histoire du Canada (I, 194, ed. 1866), that the sedentary and the migratory Ottawa together waged war against the Asistagueronon, who were 9 or 10 days' journey by canoe from the Ottawa, a distance which he estimated at "about 200 leagues and more of travel."

Before the Sauk became known as an independent tribe, it is evident that they formed a part of this group of important Algonquian communities, which was called by the Hurons and cognate peoples "Asistagueronon," and by the French, "Nation or People of the Fire," a translation of the former appellative. In order therefore to understand clearly the ethnic relations of the Sauk, it will be necessary to review the earliest known facts relating to this interesting group of tribes. So far as known, the Sauk were first mentioned independently in the Jesuit Relation for 1640 (35, ed. 1858) under the generic Huron name Hvattoehronon, i. e. 'people of the sunset,' or briefly, 'westerners.' They were here mentioned among a number of other tribes along with the Foxes (Skenchiohronon), the Potawatomi (Attistaehronon), the Kickapoo (Ontarahronon, 'lake people'), the Mascoutens (Oherokouaehronon, 'people of the place of grass'), the Winnebago (Aoueatsiouaenhronon, 'saline or brackish water people'), and the Crane band of the Miami (Attochingochronon). The following citations from the Jesuit Relations embody some of the evidence that the Sauk, the Potawatomi (q. v.), and the Nation of the Fork, were generally comprised in the Huron ethnic appellative Asistagueronon, i. e. 'People of the Place of Fire,' which is the literal signification of the tribal name Potawatomi.

Father Allouez, the first person to describe the Sauk, wrote in 1667 that they were more savage than all the other peoples he had met; that they were a populous tribe, although they had no fixed dwelling place, being wanderers and vagabonds in the forests. He was told that if they or the Foxes found a person in an isolated place they would kill him, especially if he were a Frenchman, for they could not endure the sight of the whiskers of the European. Yet, two years later he reported that the first place in which he began to give religious instruction was in a village of the "Ousaki," situated at the DePere Rapids, Wis., wherein he found several tribes in winter quarters, namely, the "Ousaki, the Pouteouatami, the Outagami [Foxes], and the Ovenibigoutz [Winnebago]— about 600 souls." Allouez adds that a league and a half away there was another village of about 150 persons; that at 4 leagues farther away there was another of about 100 persons; that at 8 leagues away there was another of about 300 persons, situated on the opposite side of the bay; that at 25 leagues, at a place called Ouestatinong, dwelt the Foxes, and that at a day's journey from this tribe dwelt the Makskouteng [Mascoutens] and the Oumami [Miami], the latter being reputed to be a band of the Illinois. The Indians of this region, the Father reported, were "more barbarous than usual," having no ingenuity, not knowing even how "to make a bark dish or a ladle," using shells instead.

In the Jesuit Relation for 1658 (21, ed. 1858) Father Ragueneau reported what he had learned concerning the upper lake tribes from Father Bruillettes, a skilful and accomplished Huron and Algonquian linguist, who in listing these tribes used to some extent the knowledge of these communities obtained by Radisson and Groseilliers, who had then but recently discovered and visited a number of them. In the descriptive list of these tribes cited by Father Ragueneau, the following statements are pertinent here: "The third nation is distant about 3 days' journey by water from the town of St Michel, going inland. It is composed of the Makoutensak and the Outitchakouk [i. e. the Crane Miami]. The two Frenchmen [probably Radisson and Groseilliers] who have traveled in those countries say that these people are of a very mild nature." . . . "The fourteenth nation has 30 towns, inhabited by the Atsistagherronnons. They are southwest a quarter south at 6 or 7 days' journey from St Michel. The Onondaga have recently declared war against them." This is presumptive evidence from seemingly competent authority that the ethnic names Mascoutens and Atsistagherronnons were not in 1658 by any means synonymous or convertible epithets, and that therefore the peoples designated by them were not identical. This confusion as to names in question persisted until about 1671, as the following citations will show. In the Jesuit Relation for 1670 (99, ed. 1858) Father Allouez stated that "We entered the river which leads to the Machkoutench, called Assista Ectaeronnons, Nation of the Fire, by the Hurons"; but in the Relation for the following year (p. 45) Father Allouez stated that "The Nation of the Fire bears this name by an error, properly calling themselves Maskoutench, which signifies a land cleared of trees, such as is that which these people inhabit; but because by the change of a few letters which one makes, this same word signifies fire, it follows that one calls them the Nation of the Fire." There is in each of these statements an error which was due directly to the process of the gradual elimination of tribes becoming known from a group of unknown peoples or tribes which bore a generic name "people of the place of fire," derived from the specific name of an important one of these tribes, the Potawatomi (q. v.), whose name signifies literally, 'people of the place of fire.' This confounding of several tribes one with another, and the consequent misapplication of specific and generic names, were made evidently not by the Hurons but by French traders and missionaries.

In the Jesuit Relation for 1671 (25, ed. 1858) Father Dablon, speaking of Green bay, Wisconsin, wrote that the Menominee, the Sauk, the Potawatomi, and other neighboring tribes, "being driven from their own countries, which are the lands southward near Missilimakinac, have taken refuge at the head of this bay, beyond which one can see inland the 'Nation of the Fire,' or Mathkoutench, with one of the Illinois tribes called Oumiami, and the Foxes." And in the same Relation (p. 37), he said: "The three nations who are now in the bay of the Winnebago as strangers resided on the mainland which is s. of this island [i. e. Missilimakinac]— some on the shores of the Lake of the Illinois [i. e. Michigan], others on those of the Lake of the Hurons. A part of those who call themselves Salteurs [Chippewa] possessed lands on the mainland toward the w. . . . Four villages of the Ottawa also had their lands in these quarters, but especially those who bore the name of the island, calling themselves Missilimakinac, and who were so numerous that some of those who are still living [1670] assert that they composed 30 villages, and that they had enclosed themselves in a fort a league and a half in circuit, when the Iroquois, flushed with a victory gained over 3,000 men of this tribe who had carried the war even into the country of the Mohawk, came to defeat them." Further (p. 42), the Father relates: "Four nations make their abode here, namely, those who bear the name

Puants [i. e., the Winnebago], who have always lived here, as it were, in their own country, and who, having been defeated by the Illinois, their enemies, have been reduced from a very flourishing and populous people to nothing; the Potawatomi, the Sauk, and the Nation of the Fork (*de la Fourche*) also live here, but as strangers, the fear of the Iroquios having driven them from their lands, which are between the Lake of the Hurons and that of the Illinois." There can be little if any doubt that in these citations the names "Iroquois" and "Mohawk" should be replaced by "Neuters," who to these fugitive tribes were known also as 'Nadō'weg' (see *Nadowa*); otherwise established facts are contravened by these statements, and it has already been shown that the "Neutre Nation" aided the Ottawa against the tribes on the shores of L. Huron. The foregoing quotations make it evident that the Potawatomi, the Sauk, and the 'Nation of the Fork' were included in the Asistagueronon of Champlain and Sagard, represented by them as dwelling in 1616 on the western shore lands of L. Huron and farther westward. Thus far no evidence has been adduced to show that Mascoutens and Asistagueronon were at first convertible or synonymous appellatives.

Further, Father Dablon, in the Jesuit Relation for 1670 (79, ed. 1858), said with reference to the Sault Sainte Marie: "The first and native inhabitants of this place are those who call themselves Pahouiting8ach Irini, whom the French name Saulteurs, because these are they who dwell at the Sault, as in their own country, the others being there only by adoption; they number only 150 souls, but they have united with three other tribes, who number more than 550 persons, to whom they have made a cession of the rights of their native country; they also reside there fixedly, except during the time in which they go to hunt. Those whom one calls the Nouquet range for that purpose southward of L. Superior, whence they came originally, and the Outchibous [Chippewa] with the Marameg, northward of the same lake, which they regard as their own proper country."

From the Jesuit Relation for 1644 it is learned that the long struggle between the so-called "Neutral Nation" and the "Nation du Feu" at that time was still maintained with unabated fury. Father Jerome Lallemant (Jes. Rel. 1644, 98, ed. 1858) states that in the summer of 1642 the Neuters with a force of 2,000 warriors advanced into the country of the "Nation du Feu" and attacked a town of this tribe which was strongly defended by palisades and manned by 900 resolute warriors; that these patriots withstood

the assaults of the besiegers for 10 days, but that at the end of this time the devoted place was carried. Many of its defenders were killed on the spot, and 800 captives—men, women, and children—were taken; and 70 of the best warriors among the prisoners were burned at the stake, the merciless victors putting out the eyes and cutting away the lips of all the old men and leaving them thus to die miserably. The Father adds the interesting statement that "this Nation of the Fire is more populous than all the Neutral Nation, all the Hurons, and all the Iroquois, enemies of the Hurons, put together; it consists of a large number of villages wherein the Algonquin language is spoken." This last citation is further proof that the term "Fire Nation," or "Nation of the Place of Fire," at that period was applied in a broad general sense rather than in a specific one. Apparently it embraced all the tribes formerly dwelling in the eastern peninsula of the present state of Michigan, and later removed to the N. and W. shores of the present L. Michigan, and still later it embraced some of the Illinois tribes. From the Jesuit Relation for 1642, (97, ed. 1858) it is learned that the Saulteurs informed the Jesuit fathers that "a certain tribe more distant [than the Sault Sainte Marie from the Huron mission], which they call Pouteatami, had abandoned its country and had come to take refuge with the inhabitants of the Sault to escape from some other hostile tribe that vexes them with ceaseless wars." This shows that the Potawatomi were then westward from the home of the Saulteurs, and that their emigration from the Michigan peninsula was not then of many years' standing.

It has been shown from historical data that for a long period before 1651 the Neuters and the Ottawa together waged bitter warfare against a group of tribes which became known to the French writers as Gens de Feu, or 'People of the Fire,' and as Asistagueronon, or 'People of the Place of Fire,' and later as the Mascoutens, by an error, the last name meaning, as an appellative, 'People Dwelling on Small Prairies.' There is no known historical data showing that, during the time that the Ottawa and the Neuters occupied the peninsula N. of L. Erie, the Iroquois, specifically so called, carried on any warlike operations against tribes dwelling westward of the two just mentioned. The fact is that the name Nadoweg, or Nadō'weg, was a general name of hateful significance which was applied by Algonquian tribes generally to any people of Iroquoian stock, as the Neuters, the Tionontati, and the Hurons. Now, inasmuch as the Neuters with their allies, the Ottawa, encountered their enemies on the western "shores" of L. Huron, i. e., in the present Michigan peninsula, and as it is known that as late as 1642 the Neuters sent into this region a force of 2,000 warriors which destroyed a stronghold of their enemies, it can be said with propriety that the Algonquian tribes formerly inhabiting the peninsula were driven therefrom by the Nadŏ'weg, meaning, conclusively it would seem, the Neuters, but understood by the French missionaries and writers to signify the "Iroquois," properly so called. Hence, the confusion regarding the invaders who drove out the tribes formerly dwelling westward of L. Huron. But it is also true that after the total defeat of the Neuters in 1651 by the "true" Iroquois, or League of Five Nations, these latter tribes came in touch at once with the tribes which had been at war against the Neuters, and in some cases naturally the Iroquois inherited the quarrels of the Neuters. The Iroquois proper did not, therefore, drive out the Potawatomi, the Sauk, the Foxes, and the other fugitive tribes from their ancient territories w. of L. Huron, for the Potawatomi were in Wisconsin as early as 1634, when Nicolet found them there. It was nearly 20 years later that the "true" Iroquois advanced into the lake region in pursuit of the Hurons, the Tionontati, and the Neuter fugitives, fleeing from the ruins of their towns and homes.

It seems clear that the tribes of the Algonquian stock formerly inhabiting the northern peninsula of Michigan were driven out by the Neuters and the Ottawa, their allies. It is erroneous to assume that the fugitive tribes retreated first southward and then westward around the southern end of L. Michigan, directly across rather than directly away from the line of attack from the E. along Detroit and St Clair rs. It is learned from Perrot that the Neuters occupied Detroit r. Most Indians who have been forced to retire from a battlefield or from their homes have shown that they were past-masters in the art of eluding a pursuing foe, and it has not been shown that the Sauk, the Potawatomi, the Rasawakoueton or Fork tribe, and their allies, were devoid of this characteristic trait. It is not probable, therefore, that the Sauk, starting from the shores of Saginaw bay, deliberately exposed their flank and rear to the direct attacks of the Neuters over a march exceeding 300 m. The more probable course of the retreat of the Sauk and their allies from the Michigan peninsula was evidently northwestward across Mackinaw straits into northern Michigan, thence westward to the region

around Green bay and Fox r., where they were first found by the early French explorers.

From the Jesuit Relation for 1666–67 it is learned that bands of the Sauk and Foxes were dwelling in the vicinity of Shaugawaumikong (La Pointe) and that Father Allouez preached to them and baptized some of their children.

During 1671–72 the expatriated Hurons, composed largely of the Tionontati and the (Black) Squirrel band of the Ottawa (Sinagos), having perfected preparations, together marched against the Sioux, who were at peace with them. On their way they succeeded in corrupting the Sauk with presents, and the Foxes and Potawatomi also were induced to join the expedition. The united tribes mustered about 1,000 warriors for this raid, nearly all of whom were armed with guns and provided with ammunition which the first two tribes had obtained in Montreal during the previous year. As a precautionary measure they had moved their villages back to Michilimackinac and Manitoulin id. As soon as this force reached the Sioux country, it fell upon some small villages, putting the men to flight and capturing the women and children. Fugitives soon spread the alarm in all the allied villages of the Sioux, whence issued swarms of warriors who attacked the enemy so vigorously that the latter were forced to abandon a fort which they had commenced to erect and to flee in consternation. The Sioux pursued them so closely that they were enabled to kill many of the fugitives, some of whom threw away their arms to expedite their flight. These losses and those caused by hunger and the rigor of the weather resulted in the practical annihilation of the allies; the Foxes, the Kiskakon, and the Potawatomi, being less inured to the stress of warfare than the others, did not lose many warriors on this occasion, because they fled at the beginning of the combat. The Hurons, the Squirrel band of the Ottawa, and the Sauk, however, distinguished themselves by their courage and prowess, and by their stubborn resistance materially aided the others in making their escape. In the retreat, which was turned to a rout by the furious pursuit of the Sioux, the confusion became so great that many of the fugitives, driven by privation and hunger, were compelled to eat one another. The chief of the Squirrel band of the Ottawa was captured by the Sioux and condemned to torture by fire. They broiled pieces of his flesh and forced him to eat them. He and his brother-in-law, the Sauk chief, were thus fed until their death at the stake. The rest of the prisoners were shot to death with arrows.

Bacqueville de la Potherie says that in

1665–66 the Potawatomi took the southern, the Sauk the northern, part of Green bay, and the Winnebago, who were not fishermen, went into the forest to live on venison and bear meat. In the spring the Foxes notified the Sauk that they had established themselves in quarters 30 leagues from the bay, forming a settlement of about 600 lodges. The French, for prudent reasons, left to the Sauk the trade in peltries with the Foxes, since they could the more quietly deal with the Sauk in the autumn.

In 1721 the Sauk were still resident at Green bay, but owing to growing difficulties with the Foxes, they were on the point of removing to the St Joseph r. At this time their village was situated on the left bank of Fox r., near its mouth. Although consisting only of a small number of persons at this period, the Sauk had separated into two factions, of which one was attached to the Foxes and the other to the Potawatomi and the French. It was these latter who constituted the bulk of the village mentioned above.

In 1725 the Sauk, in sympathy with the Foxes and the Sioux, were preparing to attack the Illinois.

According to a letter of Beauharnois, dated July 21, 1729 (Wis. Hist. Coll., XVII, 63), the Sauk and the Potawatomi of St Joseph r., along with the Ottawa and the Chippewa of Michilimackinac, the Miami, Wea, and Hurons, together with the Potawatomi and Ottawa of Detroit, went to Montreal to inform him what had occurred concerning the Foxes, against whom they were then at war, and to learn what he desired them to do further. The Sauk, whose village was situated probably on the w. side of Fox r., near the site of the present city of Green Bay, Wis., gave in 1733 asylum to some refugee Foxes. When the Sieur De Villiers, the younger, attempted after a formal demand for the surrender of the Foxes by the Sauk to take them by force, the Sauk resisted and killed De Villiers and Monsieur De Repentigny and several other Frenchmen, thus repulsing the detachment of French and Indian allies. Three days later the Sauk evacuated their fort by night. They were pursued by the French and their Indian allies—the Ottawa, the Menominee, and the Chippewa—under the ensign, the Sieur De Villiers, who overtook the Sauk and the Foxes probably at what is now called Little Butte des Morts, near the present Appleton. De Villiers at once attacked the Sauk, and after several hours of fighting defeated them. The Sauk lost 20, the Foxes 9, and among the injured 9 others were mortally wounded. Among the French 13 officers and men were wounded and 2 were killed; the Ottawa lost 9 men, including their head chief; the Chippewa loss was 2 killed and 4 wounded.

The Marquis de Beauharnois, the governor of Canada, at once gave orders to attack the Sauk and the remaining Foxes to avenge the shedding of French blood. The death of De Villiers, who was the victor at LeRocher in 1730, led to two important events—first, the close confederation of the Sauk and the Foxes, and second, the removal of the united tribes from the territory of Wisconsin to the land of the Iowa, w. of the Mississippi. Previous to the events leading up to this migration the Sauk had ostensibly been allies of the French, even taking part in the war against the Foxes, but they had nevertheless clandestinely given aid and comfort to the devoted Foxes. From this period the united tribes became known as the Sauk and Foxes.

In 1777 the Spanish authorities at San Luis de Ylinneses knew the Sauk as one of the tribes that came from the English district "to receive presents at this post; that they had 400 warriors, and that they were kindly disposed toward the Spanish," for although "frequent bands" had visited "this village," they had caused no trouble. In 1780 Francisco Cruzat, a Spanish officer, wrote to Governor Bernardo Galvez, of Louisiana, that he had caused the Sauk to surrender to him two English banners and thirteen medals which they desired to be replaced with Spanish medals. Cruzat accordingly afterward made the exchange in order that he might "content said chiefs."

In the instructions for the Spanish Governor of St Louis, dated Feb. 15, 1781 (Wis. Hist. Coll., XVIII, 419, 1908), the writer thereof said: "I believe it is excellent for Your Grace to have distinguished the zeal and affection of the Sac tribe who have so generously lent to our district in circumstances of so little advantage [to them]. . . . On this occasion, 16 medals are sent and 10 flags with 16 letters patent which Your Grace is to distribute among the chiefs of the Sac tribe, who, according to Your Grace's advice of the 28th of September, surrendered 13 English medals and three banners . . . I hope that in spite of the great presents which are distributed by the English among these tribes, and notwithstanding the small sum that we have, their hopes will prove empty, even though the [English] governor descend from Michilimakinak, which I doubt. At all events, the zeal, honor, and activity of Your Grace promises me a happy result on our part in their boasted attack on those settlements next Spring. I approve the determination which Your Grace took with the tribes of the Misuri, in making them hand over the two English banners which had been introduced among them. Chuteau [Chouteau] delivered me the 14 medals and 5 English flags which Your Grace recovered from the Sac and Pus [Potawatomi] tribes, as I have said, they were replaced on this occasion." These extracts show the good effect of the Spanish policy in restraining the extreme western tribes from following English agents against the American colonists.

Among the tribes of the Illinois country, the Sauk in 1769 received presents from the Spaniards.

In 1766 Carver found the chief town of the Sauk on Wisconsin r., probably on the site of Prairie du Sac; it consisted of about 90 lodges and 300 warriors.

From the journal of Peter Pond, 1773–75 (Wis. Hist. Coll., xviii, 335 et seq.), the following citation concerning the habits and customs of the Sauk is made: "These People are Cald Saukeas. They are of a Good Sise and Well Disposed—Les Inclind to tricks and Bad manners than thare Nighbers. Thay will take of the traders Goods on Creadit in the fall for thare youse. In Winter and Except for Axedant thay Pay the Deapt Verey Well for Indans I mite have sade Inlitend or Sivelised Indans which are in General made worse by the Operation. . . . Sum of thare Huts are Sixtey feet Long and Contanes Several fammalayes. . . . In the fall of ye Year thay Leave thare Huts and Go into the Woods in Quest of Game and Return in the Spring to thare Huts before Planting time. The Women Rase Grate Crops of Corn, Been, Punkens, Potatoes, Millans and artikels—the Land is Exaleant—and Clear of Wood Sum Distans from the Villeag. Thare [are] Sum Hundred of Inhabitants. Thare amusments are Singing, Dancing, Smokeing, Matcheis, Gaming, Feasting, Drinking, Playing the Slite of Hand, Hunting and thay are famas in Mageack. Thay are Not Verey Gellas of thare Women. In General the Women find meanes to Grattafy them Selves without Consent of the Men." Pond adds that the Sauk warriors often joined the war parties of neighboring tribes against the Indians on Missouri r. and westward; that sometimes they went to the vicinity of Santa Fé, New Mexico, and captured Spanish horses, of which he had seen a large number.

A Sauk band, which later became known as the Missouri River Sauk, had been for some time in the habit of wintering near the post of St Louis on the Missouri. One winter, about 1804, the head-men of this band were drawn into negotiations with Government officials at the post. It is an open question if these leaders knew what they were doing. At any rate the band became a party to negotiations, which in time were to lead to the undoing of the Sauk and Foxes, by which these

tribes were to relinquish all claim to territory in Wisconsin, Illinois, and Missouri. The knowledge of what the Missouri River band had done naturally incensed the rest of the people. It was then that the band realized what it had done, but it was too late. Knowing the temper of the people, the band remained away, and it has continued to do so ever since. The Foxes became so angry with the Sauk for letting one of their bands act for all the people that they began at once to draw away from the Sauk, and in the course of a generation they had moved over into their hunting grounds in Iowa. Other agreements were entered into with the three divisions of these people before the treaty of 1804 was finally carried out. Out of all this, in connection with the

SAUK MAN

general unrest of the tribes of this region, arose the so-called Black Hawk war in 1832. It is customary to lay the cause of this conflict to the refusal of the Sauk to comply with the terms of agreement they had entered into with the Government with reference particularly to the lands on Rock r. in Illinois. Be that as it may, the actual fighting between the Sauk and the Government was of a rather feeble character. But the fighting between the Sauk on the one hand and the Sioux, Omaha, and Menominee on the other was extremely severe. These tribes, together with the Potawatomi and Winnebago, had previously sent emissaries to the Sauk urging them on to fight the whites and at the same time promising immediate assistance. The Potawatomi were the most persistent in this matter; they had prophets in the camp of the Sauk preaching restoration of the old hunting grounds, the return of the game, and the sudden miraculous destruction of the whites; but when hostilities began, their chief, Shabonee (q. v.), was the first to warn the whites against the Sauk. Among the Sauk at this time was an able man of the Thunder clan known to the whites under the name of Black Hawk (q. v.). He was not a chief, but had gained a good record for bravery and leadership in war. He was deeply religious, and thoroughly patriotic. He had fought under Tecumseh and had become imbued with some of the ideas of the great Shawnee. About this man rallied the hostile Sauk. He first tried holding the Sauk in check until he could

SAUK WOMAN

count on the combined help of the Kickapoo and Foxes, but the fighting got under way before he was ready. The Sauk were thoroughly beaten, and sought refuge among the Foxes in Iowa. Considerable resentment was felt against the Winnebago for having delivered Black Hawk over to the whites when he had come to them seeking refuge; and the same feeling was entertained toward the Potawatomi for going over to the whites. For some time previous to this trouble there had been intimate relationship between the Sauk and these two tribes. This conflict practically broke the power of the Sauk and Foxes. They united again in Iowa, this time to avenge themselves against the Sioux, Omaha, and Menominee, whom they chastised in lively

fashion, but not enough to satisfy their desires. So constantly harassed were the Sioux that they finally left Iowa altogether, and the Menominee withdrew northward where they continued to remain. In 1837 the Sauk and Foxes made the last of their various cessions of Iowa lands, and were given in exchange a tract across the Missouri in Kansas. Here they remained practically as one people for about 20 years. But internal dissensions, due largely to Keokuk (q. v.), were causing them to grow apart. They maintained separate villages, the Sauk in one and the Foxes in another. One summer about the years 1857–59, the leading Foxes returned from a buffalo hunt and found that during their absence the Sauk had made a treaty with the Government by the terms of which the Sauk and Foxes were to take up lands in severalty and sell the remainder, the whole transaction having been negotiated by whites to get possession of the Indians' land for purposes of speculation. The Fox chief refused to ratify the agreement on behalf of the Foxes, and for so doing was deprived of his chieftainship; but the Foxes did not recognize the act of the agent deposing their chief. In the fall the Fox chief went away to Iowa, and with him most of the Foxes. An incident occurring shortly before this time, i. e., in 1854, had much to do with hastening the departure of many of the Foxes for Iowa. While on a buffalo hunt a party of about 50 men were attacked by a large force of Plains Indians, consisting, it is said, of Cheyenne, Arapaho, Kiowa, and Comanche. The Foxes were armed with "Kentucky rifles," while the others had only bows and arrows. Retreating upon a rise of ground where approach was possible from only one direction, the Foxes beat off their assailants, inflicting heavy loss. On their return home they became uneasy lest the Government, on learning the news of the slaughter, might deal sternly with them, and so they quietly stole off to Iowa. A few Foxes had never gone to Kansas, but had remained in Iowa. Some had returned before the main exodus of 1859. They finally found a place on Iowa r., near Tama City, where they bought a small piece of land. This has been added to from time to time till they now have more than 3,000 acres which they hold in common. They have nothing more to do with the Sauk politically. In 1867 the Sauk ceded their lands in Kansas and in exchange were given a tract in Indian Ter. In 1889 they took up lands in severalty and sold the remainder to the Government.

Language.—It is not yet possible to determine the dialectic position of the

Sauk, in particular their position with reference to other dialects of the Central Algonquian group from the standpoint of mutual intelligibility. An approximate order of relationship may be tentatively offered. The Sauk is intimately related first to the Fox and then to the Kickapoo. The Shawnee probably comes next.

Material culture.—The culture of the Sauk was that of the eastern wooded area. They were a canoe people while they were in the country of the Great Lakes, using both the birch-bark canoe and the dugout. They still retain the dugout, and learned the use and construction of the bull-boat on coming out upon the plains. They practised agriculture on an extensive scale; they cultivated the ground for maize, squashes, beans, and tobacco. Despite their fixed abodes and villages they did not live a sedentary life altogether, for much of the time they devoted to the chase, hunting game and fishing almost the whole year round. They were acquainted with wild rice, and hunted the buffalo. In the Black Hawk war the Sauk had 450 horsemen who were mounted on well-trained horses and who often worsted a much larger number of U. S. cavalry. Horses were not extensively used in agricultural pursuits until after 1837. Their abode was the bark house in warm weather and the oval flag-reed lodge in winter; the bark house was characteristic of the village. Every gens had one large bark house wherein were celebrated the festivals of the gens. In this lodge hung the sacred bundles of the gens, and here dwelt the priests that watched over them. It is said that some of these lodges were of the length required to accommodate five fires. The ordinary bark dwelling had but a single fire, which was at the center.

Social organization.—Society was rather complex. In the days when the tribe was much larger there were numerous gentes. There may be as many as 14 gentes yet in existence. These are: Trout, Sturgeon, Bass, Great Lynx or Fire Dragon, Sea, Fox, Wolf, Bear, Bear-potato, Elk, Swan, Grouse, Eagle, and Thunder. It seems that at one time there was a more rigid order of rank both socially and politically than at present. For example, chiefs came from the Trout and Sturgeon gentes, and war chiefs from the Fox gens; and there were certain relationships of courtesy between one gens and another, as when one acted the rôle of servants to another, seen especially on the occasion of a gens ceremony. Marriage was restricted to men and women of different gentes, and was generally attended with an exchange of presents between the families of the pair. Woman

as a rule was paid formal courtship before marriage. In the case of death, a man might marry the sister of his deceased wife, or a widow might become the wife of the brother of her dead husband. Polygamy was practised, but was not usual; it was a privilege that went with wealth and social prestige. A child followed the gens of the father, but it frequently happened that the mother was given the right to name; in that case the child took a name peculiar to the gens of the mother but was yet in the gens of the father. But for this practice the gens of an individual could generally be known from the nature of the name. The name is intimately connected with the gens; for example, a name meaning 'he that moves on ahead flashing light' refers to lightning, and is a name peculiar to the Thunder gens. Besides the grouping into gentes, the tribe was further divided into two great social groups or phratries: Kīshkōᵃ and Oshkashᵃ. The painting color of the first was white clay, and that of the second was charcoal. A child entered into a group at birth, sometimes the father, sometimes the mother determining which group. The several groups engaged one another in all manner of contests, especially in athletics. The Sauk never developed a soldier society with the same degree of success as did the Foxes, but they did have a buffalo society; it is said that the first was due to contact with the Sioux, and it is reasonable to suppose that the second was due to influence also from the Plains. There were a chief and a council. As stated, the chiefs came from the Trout and Sturgeon gentes, and the council consisted of these, the war-chiefs or heads of families, and all the warriors. Politically the chief was little more than a figurehead, but socially he occupied first place in the tribe. Not infrequently, however, by force of character and by natural astuteness in the management of tribal affairs the chief might exercise virtually autocratic power. Furthermore, his person was held sacred, and for that reason he was given loyal homage.

Religion.—The religion of the Sauk is fundamentally the belief in what are now commonly known as manitos. The sense of the term is best given by the combined use of the two words "power" and "magic." The world is looked on as inhabited by beings permeated with a certain magic force, not necessarily malicious and not necessarily beneficent, the manifestation of which might produce one or the other effect. Objects in nature held to be endowed with this force become the recipients of varying degrees of adoration. A child is early taught to get into personal relation with some manito by means of fasting and vigil to secure his tutelary or genius. The manitos of Sauk mythology and religious worship are represented in all nature. They are human beings, animals, birds, fishes, reptiles, insects, plants, fire, water, and all the elements personified. The mythology of the Sauk is rich with fables of anthropomorphic beasts and beings. The principal myth is concerned with the god of life, called Nanabozho by cognate tribes, with the flood, and with the restoration of the earth.

The Sauk had numerous ceremonies, social and religious. Some of these they still retain. The chief two religious ceremonies still in existence are the gens festivals and the secret rite of the Midewiwin, or Grand Medicine Society. The gens festival is held twice a year—in the spring, when thanksgiving is offered to the manitos for the new season, and in the summer after the fields ripen. The meeting of the Midewiwin is generally held but once a year, during the spring, when a ceremony is conducted by a group composed of men and women bound together by vows of secrecy. This society is entered by initiation and the payment of a fee, and the ceremony is conducted with an elaborate ritual on the occasion of the admittance of a new member, who takes the place of one who has died during the preceding year. Next in importance to these are the rites connected with death and adoption. To express grief for dead kindred, they blackened their faces with charcoal, fasted, and abstained from the use of vermilion and of ornaments in dress. The Sauk practised four different methods of burial: (1) the corpse was laid away in the branches of a tree or upon a scaffold; (2) it was placed in a sitting posture, with the back supported, out on the open ground; (3) it was seated in a shallow grave with all but the face buried and a shelter was placed over the grave; (4) there was complete burial in the ground. The ghost world is said to be in the W. beyond the setting sun, and thither it is said the people go after death. The brother of the culture-hero is master of the ghost world, while the culture-hero himself is said to be at the N., in the region of snow and ice. The Sauk are looking for his return, when they believe the world will come to an end, and they and the culture-hero will go to join his brother.

The close relations of the Sauk with the Foxes in historical times make it difficult to form more than an approximate estimate of their numbers in the past, but it is probable that the population of the tribe never exceeded 3,500 souls. When first known to history, i. e. in 1650, the Sauk and Foxes together numbered probably 6,500 (Sauk 3,500, Foxes 3,000). Perrot, writing in the first quarter of the 18th century, says that the Potawatomi, the Sauk, and the Foxes composed a body of more than 1,000 warriors. The principal estimates of the Sauk alone are: 750 persons in 1736; 1,000 (1759); 2,000 (1766); 2,250 (1783); 2,850 (1810); 4,800 (Beltrami, 1825); and 2,500 (1834). The two tribes together have been estimated at 3,000 (1820); 6,400 (1825); 5,300 (1834); 5,000 (1837). The estimates of the combined tribes indicate that the Foxes (q. v.) were the more numerous, but these appear to be incorrect. In 1885 the two tribes had a total population of about 930, of whom 457 were in Indian Ter., 380 (who claimed to be Foxes only) were at Tama, Iowa, and 87 in s. e. Nebraska; in addition there were a few at the various Indian schools. The Report of the Commissioner of Indian Affairs for 1909 gives 352 persons (almost all Foxes) at the Sauk and Fox agency, Iowa, 536 (chiefly Sauk) at the Sauk and Fox agency in Oklahoma, and 87 Sauk and Foxes (chiefly Sauk) in Kansas, a total Sauk and Fox population of 975.

The Sauk made or were parties to the following treaties with the United States: Treaty of Ft Harmar, Jan. 9, 1789; St Louis, Mo. (Sauk and Fox), Nov. 3, 1804; Portage des Sioux, Mo. (Sauk of Missouri), Sept. 13, 1815; St Louis, Mo., May 13, 1816; Ft Armstrong, Ill. (Sauk and Fox), Sept. 3, 1822; Washington, D. C. (Sauk and Fox), Aug. 4, 1824; Prairie du Chien, Wis. (Sauk and Fox), Aug. 19, 1825, and July 15, 1830; Ft Armstrong, Ill. (Sauk and Fox), Sept. 21, 1832; Ft Leavenworth, Mo. (Sauk and Fox), Sept. 17, 1836; near Dubuque, Iowa (Sauk and Fox), Sept. 27 and 28, 1836; Washington, D. C. (Sauk and Fox), Oct. 21, 1837; ditto (Sauk and Fox of Missouri), same date and place; Sauk and Fox agency, Ia. (Sauk and Fox), Oct. 11, 1847; Washington, D. C. (Sauk and Fox of Missouri), May 18, 1854; Sauk and Fox agency, Kan. (Sauk and Fox), Oct. 1, 1859; Nemaha agency, Nebr. (Sauk and Fox), Mar. 6, 1861; and Washington, D. C. (Sauk and Fox), Feb. 18, 1867.

For more detailed information concerning the many petty wars, alliances, and migrations of the Sauk and their interrelations with the French and neighboring Indian tribes, consult Bacqueville de la Potherie, Histoire de L'Amérique Septentrionale, 1753; Perrot, Mémoire sur les Mœurs, Coustumes et Relligion des Sauvages de l'Amérique Septentrionale, 1864; Jesuit Relations, i–iii, 1858, also Thwaites edition, i–lxxiii, 1896–1901; the Collections of the State Historical Society of Wisconsin; Laverdière, Œuvres de Champlain, 1870; Sagard Theodat, Histoire du Canada, I–IV, 1866; Sagard Theodat, Voyage du Pays des Hurons, I–II, 1865.   (J. N. B. H.)

Asaukees.—Ramsey in Ind. Aff. Rep. 1849, 73, 1850. **Assegunaigs.** — Schoolcraft, Ind. Tribes, I, 191, 1851.—**Hotĭ'nestakoⁿ'.**—Hewitt, Onondaga MS., B. A. E.,1888 (Onondaga name).— Jes. Rel., index, 1858. **Hvattoehronon.**—Jes. Rel. 1640, 35, 1858. **Jakis.**—Rasles (*ca.* 1723) in Mass. Hist. Soc. Coll., 2d s., VIII, 251, 1819 (misprint?). **Osagi.**—Baraga, Eng.-Otch. Dict., 218, 1878 (Chippewa form). **Osáki.**—Gatschet, Potawatomi MS., 1878 (Potawatomi name; pl. Osákĭk). **Osankies.**—Ramsay in Ind. Aff. Rep. 1849, 74, 1850 (misprint). **Osaugeeg.**—Tanner, Narr., 315, 1830 (Ottawa name). **Osaukies.**—Ramsey in Ind. Aff. Rep. 1849, 77, 1850. **O'-saw-kee.**—Lewis and Clark, Discov., 29, 1806. **Satoeronnon.**—Potier, Huron MS. Grammar, *ca.* 1762 (Huron name). **Ouatoieronon.**—Ibid. **Ousaki.**—Jes. Rel. 1667, 21, 1858. **Ousakiouek.**—Ibid. **Ozaukie.**—Parker, Minn. Handbook, 13, 1857. **Quatokeronon.**—Potier, Huron MS. Grammar, *ca.* 1762 (another Huron name). **Saäkies.**—Long, Exped. St Peters R., II, 450, 1824. **Saaskies.**—Boudinot, Star in the West, 128, 1816 (misprint). **Saasskies.**—Ibid., 107 (misprint). **Sachi.**—York (1700) in N. Y. Doc. Col. Hist., IV, 749, 1854. **Sacks.**—Harris, Tour, 195, 1805. **Sacky.**—Coxe, Carolana, 48, 1741. **Sacs.**—Doc. of 1695 in N. Y. Doc. Col. Hist., IX, 619, 1855. **Sagaseys.**—Croghan (1759) in Rupp,West. Pa., 146, 1846. **Sagíwa.**—Gatschet, Kaw MS. vocab., 27, 1878 (Kansa name). **Sakawes.**—Pike Exped., Coues ed., I, 101, 1895. **Sakies.**—Ibid. **Sakes.**—Lords of Trade (1721) in N. Y. Doc. Col. Hist., V, 622, 1855. **Sʻá̇-kė̇-wʻė̇.**—Long, Exped. St Peters R., I, 218, 1824 (own name). **Sakewi.**—Ibid., II, 450. **Saki.**—Jes. Rel. 1670, 98, 1858. **Sa-ki-yû.**—Grayson, Creek MS. vocab., B. A. E., 1885 (Creek name for united Sauk and Foxes). **Saks.**—McKenney and Hall., Ind. Tribes, III, 79, 1854. **Saky.**—Jes. Rel. 1670, 96, 1858. **Sankewi.**—Tanner, Narr., 315, 1830 (misprint?). **Sanks.**—Jones, Ojebway Inds., 69, 1861 (misprint). **Saques.**—Vater, Mith., pt. 3, sec. 3, 266, 1816. **Saquis.**—La Harpe (1700) in French, Hist. Coll. La., III, 23, 1851. **Sauckeys.**—De Butts (1795) in Am. State Pap., Ind. Aff., I, 567, 1832. **Saucs.**—De Smet, Oregon Miss., 161, 1847. **Saugies.**—Old map in Lapham, Inds. of Wis., 16, 1870. **Sauk.**—Pike Exped., I, app., 20, 1810. **Saukees.**—Lewis and Clark, Discov., 15, 1806. **Saukeys.**—Clark (1809) in Am. State Pap., Ind. Aff., I, 798, 1832. **Saukies.**—Edwards (1788) in Mass. Hist. Soc. Coll., 1st s., IX, 92, 1804. **Sawkee.**—Pike, Trav., 134, 1811. **Sawkeys.**—Johnston (1810) in Am. State Pap., Ind. Aff., I, 799, 1832. **Sawkies.**—Volney, View of U. S. A., 352, 1804. **Sawkis.**—Vater, Mith., pt. 3, sec. 3, 266, 1816. **Saxes.**—Goldthwait (1766) in Mass. Hist. Soc. Coll., 1st s., X, 122, 1809. **Scungsicks.**—Albany conf. (1726) in N. Y. Doc. Col. Hist., V, 791, 1855 (apparently given as the Iroquois name for the Sauk; the Foxes are called Quacksis in the same doc.; Hewitt thinks the form may be intended for *Skenchiohronon* 'Fox,' the Huron name for the Foxes, and possibly for the united tribes). **Shakies.**—Croghan (1759) quoted by Jefferson, Notes, 143, 1825. **Shàkirs.**—Hutchins (1768), ibid. (misprint). **Shockays.**—Croghan (1765) in Monthly Am. Jour. Geol., 272, 1831. **Shockeys.**—Croghan (1759) quoted by Rupp, West. Pa., app., 132, 1846. **Shougheys.**—Croghan (1760) in Mass. Hist. Soc. Coll., 4th s., IX, 250, 1871. **Skakies.**—Inlay, West. Ter., 290, 1797 (misprint). **Sokkie.**—Dalton (1783) in Mass. Hist. Soc. Coll., 1st s., X, 123, 1809. **Taukies.**—Lewis, Trav., 37, 1809 (misprint). **Za'-ke.**—Riggs, Dak. Gram. and Dict., 275, 1852 (Santee and Yankton Sioux name).

Saukaulutuchs. Reported to be the name of a small band of Indians in the interior of Vancouver id. They traded with the Nootka and are said to have spoken the same language; from the latter circumstance the Nootka had a superstition that they were the spirits of their dead.

Säa-Käalituck.—Mayne, Brit. Col., 180, 1861. **Saukaulutuchs.**—Keane in Stanford, Compend., 534, 1878. **Sau-kau-lutuck.**—Lord, Nat. in Brit. Col., I, 158, 1866.

Sauk-eye. See *Sockeye*.

Sauktich. A Squawmish village community inhabiting Hat id., Howe sd., Brit. Col.

Sau'qtito.—Hill-Tout in Rep. Brit. A. A. S., 474, 1900.

Sault au Recollet (French: 'rapids of the Récollet,' because a Récollet missionary was drowned there early in the 17th century). A Catholic Iroquois mission village near the mouth of Ottawa r., in Two Mountains co., Quebec, established in 1696 by converts from The Mountain. In 1704 the rest of the Indians at The Mountain removed to the new mission. In 1720 the settlement was abandoned, and the inhabitants, numbering about 900, built a new village at Oka (q. v.).   (J. N. B. H.)

Annunciation.—Shea, Cath. Miss., 329, 1855 (mission name bestowed in 1704). **Lorette.**—Ibid., 329 (first mission name; see also *Lorette*). **Sault au Recolet.**—Vaudreuil (1711) in N. Y. Doc. Col. Hist., IX, 860, 1855. **Sault au Recollet.**—Shea, Cath. Miss., 328, 1855. **Saut au Récollet.**—Vaudreuil (1717) in N. Y. Doc. Col. Hist., IX, 961, 1855.

Saumingmiut ('inhabitants of the left side'). A subtribe of the Okomiut Eskimo of Baffin land, inhabiting the extremity of Cumberland penin. Their villages are Kekertaujang and Ukiadliving. Pop. 17 in 1883. See Boas in Trans. Anthr. Soc. Wash., III, 96, 1885.

Shaumeer.—Kumlien in Bull. Nat. Mus., no. 15, 15, 1879. **SSaumingmiut.**—Boas in Deutsche Geog. Blätt., VII, 34, 1885.

Sauniktumiut. An Eskimo tribe on the coast of Hudson bay, s. of the Kinipetu, in the region of Port Churchill; pop. 178 in 1902.—Boas in Bull. Am. Mus. Nat. Hist., XV, 6, 1901; 378, 1907.

Saunutung. A spring settlement of the Kinguamiut Eskimo at the entrance to Nettilling fiord, Baffin land.—Boas in 6th Rep. B. A. E., map, 1888.

Sauquonckackock. A Pequot village in 1638, on the w. bank of Thames r., below Mohegan, New London co., Conn., occupied by a portion of the conquered tribe subject to the Mohegan.—Williams (1638) in Mass. Hist. Soc. Coll., 4th s., VI, 251, 1863.

Sauwontiats (*Sau-won'-ti-ats*). A Paiute band formerly in or near Moapa valley, s. E. Nev.; pop. 92 in 1873.—Powell in Ind. Aff. Rep. 1873, 50, 1874.

Saveata. See *Sabeata*.

Savinnars. Given as a tribe on Vancouver id., N. of Nootka sd. Unidentified, but undoubtedly either a Nootka tribe or the Nootka name of a Kwakiutl tribe.

Savinards.—Armstrong, Oregon, 136, 1857. **Savinnars.**—Jewitt, Narr., 36, 1849.

Savoyan. A name of the goldthread (*Coptis trifoliata*) and of certain species of bedstraw (*Galium boreale*, etc.), which has come into American English through the *savoyane* of Canadian French. The Indians used the root of *Coptis trifoliata* to make a yellow dye for their baskets, porcupine-quills, skins, etc. The word is derived from the Algonquian term for the goldthread, represented by the Nipissing-Chippewa *atisawaiân*, literally meaning 'skin dye,' from *atiso*, 'to be dyed,' and *waiân*, 'skin.' (A. F. C.)

Sawagativa (*Sa-wa'-ga-ti-va*, 'large hill'). A Paviotso tribe formerly about Winnemucca, N. Nev.—Powell, Paviotso MS., B. A. E., 1881.

Sawamish. A Salish division on Totten inlet, at the S. end of Puget sd., Wash. Not to be confounded with Samamish.
Sah-wah-mish.—Starling in Ind. Aff. Rep., 171, 1852. Sa-wa-mish.—Gibbs in Pac. R. R. Rep., I, 435, 1855.

Sawani. A subtribe or division of the Cholovone, E. of lower San Joaquin r., Cal.
Sawani.—Pinart, Cholovone MS., 1880. Saywamines.—Hale, Ethnol. and Philol., VI, 630, 1846. Seywamines.—Bancroft, Nat. Races, I, 450, 1874. Suraminis.—Taylor in Cal. Farmer, June 8, 1860.

Sawanogi (Creek form of *Shawano*, or *Shawnee*). A former town of Shawnee Indians incorporated with the Creek confederacy, situated on the S. side of Tallapoosa r., in Macon co., Ala. It is mentioned in Bartram's list in 1773, and again by Hawkins in 1799, at which time its people still retained their distinctive language and tribal customs. A few Yuchi were living with them. From a statement by Adair (Am. Inds., 410, 1775) it is probable that they had joined the Creeks about the middle of the 18th century. See *Shawnee.* (J. M.)

Saway-yanga. A former Gabrieleño rancheria near San Fernando mission, Los Angeles co., Cal.—Taylor in Cal. Farmer, May 11, 1860.

Sawcunk (Delaware: *Sâkunk*, 'at-the-mouth (of a stream).' A former important village on the N. bank of Ohio r. near the mouth of Beaver cr., about the site of the present Beaver, Beaver co., Pa. It was a fur-trading station of note, and after the establishment of Ft Duquesne the French erected houses there for the Delaware, Shawnee, and Mingo inhabitants. Sawcunk was the home of Shingass, noted for his hostility toward the frontier settlements. It was abandoned when the English took Ft Duquesne in 1758.
Beaver Creek.—Weiser (1748) quoted by Rupp, West. Penn., app., 14, 1846. Sacoung.—Post (1758) quoted by Proud, Penn., II, app., 124, 1798. Sackung.—Ibid., 122. Sacunck.—Ibid., 92. Sankonk.—Post (1758) quoted by Rupp, op. cit., app., 81. Sawcung.—Post quoted by Proud, op. cit., app., 105, 1798. Sawcunc.—Ibid., 80. Sawkunck.—Post quoted by Rupp, op. cit., app., 96. Sawkung.—Ibid., 106. Sawkunk.—Ibid., 87. Shingas's Old Town.—Thwaites, Early Western Trav., I, 26, note, 1904. Sohkon.—Ibid. Sŏh'koon.—Alden (1834) in Mass. Hist. Soc. Coll., 3d s., VI, 145, 1837.

Saweachic ('place of many pines'). A Tarahumare rancheria 25 m. E. of Chinatu, w. Chihuahua, Mexico.—Lumholtz, inf'n, 1894.

Sawkin. A Delaware village on the E. bank of Delaware r., in New Jersey, in 1675.—Newcastle conf. (1675) in N. Y. Doc. Col. Hist., XII, 523, 1877.

Sawkwey. See *Sockeye.*

Sawmehnaug (probably the chief's name). A village, probably Potawatomi, on Fox r., Ill., on a tract sold in 1833.—Treaty of Prairie du Chien (1829) in U. S. Ind. Treat., 162, 1873.

Sawokli (*sâwi* 'raccoon', *úkli* 'town'). A former Hitchiti town in the open pine forest on the w. bank of Chattahoochee r., in N. E. Barbour co., Ala., 6 m. below Oconee. In 1832 it had 2 chiefs and 56 families. (A. S. G.)
Chau-woo-e-lau-hatchee.—Royce in 18th Rep. B. A. E., Ala. map, 1900. Chawaccola Hatchu.—U. S. Ind. Treat. (1827), 421, 1837. Chewackala.—Swan (1791) in Schoolcraft, Ind. Tribes, V, 262, 1855. Che-wak-a-to.—Sen. Ex. Doc. 425, 24th Cong., 1st sess., 215, 1836. Che wok o lee.—Schoolcraft, Ind. Tribes, IV, 580, 1854. Chowockolo.—H. R. Doc. 452, 25th Cong., 2d sess., 49, 1838. Chowocolo.—Taylor, ibid., 61. Ehawho-ka-les.—Morse, Rep. to Sec. War, 364, 1822. Great Sáwokli.—Gatschet, Creek Migr. Leg., I, 144, 1884. Great Swaglaw.—Bartram, Travels, 462, 1791. Sabacola.—Barcia, Ensayo (1718), 336, 1723. Sá-ukli.—Gatschet, op. cit., I, 144. Sau-woo-ge-lo.—Hawkins (1799), Sketch, 65, 1848. Sau-woo-ge-to.—Royce in 18th Rep. B. A. E., Ga. map, 1899. Sawakola.—Adair, Am. Inds., 257, 1775. Sáwokli.—Gatschet, op. cit., I, 144. Shogleys.—McKenney and Hall, Ind. Tribes, III, 80, 1854. Shogteys.—Romans, Florida, I, 59, 1775. Sonwuckolo.—H. R. Ex. Doc. 276, 24th Cong., 1st sess., 308, 1836. Souckelas.—Boudinot, Star in West, 128, 1816. Souikilas.—French trader in Smith, Bouquet Exped., 70, 1766. Soulikilas.—Bouquet (1764) quoted by Jefferson, Notes, 145, 1825. Souwagoolo.—U. S. Ind. Treat. (1814), 162, 1837. Souwogoolo.—Ibid. Sowoccolo.—Schoolcraft, Ind. Tribes, IV, 578, 1854. So-wok-ko-los.—Drake, Bk. Inds., bk. IV, 1848. Suoculo.—U. S. Ind. Treat. (1827), 420, 1837. Swaggles town.—Am. State Papers, Ind. Aff. (1793), I, 383, 1832. Swaglaw.—Form cited by Gatschet, Creek Migr. Leg., I, 144, 1884. Swaglers.—Robin, Voy., I, map, 1807. Swagles.—McCall, Hist. Georgia, I, 364, 1811. Swales.—Harris, Voy. and Trav., II, 335, 1802.

Sawokliudshi ('little Sawokli'). A former Hitchiti town on the E. bank of Chattahoochee r., Quitman co., Ga., 4 m. below Oconee. It contained about 20 families in 1799.
Little Sáwokli.—Gatschet, Creek Migr. Leg., I, 144, 1884. Little Swaglaw.—Bartram, Travels, 462, 1791. Sau-woog-e-loo-ohe.—Hawkins (1799), Sketch, 66, 1848. Sawokli-ū'dshi.—Gatschet, op. cit. Swgahatchies.—Robin, Voy., I, map, 1807.

Saws. The aborigines employed primitive forms of the saw in shaping metal, stone, bone, and other hard substances. The chief use, however, was that of dividing portions of the raw material intended for further elaboration. These implements took many forms, and their use involved two distinct processes—one in which the saw employed was harder than the material sawed and was operated by direct abrasion, and the other in which the implement was softer than the material cut, sharp sand being introduced as the abrading agent. The former were usually thin pieces of hard stone, the edges of which were notched by chipping; doubtless other flaked implements, such as knives and spearheads, served on occasion for kindred purposes. Later saws were thin pieces or strips of almost any available material, beneath which the sand was moved back and forth or into the under surfaces of which the grains became imbedded, thus forming a kind of rasp or file. The dividing of masses of the harder stones was of course a tedious process and required great patience, but that the work was effective is shown by many specimens. The cutting of portions of jade for use in the manufacture of adzes and other implements by the natives of Alaska serves to illustrate this. See *Stonework*. (w. h. h.)

Sawuara. Given as a Karok settlement of two houses on the e. bank of Klamath r., not far below Orleans bar, n. w. Cal. Sa-ron-ra.—McKee (1851) in Sen. Ex. Doc. 4, 32d Cong., spec. sess., 194, 1853. Sa-vour-ras.—Ibid., 215. Sa-vow-ra.—Ibid., 161. Sa-wa-rahs.—Meyer, Nach dem Sacramento, 282, 1855. Shah-woo-rum.—Gibbs, MS. Miscel., B. A. E., 1852.

Sayenqueraghta ('Smoke Revanishes,' also known as Old King and Old Smoke). A Seneca chief during the Revolutionary period. His place of residence was on Smoke cr., 5 or 6 m. s. of Buffalo, N. Y. He is first mentioned by Zeisberger in 1750 (Conover, Sayenqueraghta, 2, 1885). His name appears in the treaty of Johnson Hall, N. Y., Apr. 3, 1764; he also figured at the Easton treaty of 1758, and was prominent in most of the conferences of his tribe and of the Six Nations up to 1775. He was speaker in 1774, commanded the Seneca at Oriskany, and led them at Wyoming. Mrs Campbell spoke of him in 1779 as "Guyanguahto, or, as he was commonly called, Grahta, the Seneca King." His death occurred before 1788. Although wielding great influence over his tribe as head-chief, he was not an elected or hereditary chief, but held office at the dictation of the British government and with the willing consent of his people. (c. t.   w. m. b.)

Sayokinck. A Chumashan village formerly on Arroyo Burro, near Santa Barbara, Cal. Sayokenek.—Bancroft, Nat. Races, I, 459, 1874. Sayokinck.—Taylor in Cal. Farmer, Apr. 24, 1863.

Sazeutina. A Nahane tribe inhabiting the region between Dease and Black rs., Brit. Col. In 1887 they numbered 94. Petitot considered them an outlying eastern offshoot of the Sekani. Sa-zē-oo-ti-na.—Dawson in Rep. Geol. Surv. Can. 1887-8, 200B, 1889. Sicanees.—Dall in Cont. N. Am. Ethnol., I, 33, 1877 (so called by traders). Thè-kka-'nè.—Petitot, Autour du lac des Esclaves, 362, 1891. Thikanies.—Hardisty in Smithson. Rep. 1866, 311, 1872.

Scabbards. See *Receptacles*.

Scalping. The common name for the Indian practice of removing a portion of the skin, with hair attached, from an enemy's head, for trophy purposes. The word scalp is derived from an old Low German word signifying a shell or sheath. The equivalent word in the various Indian languages commonly refers either to skin or hair.

The practice is not exclusively an Indian one, having been noted among the ancient Scythians as far back as the time of Herodotus. Neither was it common to all the American tribes, as so often supposed. On the contrary, recent researches by Friederici indicate that it was confined originally in North America to a limited area in the e. United States and the lower St Lawrence region, about equivalent to the territory held by the Iroquoian and Muskhogean tribes and their immediate neighbors. It was absent from New England and much of the Atlantic Coast region, and was unknown until comparatively recent times throughout the whole interior and the Plains area. It was not found on the Pacific coast, in the Canadian N. W., or in the Arctic region, or anywhere s. of the United States, with the exception of an area in the Gran Chaco country of South America. Throughout most of America the earlier trophy was the head itself. The spread of the scalping practice over a great part of central and western United States was a direct result of the encouragement in the shape of scalp bounties offered by the colonial and more recent governments, even down to within the last fifty years, the scalp itself being superior to the head as a trophy by reason of its lighter weight and greater adaptability to display and ornamentation.

The operation of scalping was painful, but by no means fatal. The impression that it was fatal probably arises from the fact that the scalp was usually taken from the head of a slain enemy as a token of his death, but among the Plains tribes the attacking party frequently strove to overpower his enemy and scalp him alive, to inflict greater agony before killing him, and frequently also a captured enemy was scalped alive and released to go back thus mutilated to his people as a direct defiance and as an incitement to retaliation. The portion taken was usually a small circular patch of skin at the root of the scalplock just back of the crown of the head. The "scalplock" itself was the small hair braid which hung from the back of the head, as distinguished from the larger side braids. It was usually decorated with beads or other ornaments. When opportunity offered the whole top skin of the head, with the hair attached, was removed, to be divided later into smaller scalplocks for decorating war-shirts, leggings, etc. The operation was performed by making a quick knife stroke around the head of the fallen enemy, followed by a strong tug at the scalplock. The teeth also were sometimes used in the pulling process, and the victor usually knelt with knee pressed down upon the back of his victim stretched face downward. The one who took the scalp was not necessarily the same one who had killed the victim; neither was the number of scalps, but rather of *coups* (q. v.), the measure of the warrior's prowess. The fresh scalp was sometimes soon afterward offered as a sacrifice to the sun, the water, or some other divinity. In the former case it was held up to the sun, with a short prayer by the owner, and then carefully stretched on a buffalo-chip and thus left on the prairie. When sacrificed to the water the scalp was thrown into the river after a similar prayer. When preserved for a time, as was most usual, the scalp was cleaned of the loose flesh on its under side, and then stretched by means of sinew cords around its circumference within a hoop of about 6 in. diameter, tied at the end of a light rod. When dry the skin side was painted either entirely red, or one half red and the other half black. The hair was carefully rebraided and decorated with various ornaments. It was carried thus by the women in the triumphal scalp dance on the return of the successful war-party to the home camp and then, having served its first purpose, was retained as a bridle pendant by the warrior, deposited with the tribal "medicine," or thrown away in some retired spot.

The many ceremonies, taboos, and beliefs in connection with scalps and scalping are too numerous for treatment within the limits of a brief article. For a discussion of the whole subject the reader should consult Friederici, (1) Skalpieren und ähnliche Kriegsgebräuche in Amerika, Braunschweig, 1906, (2) in Smithson. Rep. 1906, 1907.

The numerous popular misconceptions in connection with the scalping practice may be recapitulated in a series of negatives. The custom was not general, and in most regions where found was not even ancient. The trophy did not include any part of the skull or even the whole scalp. The operation was not fatal. The scalp was not always evidence of the killing of an enemy, but was sometimes taken from a victim who was allowed to live. It was not always taken by the same warrior who had killed or wounded the victim. It was not always preserved by the victor. The warrior's honors were not measured by the number of his scalps. The scalp dance was performed, and the scalps carried therein, not by the men, but by the women. See *Hair dressing*. (J. M.)

Scaltalpe. A Chinookan village a short distance above the cascades of Columbia r., Oreg.—Lee and Frost, Oregon, 176, 1844.

Scandaouati, Scandawati. See *Skandawati*.

Scandinavian influence. The discovery of Greenland by the Norsemen in 985 A. D. and their occasional voyages southward apparently as far as Nova Scotia, together with their colonization of Greenland for most of the period between 1000 and 1500, form an episode in the precolumbian period the influence of which on the natives has been confined almost exclusively to the Eskimo of Greenland and the coast of Labrador. It is now the generally accepted belief that the Markland of the Icelandic historians was Newfoundland, and Vineland a part of Nova Scotia. Storm states that he would identify the inhabitants of Vineland with the Indians—Beothuk or Micmac (Reeves, Finding of Wineland the Good, 176, 1895). The long contact of Scandinavian settlers with the Eskimo of Greenland, although having no marked effect on the habits and customs of the latter in the historic era, has had some influence in this direction. The contact began about 1000, and by 1450 the colonies had ceased to make reports to the home country and were forgotten by the civilized world. They were probably exterminated or absorbed by the natives. Rink (Tales and Trad. of Eskimo, 75, 1875) goes so far as to say: "The features of the natives in the southern part of Greenland indicate a mixed descent from Scandinavians and Eskimo, the former, however, not having left the slightest sign of any influence on the nationality or culture of the present natives." Mason (Am. Anthr. XI, 356, 1898) suggests that the well-known skill of the Eskimo in ivory-carving and etching has arisen since contact with the whites, and is due to the introduction of iron; but Boas (Bull. Am. Mus. Nat. Hist., XV, 367, 1901) considers that the resemblance of Eskimo art to the birch-bark art of the Indians indicates that such origin is impossible, though European influence may account for some of its exuberant development. With the mission of Egede in 1721 began the Christianizing of the Eskimo of the w. coast of Greenland and the institution of schools, charitable and judicial institutions, etc., which have resulted in what is called their civilization (see *Missions*). Intoxicating liquors have largely been kept from them, but the introduction of firearms has caused deterioration of their ancient skill in fishing and hunting. The adoption of writing, according to some, has impaired the ability of the Eskimo as kaiakers. The abolition of native laws and authority has led, Rink observes, to "a kind of self-abasement and disheartening." Another result of European contact is the tendency to make the houses smaller and the impairment of the power of the head of the family. From the earliest times "Europeans of the working classes have intermarried with native women, and formed their household after the Greenland model, with merely a few European improvements." The presence of a few Scandinavian words, for example, *kunia* 'wife,' in the jargon of the Pt Barrow Eskimo and whites, is due to Danish rather than to Norse influence. Another Danish loanword employed in the east may be cited— *tupak*, 'tobacco.'

Scandinavian influence is represented also by the results of the Swedish settlements in New Jersey during the period 1638–55, after the Swedes had driven out the English colonists and before they were themselves subjected by the Dutch and succeeded by Lutheran missionaries. As the labors of Campanius, Biörck, Hesselius, and others show, the Swedes came into very close contact with the Indians (Nelson, Ind. of New Jersey, 1894), and the American dialect of Swedish adopted several names of plants and animals from the Indian tongues of the region. As Nelson notes (ibid., 77), Biörck's *Dissertatio Gradualis*, published in 1731, contains valuable material bearing on the subject of the religion of the tribes of Delaware r.

Consult, in addition to the works above cited, Durrett in Filson Club Pub. 23, 1908; Egede, Description of Greenland, 1745; Fischer, Discoveries of the Norsemen in America, 1903; Fowke in Am. Anthr., II, 1900; Iowa Jour. Hist. and Pol., III, no. 1, 1905; Leland, Algonquin Legends, 1885; Stefánsson in Am. Anthr., VIII, no. 2, 1906.   (A. F. C.)

Scanonaenrat. A former Huron village situated between Nottawasaga bay and L. Simcoe, Simcoe co., Ontario. It was occupied by the Tohontaenrat, one of the four Huron tribes. The Jesuit mission of St Michel was established there. In 1649, on the overthrow of the Hurons, the Tohontaenrat abandoned their village in a body and were incorporated with the Seneca.   (J. N. B. H.)
Sainct Michel.—Jes. Rel. 1641, 81, 1858. Scanonaenrat.—Ibid. 1636, 77, 1858. Scanonaentat.—Ibid. 1639, 72, 1858. Scanonaerat.—Shea quoted by Schoolcraft, Ind. Tribes, IV, 204, 1854. Scanonahenrat.—Champlain, Œuvres, IV, 80, note, 1870. Scanouaenrat.—Jes. Rel. 1635, 85, 1858. St. Michael's.—Shea, Cath. Miss., 192, 1855.

Scarface Charley. A celebrated warrior, best known through his connection with Capt Jack, or Kintpuash, during the Modoc war of 1873. By the natives he was known as Chíkchikam-Lupalkuelátko, meaning 'wagon scar-faced,' whence the name by which he was known to the whites by reason of a disfigurement caused

by his having been run over by a mail stage when a child. Capt Jack spoke of him as a relative, but it is said also that he was a Rogue River Indian of the Tipsoe Tyee (Bearded Chief's) band and joined Capt Jack some years prior to the war of 1873, when 22 years of age. Scarface was among those who taunted Jack when, after the first attack and repulse of the white soldiers, he was disposed to enter into a treaty of peace. When the Modoc became angered during Judge Steele's last visit to them in the lavabeds, Scarface and Capt Jack saved the life of Steele by guarding him during the night; and when Odeneal and Dyar visited the Modoc, Jan. 27, 1873, on behalf of the Commissioner of Indian Affairs, Scarface would have killed them on the spot had he not been restrained by Jack. He was also the first to fire on the troops when Capt Jackson attempted the arrest of Jack's band on Jan. 28.

Rev Dr Thomas, who was killed in the peace commission massacre, on the day before his death called Scarface Charley the "Leonidas of the lava-beds." He was never known to be guilty of any act not authorized by the laws of legitimate warfare, and entered his earnest protest against the killing of Gen. Canby and Dr Thomas. He led the Modoc against Maj. Thomas and Col. Wright when the troops were so disastrously repulsed with a loss of about two-thirds in killed and wounded. Wearied of the slaughter, he is said to have shouted to the survivors, "You who are not dead had better go home; we don't want to kill you all in a day!" Later he said, "My heart was sick at seeing so many men killed."

Scarface Charley was one of the witnesses called to testify in behalf of the Modoc prisoners during their trial in July following. He was sent with other prisoners successively to Ft D. A. Russell, Wyo., Ft McPherson, Neb., and the Quapaw agency, Ind. Ter., where he died about Dec. 3, 1896. For his portrait, see *Modoc*.

Scarification. Scarification consists in cutting the skin with any suitable instrument for the purpose of extracting blood, producing suffering, or bringing about a scar. It is known among probably all American tribes from remote antiquity. Its objects were (1) medicinal, a small or a moderate quantity of blood being drawn principally for the purpose of relieving local pain; (2) ceremonial, or emotional; and (3) cosmetic.

Medicinal scarification was widely practised among the Indians of North America from prehistoric times, and was much in favor; it is still observed by some of the tribes of northern and southwestern United States. The ceremonial form, much less common than the medicinal, was practised principally for the purpose of inuring young men to suffering; while emotional scarification was observed, especially among some of the tribes of the plains, of the N.w. coast, and California, by both men and women on the death of a spouse or other near relative. Cosmetic scarifying, allied to tattooing and probably of ceremonial origin, is reported from among the Tlingit of the N. Pacific coast.

The instruments used for scarification were sharp objects, such as knives, arrowpoints, chips of stone or obsidian (and later of glass), thorns, porcupine quills, shells, awls, teeth, and finally objects of metal, the material of the implement being determined by the available supply. In exceptional cases the scarifying instrument was of symbolic significance.

Probably all the Indians by whom medicinal scarification was practised recognized the difference between merely scarifying the skin and opening a vein, the latter treatment also being given in some localities. When white physicians first went among the Indians they were often asked to employ bleeding, in the belief that it was of general benefit in almost all cases of illness. Following the scarification, when the blood ceased to flow the wound was usually covered with a substance believed to facilitate healing. On rare occasions the flow of blood from the incision was accelerated by sucking.

Consult Bancroft, Native Races, 1874–75; Bossu, Travels, II, 24–25, 1771; Champlain, Œuvres, III, 191, 1870; Cox, Adventures, I, 248, 1831; Harmon, Journal, 182, 1820; Hrdlička in Bull. 34, B. A. E., 1908; Hunter, Captivity, 1823; Jesuit Relations, Thwaites ed., 1896–1901; Lafitau, Mœurs des Sauvages Américquains, II, 1724; Lahontan, New Voy., II, 1703; La Perouse, Voy., II, 223, 1797; Le Moyne, Narr., Boston ed., 8, 1875; Rush, Enquiry into Nat. Hist. Med. among Ind., 30, 1774; Yarrow in 1st Rep. B. A. E., 1881.

Scarouady (*Skaronʻhiǎ′dǐʻ*, 'on the other side of the sky.'—Hewitt). An Oneida chief, sometimes called Half-King, who came into prominence about the middle of the 18th century. He was known among the Delawares as Monacatuatha, or Monakaduto. He is mentioned as early as 1748, and in 1753 was present at the Carlisle treaty. The following year he succeeded Half-King Scruniyatha in the direction of affairs at Aughwick, Pa. (Pa. Archiv., 1st s., II, 114, 1853), whither he removed from Logstown to escape the influence of the French. On Jan. 7, 1754, he was in Philadelphia, on his way to the Six Nations with a message from the Governor of Virginia, and also by the desire of the Indians of Pennsylvania to ask the former to send deputies to a conference with the Governor. He was with Braddock at the time of his defeat, having made in the preceding May a speech to the Indians at Ft Cumberland urging them to join Braddock in his expedition. In 1756 he seems to have been attending conferences and making speeches, mostly in behalf of peaceful measures, in some of these efforts being joined by Andrew Montour (q. v.). One of his speeches was made July 1, 1756, at the conference of the Six Nations with Sir William Johnson in behalf of the Shawnee and Delawares (N. Y. Doc. Col. Hist., VII, 148, 1856). Mention is made in the same year of his son who had been taken prisoner by the French and afterward released, and who soon thereafter visited and conferred with Johnson. Scarouady was a firm friend of the English colonists, and as strong an enemy of the French. He was an orator of considerable ability, and was the leading speaker at the numerous conferences he attended. His home was on the Ohio r. in w. Pennsylvania, where he exercised jurisdiction over the western tribes similar to that of Shikellimay over those in central Pennsylvania.   (c. t.)

Scaticook. (Properly *Pʻskáʻtikuk*, 'at the river fork,' here referring to the junction of Ten-mile and Housatonic rs. According to Eunice Mahwee, an aged Scaticook woman, in 1859, a corruption of Mohegan *Pishgachtikuk*, with the same meaning.) An Indian settlement and reservation on Housatonic r., a few miles below the present Kent, Litchfield co., Conn. It was established by Gideon Mauwehu or Mahwee, a Pequot Indian from the lower Housatonic, who, about the year 1730, removed with a few followers to the present Dover Plains, N. Y., but within a year or two again removed a few miles farther E. and established himself on the Housatonic. Here he invited his old friends of the broken tribes lower down the river to join him, and they did so in considerable numbers, calling the new settlement Scaticook. They were chiefly of the Paugusset, Uncowa, and Potatuc tribes. In 1743 the Moravians, who were at work among the neighboring Mahican of New York, established a mission at Scaticook, which at one time had about 150 baptized converts, but in consequence of difficulties with the white settlers the missions both here and at Shecomeco, of the Mahican tribe, were discontinued in 1746, and the missionaries with many of the converts removed to Pennsylvania. Those from Scaticook wasted by disease in the new location, in consequence of which most of the survivors soon returned to their former settlement; but the mission was not established, and they fell under neglect and poverty. They took no part in the French and Indian war, being too far reduced, as in 1752 they numbered but 18 families. Mauwehu died about 1755. In 1786 they numbered 71, and in 1801 only 35, but the latter figure probably does not include absentees. In 1849 there were only 8 or 10 of full blood and 20 or 30 of mixed blood. In 1903 there remained on the reservation, according to Speck, but one reputed full blood, with 14 others of negro mixture; there were besides a number of others of mongrel breed absent from the reservation. Eunice Mahwee, the last descendant of the founder, died about 1870. One man only still retained any knowledge of the language a few years ago. They have entirely lost the Indian arts and customs, except for

SCATICOOK MAN (F. G. SPECK, PHOTO.)

the making of baskets and bows and arrows. They are not to be confounded with the Indians of Scaticook, Rensselaer co., N. Y. (q. v.). Consult De Forest, Indians of Conn., 1851; Prince and Speck in Proc. Am. Philos. Soc., XLII, no. 174, 1903. (J. M.)

Pachgatgoch.—Loskiel, Hist. Miss. United Brethren, II, 183, 1794. Patchgatgoch.—Day, Penn., 185, 1843. Pisgachtigok.—Ruttenber, Tribes Hudson R., 195, 1872. Pishgachtigok.—Ibid. Scachtacook.—De Lancey (1754), in N. Y. Doc. Col. Hist., VI, 909, 1855. Scaghkooke.—Marshall (1749), ibid., 518. Schaachkook.—Albany conf. (1737) ibid., 109. Schaacticook.—Albany conf. (1754), ibid., 884. Scotticook.—Niles (ca. 1761) in Mass. Hist. Soc. Coll., 4th s., v, 507, 1861. Seachcook.—Albany conf. (1737) in N. Y. Doc. Col. Hist., VI, 108, 1855 (misprint).

Scaticook. A village on E. bank of Hudson r. near the mouth of Hoosac r., Rensselaer co., N. Y. It seems to have been originally a Mahican village, but first acquired prominence about 1676

through the settlement there of a body of fugitive Pennacook, Nipmuc, Wampanoag, Narraganset, Pocomtuc, and other refugees from New England, who had been driven out through King Philip's war in 1675. They were soon joined by others, who were encouraged to settle there by the New York authorities, and in 1702 they numbered about 1,000. They had, besides Scaticook, a village near Albany, and were regarded as under the protection of the Mohawk. The Mahican and the immigrant body each preserved its identity. The New York government endeavored to induce the Pennacook at St Francis in Canada to join the Scaticook settlement, while, on the other hand, the French and the St Francis Indians were striving to draw off the Scaticook to Canada. The latter were so far successful that the settlement soon decreased steadily, chiefly through emigration to St Francis and Caughnawaga, until in 1721 not more than 200 persons remained. At the beginning of the French and Indian war these were further reduced to about 50, who joined a party of St Francis Indians in a hostile expedition against the Massachusetts frontier in the year 1754, after which they went with them to Canada. (J. M.)

River Indians.—Doc. of 1709 in N. Y. Doc. Col. Hist., V, 140, 1855. Scaacticook.—Albany conf. (1754), ibid., VI, 880, 1855. Scaahkook.—Doc. of 1724, ibid., V, 722, 1855. Scaakticook.—Albany conf. (1754), ibid., VI, 880, 1855. Scachhook.—Livingston (1702), ibid., IV, 984, 1854. Scachkoke.—Livingston, ibid., 996. Scachkooks.—Livingston, ibid. Scackhook.—Albany conf. (1714), ibid., V, 388, 1855. Scackkook.—Albany conf. (1714), ibid., 387. Scaghtakooks.—Clark, Onondaga, I, 18, 1849. Scaghtieoke.—Kendall, Trav., I, 242, 1809. Scaghtikoke.—Macauley, N. Y., II, 10, 1829. Scagticookes.—Schoolcraft, Ind. Tribes, VI, 200, 1857. Scahcooks.—Drake, Ind. Chron., 162, 1836. Scahkooks.—Colden (1727), Five Nat., 95, 1747. Scahook.—Writer of 1690 quoted by Ruttenber, Tribes Hudson R., 178, 1872. Scatacook.—Penhallow (1726) in N. H. Hist. Soc. Coll., I, 101, 1824. Scatakook.—Dudley (1721) in Mass. Hist. Soc. Coll., 2d s., VIII, 244, 1819. Scaticook.—Kendall, Trav., I, 242, 1809. Scattacook.—Church (1716) quoted by Drake, Ind. Wars, 50, 1825. Scattakooks.—Am. Pioneer, II, 191, 1843. Scautacook.—Wainwright (1735) in Me. Hist. Soc. Coll., IV, 123, 1856. Scauticook.—Kidder, ibid., VI, 238, 1859. Schaahkook.—Schuyler (1699), ibid., IV, 575, 1854. Schaahook.—Albany conf. (1728) in N. Y. Doc. Col. Hist., V, 868, 1855. Schaakook.—Albany conf. (1726), ibid., V, 798, 1855. Schachkook.—Winthrop (1700), ibid., IV, 612, 1854. Schachticook.—Schuyler (1691), ibid., III, 800, 1853. Schackhook.—Clarkson (1691), ibid., 816. Schackooke River Indians.—Wessells (1696), ibid., IV, 248, 1854. Schackwock.—Gouverneur (1690), ibid., III, 713, 1853. Schacook.—Doc. of 1709, ibid., V, 140, 1855. Schactecoke.—Kendall, Trav., I, 241, 1809. Schacthook.—Bellomont (1700) in N. Y. Doc. Col. Hist., IV, 637, 1854. Schacticoke.—Kendall, Trav., I, 241, 1809. Schactikook.—Boudinot, Star in the West, 128, 1816. Schaggkooke.—Courtland (1688) in N. Y. Doc. Col. Hist., III, 562, 1853. Schaghkoos.—Bayard (1689), ibid., 611. Schaghtacooks.—Esnauts and Rapilly Map, 1777. Scnaghticoke.—Hayward, Gaz. U. S., 571, 1853. Schagkook.—Courtland (1688) in N. Y. Doc. Col. Hist., III, 561, 1853. Schagtihoke.—Wessells (1692) in N. Y. Doc. Col. Hist., III, 817, 1853. Schahkook.—Schuyler (1699), ibid., IV, 576, 1854. Schahook.—Council of 1683 quoted by Ruttenber, Tribes Hudson R., 176, 1872. Schakkook.—Livingston (1700) in N. Y. Doc. Col. Hist., IV, 744, 1854. **Schakook.**—Writer of about 1700 quoted by Ruttenber, op. cit., 186. **Schathsooke.**—Schuyler (1688) in N.Y. Doc. Col. Hist., III, 564,1853. **Schaticoke.**—Macauley, N. Y., II, 385, 1829. **Schaticook.**—Schuyler (1691) in N. Y. Doc. Col. Hist., III, 801, 1853. **Schauhtecogue.**—Albany charter (1686),ibid., v, 388, 1855. **Schauwunks.**—Macauley, N. Y., II, 385, 1829. **Seaticook.**—Rafinesque in Marshall, Ky., I, introd., 42, 1824 (misprint). **Shaachkook.**—Colden (1738) in N. Y. Doc. Col. Hist.,VI, 126, 1855. **Shaak-kooke.**—Bellomont (1700), ibid.,IV, 759, 1854. **Shachkook.**—Winthrop (1700), ibid., 612. **Shachook.**—Cornbury (1703), ibid., 1057. **Shackhokes.**—Markham (1691),ibid.,III, 809, 1853. **Shackhook.**—Schuyler (1701), ibid., IV. 835, 1854. **Shaktakook.**—Jefferys, Fr. Doms., pt. 1, map, 1761. **Skaachkook.**—Livingston (1710) in N. Y. Doc. Col. Hist., v, 223, 1855. **Skaahkook.**—Doc. of 1710, ibid., 219. **Skachcook.**—Livingston (1702), ibid., IV, 991, 1854. **Skachhooke.**—Livingston(1703),ibid.,1068. **Skachkock.**—Livingston (1702), ibid.,991. **Skachkoke.**—Livingston (1700), ibid., 652. **Skachkook.**—Livingston (1687), ibid., III, 481, 1853. **Skachticookes.**—Tryon (1774), ibid., VIII, 451, 1857. **Skackkook.**—Bellomont (1698), ibid., IV, 364, 1854. **Skackoor.**—Bellomont (1698) quoted by Ruttenber, Tribes Hudson R., 166, 1872. **Skacktege.**—Doc. of 1711 in N. Y. Doc. Col. Hist., v, 281, 1855. **Skaghhook.**—Albany conf. (1722),ibid., 661. **Skaticok.**—Albany conf. (1754), ibid., VI, 879, 1855. **Skattock.**—Rupp, West. Penn., app., 75, note, 1846. **SkoohHook.**—Livingston (1702) in N. Y. Doc. Col. Hist., IV, 984, 1854. **Skotacook.**—Stiles (1761) in Mass. Hist. Soc. Coll., 1st s., x, 105, 1809.

Schachipkaka. See *Dekaury, Konoka.*

Schachuhil (so called because the dead were carried down from this place to a village below, called Chutil, to be buried). A former village of the Pilalt, a Cowichan tribe of lower Chilliwack r., Brit. Col. **Stcā'tcūHil.**—Hill-Tout in Ethnol. Surv. Can., 48, 1902. **Tcā'tcōHil.**—Boas in Rep. Brit. A. A. S., 454, 1894.

Schaeken (*S'tcaēkEn*). A village of the Ntlakyapamuk on Fraser r., above Lytton, Brit. Col.—Hill-Tout in Rep. Ethnol. Surv. Can., 4, 1899.

Schekaha (*Shinuk-kaha*, 'lying in the sand,' or 'sand town'). A former Choctaw village situated about 7 m. N. E. of Philadelphia, Neshoba co., Miss.—Halbert in Pub. Miss. Hist. Soc., VI, 428, 1902. **Schekaha.**—Romans, Florida, map, 1775. **Schekahaw.**—West Florida Map, ca. 1775.

Schenectady ('on that side of the pinery', referring to the large number of pines formerly growing between Albany and Schenectady). According to Macauley, the Ohnowalagantles, whom he calls a clan of the Mohawk, lived at Schenectady, which was situated about 17 m. w. of Albany, N. Y. He adds that the Schaunactadas, apparently only another form of the name Schenectady, whom he calls a clan of the Mohawk, dwelt along the Hudson at Albany and southwardly. The lands of Schenectady were purchased from the Mohawk by Arent Van Corlaer and others in 1662, and the present city founded. It suffered severely during the later Indian wars, and in 1690 it was attacked by French and Indians and many of its inhabitants were massacred. **Ohnowalagantles.**—Macauley, Hist. N. Y., II, 295, 1829. **O-no-ä-lä-gōne'-na.**—Morgan, League Iroq., app. A, 138, 1904. **Schaunactadas.**—Macauley, op. cit.

Schepinaikonck. A former Minisink village, perhaps in Orange co., N. Y.—Van der Donck (1656) quoted by Ruttenber, Tribes Hudson R., 96, 1872.

Schilks (*Stcilks*, 'sling'). A Squawmish village community on the E. side of Howe sd., Brit. Col.—Hill-Tout in Rep. Brit. A. A. S., 474, 1900.

Schink (*Stcink·*). A Squawmish village community at Gibson's landing, on the w. side of Howe sd., Brit. Col.—Hill-Tout in Rep. Brit. A. A. S., 474, 1900.

Schipston. A former village, probably of the Delawares, at the head of Juniata r., Pa.—Pouchot map (1758) in N. Y. Doc. Col. Hist., x, 694, 1858.

Schira. The extinct Crow clans of Sia and San Felipe pueblos, N. Mex. **Schilrá-háno.**—Hodge in Am. Anthr., IX, 350, Oct. 1896 (San Felipe name). **Shíra-háno.**—Ibid. (Sia name; *háno* = 'people').

Schischlachtana ('deceivers like the raven,' the raven being the primary instructor of man). A Knaiakhotana clan of Cook inlet, Alaska.—Richardson, Arct. Exped., I, 407, 1851.

Schist. A term applied to fissile and foliated rocks which, although often massive in appearance, split readily in one direction owing to parallel arrangement of the constituent minerals. They are quite variable in composition and are referred to as mica, hornblende, chlorite, or quartz-schist, according to the predominance of the particular mineral. The schists were commonly referred to as slates by early geologists, but the latter term is now confined especially to those varieties that split with considerable regularity. Schists are widely distributed and were extensively used by the native tribes in the manufacture of implements. A majority of the grooved axes and many of the celts, gouges, and other articles, including spear and arrow heads of E. United States, are made of this material. The color is usually gray. In texture the schists are exceedingly varied, but the tribes made use only of the hard and tough varieties. (w. H. H.)

Schloss. The local name for a body of Upper Lillooet around Seton lake, interior of British Columbia; pop. 34 in 1909. **Schloss.**—Can. Ind. Aff. Rep., pt. II, 72, 1902. **Slosh.**—Ibid., pt. I, 277.

Schodac (*M'skatak*, 'at the prairie.'—Hewitt). The ancient Mahican capital, situated on the E. bank of Hudson r., on the site of Castleton, Rensselaer co., N. Y., which derives its name from the palisaded village formerly existing on the height. It was occupied as late as 1664. The council fire was afterward removed to Westenhuck (see *Stockbridge*) in the Housatonic valley. (J. M.) **Pempotawuthut.**—Hoyt, Antiq. Res., 90, 1824. **Pempotowwuthut, Muhhecanneuw.**—Holmes in Mass. Hist. Soc. Coll., 1st s., IX, 100, 1804 (trans. 'fireplace of the Muhheakunnuk Indians'). **Schodac.**—

Ruttenber, Tribes Hudson R., 41, 1872. **Schotack.**—Livingston (1678) in N. Y. Doc. Col. Hist., XIII, 515, 1881. **Schotax.**—Doc. of 1677 cited by Ruttenber, Ind. Geog. Names, 59, 1906.

Schoenbrunn (Ger.: 'beautiful spring'). A Moravian town, of Munsee Indians, situated about 2 m. below the site of New Philadelphia, Ohio. Zeisberger went from the station (Friedensstadt), on Beaver r., Pa., to Tuscarawas r., where the three stations of Schoenbrunn, Gnadenhuetten, and Salem were established. The Moravian Indians moved from the Beaver to these villages in 1773. The first meetinghouse and schoolhouse in the present state of Ohio were built at this station, which was also the birthplace of the first white child born within the state. The Indian village was a prosperous settlement. The Revolution brought these villages on the line between the British at Detroit and the Americans at Ft Pitt. In Aug. 1781 De Peyster, the commander at Detroit, becoming convinced that these Indians were giving information of the British movements, sent Capt. Matthew Elliott with a party of Wyandot, Delawares, and Shawnee, and a small band of French-Canadians, to remove these Indians to Sandusky, a task which they performed with great harshness, the Indians being robbed of nearly everything they had. When the Moravians were massacred at Gnadenhuetten (q. v.) in Mar. 1782, the village at Schoenbrunn was burned by the same troop of Pennsylvanians under Col. Williamson. There was also a small settlement on the opposite side of the river called New Schoenbrunn, which was established in 1779 and destroyed in 1782. Consult Loskiel, Hist. Missions, pt. 3, 177–182, 1794; Butterfield, Washington-Irvine Corr., 100–102, 1882; Archives Pa., IX, 523–525, 1854.   (G. P. D.)

Schoenbrunn.—Loskiel, Hist. Miss. United Breth., pt. 3, 75, 1794. **Schonbrunn.**—Howe, Hist. Coll. Ohio, II, 691, 1896. **Shoenbrun.**—Harris, Tour, 134, 1805. **Weelhick Thuppek.**—Connolly, Heckewelder's Narr., 233, 1907 (Delaware translation of German name).

Schoharie ('the driftwood', or 'the floating driftwood.'—Hewitt). A Mohawk village formerly near the present Schoharie, Schoharie co., N. Y.

Fort Kouari.—Document ca. 1758 in N. Y. Doc. Col. Hist., X, 676, 1858 (fort). **Schoaries.**—Goldthwait (1766) in Mass. Hist. Soc. Coll., 1st s., X, 121, 1809. **Schohare.**—Johnson (1756) in N. Y. Doc. Col. Hist., VII, 91, 1856. **Schoharie.**—Tryon (1774), ibid., VIII, 451, 1857. **Schoherie.**—Johnson (1757), ibid., VII, 278, 1856. **Schohery.**—Zeisberger MS. (1750) quoted by Conover, MS. Kan. and Geneva. **Scohare.**—Johnson (1763) in N. Y. Doc. Col. Hist., VII, 582, 1856. **Scoharee.**—Ft Johnson Conference (1756), ibid., 105. **Scoharies.**—Johnson (1747), ibid., VI, 361, 1855. **Sko-har'-le.**—Morgan, League Iroq., 473, 1851 (correct form).

Schoherage. A former Iroquois village, apparently under Oneida jurisdiction, situated, according to the Brion de la Tour map, 1781, on the w. bank of the E. branch of Susquehanna r., below Tuskokogie. This is probably an error for Chenango r. in New York.

Schohoragé. A former Iroquois village, placed on the w. bank of the Susquehanna, a short distance above Oquaga (q. v.), in New York.—Esnauts and Rapilly Map, 1777.

Schonchin. The recognized head-chief of the Modoc at the time of the Modoc war of 1872–73. In 1846 the Modoc numbered 600 warriors, governed by Schonchin, whose authority seems even then to have been disputed on the ground that he was not an hereditary chief. He took an active part in the early hostilities between the Modoc and the whites, and admitted that he did all in his power to exterminate his enemies. Hostilities were continued at intervals until 1864, when a treaty was made with the Modoc by the provisions of which they agreed to go on a reservation with the Klamath Indians. At this council the Modoc were represented by Schonchin and his younger brother, known as Schonchin John. To the credit of the old chief it is said that after signing the treaty no act of his deserved censure. He went with his people on the land allotted to them, and at the time of the outbreak under Kintpuash (q. v.), or Captain Jack, remained quietly on the reservation in charge of his peaceful tribesmen. His brother John, following Captain Jack, withdrew from the reservation and took up his abode on Lost r., the former home of the tribe. The old chief made every effort to induce Jack to return, but the latter steadfastly refused, on the ground that he could not live in peace with the Klamath. In order to remove every obstacle to the return of the fugitives, the reservation was divided into distinct agencies, a district being set apart exclusively for the Modoc. To this new home old Schonchin was removed with his people, and a portion of Captain Jack's band took up their abode with him. The rest, including Schonchin John, fled to the lava beds, and from this stronghold waged a destructive war. It is believed that Schonchin John, more than any other member of the tribe, was influential in keeping up the strife. He repeatedly advised continuing the fight when Jack would have made peace, and he is considered responsible for many of the inhuman acts committed. In 1873 a peace commission was appointed to deal with the Indians, and a meeting with them was arranged for April 11. To this meeting the Indians agreed to send a number of men equal to that of the commission, and that all should go unarmed.

The commission were divided as to the advisability of keeping the appointment. Commissioners Dyar and Meacham suspected treachery and were of the opinion that it was not safe, while General Canby and Dr Thomas, a Methodist minister, insisted that it was plainly their duty to go. The four commissioners, accompanied by an interpreter and his Indian wife, proceeded to the place of appointment, and, being met by eight Indians, fully armed, it was evident that they had fallen into a trap. The council was opened with brief speeches by Thomas and Canby offering the terms of peace, only to be interrupted by Schonchin John, who angrily commanded, "Take away your soldiers and give us Hot Creek for a home!" Before the commissioners could reply, at a signal from Jack the Indians fell upon the white men. Canby and Thomas were shot to death, Dyar fled and escaped, and Meacham was shot five times by Schonchin John, but finally recovered. As a result of this massacre military operations were resumed with great activity, and after a few severe engagements Jack was dislodged from the lava beds and with his party surrendered on June 1. Gen. Davis decided to hang the leaders forthwith, Schonchin John among the number. While the scaffolds were being prepared word was received from Washington that the condemned men must be tried by a military commission. The prisoners were found guilty of murder and assault to kill, in violation of the rules of war, and sentenced to be hanged, but sentences of two of them were commuted to imprisonment for life. Schonchin John was one of those who were hanged. The execution took place at Ft Klamath, Oct. 3, 1873. In a speech made by Schonchin immediately before his death he declared that his execution would be a great injustice, that his "heart was good," and that he had not committed murder. He asked that his children should be sent to his brother Schonchin, who was still at Yainax on the reservation, and who would "bring them up to be good." Bancroft says that Schonchin John was striking in appearance, with a sensitive face, showing in its changing expression that he noted and felt all that was passing about him. Had he not been deeply wrinkled, though not more than 45 years of age, his countenance would have been rather pleasing. (F. S. N.)

Schoneschioronon ('beautiful-hillside people.'—Hewitt). A clan of the Iroquois, q. v.—French writer (1666) in N. Y. Doc. Col. Hist., IX, 47, 1855.

Schoomadits. An unidentified tribe of Vancouver id., probably Nootka.
Schoomadits.—Jewitt, Narr., 36, 1849. Shoomads.—Armstrong, Oregon, 136, 1857.

Schoyerre. A former Seneca settlement on the w. side of Seneca lake, probably in Ontario or Yates co., N. Y. It contained 18 houses when destroyed by Gen. Sullivan in 1779.—Grant (1779) quoted by Conover, Kan. and Geneva MS., B. A. E.

Schuelstish. A former Salish division on Columbia r., Wash. According to Stevens it formed one of the 8 Spokan bands in 1853.
Schee-et-st-ish.—Stevens in Ind. Aff. Rep., 429, 1854. Schu-el-stish.—Gibbs in Pac. R. R. Rep., I, 414, 1855.

Schurye. A Cowichan village on lower Fraser r., just above Sumass lake, Brit. Col. Pop. 27 in 1894, the last time it was enumerated separately.
Schuary.—Can. Ind. Aff. Rep. 1894, 276, 1895. Schurye.—Ibid., 1880, 316, 1881. Schuye.—Brit. Col. map, Ind. Aff., Victoria, 1872.

Scitadin. A village on the St Lawrence, in 1535, below the site of Quebec.—Cartier, Bref Récit, 32, 1863.

Sconassi. A former village with a mixed population under Iroquois jurisdiction, situated in 1746, according to D'Anville's map of that date, on the w. side of Susquehanna r., below the w. branch of the Susquehanna, probably in Union co., Pa.
Sionassi.—Nouvelle Carte Particulière de l'Amérique, n. d.

Scorse Ranch ruins. A group of pueblo ruins on the s. side of Leroux wash, in the broken country along the N. flank of the Holbrook mesa, 16 to 20 m. N. E. of Holbrook, Ariz. The pottery, of which there are 175 pieces in the National Museum, is chiefly of coarse gray and undecorated brown ware, vases with handles being largely represented, and resembles the ancient Zuñi earthenware more closely than it does any other type.—Hough in Rep. Nat. Mus. 1901, 307, 1903.

Scotch. See *English influence*.

Scoutash's Town. A former Mingo or Shawnee village, named after a chief, near Lewistown, Logan co., Ohio, on a tract ceded by treaty of July 20, 1831, when the occupants removed to Indian Ter.
Scoutashs town.—Maumee treaty, Sept. 29, 1817, in U. S. Ind. Treat., Kappler ed., II, 105, 1903.

Scowlitz. A Cowichan tribe living at a town of the same name at the mouth of Harrison r., Brit. Col. Pop. 52 in 1904, 42 in 1909.
Harrison Mouth.—Can. Ind. Aff. Rep. 1891, 248, 1892. Scowlitz.—Can. Ind. Aff. Rep., 160, 1901. Sk·au'elitsk.—Boas in Rep. 64th Meeting Brit. A. A. S., 454, 1894. Skowliti.—Brit. Col. map, Ind. Aff., Victoria, 1872.

Scrapers. Implements of the scraper class are indispensable adjuncts of the arts of life among primitive peoples. They take varied forms, serve many important purposes, and are made of every available material—animal, vegetal, and mineral. It is observed that although the shapes are often highly specialized, these implements have never risen above the homely realm of the simply useful arts as have some of the implements associated with war and the chase. In their use they have much in common with the knife, the gouge, and the adz, as well as with the abrading implements proper, by the aid of which objects of many kinds were given their final shape and finish. Any sharp-edged stone or fragment of bone, shell, or hard wood could be employed in sharpening or treating materials less refractory than themselves. Stone was of most general application, and fragments and flakes of suitable shape were selected and used or were modified by chipping to increase their effectiveness. The most common form was made from a substantial flake, straight or slightly concave on one side and convex on the other, by removing a few chips around the broad end on the convex side, thus giving a keen, curved scraping edge. Another variety is shaped like a short-bladed spear-head, with stem or notches for hafting, the edge, generally rounded in outline, being either beveled or sharpened equally from both sides. In many cases broken spearpoints and knives were sharpened across the broken end by the removal of a few flakes, giving the necessary scraping edge. These implements were hafted by inserting the stem in the end of a piece of wood or bone, and fixing it with some kind of cement, or by attaching it with cords or thongs to the properly notched end of the handle. With some of the tribes, especially the Eskimo, the handle was elaborated in various artistic ways to fit the hand and to accommodate the thumb and fingers; and on the plains the years of children were recorded by means of tally marks on the handle. Scrapers shaped

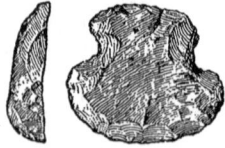

QUARTZ SCRAPER; DIST. COL. (1-2)

QUARTZITE SCRAPER; DIST. COL. (1-2)

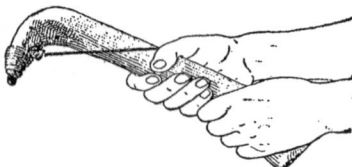

USE OF SCRAPER IN HIDE-DRESSING; SIOUX

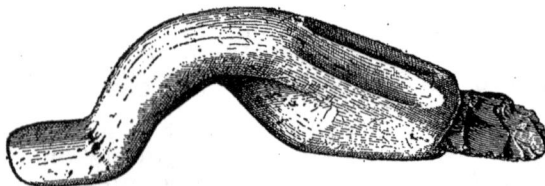

ESKIMO SCRAPER; LENGTH, 5 IN. (MURDOCH)

in part or in whole by pecking and grinding are common. Many of these take the celt or adz form, being beveled after the manner of the latter, with which implement, in both form and use, they imperceptibly blend. Among the uses of the scraper that of dressing hides probably took first place (see Skin-dressing). But its services in shaping many varieties of articles of wood, bone, horn, antler, shell, and soft stone were varied and important.

Scrapers are described, among others, by Boas in 6th Rep. B. A. E., 1888; Fowke in 13th Rep. B. A. E., 1896; Holmes in 15th Rep. B. A. E., 1897; Jones, Antiq. So. Inds., 1873; Moorehead, Prehist. Impls., 1900; Murdoch in 9th Rep. B. A. E., 1892; Nelson in 18th Rep. B. A. E., 1899; Niblack in Rep. Nat. Mus. 1886, 1889; Rau in Smithson. Cont., XXII, 1876;

HUDSON BAY ESKIMO SCRAPER. (TURNER)

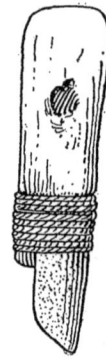

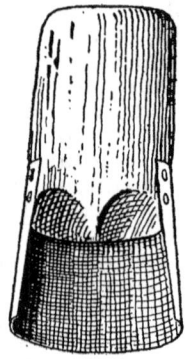

a   b

CENTRAL ESKIMO SCRAPERS: a, STONE; b, SHEET TIN. (BOAS)

Thruston, Antiq. Tenn., 1897; Turner in 11th Rep. B. A. E., 1894. (W. H. H.)

Scruniyatha. See Half King.

Sculpture and Carving. The sculptural arts in their widest significance may be regarded as including the whole range of the nonplastic shaping arts, their processes and products; but as here considered they relate more especially to the higher phases of the native work, those which rise above the mere utilitarian level into the realm of esthetic expression, thus serving to illustrate the evolution of sculpture the fine art. The shaping arts in nonplastic materials, in their ethnological and technical bearings, are treated under appropriate heads (see, Bone-work, Shell-work, Stone-work, Wood-work). The native tribes N. of

Mexico had made very decided progress in the sculptural arts before the arrival of the whites, and in more recent times the tribes of British Columbia and Alaska have produced carvings of very considerable merit. The acquisition of implements of steel has no doubt contributed to the success of this work. The carvings of the Haida, Tlingit, Kwakiutl,

HAIDA SLATE PIPE.   THE BEAR MOTHER, IN
(NIBLACK)   BLACK SLATE; HAIDA.
                  (NIBLACK) (1-4)

and other tribes, in wood, bone, ivory, and slate are remarkable for their artistic qualities and perfection of execution, displaying more than a mere suggestion of the masterly qualities of the prehistoric work of the tribes of Mexico and Central America (Niblack, Boas). A carving in black slate by a member of the Haida

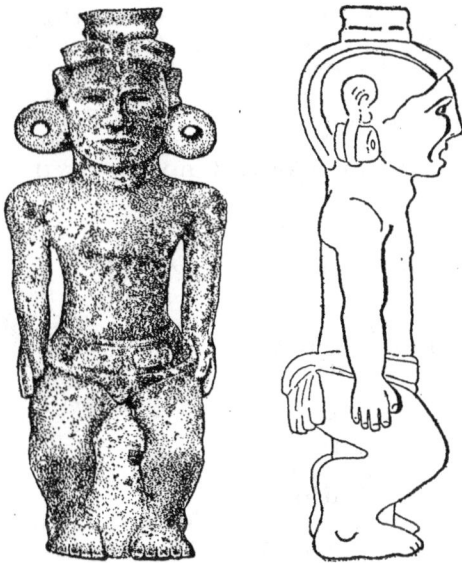

PIPE, STONE; OHIO MOUND; HEIGHT, 8 IN. (MILLS)

tribe, representing the "bear mother" (Swan), is not surpassed in spirit and expression by any known work N. of Mexico. However, like the totem-pole models, masks, rattles, dishes, boxes, and tobacco pipes which excite our admiration, it was executed with steel tools and at a time when the influence of the art of the white man had no doubt come to be somewhat decidedly felt. The Eskimo have exercised their very pronounced genius for realistic carving in ivory and bone, and to some extent in stone and wood. Their representations of animal forms in the round are often admirable, although usually applied to objects that serve some practical purpose (Turner, Boas, Nelson, Murdoch, Hoffman). The Pueblo tribes are not especially accom-

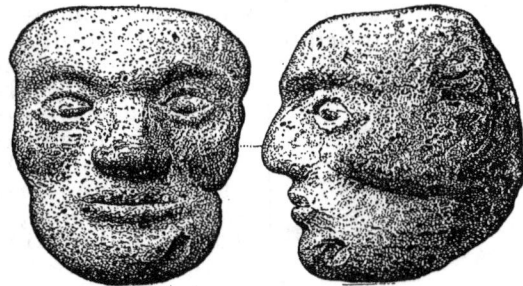

HUMAN HEAD, STONE; NEW YORK (1-6)

plished in sculpture, notwithstanding the facts that they stand alone as builders in stone and have exceptional skill and taste in modeling in clay. Their small animal fetishes in several varieties of stone are interesting, but very elementary as works of art, and the human figure, as illustrated by the wooden katcinas of the Hopi, is treated in an extremely primitive manner. The ancient Pueblos were hardly more skillful in these branches (Cushing, Stevenson, Fewkes). The prehistoric sculpture of the Pacific states had barely advanced beyond the elaboration of utensils, although these were often well executed. Worthy of especial attention, however, are certain ape-like heads found in Oregon and Washington, believed by some to represent the seal or sealion rather

STONE FIGURE; TENNESSEE (1-8)

than any exotic form (Terry). Carvings in wood, stone, bone, horn, and shell, among the historic natives of E. United States, are deserving of slight notice except in so far as they illustrate the very beginnings of sculptural effort. The mound-building tribes of precolumbian times made somewhat ambitious attempts at the portrayal of the human form in the round, and expended much time in the shaping of tobacco pipes in many varieties of hard stone. In these the forms of various quadrupeds, reptiles, and birds were executed in such close approximation to nature that in some cases the species can be recognized with reasonable certainty (Henshaw). In no section, so far as can be determined, was portraiture of the human face very successfully attempted, and the idea of statuary for statuary's sake had probably not been conceived. The life forms shaped were generally the embodiment of mythic personages or beings of importance in the mythology of the people. They are forcefully, but formally or conventionally, presented. It is believed that the native artist drew, modeled, or carved not with the subject before him, but relying upon the traditional conception of the particular subject, the mythological characters being of greater importance to him than the literal or specific rendering of any original. The shortcomings of these sculptures as works of representative art were thus not due to lack of capacity to imitate nature correctly, but resulted rather from the fact that exact imitation of nature was not essential to the native conception of the requirements of the art (Squier and Davis, Schoolcraft, Henshaw, Thomas). The carvings in bone and shell of these tribes present few art features of particular interest, excepting in the designs which were engraved on gorgets and other forms of personal ornaments.

Technologically considered, sculpture includes all representative work in the round and in relief of all degrees, the lower forms connecting with the bolder phases of the engraver's art (see *Engraving*). In the period before the arrival of the whites the shaping processes employed implements of stone chiefly, but copper and bone were employed to some extent. These tools, however, were more efficient than those unacquainted with their operation would at first imagine. The brittle materials were shaped by fracturing with stone hammers and by pressure with implements of bone or horn. Hard and tough stones were reduced by pecking with stone hammers and by saw-

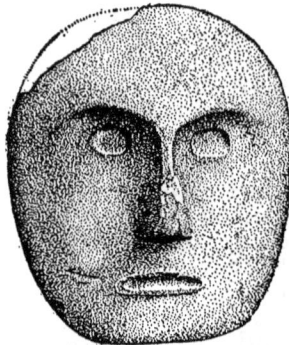

STONE PIPE; OHIO: HEIGHT, 2 IN. (SQUIER AND DAVIS)

STONE MASKETTE; OHIO

ing and drilling with wood and bone or copper tools, aided by fine sand, but soft stones, such as steatite, were cut with stone saws, chisels, and knives. The forms were elaborated and specialized by grinding and finished by rubbing. (See *Art*.)

Native sculpture is referred to and somewhat fully illustrated in numerous works: Ann. Archæol. Rep. Ontario, 1888–1906; Boas in Bull. Am. Mus. Nat. Hist., IX, 1897; XV, pt. 1, 1901; Cushing in Proc. Am. Philos. Soc., XXXV, 1897, Dellenbaugh, North Americans of Yesterday, 1901; Fowke, Archæol. Hist. Ohio, 1902; Henshaw, Holmes, Thomas, Fowke, Cushing, Stevenson, Fewkes, Boas, Turner, Nelson, Murdoch, Dall, in Rep. B. A. E.; Jones, Antiq. So. Inds., 1873; McGuire in Am. Anthr., Oct. 1894, Moore, in Jour. Acad. Nat. Sci. Phila.; Moorehead, Prehist. Impls., 1900; Rau in Smithson. Cont. Knowl., XXII, 1876; Schoolcraft, Ind. Tribes, 1851–57; Smith in Bull. Am. Mus. Nat. Hist., XX, 1904; Squier and Davis, Ancient Monuments, 1848; Swan in Smithson. Cont. Knowl., XXI, 1874; Terry, Sculptured Anthropoid Ape Heads, 1891; Thruston, Antiq. of Tenn., 1897; Boas, Wilson, Hoffman, Hough, Niblack, in Rep. Nat. Mus. and Smithson. Inst. (W. H. H.)

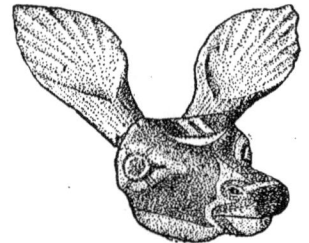

STONE VESSEL; ALA. DIAM. OF BOWL, 11 3-4 IN. (MOORE)

DEER HEAD OF WOOD; FLORIDA. (CUSHING)

Scup. See *Scuppaug.*

Scuppaug. A name current in parts of New England, Rhode Island in particular, for the porgy (*Pagrus argyrops*), a fish of the Atlantic Coast waters, known also as scup, a reduction of *scuppaug*, which is itself a reduction of *mishcŭp-paŭog* (plural of mishcŭp, q. v.), called breame in the Narraganset vocabulary of Roger Williams (1643). The word *scuppaug* appears also as *skippaug*. (A. F. C.)

Scuppernong. The name of a small and unimportant river in Tyrrell co., N. C., raised from obscurity through the application of its name to a whitish grape (a variety of *Vitis rotundifolia*, Michx., the muscadine grape; the *messamin* of Capt. John Smith), discovered near Columbia (the county seat), on its E. shore, in the 18th century, by two men named Alexander. This variety, which subsequently became somewhat famous as a table and wine grape, was called at first the "white grape" by its discoverers, who afterward changed the name, owing to its indefiniteness, to that of the river on which it was found. The name of the river (which is also that of the lake in which it has its source) was originally the Indian designation of the swampy land along its borders, viz, *äskŭp'onong*, 'at (or in) the place (or country) of the *äskŭpo*,' the Southern Algonquian name of the *Magnolia glauca*, a small tree growing in swamps (or "bays," as magnolia swamps are called in North Carolina) from New Jersey to Florida, and popularly known as sweet bay, swamp bay, swamp sassafras, bay laurel, etc. This species of magnolia is the tree that Capt. Arthur Barlow in his account of Wokokon id. (1584) refers to as "the tree that beareth the rine [rind] of blacke sinamon," and compares to another magnolia now known as *Drimys Winteri;* and that Thomas Hariot, in his Brief and True Report (1588), mentions under the Indian name of *ascopo*, and likens to the "cassia lignea" (*Canella alba*) of the West Indies.　　　(W. R. G.)

Scuteeg. See *Squeteague.*

Scyo. Mentioned by Laet (Heylyn, Cosmog., 969, 1703) as one of the provinces of Quivira (q. v.); apparently imaginary.

Se. The Bluebird clan of the Tewa pueblo of San Ildefonso, N. Mex.
Se-tdóa.—Hodge in Am. Anthr., IX, 349, 1896 (*tdóa*='people').

Seakop. A Salish village or band under Fraser superintendency, Brit. Col.—Can. Ind. Aff. Rep., 78, 1878.

Seama. A former village, whose inhabitants were probably Salinan, connected with San Antonio mission, Monterey co., Cal.—Taylor in Cal. Farmer, Apr. 27, 1860.

Seamysty. According to Gairdner (Jour. Geog. Soc. Lond., XI, 255, 1841) a Chinookan tribe living at the mouth of Cowlitz r., Oreg., before 1835. It was undoubtedly a band or division of the Skilloot and closely related to the Cooniac band.　　　(L. F.)
Cia'mēctix·.—Boas, inf'n, 1905. Lctā'mēctîx·.—Boas, Kathlamet Texts, 6, 1901. Noowootsoo.—Boas, inf'n, 1905.

Seantre. A band, belonging probably

to the Moquelumnan stock, formerly living on Merced r., central Cal.—Wessells (1853) in H. R. Ex. Doc. 76, 34th Cong., 3d sess., 30, 1857.

Seasons. See *Calendar.*

Seats. See *Furniture.*

Seattle (properly *Seathl*). A chief of the Dwamish and allied tribes of Puget sd., Wash.; born perhaps about 1790, died on Port Madison res., in the same neighborhood, June 7, 1866. He was the first signer of the Port Elliott treaty of 1855, by which the Puget sd. tribes submitted to agency restrictions. In the general outbreak of 1855–58 he maintained a friendly attitude. Through the efforts of the French missionaries he became a Catholic and inaugurated regular morning and evening prayers in his tribe, which were continued by his people after his death. In appearance he is described as dignified and venerable, with a bearing reminding one somewhat of Senator Benton. The town of Seattle was named from him, and in accordance with local Indian belief that the mention of a dead man's name disturbs the rest of the spirit, the old man was accustomed to levy a small tribute on the citizens as compensation in advance. A monument was erected over his grave by the people of Seattle in 1890. See Bancroft, Hist. Wash., Idaho and Mont., 1890; Ind. Aff. Rep. 1904, 357, 1905.　　　(J. M.)

Seawan, Seawant. See *Sewan.*

Sebaik ('at the water-passage.'—Gatschet). A Passamaquoddy village at Pleasant Point on Passamaquoddy bay, near Perry, Washington co., Me. It was settled by the Indians who came across Passamaquoddy bay from Gunasquamekook.
Pleasant Point.—Vetromile, Abnakis, 19, 1866. Point Pleasant.—Shea, Cath. Miss., 158, 1855. Seboiak.—Kellogg in Mass. Hist. Soc. Coll., 3d s., III, 181, 1833. Siba-igewi.—Gatschet, Penobscot MS., B. A. E., 1887 (Penobscot name). Sybaik.—Vetromile, Abnakis, 55, 1866. Sybayks.—Kidder in Me. Hist. Soc. Coll., VI, 232, 1859. Tchibaique.—Romagné, Ind. Prayer Book, title, 1804.

Secacawoni. A tribe or village of the Powhatan confederacy on the s. bank of the Potomac in Northumberland co., Va. In 1608 the inhabitants numbered about 120. The village was situated at the mouth of Coan r.
Cecocawanee.—Bozman, Md., I, 118, 1837. Cecocawonee.—Simons in Smith (1629), Va., I, 177, reprint of 1819. Cekacawone.—Smith, ibid., II, 78. Cekakawwon.—Strachey (1612), Va., 38, 1849. Chicocoan.—Bozman, Md., II, 308, 1837. Sakacawone.—Ibid., I, 138, 1837. Se-ca-ca-co-nies.—Macauley, N. Y., II, 166, 1829. Secacaonies.—Jefferson, Notes, 128, table, 1802. Secakoonies.—Boudinot, Star in the West, 128, 1816. Sekacawone.—Smith, Va., I, 118, repr. 1819. Sekacowones.—Laet, Nouv. Monde, 85, 1640.

Secatoag ('burned land.'—Gerard). A tribe or band on the s. coast of Long Id., N. Y., in Suffolk co., occupying the district between Oyster Bay and Patchogue. Their principal village was near Islip. They were nearly extinct when the island was first settled by whites.

Seacotauk.—Doc. of 1677 in N. Y. Doc. Col. Hist., XIV, 728, 1883. Seaketaulke.—Doc. of 1677, ibid., 733. Secatague.—Wood quoted by Macauley, N. Y., II, 253, 1829. Secataug.—Ibid. Secatogue.—Thompson, Long Id., 68, 1839. Secatoket.—Ibid., I, 442, 1843. Secatong.—Treaty of 1656 quoted by Ruttenber, Tribes Hudson R., 125, 1872. Secoutagh.—Doc. of 1657 in N. Y. Doc. Col. Hist., II, 5, 1858. Sequatake.—Thompson, Long Id., I, 448, 1843. Sequatogue.—Deed of 1696 quoted by Thompson, ibid., 446. Sequetauke.—Doc. of 1676 in N. Y. Doc. Col. Hist., XIV, 711, 1883. Si-ca-tugs.—Macauley, N. Y., II, 164, 1829. Sicketauyhacky.—Doc. of 1645 in N. Y. Doc. Col. Hist., XIV, 60, 1883. Sicketawach.—Doc. of 1656, ibid., 369. Sicketawagh.—Ibid. Sicketeuwhacky.—Deed of 1639, ibid., 15. Sicketewackey.—Van der Donck (1656) quoted by Ruttenber, Ind. Geog. Names, 82, 1906. Siketeuhacky.—Doc. of 1644 in N. Y. Doc. Col. Hist., XIV, 56, 1883.

Secawgo. A tribe or band which in 1807 attended a conference at Greenville, Ohio; perhaps the Potawatomi living near Chicago, Ill.

Lecawgoes.—Blue Jacket (1807) quoted by Brice, Ft Wayne, 173, 1868 (misprint). Secawgoes.—Blue Jacket (1807) quoted by Drake, Tecumseh, 94, 1852.

Seccasaw. A Massachuset village in 1614 on the coast of Massachusetts, in the N. part of Plymouth co.

Secassaw.—Smith (1629), Va., II, 183, repr. 1819. Seccasaw.—Smith (1616) in Mass. Hist. Soc. Coll., 3d s., VI, 108, 1837.

Seccherpoga (probably intended for Lutchapoga). Mentioned by Webb (H. R. Doc. 80, 27th Cong., 3d sess., 47, 1843) as a band of Indians living in Florida; they doubtless formed part of the Seminole tribe.

Secharlecha (*Sidshálidsha*, 'under a blackjack [*Quercus Catesbæi*] tree.'—Gatschet). A former Lower Creek settlement where a council of the Lower Creeks was held in Nov. 1832; not otherwise known.

Secharlecha.—Seale in H. R. Doc. 452, 25th Cong., 2d sess., 50, 1838. See-char-litch-ar.—Schoolcraft, Ind. Tribes, IV, 579, 1854.

Sechi. A Kawia village in Cahuilla valley, s. Cal. Agua Caliente, one name for this place, has been extended to designate a reservation, Agua Caliente No. 2, which comprises 3,844 acres of patented desert land, on which there were 31 Indians in 1903 under the San Jacinto agency, and 43 in 1909 under the Malki school superintendency.

Agua Caliente.—Barrows, Ethno-Bot. Coahuilla, 33, 1900. Palm Springs.—Ind. Aff. Rep. 1902, 175, 1903. Se-chi.—Barrows, op. cit. Techáhet.—Schumacher in Peabody Mus. Rep., XII, 521, 1880 (probably the correct identification, the author being evidently wrong in placing the people he refers to, in Los Angeles co., where there are no Kawia).

Sechukhtun (*Se-tcuq'-tún*). A former village of the Chastacosta on Rogue r., Oreg.—Dorsey in Jour. Am. Folk-lore, III, 234, 1890.

Secmoco (*Sek-mo-ko'*). A tribe represented at San Antonio de Valero mission, Texas, between 1730 and 1741. The parents of an adult gentile woman baptized

there in 1730 were a Secmoco and a Papanac (Valero Bautismos, 1730, 1737, 1741, MS.). Cf. *Sinicu*.   (H. E. B.)

Sencase.—Valero Bautismos, op. cit., 1737 (identical?) Sepuncó.—Ibid., 1730.

Secobec. A village of the Powhatan confederacy in 1608, on the s. bank of the Rappahannock, in Caroline co., Va.

Secobeck.—Smith (1629), Va., I, map, repr. 1819.

Seconchqut. A village on Marthas Vineyard, off the coast of Massachusetts, in 1698.—Doc. of 1698 in Mass. Hist. Soc. Coll., 1st s., X, 131–132, 1809.

Secotan (apparently a substantive meaning 'burned place,' from a verb signifying 'it burns'; cf. *Secatoag*.—Gerard). An Algonquian tribe occupying in 1584 the peninsula between Albemarle sd. and lower Pamlico r., with the adjacent islands, the territory now embraced in Washington, Tyrrell, Dare, Beaufort, and Hyde cos., N. C. In later times the same territory was occupied by the Machapunga, Pamlico, and Hatteras, who may have been the descendants of the Secotan. From the statements of White, who accompanied the early Raleigh expeditions, these Indians were of medium stature; they dressed in loose mantles of deerskin, and wore summer aprons of the same about the loins, in front only on the men, but before and behind on the women. The men cut their hair close on the sides of the head, leaving a crest from the forehead back to the neck; that of the women, being comparatively short, thin, and soft, was clipped in front. The arms, legs, and cheeks of the women and parts of the body of the men were tattooed to a limited extent. The Secotan believed in the immortality of the soul and in numerous deities called "Mantoac [i.e. *man'toak*, pl. of *manito*, the first mention of the word in English], but of different sortes and degrees; one only chiefe and great God, which hath bene from all eternitie." Their towns are described as small, and near the seacoast but few; some containing 10 or 12 houses, some 20, the greatest seen having but 30. Some of these were inclosed "with barks of trees made fast to stakes, or els with poles onely fixed upright and close one by another." Their houses were oblong and consisted of a framework of poles set in the ground and lashed with cross-pieces; the roof was rounded, covered with bark or rush mats. The Secotan people were comparatively well advanced in agriculture, cultivating not only maize, of which they had three varieties, but two leguminous plants which the English called peas and beans, and melons, pumpkins, gourds, etc. They drew a large part of their subsistence from the waters, being expert fishermen, spearing fish, and also capturing them in "a kind of wear made of reedes, which in that country are very strong." For synonyms, see the village, following.   (J. M.)

Secotan. The chief Secotan village in the 16th century, situated on the N. bank of Pamlico r. in the present Beaufort co., N. C. For an illustration from White's drawing, see *Habitations*.

Assamacomoe.—Raleigh (1589) quoted by Martin, N. C., I, 33, 1829 (perhaps a corruption of Dasamonquepeuc). **Secota.**—De Bry, map (*ca.* 1585) in Hawks, N. C., I, 1859. **Secotan.**—Barlowe (1584), ibid., 87. **Sequotan.**—Ibid., 86. **Sicopan.**—Schoolcraft, Ind. Tribes, VI, 92, 1857 (misprint). **Wangadacea.**—Martin, N. C., I, 33, 1829. **Wingadocea.**—Martin, N. C., I, 10, 1829. **Wingandacoa.**—Barlowe (1584) quoted by Hawks, N. C., I, 78, 1859 (said by Raleigh to mean "you wear good clothes," the reply of the natives to questions of the English and mistaken by them for the name of the country). **Wingandagoa.**—Strachey (1612), Va., 143, 1849. **Winginans.**—Rafinesque in Marshall, Ky., introd., I, 36, 1824. **Winginas.**—Ibid., 27.

Secowocomoco. A former Algonquian tribe or subtribe of Maryland, living on Wicomico r. in St Mary and Charles cos. In 1608 their village was on the E. bank of Wicomico r. at its junction with the Potomac in St Mary co., and was estimated to contain 50 warriors. They are distinct from the Wicomoco. They are the tribe among whom the first Maryland colonists landed and made their primary settlement. At that time (1634) they had their village on St Marys r., but soon afterward abandoned it, nominally for the benefit of the English, but more likely on account of the frequent inroads of the Conestoga. It is probable that this and other small tribes in this section of Maryland formed parts of or were closely connected with the Conoy. In 1651 they with other tribes were removed to a reservation at the head of Wicomico r.

According to White (Relatio Itineris) they were very tall and well proportioned; they painted their faces dark blue above the nose and red below, or the reverse. Their hair was gathered in a knot at the left ear and fastened with a band. Their houses were built "in an oblong oval shape." Their chief deity was named Ochre, and they also paid a kind of adoration to corn and fire. For subsistence they depended largely on agriculture.

Cecomocomoco.—Smith (1629), Va., I, map, repr. 1819 (misprint). **Secowocomoco.**—Ibid., 118. **Wicomocons.**—Bozman, Md., II, 421, 1837. **Yaocomico.**—White (*ca.* 1634), Relatio Itineris, 36, 1874 (apparently the chief's name). **Yaocomoco.**—Ibid. **Yaomacoes.**—Shea misquoting Bozman in Alsop, Md., 119, note, 1880. **Yoamaco.**—Harris, Voy. and Trav., II, 259, 1705. **Yoamacoes.**—Bozman, Md., II, 29, 1837.

Secret societies. Societies or brotherhoods of a secret and usually sacred character existed among very many American tribes, among many more, doubtless, than those from which there is definite information.

On the Plains the larger number of these were war societies, and they were graded in accordance with the age and attainments of the members. The Buffalo society was a very important body devoted to healing disease. The Omaha and Pawnee seem to have had a great number of societies, organized for all sorts of purposes. There were societies concerned with the religious mysteries, with the keeping of records, and with the dramatization of myths, ethical societies, and societies of mirth-makers, who strove in their performances to reverse the natural order of things. We find also a society considered able to will people to death, a society of "big-bellied men," and among the Cheyenne a society of fire-walkers, who trod upon fires with their bare feet until the flames were extinguished.

According to Hoffman the Grand Medicine society, or Midewiwin, of the Chippewa and neighboring tribes, was a secret society of four degrees, or lodges, into which one could be successively inducted by the expenditure of a greater and greater amount of property on the accompanying feasts. As a result of these initiations the spiritual insight and power, especially the power to cure disease, was successively increased, while on the purely material side the novitiate received instruction regarding the medicinal virtues of many plants. The name of this society in the form *medeu* occurs in Delaware, where it was applied to a class of healers. In the neighborhood of New York bay there was a body of conjurers who "had no fixed homes, pretended to absolute continence, and both exorcised sickness and officiated at the funeral rites." Their name is interpreted by Brinton to mean "Great Snake," and they participated in certain periodical festivals where "a sacrifice was prepared, which it was believed was carried off by a huge serpent."

In the S. W. each Pueblo tribe contains a number of esoteric societies, which mediate between men and the zoömorphic beings of Pueblo mythology. At Zuñi there are 13 of these societies, and they have to do especially with healing, either collectively in their ceremonies or through individual members. They also endeavor to bring rain, but only by means of the influence which the beast gods are able to exert over the anthropic beings who actually control it. Rain-bringing itself is properly the function of the rain priests and of the Kótikilli society, the latter consisting of Zuñi of the male sex, and occasionally some females. Admission to this is necessary in order that one may have access after death to the dance-house of the anthropic gods. There are six divisions of the Kótikilli, holding their ceremonies in as many kivas corresponding to the six world-quarters, and in their performances members wear masks representing the anthropic beings, which they are then supposed actually to embody, although they sing to them at the same time in order to bring showers. The Rain priesthood and the Priesthood of the Bow are considered under the caption *Shamans and Priests*, but they may be classed also as brotherhoods concerned respectively with rain-making and war (see Stevenson in 23d Rep. B. A. E., 1905).

At Sia the Society of the Cougar presides over hunting, and there is also a Warrior society. Parents apply to have their children admitted into a society, or a person who has been cured by the society may afterward be taken in. A person may belong to more than one society, and most of the societies also consist of two or more orders, the most important "being that in which the members are endowed with the anagogics of medicine."

Since the Hopi clans have been shown by Fewkes to have been originally independent local groups, the secret society performances among them would appear to be nothing more than the rituals of the various groups, the societies themselves being the members of the groups owning such rituals and certain others that have been granted a right to participate. The principal war society, however, has resulted from a fusion of the warriors or war societies of all the clans of the Hopi pueblos except one. Besides the two war societies, and two societies devoted to the curing of diseases, all of these brotherhoods devote themselves to bringing rain and stimulating the growth of corn. Each is headed by a chief, who is the clan chief as well and the oldest man in his clan, and contains several subordinate chiefs, while the oldest woman of the clan occupies a conspicuous place.

The Californian Maidu had a society into which certain boys chosen by the old men were annually admitted. The societies were called Yĕponi, and included all the men of note in the tribe. "The ceremonies were more or less elaborate, involving fasts, instruction in the myths and lore of the tribe by the older men, and finally a great feast and dance at which the neophytes for the first time performed their dances, which were probably received through visions." (Dixon, Maidu Myths, 1902.) Each village or group of villages commonly had a separate branch of the society under a leader called Húku, who was one of the most important personages in the place, being frequently called upon to settle disputes that could not otherwise be composed, lead a war-party, or determine when the people should go to gather acorns. He was usually a shaman also, and was then considered more powerful

than any other, for which reason he was looked to, to make rain, insure good supplies of acorns and salmon, keep his people in good health, and destroy their enemies by means of diseases. He was the keeper of a sacred cape made of feathers, shells, and pieces of stone, which was made for him by the previous leader and would kill anyone else who touched it. He was appointed by the most noted shaman in the society, who pretended that he had been instructed in a dream, and usually held office as long as he chose, though he might be deposed. Powers quotes a local authority to the effect that there was a secret society among the Pomo which conjured up infernal horrors for the purpose of "keeping their women in subjection," and they are also said to have had regular assembly houses, but the account of this society is evidently garbled and distorted.

The sense of supernatural as distinguished from purely secular relationships received its logical recognition among the Kwakiutl of the coast of British Columbia in a division of the year into a sacred and a profane period, during each of which the social organization and along with it personal appellations of the tribe changed completely. In the first place, a distinction was made between present members of the secret societies, called "seals," and the *quéqutsa*, those who were for the time being outside of them. These latter were furthermore divided, in accordance with sex, age, and social standing, into several bodies which received names generally referring to animals.

The "seals," on the other hand, were subdivided into societies in accordance with the supernatural beings supposed to inspire the various members. All of those whose ancestors had had an encounter with the same supernatural being were thus banded together, and, since only one person might represent each ancestor, the number in a society was limited, and one might join only on the retirement of a member. Every secret society had its own dances, songs, whistles, and cedar-bark rings. The right to a position in a secret society might be acquired by killing a person of some foreign tribe and taking his paraphernalia, or for one's son by marrying the daughter of him who possessed it. At the time of initiation the novice was supposed to be carried away for a season by the spirit which came to him, and after his return he usually went through the different houses in the town accompanied by other members of the society who had been initiated previously. In case his spirit were a violent one, he might break up boxes, canoes, etc., which the giver of the feast had to replace. The most important part of these societies were the ones inspired by the cannibal spirit, the origin of which has been traced by Boas to the Heiltsuk tribe and to customs connected with war.

From the Kwakiutl and Heiltsuk these secret society dances spread northward and southward. The Nootka are said to have had two principal secret society performances, the Dukwally (i. e. *ъ̄'koala*), or Thunder-bird ceremony, supposed to have been obtained from the wolves, and the Tsáyeq (Kwakiutl *Ts'ā'eqa*), or Tsiahk, into which a patient was initiated when the shaman had not succeeded in curing him. According to Swan the latter was performed after the patient had seen a dwarfish spirit with long, yellowish hair and four horns on his head who promised relief if the ceremonies were performed.

The Songish of British Columbia have two societies called Tciyī'wan and Xʌnxʌnī'tʌl, obtained from the Nootka. The first is open to anybody and consists of five subordinate societies. That to which a man belongs depends on the dream he has after retiring into the woods. Unlike the other, only rich people can become members of the Xʌnxʌnī'tʌl, as heavy payments are exacted for initiation. The Xʌnxʌnī'tʌl novice also obtains his guardian spirit in the woods, after which he performs his first dance with masks and cedar-bark ornaments. Among the coast Salish of Fraser valley is found a brotherhood or society called Sqoíaqī, which enjoys special prerogatives and possesses certain emblems and dances. Bellacoola secret societies are closely bound up with the festivals and the tribal organization. They are of two varieties, the Sisaúkʿ, obtained from a being of that name who resides in the sun, and the Kū'siut, which were derived from a female spirit who lives in a cave in the woods and comes out only in winter when the feasts are about to be held. He who sees her has to invite people to dance the Kū'siut. There are several different societies or degrees of this, however, corresponding to the highest ones among the Kwakiutl. The dances, masks, etc., used at such times, and only then, seem to be the special property of the different clans, but right to wear them has to be acquired by the individuals.

The Tsimshian societies were all received from the Heiltsuk through Kitkatla, but according to Niska tradition they were obtained by the former from a man who went to live among the bears. There are said to have been five or six of these societies among the latter people, and the number of places in each was limited. The performances were similar to those seen among the Kwakiutl, except that they were not so elaborate.

57009°—Bull. 30, pt 2—12——32

The Haida have had secret societies only during the last 100 or 150 years. The entire performance consisted in the supposed possession of the novice by some one of a number of spirits, who carried the youth away and made him act the way the spirit himself was supposed to act. Some of these ways of acting were introduced, while others were in accordance with native conceptions. They were largely the property of certain chiefs who would allow only their own families to use them. Among the Tlingit the societies appear to have been employed in a very similar manner, but with the northern Tlingit they had barely made their appearance.

Consult Boas (1) in Rep. Nat. Mus. for 1895, 1897, (2) in Mem. Am. Mus. Nat. Hist., II, Anthr. I, 1898; Boas and Hill-Tout in Reps. B. A. A. S.; Boas, Cushing, Fewkes, Hoffman, Dorsey, and Mrs Stevenson in Reps. B. A. E.; Brinton, Lenape Leg., 1885; Curtis, N. Am. Ind., I–V, 1907–09; Cushing in Pop. Sci. Mo., June 1882; Dixon in Bull. Am. Mus. Nat. Hist., XVII, pt. II, 1902, and pt. III, 1905; Powers in Cont. N. A. Ethnol., III, 1877; Warren in Coll. Minn. Hist. Soc., V, 1885.   (J. R. S.)

Seechelt (*Sī'ciatl*). A Salish tribe on Jervis and Seechelt inlets, Nelson id., and the s. part of Texada id., Brit. Col. They speak a distinct dialect and are thought by Hill-Tout on physical grounds to be related to the Lillooet. Anciently there were 4 divisions or septs — Kunechin, Tsonai, Tuwanek, and Skaiakos—but at present all live in one town, called Chatelech, around the mission founded by Bishop Durieu, who converted them to Roman Catholicism. The Kunechin and Tsonai are said to be of Kwakiutl lineage. Pop. 236 in 1902, according to the Canadian Department of Indian Affairs, and 325 according to Hill-Tout. The former authority gives 244 in 1909.   (J. R. S.)
Nī'ciatl.—Boas in 5th Rep. N. W. Tribes Can., 10, 1889 (Comox name). Seashelth.—Brit. Col. map, Ind. Aff., Victoria, 1872. Seehelts.—Mayne, Brit. Col., 144, 1862. Seshal.—Tolmie and Dawson, Vocabs. Brit. Col., 119B, 1884. She-shell.—Can. Ind. Aff., 308, 1879. Sī'cätl.—Boas, op. cit. (Nanaimo name). Sī'ciatl.—Ibid. (own name).

Seechkaberuhpaka ('prairie chicken'). A band of the Hidatsa (q. v.).
Prairie Chicken.—Morgan, Anc. Soc., 159, 1877. Prairie hen.—Matthews, Ethnog. Hidatsa, 207, 1877. Seeh-ka-be-ruh-pä'-ka.—Morgan, op. cit. Sitskabinohpaka.—Matthews, inf'n, 1885. Tsitska' dʠo-qpa'-ka.—Dorsey in 15th Rep. B. A. E., 242, 1897. Tsí tska do hpa-ka.—Matthews, Ethnog. Hidatsa, op. cit.

Seeharongoto (*See-har-ong'-o-to*, 'drawing down hill'). A subdivision of the Wolf clan of the Delawares.—Morgan, Anc. Soc., 172, 1877.

Seek's Village. A former Miami village, named from the chief, on Eel r., about 3 m. from Columbia City, in Whitley co.,

Ind. The tract was sold in 1838. According to Indian information obtained by J. P. Dunn, the chief's name was Zeke and his father was a German. His Miami name was Maconsaw, 'Young Beaver,' and this name was sometimes given to the village.

Seethltun (Chasta Costa: *Se-eçl-tún,* 'people using salmon weirs'). The Takelma village nearest the Chastacosta, on the s. side of Rogue r., Oreg.—Dorsey in Jour. Am. Folk-lore, III, 235, 1890.

Seginsavin. A former Potawatomi village, named from its chief, on Rouge r., near Detroit, Mich. The tract was sold in 1827.
Seginsairn's Village.—Treaty of 1827 in U. S. Ind. Treat., 674, 1873. Seginsavin's village.—Brown, West. Gaz., 159, 1817. Seginservin's village.—Detroit treaty (1807) in Am. St. Papers, Ind. Aff., I, 747, 1832. Seginsiwin's village.—Detroit treaty (1807) in U. S. Ind. Treat., 194, 1873.

Sego. A bulbous root (*Calochortus luteus*) found particularly in Utah and used for food by the Indians: from the word for bulbous roots of this sort in the Paiute language. (A. F. C.)

Segocket. An Abnaki village about 1614, near the mouth of Penobscot r., Me.
Segocket.—Smith (1616) in Mass. Hist. Soc. Coll., 3d s., VI, 97, 1837. Segohquet.—Strachey (ca. 1612), Va., 167, 1849.

Segotago. An Abnaki village in 1614, probably near the mouth of Kennebec r., Me.—Smith (1616) in Mass. Hist. Soc. Coll., 3d s., VI, 107, 1837.

Segunesit. A former Nipmuc village in N. E. Connecticut, whose warriors gathered with other hostile Indians in 1675 at Manexit.—Quanapaug (1675) in Mass. Hist. Soc. Coll., 1st s., VI, 205, 1800.

Segwallitsu. Given by Gibbs (Cont. N. A. Ethnol., I, 178, 1877) as a band of the Nisqualli. The name is not found elsewhere.

Segwarusa. See *Saghwareesa.*

Seh. The Eagle clan of Jemez pueblo, New Mexico. A corresponding clan existed also at the former related pueblo of Pecos.
Seé+.—Hodge in Am. Anthr., IX, 350, 1896 (Pecos form; +=ash='people'). Sehtsaásh.—Hodge, Ibid. (Jemez form). Se-peh.—Hewett, ibid., n. s., VI, 431, 1904 (Pecos form).

Sehachpeya (*Seh-ach-pe-ya*). A former Hupa village on the w. bank of Trinity r., Cal., below the mouth of Willow cr.—Gibbs, MS., B. A. E., 1852.

Sekamish. A Salish division formerly on White r., N. w. Wash., now on Port Madison res.
Se-ka-mish.—Gibbs in Pac. R. R. Rep., I, 436, 1855. Sk-Khabish.—Mallet in Ind. Aff. Rep., 198, 1877. St-ka-bish.—Ibid. St-káh-mish.—Treaty of 1855 in U. S. Ind. Treaties, 378, 1873. St. Kalmish.—Ross in Ind. Aff. Rep. 1869, 135, 1870. St'kamish.—Gibbs in Cont. N. A. Ethnol., I, 179, 1877.

Sekani ('dwellers on the rocks'). A group of Athapascan tribes living in the valleys of upper Peace r. and its tributaries and on the w. slope of the Rocky mts., Brit. Col. Morice says they were formerly united into one large tribe, but on account of their nomadic habits have gradually separated into smaller distinct tribes having no affiliation with one another. Harmon (Jour., 190, 1820) said that they came from E. of the Rocky mts., where they formed a part of the Tsattine. Gallatin (Trans. Am. Antiq. Soc., II, 20, 1836) gave their habitat as the headwaters of Peace r. Dunn (Hist. Oreg., 79, 1844) located them in the mountains near Nahanni r. Wilkes (U. S. Explor. Exped., IV, 451, 1845) said they ranged about Ft Simpson, E. of the Taculli and beyond the Rocky mts. McLean (Hudson's Bay, I, 235, 1849) found some at McLeod lake in 1849. Richardson (Arct. Voy., II, 31, 1851) placed them between Stikine and Skeena rs. Taylor (Cal. Farmer, July 19, 1862) described them as being in the mountains between McLeod and Connolly lakes. According to Hind (Labrador Penin., II, 261, 1863) they inhabited the foot of the Rocky mts. N. w. of Peace r. and a part of New Caledonia w. of the Rocky mts., resorting to Fts Dunvegan, Halkett, and Liard. Pope (MS., B. A. E.) located them w. of Tatlah lake, Brit. Col. Petitot (Dict. Dènè-Dindjié, xx, 1876) said that most of them were near the trading posts on Fraser r., a small number only frequenting the Peace and Liard, where they have a reputation for great savageness. Morice (Proc. Canad. Inst., 112, 1889) says they roam over the Rocky mts. on both slopes and the adjacent forests and plains from about 54° to 60° N. They are of much slighter build and shorter in stature than any of the neighboring tribes, from whom they otherwise differ but little except that their bands are numerous and not closely organized socially. Morice describes them as slender and bony, in stature below the average, with narrow forehead, prominent cheek-bones, small, deeply sunk eyes, the upper lip very thin, the lower protruding, the chin very small, and the nose straight. Fathers appear like children, and none are corpulent and none bald. Petitot describes them as built like Hindus, light of color, with fine black almond eyes, large and of oriental limpidity, firm noses, the mouth large and voluptuous. Many of the males are circumcised. The women wear rings in their noses. These people are very barbarous and licentious. Their complete isolation in the Rocky mts. and their reputation for merciless and cold-blooded savagery cause them to be dreaded by other tribes. Their manner of life is miserable. They do without tents, sleeping in brush huts open to the weather. Their only clothing consists of coats and breeches of mountain-goat or bighorn skins, the hair turned outside or next to the skin according to the season. They cover themselves at night with goat-skins sewed together, which communicate to them a strong odor, though less pungent than the Chipewyan receive from their smoked elk skins. Petitot (Autour du lac des Esclaves, 309, 1891) pronounces them the least frank and the most sullen of all of the Tinneh. They are entirely nomadic, following the moose, caribou, bear, lynx, rabbits, marmots, and beaver, on which they subsist. They eat no fish and look on fishing as an unmanly occupation. Their society is founded on father-right. They have no chiefs, but accept the council of the oldest and most influential in each band as regards hunting, camping, and traveling (Morice, Notes on W. Dénés, 28, 1893). When a man dies they pull down his brush hut over the remains and proceed on their journey. If in camp, or in the event of the deceased being a person of consequence, they make a rough coffin of limbs and erect a scaffolding for it to rest on, covering it usually with his birch-bark canoe inverted; or, on the death of an influential member of the tribe, a spruce log may be hollowed out for a coffin and the remains suspended therein on the branches of trees. Sometimes they hide the corpse in an erect position in a tree hollowed out for the purpose. They keep up the old practice of burning or casting into a river or leaving suspended on trees the weapons and clothing of the dead person. When a member of the band was believed to be stricken with death they left with him what provisions they could spare and abandoned him to his fate when the camp broke up. They are absolutely honest. A trader may go on a trapping expedition, leaving his store unlocked without fear of anything being stolen. Natives may enter and help themselves to powder and shot or any other articles they require out of his stock, but every time they leave the exact equivalent in furs (Morice).

Morice (Trans. Can. Inst., 28, 1893) divides the Sekani into 9 tribes, each being composed of a number of bands having traditional hunting grounds the limits of which, unlike those of their neighbors, are but vaguely defined. It is not uncommon for them to trespass on the territory of one another without molestation, an unusual custom among the tribes of the N. W. The tribes are as follows: (1) Yutsutkenne, (2) Tsekehneaz, (3) Totatkenne, (4) Tsatkenne (Tsattine), (5) Tsetautkenne, (6) Sarsi, (7) Saschutkenne, (8) Otzenne, (9) Tselone. Besides these there is an eastern division, the Thekkane.

Drake (Bk. Inds., xi, 1848) gave their number as 1,000 in 1820. Dawson (Rep. Can. Inst., 200B, 1889) said that in 1888 there were 78 near Ft Liard and 73 near Ft Halkett, making 151 in the Mackenzie r. region. Morice (Proc. Can. Inst., 113, 1889) said that they numbered 500 in 1887, not more than 250 of them being in British Columbia. The same authority (Notes on W. Dénés, 16, 1893) estimated the total population of the Sekani group at 1,300; the Sekani proper, on both sides of the Rocky mts., numbering 500, the Tsattine 700, and the Sarsi 100. In 1909 the Sarsi (q. v.) alone were officially reported to number 197.

Al-ta-tin.—Dawson in Rep. Geol. Surv. Can., 192B, 1887. **Lhtaten.**—Morice in Proc. Can. Inst., 118, 1889 ('inhabitants of beaver dams': applied also to Nahane). **T'tat-'tenne.**—Morice, Notes on W. Dénés, 29, 1893 ('people of the beaver dams': Takulli name.) **Rocky Mountain Indians.**—Bancroft, Nat. Races, I, map, 35, 1882. **Sécanais.**—Petitot in Jour. Roy. Geog. Soc., 651, 1883 ('men who live on the mountain'). **Secunnie.**—Hale, Ethnol. and Philol., 202, 1846. **Sékanais.**—Petitot, Dict. Dènè-Dindjié, xx, 1876. **Sékanais toenè.**—Morice in Proc. Can. Inst., 113, 1889. **Sékan'-es.**—Petitot, MS. vocab., B. A. E., 1869. **Sicannis.**—Bancroft, Nat. Races, I, 115, 1874. **Sicanny.**—Pope, MS. vocab., B. A. E., 1865. **Sicaunies.**—Harmon, Jour., 190, 313, 1820. **Siccane.**—Can. Ind. Aff., 91, 1876. **Siccanies.**—Taylor in Cal. Farmer, July 19, 1862. **Siccannies.**—Hind, Labrador Penin., II, 261, app., 1863. **Siccony.**—Ross, MS. notes on Tinne, B. A. E. **Sickanies.**—Ross in Smithson. Rep. 1866, 309, 1872. **Sickannies.**—Ross, MS. vocab., B. A. E. **Siconi.**—Wilkes, U. S. Expl. Exped., IV, 451, 1845. **Sikanis.**—Duflot de Mofras, Expl. de l'Oregon, II, 339, 1844. **Sikanni.**—Latham in Trans. Philol. Soc. Lond., 71, 1856. **Sikannies.**—Keane in Stanford, Compend., 535, 1878. **Sikennies.**—Ibid., 464. **Thœcanies.**—Dunn, Hist. Oregon, 79, 1844. **Thé-ké-né.**—Petitot, MS. vocab., B. A. E., 1865 ('dwellers on the mountains'). **The'-kĕn-nĕh.**—Ross, MS. notes on Tinne, B. A. E. **Thé-ké-ottiné.**—Petitot, MS. vocab., B. A. E., 1865. **Thè-khènè.**—Petitot in Bull. Soc. Géog. Paris, chart, 1875. **Thè-kk'a-nè.**—Petitot, Autour du lac des Esclaves, 362, 1891 ('people on the mountain'). **Thè-kka-nè.**—Petitot, Dict. Dènè-Dindjié, xx, 1876. **Thè-kké-Ottiné.**—Petitot in Jour. Roy. Geog. Soc., 651, 1883. **Thickcannies.**—Hind, Labrador Penin., II, 261, 1863. **Thikanies.**—Hardisty in Smithson. Rep. 1866, 311, 1872. **Tsekanie.**—McLean, Hudson's Bay, I, 235, 1849. **Tsé'kéhne.**—Morice, Notes on W. Dènès, 19, 1893. **Tsekenné.**—Morice in Proc. Can. Inst., 112, 1889 ('inhabitants of the rocks'). **Tsikanni.**—Latham, Nat. Hist. Man, 306, 1850. **Tsitka-ni.**—Richardson, Arct. Exped., II, 31, 1851.

Sekhatsatunne (*Se-qa'-ts'ă γûnnĕ*). A former village of the Chastacosta, on the N. bank of Rogue r., Oreg.—Dorsey in Jour. Am. Folk-lore, III, 234, 1890.

Sekhushtuntunne (*Se-qûc-tûn γûnnĕ*, 'people at the big rocks'). A band of the Mishikhwutmetunne formerly living on Coquille r., Oreg.—Dorsey in Jour. Am. Folk-lore, III, 232, 1890.

Sekumne (*Se-kum'-ne*). A former Maidu village on the right bank of American r., about 10 m. above Sacramento, Cal.

Lacomnis.—Taylor in Cal. Farmer, June 8, 1860. **Secumnes.**—Hale, Ethnol. and Philol., 631, 1846. **Secumni.**—Latham in Proc. Philol. Soc. Lond., VI, 79, 1854. **Sekamne.**—Hale, op. cit., 222. **Sekomne.**—Hale misquoted by Bancroft, Nat. Races, I, 450, 1874. **Sekume.**—Latham, Opuscula, 313, 1860. **Sekumne.**—Dixon in Bull. Am. Mus. Nat. Hist., XVII. pt. 3, pl. 38. 1905. **Sekúmne.**—Hale, op. cit., 631. **Sicumnes.**—Ibid., 630,

Sekwu (*Sek'-wu*). The Klikitat name of a village at the forks of Cowlitz r., Wash., in 1863, presumably belonging to the Cowlitz tribe.—Gibbs, MS. no. 248, B. A. E.

Selalkwo (*Sel-al'-kwo*). A Salish village, about 1863, below the forks of Dwamish r., Wash., and probably below the junction of White and Green rs.—Gibbs, MS. no. 248, B. A. E.

Selawigmiut. A tribe of Alaskan Eskimo living on Selawik lake, E. of Kotzebue sd., Alaska. They numbered 100 in 1880.
Chilivik.—Zagoskin, Descr. Russ. Poss. Am., I, 74, 1847. Seelawik Mutes.—Kelly, Arct. Eskimos, chart, 1890. Selawigamute.—Petroff in 10th Census, Alaska, 4, 1884. Selāwig'mūt.—Dall in Cont. N. A. Ethnol., I, 12, 1877. Silawïñmiun.—Murdoch in 9th Rep. B. A. E., 44, 1892. Sulawig-meuts.—Hooper, Cruise of Corwin, 26, 1881.

Seldovia (Russian: 'herring'). A Kaniagmiut Eskimo village on the s. side of Kachemak bay, w. coast of Kenai penin., Alaska. Pop. 74 in 1880; 99 in 1890. (Petroff, 10th Census, Alaska, 29, 1884.)

Selelot (*Sẹl'ẹlōt*). A Squawmish division living on Burrard inlet, coast of British Columbia.—Boas, MS., B. A. E., 1887.

Selenite. See *Gypsum*.

Seleuxa. A former Seminole town at the head of Ocilla r., probably in Madison co., Fla.—H. R. Ex. Doc. 74 (1823), 19th Cong., 1st sess., 27, 1826.

Selikwayi (*Selikwä'yĭ*). A Cherokee settlement, about the time of the removal of the tribe to the W. in 1839, on Sallacoa cr., probably at or near the present Sallacoa, Cherokee co., N. w. Ga. The name is that of a small green snake, and of a tall broad-bladed grass bearing a fancied resemblance to it. (J. M.)
Sallicoah.—Doc. of 1799 quoted by Royce in 5th Rep. B. A. E., 144, 1887.

Selkuta (*Sel-ku'-ta*). A Bellacoola village on the N. side of the mouth of Bellacoola r., Brit. Col.—Boas in Mem. Am. Mus. Nat. Hist., II, 49, 1898.

Sels ('food-steamers'). The name applied, probably contemptuously, to a Haida family of low social rank which formed a subdivision of the Hlgahetgulanas. It is related that the people of this family were so much in the habit of steaming food that one of their women once said, "We shall be called 'food-steamers'"; and so it happened. Low-class people in other families seem to have received the same name.—Swanton, Cont. Haida, 270, 1905.

Seltsas (*Selts'ā's*). A Katsey summer village at the head of Pitt lake, which drains into lower Fraser r., Brit. Col.—Boas in Rep. Brit. A. A. S., 454, 1894.

Semeckamenee. See *Sewackenaem*.

Semehau (*Semexā'u*, 'little lynx'). A village of the Spences Bridge band of Ntlakyapamuk on the N. side of Thompson r., 32 m. from Lytton, Brit. Col.—Teit in Mem. Am. Mus. Nat. Hist., II, 173, 1900.

Semiahmoo. A Salish tribe living about the bay of the same name in N. w. Washington and s. w. British Columbia. In 1843 they numbered 300, and in 1909 there were 38 of the tribe on the Canadian side.
Birch Bay.—Farnham, Trav., 111, 1843. Samamhoo.—Can. Ind. Aff., 308, 1879. Semiahmoo.—Wilson in Jour. Ethnol. Soc. Lond., 278, 1866. Semiā'mō.—Boas in 5th Rep. N. W. Tribes, Can., 10, 1889. Sem-mi-an-mas.—Fitzhugh in Ind. Aff. Rep. 1857, 328, 1858. Shimiahmoo.—Gibbs in Pac. R. R. Rep., I, 433, 1855. Simiahmoo.—Gibbs, Clallam and Lummi, 6, 1863. Simiamo.—Tolmie and Dawson, Vocabs. Brit. Col., 119B, 1884. Skim-i-ah-moo.—Gibbs in Pac. R. R. Rep., I, 436, 1855.

Seminole (Creek: *Sim-a-no'-le*, or *Isti simanóle*, 'separatist', 'runaway'). A Muskhogean tribe of Florida, originally made up of immigrants from the Lower Creek towns on Chattahoochee r., who moved down into Florida following the destruction of the Apalachee (q. v.) and other native tribes. They were at first classed with the Lower Creeks, but began to be known under their present name about 1775. Those still residing in Florida call themselves Ikaniúksalgi, 'peninsula people' (Gatschet).

The Seminole, before the removal of the main body to Indian Ter., consisted chiefly of descendants of Muscogee (Creeks) and Hitchiti from the Lower Creek towns, with a considerable number of refugees from the Upper Creeks after the Creek war, together with remnants of Yamasee and other conquered tribes, Yuchi, and a large negro element from runaway slaves. When Hawkins wrote, in 1799, they had 7 towns, which increased to 20 or more as they overran the peninsula.

While still under Spanish rule the Seminole became involved in hostility with the United States, particularly in the War of 1812, and again in 1817–18, the latter being known as the first Seminole war. This war was quelled by Gen. Andrew Jackson, who invaded Florida with a force exceeding 3,000 men, as the result of which Spain ceded the territory to the United States in 1819. By treaty of Ft Moultrie in 1823, the Seminole ceded most of their lands, excepting a central reservation; but on account of pressure from the border population for their complete removal, another treaty was negotiated at Paynes Landing in 1832, by which they were bound to remove beyond the Mississippi within 3 years. The treaty was repudiated by a large proportion of the tribe, who, under the leadership of the celebrated Osceola (q. v.), at once prepared for resistance. Thus began the second Seminole war in 1835, with the killing of Emathla, the principal signer of the removal treaty, and of Gen. A. R. Thompson, who had been instrumental in applying pressure to those who opposed the arrangement. The war lasted nearly 8 years, ending in Aug. 1842, with the practical expatriation of the tribe from Florida for the W., but at the cost of the lives of nearly 1,500 American troops and the expenditure of $20,000,000. One incident was the massacre of Maj. F. L. Dade's command of 100 men, only one man escaping alive. The Seminole negroes took an active part throughout the war.

Those removed to Oklahoma were subsequently organized into the "Seminole Nation," as one of the so-called Five Civilized Tribes. In general condition

SEMINOLE MAN (MACCAULEY)

and advancement they are about on a level with their neighbors and kinsmen of the Creek Nation. In common with the other tribes they were party to the agreement for the opening of their lands to settlement; and their tribal government came to an end in Mar. 1906. In 1908 they were reported officially to number 2,138, largely mixed with negro blood, in addition to 986 "Seminole freedmen." A refugee band of Seminole, or, more properly, Seminole ne-

groes, is also on the Mexican side of the Rio Grande in the neighborhood of Eagle Pass, Texas.

The Seminole still residing in the s. part of Florida, officially estimated at 358 in 1900, but reduced to about 275 in 1908, remain nearly in their original condition. Within the last few years the Government has taken steps to secure to them a small permanent reservation to include their principal settlements. In general characteristics they resemble the Creeks, from whom they have descended. The best account of their present status is that of MacCauley in the 5th Rep. B. A. E., 1887. Consult also Bartram, Travels, ed. 1792; Dimock in Collier's Weekly, Oct. 17, 1908; Fairbanks, Florida, 1901; Gatschet, Creek Migr. Leg., I, II, 1884–88; Sprague, Hist. Fla. War, 1848.

Their towns and bands were Ahapopka, Ahosulga, Alachua, Alafiers, Alapaha, Alligator, Alouko, Apukasasocha, Asapalaga, Attapulgas, Beech Creek, Big Cypress Swamp, Big Hammock, Bowlegs' Town, Bucker Woman's Town, Burges Town, Calusahatchee, Capola, Catfish Lake, Chefixico's Old Town, Chetuckota, Chiaha, Chicuchatti, Choconikla, Chohalaboohhulka, Chokoukla, Coe Hadjo's Town, Cohowofooche, Cow Creek, Cuscowilla, Etanie, Etotulga, Fish-eating Creek, Fowl Town, Hatchcalamocha, Hiamonee, Hitchapuksassi, Hitchitipusy, Homosassa, John Hicks' Town, Jolee, Lochchiocha, Loksachumpa, McQueen's Village, Miami River, Mikasuki, Mosquito Indians, Mulatto Girl's Town, Negro Town, New Mikasuky, Notasulgar, Ochisialgi, Ochuceulga, Ochupocrassa, Ocilla, Oclackonayahe, Oclawaha, Ohathtokhouchy, Okehumpkee, Oktahatke, Oponays, Owassissas, Payne's Town, Pea Creek Band, Picolata, Pilaklikaha, Pilatka, Phillimees, Pinder Town, Red Town, Sampala, Santa Fé, Sarasota, Seccherpoga, Seleuxa, Sitarky, Spanawatka, Suwanee, Talahassee, Talofa Okhase, Taluachapko-apopka, Tattowhehallys, Toctoethla, Tohopekaliga, Toloawathla, Toponanaulka, Totstalahoeetska, Tuckagulga, Tuslalahockaka, Wacahoota, Wakasassa, Wasupa, Wechotookme, Weechitokha, Welika, Wewoka, Willanoucha, Withlacoochee, Withlacoochee talofa, Withlako, Yalacasooche, Yalaka, Yolanar, Yumersee (Yamasee). (J. M.)

Ikanafáskalgi.—Gatschet, Creek Migr. Leg., I, 66, 1884 ('people of the pointed land': Creek name, from *Ikan-fáski*, 'the pointed land,' referring to Florida peninsula; *algi* 'people'). **Ikaniúksalgi.**—Ibid. ('Peninsula people,' own name, from *ikana* 'land,' *in-yúksa* 'its point, i. e. point of land, or peninsula'). **Ishti semoli.**—Brinton, Florida Penin., 145, 1859. **Isti simanóle.**—Gatschet, Creek Migr. Leg., I, 66, 1884 (= 'separatist,' 'runaway'). **Isty-semole.**—Gallatin in Trans. Am. Antiq. Soc., II, 94, 1836 (improperly translated 'wild men'). **Lower Creeks.**—Knox (1789) in Am. St. Papers, Ind. Aff., I, 15, 1832 (here used to designate the Seminole as emigrants from the Lower

Creeks proper). **Semanole.**—Gatschet, Creek Migr. Leg., I, 66, 1884 (or Isti semanóle). **Seminola.**—Ramsay (1795) in Mass. Hist. Soc. Coll., 1st s., IV, 99, 1795. **Seminoleans.**—Conrad in H. R. Doc. 285, 25th Cong., 2d sess., 2, 1838. **Seminoles.**—Lincoln (1789) in Am. State Papers, Ind. Aff., I, 78, 1832. **Seminolie.**—Keane in Stanford, Compend., 535, 1878. **Seminolúlki.**—ten Kate, Reizen in N. A., 412, 1885 ('the people that are wild': Creek name). **Seminu'niak.**—Gatschet, Fox MS., B. A. E., 1882 (Fox name). **Simanō'lalgi.**—Gatschet, Creek Migr. Leg., I, 67, 1884 (Creek name). **Simanō'la'li.**—Ibid. (Hitchiti name). **Sim-e-lo-le.**—Hawkins (1799), Sketch, 25, 1848 (trans. 'wild'). **Sim-e-no-le.**—Ibid. **Simenolies.**—Ibid. **Similoculgee.**—Schoolcraft, Ind. Tribes, IV, 380, 1854 (Creek name). **Siminole.**—Bartram, Travels, 21, 1792. **Simonde.**—Woodward, Reminisc., 25, 1859 (misprint). **Simonolays.**—Milfort, Mémoire, 120, 1802. **Sĭm-û-no-lĭ̆.**—Grayson, Creek MS. vocab., B. A. E., 1885 (Creek name). **Tallaháski.**—Gatschet, Creek Migr. Leg., I, 66, 1884 (so called "from their town Tallahassie"). **Ungiayó-rono.**—Gatschet, ibid. ('peninsula people': Huron name). **Wild Creeks.**—Ellicott, Journal, 246–7, 1799.

Semonan. A former tribe noted by Massanet as on the road from Coahuila to the Texas country in 1690. They are possibly the Tsepcoen of Joutel.

Semonan.—Massanet, Dictamen Fiscal, Nov. 30, 1716, MS. **Tsepcoen.**—Joutel in Margry, Déc., III, 289, 1878 (identical?). **Tsepechoen frercuteas.**—Barcia, Ensayo, 271, 1723 (=Tsepcoen and Serecoutcha). **Tsepehoen.**—Joutel, Jour., 90, 1719. **Tsepehouen.**—Ibid., 114.

Sempoapi (*Sem-po-a-pi*). The Tewa name of a ruined Tano pueblo of the compact, communal type, situated near Golden, Santa Fé co., N. Mex. According to Bandelier (Ritch, N. Mex., 201, 1885; Arch. Inst. Papers, IV, 108, 1892) it was abandoned probably in 1591 on account of a raid by other Indians.

Valverde.—Bandelier, op. cit.

Senan ('bird'). A Yuchi clan.

Senä'ⁿtahá.—Gatschet, Uchee MS., B. A. E., 70, 1885 (= 'bird clan').

Senap. See *Sannup*.

Senasqua (equivalent of Delaware *lenaskqual*, 'original grass,' i. e. grass which was supposed to have grown on the land from the beginning.—Ruttenber). A former Kitchawank fortified village on Hudson r., at the mouth of Croton r., in Westchester co., N. Y. It may be identical with Kitchawank village.—Ruttenber (1) Tribes Hudson R., 79, 1872, (2) Ind. Geog. Names, 29, 1906.

Senati. A Tatsakutchin village on the N. side of Yukon r., Alaska, above the mouth of Tanana r.

Senatuch. Mentioned by Grant (Jour. Roy. Geog. Soc., 293, 1857) as a Nootka tribe on the s. w. coast of Vancouver id.

Seneca ('place of the stone,' the Anglicized form of the Dutch enunciation of the Mohegan rendering of the Iroquoian ethnic appellative *Oneida*, or, strictly, *Onĕñiute'ā'kă'*, and with a different ethnic suffix, *Onĕñiute'roñ'noⁿ'*, meaning 'people of the standing or projecting rock or stone'). A prominent and influential tribe of the Iroquois (q. v.). When first known they occupied that part of w. New York between Seneca lake and Geneva r.,

having their council fire at Tsonontowan, near Naples, in Ontario co. After the political destruction of the Erie and Neuters, about the middle of the seventeenth century, the Seneca and other Iroquois people carried their settlements westward to L. Erie and southward along the Alleghany into Pennsylvania. They also received into their tribe a portion of these conquered peoples, by which accessions they became the largest tribe of the confederation and one of the most important. They are now chiefly settled on the Allegany, Cattaraugus, and Tonawanda res., N. Y. A portion of them remained under British jurisdiction after the declaration of peace and live on Grand River res., Ontario. Various local bands have been known as Buffalo, Tonawanda, and Cornplanter Indians; and the Mingo, formerly in Ohio, have become officially known as Seneca from the large number of that tribe among them. No considerable number of the Seneca ever joined the Catholic Iroquois colonies.

In the third quarter of the 16th century the Seneca was the last but one of the Iroquois tribes to give its suffrage in favor of the abolition of murder and war, the suppression of cannibalism, and the establishment of the principles upon which the League of the Iroquois was founded. However, a large division of the tribe did not adopt at once the course of the main body, but, on obtaining coveted privileges and prerogatives, the recalcitrant body was admitted as a constituent member in the structure of the League. The two chiefships last added to the quota of the Seneca were admitted on condition of their exercising functions belonging to a sergeant-at-arms of a modern legislative body as well as those belonging to a modern secretary of state for foreign affairs, in addition to their duties as federal chieftains; indeed, they became the warders of the famous "Great Black Doorway" of the League of the Iroquois, called *Ka'nho'hwădjï'gō'nă'* by the Onondaga.

In historical times the Seneca have been by far the most populous of the five tribes originally composing the League of the Iroquois. The Seneca belong in the federal organization to the tribal phratry known by the political name *Hoñdoñnis'hĕⁿ'*, meaning, 'they are clansmen of the fathers,' of which the Mohawk are the other member, when the tribes are organized as a federal council; but when ceremonially organized the Onondaga also belong to this phratry (see *Government*). In the federal council the Seneca are represented by eight federal chiefs, but two of these were added to the original six present at the first federal council, to give representation to that part of the tribe which had at first refused to join the League. Since the organization of the League of the Iroquois, approximately in the third quarter of the

A SENECA

16th century, the number of Seneca clans, which are organized into two phratries for the performance of both ceremonial and civil functions, have varied. The names of the following nine have been recorded: Wolf, *Hoñnat 'haiioñ'nĭ'*; Bear, *Hodidjioñni'gā'*; Beaver, *Hodigĕⁿ'gegā'*; Turtle, *Hadiniă''dĕñ'*; Hawk, *Hadi'-shwĕⁿ'gaiiu'*; Sandpiper, *Hodi'ne'si'iu'*, sometimes also called Snipe, Plover, and Killdee; Deer, *Hadinioñ'gwaiiu'*; Doe, *Hodinoⁿ'deogā'*, sometimes *Hoñnoñt'-goñdjĕⁿ'*; Heron, *Hodidaioⁿ'gā'*. In a list of clan names made in 1838 by Gen. Dearborn from information given him by Mr Cone, an interpreter of the Tonawanda band, the Heron clan is called the Swan clan with the native name given above. Of these clans only five had an unequal representation in the federal council of the League; namely, the Sandpiper, three, the Turtle, two, the Hawk, one, the Wolf, one, and the Bear, one.

One of the earliest known references to the ethnic name Seneca is that on the Original Carte Figurative, annexed to the Memorial presented to the States-General of the Netherlands, Aug. 18, 1616, on which it appears with the Dutch plural as Sennecas. This map is remarkable also for the first known mention of the ancient

Erie, sometimes called Gahkwas or Kahkwah; on this map they appear under the name last cited, *Gachoi* (ch = kh), and were placed on the N. side of the W. branch of the Susquehanna. The name did not originally belong to the Seneca, but to the Oneida, as the following lines will show.

In the early part of Dec. 1634, Arent Van Curler (or Corlaer), the commissary or factor of the Manor of Rensselaerwyck (his uncle's estate), set out from Ft Orange, now Albany, N. Y., in the interest of the fur-trade, to visit the Mohawk and the Sinnekens. Strictly speaking, the latter name designated the Oneida, but at this time it was a general name, usually comprising the Onondaga, the Cayuga, and the Seneca, in addition. At that period the Dutch and the French commonly divided the Five Iroquois tribes into two identical groups; to the first, the Dutch gave the name Maquas (Mohawk), and to the latter, Sinnekens (Seneca, the final –*ens* being the Dutch genitive plural), with the connotation of the four tribes mentioned above. The French gave to the latter group the general name "les Iroquois Superieurs", "les Hiroquois d'en haut", i. e. the Upper Iroquois, "les Hiroquois des pays plus hauts, nommés Sontouaheronnons" (literally, 'the Iroquois of the upper country, called Sontouaheronnons'), the latter being only another form of "les Tsonnon-

SENECA WOMAN—THE DAUGHTER OF GEN. ELI S. PARKER

touans" (the Seneca); and to the first group the designations "les Iroquois inférieurs" (the Lower Iroquois), and "les Hiroquois d'en bas, nommés Agnechronnons'' (the Mohawk; literally, 'the Iroquois from below, named Agnechronnons'). This geographical rather than political division of the Iroquois tribes, first made by Champlain and the early Dutch at Ft Orange, prevailed until about the third quarter of the 17th century. Indeed, Governor Andros, two years after Greenhalgh's visit to the several tribes of the Iroquois in 1677, still wrote, "Ye Oneidas deemed ye first nation of sineques." The Journal of Van Curler, mentioned above, records the interesting fact that during his visit to the tribes he celebrated the New Year of 1635 at a place called *Enneyuttehage* or *Sinnekens*. The first of these names was the Iroquois, and the second, the Mohegan, name for the place, or, preferably, the Mohegan translation of the Iroquois name. The Dutch received their first knowledge of the Iroquois tribes through the Mohegan. The name *Enneyuttehage* is evidently written for *Onĕñiute'agä'/ge'*, 'at the place of the people of the standing (projecting) stone.' At that date this was the chief town of the Oneida. Van Curler's Journal identifies the name *Sinnekens* with this town, which is presumptive evidence that it is the Mohegan rendering of the Iroquois local name *Onĕñ'iute'*, 'it is a standing or projecting stone', employed as an ethnic appellative. The derivation of *Sinnekens* from Mohegan appears to be as follows: *a'sinni*, 'a stone, or rock', *–ika* or *–iga*, denotive of 'place of', or 'abundance of', and the final *–ens* supplied by the Dutch genitive plural ending, the whole Mohegan synthesis meaning 'place of the standing stone'; and with a suitable pronominal affix, like *o–* or *wă–*, which was not recorded by the Dutch writers, the translation signifies, 'they are of the place of the standing stone.' This derivation is confirmed by the Delaware name, *W'tassone*, for the Oneida, which has a similar derivation. The initial *w–* represents approximately an *o*-sound, and is the affix of verbs and nouns denotive of the third person; the intercalary *–t–* is merely euphonic, being employed to prevent the coalescence of the two vowel sounds; and it is evident that *assone* is only another form of *a'sinni*, 'stone', cited above. Hence it appears that the Mohegan and Delaware names for the Oneida are cognate in derivation and identical in signification. Heckewelder erroneously translated *W'tassone* by 'stone pipe makers.'

Thus, the Iroquois *Onĕñiute'ă'gă'*, the Mohegan *Sinnekens*, and the Delaware *W'tassone* are synonymous and are homologous in derivation. But the Dutch, followed by other Europeans, used the Mohegan term to designate a group of four tribes, to only one of which, the

Oneida, was it strictly applicable. The name *Sinnekens*, or *Sennecaas* (Visscher's map, *ca.* 1660), became the tribal name of the Seneca by a process of elimination which excluded from the group and from the connotation of the general name the nearer tribes as each with its own proper native name became known to the Europeans. Obviously, the last remaining tribe of the group would finally acquire as its own the general name of the group. The Delaware name for the Seneca was *Meχaχtĭn'nĭ* (the *Maechachtinni* of Heckewelder), which signifies 'great mountain'; this is, of course, a Delaware rendering of the Iroquois name for the Seneca, *Djiionoñdowănĕñ'/ăkă'*, or *Djiionoñdowănĕñ'roñ'no*n', 'People of the Great Mountain.' This name appears disguised as *Trudamani* (Cartier, 1534–35), *Entouhonorons*, *Chouontouaroüon* = *Chonontouaronon* (Champlain, 1615), *Ouentouaronons* (Champlain, 1627), and *Tsonontouan* or *Sonontouan* (Jes. Rel., *passim*).

Previous to the defeat and despoliation of the Neuters in 1651 and the Erie in 1656, the Seneca occupied the territory drained by Genesee r., eastward to the lands of the Cayuga along the line of the watershed between Seneca and Cayuga lakes.

The political history of the Seneca is largely that of the League of the Iroquois, although owing to petty jealousies among the various tribes the Seneca, like the others, sometimes acted independently in their dealings with aliens. But their independent action appears never to have been a serious and deliberate rupture of the bonds uniting them with the federal government of the League, thus vindicating the wisdom and foresight of its founders in permitting every tribe to retain and exercise a large measure of autonomy in the structure of the federal government. It was sometimes apparently imperative that one of the tribes should enter into a treaty or other compact with its enemies, while the others might still maintain a hostile attitude toward the alien contracting party.

During 1622 the Montagnais, the Algonkin, and the Hurons sought to conclude peace with the Iroquois (*Yroquois* = Mohawk division?), because "they were weary and fatigued with the wars which they had had for more than 50 years." The armistice was concluded in 1624, but was broken by the continued guerrilla warfare of the Algonkin warriors; for this reason the Seneca ("Ouentouoronons d'autre nation, amis desdits Yrocois") killed in the "village of the Yrocois" the embassy composed of a Frenchman, Pierre Magnan, and three Algonquian ambassadors. This resulted in the renewal of the war. So in Sept. 1627, the Iroquois, including the Seneca, declared war against the Indians and the French on the St Lawrence and its northern affluents by sending various parties of warriors against them.

From the Jesuit Relation for 1635 (p. 34, 1858) it is learned that the Seneca, after defeating the Hurons in the spring of 1634, made peace with them. The Hurons in the following year sent an embassy to Sonontouan, the chief town of the Seneca, to ratify the peace, and while there learned that the Onondaga, the Oneida, the Cayuga, and the Mohawk were desirous of becoming parties to the treaty.

In 1639 the war was renewed by the Hurons, who in May captured 12 prisoners from the Seneca, then regarded as a powerful people. The war continued with varying success. The Jesuit Relation for 1641 (p. 75, 1858) says the Seneca were the most feared of the enemies of the Hurons, and that they were only one day's journey from Ongniaahra (Niagara), the most easterly town of the Neuters. The Relation for 1643 (p. 61) says that the Seneca (i. e. "les Hiroquois d'en haut"), including the Cayuga, the Oneida, and the Onondaga, equaled, if they did not exceed, in number and power the Hurons, who previously had had this advantage; and that the Mohawk at this time had three villages with 700 or 800 men of arms who possessed 300 arquebuses that they had obtained from the Dutch and which they used with skill and boldness. According to the Jesuit Relation for 1648 (p. 49, 1858), 300 Seneca attacked the village of the Aondironnons, and killed or captured as many of its inhabitants as possible, although this people were a dependency of the Neuters who were at peace with the Seneca at this time. This affront nearly precipitated war between the Iroquois and the Neuters.

The Seneca warriors composed the larger part of the Iroquois warriors who in 1648–49 assailed, destroyed, and dispersed the Huron tribes; it was likewise they who in 1649 sacked the chief towns of the Tionontati, or Tobacco tribe; and the Seneca also took a leading part in the defeat and subjugation of the Neuters in 1651 and of the Erie in 1656. From the Journal des PP. Jésuites for 1651–52 (Jes. Rel., Thwaites' ed., XXXVII, 97, 1898) it is learned that in 1651 the Seneca, in waging war against the Neuters, had been so signally defeated that their women and children were compelled to flee from Sonontowan, their capital, to seek refuge among the neighboring Cayuga.

In 1652 the Seneca were plotting with the Mohawk to destroy and ruin the French settlements on the St Lawrence.

Two years later the Seneca sent an embassy to the French for the purpose of making peace with them, a movement which was probably brought about by their rupture with the Erie. But the Mohawk not desiring peace at that time with the French, perhaps on account of their desire to attack the Hurons on Orleans id., murdered two of the three Seneca ambassadors, the other having remained as a hostage with the French. This act almost resulted in war between the two hostile tribes; foreign affairs, however, were in such condition as to prevent the beginning of actual hostility. On Sept. 19, 1655, Fathers Chaumonot and Dablon, after pressing invitations to do so, started from Quebec to visit and view the Seneca country, and to establish there a French habitation and teach the Seneca the articles of their faith.

In 1657 the Seneca, in carrying out the policy of the League to adopt conquered tribes upon submission and the expression of a desire to live under the form of government established by the League, had thus incorporated eleven different tribes into their body politic.

In 1652 Maryland bought from the Minqua, or Susquehanna Indians, i. e. the Conestoga, all their land claims on both sides of Chesapeake bay up to the mouth of Susquehanna r. In 1663, 800 Seneca and Cayuga warriors from the Confederation of the Five Nations were defeated by the Minqua, aided by the Marylanders. The Iroquois did not terminate their hostilities until famine had so reduced the Conestoga that in 1675, when the Marylanders had disagreed with them and had withdrawn their alliance, the Conestoga were completely subdued by the Five Nations, who thereafter claimed a right to the Minqua lands to the head of Chesapeake bay.

In 1744 the influence of the French was rapidly gaining ground among the Seneca; meanwhile the astute and persuasive Col. Johnson was gradually winning the Mohawk as close allies of the British, while the Onondaga, the Cayuga, and the Oneida, under strong pressure from Pennsylvania and Virginia, sought to be neutral.

In 1686, 200 Seneca warriors went w. against the Miami, the Illinois in the meantime having been overcome by the Iroquois in a war lasting about five years. In 1687 the Marquis Denonville assembled a great horde of Indians from the region of the upper lakes and from the St Lawrence— Hurons, Ottawa, Chippewa, Missisauga, Miami, Illinois, Montagnais, Amikwa, and others—under Durantaye, DuLuth, and Tonti, to serve as an auxiliary force to about 1,200 French and colonial levies, to be employed in attacking and destroying the Seneca. Having reached Irondequoit, the Seneca landing-place on L. Ontario, Denonville built there a stockade in which he left a garrison of 440 men. Thence advancing to attack the Seneca villages, he was ambushed by 600 or 800 Seneca, who charged and drove back the colonial levies and their Indian allies, and threw the veteran regiments into disorder. Only by the overwhelming numbers of his force was the traitorous Denonville saved from disastrous defeat.

In 1763, at Bloody Run and the Devil's Hole, situated on Niagara r. about 4 m. below the falls, the Seneca ambushed a British supply train on the portage road from Ft Schlosser to Ft Niagara, only three escaping from a force of nearly 100. At a short distance from this place the same Seneca ambushed a British force composed of two companies of troops who were hastening to the aid of the supply train, only eight of whom escaped massacre. These bloody and harsh measures were the direct result of the general unrest of the Six Nations and the western tribes, arising from the manner of the recent occupancy of the posts by the British, after the surrender of Canada by the French on Sept. 8, 1760. They contrasted the sympathetic and bountiful paternalism of the French régime with the neglect and niggardliness that characterized the British rule. Such was the state of affairs that on July 29, 1761, Sir Wm. Johnson wrote to General Amherst: "I see plainly that there appears to be an universal jealousy amongst every nation, on account of the hasty steps they look upon we are taking towards getting possession of this country, which measures, I am certain, will never subside whilst we encroach within the limits which you may recollect have been put under the protection of the King in the year 1726, and confirmed to them by him and his successors ever since and by the orders sent to the governors not to allow any one of his subjects settling thereon . . . but that it should remain their absolute property." But, by the beginning of the American Revolution, so well had the British agents reconciled them to the rule of Great Britain that the Seneca, together with a large majority of the people of the Six Nations, notwithstanding their pledges to the contrary, reluctantly espoused the cause of the British against the colonies. Consequently they suffered retribution for their folly when Gen. Sullivan, in 1779, after defeating their warriors, burned their villages and destroyed their crops.

There is no historical evidence that the Seneca who were on the Ohio and the s. shore of L. Erie in the 18th and 19th centuries were chiefly an outlying colony from the Iroquois tribe of that name dwelling in New York. The significant fact that in historical times their affiliations were never with the Iroquois, but rather with tribes usually hostile to them, is to be explained on the presumption that they were rather some remnant of a subjugated tribe dependent on the Seneca and dwelling on lands under the jurisdiction of their conquerors. It is a fair inference that they were largely subjugated Erie and Conestoga. Regarding the identity of these Indians, the following citation from Howe (Hist. Coll. Ohio, II, 574, 1896) is pertinent: "The Senecas of Sandusky—so-called—owned and occupied 40,000 acres of choice land on the E. side of Sandusky r., being mostly in this [Seneca] and partly in Sandusky co. Thirty thousand acres of this land was granted to them on the 29th of September, 1817, at the treaty . . . of Maumee Rapids. . . . The remaining 10,000 acres, lying s. of the other, was granted by the treaty at St Mary's, . . . 17th of September, 1818." By the treaty concluded at Washington Feb. 28, 1831, these Seneca ceded their lands in Ohio to the United States and agreed to emigrate s. w. of Missouri, on Neosho r. The same writer states that in 1831 "their principal chiefs were Coonstick, Small Cloud Spicer, Seneca Steel, Hard Hickory, Tall Chief, and Good Hunter, the last two of whom were their principal orators. The old chief Good Hunter told Henry C. Brish, their subagent, that this band [which numbered 390 in 1908] were in fact the remnant of Logan's tribe, . . . and says Mr Brish in a communication to us: 'I cannot to this day surmise why they were called Senecas. I never found a Seneca among them. They were Cayugas—who were Mingoes—among whom were a few Oneidas, Mohawks, Onondagas, Tuscarawas, and Wyandots.'" The majority of them were certainly not Cayuga, as Logan was Conestoga or Mingo on his maternal side.

In 1677 the Seneca had but four villages, but a century later the number had increased to about 30. The following are the better known Seneca towns, which, of course, were not at all contemporary. Canadasaga, Canandaigua, Caneadea, Catherine's Town, Cattaraugus, Chemung, New Chemung, Old Chemung, Chenango, Cheronderoga, Chinoshageh, Condawhaw, Connewango, Dayoitgao, Deonundagae, Deyodeshot, Deyohnegano, Deyonongdadagana, Dyosyowan, Gaandowanang, Gadaho, Gahato, Gahayanduk, Ganagweh, Ganawagus, Ganeasos, Ganedontwan, Ganogeh, Ganondasa, Ganos, Ganosgagong, Gaonsagaon, Gaousge,

Gaskosada, Gathtsegwarohare, Geneseo, Gistaquat, Gwaugweh, Honeoye, Joneadih, Kanagaro (3), Kanaghsaws, Kannassarago, Kashong, Kaskonchiagon, Kaygen, Keinthe, Newtown, Oatka, Ongniaahra, Onnahee, Onoghsadago, Onondarka, Owaiski, Sheshequin, Skahasegao, Skoiyase, Sonojowauga, Tekisedaneyont, Tioniongarunte, Tonawanda, Totiakton, Tsonontowanen, Yorkjough, Yoroonwago.

The earliest estimates of the numbers of the Seneca, in 1660 and 1677, give them about 5,000. Later estimates of the population are: 3,500 (1721); 1,750 (1736); 5,000 (1765); 3,250 (1778); 2,000 (1783); 3,000 (1783), and 1,780 (1796). In 1825 those in New York were reported at 2,325. In 1850, according to Morgan, those in New York numbered 2,712, while about 210 more were on Grand River res. in Canada. In 1909 those in New York numbered 2,749 on the three reservations, which, with those on Grand r., Ontario, would give them a total of 2,962. The proportion of Seneca now among the 4,071 Iroquois at Caughnawaga, St Regis, and Lake of Two Mountains, Quebec, can not be estimated. (J. N. B. H.)

Anantooeah.—Adair quoted by Mooney in 19th Rep. B. A. E., 509, 1900 (from Ani'-Nûn'dăwe'gĭ, the Cherokee name). **Ani'-Nûn'dăwe'gĭ.**—Mooney, ibid. (Cherokee name, sing. Nûn'dăwe'gĭ; also applied to the Iroquois generally). **Ani'-Sĕ'nĭkă.**—Ibid. (one of the Cherokee names). **Antouhonorons.**—Champlain (1616), Œuvres, IV, 75, 1870. **Antouoronons.**—Map of 1632, ibid., v, ii, 1870 (cf. *Entouohonoron*). **Antovorinos.**—Freytas, Peñalosa, Shea trans., 52, 83, 1882. **Assikanna.**—Gatschet, Fox MS., 1882 (Fox name; extended to the whole of the Six Nations). **Ceneca's.**—Document of 1719 in N. Y. Doc. Col. Hist., v, 528, 1855. **Chenandoanes.**—Mallery in Proc. A. A. A. S. 1877, XXVI, 352, 1878. **Chit-o-won-e-augh-gaw.**—Macauley, N. Y., II, 185, 1829. **Chonontouaronon.**—Shea in Charlevoix, New France, II, 28, note, 1866. **Chonuntoowaunees.**—Edwards (1751) in Mass. Hist. Soc. Coll., 1st s., X, 146, 1809. **Chouontouaroüon.**—Champlain (1615), Œuvres, IV, 34, 1870. **Ciniques.**—Old form quoted by Conover, MS. Hist. of Kanadesaga and Geneva. **Cinnakee.**—McKendry (1779) in Conover, ibid. **Cinnigos.**—Document of 1677 in N. Y. Doc. Col. Hist., IX, 227, 1855. **Cyneper.**—Hyde (1712) in N. C. Rec., II, 900, 1886. **Cynikers.**—Hubbard (1680) in Mass. Hist. Soc. Coll., 2d s., v, 33, 1815. **Djonontewake.**—Hale, letter, B. A. E., Mar. 6, 1879 (Mohawk name). **Entouhonorono.**—Champlain (1620), Voy., I, 331, 1830. **Entouhonorons.**—Champlain, Œuvres, IV, 32, 1870. **Entouohonorons.**—Shea in Charlevoix, New France, II, 28, note, 1866. **Entwohonoron.**—Ibid. **Ganochgeritáwe.**—Pyrlæus (*ca.* 1750) quoted in Am. Antiq., IV, 75, 1882 (a chief's name). **Honan-ne-ho'-ont.**—Morgan, League Iroq., 97, 1851 ('the doorkeeper'). **Honnonthauans.**—Bollan (1748) in Mass. Hist. Soc. Coll., 1st s., VI, 132, 1800. **Honuχ-shiniondi.**—Gatschet, Tuscarora MS., 1885 ('he makes a leaning house': a name of the Iroquois confederation). **Ieuontowanois.**—Weiser (1748) in Drake, Bk. Inds., bk. 5, 97, 1848. **Isonnontoans.**—Barton, New Views, app., 6, 1798. **Isonnontonans.**—Hennepin, Cont. of New Discov., 93, 1698. **Isonontouanes.**—La Hontan (1703) as quoted by Pownall (1754) in N. Y. Doc. Col. Hist., VI, 896, 1855. **Jeneckaws.**—Dalton (1783) in Mass. Hist. Soc. Coll., 1st s., X, 123, 1809 (misprint). **Jenontowanos.**—Mallery in Proc. A. A. A. S. 1877, XXVI, 352, 1878. **Lenekees.**—Bacqueville de la Potherie, IV, 128, 1753 (misprint). **Năn-tẹ-wĕ'-ki.**—ten Kate, Synonymie, 11, 1884 (Cherokee name). **Nation de la Grande Montagne.**—Jes. Rel. for 1669, 16, 1858 (cf. *Tsonontowan*). **Noⁿto-wa-ka.**—Hewitt, Seneca MS.

vocab., B. A. E., 1883 (Tuscarora name). **Nottawagees.**—Glen (1750) quoted in Conover, MS. Kan. and Geneva. **Nun-da-wä'-o-no.**—Morgan, League Iroq., 51, 1851 ('the great hill people': own name). **Nundawaronah.**—Mallery in Proc. A. A. A. S. 1877, XXVI, 352, 1878. **Nûn'dăwe'gĭ.**—Mooney in 19th Rep. B. A. E., 509, 1900 (Cherokee name, sing. form; cf. *Ani'-Nûn'dăwe'gĭ,* above). **Nundowaga.**—Gatschet, Seneca MS., 1883. **Ondawagas.**—Treaty (1789) in Am. St. Papers, Ind. Aff., I, 512, 1832 (not to be confounded with the Onondaga). **Onughkaurydaaug.**—Weiser (1748) in Drake, Bk. Inds., bk. 5, 97, 1848 (name of a chief). **Onundawaga.**—Schoolcraft, Ind. Tribes, IV, 199, 1854. **Onuntewakaa.**—Hale, letter, B. A. E., Mar. 6, 1879. **Ossikanna.**—Gatschet, Fox MS., B. A. E., 1882 (Fox name; applied also to all the Six Nations; plural, Ossikannehak). **Ouentouoronons.**—Champlain (1615), Œuvres, VI, 143, 1870. **Padowagas.**—Drake, Bk. Inds., x, 1848 (misprint for Nadowagas). **Paisans, Les.**—Greenhalgh (1677) in N. Y. Doc. Col. Hist., III, 252, 1853 (so called by French). **Sannagers.**—Brickell, N. C., 320, 1737. **Sant8eronons.**—Jes. Rel. 1643, 61, 1858. **Seanecas.**—Brockholls (1682) in N. Y. Doc. Col. Hist., XIII, 555, 1881. **Senacaes.**—Writer of 1676 in Mass. Hist. Soc. Coll., 4th s., IX, 167, 1871. **Senacars.**—Mason (1684) in N. H. Hist. Soc. Coll., II, 200, 1827. **Senacas.**—Weiser (1748) in Thwaites, Early West. Trav., I, 31, 1904. **Senakees.**—Niles (1760) in Mass. Hist. Soc. Coll., 4th s., v, 332, 1861. **Senecaes.**—Coxe, Carolana, 55, 1741. **Senecas.**—Brockholls (1682) in N. Y. Doc. Col. Hist., XIII, 555, 1881. **Senecca.**—Council of 1726 in N. C. Rec., II, 640, 1886. **Seneckes.**—Winthrop (1664) in Mass. Hist. Soc. Coll., 4th s., VI, 531, 1863. **Senecques.**—Greenhalgh (1677) in N. Y. Doc. Col. Hist., III, 251, 1853. **Senegars.**—Brickell (1737) in Haywood, Tenn., 224, 1823. **Senekaas.**—Esnauts and Rapilly map, 1777. **Senekaes.**—Bellomont (1698) in N. Y. Doc. Col. Hist., IV, 370, 1854. **Senekas.**—Dongan (*ca.* 1687), ibid., III, 428, 1853. **Senekées.**—Louis XIV (1699) ibid., IX, 698, 1855. **Senekers.**—Ibid. 697. **Senekes.**—Dongan (1687), ibid., III, 514, 1853. **Senekies.**—Livingston (1720), ibid., v, 565, 1855. **Senekoes.**—Gale (1711) in N. C. Rec., I, 828, 1886. **Senequaes.**—Ingoldsby (1691) in N. Y. Doc. Col. Hist., III, 792, 1853. **Senequas.**—Spotswood (1712) in N. C. Rec., I, 861, 1886. **Seneques.**—Greenhalgh (1677) in N. Y. Doc. Col. Hist., III, 252, 1853. **Senequois.**—Conover, MS. Hist. of Kanadesaga and Geneva (old form). **Senicaes.**—Pateshall (1684) in Me. Hist. Soc. Coll., v, 90, 1857. **Senikers.**—Marshe (1744) in Mass. Hist. Soc. Coll., 1st s., VII, 197, 1801. **Sennagars.**—Catesby, Nat. Hist. Car., II, xiii, 1743. **Sennakas.**—Colden, Five Nations, 42, 1727, quoted in Conover, MS. Kanadesaga and Geneva. **Sennakers.**—Penhallow (1699) in N. H. Hist. Soc. Coll., I, 134, 1824. **Sennecas.**—Map of 1614 (?) in N. Y. Doc. Col. Hist., I, 1856. **Sennecca.**—Council of 1725 in N. C. Rec., II, 570, 1886. **Senneches.**—Penhallow (1726) in N. H. Hist. Soc. Coll., I, 41, 1824. **Senneckes.**—Clinton (1745) in N. Y. Doc. Col. Hist., VI, 275, 1855. **Sennecks.**—Livingston (1698), ibid., IV, 341, 1854. **Sennekaes.**—Livingston (1691), ibid., 781. **Sennekas.**—Dongan (1687), ibid., III, 476, 1853. **Sennekees.**—Document of 1712, ibid., v, 588, 1855. **Sennekies.**—Livingston (1720), ibid., 569. **Senneks.**—Dudley (1721) in Mass. Hist. Soc. Coll., 2d s., VIII, 244, 1819. **Sennekus.**—Ibid. **Sennequans.**—Conover, MS. Hist. of Kanadesaga and Geneva (old form). **Sennequens.**—Document of 1656 in N. Y. Doc. Col. Hist., XIV, 374, 1883. **Senneques.**—Livingston (1691), ibid., III, 782, 1853. **Sennickes.**—Salisbury (1678), ibid., XIII, 531, 1881. **Sennicks.**—Document of 1698, ibid., IV, 337, 1854. **Senontouant.**—Tonti (1689) in Margry, Déc., III, 564, 1878. **Senottoway.**—Document of 1713 in N. C. Rec., II, 1, 1886. **Sha-de-ka-ron-ges.**—Macauley, N. Y., II, 176, 1829 (a chief's name). **Shinikes.**—Livingston (1711) in N. Y. Doc. Col. Hist., v, 272, 1855. **Sianekees.**—Albany Conference (1737), ibid., VI, 99, 1855. **Sikne.**—Gatschet, Potawatomi MS., 1878 (Potawatomi name; plural, Sekne-eg). **Simmagons.**—Martin, N. C., I, 128, 1829. **Sinacks.**—Phillips (1692) in N. Y. Doc. Col. Hist., III, 837, 1853. **Sinagars.**—Brickell, N. C., 283, 1737. **Sinakees.**—Dongan (1687) in N. Y. Doc. Col. Hist., III, 474, 1853. **Sinakers.**—Conover, MS. Hist.

Kanadesaga and Geneva (old form). **Sinecas.**—Document of 1687 in N. Y. Doc. Col. Hist., III, 509, 1853. **Sineckes.**—Andros (1688), ibid., 555. **Sinekas.**—Albany Conference (1746), ibid., VI, 317, 1855. **Sinekees.**—Clarkson (1693), ibid., IV, 45, 1854. **Sinekes.**—Maryland Treaty (1682), ibid., III, 321, 1853. **Sinekies.**—Schuyler (1720) quoted by Conover, MS. Kanadesaga and Geneva. **Sineks.**—Bellomont (1700) quoted by Conover, ibid. **Sineques.**—Andros (1678) in N. Y. Doc. Col. Hist., III, 271, 1853. **Sinica.**—Bartram, Trav., 372, 1792. **Sinicaes.**—Dongan (ca. 1686) in N. Y. Doc. Col. Hist., III, 394, 1853. **Sinicker.**—Weiser (1737) in Schoolcraft, Ind. Tribes, IV, 332, 1854. **Sinikers.**—Weiser (1737) quoted by Drake, Bk. Inds., bk. 5, 97, 1848. **Siniques.**—Andros (1676) in N. Y. Doc. Col. Hist., XII, 558, 1877. **Sinnagers.**—Lawson (1709), N. C., 77, 1860. **Sinnakees.**—Dongan (1687) quoted by Parkman, Frontenac, 160, 1883. **Sinnakers.**—Document of 1687 in N. Y. Doc. Col. Hist., III, 431, 1853. **Sinnakes.**—Ibid. **Sinnaques.**—Ibid., 432. **Sinnecas.**—Lovelace (1669) quoted by Ruttenber, Tribes Hudson R., 68, 1872. **Sinneche.**—Albany Conference (1728) in N. Y. Doc. Col. Hist., V, 867, 1855. **Sinneck.**—Document of 1699, ibid., IV, 579, 1854. **Sinneckes.**—Ft Orange Conference (1660), ibid., XIII, 184, 1881. **Sinneco.**—Herman (1681), ibid., XII, 664, 1877. **Sinnecus.**—Beeckman (1661), ibid., 344. **Sinnedowane.**—Writer of 1673, ibid., II, 594, 1858. **Sinnek.**—Livingston (1687), ibid., III, 445, 1853. **Sinnekaes.**—Document of 1688, ibid., 565. **Sinnekas.**—Durant (1721), ibid., V, 589, 1855. **Sinnekees.**—Burnet (1720), ibid., V, 577, 1855. **Sinnekens.**—Document of 1657, ibid., XIII, 73, 1881. **Sinnekes.**—Ibid., 72. **Sinnekies.**—Schuyler (1720), ibid., V, 542, 1855. **Sinnekis.**—Livingston (1699), ibid., IV, 597, 1854. **Sinnekus.**—Document of 1659, ibid., XIII, 113, 1881. **Sinneqars.**—Conover, MS. Hist. Kanadesaga and Geneva (old form). **Sinnequaas.**—Gouvernour (1690) in N. Y. Doc. Col. Hist., III, 714, 1853. **Sinnequens.**—Ibid., XIV, 373, 1883. **Sinnequois.**—Conover, MS. Kanadesaga and Geneva (old form). **Sinnicars.**—Dongan (1687) in N. Y. Doc. Col. Hist., III, 516, 1853. **Sinnicas.**—Nottingham (1692), ibid., 823. **Sinnichees.**—Schuyler (1720), ibid., V, 549, 1855. **Sinnickes.**—Bellomont (1698), ibid., IV, 420, 1854. **Sinnickins.**—Vailliant (1688), ibid., III, 523, 1853. **Sinnicks.**—Dongan (1687), ibid., 516. **Sinnicus.**—Herrman map (1673) in Maps to accompany the Rept. of the Comrs. on the Bndry. Line bet. Va. and Md., 1873. **Sinnikaes.**—Livingston (1691) in N. Y. Doc. Col. Hist., III, 782, 1853. **Sinnikes.**—Jamison (1697), ibid., IV, 295, 1854. **Sinniques.**—Andros (1676), ibid., XII, 558, 1877. **Sinnodowannes.**—Dellius (1697), ibid., IV, 280, 1854. **Sinnodwannes.**—Ibid., 279. **Sinnokes.**—Schuyler (1687), ibid., III, 478, 1853. **Sinnondewannes.**—Blakiston (1691), ibid., 788, 1853. **Sinodouwas.**—McKenney and Hall, Ind. Tribes, III, 79, 1854. **Sinodowannes.**—Maryland treaty (1682) in N. Y. Doc. Col. Hist., III, 321, 1853. **Sinondowans.**—Colden (1727), Five Nations, 42, 1747 (here used for a part of the tribe, probably those at Nundawao). **Sniekes.**—Maryland treaty (1682) in N. Y. Doc. Col. Hist., III, 322, 1853. **Sonnontoehronnons.**—Jes. Rel. 1654, 8, 1858. **Sonnontoeronnons.**—Ibid., 1657, 2, 1858. **Sonnontouaheronnons.**—Ibid., 1653, 18, 1858. **Sonnontoüeronnons.**—Ibid., 1648, 46, 1858. **Sonnontovans.**—Coxe, Carolana, 55, 1741. **Sonontoerrhonons.**—Jes. Rel. 1635, 34, 1858. **Sonont8aëronons.**—Ibid., 1646, 3, 1858. **Sonontoüanhrronon.**—Ibid., 1637, 111, 1858. **Sonontouans.**—Denonville (1685) in N. Y. Doc. Col. Hist., IX, 282, 1855. **Sonontouehronon.**—Jes. Rel. 1640, 35, 1858. **Sonontouons.**—Colden (1724) in N. Y. Doc. Col. Hist., V, 727, 1855. **Sonontrrhonons.**—Jes. Rel. 1635, 24, 1858. **Sontouaheronnons.**—Ibid., 1652, 36, 1858. **Sontouhoironon.**—Sagard, Hist. Can. (1632), IV, 1866. **Sontouhouethonons.**—Ibid., II, 334, 1866. **S8nt8aronons.**—Jes. Rel. 1646, 34, 1858. **Sunnekes.**—Livingston (1711) in N. Y. Doc. Col. Hist., V, 272, 1855. **Syneck.**—Bellomont (1700), ibid., IV, 718, 1854. **Synekees.**—Carr (1664), ibid., III, 74, 1853. **Synekes.**—Bayard (1689), ibid., 621. **Synicks.**—Cartwright (1664), ibid., 67. **Synnekes.**—Lovelace (1669), ibid., XIII, 423, 1881. **Synneks.**—Ibid., 428. **Te-en-nenhogh-huut.**—Macauley, N. Y., II, 176, 1829 (functional name). **Te-how-nea-nyo-hunt.**—Ibid., 185.

Teuontowanos.—Drake, Bk. Inds., bk. 5, 4, 1848. **Ti''-kwă'.**—Hewitt, inf'n, 1886 ('I do not know': Tuscarora nickname for the Seneca, on account of the frequent use of this expression by the latter tribe). **Tionionhogaráwe.**—Pyrlæus (ca. 1750) quoted in Am. Antiq., IV, 75, 1882 (a chief's name). **Toe-nen-hogh-hunt.**—Macauley, N. Y., II, 185, 1829. **Tondamans.**—Cartier (1535), Bref Récit, 59, 1863 (identical; Hewitt considers this form, Toudaman, and Trudaman in Cartier, to be corruptions of Tsonondowanen, which he says was applied to the Onondaga as well as to the Seneca). **Tonnontoins.**—Pouchot map (1758) in N. Y. Doc. Col. Hist., X, 694, 1858. **Toudamans.**—Cartier (1535), Bref Récit, 59, 1863 (identical?). **To-wă''-kă'.**—Hewitt, Seneca MS. vocab., B. A. E., 1888 (common Tuscarora name, abbreviated from Noⁿtowáka). **Trudamans.**—Cartier (1535), Bref Récit, 29, 1863. **Ts-ho-ti-non-do-wă''-gă'.**—Hewitt, inf'n, 1886 (name used by the tribe; singular, Tshonondowaga). **Tsonantonon.**—Jefferys, Fr. Doms., pt. 1, map, 1761. **Tsonnonthouans.**—Ibid., 49. **T. Son-non-thu-ans.**—Macauley, N. Y., II, 176, 1829. **T. Sonnontoüans.**—Ibid. **Tsonnontoüans.**—Jes. Rel. 1669, 16, 1858. **Tsononthouans.**—Am. Pioneer, II, 192, 1843. **Tsonontooas.**—Keane in Stanford, Compend., 535, 1878. **Tsonontouans.**—Lahontan, New Voy., I, map, 1703. **Tsonontowans.**—Schoolcraft, Ind. Tribes, VI, 326, 1857. **Tsonothouans.**—Drake, Bk. Inds., XI, 1848. **Tsouonthousaas.**—Boudinot, Star in the West, 129, 1816. **Tudamanes.**—Cartier (1535), Bref Récit, 29, 1863.

Seneca (*I'sû'nigû*, not translatable, but it has no relation to the Iroquois tribal name). A former important Cherokee settlement on Keoweer., about the mouth of Conneross cr., in Oconee co., S. C. Hopewell, the country seat of General Pickens, where the famous treaty was made in 1785, was near it, on the E. side of the river.—Mooney in 19th Rep. B. A. E., 522, 1900.

Sennekaw.—Royce in 5th Rep. B. A. E., map, 1887. **Sinica.**—Bartram, Travels, 372, 1792

Seneca Town. A former village of Mingos, occupied by the remnant of Logan's band, situated on the E. side of Sandusky r., in Seneca co., Ohio, probably opposite Ft Seneca, established during the war of 1812. It was on a tract of 40,000 acres in Seneca and Sandusky cos., 30,000 acres of which were granted the "Senecas of Sandusky," so called, by treaty of Sept. 29, 1817, and 10,000 acres by treaty of Sept. 17, 1818. By treaty of Feb. 28, 1831, these Indians ceded their Ohio lands to the United States and removed to the Neosho r., Ind. Ty.

Senecu (*Se-ne-ku'*, probably from *Tzen-o-cué*, which was perhaps the aboriginal name.—Bandelier). A former pueblo of the Piro, 13 m. below Socorro, N. Mex., on the w. bank of the Rio Grande, at the site of the present village of San Antonio. It was the seat of the Spanish mission of San Antonio de Senecú founded in 1629 by Fray Antonio de Arteaga and Fray García de Zúñiga, or de San Francisco (who died at El Paso and was buried at Senecu in 1673), and contained the first church and monastery erected on the lower course of the Rio Grande in New Mexico. Regarding the fate of the village, Bandelier (Arch. Inst. Papers, IV, 250, 1892) says: "On the 23d of Jan. 1675, the Apaches surprised the pueblo of Senecú, killed its missionary, Fray Alonzo Gil de Avila, and slaughtered so many of the inhabitants of all ages and both sexes that the survivors fled in dismay to Socorro, and the pueblo remained forever deserted." Not to be confounded with the Senecu (see *Senecu del Sur*) below El Paso, in Chihuahua, which was settled about 1680 by fugitive Piro and Tigua from New Mexico, some of them being from the older Senecu. See also *Piros; Pueblos.* (F. W. H.)

Cenecu.—Davis, Span. Conq. N. Mex., 310, 1869. Renecuey.—New Mex. Doc. quoted by Bancroft, Ariz. and N. Mex., 171, 1889 (identical?). San-Antonio de Senecu.—Benavides, Memorial, 19, 1630. Sant Antonio de Senecu.—Blaeu, Atlas, XII, 61, 1667. S. Antoine de Senecu.—De l'Isle, Map Am. Sept., 1700. S. Antonio.—D'Anville, Map N. A., Bolton's ed., 1752. S. Antonio de Senaca.—Crepy, Map Amér. Sept., 1783 (?). S. Antonio de Sencen.—Brion de la Tour, Map l'Amér., 1779. S. Antonio de Seneci.—Jefferys, Am. Atlas, map 5, 1776. S. Antonio de Senecu.—De l'Isle, Carte Mexique et Floride, 1703. Senacu.—Davis, El Gringo, 123, 1857. Séne.—Doc. of 17th cent. quoted by Bandelier in Arch. Inst. Papers, IV, 251, 1892. Seneca.—Columbus Mem. Vol., 156, 1893 (misprint). Senecu.—Benavides, Memorial, 14, 1630. St. Antonio.—Shea, Cath. Miss., 80, 1855. St Antony.—Kitchin, Map N. A., 1787. Zen-ecú.—Bandelier in Arch. Inst. Papers, IV, 247, 1892 (Senecú, or). Zennecu.—Solis Miranda (1676) quoted by Bandelier, ibid., III, 131, 1890.

Senecu del Sur (Span.: 'Senecu of the South'). A pueblo on the s. E. bank of the Rio Grande, a few miles below El Paso, in Chihuahua, Mexico, inhabited by the last remnant of the Piro and Tigua who escaped from Senecu, N. Mex., during an Apache outbreak in 1675, or who were taken there from Isleta, Socorro, and Alamillo by Gov. Otermin on his retreat from Santa Fé during the Pueblo revolt of 1680. The mission of San Antonio was established there in 1682. The natives have practically lost their language and are almost completely "Mexicanized." (F. W. H.)

Cinecú.—Escudero, Not. Nuevo-Méx., 14, 1849. Ienecu.—Siguenza (1691–93) quoted by Buschmann, Neu-Mexico, 264, 1858. Jenecu.—Buschmann, ibid., 249. San Antonio of Sinolu.—Cruzate (1685) as quoted by Davis, Span. Conq. N. Mex., 337, 1869 ("supposed to be the same"). San Antonio Seneca.—Ward in Ind. Aff. Rep. 1867, 213, 1868. Saneca.—Morse, Hist. Am., map, 1798. Seneco.—Calhoun (1849) in Cal. Mess. and Corresp., 215, 1850. Senecú.—Rivera, Diario, leg. 684, 1736. Sinecu.—Bartlett, Pers. Narr., I, 149, 1854. Sinicú.—Gatschet in Mag. Am. Hist., 259, Apr. 1882 (Sinecú, or).

Senedo. According to Peyton (Hist. Augusta Co., 6, 1882), a tribe formerly on the N. fork of Shenandoah r., Va., and exterminated by the Southern Indians in 1732. The statement is of doubtful authenticity. (J. M.)

Senega. The "*Seneca* snakeroot" (*Polygala senega*), from which the Indians, and after them the whites, prepared a remedy for snake bites, etc.; from *Seneca*, the name of one of the Five Nations of the Iroquois. The *siniga* of Cherokee is probably the same word. (A. F. C.)

Senestun (*Se-nĕs'-tûn*). A band or village of the Chastacosta on Rogue r., Oreg.—Dorsey in Jour. Am. Folk-lore, III, 234, 1890.

Senijextee. A Salish tribe formerly residing on both sides of Columbia r. from Kettle falls to the Canadian boundary; they also occupied the valley of Kettle r., Kootenay r. from its mouth to the first falls, and the region of the Arrow lakes, Brit. Col. In 1909 those in the United States numbered 342, on the Colville res., Wash.

Lake Indians.—Parker, Journal, 293, 1840. Savages of the Lake.—De Smet, Letters, 37, 1843. Sen-i-jex-tee.—Winans in Ind. Aff. Rep., 22, 1870. Sinatcheggs.—Ross, Fur Hunters, II, 172, 190, 1855. Sinuitskistux.—Wilson in Jour. Ethnol. Soc. Lond., 292, 1866. S-na-a-chikst.—Dawson in Trans. Roy. Soc. Can. 1891, sec. II, 6, 1892.

Senikave. A Kaviagmiut Eskimo village on the mainland opposite Sledge id., Alaska.—11th Census, Alaska, 162, 1893.

Senisos (Span., probably referring either to *ceniza*, 'ashes,' or to *cenizo*, the white goose-foot, a plant). A former tribe in N. E. Mexico, probably Coahuiltecan, which was drawn from Nuevo Leon and in 1698 gathered into mission San Antonio Galindo Moctezuma, N. of Monclova.

Cenizos.—Revillagigedo, Carta, MS., quoted by Bancroft, Nat. Races, I, 611, 1886.

Senktl (*Senxʟ*). A Bellacoola village near the mouth of Bellacoola r., Brit. Col., "about 1 m. above Nuxa'lk·!."

SEnqtl.—Boas in 7th Rep. N. W. Tribes Can., 3, 1891. SEnxʟ.—Boas in Mem. Am. Mus. Nat. Hist., II, 49, 1900. Snihtlimih.—Tolmie and Dawson, Vocabs. Brit. Col., 122B, 1884 (perhaps refers to Snū't'ele, another town; *mih*='people of').

Sennenes. A Costanoan division or village in California.—Engelhardt, Franciscans in Cal., 331, 1897.

Senobe. See *Sannup.*

Sentethltun (*Sĕn-tĕçl-tûn*). A former village of the Tututni on the s. side of Rogue r., Oreg. Schumacher (Bull. Geol. Surv., 31, 1877) placed it at the mouth of Rogue r., making its inhabitants a part of the Tshemetunne.—Dorsey in Jour. Am. Folk-lore, III, 236, 1890.

Sepascoot. A former band called Munsee, but probably a part of the Wappinger, on the E. bank of Hudson r., at Rhinebeck, Westchester co., N. Y.—Schoolcraft in Proc. N. Y. Hist. Soc., II, 103, 1844.

Sepawi. A pueblo formerly occupied by the Tewa in the valley of El Rito cr., on the heights above the Ojo Caliente of Joseph, and 5 m. from the Mexican settlement of El Rito, N. N. Mex. Bandelier (Arch. Inst. Papers, III, 61, 1890; IV, 51 et seq., 1892) regards its ruin as the largest in New Mexico.

Se-pä-uä.—Bandelier, op. cit., IV, 17, 1892. Se-pä-ue.—Ibid., 51. Sepawi.—Hewett in Bull. 32, B. A. E., 40, 1906.

Sepawn. See *Supawn.*

Seping. The Painted Eagle clan of the Tewa pueblo of San Juan, N. Mex.

Sepiⁿ-tdóa.—Hodge in Am. Anthr., IX, 350, 1896 (*tdóa*='people').

Sepon. See *Supawn.*

Sepori. A former Pima settlement in Arizona, s. of Gila r., probably near the Sonora boundary. It contained 80 families in 1871.

Sepori.—Rudo Ensayo (*ca.* 1763), 162, 1863. Sopori.—Ibid., 193. Topony.—Ind. Aff. Rep. 1871, 365, 1872 (misprint).

Seppock. See *Shoe-pack.*

Sequallisere. See *Sequareesere.*

Sequan. A small Diegueño band in Sweetwater canyon, 20 m. from San Diego, s. Cal.; pop. 50 in 1883, 35 in 1891. The name is now given to a reservation of 640 acres, largely of non-arable land, 110 m. from Mission Tule River Agency, with 34 people in 1909.

Saquan.—H. R. Ex. Doc. 76, 34th Cong, 3d sess., 133, 1857. Sequan.—Jackson and Kinney, Rep. Mission Inds., 28, 1883. Sycuan.—Ind. Aff. Rep., II, 72, 1891. Syquan.—Ibid., 1902, 175, 1903.

Sequareesa, Sequaresere. See *Saghwareesa.*

Sequareesere. An Onondaga chief who joined in a message to Pennsylvania in 1753, was at a treaty in Montreal in 1756, and a council at Ft Johnson, N. Y., in 1757. In Aug. 1759 he was mentioned at Oswego as old Saquerisera, an Onondaga sachem. He signed the treaty negotiated at Ft Stanwix in 1768, and his name appears in Weiser's list, under the form Achseyquarresery, of those in authority in 1752 (Minutes Prov. Coun. Pa., v, 686, 1852–56). In 1750 Cammerhoff called him Sequallisere. Cf. *Saghwareesa, Sakarissa.* (w. m. b.)

Sequidongquee. A famous Seneca chief of the period of the American Revolution, called also Little Beard, and living at Little Beard's town, now Cuylerville, Livingston co., N. Y. His successor inherited both names, and the two can not always be distinguished. Their names appear on the treaties of 1790, 1797, 1815, and 1826, in various forms, as Shecanachweschegue, Saheoquiaudonqui, Sigwáahsohgwih, Checanadughtwo, etc. The Indian name may belong to the later chief alone, who is described as having been below the medium height, and a fluent speaker. (w. m. b.)

Sequim. A Clallam village on Squim bay or Port Washington, N. w. Wash. In 1887 Eells stated that there were about 40 Indians there, mostly old people.

Ft Queen.—Stevens in Ind. Aff. Rep., 450, 1854. Sequim.—Eells in Smithson. Rep., 608, 1887. Shkwin.—Gibbs, Clallam and Lummi, 20, 1863. Squim bay.—Gibbs in Pac. R. R. Rep., I, 429, 1855. Squinbay.—Stevens, op. cit. St-Queen.—Gibbs in Pac. R. R. Rep., I, 429, 1855. Swimmish.—Elder in Ind. Aff. Rep. 1867, 37, 1868. Tch-queen.—U. S. Ind. Treaties, 800, 1873. Washington harbor.—Gibbs in Pac. R. R. Rep., I, 429, 1855.

Sequoia. The big tree (*Sequoia gigantea*) or the redwood (*S. sempervirens*) of California: from *Sequoia* (q. v.), the inventor of the Cherokee alphabet, whose name in the Cherokee language is *Sikwáyi.* From the needles of the sequoia is distilled "sequoiene". (A. F. C.)

Sequoya. Inventor of the Cherokee alphabet, born in the Cherokee town of Taskigi, Tenn., about 1760; died near San Fernando, Tamaulipas, Mexico, in Aug. 1843. He was the son of a white man and a Cherokee woman of mixed blood, daughter of a chief in Echota. Besides his native name of Sikwayi, or Sequoya, he was known as George Gist, otherwise spelled Guest or Guess, the patronymic of his father, generally believed to have been a German trader. He has also been claimed as the son of Nathaniel Gist of Revolutionary note. Sequoya grew up in the tribe, quite unacquainted with English or civilized arts, becoming a hunter and trader in furs. He was also a craftsman in silverwork, an ingenious natural mechanic, and his

SEQUOYA

inventive powers had scope for development in consequence of an accident that befell him in hunting and rendered him a cripple for life. The importance of the arts of writing and printing as instruments and weapons of civilization began to impress him in 1809, and he studied, undismayed by the discouragement and ridicule of his fellows, to elaborate a system of writing suitable to the Cherokee language. In 1821 he submitted his syllabary to the chief men of the nation, and on their approval the Cherokee of all ages set about to learn it with such zeal that after a few months thousands were able to read and write their language. Sequoya, in 1822, visited Arkansas to introduce writing in the Western division of the Cherokee, among whom he took up his permanent abode in 1823. Parts of the Bible were printed in Cherokee in 1824, and in 1828 *The Cherokee Phœnix*, a weekly newspaper in Cherokee and English (see *Periodicals*), began to appear. Sequoya was sent to Washington in 1828 as an envoy of the Arkansas band, in whose affairs he bore a conspicuous part, and when the Eastern Cherokee joined the old settlers in the W. his influence and counsel were potent in the organization of the reunited nation in Indian Ter. When, in his declining years, he withdrew from active political life, speculative ideals once again possessed his mind. He visited tribes of various stocks in a fruitless search for the elements of a common speech and grammar. He sought also to trace a lost band of the Cherokee that, according to tradition, had crossed the Mississippi before the Revolution and wandered to some mountains in the W., and while pursuing this quest in the Mexican sierras he met his death. See Mooney, Myths of the Cherokee, 19th Rep., B. A. E., 108 et seq., 147, 148, 1900, and the authorities therein cited.

Sequoya League. An association incorporated "to make better Indians;" named in honor of Sequoya, the "American Cadmus," and founded as a national organization with headquarters in Los Angeles, Cal., in 1902, by Charles F. Lummis, in consultation with other persons throughout the country. The first work of the league was to secure the appointment of the Warner's Ranch Commission, which procured a model reservation for 300 Mission Indians evicted from their home under decision of the U. S. Supreme Court. The league also secured revocation, by the President, of the "hair-cut order" and secured several vital reforms in agency administration in the S. W. More recently (1904) the league, through the Los Angeles council, has supplied clothing, bedding, seed grain, and ten months' rations to the Mission Indians of the five Campo reservations in San Diego co., Cal., and has organized a concerted movement for the purchase, by the Government, of adequate lands for these Indians, who have been practically destitute for 40 years. It has also carried to headquarters the case of the Pueblo Indians of New Mexico, who were in danger of losing, through a scheme of taxation, the lands given them by the Crown of Spain and respected through all the vicissitudes of Spanish-American rule. The aim of the Sequoya League is to organize public opinion to aid the Department of the Interior; to present reliable information as to conditions in the field; and by proper influence on legislators to secure legislation with regard to the Indians,   (c. f. l.)

Serecoutcha. A village mentioned by Joutel as N. or N. w. of the Maligne (Colorado) r., Texas, in 1687. The name seems to have been given to him by the Ebahamo Indians, who were probably affiliated with the Karankawa. The locality was controlled generally by Tonkawan tribes. Possibly the Terocodames of the Spaniards.   (a. c. f.)
Fercorteha.—Charlevoix, New France, Shea ed., IV, 78, 1870. **Fercouteha.**—Joutel, Journal, Eng. trans., 90, 1719. **Serecoutcha.**—Joutel (1687) in Margry, Déc., III, 289, 1878. **Tsepechoen frercuteas.**—Barcia, Ensayo, 271, 1723 (=Tsepcoen and Serecoutcha).

Seredka (Russian: 'middle'). A former Aleut village on a bay of that name in Akun id., E. Aleutians, Alaska. Pop. 16 in 1834.
Sayraidneuskoi.—Elliott, Cond. Aff. Alaska, 225, 1875. **Seredkinskoje.**—Holmberg, Ethnog. Skizz., map, 1855. **Seredninskoe.**—Veniaminoff, Zapiski, II, 202, 1840.

Sermiligak. The northernmost known village of the northern group of East Greenland Eskimo, situated on Sermiligak fjord, lat. 65°45′.—Rink in Deutsche Geog. Blätt., VIII, 351, 1885.

Sermilik. The most southerly village of the northernmost group of East Greenland Eskimo, situated on Sermilik fjord, lat. 65° 40′.—Rink in Deutsche Geog. Blätt., VIII, 349, 1885.

Serpent. See *Snake Dance*.

Serpentine. A magnesium silicate, of greatly varying texture and color, much used by the native tribes in the manufacture of ornaments, tobacco pipes, and ceremonial objects. It is too soft for making effective implements, but in California it was much employed in the manufacture of small vessels. It is usually greenish in color, although reddish, brownish, and grayish hues and mottled effects are common. The distribution is wide and the deposits are extensive.   (w. h. h.)

Serpent Mound. A remarkable earthwork representing a serpent and usually designated the Great Serpent Mound; situated on Brush cr., in the extreme northern part of Adams co., Ohio. For an illustration, see *Mounds*. The first description and figure of this ancient work were published by Squier and Davis in 1848 (Anc. Mon., 96–98, pl. XXXV). It was subsequently repeatedly described and figured after what was given by Squier and Davis, until a new drawing and description by MacLean appeared in 1885 (Am. Antiq., VII, 44–47), and by Holmes in 1886 (Science, VIII, Dec. 31). The mound is on the middle line of a narrow, crescent-shaped spur, about 100 ft high, flanked on one side by Brush cr. and on the other by East cr. Commencing with the head, which is at the very point of the spur and is partially obliterated, and proceeding toward the tail, one comes first to an enlargement, suggestive of the enlarged neck of a cobra; this is formed by an outer wall on each side, beginning at the small head and uniting in the rear. Within is an inner wall inclosing a small oval space. On each side of the outer wall, about the middle, is an opening or gateway, and back of the interior oval is a slightly curved cross wall, extending from one side to the other. From the union of the two outer walls to the tip of the tail the serpent body is represented by a single embankment, fairly uniform in size, though diminishing gradually toward the tip, having serpentine bends, and ending with a coil of two complete turns. The height of the embankment before restoration under the auspices of the Peabody Museum varied from 2 to 3½ ft, and probably never exceeded 4 ft. The entire length, from the point of the head to the end of the tail, following the curves and bends, as measured by MacLean, is 1,330 ft; the width varies from 15 to 20 ft. The length of the oval, as given by Squier and Davis, is 160 ft, and its width 80 ft. In the middle is a low mound, about 15 ft in diameter, which has been partially excavated, revealing stones in the center, some of which appear to have been burned. The serpent form is so accurately imitated as to leave no doubt that it was the object of the builders to represent this reptile. "Beginning with a small pit at the terminal point, we follow the unfolding coil for two full turns, and then advance along the body to its highest point on the ridge. The curves are strong and even, and the body increases gradually in height and width as we advance. Upon the crest of the ridge we find ourselves at the beginning of three great double folds. Following these, we descend into a slight sag . . . and ascend again slightly to a point where the body straightens out along the ridge. Beyond this we reach the curious enlargement with its triangular and oval enclosures" (Holmes). There is nothing to be found to indicate the legs of MacLean's frog or the winglike projections of Squier and Davis's figure. The most reasonable suggestion respecting the enlargement and the oval is that of Holmes: "When we restore the neck and head of the reptile, omitted by Squier and Davis and misinterpreted by others, the strange oval takes the position of the heart, and in all probability marks the site of the ceremonies that must have been connected with this work."

The land on which the Serpent Mound is situated was purchased for the Peabody Museum; fences were built, trees planted, and defaced portions of the artificial work restored and sodded. In 1900 the trustees of Harvard College deeded the property to the Ohio Archeological and His-

torical Society, to which it now belongs. The most accurate drawing is that by Holmes, above referred to, also reproduced in the 12th Rep. B. A. E., 493, 1894. See Thomas, Cat. Prehist. Works, 161, 1891, with bibliography; Reps. Peabody Museum, 1899–1900, et seq.; Randall, Serpent Mound, 1905.   (c. t.)

Serpent Piqué. See *Olabalkebiche.*

Serper. A Yurok village on Klamath r., N. w. Cal., about 25 m. below the mouth of the Trinity, or 5 m. below Klamath P. O.

Sche-perrh.—Gibbs (1851) in Schoolcraft, Ind. Tribes, III, 138, 1853. Sehe-perrh.—Ibid., 147. Serper.—A. L. Kroeber, inf'n, 1906.

Serranos (Span.: 'highlanders', 'mountaineers'). A Shoshonean division with a common dialect, centering in the San Bernardino mts., s. Cal., N. of Los Angeles, but extending down Mohave r. at least to Daggett and N. across the Mohave desert into the valley of Tejon cr. They also occupied San Bernardino valley. Fray Francisco Garcés, in 1775–76, described the Serranos near Tejon cr., under the name Cuabajai or Cuabajay (their Mohave name), as living in large square communal houses of tule mats on a framework of willow, each family having its own fireplace; they made small baskets, flint knives, and vessels inlaid with mother-of-pearl, and conducted much trade with the natives of the coast near Santa Barbara. One of their rancherias Garcés named San Pascual. The Serranos on the upper waters of Santa Ana r. he called also by their Mohave name, Jenequich (Hanakwiche). In his time these were approachable "and of middling good heart; they are of medium stature, and the women somewhat smaller, round-faced, flat-nosed, and rather ugly; their custom in gentiledom is for the men to go entirely naked, and the women wear some sort of deerskin, with which they cover themselves, and also some small coat of otter or of hare." The same friar visited the Serranos of Mohave r., whom he designated Beñemé (from *Vanyume*, the Mohave name of this branch). These were very poor, but possessed baskets, otter and rabbit coats, and some very curious snares which they made of wild hemp. They subsisted on wild game and acorns. "As a rule they are very effeminate, and the women uncleanly, but all are very quiet and inoffensive." The Serranos formed part of the Indians brought under San Gabriel and San Fernando missions. So far as recorded the villages or rancherias of the Serranos were: Homhoabit, Jurumpa, Juyubit, Muscupiabit, San Benito, San Gorgonio, San Pascual, Tolocabi, and Yucaipa. In 1885 there were 390 Serranos attached to the Mission agency, but they are no longer separately enumerated.

Banumints.—Kroeber in Univ. Cal. Pub., Am. Arch. and Eth., IV, 134, 1907 (Chemehuevi name). **Benemé.**—Cortez (1799) in Pac. R. R. Rep., III, pt. 3, 124, 1856. **Beñemé.**—Garcés (1776), Diary, 238, 1900 (with Panamint). **Benyeme.**—Font, map (1777) in Garcés, Diary, 1900. **Ców-ang-a-chem.**—Barrows, Ethno.-Bot. Coahuilla, 19, 1900 (own name). **Cuabajái.**—Garcés, Diary, 445, 1900 (applied by Mohave to those about Tejon cr.; from Kuvahaivima). **Cuabajay.**—Ibid., 269. **Genicuiches.**—Orozco y Berra, Geog., 59, 1864. **Genigneihs.**—Domenech, Deserts N. Am., I, 441, 1860. **Genigueches.**—Garcés, (1776), Diary, 423, 1900. **Genigueh.**—Folsom, Mexico, map, 1842. **Geniguiehs.**—Taylor in Cal. Farmer, Feb. 21, 1862. **Gidanemuik.**—Kroeber in Univ. Cal. Pub., Am. Arch. and Eth., IV, 134, 1907 (Serranos of upper Tejon and Paso crs. in San Joaquin valley drainage). **Gikidanum.**—Ibid. **Gitanemok.**—Ibid. **Gitanemuk.**—Ibid. **Gitanemum.**—Ibid. **Hanakwiche.**—A. L. Kroeber, inf'n, 1905 (applied by some Yuman tribes). **Hanyuveche.**—Kroeber in Univ. Cal. Pub., Am. Arch. and Eth., IV, 135, 1907 (Mohave name). **Janequeile.**—Pike, Exped., 3d map, 1810. **Jenegueches.**—Garcés, op. cit., 466. **Jeneguechi.**—Font (1775-76) quoted by Coues, Garcés Diary, 261, 1900. **Jenequiches.**—Garcés, op. cit., 218. **Jenigueche.**—Ibid., 444. **Jenigueich.**—Font, map (1777), ibid. **Jenigueih.**—Buschmann, Spuren der Aztek Spr., 259, 1854. **Jeniguieh.**—Warren in Pac. R. R. Rep., XI, pl., 29-31, 1861. **Juníguis.**—Mayer, Mexico, II, 38, 1853. **Kaiviat-am.**—Kroeber in Univ. Cal. Pub., Am. Arch. and Eth., VIII, 35, 1908 (given by a native as their own name; from *kai-ch*, 'mountain'). **Kuvahaivima.**—Kroeber, ibid., IV, 135, 1907 (Mohave name for those about Tejon cr.; distinct from Kuvakhye). **Marangakh.**—Kroeber, ibid., 133 (so called by their southern and other neighbors). **Marayam.**—Ibid., 134 (Luiseño name). **Maringayam.**—Boas in Proc. A. A. A. S., XLIV, 261, 1895. **Maringints.**—Kroeber in Univ. Cal. Pub., Am. Arch. and Eth., IV, 133, 135, 1907 (Chemehuevi name for those s. of San Bernardino mts.). **Mayaintalap.**—Ibid., 131, 135 ('large bows': name given to Serranos of upper Tejon, Paso, and possibly Pastoria crs. by southern Yokuts). **Möhineyam.**—Ibid., 139 (name given to themselves by Mohave r. Serranos). **Panumints.**—Ibid., 134 (name given by Chemehuevi to Serranos N. of San Bernardino range toward Tehachapi mts.). **Panumits.**—Ibid. **Pitanta.**—Ibid. (Chemehuevi name for those N. of San Bernardino range in Mohave desert and on Tejon cr.). **Quabajais.**—Garcés, op. cit., 301, 435. **Quabajay.**—Ibid., 300. **Serranos.**—Garcés (1775), Diary, 197 et seq., 1900. **Takhtam.**—Gatschet in Wheeler Surv. Rep., VII, 413, 1879 (trans.: 'men'). **Tamankamyam.**—Boas in Proc. A. A. A. S., XLIV, 261, 1895 (so called by the related Agua Calientes). **Teniqueches.**—Cortez (1799) in Pac. R. R. Rep., III, pt. 3, 125, 1856. **Vanyume.**—Kroeber, op. cit., 135, 1907 (Mohave name for Mohave r. Serranos). **Witanghatal.**—Ibid. (Tubatulabal name for Tejon cr. Serranos).

Seruniyattha. See *Half King.*

Servas. A Jova pueblo in the 17th century on a small tributary of Rio Yaqui, s. e. of Nacori (of which mission it was a visita), in E. Sonora, Mexico. According to Bandelier (Arch. Inst. Papers, III, 56, 60, 1890; IV, 510, 1892) it became Christianized about 1645, and in 1678 contained 262 inhabitants, but was destroyed by the Suma and Jocome in 1690.

Santo Tomas.—Orozco y Berra, Geog., 345, 1864. **Santo Tomas de Sereba.**—Zapata (1678) quoted by Bandelier, op. cit., IV, 511, 1892. **Santo Tomas de Servas.**—Doc. of 18th century, ibid. **Sereva.**—Doc. of 18th century, ibid., 510. **Servas.**—Bandelier, ibid., III, 56, 60, 1890; IV, 510, 1892.

Service berry. See *Saskatoon.*

Servushamne. Apparently the incorrect form of the name of a former division of the Miwok that lived between Cosumne

and Mokelumne rs., Cal.—Hale, Ethnol. and Philol., 630, 1846.

Seshart. A Nootka tribe on Barclay sd. and Alberni canal, s. w. coast of Vancouver id. Its septs, according to Boas, are: Hameyisath, Kuaiath, Kutssemhaath, Maktlaiath, Nechimuasath, Neshasath, Tlasenuesath, Tseshaath, and Wanineath. Their principal village is Tsahahch. Pop. 124 in 1909.

Schissatuch.—Grant in Jour. Roy. Geog. Soc., 293, 1857. **Ses'h-aht.**—Brit. Col. map, 1872. **Seshaht.**—Sproat, Savage Life, 308, 1868. **Shechart.**—Mayne, Brit. Col., 251, 1862. **She-sha-aht.**—Can. Ind. Aff., 1880, 315, 1881. **Sishat.**—Swan, MS., B. A. E. **Suthsetts.**—Jewitt, Narr., 36, repr. 1849. **Sutsets.**—Armstrong, Oregon, 136, 1857. **Ts'ēcā'ath.**—Boas in 6th Rep. N. W. Tribes Can., 31, 1890. **Tsesaht.**—Can. Ind. Aff., pt. 2, 77, 1908. **Tsesh-aht.**—Can. Ind. Aff., 188, 1883.

Seshukwa. A former pueblo of the Jemez in New Mexico, the exact site of which is not known.

Se-shiu-qua.—Bandelier in Arch. Inst. Papers, IV, 207, 1892. **Sé-shu-kwa.**—Hodge, field-notes, B. A. E., 1895.

Sespe. A Chumashan village said by Indians to have been on Sespe cr., Ventura co., Cal. Situated near San Cayetano ranch, Saticoy r., 20 m. from the sea.

Sĕ-ĕk'-pĕ.—Henshaw, Buenaventura MS. vocab., B. A. E., 1884. **Sespe.**—Taylor in Cal. Farmer, July 24, 1863.

Sestikustun (*Sĕs'-ti-ku'-stûn*). A former Takelma village on the s. side of Rogue r., Oreg. Distinct from Chasta, Sesti, and Chastacosta.—Dorsey in Jour. Am. Folklore, III, 235, 1890.

Sesum. A former Maidu village on the w. side of Feather r., just s. of the village of Mimal, in the present Sutter co., Cal.—Dixon in Bull. Am. Mus. Nat. Hist., XVII, map, 1905.

Lishu.—Bancroft, Nat. Races, I, 450, 1874. **Sesum.**—Chever in Bull. Essex Inst., II, 28, 1870. **Sishu.**—Bancroft, op. cit. **Sisumi.**—Curtin, MS. vocab., B. A. E., 1885.

Setaaye (*Se'-ta-a'-yĕ.*) A band or village of the Chastacosta on Rogue r., Oreg.—Dorsey in Jour. Am. Folk-lore, III, 234, 1890.

Setangya (*Set-ängyä*, 'Sitting Bear'). A noted Kiowa chief and medicine-man, and leader of the principal war society of the tribe. Commonly known to the whites as Satank. He was born in the Blackhills region about the year 1810, his paternal grandmother having been a Sarsi woman. He became prominent at an early age, and is credited with having been a principal agent in negotiating the final peace between the Kiowa and the Cheyenne about 1840. His name heads the list of signers of the noted Medicine Lodge treaty of 1867. In 1870 his son was killed by the whites while raiding in Texas. The father went down into Texas, gathered the bones into a bundle, and brought them back, thenceforth carrying them about with him upon a special horse until himself killed about a year later. On May 17, 1871, in company with Settainte (q. v.) he led an attack on a wagon train in Texas, by which 7 white men lost their lives. On making public boast of the deed to the agent at Ft Sill, in the present Oklahoma, shortly afterward, he and two others were arrested by military authority to be sent to Texas for trial. Setangya, however, refused to be a prisoner, and deliberately inviting death, sang his own death song, wrenched the fetters from his wrists, and drawing a concealed knife sprang upon the guard and was shot to death by the troops surrounding him. He was buried in the military cemetery at Ft Sill. (J. M.)

Setaslema ('people of the rye prairie'). A Yakima band formerly living on Setass cr., a w. tributary of Yakima r. on the Yakima res., Wash.

Setasura. An ancient Jova pueblo at or near the site of the former settlement of Servas, in E. Sonora, Mexico. It was abandoned prior to 1678, probably on account of Apache depredations.
Setasura.—Zapata (1678) quoted by Bandelier in Arch. Inst. Papers, IV, 511, 1892. Setusura.—Zapata (1678) quoted by Bancroft, No. Mex. States, I, 513-14, 1884.

Setauket. An Algonquian tribe formerly occupying the N. shore of Suffolk co., Long id., N. Y., from Stony Brook to Wading r. They sold their last remaining lands in 1675.
Satauket.—Wood quoted by Macauley, N. Y., II, 252, 1829. Seaquatalke.—Andros (1675) in N. Y. Doc. Col. Hist., XIV, 709, 1883. Seaquetalke.—Ibid. Seatakot.—Winthrop (1673) in Mass. Hist. Soc. Coll., 3d s., X, 92, 1849. Seatalcott.—Nicolls (1666) in N. Y. Doc. Col. Hist., XIV, 576, 1883. Seatalcutt.—Doc. of 1681, ibid., 762. Seatalkot.—Doc. of 1673, ibid., II, 602, 1858. Sea-Talkott.—Doc. of 1668, ibid., XIV, 605, 1883. Seataucok.—Doc. of 1673, ibid., II, 583, 1858. Seatauk.—Topping (1675), ibid., XIV, 708, 1883. Seatauke.—Doc. of 1676, ibid., 711. Sea-tolcotts.—Macauley, N. Y., II, 164, 1829. Seetauke.—Deed of 1664 quoted by Thompson, Long Id., I, 410, 1843. Setaket.—Underhill (1665) in Mass. Hist. Soc. Coll., 4th s., VII, 190, 1865. Setalcket.—Doc. of 1673 in N. Y. Doc. Col. Hist., II, 584, 1858. Setauck.—Underhill (1660) in Mass. Hist. Soc. Coll., 4th s., VII, 185, 1865. Setauk.—Record of 1661 quoted by Thompson, Long Id., I, 408, 1843. Setauket.—Deed of 1675 quoted by Thompson, ibid., 264, 1839. Setokett.—Gardiner (1660) in Mass. Hist. Soc. Coll., 4th s., VII, 65, 1865. Setuket.—Winthrop (ca. 1660), ibid.

Setauket. The principal village of the Setauket, near the present Setauket, Long id., N. Y.
Setawkett.—Allyn (1664) in N. Y. Doc. Col. Hist., III, 86, 1853.

Setlia (*Sĕ'lia*). A Bellacoola town at the entrance of S. Bentinck Arm, coast of British Columbia.
Sĕ'Lia.—Boas in Mem. Am. Mus. Nat. Hist., II, 48, 1898. Sitleece.—Whymper, Alaska, 55, 1869.

Setokwa. A former village of the Jemez, situated about 2 m. s. of their present pueblo, in New Mexico.
Setokwa.—Hodge, field-notes, B. A. E., 1895. Se-to-qua.—Bandelier in Arch. Inst. Papers, IV, 207, 1892.

Seton Lake. The local name for a body of Upper Lillooet around a lake of this name in the interior of British Columbia, subsequently subdivided into the Enias, Mission, Niciat, and Schloss.
Seaton Lake.—Can. Ind. Aff., 279, 1894. Seton Lake.—Ibid., 1884, 190, 1885.

Setsi (*Sĕ'tsĭ*, of lost meaning). A traditional Cherokee settlement on the s. side of Valley r., about 3 m. below Valleytown, in Cherokee co., N. C. There is a mound at this place.—Mooney in 19th Rep. B. A. E., 531, 1900.

Setsurgheake (*Sĕ'-tsŭ-rxe-a'-γĕ*). A former village of the Chastacosta on Rogue r., Oreg.—Dorsey in Jour. Am. Folk-lore, III, 234, 1890.

Settainte. See *Satanta*.

Setthatun (*Se-t'ca'-tŭn*, probably 'where there are many rocks'). A band of the Chetco on the s. side of Chetco r., Oreg.—Dorsey in Jour. Am. Folk-lore, III, 236, 1890.

Settulushaa. See *Old Knife*.

Seuvarits. A division of Ute formerly occupying the Castle valley country in w. central Utah. Powell found 144 on the Uinta res. in 1873. They are now grouped with other bands under the name of Uinta Indians.
Asivoriches.—Collins in Ind. Aff. Rep., 125, 1861. Cheveriches.—Simpson (1859), Rep. of Expl. Across Utah, 35, 459, 1876. Ciba-riches.—Graves in Ind. Aff. Rep., 386, 1854. Elk Mountain Utes.—Head in Ind. Aff. Rep. 1867, 174, 1868. Elk Mountain Yutas.—Burton, City of Saints, 578, 1861. Fish Utes.—Tourtellotte in Ind. Aff. Rep., 142, 1870. Seu-a-rits.—Sen. Ex. Doc. 42, 43d Cong., 1st sess., 14, 1874. Seuv-a-rits.—Powell in Ind. Aff. Rep. 1873, 42, 1874. She-ba-retches.—Head in Ind. Aff. Rep., 149, 1868. Sheberetches.—Tourtellotte in Ind. Aff. Rep., 142, 1870. She-be-riches.—Powell in Smithson. Rep. 1874, 41, 1875. She-be-Ucher.—Tourtellotte in Ind. Aff. Rep. 1869, 231, 1870. Suivirits.—Mallery in Proc. A. A. A. S., 353, 1877.

Sevege. A former town, apparently under Oneida jurisdiction, situated, according to the Brion de la Tour map, 1781, a short distance above Owego, on the w. side of the E. branch of Susquehanna r., N. Y.

Seven Council Fires. The league of the Dakota (q. v.) existing previous to the migration of the Teton from Minnesota to Missouri r., and commemorated later in ceremony and tradition. The members of the league in the order of seniority were: 1. Mdewakanton; 2. Wahpekute; 3. Sisseton; 4. Wahpeton; 5. Yankton; 6. Yanktonai; 7. Teton. The Assiniboin, who had separated from the Yanktonai before the historic period, constituted a distinct and hostile tribe.
Ochénté Shakóán.—Long, Exped. St Peter's R., I, 377, 1824 ('nation of seven fires'). Ochente Shakoans.—Gallatin in Trans. Am. Antiq. Soc., II, 121, 1836. Ocheti Shaowni.—Warren, Dacota Country, 15, 1856. Seven Council Fires.—Ibid. Seven Fires.—Gallatin, op. cit.

Seven Houses. A former Delaware village in Beaver co., Pa., near the ford of Beaver cr. just above the mouth. About 7 houses remained after the defeat of the Indians at Bushy Run in 1763, when they forsook all their settlements in this part of the country.—Smith, Bouquet Exped., 10, 1766.

Seven Islands. A Montagnais trading and mission station on the N. shore of the gulf of St Lawrence, near the mouth of Moisie r., Quebec. In 1884 the inhabitants numbered 269; in 1909, 360.
Sept Isles.—Boucher in Can. Ind. Aff. 1884, pt. I, 37, 1885. Seven Islands.—Ibid., 185.

Seven Nations of Canada. The 7 tribes signified are the Skighquan (Nipissing), Estjage (Saulteurs), Assisagh (Missisauga), Karhadage, Adgenauwe, Karrihaet, and Adirondax (Algonkins). The 4th, 5th, and 6th are unidentified. These are the peoples mentioned in N. Y. Doc. Col. Hist., IV, 899, 1854. In the Mass. Hist Soc. Coll., 3d s., v, 78, 1836, the Caughnawaga are not included in the 7 tribes there mentioned.
Seven Castles.—Knox (1792) in Am. St. Papers, Ind. Aff., I, 235, 1832. Seven Nations of Canada.— Maumee council (1793), ibid. Seven nations of Indians inhabiting lower Canada.—Rep. in Williams, Vermont, II, 291, 1809. Seven nations of Lower Canada Indians.—Caughnawaga address (1798), ibid., 233–234. "Seven Tribes" on the River St. Lawrence.—Mass. Hist. Soc. Coll. 3d s., v, 78, 1836.

Sevilleta (Span.: 'Little Seville,' so called on account of its resemblance in situation to the Spanish city). A former pueblo of the Piro on the E. bank of the Rio Grande, about 20 m. above Socorro, N. Mex.; visited by Oñate in 1598 and named by him Nueva Sevilla. It was subsequently depopulated and destroyed by other tribes, probably Apache, with whom the inhabitants were at war, but it was resettled between 1626 and 1630, when it became the seat of the Franciscan mission of San Luis Obispo, having a number of other Piro pueblos as visitas. At this time it was mentioned as the most northerly of the Piro villages. In 1693 Vetancurt reported it to contain only 3 families, the remainder having fled with the Spaniards to El Paso at the outbreak of the Pueblo revolt in 1680. On the return of Gov. Otermin in 1681 he found the pueblo abandoned and almost in ruins; it was never resettled by Indians. Not to be confounded with Cebolleta in any of its various forms. Consult Bandelier in Arch. Inst. Papers, IV, 239, 1892. See also *Piros, Pueblos.*   (F. W. H.)
New Sevilla.—Bandelier, op. cit., 238 (transl. of Oñate's Nueva Sevilla). Nueva Sevilla.—Oñate (1598) in Doc. Inéd., XVI, 252, 1871. San Lodovic.— Columbus Memorial Vol., 156, 1893. San-Luis de Seuilleta.—Benavides, Memorial, 19, 1630. Sebollita.—Davis, Span. Conq. N. Mex., 313, 1869. Semillete.—Humboldt, New Spain, II, 309, 1811. Seuilleta.—Benavides, op. cit., 14. Sevilleta.— Vetancurt (1696) in Teatro Mex., III, 310, 1871; Rivera, Diario, leg. 756, 1736. Sevillete.—Shea, Cath. Miss., 82, 1850. Sevilletta.—Sanson, L'Amérique, map, 27, 1657. Sibillela.—Pike, Explor. Travels, map, 1811. Sibilleta.—Pike, Exped., app., pt. III, 7, 1810. Sivilleta.—Benavides, op. cit., 16. S. Luis Obispo Sevilleta.—Benavides (1630) cited by Bancroft, Ariz. and N. Mex., 163, 1889.

Sewaathlchutun (*Se'-wa-açl-tcû'-tûn*). A Takelma band or village on the s. side of Rogue r., Oreg.—Dorsey in Jour. Am. Folk-lore, x, 235, 1890.

Sewackenaem. An Esopus chief at the council of 1658; called Semeckamenee and Sewackemamo at the peace treaty of 1660, and Seweckenamo in 1664 and 1667. Sewackenamie as sachem renewed a deed in 1674, and signed a renewal in 1681. He also acknowledged his mark in 1669, and was one of the 5 Esopus sachems at the treaty of that year. Sewakonama also signed an agreement with Gov. Nicolls in 1665. See N. Y. Doc. Col. Hist., XIII, 93, 150, 400, 533, 1851.   (W. M. B.)

Sewan. A name among the Dutch settlers of New Netherland (whose traders obtained it from Rhode Island) for the Indian shell money called by the English settlers of Massachusetts *wampum* and *peag* (q. v.). The name *sewan* is first mentioned in a letter written by De Rasières in 1627. Spelled *zeawant* by Montanus (1671), and *seawan* and *seawant* by other writers. The word is from Narraganset *siwân*, 'scattered,' from *siweu*, 'he scatters.' The shell money that bore this name among the Indians was unstrung and passed from hand to hand, by count, in a loose state, one dark purple bead being worth two white ones. The Dutch applied the name indiscriminately to the beads in a loose or scattered and strung state. See *Roanoke.*   (W. R. G.)

Sewapoo. A tribe or band that lived about Delaware bay; probably a Delaware band in s. New Jersey.—De Laet (1633) in N. Y. Hist. Soc. Coll., 2d s., I, 315, 1841.

Sewathen. A Cowichan tribe formerly living on the coast of British Columbia s. of the mouth of Fraser r. They are now on a reservation near Pt Roberts, called Chewassan from the name of the tribe. Pop. 50 in 1909.
Isowasson.—Can. Ind. Aff., 74, 1878. SEwā'çEn.— Hill-Tout in Ethnol. Surv. Can., 54, 1902. Stauāçen.—Boas, MS., B. A. E., 1887. Stcuwā'oEl.— Boas in Rep. 64th Meeting B. A. A. S., 454, 1894 (given as a town). Tche-wassan.—Can. Ind. Aff., 277, 1894. Tsawwassen.—Ibid., pt. II, 75, 1904. Tsonassen.—Ibid., pt. I, 189, 1883. Tsowassan.— Ibid., 316, 1880.

Seweckenamo. See *Sewackenaem.*

Sewee. A small tribe, supposedly Siouan, formerly living in E. South Carolina. According to Rivers (Hist. So. Car., 36, 1856) they occupied the lower part of Santee r. and the coast westward to the divide of Ashley r., about the present Monks Corner, Berkeley co., where they adjoined the Etiwaw. Nothing is known of the language, but judging by their alliances and their final incorporation with the Catawba they are assumed to have been Siouan. Lawson, who met them in 1701, when they were living at the mouth of Santee r., states that they had been a large tribe, but had been wasted by alcohol and smallpox, which disease was commonly fatal because the afflicted plunged into cold water to alleviate the fever. At Sewee bay he found a deserted village, Avendaughbough, which may have been one of their towns. Lawson says that they undertook to send a fleet of canoes to England in charge of most of their able-bodied men, for the purpose of trade; a storm swamped most of the canoes, and the survivors were rescued by an English ship and sold as slaves in the West Indies. In 1715 there remained but one village of 57 souls. The Yamasee war of that year probably put an end to their separate existence as a tribe, forcing the survivors to join the Catawba. An anonymous old chronicle published by Rivers (Hist. So. Car., 38, 1874) states that they belonged to the Cusabo tribes. Consult Mooney, Siouan Tribes of the East, Bull. B. A. E., 1894.

Seawees.—Doc. of 1719 in Rivers, Hist. So. Car., 93, 1874. Seewas.—Ibid., 38, 1856. Sewee.—Purcell, Map of Va., 1795. Sewees.—Lawson (1701), Hist. Car., 24, 1860. Sewoe.—Moll, Map Car. (1720), no. 98 in Am. maps, I (misprint).

Sewellel. One of the names of a species of rodent (*Haplodon rufus*) peculiar to a limited area in the Oregon-British Columbia region and regarded by some authorities as a sort of connecting link between the beaver and the squirrel. Lewis and Clark (Trav., III, 39, 1817) state that *sewellel* is the name given by the natives. To the trappers and hunters this animal was known also as boomer, mountain beaver, etc. Another native name subsequently used by the whites is *showt'l* (q. v.). According to Gibbs (Pac. R. R. Rep., XII, pt. 2, 126, 1860) *sewellel* is a corruption of *shewallal*, the Chinook name for a robe made of the skins of these animals, the animal itself being called *ogwoollal*. (A. F. C.)

Sewickley. A former village of the Shawnee, called by the early Indian traders Asswikales (see *Hathawekela*), later shortened to Swickleys, situated on the N. side of the Allegheny r., about 12 m. above Pittsburg, near the site of Springdale, Allegheny co., Pa. In the notes given in the table of distances by James Le Tort before the Pennsylvania Council (1731), he speaks of 50 families of these Asswikales "lately from Carolina to Potowmack, & from thence thither; making 100 men; Aqueloma, their Chief" (Arch. Pa., I, 302, 1852; see also letter of Davenport, ibid., 299). These Shawnee, a short time before, had settled on the w. branches of the Susquehanna, whence they moved to the Conemaugh, then down the Kiskiminetas to the Allegheny At the time the village on this river was visited by Le Tort, various French traders had been among the Indians, among

them "Cavalier," who had taken a number of the Shawnee to Montreal, where they had been kindly treated and given presents. The next year, about 1730, several of the Shawnee chiefs visited the French governor, who sent back to the Allegheny five blacksmiths to mend the guns and hatchets of the Indians in the settlement. This led to a request that the English authorities send a blacksmith to the Allegheny to render similar service.

A number of these Shawnee were located along the streams in Westmoreland co., hence the name for Sewickley cr., Sewickley settlement, etc. The town on the Allegheny is noted on Bonnecamp's map of 1749 as "Ancien Village des Chaouanons", through which place Celeron de Bienville passed in that year. After the English occupancy of the Ohio in 1758, the village was occupied by a few Mingo and friendly Delawares. After Pontiac's conspiracy in 1763 all the Indian villages near Ft Pitt were abandoned, although a few Indians lived at this locality at a later date. (G. P. D.)

Sewickly's old T.—Evans map, 1755. Sewicklys Old Town.—Scull map, 1770; Pownall map, 1776. Village des Chaouanons.—Bonnecamp map, 1749.

Seyupa. A former pueblo of the Pecos tribe, more commonly known as El Gusano (Span.: 'The Worm'), situated a few miles S. E. of Pecos, at the present site of the village of Fulton, San Miguel co., N. Mex. In the opinion of Bandelier it is not unlikely that this pueblo was occupied, together with Kuuanguala (q. v.), at the time of Espejo's visit in 1583; and, indeed, if the pueblo of Seipa mentioned by Castañeda of Coronado's expedition in 1540 is identical, it was occupied when New Mexico was first visited by the Spaniards. (F. W. H.)

El Gusano.—Bandelier in Arch. Inst. Papers, III, 128, 1890. Seipa.—Castañeda (1541) in Ternaux-Compans, Voy., IX, 182, 1838 (identical?). Se-yu-pä.—Bandelier, op. cit., IV, 128, 1892. Se-yu Paela.—Ibid., III, 128, 1890. Se-yu-pä-lo.—Ibid., IV, 128, 1892.

Sfaganuk. A Kaialigmiut Eskimo village between Dall lake and Etolin str., Alaska.

Sfaganugamute.—Petroff, Alaska, map, 1880. Sfoganugamiut.—Nelson quoted by Baker, Geog. Dict. Alaska, 1902. Sfugunugumut.—Nelson in 18th Rep. B. A. E., map, 1899.

Sganatees ('the very long town'). A former village, probably of the Tuscarora, situated in 1752 on the "main road to Onondaga," about 10 miles w. of "Old Oneida," N. Y. (J. N. B. H.)

Ganatisgowa.—De Schweinitz, Life of Zeisberger, 55, 1870 (='the great long town'). Sganatees.—Ibid., 712.

Sgilgi (*Sgĭ'lgĭ*, 'plenty of scoters'). A Haida town of the Saki-kegawai family, formerly in an inlet on the s. w. coast of Moresby id., Queen Charlotte ids., Brit. Col. It was the most important Ninstints town on the w. coast, and its chief became town chief of Ninstints.—Swanton, Cont. Haida, 277, 1905.

Sha. The doubtful Snake clan of the Yuchi.

Ca.—Speck, Yuchi Inds., 70, 1909 (c=sh).

Shaa. A Yurok village on lower Klamath r., close to Kepel and about 12 m. below the mouth of Trinity r., N. w. Cal.

Shaa.—A. L. Kroeber, inf'n, 1907. Schaitl.—Gibbs (1851) in Schoolcraft, Ind. Tribes, III, 138, 1853.

Shabanshksh (*Cábanckc*). A former village of the Tlakluit 1 m. below The Dalles of Columbia r., Wash.   (E. S.)

Shabawywyagun (*Shábwéwéagän*, from *shábo*, *shábw*, 'through,' 'from side to side'; *-wéwé*, 'sound'; *-agän*, nominal formative: 'sound heard from one side to another': a sound heard through other sounds.—Gerard). An Ottawa village about the year 1800, apparently on the E. shore of L. Michigan.

Chab-way-way-gun.—Prairie du Chien Treaty (1829) in U. S. Ind. Treat., 164, 1873. Shab-a-wy-wy-a-gun.—Tanner, Narr., 37, 1830.

Shabonee (the name is in dispute; by some he is said to have been named from Capt. Jacques de Chambly; by others the name is said to be of Potawatomi derivation and to signify 'built like a bear'). A Potawatomi chief, grand nephew of Pontiac, born on Maumee r., Ill., in 1775; died in Morris, Grundy co., Ill., July 17, 1859. His father was an Ottawa who fought under Pontiac. The son, who was a man of fine parts and magnificent presence, emigrated at an early age with a part of his tribe to Michigan, and, becoming one of Tecumseh's lieutenants, fought by his side when he was killed at the battle of the Thames. Incensed at the treatment of the Indian allies by the British commander, he and Sauganash transferred their allegiance to the Americans. Joining the Potawatomi, among whom he married, he was chosen peace chief of the tribe and was their spokesman at the council with the representatives of the Government at Chicago in Aug. 1836. In the Winnebago and Black Hawk wars he performed invaluable services for the white pioneers, time and again saving the settlements from destruction by timely warnings. When the Winnebago rose in 1827 he visited the Potawatomi villages to dissuade them from taking up arms, and at the village of Geneva Lake, Wis., he was made a prisoner and threatened with death. As the white man's friend he encountered the ill will of a large part of the Indians, but his influence over his own tribe was sufficient to restrain it from joining in a body the forces of Black Hawk, who twice went to Shabonee and tried to enlist him in his cause. At a council of the allied tribes in Feb. 1832, Shabonee espoused the cause of the whites and endeavored to convince Black Hawk that his proposed uprising would only bring disaster to the

Indians. Unsuccessful in his endeavor, he and his son mounted their ponies at midnight, and starting from a point near the present Princeton, Ill., warned the settlers both E. and w. of the intended outbreak, Shabonee finally reaching Chicago in time to put the inhabitants on their guard. The Sauk and Foxes in revenge attempted many times to murder him, and killed his son and his nephew. When under the treaties of 1836 the Potawatomi migrated beyond the Mississippi, Shabonee went with them, but returned shortly to the two sections of land at his village "near the Pawpaw Grove," in De Kalb co., which the Government had awarded him under the treaties of July 29, 1829, and Oct. 20,

SHABONEE

1832, as a reward for his services. At the solicitation of his tribe he joined them again, but pined for civilization, and in 1855 again returned only to find that speculators had bought at public sale his two sections of land on the ground that he had abandoned it. The citizens of Ottawa, Ill., then bought him a small farm on the s. bank of Illinois r., 2 m. above Seneca, Grundy co., on which he passed his remaining years. He received an annuity of $200 from the Government for his services in the Black Hawk war, which, with contributions from friends, kept him from want. A monument, consisting of a large granite bowlder, was erected over his grave in Evergreen Cemetery, at

Morris, Ill., Oct. 23, 1903. Shabonee's name is appended to the treaties of Prairie du Chien, Wis., Aug. 19, 1825, and July 29, 1829; Camp Tippecanoe, Ind., Oct. 20, 1832; and Chicago, Sept. 26, 1833. He was married three times, the last two wives living with him at the same time. He was succeeded as chief by his grandson, Smoke. See Matson, Memories of Shaubena, 1880.

Shabwasing. A Chippewa band in 1851, probably in lower Michigan.—Smith in Ind. Aff. Rep., 53, 1851.

Shackaconia. A tribe of the Mannahoac confederacy, formerly living on the s. bank of the Rappahannock, in Spotsylvania co., Va. Their principal village bore the same name.
Shackaconias.—Strachey (1612), Va., 104, 1849. Shackakonies.—Jefferson, Notes, 129, 1802. **Shakahonea.**—Simons in Smith (1629), Va., I, 186, 1819.

Shackamaxon (of doubtful meaning). A Delaware village on the site of Kensington, now a part of Philadelphia, Pa. At this place Penn made his treaty with the Indians in 1682.
Schachamesink.—Heckewelder Narr., Connelley ed., 554, 1907 (given as Delaware form; German spelling). **Shackamaxon.**—Proud, Penn., I, 143, 1797. **Shackaxons.**—Boudinot, Star in the West, 128, 1816. **Shakamaxon**—Proud, op. cit. **Shakhamexunk.**—Deed of 1676 in N. Y. Doc. Col. Hist., XII, 550, 1877 (identical?). **Shakhamuxunck.**—Doc. of 1679, ibid., 620. **Shorbanaxon.**—Rupp, West. Penn., 27, 1846 (misprint).

Shadjwane (*Shadjwané*). The Rabbit clan of the Yuchi (q. v.).—Speck, Yuchi Inds., 70, 1909.

Shaganappi. Thongs of rawhide used for rope or cord. *Shaganappi*, or "Northwest iron," was an important factor in the economic development of the N. W., where it was a godsend to the mixed-bloods and white settlers. Out of it was made the harness of the famous Red river carts and of the dog sleds of the country to the northward. It was one of the most important gifts from the Indian to the white man. A variety of spellings of this word exists, as shaganappi, shaggineppi, and shaggunappy. It is derived from *pisaganâbiy*, *pishaganâpi*, in the Cree dialects of Algonquian, the corresponding Chippewa word being *bishaganâb*, signifying 'a thong of rawhide.' Gerard gives the Wood Cree word as *pishaganâbii*, from *pishagan* 'hide' (lit. 'what is flayed'), *âbii* 'cord', 'string', 'rope.' It has been said that "shaganappi and Scotchmen made the Northwest." A corresponding term is *babiche* (q. v.), though it is not of such importance as the other.   (A. F. C.)

Shagoyewatha. See *Red Jacket*.

Shagsowanoghroona (Iroquois name). A tribe or band, probably Algonquian, living in Canada in 1759.—Canajoharie conf. (1759) in N. Y. Doc. Col. Hist., VII, 393, 1856.

Shahaka (*She'-he-ke*, 'Coyote'). A Mandan chief, more commonly known as Le Gros Blanc, or Big White; born about 1765. He was principal chief of Metutahanke, the "Lower Village" of the Mandan, on the Missouri below the mouth of Knife r., and rendered friendly service to Lewis and Clark while at Ft Mandan in the winter of 1804–5, in recognition of which he was given a medal. Brackenridge described him as a fat man, of mild and gentle disposition, not much distinguished as a warrior, "and extremely talkative, a fault much despised amongst the Indians"; and, again, as "a fine looking Indian, and very intelligent—his complexion fair, very little different from that of a white man much exposed to the

SHAHAKA

sun." When the expedition returned to the Missouri from the Pacific, Lewis and Clark persuaded Shahaka to accompany them to St Louis with a view of making a visit to President Jefferson, and Jefferson later invited Lewis to visit Monticello with Shahaka for the purpose of showing the latter his collection of Indian objects from the N. W. Shahaka remained in the E. for a year, and while there, evidently in Philadelphia, St Mémin made a portrait of him with the aid of a physionotrace, the original of which (see illustration) now belongs to the American Philosophical Society of Philadelphia. Shahaka left St Louis for his home in May 1807, the party consisting of himself and his squaw-man interpreter, Réné Jessaume, with their wives and one child each, escorted by 2 noncommissioned officers and 11 privates under the command of Ensign Nathaniel Pryor, who, as a sergeant, had accompanied the expedition of Lewis and Clark. There ascended the Missouri at the same time a deputation of 24 Sioux, including 6 children, who were provided with a separate escort; and also 2 trading parties, one of which, consisting of 32 men under Pierre Chouteau, was designed to traffic with the Mandan. The expedition proceeded slowly up the Missouri, reaching the lower Arikara village on Sept. 9, where it was learned that the Mandan and the Arikara were at war. The demand of the chief of the upper Arikara village that Shahaka go ashore with him being refused, the Indians became insolent and aggressive, and afterward opened fire on the boats, which was returned. Pryor then ordered a retreat downstream, but the Indians followed along shore, killing one of the Sioux, mortally wounding one of Chouteau's men, and wounding several others, including Jessaume. Pryor now proposed to Shahaka that they attempt to cover the rest of the distance— about 3 days' journey—by land, but this the Mandan refused to do on account of the incumbrance of the women and children and the wounded condition of their interpreter, whereupon the party returned to St Louis. By an agreement entered into with the Missouri Fur Co. in the spring of 1808 for the safe conduct of the Indians to their home, another expedition, consisting of about 150 men having Shahaka and his companions in charge, started from St Louis about the middle of May 1809, and although the Sioux at first showed a disposition to be troublesome the Arikara were found to be friendly and the party reached its destination Sept. 24, laden with presents. Shahaka fell into disrepute among his people by reason of what were regarded as extravagant tales of his experiences among the whites. He was killed in a fight with the Sioux on an occasion when he went out to watch his people drive them off. Shahaka's wife was Yellow Corn; his son was White Painted House, whose son was Tobacco, whose son (Shahaka's great grandson) is Gun that Guards the House, who is still living and who preserves, with Shahaka's medal bearing date 1797, the story of his great grandfather's exploits. Consult Orig. Jour. Lewis and Clark, passim, 1904–5; Chittenden, Am. Fur Trade, 1902; Coues in Annals of Iowa, 3d s., I, 613, 1895; Brackenridge, Views of La., 1814; Bradbury, Travels, 2d ed., 1819; N. Dak. Hist. Soc. Coll., II, 470–473, 1908. (F. W. H.)

Shahala (*Saxala*, 'above'). A name given by Lewis and Clark to the Chinook-

an tribes living on Columbia r. from Sauvies id. to the Cascades in Oregon. They estimated the number at 2,800, in 62 houses, and mention the following tribes: Neerchokioon, Clahclellah, Wahclellah, and Yehuh. Katlagakya was the native name for the Indians of this region. See *Watlala*.   (L. F.)

Cath-le-yach-ē-yachs.—Ross, Adventures, 111, 1849. Katlagakya.—Framboise quoted by Gairdner in Jour. Geog. Soc. Lond., XI, 255, 1841. Sah-halah.— Orig. Jour. Lewis and Clark, IV, 252, 1905. Saxala.—Boas, inf'n, 1905. Shahala.—Orig. Jour. Lewis and Clark, VI, 67, 1905. Shahalahs.—Am. Pioneer, II, 191, 1843. Shahana.—Kelley, Oregon, 68, 1830. Shah-ha-la.—Orig. Jour. Lewis and Clark, IV, 236, 1905 (also Shâh-ha-la, p. 223). Sha-la-la.—Gibbs in Pac. R. R. Rep., I, 417, 1855 (error).

Shahanik (*Sha'xanîx*, 'little rock'). A village of the Nicola band of Ntlakyapamuk near Nicola r., 16 m. above Spences Bridge, Brit. Col.; pop. 81 in 1901, the last time the name appears.

Ca'xanîx.—Teit in Mem. Am. Mus. Nat. Hist., II, 174, 1900. CQokunQ.—Hill-Tout in Rep. Ethnol. Surv. Can., 4, 1899. Shahahanih.—Can. Ind. Aff., 308, 1887. Shahshanih.—Ibid., 269, 1889. Sh-ha-ha-nih.—Ibid., 196, 1885. Shhahanik.—Ibid., pt. II, 166, 1901.

Shahaptian Family (from *Sáptini*, pl. *Saháptini*, the Salish name for the Nez Percés). An important linguistic family occupying what is now s. w. Idaho, s. E. Washington, and N. E. Oregon. The earlier territory of the Shahaptian tribes extended from the Rocky mts. to the Cascade range, and from the Yakima r. basin to the Blue mts. of Oregon. This territory was overstepped at various times, particularly by the Klikitat in the w., who crossed the Cascades and occupied the headwaters of Cowlitz, Lewis, and White Salmon rs., and even pushed temporarily as far s. as Willamette valley after the depopulation of that region by fever in 1829 (see *Chinookan*). Along Columbia r. Shahaptian villages extended nearly to The Dalles, where they were checked by the Chinook, who had pushed to that point from the coast. To the E. occasional hunting parties crossed the Rockies, but no permanent settlements were formed. (Consult the linguistic map in Part 1.)

The Shahaptian family is well defined linguistically, except possibly in its southern habitat where it may prove to be connected with the Waiilatpuan and Shastan families, and possibly the Lutuamian. In customs and habits its tribes were fairly homogeneous. Family organization was loose and showed no traces of a clan system. Village communities of varying size were the rule, but were prevented from normal development by the seasonal changes of residence necessitated by the character of the food supply. Chiefs were local in authority except in times of emergency. Salmon was the staple article of food, but at the time of the Lewis and Clark expedition in 1804–05 hunting various kinds of game was common, and this had probably been much advanced by the introduction of horses. Roots and berries also were much used as food, but no agriculture was evident. The Shahaptian tribes have always had a high reputation for bravery and, except for certain sporadic outbreaks, have been friendly with the whites.

The following principal divisions of the stock are usually considered as separate tribes: Klikitat, Nez Percés, Paloos, Tenino, Tyigh, Umatilla, Wallawalla, and Yakima. A large number of smaller divisions are often spoken of as independent tribes, but which are really subordinate bands of one or another of the tribes named. Of these smaller bands those most frequently met with in literature are: Akaitchis, Atanumlema, Chimnapum, Des Chutes, Klinquit, Kowasayee, John Day, Liaywas, Ochechote, Pisko, Pishquitpah, Shyik, Skinpah, Sokulk, Tilkuni, Tushepaw, Wahowpun, and Wiam. (H. W. H. L. F.)

Saituka.—See under this caption. Sciatogas.—Stuart in Nouv. Ann. Voy., XII, 42, 1821. Scietogas.—Coues, Henry-Thompson Jour., 818, 1897. Shatasla.—Ibid., 827. Shyatogoes.—Cox, Advent., 239, 1832. Shy-to-gas.—Ross, Fur Hunters, I, 264, 1855. Thy-eye-to-ga.—Brackenridge, Views of La., 302, 1815.

Family Synonymy: ✕Shahaptan.—Scouler in Jour. Roy. Geog. Soc., XI, 225, 1841 (three tribes: Shahaptan, or Nez-percés, Kliketat, Okanagan; the latter being Salishan). <Shahaptan.—Prichard, Phys. Hist. Mankind, v, 428, 1847 (two classes: Nez-percés proper of mountains, and Polanches of plains; includes also Kliketat and Okanagan). >Sahaptin.—Hale in U. S. Expl. Exped., VI, 198, 212, 542, 1846 (Shahaptin or Nez-percés, Wallawallas, Pelooses, Yakemas, Klikatats); Gallatin in Trans. Am. Ethnol. Soc., II, pt. 1. c, 14, 1848 (follows Hale); Gallatin, ibid., 77 (Nez-percés only); Berghaus (1851), Physik. Atlas, map 17, 1852; Gallatin in Schoolcraft, Ind. Tribes, III, 402, 1853 (Nez-percés and Wallawallas); Dall, after Gibbs, in Cont. N. A. Ethnol., I, 241, 1877 (includes Taitinapam and Kliketat). >Saptin.—Prichard, Phys. Hist. Mankind, v, 428, 1847 (or Shahaptan). <Sahaptin.—Latham, Nat. Hist. Man, 323, 1850 (includes Wallawallas, Kliketat, Proper Sahaptin or Nez-percés, Pelús, Yakemas, Cayús?); Latham in Trans. Philol. Soc. Lond., 73, 1856 (includes Waiilatpu); Buschmann, Spuren der aztek. Sprache, 614, 615, 1859; Latham, Opuscula, 340, 1860 (as in 1856); Latham, El. Comp. Philol., 440, 1862 (vocabularies of Sahaptin, Wallawalla, Kliketat); Keane in Stanford, Compend., Cent. and So. Am., app., 460, 474, 1878 (includes Palouse, Walla Wallas, Yakimas, Tairtlas, Kliketats or Pshawanwappams, Cayuse, Mollale; the two last are Waiilatpuan). =Sahaptin.—Gatschet in Mag. Am. Hist., 168, 1877 (defines habitat and enumerates tribes of); Gatschet in Beach, Ind. Miscel., 443, 1877; Bancroft, Nat. Races, III, 565, 620, 1882. >Shahaptani.—Tolmie and Dawson, Comp. Vocabs. Brit. Col., 78, 1884 (Whulwhaipum tribe). >Nez-Percés.—Prichard, Phys. Hist. Mankind, v, 428, 1847 (see *Shahaptan*, above); Keane in Stanford, Compend., Cent. and So. Am., app., 474, 1878 (see his *Sahaptin*). ✕Selish.—Dall, after Gibbs, in Cont. N. A. Ethnol., I, 241, 1877 (includes Yakama, which belongs here). =Shahaptian.—Powell in 7th Rep. B. A. E., 126, 1891.

Shahwundais ('God of the South,' who makes the summer.—J. Jones). A converted Chippewa, generally known as John Sunday, who took an active part in the Methodist missionary work among his people during the early and middle parts of the 19th century. Peter Jones (Hist. Ojeb. Inds., 200, 1861) says he belonged to the Mink "tribe" (probably the Marten gens of Warren). His home, and probably the place of his birth, about 1796, was Alnwick district, Northumberland co., Ont. In 1823 John and Peter Jones, the latter the author of the History of the Ojebway Indians, were converted at the Methodist mission on Credit r., near Rice lake, Northumberland co. The brothers commenced teaching their people, and with other missionaries in 1826–27 held a camp-meeting near Coburg, at which Sunday was converted. He began at once to learn to read and write, was ordained as a minister, and entered actively into missionary work among the Chippewa. With George Copway and other native preachers he went on several missionary tours to the Chippewa about L. Superior. They established a permanent mission in 1833 at L'Anse on Keweenaw bay, Mich., and another in 1835 at Ottawa Lake, in the same state. Sunday appears to have devoted some time to special work among the Saulteurs at Sault Ste Marie, where his preaching was so highly regarded that women bearing children in their arms forded streams to reach the meeting place (Jones, op. cit., 227). It was about this period that the Rev. Wm. Case, who had been influential in bringing Sunday into the church, took him on a tour of the States for the purpose of raising funds for the Canadian missions. At the general council of the Christian Chippewa and Ottawa, held at Saugeen, Ont., in 1845, Sunday was present, and his eloquence on this occasion has received special mention. Copway (Life, Hist. and Trav., 197, 1847) says he was "uncommonly eloquent"; Jones (op. cit., 201) says he was "particularly happy in his address at this meeting, and towards the close, thrilled and astonished all present by the ingenuity and power of his appeals." After this he is not mentioned, though he was probably living as late as 1855. Copway speaks of him as a chief, and he signs as chief the report made by him and one Simpson as commissioners of Alnwick in 1842. (c. t.)

Shakaik (*Shā'kaik*, 'many rattlesnakes'). A Pima village on the N. side of the Gila, N. w. of Casa Blanca, s. Ariz.—Russell in 26th Rep. B. A. E., 23, 1908.

Shakallamy. See *Shikellamy.*

Shakan (*Caxā'n*). A summer village of the Henya on the N.w. coast of Prince of Wales id., Alaska, whither they used to go for fish eggs.

Caxan.—Swanton, field notes, B. A. E., 1904. Tsī'choān.—Krause, Tlinkit Ind., 120, 1885.

Shakchukla (*Shak-chuk'-la*, 'crayfish

people'). A Choctaw clan of the Watakihulata phratry.—Morgan, Anc. Soc., 162, 1878.

Shakehand. Principal chief of the Yankton Sioux in 1804. He was the leader in the council with Lewis and Clark, held opposite the present city of Yankton, S. Dak., when the explorers were going up the Missouri r. He had previously visited Mackinaw and St Louis. (D. R.)

Shakes' Village. A summer camp of the head Stikine chief Cĕks, on Etolin id., Alaska; pop. 38 in 1880.—Petroff in Tenth Census, Alaska, 32, 1884.

Shakian ('beaver'). A Yuchi clan.
Cagä^n'.—Speck, Yuchi Inds., 70, 1909 ($c = sh$). Shákiä^n tahá.—Gatschet, Uchee MS., B. A. E., 71, 1885 (='beaver clan').

Shakkeen. A (former?) Salish village or band under Fraser superintendency, Brit. Col.—Brit. Col. map, Ind. Aff., Victoria, 1872.

Shakopee (*Shakpe*, 'six'). The name of a succession of chiefs of the Mdewakanton Sioux, residing on Minnesota r. not far from the present town of Shakopee, Scott co., Minn. Three men of the name are mentioned in succession. The first met Maj. S. H. Long at the mouth of the Minnesota in 1817, when he came up to distribute the presents which Lieut. Z. M. Pike had contracted to send them 12 years earlier, and Long found him very offensive. This Shakopee was succeeded by his son, who was known as Eaglehead Shakopee, and he by his son Little Six (Shakopeela), who was a leader in the Minnesota massacre of 1862. See *Taoapa*. (D. R.)

Shakori. A small tribe associated with the Eno and Adshusheer in North Carolina in the 17th century. It is doubtful, from their physical characteristics, whether they were of Siouan stock, though they were allied with Siouan tribes. As the Shakori were constantly associated with the Eno they were probably linguistically related to them. They are first mentioned by Yardley (1654), who says a Tuscarora Indian described to him among other tribes of the interior "a great nation called Cacores," of dwarfish stature, not exceeding that of boys of 14 years, yet exceedingly brave and fierce in fight and active in retreat, so that even the powerful Tuscarora were unable to conquer them. They were then near neighbors of the Eno. Lederer (1672) found the villages of the two tribes about 14 m. apart, that of the Shakori being farthest w. In 1701 Lawson found the two tribes confederated, and the Adshusheer with them. Their village, which he calls Adshusheer, was on Eno r. about 14 m. E. of the Occaneechi village, probably a short distance N. E. of the present Durham, N. C.

They resembled the Eno in their customs. According to Col. Barnwell, commander in the Tuscarora war of 1711, they are identical with the Sissipahaw. Consult Mooney, Siouan Tribes of the East, Bull. B. A. E., 1894.
Cacores.—Yardley (1654) in Hawks, N. Car., II, 19, 1858. Schoccories.—Lawson (1701), Hist. Car., 384, 1860. Shabor.—Hawks, N. Car., II, map, 1858 (misprint). Shacco.—Byrd (1733), Hist. Dividing Line, II, 2, 1866. Shacioes.—Barnwell (1711) in S. C. Hist. and Geneal. Mag., IX, 31, 1908. Shackory.—Byrd, op. cit., 15. Shakor.—Lederer, Discov., map, 1672. Shoccories.—Lawson (1701), Hist. Car., 96, 1860.

Shakshakeu ('great heron'). A subphratry or gens of the Menominee.—Hoffman in 14th Rep. B. A. E., 42, 1896.

Shaktabsh. A body of Salish who lived on Port Washington bay, Kitsap co., Wash.; now on Port Madison res.
Shak-tabsh.— Boulet, letter, Mar. 22, 1886. S'hak-tabsh.—Mallet in Ind. Aff. Rep., 198, 1877.

Shaktoligmiut (*Shakto'ligmūt*). A subdivision of the Malemiut Eskimo of Alaska, whose village is Shaktolik.
Chakhtogmut.—Zagoskin, Descr. Russ. Poss. Am., pt. 1, 72, 1847. Shakto'ligmūt.—Dall in Cont. N. A. Ethnol., I, 16, 1877. Tchakh-toligmiouth.—Zagoskin in Nouv. Ann. Voy., 5th s., XXI, map, 1850.

Shaktolik. A Malemiut village on the E. coast of Norton sd., Alaska, inhabited by descendants of the native tribe and invaders from Kotzebue sd.
Shaklolik.—Post-route map, 1903. Shaktolik.—Dall in Cont. N. A. Ethnol., I, 16, 1877. Shaktolit.—11th Census, Alaska, 165, 1893.

Shakwabaiyaki ('blue or green running water pueblo'). A ruined pueblo, formerly occupied by the ancestors of the Hopi, situated opposite Hardy station on the Santa Fé Pacific R. R., near the mouth of Chevlon cr., Ariz.
Blue Running Water pueblo.—Fewkes in 22d Rep. B. A. E., 31, 1904. Cakwabaiyaki.—Ibid., 23 (Hopi name). Chevlon ruin.—Ibid., 23.

Shakwalengya. The Blue or Green Flute clan of the Ala (Horn) phratry of the Hopi.
Cakwaleñya wiñwû.—Fewkes in 19th Rep. B. A. E., 583, 1901 (*wiñwû* = 'clan'). Ca-kwa'-len-ya wüñwü.—Fewkes in Am. Anthr., VII, 401, 1894.

Shalawa. A Chumashan village located by Taylor near Santa Inés mission, Cal.; given by Ventura Indians as formerly between Santa Barbara and Carpenteria, in the locality now called La Matanza.
Cál-a-wa.—Henshaw, Buenaventura MS. vocab., B. A. E., 1884. Shalawa.—Taylor in Cal. Farmer, May 4, 1860. Shhalwaj.—Henshaw, op. cit.

Shalikuwewich (*Cal-i-ku-we'-witc*). A former Chumashan village at a place called Las Lajas, on the coast in Ventura co., Cal.—Henshaw, Buenaventura MS. vocab., B. A. E., 1884.
Shalicuwewech.—Henshaw, op. cit.

Shalkahaan (*Cálkáháán*). A former Chumashan village in the interior of Ventura co., Cal., at a locality called La Cañada del Salto.—Henshaw, Buenaventura MS. vocab., B. A. E., 1884.
Sholchohoon.—Henshaw, op. cit.

Shallattoo (Yakima: *W'shä'nătu*, 'huckleberry', the name of a site on Yakima r. above Ellensburg). A tribe, numbering

100 persons, first visited by Lewis and Clark in 1805 and described as living on Cataract r., in the present Washington. Mooney regards them as a division of the Pisquows.

Lower Yakima.—Gibbs in Pac. R. R. Rep., I, 417, 1855. **Shallates.**—Lewis and Clark Exped., Coues ed., 958, 1893. **Shallatolos.**—Robertson, Oregon, 129, 1846. **Shal-lat-tas.**—Lewis and Clark Exped., I, map, 1817. **Shallattoos.**—Ibid., II, 595, 1817. **Shal-lat-tos.**—Ibid., I, map, 1814. **Shal-tat-tos.**—Lewis and Clark misquoted by Gibbs, op. cit. **W'shä'nătu.**—Mooney in 14th Rep. B. A. E., 736, 1896.

Shallon. A name for the fruit of *Gaultheria shallon*, mentioned first in Allen's History of Lewis and Clark's Expedition, 1814. The name, also spelled *shallun*, is a corruption of Chinook *kl'kwushálla*. (W. R. G.)

Shallyany's Village. A summer camp of a Stikine chief named Căĭyä'nî, on Stikine r., Alaska; pop. 24 in 1880.—Petroff, 10th Census, Alaska, 32, 1882.

Shamans and Priests. Mediators between the world of spirits and the world of men may be divided into two classes: The shamans, whose authority was entirely dependent on their individual ability, and the priests, who acted in some measure for the tribe or nation, or at least for some society.

Shaman is explained variously as a Persian word meaning 'pagan', or, with more likelihood, as the Tungus equivalent for 'medicine-man', and was originally applied to the medicine-men or exorcists in Siberian tribes, from which it was extended to similar individuals among the Indian tribes of America.

Among the Haida and Tlingit, shamans performed practically all religious functions, including, as usual, that of physician, and occasionally a shaman united the civil with the religious power by being a town or house chief also. Generally speaking, he obtained his position from an uncle, inheriting his spiritual helpers just as he might his material wealth; but there were also shamans who became such owing to natural fitness. In either case the first intimation of his new power was given by the man falling senseless and remaining in that condition for a certain period. Elsewhere in North America, however, the sweat bath was an important assistant in bringing about the proper psychic state, and certain individuals became shamans after escaping from a stroke of lightning or the jaws of a wild beast. When treating a patient or otherwise performing, a N. W. coast shaman was supposed to be possessed by a supernatural being whose name he bore and whose dress he imitated, and among the Tlingit this spirit was often supported by several minor spirits which were represented upon the shaman's mask and strengthened his eyesight, sense of smell,

etc. He let his hair grow long, never cutting or dressing it. When performing he ran around the fire very rapidly in the direction of the sun, while his assistant beat upon a wooden drum and his friends sang the spirit songs and beat upon narrow pieces of board. Then the spirit showed him what he was trying to discover, the location of a whale or other food animal, the approach of an enemy, or the cause of the sickness of a patient. In the latter case he removed the object that was causing pain by blowing upon the affected part, sucking at it, or rubbing a charm upon it. If the soul had wandered, he captured and restored it, and in case the patient had been bewitched he revealed the name of the offender and directed how he was to be handled. Payment for his services must always be made in advance, but in case of failure it was usually returned, while among some tribes failure was punished with death. Shamans also performed sleight-of-hand feats to show their power, and two shamans among hostile people would fight each other through the air by means of their spirits, while no war party started off without one.

The ideas behind shamanistic practices in other American tribes were very much the same as these, but the forms which they took varied considerably. Thus instead of being actually possessed, Iroquois shamans and probably others controlled their spirits objectively as if they were handling so many instruments, while Chitimacha shamans consulted their helpers in trances.

Among the Nootka there were two classes of shamans, the *Ucták-u*, or 'workers', who cured a person when sickness was thrown upon him by an enemy or when it entered in the shape of an insect, and the *K·ok·oā'tsmaah*, or 'soul workers', especially employed to restore a wandering soul to its body.

The Songish of the southern end of Vancouver id. also had two sorts of shamans. Of these the higher, called the *squnä'am*, acquired his power in the usual way by intercourse with supernatural beings, while the *sī'oua*, who was usually a woman, received her knowledge from another *sī'oua*. The former answered more nearly to the common type of shaman, while the function of the latter was to appease hostile powers, to whom she spoke a sacred language. She was also applied to by women who desired to bear children, and for all kinds of charms.

Among the interior Salish the initiation of shamans and warriors seems to have taken place in one and the same manner, i. e. through animals which became the novices' guardian spirits. Kutenai shamans had special lodges in the camp larger than the rest, in which they prayed and invoked the spirits.

The Hupa of California recognized two sorts of shamans: the dancing shamans, who determined the cause of disease and the steps necessary for recovery, and other shamans, who after locating the trouble removed it by sucking. Mohave shamans usually receive their powers directly from Mastamho, the chief deity, and acquire them by dreaming rather than the more usual methods of fasting, isolation, petition, etc. Dixon records this latter feature also among the Shasta. The Maidu seem to have presented considerable variations within one small area. In some sections heredity played little part in determining who should become a shaman, but in the N. E. part of the Maidu country all of a shaman's children were obliged to take up his profession or the spirits would kill them. There were two sorts of shamans—the shaman proper, whose functions were mainly curative, and the "dreamer," who communicated with spirits and the ghosts of the dead. All shamans were also dreamers, but not the reverse. During the winter months the dreamers held meetings in darkened houses, where they spoke with the spirits much like modern spirit mediums. At other times the shamans of the foothill region met to see which was most powerful, and danced until all but one had dropped out. One who had not had a shaman for a parent had to go into the mountains to a place where some spirit was supposed to reside, fast, and go through certain ceremonies, and when a shaman desired to obtain more powerful helpers than those he possessed he did the same. Shamans in this region always carried cocoon rattles.

Hoffman enumerates three classes of shamans among the Chippewa, in addition to the herbalist or doctor, properly so considered. These were the *wâbĕnō'*, who practised medical magic, the *jĕs'-sakkĭ'd*, who were seers and prophets deriving their power from the thunder god, and the *midē'*, who were concerned with the sacred society of the *Midē'wiwin*, and should rather be regarded as priests.

These latter were evidently represented among the Delawares by the *medeu*, who concerned themselves especially with healing, while there was a separate class of diviners called *powwow*, or 'dreamers.'

Unlike most shamans, the *angakunirn* of the Central Eskimo communicated with their spirits while seated. It was their chief duty to find out the breaking of what taboos had caused sickness or storms.

As distinguished from the calling of a shaman, that of a priest was, as has been said, national or tribal rather than individual, and if there were considerable ritual his function might be more that of leader in the ceremonies and keeper of the sacred myths than direct mediator between spirits and men. Sometimes, as on the N. W. coast and among the Eskimo, the functions of priest and shaman might be combined, and the two terms have been used so interchangeably by writers, especially when applied to the Eastern tribes, that it is often difficult to tell which is the proper one.

Even where shamanism flourished most there was a tendency for certain priestly functions to center around the town or tribal chief. This appears among the Haida, Tlingit, Tsimshian, and Kwakiutl in the prominent part the chiefs played in secret society performances, and a chief of the Fraser r. coast Salish was even more of a high priest than a civil chief, leading his people in all religious functions.

Most of the tribes of the eastern plains contained two classes of men that may be placed in this category. One of these classes consisted of societies which concerned themselves with healing and applied definite remedies, though at the same time invoking superior powers, and to be admitted to which a man was obliged to pass through a period of instruction. The other was made up of the one or the few men who acted as superior officers in the conduct of national rituals, and who transmitted their knowledge concerning it to an equally limited number of successors. Similar to these, perhaps, were the priests of the Midē'wiwin ceremony among the Chippewa, Menominee, and other Algonquian tribes.

According to Bartram, "besides several juniors or graduates" there was a high priest in every Creek town. These were persons of consequence and exercised great influence in the state, particularly in military affairs. They would "foretell rain or drought and pretend to bring rain at pleasure, cure diseases, and exorcise witchcraft, invoke or expel evil spirits, and even assume the power of directing thunder and lightning." The Natchez state was a theocracy in which the head chief, or "Great Sun," being directly descended from the national lawgiver who had come out of the sun, was ex-officio high priest of the nation, although the guardian of the temple seems to have relieved him partially of his priestly duties. The rest of the Suns shared in their functions to a minor degree, they forming a sacred caste.

Doubtless the most highly developed priesthood N. of Mexico, however, is among the Pueblos of New Mexico and Arizona, where it controls the civil and military branches of the tribe, transforming it into a theocratic oligarchy. The rain priesthood is a body almost entirely composed of men whose duty it is ·by secret prayers and fasts to bring plentiful supplies of rain. The priesthood of the bow is really a war society whose ceremonies are held to give thanks for abundant crops, or, after a scalp had been taken, to bring about rain through the pleasure that the taking of this scalp gives to the anthropic gods, the controllers of the rain. The two head priests of the bow and the rain priests of the six cardinal points form the fountain head of all authority and the court of last appeal in Zuñi. Each of these, except the priest of the zenith, has several assistants, and the priestess of fecundity, the female assistant of the priest of the north, who stands highest in rank, possesses very great authority. Below these are the society of Kótikilli and the esoteric societies. All male Zuñi and very rarely some females are admitted into the former, which deals directly with the anthropic gods and whose ceremonials are for the purpose of bringing rain. The esoteric societies, however, have to do mainly with the zoic or beast gods and are primarily healing societies. A patient may be treated by them at the time of the ceremonies or he may send for a single member. These societies also hold very important ceremonies to bring rain, but they effect this mediately through the influence which the beast gods are supposed to exert upon the anthropic gods. The active members of these societies, including the Kótikilli also, in contradistinction to the rain and war priests, are called by a special name "theurgists," but their functions approach nearer to those of priests than of shamans (Stevenson).

Consult Bartram, Travels, 1791; Boas, Bourke, Cushing, Dorsey, Hoffman, Mooney, Russell, and Mrs Stevenson in Reps. B. A. E.; Boas in Reps. Brit. Asso. Adv. Sci.; Boas in Rep. Nat. Mus. 1895, 1897; Brinton, The Lenâpé and their Legends, 1885; Chamberlain in Jour. Am. Folk-lore, xiv, no. 53, 1901; Curtis, N. Am. Ind., 1907–09; Cushing in Pop. Sci. Mo., June 1882; Dixon in Jour. Am. Folk-lore, xvii, no. 64, 1904; Gatschet, Creek Migr. Leg., i, ii, 1884–88; Goddard, Life and Culture of the Hupa, 1903; Krause, Tlinkit Ind., 1885; Kroeber in Am. Anthr., iv, 2, 1902; Teit in Mem. Am. Nat. Hist., ii, no. iv, 1900; Teit and Swanton in Mem. Am. Mus. Nat. Hist., ii and v, 1905.   (J. R. S.)

Shamapa. A tribe, band, or village of the ancient Powhatan confederacy, on Pamunkey or York r., Va., numbering about 500 early in the 17th century.— Strachey (1612), Va., 62, 1849.

Shamokin (probably from Lenape *Shámókenk*, 'where horns, or antlers, are plenty.'—Gerard). The largest and most important Indian settlement in Pennsylvania after the dispersion of the Delawares and during the first half of the 18th century. The old Indian village was situated a short distance from the forks of the Susquehanna, on the N. E. branch. Later the settlement was on both sides of the river, including the island, at the site of Sunbury, Northumberland co. Before the historic period the location had evidently been a stopping place for the Iroquois on returning from their raids into the country of the Cherokee and Catawba. Here they met, as they did in later days, to hold their last celebration before their return to their villages in New York. It was the most strategic location in the province for an Indian settlement, since from this point all the region of the Potomac, the Delaware, and the Ohio could be easily reached; to gain the Ohio country but a short portage was necessary from Canoe Place to Kittanning. The forks of the Susquehanna thus became the point of convergence of the various trails leading to the Potomac, Wyoming, and the Ohio. The population was made up of Delawares, Shawnee, and Iroquois. The Shawnee came into the province from the S. in 1698, and soon began to settle along the Susquehanna and its branches. By 1727, when they first commenced to go westward to the Ohio, a large number of them was settled at Shamokin. In the following year the Onondaga council appointed Shikellamy (q. v.) to act as the deputy of the Iroquois at Shamokin, with instructions to have special oversight of the Shawnee (Archives Pa., i, 228, 1852). From this time until 1755 Shamokin was regarded as the Indian capital of the province; it was not only headquarters of the Iroquois influence, but also was the residence of Allummapees, the "king" of the Delawares. At the council in Philadelphia in the summer of 1742 the various disputes concerning land sales on the Susquehanna were brought up by the Delawares. In a stinging reply to the Delaware complaints, Canassatego, the Iroquois chief, ordered the Delawares to remove from their lands to Shamokin or Wyoming and to have nothing whatever to do with the sales of lands in the future (Col. Rec. Pa., iv, 579–80, 1851). They never forgot this reproach, and went to Shamokin and Wyoming to consider their wrongs and to listen to the Shawnee warriors who were seeking to have them remove to the Ohio. Count Zinzendorf, under the guidance of Conrad Weiser, visited Shamokin in the fall of 1742, where he met Shikellamy, with whom he held several conferences. A friendship sprang up between the Iroquois deputy and the Moravian Brethren which lasted during the life of the wise chief, who was one of the most conservative of the leaders of the Six Nations. Zinzendorf was very much interested in the Iroquois vicegerent, and wrote much about this visit to Shamokin in his journal (Mem. Moravian Church, 84 et seq., 1870). Various missionaries of the Moravian Church labored at Shamokin from this time until its abandonment in 1755, among them being Mack, Post, Pyrlæus, and Zeisberger. During these days the Indian settlement had a bad reputation. Martin Mack, who with his wife was obliged to flee to the woods nearly every night from the drunken savages, said that it "was the very seat of the Prince of Darkness." David Brainerd, who visited the village each year, said in 1745: "The town lies partly on the east and west shores of the river and partly on the island. It contains upwards of 50 houses and 300 inhabitants. The Indians of the place are accounted the most drunken, mischievous, and ruffianlike fellows of any in these parts—about one-half are Delawares and the others are Senecas and Tutelars" (Mem. Moravian Church, 67, 1870). At the council at Philadelphia in 1744 the Delawares stated that the Shawnee had removed to the Ohio, chiefly through the influence of Peter Chartier (Col. Rec. Pa., IV, 757, 1851). In the year before a number of the Conoy Indians had removed to Shamokin (ibid., 657). In 1747 the Moravians built a smithy in the village at the request of Shikellamy. The Delaware "king," Allummapees, died in 1747, and Shikellamy, the Iroquois deputy, died in the year following. In 1749 all the Indians were obliged to leave Shamokin for want of provisions (Arch. Pa., II, 23, 1852). Taghneghdoarus, Shikellamy's eldest son, at the request of Weiser, became the deputy of the Iroquois in the province (see Weiser's Journals of his three visits to Shamokin in 1743, 1744, in Col. Rec. Pa., IV, 640, 646, 680, 1851). At the treaty of Albany (1754) the Iroquois reserved the lands at Shamokin and Wyoming as their hunting grounds (ibid., VI, 119, 1851). John Shikellamy, the eldest son of the old Oneida vicegerent, was appointed to look after these lands and all Iroquois affairs in the province. Gov. Morris, in a letter to Gen. Shirley, tells of the Indian raids near Shamokin and gives a description of the location as suitable for a fort (ibid., 665). In 1755, after Braddock's defeat, the entire region was at the mercy of the hostile Delawares and Shawnee. The former, who were faithful to the English, were obliged to leave Shamokin. Scarouady, at the council in Philadelphia in the fall of 1755, spoke very plainly concerning the situation, and said that if the English "will not fight with us we will go somewhere else" (ibid., 686). In the winter of 1755 Gov. Morris spoke of his intention of building a fort at Shamokin to protect the frontier (ibid., 701). At the council at Carlisle (1756), The Belt, a Delaware chief, asked that a fort be built at Shamokin for the protection of the friendly Indians and as a place of refuge for their wives and children when they were away (ibid., VII, 6, 1851). This request was repeated at the council at Philadelphia in the spring (ibid., 54). At a council held in April (1756) Scarouady spoke of the importance of the English having a fort at this place to which the friendly Indians could go (ibid., 80). He later informed the governor that he and all the women and children were going to Onondaga, and that they would return when a fort was built at Shamokin (ibid., 90). In May, Gov. Morris was at Harris Ferry, on his way to Shamokin, where a fort was to be built. During the spring and summer of 1756 the fort was built on the E. bank of the Susquehanna, just below the junction of the North and West branches, at the upper end of the present Sunbury. The French realizing the necessity of holding this point, sent an expedition in the fall of 1756 to build a fort at the place. They reached the mouth of Loyal Sock cr., and finding the force at work building Ft Augusta, retreated. Col. Clapham, who had charge of the building of the fort, was succeeded by Col. James Burd (see Archives Pa., 2d s., II, 745–820, 1890). In June, 1756, just previous to the coming of the English force to build the fort, all the houses in the place were burned by hostile Indians (Col. Rec. Pa., VII, 154, 1851). Various Indian agents were appointed to reside at Ft Augusta during this period (ibid., VIII, 99, 128, 501, 1852). A number of important conferences were held with the Indians at Ft Augusta by Col. Francis in 1769 (ibid., IX, 610–620, 1852). After the conclusion of the French and Indian war the clamor of the "peace at any price" element in the province led to the dismantling of the fort. The conditions along the frontiers were deplorable; nearly the entire region on the West branch was entirely deserted. After the commencement of the Revolution the fort became the military headquarters for the upper Susquehanna, and during the entire period the authorities at the fort were kept busy. The massacre of Wyoming and the Big Runaway filled Ft Augusta with people who had left their homes to escape the fury of the Indians.

See Frontier Forts of Pa., I, 356 et seq., 1895; Meginness, Otzinachson, 1857; Egle, Hist. of Pa., 998, 1883.   (G. P. D.)

Fort Augusta.—Scull map, 1759, 1770. **Fort Schamookin**—Leroy (1755) in Arch. Pa., 2d s., VII, 403, 1878. **Samokin.**—Lattre map, 1784. **Schachaméki.**—Heckewelder in Trans. Am. Philos. Soc., n. s., IV, 363, 1834 (trans. 'the place of eels'; supposed by some Indians to be the proper name). **Schachhenamendi.**—Heckewelder quoted by Connelley, Heckewelder's Narr., 144, 1907. **Schahamoki.**—Ibid. ('the place where gun barrels are straightened': name given after Nutamees, a Delaware gunsmith, settled there). **Shahamóki.**—Heckewelder in Trans. Am. Philos. Soc., op. cit. (Delaware pronunciation). **Shahamókink.**—Ibid. **Shahomaking.**—Allummapees (1727) quoted in Arch. Pa., I, 214, 1852. **Shamaken.**—Blunston (1728), ibid., 214. **Shamochan.**—Burd (1757) in Arch. Pa., 2d s., II, 665, 1890. **Shamoken.**—Weiser (ca. 1740) quoted by Boudinot, Star in the West, 268, 1816. **Shamokin.**—Colden (1727), Five Nat., app., 115, 1747. **Shamoking.**—Doc. of 1759 quoted by Rupp., Northampton Co., 50, 1845. **Shaumoking.**—Brainerd (1745) quoted by Day, Penn., 525, 1843. **Shawmokin.**—Harris (1754) in Arch. Pa., II, 178, 1852. **Shomhomokin.**—Weiser (1744) in Arch. Pa., I, 661, 1852. **Shomoken.**—Bard (1755) in Border Wars, 1839. **Shomokin.**—Weiser (1745) in Arch. Pa., I, 673, 1852. **Shomoko.**—Zeisberger (1750) quoted by Conover, Kan and Geneva MS., B. A. E. **Siamocon.**—Zadowsky (1728) in Arch. Pa., I, 227, 1852. **Skamoken.**—Vaudreuil (1757) in N. Y. Doc. Col. Hist., X, 588, 1858. **Skamokin.**—Ibid., 589. **Tsinaghse.**—N. Y. Doc. Col. Hist., VII, 47, note, 1856. **Tsnasogh.**—Ft Johnson Conf. (1756), ibid. **Zinachson.**—Weiser (1747) in Col. Rec. Pa., v, 84, 1851.

Shana. The Eagle clan of the Yuchi.
Ca.—Speck, Yuchi Inds., 70, 1909 (c=sh). **Shátaha.**—Gatschet, Uchee MS., B. A. E., 71, 1885.

Shanamkarak. A Karok village on the E. bank of the large rapids in Klamath r., a mile or two below the mouth of Salmon r., N. W. Cal. It had 5 houses in 1852, was an important fishing place, and part of the annual salmon ceremony belonging to the village of Amaikiara, on the opposite side of the river, was performed there.
Asha-náhm-ka.—Gibbs, MS. Misc., B. A. E., 1852. **Eh-qua-nek.**—Gibbs (1851) in Schoolcraft, Ind. Tribes, III, 151, 1853 (Yurok name). **He-conecks.**—McKee (1851) in Sen. Ex. Doc. 4, 32d Cong., spec. sess., 211, 1853. **Ikwanek.**—Gibbs, MS., B. A. E., 1851. **Ke-ko-neck.**—McKee, op. cit., 164. **Shanamkarak.**—A. L. Kroeber, inf'n, 1907.

Shanel. A former Pomo settlement in Potter valley, Cal., on the E. bank of Russian r., about a mile N. of Centerville. The name has also been applied to a village near the American town of Hopland. Distinct from Shnalkaya. See *Salan Pomo.*
Cane'l.—Barrett, Ethno-Geog. Pomo, 141, 1908 (c=sh). **Sah-nel.**—Gibbs in Schoolcraft, Ind. Tribes, III, 112, 1853. **Sai-nals.**—McKee (1851) in Sen. Ex. Doc. 4, 32d Cong., spec. sess., 144, 1853. **Sai-nels-chas-kaw.**—Ibid., 145. **Sanels.**—Powers quoted by Bancroft, Nat. Races, I, 451, 1874. **See'l.**—Barrett, op. cit. **Se-nel'.**—Powers in Cont. N. A. Ethnol., III, 168, 1877. **Shanelpoma.**—J. W. Hudson, inf'n, 1906.

Shangke. The Dog or Wolf gens of the Quapaw.
Cañᵭe' nikaci'ᵭa.—Dorsey in 15th Rep. B. A. E., 229, 1897.

Shanhaw A former Choctaw town in Mississippi, belonging to the "Sixtowns" district.—West Fla. map, ca. 1775.

Shannopin's Town. A former Delaware village on Allegheny r., about 2 m. above the junction with the Monongahela, within the limits of the present city of Pittsburg, Pa., between Penn ave. and the river, and N. of Thirtieth st. The locality was occupied by about 20 families of Delawares in 1730, and was named for the chief, Shanopin, who lived there at that time. On account of its situation on the trail between the Susquehanna, Ohio, Beaver, and Muskingum rs., it was much frequented by Indian traders. In April 1730 Gov. Gordon of Pennsylvania received a letter from the chiefs of the Delawares at "Alleegaeening on the Main road," written by Edmund Cartledge, James Le Tort, and Joseph Davenport (three prominent traders), telling of the death of a trader named John Hartt, and requesting that something be done to put a stop to the unrestricted sale of rum and the coming of so many traders into "the woods." This letter was signed by mark by "Shawannoppan" and others (Arch. Pa., I, 255, 1852). The same traders also wrote to the Governor informing him of the abuse of the Indian trade caused by the sale of rum, the Indians buying it with their peltries and being unable to pay their debts to the traders who made the complaint. These Delawares then owed the traders about £2,000 for goods which they had purchased (ibid., 261). Thus early began the trouble among the rival traders on the Ohio, chiefly through the sale of liquor. Conrad Weiser passed through the place on his way to Logstown in 1748, the Indians treating him with kindness (Col. Rec. Pa., v, 348, 1851), and Shanopin attended the conference at that place. The expedition of Celeron de Bienville in the following year also stopped at the place, which is noted on Bonnecamp's map as "Village du Loups." Christopher Gist, the agent of the Ohio Company, likewise stopped here in 1750 on his way to the Muskingum, and recorded in his journal: "The River Ohio is 76 Poles wide at Shannopin Town: There are about twenty Families in this town" (Darlington, Gist's Jour., 34, 1893). In Lewis Evans's Analysis of Map of the Middle Colonies (1775), he says (p. 25): "At Shannopins there is a fording place in very dry times and the lowest down the river." The fording place, which Gist crossed, was at this point, where the Indian trail crossed the Allegheny, then ran along near the location of East and West Ohio sts. to Beaver ave. and on to Logstown (see Gist's map). Washington and Gist were both at the village in the winter of 1753, when on their way to the French fort at Venango. They swam their horses across the Allegheny at this point, and spent the night on that side of the river, the next day going on to Logstown (Darlington, Gist's Jour., 81, 1893; Washington's Jour. of 1753 in Olden Time, I, 12–26, 1846; Sparks, Writings of Wash., II, 432–447, 1834). According to Ensign Ward's deposition the French under Contracœur were first noticed by him as they descended the river "at Shanopins Town about two Miles distant from the Fort the 17th. of April last" (Darlington, Gist's Jour., 275, 1893). George Croghan, when on his way to Logstown in 1754, was overtaken at this point by Andrew Montour and John Patten, who were on their way to the western Indians with the two Shawnee prisoners who had been released from jail in Charleston, S. C. (Col. Rec. Pa., v, 731, 1851), Croghan noting that "from Lowril Hill to Shanopens is butt 46 Miles" (Arch. Pa., II, 132, 1852). The place is mentioned also in the table of distances as given by John Patten (Col. Rec. Pa., v, 750, 1851). In the examination of Mr West before the Provincial Council, in 1754, he said: "Col. Joshua Fry . . took an observation on the 16th of June 1752, at a Place about a Mile North of Shanoppin Town, and found the Sun's Meridian Altitude to be 72^d 54° . . . Latitude 40^d 29°'' (ibid., 751). Richard Peters, in his letter of information to the Governor concerning the distances to the Ohio, says "Who [the traders] all agree that it is 34 Miles from Laurel Hill to Shanoppin, and from Shanoppin to Weningo 34 Miles by what Mr. Patten and Mr. West have heard" (ibid., 759). According to the statement of Lewis Montour, this was the place of residence of the Half King (Tanacharison) and Scarouady in 1753 (Col. Rec. Pa., v, 702). General Forbes's army passed by the site in 1758, on its way to the ruins of Ft Duquesne. At that time many of the bodies of the Scotch Highlanders of Grant's ill-fated detachment were found along the river front, where they had been tortured to death.

The Delaware chief after whom the village was named is first noticed in the letter from James Le Tort, above noted. He was present at the council in Philadelphia in 1740, at which time he is spoken of as "Schahanapan" (Col. Rec. Pa., IV, 447, 1851). His name appears attached to several letters as "Shawannoppan" (Arch. Pa., I, 255, 1852). He wrote a letter to Gov. Gordon in 1732, thanking him for the present of a cask of rum (ibid., 341). He died between 1749 and 1751, as Gov. Hamilton, in a letter sent to the Indians at Logstown by Croghan and Montour in the latter year, says: "Shawanapon and Others are since dead" (Col. Rec. Pa., v, 519, 1851).   (G. P. D.)

Alleegaeening—Letter of 1730 in Arch. Pa., I, 255, 1852. Allegaeniny.—Doc. of 1730 cited by Darlington, Christopher Gist's Jour., 93, 1893. Schahanapan.—Doc. of 1740 in Col. Rec. Pa., IV, 447, 1851. Shanapins.—Washington (1753), Jour., 13, 1865. Shanapin's town.—Washington (1753) quoted by Rupp, W. Penn., app., 46, 1846. Shanappins T.—Pownall map, 1775. Shannapins.—Washington, Jour., 37, 1865. Shannopen T.—Evans map, 1755. Shannopini Town.—Gist (1750) in Darlington, Gist's Jour., 33, 1893. Shannopin's Town.—Ibid., 34. Shannopin's town.—Gist (1753), ibid., 80. Shannopin Town.—Gist (1750), ibid., 34. Shanopens.—Croghan (1754) in Arch. Pa., II, 132, 1852. Shanopins.—Washington (1753), Jour., op. cit., 39. Shanoppin.—Patten (1754) in Col. Rec. Pa., v, 750, 1851. Shanoppin's T.—Evans map, 1755. Shanoppin's Town.—Croghan (1754) in Thwaites, Early West. Trav., I, 74, 1904; Patten, op. cit. Shawanapon.—Pa. Hist. Soc. Coll., I, 29, 1851. Shawanasson.—Col. Rec. Pa., v, 355, 1851. Shawannoppan.—Arch. Pa., I, 255, 1852. Village du Loups.—Bonnecamp map, 1749.

Shanwappom (Yakima: *Pshwánăpŭm*, 'shoal people'). A tribe of 400 persons found by Lewis and Clark in 1805 on the headwaters of Cataract (Klikitat) and Tapteel rs., in the present Washington. Mooney classes them as a division of the Pisquows, stating that their Yakima name refers to a shoal in Yakima r. above Ellensburg.

Chamoappans.—Robertson, Oregon, 129, 1846. Chanwappan.—Lewis and Clark Exped., I, map, 1814. Ketetas.—Stevens quoted by Mooney in 14th Rep. B. A. E., 736, 1896. K''tätäs.—Mooney, ibid. (sig. 'shoal'). K''tätäs-lĕ'ma.—Ibid. (='shoal people'). Pschwan-wapp-am.—Gibbs in Pac. R. R. Rep., I, 407, 1855 (name of country around main branch of Yakima r., sometimes assumed by the Indians). Pshwa'năpûm.—Mooney, op. cit. ('shoal people': Yakima name). Shanwappoms.—Lewis and Clark Exped., Coues ed., 1255, 1893. Shanwap-pums.—Ibid., 958.

Shapashkeni (*Shapashχē'ni*, from *shápash*, 'sun,' 'moon'; *χē'ni*, 'place of'). A Modoc settlement on the s. e. side of Little Klamath lake, N. Cal. There are rocks there shaped like crescents, hence the Modoc believed that the moon and the sun once lived there.—Gatschet in Cont. N. A. Ethnol., II, pt. I, xxxii, 1890.

Shapata ('raccoon'). A gens of the Shawnee. The Shawnee name for raccoon is *ethipate*, of which *shapata* is seemingly a corruption.

Shapeinihkashina ('beaver people'). A social division of the Osage, said to be a subgens of the Washashe.

ρa'de iniͺk'ăciⁿ'a.—Dorsey in 15th Rep. B. A. E., 235, 1897. Beaver.—Keane in Stanford, Compend., 470, 1878.

Shappa. See *Red Thunder.*

Shash. A former Yaquina village on the N. side of Yaquina r., Oreg.

Cac.—Dorsey in Jour. Am. Folk-lore, III, 229, 1890 (c=sh).

Shasta (from *Sŭsti'ka*, apparently the name of a well-known Indian of the tribe living about 1840 near the site of Yreka). A group of small tribes or divisions forming the Shastan linguistic family of N. California and formerly extending into Oregon. The area occupied by the Shasta is quite irregular, and consists of one main and three subsidiary areas. The main body, comprising the Iruwaitsu, Kammatwa, Katiru, and Kikatsik, with whom there was little diversity in language, occupied Klamath r. from Klamath Hot Springs to Happy Camp, the N. half of Shasta valley, the whole of Scott valley, and the upper part of the S. part of Salmon r. During the last hundred years, at least, they inhabited also the valley of Stewart r. in Oregon from its source to the junction of Rogue r. The three subsidiary groups, consisting of the Konomihu, New River Indians, and Okwanuchu, occupied the forks of the Salmon, the head of New r., and McCloud and upper Sacramento rs. and Squaw cr. These subsidiary groups are now practically extinct. For the distribution of the component divisions see under their respective names. The culture and customs of the Shasta seem to have

AN AGED SHASTA

been much the same throughout this area, but linguistically they were divided into four groups speaking divergent dialects. Little record has been preserved of their characteristics, and with their decrease in numbers and proximity to civilization, they have lost practically all their native customs. They were a sedentary people, living in small villages, composed of rectangular, semisubterranean plank houses, similar to those in use by the Indians on the coast immediately to the w. Their food was largely vegetal, made up of acorns, seeds, and roots; but fish, particularly salmon, was an important factor in the food supply. The salmon were caught by net, weir, trap, and spear, and were dried and preserved for winter food. Their arts were few. Dugout canoes of

rather broad, clumsy type, similar to those used nearer the mouth of the Klamath, were in use. The bow was the chief weapon. Carving was practically limited to rude spoons of wood and bone, painting was little used, and basketry was not developed to any great extent, being confined chiefly to basket caps for the women and small food baskets of simple form and ornament. There was no clan organization, and the village seems to have been the unit, as elsewhere in California. Their religious beliefs and ceremonials seem to have been only in small part similar to the tribes to the E. and w. of them, but their mythology is not as rich as that of the Maidu, Wintun, or other of the northern California linguistic groups. The first contact of the Shasta with the whites was with fur traders, who early in the 19th century trapped in their territory. With the opening of the trade route from Oregon to California by way of Sacramento valley in the middle of the 19th century, the Shasta came more into contact with civilization, and the development of gold mining in the 60's hastened the process of their extinction, for they soon succumbed to the unfavorable environment of the mining camp. There are fewer than a score now living, some on the Grande Ronde res. in Oregon, the others scattered about their former territory. The names Idakariuke, Ikaruck, and Kosetah have been mentioned, largely through misunderstanding, as those of Shasta divisions and villages. Consult Dixon, (1) in Bull. Am. Mus. Nat. Hist., XVII, pt. 5, 1907; (2) in Am. Anthr., X, no. 2, 1908.   (R. B. D.)

Chester Valley Indians.—Spaulding in H. R. Rep. 830, 27th Cong., 2d sess., 59, 1842 (probably identical; Chester = Shasta). Chestes.—Allen, Ten Years in Oregon, 128, 1850. Ekpimi.—Curtin, Ilmawi vocab., B. A. E., 1889 (Ilmawi name). Mashukhara.—A. L. Kroeber, inf'n, 1903 (Karok name). Rogue river.—Dart (1851) in Schoolcraft, Ind. Tribes, III, 632, 1853 (Shasta, or). Sai'-wash.—Powers in Cont. N.A. Ethnol., III, 243, 1877. Saste.—Hale in U. S. Expl. Exped., VI, 218, 1846. Shasta.—Dart (1851) in Schoolcraft, Ind. Tribes, III, 632, 1853 (or Rogue River). Shasteecas.—Powers in Overland Mo., XII, 530, 1874. Shastika.—Powers in Cont. N. A. Ethnol., III, 243, 1877. Shasty.—Farnham, Travels, 93, 1843. Tishravarahi.—A. L. Kroeber, inf'n, 1903 (Karok name for the Shasta language). Wai-ri'-ka.—Powers in Cont. N. A. Ethnol., III, 243, 1877. Wülx.—Sapir in Am. Anthr., IX, 252, 1907 ('enemies': Takelma name).

Shastan Family (adapted from *Shasta*, q. v., the name of one of its divisions). A linguistic stock comprising two principal groups, the Sastean and the Palaihnihan of Powell, which until recently (Dixon in Am. Anthr., VII, 213, 1905, and in Internat. Cong. Amér., 1906, Quebec, 1907) were regarded as distinct families. The area occupied by the Shasta division was the Klamath valley in N. California and s. Oregon, extending, in the northern part, up the valleys of Jenny and Cottonwood crs. and over the entire valley of Stewart r. to its mouth; from here they controlled the area along Rogue r., above the mouth of the Stewart, to Little Butte cr., as well as the basin of the latter stream, which heads near the base of Mt Pit.   Another tribe, the Konomihu, determined by Dixon to be related to the Shasta group, occupied the region about the Forks of Salmon in California, extending for 7 m. up the s. fork and 5 m. up the N. fork, while above them, on the upper courses of the two forks and extending over the divide into the head of New r., resided the related New River tribe.   Still another Shasta tribe, known as Okwanuchu, formerly occupied the head of Sacramento r. down as far as Salt cr. and the upper part of the McCloud as far down as Squaw cr., together with the valley of the latter stream.

The other division of the family, hitherto known as the Palaihnihan or Pit River Indians, consisting of the Achomawi, Astakiwi, Atsugewi, Atuami, Chumawi, Hantiwi, Humawhi, and Ilmawi, occupied chiefly the area drained by Pit r. in extreme N. California.   For further information see under the tribal names.

>Saste.—Hale in U. S. Expl. Exped., VI, 218, 1846. Gallatin in Trans. Am. Ethnol. Soc., II, pt. 1, c, 77, 1848.   Berghaus (1851), Physik. Atlas, map 17, 1852.   Buschmann, Spuren d. aztek. Sprache, 572, 1859.   >Palaihnih.—Hale in U. S. Expl. Exped., VI, 218, 569, 1846 (used in family sense).   >Palaik.—Hale in U. S. Expl. Exped., VI, 199, 218, 569, 1846 (southeast of Lutuami in Oregon)   Gallatin in Trans. Am. Ethnol. Soc., II, pt. 1, 18, 77, 1848.   Latham, Nat. Hist. Man, 325 1850 (southeast of Lutuami).   Berghaus (1851), Physik. Atlas, map 17, 1852.   Latham in Proc. Philol. Soc. Lond., VI, 82, 1854 (cites Hale's vocab.).   Latham in Trans. Philol. Soc. Lond., 74, 1856 (has Shoshoni affinities).   Latham, Opuscula, 310, 341, 1860.   Latham, El. Comp. Philol., 407, 1862.   >Shasty.—Hale in U. S. Expl. Exped., VI, 218, 1846 (=Saste).   Buschmann, Spuren d. aztek. Sprache, 572, 1859 (=Saste).   >Shasties.—Hale in U.S. Expl. Exped., VI, 199, 569, 1846 (=Saste).   Berghaus (1851), Physik. Atlas, map 17, 1852.   >Palainih.—Gallatin in Trans. Am. Ethnol. Soc., II, pt. 1, c, 1848 (after Hale).   Berghaus (1851), Physik. Atlas, map 17, 1852.   >Shasti.—Latham, Nat. Hist. Man, 325, 1850 (southwest of Lutuami).   Latham in Proc. Philol. Soc. Lond., VI, 82, 1854.   Latham, ibid., 74, 1856.   Latham, Opuscula, 310, 341, 1860 (allied to both Shoshonean and Shahaptian families).   Latham, El. Comp. Philol., 407, 1862.   >Shasté.—Gibbs in Schoolcraft, Ind. Tribes, III, 422, 1853 (mentions Watsa-he'-wa, a Scott r. band).   >Sasti.—Gallatin in Schoolcraft, Ind. Tribes, III, 402, 1853 (=Shasties).   >Pulairih.—Ibid. (obvious typographical error; quotes Hale's Palaiks).   >Pit River.—Powers in Overland Monthly, 412, May 1874 (three principal tribes: Achomáwes, Hamefcuttelies, Astakaywas or Astakywich).   Gatschet in Mag. Am. Hist., 164, 1877 (gives habitat; quotes Hale for tribes).   Gatschet in Beach, Ind. Misc., 439, 1877.   >A-cho-mâ'-wi.—Powell in Cont. N. A. Ethnol., III, 601, 1877 (vocabs. of A-cho-mâ'-wi and Lutuami).   Powers, ibid., 267 (general account of tribes; A-cho-mâ'-wi, Hu-mâ'-whi, Es-ta-ke'-wach, Han-te'-wa, Chu-mâ'-wa, A-tu-a'-mih, Il-mâ'-wi).   >Shasta.—Powell in Cont. N. A. Ethnol., III, 607, 1877.   Gatschet in Mag. Am. Hist., 164, 1877.   Gatschet in Beach, Ind. Misc., 438, 1877.   >Shas-ti'-ka.—Powers in Cont. N. A. Ethnol., III. 243, 1877.   <Klamath.—Keane in Stanford, Compend., Cent. and So. Am., app., 460, 475, 1878 (includes

Palaiks and Shastas).   >Shasta.—Bancroft, Nat. Races, III, 565, 1882 (contains Palaik, Watsahewah, Shasta).   >Palaihnihan.—Powell in 7th Rep. B. A. E., 97, 1891.   >Sastean.—Ibid., 105.   =Shasta-Achomawi.—Dixon in Am. Anthr., VII, 213, 1905.

Shatane ('wildcat').   A Yuchi clan.
Cadᵍané.—Speck, Yuchi Inds., 70, 1909 (c=sh).
Shátane tahá.—Gatschet, Uchee MS., B. A. E., 70, 1885 (='wildcat clan').

Shatara.   A former Chickasaw town in N. Mississippi, forming part of a large settlement of 5 towns.—Adair, Am. Inds., 353, 1775.

Shateiaronhia.   See *Leatherlips.*

Shathiane ('fox').   A Yuchi clan.
Catiené.—Speck, Yuchi Inds., 70, 1906 (c=sh).
Shat'hiané tahá.—Gatschet, Uchee MS., B.A.E., 71, 1885 (='fox clan').

Shaubena.   See *Shabonee.*

Shaugawaumikong (*Shágawámikáng*, or *Jágawámikáng*, from *shágaw* 'narrow', *ámika* 'there is a lake-bottom', *-ng* 'at': 'where there is a long shallow place in the lake where the waves break.'—Baraga).   One of the most ancient Chippewa villages, situated on Long id., formerly known as Chaquamegon peninsula, on the coast of L. Superior, in Ashland co., Wis.   On account of the inroads of the Sioux, the village was at one time removed to the adjacent Madeleine id., about where La Pointe now is.   For a long time it was the only village of the Chippewa excepting Pawating, but was finally abandoned for superstitious reasons.   In 1665 the Jesuits established on Long id., among the Huron, Tionontati, and Ottawa then residing there, the mission of La Pointe du St Esprit.   Numbers from the surrounding Algonquian tribes soon joined the mission, which flourished until broken up by the Sioux in 1670.   At the beginning of the 19th century the village was on the mainland near the site of Bayfield, Wis.   In later times it has commonly been known as La Pointe. (J. M.)
Cágawámi'káng.—Wm. Jones, inf'n, 1905 (correct Chippewa form; c=sh).   Chagaouamigong.—Jes. Rel. for 1670, 78, 1858.   Chagoamigon.—De Bougainville (1757) in N. Y. Doc. Col. Hist., x, 608, 1858.   Chagoimegon.—Schoolcraft quoted by Warren in Minn. Hist. Soc. Coll., v, 252, 1885.   Chagouamigon.—Neill in Minn. Hist. Soc. Coll., v, 403, 1885.   Chagᵍamigon.—Doc. of 1695 in N. Y. Doc. Col. Hist., IX, 609, 1855.   Chagoüamigong.—Jes. Rel. for 1667, 9, 1858.   Chagouemig.—Henry, Trav., 195, 1809.   Chagouemigon.—Ibid., 198.   Chegoimegon.—Hall, N.W. States, 129, 1849.   Lapointe.—Schoolcraft, op. cit.   La Pointe band.—La Pointe treaty (1854) in U. S. Ind. Treat., 223, 1873.   Lapointe du St Esprit.—Shea, Cath. Miss., 358, 1855.   La Pointe Chagauamegou.—Chauvignerie (1736) as quoted by Schoolcraft, Ind. Tribes, III, 556, 1853 (misprint).   Mission of the Holy Ghost.—Jefferys, Fr. Doms., pt. 1, 19, 1761.   Monengwanekan.—Baraga, Otch. Gram., 12, 1878.   Moningwanekan.—Baraga, Eng.-Otch. Dict., 154, 1878 (Chippewa name of La Pointe).   Shagawamigong.—Kelton, Ft Mackinac, 146, 1884.   Shag-a-waum-ik-ong.—Warren (1852) in Minn. Hist. Soc. Coll., v, 52, 1885.   Shaug-ah-waum-ik-ong.—Ibid., 86.   Shaug-a-waum-ik-ong.—Ibid., 48.   Shaugha-waum-ik-ong.—Ibid., 219.   Shaugwamegin.—Schoolcraft quoted by Neill in Minn. Hist. Soc. Coll., v, 403, 1885.

Shaukimmo.   One of the aboriginal divisions of Nantucket id., Mass.   It apparently included a portion of the interior, s. of Nantucket harbor. See Mass. Hist. Soc. Coll., 2d s., III, 25, 1815.

Shavehead. A well known Potawatomi chief, so named by the whites because, like many of his ancestors, he kept the hair shaved from the greater part of his scalp. The dates of his birth and death are not known, but he lived during the early part of the 19th century in the s. E. part of Cass co., Mich. As a warrior Shavehead was the terror of the vicinity, feared by both whites and Indians. He participated in many battles and manifested a determined hatred for the whites, openly boasting of the scalps he had taken, and wearing them as trophies about his person. It was reported, although probably with great exaggeration, that he possessed a string of 99 white men's tongues. Many incidents of Shavehead's vindictiveness are related. After the mail stages had begun to run on the Chicago road, Shavehead, claiming the rights of his people as proprietors of the soil, established himself at a ferry of St Joseph r., near Mottville, and demanded tribute from every one who crossed, especially the settlers who were compelled to use this route to the nearest grist mill. Finally, exasperated beyond endurance, one of the settlers caught the Indian unaware and administered a severe beating, which had the effect of curing his depredations, but making him more sullen. He is described in his old age as being tall and erect, quite dark, and with not a hair on his head. Both a lake and a prairie bear his name.

Several stories are told of the manner of Shavehead's death, but they can not be substantiated. One is that the old chief, while boasting of his part in the massacre at Ft Dearborn, Chicago, in 1812, was recognized by a surviving soldier, who followed him out of the village, and, it is supposed, murdered him. Another account states that after significantly saying that there was no longer game enough for both the Indian and the white man, he was killed by a white hunter who had been his companion on many hunting expeditions. The last and more probable story is that he died, enfeebled by age and poverty, and was buried in a hollow log in the forest. Settlers visited his grave and severed his head from his body, and his skull was said in 1889 to be in the collection of the pioneers of Van Buren co. One of Shavehead's sons died in prison under a life sentence for murder. See Coll. Mich. Pion. and Hist. Soc., v, 1884; xiv, 1890; xxviii, 1900. (F. S. N.)

Shawakhtau. The name, in the Yaudanchi dialect of Yokuts, of a place on Tule r., Cal., above Springville, where the Yaudanchi frequently wintered.
Sa-wakh'-tu.—Powers in Cont. N. A. Ethnol., III, 370, 1877 (given as a tribal name). Shawakhtau.— A. L. Kroeber, inf'n, 1906.

Shawala ('Shawnee'). A band of the Brulé Teton Sioux, descended from a Shawnee chief adopted into the tribe.
Cawala.—Dorsey in 15th Rep. B. A. E., 218, 1897 (c=sh). Sawala.—Ibid.

Shawangunk (shăw 'side,' ong 'hill,' unk locative: 'at or on the hillside.'—Gerard). An important fortified Waranawonkong village near the site of Tuthill, Ulster co., N. Y. It was destroyed by the Dutch in 1663.
Chauwanghungh.—Doc. of 1684 cited by Ruttenber, Ind. Geog. Names, 140, 1906. Chauwangung.—Doc. of 1686, ibid. Chawangon.—Deed of 1684 quoted by Ruttenber, Tribes Hudson R., 388, 1872. Chawangung.—Patent of 1686, ibid. Shawangung.— Doc. of 1709 cited by Ruttenber, Ind. Geog. Names, 141, 1906. Shawangunk.—Dutch record (ca. 1660) cited by Ruttenber, Tribes Hudson R., 388, 1872. Showangunck.—Doc. of 1723 cited by Ruttenber, Ind. Geog. Names, 141, 1906.

Shawi ('raccoon'). A Chickasaw clan of the Ishpanee phratry.
Shä-u-ee.—Morgan, Anc. Soc., 163, 1878. Shăwi.— Gatschet, Creek Migr. Leg., I, 96, 1884.

Shawiangto. A former small village of the Tuscarora, containing about a dozen houses, situated on the w. side of the Susquehanna, not far from the present Windsor, Broome co., N. Y. It was burned by Gen. Clinton, Aug. 17, 1779. In 1778 there appear to have been four villages of the Tuscarora not far below Oquaga, in the same county. (J. N. B. H.)

Shawiti. The Parrot clans of the Keresan pueblos of Laguna, Acoma, Santa Ana, San Felipe, and Sia, N. Mex. That of Laguna claims to have come originally from Zuñi, while the Parrot clan of Acoma formed a phratry with the Hapanyi (Oak) and Tanyi (Calabash) clans. (F. W. H.)
Sha'-wi-ti.—Stevenson in 11th Rep. B. A. E., 19, 1894 (Sia form). Shăwiti-hánoch.—Hodge in Am. Anthr., IX, 351, 1896 (Laguna form; hánoch= 'people'). Shăwiti-hánoqch.—Ibid. (Acoma form). Shô'wati-hano.—Ibid. (San Felipe form). Shô'witi-háno.—Ibid. (Sia and Santa Ana form).

Shawnee (from shawŭn, 'south'; shawŭnogi, 'southerners.'—W. J.). Formerly a leading tribe of South Carolina, Tennessee, Pennsylvania, and Ohio. By reason of the indefinite character of their name, their wandering habits, their connection with other tribes, and because of their interior position away from the traveled routes of early days, the Shawnee were long a stumbling block in the way of investigators. Attempts have been made to identify them with the Massawomec of Smith, the Erie of the early Jesuits, and the Andaste of a somewhat later period, while it has also been claimed that they originally formed one tribe with the Sauk and Foxes. None of these theories, however, rests upon sound evidence, and all have been abandoned. Linguistically the Shawnee belongs to the group of Central Algonquian dialects, and is very closely related to Sauk-Fox. The name "Savanoos," applied by the early Dutch writers to the Indians living upon the E. bank of Delaware r., in New Jersey,

SHAWNEE MAN

did not refer to the Shawnee, and was evidently not a proper tribal designation, but merely the collective term, "southerners," for those tribes southward from Manhattan id., just as Wappanoos, "easterners," was the collective term for those living toward the E. Evelin, who wrote about 1646, gives the names of the different small bands in the s. part of New Jersey, while Ruttenber names those in the N., but neither mentions the Shawnee.

The tradition of the Delawares, as embodied in the *Walum Olum*, makes themselves, the Shawnee, and the Nanticoke, originally one people, the separation having taken place after the traditional expulsion of the Talligewi (Cherokee, q. v.) from the N., it being stated that the Shawnee went S. Beyond this it is useless to theorize on the origin of the Shawnee or to strive to assign them any earlier location than that in which they were first known and where their oldest traditions place them—the Cumberland basin in Tennessee, with an outlying colony on the middle Savannah in South Carolina. In this position, as their name may imply, they were the southern advance guard of the Algonquian stock. Their real history begins in 1669–70. They were then living in two bodies at a consid-

erable distance apart, and these two divisions were not fully united until nearly a century later, when the tribe settled in Ohio. The attempt to reconcile conflicting statements without a knowledge of this fact has occasioned much of the confusion in regard to the Shawnee. The apparent anomaly of a tribe living in two divisions at such a distance from each other is explained when we remember that the intervening territory was occupied by the Cherokee, who were at that time the friends of the Shawnee. The evidence afforded by the mounds shows that the two tribes lived together for a considerable period, both in South Carolina and in Tennessee, and it is a matter of history that the Cherokee claimed the country vacated by the Shawnee in both states after the removal of the latter to the N. It is quite possible that the Cherokee invited the Shawnee to settle upon their eastern frontier in order to serve as a barrier against the attacks of the Catawba and other enemies in that direction. No such necessity existed for protection on their northwestern frontier. The earliest notices of the Carolina Shawnee represent them as a warlike tribe, the enemies of the Catawba and others, who were also the enemies of the Cherokee. In Ramsey's Annals of Tennessee is the statement, made by a Cherokee chief in 1772, that 100 years previously the Shawnee, by permission of the Cherokee, re-

SHAWNEE WOMAN

moved from Savannah r. to the Cumberland, but were afterward driven out by the Cherokee, aided by the Chickasaw, in consequence of a quarrel with the former tribe. While this tradition does not agree with the chronologic order of Shawnee occupancy in the two regions, as borne out by historical evidence, it furnishes additional proof that the Shawnee occupied territory upon both rivers, and that this occupancy was by permission of the Cherokee. De l'Isle's map of 1700 places the "Ontouagannha," which here means the Shawnee, on the headwaters of the Santee and Pedee rs. in South Carolina, while the "Chiouonons" are located on the lower Tennessee r. Senex's map of 1710 locates a part of the "Chaouenons" on the headwaters of a stream in South Carolina, but seems to place the main body on the Tennessee. Moll's map of 1720 has "Savannah Old Settlement" at the mouth of the Cumberland (Royce in Abstr. Trans. Anthr. Soc. Wash., 1881), showing that the term Savannah was sometimes applied to the western as well as to the eastern band.

The Shawnee of South Carolina, who included the Piqua and Hathawekela divisions of the tribe, were known to the early settlers of that state as Savannahs, that being nearly the form of the name in use among the neighboring Muskhogean tribes. A good deal of confusion has arisen from the fact that the Yuchi and Yamasee, in the same neighborhood, were sometimes also spoken of as Savannah Indians. Bartram and Gallatin particularly are confused upon this point, although, as is hardly necessary to state, the tribes are entirely distinct. Their principal village, known as Savannah Town, was on Savannah r., nearly opposite the present Augusta, Ga. According to a writer of 1740 (Ga. Hist. Soc. Coll., II, 72, 1842) it was at New Windsor, on the N. bank of Savannah r., 7 m. below Augusta. It was an important trading point, and Ft Moore was afterward built upon the site. The Savannah r. takes its name from this tribe, as appears from the statement of Adair, who mentions the "Savannah r., so termed on account of the Shawano Indians having formerly lived there," plainly showing that the two names are synonyms for the same tribe. Gallatin says that the name of the river is of Spanish origin, by which he probably means that it refers to "savanas," or prairies, but as almost all the large rivers of the Atlantic slope bore the Indian names of the tribes upon their banks, it is not likely that this river is an exception, or that a Spanish name would have been retained in an English colony. In 1670, when South Carolina was first settled, the Savannah were one of the principal tribes southward from Ashley r. About 10 years later they drove back the Westo, identified by Swanton as the Yuchi, who had just previously nearly destroyed the infant settlements in a short but bloody

war. The Savannah seem to have remained at peace with the whites, and in 1695, according to Gov. Archdale, were "good friends and useful neighbors of the English." By a comparison of Gallatin's paragraph (Trans. Am. Antiq. Soc., II, 66, 1836) with Lawson's statements (Hist. Car., 75, 279–280, ed. 1860) from which he quotes, it will be seen that he has misinterpreted the earlier author, as well as misquoted the tribal forms. Lawson traveled through Carolina in 1701, and in 1709 published his account, which has passed through several reprints, the last being in 1860. He mentions the "Savannas" twice, and it is to be noted that in each place he calls them by the same name, which, however, is not the same as any one of the three forms used by Gallatin in referring to the same passages. Lawson first mentions them in connection with the Congaree as the "Savannas, a famous, warlike, friendly nation of Indians, living to the south end of Ashley r." In another place he speaks of "the Savanna Indians, who formerly lived on the banks of the Messiasippi, and removed thence to the head of one of the rivers of South Carolina, since which, for some dislike, most of them are removed to live in the quarters of the Iroquois or Sinnagars [Seneca], which are on the heads of the rivers that disgorge themselves into the bay of Chesapeak." This is a definite statement, plainly referring to one and the same tribe, and agrees with what is known of the Shawnee.

On De l'Isle's map, also, we find the Savannah r. called "R. des Chouanons," with the "Chaouanons" located upon both banks in its middle course. As to Gallatin's statement that the name of the Savannahs is dropped after Lawson's mention in 1701, we learn from numerous references, from old records, in Logan's Upper South Carolina, published after Gallatin's time, that all through the period of the French and Indian war, 50 years after Lawson wrote, the "Savannahs" were constantly making inroads on the Carolina frontier, even to the vicinity of Charleston. They are described as "northern savages" and friends of the Cherokee, and are undoubtedly the Shawnee. In 1749 Adair, while crossing the middle of Georgia, fell in with a strong party of "the French Shawano," who were on their way, under Cherokee guidance, to attack the English traders near Augusta. After committing some depredations they escaped to the Cherokee. In another place he speaks of a party of "Shawano Indians," who, at the instigation of the French, had attacked a frontier settlement of Carolina, but had been taken and imprisoned. Through a reference by Logan it is found that these prisoners are called Savannahs in the records of that period. In 1791 Swan mentions the "Savannas" town among the Creeks, occupied by "Shawanese refugees."

Having shown that the Savannah and the Shawnee are the same tribe, it remains to be seen why and when they removed from South Carolina to the N. The removal was probably owing to dissatisfaction with the English settlers, who seem to have favored the Catawba at the expense of the Shawnee. Adair, speaking of the latter tribe, says they had formerly lived on the Savannah r., "till by our foolish measures they were forced to withdraw northward in defence of their freedom." In another place he says, "by our own misconduct we twice lost the Shawano Indians, who have since proved very hurtful to our colonies in general." The first loss referred to is probably the withdrawal of the Shawnee to the N., and the second is evidently their alliance with the French in consequence of the encroachments of the English in Pennsylvania. Their removal from South Carolina was gradual, beginning about 1690 and continuing at intervals through a period of more than 30 years. The ancient Shawnee villages formerly on the sites of Winchester, Va., and Oldtown, near Cumberland, Md., were built and occupied probably during this migration. It was due mainly to their losses at the hands of the Catawba, the allies of the English, that they were forced to abandon their country on the Savannah; but after the reunion of the tribe in the N. they pursued their old enemies with unrelenting vengeance until the Catawba were almost exterminated. The hatred cherished by the Shawnee toward the English is shown by their boast in the Revolution that they had killed more of that nation than had any other tribe.

The first Shawnee seem to have removed from South Carolina in 1677 or 1678, when, according to Drake, about 70 families established themselves on the Susquehanna adjoining the Conestoga in Lancaster co., Pa., at the mouth of Pequea cr. Their village was called Pequea, a form of Piqua. The Assiwikales (Hathawekela) were a part of the later migration. This, together with the absence of the Shawnee names Chillicothe and Mequachake E. of the Alleghanies, would seem to show that the Carolina portion of the tribe belonged to the first named divisions. The chief of Pequea was Wapatha, or Opessah, who made a treaty with Penn at Philadelphia in 1701, and more than 50 years afterward the Shawnee, then in Ohio, still preserved a copy of this treaty. There is no proof that they had a part in Penn's first treaty in 1682. In 1694, by invitation of the Delawares and their allies, another large party came from the S.—probably from Carolina—

and settled with the Munsee on the Delaware, the main body fixing themselves at the mouth of Lehigh r., near the present Easton, Pa., while some went as far down as the Schuylkill. This party is said to have numbered about 700, and they were several months on the journey. Permission to settle on the Delaware was granted by the Colonial government on condition of their making peace with the Iroquois, who then received them as "brothers," while the Delawares acknowledged them as their "second sons," i. e. grandsons. The Shawnee to-day refer to the Delawares as their grandfathers. From this it is evident that the Shawnee were never conquered by the Iroquois, and, in fact, we find the western band a few years previously assisting the Miami against the latter. As the Iroquois, however, had conquered the lands of the Conestoga and Delawares, on which the Shawnee settled, the former still claimed the prior right of domain. Another large part of the Shawnee probably left South Carolina about 1707, as appears from a statement made by Evans in that year (Day, Penn, 391, 1843), which shows that they were then hard pressed in the S. He says: "During our abode at Pequehan [Pequea] several of the Shaonois Indians from ye southward came to settle here, and were admitted so to do by Opessah, with the governor's consent, at the same time an Indian, from a Shaonois town near Carolina came in and gave an account that four hundred and fifty of the flat-headed Indians [Catawba] had besieged them, and that in all probability the same was taken. Bezallion informed the governor that the Shaonois of Carolina—he was told—had killed several Christians; whereupon the government of that province raised the said flat-headed Indians, and joined some Christians to them, besieged and have taken, as it is thought, the said Shaonois town." Those who escaped probably fled to the N. and joined their kindred in Pennsylvania. In 1708 Gov. Johnson, of South Carolina, reported the "Savannahs" on Savannah r. as occupying 3 villages and numbering about 150 men (Johnson in Rivers, S. C., 236, 1856). In 1715 the "Savanos" still in Carolina were reported to live 150 m. N. W. of Charleston, and still to occupy 3 villages, but with only 233 inhabitants in all. The Yuchi and Yamasee were also then in the same neighborhood (Barnwell, 1715, in Rivers, Hist. S. C., 94, 1874).

A part of those who had come from the S. in 1694 had joined the Mahican and become a part of that tribe. Those who had settled on the Delaware, after remaining there some years, removed to the Wyoming valley on the Susquehanna and established themselves in a village on the w. bank near the present Wyoming, Pa. It is probable that they were joined here by that part of the tribe which had settled at Pequea, which was abandoned about 1730. When the Delawares and Munsee were forced to leave the Delaware r. in 1742 they also moved over to the Wyoming valley, then in possession of the Shawnee, and built a village on the E. bank of the river opposite that occupied by the latter tribe. In 1740 the Quakers began work among the Shawnee at Wyoming and were followed two years later by the Moravian Zinzendorf. As a result of this missionary labor the Shawnee on the Susquehanna remained neutral for some time during the French and Indian war, which began in 1754, while their brethren on the Ohio were active allies of the French. About the year 1755 or 1756, in consequence of a quarrel with the Delawares, said to have been caused by a childish dispute over a grasshopper, the Shawnee abandoned the Susquehanna and joined the rest of their tribe on the upper waters of the Ohio, where they soon became allies of the French. Some of the eastern Shawnee had already joined those on the Ohio, probably in small parties and at different times, for in the report of the Albany congress of 1754 it is found that some of that tribe had removed from Pennsylvania to the Ohio about 30 years previously, and in 1735 a Shawnee band known as Shaweygria (Hathawekela), consisting of about 40 families, described as living with the other Shawnee on Allegheny r., refused to return to the Susquehanna at the solicitation of the Delawares and Iroquois. The only clue in regard to the number of these eastern Shawnee is Drake's statement that in 1732 there were 700 Indian warriors in Pennsylvania, of whom half were Shawnee from the S. This would give them a total population of about 1,200, which is probably too high, unless those on the Ohio are included in the estimate.

Having shown the identity of the Savannah with the Shawnee, and followed their wanderings from Savannah r. to the Ohio during a period of about 80 years, it remains to trace the history of the other, and apparently more numerous, division upon the Cumberland, who preceded the Carolina band in the region of the upper Ohio r., and seem never to have crossed the Alleghanies to the eastward. These western Shawnee may possibly be the people mentioned in the Jesuit Relation of 1648, under the name of "Ouchaouanag," in connection with the Mascoutens, who lived in N. Illinois. In the Relation of 1670 we find the "Chaouanon" mentioned as having visited the Illinois the preceding year, and they are described as living some distance to the S. E. of the latter. From this period until

their removal to the N. they are frequently mentioned by the French writers, sometimes under some form of the collective Iroquois name Toagenha, but generally under their Algonquian name Chaouanon. La Harpe, about 1715, called them Tongarois, another form of Toagenha. All these writers concur in the statement that they lived upon a large southern branch of the Ohio, at no great distance E. of the Mississippi. This was the Cumberland r. of Tennessee and Kentucky, which is called the River of the Shawnee on all the old maps down to about the year 1770. When the French traders first came into the region the Shawnee had their principal village on that river near the present Nashville, Tenn. They seem also to have ranged northeastward to Kentucky r. and southward to the Tennessee. It will thus be seen that they were not isolated from the great body of the Algonquian tribes, as has frequently been represented to have been the case, but simply occupied an interior position, adjoining the kindred Illinois and Miami, with whom they kept up constant communication. As previously mentioned, the early maps plainly distinguish these Shawnee on the Cumberland from the other division of the tribe on Savannah r.

These western Shawnee are mentioned about the year 1672 as being harassed by the Iroquois, and also as allies and neighbors of the Andaste, or Conestoga, who were themselves at war with the Iroquois. As the Andaste were then incorrectly supposed to live on the upper waters of the Ohio r., the Shawnee would naturally be considered their neighbors. The two tribes were probably in alliance against the Iroquois, as we find that when the first body of Shawnee removed from South Carolina to Pennsylvania, about 1678, they settled adjoining the Conestoga, and when another part of the same tribe desired to remove to the Delaware in 1694 permission was granted on condition that they make peace with the Iroquois. Again, in 1684, the Iroquois justified their attacks on the Miami by asserting that the latter had invited the Satanas (Shawnee) into their country to make war upon the Iroquois. This is the first historic mention of the Shawnee—evidently the western division—in the country N. of the Ohio r. As the Cumberland region was out of the usual course of exploration and settlement, but few notices of the western Shawnee are found until 1714, when the French trader Charleville established himself among them near the present Nashville. They were then gradually leaving the country in small bodies in consequence of a war with the Cherokee, their former allies, who were assisted by the Chickasaw. From the statement of Iberville in 1702 (Margry, Déc., IV, 519, 1880) it seems that this was due to the latter's efforts to bring them more closely under French influence. It is impossible now to learn the cause of the war between the Shawnee and the Cherokee. It probably did not begin until after 1707, the year of the final expulsion of the Shawnee from South Carolina by the Catawba, as there is no evidence to show that the Cherokee took part in that struggle. From Shawnee tradition the quarrel with the Chickasaw would seem to be of older date. After the reunion of the Shawnee in the N. they secured the alliance of the Delawares, and the two tribes turned against the Cherokee until the latter were compelled to ask peace, when the old friendship was renewed. Soon after the coming of Charleville, in 1714, the Shawnee finally abandoned the Cumberland valley, being pursued to the last moment by the Chickasaw. In a council held at Philadelphia in 1715 with the Shawnee and Delawares, the former, "who live at a great distance," asked the friendship of the Pennsylvania government. These are evidently the same who about this time were driven from their home on Cumberland r. On Moll's map of 1720 we find this region marked as occupied by the Cherokee, while "Savannah Old Settlement" is placed at the mouth of the Cumberland, indicating that the removal of the Shawnee had then been completed. They stopped for some time at various points in Kentucky, and perhaps also at Shawneetown, Ill., but finally, about the year 1730, collected along the N. bank of the Ohio r., in Ohio and Pennsylvania, extending from the Allegheny down to the Scioto. Sawcunk, Logstown, and Lowertown were probably built about this time. The land thus occupied was claimed by the Wyandot, who granted permission to the Shawnee to settle upon it, and many years afterward threatened to dispossess them if they continued hostilities against the United States. They probably wandered for some time in Kentucky, which was practically a part of their own territory and not occupied by any other tribe. Blackhoof (Catahecassa), one of their most celebrated chiefs, was born during this sojourn in a village near the present Winchester, Ky. Down to the treaty of Greenville, in 1795, Kentucky was the favorite hunting ground of the tribe. In 1748 the Shawnee on the Ohio were estimated to number 162 warriors or about 600 souls. A few years later they were joined by their kindred from the Susquehanna, and the two bands were united for the first time in history. There is no evidence that the

western band, as a body, ever crossed to the E. side of the mountains. The nature of the country and the fear of the Catawba would seem to have forbidden such a movement, aside from the fact that their eastern brethren were already beginning to feel the pressure of advancing civilization. The most natural line of migration was the direct route to the upper Ohio, where they had the protection of the Wyandot and Miami, and were within easy reach of the French.

For a long time an intimate connection existed between the Creeks and the Shawnee, and a body of the latter, under the name of Sawanogi, was permanently incorporated with the Creeks. These may have been the ones mentioned by Pénicaut as living in the vicinity of Mobile about 1720. Bartram (Travels, 464, 1792), in 1773, mentioned this band among the Creeks and spoke of the resemblance of their language to that of the Shawnee, without knowing that they were a part of the same tribe. The war in the N. W. after the close of the Revolution drove still more of the Shawnee to take refuge with the Creeks. In 1791 they had 4 villages in the Creek country, near the site of Montgomery, Ala., the principal being Sawanogi. A great many also joined the hostile Cherokee about the same time. As these villages are not named in the list of Creek towns in 1832 it is possible that their inhabitants may have joined the rest of their tribe in the W. before that period. There is no good evidence for the assertion by some writers that the Suwanee in Florida took its name from a band of Shawnee once settled upon its banks.

The history of the Shawnee after their reunion on the Ohio is well known as a part of the history of the Northwest territory, and may be dismissed with brief notice. For a period of 40 years—from the beginning of the French and Indian war to the treaty of Greenville in 1795—they were almost constantly at war with the English or the Americans, and distinguished themselves as the most hostile tribe in that region. Most of the expeditions sent across the Ohio during the Revolutionary period were directed against the Shawnee, and most of the destruction on the Kentucky frontier was the work of the same tribe. When driven back from the Scioto they retreated to the head of the Miami r., from which the Miami had withdrawn some years before. After the Revolution, finding themselves left without the assistance of the British, large numbers joined the hostile Cherokee and Creeks in the S., while a considerable body accepted the invitation of the Spanish government in 1793 and settled, together with some Delawares, on a tract near Cape Girardeau, Mo., between the Mississippi and the Whitewater rs., in what was then Spanish territory. Wayne's victory, followed by the treaty of Greenville in 1795, put an end to the long war in the Ohio valley. The Shawnee were obliged to give up their territory on the Miami in Ohio, and retired to the headwaters of the Auglaize. The more hostile part of the tribe crossed the Mississippi and joined those living at Cape Girardeau. In 1798 a part of those in Ohio settled on White r. in Indiana, by invitation of the Delawares. A few years later a Shawnee medicine-man, Tenskwatawa (q. v.), known as The Prophet, the brother of the celebrated Tecumseh (q. v.), began to preach a new doctrine among the various tribes of that region. His followers rapidly increased and established themselves in a village at the mouth of the Tippecanoe r. in Indiana. It soon became evident that his intentions were hostile, and a force was sent against him under Gen. Harrison in 1811, resulting in the destruction of the village and the total defeat of the Indians in the decisive battle of Tippecanoe. Tecumseh was among the Creeks at the time, endeavoring to secure their aid against the United States, and returned in time to take command of the N. W. tribes in the British interest in the War of 1812. The Shawnee in Missouri, who formed about half of the tribe, are said to have had no part in this struggle. By the death of Tecumseh in this war the spirit of the Indian tribes was broken, and most of them accepted terms of peace soon after. The Shawnee in Missouri sold their lands in 1825 and removed to a reservation in Kansas. A large part of them had previously gone to Texas, where they settled on the headwaters of the Sabine r., and remained there until driven out about 1839 (see *Cherokee*). The Shawnee of Ohio sold their remaining lands at Wapakoneta and Hog Creek in 1831, and joined those in Kansas. The mixed band of Seneca and Shawnee at Lewistown, Ohio, also removed to Kansas about the same time. A large part of the tribe left Kansas about 1845 and settled on Canadian r., Indian Ter. (Oklahoma), where they are now known as Absentee Shawnee. In 1867 the Shawnee living with the Seneca removed also from Kansas to the Territory and are now known as Eastern Shawnee. In 1869, by intertribal agreement, the main body became incorporated with the Cherokee Nation in the present Oklahoma, where they are now residing. Those known as Black Bob's band refused to remove from Kansas with the others, but have since joined them.

The Shawnee have 5 divisions, which may be regarded as phratries, or perhaps as originally distinct tribes, and the members of these divisions occupied different sides of the council house in their public assemblies. Their names are Chilahcahtha (Chillicothe), Kispokotha (Kispogogi), Spitotha (Mequachake?), Bicowetha (Piqua), and Assiwikale (Hathawekela). The villages of the tribe have generally taken their names from these divisions. The Woketamosi division mentioned by Heckewelder is probably one of these, but is not the Piqua.

According to Morgan (Anc. Soc., 168, 1877) the Shawnee have 13 clans, as follows: M'-wa-wä', wolf; Ma-gwä', loon; M'-kwä', bear; We-wä'-see, buzzard; M'-se'-pa-se, panther; M'-ath-wa', owl; Pa-la-wä', turkey; Psake-the', deer; Shapä-tä', raccoon; Na-ma-thä', turtle; Mana-to', snake; Pe-sa-wä', horse; Pä-täke-e-no-the', rabbit. The Turtle clan occupies an important place in their mythologic traditions. At a conference in 1793 the Shawnee signed with the snake totem.

The early estimates of the numbers of the Shawnee are only partial, owing to the fact that the tribe was not united. The highest estimate given is that of 1817, which places them at 2,000 souls. Others are 1,750 (1732); 1,000 (1736); 1,500 (1759, 1765, 1778, 1783, 1794, 1812); 1,900 on Auglaize r. (1794); 1,600 (1812; one-half in Missouri). In 1909 the Eastern Shawnee numbered 107; the Absentee Shawnee 481; and those incorporated with the Cherokee Nation about 800, making, with a few individuals, resident Cherokee, a present total of about 1,400 for the tribe, a considerable decrease in the last twenty years.

The following were Shawnee villages: Bulltown, Canasoragy, Catawissa, Chillicothe (several), Conedogwinit, Cornstalk's Town, Girty's Town, Grenadier Squaw's Town, Hog Creek, Kagoughsage, Kickenapawling, Kishacoquillas, Lewistown (with Mingos), Lick Town (?), Logstown (mixed), Long Tail, Lowertown, Mequachake (several), Nawake (?), Old Shawnee Town, Peixtan (mixed), Pigeon Town, Piqua (Pequea; several), Sawanogi, Scoutash, Shawneetown (Ill.), Sonnioto, Standing Stone, Tippecanoe, Wapakoneta, Will's Town, Wyoming (mixed). (J. M.)

Ani'-Sawănu'gĭ.—Mooney in 19th Rep. B. A. E., 509, 1900 (Cherokee name). **Cacahouanous.**—Joutel (1687) in French, Hist. Coll. La., I, 185, 1846 (identical?). **Cawălă.**—Dorsey, inf'n, 1886 (Sioux name for the Shawnee; applied also to a Teton division descended from an adopted Shawnee chief; *c=sh*). **Cawana.**—Dorsey, Dhegiha MS. dict., 1878; Osage MS. vocab., 1883, B. A. E. (Omaha, Ponca, and Osage name; *c=sh*). **Chaganons.**—Tonti (*ca.* 1680) in French, Hist. Coll. La., I, 69, 1846 (misprint). **Chaguanos.**—Alegre, Hist. Comp. Jesus, I, 336, 1841 (Spanish form). **Chanousanons.**—Letter of 1756 in N. Y. Doc. Col. Hist., X, 469, 1858 (misprint). **Chaonanons.**—Domenech, Deserts, I, 440, 1860 (misprint). **Chaoni.**—Vater, Mith., pt. 3, sec. 3, 351, 1816. **Chaouannons.**—Montreal Conf. (1756) in N. Y. Doc. Col. Hist., X, 506, 1858. **Chaoüanon.**—Gravier (1670) in Jes. Rel., III, 91, 1858. **Chaoüa-**

nong.—Jes. Rel. 1672, 25, 1858. **Chaouanonronron.**—Charlevoix, Hist. Nouv. France, Shea trans., III, 175, note, 1868. **Cha8anons.**—Denonville (1688) in N. Y. Doc. Col. Hist., IX, 383,1855. **Chaouanos.**—La Tour map, 1782. **Chaoüanoüa.**—Gravier (1700) quoted by Shea, Early Voy., 120, 1861. **Chaouans.**—Hind, Lab. Penin., I, 5, 1863 (identical?). **Chaouennons.**—Lamberville (1684) in N. Y. Doc. Col. Hist., IX, 226, 1855. **Chaouenon.**—Hennepin, Cont. of New Discov., 34, 1698. **Chaouens.** — Ibid., 17. **Chaounons.** — Montcalm (1757) in N. Y. Doc. Col. Hist., X, 554,1858. **Chaouoinons.** — Vaudreuil (1760), ibid., X, 1094, 1858. **Chaovanons.**—Crepy, map, ca. 1755. **Chaovenon.**—Hennepin, Cont. of New Discov., 48a, 1698. **Chaowanons.**—d'Abbadie (1765) in N. Y. Doc. Col. Hist., X, 1160, 1858. **Charanons.**—Shea, Rel. M. Miss., 28,1861 (misprint). **Chasunous.**—McIntosh, Origin N. Am. Inds., 201, 1853 (misprint). **Chauanons.**—Doc. of 1668 quoted by French, Hist. Coll. La., II, 137, 1875. **Chauenese.**—Colden (1764) in N. Y. Doc. Col. Hist., VII, 624, 1856. **Chauenous.**—Chauvignerie (1736) quoted by Schoolcraft, Ind. Tribes, III, 555, 1853. **Chaunis.**—Vater, Mith., pt. 3, sec. 3, 351, 1816. **Chaunys.**—Ann. de la Prop. de la Foi, II, 380, 1841. **Chavanons.**—Alcedo, Dic. Geog., II, 630, 1787. **Chavouanons.**—Sheldon, Early Hist. Mich., 228, 1856. **Chawanoes.**—Coxe, Carolana, 12, 1741. **Chawanons.**—Doc. of 1759 in N. Y. Doc. Col. Hist., X, 974, 1858. **Chawenons.**—Vaudreuil (1758, incorrectly 1759), ibid., 925. **Cherermons.**—Lamberville (1686), trans., ibid., III, 488, 1853 (probably a misreading by the translator). **Chiouanons.**—Gallinée (1669) in Margry, Déc., I, 116, 1875. **Chonanons.**—Céloron (1749) in Rupp, West. Pa., 36, 1846 (misprint). **Chouanongs.**—Boudinot, Star in the West, 126,1816. **Chouanons.**—Iberville (1702) in Margry, Déc., IV, 519, 1880. **Chouanous.**—Vaugondy map, 1778. **Chouenons.**—Memoir of 1706 in N. Y. Doc. Col. Hist., IX, 799, 1855. **Chouesnons.**—La Salle (1681) in Margry, Déc., II, 159, 1877. **Chuanoes.**—Albany Conf. (1722) in N. Y. Doc. Col. Hist., V, 675,1855. **Chuoanous.**—Marquette (ca. 1673), Discov., 341, 1698. **Ontwaganha.**—For forms of this name, applied to the Shawnee, see *Ontwaganha*. **Oshawanoag.**—Tanner, Narr., 315, 1830 (Ottawa name). **Ouchaouanag.**—Jes. Rel. 1648, XXXIII, 151, 1898 (possibly identical). **Ouchawanag.**—Smith in Hist. Mag., 1st s., X, 1, 1866. **Sabanoes.**—MS. Doc. of 1835 in Texas State archives. **Saguanós.**—MS. Doc. of 1832 in Texas State archives (Spanish form). **Sah-wau-noo.**—Macauley, N. Y., II, 166, 1829. **Santanas.**—Drake, Tecumseh, 9–11, 1852 (misprint for Satanas). **Sarannahs.**—Archdale (1707) quoted by Carroll, Hist. Coll. S. C., II, 89, 1836 (misprint for Savannahs). **Sarannas.**—Archdale misquoted by Oldmixon (1708) in Carroll, ibid., 458. **Satanas.**—Colden (1727), Five Nations, 23, 1747 (perhaps a misprint for Sabanas). **Satans.**—Ruttenber, Tribes Hudson R., 181, 1872. **Sauouans.**—Macauley, N. Y., II, 180, 1829. **Sauounons.**—Ibid., 114. **Sau-va-no-gee.**—Hawkins (1799), Sketch, 25, 1848. **Sauwanew.**—Map of 1614 in N. Y. Doc. Col. Hist., I, 1856 (here used as a collective term for the tribes on the Delaware s. of Manhattan id.). **Sauwanous.**—Alcedo, Dic. Geog., IV, 525, 1788 (the Shawnee town with the Creeks). **Sau-wa-no-gee.**—Hawkins (1799), Sketch, 34, 1848 (applied more particularly to the Shawnee town incorporated with the Creeks). **Savanahs.**—Homann Heirs map, ca. 1730 (in Carolina). **Savanaus.**—Soc. Geog. Mex., 268, 1870. **Savannahs.**—Johnson (1708) in Rivers, S. C., 236,1856. **Savannas.**—Lawson (1709), Hist. Car., 75, 1860 (applied also to the Maskegon; on Lattré's U. S. map of 1784 applied to the Shawnee among the Creeks). **Savannechers.**—Haywood, Tenn., 222, 1823. **Savannehers.**—Ibid., 223. **Savannuca(s).**—Bartram, Trav., 461–464, 1792 (the Shawnee band and town incorporated with the Creeks). **Savanoes.**—Drake, Tecumseh, 11–12, 1852. **Savanore.**—Randolph (1689) in Rivers, S. C., 448, 1856 ("the Savanore Town" on Savannah r.). **Savanos.**—Early Dutch writers cited by Ruttenber, Tribes Hudson R., 333, 1872 (here used as a collective term for the tribes s. of Manhattan id. On page 51 Ruttenber quotes the form as Savanoos. The same form is used for the Shawnee on Savannah r. in 1715 by Barnwell (1715) in Rivers, Early Hist. S. C., 94, 1874). **Sawála.**—Riggs-Dorsey, Da-

kota-Eng. Dict., 441, 1890 (Sioux, i. e. Teton Sioux name). **Sawana.**—Lattré map, 1784 (old Shawnee village on upper Potomac). **Sawanee.**—Drake, Bk. Inds., bk. 5, 68, 1848. **Sawanees.**—Putnam, Mid. Tenn., 365, 1859. **Sáwano.**—Gatschet, Shawnee and Tonkawa MSS., B. A. E., 1884 (correct Shawnee form; plural, Sawanógi. The Tonkawa use the same name for the tribe, and also for the Delawares, because the two tribes live together). **Sawanógi.**—Gatschet, Creek Migr. Leg., I, 143, 1884 (Creek form, applied more particularly to the Shawnee town incorporated with the Creeks). **Sa-wä-no'-o-no.**—Morgan, League Iroq., 268, 1851 (Seneca name). **Sawanoos.**—De Laet (1633) in Brinton, Lenape Leg., 31, 1885 (used not as a tribal, but as a collective term for the Indians living then on Delaware r. southward from Manhattan id.). **Sawanos.**—Barton, New Views, XXXII, 1798. **Sawa'nu-háka.**—Gatschet, Tuscarora MS., 1885 (Tuscarora name). **Sa-wa-nu'-ka.**—ten Kate, Synonymie, 11, 1884 (Cherokee name). **Sa-wanwa.**—Smith, Memoir of Fontaneda, 33, 47, 1854 (given as their own name; pl. Sa-wan-wa ki). **Sä-wan-wä-kee.**—Morgan, Consang. and Affin., 288, 1871. **Sawonocas.**—Creek talk (1793) in Am. St. Papers, Ind. Aff., I, 383, 1832. **Sa-wû-no-kî.**—Grayson, Creek MS. vocab., B. A. E., 1885 (Creek name). **Sawwanew.**—Map of 1614 cited by Brinton, Lenape Leg., 30, 1885 (used locally to designate the Indians on Delaware r., southward from Manhattan id.). **Sawwannoo.**—Barton, New Views, XXXII, 1798. **Sawwanoo.**—Vater, Mith., pt. 3, sec. 3, 349, 1816. **Schaouanos.**—Duflot de Mofras, Oregon, I, 379, 1844. **Schavanna.**—Albany Conf. (1737) in N. Y. Doc. Col. Hist., VI, 103, 1855. **Schaveno.**—Ibid., 99. **Schawanese.**—Güssefeld, map, 1784. **Schawanno.**—Heckewelder (1798) in Barton, New Views, app., 3, 1798. **Scha,wan,ooes.**—Clinton (1750) in N. Y. Doc. Col. Hist., VI, 548, 1855. **Schawenoes.**—Albany Conf. (1787), ibid., 105. **Schawenons.**—Ann. de la Prop. de la Foi, III, 569, 1828. **Schawnoah.**—La Tour map, 1779. **Serannas.**—Hewatt quoted by Gallatin in Trans. Am. Antiq. Soc., II, 66, 1836 (misprint for Savannas). **Sewanne.**—Putnam, Mid. Tenn., 365, 1859. **Shamanese.**—La Tour map, 1782 (misprint: "Old Shamanese Town," about opposite Wyoming, Pa.). **Shanaws.**—Homann Heirs map, 1756. **Shannoahs.**—Washington (1753), Jour., 21, 1865. **Shanoas.**—Ibid. **Shañwans.**—Schuyler (1694) in N. Y. Doc. Col. Hist., IV, 98, 1854. **Shaonois.**—Evans (1707) in Day, Penn., 391, 1843. **Shaononons.**—Boudinot, Star in the West, 100, 1816. **Shauanos.**—Smith in Beach, Ind. Miscel., 120, 1877. **Shaunas.**—Croghan (1760) in Mass. Hist. Soc. Coll., 4th s., IX, 246, 1871. **Shauwaunoes.**—Brainerd (1746) in Day, Penn., 526, 1843. **Shavanos.**—Post (1758) in Proud, Pa. II, app., 129, 1798. **Shaw.**—Vater, Mith., pt. 3, sec. 3, 247, 1816 (mistake?). **Shawahahs.**—Livingston (1717) in N. Y. Doc. Col. Hist., V, 486, 1855 (the Shawnees seem to be designated). **Shawana.**—Lewney (ca. 1760) in Mass. Hist. Soc. Coll., 4th s., V, 437, 1861. **Shawanahaac.**—Doc. of 1788 quoted by Mayer, Logan and Cresap, 67, 1867. **Shawanahs.**—Lindesay (1751) in N. Y. Doc. Col. Hist., VI, 706, 1855. **Shawanapi.**—Squier in Beach, Ind. Miscel., 29, 1877. **Shawanaws.**—Dalton (1783) in Mass. Hist. Soc. Coll., 1st s., X, 123, 1809. **Shawane.**—Croghan (1754) in Rupp, West. Pa., app., 51, 1846 ("Lower Shawanetown"). **Shawanees.**—Records (1731) in Day, Penn., 525, 1843. **Shawaneise.**—Johnson (1757) in N. Y. Doc. Col. Hist., VII, 279, 1856. **Shawanese.**—Penn. Records (1701) in Day, Penn., 390, 1843. **Shawanesse.**—Proud, Pa., II, 296, 1798. **Shawaneu.**—Gallatin in Drake, Tecumseh, 9, 1852. **Shawanies.**—Campbell (1761) in Mass. Hist. Soc. Coll., 4th s., IX, 423, 1871. **Shawanna.**—Penn's Treaty (1701) in Proud, Pa., I, 428, 1797. **Shawannohs.**—Quoted by Brinton, from Smith's Fontaneda, in Hist. Mag., 1st s., X, 1, 1866. **Shawannos.**—Vater, Mith., pt. 3, sec. 3, 245, 1816. **Sháwano-Algonkins.**—Gatschet, Creek Migr. Leg., I, 143, 1884. **Shawanoes.**—Doc. of 1692 in Ruttenber, Tribes Hudson R., 180–181, 1872. **Shawanœese.**—Brown, West. Gaz., 289, 1817. **Shawanœse.**—Ibid., 326. **Shawánoh.**—Adair, Am. Inds., 155,1775. **Shawanois.**—Penn. Records (1707) in Day, Penn., 391, 1843. **Shawanons.**—De Smet, Letters, 38, 1843. **Sháwanos.**—Gatschet, Creek Migr. Leg., I, 143, 1884 (applied to the settlement among the Creeks). **Shawano's.**—Ft Johnson Conf. (1756) in N. Y. Doc. Col. Hist., VII, 214, 1856. **Shawanose.**—Loskiel, Hist. Miss. Unit. Breth., pt. 1, 2, 1794. **Shawanous.**—McKenney and Hall, Ind. Tribes, III, 79, 1854. **Shawanowi.**—Walam Olum (1833) in Brinton, Lenape Leg., 204, 1885. **Shawans.**—Schuyler (ca.1693) in Ruttenber, Tribes Hudson R., 180–181, 1872. **Shawenoes.**—Albany Conf. (1737) in N. Y. Doc. Col. Hist., VI, 107, 1855. **Shawnees.**—Stuart (1775) in Gibbes, Doc. Hist. Am. Rev., I, 160, 1855. **Shawneese.**—Campbell (1761) in Mass. Hist. Soc. Coll., 4th s., IX, 424, 1871. **Shawnese.**—Croghan (1750) in Rupp, West. Pa., app., 28, 1846. **Shawnesse.**—Croghan (1765) in Monthly Am. Jour. Geog., 257, 1831. **Shawneys.**—Cowley (1775) in Archives of Md., Journal of the Md. Convention, 94, 1892. **Shawno.**—Mandrillon, Spectateur Américain, map, 1785. **Shawnoah.**—Morse, N. Am., map, 1798. **Shawnoes.**—Esnauts and Rapilly map, 1777. **Shawonese.**—Thomas (1745) in Rupp, West. Pa., app., 24, 1846. **Shawoniki.**—Rafinesque, Am. Nations, I, 139, 1836 (Delaware name). **Shawonoes.**—Pike, Trav., 102, 1811. **Shaw-un-oag.**—Warren (1852) in Minn. Hist. Soc. Coll., v, 32, 1885. **Showammers.**—New York Conf. (1753) in N. Y. Doc. Col. Hist., VI, 782, 1855. **Showanhoes.**—Livingston (1711), ibid., v, 272, 1855. **Showannees.**—Clarkson (1694), ibid., IV, 90, 1854. **Showannoes.**—Clarkson (1693), ibid., 43. **Showanoes.**—Schuyler (1694), ibid., 96. **Showonese.**—Weiser (1748) in Rupp, West. Pa., app., 14, 1846. **Showonoes.**—Livingston (1700) in N. Y. Doc. Col. Hist., IV, 651, 1854. **Shwanoes.**—Castor Hill Treaty (1832) in U. S. Ind. Treaties, 377, 1873. **Sirinueses.**—Barcia, Ensayo, 313, 1723 (probably identical). **Sowanakas.**—Woodward, Remin., 94, 1859. **Sowanokas.**—Ibid., 25. **Sowanokees.**—Ibid., 29. **Sow-on-no.**—Whipple, Pac. R. R. Rep., III, pt. 3, 61, 1856 (pl. Sow-on-o-ki). **Suwanoes.**—De Laet (1633) in Vater, Mith., pt. 3, sec. 3, 349, 1816 (used here as a collective name for the tribes southward from Manhattan id.). **Toagenha.**—For forms of this name as applied to the Shawnee, see *Ontwaganha*.

Shawnee Cabins. A prominent landmark on the traders' trail between Rays Town (Bedford, Pa.) and the Ohio r. in the 18th century, situated 8 m. w. of the site of Bedford and not far from the present Schellburg. It was first settled by the Shawnee as they came northward from the Potomac early in the 18th century, and was a well-known point on the Indian trail when the traders of Pennsylvania commenced to visit the Ohio. James Le Tort was perhaps the first trader to go westward over this route, having traversed it as early as 1701; in 1712 he was granted a license as a trader by the Provincial Council (Col. Rec. Pa., II, 562, 1852). Conrad Weiser passed through in 1748 on his way to Logstown (ibid., v, 348, 1851). The locality is noted on all early maps of Pennsylvania and is mentioned in nearly all the traders' journals. (G. P. D.)

Shawana Cabbins.—John Harris (1754) in Arch. Pa., II, 135, 1852. **Shawane Cabbins.**—Scull map, 1759. **Shawanoe Cabbins.**—Hutchins map, 1764. **Shawonese Cabbins.**—Weiser (1748) in Arch. Pa., II, 13, 1852.

Shawnee haw. A North Carolina name for the possum haw, *Viburnum nudum*.

Shawnee Prophet. See *Tenskwatawa*.

Shawnee salad. The leaves of *Hydrophyllum macrophyllum*, which are eaten as "greens" in the W. in early spring.

Shawneetown. A Shawnee village on the w. bank of the Ohio r., about the present Shawneetown, Gallatin co., Ill.

Putnam (Mid. Tenn., 365, 1859) says the tribe occupied it after being driven from Cumberland r. by the Chickasaw. It was situated within the limits of the territory ceded by the Piankashaw to the U. S. by the Vincennes treaty of Dec. 30, 1805, but was already abandoned at the time of Croghan's visit in 1765.

Old Shawnesse Village.—Croghan (1765) in Thwaites, Early West. Trav., I, 136, 1904. **Shawanee town.**—Cuming, Tour, 241, 1810.

Shawneetown. A small settlement between Sayre, Pa., and Waverly, N. Y., occupied a short time by a few Shawnee families.

Town of Shawnee.—Proc. Wyo. Hist. and Geol. Soc., IX, 203, 1905.

Shawnee wood. A western name for *Catalpa speciosa*.

Shawomet ('neck of land'). A former village of the Wampanoag near the present Somerset, Bristol co., Mass.

Mishawomet. — Drake, Ind. Chron., 157, 1836. **Mshawomet.**—Holden (1643) in Mass. Hist. Soc. Coll., 3d s., I, 6, 1825. **Shawamet.**—Barber, Hist. Coll., 139, 1839. **Shewamett.**—Cole (1670) in Mass. Hist. Soc. Coll., 1st s., VI, 211, 1800. **Showamet.**—Hazard, ibid., 2d s., VI, 507, 1815.

Shawomet. A former village of the Narraganset near the present Warwick, Kent co., R. I.

Mishowomett.—Williams (1658) in R. I. Col. Rec., I, 391, 1856. **Shaomet.**—Hubbard (1680) in Mass. Hist. Soc. Coll., 2d s., VI, 507, 1815. **Shawomet.**—Warner (1644) in R. I. Col. Rec., I, 140, 1856. **Shawomut.**—Jones, Ind. Bul., 16, 1867. **Showomut.**—Arnold (1651) in R. I. Coll. Rec., I, 234, 1856.

Shaya. The Squirrel clan of the Yuchi, q. v.

Čáya.—Speck, Yuchi Inds., 70, 1909 (c=sh).

Shaytee's Village (*She'-te*, 'pelican'.—Gerard). A former village, probably Potawatomi, named from a chief, on Fox r., Ill., on a tract of land sold in 1833.

She. A prehistoric ruined pueblo of the compact, communal type, situated about 5 m. s. of Galisteo, in Santa Fé co., N. Mex. The Tano claim that it was a village of their tribe.

Pueblo de Shé.—Bandelier in Ritch, N. Mex., 201, 1885. **Shé.**—Bandelier in Arch. Inst. Papers, IV, 106, 1892.

Sheaksh ('new water'). A Niska village site on the s. bank of Nass r., Brit. Col., 5 m. above the canyon, at the mouth of a stream that came into existence after the eruption that is visible at this point. Several modern fishing houses mark the site. (G. T. E.)

Shecalamy. See *Shikellamy*.

Shecarachweschgue. See *Sequidongquee*.

Shecomeco ('great village,' from *kitchi* 'great,' 'superior,' *comoco* 'land' with definite boundaries, hence 'settlement,' 'house,' etc.—Gerard). A village belonging to the Wawyachtonoc division of the Mahican, situated about 2 m. s. of the present Pine Plains, Dutchess co., N. Y. The Moravians established a mission there in 1740, but in 1746 the Indians removed to Friedenshuetten, and afterward to Gnadenhuetten.

Chic′omi′co.—Trumbull, Ind. Names Conn., 66, 1881. Chĭ′-cō̆-mĭ′-co.—Connolley in Heckewelder, Narr., 117, 1907 (Indian pronunciation). Sháco-mico.—Ruttenber, Tribes Hudson R., 86. 1872. Shecomeco.—Inscription (1746) quoted by Rupp, Northampton Co., 82, 1845. Shecomeka.—Hecke-welder (1740–1808), Narr., 117, 1907. Shekomeko.—Loskiel, Hist. Miss. Unit. Breth., pt. 2, 9, 1794. Shicomiko.—Trumbull, op. cit., 67.

Shediac. A Micmac village or band in 1670 at the present Shediac, on the E. coast of New Brunswick.
Chedaik.— Vaudreuil (1755) in N. Y. Doc. Col. Hist., x, 359, 1858. Gediak.— Frye (1760) in Mass. Hist. Soc. Coll., 1st s., x, 115, 1809. Jediuk.—Stiles (1761), ibid., 116.

Sheethltunne (*Ce-ĕçl-t̄ûnnĕ*). A band or village of the Chastacosta on the N. bank of Rogue r., Oreg.; or perhaps the Tak-elma village on the opposite bank.—Dor-sey in Jour. Am. Folk-lore, III, 234, 1890.

Shegoashkwu. The Yurok name of a Karok village below Orleans Bar, Kla-math r., N. w. Cal.

Shehees. A band, probably of the Cala-pooya, mentioned by Ross (Advent., 236, 1849).

Sheheké, Shekeke. See *Shahaka.*

Shekallamy, Shekellamy. See *Shikel-lamy.*

Shell, Shellwork. Shell was a favorite material with the aborigines all over America for the manufacture of imple-ments, utensils, and ornaments; and shells in their natural state or merely notched or perforated for attachment were, on account of their beauty of form and color (Marginella, Olivella, Natica, etc.), extensively used for personal em-bellishment. Among the tribes N. of

SPOON OF UNIO SHELL; OHIO

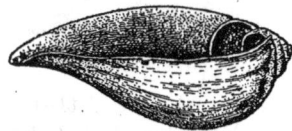

CUP MADE OF CONCH SHELL; ILLINOIS (1-6)

Mexico clam and mussel shells (Venus, Mya, Anodon, Unio, etc.) served for cups and spoons, were hafted for scraping and digging, and worked up into fish-hooks, knives, and other minor imple-ments. The large conchs (Strombus, Cassis, Fulgur, etc.) were used as drink-ing vessels after the interior portions had been removed, and in Florida they were hafted as clubs and picks. In many sec-tions the thick walls were cut up to be shaped by tedious processes of scraping, grinding, and drilling with stone tools into celts, adzes, gouges, scrapers, and plummets. Ornaments of shell were ex-ceedingly varied in form, and the clam, unio, conch, and many of the larger shells in the E., and like forms, and more especially the beautiful abalone (Hali-otis) of the Pacific coast, were cut up,

trimmed, ground, and polished and per-forated for beads, pins, pendants, and breastplates or gorgets. The column of the conch was cut up into sections and ground down into rude beads. Much skill was shown in boring these, and cylinders 3 in. or more in length were perforated longitudinally by means of drills of un-known make. Along the Atlantic coast

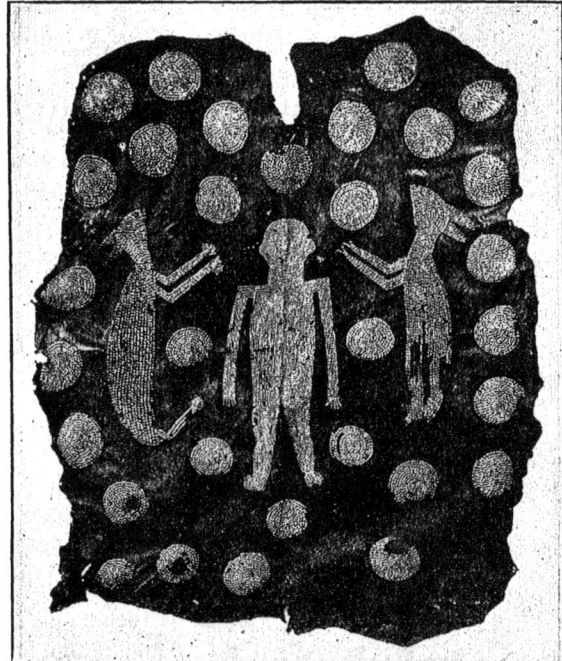

SKIN CLOAK DECORATED WITH DESIGNS WORKED OUT IN SMALL SHELLS; VIRGINIA INDIANS

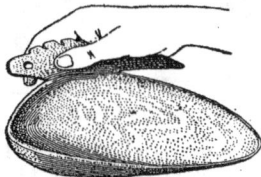

clam shells (*Venus mercenaria*) were made into small cylindrical beads, which were strung as necklaces and woven into belts, and in colonial times served as a medium of exchange (see *Wampum*). A most in-teresting example of the use of small shells for ornament is given by Tylor (Internat. Archiv f. Ethnog., I, 215, 1888) and Bush-nell (Am. Anthr., IX, 38–39, 1907). It is a deerskin mantle, on which figures of a man and two quadru-peds, accompanied by a number of round figures, are worked in margi-nella shells. The specimen has been in English hands

SHELL CELT; FLORIDA (1-4)

for upward of 250 years, and was ob-tained by early colonists from the Pow-hatan Indians. Bivalve shells from the Pacific coast, and also possibly from the Gulf of Mexico, were much used by the tribes of the Pueblo region for various ornaments, and especially for beads, which were very highly prized.

Some of the objects were neatly carved, the frog being frequently imitated in pendant ornaments. Dentalium shells were strung as beads by the coast tribes, and

PORTIONS OF SHELLS USED FOR ORNAMENTS AND IMPLEMENTS

formed an important article of trade with those of the interior. On the Pacific coast the larger varieties of clam shell (Tivela, Saxidomus) were employed in the manu-

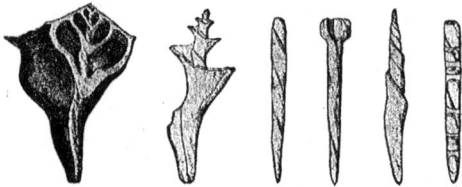

USE OF THE COLUMN OF THE CONCH SHELL

facture of beads and other objects, and the abalone was in universal demand for personal ornaments; and baskets and other objects of use and ornament were decked with pendants made of it. This shell was in very general use for settings and inlaying, and was and is employed for these purposes with excellent effect by the tribes of the N. W. coast. The opercule of a spe-

SHELL PINS; TENNESSEE MOUNDS (a, 1-2; b, 2·9)

cies of Turbinidæ (*Pachypoma inequale*) was also used in like manner by the tribes of the N. W. coast.

Probably the most effective and important ornaments of shell employed by

MANNER OF BORING SHELL BEADS

the mound-building tribes were disks, highly polished, carved, or engraved with designs, and suspended on the chest or from the ears. The designs on these are

especially noteworthy, many being evidently symbolic and depicting serpents, birds, spiders, dancing figures in elaborate costume, etc. Some of these, found in mounds in the middle Mississippi valley region, have designs closely resem-

MAKING SHELL BEADS, CALIFORNIA INDIANS

bling Mexican work, although undoubtedly of local manufacture.

Shells and objects made of shell served as an important feature of trade between the coast and inland tribes, and in many localities were used as money. The conch

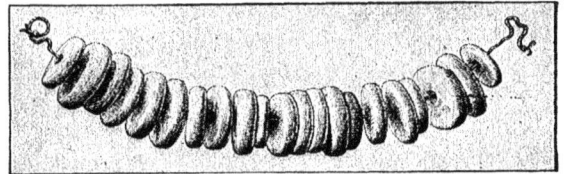

SHELL BEADS FROM GEORGIA MOUNDS (1-2)

shells of the Atlantic coast and the Gulf of Mexico are found in mounds in the upper Mississippi valley, and even in Manitoba, and shells from the Pacific were in common use as far inland as the Rocky mts. We learn from historical

WAMPUM BELT; ONONDAGA

sources that some varieties of shell, including the conch, were employed by the natives of the E., S., and S. W. for trumpets, and also on occasion in ceremony and as votive offerings. Fossil shells, many of which are quite equal in beauty of form and color to the living species, were much prized by the Indians; they served as fetishes and charms, and are

SHELL PENDANTS: *a*, NEW YORK; *b*, ARIZONA (1-2)

found on altars or shrines and in the kits of medicine-men. Some varieties of shell, especially those derived from the sea, appear to have had special significance with

SHELL PENDANTS WITH ENGRAVED DESIGNS (*a*, DIAM. 4 1-4 IN.; *b*, TENNESSEE, 1-6)

the tribes of the far interior. They were buried with the dead, or were sacrificed on altars and before shrines. Beads and other ornaments of shell, and like forms

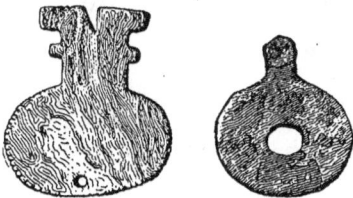

SHELL PENDANTS; CALIFORNIA

made in imitation of shell, were manufactured for trade by the whites, and are still in common use by the tribes of the farthest inland. (See *Beads, Peag, Roanoke, Runtee, Sewan, Wampum.*)

Consult Ann. Archæol. Reps. Ontario, 1888–1907; Beauchamp in Bull. N. Y. State Mus., 8, no. 41; Beverley, Virginia, 1705; Dixon in Bull. Am. Mus. Nat. Hist., XVII, pt. 3, 1905; Dunning quoted by Putnam in 5th Rep. Peabody Mus., 1872; Fewkes (1) in 22d Rep. B. A. E., 1903, (2) in Am. Anthr., IX, Nov. 1896; Fowke, Archæol. Hist. Ohio, 1902; Goddard in Univ. Cal. Pub., Am. Archæol. and Ethnol., I, no. 1, 1903; Holmes in 2d Rep. B. A. E., 1883; C. C. Jones, Antiq. So. Inds., 1873; J. Jones in Smithson. Cont. Knowl., XXII, 1876; Lawson, Hist. Carolina, 1714; Moore, various memoirs in Proc. Acad. Nat. Sci. Phila.; Moorehead, Prehist. Impls., 1900; Powers in Cont. N. A. Ethnol., III, 1877; Putnam in Proc. Bost. Soc. Nat. Hist., XXIV, ——, Rau (1) in Smithson. Rep. 1874, 1875, (2) Archæol. Coll. Nat. Mus., 1876;

Sapir in Am. Anthr., IX, no. 2, 1907; Schoolcraft, Indian Tribes, 1851–54; Schumacher in Peabody Mus. Reps.; Stearns in Nat. Mus. Rep. 1887, 1889; Thomas in 12th Rep. B. A. E., 1894; Thruston, Antiq. of Tenn., 1897; Tooker, Algonq. Ser., IV, 16, 17, 25, 1901; Roger Williams in R. I. Hist. Soc. Coll., I, 133, 1827; Woodward, Wampum, 1878; Wyman (1) in Am. Nat., II, nos. 8, 9, 1868, (2) in Mem. Peabody Acad. Sci., I, no. 4, 1875; Yarrow in G. and G. Surv. West of 100th Merid., VII, 1879.   (W. H. H.)

Shell-heaps. A term applied to deposits of refuse resulting from the consumption of shellfish as food. Kindred deposits, known ordinarily as "kitchen middens," accumulate on all inhabited sites, and are among the most widely distributed and permanent remains left by primitive peoples. For these reasons, and because they necessarily contain examples of almost every variety of the durable handiwork of the peoples concerned in their accumulation, they are of the highest value to the student of prehistoric times. The percentage of waste resulting from the consumption of shellfish, such as oysters, clams, mussels, and conchs, is very great, and the accumulations on many sites are so extensive as to excite the wonder of those who encounter them for the first time. The deposits, however, are not always mere random accumulations, for during the period of deposition, and subsequently, the materials have been utilized in the erection of mounds for residence and defense and as depositories for the dead (see *Mounds*). Many of the most notable shell-mounds are the result of long periods of gradual deposition and building, during which they served alternately for residence and burial, and, in the S., perhaps also as sites for temples and fortifications. Since the occupancy of the country by the whites, the destruction of these deposits of shell has gone forward with great rapidity. They have been burned for lime and for fertilizer; have been used in vast quantities for the building of roads, as at St Augustine, Mobile, and New Orleans, and have been leveled by the plow on innumerable sites. The most extensive deposits of shell refuse are found along the salt-water shores, and especially within tidewater bays, rivers, and inlets where the clam, and especially the oyster, abound, and in inland valleys where the fresh-water mollusks, the mussel, vivipara, etc., thrive. Along some of the shores they are almost continuous for many miles, but, as a rule, they do not extend very far back from the landing places. Deposits covering 10 or even 20 acres are not uncommon, but the depth is usually not great save over limited areas, where they rise frequently to 20 feet, and in cases to 30 feet or more. Though sometimes approximately homogeneous throughout, there are generally evidences of stratification in the greater deposits, and layers of earth and other refuse are intercalated with the shells. In some cases the lower strata are in an advanced stage of decay, indicating the lapse of a long period of time since their deposition.

The cultural contents of the normal middens furnish a very striking record of the arts and industries, habits, and customs of the tribes concerned in their accumulation. Ordinary implements of stone, bone, shell, wood, and metal are embedded with the shells, and it is not unusual to encounter at various levels traces of ancient lodge sites, each marked by a central fireplace encircled by accumulations of dark earth and ridges of shell refuse. Lodge-site depressions are also traceable on the surface of the heaps where the plow has not effaced them. It is observed that in some of the deposits remains of art are rare or apparently absent, while in others of equal size and possibly greater antiquity artifacts are plentiful. Fragmentary earthenware is abundant in many of the heaps of eastern United States and usually corresponds somewhat closely with that of the village sites of the general region; but in the salt-water accumulations the pottery is often exceptionally rude in make. This may be measurably accounted for on the theory that the shell-heap sites were in many cases not permanent abodes and that inferior vessels were constructed for local and temporary use.

The shell-heaps of New England, New Brunswick, Nova Scotia, and Prince Edward id. are numerous and cover considerable areas, but usually have no great depth. (See *Peninsular Shellmound*, *Whaleback Shellmound*.) They contain shells of several varieties, including the oyster to a limited extent, the common clam (*Mya arenaria*), the quahog (*Venus mercenaria*), the scallop, the mussel, the cockle, the whelk, and other varieties (Chase, Mercer, Morse, Rau, Wyman). The deposits include vast numbers of the simple implements, utensils (including some pottery), and ornaments of the tribes, and these are well represented in the collections of the Peabody Museum, the American Museum of Natural History, and the National Museum. The theory that the Eskimo formerly occupied the coast as far s. as Maine has led to the search for definite traces of this people in the shell-heaps, but so far no decisive evidence has been obtained. The shell-heaps of New York and New Jersey closely resemble those of New England, and have been described by Abbott, Leidy, Rau, and Tooker. Those of Mary-

land, Virginia, and the Carolinas are numerous and extensive. The oyster-shell deposits at Popes cr. on the Potomac, for example, cover 30 acres or more, and were 15 ft in depth over a considerable area before the removal of shells for fertilizing purposes began (Holmes, Reynolds). Equally important deposits occur along the shores of the Chesapeake, as at Still pond, on the eastern shore (Jordan). A mound situated on Stallings id. in the Savannah r., below Augusta, Ga., affords an excellent illustration of the use of midden deposits in the construction of burial mounds. It is described as 15 ft in height and 120 by 300 ft in horizontal extent; as consisting of mussel, clam, and snail (Paludina) shells, and as containing hundreds of skeletons deposited in successive layers (C. C. Jones). The shell-heaps of the Georgia coast are not particularly noteworthy, but the coast of Florida abounds in these deposits, those at Turtle mound, Charlotte Harbor, and Cedar Keys being of gigantic proportions. Those along the Atlantic coast of the peninsula are composed chiefly of oyster shells; but on the w. coast, besides the oyster there are several genera of the conchs, including Busycon, Strombus, Fulgur, Fasciolaria, and other shells (Brinton, Cushing, Moore, Wyman). One mound on Tampa bay is upward of 30 ft in height and covers an island of 8 acres in extent. The deposits of the northern margin of the gulf. in Louisiana and Mississippi, described by Foster, Lyell, Moore, Vanuxem, and others, include, besides the oyster, particularly the clam (*Gnathodom cuneatus*).

The inland fresh-water shell-heaps of Florida are composed of distinct genera of shells—Ampullaria, Paludina, Unio, etc. On St Johns r. a fresh-water snail (*Vivipara georgiana*) is everywhere the principal, and in many cases the almost exclusive, species. Many of the deposits are of great size, although they are accumulations of kitchen refuse pure and simple. The mound at Bluffton has 30 acres of shells and reaches a height of 25 ft above the river level (Moore). Mount Taylor and others are of nearly equal importance. All contain examples of such artifacts of stone, shell, bone, and metal as were used by the shell-heap people. Stone implements are rather rare, and pottery occurs in considerable quantities in most of the deposits, especially on and near the surface. Many of the shell-heaps, especially of Florida, present the appearance of great age, and the growth on them of live oaks of the largest size indicates that the deposits had reached their present dimensions before, perhaps long before, the discovery of America. It is also noted that the shells at the lower levels have become consolidated, and that bones embedded with them have lost their organic matter (Wyman), conditions indicative of very considerable age. Great age is also suggested by changes in the river courses, the erosion of bluffs, and the formation of swamps since the period of the midden accumulation, as well as by changes in the character of the shells themselves. Dr Pilsbry, discussing the bearing of the observed faunal changes on the question of antiquity, states that there was a marked change in the characteristics of the shells during the period of formation of certain of the shell-fields. At the lower levels in the Juniper cr. mounds,

Mr Moore states that in the shell-mounds he has observed no evidence of a succession of distinct peoples or widely variant cultures; that certain of the great mounds contain no pottery whatever; that in others pottery-making came in during the period of their accumulation, while in still others earthenware is distributed in somewhat varying forms with the different layers from base to summit. There is, he believes, satisfactory evidence of progress in culture, and, withal, evidence of great age, not, however, of a nature to lead to the belief that the occupancy of Florida extended to a previous geological period. As a result of

SHELL-HEAP, POPES CREEK, MD., AS EXCAVATED FOR FERTILIZING PURPOSES. 100 YARDS BACK FROM THE BLUFF FACE

for example, a dominant species of the shells used is the normal *Vivipara georgiana*. Near the surface a divergent form (altior) appears and prevails. At another point a variety known as limnothauma appears, the most strongly characterized individuals being at or near the surface. "We have no definite standards whereby to measure the time required for the evolution of new species or varieties and their establishment as dominant local forms; but judging by the amount of change in the mollusca since the deposition of such post-Glacial deposits as the Loess, we can not escape the conclusion that a long period is indicated."—H. A. Pilsbry, in a letter addressed to Clarence B. Moore, in response to inquiries.

the investigations of Wyman and Moore an estimate of a thousand years may safely be given as a minimum for the occupancy of Florida by the aborigines.

The shell-heaps of the rivers flowing into the Gulf on the N., and those of the eastern tributaries of the Mississippi, are numerous and extensive. They are composed of the local fresh-water shells, especially the mussels (Unio) and snails (Paludina), and contain characteristic art remains of the region, and in very many cases the osseous remains of the vertebrate animals utilized for food. On the Tennessee and Cumberland rs., especially in their middle courses, are extensive deposits that reach a depth of 10 ft or more. They have not been adequately studied and described, but have received casual attention by a number of authors (Foster, Maximilian, Stelle, Lyell, Mac-Lean, Thruston, Jos. Jones, Thomas, Mc-Whorter). Midden deposits do not occur to any great extent about the shores of the Great Lakes or along the rivers of the middle west and the Rocky mtn. region, but are numerous and important on the Pacific coast. Between s. California and

PARTIAL SECTION OF THE POPES CREEK SHELL-HEAP. SHOWING THE UNIFORM CHARACTER OF THE SHELLS

Alaska the shells are the mussel, oyster, clam, haliotis, nautilus, and other less conspicuous varieties (Bancroft, Dall, Eells, Schumacher, Yarrow, Yates, and authors in Univ. Cal. Pub. in Am. Archæol. and Ethnol.).

The shell-heaps of Alaska have been described by Dall and are remarkable as representing 3 successive periods of occupancy: the first, designated the littoral period, is characterized by the almost exclusive use of the *Echinus dröbachiensis*

and the absence of human handiwork; the second is called the fishing period, the deposits being composed largely of fish bone and containing traces of very primitive forms of stone implements; and the third is called the hunting period, in which the food supply was much varied, including prominently the game animals of the region, the culture having approached that of the Alaskan tribes of the historic period. The deposits are numerous, but do not compare in extent with those of the more southerly shores. Dr Dall, weighing the evidence carefully, reaches the conclusion that a period approximating 3,000 years is represented.

Consult Abbott, Prim. Indust., 1881; Bancroft, Native Races, v, 1882; Brinton, Floridian Peninsula, 1859; A. W. Chase, Oregon Shell Mounds (MS. in B. A. E.); H. E. Chase in Smithson. Rep. 1882, 1884; Cushing in Proc. Am. Philos. Soc., xxv, 1896; Dall in Cont. N. A. Ethnol., i, 1877; Fewkes in Am. Antiq., xviii, 1896; Foster, Prehist. Races, 1878; Holmes in Am. Anthr., ix, no. 1, 1907; C. C. Jones, Antiq. So. Inds., 1873; J. M. Jones in Foster's Prehist. Races, 1878; Jordan in The Archeologist, iii, 1895; Le Baron in Smithson. Rep. 1882, 1884; Lyell, Second Visit to the U. S., 1849; Matthew in Bull. Nat. Hist. Soc. New Brunswick, no. iii, 1884; McGuire in Trans. Anthr. Soc. Wash., 1880; McLean in Smithson. Rep. 1882, 1884; McWhorter in Smithson. Rep. 1874, 1875; Mercer in Pub. Univ. Pa., vi, 1897; Moore, (1) various memoirs in Proc. Acad. Nat. Sci. Phila., 1894–1910, (2) in Am. Nat., xxvi, no. 311, 1892; Nelson in Univ. Cal. Pub., Am. Arch. and Eth., vii, nos. 4–5, 1909–1910; Peale in Smithson. Rep. 1872, 1873; Rau in Smithson. Rep. 1864, 1865, and in Smithson. Cont., xxv, 1884; Reynolds in Trans. Anthr. Soc. Wash., 1880, and in Am. Anthr., ii, no. 3, 1889; Schumacher in Smithson. Rep. 1874, 1875; Smith in Mem. Am. Mus. Nat. Hist., iv, Anthr. ser. iii, 1903; Stelle in Smithson. Rep. 1870, 1871; Thomas in 12th Rep. B. A. E., 1894; Thruston, Antiq. Tenn., 1897; Vanuxem in Proc. Am. Asso. Geol., 2d sess. 1841, 1843; Wyman (1) in Am. Nat., ii, nos. 8 and 9, 1868, (2) in Mem. Peabody Acad. Sci., i, no. 4, 1875; Yarrow in Surv. W. 100th Merid., vii, 1879. (w. h. h.)

Shemaukan (*Shimảgản*, 'lance,' 'sword.'—Gerard). The largest of the Cree bands in 1856, at which period they occupied 350 tipis. They roamed and hunted in the Cypress and Prickly-pear mts., s. w. Assiniboia, Canada, but occasionally visited Missouri r. for trade. They took their name from a chief, otherwise known as The Lance.

She-mau-káu.—Hayden, Ethnog. and Philol. Mo. Val., 237, 1862 (misprint).

Shemps. A Squawmish village community on the left bank of Squawmisht r., Brit. Col.

Cēmps.—Hill-Tout in Rep. Brit. A. A. S., 474, 1900 (c=sh).

Shenango. The name of several Indian settlements, widely separated in situation. One was on the N. bank of the Ohio r., a short distance below the site of the present Economy, Beaver co., Pa., and at one time was an important trading-post, but after the capture of Ft Duquesne and the erection of Ft Pitt by the English in 1758, it gradually lost its importance, and early in the Revolutionary war it was wholly abandoned. It was at this place, called by them Logs Town, that Weiser and Croghan held in 1748 the first treaty with the western Indians, which apparently led to Céloron's expedition to the Ohio in the following year. This French expedition awakened Virginia to the great importance of retaining possession of the Ohio country; her activity in this direction in turn resulted in the French and Indian war six years later. In 1749 Céloron, with his expedition to the Ohio, found about 50 lodges there, while Bonnecamps estimated 80, occupied by "Iroquois, Shawnee, and Loups; also Iroquois from the Sault St Louis and Lake of the Two Mountains, with some Nippissingues, Abenakis, and Ottawas." Bonnecamps says that "we called it Chiningué, from its vicinity to a river of that name." At the time of this expedition it had been established for only 5 or 6 years, and was occupied almost wholly by Iroquois. General Wayne with his "Legion of the United States" encamped on its site from Nov. 1792 to Apr. 20, 1793, from which fact it became known as Legionville.

Probably following the Nuremberg map of 1756, Mitchell's map of 1755, and D'Anville's map of about 1775, the name was applied to the site of Warren, Pa., a place on which Céloron found a village called Kananouangon (Conewango) with 12 or 13 cabins (N. Y. Doc. Col. Hist., x, 249, 1858). Parkman makes the statement that at different times in the Ohio valley there have been 3 distinct villages called Shenango: one situated at the junction of the Conewango and the Allegheny, then the first one described above, and the third, some distance up the Big Beaver, near the Kuskuski of Hutchins' map of 1764, on which it is written Shaningo, being about 60 m. from Ft Pitt (Jes. Rel., Thwaites ed., LXIX, note 40, 1900). Shenango is also a form of Chenango (q: v.), the name of a former Iroquois town in Broome co., N. Y., situated on Chenango r., 4 m. above its junction with the Susquehanna, and which was evacuated and partly burned by the Indians in the winter of 1778–79. It contained about 20 cabins. Halsey (Old N. Y. Frontier, 276, map, 1901) locates two villages where only one has hitherto been recognized as Shenango, the one on the Chenango r. about 4 m. above, and the other just below its junction with the Susquehanna. The one he writes Otseningo, and the other Ochenang on the map and Chenang in the text. See *Logstown*. (J. N. B. H.)

Chenang.—Halsey, Old New York Frontier, 276, 1901. **Chenango.**—Jes. Rel., Thwaites ed., index, item Logstown, 1900. **Cheningo.**—McKendry in Jour. Mil. Exped. Maj. Gen. Sullivan (1779), 202, 1887 (Chenango, N. Y., site). **Cheningué.**—Mitchell, map (1755), cited in N. Y. Doc. Col. Hist., x, 249, 1858 (Warren site). **Chinango.**—Beatty in Jour. Mil. Exped. Maj. Gen. Sullivan (1779), 24, 1887 (Chenango, N. Y., site). **Chingué.**—Jes. Rel., Thwaites ed., index, item Logstown, 1900. **Kananouangon.**—Bonnecamps (1749) in Jes. Rel., ibid., LXIX, 165, 1900 (Conewango=Warren site). **Legionville.**—Ibid., index, item Logstown. **Ochenang.**—Halsey, Old New York Frontier; map, 1901. **Shaningo.**—Bouquet, Exped. (1764), 149, and map, 1868 (Beaver cr. site). **Shenango.**—Jes. Rel., Thwaites ed., index, item Logstown. **Zeninge.**—Loskiel, Hist. Miss. United Brethren, pt. III, 8, 1794 (Chenengo, N. Y., site). For other synonyms, see *Chenango* and *Logstown*.

Shennosquankin. One of the 3 bands of Similkameen Okinagan in British Columbia, numbering in all 179 in 1909.

Shennoquankin.—Can. Ind. Aff., pt. II, 166, 1901. Shenhoskuankin.—Ibid., 419, 1898. Shen-nos-quan-kin.—Ibid., 191, 1883.

Sheo. An unidentified division of the Oglala Sioux, mentioned by Lewis and Clark (Discov., 34, 1806).

Shequallisere. See *Saghwareesa*.

Sheshalek ('white whale passage'). A Kowagmiut Eskimo summer village on the N. shore of Kotzebue sd., near the mouth of Noatak r., where Kowagmiut, Selawigmiut, Malemiut, and Nunatogmiut meet Kaviagmiut, Kinugumiut, and other traders from the coast and islands to exchange furs for oil and walrus hides, and for rifles, cartridges, drilling, alcohol, and tobacco obtained from the Chukchi of Siberia, who have traded ivory and whalebone for them with whalemen. Pop. 100 in 1880.

Sesūalik.—Beechey, Narr., chart, 1831. Sheshale-gamute.—Petroff in 10th Census, Alaska, 4, 1884. Sheshoalik.—11th Census, Alaska, 137, 1893. She-shore-lik.—Hooper, Cruise of Corwin, 44, 1881.

Sheshebe ('duck'). A gens of the Chippewa.

Muk-ud-a-shib.—Warren (1852) in Minn. Hist. Soc. Coll., v, 45, 1885 ('black duck'). She-shebe'.—Morgan, Anc. Soc., 166, 1877. Sheshebug.—Tanner, Narr., 315, 1830. Shiship.—Gatschet, Ojibwa MS., B. A. E., 1882.

Sheshequin (Lenape *Shĕshĕkwan*, cognate with Nipissing and Montagnais *shishíkwan*, Prairie Cree *sísĭkwan*, Chippewa *jishĭg-wan*, Menominee *sísĭkwan*, Southern Renape *tshĕtshĭnkwan*, etc., a gourd rattle used by Indians in their ceremonies. With the locative suffix, *Shĕshĕkwanĭnk*, 'at the gourd rattle.' The name probably had reference to some practices of the pagan Indians who lived at the place so named.—Gerard). A former Iroquois town with a mixed population, dominantly Seneca, but including also Delawares or Munsee, situated in 1772 about 6 m. below Tioga Point, Bradford co., Pa. It was the home of the notorious Queen Esther, the "fiend of Wyoming," who about this time removed northward 6 m., forming a new settlement that later became known as Queen Esther's Town, and which was destroyed by Col. Hartley in 1778, whereupon the Queen fled, probably to Chemung, Chemung co., N. Y. Sheshequin was situated on the E. side of Susquehanna r., on the site of the present Ulster, Bradford co., Pa., and was divided into two parts by Cash cr., the northern part being heathen, the southern Moravian Christian Indians; it was the former who removed 6 m. higher, while the latter went to Friedensstadt. See *Queen Esther's Town*.   (J. N. B. H.)

Old Sheshequin.—Craft in Proc. and Coll. Wyo. Hist. and Geol. Soc., IX, 200, 1906. **Schechschiquanuk.**—Brinton, Lenape Leg., 79, 1885. **Sheschequon.**—Heckewelder in Trans. Am. Philos. Soc., n. s., IV, 386, 1834. **Sheshecununk.**—Craft in Proc. and Coll. Wyo. Hist. and Geol. Soc., IX, 202–4, 1906. **Sheshequin.**—Day, Penn.,139, 1843. **Tschechschequannink.**—Loskiel, Hist. Miss. Unit. Breth., pt. 3, 77, 1794. **Tschechschequanüng.**—Roth (1772) quoted by Brinton, Lenape Leg., 79, 1885. **Tschechsequannink.**—Rupp, W. Penn., app., 359, 1846.

Shetak Captives. A party consisting of two women, Mrs John Wright and Mrs William J. Duly, with two children each, two daughters of Thomas Ireland, and Lillie Everett, captured by White Lodge at Lake Shetak, Murray co., Minn., on Aug. 20, 1862, and carried away to the Missouri r., where, after great hardship, they were rescued by the "Fool Soldier Band," consisting of 11 young Teton Sioux, opposite the mouth of Grand r., in Walworth co., S. Dak., Nov. 20 of the same year.   (D. R.)

Shevenak. A Kuskwogmiut Eskimo village on the left bank of Kuskokwim r., Alaska. Pop. 58 in 1880; 62 in 1890.

Shevenagamute.—Nelson quoted by Baker, Geog. Dict. Alaska, 1901. **Shovenagamute.**—Petroff, Rep. on Alaska, 53, 1884.

Shgwaliksh (*Cgwálikc*, Tlakluit name). A former village of either the Tlakluit or the Klikitat, about 3 m. below The Dalles of Columbia r., Wash.   (E. S.)

Shiankya. The Mountain Lion clan of the former pueblo of Pecos, N. Mex.

Shi-añ-hti.—Hewett in Am. Anthr., n. s., VI, 431, 1904. **Shiañk'yá+.**—Hodge, ibid., IX, 351, 1896.

Shickalamy, Shick Calamy, Shickelimy. See *Shikellamy*.

Shickshack. A Winnebago chief, prominent in the history of the Sangamon country in Illinois, whose name is said to signify 'rising sun.' He is first heard of in 1819, having come down from the N. to the Sangamon country to avoid the constant hostility between his people and the Chippewa; here he made many

friends among the white settlers. In 1820 he was chief of a band of about 40 families with a village on the s. side of Sangamon r., 25 m. above its mouth, and about 12 m. w. of New Salem, Ill. A high, dome-shaped hill near the Indian village was called "Shickshack's Knob," and is still known by that name. In 1827, on hearing of the trouble between the Indians and the whites, which culminated in the Black Hawk war, Shickshack and his people departed for the northern part of the state. He was seen at Dixon's Ferry in 1832, where he had come, he explained, to meet some of his old friends among the soldiers, and it is said that he was among the friendly Winnebago who captured Black Hawk and placed him in the custody of United States troops. At the close of the war the Winnebago concluded a treaty with the United States and removed w. of the Mississippi, finally settling in Kansas, and it is supposed that Shickshack and his immediate followers accompanied them. In appearance Shickshack was erect, muscular and active, of medium height and weight; his expression, harsh and unpleasant, did not accord with his jovial and sympathetic disposition. He had two wives, one a Winnebago and one a Kickapoo, and four children. Mrs Mary Catherwood has made him a prominent character in her novel, "Spanish Peggy," in which she represents him as the intimate friend of Abraham Lincoln. See Snyder in Jour. Ill. State Hist. Soc., II, no. 3, 1909.

Shiegho. A Pomo tribe or village near Hopland, Mendocino co., Cal.; associated with the Shokhowa.

Seacos.—Bancroft, Nat. Races, I, 449, 1882. **Shiegho.**—A. L. Kroeber, inf'n, 1904. **Sí-a-ko.**—Powers in Cont. N. A. Ethnol., III, 172, 1877.

Shields. The shield was a regular part of the defensive equipment of the Indian warrior of the open country of the plains and the arid S. W., as well as farther s. in Mexico, but was found only occasionally among the Eastern tribes, not being adapted to use in a region of timber and thick undergrowth. Shields of bark or netted willow or cane are mentioned among the Iroquois, the Virginia tribes, and the Carolina tribes as far back as De Soto's expedition, 1539. The cuirass and other forms of body armor took the place of the shield among the eastern and northern tribes generally on the Arctic coast and in the Canadian N. W., and along the Pacific coast southward into California, and were found also among the Pueblos, and more anciently among the Navaho. (See *Armor*.)

The shield of the equestrian warrior of the plains was round, varying from 12 to 26 in. in diameter, and averaging about

17 in. The ordinary material was thick buffalo hide, with one or two covers of soft dressed buffalo, elk, or deer skin, but a few instances are known of shields of netted rods covered with soft dressed skin, the supposed protecting power in such cases being wholly due to the "medicine." The design upon the outside cover was different from that upon the inside cover, which last was exposed only at the moment of going into the fight, by loosening and throwing back the outside cover. The protecting "medicine" and the head and bridle pendant were usually kept between the two covers. The shield was carried upon the left arm by means of a belt passing over the shoulder, in such a way as to permit the free use of the left hand to grasp the bow, or could be slung around to the back in a retreat. It was sufficient to stop an arrow or turn the stroke of a lance, but afforded but slight protection against a bullet. The Pima, Navaho, and Pueblo shield, intended for use on foot rather than on horse, was usually of large size, cut from a single piece of thick hide, without cover, and was sometimes fitted with a wooden hand-grasp on the inner side. In ancient times Pueblo shields were made also of basketry. The Pima shield was frequently painted with a design resembling the swastika cross, a favorite symbol in the tribe. The shields of the Zuñi

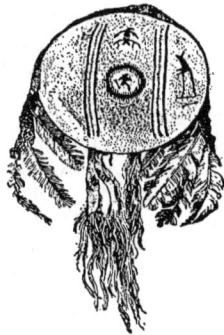

ARAPAHO SHIELD OF RAW-HIDE; DIAM. 18 IN.

Priests of the Bow seem to have been intended for ceremonial purposes rather than for war.

The shield of the Plains warrior constituted his most sacred possession from the time when it was made for him, or given to him soon after his first encounter with the enemy, until it was laid under his head in the grave, unless before that time bestowed on some worthy younger warrior or left as a precious sacrifice at the grave of wife or child. Every shield originated from a dream, in which the dreamer was told by the spirit how many shields he might make, how they must be painted and decorated, how the owner must paint and otherwise decorate himself and his pony, and what taboos and other sacred obligations he must observe through life in order to obtain the protection of the shield spirit, which might be a bird, a quadruped, a being of the tribal pantheon, or one of the personified powers of nature. The owner rarely made his own shield,

but received it from the dreamer, usually an old warrior or recognized medicine-man, who made it on request as he had been instructed, for a definite compensation in horses, blankets, or other property. The hide used for the purpose was taken from the neck of the buffalo bull, and was made exceptionally thick and tough by shrinking it, while wet, over a fire built in a hole in the ground. The cutting, painting, and decorating with feathers and other pendants were all matters of much ceremony, in which the maker was assisted by the candidate and by other shield owners, usually those carrying shields of the same pattern. During the progress of the work the young man was instructed in all the obligations connected with the shield, and at its completion the shield was formally consecrated in a sweat-house built for the purpose, and the whole ceremony concluded with a feast. The obligations included certain taboos, prayers, songs, and war cries, with a specific method of caring for the shield when in camp and of uncovering it before going into the fight. When not in use it was hung upon a tripod, usually facing the sun, or tied upon an upright pole. (J. M.)

Shifunin ('black-eye people,' probably referring to corn with black grains). One of the two divisions or fraternities of the people of the pueblo of Isleta, N. Mex. See *Churán*.
Shi-fu-nï'n.—Hodge, field notes, B. A. E., 1895.

Shigom. A Pomo village just N. of what is known as Morrison's Landing, on the E. shore of Clear lake, Lake co., Cal. The present village stands about ½ m. N. of the old village of the same name, to which Gibbs attributed a population of 91 in 1851. It is now occupied by not more than a dozen people. (S. A. B.)
Che-com.—McKee (1851) in Sen. Ex. Doc. 4, 32d Cong., spec. sess., 136, 1853. Cigom.—Barrett in Univ. Cal. Pub. in Am. Archæol. and Ethnol., VI, no. 1, map, 1908 (c = sh). She-kom.—Gibbs (1851) in Schoolcraft, Ind. Tribes, III, 109, 1853. Shigom.—S. A. Barrett, inf'n, 1907.

Shikag. See *Skunk*.

Shikallamy. See *Shikellamy*.

Shike. The extinct Star clan of Sia pueblo, N. Mex.
Shi-kĕ.—Stevenson in 11th Rep. B. A. E., 19, 1894. Shĭkĕ-hano.—Hodge in Am. Anthr., IX, 352, 1896 (háno = 'people').

Shikeldaptikh (*Ciq!E.ldaptix*, 'there is a gap or gulch'). A former village of the Tlakluit, ½ m. below The Dalles of Columbia r., Wash. (E. S.)

Shikellamy (a highly Anglicized form of the Delaware translation of the Oneida chieftain title *Oñgwateronʻhiatʻʻhe* (Ungquaterughiathe), signifying 'It has caused the sky to be light or bright for us.' The cognate form of the Delaware term is *Kijikánamáwew* (n = Delaware l), meaning 'He causes it to be light or daylight for him,' or 'He lights, enlightens him.' The forms of the name ending in *us* (see below) are due to a Latinism by the Moravian writers rather than to the original native form of the name. Those ending in *o*, *a*, or *y* are forms employed by English writers, and probably are approximately nearer the original native term than those ending in *us*. Another Iroquoian name applied to this chieftain is Swataney, a highly Anglicized form of *Oñkhi'swathe''tani'*, signifying 'He causes it to be light for us,' and, figuratively, 'He enlightens it for us,' or as an appellative, 'Our Enlightener'). An Oneida chieftain. According to Bartram he was "an adopted Frenchman," born in Montreal, who had been captured and adopted by the Oneida, although he claimed to be a Cayuga. He was the exponent of the colonial policy of the great federal Iroquois council at Onondaga, and was sent by it to the forks of the Susquehanna in 1728 to conserve the interests of the Six Nations in the valley of the Susquehanna and to keep watch over the tributary Shawnee and Delaware Indians. He was a man of great dignity, sobriety, and prudence, and at all times showed marked kindness to the whites, especially to the missionaries. In the execution of his trust Shikellamy conducted many important embassies between the government of Pennsylvania and the Iroquois council at Onondaga, and he also attended many if not most of the councils held at Philadelphia, Conestoga, and elsewhere in the performance of his duties. The importance of his office is evident from the fact that the valley of the Susquehanna, after the Conestoga were subjugated in 1676 by the Iroquois, was assigned by the Five Nations of Iroquois as a hunting ground to the Shawnee, Delawares, Conoy, Nanticoke, Munsee, Tutelo, Saponi, and Conestoga tribes. When the Mohawk sold the Wyoming region in Pennsylvania to the Susquehanna Land Co., although this tribe had never aided in the conquests made in this valley, the council at Onondaga began to realize that this section, with its valuable lands and many dependent tribes, was worthy of careful attention; hence these tribes were made to understand that in the future they must transact all business with the proprietary government solely through their deputy. With his residence fixed at Shamokin (now Sunbury), Pa., Shikellamy was promoted in 1745 to the full vicegerency over the tributary tribes in the Susquehanna valley, and intricate and important interests committed to him received the care of an astute statesman and diplomat. The effects of the liquor traffic on the Indians led to prohibitory decrees on the part of the government of Penn-

sylvania, and later, evidently through the influence of traders, when these prohibitory measures became lax, Shikellamy in 1731 delivered an ultimatum to the Pennsylvania government to the effect that unless the liquor trade should be better regulated with regard to its sale among his people, friendly relations between the proprietary government and the Six Nations would cease. As the difficulties arising from the sale of liquor had forced a large number of Shawnee to migrate from the Susquehanna to the Ohio r. in 1730, and as French emissaries were taking advantage of this condition to alienate the Shawnee from the English interest, the Governor decided in 1731 to send Shikellamy, "a trusty, good man, and a great lover of the English," to Onondaga to invite the Six Nations to Philadelphia, with a view of securing the friendship and alliance of the Six Nations in order to keep the Shawnee in the English interest; but owing to the mistrust the Six Nations had of the motives of the English, they did not send a deputation until August, 1732, and even then there were delegates from only three of the tribes, who professed to speak for the others, consequently the conference was unsatisfactory. In 1736 Shikellamy's influence was enlisted to bring about a conference in which would be represented the entire confederation of the Six Nations, and in less than two months' time Conrad Weiser was enabled to inform the Governor of Pennsylvania that more than a hundred chiefs of the Iroquois with their retinues were on their way to Philadelphia. By this treaty of 1736 the Six Nations, in consideration of a large consignment of merchandise, deeded all their Susquehanna lands s. and e. of the Blue mtns. Some weeks later, when nearly all the leading Indians had departed, another deed was prepared and signed by the remaining Indians, which purported to include the lands ostensibly claimed by the Six Nations within the drainage of Delaware r. s. of the Blue mtns.—a treaty that, says Walton, "established a precedent for an Iroquois claim to lands owned by the Delaware Indians," a claim that had never hitherto been advanced. "No doubt," says Walton, "Shikelimy was the Indian agent who accomplished this, and that he used Conrad Weiser to bring it to pass. Weiser helped Shikelimy sow the seed which drenched Pennsylvania in blood from 1755 to 1764. In permitting this second deed Pennsylvania started that series of events with the Delawares which cost her one of the most remarkable Indian invasions in colonial history. And at the same time by securing this and thus conciliating the Iroquois, and holding the key to their future attitude, Weiser and the proprietary government made a future nation possible. Pennsylvania suffered that a nation might live. She brought upon herself after many years a Delaware war, but escaped a Six-Nation war, a French alliance with the Iroquois, and the threatening possibility of the destruction of all the English colonies on the coast.'' Shikellamy did not sign the treaty of 1744, because, it appears, he was determined not to recognize the claims of Maryland to lands N. of the disputed boundary.

Weiser had many good reasons for regarding Shikellamy as the key to the secret policies of the council of the Iroquois at Onondaga, hence in 1745, when Shikellamy was requested by Governor Thomas to visit Onondaga for the purpose of inducing the Six Nations to agree to a peace with the Catawba, Weiser took an offering with which to ''wipe away'' the faithful old chieftain's tears for the death of his son, ''Unhappy Jake,'' among the Catawba; for until this was done the chieftain could not devote attention to public affairs. Having thus comforted the aged chieftain, he set out in company with Andrew Montour, Shikellamy and son, in May, 1745, for Onondaga, where he was kindly received, but was able to learn only that the Six Nations favored peace with the Catawba.

On the acquisition of firearms by the Indians, the smiths of the white people became a necessity to the Indian hunter and warrior. On account of the remoteness of these conveniences from the Indian country, Shikellamy persuaded the colonial government to establish a forge at Shamokin. This was granted on condition that the Indians would permit the Moravians to begin a mission at that place, which the missionaries regarded as the greatest stronghold of paganism. To this proposal Shikellamy readily consented, and in April, 1747, a smithy and a mission house were erected there. A year later, Zeisberger, who had become proficient in the Mohawk tongue, became an assistant missionary at Shamokin, and while there began the preparation of an Onondaga dictionary under the interested instruction of Shikellamy. During this year (1748) Shikellamy received from Count Zinzendorf a silver knife, fork, and spoon, and an ivory drinking cup richly mounted in silver, accompanied with a message entreating him to hold fast to the gospel which he had heard from the count's own lips. This resulted in the conversion of Shikellamy at Bethlehem shortly afterward; he was not baptized by the Moravians, however, because he had been baptized many years before by a Jesuit priest in Canada. On his way to Shamokin he fell ill of fever and ague

at Tulpehocking and had barely strength to reach his home. Zeisberger, who had returned to his post, ministered to the stricken chieftain until his death, Dec. 6, 1748. The colonial government sent a message of condolence, with the usual presents to the family, and requested the eldest son of Shikellamy, John or Thachnechtoris (Taghneghdoarus) to serve as the Iroquois deputy governor until the council at Onondaga could make a permanent appointment. Another son of Shikellamy was James Logan (q. v.).

Consult De Schweinitz, Life and Times of David Zeisberger, 1870; Walton, Conrad Weiser and the Indian Policy of Colonial Pennsylvania, 1900; Bartram, Observations, 1751; Pennsylvania Archives, I–IV, 1852–56; Minutes of the Provincial Council of Pennsylvania, I–V, 1852–56; Crantz, History of the United Brethren, 1780; Jefferson, Notes on Virginia, 1802; Mayer, Tah-gah-jute or Logan and Cresap, 1867.   (J. N. B. H.)

Shakallamy.—Pa. Arch., I, 228, 1852–56. Shecalamy.—Ibid., 494. Shekallamy.—Min. Prov. Coun. Pa., III, 409, 1852–56. Shekellamy.—Ibid., 506. Shickalamy.—Ibid., V, 80. Shick Calamy.—Pa. Arch., I, 650, 1852–56. Shickelimy.—Ibid., 673. Shikallamy.—Min. Prov. Coun. Pa., III, 404, 1852–56. Shikelimo.—Ibid., IV, 584. Shikellemus.—Crantz, Hist. United Brethren, 269, 1780. Shikellima.—Min. Prov. Coun. Pa., III, 334, 1852–56. Shikellimus.—Jefferson, Notes, 356, 1802. Shikellimy.—Min. Prov. Coun. Pa., IV, 641, 1852–56. Shykelimy.—Pa. Arch., I, 499, 1852–56. Sicalamous.—Ibid., 648. Swatana.—De Schweinitz, Life of Zeisberger, 109, 1870. Swataney.—Min. Prov. Coun. Pa., III, 435, 1852–56. Takashwangaroras.—Ibid., IV, 80 (='the saw-mill'). Ungquaterughiathe.—Ibid., 584.

Shikshichela ('bad ones of different kinds'). A band common to the Sans Arcs, Miniconjou, and Hunkpapa Sioux. Cikcitcela.—Dorsey in 15th Rep. B. A. E., 219, 220, 221, 1897. Sikśićela.—Ibid.

Shikshichena ('bad ones of different kinds'). A band of the Upper Yanktonai Sioux. Cikcitcena.—Dorsey in 15th Rep. B. A. E., 218, 1897. Sikśićena.—Ibid.

Shilekuatl (*Cilɛk'uā'tl*). A Cowichan town at Yale, Brit. Col., belonging to the Tsakuam tribe (q. v.). Probably the Indian name for Yale. Pop. 77 in 1909. Cilɛk'uā'tl.—Boas in Rep. Brit. A. A. S., 454, 1894. Lichaltchingko.—Brit. Col. Map, Ind. Aff., Victoria, 1872. Yale.—Can. Ind. Aff., 74, 1878.

Shilkhotshi. A former Yaquina village on the s. side of Yaquina r., Oreg. Cil-qo'-ʒoi.—Dorsey in Jour. Am. Folk-lore, III, 229, 1890.

Shimmoah ('a spring'). A former village on Nantucket id., off the s. coast of Massachusetts. Shimmoah.—Writer of 1807 in Mass. Hist. Soc. Coll., 2d s., III, 25, 1815. Shimmuo.—S. D., ibid., X, 174, 1823.

Shimpshon. A body of Salish of Kamloops agency, Brit. Col.; pop. 186 in 1884, the last time the name appears. Shimps-hon.—Can. Ind. Aff. 1884, 188, 1885.

Shinagrua. A Nunatogmiut Eskimo village on the Arctic coast, close to Anxiety pt., Alaska.

Shinagrua.—Coast Surv. map 20, 1869. **Shiningrua.**—Dall in Cont. N. A. Ethnol., I, map, 1877.

Shinalutaoin ('scarlet cloth earrings'). A band of the Sans Arcs Sioux. **Cina-luta-oi^n.**—Dorsey in 15th Rep. B. A. E., 219, 1897. **Śina-luta-oiŋ.**—Ibid.

Shinana. A ruined pueblo, probably of the Tigua, on the Rio Grande, in the vicinity of Albuquerque, N. Mex.—Loew (1875) in Wheeler Surv. Rep., VII, 338, 1879.

Shinats. A former summer village of the Laguna tribe, situated 3½ m. s. of the present Laguna pueblo, N. Mex. It is said to have been abandoned on account of Apache depredations. (F. W. H.)

Shingabawassin (*Shingábewasin*, 'reclining human figure of stone.'—W. J.). A Chippewa chief of the Crane gens, born about 1763, and prominent during the first quarter of the 19th century. He was the eldest son of Maidosagee, the son of Gitcheojeedebun. His residence, during most of his years at least, was on the banks of St Mary's r., Mich., at the outlet of L. Superior. His life, so far as known, was characterized by but few marked incidents, though largely spent in behalf of the welfare of his people. During his younger days he took an active part in the war expeditions of his band, especially those against the Sioux, but after assuming the responsibilities of his official life he became a strong advocate of peace. At the councils convened for the purpose of entering into treaties, especially those at Prairie du Chien in 1825, Fond du Lac in 1826, and Butte des Mortes in 1827, he was the leading speaker and usually the most important person among the Indian delegates. He seems to have risen, to a large extent, above the primitive beliefs of his people, and even went so far in one of the councils as to advise making known to the whites the situation of the great copper deposits, although these were regarded by the Indians as sacred. A favorite scheme which he advanced and vigorously advocated, but without effect, was to have the United States set apart a special reservation for the half-breeds. In addition to the treaties mentioned Shingabawassin signed the treaty of Sault Ste Marie, June 11, 1820. He died between 1828 and 1837, and was succeeded as chief of the Crane gens by his son Kabay Noden. Consult Schoolcraft, Pers. Mem., 1851; McKenney and Hall, Ind. Tribes, I, 1854; Warren, Hist. Ojebways, 1885. (C. T.)

Shiniak. A Kuskwogmiut Eskimo village on the E. shore at the head of deepwater navigation in Kuskokwim bay, Alaska, where the Moravian missionaries have a warehouse. Pop. 40 in 1880; 7 in 1890.
Shineyagamute.—Petroff in 10th Census, Alaska, 17, 1884. **Shiniagmiut.**—Sarichef's atlas (1826) quoted by Baker, Geog. Dict. Alaska, 1901. **Shinyagamiut.**—11th Census, Alaska, 101, 1893.

Shinnapago. A Kaviagmiut Eskimo village at Port Clarence, Alaska.—11th Census, Alaska, 162, 1893.

Shinnecock. An Algonquian tribe or band on Long id., N. Y., formerly occupying the s. coast from Shinnecock bay to Montauk pt. Many of them joined the Brotherton Indians in New York. About 150 still remain on a reservation of 750 acres, 3 m. w. of Southampton, having intermarried with negroes until their aboriginal character is almost obliterated. Nowedonah, brother of the noted Wyandanch, was once their chief, and on his death his sister, wife of Cockenoe, became his successor. In Dec. 1876, 28 Shin-

SHINNECOCK MAN (HARRINGTON, PHOTO. COURTESY OF "SOUTHERN WORKMAN")

necock men lost their lives in an attempt to save a ship stranded off Easthampton, since which time a number, especially the younger people, have left the reservation and become scattered. They have a Presbyterian and an Adventist church; the men gain a livelihood by employment as farm-hands, baymen, berrypickers, etc., and the women as laundresses. A few families make and sell baskets and a sort of brush made of oak splints; there is almost no agriculture. They have lost all their old customs, and but few words of their native language survive even in the memory of the oldest people, although it was in more or less general use 60 or 70 years ago. Consult Harrington in Jour.

Am. Folk-lore, XVI, 37–39, 1903, and in So. Workman, XXXII, no. 6, 1903.

SHINNECOCK WOMAN (HARRINGTON, PHOTO. COURTESY OF "SOUTHERN WORKMAN")

Mochgonnekouck.—W. W. Tooker, inf'n, 1907 (Dutch name). **Shinacock.**—Gardener (1660) in Mass. Hist. Soc. Coll., 3d s., III, 156, 1833. **Shinecock.**—Deed of 1648 quoted by Thompson, Long Id., 181, 1839. **Shinicooks.**—Clark, Onondaga, I, 18, 1849. **Shinicooks.**—Keane in Stanford, Compend., 535, 1878. **Shinikooks.**—Drake, Bk. Inds., xi, 1848. **Shinnacock.**—Doc. of 1667 in N. Y. Doc. Col. Hist., XIV, 601, 1883. **Shinnecock.**—Deed of about 1640 quoted by Thompson, Long Id., 207, 1839. **Sinnacock.**—Doc. of 1667 in N. Y. Doc. Col. Hist., XIV, 602, 1883. **Skinnacock.**—Doc. of 1667, ibid., 600. **Southampton Indians.**—Gardiner (1660) in Mass. Hist. Soc. Coll., 3d s., III, 154, 1833. **Southton.**—Doc. of 1676 in N. Y. Doc. Col. Hist., XIV, 711, 1883.

Shipapulima (Zuñi: 'mist - enveloped town,' from *shipia* 'mist', *úlin* 'surrounding', *imona* 'sitting place of.'—Cushing). The Zuñi name of the traditional place of origin as well as the final resting place of the Zuñi, Keresan, and other Pueblo tribes, whence came the gods who taught them their arts, agriculture, and ceremonies. By the Zuñi it is said to be a group of pueblo ruins on the Rio Mancos, a tributary of the San Juan, in s. w. Colo.; to the Rio Grande pueblos (called by them Cibobe) and the Jemez (to whom it is known as Uabunatota) it is a lagoon in the same locality. See Bandelier, cited below; Cushing in 13th Rep. B. A. E., 1896; Cushing, Zuñi Folk Tales, 1900.
Black Lake of Tears.—Lummis, Land of Poco Tiempo, 136, 1893. **Cibobe.**—Bandelier in Arch. Inst. Papers, III, 66, 303, 1890 (Shi-Pap-u, or). **Colela.**—MS. of 18th century quoted by Bandelier, ibid., IV, 30, 1892. **Copiala.**—Ibid. **O-jang-ge P'hoquing-ge.**—Ibid. (name given by Tewa of San Juan). **Shee-p'ah-póon.**—Lummis, Man Who Married the Moon, 233, 1894 (Tigua name). **Shi'-pàp.**—Whipple, Pac. R. R. Rep., III, pt. 3, map, 10, 1856. **Shi-Pap-u.**—Bandelier, op. cit., III, 66, 1890 (or Cibobe). **Shi-p'a-pú.**—Lummis, Land of Poco Tiempo, 75, 1893. **Shí-pä-pu-li-ma.**—Cushing in 2d Rep. B. A. E., 16, 1883. **Shi-pap-ulima.**—Bandelier quoted in Arch. Inst. Rep., v, 40, 1884. **Shipa-puyna.**—Bandelier in Arch. Inst. Papers, IV,

30, 1892 (Santa Clara Tewa name). **Shipop.**—Meline, Two Thousand Miles, 202, 1867. **Ua-bunatota.**—Bandelier in Arch. Inst. Papers, IV, 207, 1892 (Jemez name).

Shipaulovi (from *shipaulavitu*, 'mosquitoes,' because its largest clan consists of part of the people who formerly lived at Homolobi, which was abandoned on account of the mosquitoes (Voth, Trad. Hopi, 61, 1905). One of the 6 pueblos of the Hopi (q. v.), situated on the Middle mesa of Tusayan, N. E. Arizona. According to Stephen it was built by Walpi people who had intermarried with those of Mishongnovi, and according to Voth the population was considerably augmented by the Forehead clan of Homolobi after the refusal of the inhabitants of Shongopovi to receive them, and to have been further increased within historic times by the removal of people from Shongopovi on account of their fear of the Spaniards after killing the missionaries and destroying their mission in 1680. In 1782 Morfi (see Fewkes in 17th Rep. B. A. E., 579, 1898) reported Shipaulovi to contain only 14 families, a reduction apparently due to a story circulated by a Shongopovi chief that the Spaniards would again make their appearance, causing many of the Shipaulovi people to move to Shongopovi. The present population is about 125.   (F. W. H.)

Áh-lé-là.—Whipple in Pac. R. R. Rep., III, pt. 3, 13, 1856 (Zuñi name). **Ahlelq.**—Whipple, misquoted by Donaldson, Moqui Pueblo Inds., 3, 1893. **Cĕ-pa'-le-ve'.**—ten Kate, Synonymie, 6, 1884 (native name; mistranslated 'house of peaches'). **Cipaulire.**—Moffet in Overland Mo., 2d s., 243, Sept. 1889. **Ci-pau'-lo-vi.**—Fewkes in Am. Anthr., v, 105, 1892. **Cipoliva.**—Shipley in Ind. Aff. Rep., 310, 1891. **Ci-pow-lovi.**—Ibid., lxxx, 1886. **Clipalines.**—Corbin (1891) in Donaldson, Moqui Pueblo Inds., 37, 1893 (misprint). **Guipaolave.**—Escudero, Not. de Chihuahua, 231, 1834. **Guipaulavi.**—Cortez (1799) in Pac. R. R. Rep., III, pt. 3, 121, 1856. **Inparavi.**—Calhoun quoted by Donaldson, op. cit., 14. **Juparivi.**—Schoolcraft, Ind. Tribes, I, 519, 1853. **Qset-so-kít-pee-tsée-lee.**—Eaton, ibid., IV, 220, 1854 (Navaho name; cf. *Tse-itso-kit'-bit-si-li*, below). **Sesepaulaba.**—Garcés (1776), Diary, 394, 1900 (Yavapai form). **Sesepaulabe.**—Garcés quoted by Bandelier in Arch. Inst. Papers, III, 135, 1890. **Shapalawee.**—Taylor in Cal. Farmer, Apr. 10, 1863. **Shapan-la-vi.**—Ward (1861) quoted by Donaldson, op. cit., 14. **Shapanlobi.**—Taylor, op. cit., June 19, 1863. **Sha-pau-lah-wee.**—Ives, Col. Riv., map, 1861. **She-banlavi.**—Loew in Rep. Geog. Surv. W. 100th Merid., 178, 1875. **Shebaula-vi.**—Loew in Pop. Sci. Mo., v, 352, July 1874. **Shebaúlavi.**—Gatschet in Mag. Am. Hist., 260, Apr. 1882. **She-bo-pav-wee.**—French, Hist. Coll. La., II, 175, 1875. **Sheeponarleeve.**—Eastman (1853) misquoted by Donaldson, op. cit., 14. **Sheepowarleeve.**—Eastman, map in Schoolcraft, Ind. Tribes, IV, 24, 1854. **Shepálavé.**—ten Kate, Reizen, 454, 1885 (mistransl. *perzikenhuis*, 'peach house'). **Shepalawa.**—Beadle, Undeveloped West, 576, 1873. **She-pa-la-wee.**—French, Hist. Coll. La., II, 175, 1875. **She-pau'-lave.**—Barber in Am. Nat., 730, Dec. 1877. **Shepauliva.**—Clark and Zuck in Donaldson, op. cit., 14. **Shepolavi.**—Mason, ibid. **She-powl-a-we.**—Palmer in Ind. Aff. Rep., 133, 1870. **Shi-pau-a-luv-i.**—Powell in Scribner's Mag., 203, Dec. 1875. **Shipau-i-luv-i.**—Ibid., 202. **Shi-pau'-la-vi.**—Barber in Am. Nat., 730, Dec. 1877. **Shi-pav-i-luv-i.**—Powell in Scribner's Mag., 196, map, Dec. 1875. **Shi-powl-ovi.**—Stephen quoted by Donaldson, op.

cit., 14. **Shu-par-la-vay.**—Irvine in Ind. Aff. Rep., 160, 1877. **Shupaúlavi.**—Voth, Traditions of the Hopi, 61, 1905. **Shupowla.**—Bourke misquoted by Donaldson, op. cit., 14. **Shupowlewy.**—Bourke, Moquis of Ariz. 226, 1884. **Suponolevy.**—Bourke in Proc. Am. Antiq. Soc., n. s., I, 244, 1882. **Supowolewy.**—Bourke, Moquis of Ariz., 136, 1884. **Tse-itso-kǐt'-bǐt-si'-li.**—Stephen, MS., B. A. E., 1879 ('miserable dwellings at': Navaho name). **Wáki.**—Voth, Traditions of the Hopi, 61, 1905 (former name; sig. 'refuge house'). **Xipaolabi.**—Dominguez and Escalante (1776) in Doc. Hist. Mex., 2d s., I, 548, 1854.

Shipololonkaia (*Shi-po-lo-lon K'ai-a*, 'place of misty waters'). The traditional fourth resting place of the Zuñi on their eastward migration.—Cushing in Millstone, IX, 2, Jan. 1884.

Shiptetza (correctly *Shíptatsĕ*, referring to the glancing of an arrow when it strikes a buffalo's ribs.—Curtis). A band of the Crow tribe.
Bear's Paw Mountain.—Morgan, Anc. Soc., 159, 1877. **Shíptatsĕ.**—Curtis, N. Am. Ind., IV, 38, 45, 1909. **Ship-tet-sa.**—Culbertson in Smithson. Rep. 1850, 144, 1851. **Ship-tet'-zä.**—Morgan, op. cit.

Shishaiokoi (*Cīcai'ōǫoi*). A Squawmish village community on the E. coast of Howe sd., Brit. Col.—Hill-Tout in Rep. Brit. A. A. S., 474, 1900.

Shishalap (*Shi-shá'-láp*). Two Chumashan villages: one formerly between Pt Conception and Santa Barbara, Cal., in the locality now called El Cajo Viejo; the other near San Buenaventura, Ventura co., at a place later called Frente de la Calle de Fezueroa.
Chichilop.—Taylor in Cal. Farmer, July 24, 1863. **Ci-câ'-lâp.**—Henshaw, Buenaventura MS. vocab., B. A. E., 1884 (*c=sh*).

Shishlamau (*Cic-lá-má'-u*, pron. *Shish-lá-má'-u*). A Chumashan village formerly existing near Hueneme, Ventura co., Cal.—Henshaw, Buenaventura MS. vocab., B. A. E., 1884.

Shishmaref (after Lieut. Shishmaref, who accompanied Kotzebue in 1816). A Kinugumiut Eskimo village at Shishmaref cape, Alaska.—Post-route map, 1903.

Shitaimu. A former pueblo of the Eagle clan of the Hopi, situated on the summit of a large mound E. of Mishongnovi, Arizona, where traces of numerous small-roomed houses are found. The uneven summit of the mound is about 300 by 200 ft, and the village seems to have been built in the form of an irregular ellipse, but the ground-plan is very obscure.
Shi-tái-mu.—Stephen and Mindeleff in 8th Rep. B. A. E., 28, 1891. **Shitaimuvi.**—Mindeleff, ibid., 48. **Shitaumû.**—Fewkes in 17th Rep. B. A. E., 581, 1898.

Shiu. The Eagle clan of Isleta pueblo, N. Mex.
Shíu-t'aínin.—Lummis quoted by Hodge in Am. Anthr., IX, 350, 1896 (*t'aínin*='people').

Shiuguermi. A Costanoan village situated in 1819 within 10 m. of Santa Cruz mission, Cal.—Taylor in Cal. Farmer, Apr. 5, 1860.

Shiuwauk (*Ci'-u-wa'-ŭk*). An Alsea village on the N. side of Alsea r., Oreg.—

Dorsey in Jour. Am. Folk-lore, III, 230, 1890.

Shivwits. A Paiute tribe formerly inhabiting the plateau bearing their name in N. W. Arizona, and numbering 182 in 1873. There are now (1909) 118 Shivwits in the s. w. corner of Utah, near St George, where they have about 70 acres of tillable land, with adjacent land suitable for pasturage, while others are said to be on the Moapa res. in Nevada.
Cehmeque-sabinta.—Cortez (1799) in Pac. R. R. Rep., III, pt. 3, 126, 1856. **Chemeguabas Sevintas.**—Garcés (1776), Diary, 472, 1900. **Chemegue-seviota.**—Orozco y Berra, Geog., 59, 1864. **Chemegué Sevínta.**—Garcés, op. cit., 444. **Chevet.**—Arricivita quoted by Bancroft, Nat. Races, III, 686, 1882. **Kohoaldje.**—Kroeber in Univ. Cal. Pub., Am. Archæol. and Ethnol., VI, 107, 1907 (Mohave name). **Lee-Biches.**—Beadle, Undeveloped West, 658, 1873. **Paranükh.**—Kroeber, op. cit. (Chemehuevi name). **Savints.**—Hinton, Handbook to Arizona, 353, 1878. **Seviches.**—Hoffman in 10th Rep. Hayden Surv., 461, 1878. **Sevinta.**—Escudero, Not. Estad. de Chihuahua, 228, 1834. **Sheavwits.**—Powell and Ingalls in Ind. Aff. Rep. 1873, 42, 50, 1874. **Sherwits.**—Ingalls in H. R. Ex. Doc. 66, 42d Cong., 3d sess., 2, 1873. **Shi'-vwits.**—Powell and Ingalls, op. cit., 50. **Sivinte.**—Kroeber, op. cit. (another Mohave name). **Sivits.**—Ibid. (another Chemehuevi name). **Virgin River Paiutes.**—Ibid.

Shiwanu. The Ant clan of the Ala (Horn) phratry of the Hopi.
Ci'-wa-nü wüñ-wü.—Fewkes in Am. Anthr., VII, 401, 1894 (*wüñ-wü*=clan).

Shiyosubula ('sharp-tailed grouse'). A band of the Brulé Teton Sioux.
Ciyo-subula.—Dorsey in 15th Rep. B. A. E., 218, 1897. **Siyo-subula.**—Ibid.

Shiyotanka ('prairie chicken'). A band of the Brulé Teton Sioux.
Ciyo-tañka.—Dorsey in 15th Rep. B. A. E., 218, 1897. **Pheasants.**—Culbertson in Smithson. Rep. 1850, 141, 1851. **Siyo-tañka.**—Dorsey, op. cit.

Shkagech (*Cgágɛtc*, 'her nose'). A former village of the Tlakluit on Columbia r., Wash.   (E. S.)

Shkanatulu. The extinct Lizard clan of the pueblo of Sia, N. Mex.
Shkanátulu-háno.—Hodge in Am. Anthr., IX, 351, 1896 (*háno*='people').

Shkashtun (*Ckac'-tún*). A Takelma band or village on the s. side of Rogue r., Oreg., between Hashkushtun and Leaf cr.—Dorsey in Jour. Am. Folk-lore, III, 235, 1890.

Shkonana (*Cq!ó'nana*). A former village of the Tlakluit opposite Crates Point on Columbia r., Wash.   (E. S.)

Shkuet (*C'kŭēt*). A village of the Ntlakyapamuk on Fraser r., near Spuzzum, Brit. Col.—Hill-Tout in Rep. Ethnol. Surv. Can., 5, 1899.

Shkuokem (*Ckŭō'kɛm*, 'little hills'). A village of the Ntlakyapamuk on Fraser r., above Spuzzum, Brit. Col.—Hill-Tout in Rep. Ethnol. Surv. Can., 5, 1899.

Shkutch (*Ckŭtc*). A former Siuslaw village on Siuslaw r., Oreg.—Dorsey in Jour. Am. Folk-lore, III, 230, 1890.

Shlalki (*C'lä'lki*). An insignificant Chilliwack village in s. British Columbia—Hill-Tout in Rep. Ethnol. Surv. Can., 4, 1902.

Shmoqula. See *Smohalla.*

Shnalkeya (*shnal*, 'head of the lake'; *keya* refers to the head-crest of the quail). A small Kulanapan tribe living near the town of Upper Lake, at the head of Clear lake, Cal.—J. W. Hudson, inf'n, 1906.
Oha-net-kai.—McKee (1851) in Sen. Ex. Doc. 4, 32d Cong., spec. sess., 136, 1853. **Shanel-kaya.**—Gibbs (1851) in Schoolcraft, Ind. tribes, III, 109–110, 1853.

Shobarboobeer. Given by Lewis and Clark as a Shoshoni band, numbering 1,600, living high up on the N. w. side of Multnomah (Willamette) r., Oreg. The name is not identifiable, but it is in territory of the Mono-Paviotso dialectic division of the stock, as the authors supposed the Willamette to rise in the interior, far to the E. of the Sierras.
Sho-bar-boo-be-er.—Orig. Jour. Lewis and Clark, VI, 119, 1905. **So-so-bâ.**—Lewis and Clark, Discov., 60, 1806. **So-so'-bu-bar.**—Ibid., 63.

Shobonier. A Potawatomi village near the present Shabbona, De Kalb co., N. E. Illinois, about 1830; named from the chief. See *Shabonee.*
Shab-eh-nay.—Prairie du Chien treaty (1829) in U. S. Ind. Treat., 162, 1873. **Shab-eh-nay's Vill.**—Royce in 18th Rep. B. A. E., Ill. map, 1899. **Shobon-ier.**—Tippecanoe treaty (1832) in U. S. Ind. Treat., 698, 1873.

Shobotarcham. A Maricopa rancheria on the Rio Gila, Ariz., in 1744.—Sedelmair (1744) cited by Bancroft, Ariz. and N. Mex., 366, 1889.

Shodakhai Pomo ('east valley people'). A name applied to the Pomo living in what is known as Coyote valley, along the lower course of the E. fork of Russian r., about 4 m. N. E. of Ukiah, Mendocino co., Cal. Shodakhai was the name of a temporary modern village near the center of this valley. (s. A. B.)
Oódakai.—Barrett in Univ. Cal. Pub., Am. Archæol. and Ethnol., VI, no. 1, map, 1908. **Shodakhai pomo.**—S. A. Barrett, inf'n, 1907. **Sho-do Kai Po'-mo.**—Powers in Cont. N. A. Ethnol., III, 155, 1877.

Shoe-pack. "A moccasin having a sole turned up and sewed to the upper. Though now made of leather, the *pac* as used by the Indians . . . was made of hide boiled in tallow and wax, or of tawed hide subsequently stuffed with tallow and wax" (E. H. Knight, s. v. *Pac, Pack*, with a cross-reference to *Shoe-pack*, in Amer. Mechan. Dict., 1876). The Century Dictionary defines *shoepack* as a shoe made of leather without a separate sole, or in the manner of a moccasin, but of tanned leather. The word is of Lenape (Delaware) origin. In an old vocabulary of Lenape words used by the Indians of New Jersey, the word *seppock* is defined as 'shoes'. In the Lenape-English dictionary the name for 'shoe' is given as *machtschipak* (German orthography), which really means 'bad [*machtschi*] shoe'', and the name for 'bad shoes' as *machtalipaqual*, lit. 'bad-hole-shoes' (i. e. shoes bad because of holes). From this plural it appears that the Lenape name of a kind of shoe differing

from the ordinary moccasin was *paku*, or in the Unami dialect, *pathko*. *Shoepack*, then, is an accommodated spelling of the abbreviation *shǐpak* designed to give the word a semblance of meaning in English. (w. r. g.)

Shohoaigadika (*Shóhoaigadíka*). One of the Shoshoni divisions said to live near Salmon r., a branch of Snake r. in w. Idaho.
Cottonwood-Salmon-Eaters.—Hoffman in Proc. Am. Philos. Soc., XXIII, 298, 1886. **Shóhoaigadíka.**—Ibid.

Shohoita. The Deer clan of the Zuñi of New Mexico.
Shóhoita-kwe.—Cushing in 13th Rep. B. A. E., 368, 1896 (*kwe*='people').

Shohopanaiti (*Shóhopanaíti*, 'Cottonwood Bannock'). A band of the Bannock.
Cottonwood Banaks.—Hoffman in Proc. Am. Philos. Soc., XXIII, 299, 1886. **Shóhopanaíti.**—Ibid.

Shohu. One of the clans of the Pakab (Reed) phratry of the Hopi.
Oohu wiñwû.—Fewkes in 19th Rep. B. A. E., 584, 1900. **Co-hü wüñ-wû.**—Fewkes in Am. Anthr., VII, 403, 1894.

Shokfak. A Kuskwogmi̇̄t Eskimo village on a lake in the tundra N. of Kuskokwim bay, Alaska.
Chokfaktoligamute.—Spurr (1898) quoted by Baker, Geog. Dict. Alaska, 1902. **Chokfoktolegha-gamiut.**—11th Census, Alaska, 164, 1893. **Tshokfachtolígamut.**—Post (1898) quoted by Baker, op. cit.

Shokhowa. A division or village of the Pomo, near Hopland, Mendocino co., Cal., associated with the Shiegho.
Socoas.—Powers quoted by Bancroft, Nat. Races, I, 449, 1874. **So-kó-a.**—Powers in Cont. N. A. Ethnol., III, 172, 1877.

Shoktangihanehetchinsh. A former Chitimacha village on an inlet of Grand lake, about 3 m. N. of Charenton, La. Their central house for religious dances, or at least one such house, and the burial ground of their chiefs were in this locality.
Shóktangi háne hetchi'nsh.—Gatschet in Trans. Anthr. Soc. Wash., II, 151, 1883.

Shokumimlepi ('wild-potato place'). A former Nishinam village in the valley of Bear r., which is the next stream N. of Sacramento, Cal.
Shokumi'mleppe.—Powers in Overland Mo., XII, 22, 1874.

Shomakoosa. The Prairie Wolf gens of the Kansa, according to Morgan, but not given by Dorsey in his latest list of the Kansa gentes.
Oüⁿmikase.—Dorsey, Kansa MS. vo ab., B. A. E., 1882. **Prairie Wolf.**—Morgan, Anc. Soc., 156, 1878. **Sho'-ma-koo-sa.**—Ibid.

Shomamish. A division of Salish occupying Vashon id., Puget sd., Wash.
Homamish.—Lane in Sen. Ex. Doc. 52, 31st Cong., 1st sess., 173, 1850. **S'Homahmish.**—Stevens in H. R. Ex. Doc. 37, 34th Cong., 3d sess., 45, 1857. **S'Homamish.**—Treaty of 1854 in U. S. Ind. Treaties, 561, 1873. **Sho-mam-ish.**—Starling in Ind. Aff. Rep., 170, 1852. **S'slo-ma-mish.**—Gibbs in Pac. R. R. Rep., I, 435, 1855.

Shonchin. See *Schonchin.*

Shongopovi ('place of *chumoa*,' a variety of grass). A Hopi pueblo of the Middle mesa of Tusayan, N. E. Ariz., built probably about 1680. The earlier pueblo, which bore the same name, was situated on a ridge of foothills E. of the present town, near an ancient spring. It was one of the original villages of the Hopi, and the seat of the Franciscan mission of San Bartolomé, established about 1629, with Mishongnovi as its visita. The population of Shongopovi was about 160 in 1870, 193 in 1882, and 224 in 1891. See Fewkes in 17th Rep. B. A. E., 582, 1898; Mindeleff in 8th Rep. B. A. E., 73, 1891. (F. W. H.)

Ci-mo-pave.—Ind. Aff. Rep., lxxx, 1886. Ci-mó-pavi.—Fewkes in Bull. Essex Inst., xxiv, 114, 1892. Ci-motk-pivi.—Shipley in Ind. Aff. Rep., 310, 1891. Comupavi.—Oñate (1598) in Doc. Inéd., xvi, 207, 1871. Cuñopavi.—Fewkes in Am. Anthr., vii, 394, 1894. Iogopani. — Bowles, Map America, 1750 (?). Iogopapi.—De l'Isle, Carte de Mex. et Flor., 1703. Jongoapi.—Humboldt, Atlas Nouv. d'Espagne, carte 1, 1811. Jongopabi. — Vargas (1692) quoted by Davis, Span. Conq. N. Mex., 367, 1869. Jongopai.—Ruxton in Jour. Ethnol. Soc. Lond., ii, 182, 1850. Jongopavi.—Davis, El Gringo, 115, 1857. Jon-jon-cali.—Escudero, Not. Estad. de Chihuahua, 231, 1834. Kin-nas-ti.—Stephen, MS., B. A. E., 1887 ('houses built round a court': Navaho name). Kiu-ahs-dée.—Eaton in Schoolcraft, Ind. Tribes, iv, 220, 1854 (a Navaho name). Samoupavi.—Calhoun quoted by Donaldson, Moqui Pueblo Inds., 14, 1893. San Bartolome de Jongopavi.—Fewkes in Am. Anthr., vi, 394, 1894. San Bartoloméde Jougopavi.—Bancroft, Ariz. and N. Mex., 349, 1889. San Bartolomé de Xongopabi.—Vetancurt (1694) in Teatro Am., iii, 321, 1871. San Bartolomé de Xongopavi.—Vetancurt (1694), Menolog. Fran., 274, 1871. San Bernardo de Jongopabi.—Vargas (1692) quoted by Davis, Span. Conq. N. Mex., 369, 1869. S. Bernabé Jongopavi.—Vargas (1692) quoted by Bancroft, Ariz. and N. Mex., 201, 1889. She-mo-pa'-ve.—Jackson quoted by Barber in Am. Nat., 730, Dec. 1887. Shi-ma-co-vi.—Cushing in Atl. Monthly, 368, Sept. 1882. Shimopavi.—Bandelier in Arch. Inst. Papers, iii, 258, 1890. Shimopova.—Clark and Zuck in Donaldson, Moqui Pueblo Inds., 14, 1893. Shomonpavi.—Taylor in Cal. Farmer, June 19, 1863. Shomoparvee.—Eastman, map in Schoolcraft, Ind. Tribes, iv, 25, 1854. Shongápavé.—ten Kate, Reizen in N. A., 245, 1885. Shong'-a-pa-vi.—Powell in Scribner's Mag., 196, Dec. 1875. Shongápavi.—Voth, Traditions of the Hopi, 61, 1905. Shongoba-vi.—Loew in Pop. Sci. Month., v, 352, July, 1874. Shongópavi.—Gatschet in Mag. Am. Hist., 260, Apr. 1882. Show-mowth-pa.—Domenech, Deserts N. A., i, 185, 1860. Shu-mo-pa-vay.—Irvine in Ind. Aff. Rep., 160, 1877. Shú-müth-pà.—Whipple in Pac. R. R. Rep., iii, pt. iii, 13, 1856. Shú-müth-pài-ò-wà.—Ibid. (Zuñi name). Shung-a-pá-vi.—Barber in Am. Nat., 730, Dec. 1877. Shung-o-pah-wee.—Ives, Colorado Riv., map, 1861. Shung-o-pa-we.—Palmer in Ind. Aff. Rep., 133, 1870. Shungopawee.—Taylor in Cal. Farmer, Apr. 10, 1863. Shung-op-ovi.—Stephen in Donaldson, Moqui Pueblo Inds., 14, 1893. Shuñopovi.—Fewkes in 17th Rep. B. A. E., 582, 1898. Songoapt.—Pike, Exped., 3d map, 1810. Sumonpavi.—Schoolcraft, Ind. Tribes, i, 519, 1853. Sumo-porvy.—Bourke in Proc. Am. Antiq. Soc., n. s., i, 244, 1881. Sumopowy.—Bourke, Moquis of Ariz., 227, 1884. Sumopoy.—Bourke misquoted by Donaldson, Moqui Pueblo Inds., 14, 1893. Xangopany.—Jefferys, Am. Atlas, map 5, 1777. Xommapavi.—Vargas (1692) quoted by Bancroft, Ariz. and N. Mex., 201, 1889. Xongopabi.—Morfi (1782) quoted by Bandelier in Arch. Inst. Papers, iii, 135, 1890. Xongopani.—D'Anville, map Am. Sept., 1746. Xongopaui.—Alcedo, Dic. Geog., v, 372, 1789. Xongopavi—Villa-Señor, Theatro Am., ii, 425, 1748. Xougopavi.—Cortez (1799) quoted in Pac. R. R. Rep., iii, pt. 3, 121, 1856. Xumupamí.—Oñate (1598) in Doc. Inéd., xvi, 137, 1871. Xumupani.—Bandelier in Arch. Inst. Papers, iv, 369, 1892.

Shonivikidika (*Shónivikidíka*, 'sunflower-seed eaters'). One of the former divisions of the Shoshoni.

Shónivikidíka.—Hoffman in Proc. Am. Philos. Soc., xxiii, 298, 1886. Sun-Flower-Seed-Eaters.—Ibid.

Shookany. Probably a band of the Calapooya.

Shook-any.—Ross, Adventures, 236, 1849.

Shooyoko (*Sho'-o-yo-ko*). A Hopi clan. The name probably has some relation to Showongwu, a mythological personage.

Cooyoko.—Dorsey and Voth, Mishongnovi Ceremonies, 175, 1902 (c=sh).

Shopakia (*Sho'pak'ia*). A ruined village pertaining to the Zuñi, situated 5 m. N. of Zuñi pueblo, N. Mex.—ten Kate, Reizen in N. A., 291, 1885. Cf. *Heshokta*.

Shopeshno. A Chumashan village, formerly near Santa Inés mission, Santa Barbara co., Cal.—Taylor in Cal. Farmer, May 4, 1860.

Shoremee. A Costanoan village, situated in 1819 within 10 m. of Santa Cruz mission, Cal.—Taylor in Cal. Farmer, Apr. 5, 1860.

Short Bull. A Brulé Sioux, born on the Niobrara r. about 1845. He came into prominence in 1890 when chosen one of the Sioux delegation to visit Wovoka, the Indian "Messiah," at Pyramid lake, Nev. On his return he represented himself as the special vicar of Wovoka, and later, after having been imprisoned by the Federal authorities, assumed to be the "Messiah" himself. He had great vogue with the Sioux for several months during the Ghost Dance craze, but with the abatement of the excitement fell into disrepute. He resides at Pine Ridge agency, S. Dak., and affiliates with the Congregationalists. (D. R.)

Short Hair Band. An Oglala Sioux band, possibly the same as Peshla.—Schoolcraft, Ind. Tribes, iii, 629, 1853.

Shoshoko ('walkers'). A collective name of indefinite application attached to the poorer bands and individuals of the Shoshoni who did not happen to own horses, and were, temporarily at least, "walkers." As they could not hunt the buffalo and were dependent on humbler modes of livelihood, they were frequently termed "Diggers," though the latter term was really no more applicable to them than to many others who bore it. The term Shoshoko has frequently been taken to designate a definite division or tribe of the Shoshoni; in reality it is not a tribal designation at all. (H. W. H.)

Chochocois.—Webb, Altowan, i, 42, 1846. Diggers.—Irving, Astoria, 257, 1849. Gens de Pitié.—Maximilian, Travels, 509, 1843. Les Radiqueurs.—Ibid. Muradiços.—Ibid. (so called by Spaniards). Root Diggers.—Farnham, Travels, 74, 1843. Root Eaters.—Irving, Astoria, 257, 1849. Sho-sho-co.—Gebow, Sho-sho-nay Vocab., 17, 1868 (Shoshoni name). Sho-sho-coes.—Wilson (1849) in Cal. Mess. and Corresp., 109, 1850. Shoshokoes.—Irving, Rocky Mts., ii, 48, 1837. Sho-sho-kos.—Lander in Sen. Ex. Doc. 42, 36th Cong., 1st sess., 133, 1860. Shuckers.—Irving, Astoria, 257, 1849. Snake Root Diggers.—Farnham, Travels, 75, 1843. Sosokos.—Schoolcraft, Ind. Tribes, v, 199, 1855. Walkers.—Wilson, op. cit. Western Shoshonees.—Lander in

Sen. Ex. Doc. 42, 36th Cong., 1st sess., 133, 1860 (so called by mountaineers).

Shoshonean Family. The extent of country occupied renders this one of the most important of the linguistic families of the North American Indians. The area held by Shoshonean tribes, exceeded by the territory of only two families—the Algonquian and the Athapascan,—may thus be described: On the N. the s. w. part of Montana, the whole of Idaho s. of about lat. 45° 30′, with s. E. Oregon, s. of the Blue mts., w. and central Wyoming, w. and central Colorado, with a strip of N. New Mexico; E. New Mexico and the whole of N. w. Texas were Shoshonean. According to Grinnell, Blackfoot (Siksika) tradition declares that when the Blackfeet entered the plains s. of Belly r. they found that country occupied by the Snakes and the Crows. If this be true, s. w. Alberta and N. w. Montana were also Shoshonean territory. All of Utah, a section of N. Arizona, and the whole of Nevada (except a small area occupied by the Washo) were held by Shoshonean tribes. Of California a small strip in the N. E. part E. of the Sierras, and a wide section along the E. border s. of about lat. 38°, were also Shoshonean. Shoshonean bands also lived along the upper courses of some of the streams flowing into the San Joaquin. Toward the broken southern flanks of the Sierras, Shoshonean territory extended across the state in a wide band, reaching N. to Tejon cr., while along the Pacific the Shoshoni occupied the coast between lat. 33° and 34°.

From the wide extent of country thus covered, and its varied climatic and topographic features, the habits of the peoples occupying it might be expected to vary considerably, and such is indeed the case. The Hopi, in particular, differ so widely from the rest that they have little in common with them but linguistic affinity. On the N. and along the entire E. border of the territory, where lived the Shoshoni, Bannock, Ute, and Comanche divisions, their habits were essentially those of the hunting Indians generally. None of them cultivated the soil, and all derived the larger part of their subsistence from the pursuit of large game. The Comanche alone can be said to have been buffalo Indians, though buffalo were pursued more or less by all the tribes mentioned. Horses early became abundant among them. In general character they were fierce and warlike.

To the w. of the Rocky mts., in Idaho, w. Utah, Arizona, Nevada, California, and Oregon, the Shoshoneans were of a different character. The country occupied by many of them is barren in the extreme, largely destitute of big game, and of such character generally as to compel its aboriginal inhabitants to resort to humble methods of procuring subsistence. Rabbits and small game generally, fish, roots, and seeds formed the chief support of these tribes, among which were included the representatives of the family that possessed the rudest and simplest culture. It was chiefly to these tribes individually and collectively that the opprobrious name of "Diggers" was applied. These are the tribes, also, which were called by the settlers and by many writers, Paiute. Representing as a class, as they undeniably do, a culturally low type of Indian, they were by no means so low as many writers of repute have asserted. They have been represented as closely approaching the brutes in their mode of life, and, like them, of passing the winter in a semitorpid state in holes in the ground, from which they crawled forth in spring to eat grass upon hands and knees. Of all men they have been said to be the lowest. Such pictures of their condition are nonsensical. They are not true of them to-day, when, decimated in numbers and with tribal organization broken up, the remnants of many of the tribes have been forced to a precarious and parasitic mode of livelihood obtained from the whites. Still less are they true of their former condition when living under their own social organizations. The inhospitable nature of their country compelled them, it is true, to a less adventurous and humbler mode of life than their eastern brethren, who possessed a more richly endowed country. However, they made and used bows and arrows, basketry, and in parts pottery; and, more important than all, a number of the tribes, as the Paiute of Corn cr., Utah, the Gosiute of Utah, the Chemehuevi of the Rio Colorado, and some of the Nevada tribes, practised a rude agriculture.

The Hopi of N. E. Arizona, who had made further progress toward civilization than any other of the Shoshonean tribes, had become true village Indians. Long contact and probably considerable blood-amalgamation have given them the physical type of their neighbors of the S. W., and have made them an integral part of the well-defined and highly specialized Pueblo culture. They derive their subsistence mainly from agriculture, and are skilful potters and weavers.

Over the wide expanse of territory above indicated the Shoshoneans were split into a number of major divisions, each composed of numerous bands speaking a great number of related dialects.

On linguistic grounds, as determined by Kroeber, it is found convenient to classify the Shoshonean family as follows:

I. HOPI.

II. PLATEAU SHOSHONEANS: (a) *Ute-*

Chemehuevi: Chemehuevi, Kawaiisu, Paiute, Panamint, Ute, and some of the Bannock; (b) *Shoshoni-Comanche:* Comanche, Gosiute, Shoshoni; (c) *Mono-Paviotso:* Mono, Paviotso, part of the Bannock, and the Shoshoneans of E. Oregon.

III. KERN RIVER SHOSHONEANS.

IV. SOUTHERN CALIFORNIA SHOSHONEANS: (a) *Serrano,* (b) *Gabrieleño,* (c) *Luiseño-Kawia:* Agua Caliente, Juaneño, Kawia, Luiseño.

For the smaller divisions see under the several subordinate heads.

The genetic relationship of the Shoshonean languages with those of the Piman and Sonoran group, and of the Nahuatl or Aztec group in Mexico, was investigated by Buschmann in the middle of the last century. Powell has since regarded the Shoshonean group as constituting a distinct family, but others, including Brinton, Chamberlain, and Kroeber, have maintained that it is only part of a larger family, which they have designated Uto-Aztekan.

In addition to the writings cited below, consult Kroeber, Shoshonean Dialects of California, Univ. Cal. Pub., Am. Archæol. and Ethnol., IV, no. 3, 1907. (H. W. H.)

>**Shoshonees.**—Gallatin in Trans. Am. Antiq. Soc., II, 120, 133, 306, 1836 (Shoshonee or Snake only); Hale in U. S. Expl. Exped., VI, 218, 1846 (Wihinasht, Pánasht, Yutas, Sampiches, Comanches); Gallatin in Trans. Am. Ethnol. Soc., II, pt. 1, c, 77, 1848 (as above); Gallatin, ibid., 18, 1848 (follows Hale; see below); Gallatin in Schoolcraft, Ind. Tribes, III, 402, 1853; Turner in Pac. R. R. Rep., III, pt. 3, 55, 71, 76, 1856 (treats only of Comanche, Chemehuevi, Cahuillo); Buschmann, Spuren der aztek. Sprache, 552, 649, 1859. >**Shoshoni.**—Hale in U. S. Expl. Exped., VI, 199, 218, 569, 1846 (Shoshóni, Wihinasht, Pánasht, Yutas, Sampiches, Comanches); Latham in Trans. Philol. Soc. Lond., 73, 1856; Latham, Opuscula, 340, 1860. >**Schoschonenu Kamantschen.**—Berghaus (1845), Physik. Atlas, map 17, 1848; ibid., 1852. >**Shoshones.**—Prichard, Phys. Hist. Mankind, V, 429, 1847 (or Snakes, both sides Rocky mountains and sources of Missouri). =**Shóshoni.**—Gatschet in Mag. Am. Hist., 154, 1877; Gatschet in Beach, Ind. Miscel., 426, 1877. <**Shoshone.**—Keane in Stanford, Compend., Cent. and So. Am., app., 460, 477, 1878 (includes Washoes of a distinct family); Bancroft, Nat. Races, III, 567, 661, 1882. >**Snake.**—Gallatin in Trans. Am. Antiq. Soc., II, 120, 133, 1836 (or Shoshonees); Hale in U. S. Expl. Exped., VI, 218, 1846 (as under Shoshonee); Prichard, Phys. Hist. Mankind, V, 429, 1847 (as under Shoshones); Turner in Pac. R. R. Rep., III, pt. 3, 76, 1856 (as under Shoshonees); Buschmann, Spuren der aztek. Sprache, 552, 649, 1859 (as under Shoshonees). <**Snake.**—Keane in Stanford, Compend., Cent. and So. Am., app., 477, 1878 (contains Washoes in addition to Shoshonean tribes proper). >**Kizh.**—Hale in U. S. Expl. Exped., VI, 569, 1846 (San Gabriel language only). >**Netela.**—Hale, ibid., 569, 1846 (San Juan Capistrano language). >**Paduca.**—Prichard, Phys. Hist. Mankind, V, 415, 1847 (Cumanches, Kiawas, Utas); Latham, Nat. Hist. Man., 310, 326, 1850; Latham (1853) in Proc. Philol. Soc. Lond., VI, 73, 1854 (includes Wihinast, Shoshoni, Uta); Latham in Trans. Philol. Soc. Lond., 96, 1856; Latham, Opuscula, 300, 360, 1860. <**Paduca.**—Latham, Nat. Hist. Man., 346, 1850 (Wihinast, Bonaks, Diggers, Utahs, Sampiches, Shoshonis, Kiaways, Kaskaias?, Keneways?, Bald-heads, Cumanches, Navahoes, Apaches, Carisos); Latham, El. Comp. Philol., 440, 1862 (defines area; cites vocabs. of Shoshoni, Wihinasht, Uta, Comanch, Piede or Pa-uta, Chemuhuevi, Cahuillo, Kioway, the latter not belonging here). >**Cumanches.**—Gallatin in School-

craft, Ind. Tribes, III, 402, 1853. >**Netela-Kij.**—Latham (1853) in Trans. Philol. Soc. Lond., VI, 76, 1854 (composed of Netela of Hale, San Juan Capistrano of Coulter, San Gabriel of Coulter, Kij of Hale). >**Capistrano.**—Latham in Proc. Philol. Soc. Lond., 85, 1856 (includes Netela of San Luis Rey and San Juan Capistrano, the San Gabriel or Kij of San Gabriel and San Fernando). =**Shoshonean.**—Powell in 7th Rep. B. A. E., 108, 1891.

Shoshoni. The most northerly division of the Shoshonean family. They formerly occupied w. Wyoming, meeting the Ute on the s., the entire central and southern parts of Idaho, except the territory taken by the Bannock, N. E. Nevada, and a small strip of Utah w. of Great Salt lake. The Snake r. country in

URIEWISHI, A SHOSHONI

Idaho is, perhaps, to be considered their stronghold. The northern bands were found by Lewis and Clark in 1805, on the headwaters of the Missouri in w. Montana, but they had ranged previously farther E. on the plains, whence they had been driven into the Rocky mts. by the hostile Atsina and Siksika, who already possessed firearms. Nowhere had the Shoshoni established themselves on the Columbia, although they reached that river on their raiding excursions.

The origin of the term Shoshoni appears to be unknown. It apparently is not a Shoshoni word, and although the name is recognized by the Shoshoni as applying to themselves, it probably originated among some other tribe. The Cheyenne name for the Comanche, who speak the Shoshoni language, is *Shĭshĭ-noats-hitäneo*, 'snake people'; but they have a different name for the Shoshoni. The term Snake seems to have no etymological connection with the designation Shoshoni. It has been variously and frequently applied to the northern bands of the Shoshoni, especially those of Oregon. By recent official usage the term Snake has been restricted to the Yahuskin and Walpapi of Oregon. Hoffman was of the opinion that the name Snake comes from a misconception of the sign for Snake Indian, made by a serpentine motion of the hand with the index finger extended. This he thought really has reference to

SHOSHONI WOMEN AND CHILD

the weaving of the grass lodges of the Shoshoni, a reasonable assumption, since they are known as "grass-house people," or by some similar name, among numerous tribes.

The more northerly and easterly Shoshoni were horse and buffalo Indians, and in character and in warlike prowess compared favorably with most western tribes. To the w. in western Idaho along Snake r. and to the s. in Nevada the tribes represented a lower type. Much of this country was barren in the extreme and comparatively devoid of large game, and as the nature of the country differed, so did the inhabitants. They depended for food to a large extent on fish, which

was supplemented by rabbits, roots, nuts, and seeds. These were the Indians most frequently called "Diggers." They were also called Shoshokos, or "Walkers," which simply means that the Indians so called were too poor to possess horses, though the term was by no means restricted to this section, being applied to horseless Shoshoni everywhere.

None of these Shoshoni were agriculturists. In general the style of habitations corresponded to the two types of Shoshoni. In the N. and E. they lived in tipis, but in the sagebrush country to the w. they used brush shelters entirely, and Bonneville found the tribes of Snake r. wintering in such shelters without roofs, being merely half circles of brush, behind which they obtained an imperfect protection from wind and snow. There were many dialects among the Shoshoni, corresponding to the greater or less degree of isolation of the several tribes. They presented, however, no essential differences and were all mutually intelligible.

In 1909 there were in Idaho 1,766 Shoshoni and Bannock under the Ft Hall school (of whom 474 had recently been transferred from the old Lemhi res.), and about 200 not under official supervision; in Nevada there were 243 under the Western Shoshoni school, and about 750 not under agency or school control; In Wyoming, under the Shoshoni school, there were 816, formerly known as Washaki's band, from its chief. Deducting about 500 Bannock from these figures, the total Shoshoni population approximates 3,250. The Shoshoni divisions, so far as known, were: Hohandika, Shobarboobeer, Shohoaigadika, Shonivikidika, Tazaaigadika, Towahnahiooks, Tukuarika, Tussawehe, Washaki, Wihinasht, and Yahandika. See also *Pohoi*.   (H. W. H.)

Aliatan.—For forms of this name, see *Ietan*. Bik-ta′-she.—Hayden, Ethnog. and Philol. Mo. Val., 402, 1862 ('grass lodges': Crow name). Chochones.—Ind. Aff. Rep. 1873, 192, 1874. Choshon-nê.—Orig. Jour. Lewis and Clark, II, 367, 1905. E-wu-ha′-wu-si.—Hayden, op. cit., 326 (='people that use grass and bark for their lodges or huts': Arapaho name). Gens de Serpent.—Orig. Jour. Lewis and Clark, VI, 106, 1905. Gens des Serpent.— Lewis and Clark, Discov., 60, 1806 (so called by the French). Gens du Serpent.—La Verendrye (1742) in Margry, Déc., VI, 601, 1886. Ginebigônini.—Baraga, Otchipwe-Eng. Dict., 136, 1880 (pl. Ginebigóniniwog, 'snake men': Chippewa name). Grass House People.—Mooney, Cheyenne Inds., 422, 1907 (translation of Kiowa name). Indiens-Serpents.—Gass, Voyage, 185, 1810. Kinebikowininiwak.—Cuoq, Lexique Algon., 167, 1886 ('serpents': Algonkin name). Må-bůo-shǒ-rǒch-pǎn-gǎ.—Long, Exped. Rocky Mts., II, lxxxiv, 1823 (Hidatsa name). Miká-atí.—Curtis, N. Am. Ind., IV, 186, 1909 ('grass lodge': Hidatsa name). Mi′-kyashě.—Ibid., 180 (Crow name, with same meaning). Nation of the Snake.—Jefferys, French Dom. Am., I, map, 1741. Pe-ji′-wo-ke-ya-o-ti.— Cook, Yankton MS. vocab., B. A. E., 184, 1882 (='those dwelling in grass lodges': Yankton name). Pezhí-wokeyotila.—Curtis, N. Am. Ind.,

III, 141, 1908 ('grass-thatch dwellers': Teton Sioux name). **Pi-ói′-kse-ni-tup′-i-o.**—Hayden, Ethnog. and Philol. Mo. Val., 264, 1862 (Blackfoot name). **Serpents.**—Smet, Letters, 62, 1843. **Shashones.**—Orig. Jour. Lewis and Clark, VI, 340, 1905. **Shirry-dikas.**—Ross, Fur Hunters, I, 249, 1855 ('dog-eaters': given as a division of the Snakes, but evidently confused with the Arapaho). **Sho-shon.**—Clarke in Jour. Anthr. Inst. G. B., IV, 160, 1875. **Sho-Sho-nay.**—Gebow, Sho-sho-nay Vocab., 10, 1868 (Shoshoni name). **Sho-sho-ne.**—Gass, Journal, 210, 1807. **Shoshonee.**—Lewis and Clark Exped., II, 587, 1817. **Sho-shones.**—Orig. Jour. Lewis and Clark, v, 94, 1905. **Shoshoni.**—Lewis and Clark Exped., II, 587, 1817. **Shos-shone.**—Ruxton, Adventures, 243, 1848. **Shossoonies.**—Scouler (1846) in Jour. Ethnol. Soc. Lond., I, 239, 1848. **Shothones.**—Coke, Ride over Rocky Mts., 294, 1852. **Shúⁿshun-wichăsha.**—Curtis, N. Am. Ind., III. 141, 1908 ("the first part of the word is doubtless an attempt to say *Shoshoni*"). **Siŋ-te′-ḣda wi-ca-śa.**—Cook, Yankton MS. vocab., B. A. E., 184, 1882 (= 'Rattlesnake Indians': Yankton name). **Sisízhă-nĭn.**—Curtis, N. Am. Ind., v, 154, 1909 ('rattlesnake men': Atsina name). **Snake Diggers.**—Johnson and Winter, Route Across Rocky Mts., 111, 1846. **Snake Indians.**—Writer of 1786 in Mass. Hist. Soc. Coll., 1st s., III, 24, 1794. **Snegs.**—Beltrami, Pilgrimage, II, 282, 1828. **Snóă.**—Gatschet, MS., B. A. E. (Okinagan name). **Soshawnese.**—Porter in Schoolcraft, Ind. Tribes, III, 597, 1853. **Sosho-nees.**—Frignet, La Californie, 273, 1867. **Sosho-nes.**—Smet, Letters, 36, 1843. **So′-so-i-ha′-ni.**—Hayden, op. cit., 290 (Cheyenne name). **So-so-na.**—Lewis and Clark, Discov., 63, 1806. **Sosone.**—Orig. Jour. Lewis and Clark, II, 329, 1905. **Soso-nee.**—Ibid., IV, 70. **Sosonees.**—Ibid., II, 244. **Sosones.**—Ibid., IV, 77. **Sosone′s.**—Ibid., 38. **So′-so-ni.**—Hayden, op. cit., 290 (Cheyenne name). **Su′-su-ne.**—Cook, Yankton MS. vocab., B. A. E., 184, 1882 (Yankton name). **Wahkiruxkanu-manke.**—Will and Spinden, Mandans, 217, 1906 (Mandan name). **Wákidoňka-numak.**—Curtis, N. Am. Ind., v, 148, 1909 ('snake man': Mandan name). **Wěs′ănikaciⁿga.**—Dorsey, Çegiha MS. Dict., B. A. E., 1878 ('snake people': Omaha and Ponca name). **Zuzéća wi-óáśa.**—Bushotter, inf'n, 1887 ('snake people': Teton Sioux name).

Shotlemamish. A body of Salish on Case inlet, at the s. w. extremity of Puget sd., Wash.

Hotlimamish.—Schoolcraft, Ind. Tribes, v, 700, 1855. **Hottimamish.**—Lane in Sen. Ex. Doc. 52, 31st Cong., 1st sess., 173, 1850. **Hottunamish.**—Lane in Ind. Aff. Rep., 162, 1850. **Scootle-mam-ish.**—Starling, ibid., 171, 1852. **S'Hotle-ma-mish.**—Stevens, ibid., 458, 1854. **S'Hotlmahmish.**—Stevens in H. R. Ex. Doc. 37, 34th Cong., 3d sess., 45, 1857. **S'hotlma-mish.**—Dall, after Gibbs, in Cont. N. A. Ethnol., I, 241, 1877. **S'Kosle-ma-mish.**—Gibbs in Pac. R. R. Rep., I, 435, 1855. **Sroo-tle-mam-ish.**—Starling in Ind. Aff. Rep., 170, 1852.

Shoto. A Chinookan tribe or division found in 1806 by Lewis and Clark on the N. side of Columbia r., a short distance from the stream and nearly opposite the mouth of the Willamette. Their estimated number was 460, in 8 houses.

Shoto.—Lewis and Clark Exped., II, 472, 1814. **Sho-toes.**—Orig. Jour. Lewis and Clark, IV, 219, 1905.

Showtl. A name of a species of rodent (*Haplodon rufus*) of parts of the Oregon-British Columbia region, known as the *sewellel* (q. v.), or *shavl′l*, the name of this animal in the Nisqualli and closely related Salishan dialects. (A. F. C.)

Showtucket (Mohegan: *nashauetuk-ut*, 'between the rivers.'—Trumbull). A village in the fork of the Shetucket and Quinebaug rs., near Lisbon, New London co., Conn. Before King Philip's war (1675) it was occupied by a Mohegan band. After the war, in 1678, a band of friendly Indians from various tribes was settled there, known as "Surrenderers," but after a few years the village was abandoned on account of the opposition of Uncas. (J. M.)

Shatetucket.—Leete (1665) in Mass. Hist. Soc. Coll., 4th s., VII, 556, 1865. **Shatuckett.**—Pynchon (1700) in N. Y. Doc. Col. Hist., IV, 616, 1854. **Shatuskett.**—Owaneco (1700), ibid., 615. **Showtucket.**—Caulkins, Norwich, 50, 1866. **Surrenderers.**—Ibid., 256.

Shregegon. A Yurok village on lower Klamath r., about a mile above the mouth of Pekwan cr., N. w. Cal.

Sca-goines.—McKee (1851) in Sen. Ex. Doc. 4, 32d Cong., spec. sess., 162, 1853. **Schre-gon.**—Gibbs (1851) in Schoolcraft, Ind. Tribes, III, 138, 1853. **Ser-a-goines.**—Meyer, Nach dem Sacramento, 282, 1855. **Seragoins.**—McKee, op. cit., 193. **Ser-a-goins.**—Ibid., 194. **Serragoin.**—Schoolcraft, Ind. Tribes, III, 422, 1853. **Shregegon.**—A. L. Kroeber, inf'n, 1906. **Sira-grins.**—McKee, op. cit., 161. **Sri′-gon.**—Powers in Cont. N. A. Ethnol., III, 44, 1877.

Shrines. Places where sacred offerings are deposited or cult images or objects are set up. They are fixed or portable, the former often being altar shrines (see *Altar*), or consist of stone boxes inclosing sacred objects. The latter class includes the sacred bundles of the Pawnee, Papago, Hopi, and other tribes (see *Palladium*).

Shrines are common to many tribes N. of Mexico, but perhaps among none do they now enter more into the religious life of the people than among the Pueblos, particularly among the Hopi, whose shrines will here be described as typical:

Among these people any special spot consecrated to supernatural beings, where prayer offerings to them are made, is called a *pahoki*, or 'prayer house,' generally translated 'shrine.' There are about a hundred shrines at or near the pueblo of Walpi, half of which have special names. They are situated on the mesa, among the foothills, at springs, and near the ruins of ancestral villages. Certain of these places of offering have no special names, but are called "rain-cloud shrines," or "world-quarter shrines," because situated at the four cardinal directions from the pueblo. A Hopi shrine differs from an altar in being a place in which the offerings remain permanently, or until they or their essence are supposed to be removed by the gods.

Every great ceremony has its special shrine, but in some of them prayer offerings are made in all ceremonies. Many shrines have nothing to mark them except prayer sticks (q. v.). Common forms of shrines are circles of small stones or even a single stone, caves or clefts, a natural depression in a bowlder, or any object symbolically marked. The most elaborate shrines are sealed stone inclosures, sometimes painted with symbols, and containing symbolic representations of supernatural beings, idols, water-worn stones, or fossils. Shrines may be classified either on the basis of their form and contents or on that of the supernatural beings to which they are dedicated. Of the latter, among the Hopi, there are those of the Earth and Sky gods, Kachina shrines, and shrines of numerous lesser supernatural beings.

The most elaborate Earth-goddess shrine at the East mesa of the Hopi is that of Talatumsi, situated in the foothills E. of Walpi. It is a sealed chamber in which is a seated idol of the Dawn Woman. The slab ordinarily closing the entrance is removed every November, during the New Fire ceremony, when offerings are placed near it; and every 4 years the idol is taken from the shrine and carried to the village. The shrine of Kokyanwuqti, Spider Woman, another name for the Earth goddess, is a simple stone inclosure. The shrine of Masauu, the god of the Underworld, is situated in the foothills w. of Walpi, and consists of a small pile of stones and twigs. The shrine of Tuwapontumsi, another Earth goddess, contains a petrified log surrounded by slabs of stone. There are numerous shrines of the Sky god in the vicinity of Walpi, but they are generally of very simple construction.

Sun shrines among the Hopi are simple circles of stone, with openings toward the point where the sun rises at the time of the summer solstice. A shrine at "Wala," a gap in East mesa, toward the top of the trail to Hano pueblo, containing a coiled stone, or natural cast of a shell, may be considered a Sun shrine. The Sky-serpent god, Palulukong, has several shrines, among which may be mentioned the two great springs in the foothills E. of Walpi and Hano.

The Kachina shrine is a closed receptacle constructed of slabs of stone set on edge. It is situated in the foothills w. of Walpi, and is ceremonially opened and closed every July. Individual clans have their special shrines where offerings are made to their tutelary ancients. Raincloud and world-quarter shrines are of the simplest construction, commonly consisting of circles of small stones.

Shrines sometimes mark places where mythological events are said to have happened; thus the shrine of the so-called Heart-Contained-Here, in the foothills E. of Walpi, is supposed to contain the heart of a god who won a mythic footrace. Those who aspire to speed in these races worship at this shrine.

Human or animal images of wood and stone, concretionary or botryoidal stones, carved stone slabs, and fossil shells are among the permanent objects, not offerings, found in Hopi shrines. The temporary offerings on shrines are prayer meal and pollen, sticks, clay effigies of small animals, miniature bowls and vases of water, small bows and arrows, small dolls, turquoise, shells, and other objects.

Some shrines are known by the character of their offerings; thus, a warrior's shrine contains netted shields, bows, and arrows; an eagle shrine, painted wooden imitations of eagle's eggs. Places where ceremonial paraphernalia are kept partake of the sacred nature of a shrine, and caves resorted to for prayer are considered in the same light. All springs of water are places of prayer offerings, and each has a shrine either near by or remote.

Zuñi "prayer houses" are no less numerous and instructive than those of the Hopi, and are of the same general character, although several differ in form from those above mentioned. The best known Zuñi shrine, that of Hepatina, lies near the village and is said to be consecrated to the center of the earth, in which spot it is supposed to stand. It is a tri-chambered stone inclosure with an opening to the E. surmounted by strangely formed stones. There are numerous shrines on the mesa of Taaiyalone, among which that of the Twin War Gods of the Zuñi is the most characteristic.

The most notable of the many shrines of the Rio Grande pueblos are the stone pumas of Cochiti.

Consult Curtis, N. Am. Ind., I–V, 1907–09; Dorsey and Voth in Field Columbian Mus. Pubs., Anthr. ser., III, nos. 1 and 3, 1901, 1902; Fewkes (1) in Jour. Am. Ethnol. and Archæol., I, 1891; II, 1892; IV, 1894; (2) in 17th Rep. B. A. E., 1898; (3) in Jour. Am. Folk-lore, V, 196, 1892; (4) in Am. Anthr., VIII, 346, 1906; Starr in Am. Antiq., XXII, no. 4, 1900; Stevenson in 11th and 23d Rep. B. A. E., 1893, 1904; Pepper and Wilson, Hidatsa Shrine, Mem. Am. Anthr. Asso., II, pt. 4, 1908. (J. W. F.)

Shruhwi. The Rattlesnake clans of the Keresan pueblos of Laguna, Acoma, Cochiti, and Sia, N. Mex. The Laguna clan came originally from Sia, and forms a phratry with the Hatsi (Earth), Skurshka (Water-snake), and Meyo (Lizard) clans of that pueblo. The Rattlesnake clan of Cochiti is extinct. (F. W. H.)
Shqúwï-hánoqᶜʰ.—Hodge in Am. Anthr., IX, 352, 1896 (Acoma form; hánoqᶜʰ='people'). Shrúhwi-hanuch.—Ibid. (Cochiti form). Sqówi-hánoᶜʰ.—Ibid. (Laguna form). Squ-háno.—Ibid. (Sia form).

Shrutsuna. The Coyote clans of the Keresan pueblos of Laguna, Santa Ana, Sia, San Felipe, and Cochiti, N. Mex. Part of the Laguna clan claims to have come from Zuñi and part from Sia. Compare the Laguna (Tsŭ'shki) and Zuñi (Súski) names of these clans, the two peoples belonging to distinct linguistic families. (F. W. H.)

Shrótsona-háno.—Hodge in Am. Anthr., IX, 350, 1896 (San Felipe form; *háno*='people'). **Shrútsuna-hánuch.**—Ibid. (Cochiti form). **Shurts-ŭnna.**—Stevenson in 11th Rep. B. A. E., 19, 1894 (Sia form). **Shutsón-háno.**—Hodge, op. cit. (Santa Ana form). **Shútsun'-háno.**—Ibid. (Sia form). **Shutzuna.**—Bandelier, Delight Makers, 251, 1890. **Tsŭshki-háno**ch.—Hodge, op. cit. (Laguna form).

Shu ('fish'). A Yuchi clan.
Cu.—Speck, Yuchi Inds., 70, 1909 (*c=sh*). **Shútahá.**—Gatschet, Uchee MS., B. A. E., 70, 1885 (='fish clan').

Shubenacadie (*Shubenakádi*, 'plenty of ground-nuts(?).—Trumbull). A Micmac village and reservation at the head of Shubenacadie r., N. of Halifax, Nova Scotia. Pop. 100 in 1909.
Chibenaccadie.—Doc. of 1746 in N.Y. Doc.Col. Hist., X, 70, 1858. **Chigabennakadik.**—Frye (1760) in Mass. Hist. Soc. Coll., 1st s., X, 115, 1809. **Shubenakadie.**—Rand, Micmac Reading Bk., 81, 1875. **Shubenecadie.**—Macdonald in Can. Ind. Aff. for 1884, xxix, 1885.

Shufina (strictly *Tsiphenu*, 'dark-colored obsidian flakes,' from *tsi*, 'obsidian flakes,' *phenu*, 'dark'; in the Santa Clara Tewa dialect the form is *Tsifeno*.—J. P. Harrington). A small ancient pueblo ruin on a castle-like mesa of tufa, N. w. of Puye and separated from it by Santa Clara canyon, N. Mex. The s. face of the mesa is honeycombed with cliff-dwellings, cut in the rock. While according to Santa Clara tradition these lodges have been occupied within the historic period, they doubtless date from a time prior to the advent of the first Spaniards in the 16th century. See 7th Rep. B. A. E., xxi, 1891; Bandelier, (1) Delight Makers, 378, 1890, (2) in Arch. Inst. Papers, IV, 66, 1892; Hewett (1) in Am. Anthr., VI, no. 5, 1904, (2) in Bull. 32, B. A. E., 1906, (3) in Out West, xxxi, 693–719, 1909. (F. W. H.)
Shu Finne.—Bandelier, op. cit. **Tsifeno.**—Harrington in Out West, xxxi, 702, 1909 (Santa Clara Tewa form). **Tsiphenu.**—Ibid. (San Ildefonso Tewa form).

Shuhlanan ('otter'). A Yuchi clan.
Cūlané.—Speck, Yuchi Inds., 70, 1909 (*c=sh*). **Shu'laná**ⁿ **tahá.**—Gatschet, Uchee MS., B. A. E., 71, 1885 (='otter clan').

Shuimp (*Cŭimp*, 'strong'). A head village of the Ntlakyapamuk just above Yale, Fraser r., Brit. Col.—Hill-Tout in Rep. Ethnol. Surv. Can., 5, 1899.

Shukhata ('opossum [town],' from *shukhúta*, opossum, lit. 'white hog'). A former Choctaw town on the site of the present Columbus, Ala.—Halbert in Pub. Ala. Hist. Soc., Misc. Coll., I, 431, 1901.

Shukhtutakhlit (*Shu-qtu'-ta-qlit'*, 'man-eaters': Kaniagmiut name). A division of the Ahtena on Copper r., Alaska, next below the Kangikhlukhmut.—Hoffman, MS., B. A. E., 1882.

Shuku. A Chumashan village stated by Indians to have been formerly at the Rincon, Santa Barbara co., Cal. Placed by Taylor near Santa Inés mission.
Pueblo de las Canoas.—Cabrillo, Narr. (1542), in Smith, Colec. Doc. Fla., 181, 1857. **Shucu.**—Taylor in Cal. Farmer, Apr. 17, 1863. **Shukku.**—Ibid., May 4, 1860. **Shu-kú.**—Henshaw, Buenaventura

MS. vocab., B. A. E., 1884. **Xuco.**—Cabrillo, Narr. (1542), in Smith, op. cit., 181. **Xucu.**—Rep. Geog. Surv. W. 100th Mer., VII, 307, 1879.

Shulya ('beaver'). Given by Bourke (Jour. Am. Folk-lore, II, 181, 1889) as a gens of the Mohave, q. v.

Shumasitcha (Keresan: 'the corpse on the summit'). A ruin of unknown origin on a mesa w. of Rito, near Hasatch, N. Mex. In modern times it has been temporarily occupied by the Laguna Indians, during their wars with the Navaho and Apache, as a stronghold for the protection of their flocks. So called from the fact that the corpse of a herder, who had been killed by a wild animal, was once found on the highest point of the mesa.—Pradt quoted by Hodge in Am. Anthr., IV, 346, 1891.

Shumig. A former Yurok village on the N. W. coast of California, at Patrick's Point, 5 or 6 m. N. of Trinidad. It was not inhabited in historic times, except as a camp site, but is important in mythology.

Shuminkyaiman (*Shu'-mingk'ya-i'man*: *Shu'-me-k'u-li*, the mythic man-bird of the Ka'ka or esoteric Shu'-me-kwe; *ink'ya*, 'region anciently frequented by, acted in,' etc.; *i'man*, 'home of,' 'sitting place of'). A hill and section of country where the Shumekuli being of Zuñi mythology was captured by the Shaalako; situated about 13 m. s. of Zuñi pueblo, N. Mex. The whole country thereabout is covered with the stone-hut foundations attributed to the Pewikwithltchu (q. v.) (F. H. C.)
Shuminkia.—Fewkes in Jour. Am. Ethnol. and Archæol., I, 100, 1891 (given as name of ruins).

Shumnac (*Shum'-nac*). A former Tigua pueblo, E. of the Rio Grande, in the vicinity of the present Mexican settlements of Chilili, Tajique, and Manzano, N. Mex.—Lummis in Scribner's Mo., 469, Apr. 1893.

Shumway Ruin. A ruined prehistoric pueblo near the town of Shumway, 40 m. s. of Holbrook, Ariz. It consists of a long house group, 2 rooms deep, and a parallel group having a wing at right angles at one end, and between these groups a plaza.—Hough in Rep. Nat. Mus. 1901, 302, pl. 22, 1903.

Shunaiki. A ruined village claimed to have been inhabited by the ancestors of the people of the present pueblo of Laguna, N. Mex.; situated about 3 m. w. of the latter. (F. W. H.)

Shungikcheka ('common dogs'). A band of the Yanktonai Sioux.
Cŭn-iktceka.—Dorsey in 15th Rep. B. A. E., 218, 1897. **Suŋ ikćeka.**—Ibid.

Shungikikarachada ('they who call themselves from the original dog'). A Winnebago gens.
Øe-go'-ni-na.—Dorsey in 15th Rep. B. A. E., 240, 1897 ('wolf': archaic name). **Cŭñk i-ki'-ka-ra'-tca-da.**—Ibid. **Cŭñk-tcañk' i-ki'-ka-ra'-tca-da.**—

Ibid.   **Shonk-chun'-ga-dă.**—Morgan, Anc. Soc., 157, 1877

Shungkahanapin ('wears a dogskin around the neck,' i. e. 'dog necklace') A band of the Brulé Teton Sioux.
Cŭñkaha-nap'iⁿ.—Dorsey (after Cleveland) in 15th Rep. B. A. E., 219, 1897.   Suŋkaha napin.—Ibid.

Shungkayuteshni ('eat no dogs'). A band of the Miniconjou Sioux.
Cuñka-yute-cni.—Dorsey in 15th Rep. B. A. E., 220, 1897.   Ho-tum'-mi'-hu-is.—Hayden, Ethnog. and Philol. Mo. Val., 290, 1862 (Cheyenne name).   Shunk'-a-yu-tĕsh'-ni.—Ibid., 376.   Suŋka yute-śni.—Dorsey in 15th Rep. B. A. E., 220, 1897.   **Those that eat no dogs.**—Culbertson in Smithson. Rep. 1850, 142, 1851.

Shunkukedi (named from an island called *Shăn*, 'old'). A Tlingit division of the Wolf phratry, living at Klawak, Alaska. The name of this clan is sometimes applied, in the form Shunkukedina ('Shunkukedi nation'), to the entire Wolf phratry.
Cê'ngoqedî'na.—Swanton, field notes, B. A. E., 1904.   Schengo-kĕdi.—Krause, Tlinkit Ind., 116, 1885.

Shup. A former Chumashan village near Carpenteria, Santa Barbara co., Cal., N. of El Rincon.
Cûp.—Henshaw, S. Barbara MS. vocab., B. A. E., 1884 (c=sh).

Shupauk. A former Yaquina village on the s. side of Yaquina r., Oreg.
Cu'-dauk.—Dorsey in Jour. Am. Folk-lore, III, 229, 1890 (c=sh).

Shuqualak. A former Choctaw town or division in Noxubee co., Miss.—Gatschet, Creek Migr. Leg., I, 109, 1884.

Shurmuyu. The Turquoise clan of the Tigua pueblo of Isleta, N. Mex.
Shurmúyu-t'aínïn.—Lummis quoted by Hodge in Am. Anthr., IX, 352, 1896 (t'aínïn='people').

Shushuchi. A former Chumashan village between Pt Conception and Santa Barbara, Cal., in the locality now called La Fuemada.
Cu'-cu-tci.—Henshaw, Buenaventura MS. vocab., B. A. E., 1884 (c=sh).

Shustak's Village. A camping place of a Stikine chief named Shastaak (ᏟAct!aă'k), on Etolin id., Alaska; pop. 38 in 1880.—Petroff in 10th Census, Alaska, 32, 1884.

Shuswap (strictly *Sequa'pmuq*). The most important Salishan tribe of British Columbia, formerly holding most of the territory between the Columbia r. watershed and Fraser r., including the basin of Thompson r. above Ashcroft, embracing Shushwap or Adams lakes, and extending N. to include Quesnel lake. They now occupy a number of small village reservations attached to the Kamloops-Okanagan and Williams Lake agencies, together with a small band, descendants of Chief Kinbasket, for about 60 years past permanently settled among the Kutenai. On the N. they border the Tsilkotin, an Athapascan tribe; on the s. and w. the kindred Okanagan, Ntlakyapamuk, and Lillooet. They have probably dwindled at least one-half since the advent of the miners in their country half a century ago, but still number more than 2,100, in

the following bands: *Kamloops-Okanagan Agency*—Adams Lake, Ashcroft, Bonaparte, Deadman's Creek, Kamloops, Neskainlith or Halaut, North Thompson, Little Shushwap Lake, Spallumcheen; *Williams Lake Agency*—Alkali Lake, Canoe Creek, Clinton, Dog Creek, Fountain (occupied chiefly by Lillooet), High Bar, Pavilion, Soda Creek, Williams Lake; *Kootenay Agency*—Kinbasket.

Consult Dawson in Trans. Roy. Soc. Canada, IX, sec. II, 1892; Teit in Mem. Am. Mus. Nat. Hist., II, Anthr. I, no. 4, 1900; Ann. Rep. Can. Ind. Aff.; Boas in 6th Rep. N. W. Tribes Can., 1891.   (J. M.)
Atenas.—Morse, Rep. to Sec. War, 371, 1822 (the variants of this are from the Takulli word meaning 'stranger').   Atnahs.—Gallatin in Trans. Am. Antiq. Soc., II, 16, 134, 1836.   At-naks.—Mayne, Brit. Col., 296, 1861.   Atnans.—De Smet, Oregon Miss., 100, 1847.   Atnas.—Drake, Bk. Inds., vi, 1848.   Clulwarp.—Fitzhugh in Ind. Aff. Rep. 1857, 328, 1858.   Ka-la-muh.—Mackay quoted by Dawson in Trans. Roy. Soc. Can., sec. II, 7, 1891 ('the people': own name).   Schouchouaps.—Duflot de Mofras, Oregon, II, 337, 1844.   Se-huapm-uh.—Mackay, op. cit., 4.   SeQuapmuQ.—Boas in 6th Rep. N. W. Tribes Can., 80, 1890.   Shewhap.—Anderson quoted by Gibbs in Hist. Mag., VII, 77, 1863.   Shewhapmuch.—Ibid., 73, 76.   Shewhapmuh.—Tolmie and Dawson, Vocabs. Brit. Col., 124B, 1884.   Shewhapmukh.—Gibbs in Shea's Lib. Am. Ling., XI, vii, 1860-3.   She-whaps.—Ross, Adventures, 151, 1849.   Shoo-schawp.—Kane, Wanderings, 155, 1859.   Shooshaps.—Parker, Journal, 299, 1840.   Shooswabs.—Taylor in Cal. Farmer, July 19, 1862.   Shoo-whā'-pa-mooh.—Dawson in Trans. Roy. Soc. Can., sec. II, 4, 1891.   Shoushwaps.—Hale in U. S. Expl. Exped., VI, 198, 1846.   Shouwapemoh.—De Smet, Oregon Miss., 63, 1847.   Shouwapemot.—Ibid., 100.   Shushwaps.—Hale, op. cit., 205, 1846.   Shushwapumsh.—Ibid.   Shuswap-much.—Mayne, Brit. Col., 296, 1861.   Shuswaps.—Ibid.   Sioushwaps.—De Smet, Oregon Miss., 137, 1847.   Sockacheenum.—Brit. Adm. Chart, no. 1917.   Soushwaps.—Prichard, Phys. Hist., v, 427, 1847.   SQua'pamuQ.—Boas in 5th Rep. N. W. Tribes Can., 10, 1889.   Sü'Quapmuq.—Boas in 6th Rep. N. W. Tribes Can., 80, 1890.   Thompson river Indians.—Taylor in Cal. Farmer July 19, 1862.   Tlitk·atEwū'mtlat.—Boas in 5th Rep. N. W. Tribes Can., 10, 1889 ('without shirts and trousers': Kutenai name).   Towapummuk.—Brit. Col. map, Ind. Aff., Victoria, 1872.

Shuta. The extinct Crane clan of Sia pueblo, N. Mex.
Shu'ta.—Stevenson in 11th Rep. B. A. E., 19, 1894.   Shúta-hano.—Hodge in Am. Anthr., IX, 350, 1896 (hano='people').

Shutamul (*Shu'-ta-mūl*). A former Nishinam village in the valley of Bear r., which is the next stream N. of Sacramento, Cal.
Shootamool.—Powers in Overland Mo., XII, 22, 1874.   Shu'-ta-mūl.—Powers in Cont. N. A. Ethnol., III, 316, 1877.

Shutaunomanok. A Pomo village on what is known as Buckingham id., in lower Clear lake, Cal.
Cho-tan-o-man-as.—Gibbs in Schoolcraft, Ind. Tribes, III, 110, 1853.   Shutaunomanok.—A. L. Kroeber, inf'n, 1903 (name in Upper Clear Lake dialect).

Shuuk ('much water'.—ten Kate). A (former?) Pima village on the Gila r. res., s. Ariz.
Shootk.—ten Kate quoted by Gatschet, MS., B. A. E., 199, 1888.   Shu-uk.—Dudley in Ind. Aff. Rep. 1871, 58, 1872.

Shuwalashu. A former Chumashan village at a place called Cañada de los Alisos, Ventura co., Cal.

Cu′-wa-la-ou.—Henshaw, Buenaventura MS. vocab., B. A. E., 1884 (c=sh).

Shuwalethet (*Cuwā′lɛçɛt*). A winter village of the Katsey tribe of Cowichan at the s. end of Pitt lake, near lower Fraser r., Brit. Col.—Boas in Rep. 64th Mtg. Brit. A. A. S., 454, 1894.

Shuwimi. The Turquoise clans of the Keresan pueblos of Laguna, Sia, San Felipe, and Cochiti, N. Mex. The Turquoise clan of Laguna claims to have come originally from Sandia. The corresponding clans in Sia and San Felipe are extinct. According to Bandelier (Arch. Inst. Papers, III, 301, 1890) this clan, since the beginning of the 19th century, seems to represent what may be called the conservative element among the Rio Grande Keresan tribes. Cf. *Tanyi.* (F. W. H.)

Shíuwimi-háno.—Hodge in Am. Anthr., IX, 352, 1896 (Sia form). Shúwhami-hánuch.—Ibid.(Cochiti form). Shúwimi-háno.—Ibid. (San Felipe form). Shŭ′wimi-hánoᶜʰ.—Ibid. (Laguna form). Shyuamo.—Bandelier, op. cit.

Shuyakeksh ('leaping place'). A former Klamath settlement near the N. end of Nilaks mts. and the shore of upper Klamath lake, Oreg. So called because here the Indians were accustomed to leap for amusement over large fallen rocks. Pop. 92 in 1877.

Linkville Indians.—Gatschet in Cont. N. A. Ethnol., II, pt. II, 370, 1890. Shuhiaχiä′gish.—Ibid. Shuyakē′kish.—Ibid., 369. Shuyakē′ksh.—Ibid. Shuyakē′kshni.—Ibid., 370 (name of people). Shuyakē′kshni máklaks.—Ibid. (ditto). Shuyakē′ksi.—Ibid., pt. I, xxx. Shuyéakēks.—Ibid., pt. II, 369. Shúyikēks.—Ibid., 369–70. Suhiaχē′gish.—Ibid., 370. Tsúyakēks.—Ibid. Tsuyakē′ksni.—Ibid.(name of people).

Shyik. One of the tribes participating in the Yakima treaty of June 9, 1855, and placed on the reservation of that name in Washington. It is not identifiable.

Shyicks.—Keane in Stanford, Compend., 535, 1878. Shyiks.—Camp Stevens treaty of 1855 in U. S. Stat. at Large, XII, 951, 1863.

Shykelimy. See *Shikellamy.*

Sia (from *Tsia*, the native name). A small Keresan tribe inhabiting a single pueblo on the N. bank of Jemez r., about 16 m. N. w. of Bernalillo, N. Mex. Castañeda (1541) mentioned one village of the tribe, but 42 years later Espejo visited their "province," which he called Punames (q. v.), describing it as containing 5 pueblos, of which Sia was the largest. Oñate (1598) mentions only Tria or Trios, which is apparently identical with Sia. Opposite the present Sia are the remains of a pueblo called Kakanatzatia, while N. of the town lies another ruined village known as Kohasaya. It is not improbable that at least one of these was among the 5 settlements alluded to by Espejo in 1583, although the Indians now claim that they occupy the same site as in the days of Coronado.

Sia engaged with the other Pueblos in the revolt against Spanish authority in 1680, making a determined stand in their village until Aug. 1689, when they were assaulted by Domingo de Cruzate, the pueblo being completely wrecked and the tribe decimated in the most bloody engagement of the Pueblo rebellion. The friendly attitude of these Indians toward the Spaniards from this time to the close of the revolt in 1696 created considerable friction between them and the people of Jemez and Cochiti. Sia was the seat of a Spanish mission from an early date, hav-

SIA WATER CARRIER

ing Jemez and Santa Ana as its visitas after 1782. According to Bandelier the pueblo doubtless owes its decline since the revolt to the constant inter-killing going on for the supposed evil practice of witchcraft. Pop. 106 in 1890, 119 in 1910. As is to be expected in a tribe that has lost so much in population within the period of reliable tradition, many of the clans once represented are now extinct. Those

marked with an asterisk in the following
list no longer exist: Yaka (Corn), Dyami
(Eagle), Kohai (Bear), Osach (Sun),
Tyupi (Badger), Squ (Rattlesnake), Shu-
tsun (Coyote), Tsits (Water), Tsi (Wild
Turkey), Kuts (Antelope), Dyani (Deer),
*Ishtowa (Arrow), *Mina (Salt), Showiti
(Parrot), Hakan (Fire), *Hohoka (Dove),
*Hapan (Oak), Hami (Tobacco), *Cha-
natya (Pegwood?), *Shiuwimi (Turquoise), Choshka (Roadrunner), *Shkanatulu (Lizard), Tanyi (Calabash), *Mu-
shach (Buffalo), *Tyaia (Piñon), *Sii

SIA SNAKE PRIEST

(Ant), *Akuch (Ivy), *Henuti (Cloud),
*Schira (Crow), *Spia (Hawk), *Shike
(Star), *Tawash (Moon), *Mokaich
(Mountain-lion), *Shuta (Crane), *Wa-
pon (Shell bead), *Yaunyi (Stone [gran-
ite?]), *Washpa (Dance-kilt).

Consult Bandelier in Arch. Inst. Papers, III, 260, 1890, IV, 194 et seq., 1892;
Stevenson in 11th Rep. B. A. E., 1894. See
also *Keresan Family, Pueblos*. (F. W. H.)

Asuncion.—Bancroft, Ariz. and N. Mex., 281, 1889. Chea.—Simpson in Smithson. Rep. 1869, 339, 1871. Chia.—Castañeda (1596) in Ternaux-Compans, Voy., IX, 110, 1838; Jaramillo, ibid., 371. Cia.—Mendoça (1586) in Hakluyt, Voy., 461, 469, 1600. Cice.—Calhoun in Cal. Mess. and Corresp., 215, 1850 (misprint). Cilla.—Davis, Span. Conq. N. Mex., 202, 1869 (or Cia). Ciya.—Bancroft, Ariz. and N. Mex., 58, 1889 (given as Spanish-Mexican name; also Siya). Cla.—Pike, Explor. Travels, map, 1811 (misprint). Ël-ke-ai'.—Hodge, field notes, B. A. E., 1895 (Picuris name). Lia.—Brevoort, New Mexico, 20, 1874 (misprint). N. S. de la Assunscion de Zia.—Donaldson, Moqui Pueblo Inds., 91, 1893. N. S. de la Asumpcion de Zia.—Alencaster (1805) in Prince, N. Mex., 37, 1883. Nuestra Señora de la Assumpsion de Zia.—Ward in Ind. Aff. Rep. 1867, 213, 1868 (full mission name). O-ku-wa'-ri.—Hodge, field notes, B. A. E., 1895 ('place of the sand dunes': Tewa name). Pia.—Kern in Schoolcraft, Ind. Tribes, IV, 39, 1854 (misprint). Sai'-a-kwa.—Hodge, field notes, B. A. E., 1895 (Jemez name). Sai'-o-kwâ.—Ibid. (Pecos name). Sant Pedro y Sant Pablo.—Oñate (1598) in Doc. Inéd., XVI, 254, 1871 (Tria or; doubtless identical; the first saint name applied). Sayaqúa-kwá.—Stevenson, Pecos MS. vocab., B. A. E., 1887 (Pecos name of the pueblo). Sia.—Espejo (1583) in Doc. Inéd., XV, 178, 1871. Siay.—Ibid., 115. Silla.—Parke, map of New Mexico, 1851. Sille.—Lane (1854) in Schoolcraft, Ind. Tribes, V, 689, 1855. Siya.—Bancroft, Ariz. and N. Mex., 58, 1889 (cf. Ciya, above). Tlascala.—Bustamante and Gallegos (1582) in Doc. Inéd., XV, 85, 1871 (Bancroft, Ariz. and N. Mex., 77, 1889, thinks it may possibly be identical). Tlaxcala.—Ibid., 92. Tlogi.—Curtis, N. Am. Ind., I, 138, 1907 ('hairy': Navaho name). Tria.—Oñate (1598) in Doc. Inéd., XVI, 115, 254, 1871. Trios.—Ibid., 102. Tse-a.—Loew cited by Gatschet, Zwölf Sprachen, 41, 1876. Tse-ah.—Simpson in Rep. Sec. War, 143, 1850. Tsia.—Loew in Wheeler Surv. Rep., VII, 345, 1879. Tŭnavwá.—Hodge, field notes, B. A. E., 1895 (Sandia name). Tŭnawák.—Ibid. (Isleta name). Tzia.—De l'Isle, Carte Mex. et Floride, 1703. Tzi-a.—Bandelier in Arch. Inst. Papers, III, 260, 1890. Zea.—Meriwether (1856) in H. R. Ex. Doc. 37, 34th Cong., 3d sess., 146, 1857. Zíá.—Villagran, Hist. Nueva Mex., 155, 1610.

Siaguan. One of the tribes, probably
Coahuiltecan, at San Juan Bautista and
San Francisco Solano missions, Texas, at
the opening of the 18th century. At San
Francisco Solano this was one of the four
original tribes when it was founded in
Mar. 1700; the others were the Sarames
(Xarames), Paiaguanes, and Panacs.
They all evidently spoke the same language, and came from N. of the Rio Grande
(Autos, XXVIII, MS.). In 1738 Indians of
this tribe were at San Bernardo mission
(Portillo, Apuntes, 289). After Solano
mission was transferred to San Antonio,
Texas, numbers of the tribe were baptized
there, and some were still living there as
late as 1760 (Valero Entierros, partida
1107, MS.; see also baptismal and marriage records of Valero). It is not certain that the Siaban were distinct from
this tribe, but there are indications that
they were. If distinct, they were closely
allied with and had essentially the same
history as the Siaguan. (H. E. B.)

Chiaguan.—Valero Bautismos, partida 78, 1720, MS. Chiguan.—Ibid., 197, 1727. Ciaguan.—Ibid., 219, 1730. Sciaguan.—Valero Entierros, 67, 1728, MS. Siaban.—Ibid., 1704 (identical?). Siaguan.—Valero Bautismos, 213, 1728. Siaguane.—Ibid., 157, 1726. Xhiahuam.—Ibid., 440, 1737. Xhiahuan.—Ibid., 441, 1738. Xiguan.—Ibid., 208, 1728. Zhiaguan.—Ibid., 446, 1738. Ziaban.—Valero Entierros, 1704 (identical?). Ziaguan.—Ibid., 88, 1728.

Siamannas ('hunters'). A name applied generally to the interior Indians by those of Washington and British Columbia. This form of the word was used for some Salish on Whatcom and Siamanna lakes, N. W. Wash. Similarly the Ntlakyapamuk were called *Somena* by the Cowichan, while *Swádabsh*, which was applied by the Nisqualli to the Shahaptian Klikitat and Yakima, is said to have the same meaning. (Gibbs in Cont. N. A. Ethnol., I, 341, 1877). This last, however, resembles *Swedebish*, a name given to one of the Skagit tribes on Whidbey id., Puget sd. Cf. *Samamish.* (J. R. S.)
Saw-meena.—Anderson quoted by Gibbs in Hist. Mag., VII, 73, 1863. SEmā'mila.—Teit in Mem. Am. Mus. Nat. Hist., II, 167, 1900. Sia-man-nas.—Fitzhugh in Ind. Aff. Rep. 1857, 329, 1858. Si-him-e-na.—Mahoney (1869), ibid., 70, 576, 1869 (or Stick Indians). Some-na.—Dawson in Trans. Roy. Soc. Can. 1891, sec. II, 6, 1892.

Siansi. A tribe or subtribe, formerly of San Antonio de Valero, some of whose members lived in 1706 and 1707 at San Francisco Solano mission, near the Rio Grande, in Coahuila, Mexico.—Valero Bautismos, 1707; Entierros, 1706, 1707, MSS. cited by H. E. Bolton, inf'n, 1907.

Siapkat (*Si'ápkat*). A division of the Pisquows who probably lived originally at a place of the same name on the E. bank of the Columbia, about Bishop rock and Milk cr., below Wenatchee r., Wash., but are now in Kittitas co. They were a party to the treaty of June 9, 1855, and in 1876 were reported as one of the bands on the Yakima res.
Seapcat.—Ind. Aff. Rep. 1856, 266, 1857. Seapeats.—Keane in Stanford, Compend., 534, 1878 (misprint). Si'ápkat.—Mooney in 14th Rep. B. A. E., 737, 1896.

Siasconsit. One of the aboriginal divisions of Nantucket id., Mass. It probably included the site of the present Siasconset. See Mass. Hist. Soc. Coll., 2d s., III, 25, 1815.

Siatlhelaak (*Siatlqēlā'aq*). A division of the Nuhalk, a branch of the Bellacoola of the coast of British Columbia.—Boas in 7th Rep. N. W. Tribes Can., 3, 1891.

Sibagna. A former Gabrieleño rancheria in Los Angeles co., Cal., on the site of San Gabriel mission (Ried, 1852, quoted by Taylor in Cal. Farmer, June 8, 1860). Cf. *Toviscanga.*

Sibagoida. A rancheria in Arizona, probably of the Maricopa, visited by Kino and Mange in 1699 (Mange cited by Bancroft, Ariz. and N. Mex., 358, 1889). Cf. *Sicoroidag.*

Sibirijoa. A former settlement of the Tehueco on Rio del Fuerte, about lat. 26° 40′, N. W. Sinaloa, Mexico. Hardy mentions it as a Mayo pueblo, which is improbable, although it may have contained some members of that tribe.
Sibirijoa.—Orozco y Berra, Geog., map, 1864. Sivilihóa.—Hardy, Trav in Mex., 438, 1829. Sivirijoa.—Orozco y Berra, op. cit., 332. Zibirgoa.—Kino, map (1702), in Stöcklein, Neue Welt-Bott, 1726.

Sibrepue (*Sibupue ?*). A Maricopa rancheria on the Rio Gila, Ariz., in 1744.—Sedelmair (1744) cited by Bancroft, Ariz. and N. Mex., 366, 1889.

Sibubapa. A branch of the Nevome, of Sonora, Mexico, which inhabited the pueblo of Suaqui.
Sibubapas.—Orozco y Berra, Geog., 58, 351, 1864. Simupapas.—Hamy in Bull. Soc. d'Anthrop. de Paris, 786, 1883.

Sicalamous. See *Shikellamy.*

Sicca. A former village, presumably Costanoan, connected with Dolores mission, San Francisco, Cal.—Taylor in Cal. Farmer, Oct. 18, 1861.

Siccameen. A Cowichan tribe on Oyster bay, S. E. Vancouver id.; pop. 40 in 1906, 30 in 1909.
Ceqemén.—Boas, MS., B. A. E., 1887. Siccameen.—Can. Ind. Aff., pt. II, 164, 1901. Sickameen.—Ibid., 120, 316, 1880. Sick-a-mun.—Ibid., 308, 1879. Tickarneens.—Ibid., lix, 1877.

Sichanetl (*Sitca'nētl*). A Songish division at Oak bay, S. end of Vancouver id.—Boas in 6th Rep. N. W. Tribes Can., 17, 1890.

Sichanghu ('burnt thighs'). A band of the Brulé Teton Sioux.
Sitca[n]xu.—Cleveland quoted by Dorsey in 15th Rep. B. A. E., 218, 1897.

Sichomovi ('place of the wild currant-bush mound'). A pueblo of the Hopi on the East mesa of Tusayan, between Hano and Walpi, N. E. Ariz. It was built about 1750 by a colony of Badger people from Walpi, later joined by a group of Tanoan clans of the Asa phratry from the Rio Grande in New Mexico, who were invited by the Hopi to aid them in resisting the invasions of the Ute. In 1782 it contained about 15 families; the population was 91 in 1870, 120 in 1882, 107 in 1891. It now numbers about 100. See Mindeleff in 8th Rep. B. A. E., 62, 1891; Fewkes in 17th Rep. B. A. E., 578, 1898.
Chemovi.—Schoolcraft, Ind. Tribes, I, 519, 1853. Ci-cho-mo-oi.—Ward (1861) misquoted by Donaldson, Moqui Pueblo Inds., 14, 1893. Cichomovi.—Taylor in Cal. Farmer, June 19, 1863. Citcumave.—Moffet in Overland Month., 2d s., 243, Sept. 1889 Ci-tcum-wi.—Shipley in Ind. Aff. Rep., 310, 1891. It-t'ha'gi.—Stephen, MS., B. A. E., 1887 ('Halfway house': Navaho name). Saránai.—Hodge, field notes, B. A. E., 1895 (Isleta name). Se-choma-we.—Palmer in Ind. Aff. Rep., 133, 1870. Sechumevay.—Jackson in 10th Rep. Hayden Surv., 450, 1878. Se-chum'-e-way.—Barber, after Jackson, in Am. Nat., 730, Dec. 1877. See-chomah-wee.—Ives, Colo. Riv., map, 1861. Se-tco'-mo-we.—ten Kate, Synonymie, 6, 1884 (trans. 'white house'). Setshómavé.—ten Kate, Reizen, 454, 1885 (trans. 'wit huis'). Setshómové.—Ibid., 245. Sheeourkee.—Eastman, map in Schoolcraft, Ind. Tribes, IV, 24–25, 1854. Shi-choam-a-vi.—Powell in Scribner's Mag., 196, 202, Dec. 1875. Shí-wĭn-è-wà.—Whipple, Pac. R. R. Rep., III, pt. 3, 13, 1856 (Zuñi name). Shí-wĭn-nà.—Ibid. (confused with Zuñi). Shu-chum-a-vay.—Irvine in Ind. Aff. Rep., 160, 1877. Shu-sho-no-vi.—Fewkes in Jour. Am. Folk-lore, IV, 132, 1891. Si-ohoan-avi.—Powell quoted by Donaldson, Moqui Pueblo Inds., 14, 1893. Sichomivi.—Bandelier in Arch. Inst. Papers, III, 258, 1890. Sichomovi.—Fewkes in 17th Rep. B. A. E., 578, 1898. Si-chum'-a-vi.—Barber in Am. Nat., 730, Dec. 1877. Sichumnavi.—Donaldson, Moqui Pueblo Inds., 4, 1893. Sichumniva.—Clark and Zuck, ibid., 14. Sichumovi.—

Mindeleff in 8th Rep. B. A. E., 62, 1891. **Sickmu-nari.**—Ten Broeck (1852) in Donaldson, Moqui Pueblo Inds., 26, 1893. **Sionimone.**—Fewkes in 17th Rep. B. A. E., 642, 1898 ('Zuñi court': Tewa name, because of its resemblance to Zuñi). **Sitchom-ovi.**—Stephen in Donaldson, Moqui Pueblo Inds., 14, 1893. **Sitcomovi.**—Fewkes in Am. Anthr., VII, 394, 1893. **Si-tcum'-o-vi.**—Fewkes, ibid., V, 106, 1892. **Siwinna.**—Bancroft, Ariz. and N. Mex., 137, 1889 (misquoting Whipple). **Suchongnewy.**—Bourke, Moquis of Ariz., 226, 1884. **Tsitsumevi.**—Loew (1875) in Wheeler Surv. Rep., VII, 345, 1879. **Tsi-tsumo-vi.**—Loew in Pop. Sci. Month., V, 352, July 1874. **Tsitúmovi.**—Gatschet in Mag. Am. Hist., 260, Apr. 1882.

Sichteyhacky (prob. 'place of salt.'—Hewitt). A former village on Long id., N. Y., probably near the w. end (Doc. of 1645 in N. Y. Doc. Col. Hist., XIV, 60, 1883). Evidently distinct from Secatoag, q. v.

Sicobutovabia. A former rancheria, apparently Papago, visited by Kino and Mange in 1701; situated on the Rio Salado, 20 m. below Sonoita, in N. W. Sonora, Mexico.

Sicobutovabia.—Kino (1701) cited by Bancroft, No. Mex. States, I, 495, 1884. Totonat.—Ibid.

Siconesses (perhaps from *tschiconesink*, 'where it was forcibly taken away'). A division of the New Jersey Delawares formerly living on the E. bank of Delaware r., a short distance above the present Salem, N. J.

Seckoneses.—Sanford, U. S., cxlxi, 1819. **Sickoneysincks.**—Alrichs (1659) in N. Y. Doc. Col. Hist., II, 71, 1858. **Siconescinque.**—Van Sweeringen (1684), ibid., III, 342, 1853. **Siconysy.**—De Laet (*ca.* 1633) in N. Y. Hist. Soc. Coll., 2d s., I, 315, 1841. **Sikonesses.**—Evelin (1648) quoted by Proud, Penn., I, 113, 1797.

Sicoroidag. A Maricopa rancheria on the Gila r., Ariz., below Tucsani, in Spanish colonial times. Cf. *Sibagoida*.

Sicoroidag.—Kino, map (1701), in Bancroft, Ariz. and N. Mex., 360, 1889. **S. Matthœus de Sicoroidag.**—Kino, map (1702), in Stöcklein, Neue Welt-Bott, 74, 1726.

Sidaru. The chief Sidarumiut village, between Wainwright inlet and Pt Belcher, Alaska. They formerly lived at Nunaria.

Sedard.—Baker, Geog. Dict. Alaska, 560, 1906 (quoted form). **Sedars.**—Ibid. **Sezaro.**—Ibid. **Sida'ru.**—Murdoch in 9th Rep., B. A. E., 44, 1892.

Sidarumiut. A tribe of Eskimo w. of Pt Barrow, Alaska. They have much social intercourse with the Nuwukmiut, with whom they intermarry frequently. In 1890 they numbered 47. The villages are Atnik, Attenok, Charnrokruit, Nunaria, Perignak, Pinguishuk, Sidaru.

Setorokamiut.—11th Census, Alaska, 162, 1893. **Sezaro Mutes.**—Kelly, Arct. Eskimos, map, 1890. **Sidarú.**—11th Census, Alaska, 154, 1893. **Sida'rumiun.**—Murdoch in 9th Rep. B. A. E., 44, 1892.

Siechem (*Sīē'tcɛm*, 'sandy'). A Squawmish village community on the right bank of Squawmisht r., Brit. Col.—Hill-Tout in Rep. Brit. A. A. S., 474, 1900.

Siemas. Mentioned as a Pueblo tribe of New Mexico by Mota-Padilla (1742), Hist. Nueva Galicia, 515, 1870.

Sienite. A massive igneous rock, resembling granite in appearance, but distinguished from it especially by the almost total absence of quartz in its composition. It is heavy and tough, and thus came to be used by the aborigines for the manufacture of their heavier implements, especially axes and the larger hammers. (w. h. h.)

Sierra Blanca (Span.: 'white mountain'). A Papago village, probably in Pima co., s. Ariz., with 50 inhabitants in 1858.

Sarra Blanco.—Davidson in Ind. Aff. Rep., 135, 1865. **Sierra Blanca.**—Bailey, ibid., 208, 1858.

Signals. The system of long-distance signaling in use among many tribes may be regarded as supplementary to the sign language (q. v.), and many of the signals were but adaptations of the corresponding gesture signs on a larger scale. Long-distance signals were naturally most in use and most highly systematized in the open country of the plains and the S. W., where the atmosphere is usually clear and the view unobstructed, and to a lesser degree along certain sandy beaches, as in Florida; but were rarely used, and then only in the simplest fashion, in the forest region or along such shores as that of the N. W. coast, where cloudiness was the prevailing atmospheric condition.

Signals were commonly conveyed by means of smoke, fire, or the movements of men either mounted or on foot. Their most frequent purpose was to indicate the presence of game or of danger, or to define the intentions of an approaching party. Signals by means of fires built at convenient observation points were most frequent at night and along the coast, and were usually simple alarm fires, serving rather to announce the event than to disclose its nature. The fire might mean the stranding of a whale or the approach of a boatload of strangers, and the watchers in the distant village at once prepared for either emergency, according to their expectation. If they were on the lookout for food or plunder they came prepared; if they dreaded an enemy they fled until they thought the danger had passed. The narratives of the early explorers along the southern coasts make frequent allusions to such signal fires. Methods of setting fire to an enemy's camp or fortified village by means of lighted combustibles attached to arrows were in general use down to a recent period, but the statement by one author that the Sioux had an elaborate system of signaling at night by means of fiery arrows requires confirmation.

Smoke signals by day were used over a wide area of the western country, and were reduced to a regular system by means of which many different details of information could be conveyed across miles of distance. The fire was built on some commanding elevation, the combustible used being damp grass, weeds, cedar tops, or some similar material which would burn slowly and throw out a dense smoke. The fire, after having been lighted, was first allowed to burn for some time without hindrance until it was evident or probable that it had attracted the attention of those at a distance for whom it was intended. The signaler then proceeded with the message by throwing his blanket over the smoldering pile so as to confine the smoke, and then withdrawing it, allowing a single balloon-like puff of smoke to ascend toward the sky. This was repeated again and again until by the number, length, or continued succession of the smoke puffs the watchers in camp knew whether buffalo or an approaching enemy had been discovered, whether they must flee for safety, or hurry with all speed to the attack or rescue. The signal was the more surely noted by reason of the fact that the Indians were almost constantly on the watch and that certain commanding lookout points in the neighborhood of every regular camping place were recognized as regular signal stations. Returning war parties among the Pima and some other tribes of that region were accustomed to give advance notice of the number of scalps taken by means of a corresponding number of fires built within view of the home camp. Among the Omaha the returning successful war party sent up smoke signals when near the home camp, while on coming in sight of their friends the number of warriors lost was indicated by having the same number of men turn successively to one side and drop to the ground (La Flesche). The Apache sent up fire signals by firing the resinous spines on the tall trunks of the giant saguaro cactus (*Cereus giganteus*). The timber tribes of the E., on the contrary, made similar announcement by means of the long-drawn scalp halloo.

Motion signals were made either on horse or foot, and frequently with the aid of the blanket which the Indian warrior almost always wore about his shoulders or twisted around his waist. In many cases, as has been said, they were simply adaptations from the ordinary sign language, and were frequently extremely picturesque in execution. The ordinary signal of "discovery" was made by riding in a circle, not because the circle in itself indicated anything in this connection, but because such a movement was most sure to be distinguishable from any direction. When it was seen from the bustle in camp to have attracted attention, it was followed by the specific signal for "buffalo" or "enemy," the two most constant ideas in the mind of the western nomad. The buffalo sign might be made to do duty for any other large game or even in late times for a

herd of range cattle, while the absence of either sign after the discovery signal indicated the proximity of a friendly party. The "buffalo" signal was made by holding the open blanket at the two corners with the arms outstretched above the head and gracefully bringing it down toward the ground. The "enemy" signal was made by confused and rapid riding back and forth after the first discovery signal. It was also made by waving the outstretched blanket several times rapidly above the head. Among the Omaha and some other tribes the "discovery" signal was made by riding from side to side, or by running in the same way, if on foot, the motion being known by terms signifying approximately "showing" or "zigzagging." The false or dishonest making of this signal was severely punished (La Flesche). The "alarm" signal was made by throwing the blanket into the air several times in quick succession. The signal for "coast clear" was given by gently waving the open blanket from side to side in front of the body. Returning war parties or parties of scouts often with robe or blanket signaled success or failure, and in the latter case the number of men that the party had lost. Other signals, more or less easily understood, indicated "come," "halt," "friend," "defiance," etc. On those accidental occasions where the discoverer was without either horse or blanket, he might give the alarm from a distance by throwing up handfuls of dust. The Sioux, and perhaps other northern plains tribes, in later times had a system of heliograph signals by means of mirrors.

The drum signal, for calling the people together on ceremonial occasions and for marking the changes in the performance, was probably universal. Signal calls, as the "journey halloo" of an expedition on starting out, the "scalp halloo," the "death halloo," etc., were in general use among the Eastern tribes. On Kodiak and the Aleutian ids. of Alaska, according to Miss A. C. Fletcher, strangers halted at a recognized station to signal to the distant village and then sat down to await the arrival of the receiving party, occupying themselves in the meantime in fashioning stone lamps from material always kept on deposit at such places. Farther s. along the same coast, as early as 1787, explorers noted the peace signal made from an approaching canoe by blowing into the air the white down feathers of the eagle, or displaying a tuft of white feathers from a pole set up at the head of the canoe. The various social signals, used by children at play, by lovers, and by others in the home camps, were too diverse for description.

Closely akin to signals were the various trail marks used to indicate the passing of a traveler or party, the occurrence of some notable incident, etc. These varied from the simple bending of a twig, blazing of a tree, or piling of stones, to the elaborate pictograph set in some conspicuous place, or the symbolic declaration of war among the Eastern tribes, particularly in the Gulf states, by setting up red-painted arrows along the trail near the enemy's village, along with the totemic symbol of the attacking tribe, or leaving in plain view a red-painted tomahawk with a scalp attached.   (J. M.)

Sign language. A system of gestures in use by the Indians of the plains for intercommunication among tribes speaking different languages. Traces of such a system have been found among the former tribes of E. United States, in the Canadian northwest, and in Mexico, but as commonly known the sign language belongs to the tribes between the Missouri and the Rocky mts. and from Fraser r., Brit. Col., s. to the Rio Grande. It seems never to have extended w. of the mountains, excepting among the Nez Percés and other tribes accustomed to make periodic hunting excursions into the plains, nor to have attained any high development among the sedentary tribes in the eastern timber region, being superseded in these sections by some mother dialect or trade jargon. In the great treeless area of the plains, stretching nearly 2,000 m. from N. to S. and occupied by tribes of many different stocks, all constantly shifting about in pursuit of the buffalo herds and thus continually brought into friendly meeting or hostile collision, the necessities of nomadic life resulted in the evolution of a highly developed system of gesture communication which, for all ordinary purposes, hardly fell short of the perfection of a spoken language.

In its evolution the sign language appears to have followed the same lines along which, according to the theory of most philologists, human speech developed, viz, a gradual progress from the representative to the conventional, from the picture to the arbitrary symbol, the sign language, however, being still chiefly in the representative or pantomimic stage. It may, in fact, be described as a motional equivalent of the Indian pictograph, the conventional sign being usually a close reference to the predominant characteristic of the object in shape, habit, or purpose. The signs are made almost entirely with the hands, either one or both. Minor differences exist, like dialects in spoken languages, the differences being naturally greatest at the two extremes of the sign-language area, but even with these slight dissimilarities a Sioux or a Blackfoot from the

upper Missouri has no difficulty in communicating with a visiting Kiowa or Comanche from the Texas border on any subject from the negotiating of a treaty to the recital of a mythic story or the telling of a hunting incident. The claim of any particular tribe to having invented the system may be set down as mere boasting, but it is universally admitted that the Crows, Cheyenne, and Kiowa are most expert in its use; and the tribes E. and W. of the central area, viz, the Omaha, Kansa, Osage, and others near the Missouri, and the Ute and Shoshoni in the mountains, know less of it. In fluent grace of movement a conversation in the sign language between a Cheyenne and a Kiowa is the very poetry of motion.

As has been stated, the signs in every case are founded on some tangible or symbolic characteristic, although by abbreviation or "wearing down," as in a spoken language, the resemblance has frequently been obscured and conventionalized. Thus the sign for *man* is made by throwing out the hand, back outward, with index finger extended upward, apparently having reference to an old root word in many Indian languages which defines *man* as the erect animal. *Woman* is indicated by a sweeping downward movement of the hand at the side of the head, with fingers extended toward the hair to denote long flowing hair or the combing of flowing locks. A *white man* is distinguished as the hat wearer, either by drawing the index finger across the forehead or by clasping the forehead with outstretched thumb and index finger. For *Indian* the speaker rubs the back of his left hand, or, perhaps, his cheek, with the palm of the right to indicate a person whose skin is of the same color. The sign having obtained this conventional meaning, it may be used equally by a white man to convey the same idea. Each tribe is designated by a special sign combination, usually the equivalent of the common name in the various spoken languages. Thus for *Blackfoot* the speaker touches his moccasin and then rubs his fingers upon something black. For *Ute* he makes the sign for black man. For *Pawnee*, the "Wolf people" of the Plains tribes, he throws up the right hand, with two fingers apart and pointing upward and forward, at the side of his head, to indicate erect ears of a wolf, following this with the sign for man, as already explained. Another suggested interpretation is "Horn people" from a peculiar scalp-lock formerly worn by the Pawnee. A *tipi* is shown by bringing both index fingers together like an inverted V ($\wedge$), to indicate the conical shape and the crossing of the poles. An ordinary house would be distinguished by adding the sign for white man. The *buffalo*, and in later days a *cow*, is indicated by crooking the index finger at the side of the head to resemble a horn. A *dog* is indicated by drawing the hand, with first and second fingers spread apart, across in front of the body, typifying the old time travois dragged by the animal when used as a beast of burden.

Eating and *drinking* are indicated by signs easily intelligible. *Sleeping* is indicated by inclining the head to one side, with the open palm held just below, typifying the recumbent attitude of repose. As days, or rather nights, are counted by "sleeps," the same sign may mean a *day* when used in connection with enumeration, indicated by the motion of counting upon the fingers. In the same way *cold* is indicated by a shivering movement of the clenched hands in front of the body, and as Indians count years by winters or "cold" seasons, it signifies also a *year* in another context. The hand upright and turned upon the wrist, with fingers apart and extended, indicates the *question sign*, and a somewhat similar but slower gesture means *vacillation*, i. e. *may be*.

Reduced to action, the question, "How old are you?" becomes (1) point finger at subject=*you;* (2) cold sign=*winter, year;* (3) counting sign=*number;* (4) question sign=*how many?* An expert can go through the whole movement in about the time required to put the spoken question, with the advantage that he can be understood by an Indian of any language from Canada to Texas.

Some signs are beautifully symbolic. Thus, *fatigue* is shown by a downward and outward sweep of the two hands in front of the body, index fingers extended, giving a gesture-picture of utter collapse. *Bad* is indicated by a motion of throwing away; *truth* by signs for straight talk, and *falsehood* by the talk sign, with another for *different directions*, i. e. "talking two ways."

Besides the hand gestures, there is also a signal system for communicating on war or hunting expeditions by means of smoke, waving of a blanket, riding in a circle, etc., to indicate discovering enemies, buffalo, advance, retreat, etc. See *Signals*.

The best practical treatise on the subject is Capt. W. P. Clark's Indian Sign Language, 1885. A philosophic and comparative presentation is given by Col. Garrick Mallery in 1st Rep. B. A. E., 1881.   (J. M.)

Siguniktawak ('inhabitants of C. Chignecto,' from *sigunikt*, 'foot cloth,' the native name of the cape). A Micmac band on a reservation near Parrsborough, Cumberland co., Nova Scotia. The number connected with the agency was 95 in 1909.

Siguniktawak. A Micmac band in Pictou co., Nova Scotia (Rand, Micmac Reading Bk., 81, 1875). The Micmac now in this county occupy the Fisher's Grant and Indian Island reserves and numbered 174 in 1909.

Sigwaahsohgwih. See *Sequidongquee*.

Sihasapa ('black feet', so called because they wore black moccasins). A small division of the Teton Sioux. The name, like the names of some other Teton tribes, does not appear to have come into notice

PEZHI, "GRASS," A SIHASAPA OR BLACKFOOT SIOUX

until a recent date, no mention being made of it by Lewis and Clark, Long, or earlier authorities. Catlin in his Letters and Notes, written during his stay among the northwestern Indians (1832–39), mentions the Blackfoot Sioux. In a note to De Smet's Letters (1843) they were estimated to number 1,500. Culbertson (Smithson. Rep. 1850, 141, 1851) estimated the tribe at 450 lodges, an exaggeration, and mentions five bands or subtribes, but does not locate them. It was not until Gen. Warren and Dr.

Hayden visited their country that definite information in regard to them was obtained. The former (1856) makes the following brief notes: "Sihasapas Blackfeet. Haunts and homes same as the Unkpapas; number, 165 lodges. These two bands have very little respect for the power of the whites. . . . Many of the depredations along the Platte are committed by the Unkpapas and Sihasapas, whose homes are farther from it than those of any other of the Titonwans." Hayden (1862) says that they, the Hunkpapa and Sans Arcs, "occupy nearly the same district, and are so often encamped near each other, and otherwise so connected in their operations, as scarcely to admit of being treated of separately. That part of the country under their control lies along the Moreau, Cannonball, Heart, and Grand rs., seldom extending very high up on Grand r., but of late years reaching to the Little Missouri [in North Dakota]. Although the bands just mentioned are often stationed near each other, they are sometimes found several days' journey apart, and each is headed by its own chief." His estimate is 220 lodges. Subsequently the Sihasapa were gathered partly at Cheyenne River res., S. Dak., and partly at Standing Rock res., N. Dak. The number on the former in 1878 was 224, and on the latter 590, a total of 814. They are no longer separately reported. J. O. Dorsey mentions the following bands: 1, Sihasapakhcha; 2, Kanghishunpegnaka; 3, Glaglahecha; 4, Wazhazhe; 5, Hohe; 6, Wamnughaoin. Swift (1884) gives the same divisions, except that he omits Glaglahecha and includes Tizaptan. The first and third were given in a list of bands by Culbertson (1850), who enumerates also the Cuts, Those That Camp Next To The Last, Tashunkeota, and Devil's Medicineman Band.

Blackfeet.—Culbertson in Smithson. Rep. 1850, 105, 1851. Blackfeet Dakotas.—Hayden, Ethnog. and Philol. Mo. Val., 290, 1862. Black-feet Scioux.—De Smet, Letters, 23, 1843. Blackfeet Sioux.—Stanley in Poole, Among the Sioux, app., 232, 1881. Blackfeet Tetons.—Corliss, Lacotah MS. vocab., B. A. E., 107, 1874. Blackfoot Dakotas.—Morgan in N. Am. Rev., 44, Jan. 1870. Blackfoot Sioux.—Catlin, N. Am. Inds., I, 223, 1844. Moh-ta'-wa-tata'-ni-o.—Hayden, Ethnog. and Philol. Mo. Val., 290, 1862 (Cheyenne name). Se-ä'-sä-pä.—Morgan, Systems of Consang., 284, 1871. Se-ash-ha-pa.—Brackett in Smithson. Rep. 1876, 466, 1877. Sihasapa.—Riggs, Dak. Gram. and Dict., vii, 1852. Si-há-sa-pa.—Brackett in Smithson. Rep. 1876, 466, 1877. Sisapapa.—Blackmore in Jour. Ethnol. Soc. Lond., I, 302, 1869 (misprint).

Sihasapakhcha (Blackfeet proper). A Sihasapa band.

Black footed ones.—Culbertson in Smithson. Rep. 1850, 141, 1851. Siha-sapa-qtca.—Dorsey in 15th Rep. B. A. E., 219, 1897. Sihasapa-rca.—Swift, letter to Dorsey, 1884.

Sihimi. A former Chumashan village near Purísima mission, Santa Barbara co., Cal.—Taylor in Cal. Farmer, Oct. 18, 1861.

Sihu. The Flower or Bush clan of the Hopi, q. v.

Sihu winwû.—Fewkes in 19th Rep. B. A. E., 583, 1901 (winwü='clan'). Si'-hü wün-wü.—Fewkes in Am. Anthr., VII, 404, 1894.

Sihuicom. A former Chumashan village near Santa Barbara, Cal.—Taylor in Cal. Farmer, Apr. 24, 1863.

Sii (Si'-i). The Ant clans of the Keresan pueblos of Acoma, Sia, and San Felipe, N. Mex. Those of Acoma and Sia are extinct. The forms of the name thus vary in pronunciation: Acoma, Siíhánoq^ch; Sia, Sii-háno; San Felipe, Siíháno (háno, etc., = 'people').—Hodge in Am. Anthr., IX, 348, 1896.

ʋZi-i.—Stevenson in 11th Rep. B. A. E., 19, 1894 (Sia form).

Sijame. A tribe, either Tonkawan or Coahuiltecan, represented in considerable numbers between 1719 and 1763 at San Antonio de Valero mission, Texas. It was mentioned as early as 1716 by Espinosa, who encountered some of its members in a rancheria in central Texas with Pamaya, Payaya, Xarame, and others (Diario, MS. in Archivo Gen., Prov. Intern., CLXXXI). In 1727 Rivera listed them as a tribe of Coahuila, which, if he were correct, would place them w. of San Antonio (Diario, leg. 2763, 1736). They are also given by Orozco y Berra as a Coahuila tribe (Geog., 306, 1864), but other evidence seems rather to place them farther E.

A child of gentile Sijames was baptized at San Antonio de Valero as early as 1719, the second year of the mission's existence (Valero Bautismos, partida 47, 1719). Baptisms of members of the tribe are recorded there as late as 1761, and burials as late as 1763 (ibid., partida 1469; Entierros, partida 1212). Before 1740 the number of the tribe coming to the mission was small, but in that year they entered in considerable numbers, apparently coming with the Sana, Mayeye, Emet, Tuu, Ervipiame, Caguas (Cavas), Zorquan, and others. This close association with the tribes named is an indication of a central Texas habitat and of Tonkawan affiliation. On this point see *Sana*. A considerable list of personal names of members of the above tribes has been preserved and will probably make it possible to settle definitely their linguistic affinity. Names of some members of the Sijame tribe, represented by Spanish orthography, were as follows: Pererqueguita, Amatmesat, Teamo, Cinmaiaia, Apenujume, Pautenejera, Tecumerea, Ostaia, Pozoa, Maiaya, Comecaguagua, and Ameterajera. All but the last two names were of men or boys, these two being of women. (H. E. B.)

Cijame.—Valero Bautismos, partida 492, 1739 MS. Gijames.—Morfi (1777) quoted by Bancroft, Nat. Races, I, 611, 1886. Hijames.—Revillagigedo (1793), ibid. Sicxacames.—Orozco y Berra, Geog., 302, 1864. Sijame.—Espinosa, Diario, 1716, MS. Sixame.—Valero Bautismos, partida 114, 1722.

Xijame.—Ibid., 331, 1731.   Xixame.—Valero Entierros, partida 182, 1732.   Zijame.—Valero Bautismos, partida 526, 1741.

Sikak. See *Skunk*.

Sikanasankian (*S!íkɅnas!ā′nk!í-ān*,
'small-black-bear town'). A Tlingit
town of the Taku people, on Taku inlet,
Alaska.   (J. R. S.)

Sikitipuc. A former Chumashan village near Santa Inés mission, Santa Barbara co., Cal.—Taylor in Cal. Farmer,
Oct. 18, 1861.

Siknahadi ('people of Sinak'). A Tlingit division of the Wolf phratry, at Wrangell, Alaska. They are said to have received their name from a place called
S!ī′nɅx, where they stopped on their way
from the N.   (J. R. S.)
Sick-naa-hulty.—Kane, Wand. in N. A., app., 1859.
Siknaq'a′dē.—Boas. 5th Rep. N. W. Tribes Can.,
25, 1889.   S!īknaxa′dî.— Swanton, field notes,
B. A. E., 1904.   Ssĭk-nachădí.—Krause, Tlinkit
Ind., 120, 1885.

Sikokitsimiks ('black doors'). A band
of the Piegan division of the Siksika.
Black Doors.—Grinnell, Blackfoot Lodge Tales,
225, 1892.   Si-kŏh′-i-tsim.—Hayden, Ethnog. and
Philol. Mo. Val., 264, 1862 (trans. 'band with black
doors').   Sik′-o-kĭt-sim-iks.—Grinnell, op. cit.,
209.

Sikopoksimaiks ('black-fat roasters').
A band of the Piegan division of the
Siksika.
Black Fat Roasters.—Grinnell, Blackfoot Lodge
Tales, 225, 1892.   Sik-o-pok′-si-maiks.—Ibid., 209.

Sikosuilak. A settlement of the Sikosuilarmiut Eskimo E. of King cape, Baffin
land.
Sikosuilaq.—Boas in 6th Rep. B. A. E., 421, 1888.

Sikosuilarmiut ('inhabitants of the
shore without an ice floe'). An Eskimo
tribe inhabiting the region about King
cape, s. w. Baffin land. They are settled
in two places, Nurata and Sikosuilak.
Sekoselar.—Gilder, Schwatka's Search, 181, 1881.
Sekoselar Innuits.—Nourse, Am. Explor., 200, 1884.
Sicosuilarmiut.—Boas in Trans. Anthr. Soc.
Wash., 95, 1884.   Sikosuilarmiut.—Boas in 6th Rep.
B. A. E., 421, 1888.   Ssikossuilar-miut.—Boas in
Deutsche Geog. Blätt., VIII, no. 1, 1885.

Siksahpuniks ('black blood'). A band
of the Kainah division of the Siksika.
Blackblood.—Grinnell, Blackfoot Lodge Tales, 209,
1892.   Siks-ah′-pun-iks.—Ibid.

Siksatok. A former Aleut village on
Agattu id., Alaska, one of the Near id.
groups of the Aleutians, now uninhabited.

Siksika ('black feet', from *siksinam*
'black', *ka* the root of *oqkatsh* 'foot'. The
origin of the name is disputed, but it is
commonly believed to have reference to
the discoloring of their moccasins by the
ashes of the prairie fires; it may possibly
have reference to black-painted moccasins,
such as were worn by the Pawnee, Sihasapa, and other tribes). An important
Algonquian confederacy of the northern
plains, consisting of three subtribes, the
Siksika proper or Blackfeet, the Kainah or
Bloods, and the Piegan, the whole body
being popularly known as Blackfeet. In
close alliance with these are the Atsina
and the Sarsi.

Within the recent historic period, until
gathered upon reservations, the Blackfeet held most of the immense territory
stretching almost from North Saskatchewan r., Canada, to the southern head-
streams of the Missouri in Montana, and
from about lon. 105° to the base of the
Rocky mts. A century earlier, or about
1790, they were found by Mackenzie occupying the upper and middle South Saskatchewan, with the Atsina on the lower
course of the same stream, both tribes
being apparently in slow migration toward
the N. W. (Mackenzie, Voy., lxx–lxxi,
1801). This would make them the van-
guard of the Algonquian movement from
the Red r. country. With the exception
of a temporary occupancy by invading
Cree, this extreme northern region has
always, within the historic period, been
held by Athapascan tribes. The tribe is
now settled on three reservations in Alberta, Canada, and one in N. W. Montana,
about half being on each side of the inter-
national boundary.

So far as history and tradition go, the
Blackfeet have been roving buffalo
hunters, dwelling in tipis and shifting
periodically from place to place, without
permanent habitations, without the pottery art or canoes, and without agriculture excepting for the sowing and gathering of a species of native tobacco. They
also gathered the camas root in the foothills. Their traditions go back to a time
when they had no horses and hunted their
game on foot; but as early as Mackenzie's
time, before 1800, they already had many
horses, taken from tribes farther to the
s., and later they became noted for their
great horse herds. It is entirely probable that their spread over the plains
region was due largely to the acquisition
of the horse, and, about the same time, of
the gun. They were a restless, aggressive,
and predatory people, and, excepting for
the Atsina and Sarsi, who lived under
their protection, were constantly at war
with all their neighbors, the Cree, Assiniboin, Sioux, Crows, Flatheads, and Kutenai. While never regularly at war with
the United States, their general attitude
toward Americans in the early days was
one of hostility, while maintaining a
doubtful friendship with the Hudson's
Bay Co.

Their culture was that of the Plains
tribes generally, although there is evidence of an earlier culture, approximately
that of the Eastern timber tribes. The 3
main divisions seem to have been independent of each other, each having its
own Sun dance, council, and elective head-
chief, although the Blackfeet proper appear to have been the original nucleus.
Each of the 3 was subdivided into a number of bands, of which Grinnell enumerates 45 in all. It has been said that these

bands were gentes, but if so, their gentile character is no longer apparent. There is also a military and fraternal organization, similar to that existing in other Plains tribes, known among the Blackfeet as the *Ikunuhkahtsi*, or 'All Comrades,' and consisting formerly, according to Grinnell, of at least 12 orders or societies, most of which are now extinct. They have a great number of dances—religious, war, and social—besides secret societies for various purposes, together with many "sacred bundles," around each of which centers a ritual. Practically every adult has also his personal "medicine." Both sexes may be members of some societies. Their principal deities are the Sun, and a supernatural being known as Napi, 'Old Man,' who may be an incarnation of the same idea. The dead are usually deposited in trees or sometimes laid away in tipis erected for the purpose on prominent hills.

As usual, many of the early estimates of Blackfoot population are plainly unreliable. The best appears to be that of Mackenzie, who estimated them about 1790 at 2,250 to 2,500 warriors, or perhaps 9,000 souls. In 1780–81, in 1837–38, in 1845, in 1857–58, and in 1869 they suffered great losses by smallpox. In 1864 they were reduced by measles, and in 1883–84 some 600 of those in Montana died of sheer starvation in consequence of the sudden extinction of the buffalo coincident with a reduction of rations. The official Indian report for 1858 gave them 7,300 souls, but another estimate, quoted by Hayden as having been made "under the most favorable circumstances" about the same time, gives them 2,400 warriors and 6,720 souls. In 1909 they were officially reported to number in all 4,635, viz: Blackfoot agency, Alberta, 795; Blood agency, Alberta, 1,174; Piegan agency, Alberta, 471; Blackfoot agency (Piegan), Montana, 2,195.

Consult Grinnell, Blackfoot Lodge Tales, 1892; Hayden, Ethnog. and Philol. Mo. Val., 1862; Schultz, My Life as an Indian, 1907; Wissler (1) in Ontario Archæol. Rep. for 1905, 1906, (2) in Anthr. Pap. Am. Mus. Nat. Hist., v, pt. 1, 1910. (J. M.)

Ah-hi'-tä-pe.—Morgan, Consang. and Affin., 289, 1871 (former name for themselves; trans. 'bold people'). **Ayatchinini.**—Baraga, Eng.-Otch. Dict., 29, 1878 (Chippewa name). **Ayâtchiyiniw.**—Lacombe, Dict. Langue Cris, 325, 1864 ('stranger,' 'alien,' 'enemy': Cree name for Siksika, Bloods, and Piegan). **Beaux Hommes.**—Dobbs, Hudson Bay, 35, 1744. **Blackfeet.**—Writer of 1786 in Mass. Hist. Soc. Coll., 1st s., III, 24, 1794. **Blackfoot.**—Lewis and Clark, Discov., 58, 1806. **Carmeneh.**—Crow MS. vocab., B. A. E. (Crow name). **Choch-Katit.**—Maximilian, Trav., II, 247, 1841 (Arikara name). **Chokitapia.**—L'Heureux in Jour. Anthr. Inst., G. B., 162, Nov. 1885. **Cuskœtehwaw-thesseetuck.**—Franklin, Journ. Polar Sea, 97, 1824. **É-chĭp-é-tä.**—Long, Exped. Rocky Mts., II, lxxix, 1823 (Crow name). **Erchipeetay.**—Gallatin in Trans. Am. Antiq. Soc., II, 377, 1836

(Crow name). **High-minded people.**—Morgan, Consang. and Affin., 289, 1871. **Ish-te-pit'-e.**—Hayden, Ethnog. and Philol. Mo. Val., 402, 1862 (Crow name). **Issi-Chupicha.**—Maximilian, Trav., II, 234, 1841 (Hidatsa name; French form). **Issi-Schüpischa.**—Ibid. (Hidatsa name; German form). **Itsisihisa.**—Matthews, Hidatsa Inds., 217, 1877 (Hidatsa name). **Ĭ tsi śí pi śa.**—Ibid., 162 (Hidatsa name: 'black feet,' from *śipiśa* 'black,' and *ĭtsi* 'foot'). **It-zĕ-sŭ-pĕ-shä.**—Long, Exped. Rocky Mts., II, lxxxiv, 1823 (Hidatsa name). **Katœ.**—Wilson, Rep. on N. W. Tribes to Brit. A. A. S. 11, 1888 (Sarsi name). **Ka-wi'-na-han.**—Hayden, Ethnog. and Philol. Mo. Val., 326, 1862 ('black people': Arapaho name). **Makadewana-ssidok.**—Gatschet, Ojibwa MS., B. A. E., 1882 (Chippewa name). **Mämakatä'wana-si'tä'-ak.**—Gatschet, Fox MS., B. A. E., 1882 (Fox name). **Mkatewetitéta.**—Gatschet, Shawnee MS., B. A. E., 1879 (Shawnee name; pl. Mkatewetitetchki). **Mukkudda Ozitunnug.**—Tanner Narr., 316, 1830 (Ottawa name). **Netsepoyè.**—Hale in Rep. Brit. A. A. S. 1885, 707, 1886 ('people who speak one language': name sometimes used by the confederacy). **Pahkee.**—Lewis and Clark, Exped., I, 408, 1814 (Shoshoni name). **Paìk.**—Gebow, Snake Vocab., 7, 1868. **Par'-keeh.**—Stuart, Montana As It Is, 23, 1865. **Patas-negras.**—Barriero, Ojeada sobre Nuevo México, app., 10, 1832. **Pawkees.**—Lewis and Clark, Exped., I, 418, 1814. **Peíki.**—Gebow, Snake Vocab., 7, 1868. **Pieds-noirs.**—De Smet, Miss., 84, 1844. **Pike.**—Gebow, Snake Vocab., 7, 1868 (Shoshoni name). **Po'-o-mas.**—Hayden, Ethnog. and Philol. Mo. Val., 290, 1862 ('blankets whitened with earth': Cheyenne name). **Sähä'ntlä.**—A. F. Chamberlain, inf'n, 1903 ('bad people': Kutenai name). **Sâketûpiks.**—McLean, Inds., 130, 1889. **Sasitka.**—Schoolcraft, Ind. Tribes, VI, 688, 1857. **Sat-siaqua.**—Robinson, Gt. Fur Land, 187, 1879. **Satsikaa.**—Hale, Ethnol. and Philol., 219, 1846. **Sawketakix.**—Hale in Rep. Brit. A. A. S. 1885, 707, 1886 ('men of the plains': name sometimes used by themselves). **Saxœ-kœ-koon.**—Franklin, Journ. Polar Sea, 97, 1824. **S'chkoé.**—Mengarini, Kalispelm Dict., B. A. E., 1877 (Kalispel name; abbreviated form). **S'chkoéishin.**—Ibid. (Kalispel name, from *kodi,* 'black'). **Schwarzfüssige.**—Güssefeld, map, 1797. **Seksekai.**—Maximilian, Trav., 245, 1843. **Sicá'bê.**—Dorsey, Kansas MS. vocab., B. A. E., 1882 (Kansa name). **Si-ha'-sa-pa.**—Cook, Yankton MS. vocab., B. A. E., 1882 ('black feet': Yankton name). **Sikcitano.**—Can. Ind. Aff., 125, 1902. **Siksekai.**—Maximilian, Trav., 245, 1843. **Sik-si-ka'.**—Hayden, Ethnog. and Philol. Mo. Val., 264, 1862. **Siksikai.**—Maximilian (1839) quoted by Hayden, ibid., 256. **Sikskékuanak.**—Hale, Ethnol. and Philol., 219, 1846. **Sitkeas.**—Schoolcraft, Ind. Tribes, III, 252, 1853. **Six-he-kie-koon.**—Henry, MS. vocab., 1808. **Sixikau'a.**—Tims, Blackfoot Gram. and Dict., 112, 1889. **Skuäíshèni.**—Gatschet, Okinagan MS., B. A. E., 1883 ('black foot': Salish name). **Stχuaíχn.**—Ibid. ('black': Okinagan name). **Toñkoñko.**—Mooney in 17th Rep. B. A. E., I, 426, 1898 ('black legs': Kiowa name). **Tuhu'vti-ómokat.**—Gatschet, Comanche MS., B. A. E., 1884 (Comanche name, from *tuhúvti* 'black'). **Wateni'hte.**—Gatschet, Arapaho MS., B. A. E., 1882 (Arapaho name). **Yatcheé-thinyoowuc.**—Richardson quoted by Franklin, Journ. Polar Sea, 96, 1824 ('strangers': Cree name for several tribes, including the Siksika).

Siksika. A tribe of the Siksika confederacy (q. v.). They now live on a reservation in Alberta, Canada, on upper Bow r., and are officially known as the Running Rabbit and Yellow Horse bands. They were divided into the following subtribes or bands: Aisikstukiks, Apikaiyiks, Emitahpahksaiyiks, Motahtosiks, Puhksinahmahyiks, Saiyiks, Siksinokaks, Tsiniktsistsoyiks. Pop. 942 in 1902, 795 in 1909.

Siksinokaks ('black elks'). A subtribe or band of the Kainah division of the

Siksika or Blackfeet, and also of the Siksika proper.

Black Elks.—Grinnell, Blackfoot Lodge Tales, 208, 209, 1892. **Sik-si-no′-kai-īks.**—Hayden, Ethnog. and Philol. Mo. Val., 264, 1862. **Siks-in′-o-kaks.**—Grinnell, op. cit.

Siksinokaks. A subtribe or band of the Siksika.

Siks-in′-o-kaks.—Grinnell, Blackfoot Lodge Tales, 208, 1892.

Siktokkis. A town of the Ahousaht Nootka on the N. arm of Clayoquot sd., Vancouver id. It was destroyed by Admiral Denham in Oct. 1864 in punishment for the killing of the crew of the trading schooner *Kingfisher*.

Sik-tok-kis.—Sproat, Savage life, 197, 1868.

Sikutsipumaiks ('black patched moccasins'). A band of the Piegan division of the Siksika or Blackfeet.

Black Patched Moccasins.—Grinnell, Blackfoot Lodge Tales, 225, 1892. **Si-ka′-tsi-po-maks.**—Hayden, Ethnog. and Philol. Mo. Val., 264, 1862 (trans. 'band with black patched moccasins'). **Sik-ut′-si-pum-aiks.**—Grinnell, op. cit., 209.

Sikwayi. See *Sequoya.*

Sikyachi. The name of two distinct Yellow Bird clans of the Hopi, one belonging to the Kachina, the other to the Kokop phratry.

Si-kya′-tci.—Stephen in 8th Rep. B. A. E., 39, 1891. **Sikyatci wiñwû.**—Fewkes in 19th Rep. B. A. E., 584, 1900. **Si-kya-tci wüñ-wü.**—Fewkes in Am. Anthr., VII, 404, 1894.

Sikyataiyo. The Yellow Fox clan of the Hopi.

Si-kah-ta-ya.—Dorsey and Voth, Mishongnovi Ceremonies, 175, 1902. **Sikáhtayo.**—Voth, Hopi Proper Names, 105, 1905. **Sikyataiyo wiñwû.**—Fewkes in 19th Rep. B. A. E., 584, 1900. **Si-kya′-tai-yo wüñ-wû.**—Fewkes in Am. Anthr., VII, 403, 1894.

Sikyatki ('yellow house'). A prehistoric pueblo of the Firewood (Kokop) people of the Hopi, situated on two rocky knolls at the E. base of the Walpi mesa of Tusayan, N. E. Arizona. According to tradition it was built by the Firewood clans after the abandonment of their pueblo of Tebugkihu, and in turn was destroyed by warriors from Walpi and possibly from other Hopi pueblos. See Fewkes in Am. Anthr., VII, 396, 406, 1894, and in 17th Rep. B. A. E., 631–744, 1898; Mindeleff in 8th Rep. B. A. E., 20, 1891.

Si-kā′k-i.—Fewkes in Am. Anthr., V, 10, 1892.

Silela (*Ts'ä′-lil-ä*). A former village of the Kuitsh on lower Umpqua r., w. Oreg. Mentioned by Lewis and Clark in 1806 as a tribe of 1,200.

Isalleet.—Gairdner (1835) in Jour. Geog. Soc. Lond., XI, 256, 1841. **Sahlalah.**—McVickar, Hist. Exped. Lewis and Clark, II, 383, 1842. **Shalalahs.**—Lewis and Clark, Exped., II, 119, 1814. **Shallalah.**—Ibid., 474. **Silela.**—Dorsey in Jour. Am. Folk-lore, III, 231, 1890. **Tsalél.**—Hale, Ethnol. and Philol., 221, 1846. **Ts'ä′-lil-ä.**—Dorsey in Jour. Am. Folk-lore, III, 231, 1890. **Tsan tchä′lila amím.**—Gatschet, Lakmiut MS., B. A. E., 105 (Lakmiut-Kalapuya name for Indians at mouth of Umpqua r.).

Siletz. A former Salishan tribe on a river of the same name in N. w. Oregon. It was the southernmost Salishan tribe on the coast. Latterly the name was extended to designate all the tribes on the Siletz res. in Oregon, which belong to the Athapascan, Yakonan, Kusan, Takilman, Shastan, and Shahaptian linguistic families.

Celetse.—Gibbs, MS. Notes, B. A. E., 1856. **Neselitch.**—Gairdner (1835) in Jour. Geog. Soc. Lond., XI, 255, 1841. **Sai-lĕto′.**—Dorsey, Tutu MS., B. A. E., 1884. **Sai-lĕto′-ĭc-me′-ɥûnnĕ.**—Dorsey, Naltûnneɥûnnĕ MS. vocab., B. A. E., 1884. **Siletz.**—Dorsey (1884) in Jour. Am. Folk-lore, III, 227, 1890. **Tsä Shnádsh amím.**—Gatschet, Lakmiut-Kalapuya MS., B. A. E., 105 (Lakmiut name).

Silimastus. A former Chumashan village near Purísima mission, Santa Barbara co., Cal.—Taylor in Cal. Farmer, Oct. 18, 1861.

Silimi. A former Chumashan village near Purísima mission, Santa Barbara co., Cal.—Taylor in Cal. Farmer, Oct. 18, 1861.

Silino. A former Chumashan village near Purísima mission, Santa Barbara co., Cal.—Taylor in Cal. Farmer, Oct. 18, 1861.

Silisne. A former Chumashan village near Purísima mission, Santa Barbara co., Cal.—Taylor in Cal. Farmer, Oct. 18, 1861.

Siliwihi. A former Chumashan village on Santa Rosa id., coast of California, E. of the harbor.—Henshaw, Buenaventura MS. vocab., B. A. E., 1884.

Silkhkemechetatun (*Sil′-qke-me′-tce-ta′-tûn*). A band or village of the Chastacosta on the N. side of Rogue r., Oreg.—Dorsey in Jour. Am. Folk-lore, III, 234, 1890.

Sillanguayas. A tribe given by Rivera in 1727 and by Orozco y Berra in 1864 as natives of Coahuila (Rivera, Diario, leg. 2763, 1736; Orozco y Berra, Geog., 306, 1864).

Siyanguayas.—Orozco y Berra, op. cit.

Sillery. A Jesuit mission village established in 1637 on St Lawrence r., a few miles above Quebec, Canada. The Algonkin and Montagnais were first gathered there and were joined at the close of King Philip's war in 1679 by Abnaki from Kennebec r. in Maine in such numbers that it soon became virtually an Abnaki village. In 1683–85 the inhabitants removed to St Francis, and the village was deserted. (J. M.)

Kamiskwawāngachit.—Vetromile in Me. Hist. Soc. Coll., VI, 213, 1859 ('where they catch salmon with the spear': Abnaki name). **Sciller.**—Lahontan (1703) quoted by Richardson, Arct. Exped., II, 39 1851. **Silem.**—Jefferys, Fr. Doms., pt. 1, map, 1761 (misprint). **Sillerie.**—Doc. of 1759 in N. Y. Doc. Col. Hist., X, 1037, 1858. **Sillery.**—Denonville (1687), ibid., IX, 354, 1855. **St. Joseph.**—Vetromile, op. cit. (mission name). **Syllery.**—Jefferys, Fr. Doms., pt. 1, 10, 1761.

Silongkoyo. A former Maidu village at Quincy, Plumas co., Cal.—Dixon in Bull. Am. Mus. Nat. Hist., XVII, map, 1905.

Silpoponemew. A former Chumashan village at San Antonio, about 4 m. from Santa Barbara mission, Cal.—Taylor in Cal. Farmer, May 4, 1860.

Silver. At the time of the discovery silver had not come into general use among the aborigines N. of Mexico. The native metal is found sparingly in many localities, notably in small bits in direct association with native copper in the L. Superior region, from which source a limited supply probably was obtained. Finds of objects of silver in the older mounds are rare. An interesting occurrence of silver in a mound in Pickaway co., Ohio, is mentioned by Fowke. In a stone box, 3½ in. long and 3 in. deep, made of the halves of two concretions fitted together, were five nuggets of silver about the size of small walnuts. Three were coated with black paint and 2 with reddish ocher. Prof. Putnam describes a number of objects of copper from the Turner mound, in Hamilton co., Ohio, plated with thin sheets of silver; and Dr Thomas illustrates 2 small, neatly cut objects of sheet silver which were found wrapped about a bit of cane along with a burial in a mound in Warren co., Pa. An interesting find of silver-plated objects in connection with a burial is described by Dr S. P. Hildreth and quoted by Squier. These consisted of large circular bosses composed of copper overlaid with a thick plating of silver on a ribbed plate of silver 2 in. in breadth and 6 in. length. Hildreth regarded these as probably part of a sword scabbard, but it is more likely that they are aboriginal ornaments. A number of disks and tablets of thin sheet silver and some other objects have been found in Florida, but it is believed that in the main they are recent, the metal having been derived from foreign sources—either from Europe direct or from vessels wrecked on the coast of Florida on the homeward voyage from Mexico. It is observed that some of these objects are alloyed with copper and gold in different proportions, and this is confirmative of western origin, alloys of gold, silver, and copper being common in middle America.

Some of the native tribes, under the influence of the whites, have turned their attention to silver working, and the Navaho and some of the Pueblos in Arizona and New Mexico, employing methods learned from the Mexicans, make many objects of use and ornament. The Iroquois, and the Haida and other N. W. coast tribes are also skilful metal workers, producing many tasteful ornaments, such as bracelets and pendants ornamented with engravings of mythical subjects. Silver was early introduced by colonial traders, and objects of this metal of European make are frequently found in the mounds, as well as on village sites in many sections of the country. These include necklaces, bracelets, brooches, lockets, rings, and especially crosses. See *Metal-work, Ornament.*

Consult Beauchamp in Bull. 73, N. Y. State Mus., 1903; Culin in Museum Notes, Brooklyn Inst., III, no. 7, 1908; Douglas in Am. Antiq., VII, no. 3, 1885; Fowke, Archæol. Hist. Ohio, 1902; Harrington, Iroquois Silverwork, Anthr. Pap. Am. Mus. Nat. Hist., I, pt. VI, 1908; Jones, Antiquities of Southern Indians, 1873; Kunz in Am. Antiq., IX, no. 4, 1887; Matthews in 2d Rep. B. A. E., 1883; Niblack in Nat. Mus. Rep. 1888, 1890; Putnam in 16th Rep. Peabody Mus., 1884; Rau, Archæol. Coll. Nat. Mus., 1876; Squier, Antiquities of N. Y. and the West, 1851; Thomas in 12th Rep. B. A. E., 1894. (w. h. h.)

Silver Bay. A summer camp of the Sitka, on Baranof id., Alaska; pop. 39 in 1880.—Petroff in Tenth Census, Alaska, 32, 1884.

Silver Bluff. A former Yuchi village on Savannah r. in Barnwell co., S. C., probably identical with Cofitachiqui of the De Soto narratives.—Georgia tract (1740) in Force, Tracts, I, 6, 1836.

Simaomo. A central Texas tribe or group, apparently Tonkawan, frequently mentioned by the Spaniards under the name of Cantona, or some variation of this name, in the later 17th and early 18th century records, but suddenly disappearing thereafter. It is quite probably a tribe known in later times by some other name, and one document seems to connect it with the Yojuane (q. v.). They are apparently distinct from the Indians referred to by the French writers as Canohatinno (see *Kanohatino*), for the latter were hostile to the Hasinai (Caddo), which evidently was not the case with the Simaomo.

The Cantona were definitely mentioned by Massanet in 1691 as one of the tribes living E. of Arroyo del Cibolo and speaking a language different from that of the Coahuiltecan tribes to the w. of that stream (Diario, MS. in Mem. de Nueva España, XXVII, 98). Tribes mentioned in the same connection were the Sanas, Emet, and Cavas. In the same year Jesus María, missionary among the Nabedache (q. v.), included the tribe, which he called the Cantauhaona, in his list of Texas, or "allies," living s. w. of his mission on the Neches (Relación, MS.). In 1692 it was proposed by Don Gregorio de Salinas, who had crossed Texas four times, that the missionaries among the Nabedache should retire to the Colorado and induce that tribe to settle between the Colorado and the Brazos "with the Cantona nation, which, for another name, is called Simaomo. They are a large nation and are friends of these [Nabedache] . . . They are together most of the year hunting buffalo, for which this is the center" (Salinas, Compendio de puntos, etc., 1692, MS.). In 1692 the Cantona were met on the Colorado by Terán (autos of the Terán Expedition, MS.). In 1693 Joseph Urrutia, later captain at San Antonio, was left disabled at the Colorado r. when the Spaniards retired. Being found by a body of "Cantujaunás, Toos, and Yemes [Emets]," he was rescued by the great chief Cantujauná, and taken to his rancheria, where he lived 7 years, becoming head-chief in their wars with the Apache, against whom, he claimed, he sometimes led 10,000 or 12,000 men (Urrutia to the Viceroy, July 4, 1733, MS.). Information recorded in 1709 connects the names Cantona and Simaomo with Yojuane. In April of that year Fr. San Buenaventura y Olivares and Fr. Isidro Felix de Espinosa were visited at the Colorado by a band of Indians composed mainly of "Yojuan," with some "Simomo" and "Tusolivi." Among them was the old Cantona chief known to the Spaniards since 1691, whom Espinosa now calls "the chief Canttona" and "the chief of the Yojuanes, called Canttona" (Diary, 1709, MS.). From this it would seem that the tribe formerly known as Cantona had been so called from the name of the principal chief, which was a common practice with the Spaniards. On the other hand, one can not fail to note the resemblance between the last part of the name Cantujauná and the tribal name Yojuan. The missionaries made a visit to the rancheria of these tribes, which was near by, and estimated its population at 2,500. They were on friendly terms with the Hasinai, to whom they agreed to carry a message (Espinosa, op. cit.). In 1716 Espinosa met Cantona Indians in a rancheria near the Brazos, with members of numerous other tribes (Diary, entries for June 10–13). Except for the baptism of one Cantona Indian in 1725 at the Ervipiame mission, this is the last we hear of the tribe under that name, though their old associates, the Emet, Too, Sanos, Cavas, and others are known much later. The passage in the diary of Espinosa, cited above, and the statement of Urrutia, cause one to wonder if the

Cantona were not a branch of the Yojuane more frequently heard of farther N. but who entered the San Xavier missions in this region in 1749. (H. E. B.)

Cantanual.—Valero Baptisms, 1725, MS. Cantauhaona.—Jesus María, Relación, 12, 1691, MS. Cantona.—Massanet, Diary, in Mem. de Nueva España, XXVII, 98, 1691, MS. Cantonáes, Espinosa (1716), op. cit. Cantujuaná.—Urrutia (1733), op. cit. Cantuna.—Terán, Descripción (1692) in Mem. de Nueva España, XXVII, 29, 42, MS. Simaomo.—Salinas, op. cit., 1692. Simomo.—Espinosa (1709), op. cit.

Simi. A former Chumashan village, said by Indians to have been situated on the Rancho of Simi, Ventura co., Cal. Cf. *Somo.*

Ci-mi'-i.—Henshaw, Buenaventura MS. vocab., B. A. E., 1884. Simi.—Taylor in Cal. Farmer, July 24, 1863.

Similkameen. The local name for several bands of Okinagan on a river of the same name, a N. w. tributary of the Okanagan, Brit. Col. Under the term "Similkameen group" are classed 3 or 4 villages in the Canadian Reports of Indian Affairs, namely, Shennosquankin, Keremeus, Chuckuwayha, and subsequently Ashnola, having an aggregate population of 179 in 1906. These Indians are also divided into Lower and Upper Similkameen, with 135 and 44 inhabitants respectively in 1909.

Chitwout Indians.—Brit. Col. Map, Ind. Aff., Victoria, 1872 (in two villages on Similkameen r.). Sa-milk-a-nuigh.—Ross, Adventures, 290, 1849. Similkameen.—Can. Ind. Aff., 74, 1878. Similkameen.—Ibid., 364, 1897. Smelkameen.—Ibid., 309, 1879. Smîlê'qamux.—Teit in Mem. Am. Mus. Nat. Hist., II, 167, 1900 (= 'people of Similkameen'). Smilkameen.—Can. Ind. Aff. 1880, 317, 1881. Smilkamīn.—Gatschet, MS., B. A. E. (Salish name). Smilkěmíχ.—Ibid.

Simomo (*Si-mo'-mo*). An important and populous Chumashan village formerly N. of the estero near Pt Mugu, Ventura co., Cal. Perhaps the same as Somo.—Henshaw, Buenaventura MS. vocab., B. A. E., 1884.

Sinaesta. A village of the Calusa situated on the s. w. coast of Florida, about 1570.

Sinacsta.—Fontaneda as quoted by Shipp, De Soto and Fla., 586, 1881. Sinaesta.—Fontaneda Memoir (*ca.* 1575), Smith trans., 19, 1854.

Sinago ('gray squirrel,' from (Chippewa) *assánago*, correlative of *missánig*, 'black squirrel,' 'great or large squirrel,' from *missi* and *anigus.*—Hewitt). A subtribe of the Ottawa, second in importance only to the Kishkakon. They were in 1648 on the s. shore of L. Huron. During the subsequent wanderings of the tribe they are usually found in the company of the Kishkakon. According to the Walam Olum the Delawares were once at war with them.

Cynagos.—La Potherie, Hist. Am., II, 48, 1753. Outa8esinagos.—Frontenac (1682) in N. Y. Doc. Col. Hist., IX, 176, 1855. Outaouae Sinagos.—Frontenac (1682), ibid., 182. Outa8ais-Cinago.—Doc. of 1695, ibid., 606. Outaoüaks Sinagaux.—Jes. Rel. for 1670, 87, 1858. Outaouasinagouk.—Jes. Rel. for 1648, 62, 1858. Outawas Sinagos.—Neill in Minn. Hist. Soc. Coll., V, 413, 1885. Ouxeinacomigo.—La Chesnaye (1697) in Margry, Déc., VI, 6, 1886 (misprint). Sinago.—Cadillac (1695), ibid., V, 80, 1883. Sinagoux.—Lapham, Inds. Wis., 4, 1870. **Sinako.**—Brinton, Lenape Leg., 206, 1885. **Singos.**—Charlevoix (1744), New Fr., v, 143, 1871. **Sinojos.**—Chauvignerie (1736) quoted by Schoolcraft, Ind. Tribes, III, 554, 1853. **Towecenegos.**—York (1700) in N. Y. Doc. Col. Hist., IV, 749, 1854.

Sinaloa (said to be contracted from *sina*, a species of pitahaya; *lobala*, 'a round object': hence 'round pitahaya'). A division of the Cahita group of the Piman family, inhabiting principally N. Sinaloa and S. E. Sonora, Mexico, on the western slopes of the sierras, about the headwaters of Rio del Fuerte. There is considerable confusion among early writers respecting the application of the name. Hervas (Cat. Leng., I, 322, 1800) identifies the Cinoloa people with the Yaqui, although Ribas (Hist. Trium., 142, 1645) had considered them a distinct tribe living on the headwaters of Rio del Fuerte. The name has also been applied synonymously with Cahita. The Sinaloa were described in 1645 as being able to muster 1,000 warriors. Their idiom was closely related to, if not identical with, that of the Tehueco. They were probably absorbed by stronger allied tribes. (F. W. H.)
Cinaloas.—Ribas, Hist. Trium., 142, 1645. **Sinaloa.**—Orozco y Berra, Geog., 58, 1864. **Sinoloa.**—Castañeda (1596) in 14th Rep. B. A. E., 515, 1896 (referring to their settlement).

Sinapa. A Calusa village on the S. W. coast of Florida, about 1570.—Fontaneda Memoir (*ca.* 1575), Smith trans., 19, 1854.

Sinar. A Kinugumiut Eskimo village near Pt Clarence, Alaska.
Sinarmete.—Jackson, Reindeer in Alaska, map, 145, 1896.

Sinarghutlitun (*Si'-na-rxŭt-li'-tŭn*, 'cataract village'). A band or village of the Chastacosta on the N. side of Rogue r., Oreg.—Dorsey in Jour. Am. Folk-lore, III, 234, 1890.

Sindas-kun (*Si'ndas kun*, 'village on a point always smelling'). A Haida town in the Ninstints country belonging to the Kaidju-kegawai.—Swanton, Cont. Haida, 277, 1905.

Sindatahls (*Si'ndᴧt!als*, 'gambling place'). A Haida town of a branch of the Kuna-lanas family called Djus-hade, formerly near Tsoo-skahli, an inner expansion of Masset inlet, Queen Charlotte ids., Brit. Col.—Swanton, Cont. Haida, 281, 1905.

Sinegainsee (*Sine-gain'-see*, 'creeping thing', i. e. 'snake'). A clan of the Hurons.—Morgan, Anc. Soc., 153, 1877.

Sinew. The popular term for the tendonous animal fiber used by the Indians chiefly as thread for sewing purposes. The fiber thus used is not, as commonly supposed, the tendon from the legs, but the large tendon, about 2 feet in length, lying along each side of the backbone of the buffalo, cow, deer, or other animal,

just back of the neck joint. The tendons were stripped out and dried, and when thread was needed were hammered to soften them and then shredded with an awl or a piece of flint. Sometimes the tendon was stripped of long fibers as needed, and often the tendons were shredded fine and twisted in the same way as agave fiber. The Eskimo had a twister like that used by the Pima, and commonly plaited the fibers into fine sennit; but most other tribes simply twisted it with the hands or on the thigh. Practically all the sewing of skins for costume, bags, pouches, tents, boats, etc., was done with sinew, as was embroidery with beads and quills. For binding together parts of woodwork sinew was even more valuable than rawhide. One of the more remarkable of its many uses was as a spring in an Alaskan Eskimo fox trap of Siberian origin. The elasticity of sinew was known to many tribes, who applied this material to the backs of bows, either as a series of cords lashed on and twisted by means of ivory keys (Eskimo), or by fastening a layer of shredded sinew to the back of the bow with glue, a method employed by the Pacific Coast tribes and some others. The enormously strong sinew bowstring enabled the Indians to employ powerful bows. The Klamath recurving bow, for instance, will snap any cord of vegetal material as if it were pack thread.

Another important use of sinew was in feathering and pointing arrows. Some tribes set arrowheads in such a way that the sinew binding would soften in the wound so that the head would remain when the shaft was withdrawn. By moistening the end of the sinew in binding the feather to the shaft, and in similar light work, it was made to hold fast without the use of glue. Fishing lines and cords for harpoons, etc., were frequently of sinew; the rope over which hides were worked in tanning was ordinarily made of this material, and arrowpoints were once made entirely of buffalo sinew by the Hidatsa. At present the pair from a single cow is commonly rated among the Plains tribes at 50 cents. (W. H.)

Singa (*Si'ñga*, 'winter [village]'). A Haida town, of the Kas-lanas family, situated on the N. side of Tasoo harbor, W. coast of Moresby id., Queen Charlotte ids., Brit. Col.—Swanton, Cont. Haida, 280, 1905.

Sinicon. A former Chumashan village near Santa Barbara, Cal.—Taylor in Cal. Farmer, Apr. 24, 1863.

Sinicu. A tribe or subtribe represented at San Antonio de Valero mission, Texas, between 1728 and 1739. It may be identical with the Secmocó tribe (q. v.), members of which were there at the same time. Cf. *Senecu*.   (H. E. B.)

Censoc.—Valero Bautismos, 1739, MS. Censoo.— Ibid. Seniczo.—Ibid., 1728. Senixzo.—Ibid., 1728.

Sinimiut. A Central Eskimo tribe on Pelly bay, Canada. They live on muskox and salmon like the tribes of Hudson bay, and have also an abundance of seals. They numbered 45 in 1902.

Pelly Bay Eskimo.—Ausland, 653, 1885. Sinamiut.—Boas in Bull. Am. Mus. Nat. Hist., xv, pt. 2, 377, 1907. Sinimijut.—Boas in Zeitschr. Ges. f. Erdk., 226, 1883. Sinimiut.—Boas in 6th Rep. B. A. E., 451, 1888.

Siningmon. A Kaviagmiut Eskimo village on Golofnin bay, Alaska.—11th Census, Alaska, 162, 1893.

Sinkers. Primitive fishermen everywhere weight their lines and nets with stones. These are usually pebbles or other suitable bits of stone, grooved or notched for attachment by means of cords. Those now in use by the Indian tribes, as well as by the whites, correspond with specimens found in large numbers along the banks of streams and the shores of lakes and other large bodies of water. Larger specimens of the same general shape become anchors (q. v.) on occasion, and the better finished forms pass by imperceptible gradations into the very large group of objects classed as plummets (q. v.), and, in another direction, into the stone clubheads of the Plains tribes (see *Weapons*). Adair states that the Southern Indians, having placed a trap in the bed of the stream, drove the fish toward it by means of a rope made of long grape vines to which were attached stones at proper distances, men placed on opposite sides

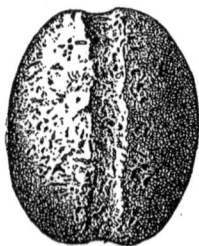

SINKER; N. Y. (1-3)

SINKER OF GRANITE; R. I.   SINKER OF STEATITE; N. C. (1-2)

of the stream dragging the weighted rope along the bottom. The extent to which nets (q. v.) were used by the Indians of the Middle Atlantic states is not known; but the impressions of nets of varying degrees of fineness on pottery show at least that nets were in common use.

Consult Abbott, Prim. Indust., 1881; Adair, Hist. Am. Inds., 1775; Beauchamp in Bull. N. Y. State Mus., IV, no. 16, 1897; Jones, Antiq. Southern Inds., 1873; Rau, Prehist. Fishing, Smithson. Cont., xxv, 1884.   (W. H. H.)

Sinkiuse. A former division of Salish, under Chief Moses, living on the E. side of Columbia r. from Ft Okinakane to the neighborhood of Pt Eaton, Wash. Hale classed them as a division of the Pisquows. Pop. 355 in 1905, 299 in 1908, 540 (with others?) in 1909.

Columbias.—Mooney in 14th Rep. B. A. E., 734, 1896. Isle-de-Peins.—Nesmith in Ind. Aff. Rep., 219, 1858. Isle-de-peiree.—Owen, ibid., 268. Isle-de-Pierre.—Shaw in H. R. Ex. Doc. 37, 34th Cong., 3d sess., 113, 1857. Linkinse.—Bancroft, Nat. Races, I, 316, 1874 (misprint) Moses band.—Ind. Aff. Rep. 1904, 610, 1905. Sinakaiausish.—Hale in U. S. Expl. Exped., VI, 211, 1846. Sinkáyus.— Gatschet, Salish MS., B. A. E. (Salish name). Sinki-use.—Winans in Ind. Aff. Rep., 23, 1870- Snχáyus.—Gatschet, Salish MS., B. A. E. (Salish name).

Sinklezin (Navaho name). An ancient pueblo ruin situated on the highest point of a peninsula-like mesa jutting into Chaco canyon from the s., about ¾ m. s. of Pueblo Bonito, N. W. N. Mex. It is built of dull-brown sandstone, rectangular in form but very irregular, a semicircular tier of rooms on the s. inclosing a large court. The dimensions of the structure are 135 ft E. and W. by 183 ft N. and s. The E. wing is 50 by 75 ft, the w. 30 by 58 ft. A wing 30 ft wide extends 40 ft to the s. The semicircular tier of rooms was 360 ft long, 9 ft wide, and 2 stories high; 72 ft of this tier is still (1902) standing about 12 ft high. The walls throughout vary from 20 to 30 in. thick. The rooms are long and narrow, 5½ by 21½ ft being a common size. There are 5 circular kivas in the building, varying from 6 to 25 ft in diameter. The masonry is of alternating bands of fine and coarse stone and dressed blocks chinked with fine tablets, the arrangement being very irregular. Portions of the third story remain standing. The original height was probably 4 stories.   (E. L. H.)

Sinkyone. An Athapascan group formerly living on the lower part of the South fork of Eel r., Humboldt co., Cal., having settlements on Bull and Salmon crs. They also held the country down to the coast at Shelter cove and s. to Usal. This section has been popularly known as the Usal (a Pomo term), that on Bull cr. and South fork as the Lolanko (from the name of a locality). They lived for a time on Smith River res., afterward being transferred to Hoopa res. on Trinity r., from which place a few survivors returned in the early seventies and are now living near their old homes. They lived in conical houses of bark, dressed much as the tribes about them, and made baskets by twining. They burned their dead. They differed but little from the Wailaki in language.   (P. E. G.)

Bay-ma-pomas.—Tobin in Ind. Aff. Rep. 1857, 405, 1858.

Sinnonquiresse ('Very long wampum string.'—Hewitt). A Mohawk chief, the speaker at Albany in 1691, 1696, 1700, and 1701, signing the Beaver land treaty in the latter year. He was examined about Dellius in 1699, and was at Albany in 1702. Possibly Tananguriss at the Albany council of Sept. 4, 1691, is the same person. The Indian Sinonneequerison, who signed a deed in 1714, seems a later chief. In 1711 M. de Longueuil was called Sinonquirese. See N. Y. Doc. Col. Hist., III, 805, 807, 1853; IV, 237, 540, 910, 1854. (w. m. b.)

Sinopah (*Sĭn'-o-pah*, 'kit-foxes', 'Piegans'). A society of the Ikunuhkatsi, or All Comrades, in the Piegan tribe of the Siksika. It is now obsolete among the Piegan, but still existed with the Kainah in 1892.—Grinnell, Blackfoot Lodge Tales, 221, 1892.

Sinoquipe ('birthplace of warriors'). A pueblo of the Opata and the seat of a Spanish mission founded in 1646; situated in lat. 30° 10′, lon. 110°, on the upper Rio Sonora below Arispe, Sonora, Mexico. Pop. 367 in 1678, 91 in 1730.
Cenokipe.—Kino, map (1702) in Stöcklein, Neue Welt-Bott, 74, 1726. Cinoquipe.—Hardy, Travels, 442, 1829. San Ignacio de Soniquipa.—Orozco y Berra, Geog., 343, 1864. San Ignacio Sinoquipe.—Rivera (1730) quoted by Bancroft, No. Mex. States, I, 514, 1884. S. Ignacio Sinoquipe.—Zapata (1678), ibid., 246. Sinoquipe.—Hrdlička in Am. Anthr., VI, 72, 1904.

Sinslikhooish. A division of Salish that occupied, according to Gibbs, the great plain above the crossing of Cœur d'Alène r., Idaho.
Sin-slih-hoo-ish.—Stevens in Ind. Aff. Rep., 428, 1854. Sin-slik-hoo-ish.—Gibbs in Pac. R. R. Rep., I, 414, 1855.

Sintagallesca. See *Spotted Tail*.

Sintaktl (*Sĭnta'kl*, 'reached the bottom', or 'bottom of the hill'). A Ntlakyapamuk village 30 or 40 m. above Yale, on the w. side of Fraser r., Brit. Col.
O'nta'k'tl.—Hill-Tout in Rep. Ethnol. Surv. Can., 5, 1899. Shuitackle.—Can. Ind. Aff., 79, 1878. Sînta'kL.—Teit in Mem. Am. Mus. Nat. Hist., II, 169, 1900.

Sintootoolish. A division of Salish living, according to Gibbs, on Spokane r., N. Idaho, above the forks.
Middle Spo-ko-mish.—Winans in Ind. Aff. Rep., 23, 1870. Sin-too-too.—Ibid. Sintootoolish.—Gibbs in Pac. R. R. Rep., I, 414, 1855. Sintou-tou-oulish.—Parker, Journal, 298, 1840.

Sintsink (abbr. and corrupt. of Delaware *Assinesink*, 'at the small stone.'—Gerard. Cf. *Ossingsing*). A Wappinger tribe or band on the E. bank of Hudson r., about the present Ossining, N. Y. Villages, Ossingsing and Kestaubuinck.
Sing-sings.—Schoolcraft, Ind. Tribes, VI, 119, 1857. Sinksink.—Deed of 1685 quoted by Ruttenber, Tribes Hudson R., 366, 1872. Sinsinoks.—Stuyvesant (1663) in N. Y. Doc. Col. Hist., XIII, 302, 1881. Sinsinoqs.—Doc. of 1663, ibid., 303. Sinsing.—Van der Donck (1658) quoted by Ruttenber, op. cit., 72. Sintsings.—Treaty of 1645 in N. Y. Doc. Col. Hist., XIII, 18, 1881. Sint-sings.—Breeden Raedt quoted by Ruttenber, op. cit., 108. Sint-Sinks.—Ibid., 79. Sintsnioks.—Treaty of 1645 quoted by Winfield, Hudson Co., 45, 1874 (misprint).

Sinuk. A Kaviagmiut Eskimo village on the N. shore of Pt Clarence, Alaska; pop. 36 in 1880, 12 in 1890.

Singick.—11th Census, Alaska, 165, 1893. Siniogamut.—Nelson in 18th Rep. B. A. E., map, 1899. Siniogamute.—Petroff, Rep. on Alaska, 59, 1880.

Sinyu. An Utkiavinmiut Eskimo summer village inland from Pt Barrow, Alaska.
Sĭ'nnyû.—Murdoch in 9th Rep. B. A. E., 83, 1892.

Siocotchmin. A Costanoan village situated in 1819 within 10 m. of Santa Cruz mission, Cal.—Taylor in Cal. Farmer, Apr. 5, 1860.

Siorartijung. A spring settlement of Padlimiut Eskimo on the coast s. of Home bay, Baffin land, Canada.—Boas in 6th Rep. B. A. E., map, 1888.

Siouan Family. The most populous linguistic family N. of Mexico, next to the Algonquian. The name is taken from a term applied to the largest and best known tribal group or confederacy belonging to the family, the Sioux or Dakota, which, in turn, is an abbreviation of Nadowessioux, a French corruption of *Nadowe-is-iw*, the appellation given them by the Chippewa. It signifies 'snake,' 'adder,' and, by metaphor, 'enemy.' See *Dakota*.

Before changes of domicile took place among them, resulting from contact with whites, the principal body extended from the w. bank of the Mississippi northward from the Arkansas nearly to the Rocky mts., except for certain sections held by the Pawnee, Arikara, Cheyenne, Arapaho, Blackfeet, Comanche, and Kiowa. The Dakota proper also occupied territory on the E. side of the river, from the mouth of the Wisconsin to Mille Lacs, and the Winnebago were about the lake of that name and the head of Green bay. Northward Siouan tribes extended some distance into Canada, in the direction of L. Winnipeg. A second group of Siouan tribes, embracing the Catawba, Sara or Cheraw, Saponi, Tutelo, and several others, occupied the central part of North Carolina and South Carolina and the piedmont region of Virginia (see Mooney, Siouan Tribes of the East, Bull. B. A. E., 1894), while the Biloxi dwelt in Mississippi along the Gulf coast, and the Ofo on Yazoo r. in the same state.

According to tradition the Mandan and Hidatsa reached the upper Missouri from the N. E., and, impelled by the Dakota, moved slowly upstream to their present location. Some time after the Hidatsa reached the Missouri internal troubles broke out, and part, now called the Crows, separated and moved westward to the neighborhood of Yellowstone r. The Dakota formerly inhabited the forest region of s. Minnesota, and do not seem to have gone out upon the plains until hard pressed by the Chippewa, who had been supplied with guns by the French. According to all the evidence available, traditional and otherwise, the so-called Chiwere tribes—Iowa, Oto, and Missouri—separated from the Winnebago or else moved westward to the Missouri from the same region. The five remaining tribes of this group—Omaha, Ponca, Osage, Kansa, and Quapaw—which have been called Dhegiha by Dorsey, undoubtedly lived together as one tribe at some former time and were probably located on the Mississippi. Part moving farther down became known as "downstream people," Quapaw, while those who went up were the "upstream people," Omaha. These latter moved N. w. along the river and divided into the Osage, Kansa, Ponca, and Omaha proper. As to the more remote migrations that must have taken place in such a widely scattered stock, different theories are held. By some it is supposed that the various sections of the family have become dispersed from a district near that occupied by the Winnebago, or, on the basis of traditions recorded by Gallatin and Long, from some point on the N. side of the Great Lakes. By others a region close to the eastern Siouans is considered their primitive home, whence the Dhegiha moved westward down the Ohio, while the Dakota, Winnebago, and cognate tribes kept a more northerly course near the Great Lakes. The tribes of the Manahoac confederacy were encountered by Capt. John Smith in 1608, but after that time all of the eastern Siouans decreased rapidly in numbers through Iroquois attacks and European aggression. Finally the remnants of the northern tribes, consisting chiefly of Tutelo and Saponi, accompanied the Tuscarora northward to the Iroquois and were adopted by the Cayuga in 1753. On the destruction of their village by Sullivan in 1779 they separated, the Saponi remaining with the Cayuga in New York, while the Tutelo fled to Canada with other Cayuga. From the few survivors of the latter tribe, Hale and J. O. Dorsey obtained sufficient material to establish their Siouan connections, but they are now almost extinct. The fate of the Saponi is probably the same. The southern tribes of this eastern Siouan group consolidated with the Catawba, and continued to decrease steadily in numbers, so that at the present time there are only about 100 remaining of the whole confederated body. Some of the eastern Siouan tribes may have been reached by De Soto; they are mentioned by the Spanish captain Juan Pardo, who conducted an expedition into the interior of South Carolina in 1567.

The Biloxi were first noted by Iberville, who found them in 1699 on Pascagoula r., Miss. In the next century they moved N. w. and settled on Red r., La., where the remnant was found by Gatschet in 1886 and their affinities determined. These people reported that another section had moved into Texas and joined the Choctaw.

The Ofo, called Ushpi by their neighbors, are first mentioned by Iberville in 1699, but were probably encountered the year preceding by the missionaries De Montigny, Davion, La Source, and St Cosme, though not specifically mentioned. Unlike the other Yazoo tribes, they sided with the French in the great Natchez war and continued to live near the Tunica Indians. Their Siouan affinity was demonstrated by Swanton in 1908 through a vocabulary collected from the last survivor.

The first known meeting between any western Siouans and the whites was in 1541, when De Soto reached the Quapaw villages in E. Arkansas. The earliest notice of the main northwestern group is probably that in the Jesuit Relation of 1640, where mention is made of the Winnebago, Dakota, and Assiniboin. As early as 1658 the Jesuit missionaries had heard of the existence of 30 Dakota villages in the region N. from the Potawatomi mission at St Michael, about the head of Green bay, Wis. In 1680 Father Hennepin was taken prisoner by the same tribe.

In 1804–05 Lewis and Clark passed through the center of this region and encountered most of the Siouan tribes. Afterward expeditions into and through their country were numerous; traders settled among them in numbers, and were followed in course of time by permanent settlers, who pressed them into narrower and narrower areas until they were finally removed to Indian Territory or confined to reservations in the Dakotas, Nebraska, and Montana. Throughout all this period the Dakota proved themselves most consistently hostile to the intruders. In 1862 occurred a bloody Santee uprising in Minnesota that resulted in the removal of all of the eastern Dakota from that state, and in 1876 the outbreak among the western Dakota and the cutting off of Custer's command. Later still the Ghost-dance religion (q. v.) spread among the Sioux proper, culminating in the affair of Wounded Knee, Dec. 29, 1890.

It is impossible to make statements of the customs and habits of these people that will be true for the entire group. Nearly all of the eastern tribes and most of the southern tribes belonging to the western group raised corn, but the Dakota (except some of the eastern bands) and the Crows depended almost entirely on the buffalo and other game animals, the buffalo entering very deeply into the economic and religious life of all the tribes of this section. In the E. the habitations were bark and mat wigwams, but on the plains earth lodges and skin tipis were used. Formerly they had no domestic animals except dogs, which were utilized in transporting the tipis and all other family belongings, including children (see *Travois*), but later their place was largely taken by horses, the introduction of which constituted a new epoch in the life of all Plains tribes, facilitating their migratory movements and the pursuit of the buffalo, and doubtless contributing largely to the ultimate extinction of that animal.

Taking the reports of the United States and Canadian Indian offices as a basis and making a small allowance for bands or individuals not here enumerated, the total number of Indians of Siouan stock may be placed at about 40,800.

The Tutelo, Biloxi, and probably the rest of the eastern Siouan tribes were organized internally into clans with maternal descent; the Dakota, Mandan, and Hidatsa consisted of many non-totemic bands or villages, the Crows of non-totemic gentes, and the rest of the tribes of totemic gentes.

The Siouan family is divided as follows:

I. Dakota-Assiniboin group: 1, Mdewakanton; 2, Wahpekute (forming, with the Mdewakanton, the Santee); 3, Sisseton; 4, Wahpeton; 5, Yankton; 6, Yanktonai; 7, Teton (a) Sichangu or Brulés, (b) Itazipcho or Sans Arcs, (c) Sihasapa or Blackfeet, (d) Miniconjou, (e) Oohenonpa or Two Kettles, (f) Oglala, (g) Hunkpapa; 8, Assiniboin.

II. Dhegiha group: 1, Omaha; 2, Ponca; 3, Quapaw; 4, Osage (a) Pahatsi, (b) Utsehta, (c) Santsukhdhi; 5, Kansa.

III. Chiwere group: 1, Iowa; 2, Oto; 3, Missouri.

IV. Winnebago.

V. Mandan.

VI. Hidatsa group: 1, Hidatsa; 2, Crows.

VII. Biloxi group: 1, Biloxi; 2, Ofo.

VIII. Eastern division: 1, Monacan group, almost extinct: A, Monacan confederacy—(a) Monacan, (b) Meipontsky, (c) Mohemencho; B, Tutelo confederacy—(a) Tutelo, (b) Saponi, (c) Occaneechi; C, Manahoac confederacy—(a) Manahoac, (b) Stegaraki, (c) Shackaconia, (d) Tauxitania, (e) Ontponea, (f) Tegninateo, (g) Whonkentia, (h) Hassinunga; D, Catawba group—(a) Catawba, (b) Woccon, (c) Sissipahaw, (d) Cape Fear Indians (?), (e) Warrennuncock (?), (f) Adshusheer, (g) Eno, (h) Waxhaw, (i) Sugeree, (j) Santee, (k) Wateree (?), (l) Sewee (?), (m) Congaree (?), all extinct except the Catawba; E, (a) Cheraw, (b) Keyauwee, both extinct; F, (a) Pedee (?),

(b) Waccamaw (?), (c) Winyaw (?), (d) Hooks (?), (e) Backhooks (?), all extinct.　　　　(C. T.　J. R. S.)

>**Dacotan.**—Lapham, Inds. Wis., 6, 1870. >**Dakotan.**—Powell in 1st Rep. B. A. E., xvii, xix, 1881. >**Sioux.**—Gallatin in Trans. Am. Antiq. Soc., II, 121, 306, 1836; Prichard, Phys. Hist. Mankind, v, 408, 1847 (follows Gallatin); Gallatin in Trans. Am. Ethnol. Soc., II, pt. 1, xcix, 77, 1848 (as in 1836); Berghaus (1845), Physik. Atlas, map 17, 1848; ibid., 1852; Gallatin in Schoolcraft, Ind. Tribes, III, 402, 1853; Berghaus, Physik. Atlas, map 72, 1887. >**Sioux.**—Latham, Nat. Hist. Man, 333, 1850 (includes Winebagoes, Dakotas, Assineboins, Upsaroka, Mandans, Minetari, Osage); Latham in Trans. Philol. Soc. Lond., 58, 1856 (mere mention of family); Latham, Opuscula, 327, 1860; Latham, El. Comp. Philol., 458, 1862. >**Sioux-Osages.**—Balbi, Atlas Ethnogr., 55, 1826. >**Catawbas.**—Gallatin in Trans. Am. Antiq. Soc., II, 87, 1836 (Catawbas and Woccons); Bancroft, Hist. U. S., III, 245, and map, 1840; Prichard, Phys. Hist. Mankind, v, 399, 1847; Gallatin in Trans. Am. Ethnol. Soc., II, pt. 1, xcix, 77, 1848; Keane in Stanford, Compend., Cent. and So. Am., app., 460, 473, 1878. >**Catahbas**—Berghaus (1845), Physik. Atlas, map 17, 1848; ibid., 1852. **Catawba.**—Latham, Nat. Hist. Man, 334, 1850 (Woccoon are allied); Gallatin in Schoolcraft, Ind. Tribes, III, 401, 1853. >**Kataba.**—Gatschet in Am. Antiq., IV., 238, 1882; Gatschet, Creek Migr. Leg., I, 15, 1884; Gatschet in Science, 413, Apr. 29, 1887. >**Woccons.**—Gallatin in Trans. Am. Antiq. Soc., II, 306, 1836 (numbered and given as a distinct family in table, but inconsistently noted in footnote where referred to as Catawban family). >**Dahcotas.**—Bancroft, Hist. U. S., III, 243, 1840. >**Dakotas.**—Hayden, Ethnog. and Philol. Mo. Val., 232, 1862 (treats of Dakotas, Assiniboins, Crows, Minnitarees, Mandans, Omahas, Iowas). >**Dacotah.**—Keane in Stanford, Compend., Cent. and So. Am., app., 460, 470, 1878 (the following are the main divisions given: Isaunties, Sissetons, Yantons, Teetons, Assiniboines, Winnebagos, Punkas, Omahas, Missouris, Iowas, Otoes, Kaws, Quappas, Osages, Upsarocas, Minnetarees). >**Dakota.**—Berghaus, Physik. Atlas, map 72, 1887. =**Siouan.**—Powell in 7th Rep. B. A. E., 111, 1891.

Sipanum. A former village, presumably Costanoan, connected with Dolores mission, San Francisco, Cal.—Taylor in Cal. Farmer, Oct. 18, 1861.

Sipiwithiniwuk ('river people'). A division of the Sakawithiniwuk, or Wood Cree.

Siplichiquin. A former village, presumably Costanoan, connected with Dolores mission, San Francisco, Cal.—Taylor in Cal. Farmer, Oct. 18, 1861.

Sipsisseway. See *Pipsissewa*.

Sipuca. A former Chumashan village near Purísima mission, Santa Barbara co., Cal.—Taylor in Cal. Farmer, Oct. 18, 1861.

Sipushkanumanke ('grouse people'). A Mandan gens according to Morgan (Anc. Soc., 158, 1877); according to Matthews (Ethnog. Hidatsa, 14, 1877), who is evidently correct, a large band.

Grouse Men.—Matthews, Ethnog. Hidatsa, 14, 1877. **Nu-mah-ká-kee.**—Catlin, Okeepa, 5, 44, 1867. **People of the Pheasants.**—Bowen, Am. Discov. by the Welsh, 126, 1876. **Peuple de Faisans.**—Domenech, Deserts N. Am., II, 36, 1860. **Prairie Chicken.**—Morgan, Anc. Soc., 158, 1877. **Prairie-hen People.**—Matthews, op. cit. **Prairie hens.**—Maximilian, Trav., 335, 1843. **See-pohs-ka-mi-mah-ka-kee.**—Bowen, op. cit. **See-poosh'-kä.**—Morgan, op. cit. **Siposka-numakaki.**—Matthews, op. cit. **Si-pu'-cka nu-mañ'-ke.**—Dorsey in 15th Rep. B. A. E., 241,

1897.	**Sipuske-Numangkake.**—Maximilian, Trav., 335, 1843.

Sirmiling. A winter settlement of the Akudnirmiut Eskimo on the N. coast of Baffin land, near the N. W. end of Home bay.

Sirmilling.—Boas in 6th Rep. B. A. E., map, 1888.

Sirunues. Mentioned by Barcia (Ensayo, 328, 1723) as a tribe living on the borders of New Mexico. Unidentified, unless possibly intended for Zuñi.

Sisa (*Sis'-á*). A large Chumashan village formerly in a canyon near Santa Paula, Ventura co., Cal.—Taylor in Cal. Farmer, July 24, 1863; Henshaw, Buenaventura MS. vocab., B. A. E., 1884.

Sisaguk. A former Aleut village on Unimak, Aleutian ids., Alaska; pop. 91 in 1833.

Schischaldenskoje.—Holmberg, Ethnol. Skizz., map, 1855. Sheeshaldenskoi.—Elliott, Cond. Aff. Alaska, 225, 1875. Shishaldin.—Petroff in 10th Census, Alaska, 35, 1884. Shishaldinski.—Baker, Geog. Dict. Alaska, 577, 1906 (Russian name). Shishaldinskoe.—Veniaminof, Zapiski, II, 203, 1840. Sisaguk.—Holmberg, Ethnol. Skizz., map, 1855.

Sisahiahut. A former Chumashan village near Santa Barbara, Cal.—Taylor quoted by Bancroft, Nat. Races, I, 459, 1874.

Siscastac. A former village, presumably Costanoan, connected with Dolores mission, San Francisco, Cal.—Taylor in Cal. Farmer, Oct. 18, 1861.

Siscowet, Siscowit. See *Siskawet*.

Sisibotari. A branch of the Nevome in s. central Sonora, Mexico; so called from their chief. Described by Ribas (Hist. Triumphos, 380, 1645) as the most peaceable and cultivated of the tribes encountered up to that time; they differed much from the Yaqui and Mayo in dress, the men wearing short mantles in summer and long cloaks of cotton and agave thread in winter, and the women petticoats of highly dressed and painted skins or of cotton and agave, and also aprons, in summer, to which, in winter, was added a garment like a bishop's gown (*roqueta*). Their houses were of a kind of adobe unmixed with straw. Their dances are described as having been very gay but modest.

Sisichii. A former Chumashan village in "Dos Pueblos," near Santa Barbara, Cal. (Taylor quoted by Bancroft, Nat. Races, I, 459, 1874.) Cf. *Lisuchu, Sisuchi*.

Sisika. The Swallow clan of San Felipe pueblo, N. Mex. It was almost extinct in 1895.

Sísika-háno.—Hodge in Am. Anthr., IX, 352, 1896 (*háno* = 'people').

Sisintlae (*Si'sînLaē*, 'the Sî'nLaēs'). The name of gentes among the Goasila, Nakoaktok, Nimkish, Tlauitsis, and true Kwakiutl.

Séntlaē.—Boas in Petermanns Mitteil., pt. 5, 130, 1887. Si'sînLaē.—Boas in Rep. Nat. Mus. 1895, 330, 1897.

Sisitcanogna. A former Gabrieleño rancheria in Los Angeles co., Cal., at a local-ity later known as Pear Orchard.—Ried (1852) quoted by Taylor in Cal. Farmer, June 8, 1860.

Sisjulcioy (from *Shi-shá'-we-ku-i*). A former Chumashan village on the coast in Ventura co., Cal., in a locality now called Punta Gorda.

Ci-câ'wo-ku-i.—Henshaw, Buenaventura MS. vocab., B. A. E., 1884. Sisjulicoy.—Taylor in Cal. Farmer, July 24, 1863.

Siskawet. A name, with many variants, such as *siskowet, siskiwit, siskowit, siskwoet, ciscovet*, etc., for *Salvelinus namaycush*, var. *siscowet*, a large thick-bodied salmon of the deep waters of L. Superior. Its flesh possesses a fine flavor, but is so fat and oily as to render it almost unfit for food until after it has been salted and pickled. After it has been cured with salt, the fish commands in the market double the price of the Mackinaw salmon, of which it is now regarded as a variety. It is taken in large quantities by the Canadian French and by Indian fishermen by means of the torch and spear. The name is a Canadian French contraction and corruption of the cumbersome Chippewa name *pemitewiskawet*, 'that which has oily flesh.' The suffix *-skawet* is the participial form of the verbal suffix *-skawe*, denoting that a fish has flesh of a character denoted by the attributive prefix. The flesh of other animals is denoted by the suffix *-shkiwe*. (W. R. G.)

Siskhaslitun (*Sis'-qas-li'-tún*). A former village of the Chetco on the s. side of Chetco r., Oreg.—Dorsey in Jour. Am. Folk-lore, III, 236, 1890.

Siskiwit, Siskowit, Siskwoet. See *Siskawet*.

Sisolop. A former Chumashan village near Purísima mission, Santa Barbara co., Cal.—Taylor in Cal. Farmer, Oct. 18, 1861.

Sissabanonase. A former Chumashan village near Santa Barbara mission, Cal.—Taylor in Cal. Farmer, Apr. 24, 1863.

Sisseton ('lake village'). One of the seven original tribes of the Dakota. They appear to have formed a link between the eastern and western tribes, though generally included in the eastern division, with which they seem to have the closest affinity. Riggs says that the intercourse between the Mdewakanton on the Mississippi and lower Minnesota rs. and the Wahpeton, Wahpekute, and a part of the Sisseton has been so constant that but slight differences are discoverable in their manner of speaking, though the western Sisseton show greater difference in their speech. This tribe was in existence at the coming of the whites. Rev. T. S. Williamson, who was well acquainted with the history, traditions, languages, and customs of the eastern Dakota, says: "From what was written on this subject by Hennepin, La Hontan,

Le Sueur, and Charlevoix, and from the maps published under the superintendence of these authors, it is sufficiently clear that in the latter part of the 17th century the principal residence of the Isanyati Sioux [Mdewakanton, Wahpeton, Wahpekute, and Sisseton] was about the headwaters of Rum r., whence they extended their hunts to St Croix and Mississippi rs., and down the latter nearly or quite as far as the mouth of the Wisconsin.'' (Minn. Hist. Soc. Coll., I, 295, 1872.) The first recorded mention of the tribe is probably that of Hennepin (Descr. La., 1683), who said that in the neighborhood of Mille Lacs were many other lakes, whence issue several rivers, on the banks of which live the Issati, Nadouessans Tinthonha (Teton), Oudebathon (Wahpeton) River people, Chongaskethon (Sisseton), and other tribes, all comprised under the name Nadouessiou. This locates the tribe in 1680 in the vicinity of Mille Lacs, not in the region of Rainy lake, as Hennepin's map appears to place them. In the Prise de Possession of May 1689, they are mentioned as living, the greater part of them, in the neighborhood of the Mdewakanton, in the interior N. E. of the Mississippi. Du Luth, who was in that region as early as July 1679, found them in the vicinity of the Wahpeton. The statement that a part of the tribe was in the vicinity of Mille Lacs at the time of Hennepin's visit (1680) indicates that the division into the two bands had already taken place. Pike states that the two divisions, the Kahra and the Sisseton proper, hunted eastward to the Mississippi and up that river as far as Crow Wing r. Long (Exped. St Peters R., 1824) names the divisions the Miakechakesa and Kahra, giving as the number of the latter 1,500, and that of the former 1,000. Lewis and Clark (1804) located them on the headwaters of Minnesota r. Schermerhorn, following Pike, said they were on the upper parts of Red r. of L. Winnipeg, and that they roved on the Mississippi and also on Crow Wing r., which was the boundary between them and the Chippewa. Brown (1817) gave their habitat as on Minnesota r. up to Big Stone lake. According to Ramsey (1849) they then claimed all the lands w. of Blue Earth r. to James r., S. Dak. Their principal village was located near L. Traverse. In 1854 the distributing point of annuities for the Sisseton and Wahpeton was then at Yellow Medicine r. Subsequently they were gathered on a reservation.

Lewis and Clark estimated the number of warriors in 1804 at 200, and a total population of about 800. According to Neill they numbered 2,500 in 1853. The combined population of the Sisseton and Wahpeton at L. Traverse res. in 1886 was 1,496. In 1909 there were 1,936 of both tribes at the Sisseton agency, S. Dak., and in North Dakota 980 Sisseton, Wahpeton, and Pabaksa, representing bands that fled thither after the Minnesota massacre of 1862.

Two subdivisions were mentioned by Pike (1811) and Long (1824), the Miakechakesa, or Sisseton proper, and the Kahra. Rev. S. R. Riggs, in a letter to Dorsey (1882), gives the following bands: Chanshdachikana; Tizaptan; Okopeya-Amdowapuskiyapi; Basdecheshni; Ka; pozha; Ohdihe. Rev. E. Ashley, in a letter to Dorsey (1884), gives these, with the exception of the first, named from

LITTLE SHORT-HORN, A SISSETON

chief Sleepyeye, and adds the following: Witawaziyataotina; Itokakhtina; Kakhmiatonwan; Maniti; Keze; Chankute. Bands that can not be identified with any of these are the Grail and Little Rock bands, Mechemeton, Red Iron band, and the Traverse des Sioux and Wabey bands.

The Sisseton made or joined in the following treaties with the United States: Prairie du Chien, Mich. Ter., July 15, 1830; St Peters, Minn., Nov. 30, 1836; Traverse des Sioux, Minn. Ter., July 23, 1851; Washington, D. C., June 19, 1858; Feb. 19, 1867; Lake Traverse res., Dak. Ter., Sept. 20, 1872 (unratified); agreement at Lac Traverse agency, Dak. Ter., May 2, 1873. By resolution of the Senate, June 27, 1860, the right and title of certain bands of Sioux, including the Sisseton, to lands embraced in the reservation on Minnesota r., were confirmed.

Chongas Kabi.—Bacqueville de la Potherie, Hist. Am., II, map, 1753 ('nation des forts'). **Chongaskaby.**—Hennepin, New Discov., map, 1698. **Cissitons.**—Lewis and Clark, Exped., II, 442, 1814. **Kienketons.**—Badin in Ann. de la Prop. de la Foi, IV, 536, 1843 (possibly identical). **Marsh Village Dakotas.**—Riggs, Dak. Gram. and Dict., xvi, 1852. **Marsh Villagers.**—Minn. Hist. Soc. Coll., II, pt. 2, 84, 1864. **Sankaskitons.**—Lahontan (1688) quoted by Ramsey in Ind. Aff. Rep. 1849, 72, 1850. **Saussetons.**—Pike quoted by Schermerhorn in Mass. Hist. Soc. Coll., 2d s., II, 40, 1814. **Schahswintowaher.**—Balbi, Atlas Ethnog., 55, 1826. **Seeseetoan.**—Sioux petition (1852) in Sen. Ex. Doc. 29, 32d Cong., 2d sess., 3, 1853. **See-see-ton.**—Treaty of 1853 in U. S. Ind. Treaties, 879, 1873. **Seeseetwaun.**—Ramsey in Minn. Hist. Soc. Coll., I, 47, 1856. **See-see-wan.**—Ramsey (1853) in Sen. Ex. Doc. 61, 33d Cong., 1st sess, 324, 1854. **Seesetoan.**—Marshall (1852) in Sen. Ex. Doc. 29, 32d Cong., 2d sess., 8, 1853. **Seese-ton.**—Sweetser in Sen. Rep. 90, 36th Cong., 1st sess., 1, 1860. **Se-see-toans.**—Ind. Aff. Rep., 15, 1858. **Se-see-t'wawns.**—Ramsey in Ind. Aff. Rep. 1849, 84, 1850 (pronunciation). **Sesetons.**—Prescott in Schoolcraft, Ind. Tribes, II, 185, 1852. **Sesiton Sioux.**—Prescott in Ind. Aff. Rep., 279, 1854. **Sessatone.**—Brackenridge, Views of La., 78, 1815. **Sessatons.**—Schoolcraft, Ind. Tribes, VI, 350, 1857. **Sesseton.**—Prescott in Schoolcraft, Ind. Tribes, II, 155, 1852. **Shahsweentowahs.**—Carver, Trav., 60, 1778. **Shiveytown.**—Doc. 1786 in Mass. Hist. Soc. Coll., 1st s., III, 24, 1794. **Sinsitwans.**—Ramsey in Ind. Aff. Rep. 1849, 72, 1850. **Sisatoone.**—Arrowsmith, Map N. Am., 1795, ed. 1814. **Sisatoons.**—Lewis and Clark, Exped., I, 166, 1814. **Siseton.**—Prescott in Ind. Aff. Rep., 283, 1854. **Sisetwans.**—Ramsey in Ind. Aff. Rep. 1849, 72, 1850. **Sisin-towanyan.**—Williamson in Minn. Geol. Rep. for 1884, 110. **Sisi toan.**—Long, Exped. St. Peters R., I, 378, 1824. **Sisitons.**—Lewis and Clark, Exped., II, 459, 1814. **Si-si'-toŋ-waŋ.**—Riggs, Dak. Gram. and Dict., 186, 1852. **Si-si-ton-wans.**—Ramsey in Ind. Aff. Rep. 1849, 84, 1850. **Si-si-t'wans.**—Ibid., 74. **Sissaton.**—Gale, Upper Miss., 229, 1867. **Sissatones.**—Lewis and Clark, Discov., 24, 1806. **Sisseton.**—U. S. Stat. at Large, XII, 1037, 1863. **Sissetoans.**—Neill, Hist. Minn., 122, 1858. **Sisseton.**—U. S Ind. Treaties, 640, 1826. **Sissetong.**—Treaty of 1831 in U. S. Stat. at Large, VII, 328, 1846. **Sissetonwan.**—Neill, Hist. Minn., 80, 1858. **Sissitoan.**—Ind. Aff. Rep. 1856, 38, 1857. **Sissiton.**—Nicollet, Rep. on Upper Miss. R., 13, 1843. **Sissitongs.**—Schoolcraft, Trav., 307, 1821. **Sissit'wan.**—Ramsey in Ind. Aff. Rep. 1849, 75, 1850. **Sistasoona.**—Coyner, Lost Trappers, 70, 1847. **Sistasoone.**—Lewis and Clark, Exped., I, 62, 1814. **Sistons.**—Balbi, Atlas Ethnogr., 55, 1826. **Si-'twans.**—Ramsey in Ind. Aff. Rep. 1849, 74, 1850. **Songasketons.**—Domenech, Deserts N. Am., II, 26, 1860. **Songaskicons.**—Du Luth (1679) quoted by Neill, Hist. Minn., 122, 1858. **Songasquitons.**—Le Sueur (1700) in Margry, Déc., VI, 86, 1886. **Songastikons.**—Du Lhut (1678) in Margry, Déc., VI, 22, 1886. **Songats.**—Harris, Coll. Voy. and Trav., I, map, 1705. **Songatskitons.**—Crepy (ca. 1783), Carte gé. de l'Am. Septent. **Songeskitons.**—Doc. of 1689 in N. Y. Doc. Col. Hist., IX, 418, 1855. **Songeskitoux.**—Perrot (1689) in Minn. Hist. Soc. Coll., II, pt. 2, 31, 1864. **Songestikons.**—French, Hist. Coll. La., II, 122, 1875. **Sonkaskitons.**—Lahontan, New Voy., I, 231, 1703. **Sougaskicons.**—Du Luth (1679) in N. Y. Doc. Col. Hist., IX, 795, 1855. **Sousitoons.**—Lewis and Clark Exped., I, 101, note, 1893. **Susseetons.**—Ind. Aff. Rep., 495, 1839. **Sussetongs.**—Brown, West. Gaz., 208, 1817. **Sussetons.**—Snelling, Tales of Northwest, 39, 1830 (trans.: 'people who end by curing'). **Sussetonwah.**—Prescott (1847) in Schoolcraft, Ind. Tribes, II, 168, 1852. **Sussitongs.**—Pike, Exped., 49, 1810.

Sissipahaw. A former small tribe of North Carolina, presumably Siouan, from their alliance and associations with known Siouan tribes. They must have been an important tribe at one time, as Haw r., the chief head stream of Cape Fear r., derives its name from them, and the site of their former village, known in 1728 as Haw Old Fields, was noted as the largest body of fertile land in all that region. It was probably situated about the present Saxapahaw on Haw r., in the lower part of Alamance co., N. C. They were mentioned by Lawson in 1701, but he did not meet them. Nothing more is known of them beyond the general statement that they and other tribes of the region joined the Yamasee against the English in the war of 1715. (J. M.)

Sauxpa.—Vandera (1569) in Smith Colec. Doc. Fla., 17, 1857 (probably identical). **Saxapahaw.**—Bowen, Map Brit. Am. Plantations, 1760. **Sippahaws.**—Martin, Hist. No. Car., I, 129, 1829. **Sissipahau.**—Lawson (1701), Hist. Carolina, 94, 1860. **Sissispahaws.**—Latham, Varieties of Man, 334, 1850.

Sisuch. A former Chumashan village near Santa Barbara, Cal.—Taylor in Cal. Farmer, Apr. 24, 1863.

Sisuchi. A former Chumashan village near Santa Inés mission, Santa Barbara co., Cal. (Taylor in Cal. Farmer, Oct. 18, 1861). Cf. *Lisuchu, Sisithii.*

Sitaptapa (*Si-tá'p-tá-pá*). A former Chumashan village on or near the site of the present town of Nordhoff, Ventura co., Cal.—Henshaw, Buenaventura MS. vocab., B. A. E., 1884.

Sitarky. A former Seminole village between Camp Izard and Ft King, w. Fla.; doubtless named from its chief.

Sitarky's.—H. R. Doc. 78, 25th Cong., 2d sess., map, 768–769, 1838.

Sitiku (*Si'tikŭ'*, or *Sŭ'tăgŭ'*). A former Cherokee settlement on Little Tennessee r., at the entrance of Citico cr., in Monroe co., Tenn. The name, which can not be translated, is commonly spelled Citico, but appears also as Sattiquo, Settico, Settacoo, Sette, Sittiquo, etc.—Mooney in 19th Rep. B. A. E., 531, 1900.

Settacoo.—Timberlake, Memoirs, map, 1765. **Sette.**—Bartram, Travels, 371, 1792 (identical?). **Sittiquo.**—Doc. of 1755 quoted by Royce in 5th Rep. B. A. E., 142, 1887.

Sitintajea. A former rancheria connected with Dolores mission, San Francisco, Cal.—Taylor in Cal. Farmer, Oct. 18, 1861.

Sitka (prob. meaning 'on Shi,' the native name of Baranof id.). A Tlingit tribe, named from their principal town, on the w. coast of Baranof id., Alaska. Their territory extends over all of this island and over the southern part of Chichagof. Pop. 721 in 1880, of whom 540 were in Sitka town; 815 in 1890. Former towns in the Sitka territory were Dahet, Keshkunuwu, Kona, Kustahekdaan, Tlanak, and Tluhashaiyikan. Silver Bay was a summer camp. Social divisions were Kagwantan, Katagwadi, Katkaayi, Kiksadi, Kokhittan, and Tluknahadi. See *Old Sitka.* (J. R. S.)

S-chitcha-chon.—Langsdorff, Voy., II, 128, 1814.

Schĭtka.—Holmberg, Ethnol. Skizz., map, 142,1855.
Schitka-kŏn.—Krause, Tlinkit Ind., 118, 1885.
Schitkhakhóãn.—Ibid., 11. Seethenskie.—Elliott, Cond. Aff. Alaska, 227, 1875 (transliterated from Veniaminoff). Sitca.—Latham in Jour. Ethnol. Soc. Lond., I, 163, 1848. Sitcha. — Holmberg, Ethnol. Skizz., map, 142, 1855. Sitka-kwan.—Dall in Proc. A. A. A. S. 1869, 269, 1870. Sitka-qwan.—Emmons in Mem. Am. Mus. Nat. Hist., III, 232, 1903. Sitkas.—Colyer in Ind. Aff. Rep. 1869, 572, 1870. Sitkhinskoe.—Veniaminoff, Zapiski, II, pt. III, 30, 1840.

Sitkoedi (*S! ĭtqoe′dĭ*, 'people of Sitko'). A division of the Tlingit at Sumdum, Alaska, of the Wolf phratry. (J. R. S.)

Sitlintaj. A former rancheria connected with Dolores mission, San Francisco, Cal.—Taylor in Cal. Farmer, Oct. 18, 1861.

Sitnazuak. A village of the Kaviagmiut Eskimo w. of C. Nome, Alaska; pop. 20 in 1880.
Chitashuak.—Jackson in Rep. Bur. of Ed., map, 1894. Chitnashuak.—Petroff in 10th Census, Alaska, 11, 1884.

Sitolo. A former Chumashan village near Purísima mission, Santa Barbara co., Cal.
Sautatho.—Taylor in Cal. Farmer, Oct. 18, 1861. Sitolo.—Ibid.

Sitsimé. Said to be the name applied to themselves by the inhabitants of the Keresan (Queres) pueblos of Acoma and Laguna (q. v.), with their outlying villages, w. central N. Mexico. The language of these pueblos differs slightly in dialect from that of the Rio Grande Queres, as well as from each other.
Kan-ayko.—Loew (1876) in Wheeler Surv. Rep., VII, 345, 1879 (misprint *n* for *u;* cf. *Laguna*). Kawaíko.—Ibid., 418. Sis-stsi-mé.—Ibid., 345. Sistsi-mé.—Loew in Ann. Rep. Wheeler Surv., app. LL., 178, 1875. Sitsimé.—Loew in Wheeler Surv. Rep., VII, 418, 1879. Tse-mo-é.—Ibid., 339 (another form).

Sits-in-the-Middle. See *Many Horses.*

Sitting Bull (*Tataⁿka Yotaⁿka,* 'sitting buffalo bull'). A noted Sioux warrior and tribal leader of the Hunkpapa Teton division, born on Grand r., S. Dak., in 1834, his father being Sitting Bull, alias Four Horns, a subchief. As a boy he was first known as Jumping Badger. He manifested hunting ability when but 10 years of age, in the pursuit of buffalo calves. When he was 14 he accompanied his father on the warpath against the Crows and counted his first coup on the body of a fallen enemy. On the return of the party his father made a feast, gave away many horses, and announced that his son had won the right to be known henceforth by his own name. According to the native interpretation of a Dakota winter count his name was Four Horn, and was changed to Sitting Bull when he "made medicine" in 1857. The name is quite common among the Plains tribes. He rapidly acquired influence in his own band, being especially skilful in the character of peacemaker. He took an active part in the Plains wars of the '60's, and first became widely known to the

whites in 1866, when he led a memorable raid against Ft Buford. Sitting Bull was on the warpath with his band of followers from various tribes almost continuously from 1869 to 1876, either raiding the frontier posts or making war on the Crows or the Shoshoni, especially the former. His autographic pictorial record in the Army Medical Museum at Washington refers chiefly to contests with the Crows and to horse stealing.

SITTING BULL

His refusal to go upon a reservation in 1876 led Gen. Sheridan to begin against him and his followers the campaign which resulted in the surprise and annihilation of Custer's troop on Little Bighorn r., Mont., in June. During this battle, in which 2,500 to 3,000 Indian warriors were engaged, Sitting Bull was in the hills "making medicine," and his accurate foretelling of the battle enabled him "to come out of the affair with higher honor than he possessed when he went into it" (McLaughlin). After this fight the hostiles separated into two parties. Sitting Bull, in command of the western party, was attacked by Gen. Miles and routed; a large number of his followers surrendered, but the remainder of the band, including Sitting Bull himself, escaped to Canada, where they remained until 1881, when he surrendered at Ft Buford under promise of amnesty and was confined at Ft Randall until 1883. Although he had surrendered and gone upon a reservation,

Sitting Bull continued unreconciled. It was through his influence that the Sioux refused to sell their land in 1888; and it was at his camp at Standing Rock agency and at his invitation that Kicking Bear organized the first Ghost dance on the reservation. The demand for his arrest was followed by an attempt on the part of some of his people to rescue him, during which he was shot and killed by Sergeants Red Tomahawk and Bullhead of the Indian police, Dec. 15, 1890. His son, Crow Foot, and several others, with six of the Indian police, were also killed in the struggle. Although a chief by inheritance, it was rather Sitting Bull's success as an organizer and his later reputation as a sacred dreamer that brought him into prominence. According to McLaughlin, "his accuracy of judgment, knowledge of men, a student-like disposition to observe natural phenomena, and a deep insight into affairs among Indians and such white people as he came into contact with, made his stock in trade, and he made 'good medicine.'" He stood well among his own people, and was respected for his generosity, quiet disposition, and steadfast adherence to Indian ideals. He had two wives at the time of his death (one of whom was known as Pretty Plume), and was the father of 9 children. His eldest son was called Louis.

Consult Dunn, Massacres of the Mts., 1886; Finerty, War Path and Bivouac, 1890; W. F. Johnson, Life of Sitting Bull, 1891; McLaughlin, My Friend the Indian, 1910; Mooney in 14th Rep. B. A. E., 1896; Walker, Campaigns of General Custer and Surrender of Sitting Bull, 1881.

Sittintac. A former rancheria connected with Dolores mission, San Francisco, Cal.—Taylor in Cal. Farmer, Oct. 18, 1861.

Situchi. A former Chumashan village situated near Santa Inés mission, Santa Barbara co., Cal.—Taylor in Cal. Farmer, Oct. 18, 1861.

Siuktun. A Chumashan village given by Taylor as having been situated near Santa Inés mission, Santa Barbara co., Cal., and said by the Ventura Indians to have been on the harbor of Santa Barbara.
Seyuktoon.—Taylor in Cal. Farmer, May 4, 1860. Si-úk-tun.—Henshaw, Buenaventura MS. vocab., B. A. E., 1884.

Siupam (or Suipam?). A tribe met by Fr. San Buenaventura y Olivares and Fr. Espinosa in Apr. 1709, at San Pedro Springs, San Antonio, Texas. The rancheria in which they were living was composed of this tribe, Chaulamas, and Sijames, and was estimated by Fr. Espinosa at 1,000 persons. (The Chaulamas were probably the Xarames, for in the Spanish of that day ch and x, as well as l and r, were frequently interchangeable. Moreover, this was the home of the Xarames.) The Pampopas, who had accompanied the padres from Medina r., remained at the rancheria when the latter continued their journey northeastward (Fray Isidro Felis de Espinosa Diario, 1709, MS). When the missionaries returned a few days later the rancherias had been moved down-stream, an indication of the unfixed character of their villages. The tribe is perhaps the same as the Siguipam, of the Texas coast country, who later were at San Francisco de la Espada mission. In 1754 a portion of the tribe deserted to the Rio Grande missions, but were brought back by Fr. Bartholomé García (MS. in Arch. Col. Santa Cruz, K. Leg. 19, no. 34). See *Seguipam.* (H. E. B.)

Siuslaw. A small Yakonan tribe formerly living on and near Siuslaw r., w. Oreg. It is now nearly extinct, a few survivors only being on the Siletz res. The following were the former villages of the Siuslaw as ascertained by Dorsey in 1884 (Jour. Am. Folklore, III, 230, 1890): Khaikuchum, Khachtais, Hauwiyat, Kumiyus, Khalakw, Khakhaich, Hilakwitiyus, Thlachaus, Kwsichichu, Mithlausmintthai, Stthukhwich, Chimuksaich, Waitus, Shkutch, Paauwis, Pilumas, Tiekwachi, Kumkwu, Tsatauwis, Kwuskwemus, Kwulhauunnich, Thlekuaus, Kwultsaiya, Pithlkwutsiaus, Wetsiaus, Kuskussu, Kupimithlta, Tsahais, Matsnikth, Pia, Khaiyumitu, Yukhwustitu, Kwunnumis, Tsiekhaweyathl.

Cai-yu'-clă.—Dorsey, Alsea MS. vocab., B. A. E., 1884 (Alsea name). K'ọu-qwĭọ' ᴣŭnnĕ.—Dorsey, Naltûnnetûnnĕ MS. vocab., B. A. E., 1884 (Naltunne name). K'qlo-qweọ ᴣŭnnĕ.—Dorsey, Chasta Costa MS. vocab., B. A. E., 1884 (Chastacosta name). Linslow.—Drew (1855) in H. R. Ex. Doc. 93, 34th Cong., 1st sess., 94, 1856. Sainstkla.—Hale in Wilkes Expl. Exped., VI, 204, 1846. Saiustkla.—Ibid., 221. Sai-yu'-sla-me' ᴣŭnnĕ.—Dorsey, Chetco MS. vocab., B. A. E., 1884 (Chetco name). Sai-yŭs'-t'ọû-me' ᴣŭnnĕ.—Dorsey, Naltûnnetûnnĕ MS. vocab., B. A. E., 1884 (Naltunne name). Saliûtla.—Parker, Journal, 257, 1840. Sayonstla.—Framboise quoted by Gairdner (1835) in Jour. Geog. Soc. Lond., XI, 255, 1841. Sayousla.—Brooks in Ind. Aff. Rep. 1862, 299, 1863. Sayouslaw.—Ind. Aff. Rep., 479, 1865. Sayúskla.—Gatschet in Globus, XXXV, no. 11, 168, 1879. Sayústkla.—Gatschet in Beach, Ind. Misc., 441, 1877. Scinslaw.—Manypenny (1856) in H. R. Ex. Doc. 37, 34th Cong., 3d sess., 9, 1857. Sciuslau.—Gibbs, Obs. on Coast Tribes of Oreg., MS., B. A. E. Seinslaw Eneas.—Dole in Ind. Aff. Rep., 220, 1861. Senslaw Eneas.—Ibid., 1863, 510, 1864. Senslaws.—Ibid., 1857, 321, 1858. Sheastuckles.—Lewis and Clark, Exped., II, 474, 1814. Sheastukles.—Morse, Rep. to Sec. War, 371, 1822. Shiastuckles.—Lewis and Clark, Exped., II, 118, 1814. Sinselan.—Ind. Aff. Rep. 1867, 62, 1868. Sinselano.—Ibid., 1871, 682, 1872. Sinselau.—Ibid., 1867, 67, 1868. Sinselaws.—Harvey, ibid., 1868, 79, 1864. Siouslaws.—H. R. Rep. 98, 42d Cong., 3d sess., 428, 1873. Siusclau.—Gibbs, Obs. on Coast Tribes of Oreg., MS., B. A. E. Siuselaws.—Ind. Aff. Rep., 470, 1865. Siuslaw.—Drew, ibid., 1857, 359, 1858. Suislaws.—Bancroft, Nat. Races., I, 250, 1882. Syouslaws.—Ind. Aff. Rep. 1856, 106, 1857. Tsaná-uta am'im.—Gatschet, Lakmiut MS., B. A. E., 105 (Lakmiut name). Tsashtlas.—Domenech, Deserts, I, map, 1860.

Sivinganek. A village of the Angmagsalingmiut Eskimo in Sermilik fjord, E.

SIVÍNGARÑARSÍK—SKAÍAKOS

585

BULL. 30]

Greenland; pop. 31 in 1884.—Meddelelser om Grönland, x, map, 1888.

Sivingarnarsik. A village of the Angmagsalingmiut Eskimo in Sermilik fjord, E. Greenland; pop. 31 in 1884.
Sivinganarsik.—Meddelelser om Grönland, x, map, 1888. Sivingarnasik.—Ibid., expl. of map.

Siwanoy (from their having been a seacoast people, their name may be a corruption of *Siwanak*, 'salt people,' a dialectic form of *Suwanak*, a name applied by the Delawares to the English.—Gerard). One of the principal tribes of the Wappinger confederacy, formerly living along the N. shore of Long Island sd. from New York to Norwalk, Conn., and inland as far at least as White Plains. They were one of the seven tribes of the seacoast and had a number of villages, the principal one in 1640 being Poningo. (J. M.)
Sewonkeeg.—Owaneco (1700) in N. Y. Doc. Col. Hist., IV, 614, 1854 (trans.: 'western Indians'). Siwanoos.—De Laet (1633) in N. Y. Hist. Soc. Coll., 2d s., I, 296, 1841. Siwanoys.—Ruttenber, Tribes Hudson R., 81, 1872. Sywanois.—Map of 1616 in N. Y. Doc. Col. Hist., I, 13, 1856.

Siwapi. The Sage (*Chrysothamnus howardii*) clan of the Patki (Water-house) phratry of the Hopi.
Shiwáhpi.—Voth, Hopi Proper Names, 105, 1905. Si-vwa'-pi.—Stephen in 8th Rep. B. A. E., 39, 1891. Sivwapi wiñwû.—Fewkes in 19th Rep. B. A. E., 583, 1900 (*wiñwû*='clan').

Siwim Pakan. A former Maidu village a few miles N. of Kelsey, Eldorado co., Cal.—Dixon in Bull. Am. Mus. Nat. Hist., XVII, map, 1905.

Six. See *Shakopee*.

Siyante. A former Miwok village on Tuolumne r., Tuolumne co., Cal.
Li-yan-to.—Barbour in Sen. Ex. Doc. 4, 32d Cong., spec. sess., 252, 1853. Segantes.—Ibid., 69. Si-yan-te.—Johnson in Schoolcraft, Ind. Tribes, IV, 407, 1854. Si-yan-ti.—Johnston in Sen. Ex. Doc. 61, 32d Cong., 1st sess., 22, 1852. Si-yau-te.—McKee et al. (1851) in Sen. Ex. Doc. 4, 32d Cong., spec. sess., 74, 1853. Typoxies.—Johnson in Schoolcraft, op. cit. (so called from their chief).

Siyita (*Sīyi'ta*). A Cowichan tribe whose village was Skuhamen, at Agassiz, on lower Fraser r., Brit. Col.—Boas in 64th Rep. Brit. A. A. S., 454, 1894.

Skaddal. A tribe numbering 200 persons, found by Lewis and Clark in 1806 on Cataract (Klikitat) r., 25 m. N. of Big Narrows, in the present Washington, and mentioned by Robertson in 1846, under the name Saddals, as numbering 400. They subsisted by hunting deer and elk, and traded with the Eneeshur and Skilloot for prepared fish. Classed by Mooney as a division of the Pisquows living about Boston cr. and Kahchass lake, at the head of Yakima r.
Lower Yakima.—Gibbs in Pac. R. R. Rep., I, 417, 1855. Saddals.—Robertson (1846) in H. R. Ex. Doc. 76, 30th Cong., 1st sess., 9, 1848. Scad-dals.—Lewis and Clark Exped., Coues ed., III, 958, 1893. Skaddal.—Ibid., Allen ed., II, 475, 1814. Skaddals nation.—Ibid., Coues ed., III, 1255, 1893. Skaddat.—Clark (1806) in Orig. Jour. Lewis and Clark, IV, 311, 1905. Skad-dats.—Ibid., 307. Skad-datts.—Ibid., 296. Ska'utăl.—Mooney in 14th Rep. B. A. E., 736, 1896.

Skae (*Sqa-i*). A Haida town of the Kaidju-kegawai, formerly close to C. St James, at the s. end of Queen Charlotte ids., Brit. Col. It is said to have been so named because its inhabitants here skinned the sea lions which they killed on the Isles Kerouart.—Swanton, Cont. Haida, 277, 1905.

Skagit. A body of Salish on a river of the same name in Washington, particularly about its mouth, and on the middle portion of Whidbey id., especially at Penn's cove. According to Gibbs the population of the Skagit proper in 1853 was about 300. They are now on Swinomish res., Wash. Gibbs makes this division include the Kikiallu, Nukwatsamish, Towahha, Smalihu, Sakumehu, Miskaiwhu, Miseekwigweelis, Swinamish, and Skwomamish; but probably nothing more is meant by this classification than that the dialects of the several divisions were nearly related and the geographical position close. Nothing like political union appears to have existed among them.
Hum-a-luh.—Mackay quoted by Dawson in Trans. Roy. Soc. Can., sec. II, 7, 1891 ('the people': own name). Sachet.—Wilkes, U. S. Expl. Exped., IV, 149, 1844. Sacket.—De Smet, Oregon Miss., 34, 1847. Scad-jat.—Mallet in Ind. Aff. Rep., 198, 1877. Scatchae.—Gibbs (misquoting Wilkes) in Pac. R. R. Rep., I, 435, 1855. Scatchat.—Stevens in Ind. Aff. Rep., 459, 1854. Shatchet.—Farnham, Travels, 111, 1843. Skadjats.—De Smet, Oregon Miss., 61, 1847. Skadjets.—Schoolcraft, Ind. Tribes, v, 701, 1857. Skagats.—Lane in Sen. Ex. Doc. 52, 31st Cong., 1st sess., 173, 1850. Skaget.—Hill in H. R. Doc. 37, 34th Cong., 3d sess., 79, 1857. Skagit.—Gibbs in Pac. R. R. Rep., I, 433, 1855. Sk'a'-jub.—McCaw, Puyallup MS. vocab., B. A. E., 1885 (Puyallup name).

Skagway (*Cqague'*, a term that does not bear popular interpretation). A former Chilkat town at the head of Lynn canal, now noted as the terminus of the Yukon and White Horse railroad.
Cqague'.—Swanton, field notes, B. A. E., 1904. Sohkagué.—Krause (1882) quoted by Baker, Geog. Dict. Alaska, 580, 1906. Shkagway.—Nichols (1891), ibid. Skaguay.—Baker, ibid. Skagwa.—Ibid.

Skahakmehu ('numerous tribe'). A Salish division that resided where the Port Madison (Wash.) mill now stands, but now on Port Madison res.
Ska-hak-bush.—Mallet in Ind. Aff. Rep., 198, 1877. Ska-hak-mehu.—Boulet in letter, Mar. 22, 1886.

Skahasegao (*Skä-hase'-gä-o*). An ancient Seneca village on the site of Lima, Livingston co., N. Y.—Morgan, League Iroq., 314, 468, 1851.

Skahene-hadai (*Sqahē'ne xā'da-i*, 'Ska river people'). A subdivision of the Chaahl-lanas, a Haida family of the Eagle clan living in Alaska. Skahene is said to mean, in Tlingit, 'to cry over a river,' and it is related that at a time when this branch was almost exterminated they went up on a mountain above this river and cried.—Swanton, Cont. Haida, 276, 1905.

Skaiakos (*Sqaí'aqōs*). A Seechelt sept with many settlements but no fixed abode (Hill-Tout in Jour. Anthr. Inst., 23, 1904). For general habitat see *Seechelt*.

Skaialo (*Sqaid′lō*). A Chilliwack village in s. British Columbia, with 16 inhabitants in 1909.

Isquahala.—Can. Ind. Aff., 78, 1878. Sqaiâ′lo.—Hill-Tout in Ethnol. Surv.Can.,4,1902. Squehala.—Can. Ind. Aff., 309, 1879. Squiahla.—Ibid., pt. II, 160, 1901. Squihala.—Ibid., 74, 1878.

Skaiametl. A Kwantlen village at New Westminster, on Fraser r., Brit. Col. Pop. 45 in 1909, including Kikait.

New Westminster.—Can. Ind. Aff., pt. II, 72, 1902. SQai′amEtl.—Hill-Tout in Ethnol. Surv. Can., 54, 1902. Tcē′tstlEs.—Boas in Rep. B. A. A. S.,454,1894.

Skaiets (*Sqai′Ets*). A Kwantlen village on Stave r., an affluent of lower Fraser r., Brit. Col.—Hill-Tout in Ethnol. Surv. Can., 54, 1902.

Skaischiltnish. A Salish division living, according to Gibbs, at the old Chimakum mission on Spokane r., Wash. Pop. of "Lower Spokan," 301 in 1908.

Chekasschee.—Bancroft, Nat. Races, I, 315, 1874. Che-kiss-chee.—Winans in Ind. Aff. Rep., 23, 1870. Lower Spokan.—Ind. Aff. Rep., 702, 1901 Lower Spokanes.—Winans, op. cit. Skai-schil-t′nish.—Gibbs in Pac. R. R. Rep., I, 414, 1855.

Skaito. A camp on the w. coast of the Queen Charlotte ids., Brit. Col., occupied by Haida at the time of the gold excitement at Gold Harbor in 1852–60. It is sometimes spoken of erroneously as a town and confused with Kaisun and Chaahl.

Kai-shun.—Dawson, Q. Charlotte Ids., 168B, map., 1878 (misapplied). Sqai′-tāo.—Swanton, Cont. Haida, 280, 1905. Tlg·â′it.—Boas, 12th Rep. N. W. Tribes, Can., 24, 1898 (misapplied).

Skakaiek (*Sqāqai′Ek*). A Squawmish village community on the right bank of Squawmisht r., Brit. Col.—Hill-Tout in Rep. Brit. A. A. S., 474, 1900.

Skakhaus (*Sk′a′-quas*). A Kuitsh village on lower Umpqua r., Oreg.—Dorsey in Jour. Am. Folk-lore, III, 231, 1890.

Skaleksum. The Lummi name of one of their temporary fishing villages on the w. side of Lummi id., Whatcom co., Wash.

Skáleksun.—Gibbs, MS. no. 248, B. A. E. Sky-lak-sen.—Fitzhugh in H. R. Ex. Doc. 87, 34th Cong., 3d sess., 75, 1857.

Skamoynumachs (*Ska-moy-num-achs*). Given by Ross (Advent., 289, 1849) as one of the Okinagan tribes, but the name is not met with elsewhere.

Skanahwahti ('beyond the stream.'—Hewitt). An Onondaga, known generally to the whites as John Buck, the firekeeper of his tribe in Canada; died about 1893 at Brantford, Ontario. He gave Horatio Hale valuable aid in preparing the Iroquois Book of Rites (1883), and was much esteemed. He was official keeper and interpreter of the tribal wampum. See *Skandawati*.   (w. m. b.)

Skanapa. A former Choctaw town noted by d'Anville. It was on the E. side of the head of a tributary of the Sukenatcha, probably Running Tiger cr., Kemper co., Miss.—Halbert in Pub. Miss. Hist. Soc., VI, 432, 1902.

Skanapa.—d'Anville's map in Hamilton, Colonial Mobile, 158, 1897. Skanappa.—Halbert, op. cit. Skunnepaw.—West Florida Map, ca. 1775.

Skandawati ('beyond the stream'). An Onondaga chief, of the Turtle clan, who led an embassy to the Hurons in Oct. 1647. He returned 15 Huron prisoners and bore 7 great belts. Early in the following year the Hurons sent a new embassy, and Skandawati and another remained as hostages. The Mohawk destroyed the party, and Skandawati was so mortified that he killed himself. The other had a like sense of honor, but was less rash. His name appears also as Scandaouati (Jes. Rel. 1648, 56, 1858) and Scandawati (Hale, Iroq. Book Rites, 160, 1883). Cf. *Skanahwahti*. (w.m.b.)

Skaniadariio (Seneca: *Skaniadai′io*', 'it is a very fine lake,' commonly rendered "Handsome Lake"). A former federal chief of the Seneca; born at the village of Ganawagus, near Avon, in the Genesee valley, N. Y., about 1735; died at Onondaga, near Syracuse, in 1815. By birth he belonged to the Turtle clan, and was a half-brother of Cornplanter (q. v.) on his father's side. Although thus closely related to Cornplanter, he did not, like his illustrious half-brother, acquire marked distinction during the American Revolution, which was one of the most trying periods in the history of the Seneca and their confederates. On the contrary, the greater part of his life was spent in dissipation and idleness; but late in life, realizing that the worst curse of his race was the evil of drunkenness and the traffic in liquor, he sought to establish a better system of morals among his people, who were then passing through a transition period between their ancient mode of life and modern civilization. His precepts and teachings, based largely on the ancient custom and faith, but recast to adjust them to the new conditions, contemplated the regulation of family life by pointing out the respect and duties that should sub-ist between husband and wife and between parents and children, and the need of chastity and continence, and by the inculcation of habits of industry and thrift. About 1796, while living at Connewango on Allegheny r., at Warren, Pa., Skaniadariio was prostrated, it is said, by epilepsy and partial paralysis. For four years he lay suffering, and having lost all hope of recovery, resigned himself to death. According to his own story, one afternoon he heard voices calling him out. He arose in spirit and went outside, where, at a short distance from the house among some shrubbery, he saw four spirits in human shape, who assured him that they were merely messengers to him from the Artificer of Life. Of these, three bore shrubs in their hands, on which hung several kinds of fruit, which he was told to eat, when he was at once restored by their magical efficacy. Thereupon the messengers revealed to him by means of a great number of precepts the will of the Artificer of Life, on a variety of subjects; he was further told to promulgate these teachings among the tribes of the Iroquois, and was led by the messengers into the white man's hell, in order to permit him to witness the punishments that are in store for the lawless and the drunkard, the better to enable him to warn his people of the need of reform. The watchers at his bedside thought he was dead, but after a long trance he suddenly arose, and from that time rapidly recovered health. He visited the several Iroquois villages from year to year, preaching his new doctrines with power and eloquence. It is reported that many so-called pagans gave up their dissolute habits, becoming sober and moral men and women, among whom "discord and contention gave place to harmony and order, and vagrancy and sloth to ambition and industry." It was this reformed religion of Handsome Lake, or the so-called paganism of the modern Iroquois, that has so steadfastly resisted the advance of Christianity and education among the Iroquois tribes. At the present time the seat of this faith is in Canada, on the Grand River res., where it has about 1,200 adherents; but there are small bodies who still profess to follow the precepts of Handsome Lake dwelling on the Cattaraugus and the Allegany res., and on the Onondaga res. in New York. Each autumn these "pagans" assemble to hear the doctrines of Skaniadariio preached to them. In 1802, Skaniadariio with a number of associates visited Washington to explain to President Jefferson the nature of their doctrine in order to receive recognition of it by the Government for the purpose of counteracting the inroads of Christianity. The President, through the Secretary of War, commended the new doctrines in a letter, which was mistaken by the Seneca for a license permitting Skaniadariio to preach his new faith to the Indians.　　　(J. N. B. H.)

Skannayutenate (probably from *Skanĕñyuté'*, 'rock again protrudes.'—Hewitt). A Cayuga village, destroyed by Gen. Sullivan in 1779. It was on the w. side of Cayuga lake, N. E. of the present village of Canoga, Seneca co., N. Y., and nearly opposite the Cayuga towns on the E. The lake is narrow there, and the Cayuga occupied both shores.　(W. M. B.)

Skanowethltunne (*Ska-no'-wĕçl ʇûn'nĕ*). Given as a Takelma band or village on the s. side of Rogue r., Oreg.—Dorsey in Jour. Am. Folk-lore, III, 235, 1890.

Skanuka (*Sχa-nu-χā*). A name applied by Dawson (Queen Charlotte Ids., 134, 1880) to one of the four clans into which he erroneously supposed the Haida to be divided. It may be otherwise spelled Sg·anag·wa, and is the native term for "supernatural power." Dawson translates it "killer-whale," but the more usual name for the killer-whale is *sg·ana*, though this animal was indeed so named because it was held to be supernatural. Dawson's mistake arose from the fact that the Tsimshian of the mainland opposite are divided into four clans, and among the Haida the killer-whale is a very important crest belonging to one of the two clans.　　　(J. R. S.)

Skaos (*Sq!a'os*, probably 'salmonberry bushes'). A Haida town of the Sagualanas family at the entrance to Naden harbor, Graham id., Brit. Col.—Swanton, Cont. Haida, 281, 1905.

Skappa ('sandy land'). A Ntlakyapamuk village on the E. bank of Fraser r., near Boston Bar, Brit. Col. Pop. 17 in 1909. Sk·āpa.—Hill-Tout in Rep. Ethnol. Surv. Can., 4, 1899. Skappah.—Can. Ind. Aff., 309, 1879. Skepah.—Ibid., 78, 1878. Skopah.—Brit. Col. map, Ind. Aff., Victoria, 1872. Skuppa.—Can. Ind. Aff. Rep. 1904, sec. II, 71, 1905. Skuppah.—Ibid., map, 1891.

Skasahah. A band of Cowichan on Vancouver id., numbering 20 in 1882, the last time their name appears. Ska-sah-ah.—Can. Ind. Aff., 258, 1882.

Skatalis. An Ahtena village near the mouth of Copper r., Alaska; probably the original Alaganik. Sákhalis.—Allen, Rep. on Alaska, 38, 1887. Skatalis.—Ibid., 120.

Skatehook (from *peskatekuk*, 'at the river fork.'—Gerard). A Westenhuck village on Housatonic r. near the present Sheffield, Berkshire co., Mass. In 1736 the inhabitants removed to Stockbridge, a few miles up the river. Skatehook.—Barber, Hist. Coll. Mass., 94, 1841. Statehook.—Hoyt, Antiq. Res., 209, 1824.

Skauishan. A Squawmish village community on the right bank of Squawmisht r., w. Brit. Col. Skáocin.—Boas, MS., B. A. E., 1887. 'Skaui'can.—Hill-Tout in Rep. Brit. A. A. S., 474, 1900.

Skaukel. A Chilliwack village in s. British Columbia, with 30 inhabitants in 1909. Skaukē'l.—Hill-Tout in Rep. Ethnol. Surv. Can., 4, 1902. Skokale.—Can. Ind. Aff., 316, 1880. Skolale.—Brit. Col. map, Ind. Aff., Victoria, 1872. Skulkayn.—Can. Ind. Aff., pt. 2, 45, 1909. Skulkayu.—Ibid., pt. II, 160, 1901.

Skauton. A village near Sandwich, Barnstable co., Mass., in 1685. It seems to have been on Buzzards bay, and was probably subject to either the Wampanoag or the Nauset.—Hinckley (1685) in Mass. Hist. Soc. Coll., 4th s., v, 133, 1861.

Skeakunts (*Sk·ē'akunts*). A Squawmish village community on Burrard inlet, Brit. Col.—Hill-Tout in Rep. Brit. A. A. S., 474, 1900.

Skeawatsut (*Skē′awasut*). A Squawmish village community at Pt Atkinson, E. side of Howe sd., Brit. Col.—Hill-Tout in Rep. Brit. A. A. S., 474, 1900.

Skecheramouse. A former division of the Salish living on the Colville trail, Wash. Stevens calls them a band of Spokan.
Ske-chei-a-mouse.—Gibbs in Pac. R. R. Rep., I, 414,1855. Ske-cher-a-mouse.—Stevens in Ind. Aff. Rep., 429, 1854.

Skedans (corrupted from *Gidansta*, 'from his daughter,' the name of its chief). An important Haida town of the Kagials-kegawai family, formerly on a point of land which extends into Hecate str. from the E. end of Louise id., Queen Charlotte ids., Brit. Col. The town was known to its inhabitants as Kona or Huadji-lanas. They were always on the best of terms with those of the Tsimshian town of Kitkatla, whence they imported many new customs and stories into the Haida country. John Work, 1836–41, assigned to this town 30 houses and 738 inhabitants. The old people remember 27 houses; in 1878 Dawson noted about 16 houses. It has been abandoned for several years, though a number of housepoles are still standing.   (J. R. S.)
Kiddan.—Keane in Stanford, Compend., app., 473, 1878. Koona.—Swan in Smithson. Cont., XXI, 5, 1876. K.'u′na.—Boas, 12th Rep. N. W. Tribes Can., 24, 1898. Kwun Hāadē.—Harrison in Proc. Roy. Soc. Can., sec. II, 125, 1895. Q!ō′na.—Swanton, Cont. Haida, 278, 1905. Skedans.—Dawson, Q. Charlotte Ids., 169B, 1880. Skeeidans.—Schoolcraft, Ind. Tribes, V, 489, 1855. Skidans.—Boas, op. cit. (misprint from Dawson). Skidanst.—Harrison, op. cit. Skiddan.—Poole, Q. Charlotte Ids., 309, 1872. Xū′Adji lnagā′-i.—Swanton, op. cit., 120.

Skeinah (contr. of *Uñskiniyĭ*). A Cherokee settlement on Toccoa r., in the present Fannin co., N. Ga., about the period of the removal of the tribe in 1839. From a confusion of the name with the Cherokee *askina*, an evil spirit or malevolent ghost, it has sometimes been rendered "Devil Town."

Skekaitin (*SkEka′itĭn*, 'place of coming up above, or reaching the top'). A village of the Upper Fraser band of Ntlakyapamuk, on the w. side of Fraser r., 43 m. above Lytton, Brit. Col.
Skāikai′Eten.—Hill-Tout in Rep. Ethnol. Surv. Can., 4, 1899. SkEka′itĭn.—Teit in Mem. Am. Mus. Nat. Hist., II, 172, 1900.

Skelautuk (*SqEla′utuQ*, 'painted house,' on account of a painted post in a house there). A former village or camp of the Pilalt, a Cowichan tribe on lower Chilliwack r., Brit. Col.—Hill-Tout in Ethnol. Surv. Can., 48, 1902.

Skeleton. See *Anatomy*.

Skelsh (*Sqēlc*, 'standing up,' referring to "Siwash rock"). A Squawmish village community on Burrard inlet, Brit. Col.—Hill-Tout in Rep. Brit. A. A. S., 475, 1900.

Skelten (*SqE′ltEn*). A village of the Ewawoos tribe of the Cowichan on lower Fraser r., Brit. Col., 2 m. above Hope.—Boas in Rep. Brit. A. A. S., 454, 1894.

Skena (*Sqē′na*). A Haida town prominent in the family stories, situated just s. of Sand Spit pt., Moresby id., Brit. Col. According to tradition it was composed of 5 rows of houses, each occupied by a single family of the Raven clan. These 5 are said to have been the Tadji-lanas, Kuna-lanas, Yaku-lanas, Koetas, and Stlenga-lanas. The Daiyuahl-lanas claimed that their own chief was chief of the town.—Swanton, Cont. Haida, 279, 1905.

Skenandoa (*Skĕñnoñ′don*, 'deer.'—Hewitt). A noted Oneida chief who died at Oneida Castle, Tryon co., N. Y., Mar. 11, 1816, reputed to be 100 years of age; in all probability, however, he was not so old, otherwise he would have been nearly 70 years of age before appearing in history. He is described as a tall, robust man of intelligent appearance. During the first part of his life he was addicted to drink. In 1775, while at Albany attending to business in behalf of his tribe, he became drunk and the next morning found himself in the street, everything of value, including the sign of his chieftainship, having been taken from him. Feeling the disgrace, he resolved never again to become intoxicated, a resolution which he strictly maintained during his remaining years. He seems to have been reformed and brought into the church chiefly through the influence of Rev. Samuel Kirkland, missionary to the Oneida, to whom Skenandoa was so greatly attached that he asked to be buried by the side of the latter in the cemetery at Clinton, N. Y. He was the friend of the colonists previous to the Revolution, and during the war staunchly espoused the cause of the people of the United States. He watched and aided in repelling Canadian invasions, and on one occasion preserved from massacre the people of the settlements at German Flats, Herkimer co., N. Y. It was chiefly through his influence that the Oneida declaration of neutrality in the Revolutionary war was issued in May 1775, bearing the names of Skenandoa (Johnko' Skeanendon) and eleven other principal men of the tribe (Stone, Life of Brant, I, 63, 1838). His name in various forms is signed, always by his mark, to deeds of cession, treaties, agreements, etc., with the state of New York between 1790 and 1811, and to the treaty with the United States, Dec. 2, 1794. He became blind and is credited with saying that he was "an old hemlock, dead at the top." Lewis H. Morgan, the ethnologist, sometimes wrote under the pen-name Skenandoah.   (C. T. W. M. B.)

Skhakhwaiyutslu (*Sqa′-qwai yu′-tslu*). An Alsea village on the s. side of Alsea r., Oreg.—Dorsey in Jour. Am. Folk-lore, III, 230, 1890.

Skichistan. A Shuswap village on

Deadman r., a N. affluent of Thompson r., Brit. Col. Population of all Deadman's r. Indians, 117 in 1909.

Dead Man's Creek.—Can. Ind. Aff., 259, 1882 (includes all the other Shuswap on this river). Sket-shiotin.—Ibid., 189, 1883. Skichistan.—Ibid., pt. II, 166, 1901. Ski-shis-tin.—Dawson in Trans. Roy. Soc. Can., sec. II, 44, 1891. Stichistan band.—Can. Ind. Aff., 240, 1902.

Skicoak (possibly a contraction of Virginia Algonquian (Renape) *Maskikok*, 'swamp people.'—Gerard). A large village in 1584, possibly Siouan, on Roanoke r., about 6 days' travel above the mouth of Albemarle sd., probably in Virginia. It may have been identical with Occaneechi.

Skicoack.—Amadas (1585) in Smith (1629), Va., I, 83, 1819. Skicoak.—Strachey (1612), Va., 143, 1849. Skihoah.—Martin, N. C., I, 12, 1829.

Skidai-lanas (*Skidā'-i lā'nas*, 'powerless town-people'). A Haida family of the Eagle clan, belonging to the geographic group known as Gunghet-haidagai, or Ninstints people. It is said to have been a branch of the Gunghet-kegawai, and owned the ancient town of Hlgadun.—Swanton, Cont. Haida, 272, 1905.

Skidaokao (*Ski'daoqao*, 'eggs of Ski'-dao'). One of the principal Haida families of the Raven clan on Masset inlet, Brit. Col., said to have been named from a man called Skidao. Formerly these people lived with several other families in the town of Naikun, whence they moved to Masset and owned the town, now known by that name, until very recent times.   (J. R. S.)

Ski'daoqao.—Swanton, Cont. Haida, 271, 1905. Skidoukou.—Harrison in Proc. Roy. Soc. Can., sec. II, 125, 1895. Skyit'au'k·ō.—Boas, 12th Rep. N. W. Tribes Can., 23, 1898.

Skidegate. One of the two or three inhabited Haida towns on Queen Charlotte ids., Brit. Col.; situated at the entrance to an inlet of the same name on its N. shore. The native names for this town were Hlgaiu and Hlgagilda, Skidegate being the corruption by whites of a name of the chief, Sgedagits (Sgē'dagîts). Anciently owned by the Hlgaiu-lanas, it was given over to the Gitins, according to tradition, in payment for an injury received by a member of the latter family. According to John Work there were 48 houses between the years 1836 and 1841, with 738 people. The last row of native houses which stood here numbered only 20, which would give a population of 300 to 400. In 1909 there were 239 people, living almost entirely in houses patterned after those of the whites. There is a Methodist mission at Skidegate, and the Salvation Army has some followers. All the people are nominally Christians. The name of this town has been adopted to designate the Skittagetan family (q. v.).   (J. R. S.)

Hyo-hai-ka.—Dawson, Q. Charlotte Ids., 165, 1880 (given as native name; possibly intended for "Hlgai-u"). Illth-cah-getla.—Deans, Tales from Hidery, 58, 1899. Kil-hai-oo.—Dawson, op. cit., 165. Łgagî'-lda.—Swanton, Cont. Haida, 279, 1905 (native name). Łgā-iū'.—Ibid., 279. Lthagild.—Harrison in Proc. Roy. Soc. Can., sec. II, 125,

1895. Sketigets.—Dunn, Hist. Oregon, 281, 1844. Skid-a-gate.—Poole, Q. Charlotte Ids., 309, 1872. Skid-de-gates.—Dawson, op. cit., 173. Skiddegeet.—Scouler (1846) in Jour. Ethnol. Soc. Lond., I, 233, 1848. Skidegate-Hāadē.—Harrison in Proc. Roy. Soc. Can., sec. II, 125, 1895. Skidegat's town.—Deans, Tales from Hidery, 4, 1899. Skidegattz.—Schoolcraft, Ind. Tribes, III, 402, 1853. Skidigate.—Can. Ind. Aff., 128, 1879. Skit'-a-get.—Gibbs in Cont. N. A. Ethnol., I, 136, 1877. Skit-e-gates.—Kane, Wand. N. Am., app., 1859. Skit-ei-get.—Dawson, op. cit., 165. Skittagete.—Gallatin in Trans. Am. Ethnol. Soc., II, 77, 1848. Skittagets.—Gallatin, ibid., pt. 1, c. Skitt de gates.—Schoolcraft, Ind. Tribes, V, 489, 1855. Skittegas.—Scouler in Jour. Geog. Soc. Lond., XI, 219, 1841. Skittegats.—Scouler (1846) in Jour. Ethnol. Soc. Lond., I, 233, 1848. Skittgetts.—Anderson quoted by Gibbs in Hist. Mag., 74, 1863. Tlk·āgîlt.—Boas, 12th Rep. N. W. Tribes Can., 24, 1898.

Skidi (probably from *tskiri*, 'wolf,' or *skirirara*, 'wolves standing in water,' referring to a tribal tradition). One of the tribes of the Pawnee confederacy (q. v.), sometimes called Wolf Pawnee, and by the French Pawnee Loup. That the Skidi were closely associated with the idea of the wolf is evident from the sign language, in which they are designated by the sign for that animal. The speech of the Skidi differed slightly from that of the other 3 Pawnee tribes. According to tradition the Skidi and Arikara were once united, but became separated during the northward migration, the Arikara keeping to the Missouri valley and the Skidi settling on Loup r., Nebr., where finally the other 3 Pawnee tribes built their villages. The wanderings and adventures of the Skidi are matters of tradition rather than of history. They have so long regarded the valley of the Loup as their home that they have located in that vicinity the supernatural underground dwellings of the mythic animals which preside over the ceremonies of their secret societies. When first known to the white race the Skidi were farther N. than the other 3 Pawnee tribes. Tradition indicates that this tribe was the first to push northward from their old home in the S. W. There are stories of the Skidi having been conquered by the other Pawnee tribes, but these may refer rather to local tribal quarrels and not imply subjugation, for the Skidi have ever kept their distinctive organization and have tenaciously preserved their tribal rites with their esoteric teachings.

According to information obtained by Bolton from Spanish manuscript sources, a part of the Skidi (or "Pani-Maha," as they were called) moved southward and about 1770 approached the Texas border. One of the conditions of the general peace that was established between the Spaniards and the northern Texas tribes in 1772 was that these tribes should consent to be moved s., away from the influence of the Pani-Maha (Viceroy to the King of Spain, Nov. 26, 1772, MS. in Archivo Gen., Corr. of Viceroys, Bucareli no.

654). About 1777 a group of the Pani-Maha joined the Taovayas (Tawehash) settlement. When Mezières was there in 1778 they had temporarily withdrawn, but he urged them to return, which they did within a year. From this time on they seem to have formed an important part of the Taovayas settlement, which was called by Sibley, in 1805, that of the "Panis or Towiaches" (Hist. Sketch, 1806). A Mexican map of 1862 shows a "Pannis" village near the head of Sulphur cr., N. E. Texas (Map no. 1020, Sec. de Cartografía, Depto de Fomento, Mexico).

During the two centuries prior to their removal from Nebraska to Indian Ter. in 1874 the Skidi, in common with the other Pawnee tribes, fought to hold their hunting grounds against intruders, and to that end strove for the possession of horses. The securing of this class of booty was the chief incentive of war parties, and the possession of ponies became the sign of wealth. The history of the Skidi does not differ materially from that of the other Pawnee tribes. They joined in the treaties with the United States, served as scouts in its army, and followed their kindred to Oklahoma, where they live to-day, owning lands in severalty as citizens of the United States. There were no missions established especially for the Skidi; they were included in those maintained for all the Pawnee.

The organization of the Skidi is perhaps more fully carried out in accordance with the religious beliefs of the people than that of the other Pawnee tribes. They say they were organized by the stars, which powers "made them into families and villages, taught them how to live and how to perform their ceremonies." Five villages formed the central group. The village at the w. led in religious ceremonies and had no secular function except in times of dire distress. The other 4 villages of the group were situated as at the corners of a square, the sides of which faced the cardinal directions. Following an established rotation, each village led in tribal affairs during one year—a winter and a summer. The position of these 5 villages and of the other 17 of the tribe were all fixed by the position of the stars which had given them their shrines and ceremonies, so that the Skidi villages on the earth were like a reflection of their stars in the heavens. The star gave its name to the shrine, and the village took its name from the shrine or from some incident connected with its bestowal by the star. A secular name indicative of locality was sometimes added. The shrine was given by the star to a certain man, and his descendants became its hereditary keepers.

The immediate care and protection of the shrine devolved on a woman descendant. The ceremonies and rituals pertaining to the shrine were in charge of a priesthood, into which anyone of good character might enter after instruction and the performance of certain duties.

To the Skidi the universe was dual—male and female—and on the conjunction of these two forces depended the perpetuation of all forms of life. A ceremony exemplifying this belief, in which was the sacrifice of a girl, typical of the evening star, to the masculine morning star, was peformed among the Skidi as late as the first quarter of the 19th century (see *Petalesharo*). The various ceremonies of the villages began with the first thunder in the spring and closed when the winter sleep set in. The social customs and avocations of the Skidi did not differ from those of the other Pawnee tribes.

Consult G. A. Dorsey, Traditions of the Skidi, 1904; Dunbar, Pawnee Indians, 1880–82; Fletcher, (1) The Hako, in 22d Rep. B. A. E., 1903, (2) in Am. Anthr., IV, 730, 1902; Grinnell, Pawnee Hero Stories, 1889.   (A. C. F.)

Ckíɸi.—Dorsey, Osage MS. vocab., B. A. E., 1883 (Osage name). **Ckíyi.**—Dorsey, Kansa MS. vocab., B. A. E., 1882 (Kansa name). **Indiens-Loups.**—Gass, Voy., 22, 1810. **La Loup.**—Orig. Jour. Lewis and Clark, VI, 86, 1905. **Loos.**—Gass, Jour., 23, 1807. **Lou.**—Orig. Jour. Lewis and Clark, VI, 86, 1905. **Loupes.**—Lewis, Travels, 15, 1809. **Loup Pawnees.**—Prichard, Phys. Hist. Man, V, 412, 1847. **Loups.**—Lewis and Clark Discov., 15, 1806. **Mahah.**—Sage, Scenes in Rocky Mts., 153, 1846. **Mahas.**—Gregg, Comm. Prairies, II, 301, 1844. **ɟaɸiⁿ-mahaⁿ.**—Dorsey, Çegiha MS. dict., B. A. E., 1879 (Omaha name). **Pahi Mahas.**—Gallatin in Schoolcraft, Ind. Tribes, III, 397, 1853. **Pammahas.**—McKenney and Hall, Ind. Tribes, III, 80, 1854. **Panemaha.**—Boudinot, Star in West, 128, 1816. **Pania Loups.**—Lewis and Clark Discov., 62, 1806. **Pania Luup.**—Orig. Jour. Lewis and Clark, V, 381, 1905. **Pania Lousis.**—Ibid., VII, 314. **Panias Loups.**—Lewis and Clark, Travels, 15, 1807. **Panimachas.**—Barcia, Ensayo, 298, 1723. **Panimaha.**—Douay (1687) quoted by Hayden, Ethnog. and Philol. Mo. Val., 346, 1862. **Panimaha's.**—Coxe, Carolana, 16, 1741. **Pani-Mahaws.**—Schoolcraft, Ind. Tribes, III, 399, 1853. **Pa-ni-mahû.**—Grayson, Creek MS. vocab., B. A. E., 1885 (Creek name). **Panimakas.**—Jefferys, French Dom. Am., I, 139, 1761. **Panimalia.**—Ibid., I, Canada map. **Panimalis.**—Alcedo, Dic. Geog., IV, 52, 1788. **Panimoas.**—Barcia, Ensayo, 291, 1723. **Panimoha.**—Hennepin, New Discov., pt. II, 47, 1698. **Panislousa.**—Crepy, Carte Gén. de l'Amérique Sept., n. d. **Panismahans.**—La Salle (1687) quoted by Shea, Early Voy., 28, 1861. **Panis Mahas.**—Lewis, Travels, 15, 1809. **Panivacha.**—McKenney and Hall, Ind. Tribes, III, 81, 1854 (probably identical). **Pannamaha.**—Coxe, Carolana, map, 1741. **Pannimalia.**—Bowles, Map of America, after 1750. **Pants Mahas.**—Lewis and Clark, Journal, 17, 1840. **Papia Louisis.**—Lewis, Travels, 24, 1809. **Paunee Loups.**—H. R. Ex. Doc. 117, 19th Cong., 1st sess., 7, 1826. **Pawnee Loup.**—Irving, Ind. Sketches, II, 13, 1835. **Pawnee Loupes.**—Drake, Bk. Inds., bk. V, 181, 1841. **Pawnee Mahas.**—Long, Exped. Rocky Mts., I, 300, 1823. **Pawnee Mahaw.**—Pike, Exped., 143, 1810. **Pawnee Marhar.**—Treaty of 1812 in U. S. Ind. Treaties, 644, 1873. **Pawnee Mohaw.**—Ind. Aff. Rep., 904, 1847. **Pawnee O'Mahaws.**—Hildreth, Dragoon Campaigns, 163, 1836. **Pawneeomawhaws.**—Long, Exped. Rocky Mts., II, lxxxv, 1823. **Pawnee O'Mohaws.**—Hildreth, op. cit., 169. **Pawnees Loups.**—Lewis and Clark Exped., I, 33,

1814. **Pawnemahas.**—Long, Exped. Rocky Mts., I, 159, 1823. **Páyiⁿ-maⁿhaⁿ'.**—Dorsey, Osage MS. vocab., B. A. E., 1883 ('Upstream Pawnees': Osage name). **Så-ṭjěr-ŏ-pån-gå.**—Long, Exped. Rocky Mts., II, lxxxiv, 1823 (Hidatsa name). **Scidi.**—Iapi Oaye, XIII, no. 2, 6, Feb. 1884 (Dakota name). **Sói'li.**—Riggs in Cont. N. A. Ethnol., VII, 441, 1892 (Teton name). **Skee'-e-ree.**—Lewis and Clark Discov., 19, 1806. **Skee'-de.**—Morgan in Smithson. Cont., XVII, 196, 1871. **Skeedee.**—Ind. Aff. Rep., 213, 1861. **Skee-e-ree.**—Am. State Papers, Ind. Aff., I, 709, 1832. **Skeeree.**—Long, Exped. Rocky Mts., I, 478, 1823. **Skere.**—Ibid., II, 365. **Skerreh.**—Rafinesque, Amer. Nations, I, 24, 1836. **Ski'-di.**—Dunbar in Mag. Am. Hist., IV, 244, 1880 (*Tski'-ri*='wolf'). **Steelar.**—Corliss, Lacotah MS. vocab., B. A. E., 106, 1874 (Teton name). **Stili.**—Ind. Aff. Rep., 179, 1875 (Teton name). **Wolf Indians.**—Gass, Jour., 23, 1807. **Wolf Pawnees.**—Lewis and Clark Exped., I, 33, 1814. **Wolves.**—Lewis and Clark Discov., 19, 1806.

Skidirahru (*Tskiri rah'ru*, 'the wolves standing in the pools'). A band of the Skidi Pawnee, so named by other Skidi because long ago, while camped on Loup r., Nebr., they obtained so much meat while an immense buffalo herd was crossing that they began to take only the hides, leaving the carcasses on the river ice, which, melting, formed small pools, around which many wolves gathered.—Grinnell, Pawnee Hero Stories, 238, 1889. **Skidi rah'ru.**—Grinnell, Pawnee Hero Stories, 238, 1889. **Tskiri rah'ru.**—F. Boas, inf'n, 1907.

Skihwamish (*skaikh* 'inland', *-mish* 'people': 'people living inland'). A Salish division on a river of same name and on the upper branches of the Snohomish, in Washington.

Skai-na-mish.—Ross in Ind. Aff. Rep. 17, 1870. **Skai-wha-mish.**—Pt. Elliott treaty (1855) in U. S. Ind. Treaties, 378 1873. **Skawhahmish.**—Maynard in H. R. Ex. Doc. 37, 34th Cong., 3d sess., 86, 1857. **Ska-whamish.**—Ibid. **Skea-wa-mish.**—Starling in Ind. Aff. Rep., 170, 1852. **Skeysehamish.**—De Harley in Schoolcraft, Ind. Tribes, V, 701, 1855. **Skey-wah-mish.**—Jones (1853) in H. R. Ex. Doc. 76, 34th Cong., 3d sess., 5, 1857. **Skeywhamish.**—Lane in Sen. Ex. Doc. 52, 31st Cong., 1st sess., 173, 1850. **Skihwamish.**—Gibbs quoted by Dall in Cont. N. A. Ethnol., I, 241, 1877. **Skiwhamish.**—Gibbs, ibid., 179. **Sky-wa-mish.**—Gibbs in Pac. R. R. Rep., I, 436, 1855.

Skil. A local name of the black candlefish (*Anoplopoma fimbria*), an excellent food fish of the waters of the N. Pacific coast, particularly about Queen Charlotte ids., Brit. Col. The word is derived from *sqil*, the name of this fish in the Haida language.   (A. F. C.)

Skilak. A Knaiakhotana village, of 44 inhabitants in 1880, on the s. side of Skilak lake, Kenai penin., Alaska.
Skilakh.—Petroff in 10th Census, Alaska, 29, 1884.

Skilloot. A Chinookan tribe found by Lewis and Clark in 1806 residing on both sides of Columbia r. in Washington and Oregon, above and below the entrance of Cowlitz r., and numbering in all 2,500 souls. The Hullooetell may have been a band of them (Orig. Jour. Lewis and Clark, III, 196; VI, 68, 117, 1905). They were among the tribes almost exterminated by the fever epidemic of 1823. Later their principal village was Cooniac,

at Oak Point, Wash. In 1850 Lane placed their number at 200, but as a tribe they disappeared from view a few years later. The Seamysty appear to have been a division.   (L. F.)
Caloait.—Lane in Schoolcraft, Ind. Tribes, I, 521, 1853. **Calooit.**—Lane in Ind. Aff. Rep., 161, 1850. **Caloort.**—Lane in Sen. Ex. Doc. 52, 31st Cong., 1st sess., 172, 1850. **Chilook.**—Gass, Jour., 191, 1807. **Kolnit.**—Gairdner in Jour. Geog. Soc. Lond., XI, 255, 1841. **Kreluits.**—Franchère, Voy., 105, 1854. **Skillools.**—Boudinot, Star in the West, 128, 1816. **Skilloot.**—Lewis and Clark Exped., II, 63, 1814. **Skillute.**—Ibid., I, map, 1814. **Skillutes.**—Wilkes, Hist. Oregon, 44, 1845. **Skillutts.**—Robertson, Oregon, 129, 1846.

Skin. See *Anatomy*.

Skin and Skin dressing. In the domestic economy of the Indians skins were his most valued and useful property, as they became later his principal trading asset, and a mere list of the articles made of this material would embrace nearly half his earthly possessions. Every kind of skin large enough to be stripped from the carcass of beast, bird, or fish was used in some tribe or another, but those in most general use were those of the buffalo, elk, deer, antelope, beaver, ermine, certain large birds in ceremonial costumes, the jackrabbit in the Paiute country, the seal and walrus, with the salmon and wolffish, among the Eskimo.

Among the principal belongings made in whole or in part from skins may be named tipis, parflèche boxes, feather boxes, bed covers,

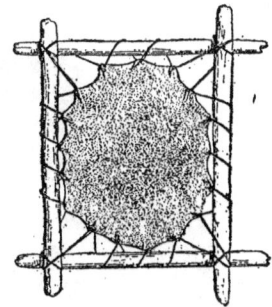

ESKIMO METHOD OF MOUNTING SEAL-SKIN (NELSON)

pillows, tobacco pouches, medicine bags, pounding hides (upon which to mash and spread out berries, pemmican, etc.), saddle blankets, horse and dog harness, the bullboat of the upper Missouri tribes, the kaiak of the Eskimo; fishing lines, nets, etc.; clothing in all its parts, from robes and shirts to leggings and moccasins; shields, body armor, pictograph records, ceremonial masks, and cradles.

The methods employed for dressing skins were very much the same everywhere N. of Mexico, the difference being chiefly in the chemicals used and in the amount of labor given to the task. Among the Plains tribes, with which the art is still in constant practice nearly according to the ancient method, the process consists of 6 principal stages, viz, fleshing, scraping, braining, stripping, graining, and working, for each of which a different tool is required. When skins are dressed for robes the hair is not removed. A number of hides are usually dressed at the same time, the women working together in the open air. Sunshine, without too great heat, is essential for the best result.

The fleshing process begins as soon as possible after the hide is stripped from the carcass, while the skin is still soft and moist. The hide is staked out upon the ground, fleshy side up, when two women, working together, scrape off the flesh and fat by means of a sort of gouge with serrated edge, anciently made from the leg bone of some large animal, for which is now substituted a similar iron instrument procured from the traders. By means of a loop going over the wrist the strength of the blow is increased, the worker kneeling or bending over the skin.

Next comes the scraping, a very laborious process, the instrument used being a sort of short adz, made of wood or elkhorn, with a blade of stone or iron set at a right angle to the handle. Several

METHOD OF MOUNTING BUFFALO-HIDE BY WESTERN TRIBES

women work together. The hide is staked out, hair side up, with a bed of old dressed skin under it to break the force of the blow, and thus prevent tearing, as well as to keep the dressed surface clean. Each side is scraped in turn, the final scraping being the more delicate operation. The hair and the skin shavings are saved for filling pillows, or are sometimes boiled into soup.

Then comes the braining process, in which the skin is thoroughly anointed with a mixture of cooked brains and liver, grease, and pounded soaproot (yucca), all mixed together and applied with a sponge of soaproot fiber. A little salt is frequently added. The liver is hashed, or sometimes chewed, to render it fine enough before cooking, and approximately the whole brain and liver of the animal are required to dress its hide. The braining is an easy and rapid process,

after which a bundle of dried grass is laid in the center of the hide and saturated with hot water, when the corners of the hide are brought together over it in bag fashion, and the skin tightly twisted into a solid ball, and hung up to soak overnight for the next process. According to Schoolcraft (Narr. Jour., 323, 1821), the eastern Sioux dressed their buffalo skins with a decoction of oak bark, which he surmises may have been an idea borrowed from the whites. According to La Flesche, liver is not used in the dressing process by the Ponca, Omaha, and Oto, and meat broth is sometimes substituted for brains, while the hide is soaked in the running stream overnight. The Maricopa of s. Arizona use the castor bean in the tanning process.

Next comes the stripping, intended to squeeze out the surplus moisture and the dressing mixture. The dampened hide is first opened out and twisted into a rope in order to expel as much moisture as can be thus dislodged, after which it is stretched tightly, at an angle of about 45 degrees, in a frame consisting of a crosspiece supported by 2 stout forked poles, the lower end of the skin being staked to the ground. The stripping is done by 2 women working together, the instrument being a broad blade about 6 in. long, set in a bone handle, and much resembling a small hoe blade. The ancient tool was of stone. The instrument being grasped horizontally in both hands, with the blade pressing heavily upon the skin, it is drawn steadily from top to bottom, causing a thin stream of water to ooze out before the blade as it descends. As one woman nears the bottom her partner follows along the same track, before the moisture can work back under the blade. In this way the work goes on to the end over the whole surface of the skin, after which the skin is left suspended in the frame to dry and bleach until it is ready for graining. This is done with a globular piece of bone, as large as can be conveniently held in the hand, cut from the spongy portion of the humerus of a buffalo or other large animal. With this the whole surface of the skin is rubbed as with sandpaper to reduce the hide to uniform thickness and smoothness and to remove any hanging fibers. After this the breaks and holes are repaired with an awl and sinew thread. According to La Flesche, the semiagricultural Omaha and Pawnee also rub corn-meal over the skin to hasten the drying process.

Then comes the process of working or softening, to render the skin pliable. This is done by drawing the skin for some time in seesaw fashion across a rope of twisted sinew stretched between two trees a few feet apart. It is sometimes drawn first around the trunk of a rough-barked tree for a short time, two women again working together, one at each end of the skin; this treatment gives the skin its final softness. Afterward it is cleaned with a wash of white chalk clay in water, put on thick with a bunch of root fiber or dried grass for a brush, and brushed off when dry.

For parflèche purposes the tanning process is omitted. For making shields the hide is shrunk over a fire until it is of twice its original thickness and correspondingly tougher, being sometimes anointed before the operation, as already described. The process for deer skins and smaller skins is naturally less laborious than for buffalo (or cow) hides, and skins of panthers, wildcats, etc., intended for quivers, boys' coats, and pouches, are dressed with the hair on. Among the coast tribes the scraper is frequently a mussel shell or an oyster shell. In California and along the Pacific coast generally a rib bone is used, and the skin is laid over an inclined log instead of being staked on the ground. In the eastern timber country and in the Arctic region hides are usually smoked to render them impervious to moisture, and urine takes the place of soaproot in the dressing mixture. Bleaching is effected by the action of the sun's rays on wet skins. Among the Eskimo, for lack of summer sunshine the skin is sometimes dried over the fire or by wrapping it around the human body. Skins of the seal and walrus, and of birds and fish, all require special processes, while for intestines, pericardiums, and other internal membranes, used as water jars, paint bags, etc., the preparation is limited to softening and dyeing. It is doubtful if skin dyeing was commonly practised in former times, although every tribe had some method of skin painting. The Omaha, however, according to La Flesche, procured a dark-blue or black dye by combining the bark of the white maple with pulverized and roasted yellow ocher. The Plains tribes use the juice from the leaf of the prickly pear as a mordant to fix the painted design, and obliterate it, when so desired, by rubbing it over with a piece of roasted liver.

The process of preparing skins, as described above, pertains more particularly to the northern and western tribes of the United States. The Choctaw, Cherokee, and probably all the tribes that inhabited the area eastward from the Mississippi to the Atlantic and s. of the Algonquian tribes, followed a somewhat different method, which is thus described by David I. Bushnell, jr., as witnessed by him among the Choctaw of Louisiana:

57009°—Bull. 30, pt 2—12——38

The skin to be dressed is first soaked in water several hours or during a night. Being removed from the water it is placed over a log which has been smoothed so as to form an even surface. While in this position the hair or fur is removed by being scraped with an instrument resembling a drawknife, now made by inserting a metal blade in a long wooden handle. Next the skin is placed in a wooden mortar, together with a mixture of corn-meal, eggs, and a small quantity of water. It is then beaten with a wooden pestle until it becomes thoroughly saturated with the mixture. This conforms with the statement made by Lawson more than two centuries ago, when he wrote of the Indians of Carolina. With regard to their method of dressing skins, he alluded to "young Indian corn beaten to a pulp," used in the place of the brains of animals, to soften the skins. The combination of eggs and corn-meal would probably affect the skins in the same manner as green corn. After the process of beating or pounding, the skin is stretched on a perpendicular frame, consisting of two uprights and two horizontal bars. It is then scraped and rubbed until dry, the instrument consisting of a piece of metal set in a wooden handle extending in the same direction. When dry, the skin is removed from the frame; but it is then stiff. It is softened by being pulled back and forth over a stake driven into the ground, the top of the stake having previously been rounded and smoothed to prevent tearing the skin. This process of dressing a skin makes it very white and soft.

If a skin is to be smoked, a pit is first dug in the ground. A fire is then made in the pit and allowed to burn until a mass of hot ashes and glowing embers accumulates. Pieces of damp, rotten oak are placed on the ashes, causing a dense smoke. The skin, being previously dressed as described, is stretched over the pit and allowed to remain in the smoke two or three hours.

If the skin is to be dressed with the hair or fur remaining, it is first softened with a little clear water, after which it is spread over a log and scraped on the inner surface to remove all particles of flesh. The inside is then thoroughly rubbed with a mixture of eggs, corn-meal, and water, great care being taken not to wet the outside or fur. When the skin is nearly dry it is worked back and forth over the smooth and rounded top of a stake driven in the ground.

There are but few detailed descriptions of the skin-dressing processes of the tribes within the limits of the United States. Among these is Lawson's account of the method formerly in use in Carolina (Hist.

Car., 338, reprint 1860), Kroeber's account of the Arapaho process (Bull. Am. Mus. Nat. Hist., XVIII, pt. 1, 1902), and Wissler's for the Siksika (Ontario Archæol. Rep. for 1906). Good descriptions of Eskimo methods are given by Boas, Murdoch, and Nelson in the 6th, 9th, and 18th Reps. respectively of the B. A. E.; of the Nascapee process by Turner in 11th Rep. B. A. E.; of the British Columbia method by Teit in Mem. Am. Mus. Nat. Hist., II, pt. 4, 1900; and of that used by the Chukchi of N. E. Siberia by Bogoras in vol. VII, pt. 1, of the same series. Consult also Bushnell in Bull. 48, B. A. E., 1909; Mason in Rep. Nat. Mus. 1889, 552, 1891; N. Dak. Hist. Soc. Coll., I, 455, 1906; Shufeldt in Proc. Nat. Mus. 1888, XI, 1889; Spinden in Mem. Am. Anthr. Asso., II, pt. 3, 1908.　(J. M.)

Skingenes (*Sk·iñgē′nes*). A Songish band living on Discovery id., s. end of Vancouver id. Pop. 26 in 1909.
Discovery Island (Indians).—Can. Ind. Aff., pt. 2, 66, 1902. Sk·iñgē′nes.—Boas in 6th Rep N. W. Tribes Can., 17, 1890.

Skinpah (Tenino: *skin*, 'cradle'; *pä*, locative: 'cradle place'). A small Shahaptian tribe speaking the Tenino dialect and formerly living on the N. bank of Columbia r. opposite the mouth of the Des Chutes, in Klickitat co., Wash. They were included in the Yakima treaty of 1855 and placed on the reservation of that name. Their number is unknown.
Saw-paw.—Ross, Fur Hunters, I, 186, 1855. Skeen.—Kane, Wand. in N. A., 263, 1859. Skin.—Robie in Ind. Aff. Rep. 1857, 352, 1858. Skin.—Gibbs in Pac. R. R. Rep., I, 410, 1855. Skĭ′npä.—Mooney in 14th Rep. B. A. E., 740, 1896. Skin-pah.—U. S. Stat. at Large, XII, 951, 1863. Tekin.—Lee and Frost, Oregon, 176, 1844 (misprint).

Skistlainai-hadai (*Sk!í′sʟa-ina-ixadā′-i*, 'people of the house where they always have plenty of food'). A subdivision of the Yaku-lanas, a Haida family of the Raven clan; probably named from a house.—Swanton, Cont. Haida, 271, 1905.

Skitswish. A Salish tribe on a river and lake of the same name in N. Idaho. The name Cœur d'Alène (French 'Awl-heart'), by which they are popularly known, was originally a nickname used by some chief of the tribe to express the size of a trader's heart. The Skitswish bear a high reputation for industry, self-respect, and good behavior. In 1909 533 were enumerated as belonging to the Cœur d'Alène res., Idaho.
Coeur, and Alenes.—Scouler (1846) in Jour. Ethnol. Soc. Lond., I, 238, 1848. Cœur d'Aléne.—Parker, Journal, 293, 1840. Cœur d'Eleine.—Stevens in H. R. Doc. 46, 33d Cong., 1st sess., 77, 1854. Cœur d'Eliene.—Ibid. Cœur d'Eline.—Ibid. Cœur d'Helene.—Lane in Sen. Ex. Doc. 52, 31st Cong., 1st sess., 170, 1850. Cœurs d'Aleines.—Mayne, Brit. Col., 296, 1862. Cœurs d'aliene.—De Smet, Letters, 170, 1843. Cœurs d'Helene.—Lane in Ind. Aff. Rep., 159, 1850. Cœurs-pointus.—Domenech, Deserts, I, 441, 1860. Conerd Helene.—Lane in Schoolcraft, Ind. Tribes, I, 521, 1853. Couer d'Alienes.—Dart in Ind. Aff. Rep., 216, 1851. Cour d'Aleine.—Nicolet, Oregon, 143, 1846. Cour d'Alenes.—Cain

in Ind. Aff. Rep., 210, 1860. Cour d'Aline.—Robertson (1846) in H. R. Ex. Doc. 76, 30th Cong., 1st sess., 8, 1848. Cour De Lion.—Johnson and Winter, Rocky Mts., 34, 1846. Les Cœurs d'Alênes.—Cox, Columbia R., II, 150, 1831. Needle Hearts.—Domenech, Deserts, II, 262, 1860. Painted Heart Indians.—Saxton in Pac. R. R. Rep., I, 257, 1855 (misprint). Pointed Hearted Indians.—Wright in Sen. Ex. Doc. 32, 35th Cong., 2d sess., 37, 1859. Pointed-hearts.—Cox, Columbia R., II, 131, 1850. Printed Hearts.—Lane in Ind. Aff. Rep., 159, 1850 (misprint). Q'ma'shpäl.—Mooney in 14th Rep. B. A. E., 733, 1896 ('camas people': Yakima name). S'chízui.—Giorda, Kalispel Dict., I, 494, 1877–79. Sh-chee-tsoo-ee.—A. T. Richardson, inf'n, 1907 (name as pronounced by a Skitswish). Skee-cha-way.—Ross in Ind. Aff. Rep., 23, 1870. Skeelsomish.—Kelley, Oregon, 68, 1830. Skeetsomish.—Lewis and Clark Exped., II, 475, 1814. Skeetsonish.—Cass (1834) quoted by Schoolcraft, Ind. Tribes, III, 609, 1855. Sketsomish.—Lewis and Clark Exped., I, map, 1814. Sketsui.—Wilkes, U. S. Expl. Exped., IV, 449, 1845. Skit-mish.—Stevens in Ind. Aff. Rep., 460, 1854. Skitsaih.—Gallatin quoted by Schoolcraft, Ind. Tribes, III, 402, 1853. Skitsaish.—H. R. Ex. Doc. 76, 30th Cong., 1st sess., 7, 1848. Skitsämŭq.—Mooney in 14th Rep. B. A. E., 733, 1896 (Paloos name). Skítsui.—Gatschet, MS., B. A. E. (Okinagan name). Skitsuish.—Hale in U. S. Expl. Exped., VI, 209, 1846. Skitswish.—Gibbs in Pac. R. R. Rep., I, 415, 1855. Stohitsui.—Gatschet, op. cit. ("Flathead" name). Stiel Shoi.—De Smet, Letters, 216, 1843. Stietshoi.—Mooney in 14th Rep. B. A. E., 733, 1896.

Skittagetan Family. The name applied to a linguistic family composed of the Indians usually known as Haida (q. v.). It was taken from *Sgē′dagits*, a name of one of the Haida town chiefs, which seems to mean 'son of the chiton' [mollusk]. This was first erroneously applied to the town of Hlgagilda, of which he was head chief, and later, under the form Skittagets (see *Skidegate*), was applied by Gallatin to the people speaking this language, whence it was adopted by Powell.
=Haida.—Tolmie and Dawson, Comp. Vocabs., 15B, 1884. =Haidah.—Scouler in Jour. Roy. Geog. Soc., XI, 224, 1841. >Hai-dai.—Work quoted by Kane, Wand. in N. A., app., 1859. =Hidery.—Deans, Tales from Hidery, passim, 1899. <Hydahs.—Keane in Stanford, Compend., app., 460, 1878. >Kygáni.—Dall in Proc. A. A. A. S., 269, 1869. ×Nootka.—Bancroft, Nat. Races, III, 564, 1882. × Northern.—Scouler, op. cit. > Queen Charlotte's Island.—Gallatin in Trans. Am. Antiq. Soc., II, 15, 306, 1836. >Skidegattz.—Gallatin in Schoolcraft, Ind. Tribes, III, 402, 1853. >Skittagets.—Gallatin in Trans. Am. Ethnol. Soc., II, pt. 1, c, 1848. =Skittagetan.—Powell in 7th Rep. B. A. E., 118, 1891.

Skittok. A Knaiakhotana village on Kaknu r., Alaska, forming part of the Kenai settlement.
Chkituk.—11th Census, Alaska, 70, 1893. Shittok.—Post route map, 1903.

Sklau (*S′k·lau′*, 'beaver'). A Squawmish village community on the left bank of Squawmisht r., Brit. Col.—Hill-Tout in Rep. Brit. A. A. S., 474, 1900.

Skoachais (*Sk·ōātcai′s*, 'deep hole in water'). A Squawmish village community on Burrard inlet, Brit. Col.—Hill-Tout in Rep. B. A. A. S., 475, 1900.

Skogari. The Tutelo village in 1748; situated on the N. branch of the Susquehanna, in the present Columbia co., Pa. At the date named it was "the only town on the whole continent inhabited by Tutelees, a degenerate remnant of thieves and drunkards (De Schweinitz, Life of Zeisberger, 149, 1870). It was to this village that the Tutelo moved from Shamokin.

Skohwak (*Skoxwā'k*, 'skinny [people]'.—Hill-Tout). A village of the Ntlakyapamuk, on the w. side of Fraser r., about 15 m. above Yale, Brit. Col. Pop. 11 in 1897, the last time the name appears.
Skoxwā'k.—Teit in Mem. Am. Mus. Nat. Hist., II, 169, 1900. Skuhuak.—Can. Ind. Aff. 1892, 312, 1893. Skuōūa'k·k.—Hill-Tout in Rep. Ethnol. Surv. Can., 5, 1899. Skuwha.—Can. Ind. Aff. 1886, 230, 1887. Skuwka.—Ibid., 277, 1894.

Skoiyase ('place of whortleberries.'—Morgan.) A former Seneca village at the site of Waterloo, Seneca co., N. Y. It was destroyed by a detachment of Gen. Sullivan's army, under Col. John Harper, Sept. 8, 1779. At that time it contained about 18 houses, and was surrounded by orchards of peach and apple trees. On Sept. 3, 1879, the centennial of this event was celebrated, at which time a monument was erected in the village park at Waterloo. (G. P. D.)
Long Falls.—Fellows (1779) in Conover, Kan. and Geneva MS., B. A. E. Sauyou.—Grant (1779) in Jour. Mil. Exped. Gen. Sullivan, 142, 1887. Sä'-yase.—Morgan, League Iroq., 394, 1851 (Seneca and Onondaga name). Scauwaga.—Jenkins (1779) in Jour. Mil. Exped. Gen. Sullivan, 174, 1887. Scawyace.—Ibid., 142. Scharoyos.—Pa. Mag. Hist., 18, 1904. Schoyerre.—Grant, op. cit., 111. Secawyace.—N. Y. Ind. Problem, 224, 1889. Shaiyus.—Norris (1779) in Jour. Mil. Exped. Gen. Sullivan, 235, 1887 (or Large Falls). Skaigee.—Dearborn (1779) quoted by Conover, Kan. and Geneva MS., B. A. E. Skä'-yase.—Morgan, League Iroq., 394, 1851 (Tuscarora and Mohawk name). Skayes.—N. Y. Ind. Problem, 216, 220, 1889. Skoi-yase.—Morgan, League Iroq., 470, 1851 (Cayuga name). Skō-ne'-ase.—Ibid., 394 (Oneida name).

Skoka. A name among herbalists for the skunk-cabbage (*Symplocarpus fœtidus*), "skoka of the Indians" (Rafinesque, 1830). The name is probably short for Lenape (Delaware) *s'kākawûnsh*, 'skunk-weed'. (W. R. G.)

Skoke. A New England name for the pokeberry (*Phytolacca decandra*). Probably derived from Massachuset *m'skok*, 'that which is red' (Trumbull), or *m'skwak*. (W. R. G.)

Skokomish ('river people'). A body of Salish who, according to Eells, form one of three subdivisions of the Twana (q. v.). They lived at the mouth of Skokomish r., which flows into the upper end of Hoods canal, Wash., where a reservation of the same name has been set aside for them. They officially numbered 203 in 1909, but this figure includes the two other subdivisions of the Twana.
Hokamish.—Lane quoted by Schoolcraft, Ind. Tribes, I, 521, 1853. Kokomish.—Ind. Aff. Rep., 302, 1877. Scocomish.—Wilkes, U. S. Expl. Exped., IV, 410, 1845. Skâ-kâ-bǐsh.—Eells in Smithson. Inst. Rep., pt. I, 605, 1887 (Twana name). Ska-ka-mǐsh.—Ibid. (Clallam name). Skakobish.—Eells, letter, B. A. E. (Nisqualli name). Skaquah-mish.—Stevens in H. R. Ex. Doc. 37, 34th Cong.,

3d sess., 46, 1857. Skaquamish.—Taylor in Cal. Farmer, June 12, 1863. Skasquamish.—Ind. Aff. Rep. 1862, 359, 1863. Skiquamish.—Stevens, op. cit. Skokamish.—Gibbs in Pac. R. R. Rep., I, 431, 1855. Skŏ-kŏbĉ.—McCaw, Puyallup MS. vocab., B. A. E., 1885 (Puyallup name). Skokomish.—Lane in Ind. Aff. Rep., 162, 1850. Sko-ko-nish.—U. S. Ind. Treaties, 800, 1873. S'Komish.—Watkins in Sen. Ex. Doc. 20, 45th Cong., 2d sess., 3, 1878. Sko-sko-mish.—Starling in Ind. Aff. Rep., 170, 1852.

Skolai (from *Nikolai*, the chief's name). An Ahtena village on Nizina r., Alaska, near the mouth of Chitistone r., lat. 61° 21′, lon. 143° 17′.
Nicolai's village.—Allen, Rep., 128, 1887. Nikolai.—Baker, Geog. Dict. Alaska, 299, 1901.

Skonchin, Skontchish. See *Schonchin*.

Skonon (*Skŏ'nŏn*). A former Chumashan village near Santa Barbara, Cal., in the locality now called Arroyo del Burro.—Henshaw, Buenaventura MS. vocab., B. A. E., 1884.

Skooke ('snake'). A gens of the Abnaki.
Skog.—J. D. Prince, inf'n, 1905 (modern St Francis Abnaki form). Skooke.—Morgan, Anc. Soc., 174, 1877.

Skookum Chuck ('strong water'). The local name for a body of Salish of Fraser River agency, Brit. Col.; pop. 102 in 1909.
Skookum Chuck.—Can. Ind. Aff., pt. 2, 160, 1901. Skukem Chuck.—Ibid., 187, 1884.

Skopamish. A body of Salish formerly living on upper Green r., Wash., a tributary of White r., but now on Muckleshoot res. Pop. 222 in 1863; at present unknown.
Green River Indians.—Gosnell in Ind. Aff. Rep., 338, 1857. Neccope.—Simmons, ibid., 395, 1859. Nescope.—Taylor in Cal. Farmer, June 12, 1863. Niskap.—Gosnell in Ind. Aff. Rep., 244, 1858. Nooscope.—Ibid., 338, 1857. Sko-pabsh.—Mallet, ibid., 198, 1877. Skopahmish.—Gibbs in Cont. N. A. Ethnol., I, 179, 1877. Skope-áhmish.—U. S. Ind. Treat., 378, 1873. Skope-a-mish.—Ind. Aff. Rep., 17, 1870. White River Indians.—Gosnell in Ind. Aff. Rep., 244, 1858 (evidently intended for Green r.; see Gosnell, op. cit., 338, 1857).

Skoton. One of the names applied to the Athapascans formerly dwelling on or near Rogue r., Oreg. They were included by Parker (Jour., 257, 1840) among the Umpqua. The treaty of Nov. 18, 1854 (Sen. Ex. Doc. 48, 34th Cong., 3d sess., 10, 1854) was made by the Chasta, Scoton, and Umpqua, all of w. Oregon. The Skoton were divided into the Cownantico, Sacheriton, and Naalye. In 1875 (Ind. Aff. Rep., 177, 1875) they numbered 36 on Grande Ronde res. and 166 on Siletz res. See *Chasta-Skoton*.
Sconta.—Parker, Jour., 257, 1840. Scotons.—Ind. Aff. Rep., 219, 1856.

Skowl. Given by Petroff (10th Census, Alaska, 32, 1884) as the name of a town near Kasaan, Alaska. The word is undoubtedly a corruption of *Sqa'oal*, the name of a chief of Kasaan. If any place was so named, it was probably a small summer town or camp. (J. R. S.)

Skowtous. A division of the Ntlakyapamuk in the neighborhood of Nicola lake, Brit. Col.—Mayne, Brit. Col., 113, 1862.

Sktahlejum. A division of Salish, sometimes rated as a subdivision of the Snohomish, on the upper waters of Snohomish r., Wash.

Sk-tah-le-gum.—Gibbs in Pac. R. R. Rep., I, 436, 1855. Sk-tah-le-jum.—Stevens in Ind. Aff. Rep., 458, 1854. Sk-táh-le-jum.—U. S. Ind. Treaties, 378, 1873. Skuck-stan-a-jumps.—Starling in Ind. Aff. Rep., 170, 1852. Stak-ta-le-jabsh.—Mallet, ibid., 198, 1877.

Sktehlmish. A division of Salish on Dwamish lake and r., Wash.

S'ke-tehl-mish.—Gibbs in Pac. R. R. Rep., I, 436, 1855. S'ketēhmish.—Schoolcraft, Ind. Tribes, v, 703, 1857. Sk-táhl-mish.—U. S. Ind. Treaties, 378, 1873. Sk'tehlmish.—Gibbs in Cont. N. A. Ethnol., I, 241, 1877.

Skudus (*Sk!ū'dᴀs*, a word used when one misses a thing by arriving too late). A Haida town of the Djiguaahl-lanas family on the N. side of Lyell id., Queen Charlotte ids., Brit. Col.—Swanton, Cont. Haida, 278, 1905.

Skuhamen (*Squhä'mᴇn*). A village of the Siyita tribe of Cowichan, at Agassiz, on lower Fraser r., Brit. Col.—Boas in 19th Rep. N. W. Tribes Can., 454, 1894.

Skuingkung (*Squi'ñquñ*). A Songish band at Victoria, Brit. Col.—Boas in 6th Rep. N. W. Tribes Can., 17, 1890.

Skukskhat (*Skuksxat*, 'sucker mouth'). A former village of the Tlakluit below The Dalles of Columbia r., Wash. (E. S.)

Skull. See *Anatomy*.

Skulteen. A body of Salish of Fraser River agency, Brit. Col. Pop. 122 in 1896, the last time the name appears.

Skumeme (*Skû-mē'-me*). A former village of the Tututni on the s. side of Rogue r., Oreg., at its mouth.—Dorsey in Jour. Am. Folk-lore, III, 236, 1890.

Skumin (*Sk·ūmi'n*, 'keekwilee-house,' the term *keekwilee* meaning 'low,' or 'under,' probably referring to the semisubterranean houses of the N. W. interior.) A Squawmish village community on the left bank of Squawmisht r., Brit. Col.—Hill-Tout in Rep. Brit. A. A. S., 474, 1900.

Skunk. (1) The common name of a member of American musteloid carnivorous mammals (*Mephitis mephitica*), first appearing in English in the 17th century. The earliest citation is by Wood in his New England's Prospect (1634). This author, as well as Josselyn (1638–63), uses the form *squnck*, which Trumbull (Natick Dict., 155, 1903) connects with the Abnaki *ségaⁿkw*. The Cree *sikák*, the Chippewa *shikág*, etc., are cognate Algonquian words. The word came into English from Abnaki (Kennebec), in which the second syllable is nasalized. (2) Any other species of the genus *Mephitis*, and, by extension, any species of the genera *Spilogale* and *Conepatus*. After the skunk have been named skunk-bear (the wolverene), skunk blackbird or skunk-bird (the bobolink), skunk-bill (the surfscoter), skunk-cabbage or skunkweed

(*Symplocarpus fœtidus*; see *Skoke*), skunkhead or skunktop (pied duck, or the surf-scoter), skunk-porpoise (*Lagenorhyncus acutus*), skunk-spruce (*Picea canadensis*), skunkery or skunk-farm (a place where skunks are kept or bred for profit). (3) Among derived meanings are: "a vile, mean, good-for-nothing, or lowdown fellow," the corresponding adjective being skunky or skunkish. Also there is the verb to skunk, having the senses: (*a*) to defeat utterly, without the other party scoring at all; (*b*) to get no votes in an election; (*c*) to leave without paying one's bills. *Sea-skunk* is a term which is applied to a certain type of motor-boats. (A. F. C. W. R. G.)

Skunk-cabbage. See *Skoke*.

Skurghut (*Sku'-rxût*). A band or village of the Chastacosta on the N. side of Rogue r., Oreg.—Dorsey in Jour. Am. Folk-lore, III, 234, 1893.

Skurshka. The Water-snake clan of the pueblo of Laguna, N. Mex. Its members claim to have come originally from Sia. The clan forms a phratry with the Sqowi (Rattlesnake), Hatsi (Earth), and Meyo (Lizard) clans. (F. W. H.)

Shŭ'rshka-hánoᶜʰ.—Hodge in Am. Anthr., IX, 352, 1896 (misprint *sh* for *sk*; *hánoch*='people').

Skutuksen (*Sk·u'tuksᴇn*, 'promontory'). A Squawmish village community on the E. side of Howe sd., Brit. Col.—Hill-Tout in Rep. Brit. A. A. S., 474, 1900.

Skuzis ('jumping'). A Ntlakyapamuk village on Fraser r. above Spuzzum, Brit. Col.; pop. 33 in 1901, the last time the name appears.

Scuzzy.—Can. Ind. Aff., 418, 1898. Sku'zis.—Hill-Tout in Rep. Ethnol. Surv. Can., 5, 1899. Skuzzy.—Can. Ind. Aff., pt. II, 164, 1901.

Skwah. A Chilliwack village in s. British Columbia; pop. 104 in 1909.

Skwah.—Can. Ind. Aff., pt. 2, 160, 1901. Squah.—Ibid., 74, 1878. Squah-tta.—Gibbs, MS. vocab., B. A. E.

Skwahladas (*Sqoā'ladas*). A Haida family of the Raven clan, living on the w. coast of Queen Charlotte ids., Brit. Col. The meaning of the name is uncertain, but it has been suggested that it may indicate that they were successful fishermen. This family generally lived with the Hlgahetgu-lanas, but at one time had independent towns opposite Hippa id. and in Rennell sd. There part of them came to be known as Nasto-kegawai. Originally they seem to have formed one family with the Djahuiskwahladagai. (J. R. S.)

Skoa'tl'adas.—Boas, 12th Rep. N. W. Tribes Can., 24, 1898. Sqoā'ladas.—Swanton, Cont. Haida, 270, 1905.

Skwailuh ('hoar frost'). A Shuswap town on Pavilion cr., an E. affluent of upper Fraser r., Brit. Col.; pop. 68 in 1909.

Papillion.—Taylor in Cal. Farmer, July 19, 1862. Pavilion.—Can. Ind. Aff., pt. II, 162, 1901. Pavillon.—Teit in Mem. Am. Mus. Nat. Hist., II, 166, map, 1900. Skwai'-luh.—Dawson in Trans. Roy. Soc. Can., 1891, sec. II, 44, 1892.

Skwaius (*Sk·wai'us*). A Squawmish village community on Burrard inlet, Brit. Col.—Hill-Tout in Rep. Brit. A. A. S., 475, 1900.

Skwala (*Sk·wä'la*). A former village or camp of the Pilalt, a Cowichan tribe on lower Chilliwack r., Brit. Col.; so named from a slough on which it was situated.—Hill-Tout, Ethnol. Surv. Can., 48, 1902.

Skwauyik (*Skwa'uyix*). A Ntlakyapamuk village on the w. side of Fraser r., Brit. Col.—Teit in Mem. Am. Mus. Nat. Hist., ii, 169, 1900.

Skwawalooks. A Cowichan tribe on lower Fraser r., below Hope, Brit. Col.; pop. 16 in 1909.
Shawahlook.—Can. Ind. Aff. 1904, sec. ii, 75, 1905. Skawah-looks.—Ibid., 1894, 277, 1895. Skowall.—Ibid., 79, 1878. Skwawahlooks.—Ibid., pt. 2, 160, 1901.

Skway. A Chilliwack village on Skway r., which empties into the lower Fraser, Brit. Col.; pop. 27 in 1909.
Skway.—Can. Ind. Aff., pt. 2, 160, 1901. SQai.—Hill-Tout in Rep. Ethnol. Surv. Can., 4, 1902. Squay.—Ibid., 276, 1894. Squay-ya.—Brit. Col. map, Ind. Aff., Victoria, 1872. Syuay.—Can. Ind. Aff., 188, 1884.

Skweahm. A Nicomen winter village on Nicomen slough, near lower Fraser r., Brit. Col.; pop. 27 in 1909.
Skuyā'm.—Boas in Rep. Brit. A. A. S., 454, 1894. Skweahm.—Can. Ind. Aff., 160, 1901. Squeam.—Ibid., 313, 1888.

Skwealets (*Skwēā'lĕts*, 'coming in of the water'). An abandoned Chilliwack village on upper Chilliwack r., Brit. Col.—Hill-Tout in Ethnol. Surv. Can., 4, 1902.

Skwiteague. See *Squeteague.*

Slaaktl (*Slā'axʟ*). A Bellacoola village on Bellacoola r., Brit. Col., above Snutlelatl.
Slā'aqtl.—Boas in 7th Rep. N. W. Tribes Can., 3, 1891. Slā'axʟ.—Boas in Mem. Am. Mus. Nat. Hist., ii, 49, 1898.

Slahaltkam ('upper country'). A Shuswap village at the foot of Little Shuswap lake, interior of British Columbia. It gives its name to a band which includes the people of this village and those of Kwikooi. Pop. 88 in 1906, 96 in 1909.
Haltham.—Can. Ind. Aff., pt. 2, 166, 1901. Halthum.—Ibid., 363, 1897. Haltkam.—Ibid., 312, 1892. Halt-kum.—Ibid., 1885, 196, 1886. Little Lake Shuswap.—Ibid., pt. ii, 68, 1902. Sahhahltkum.—Ibid., 47, suppl., 1902. Sla-halt-kam.—Dawson in Trans. Roy. Soc. Can., sec. ii, 44, 1891.

Slana. An Ahtena village at the confluence of Slana and Copper rs., Alaska.

Slank. A word said to be of Indian origin, but of doubtful etymology, defined by Nelson (Inds. of N. J., 129, 1894) as "a name applied in the neighborhood of Paterson to a small body of water setting back like a bay along the shores of a river."

Slate. This material, which is widely diversified in character, was in very general use by the tribes n. of Mexico for the manufacture of utensils, implements, ornaments, and carvings in general. The typical slates are characterized by their laminated structure, and these were used to some extent, especially for implements; but the more massive varieties, such as the greenish striped slates of the Eastern states, the argillite (q. v.) of New Jersey, Pennsylvania, and the states to the s., and the black slate of the N. W. coast, were usually preferred. Argillite was much used by the tribes of the Delaware and Susquehanna valleys, and an ancient quarry of this material, located at Point Pleasant, Pa., has been described by Mercer (see *Quarries*). Material from this and corresponding quarries was used mainly for flaked implements, including leaf-shaped blades, knives, and arrow heads and spear heads, and these are widely distributed over the middle Atlantic states. The fine-grained greenish and striped slates of the Eastern and Middle states and Canada were extensively employed in the manufacture of several varieties of objects of somewhat problematic use, including banner stones, bird-shaped stones, and perforated and sculptured tablets. It is probable that, like the green agates and jadeites of Mexico, some varieties of this stone had special significance with the native tribes. The tribes of the N. W. coast employ a fine-grained black slate in their very artistic carvings, which the Haida obtain chiefly from deposits on Slate cr., Queen Charlotte ids. This slate has the desirable quality of being soft and easily carved when freshly quarried, and of growing harder with time. It is black and takes an excellent polish. See *Sculpture, Totem-poles.*

References to the use of slate occur in many works relating to ethnology and archeology, but are not sufficiently important to be given in full. Worthy of special mention are Mercer in Pub. Univ. Penn., vi, 1897; Niblack in Nat. Mus. Rep. 1888, 1890; Squier and Davis, Ancient Monuments, 1848. (w. h. h.)

Slavery. It may be doubted whether slavery, though so widespread as to have been almost universal, existed anywhere among very primitive peoples, since society must reach a certain state of organization before it can find lodgment (see *Social organization*). It appears, however, among peoples whose status is far below that of civilization.

Among the Eskimo, slavery appears to have been wholly unknown, although in the part of Alaska immediately n. of the Tlingit, where the Eskimo borrowed much of Indian culture and arts, it is possible that it existed in some form, as Bancroft affirms. Dall discovered no traces of slavery in Alaska, and doubts if it ever existed there. If the institution ever gained a foothold among the Eskimo it was foreign to their own culture and habits, was of comparatively recent introduction, and was practised only in a much modified form.

Beginning with the Tlingit, slavery as an institution existed among all the N. W. coast Indians as far as California. It practically ceased with s. Oregon, although the Hupa, of Athapascan stock, and the Nozi (Yanan), both of N. California, practised it to some extent, according to Powers. Among the former, a bastard became the slave for life of one of the male relatives of the mother and was compelled to perform menial service; nor could he or she marry a free person. Such slaves seem to have been entitled to purchase freedom, provided they could accumulate sufficient wealth. Both the Klamath and the Modoc seem to have had slavery in some form. The Klamath word for slave is *lugsh*, from *luktha*, 'to carry a load,' indicating that the slaves were the carriers of the tribe (Gatschet). The institution had found its way up Columbia r. also, at least as far as Wallawalla r., where it was known to the Cayuse of Waiilatpuan, and to the Nez Percés of Shahaptian stock. From the W. coast it appears to have passed far into the interior, where it was practised, probably in a much modified form, by the Indians of the Mackenzie r. region. It is said that the Etchareottine were called *Awokànak*, 'slaves', by their Cree neighbors, an epithet which in its French and Indian forms came to be the name (Slave or Slavey) under which they are best known.

The N. W. region, embracing the islands and coast occupied by the Tlingit and Haida, and the Chimmesyan, Chinookan, Wakashan, and Salishan tribes, formed the stronghold of the institution. As we pass to the eastward the practice of slavery becomes modified, and finally its place is taken by a very different custom. Among the tribes mentioned, slavery seems to have existed long enough to have secured a prominent place in mythology and to have materially modified the habits and institutions of the people. It was no doubt the origin of ideas of caste and rank widespread among tribes of the N. W. coast, but comparatively unknown elsewhere among our Indians. It varied considerably among different tribes, the most essential characteristics, however, being similar, as was the general mode of life of the peoples practising it. The above-named were fishing tribes and expert canoemen, depending for food far more on the products of sea fisheries than on game. All lived in settled villages. With all, the essential condition of rank and position was wealth, not renown gained in war. The slaves consisted of prisoners taken from neighboring tribes, chiefly women and children; and, among most

tribes, of their descendants. Over most of the area in question there appears to have been a regular traffic in slaves, the source of a considerable part of the private wealth. Jewett states in his Narrative (1815) that a Nootka chief had in his house "nearly fifty male and female slaves, no other chief having more than twelve." Simpson estimated that slaves formed one-third of the population of the Tlingit. The price of an adult slave was about $500 in blankets; of a child, 50 blankets, about $150.

Servitude in the N. W. appears to have been of a rather mild type. Slaves, as a rule, were well fed and well treated, as was natural with valuable property. The condition of the bondman indeed seems generally to have been little inferior to that of his master, whom he assisted in paddling, fishing, and hunting, even in making war on neighboring tribes. Expeditions were often undertaken for the primary purpose of slave catching. The slaves made or helped make canoes, cut wood, carried water, aided in building houses, etc. Enslaved women and children were household drudges, performing the laborious and menial tasks which elsewhere fell to the lot of free women. The distinction between the slave and the free man was especially sharply drawn in all ceremonial practices, from which slaves were rigidly excluded, and generally also with regard to marriage, for the slave usually could not mate with a free man or woman, though the Makah men, Swan asserts, frequently married female slaves. The male offspring of such marriages seem to have occupied an equivocal position between free men and slaves. Slaves seem to have had no well-defined rights; they could not own property and were subject to the caprices of their owners, who had power of life and death over them. Among the Tlingit it was customary to kill slaves and to bury their bodies beneath the corner-posts of the chiefs' houses at the time when they were erected; but this does not appear to have been done by the Haida. At other times they were given away or freed to show that their owner was so wealthy he could easily afford to part with them. Swan states that when a chief died among the Makah his favorite slaves were killed and buried with him.

Punishment for shortcomings was sometimes severe, the owner of a slave being responsible to no one. Occasionally slaves were killed outright in moments of passion.

Investigation of slavery among the tribes of the Great Plains and the Atlantic slope is difficult. Scattered through early histories are references to the subject, but such accounts are usually devoid of details, and the context often proves them to be based on erroneous conceptions. Had slavery existed among the Eastern and Southern tribes, we should find in the mass of documentary history as full accounts of the practice as there is concerning the less-known tribes of the N. W. coast. The unsatisfactory character of the references should make us cautious in accepting statements regarding the existence of slavery. The early French and Spanish histories, it is true, abound in allusions to Indian slaves, even specifying the tribes from which they were taken, but the terms "slave" and "prisoner" were used interchangeably in almost every such instance. Hennepin, in his account of his own captivity among the Sioux, uses these terms as equivalent, and speaks of himself as a slave, though his story clearly shows that he had been adopted by an old chief in the place of a lost son. With the exception of the area above mentioned, traces of true slavery are wanting throughout the region N. of Mexico. In its place is found another institution that has often been mistaken for it. Among the North American Indians a state of periodic intertribal warfare seems to have existed. Disputes as to the possession of land, retaliation for acts of violence, and blood revenge were the alleged causes; but underlying all was the fierce martial spirit of the Indian which ever spurred him from inglorious peace to stirring deeds of war. In consequence of such warfare tribes dwindled through the loss of men, women, and children killed or taken captive. Natural increase was not sufficient to make good such losses; for while Indian women were prolific, the loss of children by disease, especially in early infancy, was very great. Hence arose the institution of adoption. Men, women, and children, especially the latter two classes, were everywhere considered spoils of war. When a sufficient number of prisoners had been tortured and killed to glut the savage passions of the conquerors, the rest of the captives were adopted, after certain preliminaries, into the several gentes, each newly adopted member taking the place of a lost husband, wife, son, or daughter, and being invested with the latter's rights, privileges, and duties. It sometimes happened that small parties went out for the avowed purpose of taking captives to be adopted in the place of deceased members of families. John Tanner, a white boy thus captured and adopted by the Chippewa, wrote a narrative of his Indian life that is a mine of valuable and interesting information. Adoption occasionally took place on a large scale, as, for instance, when the Tuscarora and the Tutelo, on motion of their sponsors in the federal council, were formally adopted as offspring by the Oneida, the Delawares as cooks (an honorable position) by the Mohawk, and the Nanticoke, as offspring by the Seneca. In this way these alien tribes acquired citizenship in the Iroquois League; they were said to be "braces" to the "Extended Cabin," the name by which the Iroquois designated their commonwealth. (See *Adoption, Captives*).

Nor is it impossible that slaveholding tribes might have substituted adoption. Indications of the manner in which such change might have been effected may be found among the Tlingit and other N. W. Coast tribes, who not only freed their slaves on occasions, but made them members of the tribe. They also sometimes married slaves, which was tantamount to adoption. Wherever slavery did not exist, adoption seems to have been universally practised. Except that prisoners of war were necessary to recruit both institutions, the two are very unlike. The slave of the N. W. coast held absolutely no status within the tribe, whether he came into possession of the individual as the result of war or was bought as a slave from a neighboring tribe. Whatever privileges were his were granted as a favor, not as a right. On the other hand, the adopted person was in every respect the peer of his fellow-tribesmen. If he proved equal to the position assigned him in the tribe, and improved his opportunities, his advancement was sure, and he might aspire to any office attainable by the individual into whose place he had been adopted. If the new member of the tribe proved a poor hunter, a poor provider, or, above all, if he lacked courage, his position was not enviable: he was despised, and treated according to his demerits, probably worse than if he had been born a member of the tribe. Still there was nothing in his position or treatment to justify the statement that he was a slave, and his ignominy and shame were probably not greater than were usually incurred by the poor and worthless. It was the usual custom to depose the coward from man's estate, and, in native metaphor, to "make a woman" of him. Such persons associated ever after with the women and aided them in their tasks. Such was the custom among the Pawnee, as recorded by Grinnell (Pawnee Hero Stories, 26, 1893), who also gives a still more curious custom, by which young men who had not attained any special standing in the tribe lived as servants in the families of men of position and influence, and performed many offices almost menial. Dunbar speaks of these servants as being parasites and as usually being the most worthless members of the tribes (Pawnee Indians, 1880).

In most tribes polygamy was permitted, and it was a common practice for men to take to wife female captives. As a legal wife such a woman was entitled to the same privileges as her married sisters in the tribe, but her actual treatment depended largely upon her capacities and her personal popularity. When she was introduced into a family where there already were several wives, jealousy was easily aroused, and the new wife was likely to be abused and driven to menial tasks. No doubt such women were often assumed to be slaves by the casual observer.

European influence materially modified almost every art and practice of the Indian. No sooner had the border wars begun than the natives discovered a higher value for the white prisoners of war than adoption. Although white men and children were adopted into Indian tribes and lived and died with them, the ransom offered in ready money, in whisky, or in powder and guns changed the status of the white captive. He was very generally held in captivity for ransom, or taken to the French, English, or Spanish, according to his nativity, and disposed of for a cash payment. Cases were not rare in which white captives were redeemed and sent back to their friends even after formal adoption into a tribe. The practice of redeeming captives was favored by the missionaries and settlers with a view of mitigating the hardships of Indian warfare. The spread of Indian slavery among the tribes of the central region was due in part to the efforts of the French missionaries to induce their red allies to substitute a mild condition of servitude for their accustomed practice of indiscriminate massacre, torture, and cannibalism (see Dunn, Indiana, 1905). During the interval between his captivity and redemption, usually lasting months, occasionally several years, the white captive, unless adopted, was made to do menial tasks, and his lot was hard. The white prisoner, indeed, unless very young, rarely proved satisfactory as an adopted member of the tribe. He did not often take kindly to Indian life, was quick to seize an opportunity to escape, and was always welcomed back by his friends, whereas in the case of the Indian, adoption severed all former social and tribal ties. The adopted Indian warrior was forever debarred from returning to his own people, by whom he would not have been received. His fate was thenceforth inextricably interwoven with that of his new kinsmen.

The Southeastern Indians—Cherokee, Creeks, Choctaw, and Chickasaw—soon after the settlement of the country by Europeans came into possession of runaway negro slaves. The Indians were quick to perceive their value as servants, and we soon find them buying and selling black slaves. There is nothing to show that this introduction of black slaves among the Muskhogean tribes and others materially changed the status of the Indian prisoner of war. The Seminole of Florida married many negro runaways, whose position seems to have been in all respects like that of other members of the tribe. There were, indeed, among the Seminole several settlements of runaway negro slaves who had their own chiefs and seem to have been a recognized part of the tribe.

Europeans made a practice of enslaving or selling into slavery captive Indians. Carolina was early made by the Spaniards a hunting ground for Indian slaves, who were deported to Cuba. Numbers of the male children of the conquered Pequot were transported to the West Indies from Massachusetts and sold into slavery, while the women and girls were scattered among white families (Bradford in Coll. Mass. Hist. Soc., III, 360, 1856). The English settlers of South Carolina practised the enslavement of Indians on a large scale, and during the years 1702–1708 sent out three expeditions against the Yamasee, Apalachee, and Timucua, of N. Florida. They carried back to Charleston almost the entire population of 7 large towns, in all, some 1,400 persons, who were sold as slaves to the Carolina settlers or distributed among the Creeks, who assisted in the enterprise. Indeed, in the early days of the colonies the enslavement of Indians by settlers seems to have been general. See *Adoption, Social Organization.*   (H. W. H.)

Slaves. An ethnic and linguistic Athapascan group comprising, according to Petitot (Dict. Dènè Dindjié, xx, 1876), the Etchareottine, Thlingchadinne, and Kawchodinne. He included also the Etagottine of the Nahane group. The Etchareottine are specifically designated by this term, which originated with the Cree, who captured them in forays, and the tribe nearest to the Cree, the Etchaotine, are called Slaves proper.

Sleds. The Eskimo and the Indians N. of lat. 40° used as a vehicle for travel and transportation, complementary to the skin boat and the bark canoe, the sled drawn by man and dog over snow and ice. The Eskimo make long journeys, using boat and sled alternately. Sleds differ in construction, shape, and use according to the materials, the ingenuity of the people, the nature of the ice and snow, the journeys to be made, and the loads to be hauled. The simplest forms are smooth, flat substances, sometimes even blocks of ice; there is one consisting of a few plates of baleen stitched together; others are elaborately constructed. Uniform widths were adopted to enable them to follow the same tracks. Owing to frost and strain treenails and pegs were little used in construction; only lashings of good

CENTRAL ESKIMO SLEDGE (BOAS)

rawhide thongs would hold them together. In the use of these the makers were as ingenious at seizing and making knots as the Pacific islanders. The parts of a sled are the runners, shoes, crossbars, handles, lashings, lines, traces, toggles, packing, webbing, and braces. These belong to the fully equipped sled, which is a marvel of convenience, but some of them may be wanting. There are four plans of construction besides numerous makeshifts: (1) The bed lashed to solid runners; (2) the bed on pairs of bent sticks spliced together or arched and fastened below to runners; (3) the bed resting on a square mortised frame, probably an introduced type; (4) the bed flat on the ground, the toboggan. In the E., the Eskimo, being in some places poorly provided with wood, made sled runners

DOG HARNESS, CENTRAL ESKIMO (BOAS)

of porous bone, pieces of which, cut to shape and pierced, were sewed together neatly. The shoeing consisted of short strips of ivory or smooth bone, pierced and fastened on with treenails or thongs, which were countersunk to prevent abrading. When in use the shoes and runners were coated with ice or often with blood and salt. Boas figures a complete sled

from Cumberland gulf, and Mason a much pieced and perforated runner from Greenland, brought by Dr Kane. In the Mackenzie r. district were brought together the riding and freighting toboggan, the framed sleds of the Kutchin, and varieties with solid wooden runners. The greatest variety of forms, figured and described by Murdoch and Nelson, were found in Alaska. The main types are the low, flat sled without a rail, for carrying bulky objects and umiaks, and the built-up sled with a high rail on each side for loads of smaller articles and camp equipage. Murdoch describes a shoe of ice, 1 ft high and 6 in. wide, placed by the Pt Barrow Eskimo on the runners. Nelson figures the details of the two types of sled about Bering str., together with the whip, breast-board, swivels, and line attachers.

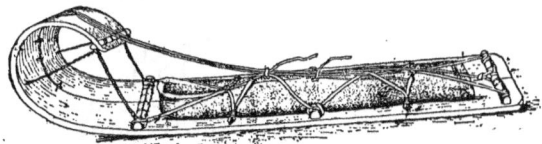

CANADIAN TOBOGGAN (MASON)

Consult Boas in 6th Rep. B. A. E., 1888; Dall, Alaska, 1870; Mason in Rep. Nat. Mus. 1894, 1896; Murdoch in 9th Rep. B. A. E., 1892; Nelson in 18th Rep. B. A. E., 1901; Stites, Economics of the Iroquois, 1905; Turner in 11th Rep. B. A. E., 1894.　　　　　　　　　　　(o. t. m.)

Sleeping Wolf (proper name *Gui-k'ati*, 'Wolf lying down'). Second chief of the Kiowa, a delegate to Washington in 1872, and a prominent leader in the outbreak of 1874–75. He was shot and killed in a quarrel with one of his own tribe in 1877. The name is hereditary in the tribe and has been borne by at least 5 successive individuals, the first of whom negotiated the permanent peace between the Kiowa and Comanche about 1790.　　　　　　　　　　(j. m.)

Sleepy Eyes (*Ishtaba*, or *Ishtahumba*). A chief of the Lower Sisseton Sioux, of the Chansdachikana band (not a Teton, as is sometimes said), born on Minnesota r. near the present site of Mankato; he lived most of his years on the lake which bears his name in Brown co., Minn. He was prominent in the affairs of his tribe contemporary with the relinquishment of their lands in Minnesota and the removal to the reservations on the upper Minnesota from 1850 to 1865. Sleepy Eyes became chief between 1822 and 1825, evidently succeeding Wahkanto. He was a frequent and friendly visitor at the home of Rev. S. R. Riggs, the renowned missionary. Heard states that a party of his people participated in the massacre of the whites at the Lake Shetek settlement in

1862. He is described in 1836 (McKenney and Hall, Ind. Tribes, II, 109, 1854) as large and well proportioned, of rather dignified appearance, good natured and plausible, but as having never been distinguished as a warrior or hunter. He signed the treaties of Prairie du Chien, Aug. 19, 1825, and July 15, 1830; St. Peters, Nov. 30, 1836; and Traverse des Sioux, July 23, 1851. The last treaty was signed also by "Sleepy Eyes young," probably a son. Sleepy Eyes died in Roberts co., S. Dak., but many years after his death his remains were disinterred and removed to Sleepyeye, Minn., where they were reburied under a monument erected by the citizens. (D. R. C. T.)

Sliammon. A Salish tribe on Malaspina inlet, Brit. Col., speaking the Comox dialect; pop. 107 in 1909.
Klaamen.—Brit. Col. Map, Ind. Aff., Victoria, 1872 (given as N. of Malaspina inlet). Sliammon.—Can. Ind. Aff., pt. II, 160, 1901. Tlaämen.—Boas, MS., B. A. E., 1887.

Slings. Slings made of the skins of animals and of textile materials variously woven and plaited were in use among the ancient aborigines of Middle and South America, and are still employed by the more primitive tribes. There appears to be no absolute proof, however, that the sling was known to the northern tribes before the discovery of America, although it has been assumed that certain pellets of baked clay found in numbers in California mounds were intended for this use. The slings found in collections, although showing in their materials and manufacture some local tribal characteristics, were adopted from Europeans and had no employment other than for youthful sports. (W. H.)

Slokoi. A Squawmish village community on the right bank of Squawmisht r., Brit. Col.—Hill-Tout in Rep. Brit. A. A. S., 474, 1900.

Slubeama. Given as a division of Salish numbering 400 and living N. of Whidbey id., on a river of the same name.
Slub-e-a-ma.—Jones (1853) in H. R. Ex. Doc. 76, 34th Cong., 3d sess., 5, 1857.

Slumach. A band of the Katsey (q. v.) in British Columbia; pop. 69 in 1896, when last separately enumerated.
Slumach.—Can. Ind. Aff., 276, 1894. Slumagh.—Ibid., 313, 1888.

Smackshop. A band of the Chilluckittequaw living in 1806 on Columbia r. from the mouth of Hood r. to The Dalles. Their estimated number was 800.
Sinacsops.—Wilkes, Hist. Oregon, 44, 1845. Smackshops.—Orig. Jour. Lewis and Clark, VI, 67, 1905. Smacshop.—Lewis and Clark Exped., map, 1893. Smacsops.—Robertson, Oregon, 129, 1846. Smakshop.—Ind. Aff. Rep., 460, 1854. Smascops.—Robertson in H. R. Ex. Doc. 76, 30th Cong., 1st sess., 9, 1848. Smockshop.—Morse, Rep. to Sec. War, 370, 1822. Smokshops.—Am. Pioneer, II, 191, 1843. Weocksockwillacum.—Lewis and Clark Exped., II, 239, 1814. We-ock-sock, Willacum.—Orig. Jour. Lewis and Clark, IV, 280, 1905. Wil-la-cum.—Ibid., 282.

Smalihu. A Salish division on a branch of Skagit r., N. W. Wash.; generally classed as a Skagit subtribe.
Sma-lèh-hu.—Stevens in Ind. Aff. Rep., 458, 1854. Sma-lih-hu.—Gibbs in Pac. R. R. Rep., I, 436, 1855. Smali-hu.—Gibbs in Cont. N. A. Ethnol., I, 180, 1877.

Smelakoa (*Smẹlä′kōä*). A Squawmish village community on Burrard inlet, Brit. Col.—Hill-Tout in Rep. Brit. A. A. S., 475, 1900.

Smith, Nimrod Jarrett (known to his people as *Tsálătíhí*, an attempt at the sound of "Jarrett"). A mixed-blood Cherokee, for a number of years chief of the Eastern band, residing on a reservation in w. North Carolina. His father, Henry Smith, was a half-breed, while his mother was of full blood. Chief Smith was born on Valley r., near the present Murphy, N. C., about 1838. He received a fair education, which he supplemented from his own resources in later years. Shortly after the outbreak of the Civil War he enlisted, with a considerable number of the East Cherokee, in the Thomas Confederate Legion, organized by Col. W. H. Thomas, a Cherokee trader, and served to the close of the war as sergeant of his Indian company. Some 10 years later he was elected principal chief of the Eastern band, which office he held by successive reelections almost to the time of his death. During all these years he was an active worker on behalf of his people, both at home and in Washington, and always at great personal sacrifice to himself, as by reason of the refusal of the band to join the main body of the tribe in the W. they were denied any share in the tribal funds, so that most of his service was performed at his own expense. Through his efforts the first schools were established among the East Cherokee and the landed interests of the tribe were established on a secure basis. He died in Aug. 1893. In person Smith was of manly and lovable disposition, dignified bearing, and magnificent physique, being 6 ft 4 in. in height. He was a master of both Cherokee and English. His wife was a white woman, formerly Miss Mary Guthrie. (J. M.)

Smoen (*Smō′ẹn*). The highest gens or band of the Bellacoola people of Nutlel, Brit. Col.—Boas in 7th Rep. N. W. Tribes Can., 6, 1891.

Smohalla. An Indian prophet and teacher, the originator of a religion current among the tribes of the upper Columbia r. and adjacent region in Washington, Oregon, and Idaho, whence the name "Smohallah Indians" sometimes applied. The name, properly *Shmoqŭla*, signifies "The Preacher," and was given to him after he became prominent as a religious reformer. He belonged to the Sokulk, a small tribe cognate to the Nez Percés and centering about Priest rapids on the Columbia in E. Washington. He was born about 1815 or 1820, and in his boyhood frequented a neighboring Catholic mission, from which he evidently derived some of his ceremonial ideas. He distinguished himself as a warrior, and began to preach about the year 1850. Somewhat later, in consequence of a quarrel with a rival chief, he left home secretly and absented himself for a long time, wandering as far s. as Mexico and returning overland through Nevada to the Columbia. On being questioned he declared that he had been to the spirit world and had been sent back to deliver a message to the Indian race. This message, like that of other aboriginal prophets, was, briefly, that the Indians must return to their primitive mode of life, refuse the teachings or the things of the white man, and in all their actions be guided by the will of the Indian God as revealed in dreams to Smohalla and his priests. The doctrine found many adherents, Chief Joseph and his Nez Percés being among the most devoted believers. Smohalla has recently died, but, in spite of occasional friction with agency officials, the "Dreamers," as they are popularly called, maintain their religious organization, with periodical gatherings and an elaborate ceremony. See Mooney, Ghost Dance Religion, 14th Rep. B. A. E., 1896. (J. M.)

Smok (*Smŏk*). A Squawmish village community on the left bank of Squawmisht r., Brit. Col.—Hill-Tout in Rep. Brit. A. A. S., 474, 1900.

Smoking. For more than a century after the discovery of America nearly all the early voyagers remarked on a curious practice, described as "a fumigation of a peculiar kind," that they found prevailing in some form almost everywhere in North America. It is narrated that "the Spaniards were honored as though they had been deities." Cortés is reported to have been received with incense, and it was said by one chronicler that he was "met by persons carrying vessels with lighted coals to fumigate him." The natives were said to burn incense to or to fumigate their idols, and the priests to "prepare themselves by smoking to receive the devil's oracles." These and many similar expressions indicate that the practice of smoking was not understood by Europeans. The cigar or the cigarette was used throughout Spanish America. Montezuma and other chiefs of Mexico were said "to compose themselves to sleep by smoking." Alarcon, in 1540, found the natives on the lower Colorado using "small reeds for making perfume," likening them to "the Indian *tobagos* of New Spain." Jacques Cartier found the practice of

smoking to prevail on the lower St Lawrence. Champlain refers to the native assemblies as *tabagies*. Hariot says the natives took the fumes of smoke as a cure for disease, and that they knew nothing of many ailments "wherewith we in England are oftentimes afflicted." Tobacco or some mixture thereof was invariably smoked in councils with the whites and on other solemn occasions.

CEREMONIAL SMOKING; PAWNEE (G. A. DORSEY)

No important undertaking was entered upon without deliberation and discussion in a solemn council at which the pipe was smoked by all present. The remarkable similarity in smoking customs throughout the continent proves the great antiquity of the practice. The custom of offering incense was not restricted to men, for women also, in certain localities, are said to have offered incense to idols. It was not necessarily a religious act; it was observed as a compliment to "lords and ambassadors." The women of Cartagena, we are told,

FLORIDA INDIAN SMOKING (DE BRY)

about 1750, could offer no higher courtesy to a person than to light his tobacco for him. The Hopi, in their ceremonies, offer smoke to their sacred images, and the ceremonies of the pipe are observed with great decorum; the head chief is attended by an assistant of nearly equal rank, who ceremoniously lights the pipe, and with certain formalities and set words hands it to the chief, who blows the smoke to the world-quarters and over the altar as a preliminary to his invocation. In religious ceremonies in general the priest usually blows the smoke over the altar to the world-quarters. In the councils of some tribes the pipe was handed to the head chief by the official pipe keeper; after lighting it he handed it on, and it was passed around in the council house, usually from left to right, until each one had smoked and thus fitted himself for serious deliberation. Among some tribes the pipe, in being passed from one individual to another during a ceremony, is differently grasped and held, according to the nature of the ceremony or to the taboo obligation of the individual. Among other tribes the decoration of pipes, and especially of the pipe stems, has great ceremonial and ethnic significance; even the attachment holding the pipe to the stem is fixed with special care, and the early death of an individual, or other calamity, it was believed, would ensue were the pipe dropped from the stem during a ceremony. Every individual engaging in war, hunting, fishing, or husbandry, and every clan and phratry made supplication to the gods by means of smoke, which was believed to bring good and to arrest evil, to give protection from enemies, to bring game or fish, allay storms, and protect one while journeying.

Smoking was early introduced from America into Europe and spread to the most distant parts of the world with astonishing rapidity until it encircled the globe, returning to America by way of Asia. It should be said, however, that the act of inhaling and exhaling smoke through a tube for medicinal purposes was certainly known to the ancients in Europe and Asia from a time antedating the Christian era. The fear that smoking would cause degeneration of the race or affect injuriously the revenues of the government caused stringent edicts to be passed against the use of tobacco, the violation of which was punished sometimes with death.

See *Pipes*, *Tobacco*, and the authorities thereunder cited. (J. D. M.)

Smulkamish. A small band of Salish formerly on upper White r., Wash., associated with the Skopamish; afterward on Muckleshoot res. Pop. about 183 in 1870, but no longer separately enumerated.

S'Balahco.—Gosnell in Ind. Aff. Rep., 338, 1857. Smalh.—Ross, ibid., 1869, 135, 1870. Smalh-kah-mish.—Treaty of 1855 in U. S. Ind. Treaties, 378, 1873. Smel-ka-mish.—Stevens in Ind. Aff. Rep., 458, 1854. Smulcoe.—Gosnell, ibid., 244, 1855. Smul-ka-mish.—Gibbs in Pac. R. R. Rep., I, 436, 1855. Sobal-ruck.—Ross in Ind. Aff. Rep., 17, 1870 (probably identical). White River Indians.—Gosnell in Ind. Aff. Rep., 338, 1857.

Smuttuns. Said to be a division of Sa-

lish contiguous to the Nooksak, near the N. W. boundary of Washington.—Fitzhugh in Ind. Aff. Rep. 1857, 328, 1858.

Smutty Bear. A head-man of the Yankton Sioux, who first appears as a signer of the treaty of Portage des Sioux in 1815. He signed also the trade and intercourse treaty at Ft Kiowa in 1825, and the treaty relinquishing title to the Yankton lands in 1858. Soon after, however, he led a strong faction of his tribe in hostility to the treaty, but was out-maneuvered by his contemporary chief, Struck-by-the-Ree. After the removal of the tribe to their reservation near Ft Randall, S. Dak., in 1859, Smutty Bear, then very old, lost his influence and soon died. (D. R.)

Snakaim. An unidentified body of Ntlakyapamuk on or near Fraser r., Brit. Col. Pop. 40 in 1901, the last time the name appears.

S-na-ha-em.—Can. Ind. Aff. 1885, 196, 1886. Snahaim.—Ibid. 1886, 230, 1887. Snahain.—Ibid. 1897, 363, 1898. Snakaim.—Ibid., pt. II, 166, 1901.

Snake dance. A noteworthy ceremony of the Hopi Indians of Arizona, in which live snakes are carried. It is held every 2 years, alternating with the Flute ceremony, in the Hopi pueblos of Walpi, Mishongnovi, Shipaulovi, Shumopovi, and Oraibi, by the Snake and Antelope fraternities conjointly about Aug. 20. Each fraternity meets in separate underground kivas, and each holds a public "dance" at the conclusion of certain secret rites conducted during the preceding 8 days. The striking features of the complicated secret rite are the gathering of snakes from the world-quarters, the making of the sand altar, the snake washing, the snake drama, and the races which occur on the mornings of the days of the public "dance" of the Snake fraternity. In the afternoon the Antelope celebrants file from their kiva, painted and attired in the traditional costume consisting of headdress, necklace, bandolier, armlets, kilt, anklets, moccasins, and a tortoise-shell rattle bound to the knee, and march to the plaza, about which they circle four times, each man stamping on a small board set in the ground in notification to the beings of the underworld that a ceremony is going on. They then form in line on each side of a small shelter of cottonwood boughs, called a *kisi*, erected at the margin of the plaza, and sound their rattles. The Snake priests follow in the same order and form in line, facing the Antelope priests. A low chant begins, gradually intensifying in volume; the lines sway in undulating curves, the motion increases with the chant until the movement culminates in a dance-like restrained leap. The snake dancers at once form in groups of three and dance with a hopping step until they arrive before the *kisi* where the snakes and snake passer are concealed. The carrier drops to his knees and receives a snake, grasps it by the middle in his mouth, and, rising, dances four times around the plaza, when he drops the snake, which is immediately picked up by the collector. The carrier then returns to the *kisi*, obtains another snake, and goes through the same process. The carrier is assisted by a companion, who passes one hand over his shoulder and

HOPI ANTELOPE PRIEST, SNAKE DANCE

waves before the snake, with the other hand, a snake whip, consisting of a short staff to which are attached two eagle feathers; this is for the purpose of causing the snakes to uncoil and run, when they are picked up with great celerity. While the dance is progressing a group of women and maidens in picturesque costume stand at one side of the plaza and sprinkle the dancers with sacred meal from basket trays.

When the snakes have all been carried, the participants pause while a "six-directions picture" in sacred corn-meal is drawn on the ground. At a signal the collectors throw the snakes on the meal; then a wild scramble ensues, and one by one the priests emerge with snakes in their hands and rush down the rocky trail of the mesa to release the reptiles at various points below the pueblo. Returning, the priests are given an emetic drink, made from herbs, and undergo a thorough purification. The ceremony closes with feasting and games by the entire populace.

The Snake dance is celebrated principally as a prayer for rain. The legend as to its origin recounts that the children of the union of the Snake Hero and the Snake Maid were transformed into snakes, hence snakes are regarded by the Hopi as their elder brothers and are thought to be powerful in compelling the nature gods to bring rain. For this purpose they are set free at the close of the ceremony. The snake rite is thought to have been originally an observance of the ancient Snake clan, which furnishes the chief of the society. The ceremony is believed to represent an agreement between the Snake and Antelope clans to hold joint celebration of their respective rites, which no doubt conflicted when the clans originally came to live together. Some rivalry is still observable in connection

HOPI SNAKE PRIEST (SANTA FÉ RAILWAY)

with the assumed efficiency of the rain charms of the two societies. Two species of rattlesnake and the bull and the whip snake are carried in the dance. The latter two are not venomous. The celebrants are rarely bitten by the dangerous snakes, a fact due largely to careful handling and to the "herding" to which the snakes have been subjected between the time when they are gathered and the dance. The Snake dance formerly must have been widely distributed among the Pueblo tribes, as remnants of it are found at Zuñi, Laguna, Acoma, Sia, and Cochiti, and among other Rio Grande villages. That it was practised in Mexico is evidenced by a picture in Sahagun's Historia. The Yokuts of California held a rattlesnake ceremony, *Tatulowis*, which from Powers' description (Cont. N. A. Ethnol.,

III, 380, 1877) was similar in some respects to the Hopi dance.

For detailed information see Bourke, Snake Dance of the Moquis of Arizona, 1884; Dorsey and Voth, Mishongnovi Ceremonies of the Snake and Antelope Fraternities, Field Columbian Mus. Pub.,

HOPI SNAKE DANCE

Anthr. ser., III, no. 3, 1902; Fewkes, Snake Ceremonials at Walpi, Jour. Am. Ethnol. and Archæol., IV, 1894, and Tusayan Snake Ceremonies, 16th Rep. B. A. E., 1897; Hodge, Pueblo Snake Ceremonials, Am. Anthr., IX, 1896; Hough, Moki Snake Dance, 1898; Stevenson, The Sia, in 11th Rep. B. A. E., 1894.   (w. h.)

Snake River. A Chippewa band on Mille Lac res., Minn.—Ind. Aff. Rep., 250, 1877.

Snakes. A name applied to many different bodies of Shoshonean Indians, but most persistently to those of E. Oregon, to which the following synonyms refer. These Indians form one dialectic group with the Paviotso of w. Nevada and the Mono of s. E. California. The principal Snake tribes were the Walpapi and the Yahuskin. For others, see *Mono-Paviotso, Shoshonean Family.*   (j. r. s.)

Aígspaluma.—Gatschet in Cont. N. A. Ethnol., II, pt. 1, xxxiii, 1890 ('Chipmunk people'; applied by the Warm Springs Indians to Oregon Shoshoni and Klamath). **Saí'-du-ka.**—Powers, Inds. W. Nevada, MS., B. A. E., 1876. **Sä′t.**—Gatschet, MS., B. A. E. (Klamath and Modoc name for all Shoshonean Indians; sig. 'unclean,' 'disheveled,' 'of low character'). **Shā′t.**—Ibid. **Shïtaikt.**—Mooney, inf'n, 1900 (Tenino name, especially for the Shoshoneans of Warm Springs, Oreg.). **Shne′-gitsuish.**—Gatschet, MS., B. A. E. (Shasta name for a "Snake" Indian). **Shoshoni.**—Lewis and Clark Exped., II, 594, 1817.

Snakestown. A former village, perhaps of the Delawares, on Muskingum r., Ohio, in 1774.—McKee (1774) quoted by Rupp, W. Penn., app., 211, 1846.

Snakwametl (*Snā′kwamEtl*). A village belonging to the Snonkweametl, an extinct tribe of Cowichan on lower Fraser r., Brit. Col.—Hill-Tout in Rep. Ethnol. Surv. Can., 54, 1902.

Snapa ('burnt place,' according to Teit; 'barren or bare place,' according to Hill-Tout). A village of the Spences Bridge band of Ntlakyapamuk, 1½ m. back from the s. side of Thompson r. and 42 m. above Lytton, Brit. Col. Pop. 17 in 1897, the last time it was enumerated separately.

Black Cañon.—White men's name. **O'npâ.**—Hill-Tout in Rep. Ethnol. Surv. Can., 4, 1899. **Nepa.**—Can. Ind. Aff., 230, 1886. **Snapa′.**—Teit in Mem. Am. Mus. Nat. Hist., II, 173, 1900.

Snares. See *Fishing, Hunting, Traps.*

Snauk. A Squawmish village community at False cr., Burrard inlet, Brit. Col.; pop. 47 in 1909.

False Creek.—Can. Ind. Aff., pt. II, 72, 1902. **Snauq.**—Hill-Tout in Rep. Brit. A. A. S., 475, 1900.

Snihuax. A former Chumashan village near Santa Barbara, Cal.—Taylor in Cal. Farmer, Apr. 24, 1863.

Snohomish. A Salish tribe formerly on the s. end of Whidbey id., Puget sd., and on the mainland opposite at the mouth of Snohomish r., Wash. Pop. 350 in 1850. The remnant is now on Tulalip res., Wash., mixed with other broken tribes.

Ashnuhumsh.—Gatschet, Kalapuya MS., B. A. E., 71 (Kalapuya name). **Sdo-hobé.**—McCaw, Puyallup MS. vocab., B. A. E. (Puyallup name). **S'do-ho-bish.**—Mallet in Ind. Aff. Rep., 198, 1877. **Sinahamish.**—Lane in Sen. Ex. Doc. 52, 31st Cong., 1st sess., 173, 1850. **Sinahōmās.**—Kane, Wand. in N. A., 240, 1859. **Sin-a-ho-mish.**—Gibbs in Pac. R. R. Rep., I, 436, 1855. **Sinahoumez.**—Duflot de Mofras, Oregon, II, 335, 1844 (evidently includes many other tribes). **Sineramish.**—Lane in Ind. Aff. Rep., 162, 1850. **Sinnamish.**—Lane in Sen. Ex. Doc. 52, 31st Cong., 1st sess., 173, 1850 (mentioned distinctly from the "Sinahamish"). **Sno-dom-ish.**—Fay in Ind. Aff. Rep., 238, 1858. **Sno-ho-mish.**—Treaty of 1855 in U. S. Ind. Treaties, 378, 1873. **Sunahúmes.**—Hale in U. S. Expl. Exped., VI, 221, 1846.

Snonkweametl (*Snonkwe′amEtl*). An extinct Cowichan tribe on lower Fraser r., Brit. Col.; their village was Snakwametl.—Hill-Tout in Ethnol. Surv. Can., 54, 1902.

Snonowas. A Salish tribe around Nanoose bay, E. coast of Vancouver id. They speak the Cowichan dialect, and numbered 14 in 1909.

Nanoos.—Tolmie and Dawson, Vocabs. Brit. Col., 120B, 1884. **Nanoose.**—Mayne, Brit. Col., 243, 1861. **Snōnōos.**—Boas, MS., B. A. E., 1887. **Snonowas.**—Can. Ind. Aff., pt. II, 164, 1901. **Sno-no-wus.**—Ibid., 417, 1898. **Sno-uo-wus.**—Ibid., 270, 1889.

Snoqualmu. A Salish division which formerly occupied the upper branches of a river of the same name in Washington and which numbered 225 in 1857. The remnant of these Indians is now on Tulalip res., with other broken tribes.

Sdok′-al-bĭhw.—McCaw, Puyallup MS. vocab., B. A. E., 1885 (Puyallup name). **Sdo-qual-bush.**—Mallet in Ind. Aff. Rep., 198, 1877. **Sno-kwāl-mi-yŭkh.**—Gibbs in Cont. N. A. Ethnol., I, 342, 1877 (full form of name; *miukh*=locative). **Snokwalmū.**—Gibbs, ibid., 179. **Snoqualamick.**—Lane in Sen. Ex. Doc. 52, 31st Cong., 1st sess., 173, 1850. **Sno-qual-a-mick.**—Jones (1853) in H. R. Ex. Doc. 76, 34th Cong., 3d sess., 5, 1857. **Sno-qual-a-muhe.**—Starling in Ind. Aff. Rep., 171, 1852. **Sno-qual-a-muke.**—Ibid., 170. **Snoqualimich.**—Schoolcraft, Ind. Tribes, V, 701, 1855. **Sno-qualimick.**—Lane in Sen. Ex. Doc. 52, 31st Cong., 1st sess., 167, 1850.

Snoqualimick.—Ibid., 174. Snoqualmie.—Stevens in H. R. Ex. Doc. 37, 34th Cong., 3d sess., 33, 1857. Sno-qual-mie.—Fay in Ind. Aff. Rep., 238, 1858. Snoquálmoo.—U. S. Ind. Treaties, 378, 1873. Snoqual-mook.—Gibbs in Pac. R. R. Rep., I, 436, 1855.

Snoquamish. A Salish division about Pt Orchard, Kitsap co., w. Wash.; pop. about 500 in 1850.

Shoquamish.—Lane in Ind. Aff. Rep., 162, 1850. Sno-qua-mish.—Starling in ibid., 170, 1852.

Snowshoes. Devices worn on the feet to enable the Eskimo and the Indian to walk over snow and very soft ground in hunting, pulling sleds, driving dog teams, and gathering food. The parts of a snowshoe are the wooden rim, toe and heel crossbar of wood or rawhide, extra strengthening bars, foot netting in large meshes with a stout thong for the foot to rest upon, toe and heel netting closely meshed with babiche or twisted sinew, which, however, is not always present, and foot lines for attaching the shoe. The size of the mesh varies, a coarser mesh being used for wet, soft snow. Snowshoes differ in materials, form, fineness, and decoration from place to place and from tribe to tribe. Wooden skees, such as were used in the Eastern continent, were absent, though Turner found the Indians of Whale r., Labrador, wearing shoes of thin spruce board, and the toboggan of Canada is a double skee for freight or passenger. Snowshoes vary greatly in shape, being round, elliptical, pointed oval, pointed at both ends, or irregular. The toe may be flat or upturned; the heel rounded, pointed, or widened into a trailer. The best examples are made in rights and lefts. The separate forms so differ locally that they almost equal in number the tribes wearing them. This can be shown best by figures (see Dall, Dixon, Mason, Murdoch, Nelson, and Turner). Especial attention is paid to the footing and foot lines. The netting under the foot is arranged with a view to the greatest comfort, the ball of the foot being firmly supported and the toes

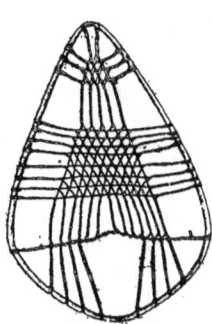

COLUMBIA RIVER (MASON)   ESKIMO, ALASKA (MASON)

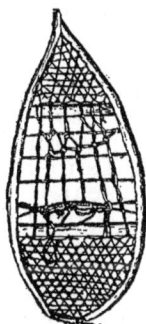

having free play. In putting on the shoe the hands are not used, the foot being thrust into the ankle loop fastened at a right angle to the frame, after which, by a dexterous twist, the toe is thrust under its loop. The snowshoer walks with a long, swinging stride, lifting the toe and letting the tail or heel drag. Among the eastern Eskimo,

who live outside of the tree zone, the snowshoe is very crude; the frames are small, made sometimes of bone, and the webbing is very coarse, but in the W. there is greater variety between the coarse and the finer types. The rim consists of two willow stems, thickest in the middle, elliptical in section, the long axis being vertical, and keeled on the inner face, except between the toe and heel bars. These stems are joined in front by a long lap splice held together by stitching with thongs. At the heel the ends are prolonged into a

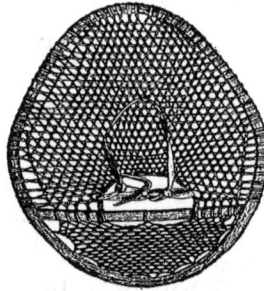

NASCAPEE, LABRADOR (MASON)   KLAMATH (MASON)

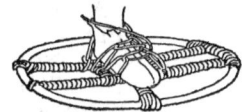

slight tail and the ends sewed together. The method of putting on the netting is elaborate. The Athapascan tribes adjoining the western Eskimo inland use fine-meshed shoes with upturned toes. The Kutchin on Mackenzie r. wear a round upturned snowshoe of 3 sizes, the largest for moose hunting, one of half size, and the traveling shoe. South of them for an indefinite distance, even into N. United States, was found the pointed elliptical type. Farther E. were used flat shoes with square fronts, having trailers; and in Labrador flat shoes of immense sizes and widths, with round beaver-tail and swallow-tail heels (Turner). In the Pacific states the simplest forms prevailed as far s. as N. California. The rim was round or slightly oval, flat, and not always regular; toe and heel bars were replaced with stout rawhide rope, and netting was of the simplest kind. These approximate most closely to the eastern Asiatic forms. The foot lacing in some binds closely down both toe and heel. With the snowshoe in Alaska goes a staff, having a spike and a little snowshoe at the lower end.

Consult Dixon in Bull. Am. Mus. Nat. Hist., XVII, 162, 1905; Mason in Nat. Mus. Rep. 1894, 381–410, 1896; Murdoch in 9th Rep. B. A. E., 344–352, 1892; Nelson in 18th Rep. B. A. E., 1899; Stites, Economics of the Iroquois, 1905; Turner in 11th Rep. B. A. E., 1889. (O. T. M.)

Snutele (*Snū′t′ᴇle*). A Bellacoola village on Bellacoola r., Brit. Col., above Tsomootl.—Boas in Mem. Am. Mus. Nat. Hist., II, 49, 1898.

Snutlelatl (*Snū′ʟ′ᴇlaʟ*). A Bellacoola village on Bellacoola r., Brit. Col., above Stuik.

Snū′ʟ′ᴇlaʟ.—Boas in Mem. Am. Mus. Nat. Hist., II, 49, 1898. Snū′tl′ᴇlatl.—Boas in 7th Rep. N. W. Tribes Can., 3, 1891.

Soacatino. A district visited by the troops of Moscoso, of the De Soto expedition, in 1542. It lay w. of Mississippi r., bordering on the Eyeish and Anadarko, probably near the middle course of Red r. The Spaniards expected to find a large and rich province, but it was a thick forest, where the people lacked food; hence they abandoned the hope of reaching Mexico by land and returned to the Mississippi. The natives evidently belonged to the Caddoan family. Cf. *Doustioni.*
Soacatina.—Harris, Voy. and Trav., I, 810, 1705. Soacatino.—Gentl. of Elvas (1557) in French, Hist. Coll., La., II, 198, 1850. Xacatin.—Biedma in Bourne, Narr. De Soto, II, 37, 1904. Xuacatin.—Biedma (1544) in French, Hist. Coll. La., II, 108, 1850. Xuacatino.—Ibid.

Soapstone. See *Steatite.*

Soba. A large body of Papago, named after their chief, centering around Caborca, N. w. Sonora, Mex., in the latter part of the 17th century, when they were said to number 4,000. They may have been identical with the Piato. Their other villages were Batequi, Mata, Pitic, and San Ildefonso.   (F. W. H.)
Sobas.—Kino (1692) in Doc. Hist. Mex., 4th s., I, 226, 1856. Tobas.—Villa-Señor, Theatro Am., II, 391, 1748 (misprint). Zopex.—Burton (1847) in Cal. Mess. and Corresp., 312, 1850 (identical?).

Sobaipuri. A Piman tribe formerly inhabiting the main and tributary valleys of San Pedro and Santa Cruz rs., between lon. 110° and 111°, and the Rio Gila between the mouth of the San Pedro r. and the ruins of Casa Grande, and possibly eastward of this area in s. Arizona. Missions were established among them by the Spaniards in the latter part of the 17th and beginning of the 18th centuries at Guevavi, Suamca, and San Xavier del Bac, to which numerous visitas were attached. According to Bourke "the Apaches have among them the Tze-kinne, or Stone-house people, descendants of the cliff-dwelling Sòbaypuris, whom they drove out of Aravypa cañon and forced to flee to the Pimas for refuge about a century ago" (Jour. Am. Folk-lore, 114, Apr.-June 1890); and Bandelier (Arch. Inst. Papers, III, 102, 1890) states that "the Apaches caused the Sobaypuris to give up their homes on the San Pedro and to merge into the Pápagos." It would seem, therefore, that the extinction of the Sobaipuri as a tribe was due to depredations by the Apache and that their remnant was absorbed by the Papago, their western neighbors, of whom indeed they may have been but a part. In later years the Papago occupied at least one of the former Sobaipuri towns—San Xavier del Bac.

Former settlements ascribed to the Sobaipuri are: Alamos, Aribaiba, Babisi, Baicadeat, Busac, Camani, Causac, Comarsuta, Esqugbaag, Guevavi, Jaumalturgo(?),

Jiaspi, Muiva, Ojio, Optuabo, Quiburi, Quiquiborica, Reyes, San Angelo, San Clemente, San Felipe, San Salvador, Santa Eulalia, San Xavier del Bac, Sonoita, Suamca, Tubo, Tumacacori, Turisai, Tusonimon, and Tutoida.   (F. W. H.)
Rsársaviñâ.—Russell, Pima MS., B. A. E., 16, 1902 ('spotted': Pima name). Sabagui.—Pimentel, Lenguas de Mex., II, 94, 1865 (given as the name of a Pima dialect; possibly Sobaipuri). Sebaipuris.—Aguirre (1764) in Doc. Hist. Mex., 4th s., I, 125, 1856 (misprint; also Sobaipuris). Sobahipuris.—Rudo Ensayo (1763), 17, 103, 1863. Sobaihipure.—Pimentel, Lenguas, I, 377, 1874. Sobaiporis.—De l'Isle, Carte Mex. et Floride, 1703. Sobaipotis.—Kino, map (1702) in Stöcklein, Neue Welt-Bott, 74, 1726. Sobaipures.—Mota-Padilla (1742), Hist. Conq. Nueva Galicia, 361, 1870. Sobaipuris.—Kino (1692) in Doc. Hist. Mex., 4th s., I, 226, 1856. Sobaipuris Pimas.—Villa-Señor, Theatro Am., II, 408, 1748. Sobaypures.—Venegas, Hist. Cal., II, 202, 1759. Sobaypuris.—Villa-Señor, op. cit., 396. Subaipures.—Arricivita, Crón. Seráf., II, 410, 1792. Subaipuris.—Garcés (1776), Diary, 386, 1900.

Soccorondo. A former rancheria, presumably Esselenian, connected with San Carlos mission, Cal.—Taylor in Cal. Farmer, Apr. 20, 1860.

Social organization. North American tribes contained (1) subdivisions of a geographic or consanguineal character; (2) social and governmental classes or bodies, especially chiefs and councils, with particular powers and privileges; and (3) fraternities of a religious or semi-religious character, the last of which are especially treated under *Secret societies.*

Tribes may be divided broadly into those in which the organization was loose, the subdivisions being families or bands and descent being counted prevailingly in the male line, and those which were divided into clearly defined groups called gentes or clans, which were strictly exogamic. Among the former may be placed the Eskimo; the eastern branch of the northern Athapascans; the Cree, Montagnais, Nascapee, Micmac, and Cheyenne, among the Algonquians; the northern Caddoan tribes; the Kiowa; most of the Shoshonean tribes; the Apache, and nearly all of the peoples of California, Oregon, Washington, s. Texas, and s. British Columbia; among the latter the Haida, Tlingit, Tsimshian, Heiltsuk, and western Athapascans; the Pueblos, Navaho, a few s. California tribes, and the majority of tribes in the Atlantic and Gulf states.

Where clans exist the distinctive character of each is very strongly defined, and a man can become a member only by birth, adoption, or transfer in infancy from his mother's to his father's clan, or vice versa. Each clan generally possessed some distinctive tutelary from which the majority of the persons belonging to it derived their names, certain rights, carvings, and ceremonies in common, and often the exclusive right to a tract of land. Although the well-defined caste system of the N. Pacific coast, based on property and the institution of slavery, does not seem to have had a parallel elsewhere N. of Mexico except perhaps among the Natchez, bravery in war, wisdom in council, oratorical, poetical, or artistic talents, real or supposed psychic powers—in short, any variety of excellence whatever served in all Indian tribes to give one prominence among his fellows, and it is not strange that popular recognition of a man's ability sometimes reacted to the benefit of his descendants. Although it was always a position of great consequence, leadership in war was generally separate from and secondary to the civil chieftainship. Civil leadership and ceremonial primacy were much more commonly combined. Among the Pueblos all three are united, forming a theocracy. Councils of a democratic, unconventional kind, in which wealthy persons or those of most use to the tribe had the greatest influence, were universal where no special form of council was established.

An Eskimo tribe consisted of those households that hunted or fished in the same geographical region and wintered in one village, or in several villages not far apart. Government was carried on by the heads of houses, and usually there was a headman in the tribe whose word had weight in matters connected with hunting and fishing. A class of helpers was composed of "bachelors without any relations, cripples who were not able to provide for themselves, or men who had lost their sledges and dogs" (Boas, Central Eskimo, 1888). A young man generally lived with his wife's family, much under their control, until the death of his parents-in-law. If he or his wife died meantime, their children remained with her people. When a man had once established his household independently, however, he was the head of it, and on his death his principal possessions went to the eldest of his sons, born to him or adopted, who had not an independent position. In so simple an organization as this we see the basis on which very important structures were elsewhere built. Nelson claims to have found traces of totemism among the Alaskan Eskimo, but it was probably imported from the Indians to the s. and does not appear to have taken deep root in the social life.

Among the more eastern Athapascan tribes the social organization is said to have been of a similar loose, paternal type. The Paiute and some other Shoshonean tribes consisted of bands, each governed by a chief, which occupied and took their names from particular localities. There were also chiefs whose authority extended, probably in a very indefinite form, over a number of others.

Throughout California, except in one small area, subdivisions were also local, and descent was paternal, so far as it was distinguished at all. Hupa men, for instance, usually resided throughout life in the town where they were born, while the women went elsewhere to live with their husbands, the towns being in practice chiefly exogamic, though there was no recognized requirement of exogamy. A man more often married a woman from outside of his village than one born there, only because the chances were that the majority of women in his own village were his actual blood-relations. Headship among them depended on wealth, and might be lost with it. Amount of property also determined headship over the villages of an entire district when they united for war or for ceremonial observances.. The Mohave also reckoned descent through the father, and there are indications of a nascent or decadent gentile system. Among the Hupa, Yurok, Karok, and other tribes of N. W. California slavery was a recognized institution, though the number of slaves was small.

The coast people of Oregon and Washington were organized on the basis of village communities similar to those of California, but slavery occupied a more prominent position in the social fabric and its importance increased northward, the institution extending as far, at least, as Copper r., Alaska (see *Slavery*). The Salish tribes of the interior of British Columbia consisted of many village communities, for the greater part independent of one another. Civil, military, and religious matters were each directed by different persons whose special fitness had been recognized, and though the succession usually passed from father to son, the actual selection rested with the people. In the selection of a civil chief, property was the determining factor. The few totemic devices or crests found in this region were inherited by all of the original owner's blood relations in both the male and female lines. A chief, like the noted Seattle, was sometimes found ruling over his mother's instead of his father's people, and a man was often known by a different name in his mother's town from that he bore in his father's.

Freemen among the coast Salish were divided into nobles, middle-class men, and servants. Below the last were the slaves captured in war. Servants were either poor relations of the better classes or members of formerly independent divisions reduced by war or otherwise to a servile condition, yet not actually enslaved. A chief might be displaced, but his office was usually hereditary from father to son, and it carried with it leadership in ceremonial matters, though not in war. According to Hill-Tout many of the larger Salish tribes recognized the paramount authority of one among the various local chiefs.

The Nootka tribes of the w. coast of Vancouver id. were subdivided into septs, or gentes, each possessing a single crest and ruled by a head chief. A council formed of these head chiefs determined the action of the tribe, and the chief of the sept that was highest in rank exercised some influence over the rest. Membership in the septs did not involve marriage prohibition, which was confined to real blood relationship, marriage within the sept being otherwise permissible. Chieftainships are said to have descended from father to son, but when persons of different septs married, the children belonged to the one higher in rank.

Although related by language to the Nootka, the Kwakiutl system differed considerably. Each division composing a Kwakiutl tribe was thought to be descended from an ancestor who had set up his house at a definite place, and it is probable that these divisions were originally local groups like those of the Salish, though some of them have now spread among several different tribes. Descent appears originally to have been paternal, but a man might obtain new crests and membership in a different gens for his son by marrying the daughter of another man who had them. This, however, may have been due to the influence of the more northern tribes having maternal descent.

The tribes possessing a well-defined clan system are divided into three groups— the North Pacific, Southwestern, and Eastern. All of the first group had two or more phratries, each named after some animal or bird and subdivided into a number of clans ruled over by chiefs. Unless there was a more powerful clan at the same place a family chief was also chief of his town. In some cases a clan was divided, having chiefs in different towns. The lowest unit was the house group, consisting of a family in the European sense, including remote relations together with servants and slaves over which ruled the house chief or householder. As among the tribes farther s., there were also low-caste groups, which formed a large part of the servant class. The principal power rested with the town chiefs, but depended on their ability to maintain their superiority in riches. A house chief might displace a family chief, and the chief of a different family could supplant a town chief.

The Pueblos had a large number of small clans, organized on a theocratic basis with special rituals and special lead-

ers in the rituals, and in some pueblos, as Zuñi, Laguna, Acoma, and the Hopi villages, there existed also phratries. In some towns, at least, a man was not permitted to marry into either the clan of his mother or that of his father, but since the advent of missionaries, in consequence of the reduction in numbers which has taken place and as a result of their teachings, this law has been often set aside in recent years.

The Zuñi are divided into a large number of clans, and many offices are always filled with reference to these. A boy or a girl is regarded as belonging to the mother's clan, but is spoken of as a "child" of the father's clan, and marriage into either of these is practically prohibited. Land, along with most other kinds of property, is owned by individuals and passes to the daughters in preference to the sons. The government of the entire state is hierarchic, the supreme authority resting in a body consisting of the rain priests of the six cardinal points— N., S., E., W., zenith, and nadir—the priestess of fecundity, assistant of the priest of the N., and the two head war priests. The priest of the N. is first among these and may be considered the high priest of Zuñi. Each of the male priests above enumerated, except the priest of the zenith, has assistants who usually succeed him and one another in regular order, but whose original appointment as assistants rests practically with their principal, although ostensibly he was appointed by the body of nine. The civil governor, his lieutenant, and the four assistants of each are nominated by the six rain priests and two war priests, though outside pressure may be brought to bear for or against this or that candidate. Although the governor attends to most civil matters, the appointing body acts as a final court of appeal in matters of extreme importance. His term of office is for one year, but he is eligible for reelection. War expeditions were formerly in the hands of the war priesthood under control of the two priests just referred to (Stevenson).

Sia is governed by two priests, with their vicars or intended successors. One priest has control over civil matters, the other over war and hunting. These offices are elective, the choice being limited to members of certain clans. Although the determinations reached by the two head priests and their vicars are referred to the heads of the ceremonial societies for confirmation, this is a mere matter of courtesy. They hold their positions for life and have the appointment of the subordinate officers who carry out their instructions. In Taos and a few other pueblos descent was patrilineal.

Like their neighbors, the Pueblos, the

Navaho were divided into numerous clans, with female descent and prohibition of marriage within the mother's and the father's clans. In addition there were several sets of clans which could not intermarry and thus constituted phratries analogous to those of Eastern tribes. Matthews considers it probable that the Navaho clans had a local rather than a totemic origin, and this may be true of most of the Pueblo clans.

Among the Plains Indians the Omaha had a highly organized social system. The tribe was divided into 10 gentes called "villages," with descent through the father, each of which had one head chief. Seven of these chiefs constituted a sort of oligarchy, and two of them, representing the greatest amount of wealth, exercised superior authority. The functions of these chiefs were entirely civil; they never headed war parties. Below them were two orders of warriors, from the higher of which men were selected to act as policemen during the buffalo hunt. Under all were those who had not yet attained to eminence. During the buffalo hunts and great ceremonials the tribe encamped in a regular circle with one opening, like most other Plains tribes. In it each gens and even each family had its definite position. The two halves of this circle, composed of five clans each, had different names, but they do not appear to have corresponded to the phratries of more eastern Indians. A man was not permitted to marry into the gens of his father, and marriage into that of his mother was rare and strongly disapproved. Other Plains tribes of the Siouan family probably were organized in much the same manner and reckoned descent similarly. The Dakota are traditionally reputed to have been divided at one time into seven council fires, each of which was divided into two or three major and a multitude of minor bands. Whatever their original condition may have been, their organization is now much looser than that of the Omaha.

Most of the southern Caddoan tribes reckoned descent through the mother. The Caddo proper, who came from a timber country, had 10 clans with maternal descent.

The social organization of the western and northern Algonquian tribes is not well known. The Siksika have numerous subdivisions which have been called gentes; they are characterized by descent through the father, but would appear to be more truly local groups. Each had originally its own chief, and the council composed of these chiefs selected the chief of the tribe, their choice being governed rather by the character of the person than by his descent. The head chief's authority was made effective largely through the voluntary cooperation of several societies. The Chippewa, Potawatomi, Menominee, Miami, Shawnee, and Abnaki in historic times have had gentes, with paternal descent, which Morgan believed had developed from a maternal stage owing to white influence; but this theory must be viewed with caution, inasmuch as there never has been a question as to the form of descent among the Delawares, who were subjected to white influences at an earlier date than most of those supposed to have changed.

The Delawares consisted of three subtribes, called by geographic names from the regions occupied by them, each characterized by a special totem. Over each presided a head chief, said to have been elected by the heads of the other divisions; but more probably they merely inducted him into office. The chief of the Unami is said to have been ordinarily first in dignity. These chiefs were assisted by councils, composed of heads of wealthy families and prominent warriors; but their authority was almost entirely confined to civil matters. "War was declared by the people at the instigation of the 'war captains,' valorous braves of any birth or family who had distinguished themselves by personal prowess, and especially by good success in forays against the enemy" (Brinton, The Lenape, 1885). According to Morgan, each of the three tribes was subdivided into twelve groups, probably consanguineous, though it is uncertain whether they were geographic or totemic.

The towns constituting the Creek confederacy were composed of members of various clans, and each was ruled by a civil chief, or *miko*, assisted by two councils. The chief was elected for life from a particular clan, and appointed the head war chief of the town. The town council advised the *miko* on questions of intertribal policy as well as the appointment of minor officers, while the council of old men concerned itself with internal questions, such as those connected with the raising of corn. Below these ranked the "beloved men," and then the common people. Subordinate to the "great warrior" were two grades of war leaders. Members of the same clan are said to have occupied houses adjoining one another, and in the larger towns all these surrounded a central square, in which were the houses of the chiefs, the council houses, and the playground. It is known that some clans could not intermarry, and thus constituted phratries. The part which clans and phratries played in the composition of the councils, the appointment of officers, and the order of business has not been determined. The confederacy was so loosely constituted that decisions for war or peace rested directly with the individual towns. In cases where numbers of towns decided to go to war together they appointed a head war chief for themselves.

The Natchez were divided into two castes, called by the French nobility and *puants*. The first was again divided into suns, nobles, and honored men, the individuals of each of which were compelled to marry among the *puants*. Children of the women of the three noble classes belonged to the class of the mother, and children of the honored men by *puant* women also belonged to their mother's class. Children of *puant* women and sun men, however, belonged to the middle class of nobles, while children of *puant* women and noble men belonged to the honored. By the exhibition of superior qualities a man could raise himself from the *puants* as far at least as the middle class of nobles. The highest chief, or Great Sun, derived his power from the mythic lawgiver of the nation. Thus the state constituted a theocracy resembling that of the Quichua of Peru.

The most advanced social organization north of the Pueblo country was probably that developed by the Iroquois confederated tribes. Each tribe consisted of two or more phratries, which in turn embraced one or more clans, named after various animals or objects, while each clan consisted of one or more kinship groups called *ohwachira*. When the tribes combined to form the confederacy called the Five Nations they were arranged in three phratries, of two, two, and one tribes respectively. There were originally 48 hereditary chieftainships in the five tribes, and subsequently the number was raised to 50. Each chieftainship was held by some one *ohwachira*, and the selection of a person to fill it devolved on the child-bearing women of the clan to which it belonged, more particularly those of the *ohwachira*, which owned it. The selection had to be confirmed afterward by the tribal and league councils successively. With each chief a vice-chief was elected, who sat in the tribal council with the chief proper, and also acted as a leader in time of war, but the chief alone sat in the grand council of the confederacy. See *Clan and Gens; Government*.

Consult Boas, Dorsey, Murdoch, Nelson, Powell, Mrs Stevenson, and Turner in Reports B. A. E.; Boas (1) in Reports Brit. A. A. S. from 1889; (2) in Rep. Nat. Mus. 1895, 1897; Brinton, Lenape and their Legends, 1885; Cushing in Pop. Sci. Mo., L, June 1882; Dixon in Bull. Am. Mus. Nat. Hist., XVII, pt. 3, 1905; Gatschet, Creek Migration Legend, 1884, 1888; Goddard, Life and Culture of the Hupa, Univ. Cal. Pub., I, 1903; Grinnell, Blackfoot Lodge Tales, 1892; Krause, Tlinkit Ind., 1885; Kroeber (1) in Am. Anthr., IV, no. 2, 1902, (2) in Bull. Am. Mus. Nat. Hist., XVIII, pt. 1, 1902; Loskiel, Hist. Missions United Brethren, 1794; Matthews, Navaho Legends, 1897; Morgan, Ancient Society, 1877; Morice in Trans. Roy. Soc. Can., X, 1905; Powell and Ingalls, Rep. regarding the Indians of Utah, 1874; Teit in Mem. Am. Mus. Nat. Hist., II, no. 4, 1900.   (J. R. S.)

Societies. See *Medicine and Medicinemen; Secret societies*.

Sockeye. One of the names of the Fraser r. salmon, blueback, or redfish (*Salmo nerka*) of the N. Pacific coast. The word is a corruption by folk etymology of *suk-kegh*, the name of this fish in one of the Salishan dialects of the N. W. Pacific coast. It is spelled also *sugk-eye, sawk-wey, sauk-eye*, etc., confirming the derivation.   (A. F. C.)

Sockobeck. A village of the Powhatan confederacy situated in 1608 on the N. bank of Rappahannock r. in King George co., Va.—Smith (1629), Va., I, map, repr. 1819.

Soco. A Calusa village on the S. W. coast of Florida, about 1570.
Soco.—Fontaneda Memoir (*ca.* 1575), Smith trans., 19, 1854. Sogo.—Fontaneda in Ternaux-Compans, Voy., XX, 22, 1841. Togo.—Fontaneda as quoted by Shipp, De Soto and Fla., 586, 1881.

Socoisuka. Mentioned by Taylor (Cal. Farmer, June 22, 1860) as a subdivision of the so-called Thamien group of the Costanoan Indians of the coast of central California.

Socorro (Span.: 'succor'). A former pueblo of the Piro on the site of the present town of Socorro, on the Rio Grande in New Mexico. So named by Oñate, in 1598, because of the friendly reception of the Spaniards by the inhabitants, who gave them a large quantity of corn. It was the seat of the Franciscan mission of Nuestra Señora del Socorro from 1626, and contained a church and monastery. At the outbreak of the Pueblo revolt in 1680 its population was 600, but most of the inhabitants followed the Spaniards, with whom they were friendly, to El Paso, and afterward established a village bearing the same name (distinguished as Socorro del Sur) below that place on the Rio Grande in Texas. The walls of the old church were standing in 1692, and the ruins of the village were still visible in 1725, but no trace of the former settlement is now to be seen. Consult Bandelier in Arch. Inst. Papers, IV, 241 et seq., 1892. See also *Piros, Pueblos*.   (F. W. H.)
N. D. du Secour.—Vaugondy, Carte Amér., 1778. Nra Sra del Socorro.—Benavides (1630) quoted by Bancroft, Ariz. and N. Mex., 163, 1889. Pilabo.—

Benavides, Memorial, 16, 1630 (aboriginal name of pueblo). **Pilaho.**—Columbus Mem. Vol., 156, 1893 (misprint). **Pilopué.**—Oñate (1598) in Doc. Inéd., XVI, 115, 1871 (identified by Bandelier, Arch. Inst. Papers, IV, 241, 1892). **Socora.**—Johnston in Emory, Recon., 570, 1848. **Socoro.**—Gallegas (1844), ibid., 478. **Socorra.**—Ogilby, America, map, 1671. **Socorre.**—Domenech, Deserts of N. A., I, map, 1860. **Socorro.**—Oñate (1598) in Doc. Inéd., XVI, 251, 1871 (earliest form).

Socorro del Sur ('Socorro of the South,' in contradistinction from Socorro (q. v.) in New Mexico). A small pueblo on both sides of the Rio Grande, a few m. below El Paso, Tex., the inhabitants of which, now completely Mexicanized, belonged to the Piro tribe, although there is evidence (Bancroft, Ariz. and N. Mex., 191, 1889) that Tano and Jemez people were among them. It was established in 1680–81 by Gov. Otermin with fugitive Indians chiefly from Socorro, N. Mex. It became the seat of a Spanish mission in 1682. See *Piros, Pueblos*. (F. W. H.)

Nª Señora del Socorro.—De l'Isle, Carte Mex. et Floride, 1703. **Nra del Socorro.**—Otermin (1682) cited by Bancroft, Ariz. and N. Mex., 191, 1889. **N. Senora del Socorro.**—Jefferys, Am. Atlas, map 5, 1776. **Nuestra Señora del Socorro.**—Vetancurt (1696) in Teatro Mex., III, 309, 1871. **Soccorro.**—Villa-Señor, Theatro-Am., II, 360, 1748. **Socorro.**—Calhoun in Cal. Mess. and Corresp., 211, 1850. **Socorro.**—Rivera, Diario, leg. 684, 1736. **Socorro del Sur.**—Bandelier in Arch., Inst. Papers, III, 86, 1890.

Soda Creek. A Shuswap village or band situated on upper Fraser r. between Alexandria and the mouth of Chilcotin r., Brit. Col.; pop. 81 in 1909.—Can. Ind. Aff. Reps.

Sodoms. An Iroquois village placed on the Esnauts and Rapilly map, 1777, s. w. of Oswego, N. Y. The name is probably a misprint of Sodus.

Soenadut. A Maricopa rancheria on the Rio Gila, Ariz., in 1744.—Sedelmair (1744) cited by Bancroft, Ariz. and N. Mex., 366, 1889.

Sofki, Sofkey. A thin sour corn gruel prepared by the Creek and other Indians formerly of the Gulf region, from corn, water, and lye. There are three kinds of the liquid: plain, sour, and white. The corn is pounded into a coarse meal, which is fanned in order to remove the broken grains and husks. Two quarts of the meal are put into a gallon pot of hot water, which is placed over a fire and allowed to boil. A perforated vessel is filled with clean wood ashes, on which water is poured to form a lye. The lye as it percolates through the ashes drops into the meal and water and turns the mixture yellow. Water is kept on the *sofki* for hours at a time, and, finally, after the mixture has become very thick, it is removed and allowed to cool. A half-dozen "blue dumplings" (a very palatable cornmeal preparation) are almost a necessary accompaniment of a mug of *sofki*. Pounded hickory-nuts are frequently added to the mixture, and marrow too, to improve the flavor. The vessel which is used expressly for preparing the meal

is called a "sofki dish." The Yuchi name for *sofki* is *tsoshi*. The word is derived from the Creek dialect of the Muskhogean language. The Cherokee know it as *kanahena* (Mooney). (W. R. G.)

Sogup. Given by Cortez (Pac. R. R. Rep., III, pt. 3, 120, 1856) as one of 4 bands of the Ute, within or near the province of New Mexico in 1799.

Sohonut. Mentioned by Royce (18th Rep. B. A. E., 782, 1899), together with a number of other tribes, as ceding all their lands except a strip between Tejon pass and Kern r., Cal. They may have been Yokuts (Mariposan), Chumashan, or Shoshonean, but are not identified.

Soiones ('long wampum belt.'—Hewitt). An Onondaga chief who was leader of the embassy to the Hurons in 1647. He was a "Huron by nation, but so naturalized among the enemies within a number of years, that there is no Iroquois who has made more massacres in this country nor worse attacks than he." He brought three Huron captives from Onondaga (Jes. Rel. 1648, 56, 1858).

Sokchit. Seemingly the Yurok name of a small Hupa village on Trinity r., Cal.

Soc-kail-kit.—McKee (1851) in Sen. Ex. Doc. 4, 32d Cong., spec. sess., 194, 1853. **Socktish.**—A. L. Kroeber, inf'n, 1907 (a name sometimes applied). **Sokchit.**—Ibid., 1904. **So-kéa-keit.**—Gibbs in Schoolcraft, Ind. Tribes, III, 139, 1853. **Sok-kail-kit.**—Meyer, Nach dem Sacramento, 282, 1855. **Soktich.**—A. L. Kroeber, inf'n, 1907.

Sokoki (apparently a contraction of Abnaki *Sákukiak*, 'people at the outlet.'—Gerard. See *Abnaki*). A tribe closely connected with the Abnaki and probably a part of the confederacy. Vetromile considered them as distinct (Me. Hist. Soc. Coll., VI, 211, 1859). He says: "Only five nations are reckoned in New England and Acadia, namely, the Mohegans, the Sokoquis, the Abnakis, the Etchimins, and the Micmacs." He and Ruttenber (Tribes Hudson R., 85, 1872) place them in the Mahican group. On the other hand, Williamson (Hist. Maine, 1832) and Maurault say they belonged to the Abnaki group, which is probably the correct conclusion. The Pequawket and Ossipee, on the upper Saco, were apparently branches of this tribe (Kidder in Me. Hist. Soc. Coll., VI, 235, 1859). The tribe, including these, occupied the banks of Saco r., Me., the Sokoki being nearest to the mouth. Ruttenber believed they had occupied the w. bank of Hudson r. above Mohawk r. until driven out by the Mohawk in 1626. There is no reason to doubt, however, that the Indians Champlain found in 1604 at the mouth of the Saco, were of this tribe. Smith (1616) mentions Sowocatuck, perhaps their chief village. Champlain has preserved the name of one of the sachems of this people, Marchim, of Casco bay, "who had the reputation of being one of the bravest men of his country, and he had a fine manner, and all his gestures and movements were grave and dignified, savage though he was." The Sokoki are described by Gorges in 1658 as enemies of the Abnaki. They participated in King Philip's war in 1675, and some of them fled to Scaticook on the Hudson at its close. In 1725 the rest of the tribe retired to St Francis, Canada, with the Pequawket and others.   (J. M. C. T.)

Assok8ekik.—Jes. Rel. for 1646, 3, 1858. Chouacoët.—Jes. Rel. for 1611, 15, 1858. Onejagese.—Ft Orange conf. (1663) in N. Y. Doc. Col. Hist., XIII, 298, 1881 (Iroquois name). Patsuikets.—Maurault, Hist. des Abenakis, 5, 1866. Sacoes.—Willis (1830) in Me. Hist. Soc. Coll., I, 215, 1865. Saco Indians.—Niles (ca. 1761) in Mass. Hist. Soc. Coll., 3d s., VI, 206, 1837. Sawocotuck.—Smith (1629), Va., II, 193, reprint of 1819. Soccokis.—Lahontan, New Voy., I, 230, 1703. Soccoquis.—Monseignat (1689) in N. Y. Doc. Col. Hist., IX, 471, 1855. Soccouky.—Agean (1699) in Margry, Déc., VI, 115, 1886. Sockegones.—Gorges (1658) in Me. Hist. Soc. Coll., VII, 99, 1876. Sockhigones.—Gorges (1658) in Mass. Hist. Soc. Coll., 3d s., VI, 90, 1837. Socokis.—Drake, Bk. Inds., bk. 3, 102, 1848. Socoquiois.—Jes. Rel. for 1643, 44, 1858. Socoquis.—Talon (1670) in N. Y. Doc. Col. Hist., IX, 66, 1855. Socoquois.—Doc. of 1696, ibid., 650. Socouky.—Agean (1699) in Margry, Déc., VI, 119, 1886. Sohokies.—Keane in Stanford, Compend., 536, 1878 (misprint). Sokakies.—Macauley, N. Y., II, 405, 1829. Sokokies.—Colden (1727) quoted by Richardson, Arct. Exped., II, 39, 1851. Sokokiois.—Jes. Rel. for 1643, 67, 1858. Sokokis.—Cadillac (1694) in N. Y. Doc. Col. Hist., IX, 580, 1855. Sokoquiois.—Jes. Rel. for 1646, 3, 1858. Sokoquis.—French letter (1651) in N. Y. Doc. Col. Hist., IX, 5, 1855. Sok8akiaks.—Maurault, Hist. des Abenakis, 5, 1866. Sokoueki.—Jes. Rel. for 1653, 26, 1858. Soquachjck.—Ft Orange conf. (1663) in N. Y. Doc. Col. Hist., XIII, 298, 1881. Soquackicks.—Dareth (1664), ibid., 381. Soquatucks.—Ruttenber, Tribes Hudson R., 41, 1872. Soquokis.—Doc. of 1697 in N. Y. Doc. Col. Hist., IX, 669, 1855. Soquoquis.—Memoir (1706), ibid., 796. Soquoquisii.—Du Creux (1660) quoted by Vetromile in Me. Hist. Soc. Coll., VI, 210, 1859. Sowocatuck.—Smith (1616) in Mass. Hist. Soc. Coll., 3d s., VI, 108, 1837. Sowocotuck.—Smith (1616), ibid., 117. Sowquackick.—Pynchon (1663) in N. Y. Doc. Col. Hist., XIII, 308, 1881.

Sokulk. A small Shahaptian tribe located by Lewis and Clark on Columbia r., above the mouth of the Snake. They are known to the Nez Percés and Yakima as Wanapum, and their principal village is on the w. bank of the Columbia, at the foot of Priest rapids, Wash. The tribe has attracted some notice of late years from the fact that the noted religious leader and prophet Smohalla (q. v.) was their chief. The tribe was never included in any treaty and consequently is not officially recognized. Their number is estimated as between 150 and 200. (L. F.)

Lekulks.—Robertson, Oregon, 129, 1846. Lokulk.—Schoolcraft, Ind. Tribes, III, 609, 1853. Priest's Rapids.—Gibbs in Pac. R. R. Rep., I, 417, 1855. Sokulk.—Lewis and Clark Exped., I, map; II, 12, 1814. Wa'napûm.—Mooney in 14th Rep. B. A. E., 735, 1896 (name given by cognate tribes).

Sokut Menyil ('deer moon'). A Kawia village in Cahuilla valley, on the Torres res., s. Cal., said to have been so named because it was once a famous place in which to hunt deer by moonlight.

Martinez.—Barrows, Ethno.-Bot. Coahuilla Ind., 33, 1900. So-kut Men-yil.—Ibid.

Solakiyu (*So'-lak-i-yu*). A former Nishinam village in the valley of Bear r., which is the next stream N. of Sacramento, Cal.

Solackeyu.—Powers in Overland Mo., XII, 22, 1874. So'-lak-i-yu.—Powers in Cont. N. A. Ethnol., III, 316, 1877.

Soldier. In the strict sense of the word the soldier did not exist in any of the tribes N. of Mexico, for among the aborigines there was no paid war force. Neither was there any group of men who served as an organized police to maintain order within the tribe, nor was there any body of men assigned, as in an army, to defensive or aggressive warfare. These duties, which are distinct in coordinated society, in the tribe were laid on every able-bodied man, who from his youth had been trained in the use of weapons, taught to be ready at a moment's notice to defend his home and to be the protector of the women and children. There was no school in which the men were drilled to act and move together. The methods of fighting were handed down by tradition, and boys and young men gained their first knowledge of the warrior's tactics chiefly from experiences related about the winter fire. Every village or camp was liable to attack, and their ever-present danger from enemies influenced the training and avocation of young men and determined the position near the door of the lodge, where they would be first to meet an intruding foe. There was, however, a class of men, warriors of approved valor, to whom were assigned special duties, as that of keeping the tribe in order during the annual hunt or at any great ceremonial where order was strictly to be enforced. It is this class which English-speaking observers have called "soldiers," for their power and prestige in the tribe corresponded more nearly with the rank held by the army than by any other set of men. The name by which this class of warriors was known in the language of some tribes meant "difficult to break or destroy," in other tribes "seizers" or "catchers," i.e. those who make captive. The first refers not only to the invincible courage of the men in war and in executing unswerving justice, but to their wealth upon which they could draw for generous contribution when a tribal appeal was made. If at any time one of these men should offend and be subject to punishment, which was frequently by flogging, only the man of equal or superior war honors could strike the heavy blows; a man of fewer honors could only *touch* the offender whose rank was higher than his own. In many tribes warriors were members of a society in which were orders or degrees.

The youth entered the lowest and gradually won promotion by his acts. Each degree or order had its insignia, and there were certain public duties to which it could be assigned. Every duty was performed without compensation, honor being the only reward. These societies were under the control of war chiefs and exercised much influence in tribal affairs. In other tribes war honors were won through the accomplishment of acts, all of which were graded, each honor having its peculiar mark or ornament which the man could wear after the right had been publicly accorded him. There were generally six grades of honors. It was from the highest grade that the "soldier" spoken of above was taken. See *Coup, Military Societies, War and War Discipline.* (A. C. F.)

Soldier's Village. A Potawatomi village, called after a chief, in N. Illinois in 1832.—Tippecanoe treaty (1832) in U. S. Ind. Treat., 698, 1873.

Soledad (Span. 'solitude,' 'comfortlessness,' abbr. of *Nuestra Señora de la Soledad,* 'Our Lady of Solitude'). Formerly a Huichol village, but now a Mexican settlement, situated about 15 m. N. w. of Mezquitic, beyond the present limits of the Huichol country, in Jalisco, Mexico.—Lumholtz, Unknown Mex., II, 112, 1902.

Soledad Indians. A collective term used to designate the Indians of several distinct linguistic families that lived within the territory or under the authority of Soledad mission, Monterey co., Cal. They were Costanoan and probably Esselen and Salinan, together with Yokuts neophytes brought from the region of Tulare lake.
La Soledad.—Hale in U. S. Expl. Exped., VI, 633, 1846. Soledad.—Taylor in Cal. Farmer, Apr. 20, 1860.

Solocka. A town of mixed population, under Oneida jurisdiction, situated, according to Evans' map of 1756, about 60 m. above Shamokin, on a creek issuing from the Great Swamp N. of the Cashuetunk mts. in Pennsylvania. On Pownall's map of 1776 it is placed on the left bank of the Susquehanna, above the mouth of Tunkhannock cr. (J. N. B. H.)

Somehulitk (*Sŏ'mexulitx*). A Heiltsuk tribe living at the upper end of Wikeno lake, Brit. Col.; the name is applied also to one of its clans.—Boas in Nat. Mus. Rep. 1895, 328, 1897.

Somenos. A Salish tribe in Cowitchin valley, S. E. Vancouver id., speaking the Cowichan dialect; pop. 100 in 1909.
Sā'menos.—Boas, MS., B. A. E., 1887. Soieenos.—Can. Ind. Aff., IX, 1877. So-me-nau.—Ibid., 308, 1879. Somenos.—Ibid., pt. II, 164, 1901.

Somhotnechau. A Wikeno village on Rivers inlet, Brit. Col.
Somhótnehau.—Boas, MS. field notes. Sŏmχótnechau.—Boas in Petermanns Mitteil., pt. 5, 130, 1887.

Somo. A former Chumashan village near some hills of the same name in Ventura co., Cal. Cf. *Simi.*
Somes.—Taylor in Cal. Farmer, July 24, 1863.—Somo.—Ibid. S'o-mus+.—Henshaw, Buenaventura MS. vocab., B. A. E., 1884.

Sona. Mentioned by Oviedo (Hist. Gen. Indies, III, 628, 1853) as one of the provinces or villages, probably on the South Carolina coast, visited by Ayllon in 1520.

Sonagna. A former Gabrieleño village in Los Angeles co., Cal., at a locality later called White's ranch.—Ried (1852) quoted by Taylor in Cal. Farmer, June 8, 1860.

Sonaque. A former tribe noted by Massanet (Dictamen Fiscal, MS., Nov. 30, 1716) on the road from Coahuila to the Texas country in 1690. It was probably of Coahuiltecan stock.

Sonayan. A former tribe noted by Massanet (Dictamen Fiscal, MS., Nov. 30, 1716) on the road from Coahuila to the Texas country in 1690. It was probably of Coahuiltecan stock and possibly identical with the Kouyam (q. v.), or Kouayon, of Joutel.

Soneto. A former village connected with San Francisco Solano mission, Cal.—Bancroft, Hist. Cal., II, 506, 1886.

Songish (adapted by the whites from *Stsā'ñges,* the name of one of their septs). A Salish tribe about Victoria, Vancouver id., and on the w. shore of San Juan id., who call themselves Lkungen. This tribe gives its name to a Salish dialect spoken also by the Sanetch and Sooke of Vancouver id., by the Clallam of the s. side of Juan de Fuca str., and by the Samish, Semiahmoo, and Lummi of the coast s. of the Fraser delta. Population of the Songish proper, including Cheerno, Discovery id., Esquimalt, and Songish bands, 182 in 1906. Those speaking the Songish dialect number about 1,000. Their bands are Chikauach, Chkungen, Kekayaken, Kltlasen, Ksapsem, Kukoak, Kukulek, Lelek, Sichanetl, Skingenes, Skuingkung, and Stsanges. (J. R. S.)
Etzāmish.—Tolmie and Dawson, Vocabs. Brit. Col., 119B, 1884 (so called by the tribes of the s. part of Puget sd.). Hue-lang-uh.—Mackay quoted by Dawson in Trans. Roy. Soc. Can., sec. II, 7, 1891 ('the people': own name). Lkū'men.—Boas in 6th Rep. N. W. Tribes Can., 11, 1890 (Nanaimo name). Lkū'mEn.—Boas in 5th Rep. N.W. Tribes Can., 10, 1889. Lku'ngEn.—Ibid. (own name). Lkū'ñgEn.—Boas, 6th Rep., 11, 1890. Lχúñgen.—Boas, MS., B. A. E., 1887. Songars.—Brit. Col. map, Ind. Aff., Victoria, 1872 (given as a settlement N. of Victoria). Songees.—Taylor in Cal. Farmer, July 19, 1862. Songhies.—Mayne, Brit. Col., 73, 1862. Songish.—Hoffman quoted by Powell in 6th Rep. B. A. E., xlii, 1888. Thongeith.—Sproat, Savage Life, 311, 316, 1868 (an alternative for Kowitchan as the designation of the Salish of Vancouver id.). Tsaumas.—Wilson in Jour. Ethnol. Soc. Lond., 278, 1866. Tsaumass.—Ibid., 286. Tsong.—Gibbs in Cont. N. A. Ethnol., I, 177, 1877.

Songs. See *Music and Musical instruments; Nith-songs.*

Sonnioto. A former Shawnee village at the mouth of Scioto r., Ohio; perhaps the same as Lowertown.
Scioto.—Rafinesque in Marshall, Ky., I, introd., 31, 1824. Sinhioto.—Bonnécamps (1749) in Jes. Rel., LXIX, 177, 1900. Sonnioto.—Doc. of 1748 in N. Y. Doc. Col. Hist., X, 138, 1858. Souyoto.—Vaudreuil (1760), ibid., 1094. St. Yotoc.—Thwaites in Jes. Rel., LXIX, 298, 1900 (a French form).

Sonoita. A Papago rancheria on the headwaters of the Rio Salado of Sonora, just below the Arizona-Sonora boundary. It was visited in 1699 by the Jesuit Father Kino, who applied to it the name San Marcelo. It afterward became a mission, the name of which, apparently in May 1751, was changed to San Miguel in accordance with the wish of the Marques de Villapuente, who, at his death in 1739, endowed this mission and that of Busanic. In the same year (1751), during the Pima revolt against the Spaniards, the mission was destroyed and its missionary, Heinrich Ruen, killed by the natives. In 1776, when visited by Anza and Font, it was still in ruins. In 1865 the settlement contained 50 Papago families, commonly known as "Sand Papagos." (F. W. H.)
Arroyo del Sonoitac.—Anza and Font (1776) quoted by Bancroft, Ariz. and N. Mex., 393, 1889. Carizal.—Kino, map (1701), ibid., 360. La Sone.—Audubon (1849), Western Jour., 147, 1906. San Marcelo.—Mange (1699) in Doc. Hist. Mex., 4th s., I, 318, 1856. San Marcelo del Sonoita.—Ibid., 319. San Marcelo del Xonuida.—Writer of 1702 (?), ibid., V, 139, 1857. San Miguel de Sonoitac.—Doc. of 1764 quoted by Bandelier in Arch. Inst. Papers, III, 73, 1890. San Miguel de Ssonoitag.—Rudo Ensayo (ca. 1763), 102, 1863. Sedge.—Venegas, Hist. Cal., I, map, 1759. S. Marcellus.—Kino, map (1702), in Stöcklein, Neue Welt-Bott, 74, 1726. S. Marcelo de Sonoitac.—Anza and Font (1780) quoted by Bancroft, Ariz. and N. Mex., 393, 1889. S. Marcelo Sonoydag.—Kino (1698) cited by Bancroft, No. Mex. States, I, 266, 1884. S Mateo Soroydad.—Kino misquoted by Alegre, ibid. Soni.—Box, Advent., 267, 1869 (probably identical). Sonoaitac.—Arricivita, Crón. Seráf., II, 421, 1792. Sonoi.—Garcés (1771) cited by Coues, Garcés Diary, 31, 1900. Sonoitac.—Garcés (1776), Diary, 455, 1900. Sonorita.—Poston misquoted by Browne, Apache Country, 291, 1869. Sonoytac.—Och (1756), Journey to the Missions, I, 71, 1809. Xonoidag.—Writer of 1702 (?), op. cit., 143. Zoñi.—Orozco y Berra, Geog., 348, 1864 (probably identical).

Sonoita. A former rancheria of the Sobaipuri and a visita of the mission of Guevavi (from which it was situated 7 leagues, E. N. E.), on Rio Santa Cruz, N. of the present town of Nogales, S. Ariz. Pop. 91 in 1760. It became a visita of Tubutama in 1764, and was deserted before 1784. (F. W. H.)

Sonojowauga ('at Big Kettle's,' referring to a chief.—Hewitt). A former Seneca village on the E. bank of Genesee r., on the site of Mt Morris, Livingston co., N. Y.
Big Kettle.—Morgan, League Iroq., 437, 1851. Shanawageras.—Phelps deed (1788) in Am. St. Papers, Ind. Aff., I, 210, 1832 (probably identical). So-no'-jo-wau-ga.—Morgan, op. cit.

Sonoma (from the Yukian Wappo terms so or tso, 'ground,' and noma, 'place,' 'location'). A name probably applied first by the Franciscan fathers to the vicinity of what is now the site of the

town of Sonoma, Sonoma co., Cal., where the last mission in California was established (See San Francisco Solano). It is said that they took the name from that of one of the chiefs among the neophytes whom the fathers gathered about them at their mission, but it is not definitely known to what stock this chief belonged. The name, however, came to be applied to all the Indians of the mission and vicinity, and as there were people here of at least four or five distinct stocks, it is easy to account for statements made by such early writers as Chamisso, who says that the "Sonomi" spoke a language similar to the "Tamal," that is, a Miwok or Moquelumnan dialect. In fact the mission of Sonoma was situated in territory formerly belonging to Indians of this stock, and it is probable that a very considerable number of its converts were Moquelumnan Indians. The Sonomo, or Sonomi, mentioned by Taylor on the authority of settlers as speaking a dialect similar to that of the Suisun, were a later immigration into the valley; these were Wintun brought in to the mission from the vicinity of what is now Solano co. (S. A. B.)
Sonomas.—Taylor in Cal. Farmer, Mar. 30, 1860. Sonomellos.—Ibid. Sonomi.—Chamisso in Kotzebue, Voy., III, 51, 1821. Sonomos.—Taylor, op. cit. Sonons.—Choris, Voy. Pitt., 6, 1822.

Sonomaite. A mineral, named from Sonoma (q. v.), the county in California where it was discovered.

Sonsa. The Badger clan of the pueblo of Jemez, N. Mex. The corresponding clan at the former pueblo of Pecos was called So'hl, but it is now extinct.
Sonsaásh.—Hodge in Am. Anthr., IX, 349, 1896 (ash = 'people').

Sons of Tammany. See Red Men, Improved Order of.

Sooke. A Salish tribe, speaking the Songish dialect, about an inlet of the same name at the S. E. end of Vancouver id.; pop. 28 in 1909.
Achiganes.—De Smet, Oregon Miss., 192, 1847. Sâ'ok.—Boas in 6th Rep. N. W. Tribes Can., 11, 1890. Sock Indians.—De Smet, Oregon Miss., 192, 1847. Sôk.—Tolmie and Dawson, Vocabs. Brit. Col., 120B, 1884. Sokes.—Grant in Jour. Roy. Geog. Soc., 293, 1857. Sooke.—Can. Ind. Aff., pt. II, 164, 1901. Tsohke.—Gibbs in Cont. N. A. Ethnol., I, 177, 1877.

Soonkakat. A Koyukukhotana village of 12 inhabitants on the left bank of the Yukon, below Nulato, Alaska.
Soonkakat.—Petroff in 10th Census, Alaska, 12, 1884. Súnkā'kāt.—Dall, Alaska, 28, 1877. Yukochakat.—Petroff, map of Alaska, 1880. Yukokakat.—Ibid. Yukokokat.—Ibid.

Sopaktalgi ('toad people'). A clan of the Creeks.
Sopáktalgi.—Gatschet, Creek Migr. Leg., I, 155, 1884. So-päk'-tŭ.—Morgan, Anc. Soc., 161, 1877.

Sopone. A former Chumashan village near Santa Barbara, Cal.
Missopeno.—Taylor in Cal. Farmer, Apr. 24, 1863. Sopone.—Ibid. Sopono.—Cabrillo, Narr. (1542), in Smith, Colec. Doc. Fla., 181, 1857.

Soquee (corruption of Sŭkwi'yĭ, or Sukí'-yĭ; abbreviated Sŭkwi and Suki). A former Cherokee settlement on Soquee r., a headstream of the Chattahoochee, near Clarkesville, Habersham co., Ga. The name has lost its meaning.—Mooney in 19th Rep. B A. E., 530, 1900.

Saukee.—Doc of 1799 quoted by Royce in 5th Rep B. A. E., 144, 1887. Sookee.—Mooney op. cit. (sometimes so written)

Sora. The Carolina rail (*Rallus carolinus*). This word, spelled also *soree*, is said to be derived from one of the Indian languages of s. E. United States, and also to be of negro derivation, *sora* in one of the African dialects meaning 'to rise.'

Sorcery. See *Oyaron, Witchcraft.*

Soree See *Sora.*

Sorrochos A village situated on an inlet of the E. coast of Florida, N. of C. Cañaveral, in the 16th century.—De Bry map (1591) in Le Moyne, Narr., Appleton trans., 1875.

Soshka The native name of the Chaparral Cock, or Road-runner, clans of the Keresan pueblos of Laguna, Acoma, Sia, and San Felipe, N. Mex. The clan at Laguna claims to have come originally from Zuñi (cf. *Poyi*), while that of Acoma forms a phratry with the Dyami (Eagle) clan.   (F. W. H.)

Chösh'ka-háno.—Hodge in Am. Anthr, IX, 349, 1896 (Sia form; *háno*='people'). Shásk'hánoqᶜʰ.—Ibid (Acoma form). Shiáska-hánoᶜʰ.—Ibid. (Laguna form). Sösh'ka-háno.—Ibid. (San Felipe form).

Sotonoemu. A former Chumashan village near Santa Inés mission, Santa Barbara co., Cal.—Taylor in Cal. Farmer, Oct. 18, 1861.

Sotstl (*Sŏtsʟ*). A Bellacoola town at the mouth of Salmon r., coast of British Columbia. The people of this town and those of Satsk, who together are called Kinisquit, numbered 63 in 1909.

Nūt-ęl.—Boas in Petermanns Mitteil., pt. 5, 130, 1887 Nūtl'ᴇ'l.—Boas in 7th Rep. N.W. Tribes Can., 3, 1891. Rascals' Village.—Mackenzie, Voy., 339, 1802; Mayne, Brit. Col., 146, 1862 (so named by Mackenzie from the treatment received there). Sŏtsʟ.—Boas in Mem. Am. Mus. Nat. Hist., II, 49, 1900.

Souanetto. An unidentified village or tribe mentioned to Joutel in 1687 (Margry, Déc., III, 409, 1878), while he was staying with the Kadohadacho on Red r. of Louisiana, by the chief of that tribe, as being among his enemies.

Souhegan. A tribe or band of the Pennacook confederacy, formerly living on Souhegan r. in Hillsborough co., N. H. Their principal village may have been near the present Amherst, which was formerly called Souhegan.

Nacooks.—Potter in Schoolcraft, Ind. Tribes, V, 221, 1855. Natacooks.—Potter, ibid. (trans. 'clearing'). Nattukkog.—Hogkins (1685) in N. H. Hist. Soc. Coll., I, 221, 1824. Saugehans.—Keane in Stanford, Compend., 534, 1878 (misprint). Souhegans.—Potter, op. cit. Sowahegen Indians.—Eliot (1651) in Mass. Hist. Soc. Coll., 3d s., IV, 123, 1834.

Soul. The ideas relating to the soul are based principally on three mental processes: the formation of the concept of

"power of acting" resident in a body, but distinct from the existence of the body; the formation of concepts due to the subjective feelings connected with imagery; and that of others due to the objective impressions made by memory images. Owing to these distinct sources from which the ideas combined under the term "soul" spring, they show considerable diversity of form. The principal concept representing the first-named group of ideas is that of "life," with which the power of acting is bound up—either the life of the whole body, or that of parts of the body or of special organs. Thus the Hidatsa and the Fraser River tribes of British Columbia believe in several souls, the loss of one of which causes partial loss of life, i. e. sickness, while the loss of all, or of the principal one, entails death. In other cases the "life" is associated with the vital organs, such as blood and breath, the loss of which causes death; but this particular idea is not strongly developed among the American aborigines. It is not necessary that this "life" should be considered in anthropomorphic form.

Another concept of the "soul" is based on the association of the phenomena of will power, which are conceived of as separate from the body acting in accordance with the dictates of the will. These associations are expressed particularly in the beliefs relating to "will-souls" of animals and inanimate objects, and in those of guardian spirits that carry out the wishes of their owners.

The forms that these ideas regarding the soul assume are deeply influenced by the second and third groups of mental processes already referred to. The power of imagery, which is inherent in every person, manifests itself in memory images, in the conceptions of fancy, in dreams, and in hallucinations. The subjective impressions of imagery find expression most readily in the creation of an image which has an entity similar to the self, but separate from it, able to leave the body and to visit distant places and to see past and future. This entity, although similar to the self, is nevertheless not discernible to our senses. In this group of ideas may be classed the belief of the Nootka in the soul of a person in the form of a tiny man, and the similar beliefs of the Hurons and the Eskimo.

Objectively, imagery shows us distant objects as present, and thus the same twofold existence that is experienced by the self appears to belong to the outer world; and it is of particular importance to note that things gone and past, like the dead, may appear in one's mental images in full vigor. Thus the three lines of thought lead to the belief in souls separate from the body, often in human form, and continuing to exist after death.

The lack of tangibility of the soul has led everywhere among Indians to the belief that it is visible to shamans only, or at least that it is like a shadow (Algonquian), like an unsubstantial image (Eskimo), or that its trail and footprints only can be seen (Shasta), or that it glides through the air without touching the earth (Omaha). Peculiar is the notion of the soul as a butterfly or a bird (Tsimshian, Bellacoola), which, however, is not so common in America as in other parts of the world. This idea is probably derived from independent psychological sources. The same is probably the case with the mythic notion of the "life" which is kept outside of the body, in a box, a hat, in the form of a thread, etc., and the destruction of which terminates the life of its owner (N. W. coast, California); and of the identification of the soul of the dead with the owl, which is of almost universal occurrence. Perhaps the flitting motions of the owl, combined with its human likeness, have associated themselves with the idea of the unsubstantial soul. Among the Eskimo the memory image attached to the name is so strong that the name has a separate entity and is considered a soul which enters the person who is given the name of the deceased.

The beliefs relating to the soul's existence after death are very uniform, not only in North America, but all over the world. The souls live in the land of the dead in the form that they had in life, and continue their former occupations. Detailed descriptions of the land of the dead are found among almost all American tribes. Often the physical conditions in the land of the dead are the reverse of those in our world: when it is night here, it is day there; when it is summer here it is winter there. The Eskimo tribes believe in several worlds of this kind. Those who suffer violent deaths go to the sky, while those who die of sickness go to another world. The Indians of Vancouver id. believe that the villages of the dead are near their own villages, but invisible; but the most common notion is that of the world of the ghosts lying in the distant west beyond a river which must be crossed by canoe. This notion is found on the western plateaus and on the Plains. The Algonquians believe that the brother of the culture hero lives with the souls of the dead. Visits to the world of the dead by people who have been in a trance are one of the common elements of American folklore. They have been reported from almost all over the continent. See *Mythology, Religion.* (F. B.)

Souligny. A war chief of the Menominee tribe, born in 1785. His grandfather was one Souligny, an early French trader, who married a Menominee woman. In 1812 Souligny was one of a large party of Sioux, Winnebago, and Menominee which, under the British colonel, Robert Dickson, captured the fort at Mackinaw from the Americans. The following year Souligny with about 50 warriors, and White Elk, a chief of distinction, united with Tecumseh in time to participate in the battle of Ft Meigs, on Miami r., Ohio. He took an active part in the battle at Mackinaw, Mich., in which the American commander, Major Holmes, was killed; he also served in Stambaugh's expedition.

SOULIGNY (1785-1864), HEAD WAR CHIEF OF THE MENOMINEE (WIS. HIST. SOC.)

Although he fought against the Americans during the War of 1812, in the Black Hawk war of 1837 he espoused their cause. In Mar. 1855 Souligny and Oshkosh, another Menominee chief, visited the office of the *Milwaukee Sentinel* and asked that the editor give publicity to their petition for the return of an Indian child who had been kidnapped by the whites. At this time Souligny was 70 years of age, but spoke with all the energy of one in the prime of life. He is described as being a stout, good-looking man, despite the loss of an eye. He died of erysipelas in Dec. 1864, at his home on the w. bank of Wolf r., Wis., at what is known as the Great Falls. His portrait, painted by Samuel Brookes, is in possession of the Wisconsin Historical Society at Madison.   (F. S. N.)

Sounikaeronon. The Iroquois name for a tribe defeated by them a few years before 1682 (La Salle in Margry, Déc., II, 237, 1877). In this name *ronon* is the tribal suffix.

Soupnapka. A former Delaware village on the E. bank of Delaware r. in New Jersey.—Newcastle conf. (1675) in N. Y. Doc. Col. Hist., XII, 523, 1877.

Souscoc. A former Chumashan village near Santa Inés mission, Santa Barbara co., Cal.—Taylor in Cal. Farmer, Oct. 18, 1861.

South Andrian Band. A band of Shuswap, formerly known as the Adam's Lake band.—Can. Ind. Aff., 74, 1878.

Southern Ute. The general official designation of the Ute (q. v.) under the Ft Lewis and Southern Ute school superintendency, s. w. Colorado, on a reservation comprising 483,750 acres. They comprise the Capote, Moache, and Wiminuche bands, with an aggregate population of 806 in 1909. They are decreasing in numbers.

The Wiminuche are the strongest numerically (454 individuals), and occupy the s.w. portion of the reservation, near Mesa Verde; they are the "unallotted" part of the tribe and endeavor to remain as far as possible in a primitive state. The Moache, next in population, and the Capote, are settled about Ignacio; their lands have been allotted in severalty, they do some farming with Government aid, and are somewhat more civilized than the Wiminuche.

Of the early history of the Southern Ute but little is known; they occupied portions of Utah, Colorado, and New Mexico, and possibly even Arizona. In 1775 Father Escalante visited them, describing them as "inhabiting the region north of the Moquis." Toward the middle of the 19th century they were estimated at 200 lodges, with from 1,400 to 2,000 souls. They have occupied their present reservation since 1863.

The Southern Ute are neither industrious nor wealthy. The family property consists at best of a tent, a few ponies, a wagon, and a few head of cattle, sheep, or goats. The aged members of the Wiminuche band are still receiving rations, while the Moache and Capote about Ignacio are assisted in other ways. They live, by preference, in tipis or brush shelters; only a few of those at Ignacio have houses of adobe. The furnishings of the dwelling are of the rudest description, consisting chiefly of a quantity of rags, a soiled cotton blanket or two, one or two water-gourds, and sometimes a sheep skin or a goat skin. Other individual property may consist of a saddle, bow and arrows, or a

gun or revolver, a few cups, pans, cans, and a bag containing extra clothing and ornaments. The middle of the dwelling is occupied by a small fireplace. Among the Wiminuche the tipis are often moved from place to place, while the huts are abandoned or destroyed.

The people all dress to-day chiefly in the clothing of civilization; the blanket, or in its absence a calico shawl, is still a favorite part of the costume. The women often wear leather belts. Decoration is more highly regarded than clothing and consists chiefly of objects covered with beadwork, as pouches, knife-scabbards, belts, etc., of necklaces, and sometimes breast-plates of porcupine quills. Medallions and badges, and copper or silver earrings, are much in favor among the men. Both sexes wear deerskin moccasins ornamented with beadwork. A sombrero decorated with a ribbon or a feather, is preferred by the men as a head-covering. The men wear their hair in two braids, hanging over the chest; some of the men wear another small braid depending from the middle of the scalp. The women wear the hair loose, cut above the brows and at the back to convenient length.

The occupations of these people are few. Once subsisting by the chase, they are not good laborers, nor do they take kindly to farming. They are neither weavers nor potters, and only a limited trade is conducted with other tribes. Indolence is characteristic of the younger men, and it is apparent that the tribe is passing through a period of degradation. The family life is of a rather low order. Marriage is easily contracted and as easily dissolved, and the custom of exchanging wives is said to occur. Polygyny is practised, though to a lesser extent than formerly. The morals of the Wiminuche particularly are bad. Gambling is prevalent, a woman often neglecting her children for a game of cards. The aged are neglected by their offspring, being suffered to shift for themselves. The natural abilities of the people, however, are not inferior to those of other tribes. The children are bright, and considerable artistic talent is exhibited by both men and women. The tribe preserves remnants of what may have been a clan organization, and each band recognizes a distinct chief. In important matters the families act together. Intermarriage among the three bands is not prohibited. Friendship exists and visits are exchanged between the Southern Ute and the Cheyenne and Arapaho. Little progress has been made toward Christianity. They still practise a few ceremonies and perform a few dances, among the latter being a "bear dance," which takes place in spring. They dispose of the dead as soon as possible either by burying in the ground or, preferably, by depositing the remains in crevices in the rocks, the situation of which is carefully guarded. The dwelling of the deceased, with all his property, is burned. An observance still common among both sexes is face painting in many colors and designs, to some extent symbolic. Physically the people exhibit a characteristic physiognomy, which, with their hair-dress, makes them easy of recognition as Southern Ute. They are short in stature, and the men are considerably inclined to obesity. In color they are moderately brown or yellowish brown. Few of the young women are handsome, and the old ones usually are very ugly. The hair shows the usual Indian characteristics; the beard, as among most tribes, is eradicated. Measurements of 50 male adults indicate an average height of 166.8 cm. The cephalic index shows a rather wide range, with a predominance of mesocephaly. The tribe is less pure in blood than the more northerly Ute. (A. H.)

Zuidelijke Utes.—ten Kate, Reizen in N. A., 314, 1885 (Dutch form).

Southern Workman. See *Hampton Normal and Agricultural Institute.*

Southwood Indians. An evident misprint for Southward Indians, referring to those s. of Ohio r.—Croghan (1750) in Kauffman, West. Pa., app., 27, 1851.

Sowi. The Jackrabbit clan of the Hopi.
So'-wi.—Stephen in 8th Rep. B. A. E., 39, 1891. **Sowi wiñwû.**—Fewkes in 19th Rep. B. A. E., 583, 1900. **Sui.**—Bourke, Snake Dance, 117, 1884.

Sowiinwa. The Deer clan of the Ala (Horn) phratry of the Hopi.
Shu-húi-ma.—Bourke, Snake Dance, 117, 1884. **So-wi'-in-wa wüñ-wü.**—Fewkes in Am. Anthr., VII, 401, 1894 (*wüñ-wü*=clan). **Sowinû wiñwû.**—Fewkes in 19th Rep. B. A. E., 583, 1891. **So'-wiñ-wa.**—Stephen in 8th Rep. B. A. E., 38, 1891.

Soyennow. According to Lewis and Clark, a division of the Chopunnish (see *Nez Percés*) on the N. side of the upper Clearwater in Idaho. Their number was given as 400 in 1805. They were probably a band of the Paloos.
Sagennom.—Schoolcraft, Ind. Tribes, III, 570, 1853. **Soyennom.**—Lewis and Clark Exped., II, 471, 1814. **So-yen-now.**—Orig. Jour. Lewis and Clark, VI, 115, 1905. **Tätqu'nma.**—Mooney in 14th Rep. B. A. E., 745, 1896 (proper form, whence Thatuma hills).

Soyopa. A rancheria of the Nevome, which contained also some Eudeve (Orozco y Berra, Geog., 351, 1864), and forming, in 1730-64(?), a visita of the mission of Onabas (q. v.). Situated on an upper branch of the Yaqui r., lat. 29° 5', lon. 109° 20', Sonora, Mexico.
S. Joseph de Soyôpa.—Rivera, Diario, leg. 1382, 1736. **Sopopo.**—Rivera (1730) misquoted by Bancroft, No. Mex. States, I, 514, 1884. **Soyopa.**—Rudo Ensayo (*ca.* 1762), 124, 1863.

Spades. See *Hoes and Spades.*

Spade-stones. Prehistoric objects of polished stone, the purpose of which has not been determined, but as they are symmetrically shaped, carefully finished, and rarely show decided marks of use, and besides are sometimes made of soft stone of several varieties, archeologists are disposed to assign them to ceremonial use. The name has been given them because they resemble somewhat ordinary spades, although some varieties are as much like blades of axes, hoes, or shovels. This name will serve as well as any other for purposes of description. For the present, all of these objects may be grouped between the two extremes of

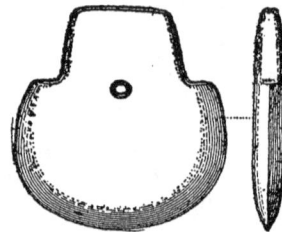
GREENSTONE; NORTH CAROLINA (1-6)

form, the hoe or ax shaped variety with broad, thick blade and short stem, and the long-shafted variety with small, somewhat rudimentary blade. Many of the intermediate forms, being rather short and thick, approach the celt in appearance. The recent discovery by Moore of specimens of the short, broad-bladed variety retaining traces of hafting has led to the suggestion that these, and possibly the whole group of objects here considered, are ceremonial derivatives of the celt. The longer-shafted forms correspond in general appearance to the long-shafted copper celts found by Moore in Southern mounds. A number of these objects are said to show effects of use in scraping, digging, or other service resulting in abrasion of the blade, and

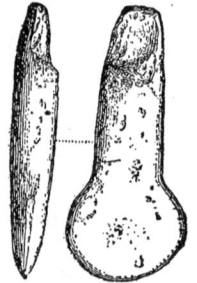
WISCONSIN (1-6)

C. C. Jones, describing specimens in his own collection, takes the view that they were scrapers; but it seems possible that the wear in such cases may be the result of secondary use by persons not acquainted with the original, normal functions of the objects. A characteristic feature of the broad, short forms is a perforation, which occurs generally near the upper part of the blade and occasionally well up the shaft. A few have the perforation near the top, giving the appearance of a pendant ornament. A characteristic feature of the slender-shafted variety is the occurrence of a number of small notches in the margin of the upper part of the blade.

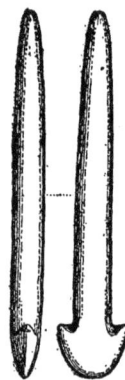
CHLORITIC STONE; ARKANSAS (1-10)

These objects are not numerous in any section, but the various types are widely distributed over the country E. of the great plains. The short, broad-bladed form prevails in the Southern states, and the small-bladed, long-handled variety in the N. and N. W. They occur generally in mounds in connection with burials. See *Problematical objects*.

Consult Brown in Wis. Archeologist, II, no. 1, 1902; Fowke in 13th Report B. A. E., 1896; Jones, Antiq. So. Inds., 1873; Moore in Am. Anthr., n. s., v, no. 3, 1903, and in various numbers of Jour. Acad. Nat. Sci. Phila.; Moorehead, Prehistoric Impls., 1900; Rau in Smithson. Cont., XXII, 1876; Thruston, Antiq. of Tenn., 1897.   (W. H. H.)

Spahamin (*Spa'xEmîn*, 'shavings,' 'cuttings,' as of wood or bone). An Okinagan village situated at Douglas lake, 11 m. from Kwilchana, Brit. Col. Its people associate much with the Ntlakyapamuk, whose language they speak as well as their own; they numbered 189 in 1909, probably including some Ntlakyapamuk.

Douglas Lake.—White men's name. **Nicola (Upper).**—Can. Ind. Aff., pt. I, 243, 1902. **Spah-a-man.**—Can. Ind. Aff., pt. I, 189, 1884. **Spa-ha-min.**—Ibid., 271, 1889. **Spa'xEmîn.**—Teit in Mem. Am. Mus. Nat. Hist., II, 174, 1900. **Upper Nicola.**—Can. Ind. Aff., pt. II, 68, 1902 (includes some Ntlakyapamuk villages).

Spaim (*Spa'-im*, 'flat land,' 'open flat' [Teit]; 'pleasant, grassy, flowery spot' [Hill-Tout]). A Ntlakyapamuk village on the E. side of Fraser r., Brit. Col.; pop. 27 in 1897.

Spa'im.—Teit in Mem. Am. Mus. Nat. Hist., II, 169, 1900. **Spayam.**—Can. Ind. Aff., 418, 1898 ("Chomok-Spayam"). **Spē'im.**—Hill-Tout in Rep. Ethnol. Surv. Can., 5, 1899. **Speyam.**—Can. Ind. Aff., 230, 1884.

Spallamcheen. A body of Shuswap on a branch of Thompson r., Brit Col., at first under the Okanagan agency, afterward under that of Kamloops. Pop. 144 in 1904, 162 in 1909.

Spallamcheen.—Can. Ind. Aff., pt. II, 166, 1901. **Spallum-acheen.**—Ibid., 191, 1888. **Spallumcheen.**—Ibid., 363, 1897. **Spelemcheen.**—Ibid., 317, 1880. **Spellamcheen.**—Ibid., 313, 1892. **Spellammachum.**—Ibid., 79, 1878.

Spamagelabe. See *Spemicalawba*.

Spanawatka. A former Seminole town 2 m. below Iola, on the w. side of Apalachicola r., Calhoun co., Fla.—H. R. Ex. Doc. 74 (1823), 19th Cong., 1st sess., 27, 1826.

Spanguliken. A word in use in several parts of the State of New York formerly inhabited by the Delawares as a term for a conceited or a vain person, and for a "know-it-all." The word is a corruption of Lenape *äspinguliechsin*, meaning 'to raise the eyes in speaking,' that is, to be supercilious. It corresponds pretty well to Latin *superciliosus*, from *supercilium*, 'haughtiness,' as expressed by raising the eyebrows (from *super*, 'above,' and *cilium*, 'eyebrow,' 'eyelid').   (W. R. G.)

Spanish influence. The influence of the Spaniards on the aborigines of America N. of Mexico was very marked along the whole southern border from Florida to California; but it was most notable in the W., where greater numbers of aborigines were present to be affected by the processes of colonization. Elsewhere in North America the Spanish adventurers and fishermen left slight evidences of their sojourn. A trace of Spanish influence, through Basque fishermen, is found in the early accounts of the Micmac (Lescarbot, Hist. Nouv. France, 668, 1612), where a few words of Spanish or of Basque origin were preserved in the jargon used between natives and Europeans.

On the opposite side of the continent the people of Vancouver id. were affected by the Spanish settlements in California, for some of the Indians of this coast were brought down to the Catholic missions. Contrary to a widespread belief, there is no Spanish element in the Chinook jargon. In Florida, where Spanish domination extended over two centuries, the Indian tribes of the northern and central sections were much influenced by the European colonists, as appears from Margry, Dickenson, and other documentary sources. This was particularly true of the Apalachee and the Timucua, whose prosperity continued until the destruction of the missions by the English and their Indian allies between 1702 and 1708, after which the ruin of the native tribes was completed by the inroads of the Creeks. The vocabularies of all the Southern tribes show Spanish influence, as, for example, the word *waka*, for *vaca*, 'cow'. The Eno of North Carolina in 1654 met with Spaniards who had come from the gold regions of the southern Alleghanies (Mooney, Siouan Tribes of the East, 58, 1894), while Spanish intimacy in South Carolina began as early as the establishment of the post at Santa Elena in 1567. Spanish slavers decimated the minor tribes of the Carolina and Georgia coast. In Texas as many as 10,000 Indians were gathered into the missions, some of whose massive buildings still remain in fair preservation, and a considerable strain of blood of the Mexican element of to-day is known to be of Indian origin. Spanish blood, introduced by capture, enters to some extent into the composition of most of the southern Plains tribes, as well as of the Apache, and the Spanish language is still a frequent means of intertribal communication in many parts of the S. W. The Caddo of Louisiana, as early as 1688, according to Tonti, called the horse *cavali*, evidently from the Spanish *caballo*, which word has furnished the name of this animal to many Southwestern tribes. The effects of the Spanish occupancy of the S.W. have been discussed in detail by Bandelier (Papers Arch. Inst. Am.), Blackmar (Spanish Colonization in the S. W., 1890; Spanish Institutions of the S. W., 1891, and Bancroft (History of the Pacific States). The fame of the so-called Seven Cities of Cibola and the quest for gold led the Spaniards northward from Old Mexico as early as 1539. Within the present bounds of Arizona the permanent results of Spanish occupancy were of consequence through the planting of Jesuit missions in the southern part of the territory, in the latter part of the 17th century, where the Pima and Papago were chiefly concerned. The expulsion of the Jesuits in 1767 and the transfer of authority to the Franciscans affected the Indians unfavorably, at first, but the missions prospered again later, and the famous church of San Xavier del Bac (q. v.) still stands as a monument to their skill and energy. The unsatisfactory condition of affairs in Mexico, the constant incursions of the Apache, and the neglect of the outlying garrisons caused the missions almost to cease their activity by 1830, and in 1853, by the Gadsden purchase, s. Arizona passed into the possession of the United States.

On the Hopi of N. E. Arizona the Spaniards made no such deep impression as on the Pueblos of the Rio Grande, chiefly for the reason that missions were not reestablished among the former after the Pueblo rebellion of 1680–92. Nevertheless, the introduction of horses, burros, sheep, goats, cattle, wheat, peaches, firearms, the cart, the wooden plow, iron axes, adzes, and other tools, and probably the handloom, had marked effect on the daily life of the people even if it did not affect their religious beliefs and practices. The introduction of sheep alone had an important result, no small measure of which was the complete changing of the Navaho, once largely a predatory tribe like their Apache cousins, into a pastoral people. In New Mexico the influence of the Spaniards was more lasting and far-reaching than in Arizona. The Europeans were welcomed at first and hospitably received, the natives even taking kindly to the new religion of the missionaries as powerful "new medicine," adding to their own ancient rites and ceremonies those of the Roman Catholic church and even sincerely adopting the latter so long as the protection of the Spaniards against the predatory tribes was effective. The Indians, it should be said, were not affected by the Inquisition, being regarded as minors so far as religious matters were concerned. Not only is the outward form of Christianity preserved among the New Mexican Pueblos, but for many

things they hold the Christian religion to be the only potent magic, "God being regarded as an outside spiritual being who can do much good within a certain sphere of action and great harm if interfered with from the other side of the house" (Bandelier, inf'n, 1905). Tools of Spanish proveniance largely replaced the wooden dibble, greatly facilitating agriculture; the Spanish cart, however clumsy, was a vast improvement over the former method of transporting the harvest on the back; while the horse, the mule, and the burro promoted travel and traffic to a degree almost beyond reckoning, and supplied the machinery for threshing the wheat, that was unknown before the Spaniards came. The houses also show the effect of Spanish influence when compared with the ruins of ancient dwellings. The horse making it possible to transport longer beams, the rooms are more capacious than formerly. Wooden doors and windows, molded adobe bricks, chimneys, and probably surface ovens also owe their origin to the Spaniards, as do likewise doorways to the lower rooms, access to which was formerly gained through the roof until the presence of the whites made no longer necessary this device for protection against predatory enemies. The Spaniards made some changes in the method of government of the New Mexican Pueblos, causing each to elect annually a governor and other civil officers, a custom still prevailing, although the governor is usually selected by the caciques, and is not much more than their mouthpiece.

From Bourke's résumé of "The Laws of Spain in their Application to the American Indians" (Am. Anthr., VII, 193, 1894) we gain a more favorable view of the disposition of the Spanish authorities than is generally entertained. The Spaniards accepted more or less assimilation, and "left upon the American continent communities of aborigines whose social and moral condition has been most appreciably improved by the introduction of horses, cattle, sheep, goats, hogs, and chickens, the planting of orchards of peaches, oranges, and other fruits, as well as vineyards, and instruction in such new trades as carpentry, saddlery, blacksmithing, and wagon making, or the improvement of such prehistoric handicrafts as stone masonry, weaving, basket-making, and pottery." As Bourke points out, some of these Spanish laws continue still to be observed in the Indian pueblos. In the villages of New Mexico, for example, the Indians sell in their own markets and not to those they meet on the way thither. As Bandelier (Papers Arch. Inst. Am., 188–319, 1890) and Lummis (Spanish Pioneers,

1893) have shown, the charges against the Spaniards of enslaving the Indians in the mines have not been sustained, such servitude being contrary to the letter and the spirit of the law. Moreover, captives and slaves were often redeemed from the wilder tribes, as the villages of Genizaros established before 1648 at Abiquiu and afterward at Tomé and Belen on the Rio Grande prove. The Protectores de los Indios, at first the prelates of the country, performed somewhat the same functions as our Indian agents. The system of pueblo grants had its advantages for the Indians, and many of the Spanish enactments "enlarged their scope of vision and fostered the thought of individuality." The industrial training of the Franciscans began early, and though to-day some of the Pueblos have the tools and appliances of medieval Spain—the old plow, the two-wheeled cart, the clumsy iron ax, and the crude saw—even these constituted a considerable advance over primitive implements—the digging stick, fire-drill, etc., while the addition of numerous domesticated animals and plants made possible progress in various ways. Bandelier is of the opinion that "in many respects the Apache, Comanche, the Navaho above all, owe more to European culture introduced by Spain than the Pueblos." The introduction of the horse made speedy travel possible and the acquisition of fire-arms enabled some of these Indians to compete on fairly even terms with the whites. As a result of white contact the Indians of the New Mexico pueblos abandoned for a time the making of blankets, an art learned from them by the Navaho, who attained great skill in it, and paid less attention to the elaboration of their pottery. These facts, as Bandelier observes, may be evidences, not of decadence, but of progress. Of the general intent and effect of Spanish laws relating to the Indian, Bandelier, it may be observed, takes the same sympathetic view as do Lummis and Bourke.

While the Pueblos of New Mexico had their missions, and the fathers often acquitted themselves heroically in their hard labors, California was the scene of the exploitation of the mission idea on a scale impossible where the Indians themselves were of the character and social condition exemplified among the Pueblos. The first Spanish colony in California proper was established at San Diego in 1769 as a result of the expedition of Galvez. By 1834 there were 21 missions, extending in an irregular line for more than 600 m. along the coast, linking together the most fertile valleys of California. Connected with these missions were 30,650 Indians; the cattle numbered 424,000; the bushels of grain harvested, 100,000;

the value of the product, $2,000,000; the movable stock, apart from buildings, orchards, vineyards, etc., $3,000,000; annual income of the pious fund, $50,000. Eight years later only 4,450 Indians remained and other things had declined in proportion. Secularization of the missions by the Mexican Government was in part responsible for this, though previous individual and temporary abuses and vacillation in policy, as for example the changes from one religious order to another or transfer of the missions to the care of secular ecclesiastics or of political officers, were often detrimental. By the time of the American occupancy in 1846 the decline was complete; "a small number of the natives were still living at the missions, but the majority had returned to their rancherias in the mountains and districts remote from the settlements." Since then some of the missions have crumbled to dust and many of the Indian tribes have vanished with them or linger only in insignificant numbers, but the buildings and other remains evidence the extent of this remarkable, though in the end unsuccessful, attempt to make over thousands of the aborigines of the New World. The influence of Spain can be seen among them still, but they were too much domesticated, and the change from the friar and the priest to the Anglo-Saxon pioneer, the cowboy, and the miner proved too masterful for them. What the Spaniards accomplished in California in the brief space of 50 years was a marvel, but an evanescent one. The results of Indian labor can be seen over all California, but the sons and daughters of the workers are no more. The story of the Spanish missions of California, New Mexico, and Texas will ever be one of the most interesting in the annals of American history. See *California Indians, Mission Indians, Missions, Pueblos.*   (A. F. C.)

Spapak (*Spāpa'k·*). A Squawmish village community on the right bank of Squawmisht r., Brit. Col.—Hill-Tout in Rep. Brit. A. A. S., 474, 1900.

Spapium (*Spapī'um*, 'level grassy land'). A Ntlakyapamuk village on a river bench opposite Lytton, Brit. Col.; pop. 84 in 1901.
Spa-ki-um.—Can. Ind. Aff., 196, 1885 (misprint). Spapiam.—Ibid., 312, 1892. Spapī'um.—Hill-Tout in Rep. Ethnol. Surv. Can., 5, 1889.

Spatlum. A name which, with variants *spatulum, spatlam,* and *spætlum,* has long been applied to the "bitter-root," *Lewisia rediviva,* a succulent perennial of upper Oregon, the root of which is highly prized by the Indians as an article of food. As the root is very small, it requires much labor to gather a bagful, which commands the price of a horse. The plant was observed in use among the natives by Lewis and Clark, and its supposed name was obtained from Lewis's manuscript by Pursh, who gives it as spatlum ("*Spatlum Aboriginorum*"). The name, which is Salishan, is here a misapplication, since *spatlûm* in the Comox dialect (*spätlûm* in the Kwantlin) is the name for tobacco. (W. R. G.)

Spatsatlt (*Spatsā'tlt*). A Bellacoola band at Talio (q. v.), Brit. Col.—Boas in 7th Rep. N. W. Tribes Can., 3, 1891.

Spatsum (contracted from *Spa'ptsEn*, 'little Indian hemp place'). A village of the Spences Bridge band of Ntlakyapamuk on the s. side of Thompson r., 35 m. above Lytton, Brit. Col. (Teit in Mem. Am. Mus. Nat. Hist., II, 173, 1900). Pop. 135 in 1901.
Apaptsim.—Can. Ind. Aff., 363, 1897 (misprint). Cpa'ptsEn.—Hill-Tout in Rep. Ethnol. Surv. Can., 4, 1899. S-pap-tsin.—Can. Ind. Aff., 196, 1885. Spatsim.—Ibid., 419, 1898. Spatsum.—Teit, op. cit.

Spear. See *Lance*.

Spearheads. See *Arrowheads*.

Spemicalawba ('High Horn,' from *spûmûk*, 'high'; the common spelling of the name). A Shawnee chief, known to the whites as Captain James Logan. His mother was Tecumtha's (Tecumseh's) sister. When a boy, in 1786, he was captured by Gen. Logan, of Kentucky, while the latter was on an expedition against the Ohio tribes. The general took the boy into his own family, sent him to school, gave him his own name, and then sent him back to his tribe. The result was that Logan thenceforth was the firm friend of the whites. He afterward married an Indian woman, who, like himself, had been taken under similar conditions and resided with the family of Col. Hardin, of Kentucky, for several years. He endeavored unsuccessfully to dissuade Tecumtha from hostilities, and in the War of 1812 enlisted on the side of the Americans, doing good service as a scout and spy in the Ohio region. His good faith having been called into question on one occasion when his party had retreated before a superior force, he determined to prove his loyalty, and setting out with two Indian companions down the Maumee r., encountered near the rapids the British Captain Elliot with 5 Indians, who claimed Logan's party as prisoners. Watching an opportunity, Logan's men attacked the others, killing Elliot and two of his Indians, but with the dangerous wounding of Logan and one of his men. Taking their enemies' horses, they made their way to the camp of the American General Winchester, where Logan died two days after, Nov. 24, 1812. He was buried with the honors due his rank and received warm eulogies from Gen. Winchester and Maj. Hardin. In person he is described as of fine physique, with features expressive of courage, intelligence, good humor, and sincerity. His usual residence was at the Shawnee town of Wapakoneta, Ohio. Logansport, Ind., takes its name from him. His name occurs also as Spamagelabe. (J. M.)

Spences Bridge Band. One of 4 subdivisions of Ntlakyapamuk occupying the banks of Thompson r., Brit. Col., from about 8 m. below Spences Bridge nearly to Ashcroft.—Teit in Mem. Am. Mus. Nat. Hist., II, 170, 1900.
Nkamtci'nEmux.—Teit, op. cit. ('people of the entrance'; more strictly applied to the Indians immediately about Spences Bridge).

Spia. The extinct Hawk clan of Sia pueblo, N. Mex.
Spía-háno.—Hodge in Am. Anthr., IX, 351, 1896 (*háno* = 'people').

Spichehat. A tribe or village formerly in the country between Matagorda bay and Maligne (Colorado) r., Texas. The name seems to have been given to Joutel in 1687 by the Ebahamo, a tribe probably closely affiliated with the Karankawa, which dwelt in this region. See Gatschet, Karankawa Inds., Peabody Mus. Papers, I, 23, 35, 1891. (A. C. F.)
Espicheates.—Barcia, Ensayo, 271, 1723. Spicheats.—Joutel (1687) in French, Hist. Coll. La., I, 137, 1846. Spicheets.—Shea, note in Charlevoix, New France, IV, 78, 1870. Spichehat.—Joutel (1687) in Margry, Déc., III, 288, 1878.

Spike-buck Town. A former Cherokee settlement on Hiwassee r., at or near the present Hayesville, Clay co., N. C.
Spike Bucktown.—Royce in 5th Rep. B. A. E., map, 1887.

Spine-back Stones. A descriptive term for a number of objects of stone, the use of which is problematical. They are somewhat related in their form to the pierced tablets and the boat-shaped stones (q. v.), and have two perforations for attachment or suspension.

SPINE-BACK STONE; GREENISH BANDED SLATE; OHIO (LENGTH 4 5-8 IN.)

Nearly all are made of slate, and are neatly shaped and polished. In length they vary from 4 to 6 in. The under side is flattish and the ends are unequal, one being pointed and the other blunt and often sloping upward, while the convex back rises into a somewhat pronounced knob, or spine, which is doubtless reminiscent of some characteristic animal feature. These interesting objects are suggestive of the small carvings representing the spine back whale found in ancient graves of California. See *Problematical objects*. (W. H. H.)

Spinning. See *Weaving*.

Spirit Walker. A chief of the Wahpeton Sioux, born at Lacquiparle, Minn., about 1795. He was early converted to Christianity and was friendly in the Sioux outbreak of 1862, but fled to Dakota after the defeat of Little Crow. Mrs Marble, the Spirit Lake captive of 1857, was rescued by Grayfoot and Sounding Heavens, sons of Spirit Walker.   (D. R.)

Spitotha. One of the 5 original divisions or bands of the Shawnee (W. H. Shawnee in Gulf States Hist. Mag., I, 415, 1903). Evidently distinct from Kispokotha, but probably the same as Mequachake, q. v.

Spokan. A name applied to several small bodies of Salish on and near Spokane r., N. E. Wash. According to Gibbs the name was originally employed by the Skitswish to designate a band at the forks of the river, called also Smahoomenaish. By the whites it was extended to cover several nearly allied divisions, which Gibbs enumerates as follows: Sin-slik-hoo-ish, Sintootoolish, Sma-hoo-men-a-ish (Spokenish), Skai-schil-t'nish, Ske-chei-a-mouse, Schu-el-stish, Sin-poil-schne, Sin-shee-lish. The last two were claimed by the Okinagan also. All of them are now held to be separate divisions and not bands of one tribe. The population was estimated by Lewis and Clark in 1805 at 600 in 30 houses, and by Gibbs in 1853 at 450. In 1908 there were 301 "Lower Spokan" and 238 "Upper Spokan" under Colville agency, Wash., and 95 Spokan on Cœur d'Alène res., Idaho; total, 634. In 1909 the entire number of Spokan in Washington was 509, while those in Idaho numbered 104.

Flat Heads.—Dart in Ind. Aff. Rep., 216, 1851 (so called because their heads were left in the natural state. (See *Flatheads*.) Lar-li-e-lo.—Lewis and Clark Exped., I, map, 1814. Lartielo.—Ibid., II, 475, 1814. Lar-ti-e-to's Nation.—Orig. Jour. Lewis and Clark, VI, 119, 1905. Ne-com-ap-oe-lox.—Suckley in Pac. R. R. Rep., I, 300, 1855. Sälst sхästsít-lini.—Gatschet, MS., B. A. E. (Okinagan name for the Lower Spokan at Little Spokane Falls; ='people with bad heads'). Sar-lis-lo.—Gibbs in Pac. R. R. Rep., I, 417, 1855 (the Lar-ti-e-lo of Lewis and Clark). Sin-ee-guo-men-ah.—Winans in Ind. Aff. Rep., 23, 1870 (applied here to the Upper Spokan). Sin-ha-ma-mish.—Gibbs in Pac. R. R. Rep., I, 418, 1855. Sin-hu.—Morgan, Consang. and Affin., 290, 1871 ('people wearing red paint on their cheeks': own name). Sinhuman-ish.—Schoolcraft, Ind. Tribes, III, 632, 1853. Sinkoman.—Gibbs in Pac. R. R. Rep., I, 414, 1855 (Kutenai name). Sinkumana.—Gatschet, MS., B. A. E. (Pend d'Oreille [Kalispel] name). Ska-moy-num-achs.—Ross, Adventures, 289, 1849 (Kutenai name). Sma-hoo-men-a-ish.—Gibbs in Pac. R. R. Rep., I, 414, 1855 (=Spokan proper). Snxú-mina.—Gatschet, MS., B. A. E. (Okinagan name for Upper Spokan). Spogans.—Meek in H. R. Ex. Doc. 76, 30th Cong. 1st sess., 10, 1848. Spokains.—McVickar, Exped. Lewis and Clark, II, 386, note, 1842 (probably used for Spokan proper). Spokan.—Parker, Journal, 292, 1840. Spokane.—Ibid., 292. Spo-kehmish.—Stevens in Ind. Aff. Rep., 429, 1854. Spokehnish.—Gibbs in Pac. R. R. Rep., I, 414, 1855. Spokein.—Parker, op. cit., 285. Spokens.—Robertson, Oregon, 129, 1846. Spo-kih-nish.—Stevens in Ind. Aff. Rep., 428, 1854. Spokineish.—Winans, ibid., 22, 1870. Spokines.—Johnson and Winter, Rocky Mts., 34, 1846. Spoko-mish.—Mooney in 14th Rep. B. A. E., 732, 1896. Spukä'n.—Gatschet, MS., B. A. E. (Klamath and Modoc name). Tsakaïtsetlins.—Domenech, Deserts, I, 444, 1860. Tsakaitsitlin.—Hale in U. S. Expl. Exped., VI, 205, 569, 1846. Upper Spokanes.—Winans in Ind. Aff. Rep., 23, 1870 (applies to Spokan proper). Zingomenes.—De Smet, Oregon Miss., 108, 1847.

Spookow. A Chumashan village formerly on the beach N. of San Buenaventura mission, Ventura co., Cal.—Taylor in Cal. Farmer, May 4, 1860.

Spools. Small prehistoric objects somewhat resembling spools, the purpose of which is unknown. They are nearly cylindrical, with incurved sides, perforated lengthwise at the center, and are made in most cases of sandstone, a few specimens being of baked clay. Their length varies from 1 to 2½ in. and their diameter rarely exceeds 2 in. The surface is always covered with incised lines arranged in what is apparently intended for a definite order or design, but no two are alike. They are not numerous, and, with the exception of a few from Ross co., Ohio, all are from counties bordering the Ohio r. between the Big Sandy and the Miami. Consult Fowke, Archæol. Hist. Ohio, 1902; Moorehead, Prehist. Impls., 1900; Squier and Davis, Ancient Monuments, 1848; Thruston, Antiq. of Tenn., 1897.   (G. F.)

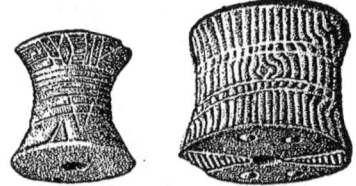
SPOOL-SHAPED STONES; OHIO (FOWKE)

Spoon de Kaury. See *Dekaury, Choukeka*.

Spoons and Ladles. Utensils for carrying liquid food or water to the mouth or from one vessel to another were found among all tribes of the United States. They were made of a wide variety of materials, as stone, shell, bone, horn, antler, ivory, wood, gourd, bark, basketry, and pottery were employed. In size they exceeded European utensils of this class. Beverley (Hist. Va., 154, 1722) thus refers to them: "The spoons which they eat with, do generally hold half a pint; and they laugh at the English for using small ones, which they must be forced to carry so often to their mouths, that their arms are in danger of being tired, before their Belly."

The animals supplying the most materials for spoons, dippers, and ladles were the mountain sheep and mountain goat. All the tribes living in the habitat of these animals utilized their horns for this purpose, and the manufactured products were distributed widely in trade among neighboring tribes. Specimens have been gathered among the Pueblos, Havasupai, Ute, Cheyenne, and Sioux, the Salishan and northern Algonquian tribes, and the N. W. Coast and Athapascan tribes. Among the southern Rocky Mountain Indians these utensils were rude, but the northern tribes made them works of art, softening the horn and bending and shaping it over forms by means of heat, and carving and inlaying the material with great skill. Spoons were also made from the horns of the buffalo. After cattle were introduced their horns were substituted, especially among the Plains tribes, for those of the disappearing wild animals.

Antler spoons.—A few tribes of N. California and Columbia r. used spoons made of antler. The Hupa spoons are characteristic and well made, and men's and women's spoons are of different shapes. The Eskimo sometimes made small spoons from antler, and in rare cases employed bone or ivory, though these materials are hard to work. Some of their fat-scrapers resemble spoons, and they used narrow bowl spoons as marrow extractors.

Wooden spoons and ladles.—The majority of spoons, dippers, and ladles were made of wood. The Eskimo and northern Athapascan tribes produced a variety of such utensils that exhibited some degree of art; but the tribes of the N. W. coast and of s. Alaska surpassed all others in the variety, grace of form, and decoration of these as well as other domestic objects. The tribes of the S. W. utilized wood to some extent for spoons and ladles, but these were always rude and were generally fashioned from knots. There is remarkable uniformity in the shape of utensils of this class among the Eastern and Southern Indians from New York to Florida. They all had the pointed bowl, a form which occurs in no other part of the United States.

Gourds.—The gourd, like the decayed knot, is a natural dipping instrument, and its use as such readily suggested itself. Gourds were extensively used and their forms were often repeated in pottery.

Shell spoons and dippers.—Wherever shells were available they were used in their natural form as dippers and were wrought into spoons. Spoons of shell, artistically worked, have been found in the mounds of Kentucky, Tennessee, Arkansas, and Ohio.

Pottery ladles and spoons.—Numerous objects of this class are found on the ancient sites of pottery-making tribes, and the Pueblo Indians, especially the Hopi, still manufacture them in great variety. In general the spoons follow the older elliptic shallow forms cut from gourds, while the dippers are characteristic, having a tubular or trough-like handle and an ample bowl, the latter sometimes saucer-shaped, but generally of the form of a small food bowl. The handles are often decorated with bands or short lines of color, and the terminal end is frequently modeled in the form of an animal's head. Cups with a small loop handle were and are common among the Hopi. See *Receptacles.*		(w. h.)

Spotted Arm. An influential Winnebago chief, born about 1772, known among his tribesmen as Manahketshumpkaw, and sometimes called Broken Arm by the whites, from the fact that he had been severely wounded in the arm at the siege of Ft Meigs in 1813, where he distinguished himself. It was his custom in after years to paint the scar in representation of a fresh wound. Spotted Arm was a signer of the Green Bay treaty in 1828, and during the Black Hawk war in 1832 he was one of three important headmen held by the whites as hostages for the good behavior of the Winnebago. He is described as having been stoop-shouldered and ill-shaped, but as possessing a mild and agreeable temperament. His village, known as Spotted Arm's village, was situated near the present Exeter, Green co., Wis. He died a few years after the Black Hawk war, having removed with his people to their new lands beyond the Mississippi after the Rock Island treaty of 1832. See Wis. Hist. Soc. Coll., VIII, 1879; X, 1888.

Spotted Tail (*Sinte-galeshka*). A Brulé Teton Sioux chief, born about 1833 near Ft Laramie, Wyo. He was not a chief by birth, but rose by dint of his fighting qualities. He won his wife in a duel with a subchief and proved his prowess in battle, so that when the head chief died the tribe passed over the hereditary claimant and aspirants of riper years and experience in favor of the young warrior. He had borne a conspicuous part in the destruction of Lieut. Grattan's detachment in 1854 when it entered the Brulé camp to arrest an Indian who had taken an old cow abandoned by some emigrants, and in the subsequent depredations on the Oregon trail. After signal punishment was inflicted on the tribe by Gen. Harney at Ash Hollow, w. Nebr., Spotted Tail and two others of the murderers, whose surrender was demanded, surprised the soldiers at Ft Laramie by marching in, arrayed in war dress and chanting their death songs, to give themselves up in order that the tribe might be spared. He regained his freedom and was chief of the Lower Brulés in 1865, when commissioners treated with the Sioux for a right of way through Montana, and was in favor of the treaty, though neither he nor any other prominent chief signed, while Red Cloud, the Oglala chief, led the party that opposed the cession of the overland route to the Montana mines. With the other chiefs he signed the treaty of Apr. 29, 1868, accepting for the Teton a reservation embracing all the present South Dakota w. of Missouri r., and assenting to the construction of a railroad, the Government acknowledging as unceded Indian territory the sections of Wyoming and Montana N. of the North Platte as far w. as Bighorn mts. and abandoning the road to the mines, with Ft Phil. Kearny, where the massacre of Lieut. Col. William J. Fetterman's command had occurred on Dec. 21, 1866, and Ft

SPOTTED TAIL

Reno near the head of Powder r. When gold was discovered in the Black hills, Spotted Tail and Red Cloud, who were recognized as the chiefs at the respective agencies called by their names, arranged to go to Washington to negotiate a sale of the mineral rights; and thoroughly to inform himself of the value of the minerals, Spotted Tail visited the hills, hung around the camps of the prospectors, listened to their talk, and conceived the idea therefrom that the mines were immensely valuable. Under the treaty of 1868 the chiefs could not make treaties for sale of lands, hence commissioners were sent to the Indians, finding that Spotted Tail had raised the Indian expectations so high that sixty million dollars were demanded for the concession. The Government could not agree to this, hence no treaty was made that year, and miners were permitted by the troops to pass into the Black hills without hindrance. Then all the young men on the reservations joined the hostiles. Red Cloud was suspected of disloyalty, and in the course of the campaign that followed the Custer disaster in 1876, Spotted Tail was appointed chief of all the Indians at both agencies, and negotiated the settlement by which his nephew, Crazy Horse, came

in from Powder r. and surrendered in the spring of 1877. Spotted Tail was killed near Rosebud agency, S. Dak., Aug. 5, 1881, by a tribesman named Crow Dog. The facts relating to the killing are in dispute, but there is not much question that Spotted Tail, at the time, was leading a hostile party against Crow Dog, who deemed his life in peril and shot in self-defense. (F. H. D. R.)

Spring Frog. See *Tooantuh.*

Spring Garden Town. A former town in the Seminole country, settled by Yuchi under chief Billy; situated above L. George, Fla.—Bell in Morse, Rep. to Sec. War, 308, 1822.

Spring Place. A Cherokee mission station established by the Moravians Steiner and Byhan, in 1801, in Murray co., N. W. Ga., and continued in operation until the extension of the Georgia laws over the Cherokee territory in 1834. (J. M.)

Spruce-tree House. A ruined cliff-dwelling, situated in the Mesa Verde National Park, about 25 m. from Mancos, Colo. Next to Cliff Palace, this ruin is the largest cliff-house in Colorado. It occupies a great natural cave in the E. wall of Spruce-tree canyon, a branch of Navaho canyon, and receives its name from a large spruce tree that formerly stood near by. The curved front wall of the structure measures 218 ft long; the breadth of the ruin is 89 ft, and its longest axis is about N. and S. This ruin has 114 secular rooms, 8 subterranean kivas, and a roofless kiva sometimes called a warriors' room. Many of the dwelling chambers are 3 stories high, several filling the interval from the floor to the roof of the cave. It is estimated that the population of Spruce-tree House was 350. The period of occupancy and the causes of depopulation are unknown, but there is no doubt that the buildings are prehistoric.

The kivas of Spruce-tree House as a rule are arranged at equal distances along the front of the cave; they average about 15 ft in diameter. They are circular or oval in form, and subterranean in position, their tops being level with the adjoining plazas. Entrance to kivas was gained probably by means of notched logs or ladders through hatchways in the roofs. There were also subterranean passageways communicating with neighboring plazas or rooms. Each kiva has a ventilator by which fresh air is introduced and distributed at the floor level, a central fireplace, and a small symbolic opening, or *sipapu*, in the floor, representing the entrance into the underworld. The roof is elaborately constructed in vaulted form, its beams being placed crosswise, the outer ones resting on six vertical pilasters, or pedestals, supported by a banquette surrounding the room and raised about

3 ft from the floor. The roof covering is cedar bast, and clay hardened by stamping.

The dwelling rooms are circular, rectangular, and triangular in form, arranged in rows or clusters near the kivas, generally inclosing plazas or dance places. Some of the rooms have fireplaces, doors, windows, and plastered floors. The roofs of several rooms are as well preserved as when first constructed. In the rear of the dwelling rooms are found storage places and granaries. Some of these back rooms had their entrances closed and sealed, and were used as ossuaries, or intramural receptacles for the dead, while the village was inhabited. In addition to the kivas there are two other rooms that may have served for ceremonial purposes; these have no pedestals or roof supports, and are not subterranean. The walls of both the kivas and the dwelling rooms are plastered, and decorated with colored designs, among the latter being representations of birds, mountain-sheep, butterflies, and rain-clouds.

In the rear of the ruin there are two large open spaces inclosed by walls of buildings. These are dark, and the floors were covered with débris containing many relics of the former inhabitants. A well-preserved mummy of an adult wrapped in cloth, in a sitting position, with knees brought to the chin, is said to have been found in this débris. There are also fragments of calcined human bones, indicating cremation. Three infants partially mummified and the skeleton of an adult were buried under the floor of one of the rooms. From the position of the skeletons it is supposed that intramural interments were made at different periods. Beautiful specimens of black-and-white pottery, fine cloth made of agave and cotton fibers, basketry, lignite gorgets,

SPRUCE-TREE HOUSE, BEFORE REPAIR

and stone and wooden objects have been found. The rooms of Spruce-tree House were cleaned out and their fallen walls repaired under direction of the Secretary of the Interior, in 1908. All the rooms were numbered and labeled, and appro-

priate explanations of doubtful structures provided. There are several fine groups of pictographs and two ancient stairways cut into the cliffs in its vicinity.

SPRUCE-TREE HOUSE, AFTER REPAIR, 1908

Consult Birdsall in Bull. Am. Geog. Soc., XXIII, no. 4, 584, 1891; Chapin in Appalachia, May, 1890; Fewkes, (1) Antiq. Mesa Verde Nat. Park, Bull. 41, B. A. E., 1909; (2) Report to Sec. Int., 1909; H. R. Rep. 3703, 58th Cong., 3d sess., 1905; Nordenskiöld, Cliff Dwellers of Mesa Verde, 1893. (J. W. F.)

Spukpukolemk (*Spuqpuqō'lɛmq*). A band of the Nuhalk, a subdivision of the Bellacoola on the coast of British Columbia.
Mā'lakyilatl.—Boas in 7th Rep. N. W. Tribes Can., 3, 1891 (secret society name). SpuQpuQō'lɛmQ.—Ibid.

Sputuishkeni ('at the diving place'). A Modoc settlement or camping place on Lower Klamath lake, N. Cal. So called because frequented by young men for the purpose of plunging into the water as a part of their initiation ceremonies.
Sputuishχē'ni.—Gatschet in Cont. N. A. Ethnol., II, pt. I, xxxii, 1890.

Spuzzum ('little flat.'—Teit). The nearest to the sea of the important towns of the Ntlakyapamuk, lying on the w. side of Fraser r., Brit. Col., 9 m. above Yale, 2 m. below Spuzzum station, Canadian Pacific R. R., and 110 m. from the Pacific. Pop. 156 in 1909.
Cpu'zum.—Hill-Tout in Rep. Ethnol. Surv. Can., 5, 1899. Spô'zêm.—Teit in Mem. Am. Nat. Hist., II, 169, 1900. Spuggum.—Can. Ind. Aff., 196, 1885 (misprint). Spu'zum.—Hill-Tout, op. cit. Spuzzam.—Can. Ind. Aff., 269, 1889. Spuzzum.—Ibid., pt. II, 164, 1901.

Squacum. A band of Salish, probably of the Ntlakyapamuk, in British Columbia.—Can. Ind. Aff., 79, 1878.

Squam. A yellow oilskin hat worn by sailors and fishermen (Stand. Dict., 1895), from *Annisquam*, the name of a village in Essex co., Mass. One of the traditional significations of this name is 'top of a rock,' for which Eliot gives, in the Massachuset dialect of Algonquian, *wanashquompskqut* (quoted by Trumbull, Natick Dict., 181, 1903), the first component of which is *wanashque*, 'on the top of,' the second *ompsq*, 'rock'; the *ut* is locative. There is also a squam duck. (A. F. C.)

Squam. One of the aboriginal divisions of Nantucket id., Mass.—Mass. Hist. Soc. Coll., 2d s., III, 25–26, 1815.

Squamish. The name given by the Canadian Department of Indian Affairs to that portion of the Squawmish living on Howe sd., Brit. Col. Pop. 31 in 1909. Shw-aw-mish.—Can. Ind. Aff., 276, 1894 (probably a misprint). Skw-amish.—Ibid., 358, 1895. Skwawmish.—Ibid., 308, 1879. Squamish.—Ibid., 195, 1885.

Squamscot. A part of the Pennacook confederacy, called a tribe, which formerly lived on Exeter r., probably about the present site of Exeter, Rockingham co., N. H.—Potter in Schoolcraft, Ind. Tribes, v, 222, 1856.

Squando. An Abnaki sachem of the Sokoki, known generally as the "Sagamore of Saco." He was credited with seeing visions and was called by Mather "a strange, enthusiastical sagamore." His wife and child had been insulted by the English, and he took part in the war of 1675–76 and in the burning of Saco. He signed the treaty of Cocheco. (A. F. C.)

Squannaroo (Yakima: *Skwánănă*, 'whirlpool'). A body of Indians, numbering 120 persons, found by Lewis and Clark in 1805 on Cataract r., Wash., N. of the Big Narrows. According to Mooney they are a division of the Pisquows, and their Yakima name refers strictly to a point on Yakima r. about opposite the entrance to Selah cr., their village being on the w. bank of the river. The same authority states also that they may possibly speak the language of the Atanumlema, a neighboring Shahaptian tribe. Lower Yakima.—Lewis and Clark quoted by Gibbs in Pac. R. R. Rep., I, 417, 1855. Skwa'nănă.—Mooney in 14th Rep. B. A. E., 736, 1896. Spearmaros.—Robertson (1846) in H.R.Ex. Doc. 76, 30th Cong., 1st sess., 9, 1848. Squam-a-cross.—Lewis and Clark quoted by Stevens in Ind. Aff. Rep., 460, 1854. Squam-a-ross.—Lewis and Clark quoted by Gibbs, op. cit. Squan-nan-os.—Lewis and Clark Exped., Coues ed., 958, 1893. Squannaroos.—Lewis and Clark Exped., II, 595, 1817. Squannor-oss.—Ibid., I, map, 1817. Squan-nun-os.—Orig. Jour. Lewis and Clark, IV, 307, 1905.

Squantersquash. An early name for the squash, the latter word being a reduction of the longer one; spelled also "squontersquash." See *Squash*. (A. F. C.)

Squanto. A Wampanoag (Drake, Inds. of N. Am., 69, 1880) who is said to have been the only person in Patuxet that escaped the plague of 1619. He was a friend of the English, and did them much service besides acting as interpreter and guide, though he seems to have been also at one time the agent or spy of Caunbitant, sachem of Mattapoisett. He died at Chatham in 1622. The name Squanto was contracted from Tisquantum. (A. F. C.)

Squantum. A word still in use in parts of New England in the sense of a merrymaking, a picnic, a shore dinner, a good time, a high old time, or the like. Osgood (New Eng., 61, 1883) states: "The *squantum* is a peculiar institution of this island [Nantucket], being an informal picnic on the beach sands, where the dinner is made of fish and other spoils of the sea." Bartlett (Dict. of Americanisms, 1877), says, "probably from Indian place-names (Squantum), as in or near Quincy, Mass." The place name Squantum is said to be derived from Tisquantum, or Tasquantum, the appellation of a Massachusetts Indian, generally known to the settlers about Plymouth as Squantum or Squanto (q. v.). In all probability the word goes back to this personal name in the Massachuset dialect of Algonquian, signifying 'door,' 'entrance,' like the cognate Delaware *eshkande*, Chippewa *ishkwandem*, Nipissing *ishkwandem* or *ishkwand*, and Cree *iskwátem*. (A. F. C.)

Squash. The common name of several species of the genus *Cucurbita*. These vegetables were cultivated by the Algonquian Indians of N. E. North America before the coming of the whites, who inherited both thing and name. Roger Williams (Key to Lang. of Amer., 103, 1643) says: "*Askútasquash*, their vine-apples, which the English from them call *squashes*." Josselyn (N. E. Rarities, 57, 1672) speaks of "*squashes* . . . more truly *squontersquashes*, a kind of melon, or rather gourd." Wood (N. E. Prospect, 761, 1634) says of the aborigines of Massachusetts that "in summer, when their corne is spent, 'Isquontersquashes' is their best bread, a fruit like a young Pumpion." Eliot (1663) in his Bible renders "cucumbers" by *askoot-asquash*, which is the Massachuset form of the Narraganset word cited by Williams. Squashes were so spoken of by the Indians because, as some of the early chroniclers remarked, "you may eat them green, and never after they are ripe." *Askutasquash* signifies literally 'vegetables eaten green,' inan. pl. of *askutasq*; from the root *ask* (1) 'to be green,' (2) 'to be raw,' (3) 'to be immature.' From the squash have been named: Squash-beetle (*Diabrotica vittata*), squash-vine borer (*Trochilium cucurbitæ*), squash-bug (*Anasa tristis*), Hubbard squash, crookneck squash, summer squash, winter squash, squash gourd, squash melon, squash vine, etc. (A. F. C. W. R. G.)

Squash. A name mentioned by Buffon, and by Webster on the authority of Goldsmith, as that of the brown coati, *Nasua narica*. The word is a corruption of the Tupi (South American) name of the animal. (W. R. G.)

Squaw. An Indian woman. From Narraganset *squaw*, probably an abbreviation of *eskwaw*, cognate with the Delaware *ochqueu*, the Chippewa *ikwé*, the Cree *iskwew*, etc. As a term for woman *squaw* has been carried over the length and breadth of the United States and Canada, and is even in use by Indians on the reservations of the W., who have taken it from the whites. After the squaw have been named: Squawberry (the partridge berry), squaw bush (in various parts of the country, *Cornus stolonifera, C. sericea,* and *C. canadensis*), squaw carpet (a California name of *Ceanothus prostratus*), squaw fish (a species of fish found in the N. W.), squaw flower (*Trillium erectum*, called also squaw root), squaw man (an Indian who does woman's work; also a white man married to an Indian woman and living with her people), squaw mint (the American pennyroyal), squawroot (in different parts of the country, *Trillium erectum*, the black and the blue cohosh, *Conopholis americana*, and other plants), squaw sachem (a term in vogue in the era of New England colonization for a female chief among the Indians), squaw vine (a New England name for the partridge berry), squawweed (*Erigeron philadelphicum* and *Senecio aureus*), squaw winter (a term in use in parts of the Canadian N. W. to designate a mild beginning of winter). A species of duck (*Harelda glacialis*) is called old squaw.   (A. F. C.)

Squawkeag ('red earth or land.'—Hewitt). A tribe or band formerly occupying a considerable territory on both banks of Connecticut r., in Franklin co., Mass. Their principal village, of the same name, was near the present Northfield. Some of them were still there in 1688.

Soquagkeeke.—Courtland (1688) in N. Y. Doc. Col. Hist., III, 562, 1853. Squaheag.—Rowlandson (ca. 1676) quoted by Drake, Trag. Wild., 32, 1841. Squakeage.—Winthrop (1664) in Mass. Hist. Soc. Coll., 4th s., VI, 531, 1863. Squakeays.—Gookin (1674), ibid., 1st s., I, 160, 1806 (misprint). Squakheag.—Pynchon (1677) in N. Y. Doc. Col. Hist., XIII, 511, 1881. Squakheig.—Writer of 1676 quoted by Drake, Ind. Chron., 123, 1836. Squakkeag.—Drake, Bk. Inds., III, 31, 1848. Squawkeague.—Hubbard (1792) in Mass. Hist. Soc. Coll., 1st s., II, 30, 1810. Squawkheag.—Sewall (1688), ibid., 4th s., VIII, 519, 1868.

Squawkihow (the Iroquois adaptation of *Muskwaki*, the Fox name for themselves; the *m*-sound not occurring in the phonetic elements of the Iroquois tongues; there was left *squawkie*, commonly pronounced *skwahkiha* by the Iroquois. The signification of *Muskwaki* is 'red earth,' and it may have been originally employed in contradistinction to *Osauaki* or *Osawki*, 'yellow earth,' the base of the tribal name Sauk). A colony of immigrant and captive Fox Indians, who dwelt, when first known, at Gathtsegwarohare (Gaghegwalahala, Cassawauloughly, Gaghaheywarahera, Gathseowalohare, etc.), a village consisting of about 25 cabins, situated on the E. side of Canaseraga cr., 2 m. from its confluence with Genesee r., N. Y., and there-

fore only a few miles s. of Geneseo (Chenussio), the principal town of the Seneca. With its extensive fields of corn, and gardens of beans, squashes, and tobacco, it was destroyed, Sept. 14, 1779, by the army of Gen. Sullivan. The importance of this colony of "Squ-agh-kie Indians" may be inferred from the fact that at the Niagara treaty negotiated by Col. Butler in 1776 they "figured as a separate nation."

In 1652–53, immediately after the dispersion and political extinction of the Hurons, the Tionontati, and the Neutrals in 1648–51, the Iroquois while in pursuit of the fugitive remnants of these people extended their western sphere of action to the region around L. Michigan. The result of this was to bring them into contact with the Fox (Muskwaki) Indians among others, a part of whom later became involved in war with the French and the surrounding tribes. This state of affairs brought about a quasi-alliance between the isolated Fox tribe and the English, and the allies of the latter, the Iroquois. In the subsequent struggle between the French and the Indian tribes under their protection on the one hand and the Fox tribe on the other, the latter were finally overpowered and severely chastised. "The destruction of two Mascoutin and Ottagamie [Muskwaki] villages is one of the principal reasons which induces me to send this express canoe," wrote Du Buisson, the French commander at Detroit, in 1712. "They received many presents," he continued, "and some belts from the English, to destroy the post of Ft Pontchartrain [Detroit], and then to cut our throats and those of our allies, particularly the Hurons and Ottawas, residing upon Detroit r.; and after that these wretches intended to settle among the English and devote themselves to their service. It is said that the band of Oninetonam and that of Mucatemangona have been received among the Iroquois and have established a village upon their lands. This information has been brought by three canoes of Outagamis." (Wis. Hist. Coll., XVI, 268, 1902.) Some time in the 80's Dr M. H. Mills communicated to the *Rochester* (N. Y.) *Union* a tradition that identifies the "Squawkiehah Indians" with the Sauk and Fox (Conover, Kanadesaga and Geneva MS.).

There are many references showing conclusively that the Iroquois and the Foxes on the one hand were making common cause against the French and their allies on the other, and it is also learned that in 1741 the Foxes had an understanding with the Iroquois that if the Foxes should be compelled to leave their villages, they could find a safe asylum among the Iroquois. The confused and untrustworthy statements concerning the Squawkihow and the Missisauga (Twakanha) Indians made by David Cusick in his History of the Six Nations (1828) have misled most authors who have attempted to identify the Squawkihow. Thus, Macauley (Hist. N. Y., 180, 1829) identifies them with the Shawnee, and says that the Squawkihow inhabited the banks of Genesee r. before the Seneca and the Erie possessed the country. In Butler's Niagara treaty with various Indian tribes the "Squaghkie" Indians figured as a separate tribe, as above mentioned.

For 16 m. below Portage, N. Y., the channel of Genesee r. lies at the bottom of a deep gorge whose banks in some places rise nearly 700 ft, and in the town of Leicester, Livingston co., the stream breaks forth from the side of the mountain cliff. This opening in the valley, forming a striking feature of the landscape, was called by the Seneca Indians Dayoitgao (*Deioitgĕn'/on'*, 'there it issues'). In the spring of 1780, Guy Johnson, in assigning the dispersed Iroquois tribes new homes, placed the dependent Squawkihow on the w. side of Genesee r., at Dayoitgao, near the present Mt Morris, and it is this place that has retained the name "Squawkie Hill." (J. N. B. H.)

Squ-agh-kie Indians.—Harris in Buffalo Hist. Soc. Pub., VI, 431, 1903. Squakies.—Ibid. Squatchegas.—Sullivan's Rep. in Jour. Mil. Exped. against Six Nations, 1779, 300, 1887. Squatehokus.—Ibid., 266. Squawkey.—Proctor (1791) in Archives of Pa., 2d s., II, 472, 1890. Squawkihows.—Cusick, Hist. Six Nations, 20, 1828. Tchoueragak.—Clark in Cayuga Co. Hist. Soc. Coll., no. 1, 52, 1879 (Onondaga name; probably from a suggested erroneous identification).

Squaw-man. See *Squaw.*

Squawmish. A Salishan tribe on Howe sd. and Burrard inlet, N. of the mouth of Fraser r., Brit. Col. Their former village communities or bands were Chakkai, Chalkunts, Chants, Chechelmen, Chechilkok, Chekoalch, Chewas, Chiakamish, Chichilek, Chimai, Chukchukts, Ekuks, Etleuk, Hastings Sawmill Indians, Helshen, Homulchison, Huikuayaken, Humelsom, Ialmuk, Ikwopsum, Itliok, Kaayahunik, Kaksine, Kapkapetlp, Kauten, Kekelun, Kekios, Kekwaiakin, Kelketos, Ketlalsm, Kiaken, Kicham, Koalcha, Koekoi, Koikoi, Kolelakom, Komps, Kotlskaim, Kuakumchen, Kukutwom, Kulaken, Kulatsen, Kwanaken, Kwichtenem, Kwolan, Male (shared with the Musqueam), Mitlmetlelch, Nkukapenach, Nkuoosai, Nkuoukten, Npapuk, Npokwis, Nthaich, Papiak, Poiam, Pokaiosum, Sauktich, Schilks, Schink, Selelot, Shemps, Shishaiokoi, Siechem, Skakaiek, Skauishan, Skeakunts, Skeawatsut, Skelsh, Sklau, Skoachais, Skumin, Skutuksen, Skwaius, Slokoi, Smelakoa, Smok, Snauk, Spapak, Stamis, Stetuk, Stlaun, Stoktoks, Stotoii, Suntz, Sutkel, Swaiwi, Swiat, Thetsaken, Thetuksem, Thetusum, Thotais, Tktakai, Tlakom, Tlastlemauk, Tleatlum, Toktakamai, Tseklten, Tumtls, Ulksin, and Yukuts. There were a few more at the upper end of Burrard inlet. Only six villages are now inhabited: Burrard Inlet, No. 3 reserve, False Creek (see Snauk), Kapilano (see Homulchison Mission, Burrard inlet), Seymour Creek (see Chechilkok), and Squamish. (Consult Hill-Tout in Rep. B. A. A. S., 472–549, 1900.) The total population of the Squawmish was 174 in 1909. (J. R. S.)

Skoomic.—Boas in 6th Rep. N. W. Tribes Can., map, 1890. Sk·qoā'mic.—Boas in 5th Rep., ibid., 10, 1889 (Comox name). Sk qō'mic.—Ibid. Skwāmish.—Tolmie and Dawson, Vocabs. Brit. Col., 119B, 1884. Sqnamishes.—Sage, Rocky Mtns., 221, 1846. Squamisht.—Brit. Col. Map, Ind. Aff., Victoria, 1872. Squawmisht.—Mayne, Brit. Col., 243. 1862. Squohamish.—Brit. Adm. Chart, no. 1917, 1862. Sxqōmic.—Boas, MS., B. A. E., 1887.

Squaw Sachem of Pocasset. See *Wetamoo.*

Squawtits. A Cowichan tribe on lower Fraser r., Brit. Col., between Agassiz and Hope. Pop. 47 in 1909.

Squatils.—Can. Ind. Aff., 309, 1879. Squatits.—Brit. Col. Map, Ind. Aff., Victoria, 1872. Squattets.—Can. Ind. Aff. 1889, 268, 1890. Squawtas.—Trutch, Map of Brit. Col., 1870. Squawtits.—Can. Ind. Aff., pt. 2, 160, 1901.

Squaxon. A Salish division on the peninsula between Hoods canal and Case inlet, Wash., under the Puyallup school superintendency. Pop. 98 in 1909.

Guak-s'n-a-mish.—Gibbs in Pac. R. R. Rep., I, 435, 1855. Iquahsinawmish.—Lane in Ind. Aff. Rep., 162, 1850. Quach-snah-mish.—Jones (1853) in H. R. Ex. Doc. 76, 34th Cong., 3d sess., 5, 1857. Quackena-mish.—Starling in Ind. Aff. Rep., 170, 1852. Quák-s'n-a-mish.—Stevens, ibid., 458, 1854. Quashsua-mish.—Starling, op. cit., 171. Skwahw-sda+bé.—McCaw, MS. vocab., B. A. E., 1885 (Puyallup name). Skwâk-sin.—Eells in letter, B. A. E., Feb. 1886 (own name). Skwak-sin-a-mish.—Ibid. Skwawksen.—Gibbs, MS. no. 248, B. A. E. ("properly the portage from Hood's canal to Case's inlet"). Skwawksin.—Gibbs in Cont. N. A. Ethnol., I, 178, 1877. Skwawksnamish.—Ibid. Squahksen.—Gibbs, MS. no. 248, B. A. E. Squah-sin-awmish.—Lane in Sen. Ex. Doc. 52, 31st Cong., 1st sess., 173, 1850. Squakshin.—Watkins in Sen. Ex. Doc. 20, 45th Cong., 2d sess., 4, 1878. Squakskin.—Ind. Aff. Rep. 1856, 265, 1857. Squaks'na-mish.—Tolmie quoted by Gibbs in Pac. R. R. Rep., I, 434, 1855. Squa-sua-mish.—Starling in Ind. Aff. Rep., 171, 1852. Squawskin.—Treaty of 1855 in U. S. Ind. Treat., 561, 1873. Squaxins.—Keene in Stanford, Compend., 536, 1878. Squaxon.—Ind. Aff. Rep. 1901, 702, 1902. Squorins.—Sen. Misc. Doc. 53, 45th Cong., 3d sess., 78, 1879. Squoxsin.—Stevens in H. R. Ex. Doc. 37, 34th Cong., 3d sess., 45, 1857.

Squeteague. The weakfish (*Otolithus regalis*), a very useful species of fish, since its flesh, which is rich and gelatinous when fresh, affords a delicate article of food, while from its swimming bladder can be made an excellent fish glue or isinglass. The latter fact was discovered by the Narraganset, who used the "sounds" of the fish for making a glutinous substance which they used for the same purpose for which glue would be employed, hence the name *pĕsäkweteauaq*, 'they make glue' (the subject of the verb being the "sounds" of the fish taken as animate), contracted to *p's'kwĕteauaq, s'kwĕteauaq,* and *skweteague.* Among other spellings of the name are squettee, squiteeg, squitie, succoteague, skwiteague, scuteeg, and squit.   (W. R. G.)

Squettee. See *Squeteague.*

Squiatl. A body of Salish on Eld inlet, at the extreme s. end of Puget sd., Wash. Pop. 45 in 1853; no longer separately enumerated.
Skwai-aitl.—Gibbs in Cont. N. A. Ethnol, I, 178, 1877. Squa-aitl.—Gibbs in Pac. R. R. Rep., I, 435, 1855. Squai-aitl.—Stevens in Ind. Aff. Rep., 458, 1854. Squeit-letoh.—Simmons, ibid., 226, 1858 (one of the Medicine Creek treaty bands). Squi-aitl.—Treaty of 1855 in U. S. Ind. Treat., 561, 1873. Squiatl.—Ind. Aff. Rep., 265, 1856.

Squierhonon. An unidentified tribe, probably Algonquian, dependent on the Hurons.—Sagard (1636), Hist. Can., Huron Dict., IV, 1866.

Squit, Squiteeg, Squitie. See *Squeteague.*

Squnck. See *Skunk.*

Squontersquash. See *Squantersquash.*

Srattkemer. A body of Salish belonging to Kamloops agency, Brit. Col. Pop. 230 in 1884, the last time the name appears.
Sratt-kemer.—Can. Ind. Aff., 188, 1884.

Ssalayme. A former village, presumably Costanoan, connected with Dolores mission, San Francisco, Cal.—Taylor in Cal. Farmer, Oct. 18, 1861.

Ssichitca. A former village, presumably Costanoan, connected with Dolores mission, San Francisco, Cal.—Taylor in Cal. Farmer, Oct. 18, 1861.

Ssipudca. A former village, presumably Costanoan, connected with Dolores mission, San Francisco, Cal.—Taylor in Cal. Farmer, Oct. 18, 1861.

Ssiti. A former village, presumably Costanoan, connected with Dolores mission, San Francisco, Cal.—Taylor in Cal. Farmer, Oct. 18, 1861.

Ssogereate. A former village, presumably Costanoan, connected with Dolores mission, San Francisco, Cal.—Taylor in Cal. Farmer, Oct. 18, 1861.

Ssupichum. A former village, presumably Costanoan, connected with Dolores mission, San Francisco, Cal.—Taylor in Cal. Farmer, Oct. 18, 1861.

Sta. For references beginning with this abbreviation, see *Santa.*

Stabber. See *Pashipaho.*

Stadacona. A village occupying the site of Quebec, on St Lawrence r., Canada, visited by Cartier in 1535. The village had disappeared when Champlain ascended the river 70 years later.
Stadacona.—Hind, Lab. Penin., II, 6, 1863. Stada-cone.—Cartier (1545), Relation, 32, ½, 1863. Tada-cone.—Vallard, Atlas (ca. 1543) in Me. Hist. Soc. Coll., I, 354, 1869.

Stagilanas (*Stā'gĭ lā'nas,* 'Stā'gĭ town-people'). A Haida family of the Eagle clan. It was one of those of Ninstints (Gunghet-haidagai), and is said to have been part of the Gunghet-kegawai.—Swanton, Cont. Haida, 272, 1905.

Stahehani (*Staxĕha'ni,* 'this side of the ear or cliff.'—Teit). A Ntlakyapamuk village on the E. side of Fraser r., Brit. Col., between Keefer's station and Cisco.
Stacīa'nĭ.—Hill-Tout in Rep. Ethnol. Surv. Can., 5, 1899. Staxĕha'nĭ.—Teit in Mem. Am. Mus. Nat. Hist., II, 169, 1900.

Stahlouk. A former band of Salish, probably Cowichan, of Fraser superintendency, Brit. Col.—Can. Ind. Aff., 138, 1879.

Staitan. "Staitan or Kite Indians," mentioned by Lewis and Clark in 1804 as one of the small tribes about whom little more than the name was known, roving on the heads of Platte and Cheyenne rs. The narrative continues: "They have acquired the name of Kites from their flying—that is, their being always on horseback, and the smallness of their numbers is to be attributed to their extreme ferocity; they are the most warlike of all the western Indians; they never yield in battle; they never spare their enemies; and the retaliation of this barbarity has almost extinguished the nation." They are estimated at 40 lodges, 100 warriors, 400 souls. They are elsewhere represented as neighbors and friends of the Cheyenne and the Kanenavish (Arapaho).

They are probably the Sutaio (q. v.), formerly a distinct tribe, but now incorporated with the Cheyenne. The Cheyenne form for 'Sŭtai man' would be *Sŭtai'-itä'n,* pl. *Sŭtai'-itä'neo.* They are not the Crows, as has sometimes been supposed from the coincidence of the name Kites, neither are they identical with the Cheyenne as Mooney at one time supposed (Ghost Dance, 1023, 1896). By careless copying, the name appears also as Stactan, Stailan, and even Marlain; but the original and only authority rests with Lewis and Clark.   (J. M.)
Kite Indians.—Lewis and Clark (1804), Trav., I, 58, Coues ed., 1893. Kites.—Ibid. Marlain.—Cossin in H. R. Ex. Doc. 117, 20th Cong., 2d sess., 100, 1829. Marlin.—Cass (1834) quoted by Schoolcraft, Ind. Tribes, III, 609, 1853. Stactan.—Sibley, Hist. Sketches, 25, 1806. Stá-e-tan.—Ibid., 38 (their own name). Staetons.—Lewis, Trav., 15, 1809. Sta-he-tah.—Hunter, Captivity, 62, 1823. Stailans.—Sen. Ex. Doc. 72, 20th Cong., 2d sess., 104, 1829. Staitans.—Morse, Rep. to Sec. War, 366, 1822.

Staiya (*Sta-iya*). A settlement just below Lytton, Brit. Col., on the E. bank of Fraser r. Its position corresponds very nearly to that of Cisco, a Ntlakyapamuk village.—Brit. Col. map, Ind. Aff., Victoria, 1872.

Staktabsh ('forest people'). Given as a band of Salish on Tulalip res., Wash. (Mallet in Ind. Aff. Rep., 198, 1877), but strictly a name applied to the inland people by those of the coast.

Stalactite, Stalagmite. See *Gypsum, Marble.*

Stalame. A chief or tribe in alliance with the chief of Audusta (Edisto), S. C., and in friendly relations with the French in 1562; possibly the Stono. The village indicated on the De Bry map of 1591 is described as 15 leagues by water N. from the French fort near Port Royal. See De Bry (1591) in Le Moyne, Narr., Appleton trans., 1875; Laudonnière (1564) in French, Hist. Coll. La., 201, 1869.

Stamis. A Squawmisht village on the left bank of Squawmisht r., w. Brit. Col.
Sta-amus.—Brit. Adm. chart, no. 1917. **Stămas.—** Boas, MS., B. A. E., 1887. **Stā'mis.—**Hill-Tout in Rep. Brit. A. A. S., 474, 1900.

Standing Bear (Mo^n-chu-no^n-zhi^n). A Ponca chief of whom little was known until the removal of his people from N. Nebraska to Indian Ter. because the reservation confirmed to them by treaty had been included in the land granted to the Sioux. When the order for removal was given, Jan. 15, 1877, Standing Bear strongly opposed it, but in February he and nine other chiefs were taken s. to choose a reservation. They followed the official, but would not select a place. Their wearisome journey brought them to Arkansas City, Kans., whence they asked to be taken home; being refused, they started back afoot, with a few dollars among them and a blanket each. In 40 days they had walked 500 m., reaching home Apr. 2, to find the official there unwilling to listen to protests and determined to remove the people. He called the military, and the tribe, losing hope, abandoned their homes in May. Standing Bear could get no response to his demand to know why he and his people were arrested and treated as criminals when they had done no wrong.

The change of climate brought great suffering to the Ponca; within the year a third of the tribe had died and most of the survivors were ill or disabled. A son of Standing Bear died. Craving to bury the lad at his old home, the chief determined to defy restraint. He took the bones of his son and with his immediate following turned northward in Jan. 1879, and in March arrived destitute at the Omaha res. Asking to borrow land and seed, his request was granted, and the Ponca were about to put in a crop when soldiers appeared with orders to arrest Standing Bear and his party and return them to Indian Ter. On their way they camped near Omaha, where Standing Bear was interviewed by T. H. Tibbles, a newspaper correspondent, and accounts of their grievances appearing in the Omaha newspapers, the citizens became actively interested and opened a church where to a crowded house the chief repeated his story. Messrs Poppleton and Webster proffered legal services to the prisoners and in their behalf sued out a writ of *habeas corpus*. The United States denied the prisoners' right to the writ on the ground that they were "not persons within the meaning of the law." On

Apr. 18 Judge Dundy decided that "an Indian is a person within the meaning of the law of the United States," and therefore had a right to the writ when restrained in violation of law; that "no rightful authority exists for removing by force any of the prisoners to the Indian Territory," and therefore, "the prisoners must be discharged from custody."

Standing Bear and his band returned to N. Nebraska. In the winter of 1879–80, accompanied by Susette La Flesche ("Bright Eyes," q. v.) and Francis La Flesche, as interpreters, with T. H. Tibbles, Standing Bear visited the cities of the E., where, by relating his story of the

'STANDING BEAR

wrongs suffered, he won attention and sympathy. Many people wrote to the President and to other executive officials of the Government, and to members of Congress, protesting against unjust treatment of Indians. In the spring of 1880 the Senate appointed a committee to investigate the Ponca removal, the report of which confirmed the story of Standing Bear, and a satisfactory adjustment was effected. Better lands were given those Ponca who chose to remain in Indian Ter.; payment was made to all who had lost property, and a home was provided for Standing Bear and his followers at their old reservation. Here, in Sept. 1908, after having been instrumental in bringing about a change of Governmental policy toward all Indians and their homes, the chief died at the age of 79 and was buried among the hills overlooking the village site of his ancestors. (F. L.)

Standing Peach Tree. A former Cherokee settlement on Chattahoochee r., at the mouth of Peachtree cr., N. W. of Atlanta, Ga.—Royce in 5th Rep. B. A. E., map, 1887.

Standing Stone. A famous Indian landmark on the right bank of a creek of the same name, on the Kittanning trail, at the site of the present Huntingdon, Huntingdon co., Pa. The "standing stone" is described by John Harris (1754) as being 14 ft high and 6 in. square, and covered with Indian pictographs. It was highly venerated by the Indians, and is supposed to have been erected by one of the tribes of the Iroquois. After the treaty of 1754 the stone was carried away by the Indians. A similar one was erected on the same spot, which soon became covered with the names and initials of the Indian traders who passed by.

Conrad Weiser, in his mission to the Ohio Indians at Logstown in 1748, passed near the place, which he mentions in his Journal as "the Standing Stone" (Col. Rec., Pa., v, 348, 1851). There is no evidence that this place was ever the site of an Indian settlement. Many Indian objects have been found in the vicinity of the "standing stone," which may have been a meeting place of the Indians after returning from their raids and hunts. A settlers' fort was begun at the locality in 1762, but was abandoned soon after the commencement of the Indian hostilities, when all the settlers in that region fled to Carlisle. At the beginning of the Revolution this fort was rebuilt. In 1778 it was a meeting place for the Tories of Sinking valley, on their way to Kittanning, who, according to various letters from the frontier, "drove away the inhabitants of Standing Stone town" (Frontier Forts of Pa., I, 584, 1895). The only "Indian massacre" near Standing Stone was on June 19, 1777, at the Big Spring, some miles W. of the fort, when a band of hostile Indians killed a boy named Donnelly. The inhabitants during this period were in a constant state of alarm, and frequently fled to the various posts for protection from the Indians.

Rev. Dr William Smith, provost of the University of Pennsylvania, laid out a town on the site of Standing Stone in 1767, to which he gave the name of Huntingdon, in honor of Selina, Countess of Huntingdon (England), who had made a gift to the university. The old name, however, clung to the place for years afterward. Nearly all the traders and military officers of the 18th century use the old name. It is marked "Standing Stone" on Lewis Evans' maps of 1755 and 1770; "Standing Stone, Hunt-

ington," on the Pownall map of 1776. For other references see Egle, Hist. Pa., 779, 1883; Walton's Conrad Weiser, 186, 1900.   (G. P. D.)

Stand Watie (native name *De'gătă'gă*, conveying the meaning that two persons are standing together so closely united in sympathy as to form but one human body). A noted Cherokee Indian, son of Uweti and brother of Elias Boudinot (q. v.), and after his death a leader of the party which had signed the removal treaty of New Echota. On the outbreak of the Civil War he and his party were the first to ally themselves with the South, and he was given command of one of two Cherokee regiments which joined the Confederate forces and participated in the battle of Pea Ridge and in other actions. Later he led his regiment back to Indian Ter., and in conjunction with Confederate sympathizers from other tribes laid waste the fields and destroyed the property of the Indians who espoused the Federal cause. In revenge for the death of his brother he burned the house of John Ross, the head chief. He is further noted as one of the principal authorities for the legends and other material collected by Schoolcraft among the Cherokee. See Mooney in 19th Rep. B. A. E., 1900.

Star Band. An unidentified band of the Mdewakanton Sioux.—Ind. Aff. Rep., 282, 1854.

Staria Selenie (Russian: 'old settlement'). A Chnagmiut Eskimo village on the lower Yukon, Alaska. Pop. 55 in 1880.
Staraie Selenie.—Petroff in 10th Census, Alaska, 12, 1884.   Staria Selenie.—Petroff, Rep. on Alaska, 57, 1880.

Starik (Russian: 'old'). A Chnagmiut Eskimo village on the s. bank of Yukon r., Alaska, above the head of the delta. Pop. 90 in 1880.
Sarikvihpak.—Post route map, 1903.   Starik.—Baker, Geog. Dict. Alaska, 1902.   Starikvikhpak.—Petroff in 10th Census, Alaska, 12, 1884 (Old Kwikpak).   Stari-kwikhpak.—Petroff, Rep. on Alaska, 57, 1880.   Starry Kwikhpák.—Dall, Alaska, 229, 1870.

Starnatan. A village on the St Lawrence, just below the site of Quebec, in 1535.—Cartier (1535), Bref. Récit., 32, 1863.

Stasaos-kegawai (*Stasa'os qē'gawa-i*, 'those born on the Stasaos coast'). A Haida family of the Raven clan who were in the habit of camping on the N. side of the w. entrance of Skidegate channel, and were so called from the name of the shore there (Stasaos). They were probably a subdivision of the Hlgahetgu-lanas. A minor division of the Stasaos-kegawai was called Gunghet-kegawai.—Swanton, Cont. Haida, 270, 1905.
Stasausk·ē'owai.—Boas, 12th Rep. N. W. Tribes Can., sec. II, 24, 1898.

Stasaos-lanas (*Stasa'os lā'nas*, 'people of Stasaos coast'). A Haida family of the Eagle clan that received its name from a strip of coast along the N. side of the channel between the largest two of the Queen Charlotte ids., Brit. Col. Probably they were originally a part of the Kaiahl-lanas, with whom they used to go about.—Swanton, Cont. Haida, 274, 1905.

Stashum (*Sta-shum*). A former Lummi village on Waldron id., Wash.—Gibbs, Clallam and Lummi, 39, 1863.

Statannyik (*Stā'tánnyĭk*, 'many ants'). A Pima village on the S. bank of the Gila, S. Ariz., between Vaaki (Casa Blanca) and Huchiltchik. It may be identical with Hormiguero (q. v.).
Stâ'tânnyĭk.—Russell in 26th Rep. B. A. E., 23, 1908. Staw-to-nik.—Dudley in Ind. Aff. Rep. 1871, 58,1872. Stotonik.—ten Kate cited by Gatschet, MS., B. A. E., xx, 199, 1888.

Stature. See *Anatomy*.

Stawas-haidagai (*St!awā's xā'-idaga-i*, 'witch people'). A Haida family of the Eagle clan. While these people were living near the Kogahl-lanas the screech-owls (*st!ao*) were heard to call so much from their side of the creek that a boy in the town opposite said they ought to be called 'Witch people' (*St!awā's xā'-idaga-i*). This story was probably told to alleviate the application of a rather harsh name. They had the same traditional origin as the Kona-kegawai, Djiguaahl-lanas, and Kaiahl-lanas. All of them lived in the town of Cumshewa, which was owned by their chief. There were three local subdivisions, the Heda-haidagai, Sa-haidagai, and Kahligua-haidagai.—Swanton, Cont. Haida, 273, 1905.

Steatite. A soft, tough, talcose rock, commonly called soapstone, occurring in massive bodies in connection with other metamorphic rocks, and much used by the Indian tribes N. of Mexico for implements, utensils, and ornaments. It was employed for the manufacture of cooking utensils because of its resistance to the destructive action of fire, and for various minor utensils and ornaments because readily carved with stone tools and susceptible of a high polish. The color is usually a somewhat greenish gray, but when polished and subjected to long-continued handling it becomes almost black, presenting an attractive appearance. This material is of very general distribution. It occurs in numberless places in the Appalachian highland, extending into New England, New Brunswick, and Canada in the N. and into the Gulf states in the S. (see *Mines and Quarries*). Deposits occur in Wyoming and other states along the Great Divide, and in California it was extensively mined, especially on Santa Catalina id., off the coast of Santa Barbara co. (Schumacher, Holmes). It is in general use among the Eskimo, some of their sources of supply being Cumberland sd., Wager r., and Greenland. Steatite was quarried from the massive deposits by means of stone picks and chisels, and the various shapes were roughed out with the same implements, many of which were left on the quarry sites and on dwelling sites where the utensils were specialized. The implements used in carving were probably hafted, but the manner of hafting is unknown. In E. United States a common form of soapstone utensils was a heavy oblong basin, from a few inches to 20 or more in length, about half as wide, and a few inches in depth, having rudely carved projections at the ends for handles. These crude vessels are believed to have been used for cooking. In this section the material was in general use for various minor

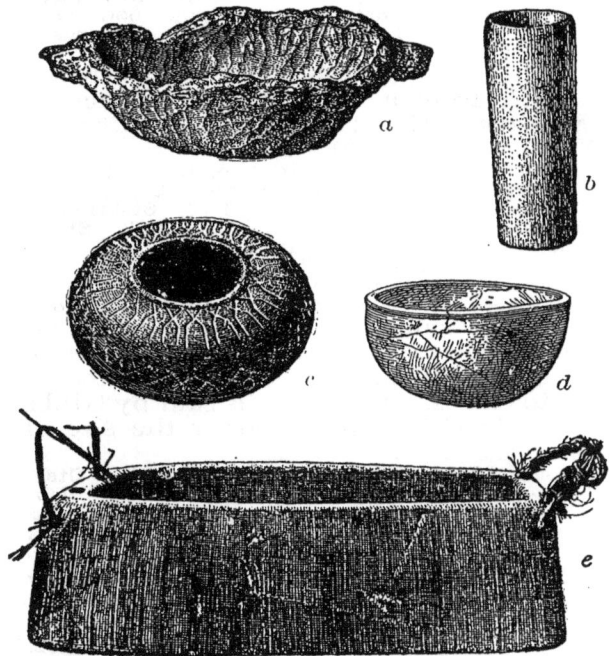

STEATITE VESSELS: *a*, VIRGINIA; *b, c, d*, CALIFORNIA; *e*, ALASKA

carvings, and especially for tobacco pipes, many elaborate and tasteful examples of which have been obtained from ancient mounds and village sites. In California steatite was employed in the manufacture of utensils of many kinds, notably the globular ollas of the southern part of the state, baking plates, tobacco pipes, personal ornaments, fetiches, and various objects of unknown use. In the Arctic regions it is of the greatest value to the Eskimo, by whom it is used in making lamps. On account of the ease with which this material is carved it has been freely used in the manufacture of imitations of the aboriginal work, and fraudulent specimens are frequently offered for sale. See *Chisels, Mines and Quarries, Picks, Stonework*.

Consult Abbott in Wheeler Survey Rep., VII, 1879; Boas in 6th Rep. B. A. E., 1888; Bushnell in Am. Anthr., x, no. 4, 1908; Holmes (1) in Am. Anthr., II, no. 4, 1890, (2) in 15th Rep. B. A. E., 1897, (3) in Rep. Nat. Mus. 1900, 1902; Hough in Rep. Nat. Mus. 1896, 1898; Kengla, Archæology of the District of Columbia, 1883; McGuire in Trans. Anthr. Soc. Wash., II, 1883; Niblack in Rep. Nat. Mus. 1888, 1890; Putnam in 11th Rep. Peabody Mus., 1878; Reynolds in 13th Rep. Peabody Mus., 1880; Schumacher in 11th and 12th Reps. Peabody Mus., 1878. (w. h. h.)

Stegaraki. A tribe of the Mannahoac confederacy, living in 1608 on Rapidan r., in Orange co., Va.
Stegara.—Smith (1629), Va., I, map, 1819. Stegarakes.—Ibid., 134. Stegarakies.—Jefferson, Notes, 139, 1801. Stegerakies.—Boudinot, Star in the West, 128, 1816. Stegora.—Simons in Smith (1629), Va., I, 186, 1819. Stenkenocks.—Spotswood (1722) in N. Y. Doc. Col. Hist., v, 673, 1855. Stogaras.—Strachey (ca. 1612), Va., 104, 1809.

Stehtlum (Stût-lûm, 'a shovel-nosed canoe', from a fancied resemblance of the cape.—Eells). A Clallam village at New Dungeness, Wash.
False Dungeness.—Gibbs in Pac. R. R. Rep., I, 429, 1855 (should be Dungeness). Stehl-lum.—Stevens in Ind. Aff. Rep., 457, 1854. Stehtlum.—Gibbs in Cont. N. A. Ethnol., I, 177, 1877. Stentlum.—Gibbs in Pac. R. R. Rep., I, 435, 1855. Stetchtlum.—U. S. Ind. Treaties, 800, 1873. Stete-tlûm.—Eells, letter to B. A. E., May 21, 1886. Stét-lum.—Gibbs, Clallam and Lummi, 20, 1863.

Stehtsasamish. A division of Salish on Budds inlet, near the present site of Olympia, Wash.; pop. 20 in 1854, according to Gibbs. Stéhchass is said by Gibbs to be the Nisqualli name for the site of Olympia itself.
Stéh-cha-sá-mish.—Ind. Aff. Rep., 458, 1854. Stehchass.—Treaty of 1854 in U. S. Ind. Treaties, 561, 1873. Stehchop.—Ind. Aff. Rep., 265, 1856. Stehtsasamish.—Gibbs in Cont. N. A. Ethnol., I, 178, 1877. Stekohar.—Ross in Ind. Aff. Rep., 135, 1869. Stell-cha-sa-mish.—Gibbs in Pac. R. R. Rep., I, 435, 1855. Stetch-as.—Simmons in Ind. Aff. Rep., 226, 1858. Stitchafsamish.—Lane (1849) in Sen. Ex. Doc. 52, 31st Cong., 1st sess., 173, 1850. Stitchasaw-mich.—Starling in Ind. Aff. Rep., 171, 1852. Stitcheo-saw-mish.—Ibid., 170. Turn Water.—Ibid. (misprint of Tumwater).

Steilacoomamish. A band of Salish on Steilacoom cr., N. W. Wash. They are closely related to the Nisqualli.
Stailakū-mamish.—Gibbs quoted by Dall in Cont. N. A. Ethnol., I, 241, 1877. Steilacoom.—Treaty of 1854 in U. S. Ind. Treaties, 561, 1873. Steila-coom-a-mish.—Gibbs in Pac. R. R. Rep., I, 435, 1855. Steilakūmahmish.—Gibbs in Cont. N. A. Ethnol., I, 178, 1877.

Stella ('the cape'). A Natliatin village at the entrance of Stelako r. into Fraser lake, Brit. Col.; pop. 42 in 1902, 60 in 1909.
Stelaoten.—De Smet, Oregon Miss., 100, 1847. Stel-a-tin.—Dawson in Can. Geol. Surv. 1879–80, 30B, 1881. Stella.—Morice, Notes on W. Dénés, 25, 1892. Stillâ.—Harmon, Jour., 244, 1820.

Stella. The village of the Tautin, on Fraser r., lat. 52° 40′, Brit. Col.
Alexandria.—Ind. Aff. Can., 138, 1879. Stélla.—Morice in Trans. Roy. Soc. Can., 109, 1892.

Stella. A Tsilkotin village on the right bank of Fraser r., near Alexandria,

Brit. Col.—Morice in Trans. Roy. Soc. Can., 109, 1892.

Steloglamo. A former village, probably Salinan, connected with San Antonio mission, Monterey co., Cal.—Taylor in Cal. Farmer, Apr. 27, 1860.

Stetuk (Stétūqk·). A Squawmish village community on Burrard inlet, Brit. Col.—Hill-Tout in Rep. Brit. A. A. S., 475, 1900.

Stiahta. See Roundhead.

Stick Indians (from stick, meaning 'tree,' or 'wood,' in the Chinook jargon). A term universally applied by certain N. W. Coast tribes to any Indians from the interior; that is, to those who live back in the woods. It is more commonly used on the coasts of Alaska and British Columbia to refer to the Athapascan tribes E. of the Coast range, but it was used also by the Chinook and other Oregon and Washington tribes to designate the Salish and Shahaptian tribes of Columbia r. and Puget sd. (L. F.)
Si-him-e-na.—Mahoney in Sen. Ex. Doc. 68, 41st Cong., 2d sess., 20, 1870. Thick-wood Indians.—Franklin, Journ. Polar Sea, 262, 1824. Thick Wood Indians.—Simpson quoted by Morgan in Beach, Ind. Miscel., 179, 1877.

Stikayi (Stikä'yi). The name of three distinct Cherokee settlements: (1) on Sticoa cr., near Clayton, Rabun co., Ga.; (2) on Tuckasegee r., at the old Thomas homestead, just above the present Whittier, in Swain co., N. C.; (3) on Stekoa cr. of Little Tennessee r., a few miles below the junction of Nantahala, in Graham co., N. C. The word has lost its meaning. It is variously spelled Stecoe, Steecoy, Stekoah, Stickoey, etc.—Mooney in 19th Rep. B. A. E., 532, 1900.
Steecoy.—Doc. of 1755 quoted by Royce in 5th Rep. B. A. E., 143, 1887. Stekoa.—Royce in 18th Rep. B. A. E., map 54, 1899. Sticcoa.—Royce in 5th Rep., op. cit., map.

Stikine. A Tlingit tribe on and near the mouth of the river which bears its name. Pop. 1,300 in 1840, 317 in 1880, 255 in 1890. Their winter town is Katchanaak (Wrangell); their ancient village was Kahltcatlan (Old Wrangell). Shake's Village, Shallyany's Village, and Shustak's Village are also mentioned. The following social divisions are found here: Hehlkoan, Hokedi, Kaskakoedi, Katchadi, Kayashkidetan, Kiksadi, Nanyaayi, Siknahadi, Tahlkoedi, and Tihittan.
Shikene.—Peirce in H. R. Rep. 830, 27th Cong., 2d sess., 62, 1842 (village). Stach'in.—Holmberg, Ethnog. Skizz., map, 142, 1855. Stackeenes.—Borrows in H. R. Ex. Doc. 197, 42d Cong., 2d sess., 4, 1872. Stakeen.—Borrows in Sen. Ex. Doc. 67, 41st Cong., 2d sess., 9, 1870. Stakhin.—Petroff in 10th Census, Alaska, 32, 1884. Stak-hīn-kŏn.—Krause, Tlinkit Ind., 120, 1885. Stākhin'-kwān.—Dall in Cont. N. A. Ethnol., I, 38, 1877. Stakhinskoe.—Veniaminoff, Zapiski, II, pt. III, 30, 1840. Stakin.—Eleventh Census, Alaska, 158, 1893. Stekini.—Kane, Wand. in N. A., app., 1859. Stickens.—Crosbie in H. R. Ex. Doc. 77, 36th Cong., 1st sess., 7, 1860. Stickienes.—Beardslee in Sen. Ex. Doc. 105, 46th Cong., 1st sess., 29, 1880. Stickine.—Borrows (1869) in Sen. Ex. Doc. 67, 41st Cong., 2d sess., 2, 1870. Stikin.—Boas, 5th Rep. N. W. Tribes Can., 25, 1889. Stikines.—Scott (1859) in H. R. Ex. Doc. 65, 36th Cong., 1st sess., 115, 1860. Stohen-

skie.—Elliott, Cond. Aff. Alaska, 228, 1875 (transliterated from Veniaminoff). **Sucheen.**—George in Sen. Ex. Doc. 105, 46th Cong., 1st sess., 29, 1880.

Stillaquamish. A division of Salish formerly living on a river of the same name in N. W. Washington. They are a branch of, or closely related to, the Snohomish, and are now on Tulalip res., but their number is not separately reported. **Steilaquamish.**—Gibbs in Pac. R. R. Rep., I, 432, 1855. **Steil-la-qua-mish.**—Jones (1853) in H. R. Ex. Doc. 76, 34th Cong., 3d sess., 5, 1857. **Stilla-quamish.**—Starling in Ind. Aff. Rep., 170, 1852. **Stolo-qua-bish.**—Mallet, ibid., 198, 1877. **Stoluch-quamish.**—Gibbs, op. cit. **Sto-luch-wámish.**—Ind. Aff. Rep., 458, 1854. **Stoluch-wa-mish.**—Gibbs, op. cit., 436. **Sto-luck-qua-mish.**—Stevens in Ind. Aff. Rep., 454, 1854. **Stoluck-whá-mish.**—Treaty of 1855 in U. S. Ind. Treaties, 378, 1873. **Stolutswhamish.**—Gibbs in Cont. N. A. Ethnol., I, 179, 1877.

Stipu. A Chumashan village formerly near Purísima mission, Santa Barbara co., Cal.—Taylor in Cal. Farmer, Oct. 18, 1861.

Stlaun (*Stlāu'n*). A Squawmish village community on Burrard inlet, Brit. Col.—Hill-Tout in Rep. Brit. A. A. S., 475, 1900.

Stlaz (*SLaz*, or *SLêtz*, having reference to a place where the Indians obtained a mineral earth with which they covered the face to prevent it from chapping.—Hill-Tout). A village of the Spences Bridge band of Ntlakyapamuk at a place called Cornwalls, near Ashcroft, a mile back from Thompson r., on the N. side, about 45 m. above Lytton, Brit Col. Pop. 45 in 1909. **Ashcroft.**—Can. Ind. Aff., suppl., 47, 1902. **Cornwalls.**—Can. Ind. Aff., 138, 1879 (white men's name). **Sk'lalc.**—Hill-Tout in Rep. Ethnol. Surv. Can., 4, 1899. **SLaz.**—Teit in Mem. Am. Mus. Nat. Hist., II, 173, 1900. **Slêtz.**—Ibid. **Stahl.**—Can. Ind. Aff., 308, 1887. **Stahl-lch.**—Ibid., 230, 1886. **Stlahl.**—Dawson in Trans. Roy. Soc. Can., sec. II, 44, 1891. **Stlahlilitch.**—Can. Ind. Aff., 196, 1885.

Stlenga-lanas (*SL!e'ña lā'nas*, 'rear town people'). A great Haida family of the Raven clan living along the N. coast of the Queen Charlotte ids., Brit. Col. According to tradition they received their name from having occupied the row of houses farthest back from the coast in the legendary town of Skena. It seems more likely that they became a separate family while at Naikun. There were several subdivisions, the Dostlan-lnagai, Aostlan-lnagai, Teesstlan-lnagai, and Yagunstlan-lnagai.—Swanton, Cont. Haida, 271, 1905. **Stl'EngE lā'nas.**—Boas, 12th Rep. N. W. Tribes Can., 22, 1898. **Stling Lennas.**—Harrison in Proc. Roy. Soc. Can., sec. II, 124, 1895.

Stlep (*St'lEp*, 'home country'). An abandoned Chilliwack village on upper Chilliwack r., Brit. Col.; so called because the old communal houses of the tribe were situated there.—Hill-Tout in Ethnol. Surv. Can., 4, 1902.

Stlindagwai (*SL!i'ndagwa-i*, 'the village deep in the inlet'). A Haida town of the Hagi-lanas family in an inlet on the w. coast of Moresby id., not far from Houston Stewart channel, Brit. Col.—Swanton, Cont. Haida, 277, 1905.

Sto. For all references beginning with this abbreviation, see *Santo.*

Stoam Ohimal (*Sto'am O'himal*, 'white ants'). A phratral group of the Pima, comprising the Apap and Apuki gentile organizations.—Russell, Pima MS., B. A. E., 1903. **Coyote People.**—Russell, in 26th Rep. B. A. E., 197, 1908. **Sto'am O'himal.**—Ibid. **White People.**—Ibid.

Stockbridge. A mission village into which the Stockbridges were collected about 1736 on the site of the present Stockbridge, Berkshire co., Mass. It prospered and soon had a population of about 500, but in 1787 it was abandoned.

Stockbridge. The former village of the Stockbridges on the site of the present Stockbridge, Madison co., N. Y., to which these Indians removed by invitation of the Oneida in 1785. **Ah-gote'-sa-ga-näge.**—Morgan, League Iroq., 473, 1851 (Oneida name). **Anatsagane.**—Brion de la Tour map, 1781.

Stockbridge. The village of the Stockbridges on the site of the present Stockbridge, Calumet co., Wis.

Stockbridges. A tribe of the Mahican confederacy, first known under the name Housatonic. They occupied part of the valley of Housatonic r., in s. Berkshire

NAUNNAUPTAUK, JOHN JACOBS—STOCKBRIDGE

co., Mass. Their principal village, Westenhuck, was for a long time the capital of the Mahican after the removal of the council fire from Schodac. They had another village at Skatehook. In 1734 Sergeant began missionary work among them, and two years later the several bands were collected on a tract reserved for their use by the Colonial government. After the village of Stockbridge was established they were known as Stockbridge Indians. The French and Indian war, which broke out in 1754, proved disastrous to the Stockbridges. Many of them joined the English army and their town suffered from marauding parties, so that at the close of the war there were only about 200 remaining. The whites were also closing in around them, and in 1785 the dispirited remnant, accepting an invitation of the Oneida, removed to a tract on Oneida cr. in Madison and Oneida cos., N. Y., where a new village sprang up (see *Stockbridge*, above). The removal required two years. Under the protection of the Oneida the Stockbridges again increased, and in 1796 numbered 300. In 1833, with the Oneida and Munsee, they removed to a tract at the head of Green bay, Wis., which had been purchased from the Menominee. Here they became incorporated with the Munsee, and the two tribes have since formed one body. From the time of their leaving New York the tribe has divided on questions in regard to land and citizenship. After interminable negotiations with the state and national governments the matter is still unsettled. In 1839 the Stockbridges and Munsee, then numbering about 420, sold half of their reservation and agreed to remove to lands that were to be assigned to them w. of the Mississippi. On the remaining land a town was laid out, on the E. shore of Winnebago lake, where it was intended to settle such as desired to become citizens. About 80 removed to the Missouri r. and remained for a time near Leavenworth, Kans. The arrangement proved unsatisfactory, and they were once more brought together and the tribal government restored. In 1856 they removed, with the exception of a number who desired to become citizens, to a reservation w. of Shawano, Shawano co., Wis., where in 1909 the united tribes, including the Munsee, numbered 582 souls. There are also some who have become citizens near their former home on Winnebago lake.

The Stockbridges entered into treaties with the United States at Oneida, N. Y., Dec. 2, 1794; Green Bay, Wis., Oct. 27, 1832; Buffalo Creek, N. Y., Jan. 15, 1838; Stockbridge, Wis., Sept. 3, 1839; Nov. 24, 1848; Feb. 5, 1856.   (J. M.)

Ausotunnoog.—Macauley, N. Y., II, 171, 1829. **Hoosatunnuk.**—Schoolcraft, Ind. Tribes, VI, 734, 1857. **Housatannuck.**—Gallatin in Trans. Am. Antiq. Soc., II, 35, 1836. **Housatonic Indians.**—Hoyt, Antiq. Res., 225, 1824. **Housatonnoc.**—Barber, Hist. Coll. Mass., 99, 1839. **Houssatonnoc Indians.**—Wainwright (1735) in Me. Hist. Soc. Coll., IV, 123, 1856. **Houssatunnuck.**—Hawley (1794) in Mass. Hist. Soc. Coll., 1st s., III, 192, 1794. **Muhheconnuk.**—Sen. Doc. 189, 27th Cong., 2d sess., 19, 1842. **Muhhekanew.**—Edwards quoted by Gallatin in Trans. Am. Antiq. Soc., II, 35, 1836. **Ousatannock**

Indians.—Mass. Hist. Soc. Coll., 2d s., x, 124, note. 1823. **Ousatunnuck.**—Trumbull, Conn., II, 72, 1818, **Ousetannuck.**—Wadsworth (1694) quoted by Hoyt, Antiq. Res., 163, 1824. **Oustonnoc.**—Stiles (*ca.* 1762) in Mass. Hist. Soc. Coll., 1st s., x, 112, 1809.

Stocks. See *Linguistic families.*

Stogie. (1) A sort of cigar, a long cheroot, the name of which is said to be derived from the place-name Conestoga, Pa., where these cigars were first made. The form *stoga* would seem to confirm this etymology. (2) Conestoga (q. v.) is an ethnic appellation of one of the Iroquoian tribes, the word itself being of Iroquois derivation.   (A. F. C.)

Stoktoks. A Squawmish village community on Howe sd., Brit. Col.
St'o'ktoks.—Hill-Tout in Rep. Brit. A. A. S., 474, 1900. **St'ōx.**—Boas, MS., B. A. E., 1887.

Stone age. See *Antiquity, Archeology.*

Stone-axe ruin. A prehistoric pueblo ruin 4½ m. E. of the central Petrified Forest, on the N. slope, near the Little Colorado and Puerco divide, about 30 m. E. of Holbrook, in Apache co., Ariz.; so named from the numerous axes of actinolite that have been found on its surface. The ruin was excavated in 1901 by Dr Walter Hough, of the National Museum, who, from the artifacts recovered, regards the structure as of Hopi origin. See Nat. Mus. Rep. 1901, 320–25, 1903.

Stone-boiling. See *Food.*

Stone Tsilkotin. A body of Tsilkotin of Williams Lake agency, Brit. Col. Pop. 106 in 1901; 96 in 1909.
Stone.—Can. Ind. Aff. 1887, 310, 1888. **Stones.**—Can. Ind. Aff. 1901, pt. II, 162, 1901.

Stonework. Primitive men doubtless first used stones in their natural form for throwing, striking, and abrading; but as use continued, a certain amount of adventitious shaping of the stones employed necessarily took place, and this probably suggested and led to intentional shaping. Men early learned to fracture brittle stones to obtain cutting, scraping, and perforating implements; and flaking, pecking, cutting, scraping, and grinding processes served later to modify shapes and to increase the convenience, effectiveness, and beauty of implements. Much has been learned of the course of progress in the stone-shaping arts from the prehistoric remains of Europe, and studies of the work of the native American tribes, past and present, are supplying data for a much more complete understanding of this important branch of primitive activity. It is not believed that the course of events in the development of art in stone was uniform with all peoples, for the materials available in the different countries are so unlike that uniformity would be quite out of the question. It may be reasonably assumed, however, that with average lithic resources the simpler processes and those giving required results most directly would take precedence, and the more complex processes—those requiring higher intelligence and greater skill—would follow. In America, although there has doubtless been, generally speaking, progress from simpler to more complex conditions of stone art, no definite separation of an early and a late, a paleolithic and a neolithic, a chipped and a polished stone age, has been recognized. See *Neolithic age, Paleolithic implements*.

The Americans N. of Mexico were still well within the stone stage of culture. Metal had come somewhat into use, but in no part of the country had it taken in a very full measure the place of stone. According to the most approved views regarding Old World culture history the metal age was not definitely ushered in until bronze and iron came into common use, not only as shaping implements but as shaped product. With stone implements the more cultured tribes of middle America had constructed handsome buildings and executed sculptures of a high order of merit, but N. of Mexico the results were of a much less pretentious kind. Only one group of tribes, the Pueblos, had made intelligent and extensive use of stone in building (see *Architecture, Cliff dwellings, Habitations, Pueblos*), although the mound-builders, the Eskimo, and others employed it for this purpose in a limited way. Numerous tribes, however, had entered the field of sculpture, especially as applied to the shaping of objects of utility and common use; but the work extended also to the shaping of personal ornaments and of symbolic objects connected with religious beliefs and ceremonies. See *Sculpture*.

No extensive region in America is without stone of one or more varieties, and the resources usually are varied and vast. The raw materials were obtained from the surface supply, or, where that was not available in sufficient quantities, they were quarried from the beds in place. See *Mines and Quarries*.

The varieties employed by the primitive tribes are very numerous, and being of special interest in this connection the following are briefly described under separate heads: Actinolite, agate (chalcedony), alabaster (gypsum), amber, andesite, argillite, basalt, calcite, cannel coal (jet), catlinite, chalcedony, chert (chalcedony), chlorite, flint, granite, gypsum, hematite, iron, jade (nephrite), jasper, jet, lignite (jet), limonite (hematite), marble, mica, muscovite (mica), nephrite, novaculite, obsidian, onyx (marble), pectolite, porphyry, pyrites, quartz, quartzite, rhyolite, schist, selenite (gypsum), serpentine, sienite, slate, soapstone (steatite), stalactite (marble), stalagmite (marble), steatite, talc (steatite), trachyte, travertine (marble), turquoise, utahlite.

The processes employed in shaping these materials by the American tribes, and, for that matter, by the whole primitive world, are: (1) fracturing processes, variously known as breaking, spalling, chipping, flaking; (2) crumbling processes, as battering, pecking; (3) incising or cutting processes; (4) abrading processes, as sawing, drilling, scraping, and grinding, and (5) polishing processes. The implements used in or connected with the shaping work are described separately under the following heads: *Abrading implements, Anvils, Arrowheads; Arrows, Bows, and Quivers; Chisels, Drills and Drilling, Flaking implements, Hammers, Knives, Pecking implements, Picks, Polishing implements, Saws, Scrapers*.

Of later years the operation of the primitive stone-shaping processes has received much attention on the part of archeologists, and the mystery formerly surrounding some of them has been well cleared away. Implements of stone and bone in skilled hands are demonstrated to be as effective in shaping stone as bronze or iron, and the methods most commonly employed by the tribes may be briefly outlined. Implements shaped by the chipping or flaking processes present a wide range of size, form, and finish, and include principally arrowheads, spearheads, lance heads, harpoon heads, knives, scrapers, drills, hoes, spades, and unspecialized blades. These objects are largely leaf-shaped or were specialized from leaf-shaped blades, and the getting out of these blades was one of the most arduous and difficult tasks undertaken by the native artisan. In shaping the blades a suitable piece of brittle stone, preferably a flattish pebble, bowlder, flake, or fragment was selected, and with a hammerstone of proper weight, usually globular or discoidal in form and generally not hafted, chips were removed by means of vigorous blows about the periphery, alternating the faces. The utmost skill of the operator was exerted to cause the flakes to carry from the point of percussion near the edge across and beyond the middle of the sides of the stone; failure in this resulted in the formation of a high ridge or node on one or both faces of the blade, which effectually prevented the proper development of the form.

If breakage or imperfect fracture did not intervene, the skilled workman in a few moments had roughed out a leaf-like blade of requisite thinness, and when the work had proceeded as far

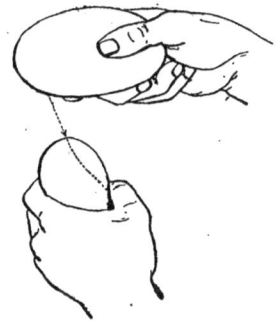

USE OF THE FLAKING HAMMER—FIRST STEP IN BOWLDER WORKING

as convenient with the hammerstone, if further elaboration were desired, the pressure implement, usually a bit of hard bone or antler, suitably hafted, was resorted to. By means of strong, abrupt pressure at the proper points, first on one side and then on the other, the flakes were detached, margins were trimmed, stems formed, notches made, points sharpened, and the specialization completed. Utilizing flakes or fragments of suitable shape, the smaller projectile points, drills, scrapers, and knife blades could be completed in a few minutes, but the difficulty increased with increase in size. The larger blades, some of which are upward of 2 ft in length, required skill of a high order for their successful

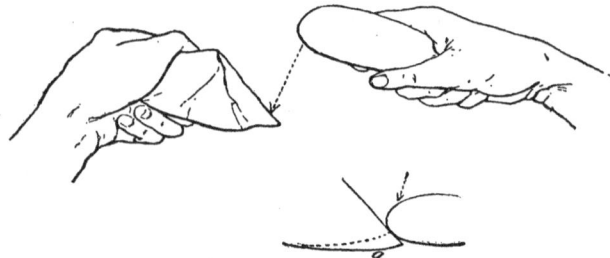

USE OF THE FLAKING HAMMER—BEGINNING ON THE SECOND SIDE IN BOWLDER WORKING

elaboration. In making small implements from fragments of proximate form, such as flakes or spalls, the hammer is not required, the work being readily accomplished

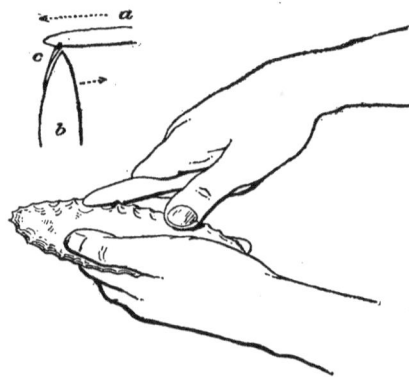

FREEHAND USE OF THE BONE FLAKING IMPLEMENT

with the bone point. It is to be observed, however, that the pressure flaker is available only with brittle stone and on forms having rather thin and sharp edges. Fracture processes varied much in detail from those here sketched.

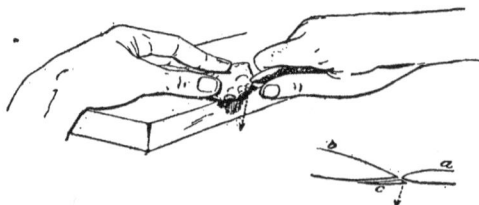

FLAKING WITH BONE OR METAL POINT, USING A REST

In some cases the flakes were removed by setting a punch-like implement upon the proper point and striking it with a mallet, and the larger work was accomplished by means of strong leverage or heavy strokes, the appliances being too

vaguely described by those making the record to convey a clear conception of the operations. The manner of resting and holding the stone and the method of applying the percussion and pressure implements differed with the different tribes, but the principles involved are apparently about the same with all. The fracture processes served also to produce emergency implements of almost every class—axes, celts or hatchets, picks, adzes, gouges, hammers, etc.; and this is true not only with the more primitive tribes but with all peoples using stone in the arts. It may be further noted that the flaking hammer was often employed to rough out the forms of many implements, as celts, axes, and adzes, designed to be elaborated and finished by pecking and grinding. See Cores, Flakes, Flaking implements, Hammers.

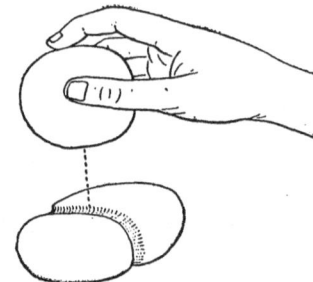

USE OF THE PECKING HAMMER

Many varieties of stone can not be shaped by fracture or can be shaped only imperfectly, and the aborigines resorted to the process of battering or pecking to secure the desired results. It was formerly supposed that this was a very tedious work and that the shaping of a celt or an ax required much time, but the experiments of McGuire and others

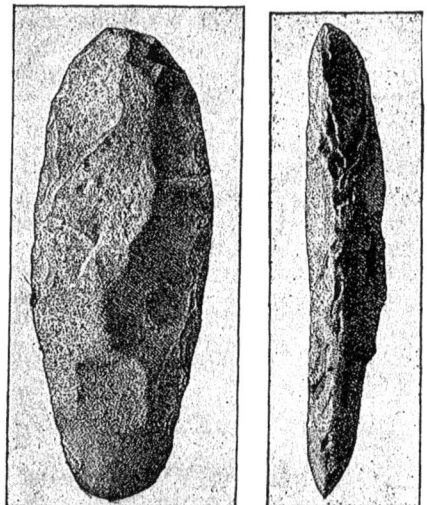

CHISEL USED IN CUTTING STEATITE

have shown that the work may be comparatively rapid and that by repeated blows of the hammerstone the toughest and hardest materials may readily be reduced to the desired shapes. Beginning with a bowlder or fragment of proximate shape or with a form roughed out by flaking, the primitive operator attacked the surface, crumbling the parts to be removed by rapid blows, and continued the work until the shape was so far perfected as to be ready for the grinding and polishing processes which followed. This pecking work is the prototype of the bush-hammering and the machine-chisel work of the civilized stonecutter. The leading varieties of articles shaped in part or in whole by this process are celts, axes, adzes, gouges, mortars, pestles, various culinary utensils, pipes, ornamental and ceremonial objects, and sculptures generally. See *Pecking implements.*

PIECE OF JADE, SHOWING RESULTS OF SAWING AND BREAKING

Incising processes were much employed by the native tribes. Knives, chisels, and other edged tools of stone served to carve all the softer varieties, the most universally available of these being soapstone or steatite (q. v.). Others are cannel coal, lignite, chalk, serpentine, and calcite. Chisels or edged stone picks were used in cutting out masses of soapstone in the quarry and in shaping the vessels and other large objects made from them. See *Chisels, Knives, Picks.* Abrading and smoothing processes were also of first importance to the tribes in shaping and finishing articles of stone. These employed the various grinding, sawing, drilling, and polishing tools. Drilling with pointed and tubular drills was constantly resorted to, as in the making of tobacco pipes and certain forms of ornaments and cere-

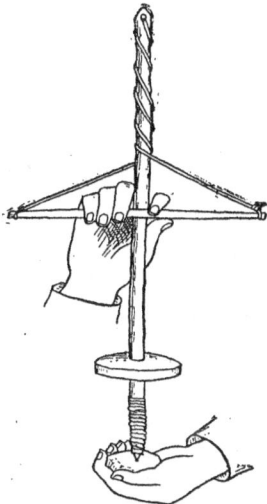

USE OF THE PUMP DRILL IN BORING

monial objects. See *Abrading implements, Drills and Drilling, Polishing implements, Saws, Scrapers.*

The following groups of products of the stone using and shaping arts are described under separate heads, viz: (1) *Buildings:* Pueblos (towns), cliff-dwellings, habitations, kivas, fortifications, tombs; (2) *Im-*

plements and utensils: Abrading implements, adzes, anchors, anvils; arrows, bows, and quivers; arrowheads, awls, axes, baking stones, boxes, celts, chisels, daggers, drills, flakes, flaking implements, gouges, hammers, hatchets, hoes and spades, knives, lamps, lances, metates, mortars, mullers, pestles, picks, pincers, pipes, polishing implements, cups, dishes, ladles, receptacles, saws, scrapers, sinkers, slings, spearheads, tomahawks, wedges; (3) *Ornaments:* Beadwork, gorgets, labrets, mosaics, pendants; (4) *Ceremonial objects:* Batons, masks, pipes; (5) *Problematical objects:*

GRINDING STONE

Banner-stones, bird-stones, boat-stones, cache disks and blades, cones, flaked stones (eccentric forms), footprint sculptures, hemispheres and spheres, hook stones, inscribed tablets, notched plates, pierced tablets, plummets, perforated

a

b

UNFINISHED STEATITE VESSEL SHOWING CHISEL MARKS

stones, sculptures (eccentric forms), spade-stones, spools, tubes.

Besides the shaped product above dealt with, the shaping of stone gives rise to another class of results of particular importance in the history of stone art and especially deserving of the attention of students who would intelligently discriminate stone-age phenomena. These are the various forms of rejectage of manufacture. In getting out stone where large bodies are dealt with, the first step is that of dividing the masses by heavy blows, and the resultant forms are blocks, fragments, and splinters of diversified shape and size. From these suitable pieces are selected for specialization; the remainder are refuse. When selected pieces are under treatment by percussive processes the blows of the hammer remove flakes, chips, and spalls, and these become refuse; when other portions are under treatment by pressure processes, minute flakes or chips are produced and become refuse. When a suitable mass of the material is selected from which to remove flakes designed for use as knives or other implements or for further elaboration, a nucleus or core results and this also becomes refuse (see *Cores*). Again, the portion of stone in process of shaping and partly shaped often breaks under the blows of the hammer or the pressure of the flaking tool and the pieces become refuse; and still more notably the piece being shaped does not develop properly and becomes unmanageable under the hammer or pressure flaker, and, being irreparably faulty, is rejected and becomes refuse. The last-mentioned abortive forms or failures are varied in shape and may or may not resemble closely the final forms which it was intended they should take. The term "turtleback" is applied to such of these rejected forms as have a faceted upper surface and a smoother under surface, suggesting the carapace of a turtle. It is these rejected defective forms, showing as they do clear evidence of design, that have led to much misapprehension because ignorant persons have mistaken them for actual implements and have attempted to classify them as such, assigning them to particular uses or periods suggested by their form. The various classes of rejectage here described—fragments, splinters, flakes, chips, cores, fragments resulting from breakage of partly shaped forms, and unbroken abortive forms, as

THE "TURTLEBACK," A BOWLDER WORKED ON ONE SIDE

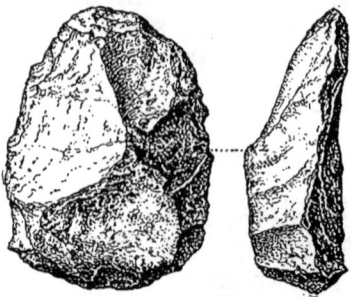

REJECT OF BLADE WORKING, ABANDONED ON ACCOUNT OF HUMP ON ONE FACE

well as broken and abandoned hammerstones—are usually left on the shaping sites. In bulk this rejectage far exceeds that of the accepted product—the output proper of the shop work. Other processes, as pecking, cutting, and grinding, also result in rejectage, but not to an equal extent with the fracture process, and the rejectage is seldom especially noteworthy except on soapstone quarry sites, where much breakage occurred during the process of roughing out the larger utensils.

The knowledge acquired in recent years through experiments in stone-shaping processes has led unfortunately to the manufacture of fraudulent imitations of aboriginal implements and sculptures for commercial purposes, and so great is the skill acquired in some cases that it is exceedingly difficult to detect the spurious work; there is thus much risk in purchasing objects whose pedigree is not fully ascertained. See *Pseudo-Indian*.

Works that may be consulted on this subject are very numerous, and only a few of the principal authorities are here cited; these, however, will enable the inquirer to find such other publications as are of value. Abbott (1) Prim. Indus., 1881; (2) in Surv. W. 100th Merid., VII, 1879; Bailey in Bull. Nat. Hist. Soc. N. B., no. VI, 1887; Beauchamp in Bull. N. Y. State Mus., IV, no. 18, 1897; Boas in Bull. Am. Mus. Nat. Hist., XV, pt. 1, 1901; Boyle in Ann. Archæol. Reps. Ontario, 1888–1905; Cushing (1) in Am. Anthr., VIII, no. 4, 1895; (2) in Proc. A. A. A. S., XLIV, 1896; Dawson in Can. Rec. Sci., II, no. 6, 1887; Dellenbaugh, N. Americans of Yesterday, 1901; Dixon in Bull. Am. Mus. Nat. Hist., XVII, pt. 3, 1905; Dorsey in Pub. Field Col. Mus., Anthr. ser., II, no. 4, 1900; Evans, Ancient Stone Implements of Great Britain, 1872; Foster, Prehist. Races, 1878; Fowke (1) in 13th Rep. B. A. E., 1896; (2) in the Archæologist, II, 1894, and III, 1895, (3) Archæol. Hist. Ohio, 1902; Holmes (1) in Bull. 21, B. A. E., 1894; (2) in 15th Rep. B. A. E., 1897; (3) in Proc. A. A. A. S., XLIII, 1895; (4) in Am. Anthr., III, no. 4, 1890; (5) ibid., IV, nos. 1 and 4, 1891; C. C. Jones, Antiq. Southern Indians, 1873; Jos. Jones in Smithson. Cont., XXII, 1876; Kunz, Gems and Precious Stones, 1890; McGuire (1) in Rep. Nat. Mus. 1894, 1896; (2) in Am. Anthr., IV, no. 3, 1893; (3) ibid., IX, no. 7, 1896; MacLean, Mound Builders, 1879; Matthew in Bull. Nat. Hist. Soc. N. B., no. III, 1884; Mercer (1) in Rep. of Madrid Commission, 1892; (2) in Pub. Univ. Pa., VI, 1897; Moore in Jour. Acad. Nat. Sci. Phila., 1894–1909; Moorehead, (1) Prehist. Impls., 1900; (2) Prim. Man in Ohio, 1892; Nordenskiöld, Cliff Dwellers of the Mesa Verde, 1893;

Phillips in Am. Anthr., n. s., II, no. 1, 1900; Proudfit in Am. Anthr., II, no. 3, 1889; Rau, Archæol. Colls. Nat. Mus., 1876; Reynolds in 12th Rep. Peabody Mus., 1880; Schumacher (1) in Surv. W. 100th Merid., VII, 1879; (2) in Bull. Surv. of Terr., III, no. 3, 1877; (3) in 11th Rep. Peabody Mus., 1878; Smith (1) in Mem. Am. Mus. Nat. Hist., IV, Anthr. III, 1903; (2) ibid., II, Anthr. I, 1899; (3) ibid., Anthr. I, pt. VI, 1900; Snyder in The Antiquarian, I, pt. 9, 1897; Squier and Davis in Smithson. Cont., I, 1848; Stevens, Flint Chips, 1870; Teit in Mem. Am. Mus. Nat. Hist., II, 1900; Thruston, Antiq. of Tenn., 1897; Wilson in Nat. Mus. Rep. 1897, 1899; Wyman in Mem. Peabody Acad. Sci., I, no. 4, 1875.   (w. h. h.)

Stonington. A former Pequot village in New London co., Conn. In 1825 there were 50 Indians there.

Stono. A tribe formerly residing in the neighborhood of the present Charleston, S. C., probably about Stono r. They may be identified with the Stalame of the French explorer Laudonnière in 1562, mentioned as confederated with Audusta (Edisto). In the English colonial documents the Stono and Westo are named together as at war with the Carolina settlers in 1664, 1669–71, and again in 1674, in consequence of raids made on them by the whites for the purpose of procuring slaves, but this association is due to nothing more perhaps than similarity between the names. If it actually existed, they must have retired among the Creeks along with the Westo (Yuchi). Consult Gatschet, Creek Migr. Leg., I, 1884; Mooney, Siouan Tribes of the East, Bull. B. A. E., 1894.   (a. s. g.   j. r. s.)
Stono.—Rivers, Hist. S. C., 38, 1856. Stonoes.—Hewat, Hist. Acc. S. C. and Ga., I, 51, 1779.

Storage and Caching. The storage of articles and supplies appears to have been quite general throughout America, and the practice of caching, or hiding, things not less so. The extent of this custom indicates its ancient origin, a conclusion strengthened by the discovery of large deposits of articles of stone which in many instances show partial disintegration and other indications of great age. Hoards of stone axes have been found in New Jersey, ceremonial implements in Florida, tobacco pipes in Ohio, and leaf-shaped blades along the greater part of the Atlantic seaboard. Many authors have described the methods employed by the Indians in the storage and caching of things, the process often evidencing great ingenuity in concealment. The season, the temperature, the locality, and the time required to make a cache were important considerations. When time allowed, some things were sewed in skins and suspended on trees or hidden in hollow tree trunks; others were buried under shelving rocks or in carefully prepared holes in the ground. Owing to seasonal journeys of large numbers of persons in search of food or other supplies, many things had to be left behind which, because of their weight or bulk, would add to the difficulty of movement. Caching was resorted to in order to prevent the hidden things from being disturbed by wild beasts, stones often being piled over the cache; or, when the deposit was of food or clothing, fires were built in order that the ashes should hide surface indications and thus keep enemies from disturbing the deposit; or, in other cases, the sod was carefully removed and replaced after the cache was completed; or, if the land was sandy, water was poured over the surface to conceal indications of the ground having been disturbed. The term *cache*, from the French *cacher*, 'to hide,' has been very generally adopted by the whites, who have not been slow to accept and practise this primitive method of hiding things intended to be reclaimed.

Martin Frobisher (1578), according to Dionese Settle, found that the natives in Baffinland hid their provisions, "both fish and flesh, in great heaps of stone," a practice still generally followed in the frozen north. Jacques Cartier (1535) found the natives on the St Lawrence to have vessels "as big as any butt or tun" in which to keep their fish that had been dried in the summer; these people are also said to have kept their corn in garrets on top of their houses. Pierre Biard refers in 1616 to winter storehouses in Canada wherein the natives kept smoked meat, roots, shelled acorns, peas, beans, etc., which they first put into sacks, and these in large pieces of bark that they then suspended from interlacing branches of two trees, so that neither rats nor dampness could injure them. Biard refers also to the corn he ate in going upstream, which the natives sought in secluded places where they had hidden it in little caches of birch-bark when they went down the river. The Jesuit Relations record many instances of this general habit, while on war, trading, and other expeditions, of caching food, to be used on the return journey. Many instances are related of the loss of caches by robbery, through forgetfulness of their locations, or through injury by weather, and of great suffering caused thereby.

Champlain, in 1603, spoke of pits dug in slopes of the seacoast to a depth of 5 or 6 ft, in which sacks made from plants and filled with grain were placed and covered with sand, "which keep as well as our granaries."

Formerly in Oregon, Washington, and British Columbia dried fish were stored by the Indians of Columbia and Fraser rs. in caches built of split cedar planks supported on the branches of trees far above the ground. The Kalispel cached their stores of dried berries on little islands in Pend d'Oreille lake. The berries were placed in reed bags and were protected from the weather by small log houses built over them (Grinnell). On the N. W. coast, according to Boas, clams taken from strings of cedar bark, on which they had been dried, were stored for future use. Lewis and Clark, in 1804, found at the falls of Columbia r. that dried fish were pounded between two stones and then placed in baskets made of grass and rushes and lined with salmon skin; the fish was then pressed down and covered with fishskins, each basket weighing from 90 to 100 pounds. They describe a cache on Missouri r. made by first removing the soil from a circle 20 in. across and then excavating a pit which was gradually enlarged to a diameter of 6 or 7 ft, having the form of a kettle; this hole was lined on the bottom and sides with sticks, and then filled with skins which it was desired to preserve, after which the sod was replaced and the surface made to appear as natural as possible. This is a typical method among the Plains Indians and Southwestern tribes. These explorers refer also to buying corn in ears from the Mandan, who dug it up in front of their lodges, where it had been buried the winter before.

The ancient Zuñi are said by Mindeleff to have rolled up huge snowballs, which they melted in reservoirs to obtain water, their arid environment having taught them to use such an expedient to increase the supply. Chroniclers of the Coronado expedition refer to a habit of the Hopi of taking along with them, when crossing the desert, a number of women laden with water in gourds, which receptacles they buried along the way for use on the return journey.

The natives of the Pacific coast keep acorns in brush storehouses and store pine seeds in granaries on top of their houses. The Indians of this region make vessels of rushes, plastered inside and outside with piñon gum and pitch, for holding liquids and seeds. Thomas Hariot, in 1585, refers to the natives of Florida hardening their meat in smoke in order to "preserve the same for winter use." John Smith (1608) speaks of the Virginia Indians as drying their fish in the Spanish fashion, as was done in the West Indies. Smith refers also to dried walnuts, chestnuts, acorns, and chinquapins which the natives gathered in the

winter and kept in great baskets. John Lawson (1714) speaks of "other sorts of cabins," which were without windows, that were used for granaries and for storing skins and other merchandise. The Southern Indians, according to the same authority, made cribs wherein they preserved their corn from injury; these were erected on posts and were daubed inside and outside with loam or clay, being tight enough to keep out the smallest vermin. Oysters and clams were dried on strings and stored for future use. Mesquite beans, piñon nuts, acorns, filberts, and hickory nuts in their respective habitats were stored in brush inclosures, which were presumably the originals of the slatted corncribs of the present day. The Gulf tribes built houses raised upon poles for the purpose of storing grain. All Plains Indians dry and store fruits and nuts of various sorts. The Pima bury watermelons in sand and make immense basketry cribs for storing grain, as do also the Apache, the Tarahumare, and other tribes of the S. W.

Consult Brown (1) in Records of the Past, IV, pt. 3, Mar. 1905; (2) in Wis. Archeol., VI, no. 2, 1907; Champlain, Œuvres, 1870; Hakluyt, Voy., III, 1810; Jesuit Relations, ed. 1858; Joutel, Jour., 1713; Lawson, Hist. Carolina, ed. 1860; Orig. Jour. Lewis and Clark, 1904–05; Lumholtz, Unknown Mexico, 1902; Mass. Hist. Soc. Coll., 2d s., IX, 1822; Mindeleff, Study of Pueblo Architecture, 8th Rep. B. A. E., 1891; Rau, North American Stone Implements, Smithson. Rep., 1872; Rep. Brit. A. A. S., 1890; Russell in 26th Rep. B. A. E., 1908; Sagard, Grand Voyage du pays des Hurons, 1865; Smith, History of Virginia, 1819; Stites, Economics of the Iroquois, 1905; Wheeler, Rep. U. S. G. and G. Surv. W. 100th Mer., VII, 1879; Winship, Coronado Exped., 14th Rep. B. A. E., pt. 1, 1896.   (J. D. M.)

Stotoii (*Stŏ′toïi*, 'leaning over [a cliff]'). A Squawmish village community on the right bank of Squawmisht r., Brit. Col.—Hill-Tout in Rep. Brit. A. A. S., 474, 1900.

Stott Ranch ruin. A prehistoric ruined pueblo on Stott ranch, a few m. w. of Pinedale, Navajo co., Ariz.—Fewkes in 22d Rep. B. A. E., 167, 1904.

Stratten. The local name for a band of Salish of Fraser superintendency, Brit. Col.—Can. Ind. Aff. Rep., 79, 1878.

Straw Town. See *Onondakai*.

Struck-by-the-Ree (*Palaneapape*). The head-chief of the Yankton Sioux at the period of the relinquishment of their lands in 1859 and until his death; born at Yankton, S. Dak., Aug. 30, 1804, while Lewis and Clark were encamped there. Capt. Lewis, on learning that a male child had been born in the camp, sent for it, and, wrapping it in the Stars and

Stripes, declared it to be "an American." Growing to manhood with the tradition of his christening upon him, Struck-by-the-Ree took great pride in his "Americanism," and was always a staunch friend of the whites. His greatest service was in 1862, during the time of the panic due to the outbreak and massacre in Minnesota, when, by his influence, he kept his tribe from joining the hostiles and actually threw a cordon of his warriors across South Dakota from Ft Randall to the Sioux as a barrier between the hostiles and the white settlements. He died July 29, 1888.   (D. R.)

Stryne. A Ntlakyapamuk village on the w. side of Fraser r., 5 m. above Lytton, Brit. Col. Pop. 57 in 1901, the last time the name appears.
Stā-ai'-in.—Dawson in Trans. Roy. Soc. Can., sec. II, 44, 1891. Sta'iEn.—Teit in Mem. Am. Mus. Nat. Hist., II, 172, 1900. Stain.—Hill-Tout in Rep. Ethnol. Surv. Can., 4, 1899. Strain.—Teit, op. cit. Stryen.—Brit. Col. map, Ind. Aff., Victoria, 1872. Stryne.—Can. Ind. Aff., 164, 1901. Stryne-Nqakin.—Ibid., 418, 1898 (two town names combined). Strynne.—Ibid., 269, 1889. Stryune.—Ibid., 434, 1896. Styne Creek.—Teit, op. cit. (white men's name).

Stsababsh (*S'tsa-babsh*). A Salish band living among the Dwamish lakes, Wash.—Boulet in letter, B. A. E., Mar. 22, 1886.

Stsanges (*Stsâ'ñges*). A Songish band between Esquimalt and Beecher bay, s. end of Vancouver id. Pop. 103 in 1904, 96 in 1909. Songish, the name given to this tribe by whites, is corrupted from the name of this band.
Songhees.—Can. Ind. Aff., pt. II, 164, 1901. Stsâ'ñges.—Boas in 6th Rep. N. W. Tribes Can., 17, 1890.

Stskeitl (*Stsk·ē'iL*). A Bellacoola town on the s. side of Bellacoola r., Brit. Col., near its mouth. It is one of the 8 villages called Nuhalk.
Stskē'etl.—Boas in 7th Rep. N. W. Tribes Can., 3, 1891. Stsk·ē'iL.—Boas in Mem. Am. Mus. Nat. Hist., II, 49, 1898.

Stthukhwich. A Siuslaw village on Siuslaw r., Oreg.
St'çu'-qwĭtc.—Dorsey in Jour. Am. Folk-lore, III, 230, 1890.

Stucabitic. A Maricopa rancheria on the Rio Gila, Ariz., in 1744.
Stucabitic.—Orozco y Berra, Geog., 348, 1864. Stue Cabitic.—Sedelmair (1744) cited by Bancroft, Ariz. and N. Mex., 366, 1889.

Stuckre. An unidentified Salishan band formerly at or about Port Madison Mills, w. Wash. Called "northern or Stuck-re Indians."—Maynard (1855) in Sen. Ex. Doc. 26, 34th Cong., 1st sess., 67, 1856.

Stucu. A Chumashan village formerly near Santa Inés mission, Santa Barbara co., Cal.—Taylor in Cal. Farmer, Oct. 18, 1861.

Stugarok. A Nushagagmiut Eskimo village on Nushagak bay, Alaska, where there is a salmon cannery. Pop. 7 in 1890.—11th Census, Alaska, 95, 1893.

Stuichamukh. An Athapascan tribe, now absorbed into the surrounding Salishan tribes, that inhabited upper Nicola valley,

Brit. Col. They have been supposed to be descendants of a war party of Tsilkotin (McKay in Dawson, Notes on Shuswap of Brit. Col., Trans. Roy. Soc. Can., IX, sec. 2, 23, 1891), but the evidence of their long occupancy of Nicola and Similkameen valleys has led Boas (10th Rep. N. W. Tribes, Rep. Brit. A. A. S., sec. 2, 33, 1895) to consider them the northernmost of the isolated Athapascan bands found along the Pacific coast. Four or five generations back they lived in three subterranean lodges, indicating a population of between 120 and 150.
SEi'lEqamuQ.—Boas in 10th Rep. N. W. Tribes, 32, 1905, ('people of the high country': Ntlakyapamuk name). Smîlê'kamuQ.—Ibid. (another Ntlakyapamuk name). Stûwi'HamuQ.—Ibid.

Stuik (*Stū'ix·*). A Bellacoola village on Bellacoola r., Brit. Col., 28 m. from its mouth.
Stū'.iH.—Boas in 7th Rep. N. W. Tribes Can., 3 1891. Stū'îx·.—Boas in Mem. Am. Mus. Nat. Hist., II, 49, 1898.

Stuikishkeni (*Stuikishχē'ni*, 'where the canoes are drawn on shore'). A Modoc settlement on the N. side of Little Klamath lake, Oreg.—Gatschet in Cont. N. A. Ethnol., II, pt. I, xxxii, 1890.

Stukamasoosatick. A former Pima village on the Gila r. res., s. Ariz.—Dudley in Ind. Aff. Rep. 1871, 58, 1872.

Stulnaas-hadai (*StAl na'as xā'da-i*, 'steep-house people'). A subdivision of the Chaahl-lanas, a Haida family settled in Alaska; named from one of its houses.—Swanton, Cont. Haida, 276, 1905.

Stumiks (*Stŭ'mĭks*, 'bulls'). A society of the Ikunuhkatsi, or All Comrades, in the Piegan tribe; it has been obsolete since about 1840.—Grinnell, Blackfoot Lodge Tales, 221, 1892.

Stung Serpent. See *Olabalkebiche*.

Stunhlai (*StA'nta-i*, said to refer to "any fat game or fish brought in"). A Haida town on the N. w. coast of Moresby id., Brit. Col., occupied anciently by the Kas-lanas.—Swanton, Cont. Haida, 280, 1905.

Stuntusunwhott. A former Tolowa village on Smith r., Cal.
Stŭn-tūs-un-whott.—Hamilton, Hay-narg-ger MS. vocab., B. A. E.

Stustas (*Sta'stas*). One of the most important Haida families of the Eagle clan. The name is that given to salmon eggs after the young fish have begun to take form in them. There is a story that this family was once reduced to a single woman, but subsequently increased very rapidly from her children; for that reason they were likened to spawning salmon. The family is known also as *Sā'ñgaLlā'nas*, referring to sea-birds called *sañg;* when these birds find any food on the surface of the sea, all swoop down upon it, making a great noise, and their actions are likened to those of people at potlatches made by this family. According to tradition, part of the Stustas, including that to which the chief himself belonged, came down from Stikine r. in the Tlingit country, while the rest were from the country of the Nass people. Edenshaw (q. v.), the name of the chief, was also brought along from the Stikine. A chief of this family was very friendly to the whites, and it was largely through his influence that a mission was established at Masset. The Stustas land lay principally around Naikun and in Naden harbor, but their chief town was Kiusta, on the coast opposite North id. There were many subdivisions: Kawas, Kangguatl-lanas, Hlielung-keawai, Hlielung-stustae, Naikun-stustae, Chawagis-stustae, and the Yadus of Alaska, the last being still further subdivided.   (J. R. S.)

Sā′ṅgaL lā′nas.—Swanton, Cont. Haida, 275, 1905. Shongalth Lennas.—Harrison in Proc. Roy. Soc. Can. 1895, sec. II, 125, 1895. Stastas.—Ibid.

Suahpi. One of the Diegueño rancherias represented in the treaty of 1852 at Santa Isabel, s. Cal.—H. R. Ex. Doc. 76, 34th Cong., 3d sess., 132, 1857.

Suahuaches. A former tribe encountered by Salinas in 1693 on the road from Coahuila to San Francisco mission, Texas.—Salinas (1693) in Dictamen Fiscal, Nov. 30, 1716, MS.

Suamca. A Jesuit mission, founded by Father Kino among the Sobaipuri about 1687 (the Rudo Ensayo says in 1730); situated on the headwaters of Rio Santa Cruz, in the vicinity of Terrenate, Sonora, Mexico, just below the Arizona-Sonora boundary. In 1697 Bernal reported it to be in a prosperous condition; in 1731 it had several rancherias. Villa-Señor mentions it as a mission in 1748, and it was still in existence in 1767, at which date the population was 114. Quiburi, Optuabo, Esqugbaag, Baibcat, Turisai, and Babisi were its visitas.   (F. W. H.)

Santa María de Suamca.—Roche (1768) in Doc. Hist. Mex., 4th s., II, 391, 1856. Santa María de Suanca.—Croix (1769), ibid., 10. Santa María Magdalena Soanca.—Orozco y Berra, Geog., 347, 1864. Santa Maria Soamca.—Rudo Ensayo (ca. 1762), 148, 160, 1863. Santa María Soamnca.—Keler (1752) in Doc. Hist. Mex., 4th s., I, 28, 1856. Santa Maria Soanca.—Villa-Señor, Theatro Am., pt. 2, 403, 1748. S. Maria de Sucunca.—Venegas Hist. Cal., I, map, 1759. Sta. María.—Kino (1697) in Doc. Hist. Mex., 4th s., I, 276, 1856. Suamca.—Venegas, Hist. Cal., II, 177, 191, 1759.

Suanas. A former tribe, probably Coahuiltecan, met by Salinas on the road from Coahuila to San Francisco mission, Texas, in 1693.—Salinas (1693) in Dictamen Fiscal, Nov. 30, 1716, MS.

Suangna. A former Gabrieleño rancheria in Los Angeles co., Cal., on the coast near Palos Verdes or Cerritos, at a locality later called Suanga.

Shua-vit.—Kroeber in Univ. Cal. Pub., Am. Archeol. and Ethnol., VIII, 39, 1908 (native form.) Suagna.—Reid (1852) quoted by Taylor in Cal. Farmer, June 8, 1860. Suang-na.—Reid quoted by Hoffman in Bull. Essex Inst., XVII, 2, 1885.

Suaqui. One of the principal pueblos of the Nevome and seat of a Spanish mission founded in 1619. Situated near the lower Yaqui r., 20 m. w. of Onava, Sonora, Mexico. Pop. 415 in 1678, 42 in 1730. Its inhabitants were called Sibubapas.

S. Ignacio Subaque.—Zapata (1678) in Doc. Hist. Mex., 4th s., III, 358, 1857. Suaqui.—Rivera (1730) quoted by Bancroft, No. Mex. States, I, 513, 1884. Zuake.—Kni, map (1702), in Stöcklein, Neue Welt-Bott, 74, 1726. Zuaqui.—Rudo Ensayo (ca 1762), 125, 1863.

Subazama. A former village, probably Salinan, connected with San Antonio mission, Monterey co., Cal.—Taylor in Cal. Farmer, Apr. 27, 1860.

Subchiam. A former village, presumably Costanoan, connected with Dolores mission, San Francisco, Cal.—Taylor in Cal. Farmer, Oct. 18, 1861.

Succaah. A band, probably Moquelumnan, formerly living in San Joaquin valley, or to the northward, in California.

Lukahs.—Johnston in Sen. Ex. Doc. 61, 32d Cong., 1st sess., 20, 1852. Suc-ca-ah.—Ryer, ibid., 21. Suc-co-ah.—Ryer in Sen. Ex. Doc. 4, 32d Cong., spec. sess., 199, 1853.

Succanash. See *Succotash.*

Succonesset. A village of Praying Indians in 1685, near Falmouth, Barnstable co., Mass. The inhabitants were probably subject to either the Wampanoag or the Nauset.

Saccanesset.—Writer about 1767 in Mass. Hist. Soc. Coll., 2d s., III, 14, 1846. Sokones.—Bourne (1764), ibid., 1st s., I, 198, 1806. Sokonesset.—Freeman (1792), ibid., 231. Succonesset.—Freeman (1802), ibid., VIII, 152, 1802. Succonet.—Mourt (1622), ibid., 262. Succonusset.—Ibid., I, 198, note, 1806. Suckanessett.—Hinckley (1685), ibid., 4th s., V, 133, 1861.

Succotash. A corruption of a Narraganset name for an ear of corn, long misapplied by English-speaking people to a preparation of green corn cut from the cob, and transversely cut string-beans or shelled lima-beans boiled with the addition of milk, butter, and seasoning. Roger Williams (1643) gives *msickquatash* (*m'sikwatash*) as the name for a boiled ear of corn, although the word signifies simply an ear of corn whether boiled or raw. Just when the name in a slightly more corrupt form was misapplied is not certain, since a gap occurs in the history of the word between 1643 and 1778, when it appears, in the form of "succatash," in Carver's Travels, a widely-read book in the time of its author. Carver describes "succatash" as a dish composed of corn, beans, and bear's flesh. The word is next mentioned by Jeremy Belknap (1792) in the form "succotash." The Narraganset word *m'sikwatash* means 'the grains are whole (or entire),' i. e. not cracked or broken by pounding. The Caniba (Norridgewock) name *mesikutar* has the same meaning ("blé qui n'est pas pilé."—Râle). The old Abnaki inanimate plural was *r* instead of *sh*. The aboriginal name for the preparation that we call *succotash* has been lost. The form of the name would have been determined by the preponderance of corn or of beans in the stew, as may have been the case, since no Algonquian word can be formed to indicate that more than one vegetable is contained in a stew or soup. (W. R. G.)

Suchigin. A former village, presumably Costanoan, connected with Dolores mission, San Francisco, Cal.—Taylor in Cal. Farmer, Oct. 18, 1861.

Suchui. A former village, presumably Costanoan, connected with Dolores mission, San Francisco, Cal.
Suchni.—Bancroft, Nat. Races, I, 453, 1874. Suchui.—Taylor in Cal. Farmer, Oct. 18, 1861.

Suckatash. See *Succotash*.

Sudac. A Maricopa rancheria on the Rio Gila, Ariz., in 1744.—Sedelmair (1744) cited by Bancroft, Ariz. and N. Mex., 366, 1889.

Sudacsasaba. A Maricopa settlement on the Gila r., Ariz., in the 18th century.
Sudacsasaba.—Rudo Ensayo (ca. 1762), 22, 1863. Sudacsassaba.—Orozco y Berra, Geog., 348, 1864.

Sudacson. A former Pima settlement on the Rio Gila, Pinal co., Ariz., between Casa Grande and a point 10 leagues below. It was visited by Kino in 1698, possibly as early as 1694, and named by him Encarnación. It was not far from the present Sacaton. According to Font the population was 5,000(?) in 1775. See Bartlett, below.
Encarnacion.—Bancroft, No. Mex. States, I, 259, note, 1884. Encarnacion Sutaquison.—Anza and Font (1780) quoted by Bancroft, Ariz. and N. Mex., 392, 1889. La Encarnacion.—Venegas, Hist. Cal., I, 297, 1759. La Encarnacion del Sutaquison.—Garcés (1775), Diary, 106, 1900. Sudacson.—Rudo Ensayo (ca. 1762), 21, 1863. Sutaguison.—Bartlett, Pers. Narr., II, 268, 1854. Sutaquisan.—Humboldt, Kingdom of New Spain, II, 303, 1811 (also Sutaquizan; see index, vol. iv). Sutaquisau.—Squier in Am. Rev., II, 512, Nov. 1848. Sutaquison.—Garcés (1775), Diary, 109, 1900.

Sudagunachte. See *Sadekanaktie*.

Sugar. See *Maple sugar*.

Sugarcane. A Shuswap village on the E. side of Fraser r., Brit. Col.—Morice in Trans. Can. Inst. 1892–93, IV, 22, 1895.

Sugeree. A small tribe, supposed to have been Siouan, that lived near the Waxhaw in Mecklenburg co., N. C., and York co., S. C. They occupied a fertile district and, according to Lawson (Hist. Car., 76, 1860), inhabited many towns and settlements. They were doubtless greatly reduced by the Yamasee war of 1715 and later merged in the Catawba.
Sagans.—Bowles, New Pocket map of U. S., 1783. Satarees.—Popple's map, n. d. Sugans.—Vaugondy's map, 1778. Sugaus.—Bowen's map, 1760. Suturees.—War map (1715) in Winsor, Hist. Am., V, 346, 1887.

Sugk-eye. See *Sockeye*.

Sugwaundugahwininewug (*Sägwándäga-wininiwäg*, 'men of the dense-wooded forest.'—Gerard). A Chippewa band, commonly known as Bois Fort Chippewa, living in the coniferous forest region W. of L. Superior, in Minnesota. They

numbered 640 in 1909 and occupy lands allotted in severalty from a reservation formerly consisting of 107,519.42 acres.
Boise Forte.—Ind. Aff. Rep., 332, 1873. Bois Forts.—Warren (1852) in Minn. Hist. Soc. Coll., V, 85, 1885. Hardwoods.—Ibid. Sagantwaga-wininiwak.—Gatschet, Ojibwa MS., B. A. E., 1882. Sagwandagawinini.—Baraga, Eng.-Otch. Dict., 109, 1878 (trans. 'Indian from the thick forests': Chippewa form). Sagwändägawininiwąg.—Wm. Jones, inf'n, 1905. Sakâwiyiniw.—Baraga, op. cit. Sug-wau-dug-ah-win-in-e-wug.—Warren (1852) in Minn. Hist. Soc. Coll., V, 85, 1885. Sug-waun-dug-ah-win-ine-wug.—Warren in Schoolcraft, Ind. Tribes, II, 139, 1852 (trans. 'men of the thick fir woods'). Sug-wun-dug-ah-win-in-e-wug.—Ramsey in Ind. Aff. Rep., 90, 1850. Thick Woodsmen.—Warren in Schoolcraft, Ind. Tribes, II, 139, 1852. Waub-ose.—Warren (1852) in Minn. Hist. Soc. Coll., V, 86, 1885 ('rabbits': so called by other Chippewa on account of their unwarlike disposition).

Suhinimiut ('people of the sun,' that is, living in the east). A tribe of Labrador Eskimo extending from Koksoak r. E. to C. Chidley and thence S. to Hamilton inlet. A part have long been Christianized by Moravian missionaries, but those of the northern districts still retain their heathen customs. Girls are tattooed at the age of puberty, though less elaborately than formerly; they are then forced into marriage, and early show the effects of their harsh and laborious life. Children are few and weak. Many men have two wives, the wealthy several. The aged and the diseased are frequently deserted, sometimes quietly strangled. An unlucky woman is driven out into the wilderness. A bad man is not admitted into the houses, and if he commits murder the others stone him to death. Blood vengeance is incumbent on the next of kin. The people are of the stature of Europeans and very muscular. Their legs are disproportionately short and malformed, owing probably to the habit of carrying infants in the hood. There is a recognized elder in the community, yet he is controlled by the angekok. These conjurers, who pretend to propitiate the malevolent spirits of nature and each man's evil spirit, work much harm, often separating man and wife on the plea that their union causes ill luck. The people often devour deer meat raw, though they prefer cooked food. The complexion of these Eskimo shows much variation; those who are bleached almost white in winter become quickly browned by exposure to the summer sun.

Subtribes are the Koksoagmiut, Kangivamiut, and Kilinigmiut. The mission stations are Hebron, Hopedale, Nachvak, Nain, Okak, Ramah, and Zoar. A native village on the N. coast is Aukpatuk.
Sûhĭnĭmyut.—Turner in 11th Rep. B. A. E., 176, 1894. Sukhinimyut.—Turner in Trans. Roy. Soc. Can., V, 104, 1888.

Suhub. The Cottonwood clan of the Hopi.
Si-he'-bi.—Stephen in 8th Rep. B. A. E., 39, 1891. Sühüb wiñwû.—Fewkes in 19th Rep. B. A. E., 584,

1900. **Sü-hüb wüñ-wû.**—Fewkes in Am. Anthr., VII, 404, 1894.

Suiesia. A Chumashan village formerly near Santa Inés mission, Santa Barbara co., Cal.—Taylor in Cal. Farmer, Oct. 18, 1861.

Suisun (probably 'big expanse'). A former Patwin division, probably only a village, on Suisun bay, Solano co., Cal. **Soisehme.**—Taylor in Cal. Farmer, Oct. 18, 1861. **Soo-i-soo-nes.**—Ibid., Mar. 30, 1860. **Souissouns.**—Choris, Voy. Pitt., 6, 1822. **Su-i-sun′.**—Powers in Cont. N. A. Ethnol., III, 218, 1877. **Suysum.**—Chamisso in Kotzebue, Voy., III, 51, 1821.

Suk (*S′ŭk*, 'valley,' 'depression'). A Ntlakyapamuk village on the E. side of Fraser r., Brit. Col., below Keefer station, C. P. R. R. The population of this place and the neighboring village of Kimus, with which later reports of Indian affairs have combined it, was 74 in 1901, since which date neither is mentioned. **Cûk′.**—Hill-Tout in Ethnol. Surv. Can., 5, 1899. **Sheooke.**—Can. Ind. Aff., 189, 1883. **Shoouk.**—Brit. Col. map, Ind. Aff., Victoria, 1872. **Snuk.**—Can. Ind. Aff., 363, 1897. **Sook-kamus.**—Ibid., pt. II, 164, 1901. **S′ûk.**—Teit in Mem. Am. Mus. Nat. Hist., II, 169, 1900. **Sunk.**—Can. Ind. Aff., 269, 1889. **Suuk.**—Ibid., 230, 1886. **Suuk-kamus.**—Ibid., 418, 1898.

Sukaauguning. A Chippewa village formerly on Pelican lake, Oneida co., Wis. **Pelican Lake band.**—Warren (1852) in Minn. Hist. Soc. Coll., V, 315, 1885. **Sa′ka·ō′gaming.**—Wm. Jones, inf′n, 1905. **Suk-a-aug-un-ing.**—Warren, op. cit.

Sukanom. A division of the Yuki of N. California, living s. of the Ukomnom of Round valley.

Sukaispoka (*Sŭka-ĭspóga*, 'hog-killing place'). A small Upper Creek town formerly in Cleburne co., Ala., on the w. bank of Tallapoosa r., 12 m. above Oakfuskee, to which town it was subordinate and to which the inhabitants moved prior to the year 1799.   (A. S. G.) **Hog Range.**—Gatschet, Creek Migr. Leg., I, 144, 1884 (traders′ name). **Hog range.**—Hawkins (1799), Sketch, 48, 1848. **Shuckospaga.**—Alcedo, Dic. Geog., IV, 547, 1788. **Shuckospoja.**—Bartram, Trav., I, map, 1799. **Soguspogus.**—Swan (1791) in Schoolcraft, Ind. Tribes, V, 262, 1855. **Sokaspoge.**—Bartram, op. cit., 461, 1792. **Sooc-he-ah.**—Hawkins, op. cit. **Suche-poga.**—Sen. Ex. Doc. 425, 24th Cong., 1st sess., 215, 1836. **Suka-ishpógi.**—Gatschet, op. cit. **Suka-ispóka.**—Ibid.

Sukechunetunne. A band or village of the Chastacosta on the N. side of Rogue r., Oreg. **Sû-ꭓe′-tcû-ne′ tûnně.**—Dorsey in Jour. Am. Folklore, III, 234, 1890.

Sukhutit ('black mouths'). A former Arikara band under chief Sutaka, White Shield. **Blackmouths.**—Culbertson in Smithson. Rep. 1850, 143, 1851. **Sûh-ut′-it.**—Hayden, Ethnog. and Philol., 357, 1862.

Sukiaug (meaning doubtful). An Algonquian tribe formerly occupying a considerable territory on both sides of Connecticut r. about Hartford, Conn. Their principal village, of the same name, was near the present Hartford. In 1730 they removed to Farmington.   (J. M.)

Sekioge.—Goodwin (1636) in Mass. Hist. Soc. Coll., 4th s., VII, 44, 1865. **Sicaock.**—Ludlowe (1637), ibid., 2d s., VIII, 235, 1819. **Sicaogg.**—Writer about 1642, ibid., 3d s., III, 161, 1833. **Suokiang.**—Hubbard (1680), ibid., 2d s., V, 307, 1815. **Suckiaug.**—Kendall, Trav., I, 142, 1809. **Suckieag.**—Writer of 1815 in Mass. Hist. Soc. Coll., 2d s., III, 182, 1846. **Sukiaugk.**—Stiles (1761), ibid., 1st s., X, 105, 1809.

Sukinatchi (*Shukha-in-hacha*, 'hog its river'). Given by Gatschet (Creek Migr. Leg., I, 109, 1884) as a former Choctaw settlement in Lowndes and Kemper cos., Miss. The mention of Lowndes co. must be a mistake, the name probably referring to those Choctaw living along Sukinatchie or Sookanatchie cr., in Kemper co. Halbert does not use this as the name of a town, and evidently it is a general term. **Factory Indians.**—Gatschet, op. cit. **Senachas.**—N. Y. Doc. Col. Hist., X, 951, 1858. **Shuk-hu-natchee.**—Rutherford in Ind. Aff. Rep., 877, 1847. **Sook-e-nook-e.**—H. R. Ex. Doc. 138, 23d Cong., 2d sess., 14, 1835. **Su-quah-natch-ah.**—U. S. Stat., IX, 114, 1851.

Sukkertoppen. A Danish mission and Eskimo settlement in w. Greenland, lat. 65° 20′.—Nansen, Across Greenland, II, 29, 1890.

Sukkwan (said to be from Tlingit *suq-qo-ăn*, 'grassy town'). A Haida town of the Koetas family, formerly on Cordova bay, in the Kaigani country, Alaska. In 1836–41 John Work stated the number of houses here was 14 and the number of people 229. Former inhabitants of this town can now recall 7 houses. Petroff in 1880–81 gave the number of people as 141. The town is now abandoned. **Sakoā′n.**—Boas, Twelfth Rep. N. W. Tribes Can., 26, 1898. **Shakan.**—Petroff in 10th Census, Alaska, 32, 1884. **Shākwan Hāadē.**—Harrison in Proc. Roy. Soc. Can., sec. II, 125, 1895. **Shaw-a-gan.**—Dawson, Q. Charlotte Ids., 173B, 1880 (after Work, 1836–41). **Shou a gan.**—Schoolcraft, Ind. Tribes, V, 489, 1855 (after Work). **Show-a-gan.**—Kane, Wand. N. A., app., 1859 (after Work). **Ssokŏān hādē.**—Krause, Tlinkit Ind., 304, 1885. **Sukkwan.**—U. S. Coast Surv. map of Alaska, s. E. sec., no. 8050. **Suqqo-ān.**—Swanton in 26th Rep. B. A. E., 408, 1908.

Suko. The Sun gens of the Caddo.—Mooney in 14th Rep. B. A. E., 1093, 1896.

Sukshultaatanom. A branch of the Yuki of N. California possessing the N. fork of the Middle fork of Eel r. and Hull cr.

Suktaloosa ('black bluff'). A former temporary settlement of the Koasati, on the w. bank of Tombigbee r., E. Miss. It was abandoned in 1722. **Coosada Sackla Loosa.**—West Fla. map, ca. 1775. **Seekta Loosa.**—Romans, Florida, I, 334, 1775. **Sukta loosa.**—Ibid., 332.

Suktaloosa. A former temporary settlement of the Koasati on Tombigbee r. below the mouth of Sukenatcha cr., Ala.—Romans, Fla., 326, 1775.

Suktanakamu (*Sŭk′-ta-na-ka′-mu*). One of the Chumashan villages formerly near Santa Inés mission, Santa Barbara co., Cal.—Henshaw, Santa Inez MS. vocab., B. A. E., 1884.

Sulapin (*Sul′-ă-pĭn*). A Chumashan village formerly in Ventura co., Cal.—

Henshaw, Buenaventura MS. vocab., B.
A. E., 1884.

Suliga. An unidentified village in central Florida, lat. 28° 30′, near a small lake.—Bartram, Voy., I, map, 1799.

Sulujame. A tribe, apparently Coahuiltecan, which was represented at San Antonio de Valero mission, Texas, as early as 1726 and as late as 1741. Their Coahuiltecan affiliation is inferred from their close association with the Xarame and the Patagua.   (H. E. B.)
Chrelejan.—Valero Baptisms, partida 578, 1747, MS. Chulajam.—Ibid., partida 331, 1731. Chulajame.—Ibid., partida 448, 1738. Chuluaam.—Ibid., partida 351, 1731. Sulajame.—Ibid., partida 157, 1726. Zolajan.—Ibid., partida 236, 1728. Zolojan.—Ibid., partida 96, 1729. Ztolam.—Ibid., partida 219, 1728. Zulaja.—Valero Marriages, partida 135, 1736. Zulajan.—Ibid., partida 150, 1740.

Sulu-stins (*Sū'lu stins*). A former Haida town of the Do-gitunai family, on the E. coast of Hippa id., Queen Charlotte ids., Brit. Col.
Skao nAns.—Swanton, Cont. Haida, 281, 1905. Sūlu stīns.—Ibid.

Suma. A semi-nomadic tribe, one branch of which formerly occupied the region of the Casas Grandes in Chihuahua, Mexico, and the other the vicinity of El Paso, Tex. The latter are mentioned in 1659, under the name Zumanas, as forming part of the mission population of San Lorenzo (q. v.), but the name Sumas is used by Benavides as early as 1630. Vetancurt (*ca.* 1696) speaks also of the Zumas and Zumanas as living somewhat below El Paso, and Bandelier apparently classifies the former at least as the Suma. The names Zumanas and Jumanos seem to have been confused. At the instigation of the Pueblo Indians taken from the N. to El Paso by Gov. Otermin when retreating from Santa Fé, N. Mex., during the Pueblo revolt of 1680, this branch of the Suma became hostile to the whites and induced the friendly Mansos to join them, with their confederates the Jano, in their outbreak of 1684. The Spaniards succeeded in reducing them two years later, forming them into several settlements about El Paso, but San Lorenzo was the only one that endured. In 1744 the tribe comprised 50 families; in 1765 only 21 families remained, the decrease in population being doubtless due to smallpox. Only one of the tribe was known to be living (at Senecú, Mexico) in 1897.

The mission of Casas Grandes was established among the southern branch of the tribe about 1664. At this time and for many years later they confederated with the Apache and Jocome in their depredations against the Piman tribes to their westward, particularly the Opata. The extermination of the Suma was probably due to Apache hostility. According to Orozco y Berra (p. 327) they spoke the Piro dialect, but there seems to be

no warrant for this classification, and their linguistic affinities are not known. See Bandelier in Arch. Inst. Papers, III, 86–91, 1890.   (F. W. H.)
Bumas.—Doc. of 18th cent. quoted by Bandelier in Arch. Inst. Papers, IV, 525, 1893 (misprint). Sumas.—Benavides, Memorial, 7, 1630. Sumes.—Linschoten, Descr. de l'Amer., map 1, 1638. Sunas.—Ribas (1645) quoted by Bandelier in Arch. Inst. Papers, III, 89, 1890. Yumas.—Arlegui (1660-65) quoted by Bandelier, ibid., (misprint). Zumanas.—Garcia de San Francisco (1659) quoted by Bandelier, ibid., 87 (distinct from Jumanos). Zumas.—Vetancurt (1696) in Teatro Mex., III, 308, 1871; 18th cent. doc. quoted by Bandelier in Arch. Inst. Papers, III, 88, 1890.

Sumass. A Cowichan tribe on the lake and river of the same name, which are tributary to lower Frazer r., Brit. Col. Until 1894 three divisions or villages called by this name, and numbered 1, 2, and 3, appeared in the reports of the Canadian Department of Indian Affairs, having populations, respectively, of 30, 57, and 53 in 1893. Their total number in 1909 was given as 50.
Semáç.—Boas, MS., B. A. E., 1887. Smess.—Mayne, Brit. Col., 295, 1862. Sumas.—Can. Ind. Aff., 300, 1893. Sumass.—Ibid., 160, 1901. Su-mat-se.—Fitzhugh in U. S. Ind. Aff. Rep. 1857, 328, 1858.

Sumaun. Given as a Karok village on Klamath r., N. w. Cal., inhabited in 1860.
Sum-maun.—Taylor in Cal. Farmer, Mar. 23, 1860.

Sumdum. A small Tlingit tribe occupying a village of the same name at Port Houghton, Alaska. The population was 150 in 1868, but is now only about 50. Sitkoedi is a social division.   (J. R. S.)
Samdan.—Kane, Wand. in N. A., app., 1859. S!aodā'n.—Swanton, field notes, B. A. E., 1904. Soundun.—Petroff in 10th Census, Alaska, 32, 1884. Sumdum.—Porter in 11th Census, Alaska, 3, 1893. Sundowns.—Scott in Ind. Aff. Rep., 314, 1868.

Sumpitan. See *Blowgun*.

Sunananahogwa (*Su-nu-na' na-ho'-gwa*). A Paviotso tribe formerly on Reese r., central Nevada.—Powell, Paviotso MS., B. A. E., 1881.

Sunchaque. A former village, presumably Costanoan, connected with Dolores mission, San Francisco, Cal.—Taylor in Cal. Farmer, Oct. 18, 1861.

Sun dance. The Sun dance was a ceremony confined to the Plains tribes. It was performed by the Arapaho, Cheyenne, Siksika, and Cree of Algonquian stock; the Dakota, Assiniboin, Mandan, Crows, Ponca, and Omaha of Siouan stock; the Pawnee of Caddoan stock; the Kiowa; and the Shoshoni and Ute of Shoshonean stock. In its ceremonial forms the Sun dance of all these tribes seems related, and it may be regarded as a summer solstice ceremony, though in many tribes this element is largely or entirely obscured. The fundamental object of the ceremony seems to have been the overcoming of certain cosmic elements.

In all of the tribes the ritual is subordinated to the drama; the former never predominates, as it does in the star cult of the Pawnee ceremonies. The ritual, when present, is chanted, and consists of groups of songs, generally eight in number. As a rule these songs are sung on the night of the entrance into the lodge of the Sun dance.

The time of the ceremony is summer, varying from early to late in the season, and it may even be held in the autumn. Among some tribes, as the Siouan, the ceremony is annual, and is in charge of a self-perpetuating priesthood, apparently under the control of the war chief. In other tribes, especially those of Algonquian stock, the performance of the ceremony is dependent on a vow or a pledge made by an individual who hopes by such performance to ward off sickness from himself or from some member of his family, although other reasons for making the vow exist, the most common of these being to avert lightning.

The participants in the ceremony among the Siouan tribes, besides the priesthood, are selected and compelled to perform by the priests. In other tribes, as for example the Arapaho, the participants, other than the priests (who are those that have vowed the ceremony in former years), are those who have made minor vows, and whose participation is hence voluntary. Among such tribes the chief priest is chosen by the friends of the votary of the ceremony.

The duration of the ceremony varies among the different tribes, 8 days being the most common period. The period is largely dependent, however, on the number of fasting and dancing days, the preliminary days being 3 or 4 in number, and the dancing days from 1 to 4, though formerly, it would seem, 4 was the common number.

Among all tribes there is a division of the ceremony into secret rites and a public performance. The secret rites, occupying from 1 day to 4 days, are held in a tipi of preparation, which occupies a position alone in the camp circle. In at least one tribe there are four such tipis of preparation, each in charge of a leader. By the time of the erection of the secret tipi or tipis the camp circle has been formed in the shape of a horseshoe with the opening to the E.; here is camped the entire tribe, the arrangement of the family tipis being according to a fixed system. Within the secret tipi the priests congregate each day and spend their time in the performance of certain rites, consisting of smoking, feasting, praying, and the preparation of objects that are to be used upon the altar or worn during the public performance. On the last day of the secret rites a great lodge is built in the center of the camp circle, the selection of the site being the office of a special individual and attended with rites. The

gathering of suitable timber for the lodge and its erection are usually done by one or more warrior organizations. The selection of the center pole is accompanied with special rites and usually is in charge of the most noted warrior or warriors of the tribe. The lodge varies from a roofless inclosure with a tall center pole, as among the Siouan tribes, to a partially covered structure, consisting of an outer row of forked uprights connected by cross-bars, from which rafter poles extend to the fork of the center pole. The lodge is from 60 to 100 ft. in diameter, and is always provided with an opening toward the E. On the completion of the lodge, generally late in the afternoon, the priests formally abandon the secret tipi of preparation, and reside until the termination of the ceremony in the Sun-dance lodge proper. On this night the lodge is formally dedicated, often with elaborate rites; the warrior societies parade, and the chiefs signalize the bravery of certain young men of the tribe by specially designating them by name. On the morning following the erection of the lodge the altar is set up near its western side. The altar varies from the simple buffalo skull and pipe on a cleared circle of earth, as among the Ponca, to an elaborate arrangement of a buffalo skull, an excavation with a dry sand-painting, upright sticks with rainbow symbols, and various bushes and young trees, as among the Cheyenne. On the completion of the altar the priests decorate the bodies, naked except for a loin cloth, of those who are to dance; these, together with the priests, have taken neither food nor drink since the preceding night. After the dancers have been painted, and decked with sage or willow wreaths about the head, neck, waist, wrists, and ankles, the dancers, forming in line, dance toward the center pole, representing the sun, blowing whistles made of the wing-bones of eagles to accompany Sun-dance songs, which are sung by musicians seated about a large drum at the southern side of the entrance. After an interval, which may be a day, the paint is removed and renewed, and the ceremony is resumed, and to the end the dancers thus alternately dance and rest. At the close of the performance the dancers in some tribes take an emetic, drink medicine-water, break their fast, and then enter the sweat-lodge. In all tribes, so far as known, the lodge with its accompanying altar is abandoned to the elements, for it is considered sacred and may not be disturbed. Among several taboos of the ceremony, one most frequent and almost universal is that forbidding the presence of menstruating women.

In the majority of tribes one of the most common rites of the public performance is that of voluntary self-laceration or torture. The two most common forms of torture were (1) to attach the free end of a reata that had been fastened to the center fork of the lodge, to a skewer inserted in the loose skin of the breast, and (2) to drag around inside the camp circle one or more buffalo-skulls by a reata the other end of which was attached to a skewer inserted in the back. In some tribes a small piece of flesh was cut from the arm or shoulder of the dancer and was offered with tobacco seeds at the foot of the center pole. The amount of torture performed seems to have been greatest among the Cheyenne and Mandan. Torture in any form was not tolerated by the Kiowa; indeed, the appearance of blood at any stage of the ceremony was regarded by them as an ill omen, and it is said sometimes to have caused the ceremony to cease.

A form of sacrifice other than torture, consisting in the offering of the cast-off clothing of children or adults to the lodge on the last day, was practised by several tribes, especially those of Algonquian stock.

The ceremony of the Sun dance abounds in symbolism, no rite being performed except in a prescribed manner. There seems to have been universal veneration of the four cardinal points. The sun, or a god spoken of as the "great mystery," "great medicine," or "man above," was even more prominent, being symbolized by the center pole. The salient features of the symbolism may be epitomized as follows: The tipi of secret preparation corresponds to the sacred mountain to which the originator of the ceremony repaired when in distress and there learned the mysteries of the ceremony. The rites of the secret tipi represent the acts performed originally in the sacred mountain, and hence are a kind of rehearsal. The secret tipi is often spoken of as the "rabbit" or "lone" tipi or the "morning star." The camp circle symbolizes the constellation Corona Borealis, which is frequently spoken of by the Plains tribes as the camp circle of the gods above. Again, the camp circle may be regarded as symbolizing the horizon, standing for the universe. The lodge itself represents this earth, as the home of man. The altar symbolizes the essence of life or spring of fertilization. In the fork of the center pole was the nest of the thunderbird. Into the nest a digging stick was usually thrust, symbolic of that used by the woman who in the well-known tale climbed to the sky in pursuit of a porcupine and later gave birth to the Sun Boy. While the center pole itself, with its bands of red and black paint, is symbolic of earth and heaven, and typifies the supreme

medicine or mystery, it may be regarded as symbolizing also, especially at the time of its capture, the common enemy of the tribe. The Cheyenne declare, indeed, that from the fork of the center pole was formerly suspended alive an enemy captured in war. The dancers collectively overcome an enemy, generally the sun, and by their medicine compel the thunderbird to release rain. The wreaths worn by dancers are symbols of the sun, and the four old men in the dance represent the gods of the four world-quarters, while the paints applied to the body, usually four in number, are progressive in their virtue, generally culminating in a black paint, which may be regarded as defying the rain to wash it off. The painted designs are symbols of the sun, the moon, the morning star, and the gods of the four world-quarters. The whistling symbolizes the breath, or life, of man, and at the same time the cry of the thunderbird. Vomiting and sweating are employed as purification rites. The fasting and the self-inflicted torture are penance, done to obtain special favor of the gods, and represent the fast of the originator of the ceremony.

In the ritual of the Sun dance it is related that once in a period of famine an individual wandered forth with a female companion in behalf of his tribe, encountered a deity, fasted, learned the ceremony, returned to the tribe, caused the ceremony to be performed, and thus brought relief from famine through the appearance of the buffalo. The ceremony accordingly may be regarded as one of rebirth or reanimation. In the tribes which have this ritual the one who has made the vow at a stated period of the ceremony offers his wife to the chief priest, thus exemplifying the act of the originator of the ceremony, who offered his companion to the one from whom he obtained the ceremony.

The Sun dance, being strongly opposed by the missionaries because it was utterly misunderstood, and finding no favor in official circles, has been for many years an object of persecution, and in consequence is extinct among the Dakota, the Crows, and the Mandan, of the Siouan stock, and among the Pawnee and the Kiowa. It is still performed by the Cree, Siksika, Arapaho, Cheyenne, Assiniboin, Ponca, Shoshoni, and Ute. Its disappearance among certain of these tribes, such as the Ponca, is near at hand, for it has lost part of its rites and has come to be largely a spectacle for gain rather than a great religious ceremony.

The Sun dance was not only the greatest ceremony of the Plains tribes, but was a condition of their existence. More than any other ceremony or occasion, it furnished the tribe the opportunity for the expression of emotion in rhythm, and was the occasion of the tribe becoming more closely united. It gave opportunity for the making and renewing of common interests, the inauguration of tribal policies, and the renewing of the rank of the chiefs; for the exhibition, by means of mourning feasts, of grief over the loss of members of families; for the fulfilment of social obligations by means of feasts; and, finally, for the exercise and gratification of the emotions of love on the part of the young in the various social dances which always formed an interesting feature of the ceremony. With the disappearance of tribal organization and tribal interests, there is no doubt of the ultimate doom of the Sun dance. See *Ceremony*, *Dance*, *Mythology*, *Religion*.   (G. A. D.)

Sunday, John. See *Shahwundais*.

Sungkitsaa. The Turquoise clan of the pueblo of Jemez, N. Mex. A corresponding clan existed also at the former related pueblo of Pecos.
Suⁿkítsaá.—Hodge in Am. Anthr., IX, 352, 1896 (Jemez form). Suⁿtí+.—Ibid. (Pecos form; += *ash*='people').

Sunik. A former Aleut village on Agattu id., Alaska, one of the Near id. group of the Aleutians, now uninhabited.

Sunk Squaw. See *Magnus*.

Sunsunnestunne ('people at the small beach'). A band of the Mishikhwutmetunne on Coquille r., Oreg.
Sûn'-sûn-nĕs' ꭲunnĕ'.—Dorsey in Jour. Am. Folklore, III, 232, 1890.

Suntaho. A Chumashan village formerly near Purísima mission, Santa Barbara co., Cal.—Taylor in Cal. Farmer, Oct. 18, 1861.

Sunteacootacoot(*Sun-tea-coot-a-coot*). An unidentified body of Salishan Indians said by Ross (Fur Hunters, I, 145, 1855) to have lived between Thompson and Fraser rs., Brit. Col.

Suntz. A Squawmish village community on Burrard inlet, Brit. Col.—Hill-Tout in Rep. Brit. A. A. S., 474, 1900.

Sunum. Given as a Karok village on Klamath r., N. W. Cal., inhabited in 1860.
Sun-num.—Taylor in Cal. Farmer, Mar. 23, 1860.

Sunusi (*Sū'-nū-si*). A former Maidu village on Sacramento r., near Jacinto, Butte co., Cal.   (R. B. D.)

Sunvalluk. A small Kaviagmiut Eskimo village on the coast opposite Sledge id., Alaska.—11th Census, Alaska, 162, 1893.

Suolanocha. A former Lower Creek town on Flint r. (?), formerly part of the Creek confederacy. In 1773 the inhabitants are said to have spoken the Creek and "Stincard languages."—Bartram, Trav., 462, 1791.

Supaen. See *Supawn*.

Supasip. Given as a Karok village on Klamath r., N. W. Cal., inhabited in 1860.
Soo-pas-ip.—Taylor in Cal. Farmer, Mar. 23, 1860.

Supawn. According to Bartlett (Dict. of Americanisms, 681, 1877) "a name in common use in New England, New York, and other northern states for boiled Indian meal." The word is applied to hasty pudding, mush, corn-meal boiled and eaten with milk, etc. *Supawn*, spelled also sepawn, sepon, supaen, suppawn, etc., by earlier writers, is derived from *sapaun* in the Massachuset dialect of Algonquian, signifying 'softened by water.' The word *samp* is from the same radical.   (A. F. C.)

Suphko. An unidentified town formerly near the mouth of Tallapoosa r., Ala., above Atasi.—Robin, Voy., II, map, 1807.

Suppaen, Suppawn. See *Supawn*.

Suquamish. A Salish division on the w. side of Puget sd., Wash. According to Paige (Ind. Aff. Rep., 329, 1857) they claimed the land from Appletree cove in the N. to Gig harbor in the S. Seattle, who gave his name to the city, was chief of this tribe and the Dwamish in 1853. Pop. 441 in 1857, 180 in 1909.
Lugua-mish.—Stevens in Ind. Aff. Rep., 453, 1854 (frequently used for Suquamish). **Port Madison.**—Ind. Aff. Rep., 180, 1907. **Port Orchard.**—Farnham, Travels, 112, 1843. **Seattle.**—Page (1856) in H. R. Ex. Doc. 37, 34th Cong., 3d sess., 82, 1857. **Soquamish.**—Schoolcraft, Ind. Tribes, V, 700, 1855. **Squamish.**—Taylor in Cal. Farmer, June 12, 1863. **Squawmish.**—Farnham, Travels, 111, 1843. **Sukwámes.**—Hale, Ethnol. and Philol., 221, 1846. **Sŭkwamish.**—Gibbs in Cont. N. A. Ethnol., I, 179, 1877. **Suquahmish.**—Stevens in H. R. Ex. Doc. 37, 34th Cong., 3d sess., 46, 1857. **Suquamish.**—Wilkes, U. S. Expl. Exped., IV, 410, 1845. **Swo-Kwabish.**—Mallet in Ind. Aff. Rep., 198, 1877 (given as subordinate to Dwamish).

Surghustesthitun ('where the black bear lay down'). A former village of the Chastacosta on the N. side of Rogue r., Oreg.
Sû-rxûs' tĕ-st'hi'-tûn.—Dorsey in Jour. Am. Folklore, III, 234, 1890.

Suricuama. A village, presumably Costanoan, formerly connected with San Juan Bautista mission, Cal.—Engelhardt, Franc. in Cal., 398, 1897.

Suscol. A village of an uncertain tribe, but probably Moquelumnan, on what was known in 1860 as the Suscol ranch, E. of Napa, Napa co., Cal.—Taylor in Cal. Farmer, Mar. 30, 1860.

Sus-haidagai (*Sūs xā'-idᴀga-i*, 'lake people'). A subdivision of the Kona-kegawai, a Haida family of the Eagle clan. They owned the town of Hlgaedlin and received their name from a lake which lies inland from Skedans bay, Brit. Col.—Swanton, Cont. Haida, 273, 1905.

Sushitna. A Knaiakhotana settlement on Susitna r., Cook inlet, Alaska, consisting of 2 villages, one containing 44, the other 46 persons in 1880; 142 people and 27 houses in 1890.
Sushetno.—Petroff in 10th Census, Alaska, 29, 1884. Susitna.—Baker, Geog. Dict. Alaska, 608, 1906.

Sushltakhotthatunne ('people back toward the head of the stream'). A band of the Mishikhwutmetunne formerly residing near the head of Coquille r., Oreg.

Sûʻol-taʻ-qo-tʻọaʻ ẓûnněʻ.—Dorsey in Jour. Am. Folk-lore, III, 232, 1890.

Susk. More correctly Sisk, the Haida name for Frederick id., off the N. W. coast of Graham id., Queen Charlotte ids., Brit. Col. Dawson (Q. Charlotte Ids., 171, 1880) wrongly supposed it to be the name of a town as well, his informants probably referring to Te, which once stood on the mainland opposite.   (J. R. S.)

Suski. The Coyote clan of Zuñi pueblo, N. Mex.

Súski-kwe.—Cushing in 13th Rep. B. A. E., 368, 1896 (kwe='people').

Susksoyiks ('band with hairy mouths'). A band of the Piegan tribe of the Siksika, probably extinct.

Sus-kso'-yiks.—Hayden, Ethnog. and Philol. Mo. Val., 264, 1862.

Susolas. A tribe seen by Cabeza de Vaca (Smith's trans., 72, 84, 1851) during his sojourn in Texas in 1527–34, that lived opposite the Atayos (Toho?), with whom they were at war. During the season of gathering prickly-pears they were associated with other tribes of the vicinity which spoke different tongues. So far as known the tribe is extinct.

Lusolas.—Cabeça de Vaca, op. cit., 72. Susolas.—Ibid., 121. Susoles.—Davis, Span. Conq. N. Mex., 82, 1869.

Susquehanna. A town and a tribe of the Iroquoian stock, situated in 1608 on the lower portion of the Susquehanna r. and its affluents. The original form of the name used by Capt. John Smith was *Sasquesahannocks* in his text and *Sasquesahanough* on his map. He first heard the name from Tockwock, Nanticoke, or Powhatan speakers of the Algonquian tongue, while exploring the waters of upper Chesapeake bay and its affluents, as the designation of a mighty people who dwelt on the Susquehanna two days journey "higher than our barge could pass for rocks." Of this people Smith wrote: "Such great and well-proportioned men are seldom seen, for they seemed like giants to the English, yea to their neighbors;" also that they were scarcely known to Powhatan, could muster nearly 600 able men, and lived in palisaded towns to defend themselves from the "Massawomeckes, their mortal enemies." Meeting at the head of the bay 60 of their warriors, five of their chiefs did not hesitate to board his barge. Although in his text Smith does not mention the names of any Susquehanna towns, he nevertheless places on his map 6 towns with "king's houses" under the general rubric "Sasquesahanough." The six are Sasquesahanough, Quadroque, Attaock, Tesinigh, Utchowig, and Cepowig. It is difficult to locate these towns correctly on a modern map; the foregoing names are evidently highly conventionalized forms of the origi-

nal native terms. Unfortunately Smith furnishes but little information regarding these people beyond a description of their bearing, size, and implements, and a general statement as to their habitat and their enemies, the most formidable of the latter being the famous "Massawomeckes."

Alsop (1666) says that the Christian inhabitants of Maryland regarded the Susquehanocks as "the most noble and heroic nation of Indians that dwell upon the confines of America," and that the other Indians "by a submissive and tributary acknowledgment" held them in like esteem, for he adds that being for the most part great warriors, they "seldom sleep one summer in the quiet arms of a peaceful rest, but keep (by their present power, as well as by their former conquest) the several nations of Indians round about them, in a forceable obedience and subjection." He declares also that men, women, and children in both summer and winter went practically naked; that they painted their faces in red, green, white, and black stripes; that their skins were naturally light in color, but were changed to a dark cinnamon hue "by the several dyeings of roots and barks"; that the hair of the head was black, long, and coarse, but that the hair growing on other parts of the body was removed by pulling it out hair by hair; that some tattooed their bodies, breasts, and arms with outlines of beasts and other objects.

Hitherto no information concerning a clan system among the Susquehanna has been available in ethnologic literature; but in the Proceedings of the Council of Maryland for 1636–1667 (pp. 421, 550) the names of the "Sassqsahannough" chiefs and delegates, and also those of the several clans to which they belonged, appear in the minutes of a treaty concluded at Spes Utia, May 16, 1661, in behalf of the Lord Proprietary of Maryland and of the Susquehanna Indians, and at a conference held at St Johns, June 29, 1666. The names of the Susquehanna delegates to the former were: "Dahadaghesa of the great Torripine family, Sarangararo of the Wolf family, Waskanecqua of the Ohongeoquena nation, Kagoregago of the Unquehiett nation, Saraqundett of the Kaiquariegahaga nation, Uwhanhierelera of the Usququhaga nation, and Waddon hago of the Sconondihago nation; but among the signatures appears the name Andra Sonque without that of his clan or nation. It was at this treaty that the Maryland authorities agreed to send 50 soldiers to aid the Susquehanna against the Seneca (here called Cynaco, Nayssone, or Naijssone), in consequence of which Capt. Odber was ordered to cause some "spurs and flankes" to be laid out for the defense of the Susquehanna fort and inmates, "whom you are upon all occasions to assist against the assaults of their enemies." At the conference of June 29, 1666, at St Johns, Wastahanda Hariguera of the Terrapin or Turtle clan, and Gosweinquecrakqua of the Fox clan, war chiefs of the Susquehanna, brought Wanahedana to justice, "lest the crime of one be imputed to the whole tribe," and asked assistance from the governor "at this time," for they had lost a large number of men who were ranging about the head of Patapsco and other rivers to secure the English plantations from the Seneca, who, they declared, were resolved to storm the Susquehanna fort in the following August and then fall upon the English; and they also agreed to deliver the "King of Potomack his two sonns" to Major Goldsmyth. At the former treaty it was stipulated also that 6 Susquehanna warriors should act as dispatch bearers.

On July 28, 1663, the Maryland authorities gave to Civility and the rest of the Susquehanna Indians 2 barrels of powder, 200 pounds of lead, and their own choice of one of two small cannon. At this conference Wastahandow of the Turtle clan declared that it was not "the Sasquesahanoughs" but the Seneca who began the war, for the Seneca had killed the Susquehanna ambassadors and had robbed them of 70 belts of wampum; and he declared that their enemies (such of the Iroquois tribes as were engaged in making war on them) mustered about 1,460 warriors, while the Susquehanna had about 700 fighting men.

In the writings of Swedish and Dutch authors many references are found to a people called therein Minquas, Minquosy, or Machoeretini (in De Laet), Mengwe, or Mingo, names which were evidently bestowed on them by the Algonquians of the lower Delaware r. and bay. It would seem that in the earliest application of the names Susquehanna and Minqua they denoted a tribe or group of allied tribes which from 1608 to 1633 waged relentless war against the Algonquian tribes on and about the lower portion of Potomac r. and Delaware r. and bay. De Vries says that on Feb. 11, 1633, when he and a small crew were in the Delaware r. opposite Ft Nassau, 50 Indians came over the river from the fort and spoke to him and his men. He states that these were Minquas dwelling among "the English of Virginia," and that, numbering 600 warriors, they had come on a warlike expedition, but that they were friendly with him and his men; that while in that immediate vicinity two days later, three Indians of the Armewamen came to him and reported that they were fugi-

tives from the Minquas, who had killed some of their people, plundered them of their corn, and burned their houses, and that these Minquas had killed 90 men of the Sankiekens (Sankhikans); also that the Minquas had returned to their own country. But subsequent to this period these two names, Susquehanna and Minqua, especially the latter, had acquired a broader and more comprehensive signification. Van der Donck, writing prior to 1653, says, "With the Minquas we include the Senecas, the Maquas, and other inland tribes."

On July 24, 1608, Capt. John Smith began his exploration of Susquehanna r., completing the work on Sept. 8 of the same year. As already stated, in his text he calls the Indians he found inhabiting the river, Sasquesahannocks, but on his map he recorded the name Sasquesahanoughs, and the name of their town Sasquesahanough. The exact situation of this town is not definitely known, but a satisfactory approximation may be made. Smith said that it was "two days' journey higher than our barge could pass for rocks." The rocks are at Port Deposit, Md., and 40 or 50 m. above this point may be tentatively taken as the approximate situation of the town. Smith locates it on the E. side of the Susquehanna, a short distance above the confluence of a feeder from the w. side. It is matter of record that a "Sasquehanocks new-town" existed about 1648 where "some falls below hinder navigation," and that in 1670 Augustine Herrman located Canooge, "the present Sassquahana Indian fort," on the w. bank just above the "greatest fall" (the present Conewago falls); and they also had a palisaded town at the mouth of the Octoraro, probably as early as 1662, so that the Susquehanna of 1608 may probably have been in the vicinity of the Conewago falls. In Smith's text a remarkable silence is maintained as to the names of any other towns of the Susquehanna, but on his map he places five other towns with king's houses: Attaock, Quadroque, Tesinigh, Utchowig, and Cepowig, and with the single exception of Cepowig, which is located on the E. side of the main stream of Willowbye's r., all these towns are located on the Susquehanna or on some of its affluents. Since no Indians were found along the upper portion of the w. shore of the bay, there can be little doubt that Cepowig was a Susquehanna town, for an early writer in a general recapitulation of names and situations of tribes says that "the Sasquesahanoes are on the Bolus river." The "Bolus r." of Smith is the present Patapsco, which flows into Chesapeake bay at Baltimore. This would seem to indicate that Cepowig, located by Smith on Willowbye's r., which is apparently only a continuation of what is to-day Bush r. (unless it was placed there instead of on the Patapsco by an engraver's inadvertence), was at all events well within the "Sasquesahanough" country. Under the circumstances it is a question whether these five towns, which were not mentioned in the text of Smith, are to be regarded as Susquehanna towns rather than as the chief towns of allied or neighboring tribes. With the meager data supplied by their position on the Smith map, it is difficult to assign them a definite geographical position on a modern map. One of the interpretations of the indicative marks places Cepowig in the vicinity either of Westminster, Md., or of Gettysburg, Pa.; Quadroque about Middletown; Tesinigh about Lebanon; Attaock about York; and Utchowig in the region of Carlisle. The other broader and, perhaps, intended view would locate Attaock in the region of Juniata r., Quadroque at the forks at Northumberland, Tesinigh on the North branch in the region of Wyoming, and Utchowig on the West branch in the vicinity of Lockhaven. Marked with "king's houses," they may have indicated the seats of neighboring tribes, whether allied or hostile.

From the data found in Smith it is difficult to form a satisfactory estimate of the population of the Susquehanna at that early date. Smith said that the "Sasquesahannocks" could muster "near 600 able and mighty men," who where entrenched in palisaded towns "to defend them from the Massawomeckes, their mortal enemies." To these people, whom Smith designated by the name "Sasquesahanough," modernized to Susquehanna, the Dutch and Swedes on Delaware r. and bay applied the name Minqua, or Mincquaas, with its many variants, which the English adopted with a wider and varying application, under the form Mingo. De Vries, in Feb., 1633, while cruising in the vicinity of Ft Nassau on Delaware r., encountered a detachment of 50 Indians from a larger body consisting of 600 men. Crossing the river from the fort, they came alongside his yacht and spoke to him and his men in a friendly manner. He learned that they were Minquas who dwelt "among the English of Virginia," and who had come on a warlike expedition. The next day, while sailing up the river, he met three Armewamen Indians who declared to him that they were fugitives from the Minquas who had killed some of their people, as above mentioned. The trio had left the main body of their people with the women and children five or six hours journey distant, and had come

there to learn in what way the Minqua had gone; they declared that 90 men of the Sankhikans (Sankiekens) had been killed by these Minqua and that the Minqua had returned to their country (Coll. N. Y. Hist. Soc., 2 s., III, pt. I, 31–32, 1857). This indicates that the people called Minqua or Sasquesahanna in 25 years had not lost their military strength, although they were engaged in continual wars with the Algonquian tribes on Delaware r. and bay, and on the Potomac. Hence it would appear that Smith's statement that they could muster in 1608 nearly 600 men did not include those belonging to the five towns exclusive of Sasquesahanough. They were in 1608 waging war on the Massawomeckes.

On Aug. 18, 1616, Captain Hendricksen reported to the New Netherland Provinces his discovery of certain lands, a bay and three rivers, lying from 38° to 40° N. lat.; that there he traded for "sables, furs, robes, and other skins," and that he also traded for and bought from the inhabitants, the Minquaes, "three persons, being people belonging to this company, which three persons were employed in the service of the Mohawks and Machicans, giving for them kettles, beads, and merchandise" (N. Y. Doc. Col. Hist., I, 14, 1854). This is perhaps the first notice of the name Minqua on record, if its use on the map accompanying this report be excepted. The map bears date 1614 (Oct. 11) and is the famous "Carte Figurative." It is the first known attempt to portray geographically the Susquehanna r. and valley with the tribes of Indians dwelling in the region covered; the map, in fact, includes the region now within New York and Pennsylvania, and represents the Susquehanna as an outlet of L. Ontario. A legend on the map says that the data concerning the location of rivers and the position of the tribes were obtained from Kleynties and his comrade, which they had acquired in an expedition from the Mohawk (Maquaas) into the interior and along the New r. (Susquehanna) downward to the Ogehage, who are identified as the "enemies of the aforesaid northern tribes"; and, further, that the positions of the tribes (Sennecas, Gachoos, Capitannasses, and Jottecas) should be indicated as considerably farther to the w. On the above-mentioned map the "Sennecas" are located some distance N. of a branch of the river which was evidently intended to represent Chemung r. of to-day; lower down, on what represented the West branch of the Susquehanna, on the s. side, the "Gachoos" are placed, with four designs denoting lodges (towns); on what probably represents the present Juniata r., on the N. side, some distance from the confluence with the Susquehanna, the Capitannasses are placed, with seven designs denoting towns arranged some distance apart along the course of the river; s. and slightly farther w. into the interior the "Iottecas" (Jottecas) are placed, with five designs representing towns set close together; and much farther down, on the w. side, a short distance below the confluence of a branch on the E. side, probably Conestoga cr., the "Mincquaas" are placed, with four palisaded towns, three of which are marked with two towns and one with four. The name "Mincquaas" occurs on the E. side of the Susquehanna a short distance above the branch last mentioned, but without any designs denotive of lodges or towns. The four palisaded towns were probably not far from the present Conewango r. and falls of the Susquehanna. This disposition of the tribes on the Susquehanna shows that the name "Mincquaas" was originally applied specifically to the people who dwelt in the same general position as those whom Smith called "Sasquesahanoughs." The Mohawk (Maquaas), with five closely set designs of lodges, are placed on the N. side of what purports to be an affluent of L. Ontario, in a relatively correct geographical position; on the opposite side of the river occurs the name "Canoomakers," which is apparently miswritten for Caughnawaga. This map exhibits a noteworthy knowledge of the interior of the region now comprised in New York and Pennsylvania, and of the names and position of the several Indian tribes inhabiting it. This name later came to include many tribes and remnants of tribes which dwelt of their own accord or were forced to dwell in the valley of Susquehanna r., but the period must be known before it is possible to state the names of the tribes inhabiting that stream. For during the middle decades of the 17th century all the tribes dwelling along this r. at the time of its discovery were destroyed as political entities and removed by the Iroquois.

In 1647, learning that the Hurons were being worsted by the Iroquois, the Susquehanna or Conestoga offered them diplomatic and military assistance, backed by a force of 1,300 warriors in a single palisaded town, who had been trained by three Swedish soldiers in the use of guns and in European tactics (Bozman, Hist. Md., II, 273, 1837; Proud, Hist. Pa., I, 111, 1897). This proffered aid was accepted by the hard-pressed Hurons, who sent at once an embassy to the Susquehanna or Conestoga capital. The Susquehanna lost no time in sending ambassadors, with suitable wampum belts and presents, to the Iroquois federal council at Onondaga, for the purpose of ending the war and establishing peace between the Hurons and the Iroquois; but the Iroquois refused the mediation and the war continued. On the other hand, the Hurons, sunk in a hopeless lethargy, did not actively seek to avail themselves of the Susquehanna aid, and so in less than 18 months they were entirely defeated and dispersed by the Iroquois.

From about 1630 to 1644 the Susquehanna waged a relentless war southward from their homes against the Yaomacos, the Piscataway, and the Patuxent (Bozman, op. cit., II, 161, 1837), and they created so much trouble for the colonists that Gov. Calvert, in 1642, by proclamation, declared them public enemies. Holm (Descr. New Sweden, Mem. Hist. Soc. Pa., III, 157, 1834), says that the Minques or Minckus live on a "high mountain, very steep and difficult to climb; there they have a fort or square building, surrounded with palisades, in which they reside. . . . There they have guns, and small cannon, with which they shoot and defend themselves, and take them when they go to war." He says that this place was situated 12 Swedish or 54 English m. from the Swedish settlements, and that they had forced the surrounding tribes to be subject and tributary to them, "so that they dare not stir, much less go to war against them."

In 1652, having maintained for a number of years friendly intercourse with their European neighbors, the Susquehanna, in the presence of a Swedish commissioner, through their chiefs, Sawahegeh, Auroghteregh, Scarhuhadigh, Rutchogah, and Nathheldaneh, ceded to Maryland all their territory from the Patuxent r. to Palmer's id., and from Choptank r. to the N. E. branch, N. of Elk r.

Early in Apr. 1663, the Onondaga, Cayuga, and Seneca, in pressing more vigorously the war which had been waging for a number of years, dispatched an expedition of 800 men against Susquehanna itself (properly called Andastoé, by the Jesuit Relations). The narrative is indefinite as to the situation of the objective point of the expedition. Erroneously adopting the geography of the "Carte Figurative," it states that this Iroquois army embarked on L. Ontario, and near one of its extremities came to a large river leading without rapids or falls to the very gates of Susquehanna (Andastogue). On arriving there, after a voyage of more than 100 leagues on the river, they found the town defended on one side by the stream and on the others by trunks of large trees; it was flanked by two bastions constructed in accordance with European methods, and was also furnished with some pieces of artillery.

The Iroquois consequently abandoned the idea of making an assault. In attempting to outwit the Susquehanna by a transparent ruse, 25 of their men were admitted into the fort; but these were at once seized, placed on scaffolds in sight of their own army, and burned to death. The humiliated Iroquois force retired to act on the defensive. At home the Iroquois tribes were at this time menaced by three scourges—their Susquehanna (Conestoga) enemies, the smallpox (which was carrying off not only women and children but many men, thus leaving, it is said, their villages nearly deserted and their lands untilled), and, consequently, by famine. The situation of the Susquehanna fort at this date was probably above the falls at Conewango, and may have been the Canooge of Herrman's map of 1673.

Brebeuf (Jes. Rel. 1635, 33, 1858) rejoices that the Huron or Wendat tongue, which he thoroughly understood, was spoken by about 12 populous sedentary tribes dwelling s. of the French settlements. Of these the following are of interest in the present connection: The Andastoerrhonons, the Scahentoarrhonons, the Rhiierrhonons, and the Ahouenrochrhonons. From the long and important list of tribes found in the Jesuit Relation for 1640 (35,1858), which is apparently a slightly enlarged enumeration of the one just cited, it is found that the name Akhrakvaeronon appears in place of Scahentoarrhonons. These four tribes have been identified as the Conestoga, the people of the Great Flats or Wyoming, the Erie, and the Wenroh, the last a tribe which migrated to and became incorporated with the Hurons in 1639. The Scahentoarrhonons were probably the Massawomeckes of Smith. The name itself is derived from other forms, among which are Andasto'eronon and Gandasto'eronon, which appear in Mohawk as Ganastohgeronon. Du Creux, in his Latin map of 1660, translates this name by "Natio perticarum," meaning simply "Pole or (roof-) pole tribe." This is not satisfactory, as no account is taken of the incorporated verb -o', 'to be immersed,' 'to be contained in'; and there is a question as to the identification of the nominal element as *kanasta*', 'roof-pole,' for *ka'nestă*', 'mud,' 'clay,' is equally possible. Conestoga or Conestogues is the Anglicized form of the French spellings.

In 1615 Champlain sent his interpreter Brulé to one of the allied tribes of the Hurons, which lived on the Susquehanna three days journey from the Seneca (meaning the four western Iroquois tribes). From the Bear nation of the Hurons, Champlain learned that this allied tribe was very warlike and possessed only three among more than twenty towns which were hostile to them; that the year before they had captured three Dutchmen who were assisting their enemies and whom they permitted to go without harm, for they thought the Dutchmen were French, the allies of the Hurons. Brulé did not report to Champlain until 1618, and from him the latter learned that the chief town of the tribe visited by Brulé, called Carantouan, was defended by 800 warriors, was only 7 days journey from where the Dutch traded, in lat. 40°, and that along the river below it were "many powerful and warlike nations, carrying on wars against each other." On the Champlain map of 1632 this tribe is called "Carantouanais." A noteworthy correspondence is found in the number of towns assigned to this tribe by Champlain and the number assigned to the Massawomeckes by Smith. Champlain said that the tribe had three towns, although he named only one after Brulé reported to him; and Smith on his map under the legend "Massawomecks" places three kings' houses, which are evidently intended for towns, as he names one Massawomeck. Concerning the Massawomeckes, Smith learned that "beyond the mountains from whence is the head of the river Patawomeke, the savages report, inhabit their most mortal enemies, the Massawomekes, upon a great salt water," and that this people were a great nation and very populous; and that "the heads of all those rivers, especially the Pattawomekes, the Pautuxuntes, the Sasquesahanocks, the Tockwoughes, are continually tormented by them." While exploring Chesapeake bay he met 7 canoes full of these Indians; and judging by their "targets, baskets, swords, tobacco pipes, platters, bows and arrows," and other things, he decided that "they much exceeded them of our parts." Noting their dexterity in the management of their canoes, "made of the barks of trees, sewed together with bark, and well luted with gum," he concluded that they were seated on some great water. He says that they were "much extolled" by the Nanticoke and their neighbors. He also learned that they had "so many men that they made warre with all the world," and that the Massawomeckes were "higher up in the mountains." These references to the presence of mountains in the country of the Massawomeckes well describe the mountainous regions of upper Susquehanna r. and its branches. As *Scahentowanen* in "Scahentowanen-rhonon" signifies 'It is a very great plain,' and was the Huron and Iroquois name of the Wyoming plain or flats in Pennsylvania, it seems probable ·

that Heckewelder's suggested derivation of the name Wyoming from a Delaware or cognate term is merely a translation of the Iroquoian term. Heckewelder says, *M'cheuómi* or *M'cheuwámi* "signifieth extensive level flats," and because of the large falls on this river, it is called, he says, "M'chweuwami Sipu" by the Delawares, and "Quahonta" by the Six Nations, which is the nominal stem in the Iroquoian term in question. The locative of the Delaware term would be *M'cheuóming*, or *M'cheuwáming*, meaning 'at the great flats, or plain,' which the English have changed into "Wyoming." The animate plural added to the first of these examples would produce *M'cheuómek*, which Smith heard from another dialect as "Massawomecke." This seems to confirm the suggestion that the "Massawomecks" of Smith were identical with the "Scahentoarrhonons" of the Jesuit Relation for 1635. It has been seen that Akhrakvaeronon, of which *Atra'kwae'ronnons* is a well-known dialectic variation in Huron (in which *kh=t*), is a synonym of *Scahentoarrhonons*, and so it is possible to show that these people of Wyoming were destroyed by the Iroquois in 1652. Two entries in the Journal des PP. Jésuites for 1652 explain this; the entry for June 5 says that "the Iroquois, having gone during the winter in full force against the *Atra'kwae'ronnons* or *Andasto'e'ronnons*, had had the worst of it," but that for July 3 says the news was "the capture of Atra'kwa'e [=*Atra'kwaye*] by the Iroquois Nations, to the number of a thousand. They have carried off 5 or 6 hundred—chiefly men. The Mohawk lost in this expedition 10 men; the other cantons, some 20, some 30—all together, 130." The identification of *Atra'kwa'e* with *Andasto'e'* in the foregoing citations is probably due to a misconception of the relator. From the Journal des PP. Jésuites for 1651 (Apr. 22) it is learned that in the autumn of 1650, 1,500 Iroquois had attacked the Neutrals and had taken one of their towns, but that the Neutrals, led by the Tohontaenrat, the Deer tribe of the Hurons, named the White-eared, fell on the retreating Iroquois and killed or captured 200; that, notwithstanding this reverse, 1,200 Iroquois returned thither during the winter of 1651 to avenge their loss. The Journal for Apr. 7, 1652 says only 600 Iroquois struck this blow. In the same Journal for 1652 (Apr. 19) it is stated that the Neutrals have formed an alliance with those of Andasto'e' (=Kanasto'ge) against the Iroquois; that the Seneca, going to war against the Neutrals, had been defeated, and as a consequence the women had been compelled to leave Sonnontouan (the Seneca capital) and withdraw to the Cayuga; and that during

the winter the Mohawk had gone to war toward Andasto'e', the result being unknown. The Jesuit Relation for 1651 (chap. II, ed. 1858) gives the information that the Iroquois for a year past had turned their arms against the Neutrals and had met with some success, taking two frontier towns, in one of which were 1,600 men. One was taken in the autumn of 1650, and the other in the early spring of 1651; the destruction of life was great, especially among the aged and the children, and the number of captives, particularly young women, was very large. This loss brought about the total dispersal of the Neutrals, but did not result by any means in the total extinction of the people of that nation, as the following citation from the Journal des PP. Jésuites for 1653 clearly indicates, when considered in connection with the reputed alliance of the Neutrals with the Conestoga, mentioned above, giving some insight into the state of affairs in regard to the Erie and allied tribes southward. "All the Algonquian Nations are assembling, with what remains of the Tobacco Nation and of the Neutral Nation, at *Ayotonatendiye* [i. e., At Potawatomi Place], 3 days' journey above the Sault *Skiaye* [i. e., Sault Ste Marie], toward the south. Those of the Tobacco Nation have wintered at *Teyaonto'rayi* [i. e., At Michilimackinac]; the Neutrals, to the number of 800, at *Sken'chioye* [i. e., At the Place of the Foxes, being s. of Detroit], toward *Teyo'chanontian* [Detroit]; these two nations are to betake themselves next autumn to the "Place of the Potawatomi, where even now they number a thousand men, to wit, 400 Potawatomi, 200 Ottawa or Cheveux Relevez, 100 Winnebago, people from the Nation of A'chawi, 200 Chippewa, and 200 Missisauga and allies. *A'chawi* is the one who is directing all this affair." (In the italicized native words the letter *y* has been substituted for the inverted comma of the original.) Of all the tribes which at this period became involved in war with the Iroquois, the Erie and allies apparently do not appear in this complot of the enemies of the Iroquois. But it is very probable that the Erie here appear under the name *Achawi*, or *A'chawi*, which was seemingly their Algonquian appellation. And it may be that this name is a form of Smith's *Utchowig*, the final *g* being the animate plural sign. It is evidently a translation of the Iroquois-Huron name *Rhiierrhonon* and cognate forms (see *Erie*), which signify, apparently, 'People of the place of panthers,' or possibly of wildcats, the name being generic for both of these animals. For wildcat, Smith gives *utchunquoyes*, Strachey gives *utchoonggwai* for a cat or a wild beast much larger and spotted black under the belly like a lynx, and *uttacawai* for "lyon," which of course was probably intended for panther, and the native terms employed by him are evidently cognate. From the Jesuit Relation for 1647–48, in reference to the Rhiierrhonon, it is learned that the s. shores of L. Erie were formerly inhabited "by certain tribes whom we call the Nation of the Cat; they have been compelled to retire far inland to escape their enemies, who are farther west"; and further that they had a number of fixed towns, as they cultivated the soil. This would indicate that before this date the Erie had been forced eastward into the region along the w. branch of the Susquehanna or the upper waters of the Allegheny. Now, it was from this latter region that the Wenrohronon, an allied tribe of the Neutrals, emigrated in 1639 to the Huron country. Of these, Father Du Peron wrote, Apr. 27, 1639: "We have a foreign nation taking refuge here both on account of the Iroquois, their enemies, and of the epidemic, which is still causing them great mortality; nearly all of them are baptized before death." And Bressani (Relation for 1653, Thwaites' ed., 39, 141), writing of the Wenrohronon (Ahouenrochrhonons), said that they had then recently come into the Huron country and "had formerly traded with the English, Dutch, and other heretical Europeans." At this point it may be well to cite some information concerning a little-known people, called the Black Minquas, who apparently dwelt in the region now under consideration, that s. E. of L. Erie and the Juniata, and the w. branch of the Susquehanna. Some interesting data are obtained from an extended legend appearing on Herrman's map of Virginia and Maryland, prepared in 1670 and issued in 1673. Beyond the Alleghany mts. all the streams flow westward either into "the Bay of Mexico or the West Sea," especially the first one discovered, "a very great River, called the Black Mincquaas River" (i. e., the Ohio), whereon lived the tribe of that name. There was a branch (the Conemaugh) of the "Black Mincquaas River" opposite a branch (the Juniata) of the Susquehanna r., which entered the main stream of the Susquehanna some leagues above the "Sassquahana forte," placed by the map on the right bank near "the greatest fal, . . . where formerly those Black Mincquaas came over as far as Delaware to trade"; but that "the Sassquahana and Sinnicus Indians went over and destroyed that very great nation." Van der Donck mentions these Indians, assigning them a general position and stating: "The beavers are mostly taken far inland, there be-

ing few of them near the settlements— particularly by the Black Minquas, who are thus named because they wear a black badge on their breast, and not because they are really black." One other reference to these people is found in Beekman's Letter of Dec. 23, 1662 (Pa. Archives, 2d s., VII, 695, 1878), wherein the statement is made that 5 Minquas (Susquehanna) chiefs informed him that they expected shortly the assistance of 800 Black Minquas, of whom 200 had already arrived, so that they were fully resolved to carry the war into the country of the Seneca and to attack their forts; and they requested that the white people furnish them with munitions of war when payment was made for them. Hazard (Annals of Pa., 2d s., 342, 1850) evidently errs in calling these allies of the Susquehanna "Swedish Minquas," probably because he did not know that the Erie or some of their allied tribes bore this name.

It is thus seen that the number and position of the tribes marked on the "Carte Figurative" confirm in large measure the view that the names of places with kings' houses placed on Smith's map under the general rubric "Sasquesahanoughs" were those of independent tribes or of the chief towns of such tribes in the valley of the Susquehanna. It was perhaps the lack of definite knowledge concerning them that compelled Smith to be silent about them in his text. With the final subjugation of the Susquehanna, representing the remnants of the tribes dwelling above them, in 1676, this period of the history of the Susquehanna valley is closed.

Subsequent to the year 1700 the valley of the Susquehanna became the habitat of many of the tribes subject to the Iroquois. The Shawnee, Conoy, Nanticoke, Delawares, Munsee, Mahican, Saponi, Tutelo, Tuscarora, and 12 or 15 other tribes were settled here at one time or another under the jurisdiction of the Five Nations.

For sources and further details, consult Alsop, Character of the Prov. of Maryland, in Gowans' Bibl. Am. No. 5, 1869; De Vries in N. Y. Hist. Soc. Coll., 2d s., III, pt. I, 1858; Jesuit Relations, Thwaites ed., 1896–1901; Md. Archives, 1636–1667; Pa. Archives, 2d s., v, 1877; VII, 1878; Smith, Works, Arber ed., 1884; Strachey, Hist. Travaile into Virginia, 1849; Van der Donck, Description of New Netherland, in N. Y. Hist. Soc. Coll., 2d s., I, 1841. See also *Conestoga, Erie, Meherrin, Minqua, Neutrals*, and their respective synonyms.   (J. N. B. H.)

Susuquey. A Chumashan village w. of Pueblo de las Canoas (San Buenaventura), Ventura co., Cal., in 1542.

Susaguey.—Taylor in Cal. Farmer, Apr. 17, 1863. Susuquey.—Cabrillo, Narr. (1542), in Smith, Colec. Doc. Fla., 181, 1857.

Sutaio (singular, *Sŭ'tai;* the several attempted Cheyenne etymologies are of doubtful value, as the word is probably not of Cheyenne origin). An Algonquian tribe, residing in the 18th century, according to tradition, about James r., S. Dak., who were at war with the Cheyenne, their eastern neighbors, to whom they were closely related linguistically. The two tribes finally formed an alliance and crossed the Missouri together to the w., the Sutaio leading the advance. The Sutaio rapidly declined, but kept their separate identity until about the year 1850, when they were absorbed by the Cheyenne. They exist now only as a division of that tribe. They are probably identical with the Staitan (q. v.) of Lewis and Clark. See *Cheyenne.*   (J. M.)
Half-Cheyenne band.—Dorsey in Field Columb. Mus. Pub. no. 99, 19, 1905. Sotaeo.—Petter in Mem. Am. Anthr. Asso., I, pt. 6, 476, 1907 (sing., *Sota*). Suh'tai.—Grinnell, Social Org. Cheyennes, 136, 1905. Su'tai.—ten Kate, Synonomie, 9, 1884. Sŭtaío.—Mooney, Cheyenne Inds., 369, 1907. Sŭ'tasi'na.—Mooney, Ghost Dance, 1025, 1896 ('children, i. e., race, of the Sutaio': another form). Sŭta'ya.—Ibid. Sutayo.—Dorsey in Field Columb. Mus. Pub. no. 103, 62, 1905. Sŭ'ti.—Grinnell in Am. Anthr., 163, 1892.

Sutali (*Sútalĭ,* 'six'). A former Cherokee settlement, named from a chief, on Etowah r., probably in s. w. Cherokee co., Ga.
Sixes Old Town.—Royce in 5th Rep. B. A. E., map, 1887.

Sutkel ('*Sĭ'k·qē'l*). A Squawmish village community on Burrard inlet, Brit. Col.—Hill-Tout in Rep. Brit. A. A. S., 475, 1900.

Sutkum. A Kaniagmiut Eskimo village on Sutwik id., off the s. coast of Alaska penin., Alaska; pop. 25 in 1880.
Sutkhoon.—Petroff in 10th Census, Alaska, 28, 1884.

Suwanee. A former Seminole town on the w. bank of Suwannee r., Lafayette co., Fla. It was deserted as early as 1763 and was afterward rebuilt, but was destroyed in the Seminole war of 1818. There is a village called Old Town on its site.   (A. S. G.)
Old Suwany Town.—Bell in Morse, Rep. to Sec. War, 306, 1822. Souhane.—Penière quoted by Morse, ibid., 149, 311. Suahnee.—Drake, Ind. Chron., 200, 1836. Suanee Old Town.—Ibid., 217. Suwanee Old Town.—Butler (1836) in Sen. Doc. 278, 26th Cong., 1st sess., 14, 1840.

Suwanee (*Suwa'nĭ,* said to be a Creek word). A former Cherokee settlement on Chattahoochee r., about the present Suwanee, Gwinnett co., Ga.—Mooney in 19th Rep. B. A. E., 532, 1900.

Suwanee lily. A popular name in South Carolina and Florida for *Zephyranthes atamasco.*

Suwuki Ohimal (*Sŭwŭ'kĭ O'himal,* 'red ants'). A phratral group of the Pima, comprising the Akol, Maam, and Vaaf gentile organizations.—Russell, Pima MS., B. A. E., 313, 1903.

Red people.—Russell in 26th Rep. B. A. E., 197, 1908. Sŭwŭ'kĭ O'himal.—Ibid. Vulture people.—Ibid.

Suya. A settlement, apparently of the Opata, in the valley of Sonora r., Sonora, Mexico, visited by Coronado in 1540, on his way to Cibola. An outpost was established there on the removal of the Spanish force from Corazones. The town having become weakened by desertions while Coronado was in the northern country, as well as by the death of Melchior Diaz, its commander, the natives attacked it, killed some of the Spanish and Indian occupants, and burned the settlement to the ground. See Winship in 14th Rep. B. A. E., 399 et seq., 1896.

Svartehuk. An Eskimo settlement on Salmon r., lat. 74°, w. Greenland.—Kane, Arctic Explor., II, 124, 1856.

Swahyawanah. A Cayuga town near Kendaia, at the N. E. corner of the present Romulus, Seneca co., N. Y. It was destroyed by Sullivan's army in 1779.—Cook, Jour. Sullivan Exped., 77, 1887.

Swaiwi (*Swai'wĭ*). A Squawmish village community on Burrard inlet, Brit. Col.—Hill-Tout in Rep. Brit. A. A. S., 475, 1900.

Swalash. Said to be a band of Salish (perhaps one of the Lummi subdivisions) on Orcas id. of the San Juan group, N. W. Wash.; now on Lummi res.
Swalarh.—Boulet letter, B. A. E., Mar. 22, 1886. Swa-lash.—Mallet in Ind. Aff. Rep., 198, 1877.

Swampy Ground Assiniboin. A division of the Assiniboin (Coues, Henry Thompson Jour., II, 523, 1897). Henry (1808) says that they "inhabit the strong wood w. of Fort Augustus, along Panbian [Pembina] r., never frequent the plains, and are excellent beaver hunters. Formerly they were very numerous, but frequent murders among themselves, and the ravages of the smallpox have reduced their number to about 30 tents. They are fully as much addicted to spirituous liquor as the Saulteurs."

Swastika. See *Cross.*

Swatana, Swataney. See *Shikellamy.*

Sweating and Sweat-houses. Few practices were so nearly universal among the Indians as the sweat-bath, probably known to every tribe N. of Mexico, although along the N. W. coast s. of the Eskimo territory it seems to have been superseded by bathing in the sea. The sweat-lodge is to this day common in most Indian villages and camps.

The type of the ordinary sweat-house seems to have been everywhere the same. Willow rods or other pliant stems were stuck into the ground and bent and fastened with withes into a hemispherical or oblong framework, which generally was large enough to accommodate several persons. A hole was dug conveniently near the door into which stones, usually heated outside, were dropped by means of forked sticks. These were sprinkled with water to generate steam. A temporary covering of blankets or skins made the inclosure tight. This was the sweat-house in its simplest form. The Delawares of Pennsylvania, according to Loskiel (Hist. Miss. United Breth., pt. 1, 108–9, 1794) in the 18th century had "in every town an oven, situated at some distance from the dwellings, built either of stakes and boards covered with sods, or dug in the side of a hill, and heated with some red-hot stones."

The construction of a sweat-house was usually attended with many rules and observances. Among the Ntlakyapamuk or Thompson Indians (Teit), the door must always face the E. Among the Kiowa (Mooney) the framework consisted always of twelve supports. Formerly among the southern Plains tribes a buffalo skull was placed on a small mound in front of the sweat-house, the mound being formed of earth excavated from the fireplace. In no tribe was the sweat-lodge made except according to prescribed rules.

In permanent villages a more roomy and substantial house was made, and the stout framework was covered by the Ntlakyapamuk with bark or pine-needles and with earth. Among the Eskimo, according to Nelson, a kashim was used for the sweat-bath, a large permanent structure that was the "center of social and religious life" in every village. In California the sweat-house was a permanent structure, semisubterranean or earth-covered. Except in the extreme N. E. part of the state, heat was produced directly by a fire, never by steam. In some cases the sweat-house was more or less merged with the communal ceremonial chamber, the same structure being used for both purposes. Like the Pueblo kiva, it sometimes partook of the character of a men's club-house or working or lounging place. It was sometimes entered or used by women for ceremonial purposes, but never for sweating. In N. w. California it was the regular sleeping place of adult males, who never passed the night in the living house. The use of the sweat-house in California was always more or less associated or tinged with religious motives, but the fact that it was a regular practice, and with some groups a daily habit, must not be lost sight of (Kroeber).

Among the Indian tribes methods of sweating seem to have been everywhere very similar. After a half-hour or more spent in the steaming air of the sweat-house, the bather plunged into the cold water of a stream, when one was near, and thus the function was ended. Among the Eskimo hot air was used in place of steam, and in Zuñi, and probably in the pueblos

generally, hot stones near the body furnished the heat. The practice of scraping the body with wooden or bone scrapers before leaving the sweat-house was common, and was perhaps simply a measure of cleanliness, for Beechey records that the Kaniagmiut Eskimo near Cook inlet do not employ scrapers, but rub themselves after the bath with grass and twigs.

There seem to have been three distinct purposes for which sweating was practised. First, it was a purely religious rite or ceremony for the purpose of purifying the body and propitiating spirits. A sweat-bath was always undergone by warriors preparing for war; among

NAVAHO SWEAT-HOUSE (STEVENSON)

many tribes, by boys at the puberty age; and, perhaps generally, before any serious or hazardous undertaking. Such ceremonial baths were almost always attended by scarification or the mutilation of some part of the body. Teit states of the Ntlakyapamuk that while in the sweat-house the hunter "sang to his spirit." No doubt the offering of prayers in the sweat-house for success in various enterprises was a general custom. The religious motive probably gave rise to the practice, and it was by far the most important in the estimation of the Indian. Second, sweating was important in medical practice for the cure of disease. The underlying idea was doubtless analogous to its religious and ceremonial use, since it was intended to influence disease spirits and was usually prescribed by the shaman, who sang outside and invoked the spirits while the patient was in the sweat-house. It was sometimes the friends and relatives of the sick person who, assembled in the sweat-house, sang and prayed for the patient's recovery. Among the Plains tribes all priests who perform ceremonies have usually to pass through the sweat-house to be purified, and the sweating is accompanied by special rituals (Miss Fletcher). Whether the Indian's therapeutic theory was rational or irrational, sweating was an efficacious remedy in many diseases to which he was subject, though used with little discrimination. Third, it was often purely social and hygienic—a number of individuals entered the sweat-house together, apparently actuated only by social instinct and appreciation of the luxury of a steam bath. Boller says that the Sioux, after severe exertions on a hunt, resorted to the steam bath as a means of invigorating their tired bodies. This practice seems to have been very common among the Plains tribes. Mooney states that among the Kiowa, Arapaho, and Cheyenne sweating was an almost daily custom, frequently having no other purpose than to give pleasure. It is possible that this practice is modern and that the sweatbath has lost some of its primitive importance and sacredness.   (H. W. H.)

Sweteti (*Swe-tĕt-ĭ*). A Chumashan village formerly near Santa Barbara, Cal., in the locality later called La Salina.—Henshaw, Buenaventura MS. vocab., B. A. E., 1884.

Swiat (*Swĭ′at*). A Squawmish village community on the w. side of Howe sd., Brit. Col.—Hill-Tout in Rep. Brit. A. A. S., 474, 1900.

Swift Bird. The half-Indian son of Chapelle, a trader of note on the Missouri, whose wife was a Teton Sioux; born at Chappelle cr., Hughes co., S. Dak., about 1842. He lived the Indian life with his mother's people, and was a member of the noted "Fool Soldier Band" that rescued the Shetak captives from White Lodge in Nov. 1862. Swift Bird was an intelligent, peace-loving man, a sub-chief and a recognized authority on the historical happenings about old Ft Pierre. He died in 1905.   (D. R.)

Swino (*Swĭ′-nö*). A Chumashan village formerly in Ventura co., Cal., at a locality now called Punta de la Loma.—Henshaw, Buenaventura MS. vocab., B. A. E., 1884.

Swinomish. Said to be a subdivision of the Skagit, formerly on Whidbey id., N. w. Wash., now under the Tulalip school superintendency. The Skagit and Swinomish together numbered 268 in 1909.
Sba-lush.—Mallet in Ind. Aff. Rep., 198, 1877.

Swords. A term sometimes applied to certain long blades of flaked stone made and used by the aborigines. Such are the wonderful blades of chalcedony and obsidian employed ceremonially by certain California tribes, and the equally remarkable flint blades of the middle Mississippi Valley region. As none of these stone blades are so specialized as fully to warrant the use of the term "sword" in describing them, all are therefore classed as knives (q. v.). In early colonial literature frequent mention is made of the wooden swords of the tribes; but these weapons appear to have had nothing in their shape or manner of use to distinguish them from the flattish-bladed clubs intended to break or bruise rather than

to cut or pierce. The term tomahawk is sometimes used as synonymous with sword, as in the words of Strachey, who, referring to the weapons of the Virginia Indians, says: "Their swordes be made of a kind of heavy wood which they have, much like such wooden instruments as our English women swingle their flax withall, and which they call monococks, as the salvadges in Bariena, in the West Indies, call their(s) macanas, and be alike made; but oftentymes they use for swordes the horne of a deare put through a piece of wood in forme of a pickaxe. Some use a long stone sharpened at both ends, thrust through a handle of wood in the same manner, and these last they were wont to use instead of hatchetts to fell a tree, or cut any massy thing in sonder; but now, by trucking with us, they have thowsands of our iron hatchetts, such as they be" (Strachey, Virginia, Hakluyt Soc. Pub., VI, 106, 1849). See *Daggers, Knives, Obsidian.*   (W. H. H.)

Syilalkoabsh (*S′yi-lal-ko-absh*). A Salish band, said to be subordinate to the Skopamish of Green r., w. Wash. (Mallet in Ind. Aff. Rep., 198, 1887). They are now with the Muckleshoot under the Tulalip school superintendency, but their number is not separately reported.

Symbolism. A symbol is an object or an action which conveys a meaning distinct from the actual concept corresponding to the object or to the action. By symbolism is meant either the quality of an object or action of having a symbolic meaning besides its proper meaning, or the tendency to connect symbolic meanings with objects or actions.

The symbolic tendencies of the North American Indians are very highly developed. They are strongest among the Indians of the S. W., of the Plains, and of the N. W. coast, and, on the whole, decrease in intensity toward the western plateaus and the N. Symbolism is found particularly in art, ritual, and mythology. One of the most characteristic aspects of primitive symbolism is found in decorative art, which at times serves purely decorative ends, but frequently is symbolic. The degree of symbolism varies considerably in different areas. In the semirealistic art of the N. Pacific coast, characteristic parts of animals are utilized as symbols of the whole animal—the beaver's incisors for the beaver, the killer-whale's fin for the killer-whale. Cases in which remoter associations prevail are few and uncertain. The joint, represented by the "eye" pattern, stands sometimes for the idea "power of motion." In California and in the interior of British Columbia, where highly developed geometrical decoration of basketry occurs, the symbolic significance is ordinarily so slight that we may rather speak of pattern names than of symbolic meaning of design. The triangle may be called a mountain; a zigzag line, a snake; a meandric pattern, waves of the sea; a rectangular line, the leg of a lizard; a series of acute angles, flying birds. Similar names occur in the folk-art of more advanced people. Thus the Shetland islanders give their patterns names of "flowers"; and thus has the Mexican woman names for her patterns in drawn-work. It is hardly possible to draw a sharp line between pattern names and a stronger feeling for symbolic significance of a design. That the tendency is markedly present in California and on the plateaus of British Columbia is shown, for instance, by rock-paintings in which a semicircular line with ray-like divergent lines represents an unfinished basket, and symbolizes industry and perseverance; or in the decoration of war-axes, which represent the woodpecker and symbolize the striking-power of its beak.

Symbolic significance is much more highly developed on the Great Plains, and still more in the S. W. Its development in this area is so peculiar that it seems likely that one must look for the origin of this strong symbolistic tendency in the relations between the Mississippi basin and the S. The decorative elements of which designs are composed are largely triangles and squares, but their meanings show an endless variety. Thus the triangle or semicircle, with a number of lines descending from its base, conveys the idea to the Pueblo Indian of the beneficent rain-cloud and raindrops; or, to the Plains Indian, of a mountain and springs streaming down from it; to other tribes, the idea of the bear's foot, and thus of the bear himself. A straight line in dark color, interrupted by a few light spots, may be a trail on the prairie interrupted by gulches, or the path of life. Each tribe has its own style of symbolic interpretation of similar designs. In the S. W., ideas relating to rain, water, and fertility prevail; among the Sioux men the symbolic significance relates to war; among the Shoshoni, geometric designs tend to become pictures of events happening in a certain geographic environment; but more abstract ideas, like prayers for life, thoughts, etc., are not absent. The more important in the social or religious life of a people an object is, the more important also is the symbolic value of its decoration.

The question as to whether the symbolic ornament should be considered as a conventionalized representation of the symbol which was originally shown in a realistic manner, or whether the geometrical ornament was given a symbolic meaning by reinterpretation, has been much discussed. There is little doubt that both lines of development have occurred with great frequency, but that reinterpretation has been more common in North America. This may be inferred from the similarity of style in different parts of the continent, and the variety of symbolic interpretation.

In a few cases the symbolic interpretation of decorative elements has become so definitely fixed that we may recognize the beginnings of ideographic writing. Cases of this kind are found in the so-called "calendar histories" of North American Indians, and also in symbolic objects used in definite ceremonials. Thus the associations between the colors and certain quarters of the world among the Southern tribes; between red and blood among the Sioux (see *Color symbolism*); between an arrow and prayer among the Huichol; that of the triangle as rain-cloud in the S. W.—seem so fixed that their symbolic significance may be read without hesitation.

Symbolism is not confined to decorative art, but appears also in other arts. In music, rhythm has very often symbolic significance; as, for instance, in the ⅝ rhythm of the N. Pacific coast, which is confined strictly to songs of the highest societies of the winter-dances. The burden of songs is almost always associated with definite ideas conveyed by the song. It is not certain whether or not a symbolic meaning of musical phrases and scales exists in America.

The dance is very often symbolic in so far as motion or gestures are associated with distantly related concepts: like the crouching of a dancer to express his submissiveness, heavy steps symbolizing the weight of the wealth that he carries; or a circuit contrary to the custom of the tribe, signifying his greatness, which permits him to disregard the customs of everyday life.

Symbolism in poetry is highly developed; and it is found that very often the meaning of songs is entirely unintelligible unless its symbolic meaning is explained. There is hardly an exception to this rule among the songs of American Indians, even among tribes that have no strongly developed symbolism in decorative art. The numerous songs of the Hako ceremony of the Pawnee and those of the ceremonials of the N. W. coast are examples of symbolism of poetry.

Symbolism plays an important part in rituals in so far as acts signify or are intended to bring about a result different from the act itself. Thus, smoking is a symbol of prayer, the shooting of an arrow symbolizes the sending of a prayer to the deity, painting with red paint signifies the bestowal of vigor, playing cat's-cradle symbolizes capture of the sun, success in gambling symbolizes the success of the player in other undertakings. In many cases the objects used in rituals are themselves symbols. On the N. Pacific coast, cedar-bark dyed red is the symbol of the winter-dance; cedar-bark undyed, the symbol of purification; the skin head-dress, that of the summer season; among the Pawnee the corn symbolizes "the omniscience which the earth is believed to possess" (Fletcher in 22d Rep. B. A. E., 289, 1904). The flat pipe of the Arapaho, the sacred bundles of the Plains Indians, the sacred objects of the Pueblos—all are symbols of supernatural powers or of supernatural beings (see *Palladium*). Among those tribes that possess an elaborate systematized cult, the symbolism of rituals is often highly developed; so much so, that the whole ritual may represent elaborate mythical concepts.

In magic, purely symbolic actions are not so frequent. A symbolic action performed on an object connected in some real or imaginary material way with the person or animal to be affected contains a new psychological element not present in the concept of symbolism. The swinging of a bullroarer in which is contained a hair of the person to be affected, and which is believed to produce dizziness, is a case of sympathy rather than of symbolism, although it contains clearly a symbolic element.

Whether or not mythology may be considered as primarily symbolic is a question difficult to decide. If myths, in their original forms, are attempts to explain nature, they must have contained important symbolic elements; but the present condition of American mythology, even among those tribes that possess an elaborate systematic mythology, does not favor this theory. The symbolic significance of the myth seems rather adventitious than primary, in the same manner in which the symbolic significance of decorative art seems more often rather adventitious than due to a development from realistic form to conventional form. In many cases the primary element seems to be the tale; the adventitious element, the symbolic interpretation of the tale. It seems that with the strong growth of ritual and its symbolic actions the symbolic significance of mythology develops, and that the priests in charge of rituals are largely responsible for the wealth of symbolism of the mythology of the southern plains and of the Pueblo region. In all other cases American myths seem to be taken in a remarkably matter-of-fact way.

It appears, therefore, that American symbolism is much more a phenomenon of action than of opinion; that it develops most strongly in artistic productions and in religious rites. (F. B.)

Sypouria. An unidentified Southern "nation" and river, perhaps mythical. The Sypouria r. is marked on Coxe's map (Carolana, 12, 1741) as a w. affluent of the Meschacébé (Mississippi), joining it below the territory of the Mosopelea tribe, and 15 leagues above Chongue r., which flows into it from the E. The name is possibly another form of Mosopelea (q.v.).